Ranking The Albums

Ranking the Albums
The Stereo LP Era: 1963-1989

A complete catalog of all the acts and albums appearing on the Billboard album charts

Bill Carroll

Cover Art by Lighthouse 24

Ranking the Albums The Stereo LP Era: 1963-1989

Published by Carroll Applied Science, LLC
Dallas, TX

Please visit the website at **http://ranking.rocks** for more information or to contact the author.

Ranking the Albums The Stereo LP Era: 1963-1989
Bill Carroll

1. Title 2. Author 3. Popular Music/History

Library of Congress Control Number: 2020914523

ISBN-13: 978-0-578-73930-4

Praise for **Ranking the Albums:**

"Bill Carroll has documented the most important transition in the history of recorded sound: our world going from 45 to 33! The hole got smaller but the adventure of discovery expanded. This is the biography of the albums that we listened to in the car on cassette and 8-track...the vinyl that populated our parties and dorm rooms...the LP's that are the very art of our lives. And you can read the whole book without getting up to flip it to side two!"

Lou Simon, VP/Music Programming, host of The Diner, Sirius XM Radio

"Warning: May cause getting out your favorite albums and experiencing them again - whether soundtracks, live concerts, or those you bought just to get the long version of that one song!"

- Rich Appel, Host of the worldwide-syndicated radio show *That Thing with Rich Appel*

"To all deep-divers of album chart lore: Take a deep breath before plunging into Bill's Ranking the Albums to keep from feeling sucker punched by all its buried treasure. I challenge anyone to find an album reference as densely filled with information presented in as novel yet accessible a way as this volume has done. You'll be rewarded with handfuls of pearls of fascinating stats and "I didn't know that!" moments whenever you come up for air from the pages of *Ranking the Albums*."

Dann Isbell, author of *Ranking the '60s* and *Ranking the '70s*.

To Dann Isbell and Lou Simon
Mentors, friends and fellow chart-hounds.

"Trying to make a living off an elpee's worth of toons..."
--Todd Rundgren

CONTENTS

Cont'd

The Appendix

FOREWORD

Life at 33 1/3

By Fred Bronson
Author and Billboard journalist

The month of June, 1948 should be in the Innovation Hall of Fame – if there is such a thing. The prototype of TV Guide was introduced on newsstands, the first drive-in theater where you could land a plane and watch a movie opened (was it also the last?) and Columbia Records introduced a new format, the 33 1/3 long-playing album, copyrighted by the label as "LP."

There had been 33 1/3 discs before label president Goddard Lieberson announced the new kind of recording at the June 18, 1948 press conference held at the Waldorf-Astoria in New York City, but the format hadn't been viable (blame it on poor sound, grooves that were too wide and short playing times) and was considered a failure. Columbia's initial batch of releases with improved technology were mostly classical, but there were some pop albums too, including one by Frank Sinatra.

Billboard introduced a weekly pop album sales chart on March 24, 1956, just one day after Elvis Presley released his first album. Most of the titles in those early days of the chart were middle-of-the-road artists, or soundtracks and Broadway cast albums. Harry Belafonte had the biggest-selling album of 1956, while the cast album of *My Fair Lady* and the soundtrack to *The King and I* also sold well. Elvis represented the new sound of rock 'n' roll, with his eponymously-titled debut album occupying pole position for 10 weeks.

Despite the success of Elvis, for the next few years, the album chart was not dominated by rock 'n' roll. In 1963, comedy albums ruled the mono charts, with No. 1 albums by Vaughn Meader (*The First Family*) and Allan Sherman (*My Son, The Celebrity*), while the soundtrack to the movie adaptation of *West Side Story* had a lengthy run in pole position on the stereo chart. Once the mono and stereo charts were combined into one tally the week of Aug. 17, Andy Williams continued his reign from both separate charts with *Days of Wine and Roses*, but one week later, Motown scored its first No. 1 album, *Recorded Live: The 12-Year-Old Genius* by Little Stevie Wonder. Still, the chart was often led by artists who were considered "easy listening," like Louis Armstrong, Barbra Streisand, Herb Alpert & the Tijuana Brass and Frank Sinatra, plus soundtracks like *Mary Poppins* and *The Sound of Music*.

As the Billboard 200 took its place alongside the Hot 100 as the magazine's most important charts, the list of best-selling albums slowly evolved. The days of albums that contained some hit singles and mostly filler material faded away as artists put more thought into their work and came up with cohesive themes and even concept albums. The Beatles reached a turning point with *Sgt. Pepper's Lonely Hearts Club Band*, their most praised album to date when it was released in 1967.

By 1968, the album chart was filled with recordings that weren't just 12-inch pieces of vinyl, but works of art, like *Bookends* by Simon & Garfunkel, *Waiting for the Sun* by the Doors, *Wheels of Fire* by Cream, *Cheap Thrills* by Big Brother & the Holding Company and *Electric Ladyland* by the Jimi Hendrix Experience. As the decade was coming to a close, the Who released their major opus, the rock opera *Tommy*.

Albums continued to mature in the '70s, a decade that produced some of the most classic albums of all time, including Carole King's *Tapestry*, Neil Young's *Harvest*, Marvin Gaye's *What's Going On*, Elton John's *Goodbye Yellow Brick Road* , Fleetwood Mac's *Rumours*, the Eagles' *Hotel California* and a pack of Steve Wonder LPs: *Talking Book*, *Innervisions*, *Fulfillingness' First Finale* and *Songs in the Key of Life*.

As technology has advanced, the Billboard charts have kept up with the times. For decades, the album chart relied only on sales information, whether it was sales of vinyl albums, or albums and cassettes, or albums, cassettes and 8-tracks, or albums, cassettes, 8-tracks and CDs. Downloads were eventually added to the mix and today the formula is so complicated that it takes an entire paragraph to explain what goes into compiling the weekly survey: "The Billboard 200 chart ranks the most popular albums of the week in the U.S. based on multi-metric consumption as measured in equivalent album units. Units comprise album sales, track equivalent albums (TEA) and streaming equivalent albums (SEA). Each unit equals one album sale, or 10 individual tracks sold from an album, or 3,750 ad-supported or 1,250 paid/subscription on-demand official audio and video streams generated by songs from an album."

Got it?

As a long-time chart follower and fan, when confronted by someone who believes that you can't compare the current charts to the charts of yesteryear, I offer my thoughts: no matter the recording technology and no matter the methods of assembling the charts, there is a constant: every week there is an album that ranks No. 1, and another that ranks No. 2, and so on. And so I am grateful to Bill Carroll for doing the work that has resulted in his outstanding *Ranking the Albums*, a tome that will take its place on my bookshelf of reference works that I constantly rely on. Thank you Bill, for your dedication and for asking me to write this foreword.

How To Use This Book/FAQs

The information used to compile this book consists of Album Title, Act and Chart Position week by week for all albums entering the Billboard consolidated Mono and Stereo album chart between August 17, 1963 and December 31, 1989. All the other quantities are derived from these data. Descriptive information about albums and acts is found from various sources, including act websites and Wikipedia.

There are three major sections of this book and they interoperate: the Acts Section, the Albums Section and the Acts With Albums Section. There are four major lists with the Albums ranked, the Albums in alphabetical order, the Acts Ranked and the Acts in alphabetical order, along with their albums. Additionally, there are a number of specialized lists, including the top albums for each year and the top acts for each year and the decades.

Not all the album-specific information is contained in every list—that would have made the book four times as large; but it allows you to start with either an album title, an act or a ranking and find all the relevant information in the various lists.
For example:

Q: What was the rank of Sgt. Pepper's Lonely Hearts Club Band?
A: Rank? Sergeant. Oh, sorry. Did you mean the original album or the movie Soundtrack? If all you know is the album name, start with the Album Alphabetical list. It has the Title, the Act and the Rank.

Q: I meant the Beatles album.
A: Fine. As you can see, it ranked 19. The Soundtrack ranked 1079.

Q: What was the number 20 album, then?
A: Go to the Albums, Rank Order list. Appetite For Destruction by Guns N' Roses.

Q: I hated that album. Why did you rank it so high?
A: Remember, this is not about what is good or bad, it's about what charted strongly.

Q: OK. What other Beatle albums charted?
A: Go to the Acts With Albums Section and look up The Beatles (under B—the words a, an and the are not used for alphabetical order). There you will find The BEATLES along with their Act ranking (1) their highest peak with any album (1) and the number of their albums that made the Top 10, Top 40, and the chart itself [23|27|37]. First album under the heading is Sgt. Pepper's and you will find its year of entry, (67), Peak and Weeks at Peak, 1(15), and weeks in the Top 10, Top 40 and in Total [33|63|175]. Finally there is the score.

Q: Let's try one more. Where did the Bee Gees rank as a group?
A: Start with the Acts in Alphabetical order because it also has rank.

Q: Right. I see they're number 14. Who was 13?
A: Go To the Acts, Rank Order list. It was Bob Dylan.

Q: There's so much stuff here. Are there any mistakes?
A: Probably. I hope you look hard enough to find them and let me know where they are. Contact me through http://ranking.rocks.

Acts with Their Albums

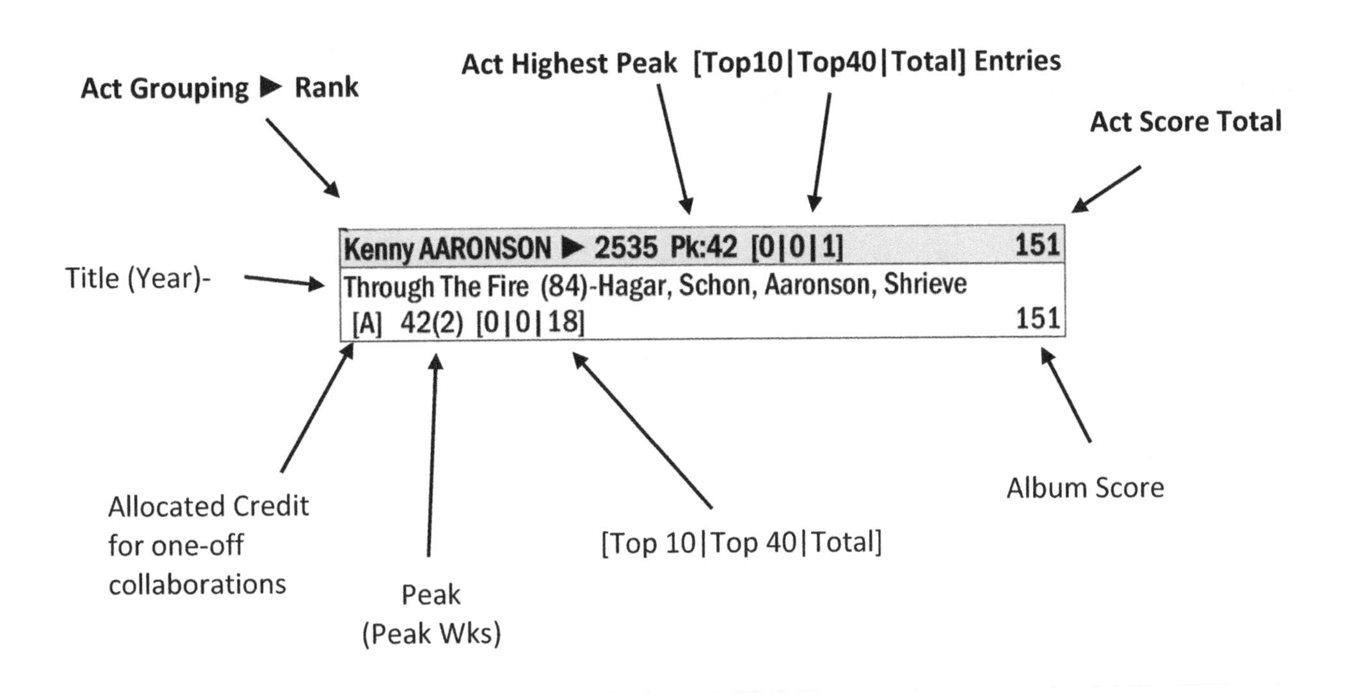

*Act is reproduced if different from grouping name. Allocated credit is used for infrequent or one-off collaborations rather than creating a new Grouping. In this case, credit is divided among the underlying Groupings. See "Methodology" in the appendix.

Act ▶ Highest Peak [Top10s|Top40s|Total]
Title (Yr) Peak(Wk) [T10 Wk|T40Wk|TotalWk] **Score**

A

Kenny AARONSON ▶ 2535 Pk:42 [0|0|1] 151
Through The Fire (84)-Hagar, Schon, Aaronson, Shrieve [A] 42(2) [0|0|18] 151

ABBA ▶ 261 Pk:14 [0|5|10] 13632
The Album (78) 14(2) [0|17|41] 2946
Super Trouper (80) 17(3) [0|16|38] 2763
Arrival (77) 20(2) [0|9|50] 2238
Voulez-Vous (79) 19(2) [0|12|27] 1925
Greatest Hits (76) 48(1) [0|0|61] 1814
The Visitors (82) 29(2) [0|6|17] 844
The Singles (The First Ten Years) (82) 62(6) [0|0|18] 496
Greatest Hits Vol.2 (79) 46(2) [0|0|14] 462
Waterloo (74) 145(1) [0|0|8] 113
Abba (75) 174(1) [0|0|3] 31.3

Gregory ABBOTT ▶ 995 Pk:22 [0|1|2] 1961
Shake You Down (86) 22(1) [0|16|36] 1838
I'll Prove It To You (88) 132(2) [0|0|9] 123

ABC ▶ 551 Pk:24 [0|2|4] 5377
The Lexicon Of Love (82) 24(10) [0|20|39] 2473
How To Be A...Zillionaire! (85) 30(2) [0|15|41] 1871
Alphabet City (87) 48(3) [0|0|25] 662
Beauty Stab (83) 69(2) [0|0|14] 371

Paula ABDUL ▶ 179 Pk:1 [1|1|1] 19418
Forever Your Girl (88) 1(10) [64|78|175] 19418

-- Abnuceals Emuukha Electric Symphony Orchestra And Chorus: See Zappa, Frank

Colonel ABRAMS ▶ 2304 Pk:75 [0|0|1] 214
Colonel Abrams (86) 75(2) [0|0|11] 214

ACCEPT ▶ 1404 Pk:74 [0|0|4] 968
Balls To The Wall (84) 74(1) [0|0|26] 459
Metal Heart (85) 94(2) [0|0|14] 265
Russian Roulette (86) 114(2) [0|0|9] 137
Eat The Heat (89) 139(2) [0|0|9] 107

AC/DC ▶ 94 Pk:1 [3|8|13] 30779
Back In Black (80) 4(3) [23|45|131] 10402
Dirty Deeds Done Dirt Cheap (81) 3(6) [12|19|55] 5829
For Those About To Rock (We Salute You) (81) 1(3) [12|16|30] 4377
Highway To Hell (79) 17(2) [0|11|83] 3255
Blow Up Your Video (88) 12(1) [0|12|24] 1815
Flick Of The Switch (83) 15(2) [0|11|23] 1466
Who Made Who (Soundtrack) (86) 33(4) [0|6|42] 1419
Fly On The Wall (85) 32(2) [0|5|30] 1041
Powerage (78) 133(2) [0|0|17] 286
'74 Jailbreak (84) 76(2) [0|0|14] 268
High Voltage (81) 146(1) [0|0|19] 263
If You Want Blood You've Got It (78) 113(1) [0|0|14] 237
Let There Be Rock (77) 154(1) [0|0|11] 122

ACE ▶ 922 Pk:11 [0|1|3] 2260
Five-A-Side (An Ace Album) (75) 11(1) [0|11|22] 2156
Time For Another (75) 153(1) [0|0|6] 79.8
No Strings (77) 170(1) [0|0|2] 24.3

ACE SPECTRUM ▶ 2713 Pk:138 [0|0|1] 112
Low Rent Rendezvous (75) 138(1) [0|0|7] 112

David ACKLES ▶ 2825 Pk:167 [0|0|1] 91
American Gothic (72) 167(1) [0|0|10] 91.2

Act ▶ Highest Peak [Top10s|Top40s|Total]
Title (Yr) Peak(Wk) [T10 Wk|T40Wk|TotalWk] **Score**

Barbara ACKLIN ▶ 2914 Pk:146 [0|0|1] 78
Love Makes A Woman (68) 146(2) [0|0|5] 78.5

Bryan ADAMS ▶ 182 Pk:1 [3|3|4] 18844
Reckless (84) 1(2) [40|66|83] 11440
Cuts Like A Knife (83) 8(3) [6|24|89] 4109
Into The Fire (87) 7(1) [5|23|33] 3091
You Want It, You Got It (82) 118(1) [0|0|13] 204

ADC BAND ▶ 2534 Pk:139 [0|0|1] 151
Long Stroke (78) 139(2) [0|0|9] 151

Nat ADDERLEY Sextet ▶ 1797 Pk:75 [0|0|1] 488
Soul Zodiac (72)-Nat Adderley Sextet and Rick Holmes 75(1) [0|0|20] 488

"Cannonball" ADDERLEY Quintet ▶ 890 Pk:13 [0|1|9] 2434
Mercy, Mercy, Mercy! (67) 13(2) [0|9|27] 1705
Country Preacher (70) 136(1) [0|0|22] 314
Phenix (75)-Cannonball Adderley 121(2) [0|0|8] 150
Why Am I Treated So Bad! (67) 154(1) [0|0|12] 133
Inside Straight (73) 179(1) [0|0|5] 40.5
The Black Messiah (72)-Cannonball Adderley 167(1) [0|0|3] 36.8
The Price You Got To Pay To Be Free (71) 169(2) [0|0|2] 27.1
74 Miles Away - Walk Tall (67) 186(1) [0|0|2] 14.8
Experience In E, Tensity, Dialogues (70) 194(2) [0|0|2] 13.9

ADDRISI BROTHERS ▶ 2182 Pk:118 [0|0|2] 266
Addrisi Brothers (77) 118(1) [0|0|14] 215
We've Got To Get It On Again (72) 137(1) [0|0|3] 50.9

King Sunny ADE & His AFRICAN BEATS ▶ 1682 Pk:91 [0|0|2] 598
JuJu Music (83) 111(1) [0|0|29] 423
Synchro System (83) 91(1) [0|0|10] 175

The ADVENTURES ▶ 2882 Pk:144 [0|0|1] 82
The Sea Of Love (88) 144(1) [0|0|9] 82.1

AEROSMITH ▶ 61 Pk:3 [2|10|14] 40371
Pump (89) 5(3) [30|54|110] 8649
Toys In The Attic (75) 11(1) [0|30|128] 7586
Permanent Vacation (87) 11(4) [0|52|67] 5898
Rocks (76) 3(3) [10|21|53] 5740
Aerosmith (73) 21(2) [0|8|59] 2229
Live! Bootleg (78) 13(2) [0|13|22] 2223
Night In The Ruts (79) 14(2) [0|12|19] 1808
Draw The Line (77) 11(3) [0|8|20] 1694
Get Your Wings (74) 74(1) [0|0|86] 1634
Done With Mirrors (85) 36(3) [0|5|28] 956
Aerosmith's Greatest Hits (80) 53(3) [0|0|40] 835
Rock In A Hard Place (82) 32(4) [0|6|19] 734
Classics Live (86) 84(1) [0|0|12] 236
Gems (88) 133(1) [0|0|11] 148

AFRIQUE ▶ 2828 Pk:152 [0|0|1] 91
Soul Makossa (73) 152(1) [0|0|8] 90.9

AFTER 7 ▶ 1021 Pk:35 [0|1|1] 1864
After 7 (89) 35(1) [0|4|72] 1864

AFTER THE FIRE ▶ 1356 Pk:25 [0|1|1] 1034
ATF (83) 25(3) [0|8|20] 1034

A-HA ▶ 745 Pk:15 [0|1|3] 3302
Hunting High And Low (85) 15(2) [0|25|47] 2928
Scoundrel Days (86) 74(2) [0|0|20] 308
Stay On These Roads (88) 148(2) [0|0|6] 66.0

AIR SUPPLY ▶ 222 Pk:7 [2|5|6] 15837
The One That You Love (81) 10(4) [4|25|60] 5042

Act ▶ Highest Peak [Top10s|Top40s|Total]
Title (Yr) Peak(Wk) [T10 Wk|T40Wk|TotalWk] **Score**

Lost In Love (80) 22(3) [0|19|104] 4355
Greatest Hits (83) 7(1) [8|26|51] 3820
Now And Forever (82) 25(3) [0|8|38] 1443
Air Supply (85) 26(4) [0|8|21] 997
Hearts In Motion (86) 84(2) [0|0|9] 180

AIRTO ▶ 2847 Pk:114 [0|0|1] 88
In Concert (74)-Deodato/Airto [A] 114(1) [0|0|9] 88.0

Jan AKKERMAN ▶ 3141 Pk:192 [0|0|3] 47
Profile (73) 192(2) [0|0|4] 23.8
Tabernakel (74) 195(1) [0|0|2] 11.9
Jan Akkerman (78) 198(1) [0|0|2] 11.3

ALABAMA ▶ 129 Pk:10 [1|6|12] 24744
Feels So Right (81) 16(2) [0|42|161] 8135
Mountain Music (82) 14(2) [0|20|114] 4690
The Closer You Get (83) 10(1) [1|15|70] 3270
Roll On (84) 21(2) [0|17|62] 2447
Greatest Hits (86) 24(3) [0|15|38] 1740
40 Hour Week (85) 28(3) [0|5|40] 1203
Just Us (87) 55(1) [0|0|28] 748
The Touch (86) 42(1) [0|0|30] 734
My Home's In Alabama (80) 71(1) [0|0|21] 614
Southern Star (89) 62(2) [0|0|21] 558
Live (88) 76(3) [0|0|19] 414
Christmas (85) 75(2) [0|0|9] 191

The ALARM ▶ 740 Pk:39 [0|1|6] 3365
Strength (85) 39(3) [0|3|36] 1304
Declaration (84) 50(2) [0|0|22] 709
Eye Of The Hurricane (87) 77(2) [0|0|30] 574
The Alarm (83) 126(1) [0|0|37] 388
Change. (89) 75(1) [0|0|23] 349
Electric Folklore Live (88) 167(2) [0|0|5] 40.8

Morris ALBERT ▶ 1180 Pk:37 [0|1|2] 1389
Feelings (75) 37(2) [0|2|31] 1273
Morris Albert (76) 135(1) [0|0|7] 116

Gerald ALBRIGHT ▶ 3254 Pk:181 [0|0|1] 33
Just Between Us (88) 181(2) [0|0|5] 32.7

AL B. SURE! ▶ 741 Pk:20 [0|1|1] 3363
In Effect Mode (88) 20(1) [0|25|54] 3363

ALCATRAZZ ▶ 1859 Pk:128 [0|0|3] 434
No Parole From Rock 'n' Roll (84) 128(1) [0|0|18] 174
Disturbing The Peace (85) 145(2) [0|0|16] 154
Live Sentence (84) 133(1) [0|0|10] 106

Ronnie ALDRICH ▶ 2975 Pk:169 [0|0|1] 69
Love Story (71) 169(1) [0|0|6] 68.9

ALICE COOPER (Grp) ▶ 183 Pk:1 [4|6|7] 18831
Billion Dollar Babies (73) 1(1) [10|23|50] 4898
Killer (71) 21(2) [0|16|54] 4153
School's Out (72) 2(3) [6|15|32] 3734
Alice Cooper's Greatest Hits (74) 8(1) [2|10|23] 2081
Love It To Death (71) 35(2) [0|6|38] 1999
Muscle Of Love (73) 10(2) [2|10|21] 1921
Pretties For You (69) 193(2) [0|0|6] 44.8

ALICE COOPER (Solo) ▶ 298 Pk:5 [1|3|10] 11705
Welcome To My Nightmare (75) 5(1) [10|17|37] 4253
Trash (89) 20(2) [0|22|43] 2735
Alice Cooper Goes To Hell (76) 27(1) [0|7|32] 2077
Lace And Whiskey (77) 42(2) [0|0|16] 737
Flush The Fashion (80) 44(2) [0|0|17] 651
Constrictor (86) 59(1) [0|0|21] 460

<table>
<tr><th>Act ▶ Highest Peak [Top10s|Top40s|Total]
Title (Yr) Peak(Wk) [T10 Wk|T40Wk|TotalWk]</th><th>Score</th></tr>
<tr><td>ALICE COOPER ▶ (Solo) Continued</td><td></td></tr>
<tr><td>From The Inside (78) 60(1) [0|0|11]</td><td>320</td></tr>
<tr><td>Raise Your Fist And Yell (87) 73(2) [0|0|15]</td><td>274</td></tr>
<tr><td>The Alice Cooper Show (77) 131(1) [0|0|6]</td><td>100</td></tr>
<tr><td>Special Forces (81) 125(2) [0|0|5]</td><td>97.8</td></tr>
<tr><td>ALIVE 'N KICKIN' ▶ 3068 Pk:129 [0|0|1]</td><td>56</td></tr>
<tr><td>Alive 'N Kickin' (70) 129(1) [0|0|3]</td><td>56.5</td></tr>
<tr><td>Davie ALLAN And The ARROWS ▶ 717
Pk:17 [0|1|3]</td><td>3515</td></tr>
<tr><td>The Wild Angels (Soundtrack) (66)
17(2) [0|13|71]</td><td>3165</td></tr>
<tr><td>The Wild Angels, Vol. II (Soundtrack) (67)
94(1) [0|0|18]</td><td>328</td></tr>
<tr><td>Devil's Angels (Soundtrack) (67) 165(1) [0|0|2]</td><td>21.6</td></tr>
<tr><td>Deborah ALLEN ▶ 1944 Pk:67 [0|0|1]</td><td>379</td></tr>
<tr><td>Cheat The Night (83) 67(1) [0|0|20]</td><td>379</td></tr>
<tr><td>Donna ALLEN ▶ 2514 Pk:133 [0|0|1]</td><td>156</td></tr>
<tr><td>Perfect Timing (87) 133(1) [0|0|13]</td><td>156</td></tr>
<tr><td>Peter ALLEN ▶ 2031 Pk:123 [0|0|3]</td><td>336</td></tr>
<tr><td>Bi-Coastal (80) 123(1) [0|0|20]</td><td>260</td></tr>
<tr><td>Not The Boy Next Door (83) 170(2) [0|0|6]</td><td>45.7</td></tr>
<tr><td>I Could Have Been A Sailor (79) 171(2) [0|0|3]</td><td>30.2</td></tr>
<tr><td>Woody ALLEN ▶ 2203 Pk:63 [0|0|1]</td><td>253</td></tr>
<tr><td>Woody Allen (64) 63(2) [0|0|11]</td><td>253</td></tr>
<tr><td>Duane ALLMAN ▶ 1037 Pk:28 [0|1|2]</td><td>1804</td></tr>
<tr><td>An Anthology (72) 28(1) [0|6|26]</td><td>1263</td></tr>
<tr><td>An Anthology, Vol. II (74) 49(1) [0|0|16]</td><td>541</td></tr>
<tr><td>Gregg ALLMAN ▶ 738 Pk:13 [0|1|2]</td><td>3392</td></tr>
<tr><td>Laid Back (73) 13(1) [0|17|39]</td><td>2934</td></tr>
<tr><td>The Gregg Allman Tour (74) 50(1) [0|0|12]</td><td>458</td></tr>
<tr><td>Gregg ALLMAN Band ▶ 1007 Pk:30 [0|1|3]</td><td>1918</td></tr>
<tr><td>I'm No Angel (87) 30(3) [0|6|28]</td><td>1183</td></tr>
<tr><td>Playing Up A Storm (77) 42(1) [0|0|12]</td><td>579</td></tr>
<tr><td>Just Before The Bullets Fly (88) 117(2) [0|0|11]</td><td>157</td></tr>
<tr><td>ALLMAN BROTHERS Band ▶ 119
Pk:1 [4|8|16]</td><td>26611</td></tr>
<tr><td>Brothers And Sisters (73) 1(5) [15|24|56]</td><td>7279</td></tr>
<tr><td>Eat A Peach (72) 4(2) [10|29|48]</td><td>5683</td></tr>
<tr><td>At Fillmore East (71) 13(1) [0|11|47]</td><td>3136</td></tr>
<tr><td>Enlightened Rogues (79) 9(4) [5|13|24]</td><td>2714</td></tr>
<tr><td>Win, Lose Or Draw (75) 5(2) [5|8|14]</td><td>2076</td></tr>
<tr><td>Beginnings (73) 25(1) [0|6|55]</td><td>1945</td></tr>
<tr><td>Idlewild South (70) 38(1) [0|2|22]</td><td>1041</td></tr>
<tr><td>Reach For The Sky (80) 27(2) [0|6|13]</td><td>940</td></tr>
<tr><td>The Road Goes On Forever,
A Collection Of Their Greatest Recordings (75)
43(1) [0|0|14]</td><td>569</td></tr>
<tr><td>Brothers Of The Road (81) 44(1) [0|0|12]</td><td>524</td></tr>
<tr><td>Wipe The Windows-Check The Oil-Dollar Gas (76)
75(2) [0|0|10]</td><td>265</td></tr>
<tr><td>Dreams (89) 103(2) [0|0|11]</td><td>165</td></tr>
<tr><td>Duane & Gregg Allman (72) 129(1) [0|0|8]</td><td>147</td></tr>
<tr><td>Early Allman (73)-Allman Joys 171(1) [0|0|8]</td><td>72.5</td></tr>
<tr><td>The Allman Brothers Band (70) 188(1) [0|0|5]</td><td>36.5</td></tr>
<tr><td>The Best Of The Allman Brothers Band (81)
189(1) [0|0|3]</td><td>18.5</td></tr>
<tr><td>Marc ALMOND ▶ 2684 Pk:144 [0|0|1]</td><td>118</td></tr>
<tr><td>The Stars We Are (89) 144(2) [0|0|11]</td><td>118</td></tr>
<tr><td>Herb ALPERT ▶ 412 Pk:6 [1|3|8]</td><td>7901</td></tr>
<tr><td>Rise (79) 6(1) [7|19|39]</td><td>3939</td></tr>
<tr><td>Keep Your Eye On Me (87) 18(3) [0|17|31]</td><td>1954</td></tr>
<tr><td>Beyond (80) 28(2) [0|4|12]</td><td>735</td></tr>
<tr><td>Fandango (82) 100(2) [0|0|26]</td><td>414</td></tr>
<tr><td>Magic Man (81) 61(1) [0|0|10]</td><td>362</td></tr>
<tr><td>Herb Alpert/Hugh Masekela (78)-
Herb Alpert/Hugh Masekela [A] 65(1) [0|0|19]</td><td>281</td></tr>
<tr><td>Blow Your Own Horn (83) 120(1) [0|0|8]</td><td>123</td></tr>
</table>

<table>
<tr><th>Act ▶ Highest Peak [Top10s|Top40s|Total]
Title (Yr) Peak(Wk) [T10 Wk|T40Wk|TotalWk]</th><th>Score</th></tr>
<tr><td>Wild Romance (85) 151(2) [0|0|10]</td><td>93.3</td></tr>
<tr><td>Herb ALPERT & The TIJUANA BRASS ▶ 6
Pk:1 [8|11|18]</td><td>93850</td></tr>
<tr><td>Whipped Cream & Other Delights (65)-
Herb Alpert's Tijuana Brass 1(8) [61|141|185]</td><td>22164</td></tr>
<tr><td>!!Going Places!! (65) 1(6) [48|107|164]</td><td>17192</td></tr>
<tr><td>What Now My Love (66) 1(9) [32|60|129]</td><td>12888</td></tr>
<tr><td>S.R.O. (66) 2(6) [19|38|85]</td><td>8579</td></tr>
<tr><td>South Of The Border (65) 6(1) [3|52|163]</td><td>7622</td></tr>
<tr><td>Beat Of The Brass (68) 1(2) [16|28|54]</td><td>7403</td></tr>
<tr><td>Sounds Like... (67) 1(1) [12|36|53]</td><td>6677</td></tr>
<tr><td>Herb Alpert's Ninth (67) 4(2) [10|18|49]</td><td>4113</td></tr>
<tr><td>Herb Alpert's Tijuana Brass, Volume 2 (66)-
Herb Alpert's Tijuana Brass 17(1) [0|13|56]</td><td>2265</td></tr>
<tr><td>Warm (69) 28(3) [0|7|26]</td><td>1630</td></tr>
<tr><td>The Brass Are Comin' (69) 30(1) [0|5|20]</td><td>1087</td></tr>
<tr><td>Greatest Hits (70) 43(1) [0|0|32]</td><td>1024</td></tr>
<tr><td>You Smile-The Song Begins (74) 66(1) [0|0|11]</td><td>360</td></tr>
<tr><td>Coney Island (75) 88(1) [0|0|10]</td><td>252</td></tr>
<tr><td>Summertime (71) 111(1) [0|0|10]</td><td>220</td></tr>
<tr><td>Bullish (84) 75(1) [0|0|10]</td><td>201</td></tr>
<tr><td>Solid Brass (72) 135(1) [0|0|9]</td><td>151</td></tr>
<tr><td>Foursider (73) 196(1) [0|0|4]</td><td>20.8</td></tr>
<tr><td>ALPHAVILLE ▶ 2663 Pk:174 [0|0|2]</td><td>120</td></tr>
<tr><td>Forever Young (84) 180(1) [0|0|15]</td><td>82.1</td></tr>
<tr><td>Afternoons In Utopia (86) 174(1) [0|0|6]</td><td>38.4</td></tr>
<tr><td>Dave ALVIN ▶ 2444 Pk:116 [0|0|1]</td><td>174</td></tr>
<tr><td>Romeo's Escape (87) 116(1) [0|0|13]</td><td>174</td></tr>
<tr><td>AMAZING RHYTHM ACES ▶ 1553
Pk:114 [0|0|6]</td><td>724</td></tr>
<tr><td>Toucan Do It Too (77) 114(1) [0|0|11]</td><td>199</td></tr>
<tr><td>Burning The Ballroom Down (78)
116(2) [0|0|9]</td><td>170</td></tr>
<tr><td>Stacked Deck (75) 120(1) [0|0|8]</td><td>137</td></tr>
<tr><td>The Amazing Rhythm Aces (79) 144(1) [0|0|7]</td><td>96.3</td></tr>
<tr><td>Too Stuffed To Jump (76) 157(1) [0|0|7]</td><td>92.6</td></tr>
<tr><td>How The Hell Do You Spell Rythum (80)
175(1) [0|0|3]</td><td>29.6</td></tr>
<tr><td>AMBOY DUKES ▶ 1601 Pk:74 [0|0|4]</td><td>680</td></tr>
<tr><td>Journey To The Center Of The Mind (68)
74(2) [0|0|23]</td><td>535</td></tr>
<tr><td>Survival Of The Fittest/Live (71)-
Ted Nugent And The Amboy Dukes
129(2) [0|0|5]</td><td>103</td></tr>
<tr><td>The Amboy Dukes (68) 183(1) [0|0|4]</td><td>26.7</td></tr>
<tr><td>Marriage On The Rocks/Rock Bottom (70)
191(1) [0|0|2]</td><td>14.7</td></tr>
<tr><td>AMBROSIA ▶ 509 Pk:19 [0|3|5]</td><td>6084</td></tr>
<tr><td>One Eighty (80) 25(1) [0|7|33]</td><td>1910</td></tr>
<tr><td>Life Beyond L.A. (78) 19(2) [0|9|29]</td><td>1840</td></tr>
<tr><td>Ambrosia (75) 22(1) [0|8|33]</td><td>1835</td></tr>
<tr><td>Somewhere I've Never Travelled (76)
79(1) [0|0|17]</td><td>386</td></tr>
<tr><td>Road Island (82) 115(2) [0|0|7]</td><td>113</td></tr>
<tr><td>AMERICA ▶ 100 Pk:1 [5|8|14]</td><td>29659</td></tr>
<tr><td>America (72) 1(5) [13|22|40]</td><td>6744</td></tr>
<tr><td>History/America's Greatest Hits (75) 3(6)
[12|22|63]</td><td>6466</td></tr>
<tr><td>Holiday (74) 3(1) [7|17|53]</td><td>4445</td></tr>
<tr><td>Hearts (75) 4(1) [6|17|44]</td><td>3874</td></tr>
<tr><td>Homecoming (72) 9(4) [4|16|32]</td><td>2887</td></tr>
<tr><td>Hideaway (76) 11(3) [0|8|22]</td><td>1839</td></tr>
<tr><td>View From The Ground (82) 41(8) [0|0|28]</td><td>1020</td></tr>
<tr><td>Hat Trick (73) 28(1) [0|5|18]</td><td>920</td></tr>
<tr><td>Harbor (77) 21(2) [0|4|14]</td><td>901</td></tr>
<tr><td>Your Move (83) 81(1) [0|0|14]</td><td>246</td></tr>
<tr><td>America/Live (77) 129(2) [0|0|7]</td><td>111</td></tr>
<tr><td>Silent Letter (79) 110(1) [0|0|6]</td><td>109</td></tr>
</table>

<table>
<tr><th>Act ▶ Highest Peak [Top10s|Top40s|Total]
Title (Yr) Peak(Wk) [T10 Wk|T40Wk|TotalWk]</th><th>Score</th></tr>
<tr><td>Alibi (80) 142(2) [0|0|6]</td><td>77.6</td></tr>
<tr><td>Perspective (84) 185(1) [0|0|3]</td><td>19.5</td></tr>
<tr><td>AMERICAN BREED ▶ 2435 Pk:99 [0|0|1]</td><td>177</td></tr>
<tr><td>Bend Me, Shape Me (68) 99(1) [0|0|10]</td><td>177</td></tr>
<tr><td>AMERICAN DREAM ▶ 3460 Pk:194 [0|0|1]</td><td>13</td></tr>
<tr><td>The American Dream (70) 194(2) [0|0|2]</td><td>13.3</td></tr>
<tr><td>AMERICAN FLYER ▶ 2068 Pk:87 [0|0|2]</td><td>316</td></tr>
<tr><td>American Flyer (76) 87(1) [0|0|10]</td><td>260</td></tr>
<tr><td>Spirit Of A Woman (77) 171(1) [0|0|5]</td><td>55.9</td></tr>
<tr><td>Ed AMES ▶ 324 Pk:4 [1|3|13]</td><td>10582</td></tr>
<tr><td>My Cup Runneth Over (67) 4(3) [10|19|81]</td><td>4722</td></tr>
<tr><td>Who Will Answer? And Other Songs Of Our Time
(68) 13(1) [0|18|50]</td><td>2821</td></tr>
<tr><td>When The Snow Is On The Roses (67)
24(1) [0|8|25]</td><td>1277</td></tr>
<tr><td>Time, Time (67) 77(2) [0|0|38]</td><td>556</td></tr>
<tr><td>The Best Of Ed Ames (69)
119(1) [0|0|16]</td><td>347</td></tr>
<tr><td>A Time For Living, A Time For Hope (69)
114(2) [0|0|14]</td><td>274</td></tr>
<tr><td>Apologize (68) 135(2) [0|0|14]</td><td>204</td></tr>
<tr><td>More I Cannot Wish You (66) 90(1) [0|0|7]</td><td>172</td></tr>
<tr><td>The Windmills Of Your Mind (69)
157(2) [0|0|6]</td><td>78.7</td></tr>
<tr><td>Love Of The Common People (70)
172(1) [0|0|6]</td><td>63.6</td></tr>
<tr><td>The Hits Of Broadway And Hollywood (68)
186(2) [0|0|6]</td><td>48.4</td></tr>
<tr><td>Sing Away The World (70) 194(1) [0|0|2]</td><td>12.0</td></tr>
<tr><td>The Songs Of Bacharach And David (71)
199(1) [0|0|1]</td><td>5.8</td></tr>
<tr><td>Nancy AMES ▶ 2411 Pk:133 [0|0|2]</td><td>183</td></tr>
<tr><td>Latin Pulse (66) 133(1) [0|0|8]</td><td>132</td></tr>
<tr><td>This Is The Girl That Is (64) 133(1) [0|0|4]</td><td>51.8</td></tr>
<tr><td>Gene AMMONS ▶ 3361 Pk:174 [0|0|1]</td><td>23</td></tr>
<tr><td>The Boss Is Back! (70) 174(1) [0|0|2]</td><td>22.7</td></tr>
<tr><td>Géza ANDA ▶ 2143 Pk:115 [0|0|1]</td><td>283</td></tr>
<tr><td>Mozart: Piano Concertos Nos. 17 & 21 (68)
115(1) [0|0|17]</td><td>283</td></tr>
<tr><td>Eric ANDERSEN ▶ 2115 Pk:113 [0|0|2]</td><td>294</td></tr>
<tr><td>Be True To You (75) 113(1) [0|0|9]</td><td>186</td></tr>
<tr><td>Blue River (72) 169(1) [0|0|11]</td><td>109</td></tr>
<tr><td>Carl ANDERSON ▶ 2247 Pk:87 [0|0|1]</td><td>235</td></tr>
<tr><td>Carl Anderson (86) 87(2) [0|0|12]</td><td>235</td></tr>
<tr><td>John ANDERSON ▶ 1931 Pk:58 [0|0|2]</td><td>387</td></tr>
<tr><td>Wild & Blue (83) 58(1) [0|0|12]</td><td>344</td></tr>
<tr><td>All The People Are Talkin' (83) 163(1) [0|0|5]</td><td>42.8</td></tr>
<tr><td>Jon ANDERSON ▶ 1471 Pk:47 [0|0|4]</td><td>858</td></tr>
<tr><td>Olias Of Sunhillow (76) 47(1) [0|0|13]</td><td>634</td></tr>
<tr><td>Song Of Seven (80) 143(1) [0|0|11]</td><td>149</td></tr>
<tr><td>3 Ships (85) 166(2) [0|0|5]</td><td>39.1</td></tr>
<tr><td>Animation (82) 176(1) [0|0|5]</td><td>35.2</td></tr>
<tr><td>--Anderson, Bruford, Wakeman, Howe see: Yes</td><td></td></tr>
<tr><td>Laurie ANDERSON ▶ 1488 Pk:60 [0|0|5]</td><td>834</td></tr>
<tr><td>Mister Heartbreak (84) 60(2) [0|0|19]</td><td>478</td></tr>
<tr><td>Big Science (82) 124(1) [0|0|12]</td><td>146</td></tr>
<tr><td>Home Of The Brave (Soundtrack) (86)
145(2) [0|0|12]</td><td>109</td></tr>
<tr><td>Strange Angels (89) 171(1) [0|0|12]</td><td>77.3</td></tr>
<tr><td>United States Live (85) 192(1) [0|0|5]</td><td>22.4</td></tr>
<tr><td>Lynn ANDERSON ▶ 725 Pk:19 [0|1|10]</td><td>3488</td></tr>
<tr><td>Rose Garden (71) 19(3) [0|12|33]</td><td>2483</td></tr>
<tr><td>You're My Man (71) 99(1) [0|0|14]</td><td>363</td></tr>
<tr><td>Lynn Anderson's Greatest Hits (72)
129(1) [0|0|14]</td><td>200</td></tr>
<tr><td>Cry (72) 114(1) [0|0|9]</td><td>163</td></tr>
<tr><td>How Can I Unlove You (71) 132(2) [0|0|5]</td><td>94.1</td></tr>
<tr><td>Listen To A Country Song (72) 160(2) [0|0|7]</td><td>74.6</td></tr>
</table>

Act ► Highest Peak [Top10s | Top40s | Total] Title (Yr) Peak(Wk) [T10 Wk | T40Wk | TotalWk]	Score
Lynn ANDERSON ► *Continued*	
The World Of Lynn Anderson (71) 174(1) [0|0|4]	39.7
The Best Of Lynn Anderson (69) 180(1) [0|0|3]	32.1
Top Of The World (73) 179(1) [0|0|3]	25.1
With Love, From Lynn (69) 197(2) [0|0|2]	13.7
Michael ANDERSON ► 3512 Pk:194 [0|0|1]	**10**
Sound Alarm (88) 194(2) [0|0|2]	10.3
ANDREWS SISTERS ► 2161 Pk:126 [0|0|4]	**274**
The Best Of The Andrews Sisters (73) 126(1) [0|0|9]	151
Over Here! (Original Cast) (74) 137(1) [0|0|3]	59.1
Boogie Woogie Bugle Girls (73) 167(1) [0|0|7]	58.2
In The Mood (74) 198(1) [0|0|1]	6.0
ANGEL ► 1300 Pk:55 [0|0|6]	**1139**
White Hot (78) 55(1) [0|0|13]	533
On Earth As It Is In Heaven (77) 76(1) [0|0|12]	277
Helluva Band (76) 155(1) [0|0|10]	130
Angel (75) 156(2) [0|0|6]	80.5
Live Without A Net (80) 149(1) [0|0|4]	62.2
Sinful (79) 159(1) [0|0|5]	56.3
ANGEL CITY ► 2308 Pk:133 [0|0|3]	**213**
Darkroom (80) 133(1) [0|0|6]	101
Face To Face (80) 152(2) [0|0|7]	73.6
Night Attack (82) 174(1) [0|0|5]	38.2
The ANGELS ► 1648 Pk:33 [0|1|1]	**621**
My Boyfriend's Back (63) 33(2) [0|3|14]	621
ANIMAL LOGIC ► 2118 Pk:106 [0|0|1]	**292**
Animal Logic (89) 106(1) [0|0|21]	292
The ANIMALS/Eric BURDON & The ANIMALS ► 227 Pk:6 [2|4|17]	**15402**
The Best Of The Animals (66)-The Animals 6(3) [7|51|113]	7333
Animalization (66)-The Animals 20(2) [0|13|30]	1672
The Animals (64)-The Animals 7(3) [4|15|27]	1667
Animalism (66)-The Animals 33(2) [0|3|22]	823
Animal Tracks (65)-The Animals 57(1) [0|0|25]	726
The Twain Shall Meet (68)- Eric Burdon & The Animals 79(1) [0|0|29]	716
Winds Of Change (67)- Eric Burdon & The Animals 42(2) [0|0|20]	639
The Best Of Eric Burdon And The Animals, Vol. II (67)-Eric Burdon & The Animals 71(1) [0|0|24]	450
Before We Were So Rudely Interrupted (77)- The Animals 70(2) [0|0|11]	319
Ark (83)-The Animals 66(1) [0|0|10]	268
Love Is (69)- Eric Burdon & The Animals 123(2) [0|0|10]	198
Eric Is Here (67)- Eric Burdon And The Animals 121(1) [0|0|13]	193
The Animals On Tour (65)- The Animals 99(1) [0|0|9]	153
Every One Of Us (68)- Eric Burdon & The Animals 152(2) [0|0|8]	109
The Greatest Hits Of Eric Burdon And The Animals (69)-Eric Burdon & The Animals 153(1) [0|0|6]	98.2
Rip It To Shreds-The Animals Greatest Hits Live (84)-The Animals 193(2) [0|0|4]	19.6
The Best Of The Animals(2) (73)-The Animals 188(2) [0|0|2]	15.3
ANIMOTION ► 1059 Pk:28 [0|1|3]	**1720**
Animotion (85) 28(1) [0|7|30]	1200
Strange Behavior (86) 71(2) [0|0|14]	287
Animotion(2) (89) 110(1) [0|0|17]	232
Paul ANKA ► 444 Pk:9 [1|3|13]	**7180**
Anka (74) 9(2) [3|16|28]	3025
Times Of Your Life (75) 22(2) [0|9|25]	1862
Feelings (75) 36(2) [0|3|29]	1189

Act ► Highest Peak [Top10s | Top40s | Total] Title (Yr) Peak(Wk) [T10 Wk | T40Wk | TotalWk]	Score
The Painter (76) 85(1) [0|0|15]	415
Goodnight My Love (69) 101(2) [0|0|11]	250
Paul Anka Gold (74) 125(1) [0|0|9]	161
Walk A Fine Line (83) 156(1) [0|0|8]	74.9
Listen To Your Heart (78) 179(1) [0|0|7]	59.5
Both Sides Of Love (81) 171(2) [0|0|6]	58.8
Paul Anka (72) 188(1) [0|0|4]	28.0
Jubilation (72) 192(2) [0|0|4]	24.4
The Music Man (77) 195(2) [0|0|3]	20.0
Life Goes On (69) 194(1) [0|0|2]	13.9
ANNETTE ► 1898 Pk:39 [0|1|1]	**408**
Annette's Beach Party (63) 39(1) [0|1|13]	408
ANN-MARGRET ► 2675 Pk:83 [0|0|2]	**118**
Beauty And The Beard (64)- Al Hirt & Ann-Margret [A] 83(2) [0|0|9]	94.4
David Merrick Presents Hits From His Broadway Hits (64)- John Gary/Ann-Margret [A] 141(1) [0|0|4]	24.0
Adam ANT ► 646 Pk:16 [0|1|5]	**4268**
Friend Or Foe (82) 16(3) [0|16|36]	2159
Kings Of The Wild Frontier (81)- Adam And The Ants 44(2) [0|0|35]	1122
Strip (83) 65(3) [0|0|26]	527
Prince Charming (81)- Adam And The Ants 94(2) [0|0|21]	377
Vive Le Rock (85) 131(2) [0|0|7]	83.1
ANTHRAX ► 772 Pk:30 [0|1|4]	**3124**
I'm The Man (87) 53(1) [0|0|40]	1066
State Of Euphoria (88) 30(2) [0|5|36]	1043
Among The Living (87) 62(2) [0|0|36]	795
Spreading The Disease (85) 113(1) [0|0|18]	221
ANVIL ► 3513 Pk:191 [0|0|1]	**10**
Strength Of Steel (87) 191(1) [0|0|2]	10.2
AORTA ► 2819 Pk:167 [0|0|1]	**93**
Aorta (69) 167(1) [0|0|8]	92.6
APOLLONIA 6 ► 2008 Pk:62 [0|0|1]	**348**
Apollonia 6 (84) 62(2) [0|0|17]	348
APOLLO 100 ► 1674 Pk:47 [0|0|1]	**603**
Joy (72) 47(2) [0|0|16]	603
APPALOOSA ► 3192 Pk:178 [0|0|1]	**42**
Appaloosa (69) 178(2) [0|0|4]	41.6
Carmen APPICE ► 1605 Pk:12 [0|1|1]	**673**
Jeff Beck, Tim Bogert, Carmine Appice (73)- Beck, Bogert & Appice [A] 12(1) [0|11|27]	673
APRIL WINE ► 651 Pk:26 [0|2|6]	**4241**
The Nature Of The Beast (81) 26(1) [0|12|34]	2119
Harder...Faster (79) 64(3) [0|0|40]	865
Power Play (82) 37(2) [0|3|20]	735
Animal Grace (84) 62(1) [0|0|12]	291
First Glance (79) 114(2) [0|0|11]	205
Walking Through Fire (85) 174(2) [0|0|4]	25.7
AQUARIAN DREAM ► 2875 Pk:154 [0|0|1]	**83**
Norman Connors Presents Aquarian Dream (76) 154(1) [0|0|6]	83.5
The AQUARIANS ► 3446 Pk:192 [0|0|1]	**15**
Jungle Grass (69) 192(1) [0|0|2]	15.4
ARABIAN PRINCE ► 3521 Pk:193 [0|0|1]	**10**
Brother Arab (89) 193(1) [0|0|2]	9.6
The ARBORS ► 3275 Pk:144 [0|0|1]	**31**
A Symphony For Susan (67) 144(2) [0|0|2]	30.9
ARCADIA ► 1352 Pk:23 [0|1|1]	**1039**
So Red The Rose (85) 23(2) [0|9|17]	1039
The ARCHIES ► 946 Pk:66 [0|0|5]	**2136**
Everything's Archie (69) 66(1) [0|0|36]	1080
The Archies (68) 88(1) [0|0|21]	510

Act ► Highest Peak [Top10s | Top40s | Total] Title (Yr) Peak(Wk) [T10 Wk | T40Wk | TotalWk]	Score
The Archies Greatest Hits (70) 114(2) [0|0|12]	283
Jingle Jangle (70) 125(2) [0|0|10]	172
Sunshine (70) 137(1) [0|0|6]	89.4
AREA CODE 615 ► 3295 Pk:191 [0|0|1]	**29**
Area Code 615 (69) 191(2) [0|0|4]	28.7
ARGENT ► 1029 Pk:23 [0|1|5]	**1843**
All Together Now (72) 23(3) [0|7|23]	1403
In Deep (73) 90(2) [0|0|11]	255
Nexus (74) 149(1) [0|0|6]	79.3
Encore-Live In Concert (75) 151(2) [0|0|4]	69.8
Circus (75) 171(2) [0|0|3]	35.9
ARMADA Orchestra ► 3470 Pk:196 [0|0|1]	**13**
The Armada Orchestra (76) 196(2) [0|0|2]	12.6
ARMAGEDDON ► 2896 Pk:151 [0|0|1]	**80**
Armageddon (75) 151(1) [0|0|6]	80.4
Joan ARMATRADING ► 530 Pk:28 [0|2|11]	**5610**
Me Myself I (80) 28(2) [0|5|23]	1145
Joan Armatrading (76) 67(2) [0|0|27]	799
Show Some Emotion (77) 52(2) [0|0|21]	770
The Key (83) 32(1) [0|3|22]	696
Walk Under Ladders (81) 88(2) [0|0|32]	660
Secret Secrets (85) 73(1) [0|0|19]	392
Sleight Of Hand (86) 68(1) [0|0|16]	353
How Cruel (79) 136(1) [0|0|18]	278
The Shouting Stage (88) 100(1) [0|0|13]	201
To The Limit (78) 125(2) [0|0|12]	181
Track Record (84) 113(1) [0|0|10]	135
ARMORED SAINT ► 1717 Pk:108 [0|0|3]	**565**
Delirious Nomad (85) 108(2) [0|0|19]	232
Raising Fear (87) 114(2) [0|0|12]	177
March Of The Saint (84) 138(2) [0|0|16]	156
Louis ARMSTRONG ► 407 Pk:1 [1|1|1]	**8075**
Hello Dolly! (64) 1(6) [19|48|74]	8075
Eddy ARNOLD ► 284 Pk:7 [1|5|17]	**12308**
My World (65) 7(3) [6|28|58]	4040
The Best Of Eddy Arnold (67) 34(2) [0|2|57]	1493
I Want To Go With You (66) 26(1) [0|5|28]	1219
Somebody Like Me (66) 36(1) [0|2|30]	996
Turn The World Around (67) 34(1) [0|5|36]	957
The Romantic World Of Eddy Arnold (68) 56(2) [0|0|32]	844
The Last Word In Lonesome (66) 46(1) [0|0|22]	634
Lonely Again (67) 57(1) [0|0|24]	597
Songs Of The Young World (69) 77(1) [0|0|13]	399
Walkin' In Love Land (68) 70(1) [0|0|13]	378
The Everlovin' World Of Eddy Arnold (68) 122(2) [0|0|21]	324
The Warmth Of Eddy (69) 116(1) [0|0|8]	175
Cattle Call (63) 131(1) [0|0|5]	68.4
The Glory Of Love (69) 167(1) [0|0|5]	65.4
Portrait Of My Woman (71) 141(2) [0|0|4]	59.0
The Best Of Eddy Arnold, Volume II (70) 146(2) [0|0|2]	36.8
Love & Guitars (70) 191(2) [0|0|3]	22.0
ARPEGGIO ► 1888 Pk:75 [0|0|1]	**413**
Let The Music Play (79) 75(3) [0|0|16]	413
Steve ARRINGTON'S HALL OF FAME ► 1947 Pk:101 [0|0|3]	**377**
Steve Arrington's Hall Of Fame: I (83) 101(1) [0|0|17]	247
Positive Power (84) 141(1) [0|0|9]	102
Dancin' In The Key Of Life (85)- Steve Arrington 185(2) [0|0|5]	27.9
ART IN AMERICA ► 3380 Pk:176 [0|0|1]	**21**
Art In America (83) 176(1) [0|0|3]	20.9

Act ▶ Highest Peak [Top10s|Top40s|Total]
Title (Yr) Peak(Wk) [T10 Wk|T40Wk|TotalWk] — Score

ARTISTS UNITED AGAINST APARTHEID ▶ 1549 Pk:31 [0|1|1] — 726
Sun City (85) 31(2) [0|5|18] — 726

ART OF NOISE ▶ 1100 Pk:53 [0|0|4] — 1604
In Visible Silence (86) 53(2) [0|0|30] — 977
The Best Of The Art Of Noise (88) 83(1) [0|0|14] — 271
(Who's Afraid Of?) The Art Of Noise! (84) 85(3) [0|0|13] — 264
In No Sense? Nonsense! (87) 134(1) [0|0|9] — 92.8

The A's ▶ 2893 Pk:146 [0|0|1] — 81
A Woman's Got The Power (81) 146(1) [0|0|7] — 80.9

ASHFORD & SIMPSON ▶ 385 Pk:20 [0|4|14] — 8599
Is It Still Good To Ya (78) 20(1) [0|12|28] — 2148
Solid (84) 29(2) [0|10|36] — 1459
Send It (77) 52(1) [0|0|46] — 1434
Stay Free (79) 23(3) [0|9|23] — 1380
Street Opera (82) 45(3) [0|0|20] — 641
A Musical Affair (80) 38(2) [0|2|12] — 530
Real Love (86) 74(2) [0|0|18] — 331
High-Rise (83) 84(1) [0|0|12] — 247
Gimme Something Real (73) 156(1) [0|0|13] — 141
Love Or Physical (89) 135(2) [0|0|8] — 108
Performance (81) 125(1) [0|0|6] — 96.5
Come As You Are (76) 189(2) [0|0|4] — 31.8
So So Satisfied (77) 180(1) [0|0|3] — 27.4
I Wanna Be Selfish (74) 195(1) [0|0|4] — 23.9

ASHTON, GARDNER & DYKE ▶ 3132 Pk:178 [0|0|1] — 49
Resurrection Shuffle (71) 178(1) [0|0|6] — 48.7

ASIA ▶ 288 Pk:1 [2|2|3] — 12094
Asia (82) 1(9) [27|35|64] — 9795
Alpha (83) 6(4) [5|11|25] — 1881
Astra (85) 67(3) [0|0|17] — 418

ASLEEP AT THE WHEEL ▶ 2237 Pk:136 [0|0|4] — 240
Texas Gold (75) 136(1) [0|0|8] — 143
The Wheel (77) 162(1) [0|0|4] — 52.2
Wheelin' And Dealin' (76) 179(2) [0|0|3] — 30.6
Framed (80) 191(1) [0|0|2] — 13.9

The ASSOCIATION ▶ 192 Pk:4 [3|6|10] — 18121
Greatest Hits (68) 4(3) [10|23|75] — 6883
Insight Out (67) 8(1) [4|25|68] — 4254
And Then...Along Comes The Association (66) 5(1) [7|15|59] — 3303
Birthday (68) 23(1) [0|6|26] — 1395
The Association (69) 32(1) [0|4|17] — 782
Renaissance (67) 34(1) [0|3|15] — 676
Goodbye, Columbus (Soundtrack) (69) 99(2) [0|0|18] — 381
The Association "Live" (70) 79(1) [0|0|12] — 366
Stop Your Motor (71) 158(1) [0|0|4] — 52.5
Waterbeds In Trinidad! (72) 194(2) [0|0|5] — 27.7

Jon ASTLEY ▶ 2759 Pk:135 [0|0|1] — 103
Everybody Loves The Pilot (Except The Crew) (87) 135(2) [0|0|10] — 103

Rick ASTLEY ▶ 480 Pk:10 [1|2|2] — 6522
Whenever You Need Somebody (88) 10(2) [2|39|60] — 5157
Hold Me In Your Arms (89) 19(3) [0|10|23] — 1365

The ASTRONAUTS ▶ 2258 Pk:100 [0|0|2] — 230
Everything Is A-OK! (64) 100(1) [0|0|9] — 160
Competition Coupe (64) 123(1) [0|0|5] — 69.6

ASWAD ▶ 3125 Pk:173 [0|0|1] — 49
Distant Thunder (88) 173(3) [0|0|7] — 49.1

Chet ATKINS ▶ 1357 Pk:64 [0|0|11] — 1034
Chet Atkins Picks On The Beatles (66) 112(1) [0|0|13] — 209
Guitar Country (64) 64(1) [0|0|8] — 192
Teen Scene (63) 93(1) [0|0|6] — 117
It's A Guitar World (67) 148(2) [0|0|9] — 112
Stay Tuned (85) 145(2) [0|0|13] — 109
Solid Gold '69 (69) 150(1) [0|0|7] — 90.9
Yestergroovin' (70) 139(1) [0|0|5] — 78.9
From Nashville With Love (66) 140(1) [0|0|4] — 61.3
Chester & Lester (76)-Chet Atkins And Les Paul [A] 172(2) [0|0|5] — 26.2
Solo Flights (68) 184(1) [0|0|3] — 23.5
Class Guitar (68) 189(2) [0|0|2] — 13.6

Chet ATKINS/BOSTON POPS Orchestra ▶ 1716 Pk:62 [0|0|2] — 568
The "Pops" Goes Country (66)-Chet Atkins/Boston Pops/Arthur Fiedler 62(2) [0|0|23] — 507
Chet Picks On The Pops (69)-Chet Atkins/Boston Pops/Arthur Fiedler 160(1) [0|0|4] — 61.0

ATLANTA ▶ 2833 Pk:140 [0|0|1] — 90
Pictures (84) 140(2) [0|0|7] — 90.1

ATLANTA DISCO BAND ▶ 2865 Pk:172 [0|0|1] — 85
Bad Luck (76) 172(1) [0|0|9] — 85.4

ATLANTA RHYTHM SECTION ▶ 343 Pk:7 [1|3|10] — 9842
Champagne Jam (78) 7(2) [5|15|40] — 3722
A Rock And Roll Alternative (77) 11(1) [0|14|39] — 2926
Underdog (79) 26(3) [0|7|21] — 1315
Are You Ready! (79) 51(2) [0|0|12] — 404
The Boys From Doraville (80) 65(2) [0|0|11] — 354
Quinella (81) 70(1) [0|0|16] — 351
Third Annual Pipe Dream (74) 74(1) [0|0|12] — 325
Red Tape (76) 146(2) [0|0|15] — 212
Dog Days (75) 113(2) [0|0|9] — 176
Atlanta Rhythm Section (77) 154(1) [0|0|4] — 57.4

ATLANTIC STARR ▶ 422 Pk:17 [0|3|8] — 7569
As The Band Turns (85) 17(2) [0|14|68] — 2457
All In The Name Of Love (87) 18(1) [0|15|31] — 1929
Brilliance (82) 18(2) [0|7|29] — 1239
Radiant (81) 47(1) [0|0|30] — 995
Yours Forever (83) 91(1) [0|0|28] — 381
Atlantic Starr (78) 67(1) [0|0|13] — 380
Straight To The Point (79) 142(2) [0|0|7] — 104
We're Movin' Up (89) 125(2) [0|0|6] — 84.5

ATOMIC ROOSTER ▶ 1639 Pk:90 [0|0|3] — 629
Death Walks Behind You (71) 90(2) [0|0|15] — 417
Made In England (72) 149(1) [0|0|8] — 110
In Hearing Of Atomic Rooster (71) 167(1) [0|0|9] — 102

AUDIENCE ▶ 3153 Pk:175 [0|0|1] — 46
Lunch (72) 175(2) [0|0|5] — 46.1

AUDIO TWO ▶ 3321 Pk:185 [0|0|1] — 26
What More Can I Say? (88) 185(2) [0|0|4] — 26.2

Barbara Ann AUER ▶ 2481 Pk:145 [0|0|1] — 165
Aerobic Dancing (81) 145(2) [0|0|15] — 165

Brian AUGER ▶ 735 Pk:41 [0|0|11] — 3393
Straight Ahead (74)-Brian Auger's Oblivion Express 45(2) [0|0|20] — 933
Closer To It! (73)-Brian Auger's Oblivion Express 64(2) [0|0|31] — 793
Streetnoise (69)-Julie Driscoll/Brian Auger & The Trinity 41(1) [0|0|16] — 743
Live Oblivion, Vol. 1 (74)-Brian Auger's Oblivion Express 51(1) [0|0|13] — 464
Reinforcements (75)-Brian Auger's Oblivion Express 115(1) [0|0|8] — 167
Happiness Heartaches (77)-Brian Auger's Oblivion Express 127(2) [0|0|5] — 99.2
Second Wind (72)-Brian Auger's Oblivion Express 170(2) [0|0|7] — 64.3
Best Of Brian Auger (77) 151(2) [0|0|3] — 50.0
Live Oblivion, Vol. 2 (76)-Brian Auger's Oblivion Express 169(1) [0|0|4] — 44.6
Befour (70)-Brian Auger & The Trinity 184(1) [0|0|3] — 19.5
Jools & Brian (69)-Julie Driscoll/Brian Auger & The Trinity 194(1) [0|0|2] — 15.5

AURRA ▶ 1448 Pk:38 [0|1|2] — 893
A Little Love (82) 38(2) [0|3|15] — 619
Send Your Love (81) 103(1) [0|0|13] — 274

Patti AUSTIN ▶ 886 Pk:36 [0|1|4] — 2452
Every Home Should Have One (81) 36(8) [0|11|44] — 1862
Patti Austin (84) 87(1) [0|0|18] — 314
Havana Candy (77) 116(3) [0|0|13] — 253
Gettin' Away With Murder (85) 182(1) [0|0|4] — 22.7

AUTOGRAPH ▶ 1047 Pk:29 [0|1|3] — 1753
Sign In Please (85) 29(2) [0|12|29] — 1278
That's The Stuff (85) 92(2) [0|0|15] — 244
Loud And Clear (87) 108(2) [0|0|15] — 231

AUTOMATIC MAN ▶ 2099 Pk:109 [0|0|2] — 303
Visitors (77) 109(1) [0|0|8] — 163
Automatic Man (76) 120(1) [0|0|7] — 140

AVERAGE WHITE BAND/AWB ▶ 236 Pk:1 [3|8|10] — 14891
AWB (74)-Average White Band 1(1) [9|17|43] — 5109
Cut The Cake (75)-Average White Band 4(1) [9|11|24] — 3219
Soul Searching (76)-Average White Band 9(1) [2|10|32] — 2478
Person To Person (77)-Average White Band 28(1) [0|5|18] — 1074
Warner Communications (78)-Average White Band 28(2) [0|5|17] — 1020
Feel No Fret (79)-Average White Band 32(1) [0|3|15] — 664
Put It Where You Want It (75)-Average White Band 39(2) [0|2|13] — 620
Benny And Us (77)-Average White Band & Ben E. King [A] 33(2) [0|5|21] — 456
Shine (80)-Average White Band 116(2) [0|0|12] — 232
Volume VIII (80)-Average White Band 182(1) [0|0|2] — 18.1

AXE ▶ 1875 Pk:81 [0|0|2] — 421
Offering (82) 81(3) [0|0|20] — 358
Nemesis (83) 156(1) [0|0|6] — 62.4

Hoyt AXTON ▶ 3060 Pk:171 [0|0|2] — 58
Fearless (76) 171(1) [0|0|4] — 41.9
Southbound (75) 188(1) [0|0|2] — 16.2

Roy AYERS ▶ 938 Pk:33 [0|1|7] — 2189
Let's Do It (78) 33(1) [0|3|13] — 690
You Send Me (78) 48(2) [0|0|15] — 549
Fever (79) 67(1) [0|0|15] — 451
No Stranger To Love (79) 82(1) [0|0|18] — 378
Feeling Good (82) 160(1) [0|0|7] — 66.8
Love Fantasy (80) 157(1) [0|0|3] — 42.4
Africa, Center Of The World (81) 197(2) [0|0|2] — 11.5

Act ▶ Highest Peak [Top10s|Top40s|Total]
Title (Yr) Peak(Wk) [T10 Wk|T40Wk|TotalWk] Score

Roy AYERS UBIQUITY ▶ 926 Pk:51 [0|0|6] 2232
Everybody Loves The Sunshine (76) 51(1) [0|0|17] 733
Lifeline (77) 72(2) [0|0|25] 660
Mystic Voyage (76) 90(1) [0|0|18] 388
Vibrations (77) 74(2) [0|0|12] 331
Starbooty (78)-Ubiquity 146(1) [0|0|4] 65.0
Change Up The Groove (74) 156(1) [0|0|4] 54.0

AZTECA ▶ 2746 Pk:151 [0|0|1] 105
Azteca (73) 151(2) [0|0|9] 105

AZTEC CAMERA ▶ 2343 Pk:129 [0|0|4] 202
High Land, Hard Rain (83) 129(1) [0|0|10] 124
Knife (84) 175(2) [0|0|6] 39.8
Aztec Camera (85) 181(2) [0|0|3] 21.6
Love (87) 193(3) [0|0|3] 16.6

AZTEC TWO STEP ▶ 3248 Pk:181 [0|0|1] 33
Two's Company (76) 181(2) [0|0|4] 33.5

B

BABE RUTH ▶ 2006 Pk:75 [0|0|3] 349
Babe Ruth (75) 75(1) [0|0|7] 242
Stealin' Home (75) 169(2) [0|0|6] 56.0
First Base (73) 178(2) [0|0|6] 50.6

BABYFACE ▶ 598 Pk:14 [0|1|1] 4740
Tender Lover (89) 14(1) [0|41|61] 4740

BABYLON A.D. ▶ 1839 Pk:88 [0|0|1] 450
Babylon A.D. (89) 88(1) [0|0|28] 450

The BABYS ▶ 615 Pk:22 [0|2|6] 4600
Head First (79) 22(2) [0|10|25] 1615
Broken Heart (77) 34(3) [0|4|26] 1392
Union Jacks (80) 42(1) [0|0|22] 916
On The Edge (80) 71(2) [0|0|15] 373
The Babys (77) 133(2) [0|0|13] 206
Anthology (81) 138(1) [0|0|7] 98.3

Burt BACHARACH ▶ 545 Pk:18 [0|1|5] 5460
Make It Easy On Yourself (69) 51(2) [0|0|87] 2425
Burt Bacharach (71) 18(2) [0|12|24] 2088
Reach Out (67) 96(1) [0|0|65] 849
Burt Bacharach's Greatest Hits (74) 173(2) [0|0|5] 52.2
Living Together (74) 181(1) [0|0|6] 45.7

The BACHELORS ▶ 1757 Pk:70 [0|0|4] 515
Presenting: The Bachelors (64) 70(1) [0|0|16] 304
Marie (65) 89(1) [0|0|6] 124
No Arms Can Ever Hold You (65) 136(1) [0|0|4] 51.5
Back Again (64) 142(2) [0|0|3] 35.7

BACHMAN-TURNER OVERDRIVE ▶ 163 Pk:1 [3|5|11] 20790
Not Fragile (74) 1(1) [15|25|50] 7020
Bachman-Turner Overdrive II (74) 4(2) [11|35|75] 6892
Four Wheel Drive (75) 5(2) [4|9|22] 2340
Bachman-Turner Overdrive (73) 70(1) [0|0|68] 1602
Head On (76) 23(2) [0|7|21] 1314
Best Of B.T.O. (So Far) (76) 19(2) [0|6|15] 1203
Freeways (77) 70(1) [0|0|9] 259
Street Action (78)-BTO 130(1) [0|0|4] 74.6
Rock N' Roll Nights (79)-BTO 165(2) [0|0|4] 47.7
Bachman-Turner-Bachman As Brave Belt (75) 180(1) [0|0|3] 28.4
Bachman Turner Overdrive(2) (84) 191(1) [0|0|2] 10.6

BACK STREET CRAWLER ▶ 1663 Pk:85 [0|0|3] 609
Crawler (77)-Crawler 85(1) [0|0|13] 338
The Band Plays On (75) 111(2) [0|0|10] 190

Act ▶ Highest Peak [Top10s|Top40s|Total]
Title (Yr) Peak(Wk) [T10 Wk|T40Wk|TotalWk] Score

2nd Street (76) 140(1) [0|0|5] 81.5

BAD COMPANY ▶ 166 Pk:1 [4|6|9] 20639
Desolation Angels (79) 3(2) [14|24|37] 5595
Bad Company (74) 1(1) [8|15|64] 5083
Run With The Pack (76) 5(2) [6|15|28] 3069
Straight Shooter (75) 3(1) [5|11|33] 3006
Burnin' Sky (77) 15(2) [0|8|24] 1784
Rough Diamonds (82) 26(3) [0|6|18] 920
Dangerous Age (88) 58(2) [0|0|40] 904
Fame And Fortune (86) 106(2) [0|0|9] 140
10 From 6 (86) 137(1) [0|0|14] 138

BAD ENGLISH ▶ 822 Pk:21 [0|1|1] 2809
Bad English (89) 21(2) [0|22|52] 2809

BADFINGER ▶ 692 Pk:28 [0|2|8] 3810
Straight Up (71) 31(1) [0|3|32] 1669
No Dice (70) 28(2) [0|5|15] 1012
Magic Christian Music (70) 55(1) [0|0|17] 620
Airwaves (79) 125(1) [0|0|8] 153
Ass (73) 122(1) [0|0|8] 124
Wish You Were Here (74) 148(1) [0|0|6] 91.4
Say No More (81) 155(1) [0|0|6] 77.3
Badfinger (74) 161(1) [0|0|5] 63.3

BADGER ▶ 2962 Pk:167 [0|0|1] 70
One Live Badger (73) 167(1) [0|0|8] 70.4

BADLANDS ▶ 1560 Pk:57 [0|0|1] 720
Badlands (89) 57(2) [0|0|26] 720

Joan BAEZ ▶ 149 Pk:7 [2|9|22] 22203
Diamonds & Rust (75) 11(1) [0|17|46] 3801
Joan Baez/5 (64) 12(2) [0|28|66] 3336
Joan Baez In Concert, Part 2 (63) 7(3) [8|23|36] 3108
Blessed Are ... (71) 11(2) [0|10|23] 2387
Farewell, Angelina (65) 10(1) [1|9|27] 1298
Any Day Now (69) 30(3) [0|5|20] 1163
Come From The Shadows (72) 48(2) [0|0|24] 1027
David's Album (69) 36(2) [0|2|14] 906
From Every Stage (76) 34(1) [0|3|17] 806
Joan (67) 38(2) [0|2|20] 769
Baptism (68) 84(2) [0|0|25] 668
Gulf Winds (76) 62(1) [0|0|17] 625
Blowin' Away (77) 54(1) [0|0|14] 506
The Best Of Joan Baez (63) 45(1) [0|0|18] 458
One Day At A Time (70) 80(1) [0|0|14] 416
The First 10 Years (70) 73(2) [0|0|11] 348
The Best Of Joan C. Baez (77) 121(2) [0|0|8] 152
Honest Lullaby (79) 113(2) [0|0|7] 137
Where Are You Now, My Son? (73) 138(1) [0|0|9] 116
Hits/Greatest & Others (73) 163(1) [0|0|8] 76.7
Carry It On (Soundtrack) (72) 164(2) [0|0|5] 56.8
The Joan Baez Ballad Book (72) 188(1) [0|0|7] 42.2

Philip BAILEY ▶ 947 Pk:22 [0|1|3] 2136
Chinese Wall (84) 22(3) [0|11|35] 1633
Continuation (83) 71(1) [0|0|14] 290
Inside Out (86) 84(2) [0|0|11] 213

Razzy BAILEY ▶ 3139 Pk:176 [0|0|2] 47
Feelin' Right (82) 176(1) [0|0|4] 28.7
Makin' Friends (81) 183(2) [0|0|2] 18.7

Scott BAIO ▶ 3336 Pk:181 [0|0|1] 25
Scott Baio (82) 181(2) [0|0|4] 25.2

BAJA MARIMBA BAND ▶ 813 Pk:54 [0|0|10] 2846
Watch Out! (66) 54(1) [0|0|43] 1103
Heads Up! (67) 77(1) [0|0|44] 752
For Animals Only (66) 102(1) [0|0|16] 256

Act ▶ Highest Peak [Top10s|Top40s|Total]
Title (Yr) Peak(Wk) [T10 Wk|T40Wk|TotalWk] Score

Those Were The Days (69)-Julius Wechter and the Baja Marimba Band 117(1) [0|0|10] 236
Baja Marimba Band (64) 88(2) [0|0|12] 189
Fowl Play (68)-Julius Wechter and the Baja Marimba Band 168(1) [0|0|9] 90.3
Do You Know The Way To San Jose? (68)-Julius Wechter and the Baja Marimba Band 171(1) [0|0|8] 87.3
Greatest Hits (70)-Julius Wechter and the Baja Marimba Band 180(1) [0|0|6] 52.9
Baja Marimba Band Rides Again (65) 123(1) [0|0|3] 45.1
Fresh Air (69)-Julius Wechter and the Baja Marimba Band 176(1) [0|0|3] 34.4

Anita BAKER ▶ 220 Pk:1 [1|2|3] 15908
Rapture (86) 11(2) [0|72|157] 9452
Giving You The Best That I Got (88) 1(4) [18|28|42] 6333
The Songstress (83) 139(2) [0|0|11] 123

MARIACHI BRASS ▶ 2987 Pk:120 [0|0|1] 67
A Taste Of Tequila (66)-Mariachi Brass Feat. Chet Baker 120(1) [0|0|4] 67.3

George BAKER Selection ▶ 2294 Pk:107 [0|0|2] 219
Little Green Bag (70) 107(1) [0|0|6] 129
Paloma Blanca (76) 153(2) [0|0|7] 90.6

Ginger BAKER's Air Force ▶ 1540 Pk:33 [0|1|1] 745
Ginger Baker's Air Force (70) 33(2) [0|3|15] 745

BAKER GURVITZ ARMY ▶ 2494 Pk:140 [0|0|2] 161
The Baker Gurvitz Army (75) 140(1) [0|0|7] 98.4
Elysian Encounter (75) 165(2) [0|0|5] 62.9

BALAAM AND THE ANGEL ▶ 3344 Pk:174 [0|0|1] 25
Live Free Or Die (88) 174(1) [0|0|3] 24.6

BALANCE ▶ 2603 Pk:133 [0|0|1] 134
Balance (81) 133(1) [0|0|12] 134

Long John BALDRY ▶ 1725 Pk:83 [0|0|2] 559
It Ain't Easy (71) 83(1) [0|0|18] 510
Everything Stops For Tea (72) 180(1) [0|0|6] 48.7

Marty BALIN ▶ 1315 Pk:35 [0|1|2] 1114
Balin (81) 35(2) [0|3|23] 1063
Lucky (83) 156(2) [0|0|6] 51.2

Russ BALLARD ▶ 2389 Pk:147 [0|0|3] 189
Russ Ballard (84) 147(2) [0|0|13] 139
The Fire Still Burns (85) 166(2) [0|0|4] 35.2
Barnet Dogs (80) 187(1) [0|0|2] 14.9

BALLIN' JACK ▶ 3049 Pk:180 [0|0|1] 59
Ballin' Jack (71) 180(1) [0|0|8] 59.3

BALTIMORA ▶ 1847 Pk:49 [0|0|1] 446
Living In The Background (86) 49(2) [0|0|17] 446

BALTIMORE And OHIO MARCHING BAND ▶ 3333 Pk:177 [0|0|1] 25
Lapland (68) 177(1) [0|0|3] 25.5

BANANARAMA ▶ 667 Pk:15 [0|2|5] 4094
True Confessions (86) 15(2) [0|11|28] 1497
Bananarama (84) 30(5) [0|7|36] 1349
Wow! (87) 44(2) [0|0|26] 727
Deep Sea Skiving (83) 63(1) [0|0|19] 437
Greatest Hits Collection (88) 151(2) [0|0|9] 84.8

The BAND ▶ 193 Pk:5 [3|8|10] 17981
The Band (69) 9(1) [1|24|49] 5473
Rock Of Ages (72) 6(2) [7|14|28] 2929
Stage Fright (70) 5(1) [4|14|22] 2635
Music From Big Pink (68) 30(1) [0|7|40] 1452
The Last Waltz (Soundtrack) (78) 16(2) [0|8|20] 1452

Act ► Highest Peak [Top10s|Top40s|Total]
Title (Yr) Peak(Wk) [T10 Wk|T40Wk|TotalWk] — **Score**

The BAND ► *Continued*
Moondog Matinee (73) 28(1) [0|6|20] — 1062
Northern Lights-Southern Cross (75) 26(1) [0|5|19] — 1042
The Best Of The Band (76) 51(2) [0|0|14] — 515
Islands (77) 64(2) [0|0|10] — 315

BAND Of The BLACK WATCH ► 3151 Pk:164 [0|0|1] — 46
Scotch On The Rocks (76) 164(1) [0|0|4] — 46.2

Moe BANDY ► 3391 Pk:170 [0|0|1] — 20
Hey Joe, Hey Moe (81)-Moe Bandy & Joe Stampley [A] 170(1) [0|0|4] — 20.0

BANG ► 2751 Pk:164 [0|0|1] — 104
Bang (72) 164(1) [0|0|10] — 104

The BANGLES ► 344 Pk:2 [1|2|3] — 9839
Different Light (86) 2(2) [9|45|82] — 6569
Everything (88) 15(2) [0|19|42] — 2818
All Over the Place (84) 80(2) [0|0|30] — 452

BANGOR FLYING CIRCUS ► 3437 Pk:190 [0|0|1] — 16
Bangor Flying Circus (69) 190(2) [0|0|2] — 16.2

BANG TANGO ► 1497 Pk:58 [0|0|1] — 813
Psycho Cafe (89) 58(2) [0|0|39] — 813

Peter BANKS ► 2808 Pk:152 [0|0|1] — 96
Two Sides Of Peter Banks (73) 152(1) [0|0|8] — 95.8

Tony BANKS ► 3158 Pk:171 [0|0|1] — 46
A Curious Feeling (79) 171(1) [0|0|5] — 45.6

Frank BARBER Orchestra ► 2170 Pk:94 [0|0|1] — 269
Hooked On Big Bands (82) 94(3) [0|0|16] — 269

Gato BARBIERI ► 1027 Pk:66 [0|0|6] — 1850
Caliente! (76) 75(1) [0|0|32] — 811
Ruby, Ruby (77) 66(1) [0|0|20] — 593
Euphoria (79) 116(1) [0|0|9] — 179
Tropico (78) 96(1) [0|0|7] — 159
Last Tango In Paris (Soundtrack) (73) 166(1) [0|0|7] — 66.3
Chapter Three - Viva Emiliano Zapata (74) 160(2) [0|0|3] — 41.8

Keith BARBOUR ► 3066 Pk:163 [0|0|1] — 57
Echo Park (69) 163(2) [0|0|4] — 56.6

BARCLAY JAMES HARVEST ► 3261 Pk:174 [0|0|1] — 32
Octoberon (77) 174(1) [0|0|3] — 32.2

Pete BARDENS ► 3088 Pk:148 [0|0|1] — 54
Seen One Earth (87) 148(2) [0|0|5] — 53.6

BARDEUX ► 2132 Pk:104 [0|0|2] — 286
Bold As Love (88) 104(2) [0|0|12] — 200
Shangri-La (89) 133(2) [0|0|7] — 85.8

Bobby BARE ► 2695 Pk:119 [0|0|2] — 115
500 Miles Away From Home (64) 133(1) [0|0|5] — 68.6
"Detroit City" And Other Hits (63) 119(1) [0|0|3] — 46.0

The BAR-KAYS ► 477 Pk:35 [0|1|12] — 6588
Injoy (79)-Bar-Kays 35(3) [0|4|24] — 1054
Nightcruising (81)-Bar-Kays 55(2) [0|0|29] — 912
Flying High On Your Love (77)-Bar-Kays 47(2) [0|0|23] — 794
Too Hot To Stop (76)-Bar-Kays 69(1) [0|0|22] — 703
Propositions (82)-Bar-Kays 51(3) [0|0|29] — 683
Dangerous (84)-Bar-Kays 52(1) [0|0|22] — 555
As One (80)-Bar-Kays 57(1) [0|0|16] — 476
Money Talks (78)-Bar-Kays 72(2) [0|0|15] — 430
Light Of Life (78)-Bar-Kays 86(1) [0|0|17] — 404
Black Rock (71)-Bar-Kays 90(2) [0|0|12] — 296
Contagious (87)-Bar-Kays 110(2) [0|0|14] — 163
Banging The Wall (85)-Bar-Kays 115(2) [0|0|9] — 118

Jimmy BARNES ► 1823 Pk:104 [0|0|2] — 466
Freight Train Heart (88) 104(3) [0|0|15] — 248
Jimmy Barnes (86) 109(2) [0|0|16] — 219

BARRABAS ► 2774 Pk:149 [0|0|1] — 101
Heart Of The City (75) 149(1) [0|0|7] — 101

Syd BARRETT ► 3112 Pk:163 [0|0|1] — 51
The Madcap Laughs (74) 163(2) [0|0|4] — 50.9

Claudja BARRY ► 1980 Pk:101 [0|0|2] — 363
Boogie Woogie Dancin' Shoes (79) 101(1) [0|0|10] — 219
Claudja (78) 131(2) [0|0|10] — 144

Len BARRY ► 2224 Pk:90 [0|0|1] — 244
1-2-3 (65) 90(1) [0|0|13] — 244

Lou Ann BARTON ► 2726 Pk:133 [0|0|1] — 109
Old Enough (82) 133(1) [0|0|9] — 109

BASIA ► 878 Pk:36 [0|1|1] — 2498
Time And Tide (88) 36(1) [0|3|77] — 2498

Count BASIE ► 1758 Pk:69 [0|0|8] — 515
Ella And Basie! (63)-Ella & Basie [A] 69(1) [0|0|20] — 212
Arthur Prysock/Count Basie (66)-Arthur Prysock/Count Basie [A] 107(1) [0|0|13] — 116
Li'l Ol' Groovemaker...Basie! (63) 123(1) [0|0|5] — 78.9
The Board Of Directors (68)-Count Basie & The Mills Brothers [A] 145(1) [0|0|6] — 34.1
Broadway - Basie's Way (66) 143(1) [0|0|2] — 29.2
Our Shining Hour (65)-Sammy Davis-Count Basie [A] 141(1) [0|0|4] — 24.1
More Hits Of The 50's And 60's (64) 150(1) [0|0|1] — 12.0
Manufacturers Of Soul (68)-Jackie Wilson And Count Basie [A] 195(2) [0|0|3] — 9.0

Toni BASIL ► 1148 Pk:22 [0|1|1] — 1472
Word Of Mouth (82) 22(7) [0|9|30] — 1472

Fontella BASS ► 2498 Pk:93 [0|0|1] — 160
The New Look (66) 93(1) [0|0|8] — 160

Shirley BASSEY ► 952 Pk:60 [0|0|10] — 2134
Never, Never, Never (73) 60(1) [0|0|19] — 548
Something Else (71) 123(1) [0|0|24] — 397
I Capricorn (72) 94(2) [0|0|13] — 321
Shirley Bassey Is Really "Something" (70) 105(1) [0|0|13] — 277
Shirley Bassey Belts The Best! (65) 85(1) [0|0|9] — 161
Live At Carnegie Hall (73) 136(1) [0|0|8] — 129
Love, Life & Feelings (76) 149(1) [0|0|8] — 109
Nobody Does It Like Me (74) 142(1) [0|0|6] — 86.6
And I Love You So (72) 171(1) [0|0|8] — 78.3
Good, Bad But Beautiful (75) 186(1) [0|0|3] — 26.2

BATDORF & RODNEY ► 2334 Pk:140 [0|0|2] — 204
Life Is You (75)-Batdorf And Rodney 140(2) [0|0|10] — 157
Batdorf & Rodney (72) 185(1) [0|0|7] — 47.6

BAUHAUS ► 3120 Pk:169 [0|0|1] — 50
Swing The Heartache - The BBC Sessions (89) 169(1) [0|0|6] — 49.8

BAY CITY ROLLERS ► 526 Pk:20 [0|4|6] — 5777
Bay City Rollers (75) 20(2) [0|9|35] — 2107
Dedication (76) 26(1) [0|7|25] — 1363
It's A Game (77) 23(2) [0|7|11] — 971
Rock N' Roll Love Letter (76) 31(1) [0|4|16] — 932
Greatest Hits (77) 77(1) [0|0|11] — 317
Strangers In The Wind (78) 129(1) [0|0|4] — 86.5

BEACH BOYS ► 21 Pk:1 [12|18|38] — 59702
Endless Summer (74) 1(1) [6|19|156] — 6903
Beach Boys Concert (64) 1(4) [20|40|62] — 6309
All Summer Long (64) 4(5) [16|38|49] — 4899
The Beach Boys Today! (65) 4(6) [14|29|50] — 4482
Best Of The Beach Boys (66) 8(1) [6|18|78] — 3529
Summer Days (And Summer Nights!!) (65) 2(1) [10|17|33] — 3318
Little Deuce Coupe (63) 4(2) [8|20|46] — 3127
Surfer Girl (63) 7(2) [4|18|56] — 3030
Pet Sounds (66) 10(1) [1|21|44] — 2810
Spirit Of America (75) 8(2) [4|13|43] — 2808
Shut Down, Volume 2 (64) 13(2) [0|22|38] — 2630
15 Big Ones (76) 8(1) [3|12|27] — 2437
Beach Boys' Party! (65) 6(1) [4|14|24] — 1962
Surf's Up (71) 29(1) [0|7|17] — 1232
Good Vibrations/Best Of The Beach Boys (75) 25(2) [0|5|23] — 1113
The Beach Boys In Concert (73) 25(1) [0|5|24] — 1104
Holland (73) 36(1) [0|3|30] — 1051
Wild Honey (67) 24(2) [0|9|15] — 991
Smiley Smile (67) 41(1) [0|0|21] — 786
Pet Sounds/Carl And The Passions - So Tough (72) 50(2) [0|0|20] — 771
Best Of The Beach Boys, Vol. 2 (67) 50(2) [0|0|22] — 557
Still Cruisin' (89) 46(1) [0|0|22] — 556
Wild Honey & 20/20 (74) 50(1) [0|0|11] — 482
The Beach Boys (85) 52(3) [0|0|14] — 429
20/20 (69) 68(1) [0|0|11] — 395
Beach Boys '69 (The Beach Boys Live In London) (76) 75(2) [0|0|10] — 305
L.A. (Light Album) (79) 100(1) [0|0|13] — 288
Love You (77) 53(1) [0|0|7] — 267
Made In U.S.A. (86) 96(1) [0|0|12] — 206
Friends (68) 126(1) [0|0|10] — 176
Keepin' The Summer Alive (80) 75(1) [0|0|6] — 157
Friends & Smiley Smile (74) 125(2) [0|0|6] — 128
Close-Up (69) 136(2) [0|0|6] — 125
Best Of The Beach Boys, Vol. 3 (68) 153(1) [0|0|6] — 89.4
Ten Years Of Harmony (1970-1980) (81) 156(1) [0|0|8] — 76.0
M.I.U. Album (78) 151(3) [0|0|4] — 68.1
Sunflower (70) 151(1) [0|0|4] — 64.5
Sunshine Dream (82) 180(3) [0|0|6] — 41.4

BEACON STREET UNION ► 1738 Pk:75 [0|0|2] — 535
The Eyes Of The Beacon Street Union (68) 75(3) [0|0|16] — 429
The Clown Died In Marvin Gardens (68) 173(1) [0|0|10] — 106

The BEARS ► 3133 Pk:159 [0|0|1] — 49
Rise And Shine (88) 159(1) [0|0|5] — 48.6

BEAST ► 3451 Pk:195 [0|0|1] — 15
Beast (69) 195(2) [0|0|2] — 14.7

BEASTIE BOYS ► 372 Pk:1 [1|2|2] — 8839
Licensed To Ill (86) 1(7) [19|37|68] — 7721
Paul's Boutique (89) 14(2) [0|8|15] — 1118

BEAT FARMERS ► 2350 Pk:131 [0|0|3] — 199
The Pursuit Of Happiness (87) 131(1) [0|0|8] — 96.7
Van Go (86) 135(2) [0|0|9] — 85.9
Tales Of The New West (85) 186(1) [0|0|3] — 16.5

<table>
<tr><th>Act ▶ Highest Peak [Top10s|Top40s|Total]
Title (Yr) Peak(Wk) [T10 Wk|T40Wk|TotalWk]</th><th>Score</th></tr>
<tr><td>The BEATLES ▶ 1 Pk:1 [23|27|37]</td><td>169751</td></tr>
<tr><td>Sgt. Pepper's Lonely Hearts Club Band (67) 1(15) [33|63|175]</td><td>17889</td></tr>
<tr><td>Abbey Road (69) 1(11) [27|32|129]</td><td>15679</td></tr>
<tr><td>The Beatles [White Album] (68) 1(9) [15|25|155]</td><td>13693</td></tr>
<tr><td>A Hard Day's Night (Soundtrack) (64) 1(14) [28|40|51]</td><td>9013</td></tr>
<tr><td>Meet The Beatles! (64) 1(11) [21|27|71]</td><td>8283</td></tr>
<tr><td>The Beatles 1967-1970 (73) 1(1) [11|21|169]</td><td>8202</td></tr>
<tr><td>Magical Mystery Tour (Soundtrack) (67) 1(8) [14|30|91]</td><td>8172</td></tr>
<tr><td>Help! (Soundtrack) (65) 1(9) [15|33|44]</td><td>6986</td></tr>
<tr><td>Let It Be (Soundtrack) (70) 1(4) [10|20|59]</td><td>6889</td></tr>
<tr><td>Beatles '65 (65) 1(9) [16|38|71]</td><td>6884</td></tr>
<tr><td>The Beatles 1962-1966 (73) 3(2) [8|18|164]</td><td>6830</td></tr>
<tr><td>Revolver (66) 1(6) [14|24|77]</td><td>6808</td></tr>
<tr><td>Rubber Soul (65) 1(6) [14|39|59]</td><td>6749</td></tr>
<tr><td>Something New (64) 2(9) [18|28|41]</td><td>5426</td></tr>
<tr><td>Introducing...The Beatles (64) 2(9) [15|26|49]</td><td>5276</td></tr>
<tr><td>The Beatles' Second Album (64) 1(5) [15|26|55]</td><td>5191</td></tr>
<tr><td>Hey Jude (70) 2(4) [11|17|33]</td><td>4999</td></tr>
<tr><td>Beatles VI (65) 1(6) [13|21|41]</td><td>4898</td></tr>
<tr><td>"Yesterday" And Today (66) 1(5) [9|15|31]</td><td>4104</td></tr>
<tr><td>Yellow Submarine (Soundtrack) (69) 2(2) [6|12|25]</td><td>3755</td></tr>
<tr><td>Rock 'N' Roll Music (76) 2(2) [9|13|30]</td><td>3564</td></tr>
<tr><td>The Beatles At The Hollywood Bowl (77) 2(2) [4|8|17]</td><td>2503</td></tr>
<tr><td>The Beatles' Story (64) 7(4) [5|9|17]</td><td>1335</td></tr>
<tr><td>Love Songs (77) 24(2) [0|7|31]</td><td>1319</td></tr>
<tr><td>Rarities (80) 21(1) [0|9|15]</td><td>1091</td></tr>
<tr><td>Reel Music (82) 19(3) [0|8|12]</td><td>869</td></tr>
<tr><td>The American Tour With Ed Rudy (64) 20(2) [0|9|13]</td><td>818</td></tr>
<tr><td>The Early Beatles (65) 43(1) [0|0|35]</td><td>807</td></tr>
<tr><td>20 Greatest Hits (82) 50(2) [0|0|28]</td><td>693</td></tr>
<tr><td>The Beatles With Tony Sheridan And Their Guests (64) 68(2) [0|0|14]</td><td>295</td></tr>
<tr><td>Songs, Pictures And Stories Of The Fabulous Beatles (64) 63(1) [0|0|11]</td><td>233</td></tr>
<tr><td>The Beatles Featuring Tony Sheridan - In The Beginning (Circa 1960) (70) 117(2) [0|0|7]</td><td>139</td></tr>
<tr><td>The Beatles Live! At The Star-Club In Hamburg, Germany; 1962 (77) 111(1) [0|0|7]</td><td>128</td></tr>
<tr><td>Past Masters - Volume 2 (88) 121(2) [0|0|7]</td><td>104</td></tr>
<tr><td>Past Masters - Volume 1 (88) 149(2) [0|0|6]</td><td>60.8</td></tr>
<tr><td>Jolly What! The Beatles & Frank Ifield (64)-The Beatles/Frank Ifield [A] 104(1) [0|0|6]</td><td>50.7</td></tr>
<tr><td>The Beatles vs. The Four Seasons (64)-The Beatles/Four Seasons [A] 142(1) [0|0|3]</td><td>17.8</td></tr>
<tr><td>BEAU BRUMMELS ▶ 1384 Pk:24 [0|1|3]</td><td>989</td></tr>
<tr><td>Introducing The Beau Brummels (65) 24(1) [0|7|21]</td><td>950</td></tr>
<tr><td>The Beau Brummels (75) 180(2) [0|0|3]</td><td>29.1</td></tr>
<tr><td>Triangle (67) 197(1) [0|0|2]</td><td>9.9</td></tr>
<tr><td>Jean BEAUVOIR ▶ 2185 Pk:93 [0|0|1]</td><td>265</td></tr>
<tr><td>Drums Along The Mohawk (86) 93(2) [0|0|15]</td><td>265</td></tr>
<tr><td>BE BOP DELUXE ▶ 1240 Pk:65 [0|0|4]</td><td>1254</td></tr>
<tr><td>Live! In The Air Age (77) 65(1) [0|0|15]</td><td>495</td></tr>
<tr><td>Sunburst Finish (76) 96(2) [0|0|17]</td><td>344</td></tr>
<tr><td>Drastic Plastic (78) 95(2) [0|0|9]</td><td>222</td></tr>
<tr><td>Modern Music (76) 88(1) [0|0|8]</td><td>193</td></tr>
<tr><td>Jeff BECK ▶ 318 Pk:4 [1|7|8]</td><td>10683</td></tr>
<tr><td>Blow By Blow (75) 4(1) [4|11|25]</td><td>2731</td></tr>
<tr><td>Truth (68) 15(1) [0|14|33]</td><td>2689</td></tr>
<tr><td>Wired (76) 16(1) [0|9|25]</td><td>1931</td></tr>
</table>

<table>
<tr><th>Act ▶ Highest Peak [Top10s|Top40s|Total]
Title (Yr) Peak(Wk) [T10 Wk|T40Wk|TotalWk]</th><th>Score</th></tr>
<tr><td>There And Back (80) 21(2) [0|8|20]</td><td>1358</td></tr>
<tr><td>Jeff Beck, Tim Bogert, Carmine Appice (73)-Beck, Bogert & Appice [A] 12(1) [0|11|27]</td><td>673</td></tr>
<tr><td>Flash (85) 39(2) [0|2|18]</td><td>652</td></tr>
<tr><td>Jeff Beck With The Jan Hammer Group Live (77)-Jeff Beck With The Jan Hammer Group [A] 23(1) [0|6|15]</td><td>497</td></tr>
<tr><td>Jeff Beck's Guitar Shop (89)-Jeff Beck With Terry Bozzio & Tony Hymas [A] 49(2) [0|0|18]</td><td>152</td></tr>
<tr><td>Jeff BECK Group ▶ 644 Pk:15 [0|2|3]</td><td>4285</td></tr>
<tr><td>Beck-Ola (69) 15(3) [0|8|21]</td><td>1841</td></tr>
<tr><td>Jeff Beck Group (72) 19(2) [0|9|26]</td><td>1694</td></tr>
<tr><td>Rough And Ready (71) 46(2) [0|0|16]</td><td>750</td></tr>
<tr><td>Joe BECK ▶ 2941 Pk:140 [0|0|1]</td><td>73</td></tr>
<tr><td>Beck (75) 140(1) [0|0|5]</td><td>73.4</td></tr>
<tr><td>--Bee, Celi see: Celi Bee</td><td></td></tr>
<tr><td>--Beefheart, Captain see: Captain Beefheart</td><td></td></tr>
<tr><td>BEE GEES ▶ 14 Pk:1 [8|15|25]</td><td>69117</td></tr>
<tr><td>Saturday Night Fever (Soundtrack) (77) 1(24) [35|54|120]</td><td>19144</td></tr>
<tr><td>Spirits Having Flown (79) 1(6) [18|26|55]</td><td>8229</td></tr>
<tr><td>Here At Last...Bee Gees...Live (77) 8(1) [4|31|90]</td><td>6803</td></tr>
<tr><td>Children Of The World (76) 8(3) [5|27|63]</td><td>5355</td></tr>
<tr><td>Main Course (75) 14(1) [0|22|75]</td><td>4461</td></tr>
<tr><td>Bee Gees Greatest (79) 1(1) [13|17|32]</td><td>4406</td></tr>
<tr><td>Best Of Bee Gees (69) 9(1) [3|16|49]</td><td>4241</td></tr>
<tr><td>Bee Gees' 1st (67) 7(1) [5|18|52]</td><td>3047</td></tr>
<tr><td>Staying Alive (Soundtrack) (83) 6(2) [6|14|27]</td><td>2100</td></tr>
<tr><td>Odessa (69) 20(3) [0|10|25]</td><td>1972</td></tr>
<tr><td>Idea (68) 17(3) [0|7|27]</td><td>1886</td></tr>
<tr><td>Horizontal (68) 12(1) [0|7|22]</td><td>1349</td></tr>
<tr><td>Bee Gees Gold, Volume One (76) 50(1) [0|0|33]</td><td>1071</td></tr>
<tr><td>Trafalgar (71) 34(1) [0|6|14]</td><td>966</td></tr>
<tr><td>2 Years On (71) 32(2) [0|5|14]</td><td>857</td></tr>
<tr><td>To Whom It May Concern (72) 35(1) [0|3|14]</td><td>697</td></tr>
<tr><td>Living Eyes (81) 41(3) [0|0|12]</td><td>598</td></tr>
<tr><td>Rare Precious & Beautiful (68) 99(1) [0|0|12]</td><td>346</td></tr>
<tr><td>Life In A Tin Can (73) 69(2) [0|0|13]</td><td>344</td></tr>
<tr><td>One (89) 68(2) [0|0|13]</td><td>331</td></tr>
<tr><td>Best Of Bee Gees, Vol. 2 (73) 98(1) [0|0|16]</td><td>320</td></tr>
<tr><td>Cucumber Castle (70) 94(2) [0|0|8]</td><td>218</td></tr>
<tr><td>Rare Precious & Beautiful, Volume 2 (70) 100(1) [0|0|8]</td><td>177</td></tr>
<tr><td>E-S-P (87) 96(2) [0|0|9]</td><td>152</td></tr>
<tr><td>Mr. Natural (74) 178(1) [0|0|5]</td><td>45.3</td></tr>
<tr><td>Harry BELAFONTE ▶ 1066 Pk:17 [0|1|8]</td><td>1697</td></tr>
<tr><td>Belafonte At The Greek Theatre (64) 17(1) [0|10|20]</td><td>1149</td></tr>
<tr><td>In My Quiet Room (66) 82(1) [0|0|10]</td><td>220</td></tr>
<tr><td>An Evening With Belafonte/Makeba (65)-Harry Belafonte & Miriam Makeba [A] 85(1) [0|0|11]</td><td>113</td></tr>
<tr><td>Ballads, Blues And Boasters (64) 103(1) [0|0|7]</td><td>104</td></tr>
<tr><td>An Evening With Belafonte/Mouskouri (66)-Harry Belafonte & Nana Mouskouri [A] 124(1) [0|0|8]</td><td>58.8</td></tr>
<tr><td>Calypso In Brass (67) 172(1) [0|0|2]</td><td>20.0</td></tr>
<tr><td>Homeward Bound (70) 192(1) [0|0|3]</td><td>19.7</td></tr>
<tr><td>Belafonte On Campus (67) 199(1) [0|0|3]</td><td>13.0</td></tr>
<tr><td>Adrian BELEW ▶ 1877 Pk:82 [0|0|3]</td><td>420</td></tr>
<tr><td>Mr. Music Head (89) 114(1) [0|0|11]</td><td>173</td></tr>
<tr><td>Lone Rhino (82) 82(2) [0|0|9]</td><td>172</td></tr>
<tr><td>Twang Bar King (83) 146(2) [0|0|7]</td><td>75.4</td></tr>
</table>

<table>
<tr><th>Act ▶ Highest Peak [Top10s|Top40s|Total]
Title (Yr) Peak(Wk) [T10 Wk|T40Wk|TotalWk]</th><th>Score</th></tr>
<tr><td>Archie BELL & The DRELLS ▶ 1721 Pk:95 [0|0|3]</td><td>562</td></tr>
<tr><td>Dance Your Troubles Away (76) 95(1) [0|0|20]</td><td>390</td></tr>
<tr><td>Tighten Up (68) 142(1) [0|0|8]</td><td>129</td></tr>
<tr><td>There's Gonna Be A Showdown (69) 163(1) [0|0|3]</td><td>44.0</td></tr>
<tr><td>Maggie BELL ▶ 2015 Pk:122 [0|0|2]</td><td>344</td></tr>
<tr><td>Queen Of The Night (74) 122(1) [0|0|13]</td><td>206</td></tr>
<tr><td>Suicide Sal (75) 130(2) [0|0|8]</td><td>139</td></tr>
<tr><td>Vincent BELL ▶ 2220 Pk:75 [0|0|1]</td><td>246</td></tr>
<tr><td>Airport Love Theme (70) 75(2) [0|0|8]</td><td>246</td></tr>
<tr><td>William BELL ▶ 1959 Pk:63 [0|0|1]</td><td>373</td></tr>
<tr><td>Coming Back For More (77) 63(2) [0|0|12]</td><td>373</td></tr>
<tr><td>BELLAMY BROTHERS ▶ 2059 Pk:69 [0|0|1]</td><td>320</td></tr>
<tr><td>Bellamy Brothers (76) 69(2) [0|0|12]</td><td>320</td></tr>
<tr><td>BELL And JAMES ▶ 1327 Pk:31 [0|1|2]</td><td>1089</td></tr>
<tr><td>Bell & James (79)-Bell & James 31(1) [0|4|19]</td><td>1006</td></tr>
<tr><td>Only Make Believe (79)-Bell & James 125(2) [0|0|4]</td><td>83.4</td></tr>
<tr><td>Regina BELLE ▶ 1184 Pk:63 [0|0|2]</td><td>1384</td></tr>
<tr><td>Stay With Me (89) 63(2) [0|0|44]</td><td>1106</td></tr>
<tr><td>All By Myself (87) 85(1) [0|0|15]</td><td>278</td></tr>
<tr><td>BELLE STARS ▶ 3502 Pk:191 [0|0|1]</td><td>11</td></tr>
<tr><td>The Belle Stars (83) 191(1) [0|0|2]</td><td>11.2</td></tr>
<tr><td>The BELLS ▶ 2004 Pk:90 [0|0|1]</td><td>350</td></tr>
<tr><td>Fly, Little White Dove, Fly (71) 90(1) [0|0|14]</td><td>350</td></tr>
<tr><td>Pat BENATAR ▶ 81 Pk:1 [3|8|9]</td><td>34030</td></tr>
<tr><td>Crimes Of Passion (80) 2(5) [29|38|93]</td><td>11064</td></tr>
<tr><td>Precious Time (81) 1(1) [14|30|54]</td><td>6605</td></tr>
<tr><td>In The Heat Of The Night (79) 12(2) [0|15|122]</td><td>5547</td></tr>
<tr><td>Get Nervous (82) 4(5) [12|27|46]</td><td>4128</td></tr>
<tr><td>Live From Earth (83) 13(2) [0|16|34]</td><td>2147</td></tr>
<tr><td>Tropico (84) 14(4) [0|15|22]</td><td>1780</td></tr>
<tr><td>Wide Awake In Dreamland (88) 28(2) [0|10|29]</td><td>1272</td></tr>
<tr><td>Seven The Hard Way (85) 26(4) [0|9|20]</td><td>1004</td></tr>
<tr><td>Best Shots (89) 67(1) [0|0|20]</td><td>483</td></tr>
<tr><td>Tony BENNETT ▶ 353 Pk:18 [0|4|21]</td><td>9576</td></tr>
<tr><td>Tony's Greatest Hits, Vol. III (65) 20(1) [0|18|42]</td><td>2192</td></tr>
<tr><td>The Movie Song Album (66) 18(2) [0|12|29]</td><td>1804</td></tr>
<tr><td>This Is All I Ask (63) 24(1) [0|8|30]</td><td>1288</td></tr>
<tr><td>The Many Moods Of Tony (64) 20(2) [0|8|24]</td><td>1139</td></tr>
<tr><td>If I Ruled The World - Songs For The Jet Set (65) 47(2) [0|0|22]</td><td>642</td></tr>
<tr><td>Who Can I Turn To (64) 42(2) [0|0|19]</td><td>616</td></tr>
<tr><td>A Time For Love (66) 68(1) [0|0|18]</td><td>512</td></tr>
<tr><td>Love Story (71) 67(2) [0|0|13]</td><td>369</td></tr>
<tr><td>When Lights Are Low (64) 79(1) [0|0|12]</td><td>205</td></tr>
<tr><td>Tony Sings The Great Hits Of Today! (70) 144(1) [0|0|11]</td><td>150</td></tr>
<tr><td>With Love (72) 167(2) [0|0|14]</td><td>140</td></tr>
<tr><td>I've Gotta Be Me (69) 137(2) [0|0|5]</td><td>97.2</td></tr>
<tr><td>Tony Bennett's Greatest Hits, Volume IV (69) 174(1) [0|0|8]</td><td>84.2</td></tr>
<tr><td>For Once In My Life (68) 164(1) [0|0|7]</td><td>67.3</td></tr>
<tr><td>Tony Bennett's All-Time Greatest Hits (72) 175(2) [0|0|7]</td><td>66.6</td></tr>
<tr><td>The Art Of Excellence (86) 160(2) [0|0|8]</td><td>62.2</td></tr>
<tr><td>Tony Makes It Happen! (67) 178(1) [0|0|6]</td><td>47.2</td></tr>
<tr><td>The Good Things In Life (72) 196(3) [0|0|6]</td><td>33.4</td></tr>
<tr><td>Summer Of '42 (72) 182(2) [0|0|4]</td><td>33.2</td></tr>
<tr><td>Tony Bennett's "Something" (70) 193(1) [0|0|2]</td><td>14.2</td></tr>
<tr><td>Get Happy with the London Philharmonic Orchestra (71) 195(1) [0|0|2]</td><td>13.5</td></tr>
<tr><td>Marc BENNO ▶ 1965 Pk:70 [0|0|2]</td><td>369</td></tr>
<tr><td>Asylum Choir II (71)-Leon Russell & Marc Benno [A] 70(2) [0|0|20]</td><td>288</td></tr>
<tr><td>Ambush (72) 171(2) [0|0|8]</td><td>81.1</td></tr>
</table>

Act ► Highest Peak [Top10s|Top40s|Total] — Score
Title (Yr) Peak(Wk) [T10 Wk|T40Wk|TotalWk] — Score

David BENOIT ► 1867 Pk:101 [0|0|3] — 430
Urban Daydreams (89) 101(2) [0|0|14] — 222
Every Step Of The Way (88) 129(2) [0|0|14] — 191
Waiting For Spring (89) 187(1) [0|0|3] — 16.9

George BENSON ► 93 Pk:1 [5|7|18] — 30929
Breezin' (76) 1(2) [15|22|78] — 8344
Give Me The Night (80) 3(2) [10|20|38] — 4441
Weekend In L.A. (78) 5(3) [10|19|38] — 4426
In Flight (77) 9(2) [3|17|35] — 3477
Livin' Inside Your Love (79) 7(2) [5|13|26] — 2783
The George Benson Collection (81) 14(2) [0|14|26] — 2205
In Your Eyes (83) 27(1) [0|11|35] — 1711
20/20 (85) 45(3) [0|0|32] — 809
Good King Bad (76) 51(2) [0|0|16] — 649
Bad Benson (74) 78(1) [0|0|19] — 515
While The City Sleeps... (86) 77(1) [0|0|24] — 440
Collaboration (87)-George Benson/Earl Klugh [A] 59(2) [0|0|31] — 389
Twice The Love (88) 76(2) [0|0|10] — 231
Other Side Of Abbey Road (76) 125(1) [0|0|8] — 151
George Benson In Concert-Carnegie Hall (77) 122(1) [0|0|8] — 148
Benson & Farrell (76)- George Benson & Joe Farrell [A] 100(1) [0|0|8] — 81.2
Tenderly (89) 140(2) [0|0|6] — 73.1
Tell It Like It Is (69) 145(2) [0|0|3] — 57.7

Brook BENTON ► 125 Pk:27 [0|1|4] — 1223
Brook Benton Today (70) 27(1) [0|4|23] — 1144
Laura (What's He Got That I Ain't Got) (67) 156(1) [0|0|4] — 50.3
Do Your Own Thing (69) 189(1) [0|0|2] — 17.7
Home Style (70) 199(2) [0|0|2] — 11.3

Gertrude BERG ► 2445 Pk:131 [0|0|1] — 174
How To Be A Jewish Mother (65) 131(1) [0|0|12] — 174

BERLIN ► 801 Pk:28 [0|2|3] — 2939
Pleasure Victim (83) 30(1) [0|11|34] — 1250
Love Life (84) 28(2) [0|4|30] — 1186
Count Three And Pray (86) 61(2) [0|0|20] — 503

Shelley BERMAN ► 2558 Pk:88 [0|0|1] — 147
The Sex Life Of The Primate (And Other Bits Of Gossip) (64) 88(1) [0|0|8] — 147

Herschel BERNARDI ► 2921 Pk:138 [0|0|1] — 77
Fiddler On The Roof (66) 138(1) [0|0|5] — 77.0

Leonard BERNSTEIN ► 1388 Pk:53 [0|0|2] — 985
Mass (from the Liturgy of the Roman Mass) (71) 53(1) [0|0|20] — 604
West Side Story (85) 70(2) [0|0|20] — 381

Chuck BERRY ► 506 Pk:8 [1|3|8] — 6114
The London Chuck Berry Sessions (72) 8(3) [7|20|47] — 4034
Chuck Berry's Greatest Hits (64) 34(2) [0|3|21] — 752
Chuck Berry On Stage (63) 29(1) [0|2|17] — 588
Chuck Berry's Golden Decade (67) 72(1) [0|0|20] — 395
Chuck Berry's Golden Decade, Vol. 2 (73) 110(1) [0|0|8] — 151
St. Louis To Liverpool (64) 124(1) [0|0|7] — 95.5
Bio (73) 175(1) [0|0|6] — 50.6
St. Louie To Frisco To Memphis (72) 185(2) [0|0|7] — 48.6

Karen BETH ► 2980 Pk:171 [0|0|1] — 68
The Joys Of Life (69) 171(2) [0|0|6] — 68.2

Dickey BETTS ► 987 Pk:19 [0|2|4] — 1973
Highway Call (74)-Richard Betts 19(2) [0|7|16] — 1266
Dickey Betts & Great Southern (77)-Dickey Betts & Great Southern 31(1) [0|2|12] — 620
Atlanta's Burning Down (78) 157(2) [0|0|5] — 63.7
Pattern Disruptive (88)-The Dickey Betts Band 187(2) [0|0|4] — 23.7

The B-52s ► 267 Pk:4 [1|4|7] — 13148
Cosmic Thing (89) 4(1) [22|41|65] — 7172
The B-52's (79) 59(2) [0|0|74] — 2154
Wild Planet (80) 18(1) [0|9|27] — 1586
Whammy! (83) 29(2) [0|6|26] — 962
Mesopotamia (82) 35(2) [0|4|18] — 660
Party Mix! (81) 55(2) [0|0|11] — 401
Bouncing Off The Satellites (86) 85(2) [0|0|15] — 214

BIDDU Orchestra ► 3241 Pk:170 [0|0|1] — 34
Biddu Orchestra (76) 170(1) [0|0|3] — 34.4

BIG AUDIO DYNAMITE ► 1253 Pk:85 [0|0|4] — 1227
This Is Big Audio Dynamite (85) 103(2) [0|0|35] — 507
No. 10, Upping Street (86) 119(2) [0|0|23] — 265
Megatop Phoenix (89) 85(1) [0|0|13] — 259
Tighten Up Vol. '88 (88) 102(1) [0|0|12] — 196

BIG BROTHER And The HOLDING COMPANY ► 302 Pk:1 [1|1|5] — 11287
Cheap Thrills (68) 1(8) [19|29|66] — 10453
Big Brother & The Holding Company (67) 60(2) [0|0|30] — 653
Be A Brother (70) 134(2) [0|0|6] — 104
How Hard It Is (71) 157(1) [0|0|3] — 42.0
Big Brother & The Holding Company(2) (71) 185(1) [0|0|4] — 35.0

BIG COUNTRY ► 700 Pk:18 [0|1|5] — 3673
The Crossing (83) 18(2) [0|18|42] — 2443
The Seer (86) 59(2) [0|0|17] — 482
Steeltown (84) 70(4) [0|0|17] — 403
Wonderland (84) 65(2) [0|0|12] — 293
Peace In Our Time (88) 160(2) [0|0|6] — 52.9

BIG PIG ► 2047 Pk:93 [0|0|1] — 330
Bonk (88) 93(2) [0|0|17] — 330

BILLION DOLLAR BABIES ► 3492 Pk:198 [0|0|1] — 12
Battle Axe (77) 198(1) [0|0|2] — 11.8

BILLY SATELLITE ► 2963 Pk:139 [0|0|1] — 70
Billy Satellite (84) 139(2) [0|0|6] — 70.3

BIONIC BOOGIE ► 2023 Pk:88 [0|0|1] — 339
Bionic Boogie (78) 88(1) [0|0|16] — 339

Jane BIRKIN & Serge GAINSBOURG ► 3477 Pk:196 [0|0|1] — 12
Je T'Aime (Beautiful Love) (70)- Jane Birkin Serge Gainsbourg 196(2) [0|0|2] — 12.5

Elvin BISHOP ► 679 Pk:18 [0|2|5] — 3923
Struttin' My Stuff (76) 18(2) [0|8|34] — 1815
Juke Joint Jump (75) 46(2) [0|0|17] — 818
Raisin' Hell (77) 38(2) [0|2|12] — 575
Let It Flow (74) 100(1) [0|0|17] — 422
Hometown Boy Makes Good (76) 70(1) [0|0|12] — 293

Stephen BISHOP ► 992 Pk:34 [0|2|2] — 1965
Careless (77) 34(2) [0|3|32] — 1005
Bish (78) 35(2) [0|4|19] — 960

BIZ MARKIE ► 1408 Pk:66 [0|0|2] — 960
The Biz Never Sleeps (89)-The Diabolical Biz Markie 66(2) [0|0|30] — 640
Goin' Off (88) 90(2) [0|0|18] — 319

Bill BLACK'S Combo ► 2557 Pk:139 [0|0|4] — 147
Solid And Raunchy The 3rd (69) 168(1) [0|0|4] — 52.9
Plays Tunes By Chuck Berry (64) 143(1) [0|0|4] — 46.2
Bill Black's Combo Goes Big Band (64) 139(2) [0|0|3] — 37.3
Bill Black's Greatest Hits (67) 195(2) [0|0|2] — 10.5

Clint BLACK ► 699 Pk:31 [0|1|1] — 3718
Killin' Time (89) 31(1) [0|6|143] — 3718

Stanley BLACK ► 3238 Pk:148 [0|0|1] — 35
Music Of A People (65)-Stanley Black With The London Festival Orch. And Chor. 148(2) [0|0|3] — 34.5

33The BLACKBYRDS ► 430 Pk:16 [0|3|8] — 7415
City Life (75) 16(1) [0|9|40] — 2376
Flying Start (74) 30(1) [0|7|39] — 2018
Unfinished Business (76) 34(1) [0|4|24] — 1152
Action (77) 43(1) [0|0|30] — 1087
The Blackbyrds (74) 96(1) [0|0|23] — 465
Better Days (81) 133(1) [0|0|11] — 160
Cornbread, Earl And Me (Soundtrack) (75) 150(2) [0|0|6] — 79.8
Night Grooves (79) 159(1) [0|0|7] — 77.4

BLACKFOOT ► 797 Pk:42 [0|0|5] — 2967
Strikes (79) 42(2) [0|0|41] — 1420
Tomcattin' (80) 50(1) [0|0|20] — 722
Marauder (81) 48(2) [0|0|12] — 524
Siogo (83) 82(1) [0|0|13] — 263
Vertical Smiles (84) 176(3) [0|0|5] — 38.4

BLACK IVORY ► 2455 Pk:158 [0|0|2] — 172
Don't Turn Around (72) 158(2) [0|0|9] — 117
Baby, Won't You Change Your Mind (73) 188(2) [0|0|9] — 55.1

BLACKJACK ► 2605 Pk:127 [0|0|1] — 133
Blackjack (79) 127(1) [0|0|7] — 133

BLACK 'N BLUE ► 1727 Pk:110 [0|0|3] — 556
Nasty, Nasty (86) 110(1) [0|0|20] — 291
Black 'N' Blue (84) 116(2) [0|0|11] — 143
In Heat (88) 133(2) [0|0|9] — 122

BLACK OAK ARKANSAS ► 810 Pk:52 [0|0|10] — 2887
High On The Hog (73) 52(1) [0|0|22] — 661
Street Party (74) 56(1) [0|0|12] — 475
If An Angel Came To See You, Would You Make Her Feel At Home? (72) 93(2) [0|0|19] — 439
Raunch 'N' Roll (73) 90(1) [0|0|16] — 379
X-Rated (75) 99(2) [0|0|17] — 320
Keep The Faith (72) 103(1) [0|0|10] — 201
Black Oak Arkansas (71) 127(1) [0|0|12] — 188
Ain't Life Grand (75) 145(2) [0|0|8] — 128
Balls Of Fire (76) 173(3) [0|0|7] — 82.1
Live! Mutha (76) 194(1) [0|0|2] — 13.7

BLACK PEARL ► 2588 Pk:130 [0|0|2] — 138
Black Pearl (69) 130(1) [0|0|5] — 123
Black Pearl-Live! (70) 189(1) [0|0|2] — 15.2

BLACK SABBATH ► 140 Pk:8 [1|10|16] — 22920
Paranoid (71) 12(3) [0|34|70] — 5864
Master Of Reality (71) 8(2) [5|17|43] — 4105
Black Sabbath (70) 23(2) [0|10|65] — 2645
Black Sabbath, Vol. 4 (72) 13(1) [0|13|31] — 2382
Sabbath Bloody Sabbath (74) 11(1) [0|11|32] — 2195
Heaven And Hell (80) 28(3) [0|9|24] — 1367
Mob Rules (81) 29(3) [0|8|18] — 922
Sabotage (75) 28(2) [0|4|14] — 837
Born Again (83) 39(1) [0|2|16] — 503
Live Evil (83) 37(4) [0|4|12] — 483
We Sold Our Souls For Rock 'n' Roll (76) 48(1) [0|0|10] — 437
Technical Ecstasy (76) 51(1) [0|0|12] — 397
Never Say Die! (78) 69(2) [0|0|14] — 362
Seventh Star (86)-Black Sabbath Featuring Tony Iommi 78(2) [0|0|11] — 235
Headless Cross (89) 115(1) [0|0|8] — 126
The Eternal Idol (87) 168(1) [0|0|6] — 58.8

<table>
<tr><th>Act ▶ Highest Peak [Top10s|Top40s|Total]
Title (Yr) Peak(Wk) [T10 Wk|T40Wk|TotalWk]</th><th>Score</th></tr>
<tr><td>BLACK UHURU ▶ 2918 Pk:146 [0|0|1]</td><td>78</td></tr>
<tr><td>Chill Out (82) 146(1) [0|0|7]</td><td>77.7</td></tr>
<tr><td>Ruben BLADES ▶ 3087 Pk:156 [0|0|1]</td><td>54</td></tr>
<tr><td>Nothing But The Truth (88) 156(2) [0|0|6]</td><td>53.6</td></tr>
<tr><td>Jack BLANCHARD & Misty MORGAN ▶ 3202 Pk:185 [0|0|1]</td><td>39</td></tr>
<tr><td>Birds Of A Feather (70) 185(1) [0|0|5]</td><td>39.5</td></tr>
<tr><td>Bobby BLAND ▶ 1664 Pk:119 [0|0|7]</td><td>609</td></tr>
<tr><td>His California Album (73)-Bobby Blue Bland 136(1) [0|0|19]</td><td>283</td></tr>
<tr><td>Ain't Nothing You Can Do (64) 119(1) [0|0|8]</td><td>118</td></tr>
<tr><td>Dreamer (74) 172(1) [0|0|7]</td><td>72.7</td></tr>
<tr><td>Get On Down With Bobby Bland (75) 154(2) [0|0|5]</td><td>65.4</td></tr>
<tr><td>Reflections In Blue (77) 185(1) [0|0|4]</td><td>29.3</td></tr>
<tr><td>Come Fly With Me (78) 185(1) [0|0|3]</td><td>23.8</td></tr>
<tr><td>I Feel Good, I Feel Fine (79) 187(2) [0|0|2]</td><td>16.0</td></tr>
<tr><td>The BLASTERS ▶ 1048 Pk:36 [0|1|4]</td><td>1750</td></tr>
<tr><td>The Blasters (82) 36(3) [0|4|30]</td><td>1135</td></tr>
<tr><td>Hard Line (85) 86(2) [0|0|19]</td><td>350</td></tr>
<tr><td>Non Fiction (83) 95(1) [0|0|8]</td><td>138</td></tr>
<tr><td>Over There (Live At The Venue, London) (82) 117(4) [0|0|8]</td><td>126</td></tr>
<tr><td>BLIND FAITH ▶ 451 Pk:1 [1|1|1]</td><td>7080</td></tr>
<tr><td>Blind Faith (69) 1(2) [14|20|45]</td><td>7080</td></tr>
<tr><td>BLODWYN PIG ▶ 2401 Pk:96 [0|0|2]</td><td>186</td></tr>
<tr><td>Getting To This (70) 96(1) [0|0|5]</td><td>111</td></tr>
<tr><td>Ahead Rings Out (69) 149(1) [0|0|5]</td><td>74.4</td></tr>
<tr><td>BLONDIE ▶ 219 Pk:6 [2|5|6]</td><td>15962</td></tr>
<tr><td>Parallel Lines (78) 6(3) [5|16|103]</td><td>5717</td></tr>
<tr><td>Autoamerican (80) 7(5) [9|23|34]</td><td>4533</td></tr>
<tr><td>Eat To The Beat (79) 17(3) [0|19|51]</td><td>3570</td></tr>
<tr><td>The Best Of Blondie (81) 30(2) [0|11|23]</td><td>1318</td></tr>
<tr><td>The Hunter (82) 33(2) [0|4|12]</td><td>430</td></tr>
<tr><td>Plastic Letters (78) 72(1) [0|0|17]</td><td>393</td></tr>
<tr><td>BLOODROCK ▶ 582 Pk:21 [0|2|6]</td><td>4956</td></tr>
<tr><td>Bloodrock 2 (70) 21(3) [0|8|37]</td><td>2334</td></tr>
<tr><td>Bloodrock 3 (71) 27(5) [0|8|23]</td><td>1457</td></tr>
<tr><td>Bloodrock Live (72) 67(1) [0|0|22]</td><td>661</td></tr>
<tr><td>Bloodrock Passage (72) 104(2) [0|0|14]</td><td>255</td></tr>
<tr><td>Bloodrock U.S.A. (71) 88(1) [0|0|7]</td><td>196</td></tr>
<tr><td>Bloodrock (70) 160(2) [0|0|5]</td><td>53.2</td></tr>
<tr><td>BLOODSTONE ▶ 937 Pk:30 [0|1|5]</td><td>2189</td></tr>
<tr><td>Natural High (73) 30(1) [0|7|36]</td><td>1357</td></tr>
<tr><td>Unreal (74) 110(1) [0|0|22]</td><td>435</td></tr>
<tr><td>We Go A Long Way Back (82) 95(2) [0|0|11]</td><td>192</td></tr>
<tr><td>I Need Time (74) 141(1) [0|0|8]</td><td>118</td></tr>
<tr><td>Riddle Of The Sphinx (75) 147(2) [0|0|6]</td><td>87.0</td></tr>
<tr><td>BLOOD, SWEAT & TEARS ▶ 74 Pk:1 [3|5|10]</td><td>35654</td></tr>
<tr><td>Blood, Sweat & Tears (69) 1(7) [50|66|109]</td><td>23126</td></tr>
<tr><td>Blood, Sweat & Tears 3 (70) 1(2) [11|19|41]</td><td>5566</td></tr>
<tr><td>B, S & T; 4 (71) 10(2) [2|11|23]</td><td>2413</td></tr>
<tr><td>Blood, Sweat & Tears Greatest Hits (72) 19(2) [0|6|27]</td><td>1413</td></tr>
<tr><td>Child Is Father To The Man (68) 47(2) [0|0|55]</td><td>1158</td></tr>
<tr><td>New Blood (72) 32(1) [0|7|17]</td><td>997</td></tr>
<tr><td>New City (75) 47(2) [0|0|13]</td><td>518</td></tr>
<tr><td>No Sweat (73) 72(2) [0|0|12]</td><td>338</td></tr>
<tr><td>Mirror Image (74) 149(1) [0|0|6]</td><td>82.0</td></tr>
<tr><td>More Than Ever (76) 165(2) [0|0|3]</td><td>42.4</td></tr>
<tr><td>Bobby BLOOM ▶ 3074 Pk:126 [0|0|1]</td><td>56</td></tr>
<tr><td>The Bobby Bloom Album (70) 126(1) [0|0|3]</td><td>56.1</td></tr>
<tr><td>Mike BLOOMFIELD ▶ 1006 Pk:12 [0|2|4]</td><td>1922</td></tr>
<tr><td>It's Not Killing Me (69)-Michael Bloomfield 127(1) [0|0|5]</td><td>94.9</td></tr>
<tr><td>The Live Adventures Of Mike Bloomfield And Al Kooper (69)-Mike Bloomfield/Al Kooper [A] 18(2) [0|10|20]</td><td>959</td></tr>
<tr><td>Super Session (68)-Mike Bloomfield/Al Kooper/Steve Stills [A] 12(1) [0|10|37]</td><td>799</td></tr>
<tr><td>Triumvirate (73)-Mike Bloomfield/John Paul Hammond/Dr. John [A] 105(1) [0|0|12]</td><td>209</td></tr>
<tr><td>Kurtis BLOW ▶ 1285 Pk:71 [0|0|6]</td><td>1175</td></tr>
<tr><td>Ego Trip (84) 83(2) [0|0|37]</td><td>612</td></tr>
<tr><td>Kurtis Blow (80) 71(1) [0|0|10]</td><td>283</td></tr>
<tr><td>America (85) 153(3) [0|0|15]</td><td>136</td></tr>
<tr><td>Deuce (81) 137(1) [0|0|5]</td><td>89.2</td></tr>
<tr><td>Tough (82) 167(2) [0|0|5]</td><td>46.3</td></tr>
<tr><td>Kingdom Blow (86) 196(2) [0|0|2]</td><td>8.6</td></tr>
<tr><td>BLOWFLY ▶ 1909 Pk:82 [0|0|1]</td><td>401</td></tr>
<tr><td>Blowfly's Party [X-Rated] (80) 82(2) [0|0|20]</td><td>401</td></tr>
<tr><td>BLOW MONKEYS ▶ 1460 Pk:35 [0|1|2]</td><td>876</td></tr>
<tr><td>Animal Magic (86) 35(2) [0|5|18]</td><td>769</td></tr>
<tr><td>She Was Only A Grocer's Daughter (87) 134(2) [0|0|8]</td><td>107</td></tr>
<tr><td>BLUE CHEER ▶ 836 Pk:11 [0|1|4]</td><td>2748</td></tr>
<tr><td>Vincebus Eruptum (68) 11(3) [0|11|27]</td><td>1897</td></tr>
<tr><td>New! Improved! Blue Cheer (69) 84(2) [0|0|14]</td><td>424</td></tr>
<tr><td>Outsideinside (68) 90(1) [0|0|16]</td><td>389</td></tr>
<tr><td>The Original Human Being (70) 188(1) [0|0|5]</td><td>38.1</td></tr>
<tr><td>BLUE MAGIC ▶ 934 Pk:45 [0|0|4]</td><td>2206</td></tr>
<tr><td>Blue Magic (74) 45(1) [0|0|34]</td><td>1234</td></tr>
<tr><td>Thirteen Blue Magic Lane (75) 50(1) [0|0|12]</td><td>474</td></tr>
<tr><td>The Magic Of The Blue (74) 71(1) [0|0|13]</td><td>443</td></tr>
<tr><td>Mystic Dragons (76) 170(1) [0|0|5]</td><td>55.5</td></tr>
<tr><td>BLUE MERCEDES ▶ 3144 Pk:165 [0|0|1]</td><td>47</td></tr>
<tr><td>Rich And Famous (88) 165(2) [0|0|5]</td><td>46.8</td></tr>
<tr><td>BLUE MURDER ▶ 1871 Pk:69 [0|0|1]</td><td>425</td></tr>
<tr><td>Blue Murder (89) 69(2) [0|0|21]</td><td>425</td></tr>
<tr><td>BLUE ÖYSTER CULT ▶ 345 Pk:22 [0|5|14]</td><td>9809</td></tr>
<tr><td>Agents Of Fortune (76) 29(1) [0|9|35]</td><td>2186</td></tr>
<tr><td>Fire Of Unknown Origin (81) 24(2) [0|11|31]</td><td>1923</td></tr>
<tr><td>On Your Feet Or On Your Knees (75) 22(2) [0|4|13]</td><td>953</td></tr>
<tr><td>Cultosaurus Erectus (80) 34(2) [0|3|16]</td><td>775</td></tr>
<tr><td>Mirrors (79) 44(2) [0|0|17]</td><td>730</td></tr>
<tr><td>Extraterrestrial Live (82) 29(2) [0|5|19]</td><td>714</td></tr>
<tr><td>Some Enchanted Evening (78) 44(1) [0|0|12]</td><td>565</td></tr>
<tr><td>Spectres (77) 43(2) [0|0|14]</td><td>491</td></tr>
<tr><td>Secret Treaties (74) 53(1) [0|0|14]</td><td>444</td></tr>
<tr><td>Club Ninja (86) 63(2) [0|0|14]</td><td>337</td></tr>
<tr><td>The Revolution By Night (83) 93(1) [0|0|16]</td><td>313</td></tr>
<tr><td>Tyranny And Mutation (73) 122(1) [0|0|13]</td><td>204</td></tr>
<tr><td>Imaginos (88) 122(1) [0|0|8]</td><td>112</td></tr>
<tr><td>Blue Öyster Cult (72) 172(1) [0|0|8]</td><td>63.7</td></tr>
<tr><td>BLUES BROTHERS ▶ 449 Pk:1 [1|2|4]</td><td>7128</td></tr>
<tr><td>Briefcase Full Of Blues (78) 1(1) [13|16|29]</td><td>4763</td></tr>
<tr><td>The Blues Brothers (Soundtrack) (80) 13(2) [0|12|19]</td><td>1874</td></tr>
<tr><td>Made In America (80) 49(1) [0|0|12]</td><td>445</td></tr>
<tr><td>The Best Of The Blues Brothers (82) 143(2) [0|0|3]</td><td>45.4</td></tr>
<tr><td>BLUES IMAGE ▶ 1963 Pk:112 [0|0|2]</td><td>370</td></tr>
<tr><td>Blues Image (69) 112(1) [0|0|9]</td><td>200</td></tr>
<tr><td>Open (70) 147(2) [0|0|13]</td><td>170</td></tr>
<tr><td>BLUES MAGOOS ▶ 1109 Pk:21 [0|1|2]</td><td>1578</td></tr>
<tr><td>Psychedelic Lollipop (66) 21(1) [0|5|32]</td><td>1219</td></tr>
<tr><td>Electric Comic Book (67) 74(1) [0|0|16]</td><td>358</td></tr>
<tr><td>BLUES PROJECT ▶ 1022 Pk:52 [0|0|4]</td><td>1857</td></tr>
<tr><td>Projections (66) 52(2) [0|0|36]</td><td>1092</td></tr>
<tr><td>Live At The Cafe Au Go Go (66) 77(1) [0|0|21]</td><td>474</td></tr>
<tr><td>The Blues Project Live At Town Hall (67) 71(1) [0|0|11]</td><td>279</td></tr>
<tr><td>Best Of The Blues Project (69) 199(1) [0|0|2]</td><td>12.0</td></tr>
<tr><td>BLUE SWEDE ▶ 1912 Pk:80 [0|0|1]</td><td>398</td></tr>
<tr><td>Hooked On A Feeling (74) 80(1) [0|0|17]</td><td>398</td></tr>
<tr><td>BOBBY And The MIDNITES ▶ 2765 Pk:158 [0|0|2]</td><td>102</td></tr>
<tr><td>Bobby & The Midnites (81) 158(2) [0|0|7]</td><td>72.8</td></tr>
<tr><td>Where The Beat Meets The Street (84) 166(1) [0|0|4]</td><td>29.3</td></tr>
<tr><td>BOBBY JIMMY & The CRITTERS ▶ 3542 Pk:200 [0|0|1]</td><td>4</td></tr>
<tr><td>Roaches: The Beginning (86) 200(1) [0|0|1]</td><td>3.6</td></tr>
<tr><td>Willie BOBO ▶ 2711 Pk:137 [0|0|1]</td><td>112</td></tr>
<tr><td>Spanish Grease (66) 137(1) [0|0|8]</td><td>112</td></tr>
<tr><td>BODEANS ▶ 1486 Pk:86 [0|0|3]</td><td>839</td></tr>
<tr><td>Outside Looking In (87) 86(2) [0|0|20]</td><td>345</td></tr>
<tr><td>Love & Hope & Sex & Dreams (86) 115(2) [0|0|19]</td><td>254</td></tr>
<tr><td>Home (89) 94(2) [0|0|13]</td><td>240</td></tr>
<tr><td>Angela BOFILL ▶ 595 Pk:34 [0|2|5]</td><td>4774</td></tr>
<tr><td>Angel Of The Night (79) 34(1) [0|8|33]</td><td>1773</td></tr>
<tr><td>Too Tough (83) 40(3) [0|3|32]</td><td>984</td></tr>
<tr><td>Angie (79) 47(1) [0|0|26]</td><td>920</td></tr>
<tr><td>Something About You (81) 61(4) [0|0|22]</td><td>681</td></tr>
<tr><td>Teaser (83) 81(1) [0|0|21]</td><td>416</td></tr>
<tr><td>Tim BOGERT ▶ 1606 Pk:12 [0|1|1]</td><td>673</td></tr>
<tr><td>Jeff Beck, Tim Bogert, Carmine Appice (73)-Beck, Bogert & Appice [A] 12(1) [0|11|27]</td><td>673</td></tr>
<tr><td>Hamilton BOHANNON ▶ 1677 Pk:58 [0|0|1]</td><td>601</td></tr>
<tr><td>Summertime Groove (78) 58(1) [0|0|19]</td><td>601</td></tr>
<tr><td>Tommy BOLIN ▶ 1814 Pk:96 [0|0|2]</td><td>474</td></tr>
<tr><td>Teaser (75) 96(2) [0|0|14]</td><td>285</td></tr>
<tr><td>Private Eyes (76) 98(1) [0|0|8]</td><td>189</td></tr>
<tr><td>--Bolling, Claude see Rampal, Jean-Pierre</td><td></td></tr>
<tr><td>Michael BOLTON ▶ 249 Pk:3 [1|1|3]</td><td>14229</td></tr>
<tr><td>Soul Provider (89) 3(3) [21|50|202]</td><td>12887</td></tr>
<tr><td>The Hunger (87) 46(1) [0|0|41]</td><td>1145</td></tr>
<tr><td>Michael Bolton (83) 89(1) [0|0|13]</td><td>198</td></tr>
<tr><td>Angelo BOND ▶ 3379 Pk:179 [0|0|1]</td><td>21</td></tr>
<tr><td>Bondage (75) 179(1) [0|0|2]</td><td>20.9</td></tr>
<tr><td>Johnny BOND ▶ 3222 Pk:142 [0|0|1]</td><td>37</td></tr>
<tr><td>Ten Little Bottles (65) 142(1) [0|0|3]</td><td>37.2</td></tr>
<tr><td>Gary (U.S.) BONDS ▶ 1014 Pk:27 [0|1|2]</td><td>1893</td></tr>
<tr><td>Dedication (81)-Gary U.S. Bonds 27(2) [0|7|20]</td><td>1338</td></tr>
<tr><td>On The Line (82)-Gary U.S. Bonds 52(2) [0|0|17]</td><td>555</td></tr>
<tr><td>BONEY M ▶ 2448 Pk:134 [0|0|1]</td><td>174</td></tr>
<tr><td>Nightflight To Venus (78) 134(2) [0|0|10]</td><td>174</td></tr>
<tr><td>BONHAM ▶ 1306 Pk:38 [0|1|1]</td><td>1131</td></tr>
<tr><td>The Disregard Of Timekeeping (89) 38(1) [0|3|29]</td><td>1131</td></tr>
<tr><td>BON JOVI ▶ 99 Pk:1 [2|3|4]</td><td>29706</td></tr>
<tr><td>Slippery When Wet (86) 1(8) [46|60|94]</td><td>14801</td></tr>
<tr><td>New Jersey (88) 1(4) [22|52|76]</td><td>9744</td></tr>
<tr><td>7800 Degrees Fahrenheit (85) 37(3) [0|5|104]</td><td>2896</td></tr>
<tr><td>Bon Jovi (84) 43(2) [0|0|86]</td><td>2265</td></tr>
<tr><td>Karla BONOFF ▶ 731 Pk:31 [0|1|3]</td><td>3427</td></tr>
<tr><td>Restless Nights (79) 31(2) [0|8|26]</td><td>1266</td></tr>
<tr><td>Karla Bonoff (77) 52(1) [0|0|40]</td><td>1115</td></tr>
<tr><td>Wild Heart Of The Young (82) 49(1) [0|0|35]</td><td>1046</td></tr>
<tr><td>BONZO DOG BAND ▶ 3511 Pk:199 [0|0|1]</td><td>10</td></tr>
<tr><td>Let's Make Up And Be Friendly (72) 199(2) [0|0|2]</td><td>10.3</td></tr>
<tr><td>BOOGIE BOYS ▶ 1570 Pk:53 [0|0|3]</td><td>710</td></tr>
<tr><td>City Life (85) 53(2) [0|0|17]</td><td>448</td></tr>
</table>

<table>
<tr><th>Act ▶ Highest Peak [Top10s | Top40s | Total]
Title (Yr) Peak(Wk) [T10 Wk | T40Wk | TotalWk]</th><th>Score</th></tr>
<tr><td>BOOGIE BOYS ▶ Continued</td><td></td></tr>
<tr><td>Romeo Knight (88) 117(2) [0|0|11]</td><td>164</td></tr>
<tr><td>Survival Of The Freshest (86)
124(2) [0|0|9]</td><td>97.4</td></tr>
<tr><td>BOOGIE DOWN PRODUCTIONS ▶ 1288
Pk:36 [0|1|2]</td><td>1170</td></tr>
<tr><td>Ghetto Music: The Blueprint Of Hip Hop (89)
36(2) [0|4|17]</td><td>693</td></tr>
<tr><td>By All Means Necessary (88) 75(1) [0|0|23]</td><td>477</td></tr>
<tr><td>Chuckii BOOKER ▶ 2550 Pk:116 [0|0|1]</td><td>148</td></tr>
<tr><td>Chuckii (89) 116(1) [0|0|10]</td><td>148</td></tr>
<tr><td>BOOKER T. & PRISCILLA ▶ 2499
Pk:106 [0|0|2]</td><td>160</td></tr>
<tr><td>Booker T. & Priscilla (71) 106(1) [0|0|6]</td><td>134</td></tr>
<tr><td>Home Grown (72) 190(1) [0|0|4]</td><td>26.0</td></tr>
<tr><td>BOOKER T. & The M.G.'s ▶ 603
Pk:35 [0|1|10]</td><td>4711</td></tr>
<tr><td>Melting Pot (71) 3(1) [0|0|38]</td><td>1626</td></tr>
<tr><td>Hip Hug-Her (67) 35(1) [0|4|29]</td><td>1013</td></tr>
<tr><td>The Booker T. Set (69) 53(1) [0|0|18]</td><td>747</td></tr>
<tr><td>Uptight (Soundtrack) (69) 98(1) [0|0|27]</td><td>581</td></tr>
<tr><td>McLemore Avenue (70) 107(1) [0|0|15]</td><td>229</td></tr>
<tr><td>Soul Limbo (68) 127(1) [0|0|9]</td><td>173</td></tr>
<tr><td>The Best Of Booker T. & The MG's (68)-
167(2) [0|0|11]</td><td>132</td></tr>
<tr><td>Booker T. & The M.G.'s Greatest Hits (70)-
132(1) [0|0|8]</td><td>127</td></tr>
<tr><td>Back To Back (67)-The Mar-Keys/Booker T. &
The MG's [A] 98(2) [0|0|4]</td><td>46.4</td></tr>
<tr><td>Doin' Our Thing (68)
176(1) [0|0|4]</td><td>34.8</td></tr>
<tr><td>BOOK OF LOVE ▶ 2853 Pk:156 [0|0|1]</td><td>87</td></tr>
<tr><td>Lullaby (88) 156(2) [0|0|10]</td><td>87.3</td></tr>
<tr><td>Taka BOOM ▶ 3178 Pk:171 [0|0|1]</td><td>43</td></tr>
<tr><td>Taka Boom (79) 171(2) [0|0|4]</td><td>43.3</td></tr>
<tr><td>BOOMTOWN RATS ▶ 1495 Pk:103 [0|0|4]</td><td>814</td></tr>
<tr><td>The Fine Art Of Surfacing (79)
103(2) [0|0|16]</td><td>349</td></tr>
<tr><td>A Tonic For The Troops (79)
112(1) [0|0|13]</td><td>290</td></tr>
<tr><td>Mondo Bongo (81) 116(2) [0|0|8]</td><td>152</td></tr>
<tr><td>In The Long Grass (85) 188(1) [0|0|4]</td><td>22.7</td></tr>
<tr><td>Daniel BOONE ▶ 2661 Pk:142 [0|0|1]</td><td>121</td></tr>
<tr><td>Beautiful Sunday (72) 142(2) [0|0|9]</td><td>121</td></tr>
<tr><td>Debby BOONE ▶ 855 Pk:6 [1|1|2]</td><td>2629</td></tr>
<tr><td>You Light Up My Life (77)
6(3) [6|10|37]</td><td>2560</td></tr>
<tr><td>Midstream (78) 147(1) [0|0|5]</td><td>68.7</td></tr>
<tr><td>BOOTSY'S RUBBER BAND ▶ 538
Pk:16 [0|2|6]</td><td>5537</td></tr>
<tr><td>Ahh... The Name Is Bootsy, Baby (77)
16(4) [0|12|23]</td><td>2108</td></tr>
<tr><td>Bootsy? Player Of The Year (78)
16(2) [0|10|24]</td><td>1658</td></tr>
<tr><td>Stretchin' Out In Bootsy's Rubber Band (76)
59(1) [0|0|27]</td><td>982</td></tr>
<tr><td>This Boot Is Made For Fonk-n (79)
52(1) [0|0|9]</td><td>411</td></tr>
<tr><td>Ultra Wave (80)-Bootsy 70(3) [0|0|9]</td><td>281</td></tr>
<tr><td>The One Giveth, The Count Taketh Away (82)-
William "Bootsy" Collins 120(1) [0|0|8]</td><td>96.0</td></tr>
<tr><td>BOSTON ▶ 122 Pk:1 [3|3|3]</td><td>25724</td></tr>
<tr><td>Boston (76) 3(6) [30|49|132]</td><td>14152</td></tr>
<tr><td>Third Stage (86) 1(4) [20|29|50]</td><td>6153</td></tr>
<tr><td>Don't Look Back (78)
1(2) [11|13|45]</td><td>5419</td></tr>
<tr><td>BOSTON POPS Orchestra/Arthur FIEDLER
▶ 1175 Pk:18 [0|1|11]</td><td>1402</td></tr>
<tr><td>"Pops" Goes The Trumpet (64)-
Al Hirt & Boston Pops Orchestra [A]
18(1) [0|12|31]</td><td>692</td></tr>
</table>

<table>
<tr><th>Act ▶ Highest Peak [Top10s | Top40s | Total]
Title (Yr) Peak(Wk) [T10 Wk | T40Wk | TotalWk]</th><th>Score</th></tr>
<tr><td>Peter And The Commissar (64)-Allan Sherman/
Boston Pops Orchestra/Arthur Fiedler [A]
53(1) [0|0|14]</td><td>185</td></tr>
<tr><td>Nero Goes "Pops" (65)-Peter Nero/
Boston Pops Orchestra [A] 86(1) [0|0|16]</td><td>147</td></tr>
<tr><td>Up Up And Away (68)-Boston Pops Orchestra
157(1) [0|0|7]</td><td>109</td></tr>
<tr><td>Saturday Night Fiedler (79)-
Boston Pops Orchestra 147(1) [0|0|6]</td><td>82.8</td></tr>
<tr><td>Concert In The Park (63)-Boston Pops Orchestra
116(2) [0|0|4]</td><td>61.9</td></tr>
<tr><td>Arthur Fiedler "Superstar" (71)-
Boston Pops Orchestra Arthur Fiedler
174(1) [0|0|5]</td><td>56.6</td></tr>
<tr><td>The Duke At Tanglewood (66)-Duke
Ellington/Boston Pops Orchestra/Arthur Fiedler
[A] 145(1) [0|0|3]</td><td>19.7</td></tr>
<tr><td>The Music Of Paul Simon (72)-Boston Pops
Orchestra 196(2) [0|0|3]</td><td>18.0</td></tr>
<tr><td>Glenn Miller's Biggest Hits (69)-Boston Pops
Orchestra 192(1) [0|0|2]</td><td>15.4</td></tr>
<tr><td>Fabulous Broadway (71)-Boston Pops Orchestra
190(1) [0|0|2]</td><td>15.0</td></tr>
<tr><td>BOSTON POPS Orchestra/John WILLIAMS
▶ 2633 Pk:155 [0|0|2]</td><td>127</td></tr>
<tr><td>Swing, Swing, Swing (86) 155(2) [0|0|8]</td><td>78.6</td></tr>
<tr><td>Pops In Space (80) 181(1) [0|0|6]</td><td>48.0</td></tr>
<tr><td>--Boston Pops Orchestra: See also Chet Atkins</td><td></td></tr>
<tr><td>BOSTON SYMPHONY Orchestra ▶ 2222
Pk:82 [0|0|1]</td><td>244</td></tr>
<tr><td>Mozart: Requiem Mass (64) 82(2) [0|0|12]</td><td>244</td></tr>
<tr><td>BOURGEOIS TAGG ▶ 1831 Pk:84 [0|0|2]</td><td>457</td></tr>
<tr><td>YoYo (87) 84(1) [0|0|21]</td><td>384</td></tr>
<tr><td>Bourgeois Tagg (86) 139(2) [0|0|7]</td><td>72.5</td></tr>
<tr><td>David BOWIE ▶ 67 Pk:3 [6|15|28]</td><td>38179</td></tr>
<tr><td>Let's Dance (83) 4(1) [16|35|68]</td><td>6138</td></tr>
<tr><td>Young Americans (75) 9(2) [3|17|51]</td><td>3974</td></tr>
<tr><td>Station To Station (76) 3(2) [9|13|32]</td><td>3525</td></tr>
<tr><td>Diamond Dogs (74) 5(2) [4|10|25]</td><td>2476</td></tr>
<tr><td>Changesonebowie (76) 10(1) [1|8|39]</td><td>2467</td></tr>
<tr><td>Scary Monsters (80) 12(2) [0|12|27]</td><td>2118</td></tr>
<tr><td>Space Oddity (72) 16(1) [0|10|36]</td><td>2014</td></tr>
<tr><td>The Rise And Fall Of Ziggy Stardust And
The Spiders From Mars (72) 75(1) [0|0|81]</td><td>2014</td></tr>
<tr><td>David Live (74) 8(1) [3|8|21]</td><td>1991</td></tr>
<tr><td>Low (77) 11(2) [0|7|19]</td><td>1651</td></tr>
<tr><td>Tonight (84) 11(2) [0|12|24]</td><td>1546</td></tr>
<tr><td>Aladdin Sane (73) 17(2) [0|8|22]</td><td>1365</td></tr>
<tr><td>Bowie Pin Ups (73) 23(1) [0|9|21]</td><td>1266</td></tr>
<tr><td>Lodger (79) 20(2) [0|8|15]</td><td>1265</td></tr>
<tr><td>Never Let Me Down (87) 34(1) [0|4|26]</td><td>1035</td></tr>
<tr><td>"Heroes" (77) 35(1) [0|3|19]</td><td>561</td></tr>
<tr><td>Stage (78) 44(1) [0|0|13]</td><td>549</td></tr>
<tr><td>Changestwobowie (81) 68(1) [0|0|18]</td><td>441</td></tr>
<tr><td>The Man Who Sold The World (72)
105(1) [0|0|23]</td><td>407</td></tr>
<tr><td>Ziggy Stardust-The Motion Picture (Soundtrack)
(83) 89(1) [0|0|15]</td><td>263</td></tr>
<tr><td>Hunky Dory (72) 93(2) [0|0|16]</td><td>261</td></tr>
<tr><td>Sound + Vision (89) 97(1) [0|0|16]</td><td>195</td></tr>
<tr><td>Labyrinth (Soundtrack) (86)
68(2) [0|0|8]</td><td>179</td></tr>
<tr><td>Golden Years (83) 99(1) [0|0|9]</td><td>152</td></tr>
<tr><td>Images 1966-1967 (73) 144(1) [0|0|9]</td><td>114</td></tr>
<tr><td>Christiane F. (Soundtrack) (82) 135(2) [0|0|7]</td><td>74.4</td></tr>
<tr><td>Fame And Fashion -
David Bowie's All Time Greatest Hits (84)
147(1) [0|0|6]</td><td>72.6</td></tr>
<tr><td>David Bowie Narrates Prokofiev's "Peter And The
Wolf" (78)-David Bowie/Philadephia Orchestra/
Eugene Ormandy [A] 136(1) [0|0|8]</td><td>65.2</td></tr>
</table>

<table>
<tr><th>Act ▶ Highest Peak [Top10s | Top40s | Total]
Title (Yr) Peak(Wk) [T10 Wk | T40Wk | TotalWk]</th><th>Score</th></tr>
<tr><td>BOW WOW WOW ▶ 1524 Pk:67 [0|0|4]</td><td>762</td></tr>
<tr><td>The Last Of The Mohicans (82) 67(1) [0|0|22]</td><td>366</td></tr>
<tr><td>When The Going Gets Tough, The Tough Get Going
(83) 82(1) [0|0|13]</td><td>264</td></tr>
<tr><td>I Want Candy (82) 123(1) [0|0|9]</td><td>119</td></tr>
<tr><td>See Jungle! See Jungle! Go Join Your Gang Yeah!
City All Over, Go Ape Crazy (81) 192(2) [0|0|2]</td><td>12.9</td></tr>
<tr><td>BOX OF FROGS ▶ 1635 Pk:45 [0|0|2]</td><td>635</td></tr>
<tr><td>Box Of Frogs (84) 45(3) [0|0|20]</td><td>613</td></tr>
<tr><td>Strange Land (86) 177(2) [0|0|3]</td><td>22.0</td></tr>
<tr><td>BOX TOPS ▶ 918 Pk:45 [0|0|4]</td><td>2276</td></tr>
<tr><td>The Box Tops Super Hits (68) 45(1) [0|0|26]</td><td>1041</td></tr>
<tr><td>Cry Like A Baby (68) 59(2) [0|0|19]</td><td>569</td></tr>
<tr><td>Dimensions (69) 77(2) [0|0|11]</td><td>349</td></tr>
<tr><td>The Letter/Neon Rainbow (67) 87(1) [0|0|15]</td><td>317</td></tr>
<tr><td>Tommy BOYCE & Bobby HART ▶ 2667
Pk:109 [0|0|2]</td><td>120</td></tr>
<tr><td>I Wonder What She's Doing Tonite? (68)
109(1) [0|0|5]</td><td>116</td></tr>
<tr><td>Test Patterns (67) 200(1) [0|0|1]</td><td>4.3</td></tr>
<tr><td>Charles BOYER ▶ 3349 Pk:148 [0|0|1]</td><td>24</td></tr>
<tr><td>Where Does Love Go (66) 148(1) [0|0|2]</td><td>24.4</td></tr>
<tr><td>BOY GEORGE ▶ 2318 Pk:126 [0|0|2]</td><td>210</td></tr>
<tr><td>High Hat (89) 126(1) [0|0|11]</td><td>154</td></tr>
<tr><td>Sold (87) 145(2) [0|0|5]</td><td>56.4</td></tr>
<tr><td>Terence BOYLAN ▶ 3309 Pk:181 [0|0|1]</td><td>27</td></tr>
<tr><td>Terence Boylan (77) 181(2) [0|0|3]</td><td>27.4</td></tr>
<tr><td>BOY MEETS GIRL ▶ 1360 Pk:50 [0|0|2]</td><td>1034</td></tr>
<tr><td>Reel Life (88) 50(2) [0|0|26]</td><td>824</td></tr>
<tr><td>Boy Meets Girl (85) 76(2) [0|0|11]</td><td>210</td></tr>
<tr><td>The BOYS ▶ 1204 Pk:33 [0|1|1]</td><td>1335</td></tr>
<tr><td>Messages From The Boys (88) 33(2) [0|7|36]</td><td>1335</td></tr>
<tr><td>BOYS CLUB ▶ 2165 Pk:93 [0|0|1]</td><td>271</td></tr>
<tr><td>Boys Club (88) 93(2) [0|0|16]</td><td>271</td></tr>
<tr><td>BOYS DON'T CRY ▶ 1750 Pk:55 [0|0|1]</td><td>520</td></tr>
<tr><td>Boys Don't Cry (86) 55(3) [0|0|19]</td><td>520</td></tr>
<tr><td>Terry BOZZIO ▶ 2531 Pk:49 [0|0|1]</td><td>152</td></tr>
<tr><td>Jeff Beck's Guitar Shop (89)-Jeff Beck With Terry
Bozzio & Tony Hymas [A] 49(2) [0|0|18]</td><td>152</td></tr>
<tr><td>BRADY BUNCH ▶ 2033 Pk:108 [0|0|1]</td><td>335</td></tr>
<tr><td>Meet The Brady Bunch (72) 108(1) [0|0|19]</td><td>335</td></tr>
<tr><td>Billy BRAGG ▶ 3539 Pk:198 [0|0|1]</td><td>5</td></tr>
<tr><td>Workers Playtime (88) 198(1) [0|0|1]</td><td>4.6</td></tr>
<tr><td>BRAINSTORM ▶ 2303 Pk:145 [0|0|1]</td><td>214</td></tr>
<tr><td>Stormin' (77) 145(2) [0|0|16]</td><td>214</td></tr>
<tr><td>Bonnie BRAMLETT ▶ 3097 Pk:168 [0|0|1]</td><td>52</td></tr>
<tr><td>It's Time (75) 168(2) [0|0|5]</td><td>52.1</td></tr>
<tr><td>BRAM TCHAIKOVSKY ▶ 1302 Pk:36 [0|1|3]</td><td>1137</td></tr>
<tr><td>Strange Man, Changed Man (79)
36(1) [0|4|18]</td><td>850</td></tr>
<tr><td>Pressure (80) 108(1) [0|0|10]</td><td>188</td></tr>
<tr><td>Funland (81) 158(1) [0|0|8]</td><td>100</td></tr>
<tr><td>The BRANDOS ▶ 2197 Pk:108 [0|0|1]</td><td>258</td></tr>
<tr><td>Honor Among Thieves (87) 108(2) [0|0|19]</td><td>258</td></tr>
<tr><td>BRAND X ▶ 2338 Pk:125 [0|0|3]</td><td>203</td></tr>
<tr><td>Moroccan Roll (77) 125(1) [0|0|8]</td><td>126</td></tr>
<tr><td>Product (79) 165(2) [0|0|6]</td><td>54.8</td></tr>
<tr><td>Unorthodox Behaviour (76) 191(2) [0|0|3]</td><td>22.2</td></tr>
<tr><td>Laura BRANIGAN ▶ 537 Pk:23 [0|3|5]</td><td>5558</td></tr>
<tr><td>Self Control (84) 23(2) [0|19|45]</td><td>2270</td></tr>
<tr><td>Branigan (82) 34(5) [0|9|36]</td><td>1260</td></tr>
<tr><td>Branigan 2 (83) 29(1) [0|5|37]</td><td>1216</td></tr>
<tr><td>Touch (87) 87(3) [0|0|28]</td><td>462</td></tr>
<tr><td>Hold Me (85) 71(3) [0|0|15]</td><td>351</td></tr>
<tr><td>John BRANNEN ▶ 2583 Pk:156 [0|0|1]</td><td>140</td></tr>
<tr><td>Mystery Street (88) 156(1) [0|0|14]</td><td>140</td></tr>
</table>

Act ▶ Highest Peak [Top10s | Top40s | Total] Title (Yr) Peak(Wk) [T10 Wk | T40Wk | TotalWk]	Score
BRASS CONSTRUCTION ▶ 544 Pk:10 [1 | 2 | 8]	**5473**
Brass Construction (76) 10(1) [1 | 13 | 35]	3002
Brass Construction II (76) 26(3) [0 | 9 | 22]	1394
Brass Construction 5 (79) 89(1) [0 | 0 | 20]	439
Brass Construction III (77) 66(2) [0 | 0 | 14]	369
Attitudes (82) 114(3) [0 | 0 | 8]	94.2
Brass Construction 6 (80) 121(2) [0 | 0 | 5]	90.2
Conversations (83) 176(1) [0 | 0 | 6]	45.8
Brass Construction IV (78) 174(1) [0 | 0 | 4]	38.2
BRASS RING ▶ 2361 Pk:109 [0 | 0 | 3]	**195**
Love Theme From The Flight Of The Phoenix (66)-The Brass Ring featuring Phil Bodner 109(1) [0 | 0 | 8]	145
Sunday Night At The Movies (67)-The Brass Ring featuring Phil Bodner 157(1) [0 | 0 | 3]	37.8
The Dis-Advantages Of You (67)-The Brass Ring featuring Phil Bodner 193(1) [0 | 0 | 2]	11.6
BREAD ▶ 172 Pk:2 [2 | 7 | 8]	**20310**
The Best Of Bread (73) 2(1) [8 | 23 | 119]	6903
Baby I'm-A Want You (72) 3(1) [10 | 20 | 56]	5112
Guitar Man (72) 18(1) [0 | 16 | 29]	2192
On The Waters (70) 12(2) [0 | 8 | 32]	2097
Manna (71) 21(3) [0 | 10 | 25]	1963
Lost Without Your Love (77) 26(2) [0 | 6 | 16]	1024
The Best Of Bread, Volume Two (74) 32(2) [0 | 3 | 18]	848
Bread (69) 127(1) [0 | 0 | 9]	169
BREAKFAST CLUB ▶ 1393 Pk:43 [0 | 0 | 1]	**978**
The Breakfast Club (87) 43(2) [0 | 0 | 30]	978
BREAKWATER ▶ 2620 Pk:141 [0 | 0 | 2]	**129**
Splashdown (80) 141(1) [0 | 0 | 5]	74.3
Breakwater (79) 173(3) [0 | 0 | 5]	54.5
BREATHE ▶ 906 Pk:34 [0 | 1 | 1]	**2350**
All That Jazz (88) 34(3) [0 | 8 | 51]	2350
BRECKER BROTHERS ▶ 1505 Pk:82 [0 | 0 | 4]	**794**
Back To Back (76) 82(2) [0 | 0 | 16]	411
The Brecker Brothers (75) 102(1) [0 | 0 | 13]	255
Don't Stop The Music (77) 135(1) [0 | 0 | 6]	98.6
Straphangin' (81) 176(2) [0 | 0 | 3]	30.6
Beverly BREMERS ▶ 2604 Pk:124 [0 | 0 | 1]	**134**
I'll Make You Music (72) 124(1) [0 | 0 | 8]	134
BRENDA & The TABULATIONS ▶ 3374 Pk:191 [0 | 0 | 1]	**22**
Dry Your Eyes (67) 191(1) [0 | 0 | 4]	21.6
BREWER And SHIPLEY ▶ 1119 Pk:34 [0 | 1 | 4]	**1553**
Tarkio (71) 34(2) [0 | 3 | 26]	1374
Shake Off The Demon (71) 164(2) [0 | 0 | 8]	89.6
Rural Space (73) 174(1) [0 | 0 | 7]	52.8
ST-11261 (74) 185(1) [0 | 0 | 5]	37.0
BRICK ▶ 655 Pk:15 [0 | 2 | 5]	**4216**
Brick (77) 15(1) [0 | 9 | 32]	2241
Good High (76) 19(2) [0 | 8 | 24]	1530
Summer Heat (81) 89(2) [0 | 0 | 10]	222
Stoneheart (79) 100(1) [0 | 0 | 8]	179
Waiting On You (80) 179(2) [0 | 0 | 5]	43.3
Edie BRICKELL & NEW BOHEMIANS ▶ 612 Pk:4 [1 | 1 | 1]	**4620**
Shooting Rubberbands At The Stars (88) 4(2) [8 | 28 | 54]	4620
BRIDES OF FUNKENSTEIN ▶ 1822 Pk:70 [0 | 0 | 2]	**467**
Funk Or Walk (78) 70(1) [0 | 0 | 13]	314
Never Buy Texas From A Cowboy (80) 93(2) [0 | 0 | 7]	153

Act ▶ Highest Peak [Top10s | Top40s | Total] Title (Yr) Peak(Wk) [T10 Wk | T40Wk | TotalWk]	Score
Alicia BRIDGES ▶ 1155 Pk:33 [0 | 1 | 1]	**1450**
Alicia Bridges (78) 33(2) [0 | 7 | 32]	1450
Dee Dee BRIDGEWATER ▶ 2801 Pk:170 [0 | 0 | 2]	**97**
Just Family (78) 170(1) [0 | 0 | 7]	65.9
Bad For Me (79) 182(1) [0 | 0 | 4]	31.1
Martin BRILEY ▶ 1514 Pk:55 [0 | 0 | 2]	**777**
One Night With A Stranger (83) 55(1) [0 | 0 | 22]	589
Dangerous Moments (85) 85(2) [0 | 0 | 10]	188
Johnny BRISTOL ▶ 1830 Pk:82 [0 | 0 | 2]	**459**
Hang On In There Baby (74) 82(1) [0 | 0 | 17]	351
Bristol's Creme (76) 154(1) [0 | 0 | 11]	108
BRITISH LIONS ▶ 2076 Pk:83 [0 | 0 | 1]	**313**
British Lions (78) 83(1) [0 | 0 | 15]	313
BRITNY FOX ▶ 998 Pk:39 [0 | 1 | 2]	**1956**
Britny Fox (88) 39(2) [0 | 2 | 37]	1441
Boys In Heat (89) 79(3) [0 | 0 | 23]	516
Benjamin BRITTEN ▶ 2384 Pk:68 [0 | 0 | 1]	**190**
Britten: War Requiem (63) 68(1) [0 | 0 | 8]	190
David BROMBERG ▶ 1594 Pk:104 [0 | 0 | 7]	**687**
How Late'll Ya Play 'Til (76) 104(2) [0 | 0 | 11]	244
Bandit In A Bathing Suit (78) 130(1) [0 | 0 | 9]	151
Reckless Abandon (77) 132(2) [0 | 0 | 9]	141
My Own House (79) 152(2) [0 | 0 | 4]	55.2
Wanted Dead Or Alive (74) 167(1) [0 | 0 | 5]	49.8
Midnight On The Water (75) 173(2) [0 | 0 | 3]	33.2
David Bromberg (72) 194(2) [0 | 0 | 2]	13.1
BRONSKI BEAT ▶ 1439 Pk:36 [0 | 1 | 2]	**908**
The Age Of Consent (85) 36(2) [0 | 3 | 25]	847
Truthdare Doubledare (86) 147(2) [0 | 0 | 6]	61.1
Herman BROOD ▶ 2072 Pk:122 [0 | 0 | 1]	**315**
Herman Brood & His Wild Romance (79) 122(2) [0 | 0 | 19]	315
BROOKLYN BRIDGE ▶ 119 Pk:54 [0 | 0 | 2]	**1344**
Brooklyn Bridge (69) 54(2) [0 | 0 | 30]	1190
The Second Brooklyn Bridge (69) 145(1) [0 | 0 | 8]	154
BROOKLYN, BRONX & QUEENS Band ▶ 2485 Pk:109 [0 | 0 | 1]	**164**
The Brooklyn, Bronx & Queens Band (81) 109(1) [0 | 0 | 9]	164
BROOKLYN DREAMS ▶ 2860 Pk:151 [0 | 0 | 1]	**87**
Sleepless Nights (79) 151(1) [0 | 0 | 7]	86.6
BROS ▶ 3197 Pk:171 [0 | 0 | 1]	**40**
Push (88) 171(1) [0 | 0 | 5]	40.0
BROTHERHOOD OF MAN ▶ 2925 Pk:168 [0 | 0 | 1]	**76**
United We Stand (70) 168(2) [0 | 0 | 8]	76.1
BROTHERS FOUR ▶ 1342 Pk:56 [0 | 0 | 5]	**1057**
The Big Folk Hits (63) 56(1) [0 | 0 | 20]	459
Try To Remember (65) 76(1) [0 | 0 | 15]	328
A Beatles' Songbook (The Brothers Four Sing Lennon/McCartney) (66) 97(1) [0 | 0 | 7]	142
The Honey Wind Blows (65) 118(1) [0 | 0 | 5]	75.5
More Big Folk Hits (64) 134(1) [0 | 0 | 4]	51.9
BROTHERS JOHNSON ▶ 246 Pk:5 [3 | 4 | 7]	**14486**
Look Out For #1 (76) 9(2) [4 | 24 | 49]	4485
Right On Time (77) 13(3) [0 | 26 | 31]	3695
Light Up The Night (80) 5(2) [7 | 16 | 30]	3294
Blam!! (78) 7(3) [5 | 10 | 24]	2283
Winners (81) 48(2) [0 | 0 | 13]	481
Out of Control (84) 91(1) [0 | 0 | 11]	185
Blast! (The Latest And The Greatest) (83) 138(2) [0 | 0 | 5]	62.2

Act ▶ Highest Peak [Top10s | Top40s | Total] Title (Yr) Peak(Wk) [T10 Wk | T40Wk | TotalWk]	Score
Crazy World Of Arthur BROWN ▶ 846 Pk:7 [1 | 1 | 1]	**2702**
The Crazy World Of Arthur Brown (68) 7(2) [7 | 10 | 24]	2702
Bobby BROWN ▶ 187 Pk:1 [2 | 2 | 3]	**18363**
Don't Be Cruel (88) 1(6) [45 | 69 | 97]	15398
Dance!...Ya Know It! (89) 9(3) [5 | 17 | 33]	2707
King Of Stage (86) 88(2) [0 | 0 | 17]	258
Chuck BROWN & The SOUL SEARCHERS ▶ 1506 Pk:31 [0 | 1 | 1]	**794**
Bustin' Loose (79) 31(1) [0 | 5 | 14]	794
Danny Joe BROWN ▶ 2650 Pk:120 [0 | 0 | 1]	**123**
Danny Joe Brown And The Danny Joe Brown Band (81)-Danny Joe Brown And The Danny Joe Brown Band 120(2) [0 | 0 | 7]	123
James BROWN ▶ 118 Pk:10 [1 | 14 | 48]	**26659**
Live At The Apollo, Volume II (68) 32(1) [0 | 7 | 39]	1809
It's A Mother (69) 26(1) [0 | 7 | 24]	1579
Sex Machine (70) 29(1) [0 | 6 | 31]	1538
Pure Dynamite! Live At The Royal (64) 10(1) [1 | 13 | 22]	1525
The Payback (74) 34(1) [0 | 8 | 36]	1451
Hot Pants (71) 22(2) [0 | 7 | 18]	1291
Papa's Got A Brand New Bag (65) 26(2) [0 | 8 | 27]	1247
Revolution Of The Mind - Live At The Apollo, Volume III (71) 39(2) [0 | 2 | 21]	1114
Say It Loud-I'm Black And I'm Proud (69) 53(2) [0 | 0 | 22]	1035
James Brown Plays & Directs The Popcorn (69) 40(1) [0 | 1 | 22]	918
I Can't Stand Myself (When You Touch Me) (68) 17(1) [0 | 6 | 14]	903
Black Caesar (Soundtrack) (73) 31(2) [0 | 5 | 21]	898
Hell (74) 35(2) [0 | 2 | 19]	857
There It Is (72) 60(1) [0 | 0 | 21]	805
Cold Sweat (67) 35(2) [0 | 2 | 17]	766
Live At The Garden (67) 41(2) [0 | 0 | 17]	730
I Got You (I Feel Good) (66) 36(1) [0 | 4 | 17]	699
James Brown Plays James Brown - Today & Yesterday (65) 42(1) [0 | 0 | 19]	637
Super Bad (71) 61(1) [0 | 0 | 15]	634
Ain't It Funky (70) 43(3) [0 | 0 | 12]	606
Get On The Good Foot (72) 68(2) [0 | 0 | 17]	490
Showtime (64) 61(1) [0 | 0 | 18]	430
Gettin' Down To It (69) 99(2) [0 | 0 | 14]	426
James Brown Soul Classics (72) 83(2) [0 | 0 | 16]	420
Reality (75) 56(1) [0 | 0 | 10]	404
Prisoner Of Love (63) 73(2) [0 | 0 | 17]	392
Jam/1980's (78) 121(1) [0 | 0 | 22]	341
Raw Soul (67) 88(1) [0 | 0 | 14]	273
Slaughter's Big Rip-Off (Soundtrack) (73) 92(1) [0 | 0 | 11]	231
I'm Real (88) 96(1) [0 | 0 | 14]	229
I Got The Feelin' (68) 135(1) [0 | 0 | 14]	211
It's A Man's Man's Man's World (66) 90(1) [0 | 0 | 9]	204
James Brown Plays New Breed (66) 101(1) [0 | 0 | 11]	189
Soul On Top (70) 125(1) [0 | 0 | 10]	183
Sex Machine Today (75) 103(2) [0 | 0 | 8]	181
Bodyheat (77) 126(2) [0 | 0 | 10]	159
Grits & Soul (65) 124(1) [0 | 0 | 10]	131
Get Up Offa That Thing (76) 147(2) [0 | 0 | 8]	121
It's A New Day So Let A Man Come In (70) 121(2) [0 | 0 | 6]	121
Sho Is Funky Down Here (71) 137(2) [0 | 0 | 4]	80.3
The Original Disco Man (79) 152(1) [0 | 0 | 6]	73.2

<table>
<tr><th>Act ▶ Highest Peak [Top10s|Top40s|Total]
Title (Yr) Peak(Wk) [T10 Wk|T40Wk|TotalWk]</th><th>Score</th></tr>
<tr><td>James BROWN ▶ Continued</td><td></td></tr>
<tr><td>James Brown Plays Nothing But Soul (68)
150(1) [0|0|5]</td><td>72.0</td></tr>
<tr><td>Gravity (86) 156(2) [0|0|6]</td><td>56.4</td></tr>
<tr><td>James Brown Plays The Real Thing (67)
164(2) [0|0|5]</td><td>54.0</td></tr>
<tr><td>Handful Of Soul (66) 135(1) [0|0|3]</td><td>47.8</td></tr>
<tr><td>James Brown...Live/Hot On The One (80)
170(2) [0|0|5]</td><td>45.7</td></tr>
<tr><td>Live And Lowdown At The Apollo Vol 1 (80)
163(2) [0|0|3]</td><td>36.8</td></tr>
<tr><td>Everybody's Doin' The Hustle & Dead On The
Double Bump (75) 193(1) [0|0|2]</td><td>13.9</td></tr>
<tr><td>Jim Ed BROWN ▶ 2327 Pk:81 [0|0|1]</td><td>207</td></tr>
<tr><td>Morning (71) 81(2) [0|0|9]</td><td>207</td></tr>
<tr><td>Julie BROWN ▶ 3082 Pk:168 [0|0|1]</td><td>54</td></tr>
<tr><td>Goddess In Progress (85) 168(1) [0|0|7]</td><td>54.4</td></tr>
<tr><td>Maxine BROWN ▶ 3458 Pk:195 [0|0|1]</td><td>13</td></tr>
<tr><td>We'll Cry Together (69) 195(1) [0|0|2]</td><td>13.4</td></tr>
<tr><td>Odell BROWN & THE ORGAN-IZERS ▶ 3256
Pk:173 [0|0|1]</td><td>33</td></tr>
<tr><td>Mellow Yellow (67) 173(1) [0|0|4]</td><td>32.7</td></tr>
<tr><td>Peter BROWN ▶ 715 Pk:11 [0|1|1]</td><td>3524</td></tr>
<tr><td>Fantasy Love Affair (78) 11(2) [0|19|44]</td><td>3524</td></tr>
<tr><td>Shirley BROWN ▶ 2287 Pk:98 [0|0|1]</td><td>220</td></tr>
<tr><td>Woman To Woman (75) 98(2) [0|0|11]</td><td>220</td></tr>
<tr><td>Duncan BROWNE ▶ 3100 Pk:174 [0|0|1]</td><td>52</td></tr>
<tr><td>The Wild Places (79) 174(2) [0|0|5]</td><td>51.9</td></tr>
<tr><td>Jackson BROWNE ▶ 123 Pk:1 [4|6|9]</td><td>25712</td></tr>
<tr><td>Running On Empty (78) 3(2) [17|25|65]</td><td>6523</td></tr>
<tr><td>Hold Out (80) 1(1) [13|21|38]</td><td>6411</td></tr>
<tr><td>The Pretender (76) 5(3) [5|18|35]</td><td>3859</td></tr>
<tr><td>Late For The Sky (74) 14(2) [0|12|29]</td><td>2401</td></tr>
<tr><td>Lawyers In Love (83) 8(3) [4|12|33]</td><td>2216</td></tr>
<tr><td>Lives In The Balance (86) 23(3) [0|9|31]</td><td>1582</td></tr>
<tr><td>For Everyman (73) 43(1) [0|0|38]</td><td>1395</td></tr>
<tr><td>Jackson Browne (72) 53(2) [0|0|23]</td><td>790</td></tr>
<tr><td>World In Motion (89)
45(2) [0|0|16]</td><td>536</td></tr>
<tr><td>Tom BROWNE ▶ 759 Pk:18 [0|2|5]</td><td>3204</td></tr>
<tr><td>Love Approach (80) 18(2) [0|9|26]</td><td>1795</td></tr>
<tr><td>Magic (81) 37(2) [0|2|19]</td><td>929</td></tr>
<tr><td>Yours Truly (81) 97(1) [0|0|14]</td><td>291</td></tr>
<tr><td>Rockin' Radio (83) 147(1) [0|0|12]</td><td>111</td></tr>
<tr><td>Browne Sugar (79) 147(2) [0|0|6]</td><td>78.4</td></tr>
<tr><td>BROWNSVILLE STATION ▶ 1934
Pk:98 [0|0|3]</td><td>385</td></tr>
<tr><td>Yeah! (73) 98(1) [0|0|19]</td><td>284</td></tr>
<tr><td>School Punks (74) 170(1) [0|0|8]</td><td>73.1</td></tr>
<tr><td>A Night On The Town (72) 190(1) [0|0|5]</td><td>28.7</td></tr>
<tr><td>Dave BRUBECK ▶ 3312 Pk:167 [0|0|1]</td><td>27</td></tr>
<tr><td>1975: The Duets (76)-Dave Brubeck And
Paul Desmond [A] 167(1) [0|0|5]</td><td>27.3</td></tr>
<tr><td>Dave BRUBECK Quartet ▶ 1838
Pk:81 [0|0|6]</td><td>451</td></tr>
<tr><td>Time Changes (64) 81(1) [0|0|9]</td><td>173</td></tr>
<tr><td>My Favorite Things (66) 133(1) [0|0|5]</td><td>72.4</td></tr>
<tr><td>Dave Brubeck's Greatest Hits (66)-
Dave Brubeck 134(1) [0|0|4]</td><td>64.5</td></tr>
<tr><td>Jazz Impressions Of New York (65)
142(1) [0|0|4]</td><td>50.8</td></tr>
<tr><td>Angel Eyes (65) 122(1) [0|0|3]</td><td>46.7</td></tr>
<tr><td>Brandenburg Gate: Revisited (63)
137(1) [0|0|3]</td><td>42.8</td></tr>
<tr><td>Jack BRUCE ▶ 1411 Pk:37 [0|1|6]</td><td>954</td></tr>
<tr><td>Songs For A Tailor (69) 55(2) [0|0|11]</td><td>485</td></tr>
<tr><td>B.L.T. (81)-
Jack Bruce/Bill Lordan/Robin Trower [A]
37(1) [0|3|16]</td><td>281</td></tr>
<tr><td>How's Tricks (77)-The Jack Bruce Band
153(1) [0|0|5]</td><td>69.9</td></tr>
<tr><td>Truce (82)-Jack Bruce & Robin Trower [A]
109(2) [0|0|6]</td><td>60.1</td></tr>
<tr><td>Out Of The Storm (74) 160(1) [0|0|3]</td><td>39.6</td></tr>
<tr><td>I've Always Wanted To Do This (80)-Jack Bruce
And Friends 182(1) [0|0|2]</td><td>17.7</td></tr>
<tr><td>Lenny BRUCE ▶ 3228 Pk:178 [0|0|2]</td><td>36</td></tr>
<tr><td>Lenny Bruce/Carnegie Hall (75) 178(1) [0|0|2]</td><td>20.7</td></tr>
<tr><td>The Real Lenny Bruce (75) 191(2) [0|0|2]</td><td>15.8</td></tr>
<tr><td>Bill BRUFORD ▶ 2754 Pk:123 [0|0|2]</td><td>104</td></tr>
<tr><td>One Of A Kind (79) 123(1) [0|0|5]</td><td>90.5</td></tr>
<tr><td>Gradually Going Tornado (80) 191(1) [0|0|2]</td><td>13.2</td></tr>
<tr><td>Anita BRYANT ▶ 3052 Pk:146 [0|0|1]</td><td>59</td></tr>
<tr><td>Mine Eyes Have Seen The Glory (67)
146(1) [0|0|4]</td><td>58.9</td></tr>
<tr><td>Ray BRYANT ▶ 2309 Pk:111 [0|0|2]</td><td>213</td></tr>
<tr><td>Gotta Travel On (66)-Ray Bryant Trio
111(1) [0|0|12]</td><td>196</td></tr>
<tr><td>Slow Freight (67) 193(1) [0|0|3]</td><td>16.3</td></tr>
<tr><td>Sharon BRYANT ▶ 2589 Pk:139 [0|0|1]</td><td>138</td></tr>
<tr><td>Here I Am (89) 139(1) [0|0|13]</td><td>138</td></tr>
<tr><td>Peabo BRYSON ▶ 524 Pk:35 [0|2|11]</td><td>5792</td></tr>
<tr><td>Reaching For The Sky (78) 49(2) [0|0|29]</td><td>1114</td></tr>
<tr><td>Crosswinds (78) 35(1) [0|4|26]</td><td>1099</td></tr>
<tr><td>I Am Love (81) 40(2) [0|2|24]</td><td>868</td></tr>
<tr><td>Straight From The Heart (84) 44(2) [0|0|26]</td><td>847</td></tr>
<tr><td>Don't Play With Fire (82) 55(3) [0|0|21]</td><td>497</td></tr>
<tr><td>We're The Best Of Friends (79)-Natalie Cole &
Peabo Bryson [A] 44(1) [0|0|19]</td><td>403</td></tr>
<tr><td>Paradise (80) 79(2) [0|0|16]</td><td>344</td></tr>
<tr><td>Turn The Hands Of Time (81) 82(1) [0|0|11]</td><td>289</td></tr>
<tr><td>Take No Prisoners (85) 102(2) [0|0|13]</td><td>196</td></tr>
<tr><td>The Peabo Bryson Collection (84)
168(1) [0|0|10]</td><td>74.9</td></tr>
<tr><td>Positive (88) 157(1) [0|0|6]</td><td>59.6</td></tr>
<tr><td>B.T. EXPRESS ▶ 492 Pk:5 [1|2|6]</td><td>6286</td></tr>
<tr><td>Do It ('Til You're Satisfied) (74) 5(1) [5|18|31]</td><td>3720</td></tr>
<tr><td>Non-Stop (75) 19(1) [0|8|19]</td><td>1555</td></tr>
<tr><td>Energy To Burn (76) 43(2) [0|0|12]</td><td>523</td></tr>
<tr><td>Shout! (78) 67(2) [0|0|11]</td><td>328</td></tr>
<tr><td>Function At The Junction (77) 111(2) [0|0|5]</td><td>115</td></tr>
<tr><td>1980 (80) 164(1) [0|0|4]</td><td>45.1</td></tr>
<tr><td>BUBBLE PUPPY ▶ 2960 Pk:176 [0|0|1]</td><td>70</td></tr>
<tr><td>A Gathering Of Promises (69) 176(1) [0|0|6]</td><td>70.5</td></tr>
<tr><td>Roy BUCHANAN ▶ 1209 Pk:86 [0|0|10]</td><td>1325</td></tr>
<tr><td>Second Album (73) 86(1) [0|0|13]</td><td>270</td></tr>
<tr><td>Roy Buchanan (72) 107(1) [0|0|12]</td><td>250</td></tr>
<tr><td>Loading Zone (77) 105(2) [0|0|8]</td><td>172</td></tr>
<tr><td>You're Not Alone (78) 119(2) [0|0|7]</td><td>144</td></tr>
<tr><td>That's What I Am Here For (74) 152(1) [0|0|10]</td><td>118</td></tr>
<tr><td>A Street Called Straight (76) 148(3) [0|0|7]</td><td>114</td></tr>
<tr><td>When A Guitar Plays The Blues (85)
161(1) [0|0|13]</td><td>110</td></tr>
<tr><td>In The Beginning (74) 160(1) [0|0|6]</td><td>68.2</td></tr>
<tr><td>Dancing On The Edge (86)
153(2) [0|0|8]</td><td>66.0</td></tr>
<tr><td>My Babe (81) 193(1) [0|0|2]</td><td>13.2</td></tr>
<tr><td>Lindsey BUCKINGHAM ▶ 1033
Pk:32 [0|1|2]</td><td>1817</td></tr>
<tr><td>Law And Order (81) 32(1) [0|6|24]</td><td>1282</td></tr>
<tr><td>Go Insane (84) 45(4) [0|0|16]</td><td>534</td></tr>
<tr><td>The BUCKINGHAMS ▶ 1088 Pk:53 [0|0|5]</td><td>1640</td></tr>
<tr><td>Time & Charges (67) 58(1) [0|0|23]</td><td>548</td></tr>
<tr><td>Portraits (68) 53(1) [0|0|16]</td><td>434</td></tr>
<tr><td>The Buckinghams' Greatest Hits (69)
73(1) [0|0|12]</td><td>431</td></tr>
<tr><td>Kind Of A Drag (67) 109(1) [0|0|8]</td><td>159</td></tr>
<tr><td>In One Ear And Gone Tomorrow (68)
161(1) [0|0|5]</td><td>67.5</td></tr>
<tr><td>Tim BUCKLEY ▶ 1869 Pk:81 [0|0|3]</td><td>428</td></tr>
<tr><td>Happy Sad (69) 81(1) [0|0|12]</td><td>370</td></tr>
<tr><td>Goodbye And Hello (67) 171(2) [0|0|5]</td><td>43.3</td></tr>
<tr><td>Blue Afternoon (70) 192(1) [0|0|2]</td><td>14.1</td></tr>
<tr><td>BUCKNER And GARCIA ▶ 1483
Pk:24 [0|1|1]</td><td>844</td></tr>
<tr><td>Pac-Man Fever (82)-Buckner & Garcia
24(2) [0|5|16]</td><td>844</td></tr>
<tr><td>BUCKWHEAT ▶ 3117 Pk:179 [0|0|1]</td><td>50</td></tr>
<tr><td>Movin' On (72) 179(1) [0|0|6]</td><td>50.2</td></tr>
<tr><td>BUCKWHEAT ZYDECO ▶ 2490
Pk:104 [0|0|2]</td><td>163</td></tr>
<tr><td>Taking It Home (88) 104(1) [0|0|7]</td><td>130</td></tr>
<tr><td>On A Night Like This (87) 172(1) [0|0|5]</td><td>32.7</td></tr>
<tr><td>BUD And TRAVIS ▶ 2579 Pk:126 [0|0|2]</td><td>141</td></tr>
<tr><td>Perspective On Bud & Travis (64)-Bud & Travis
129(1) [0|0|6]</td><td>81.3</td></tr>
<tr><td>Bud & Travis...In Concert (63)-Bud & Travis
126(1) [0|0|4]</td><td>59.6</td></tr>
<tr><td>BUFFALO SPRINGFIELD ▶ 784
Pk:42 [0|0|5]</td><td>3058</td></tr>
<tr><td>Retrospective/The Best Of Buffalo Springfield
(69) 42(3) [0|0|24]</td><td>1065</td></tr>
<tr><td>Last Time Around (68) 42(1) [0|0|19]</td><td>900</td></tr>
<tr><td>Buffalo Springfield Again (67) 44(1) [0|0|14]</td><td>480</td></tr>
<tr><td>Buffalo Springfield (67) 80(2) [0|0|16]</td><td>374</td></tr>
<tr><td>Buffalo Springfield(2) (73) 104(1) [0|0|13]</td><td>240</td></tr>
<tr><td>Jimmy BUFFETT ▶ 244 Pk:10 [1|6|16]</td><td>14581</td></tr>
<tr><td>Changes In Latitudes, Changes In Attitudes (77)
12(2) [0|19|42]</td><td>3750</td></tr>
<tr><td>Son Of A Son Of A Sailor (78)
10(2) [2|9|29]</td><td>2228</td></tr>
<tr><td>Volcano (79) 14(1) [0|11|28]</td><td>1857</td></tr>
<tr><td>A1A (75) 25(2) [0|4|27]</td><td>1237</td></tr>
<tr><td>Coconut Telegraph (81) 30(1) [0|4|18]</td><td>909</td></tr>
<tr><td>Somewhere Over China (82) 31(3) [0|6|15]</td><td>755</td></tr>
<tr><td>Last Mango In Paris (85) 53(3) [0|0|20]</td><td>568</td></tr>
<tr><td>One Particular Harbour (83) 59(3) [0|0|24]</td><td>545</td></tr>
<tr><td>You Had To Be There (78) 72(1) [0|0|18]</td><td>510</td></tr>
<tr><td>Hot Water (88) 46(2) [0|0|14]</td><td>487</td></tr>
<tr><td>Havana Daydreamin' (76) 65(1) [0|0|14]</td><td>429</td></tr>
<tr><td>Off To See The Lizard (89) 57(2) [0|0|13]</td><td>358</td></tr>
<tr><td>Floridays (86) 66(1) [0|0|16]</td><td>326</td></tr>
<tr><td>Songs You Know By Heart:
Jimmy Buffett's Greatest Hit(s) (85)
100(2) [0|0|24]</td><td>280</td></tr>
<tr><td>Riddles In The Sand (84) 87(1) [0|0|14]</td><td>238</td></tr>
<tr><td>Living And Dying In 3/4 Time (74)
176(2) [0|0|13]</td><td>106</td></tr>
<tr><td>The BUGGLES ▶ 3127 Pk:161 [0|0|1]</td><td>49</td></tr>
<tr><td>Adventures In Modern Recording (82)
161(2) [0|0|5]</td><td>48.9</td></tr>
<tr><td>Alex BUGNON ▶ 2574 Pk:127 [0|0|1]</td><td>142</td></tr>
<tr><td>Love Season (89) .1 127(3) [0|0|11]</td><td>142</td></tr>
<tr><td>BULGARIAN STATE RADIO &
T.V. FEMALE CHOIR ▶ 2857 Pk:165 [0|0|1]</td><td>87</td></tr>
<tr><td>Mystery Of Bulgarian Voices (88)
165(1) [0|0|10]</td><td>86.8</td></tr>
<tr><td>BULLDOG ▶ 2799 Pk:176 [0|0|1]</td><td>98</td></tr>
<tr><td>Bulldog (72) 176(1) [0|0|12]</td><td>97.5</td></tr>
<tr><td>BULLETBOYS ▶ 1138 Pk:34 [0|1|1]</td><td>1504</td></tr>
<tr><td>Bulletboys (88) 34(3) [0|5|47]</td><td>1504</td></tr>
<tr><td>Victor BUONO ▶ 1652 Pk:66 [0|0|1]</td><td>619</td></tr>
<tr><td>Heavy! (71) 66(2) [0|0|17]</td><td>619</td></tr>
<tr><td>Eric BURDON Band ▶ 1547 Pk:51 [0|0|2]</td><td>733</td></tr>
<tr><td>Sun Secrets (74) 51(1) [0|0|16]</td><td>690</td></tr>
<tr><td>Stop (75) 171(1) [0|0|5]</td><td>43.5</td></tr>
</table>

Act ▶ Highest Peak [Top10s | Top40s | Total] Title (Yr) Peak(Wk) [T10 Wk | T40Wk | TotalWk]	Score
Eric BURDON & WAR ▶ 873 Pk:18 [0 | 1 | 3]	**2522**
Eric Burdon Declares "War" (70)-Eric Burdon And War 18(3) [0 | 13 | 27]	2173
The Black-Man's Burdon (70)-Eric Burdon And War 82(1) [0 | 0 | 9]	261
Love Is All Around (76)-War Featuring Eric Burdon 140(2) [0 | 0 | 5]	88.7
Solomon BURKE ▶ 2641 Pk:140 [0 | 0 | 2]	**125**
Proud Mary (69) 140(2) [0 | 0 | 4]	87.0
The Best Of Solomon Burke (65) 141(1) [0 | 0 | 3]	38.0
Carol BURNETT ▶ 3506 Pk:199 [0 | 0 | 1]	**11**
Carol Burnett Featuring If I Could Write A Song (72) 199(2) [0 | 0 | 2]	10.9
T-Bone BURNETT ▶ 3311 Pk:188 [0 | 0 | 1]	**27**
Proof Through The Night (83) 188(2) [0 | 0 | 5]	27.3
Rocky BURNETTE ▶ 1791 Pk:53 [0 | 0 | 1]	**491**
The Son Of Rock And Roll (80) 53(1) [0 | 0 | 14]	491
BURNING SENSATIONS ▶ 3282 Pk:175 [0 | 0 | 1]	**30**
Burning Sensations (83) 175(1) [0 | 0 | 4]	29.9
George BURNS ▶ 2314 Pk:93 [0 | 0 | 1]	**211**
I Wish I Was Eighteen Again (80) 93(2) [0 | 0 | 10]	211
Kenny BURRELL ▶ 2905 Pk:108 [0 | 0 | 3]	**80**
Blue Bash! (63)-Kenny Burrell/Jimmy Smith [A] 108(1) [0 | 0 | 4]	35.8
The Tender Gender (66) 146(1) [0 | 0 | 2]	28.8
Blues-The Common Ground (68) 191(1) [0 | 0 | 2]	15.1
Glen BURTNICK ▶ 3003 Pk:147 [0 | 0 | 1]	**66**
Heroes & Zeros (87) 147(2) [0 | 0 | 6]	65.9
Jenny BURTON ▶ 3296 Pk:181 [0 | 0 | 1]	**29**
In Black And White (84) 181(2) [0 | 0 | 4]	28.7
BUS BOYS ▶ 1882 Pk:85 [0 | 0 | 2]	**416**
Minimum Wage Rock & Roll (80) 85(1) [0 | 0 | 15]	330
American Worker (82) 139(3) [0 | 0 | 7]	86.3
Kate BUSH ▶ 834 Pk:30 [0 | 1 | 5]	**2754**
Hounds Of Love (85) 30(1) [0 | 6 | 27]	1088
The Sensual World (89) 43(2) [0 | 0 | 26]	1024
The Whole Story (86) 76(1) [0 | 0 | 27]	484
The Dreaming (82) 157(2) [0 | 0 | 11]	98.8
Kate Bush (83) 148(1) [0 | 0 | 6]	59.5
Jon BUTCHER AXIS ▶ 1225 Pk:66 [0 | 0 | 5]	**1287**
Wishes (87)-Jon Butcher 77(2) [0 | 0 | 27]	532
Along The Axis (85) 66(1) [0 | 0 | 17]	340
Jon Butcher Axis (83) 91(1) [0 | 0 | 13]	228
Pictures From The Front (89)-Jon Butcher 121(3) [0 | 0 | 8]	129
Store At The Sun (84) 160(1) [0 | 0 | 6]	57.5
Jerry BUTLER ▶ 568 Pk:29 [0 | 1 | 15]	**5118**
The Ice Man Cometh (69) 29(1) [0 | 6 | 47]	2455
Ice On Ice (69) 41(1) [0 | 0 | 23]	961
The Spice Of Life (72) 92(2) [0 | 0 | 24]	551
The Sagittarius Movement (71) 123(1) [0 | 0 | 22]	381
Thelma & Jerry (77)-Thelma Houston & Jerry Butler [A] 53(1) [0 | 0 | 12]	199
Suite For The Single Girl (77) 146(1) [0 | 0 | 11]	155
Delicious Together (64)-Betty Everett & Jerry Butler [A] 102(1) [0 | 0 | 11]	89.8
Mr. Dream Merchant (68) 154(1) [0 | 0 | 7]	78.5
The Best Of Jerry Butler (70) 167(2) [0 | 0 | 5]	47.4
Gene & Jerry - One & One (71)-Gene Chandler & Jerry Butler [A] 143(2) [0 | 0 | 5]	46.9
You & Me (70) 172(1) [0 | 0 | 4]	44.8
Nothing Says I Love You Like I Love You (79) 160(1) [0 | 0 | 4]	42.9
Jerry Butler Sings Assorted Sounds (71) 186(1) [0 | 0 | 4]	34.8
Jerry Butler's Golden Hits Live (68) 178(2) [0 | 0 | 2]	18.2
The Soul Goes On (68) 195(1) [0 | 0 | 2]	12.2
Jonathan BUTLER ▶ 1183 Pk:50 [0 | 0 | 3]	**1385**
Jonathan Butler (87) 50(2) [0 | 0 | 33]	916
More Than Friends (88) 113(2) [0 | 0 | 22]	235
Introducing Jonathan Butler (86) 101(2) [0 | 0 | 16]	234
Billy BUTTERFIELD ▶ 2580 Pk:85 [0 | 0 | 1]	**141**
Just Kiddin' Around (63)-Ray Conniff & Billy Butterfield [A] 85(1) [0 | 0 | 13]	141
Paul BUTTERFIELD Blues Band ▶ 796 Pk:52 [0 | 0 | 10]	**2967**
East-West (66)-The Butterfield Blues Band 65(2) [0 | 0 | 29]	773
The Resurrection Of Pigboy Crabshaw (68)-The Butterfield Blues Band 52(2) [0 | 0 | 16]	573
In My Own Dream (68)-The Butterfield Blues Band 79(1) [0 | 0 | 17]	440
The Butterfield Blues Band/Live (71)-The Butterfield Blues Band 72(1) [0 | 0 | 12]	334
Keep On Moving (69)-The Butterfield Blues Band 102(1) [0 | 0 | 10]	253
Better Days (73)-Paul Butterfield's Better Days 145(1) [0 | 0 | 13]	148
The Paul Butterfield Blues Band (65) 123(1) [0 | 0 | 9]	140
Golden Butter/The Best Of The Paul Butterfield Blues Band (72)-The Butterfield Blues Band 136(2) [0 | 0 | 6]	107
Sometimes I Just Feel Like Smilin' (71)-The Butterfield Blues Band 124(2) [0 | 0 | 6]	101
It All Comes Back (73)-Paul Butterfield's Better Days 156(1) [0 | 0 | 8]	98.9
BUZZCOCKS ▶ 3089 Pk:163 [0 | 0 | 1]	**53**
Different Kind Of Tension (80) 163(1) [0 | 0 | 6]	53.4
Charlie BYRD ▶ 2708 Pk:129 [0 | 0 | 2]	**113**
Aquarius (69) 197(2) [0 | 0 | 4]	26.2
Let Go (69)-The Charlie Byrd Quartet 129(1) [0 | 0 | 4]	86.5
Donald BYRD ▶ 580 Pk:33 [0 | 2 | 8]	**4991**
Street Lady (74) 33(1) [0 | 3 | 28]	1243
Black Byrd (73) 36(1) [0 | 2 | 34]	1230
Places And Spaces (75) 49(2) [0 | 0 | 29]	1091
Stepping Into Tomorrow (75) 42(1) [0 | 0 | 19]	791
Caricatures (77) 60(1) [0 | 0 | 14]	440
A New Perspective (64) 110(1) [0 | 0 | 8]	122
Donald Byrd's Best (76) 167(1) [0 | 0 | 4]	47.2
Thank You...For F.U.M.L. (Funking Up My Life) (78) 191(1) [0 | 0 | 4]	26.1
Donald BYRD And 125th STREET N.Y.C. ▶ 2292 Pk:93 [0 | 0 | 1]	**220**
Love Byrd (81) 93(1) [0 | 0 | 10]	220
The BYRDS ▶ 258 Pk:6 [2 | 8 | 15]	**13819**
The Byrds' Greatest Hits (67) 6(3) [5 | 15 | 29]	2607
Mr. Tambourine Man (65) 6(3) [3 | 14 | 38]	2014
Turn! Turn! Turn! (66) 17(1) [0 | 10 | 40]	1737
Fifth Dimension (66) 24(2) [0 | 8 | 28]	1288
The Byrds (Untitled) (70) 40(2) [0 | 2 | 21]	1166
Byrds (73) 20(1) [0 | 7 | 17]	1081
Younger Than Yesterday (67) 24(1) [0 | 5 | 24]	923
Ballad Of Easy Rider (69) 36(1) [0 | 3 | 17]	751
The Notorious Byrd Brothers (68) 47(2) [0 | 0 | 19]	558
Byrdmaniax (71) 46(1) [0 | 0 | 10]	501
Preflyte (69) 84(2) [0 | 0 | 15]	409
Sweetheart Of The Rodeo (68) 77(2) [0 | 0 | 10]	317
The Best Of The Byrds (Greatest Hits, Volume II) (72) 114(1) [0 | 0 | 13]	256
Dr. Byrds & Mr. Hyde (69) 153(1) [0 | 0 | 7]	113
Farther Along (71) 152(1) [0 | 0 | 7]	97.2
David BYRNE ▶ 1455 Pk:44 [0 | 0 | 4]	**885**
Rei Momo (89) 71(2) [0 | 0 | 18]	324
My Life In The Bush Of Ghosts (81)-Brian Eno - David Byrne [A] 44(2) [0 | 0 | 13]	257
The Catherine Wheel (Original Cast) (81) 104(1) [0 | 0 | 12]	237
Music For The Knee Plays (85) 141(2) [0 | 0 | 6]	66.7
D.L. BYRON ▶ 2566 Pk:133 [0 | 0 | 1]	**145**
This Day And Age (80) 133(1) [0 | 0 | 10]	145
C	
CACTUS ▶ 1269 Pk:54 [0 | 0 | 5]	**1206**
Cactus (70) 54(2) [0 | 0 | 18]	642
One Way...Or Another (71) 88(1) [0 | 0 | 13]	330
Restrictions (71) 155(1) [0 | 0 | 10]	127
'Ot 'N' Sweaty (72) 162(2) [0 | 0 | 5]	61.6
Son Of Cactus (73)-New Cactus Band 183(1) [0 | 0 | 6]	44.7
CACTUS WORLD NEWS ▶ 3252 Pk:179 [0 | 0 | 1]	**33**
Urban Beaches (86) 179(1) [0 | 0 | 5]	33.0
John CAFFERTY & The BEAVER BROWN BAND ▶ 594 Pk:9 [1 | 2 | 3]	**4782**
Eddie & The Cruisers (Soundtrack) (83) 9(5) [6 | 24 | 62]	3552
Tough All Over (85) 40(3) [0 | 3 | 32]	1156
Eddie & The Cruisers II (Soundtrack) (89) 121(2) [0 | 0 | 6]	74.5
Tané CAIN ▶ 2546 Pk:121 [0 | 0 | 1]	**149**
Tane Cain (82)-Tane Cain 121(2) [0 | 0 | 10]	149
CALDERA ▶ 3118 Pk:159 [0 | 0 | 1]	**50**
Sky Islands (77) 159(1) [0 | 0 | 4]	50.1
Bobby CALDWELL ▶ 945 Pk:21 [0 | 1 | 3]	**2149**
Bobby Caldwell (78) 21(2) [0 | 10 | 31]	1758
Cat In The Hat (80) 113(2) [0 | 0 | 15]	239
Carry On (82) 133(1) [0 | 0 | 13]	152
J.J. CALE ▶ 941 Pk:51 [0 | 0 | 7]	**2169**
Naturally (72) 51(2) [0 | 0 | 32]	944
Troubadour (76) 84(2) [0 | 0 | 18]	369
Really (72) 92(2) [0 | 0 | 11]	261
Okie (74) 128(1) [0 | 0 | 11]	206
Shades (81) 110(1) [0 | 0 | 7]	150
5 (79) 136(1) [0 | 0 | 9]	148
Grasshopper (82) 149(1) [0 | 0 | 8]	92.9
John CALE ▶ 2961 Pk:154 [0 | 0 | 1]	**70**
Honi Soit (o nee swa) (81) 154(2) [0 | 0 | 5]	70.4
CALIFORNIA RAISINS ▶ 1395 Pk:60 [0 | 0 | 2]	**976**
The California Raisins (87) 60(2) [0 | 0 | 36]	822
Sweet, Delicious & Marvelous (88) 140(1) [0 | 0 | 15]	154
The CALL ▶ 1143 Pk:64 [0 | 0 | 4]	**1485**
Reconciled (86) 82(2) [0 | 0 | 30]	517
Let The Day Begin (89) 64(1) [0 | 0 | 22]	516
Modern Romans (83) 84(1) [0 | 0 | 15]	268
Into The Woods (87) 123(2) [0 | 0 | 13]	184
Maria CALLAS ▶ 2479 Pk:87 [0 | 0 | 1]	**166**
Bizet: Carmen (65) 87(2) [0 | 0 | 8]	166
Godfrey CAMBRIDGE ▶ 1735 Pk:42 [0 | 0 | 2]	**541**
Ready Or Not...Here's Godfrey Cambridge (64) 42(1) [0 | 0 | 13]	432
Them Cotton Pickin' Days Is Over (65) 142(1) [0 | 0 | 9]	109
CAMEL ▶ 1571 Pk:118 [0 | 0 | 5]	**707**
Moonmadness (76) 118(2) [0 | 0 | 13]	251
Breathless (79) 134(1) [0 | 0 | 10]	157
Mirage (74) 149(2) [0 | 0 | 13]	155
Rain Dances (77) 136(2) [0 | 0 | 5]	82.6
The Snow Goose (75) 162(2) [0 | 0 | 5]	61.1

Act ▶ Highest Peak [Top10s | Top40s | Total] Title (Yr) Peak(Wk) [T10 Wk | T40Wk | TotalWk]	Score
CAMEO ▶ 289 Pk:8 [1|4|13]	**12075**
Word Up! (86) 8(1) [3|31|54]	3662
Cameosis (80) 25(3) [0|10|26]	1618
She's Strange (84) 27(1) [0|9|24]	1083
Alligator Woman (82) 23(3) [0|6|24]	987
Feel Me (80) 44(1) [0|0|17]	814
Secret Omen (79) 46(1) [0|0|21]	778
Single Life (85) 58(2) [0|0|27]	671
We All Know Who We Are (78) 58(2) [0|0|23]	644
Knights Of The Sound Table (81) 44(2) [0|0|13]	564
Machismo (88) 56(1) [0|0|19]	414
Style (83) 53(1) [0|0|12]	301
Ugly Ego (78) 83(1) [0|0|15]	293
Cardiac Arrest (77) 116(1) [0|0|15]	244
Rafael CAMERON ▶ 1600 Pk:67 [0|0|2]	**680**
Cameron (80) 67(1) [0|0|18]	464
Cameron's In Love (81) 101(1) [0|0|12]	217
CAMOUFLAGE ▶ 2249 Pk:100 [0|0|1]	**235**
Voices & Images (89) 100(3) [0|0|14]	235
Glen CAMPBELL ▶ 36 Pk:1 [3|14|25]	**48249**
Wichita Lineman (68) 1(5) [22|29|46]	11245
Gentle On My Mind (67) 5(1) [14|40|76]	6843
Galveston (69) 2(1) [10|18|42]	5663
By The Time I Get To Phoenix (67) 15(4) [0|35|80]	5471
Glen Campbell - "Live" (69) 13(1) [0|14|29]	2936
Rhinestone Cowboy (75) 17(2) [0|13|30]	2409
Hey, Little One (68) 26(1) [0|4|51]	2254
Try A Little Kindness (70) 12(2) [0|11|28]	2051
A New Place In The Sun (68) 24(1) [0|5|33]	1569
Southern Nights (77) 22(2) [0|7|22]	1291
The Glen Campbell Goodtime Album (70) 27(2) [0|5|21]	1176
Glen Campbell's Greatest Hits (71) 39(1) [0|1|27]	1166
Oh Happy Day (70) 38(2) [0|3|19]	877
Norwood (Soundtrack) (70) 90(1) [0|0|13]	291
Bloodline (76) 63(2) [0|0|9]	269
The Last Time I Saw Her (71) 87(1) [0|0|9]	251
Glen Travis Campbell (72) 148(3) [0|0|13]	165
Best Of Glen Campbell (76) 116(1) [0|0|6]	128
Anne Murray / Glen Campbell (71)-Anne Murray & Glen Campbell [A] 128(1) [0|0|8]	77.7
I Knew Jesus (Before He Was A Star) (73) 154(1) [0|0|6]	71.7
Basic (78) 164(3) [0|0|5]	59.2
Reunion (The Songs Of Jimmy Webb) (74) 166(2) [0|0|5]	53.9
Live At The Royal Festival Hall (78) 171(3) [0|0|5]	51.5
It's The World Gone Crazy (81) 178(1) [0|0|3]	28.1
Bobbie Gentry & Glen Campbell (68)-Bobbie Gentry & Glen Campbell [A] 11(2) [0|13|47]	1850
CAMPER VAN BEETHOVEN ▶ 1958 Pk:124 [0|0|2]	**374**
Our Beloved Revolutionary Sweetheart (88) 124(1) [0|0|17]	238
Key Lime Pie (89) 141(3) [0|0|12]	135
CANDLEMASS ▶ 3170 Pk:174 [0|0|1]	**44**
Ancient Dreams (89) 174(2) [0|0|6]	44.1
The CANDYMEN ▶ 3384 Pk:195 [0|0|1]	**20**
The Candymen (67) 195(2) [0|0|4]	20.4
CANNED HEAT ▶ 442 Pk:16 [0|3|11]	**7227**
Boogie With Canned Heat (68) 16(2) [0|14|52]	2552
Living The Blues (68) 18(2) [0|9|17]	1612
Hallelujah (69) 37(2) [0|2|15]	763
Future Blues (70) 59(2) [0|0|19]	675
Canned Heat Cook Book (The Best Of Canned Heat) (69) 86(1) [0|0|19]	503
Canned Heat (67) 76(1) [0|0|23]	433
Historical Figures And Ancient Heads (72) 87(1) [0|0|12]	242
Hooker 'N Heat (71)-Canned Heat And John Lee Hooker [A] 73(1) [0|0|16]	222
Canned Heat Concert (Recorded Live In Europe) (71) 133(1) [0|0|9]	148
Vintage-Canned Heat (70) 173(2) [0|0|5]	56.2
Living The Blues(2) (71) 182(1) [0|0|2]	19.9
CANNIBAL And The HEADHUNTERS ▶ 3096 Pk:141 [0|0|1]	**52**
Land Of 1000 Dances (65) 141(2) [0|0|4]	52.2
Lana CANTRELL ▶ 3266 Pk:166 [0|0|1]	**31**
Lana! (68) 166(2) [0|0|2]	31.3
Jim CAPALDI ▶ 1710 Pk:82 [0|0|5]	**576**
Oh How We Danced (72) 82(1) [0|0|11]	284
Fierce Heart (83) 91(1) [0|0|12]	199
Some Come Running (88) 183(2) [0|0|8]	46.4
Short Cut Draw Blood (76) 193(1) [0|0|4]	26.6
Whale Meat Again (74) 191(1) [0|0|3]	19.9
The CAPITOLS ▶ 2260 Pk:95 [0|0|1]	**229**
Dance The Cool Jerk (66) 95(1) [0|0|12]	229
CAPTAIN & TENNILLE ▶ 254 Pk:2 [2|4|6]	**14057**
Love Will Keep Us Together (75) 2(1) [9|14|104]	6501
Song Of Joy (76) 9(2) [3|17|61]	4113
Make Your Move (79) 23(2) [0|9|24]	1476
Come In From The Rain (77) 18(1) [0|7|15]	1201
Captain & Tennille's Greatest Hits (77) 55(1) [0|0|12]	395
Dream (78) 131(2) [0|0|30]	372
CAPTAIN BEEFHEART ▶ 2190 Pk:66 [0|0|2]	**262**
Bongo Fury (75)-Frank Zappa/ Captain Beefheart/The Mothers [A] 66(1) [0|0|8]	133
The Spotlight Kid (72) 131(1) [0|0|9]	129
CAPTAIN BEEFHEART & The MAGIC BAND ▶ 2999 Pk:191 [0|0|2]	**66**
Clear Spot (72) 191(2) [0|0|7]	41.7
Unconditionally Guaranteed (74) 192(1) [0|0|4]	24.5
CAPTAIN BEYOND ▶ 1878 Pk:90 [0|0|3]	**419**
Sufficiently Breathless (73) 90(2) [0|0|10]	213
Captain Beyond (72) 134(2) [0|0|12]	186
Dawn Explosion (77) 181(2) [0|0|2]	20.5
CAPTAIN SKY ▶ 2567 Pk:157 [0|0|1]	**145**
The Adventures Of Captain Sky (79) 157(2) [0|0|12]	145
Carla CAPUANO ▶ 2874 Pk:152 [0|0|1]	**84**
Aerobic Dance Hits, Volume One (82) 152(3) [0|0|8]	84.0
Irene CARA ▶ 1265 Pk:76 [0|0|2]	**1213**
What A Feelin' (83) 77(1) [0|0|37]	798
Anyone Can See (82) 76(2) [0|0|17]	415
CARAVAN ▶ 2496 Pk:124 [0|0|1]	**161**
Cunning Stunts (75) 124(1) [0|0|10]	161
The CARAVELLES ▶ 3031 Pk:127 [0|0|1]	**62**
You Don't Have To Be A Baby To Cry (64) 127(1) [0|0|4]	61.5
Tony CAREY ▶ 1561 Pk:60 [0|0|2]	**719**
Some Tough City (84) 60(2) [0|0|24]	649
Tony Carey [I Won't Be Home Tonight] (83) 167(1) [0|0|9]	70.2
Henson CARGILL ▶ 3421 Pk:179 [0|0|1]	**17**
Skip A Rope (68) 179(1) [0|0|2]	17.3
George CARLIN ▶ 370 Pk:13 [0|5|9]	**8926**
FM & AM (72) 13(3) [0|16|35]	2901
Class Clown (72) 22(2) [0|10|35]	2176
Toledo Window Box (74) 19(2) [0|7|17]	1359
Occupation: Foole (73) 35(1) [0|5|21]	1098
An Evening With Wally Londo Featuring Bill Slaszo (75) 34(2) [0|3|15]	758
On The Road (77) 90(1) [0|0|9]	207
Indecent Exposure (Some Of The Best Of George Carlin) (79) 112(1) [0|0|8]	166
A Place For My Stuff! (81) 145(1) [0|0|13]	142
Carlin on Campus (84) 136(1) [0|0|11]	119
Belinda CARLISLE ▶ 457 Pk:13 [0|3|3]	**6991**
Heaven On Earth (87) 13(2) [0|35|51]	4078
Belinda (86) 13(1) [0|16|34]	1971
Runaway Horses (89) 37(1) [0|2|25]	943
Walter CARLOS ▶ 641 Pk:10 [1|1|4]	**4296**
Switched-On Bach (69) 10(1) [1|17|56]	4085
Walter Carlos' Clockwork Orange (72) 146(1) [0|0|9]	125
Sonic Seasonings (72) 168(2) [0|0|7]	74.5
The Well-Tempered Synthesizer (70) 199(1) [0|0|2]	11.2
Carl CARLTON ▶ 1294 Pk:34 [0|1|3]	**1159**
Carl Carlton (81) 34(2) [0|3|19]	941
Everlasting Love (75) 132(2) [0|0|7]	126
The Bad C.C. (82) 133(2) [0|0|7]	92.1
Larry CARLTON ▶ 1437 Pk:99 [0|0|7]	**912**
Sleepwalk (82) 99(1) [0|0|16]	302
Friends (83) 126(1) [0|0|11]	138
Strikes Twice (80) 138(1) [0|0|8]	124
On Solid Ground (89) 126(2) [0|0|8]	116
Larry Carlton (78) 174(2) [0|0|10]	98.4
Alone/But Never Alone (86) 141(2) [0|0|11]	98.4
Discovery (87) 180(1) [0|0|6]	36.3
Eric CARMEN ▶ 691 Pk:21 [0|1|6]	**3817**
Eric Carmen (75) 21(2) [0|8|51]	2361
Boats Against The Current (77) 45(1) [0|0|13]	556
The Best Of Eric Carmen (88) 59(1) [0|0|20]	543
Change Of Heart (78) 137(1) [0|0|12]	193
Eric Carmen (II) (85) 128(2) [0|0|10]	101
Tonight You're Mine (80) 160(1) [0|0|5]	61.5
Jean CARN ▶ 2240 Pk:122 [0|0|3]	**239**
Jean Carn (77) 122(1) [0|0|10]	162
Closer Than Close (86)-Jean Carne 162(2) [0|0|6]	47.6
Sweet And Wonderful (81) 176(1) [0|0|3]	28.8
Kim CARNES ▶ 374 Pk:1 [1|1|6]	**8833**
Mistaken Idenity (81) 1(4) [12|23|52]	6959
Voyeur (82) 49(3) [0|0|22]	583
Romance Dance (80) 57(2) [0|0|17]	553
Barking At Airplanes (85) 48(2) [0|0|14]	419
Cafe Racers (83) 97(1) [0|0|16]	223
Lighthouse (86) 116(2) [0|0|7]	94.9
The CARNIVAL ▶ 3442 Pk:191 [0|0|1]	**16**
The Carnival (69) 191(2) [0|0|2]	15.8
Mary Chapin CARPENTER ▶ 3061 Pk:183 [0|0|1]	**58**
State Of The Heart (89) 183(1) [0|0|10]	57.7
CARPENTERS ▶ 66 Pk:1 [5|7|14]	**39187**
Close To You (70) 2(1) [15|52|87]	10928
Carpenters (71) 2(2) [24|39|59]	10448
The Singles 1969-1973 (73) 1(1) [9|17|49]	4680
Now & Then (73) 2(1) [8|19|41]	4176
A Song For You (72) 4(3) [5|19|41]	3786
Horizon (75) 13(3) [0|11|18]	1952

Act ▶ Highest Peak [Top10s | Top40s | Total] Title (Yr) Peak(Wk) [T10 Wk | T40Wk | TotalWk]	Score
CARPENTERS ▶ *Continued*	
A Kind Of Hush (76) 33(2) [0 | 5 | 16]	976
Passage (77) 49(1) [0 | 0 | 18]	691
Made In America (81) 52(1) [0 | 0 | 15]	572
Voices Of The Heart (83) 46(2) [0 | 0 | 19]	548
Ticket To Ride (71) 150(2) [0 | 0 | 16]	241
Christmas Portrait (78) 145(1) [0 | 0 | 7]	100
Yesterday Once More (85) 144(2) [0 | 0 | 8]	84.0
An Old Fashioned Christmas (85) 190(1) [0 | 0 | 1]	5.5
Vikki CARR ▶ 458 Pk:12 [0 | 2 | 12]	**6983**
It Must Be Him (67) 12(2) [0 | 16 | 47]	2756
For Once In My Life (69) 29(2) [0 | 7 | 34]	1978
Vikki! (68) 63(2) [0 | 0 | 16]	532
Vikki Carr's Love Story (71) 60(1) [0 | 0 | 14]	513
En Espanol (72) 106(2) [0 | 0 | 25]	503
Nashville by Carr (70) 111(1) [0 | 0 | 8]	168
The First Time Ever (I Saw Your Face) (72) 146(1) [0 | 0 | 12]	166
Ms. America (73) 142(1) [0 | 0 | 7]	93.8
Superstar (72) 118(1) [0 | 0 | 4]	86.2
One Hell Of A Woman (74) 155(1) [0 | 0 | 5]	62.5
Live At The Greek Theatre (73) 172(1) [0 | 0 | 7]	61.9
Discovery! (64) 114(1) [0 | 0 | 4]	61.8
Paul CARRACK ▶ 1281 Pk:67 [0 | 0 | 3]	**1180**
One Good Reason (87) 67(1) [0 | 0 | 31]	704
Suburban Voodoo (82) 78(1) [0 | 0 | 14]	268
Groove Approved (89) 120(2) [0 | 0 | 18]	207
Keith CARRADINE ▶ 1744 Pk:61 [0 | 0 | 1]	**528**
I'm Easy (76) 61(1) [0 | 0 | 17]	528
Terri Lyne CARRINGTON ▶ 3119 Pk:169 [0 | 0 | 1]	**50**
Real Life Story (89) 169(1) [0 | 0 | 7]	49.9
Jim CARROLL Band ▶ 1593 Pk:73 [0 | 0 | 2]	**688**
Catholic Boy (80) 73(2) [0 | 0 | 23]	627
Dry Dreams (82) 156(2) [0 | 0 | 7]	60.6
The CARS ▶ 85 Pk:3 [4 | 7 | 7]	**32798**
Heartbeat City (84) 3(1) [31 | 48 | 69]	8802
The Cars (78) 18(2) [0 | 37 | 139]	7689
Candy-O (79) 3(4) [12 | 21 | 62]	6067
Shake It Up (81) 9(4) [7 | 24 | 41]	3973
Panorama (80) 5(4) [6 | 11 | 28]	2985
Greatest Hits (85) 12(4) [0 | 16 | 39]	2244
Door To Door (87) 26(3) [0 | 8 | 23]	1037
Carlene CARTER ▶ 2863 Pk:139 [0 | 0 | 1]	**86**
Musical Shapes (80) 139(2) [0 | 0 | 6]	85.7
Clarence CARTER ▶ 1350 Pk:44 [0 | 0 | 6]	**1040**
Patches (70) 44(2) [0 | 0 | 12]	622
The Best Of Clarence Carter (71) 103(1) [0 | 0 | 10]	262
Testifyin' (69) 138(1) [0 | 0 | 3]	64.2
The Dynamic Clarence Carter (69) 169(2) [0 | 0 | 4]	57.3
Let's Burn (81) 189(1) [0 | 0 | 3]	22.5
This Is Clarence Carter (68) 200(2) [0 | 0 | 2]	12.2
Mel CARTER ▶ 1733 Pk:62 [0 | 0 | 2]	**547**
Hold Me, Thrill Me, Kiss Me (65) 62(1) [0 | 0 | 12]	285
Easy Listening (66) 81(1) [0 | 0 | 11]	262
Ron CARTER ▶ 3229 Pk:178 [0 | 0 | 2]	**36**
A Song For You (78) 178(1) [0 | 0 | 3]	29.3
Pastels (77) 193(1) [0 | 0 | 1]	7.0
Valerie CARTER ▶ 3143 Pk:182 [0 | 0 | 1]	**47**
Just A Stone's Throw Away (77) 182(1) [0 | 0 | 5]	47.0
Johnny CASH ▶ 101 Pk:1 [2 | 3 | 22]	**29361**
Johnny Cash At San Quentin (69) 1(4) [20 | 35 | 70]	11537

Act ▶ Highest Peak [Top10s | Top40s | Total] Title (Yr) Peak(Wk) [T10 Wk | T40Wk | TotalWk]	Score
Johnny Cash At Folsom Prison (68) 13(2) [0 | 39 | 122]	7728
Hello, I'm Johnny Cash (70) 6(1) [4 | 17 | 30]	3209
Johnny Cash's Greatest Hits, Volume I (67) 82(1) [0 | 0 | 71]	1231
The Johnny Cash Show (70) 44(1) [0 | 0 | 18]	947
The World Of Johnny Cash (70) 54(1) [0 | 0 | 34]	915
The Holy Land (69) 54(2) [0 | 0 | 20]	799
I Walk The Line (64) 53(2) [0 | 0 | 17]	457
Man In Black (71) 56(1) [0 | 0 | 12]	450
Original Golden Hits, Volume I (69) 95(2) [0 | 0 | 13]	350
Orange Blossom Special (65) 49(2) [0 | 0 | 13]	342
Bitter Tears (Ballads Of The American Indian) (64) 47(1) [0 | 0 | 13]	323
Original Golden Hits, Volume II (69) 98(1) [0 | 0 | 8]	217
A Thing Called Love (72) 112(1) [0 | 0 | 9]	198
The Johnny Cash Collection (His Greatest Hits, Volume II) (71) 94(1) [0 | 0 | 8]	181
Everybody Loves A Nut (66) 88(1) [0 | 0 | 9]	179
Get Rhythm (69) 164(2) [0 | 0 | 6]	78.8
Johnny Cash: America (A 200-Year Salute In Story And Song) (72) 176(2) [0 | 0 | 7]	59.6
I Walk The Line (Soundtrack) (70) 176(2) [0 | 0 | 6]	58.9
Class Of '55 (86)-Carl Perkins, Jerry Lee Lewis, Roy Orbison, & Johnny Cash [A] 87(2) [0 | 0 | 12]	54.0
Any Old Wind That Blows (73) 188(1) [0 | 0 | 4]	26.9
Johnny Cash (69) 186(2) [0 | 0 | 2]	19.2
Johnny CASH & June CARTER ▶ 3430 Pk:194 [0 | 0 | 1]	**17**
Carryin' On With Johnny Cash & June Carter (67) 194(1) [0 | 0 | 3]	16.8
Johnny CASH And The TENNESSEE TWO/THREE ▶ 2889 Pk:181 [0 | 0 | 4]	**81**
Showtime (69)-Johnny Cash And The Tennessee Two 181(1) [0 | 0 | 4]	30.9
The Singing Story Teller (70)-Johnny Cash And The Tennessee Two 186(1) [0 | 0 | 3]	20.0
One Piece At A Time (76)-Johnny Cash And The Tennessee Three 185(1) [0 | 0 | 2]	18.0
Story Songs Of The Trains And Rivers (69)-Johnny Cash And The Tennessee Two 197(2) [0 | 0 | 2]	12.7
Rosanne CASH ▶ 848 Pk:26 [0 | 1 | 5]	**2695**
Seven Year Ache (81) 26(1) [0 | 9 | 32]	1880
Rhythm And Romance (85) 101(1) [0 | 0 | 21]	325
Somewhere In The Stars (82) 76(2) [0 | 0 | 12]	244
King's Record Shop (87) 138(1) [0 | 0 | 20]	176
Hits 1979-1989 (89) 152(1) [0 | 0 | 7]	69.1
CASHFLOW ▶ 2752 Pk:144 [0 | 0 | 1]	**104**
Ca$hflow (86)-Ca$hflow 144(2) [0 | 0 | 11]	104
CASHMAN & WEST ▶ 2844 Pk:168 [0 | 0 | 2]	**88**
A Song Or Two (72) 168(2) [0 | 0 | 8]	75.7
Moondog Serenade (73) 192(1) [0 | 0 | 2]	12.6
The CASINOS ▶ 3327 Pk:187 [0 | 0 | 1]	**26**
Then You Can Tell Me Goodbye (67) 187(1) [0 | 0 | 4]	25.8
David CASSIDY ▶ 927 Pk:15 [0 | 1 | 2]	**2232**
Cherish (72) 15(2) [0 | 8 | 23]	1480
Rock Me Baby (72) 41(1) [0 | 0 | 17]	751
Shaun CASSIDY ▶ 360 Pk:3 [2 | 3 | 3]	**9172**
Shaun Cassidy (77) 3(2) [11 | 26 | 57]	5827
Born Late (77) 6(3) [4 | 11 | 37]	2635
Under Wraps (78) 33(2) [0 | 4 | 13]	710
Jimmy CASTOR Bunch ▶ 1040 Pk:27 [0 | 1 | 4]	**1775**
It's Just Begun (72) 27(1) [0 | 6 | 23]	1170
Butt Of Course (75) 74(1) [0 | 0 | 17]	432

Act ▶ Highest Peak [Top10s | Top40s | Total] Title (Yr) Peak(Wk) [T10 Wk | T40Wk | TotalWk]	Score
E-Man Groovin' (76) 132(1) [0 | 0 | 9]	150
Phase Two (72) 192(1) [0 | 0 | 4]	23.7
CATE BROS. ▶ 2658 Pk:158 [0 | 0 | 2]	**122**
Cate Bros. (76) 158(1) [0 | 0 | 9]	103
In One Eye And Out The Other (76) 182(1) [0 | 0 | 2]	19.0
CAT MOTHER and the ALL NIGHT NEWS BOYS ▶ 1707 Pk:55 [0 | 0 | 1]	**577**
The Street Giveth...And The Street Taketh Away (69) 55(1) [0 | 0 | 15]	577
C.C.S. ▶ 3464 Pk:197 [0 | 0 | 1]	**13**
Whole Lotta Love (71) 197(2) [0 | 0 | 2]	13.0
CELI BEE And The BUZZY BUNCH ▶ 3111 Pk:169 [0 | 0 | 1]	**51**
Celi Bee & The Buzzy Bunch (77) 169(2) [0 | 0 | 5]	51.0
CENTRAL LINE ▶ 2804 Pk:145 [0 | 0 | 1]	**97**
Central Line (82) 145(2) [0 | 0 | 9]	96.6
CERRONE ▶ 1736 Pk:118 [0 | 0 | 4]	**540**
Cerrone IV - The Golden Touch (78) 118(1) [0 | 0 | 13]	231
Love In C Minor (77) 153(1) [0 | 0 | 10]	135
Cerrone 3 - Supernature (78) 129(2) [0 | 0 | 8]	121
Cerrone's Paradise (77) 162(2) [0 | 0 | 5]	52.3
Peter CETERA ▶ 837 Pk:23 [0 | 1 | 3]	**2743**
Solitude/Solitaire (86) 23(1) [0 | 17 | 43]	2156
One More Story (88) 58(3) [0 | 0 | 17]	482
Peter Cetera (82) 143(2) [0 | 0 | 10]	105
Frank CHACKSFIELD And His Orchestra ▶ 2621 Pk:120 [0 | 0 | 1]	**129**
The New Ebb Tide (64)-Frank Chacksfield And His Orch. 120(2) [0 | 0 | 9]	129
CHAD & JEREMY ▶ 683 Pk:22 [0 | 2 | 8]	**3866**
Yesterday's Gone (64) 22(1) [0 | 11 | 39]	1499
Before And After (65) 37(2) [0 | 3 | 18]	670
The Best Of Chad & Jeremy (66) 49(1) [0 | 0 | 23]	659
Distant Shores (66) 61(1) [0 | 0 | 14]	441
Chad & Jeremy Sing For You (65) 69(1) [0 | 0 | 14]	290
I Don't Want To Lose You Baby (65) 77(1) [0 | 0 | 11]	218
More Chad & Jeremy (66) 144(1) [0 | 0 | 4]	59.5
Of Cabbages And Kings (67) 186(2) [0 | 0 | 5]	28.8
CHAIRMEN OF THE BOARD ▶ 1841 Pk:117 [0 | 0 | 3]	**449**
In Session (70) 117(1) [0 | 0 | 16]	283
Give Me Just A Little More Time (70) 133(2) [0 | 0 | 10]	140
Bittersweet (72) 178(2) [0 | 0 | 3]	25.8
CHAKACHAS ▶ 2394 Pk:117 [0 | 0 | 1]	**188**
Jungle Fever (72) 117(1) [0 | 0 | 11]	188
CHAMBERS BROTHERS ▶ 467 Pk:4 [1 | 2 | 6]	**6750**
The Time Has Come (68) 4(2) [10 | 17 | 58]	4290
A New Time-A New Day (68) 16(1) [0 | 6 | 21]	1408
Love, Peace And Happiness (69) 58(1) [0 | 0 | 33]	868
New Generation (71) 145(1) [0 | 0 | 7]	86.2
The Chambers Brothers' Greatest Hits (71) 166(1) [0 | 0 | 7]	84.7
The Chambers Brothers Greatest Hits (70) 193(1) [0 | 0 | 2]	14.0
CHAMPAIGN ▶ 1161 Pk:53 [0 | 0 | 3]	**1437**
How 'Bout Us (81) 53(1) [0 | 0 | 20]	805
Modern Heart (83) 64(1) [0 | 0 | 24]	612
Woman In Flames (84) 184(2) [0 | 0 | 3]	20.2
Bill CHAMPLIN ▶ 3247 Pk:178 [0 | 0 | 1]	**34**
Runaway (82) 178(3) [0 | 0 | 4]	33.5
Gene CHANDLER ▶ 1201 Pk:47 [0 | 0 | 6]	**1344**
Get Down (78) 47(3) [0 | 0 | 20]	713

Act ▶ Highest Peak [Top10s | Top40s | Total] Title (Yr) Peak(Wk) [T10 Wk | T40Wk | TotalWk]	Score
Gene CHANDLER ▶ *Continued*	
Gene Chandler '80 (80) 87(1) [0|0|18]	413
The Gene Chandler Situation (70) 178(1) [0|0|9]	79.0
Gene & Jerry - One & One (71)-Gene Chandler & Jerry Butler [A] 143(2) [0|0|5]	46.9
Gene Chandler - Live On Stage In '65 (66) 124(1) [0|0|3]	46.4
When You're # 1 (79) 153(2) [0|0|3]	45.8
CHANGE ▶ 874 Pk:29 [0|1|5]	**2509**
The Glow Of Love (80) 29(2) [0|7|25]	1270
Miracles (81) 46(1) [0|0|22]	793
Change Of Heart (84) 102(1) [0|0|15]	202
Sharing Your Love (82) 66(2) [0|0|9]	185
This Is Your Time (83) 161(1) [0|0|7]	59.3
CHANSON ▶ 1402 Pk:41 [0|0|1]	**970**
Chanson (78) 41(1) [0|0|21]	970
Harry CHAPIN ▶ 425 Pk:4 [1|1|11]	**7478**
Verities & Balderdash (74) 4(1) [7|17|33]	3835
Heads & Tales (72) 60(1) [0|0|27]	805
Greatest Stories-Live (76) 48(2) [0|0|19]	662
Short Stories (73) 61(1) [0|0|23]	591
Sequel (80) 58(1) [0|0|15]	498
Portrait Gallery (75) 53(1) [0|0|8]	365
Dance Band On The Titanic (77) 58(1) [0|0|10]	302
On The Road To Kingdom Come (76) 87(1) [0|0|6]	157
Living Room Suite (78) 133(3) [0|0|8]	136
Sniper and Other Love Songs (72) 160(1) [0|0|8]	87.2
Legends Of The Lost And Found - New Greatest Stories Live (79) 163(1) [0|0|3]	37.8
Tracy CHAPMAN ▶ 341 Pk:1 [2|2|2]	**9969**
Tracy Chapman (88) 1(1) [18|46|61]	7949
Crossroads (89) 9(2) [4|14|26]	2020
CHARLENE ▶ 1538 Pk:36 [0|1|2]	**746**
I've Never Been To Me (82) 36(2) [0|3|20]	688
Used To Be (82) 162(1) [0|0|7]	57.5
Ray CHARLES ▶ 237 Pk:2 [2|4|23]	**14823**
Ingredients In A Recipe For Soul (63) 2(2) [14|21|36]	4154
Crying Time (66) 15(1) [0|20|36]	2251
Sweet & Sour Tears (64) 9(2) [2|11|23]	1499
A Man And His Soul (67) 77(1) [0|0|62]	1109
A Portrait Of Ray (68) 51(1) [0|0|24]	791
A Message From The People (72) 52(2) [0|0|22]	726
Ray Charles Invites You To Listen (67) 76(2) [0|0|34]	662
Volcanic Action Of My Soul (71) 52(1) [0|0|16]	640
Have A Smile With Me (64) 36(2) [0|5|16]	605
Ray's Moods (66) 52(1) [0|0|17]	580
Friendship (85) 75(1) [0|0|20]	392
True To Life (77) 78(1) [0|0|20]	376
Ray Charles Live In Concert (65) 80(1) [0|0|18]	337
A 25th Anniversary In Show Business Salute To Ray Charles (71) 152(1) [0|0|10]	159
I'm All Yours-Baby! (69) 167(1) [0|0|11]	122
Country & Western Meets Rhythm & Blues (65) 116(1) [0|0|7]	116
Porgy & Bess (76)-Ray Charles And Cleo Laine [A] 138(3) [0|0|11]	84.4
Through The Eyes Of Love (72) 186(1) [0|0|8]	56.4
Ray Charles Live (73) 182(2) [0|0|5]	39.3
Doing His Thing (69) 172(1) [0|0|3]	36.3
My Kind Of Jazz (70) 155(2) [0|0|2]	31.9
Renaissance (75) 175(1) [0|0|3]	28.5
Love Country Style (70) 192(1) [0|0|4]	26.6

Act ▶ Highest Peak [Top10s | Top40s | Total] Title (Yr) Peak(Wk) [T10 Wk | T40Wk | TotalWk]	Score
Ray CHARLES Singers ▶ 812 Pk:11 [0|1|4]	**2860**
Something Special For Young Lovers (64) 11(1) [0|15|33]	1871
Al-Di-La And Other Extra-Special Songs For Young Lovers (64) 45(1) [0|0|22]	544
Songs For Lonesome Lovers (64) 88(1) [0|0|20]	354
Songs For Latin Lovers (65) 125(1) [0|0|6]	90.7
Sonny CHARLES ▶ 2939 Pk:136 [0|0|1]	**73**
The Sun Still Shines (82) 136(2) [0|0|7]	73.4
CHARLIE ▶ 1308 Pk:60 [0|0|4]	**1128**
Lines (78) 75(1) [0|0|14]	400
Fight Dirty (79) 60(2) [0|0|10]	336
No Second Chance (77) 111(1) [0|0|15]	301
Charlie (83) 145(1) [0|0|9]	91.4
CHASE ▶ 914 Pk:22 [0|1|3]	**2289**
Chase (71) 22(1) [0|10|26]	1820
Ennea (72) 71(2) [0|0|12]	354
Pure Music (74) 155(1) [0|0|10]	116
CHEAP TRICK ▶ 194 Pk:4 [2|7|11]	**17889**
Cheap Trick At Budokan (79) 4(4) [14|30|53]	6482
Lap Of Luxury (88) 16(1) [0|28|47]	3824
Dream Police (79) 6(2) [3|10|25]	2528
One On One (82) 39(1) [0|10|27]	1245
All Shook Up (80) 24(2) [0|7|15]	985
Heaven Tonight (78) 48(1) [0|0|22]	909
Standing On The Edge (85) 35(2) [0|4|18]	704
Found All The Parts (80) 39(2) [0|2|12]	533
In Color (77) 73(1) [0|0|12]	289
Next Position Please (83) 61(1) [0|0|11]	278
The Doctor (86) 115(2) [0|0|9]	110
Chubby CHECKER ▶ 2328 Pk:104 [0|0|3]	**206**
Chubby Checker's Greatest Hits (72) 152(2) [0|0|10]	123
Chubby Checker In Person (63) 104(1) [0|0|4]	69.7
The Change Has Come (82) 186(1) [0|0|2]	13.8
CHECKMATES, LTD. ▶ 3166 Pk:178 [0|0|1]	**45**
Love Is All We Have To Give (69) 178(2) [0|0|4]	44.8
CHEECH & CHONG ▶ 173 Pk:2 [3|5|8]	**20297**
Big Bambu (72) 2(1) [12|20|111]	7459
Los Cochinos (73) 2(1) [12|29|69]	6317
Cheech And Chong (71) 28(3) [0|10|64]	3041
Cheech & Chong's Wedding Album (74) 5(1) [3|9|25]	2222
Sleeping Beauty (76) 25(2) [0|6|13]	980
Get Out Of My Room (85) 71(2) [0|0|11]	171
Up In Smoke (Soundtrack) (78) 162(1) [0|0|7]	76.7
Let's Make A New Dope Deal (80) 173(1) [0|0|3]	30.9
CHEQUERED PAST ▶ 3058 Pk:151 [0|0|1]	**59**
Chequered Past (84) 151(2) [0|0|6]	58.5
CHER ▶ 206 Pk:10 [1|7|18]	**16854**
Heart Of Stone (89) 10(2) [2|29|53]	4398
Gypsys, Tramps & Thieves (71) 16(1) [0|11|45]	3158
Cher(2) (87) 32(3) [0|8|41]	1727
All I Really Want To Do (65) 16(2) [0|10|24]	1280
Take Me Home (79) 25(2) [0|6|21]	1205
Foxy Lady (72) 43(2) [0|0|22]	1022
Half-Breed (73) 28(1) [0|4|25]	988
The Sonny Side Of Cher (66) 26(2) [0|7|19]	897
Cher (66) 59(1) [0|0|16]	555
With Love - Cher (67) 47(2) [0|0|14]	473
Dark Lady (74) 69(1) [0|0|14]	378
Cher Superpak (72) 92(1) [0|0|10]	213
Cher Superpak, Vol. II (72) 95(1) [0|0|9]	201
Bittersweet White Light (73) 140(2) [0|0|8]	110
Stars (75) 153(2) [0|0|7]	95.1

Act ▶ Highest Peak [Top10s | Top40s | Total] Title (Yr) Peak(Wk) [T10 Wk | T40Wk | TotalWk]	Score
Greatest Hits (74) 152(2) [0|0|7]	89.1
3614 Jackson Highway (69) 160(1) [0|0|3]	43.7
Cher's Golden Greats (68) 195(1) [0|0|3]	21.2
CHERRELLE ▶ 1277 Pk:36 [0|1|3]	**1185**
High Priority (86) 36(2) [0|2|30]	874
Affair (88) 106(3) [0|0|15]	220
Fragile (84) 144(1) [0|0|8]	90.8
Neneh CHERRY ▶ 1334 Pk:40 [0|1|1]	**1083**
Raw Like Sushi (89) 40(1) [0|1|35]	1083
CHIC ▶ 334 Pk:4 [2|4|7]	**10365**
C'est Chic (78) 4(4) [11|22|48]	4931
Risque (79) 5(2) [7|11|17]	2414
Chic (77) 27(1) [0|9|40]	1842
Real People (80) 30(2) [0|3|15]	784
Les Plus Grands Succes De Chic - Chic's Greatest Hits (79) 88(2) [0|0|9]	198
Take It Off (81) 124(1) [0|0|9]	158
Tongue In Chic (82) 173(2) [0|0|6]	36.9
CHICAGO ▶ 5 Pk:1 [12|18|20]	**98583**
Chicago (70) 4(5) [33|53|134]	14299
Chicago Transit Authority (69) 17(2) [0|42|171]	11343
Chicago VII (74) 1(1) [14|35|69]	7973
Chicago IX: Chicago's Greatest Hits (75) 1(5) [13|22|72]	7717
Chicago V (72) 1(9) [13|20|51]	7391
Chicago VI (73) 1(5) [10|27|73]	6934
Chicago III (71) 2(2) [10|22|63]	6848
Chicago X (76) 3(1) [16|30|44]	6723
Chicago 17 (84) 4(1) [12|44|72]	6572
Chicago At Carnegie Hall (71) 3(1) [13|18|46]	5202
Chicago VIII (75) 1(2) [11|15|29]	5049
Chicago 16 (82) 9(5) [6|18|38]	2792
Hot Streets (78) 12(1) [0|11|29]	2337
Chicago XI (77) 6(2) [4|10|20]	2251
Chicago 19 (88) 37(2) [0|4|42]	1846
Chicago 18 (86) 35(2) [0|4|45]	1402
Greatest Hits 1982-1989 (89) 37(1) [0|5|25]	818
Chicago 13 (79) 21(2) [0|5|10]	750
Chicago XIV (80) 71(2) [0|0|9]	294
Chicago - Greatest Hits, Volume II (81) 171(2) [0|0|5]	43.7
The CHIEFTAINS ▶ 2598 Pk:102 [0|0|2]	**135**
Irish Heartbeat (88)-Van Morrison & The Chieftains [A] 102(2) [0|0|13]	103
Chieftains 5 (76) 187(1) [0|0|4]	32.0
The CHIFFONS ▶ 3189 Pk:149 [0|0|1]	**42**
Sweet Talkin' Guy (66) 149(1) [0|0|3]	42.2
Desmond CHILD and ROUGE ▶ 2943 Pk:157 [0|0|1]	**73**
Desmond Child And Rouge (79) 157(1) [0|0|6]	73.0
Toni CHILDS ▶ 1325 Pk:63 [0|0|1]	**1092**
Union (88) 63(1) [0|0|45]	1092
The CHI-LITES ▶ 396 Pk:5 [1|2|10]	**8284**
A Lonely Man (72) 5(1) [6|16|36]	3349
(For God's Sake) Give More Power To The People (71) 12(1) [0|14|32]	3014
The Chi-Lites Greatest Hits (72) 55(2) [0|0|24]	719
A Letter To Myself (73) 50(1) [0|0|13]	492
Chi-Lites (73) 89(1) [0|0|14]	297
Bottoms Up (83) 98(1) [0|0|12]	219
Me And You (82) 162(2) [0|0|7]	64.7
Heavenly Body (80) 179(3) [0|0|6]	55.8
Toby (74) 181(1) [0|0|5]	43.9
Give It Away (69) 180(2) [0|0|3]	29.7

Act ▶ Highest Peak [Top10s|Top40s|Total]
Title (Yr) Peak(Wk) [T10 Wk|T40Wk|TotalWk] — Score

CHILLIWACK ▶ 1389 Pk:78 [0|0|4] — **982**
Wanna Be A Star (81) 78(1) [0|0|30] — 638
Dreams, Dreams, Dreams (77) 142(1) [0|0|13] — 194
Opus X (82) 112(2) [0|0|10] — 124
Lights From The Valley (78) 191(1) [0|0|4] — 26.2

CHINA CRISIS ▶ 2331 Pk:114 [0|0|2] — **205**
What Price Paradise (87) 114(2) [0|0|12] — 172
Flaunt The Imperfection (85) 171(1) [0|0|4] — 33.7

The CHIPMUNKS ▶ 720 Pk:14 [0|2|5] — **3507**
The Chipmunks Sing The Beatles Hits (64) 14(1) [0|11|23] — 1091
Chipmunk Punk (80) 34(2) [0|6|26] — 1024
Urban Chipmunk (81) 56(1) [0|0|35] — 1020
A Chipmunk Christmas (81) 72(2) [0|0|9] — 271
Chipmunk Rock (82) 109(1) [0|0|6] — 102

CHOCOLATE MILK ▶ 2195 Pk:161 [0|0|4] — **259**
Blue Jeans (81) 162(1) [0|0|10] — 106
Milky Way (79) 161(1) [0|0|6] — 72.9
We're All In This Together (78) 171(3) [0|0|5] — 59.5
Action Speaks Louder Than Words (75) 191(2) [0|0|3] — 21.2

The CHRISTIANS ▶ 2936 Pk:158 [0|0|1] — **74**
The Christians (88) 158(2) [0|0|8] — 74.1

CHRISTIE ▶ 2413 Pk:115 [0|0|1] — **183**
Yellow River (70) 115(1) [0|0|10] — 183

Lou CHRISTIE ▶ 2035 Pk:103 [0|0|2] — **335**
Lightnin' Strikes (66) 103(1) [0|0|14] — 246
Lou Christie (63) 124(1) [0|0|6] — 88.4

Gavin CHRISTOPHER ▶ 2153 Pk:74 [0|0|1] — **278**
One Step Closer (86) 74(3) [0|0|15] — 278

CHUNKY A ▶ 2127 Pk:71 [0|0|1] — **288**
Large And In Charge (89) 71(1) [0|0|13] — 288

The CHURCH ▶ 1122 Pk:41 [0|0|2] — **1542**
Starfish (88) 41(2) [0|0|36] — 1426
Heydey (86) 146(1) [0|0|11] — 116

CINDERELLA ▶ 278 Pk:3 [2|2|2] — **12591**
Night Songs (86) 3(3) [15|49|70] — 6880
Long Cold Winter (88) 10(5) [5|32|66] — 5711

CIRCUS OF POWER ▶ 3465 Pk:185 [0|0|1] — **13**
Circus Of Power (88) 185(1) [0|0|2] — 12.9

CITY BOY ▶ 2193 Pk:115 [0|0|3] — **261**
Book Early (78) 115(2) [0|0|9] — 187
Dinner At The Ritz (77) 170(1) [0|0|4] — 45.1
City Boy (76) 177(1) [0|0|3] — 29.0

C.J. & CO. ▶ 1534 Pk:60 [0|0|1] — **747**
Devil's Gun (77) 60(1) [0|0|23] — 747

CLANCY BROTHERS AND Tommy MAKEM ▶ 1952 Pk:60 [0|0|2] — **376**
In Person At Carnegie Hall (63) 60(1) [0|0|12] — 270
The First Hurrah! (64) 91(1) [0|0|6] — 106

CLANNAD ▶ 2360 Pk:131 [0|0|2] — **195**
Macalla (86) 131(2) [0|0|12] — 157
Sirius (88) 183(2) [0|0|5] — 38.0

Eric CLAPTON ▶ 50 Pk:1 [6|16|19] — **44038**
Slowhand (77) 2(5) [16|30|74] — 7923
Just One Night (80) 2(6) [11|19|31] — 5135
461 Ocean Boulevard (74) 1(4) [9|14|25] — 4705
History Of Eric Clapton (72) 6(2) [6|22|42] — 4002
Backless (78) 8(3) [8|17|37] — 3494
Journeyman (89) 16(1) [0|26|51] — 3472
Another Ticket (81)-Eric Clapton And His Band 7(2) [8|13|21] — 2816
No Reason To Cry (76) 15(3) [0|12|21] — 2173
Eric Clapton (70) 13(2) [0|10|32] — 1847
Money And Cigarettes (83) 16(4) [0|10|19] — 1289
August (86) 37(2) [0|5|34] — 1193
E.C. Was Here (75) 20(2) [0|7|13] — 1158
There's One In Every Crowd (75) 21(1) [0|5|14] — 1066
Behind The Sun (85) 34(1) [0|7|28] — 1065
Eric Clapton's Rainbow Concert (73) 18(2) [0|6|14] — 980
Crossroads (88) 34(2) [0|3|26] — 842
Eric Clapton At His Best (72) 87(1) [0|0|17] — 379
Clapton (73) 67(1) [0|0|11] — 286
Time Pieces -- The Best Of Eric Clapton (82) 101(2) [0|0|14] — 212

Dave CLARK Five ▶ 235 Pk:3 [4|8|13] — **14893**
The Dave Clark Five's Greatest Hits (66) 9(1) [4|20|62] — 3166
Glad All Over (64) 3(1) [10|25|32] — 3158
The Dave Clark Five Return! (64) 5(1) [7|13|22] — 1986
Coast To Coast (65) 6(1) [6|13|21] — 1773
Having A Wild Weekend (65) 15(1) [0|11|21] — 1332
American Tour (64) 11(1) [0|9|28] — 1233
Weekend In London (65) 24(1) [0|6|23] — 842
I Like It Like That (65) 32(2) [0|6|16] — 741
Try Too Hard (66) 77(1) [0|0|11] — 260
The Dave Clark Five/More Greatest Hits (66) 103(1) [0|0|7] — 141
5 By 5 (67) 119(1) [0|0|7] — 121
Satisfied With You (66) 127(1) [0|0|6] — 101
You Got What It Takes (67) 149(1) [0|0|3] — 39.2

Gene CLARK ▶ 2904 Pk:144 [0|0|1] — **80**
No Other (74) 144(2) [0|0|5] — 79.8

Petula CLARK ▶ 416 Pk:21 [0|3|14] — **7803**
Downtown (65) 21(2) [0|16|36] — 1803
These Are My Songs (67) 27(2) [0|10|27] — 1245
Petula (68) 51(2) [0|0|21] — 829
Petula Clark's Greatest Hits, Vol. 1 (68) 57(1) [0|0|17] — 692
Portrait Of Petula (69) 37(2) [0|3|11] — 642
Color My World/Who Am I (67) 49(1) [0|0|27] — 611
I Couldn't Live Without Your Love (66) 43(1) [0|0|16] — 565
I Know A Place (65) 42(2) [0|0|17] — 555
My Love (66) 68(1) [0|0|12] — 318
The Other Man's Grass Is Always Greener (68) 93(2) [0|0|23] — 317
The World's Greatest International Hits! (65) 129(2) [0|0|9] — 121
Just Pet (69) 176(1) [0|0|7] — 64.1
Warm And Tender (71) 178(1) [0|0|3] — 29.2
Memphis (70) 198(2) [0|0|2] — 11.6

Roy CLARK ▶ 1191 Pk:50 [0|0|8] — **1364**
Yesterday, When I Was Young (69) 50(1) [0|0|20] — 762
Roy Clark Country! (72) 112(1) [0|0|12] — 246
The Everlovin' Soul Of Roy Clark (70) 129(1) [0|0|9] — 149
The Best Of Roy Clark (71) 178(1) [0|0|8] — 68.2
I Never Picked Cotton (70) 176(1) [0|0|6] — 53.0
Roy Clark / Superpicker (73) 172(1) [0|0|6] — 50.0
Roy Clark / The Entertainer (74) 186(1) [0|0|3] — 24.1
The Incredible Roy Clark (71) 197(1) [0|0|2] — 12.2

Stanley CLARKE ▶ 689 Pk:34 [0|2|8] — **3828**
School Days (76) 34(1) [0|4|22] — 922
Journey To Love (75) 34(2) [0|3|19] — 909
Modern Man (78) 57(2) [0|0|19] — 580
Stanley Clarke (75) 59(2) [0|0|16] — 539
I Wanna Play For You (79) 62(1) [0|0|14] — 422
Rocks, Pebbles And Sand (80) 95(2) [0|0|11] — 233
Time Exposure (84) 149(1) [0|0|12] — 118
Let Me Know You (82) 114(2) [0|0|8] — 105

Stanley CLARKE & George DUKE ▶ 1096 Pk:33 [0|1|2] — **1615**
The Clarke/Duke Project (81) 33(4) [0|8|23] — 1491
The Clarke/Duke Project II (83) 146(1) [0|0|10] — 125

The CLASH ▶ 357 Pk:7 [1|3|8] — **9264**
Combat Rock (82) 7(5) [10|39|61] — 5485
London Calling (80) 27(3) [0|9|33] — 1770
Sandinista! (81) 24(2) [0|5|20] — 1021
Black Market Clash (80) 74(2) [0|0|16] — 398
Cut The Crap (85) 88(2) [0|0|12] — 219
Give 'Em Enough Rope (79) 128(1) [0|0|10] — 152
The Clash (79) 126(2) [0|0|6] — 121
The Story Of The Clash, Volume I (88) 142(2) [0|0|8] — 98.0

CLASSICS IV ▶ 980 Pk:45 [0|0|4] — **2001**
Traces (69) 45(2) [0|0|20] — 950
Dennis Yost & The Classics IV/ Golden Greats-Volume I (69) 50(1) [0|0|20] — 919
Spooky (68) 140(3) [0|0|7] — 112
Mamas And Papas/Soul Train (69) 196(2) [0|0|3] — 20.9

Andrew Dice CLAY ▶ 1521 Pk:94 [0|0|1] — **767**
Dice (89) 94(1) [0|0|47] — 767

Cassius CLAY ▶ 1837 Pk:61 [0|0|1] — **452**
I Am The Greatest! (63) 61(1) [0|0|20] — 452

Tom CLAY ▶ 2612 Pk:92 [0|0|1] — **132**
What The World Needs Now Is Love (71) 92(1) [0|0|5] — 132

Richard CLAYDERMAN ▶ 2899 Pk:160 [0|0|1] — **80**
Amour (84) 160(3) [0|0|9] — 80.1

Merry CLAYTON ▶ 2366 Pk:146 [0|0|2] — **194**
Keep Your Eye On The Sparrow (75) 146(2) [0|0|8] — 106
Merry Clayton (71) 180(1) [0|0|11] — 87.4

David CLAYTON-THOMAS ▶ 2714 Pk:159 [0|0|2] — **112**
David Clayton-Thomas! (69) 159(2) [0|0|8] — 89.5
David Clayton-Thomas (72) 184(1) [0|0|3] — 22.1

CLEAR LIGHT ▶ 2410 Pk:126 [0|0|1] — **184**
Clear Light (67) 126(1) [0|0|13] — 184

Johnny CLEGG & SAVUKA ▶ 2966 Pk:155 [0|0|1] — **70**
Shadow Man (88) 155(2) [0|0|7] — 70.0

Clarence CLEMONS ▶ 1807 Pk:62 [0|0|2] — **480**
Hero (85) 62(2) [0|0|18] — 441
Rescue (83) 174(1) [0|0|5] — 38.6

CLEVELAND Orchestra ▶ 3033 Pk:152 [0|0|1] — **61**
Carl Orff: Carmina Burana (75) 152(1) [0|0|4] — 61.3

Jimmy CLIFF ▶ 2211 Pk:122 [0|0|4] — **248**
The Harder They Come (Soundtrack) (75) 140(2) [0|0|8] — 137
Club Paradise (Soundtrack) (86) 122(2) [0|0|6] — 85.4
Special (82) 186(2) [0|0|2] — 13.2
Follow My Mind (75) 195(1) [0|0|2] — 12.9

Linda CLIFFORD ▶ 851 Pk:22 [0|2|5] — **2644**
If My Friends Could See Me Now (78) 22(2) [0|5|22] — 1265
Let Me Be Your Woman (79) 26(2) [0|8|17] — 1134
Here's My Love (79) 117(2) [0|0|9] — 172
I'm Yours (80) 160(1) [0|0|6] — 57.1
The Right Combination (80)- Linda Clifford & Curtis Mayfield [A] 180(2) [0|0|4] — 16.6

Act ▶ Highest Peak [Top10s | Top40s | Total]
Title (Yr) Peak(Wk) [T10 Wk | T40Wk | TotalWk] — **Score**

- **CLIMAX ▶ 3027 Pk:177 [0|0|1] — 62**
- Climax (72) 177(1) [0|0|7] — 61.9
- **CLIMAX BLUES Band ▶ 591 Pk:27 [0|2|9] — 4875**
- Gold Plated (76) 27(1) [0|6|44] — 1633
- Sense Of Direction (74) 37(2) [0|2|29] — 1495
- FM/Live (73) 107(1) [0|0|30] — 526
- Flying The Flag (81) 75(1) [0|0|16] — 395
- Stamp Album (75) 69(1) [0|0|11] — 322
- Shine On (78) 71(2) [0|0|11] — 320
- Rich Man (73) 150(1) [0|0|10] — 113
- Real To Reel (79) 170(2) [0|0|6] — 65.3
- The Climax Chicago Blues Band Plays On (70) 197(1) [0|0|1] — 6.3
- **CLIMIE FISHER ▶ 2235 Pk:120 [0|0|1] — 240**
- Everything (88) 120(1) [0|0|16] — 240
- **Patsy CLINE ▶ 1409 Pk:29 [0|1|2] — 957**
- Sweet Dreams: The Life And Times Of Patsy Cline (Soundtrack) (85) 29(2) [0|5|18] — 696
- The Patsy Cline Story (63) 74(1) [0|0|12] — 260
- **George CLINTON ▶ 1181 Pk:40 [0|1|5] — 1386**
- Computer Games (82) 40(1) [0|1|33] — 838
- You Shouldn't-Nuf Bit Fish (84) 102(1) [0|0|18] — 261
- R&B Skeletons In The Closet (86) 81(2) [0|0|12] — 216
- Some Of My Best Jokes Are Friends (85) 163(2) [0|0|6] — 50.2
- The Cinderella Theory (89) 192(1) [0|0|4] — 20.7
- **The CLIQUE ▶ 3273 Pk:177 [0|0|1] — 31**
- The Clique (70) 177(1) [0|0|3] — 30.9
- **CLUB NOUVEAU ▶ 764 Pk:6 [1|1|2] — 3188**
- Life, Love & Pain (86) 6(1) [7|18|44] — 3075
- Listen To The Message (88) 98(2) [0|0|6] — 114
- **Billy COBHAM ▶ 590 Pk:23 [0|3|9] — 4879**
- Spectrum (73) 26(1) [0|9|43] — 1990
- Crosswinds (74) 23(2) [0|6|21] — 1322
- Total Eclipse (74) 36(1) [0|1|13] — 742
- Shabazz (Recorded Live In Europe) (75) 74(2) [0|0|8] — 259
- A Funky Thide Of Sings (75) 79(1) [0|0|7] — 228
- Life & Times (76) 128(1) [0|0|8] — 136
- Live - On Tour In Europe (76)-Billy Cobham/George Duke Band [A] 99(1) [0|0|9] — 87.4
- Simplicity Of Expression-Depth Of Thought (78) 166(1) [0|0|6] — 71.1
- Inner Conflicts (78) 172(2) [0|0|4] — 43.9
- **Wayne COCHRAN ▶ 3216 Pk:167 [0|0|1] — 38**
- Wayne Cochran! (68) 167(1) [0|0|4] — 37.8
- **Tom COCHRANE/RED RIDER ▶ 1120 Pk:65 [0|0|6] — 1551**
- As Far As Siam (81)-Red Rider 65(2) [0|0|24] — 658
- Neruda (83)-Red Rider 66(4) [0|0|16] — 413
- Tom Cochrane & Red Rider (86)-Tom Cochrane & Red Rider 112(1) [0|0|12] — 178
- Victory Day (88)-Tom Cochrane & Red Rider 144(2) [0|0|13] — 143
- Breaking Curfew (84)-Red Rider 137(2) [0|0|8] — 93.3
- Don't Fight It (80)-Red Rider 146(1) [0|0|5] — 65.7
- **Bruce COCKBURN ▶ 1086 Pk:45 [0|0|6] — 1646**
- Dancing In The Dragon's Jaws (80) 45(2) [0|0|24] — 720
- Stealing Fire (84) 74(2) [0|0|31] — 517
- Humans (80) 81(2) [0|0|9] — 231
- World Of Wonders (86) 143(3) [0|0|8] — 90.3
- Bruce Cockburn Resume (81) 174(2) [0|0|5] — 49.4
- Big Circumstance (89) 182(1) [0|0|7] — 39.3

Act ▶ Highest Peak [Top10s | Top40s | Total]
Title (Yr) Peak(Wk) [T10 Wk | T40Wk | TotalWk] — **Score**

- **Joe COCKER ▶ 178 Pk:2 [1|5|14] — 19573**
- Joe Cocker! (69) 11(3) [0|26|53] — 5627
- Mad Dogs & Englishmen (Soundtrack) (70) 2(1) [8|16|53] — 4992
- I Can Stand A Little Rain (74) 11(1) [0|10|36] — 2387
- With A Little Help From My Friends (69) 35(2) [0|3|37] — 1745
- Joe Cocker (72) 30(2) [0|7|21] — 1153
- One Night Of Sin (89) 52(1) [0|0|30] — 808
- Cocker (86) 50(2) [0|0|18] — 588
- Unchain My Heart (87) 89(2) [0|0|27] — 528
- Jamaica Say You Will (75) 42(1) [0|0|10] — 429
- Luxury You Can Afford (78) 76(2) [0|0|13] — 391
- Sheffield Steel (82) 105(2) [0|0|23] — 356
- Stingray (76) 70(1) [0|0|10] — 303
- Joe Cocker's Greatest Hits (77) 114(2) [0|0|8] — 150
- Civilized Man (84) 133(1) [0|0|9] — 115
- **COCK ROBIN ▶ 1804 Pk:61 [0|0|2] — 481**
- Cock Robin (85) 61(2) [0|0|19] — 457
- After Here Through Midland (87) 166(2) [0|0|3] — 24.2
- **COCTEAU TWINS ▶ 2243 Pk:109 [0|0|1] — 236**
- Blue Bell Knoll (88) 109(2) [0|0|18] — 236
- **David Allan COE ▶ 3255 Pk:179 [0|0|1] — 33**
- Castles In The Sand (83) 179(1) [0|0|5] — 32.7
- **Dennis COFFEY ▶ 1041 Pk:36 [0|1|4] — 1775**
- Evolution (71) 36(1) [0|4|25] — 1313
- Goin' For Myself (72) 90(2) [0|0|14] — 328
- Finger Lickin Good (76) 147(2) [0|0|7] — 94.8
- Electric Coffey (73) 189(2) [0|0|6] — 39.0
- **Leonard COHEN ▶ 1282 Pk:63 [0|0|4] — 1179**
- Songs From A Room (69) 63(2) [0|0|17] — 690
- Songs Of Leonard Cohen (68) 83(2) [0|0|14] — 263
- Songs Of Love And Hate (71) 145(1) [0|0|11] — 162
- Leonard Cohen: Live Songs (73) 156(1) [0|0|5] — 64.9
- **Myron COHEN ▶ 2239 Pk:102 [0|0|1] — 239**
- Everybody Gotta Be Someplace (66) 102(1) [0|0|13] — 239
- **COLD BLOOD ▶ 825 Pk:23 [0|1|6] — 2785**
- Cold Blood (69) 23(1) [0|6|29] — 1750
- Sisyphus (71) 60(1) [0|0|13] — 389
- Thriller! (73) 97(1) [0|0|14] — 270
- First Taste Of Sin (72) 133(1) [0|0|11] — 182
- Lydia (74) 126(1) [0|0|8] — 161
- Lydia Pense & Cold Blood (76) 179(1) [0|0|4] — 33.1
- **COLD CHISEL ▶ 3012 Pk:171 [0|0|1] — 64**
- East (81) 171(2) [0|0|6] — 64.0
- **Nat King COLE ▶ 426 Pk:4 [1|3|10] — 7466**
- L-O-V-E (65) 4(3) [5|25|38] — 3271
- Unforgettable (65) 30(1) [0|11|39] — 1519
- I Don't Want To Be Hurt Anymore (64) 18(2) [0|4|45] — 1375
- My Fair Lady (64) 74(2) [0|0|23] — 407
- Looking Back (65) 60(1) [0|0|14] — 359
- Nat King Cole At The Sands (66) 74(1) [0|0|11] — 238
- Songs From "Cat Ballou" And Other Motion Pictures (65) 77(1) [0|0|9] — 194
- The Great Songs! (66) 145(1) [0|0|3] — 43.8
- The Best Of Nat King Cole (68) 187(2) [0|0|5] — 40.8
- Close-Up (69) 197(1) [0|0|3] — 18.5
- **Natalie COLE ▶ 214 Pk:8 [1|5|13] — 16168**
- Thankful (77) 16(1) [0|17|39] — 2927
- Unpredictable (77) 8(2) [4|13|28] — 2786
- Inseparable (75) 18(1) [0|8|56] — 2731
- Natalie (76) 13(1) [0|11|30] — 2646
- Everlasting (87) 42(2) [0|0|58] — 1792
- Natalie...Live (78) 31(2) [0|7|16] — 957

Act ▶ Highest Peak [Top10s | Top40s | Total]
Title (Yr) Peak(Wk) [T10 Wk | T40Wk | TotalWk] — **Score**

- Don't Look Back (80) 77(1) [0|0|22] — 601
- Good To Be Back (89) 59(2) [0|0|23] — 576
- I Love You So (79) 52(2) [0|0|15] — 574
- We're The Best Of Friends (79)-Natalie Cole & Peabo Bryson [A] 44(1) [0|0|19] — 403
- Dangerous (85) 140(2) [0|0|9] — 87.0
- Happy Love (81) 132(2) [0|0|4] — 66.8
- I'm Ready (83) 182(1) [0|0|3] — 20.6
- **Durell COLEMAN ▶ 2988 Pk:155 [0|0|1] — 67**
- Durell Coleman (85) 155(2) [0|0|7] — 67.2
- **Albert COLLINS ▶ 2907 Pk:124 [0|0|2] — 79**
- Showdown! (86)-Albert Collins, Robert Cray, Johnny Copeland [A] 124(1) [0|0|18] — 67.0
- There's Gotta Be A Change (72) 196(2) [0|0|2] — 12.1
- **Judy COLLINS ▶ 169 Pk:5 [1|8|16] — 20457**
- Wildflowers (68) 5(1) [6|18|75] — 4954
- Whales & Nightingales (70) 17(1) [0|16|35] — 2934
- Judith (75) 17(1) [0|17|34] — 2761
- Who Knows Where The Time Goes (68) 29(2) [0|11|33] — 2111
- Recollections (69) 29(1) [0|3|29] — 1273
- So Early In The Spring - The First 15 Years (77) 42(2) [0|0|27] — 1088
- Bread & Roses (76) 25(1) [0|4|20] — 1041
- Colors Of The Day/The Best Of Judy Collins (72) 37(2) [0|3|24] — 1004
- True Stories And Other Dreams (73) 27(1) [0|4|20] — 891
- In My Life (67) 46(1) [0|0|34] — 836
- Hard Times For Lovers (79) 54(2) [0|0|16] — 543
- Living (71) 64(1) [0|0|13] — 480
- Judy Collins' Fifth Album (65) 69(1) [0|0|13] — 290
- Judy Collins #3 (64) 126(1) [0|0|10] — 128
- Running For My Life (80) 142(3) [0|0|6] — 94.9
- Times Of Our Lives (82) 190(1) [0|0|5] — 28.7
- **Phil COLLINS ▶ 73 Pk:1 [4|4|4] — 36530**
- No Jacket Required (85) 1(7) [31|70|123] — 14141
- ...But Seriously (89) 1(4) [20|50|90] — 9734
- Face Value (81) 7(4) [10|26|164] — 8163
- Hello, I Must Be Going! (82) 8(5) [7|21|141] — 4492
- **COLOSSEUM ▶ 3369 Pk:192 [0|0|1] — 22**
- Colosseum Live (71) 192(2) [0|0|3] — 21.8
- **Jessi COLTER ▶ 920 Pk:10 [1|1|5] — 2261**
- I'm Jessi Colter (75) 50(2) [0|0|27] — 748
- Wanted! The Outlaws (76)-Waylon Jennings, Willie Nelson, Jessi Colter, Tompall Glaser [A] 10(2) [2|14|51] — 723
- Leather And Lace (81)-Waylon Jennings & Jessi Colter [A] 43(2) [0|0|19] — 371
- Diamond In The Rough (76) 79(1) [0|0|8] — 233
- Jessi (76) 109(3) [0|0|8] — 186
- **Alice COLTRANE ▶ 2587 Pk:79 [0|0|2] — 138**
- Illuminations (74)-Devadip Carlos Santana & Turiya Alice Coltrane [A] 79(2) [0|0|8] — 124
- Universal Consciousness (71) 190(1) [0|0|2] — 14.3
- **Chi COLTRANE ▶ 2707 Pk:148 [0|0|1] — 113**
- Chi Coltrane (72) 148(1) [0|0|10] — 113
- **John COLTRANE ▶ 3177 Pk:186 [0|0|2] — 43**
- Sun Ship (71) 186(2) [0|0|3] — 26.4
- Expression (67) 194(2) [0|0|3] — 17.0
- **Shawn COLVIN ▶ 2129 Pk:111 [0|0|1] — 287**
- Steady On (89) 111(1) [0|0|24] — 287
- **COMMANDER CODY & His LOST PLANET AIRMEN ▶ 983 Pk:58 [0|0|8] — 1988**
- Lost In The Ozone (71) 82(2) [0|0|33] — 747
- Commander Cody & His Lost Planet Airmen (75) 58(2) [0|0|10] — 358

Act ▶ Highest Peak [Top10s | Top40s | Total] Title (Yr) Peak(Wk) [T10 Wk | T40Wk | TotalWk]	Score
COMMANDER CODY... ▶ *Continued*	
Hot Licks, Cold Steel & Truckers Favorites (72) 94(1) [0|0|13]	289
Live From Deep In The Heart Of Texas (74) 105(2) [0|0|14]	259
Country Casanova (73) 104(1) [0|0|9]	182
Rock 'N Roll Again (77)-Commander Cody Band 163(1) [0|0|5]	61.8
Tales From The Ozone (75) 168(1) [0|0|6]	56.5
We've Got A Live One Here (76) 170(1) [0|0|3]	34.8
The COMMODORES ▶ 54 Pk:3 [5|12|16]	**43008**
Commodores (77)-Commodores 3(3) [19|31|53]	7441
Midnight Magic (79)-Commodores 3(2) [15|30|41]	6387
Natural High (78)-Commodores 3(8) [16|23|33]	6240
Hot On The Tracks (76)-Commodores 12(3) [0|25|39]	4400
In The Pocket (81)-Commodores 13(2) [0|19|40]	3539
Commodores Live! (77)-Commodores 3(2) [6|16|28]	3522
Heroes (80)-Commodores 7(3) [5|15|33]	3045
Nightshift (85)-Commodores 12(3) [0|15|37]	2071
Movin' On (75)-Commodores 29(1) [0|9|32]	2007
Caught In The Act (75)-Commodores 26(1) [0|5|33]	1632
Commodores' Greatest Hits (78)-Commodores 23(2) [0|6|20]	1220
All The Great Hits (82)-Commodores 37(3) [0|4|24]	854
United (86)-Commodores 101(3) [0|0|15]	235
Commodores 13 (83)-Commodores 103(1) [0|0|11]	173
Machine Gun (74)-Commodores 138(1) [0|0|9]	159
Commodores Anthology (83)-Commodores 141(1) [0|0|7]	84.5
The COMMUNARDS ▶ 1889 Pk:90 [0|0|2]	**413**
The Communards (86) 90(2) [0|0|16]	225
Red (88) 93(1) [0|0|9]	189
Perry COMO ▶ 577 Pk:22 [0|2|10]	**5055**
It's Impossible (71) 22(2) [0|12|27]	1909
And I Love You So (73) 34(1) [0|4|19]	831
The Songs I Love (63) 59(2) [0|0|18]	491
The Scene Changes (65) 47(2) [0|0|17]	470
Perry Como In Italy (66) 81(1) [0|0|16]	373
Seattle (69) 93(1) [0|0|11]	338
I Think Of You (71) 101(1) [0|0|9]	199
Lightly Latin (66) 86(1) [0|0|9]	179
Perry (74) 138(2) [0|0|10]	136
Just Out Of Reach (75) 142(1) [0|0|9]	129
COMPANY B ▶ 2995 Pk:143 [0|0|1]	**67**
Company B (87) 143(2) [0|0|6]	66.7
CONCRETE BLONDE ▶ 1923 Pk:96 [0|0|2]	**392**
Concrete Blonde (87) 96(2) [0|0|16]	242
Free (89) 148(1) [0|0|18]	150
CONEY HATCH ▶ 3471 Pk:186 [0|0|1]	**13**
Outa Hand (83) 186(1) [0|0|2]	12.6
CON FUNK SHUN ▶ 481 Pk:30 [0|2|10]	**6517**
Loveshine (78) 32(1) [0|7|19]	1165
Secrets (77) 51(2) [0|0|28]	1071
Spirit Of Love (80) 30(3) [0|5|20]	929
Candy (79) 46(2) [0|0|22]	905
Touch (80) 51(1) [0|0|19]	780
Electric Lady (85) 62(3) [0|0|26]	571
To The Max (82) 115(1) [0|0|29]	394
Con Funk Shun 7 (81) 82(1) [0|0|13]	302

Act ▶ Highest Peak [Top10s | Top40s | Total] Title (Yr) Peak(Wk) [T10 Wk | T40Wk | TotalWk]	Score
Fever (83) 105(1) [0|0|21]	285
Burnin' Love (86) 121(2) [0|0|11]	115
John CONLEE ▶ 3090 Pk:166 [0|0|1]	**53**
John Conlee's Greatest Hits (83) 166(1) [0|0|6]	53.4
Arthur CONLEY ▶ 2147 Pk:93 [0|0|3]	**281**
Sweet Soul Music (67) 93(1) [0|0|13]	254
Soul Directions (68) 185(2) [0|0|2]	17.0
Shake, Rattle & Roll (67) 193(1) [0|0|2]	10.3
The CONNELLS ▶ 2974 Pk:163 [0|0|1]	**69**
Fun & Games (89) 163(1) [0|0|10]	68.9
Harry CONNICK Jr. ▶ 930 Pk:42 [0|0|1]	**2220**
When Harry Met Sally (Soundtrack) (89) 42(2) [0|0|122]	2220
Ray CONNIFF ▶ 2581 Pk:85 [0|0|1]	**141**
Just Kiddin' Around (63)-Ray Conniff & Billy Butterfield [A] 85(1) [0|0|13]	141
Ray CONNIFF & His Orchestra & Chorus ▶ 165 Pk:3 [1|7|29]	**20729**
Somewhere My Love (66) 3(4) [17|41|90]	7273
Honey (68) 22(1) [0|9|39]	2135
It Must Be Him (68) 25(1) [0|13|41]	1710
This Is My Song (67) 30(2) [0|6|46]	1582
Invisible Tears (64) 23(1) [0|11|27]	1127
Bridge Over Troubled Water (70) 47(3) [0|0|28]	962
Music From Mary Poppins, The Sound Of Music, My Fair Lady, & Other Great Movie Themes (65) 34(2) [0|6|19]	844
Turn Around Look At Me (68) 70(1) [0|0|22]	726
Hawaiian Album (67) 39(1) [0|2|15]	547
Speak To Me Of Love (64) 50(1) [0|0|19]	452
Love Affair (65) 54(1) [0|0|16]	410
Jean (69) 103(1) [0|0|21]	384
I Love How You Love Me (69) 101(1) [0|0|14]	372
Love Story (71) 98(1) [0|0|15]	346
You Make Me Feel So Young (64) 73(1) [0|0|17]	311
Love Theme From "The Godfather" (72) 114(2) [0|0|14]	281
We've Only Just Begun (70) 120(1) [0|0|13]	242
Ray Conniff's World Of Hits (67) 78(1) [0|0|10]	231
Happiness Is (66) 80(1) [0|0|9]	179
I'd Like To Teach The World To Sing (72) 138(1) [0|0|11]	151
I Can See Clearly Now (73) 165(1) [0|0|10]	82.3
Ray Conniff's Greatest Hits (69) 158(1) [0|0|5]	80.2
Alone Again (Naturally) (72) 180(1) [0|0|10]	74.2
Friendly Persuasion (65) 141(1) [0|0|5]	61.1
Great Contemporary Instrumental Hits (71) 185(1) [0|0|5]	43.0
Concert In Stereo/ Live At The Sahara/Tahoe (70) 177(1) [0|0|5]	42.6
You Are The Sunshine Of My Life (73) 176(2) [0|0|5]	41.2
Harmony (73) 194(1) [0|0|4]	23.4
En Espanol! (67) 180(1) [0|0|2]	16.4
Norman CONNORS ▶ 931 Pk:39 [0|1|8]	**2216**
You Are My Starship (76) 39(1) [0|1|24]	947
This Is Your Life (78) 68(1) [0|0|17]	507
Romantic Journey (77) 94(2) [0|0|16]	423
Invitation (79) 137(1) [0|0|7]	122
Saturday Night Special (75) 150(2) [0|0|5]	80.3
Take It To The Limit (80) 145(1) [0|0|6]	77.3
Best Of Norman Connors & Friends (79) 175(1) [0|0|5]	48.9
Mr. C. (81) 197(1) [0|0|2]	10.0
The CONTROLLERS ▶ 2884 Pk:146 [0|0|1]	**82**
In Control (77) 146(1) [0|0|6]	82.1

Act ▶ Highest Peak [Top10s | Top40s | Total] Title (Yr) Peak(Wk) [T10 Wk | T40Wk | TotalWk]	Score
Tommy CONWELL And The YOUNG RUMBLERS ▶ 1861 Pk:103 [0|0|1]	**434**
Rumble (88) 103(1) [0|0|28]	434
Ry COODER ▶ 982 Pk:43 [0|0|9]	**1995**
Borderline (81) 43(2) [0|0|16]	729
Bop Till You Drop (79) 62(2) [0|0|15]	557
Crossroads (Soundtrack) (86) 85(3) [0|0|9]	175
Into The Purple Valley (72) 113(1) [0|0|8]	163
The Slide Area (82) 105(1) [0|0|7]	109
Get Rhythm (87) 177(1) [0|0|12]	83.1
Show Time (77) 158(1) [0|0|5]	64.9
Paradise And Lunch (74) 167(1) [0|0|6]	63.8
Chicken Skin Music (76) 177(2) [0|0|5]	50.3
Sam COOKE ▶ 693 Pk:29 [0|2|9]	**3803**
Sam Cooke At The Copa (64) 29(1) [0|5|55]	1517
Shake (65) 44(1) [0|0|23]	780
Ain't That Good News (64) 34(1) [0|3|19]	648
Night Beat (63) 62(1) [0|0|19]	424
The Best Of Sam Cooke, Volume 2 (65) 128(2) [0|0|8]	110
Try A Little Love (65) 120(1) [0|0|7]	105
Sam Cooke Live At The Harlem Square Club (85) 134(1) [0|0|8]	85.5
The Best Of Sam Cooke (65) 136(1) [0|0|6]	77.9
The Man & His Music (86) 175(1) [0|0|8]	56.1
Rita COOLIDGE ▶ 379 Pk:6 [1|2|10]	**8806**
Anytime...Anywhere (77) 6(4) [7|21|54]	5275
Love Me Again (78) 32(1) [0|5|22]	1028
The Lady's Not For Sale (72) 46(1) [0|0|24]	954
Fall Into Spring (74) 55(1) [0|0|15]	462
Satisfied (79) 95(3) [0|0|16]	271
It's Only Love (75) 85(1) [0|0|10]	247
Rita Coolidge (71) 105(1) [0|0|10]	221
Rita Coolidge/Greatest Hits (81) 107(2) [0|0|8]	162
Nice Feelin' (71) 135(1) [0|0|8]	138
Heartbreak Radio (81) 160(1) [0|0|4]	46.5
--Cooper, Alice see Alice Cooper	
Michael COOPER ▶ 1896 Pk:98 [0|0|1]	**409**
Love Is Such A Funny Game (88) 98(3) [0|0|25]	409
Pat COOPER ▶ 1245 Pk:82 [0|0|3]	**1236**
Our Hero...Pat Cooper (66) 82(1) [0|0|42]	906
Spaghetti Sauce & Other Delights (66) 84(1) [0|0|14]	314
More Saucy Stories From...Pat Cooper (69) 193(2) [0|0|2]	15.7
Julian COPE ▶ 1902 Pk:105 [0|0|3]	**406**
St. Julian (87) 105(2) [0|0|12]	175
My Nation Underground (88) 155(1) [0|0|13]	129
Julian Cope (87) 109(2) [0|0|6]	102
Johnny COPELAND ▶ 2992 Pk:124 [0|0|1]	**67**
Showdown! (86)-Albert Collins, Robert Cray, Johnny Copeland [A] 124(1) [0|0|18]	67.0
Stewart COPELAND ▶ 2635 Pk:148 [0|0|2]	**126**
The Rhythmotist (85) 148(2) [0|0|8]	78.4
Rumble Fish (Soundtrack) (83) 157(1) [0|0|5]	47.8
Chick COREA ▶ 997 Pk:42 [0|0|8]	**1957**
Leprechaun (76) 42(1) [0|0|15]	672
The Mad Hatter (78) 61(2) [0|0|14]	431
My Spanish Heart (77) 55(1) [0|0|12]	424
Friends (78) 86(2) [0|0|10]	266
An Evening With Herbie Hancock And Chick Corea (79)-Herbie Hancock And Chick Corea [A] 100(1) [0|0|8]	84.4
Three Quartets (81) 179(2) [0|0|4]	38.2
Tap Step (80) 170(2) [0|0|3]	32.1

Act ▶ Highest Peak [Top10s|Top40s|Total]
Title (Yr) Peak(Wk) [T10 Wk|T40Wk|TotalWk] **Score**

Chick COREA ▶ *Continued*
An Evening With Chick Corea & Herbie Hancock (79)-Chick Corea & Herbie Hancock [A] 175(1) [0|0|2] 9.9

CORNELIUS BROTHERS & SISTER ROSE ▶ 1221 Pk:29 [0|1|1] 1299
Cornelius Brothers & Sister Rose (72) 29(1) [0|6|25] 1299

The CORPORATION ▶ 3340 Pk:197 [0|0|1] 25
The Corporation (69) 197(2) [0|0|4] 25.0

Larry CORYELL ▶ 3370 Pk:196 [0|0|1] 22
Lady Coryell (69) 196(1) [0|0|3] 21.8

Bill COSBY ▶ 52 Pk:2 [3|10|22] 43693
Wonderfulness (66) 7(1) [5|54|106] 8093
Why Is There Air? (65) 19(1) [0|55|152] 7355
Revenge (67) 2(1) [12|28|73] 6405
Bill Cosby Is A Very Funny Fellow, Right! (64) 21(1) [0|34|128] 5024
To Russell, My Brother, Whom I Slept With (68) 7(2) [4|23|46] 3821
I Started Out As A Child (64) 32(1) [0|5|140] 3629
200 M.P.H. (68) 16(1) [0|11|25] 2263
Bill Cosby Sings/Silver Throat (67) 18(2) [0|12|26] 1688
It's True! It's True! (69) 37(1) [0|3|19] 981
The Best Of Bill Cosby (69) 51(2) [0|0|25] 778
Bill Cosby (69) 70(1) [0|0|24] 724
Those Of You With Or Without Children, You'll Understand (86) 26(2) [0|4|15] 648
8:15 12:15 (69) 62(2) [0|0|16] 642
Bill Cosby "Himself" Soundtrack) (82) 64(2) [0|0|14] 342
More Of The Best Of Bill Cosby (70) 80(1) [0|0|16] 334
Bill Cosby Is Not Himself These Days-(Rat Own, Rat Own, Rat Own) (76) 100(2) [0|0|12] 276
Bill Cosby Sings/Hooray For The Salvation Army Band! (68) 74(2) [0|0|11] 263
When I Was A Kid (71) 72(1) [0|0|8] 249
Live Madison Square Garden Center (70) 165(2) [0|0|6] 68.9
For Adults Only (71) 181(1) [0|0|7] 59.3
Fat Albert (73) 187(1) [0|0|4] 25.0
Inside The Mind Of Bill Cosby (72) 191(1) [0|0|4] 24.0

Alec R. COSTANDINOS ▶ 2075 Pk:92 [0|0|1] 313
Romeo & Juliet (78)-Alec R. Costandinos And The Synconic Orchestra 92(2) [0|0|17] 313

Elvis COSTELLO ▶ 726 Pk:28 [0|3|3] 3466
My Aim Is True (77) 32(2) [0|5|36] 1432
Spike (89) 32(1) [0|11|25] 1380
Taking Liberties (80) 28(1) [0|3|14] 654

Elvis COSTELLO & The ATTRACTIONS ▶ 340 Pk:10 [1|8|11] 9978
Armed Forces (79) 10(2) [2|11|25] 2310
Get Happy!! (80) 11(2) [0|8|15] 1463
Punch The Clock (83 24(1) [0|12|24] 1334
This Years Model (78) 30(2) [0|4|17] 954
Imperial Bedroom (82 30(3) [0|7|24] 943
Trust (81) 28(2) [0|4|15] 860
Goodbye Cruel World (84) 35(2) [0|3|21] 715
King Of America (86) 39(2) [0|3|18] 601
Almost Blue (81) 50(2) [0|0|13] 377
Best Of Elvis Costello/The Attractions (85) 116(2) [0|0|16] 224
Blood & Chocolate (86) 84(2) [0|0|11] 197

James COTTON Band ▶ 2680 Pk:146 [0|0|2] 118
100% Cotton (75) 146(1) [0|0|9] 107
The James Cotton Blues Band (67) 194(1) [0|0|2] 11.4

Josie COTTON ▶ 2778 Pk:147 [0|0|1] 100
Convertible Music (82) 147(2) [0|0|12] 100

COUCHOIS ▶ 3161 Pk:170 [0|0|1] 45
Couchois (79) 170(1) [0|0|4] 45.4

COUNT FIVE ▶ 2782 Pk:122 [0|0|1] 100
Psychotic Reaction (66) 122(1) [0|0|6] 100

COUNTRY JOE & The FISH ▶ 643 Pk:23 [0|2|10] 4289
Electric Music For The Mind And Body (67) 39(3) [0|3|38] 1210
Together (68) 23(2) [0|7|16] 1050
I-Feel-Like-I'm-Fixin'-To-Die (67) 67(1) [0|0|28] 623
Here We Are Again (69) 48(2) [0|0|11] 609
Country Joe & The Fish/Greatest Hits (70) 74(2) [0|0|9] 275
Paradise With An Ocean View (75)-Country Joe McDonald 124(1) [0|0|14] 251
C.J. Fish (70) 111(1) [0|0|9] 194
Incredible! Live! (72)-Country Joe McDonald 179(2) [0|0|4] 33.1
War, War, War (71)-Country Joe McDonald 185(1) [0|0|4] 31.5
The Life And Times Of Country Joe & The Fish From Haight-Ashbury To Woodstock (71) 197(2) [0|0|2] 13.0

The COUNTS ▶ 3474 Pk:193 [0|0|1] 13
What's Up Front That-Counts (72) 193(1) [0|0|2] 12.6

David COURTNEY ▶ 3345 Pk:194 [0|0|1] 25
David Courtney's First Day (76) 194(1) [0|0|4] 24.6

COVER GIRLS ▶ 1231 Pk:64 [0|0|2] 1271
Show Me (87) 64(1) [0|0|61] 1016
We Can't Go Wrong (89) 108(1) [0|0|19] 255

COWBOY JUNKIES ▶ 1160 Pk:26 [0|1|1] 1441
The Trinity Session (89) 26(1) [0|9|29] 1441

The COWSILLS ▶ 688 Pk:16 [0|2|6] 3844
The Cowsills In Concert (69) 16(2) [0|10|24] 2183
The Cowsills (67) 31(1) [0|7|17] 974
Captain Sad And His Ship Of Fools (68) 105(2) [0|0|12] 269
We Can Fly (68) 89(2) [0|0|14] 207
The Best Of The Cowsills (69) 127(1) [0|0|9] 205
On My Side (71) 200(1) [0|0|1] 5.8

CRABBY APPLETON ▶ 3073 Pk:175 [0|0|1] 56
Crabby Appleton (70) 175(2) [0|0|6] 56.3

CRACK THE SKY ▶ 2048 Pk:124 [0|0|4] 330
Safety In Numbers (78) 124(1) [0|0|8] 141
Animal Notes (76) 142(1) [0|0|5] 89.1
Crack The Sky (76) 161(1) [0|0|6] 69.9
From The Greenhouse (89) 186(1) [0|0|5] 30.6

Billy "Crash" CRADDOCK ▶ 2898 Pk:142 [0|0|1] 80
Rub It In (74) 142(2) [0|0|5] 80.2

Floyd CRAMER ▶ 1858 Pk:107 [0|0|5] 436
Class Of '65 (65) 107(1) [0|0|13] 192
Class Of '66 (66) 123(2) [0|0|7] 118
Here's What's Happening! (67) 166(1) [0|0|6] 57.3
Dallas (80) 170(1) [0|0|5] 44.1
The Big Ones, Volume II (70) 183(1) [0|0|3] 24.4

Les CRANE ▶ 1598 Pk:32 [0|1|1] 680
Desiderata (71) 32(2) [0|4|11] 680

Hank CRAWFORD ▶ 2576 Pk:143 [0|0|3] 141
I Hear A Symphony (76) 159(1) [0|0|7] 84.3
Hank Crawford's Back (77) 167(1) [0|0|3] 33.0
True Blue (64) 143(1) [0|0|2] 24.0

Michael CRAWFORD ▶ 3501 Pk:192 [0|0|1] 11
Songs From The Stage And Screen (88) 192(2) [0|0|2] 11.2

Randy CRAWFORD ▶ 1467 Pk:71 [0|0|6] 867
Secret Combination (81) 71(1) [0|0|19] 532
Rich And Poor (89) 159(3) [0|0|13] 107
Windsong (82) 148(1) [0|0|10] 104
Now We May Begin (80) 180(1) [0|0|7] 52.6
Nightline (83) 164(1) [0|0|5] 42.1
Abstract Emotions (86) 178(2) [0|0|4] 29.6

Robert CRAY Band ▶ 617 Pk:13 [0|2|5] 4577
Strong Persuader (86) 13(3) [0|26|49] 3174
Don't Be Afraid Of The Dark (88) 32(2) [0|7|32] 1034
False Accusations (86) 141(3) [0|0|21] 210
Bad Influence (87) 143(1) [0|0|11] 92.4
Showdown! (86)-Albert Collins, Robert Cray, Johnny Copeland [A] 124(1) [0|0|18] 67.0

CRAZY HORSE ▶ 1998 Pk:84 [0|0|2] 351
Crazy Horse (71) 84(1) [0|0|11] 285
Loose (72) 170(1) [0|0|6] 66.7
--See Also Young, Neil

Papa John CREACH ▶ 2025 Pk:94 [0|0|1] 339
Papa John Creach (72) 94(2) [0|0|14] 339

CREAM ▶ 80 Pk:1 [4|7|8] 34066
Disraeli Gears (67) 4(2) [30|50|83] 9811
Wheels Of Fire (68) 1(4) [20|30|50] 8375
Best Of Cream (69) 3(1) [13|20|44] 5962
Goodbye (69) 2(2) [8|14|26] 4361
Fresh Cream (67) 39(1) [0|1|92] 2650
Live Cream (70) 15(1) [0|9|21] 1759
Live Cream - Volume II (72) 27(1) [0|5|16] 995
Heavy Cream (72) 135(1) [0|0|10] 153

CREATIVE SOURCE ▶ 2715 Pk:152 [0|0|1] 111
Creative Source (74) 152(1) [0|0|10] 111

CREEDENCE CLEARWATER REVIVAL ▶ 33 Pk:1 [5|7|13] 49421
Cosmo's Factory (70) 1(9) [19|26|69] 10485
Bayou Country (69) 7(1) [13|37|88] 9860
Green River (69) 1(4) [15|23|88] 9555
Willy And The Poorboys (69) 3(6) [16|24|60] 7040
Pendulum (70) 5(1) [11|22|42] 4865
Creedence Gold (72) 15(1) [0|15|37] 2531
Creedence Clearwater Revival (68) 52(1) [0|0|73] 1789
Mardi Gras (72) 12(1) [0|12|24] 1763
The Concert (80) 62(1) [0|0|20] 512
More Creedence Gold (73) 61(1) [0|0|18] 456
Chronicle (The 20 Greatest Hits) (76) 100(1) [0|0|14] 331
Live In Europe (73) 143(1) [0|0|10] 118
Chronicle II (86) 165(2) [0|0|16] 115

Marshall CRENSHAW ▶ 1137 Pk:50 [0|0|3] 1506
Marshall Crenshaw (82) 50(2) [0|0|27] 776
Field Day (83) 52(1) [0|0|14] 488
Downtown (85) 110(2) [0|0|18] 242

The CRETONES ▶ 2472 Pk:125 [0|0|1] 167
Thin Red Line (80) 125(1) [0|0|10] 167

Bob CREWE Generation ▶ 2275 Pk:100 [0|0|1] 224
Music To Watch Girls By (67) 100(1) [0|0|11] 224

Peter CRISS ▶ 1338 Pk:43 [0|0|1] 1076
Peter Criss (78) 43(2) [0|0|20] 1076

The CRITTERS ▶ 3289 Pk:147 [0|0|1] 29
Younger Girl (66) 147(1) [0|0|2] 29.0

Act ▶ Highest Peak [Top10s|Top40s|Total]
Title (Yr) Peak(Wk) [T10 Wk|T40Wk|TotalWk] — **Score**

Jim CROCE ▶ 126 Pk:1 [4|4|6] — 25550
You Don't Mess Around With Jim (72) 1(5) [19|42|93] — 10154
Life And Times (73) 7(2) [8|26|84] — 5513
I Got A Name (73) 2(2) [7|26|53] — 5040
Photographs & Memories/His Greatest Hits (74) 2(2) [8|15|46] — 4349
The Faces I've Been (75) 87(1) [0|0|18] — 461
Time In A Bottle/Jim Croce's Greatest Love Songs (77) 170(1) [0|0|3] — 33.4

Steve CROPPER ▶ 3381 Pk:171 [0|0|1] — 21
Jammed Together (69)-Albert King, Steve Cropper, Pop Staples [A] 171(2) [0|0|5] — 20.7

Bing CROSBY ▶ 2026 Pk:98 [0|0|3] — 339
Bing Crosby's Greatest Hits (77) 98(2) [0|0|9] — 194
Hey Jude/Hey Bing! (69) 162(2) [0|0|8] — 108
America, I Hear You Singing (64)-Frank Sinatra/Bing Crosby/Frank Waring [A] 116(1) [0|0|7] — 36.1

David CROSBY ▶ 988 Pk:12 [0|1|2] — 1973
If I Could Only Remember My Name (71) 12(2) [0|10|18] — 1792
Oh Yes I Can (89) 104(2) [0|0|10] — 181

David CROSBY/Graham NASH ▶ 435 Pk:4 [2|3|5] — 7327
Graham Nash/David Crosby (72)-Graham Nash/David Crosby 4(3) [7|14|26] — 2912
Wind On The Water (75) 6(2) [6|12|31] — 2837
Whistling Down The Wire (76) 26(2) [0|6|15] — 1198
Crosby/Nash - Live (77) 52(1) [0|0|8] — 323
The Best Of Crosby/Nash (78) 150(1) [0|0|4] — 57.9

CROSBY, STILLS & NASH ▶ 175 Pk:2 [3|3|5] — 19840
Crosby, Stills & Nash (69) 6(3) [17|40|107] — 10638
CSN (77) 2(4) [10|20|33] — 4989
Daylight Again (82) 8(5) [6|30|41] — 3714
Allies (83) 43(2) [0|0|12] — 409
Replay (81) 122(2) [0|0|5] — 88.8

CROSBY, STILLS, NASH & YOUNG ▶ 139 Pk:1 [3|4|4] — 23012
Deja Vu (70) 1(1) [23|38|97] — 11184
4 Way Street (71) 1(1) [13|26|42] — 6910
So Far (74) 1(1) [5|12|27] — 3250
American Dream (88) 16(1) [0|11|22] — 1667

Christopher CROSS ▶ 245 Pk:6 [1|2|3] — 14517
Christopher Cross (80) 6(3) [15|81|116] — 12682
Another Page (83) 11(5) [0|11|31] — 1765
Every Turn Of The World (85) 127(1) [0|0|6] — 70.1

CROSS COUNTRY ▶ 3514 Pk:198 [0|0|1] — 10
Cross Country (73) 198(1) [0|0|2] — 10.1

CROW ▶ 1626 Pk:69 [0|0|2] — 648
Crow Music (69) 69(1) [0|0|24] — 616
Crow By Crow (70) 181(2) [0|0|4] — 32.1

CROWDED HOUSE ▶ 686 Pk:12 [0|2|2] — 3847
Crowded House (86) 12(1) [0|24|58] — 3074
Temple Of Low Men (88) 40(2) [0|2|19] — 773

Rodney CROWELL ▶ 2122 Pk:105 [0|0|3] — 290
Rodney Crowell (81) 105(1) [0|0|8] — 165
But What Will The Neighbors Think (80) 155(1) [0|0|10] — 93.2
Street Language (86) 177(1) [0|0|5] — 31.6

CROWN HEIGHTS AFFAIR ▶ 1865 Pk:121 [0|0|2] — 431
Dreaming A Dream (75) 121(1) [0|0|17] — 292
Sure Shot (80) 148(2) [0|0|12] — 138

The CRUSADERS ▶ 280 Pk:18 [0|6|18] — 12409
Street Life (79) 18(1) [0|17|39] — 2774
The 2nd Crusade (73) 45(1) [0|0|29] — 1098
Southern Comfort (74) 31(2) [0|3|23] — 1097
Chain Reaction (75) 26(2) [0|5|17] — 1091
Images (78) 34(3) [0|8|18] — 1059
Those Southern Knights (76) 38(2) [0|3|18] — 897
Rhapsody And Blues (80) 29(2) [0|4|16] — 883
Free As The Wind (77) 41(3) [0|0|15] — 787
Crusaders 1 (72) 96(1) [0|0|29] — 623
Scratch (74) 73(2) [0|0|20] — 508
Standing Tall (81) 59(2) [0|0|16] — 404
Ghetto Blaster (84) 79(2) [0|0|22] — 375
Old Socks, New Shoes...New Socks, Old Shoes (70)-The Jazz Crusaders 90(1) [0|0|16] — 342
The Best Of The Crusaders (76) 122(2) [0|0|10] — 198
Unsung Heroes (73) 173(1) [0|0|14] — 122
Royal Jam (82)-The Crusaders With B.B. King And The Royal Philharmonic Orchestra 144(1) [0|0|7] — 79.8
Pass The Plate (71) 168(2) [0|0|4] — 50.0
Powerhouse (69)-The Jazz Crusaders 184(2) [0|0|2] — 21.0

CRUZADOS ▶ 1634 Pk:76 [0|0|2] — 636
Cruzados (85) 76(2) [0|0|18] — 360
After Dark (87) 106(2) [0|0|21] — 276

CRYAN' SHAMES ▶ 2573 Pk:156 [0|0|3] — 143
Synthesis (69) 184(1) [0|0|9] — 71.6
A Scratch In The Sky (68) 156(2) [0|0|5] — 49.1
Sugar & Spice (67) 192(1) [0|0|4] — 21.9

Billy CRYSTAL ▶ 2131 Pk:65 [0|0|1] — 286
Mahvelous (85) 65(2) [0|0|13] — 286

Joe CUBA Sextet ▶ 2528 Pk:119 [0|0|2] — 152
Wanted Dead Or Alive (Bang! Bang! Push, Push, Push) (67) 131(1) [0|0|6] — 95.9
We Must Be Doing Something Right! (66) 119(1) [0|0|3] — 56.4

CUFF LINKS ▶ 2511 Pk:138 [0|0|1] — 156
Tracy (69) 138(1) [0|0|11] — 156

The CULT ▶ 611 Pk:10 [1|2|3] — 4643
Sonic Temple (89) 10(6) [6|20|33] — 2792
Electric (87) 38(3) [0|4|32] — 1278
Love (85) 87(2) [0|0|34] — 573

CULTURE CLUB ▶ 228 Pk:2 [1|4|4] — 15345
Colour By Numbers (83) 2(6) [30|38|59] — 8038
Kissing To Be Clever (83) 14(10) [0|38|88] — 5493
Waking Up With The House On Fire (84) 26(5) [0|9|20] — 1065
From Luxury To Heartache (86) 32(2) [0|6|17] — 748

Burton CUMMINGS ▶ 1136 Pk:30 [0|1|2] — 1507
Burton Cummings (76) 30(1) [0|7|20] — 1233
My Own Way To Rock (77) 51(2) [0|0|6] — 273

MIKE CURB CONGREGATION ▶ 2057 Pk:105 [0|0|3] — 323
Burning Bridges And Other Great Motion Picture Themes (71) 117(2) [0|0|8] — 183
Come Together (70) 105(1) [0|0|5] — 122
Sweet Gingerbread Man (70) 185(1) [0|0|2] — 17.6

The CURE ▶ 404 Pk:12 [0|2|7] — 8100
Disintegration (89) 12(3) [0|26|55] — 3656
Kiss Me, Kiss Me, Kiss Me (87) 35(4) [0|8|52] — 2063
Standing On A Beach -- The Singles (86) 48(2) [0|0|57] — 1287
The Head On The Door (85) 59(2) [0|0|49] — 978
The Walk (83) 177(1) [0|0|9] — 60.5
Japanese Whispers (84) 181(1) [0|0|5] — 30.1
The Top (84) 180(1) [0|0|4] — 26.0

CURIOSITY KILLED THE CAT ▶ 1695 Pk:55 [0|0|1] — 587
Keep Your Distance (87) 55(1) [0|0|29] — 587

Tim CURRY ▶ 1452 Pk:53 [0|0|2] — 890
Fearless (79) 53(2) [0|0|24] — 726
Simplicity (81) 112(2) [0|0|8] — 163

CUTTING CREW ▶ 1025 Pk:16 [0|1|2] — 1853
Broadcast (87) 16(2) [0|10|45] — 1795
The Scattering (89) 150(2) [0|0|6] — 57.1

CYMANDE ▶ 1924 Pk:85 [0|0|2] — 392
Cymande (73) 85(1) [0|0|17] — 361
Second Time Round (73) 180(1) [0|0|4] — 30.4

CYMARRON ▶ 3353 Pk:187 [0|0|1] — 24
Rings (71) 187(1) [0|0|3] — 24.0

Andre CYMONE ▶ 2624 Pk:121 [0|0|2] — 128
A.C. (85) 121(2) [0|0|8] — 104
Survivin' In The 80's (83) 185(1) [0|0|4] — 24.2

The CYRKLE ▶ 1718 Pk:47 [0|0|2] — 564
Red Rubber Ball (66) 47(2) [0|0|15] — 541
Neon (67) 164(1) [0|0|2] — 22.9

D

DA'KRASH ▶ 3396 Pk:184 [0|0|1] — 20
Da'Krash (88) 184(2) [0|0|3] — 19.7

Dick DALE and The DEL-TONES ▶ 2447 Pk:106 [0|0|1] — 174
Checkered Flag (63) 106(1) [0|0|11] — 174

DALE & GRACE ▶ 2691 Pk:100 [0|0|1] — 116
I'm Leaving It Up To You (64) 100(1) [0|0|7] — 116

Kathy DALTON ▶ 3368 Pk:190 [0|0|1] — 22
Boogie Bands & One Night Stands (74) 190(1) [0|0|3] — 21.9

Roger DALTREY ▶ 639 Pk:22 [0|2|7] — 4338
Ride A Rock Horse (75) 28(2) [0|5|23] — 1027
McVicar (Soundtrack) (80) 22(2) [0|6|15] — 962
Under A Raging Moon (85) 42(2) [0|0|26] — 777
Daltrey (73) 45(1) [0|0|20] — 757
One Of The Boys (77) 46(1) [0|0|19] — 629
Parting Should Be Painless (84) 102(2) [0|0|9] — 152
Best Bits (82) 185(2) [0|0|5] — 33.1

Michael DAMIAN ▶ 1751 Pk:61 [0|0|1] — 520
Where Do We Go From Here (89) 61(2) [0|0|27] — 520

DAMITA JO ▶ 2908 Pk:121 [0|0|2] — 79
This Is Damita Jo (65) 121(1) [0|0|4] — 58.0
If You Go Away (67) 169(1) [0|0|2] — 21.0

DAMNATION OF ADAM BLESSING ▶ 3387 Pk:181 [0|0|1] — 20
The Damnation Of Adam Blessing (70) 181(2) [0|0|2] — 20.2

Liz DAMON'S ORIENT EXPRESS ▶ 3453 Pk:190 [0|0|1] — 14
Liz Damon's Orient Express (71) 190(1) [0|0|2] — 14.1

Vic DAMONE ▶ 2332 Pk:86 [0|0|1] — 205
You Were Only Fooling (65) 86(2) [0|0|10] — 205

Vic DANA ▶ 1103 Pk:13 [0|1|3] — 1594
Red Roses For A Blue Lady (65) 13(1) [0|11|21] — 1373
More (63) 111(1) [0|0|9] — 145
Shangri-La (64) 116(1) [0|0|5] — 76.2

Dana DANE ▶ 1380 Pk:46 [0|0|1] — 998
Dana Dane With Fame (87) 46(2) [0|0|32] — 998

DANGER DANGER ▶ 1657 Pk:88 [0|0|1] — 615
Danger Danger (89) 88(1) [0|0|42] — 615

Rodney DANGERFIELD ▶ 1131 Pk:36 [0|1|2] — 1520
Rappin' Rodney (83) 36(3) [0|3|20] — 783
No Respect (80) 48(1) [0|0|19] — 737

<table>
<tr><th>Act ▶ Highest Peak [Top10s|Top40s|Total]
Title (Yr) Peak(Wk) [T10 Wk|T40Wk|TotalWk]</th><th>Score</th></tr>
<tr><td>DANGEROUS TOYS ▶ 1469 Pk:65 [0|0|1]</td><td>863</td></tr>
<tr><td>Dangerous Toys (89) 65(3) [0|0|36]</td><td>863</td></tr>
<tr><td>Charlie DANIELS Band ▶ 307 Pk:5 [1|5|12]</td><td>11056</td></tr>
<tr><td>Million Mile Reflections (79) 5(3) [5|17|43]</td><td>3838</td></tr>
<tr><td>Full Moon (80) 11(2) [0|9|33]</td><td>2276</td></tr>
<tr><td>Fire On The Mountain (74) 38(1) [0|2|34]</td><td>1429</td></tr>
<tr><td>Windows (82) 26(3) [0|6|19]</td><td>875</td></tr>
<tr><td>Saddle Tramp (76) 35(1) [0|3|18]</td><td>873</td></tr>
<tr><td>Nightrider (75) 57(1) [0|0|12]</td><td>489</td></tr>
<tr><td>Simple Man (89) 82(1) [0|0|25]</td><td>454</td></tr>
<tr><td>High Lonesome (76) 83(2) [0|0|10]</td><td>281</td></tr>
<tr><td>A Decade Of Hits (83) 84(1) [0|0|12]</td><td>243</td></tr>
<tr><td>Midnight Wind (77) 105(1) [0|0|11]</td><td>190</td></tr>
<tr><td>Honey In The Rock (73) 164(1) [0|0|9]</td><td>93.9</td></tr>
<tr><td>Homesick Heros (88) 181(2) [0|0|2]</td><td>15.5</td></tr>
<tr><td>Rick DANKO ▶ 2577 Pk:119 [0|0|1]</td><td>141</td></tr>
<tr><td>Rick Danko (77) 119(1) [0|0|8]</td><td>141</td></tr>
<tr><td>DANNY WILSON ▶ 2151 Pk:79 [0|0|1]</td><td>280</td></tr>
<tr><td>Meet Danny Wilson (87) 79(1) [0|0|16]</td><td>280</td></tr>
<tr><td>DANZIG ▶ 2637 Pk:125 [0|0|1]</td><td>126</td></tr>
<tr><td>Danzig (88) 125(2) [0|0|9]</td><td>126</td></tr>
<tr><td>Terence Trent D'ARBY ▶ 534 Pk:4 [1|1|2]</td><td>5579</td></tr>
<tr><td>Indtroducing The Hardline According To Terence Trent D'Arby (87) 4(2) [8|32|60]</td><td>5202</td></tr>
<tr><td>Terence Trent D'Arby's Neither Fish Nor Flesh (89) 61(2) [0|0|15]</td><td>377</td></tr>
<tr><td>Bobby DARIN ▶ 1986 Pk:98 [0|0|4]</td><td>358</td></tr>
<tr><td>From Hello Dolly To Goodbye Charlie (64) 107(2) [0|0|8]</td><td>132</td></tr>
<tr><td>18 Yellow Roses (63) 98(1) [0|0|5]</td><td>92.3</td></tr>
<tr><td>If I Were A Carpenter (67) 142(1) [0|0|5]</td><td>75.7</td></tr>
<tr><td>Venice Blue (65) 132(2) [0|0|4]</td><td>57.4</td></tr>
<tr><td>DARK ANGEL ▶ 3032 Pk:159 [0|0|1]</td><td>61</td></tr>
<tr><td>Leave Scars (89) 159(1) [0|0|6]</td><td>61.5</td></tr>
<tr><td>DARLING CRUEL ▶ 2952 Pk:160 [0|0|1]</td><td>72</td></tr>
<tr><td>Passion Crimes (89) 160(2) [0|0|8]</td><td>72.0</td></tr>
<tr><td>Johnny DARRELL ▶ 3214 Pk:172 [0|0|1]</td><td>38</td></tr>
<tr><td>Why You Been Gone So Long (69) 172(1) [0|0|3]</td><td>38.4</td></tr>
<tr><td>James DARREN ▶ 3389 Pk:187 [0|0|1]</td><td>20</td></tr>
<tr><td>James Darren/All (67) 187(1) [0|0|3]</td><td>20.0</td></tr>
<tr><td>Sarah DASH ▶ 3070 Pk:182 [0|0|1]</td><td>56</td></tr>
<tr><td>Sarah Dash (79) 182(1) [0|0|7]</td><td>56.4</td></tr>
<tr><td>DAVE & SUGAR ▶ 2848 Pk:157 [0|0|2]</td><td>88</td></tr>
<tr><td>That's The Way Love Should Be (77)-Dave Rowland And Sugar 157(1) [0|0|4]</td><td>50.8</td></tr>
<tr><td>Greatest Hits (81) 179(2) [0|0|4]</td><td>37.1</td></tr>
<tr><td>DAVE DEE, DOZY, BEAKY, MICK And TICH ▶ 3219 Pk:155 [0|0|1]</td><td>37</td></tr>
<tr><td>Greatest Hits (67) 155(2) [0|0|3]</td><td>37.4</td></tr>
<tr><td>DAVID & DAVID ▶ 1170 Pk:39 [0|1|1]</td><td>1413</td></tr>
<tr><td>Boomtown (86) 39(2) [0|2|38]</td><td>1413</td></tr>
<tr><td>John DAVIDSON ▶ 942 Pk:19 [0|1|6]</td><td>2169</td></tr>
<tr><td>The Time Of My Life! (66) 19(2) [0|10|24]</td><td>1469</td></tr>
<tr><td>A Kind Of Hush (67) 79(2) [0|0|12]</td><td>265</td></tr>
<tr><td>Goin' Places (68) 151(1) [0|0|10]</td><td>134</td></tr>
<tr><td>My Best To You (67) 125(1) [0|0|8]</td><td>129</td></tr>
<tr><td>John Davidson (69) 153(1) [0|0|7]</td><td>110</td></tr>
<tr><td>My Cherie Amour (69) 165(1) [0|0|5]</td><td>62.0</td></tr>
<tr><td>Dave DAVIES ▶ 1489 Pk:42 [0|0|2]</td><td>831</td></tr>
<tr><td>AFL1-3603 (80) 42(2) [0|0|14]</td><td>727</td></tr>
<tr><td>Glamour (81) 152(1) [0|0|8]</td><td>104</td></tr>
<tr><td>Danny DAVIS ▶ 3267 Pk:150 [0|0|1]</td><td>31</td></tr>
<tr><td>Danny Davis & Willie Nelson With The Nashville Brass (80)-Danny Davis And Willie Nelson With The Nashville Brass [A] 150(1) [0|0|5]</td><td>31.3</td></tr>
<tr><td>Danny DAVIS And The NASHVILLE BRASS ▶ 1064 Pk:78 [0|0|8]</td><td>1709</td></tr>
<tr><td>The Nashville Sound (69) 78(1) [0|0|24]</td><td>780</td></tr>
<tr><td>You Ain't Heard Nothin' Yet (70) 102(1) [0|0|12]</td><td>277</td></tr>
<tr><td>Movin' On (69) 141(1) [0|0|20]</td><td>264</td></tr>
<tr><td>Down Homers (70) 140(1) [0|0|12]</td><td>172</td></tr>
<tr><td>More Nashville Sounds (69) 143(1) [0|0|6]</td><td>107</td></tr>
<tr><td>Somethin' Else (71) 161(1) [0|0|3]</td><td>44.6</td></tr>
<tr><td>Super Country (71) 184(1) [0|0|4]</td><td>35.6</td></tr>
<tr><td>Turn On Some Happy! (72) 193(1) [0|0|5]</td><td>29.4</td></tr>
<tr><td>Jimmy DAVIS & JUNCTION ▶ 2740 Pk:122 [0|0|1]</td><td>107</td></tr>
<tr><td>Kick The Wall (87) 122(2) [0|0|8]</td><td>107</td></tr>
<tr><td>Mac DAVIS ▶ 392 Pk:11 [0|3|11]</td><td>8426</td></tr>
<tr><td>Stop And Smell The Roses (74) 13(2) [0|15|45]</td><td>3144</td></tr>
<tr><td>Baby Don't Get Hooked On Me (72) 11(2) [0|13|44]</td><td>2594</td></tr>
<tr><td>All The Love In The World (75) 21(2) [0|5|14]</td><td>1075</td></tr>
<tr><td>It's Hard To Be Humble (80) 69(2) [0|0|15]</td><td>437</td></tr>
<tr><td>Burnin' Thing (75) 64(2) [0|0|10]</td><td>347</td></tr>
<tr><td>Texas In My Rear View Mirror (80) 67(1) [0|0|9]</td><td>291</td></tr>
<tr><td>Mac Davis (73) 120(1) [0|0|13]</td><td>202</td></tr>
<tr><td>I Believe In Music (71) 160(1) [0|0|17]</td><td>161</td></tr>
<tr><td>Forever Lovers (76) 156(1) [0|0|9]</td><td>114</td></tr>
<tr><td>Song Painter (74) 182(1) [0|0|4]</td><td>35.5</td></tr>
<tr><td>Midnight Crazy (82) 174(1) [0|0|3]</td><td>24.3</td></tr>
<tr><td>Martha DAVIS ▶ 2464 Pk:127 [0|0|1]</td><td>170</td></tr>
<tr><td>Policy (87) 127(1) [0|0|13]</td><td>170</td></tr>
<tr><td>Miles DAVIS ▶ 626 Pk:35 [0|1|24]</td><td>4469</td></tr>
<tr><td>Bitches Brew (70) 35(2) [0|4|29]</td><td>1497</td></tr>
<tr><td>The Man With The Horn (81) 53(2) [0|0|18]</td><td>553</td></tr>
<tr><td>Seven Steps To Heaven (63) 62(1) [0|0|15]</td><td>376</td></tr>
<tr><td>Live--Evil (71) 125(2) [0|0|13]</td><td>248</td></tr>
<tr><td>Miles Davis At Fillmore (70) 123(2) [0|0|12]</td><td>176</td></tr>
<tr><td>Quiet Nights (64) 93(2) [0|0|9]</td><td>166</td></tr>
<tr><td>Miles Davis In Europe (64) 116(1) [0|0|10]</td><td>147</td></tr>
<tr><td>You're Under Arrest (85) 111(2) [0|0|12]</td><td>140</td></tr>
<tr><td>On The Corner (72) 156(1) [0|0|11]</td><td>128</td></tr>
<tr><td>Get Up With It (75) 141(1) [0|0|8]</td><td>117</td></tr>
<tr><td>My Funny Valentine (65) 138(1) [0|0|9]</td><td>114</td></tr>
<tr><td>In Concert (73) 152(1) [0|0|8]</td><td>104</td></tr>
<tr><td>In A Silent Way (69) 134(2) [0|0|6]</td><td>98.9</td></tr>
<tr><td>Decoy (84) 169(2) [0|0|11]</td><td>88.6</td></tr>
<tr><td>Tutu (86) 141(2) [0|0|10]</td><td>87.1</td></tr>
<tr><td>Star People (83) 136(1) [0|0|7]</td><td>85.8</td></tr>
<tr><td>A Tribute To Jack Johnson (Soundtrack) (71) 159(2) [0|0|8]</td><td>78.0</td></tr>
<tr><td>We Want Miles (82) 159(2) [0|0|7]</td><td>64.8</td></tr>
<tr><td>Agharta (76) 168(2) [0|0|5]</td><td>58.4</td></tr>
<tr><td>Big Fun (74) 179(1) [0|0|5]</td><td>47.1</td></tr>
<tr><td>Amandla (89) 177(2) [0|0|5]</td><td>37.8</td></tr>
<tr><td>Basic Miles - The Classic Performances Of Miles Davis (73) 189(1) [0|0|3]</td><td>20.9</td></tr>
<tr><td>Directions (81) 179(2) [0|0|2]</td><td>20.9</td></tr>
<tr><td>Water Babies (77) 190(2) [0|0|2]</td><td>15.9</td></tr>
<tr><td>Paul DAVIS ▶ 127 Pk:52 [0|0|4]</td><td>1185</td></tr>
<tr><td>Cool Night (81) 52(1) [0|0|29]</td><td>676</td></tr>
<tr><td>Singer Of Songs - Teller Of Tales (78) 82(2) [0|0|18]</td><td>374</td></tr>
<tr><td>Ride 'Em Cowboy (75) 148(1) [0|0|6]</td><td>97.2</td></tr>
<tr><td>Paul Davis (80) 173(2) [0|0|4]</td><td>37.6</td></tr>
<tr><td>Sammy DAVIS Jr. ▶ 623 Pk:11 [0|3|7]</td><td>4538</td></tr>
<tr><td>Sammy Davis Jr. Now (72) 11(1) [0|8|26]</td><td>1810</td></tr>
<tr><td>I've Gotta Be Me (69) 24(3) [0|8|25]</td><td>1606</td></tr>
<tr><td>The Shelter Of Your Arms (64) 26(2) [0|6|18]</td><td>752</td></tr>
<tr><td>Portrait Of Sammy Davis, Jr. (72) 128(1) [0|0|15]</td><td>228</td></tr>
<tr><td>Sammy's Back On Broadway (65) 104(1) [0|0|4]</td><td>76.8</td></tr>
<tr><td>Sammy Davis Jr. Salutes The Stars Of The London Palladium (64) 139(1) [0|0|3]</td><td>41.1</td></tr>
<tr><td>Our Shining Hour (65)-Sammy Davis-Count Basie [A] 141(1) [0|0|4]</td><td>24.1</td></tr>
<tr><td>Spencer DAVIS Group ▶ 1442 Pk:54 [0|0|3]</td><td>902</td></tr>
<tr><td>Gimme Some Lovin' (67) 54(3) [0|0|25]</td><td>668</td></tr>
<tr><td>I'm A Man (67) 83(1) [0|0|9]</td><td>216</td></tr>
<tr><td>Spencer Davis' Greatest Hits (68) 195(2) [0|0|3]</td><td>17.2</td></tr>
<tr><td>Tyrone DAVIS ▶ 1369 Pk:89 [0|0|7]</td><td>1019</td></tr>
<tr><td>Turn Back The Hands Of Time (70) 90(1) [0|0|11]</td><td>273</td></tr>
<tr><td>Love And Touch (76) 89(1) [0|0|9]</td><td>243</td></tr>
<tr><td>In The Mood With Tyrone Davis (79) 115(2) [0|0|12]</td><td>243</td></tr>
<tr><td>Can I Change My Mind (69) 146(1) [0|0|6]</td><td>108</td></tr>
<tr><td>Tyrone Davis (83) 137(2) [0|0|6]</td><td>63.9</td></tr>
<tr><td>I Had It All The Time (72) 182(1) [0|0|6]</td><td>45.4</td></tr>
<tr><td>Without You In My Life (73) 174(1) [0|0|6]</td><td>42.7</td></tr>
<tr><td>Wild Bill DAVIS ▶ 3484 Pk:148 [0|0|1]</td><td>12</td></tr>
<tr><td>Blue Rabbit (65)-Johnny Hodges/Wild Bill Davis [A] 148(1) [0|0|2]</td><td>12.3</td></tr>
<tr><td>DAWN/Tony ORLANDO ▶ 362 Pk:16 [0|5|11]</td><td>9150</td></tr>
<tr><td>Dawn's New Ragtime Follies (73)-Dawn Featuring Tony Orlando 43(1) [0|0|58]</td><td>1852</td></tr>
<tr><td>Greatest Hits (75)-Tony Orlando & Dawn 16(1) [0|6|32]</td><td>1816</td></tr>
<tr><td>Prime Time (74)-Tony Orlando & Dawn 16(1) [0|8|17]</td><td>1423</td></tr>
<tr><td>Tuneweaving (73)-Dawn Featuring Tony Orlando 30(1) [0|5|34]</td><td>1269</td></tr>
<tr><td>Candida (70)-Dawn 35(2) [0|3|23]</td><td>1245</td></tr>
<tr><td>He Don't Love You (Like I Love You) (75)-Tony Orlando & Dawn 20(2) [0|4|17]</td><td>1093</td></tr>
<tr><td>To Be With You (76)-Tony Orlando & Dawn 94(1) [0|0|6]</td><td>169</td></tr>
<tr><td>Skybird (75)-Tony Orlando & Dawn 93(2) [0|0|6]</td><td>153</td></tr>
<tr><td>Tony Orlando & Dawn II (75)-Tony Orlando & Dawn 165(2) [0|0|5]</td><td>60.7</td></tr>
<tr><td>Candida & Knock Three Times (75)-Tony Orlando & Dawn 170(2) [0|0|4]</td><td>46.3</td></tr>
<tr><td>Dawn Featuring Tony Orlando (71)-Dawn Featuring Tony Orlando 178(2) [0|0|2]</td><td>20.9</td></tr>
<tr><td>Doris DAY ▶ 2571 Pk:102 [0|0|1]</td><td>143</td></tr>
<tr><td>Love Him! (64) 102(1) [0|0|8]</td><td>143</td></tr>
<tr><td>Morris DAY ▶ 1140 Pk:37 [0|1|2]</td><td>1501</td></tr>
<tr><td>Color Of Success (85) 37(2) [0|3|31]</td><td>905</td></tr>
<tr><td>Daydreaming (88) 41(2) [0|0|15]</td><td>596</td></tr>
<tr><td>Cory DAYE ▶ 3145 Pk:171 [0|0|1]</td><td>47</td></tr>
<tr><td>Cory And Me (79) 171(2) [0|0|5]</td><td>46.8</td></tr>
<tr><td>Taylor DAYNE ▶ 419 Pk:21 [0|2|2]</td><td>7663</td></tr>
<tr><td>Tell It To My Heart (88) 21(1) [0|34|69]</td><td>4302</td></tr>
<tr><td>Can't Fight Fate (89) 25(1) [0|34|55]</td><td>3361</td></tr>
<tr><td>DAZZ BAND ▶ 663 Pk:14 [0|1|7]</td><td>4120</td></tr>
<tr><td>Keep It Live (82) 14(4) [0|11|34]</td><td>2100</td></tr>
<tr><td>Joystick (83) 73(2) [0|0|33]</td><td>652</td></tr>
<tr><td>Jukebox (84) 83(1) [0|0|29]</td><td>473</td></tr>
<tr><td>On The One (83) 59(3) [0|0|16]</td><td>387</td></tr>
<tr><td>Hot Spot (85) 98(2) [0|0|12]</td><td>190</td></tr>
<tr><td>Wild And Free (86) 100(2) [0|0|11]</td><td>180</td></tr>
<tr><td>Let The Music Play (81) 154(2) [0|0|11]</td><td>138</td></tr>
<tr><td>DB'S ▶ 3069 Pk:171 [0|0|1]</td><td>56</td></tr>
<tr><td>The Sound Of Music (87) 171(2) [0|0|8]</td><td>56.4</td></tr>
</table>

Act ▶ Highest Peak [Top10s | Top40s | Total] Title (Yr) Peak(Wk) [T10 Wk | T40Wk | TotalWk]	Score
DEAD BOYS ▶ 3291 Pk:189 [0|0|1]	**29**
Young, Loud And Snotty (77) 189(2) [0|0|4]	28.9
DEAD MILKMEN ▶ 2061 Pk:101 [0|0|2]	**319**
Beelzebubba (88) 101(2) [0|0|23]	267
Bucky Fellini (87) 163(1) [0|0|7]	52.6
DEAD OR ALIVE ▶ 1080 Pk:31 [0|1|4]	**1656**
Youthquake (85) 31(3) [0|6|20]	898
Mad, Bad And Dangerous To Know (86) 52(2) [0|0|25]	607
Nude (89) 106(2) [0|0|9]	141
Rip It Up (88) 195(2) [0|0|2]	10.2
Bill DEAL & The RHONDELS ▶ 3413 Pk:185 [0|0|1]	**18**
The Best Of Bill Deal & The Rhondels (70) 185(1) [0|0|2]	18.0
Paul DEAN ▶ 3509 Pk:195 [0|0|1]	**11**
Hard Core (89) 195(2) [0|0|2]	10.6
DEATH ANGEL ▶ 2735 Pk:143 [0|0|1]	**107**
Frolic Through The Park (88) 143(1) [0|0|11]	107
DeBARGE ▶ 520 Pk:19 [0|3|3]	**5860**
Rhythm Of The Night (85) 19(2) [0|24|48]	2623
All This Love (82) 24(2) [0|7|48]	1789
In A Special Way (83) 36(1) [0|5|40]	1448
Bunny DeBARGE ▶ 3206 Pk:172 [0|0|1]	**39**
In Love (87) 172(2) [0|0|5]	38.8
Chico DeBARGE ▶ 1883 Pk:90 [0|0|1]	**416**
Chico DeBarge (86) 90(2) [0|0|30]	416
El DeBARGE ▶ 1229 Pk:24 [0|1|1]	**1280**
El DeBarge (86) 24(3) [0|11|23]	1280
Chris De BURGH ▶ 950 Pk:25 [0|1|3]	**2135**
Into The Light (86) 25(2) [0|8|32]	1127
The Getaway (83) 43(2) [0|0|22]	631
Man On The Line (84) 69(1) [0|0|19]	377
Nick DeCARO ▶ 2959 Pk:165 [0|0|1]	**71**
Happy Heart (69) 165(1) [0|0|5]	70.6
Kiki DEE ▶ 1361 Pk:28 [0|1|2]	**1027**
I've Got The Music In Me (74)-The Kiki Dee Band 28(1) [0|4|18]	961
Kiki Dee (77) 159(1) [0|0|5]	65.6
Lenny DEE ▶ 3098 Pk:189 [0|0|3]	**52**
Spinning Wheel (70) 189(1) [0|0|3]	22.4
Gentle On My Mind (68) 196(2) [0|0|3]	17.3
Turn Around, Look At Me (69) 199(2) [0|0|2]	12.3
The DEELE ▶ 1259 Pk:54 [0|0|3]	**1222**
Eyes Of A Stranger (88) 54(2) [0|0|25]	813
Street Beat (84) 78(2) [0|0|19]	335
Material Thangz (85) 155(1) [0|0|8]	74.5
DEEP PURPLE ▶ 124 Pk:6 [3|9|18]	**25711**
Machine Head (72) 7(2) [6|30|118]	6452
Made In Japan (73) 6(2) [10|23|52]	4753
Who Do We Think We Are! (73) 15(3) [0|14|49]	2840
Burn (74) 9(1) [2|12|30]	2392
Perfect Strangers (84) 17(2) [0|18|32]	2024
Shades Of Deep Purple (68) 24(1) [0|10|23]	1555
Stormbringer (74) 20(2) [0|6|15]	1207
Fireball (71) 32(1) [0|3|18]	1114
The House Of Blue Light (87) 34(3) [0|4|22]	756
(Purple Passages) (72) 57(1) [0|0|20]	654
Come Taste The Band (75) 43(2) [0|0|14]	634
The Book Of Taliesyn (69) 54(2) [0|0|14]	617
Deep Purple In Rock (70) 143(1) [0|0|21]	280
Nobody's Perfect (88) 105(2) [0|0|9]	160
Made In Europe (76) 148(1) [0|0|6]	83.0
Deep Purple (69) 162(1) [0|0|6]	76.2

Act ▶ Highest Peak [Top10s | Top40s | Total] Title (Yr) Peak(Wk) [T10 Wk | T40Wk | TotalWk]	Score
Deepest Purple: The Very Best Of Deep Purple (80) 148(1) [0|0|4]	59.0
Concerto For Group And Orchestra (70)-Deep Purple/The Royal Philharmonic Orchestra [A] 149(2) [0|0|8]	54.8
Rick DEES ▶ 3017 Pk:157 [0|0|1]	**63**
The Original Disco Duck (77)-Rick Dees And His Cast Of Idiots 157(2) [0|0|5]	63.4
DEF LEPPARD ▶ 75 Pk:1 [2|3|5]	**35547**
Hysteria (87) 1(6) [78|96|133]	19758
Pyromania (83) 2(2) [38|58|116]	11178
High 'N' Dry (81) 38(1) [0|3|106]	3096
On Through The Night (80) 51(1) [0|0|51]	1134
High 'N' Dry(2) (84) 72(2) [0|0|18]	381
DeFRANCO FAMILY ▶ 1976 Pk:109 [0|0|2]	**364**
Heartbeat, It's A Lovebeat (73) 109(1) [0|0|16]	277
Save The Last Dance For Me (74) 163(1) [0|0|7]	86.2
DEJA ▶ 3245 Pk:186 [0|0|1]	**34**
Serious (87) 186(1) [0|0|6]	33.7
Desmond DEKKER And The ACES ▶ 3102 Pk:153 [0|0|1]	**52**
Israelites (69) 153(1) [0|0|3]	51.7
DELANEY & BONNIE & FRIENDS ▶ 960 Pk:29 [0|1|5]	**2086**
Delaney & Bonnie & Friends On Tour With Eric Clapton (70) 29(1) [0|6|17]	991
Motel Shot (71)-Delaney & Bonnie 65(1) [0|0|23]	552
To Bonnie From Delaney (70) 58(1) [0|0|10]	415
D&B Together (72)-Delaney & Bonnie 133(2) [0|0|6]	93.0
Accept No Substitute - The Original Delaney & Bonnie & Friends (69) 175(1) [0|0|3]	35.6
DE LA SOUL ▶ 1173 Pk:24 [0|1|1]	**1407**
3 Feet High And Rising (89) 24(2) [0|10|29]	1407
DELEGATION ▶ 1938 Pk:84 [0|0|1]	**382**
Promise Of Love (79) 84(2) [0|0|16]	382
The DELFONICS ▶ 1169 Pk:61 [0|0|5]	**1416**
The Delfonics (70) 61(1) [0|0|18]	603
The Delfonics Super Hits (69) 111(1) [0|0|19]	392
Tell Me This Is A Dream (72) 123(1) [0|0|11]	190
La La Means I Love You (68) 100(1) [0|0|6]	128
Sound Of Sexy Soul (69) 155(2) [0|0|6]	103
DEL FUEGOS ▶ 1685 Pk:132 [0|0|3]	**596**
Boston, Mass. (85) 132(1) [0|0|34]	304
Smoking In The Fields (89) 139(1) [0|0|22]	246
Stand Up (87) 167(2) [0|0|6]	45.8
DELIVERANCE ▶ 3535 Pk:196 [0|0|1]	**6**
Rural Free Delivery (73)-Eric Weissberg & Deliverance [A] 196(2) [0|0|2]	5.8
The DELLS ▶ 658 Pk:29 [0|1|12]	**4187**
The Dells vs. The Dramatics (74)-The Dells/The Dramatics [A] 156(1) [0|0|6]	42.8
There Is (68) 29(1) [0|5|29]	1186
Love Is Blue (69) 54(1) [0|0|24]	952
The Dells Greatest Hits (69) 102(2) [0|0|22]	569
Freedom Means (71) 81(1) [0|0|16]	503
Like It Is, Like It Was (70) 126(2) [0|0|12]	211
Give Your Baby A Standing Ovation (73) 99(1) [0|0|9]	183
I Touched A Dream (80) 137(1) [0|0|12]	174
The Dells Musical Menu/Always Together (69) 146(2) [0|0|10]	147
The Mighty Mighty Dells (74) 114(2) [0|0|8]	129
The Dells Sing Dionne Warwicke's Greatest Hits (72) 162(1) [0|0|5]	53.8
New Beginnings (78) 169(2) [0|0|3]	36.9

Act ▶ Highest Peak [Top10s | Top40s | Total] Title (Yr) Peak(Wk) [T10 Wk | T40Wk | TotalWk]	Score
Martin DENNY ▶ 2789 Pk:123 [0|0|1]	**99**
Hawaii Tattoo (65)-Martin Denny and His Orchestra 123(1) [0|0|7]	99.0
Sandy DENNY ▶ 3494 Pk:197 [0|0|1]	**12**
Like An Old Fashioned Waltz (74) 197(1) [0|0|2]	11.8
John DENVER ▶ 16 Pk:1 [7|14|21]	**65149**
John Denver's Greatest Hits (73) 1(3) [28|45|175]	15297
Back Home Again (74) 1(1) [23|37|96]	11102
Windsong (75) 1(2) [16|21|45]	7642
Poems, Prayers & Promises (71) 15(5) [0|31|80]	6479
An Evening With John Denver (75) 2(2) [10|19|50]	5194
Rocky Mountain High (72) 4(3) [9|27|53]	5091
Spirit (76) 7(2) [6|13|30]	3216
Farewell Andromeda (73) 16(2) [0|13|35]	2083
John Denver's Greatest Hits, Volume 2 (77) 6(1) [4|7|18]	1792
Some Days Are Diamonds (81) 32(2) [0|4|30]	1369
Rocky Mountain Christmas (75) 14(2) [0|6|16]	1146
John Denver (79) 25(2) [0|6|15]	942
I Want To Live (77) 45(1) [0|0|25]	850
Seasons Of The Heart (82) 39(2) [0|2|33]	835
Autograph (80) 39(2) [0|2|17]	791
Aerie (71) 75(3) [0|0|16]	491
It's About Time (83) 61(2) [0|0|15]	337
Dreamland Express (85) 90(2) [0|0|19]	330
Denver Christmas Gift Pak (75) 138(1) [0|0|6]	98.7
Rhymes & Reasons (69) 148(2) [0|0|3]	53.3
Take Me To Tomorrow (70) 197(1) [0|0|2]	11.7
John DENVER & The MUPPETS ▶ 1680 Pk:26 [0|1|1]	**600**
A Christmas Together (79) 26(2) [0|4|12]	600
DEODATO ▶ 496 Pk:3 [1|2|9]	**6207**
Prelude (73) 3(1) [5|13|26]	2782
Deodato 2 (73) 19(1) [0|10|35]	1875
Whirlwinds (74) 63(1) [0|0|16]	498
Love Island (78) 98(1) [0|0|17]	323
Very Together (76)-Eumir Deodato 86(1) [0|0|11]	261
Artistry (74) 102(2) [0|0|9]	188
First Cuckoo (75)-Eumir Deodato 110(1) [0|0|9]	170
In Concert (74)-Deodato/Airto [A] 114(1) [0|0|9]	88.0
Night Cruiser (80)-Eumir Deodato 186(1) [0|0|3]	23.0
DEPECHE MODE ▶ 656 Pk:35 [0|1|8]	**4189**
Music For The Masses (87) 35(2) [0|3|59]	1461
Some Great Reward (85) 51(2) [0|0|42]	896
101 (89) 45(2) [0|0|19]	551
People Are People (84) 71(1) [0|0|30]	521
Black Celebration (86) 90(2) [0|0|26]	426
Catching Up With Depeche Mode (85) 113(1) [0|0|18]	240
Speak & Spell (81) 192(1) [0|0|9]	51.1
A Broken Frame (82) 177(1) [0|0|8]	43.2
DEREK And The DOMINOS ▶ 507 Pk:16 [0|2|2]	**6098**
Layla And Other Assorted Love Songs (70) 16(1) [0|19|77]	4748
Derek & The Dominos In Concert (73) 20(1) [0|9|21]	1350
Rick DERRINGER ▶ 967 Pk:25 [0|1|5]	**2050**
All American Boy (73) 25(1) [0|8|31]	1586
Derringer Live (77) 123(2) [0|0|10]	190

Act ► Highest Peak [Top10s|Top40s|Total]
Title (Yr) Peak(Wk) [T10 Wk|T40Wk|TotalWk] — Score

Rick DERRINGER ► *Continued*
Spring Fever (75) 141(1) [0|0|8] — 120
Derringer (76)-Derringer 154(1) [0|0|9] — 118
Sweet Evil (77)-Derringer 169(1) [0|0|3] — 36.2

Teri DeSARIO ► 2117 Pk:80 [0|0|1] — 292
Moonlight Madness (80) 80(1) [0|0|13] — 292

Jackie DeSHANNON ► 1960 Pk:81 [0|0|2] — 372
Put A Little Love In Your Heart (69) 81(1) [0|0|15] — 361
Jackie (72) 196(2) [0|0|2] — 11.6

Paul DESMOND ► 2946 Pk:129 [0|0|2] — 73
Take Ten (63) 129(1) [0|0|3] — 45.4
1975: The Duets (76)-Dave Brubeck And Paul Desmond [A] 167(1) [0|0|5] — 27.3

DETECTIVE ► 1970 Pk:103 [0|0|2] — 366
It Takes One To Know One (78) 103(2) [0|0|12] — 219
Detective (77) 135(2) [0|0|9] — 146

DETROIT ► 3081 Pk:176 [0|0|1] — 55
Detroit (72) 176(1) [0|0|6] — 54.7

DETROIT EMERALDS ► 1856 Pk:78 [0|0|3] — 438
You Want It, You Got It (72) 78(2) [0|0|13] — 358
Do Me Right (71) 151(1) [0|0|3] — 47.1
I'm In Love With You (73) 181(1) [0|0|4] — 33.0

William DeVAUGHN ► 2677 Pk:165 [0|0|1] — 118
Be Thankful For What You Got (74) 165(1) [0|0|11] — 118

DEVICE ► 2109 Pk:73 [0|0|1] — 296
22B3 (86) 73(2) [0|0|16] — 296

DEVO ► 516 Pk:22 [0|2|8] — 5999
Freedom Of Choice (80) 22(2) [0|16|51] — 3023
New Traditionalists (81) 23(2) [0|6|25] — 1144
Oh No! It's Devo (82) 47(3) [0|0|20] — 556
Devo-Live (81) 50(1) [0|0|12] — 442
Q: Are We Not Men? A: We Are Devo! (78) 78(2) [0|0|18] — 430
Duty Now For The Future (79) 73(2) [0|0|10] — 254
Shout (84) 83(2) [0|0|6] — 130
Total Devo (88) 189(2) [0|0|3] — 18.5

Barry De VORZON ► 2402 Pk:133 [0|0|1] — 185
Nadia's Theme (The Young And The Restless) (76) 133(2) [0|0|12] — 185

DEXYS MIDNIGHT RUNNERS ► 1106 Pk:14 [0|1|1] — 1589
Too-Rye-Ay (83) 14(2) [0|12|24] — 1589

Dennis DeYOUNG ► 1309 Pk:29 [0|1|2] — 1127
Desert Moon (84) 29(3) [0|4|25] — 1005
Back To The World (86) 108(2) [0|0|8] — 123

DFX2 ► 2901 Pk:143 [0|0|1] — 80
Emotion (83) 143(1) [0|0|8] — 80.0

Neil DIAMOND ► 15 Pk:2 [12|21|32] — 66597
The Jazz Singer (Soundtrack) (80) 3(7) [19|32|115] — 8275
Hot August Night (72) 5(3) [9|19|78] — 5024
Moods (72) 5(3) [11|24|41] — 4630
Neil Diamond/Gold (70) 10(2) [2|19|56] — 4353
Beautiful Noise (76) 4(3) [8|16|33] — 4132
Serenade (74) 3(2) [8|19|27] — 4131
Jonathan Livingston Seagull (Soundtrack) (73) 2(1) [10|16|34] — 3874
Tap Root Manuscript (70) 13(2) [0|14|45] — 3215
I'm Glad You're Here With Me Tonight (77) 6(2) [7|14|24] — 3041
You Don't Bring Me Flowers (78) 4(3) [6|12|29] — 2963
Heartlight (82) 9(3) [4|19|34] — 2817
Stones (71) 11(2) [0|13|25] — 2428
September Morn (80) 10(3) [3|10|20] — 1793
Love At The Greek (77) 8(2) [3|9|21] — 1780
On The Way To The Sky (81) 17(2) [0|11|27] — 1772
Touching You Touching Me (69) 30(1) [0|6|47] — 1768
Neil Diamond/His 12 Greatest Hits (74) 29(1) [0|7|42] — 1754
Headed For The Future (86) 20(1) [0|11|23] — 1336
Double Gold (73) 36(1) [0|4|21] — 996
Shilo (70) 52(1) [0|0|25] — 980
Rainbow (73) 35(2) [0|4|17] — 785
Primitive (84) 35(3) [0|5|25] — 767
Brother Love's Travelling Salvation Show (69) 82(2) [0|0|25] — 762
12 Greatest Hits Vol. II (82) 48(2) [0|0|42] — 762
Neil Diamond's Greatest Hits (68) 100(1) [0|0|40] — 687
The Best Years Of Our Lives (89) 46(2) [0|0|16] — 495
Hot August Night II (87) 59(2) [0|0|17] — 450
Just For You (67) 80(1) [0|0|19] — 432
Do It! (71) 100(1) [0|0|6] — 148
And The Singer Sings His Songs (76) 102(1) [0|0|5] — 128
The Feel Of Neil Diamond (66) 137(1) [0|0|4] — 65.2
Classics The Early Years (83) 171(1) [0|0|7] — 50.8

Manu DIBANGO ► 2066 Pk:79 [0|0|1] — 317
Soul Makossa (73) 79(1) [0|0|13] — 317

The DICTATORS ► 3457 Pk:193 [0|0|1] — 14
Manifest Destiny (77) 193(1) [0|0|2] — 13.6

DIESEL ► 1798 Pk:68 [0|0|1] — 486
Watts In A Tank (81) 68(2) [0|0|24] — 486

DIFFORD & TILBROOK ► 1880 Pk:55 [0|0|1] — 418
Difford & Tilbrook (84) 55(3) [0|0|15] — 418

The DILLARDS ► 1745 Pk:79 [0|0|1] — 528
Roots And Branches (72) 79(2) [0|0|18] — 528

DILLMAN Band ► 2736 Pk:145 [0|0|2] — 107
Lovin' The Night Away (81) 145(2) [0|0|7] — 95.6
The Daisy Dillman Band (78) 198(2) [0|0|2] — 11.7

Al Di MEOLA ► 986 Pk:52 [0|0|8] — 1979
Casino (78) 52(1) [0|0|17] — 578
Elegant Gypsy (77) 58(2) [0|0|12] — 441
Electric Rendezvous (82) 55(2) [0|0|13] — 388
Splendido Hotel (80) 119(2) [0|0|14] — 280
Land Of The Midnight Sun (76) 129(2) [0|0|10] — 161
Scenario (83) 128(1) [0|0|6] — 67.9
Tour De Force - "Live" (82) 165(1) [0|0|7] — 55.6
Tirami Su (88)-Al Di Meola Project 190(1) [0|0|1] — 6.6

Al Di MEOLA/John McLAUGHLIN/ Paco De LUCIA ► 2112 Pk:97 [0|0|2] — 295
Friday Night In San Francisco (81) 97(1) [0|0|13] — 254
Passion, Grace & Fire (83) 171(2) [0|0|5] — 41.2

DINO ► 1112 Pk:34 [0|1|1] — 1569
24/7 (89) 34(3) [0|6|48] — 1569

DINO, DESI & BILLY ► 1614 Pk:51 [0|0|2] — 661
I'm A Fool (65) 51(1) [0|0|24] — 570
Our Time's Coming (66) 119(1) [0|0|6] — 90.7

DIO ► 642 Pk:23 [0|2|5] — 4291
The Last In Line (84) 23(2) [0|10|35] — 1475
Sacred Heart (85) 29(4) [0|10|29] — 1116
Holy Diver (83) 56(1) [0|0|38] — 1026
Dream Evil (87) 43(2) [0|0|11] — 384
Intermission (86) 70(2) [0|0|16] — 290

DION ► 1632 Pk:128 [0|0|6] — 642
Yo Frankie (89) 130(1) [0|0|19] — 253
Dion (68) 128(1) [0|0|11] — 230
Reunion-Live At Madison Square Garden 1972 (73) 144(1) [0|0|8] — 98.5
Dion's Greatest Hits (73) 194(1) [0|0|5] — 28.3
Suite For Late Summer (72) 197(1) [0|0|4] — 20.9
Sanctuary (72) 200(2) [0|0|2] — 10.5

DIRE STRAITS ► 131 Pk:1 [2|5|8] — 24314
Brothers In Arms (85) 1(9) [37|55|97] — 11915
Dire Straits (79) 2(1) [13|20|41] — 5417
Making Movies (80) 19(3) [0|17|31] — 2553
Communique (79) 11(2) [0|9|19] — 1787
Love Over Gold (82) 19(3) [0|8|32] — 1361
Alchemy-Dire Straits Live (84) 46(2) [0|0|18] — 499
Twisting By The Pool (83) 53(1) [0|0|15] — 413
Money For Nothing (88) 62(2) [0|0|17] — 368

Senator Everett McKinley DIRKSEN ► 1258 Pk:16 [0|1|2] — 1222
Gallant Men (67) 16(2) [0|8|16] — 1182
Man Is Not Alone (67) 148(1) [0|0|3] — 40.7

DIRTY LOOKS ► 1988 Pk:118 [0|0|2] — 355
Cool From The Wire (88) 134(2) [0|0|14] — 188
Turn Of The Screw (89) 118(1) [0|0|11] — 167

DISCO TEX & The SEX-O-LETTES ► 1266 Pk:36 [0|1|1] — 1210
Disco Tex And His Sex-O-Lettes (75)-Disco Tex & The Sex-O-Lettes Review Starring Sir Monti Rock III 36(1) [0|3|22] — 1210

DISNEYLAND AFTER DARK ► 2477 Pk:116 [0|0|1] — 167
No Fuel Left For The Pilgrims (89) 116(1) [0|0|11] — 167

DIVINYLS ► 2155 Pk:91 [0|0|1] — 277
What A Life! (85) 91(2) [0|0|18] — 277

DIXIE CUPS ► 2919 Pk:112 [0|0|1] — 78
Chapel Of Love (64) 112(1) [0|0|5] — 77.6

DIXIE DREGS ► 1150 Pk:56 [0|0|5] — 1470
Unsung Heroes (81)-The Dregs 67(2) [0|0|14] — 422
Dregs Of The Earth (80) 81(1) [0|0|17] — 389
Industry Standard (82)-The Dregs 56(2) [0|0|15] — 380
Night Of The Living Dregs (79) 111(1) [0|0|13] — 242
What If (78) 182(2) [0|0|4] — 36.6

Don DIXON ► 3028 Pk:162 [0|0|1] — 62
Most Of The Girls Like To Dance But Only Some Of The Boys Like To (87) 162(1) [0|0|8] — 61.9

D.J. JAZZY JEFF & THE FRESH PRINCE ► 500 Pk:4 [1|2|3] — 6158
He's The D.J., I'm The Rapper (88) 4(1) [10|23|55] — 4651
And In This Corner... (89) 39(4) [0|7|20] — 797
Rock The House (87) 83(3) [0|0|35] — 709

THE D.O.C. ► 1128 Pk:20 [0|1|1] — 1531
No One Can Do It Better (89) 20(2) [0|10|34] — 1531

DOCTOR And The MEDICS ► 2850 Pk:125 [0|0|1] — 88
Laughing At The Pieces (86) 125(1) [0|0|8] — 87.8

DR. BUZZARD'S ORIGINAL "SAVANNAH" BAND ► 698 Pk:22 [0|2|2] — 3742
Dr. Buzzard's Original Savannah Band (76) 22(2) [0|18|49] — 3237
Dr. Buzzard's Original Savannah Band Meets King Penett (78) 36(2) [0|3|9] — 505

DR. HOOK ► 601 Pk:41 [0|0|10] — 4711
Sloppy Seconds (72)-Dr. Hook & The Medicine Show 41(1) [0|0|31] — 984
A Little Bit More (76) 62(1) [0|0|31] — 891
Dr. Hook & The Medicine Show (72)-Dr. Hook & The Medicine Show 45(1) [0|0|23] — 800
Pleasure & Pain (78) 66(1) [0|0|34] — 749
Sometimes You Win (79) 71(2) [0|0|32] — 635
Bankrupt (75) 141(1) [0|0|16] — 208
Dr. Hook/Greatest Hits (80) 142(3) [0|0|12] — 174

Act ► Highest Peak [Top10s|Top40s|Total] Title (Yr) Peak(Wk) [T10 Wk|T40Wk|TotalWk]	Score
DR. HOOK ► *Continued*	
Players In The Dark (82) 118(3) [0|0|7]	120
Belly Up! (73)-Dr. Hook & The Medicine Show 141(1) [0|0|6]	85.2
Rising (80) 175(3) [0|0|8]	63.8
DR. JOHN ► 933 Pk:24 [0|1|6]	**2207**
In The Right Place (73) 24(2) [0|9|33]	1606
Dr. John's Gumbo (72) 112(3) [0|0|11]	218
Desitively Bonnaroo (74) 105(1) [0|0|8]	163
In A Sentimental Mood (89) 142(2) [0|0|11]	110
Triumvirate (73)-Mike Bloomfield/ John Paul Hammond/Dr. John [A] 105(1) [0|0|12]	209
The Sun, Moon & Herbs (71) 184(1) [0|0|5]	41.8
DR. J.R. KOOL and The OTHER ROXANNES ► 2316 Pk:113 [0|0|1]	**210**
The Complete Story Of Roxanne...The Album (85)- Dr. J.R. Kool & The Other Roxannes 113(1) [0|0|13]	210
DOKKEN ► 490 Pk:13 [0|3|5]	**6337**
Back For The Attack (87) 13(1) [0|15|33]	2188
Under Lock And Key (85) 32(3) [0|5|67]	1710
Tooth And Nail (84) 49(2) [0|0|74]	1562
Beast From The East (88) 33(3) [0|4|17]	715
Breaking The Chains (83) 136(1) [0|0|13]	163
Thomas DOLBY ► 622 Pk:13 [0|3|4]	**4541**
The Golden Age Of Wireless (83) 13(2) [0|13|28]	1799
Blinded By Science (83) 20(4) [0|11|31]	1559
The Flat Earth (84) 35(2) [0|3|18]	743
Aliens Ate My Buick (88) 70(1) [0|0|19]	440
Joe DOLCE ► 3246 Pk:181 [0|0|1]	**34**
Shaddap You Face (81) 181(2) [0|0|4]	33.7
Placido DOMINGO ► 1110 Pk:18 [0|1|3]	**1577**
Perhaps Love (81) 18(2) [0|8|27]	1375
My Life For A Song (83) 117(1) [0|0|11]	148
Domingo-Con Amore (82) 164(2) [0|0|6]	54.2
Fats DOMINO ► 2920 Pk:130 [0|0|2]	**77**
Here Comes...Fats Domino (63) 130(1) [0|0|4]	59.5
Fats Is Back (68) 189(2) [0|0|2]	17.7
Bo DONALDSON And The HEYWOODS ► 2000 Pk:97 [0|0|1]	**351**
Bo Donaldson And The Heywoods (74) 97(1) [0|0|16]	351
Lou DONALDSON ► 1828 Pk:141 [0|0|7]	**460**
Alligator Bogaloo (67) 141(1) [0|0|11]	135
Say It Loud! (69) 153(1) [0|0|7]	104
Hot Dog (69) 158(1) [0|0|6]	80.3
Midnight Creeper (68) 182(3) [0|0|6]	64.8
Sassy Soul Strut (73) 176(2) [0|0|4]	38.6
Sweet Lou (74) 185(1) [0|0|3]	22.3
Everything I Play Is Funky (70) 190(1) [0|0|2]	14.8
DON And The GOODTIMES ► 2930 Pk:109 [0|0|1]	**75**
So Good (67) 109(1) [0|0|4]	75.3
DONOVAN ► 150 Pk:4 [1|10|20]	**22162**
Donovan's Greatest Hits (69) 4(4) [14|33|56]	7771
Donovan In Concert (68) 18(2) [0|14|31]	2162
Sunshine Superman (66) 11(1) [0|12|29]	2000
The Hurdy Gurdy Man (68) 20(1) [0|9|20]	1832
Open Road (70) 16(2) [0|6|19]	1389
Barabajagal (69) 23(2) [0|6|24]	1335
Mellow Yellow (67) 14(2) [0|8|21]	1182
A Gift From A Flower To A Garden (68) 19(1) [0|7|22]	1181
Cosmic Wheels (73) 25(2) [0|8|20]	1174
Catch The Wind (65) 30(1) [0|4|23]	826

Act ► Highest Peak [Top10s|Top40s|Total] Title (Yr) Peak(Wk) [T10 Wk|T40Wk|TotalWk]	Score
Wear Your Love Like Heaven (67) 60(2) [0|0|15]	405
Fairytale (65) 85(1) [0|0|13]	246
The Real Donovan (66) 96(1) [0|0|7]	152
The Best Of Donovan (69) 135(1) [0|0|7]	133
Donovan P. Leitch (70) 128(1) [0|0|8]	131
7-Tease (74) 135(1) [0|0|6]	110
Essence To Essence (74) 174(1) [0|0|5]	44.1
Like It Is, Was And Evermore Shall Be (68) 177(2) [0|0|4]	37.0
Slow Down World (76) 174(1) [0|0|3]	32.3
For Little Ones (68) 185(1) [0|0|3]	20.9
DOOBIE BROTHERS ► 47 Pk:1 [8|11|12]	**44835**
Minute By Minute (78) 1(5) [16|30|87]	9288
The Captain And Me (73) 7(2) [3|33|102]	7061
What Were Once Vices Are Now Habits (74) 4(1) [10|30|62]	6848
Best Of The Doobies (76) 5(1) [8|14|93]	4564
Toulouse Street (72) 21(2) [0|9|119]	3618
One Step Closer (80) 3(3) [7|18|28]	3578
Takin' It To The Streets (76) 8(1) [3|10|44]	2991
Stampede (75) 4(2) [4|13|25]	2821
Livin' On The Fault Line (77) 10(3) [3|8|21]	1792
Cycles (89) 17(1) [0|11|20]	1414
Best Of The Doobies Vol. II (81) 39(1) [0|3|15]	696
The Doobie Brothers Farewell Tour (83) 79(1) [0|0|9]	164
The DOORS ► 42 Pk:1 [7|12|18]	**45576**
The Doors (67) 2(2) [22|53|121]	11218
Waiting For The Sun (68) 1(4) [9|14|41]	5773
Strange Days (67) 3(4) [9|23|63]	4773
The Doors Greatest Hits (80) 17(2) [0|17|99]	4507
L.A. Woman (71) 9(1) [3|22|34]	4180
The Soft Parade (69) 6(2) [9|15|28]	3805
Morrison Hotel (70) 4(4) [6|12|27]	3197
Absolutely Live (70) 8(1) [2|12|20]	2183
13 (70) 25(1) [0|7|21]	1204
The Best Of The Doors(2) (87) 32(1) [0|4|43]	1157
Alive She Cried (83) 23(2) [0|9|20]	1135
Other Voices (71) 31(1) [0|4|15]	872
Full Circle (72) 68(3) [0|0|15]	502
Weird Scenes Inside The Gold Mine (72) 55(1) [0|0|11]	404
An American Prayer -Jim Morrison (78)- Jim Morrison / The Doors 54(2) [0|0|13]	389
The Best Of The Doors (73) 158(1) [0|0|8]	94.2
Classics (85) 124(2) [0|0|7]	91.9
Live At The Hollywood Bowl (87) 154(2) [0|0|11]	91.5
Charlie DORE ► 2846 Pk:145 [0|0|1]	**88**
Where To Now (80) 145(1) [0|0|7]	88.0
DORO ► 2753 Pk:154 [0|0|1]	**104**
Force Majeure (89) 154(2) [0|0|11]	104
Lee DORSEY ► 2861 Pk:129 [0|0|1]	**86**
The New Lee Dorsey (66) 129(1) [0|0|5]	86.3
DOUBLE ► 1499 Pk:30 [0|1|1]	**809**
Blue (86) 30(1) [0|6|21]	809
DOUBLE EXPOSURE ► 2391 Pk:129 [0|0|1]	**188**
Ten Percent (76) 129(1) [0|0|11]	188
DOUCETTE ► 2813 Pk:159 [0|0|1]	**94**
Mama Let Him Play (78) 159(1) [0|0|8]	94.5
Doug E. FRESH & The GET FRESH CREW ► 2233 Pk:88 [0|0|1]	**241**
The World's Greatest Entertainer (88) 88(1) [0|0|13]	241

Act ► Highest Peak [Top10s|Top40s|Total] Title (Yr) Peak(Wk) [T10 Wk|T40Wk|TotalWk]	Score
Carl DOUGLAS ► 1444 Pk:37 [0|1|1]	**900**
Kung Fu Fighting And Other Great Love Songs (74) 37(1) [0|2|17]	900
Carol DOUGLAS ► 2251 Pk:139 [0|0|3]	**233**
Full Bloom (77) 139(1) [0|0|10]	155
Midnight Love Affair (76) 188(1) [0|0|6]	45.4
The Carol Douglas Album (75) 177(1) [0|0|3]	32.6
Mike DOUGLAS ► 1842 Pk:46 [0|0|1]	**448**
The Men In My Little Girl's Life (66) 46(1) [0|0|15]	448
Ronnie DOVE ► 1212 Pk:35 [0|1|4]	**1322**
The Best Of Ronnie Dove (66) 35(3) [0|6|21]	848
One Kiss For Old Times' Sake (65) 119(1) [0|0|14]	209
Cry (67) 121(1) [0|0|12]	171
Ronnie Dove Sings The Hits For You (66) 122(2) [0|0|5]	94.1
Lamont DOZIER ► 2437 Pk:136 [0|0|2]	**177**
Out Here On My Own (74) 136(1) [0|0|13]	159
Black Bach (75) 186(1) [0|0|2]	17.3
Pete DRAKE ► 2213 Pk:85 [0|0|1]	**247**
Forever (64)-Pete Drake And His Talking Steel Guitar 85(1) [0|0|14]	247
The DRAMATICS ► 548 Pk:20 [0|2|9]	**5438**
The Dells vs. The Dramatics (74)-The Dells/The Dramatics [A] 156(1) [0|0|6]	42.8
Whatcha See Is Whatcha Get (72) 20(1) [0|11|24]	1670
The Dramatic Jackpot (75)-Ron Banks And The Dramatics 31(1) [0|3|18]	931
Do What You Wanna Do (78) 44(1) [0|0|15]	648
Shake It Well (77) 60(1) [0|0|19]	590
Joy Ride (76) 103(1) [0|0|25]	528
A Dramatic Experience (73) 86(1) [0|0|18]	379
10 1/2 (80) 61(2) [0|0|12]	357
Drama V (75)-Ron Banks And The Dramatics 93(1) [0|0|12]	292
DREAM ACADEMY ► 1179 Pk:20 [0|1|2]	**1391**
The Dream Academy (85) 20(1) [0|9|37]	1369
Remembrance Days (87) 181(2) [0|0|3]	21.4
DREAMBOY ► 2858 Pk:168 [0|0|1]	**87**
Dreamboy (84) 168(1) [0|0|11]	86.6
DREAMS ► 2913 Pk:146 [0|0|1]	**79**
Dreams (70) 146(2) [0|0|6]	78.5
DREAMS SO REAL ► 2469 Pk:150 [0|0|1]	**169**
Rough Night In Jericho (88) 150(1) [0|0|18]	169
DREAM SYNDICATE ► 3253 Pk:171 [0|0|1]	**33**
Medicine Show (84) 171(1) [0|0|4]	32.8
D.R.I. ► 1996 Pk:116 [0|0|2]	**352**
4 Of A Kind (88) 116(2) [0|0|14]	215
Thrash Zone (89) 140(1) [0|0|13]	137
The DRIFTERS ► 1397 Pk:40 [0|1|3]	**974**
Under The Boardwalk (64) 40(2) [0|2|22]	728
The Drifters' Golden Hits (68) 122(2) [0|0|8]	142
The Good Life With The Drifters (65) 103(1) [0|0|6]	103
DRIVIN' N' CRYIN' ► 2524 Pk:130 [0|0|1]	**153**
Whisper Tames The Lion (88) 130(2) [0|0|12]	153
"D" TRAIN ► 2686 Pk:128 [0|0|1]	**117**
You're The One For Me (82) 128(2) [0|0|9]	117
Les DUDEK ► 1799 Pk:100 [0|0|2]	**486**
Ghost Town Parade (78) 100(2) [0|0|11]	250
Say No More (77) 107(1) [0|0|12]	236
George DUKE ► 685 Pk:25 [0|2|14]	**3850**
Reach For It (77) 25(2) [0|9|24]	1322
Don't Let Go (78) 39(1) [0|1|14]	776
Dream On (82) 48(2) [0|0|12]	442

Act ▶ Highest Peak [Top10s | Top40s | Total] Title (Yr) Peak(Wk) [T10 Wk | T40Wk | TotalWk]	Score
George DUKE ▶ *Continued*	
Follow The Rainbow (79) 56(2) [0 | 0 | 11]	369
The Aura Will Prevail (75) 111(2) [0 | 0 | 10]	222
Master Of The Game (79) 125(1) [0 | 0 | 11]	189
A Brazilian Love Affair (80) 119(1) [0 | 0 | 9]	150
Feel (75) 141(2) [0 | 0 | 6]	92.0
Live - On Tour In Europe (76)-Billy Cobham/ George Duke Band [A] 99(1) [0 | 0 | 9]	87.4
Guardian Of The Light (83) 147(1) [0 | 0 | 7]	73.8
I Love The Blues, She Heard My Cry (76) 169(2) [0 | 0 | 6]	60.2
Thief In The Night (85) 183(1) [0 | 0 | 5]	30.4
From Me To You (77) 192(1) [0 | 0 | 3]	20.8
Liberated Fantasies (76) 190(2) [0 | 0 | 2]	15.0
Patty DUKE ▶ 2293 Pk:90 [0 | 0 | 1]	**220**
Don't Just Stand There (65) 90(1) [0 | 0 | 12]	220
DUKE JUPITER ▶ 2450 Pk:122 [0 | 0 | 1]	**173**
White Knuckle Ride (84) 122(1) [0 | 0 | 12]	173
Robbie DUPREE ▶ 1496 Pk:51 [0 | 0 | 2]	**813**
Robbie Dupree (80) 51(1) [0 | 0 | 24]	755
Street Corner Heroes (81) 169(1) [0 | 0 | 5]	58.0
DURAN DURAN ▶ 162 Pk:4 [4 | 6 | 8]	**20851**
Seven And The Ragged Tiger (83) 8(5) [14 | 41 | 64]	5895
Rio (82) 6(7) [11 | 21 | 129]	5168
Duran Duran (83) 10(1) [1 | 14 | 87]	3007
Arena (84) 4(3) [8 | 15 | 28]	2637
Notorious (86) 12(1) [0 | 14 | 34]	1997
Big Thing (88) 24(2) [0 | 14 | 26]	1528
Decade (89) 67(1) [0 | 0 | 16]	379
Carnival (82) 98(3) [0 | 0 | 15]	240
Jimmy DURANTE ▶ 1528 Pk:30 [0 | 1 | 1]	**756**
September Song (63) 30(1) [0 | 4 | 19]	756
Ian DURY ▶ 3062 Pk:168 [0 | 0 | 1]	**57**
New Boots & Panties!!! (78) 168(2) [0 | 0 | 5]	57.5
Ian DURY And The BLOCKHEADS ▶ 2541 Pk:126 [0 | 0 | 2]	**150**
Do It Yourself (79) 126(1) [0 | 0 | 6]	103
Laughter (81) 159(1) [0 | 0 | 4]	46.6
DYKE And The BLAZERS ▶ 3331 Pk:186 [0 | 0 | 1]	**26**
The Funky Broadway (67) 186(1) [0 | 0 | 4]	25.5
Bob DYLAN ▶ 13 Pk:1 [12 | 27 | 31]	**69964**
Nashville Skyline (69) 3(4) [13 | 31 | 47]	8062
Desire (76) 1(5) [13 | 17 | 35]	5953
John Wesley Harding (68) 2(4) [10 | 21 | 52]	4807
Blood On The Tracks (75) 1(2) [9 | 14 | 24]	4750
Bringing It All Back Home (65) 6(1) [14 | 32 | 43]	4566
Bob Dylan's Greatest Hits (67) 10(1) [1 | 21 | 94]	4188
Planet Waves (74)-Bob Dylan with The Band 1(4) [7 | 12 | 21]	3836
Highway 61 Revisited (65) 3(1) [8 | 24 | 47]	3582
Slow Train Coming (79) 3(4) [6 | 13 | 26]	3127
Bob Dylan's Greatest Hits, Vol. II (71) 14(1) [0 | 17 | 36]	3021
Self Portrait (70) 4(2) [6 | 10 | 22]	2600
New Morning (70) 7(1) [3 | 12 | 23]	2443
Blonde On Blonde (66) 9(1) [2 | 15 | 34]	2252
Pat Garrett & Billy The Kid (Soundtrack) (73) 16(2) [0 | 14 | 30]	2130
The Freewheelin' Bob Dylan (63) 22(1) [0 | 14 | 32]	1720
Street-Legal (78) 11(1) [0 | 8 | 23]	1679
Bob Dylan At Budokan (79) 13(2) [0 | 7 | 25]	1495
Infidels (83) 20(5) [0 | 10 | 24]	1332
Hard Rain (76) 17(2) [0 | 5 | 12]	1050
Dylan (73) 17(1) [0 | 7 | 15]	1045

Act ▶ Highest Peak [Top10s | Top40s | Total] Title (Yr) Peak(Wk) [T10 Wk | T40Wk | TotalWk]	Score
Another Side Of Bob Dylan (64) 43(1) [0 | 0 | 41]	985
The Times They Are A-Changin' (64) 20(1) [0 | 5 | 21]	839
Oh Mercy (89) 30(2) [0 | 6 | 23]	792
Saved (80) 24(2) [0 | 5 | 11]	749
Empire Burlesque (85) 33(3) [0 | 6 | 17]	708
Biograph (85) 33(2) [0 | 2 | 22]	705
Shot Of Love (81) 33(2) [0 | 3 | 9]	531
Knocked Out Loaded (86) 53(1) [0 | 0 | 13]	353
Down In The Groove (88) 61(3) [0 | 0 | 10]	300
Dylan And The Dead (89)-Bob Dylan & The Grateful Dead [A] 37(2) [0 | 3 | 11]	224
Real Live (85) 115(2) [0 | 0 | 9]	141
Bob DYLAN And The BAND ▶ 608 Pk:3 [2 | 2 | 2]	**4661**
Before The Flood (74)-Bob Dylan/The Band 3(2) [5 | 10 | 19]	2697
The Basement Tapes (75) 7(2) [4 | 9 | 14]	1964
DYNAMIC SUPERIORS ▶ 2526 Pk:130 [0 | 0 | 1]	**152**
Pure Pleasure (75) 130(1) [0 | 0 | 10]	152
DYNASTY ▶ 1400 Pk:43 [0 | 0 | 2]	**972**
Adventures In The Land Of Music (80) 43(1) [0 | 0 | 21]	888
The Second Adventure (81) 119(2) [0 | 0 | 4]	83.4
Ronnie DYSON ▶ 1518 Pk:55 [0 | 0 | 2]	**769**
(If You Let Me Make Love To You Then) Why Can't I Touch You? (70) 55(1) [0 | 0 | 18]	675
One Man Band (73) 142(1) [0 | 0 | 7]	94.7
E	
EAGLES ▶ 20 Pk:1 [5 | 7 | 9]	**59933**
Hotel California (76) 1(8) [28 | 32 | 107]	12868
Their Greatest Hits 1971-1975 (76) 1(5) [12 | 57 | 133]	12106
The Long Run (79) 1(9) [21 | 36 | 57]	11205
One Of These Nights (75) 1(5) [18 | 43 | 56]	10702
On The Border (74) 17(1) [0 | 24 | 87]	5317
Eagles Live (80) 6(4) [7 | 16 | 26]	3172
Desperado (73) 41(1) [0 | 0 | 70]	2133
The Eagles (72) 22(1) [0 | 7 | 49]	1912
Eagles Greatest Hits: Volume 2 (82) 52(3) [0 | 0 | 15]	517
Charles EARLAND ▶ 1526 Pk:108 [0 | 0 | 4]	**759**
Black Talk! (70) 108(1) [0 | 0 | 19]	406
Odyssey (76) 155(1) [0 | 0 | 11]	146
Black Drops (70) 131(2) [0 | 0 | 10]	144
Living Black! (71) 176(1) [0 | 0 | 7]	63.3
Steve EARLE ▶ 1250 Pk:56 [0 | 0 | 2]	**1231**
Copperhead Road (88) 56(1) [0 | 0 | 28]	924
Guitar Town (86) 89(2) [0 | 0 | 20]	307
Steve EARLE And The DUKES ▶ 2196 Pk:90 [0 | 0 | 1]	**259**
Exit 0 (87) 90(1) [0 | 0 | 14]	259
EARTH OPERA ▶ 3209 Pk:181 [0 | 0 | 1]	**39**
The Great American Eagle Tragedy (69) 181(1) [0 | 0 | 4]	38.7
EARTH QUAKE ▶ 3023 Pk:151 [0 | 0 | 1]	**63**
8.5 (76) 151(1) [0 | 0 | 4]	62.8
EARTH, WIND & FIRE ▶ 29 Pk:1 [8 | 13 | 18]	**53194**
That's The Way Of The World (Soundtrack) (75) 1(3) [21 | 29 | 55]	9789
Gratitude (75) 1(3) [13 | 21 | 54]	6844
All 'N All (77) 3(6) [15 | 18 | 47]	6106
I Am (79) 3(3) [15 | 20 | 38]	5406
Spirit (76) 2(2) [9 | 18 | 30]	4953
The Best Of Earth, Wind & Fire, Vol. I (78) 6(1) [8 | 18 | 60]	4044

Act ▶ Highest Peak [Top10s | Top40s | Total] Title (Yr) Peak(Wk) [T10 Wk | T40Wk | TotalWk]	Score
Raise! (81) 5(8) [10 | 18 | 25]	3652
Open Our Eyes (74) 15(2) [0 | 18 | 37]	3222
Head To The Sky (73) 27(1) [0 | 10 | 71]	2882
Faces (80) 10(2) [2 | 12 | 21]	1942
Powerlight (83) 12(4) [0 | 12 | 21]	1518
Touch The World (87) 33(1) [0 | 6 | 28]	1083
Electric Universe (83) 40(2) [0 | 2 | 16]	638
Last Days And Time (72) 87(1) [0 | 0 | 25]	438
The Need Of Love (72) 89(1) [0 | 0 | 13]	304
Another Time (74) 97(1) [0 | 0 | 10]	215
Earth, Wind & Fire (71) 172(1) [0 | 0 | 13]	135
The Best Of Earth, Wind & Fire, Vol. II (88) 190(2) [0 | 0 | 4]	24.1
Elliot EASTON ▶ 2393 Pk:99 [0 | 0 | 1]	**188**
Change No Change (85) 99(2) [0 | 0 | 11]	188
Sheena EASTON ▶ 364 Pk:15 [0 | 4 | 7]	**9075**
A Private Heaven (84) 15(2) [0 | 22 | 35]	2682
Sheena Easton (81) 24(1) [0 | 8 | 38]	1828
You Could Have Been With Me (81) 47(1) [0 | 0 | 53]	1443
Best Kept Secret (83) 33(2) [0 | 9 | 38]	1284
The Lover In Me (88) 44(4) [0 | 0 | 26]	1067
Do You (85) 40(2) [0 | 2 | 19]	584
Madness, Money And Music (82) 85(3) [0 | 0 | 12]	187
The EASYBEATS ▶ 3258 Pk:180 [0 | 0 | 1]	**33**
Friday On My Mind (67) 180(1) [0 | 0 | 5]	32.6
EAZY-E ▶ 850 Pk:41 [0 | 0 | 1]	**2665**
Eazy-Duz-It (88) 41(1) [0 | 0 | 90]	2665
EBN-OZN ▶ 3316 Pk:185 [0 | 0 | 1]	**27**
Feeling Cavalier (84) 185(2) [0 | 0 | 4]	26.6
EBONEE WEBB ▶ 2909 Pk:157 [0 | 0 | 1]	**79**
Ebonee Webb (81) 157(2) [0 | 0 | 7]	79.0
ECHO & The BUNNYMEN ▶ 1290 Pk:51 [0 | 0 | 6]	**1170**
Echo & The Bunnymen(2) (87) 51(1) [0 | 0 | 37]	771
Ocean Rain (84) 87(1) [0 | 0 | 11]	199
Porcupine (83) 137(1) [0 | 0 | 9]	96.1
Songs To Learn & Sing (86) 158(1) [0 | 0 | 9]	70.3
Heaven Up Here (81) 184(1) [0 | 0 | 2]	16.9
Echo & The Bunnymen (84) 188(1) [0 | 0 | 3]	16.0
John EDDIE ▶ 2167 Pk:83 [0 | 0 | 1]	**271**
John Eddie (86) 83(2) [0 | 0 | 15]	271
Duane EDDY ▶ 2431 Pk:93 [0 | 0 | 2]	**178**
"Twangin'" Up A Storm! (63) 93(1) [0 | 0 | 8]	154
Lonely Guitar (64) 144(1) [0 | 0 | 2]	24.0
EDEN'S CHILDREN ▶ 3510 Pk:196 [0 | 0 | 1]	**10**
Eden's Children (68) 196(1) [0 | 0 | 2]	10.5
Graeme EDGE Band ▶ 2172 Pk:107 [0 | 0 | 2]	**269**
Kick Off Your Muddy Boots (75) 107(2) [0 | 0 | 9]	220
Paradise Ballroom (77) 164(2) [0 | 0 | 4]	48.7
Dave EDMUNDS ▶ 908 Pk:46 [0 | 0 | 7]	**2334**
Information (83) 51(2) [0 | 0 | 20]	615
Twangin... (81) 48(2) [0 | 0 | 14]	531
Repeat When Necessary (79) 54(2) [0 | 0 | 15]	501
D.E. 7th (82) 46(2) [0 | 0 | 14]	401
I Hear You Rockin' (87)-The Dave Edmunds Band 106(1) [0 | 0 | 12]	186
Riff Raff (84) 140(2) [0 | 0 | 4]	51.5
The Best Of Dave Edmunds (82) 163(1) [0 | 0 | 5]	48.6
Edward BEAR ▶ 1881 Pk:63 [0 | 0 | 2]	**416**
Edward Bear (73) 63(1) [0 | 0 | 16]	371
Close Your Eyes (73) 183(2) [0 | 0 | 6]	45.4
Dennis EDWARDS ▶ 1482 Pk:48 [0 | 0 | 1]	**845**
Don't Look Any Further (84) 48(2) [0 | 0 | 27]	845

<table>
<tr><th>Act ▶ Highest Peak [Top10s|Top40s|Total]
Title (Yr) Peak(Wk) [T10 Wk|T40Wk|TotalWk]</th><th>Score</th></tr>
<tr><td>Jonathan EDWARDS ▶ 1407 Pk:42 [0|0|2]</td><td>960</td></tr>
<tr><td>Jonathan Edwards (71) 42(2) [0|0|20]</td><td>869</td></tr>
<tr><td>Honky-Tonk Stardust Cowboy (72)
167(2) [0|0|9]</td><td>91.2</td></tr>
<tr><td>Walter EGAN ▶ 1454 Pk:44 [0|0|3]</td><td>887</td></tr>
<tr><td>Not Shy (78) 44(1) [0|0|31]</td><td>765</td></tr>
<tr><td>Fundamental Roll (77) 137(1) [0|0|6]</td><td>109</td></tr>
<tr><td>Wild Exhibitions (83) 187(1) [0|0|2]</td><td>12.9</td></tr>
<tr><td>EGG CREAM ▶ 3357 Pk:197 [0|0|1]</td><td>23</td></tr>
<tr><td>Egg Cream (77)-Egg Cream Feat. Andy Adams
197(2) [0|0|4]</td><td>23.2</td></tr>
<tr><td>EGYPTIAN LOVER ▶ 2798 Pk:146 [0|0|1]</td><td>98</td></tr>
<tr><td>On The Nile (85) 146(2) [0|0|10]</td><td>97.6</td></tr>
<tr><td>8TH DAY ▶ 2169 Pk:131 [0|0|1]</td><td>269</td></tr>
<tr><td>8th Day (71) 131(1) [0|0|16]</td><td>269</td></tr>
<tr><td>Donnie ELBERT ▶ 2710 Pk:153 [0|0|1]</td><td>112</td></tr>
<tr><td>Where Did Our Love Go (72) 153(1) [0|0|9]</td><td>112</td></tr>
<tr><td>EL CHICANO ▶ 1416 Pk:51 [0|0|5]</td><td>945</td></tr>
<tr><td>Viva Tirado (70) 51(1) [0|0|17]</td><td>583</td></tr>
<tr><td>El Chicano (73) 162(1) [0|0|16]</td><td>162</td></tr>
<tr><td>Celebration (72) 173(1) [0|0|13]</td><td>107</td></tr>
<tr><td>Revolucion (71) 178(2) [0|0|9]</td><td>74.1</td></tr>
<tr><td>Cinco (74) 194(1) [0|0|3]</td><td>19.2</td></tr>
<tr><td>EL COCO ▶ 1813 Pk:82 [0|0|1]</td><td>475</td></tr>
<tr><td>Cocomotion (77) 82(1) [0|0|23]</td><td>475</td></tr>
<tr><td>ELECTRIC FLAG ▶ 1081 Pk:31 [0|1|2]</td><td>1654</td></tr>
<tr><td>A Long Time Comin' (68) 31(1) [0|5|35]</td><td>1243</td></tr>
<tr><td>The Electric Flag (69) 76(1) [0|0|12]</td><td>412</td></tr>
<tr><td>ELECTRIC INDIAN ▶ 2278 Pk:104 [0|0|1]</td><td>222</td></tr>
<tr><td>Keem-O-Sabe (69) 104(2) [0|0|9]</td><td>222</td></tr>
<tr><td>ELECTRIC LIGHT ORCHESTRA ▶ 79
Pk:4 [5|10|14]</td><td>34118</td></tr>
<tr><td>A New World Record (76) 5(2) [7|44|69]</td><td>8133</td></tr>
<tr><td>Out Of The Blue (77) 4(4) [9|21|58]</td><td>5045</td></tr>
<tr><td>Face The Music (75) 8(1) [3|24|48]</td><td>4530</td></tr>
<tr><td>Discovery (79) 5(2) [10|17|35]</td><td>4323</td></tr>
<tr><td>Eldorado (74) 16(2) [0|17|32]</td><td>2969</td></tr>
<tr><td>Xanadu (Soundtrack) (80)-
Olivia Newton-John/Electric Light Orchestra [A]
4(3) [8|15|36]</td><td>2043</td></tr>
<tr><td>Ole ELO (76) 32(1) [0|5|43]</td><td>1908</td></tr>
<tr><td>Time (81) 16(3) [0|12|20]</td><td>1665</td></tr>
<tr><td>ELO's Greatest Hits (79) 30(3) [0|8|15]</td><td>925</td></tr>
<tr><td>On The Third Day (73) 52(1) [0|0|24]</td><td>818</td></tr>
<tr><td>Electric Light Orchestra II (73)
62(2) [0|0|22]</td><td>672</td></tr>
<tr><td>Secret Messages (83) 36(1) [0|1|16]</td><td>590</td></tr>
<tr><td>Balance Of Power (86) 49(3) [0|0|15]</td><td>484</td></tr>
<tr><td>No Answer (72) 196(2) [0|0|2]</td><td>11.5</td></tr>
<tr><td>ELECTRIC PRUNES ▶ 1887 Pk:113 [0|0|3]</td><td>413</td></tr>
<tr><td>The Electric Prunes (67) 113(1) [0|0|12]</td><td>211</td></tr>
<tr><td>Mass In F Minor (68) 135(2) [0|0|13]</td><td>166</td></tr>
<tr><td>Underground (67) 172(2) [0|0|4]</td><td>36.4</td></tr>
<tr><td>ELECTRONIC CONCEPT ORCHESTRA ▶ 3346
Pk:175 [0|0|1]</td><td>25</td></tr>
<tr><td>Electric Love (69) 175(1) [0|0|2]</td><td>24.5</td></tr>
<tr><td>ELEPHANT'S MEMORY ▶ 3479
Pk:200 [0|0|1]</td><td>12</td></tr>
<tr><td>Elephant's Memory (69) 200(2) [0|0|2]</td><td>12.4</td></tr>
<tr><td>ELEVENTH HOUSE ▶ 2482 Pk:163 [0|0|2]</td><td>164</td></tr>
<tr><td>Introducing The Eleventh House With Larry Coryell
(74) 163(1) [0|0|11]</td><td>118</td></tr>
<tr><td>Level One (75) 163(1) [0|0|4]</td><td>46.9</td></tr>
<tr><td>Larry ELGART ▶ 3243 Pk:128 [0|0|1]</td><td>34</td></tr>
<tr><td>Command Performance! Les & Larry Elgart Play
The Great Dance Hits (64)-Les & Larry Elgart [A]
128(1) [0|0|5]</td><td>34.1</td></tr>
</table>

<table>
<tr><th>Act ▶ Highest Peak [Top10s|Top40s|Total]
Title (Yr) Peak(Wk) [T10 Wk|T40Wk|TotalWk]</th><th>Score</th></tr>
<tr><td>Larry ELGART And His MANHATTAN SWING
Orchestra ▶ 1002 Pk:24 [0|1|2]</td><td>1934</td></tr>
<tr><td>Hooked On Swing (82) 24(5) [0|15|41]</td><td>1729</td></tr>
<tr><td>Hooked On Swing 2 (83) 89(2) [0|0|14]</td><td>206</td></tr>
<tr><td>Les ELGART ▶ 3244 Pk:128 [0|0|1]</td><td>34</td></tr>
<tr><td>Command Performance! Les & Larry Elgart Play
The Great Dance Hits (64)-Les & Larry Elgart [A]
128(1) [0|0|5]</td><td>34.1</td></tr>
<tr><td>Yvonne ELLIMAN ▶ 1243 Pk:40 [0|1|3]</td><td>1241</td></tr>
<tr><td>Night Flight (78) 40(2) [0|2|17]</td><td>770</td></tr>
<tr><td>Love Me (77) 68(1) [0|0|16]</td><td>416</td></tr>
<tr><td>Yvonne (79) 174(2) [0|0|6]</td><td>54.1</td></tr>
<tr><td>Duke ELLINGTON ▶ 2178 Pk:78 [0|0|3]</td><td>267</td></tr>
<tr><td>Francis A. & Edward K. (68)-Frank Sinatra &
Duke Ellington [A] 78(2) [0|0|13]</td><td>163</td></tr>
<tr><td>Ellington '65: Hits Of The 60's/
This Time By Ellington (64) 133(1) [0|0|7]</td><td>83.8</td></tr>
<tr><td>The Duke At Tanglewood (66)-
Duke Ellington/Boston Pops Orchestra/
Arthur Fiedler [A] 145(1) [0|0|3]</td><td>19.7</td></tr>
<tr><td>Joe ELY ▶ 2280 Pk:135 [0|0|2]</td><td>222</td></tr>
<tr><td>Musta Notta Gotta Lotta (81) 135(1) [0|0|11]</td><td>184</td></tr>
<tr><td>Live Shots (81) 159(2) [0|0|3]</td><td>38.0</td></tr>
<tr><td>Keith EMERSON ▶ 3306 Pk:183 [0|0|1]</td><td>28</td></tr>
<tr><td>Nighthawks (81) 183(1) [0|0|3]</td><td>27.8</td></tr>
<tr><td>EMERSON, LAKE & PALMER ▶ 153
Pk:4 [4|8|11]</td><td>22001</td></tr>
<tr><td>Trilogy (72) 5(1) [7|20|37]</td><td>3937</td></tr>
<tr><td>Brain Salad Surgery (73) 11(1) [0|16|47]</td><td>3512</td></tr>
<tr><td>Emerson, Lake & Palmer (71) 18(2) [0|18|42]</td><td>3365</td></tr>
<tr><td>Tarkus (71) 9(2) [2|11|26]</td><td>2751</td></tr>
<tr><td>Welcome Back, My Friends, To The Show That
Never Ends - Ladies and Gentlemen (74)
4(1) [5|11|24]</td><td>2531</td></tr>
<tr><td>Works, Volume 1 (77) 12(2) [0|10|26]</td><td>2442</td></tr>
<tr><td>Pictures At An Exhibition (72) 10(2) [2|12|23]</td><td>2084</td></tr>
<tr><td>Works, Volume 2 (77) 37(1) [0|3|14]</td><td>657</td></tr>
<tr><td>Love Beach (78) 55(3) [0|0|9]</td><td>346</td></tr>
<tr><td>Emerson, Lake & Palmer In Concert (79)
73(3) [0|0|10]</td><td>257</td></tr>
<tr><td>The Best Of Emerson, Lake And Palmer (80)
108(2) [0|0|7]</td><td>119</td></tr>
<tr><td>EMERSON, LAKE & POWELL ▶ 1165
Pk:23 [0|1|1]</td><td>1419</td></tr>
<tr><td>Emerson, Lake, & Powell (86) 23(3) [0|12|26]</td><td>1419</td></tr>
<tr><td>The EMOTIONS ▶ 501 Pk:7 [1|2|6]</td><td>6150</td></tr>
<tr><td>Rejoice (77) 7(3) [7|21|33]</td><td>3823</td></tr>
<tr><td>Flowers (76) 45(1) [0|0|27]</td><td>1128</td></tr>
<tr><td>Sunbeam (78) 40(3) [0|3|12]</td><td>562</td></tr>
<tr><td>Sunshine (77) 88(2) [0|0|15]</td><td>390</td></tr>
<tr><td>Come Into Our World (79) 96(3) [0|0|10]</td><td>207</td></tr>
<tr><td>New Affair (81) 168(2) [0|0|4]</td><td>39.9</td></tr>
<tr><td>ENCHANTMENT ▶ 1283 Pk:46 [0|0|3]</td><td>1179</td></tr>
<tr><td>Once Upon A Dream (78) 46(2) [0|0|21]</td><td>712</td></tr>
<tr><td>Enchantment (77) 104(1) [0|0|19]</td><td>346</td></tr>
<tr><td>Journey To The Land Of...Enchantment (79)
145(1) [0|0|8]</td><td>121</td></tr>
<tr><td>ENGLAND DAN & John Ford COLEY ▶ 697
Pk:17 [0|1|5]</td><td>3750</td></tr>
<tr><td>Nights Are Forever (76) 17(1) [0|12|31]</td><td>2640</td></tr>
<tr><td>Some Things Don't Come Easy (78)
61(2) [0|0|14]</td><td>479</td></tr>
<tr><td>Dowdy Ferry Road (77) 80(2) [0|0|15]</td><td>342</td></tr>
<tr><td>Dr. Heckle And Mr. Jive (79) 106(2) [0|0|12]</td><td>277</td></tr>
<tr><td>The Best Of England Dan & John Ford Coley (80)
194(2) [0|0|2]</td><td>12.3</td></tr>
<tr><td>ENGLISH BEAT ▶ 928 Pk:39 [0|1|4]</td><td>2223</td></tr>
<tr><td>Special Beat Service (82) 39(3) [0|3|44]</td><td>1477</td></tr>
<tr><td>What Is Beat? (83) 87(1) [0|0|22]</td><td>403</td></tr>
</table>

<table>
<tr><th>Act ▶ Highest Peak [Top10s|Top40s|Total]
Title (Yr) Peak(Wk) [T10 Wk|T40Wk|TotalWk]</th><th>Score</th></tr>
<tr><td>I Just Can't Stop It (80) 142(1) [0|0|14]</td><td>221</td></tr>
<tr><td>Wha'ppen (81) 126(1) [0|0|6]</td><td>123</td></tr>
<tr><td>Ethel ENNIS ▶ 3348 Pk:147 [0|0|1]</td><td>24</td></tr>
<tr><td>This Is Ethel Ennis (64) 147(1) [0|0|2]</td><td>24.4</td></tr>
<tr><td>Brian ENO ▶ 1913 Pk:44 [0|0|3]</td><td>398</td></tr>
<tr><td>My Life In The Bush Of Ghosts (81)-
Brian Eno - David Byrne [A] 44(2) [0|0|13]</td><td>257</td></tr>
<tr><td>Here Come The Warm Jets (74) 151(1) [0|0|6]</td><td>85.3</td></tr>
<tr><td>Before And After Science (78) 171(2) [0|0|5]</td><td>55.6</td></tr>
<tr><td>John ENTWISTLE ▶ 1589 Pk:71 [0|0|5]</td><td>692</td></tr>
<tr><td>Too Late The Hero (81) 71(2) [0|0|9]</td><td>266</td></tr>
<tr><td>Whistle Rymes (72) 138(2) [0|0|13]</td><td>184</td></tr>
<tr><td>Smash Your Head Against The Wall (71)
126(2) [0|0|9]</td><td>171</td></tr>
<tr><td>Rigor Mortis Sets In (73) 174(2) [0|0|7]</td><td>63.0</td></tr>
<tr><td>Mad Dog (75)-John Entwistle's Ox
192(1) [0|0|1]</td><td>7.7</td></tr>
<tr><td>ENUFF Z'NUFF ▶ 1586 Pk:74 [0|0|1]</td><td>693</td></tr>
<tr><td>Enuff Z'Nuff (89) 74(1) [0|0|34]</td><td>693</td></tr>
<tr><td>ENYA ▶ 1012 Pk:25 [0|1|1]</td><td>1899</td></tr>
<tr><td>Watermark (89) 25(4) [0|13|39]</td><td>1899</td></tr>
<tr><td>EPMD ▶ 1391 Pk:53 [0|0|2]</td><td>982</td></tr>
<tr><td>Strictly Business (88) 80(1) [0|0|23]</td><td>558</td></tr>
<tr><td>Unfinished Business (89) 53(3) [0|0|14]</td><td>424</td></tr>
<tr><td>ERASURE ▶ 905 Pk:49 [0|0|5]</td><td>2351</td></tr>
<tr><td>The Innocents (88) 49(1) [0|0|50]</td><td>1638</td></tr>
<tr><td>Wild! (89) 57(2) [0|0|23]</td><td>481</td></tr>
<tr><td>Crackers International (89) 73(3) [0|0|10]</td><td>198</td></tr>
<tr><td>The Two Ring Circus (88) 186(1) [0|0|3]</td><td>18.6</td></tr>
<tr><td>The Circus (87) 190(1) [0|0|3]</td><td>15.3</td></tr>
<tr><td>ERIC B. & RAKIM ▶ 1073 Pk:22 [0|1|2]</td><td>1667</td></tr>
<tr><td>Follow The Leader (88) 22(2) [0|7|16]</td><td>887</td></tr>
<tr><td>Paid In Full (87) 58(1) [0|0|38]</td><td>780</td></tr>
<tr><td>ERUPTION ▶ 2462 Pk:133 [0|0|1]</td><td>170</td></tr>
<tr><td>Eruption (78) 133(1) [0|0|13]</td><td>170</td></tr>
<tr><td>ESCAPE CLUB ▶ 1062 Pk:27 [0|1|1]</td><td>1716</td></tr>
<tr><td>Wild, Wild West (88) 27(3) [0|14|38]</td><td>1716</td></tr>
<tr><td>Coke ESCOVEDO ▶ 3190 Pk:190 [0|0|3]</td><td>42</td></tr>
<tr><td>Comin' At Ya! (76) 190(2) [0|0|3]</td><td>22.8</td></tr>
<tr><td>Coke (76) 195(1) [0|0|2]</td><td>12.7</td></tr>
<tr><td>Disco Fantasy (77) 195(1) [0|0|1]</td><td>6.5</td></tr>
<tr><td>ESQUIRE ▶ 3259 Pk:165 [0|0|1]</td><td>32</td></tr>
<tr><td>Esquire (87) 165(2) [0|0|4]</td><td>32.3</td></tr>
<tr><td>David ESSEX ▶ 1498 Pk:32 [0|1|1]</td><td>812</td></tr>
<tr><td>Rock On (74) 32(1) [0|3|21]</td><td>812</td></tr>
<tr><td>Gloria ESTEFAN/MIAMI SOUND MACHINE
▶ 213 Pk:6 [2|3|3]</td><td>16186</td></tr>
<tr><td>Let It Loose (87)-Gloria Estefan &
Miami Sound Machine 6(2) [9|48|97]</td><td>6903</td></tr>
<tr><td>Cuts Both Ways (89)-Gloria Estefan
8(2) [4|41|69]</td><td>5235</td></tr>
<tr><td>Primitive Love (85)-Miami Sound Machine
21(1) [0|34|75]</td><td>4048</td></tr>
<tr><td>Deon ESTUS ▶ 2140 Pk:89 [0|0|1]</td><td>284</td></tr>
<tr><td>Spell (89) 89(1) [0|0|15]</td><td>284</td></tr>
<tr><td>Melissa ETHERIDGE ▶ 628 Pk:22 [0|2|2]</td><td>4464</td></tr>
<tr><td>Melissa Etheridge (88) 22(1) [0|14|65]</td><td>2781</td></tr>
<tr><td>Brave And Crazy (89) 22(1) [0|10|58]</td><td>1683</td></tr>
<tr><td>Roy ETZEL ▶ 2979 Pk:140 [0|0|1]</td><td>68</td></tr>
<tr><td>The Silence (Il Silenzio) (65) 140(1) [0|0|5]</td><td>68.3</td></tr>
<tr><td>E.U. ▶ 2912 Pk:158 [0|0|1]</td><td>79</td></tr>
<tr><td>Livin' Large (89) 158(1) [0|0|9]</td><td>78.6</td></tr>
<tr><td>EUROGLIDERS ▶ 2779 Pk:140 [0|0|1]</td><td>100</td></tr>
<tr><td>This Island (84) 140(2) [0|0|11]</td><td>100</td></tr>
<tr><td>EUROPE ▶ 452 Pk:8 [1|2|2]</td><td>7064</td></tr>
<tr><td>The Final Countdown (86) 8(2) [10|42|78]</td><td>5668</td></tr>
</table>

<table>
<tr><th>Act ► Highest Peak [Top10s|Top40s|Total]
Title (Yr) Peak(Wk) [T10 Wk|T40Wk|TotalWk]</th><th>Score</th></tr>
<tr><td>EUROPE ► Continued</td><td></td></tr>
<tr><td>Out Of This World (88) 19(1) [0|11|25]</td><td>1396</td></tr>
<tr><td>EURYTHMICS ► 252 Pk:7 [2|5|8]</td><td>14127</td></tr>
<tr><td>Be Yourself Tonight (85) 9(1) [3|24|45]</td><td>3357</td></tr>
<tr><td>Touch (84) 7(3) [6|23|37]</td><td>3314</td></tr>
<tr><td>Sweet Dreams (Are Made Of This) (83) 15(3) [0|17|59]</td><td>3056</td></tr>
<tr><td>Revenge (86) 12(1) [0|15|33]</td><td>2090</td></tr>
<tr><td>We Too Are One (89) 34(2) [0|9|28]</td><td>1252</td></tr>
<tr><td>Savage (87) 41(2) [0|0|19]</td><td>653</td></tr>
<tr><td>1984 (For The Love Of Big Brother) (Soundtrack) (85) 93(1) [0|0|14]</td><td>227</td></tr>
<tr><td>Touch Dance (84) 115(1) [0|0|11]</td><td>177</td></tr>
<tr><td>Betty EVERETT ► 2835 Pk:102 [0|0|1]</td><td>90</td></tr>
<tr><td>Delicious Together (64)-Betty Everett & Jerry Butler [A] 102(1) [0|0|11]</td><td>89.8</td></tr>
<tr><td>EVERLY BROTHERS ► 1319 Pk:38 [0|1|5]</td><td>1102</td></tr>
<tr><td>EB 84 (84) 38(2) [0|3|17]</td><td>587</td></tr>
<tr><td>Born Yesterday (86) 83(4) [0|0|19]</td><td>366</td></tr>
<tr><td>The Everly Brothers' Original Greatest Hits (70) 180(1) [0|0|8]</td><td>58.6</td></tr>
<tr><td>Reunion Concert (84) 162(2) [0|0|5]</td><td>50.9</td></tr>
<tr><td>Beat & Soul (65) 141(1) [0|0|3]</td><td>40.1</td></tr>
<tr><td>EVERY MOTHERS' SON ► 2594 Pk:117 [0|0|1]</td><td>136</td></tr>
<tr><td>Every Mothers' Son (67) 117(1) [0|0|10]</td><td>136</td></tr>
<tr><td>EXILE ► 1004 Pk:14 [0|1|1]</td><td>1927</td></tr>
<tr><td>Mixed Emotions (78) 14(2) [0|8|26]</td><td>1927</td></tr>
<tr><td>EXODUS ► 1544 Pk:82 [0|0|2]</td><td>737</td></tr>
<tr><td>Pleasures Of The Flesh (87) 82(2) [0|0|20]</td><td>386</td></tr>
<tr><td>Fabulous Disaster (89) 82(1) [0|0|17]</td><td>351</td></tr>
<tr><td>EXOTIC GUITARS ► 2141 Pk:155 [0|0|3]</td><td>284</td></tr>
<tr><td>Those Were The Days (69) 167(1) [0|0|11]</td><td>130</td></tr>
<tr><td>Indian Love Call (69) 162(2) [0|0|6]</td><td>77.7</td></tr>
<tr><td>The Exotic Guitars (68) 155(1) [0|0|5]</td><td>75.5</td></tr>
<tr><td>EXPOSÉ ► 475 Pk:16 [0|2|2]</td><td>6602</td></tr>
<tr><td>Exposure (87) 16(2) [0|53|74]</td><td>4850</td></tr>
<tr><td>What You Don't Know (89) 33(2) [0|6|50]</td><td>1752</td></tr>
<tr><td>EXTREME ► 1705 Pk:80 [0|0|1]</td><td>580</td></tr>
<tr><td>Extreme (89) 80(1) [0|0|32]</td><td>580</td></tr>
<tr><td>EYE TO EYE ► 2263 Pk:99 [0|0|1]</td><td>228</td></tr>
<tr><td>Eye To Eye (82) 99(2) [0|0|15]</td><td>228</td></tr>
<tr><td>EZO ► 2886 Pk:150 [0|0|1]</td><td>82</td></tr>
<tr><td>EZO (87) 150(2) [0|0|9]</td><td>81.9</td></tr>
<tr><td>F</td><td></td></tr>
<tr><td>FABULOUS POODLES ► 1730 Pk:61 [0|0|2]</td><td>549</td></tr>
<tr><td>Mirror Stars (79) 61(4) [0|0|17]</td><td>526</td></tr>
<tr><td>Think Pink (79) 185(1) [0|0|3]</td><td>23.3</td></tr>
<tr><td>FABULOUS RHINESTONES ► 3085 Pk:193 [0|0|2]</td><td>54</td></tr>
<tr><td>The Fabulous Rhinestones (72) 193(1) [0|0|6]</td><td>35.3</td></tr>
<tr><td>Freewheelin' (73) 193(2) [0|0|3]</td><td>18.6</td></tr>
<tr><td>FABULOUS THUNDERBIRDS ► 673 Pk:13 [0|1|4]</td><td>4014</td></tr>
<tr><td>Tuff Enuff (86) 13(3) [0|25|53]</td><td>3398</td></tr>
<tr><td>Hot Number (87) 49(1) [0|0|15]</td><td>439</td></tr>
<tr><td>Powerful Stuff (89) 118(3) [0|0|7]</td><td>112</td></tr>
<tr><td>Butt Rockin' (81) 176(1) [0|0|7]</td><td>64.1</td></tr>
<tr><td>FACE TO FACE ► 2274 Pk:126 [0|0|2]</td><td>224</td></tr>
<tr><td>Face To Face (84) 126(1) [0|0|16]</td><td>179</td></tr>
<tr><td>One Big Day (88) 176(1) [0|0|7]</td><td>45.4</td></tr>
<tr><td>FACTS OF LIFE ► 2791 Pk:146 [0|0|1]</td><td>99</td></tr>
<tr><td>Sometimes (77) 146(1) [0|0|7]</td><td>98.8</td></tr>
<tr><td>Donald FAGEN ► 1044 Pk:11 [0|1|1]</td><td>1763</td></tr>
<tr><td>The Nightfly (82) 11(4) [0|10|27]</td><td>1763</td></tr>
<tr><td>FAIRGROUND ATTRACTION ► 2662 Pk:137 [0|0|1]</td><td>121</td></tr>
<tr><td>The First Of A Million Kisses (89) 137(2) [0|0|11]</td><td>121</td></tr>
<tr><td>FAIRPORT CONVENTION ► 2551 Pk:143 [0|0|3]</td><td>148</td></tr>
<tr><td>Rising For The Moon (75) 143(1) [0|0|8]</td><td>126</td></tr>
<tr><td>"Babbacombe" Lee (72) 195(1) [0|0|3]</td><td>16.7</td></tr>
<tr><td>Angel Delight (71) 200(1) [0|0|1]</td><td>5.5</td></tr>
<tr><td>Percy FAITH His Orchestra And Chorus ► 820 Pk:80 [0|0|20]</td><td>2817</td></tr>
<tr><td>Those Were The Days (69) 88(1) [0|0|14]</td><td>362</td></tr>
<tr><td>Leaving On A Jet Plane (70) 88(1) [0|0|14]</td><td>355</td></tr>
<tr><td>For Those In Love (68) 121(1) [0|0|22]</td><td>346</td></tr>
<tr><td>Angel Of The Morning (Hit Themes For Young Lovers) (68) 95(1) [0|0|11]</td><td>325</td></tr>
<tr><td>Today's Themes For Young Lovers (67) 111(1) [0|0|17]</td><td>284</td></tr>
<tr><td>Shangri-La! (63) Percy Faith And His Orchestra 80(2) [0|0|15]</td><td>252</td></tr>
<tr><td>Great Folk Themes (64) Percy Faith And His Orchestra 103(1) [0|0|12]</td><td>198</td></tr>
<tr><td>Love Theme From "Romeo & Juliet" (69) 134(1) [0|0|11]</td><td>196</td></tr>
<tr><td>More Themes For Young Lovers (64) Percy Faith And His Orchestra 110(1) [0|0|7]</td><td>108</td></tr>
<tr><td>Broadway Bouquet (65)-Magnificent Strings Of Percy Faith 101(1) [0|0|5]</td><td>93.0</td></tr>
<tr><td>Plays The Academy Award Winner Born Free And Other Great Movie Themes (67)-Percy Faith 152(2) [0|0|5]</td><td>58.1</td></tr>
<tr><td>Joy (72) Percy Faith And His Orchestra 176(1) [0|0|6]</td><td>43.9</td></tr>
<tr><td>Jesus Christ, Superstar (71) 186(1) [0|0|6]</td><td>40.7</td></tr>
<tr><td>Black Magic Woman (71)-Percy Faith And His Orchestra 184(1) [0|0|5]</td><td>37.3</td></tr>
<tr><td>The Beatles Album (70)-Percy Faith Strings 179(1) [0|0|4]</td><td>36.4</td></tr>
<tr><td>Windmills Of Your Mind (69)-Percy Faith 194(1) [0|0|4]</td><td>30.8</td></tr>
<tr><td>Day By Day (72) 197(3) [0|0|3]</td><td>16.4</td></tr>
<tr><td>I Think I Love You (71) 198(1) [0|0|2]</td><td>11.9</td></tr>
<tr><td>Held Over! Today's Great Movie Themes (70)-Percy Faith And His Orchestra 196(1) [0|0|2]</td><td>11.6</td></tr>
<tr><td>A Time For Love (71)-Percy Faith 200(2) [0|0|2]</td><td>11.2</td></tr>
<tr><td>Marianne FAITHFULL ► 816 Pk:12 [0|1|7]</td><td>2840</td></tr>
<tr><td>Marianne Faithfull (65) 12(1) [0|15|31]</td><td>1789</td></tr>
<tr><td>Broken English (80) 82(1) [0|0|15]</td><td>323</td></tr>
<tr><td>Go Away From My World (65) 81(1) [0|0|16]</td><td>303</td></tr>
<tr><td>Dangerous Acquaintances (81) 104(1) [0|0|9]</td><td>172</td></tr>
<tr><td>Marianne Faithfull's Greatest Hits (69) 171(2) [0|0|10]</td><td>121</td></tr>
<tr><td>A Child's Adventure (83) 107(2) [0|0|7]</td><td>102</td></tr>
<tr><td>Faithfull Forever... (66) 147(2) [0|0|2]</td><td>29.1</td></tr>
<tr><td>FAITH, HOPE AND CHARITY ► 2126 Pk:100 [0|0|1]</td><td>288</td></tr>
<tr><td>Faith, Hope And Charity (75) 100(1) [0|0|14]</td><td>288</td></tr>
<tr><td>FALCO ► 785 Pk:3 [1|1|2]</td><td>3057</td></tr>
<tr><td>Falco 3 (86) 3(1) [6|18|27]</td><td>2764</td></tr>
<tr><td>Einzelhaft (83) 64(1) [0|0|13]</td><td>293</td></tr>
<tr><td>Agnetha FALTSKOG ► 2429 Pk:102 [0|0|1]</td><td>180</td></tr>
<tr><td>Wrap Your Arms Around Me (83) 102(1) [0|0|11]</td><td>180</td></tr>
<tr><td>Georgie FAME ► 2949 Pk:137 [0|0|2]</td><td>72</td></tr>
<tr><td>Yeh Yeh (65) 137(1) [0|0|3]</td><td>40.5</td></tr>
<tr><td>The Ballad Of Bonnie And Clyde (68) 185(1) [0|0|4]</td><td>31.6</td></tr>
<tr><td>FAMILY ► 2820 Pk:177 [0|0|2]</td><td>92</td></tr>
<tr><td>Fearless (72) 177(1) [0|0|7]</td><td>56.3</td></tr>
<tr><td>Bandstand (72) 183(1) [0|0|5]</td><td>35.7</td></tr>
<tr><td>The FAMILY ► 1836 Pk:62 [0|0|1]</td><td>452</td></tr>
<tr><td>The Family (85) 62(2) [0|0|22]</td><td>452</td></tr>
<tr><td>FANNY ► 2348 Pk:135 [0|0|2]</td><td>200</td></tr>
<tr><td>Charity Ball (71) 150(1) [0|0|7]</td><td>104</td></tr>
<tr><td>Fanny Hill (72) 135(1) [0|0|6]</td><td>95.8</td></tr>
<tr><td>FANTASTIC FOUR ► 2039 Pk:99 [0|0|1]</td><td>333</td></tr>
<tr><td>Alvin Stone (The Birth & Death Of A Gangster) (75) 99(2) [0|0|16]</td><td>333</td></tr>
<tr><td>FANTASY ► 3383 Pk:194 [0|0|1]</td><td>20</td></tr>
<tr><td>Fantasy (70) 194(2) [0|0|3]</td><td>20.4</td></tr>
<tr><td>Donna FARGO ► 1114 Pk:47 [0|0|2]</td><td>1564</td></tr>
<tr><td>The Happiest Girl In The Whole U.S.A. (72) 47(2) [0|0|43]</td><td>1333</td></tr>
<tr><td>My Second Album (73) 104(2) [0|0|11]</td><td>231</td></tr>
<tr><td>FARQUAHR ► 3400 Pk:195 [0|0|1]</td><td>19</td></tr>
<tr><td>Farquahr (70) 195(1) [0|0|3]</td><td>19.3</td></tr>
<tr><td>Joe FARRELL ► 2892 Pk:100 [0|0|1]</td><td>81</td></tr>
<tr><td>Benson & Farrell (76)-George Benson & Joe Farrell [A] 100(1) [0|0|8]</td><td>81.2</td></tr>
<tr><td>FARRENHEIT ► 3174 Pk:179 [0|0|1]</td><td>44</td></tr>
<tr><td>Farrenheit (87) 179(1) [0|0|7]</td><td>43.8</td></tr>
<tr><td>FASTER PUSSYCAT ► 1116 Pk:48 [0|0|2]</td><td>1561</td></tr>
<tr><td>Wake Me When It's Over (89) 48(1) [0|0|41]</td><td>1099</td></tr>
<tr><td>Faster Pussycat (87) 97(2) [0|0|35]</td><td>463</td></tr>
<tr><td>FASTWAY ► 1036 Pk:31 [0|1|4]</td><td>1806</td></tr>
<tr><td>Fastway (83) 31(1) [0|6|32]</td><td>1213</td></tr>
<tr><td>All Fired Up (84) 59(2) [0|0|14]</td><td>396</td></tr>
<tr><td>On Target (89) 135(2) [0|0|10]</td><td>110</td></tr>
<tr><td>Trick Or Treat (Soundtrack) (86) 156(1) [0|0|12]</td><td>87.1</td></tr>
<tr><td>FATBACK ► 949 Pk:44 [0|0|8]</td><td>2135</td></tr>
<tr><td>Hot Box (80) 44(1) [0|0|27]</td><td>946</td></tr>
<tr><td>Fired Up 'N' Kickin' (78) 73(1) [0|0|12]</td><td>365</td></tr>
<tr><td>Fatback XII (79) 89(1) [0|0|12]</td><td>245</td></tr>
<tr><td>Tasty Jam (81) 102(1) [0|0|8]</td><td>203</td></tr>
<tr><td>14 Karat (80) 91(1) [0|0|7]</td><td>171</td></tr>
<tr><td>Raising Hell (76)-The Fatback Band 158(1) [0|0|8]</td><td>104</td></tr>
<tr><td>Gigolo (82) 148(1) [0|0|4]</td><td>56.6</td></tr>
<tr><td>Night Fever (76)-The Fatback Band 182(1) [0|0|5]</td><td>44.4</td></tr>
<tr><td>FAT BOYS ► 485 Pk:8 [1|2|7]</td><td>6422</td></tr>
<tr><td>Crushin' (87) 8(3) [4|21|49]</td><td>3405</td></tr>
<tr><td>Coming Back Hard Again (88) 33(2) [0|5|24]</td><td>988</td></tr>
<tr><td>Fat Boys (85) 48(2) [0|0|40]</td><td>824</td></tr>
<tr><td>The Fat Boys Are Back! (85) 63(2) [0|0|33]</td><td>607</td></tr>
<tr><td>Big & Beautiful (86) 62(2) [0|0|19]</td><td>440</td></tr>
<tr><td>The Best Part Of The Fat Boys (87) 108(2) [0|0|10]</td><td>136</td></tr>
<tr><td>On And On (89) 175(1) [0|0|3]</td><td>21.2</td></tr>
<tr><td>FATES WARNING ► 2041 Pk:111 [0|0|3]</td><td>333</td></tr>
<tr><td>No Exit (88) 111(3) [0|0|13]</td><td>209</td></tr>
<tr><td>Perfect Symmetry (89) 141(1) [0|0|9]</td><td>103</td></tr>
<tr><td>Awaken The Guardian (87) 191(3) [0|0|4]</td><td>21.1</td></tr>
<tr><td>FAT MATTRESS ► 2404 Pk:134 [0|0|1]</td><td>185</td></tr>
<tr><td>Fat Mattress (69) 134(2) [0|0|10]</td><td>185</td></tr>
<tr><td>FAZE-O ► 1825 Pk:98 [0|0|2]</td><td>463</td></tr>
<tr><td>Riding High (78) 98(1) [0|0|17]</td><td>412</td></tr>
<tr><td>Good Thang (78) 145(1) [0|0|3]</td><td>50.6</td></tr>
<tr><td>The FEELIES ► 3218 Pk:173 [0|0|1]</td><td>37</td></tr>
<tr><td>Only Life (88) 173(2) [0|0|5]</td><td>37.5</td></tr>
<tr><td>Don FELDER ► 3099 Pk:178 [0|0|1]</td><td>52</td></tr>
<tr><td>Airborne (83) 178(1) [0|0|8]</td><td>52.0</td></tr>
<tr><td>Wilton FELDER ► 1692 Pk:81 [0|0|3]</td><td>590</td></tr>
<tr><td>Secrets (85) 81(1) [0|0|16]</td><td>316</td></tr>
</table>

Act ▶ Highest Peak [Top10s|Top40s|Total]
Title (Yr) Peak(Wk) [T10 Wk|T40Wk|TotalWk] — Score

Wilton FELDER ▶ *Continued*
- Inherit The Wind (80) 142(1) [0|0|13] — 138
- We All Have A Star (78) 173(2) [0|0|14] — 136

José FELICIANO ▶ 260 Pk:2 [1|4|10] — 13682
- Feliciano! (68)- 2(3) [19|26|59] — 7730
- Feliciano/10 To 23 (69) 16(2) [0|13|36] — 2654
- Souled (68) 24(1) [0|4|19] — 1238
- Alive Alive-O! (69)- 29(1) [0|4|14] — 775
- Fireworks (70)-Jose Feliciano 57(1) [0|0|20] — 693
- Encore! José Feliciano's Finest Performances (71) 92(2) [0|0|10] — 244
- And The Feeling's Good (74) 136(2) [0|0|7] — 119
- That The Spirit Needs (71) 173(1) [0|0|9] — 94.7
- Compartments (73)- 156(1) [0|0|8] — 84.5
- Just Wanna Rock 'n' Roll (75) 165(1) [0|0|4] — 49.1

FELONY ▶ 3301 Pk:185 [0|0|1] — 28
- The Fanatic (83) 185(2) [0|0|5] — 28.1

FEMME FATALE ▶ 3020 Pk:141 [0|0|1] — 63
- Femme Fatale (89) 141(2) [0|0|5] — 63.0

Freddy FENDER ▶ 729 Pk:20 [0|1|5] — 3446
- Before The Next Teardrop Falls (75) 20(1) [0|11|43] — 2213
- Are You Ready For Freddy (75) 41(2) [0|0|18] — 720
- Rock 'N' Country (76) 59(1) [0|0|11] — 385
- The Best Of Freddy Fender (77) 155(2) [0|0|7] — 92.1
- If You're Ever In Texas (76) 170(2) [0|0|3] — 36.9

Rick FENN ▶ 3371 Pk:154 [0|0|1] — 22
- Profiles (85)-Nick Mason & Rick Fenn [A] 154(2) [0|0|5] — 21.8

Jay FERGUSON ▶ 1588 Pk:72 [0|0|3] — 692
- Thunder Island (78) 72(1) [0|0|12] — 338
- Real Life Ain't This Way (79) 86(2) [0|0|16] — 315
- White Noise (82) 178(3) [0|0|5] — 38.8

Maynard FERGUSON ▶ 869 Pk:22 [0|1|8] — 2538
- Conquistador (77) 22(2) [0|7|26] — 1657
- Primal Scream (76) 75(1) [0|0|14] — 328
- Carnival (78) 113(1) [0|0|9] — 205
- M.F. Horn/3 (73) 128(1) [0|0|8] — 145
- New Vintage (77) 124(2) [0|0|8] — 138
- Hollywood (82) 185(1) [0|0|4] — 26.1
- Hot (79) 188(2) [0|0|3] — 22.1
- It's My Time (80) 188(2) [0|0|2] — 15.5

FERRANTE & TEICHER ▶ 606 Pk:35 [0|1|22] — 4679
- Midnight Cowboy (69) 61(1) [0|0|26] — 748
- The People's Choice (64) 35(3) [0|6|20] — 704
- 10th Anniversary - Golden Piano Hits (69) 93(1) [0|0|27] — 619
- You Asked For It! (66) 57(1) [0|0|21] — 565
- Concert For Lovers (63) 63(1) [0|0|17] — 426
- Only The Best (65) 49(1) [0|0|13] — 408
- Getting Together (70) 97(1) [0|0|10] — 224
- The Best Of Ferrante & Teicher (71) 134(1) [0|0|9] — 147
- My Fair Lady (64) 145(2) [0|0|9] — 102
- 50 Fabulous Piano Favorites (64) 128(2) [0|0|7] — 102
- For Lovers Of All Ages (66) 119(2) [0|0|5] — 92.8
- A Man And A Woman & Other Motion Picture Themes (67) 133(2) [0|0|5] — 83.5
- Springtime (65) 130(1) [0|0|6] — 81.9
- The Ferrante And Teicher Concert (66) 134(2) [0|0|5] — 69.6

Act ▶ Highest Peak [Top10s|Top40s|Total]
Title (Yr) Peak(Wk) [T10 Wk|T40Wk|TotalWk] — Score

- The Enchanted World Of Ferrante & Teicher (64) 128(1) [0|0|5] — 65.1
- By Popular Demand (65) 120(1) [0|0|4] — 58.4
- It's Too Late (71) 172(1) [0|0|5] — 55.2
- The Music Lovers (71) 172(1) [0|0|4] — 43.3
- A Bouquet Of Hits (68) 198(1) [0|0|4] — 25.5
- Fiddler On The Roof (72) 186(1) [0|0|3] — 21.9
- Our Golden Favorites (67) 177(2) [0|0|2] — 18.7
- Love Is A Soft Touch (70) 188(2) [0|0|2] — 16.9

Bryan FERRY ▶ 1065 Pk:63 [0|0|5] — 1708
- Bete Noire (87) 63(2) [0|0|31] — 907
- Boys And Girls (85) 63(2) [0|0|25] — 574
- In Your Mind (77) 126(1) [0|0|5] — 103
- Let's Stick Together (76) 160(1) [0|0|5] — 63.0
- The Bride Stripped Bare (78) 159(2) [0|0|5] — 60.5

FESTIVAL ▶ 1569 Pk:50 [0|0|1] — 711
- Evita (80) 50(1) [0|0|18] — 711

FETCHIN BONES ▶ 3016 Pk:175 [0|0|1] — 63
- Monster (89) 175(1) [0|0|8] — 63.4

FEVER TREE ▶ 1604 Pk:83 [0|0|3] — 675
- Another Time, Another Place (68) 83(3) [0|0|13] — 344
- Fever Tree (68) 156(1) [0|0|21] — 188
- Creation (70) 97(2) [0|0|6] — 143

Sally FIELD ▶ 3217 Pk:172 [0|0|1] — 38
- The Flying Nun (67) 172(1) [0|0|4] — 37.7

Richard "Dimples" FIELDS ▶ 1238 Pk:33 [0|1|2] — 1258
- Dimples (81) 33(2) [0|4|17] — 748
- Mr. Look So Good! (82) 63(1) [0|0|20] — 510

W.C. FIELDS ▶ 958 Pk:30 [0|1|2] — 2101
- The Original Voice Tracks From His Greatest Movies (69) 30(1) [0|11|29] — 2088
- W. C. Fields On Radio (69) 197(2) [0|0|2] — 13.4

FIFTH ANGEL ▶ 2375 Pk:117 [0|0|1] — 192
- Fifth Angel (88) 117(2) [0|0|13] — 192

5TH DIMENSION ▶ 114 Pk:2 [3|8|14] — 27257
- The Age Of Aquarius (69) 2(2) [9|30|72] — 8929
- The 5th Dimension/Greatest Hits (70) 5(2) [5|18|55] — 4338
- Up, Up And Away (67) 8(2) [3|11|83] — 3162
- Portrait (70) 20(2) [0|16|50] — 2967
- Greatest Hits On Earth (72) 14(2) [0|10|24] — 1753
- Love's Lines, Angles And Rhymes (71) 17(1) [0|8|23] — 1742
- Stoned Soul Picnic (68) 21(2) [0|8|21] — 1343
- The 5th Dimension/Live!! (71) 32(2) [0|4|18] — 993
- Individually & Collectively (72) 58(2) [0|0|32] — 848
- The Magic Garden (68) 105(2) [0|0|31] — 390
- The July 5th Album (70) 63(1) [0|0|8] — 262
- Living Together, Growing Together (73) 108(1) [0|0|11] — 215
- Reflections (71) 112(2) [0|0|7] — 163
- Earthbound (75) 136(1) [0|0|8] — 152

FINE YOUNG CANNIBALS ▶ 313 Pk:1 [1|1|2] — 10909
- The Raw & The Cooked (89) 1(7) [27|40|63] — 10227
- Fine Young Cannibals (86) 49(1) [0|0|28] — 682

Tim FINN ▶ 3155 Pk:161 [0|0|1] — 46
- Escapade (83) 161(1) [0|0|5] — 45.8

Albert FINNEY ▶ 3536 Pk:199 [0|0|1] — 6
- Albert Finney's Album (77) 199(1) [0|0|1] — 5.5

FIONA ▶ 1753 Pk:71 [0|0|2] — 519
- Fiona (85) 71(1) [0|0|18] — 354
- Heart Like A Gun (89) 150(1) [0|0|16] — 165

Act ▶ Highest Peak [Top10s|Top40s|Total]
Title (Yr) Peak(Wk) [T10 Wk|T40Wk|TotalWk] — Score

Elisa FIORILLO ▶ 3014 Pk:163 [0|0|1] — 64
- Elisa Fiorillo (88) 163(2) [0|0|8] — 63.7

FIREBALLET ▶ 2800 Pk:151 [0|0|1] — 97
- Night On Bald Mountain (75) 151(1) [0|0|8] — 97.1

The FIREBALLS/ Jimmy GILMER And The FIREBALLS ▶ 1655 Pk:26 [0|1|1] — 617
- Sugar Shack (63)-Jimmy Gilmer And The Fireballs 26(1) [0|5|14] — 617

FIREFALL ▶ 470 Pk:27 [0|3|7] — 6727
- Firefall (76) 28(2) [0|14|67] — 3446
- Elan (78) 27(2) [0|7|24] — 1347
- Luna Sea (77) 27(1) [0|5|28] — 1275
- Undertow (80) 68(2) [0|0|15] — 370
- Clouds Across The Sun (81) 102(2) [0|0|13] — 250
- The Best Of Firefall (81) 186(1) [0|0|4] — 26.9
- Break Of Dawn (83) 199(1) [0|0|3] — 11.8

FIRESIGN THEATRE ▶ 1153 Pk:50 [0|0|8] — 1457
- I Think We're All Bozos On This Bus (71) 50(1) [0|0|14] — 623
- Dear Friends (72) 75(2) [0|0|11] — 316
- Don't Crush That Dwarf, Hand Me The Pliers (70) 106(2) [0|0|10] — 194
- Not Insane Or Anything You Want To (72) 115(2) [0|0|8] — 152
- Everything You Know Is Wrong (74) 147(1) [0|0|6] — 93.8
- The Tale Of The Giant Rat Of Sumatra (74) 172(1) [0|0|5] — 47.4
- Just Folks...a Firesign Chat (77) 184(1) [0|0|2] — 17.0
- How Can You Be In Two Places At Once When You're Not Anywhere At All (69) 195(1) [0|0|2] — 13.1

The FIRM ▶ 815 Pk:17 [0|2|2] — 2841
- The Firm (85) 17(2) [0|16|33] — 1884
- Mean Business (86) 22(3) [0|7|19] — 957

FIRST CHOICE ▶ 1801 Pk:103 [0|0|4] — 485
- Delusions (77) 103(2) [0|0|8] — 175
- Hold Your Horses (79) 135(1) [0|0|12] — 173
- The Player (74) 143(2) [0|0|7] — 108
- Armed And Extremely Dangerous (73) 184(1) [0|0|4] — 28.3

FISHBONE ▶ 3018 Pk:153 [0|0|1] — 63
- Truth And Soul (88) 153(1) [0|0|9] — 63.3

Eddie FISHER ▶ 1726 Pk:52 [0|0|3] — 556
- Eddie Fisher Today! (65) 52(1) [0|0|10] — 296
- Games That Lovers Play (66) 72(1) [0|0|10] — 243
- People Like You (67) 193(2) [0|0|3] — 17.7

Ella FITZGERALD ▶ 2014 Pk:69 [0|0|5] — 345
- Ella And Basie! (63)-Ella & Basie [A] 69(1) [0|0|20] — 212
- Ella Fitzgerald Sings The George And Ira Gershwin Song Books (64) 111(2) [0|0|5] — 76.9
- Hello, Dolly! (64) 146(1) [0|0|2] — 23.3
- Brighten The Corner (67) 172(1) [0|0|2] — 19.1
- Ella (69) 196(2) [0|0|2] — 13.9

FIVE AMERICANS ▶ 2229 Pk:121 [0|0|2] — 242
- Western Union (67) 121(1) [0|0|10] — 173
- I See The Light (66) 136(1) [0|0|5] — 69.5

FIVE MAN ELECTRICAL BAND ▶ 2599 Pk:148 [0|0|2] — 135
- Good-Byes & Butterflies (71) 148(1) [0|0|9] — 124
- Coming Of Age (72) 199(2) [0|0|2] — 10.8

5 SPECIAL ▶ 2345 Pk:118 [0|0|1] — 201
- Five Special (79) 118(3) [0|0|11] — 201

FIVE STAIRSTEPS ▶ 1566 Pk:83 [0|0|6] — 717
- The Invisible Man's Band (80)-The Invisible Man's Band 90(1) [0|0|14] — 346
- Stairsteps (70)-Stairsteps 83(1) [0|0|12] — 268

Act ► Highest Peak [Top10s|Top40s|Total]
Title (Yr) Peak(Wk) [T10 Wk|T40Wk|TotalWk] — **Score**

FIVE STAIRSTEPS ► *Continued*

The Five Stairsteps (67) 139(1) [0|0|4] — 62.7
Our Family Portrait (68)-The Five Stairsteps & Cubie 195(1) [0|0|3] — 14.9
Love's Happening (69)-The Five Stairsteps & Cubie 198(2) [0|0|2] — 13.1
Step By Step By Step (70)-Stairsteps 199(2) [0|0|2] — 11.6

FIVE STAR ► 1166 Pk:57 [0|0|2] — 1419

Luxury Of Life (85) 57(2) [0|0|47] — 1049
Silk And Steel (86) 80(2) [0|0|25] — 369

The FIXX ► 399 Pk:8 [1|3|6] — 8231

Reach The Beach (83) 8(2) [10|28|54] — 4454
Phantoms (84) 19(3) [0|10|29] — 1488
Walkabout (86) 30(2) [0|8|21] — 943
Shuttered Room (82) 106(1) [0|0|51] — 797
Calm Animals (89) 72(2) [0|0|18] — 446
React (87) 110(2) [0|0|7] — 103

Roberta FLACK ► 105 Pk:1 [4|8|12] — 28482

First Take (70) 1(5) [14|26|54] — 7872
Chapter Two (70) 33(1) [0|13|82] — 4728
Killing Me Softly (73) 3(2) [7|14|53] — 3825
Quiet Fire (71) 18(2) [0|21|48] — 3375
Blue Lights In The Basement (78) 8(1) [3|17|32] — 2852
Roberta Flack & Donny Hathaway (72)-Roberta Flack & Donny Hathaway [A] 3(2) [8|21|39] — 2211
Roberta Flack Featuring Donny Hathaway (80)-Roberta Flack Featuring Donny Hathaway 25(2) [0|10|24] — 1419
Feel Like Makin' Love (75) 24(2) [0|5|26] — 1242
I'm The One (82) 59(2) [0|0|21] — 535
Roberta Flack (78) 74(1) [0|0|10] — 235
Bustin' Loose (81) 161(1) [0|0|11] — 119
Oasis (89) 159(1) [0|0|8] — 69.2

Roberta FLACK & Peabo BRYSON ► 903 Pk:25 [0|1|2] — 2374

Born To Love (83)-Peabo Bryson & Roberta Flack 25(1) [0|14|42] — 1749
Live & More (80) 52(1) [0|0|19] — 626

Fannie FLAGG ► 3360 Pk:183 [0|0|1] — 23

Rally 'Round The Flagg (67) 183(1) [0|0|3] — 22.8

The FLAME ► 2900 Pk:147 [0|0|1] — 80

Queen Of The Neighborhood (77) 147(1) [0|0|5] — 80.0

FLAMING EMBER ► 3363 Pk:188 [0|0|1] — 23

Westbound #9 (70) 188(2) [0|0|3] — 22.5

FLAMIN' GROOVIES ► 2786 Pk:142 [0|0|1] — 100

Shake Some Action (76) 142(1) [0|0|7] — 100

FLASH ► 1051 Pk:33 [0|1|3] — 1743

Flash (72) 33(2) [0|5|29] — 1389
Flash In The Can (72) 121(1) [0|0|13] — 228
Out Of Our Hands (73) 135(1) [0|0|8] — 126

FLASH & THE PAN ► 1802 Pk:80 [0|0|2] — 484

Flash And The Pan (79)-Flash And The Pan 80(2) [0|0|16] — 419
Lights In The Night (80)-Flash And The Pan 159(2) [0|0|6] — 64.4

FLATT & SCRUGGS ► 2381 Pk:134 [0|0|4] — 191

Flatt And Scruggs At Carnegie Hall! (63) 134(1) [0|0|6] — 85.9
Original Theme From Bonnie & Clyde (68) 161(1) [0|0|4] — 46.6
The Story Of Bonnie & Clyde (68) 187(1) [0|0|5] — 34.8
Changin' Times Featuring Foggy Mountain Breakdown (68) 194(2) [0|0|4] — 23.3

Mick FLEETWOOD ► 1704 Pk:43 [0|0|1] — 581

The Visitor (81) 43(2) [0|0|14] — 581

Act ► Highest Peak [Top10s|Top40s|Total]
Title (Yr) Peak(Wk) [T10 Wk|T40Wk|TotalWk] — **Score**

FLEETWOOD MAC ► 12 Pk:1 [5|8|19] — 70927

Rumours (77) 1(31) [52|60|134] — 27526
Fleetwood Mac (75) 1(1) [37|68|148] — 18198
Mirage (82) 1(5) [18|21|45] — 6695
Tango In The Night (87) 7(3) [6|44|57] — 5973
Tusk (79) 4(3) [16|22|37] — 4913
Greatest Hits (88) 14(1) [0|12|26] — 1681
Fleetwood Mac Live (80) 14(3) [0|8|18] — 1524
Heroes Are Hard To Find (74) 34(1) [0|2|26] — 940
Mystery To Me (73) 67(1) [0|0|26] — 629
Bare Trees (72) 70(2) [0|0|27] — 601
Penguin (73) 49(1) [0|0|13] — 470
Kiln House (70) 69(2) [0|0|14] — 442
Then Play On (69) 109(1) [0|0|22] — 385
Fleetwood Mac In Chicago (71) 118(3) [0|0|22] — 355
Future Games (71) 91(2) [0|0|12] — 270
Vintage Years (75) 138(2) [0|0|9] — 128
Black Magic Woman (71) 143(2) [0|0|7] — 126
English Rose (69) 184(1) [0|0|6] — 54.0
Fleetwood Mac (1968) (68) 198(1) [0|0|3] — 17.0

FLESH FOR LULU ► 1892 Pk:89 [0|0|1] — 412

Long Live The New Flesh (87) 89(1) [0|0|24] — 412

The FLESHTONES ► 3175 Pk:174 [0|0|1] — 44

Roman Gods (82) 174(3) [0|0|5] — 43.8

The FLOATERS ► 868 Pk:10 [1|1|2] — 2539

Floaters (77) 10(2) [2|13|25] — 2403
Magic (78) 131(2) [0|0|8] — 136

The FLOCK ► 1359 Pk:48 [0|0|2] — 1034

The Flock (69) 48(2) [0|0|20] — 833
Dinosaur Swamps (70) 96(2) [0|0|9] — 200

A FLOCK OF SEAGULLS ► 579 Pk:10 [1|2|3] — 5042

A Flock Of Seagulls (82) 10(3) [3|25|50] — 3417
Listen (83) 16(2) [0|11|23] — 1383
The Story Of A Young Heart (84) 66(1) [0|0|10] — 242

FLOTSAM AND JETSAM ► 2862 Pk:143 [0|0|1] — 86

No Place For Disgrace (88) 143(2) [0|0|8] — 86.1

King FLOYD ► 2785 Pk:130 [0|0|1] — 100

King Floyd (71) 130(1) [0|0|5] — 100

FLYING BURRITO BROTHERS ► 1932 Pk:138 [0|0|6] — 386

The Gilded Palace Of Sin (69) 164(1) [0|0|7] — 91.7
The Flying Burrito Bros. (71) 176(1) [0|0|9] — 76.5
Close Up The Honky Tonks (74) 158(1) [0|0|5] — 65.1
Last Of The Red Hot Burritos (72) 171(1) [0|0|7] — 64.4
Flying Again (75) 138(1) [0|0|3] — 57.5
Sleepless Nights (76)-Gram Parsons And The Flying Burrito Brothers 185(1) [0|0|4] — 31.2

FLYING LIZARDS ► 2463 Pk:99 [0|0|1] — 170

The Flying Lizards (80) 99(1) [0|0|8] — 170

FLYING MACHINE ► 3021 Pk:179 [0|0|1] — 63

The Flying Machine (69) 179(2) [0|0|7] — 63.0

FOCUS ► 533 Pk:8 [1|2|8] — 5588

Moving Waves (73) 8(2) [4|21|38] — 3393
Focus 3 (73) 35(1) [0|4|22] — 1031
Hamburger Concerto (74) 66(2) [0|0|19] — 525
In And Out Of Focus (73) 104(1) [0|0|9] — 176
Dutch Masters - A Selection Of Their Finest Recordings 1969-1973 (75) 120(2) [0|0|9] — 170
Live At The Rainbow (73) 132(2) [0|0|10] — 138
Mother Focus (75) 152(2) [0|0|6] — 85.3
Ship Of Memories (77) 163(1) [0|0|7] — 69.4

Dan FOGELBERG ► 134 Pk:3 [3|9|10] — 24135

The Innocent Age (81) 6(6) [8|31|62] — 5782
Phoenix (79) 3(2) [10|27|39] — 5420
Nether Lands (77) 13(1) [0|12|39] — 2848
Souvenirs (74) 17(2) [0|11|27] — 2116
Dan Fogelberg/Greatest Hits (82) 15(4) [0|12|35] — 2056
Twin Sons Of Different Mothers (78)-Dan Fogelberg/ Tim Weisberg [A] 8(3) [5|13|35] — 1752
Windows And Walls (84) 15(3) [0|10|27] — 1593
Captured Angel (75) 23(1) [0|6|19] — 1128
High Country Snows (85) 30(2) [0|5|23] — 858
Exiles (87) 48(3) [0|0|19] — 581

John FOGERTY ► 455 Pk:1 [1|2|4] — 7021

Centerfield (85) 1(1) [15|28|51] — 5442
Eye Of The Zombie (86) 26(2) [0|6|19] — 814
The Blue Ridge Rangers (73)-The Blue Ridge Rangers 47(1) [0|0|15] — 546
John Fogerty (75) 78(1) [0|0|7] — 219

Tom FOGERTY ► 3138 Pk:180 [0|0|1] — 48

Tom Fogerty (72) 180(2) [0|0|6] — 47.6

FOGHAT ► 314 Pk:11 [0|7|13] — 10900

Fool For The City (75) 23(2) [0|7|52] — 2711
Foghat Live (77) 11(1) [0|9|29] — 1928
Stone Blue (78) 25(2) [0|7|23] — 1242
Energized (74) 34(1) [0|3|30] — 1235
Night Shift (76) 36(2) [0|2|21] — 935
Rock & Roll Outlaws (74) 40(2) [0|2|19] — 817
Boogie Motel (79) 35(1) [0|3|21] — 763
Foghat (II) (73) 67(1) [0|0|19] — 506
Foghat (72) 127(2) [0|0|22] — 275
Girls To Chat & Boys To Bounce (81) 92(1) [0|0|9] — 226
Tight Shoes (80) 106(1) [0|0|10] — 204
In The Mood For Something Rude (82) 162(1) [0|0|5] — 47.0
Zig-Zag Walk (83) 192(1) [0|0|2] — 11.0

Ellen FOLEY ► 2504 Pk:137 [0|0|2] — 158

Nightout (79) 137(1) [0|0|6] — 94.5
Spirit Of St. Louis (81) 152(2) [0|0|4] — 63.8

The FOLKSWINGERS ► 3039 Pk:132 [0|0|1] — 60

12 String Guitar! (63) 132(1) [0|0|4] — 60.4

Jane FONDA ► 540 Pk:15 [0|1|3] — 5515

Jane Fonda's Workout Record (82) 15(4) [0|27|120] — 5318
Jane Fonda's Workout Record For Pregnancy, Birth And Recovery (83) 115(1) [0|0|7] — 101
Jane Fonda's Workout Record New And Improved (84) 135(2) [0|0|10] — 96.1

Frank FONTAINE ► 1374 Pk:44 [0|0|2] — 1004

Sings Like Crazy (63) 44(2) [0|0|25] — 792
How Sweet It Is (64) 92(1) [0|0|12] — 212

The FOOLS ► 2572 Pk:151 [0|0|2] — 143

Sold Out (80) 151(1) [0|0|8] — 93.2
Heavy Mental (81) 158(1) [0|0|4] — 49.5

FOOLS GOLD ► 2160 Pk:100 [0|0|1] — 274

Fools Gold (76) 100(1) [0|0|13] — 274

Steve FORBERT ► 962 Pk:20 [0|1|4] — 2074

Jackrabbit Slim (79) 20(1) [0|6|26] — 1412
Alive On Arrival (79) 82(2) [0|0|15] — 325
Little Stevie Orbit (80) 70(1) [0|0|9] — 285
Steve Forbert (82) 159(2) [0|0|6] — 52.3

FORCE M.D.'S ► 1459 Pk:67 [0|0|3] — 877

Chillin' (86) 69(1) [0|0|25] — 509
Touch And Go (87) 67(2) [0|0|16] — 343
Love Letters (84) 185(3) [0|0|4] — 24.9

Act ▶ Highest Peak [Top10s|Top40s|Total] Title (Yr) Peak(Wk) [T10 Wk|T40Wk|TotalWk]	Score
Lita FORD ▶ 703 Pk:29 [0|1|2]	**3642**
Lita (88) 29(4) [0|23|62]	3280
Dancin' On The Edge (84) 66(2) [0|0|16]	361
Robben FORD ▶ 2421 Pk:120 [0|0|1]	**182**
Talk To Your Daughter (88) 120(2) [0|0|13]	182
"Tennessee" Ernie FORD ▶ 3459 Pk:192 [0|0|1]	**13**
America The Beautiful (70) 192(1) [0|0|2]	13.4
Julia FORDHAM ▶ 2073 Pk:118 [0|0|1]	**315**
Julia Fordham (88) 118(2) [0|0|25]	315
FOREIGNER ▶ 37 Pk:1 [6|7|7]	**47775**
4 (81) 1(10) [34|52|81]	15590
Double Vision (78) 3(8) [27|37|88]	10010
Foreigner (77) 4(5) [18|43|113]	9882
Head Games (79) 5(3) [6|22|41]	4255
Agent Provocateur (85) 4(3) [12|24|45]	3946
Inside Information (87) 15(1) [0|14|37]	2306
Records (82) 10(4) [4|12|25]	1785
FOREVER MORE ▶ 3342 Pk:180 [0|0|1]	**25**
Yours Forever More (70) 180(1) [0|0|3]	24.9
The FORTUNES ▶ 2586 Pk:134 [0|0|1]	**138**
Here Comes That Rainy Day Feeling Again (71) 134(2) [0|0|10]	138
David FOSTER ▶ 2556 Pk:111 [0|0|2]	**147**
The Symphony Sessions (88) 111(2) [0|0|8]	134
David Foster (86) 195(2) [0|0|3]	13.2
FOSTER & LLOYD ▶ 3044 Pk:142 [0|0|1]	**60**
Faster & Llouder (89) 142(1) [0|0|6]	60.0
FOTOMAKER ▶ 2163 Pk:88 [0|0|1]	**272**
Fotomaker (78) 88(2) [0|0|13]	272
The FOUNDATIONS ▶ 2198 Pk:92 [0|0|1]	**255**
Build Me Up Buttercup (69) 92(1) [0|0|11]	255
Pete FOUNTAIN ▶ 893 Pk:48 [0|0|8]	**2414**
Licorice Stick (64) 48(1) [0|0|44]	1260
New Orleans At Midnight (64) 53(1) [0|0|14]	371
Mr. Stick Man (65) 64(1) [0|0|14]	314
South Rampart Street Parade (63) 91(1) [0|0|9]	158
A Taste Of Honey (66) 100(1) [0|0|8]	148
Pete's Place (65) 121(1) [0|0|7]	101
Those Were The Days (69) 186(2) [0|0|6]	54.0
For The First Time (68)-Brenda & Pete [A] 187(2) [0|0|2]	8.1
4 BY FOUR ▶ 2984 Pk:141 [0|0|1]	**68**
4 By Four (87) 141(2) [0|0|7]	67.6
FOUR JACKS And A JILL ▶ 2945 Pk:155 [0|0|1]	**73**
Master Jack (68) 155(2) [0|0|6]	72.8
4 SEASONS ▶ 202 Pk:6 [3|8|20]	**17241**
The 4 Seasons' Gold Vault of Hits (65) 10(2) [2|22|88]	3741
Golden Hits Of The 4 Seasons (63) 15(1) [0|12|56]	2218
2nd Vault Of Golden Hits (66) 22(2) [0|10|53]	2127
Rag Doll (64) 7(1) [5|13|26]	1894
Dawn (Go Away) And 11 Other Great Songs (64) 6(2) [5|10|25]	1679
Who Loves You (75) 38(2) [0|2|31]	1408
Edizione D'Oro (The 4 Seasons Gold Edition-29 Gold Hits) (68) 37(1) [0|2|21]	1140
New Gold Hits (67) 37(1) [0|2|25]	689
Four Seasons Story (75) 51(1) [0|0|17]	529
Working My Way Back To You (66) 50(1) [0|0|15]	457
The Genuine Imitation Life Gazette (69) 85(1) [0|0|11]	349
The 4 Seasons Entertain You (65) 77(1) [0|0|13]	251

Act ▶ Highest Peak [Top10s|Top40s|Total] Title (Yr) Peak(Wk) [T10 Wk|T40Wk|TotalWk]	Score
Born To Wander (64) 84(1) [0|0|9]	176
Lookin' Back (66) 107(1) [0|0|9]	168
Big Hits By Burt Bacharach...Hal David...Bob Dylan... (65) 106(1) [0|0|10]	166
Stay & Other Great Hits (64) 100(2) [0|0|5]	87.6
More Golden Hits By The Four Seasons (64) 105(1) [0|0|5]	77.0
Helicon (77) 168(1) [0|0|5]	59.1
The Beatles vs. The Four Seasons (64)-The Beatles/Four Seasons [A] 142(1) [0|0|3]	17.8
Half & Half (70)-Frankie Valli & The 4 Seasons [A] 190(2) [0|0|2]	7.6
FOUR TOPS ▶ 142 Pk:4 [1|8|24]	**22847**
The Four Tops Greatest Hits (67) 4(1) [7|37|73]	5647
Still Waters Run Deep (70) 21(1) [0|14|42]	2937
Four Tops Live! (66) 17(1) [0|18|43]	2605
Four Tops Reach Out (67) 11(4) [0|14|59]	2530
Keeper Of The Castle (72) 33(1) [0|3|31]	1457
Four Tops Second Album (65) 20(2) [0|8|35]	1384
4 Tops On Top (66) 32(2) [0|5|22]	1015
Tonight! (81) 37(1) [0|4|21]	900
Nature Planned It (72) 50(2) [0|0|28]	823
Four Tops (65) 63(2) [0|0|27]	606
Main Street People (73) 66(2) [0|0|14]	385
Yesterday's Dreams (68) 91(1) [0|0|16]	374
4 Tops On Broadway (67) 79(2) [0|0|15]	348
Four Tops Now! (69) 74(1) [0|0|10]	335
Four Tops Greatest Hits, Vol. 2 (71) 106(1) [0|0|10]	255
Live & In Concert (74) 92(1) [0|0|9]	238
Changing Times (70) 109(1) [0|0|12]	211
Meeting Of The Minds (74) 118(1) [0|0|11]	190
The Best Of The 4 Tops (73) 103(1) [0|0|9]	170
Catfish (76) 124(2) [0|0|8]	130
Magic (85) 140(2) [0|0|9]	97.8
Indestructible (88) 149(2) [0|0|7]	71.3
Night Lights Harmony (75) 148(1) [0|0|5]	69.2
Soul Spin (69) 163(1) [0|0|6]	68.2
Kim FOWLEY ▶ 3401 Pk:198 [0|0|1]	**19**
Outrageous (69) 198(1) [0|0|3]	19.2
Samantha FOX ▶ 786 Pk:24 [0|2|3]	**3044**
I Wanna Have Some Fun (88) 37(1) [0|4|34]	1231
Touch Me (86) 24(2) [0|11|28]	1202
Samantha Fox (87) 51(1) [0|0|25]	611
Virgil FOX ▶ 3407 Pk:183 [0|0|1]	**19**
Bach Live At Fillmore East (71) 183(1) [0|0|2]	18.8
Redd FOXX ▶ 1951 Pk:87 [0|0|3]	**377**
You Gotta Wash Your Ass (76) 87(1) [0|0|13]	267
Sanford And Son (72) 155(2) [0|0|8]	93.5
Sanford & Foxx (72) 198(2) [0|0|3]	15.8
FOXY ▶ 753 Pk:12 [0|2|2]	**3240**
Get Off (78) 12(1) [0|12|27]	2286
Hot Numbers (79) 29(1) [0|6|16]	954
Peter FRAMPTON ▶ 96 Pk:1 [2|4|11]	**29896**
Frampton Comes Alive! (76) 1(10) [52|55|97]	20521
I'm In You (77) 2(4) [12|15|32]	4671
Frampton (75) 32(2) [0|3|64]	1990
Where I Should Be (79) 19(2) [0|7|16]	1195
Breaking All The Rules (81) 43(1) [0|0|13]	584
Frampton's Camel (73)-Frampton's Camel 110(1) [0|0|22]	330
Premonition (86) 80(2) [0|0|14]	274
Somethin's Happening (74) 125(1) [0|0|9]	162
When All The Pieces Fit (89) 152(2) [0|0|6]	60.4
The Art Of Control (82) 174(2) [0|0|8]	54.1
Wind Of Change (72) 177(2) [0|0|6]	53.0

Act ▶ Highest Peak [Top10s|Top40s|Total] Title (Yr) Peak(Wk) [T10 Wk|T40Wk|TotalWk]	Score
Sergio FRANCHI ▶ 2651 Pk:97 [0|0|2]	**123**
Live At The Cocoanut Grove (65) 114(1) [0|0|4]	62.5
The Dream Duet (64)-Anna Moffo & Sergio Franchi [A] 97(1) [0|0|7]	60.4
Connie FRANCIS ▶ 1052 Pk:61 [0|0|8]	**1741**
The Very Best Of Connie Francis (63) 68(1) [0|0|23]	482
Connie Francis Sings For Mama (65) 78(1) [0|0|15]	305
Greatest American Waltzes (63) 94(1) [0|0|17]	293
Mala Femmena & Connie's Big Hits From Italy (63) 70(1) [0|0|13]	251
When The Boys Meet The Girls (Soundtrack) (66) 61(1) [0|0|9]	230
Looking For Love (Soundtrack) (64) 122(1) [0|0|9]	127
In The Summer Of His Years (64) 126(1) [0|0|2]	30.0
A New Kind Of Connie... (64) 149(1) [0|0|2]	22.0
FRANKE AND THE KNOCKOUTS ▶ 991 Pk:31 [0|1|2]	**1968**
Franke & The Knockouts (81) 31(1) [0|5|27]	1518
Below The Belt (82) 48(2) [0|0|18]	449
FRANKIE GOES TO HOLLYWOOD ▶ 965 Pk:33 [0|1|2]	**2056**
Welcome To The Pleasure Dome (84) 33(5) [0|14|41]	1841
Liverpool (86) 88(2) [0|0|13]	215
Aretha FRANKLIN ▶ 18 Pk:2 [6|21|36]	**61975**
I Never Loved A Man The Way I Love You (67) 2(3) [17|28|79]	6978
Aretha: Lady Soul (68) 2(2) [16|33|52]	6779
Aretha Live At Fillmore West (71) 7(2) [4|18|34]	4367
Aretha Now (68) 3(2) [8|20|35]	4130
Who's Zoomin' Who? (85) 13(1) [0|35|51]	3951
Aretha Arrives (67) 5(5) [10|18|41]	3756
Young, Gifted And Black (72) 11(2) [0|17|31]	2870
Aretha Franklin: Soul '69 (69) 15(2) [0|12|32]	2593
Aretha's Gold (69) 18(1) [0|11|33]	2486
This Girl's In Love With You (70) 17(2) [0|13|30]	2306
Amazing Grace (72) 7(1) [3|11|23]	2145
Aretha In Paris (68) 13(2) [0|9|20]	2053
Aretha's Greatest Hits (71) 19(2) [0|10|34]	2043
Let Me In Your Life (74) 14(1) [0|11|25]	1918
Sparkle (Soundtrack) (76) 18(3) [0|11|24]	1899
Aretha (II) (86) 32(2) [0|8|39]	1604
Spirit In The Dark (70) 25(2) [0|8|22]	1413
Jump To It (82) 23(4) [0|9|30]	1328
Aretha (80) 47(3) [0|0|30]	1128
Hey Now Hey (The Other Side Of The Sky) (73) 30(2) [0|7|20]	1124
Sweet Passion (77) 49(4) [0|0|19]	826
Love All The Hurt Away (81) 36(2) [0|3|17]	729
Get It Right (83) 36(1) [0|3|18]	621
With Everything I Feel In Me (74) 57(1) [0|0|13]	507
Through The Storm (89) 55(2) [0|0|18]	415
Almighty Fire (78) 63(1) [0|0|11]	341
You (75) 83(1) [0|0|11]	309
One Lord, One Faith, One Baptism (87) 106(3) [0|0|16]	268
Aretha Franklin's Greatest Hits (67) 94(1) [0|0|14]	264
Runnin' Out Of Fools (64) 84(2) [0|0|13]	234
Yeah!!! (65) 101(1) [0|0|8]	143
Ten Years Of Gold (76) 135(1) [0|0|8]	131
In The Beginning/The World Of Aretha Franklin 1960-1967 (72) 160(2) [0|0|9]	104
La Diva (79) 146(1) [0|0|6]	88.6

<table>
<tr><th>Act ▶ Highest Peak [Top10s|Top40s|Total]
Title (Yr) Peak(Wk) [T10 Wk|T40Wk|TotalWk]</th><th>Score</th></tr>
<tr><td>Aretha FRANKLIN ▶ Continued</td><td></td></tr>
<tr><td>Soul Sister (66) 132(1) [0|0|4]</td><td>63.2</td></tr>
<tr><td>Take A Look (67) 173(2) [0|0|8]</td><td>60.1</td></tr>
<tr><td>Erma FRANKLIN ▶ 3480 Pk:199 [0|0|1]</td><td>12</td></tr>
<tr><td>Soul Sister (69) 199(2) [0|0|2]</td><td>12.4</td></tr>
<tr><td>Rodney FRANKLIN ▶ 2157 Pk:104 [0|0|3]</td><td>276</td></tr>
<tr><td>You'll Never Know (80) 104(1) [0|0|13]</td><td>243</td></tr>
<tr><td>Marathon (84) 187(1) [0|0|3]</td><td>18.2</td></tr>
<tr><td>Learning To Love (83) 190(2) [0|0|3]</td><td>14.9</td></tr>
<tr><td>Michael FRANKS ▶ 882 Pk:45 [0|0|9]</td><td>2483</td></tr>
<tr><td>Tiger In The Rain (79) 68(1) [0|0|16]</td><td>511</td></tr>
<tr><td>Objects Of Desire (82) 45(3) [0|0|14]</td><td>488</td></tr>
<tr><td>One Bad Habit (80) 83(1) [0|0|21]</td><td>392</td></tr>
<tr><td>Skin Dive (85) 137(2) [0|0|27]</td><td>300</td></tr>
<tr><td>Burchfield Nines (78) 90(1) [0|0|10]</td><td>220</td></tr>
<tr><td>Art Of Tea (76) 131(2) [0|0|13]</td><td>189</td></tr>
<tr><td>Sleeping Gypsy (77) 119(1) [0|0|9]</td><td>152</td></tr>
<tr><td>Passionfruit (83) 141(1) [0|0|11]</td><td>118</td></tr>
<tr><td>The Camera Never Lies (87) 147(1) [0|0|11]</td><td>113</td></tr>
<tr><td>Linda FRATIANNE ▶ 3076 Pk:174 [0|0|1]</td><td>56</td></tr>
<tr><td>Dance & Exercise With The Hits (82)
174(1) [0|0|7]</td><td>55.7</td></tr>
<tr><td>John FRED & His PLAYBOY BAND ▶ 2706
Pk:154 [0|0|1]</td><td>113</td></tr>
<tr><td>Agnes English (68)-
John Fred And His Playboy Band
154(1) [0|0|10]</td><td>113</td></tr>
<tr><td>FREDDIE And The DREAMERS ▶ 1205
Pk:19 [0|1|3]</td><td>1329</td></tr>
<tr><td>Freddie & The Dreamers (65)
19(2) [0|7|19]</td><td>916</td></tr>
<tr><td>Do The Freddie (65) 85(1) [0|0|12]</td><td>219</td></tr>
<tr><td>I'm Telling You Now (65) 86(2) [0|0|10]</td><td>195</td></tr>
<tr><td>FREE ▶ 730 Pk:17 [0|1|7]</td><td>3428</td></tr>
<tr><td>Fire And Water (70) 17(2) [0|11|27]</td><td>2029</td></tr>
<tr><td>Heartbreaker (73) 47(1) [0|0|16]</td><td>575</td></tr>
<tr><td>Free At Last (72) 69(1) [0|0|16]</td><td>459</td></tr>
<tr><td>Free Live! (71) 89(1) [0|0|8]</td><td>197</td></tr>
<tr><td>Best Of Free (75) 120(2) [0|0|7]</td><td>138</td></tr>
<tr><td>Highway (71) 190(1) [0|0|2]</td><td>16.0</td></tr>
<tr><td>Tons Of Sobs (69) 197(2) [0|0|2]</td><td>13.6</td></tr>
<tr><td>FREE MOVEMENT ▶ 2880 Pk:167 [0|0|1]</td><td>82</td></tr>
<tr><td>I've Found Someone Of My Own (72)
167(1) [0|0|8]</td><td>82.3</td></tr>
<tr><td>Ace FREHLEY ▶ 844 Pk:26 [0|1|3]</td><td>2715</td></tr>
<tr><td>Ace Frehley (78) 26(3) [0|10|23]</td><td>1749</td></tr>
<tr><td>Frehley's Comet (87) 43(2) [0|0|25]</td><td>849</td></tr>
<tr><td>Trouble Walkin' (89) 102(2) [0|0|9]</td><td>116</td></tr>
<tr><td>FREHLEY'S COMET ▶ 1770 Pk:81 [0|0|2]</td><td>503</td></tr>
<tr><td>Second Sighting (88) 81(3) [0|0|13]</td><td>274</td></tr>
<tr><td>Live + 1 (88) 84(2) [0|0|10]</td><td>229</td></tr>
<tr><td>David FREIBERG ▶ 2996 Pk:120 [0|0|1]</td><td>66</td></tr>
<tr><td>Baron Von Tollbooth & The Chrome Nun (73)-
Paul Kantner, Grace Slick & David Freiberg [A]
120(1) [0|0|12]</td><td>66.5</td></tr>
<tr><td>--Fresh, Doug E. See: Doug E. Fresh</td><td></td></tr>
<tr><td>Glenn FREY ▶ 561 Pk:22 [0|3|3]</td><td>5192</td></tr>
<tr><td>The Allnighter (84) 22(2) [0|14|65]</td><td>2635</td></tr>
<tr><td>No Fun Aloud (82) 32(3) [0|11|38]</td><td>1696</td></tr>
<tr><td>Soul Searching (88) 36(2) [0|7|19]</td><td>862</td></tr>
<tr><td>FRIDA ▶ 1487 Pk:41 [0|0|1]</td><td>839</td></tr>
<tr><td>Something's Going On (82) 41(2) [0|0|28]</td><td>839</td></tr>
<tr><td>Dean FRIEDMAN ▶ 3185 Pk:192 [0|0|1]</td><td>43</td></tr>
<tr><td>Dean Friedman (77) 192(2) [0|0|6]</td><td>42.9</td></tr>
<tr><td>Kinky FRIEDMAN ▶ 2671 Pk:132 [0|0|1]</td><td>120</td></tr>
<tr><td>Kinky Friedman (75) 132(1) [0|0|6]</td><td>120</td></tr>
</table>

<table>
<tr><th>Act ▶ Highest Peak [Top10s|Top40s|Total]
Title (Yr) Peak(Wk) [T10 Wk|T40Wk|TotalWk]</th><th>Score</th></tr>
<tr><td>FRIENDS OF DISTINCTION ▶ 924
Pk:35 [0|1|5]</td><td>2243</td></tr>
<tr><td>Grazin' (69) 35(1) [0|3|25]</td><td>1430</td></tr>
<tr><td>Real Friends (70) 68(1) [0|0|21]</td><td>650</td></tr>
<tr><td>Friends & People (71) 166(1) [0|0|7]</td><td>76.9</td></tr>
<tr><td>Highly Distinct (69) 173(1) [0|0|6]</td><td>54.9</td></tr>
<tr><td>Whatever (70) 179(1) [0|0|3]</td><td>30.8</td></tr>
<tr><td>FRIJID PINK ▶ 839 Pk:11 [0|1|2]</td><td>2738</td></tr>
<tr><td>Frijid Pink (70) 11(4) [0|12|30]</td><td>2597</td></tr>
<tr><td>Defrosted (70) 149(1) [0|0|12]</td><td>141</td></tr>
<tr><td>Robert FRIPP ▶ 1675 Pk:79 [0|0|3]</td><td>603</td></tr>
<tr><td>Exposure (79) 79(2) [0|0|14]</td><td>322</td></tr>
<tr><td>The League Of Gentlemen (81) 90(2) [0|0|7]</td><td>169</td></tr>
<tr><td>God Save The Queen/Under Heavy Manners (80)
110(2) [0|0|6]</td><td>112</td></tr>
<tr><td>The FROST ▶ 2209 Pk:148 [0|0|3]</td><td>250</td></tr>
<tr><td>Frost Music (69) 168(1) [0|0|10]</td><td>121</td></tr>
<tr><td>Rock And Roll Music (69) 148(1) [0|0|8]</td><td>118</td></tr>
<tr><td>Through The Eyes Of Love (70) 197(1) [0|0|2]</td><td>11.8</td></tr>
<tr><td>FROZEN GHOST ▶ 2405 Pk:107 [0|0|1]</td><td>185</td></tr>
<tr><td>Frozen Ghost (87) 107(2) [0|0|13]</td><td>185</td></tr>
<tr><td>David FRYE ▶ 867 Pk:19 [0|1|4]</td><td>2542</td></tr>
<tr><td>I Am The President (69) 19(1) [0|8|18]</td><td>1388</td></tr>
<tr><td>Richard Nixon: A Fantasy (73) 45(1) [0|0|15]</td><td>597</td></tr>
<tr><td>Richard Nixon Superstar (71) 60(2) [0|0|13]</td><td>438</td></tr>
<tr><td>Radio Free Nixon (71) 123(1) [0|0|6]</td><td>120</td></tr>
<tr><td>The FUGS ▶ 1621 Pk:95 [0|0|3]</td><td>652</td></tr>
<tr><td>The Fugs (66)-Fugs 95(2) [0|0|26]</td><td>469</td></tr>
<tr><td>It Crawled Into My Hand, Honest (68)-Fugs
167(1) [0|0|10]</td><td>120</td></tr>
<tr><td>The Fugs First Album (66)-Fugs 142(2) [0|0|4]</td><td>62.8</td></tr>
<tr><td>Bobby FULLER Four ▶ 3314 Pk:144 [0|0|1]</td><td>27</td></tr>
<tr><td>The Bobby Fuller Four (66) 144(2) [0|0|2]</td><td>27.0</td></tr>
<tr><td>FULL FORCE ▶ 2011 Pk:126 [0|0|3]</td><td>346</td></tr>
<tr><td>Guess Who's Comin' To The Crib? (87)
126(3) [0|0|11]</td><td>140</td></tr>
<tr><td>Full Force Get Busy 1 Time! (86)
141(3) [0|0|13]</td><td>138</td></tr>
<tr><td>Full Force (86) 160(2) [0|0|8]</td><td>68.4</td></tr>
<tr><td>FUN BOY THREE ▶ 2647 Pk:104 [0|0|1]</td><td>124</td></tr>
<tr><td>Waiting (83) 104(1) [0|0|7]</td><td>124</td></tr>
<tr><td>FUNKADELIC ▶ 585 Pk:16 [0|2|12]</td><td>4948</td></tr>
<tr><td>One Nation Under A Groove (78) 16(1) [0|9|22]</td><td>1631</td></tr>
<tr><td>Uncle Jam Wants You (79) 18(1) [0|6|17]</td><td>986</td></tr>
<tr><td>Maggot Brain (71) 108(1) [0|0|16]</td><td>359</td></tr>
<tr><td>Let's Take It To The Stage (75) 102(1) [0|0|16]</td><td>323</td></tr>
<tr><td>America Eats Its Young (72) 123(2) [0|0|15]</td><td>289</td></tr>
<tr><td>Hardcore Jollies (76) 96(4) [0|0|12]</td><td>287</td></tr>
<tr><td>Funkadelic (70) 126(1) [0|0|17]</td><td>266</td></tr>
<tr><td>Cosmic Slop (73) 112(1) [0|0|13]</td><td>255</td></tr>
<tr><td>Free Your Mind...And Your Ass Will Follow (70)
92(2) [0|0|10]</td><td>205</td></tr>
<tr><td>Tales Of Kidd Funkadelic (76) 103(1) [0|0|10]</td><td>186</td></tr>
<tr><td>The Electric Spanking Of War Babies (81)
105(2) [0|0|4]</td><td>98.7</td></tr>
<tr><td>Standing On The Verge Of Getting It On (74)
163(2) [0|0|5]</td><td>62.7</td></tr>
<tr><td>FUNKADELIC(2) ▶ 3024 Pk:151 [0|0|1]</td><td>63</td></tr>
<tr><td>Connections And Disconnections (81)
151(2) [0|0|4]</td><td>62.7</td></tr>
<tr><td>FUNKY COMMUNICATION COMMITTEE ▶ 3472
Pk:192 [0|0|1]</td><td>13</td></tr>
<tr><td>Baby I Want You (79) 192(1) [0|0|2]</td><td>12.6</td></tr>
<tr><td>Richie FURAY Band ▶ 2500 Pk:130 [0|0|1]</td><td>159</td></tr>
<tr><td>I've Got A Reason (76) 130(1) [0|0|8]</td><td>159</td></tr>
<tr><td>FUSE ONE ▶ 2773 Pk:139 [0|0|1]</td><td>101</td></tr>
<tr><td>Silk (82) 139(1) [0|0|8]</td><td>101</td></tr>
</table>

<table>
<tr><th>Act ▶ Highest Peak [Top10s|Top40s|Total]
Title (Yr) Peak(Wk) [T10 Wk|T40Wk|TotalWk]</th><th>Score</th></tr>
<tr><td>The FUZZ ▶ 3394 Pk:196 [0|0|1]</td><td>20</td></tr>
<tr><td>The Fuzz (71) 196(1) [0|0|3]</td><td>19.9</td></tr>
<tr><td colspan="2">G</td></tr>
<tr><td>Peter GABRIEL ▶ 272 Pk:2 [1|4|8]</td><td>12998</td></tr>
<tr><td>So (86) 2(3) [12|47|93]</td><td>7120</td></tr>
<tr><td>Peter Gabriel (III) (80) 22(2) [0|14|29]</td><td>2135</td></tr>
<tr><td>Peter Gabriel (Security) (82) 28(9) [0|12|31]</td><td>1598</td></tr>
<tr><td>Peter Gabriel (77) 38(2) [0|2|17]</td><td>742</td></tr>
<tr><td>Peter Gabriel/Plays Live (83) 44(1) [0|0|16]</td><td>510</td></tr>
<tr><td>Peter Gabriel (II) (78) 45(2) [0|0|10]</td><td>491</td></tr>
<tr><td>Passion: Music For The Last Temptation Of Christ
(Soundtrack) (89) 60(2) [0|0|14]</td><td>344</td></tr>
<tr><td>Birdy (Soundtrack) (85) 162(1) [0|0|7]</td><td>57.6</td></tr>
<tr><td>Eric GALE ▶ 2291 Pk:148 [0|0|2]</td><td>220</td></tr>
<tr><td>Ginseng Woman (77) 148(1) [0|0|12]</td><td>155</td></tr>
<tr><td>Part Of You (79) 154(1) [0|0|5]</td><td>64.6</td></tr>
<tr><td>Rory GALLAGHER ▶ 1182 Pk:101 [0|0|9]</td><td>1385</td></tr>
<tr><td>Rory Gallagher/Live! (72) 101(1) [0|0|15]</td><td>321</td></tr>
<tr><td>Photo-Finish (78) 116(1) [0|0|15]</td><td>264</td></tr>
<tr><td>Irish Tour '74 (74) 110(1) [0|0|11]</td><td>210</td></tr>
<tr><td>Against The Grain (75) 121(1) [0|0|13]</td><td>206</td></tr>
<tr><td>Calling Card (76) 163(1) [0|0|11]</td><td>119</td></tr>
<tr><td>Blueprint (73) 147(1) [0|0|7]</td><td>85.4</td></tr>
<tr><td>Top Priority (79) 140(2) [0|0|4]</td><td>68.3</td></tr>
<tr><td>Sinner...And Saint (75) 156(2) [0|0|5]</td><td>66.0</td></tr>
<tr><td>Tattoo (73) 186(1) [0|0|7]</td><td>46.5</td></tr>
<tr><td>GALLERY ▶ 1866 Pk:75 [0|0|1]</td><td>431</td></tr>
<tr><td>Nice To Be With You (72) 75(1) [0|0|15]</td><td>431</td></tr>
<tr><td>James GALWAY ▶ 2758 Pk:150 [0|0|2]</td><td>103</td></tr>
<tr><td>Annie's Song And Other Galway Favorites (79)
153(1) [0|0|5]</td><td>59.1</td></tr>
<tr><td>Sometimes When We Touch (80)-Cleo Laine &
James Galway [A] 150(1) [0|0|6]</td><td>44.2</td></tr>
<tr><td>GAMMA ▶ 1349 Pk:65 [0|0|3]</td><td>1042</td></tr>
<tr><td>Gamma 2 (80) 65(1) [0|0|19]</td><td>502</td></tr>
<tr><td>Gamma 3 (82) 72(1) [0|0|12]</td><td>288</td></tr>
<tr><td>Gamma 1 (79) 131(1) [0|0|17]</td><td>253</td></tr>
<tr><td>GANG OF FOUR ▶ 2873 Pk:168 [0|0|4]</td><td>84</td></tr>
<tr><td>Hard (83) 168(1) [0|0|4]</td><td>34.9</td></tr>
<tr><td>Songs Of The Free (82) 175(1) [0|0|3]</td><td>23.5</td></tr>
<tr><td>Solid Gold (81) 190(2) [0|0|2]</td><td>15.1</td></tr>
<tr><td>Another Day/Another Dollar (82)
195(2) [0|0|2]</td><td>10.8</td></tr>
<tr><td>GAP BAND ▶ 348 Pk:14 [0|3|9]</td><td>9708</td></tr>
<tr><td>The Gap Band III (80) 16(2) [0|17|37]</td><td>2856</td></tr>
<tr><td>Gap Band IV (82) 14(5) [0|17|52]</td><td>2837</td></tr>
<tr><td>Gap Band V- Jammin' (83) 28(1) [0|7|43]</td><td>1519</td></tr>
<tr><td>The Gap Band II (79) 42(1) [0|0|28]</td><td>1079</td></tr>
<tr><td>Gap Band VI (85) 58(2) [0|0|23]</td><td>583</td></tr>
<tr><td>The Gap Band (79) 77(2) [0|0|18]</td><td>447</td></tr>
<tr><td>Gap Gold/Best Of The Gap Band (85)
103(2) [0|0|16]</td><td>231</td></tr>
<tr><td>Gap Band VII (86) 159(1) [0|0|15]</td><td>120</td></tr>
<tr><td>Round Trip (89) 189(2) [0|0|7]</td><td>34.9</td></tr>
<tr><td>Jerry GARCIA ▶ 956 Pk:35 [0|1|5]</td><td>2121</td></tr>
<tr><td>Garcia (72) 35(2) [0|3|14]</td><td>689</td></tr>
<tr><td>Reflections (76) 42(1) [0|0|14]</td><td>639</td></tr>
<tr><td>Garcia (II) (74) 49(2) [0|0|15]</td><td>559</td></tr>
<tr><td>Run For The Roses (82) 100(2) [0|0|8]</td><td>123</td></tr>
<tr><td>Cats Under The Stars (78)-Jerry Garcia Band
114(1) [0|0|5]</td><td>112</td></tr>
<tr><td>Art GARFUNKEL ▶ 409 Pk:5 [2|3|6]</td><td>7994</td></tr>
<tr><td>Breakaway (75) 7(2) [5|15|28]</td><td>3474</td></tr>
<tr><td>Angel Clare (73) 5(1) [5|13|25]</td><td>2638</td></tr>
</table>

Act ► Highest Peak [Top10s | Top40s | Total]
Title (Yr) Peak(Wk) [T10 Wk | T40Wk | TotalWk] — Score

Art GARFUNKEL ► *Continued*
Watermark (78) 19(1) [0|9|16] 1296
Fate For Breakfast (79) 67(2) [0|0|14] 324
Scissors Cut (81) 113(1) [0|0|8] 171
Lefty (88) 134(2) [0|0|8] 91.8

Judy GARLAND ► 2770 Pk:136 [0|0|3] 101
Judy Garland's Greatest Hits (69) 161(1) [0|0|3] 45.5
The Best Of Judy Garland (64) 136(1) [0|0|2] 28.3
Judy Garland At Home At The Palace - Opening Night (67) 174(1) [0|0|3] 27.4

Judy GARLAND & Liza MINELLI ► 1689 Pk:41 [0|0|2] 591
Live At The London Palladium (65) 41(2) [0|0|14] 522
Live At The London Palladium (Condensed) (73) 164(1) [0|0|8] 69.2

Gale GARNETT ► 1734 Pk:43 [0|0|1] 544
My Kind Of Folk Songs (64) 43(1) [0|0|22] 544

Leif GARRETT ► 912 Pk:34 [0|2|4] 2299
Leif Garrett (77) 37(2) [0|3|24] 1040
Feel The Need (78) 34(2) [0|5|19] 929
Same Goes For You (79) 129(1) [0|0|22] 285
My Movie Of You (81) 185(1) [0|0|7] 45.4

Tommy GARRETT ► 1811 Pk:94 [0|0|5] 475
Maria Elena (63)-The 50 Guitars of Tommy Garrett 94(1) [0|0|8] 143
50 Guitars Go Italiano (64)-The 50 Guitars of Tommy Garrett 142(1) [0|0|2] 24.1
The Best Of The 50 Guitars Of Tommy Garrett (69)-The 50 Guitars of Tommy Garrett 147(1) [0|0|9] 169
50 Guitars In Love (66)-The 50 Guitars of Tommy Garrett 99(2) [0|0|5] 106
More 50 Guitars In Love (67)-The 50 Guitars of Tommy Garrett 168(2) [0|0|3] 33.0

John GARY ► 283 Pk:11 [0|5|14] 12365
Catch A Rising Star (63) 19(2) [0|27|63] 3242
Encore (64) 16(3) [0|11|46] 2020
The Nearness Of You (65) 11(2) [0|13|29] 1604
A Little Bit Of Heaven (65) 17(2) [0|8|33] 1308
Your All-Time Favorite Songs (65) 21(2) [0|7|25] 989
So Tenderly (64) 42(1) [0|0|28] 945
Choice (66) 51(1) [0|0|20] 573
A Heart Filled With Song (66) 73(1) [0|0|17] 458
The John Gary Carnegie Hall Concert (67) 76(2) [0|0|19] 374
Your All-Time Country Favorites (66) 65(1) [0|0|12] 313
Especially For You (67) 117(2) [0|0|14] 269
Spanish Moonlight (67) 90(1) [0|0|11] 223
David Merrick Presents Hits From His Broadway Hits (64)-John Gary/Ann-Margret [A] 141(1) [0|0|4] 24.0
Love Of A Gentle Woman (69) 192(1) [0|0|3] 23.3

GARY'S GANG ► 1853 Pk:42 [0|0|1] 440
Keep On Dancin' (79) 42(2) [0|0|10] 440

Luis GASCA ► 3415 Pk:195 [0|0|1] 18
Luis Gasca (72) 195(2) [0|0|3] 17.8

David GATES ► 1857 Pk:102 [0|0|3] 436
Never Let Her Go (75) 102(2) [0|0|9] 207
First (73) 107(1) [0|0|10] 184
Goodbye Girl (78) 165(1) [0|0|4] 44.9

Larry GATLIN/GATLIN BROTHERS Band ► 1636 Pk:102 [0|0|6] 634
Straight Ahead (79)-Larry Gatlin & The Gatlin Brothers Band 102(1) [0|0|16] 282
Oh! Brother (78) 140(2) [0|0|8] 113
Larry Gatlin's Greatest Hits Vol.1 (78) 171(1) [0|0|9] 92.4
Help Yourself (80)-Larry Gatlin & The Gatlin Brothers Band 118(1) [0|0|4] 80.4
Love Is Just A Game (78) 175(2) [0|0|5] 50.0
Not Guilty... (81)-Larry Gatlin & The Gatlin Brothers Band 184(1) [0|0|2] 16.0

Marvin GAYE ► 83 Pk:2 [6|11|26] 33535
What's Going On (71) 6(3) [10|27|53] 6199
Let's Get It On (73) 2(1) [8|18|61] 4642
Marvin Gaye Live At The London Palladium (77) 3(3) [11|19|26] 4450
I Want You (76) 4(1) [6|15|28] 3363
Midnight Love (82) 7(5) [7|13|41] 2691
Marvin Gaye Live! (74) 8(2) [4|13|28] 2663
Trouble Man (72) 14(2) [0|11|21] 1815
Here, My Dear (79) 26(2) [0|7|21] 1313
M.P.G. (69) 33(1) [0|4|18] 1191
In The Groove (68) 63(2) [0|0|27] 838
In Our Lifetime (81) 32(2) [0|4|17] 809
Diana & Marvin (73)-Diana Ross & Marvin Gaye [A] 26(1) [0|5|47] 759
Marvin Gaye Anthology (74) 61(1) [0|0|21] 512
Dream Of A Lifetime (85) 41(2) [0|0|15] 446
Marvin Gaye's Greatest Hits (2) (76) 44(2) [0|0|8] 400
Marvin Gaye's Greatest Hits (64) 72(1) [0|0|14] 266
Together (64)-Marvin Gaye & Mary Wells [A] 42(1) [0|0|16] 244
Every Great Motown Hit Of Marvin Gaye (83) 80(1) [0|0|16] 232
Moods Of Marvin Gaye (66) 118(1) [0|0|10] 177
How Sweet It Is To Be Loved By You (65) 128(2) [0|0|10] 143
Anthology (84) 109(1) [0|0|8] 124
Marvin Gaye Super Hits (70) 117(2) [0|0|6] 117
Marvin Gaye And His Girls (69) 183(1) [0|0|7] 67.5
Marvin Gaye/Greatest Hits, Vol. 2 (67) 178(1) [0|0|5] 37.2
That's The Way Love Is (69) 189(1) [0|0|3] 25.0
Motown Remembers Marvin Gaye (86) 193(1) [0|0|2] 10.1

Marvin GAYE & Tammi TERRELL ► 1077 Pk:60 [0|0|4] 1657
United (67) 69(1) [0|0|44] 973
You're All I Need (68) 60(2) [0|0|21] 637
Marvin Gaye & Tammi Terrell Greatest Hits (70) 171(1) [0|0|3] 29.3
Easy (69) 184(1) [0|0|2] 17.6

Crystal GAYLE ► 482 Pk:12 [0|2|11] 6506
We Must Believe In Magic (77) 12(2) [0|11|35] 2354
Miss The Mississippi (79) 36(2) [0|4|28] 1314
When I Dream (78) 52(1) [0|0|39] 1052
Classic Crystal (79) 62(3) [0|0|22] 725
These Days (80) 79(1) [0|0|11] 312
Hollywood, Tennessee (81) 99(2) [0|0|16] 249
True Love (82) 120(1) [0|0|12] 174
We Should Be Together (79) 128(3) [0|0|8] 138
Favorites (80) 149(1) [0|0|6] 76.9
Crystal Gayle's Greatest Hits (83) 169(1) [0|0|8] 62.0
Cage The Songbird (83) 171(1) [0|0|6] 49.9

GAYLORD & HOLIDAY ► 2956 Pk:180 [0|0|1] 72
Second Generation (76) 180(1) [0|0|8] 71.7

Gloria GAYNOR ► 515 Pk:4 [1|2|7] 6007
Love Tracks (79) 4(2) [9|15|34] 3789
Never Can Say Goodbye (75) 25(2) [0|5|15] 897
Experience Gloria Gaynor (75) 64(1) [0|0|21] 572
I Have A Right (79) 58(1) [0|0|11] 358
I've Got You (76) 107(1) [0|0|14] 325
Glorious (77) 183(1) [0|0|4] 33.5
Stories (80) 178(1) [0|0|4] 31.9

J. GEILS Band ► 171 Pk:1 [2|7|15] 20369
Freeze-Frame (81) 1(4) [19|29|70] 8234
Love Stinks (80) 18(2) [0|17|42] 2737
Bloodshot (73) 10(1) [1|14|44] 2546
Nightmares...And Other Tales From The Vinyl Jungle (74) 26(2) [0|4|22] 1138
Showtime (82) 23(3) [0|10|19] 1033
Live - Full House (72) 54(2) [0|0|26] 795
Sanctuary (78) 49(1) [0|0|22] 781
Ladies Invited (73) 51(1) [0|0|18] 655
The Morning After (71) 64(1) [0|0|17] 559
Monkey Island (77) 51(1) [0|0|17] 544
Hotline (75) 36(2) [0|2|9] 522
Live - Blow Your Face Out (76) 40(1) [0|1|11] 496
You're Gettin' Even While I'm Gettin' Odd (84) 80(3) [0|0|10] 222
Best Of The J. Geils Band (79) 129(2) [0|0|5] 93.2
The J. Geils Band (71) 195(2) [0|0|2] 13.7

Bob GELDOF ► 2618 Pk:130 [0|0|1] 129
Deep In The Heart Of Nowhere (86) 130(1) [0|0|12] 129

GENE LOVES JEZEBEL ► 1846 Pk:108 [0|0|2] 447
The House Of Dolls (87) 108(1) [0|0|22] 298
Discover (86) 155(2) [0|0|19] 149

GENERAL PUBLIC ► 993 Pk:26 [0|1|2] 1964
...All The Rage (84) 26(2) [0|11|39] 1712
Hand To Mouth (86) 83(1) [0|0|16] 251

GENESIS ► 95 Pk:3 [4|8|13] 30643
Invisible Touch (86) 3(2) [26|61|85] 9040
Abacab (81) 7(1) [6|29|64] 5305
Genesis (83) 9(1) [3|27|50] 3843
Duke (80) 11(2) [0|21|31] 3426
...And Then There Were Three... (78) 14(1) [0|8|33] 2200
Three Sides Live (82) 10(3) [3|11|25] 1758
Wind & Wuthering (77) 26(2) [0|8|21] 1382
A Trick Of The Tail (76) 31(2) [0|6|19] 1084
The Lamb Lies Down On Broadway (74) 41(1) [0|0|16] 920
Selling England By The Pound (73) 70(1) [0|0|29] 712
Seconds Out (77) 47(2) [0|0|16] 676
Genesis Live (74) 105(1) [0|0|14] 255
From Genesis To Revelation (74) 170(1) [0|0|4] 41.1

GENTLE GIANT ► 1192 Pk:48 [0|0|7] 1364
Free Hand (75) 48(1) [0|0|11] 444
The Power And The Glory (74) 78(2) [0|0|13] 375
The Missing Piece (77) 81(1) [0|0|7] 186
The Official "Live" Gentle Giant - Playing The Fool (77) 89(1) [0|0|6] 160
Interview (76) 137(3) [0|0|5] 95.9
Octopus (73) 170(1) [0|0|9] 76.5
Three Friends (72) 197(2) [0|0|5] 26.3

Bobbie GENTRY ► 494 Pk:1 [1|2|6] 6220
Ode To Billie Joe (67) 1(2) [10|18|30] 3754
Bobbie Gentry & Glen Campbell (68)-Bobbie Gentry & Glen Campbell [A] 11(2) [0|13|47] 1850
Fancy (70) 96(1) [0|0|17] 369
The Delta Sweete (68) 132(1) [0|0|12] 171
Touch 'Em With Love (69) 164(1) [0|0|4] 55.7
Bobbie Gentry's Greatest! (69) 180(1) [0|0|2] 19.4

Act ▶ Highest Peak [Top10s|Top40s|Total] Title (Yr) Peak(Wk) [T10 Wk|T40Wk|TotalWk]	Score
The GENTRYS ▶ 2374 Pk:99 [0|0|1]	**192**
Keep On Dancing (65) 99(1) [0|0|10]	192
Lowell GEORGE ▶ 2194 Pk:71 [0|0|1]	**260**
Thanks I'll Eat It Here (79) 71(2) [0|0|9]	260
GEORGIA SATELLITES ▶ 767 Pk:5 [1|1|3]	**3156**
Georgia Satellites (86) 5(1) [5|20|42]	2752
Open All Night (88) 77(2) [0|0|13]	288
In The Land Of Salvation And Sin (89) 130(2) [0|0|13]	116
GEORGIO ▶ 1673 Pk:117 [0|0|1]	**603**
Sexappeal (87) 117(1) [0|0|52]	603
GERRY And The PACEMAKERS ▶ 835 Pk:13 [0|2|5]	**2753**
Ferry Cross The Mersey (Soundtrack) (65) 13(1) [0|12|20]	1357
Gerry & The Pacemakers Greatest Hits (65) 44(2) [0|0|22]	654
Don't Let The Sun Catch You Crying (64) 29(2) [0|5|12]	513
Gerry & The Pacemakers Second Album (64) 129(2) [0|0|9]	122
I'll Be There! (65) 120(1) [0|0|7]	108
Stan GETZ ▶ 532 Pk:2 [1|2|5]	**5590**
Getz/Gilberto (64)-Stan Getz And Joao Gilberto Featuring Antonio Carlos Jobim [A] 2(2) [16|50|96]	3549
Getz Au Go Go (64)-The New Stan Getz Quartet Featuring Astrud Gilberto 24(2) [0|17|46]	1938
Reflections (64) 122(1) [0|0|6]	84.4
Sweet Rain (67) 195(1) [0|0|2]	10.0
Captain Marvel (75) 191(1) [0|0|1]	8.0
GIANT ▶ 1686 Pk:80 [0|0|1]	**595**
Last Of The Runaways (89) 80(1) [0|0|36]	595
GIANT STEPS ▶ 3269 Pk:184 [0|0|1]	**31**
The Book Of Pride (88) 184(1) [0|0|5]	31.3
Andy GIBB ▶ 350 Pk:7 [1|3|4]	**9669**
Shadow Dancing (78) 7(5) [9|15|43]	4069
Flowing Rivers (77) 19(4) [0|18|68]	3832
After Dark (80) 21(1) [0|7|15]	1099
Andy Gibb's Greatest Hits (80) 46(1) [0|0|18]	670
Barry GIBB ▶ 2425 Pk:72 [0|0|1]	**181**
Now Voyager (84) 72(2) [0|0|8]	181
Terri GIBBS ▶ 1492 Pk:53 [0|0|1]	**822**
Somebody's Knockin' (81) 53(3) [0|0|25]	822
Debbie GIBSON ▶ 274 Pk:1 [2|2|2]	**12968**
Out Of The Blue (87) 7(2) [13|45|89]	6673
Electric Youth (89) 1(5) [13|25|51]	6295
Don GIBSON ▶ 3169 Pk:134 [0|0|1]	**44**
I Wrote A Song... (63) 134(1) [0|0|3]	44.4
GIBSON BROTHERS ▶ 3422 Pk:185 [0|0|1]	**17**
Cuba (79) 185(2) [0|0|2]	17.3
Astrud GILBERTO ▶ 1372 Pk:41 [0|0|2]	**1007**
The Astrud Gilberto Album (65) 41(2) [0|0|18]	612
The Shadow Of Your Smile (65) 66(1) [0|0|18]	395
Joao GILBERTO ▶ 712 Pk:2 [1|1|1]	**3549**
Getz/Gilberto (64)-Stan Getz And Joao Gilberto Featuring Antonio Carlos Jobim [A] 2(2) [16|50|96]	3549
Nick GILDER ▶ 1232 Pk:33 [0|1|2]	**1270**
City Nights (78) 33(1) [0|5|20]	1139
Frequency (79) 127(2) [0|0|8]	130
Johnny GILL ▶ 3101 Pk:139 [0|0|1]	**52**
Perfect Combination (84)-Stacy Lattisaw & Johnny Gill [A] 139(1) [0|0|8]	51.8
GILLAN ▶ 3350 Pk:183 [0|0|1]	**24**
Glory Road (80) 183(1) [0|0|3]	24.3
Mickey GILLEY ▶ 2818 Pk:170 [0|0|2]	**93**
You Don't Know Me (81) 170(2) [0|0|6]	64.5

Act ▶ Highest Peak [Top10s|Top40s|Total] Title (Yr) Peak(Wk) [T10 Wk|T40Wk|TotalWk]	Score
That's All That Matters To Me (80) 177(2) [0|0|3]	28.5
David GILMOUR ▶ 900 Pk:29 [0|2|2]	**2390**
About Face (84) 32(3) [0|10|28]	1288
David Gilmour (78) 29(2) [0|6|18]	1102
Jim GILSTRAP ▶ 3022 Pk:179 [0|0|1]	**63**
Swing Your Daddy (75) 179(1) [0|0|7]	62.9
Nikki GIOVANNI ▶ 2518 Pk:165 [0|0|1]	**154**
Truth Is On Its Way (71) 165(2) [0|0|13]	154
GIPSY KINGS ▶ 1224 Pk:57 [0|0|2]	**1293**
Gipsy Kings (88) 57(2) [0|0|42]	965
Mosaique (89) 95(2) [0|0|19]	328
GIRLSCHOOL ▶ 3271 Pk:182 [0|0|1]	**31**
Hit And Run (82) 182(2) [0|0|5]	31.0
GIUFFRIA ▶ 1095 Pk:26 [0|1|2]	**1621**
Giuffria (84) 26(2) [0|7|29]	1272
Silk + Steel (86) 60(2) [0|0|14]	349
Philip GLASS ▶ 2085 Pk:91 [0|0|2]	**309**
Songs From Liquid Days (86) 91(2) [0|0|13]	221
Glassworks (82) 121(2) [0|0|6]	88.0
GLASS HARP ▶ 3390 Pk:192 [0|0|1]	**20**
Synergy (71) 192(1) [0|0|3]	20.0
GLASS MOON ▶ 2654 Pk:148 [0|0|1]	**123**
Glass Moon (80) 148(1) [0|0|9]	123
GLASS TIGER ▶ 814 Pk:27 [0|1|2]	**2842**
The Thin Red Line (86) 27(2) [0|28|51]	2531
Diamond Sun (88) 82(2) [0|0|15]	311
Tompall GLASER ▶ 1559 Pk:10 [1|1|1]	**723**
Wanted! The Outlaws (76)-Waylon Jennings, Willie Nelson, Jessi Colter, Tompall Glaser [A] 10(2) [2|14|51]	723
Jackie GLEASON ▶ 1581 Pk:71 [0|0|6]	**697**
How Sweet It Is For Lovers (66) 71(2) [0|0|11]	302
Today's Romantic Hits/For Lovers Only, Vol. 2 (64) 82(1) [0|0|10]	201
Today's Romantic Hits/For Lovers Only (63) 115(1) [0|0|8]	118
Silk 'N' Brass (66) 141(1) [0|0|4]	52.8
Close-Up (69) 192(1) [0|0|2]	15.5
A Taste Of Brass For Lovers Only (67) 200(2) [0|0|2]	9.0
Gary GLITTER ▶ 3067 Pk:186 [0|0|1]	**57**
Glitter (72) 186(2) [0|0|8]	56.5
Roger GLOVER ▶ 2123 Pk:101 [0|0|2]	**290**
Mask (84) 101(1) [0|0|12]	173
The Butterfly Ball And The Grasshopper's Feast (76) 142(2) [0|0|8]	117
GOANNA ▶ 3237 Pk:179 [0|0|1]	**35**
Spirit Of Place (83) 179(1) [0|0|5]	34.9
The GODFATHERS ▶ 1992 Pk:91 [0|0|2]	**353**
Birth, School, Work, Death (88) 91(2) [0|0|16]	313
More Songs About Love & Hate (89) 174(1) [0|0|6]	39.8
GODLEY & CREME ▶ 1694 Pk:37 [0|1|1]	**589**
The History Mix Vol. I (85) 37(2) [0|3|15]	589
The GODZ ▶ 3123 Pk:189 [0|0|2]	**50**
The Godz (78) 191(2) [0|0|5]	35.3
Nothing Is Sacred (79) 189(1) [0|0|2]	14.2
Louise GOFFIN ▶ 2133 Pk:87 [0|0|1]	**286**
Kid Blue (79) 87(1) [0|0|13]	286
The GO-GO'S ▶ 257 Pk:1 [2|3|3]	**13943**
Beauty And The Beat (81)-Go-Go's 1(6) [15|38|72]	9856
Talk Show (84)-Go-Go's 18(3) [0|18|32]	2131
Vacation (82)-Go-Go's 8(5) [9|10|28]	1956
Andrew GOLD ▶ 1630 Pk:81 [0|0|3]	**643**
All This And Heaven Too (78) 81(4) [0|0|14]	333

Act ▶ Highest Peak [Top10s|Top40s|Total] Title (Yr) Peak(Wk) [T10 Wk|T40Wk|TotalWk]	Score
What's Wrong With This Picture? (77) 95(1) [0|0|16]	295
Andrew Gold (76) 190(2) [0|0|2]	15.4
GOLDDIGGERS ▶ 2639 Pk:142 [0|0|1]	**125**
The Golddiggers (69) 142(1) [0|0|7]	125
GOLDEN EARRING ▶ 650 Pk:12 [0|2|8]	**4250**
Moontan (74) 12(2) [0|13|29]	2405
Cut (82) 24(2) [0|12|30]	1364
Switch (75) 108(2) [0|0|8]	199
N.E.W.S. (84) 107(1) [0|0|9]	154
To The Hilt (76) 156(1) [0|0|4]	54.1
Something Heavy Going Down - Live From The Twilight Zone (84) 158(2) [0|0|6]	46.8
Mad Love (77) 182(2) [0|0|2]	19.4
The Hole (86) 196(2) [0|0|2]	8.8
GOLDEN GATE Strings ▶ 3525 Pk:200 [0|0|1]	**9**
The Monkees Song Book (67) 200(2) [0|0|2]	8.8
Bobby GOLDSBORO ▶ 503 Pk:5 [1|1|10]	**6129**
Honey (68) 5(3) [9|22|48]	4427
Today (69) 60(1) [0|0|13]	542
Word Pictures Featuring Autumn Of My Life (68) 116(1) [0|0|13]	287
Bobby Goldsboro's Greatest Hits (70) 103(1) [0|0|10]	236
We Gotta Start Lovin' (71) 120(1) [0|0|13]	197
Muddy Mississippi Line (70) 139(2) [0|0|11]	177
Summer (The First Time) (73) 150(1) [0|0|11]	122
Come Back Home (71) 142(2) [0|0|5]	77.5
Solid Goldsboro - Bobby Goldsboro's Greatest Hits (67) 165(2) [0|0|3]	32.3
Bobby Goldsboro's 10th Anniversary Album (74) 174(1) [0|0|3]	31.2
Ian GOMM ▶ 2206 Pk:104 [0|0|1]	**253**
Gomm With The Wind (79) 104(2) [0|0|12]	253
GONZALEZ ▶ 1987 Pk:67 [0|0|1]	**355**
Shipwrecked (79) 67(2) [0|0|14]	355
Benny GOODMAN ▶ 2208 Pk:90 [0|0|2]	**251**
Together Again! (64)-Benny Goodman Quartet 90(1) [0|0|10]	198
Benny Goodman Today (71)-Benny Goodman And His Orchestra 189(1) [0|0|7]	52.3
Dickie GOODMAN ▶ 2676 Pk:144 [0|0|1]	**118**
Mr. Jaws And Other Fables (75) 144(1) [0|0|8]	118
Jerry GOODMAN & Jan HAMMER ▶ 3130 Pk:150 [0|0|1]	**49**
Like Children (75) 150(1) [0|0|3]	48.7
Steve GOODMAN ▶ 2614 Pk:144 [0|0|2]	**132**
Jessie's Jig & Other Favorites (75) 144(1) [0|0|6]	89.1
Words We Can Dance To (76) 175(1) [0|0|4]	42.4
GOOSE CREEK SYMPHONY ▶ 2854 Pk:167 [0|0|1]	**87**
Words Of Earnest (72) 167(2) [0|0|8]	87.3
Robert GORDON ▶ 1423 Pk:106 [0|0|5]	**935**
Are You Gonna Be The One (81) 117(4) [0|0|15]	301
Rock Billy Boogie (79) 106(3) [0|0|12]	288
Fresh Fish Special (78) 124(1) [0|0|7]	125
Bad Boy (80) 150(1) [0|0|9]	112
Robert Gordon With Link Wray (77)-Robert Gordon With Link Wray 142(1) [0|0|8]	109
Lesley GORE ▶ 1545 Pk:95 [0|0|6]	**734**
The Golden Hits Of Lesley Gore (65) 95(1) [0|0|24]	402
Lesley Gore Sings Of Mixed-Up Hearts (64) 125(2) [0|0|8]	115
Boys, Boys, Boys (64) 127(1) [0|0|6]	80.5

<table>
<tr><th>Act ▶ Highest Peak [Top10s|Top40s|Total]
Title (Yr) Peak(Wk) [T10 Wk|T40Wk|TotalWk]</th><th>Score</th></tr>
<tr><td>Lesley GORE ▶ Continued</td><td></td></tr>
<tr><td>My Town, My Guy & Me (65) 120(1) [0|0|4]</td><td>65.8</td></tr>
<tr><td>California Nights (67) 169(1) [0|0|5]</td><td>47.5</td></tr>
<tr><td>Girl Talk (64) 146(1) [0|0|2]</td><td>22.5</td></tr>
<tr><td>Martin L. GORE ▶ 3163 Pk:156 [0|0|1]</td><td>45</td></tr>
<tr><td>Counterfeit (89) 156(2) [0|0|5]</td><td>44.9</td></tr>
<tr><td>GORKY PARK ▶ 2001 Pk:80 [0|0|1]</td><td>350</td></tr>
<tr><td>Gorky Park (89) 80(2) [0|0|21]</td><td>350</td></tr>
<tr><td>Eydie GORME ▶ 766 Pk:22 [0|1|7]</td><td>3164</td></tr>
<tr><td>Don't Go To Strangers (66) 22(2) [0|9|37]</td><td>1472</td></tr>
<tr><td>Amor (64) 54(2) [0|0|22]</td><td>627</td></tr>
<tr><td>Softly, As I Leave You (67) 85(2) [0|0|18]</td><td>332</td></tr>
<tr><td>More Amor (65) 53(2) [0|0|11]</td><td>331</td></tr>
<tr><td>Tonight I'll Say A Prayer (70) 105(1) [0|0|12]</td><td>271</td></tr>
<tr><td>Eydie Gorme's Greatest Hits (67)
148(1) [0|0|9]</td><td>93.5</td></tr>
<tr><td>Gorme Country Style (64) 143(1) [0|0|3]</td><td>38.0</td></tr>
<tr><td>Barry GOUDREAU ▶ 2285 Pk:88 [0|0|1]</td><td>220</td></tr>
<tr><td>Barry Goudreau (80) 88(3) [0|0|8]</td><td>220</td></tr>
<tr><td>Robert GOULET ▶ 418 Pk:5 [1|5|13]</td><td>7680</td></tr>
<tr><td>My Love Forgive Me (64) 5(2) [8|18|29]</td><td>2442</td></tr>
<tr><td>Robert Goulet In Person (63) 16(2) [0|10|23]</td><td>1292</td></tr>
<tr><td>Summer Sounds (65) 31(2) [0|5|19]</td><td>860</td></tr>
<tr><td>Robert Goulet On Broadway (65)
33(2) [0|4|22]</td><td>842</td></tr>
<tr><td>Manhattan Tower/The Man Who Loves Manhattan
(64) 31(1) [0|7|22]</td><td>800</td></tr>
<tr><td>Begin To Love (65) 69(1) [0|0|16]</td><td>361</td></tr>
<tr><td>Without You (64) 72(1) [0|0|16]</td><td>312</td></tr>
<tr><td>I Remember You (66) 73(1) [0|0|12]</td><td>255</td></tr>
<tr><td>Both Sides Now (69) 135(1) [0|0|13]</td><td>250</td></tr>
<tr><td>Woman, Woman (68) 162(2) [0|0|15]</td><td>171</td></tr>
<tr><td>Robert Goulet On Broadway, Volume 2 (67)
145(1) [0|0|3]</td><td>44.2</td></tr>
<tr><td>Souvenir d'Italie (69) 174(2) [0|0|3]</td><td>36.2</td></tr>
<tr><td>I Wish You Love (70) 198(2) [0|0|2]</td><td>12.3</td></tr>
<tr><td>GO WEST ▶ 1417 Pk:60 [0|0|2]</td><td>944</td></tr>
<tr><td>Go West (85) 60(1) [0|0|35]</td><td>882</td></tr>
<tr><td>Dancing On The Couch (87) 172(1) [0|0|9]</td><td>62.2</td></tr>
<tr><td>GQ ▶ 675 Pk:13 [0|1|3]</td><td>3982</td></tr>
<tr><td>Disco Nights (79) 13(1) [0|19|35]</td><td>3146</td></tr>
<tr><td>Two (80) 46(2) [0|0|20]</td><td>741</td></tr>
<tr><td>Face To Face (81) 140(2) [0|0|8]</td><td>94.6</td></tr>
<tr><td>The GRACES ▶ 2870 Pk:147 [0|0|1]</td><td>84</td></tr>
<tr><td>Perfect View (89) 147(1) [0|0|9]</td><td>84.5</td></tr>
<tr><td>Larry GRAHAM/GRAHAM CENTRAL STATION
▶ 495 Pk:22 [0|2|11]</td><td>6208</td></tr>
<tr><td>One In A Million You (80)-Larry Graham
26(3) [0|9|24]</td><td>1475</td></tr>
<tr><td>Ain't No 'Bout-A-Doubt It (75)-
Graham Central Station 22(1) [0|6|24]</td><td>1412</td></tr>
<tr><td>Graham Central Station (74)-
Graham Central Station 48(1) [0|0|26]</td><td>856</td></tr>
<tr><td>Mirror (76)-Graham Central Station
46(1) [0|0|16]</td><td>708</td></tr>
<tr><td>Release Yourself (74)-
Graham Central Station 51(2) [0|0|18]</td><td>569</td></tr>
<tr><td>Just Be My Lady (81)-Larry Graham
46(1) [0|0|13]</td><td>495</td></tr>
<tr><td>Now Do-U-Wanta Dance (77)-
Graham Central Station 67(1) [0|0|10]</td><td>265</td></tr>
<tr><td>My Radio Sure Sounds Good To Me (78)-
Larry Graham And Graham Central Station
105(1) [0|0|11]</td><td>218</td></tr>
<tr><td>Sooner Or Later (82)-Larry Graham
142(1) [0|0|9]</td><td>107</td></tr>
<tr><td>Star Walk (79)-Larry Graham And Graham Central
Station 136(2) [0|0|4]</td><td>70.5</td></tr>
<tr><td>Victory (83)-Larry Graham 173(1) [0|0|4]</td><td>33.0</td></tr>
</table>

<table>
<tr><th>Act ▶ Highest Peak [Top10s|Top40s|Total]
Title (Yr) Peak(Wk) [T10 Wk|T40Wk|TotalWk]</th><th>Score</th></tr>
<tr><td>Lou GRAMM ▶ 1132 Pk:27 [0|1|2]</td><td>1519</td></tr>
<tr><td>Ready Or Not (87) 27(1) [0|7|26]</td><td>1094</td></tr>
<tr><td>Long Hard Look (89) 85(1) [0|0|23]</td><td>425</td></tr>
<tr><td>GRAND FUNK RAILROAD ▶ 55
Pk:2 [8|12|16]</td><td>42926</td></tr>
<tr><td>Closer To Home (70) 6(4) [12|24|63]</td><td>5948</td></tr>
<tr><td>Live Album (70) 5(2) [8|25|62]</td><td>5403</td></tr>
<tr><td>Survival (71) 6(1) [6|21|40]</td><td>4577</td></tr>
<tr><td>Shinin' On (74)-Grand Funk 5(2) [10|21|29]</td><td>4246</td></tr>
<tr><td>We're An American Band (73)-Grand Funk
2(2) [8|17|35]</td><td>4245</td></tr>
<tr><td>Grand Funk (70) 11(2) [0|15|67]</td><td>4140</td></tr>
<tr><td>E Pluribus Funk (71) 5(2) [5|15|30]</td><td>3651</td></tr>
<tr><td>On Time (69) 27(1) [0|8|55]</td><td>2581</td></tr>
<tr><td>Phoenix (72) 7(2) [3|13|27]</td><td>2563</td></tr>
<tr><td>All The Girls In The World Beware!!! (74)-
Grand Funk 10(1) [1|10|24]</td><td>2054</td></tr>
<tr><td>Mark, Don & Mel 1969-71 (72) 17(2) [0|9|27]</td><td>1625</td></tr>
<tr><td>Caught In The Act (75) 21(2) [0|5|10]</td><td>905</td></tr>
<tr><td>Born To Die (76) 47(1) [0|0|11]</td><td>465</td></tr>
<tr><td>Good Singin' Good Playin' (76) 52(1) [0|0|9]</td><td>370</td></tr>
<tr><td>Grand Funk Hits (76)-Grand Funk
126(1) [0|0|5]</td><td>88.9</td></tr>
<tr><td>Grand Funk Lives (81) 149(2) [0|0|5]</td><td>64.8</td></tr>
<tr><td>GRANDMASTER FLASH ▶ 2989
Pk:145 [0|0|2]</td><td>67</td></tr>
<tr><td>The Source (86) 145(2) [0|0|6]</td><td>62.5</td></tr>
<tr><td>Ba-Dop-Boom-Bang (87) 197(1) [0|0|1]</td><td>4.6</td></tr>
<tr><td>GRANDMASTER FLASH And The FURIOUS FIVE
▶ 1555 Pk:53 [0|0|2]</td><td>724</td></tr>
<tr><td>The Message (82)-Grandmaster Flash & The
Furious Five 53(4) [0|0|24]</td><td>706</td></tr>
<tr><td>On The Strength (88)-Grandmaster Flash & The
Furious Five 189(2) [0|0|3]</td><td>17.6</td></tr>
<tr><td>Amy GRANT ▶ 857 Pk:35 [0|1|4]</td><td>2613</td></tr>
<tr><td>Unguarded (85) 35(1) [0|4|38]</td><td>1391</td></tr>
<tr><td>Amy Grant - The Collection (86) 66(2) [0|0|33]</td><td>709</td></tr>
<tr><td>Lead Me On (88) 71(2) [0|0|13]</td><td>319</td></tr>
<tr><td>Straight Ahead (85) 133(2) [0|0|20]</td><td>193</td></tr>
<tr><td>Earl GRANT ▶ 2540 Pk:139 [0|0|4]</td><td>150</td></tr>
<tr><td>Fly Me To The Moon (64) 139(1) [0|0|5]</td><td>67.1</td></tr>
<tr><td>Trade Winds (65) 143(1) [0|0|4]</td><td>49.7</td></tr>
<tr><td>Just For A Thrill (64) 149(2) [0|0|2]</td><td>22.3</td></tr>
<tr><td>Gently Swingin' (68) 192(1) [0|0|2]</td><td>10.9</td></tr>
<tr><td>Eddy GRANT ▶ 863 Pk:10 [1|1|2]</td><td>2578</td></tr>
<tr><td>Killer On The Rampage (83) 10(3) [3|15|30]</td><td>2188</td></tr>
<tr><td>Going For Broke (84) 64(2) [0|0|17]</td><td>391</td></tr>
<tr><td>Stephane GRAPELLI ▶ 2836 Pk:108 [0|0|1]</td><td>90</td></tr>
<tr><td>Live (81)-Stephane Grappelli/David Grisman [A]
108(1) [0|0|10]</td><td>89.7</td></tr>
<tr><td>GRASS ROOTS ▶ 531 Pk:25 [0|2|7]</td><td>5597</td></tr>
<tr><td>Golden Grass (68) 25(2) [0|6|43]</td><td>2292</td></tr>
<tr><td>Leaving It All Behind (69) 36(3) [0|6|21]</td><td>1084</td></tr>
<tr><td>Their 16 Greatest Hits (71) 58(1) [0|0|20]</td><td>733</td></tr>
<tr><td>Lovin' Things (69) 73(1) [0|0|16]</td><td>490</td></tr>
<tr><td>Move Along (72) 86(1) [0|0|14]</td><td>341</td></tr>
<tr><td>More Golden Grass (70) 152(1) [0|0|27]</td><td>335</td></tr>
<tr><td>Let's Live For Today (67) 75(2) [0|0|15]</td><td>323</td></tr>
<tr><td>GRATEFUL DEAD ▶ 164 Pk:6 [1|13|25]</td><td>20748</td></tr>
<tr><td>In The Dark (87) 6(2) [7|17|34]</td><td>2807</td></tr>
<tr><td>Blues For Allah (75) 12(2) [0|9|13]</td><td>1682</td></tr>
<tr><td>Workingman's Dead (70) 27(2) [0|10|26]</td><td>1652</td></tr>
<tr><td>Grateful Dead From The Mars Hotel (74)
16(1) [0|9|20]</td><td>1560</td></tr>
<tr><td>Europe '72 (72) 24(1) [0|8|24]</td><td>1340</td></tr>
<tr><td>Go To Heaven (80) 23(2) [0|8|21]</td><td>1269</td></tr>
<tr><td>American Beauty (70) 30(1) [0|6|19]</td><td>1148</td></tr>
</table>

<table>
<tr><th>Act ▶ Highest Peak [Top10s|Top40s|Total]
Title (Yr) Peak(Wk) [T10 Wk|T40Wk|TotalWk]</th><th>Score</th></tr>
<tr><td>Wake Of The Flood (73)
18(1) [0|6|19]</td><td>1050</td></tr>
<tr><td>Shakedown Street (78) 41(1) [0|0|19]</td><td>1015</td></tr>
<tr><td>Grateful Dead (71) 25(1) [0|6|12]</td><td>983</td></tr>
<tr><td>Terrapin Station (77) 28(1) [0|4|16]</td><td>771</td></tr>
<tr><td>Reckoning (81) 43(1) [0|0|16]</td><td>720</td></tr>
<tr><td>Dead Set (81) 29(2) [0|3|11]</td><td>656</td></tr>
<tr><td>Built To Last (89) 27(1) [0|3|15]</td><td>626</td></tr>
<tr><td>The Grateful Dead (67) 73(1) [0|0|28]</td><td>623</td></tr>
<tr><td>Live/Dead (70) 64(1) [0|0|15]</td><td>476</td></tr>
<tr><td>Anthem Of The Sun (68) 87(1) [0|0|17]</td><td>382</td></tr>
<tr><td>Aoxomoxoa (69) 73(1) [0|0|11]</td><td>373</td></tr>
<tr><td>History Of The Grateful Dead, Vol. 1
(Bear's Choice) (73) 60(1) [0|0|11]</td><td>359</td></tr>
<tr><td>Steal Your Face (76) 56(1) [0|0|9]</td><td>358</td></tr>
<tr><td>The Best Of/Skeletons From The Closet (74)
75(1) [0|0|10]</td><td>258</td></tr>
<tr><td>Dylan And The Dead (89)-Bob Dylan & The
Grateful Dead [A] 37(2) [0|3|11]</td><td>224</td></tr>
<tr><td>Vintage Dead (70) 127(1) [0|0|10]</td><td>178</td></tr>
<tr><td>What A Long Strange Trip It's Been (77)
121(2) [0|0|8]</td><td>144</td></tr>
<tr><td>Historic Dead (71) 154(1) [0|0|7]</td><td>95.3</td></tr>
<tr><td>Dobie GRAY ▶ 1666 Pk:64 [0|0|3]</td><td>606</td></tr>
<tr><td>Drift Away (73) 64(1) [0|0|21]</td><td>551</td></tr>
<tr><td>Midnight Diamond (79) 174(1) [0|0|4]</td><td>33.5</td></tr>
<tr><td>Loving Arms (73) 188(2) [0|0|3]</td><td>21.5</td></tr>
<tr><td>Glen GRAY & The CASA LOMA Orchestra
▶ 2064 Pk:69 [0|0|1]</td><td>318</td></tr>
<tr><td>Today's Best (63)-Glen Gray &The Casa Loma
Orchestra 69(1) [0|0|15]</td><td>318</td></tr>
<tr><td>Charles Randolph GREAN Sounde ▶ 1234
Pk:23 [0|1|1]</td><td>1266</td></tr>
<tr><td>Quentin's Theme (69) 23(2) [0|5|15]</td><td>1266</td></tr>
<tr><td>GREASE BAND ▶ 3339 Pk:190 [0|0|1]</td><td>25</td></tr>
<tr><td>Grease Band (71) 190(2) [0|0|3]</td><td>25.0</td></tr>
<tr><td>GREAT WHITE ▶ 438 Pk:9 [1|2|5]</td><td>7283</td></tr>
<tr><td>...Twice Shy (89) 9(1) [4|26|50]</td><td>3912</td></tr>
<tr><td>Once Bitten (87) 23(2) [0|18|53]</td><td>2769</td></tr>
<tr><td>Shot In The Dark (86) 82(1) [0|0|13]</td><td>244</td></tr>
<tr><td>Recovery: Live! (88) 99(2) [0|0|12]</td><td>234</td></tr>
<tr><td>Great White (84) 144(1) [0|0|12]</td><td>125</td></tr>
<tr><td>R.B. GREAVES ▶ 2092 Pk:85 [0|0|1]</td><td>307</td></tr>
<tr><td>R.B. Greaves (70) 85(2) [0|0|14]</td><td>307</td></tr>
<tr><td>Boris GREBENSHIKOV ▶ 3524
Pk:198 [0|0|1]</td><td>9</td></tr>
<tr><td>Radio Silence (89) 198(2) [0|0|2]</td><td>9.2</td></tr>
<tr><td>Rick GRECH ▶ 3432 Pk:195 [0|0|1]</td><td>17</td></tr>
<tr><td>The Last Five Years (73) 195(1) [0|0|3]</td><td>16.6</td></tr>
<tr><td>Al GREEN ▶ 128 Pk:4 [3|8|15]</td><td>24854</td></tr>
<tr><td>I'm Still In Love With You (72) 4(2) [6|26|67]</td><td>5005</td></tr>
<tr><td>Let's Stay Together (72) 8(2) [6|20|56]</td><td>4963</td></tr>
<tr><td>Call Me (73) 10(2) [2|20|41]</td><td>3301</td></tr>
<tr><td>Al Green Explores Your Mind (74)
15(1) [0|16|33]</td><td>2759</td></tr>
<tr><td>Green Is Blues (73) 19(1) [0|11|28]</td><td>1707</td></tr>
<tr><td>Al Green/Greatest Hits (75) 17(1) [0|8|21]</td><td>1639</td></tr>
<tr><td>Livin' For You (73) 24(1) [0|8|30]</td><td>1449</td></tr>
<tr><td>Al Green Is Love (75) 28(1) [0|6|23]</td><td>1338</td></tr>
<tr><td>Al Green Gets Next To You (71) 58(1) [0|0|43]</td><td>1237</td></tr>
<tr><td>Full Of Fire (76) 59(1) [0|0|16]</td><td>489</td></tr>
<tr><td>Have A Good Time (76) 93(2) [0|0|14]</td><td>307</td></tr>
<tr><td>The Belle Album (77) 103(2) [0|0|12]</td><td>247</td></tr>
<tr><td>Soul Survivor (87) 131(1) [0|0|14]</td><td>171</td></tr>
<tr><td>Al Green's Greatest Hits Volume II (77)
134(2) [0|0|9]</td><td>147</td></tr>
<tr><td>Al Green (72) 162(1) [0|0|9]</td><td>94.3</td></tr>
</table>

Act ► Highest Peak [Top10s|Top40s|Total] Title (Yr) Peak(Wk) [T10 Wk|T40Wk|TotalWk]	Score
Grant GREEN ► 2682 Pk:151 [0|0|1]	**118**
Visions (71) 151(1) [0|0|9]	118
Jack GREEN ► 2630 Pk:121 [0|0|1]	**127**
Humanesque (80) 121(1) [0|0|8]	127
Peter GREEN ► 3213 Pk:186 [0|0|1]	**38**
Little Dreamer (80) 186(1) [0|0|5]	38.4
Norman GREENBAUM ► 1230 Pk:23 [0|1|1]	**1276**
Spirit In The Sky (70) 23(2) [0|5|25]	1276
Jack GREENE ► 1576 Pk:66 [0|0|2]	**705**
There Goes My Everything (67) 66(1) [0|0|21]	577
All The Time (67) 151(2) [0|0|12]	128
Lorne GREENE ► 1672 Pk:35 [0|1|1]	**604**
Welcome To The Ponderosa (64) 35(1) [0|4|19]	604
GREEN ON RED ► 3227 Pk:177 [0|0|1]	**37**
No Free Lunch (86) 177(1) [0|0|6]	36.6
Lee GREENWOOD ► 1525 Pk:73 [0|0|4]	**761**
Somebody's Gonna Love You (83) 73(1) [0|0|21]	410
You've Got A Good Love Comin' (84) 150(1) [0|0|20]	180
Meant For Each Other (84)-Barbara Mandrell & Lee Greenwood [A] 89(1) [0|0|13]	116
Greatest Hits (85) 163(2) [0|0|8]	54.0
Joanie GREGGAINS ► 3281 Pk:177 [0|0|1]	**30**
Aerobic Shape Up II (83) 177(1) [0|0|4]	30.0
Dick GREGORY ► 3013 Pk:182 [0|0|1]	**64**
The Light Side: The Dark Side (69) 182(1) [0|0|8]	64.0
GREY And HANKS ► 2282 Pk:97 [0|0|2]	**222**
You Fooled Me (79) 97(2) [0|0|11]	205
Prime Time (80) 195(1) [0|0|3]	16.4
Nanci GRIFFITH ► 2232 Pk:99 [0|0|1]	**242**
Storms (89) 99(1) [0|0|14]	242
GRIM REAPER ► 1354 Pk:73 [0|0|3]	**1036**
See You In Hell (84) 73(2) [0|0|27]	420
Rock You To Hell (87) 93(1) [0|0|21]	381
Fear No Evil (85) 108(1) [0|0|14]	236
GRIN ► 2709 Pk:180 [0|0|3]	**113**
1 + 1 (72) 180(1) [0|0|6]	48.4
All Out (73) 186(1) [0|0|7]	42.3
Grin (71) 192(1) [0|0|3]	22.0
GRINDER SWITCH ► 2722 Pk:144 [0|0|1]	**110**
Redwing (77) 144(3) [0|0|8]	110
David GRISMAN ► 2305 Pk:108 [0|0|3]	**214**
David Grisman - Quintet "80" (80) 152(1) [0|0|8]	96.9
Live (81)-Stephane Grappelli/David Grisman [A] 108(1) [0|0|10]	89.7
Mondo Mando (81) 174(1) [0|0|3]	27.0
Larry GROCE ► 3433 Pk:187 [0|0|1]	**17**
Junkfood Junkie (76) 187(1) [0|0|2]	16.6
Henry GROSS ► 990 Pk:26 [0|1|3]	**1971**
Plug Me Into Something (75) 26(1) [0|3|23]	1103
Release (76) 64(1) [0|0|28]	804
Show Me To The Stage (77) 176(2) [0|0|7]	63.8
Dave GRUSIN ► 999 Pk:52 [0|0|10]	**1948**
Mountain Dance (81) 74(1) [0|0|18]	515
The Electric Horseman (Soundtrack) (80)-Willie Nelson/Dave Grusin [A] 52(2) [0|0|25]	369
The Fabulous Baker Boys (Soundtrack) (89) 74(2) [0|0|13]	285
The Goonies (Soundtrack) (85) 73(2) [0|0|10]	201
Dave Grusin Collection (89) 110(3) [0|0|12]	193
Out Of The Shadows (82) 88(2) [0|0|9]	159
Migration (89) 145(1) [0|0|8]	75.4

Act ► Highest Peak [Top10s|Top40s|Total] Title (Yr) Peak(Wk) [T10 Wk|T40Wk|TotalWk]	Score
Dave Grusin and the NY/LA Dream Band (83) 181(1) [0|0|6]	38.2
Harlequin (85)-Dave Grusin & Lee Ritenour [A] 192(1) [0|0|2]	4.7
Dave Grusin and the GRP All-Stars/Live In Japan (81)-Dave Grusin and the GRP All-Stars 140(2) [0|0|7]	108
GTR ► 964 Pk:11 [0|1|1]	**2069**
GTR (86) 11(2) [0|17|26]	2069
GUADALCANAL DIARY ► 2298 Pk:132 [0|0|2]	**218**
Flip-Flop (89) 132(2) [0|0|13]	172
2 X 4 (88) 183(1) [0|0|7]	45.5
GUCCI CREW II ► 3162 Pk:173 [0|0|1]	**45**
Everybody Wants Some (89) 173(1) [0|0|6]	45.3
GUESS WHO ► 211 Pk:9 [1|4|15]	**16289**
American Woman (70) 9(4) [7|23|55]	4539
The Best Of The Guess Who (71) 12(2) [0|23|45]	4389
Share The Land (70) 14(2) [0|11|25]	2202
Wheatfield Soul (69) 45(2) [0|0|19]	968
Live At The Paramount (Seattle) (72) 39(1) [0|1|21]	952
Road Food (74) 60(1) [0|0|26]	784
So Long, Bannatyne (71) 52(1) [0|0|16]	737
Canned Wheat Packed by The Guess Who (69) 91(1) [0|0|17]	415
Flavours (75) 48(1) [0|0|9]	401
Rockin' (72) 79(1) [0|0|10]	312
Artificial Paradise (73) 110(1) [0|0|12]	229
Power In The Music (75) 87(1) [0|0|7]	191
#10 (73) 155(1) [0|0|8]	102
The Greatest Of The Guess Who (77) 173(1) [0|0|4]	41.3
The Best Of The Guess Who, Volume II (74) 186(1) [0|0|4]	26.4
Greg GUIDRY ► 2947 Pk:147 [0|0|1]	**72**
Over The Line (82) 147(1) [0|0|7]	72.4
GUNS N' ROSES ► 132 Pk:1 [2|2|2]	**24245**
Appetite For Destruction (87) 1(5) [52|78|147]	17811
G N' R Lies (88) 2(1) [18|33|53]	6434
Arlo GUTHRIE ► 376 Pk:17 [0|2|11]	**8808**
Alice's Restaurant (67) 17(2) [0|23|99]	4547
Hobo's Lullaby (72) 52(2) [0|0|38]	1186
Washington County (70) 33(1) [0|3|17]	865
Running Down The Road (69) 54(1) [0|0|19]	768
Alice's Restaurant (Soundtrack) (69) 63(1) [0|0|17]	611
Last Of The Brooklyn Cowboys (73) 87(1) [0|0|14]	309
Arlo (68) 100(2) [0|0|12]	274
Amigo (76) 133(1) [0|0|6]	106
Arlo Guthrie (74) 165(1) [0|0|10]	101
Power Of Love (81) 184(2) [0|0|3]	23.9
Together In Concert (75)-Pete Seeger/Arlo Guthrie [A] 181(1) [0|0|4]	17.7
Gwen GUTHRIE ► 2266 Pk:89 [0|0|1]	**227**
Good To Go Lover (86) 89(2) [0|0|13]	227
GUY ► 775 Pk:27 [0|1|1]	**3108**
Guy (88) 27(5) [0|13|70]	3108
GYPSY ► 1401 Pk:44 [0|0|2]	**971**
Gypsy (70) 44(1) [0|0|20]	904
In The Garden (71) 173(1) [0|0|8]	67.5

H

Act ► Highest Peak [Top10s|Top40s|Total] Title (Yr) Peak(Wk) [T10 Wk|T40Wk|TotalWk]	Score
Steve HACKETT ► 1796 Pk:103 [0|0|5]	**488**
Please Don't Touch (78) 103(2) [0|0|14]	278
Defector (80) 144(1) [0|0|6]	85.1
Spectral Mornings (79) 138(2) [0|0|4]	66.4
Cured (81) 169(2) [0|0|3]	31.7
Voyage Of The Acolyte (76) 191(1) [0|0|4]	26.3
Sammy HAGAR ► 393 Pk:14 [0|4|11]	**8404**
Three Lock Box (82) 17(2) [0|14|34]	1980
Standing Hampton (82) 28(2) [0|14|32]	1836
I Never Said Goodbye (87) 14(1) [0|11|23]	1636
VOA (84) 32(3) [0|9|36]	1571
Street Machine (79) 71(1) [0|0|13]	386
Danger Zone (80) 85(1) [0|0|12]	284
All Night Long (78) 89(1) [0|0|9]	212
Musical Chairs (78) 100(1) [0|0|11]	203
Through The Fire (84)-Hagar, Schon, Aaronson, Shrieve [A] 42(2) [0|0|18]	151
Sammy Hagar (77) 167(1) [0|0|9]	86.5
Rematch (83) 171(2) [0|0|9]	57.4
Nina HAGEN ► 2816 Pk:151 [0|0|2]	**93**
Fearless (84) 151(2) [0|0|8]	74.5
Nunsexmonkrock (82) 184(1) [0|0|3]	18.9
Merle HAGGARD ► 469 Pk:37 [0|1|20]	**6727**
Okie From Muskogee (70)-Merle Haggard And The Strangers 46(1) [0|0|52]	1623
The Fightin' Side Of Me (70) 68(2) [0|0|33]	977
Poncho & Lefty (83)-Merle Haggard/Willie Nelson [A] 37(1) [0|1|53]	754
Same Train, A Different Time (69) 67(1) [0|0|18]	740
Hag (71)-Merle Haggard And The Strangers 66(1) [0|0|15]	470
A Tribute To The Best Damn Fiddle Player In The World (Or, My Salute To Bob Wills) (70) 58(2) [0|0|9]	357
A Portrait Of Merle Haggard (69) 99(1) [0|0|11]	279
Someday We'll Look Back (71) 108(2) [0|0|10]	260
Big City (81) 161(1) [0|0|28]	232
I Love Dixie Blues...So I Recorded "Live" In New Orleans (73)-Merle Haggard And The Strangers 126(1) [0|0|11]	175
The Best Of The Best Of Merle Haggard (72) 137(1) [0|0|9]	150
Keep Movin' On (75) 129(2) [0|0|9]	148
Close-Up (69) 140(1) [0|0|6]	113
I'm A Lonesome Fugitive (67) 165(2) [0|0|10]	90.6
My Farewell To Elvis (77) 133(1) [0|0|5]	83.5
Let Me Tell You About A Song (72) 166(1) [0|0|8]	81.9
A Taste Of Yesterday's Wine (82)-Merle Haggard/George Jones [A] 123(4) [0|0|12]	80.8
Pride In What I Am (69) 189(1) [0|0|7]	54.3
Branded Man (67)-Merle Haggard And The Strangers 167(1) [0|0|4]	36.3
If We Make It Through December (74) 190(1) [0|0|3]	21.7
HAIRCUT ONE HUNDRED ► 1193 Pk:31 [0|1|1]	**1363**
Pelican West (82) 31(3) [0|7|37]	1363
Daryl HALL ► 1236 Pk:29 [0|1|2]	**1262**
Three Hearts In The Happy Ending Machine (86) 29(3) [0|6|26]	879
Sacred Songs (80) 58(2) [0|0|12]	383
Daryl HALL & John OATES ► 38 Pk:3 [4|13|16]	**47738**
H2O (82) 3(15) [33|46|68]	9556
Private Eyes (81) 5(3) [13|32|61]	6383
Voices (80) 17(1) [0|35|100]	6297
Bigger Than Both Of Us (76) 13(1) [0|35|57]	5998
Big Bam Boom (84) 5(2) [12|31|51]	4851
Rock 'N Soul Part 1 (83) 7(2) [11|28|44]	3750
Daryl Hall & John Oates (75) 17(1) [0|11|76]	3473

Act ▶ Highest Peak [Top10s|Top40s|Total]
Title (Yr) Peak(Wk) [T10 Wk|T40Wk|TotalWk] **Score**

Daryl HALL & John OATES ▶ *Continued*
Ooh Yeah! (88) 24(2) [0|7|26] 1295
X-Static (79) 33(1) [0|6|24] 1254
Abandoned Luncheonette (74) 33(1) [0|4|38] 1186
Along The Red Ledge (78) 27(2) [0|6|22] 1046
Beauty On A Back Street (77) 30(1) [0|5|17] 917
Hall & Oates Live At The Apollo With David Ruffin & Eddie Kendrick (85) 21(2) [0|8|18] 873
Livetime (78) 42(1) [0|0|10] 431
War Babies (74) 86(2) [0|0|10] 282
No Goodbyes (77) 92(1) [0|0|6] 148

Jimmy HALL ▶ 3425 Pk:183 [0|0|1] 17
Touch You (80) 183(1) [0|0|2] 17.1

John HALL Band ▶ 2365 Pk:147 [0|0|2] 194
All Of The Above (81) 158(3) [0|0|13] 143
Searchparty (83) 147(2) [0|0|5] 51.3

Tom T. HALL ▶ 2104 Pk:137 [0|0|4] 299
For The People In The Last Hard Town (74) 149(1) [0|0|11] 136
In Search Of A Song (71) 137(2) [0|0|6] 114
The Rhymer And Other Five And Dimers (73) 181(1) [0|0|4] 29.7
Songs Of Fox Hollow (75) 180(1) [0|0|2] 19.3

Chico HAMILTON ▶ 3150 Pk:145 [0|0|1] 46
Man From Two Worlds (64) 145(2) [0|0|4] 46.3

George HAMILTON IV ▶ 2434 Pk:77 [0|0|1] 177
Abilene (63) 77(1) [0|0|8] 177

HAMILTON, JOE FRANK & REYNOLDS ▶ 1440 Pk:59 [0|0|3] 907
Hamilton, Joe Frank & Reynolds (71) 59(2) [0|0|15] 551
Fallin' In Love (75) 82(1) [0|0|14] 330
Hallway Symphony (72) 191(1) [0|0|4] 25.9

Marvin HAMLISCH ▶ 431 Pk:1 [1|1|2] 7401
The Sting (Soundtrack) (74) 1(5) [15|23|41] 7349
The Entertainer (74) 170(2) [0|0|5] 52.6

Jan HAMMER Group ▶ 1780 Pk:23 [0|1|1] 497
Jeff Beck With The Jan Hammer Group Live (77)-Jeff Beck With The Jan Hammer Group [A] 23(1) [0|6|15] 497
--See also Jerry Goodman/Jan Hammer

Albert HAMMOND ▶ 1904 Pk:77 [0|0|2] 405
It Never Rains In Southern California (72) 77(2) [0|0|15] 383
The Free Electric Band (73) 193(1) [0|0|4] 21.6

Johnny HAMMOND ▶ 2090 Pk:125 [0|0|2] 307
Breakout (71) 125(1) [0|0|14] 249
Wild Horses/Rock Steady (72) 174(1) [0|0|6] 58.0

John Paul HAMMOND ▶ 2972 Pk:105 [0|0|1] 70
Triumvirate (73)-Mike Bloomfield/John Paul Hammond/Dr. John [A] 105(1) [0|0|12] 209

Herbie HANCOCK ▶ 290 Pk:13 [0|4|18] 12075
Head Hunters (74) 13(1) [0|21|47] 3602
Future Shock (83) 43(2) [0|0|65] 2229
Thrust (74) 13(1) [0|9|23] 1819
Man-Child (75) 21(1) [0|4|24] 1279
Feets Don't Fail Me Now (79) 38(1) [0|3|22] 819
Secrets (76) 49(2) [0|0|17] 584
Sunlight (78) 58(1) [0|0|13] 442
Monster (80) 94(1) [0|0|18] 361
Sound-System (84) 71(2) [0|0|14] 281
V.S.O.P. (77) 79(1) [0|0|7] 203
Mr. Hands (80) 117(1) [0|0|6] 112
Magic Windows (81) 140(1) [0|0|6] 85.2

Act ▶ Highest Peak [Top10s|Top40s|Total]
Title (Yr) Peak(Wk) [T10 Wk|T40Wk|TotalWk] **Score**

An Evening With Herbie Hancock And Chick Corea (79)-Herbie Hancock And Chick Corea [A] 100(1) [0|0|8] 84.4
Lite Me Up (82) 151(2) [0|0|6] 61.5
Sextant (73) 176(1) [0|0|6] 48.7
Treasure Chest (74) 158(1) [0|0|3] 42.3
Blow-Up (Soundtrack) (67) 192(2) [0|0|2] 12.2

John HANDY ▶ 1473 Pk:43 [0|0|2] 854
Hard Work (76) 43(2) [0|0|21] 843
Carnival (77) 200(2) [0|0|2] 11.0

Bo HANSSON ▶ 2894 Pk:154 [0|0|1] 81
Lord Of The Rings (73) 154(1) [0|0|8] 80.5

The HAPPENINGS ▶ 1805 Pk:61 [0|0|4] 480
Back To Back (67)-The Tokens/The Happenings [A] 134(1) [0|0|6] 45.4
The Happenings (66) 61(2) [0|0|12] 356
The Happenings Golden Hits! (68) 156(2) [0|0|4] 56.9
Piece Of Mind (69) 181(2) [0|0|2] 22.1

Paul HARDCASTLE ▶ 1728 Pk:63 [0|0|1] 551
Rain Forest (85) 63(2) [0|0|25] 551

HARDEN Trio ▶ 2977 Pk:146 [0|0|1] 68
Tippy Toeing (66) 146(1) [0|0|5] 68.5

Tim HARDIN ▶ 2460 Pk:129 [0|0|2] 171
Suite For Susan Moore And Damion-We Are-One, One, All In One (69) 129(1) [0|0|8] 163
Bird On A Wire (71) 189(1) [0|0|1] 8.6

Hagood HARDY ▶ 2248 Pk:112 [0|0|1] 235
The Homecoming (76) 112(3) [0|0|14] 235

HARDY BOYS ▶ 3482 Pk:199 [0|0|1] 12
Here Come The Hardy Boys (69) 199(2) [0|0|2] 12.3

HARPERS BIZARRE ▶ 1761 Pk:76 [0|0|2] 510
Anything Goes (67) 76(1) [0|0|13] 386
Feelin' Groovy (67) 108(1) [0|0|7] 124

Eddie HARRIS ▶ 805 Pk:36 [0|1|11] 2913
The Electrifying Eddie Harris (68) 36(1) [0|1|41] 1604
Plug Me In (68) 120(2) [0|0|16] 289
Is It In (74) 100(1) [0|0|11] 246
High Voltage (69) 122(1) [0|0|9] 203
I Need Some Money (75) 125(1) [0|0|9] 135
Eddie Harris Live At Newport (71) 164(1) [0|0|10] 125
E.H. in the U.K. (74) 150(1) [0|0|11] 119
Bad Luck Is All I Have (75) 133(1) [0|0|6] 110
Instant Death (72) 185(1) [0|0|7] 49.6
The Best Of Eddie Harris (70) 191(1) [0|0|3] 20.5
Silver Cycles (69) 199(1) [0|0|2] 11.9

Emmylou HARRIS ▶ 304 Pk:6 [1|6|17] 11224
Roses In The Snow (80) 26(2) [0|11|34] 1665
Evangeline (81) 22(3) [0|9|24] 1480
Elite Hotel (76) 25(1) [0|8|23] 1460
Luxury Liner (77) 21(2) [0|8|21] 1413
Quarter Moon In A Ten Cent Town (78) 29(1) [0|5|18] 924
Trio (87)-Dolly Parton, Linda Ronstadt, Emmylou Harris [A] 6(1) [3|14|48] 848
Blue Kentucky Girl (79) 43(2) [0|0|22] 783
Cimarron (81) 46(1) [0|0|20] 737
Pieces Of The Sky (75) 45(2) [0|0|15] 606
Last Date (82) 65(4) [0|0|17] 402
Profile: Best Of Emmylou Harris (78) 81(1) [0|0|17] 365
White Shoes (83) 116(1) [0|0|13] 197
Light Of The Stable: The Christmas Album (80) 102(3) [0|0|9] 196
Thirteen (86) 157(2) [0|0|6] 50.4

Act ▶ Highest Peak [Top10s|Top40s|Total]
Title (Yr) Peak(Wk) [T10 Wk|T40Wk|TotalWk] **Score**

Profile II: The Best Of Emmylou Harris (84) 176(1) [0|0|6] 36.8
The Ballad Of Sally Rose (85) 171(2) [0|0|4] 33.3
Angel Band (87) 166(2) [0|0|4] 30.1

Major HARRIS ▶ 1261 Pk:28 [0|1|2] 1218
My Way (75) 28(2) [0|3|22] 1132
Jealousy (76) 153(2) [0|0|6] 85.5

Richard HARRIS ▶ 423 Pk:4 [1|4|6] 7542
A Tramp Shining (68) 4(3) [5|16|42] 3427
Jonathan Livingston Seagull (73) 25(1) [0|9|27] 1514
The Yard Went On Forever... (68) 27(1) [0|6|15] 1158
The Prophet By Kahlil Gibran (74) 29(1) [0|5|15] 981
My Boy (71) 71(1) [0|0|14] 413
Slides (72) 181(1) [0|0|6] 48.9

Sam HARRIS ▶ 1223 Pk:35 [0|1|2] 1295
Sam Harris (84) 35(2) [0|3|29] 989
Sam-I-Am (86) 69(1) [0|0|14] 305

Don HARRISON Band ▶ 2910 Pk:159 [0|0|1] 79
Don Harrison Band (76) 159(1) [0|0|6] 78.7

George HARRISON ▶ 90 Pk:1 [6|10|14] 31599
All Things Must Pass (70) 1(7) [14|22|38] 7410
The Concert For Bangla Desh (72)-George Harrison and Friends 2(6) [10|23|41] 6165
Living In The Material World (73) 1(5) [7|15|26] 4174
Cloud Nine (87) 8(1) [9|22|31] 3080
Dark Horse (74) 4(1) [5|9|17] 2480
Thirty Three & 1/3 (76) 11(2) [0|8|21] 1965
George Harrison (79) 14(1) [0|9|18] 1708
Extra Texture (Read All About It) (75) 8(3) [5|7|11] 1587
Somewhere In England (81) 11(2) [0|7|13] 1295
Best Of George Harrison (76) 31(2) [0|4|15] 797
Wonderwall Music (69) 49(2) [0|0|16] 750
Gone Troppo (82) 108(2) [0|0|7] 100
The Best Of Dark Horse (89) 132(2) [0|0|6] 70.3
Electronic Sound (69) 191(1) [0|0|2] 17.0

Jerry HARRISON: CASUAL GODS ▶ 1793 Pk:78 [0|0|1] 489
Casual Gods (88) 78(1) [0|0|20] 489

Noel HARRISON ▶ 2642 Pk:135 [0|0|1] 125
Collage (67) 135(1) [0|0|9] 125

Wes HARRISON ▶ 2757 Pk:83 [0|0|1] 103
You Won't Believe Your Ears (63) 83(1) [0|0|5] 103

Wilbert HARRISON ▶ 3444 Pk:190 [0|0|1] 16
Let's Work Together (70) 190(2) [0|0|2] 15.7

Debbie HARRY ▶ 1301 Pk:25 [0|1|3] 1138
KooKoo (81) 25(1) [0|4|12] 803
Rockbird (86) 97(2) [0|0|13] 226
Def, Dumb & Blonde (89)-Deborah Harry 123(2) [0|0|8] 109

Corey HART ▶ 610 Pk:20 [0|2|4] 4644
Boy In The Box (85) 20(7) [0|15|37] 2253
First Offense (84) 31(3) [0|6|36] 1550
Fields Of Fire (86) 55(2) [0|0|27] 722
Young Man Running (88) 121(2) [0|0|8] 118

Freddie HART ▶ 1091 Pk:37 [0|1|4] 1625
Easy Loving (71) 37(1) [0|4|20] 1009
Bless Your Heart (72) 93(2) [0|0|14] 311
My Hang-Up Is You (72) 89(1) [0|0|11] 265
Trip To Heaven (73) 188(1) [0|0|6] 40.0

Mickey HART ▶ 3324 Pk:190 [0|0|1] 26
Rolling Thunder (72) 190(1) [0|0|4] 26.0

Act ▶ Highest Peak [Top10s | Top40s | Total] Title (Yr) Peak(Wk) [T10 Wk | T40Wk | TotalWk]	Score
John HARTFORD ▶ 2288 Pk:137 [0|0|2]	**220**
John Hartford (69) 137(1) [0|0|9]	194
Aereo-Plain (71) 193(1) [0|0|4]	26.1
KEEF HARTLEY BAND ▶ 3372 Pk:191 [0|0|1]	**22**
The Time Is Near (70) 191(2) [0|0|3]	21.7
Dan HARTMAN ▶ 1275 Pk:55 [0|0|3]	**1189**
I Can Dream About You (84) 55(3) [0|0|28]	725
Instant Replay (78) 80(2) [0|0|19]	449
Relight My Fire (80) 189(1) [0|0|2]	14.8
Sensational Alex HARVEY Band ▶ 2673 Pk:100 [0|0|2]	**119**
Live (75) 100(2) [0|0|4]	112
The Impossible Dream (75) 197(1) [0|0|1]	6.5
Annie HASLEM ▶ 2655 Pk:167 [0|0|1]	**123**
Annie In Wonderland (77) 167(1) [0|0|13]	123
Donny HATHAWAY ▶ 443 Pk:3 [1|2|5]	**7219**
Donny Hathaway Live (72) 18(2) [0|23|38]	3318
Roberta Flack & Donny Hathaway (72)-Roberta Flack & Donny Hathaway [A] 3(2) [8|21|39]	2211
Everything Is Everything (71) 73(1) [0|0|25]	788
Donny Hathaway (71) 89(1) [0|0|21]	546
Extension Of A Man (73) 69(1) [0|0|13]	357
Richie HAVENS ▶ 778 Pk:29 [0|1|13]	**3105**
Alarm Clock (71) 29(1) [0|7|34]	1533
Richie Havens On Stage (72) 55(2) [0|0|18]	565
Richard P. Havens, 1983 (69) 80(2) [0|0|11]	390
The Great Blind Degree (71) 126(1) [0|0|11]	226
Stonehenge (70) 155(1) [0|0|14]	150
End Of The Beginning (76) 157(1) [0|0|4]	55.2
Something Else Again (68) 184(1) [0|0|7]	47.1
Simple Things (87) 173(1) [0|0|4]	30.4
Portfolio (73) 182(1) [0|0|4]	29.3
Mixed Bag II (74) 186(1) [0|0|3]	22.7
Electric Havens (68) 192(1) [0|0|3]	21.4
Mixed Bag (68) 182(1) [0|0|2]	18.1
Mixed Bag(2) (70) 190(1) [0|0|2]	16.2
Edwin HAWKINS Singers ▶ 1000 Pk:15 [0|1|3]	**1940**
Let Us Go Into The House Of The Lord (69) 15(1) [0|8|23]	1835
Children (Get Together) (71) 180(1) [0|0|8]	66.3
I'd Like To Teach The World To Sing (72) 171(1) [0|0|4]	38.0
HAWKWIND ▶ 1993 Pk:110 [0|0|3]	**353**
Hall Of The Mountain Grill (74) 110(1) [0|0|12]	228
Warrior On The Edge Of Time (75) 150(1) [0|0|5]	66.8
Space Ritual/Alive In Liverpool And London (73) 179(1) [0|0|8]	57.5
Colin James HAY ▶ 2745 Pk:126 [0|0|1]	**105**
Looking For Jack (87) 126(2) [0|0|9]	105
Isaac HAYES ▶ 65 Pk:1 [4|9|21]	**39251**
Shaft (Soundtrack) (71) 1(1) [15|30|60]	8587
Hot Buttered Soul (69) 8(3) [4|36|81]	7331
The Isaac Hayes Movement (70) 8(1) [6|28|75]	5908
To Be Continued (70) 11(2) [0|20|56]	4236
Black Moses (71) 10(2) [2|15|34]	3071
Live At The Sahara Tahoe (73) 14(2) [0|11|26]	1914
Joy (73) 16(1) [0|14|27]	1890
Chocolate Chip (75) 18(2) [0|9|19]	1634
Don't Let Go (79) 39(1) [0|1|30]	1423
Groove-A-Thon (76) 45(1) [0|0|12]	548
For The Sake Of Love (78) 75(2) [0|0|18]	466
And Once Again (80) 59(1) [0|0|15]	447

Act ▶ Highest Peak [Top10s | Top40s | Total] Title (Yr) Peak(Wk) [T10 Wk | T40Wk | TotalWk]	Score
Disco Connection (76)-Isaac Hayes Movement 85(1) [0|0|17]	401
New Horizon (77) 78(1) [0|0|12]	268
In The Beginning (72) 102(1) [0|0|12]	262
A Man And A Woman (77)-Isaac Hayes & Dionne Warwick [A] 49(1) [0|0|13]	253
Royal Rappin's (79)-Millie Jackson & Isaac Hayes [A] 80(2) [0|0|19]	214
Juicy Fruit (Disco Freak) (76) 124(1) [0|0|7]	134
Tough Guys (Soundtrack) (74) 146(1) [0|0|8]	108
Truck Turner (Soundtrack) (74) 156(1) [0|0|9]	102
The Best Of Isaac Hayes (75) 165(1) [0|0|4]	52.4
Justin HAYWARD ▶ 1068 Pk:16 [0|2|3]	**1690**
Blue Jays (75)-Justin Hayward & John Lodge [A] 16(1) [0|8|23]	886
Songwriter (77) 37(1) [0|3|16]	749
Night Flight (80) 166(2) [0|0|5]	55.0
Leon HAYWOOD ▶ 1989 Pk:92 [0|0|2]	**355**
Naturally (80) 92(2) [0|0|10]	199
Come And Get Yourself Some (75) 140(1) [0|0|13]	156
Ofra HAZA ▶ 2643 Pk:130 [0|0|1]	**124**
Shaday (89) 130(2) [0|0|9]	124
Robert HAZARD ▶ 2424 Pk:102 [0|0|1]	**181**
Robert Hazard (83) 102(1) [0|0|11]	181
Lee HAZLEWOOD ▶ 1219 Pk:13 [0|1|1]	**1303**
Nancy & Lee (68)-Nancy Sinatra & Lee Hazlewood [A] 13(1) [0|18|44]	1303
Roy HEAD ▶ 2649 Pk:122 [0|0|1]	**124**
Treat Me Right (65) 122(1) [0|0|8]	124
The HEADBOYS ▶ 2225 Pk:113 [0|0|1]	**244**
The Headboys (79) 113(1) [0|0|15]	244
HEAD EAST ▶ 1056 Pk:65 [0|0|7]	**1728**
Head East Live! (79) 65(1) [0|0|14]	402
Head East (78) 78(1) [0|0|14]	385
A Different Kind Of Crazy (79) 96(1) [0|0|16]	334
Flat As A Pancake (75) 126(2) [0|0|17]	317
U.S. 1 (80) 137(1) [0|0|6]	106
Gettin' Lucky (77) 136(1) [0|0|7]	105
Get Yourself Up (76) 161(1) [0|0|6]	79.0
HEADHUNTERS ▶ 2427 Pk:126 [0|0|1]	**180**
Survival Of The Fittest (75) 126(1) [0|0|10]	180
The HEADPINS ▶ 2672 Pk:114 [0|0|1]	**119**
Line Of Fire (84) 114(1) [0|0|9]	119
Jeff HEALEY Band ▶ 969 Pk:22 [0|1|1]	**2041**
See The Light (88) 22(3) [0|8|69]	2041
HEAR 'N AID ▶ 2582 Pk:80 [0|0|1]	**140**
Hear 'N Aid (86) 80(2) [0|0|7]	140
HEART ▶ 64 Pk:1 [5|10|10]	**39475**
Heart (85) 1(1) [37|58|92]	11541
Bad Animals (87) 2(3) [18|36|50]	6177
Dreamboat Annie (76) 7(2) [3|21|100]	6018
Little Queen (77) 9(2) [3|22|41]	4503
Dog And Butterfly (78) 17(1) [0|22|36]	3764
Bebe Le Strange (80) 5(2) [4|13|22]	2426
Greatest Hits/Live (80) 13(3) [0|12|25]	2112
Magazine (78) 17(1) [0|7|25]	1698
Passionworks (83) 39(1) [0|2|21]	671
Private Audition (82) 25(2) [0|4|14]	565
HEARTSFIELD ▶ 2877 Pk:159 [0|0|1]	**83**
Foolish Pleasures (75) 159(1) [0|0|7]	83.0
Joey HEATHERTON ▶ 2506 Pk:154 [0|0|1]	**158**
The Joey Heatherton Album (72) 154(1) [0|0|13]	158
HEATWAVE ▶ 499 Pk:10 [1|3|5]	**6175**
Too Hot To Handle (77) 11(1) [0|12|45]	2892

Act ▶ Highest Peak [Top10s | Top40s | Total] Title (Yr) Peak(Wk) [T10 Wk | T40Wk | TotalWk]	Score
Central Heating (78) 10(2) [2|12|26]	2341
Hot Property (79) 38(2) [0|3|14]	614
Candles (80) 71(2) [0|0|10]	272
Current (82) 156(2) [0|0|6]	55.0
HEAVEN 17 ▶ 1463 Pk:68 [0|0|3]	**870**
Heaven 17 (83) 68(3) [0|0|28]	551
The Luxury Gap (83) 72(2) [0|0|13]	297
Pleasure One (87) 177(2) [0|0|3]	22.0
HEAVY D & The BOYZ ▶ 777 Pk:19 [0|1|2]	**3106**
Big Tyme (89) 19(3) [0|14|51]	2838
Living Large... (87) 92(2) [0|0|16]	268
Bobby HEBB ▶ 2228 Pk:103 [0|0|1]	**243**
Sunny (66) 103(1) [0|0|12]	243
Neal HEFTI ▶ 1620 Pk:41 [0|0|1]	**652**
Batman Theme (66) 41(2) [0|0|21]	652
HEINTJE ▶ 2283 Pk:108 [0|0|1]	**221**
Mama (70) 108(1) [0|0|11]	221
HELIX ▶ 1644 Pk:69 [0|0|4]	**624**
Walkin' The Razor's Edge (84) 69(2) [0|0|16]	323
Long Way To Heaven (85) 103(1) [0|0|17]	264
No Rest For The Wicked (83) 186(1) [0|0|4]	22.1
Wild In The Streets (87) 179(2) [0|0|2]	15.3
HELLO PEOPLE ▶ 2449 Pk:145 [0|0|1]	**174**
The Handsome Devils (74) 145(2) [0|0|13]	174
HELLOWEEN ▶ 1696 Pk:104 [0|0|3]	**586**
Keeper Of The Seven Keys - Part I (87) 104(1) [0|0|21]	286
Keeper Of The Seven Keys - Part II (88) 108(2) [0|0|16]	211
I Want Out-Live (89) 123(2) [0|0|7]	88.9
Levon HELM ▶ 2497 Pk:142 [0|0|1]	**160**
Levon Helm & The RCO All-Stars (77) 142(1) [0|0|10]	160
Michael HENDERSON ▶ 780 Pk:35 [0|2|7]	**3094**
In The Night-Time (78) 38(1) [0|2|28]	1044
Wide Receiver (80) 35(1) [0|5|18]	849
Goin' Places (77) 49(1) [0|0|13]	489
Do It All (79) 64(1) [0|0|12]	353
Slingshot (81) 86(2) [0|0|11]	253
Solid (76) 173(1) [0|0|7]	65.8
Fickle (83) 169(1) [0|0|5]	40.8
Skitch HENDERSON ▶ 2585 Pk:103 [0|0|1]	**139**
Skitch...Tonight! (65) 103(1) [0|0|8]	139
Jimi HENDRIX ▶ 188 Pk:3 [3|5|17]	**18349**
Band Of Gypsys (70) 5(4) [7|23|61]	5259
The Cry Of Love (71) 3(2) [7|17|39]	4351
Crash Landing (75) 5(1) [4|9|20]	2260
Rainbow Bridge (Soundtrack) (71) 15(1) [0|9|21]	1976
Hendrix In The West (72) 12(3) [0|9|19]	1932
War Heroes (72) 48(1) [0|0|18]	640
Midnight Lightning (75) 43(1) [0|0|11]	430
Sound Track Recordings From The Film Jimi Hendrix (73) 89(1) [0|0|18]	377
Rare Hendrix (72) 82(2) [0|0|11]	285
The Essential Jimi Hendrix (78) 114(2) [0|0|15]	213
The Jimi Hendrix Concerts (82) 79(2) [0|0|8]	181
Get That Feeling (67)-Jimi Hendrix and Curtis Knight [A] 75(2) [0|0|12]	152
Nine To The Universe (80) 127(1) [0|0|7]	104
The Essential Jimi Hendrix Vol.II (79) 156(2) [0|0|7]	82.6
Kiss The Sky (84) 148(1) [0|0|5]	52.2
Two Great Experiences Together! (71)-Jimi Hendrix & Lonnie Youngblood [A] 127(1) [0|0|4]	38.8
Jimi Plays Monterey (86) 192(2) [0|0|3]	15.3

Act ► Highest Peak [Top10s|Top40s|Total]
Title (Yr) Peak(Wk) [T10 Wk|T40Wk|TotalWk] — **Score**

Jimi HENDRIX EXPERIENCE ► 116 Pk:1 [4|5|6] — **26797**
Are You Experienced? (67) 5(1) [32|76|106] — 12140
Electric Ladyland (68) 1(2) [10|17|37] — 5633
Axis: Bold As Love (68) 3(3) [8|14|53] — 4033
Smash Hits (69) 6(2) [6|17|35] — 4007
Monterey International Pop Festival (70)-Otis Redding/The Jimi Hendrix Experience [A] 16(2) [0|8|20] — 751
Radio One (88) 119(2) [0|0|17] — 234

Nona HENDRYX ► 1678 Pk:83 [0|0|3] — **601**
Nona (83) 83(1) [0|0|19] — 319
Female Trouble (87) 96(2) [0|0|13] — 225
The Art Of Defense (84) 167(1) [0|0|7] — 57.4

Don HENLEY ► 240 Pk:8 [1|3|3] — **14758**
The End Of The Innocence (89) 8(1) [5|58|148] — 8388
Building The Perfect Beast (84) 13(5) [0|30|63] — 4238
I Can't Stand Still (82) 24(7) [0|20|35] — 2131

Carol HENSEL ► 866 Pk:56 [0|0|3] — **2563**
Carol Hensel's Exercise And Dance Program (81) 56(1) [0|0|55] — 1759
Carol Hensel's Exercise And Dance Program, Volume 2 (81) 70(1) [0|0|28] — 628
Carol Hensel's Exercise And Dance Program, Volume 3 (83) 104(2) [0|0|12] — 175

Ken HENSLEY ► 3030 Pk:173 [0|0|1] — **62**
Proud Words On A Dusty Shelf (73) 173(1) [0|0|7] — 61.5
An Evening With Chick Corea & Herbie Hancock (79)-Chick Corea & Herbie Hancock [A] 175(1) [0|0|2] — 9.9

Woody HERMAN ► 2871 Pk:136 [0|0|2] — **84**
Encore: Woody Herman - 1963 (63) 136(2) [0|0|4] — 59.9
Woody Herman: 1964 (64) 148(2) [0|0|2] — 24.6

HERMAN'S HERMITS ► 155 Pk:2 [3|6|10] — **21602**
The Best Of Herman's Hermits (65) 5(3) [16|27|105] — 5995
Introducing Herman's Hermits (65) 2(4) [17|26|40] — 4748
Herman's Hermits On Tour (65) 2(6) [18|24|39] — 4648
There's A Kind Of Hush All Over The World (67) 13(2) [0|13|35] — 2311
Hold On! (Soundtrack) (66) 14(2) [0|7|26] — 1471
The Best Of Herman's Hermits, Volume 2 (66) 20(2) [0|7|32] — 1339
Both Sides Of Herman's Hermits (66) 48(1) [0|0|21] — 664
Blaze (67) 75(1) [0|0|9] — 231
The Best Of Herman's Hermits, Volume III (68) 102(1) [0|0|8] — 166
Mrs. Brown, You've Got A Lovely Daughter (Soundtrack) (68) 182(1) [0|0|3] — 29.0

Patrick HERNANDEZ ► 1778 Pk:61 [0|0|1] — **498**
Born To Be Alive (79) 61(2) [0|0|15] — 498

The HESITATIONS ► 3431 Pk:193 [0|0|1] — **17**
The New Born Free (68) 193(1) [0|0|3] — 16.7

Howard HEWETT ► 2095 Pk:110 [0|0|2] — **306**
Forever And Ever (88) 110(2) [0|0|12] — 189
I Commit To Love (86) 159(2) [0|0|16] — 117

Nick HEYWARD ► 3304 Pk:178 [0|0|1] — **28**
North Of A Miracle (84) 178(2) [0|0|4] — 27.9

John HIATT ► 1557 Pk:98 [0|0|2] — **723**
Slow Turning (88) 98(3) [0|0|31] — 464
Bring The Family (87) 107(2) [0|0|17] — 259

Dan HICKS & His HOT LICKS ► 1645 Pk:67 [0|0|4] — **624**
Last Train To Hicksville...The Home Of Happy Feet (73) 67(1) [0|0|18] — 486
Where's The Money? (71) 195(2) [0|0|8] — 51.5
Striking It Rich! (72) 170(1) [0|0|5] — 48.3
It Happened One Bite (78)-Dan Hicks 165(2) [0|0|3] — 37.8

Bertie HIGGINS ► 1405 Pk:38 [0|1|1] — **966**
Just Another Day In Paradise (82) 38(2) [0|3|25] — 966

HIGH INERGY ► 1011 Pk:28 [0|1|3] — **1900**
Turnin' On (77) 28(3) [0|7|25] — 1294
Steppin' Out (78) 42(2) [0|0|13] — 530
Shoulda Gone Dancin' (79) 147(2) [0|0|5] — 77.0

The HIGHWAYMEN ► 2319 Pk:79 [0|0|1] — **210**
Hootenanny With The Highwaymen (63) 79(1) [0|0|9] — 210

Dan HILL ► 879 Pk:21 [0|1|5] — **2493**
Longer Fuse (77) 21(2) [0|8|24] — 1364
Dan Hill (75) 104(2) [0|0|17] — 378
Dan Hill(2) (87) 90(1) [0|0|19] — 315
Hold On (78) 79(3) [0|0|14] — 304
Frozen In The Night (78) 118(2) [0|0|6] — 131

Z.Z. HILL ► 2652 Pk:165 [0|0|3] — **123**
I'm A Blues Man (84) 170(2) [0|0|9] — 69.5
The Rhythm & The Blues (83) 165(1) [0|0|5] — 41.4
The Brand New Z.Z. Hill (72) 194(1) [0|0|2] — 11.8

Steve HILLAGE ► 2545 Pk:130 [0|0|1] — **149**
L (77) 130(1) [0|0|9] — 149

Chris HILLMAN ► 2747 Pk:152 [0|0|2] — **105**
Slippin' Away (76) 152(2) [0|0|6] — 84.1
Clear Sailin' (77) 188(1) [0|0|3] — 21.0

HILLSIDE SINGERS ► 2038 Pk:71 [0|0|1] — **334**
I'd Like To Teach The World To Sing (72) 71(1) [0|0|16] — 334

HIPSWAY ► 1826 Pk:55 [0|0|1] — **462**
Hipsway (87) 55(2) [0|0|18] — 462

HIROSHIMA ► 793 Pk:51 [0|0|6] — **2977**
Hiroshima (79) 51(2) [0|0|27] — 768
Another Place (85) 79(2) [0|0|45] — 736
Go (87) 75(2) [0|0|32] — 624
Odori (80) 72(1) [0|0|18] — 413
East (89) 105(2) [0|0|19] — 327
Third Generation (83) 142(1) [0|0|9] — 109

Al HIRT ► 133 Pk:3 [3|7|12] — **24139**
Honey In The Horn (63) 3(8) [24|66|104] — 10337
Cotton Candy (64) 6(2) [11|38|53] — 4430
Sugar Lips (64) 9(2) [3|20|48] — 2984
The Best Of Al Hirt (65) 13(1) [0|26|43] — 2719
That Honey Horn Sound (65) 28(3) [0|10|27] — 1185
They're Playing Our Song (66) 39(2) [0|3|18] — 720
"Pops" Goes The Trumpet (64)-Al Hirt & Boston Pops Orchestra [A] 18(1) [0|12|31] — 692
Live At Carnegie Hall (65) 47(1) [0|0|22] — 570
Al Hirt Plays Bert Kaempfert (68) 116(1) [0|0|13] — 225
The Happy Trumpet (66) 125(1) [0|0|6] — 96.6
Beauty And The Beard (64)-Al Hirt & Ann-Margret [A] 83(2) [0|0|9] — 94.4
Music To Watch Girls By (67) 127(1) [0|0|5] — 87.4

Robyn HITCHCOCK And The EGYPTIANS ► 1929 Pk:111 [0|0|2] — **388**
Globe Of Frogs (88) 111(1) [0|0|15] — 278
Queen Elvis (89) 139(1) [0|0|9] — 110

Don HO and the ALIIS ► 916 Pk:15 [0|1|6] — **2284**
Tiny Bubbles (66)-Don Ho 15(1) [0|8|50] — 2021
Don Ho-Again! (66) 117(1) [0|0|5] — 81.8
East Coast/West Coast (67) 115(1) [0|0|5] — 73.7
Don Ho-Greatest Hits! (69) 162(1) [0|0|6] — 72.1
Suck 'Em Up (69) 199(2) [0|0|3] — 18.5
The Don Ho TV Show (69)-Don Ho 188(1) [0|0|2] — 16.3

Johnny HODGES ► 3485 Pk:148 [0|0|1] — **12**
Blue Rabbit (65)-Johnny Hodges/Wild Bill Davis [A] 148(1) [0|0|2] — 12.3

Roger HODGSON ► 1500 Pk:46 [0|0|2] — **807**
In The Eye Of The Storm (84) 46(5) [0|0|22] — 757
Hai Hai (87) 163(2) [0|0|6] — 50.6

Billie HOLIDAY ► 1462 Pk:85 [0|0|3] — **870**
The Billie Holiday Story (72) 85(1) [0|0|21] — 460
Strange Fruit (73) 108(1) [0|0|16] — 275
The Original Recordings (73) 135(1) [0|0|9] — 135

Amy HOLLAND ► 2480 Pk:146 [0|0|1] — **165**
Amy Holland (80) 146(1) [0|0|14] — 165

Jennifer HOLLIDAY ► 1377 Pk:31 [0|1|2] — **1001**
Feel My Soul (83) 31(2) [0|5|22] — 825
Say You Love Me (85) 110(2) [0|0|14] — 177

The HOLLIES ► 459 Pk:11 [0|4|13] — **6950**
The Hollies' Greatest Hits (67) 11(3) [0|12|40] — 2243
Distant Light (72) 21(1) [0|5|21] — 1234
Hollies (74) 28(1) [0|2|23] — 978
He Ain't Heavy, He's My Brother (70) 32(2) [0|4|14] — 787
Evolution (67) 43(2) [0|0|14] — 500
Bus Stop (66) 75(1) [0|0|11] — 272
Romany (73) 84(1) [0|0|12] — 266
Stop! Stop! Stop! (67) 91(2) [0|0|8] — 178
Another Night (75) 123(2) [0|0|10] — 178
What Goes Around (83) 90(1) [0|0|9] — 175
The Hollies' Greatest Hits(2) (73) 157(1) [0|0|7] — 80.5
Hear! Here! (66) 145(1) [0|0|3] — 38.3
Moving Finger (71) 183(2) [0|0|2] — 19.8

Loleatta HOLLOWAY ► 3443 Pk:187 [0|0|1] — **16**
Queen Of The Night (78) 187(1) [0|0|2] — 15.8

Buddy HOLLY ► 1891 Pk:55 [0|0|1] — **412**
Buddy Holly & The Crickets 20 Golden Greats (78) 55(1) [0|0|12] — 412

HOLLY And The ITALIANS ► 3290 Pk:177 [0|0|1] — **29**
The Right To Be Italian (81) 177(2) [0|0|3] — 29.0

HOLLYRIDGE STRINGS ► 1076 Pk:15 [0|1|5] — **1657**
The Beatles Song Book (64) 15(1) [0|9|25] — 1300
The Beach Boys Song Book (64) 82(2) [0|0|12] — 237
The New Beatles Song Book (66) 142(1) [0|0|3] — 42.1
The Nat King Cole Song Book (65) 136(1) [0|0|3] — 40.5
Hits Made Famous By Elvis Presley (65) 144(2) [0|0|3] — 38.0

Eddie HOLMAN ► 1946 Pk:75 [0|0|1] — **377**
I Love You (70) 75(1) [0|0|13] — 377

Cecil HOLMES SOULFUL SOUNDS ► 2750 Pk:141 [0|0|1] — **105**
The Black Motion Picture Experience (73) 141(1) [0|0|10] — 105

Clint HOLMES ► 2373 Pk:122 [0|0|1] — **192**
Playground In My Mind (73) 122(1) [0|0|12] — 192

"Groove" HOLMES ► 1608 Pk:89 [0|0|3] — **668**
Soul Message (66)-Richard "Groove" Holmes 89(2) [0|0|26] — 528
Misty (66)-Richard "Groove" Holmes 134(1) [0|0|6] — 94.4
Living Soul (66)-Richard "Groove" Holmes 143(1) [0|0|3] — 45.9

Jake HOLMES ► 2767 Pk:135 [0|0|1] — **102**
So Close, So Very Far To Go (70) 135(1) [0|0|6] — 102

<table>
<tr><th>Act ▶ Highest Peak [Top10s|Top40s|Total]
Title (Yr) Peak(Wk) [T10 Wk|T40Wk|TotalWk]</th><th>Score</th></tr>
<tr><td>LeRoy HOLMES and His Orchestra ▶ 1307 Pk:42 [0|0|2]</td><td>1129</td></tr>
<tr><td>For A Few Dollars More And Other Motion Picture Themes (67) 42(2) [0|0|29]</td><td>1003</td></tr>
<tr><td>The Good, The Bad And The Ugly And Other Motion Picture Themes (68) 138(2) [0|0|8]</td><td>126</td></tr>
<tr><td>Rupert HOLMES ▶ 1061 Pk:33 [0|1|1]</td><td>1717</td></tr>
<tr><td>Partners In Crime (79) 33(2) [0|12|31]</td><td>1717</td></tr>
<tr><td>The HOMBRES ▶ 3313 Pk:180 [0|0|1]</td><td>27</td></tr>
<tr><td>Let It Out (Let It All Hang Out) (67) 180(2) [0|0|4]</td><td>27.1</td></tr>
<tr><td>The HONDELLS ▶ 3047 Pk:119 [0|0|1]</td><td>60</td></tr>
<tr><td>Go Little Honda (64) 119(2) [0|0|4]</td><td>59.5</td></tr>
<tr><td>The HONEYCOMBS ▶ 3359 Pk:147 [0|0|1]</td><td>23</td></tr>
<tr><td>Here Are The Honeycombs (65) 147(1) [0|0|2]</td><td>22.9</td></tr>
<tr><td>HONEY CONE ▶ 1539 Pk:72 [0|0|3]</td><td>745</td></tr>
<tr><td>Soulful Tapestry (71) 72(1) [0|0|20]</td><td>570</td></tr>
<tr><td>Sweet Replies (71) 137(2) [0|0|8]</td><td>148</td></tr>
<tr><td>Love, Peace & Soul (72) 189(1) [0|0|4]</td><td>26.5</td></tr>
<tr><td>The HONEYDRIPPERS ▶ 765 Pk:4 [1|1|1]</td><td>3186</td></tr>
<tr><td>Volume One (84) 4(2) [10|18|31]</td><td>3186</td></tr>
<tr><td>HONEYMOON SUITE ▶ 1129 Pk:60 [0|0|3]</td><td>1523</td></tr>
<tr><td>The Big Prize (86) 61(2) [0|0|35]</td><td>902</td></tr>
<tr><td>Honeymoon Suite (84) 60(2) [0|0|17]</td><td>378</td></tr>
<tr><td>Racing After Midnight (88) 86(2) [0|0|10]</td><td>243</td></tr>
<tr><td>HOODOO GURUS ▶ 1779 Pk:101 [0|0|3]</td><td>497</td></tr>
<tr><td>Magnum Cum Louder (89) 101(1) [0|0|15]</td><td>251</td></tr>
<tr><td>Blow Your Cool! (87) 120(4) [0|0|13]</td><td>176</td></tr>
<tr><td>Mars Needs Guitars! (86) 140(2) [0|0|7]</td><td>70.5</td></tr>
<tr><td>John Lee HOOKER ▶ 1222 Pk:62 [0|0|4]</td><td>1296</td></tr>
<tr><td>The Healer (89) 62(1) [0|0|38]</td><td>722</td></tr>
<tr><td>Endless Boogie (71) 126(2) [0|0|13]</td><td>237</td></tr>
<tr><td>Hooker 'N Heat (71)-Canned Heat And John Lee Hooker [A] 73(1) [0|0|16]</td><td>222</td></tr>
<tr><td>Never Get Out Of These Blues Alive (72) 130(1) [0|0|6]</td><td>114</td></tr>
<tr><td>Stix HOOPER ▶ 3086 Pk:166 [0|0|1]</td><td>54</td></tr>
<tr><td>The World Within (79) 166(1) [0|0|5]</td><td>53.6</td></tr>
<tr><td>The HOOTERS ▶ 558 Pk:12 [0|2|3]</td><td>5253</td></tr>
<tr><td>Nervous Night (85)-Hooters 12(1) [0|30|74]</td><td>4059</td></tr>
<tr><td>One Way Home (87)-Hooters 27(3) [0|5|26]</td><td>942</td></tr>
<tr><td>Zig Zag (89)-Hooters 115(1) [0|0|16]</td><td>252</td></tr>
<tr><td>Bob HOPE ▶ 3193 Pk:175 [0|0|1]</td><td>42</td></tr>
<tr><td>America Is 200 Years Old...And There's Still Hope! (76) 175(1) [0|0|4]</td><td>41.6</td></tr>
<tr><td>Mary HOPKIN ▶ 1185 Pk:28 [0|1|1]</td><td>1373</td></tr>
<tr><td>Post Card (69) 28(2) [0|7|20]</td><td>1373</td></tr>
<tr><td>Nicky HOPKINS ▶ 1531 Pk:33 [0|1|2]</td><td>753</td></tr>
<tr><td>Jamming With Edward! (72) 33(2) [0|3|11]</td><td>564</td></tr>
<tr><td>The Tin Man Was A Dreamer (73) 108(1) [0|0|10]</td><td>189</td></tr>
<tr><td>Jimmy 'Bo' HORNE ▶ 2475 Pk:122 [0|0|1]</td><td>167</td></tr>
<tr><td>Dance Across The Floor (78) 122(1) [0|0|10]</td><td>167</td></tr>
<tr><td>Lena HORNE ▶ 2315 Pk:112 [0|0|2]</td><td>211</td></tr>
<tr><td>Lena Horne: The Lady And Her Music (Original Cast) (81) 112(2) [0|0|9]</td><td>166</td></tr>
<tr><td>Lena & Gabor (70)-Lena Horne & Gabor Szabo [A] 162(1) [0|0|10]</td><td>44.1</td></tr>
<tr><td>Bruce HORNSBY And The RANGE ▶ 321 Pk:3 [2|2|2]</td><td>10643</td></tr>
<tr><td>The Way It Is (86)-Bruce Hornsby & The Range 3(4) [23|42|73]</td><td>7530</td></tr>
<tr><td>Scenes From The Southside (88)-Bruce Hornsby & The Range 5(1) [7|19|27]</td><td>3112</td></tr>
<tr><td>Vladimir HOROWITZ ▶ 1060 Pk:22 [0|1|3]</td><td>1719</td></tr>
<tr><td>Horowitz at Carnegie Hall - An Historic Return (65) 22(2) [0|8|32]</td><td>1418</td></tr>
</table>

<table>
<tr><th>Act ▶ Highest Peak [Top10s|Top40s|Total]
Title (Yr) Peak(Wk) [T10 Wk|T40Wk|TotalWk]</th><th>Score</th></tr>
<tr><td>Golden Jubilee Concert - Rachmaninoff Concerto No. 3 (78) 102(2) [0|0|14]</td><td>262</td></tr>
<tr><td>Horowitz On Television (68) 185(1) [0|0|4]</td><td>39.0</td></tr>
<tr><td>HORSLIPS ▶ 2089 Pk:98 [0|0|2]</td><td>308</td></tr>
<tr><td>Aliens (78) 98(2) [0|0|9]</td><td>182</td></tr>
<tr><td>The Man Who Built America (79) 155(1) [0|0|9]</td><td>126</td></tr>
<tr><td>HOT ▶ 2184 Pk:125 [0|0|1]</td><td>265</td></tr>
<tr><td>Hot (77) 125(1) [0|0|15]</td><td>265</td></tr>
<tr><td>HOT BUTTER ▶ 2683 Pk:137 [0|0|1]</td><td>118</td></tr>
<tr><td>Popcorn (72) 137(1) [0|0|7]</td><td>118</td></tr>
<tr><td>HOT CHOCOLATE ▶ 911 Pk:31 [0|1|5]</td><td>2310</td></tr>
<tr><td>Hot Chocolate (75) 41(2) [0|0|21]</td><td>815</td></tr>
<tr><td>Every 1's A Winner (79) 31(2) [0|4|16]</td><td>731</td></tr>
<tr><td>Cicero Park (75) 55(1) [0|0|17]</td><td>582</td></tr>
<tr><td>Going Through The Motions (79) 112(2) [0|0|6]</td><td>115</td></tr>
<tr><td>Man To Man (76) 172(2) [0|0|6]</td><td>66.9</td></tr>
<tr><td>HOTHOUSE FLOWERS ▶ 1763 Pk:88 [0|0|1]</td><td>507</td></tr>
<tr><td>People (88) 88(2) [0|0|33]</td><td>507</td></tr>
<tr><td>HOT TUNA ▶ 736 Pk:30 [0|1|8]</td><td>3393</td></tr>
<tr><td>Hot Tuna (70) 30(1) [0|5|19]</td><td>993</td></tr>
<tr><td>Burgers (72) 68(2) [0|0|23]</td><td>725</td></tr>
<tr><td>First Pull Up Then Pull Down (71) 43(1) [0|0|13]</td><td>685</td></tr>
<tr><td>America's Choice (75) 75(1) [0|0|11]</td><td>293</td></tr>
<tr><td>Double Dose (78) 92(1) [0|0|10]</td><td>229</td></tr>
<tr><td>Hoppkorv (76) 116(2) [0|0|10]</td><td>198</td></tr>
<tr><td>Yellow Fever (75) 97(1) [0|0|9]</td><td>180</td></tr>
<tr><td>The Phosphorescent Rat (74) 148(1) [0|0|7]</td><td>90.3</td></tr>
<tr><td>The HOUSEMARTINS ▶ 2369 Pk:124 [0|0|2]</td><td>194</td></tr>
<tr><td>London 0 Hull 4 (87) 124(2) [0|0|14]</td><td>153</td></tr>
<tr><td>The People Who Grinned Themselves To Death (88) 177(1) [0|0|6]</td><td>40.1</td></tr>
<tr><td>HOUSE OF FREAKS ▶ 2802 Pk:154 [0|0|1]</td><td>97</td></tr>
<tr><td>Tantilla (89) 154(1) [0|0|10]</td><td>96.8</td></tr>
<tr><td>HOUSE OF LORDS ▶ 1794 Pk:78 [0|0|1]</td><td>489</td></tr>
<tr><td>House Of Lords (88) 78(1) [0|0|27]</td><td>489</td></tr>
<tr><td>HOUSE OF LOVE ▶ 3042 Pk:156 [0|0|1]</td><td>60</td></tr>
<tr><td>The House Of Love (88) 156(1) [0|0|7]</td><td>60.2</td></tr>
<tr><td>David HOUSTON ▶ 1592 Pk:57 [0|0|4]</td><td>690</td></tr>
<tr><td>Almost Persuaded (66) 57(1) [0|0|20]</td><td>554</td></tr>
<tr><td>David (69) 143(1) [0|0|5]</td><td>88.7</td></tr>
<tr><td>Wonders Of The Wine (70) 170(2) [0|0|3]</td><td>34.9</td></tr>
<tr><td>Baby, Baby (70) 194(1) [0|0|2]</td><td>12.3</td></tr>
<tr><td>Thelma HOUSTON ▶ 701 Pk:11 [0|1|4]</td><td>3651</td></tr>
<tr><td>Anyway You Like It (76) 11(2) [0|16|37]</td><td>3022</td></tr>
<tr><td>The Devil In Me (77) 64(2) [0|0|11]</td><td>328</td></tr>
<tr><td>Thelma & Jerry (77)-Thelma Houston & Jerry Butler [A] 53(1) [0|0|12]</td><td>199</td></tr>
<tr><td>Never Gonna Be Another One (81) 144(1) [0|0|6]</td><td>102</td></tr>
<tr><td>Whitney HOUSTON ▶ 98 Pk:1 [2|2|2]</td><td>29875</td></tr>
<tr><td>Whitney Houston (85) 1(14) [46|78|162]</td><td>18282</td></tr>
<tr><td>Whitney (87) 1(11) [31|51|85]</td><td>11594</td></tr>
<tr><td>George HOWARD ▶ 1596 Pk:109 [0|0|5]</td><td>685</td></tr>
<tr><td>A Nice Place To Be (86) 109(3) [0|0|26]</td><td>383</td></tr>
<tr><td>Love Will Follow (86) 142(2) [0|0|11]</td><td>121</td></tr>
<tr><td>Reflections (88) 109(1) [0|0|8]</td><td>117</td></tr>
<tr><td>Dancing In The Sun (85) 169(2) [0|0|4]</td><td>34.7</td></tr>
<tr><td>Steppin' Out (84) 178(1) [0|0|4]</td><td>29.7</td></tr>
<tr><td>Miki HOWARD ▶ 2299 Pk:145 [0|0|2]</td><td>217</td></tr>
<tr><td>Love Confessions (88) 145(2) [0|0|16]</td><td>168</td></tr>
<tr><td>Come Share My Love (87) 171(2) [0|0|6]</td><td>48.5</td></tr>
<tr><td>Steve HOWE ▶ 1910 Pk:63 [0|0|2]</td><td>401</td></tr>
<tr><td>Beginnings (75) 63(1) [0|0|11]</td><td>359</td></tr>
<tr><td>The Steve Howe Album (80) 164(1) [0|0|4]</td><td>42.0</td></tr>
</table>

<table>
<tr><th>Act ▶ Highest Peak [Top10s|Top40s|Total]
Title (Yr) Peak(Wk) [T10 Wk|T40Wk|TotalWk]</th><th>Score</th></tr>
<tr><td>HOWLIN' WOLF ▶ 1819 Pk:79 [0|0|1]</td><td>468</td></tr>
<tr><td>The London Howlin' Wolf Sessions (71) 79(1) [0|0|15]</td><td>468</td></tr>
<tr><td>Freddie HUBBARD ▶ 1451 Pk:85 [0|0|9]</td><td>890</td></tr>
<tr><td>Windjammer (76) 85(2) [0|0|9]</td><td>260</td></tr>
<tr><td>The Baddest Hubbard (75) 127(2) [0|0|7]</td><td>122</td></tr>
<tr><td>High Energy (74) 153(1) [0|0|7]</td><td>98.4</td></tr>
<tr><td>Liquid Love (75) 149(2) [0|0|6]</td><td>89.0</td></tr>
<tr><td>Bundle Of Joy (77) 146(1) [0|0|6]</td><td>85.8</td></tr>
<tr><td>Super Blue (78) 131(2) [0|0|5]</td><td>85.1</td></tr>
<tr><td>Sky Dive (73) 165(1) [0|0|7]</td><td>70.9</td></tr>
<tr><td>Polar AC (75) 167(1) [0|0|4]</td><td>47.1</td></tr>
<tr><td>Keep Your Soul Together (74) 186(1) [0|0|5]</td><td>30.8</td></tr>
<tr><td>David HUDSON ▶ 3424 Pk:184 [0|0|1]</td><td>17</td></tr>
<tr><td>To You Honey, Honey With Love (80) 184(1) [0|0|2]</td><td>17.2</td></tr>
<tr><td>HUDSON And LANDRY ▶ 782 Pk:30 [0|2|3]</td><td>3073</td></tr>
<tr><td>Hanging In There (71) 30(2) [0|4|26]</td><td>1579</td></tr>
<tr><td>Losing Their Heads (71) 33(1) [0|4|23]</td><td>1381</td></tr>
<tr><td>Right-Off! (73) 147(1) [0|0|9]</td><td>112</td></tr>
<tr><td>HUDSON BROTHERS ▶ 2523 Pk:165 [0|0|3]</td><td>153</td></tr>
<tr><td>Ba-Fa (75) 165(2) [0|0|6]</td><td>74.1</td></tr>
<tr><td>Hollywood Situation (74) 176(2) [0|0|4]</td><td>44.7</td></tr>
<tr><td>Totally Out Of Control (74) 179(1) [0|0|4]</td><td>34.3</td></tr>
<tr><td>HUES CORPORATION ▶ 1202 Pk:20 [0|1|2]</td><td>1342</td></tr>
<tr><td>Freedom For The Stallion (74) 20(2) [0|7|18]</td><td>1261</td></tr>
<tr><td>Love Corporation (75) 147(1) [0|0|5]</td><td>81.1</td></tr>
<tr><td>Grayson HUGH ▶ 1850 Pk:71 [0|0|1]</td><td>445</td></tr>
<tr><td>Blind To Reason (88) 71(2) [0|0|24]</td><td>445</td></tr>
<tr><td>HUGO & LUIGI ▶ 3260 Pk:125 [0|0|1]</td><td>32</td></tr>
<tr><td>Let's Fall In Love (63) 125(1) [0|0|2]</td><td>32.2</td></tr>
<tr><td>HUMAN BEINZ ▶ 2062 Pk:65 [0|0|1]</td><td>319</td></tr>
<tr><td>Nobody But Me (68) 65(1) [0|0|10]</td><td>319</td></tr>
<tr><td>HUMAN LEAGUE ▶ 447 Pk:3 [1|3|5]</td><td>7148</td></tr>
<tr><td>Dare (82) 3(3) [9|20|38]</td><td>4081</td></tr>
<tr><td>Fascination! (83) 22(1) [0|8|29]</td><td>1400</td></tr>
<tr><td>Crash (86) 24(2) [0|11|25]</td><td>1236</td></tr>
<tr><td>Hysteria (84) 62(1) [0|0|13]</td><td>345</td></tr>
<tr><td>Love And Dancing (82)-The League Unlimited Orchestra 135(2) [0|0|7]</td><td>86.1</td></tr>
<tr><td>HUMBLE PIE ▶ 368 Pk:6 [1|4|9]</td><td>9007</td></tr>
<tr><td>Smokin' (72) 6(1) [4|14|34]</td><td>3010</td></tr>
<tr><td>Performance-Rockin' The Fillmore (71) 21(1) [0|8|32]</td><td>2010</td></tr>
<tr><td>Eat It (73) 13(3) [0|7|21]</td><td>1493</td></tr>
<tr><td>Lost And Found (72) 37(1) [0|4|20]</td><td>833</td></tr>
<tr><td>Rock On (71) 118(1) [0|0|23]</td><td>494</td></tr>
<tr><td>Thunderbox (74) 52(1) [0|0|14]</td><td>493</td></tr>
<tr><td>On To Victory (80) 60(1) [0|0|14]</td><td>396</td></tr>
<tr><td>Street Rats (75) 100(2) [0|0|8]</td><td>193</td></tr>
<tr><td>Go For The Throat (81) 154(1) [0|0|6]</td><td>85.4</td></tr>
<tr><td>Engelbert HUMPERDINCK ▶ 109 Pk:5 [3|9|16]</td><td>28050</td></tr>
<tr><td>Release Me (67) 7(3) [7|31|118]</td><td>6029</td></tr>
<tr><td>A Man Without Love (68) 12(2) [0|19|78]</td><td>4524</td></tr>
<tr><td>Engelbert Humperdinck (70) 5(2) [9|19|41]</td><td>4394</td></tr>
<tr><td>Engelbert (69) 12(2) [0|11|33]</td><td>2547</td></tr>
<tr><td>The Last Waltz (67) 10(2) [2|11|60]</td><td>2478</td></tr>
<tr><td>After The Lovin' (76) 17(2) [0|8|28]</td><td>1851</td></tr>
<tr><td>We Made It Happen (70) 19(2) [0|8|40]</td><td>1843</td></tr>
<tr><td>Sweetheart (71) 22(2) [0|8|24]</td><td>1726</td></tr>
<tr><td>Another Time, Another Place (71) 25(1) [0|5|15]</td><td>1041</td></tr>
<tr><td>Live At The Riviera, Las Vegas (72) 45(2) [0|0|13]</td><td>562</td></tr>
</table>

Act ▶ Highest Peak [Top10s | Top40s | Total] Title (Yr) Peak(Wk) [T10 Wk | T40Wk | TotalWk]	Score
Engelbert HUMPERDINCK ▶ *Continued*	
In Time (72) 72(1) [0 | 0 | 14]	403
His Greatest Hits (74) 103(2) [0 | 0 | 14]	300
King Of Hearts (73) 113(1) [0 | 0 | 10]	200
Miracles By Engelbert Humperdinck (77) 167(1) [0 | 0 | 5]	57.4
Christmas Tyme (77) 156(1) [0 | 0 | 4]	47.9
This Moment In Time (79) 164(1) [0 | 0 | 4]	45.7
Bobbi HUMPHREY ▶ 1023 Pk:30 [0 | 1 | 4]	**1856**
Satin Doll (74) 30(2) [0 | 4 | 18]	991
Blacks and Blues (74) 84(1) [0 | 0 | 21]	427
Freestyle (78) 89(1) [0 | 0 | 14]	336
Fancy Dancer (75) 133(2) [0 | 0 | 5]	103
Paul HUMPHREY & The COOL AID CHEMISTS ▶ 3057 Pk:170 [0 | 0 | 1]	**59**
Paul Humphrey & The Cool Aid Chemists (71) 170(1) [0 | 0 | 6]	58.8
Ian HUNTER ▶ 811 Pk:35 [0 | 1 | 7]	**2872**
You're Never Alone With A Schizophrenic (79) 35(1) [0 | 6 | 24]	1340
Ian Hunter (75) 50(1) [0 | 0 | 14]	473
Welcome To The Club (80) 69(1) [0 | 0 | 17]	423
Short Back 'N' Sides (81) 62(1) [0 | 0 | 11]	352
All Of The Good Ones Are Taken (83) 125(1) [0 | 0 | 8]	116
Y U I Orta (89)-Ian Hunter/Mick Ronson [A] 157(3) [0 | 0 | 20]	98.7
All American Alien Boy (76) 177(1) [0 | 0 | 7]	69.1
John HUNTER ▶ 2852 Pk:148 [0 | 0 | 1]	**87**
Famous At Night (85) 148(2) [0 | 0 | 9]	87.4
Chet HUNTLEY & David BRINKLEY ▶ 2733 Pk:115 [0 | 0 | 1]	**108**
A Time To Keep: 1963 (64) 115(1) [0 | 0 | 7]	108
HURRICANE ▶ 1660 Pk:92 [0 | 0 | 1]	**611**
Over The Edge (88) 92(2) [0 | 0 | 36]	611
HUSKER DU ▶ 2257 Pk:117 [0 | 0 | 2]	**231**
Warehouse: Songs And Stories (87) 117(2) [0 | 0 | 10]	127
Candy Apple Grey (86) 140(2) [0 | 0 | 10]	104
Willie HUTCH ▶ 1785 Pk:114 [0 | 0 | 5]	**495**
The Mack (Soundtrack) (73) 114(1) [0 | 0 | 16]	262
Ode To My Lady (75) 150(2) [0 | 0 | 6]	90.3
Concert In Blues (76) 163(2) [0 | 0 | 6]	59.7
Fully Exposed (73) 183(2) [0 | 0 | 6]	43.6
Foxy Brown (Soundtrack) (74) 179(1) [0 | 0 | 4]	39.1
Leroy HUTSON ▶ 2895 Pk:170 [0 | 0 | 1]	**81**
Feel The Spirit (76) 170(1) [0 | 0 | 8]	80.5
Paul HYDE And The PAYOLAS ▶ 2760 Pk:144 [0 | 0 | 1]	**103**
Here's The World For Ya (85) 144(2) [0 | 0 | 10]	103
Brian HYLAND ▶ 2701 Pk:160 [0 | 0 | 2]	**114**
Tragedy/A Million To One (69) 160(1) [0 | 0 | 5]	75.1
Brian Hyland (71) 171(1) [0 | 0 | 4]	38.6
Dick HYMAN ▶ 972 Pk:30 [0 | 1 | 5]	**2035**
Moog - The Electric Eclectics Of Dick Hyman (69) 30(3) [0 | 8 | 30]	1633
The Age Of Electronicus (69) 110(1) [0 | 0 | 11]	205
Electrodynamics (63) 117(1) [0 | 0 | 7]	112
Fabulous (64) 132(1) [0 | 0 | 5]	65.4
Mirrors - Reflections Of Today (68)-Dick Hyman and The Group 179(2) [0 | 0 | 2]	19.2
Phyllis HYMAN ▶ 849 Pk:50 [0 | 0 | 6]	**2689**
You Know How To Love Me (79) 50(1) [0 | 0 | 21]	745
Living All Alone (86) 78(2) [0 | 0 | 41]	537
Can't We Fall In Love Again (81) 57(1) [0 | 0 | 13]	467
Somewhere In My Lifetime (79) 70(1) [0 | 0 | 17]	461
Phyllis Hyman (77) 107(1) [0 | 0 | 14]	288

Act ▶ Highest Peak [Top10s | Top40s | Total] Title (Yr) Peak(Wk) [T10 Wk | T40Wk | TotalWk]	Score
Goddess Of Love (83) 112(1) [0 | 0 | 12]	191
Tony HYMAS ▶ 2532 Pk:49 [0 | 0 | 1]	**152**
Jeff Beck's Guitar Shop (89)-Jeff Beck With Terry Bozzio & Tony Hymas [A] 49(2) [0 | 0 | 18]	152
I	
Janis IAN ▶ 311 Pk:1 [1 | 3 | 8]	**10971**
Between The Lines (75) 1(1) [9 | 24 | 64]	6807
Aftertones (76) 12(2) [0 | 10 | 19]	1910
Janis Ian (67) 29(1) [0 | 4 | 28]	1090
Miracle Row (77) 45(1) [0 | 0 | 12]	526
Stars (74) 83(2) [0 | 0 | 20]	342
Janis Ian (II) (78) 120(2) [0 | 0 | 11]	212
Restless Eyes (81) 156(1) [0 | 0 | 3]	43.5
For All The Seasons Of Your Mind (67) 179(2) [0 | 0 | 5]	40.2
IAN & SYLVIA ▶ 1399 Pk:70 [0 | 0 | 6]	**972**
Early Morning Rain (65) 77(1) [0 | 0 | 18]	328
Northern Journey (64) 70(2) [0 | 0 | 12]	263
Lovin' Sound (67) 148(1) [0 | 0 | 10]	105
So Much For Dreaming (67) 130(2) [0 | 0 | 7]	102
Four Strong Winds (63) 115(1) [0 | 0 | 6]	92.1
Play One More (66) 142(1) [0 | 0 | 6]	81.3
ICEHOUSE ▶ 875 Pk:43 [0 | 0 | 4]	**2508**
Man Of Colours (87) 43(1) [0 | 0 | 44]	1358
Measure For Measure (86) 55(3) [0 | 0 | 24]	694
Icehouse (81) 82(2) [0 | 0 | 15]	370
Primitive Man (82) 129(2) [0 | 0 | 6]	85.1
ICE-T ▶ 959 Pk:35 [0 | 2 | 3]	**2096**
Power (88) 35(1) [0 | 5 | 33]	1029
The Iceberg (Freedom Of Speech... Just Watch What You Say) (89) 37(2) [0 | 3 | 28]	680
Rhyme Pays (87) 93(2) [0 | 0 | 27]	388
ICICLE WORKS ▶ 1671 Pk:40 [0 | 1 | 1]	**604**
Icicle Works (84) 40(2) [0 | 2 | 18]	604
ICON ▶ 3503 Pk:190 [0 | 0 | 1]	**11**
Icon (84) 190(1) [0 | 0 | 2]	11.2
IDES OF MARCH ▶ 1788 Pk:55 [0 | 0 | 1]	**494**
Vehicle (70) 55(1) [0 | 0 | 12]	494
Billy IDOL ▶ 256 Pk:6 [3 | 3 | 5]	**13945**
Rebel Yell (83) 6(3) [5 | 38 | 82]	5290
Whiplash Smile (86) 6(1) [5 | 21 | 47]	2968
Vital Idol (87) 10(1) [1 | 18 | 29]	2338
Billy Idol (82) 45(1) [0 | 0 | 104]	2061
Don't Stop (81) 71(1) [0 | 0 | 68]	1288
IF ▶ 2922 Pk:171 [0 | 0 | 3]	**77**
If 3 (71) 171(2) [0 | 0 | 3]	38.3
Waterfall (72) 195(2) [0 | 0 | 4]	22.8
If (70) 187(1) [0 | 0 | 2]	15.7
Frank IFIELD ▶ 3115 Pk:104 [0 | 0 | 1]	**51**
Jolly What! The Beatles & Frank Ifield (64)-The Beatles/Frank Ifield [A] 104(1) [0 | 0 | 6]	50.7
Julio IGLESIAS ▶ 468 Pk:5 [1 | 2 | 8]	**6749**
1100 Bel Air Place (84) 5(2) [11 | 21 | 34]	3337
Julio (83) 32(1) [0 | 9 | 89]	2545
Non Stop (88) 52(2) [0 | 0 | 17]	484
Libra (85) 92(2) [0 | 0 | 12]	204
In Concert (84) 159(2) [0 | 0 | 9]	82.5
From A Child To A Woman (84) 181(1) [0 | 0 | 6]	39.6
Hey! (84) 179(1) [0 | 0 | 6]	37.4
Moments (84) 191(1) [0 | 0 | 4]	19.5
ILLINOIS SPEED PRESS ▶ 2869 Pk:144 [0 | 0 | 1]	**85**
The Illinois Speed Press (69) 144(2) [0 | 0 | 4]	84.5

Act ▶ Highest Peak [Top10s | Top40s | Total] Title (Yr) Peak(Wk) [T10 Wk | T40Wk | TotalWk]	Score
ILLUSION ▶ 2942 Pk:163 [0 | 0 | 1]	**73**
Out Of The Mist (77) 163(1) [0 | 0 | 7]	73.3
The ILLUSION ▶ 1507 Pk:69 [0 | 0 | 1]	**792**
The Illusion (69) 69(1) [0 | 0 | 27]	792
IMPELLITTERI ▶ 1906 Pk:91 [0 | 0 | 1]	**404**
Stand In Line (88) 91(2) [0 | 0 | 20]	404
The IMPRESSIONS ▶ 394 Pk:8 [1 | 3 | 18]	**8403**
Keep On Pushing (64) 8(2) [6 | 21 | 34]	2831
We're A Winner (68) 35(1) [0 | 5 | 27]	1118
The Impressions (63) 43(1) [0 | 0 | 33]	1091
People Get Ready (65) 23(2) [0 | 9 | 19]	957
The Never Ending Impressions (64) 52(1) [0 | 0 | 22]	550
The Young Mods' Forgotten Story (69) 104(1) [0 | 0 | 18]	423
This Is My Country (68) 107(1) [0 | 0 | 13]	331
The Impressions Greatest Hits (65) 83(2) [0 | 0 | 15]	281
Ridin' High (66) 79(1) [0 | 0 | 10]	221
One By One (65) 104(1) [0 | 0 | 9]	156
The Best Of The Impressions (68) 172(1) [0 | 0 | 15]	140
First Impressions (75) 115(1) [0 | 0 | 5]	107
The Fabulous Impressions (67) 184(2) [0 | 0 | 11]	73.7
16 Greatest Hits (71) 180(1) [0 | 0 | 6]	49.9
Finally Got Myself Together (74) 176(1) [0 | 0 | 3]	31.5
Loving Power (76) 195(1) [0 | 0 | 3]	18.3
Times Have Changed (72) 192(2) [0 | 0 | 2]	13.3
The Vintage Years (77)-The Impressions Featuring Jerry Butler & Curtis Mayfield 199(2) [0 | 0 | 2]	11.1
INCREDIBLE BONGO BAND ▶ 3500 Pk:197 [0 | 0 | 1]	**11**
Bongo Rock (73) 197(2) [0 | 0 | 2]	11.3
INCREDIBLE STRING BAND ▶ 2171 Pk:161 [0 | 0 | 7]	**269**
The Hangman's Beautiful Daughter (68) 161(1) [0 | 0 | 9]	101
Changing Horses (69) 166(1) [0 | 0 | 3]	40.6
Wee Tam (69) 174(1) [0 | 0 | 3]	34.8
The Big Huge (69) 180(1) [0 | 0 | 3]	32.9
'U' (71) 183(1) [0 | 0 | 3]	25.6
Liquid Acrobat As Regards The Air (72) 189(1) [0 | 0 | 3]	22.3
I Looked Up (70) 196(2) [0 | 0 | 2]	12.3
The INDEPENDENTS ▶ 2631 Pk:127 [0 | 0 | 1]	**127**
The First Time We Met (73) 127(1) [0 | 0 | 9]	127
INDIGO GIRLS ▶ 1032 Pk:22 [0 | 1 | 2]	**1821**
Indigo Girls (89) 22(3) [0 | 11 | 35]	1704
Strange Fire (89) 159(1) [0 | 0 | 14]	117
INFORMATION SOCIETY ▶ 1089 Pk:25 [0 | 1 | 1]	**1635**
Information Society (88) 25(1) [0 | 9 | 38]	1635
James INGRAM ▶ 1187 Pk:46 [0 | 0 | 2]	**1372**
It's Your Night (83) 46(1) [0 | 0 | 42]	1262
Never Felt So Good (86) 123(2) [0 | 0 | 9]	110
Luther INGRAM ▶ 1422 Pk:39 [0 | 1 | 2]	**936**
If Loving You Is Wrong I Don't Want To Be Right (72) 39(1) [0 | 3 | 21]	840
I've Been Here All The Time (72) 175(1) [0 | 0 | 11]	96.9
The INMATES ▶ 1784 Pk:49 [0 | 0 | 1]	**495**
First Offence (79) 49(2) [0 | 0 | 17]	495
INNER CITY ▶ 3215 Pk:162 [0 | 0 | 1]	**38**
Big Fun (89) 162(2) [0 | 0 | 4]	37.8
INSIDERS ▶ 3179 Pk:167 [0 | 0 | 1]	**43**
Ghost On The Beach (87) 167(1) [0 | 0 | 5]	43.3
INSTANT FUNK ▶ 859 Pk:12 [0 | 1 | 4]	**2606**
Instant Funk (79) 12(1) [0 | 13 | 22]	2198

<table>
<tr><th>Act ▶ Highest Peak [Top10s | Top40s | Total]
Title (Yr) Peak(Wk) [T10 Wk | T40Wk | TotalWk]</th><th>Score</th></tr>
<tr><td>INSTANT FUNK ▶ Continued</td><td></td></tr>
<tr><td>Witch Doctor (79) 129(1) [0 | 0 | 13]</td><td>224</td></tr>
<tr><td>The Funk Is On (80) 130(2) [0 | 0 | 6]</td><td>108</td></tr>
<tr><td>Looks So Fine (82) 147(2) [0 | 0 | 7]</td><td>76.3</td></tr>
<tr><td>The INTRUDERS ▶ 1670 Pk:112 [0 | 0 | 3]</td><td>604</td></tr>
<tr><td>Save The Children (73) 133(1) [0 | 0 | 18]</td><td>260</td></tr>
<tr><td>Cowboys To Girls (68) 112(2) [0 | 0 | 9]</td><td>222</td></tr>
<tr><td>The Intruders Greatest Hits (69) 144(2) [0 | 0 | 6]</td><td>123</td></tr>
<tr><td>INXS ▶ 241 Pk:3 [1 | 2 | 6]</td><td>14731</td></tr>
<tr><td>Kick (87) 3(4) [22 | 65 | 81]</td><td>10126</td></tr>
<tr><td>Listen Like Thieves (85) 11(1) [0 | 16 | 55]</td><td>3022</td></tr>
<tr><td>Shabooh Shoobah (83) 46(3) [0 | 0 | 31]</td><td>761</td></tr>
<tr><td>The Swing (84) 52(2) [0 | 0 | 28]</td><td>735</td></tr>
<tr><td>Dekadance (83) 148(2) [0 | 0 | 6]</td><td>61.2</td></tr>
<tr><td>INXS (84) 164(1) [0 | 0 | 3]</td><td>27.0</td></tr>
<tr><td>Donnie IRIS ▶ 1102 Pk:57 [0 | 0 | 5]</td><td>1596</td></tr>
<tr><td>Back On The Streets (80) 57(1) [0 | 0 | 23]</td><td>621</td></tr>
<tr><td>King Cool (81) 84(2) [0 | 0 | 31]</td><td>587</td></tr>
<tr><td>No Muss...No Fuss (85) 115(1) [0 | 0 | 15]</td><td>211</td></tr>
<tr><td>Fortune 410 (83) 127(1) [0 | 0 | 12]</td><td>151</td></tr>
<tr><td>The High And The Mighty (82) 180(2) [0 | 0 | 4]</td><td>25.2</td></tr>
<tr><td>IRISH ROVERS ▶ 888 Pk:24 [0 | 1 | 4]</td><td>2442</td></tr>
<tr><td>The Unicorn (68) 24(2) [0 | 11 | 43]</td><td>2090</td></tr>
<tr><td>All Hung Up (68) 119(1) [0 | 0 | 8]</td><td>203</td></tr>
<tr><td>Wasn't That A Party (81)-The Rovers 157(1) [0 | 0 | 8]</td><td>95.9</td></tr>
<tr><td>Tales To Warm Your Mind (69) 182(1) [0 | 0 | 5]</td><td>53.3</td></tr>
<tr><td>IRON BUTTERFLY ▶ 111 Pk:3 [2 | 4 | 7]</td><td>27778</td></tr>
<tr><td>In-A-Gadda-Da-Vida (68) 4(1) [49 | 87 | 140]</td><td>18683</td></tr>
<tr><td>Ball (69) 3(1) [8 | 19 | 44]</td><td>5063</td></tr>
<tr><td>Metamorphosis (70) 16(1) [0 | 7 | 23]</td><td>1547</td></tr>
<tr><td>Iron Butterfly Live (70) 20(2) [0 | 6 | 23]</td><td>1298</td></tr>
<tr><td>Heavy (68) 78(1) [0 | 0 | 49]</td><td>1012</td></tr>
<tr><td>The Best Of Iron Butterfly/Evolution (71) 137(1) [0 | 0 | 6]</td><td>95.0</td></tr>
<tr><td>Scorching Beauty (75) 138(2) [0 | 0 | 6]</td><td>79.7</td></tr>
<tr><td>IRONHORSE ▶ 2689 Pk:153 [0 | 0 | 1]</td><td>116</td></tr>
<tr><td>Ironhorse (79) 153(1) [0 | 0 | 10]</td><td>116</td></tr>
<tr><td>IRON MAIDEN ▶ 309 Pk:11 [0 | 6 | 8]</td><td>10997</td></tr>
<tr><td>Piece Of Mind (83) 14(1) [0 | 14 | 45]</td><td>2309</td></tr>
<tr><td>Somewhere In Time (86) 11(1) [0 | 18 | 39]</td><td>2136</td></tr>
<tr><td>Seventh Son Of A Seventh Son (88) 12(1) [0 | 11 | 23]</td><td>1631</td></tr>
<tr><td>The Number Of The Beast (82) 33(2) [0 | 5 | 65]</td><td>1510</td></tr>
<tr><td>Powerslave (84) 21(3) [0 | 7 | 34]</td><td>1313</td></tr>
<tr><td>Live After Death (85) 19(1) [0 | 10 | 22]</td><td>1244</td></tr>
<tr><td>Killers (81) 78(1) [0 | 0 | 23]</td><td>484</td></tr>
<tr><td>Maiden Japan (81) 89(2) [0 | 0 | 30]</td><td>370</td></tr>
<tr><td>Chris ISAAK ▶ 681 Pk:7 [1 | 1 | 2]</td><td>3886</td></tr>
<tr><td>Heart Shaped World (89) 7(4) [7 | 21 | 74]</td><td>3876</td></tr>
<tr><td>Chris Isaak (87) 194(1) [0 | 0 | 2]</td><td>10.0</td></tr>
<tr><td>ISLE OF MAN ▶ 2255 Pk:110 [0 | 0 | 1]</td><td>231</td></tr>
<tr><td>Isle Of Man (86) 110(2) [0 | 0 | 18]</td><td>231</td></tr>
<tr><td>ISLEY BROTHERS ▶ 89 Pk:1 [6 | 12 | 23]</td><td>31661</td></tr>
<tr><td>The Heat Is On (75) 1(1) [11 | 21 | 40]</td><td>5866</td></tr>
<tr><td>Go For Your Guns (77) 6(2) [5 | 14 | 34]</td><td>3468</td></tr>
<tr><td>3 + 3 (73) 8(1) [3 | 13 | 37]</td><td>2841</td></tr>
<tr><td>Showdown (78) 4(3) [4 | 14 | 21]</td><td>2838</td></tr>
<tr><td>Harvest For The World (76) 9(2) [3 | 14 | 26]</td><td>2792</td></tr>
<tr><td>Go All The Way (80) 8(4) [4 | 13 | 22]</td><td>2369</td></tr>
<tr><td>Live It Up (74) 14(2) [0 | 9 | 28]</td><td>1914</td></tr>
<tr><td>Brother, Brother, Brother (72) 29(2) [0 | 8 | 33]</td><td>1642</td></tr>
<tr><td>It's Our Thing (69) 22(3) [0 | 7 | 18]</td><td>1527</td></tr>
<tr><td>Winner Takes All (79) 14(2) [0 | 7 | 20]</td><td>1464</td></tr>
<tr><td>Between The Sheets (83) 19(1) [0 | 9 | 23]</td><td>1214</td></tr>
</table>

<table>
<tr><th>Act ▶ Highest Peak [Top10s | Top40s | Total]
Title (Yr) Peak(Wk) [T10 Wk | T40Wk | TotalWk]</th><th>Score</th></tr>
<tr><td>Grand Slam (81) 28(3) [0 | 5 | 17]</td><td>946</td></tr>
<tr><td>Givin' It Back (71) 71(1) [0 | 0 | 25]</td><td>739</td></tr>
<tr><td>Inside You (81) 45(1) [0 | 0 | 13]</td><td>440</td></tr>
<tr><td>Smooth Sailin' (87) 64(2) [0 | 0 | 17]</td><td>403</td></tr>
<tr><td>Forever Gold (77) 58(1) [0 | 0 | 11]</td><td>319</td></tr>
<tr><td>The Real Deal (82) 87(3) [0 | 0 | 12]</td><td>244</td></tr>
<tr><td>Spend The Night (89)-The Isley Brothers Featuring Ronald Isley 89(1) [0 | 0 | 13]</td><td>233</td></tr>
<tr><td>The Isleys Live (73) 139(1) [0 | 0 | 13]</td><td>161</td></tr>
<tr><td>Masterpiece (85) 140(2) [0 | 0 | 12]</td><td>121</td></tr>
<tr><td>This Old Heart Of Mine (66) 140(1) [0 | 0 | 5]</td><td>70.4</td></tr>
<tr><td>The Brothers: Isley (69) 180(1) [0 | 0 | 3]</td><td>32.0</td></tr>
<tr><td>Isleys' Greatest Hits (73) 195(1) [0 | 0 | 3]</td><td>16.5</td></tr>
<tr><td>ISLEY JASPER ISLEY ▶ 1679 Pk:77 [0 | 0 | 2]</td><td>600</td></tr>
<tr><td>Caravan Of Love (85) 77(2) [0 | 0 | 26]</td><td>505</td></tr>
<tr><td>Broadway's Closer To Sunset Blvd. (85) 135(2) [0 | 0 | 10]</td><td>95.5</td></tr>
<tr><td>IT'S A BEAUTIFUL DAY ▶ 665 Pk:28 [0 | 1 | 5]</td><td>4105</td></tr>
<tr><td>It's A Beautiful Day (69) 47(2) [0 | 0 | 70]</td><td>2563</td></tr>
<tr><td>Marrying Maiden (70) 28(1) [0 | 5 | 21]</td><td>1014</td></tr>
<tr><td>Choice Quality Stuff/Anytime (71) 130(1) [0 | 0 | 16]</td><td>232</td></tr>
<tr><td>It's A Beautiful Day...Today (73) 114(1) [0 | 0 | 10]</td><td>182</td></tr>
<tr><td>It's A Beautiful Day At Carnegie Hall (72) 144(2) [0 | 0 | 9]</td><td>114</td></tr>
<tr><td>Burl IVES ▶ 2094 Pk:65 [0 | 0 | 1]</td><td>307</td></tr>
<tr><td>Pearly Shells (64) 65(1) [0 | 0 | 15]</td><td>307</td></tr>
</table>

J

<table>
<tr><td>Terry JACKS ▶ 2234 Pk:81 [0 | 0 | 1]</td><td>241</td></tr>
<tr><td>Seasons In The Sun (74) 81(1) [0 | 0 | 9]</td><td>241</td></tr>
<tr><td>Freddie JACKSON ▶ 414 Pk:10 [1 | 2 | 3]</td><td>7863</td></tr>
<tr><td>Rock Me Tonight (85) 10(1) [1 | 36 | 62]</td><td>4250</td></tr>
<tr><td>Just Like The First Time (86) 23(2) [0 | 26 | 51]</td><td>2850</td></tr>
<tr><td>Don't Let Love Slip Away (88) 48(2) [0 | 0 | 30]</td><td>762</td></tr>
<tr><td>Janet JACKSON ▶ 115 Pk:1 [2 | 2 | 4]</td><td>26849</td></tr>
<tr><td>Janet Jackson's Rhythm Nation 1814 (89) 1(4) [35 | 77 | 108]</td><td>13746</td></tr>
<tr><td>Control (86) 1(2) [37 | 77 | 106]</td><td>12415</td></tr>
<tr><td>Janet Jackson (82) 63(1) [0 | 0 | 25]</td><td>622</td></tr>
<tr><td>Dream Street (84) 147(2) [0 | 0 | 6]</td><td>66.6</td></tr>
<tr><td>Jermaine JACKSON ▶ 336 Pk:6 [1 | 3 | 11]</td><td>10083</td></tr>
<tr><td>Let's Get Serious (80) 6(3) [5 | 17 | 29]</td><td>3133</td></tr>
<tr><td>Jermaine Jackson (84) 19(3) [0 | 16 | 49]</td><td>2569</td></tr>
<tr><td>Jermaine (72) 27(1) [0 | 8 | 36]</td><td>1673</td></tr>
<tr><td>Jermaine(2) (80) 44(1) [0 | 0 | 23]</td><td>810</td></tr>
<tr><td>Precious Moments (86) 46(2) [0 | 0 | 22]</td><td>693</td></tr>
<tr><td>Let Me Tickle Your Fancy (82) 46(3) [0 | 0 | 16]</td><td>551</td></tr>
<tr><td>I Like Your Style (81) 86(1) [0 | 0 | 10]</td><td>224</td></tr>
<tr><td>Don't Take It Personal (89) 115(2) [0 | 0 | 16]</td><td>201</td></tr>
<tr><td>My Name Is Jermaine (76) 164(2) [0 | 0 | 11]</td><td>126</td></tr>
<tr><td>Come Into My Life (73) 152(1) [0 | 0 | 6]</td><td>75.0</td></tr>
<tr><td>Feel The Fire (77) 174(1) [0 | 0 | 3]</td><td>28.8</td></tr>
<tr><td>Joe JACKSON ▶ 268 Pk:4 [1 | 5 | 11]</td><td>13137</td></tr>
<tr><td>Night And Day (82) 4(6) [7 | 30 | 57]</td><td>4503</td></tr>
<tr><td>Look Sharp! (79) 20(2) [0 | 11 | 39]</td><td>2057</td></tr>
<tr><td>Body And Soul (84) 20(4) [0 | 16 | 29]</td><td>1868</td></tr>
<tr><td>I'm The Man (79) 22(1) [0 | 8 | 25]</td><td>1521</td></tr>
<tr><td>Big World (86) 34(2) [0 | 8 | 25]</td><td>1053</td></tr>
<tr><td>Beat Crazy (80) 41(1) [0 | 0 | 16]</td><td>605</td></tr>
<tr><td>Joe Jackson's Jumpin' Jive (81) 42(2) [0 | 0 | 13]</td><td>579</td></tr>
<tr><td>Blaze Of Glory (89) 61(2) [0 | 0 | 21]</td><td>363</td></tr>
<tr><td>Mike's Murder (Soundtrack) (83) 64(1) [0 | 0 | 13]</td><td>292</td></tr>
<tr><td>Live 1980/86 (88) 91(3) [0 | 0 | 12]</td><td>198</td></tr>
</table>

<table>
<tr><th>Act ▶ Highest Peak [Top10s | Top40s | Total]
Title (Yr) Peak(Wk) [T10 Wk | T40Wk | TotalWk]</th><th>Score</th></tr>
<tr><td>Will Power (87) 131(2) [0 | 0 | 8]</td><td>97.6</td></tr>
<tr><td>LaToya JACKSON ▶ 2056 Pk:116 [0 | 0 | 3]</td><td>323</td></tr>
<tr><td>LaToya Jackson (80) 116(2) [0 | 0 | 13]</td><td>230</td></tr>
<tr><td>Heart Don't Lie (84) 149(2) [0 | 0 | 6]</td><td>63.7</td></tr>
<tr><td>My Special Love (81) 175(2) [0 | 0 | 3]</td><td>29.5</td></tr>
<tr><td>Marlon JACKSON ▶ 3154 Pk:175 [0 | 0 | 1]</td><td>46</td></tr>
<tr><td>Baby Tonight (87) 175(2) [0 | 0 | 7]</td><td>46.1</td></tr>
<tr><td>Michael JACKSON ▶ 23 Pk:1 [4 | 5 | 11]</td><td>59268</td></tr>
<tr><td>Thriller (82) 1(37) [78 | 91 | 122]</td><td>25933</td></tr>
<tr><td>Off The Wall (79) 3(3) [29 | 52 | 169]</td><td>13427</td></tr>
<tr><td>Bad (87) 1(6) [39 | 54 | 87]</td><td>13217</td></tr>
<tr><td>Ben (72) 5(3) [6 | 15 | 32]</td><td>3309</td></tr>
<tr><td>Got To Be There (72) 14(2) [0 | 12 | 23]</td><td>2185</td></tr>
<tr><td>Farewell My Summer Love (84) 46(2) [0 | 0 | 15]</td><td>498</td></tr>
<tr><td>Music & Me (73) 92(1) [0 | 0 | 12]</td><td>255</td></tr>
<tr><td>Forever, Michael (75) 101(2) [0 | 0 | 9]</td><td>211</td></tr>
<tr><td>One Day In Your Life (81) 144(1) [0 | 0 | 10]</td><td>139</td></tr>
<tr><td>The Best Of Michael Jackson (75) 156(2) [0 | 0 | 5]</td><td>68.7</td></tr>
<tr><td>14 Greatest Hits (84)-Michael Jackson & The Jackson 5 [A] 168(1) [0 | 0 | 7]</td><td>25.5</td></tr>
<tr><td>Millie JACKSON ▶ 556 Pk:21 [0 | 2 | 14]</td><td>5269</td></tr>
<tr><td>Caught Up (74) 21(1) [0 | 12 | 21]</td><td>1877</td></tr>
<tr><td>Feelin' Bitchy (77) 34(1) [0 | 7 | 23]</td><td>1083</td></tr>
<tr><td>Get It Out'cha System (78) 55(3) [0 | 0 | 14]</td><td>483</td></tr>
<tr><td>Live And Uncensored (79) 94(2) [0 | 0 | 18]</td><td>360</td></tr>
<tr><td>Still Caught Up (75) 112(2) [0 | 0 | 16]</td><td>292</td></tr>
<tr><td>Royal Rappin's (79)-Millie Jackson & Isaac Hayes [A] 80(2) [0 | 0 | 19]</td><td>214</td></tr>
<tr><td>For Men Only (80) 100(1) [0 | 0 | 10]</td><td>199</td></tr>
<tr><td>Live And Outrageous (Rated XXX) (82) 113(1) [0 | 0 | 13]</td><td>195</td></tr>
<tr><td>An Imitation Of Love (86) 119(2) [0 | 0 | 17]</td><td>184</td></tr>
<tr><td>Millie Jackson (72) 166(1) [0 | 0 | 11]</td><td>106</td></tr>
<tr><td>A Moment's Pleasure (79) 144(3) [0 | 0 | 6]</td><td>96.8</td></tr>
<tr><td>I Had To Say It (81) 137(1) [0 | 0 | 4]</td><td>69.8</td></tr>
<tr><td>Lovingly Yours (77) 175(1) [0 | 0 | 6]</td><td>59.1</td></tr>
<tr><td>It Hurts So Good (73) 175(1) [0 | 0 | 6]</td><td>50.9</td></tr>
<tr><td>Rebbie JACKSON ▶ 1848 Pk:63 [0 | 0 | 1]</td><td>445</td></tr>
<tr><td>Centipede (84) 63(3) [0 | 0 | 18]</td><td>445</td></tr>
<tr><td>Walter JACKSON ▶ 1775 Pk:113 [0 | 0 | 3]</td><td>501</td></tr>
<tr><td>Feeling Good (76) 113(5) [0 | 0 | 18]</td><td>395</td></tr>
<tr><td>I Want To Come Back As A Song (77) 141(1) [0 | 0 | 5]</td><td>79.8</td></tr>
<tr><td>Speak Her Name (67) 194(1) [0 | 0 | 5]</td><td>26.2</td></tr>
<tr><td>Willis JACKSON ▶ 3065 Pk:137 [0 | 0 | 2]</td><td>57</td></tr>
<tr><td>Together Again! (66)-Willis Jackson & Jack McDuff [A] 137(1) [0 | 0 | 4]</td><td>30.1</td></tr>
<tr><td>The Way We Were (75) 182(1) [0 | 0 | 3]</td><td>26.7</td></tr>
<tr><td>JACKSON 5 ▶ 58 Pk:4 [6 | 14 | 20]</td><td>42109</td></tr>
<tr><td>Third Album (70) 4(3) [11 | 23 | 50]</td><td>6084</td></tr>
<tr><td>ABC (70) 4(2) [9 | 21 | 50]</td><td>4817</td></tr>
<tr><td>Diana Ross Presents The Jackson 5 (70) 5(1) [11 | 21 | 32]</td><td>4519</td></tr>
<tr><td>Maybe Tomorrow (71) 11(2) [0 | 14 | 41]</td><td>3527</td></tr>
<tr><td>Lookin' Through The Windows (72) 7(1) [5 | 17 | 33]</td><td>3181</td></tr>
<tr><td>Destiny (78)-The Jacksons 11(2) [0 | 15 | 41]</td><td>3181</td></tr>
<tr><td>Triumph (80)-The Jacksons 10(4) [4 | 18 | 29]</td><td>3024</td></tr>
<tr><td>Jackson 5 Greatest Hits (72)-The Jacksons 12(1) [0 | 15 | 41]</td><td>2634</td></tr>
<tr><td>Victory (84)-The Jacksons 4(3) [8 | 15 | 30]</td><td>2571</td></tr>
<tr><td>Goin' Back To Indiana (71) 16(1) [0 | 11 | 26]</td><td>2052</td></tr>
<tr><td>Dancing Machine (74)-The Jackson 5ive 16(2) [0 | 7 | 21]</td><td>1448</td></tr>
<tr><td>The Jacksons (76)-The Jacksons 36(2) [0 | 3 | 27]</td><td>1195</td></tr>
<tr><td>Jacksons Live (81)-The Jacksons 30(2) [0 | 8 | 19]</td><td>1022</td></tr>
</table>

<table>
<tr><th>Act ▶ Highest Peak [Top10s|Top40s|Total]
Title (Yr) Peak(Wk) [T10 Wk|T40Wk|TotalWk]</th><th>Score</th></tr>
<tr><td>JACKSON 5 ▶ Continued</td><td></td></tr>
<tr><td>Moving Violation (75) 36(1) [0|3|15]</td><td>744</td></tr>
<tr><td>Skywriter (73)-The Jackson 5ive 44(1) [0|0|16]</td><td>647</td></tr>
<tr><td>Get It Together (73)-The Jackson 5ive 100(1) [0|0|29]</td><td>518</td></tr>
<tr><td>Goin' Places (77)-The Jacksons 63(1) [0|0|11]</td><td>344</td></tr>
<tr><td>2300 Jackson St. (89)-The Jacksons 59(2) [0|0|11]</td><td>319</td></tr>
<tr><td>Jackson 5 Anthology (76) 84(1) [0|0|9]</td><td>256</td></tr>
<tr><td>14 Greatest Hits (84)-Michael Jackson & The Jackson 5 [A] 168(1) [0|0|7]</td><td>25.5</td></tr>
<tr><td>Lou JACOBI ▶ 3121 Pk:134 [0|0|1]</td><td>50</td></tr>
<tr><td>Al Tijuana And His Jewish Brass (66) 134(2) [0|0|3]</td><td>49.7</td></tr>
<tr><td>Debbie JACOBS ▶ 2502 Pk:153 [0|0|2]</td><td>159</td></tr>
<tr><td>Undercover Lover (79)-Debbie Jacobs-Rock 153(1) [0|0|8]</td><td>94.7</td></tr>
<tr><td>High On Your Love (80) 178(4) [0|0|7]</td><td>64.2</td></tr>
<tr><td>JADE WARRIOR ▶ 3476 Pk:194 [0|0|1]</td><td>12</td></tr>
<tr><td>Released (72) 194(2) [0|0|2]</td><td>12.5</td></tr>
<tr><td>Chris JAGGER ▶ 3297 Pk:186 [0|0|1]</td><td>29</td></tr>
<tr><td>Chris Jagger (73) 186(1) [0|0|4]</td><td>28.6</td></tr>
<tr><td>Mick JAGGER ▶ 902 Pk:13 [0|1|2]</td><td>2376</td></tr>
<tr><td>She's The Boss (85) 13(1) [0|12|29]</td><td>1708</td></tr>
<tr><td>Primitive Cool (87) 41(2) [0|0|20]</td><td>668</td></tr>
<tr><td>The JAGGERZ ▶ 1897 Pk:62 [0|0|1]</td><td>408</td></tr>
<tr><td>We Went To Different Schools Together (70) 62(1) [0|0|11]</td><td>408</td></tr>
<tr><td>The JAM ▶ 1321 Pk:72 [0|0|7]</td><td>1101</td></tr>
<tr><td>Sound Affects (81) 72(1) [0|0|11]</td><td>337</td></tr>
<tr><td>The Gift (82) 82(1) [0|0|16]</td><td>320</td></tr>
<tr><td>The Bitterest Pill (I Ever Had To Swallow) (82) 135(2) [0|0|14]</td><td>149</td></tr>
<tr><td>Setting Sons (80) 137(2) [0|0|8]</td><td>121</td></tr>
<tr><td>Dig The New Breed (83) 131(1) [0|0|9]</td><td>84.2</td></tr>
<tr><td>The Jam (81) 176(3) [0|0|7]</td><td>59.3</td></tr>
<tr><td>Beat Surrender (83) 171(1) [0|0|4]</td><td>30.6</td></tr>
<tr><td>Ahmad JAMAL Trio ▶ 2738 Pk:168 [0|0|2]</td><td>107</td></tr>
<tr><td>Cry Young (67)-Ahmad Jamal 168(1) [0|0|8]</td><td>59.8</td></tr>
<tr><td>Genetic Walk (80)-Ahmad Jamal 173(1) [0|0|5]</td><td>47.1</td></tr>
<tr><td>Bob JAMES ▶ 388 Pk:37 [0|2|17]</td><td>8517</td></tr>
<tr><td>Touchdown (78) 37(1) [0|2|29]</td><td>1218</td></tr>
<tr><td>Heads (77) 47(1) [0|0|31]</td><td>1095</td></tr>
<tr><td>Three (76) 49(2) [0|0|27]</td><td>1077</td></tr>
<tr><td>H (80) 47(3) [0|0|18]</td><td>656</td></tr>
<tr><td>BJ4 (77) 38(1) [0|2|17]</td><td>629</td></tr>
<tr><td>Double Vision (86)-Bob James/David Sanborn [A] 50(2) [0|0|64]</td><td>608</td></tr>
<tr><td>Lucky Seven (79) 42(2) [0|0|14]</td><td>523</td></tr>
<tr><td>All Around The Town (81) 66(1) [0|0|16]</td><td>467</td></tr>
<tr><td>Sign Of The Times (81) 56(1) [0|0|14]</td><td>439</td></tr>
<tr><td>Two (75) 75(1) [0|0|14]</td><td>372</td></tr>
<tr><td>One (74) 85(1) [0|0|14]</td><td>354</td></tr>
<tr><td>Hands Down (82) 72(2) [0|0|17]</td><td>289</td></tr>
<tr><td>Obsession (86) 142(1) [0|0|27]</td><td>270</td></tr>
<tr><td>The Genie (Themes & Variations From The TV Series "Taxi") (83) 77(1) [0|0|11]</td><td>239</td></tr>
<tr><td>Foxie (83) 106(1) [0|0|13]</td><td>177</td></tr>
<tr><td>12 (84) 136(2) [0|0|10]</td><td>95.4</td></tr>
<tr><td>Ivory Coast (88) 196(2) [0|0|2]</td><td>10.0</td></tr>
<tr><td>Bob JAMES & Earl KLUGH ▶ 809 Pk:23 [0|1|2]</td><td>2889</td></tr>
<tr><td>One On One (79)-Bob James/Earl Klugh 23(3) [0|13|33]</td><td>1967</td></tr>
<tr><td>Two Of A Kind (82)-Earl Klugh & Bob James 44(4) [0|0|29]</td><td>923</td></tr>
<tr><td>Etta JAMES ▶ 1658 Pk:82 [0|0|4]</td><td>614</td></tr>
<tr><td>Tell Mama (68) 82(2) [0|0|13]</td><td>255</td></tr>
<tr><td>Etta James Rocks The House (64) 96(1) [0|0|10]</td><td>181</td></tr>
<tr><td>Etta James (73) 154(1) [0|0|9]</td><td>107</td></tr>
<tr><td>Etta James Top Ten (63) 117(1) [0|0|4]</td><td>71.3</td></tr>
<tr><td>Jimmy JAMES & The VAGABONDS ▶ 2286 Pk:139 [0|0|1]</td><td>220</td></tr>
<tr><td>You Don't Stand A Chance If You Can't Dance (75) 139(1) [0|0|16]</td><td>220</td></tr>
<tr><td>Melvin JAMES ▶ 2915 Pk:146 [0|0|1]</td><td>78</td></tr>
<tr><td>The Passenger (87) 146(2) [0|0|8]</td><td>78.4</td></tr>
<tr><td>Rick JAMES ▶ 190 Pk:3 [1|6|11]</td><td>18183</td></tr>
<tr><td>Street Songs (81) 3(2) [12|27|74]</td><td>7134</td></tr>
<tr><td>Come Get It! (78) 13(1) [0|16|36]</td><td>2904</td></tr>
<tr><td>Bustin' Out Of L Seven (79) 16(3) [0|16|27]</td><td>2430</td></tr>
<tr><td>Cold Blooded (83) 16(1) [0|12|29]</td><td>1717</td></tr>
<tr><td>Throwin' Down (82) 13(4) [0|10|23]</td><td>1459</td></tr>
<tr><td>Fire It Up (79) 34(1) [0|3|20]</td><td>781</td></tr>
<tr><td>Glow (85) 50(2) [0|0|26]</td><td>759</td></tr>
<tr><td>Reflections (84) 41(2) [0|0|19]</td><td>503</td></tr>
<tr><td>Garden Of Love (80) 83(2) [0|0|10]</td><td>225</td></tr>
<tr><td>The Flag (86) 95(2) [0|0|12]</td><td>198</td></tr>
<tr><td>Wonderful (88) 148(2) [0|0|8]</td><td>72.8</td></tr>
<tr><td>Sonny JAMES ▶ 1609 Pk:83 [0|0|10]</td><td>668</td></tr>
<tr><td>The Astrodome Presents In Person Sonny James (69) 83(1) [0|0|13]</td><td>342</td></tr>
<tr><td>Empty Arms (71) 150(1) [0|0|5]</td><td>64.8</td></tr>
<tr><td>The Best Of Sonny James (66) 141(2) [0|0|4]</td><td>60.1</td></tr>
<tr><td>Only The Lonely (69) 161(1) [0|0|3]</td><td>46.3</td></tr>
<tr><td>It's Just A Matter Of Time (70) 177(1) [0|0|4]</td><td>40.1</td></tr>
<tr><td>When The Snow Is On The Roses (72) 190(1) [0|0|5]</td><td>30.4</td></tr>
<tr><td>Close-Up (69) 184(2) [0|0|3]</td><td>30.0</td></tr>
<tr><td>#1 (70) 187(1) [0|0|4]</td><td>28.7</td></tr>
<tr><td>The Sensational Sonny James (71) 197(1) [0|0|2]</td><td>12.4</td></tr>
<tr><td>My Love / Don't Keep Me Hangin' On (70) 197(2) [0|0|2]</td><td>12.4</td></tr>
<tr><td>Tommy JAMES And The SHONDELLS ▶ 448 Pk:8 [1|2|10]</td><td>7134</td></tr>
<tr><td>Crimson & Clover (69) 8(4) [5|14|35]</td><td>3415</td></tr>
<tr><td>The Best Of Tommy James & The Shondells (69) 21(1) [0|10|41]</td><td>2162</td></tr>
<tr><td>Hanky Panky (66) 46(1) [0|0|15]</td><td>499</td></tr>
<tr><td>I Think We're Alone Now (67) 74(2) [0|0|18]</td><td>451</td></tr>
<tr><td>Travelin' (70) 91(2) [0|0|9]</td><td>217</td></tr>
<tr><td>Cellophane Symphony (69) 141(1) [0|0|6]</td><td>115</td></tr>
<tr><td>Three Times In Love (80)-Tommy James 134(1) [0|0|7]</td><td>112</td></tr>
<tr><td>Christian Of The World (71) 131(2) [0|0|8]</td><td>105</td></tr>
<tr><td>Something Special! The Best Of Tommy James & The Shondells (68) 174(2) [0|0|5]</td><td>43.6</td></tr>
<tr><td>Mony Mony (68) 193(2) [0|0|2]</td><td>13.5</td></tr>
<tr><td>JAMES GANG ▶ 363 Pk:20 [0|3|11]</td><td>9136</td></tr>
<tr><td>James Gang Rides Again (70) 20(1) [0|12|66]</td><td>2788</td></tr>
<tr><td>Thirds (71) 27(2) [0|16|30]</td><td>2465</td></tr>
<tr><td>James Gang Live In Concert (71) 24(1) [0|5|16]</td><td>1060</td></tr>
<tr><td>Straight Shooter (72) 58(1) [0|0|19]</td><td>713</td></tr>
<tr><td>Yer' Album (69) 83(1) [0|0|24]</td><td>631</td></tr>
<tr><td>Passin' Thru (72) 72(1) [0|0|15]</td><td>407</td></tr>
<tr><td>The Best Of The James Gang Featuring Joe Walsh (73) 79(1) [0|0|16]</td><td>377</td></tr>
<tr><td>Bang (74) 122(1) [0|0|18]</td><td>250</td></tr>
<tr><td>Miami (74) 97(1) [0|0|10]</td><td>212</td></tr>
<tr><td>Newborn (75) 109(2) [0|0|9]</td><td>196</td></tr>
<tr><td>16 Greatest Hits (73) 181(1) [0|0|5]</td><td>38.7</td></tr>
<tr><td>JAN & DEAN ▶ 845 Pk:22 [0|3|8]</td><td>2712</td></tr>
<tr><td>The Little Old Lady From Pasadena (64) 40(1) [0|1|20]</td><td>628</td></tr>
<tr><td>Command Performance/Live In Person (65) 33(1) [0|3|16]</td><td>588</td></tr>
<tr><td>Drag City (64) 22(1) [0|2|14]</td><td>555</td></tr>
<tr><td>Dead Man's Curve/The New Girl In School (64) 80(2) [0|0|21]</td><td>367</td></tr>
<tr><td>Ride The Wild Surf (Soundtrack) (64) 66(1) [0|0|19]</td><td>351</td></tr>
<tr><td>Jan & Dean Golden Hits, Volume 2 (65) 107(1) [0|0|6]</td><td>104</td></tr>
<tr><td>Filet Of Soul (66) 127(2) [0|0|5]</td><td>81.2</td></tr>
<tr><td>Folk 'N Roll (66) 145(2) [0|0|3]</td><td>37.7</td></tr>
<tr><td>JANE'S ADDICTION ▶ 1688 Pk:103 [0|0|1]</td><td>595</td></tr>
<tr><td>Nothing's Shocking (88) 103(2) [0|0|35]</td><td>595</td></tr>
<tr><td>Chaz JANKEL ▶ 2433 Pk:126 [0|0|1]</td><td>178</td></tr>
<tr><td>Questionnaire (82) 126(1) [0|0|14]</td><td>178</td></tr>
<tr><td>Horst JANKOWSKI ▶ 1017 Pk:18 [0|1|3]</td><td>1881</td></tr>
<tr><td>The Genius Of Jankowski! (65) 18(1) [0|12|31]</td><td>1460</td></tr>
<tr><td>More Genius Of Jankowski (65) 65(1) [0|0|13]</td><td>377</td></tr>
<tr><td>So What's New? (66) 107(2) [0|0|2]</td><td>44.3</td></tr>
<tr><td>Jean Michel JARRE ▶ 1197 Pk:52 [0|0|4]</td><td>1348</td></tr>
<tr><td>Rendez-Vous (86) 52(4) [0|0|20]</td><td>553</td></tr>
<tr><td>Oxygene (77) 78(1) [0|0|19]</td><td>391</td></tr>
<tr><td>Magnetic Fields (81) 98(2) [0|0|12]</td><td>272</td></tr>
<tr><td>Equinoxe (79) 126(1) [0|0|8]</td><td>132</td></tr>
<tr><td>Al JARREAU ▶ 281 Pk:9 [1|3|10]</td><td>12394</td></tr>
<tr><td>Breakin' Away (81) 9(3) [4|20|103]</td><td>5128</td></tr>
<tr><td>Jarreau (83) 13(2) [0|12|43]</td><td>2144</td></tr>
<tr><td>This Time (80) 27(2) [0|5|35]</td><td>1635</td></tr>
<tr><td>High Crime (84) 49(2) [0|0|35]</td><td>901</td></tr>
<tr><td>All Fly Home (78) 78(2) [0|0|28]</td><td>792</td></tr>
<tr><td>Look To The Rainbow: Live In Europe (77) 49(1) [0|0|15]</td><td>599</td></tr>
<tr><td>Heart's Horizon (88) 75(2) [0|0|23]</td><td>494</td></tr>
<tr><td>L Is For Lover (86) 81(2) [0|0|28]</td><td>386</td></tr>
<tr><td>Glow (76) 132(1) [0|0|11]</td><td>199</td></tr>
<tr><td>In London (85) 125(1) [0|0|9]</td><td>115</td></tr>
<tr><td>Keith JARRETT ▶ 1817 Pk:117 [0|0|8]</td><td>470</td></tr>
<tr><td>Staircase/Hourglass/Sundial/Sand (77) 141(1) [0|0|12]</td><td>170</td></tr>
<tr><td>Byablue (77) 117(1) [0|0|6]</td><td>125</td></tr>
<tr><td>El Juicio (The Judgement) (75) 160(1) [0|0|5]</td><td>55.7</td></tr>
<tr><td>Shades (77) 174(1) [0|0|4]</td><td>40.9</td></tr>
<tr><td>Arbour Zena (76) 179(1) [0|0|3]</td><td>30.1</td></tr>
<tr><td>My Song (78) 174(1) [0|0|2]</td><td>22.9</td></tr>
<tr><td>Mysteries (76) 184(1) [0|0|2]</td><td>18.0</td></tr>
<tr><td>In The Light (76) 195(1) [0|0|1]</td><td>6.6</td></tr>
<tr><td>JASON & The SCORCHERS ▶ 1485 Pk:91 [0|0|3]</td><td>841</td></tr>
<tr><td>Still Standing (86) 91(4) [0|0|19]</td><td>328</td></tr>
<tr><td>Fervor (84) 116(1) [0|0|23]</td><td>258</td></tr>
<tr><td>Lost & Found (85) 96(1) [0|0|15]</td><td>255</td></tr>
<tr><td>Chris JASPER ▶ 3367 Pk:182 [0|0|1]</td><td>22</td></tr>
<tr><td>Superbad (88) 182(2) [0|0|3]</td><td>22.0</td></tr>
<tr><td>JAY & The AMERICANS ▶ 915 Pk:21 [0|1|6]</td><td>2284</td></tr>
<tr><td>Jay & The Americans Greatest Hits! (65) 21(1) [0|5|20]</td><td>885</td></tr>
<tr><td>Sands Of Time (69) 51(2) [0|0|21]</td><td>804</td></tr>
<tr><td>Blockbusters (65) 113(2) [0|0|17]</td><td>249</td></tr>
<tr><td>Wax Museum (70) 105(1) [0|0|11]</td><td>236</td></tr>
<tr><td>Sunday And Me (66) 141(1) [0|0|4]</td><td>55.4</td></tr>
<tr><td>Come A Little Bit Closer (64) 131(1) [0|0|4]</td><td>54.5</td></tr>
<tr><td>JAY And The TECHNIQUES ▶ 2443 Pk:129 [0|0|1]</td><td>174</td></tr>
<tr><td>Apples, Peaches, Pumpkin Pie (67) 129(1) [0|0|13]</td><td>174</td></tr>
<tr><td>Jerry JAYE ▶ 3515 Pk:195 [0|0|1]</td><td>10</td></tr>
<tr><td>My Girl Josephine (67) 195(1) [0|0|2]</td><td>10.1</td></tr>
</table>

Act ► Highest Peak [Top10s|Top40s|Total]
Title (Yr) Peak(Wk) [T10 Wk|T40Wk|TotalWk] — **Score**

Miles JAYE ► 2230 Pk:125 [0|0|2] — 242
Miles (87) 125(2) [0|0|12] — 157
Irresistible (89) 160(2) [0|0|9] — 85.3

The JB'S ► 1957 Pk:77 [0|0|2] — 375
Doing It To Death (73) 77(1) [0|0|13] — 357
Damn Right I Am Somebody (74)-Fred Wesley & The JB's 197(1) [0|0|3] — 17.3

JEFFERSON AIRPLANE/STARSHIP ► 17 Pk:1 [7|21|27] — 63716
Red Octopus (75)-Jefferson Starship 1(4) [21|32|87] — 10755
Surrealistic Pillow (67)-Jefferson Airplane 3(1) [20|29|56] — 6325
Spitfire (76)-Jefferson Starship 3(6) [13|16|38] — 5588
Earth (78)-Jefferson Starship 5(7) [12|23|34] — 5106
Knee Deep In The Hoopla (85)-Starship 7(3) [15|33|50] — 4436
Freedom At Point Zero (79)-Jefferson Starship 10(1) [1|17|28] — 3057
Volunteers (69)-Jefferson Airplane 13(2) [0|13|44] — 3005
Crown Of Creation (68)-Jefferson Airplane 6(2) [5|12|25] — 2849
The Worst Of Jefferson Airplane (70)-Jefferson Airplane 12(1) [0|14|40] — 2830
Bark (71)-Jefferson Airplane 11(2) [0|11|21] — 2382
Dragon Fly (74)-Jefferson Starship 11(1) [0|10|37] — 2371
Modern Times (81)-Jefferson Starship 26(3) [0|16|33] — 2256
Bless Its Pointed Little Head (69)-Jefferson Airplane 17(2) [0|8|20] — 1678
Winds Of Change (82)-Jefferson Starship 26(6) [0|11|31] — 1616
Long John Silver (72)-Jefferson Airplane 20(2) [0|9|21] — 1511
No Protection (87)-Starship 12(1) [0|9|25] — 1442
After Bathing At Baxter's (67)-Jefferson Airplane 17(2) [0|9|23] — 1263
Nuclear Furniture (84)-Jefferson Starship 28(4) [0|8|23] — 1140
Gold (79)-Jefferson Starship 20(2) [0|5|14] — 931
Blows Against The Empire (70)-Paul Kantner/Jefferson Starship [A] 20(3) [0|11|23] — 857
Flight Log (1966-1976) (77)-Jefferson Starship 37(1) [0|3|15] — 751
Thirty Seconds Over Winterland (73)-Jefferson Airplane 52(1) [0|0|16] — 546
Love Among The Cannibals (89)-Starship 64(2) [0|0|18] — 473
Early Flight (74)-Jefferson Airplane 110(1) [0|0|8] — 166
Jefferson Airplane Takes Off (66)-Jefferson Airplane 128(2) [0|0|11] — 144
Jefferson Airplane (89)-Jefferson Airplane 85(2) [0|0|7] — 140
2400 Fulton St. (87)-Jefferson Airplane 138(2) [0|0|9] — 101

Garland JEFFREYS ► 1239 Pk:59 [0|0|6] — 1257
Escape Artist (81) 59(4) [0|0|18] — 762
One-Eyed Jack (78) 99(1) [0|0|10] — 224
Ghost Writer (77) 140(2) [0|0|10] — 133
American Boy & Girl (79) 151(1) [0|0|5] — 67.8
Rock & Roll Adult (81) 163(2) [0|0|4] — 43.4
Guts For Love (83) 176(2) [0|0|4] — 27.6

JELLYBEAN ► 2396 Pk:101 [0|0|1] — 187
Just Visiting This Planet (87) 101(2) [0|0|11] — 187

Waylon JENNINGS ► 233 Pk:10 [1|6|17] — 15018
Greatest Hits (79) 28(1) [0|4|115] — 3978
Ol' Waylon (77) 15(2) [0|12|33] — 2323
Are You Ready For The Country (76) 34(1) [0|2|35] — 1598
Music Man (80) 36(2) [0|3|43] — 1492
What Goes Around Comes Around (79) 49(1) [0|0|28] — 919
Dreaming My Dreams (75) 49(1) [0|0|21] — 876
I've Always Been Crazy (78) 48(1) [0|0|24] — 761
Wanted! The Outlaws (76)-Waylon Jennings, Willie Nelson, Jessi Colter, Tompall Glaser [A] 10(2) [2|14|51] — 723
Black On Black (82) 39(2) [0|2|23] — 704
Waylon "Live" (76) 46(1) [0|0|17] — 653
The Ramblin' Man (74) 105(1) [0|0|17] — 372
Leather And Lace (81)-Waylon Jennings & Jessi Colter [A] 43(2) [0|0|19] — 371
It's Only Rock And Roll (83) 109(1) [0|0|11] — 148
Honky Tonk Heroes (73) 185(1) [0|0|5] — 34.6
Mackintosh & T.J. (Soundtrack) (76) 189(1) [0|0|4] — 26.3
Country-Folk (69)-Waylon Jennings & The Kimberlys [A] 169(1) [0|0|4] — 25.6
Waylon (70)-Waylon 192(2) [0|0|2] — 14.2

Waylon JENNINGS & Willie NELSON ► 852 Pk:12 [0|1|2] — 2636
Waylon & Willie (78) 12(1) [0|9|29] — 2075
WWII (82) 57(3) [0|0|22] — 561

JESUS AND MARY CHAIN ► 1950 Pk:105 [0|0|4] — 377
Automatic (89) 105(1) [0|0|25] — 303
Darklands (87) 161(2) [0|0|4] — 35.3
Psychocandy (86) 188(2) [0|0|4] — 21.5
Barbed Wire Kisses (88) 192(1) [0|0|3] — 17.6

JETBOY ► 2636 Pk:135 [0|0|1] — 126
Feel The Shake (88) 135(1) [0|0|10] — 126

JETHRO TULL ► 35 Pk:1 [7|17|22] — 48841
Aqualung (71) 7(7) [16|32|76] — 8099
War Child (74) 2(3) [16|23|31] — 6168
Thick As A Brick (72) 1(2) [10|20|46] — 5915
Living In The Past (72) 3(3) [10|21|31] — 4299
A Passion Play (73) 1(1) [6|14|32] — 3303
Benefit (70) 11(2) [0|17|41] — 2733
Songs From The Wood (77) 8(2) [4|14|22] — 2518
Stand Up (69) 20(1) [0|9|40] — 2387
Minstrel In The Gallery (75) 7(3) [5|8|14] — 1864
M.U. The Best Of Jethro Tull (76) 13(2) [0|9|23] — 1768
Too Old To Rock 'N' Roll: Too Young To Die! (76) 14(1) [0|7|21] — 1579
Heavy Horses (78) 19(2) [0|8|17] — 1379
Jethro Tull Live - Bursting Out (78) 21(1) [0|8|15] — 1229
Crest Of A Knave (87) 32(1) [0|8|28] — 1219
Stormwatch (79) 22(1) [0|5|17] — 1018
The Broadsword And The Beast (82) 19(3) [0|7|17] — 973
"A" (80) 30(2) [0|4|12] — 667
This Was (69) 62(2) [0|0|17] — 663
Rock Island (89) 56(2) [0|0|18] — 442
Under Wraps (84) 76(2) [0|0|12] — 233
20 Years Of Jethro Tull (88) 97(2) [0|0|15] — 233
Repeat-The Best Of Jethro Tull, Vol. II (77) 94(2) [0|0|6] — 154

The JETS ► 557 Pk:21 [0|2|3] — 5263
The Jets (86) 21(2) [0|25|70] — 3252
Magic (87) 35(1) [0|6|50] — 1898
Believe (89) 107(1) [0|0|7] — 113

Joan JETT & The BLACKHEARTS ► 308 Pk:2 [1|3|6] — 11020
I Love Rock 'N Roll (81) 2(3) [12|20|59] — 5608
Up Your Alley (88) 19(1) [0|18|46] — 2833
Album (83) 20(2) [0|10|20] — 1196
Bad Reputation (81) 51(4) [0|0|21] — 746
Glorious Results Of A Misspent Youth (84) 67(1) [0|0|21] — 454
Good Music (86) 105(1) [0|0|16] — 182

JIGSAW ► 1575 Pk:55 [0|0|1] — 705
Sky High (75) 55(2) [0|0|19] — 705

Jose JIMENEZ ► 3053 Pk:128 [0|0|1] — 59
Jose Jimenez In Jollywood (63) 128(1) [0|0|4] — 58.9

JIVE BUNNY & The MASTERMIXERS ► 1493 Pk:26 [0|1|1] — 818
Jive Bunny - The Album (89) 26(1) [0|6|19] — 818

J.J. FAD ► 1413 Pk:49 [0|0|1] — 953
Supersonic--The Album (88) 49(2) [0|0|30] — 953

Antonio Carlos JOBIM ► 1297 Pk:19 [0|1|4] — 1148
The Wonderful World Of Antonio Carlos Jobim (65) 57(1) [0|0|14] — 361
Wave (68) 114(1) [0|0|11] — 163
Stone Flower (71) 196(2) [0|0|2] — 13.2
Francis Albert Sinatra & Antonio Carlos Jobim (67)-Frank Sinatra & Antonio Carlos Jobim [A] 19(2) [0|6|28] — 611

JOBOXERS ► 2046 Pk:70 [0|0|1] — 330
Like Gangbusters (83) 70(2) [0|0|15] — 330

JOE & EDDIE ► 2474 Pk:119 [0|0|2] — 167
There's A Meetin' Here Tonite (64) 119(1) [0|0|7] — 114
Coast To Coast (64) 140(1) [0|0|4] — 53.0

Billy JOEL ► 9 Pk:1 [9|12|14] — 72919
The Stranger (77) 2(6) [19|70|137] — 14610
Glass Houses (80) 1(6) [25|35|73] — 11662
An Innocent Man (83) 4(5) [30|62|111] — 11007
52nd Street (78) 1(8) [22|34|76] — 10703
Storm Front (89) 1(1) [19|28|69] — 6443
The Bridge (86) 7(4) [11|29|47] — 4352
Greatest Hits Vol. I & II (85) 6(2) [9|26|65] — 4119
The Nylon Curtain (82) 7(4) [7|23|35] — 3773
Songs In The Attic (81) 8(3) [5|10|27] — 2554
Piano Man (74) 27(2) [0|7|40] — 1770
Streetlife Serenade (74) 35(1) [0|2|18] — 931
Kohuept (Live In Leningrad) (87) 38(1) [0|3|18] — 691
Turnstiles (76) 122(2) [0|0|12] — 235
Cold Spring Harbor (84) 158(1) [0|0|8] — 71.3

David JOHANSEN ► 1740 Pk:90 [0|0|4] — 534
Buster Poindexter (88)-Buster Poindexter And His Banshees Of Blue 90(1) [0|0|15] — 302
Live It Up (82) 148(2) [0|0|15] — 154
Here Comes The Night (81) 160(1) [0|0|3] — 39.3
In Style (79) 177(2) [0|0|4] — 38.0

Elton JOHN ► 4 Pk:1 [13|26|30] — 102732
Goodbye Yellow Brick Road (73) 1(8) [36|43|103] — 12843
Elton John's Greatest Hits (74) 1(10) [11|20|104] — 9369
Captain Fantastic And The Brown Dirt Cowboy (75) 1(7) [17|24|43] — 8391
Honky Château (72) 1(5) [18|25|61] — 7808
Caribou (74) 1(4) [14|20|54] — 7168
Don't Shoot Me I'm Only The Piano Player (73) 1(2) [9|27|89] — 7076
Elton John (70) 4(1) [6|28|51] — 5452
Tumbleweed Connection (71) 5(4) [9|20|37] — 4966
Madman Across The Water (71) 8(2) [4|25|51] — 4698
Rock Of The Westies (75) 1(3) [7|9|26] — 3949
Blue Moves (76) 3(3) [6|12|22] — 3289
11/17/1970 (71) 11(1) [0|12|23] — 2371
Sleeping With The Past (89) 23(1) [0|11|53] — 2337
Reg Strikes Back (88) 16(1) [0|19|29] — 2304

Act ▶ Highest Peak [Top10s | Top40s | Total] Title (Yr) Peak(Wk) [T10 Wk | T40Wk | TotalWk]	Score
Elton JOHN ▶ *Continued*	
Here And There (76) 4(2) [5|8|20]	2275
Too Low For Zero (83) 25(1) [0|13|54]	2107
Empty Sky (75) 6(1) [3|8|18]	1955
Breaking Hearts (84) 20(5) [0|14|34]	1779
21 At 33 (80) 13(2) [0|9|21]	1698
Live In Australia (With The Melbourne Symphony Orchestra) (87) 24(2) [0|8|41]	1685
Jump Up! (82) 17(3) [0|8|33]	1675
Elton John's Greatest Hits, Volume II (77) 21(3) [0|8|20]	1459
A Single Man (78) 15(2) [0|7|18]	1374
The Fox (81) 21(2) [0|5|19]	1144
"Friends" (Soundtrack) (71) 36(1) [0|4|19]	958
Ice On Fire (85) 48(2) [0|0|28]	859
The Thom Bell Sessions (79) 51(1) [0|0|18]	698
Victim Of Love (79) 35(2) [0|4|10]	574
Elton John's Greatest Hits, Volume III 1979-1987 (87) 84(2) [0|0|23]	324
Leather Jackets (86) 91(3) [0|0|9]	148
Robert JOHN ▶ 1979 Pk:68 [0|0|1]	**363**
Robert John (79) 68(1) [0|0|14]	363
JOHNNY And The DISTRACTIONS ▶ 2839 Pk:152 [0|0|1]	**89**
Let It Rock (82) 152(1) [0|0|9]	89.2
JOHNNY HATES JAZZ ▶ 1556 Pk:56 [0|0|1]	**723**
Turn Back The Clock (88) 56(1) [0|0|25]	723
Sammy JOHNS ▶ 2468 Pk:148 [0|0|1]	**169**
Sammy Johns (75) 148(1) [0|0|12]	169
Don JOHNSON ▶ 1163 Pk:17 [0|1|1]	**1426**
Heartbeat (86) 17(2) [0|11|27]	1426
Howard JOHNSON ▶ 2741 Pk:122 [0|0|1]	**106**
Keepin' Love New (82) 122(2) [0|0|9]	106
Jesse JOHNSON ▶ 891 Pk:43 [0|0|3]	**2433**
Jesse Johnson's Revue (85)-Jesse Johnson's Revue 43(5) [0|0|43]	1738
Shockadelica (86) 70(2) [0|0|20]	397
Every Shade Of Love (88) 79(2) [0|0|13]	299
Michael JOHNSON ▶ 1706 Pk:81 [0|0|2]	**580**
The Michael Johnson Album (78) 81(1) [0|0|17]	454
Dialogue (79) 157(1) [0|0|12]	126
Robert JOHNSON ▶ 2955 Pk:174 [0|0|1]	**72**
Close Personal Friend (79) 174(1) [0|0|8]	71.8
Tom JOHNSTON ▶ 2049 Pk:100 [0|0|2]	**329**
Everything You've Heard Is True (79) 100(2) [0|0|13]	243
Still Feels Good (81) 158(1) [0|0|7]	85.8
JO JO GUNNE ▶ 1214 Pk:57 [0|0|4]	**1316**
Jo Jo Gunne (72) 57(2) [0|0|22]	809
Bite Down Hard (73) 75(1) [0|0|17]	426
Jumpin' The Gunne (73) 169(1) [0|0|7]	74.3
So...Where's The Show? (74) 198(1) [0|0|1]	6.2
France JOLI ▶ 1424 Pk:26 [0|1|2]	**934**
France Joli (79) 26(1) [0|6|17]	905
Tonight (80) 175(1) [0|0|3]	28.5
JON And VANGELIS ▶ 1355 Pk:64 [0|0|3]	**1035**
The Friends Of Mr. Cairo (81) 64(1) [0|0|34]	771
Short Stories (80) 125(1) [0|0|15]	191
Private Collection (83) 148(1) [0|0|7]	73.1
David JONES ▶ 3210 Pk:185 [0|0|1]	**39**
David Jones (67)-Davy Jones 185(1) [0|0|6]	38.6
George JONES ▶ 1612 Pk:115 [0|0|7]	**665**
I Am What I Am (81) 132(1) [0|0|14]	228
Still The Same Ole Me (81) 115(2) [0|0|14]	227

Act ▶ Highest Peak [Top10s | Top40s | Total] Title (Yr) Peak(Wk) [T10 Wk | T40Wk | TotalWk]	Score
A Taste Of Yesterday's Wine (82)-Merle Haggard/George Jones [A] 123(4) [0|0|12]	80.8
I'll Share My World With You (69) 185(1) [0|0|5]	43.7
We Go Together (71)-Tammy Wynette & George Jones [A] 169(1) [0|0|6]	36.3
George Jones & Gene Pitney (65)-George Jones & Gene Pitney [A] 141(1) [0|0|4]	24.8
The Race Is On (65) 149(1) [0|0|2]	23.8
Glenn JONES ▶ 2138 Pk:94 [0|0|1]	**284**
Glenn Jones (87) 94(1) [0|0|17]	284
Grace JONES ▶ 791 Pk:32 [0|1|9]	**2986**
Nightclubbing (81) 32(2) [0|4|20]	977
Slave To The Rhythm (85) 73(4) [0|0|20]	447
Living My Life (82) 86(4) [0|0|20]	411
Portfolio (77) 109(2) [0|0|20]	371
Inside Story (86) 81(2) [0|0|16]	270
Fame (78) 97(1) [0|0|8]	189
Warm Leatherette (80) 132(1) [0|0|10]	173
Muse (79) 156(2) [0|0|7]	87.5
Island Life (86) 161(2) [0|0|7]	61.5
Howard JONES ▶ 502 Pk:10 [1|2|5]	**6130**
Dream Into Action (85) 10(1) [1|21|45]	3115
Human's Lib (84) 59(2) [0|0|43]	951
Action Replay (86) 34(1) [0|6|24]	909
One To One (86) 56(4) [0|0|21]	618
Cross That Line (89) 65(1) [0|0|22]	537
Jack JONES ▶ 303 Pk:9 [1|5|17]	**11267**
Wives And Lovers (63) 18(2) [0|24|53]	2827
The Impossible Dream (66) 9(1) [2|15|64]	2802
Dear Heart (65) 11(1) [0|11|25]	1642
Lady (67) 23(2) [0|6|25]	1006
My Kind Of Town (65) 29(1) [0|6|21]	824
Bewitched (64) 43(1) [0|0|19]	522
Where Love Has Gone (64) 62(1) [0|0|23]	452
Call Me Irresponsible (64) 98(1) [0|0|20]	308
Jack Jones Sings (66) 75(2) [0|0|12]	286
There's Love & There's Love & There's Love (65) 86(1) [0|0|13]	265
Our Song (67) 148(1) [0|0|7]	92.9
Without Her (67) 146(1) [0|0|7]	92.7
What The World Needs Now Is Love! (68) 167(2) [0|0|6]	51.2
A Time For Us (69) 183(2) [0|0|4]	35.7
For The "In" Crowd (66) 147(1) [0|0|2]	25.8
Where Is Love? (68) 195(2) [0|0|3]	19.9
If You Ever Leave Me (68) 198(1) [0|0|3]	15.5
Mick JONES ▶ 3399 Pk:184 [0|0|1]	**19**
Mick Jones (89) 184(1) [0|0|3]	19.4
Oran 'Juice' JONES ▶ 1622 Pk:44 [0|0|1]	**651**
Juice (86) 44(1) [0|0|22]	651
Quincy JONES ▶ 137 Pk:6 [3|6|13]	**23227**
The Dude (81) 10(1) [1|26|80]	6231
Body Heat (74) 6(1) [5|22|43]	4311
Back On The Block (89) 9(2) [3|22|40]	3185
Mellow Madness (75) 16(2) [0|11|30]	2019
Sounds...And Stuff Like That!! (78) 15(1) [0|9|20]	1846
Walking In Space (69) 56(1) [0|0|39]	1393
Smackwater Jack (71) 56(2) [0|0|33]	1160
Roots (Soundtrack) (77) 21(1) [0|6|14]	1081
I Heard That!! (76) 43(2) [0|0|15]	699
Gula Matari (70) 63(2) [0|0|16]	534
You've Got It Bad Girl (73) 94(1) [0|0|24]	488
The Best (82) 122(2) [0|0|17]	203
Ndeda (72) 173(2) [0|0|9]	78.2

Act ▶ Highest Peak [Top10s | Top40s | Total] Title (Yr) Peak(Wk) [T10 Wk | T40Wk | TotalWk]	Score
Rickie Lee JONES ▶ 320 Pk:3 [2|4|5]	**10651**
Rickie Lee Jones (79) 3(2) [8|24|36]	5217
Pirates (81) 5(2) [8|15|29]	3376
Flying Cowboys (89) 39(2) [0|2|25]	868
The Magazine (84) 44(2) [0|0|21]	659
Girl At Her Volcano (83) 39(1) [0|2|16]	531
Shirley JONES ▶ 2625 Pk:128 [0|0|1]	**128**
Always In The Mood (86) 128(1) [0|0|10]	128
New Band of Spike JONES ▶ 3011 Pk:113 [0|0|1]	**64**
Washington Square (63) 113(1) [0|0|4]	64.3
Steve JONES ▶ 3283 Pk:169 [0|0|1]	**30**
Fire And Gasoline (89) 169(2) [0|0|4]	29.9
Tom JONES ▶ 62 Pk:3 [4|8|18]	**40204**
Tom Jones Live In Las Vegas (69) 3(5) [18|26|51]	7828
This Is Tom Jones (69) 4(3) [11|26|43]	6974
Help Yourself (69) 5(2) [13|25|54]	6408
Tom Jones Live! (69) 13(4) [0|21|58]	4814
The Tom Jones Fever Zone (68) 14(1) [0|13|82]	4358
Tom (70) 6(2) [2|13|26]	2733
I (Who Have Nothing) (70) 23(1) [0|3|40]	1710
She's A Lady (71) 17(3) [0|9|20]	1686
Green, Green Grass Of Home (67) 65(1) [0|0|45]	920
It's Not Unusual (65) 54(2) [0|0|42]	806
Close Up (72) 64(1) [0|0|20]	675
Tom Jones Live At Caesars Palace (71) 43(1) [0|0|14]	560
Say You'll Stay Until Tomorrow (77) 76(2) [0|0|16]	359
The Body And Soul Of Tom Jones (73) 93(2) [0|0|10]	209
What's New Pussycat? (65) 114(2) [0|0|5]	85.3
Darlin' (81) 179(1) [0|0|3]	29.6
Tom Jones' Greatest Hits (74) 185(1) [0|0|4]	27.9
Tom Jones Greatest Hits(2) (77) 191(2) [0|0|3]	22.1
JONES GIRLS ▶ 1280 Pk:50 [0|0|3]	**1180**
The Jones Girls (79) 50(1) [0|0|16]	616
At Peace With Woman (80) 96(1) [0|0|24]	436
Get As Much Love As You Can (81) 155(1) [0|0|15]	128
JONZUN CREW ▶ 1821 Pk:66 [0|0|1]	**467**
Lost In Space (83) 66(1) [0|0|20]	467
Janis JOPLIN ▶ 203 Pk:1 [3|4|6]	**17145**
Pearl (71) 1(9) [15|23|42]	8905
Joplin In Concert (72) 4(2) [8|16|27]	3439
I Got Dem Ol' Kozmic Blues Again Mama! (69) 5(3) [5|16|28]	3427
Janis Joplin's Greatest Hits (73) 37(1) [0|2|22]	793
Janis (Soundtrack) (75) 54(2) [0|0|9]	372
Farewell Song (82) 104(1) [0|0|11]	208
Jerry JORDAN ▶ 2081 Pk:79 [0|0|1]	**310**
Phone Call From God (75) 79(2) [0|0|12]	310
Lonnie JORDAN ▶ 3051 Pk:158 [0|0|1]	**59**
Different Moods Of Me (78) 158(2) [0|0|5]	59.0
Stanley JORDAN ▶ 1069 Pk:64 [0|0|3]	**1685**
Magic Touch (85) 64(2) [0|0|66]	1345
Standards, Volume 1 (87) 116(2) [0|0|18]	231
Flying Home (88) 131(2) [0|0|9]	108
Margie JOSEPH ▶ 1885 Pk:67 [0|0|2]	**414**
Margie Joseph Makes A New Impression (71) 67(2) [0|0|14]	375
Sweet Surrender (74) 165(1) [0|0|3]	39.0
JOURNEY ▶ 34 Pk:1 [6|8|12]	**49037**
Escape (81) 1(1) [38|58|146]	17166
Frontiers (83) 2(9) [22|42|85]	8070

Act ► Highest Peak [Top10s|Top40s|Total] Title (Yr) Peak(Wk) [T10 Wk|T40Wk|TotalWk]	Score
JOURNEY ► *Continued*	
Raised On Radio (86) 4(2) [7|28|67]	4605
Evolution (79) 20(2) [0|22|96]	4507
Infinity (78) 21(1) [0|13|123]	3957
Departure (80) 8(2) [5|17|57]	3453
Journey's Greatest Hits (88) 10(2) [2|16|92]	3252
Captured (81) 9(4) [4|12|69]	3197
Look Into The Future (76) 100(1) [0|0|15]	349
Next (77) 85(1) [0|0|10]	252
Journey (75) 138(1) [0|0|9]	139
In The Beginning (80) 152(1) [0|0|8]	89.5
JOY DIVISION ► 2806 Pk:146 [0|0|1]	**96**
Substance (88) 146(2) [0|0|8]	95.9
JOY OF COOKING ► 1700 Pk:100 [0|0|3]	**583**
Joy Of Cooking (71) 100(2) [0|0|17]	395
Closer To The Ground (71) 136(1) [0|0|7]	131
Castles (72) 174(2) [0|0|6]	57.0
JUDAS PRIEST ► 323 Pk:17 [0|7|10]	**10585**
Screaming For Vengeance (82) 17(8) [0|22|53]	2965
Turbo (86) 17(2) [0|11|36]	1811
Defenders Of The Faith (84) 18(4) [0|12|37]	1785
Point Of Entry (81) 39(2) [0|2|25]	1229
Ram It Down (88) 31(3) [0|6|19]	876
British Steel (80) 34(2) [0|3|18]	844
Priest...Live (87) 38(2) [0|3|15]	551
Unleashed In The East (Live In Japan) (79) 70(2) [0|0|11]	363
Hell Bent For Leather (79) 128(1) [0|0|7]	131
Stained Class (78) 173(1) [0|0|3]	30.4
The JUDDS ► 640 Pk:51 [0|0|6]	**4334**
Greatest Hits (88) 76(2) [0|0|97]	1503
Rockin' With The Rhythm (85) 66(1) [0|0|57]	1113
Heartland (87) 52(2) [0|0|31]	632
Why Not Me (84) 71(1) [0|0|26]	509
River Of Time (89) 51(2) [0|0|20]	434
The Judds (84) 153(1) [0|0|15]	144
JULUKA ► 3298 Pk:186 [0|0|1]	**28**
Scatterlings (83) 186(1) [0|0|5]	28.4
Rob JUNGKLAS ► 2071 Pk:102 [0|0|1]	**315**
Closer To The Flame (86) 102(1) [0|0|22]	315
JUNIOR ► 1894 Pk:71 [0|0|2]	**411**
"Ji" (82) 71(3) [0|0|16]	371
Inside Lookin' Out (83) 177(1) [0|0|6]	39.3
JUNKYARD ► 2392 Pk:105 [0|0|1]	**188**
Junkyard (89) 105(2) [0|0|11]	188
Patrick JUVET ► 2357 Pk:125 [0|0|1]	**197**
Got A Feeling (78) 125(1) [0|0|14]	197

K

Act ► Highest Peak [Top10s|Top40s|Total] Title (Yr) Peak(Wk) [T10 Wk|T40Wk|TotalWk]	Score
Bert KAEMPFERT And His Orchestra ► 351 Pk:5 [1|4|15]	**9590**
Blue Midnight (65) 5(1) [5|27|55]	3936
Bert Kaempfert's Greatest Hits (66) 30(1) [0|6|40]	1545
The Magic Music Of Far Away Places (65) 27(1) [0|10|23]	1099
Bye Bye Blues (66) 46(1) [0|0|28]	846
Strangers In The Night (66) 39(2) [0|2|21]	739
Three O'Clock In The Morning (65) 42(1) [0|0|22]	670
The Kaempfert Touch (70) 87(1) [0|0|7]	149
Traces Of Love (69) 153(1) [0|0|10]	129
Lights Out, Sweet Dreams (63) 79(1) [0|0|6]	121
Hold Me (67) 122(1) [0|0|7]	109
The World We Knew (67) 136(1) [0|0|7]	108
Orange Colored Sky (71) 140(1) [0|0|6]	71.5
Warm And Wonderful (69) 194(1) [0|0|5]	34.2
My Way Of Life (68) 186(2) [0|0|2]	19.8
Bert Kaempfert Now! (71) 188(1) [0|0|2]	14.8
KAJAGOOGOO ► 1529 Pk:38 [0|1|2]	**755**
White Feathers (83) 38(2) [0|2|20]	734
Extra Play (85)-Kaja 185(1) [0|0|4]	21.3
KALEIDOSCOPE ► 2512 Pk:139 [0|0|1]	**156**
Incredible Kaleidoscope (69) 139(1) [0|0|8]	156
Gunter KALLMANN Chorus ► 2077 Pk:97 [0|0|2]	**311**
Serenade For Elisabeth (65) 97(2) [0|0|10]	186
Wish Me A Rainbow (66) 126(1) [0|0|8]	125
KALYAN ► 3223 Pk:173 [0|0|1]	**37**
Kalyan (77) 173(1) [0|0|4]	37.1
Big Daddy KANE ► 1326 Pk:33 [0|1|2]	**1091**
It's A Big Daddy Thing (89) 33(1) [0|4|30]	796
Long Live The Kane (88) 116(1) [0|0|19]	295
KANE GANG ► 2144 Pk:115 [0|0|1]	**282**
Miracle (87) 115(2) [0|0|20]	282
KANO ► 3356 Pk:189 [0|0|1]	**23**
New York Cake (82) 189(1) [0|0|4]	23.3
KANSAS ► 176 Pk:4 [3|7|13]	**19810**
Point Of Know Return (77) 4(2) [13|33|51]	6810
Leftoverture (76) 5(4) [7|26|42]	4802
Monolith (79) 10(2) [2|9|24]	1948
Audio-Visions (80) 26(1) [0|8|21]	1292
Vinyl Confessions (82) 16(2) [0|6|20]	1015
Two For The Show (78) 32(1) [0|6|19]	1007
Power (86) 35(2) [0|5|27]	949
Drastic Measures (83) 41(2) [0|0|21]	670
Masque (75) 70(1) [0|0|20]	565
Song For America (75) 57(2) [0|0|15]	519
In The Spirit Of Things (88) 114(2) [0|0|6]	100
Kansas (74) 174(2) [0|0|10]	88.9
The Best Of Kansas (84) 154(2) [0|0|5]	45.0
Paul KANTNER ► 1358 Pk:20 [0|1|3]	**1034**
Blows Against The Empire (70)-Paul Kantner/Jefferson Starship [A] 20(3) [0|11|23]	857
Sunfighter (71)-Grace Slick and Paul Kantner [A] 89(1) [0|0|9]	110
Baron Von Tollbooth & The Chrome Nun (73)-Paul Kantner, Grace Slick & David Freiberg [A] 120(1) [0|0|12]	66.5
KaSANDRA ► 2501 Pk:142 [0|0|1]	**159**
John W. Anderson Presents KaSandra (68) 142(2) [0|0|8]	159
KASHIF ► 1067 Pk:51 [0|0|4]	**1692**
Kashif (83) 54(2) [0|0|33]	720
Send Me Your Love (84) 51(2) [0|0|21]	545
Love Changes (87) 118(3) [0|0|19]	285
Condition Of The Heart (85) 144(2) [0|0|14]	142
KATRINA & The WAVES ► 961 Pk:25 [0|1|3]	**2082**
Katrina And The Waves (85) 25(2) [0|9|32]	1525
Waves (86) 49(2) [0|0|16]	445
Break Of Hearts (89) 122(2) [0|0|8]	112
Jorma KAUKONEN & VITAL PARTS ► 3007 Pk:163 [0|0|1]	**66**
Barbeque King (81) 163(2) [0|0|6]	65.5
John KAY ► 2380 Pk:113 [0|0|2]	**191**
Forgotten Songs & Unsung Heroes (72) 113(1) [0|0|11]	182
My Sportin' Life (73) 200(2) [0|0|2]	9.8
KAYAK ► 2164 Pk:117 [0|0|3]	**271**
Starlight Dancer (78) 117(1) [0|0|9]	166
Phantom Of The Night (79) 145(1) [0|0|7]	94.3

Act ► Highest Peak [Top10s|Top40s|Total] Title (Yr) Peak(Wk) [T10 Wk|T40Wk|TotalWk]	Score
Royal Bed Bouncer (76) 199(1) [0|0|2]	11.0
Sammy KAYE & His Orchestra ► 2547 Pk:97 [0|0|1]	**149**
Come Dance To The Hits (64) 97(1) [0|0|9]	149
The KAY-GEES ► 3534 Pk:199 [0|0|1]	**6**
Keep On Bumpin' & Masterplan (75) 199(1) [0|0|1]	5.9
KBC BAND ► 1765 Pk:75 [0|0|1]	**506**
KBC Band (86) 75(2) [0|0|24]	506
KC And The SUNSHINE BAND ► 266 Pk:4 [1|3|7]	**13222**
Part 3 (76) 13(1) [0|28|77]	5842
KC And The Sunshine Band (75) 4(2) [7|22|47]	4590
Do You Wanna Go Party (79) 50(1) [0|0|37]	1352
Who Do Ya (Love) (78) 36(4) [0|5|13]	870
KC Ten (84)-KC 93(1) [0|0|18]	267
Greatest Hits (80) 132(2) [0|0|11]	166
The Sound Of Sunshine (75)-The Sunshine Band 131(1) [0|0|8]	135
KEEL ► 1330 Pk:53 [0|0|3]	**1089**
The Final Frontier (86) 53(2) [0|0|18]	485
The Right To Rock (85) 99(1) [0|0|21]	338
Keel (87) 79(1) [0|0|13]	265
Tommy KEENE ► 2451 Pk:148 [0|0|1]	**173**
Songs From The Film (86) 148(2) [0|0|17]	173
KEITH ► 2849 Pk:124 [0|0|1]	**88**
98.6/Ain't Gonna Lie (67) 124(1) [0|0|5]	87.9
Manny KELLEM, His Orchestra And Voices ► 3504 Pk:197 [0|0|1]	**11**
Love Is Blue (68)-Manny Kellem - His Orchestra And Voices 197(1) [0|0|2]	11.0
Johnny KEMP ► 1749 Pk:68 [0|0|1]	**521**
Secrets Of Flying (88) 68(1) [0|0|19]	521
Eddie KENDRICKS ► 535 Pk:18 [0|3|9]	**5569**
Eddie Kendricks (73) 18(1) [0|8|40]	1772
Boogie Down! (74) 30(1) [0|4|17]	933
He's A Friend (76) 38(1) [0|2|19]	824
All By Myself (71) 80(2) [0|0|32]	686
The Hit Man (75) 63(1) [0|0|25]	662
For You (74) 108(1) [0|0|14]	345
People...Hold On (72) 131(2) [0|0|14]	221
Goin' Up In Smoke (76) 144(1) [0|0|7]	99.5
Vintage '78 (78) 180(1) [0|0|3]	25.8
John Fitzgerald KENNEDY ► 647 Pk:5 [2|4|10]	**4268**
That Was The Week That Was (BBC Telecast Tribute on 11/23/1963) (63)-No Artist 5(1) [2|6|15]	1192
The Presidential Years 1960-1963 (narrated by David Teig) (63) 8(2) [4|8|14]	1189
A Memorial Album (64) 18(2) [0|4|9]	518
Four Days That Shocked The World (narrated by Reid Collins) (64)-No Artist 29(2) [0|4|10]	424
The Kennedy Wit (narrated by David Brinkley) (64) 49(1) [0|0|11]	316
JFK The Man, The President (narrated by Barry Gray) (64) 42(1) [0|0|8]	284
John Fitzgerald Kennedy...As We Remember Him (narrated by Chartles Kuralt) (65) 93(1) [0|0|8]	165
John F. Kennedy - A Memorial Album (64) 101(1) [0|0|4]	72.5
The Presidential Years (1960-1963) (64) 119(2) [0|0|4]	62.9
Actual Speeches Of Franklin D. Roosevelt And John F. Kennedy (64)-Franklin D. Roosevelt And John F. Kennedy [A] 109(1) [0|0|5]	42.8
Joyce KENNEDY ► 2238 Pk:79 [0|0|1]	**240**
Lookin' For Trouble (84) 79(2) [0|0|13]	240

Act ▶ Highest Peak [Top10s|Top40s|Total] Title (Yr) Peak(Wk) [T10 Wk|T40Wk|TotalWk]	Score
Robert Francis KENNEDY ▶ 3262 Pk:187 [0|0|1]	**32**
A Memorial (69) 187(2) [0|0|4]	32.1
KENNY G ▶ 239 Pk:6 [2|3|5]	**14770**
Duotones (86) 6(2) [10|41|102]	6209
Silhouette (88) 8(1) [9|27|57]	4280
Live (89) 16(1) [0|21|122]	3642
G Force (84) 62(1) [0|0|21]	451
Gravity (85) 97(2) [0|0|12]	188
Stan KENTON ▶ 2359 Pk:146 [0|0|1]	**196**
Stan Kenton Today (72) 146(1) [0|0|14]	196
KENTUCKY HEADHUNTERS ▶ 864 Pk:41 [0|0|1]	**2571**
Pickin' On Nashville (89) 41(1) [0|0|96]	2571
Anita KERR Singers ▶ 2668 Pk:162 [0|0|2]	**120**
The Anita Kerr Singers Reflect On The Hits Of Burt Bacharach & Hal David (69) 162(1) [0|0|6]	83.3
Velvet Voices And Bold Brass (69) 172(1) [0|0|3]	36.8
Nik KERSHAW ▶ 1737 Pk:70 [0|0|2]	**539**
Human Racing (84) 70(2) [0|0|20]	406
The Riddle (85) 113(2) [0|0|10]	133
KGB ▶ 2763 Pk:124 [0|0|1]	**102**
KGB (76) 124(1) [0|0|6]	102
Chaka KHAN ▶ 439 Pk:12 [0|3|7]	**7266**
I Feel For You (84) 14(3) [0|16|49]	2332
Chaka (78) 12(3) [0|8|21]	1800
What Cha' Gonna Do For Me (81) 17(2) [0|9|18]	1482
Naughty (80) 43(4) [0|0|16]	709
Chaka Khan (82) 52(1) [0|0|18]	477
Destiny (86) 67(2) [0|0|12]	308
C.K. (88) 125(3) [0|0|12]	159
Steve KHAN ▶ 2970 Pk:157 [0|0|1]	**70**
Tightrope (78) 157(1) [0|0|5]	69.7
KICK AXE ▶ 2341 Pk:126 [0|0|1]	**202**
Vices (84) 126(2) [0|0|15]	202
KID CREOLE & The COCONUTS ▶ 2602 Pk:145 [0|0|2]	**134**
Wise Guy (82) 145(2) [0|0|12]	115
Fresh Fruit In Foreign Places (81) 180(1) [0|0|2]	18.7
KID 'N PLAY ▶ 1468 Pk:96 [0|0|1]	**865**
2 Hype (88) 96(1) [0|0|47]	865
KIDS FROM FAME ▶ 2102 Pk:98 [0|0|3]	**301**
The Kids From "Fame" Live! (83) 98(1) [0|0|11]	172
The Kids From "Fame" (82) 146(2) [0|0|8]	101
Songs (83) 181(4) [0|0|4]	28.2
Greg KIHN Band ▶ 614 Pk:15 [0|3|8]	**4606**
Rockihnroll (81) 32(1) [0|5|32]	1636
Kihnspiracy (83) 15(2) [0|12|24]	1424
Kihntinued (82)-Greg Kihn 33(3) [0|4|17]	612
Citizen Kihn (85)-Greg Kihn 51(2) [0|0|13]	421
With The Naked Eye (79) 114(1) [0|0|10]	197
Next Of Kihn (78) 145(1) [0|0|12]	148
Kihntagious (84) 121(1) [0|0|9]	113
Glass House Rock (80) 167(1) [0|0|5]	55.2
KILLER DWARFS ▶ 3104 Pk:165 [0|0|1]	**52**
Big Deal (88) 165(1) [0|0|6]	51.6
KILLING JOKE ▶ 3538 Pk:194 [0|0|1]	**5**
Brighter Than A Thousand Suns (87) 194(1) [0|0|1]	5.1
John KILZER ▶ 2307 Pk:110 [0|0|1]	**213**
Memory In The Making (88) 110(2) [0|0|15]	213

Act ▶ Highest Peak [Top10s|Top40s|Total] Title (Yr) Peak(Wk) [T10 Wk|T40Wk|TotalWk]	Score
Andy KIM ▶ 1097 Pk:21 [0|1|3]	**1613**
Andy Kim (74) 21(1) [0|6|17]	1147
Baby I Love You (69) 82(2) [0|0|14]	424
Andy Kim's Greatest Hits (74) 190(2) [0|0|6]	42.5
The KIMBERLYS ▶ 3330 Pk:169 [0|0|1]	**26**
Country-Folk (69)-Waylon Jennings & The Kimberlys [A] 169(1) [0|0|4]	25.6
Warren KIME ▶ 2130 Pk:89 [0|0|2]	**287**
Brass Impact (67)-Brass Choir Conducted By Warren Kime 89(1) [0|0|12]	241
Explosive Brass Impact (67)-Warren Kime & His Brass Impact Orchestra 177(2) [0|0|7]	45.8
Tom KIMMEL ▶ 2368 Pk:104 [0|0|1]	**194**
5 To 1 (87) 104(2) [0|0|15]	194
KING ▶ 2838 Pk:140 [0|0|1]	**90**
Steps In Time (85) 140(2) [0|0|9]	89.5
Albert KING ▶ 1720 Pk:133 [0|0|8]	**563**
Live Wire/Blues Power (68) 150(1) [0|0|10]	160
I'll Play The Blues For You (72) 140(2) [0|0|8]	121
Years Gone By (69) 133(1) [0|0|4]	86.3
Truckload Of Lovin' (76) 166(1) [0|0|6]	67.6
Lovejoy (71) 188(1) [0|0|6]	45.2
King Of The Blues Guitar (69) 194(1) [0|0|5]	35.0
Albert Live (77) 182(1) [0|0|3]	26.8
Jammed Together (69)-Albert King, Steve Cropper, Pop Staples [A] 171(2) [0|0|5]	20.7
B.B. KING ▶ 338 Pk:25 [0|3|21]	**10066**
Live In Cook County Jail (71) 25(3) [0|7|33]	1908
Completely Well (69) 38(2) [0|3|30]	1531
Indianola Mississippi Seeds (70) 26(1) [0|6|28]	1489
Live & Well (69) 56(2) [0|0|34]	1199
B.B. King In London (71) 57(1) [0|0|17]	629
To Know You Is To Love You (73) 71(2) [0|0|25]	576
Guess Who (72) 65(1) [0|0|20]	560
L.A. Midnight (72) 53(2) [0|0|17]	516
Midnight Believer (78) 124(1) [0|0|24]	357
Live At The Regal (71) 78(1) [0|0|8]	257
Take It Home (79) 112(1) [0|0|12]	244
The Best Of B.B. King (73) 101(1) [0|0|11]	202
There Must Be A Better World Somewhere (81) 131(1) [0|0|10]	180
King Size (77) 154(1) [0|0|7]	101
Lucille Talks Back (75) 140(1) [0|0|5]	91.4
Friends (74) 153(1) [0|0|6]	82.5
"Now Appearing" At Ole' Miss (80) 162(2) [0|0|4]	45.3
Love Me Tender (82) 179(1) [0|0|5]	31.1
Blues 'N Jazz (83) 172(1) [0|0|4]	29.9
Lucille (68) 192(2) [0|0|3]	22.1
The Incredible Soul Of B.B. King (70) 193(1) [0|0|2]	13.4
B.B. KING & Bobby BLAND ▶ 1272 Pk:43 [0|0|2]	**1193**
Together For The First Time...Live (74) 43(1) [0|0|20]	749
Together Again...Live (76) 73(1) [0|0|14]	444
Ben E. KING ▶ 1341 Pk:33 [0|2|2]	**1063**
Supernatural (75) 39(1) [0|1|14]	607
Benny And Us (77)-Average White Band & Ben E. King [A] 33(2) [0|5|21]	456
Carole KING ▶ 28 Pk:1 [6|8|15]	**53533**
Tapestry (71) 1(15) [46|68|302]	25830
Music (71) 1(3) [16|20|44]	7352
Rhymes & Reasons (72) 2(5) [16|20|31]	5586
Wrap Around Joy (74) 1(1) [5|13|29]	3499
Thoroughbred (76) 3(3) [8|14|21]	3360
Fantasy (73) 6(3) [5|15|37]	3155

Act ▶ Highest Peak [Top10s|Top40s|Total] Title (Yr) Peak(Wk) [T10 Wk|T40Wk|TotalWk]	Score
Simple Things (77) 17(1) [0|7|14]	1033
Really Rosie (Soundtrack) (75) 20(2) [0|4|15]	987
Writer: Carole King (71) 84(1) [0|0|27]	681
Pearls-Songs Of Goffin And King (80) 44(1) [0|0|17]	674
Her Greatest Hits (78) 47(2) [0|0|13]	628
City Streets (89) 111(1) [0|0|16]	228
Touch The Sky (79) 104(2) [0|0|9]	189
Welcome Home (78) 104(1) [0|0|8]	179
One To One (82) 119(3) [0|0|11]	153
Evelyn "Champagne" KING ▶ 514 Pk:14 [0|4|7]	**6007**
Smooth Talk (78) 14(2) [0|13|45]	2726
Get Loose (82)-Evelyn King 27(3) [0|7|32]	1044
I'm In Love (81)-Evelyn King 28(1) [0|6|18]	995
Music Box (79) 35(2) [0|3|17]	826
Face To Face (83) 91(1) [0|0|20]	280
Call On Me (80) 124(3) [0|0|7]	119
Flirt (88) 192(1) [0|0|3]	17.1
Freddie KING ▶ 2834 Pk:158 [0|0|1]	**90**
Woman Across The River (73) 158(1) [0|0|8]	89.8
Morgana KING ▶ 2176 Pk:118 [0|0|2]	**267**
With A Taste Of Honey (64) 118(2) [0|0|15]	231
New Beginnings... (73) 184(1) [0|0|5]	36.0
Rev. Martin Luther KING Jr. ▶ 1627 Pk:69 [0|0|7]	**647**
I Have A Dream (68 69(1) [0|0|8]	261
The Great March To Freedom (63)-Rev. Martin Luther King, Jr. 141(1) [0|0|9]	92.6
The March On Washington (63) 102(1) [0|0|5]	87.1
Freedom March On Washington (63) 119(1) [0|0|5]	77.3
In Search Of Freedom (68)-Rev. Dr. Martin Luther King, Jr. 150(1) [0|0|3]	47.9
In The Struggle For Freedom And Human Dignity (68) 154(1) [0|0|3]	44.7
The American Dream (68)-. 173(1) [0|0|4]	36.2
The KINGBEES ▶ 2627 Pk:160 [0|0|1]	**127**
The Kingbees (80) 160(2) [0|0|12]	127
KING BISCUIT BOY ▶ 3461 Pk:194 [0|0|1]	**13**
Official Music (70)-King Biscuit Boy with Crowbar 194(1) [0|0|2]	13.3
KING CRIMSON ▶ 562 Pk:28 [0|2|11]	**5190**
In The Court Of The Crimson King - An Observation By King Crimson (69) 28(2) [0|6|25]	1277
In The Wake Of Poseidon (70) 31(2) [0|5|13]	854
Discipline (81) 45(2) [0|0|17]	534
Larks' Tongues In Aspic (73) 61(1) [0|0|14]	416
Three Of A Perfect Pair (84) 58(2) [0|0|17]	416
Red (74) 66(2) [0|0|11]	373
Starless And Bible Black (74) 64(1) [0|0|11]	360
Beat (82) 52(2) [0|0|14]	355
Islands (72) 76(1) [0|0|12]	309
Lizard (71) 113(2) [0|0|10]	196
USA (75) 125(1) [0|0|5]	102
KING CURTIS ▶ 1389 Pk:54 [0|0|9]	**982**
Live At Fillmore West (71) 54(2) [0|0|15]	502
Soul Serenade (64) 103(1) [0|0|12]	187
King Size Soul (67) 168(4) [0|0|9]	90.7
The Great Memphis Hits (67) 185(2) [0|0|12]	78.4
Instant Groove (69) 160(2) [0|0|3]	47.8
The Best of King Curtis (68) 190(1) [0|0|4]	33.4
Everybody's Talkin' (72) 189(1) [0|0|3]	20.0
Sweet Soul (68) 198(2) [0|0|2]	11.6
Get Ready (70) 198(2) [0|0|2]	11.5
KING DIAMOND ▶ 1755 Pk:89 [0|0|3]	**516**
Them (88) 89(2) [0|0|12]	237

Act ► Highest Peak [Top10s | Top40s | Total] Title (Yr) Peak(Wk) [T10 Wk | T40Wk | TotalWk]	Score
KING DIAMOND ► *Continued*	
Abigail (87) 123(1) [0 | 0 | 13]	155
Conspiracy (89) 111(2) [0 | 0 | 8]	124
KINGDOM COME ► 865 Pk:12 [0 | 1 | 2]	**2570**
Kingdom Come (88) 12(1) [0 | 12 | 29]	2156
In Your Face (89) 49(2) [0 | 0 | 15]	413
KING FAMILY ► 1565 Pk:34 [0 | 1 | 2]	**719**
The King Family Show! (65) 34(1) [0 | 4 | 16]	680
The King Family Album (65) 142(1) [0 | 0 | 3]	38.7
KINGFISH ► 1698 Pk:50 [0 | 0 | 2]	**583**
Kingfish (76) 50(1) [0 | 0 | 9]	380
Live 'N' Kickin' (77) 103(1) [0 | 0 | 10]	203
KING HARVEST ► 2626 Pk:136 [0 | 0 | 1]	**128**
Dancing In The Moonlight (73) 136(1) [0 | 0 | 10]	128
KING RICHARD'S FLUEGEL KNIGHTS ► 3519 Pk:198 [0 | 0 | 1]	**10**
Something Super! (68) 198(2) [0 | 0 | 2]	9.9
The KINGS ► 1611 Pk:74 [0 | 0 | 2]	**665**
The Kings Are Here (80) 74(2) [0 | 0 | 26]	626
Amazon Beach (81) 170(1) [0 | 0 | 4]	38.8
The KINGSMEN ► 406 Pk:15 [0 | 3 | 5]	**8080**
The Kingsmen In Person (64) 20(1) [0 | 28 | 131]	5152
The Kingsmen, Volume II (64) 15(1) [0 | 9 | 37]	1490
The Kingsmen, Volume 3 (65) 22(2) [0 | 7 | 18]	887
The Kingsmen On Campus (65) 68(2) [0 | 0 | 17]	380
15 Great Hits (66) 87(1) [0 | 0 | 8]	171
KINGS OF THE SUN ► 2457 Pk:136 [0 | 0 | 1]	**172**
Kings Of The Sun (88) 136(1) [0 | 0 | 16]	172
KINGSTON TRIO ► 596 Pk:7 [1 | 3 | 7]	**4774**
Sunny Side! (63) 7(2) [4 | 13 | 25]	2104
Time To Think (64) 18(2) [0 | 7 | 21]	1022
Back In Town (64) 22(2) [0 | 5 | 20]	761
The Kingston Trio (Nick-Bob-John) (65) 53(1) [0 | 0 | 13]	367
Sing A Song with The Kingston Trio (64) 69(1) [0 | 0 | 14]	297
Stay Awhile (65) 126(1) [0 | 0 | 10]	135
Once Upon A Time (69) 163(1) [0 | 0 | 6]	88.5
KING SWAMP ► 2807 Pk:159 [0 | 0 | 1]	**96**
King Swamp (89) 159(1) [0 | 0 | 14]	95.8
KING'S X ► 1922 Pk:123 [0 | 0 | 2]	**392**
Gretchen Goes To Nebraska (89) 123(1) [0 | 0 | 18]	257
Out Of The Silent Planet (88) 144(1) [0 | 0 | 11]	134
KING TEE ► 2347 Pk:125 [0 | 0 | 1]	**200**
Act A Fool (89) 125(1) [0 | 0 | 15]	200
Sam KINISON ► 1643 Pk:43 [0 | 0 | 2]	**625**
Have You Seen Me Lately? (88) 43(3) [0 | 0 | 17]	594
Louder Than Hell (86) 175(1) [0 | 0 | 5]	31.2
The KINKS ► 147 Pk:9 [1 | 10 | 32]	**22538**
The Kinks Greatest Hits! (66) 9(1) [3 | 15 | 64]	2978
One For The Road (80) 14(4) [0 | 14 | 33]	2816
Give The People What They Want (81) 15(2) [0 | 9 | 36]	2399
Low Budget (79) 11(2) [0 | 10 | 18]	1846
State Of Confusion (83) 12(1) [0 | 12 | 25]	1739
Kinks-Size (65) 13(1) [0 | 11 | 29]	1542
Sleepwalker (77) 21(2) [0 | 8 | 16]	1242
Misfits (78) 40(1) [0 | 1 | 21]	1041
You Really Got Me (64) 29(1) [0 | 5 | 26]	877
Lola Versus Powerman And The Moneygoround, Part One (70) 35(1) [0 | 3 | 12]	766
Schoolboys In Disgrace (75) 45(3) [0 | 0 | 14]	600
Word Of Mouth (84) 57(3) [0 | 0 | 20]	577
Soap Opera (75) 51(1) [0 | 0 | 13]	561
Arthur (Or The Decline And Fall Of The British Empire) (69) 105(2) [0 | 0 | 20]	478
Kinks Kinkdom (65) 47(1) [0 | 0 | 17]	472
Everybody's In Show-Biz (72) 70(2) [0 | 0 | 14]	402
Think Visual (86) 81(2) [0 | 0 | 16]	332
The Kink Kronikles (72) 94(2) [0 | 0 | 13]	316
Kinda Kinks (65) 60(2) [0 | 0 | 9]	272
Muswell Hillbillies (71) 100(2) [0 | 0 | 14]	253
The Kink Kontroversy (66) 95(2) [0 | 0 | 12]	223
Preservation Act 2 (74) 114(1) [0 | 0 | 11]	181
The Road (88) 110(2) [0 | 0 | 7]	123
UK Jive (89) 122(2) [0 | 0 | 8]	99.0
Kinks' Greatest-Celluloid Heroes (76) 144(2) [0 | 0 | 5]	92.1
The Great Lost Kinks Album (73) 145(1) [0 | 0 | 5]	63.9
Face To Face (67) 135(1) [0 | 0 | 3]	50.5
Preservation Act 1 (73) 177(1) [0 | 0 | 6]	48.2
The Live Kinks (67) 162(1) [0 | 0 | 4]	44.4
Come Dancing With The Kinks/The Best Of The Kinks 1977-1986 (86) 159(1) [0 | 0 | 4]	38.8
Second Time Around (80) 177(1) [0 | 0 | 4]	35.2
Something Else By The Kinks (68) 153(2) [0 | 0 | 2]	27.5
KISS ► 71 Pk:4 [4 | 16 | 20]	**37030**
Alive! (75) 9(4) [5 | 17 | 110]	5270
Rock And Roll Over (76) 11(2) [0 | 26 | 45]	4256
Destroyer (76) 11(1) [0 | 14 | 78]	3772
Alive II (77) 7(2) [4 | 14 | 33]	3023
Love Gun (77) 4(2) [7 | 11 | 26]	2788
Dynasty (79) 9(3) [4 | 11 | 25]	2407
Animalize (84) 19(1) [0 | 17 | 38]	2076
Crazy Nights (87) 18(1) [0 | 17 | 34]	2060
Asylum (85) 20(1) [0 | 16 | 29]	1639
Smashes, Thrashes & Hits (88) 21(2) [0 | 11 | 27]	1558
Lick It Up (83) 24(2) [0 | 7 | 30]	1444
Hot In The Shade (89) 29(1) [0 | 5 | 36]	1344
Double Platinum (78) 22(2) [0 | 5 | 24]	1125
Dressed To Kill (75) 32(2) [0 | 3 | 29]	989
Creatures Of The Night (82) 45(6) [0 | 0 | 19]	752
Kiss Unmasked (80) 35(2) [0 | 4 | 14]	717
The Originals (76) 36(2) [0 | 3 | 17]	692
KISS (74) 87(1) [0 | 0 | 23]	466
Hotter Than Hell (74) 100(1) [0 | 0 | 15]	361
Music From The Elder (81) 75(1) [0 | 0 | 11]	290
KITARO ► 2640 Pk:141 [0 | 0 | 3]	**125**
My Best (86) 141(2) [0 | 0 | 10]	108
Asia (85) 191(1) [0 | 0 | 2]	10.1
Tenku (87) 183(1) [0 | 0 | 1]	7.0
KIX ► 1035 Pk:46 [0 | 0 | 2]	**1812**
Blow My Fuse (88) 46(1) [0 | 0 | 60]	1757
Cool Kids (83) 177(1) [0 | 0 | 8]	55.0
KLAATU ► 1510 Pk:32 [0 | 1 | 2]	**787**
Klaatu (77) 32(1) [0 | 3 | 11]	615
Hope (77) 83(1) [0 | 0 | 7]	173
KLEEER ► 1610 Pk:81 [0 | 0 | 3]	**666**
License To Dream (81) 81(2) [0 | 0 | 16]	447
Winners (80) 140(2) [0 | 0 | 10]	123
Taste The Music (82) 139(1) [0 | 0 | 8]	96.1
Robert KLEIN ► 3416 Pk:191 [0 | 0 | 1]	**18**
A Child Of The 50's (73) 191(1) [0 | 0 | 3]	17.7
John KLEMMER ► 877 Pk:51 [0 | 0 | 10]	**2503**
Touch (75) 90(1) [0 | 0 | 40]	583
Barefoot Ballet (76) 66(1) [0 | 0 | 16]	564
Lifestyle (Living & Loving) (77) 51(1) [0 | 0 | 17]	514
Arabesque (78) 83(1) [0 | 0 | 10]	295
Hush (81) 99(1) [0 | 0 | 9]	209
Magnificent Madness (80) 146(1) [0 | 0 | 11]	160
Brazilia (79) 172(1) [0 | 0 | 9]	81.6
Blowin' Gold (69) 176(1) [0 | 0 | 5]	53.0
Cry (78) 178(1) [0 | 0 | 3]	27.2
The Best Of John Klemmer-Volume One/Mosaic (79) 187(2) [0 | 0 | 2]	15.5
KLIQUE ► 2135 Pk:70 [0 | 0 | 1]	**285**
Try It Out (83) 70(2) [0 | 0 | 14]	285
The KLOWNS ► 3403 Pk:184 [0 | 0 | 1]	**19**
The Klowns (70) 184(2) [0 | 0 | 2]	19.0
Earl KLUGH ► 554 Pk:38 [0 | 1 | 16]	**5335**
Heart String (79) 49(1) [0 | 0 | 21]	811
Low Ride (83) 38(3) [0 | 3 | 24]	733
Crazy For You (81) 53(2) [0 | 0 | 27]	683
Dream Come True (80) 42(1) [0 | 0 | 19]	607
Wishful Thinking (84) 69(2) [0 | 0 | 23]	512
Late Night Guitar (80) 98(3) [0 | 0 | 23]	463
Collaboration (87)-George Benson/Earl Klugh [A] 59(2) [0 | 0 | 31]	389
Soda Fountain Shuffle (85) 110(1) [0 | 0 | 17]	255
Finger Paintings (77) 84(1) [0 | 0 | 8]	218
Nightsongs (84) 107(2) [0 | 0 | 17]	195
Magic In Your Eyes (78) 139(2) [0 | 0 | 9]	151
Life Stories (86) 143(2) [0 | 0 | 11]	112
Earl Klugh (76) 124(1) [0 | 0 | 6]	107
Whispers And Promises (89) 150(2) [0 | 0 | 5]	50.4
How To Beat The High Cost Of Living (Soundtrack) (80)-Hubert Laws And Earl Klugh [A] 134(2) [0 | 0 | 4]	31.9
Living Inside Your Love (76) 188(1) [0 | 0 | 2]	15.1
KLYMAXX ► 757 Pk:18 [0 | 1 | 2]	**3213**
Meeting In The Ladies Room (85) 18(3) [0 | 15 | 67]	2800
Klymaxx (86) 98(2) [0 | 0 | 31]	413
The KNACK ► 367 Pk:1 [1 | 2 | 3]	**9019**
Get The Knack (79) 1(5) [15 | 22 | 40]	7540
But The Little Girls Understand (80) | 15(1) [0 | 9 | 14]	1344
Round Trip (81) 93(2) [0 | 0 | 6]	136
The KNICKERBOCKERS ► 2948 Pk:134 [0 | 0 | 1]	**72**
Lies (66) 134(2) [0 | 0 | 5]	72.2
Curtis KNIGHT ► 2530 Pk:75 [0 | 0 | 1]	**152**
Get That Feeling (67)-Jimi Hendrix and Curtis Knight [A] 75(2) [0 | 0 | 12]	152
Gladys KNIGHT & The PIPS ► 145 Pk:9 [2 | 9 | 25]	**22628**
Imagination (73) 9(1) [2 | 33 | 61]	4850
I Feel A Song (74) 17(3) [0 | 13 | 41]	2750
Neither One Of Us (73) 9(1) [4 | 10 | 30]	2326
Claudine (Soundtrack) (74) 35(2) [0 | 3 | 34]	1395
Visions (83) 34(2) [0 | 6 | 33]	1303
If I Were Your Woman (71) 35(1) [0 | 2 | 26]	1297
All Our Love (87) 39(1) [0 | 3 | 27]	1027
2nd Anniversary (75) 24(2) [0 | 4 | 16]	933
Standing Ovation (72) 60(1) [0 | 0 | 24]	779
Best Of Gladys Knight & The Pips (76) 36(3) [0 | 4 | 15]	774
About Love (80) 48(1) [0 | 0 | 18]	711
Everybody Needs Love (67) 60(2) [0 | 0 | 24]	595
Anthology (74) 77(1) [0 | 0 | 23]	573
Still Together (77) 51(2) [0 | 0 | 21]	570
All I Need Is Time (73) 70(1) [0 | 0 | 21]	557
Gladys Knight & The Pips Greatest Hits (70) 55(1) [0 | 0 | 16]	505
Silk N' Soul (69) 136(1) [0 | 0 | 16]	329

Act ► Highest Peak [Top10s|Top40s|Total]
Title (Yr) Peak(Wk) [T10 Wk|T40Wk|TotalWk] — Score

Gladys KNIGHT & The PIPS *Continued*
Pipe Dreams (76) 94(2) [0|0|12] — 301
Nitty Gritty (69) 81(1) [0|0|10] — 285
Life (85) 126(2) [0|0|12] — 162
Knight Time (74) 139(1) [0|0|11] — 161
Touch (81) 109(1) [0|0|8] — 161
Feelin' Bluesy (68) 158(1) [0|0|13] — 143
The One And Only... (78) 145(1) [0|0|6] — 91.6
A Little Knight Music (75) 164(2) [0|0|4] — 49.1

Jean KNIGHT ► 1917 Pk:60 [0|0|2] — 395
Mr. Big Stuff (71) 60(1) [0|0|11] — 369
My Toot Toot (85) 180(1) [0|0|4] — 26.6

Jerry KNIGHT ► 2569 Pk:146 [0|0|2] — 144
Perfect Fit (81) 146(1) [0|0|6] — 77.8
Jerry Knight (80) 165(1) [0|0|7] — 65.7

Robert KNIGHT ► 3508 Pk:196 [0|0|1] — 11
Everlasting Love (67) 196(2) [0|0|2] — 10.8

Terry KNIGHT And The PACK ► 2250 Pk:127 [0|0|2] — 234
Terry Knight And The Pack (66) 127(1) [0|0|13] — 216
Mark, Don & Terry 1966-67 (72) 192(2) [0|0|3] — 18.8

K-9 POSSE ► 2216 Pk:98 [0|0|1] — 247
K-9 Posse (89) 98(3) [0|0|14] — 247

Fred KNOBLOCK ► 3176 Pk:179 [0|0|1] — 44
Why Not Me (80) 179(1) [0|0|5] — 43.5

Mark KNOPFLER ► 3528 Pk:180 [0|0|1] — 8
The Princess Bride (Soundtrack) (87) 180(1) [0|0|1] — 7.5

KOKOMO ► 2762 Pk:159 [0|0|2] — 102
Kokomo (75) 159(1) [0|0|9] — 89.5
Rise And Shine! (76) 194(1) [0|0|2] — 13.0

KONGAS ► 2543 Pk:120 [0|0|1] — 149
Africanism (78) 120(2) [0|0|8] — 149

KOOL & The GANG ► 102 Pk:10 [1|8|20] — 29155
Emergency (84) 13(1) [0|51|74] — 5376
Something Special (81) 12(2) [0|30|67] — 4669
Celebrate! (80) 10(2) [2|24|44] — 4159
Ladies' Night (79) 13(4) [0|28|45] — 4088
Wild And Peaceful (73) 33(1) [0|4|60] — 2282
In The Heart (83) 29(2) [0|11|37] — 1676
Forever (86) 25(1) [0|9|42] — 1651
As One (82) 29(4) [0|12|24] — 1353
Light Of Worlds (74) 63(3) [0|0|34] — 1049
Kool & The Gang Greatest Hits! (75) 81(1) [0|0|23] — 611
Love & Understanding (76) 68(2) [0|0|20] — 526
Spirit Of The Boogie (75) 48(2) [0|0|14] — 475
Live At The Sex Machine (71) 122(1) [0|0|19] — 359
Open Sesame (76) 110(1) [0|0|18] — 329
Everything's Kool & The Gang: Greatest Hits & More (88) 109(2) [0|0|11] — 148
The Best Of Kool And The Gang (71) 157(1) [0|0|8] — 117
Good Times (73) 142(1) [0|0|7] — 100
The Force (78) 142(1) [0|0|7] — 94.8
Live At P.J.'s (72) 171(1) [0|0|7] — 63.1
Kool Jazz (74) 187(2) [0|0|4] — 29.9

KOOL MOE DEE ► 773 Pk:25 [0|2|3] — 3121
How Ya Like Me Now (87) 35(1) [0|4|50] — 1604
Knowledge Is King (89) 25(2) [0|8|23] — 1142
Kool Moe Dee (87) 83(2) [0|0|21] — 375

Al KOOPER ► 842 Pk:12 [0|2|9] — 2719
The Live Adventures Of Mike Bloomfield And Al Kooper (69)-Mike Bloomfield/Al Kooper [A] 18(2) [0|10|20] — 959
Super Session (68)-Mike Bloomfield/Al Kooper/Steve Stills [A] 12(1) [0|10|37] — 799
I Stand Alone (69) 54(1) [0|0|13] — 610
Easy Does It (70) 105(1) [0|0|6] — 158
You Never Know Who Your Friends Are (69) 125(1) [0|0|6] — 108
Act Like Nothing's Wrong (77) 182(2) [0|0|5] — 38.6
Kooper Session (70)-Al Kooper/Shuggie Otis [A] 182(1) [0|0|5] — 19.1
New York City (You're A Woman) (71) 198(2) [0|0|3] — 18.2
A Possible Projection Of The Future/Childhood's End (72) 200(2) [0|0|2] — 9.8

The KORGIS ► 2355 Pk:113 [0|0|1] — 197
Dumb Waiters (80) 113(2) [0|0|12] — 197

Paul KOSSOFF ► 3445 Pk:191 [0|0|1] — 16
Back Street Crawler (75) 191(2) [0|0|2] — 15.5

Andre KOSTELANETZ And His Orchestra ► 2412 Pk:68 [0|0|4] — 183
New York Wonderland (64) 68(1) [0|0|7] — 141
Love Story (71) 183(1) [0|0|2] — 16.2
Sounds Of Love (69) 194(1) [0|0|2] — 13.8
Traces (69) 200(2) [0|0|2] — 12.5

Leo KOTTKE ► 1016 Pk:45 [0|0|9] — 1883
Dreams And All That Stuff (74) 45(2) [0|0|12] — 477
Ice Water (74) 69(1) [0|0|18] — 456
My Feet Are Smiling (73) 108(1) [0|0|11] — 179
Burnt Lips (78) 143(2) [0|0|12] — 175
Leo Kottke (77) 107(1) [0|0|9] — 174
Greenhouse (72) 127(2) [0|0|9] — 154
Chewing Pine (75) 114(2) [0|0|7] — 140
Mudlark (71) 168(2) [0|0|7] — 67.0
Leo Kottke 1971-76 Did You Hear Me? (76) 153(2) [0|0|4] — 60.7

KRAFTWERK ► 631 Pk:5 [1|1|7] — 4428
Autobahn (75) 5(1) [5|11|22] — 2679
Computer-World (81) 72(1) [0|0|42] — 1144
Trans-Europe Express (77) 119(1) [0|0|10] — 167
The Man-Machine (78) 130(1) [0|0|9] — 143
Electric Cafe (86) 156(2) [0|0|14] — 115
Radio-Activity (75) 140(1) [0|0|8] — 111
Ralf And Florian (75) 160(1) [0|0|5] — 68.4

Billy J. KRAMER with The DAKOTAS ► 1834 Pk:48 [0|0|1] — 455
Little Children (64) 48(1) [0|0|15] — 455

Lenny KRAVITZ ► 1567 Pk:61 [0|0|1] — 715
Let Love Rule (89) 61(1) [0|0|28] — 715

Kris KRISTOFFERSON ► 293 Pk:1 [1|3|11] — 11961
The Silver Tongued Devil And I (71) 21(2) [0|14|28] — 2314
Jesus Was A Capricorn (72) 31(1) [0|4|54] — 1905
Me And Bobby McGee (71) 43(1) [0|0|22] — 1036
Border Lord (72) 41(2) [0|0|16] — 777
Songs Of Kristofferson (77) 45(2) [0|0|18] — 616
Spooky Lady's Sideshow (74) 78(1) [0|0|14] — 426
Who's To Bless...And Who's To Blame (75) 105(2) [0|0|11] — 223
Easter Island (78) 86(2) [0|0|7] — 190
Music From Songwriter (Soundtrack) (84)-Willie Nelson & Kris Kristofferson [A] 152(2) [0|0|5] — 27.6
Surreal Thing (76) 180(1) [0|0|2] — 20.1

Kris KRISTOFFERSON & Rita COOLIDGE ► 1055 Pk:26 [0|1|3] — 1729
Full Moon (73) 26(2) [0|6|33] — 1287
Breakaway (74) 103(1) [0|0|12] — 278
Natural Act (79) 106(2) [0|0|9] — 164
A Star Is Born (Soundtrack) (76)-Barbra Streisand & Kris Kristofferson [A] 1(6) [18|28|51] — 4426

KROKUS ► 659 Pk:25 [0|2|7] — 4185
Headhunter (83) 25(2) [0|8|41] — 1468
The Blitz (84) 31(1) [0|6|27] — 967
Change Of Address (86) 45(2) [0|0|17] — 571
One Vice At A Time (82) 53(2) [0|0|20] — 517
Hardware (81) 103(1) [0|0|12] — 263
Heart Attack (88) 87(1) [0|0|11] — 232
Alive And Screamin' (86) 97(2) [0|0|12] — 166

Bob KUBAN And The IN-MEN ► 2917 Pk:129 [0|0|1] — 78
Look Out For The Cheater (66) 129(2) [0|0|5] — 77.8

KWAMÉ & A NEW BEGINNING ► 2259 Pk:114 [0|0|1] — 229
The Boy Genius (89)-Kwamé Featuring A New Beginning 114(2) [0|0|18] — 229

KWICK ► 3505 Pk:197 [0|0|1] — 11
Kwick (80) 197(1) [0|0|2] — 10.9

L

Patti LaBELLE ► 333 Pk:1 [2|3|12] — 10378
Winner In You (86) 1(1) [12|19|30] — 4001
Nightbirds (74)-Labelle 7(3) [4|11|28] — 2605
I'm In Love Again (84) 40(2) [0|2|35] — 965
Be Yourself (89) 86(1) [0|0|26] — 515
Patti (85) 72(3) [0|0|29] — 486
Patti La Belle (77) 62(1) [0|0|16] — 480
It's Alright With Me (79) 145(1) [0|0|16] — 222
Released (80) 114(1) [0|0|13] — 197
Tasty (78) 129(1) [0|0|7] — 121
The Spirit's In It (81) 156(3) [0|0|4] — 50.5
Phoenix (75)-Labelle 44(2) [0|0|13] — 473
Chameleon (76)-Labelle 94(1) [0|0|10] — 262

L.A. BOPPERS ► 2148 Pk:85 [0|0|1] — 281
L.A. Boppers (80) 85(1) [0|0|11] — 281

LACE ► 3263 Pk:187 [0|0|1] — 32
Shades of Lace (88) 187(2) [0|0|5] — 31.9

Cheryl LADD ► 2382 Pk:129 [0|0|2] — 190
Cheryl Ladd (78) 129(2) [0|0|11] — 161
Dance Forever (79) 179(2) [0|0|3] — 29.6

L.A. DREAM TEAM ► 2732 Pk:138 [0|0|2] — 108
Kings Of West Coast (86) 138(1) [0|0|7] — 77.6
Bad To The Bone (87) 162(2) [0|0|4] — 30.7

David LAFLAMME ► 3006 Pk:159 [0|0|1] — 66
White Bird (76) 159(1) [0|0|6] — 65.6

--L.A. Express see Scott, Tom

L.A. GUNS ► 895 Pk:38 [0|1|2] — 2410
Cocked & Loaded (89) 38(1) [0|1|56] — 1459
L.A. Guns (88) 50(1) [0|0|33] — 951

LAID BACK ► 2028 Pk:67 [0|0|1] — 338
...Keep Smiling (84) 67(1) [0|0|15] — 338

Cleo LAINE ► 1901 Pk:138 [0|0|6] — 407
Born On A Friday (76) 158(2) [0|0|10] — 133
Porgy & Bess (76)-Ray Charles And Cleo Laine [A] 138(3) [0|0|11] — 84.4
Cleo Laine Live!!! At Carnegie Hall (74) 157(1) [0|0|8] — 79.1
A Beautiful Thing (74) 168(2) [0|0|5] — 60.7
Sometimes When We Touch (80)-Cleo Laine & James Galway [A] 150(1) [0|0|6] — 44.2
Day By Day (74) 199(1) [0|0|1] — 5.8

Frankie LAINE ► 904 Pk:16 [0|1|4] — 2356
I'll Take Care Of Your Cares (67) 16(2) [0|9|29] — 1670
You Gave Me A Mountain (69) 55(1) [0|0|11] — 529
To Each His Own (68) 127(1) [0|0|9] — 133

Act ▶ Highest Peak [Top10s|Top40s|Total]
Title (Yr) Peak(Wk) [T10 Wk|T40Wk|TotalWk] Score

Frankie LAINE ▶ *Continued*

I Wanted Someone To Love (67) 162(2) [0|0|2] 24.1

LAKE ▶ 2136 Pk:92 [0|0|1] 285

Lake (77) 92(1) [0|0|15] 285

Greg LAKE ▶ 1743 Pk:62 [0|0|1] 533

Greg Lake (81) 62(4) [0|0|17] 533

LAKESIDE ▶ 618 Pk:16 [0|1|7] 4570

Fantastic Voyage (80) 16(2) [0|12|35] 2242

Your Wish Is My Command (82) 58(1) [0|0|23] 613

Untouchables (83) 42(2) [0|0|18] 490

Shot Of Love (79) 74(1) [0|0|19] 489

Outrageous (84) 68(2) [0|0|15] 307

Rough Riders (79) 141(3) [0|0|18] 231

Keep On Moving Straight Ahead (81) 109(4) [0|0|10] 199

Major LANCE ▶ 2101 Pk:100 [0|0|3] 302

Um, Um, Um, Um, Um, Um/The Best Of Major Lance (64) 100(1) [0|0|9] 148

Major's Greatest Hits (65) 109(1) [0|0|6] 98.8

The Monkey Time (63) 113(1) [0|0|3] 54.3

Robin LANE & The CHARTBUSTERS ▶ 3191 Pk:172 [0|0|1] 42

Imitation Life (81) 172(1) [0|0|4] 41.9

Ronnie LANE ▶ 2223 Pk:45 [0|0|1] 244

Rough Mix (77)-Pete Townshend & Ronnie Lane [A] 45(1) [0|0|12] 244

K.D. LANG ▶ 1039 Pk:69 [0|0|2] 1778

Absolute Torch And Twang (89)-k.d. lang & The Reclines 69(1) [0|0|56] 1203

Shadowland (88) 73(2) [0|0|25] 576

David LANZ ▶ 2617 Pk:125 [0|0|2] 130

Natural States (88)-David Lanz & Paul Speer [A] 125(1) [0|0|12] 91.0

Cristofori's Dream (88) 180(1) [0|0|6] 38.6

Mario LANZA ▶ 2188 Pk:87 [0|0|1] 264

The Best Of Mario Lanza (64) 87(1) [0|0|15] 264

Billy LARKIN & The DELEGATES ▶ 3332 Pk:148 [0|0|1] 26

Hole In The Wall (66) 148(1) [0|0|2] 25.5

The LARKS ▶ 3129 Pk:143 [0|0|1] 49

The Jerk (65) 143(1) [0|0|4] 48.9

Neil LARSEN ▶ 2749 Pk:139 [0|0|1] 105

High Gear (79) 139(1) [0|0|7] 105

LARSEN-FEITEN BAND ▶ 2623 Pk:142 [0|0|1] 128

Larsen-Feiten Band (80) 142(1) [0|0|10] 128

Nicolette LARSON ▶ 750 Pk:15 [0|1|4] 3266

Nicolette (78) 15(2) [0|12|37] 2121

In The Nick Of Time (79) 47(1) [0|0|21] 581

Radioland (81) 62(1) [0|0|12] 357

All Dressed Up & No Place To Go (82) 75(1) [0|0|10] 207

D.C. LaRUE ▶ 1903 Pk:115 [0|0|2] 405

The Tea Dance (77) 115(1) [0|0|11] 214

Cathedrals (76) 139(2) [0|0|13] 190

Denise LaSALLE ▶ 2520 Pk:120 [0|0|1] 154

Trapped By A Thing Called Love (72) 120(1) [0|0|9] 154

James LAST ▶ 2302 Pk:148 [0|0|3] 215

Seduction (80)-James Last Band 148(1) [0|0|8] 119

Music From Across The Way (72) 160(1) [0|0|5] 62.6

Well Kept Secret (75) 172(1) [0|0|3] 33.5

LAST POETS ▶ 951 Pk:29 [0|1|3] 2135

The Last Poets (70) 29(1) [0|7|30] 1649

This Is Madness (71) 104(1) [0|0|15] 375

Right On! (Soundtrack) (71)-The Original Last Poets 106(1) [0|0|6] 110

Act ▶ Highest Peak [Top10s|Top40s|Total]
Title (Yr) Peak(Wk) [T10 Wk|T40Wk|TotalWk] Score

Yusef LATEEF ▶ 3157 Pk:183 [0|0|1] 46

Yusef Lateef's Detroit (69) 183(1) [0|0|5] 45.7

LATIMORE ▶ 3181 Pk:181 [0|0|1] 43

It Ain't Where You Been (77) 181(1) [0|0|5] 43.1

Stacy LATTISAW ▶ 860 Pk:44 [0|0|7] 2605

Let Me Be Your Angel (80) 44(1) [0|0|28] 1063

With You (81) 46(1) [0|0|15] 601

Sneakin' Out (82) 55(4) [0|0|16] 528

Take Me All The Way (86) 131(2) [0|0|22] 189

Personal Attention (88) 153(2) [0|0|10] 93.2

Sixteen (83) 160(1) [0|0|8] 79.4

Perfect Combination (84)-Stacy Lattisaw & Johnny Gill [A] 139(1) [0|0|8] 51.8

Cyndi LAUPER ▶ 262 Pk:4 [2|3|3] 13582

She's So Unusual (83) 4(4) [21|62|96] 9304

True Colors (86) 4(2) [6|23|44] 3490

A Night To Remember (89) 37(4) [0|4|21] 788

Steve LAWRENCE ▶ 2114 Pk:73 [0|0|3] 295

Everybody Knows (64) 73(1) [0|0|9] 198

Academy Award Losers (64) 135(1) [0|0|5] 65.7

The Steve Lawrence Show (65) 133(1) [0|0|2] 30.9

Steve LAWRENCE & Eydie GORME ▶ 2296 Pk:136 [0|0|3] 218

What It Was, Was Love (69) 141(1) [0|0|6] 117

Together On Broadway (67) 136(1) [0|0|6] 77.3

Real True Lovin' (69) 188(1) [0|0|3] 24.2

Vicki LAWRENCE ▶ 1800 Pk:51 [0|0|1] 485

The Night The Lights Went Out In Georgia (73) 51(1) [0|0|14] 485

Debra LAWS ▶ 1550 Pk:70 [0|0|1] 726

Very Special (81) 70(1) [0|0|27] 726

Eloise LAWS ▶ 2690 Pk:156 [0|0|2] 116

Eloise Laws (81) 175(1) [0|0|7] 63.1

Eloise (78) 156(1) [0|0|5] 52.5

Hubert LAWS ▶ 996 Pk:42 [0|0|8] 1959

The Chicago Theme (75) 42(2) [0|0|18] 753

Say It With Silence (78) 71(2) [0|0|18] 511

Family (80) 133(1) [0|0|13] 230

Land Of Passion (79) 93(1) [0|0|8] 184

Romeo & Juliet (76) 139(1) [0|0|6] 104

Morning Star (73) 148(1) [0|0|9] 97.3

Carnegie Hall (73) 175(1) [0|0|6] 47.8

How To Beat The High Cost Of Living (Soundtrack) (80)-Hubert Laws And Earl Klugh [A] 134(2) [0|0|4] 31.9

Ronnie LAWS ▶ 543 Pk:24 [0|2|7] 5485

Friends And Strangers (77) 37(2) [0|2|28] 1138

Every Generation (80) 24(3) [0|6|19] 1049

Fever (76) 46(2) [0|0|21] 1006

Flame (78) 51(4) [0|0|22] 764

Pressure Sensitive (75) 73(1) [0|0|29] 727

Solid Ground (81) 51(2) [0|0|19] 612

Mr. Nice Guy (83) 98(1) [0|0|11] 189

Bernie LEADON-Michel GEORGIADES Band ▶ 2515 Pk:91 [0|0|1] 156

Natural Progressions (77) 91(1) [0|0|6] 156

LEAPY LEE ▶ 1809 Pk:71 [0|0|1] 476

Little Arrows (69) 71(1) [0|0|12] 476

LEATHERWOLF ▶ 2055 Pk:105 [0|0|2] 327

Leatherwolf (88) 105(1) [0|0|12] 213

Street Ready (89) 123(1) [0|0|8] 114

The LEAVES ▶ 2868 Pk:127 [0|0|1] 85

Hey Joe (66)-The Leaves 127(1) [0|0|5] 85.2

Act ▶ Highest Peak [Top10s|Top40s|Total]
Title (Yr) Peak(Wk) [T10 Wk|T40Wk|TotalWk] Score

LeBLANC & CARR ▶ 2742 Pk:145 [0|0|1] 106

Midnight Light (78) 145(1) [0|0|7] 106

LED ZEPPELIN ▶ 7 Pk:1 [10|10|10] 78767

Led Zeppelin II (69) 1(7) [24|29|98] 13989

Led Zeppelin IV (71) 2(4) [14|34|259] 13899

Led Zeppelin (69) 10(1) [1|50|95] 10151

Houses Of The Holy (73) 1(2) [14|30|99] 9285

In Through The Out Door (79) 1(7) [18|28|41] 8553

Led Zeppelin III (70) 1(4) [14|19|42] 6898

Physical Graffiti (75) 1(6) [12|15|41] 6436

Presence (76) 1(2) [9|13|30] 4218

The Song Remains The Same (Soundtrack) (76) 2(3) [7|12|48] 3843

Coda (82) 6(3) [7|9|16] 1495

Alvin LEE ▶ 142 Pk:65 [0|0|7] 931

In Flight (75) 65(2) [0|0|12] 367

Rocket Fuel (78) 115(1) [0|0|11] 211

Detroit Diesel (86) 124(2) [0|0|9] 116

Pump Iron! (75) 131(2) [0|0|5] 101

Ride On (79) 158(1) [0|0|5] 58.8

On The Road To Freedom (74)-Alvin Lee & Myron LeFevre [A] 138(1) [0|0|8] 56.3

Free Fall (80) 198(1) [0|0|4] 21.1

Brenda LEE ▶ 944 Pk:36 [0|2|8] 2156

Too Many Rivers (65) 36(2) [0|2|14] 519

Let Me Sing (63) 39(1) [0|1|13] 385

10 Golden Years (66) 70(1) [0|0|14] 300

Coming On Strong (66) 94(1) [0|0|12] 267

Johnny One Time (69) 98(1) [0|0|9] 260

Bye Bye Blues (66) 94(1) [0|0|13] 229

By Request (64) 90(1) [0|0|11] 188

For The First Time (68)-Brenda & Pete [A] 187(2) [0|0|2] 8.1

Jackie LEE ▶ 2440 Pk:85 [0|0|1] 176

The Duck (66) 85(1) [0|0|9] 176

Johnny LEE ▶ 1956 Pk:132 [0|0|2] 375

Lookin' For Love (80) 132(1) [0|0|21] 267

Bet Your Heart On Me (81) 147(1) [0|0|8] 109

Laura LEE ▶ 2352 Pk:117 [0|0|1] 197

Women's Love Rights (72) 117(1) [0|0|11] 197

Peggy LEE ▶ 1429 Pk:55 [0|0|6] 924

Is That All There Is? (69) 55(1) [0|0|18] 598

Bridge Over Troubled Water (70) 142(2) [0|0|9] 119

In The Name Of Love (64) 97(1) [0|0|6] 97.3

Pass Me By (65) 145(1) [0|0|4] 48.1

Big Spender (66) 130(1) [0|0|3] 47.2

Make It With You (70) 194(2) [0|0|2] 13.8

Myron LeFEVRE ▶ 3072 Pk:138 [0|0|1] 56

On The Road To Freedom (74)-Alvin Lee & Myron LeFevre [A] 138(1) [0|0|8] 56.3

Raymond LEFEVRE And His Orchestra ▶ 2159 Pk:117 [0|0|1] 275

Soul Coaxing (Ame Caline) (68) 117(1) [0|0|16] 275

LEFT BANKE ▶ 2181 Pk:67 [0|0|1] 266

Walk Away Renee/Pretty Ballerina (67) 67(1) [0|0|11] 266

Michel LEGRAND ▶ 2284 Pk:127 [0|0|2] 221

Brian's Song Themes & Variations (72) 127(2) [0|0|10] 171

Sarah Vaughan/Michel Legrand (72)-Sarah Vaughan/Michel Legrand [A] 173(1) [0|0|12] 49.3

Tom LEHRER ▶ 856 Pk:18 [0|1|2] 2615

That Was The Year That Was (65) 18(1) [0|19|51] 2499

An Evening Wasted With Tom Lehrer (66) 133(1) [0|0|8] 116

Act ► Highest Peak [Top10s|Top40s|Total]
Title (Yr) Peak(Wk) [T10 Wk|T40Wk|TotalWk] — **Score**

LEMON PIPERS ► 1999 Pk:90 [0|0|1] — **351**
Green Tambourine (68) 90(1) [0|0|18] — 351

John LENNON ► 337 Pk:1 [3|5|7] — **10083**
Walls And Bridges (74) 1(1) [6|11|35] — 3671
Mind Games (73) 9(3) [4|11|31] — 2321
Rock 'N' Roll (75) 6(1) [5|9|15] — 2182
The John Lennon Collection (82) 33(4) [0|8|16] — 760
Imagine: John Lennon (Soundtrack) (88) 31(1) [0|5|18] — 729
Live In New York City (86) 41(2) [0|0|11] — 376
Menlove Avenue (86) 127(2) [0|0|4] — 44.5

John LENNON & Yoko ONO ► 294 Pk:1 [1|2|7] — **11923**
Double Fantasy (80) 1(8) [22|27|74] — 9397
Milk And Honey (84) 11(1) [0|10|19] — 1381
Some Time In New York City (72) 48(2) [0|0|17] — 665
Unfinished Music No. 1: Two Virgins (69) 124(1) [0|0|8] — 184
Heart Play (84) 94(1) [0|0|12] — 179
Unfinished Music No. 2: Life With The Lions (69) 174(2) [0|0|8] — 84.7
Wedding Album (69) 178(1) [0|0|3] — 31.4

John LENNON/PLASTIC ONO BAND ► 270 Pk:1 [3|4|4] — **13107**
Imagine (71) 1(1) [12|17|45] — 5713
John Lennon/Plastic Ono Band (70) 6(1) [4|12|33] — 2885
The Plastic Ono Band - Live Peace In Toronto 1969 (70)-The Plastic Ono Band 10(2) [2|13|32] — 2690
Shaved Fish (75) 12(1) [0|6|32] — 1819

Julian LENNON ► 638 Pk:17 [0|2|3] — **4347**
Valotte (84) 17(2) [0|28|46] — 3339
The Secret Value Of DayDreaming (86) 32(2) [0|5|18] — 725
Mr. Jordan (89) 87(1) [0|0|15] — 284

LENNON SISTERS ► 2067 Pk:77 [0|0|1] — **317**
Somethin' Stupid (67) 77(1) [0|0|18] — 317

Le PAMPLEMOUSSE ► 2408 Pk:116 [0|0|1] — **184**
Le Spank (78) 116(1) [0|0|11] — 184

LEROI BROS. ► 3264 Pk:181 [0|0|1] — **32**
Open All Night (87) 181(2) [0|0|5] — 31.7

Le ROUX ► 1426 Pk:64 [0|0|4] — **929**
Last Safe Place (82) 64(2) [0|0|21] — 556
Louisiana's Le Roux (78)-Louisiana's Le Roux 135(1) [0|0|15] — 235
Up (80) 145(2) [0|0|6] — 90.0
Keep The Fire Burning (79)-Louisiana's Le Roux 162(2) [0|0|4] — 48.1

LET'S ACTIVE ► 1937 Pk:111 [0|0|3] — **383**
Big Plans For Everybody (86) 111(2) [0|0|10] — 142
Cypress (84) 138(1) [0|0|16] — 136
Afoot (84) 154(1) [0|0|11] — 105

The LETTERMEN ► 167 Pk:10 [1|8|28] — **20616**
The Lettermen!!!...And "Live!" (67) 10(5) [5|16|48] — 3145
Goin' Out Of My Head (68) 13(1) [0|14|44] — 2723
Hurt So Bad (69) 17(1) [0|11|30] — 2311
The Best Of The Lettermen (66) 17(1) [0|11|27] — 1573
The Hit Sounds Of The Lettermen (65) 13(1) [0|10|24] — 1382
Put Your Head On My Shoulder (68) 43(2) [0|0|21] — 1020
Spring! (67) 31(1) [0|4|26] — 973
Portrait Of My Love (65) 27(2) [0|5|23] — 916
A Lettermen Kind Of Love (64) 31(1) [0|3|32] — 844
Traces/Memories (70) 42(2) [0|0|23] — 766
I Have Dreamed (69) 74(1) [0|0|18] — 638
She Cried (64) 41(2) [0|0|20] — 621

Act ► Highest Peak [Top10s|Top40s|Total]
Title (Yr) Peak(Wk) [T10 Wk|T40Wk|TotalWk] — **Score**

A New Song For Young Love (66) 52(2) [0|0|15] — 474
More Hit Sounds Of The Lettermen! (66) 57(1) [0|0|17] — 474
Warm (67) 58(1) [0|0|17] — 471
Love Book (71) 88(1) [0|0|13] — 359
Special Request (68) 82(2) [0|0|14] — 354
You'll Never Walk Alone (65) 73(1) [0|0|13] — 258
The Lettermen In Concert (63) 76(1) [0|0|10] — 222
Close-Up (69) 90(1) [0|0|8] — 210
The Best Of The Lettermen, Vol. 2 (69) 128(1) [0|0|10] — 192
Reflections (70) 134(2) [0|0|11] — 177
The Lettermen Look At Love (64) 94(2) [0|0|10] — 162
Everything's Good About You (71) 119(1) [0|0|10] — 142
Lettermen 1 (72) 136(1) [0|0|6] — 96.3
Feelings (71) 192(2) [0|0|6] — 42.7
"Alive" Again...Naturally (73) 193(2) [0|0|7] — 40.4
All-Time Greatest Hits (74) 186(1) [0|0|4] — 27.9

LEVEL 42 ► 727 Pk:18 [0|2|3] — **3464**
World Machine (86) 18(2) [0|13|36] — 1841
Running In The Family (87) 23(1) [0|10|34] — 1525
Staring At The Sun (88) 128(1) [0|0|7] — 98.2

LEVERT ► 1083 Pk:32 [0|1|3] — **1649**
The Big Throwdown (87) 32(2) [0|7|24] — 943
Just Coolin' (88) 79(1) [0|0|31] — 691
Bloodline (86) 192(1) [0|0|3] — 14.5

Barbara LEWIS ► 2743 Pk:118 [0|0|1] — **106**
Baby, I'm Yours (65) 118(1) [0|0|7] — 106

Gary LEWIS And The PLAYBOYS ► 474 Pk:10 [1|3|9] — **6616**
Golden Greats (66) 10(4) [4|13|46] — 2733
This Diamond Ring (65) 26(1) [0|5|25] — 919
A Session With Gary Lewis And The Playboys (65) 18(2) [0|5|20] — 884
Hits Again! (66) 47(1) [0|0|24] — 704
Everybody Loves A Clown (65) 44(2) [0|0|16] — 528
She's Just My Style (66) 71(1) [0|0|17] — 360
(You Don't Have To) Paint Me A Picture (67) 79(1) [0|0|16] — 343
Gary Lewis Now! (68) 150(1) [0|0|9] — 118
New Directions (67) 185(1) [0|0|4] — 27.7

Huey LEWIS And The NEWS ► 112 Pk:1 [2|4|4] — **27471**
Sports (83)-Huey Lewis & The News 1(1) [42|72|158] — 15377
Fore! (86)-Huey Lewis & The News 1(1) [26|41|61] — 7433
Picture This (82)-Huey Lewis & The News 13(4) [0|14|59] — 2810
Small World (88)-Huey Lewis & The News 11(2) [0|12|30] — 1851

Jerry Lee LEWIS ► 716 Pk:37 [0|1|21] — **3517**
Class Of '55 (86)-Carl Perkins, Jerry Lee Lewis, Roy Orbison, & Johnny Cash [A] 87(2) [0|0|12] — 54.0
The Session (73) 37(1) [0|3|19] — 825
The Greatest Live Show On Earth (64) 71(2) [0|0|17] — 332
Great Balls Of Fire (Soundtrack) (89) 62(1) [0|0|10] — 276
Would You Take Another Chance On Me? (71) 115(3) [0|0|12] — 252
The "Killer" Rocks On (72) 105(1) [0|0|12] — 250
The Best Of Jerry Lee Lewis (70) 114(2) [0|0|14] — 220
The Country Music Hall Of Fame Hits, Vol. 1 (69) 127(2) [0|0|10] — 205
The Country Music Hall Of Fame Hits, Vol. 2 (69) 124(1) [0|0|10] — 197

Act ► Highest Peak [Top10s|Top40s|Total]
Title (Yr) Peak(Wk) [T10 Wk|T40Wk|TotalWk] — **Score**

Original Golden Hits - Volume 2 (69) 122(2) [0|0|5] — 128
She Still Comes Around (To Love What's Left Of Me) (69) 149(1) [0|0|7] — 125
The Golden Hits Of Jerry Lee Lewis (64) 116(1) [0|0|8] — 112
Another Place Another Time (68) 160(1) [0|0|12] — 103
Original Golden Hits - Volume 1 (69) 119(2) [0|0|4] — 102
Live At The International, Las Vegas (70) 149(1) [0|0|6] — 92.2
The Return Of Rock (65) 121(1) [0|0|5] — 73.1
Touching Home (71) 152(1) [0|0|3] — 46.7
There Must Be More To Love Than This (71) 190(1) [0|0|6] — 42.5
Memphis Beat (66) 145(1) [0|0|3] — 39.2
Jerry Lee Lewis (79) 186(1) [0|0|3] — 24.8
She Even Woke Me Up To Say Goodbye (70) 186(1) [0|0|2] — 15.0

Ramsey LEWIS ► 354 Pk:12 [0|2|22] — **9551**
Sun Goddess (74) 12(1) [0|14|30] — 2592
Wade In The Water (66) 16(2) [0|13|34] — 2188
Don't It Feel Good (75) 46(1) [0|0|22] — 849
Up Pops Ramsey Lewis (68) 52(2) [0|0|31] — 827
Maiden Voyage (68) 55(2) [0|0|20] — 595
Dancing In The Street (67) 59(1) [0|0|16] — 475
Goin' Latin (67) 95(1) [0|0|16] — 294
Salongo (76) 77(1) [0|0|11] — 288
Love Notes (77) 79(2) [0|0|10] — 238
Tequila Mockingbird (77) 111(2) [0|0|9] — 169
Funky Serenity (73) 117(1) [0|0|10] — 166
Mother Nature's Son (69) 156(2) [0|0|14] — 162
The Best Of Ramsey Lewis (70) 172(1) [0|0|12] — 108
Back To The Roots (71) 163(1) [0|0|9] — 103
Ramsey Lewis, The Piano Player (70) 157(2) [0|0|8] — 85.7
Routes (80) 173(1) [0|0|8] — 80.8
The Movie Album (67) 124(1) [0|0|4] — 71.6
Legacy (78) 149(1) [0|0|5] — 71.4
Three Piece Suite (81) 152(2) [0|0|5] — 69.2
Them Changes (70) 177(1) [0|0|7] — 57.5
The Two Of Us (84)-Ramsey Lewis & Nancy Wilson [A] 144(1) [0|0|9] — 46.5
Ramsey Lewis' Newly Recorded All-Time, Non-Stop Golden Hits (73) 198(1) [0|0|3] — 15.2

Ramsey LEWIS Trio ► 397 Pk:2 [1|2|7] — **8241**
The In Crowd (65) 2(1) [15|33|47] — 4876
Hang On Ramsey! (66) 15(2) [0|15|27] — 1732
Upendo Ni Pamoja (72) 79(1) [0|0|21] — 587
Choice! The Best Of The Ramsey Lewis Trio (65) 54(1) [0|0|19] — 490
Another Voyage (69) 139(2) [0|0|14] — 256
The Ramsey Lewis Trio At The Bohemian Caverns (64) 103(1) [0|0|13] — 208
Bach To The Blues (64) 125(1) [0|0|7] — 90.9

Webster LEWIS ► 2519 Pk:114 [0|0|1] — **154**
8 For The 80's (80) 114(1) [0|0|9] — 154

Lori LIEBERMAN ► 3236 Pk:192 [0|0|1] — **35**
Becoming (73) 192(2) [0|0|6] — 34.9

Enoch LIGHT & The LIGHT BRIGADE ► 1322 Pk:78 [0|0|13] — **1098**
Discotheque Dance...Dance...Dance (64) 84(1) [0|0|15] — 248
Dimension "3" (64) 78(1) [0|0|9] — 173
Magnificent Movie Themes (65) 105(1) [0|0|10] — 169
Rome 35/MM (64) 121(2) [0|0|7] — 96.1

Act ► Highest Peak [Top10s | Top40s | Total] Title (Yr) Peak(Wk) [T10 Wk | T40Wk | TotalWk]	Score
Enoch LIGHT/LIGHT BRIGADE ► *Continued*	
Persuasive Percussion 1966 (66) 144(2) [0 | 0 | 6]	80.3
Command Performances (64) 129(1) [0 | 0 | 4]	54.3
Big Band Hits Of The 30's & 40's! (71) 176(1) [0 | 0 | 5]	50.7
Enoch Light & The Brass Menagerie (69) 192(2) [0 | 0 | 7]	48.4
Great Themes From Hit Films (64) 143(2) [0 | 0 | 4]	47.6
Spanish Strings (67) 163(1) [0 | 0 | 4]	41.4
1963-The Year's Most Popular Themes (63) 133(1) [0 | 0 | 3]	41.3
Spaced Out (70) 191(1) [0 | 0 | 4]	27.3
Film On Film - Great Movie Themes (67) 173(1) [0 | 0 | 2]	19.8
Gordon LIGHTFOOT ► 180 Pk:1 [2 | 7 | 16]	**19172**
Sundown (74) 1(2) [8 | 23 | 42]	5326
Summertime Dream (76) 12(2) [0 | 26 | 41]	4127
Sit Down Young Stranger (70) 12(2) [0 | 12 | 37]	2614
Cold On The Shoulder (75) 10(1) [1 | 9 | 20]	1965
Endless Wire (78) 22(2) [0 | 7 | 20]	1183
Summer Side Of Life (71) 38(2) [0 | 3 | 20]	1152
Gord's Gold (75) 34(1) [0 | 4 | 24]	938
Don Quixote (72) 42(1) [0 | 0 | 17]	744
Dream Street Rose (80) 60(1) [0 | 0 | 11]	334
Old Dan's Records (72) 95(1) [0 | 0 | 12]	244
Shadows (82) 87(2) [0 | 0 | 12]	224
Sunday Concert (69) 143(1) [0 | 0 | 6]	104
The Very Best Of Gordon Lightfoot (74) 155(1) [0 | 0 | 9]	80.5
East Of Midnight (86) 165(1) [0 | 0 | 6]	51.5
Classic Lightfoot (The Best Of Lightfoot/Volume 2) (71) 178(2) [0 | 0 | 5]	47.2
Salute (83) 175(1) [0 | 0 | 5]	38.0
LIGHTHOUSE ► 1548 Pk:80 [0 | 0 | 5]	**726**
One Fine Morning (71) 80(2) [0 | 0 | 21]	490
Thoughts Of Movin' On (72) 157(1) [0 | 0 | 7]	69.4
Lighthouse Live! (72) 178(1) [0 | 0 | 7]	60.6
Sunny Days (73) 190(1) [0 | 0 | 9]	53.5
Peacing It All Together (70) 133(2) [0 | 0 | 3]	52.6
LIMAHL ► 1631 Pk:41 [0 | 0 | 1]	**642**
Don't Suppose (85) 41(1) [0 | 0 | 20]	642
The LIMELITERS ► 2210 Pk:73 [0 | 0 | 2]	**250**
Fourteen 14K Folk Songs (63) 73(1) [0 | 0 | 8]	179
More Of Everything! (64) 118(1) [0 | 0 | 5]	70.8
Bob LIND ► 3335 Pk:148 [0 | 0 | 1]	**25**
Don't Be Concerned (66) 148(1) [0 | 0 | 2]	25.4
David LINDLEY ► 1789 Pk:83 [0 | 0 | 2]	**493**
El Rayo-X (81) 83(1) [0 | 0 | 18]	449
Very Greasy (88)-David Lindley & El Rayo-X 174(1) [0 | 0 | 6]	44.4
Mark LINDSAY ► 1264 Pk:36 [0 | 1 | 3]	**1216**
Arizona (70) 36(1) [0 | 4 | 19]	921
Silverbird (70) 82(1) [0 | 0 | 10]	273
You've Got A Friend (71) 180(2) [0 | 0 | 2]	21.8
Art LINKLETTER ► 3172 Pk:143 [0 | 0 | 1]	**44**
For The Children Of The World, Art Linkletter Narrates "The Bible..In The Beginning" (Soundtrack) (66) 143(2) [0 | 0 | 3]	43.8
LINX ► 3201 Pk:175 [0 | 0 | 1]	**39**
Intuition (81) 175(1) [0 | 0 | 4]	39.5
LIONS AND GHOSTS ► 3427 Pk:187 [0 | 0 | 1]	**17**
Velvet Kiss, Lick Of The Lime (87) 187(2) [0 | 0 | 3]	17.0
LIPPS INC. ► 734 Pk:5 [1 | 1 | 2]	**3403**
Mouth To Mouth (80) 5(5) [7 | 13 | 26]	3106

Act ► Highest Peak [Top10s | Top40s | Total] Title (Yr) Peak(Wk) [T10 Wk | T40Wk | TotalWk]	Score
Pucker Up (80) 63(1) [0 | 0 | 9]	297
LISA LISA And CULT JAM ► 528 Pk:7 [1 | 1 | 3]	**5726**
Spanish Fly (87) 7(3) [7 | 29 | 48]	4194
Lisa Lisa & Cult Jam With Full Force (85)-Lisa Lisa And Cult Jam With Full Force 52(2) [0 | 0 | 66]	1280
Straight To The Sky (89) 77(3) [0 | 0 | 13]	252
The LITTER ► 3171 Pk:175 [0 | 0 | 1]	**44**
Emerge (69)-Litter 175(2) [0 | 0 | 5]	43.9
Rich LITTLE ► 1558 Pk:29 [0 | 1 | 1]	**723**
The First Family Rides Again (82) 29(2) [0 | 6 | 13]	723
LITTLE AMERICA ► 2300 Pk:102 [0 | 0 | 1]	**216**
Little America (87) 102(2) [0 | 0 | 14]	216
LITTLE ANTHONY And The IMPERIALS ► 1523 Pk:74 [0 | 0 | 4]	**764**
The Best Of Little Anthony & The Imperials (66) 97(2) [0 | 0 | 23]	384
Goin' Out Of My Head (65) 74(1) [0 | 0 | 13]	271
I'm On The Outside (Looking In) (65) 135(1) [0 | 0 | 4]	56.0
Out Of Sight, Out Of Mind (69) 172(2) [0 | 0 | 5]	53.4
LITTLE FEAT ► 460 Pk:18 [0 | 7 | 7]	**6911**
Waiting For Columbus (78) 18(2) [0 | 11 | 25]	1946
Down On The Farm (79) 29(1) [0 | 7 | 21]	1036
Let It Roll (88) 36(1) [0 | 4 | 33]	994
Time Loves A Hero (77) 34(2) [0 | 4 | 18]	948
Feats Don't Fail Me Now (74) 36(1) [0 | 2 | 16]	742
The Last Record Album (75) 36(2) [0 | 3 | 15]	641
Hoy-Hoy! (81) 39(1) [0 | 2 | 13]	604
LITTLE MILTON ► 2019 Pk:101 [0 | 0 | 3]	**342**
We're Gonna Make It (65) 101(2) [0 | 0 | 14]	226
Grits Ain't Groceries (69) 159(1) [0 | 0 | 7]	104
If Walls Could Talk (70) 197(2) [0 | 0 | 2]	12.4
LITTLE RICHARD ► 3160 Pk:184 [0 | 0 | 2]	**45**
King Of Rock And Roll (71) 193(1) [0 | 0 | 4]	26.0
Little Richard's Greatest Hits (67) 184(1) [0 | 0 | 3]	19.5
LITTLE RIVER BAND ► 277 Pk:10 [1 | 4 | 9]	**12752**
Sleeper Catcher (78) 16(2) [0 | 12 | 61]	3077
First Under The Wire (79) 10(3) [3 | 15 | 33]	2687
Time Exposure (81) 21(1) [0 | 9 | 50]	2288
Diamantina Cocktail (77) 49(1) [0 | 0 | 48]	1693
Greatest Hits (82) 33(6) [0 | 12 | 30]	1237
The Net (83) 61(1) [0 | 0 | 21]	541
Little River Band (76) 80(1) [0 | 0 | 24]	472
Backstage Pass (80) 44(1) [0 | 0 | 10]	460
Playing To Win (85)-LRB 75(3) [0 | 0 | 14]	298
LITTLE STEVEN ► 1386 Pk:55 [0 | 0 | 3]	**987**
Voice Of America (84) 55(2) [0 | 0 | 17]	472
Men Without Women (82)-Little Steven And The Disciples Of Soul 118(3) [0 | 0 | 18]	272
Freedom No Compromise (87) 80(2) [0 | 0 | 12]	242
LIVING COLOUR ► 584 Pk:6 [1 | 1 | 1]	**4950**
Vivid (88) 6(2) [8 | 28 | 76]	4950
LIVING IN A BOX ► 2371 Pk:89 [0 | 0 | 1]	**193**
Living In A Box (87) 89(2) [0 | 0 | 13]	193
LIZZY BORDEN ► 2040 Pk:133 [0 | 0 | 4]	**333**
Master Of Disguise (89) 133(1) [0 | 0 | 10]	139
Menace To Society (86) 144(2) [0 | 0 | 10]	96.9
Visual Lies (87) 146(1) [0 | 0 | 7]	67.1
Terror Rising (87) 188(1) [0 | 0 | 6]	29.8
LL COOL J ► 415 Pk:3 [2 | 2 | 3]	**7817**
Bigger And Deffer (87) 3(1) [13 | 23 | 53]	4537
Walking With A Panther (89) 6(1) [5 | 14 | 21]	2231
Radio (86) 46(3) [0 | 0 | 38]	1049

Act ► Highest Peak [Top10s | Top40s | Total] Title (Yr) Peak(Wk) [T10 Wk | T40Wk | TotalWk]	Score
Charles LLOYD Quartet ► 2935 Pk:171 [0 | 0 | 2]	**74**
Love-In (67) 171(1) [0 | 0 | 7]	49.3
Forest Flower (67) 188(2) [0 | 0 | 4]	24.9
LOBO ► 978 Pk:37 [0 | 1 | 5]	**2007**
Of A Simple Man (72) 37(1) [0 | 7 | 31]	1478
Calumet (73) 128(1) [0 | 0 | 14]	224
Introducing Lobo (71) 163(1) [0 | 0 | 15]	168
A Cowboy Afraid Of Horses (75) 151(2) [0 | 0 | 7]	102
Just A Singer (74) 183(1) [0 | 0 | 4]	34.7
John LODGE ► 1348 Pk:16 [0 | 1 | 2]	**1044**
Blue Jays (75)-Justin Hayward & John Lodge [A] 16(1) [0 | 8 | 23]	886
Natural Avenue (77) 121(1) [0 | 0 | 9]	158
Nils LOFGREN ► 843 Pk:32 [0 | 2 | 7]	**2716**
Cry Tough (76) 32(1) [0 | 3 | 16]	732
I Came To Dance (77) 36(1) [0 | 2 | 12]	581
Nils (79) 54(1) [0 | 0 | 14]	568
Night After Night (77) 44(2) [0 | 0 | 10]	405
Night Fades Away (81) 99(1) [0 | 0 | 11]	219
Nils Lofgren (75) 141(1) [0 | 0 | 9]	152
Flip (85) 150(2) [0 | 0 | 5]	56.8
Dave LOGGINS ► 1790 Pk:54 [0 | 0 | 1]	**493**
Apprentice (In A Musical Workshop) (74) 54(1) [0 | 0 | 16]	493
Kenny LOGGINS ► 230 Pk:7 [1 | 5 | 7]	**15306**
Keep The Fire (79) 16(2) [0 | 24 | 43]	3776
Nightwatch (78) 7(5) [7 | 17 | 31]	3483
High Adventure (82) 13(3) [0 | 9 | 44]	2457
Kenny Loggins Alive (80) 11(2) [0 | 11 | 31]	2402
Celebrate Me Home (77) 27(1) [0 | 7 | 33]	1932
Vox Humana (85) 41(1) [0 | 0 | 31]	940
Back To Avalon (88) 69(2) [0 | 0 | 14]	314
LOGGINS & MESSINA ► 185 Pk:5 [3 | 6 | 9]	**18720**
On Stage (74) 5(2) [9 | 16 | 37]	3837
Full Sail (73) 10(1) [1 | 17 | 49]	3243
Loggins And Messina (72) 16(1) [0 | 13 | 61]	2971
Sittin' In (72)-Kenny Loggins With Jim Messina 70(1) [0 | 0 | 113]	2771
Mother Lode (74) 8(1) [4 | 12 | 29]	2707
Native Sons (76) 16(1) [0 | 9 | 17]	1399
So Fine (75) 21(1) [0 | 8 | 13]	1163
The Best Of Friends (76) 61(1) [0 | 0 | 12]	437
Finale (77) 83(1) [0 | 0 | 8]	192
Jackie LOMAX ► 2553 Pk:145 [0 | 0 | 1]	**148**
Is This What You Want? (69) 145(2) [0 | 0 | 9]	148
Julie LONDON ► 3080 Pk:136 [0 | 0 | 1]	**55**
The Wonderful World Of Julie London (63) 136(1) [0 | 0 | 4]	54.9
LONDON SYMPHONY Orchestra ► 1667 Pk:62 [0 | 0 | 4]	**606**
Raiders Of The Lost Ark (Soundtrack) (81)-The London Symphony Orchestra/John Williams 62(1) [0 | 0 | 13]	362
A Classic Case: The Music Of Jethro Tull (86)-The London Symphony Orchestra/Ian Anderson 93(2) [0 | 0 | 13]	191
Hooked On Rock Classics (83) 145(2) [0 | 0 | 3]	35.7
Classic Rock - Volume One (79) 185(1) [0 | 0 | 2]	16.8
LONE JUSTICE ► 1207 Pk:56 [0 | 0 | 2]	**1327**
Lone Justice (85) 56(1) [0 | 0 | 25]	703
Shelter (86) 65(2) [0 | 0 | 30]	625
Claudine LONGET ► 522 Pk:11 [0 | 3 | 4]	**5858**
Claudine (67) 11(3) [0 | 22 | 54]	3541
Love Is Blue (68) 29(2) [0 | 5 | 21]	1225
The Look Of Love (67) 33(1) [0 | 6 | 29]	979
Colours (69) 155(1) [0 | 0 | 7]	113

Act ► Highest Peak [Top10s|Top40s|Total]
Title (Yr) Peak(Wk) [T10 Wk|T40Wk|TotalWk] — **Score**

LOOKING GLASS ► 2080 Pk:113 [0|0|1] — 310
Looking Glass (72) 113(2) [0|0|18] — 310

LOOSE ENDS ► 1292 Pk:46 [0|0|3] — 1166
A Little Spice (85) 46(2) [0|0|19] — 500
The Real Chuckeeboo (88) 80(3) [0|0|15] — 339
The Zagora (87) 59(2) [0|0|14] — 327

Denise LOPEZ ► 3326 Pk:184 [0|0|1] — 26
Truth In Disguise (88) 184(1) [0|0|4] — 25.8

Trini LOPEZ ► 405 Pk:11 [0|6|13] — 8087
On The Move (64) 32(1) [0|2|33] — 1277
The Latin Album (64) 18(2) [0|11|24] — 1229
The Folk Album (65) 18(1) [0|9|23] — 1177
More Trini Lopez At PJ's (63) 11(2) [0|8|19] — 1165
Live At Basin St. East (64) 30(1) [0|7|22] — 784
The Love Album (65) 32(1) [0|3|19] — 736
Greatest Hits! (66) 47(2) [0|0|11] — 421
Trini (66) 54(1) [0|0|16] — 417
The Rhythm & Blues Album (65) 46(1) [0|0|12] — 403
The Sing-Along World Of Trini Lopez (65) 101(1) [0|0|10] — 174
The Second Latin Album (66) 110(1) [0|0|8] — 150
Trini Lopez In London (67) 114(1) [0|0|6] — 97.5
Trini Lopez - Now! (67) 162(1) [0|0|7] — 57.1

Jeff LORBER ► 994 Pk:68 [0|0|7] — 1962
Private Passion (86) 68(2) [0|0|26] — 524
Galaxian (81)-Jeff Lorber Fusion 77(1) [0|0|15] — 390
It's A Fact (82) 73(2) [0|0|13] — 283
Step By Step (85) 90(2) [0|0|16] — 271
Water Sign (79)-Jeff Lorber Fusion 119(1) [0|0|14] — 203
Wizard Island (80)-Jeff Lorber Fusion 123(1) [0|0|12] — 168
In The Heat Of The Night (84) 106(1) [0|0|7] — 123

LORDAN ► 2149 Pk:37 [0|1|1] — 281
B.L.T. (81)-Jack Bruce/Bill Lordan/Robin Trower [A] 37(1) [0|3|16] — 281

LORDS Of The NEW CHURCH ► 3059 Pk:158 [0|0|1] — 58
The Method To Our Madness (85) 158(1) [0|0|7] — 58.2

LORD SUTCH And HEAVY FRIENDS ► 2036 Pk:84 [0|0|1] — 335
Lord Sutch And Heavy Friends (70) 84(2) [0|0|13] — 335

Gloria LORING ► 2103 Pk:61 [0|0|1] — 300
Gloria Loring (86) 61(2) [0|0|14] — 300

--Los Angeles Philharmonic see: Mehta, Zubin

Los BRAVOS ► 2507 Pk:93 [0|0|1] — 158
Black Is Black (66) 93(1) [0|0|7] — 158

Los INDIOS TABAJARAS ► 1013 Pk:7 [1|1|2] — 1896
Maria Elena (63) 7(2) [2|11|31] — 1708
Always In My Heart (64) 85(1) [0|0|10] — 188

Los LOBOS ► 511 Pk:1 [1|1|4] — 6046
La Bamba (Soundtrack) (87) 1(2) [11|19|44] — 4269
How Will The Wolf Survive (84) 47(3) [0|0|34] — 943
By The Light Of The Moon (87) 47(2) [0|0|32] — 802
La Pistola Y El Corazon (88) 179(2) [0|0|4] — 31.5

LOUDNESS ► 1491 Pk:64 [0|0|3] — 827
Thunder In The East (85) 74(2) [0|0|24] — 475
Lightning Strikes (86) 64(2) [0|0|16] — 331
Hurricane Eyes (87) 190(1) [0|0|4] — 20.5

LOVE ► 1210 Pk:57 [0|0|7] — 1325
Love (66) 57(1) [0|0|18] — 499
Four Sail (69) 102(1) [0|0|12] — 322
Da Capo (67) 80(1) [0|0|11] — 266
Forever Changes (68) 154(2) [0|0|10] — 94.9

Act ► Highest Peak [Top10s|Top40s|Total]
Title (Yr) Peak(Wk) [T10 Wk|T40Wk|TotalWk] — **Score**

Revisited (70) 142(1) [0|0|7] — 75.3
Out Here (69) 176(1) [0|0|5] — 42.7
False Start (70) 184(2) [0|0|3] — 26.0

LOVE AND KISSES ► 1687 Pk:85 [0|0|2] — 595
How Much, How Much I Love You (78) 85(4) [0|0|17] — 377
Love And Kisses (77) 135(2) [0|0|14] — 218

LOVE AND MONEY ► 3108 Pk:175 [0|0|1] — 51
Strange Kind Of Love (89) 175(2) [0|0|7] — 51.2

LOVE AND ROCKETS ► 762 Pk:14 [0|1|3] — 3195
Love And Rockets (89) 14(1) [0|17|26] — 1984
Earth - Sun - Moon (87) 64(2) [0|0|28] — 653
Express (86) 72(2) [0|0|30] — 558

LOVE CHILDS AFRO CUBAN BLUES Band ► 3107 Pk:168 [0|0|1] — 51
Out Among 'Em (75) 168(2) [0|0|5] — 51.5

LOVERBOY ► 158 Pk:7 [2|4|6] — 21227
Get Lucky (81) 7(2) [14|51|122] — 9866
Loverboy (81) 13(2) [0|17|105] — 4338
Keep It Up (83) 7(5) [7|22|39] — 3349
Lovin' Every Minute Of It (85) 13(5) [0|22|44] — 3011
Wildside (87) 42(1) [0|0|21] — 657
Big Ones (89) 189(1) [0|0|1] — 5.9

Lyle LOVETT ► 1501 Pk:62 [0|0|2] — 805
Lyle Lovett And His Large Band (89) 62(1) [0|0|21] — 588
Pontiac (88) 117(1) [0|0|14] — 217

LOVE UNLIMITED ► 605 Pk:3 [1|1|4] — 4693
Under The Influence Of... (73) 3(2) [5|17|44] — 3858
In Heat (74) 85(1) [0|0|27] — 667
Love Unlimited (72) 151(1) [0|0|12] — 147
He's All I've Got (77) 192(1) [0|0|3] — 21.1

LOVE UNLIMITED ORCHESTRA ► 635 Pk:8 [1|2|5] — 4356
Rhapsody In White (74) 8(2) [3|11|25] — 2231
White Gold (74) 28(1) [0|2|27] — 1472
Music Maestro Please (76) 92(1) [0|0|15] — 273
Together Brothers (Soundtrack) (74) 96(1) [0|0|10] — 207
My Sweet Summer Suite (76) 123(2) [0|0|8] — 173

Lene LOVICH ► 2053 Pk:94 [0|0|3] — 327
Flex (80) 94(1) [0|0|8] — 173
Stateless (79) 137(2) [0|0|10] — 132
No Man's Land (83) 188(1) [0|0|4] — 21.8

LOVIN' SPOONFUL ► 342 Pk:3 [2|4|9] — 9888
The Best Of The Lovin' Spoonful (67) 3(2) [9|26|52] — 4907
Daydream (66) 10(1) [1|11|31] — 1900
Hums Of The Lovin' Spoonful (66) 14(2) [0|8|26] — 1525
Do You Believe In Magic (65) 32(1) [0|7|35] — 1170
What's Up, Tiger Lily? (Soundtrack) (66) 126(2) [0|0|9] — 148
Everything Playing (68) 118(2) [0|0|7] — 95.3
The Best Of The Lovin' Spoonful, Volume 2 (68) 156(1) [0|0|5] — 59.2
You're A Big Boy Now (Soundtrack) (67) 160(1) [0|0|5] — 57.4
The Best...Lovin' Spoonful (76) 183(1) [0|0|3] — 26.6

Nick LOWE ► 973 Pk:31 [0|1|4] — 2030
Labour Of Lust (79) 31(3) [0|7|22] — 1321
Nick The Knife (82) 50(2) [0|0|14] — 438
Pure Pop For Now People (78) 127(1) [0|0|10] — 188
The Abominable Showman (83) 129(2) [0|0|7] — 82.8

Nick LOWE And His COWBOY OUTFIT ► 2051 Pk:113 [0|0|2] — 328
Nick Lowe And His Cowboy Outfit (84) 113(1) [0|0|12] — 173

Act ► Highest Peak [Top10s|Top40s|Total]
Title (Yr) Peak(Wk) [T10 Wk|T40Wk|TotalWk] — **Score**

The Rose Of England (85) 119(3) [0|0|12] — 155

L.T.D. ► 400 Pk:18 [0|4|6] — 8221
Something To Love (77) 21(2) [0|14|34] — 2471
Togetherness (78) 18(1) [0|11|26] — 1929
Shine On (80) 28(1) [0|8|28] — 1409
Devotion (79) 29(2) [0|5|24] — 1159
Love To The World (76) 52(2) [0|0|30] — 940
Love Magic (81) 83(1) [0|0|12] — 313

L'TRIMM ► 2407 Pk:132 [0|0|1] — 184
Grab It! (88) 132(2) [0|0|16] — 184

Carrie LUCAS ► 2226 Pk:119 [0|0|4] — 244
Carrie Lucas In Danceland (79) 119(2) [0|0|10] — 158
Simply Carrie (77) 183(1) [0|0|5] — 41.4
Portrait Of Carrie (81) 185(1) [0|0|3] — 23.3
Still In Love (82) 180(1) [0|0|3] — 20.9

LULU ► 1134 Pk:24 [0|1|3] — 1514
To Sir With Love (67) 24(2) [0|10|20] — 1033
New Routes (70) 88(1) [0|0|14] — 327
Lulu (81) 126(1) [0|0|10] — 153

Ray LYNCH ► 3523 Pk:197 [0|0|1] — 9
No Blue Thing (89) 197(2) [0|0|2] — 9.4

Cheryl LYNN ► 939 Pk:23 [0|1|5] — 2184
Cheryl Lynn (78) 23(1) [0|6|30] — 1578
In The Night (81) 104(3) [0|0|13] — 288
Instant Love (82) 133(2) [0|0|20] — 242
In Love (80) 167(1) [0|0|4] — 39.3
Preppie (84) 161(1) [0|0|5] — 37.0

Loretta LYNN ► 1111 Pk:80 [0|0|10] — 1571
Coal Miner's Daughter (71) 81(1) [0|0|17] — 419
Don't Come Home A Drinkin' (67) 80(1) [0|0|20] — 412
I Wanna Be Free (71) 110(1) [0|0|7] — 166
One's On The Way (72) 109(1) [0|0|9] — 157
Wings Upon Your Horns (70) 146(2) [0|0|11] — 147
You Ain't Woman Enough (67) 140(1) [0|0|9] — 103
Your Squaw Is On The Warpath (69) 168(1) [0|0|5] — 69.9
Woman Of The World / To Make A Man (69) 148(1) [0|0|4] — 62.1
Back To The Country (75) 182(1) [0|0|2] — 18.5
Love Is The Foundation (73) 183(1) [0|0|2] — 17.0

Gloria LYNNE ► 1045 Pk:27 [0|1|3] — 1757
Gloria, Marty & Strings (63) 27(1) [0|10|22] — 1033
I Wish You Love (64) 43(1) [0|0|19] — 541
Soul Serenade (65) 82(1) [0|0|10] — 184

LYNYRD SKYNYRD ► 168 Pk:5 [3|8|11] — 20576
One More From The Road (76) 9(3) [4|15|43] — 3462
Street Survivors (77) 5(2) [5|15|34] — 3443
Second Helping (74) 12(2) [0|19|45] — 3205
Gold & Platinum (79) 12(2) [0|11|65] — 2678
Lynyrd Skynyrd (pronounced leh-nerd skin-nerd) (73) 27(2) [0|4|79] — 2368
Nuthin' Fancy (75) 9(2) [3|10|20] — 2261
Skynyrd's First And...Last (78) 15(2) [0|7|18] — 1312
Gimme Back My Bullets (76) 20(2) [0|5|16] — 1086
Legend (87) 41(2) [0|0|17] — 456
Southern By The Grace Of God/Lynyrd Skynyrd Tribute Tour 1987 (88) 68(2) [0|0|11] — 246
The Best Of The Rest (82) 171(5) [0|0|7] — 59.5

Johnny LYTLE ► 3299 Pk:141 [0|0|1] — 28
The Village Caller! (66) 141(2) [0|0|2] — 28.3

▶ Highest Peak [Top10s|Top40s|Total]
Title (Yr) Peak(Wk) [T10 Wk|T40Wk|TotalWk] Score

M

M ▶ 2493 Pk:79 [0|0|1] — 162
New York-London-Paris-Munich (79) 79(2) [0|0|8] — 162

Moms MABLEY ▶ 1375 Pk:48 [0|0|6] — 1003
Out On A Limb (64) 48(1) [0|0|24] — 663
Moms Wows (64) 118(1) [0|0|10] — 139
The Funny Sides Of Moms Mabley (64) 134(1) [0|0|5] — 68.1
Moms The Word (64) 128(2) [0|0|4] — 53.2
Now Hear This (65) 133(1) [0|0|3] — 42.7
The Youngest Teenager (69) 173(1) [0|0|3] — 36.5

Tony MacALPINE ▶ 2734 Pk:146 [0|0|1] — 108
Maximum Security (87) 146(2) [0|0|11] — 108

MAC Band ▶ 2409 Pk:109 [0|0|1] — 184
Mac Band (88)-Mac Band Featuring The McCampbell Brothers 109(2) [0|0|14] — 184

Ralph MacDONALD ▶ 1247 Pk:57 [0|0|4] — 1236
The Path (78) 57(1) [0|0|17] — 607
Sound Of A Drum (76) 114(1) [0|0|16] — 275
Counterpoint (79) 110(2) [0|0|10] — 194
Universal Rhythm (84) 108(2) [0|0|10] — 160

Mary MacGREGOR ▶ 1215 Pk:17 [0|1|1] — 1316
Torn Between Two Lovers (77) 17(1) [0|7|19] — 1316

MACHO ▶ 2180 Pk:101 [0|0|1] — 266
I'm A Man (78) 101(1) [0|0|14] — 266

Lonnie MACK ▶ 1983 Pk:103 [0|0|2] — 361
Strike Like Lightning (85) 130(2) [0|0|21] — 213
The Wham Of That Memphis Man! (63) 103(1) [0|0|9] — 148

MADAME X ▶ 3186 Pk:162 [0|0|1] — 43
Madame X (87) 162(2) [0|0|5] — 42.9

MADHOUSE ▶ 2503 Pk:107 [0|0|1] — 159
8 (87) 107(2) [0|0|11] — 159

MAD LADS ▶ 3366 Pk:180 [0|0|1] — 22
The Mad, Mad, Mad, Mad, Mad Lads (69) 180(2) [0|0|2] — 22.3

MADNESS ▶ 1237 Pk:41 [0|0|4] — 1259
Madness (83) 41(1) [0|0|29] — 918
Keep Moving (84) 109(1) [0|0|8] — 141
One Step Beyond (80) 128(1) [0|0|9] — 141
Absolutely (80) 146(2) [0|0|4] — 58.9

MADONNA ▶ 69 Pk:1 [5|6|6] — 38131
Like A Virgin (84) 1(3) [33|52|108] — 10496
True Blue (86) 1(5) [25|52|82] — 8991
Like A Prayer (89) 1(6) [16|31|77] — 8128
Madonna (83) 8(3) [5|36|168] — 6893
Who's That Girl (Soundtrack) (87) 7(2) [3|13|28] — 2038
You Can Dance (87) 14(1) [0|12|22] — 1585

MAD RIVER ▶ 3441 Pk:192 [0|0|1] — 16
Paradise Bar And Grill (69) 192(2) [0|0|2] — 16.0

MADURA ▶ 3449 Pk:186 [0|0|1] — 15
Madura (71) 186(1) [0|0|2] — 15.0

Cledus MAGGARD And The CITIZEN's BAND ▶ 2592 Pk:135 [0|0|1] — 137
The White Knight (76)-Cledus Maggard And The Citizen's Band 135(2) [0|0|8] — 137

MAGIC ORGAN ▶ 2660 Pk:135 [0|0|1] — 122
Street Fair (72) 135(2) [0|0|7] — 122

MAGNIFICENT MEN ▶ 2418 Pk:89 [0|0|2] — 182
The Magnificent Men "Live!" (67) 89(1) [0|0|9] — 162
The Magnificent Men (67) 171(1) [0|0|2] — 20.0

▶ Highest Peak [Top10s|Top40s|Total]
Title (Yr) Peak(Wk) [T10 Wk|T40Wk|TotalWk] Score

Taj MAHAL ▶ 1295 Pk:84 [0|0|9] — 1156
The Real Thing (71) 84(2) [0|0|13] — 345
Giant Step/De Ole Folks At Home (69) 85(2) [0|0|9] — 253
The Natch'l Blues (69) 160(1) [0|0|14] — 166
Music Fuh Ya (Musica Para Tu) (77) 134(1) [0|0|8] — 128
Music Keeps Me Together (75) 155(1) [0|0|7] — 83.6
Mo' Roots (74) 165(1) [0|0|6] — 61.4
Happy Just To Be Like I Am (72) 181(1) [0|0|6] — 51.3
Recycling The Blues & Other Related Stuff (72) 177(2) [0|0|4] — 37.8
Oooh So Good 'N Blues (73) 190(1) [0|0|5] — 28.8

George MAHARIS ▶ 2539 Pk:77 [0|0|1] — 150
Where Can You Go For A Broken Heart? (63) 77(1) [0|0|7] — 150

MAHOGANY RUSH ▶ 1211 Pk:74 [0|0|9] — 1324
Child Of The Novelty (74) 74(2) [0|0|15] — 359
Strange Universe (75) 84(1) [0|0|13] — 315
What's Next (80)-Frank Marino And Mahogany Rush 88(1) [0|0|9] — 213
Tales Of The Unexpected (79)-Frank Marino And Mahogany Rush 129(1) [0|0|10] — 169
Frank Marino & Mahogany Rush Live (78) 129(1) [0|0|11] — 144
Maxoom (75) 159(1) [0|0|4] — 51.3
Mahogany Rush IV (76) 175(1) [0|0|3] — 31.7
Juggernaut (82)-Frank Marino 185(1) [0|0|4] — 23.0
World Anthem (77) 184(2) [0|0|2] — 18.4

MAIN INGREDIENT ▶ 870 Pk:52 [0|0|9] — 2531
Euphrates River (74) 52(1) [0|0|31] — 1240
Bitter Sweet (72) 79(2) [0|0|27] — 526
Rolling Down A Mountainside (75) 90(2) [0|0|12] — 281
Afrodisiac (73) 132(1) [0|0|13] — 195
Shame On The World (75) 158(1) [0|0|8] — 108
Tasteful Soul (71) 146(1) [0|0|9] — 100
Black Seeds (71) 176(1) [0|0|5] — 47.7
Music Maximus (77) 177(1) [0|0|3] — 29.0
The Main Ingredient L.T.D. (70) 200(1) [0|0|1] — 5.4

Miriam MAKEBA ▶ 1477 Pk:74 [0|0|5] — 853
Pata Pata (67) 74(1) [0|0|22] — 467
The World Of Miriam Makeba (63) 86(1) [0|0|10] — 185
An Evening With Belafonte/Makeba (65)-Harry Belafonte & Miriam Makeba [A] 85(1) [0|0|11] — 113
The Voice Of Africa (64) 122(1) [0|0|4] — 57.7
Miriam Makeba In Concert! (67) 182(2) [0|0|4] — 30.9

MALICE ▶ 3235 Pk:177 [0|0|1] — 35
License To Kill (87) 177(2) [0|0|6] — 35.3

Yngwie MALMSTEEN ▶ 824 Pk:40 [0|1|5] — 2794
Rising Force (85) 60(3) [0|0|43] — 734
Marching Out (85)-Yngwie J. Malmsteen's Rising Force 52(2) [0|0|28] — 721
Odyssey (88)-Yngwie J. Malmsteen's Rising Force 40(2) [0|2|18] — 674
Trilogy (86) 44(2) [0|0|23] — 587
Trial By Fire: Live In Leningrad (89) 128(2) [0|0|8] — 78.4

MALO ▶ 787 Pk:14 [0|1|4] — 3043
Malo (72) 14(1) [0|14|31] — 2371
Dos (72) 62(1) [0|0|14] — 427
Evolution (73) 101(1) [0|0|11] — 224
Ascencion (74) 188(1) [0|0|3] — 21.7

MAMA CASS ▶ 1472 Pk:49 [0|0|5] — 856
Bubble Gum, Lemonade &....Something For Mama (69) 91(2) [0|0|14] — 355

▶ Highest Peak [Top10s|Top40s|Total]
Title (Yr) Peak(Wk) [T10 Wk|T40Wk|TotalWk] Score

Dream A Little Dream (68) 87(1) [0|0|10] — 268
Dave Mason & Cass Elliot (71)-Dave Mason & Cass Elliot [A] 49(2) [0|0|7] — 160
Make Your Own Kind Of Music (69) 169(1) [0|0|6] — 65.8
Mama's Big Ones (71) 194(1) [0|0|1] — 7.2

MAMAS & The PAPAS ▶ 104 Pk:1 [4|5|9] — 28671
If You Can Believe Your Eyes And Ears (66) 1(1) [20|34|105] — 7986
The Mamas & The Papas (66) 4(7) [13|32|76] — 6311
The Mamas & The Papas Deliver (67) 2(7) [15|25|55] — 6067
Farewell To The First Golden Era (67) 5(3) [11|18|65] — 4665
The Papas & The Mamas (68) 15(1) [0|11|34] — 2131
16 Of Their Greatest Hits (69) 61(1) [0|0|26] — 742
Golden Era, Vol. 2 (68) 53(1) [0|0|13] — 524
People Like Us (71) 84(2) [0|0|8] — 217
20 Golden Hits (73) 186(2) [0|0|4] — 27.0

MAMA'S BOYS ▶ 2697 Pk:151 [0|0|2] — 114
Power & Passion (85) 151(2) [0|0|6] — 64.3
Mama's Boys (84) 172(1) [0|0|8] — 49.6

Melissa MANCHESTER ▶ 355 Pk:12 [0|4|13] — 9466
Melissa (75) 12(1) [0|11|41] — 2971
Hey Ricky (82) 19(5) [0|8|39] — 1614
Better Days & Happy Endings (76) 24(2) [0|8|17] — 1216
Don't Cry Out Loud (78) 33(1) [0|3|27] — 1033
Greatest Hits (83) 43(3) [0|0|21] — 620
Help Is On The Way (76) 60(2) [0|0|13] — 474
Melissa Manchester (79) 63(1) [0|0|21] — 418
Singin' (77) 60(3) [0|0|11] — 384
For The Working Girl (80) 68(3) [0|0|11] — 371
Home To Myself (73) 156(2) [0|0|13] — 123
Emergency (83) 135(3) [0|0|9] — 123
Mathematics (85) 144(2) [0|0|6] — 62.7
Bright Eyes (74) 159(1) [0|0|5] — 58.4

MANCHILD ▶ 2982 Pk:154 [0|0|1] — 68
Power And Love (77) 154(1) [0|0|6] — 67.7

Henry MANCINI & Doc SEVERINSEN ▶ 1729 Pk:74 [0|0|2] — 550
Brass On Ivory (72)-Henry Mancini & Doc Severinsen With Orchestra and Chorus 74(2) [0|0|19] — 527
Brass, Ivory & Strings (73)-Henry Mancini & Doc Severinsen With Orchestra and Chorus 185(1) [0|0|3] — 22.4

Henry MANCINI and His Orchestra ▶ 151 Pk:5 [3|6|27] — 22072
The Pink Panther (Soundtrack) (64) 8(2) [2|42|88] — 5336
A Warm Shade Of Ivory (69) 5(1) [6|19|42] — 4446
Charade (Soundtrack) (63) 6(3) [8|18|42] — 3236
Dear Heart And Other Songs About Love (65)-Henry Mancini And His Orchestra And Chorus 11(1) [0|11|25] — 1504
Mancini Plays The Theme From Love Story (71)-Henry Mancini And His Orchestra And Chorus 26(2) [0|4|22] — 1384
The Best Of Mancini (64) 42(1) [0|0|35] — 1007
The Concert Sound Of Henry Mancini (64) 15(2) [0|7|19] — 882
The Great Race (Soundtrack) (65) 63(2) [0|0|22] — 592
The Latin Sound Of Henry Mancini (65) 46(1) [0|0|17] — 522
Six Hours Past Sunset (69) 91(1) [0|0|16] — 394
Mancini Country (70)-Henry Mancini And His Orchestra And Chorus 91(1) [0|0|17] — 349
Mancini '67 (67) 65(1) [0|0|13] — 315

<table>
<tr><th>▶ Highest Peak [Top10s|Top40s|Total]
Title (Yr) Peak(Wk) [T10 Wk|T40Wk|TotalWk]</th><th>Score</th></tr>
<tr><td>Henry MANCINI/Orchestra ▶ Continued</td><td></td></tr>
<tr><td>The Academy Award Songs (66)-Henry Mancini And His Orchestra And Chorus 74(2) [0|0|13]</td><td>314</td></tr>
<tr><td>Mancini Concert (71) 85(1) [0|0|11]</td><td>305</td></tr>
<tr><td>Theme From "Z" And Other Film Music (70) 111(2) [0|0|17]</td><td>303</td></tr>
<tr><td>Music Of Hawaii (66)-Henry Mancini And His Orchestra And Chorus 121(2) [0|0|19]</td><td>293</td></tr>
<tr><td>Big Screen - Little Screen (72) 109(1) [0|0|15]</td><td>285</td></tr>
<tr><td>Encore! More Of The Concert Sound Of Henry Mancini (67) 126(1) [0|0|12]</td><td>182</td></tr>
<tr><td>Mancini's Angels (77)-Henry Mancini 126(1) [0|0|8]</td><td>136</td></tr>
<tr><td>Symphonic Soul (76) 159(2) [0|0|6]</td><td>77.7</td></tr>
<tr><td>Arabesque (Soundtrack) (66) 142(2) [0|0|4]</td><td>60.1</td></tr>
<tr><td>A Legendary Performer (76)-Henry Mancini And His Orchestra And Chorus 161(2) [0|0|4]</td><td>54.9</td></tr>
<tr><td>What Did You Do In The War, Daddy? (Soundtrack) (66) 148(2) [0|0|2]</td><td>28.8</td></tr>
<tr><td>The Mancini Generation (72) 195(1) [0|0|5]</td><td>27.2</td></tr>
<tr><td>Two For The Road (Soundtrack) (67) 183(1) [0|0|3]</td><td>20.6</td></tr>
<tr><td>This Is Henry Mancini (70)-Henry Mancini And His Orchestra And Chorus 196(1) [0|0|2]</td><td>12.2</td></tr>
<tr><td>The Hollywood Musicals (87)-Johnny Mathis & Henry Mancini [A] 197(2) [0|0|2]</td><td>4.4</td></tr>
<tr><td>Harvey MANDEL ▶ 2793 Pk:169 [0|0|3]</td><td>99</td></tr>
<tr><td>Cristo Redentor (69) 169(2) [0|0|4]</td><td>55.2</td></tr>
<tr><td>Righteous (69) 187(1) [0|0|3]</td><td>27.6</td></tr>
<tr><td>The Snake (72) 198(2) [0|0|3]</td><td>15.8</td></tr>
<tr><td>Howie MANDEL ▶ 3046 Pk:148 [0|0|1]</td><td>60</td></tr>
<tr><td>Fits Like A Glove (86) 148(2) [0|0|6]</td><td>59.6</td></tr>
<tr><td>Steve MANDELL ▶ 1010 Pk:1 [1|1|1]</td><td>1902</td></tr>
<tr><td>Dueling Banjos (73)-Eric Weissberg & Steve Mandell [A] 1(3) [9|14|25]</td><td>1902</td></tr>
<tr><td>MANDRE ▶ 1962 Pk:64 [0|0|1]</td><td>371</td></tr>
<tr><td>Mandre (77) 64(1) [0|0|13]</td><td>371</td></tr>
<tr><td>Barbara MANDRELL ▶ 1331 Pk:86 [0|0|8]</td><td>1088</td></tr>
<tr><td>Barbara Mandrell Live (81) 86(2) [0|0|24]</td><td>576</td></tr>
<tr><td>Moods (79) 132(1) [0|0|9]</td><td>142</td></tr>
<tr><td>Meant For Each Other (84)-Barbara Mandrell & Lee Greenwood [A] 89(1) [0|0|13]</td><td>116</td></tr>
<tr><td>In Black And White (82) 153(2) [0|0|6]</td><td>58.5</td></tr>
<tr><td>Just For The Record (79) 166(2) [0|0|5]</td><td>57.3</td></tr>
<tr><td>Spun Gold (83) 140(1) [0|0|4]</td><td>50.5</td></tr>
<tr><td>Love Is Fair (80) 175(1) [0|0|6]</td><td>46.0</td></tr>
<tr><td>The Best Of Barbara Mandrell (79) 170(2) [0|0|4]</td><td>41.3</td></tr>
<tr><td>MANDRILL ▶ 672 Pk:28 [0|1|9]</td><td>4018</td></tr>
<tr><td>Composite Truth (73) 28(1) [0|8|30]</td><td>1394</td></tr>
<tr><td>Mandrill (71) 48(1) [0|0|22]</td><td>857</td></tr>
<tr><td>Mandrill Is (72) 56(2) [0|0|24]</td><td>747</td></tr>
<tr><td>Just Outside Of Town (73) 82(1) [0|0|15]</td><td>330</td></tr>
<tr><td>Solid (75) 92(1) [0|0|14]</td><td>330</td></tr>
<tr><td>We Are One (77) 124(1) [0|0|10]</td><td>167</td></tr>
<tr><td>Beast From The East (76) 143(2) [0|0|8]</td><td>111</td></tr>
<tr><td>New Worlds (79) 154(2) [0|0|5]</td><td>69.2</td></tr>
<tr><td>The Best Of Mandrill (75) 194(1) [0|0|2]</td><td>13.3</td></tr>
<tr><td>MANFRED MANN ▶ 1583 Pk:35 [0|1|3]</td><td>694</td></tr>
<tr><td>The Manfred Mann Album (64) 35(1) [0|4|18]</td><td>598</td></tr>
<tr><td>The Five Faces Of Manfred Mann (65) 141(2) [0|0|4]</td><td>52.2</td></tr>
<tr><td>The Mighty Quinn (68) 1) [0|0|5]</td><td>44.1</td></tr>
<tr><td>MANFRED MANN'S EARTH BAND ▶ 634 Pk:10 [1|2|10]</td><td>4400</td></tr>
<tr><td>The Roaring Silence (76) 10(2) [2|11|37]</td><td>2423</td></tr>
<tr><td>Somewhere In Afrika (84) 40(2) [0|2|21]</td><td>627</td></tr>
<tr><td>Chance (81) 87(2) [0|0|16]</td><td>391</td></tr>
<tr><td>Solar Fire (74) 96(2) [0|0|15]</td><td>281</td></tr>
</table>

<table>
<tr><th>▶ Highest Peak [Top10s|Top40s|Total]
Title (Yr) Peak(Wk) [T10 Wk|T40Wk|TotalWk]</th><th>Score</th></tr>
<tr><td>Nightingales & Bombers (75) 120(1) [0|0|10]</td><td>191</td></tr>
<tr><td>Angel Station (79) 144(1) [0|0|13]</td><td>172</td></tr>
<tr><td>Watch (78) 83(1) [0|0|6]</td><td>154</td></tr>
<tr><td>Manfred Mann's Earth Band (72) 138(2) [0|0|6]</td><td>103</td></tr>
<tr><td>The Good Earth (74) 157(2) [0|0|3]</td><td>46.5</td></tr>
<tr><td>Get Your Rocks Off (73) 196(1) [0|0|2]</td><td>11.4</td></tr>
<tr><td>Chuck MANGIONE ▶ 208 Pk:2 [2|4|17]</td><td>16569</td></tr>
<tr><td>Feels So Good (77) 2(2) [11|28|88]</td><td>7254</td></tr>
<tr><td>Children Of Sanchez (78) 14(2) [0|10|44]</td><td>2562</td></tr>
<tr><td>Fun And Games (80) 8(4) [5|11|23]</td><td>2095</td></tr>
<tr><td>An Evening Of Magic - Chuck Mangione Live At The Hollywood Bowl (79) 27(1) [0|6|23]</td><td>1318</td></tr>
<tr><td>Chase The Clouds Away (75) 47(1) [0|0|19]</td><td>722</td></tr>
<tr><td>Main Squeeze (76) 86(1) [0|0|24]</td><td>558</td></tr>
<tr><td>Tarantella (81) 55(2) [0|0|15]</td><td>519</td></tr>
<tr><td>Bellavia (75) 68(1) [0|0|15]</td><td>474</td></tr>
<tr><td>Encore/The Chuck Mangione Concerts (75) 102(1) [0|0|10]</td><td>199</td></tr>
<tr><td>Love Notes (82) 83(2) [0|0|10]</td><td>192</td></tr>
<tr><td>Friends & Love...A Chuck Mangione Concert (71) 116(1) [0|0|11]</td><td>190</td></tr>
<tr><td>The Best Of Chuck Mangione (78) 105(1) [0|0|6]</td><td>135</td></tr>
<tr><td>Land Of Make Believe (73) 157(1) [0|0|12]</td><td>123</td></tr>
<tr><td>Disguise (84) 148(2) [0|0|8]</td><td>80.9</td></tr>
<tr><td>Journey To A Rainbow (83) 154(1) [0|0|7]</td><td>70.5</td></tr>
<tr><td>The Chuck Mangione Quartet (72) 180(2) [0|0|6]</td><td>49.1</td></tr>
<tr><td>Together: A New Chuck Mangione Concert (71) 194(1) [0|0|4]</td><td>26.9</td></tr>
<tr><td>The MANHATTANS ▶ 529 Pk:16 [0|2|11]</td><td>5649</td></tr>
<tr><td>Manhattans (76) 16(1) [0|12|27]</td><td>2147</td></tr>
<tr><td>After Midnight (80) 24(2) [0|10|26]</td><td>1600</td></tr>
<tr><td>It Feels So Good (77) 68(1) [0|0|20]</td><td>652</td></tr>
<tr><td>There's No Good In Goodbye (78) 78(2) [0|0|12]</td><td>323</td></tr>
<tr><td>Black Tie (81) 86(3) [0|0|10]</td><td>255</td></tr>
<tr><td>Manhattans Greatest Hits (80) 87(2) [0|0|10]</td><td>233</td></tr>
<tr><td>Forever By Your Side (83) 104(1) [0|0|8]</td><td>138</td></tr>
<tr><td>There's No Me Without You (73) 150(1) [0|0|8]</td><td>103</td></tr>
<tr><td>Love Talk (79) 141(2) [0|0|7]</td><td>99.4</td></tr>
<tr><td>That's How Much I Love You (75) 160(1) [0|0|4]</td><td>52.0</td></tr>
<tr><td>Too Hot To Stop It (85) 171(2) [0|0|6]</td><td>46.0</td></tr>
<tr><td>MANHATTAN TRANSFER ▶ 450 Pk:22 [0|2|11]</td><td>7104</td></tr>
<tr><td>Mecca For Moderns (81) 22(4) [0|13|27]</td><td>2009</td></tr>
<tr><td>The Manhattan Transfer (75) 33(1) [0|4|38]</td><td>1609</td></tr>
<tr><td>Extensions (79) 55(1) [0|0|37]</td><td>895</td></tr>
<tr><td>Vocalese (85) 74(2) [0|0|40]</td><td>641</td></tr>
<tr><td>Bodies And Souls (83) 52(2) [0|0|27]</td><td>490</td></tr>
<tr><td>Coming Out (76) 48(2) [0|0|9]</td><td>430</td></tr>
<tr><td>Brasil (87) 96(1) [0|0|19]</td><td>368</td></tr>
<tr><td>Pastiche (78) 66(2) [0|0|10]</td><td>293</td></tr>
<tr><td>The Best Of Manhattan Transfer (81) 103(2) [0|0|11]</td><td>223</td></tr>
<tr><td>Bop Doo-Wop (85) 127(2) [0|0|11]</td><td>129</td></tr>
<tr><td>The Manhattan Transfer Live (87) 187(2) [0|0|3]</td><td>17.9</td></tr>
<tr><td>Barry MANILOW ▶ 53 Pk:1 [7|13|18]</td><td>43066</td></tr>
<tr><td>Barry Manilow Live (77) 1(1) [11|26|67]</td><td>6736</td></tr>
<tr><td>This One's For You (76) 6(2) [4|27|60]</td><td>5876</td></tr>
<tr><td>Even Now (78) 3(3) [7|28|58]</td><td>5474</td></tr>
<tr><td>Tryin' To Get The Feelin' (75) 5(2) [4|15|87]</td><td>5128</td></tr>
<tr><td>Greatest Hits (78) 7(1) [3|16|75]</td><td>3851</td></tr>
<tr><td>Barry Manilow II (74) 9(1) [2|11|58]</td><td>3088</td></tr>
<tr><td>One Voice (79) 9(3) [4|15|25]</td><td>2784</td></tr>
<tr><td>If I Should Love Again (81) 14(3) [0|11|25]</td><td>2058</td></tr>
</table>

<table>
<tr><th>▶ Highest Peak [Top10s|Top40s|Total]
Title (Yr) Peak(Wk) [T10 Wk|T40Wk|TotalWk]</th><th>Score</th></tr>
<tr><td>Barry Manilow I (75) 28(2) [0|6|51]</td><td>1772</td></tr>
<tr><td>Barry (80) 15(2) [0|9|20]</td><td>1599</td></tr>
<tr><td>Here Comes The Night (82) 32(4) [0|6|27]</td><td>998</td></tr>
<tr><td>Barry Manilow/Greatest Hits-Vol. II (83) 30(2) [0|7|19]</td><td>919</td></tr>
<tr><td>2:00 A.M. Paradise Cafe (84) 28(2) [0|6|20]</td><td>851</td></tr>
<tr><td>Manilow (85) 42(3) [0|0|24]</td><td>671</td></tr>
<tr><td>Swing Street (87) 70(1) [0|0|21]</td><td>540</td></tr>
<tr><td>Barry Manilow (89) 64(2) [0|0|16]</td><td>345</td></tr>
<tr><td>Oh, Julie! (82) 69(2) [0|0|9]</td><td>196</td></tr>
<tr><td>The Manilow Collection/Twenty Classic Hits (85) 100(2) [0|0|12]</td><td>180</td></tr>
<tr><td>Herbie MANN ▶ 454 Pk:20 [0|2|22]</td><td>7044</td></tr>
<tr><td>Memphis Underground (69) 20(1) [0|17|44]</td><td>3383</td></tr>
<tr><td>Discotheque (75) 27(2) [0|3|18]</td><td>997</td></tr>
<tr><td>Push Push (71) 119(1) [0|0|23]</td><td>515</td></tr>
<tr><td>Super Mann (79) 77(1) [0|0|13]</td><td>336</td></tr>
<tr><td>Waterbed (75) 75(2) [0|0|7]</td><td>257</td></tr>
<tr><td>London Underground (74) 109(1) [0|0|10]</td><td>200</td></tr>
<tr><td>Reggae (74) 141(2) [0|0|11]</td><td>156</td></tr>
<tr><td>Live At The Whisky A Go Go (69) 139(1) [0|0|10]</td><td>150</td></tr>
<tr><td>Herbie Mann Live At Newport (63) 104(1) [0|0|8]</td><td>145</td></tr>
<tr><td>Herbie Mann & Fire Island (77) 122(1) [0|0|7]</td><td>118</td></tr>
<tr><td>Bird In A Silver Cage (77) 132(2) [0|0|7]</td><td>117</td></tr>
<tr><td>Glory Of Love (68) 151(1) [0|0|12]</td><td>115</td></tr>
<tr><td>Turtle Bay (73) 146(1) [0|0|8]</td><td>114</td></tr>
<tr><td>Our Mann Flute (66) 139(1) [0|0|6]</td><td>91.9</td></tr>
<tr><td>The Evolution Of Mann (73) 172(1) [0|0|8]</td><td>71.4</td></tr>
<tr><td>Memphis Two-Step (71) 137(1) [0|0|3]</td><td>61.5</td></tr>
<tr><td>Hold On, I'm Comin' (73) 163(1) [0|0|6]</td><td>59.2</td></tr>
<tr><td>Brazil-Once Again (78) 165(1) [0|0|5]</td><td>57.3</td></tr>
<tr><td>Standing Ovation At Newport (65) 143(2) [0|0|3]</td><td>39.6</td></tr>
<tr><td>Stone Flute (70) 184(1) [0|0|3]</td><td>23.7</td></tr>
<tr><td>Surprises (76) 178(1) [0|0|2]</td><td>20.9</td></tr>
<tr><td>The Best Of Herbie Mann (70) 189(2) [0|0|2]</td><td>16.3</td></tr>
<tr><td>Johnny MANN Singers ▶ 1376 Pk:51 [0|0|3]</td><td>1002</td></tr>
<tr><td>We Can Fly! Up-Up And Away (67) 51(2) [0|0|23]</td><td>624</td></tr>
<tr><td>Invisible Tears (64) 77(2) [0|0|15]</td><td>294</td></tr>
<tr><td>Golden Folk Song Hits, Volume Two (63) 90(1) [0|0|4]</td><td>84.0</td></tr>
<tr><td>MANNHEIM STEAMROLLER ▶ 955 Pk:36 [0|1|4]</td><td>2122</td></tr>
<tr><td>A Fresh Aire Christmas (88) 36(3) [0|4|24]</td><td>1006</td></tr>
<tr><td>Mannheim Steamroller Christmas (84) 50(1) [0|0|39]</td><td>886</td></tr>
<tr><td>Classical Gas (87)-Mason Williams & Mannheim Steamroller [A] 118(1) [0|0|19]</td><td>136</td></tr>
<tr><td>Fresh Aire VI (86) 155(1) [0|0|14]</td><td>94.1</td></tr>
<tr><td>--Mann, Manfred see: Manfred Mann</td><td></td></tr>
<tr><td>MANTOVANI ▶ 330 Pk:23 [0|4|20]</td><td>10488</td></tr>
<tr><td>Mr. Music...Mantovani (66) 27(2) [0|7|35]</td><td>1396</td></tr>
<tr><td>The Incomparable Mantovani (64) 37(1) [0|3|43]</td><td>1218</td></tr>
<tr><td>Mantovani Magic (66) 23(1) [0|8|26]</td><td>1172</td></tr>
<tr><td>The Mantovani Sound - Big Hits From Broadway And Hollywood (65) 26(1) [0|8|31]</td><td>1039</td></tr>
<tr><td>Mantovani's Golden Hits (67) 53(2) [0|0|33]</td><td>747</td></tr>
<tr><td>The Mantovani Touch (68) 64(3) [0|0|25]</td><td>704</td></tr>
<tr><td>Mantovani/Manhattan (63) 51(1) [0|0|22]</td><td>621</td></tr>
<tr><td>Mantovani/Hollywood (67) 49(1) [0|0|22]</td><td>613</td></tr>
<tr><td>Mantovani Ole (65) 41(1) [0|0|21]</td><td>593</td></tr>
<tr><td>The Mantovani Scene (69) 73(1) [0|0|17]</td><td>584</td></tr>
<tr><td>Mantovani Today (70) 77(1) [0|0|24]</td><td>511</td></tr>
<tr><td>The World Of Mantovani (69) 92(1) [0|0|17]</td><td>359</td></tr>
</table>

► Highest Peak [Top10s | Top40s | Total]
Title (Yr) Peak(Wk) [T10 Wk | T40Wk | TotalWk] **Score**

MANTOVANI ► *Continued*
From Monty, With Love (71) 105(1) [0|0|15] 294
Annunzio Paolo Mantovani (72) 156(2) [0|0|12] 136
To Lovers Everywhere U.S.A. (71) 150(1) [0|0|9] 127
Mantovani...Memories (68) 143(2) [0|0|7] 113
Mantovani/Tango (68) 148(2) [0|0|7] 108
Folk Songs Around The World (64) 135(1) [0|0|6] 73.6
Kismet (64) 134(1) [0|0|3] 42.4
Mantovani In Concert (70) 167(1) [0|0|3] 38.3

MANTRONIX ► 2533 Pk:108 [0|0|1] 152
In Full Effect (88) 108(2) [0|0|8] 152

Phil MANZANERA ► 3319 Pk:176 [0|0|1] 26
K-Scope (79) 176(1) [0|0|3] 26.3

Ray MANZAREK ► 2832 Pk:150 [0|0|1] 90
The Whole Thing Started With Rock & Roll And Now It's Out Of Control (75) 150(1) [0|0|6] 90.2

Little Peggy MARCH ► 3183 Pk:139 [0|0|1] 43
I Will Follow Him (63) 139(1) [0|0|3] 43.0

Benny MARDONES ► 1760 Pk:65 [0|0|1] 511
Never Run Never Hide (80) 65(1) [0|0|24] 511

Teena MARIE ► 491 Pk:23 [0|3|8] 6330
It Must Be Magic (81) 23(1) [0|9|25] 1680
Irons In The Fire (80) 38(3) [0|3|29] 1335
Starchild (84) 31(2) [0|9|35] 1315
Lady T (80) 45(1) [0|0|23] 706
Wild And Peaceful (79) 94(2) [0|0|20] 455
Robbery (83) 119(1) [0|0|24] 317
Naked To The World (88) 65(2) [0|0|13] 311
Emerald City (86) 81(2) [0|0|11] 212

MARILLION ► 1251 Pk:47 [0|0|4] 1229
Misplaced Childhood (85) 47(2) [0|0|35] 780
Brief Encounter (86) 67(2) [0|0|10] 227
Clutching At Straws (87) 103(2) [0|0|11] 171
Script For A Jester's Tear (83) 175(1) [0|0|7] 51.2

MARK-ALMOND ► 1151 Pk:73 [0|0|6] 1463
Mark-Almond 73 (73) 73(1) [0|0|14] 358
Mark-Almond II (72) 87(2) [0|0|16] 341
Rising (72) 103(1) [0|0|14] 283
To The Heart (76) 112(2) [0|0|14] 234
Mark-Almond (71) 154(2) [0|0|15] 188
The Best Of Mark-Almond (73) 177(2) [0|0|7] 58.4

The MARKETTS ► 1574 Pk:37 [0|1|2] 705
Out Of Limits! (64) 37(1) [0|2|14] 451
The Batman Theme (66) 82(1) [0|0|12] 255

The MAR-KEYS ► 3148 Pk:98 [0|0|1] 46
Back To Back (67)-The Mar-Keys/Booker T. & The MG's [A] 98(2) [0|0|4] 46.4

Pigmeat MARKHAM ► 2363 Pk:109 [0|0|1] 194
Here Come The Judge (68) 109(1) [0|0|9] 194

Markie, Biz see: BIZ MARKIE

Bob MARLEY And The WAILERS ► 331 Pk:8 [1|2|14] 10462
Rastaman Vibration (76) 8(2) [4|14|22] 2535
Legend (84) 54(2) [0|0|113] 2209
Exodus (77) 20(5) [0|11|24] 1910
Uprising (80) 45(1) [0|0|23] 962
Kaya (78) 50(2) [0|0|17] 628
Natty Dread (75) 92(2) [0|0|28] 508
Confrontation (83) 55(1) [0|0|15] 394
Survival (79) 70(1) [0|0|14] 374
Babylon By Bus (78) 102(2) [0|0|16] 368
Live! (76) 90(1) [0|0|9] 244
Chances Are (81)-Bob Marley 117(1) [0|0|6] 118
Rebel Music (86) 140(1) [0|0|9] 81.1

► Highest Peak [Top10s | Top40s | Total]
Title (Yr) Peak(Wk) [T10 Wk | T40Wk | TotalWk] **Score**

Burnin' (75)-The Wailers(2) 151(2) [0|0|6] 78.0
Catch A Fire (75)-The Wailers(2) 171(1) [0|0|5] 52.4

Ziggy MARLEY & The MELODY MAKERS ► 769 Pk:23 [0|2|2] 3140
Conscious Party (88)-Ziggy Marley And The Melody Makers 23(1) [0|16|42] 2220
One Bright Day (89)-Ziggy Marley And The Melody Makers 26(2) [0|8|18] 920

MARLEY MARL ► 3126 Pk:163 [0|0|1] 49
In Control Volume I (88) 163(2) [0|0|5] 49.0

The MARMALADE ► 2042 Pk:71 [0|0|1] 332
Reflections Of My Life (70) 71(2) [0|0|13] 332

Neville MARRINER ► 1190 Pk:56 [0|0|1] 1365
Amadeus (Soundtrack) (84) 56(2) [0|0|78] 1365

Branford MARSALIS ► 3079 Pk:164 [0|0|1] 55
Scenes In The City (84) 164(2) [0|0|7] 55.1

Wynton MARSALIS ► 1213 Pk:90 [0|0|6] 1317
Hot House Flowers (84) 90(2) [0|0|39] 654
Think Of One (83) 102(1) [0|0|29] 422
Black Codes (From The Underground) (85) 118(2) [0|0|10] 128
Wynton Marsalis (82) 165(1) [0|0|5] 48.4
Marsalis Standard Time: Vol. 1 (87) 153(1) [0|0|5] 45.4
J Mood (86) 185(2) [0|0|4] 20.3

MARSHALL TUCKER Band ► 271 Pk:15 [0|8|12] 13081
Carolina Dreams (77) 23(1) [0|15|36] 2565
Searchin' For A Rainbow (75) 15(2) [0|8|34] 1767
The Marshall Tucker Band (73) 29(1) [0|8|40] 1606
A New Life (74) 37(1) [0|3|28] 1208
Long Hard Ride (76) 32(2) [0|5|20] 1128
Together Forever (78) 22(1) [0|5|16] 1067
Running Like The Wind (79) 30(1) [0|3|22] 1037
Greatest Hits (78) 67(3) [0|0|32] 852
Tenth (80) 32(1) [0|5|15] 749
Where We All Belong (74) 54(2) [0|0|14] 558
Dedicated (81) 53(2) [0|0|12] 426
Tuckerized (82) 95(2) [0|0|7] 118

M + M ► 2864 Pk:163 [0|0|3] 86
Mystery Walk (84) 163(2) [0|0|4] 36.7
Danseparc (83)-Martha And The Muffins 184(1) [0|0|4] 25.1
Metro Music (80)-Martha And The Muffins 186(1) [0|0|3] 23.8

MARTHA & The VANDELLAS ► 1421 Pk:50 [0|0|7] 937
Greatest Hits (66) 50(1) [0|0|15] 418
Watchout! (67) 116(1) [0|0|8] 157
Black Magic (72)-Martha Reeves & The Vandellas 146(2) [0|0|7] 108
Ridin' High (68)-Martha Reeves & The Vandellas 167(1) [0|0|8] 74.7
Heat Wave (63) 125(1) [0|0|5] 74.4
Martha & The Vandellas Live! (67) 140(1) [0|0|5] 65.6
Dance Party (65) 139(1) [0|0|3] 39.3

MARTIKA ► 970 Pk:15 [0|1|1] 2041
Martika (89) 15(1) [0|12|39] 2041

Bobbi MARTIN ► 2670 Pk:127 [0|0|2] 120
Don't Forget I Still Love You (65) 127(1) [0|0|5] 69.9
For The Love Of Him (70) 176(1) [0|0|5] 49.9

Dean MARTIN ► 108 Pk:2 [2|11|21] 28226
Everybody Loves Somebody (64) 2(4) [16|32|49] 5739
Dean Martin's Greatest Hits! Vol. 1 (68) 26(1) [0|12|39] 2602

► Highest Peak [Top10s | Top40s | Total]
Title (Yr) Peak(Wk) [T10 Wk | T40Wk | TotalWk] **Score**

Welcome To My World (67) 20(1) [0|16|48] 2465
Gentle On My Mind (69) 14(1) [0|9|25] 2434
(Remember Me) I'm The One Who Loves You (65) 12(1) [0|16|39] 2362
Houston (65) 11(1) [0|17|34] 2347
The Door Is Still Open To My Heart (64) 9(3) [3|15|30] 1884
Dean Martin Hits Again (65) 13(1) [0|9|29] 1425
Dream With Dean (64) 15(2) [0|9|31] 1384
The Dean Martin TV Show (66) 34(1) [0|3|31] 1026
Somewhere There's A Someone (66) 40(2) [0|2|27] 864
The Hit Sound Of Dean Martin (66) 50(1) [0|0|25] 802
Happiness Is Dean Martin (67) 46(1) [0|0|25] 700
Dean Martin's Greatest Hits! Vol. 2 (68) 83(1) [0|0|21] 621
I Take A Lot Of Pride In What I Am (69) 90(2) [0|0|17] 488
For The Good Times (71) 113(1) [0|0|15] 316
The Best Of Dean Martin (66) 95(2) [0|0|13] 255
My Woman, My Woman, My Wife (70) 97(2) [0|0|12] 239
The Best Of Dean Martin, Vol. 2 (69) 145(1) [0|0|7] 126
Dino (72) 117(2) [0|0|4] 88.8
The Silencers (Soundtrack) (66) 108(1) [0|0|3] 59.4

Eric MARTIN Band ► 3507 Pk:191 [0|0|1] 11
Sucker For A Pretty Face (83) 191(1) [0|0|2] 10.8

George MARTIN & His Orchestra ► 2522 Pk:111 [0|0|1] 153
Off The Beatle Track (64)-George Martin 111(2) [0|0|10] 153

Marilyn MARTIN ► 2252 Pk:72 [0|0|1] 232
Marilyn Martin (86) 72(2) [0|0|11] 232

Moon MARTIN ► 1816 Pk:80 [0|0|2] 470
Street Fever (80) 138(3) [0|0|15] 236
Escape From Domination (79) 80(1) [0|0|11] 234

Steve MARTIN ► 361 Pk:2 [2|3|4] 9151
A Wild And Crazy Guy (78) 2(6) [10|18|26] 4946
Let's Get Small (77) 10(2) [2|12|68] 3035
Comedy Is Not Pretty! (79) 25(3) [0|5|22] 1104
The Steve Martin Brothers (81) 135(2) [0|0|4] 66.6

Nancy MARTINEZ ► 3414 Pk:178 [0|0|1] 18
Not Just The Girl Next Door (87) 178(1) [0|0|3] 17.9

Al MARTINO ► 225 Pk:8 [2|6|22] 15663
Spanish Eyes (66) 8(2) [2|26|73] 3743
Painted, Tainted Rose (63) 9(1) [3|21|44] 2792
My Cherie (65) 19(1) [0|8|47] 1791
Living A Lie (64) 13(1) [0|10|28] 1616
I Love You More And More Every Day/ Tears And Roses (64) 31(1) [0|6|25] 902
Daddy's Little Girl (67) 23(1) [0|4|21] 858
Mary In The Morning (67) 63(1) [0|0|21] 593
Love Is Blue (68) 56(1) [0|0|17] 548
We Could (65) 41(1) [0|0|15] 462
Somebody Else Is Taking My Place (65) 42(1) [0|0|12] 421
This Is Love (66) 57(1) [0|0|13] 421
The Italian Voice Of Al Martino (64) 57(1) [0|0|15] 381
The Best Of Al Martino (68) 108(2) [0|0|16] 295
This Love For You (67) 99(1) [0|0|12] 234
Love Theme From "The Godfather" (72) 138(2) [0|0|10] 159
To The Door Of The Sun (75) 129(2) [0|0|8] 132
Think I'll Go Somewhere And Cry Myself To Sleep (66) 116(1) [0|0|6] 105
This Is Al Martino (68) 129(1) [0|0|4] 66.5
My Heart Sings (70) 172(2) [0|0|6] 56.1

▶ Highest Peak [Top10s | Top40s | Total]
Title (Yr) Peak(Wk) [T10 Wk | T40Wk | TotalWk] Score

Al MARTINO ▶ *Continued*

Can't Help Falling In Love (70) 184(1) [0|0|5] 44.5
Sausalito (69) 189(2) [0|0|4] 31.5
Jean (69) 196(1) [0|0|2] 12.5

The MARVELETTES ▶ 1832 Pk:84 [0|0|2] 456

Greatest Hits (66) 84(2) [0|0|16] 342
The Marvelettes (67) 129(1) [0|0|8] 114

Groucho MARX ▶ 2312 Pk:155 [0|0|2] 212

An Evening With Groucho (72) 160(1) [0|0|15] 164
The Marx Bros. (The Original Voice Tracks From Their Greatest Movies) (69) 155(1) [0|0|3] 47.7

Richard MARX ▶ 247 Pk:1 [2|2|2] 14470

Repeat Offender (89) 1(1) [12|47|66] 7671
Richard Marx (87) 8(2) [4|63|86] 6799

MARY JANE GIRLS ▶ 829 Pk:18 [0|1|2] 2765

Only Four You (85) 18(2) [0|11|38] 1841
Mary Jane Girls (83) 56(1) [0|0|41] 924

Carolyne MAS ▶ 3310 Pk:172 [0|0|1] 27

Carolyne Mas (79) 172(1) [0|0|3] 27.4

Hugh MASEKELA ▶ 884 Pk:17 [0|1|7] 2471

The Promise Of A Future (68) 17(1) [0|10|22] 1681
Herb Alpert/Hugh Masekela (78)-Herb Alpert/Hugh Masekela [A] 65(1) [0|0|19] 281
Hugh Masekela Is Alive And Well At The Whisky (68) 90(2) [0|0|10] 179
The Boy's Doin' It (75) 132(1) [0|0|9] 137
Hugh Masekela's Latest (67) 151(2) [0|0|10] 114
I Am Not Afraid (74) 149(1) [0|0|4] 64.3
Masekela (69) 195(2) [0|0|2] 14.6

MASKED MARAUDERS ▶ 2218 Pk:114 [0|0|1] 247

The Masked Marauders (70) 114(2) [0|0|12] 247

Barbara MASON ▶ 2007 Pk:95 [0|0|3] 349

Give Me Your Love (73) 95(1) [0|0|12] 216
Yes, I'm Ready (65) 129(1) [0|0|8] 115
Love's The Thing (75) 187(2) [0|0|2] 17.5

Dave MASON ▶ 358 Pk:22 [0|4|14] 9253

Alone Together (70) 22(2) [0|10|25] 1830
Let It Flow (77) 37(1) [0|2|49] 1636
Dave Mason (74) 25(2) [0|4|25] 1279
Split Coconut (75) 27(2) [0|6|17] 906
It's Like You Never Left (73) 50(2) [0|0|28] 881
Mariposa Do Ora (78) 41(1) [0|0|19] 815
Headkeeper (72) 51(1) [0|0|14] 617
Certified Live (76) 78(1) [0|0|17] 517
Old Crest On A New Wave (80) 74(2) [0|0|10] 248
Dave Mason Is Alive! (73) 116(1) [0|0|11] 199
Dave Mason & Cass Elliot (71)-Dave Mason & Cass Elliot [A] 49(2) [0|0|7] 160
The Best Of Dave Mason (74) 183(1) [0|0|9] 72.6
Dave Mason At His Best (75) 133(2) [0|0|3] 60.5
The Very Best Of Dave Mason (78) 179(1) [0|0|4] 34.0

Harvey MASON ▶ 2578 Pk:149 [0|0|2] 141

Groovin' You (79) 149(1) [0|0|8] 117
M.V.P. (81) 186(1) [0|0|3] 24.4

Jackie MASON ▶ 2796 Pk:146 [0|0|1] 98

The World According To Me (88) 146(1) [0|0|9] 98.4

Nick MASON ▶ 3071 Pk:154 [0|0|2] 56

Nick Mason's Fictitious Sports (81) 170(2) [0|0|3] 34.6
Profiles (85)-Nick Mason & Rick Fenn [A] 154(2) [0|0|5] 21.8

MASON PROFFIT ▶ 2342 Pk:177 [0|0|3] 202

Last Night I Had The Strangest Dream (71) 186(1) [0|0|14] 107
Movin' Toward Happiness (71) 177(1) [0|0|8] 70.0

▶ Highest Peak [Top10s | Top40s | Total]
Title (Yr) Peak(Wk) [T10 Wk | T40Wk | TotalWk] Score

Bareback Rider (73) 198(2) [0|0|5] 25.0

MASS PRODUCTION ▶ 1248 Pk:43 [0|0|5] 1235

In The Purest Form (79) 43(1) [0|0|17] 659
Believe (77) 83(1) [0|0|9] 224
Massterpiece (80) 133(1) [0|0|9] 145
Welcome To Our World (77) 142(1) [0|0|10] 141
Turn Up The Music (81) 166(2) [0|0|6] 66.3

Mireille MATHIEU ▶ 2438 Pk:118 [0|0|1] 176

Mireille Mathieu (69) 118(1) [0|0|8] 176

Johnny MATHIS ▶ 135 Pk:9 [2|10|44] 23738

The Shadow Of Your Smile (66) 9(1) [2|16|45] 2530
You Light Up My Life (78) 9(3) [3|11|24] 2385
Tender Is The Night (64) 13(3) [0|16|28] 1962
Love Is Blue (68) 26(1) [0|6|40] 1700
Johnny (63) 20(2) [0|9|27] 1457
Romantically (63) 23(1) [0|7|27] 1146
Raindrops Keep Fallin' On My Head (70) 38(1) [0|2|26] 968
Love Theme From "Romeo And Juliet" (69) 52(3) [0|0|24] 967
Those Were The Days (68) 60(1) [0|0|21] 825
Love Story (71) 47(1) [0|0|18] 794
That's What Friends Are For (78)-Johnny Mathis & Deniece Williams [A] 19(2) [0|8|16] 614
This Is Love (64) 40(1) [0|1|20] 610
So Nice (66) 50(1) [0|0|18] 589
I'll Search My Heart And Other Great Hits (64) 35(1) [0|4|16] 535
The Sweetheart Tree (65) 71(1) [0|0|26] 533
Up, Up And Away (67) 60(2) [0|0|20] 529
I Only Have Eyes For You (76) 79(1) [0|0|15] 483
Feelings (75) 97(2) [0|0|21] 447
Song Sung Blue (72) 83(2) [0|0|18] 437
The First Time Ever (I Saw Your Face) (72) 71(1) [0|0|15] 432
I'm Coming Home (73) 115(1) [0|0|22] 342
Love Is Everything (65) 52(1) [0|0|11] 336
When Will I See You Again (75) 99(1) [0|0|13] 311
Close To You (70) 61(1) [0|0|9] 304
You've Got A Friend (71) 80(1) [0|0|10] 288
Me And Mrs. Jones (73) 83(1) [0|0|14] 279
Johnny Mathis' All-Time Greatest Hits (72) 141(1) [0|0|15] 224
Johnny Mathis Sings (67) 103(1) [0|0|11] 201
The Wonderful World Of Make Believe (64) 75(1) [0|0|10] 185
The Great Years (64) 88(1) [0|0|10] 160
A Special Part Of Me (84) 157(1) [0|0|19] 156
The Heart Of A Woman (74) 139(2) [0|0|7] 135
Killing Me Softly With Her Song (73) 120(2) [0|0|7] 127
The Best Days Of My Life (79) 122(2) [0|0|7] 120
Johnny Mathis In Person (72) 128(1) [0|0|7] 116
Friends In Love (82) 147(1) [0|0|9] 92.2
Mathis Is... (77) 139(2) [0|0|5] 87.2
The Best Of Johnny Mathis 1975-1980 (80) 140(2) [0|0|7] 83.9
Johnny Mathis Sings The Music Of Bacharach & Kaempfert (71) 169(1) [0|0|7] 69.8
The Impossible Dream (69) 163(1) [0|0|4] 59.2
Different Kinda Different (80) 164(1) [0|0|5] 56.6
The First 25 Years-The Silver Anniversary Album (81) 173(2) [0|0|4] 41.6
People (69) 192(1) [0|0|2] 15.7
The Hollywood Musicals (87)-Johnny Mathis & Henry Mancini [A] 197(2) [0|0|2] 4.4

David MATTHEWS ▶ 2937 Pk:169 [0|0|1] 74

Dune (77) 169(1) [0|0|7] 73.9

▶ Highest Peak [Top10s | Top40s | Total]
Title (Yr) Peak(Wk) [T10 Wk | T40Wk | TotalWk] Score

Ian MATTHEWS ▶ 1367 Pk:72 [0|0|4] 1019

Later That Same Year (71)-Matthews' Southern Comfort 72(1) [0|0|15] 477
Stealin' Home (78) 80(1) [0|0|24] 467
Valley Hi (73) 181(2) [0|0|7] 58.1
Tigers Will Survive (72) 196(1) [0|0|3] 17.8

Paul MAURIAT And His Orchestra ▶ 371 Pk:1 [1|1|9] 8880

Blooming Hits (67) 1(5) [14|25|50] 7252
Doing My Thing (69) 77(1) [0|0|18] 542
Mauriat Magic (68) 71(1) [0|0|18] 405
More Mauriat (68)-Paul Mauriat 122(1) [0|0|22] 355
Prevailing Airs (68) 142(2) [0|0|7] 124
The Soul Of Paul Mauriat (69)-Paul Mauriat 157(1) [0|0|8] 118
El Condor Pasa (71)-Paul Mauriat 180(2) [0|0|3] 31.4
L.O.V.E. (69) 186(2) [0|0|3] 27.1
Gone Is Love (70)-Paul Mauriat 184(2) [0|0|3] 25.4

AKA The MAX DEMIAN Band ▶ 3055 Pk:159 [0|0|1] 59

Take It To The Max (79) 159(2) [0|0|5] 58.8

MAX Q ▶ 3147 Pk:182 [0|0|1] 46

Max Q (89) 182(2) [0|0|8] 46.4

Robert MAXWELL ▶ 1252 Pk:17 [0|1|1] 1227

Shangri-La (64)-Robert Maxwell His Harp And Orchestra 17(1) [0|12|24] 1227

Brian MAY ▶ 2645 Pk:125 [0|0|1] 124

Star Fleet Project (83)-Brian May And Friends 125(1) [0|0|9] 124

John MAYALL ▶ 417 Pk:22 [0|3|16] 7682

The Turning Point (69) 32(2) [0|2|55] 2398
USA Union (70) 22(1) [0|5|22] 1167
Empty Rooms (70) 33(1) [0|4|19] 1034
Back To The Roots (71) 52(1) [0|0|15] 604
Blues From Laurel Canyon (69) 68(1) [0|0|17] 581
Jazz Blues Fusion (72) 64(2) [0|0|18] 573
Looking Back (69) 79(2) [0|0|12] 378
The Diary Of A Band (Volume 1 & 2) (70) 93(2) [0|0|11] 224
Moving On (72) 116(1) [0|0|11] 185
John Mayall-Live In Europe (71) 146(1) [0|0|8] 105
The Blues Alone (68) 128(1) [0|0|5] 91.1
Ten Years Are Gone (73) 157(1) [0|0|7] 81.9
Thru The Years (71) 164(1) [0|0|7] 78.7
New Year, New Band, New Company (75) 140(1) [0|0|4] 70.0
Down The Line (73) 158(1) [0|0|7] 61.8
Memories (71) 179(2) [0|0|5] 48.7

John MAYALL'S BLUESBREAKERS ▶ 1371 Pk:59 [0|0|2] 1011

Bare Wires (68) 59(2) [0|0|19] 826
Crusade (68) 135(1) [0|0|14] 185

Curtis MAYFIELD ▶ 200 Pk:1 [1|6|15] 17360

Superfly (Soundtrack) (72) 1(4) [11|30|46] 6533
Curtis (70) 19(1) [0|18|49] 3351
Curtis/Live! (71) 21(1) [0|11|38] 2481
Back To The World (73) 16(2) [0|10|26] 1745
Roots (71) 40(1) [0|1|19] 931
Sweet Exorcist (74) 39(1) [0|1|22] 844
Heartbeat (79) 42(2) [0|0|16] 615
Got To Find A Way (74) 76(2) [0|0|7] 201
There's No Place Like America Today (75) 120(1) [0|0|11] 196
Something To Believe In (80) 128(2) [0|0|10] 156
Curtis In Chicago (73) 135(1) [0|0|10] 128
Give, Get, Take And Have (76) 171(1) [0|0|8] 85.6

▶ Highest Peak [Top10s | Top40s | Total] Title (Yr) Peak(Wk) [T10 Wk | T40Wk | TotalWk]	Score
Curtis MAYFIELD ▶ *Continued*	
Curtis Mayfield/His Early Years With The Impressions (73) 180(2) [0|0|6]	45.9
Never Say You Can't Survive (77) 173(1) [0|0|3]	31.7
The Right Combination (80)-Linda Clifford & Curtis Mayfield [A] 180(2) [0|0|4]	16.6
Lyle MAYS ▶ 1948 Pk:50 [0|0|1]	**377**
As Falls Wichita, So Falls Wichita Falls (81)-Pat Metheny & Lyle Mays [A] 50(1) [0|0|21]	377
MAZARATI ▶ 2821 Pk:133 [0|0|1]	**92**
Mazarati (86) 133(1) [0|0|8]	92.0
MAZE Featuring Frankie BEVERLY ▶ 401 Pk:25 [0|6|9]	**8199**
Maze Featuring Frankie Beverly (77) 52(2) [0|0|45]	1398
Live In New Orleans (81) 34(2) [0|4|27]	1181
Golden Time Of Day (78) 27(1) [0|5|22]	1075
Joy And Pain (80) 31(1) [0|4|23]	1061
We Are One (83) 25(3) [0|5|26]	1026
Inspiration (79) 33(1) [0|3|22]	937
Can't Stop The Love (85) 45(2) [0|0|30]	695
Silky Soul (89) 37(2) [0|3|22]	670
Live In Los Angeles (86) 92(2) [0|0|11]	155
Letta MBULU ▶ 3402 Pk:192 [0|0|1]	**19**
There's Music In The Air (77) 192(1) [0|0|3]	19.1
MC5 ▶ 1241 Pk:30 [0|1|2]	**1254**
Kick Out The Jams (69) 30(2) [0|3|23]	1145
Back In The USA (70) 137(2) [0|0|7]	109
MC HAMMER ▶ 774 Pk:30 [0|1|1]	**3114**
Let's Get It Started (88) 30(1) [0|23|80]	3114
MC LYTE ▶ 2152 Pk:86 [0|0|1]	**280**
Eyes On This (89) 86(2) [0|0|20]	280
MC SHY D ▶ 3541 Pk:197 [0|0|1]	**5**
Got To Be Tough (87)-M.C. Shy D 197(1) [0|0|1]	4.5
--McAuley Schenker Group see: Schenker, Michael	
C.W. McCALL ▶ 1028 Pk:12 [0|1|3]	**1850**
Black Bear Road (75) 12(2) [0|8|19]	1637
Wolf Creek Pass (75) 143(2) [0|0|9]	145
Wilderness (76) 143(2) [0|0|4]	67.7
David McCALLUM ▶ 1200 Pk:27 [0|1|2]	**1344**
Music - A Part Of Me (66) 27(1) [0|8|24]	1095
Music: A Bit More Of Me (66) 79(1) [0|0|12]	249
Les McCANN ▶ 1977 Pk:141 [0|0|5]	**363**
Much Les (69) 169(1) [0|0|10]	130
Invitation To Openness (72) 141(1) [0|0|6]	87.1
Another Beginning (75) 166(2) [0|0|4]	49.6
Talk To The People (72) 181(2) [0|0|6]	49.5
Hustle To Survive (75) 161(1) [0|0|4]	47.4
Les McCANN & Eddie HARRIS ▶ 751 Pk:29 [0|1|2]	**3249**
Swiss Movement (69) 29(1) [0|5|38]	1948
Second Movement (71) 41(1) [0|0|27]	1301
Peter McCANN ▶ 2125 Pk:82 [0|0|1]	**289**
Peter McCann (77) 82(2) [0|0|12]	289
Paul McCARTNEY ▶ 177 Pk:1 [3|7|9]	**19611**
McCartney (70) 1(3) [13|20|47]	7209
Tug Of War (82) 1(3) [9|18|29]	3951
McCartney II (80) 3(5) [7|12|19]	2823
Pipes Of Peace (83) 15(1) [0|13|24]	1698
Flowers In The Dirt (89) 21(3) [0|6|49]	1694
Give My Regards To Broad Street (84) 21(2) [0|10|18]	1029
Press To Play (86) 30(2) [0|5|22]	710
All The Best! (87) 62(3) [0|0|17]	456

▶ Highest Peak [Top10s | Top40s | Total] Title (Yr) Peak(Wk) [T10 Wk | T40Wk | TotalWk]	Score
The McCartney Interview (81) 158(2) [0|0|3]	42.0
Paul & Linda McCARTNEY ▶ 377 Pk:2 [1|1|1]	**8807**
Ram (71) 2(2) [24|28|37]	8807
Paul McCARTNEY & WINGS/WINGS ▶ 41 Pk:1 [8|9|9]	**46521**
Band On The Run (73)-Paul McCartney And Wings 1(4) [32|40|116]	11152
Wings At The Speed Of Sound (76)-Wings 1(7) [21|27|51]	9726
Venus And Mars (75)-Wings 1(1) [8|17|77]	5972
Wings Over America (76)-Paul McCartney And Wings 1(1) [11|18|86]	5248
London Town (78)-Wings 2(6) [10|16|28]	4850
Red Rose Speedway (73)-Paul McCartney And Wings 1(3) [9|16|31]	4375
Back To The Egg (79)-Wings 8(2) [5|11|24]	2258
Wild Life (71)-Wings 10(2) [2|10|18]	1994
Wings Greatest (78)-Wings 29(1) [0|5|18]	946
Alton McCLAIN & DESTINY ▶ 1968 Pk:88 [0|0|1]	**368**
Alton McClain & Destiny (79) 88(2) [0|0|16]	368
Delbert McCLINTON ▶ 1299 Pk:34 [0|1|3]	**1146**
The Jealous Kind (80) 34(1) [0|4|28]	1011
Keeper Of The Flame (79) 146(2) [0|0|6]	77.8
Plain From The Heart (81) 181(1) [0|0|9]	56.5
Marilyn McCOO & Billy DAVIS JR. ▶ 929 Pk:30 [0|1|3]	**2222**
I Hope We Get To Love In Time (76) 30(1) [0|7|38]	1875
The Two Of Us (77) 57(1) [0|0|8]	257
Marilyn & Billy (78) 146(1) [0|0|6]	89.8
Gayle McCORMICK ▶ 3409 Pk:198 [0|0|1]	**19**
Gayle McCormick (71) 198(2) [0|0|3]	18.8
Charlie McCOY ▶ 1465 Pk:98 [0|0|3]	**869**
The Real McCoy (72) 98(2) [0|0|25]	569
Charlie McCoy (72) 120(1) [0|0|13]	236
Good Time Charlie (73) 155(1) [0|0|6]	64.2
Van McCOY ▶ 923 Pk:12 [0|1|5]	**2255**
Disco Baby (75)-Van McCoy & The Soul City Symphony 12(1) [0|9|23]	1701
Real McCoy (76) 106(1) [0|0|17]	303
The Disco Kid (75) 80(1) [0|0|7]	204
From Disco To Love (75) 181(1) [0|0|4]	34.1
The Hustle And Best Of Van McCoy (77) 193(1) [0|0|2]	13.2
The McCOYS ▶ 1711 Pk:44 [0|0|1]	**576**
Hang On Sloopy (65) 44(1) [0|0|19]	576
George McCRAE ▶ 1554 Pk:38 [0|1|2]	**724**
Rock Your Baby (74) 38(2) [0|2|15]	663
George McCrae (75) 152(1) [0|0|5]	60.6
Gwen McCRAE ▶ 2379 Pk:121 [0|0|1]	**191**
Rockin' Chair (75) 121(2) [0|0|10]	191
McCRARYS ▶ 2560 Pk:138 [0|0|1]	**147**
Loving Is Living (78) 138(2) [0|0|9]	147
Ian McCULLOCH ▶ 3527 Pk:179 [0|0|1]	**8**
Candleland (89) 179(1) [0|0|1]	8.0
Kathi McDONALD ▶ 2720 Pk:156 [0|0|1]	**111**
Insane Asylum (74) 156(1) [0|0|11]	111
Michael McDONALD ▶ 853 Pk:6 [1|1|2]	**2631**
If That's What It Takes (82) 6(6) [6|11|32]	2160
No Lookin' Back (85) 45(2) [0|0|15]	472
Brother Jack McDUFF ▶ 2024 Pk:81 [0|0|3]	**339**
Live! (63) 81(1) [0|0|14]	268
Down Home Style (69) 192(1) [0|0|6]	41.1
Together Again! (66)-Willis Jackson & Jack McDuff [A] 137(1) [0|0|4]	30.1

▶ Highest Peak [Top10s | Top40s | Total] Title (Yr) Peak(Wk) [T10 Wk | T40Wk | TotalWk]	Score
Reba McENTIRE ▶ 1337 Pk:78 [0|0|5]	**1077**
Sweet Sixteen (89) 78(1) [0|0|18]	331
The Last One To Know (87) 102(2) [0|0|20]	288
Greatest Hits (87) 139(2) [0|0|23]	210
Reba (88) 118(2) [0|0|10]	148
Live (89) 124(3) [0|0|8]	100
McFADDEN & WHITEHEAD ▶ 1226 Pk:23 [0|1|2]	**1286**
McFadden & Whitehead (79) 23(3) [0|8|17]	1208
I Heard It In A Love Song (80) 153(1) [0|0|6]	78.4
Gary McFARLAND ▶ 3341 Pk:189 [0|0|1]	**25**
America The Beautiful (69) 189(2) [0|0|3]	24.9
Bobby McFERRIN ▶ 687 Pk:5 [1|1|2]	**3846**
Simple Pleasures (88) 5(3) [7|16|55]	3562
Spontaneous Inventions (87) 103(1) [0|0|19]	284
Maureen McGOVERN ▶ 1756 Pk:77 [0|0|2]	**515**
The Morning After (73) 77(1) [0|0|16]	400
Maureen McGovern (79) 162(1) [0|0|10]	116
Bob McGRATH ▶ 2489 Pk:126 [0|0|1]	**163**
Bob McGrath From Sesame Street (70) 126(1) [0|0|11]	163
Jimmy McGRIFF ▶ 1990 Pk:130 [0|0|3]	**353**
The Worm (68) 161(1) [0|0|19]	247
Blues For Mister Jimmy (65) 130(1) [0|0|6]	83.1
Topkapi (64) 146(1) [0|0|2]	23.1
McGUFFEY LANE ▶ 3274 Pk:193 [0|0|1]	**31**
Aqua Dream (82) 193(1) [0|0|6]	30.9
Roger McGUINN ▶ 1994 Pk:92 [0|0|3]	**352**
Peace On You (74) 92(2) [0|0|6]	163
Roger McGuinn (73) 137(1) [0|0|9]	127
Roger McGuinn & Band (75) 165(2) [0|0|5]	62.9
McGUINN, CLARK & HILLMAN ▶ 1403 Pk:39 [0|1|2]	**970**
McGuinn, Clark & Hillman (79) 39(1) [0|2|19]	858
City (80)-McGuinn & Chris Hillman Featuring Gene Clark 136(2) [0|0|7]	112
McGUINNESS FLINT ▶ 2744 Pk:155 [0|0|2]	**106**
McGuinness Flint (71) 155(2) [0|0|8]	93.2
Happy Birthday, Ruthy Baby (71) 198(2) [0|0|2]	12.4
Barry McGUIRE ▶ 1616 Pk:37 [0|1|1]	**656**
Eve Of Destruction (65) 37(1) [0|3|21]	656
Maria McKEE ▶ 2264 Pk:120 [0|0|1]	**227**
Maria McKee (89) 120(2) [0|0|15]	227
McKENDREE SPRING ▶ 2156 Pk:118 [0|0|4]	**277**
Get Me To The Country (75) 118(2) [0|0|8]	160
McKendree Spring 3 (72) 163(1) [0|0|7]	82.2
Too Young To Feel This Old (76) 193(1) [0|0|3]	19.8
Second Thoughts (70) 192(2) [0|0|2]	15.1
Bob & Doug McKENZIE ▶ 984 Pk:8 [1|1|1]	**1984**
Great White North (82) 8(2) [4|13|21]	1984
Scott McKENZIE ▶ 2679 Pk:127 [0|0|1]	**118**
The Voice Of Scott McKenzie (67) 127(2) [0|0|7]	118
Rod McKUEN ▶ 1370 Pk:96 [0|0|9]	**1017**
Rod McKuen At Carnegie Hall (69) 96(2) [0|0|16]	323
New Ballads (70) 126(1) [0|0|13]	229
Greatest Hits Of Rod McKuen (69) 149(1) [0|0|10]	147
Rod McKuen's Greatest Hits-2 (70) 148(1) [0|0|8]	104
Lonesome Cities (68) 175(1) [0|0|5]	62.7
Listen To The Warm (68) 178(1) [0|0|6]	44.8
The Best Of Rod McKuen (69) 175(2) [0|0|4]	40.2
Pastorale (71) 182(1) [0|0|4]	34.7
Rod McKuen Grand Tour (71) 177(2) [0|0|3]	32.1

▶ Highest Peak [Top10s|Top40s|Total]
Title (Yr) Peak(Wk) [T10 Wk|T40Wk|TotalWk] — Score

Sarah McLACHLAN ▶ 2694 Pk:132 [0|0|1] — 115
Touch (89) 132(1) [0|0|12] — 115

Ian McLAGAN ▶ 2628 Pk:125 [0|0|1] — 127
Troublemaker (80) 125(1) [0|0|9] — 127

Malcolm McLAREN ▶ 2928 Pk:173 [0|0|2] — 76
D'ya Like Scratchin' (84) 173(2) [0|0|6] — 45.1
Fans (85) 190(2) [0|0|6] — 30.5

John McLAUGHLIN ▶ 1303 Pk:14 [0|1|4] — 1136
Love Devotion Surrender (73)-Carlos Santana & Mahavishnu John McLaughlin [A] 14(1) [0|7|24] — 747
Electric Guitarist (78)-Johnny McLaughlin 105(1) [0|0|14] — 265
Extrapolation (72) 152(2) [0|0|6] — 84.0
Belo Horizonte (81) 172(3) [0|0|4] — 39.6

John McLAUGHLIN/MAHAVISHNU ORCHESTRA ▶ 625 Pk:15 [0|1|8] — 4470
Birds Of Fire (73)-The Mahavishnu Orchestra 15(2) [0|11|37] — 2128
Apocalypse (74)-The Mahavishnu Orchestra 43(2) [0|0|14] — 692
Between Nothingness & Eternity (73)-The Mahavishnu Orchestra 41(2) [0|0|14] — 589
The Inner Mounting Flame (72)-Mahavishnu Orchestra With John McLaughlin 89(1) [0|0|26] — 476
Visions Of The Emerald Beyond (75)-The Mahavishnu Orchestra 68(1) [0|0|11] — 358
Inner Worlds (76)-Mahavishnu Orchestra John McLaughlin 118(2) [0|0|7] — 133
Electric Dreams (79)-John McLaughlin With The One Truth Band 147(1) [0|0|5] — 70.6
My Goal's Beyond (72)-Mahavishnu John McLaughlin 194(2) [0|0|4] — 23.9
--See also Di Meola, Al; Shakti

Pat McLAUGHLIN ▶ 3537 Pk:195 [0|0|1] — 5
Pat McLaughlin (88) 195(1) [0|0|1] — 5.4

Don McLEAN ▶ 295 Pk:1 [1|3|6] — 11891
American Pie (71) 1(7) [17|26|48] — 9002
Chain Lightning (81) 28(2) [0|6|21] — 1243
Don McLean (72) 23(2) [0|7|19] — 1173
Tapestry (72) 111(1) [0|0|10] — 186
Homeless Brother (74) 120(2) [0|0|8] — 152
Believers (81) 156(1) [0|0|11] — 134

James McMURTRY ▶ 2728 Pk:125 [0|0|1] — 109
Too Long In The Wasteland (89) 125(1) [0|0|9] — 109

Kristy And Jimmy McNICHOL ▶ 3010 Pk:116 [0|0|1] — 65
Kristy & Jimmy McNichol (78) 116(1) [0|0|4] — 64.7

Carmen McRAE ▶ 3303 Pk:150 [0|0|1] — 28
Alfie (67) 150(2) [0|0|2] — 27.9

Christine McVIE ▶ 1257 Pk:26 [0|1|2] — 1223
Christine McVie (84) 26(3) [0|7|23] — 1017
The Legendary Christine Perfect Album (76) 104(2) [0|0|10] — 206

MEAT LOAF ▶ 519 Pk:14 [0|1|3] — 5922
Bat Out Of Hell (77) 14(1) [0|28|82] — 5240
Dead Ringer (81) 45(2) [0|0|11] — 474
Bad Attitude (85) 74(1) [0|0|10] — 208

MECO ▶ 758 Pk:13 [0|1|6] — 3209
Star Wars & Other Galactic Funk (77) 13(2) [0|9|28] — 1899
Encounters Of Every Kind (78) 62(2) [0|0|13] — 419
The Wizard Of Oz (78) 68(2) [0|0|12] — 366
Pop Goes The Movies (82) 68(2) [0|0|9] — 239
Christmas In The Stars/Star Wars Christmas Album (80) 61(3) [0|0|6] — 200
Meco Plays Music From The Empire Strikes Back (80) 140(1) [0|0|8] — 86.5

▶ Highest Peak [Top10s|Top40s|Total]
Title (Yr) Peak(Wk) [T10 Wk|T40Wk|TotalWk] — Score

Glenn MEDEIROS ▶ 2173 Pk:83 [0|0|1] — 269
Glenn Medeiros (87) 83(2) [0|0|17] — 269

Bill MEDLEY ▶ 2814 Pk:152 [0|0|2] — 94
Soft And Soulful (69) 152(1) [0|0|4] — 64.0
Bill Medley 100% (68) 188(2) [0|0|4] — 30.4

MEGADETH ▶ 1019 Pk:28 [0|1|2] — 1870
So Far, So Good... So What! (88) 28(1) [0|6|23] — 1027
Peace Sells...But Who's Buying? (86) 76(1) [0|0|47] — 843

Zubin MEHTA/LOS ANGELES PHILHARMONIC Orchestra ▶ 2326 Pk:130 [0|0|2] — 207
Suites From Star Wars And Close Encounters Of The Third Kind (78)-Zubin Mehta, Los Angeles Philharmonic Orchestra 130(1) [0|0|8] — 123
Gustav Holst: The Planets (72)-Zubin Mehta, Los Angeles Philharmonic Orchestra 175(1) [0|0|10] — 84.1

Randy MEISNER ▶ 1220 Pk:50 [0|0|2] — 1301
One More Song (80) 50(1) [0|0|33] — 1114
Randy Meisner (82) 94(3) [0|0|11] — 187

MEL And TIM ▶ 3045 Pk:175 [0|0|1] — 60
Starting All Over Again (73) 175(1) [0|0|7] — 59.9

MELANIE ▶ 421 Pk:15 [0|3|10] — 7615
Gather Me (71) 15(1) [0|14|27] — 2640
Candles In The Rain (70) 17(3) [0|11|37] — 2416
Leftover Wine (70) 33(1) [0|4|19] — 962
Stoneground Words (72) 70(3) [0|0|20] — 593
The Good Book (71) 80(1) [0|0|10] — 322
Garden In The City (71) 115(1) [0|0|12] — 262
Melanie At Carnegie Hall (73) 109(2) [0|0|11] — 202
Four Sides Of Melanie (72) 103(1) [0|0|9] — 180
Madrugada (74) 192(1) [0|0|4] — 25.5
Melanie (69) 196(1) [0|0|2] — 13.3

John MELLENCAMP ▶ 77 Pk:1 [5|6|7] — 35005
American Fool (82)-John Cougar 1(9) [22|40|106] — 9588
Scarecrow (85) 2(3) [29|48|75] — 9110
The Lonesome Jubilee (87) 6(7) [27|37|53] — 6213
Uh-Huh (83) 9(1) [2|36|66] — 5328
Big Daddy (89) 7(1) [4|15|23] — 2048
Nothin' Matters And What If It Did (80)-John Cougar 37(2) [0|3|55] — 2032
John Cougar (79)-John Cougar 64(2) [0|0|29] — 687

Harold MELVIN And The BLUE NOTES ▶ 437 Pk:9 [1|2|7] — 7299
Wake Up Everybody (75) 9(1) [2|12|24] — 2307
To Be True (75) 26(1) [0|12|32] — 2217
Harold Melvin & The Blue Notes (72) 53(3) [0|0|31] — 861
Black & Blue (73) 57(1) [0|0|20] — 647
All Their Greatest Hits! (76) 51(2) [0|0|14] — 530
The Blue Album (80) 95(2) [0|0|20] — 397
Reaching For The World (77) 56(1) [0|0|10] — 341

MEMPHIS HORNS ▶ 2829 Pk:163 [0|0|1] — 91
The Memphis Horns Band II (78) 163(1) [0|0|9] — 90.8

MEN AT WORK ▶ 195 Pk:1 [2|2|3] — 17845
Business As Usual (82) 1(15) [31|48|90] — 12719
Cargo (83) 3(5) [14|23|49] — 4751
Two Hearts (85) 50(2) [0|0|13] — 374

Sergio MENDES ▶ 1009 Pk:27 [0|1|3] — 1904
Sergio Mendes(2) (83) 27(2) [0|10|27] — 1245
Confetti (84) 70(2) [0|0|22] — 451
Sergio Mendes (75) 105(2) [0|0|10] — 208

Sergio MENDES And BRASIL '66/'77 ▶ 170 Pk:3 [3|5|15] — 20448
Sergio Mendes & Brasil '66 (66)-Sergio Mendes & Brasil '66 7(1) [3|30|126] — 5896

▶ Highest Peak [Top10s|Top40s|Total]
Title (Yr) Peak(Wk) [T10 Wk|T40Wk|TotalWk] — Score

Look Around (68)-Sergio Mendes & Brasil '66 5(2) [9|33|51] — 5796
Fool On The Hill (68)-Sergio Mendes & Brasil '66 3(1) [5|16|30] — 4126
Equinox (67)-Sergio Mendes & Brasil '66 24(2) [0|6|46] — 1836
Crystal Illusions (69)-Sergio Mendes & Brasil '66 33(1) [0|2|17] — 1086
Ye-Me-Le (69)-Sergio Mendes & Brasil '66 71(1) [0|0|16] — 403
Greatest Hits (70)-Sergio Mendes & Brasil '66 101(2) [0|0|20] — 360
Sergio Mendes And The New Brasil '77 (77)-Sergio Mendes And The New Brasil '77 81(2) [0|0|12] — 298
Love Music (73)-Sergio Mendes & Brasil '77 116(1) [0|0|15] — 255
Stillness (71)-Sergio Mendes & Brasil '66 130(1) [0|0|9] — 162
Pais Tropical (71)-Sergio Mendes & Brasil '77 166(1) [0|0|6] — 78.1
Primal Roots (72)-Sergio Mendes & Brasil '77 164(2) [0|0|5] — 62.2
Vintage 74 (74)-Sergio Mendes & Brasil '77 176(1) [0|0|5] — 49.0
Sergio Mendes' Favorite Things (68)-Sergio Mendes 197(1) [0|0|4] — 21.9
Homecooking (76)-Sergio Mendes And Brazil '77 180(1) [0|0|2] — 19.0

MENUDO ▶ 1844 Pk:100 [0|0|2] — 447
Menudo (85) 100(2) [0|0|19] — 287
Reaching Out (84) 108(2) [0|0|12] — 160

Yehudi MENUHIN ▶ 3242 Pk:161 [0|0|1] — 34
West Meets East (67)-Yehudi Menuhin & Ravi Shankar [A] 161(1) [0|0|7] — 34.2

MEN WITHOUT HATS ▶ 876 Pk:13 [0|1|3] — 2504
Rhythm Of Youth (83) 13(3) [0|14|26] — 1887
Pop Goes The World (87) 73(2) [0|0|25] — 559
Folks Of The 80's (Part III) (84) 127(2) [0|0|4] — 57.9

Freddie MERCURY ▶ 3092 Pk:159 [0|0|1] — 53
Mr. Bad Guy (85) 159(1) [0|0|6] — 52.8

MERCY ▶ 1453 Pk:38 [0|1|1] — 889
The Mercy & Love (Can Make You Happy) (69) 38(1) [0|3|15] — 889

The MERRY-GO-ROUND ▶ 3469 Pk:190 [0|0|1] — 13
The Merry-Go-Round (67) 190(1) [0|0|2] — 12.7

MERRYWEATHER & FRIENDS ▶ 3478 Pk:199 [0|0|1] — 12
Word Of Mouth (69) 199(2) [0|0|2] — 12.4

Jim MESSINA ▶ 1527 Pk:58 [0|0|2] — 758
Oasis (79)-Jimmy Messina 58(1) [0|0|14] — 491
Messina (81) 95(3) [0|0|11] — 267

METAL CHURCH ▶ 1508 Pk:75 [0|0|2] — 792
The Dark (86) 92(1) [0|0|23] — 418
Blessing In Disguise (89) 75(1) [0|0|15] — 374

METALLICA ▶ 390 Pk:6 [1|3|6] — 8469
...And Justice For All (88) 6(2) [5|34|83] — 4977
Master Of Puppets (86) 29(2) [0|7|72] — 1587
The $5.98 E.P.: Garage Days Re-Revisited (87) 28(2) [0|8|30] — 1117
Ride The Lightning (84) 100(2) [0|0|50] — 564
Kill 'Em All(2) (88) 120(2) [0|0|8] — 136
Kill 'Em All (86) 155(2) [0|0|10] — 88.4

The METERS ▶ 1981 Pk:108 [0|0|4] — 361
The Meters (69) 108(1) [0|0|15] — 313
Fire On The Bayou (75) 179(1) [0|0|3] — 26.7
Look-Ka Py Py (70) 198(2) [0|0|2] — 11.8
Struttin' (70) 200(2) [0|0|2] — 10.4

► Highest Peak [Top10s I Top40s I Total] Title (Yr) Peak(Wk) [T10 Wk I T40Wk I TotalWk]	Score
Pat METHENY ► 1949 Pk:50 [0I0I1]	**377**
As Falls Wichita, So Falls Wichita Falls (81)-Pat Metheny & Lyle Mays [A] 50(1) [0I0I21]	377
PAT METHENY GROUP ► 593 Pk:44 [0I0I11]	**4798**
American Garage (79) 53(1) [0I0I24]	826
New Chautauqua (79)-Pat Metheny 44(1) [0I0I22]	739
Offramp (82) 50(2) [0I0I28]	637
First Circle (84) 91(2) [0I0I35]	532
Letter From Home (89) 66(2) [0I0I18]	485
Travels (83) 62(1) [0I0I17]	398
The Falcon & The Snowman (Soundtrack) (85) 54(2) [0I0I10]	315
80/81 (80)-Pat Metheny 89(1) [0I0I14]	311
Still Life (Talking) (87) 86(2) [0I0I15]	256
Pat Metheny Group (78) 123(1) [0I0I12]	174
Rejoicing (84)-Pat Metheny 116(2) [0I0I9]	126
MFSB ► 621 Pk:4 [1I2I5]	**4550**
Love Is The Message (74) 4(1) [4I14I35]	3069
Philadelphia Freedom (75) 39(1) [0I2I12]	616
Universal Love (75) 44(2) [0I0I13]	505
Summertime (76) 106(1) [0I0I9]	221
MFSB (73) 131(1) [0I0I10]	140
George MICHAEL ► 215 Pk:1 [1I1I1]	**16081**
Faith (87) 1(12) [51I69I87]	16081
Lee MICHAELS ► 555 Pk:16 [0I1I6]	**5285**
"5th" (71) 16(1) [0I12I36]	3084
Lee Michaels (69) 53(2) [0I0I26]	1009
Barrel (70) 51(2) [0I0I19]	697
Space & First Takes (72) 78(1) [0I0I13]	329
Lee Michaels Live (73) 135(1) [0I0I8]	121
Nice Day For Something (73) 172(1) [0I0I5]	44.1
Bette MIDLER ► 143 Pk:2 [3I6I11]	**22820**
Beaches (Soundtrack) (89) 2(3) [11I33I176]	8076
The Divine Miss M (72) 9(2) [2I23I76]	5034
The Rose (Soundtrack) (79) 12(3) [0I23I45]	3819
Bette Midler (73) 6(1) [5I11I27]	2369
Songs For The New Depression (76) 27(1) [0I6I15]	899
Divine Madness (Soundtrack) (80) 34(3) [0I4I14]	745
Broken Blossom (77) 51(2) [0I0I14]	571
Thighs And Whispers (79) 65(1) [0I0I17]	520
Live At Last (77) 49(1) [0I0I11]	391
No Frills (83) 60(1) [0I0I13]	357
Mud Will Be Flung Tonight! (85) 183(1) [0I0I6]	39.1
MIDNIGHT OIL ► 718 Pk:21 [0I1I3]	**3511**
Diesel And Dust (88) 21(3) [0I26I55]	3447
Red Sails In The Sunset (85) 177(2) [0I0I6]	36.6
10,9,8,7,6,5,4,3,2,1 (84) 178(1) [0I0I5]	26.9
MIDNIGHT STAR ► 513 Pk:27 [0I2I4]	**6014**
No Parking On The Dance Floor (83) 27(2) [0I30I96]	3986
Planetary Invasion (84) 32(2) [0I7I32]	1191
Headlines (86) 56(2) [0I0I27]	604
Midnight Star (88) 96(2) [0I0I15]	232
MIDNIGHT STRING QUARTET ► 770 Pk:17 [0I1I5]	**3140**
Rhapsodies For Young Lovers (66) 17(1) [0I12I59]	2273
Rhapsodies For Young Lovers, Volume Two (67) 67(1) [0I0I16]	331
Spanish Rhapsodies For Young Lovers (67) 76(1) [0I0I12]	294
Love Rhapsodies (68) 129(2) [0I0I17]	222
The Look Of Love And Other Rhapsodies For Young Lovers (68) 194(1) [0I0I3]	18.4

► Highest Peak [Top10s I Top40s I Total] Title (Yr) Peak(Wk) [T10 Wk I T40Wk I TotalWk]	Score
MIGHTY CLOUDS OF JOY ► 2674 Pk:165 [0I0I2]	**119**
It's Time (74) 165(1) [0I0I5]	60.3
Kickin' (76) 168(1) [0I0I6]	58.3
MIKE + THE MECHANICS ► 600 Pk:13 [0I2I2]	**4715**
Mike + The Mechanics (85) 26(6) [0I21I53]	2589
Living Years (88) 13(2) [0I13I37]	2127
Buddy MILES ► 420 Pk:8 [1I2I9]	**7634**
Carlos Santana & Buddy Miles! Live! (72)-Carlos Santana & Buddy Miles [A] 8(3) [8I14I33]	1579
Them Changes (70) 35(2) [0I5I74]	2822
We Got To Live Together (70) 53(2) [0I0I26]	1014
Buddy Miles Live (71) 50(1) [0I0I24]	842
A Message To The People (71) 60(1) [0I0I24]	779
More Miles Per Gallon (75) 68(1) [0I0I11]	357
Chapter VII (73)-Buddy MILES Band 123(1) [0I0I9]	141
Electric Church (69)-Buddy Miles Express 145(2) [0I0I4]	83.4
Booger Bear (74)-Buddy Miles Express 194(1) [0I0I3]	17.1
John MILES ► 1955 Pk:93 [0I0I2]	**375**
Stranger In The City (77) 93(1) [0I0I15]	328
Rebel (76) 171(1) [0I0I4]	47.1
Frankie MILLER(1) ► 1914 Pk:124 [0I0I3]	**397**
Full House (77)-Frankie Miller 124(1) [0I0I12]	210
Standing On The Edge (82)-Frankie Miller 135(2) [0I0I9]	101
Double Trouble (78)-Frankie Miller 177(1) [0I0I10]	86.5
Glenn MILLER Orchestra ► 2358 Pk:115 [0I0I1]	**196**
A Legendary Performer (75) 115(1) [0I0I9]	196
Jody MILLER ► 2281 Pk:117 [0I0I2]	**222**
He's So Fine (71) 117(1) [0I0I8]	133
Queen Of The House (65) 124(1) [0I0I6]	88.5
Mrs. MILLER ► 1263 Pk:15 [0I1I1]	**1217**
Mrs. Miller's Greatest Hits (66) 15(1) [0I10I17]	1217
Roger MILLER ► 317 Pk:4 [2I4I9]	**10727**
The Return Of Roger Miller (65) 4(2) [7I29I47]	3884
Golden Hits (65) 6(2) [10I21I57]	3805
The 3rd Time Around (65) 13(2) [0I9I24]	1472
Roger And Out (64) 37(2) [0I2I46]	1015
Words And Music (66) 108(1) [0I0I13]	232
Walkin' In The Sunshine (67) 118(2) [0I0I8]	140
Roger Miller (69) 163(1) [0I0I7]	95.4
A Tender Look At Love (68) 173(1) [0I0I8]	73.3
Roger Miller 1970 (70) 200(2) [0I0I2]	10.6
Steve MILLER Band ► 70 Pk:2 [4I10I18]	**37817**
Fly Like An Eagle (76) 3(2) [30I48I97]	11974
Book Of Dreams (77) 2(2) [13I27I68]	6696
The Joker (73) 2(1) [13I20I38]	5132
Abracadabra (82) 3(6) [12I18I33]	3819
Brave New World (69) 22(2) [0I8I26]	1738
Greatest Hits 1974-78 (78) 18(2) [0I9I18]	1469
Sailor (68) 24(1) [0I8I17]	1350
Number 5 (70) 23(1) [0I7I26]	1282
Circle Of Love (81) 26(2) [0I5I17]	994
Anthology (72) 56(2) [0I0I39]	868
Your Saving Grace (69) 38(2) [0I5I14]	796
Living In The 20th Century (86) 65(1) [0I0I23]	590
Rock Love (71) 82(2) [0I0I9]	269
Children Of The Future (68) 134(1) [0I0I18]	246
Recall The Beginning...A Journey From Eden (72) 109(1) [0I0I10]	207
Italian X Rays (84) 101(2) [0I0I10]	151

► Highest Peak [Top10s I Top40s I Total] Title (Yr) Peak(Wk) [T10 Wk I T40Wk I TotalWk]	Score
Born 2B Blue (88)-Steve Miller 108(2) [0I0I10]	149
Steve Miller Band - Live (83) 125(1) [0I0I7]	87.6
MILLIONS LIKE US ► 2795 Pk:171 [0I0I1]	**98**
...Millions Like Us (87) 171(1) [0I0I12]	98.4
MILLI VANILLI ► 242 Pk:1 [1I1I1]	**14650**
Girl You Know It's True (89) 1(7) [41I61I78]	14650
Frank MILLS ► 1291 Pk:21 [0I1I2]	**1167**
Music Box Dancer (79) 21(1) [0I5I16]	1050
Sunday Morning Suite (79) 149(1) [0I0I9]	117
Stephanie MILLS ► 339 Pk:16 [0I4I9]	**10060**
Sweet Sensation (80) 16(2) [0I22I44]	3213
What Cha Gonna Do...With My Lovin'? (79) 22(2) [0I9I34]	1842
If I Were Your Woman (87) 30(1) [0I9I36]	1353
Stephanie (81) 30(2) [0I5I23]	1171
Home (89) 82(3) [0I0I38]	743
Stephanie Mills (86) 47(2) [0I0I22]	607
Tantalizingly Hot (82) 48(6) [0I0I19]	598
I've Got The Cure (84) 73(2) [0I0I15]	267
Merciless (83) 104(1) [0I0I19]	266
MILLS BROTHERS ► 1108 Pk:21 [0I1I4]	**1581**
Fortuosity (68) 21(3) [0I10I26]	1480
Dream (69) 184(2) [0I0I5]	46.3
The Board Of Directors (68)-Count Basie & The Mills Brothers [A] 145(1) [0I0I6]	34.1
My Shy Violet (68) 190(1) [0I0I3]	20.5
Ronnie MILSAP ► 518 Pk:31 [0I3I14]	**5944**
Greatest Hits (80) 36(1) [0I4I41]	1516
There's No Gettin' Over Me (81) 31(1) [0I3I31]	1232
Out Where The Bright Lights Are Glowing (81) 89(2) [0I0I29]	696
Keyed Up (83) 36(1) [0I3I19]	672
It Was Almost Like A Song (77) 97(2) [0I0I15]	304
Inside Ronnie Milsap (82) 66(2) [0I0I14]	299
Images (79) 98(2) [0I0I15]	268
Only One Love In My Life (78) 109(2) [0I0I12]	264
Greatest Hits Vol. 2 (85) 102(2) [0I0I20]	245
Milsap Magic (80) 137(2) [0I0I13]	155
Lost In The Fifties Tonight (86) 121(2) [0I0I12]	149
A Legend In My Time (75) 138(2) [0I0I7]	107
One More Try For Love (84) 180(1) [0I0I3]	20.5
Night Things (75) 191(1) [0I0I2]	14.9
Garnet MIMMS & The ENCHANTERS ► 2776 Pk:91 [0I0I1]	**101**
Cry Baby And 11 Other Hits (63) 91(1) [0I0I5]	101
The MINDBENDERS ► 1872 Pk:58 [0I0I2]	**422**
The Game Of Love (65)-Wayne Fontana & The Mindbenders 58(1) [0I0I9]	237
A Groovy Kind Of Love (66) 92(1) [0I0I9]	185
MINISTRY ► 2034 Pk:96 [0I0I4]	**335**
With Sympathy (83) 96(1) [0I0I14]	209
The Mind Is A Terrible Thing To Taste (89) 163(3) [0I0I10]	71.8
The Land Of Rape And Honey (88) 164(2) [0I0I4]	39.6
Twitch (86) 194(2) [0I0I3]	14.3
MINK DE VILLE ► 2333 Pk:126 [0I0I4]	**205**
Return To Magenta (78) 126(2) [0I0I5]	100
Coup De Grace (81) 161(2) [0I0I5]	50.2
Le Chat Bleu (80) 163(2) [0I0I3]	38.2
Mink Deville (77) 186(1) [0I0I2]	16.3
Liza MINNELLI ► 819 Pk:19 [0I2I7]	**2830**
Liza With A "Z" (Soundtrack) (72) 19(3) [0I11I23]	1653
Liza Minnelli The Singer (73) 38(1) [0I2I20]	794
Liza! Liza! (64) 115(1) [0I0I8]	122
Results (89) 128(1) [0I0I10]	106

▶ Highest Peak [Top10s|Top40s|Total]
Title (Yr) Peak(Wk) [T10 Wk|T40Wk|TotalWk] — Score

Liza MINNELLI ▶ *Continued*
Liza Minnelli At Carnegie Hall (87) 156(2) [0|0|8] — 65.5
Live At The Winter Garden (74) 150(1) [0|0|4] — 51.2
New Feelin' (70) 158(1) [0|0|3] — 37.7
--See also: Judy Garland & Liza Minnelli

Kylie MINOGUE ▶ 1433 Pk:53 [0|0|1] — 922
Kylie (88) 53(2) [0|0|28] — 922

MINOR DETAIL ▶ 3483 Pk:187 [0|0|1] — 12
Minor Detail (83) 187(1) [0|0|2] — 12.3

MIRABAI ▶ 2716 Pk:128 [0|0|1] — 111
Mirabai (75) 128(1) [0|0|6] — 111

The MIRACLES/Smokey ROBINSON & The MIRACLES ▶ 231 Pk:7 [2|5|18] — 15173
Going To A Go-Go (65)-Smokey Robinson & The Miracles 8(2) [4|19|40] — 2801
Greatest Hits, Vol. 2 (68)-Smokey Robinson & The Miracles 7(2) [2|11|44] — 2524
Time Out For Smokey Robinson & The Miracles (69)-Smokey Robinson & The Miracles 25(2) [0|8|19] — 1477
Greatest Hits From The Beginning (65)-The Miracles 21(1) [0|14|25] — 1381
Special Occasion (68)-Smokey Robinson & The Miracles 42(2) [0|0|23] — 1185
Make It Happen (67)-Smokey Robinson & The Miracles 28(2) [0|7|23] — 1160
Away We A Go-Go (66)-Smokey Robinson & The Miracles 41(1) [0|0|27] — 1017
Flying High Together (72)-Smokey Robinson & The Miracles 46(2) [0|0|22] — 847
Live! (69)-Smokey Robinson & The Miracles 71(1) [0|0|14] — 461
1957-1972 (73)-Smokey Robinson & The Miracles 75(2) [0|0|16] — 427
A Pocket Full Of Miracles (70)-Smokey Robinson & The Miracles 56(1) [0|0|11] — 356
Four In Blue (69)-Smokey Robinson & The Miracles 78(1) [0|0|12] — 338
Smokey Robinson & The Miracles' Anthology (74)-Smokey Robinson & The Miracles 97(1) [0|0|17] — 320
One Dozen Roses (71)-Smokey Robinson & The Miracles 92(2) [0|0|10] — 282
What Love Has...Joined Together (70)-Smokey Robinson & The Miracles 97(1) [0|0|11] — 279
The Tears Of A Clown (70)-Smokey Robinson & The Miracles 143(2) [0|0|12] — 184
The Miracles On Stage (63)-The Miracles 139(1) [0|0|5] — 69.9
Doin' Mickey's Monkey (64)-The Miracles 113(1) [0|0|4] — 64.2

The MIRACLES ▶ 806 Pk:33 [0|1|6] — 2910
City Of Angels (75) 33(1) [0|10|30] — 1749
Do It Baby (74) 41(1) [0|0|21] — 784
Don't Cha Love It (75) 96(2) [0|0|9] — 208
Love Crazy (77) 117(2) [0|0|5] — 104
Renaissance (73) 174(1) [0|0|4] — 34.7
The Power Of Music (76) 178(1) [0|0|3] — 29.9

Judi Sheppard MISSETT ▶ 1974 Pk:117 [0|0|1] — 364
Jazzercise (81) 117(3) [0|0|20] — 364

MISSING PERSONS ▶ 570 Pk:17 [0|1|4] — 5098
Spring Session M (82) 17(6) [0|26|40] — 3181
Missing Persons (82) 46(2) [0|0|47] — 1124
Rhyme & Reason (84) 43(2) [0|0|16] — 609
Color In Your Life (86) 86(1) [0|0|11] — 184

MISSION U.K. ▶ 1982 Pk:108 [0|0|2] — 361
God's Own Medicine (87) 108(1) [0|0|18] — 233
Children (88) 126(2) [0|0|10] — 128

▶ Highest Peak [Top10s|Top40s|Total]
Title (Yr) Peak(Wk) [T10 Wk|T40Wk|TotalWk] — Score

MISSOURI ▶ 3211 Pk:174 [0|0|1] — 39
Welcome Two Missouri (79) 174(1) [0|0|4] — 38.5

MR. BIG ▶ 1653 Pk:46 [0|0|1] — 618
Mr. Big (89) 46(2) [0|0|18] — 618

MR. MISTER ▶ 497 Pk:1 [1|1|3] — 6196
Welcome To The Real World (85) 1(1) [12|34|58] — 5753
Go On... (87) 55(2) [0|0|17] — 389
I Wear The Face (84) 170(1) [0|0|7] — 54.0

MISTRESS ▶ 2201 Pk:100 [0|0|1] — 254
Mistress (79) 100(2) [0|0|14] — 254

Chad MITCHELL Trio ▶ 880 Pk:29 [0|2|5] — 2492
Reflecting (64) 29(1) [0|4|30] — 928
Singin' Our Mind (63) 39(1) [0|1|22] — 713
The Best Of Chad Mitchell Trio (63) 63(1) [0|0|28] — 667
The Slightly Irreverent Mitchell Trio (64)-The Mitchell Trio 128(1) [0|0|11] — 141
Typical American Boys (65)-The Mitchell Trio 130(1) [0|0|3] — 43.7

Joni MITCHELL ▶ 103 Pk:2 [3|12|15] — 29015
Court And Spark (74) 2(4) [15|31|64] — 7427
Miles Of Aisles (74) 2(1) [8|14|22] — 4070
The Hissing Of Summer Lawns (75) 4(3) [7|10|17] — 2504
Blue (71) 15(2) [0|12|28] — 2459
For The Roses (72) 11(2) [0|12|28] — 2227
Ladies Of The Canyon (70) 27(3) [0|9|33] — 2113
Hejira (76) 13(2) [0|8|18] — 1679
Mingus (79) 17(1) [0|9|18] — 1561
Clouds (69) 31(1) [0|6|36] — 1498
Wild Things Run Fast (82) 25(4) [0|5|21] — 957
Don Juan's Reckless Daughter (78) 25(2) [0|4|13] — 744
Shadows And Light (80) 38(2) [0|3|16] — 657
Chalk Mark In A Rain Storm (88) 45(2) [0|0|16] — 560
Dog Eat Dog (85) 63(5) [0|0|19] — 499
Joni Mitchell (68) 189(1) [0|0|9] — 59.6

Kim MITCHELL ▶ 2297 Pk:106 [0|0|1] — 218
Akimbo Alogo (85) 106(2) [0|0|15] — 218

Rubin MITCHELL ▶ 3355 Pk:164 [0|0|1] — 24
Presenting Rubin Mitchell (67) 164(2) [0|0|2] — 23.7

Willie MITCHELL ▶ 2548 Pk:151 [0|0|3] — 149
Soul Serenade (68) 151(1) [0|0|7] — 84.0
Willie Mitchell Live (68) 172(2) [0|0|5] — 47.6
Robbin's Nest (70) 188(1) [0|0|2] — 17.2

MOBY GRAPE ▶ 749 Pk:20 [0|2|5] — 3271
Moby Grape (67) 24(1) [0|7|27] — 1512
Wow (68) 20(1) [0|6|28] — 1405
Moby Grape '69 (69) 113(1) [0|0|10] — 206
Truly Fine Citizen (69) 157(1) [0|0|6] — 94.2
20 Granite Creek (71) 177(1) [0|0|5] — 53.4

MOCEDADES ▶ 2824 Pk:152 [0|0|1] — 91
Eres Tu "Touch The Wind" (74) 152(2) [0|0|7] — 91.2

M.O.D. ▶ 2452 Pk:151 [0|0|3] — 173
Gross Misconduct (89) 151(1) [0|0|8] — 92.7
U.S.A. For M.O.D. (87) 153(2) [0|0|5] — 45.1
Surfin' M.O.D. (88) 186(2) [0|0|6] — 35.1

MODELS ▶ 1969 Pk:84 [0|0|1] — 368
Out Of Mind Out Of Sight (86) 84(1) [0|0|18] — 368

MODERN ENGLISH ▶ 1516 Pk:70 [0|0|3] — 772
After The Snow (83) 70(1) [0|0|28] — 488
Riccochet Days (84) 93(1) [0|0|12] — 217
Stop Start (86) 154(2) [0|0|7] — 66.1

▶ Highest Peak [Top10s|Top40s|Total]
Title (Yr) Peak(Wk) [T10 Wk|T40Wk|TotalWk] — Score

Anna MOFFO ▶ 3038 Pk:97 [0|0|1] — 60
The Dream Duet (64)-Anna Moffo & Sergio Franchi [A] 97(1) [0|0|7] — 60.4

MOLLY HATCHET ▶ 512 Pk:19 [0|3|7] — 6021
Flirtin' With Disaster (79) 19(2) [0|18|48] — 2838
Beatin' The Odds (80) 25(2) [0|6|21] — 1065
Molly Hatchet (78) 64(1) [0|0|42] — 790
Take No Prisoners (81) 36(1) [0|4|14] — 645
No Guts...No Glory (83) 59(1) [0|0|20] — 416
The Deed Is Done (84) 117(2) [0|0|13] — 165
Double Trouble Live (85) 130(3) [0|0|9] — 102

MOM & DADS ▶ 1697 Pk:85 [0|0|2] — 585
The Rangers Waltz (71) 85(1) [0|0|23] — 519
In The Blue Canadian Rockies (72) 165(2) [0|0|6] — 65.9

The MOMENTS (2) ▶ 2145 Pk:132 [0|0|3] — 282
Look At Me (75)-The Moments 132(1) [0|0|8] — 129
The Moments Live at the New York State Womans Prison (71)-The Moments 147(2) [0|0|8] — 96.3
Moments Greatest Hits (71)-The Moments 184(2) [0|0|7] — 56.0

Eddie MONEY ▶ 299 Pk:17 [0|5|8] — 11661
Can't Hold Back (86) 20(3) [0|22|58] — 3034
Eddie Money (78) 37(2) [0|2|49] — 2099
No Control (82) 20(3) [0|13|44] — 2013
Life For The Taking (79) 17(2) [0|10|26] — 1842
Playing For Keeps (80) 35(1) [0|5|17] — 934
Nothing To Lose (88) 49(1) [0|0|29] — 791
Greatest Hits Sound Of Money (89) 53(1) [0|0|18] — 513
Where's The Party? (83) 67(1) [0|0|19] — 434

T.S. MONK ▶ 1638 Pk:64 [0|0|2] — 630
House Of Music (81) 64(1) [0|0|22] — 581
More Of The Good Life (82) 176(1) [0|0|8] — 48.8

Thelonious MONK ▶ 3168 Pk:127 [0|0|1] — 44
Criss-Cross (63) 127(1) [0|0|3] — 44.5

The MONKEES ▶ 31 Pk:1 [5|7|13] — 49833
The Monkees (66) 1(13) [32|49|102] — 13494
More Of The Monkees (67) 1(18) [25|45|96] — 12541
Headquarters (67) 1(1) [21|41|68] — 8689
Pisces, Aquarius, Capricorn, And Jones Ltd. (67) 1(5) [12|19|64] — 5738
The Birds, The Bees & The Monkees (68) 3(4) [9|15|50] — 4110
Then & Now...The Best Of The Monkees (86) 21(2) [0|12|34] — 1814
The Monkees Greatest Hits(2) (76) 58(1) [0|0|30] — 1019
Instant Replay (69) 32(1) [0|5|15] — 927
Head (Soundtrack) (68) 45(2) [0|0|15] — 611
The Monkees Greatest Hits (69) 89(1) [0|0|12] — 350
The Monkees Present (69) 100(1) [0|0|14] — 318
Pool It! (87) 72(2) [0|0|9] — 188
Changes (86) 152(1) [0|0|4] — 34.9

Matt MONRO ▶ 1759 Pk:86 [0|0|2] — 513
Invitation To The Movies/Born Free (67) 86(1) [0|0|22] — 467
Walk Away (65) 126(1) [0|0|3] — 45.3

Michael MONROE ▶ 3064 Pk:161 [0|0|1] — 57
Not Fakin' It (89) 161(1) [0|0|8] — 56.8

The MONROES ▶ 2723 Pk:109 [0|0|1] — 110
The Monroes (82) 109(2) [0|0|9] — 110

MONTANA Orchestra ▶ 3378 Pk:195 [0|0|1] — 21
Merry Christmas/Happy New Year's (81) 195(1) [0|0|4] — 21.2

<table>
<tr><th>► Highest Peak [Top10s | Top40s | Total]
Title (Yr) Peak(Wk) [T10 Wk | T40Wk | TotalWk]</th><th>Score</th></tr>
<tr><td>Hugo MONTENEGRO ► 680 Pk:9 [1 | 1 | 4]</td><td>3897</td></tr>
<tr><td>Music From "A Fistful Of Dollars" & "For A Few Dollars More" & "The Good, The Bad And The Ugly" (68)-Hugo Montenegro, His Orchestra And Chorus 9(1) [6 | 17 | 39]</td><td>3176</td></tr>
<tr><td>Original Music From The Man From U.N.C.L.E. (66)-Hugo Montenegro, His Orchestra And Chorus 52(1) [0 | 0 | 20]</td><td>633</td></tr>
<tr><td>Hang 'Em High (68)-Hugo Montenegro, His Orchestra And Chorus 166(2) [0 | 0 | 5]</td><td>57.3</td></tr>
<tr><td>Moog Power (69)-Hugo Montenegro, His Orchestra And Chorus 182(1) [0 | 0 | 4]</td><td>30.5</td></tr>
<tr><td>Chris MONTEZ ► 1260 Pk:33 [0 | 1 | 2]</td><td>1220</td></tr>
<tr><td>The More I See You/Call Me (66) 33(1) [0 | 4 | 24]</td><td>989</td></tr>
<tr><td>Time After Time (67) 106(2) [0 | 0 | 11]</td><td>231</td></tr>
<tr><td>Wes MONTGOMERY ► 373 Pk:13 [0 | 2 | 10]</td><td>8834</td></tr>
<tr><td>A Day In The Life (67) 13(2) [0 | 23 | 67]</td><td>4035</td></tr>
<tr><td>Down Here On The Ground (68) 38(1) [0 | 1 | 30]</td><td>1090</td></tr>
<tr><td>Tequila (66) 51(1) [0 | 0 | 32]</td><td>1021</td></tr>
<tr><td>The Best Of Wes Montgomery (67) 56(2) [0 | 0 | 38]</td><td>950</td></tr>
<tr><td>California Dreaming (67) 65(1) [0 | 0 | 32]</td><td>854</td></tr>
<tr><td>Road Song (68) 94(1) [0 | 0 | 16]</td><td>402</td></tr>
<tr><td>Bumpin' (65) 116(2) [0 | 0 | 13]</td><td>205</td></tr>
<tr><td>Jimmy & Wes The Dynamic Duo (67)-Jimmy Smith & Wes Montgomery [A] 129(2) [0 | 0 | 23]</td><td>133</td></tr>
<tr><td>Greatest Hits (70) 175(1) [0 | 0 | 9]</td><td>82.7</td></tr>
<tr><td>The Best Of Wes Montgomery, Vol. 2 (68) 187(1) [0 | 0 | 8]</td><td>63.9</td></tr>
<tr><td>MONTROSE ► 1203 Pk:65 [0 | 0 | 6]</td><td>1335</td></tr>
<tr><td>Paper Money (74) 65(1) [0 | 0 | 14]</td><td>546</td></tr>
<tr><td>Montrose (74) 133(1) [0 | 0 | 12]</td><td>211</td></tr>
<tr><td>Open Fire (78)-Ronnie Montrose 98(2) [0 | 0 | 10]</td><td>206</td></tr>
<tr><td>Warner Brothers Presents Montrose! (75) 79(1) [0 | 0 | 7]</td><td>184</td></tr>
<tr><td>Jump On It (76) 118(2) [0 | 0 | 7]</td><td>137</td></tr>
<tr><td>Mean (87) 165(2) [0 | 0 | 7]</td><td>50.2</td></tr>
<tr><td>MONTY PYTHON ► 1242 Pk:48 [0 | 0 | 6]</td><td>1252</td></tr>
<tr><td>The Monty Python Matching Tie & Handkerchief (75) 48(2) [0 | 0 | 13]</td><td>500</td></tr>
<tr><td>Monty Python's Flying Circus (75) 83(2) [0 | 0 | 15]</td><td>332</td></tr>
<tr><td>The Album Of The Soundtrack Of The Trailer Of The Film Of "Monty Python and the Holy Grail" (Soundtrack) (75) 87(2) [0 | 0 | 11]</td><td>271</td></tr>
<tr><td>Monty Python's Contractual Obligation Album (80) 164(1) [0 | 0 | 9]</td><td>95.3</td></tr>
<tr><td>Life Of Brian (Soundtrack) (79) 155(1) [0 | 0 | 2]</td><td>29.7</td></tr>
<tr><td>Monty Python Live! At City Center (76) 186(1) [0 | 0 | 3]</td><td>23.7</td></tr>
<tr><td>MOODY BLUES ► 30 Pk:1 [6 | 14 | 16]</td><td>50515</td></tr>
<tr><td>Long Distance Voyager (81) 1(3) [12 | 23 | 39]</td><td>6873</td></tr>
<tr><td>Days Of Future Passed (68)-The Moody Blues With The London Festival Orchestra 3(5) [6 | 23 | 106]</td><td>6396</td></tr>
<tr><td>Seventh Sojourn (72) 1(5) [12 | 23 | 44]</td><td>6301</td></tr>
<tr><td>Every Good Boy Deserves Favour (71) 2(3) [13 | 21 | 43]</td><td>6059</td></tr>
<tr><td>On The Threshold Of A Dream (69) 20(1) [0 | 13 | 136]</td><td>5328</td></tr>
<tr><td>A Question Of Balance (70) 3(1) [5 | 17 | 74]</td><td>4666</td></tr>
<tr><td>The Other Side Of Life (86) 9(4) [6 | 22 | 42]</td><td>3087</td></tr>
<tr><td>To Our Children's Children's Children (70) 14(3) [0 | 12 | 44]</td><td>2762</td></tr>
<tr><td>Octave (78) 13(1) [0 | 9 | 30]</td><td>2006</td></tr>
<tr><td>This Is The Moody Blues (74) 11(1) [0 | 9 | 25]</td><td>2000</td></tr>
<tr><td>In Search Of The Lost Chord (68) 23(1) [0 | 11 | 29]</td><td>1837</td></tr>
<tr><td>Caught Live + 5 (77) 26(2) [0 | 5 | 15]</td><td>1013</td></tr>
<tr><td>The Present (83) 26(3) [0 | 6 | 22]</td><td>1010</td></tr>
<tr><td>Sur La Mer (88) 38(2) [0 | 5 | 19]</td><td>852</td></tr>
</table>

<table>
<tr><th>► Highest Peak [Top10s | Top40s | Total]
Title (Yr) Peak(Wk) [T10 Wk | T40Wk | TotalWk]</th><th>Score</th></tr>
<tr><td>Greatest Hits (89) 113(1) [0 | 0 | 16]</td><td>211</td></tr>
<tr><td>Voices In The Sky-Best Of The Moody Blues (85) 132(2) [0 | 0 | 9]</td><td>114</td></tr>
<tr><td>MOOG MACHINE ► 2859 Pk:170 [0 | 0 | 1]</td><td>87</td></tr>
<tr><td>Switched-On Rock (69) 170(1) [0 | 0 | 8]</td><td>86.6</td></tr>
<tr><td>Keith MOON ► 3136 Pk:155 [0 | 0 | 1]</td><td>48</td></tr>
<tr><td>Two Sides Of The Moon (75) 155(2) [0 | 0 | 3]</td><td>47.8</td></tr>
<tr><td>The MOONGLOWS ► 3358 Pk:193 [0 | 0 | 1]</td><td>23</td></tr>
<tr><td>The Return Of The Moonglows (72) 193(1) [0 | 0 | 4]</td><td>22.9</td></tr>
<tr><td>Dorothy MOORE ► 1087 Pk:29 [0 | 1 | 2]</td><td>1642</td></tr>
<tr><td>Misty Blue (76) 29(1) [0 | 7 | 23]</td><td>1413</td></tr>
<tr><td>Dorothy Moore (77) 120(1) [0 | 0 | 13]</td><td>230</td></tr>
<tr><td>Gary MOORE ► 1714 Pk:114 [0 | 0 | 5]</td><td>569</td></tr>
<tr><td>After The War (89) 114(2) [0 | 0 | 9]</td><td>158</td></tr>
<tr><td>Wild Frontier (87) 139(1) [0 | 0 | 15]</td><td>153</td></tr>
<tr><td>Corridors Of Power (83) 149(1) [0 | 0 | 13]</td><td>144</td></tr>
<tr><td>Run For Cover (86) 146(2) [0 | 0 | 7]</td><td>73.1</td></tr>
<tr><td>Victims Of The Future (84) 172(1) [0 | 0 | 5]</td><td>40.3</td></tr>
<tr><td>Melba MOORE ► 1171 Pk:91 [0 | 0 | 9]</td><td>1411</td></tr>
<tr><td>A Lot Of Love (86) 91(2) [0 | 0 | 29]</td><td>372</td></tr>
<tr><td>Melba(2) (78) 114(1) [0 | 0 | 18]</td><td>335</td></tr>
<tr><td>The Other Side Of The Rainbow (82) 152(1) [0 | 0 | 19]</td><td>204</td></tr>
<tr><td>Never Say Never (83) 147(1) [0 | 0 | 14]</td><td>142</td></tr>
<tr><td>Read My Lips (85) 130(2) [0 | 0 | 10]</td><td>118</td></tr>
<tr><td>This Is It (76) 145(2) [0 | 0 | 5]</td><td>83.5</td></tr>
<tr><td>Look What You're Doing To The Man (71) 157(2) [0 | 0 | 5]</td><td>61.8</td></tr>
<tr><td>Melba (76) 177(1) [0 | 0 | 7]</td><td>56.6</td></tr>
<tr><td>Peach Melba (75) 176(2) [0 | 0 | 4]</td><td>37.6</td></tr>
<tr><td>Tim MOORE ► 2387 Pk:119 [0 | 0 | 2]</td><td>189</td></tr>
<tr><td>Tim Moore (74) 119(2) [0 | 0 | 9]</td><td>162</td></tr>
<tr><td>Behind The Eyes (75) 181(1) [0 | 0 | 3]</td><td>27.2</td></tr>
<tr><td>Vinnie MOORE ► 2932 Pk:147 [0 | 0 | 1]</td><td>75</td></tr>
<tr><td>Time Odyssey (88) 147(2) [0 | 0 | 7]</td><td>74.7</td></tr>
<tr><td>Michael MORALES ► 2205 Pk:113 [0 | 0 | 1]</td><td>253</td></tr>
<tr><td>Michael Morales (89) 113(3) [0 | 0 | 20]</td><td>253</td></tr>
<tr><td>Patrick MORAZ ► 2784 Pk:132 [0 | 0 | 1]</td><td>100</td></tr>
<tr><td>I (76) 132(1) [0 | 0 | 5]</td><td>100</td></tr>
<tr><td>Jane MORGAN ► 2990 Pk:134 [0 | 0 | 1]</td><td>67</td></tr>
<tr><td>Fresh Flavor (66) 134(1) [0 | 0 | 4]</td><td>67.0</td></tr>
<tr><td>Lee MORGAN ► 1256 Pk:25 [0 | 1 | 3]</td><td>1223</td></tr>
<tr><td>The Sidewinder (64) 25(3) [0 | 7 | 30]</td><td>1153</td></tr>
<tr><td>Search For The New Land (66) 143(2) [0 | 0 | 3]</td><td>45.3</td></tr>
<tr><td>Caramba! (69) 190(1) [0 | 0 | 3]</td><td>24.3</td></tr>
<tr><td>Meli'sa MORGAN ► 1227 Pk:41 [0 | 0 | 2]</td><td>1284</td></tr>
<tr><td>Do Me Baby (86) 41(1) [0 | 0 | 36]</td><td>980</td></tr>
<tr><td>Good Love (87) 108(1) [0 | 0 | 19]</td><td>304</td></tr>
<tr><td>Giorgio MORODER ► 2717 Pk:130 [0 | 0 | 1]</td><td>111</td></tr>
<tr><td>From Here To Eternity (77)-Giorgio 130(2) [0 | 0 | 7]</td><td>111</td></tr>
<tr><td>Gary MORRIS ► 3083 Pk:174 [0 | 0 | 1]</td><td>54</td></tr>
<tr><td>Why Lady Why (83) 174(1) [0 | 0 | 8]</td><td>54.3</td></tr>
<tr><td>Van MORRISON ► 276 Pk:15 [0 | 6 | 20]</td><td>12778</td></tr>
<tr><td>Saint Dominic's Preview (72) 15(3) [0 | 12 | 28]</td><td>2203</td></tr>
<tr><td>Tupelo Honey (71) 27(3) [0 | 6 | 24]</td><td>1468</td></tr>
<tr><td>Wavelength (78) 28(1) [0 | 5 | 23]</td><td>1220</td></tr>
<tr><td>His Band And The Street Choir (70) 32(2) [0 | 5 | 17]</td><td>1048</td></tr>
<tr><td>Hard Nose The Highway (73) 27(2) [0 | 6 | 19]</td><td>1039</td></tr>
<tr><td>Moondance (70) 29(2) [0 | 3 | 22]</td><td>951</td></tr>
<tr><td>Avalon Sunset (89) 91(2) [0 | 0 | 39]</td><td>716</td></tr>
<tr><td>Into The Music (79) 43(2) [0 | 0 | 13]</td><td>659</td></tr>
<tr><td>It's Too Late To Stop Now (74) 53(1) [0 | 0 | 17]</td><td>545</td></tr>
<tr><td>A Period Of Transition (77) 43(2) [0 | 0 | 11]</td><td>503</td></tr>
</table>

<table>
<tr><th>► Highest Peak [Top10s | Top40s | Total]
Title (Yr) Peak(Wk) [T10 Wk | T40Wk | TotalWk]</th><th>Score</th></tr>
<tr><td>A Sense Of Wonder (85) 61(3) [0 | 0 | 17]</td><td>444</td></tr>
<tr><td>Beautiful Vision (82) 44(2) [0 | 0 | 11]</td><td>399</td></tr>
<tr><td>Veedon Fleece (74) 53(2) [0 | 0 | 10]</td><td>383</td></tr>
<tr><td>Poetic Champions Compose (87) 90(2) [0 | 0 | 22]</td><td>348</td></tr>
<tr><td>Common One (80) 73(1) [0 | 0 | 10]</td><td>281</td></tr>
<tr><td>No Guru, No Method, No Teacher (86) 70(2) [0 | 0 | 13]</td><td>272</td></tr>
<tr><td>Inarticulate Speech Of The Heart (83) 116(1) [0 | 0 | 8]</td><td>118</td></tr>
<tr><td>Irish Heartbeat (88)-Van Morrison & The Chieftains [A] 102(2) [0 | 0 | 13]</td><td>103</td></tr>
<tr><td>Blowin' Your Mind! (67) 182(1) [0 | 0 | 7]</td><td>46.5</td></tr>
<tr><td>T.B. Sheets (74) 181(1) [0 | 0 | 4]</td><td>30.8</td></tr>
<tr><td>MORRISSEY ► 1628 Pk:48 [0 | 0 | 1]</td><td>647</td></tr>
<tr><td>Viva Hate (88) 48(2) [0 | 0 | 20]</td><td>647</td></tr>
<tr><td>Steve MORSE Band ► 2346 Pk:101 [0 | 0 | 2]</td><td>201</td></tr>
<tr><td>The Introduction (84) 101(1) [0 | 0 | 12]</td><td>180</td></tr>
<tr><td>High Tension Wires (89)-Steve Morse 182(2) [0 | 0 | 3]</td><td>20.6</td></tr>
<tr><td>Johnny & Jonie MOSBY ► 3531 Pk:197 [0 | 0 | 1]</td><td>7</td></tr>
<tr><td>Hold Me (69) 197(1) [0 | 0 | 1]</td><td>6.7</td></tr>
<tr><td>The MOTELS ► 576 Pk:16 [0 | 3 | 5]</td><td>5060</td></tr>
<tr><td>All Four One (82) 16(2) [0 | 15 | 41]</td><td>2453</td></tr>
<tr><td>Little Robbers (83) 22(4) [0 | 8 | 24]</td><td>1254</td></tr>
<tr><td>Careful (80) 45(2) [0 | 0 | 20]</td><td>746</td></tr>
<tr><td>Shock (85) 36(1) [0 | 2 | 16]</td><td>588</td></tr>
<tr><td>Motels (79) 175(1) [0 | 0 | 2]</td><td>19.5</td></tr>
<tr><td>MOTHER EARTH ► 1899 Pk:95 [0 | 0 | 3]</td><td>408</td></tr>
<tr><td>Make A Joyful Noise (69) 95(2) [0 | 0 | 9]</td><td>243</td></tr>
<tr><td>Living With The Animals (69) 144(1) [0 | 0 | 8]</td><td>153</td></tr>
<tr><td>Bring Me Home (71) 199(2) [0 | 0 | 2]</td><td>12.5</td></tr>
<tr><td>MOTHERLODE ► 2091 Pk:93 [0 | 0 | 1]</td><td>307</td></tr>
<tr><td>When I Die (69) 93(1) [0 | 0 | 12]</td><td>307</td></tr>
<tr><td>MOTHER'S FINEST ► 1579 Pk:123 [0 | 0 | 4]</td><td>703</td></tr>
<tr><td>Mother Factor (78) 123(1) [0 | 0 | 21]</td><td>357</td></tr>
<tr><td>Another Mother Further (77) 134(1) [0 | 0 | 8]</td><td>144</td></tr>
<tr><td>Mother's Finest (76) 148(2) [0 | 0 | 8]</td><td>110</td></tr>
<tr><td>Iron Age (81) 168(1) [0 | 0 | 8]</td><td>92.8</td></tr>
<tr><td>--Mothers Of Invention see: Zappa, Frank</td><td></td></tr>
<tr><td>MÖTLEY CRÜE ► 141 Pk:1 [3 | 4 | 5]</td><td>22918</td></tr>
<tr><td>Dr. Feelgood (89) 1(2) [11 | 55 | 109]</td><td>8619</td></tr>
<tr><td>Girls, Girls, Girls (87) 2(1) [12 | 26 | 46]</td><td>4702</td></tr>
<tr><td>Shout At The Devil (83) 17(2) [0 | 28 | 111]</td><td>4698</td></tr>
<tr><td>Theatre Of Pain (85) 6(1) [9 | 18 | 72]</td><td>3895</td></tr>
<tr><td>Too Fast For Love (83) 77(1) [0 | 0 | 62]</td><td>1004</td></tr>
<tr><td>MOTORHEAD ► 2174 Pk:150 [0 | 0 | 4]</td><td>269</td></tr>
<tr><td>Orgasmatron (86) 157(3) [0 | 0 | 11]</td><td>92.4</td></tr>
<tr><td>Another Perfect Day (83) 153(1) [0 | 0 | 7]</td><td>68.5</td></tr>
<tr><td>Rock 'N' Roll (87) 150(2) [0 | 0 | 6]</td><td>61.4</td></tr>
<tr><td>Iron Fist (82) 174(1) [0 | 0 | 6]</td><td>46.2</td></tr>
<tr><td>The MOTORS ► 2983 Pk:174 [0 | 0 | 1]</td><td>68</td></tr>
<tr><td>Tenement Steps (80) 174(1) [0 | 0 | 8]</td><td>67.6</td></tr>
<tr><td>Tony MOTTOLA ► 2111 Pk:85 [0 | 0 | 3]</td><td>296</td></tr>
<tr><td>Love Songs - Mexico/S.A. (65) 85(1) [0 | 0 | 13]</td><td>262</td></tr>
<tr><td>Tony Mottola's Guitar Factory (70) 189(1) [0 | 0 | 3]</td><td>19.2</td></tr>
<tr><td>A Latin Love-In (67) 198(2) [0 | 0 | 3]</td><td>14.8</td></tr>
<tr><td>MOTT THE HOOPLE ► 662 Pk:23 [0 | 3 | 7]</td><td>4121</td></tr>
<tr><td>The Hoople (74) 28(1) [0 | 7 | 23]</td><td>1356</td></tr>
<tr><td>Mott (73) 35(2) [0 | 4 | 29]</td><td>1175</td></tr>
<tr><td>Mott The Hoople Live (74) 23(1) [0 | 4 | 13]</td><td>885</td></tr>
<tr><td>All The Young Dudes (72) 89(1) [0 | 0 | 19]</td><td>414</td></tr>
<tr><td>Rock And Roll Queen (74) 112(1) [0 | 0 | 11]</td><td>213</td></tr>
<tr><td>Drive On (75)-Mott 160(1) [0 | 0 | 5]</td><td>62.2</td></tr>
<tr><td>Mott The Hoople (70) 185(1) [0 | 0 | 2]</td><td>16.7</td></tr>
</table>

► **Highest Peak [Top10s|Top40s|Total]**
Title (Yr) Peak(Wk) [T10 Wk|T40Wk|TotalWk] — **Score**

Bob MOULD ► 2476 Pk:127 [0|0|1] — **167**
Workbook (89) 127(1) [0|0|14] — 167

MOUNTAIN ► 428 Pk:16 [0|3|8] — **7419**
Mountain Climbing! (70) 17(2) [0|21|39] — 3285
Nantucket Sleighride (71) 16(1) [0|7|29] — 1818
Flowers Of Evil (71) 35(2) [0|4|16] — 915
Mountain Live (The Road Goes Ever On) (72) 63(1) [0|0|18] — 584
The Best Of Mountain (73) 72(1) [0|0|16] — 415
Avalanche (74) 102(1) [0|0|9] — 230
Twin Peaks (74) 142(2) [0|0|8] — 121
Go For Your Life (85) 166(2) [0|0|6] — 51.0

Nana MOUSKOURI ► 3056 Pk:124 [0|0|1] — **59**
An Evening With Belafonte/Mouskouri (66)-Harry Belafonte & Nana Mouskouri [A] 124(1) [0|0|8] — 58.8

MOUTH & MACNEAL ► 1860 Pk:77 [0|0|1] — **434**
How Do You Do? (72) 77(1) [0|0|16] — 434

Alphonse MOUZON ► 2805 Pk:146 [0|0|1] — **96**
Distant Lover (82) 146(3) [0|0|11] — 96.0

The MOVE ► 2969 Pk:172 [0|0|1] — **70**
Split Ends (73) 172(1) [0|0|8] — 69.8

MOVING PICTURES ► 2279 Pk:101 [0|0|1] — **222**
Days Of Innocence (82) 101(3) [0|0|16] — 222

Alison MOYET ► 1336 Pk:45 [0|0|2] — **1079**
Alf (85) 45(2) [0|0|25] — 795
Raindancing (87) 94(5) [0|0|17] — 284

MTUME ► 1101 Pk:26 [0|1|4] — **1603**
Juicy Fruit (83) 26(2) [0|7|22] — 1121
You, Me And He (84) 77(2) [0|0|19] — 302
Theater Of The Mind (86) 135(2) [0|0|8] — 90.2
In Search Of The Rainbow Seekers (80) 119(1) [0|0|4] — 89.6

Idris MUHAMMAD ► 2158 Pk:127 [0|0|1] — **276**
Turn This Mutha Out (77) 127(2) [0|0|19] — 276

Maria MULDAUR ► 432 Pk:3 [1|2|4] — **7400**
Maria Muldaur (73) 3(3) [11|21|56] — 5319
Waitress In The Donut Shop (74) 23(1) [0|6|26] — 1598
Sweet Harmony (76) 53(2) [0|0|12] — 397
Southern Winds (78) 143(3) [0|0|5] — 85.6

Martin MULL ► 3019 Pk:157 [0|0|2] — **63**
Sex & Violins (78) 157(2) [0|0|3] — 45.9
I'm Everyone I've Ever Loved (77) 184(1) [0|0|2] — 17.2

MUNGO JERRY ► 1925 Pk:64 [0|0|1] — **390**
Mungo Jerry (70) 64(1) [0|0|11] — 390

MUNICH MACHINE ► 3376 Pk:190 [0|0|1] — **21**
A Whiter Shade Of Pale (78) 190(1) [0|0|3] — 21.5

Shirley MURDOCK ► 1428 Pk:44 [0|0|2] — **928**
Shirley Murdock! (87) 44(2) [0|0|26] — 777
A Woman's Point Of View (88) 137(1) [0|0|15] — 150

Michael MURPHEY ► 666 Pk:18 [0|1|8] — **4099**
Blue Sky-Night Thunder (75) 18(1) [0|13|38] — 2744
Swans Against The Sun (75) 44(2) [0|0|13] — 683
Michael Martin Murphey (82) 69(1) [0|0|16] — 305
Lonewolf (78)-Michael Martin Murphey 99(2) [0|0|6] — 151
Geronimo's Cadillac (72) 160(1) [0|0|9] — 100
Flowing Free Forever (76) 130(1) [0|0|5] — 86.8
The Heart Never Lies (83)-Michael Martin Murphey 187(1) [0|0|3] — 17.7
Cosmic Cowboy Souvenir (73) 196(2) [0|0|2] — 11.2

Eddie MURPHY ► 664 Pk:26 [0|2|4] — **4105**
Eddie Murphy: Comedian (83) 35(1) [0|3|44] — 1323
How Could It Be (85) 26(1) [0|10|26] — 1285
Eddie Murphy (82) 52(5) [0|0|53] — 1275

► **Highest Peak [Top10s|Top40s|Total]**
Title (Yr) Peak(Wk) [T10 Wk|T40Wk|TotalWk] — **Score**

So Happy (89) 70(2) [0|0|9] — 223

Peter MURPHY ► 2269 Pk:135 [0|0|1] — **226**
Love Hysteria (88) 135(2) [0|0|19] — 226

Walter MURPHY ► 1043 Pk:15 [0|1|2] — **1772**
A Fifth Of Beethoven (76)-Walter Murphy & The Big Apple Band 15(1) [0|6|29] — 1740
Rhapsody In Blue (77) 175(1) [0|0|3] — 31.6

Anne MURRAY ► 197 Pk:12 [0|7|24] — **17584**
Ann Murray's Greatest Hits (80) 16(5) [0|17|64] — 3147
Let's Keep It That Way (78) 12(1) [0|8|52] — 2589
Love Song (74) 24(2) [0|6|33] — 1675
I'll Always Love You (79) 24(2) [0|9|23] — 1486
Snowbird (70) 41(2) [0|0|31] — 1344
New Kind Of Feeling (79) 23(2) [0|6|29] — 1327
Danny's Song (73) 39(2) [0|2|24] — 898
Country (74) 32(1) [0|2|16] — 808
Where Do You Go When You Dream (81) 55(2) [0|0|15] — 587
Something To Talk About (86) 68(2) [0|0|23] — 479
A Little Good News (83) 72(1) [0|0|24] — 473
Highly Prized Possession (74) 70(1) [0|0|13] — 422
Somebody's Waiting (80) 88(4) [0|0|15] — 408
Heart Over Mind (84) 92(1) [0|0|25] — 370
Christmas Wishes (81) 54(2) [0|0|8] — 301
A Country Collection (80) 73(1) [0|0|9] — 254
The Hottest Night Of The Year (82) 90(3) [0|0|12] — 215
Anne Murray (71) 121(2) [0|0|9] — 182
Keeping In Touch (76) 96(4) [0|0|6] — 175
Together (75) 142(1) [0|0|11] — 170
Annie (72) 143(1) [0|0|8] — 98.4
Anne Murray / Glen Campbell (71)-Anne Murray & Glen Campbell [A] 128(1) [0|0|8] — 77.7
Harmony (87) 149(2) [0|0|6] — 58.8
Talk It Over In The Morning (71) 179(1) [0|0|4] — 40.3

MUSCLE SHOALS HORNS ► 2704 Pk:154 [0|0|1] — **113**
Born To Get Down (76) 154(3) [0|0|8] — 113

MUSICAL YOUTH ► 1317 Pk:23 [0|1|2] — **1107**
The Youth Of Today (83) 23(4) [0|8|22] — 999
Different Style! (83) 144(1) [0|0|12] — 109

MUSIC EXPLOSION ► 3429 Pk:178 [0|0|1] — **17**
Little Bit O' Soul (67) 178(1) [0|0|2] — 16.9

MUSIC MACHINE ► 1973 Pk:76 [0|0|1] — **364**
(Turn On) The Music Machine (67) 76(1) [0|0|16] — 364

MUSIQUE ► 1668 Pk:62 [0|0|1] — **605**
Keep On Jumpin' (78) 62(3) [0|0|17] — 605

Alicia MYERS ► 3300 Pk:186 [0|0|1] — **28**
I Appreciate (84) 186(2) [0|0|5] — 28.1

Gary MYRICK ► 3420 Pk:186 [0|0|1] — **17**
Language (83) 186(1) [0|0|3] — 17.4

MYSTIC MOODS Orch. ► 1289 Pk:63 [0|0|12] — **1170**
One Stormy Night (66) 63(1) [0|0|14] — 340
Nighttide (66) 110(1) [0|0|10] — 200
Stormy Weekend (70) 165(1) [0|0|15] — 140
Extensions (69) 155(1) [0|0|9] — 139
Love Token (69) 165(1) [0|0|8] — 92.4
English Muffins (70) 174(2) [0|0|9] — 87.2
More Than Music (67) 157(1) [0|0|4] — 41.3
Mexican Trip (67) 164(1) [0|0|3] — 34.1
The Mystic Moods Of Love (68) 182(1) [0|0|4] — 27.8
Awakening (73) 190(1) [0|0|4] — 25.7
Emotions (68) 194(1) [0|0|3] — 23.4
Love The One You're With (72) 184(1) [0|0|3] — 20.2

► **Highest Peak [Top10s|Top40s|Total]**
Title (Yr) Peak(Wk) [T10 Wk|T40Wk|TotalWk] — **Score**

N

Jim NABORS ► 505 Pk:24 [0|2|12] — **6119**
Jim Nabors Sings Love Me With All Your Heart (66) 24(2) [0|7|56] — 2391
The Jim Nabors Hour (70) 34(2) [0|3|23] — 929
Jim Nabors By Request (67) 50(1) [0|0|40] — 833
Everything Is Beautiful (70) 124(1) [0|0|26] — 466
For The Good Times/The Jim Nabors Hour (71) 75(1) [0|0|13] — 407
Kiss Me Goodbye (68) 153(1) [0|0|26] — 302
Galveston (69) 145(2) [0|0|19] — 269
Help Me Make It Through The Night (71) 122(1) [0|0|10] — 161
The Lord's Prayer And Other Sacred Songs (68) 173(2) [0|0|12] — 145
The Way Of Love (72) 157(1) [0|0|8] — 107
The Things I Love (67) 147(1) [0|0|6] — 62.0
How Great Thou Art (71) 166(1) [0|0|4] — 47.0

The NAILS ► 3517 Pk:194 [0|0|1] — **10**
Dangerous Dreams (86) 194(2) [0|0|2] — 10.0

NAJEE ► 1156 Pk:56 [0|0|2] — **1449**
Najee's Theme (87) 56(2) [0|0|45] — 1012
Day By Day (88) 76(2) [0|0|21] — 437

NAKED EYES ► 1130 Pk:32 [0|1|2] — **1523**
Naked Eyes (83) 32(2) [0|4|42] — 1339
Fuel For The Fire (84) 83(3) [0|0|10] — 184

Graham NASH ► 800 Pk:15 [0|2|4] — **2947**
Songs For Beginners (71) 15(3) [0|11|24] — 2087
Wild Tales (74) 34(1) [0|3|14] — 678
Earth & Sky (80) 117(1) [0|0|5] — 101
Innocent Eyes (86) 136(2) [0|0|7] — 81.1

Johnny NASH ► 989 Pk:23 [0|1|3] — **1971**
I Can See Clearly Now (72) 23(2) [0|8|31] — 1624
Hold Me Tight (68) 109(1) [0|0|12] — 282
My Merry-Go-Round (73) 169(1) [0|0|6] — 64.8

NATIONAL LAMPOON ► 1715 Pk:107 [0|0|3] — **568**
Lemmings (73) 107(1) [0|0|13] — 237
Radio Dinner (72) 132(2) [0|0|12] — 179
Missing White House Tapes (74) 118(1) [0|0|8] — 152

NATURAL FOUR ► 3343 Pk:182 [0|0|1] — **25**
Heaven Right Here On Earth (75) 182(1) [0|0|3] — 24.9

NATURE'S DIVINE ► 2406 Pk:91 [0|0|1] — **185**
In The Beginning (79) 91(1) [0|0|8] — 185

NAZARETH ► 517 Pk:17 [0|2|13] — **5984**
Hair Of The Dog (75) 17(2) [0|9|40] — 2005
Close Enough For Rock 'N' Roll (76) 24(3) [0|7|14] — 1101
Malice In Wonderland (80) 41(3) [0|0|19] — 766
Expect No Mercy (77) 82(1) [0|0|16] — 375
The Fool Circle (81) 70(2) [0|0|13] — 344
No Mean City (79) 88(2) [0|0|14] — 290
'Snaz (81) 83(1) [0|0|9] — 248
Play 'N' The Game (76) 75(1) [0|0|9] — 247
Razamanaz (73) 157(2) [0|0|13] — 146
2XS (82) 122(2) [0|0|10] — 135
Hot Tracks (77) 120(2) [0|0|6] — 122
Rampant (74) 157(1) [0|0|9] — 115
Loud 'N' Proud (74) 150(1) [0|0|8] — 91.8

NAZZ ► 1379 Pk:80 [0|0|2] — **999**
Nazz Nazz (69) 80(2) [0|0|15] — 510
Nazz (68) 118(1) [0|0|26] — 489

Sam NEELY ► 2415 Pk:147 [0|0|2] — **183**
Loving You Just Crossed My Mind (72) 147(2) [0|0|11] — 131
Sam Neely-2 (73) 175(1) [0|0|6] — 51.9

► Highest Peak [Top10s|Top40s|Total] Title (Yr) Peak(Wk) [T10 Wk|T40Wk|TotalWk]	Score
NEKTAR ► 833 Pk:19 [0|2|5]	**2757**
Remember The Future (74) 19(2) [0|6|28]	1452
Down To Earth (75) 32(1) [0|3|20]	900
Recycled (76) 89(1) [0|0|14]	309
A Tab In The Ocean (76) 141(2) [0|0|4]	66.4
Magic Is A Child (77) 172(1) [0|0|3]	29.3
Rick NELSON ► 760 Pk:14 [0|2|6]	**3203**
Rick Nelson Sings "For You" (64) 14(2) [0|12|22]	1487
Garden Party (72)-Rick Nelson And The Stone Canyon Band 32(1) [0|5|18]	936
Rick Nelson In Concert (70) 54(1) [0|0|19]	655
Playing To Win (81) 153(2) [0|0|6]	84.4
Windfall (74)-Rick Nelson And The Stone Canyon Band 190(1) [0|0|4]	26.3
Rick Sings Nelson (70)-Rick Nelson And The Stone Canyon Band 196(2) [0|0|2]	13.4
Sandy NELSON ► 1646 Pk:118 [0|0|6]	**622**
Drums A Go-Go (65) 118(1) [0|0|11]	159
Live! In Las Vegas (64) 122(2) [0|0|11]	152
Drum Discotheque (65) 120(2) [0|0|8]	120
Boss Beat (66) 126(1) [0|0|7]	100
Teen Beat '65 (65) 135(2) [0|0|5]	66.2
"In" Beat (66) 148(1) [0|0|2]	25.3
Tracy NELSON ► 2923 Pk:145 [0|0|1]	**77**
Tracy Nelson (74) 145(1) [0|0|5]	76.5
Willie NELSON ► 106 Pk:2 [2|11|33]	**28455**
Always On My Mind (82) 2(4) [15|28|99]	6455
Stardust (78) 30(1) [0|3|117]	3488
Willie Nelson's Greatest Hits (& Some That Will Be) (81) 27(1) [0|6|93]	2922
Honeysuckle Rose (Soundtrack) (80)-Willie Nelson & Family 11(3) [0|13|36]	2735
Willie Nelson And Family Live (78) 32(2) [0|4|55]	1726
Red Headed Stranger (75) 28(2) [0|4|43]	1615
Somewhere Over The Rainbow (81) 31(3) [0|6|23]	1192
Willie Nelson Sings Kristofferson (79) 42(2) [0|0|25]	1061
Poncho & Lefty (83)-Merle Haggard/Willie Nelson [A] 37(1) [0|1|53]	754
Without A Song (83) 54(1) [0|0|34]	740
Wanted! The Outlaws (76)-Waylon Jennings, Willie Nelson, Jessi Colter, Tompall Glaser [A] 10(2) [2|14|51]	723
Tougher Than Leather (83) 39(1) [0|1|20]	666
Sound In Your Mind (76) 48(1) [0|0|15]	587
City of New Orleans (84) 69(1) [0|0|26]	495
One For The Road (79)-Willie Nelson And Leon Russell [A] 25(1) [0|5|18]	450
Before His Time (77) 78(2) [0|0|15]	415
The Electric Horseman (Soundtrack) (80)-Willie Nelson/Dave Grusin [A] 52(2) [0|0|25]	369
Take It To The Limit (83)-Willie Nelson With Waylon Jennings 60(1) [0|0|16]	368
San Antonio Rose (80)-Willie Nelson & Ray Price [A] 70(2) [0|0|25]	319
The Troublemaker (76) 60(1) [0|0|7]	298
To Lefty From Willie (77) 91(1) [0|0|12]	264
Pretty Paper (79) 73(1) [0|0|8]	255
Angel Eyes (84) 116(2) [0|0|7]	104
The Minstrel Man (81) 148(1) [0|0|7]	86.5
Me & Paul (85) 152(1) [0|0|7]	78.3
Willie Nelson Live (76) 149(1) [0|0|7]	76.8
Sweet Memories (79) 154(2) [0|0|5]	60.9
Danny Davis & Willie Nelson With The Nashville Brass (80)-Danny Davis And Willie Nelson With The Nashville Brass [A] 150(1) [0|0|5]	31.3
My Own Way (83) 182(1) [0|0|5]	28.1

► Highest Peak [Top10s|Top40s|Total] Title (Yr) Peak(Wk) [T10 Wk|T40Wk|TotalWk]	Score
Music From Songwriter (Soundtrack) (84)-Willie Nelson & Kris Kristofferson [A] 152(2) [0|0|5]	27.6
Phases And Stages (76) 187(2) [0|0|3]	23.8
Half Nelson (85) 178(2) [0|0|3]	20.9
What Can You Do To Me Now (75) 196(1) [0|0|3]	18.7
NENA ► 1535 Pk:27 [0|1|1]	**747**
99 Luftballons (84) 27(3) [0|6|14]	747
Peter NERO ► 632 Pk:23 [0|3|14]	**4413**
Summer Of '42 (71) 23(2) [0|10|27]	1829
Peter Nero In Person (63) 31(1) [0|3|23]	789
Reflections (64) 38(1) [0|2|26]	614
Songs You Won't Forget (64) 42(1) [0|0|21]	593
Nero Goes "Pops" (65)-Peter Nero/Boston Pops Orchestra [A] 86(1) [0|0|16]	147
The Screen Scene (66) 114(1) [0|0|6]	91.6
The First Time Ever (I Saw Your Face) (72) 172(2) [0|0|9]	82.3
The Best Of Peter Nero (65) 123(2) [0|0|4]	65.0
Sunday In New York (Soundtrack) (64) 133(1) [0|0|4]	54.8
Peter Nero-Up Close (66) 141(1) [0|0|3]	44.0
Career Girls (65) 147(1) [0|0|3]	35.6
Peter Nero Plays Love Is Blue And Ten Other Great Songs (68) 180(2) [0|0|4]	31.2
I've Gotta Be Me (69) 193(2) [0|0|3]	24.2
Peter Nero Plays Born Free And Others (67) 193(1) [0|0|2]	11.6
Michael NESMITH ► 2270 Pk:143 [0|0|3]	**225**
Infinite Rider On The Big Dogma (79) 151(2) [0|0|9]	115
Magnetic South (70)-Michael Nesmith & The First National Band 143(1) [0|0|3]	56.7
Loose Salute (71)-Michael Nesmith & The First National Band 159(1) [0|0|4]	54.1
Robbie NEVIL ► 1054 Pk:37 [0|1|2]	**1736**
Robbie Nevil (86) 37(2) [0|3|46]	1460
A Place Like This (88) 118(2) [0|0|21]	276
Ivan NEVILLE ► 2013 Pk:107 [0|0|1]	**345**
If My Ancestors Could See Me Now (88) 107(1) [0|0|23]	345
NEVILLE BROTHERS ► 1564 Pk:66 [0|0|4]	**719**
Yellow Moon (89) 66(3) [0|0|24]	583
Uptown (87) 155(1) [0|0|9]	79.3
Fiyo On The Bayou (81) 166(1) [0|0|3]	34.8
Treacherous: A History Of The Neville Brothers 1955-1985 (87) 178(2) [0|0|3]	21.5
The NEWBEATS ► 1787 Pk:56 [0|0|2]	**494**
Bread & Butter (64) 56(2) [0|0|19]	433
Run Baby Run (66) 131(1) [0|0|4]	60.8
NEW BIRTH ► 754 Pk:31 [0|1|8]	**3238**
Birth Day (73) 31(1) [0|4|29]	1124
It's Been A Long Time (73) 50(1) [0|0|31]	887
Blind Baby (75) 57(1) [0|0|17]	595
Comin' From All Ends (74) 56(1) [0|0|15]	468
Behold The Mighty Army (77) 164(1) [0|0|6]	75.0
Love Potion (76) 168(2) [0|0|4]	49.3
The Best Of The New Birth (75) 175(2) [0|0|2]	23.4
Ain't No Big Thing, But It's Growing (71) 189(2) [0|0|2]	17.1
Mickey NEWBURY ► 1701 Pk:58 [0|0|3]	**583**
'Frisco Mabel Joy (71) 58(1) [0|0|15]	501
Heaven Help The Child (73) 173(1) [0|0|5]	47.3
Lovers (75) 172(2) [0|0|3]	35.2
NEW CHRISTY MINSTRELS ► 375 Pk:9 [1|3|8]	**8821**
Ramblin' Featuring Green, Green (63) 15(1) [0|23|77]	4052
Today (64) 9(2) [2|20|34]	2283
Chim Chim Cher-ee (65) 22(1) [0|8|22]	1123

► Highest Peak [Top10s|Top40s|Total] Title (Yr) Peak(Wk) [T10 Wk|T40Wk|TotalWk]	Score
Land Of Giants (64) 48(1) [0|0|23]	594
Greatest Hits (66) 76(1) [0|0|16]	350
Cowboys And Indians (65) 62(1) [0|0|11]	276
The Wandering Minstrels (65) 125(1) [0|0|9]	128
You Need Someone To Love (70) 195(1) [0|0|2]	13.4
NEWCLEUS ► 1827 Pk:74 [0|0|1]	**460**
Jam On Revenge (84) 74(2) [0|0|28]	460
NEW COLONY SIX ► 2465 Pk:157 [0|0|3]	**170**
Revelations (68) 157(2) [0|0|6]	78.8
Colonization (67) 172(2) [0|0|7]	51.6
Attacking A Straw Man (69) 179(1) [0|0|4]	39.4
NEW EDITION ► 301 Pk:6 [1|3|5]	**11484**
Heart Break (88) 12(1) [0|37|50]	4305
New Edition (84) 6(2) [6|29|54]	4038
All For Love (85) 32(1) [0|15|48]	1967
Under The Blue Moon (86) 43(2) [0|0|23]	663
Candy Girl (83) 90(2) [0|0|33]	510
NEW ENGLAND ► 1690 Pk:50 [0|0|2]	**591**
New England (79) 50(2) [0|0|17]	555
Walking Wild (81) 176(2) [0|0|4]	36.1
NEW ENGLAND CONSERVATORY CHORUS ► 1431 Pk:65 [0|0|1]	**923**
Scott Joplin: The Red Back Book (73) 65(1) [0|0|36]	923
Bob NEWHART ► 2253 Pk:113 [0|0|2]	**232**
Bob Newhart Faces Bob Newhart (Faces Bob Newhart) (64) 113(1) [0|0|11]	158
The Windmills Are Weakening (65) 126(2) [0|0|5]	73.4
NEW KIDS ON THE BLOCK ► 174 Pk:1 [2|3|3]	**19989**
Hangin' Tough (88) 1(2) [45|71|132]	14550
New Kids On The Block (89) 25(3) [0|18|80]	3437
Merry, Merry Christmas (89) 9(1) [3|13|28]	2001
Randy NEWMAN ► 547 Pk:9 [1|2|7]	**5441**
Little Criminals (77) 9(2) [3|18|29]	3124
Good Old Boys (74) 36(2) [0|2|23]	900
Born Again (79) 41(2) [0|0|11]	495
Land Of Dreams (88) 80(1) [0|0|19]	384
Trouble In Paradise (83) 64(4) [0|0|13]	316
Sail Away (72) 163(1) [0|0|18]	200
Randy Newman/Live (71) 191(1) [0|0|3]	23.3
NEW ORDER ► 708 Pk:32 [0|2|4]	**3596**
Substance (87) 36(1) [0|7|60]	1864
Technique (89) 32(1) [0|6|28]	1165
Low-Life (85) 94(2) [0|0|22]	342
Brotherhood (86) 117(1) [0|0|21]	226
NEW RIDERS Of The PURPLE SAGE ► 737 Pk:33 [0|2|8]	**3393**
Powerglide (72) 33(2) [0|6|18]	964
New Riders Of The Purple Sage (71) 39(2) [0|2|15]	778
The Adventures Of Panama Red (73) 55(1) [0|0|18]	545
Home, Home On The Road (74) 68(1) [0|0|12]	321
Gypsy Cowboy (72) 85(1) [0|0|13]	305
Brujo (74) 68(1) [0|0|9]	288
New Riders (76) 145(1) [0|0|8]	123
Oh, What A Mighty Time (75) 144(1) [0|0|4]	68.6
NEW SEEKERS ► 1447 Pk:37 [0|1|4]	**893**
We'd Like To Teach The World To Sing (71) 37(2) [0|2|14]	645
Beautiful People (71) 136(1) [0|0|6]	120
Circles (72) 166(3) [0|0|10]	103
Pinball Wizards (73) 190(1) [0|0|4]	25.8
Juice NEWTON ► 410 Pk:20 [0|2|5]	**7920**
Juice (81) 22(3) [0|34|86]	5505
Quiet Lies (82) 20(2) [0|8|46]	1875

<table>
<tr><th>► Highest Peak [Top10s|Top40s|Total]
Title (Yr) Peak(Wk) [T10 Wk|T40Wk|TotalWk]</th><th>Score</th></tr>
<tr><td>Juice NEWTON ► Continued</td><td></td></tr>
<tr><td>Dirty Looks (83) 52(1) [0|0|15]</td><td>367</td></tr>
<tr><td>Can't Wait All Night (84) 128(2) [0|0|10]</td><td>140</td></tr>
<tr><td>Greatest Hits (84) 178(2) [0|0|5]</td><td>32.6</td></tr>
<tr><td>Wayne NEWTON ► 747 Pk:17 [0|2|10]</td><td>3280</td></tr>
<tr><td>Daddy Don't You Walk So Fast (72) 34(2) [0|5|21]</td><td>1091</td></tr>
<tr><td>Red Roses For A Blue Lady (65) 17(1) [0|8|20]</td><td>1028</td></tr>
<tr><td>Wayne Newton - Now! (66) 80(2) [0|0|21]</td><td>470</td></tr>
<tr><td>Danke Schoen (63) 55(1) [0|0|9]</td><td>226</td></tr>
<tr><td>It's Only The Good Times (67) 131(1) [0|0|13]</td><td>190</td></tr>
<tr><td>Can't You Hear The Song? (72) 164(1) [0|0|11]</td><td>110</td></tr>
<tr><td>Summer Wind (65) 114(2) [0|0|6]</td><td>92.7</td></tr>
<tr><td>One More Time (68) 186(1) [0|0|5]</td><td>33.0</td></tr>
<tr><td>The Best Of Wayne Newton (67) 194(1) [0|0|4]</td><td>20.0</td></tr>
<tr><td>Walking On New Grass (68) 196(1) [0|0|3]</td><td>19.2</td></tr>
<tr><td>Olivia NEWTON-JOHN ► 76 Pk:1 [5|12|16]</td><td>35230</td></tr>
<tr><td>Have You Never Been Mellow (75) 1(1) [12|17|31]</td><td>5700</td></tr>
<tr><td>Physical (81) 6(7) [14|27|57]</td><td>5534</td></tr>
<tr><td>If You Love Me Let Me Know (74) 1(1) [6|19|61]</td><td>5055</td></tr>
<tr><td>Olivia's Greatest Hits, Vol. 2 (82) 16(4) [0|21|86]</td><td>4032</td></tr>
<tr><td>Totally Hot (78) 7(2) [6|17|39]</td><td>3388</td></tr>
<tr><td>Xanadu (Soundtrack) (80)- Olivia Newton-John/Electric Light Orchestra [A] 4(3) [8|15|36]</td><td>2043</td></tr>
<tr><td>Olivia Newton-John's Greatest Hits (77) 13(2) [0|13|19]</td><td>2002</td></tr>
<tr><td>Come On Over (76) 13(1) [0|10|24]</td><td>1869</td></tr>
<tr><td>Clearly Love (75) 12(2) [0|6|22]</td><td>1569</td></tr>
<tr><td>Don't Stop Believin' (76) 30(2) [0|4|28]</td><td>1423</td></tr>
<tr><td>Making A Good Thing Better (77) 34(1) [0|4|16]</td><td>908</td></tr>
<tr><td>Soul Kiss (85) 29(3) [0|5|16]</td><td>685</td></tr>
<tr><td>Let Me Be There (73) 54(1) [0|0|20]</td><td>593</td></tr>
<tr><td>The Rumour (88) 67(2) [0|0|9]</td><td>216</td></tr>
<tr><td>Warm And Tender (89) 124(2) [0|0|13]</td><td>154</td></tr>
<tr><td>If Not For You (71) 158(1) [0|0|4]</td><td>58.6</td></tr>
<tr><td>NEW VAUDEVILLE BAND ► 799 Pk:5 [1|1|1]</td><td>2950</td></tr>
<tr><td>Winchester Cathedral (66) 5(3) [7|17|31]</td><td>2950</td></tr>
<tr><td>NEW YORK CITY ► 2544 Pk:122 [0|0|1]</td><td>149</td></tr>
<tr><td>I'm Doin' Fine Now (73) 122(1) [0|0|10]</td><td>149</td></tr>
<tr><td>NEW YORK DOLLS ► 2179 Pk:116 [0|0|2]</td><td>267</td></tr>
<tr><td>New York Dolls (73) 116(2) [0|0|12]</td><td>214</td></tr>
<tr><td>In Too Much Too Soon (74) 167(1) [0|0|5]</td><td>52.5</td></tr>
<tr><td>The NICE ► 2664 Pk:152 [0|0|2]</td><td>120</td></tr>
<tr><td>Keith Emerson with The Nice (72) 152(1) [0|0|8]</td><td>91.7</td></tr>
<tr><td>Five Bridges (70) 197(3) [0|0|5]</td><td>28.7</td></tr>
<tr><td>Stevie NICKS ► 160 Pk:1 [3|4|4]</td><td>21034</td></tr>
<tr><td>Bella Donna (81) 1(1) [26|45|143]</td><td>12532</td></tr>
<tr><td>The Wild Heart (83) 5(7) [11|22|52]</td><td>4401</td></tr>
<tr><td>Rock A Little (85) 12(1) [0|17|35]</td><td>2539</td></tr>
<tr><td>The Other Side Of The Mirror (89) 10(1) [1|11|21]</td><td>1562</td></tr>
<tr><td>NIGHT ► 2388 Pk:113 [0|0|1]</td><td>189</td></tr>
<tr><td>Night (79) 113(2) [0|0|10]</td><td>189</td></tr>
<tr><td>The NIGHTHAWKS ► 3184 Pk:166 [0|0|1]</td><td>43</td></tr>
<tr><td>Nighthawks (80) 166(1) [0|0|4]</td><td>42.9</td></tr>
<tr><td>Maxine NIGHTINGALE ► 1387 Pk:45 [0|0|3]</td><td>987</td></tr>
<tr><td>Lead Me On (79) 45(2) [0|0|18]</td><td>661</td></tr>
<tr><td>Right Back Where We Started From (76) 65(1) [0|0|9]</td><td>297</td></tr>
<tr><td>It's A Beautiful Thing (83) 176(2) [0|0|4]</td><td>28.3</td></tr>
<tr><td>NIGHT RANGER ► 319 Pk:10 [1|4|5]</td><td>10661</td></tr>
<tr><td>Midnight Madness (83) 15(10) [0|29|69]</td><td>4751</td></tr>
<tr><td>7 Wishes (85) 10(3) [3|25|45]</td><td>3665</td></tr>
<tr><td>Dawn Patrol (82) 38(4) [0|8|69]</td><td>1458</td></tr>
<tr><td>Big Life (87) 28(2) [0|3|18]</td><td>628</td></tr>
<tr><td>Man In Motion (88) 81(2) [0|0|8]</td><td>159</td></tr>
<tr><td>Willie NILE ► 2419 Pk:145 [0|0|2]</td><td>182</td></tr>
<tr><td>Golden Down (81) 158(1) [0|0|8]</td><td>93.8</td></tr>
<tr><td>Willie Nile (80) 145(2) [0|0|6]</td><td>88.5</td></tr>
<tr><td>NILSSON ► 300 Pk:3 [1|3|13]</td><td>11646</td></tr>
<tr><td>Nilsson Schmilsson (71) 3(3) [12|19|46]</td><td>5228</td></tr>
<tr><td>Son Of Schmilsson (72) 12(2) [0|13|31]</td><td>2432</td></tr>
<tr><td>The Point! (71) 25(1) [0|8|32]</td><td>1819</td></tr>
<tr><td>A Little Touch Of Schmilsson In The Night (73) 46(1) [0|0|17]</td><td>618</td></tr>
<tr><td>Pussy Cats (74) 60(1) [0|0|12]</td><td>375</td></tr>
<tr><td>Harry (69) 120(1) [0|0|15]</td><td>308</td></tr>
<tr><td>Knnillsson (77) 108(2) [0|0|10]</td><td>202</td></tr>
<tr><td>Son Of Dracula (Soundtrack) (74) 106(1) [0|0|9]</td><td>193</td></tr>
<tr><td>Sandman (76) 111(2) [0|0|7]</td><td>145</td></tr>
<tr><td>Duit On Mon Dei (75) 141(2) [0|0|7]</td><td>102</td></tr>
<tr><td>Greatest Hits (78) 140(1) [0|0|5]</td><td>87.0</td></tr>
<tr><td>...That's The Way It Is (76) 158(1) [0|0|6]</td><td>85.0</td></tr>
<tr><td>Aerial Pandemonium Ballet (71) 149(1) [0|0|3]</td><td>51.4</td></tr>
<tr><td>Leonard NIMOY ► 1568 Pk:83 [0|0|2]</td><td>715</td></tr>
<tr><td>Mr. Spock's Music From Outer Space (67) 83(1) [0|0|25]</td><td>453</td></tr>
<tr><td>Two Sides Of Leonard Nimoy (68) 97(2) [0|0|13]</td><td>262</td></tr>
<tr><td>999 ► 3167 Pk:177 [0|0|2]</td><td>44</td></tr>
<tr><td>The Biggest Prize In Sport (80) 177(2) [0|0|3]</td><td>30.2</td></tr>
<tr><td>Concrete (81) 192(2) [0|0|2]</td><td>14.3</td></tr>
<tr><td>9.9 ► 1930 Pk:79 [0|0|1]</td><td>387</td></tr>
<tr><td>9.9 (85) 79(1) [0|0|22]</td><td>387</td></tr>
<tr><td>1910 FRUITGUM CO. ► 2098 Pk:147 [0|0|3]</td><td>304</td></tr>
<tr><td>Indian Giver (69) 147(2) [0|0|8]</td><td>121</td></tr>
<tr><td>1,2,3 Red Light (68) 163(1) [0|0|12]</td><td>107</td></tr>
<tr><td>Simon Says (68) 162(1) [0|0|8]</td><td>77.2</td></tr>
<tr><td>The NITE-LITERS ► 2542 Pk:167 [0|0|2]</td><td>149</td></tr>
<tr><td>Morning, Noon & The Nite-Liters (71) 167(1) [0|0|13]</td><td>139</td></tr>
<tr><td>Instrumental Directions (72) 198(2) [0|0|2]</td><td>10.7</td></tr>
<tr><td>NITRO ► 2718 Pk:140 [0|0|1]</td><td>111</td></tr>
<tr><td>O.F.R. (89) 140(1) [0|0|9]</td><td>111</td></tr>
<tr><td>NITTY GRITTY DIRT BAND ► 559 Pk:28 [0|1|12]</td><td>5205</td></tr>
<tr><td>Stars & Stripes Forever (74) 28(2) [0|6|21]</td><td>1215</td></tr>
<tr><td>Uncle Charlie & His Dog Teddy (70) 66(1) [0|0|32]</td><td>894</td></tr>
<tr><td>Will The Circle Be Unbroken (72) 68(1) [0|0|32]</td><td>888</td></tr>
<tr><td>Make A Little Magic (80)-The Dirt Band 62(2) [0|0|16]</td><td>525</td></tr>
<tr><td>Dirt, Silver & Gold (76) 77(2) [0|0|13]</td><td>395</td></tr>
<tr><td>An American Dream (80)-The Dirt Band 76(1) [0|0|14]</td><td>319</td></tr>
<tr><td>Dream (75) 66(1) [0|0|9]</td><td>311</td></tr>
<tr><td>Will The Circle Be Unbroken, Vol.II (89) 95(2) [0|0|12]</td><td>209</td></tr>
<tr><td>Jealousy (81)-The Dirt Band 102(1) [0|0|9]</td><td>187</td></tr>
<tr><td>The Nitty Gritty Dirt Band (67) 151(1) [0|0|8]</td><td>98.4</td></tr>
<tr><td>All The Good Times (72) 162(1) [0|0|10]</td><td>96.5</td></tr>
<tr><td>The Dirt Band (78)-The Dirt Band 163(1) [0|0|6]</td><td>66.9</td></tr>
<tr><td>NITZINGER ► 2906 Pk:170 [0|0|1]</td><td>79</td></tr>
<tr><td>Nitzinger (72) 170(1) [0|0|8]</td><td>79.5</td></tr>
<tr><td>Don NIX ► 3410 Pk:197 [0|0|1]</td><td>19</td></tr>
<tr><td>Living By The Days (71) 197(2) [0|0|3]</td><td>18.6</td></tr>
<tr><td>Mojo NIXON & Skid ROPER ► 2911 Pk:151 [0|0|2]</td><td>79</td></tr>
<tr><td>Root Hog Or Die (89) 151(1) [0|0|7]</td><td>66.9</td></tr>
<tr><td>Bo-Day-Shus!!! (87) 189(1) [0|0|2]</td><td>11.7</td></tr>
<tr><td>No Artist ► 2446 Pk:96 [0|0|1]</td><td>174</td></tr>
<tr><td>Annie's Christmas (82) 96(4) [0|0|9]</td><td>174</td></tr>
<tr><td>Cliff NOBLES & Co. ► 3146 Pk:159 [0|0|1]</td><td>47</td></tr>
<tr><td>The Horse (68) 159(1) [0|0|3]</td><td>46.5</td></tr>
<tr><td>NOEL ► 2537 Pk:126 [0|0|1]</td><td>151</td></tr>
<tr><td>Noel (88) 126(1) [0|0|13]</td><td>151</td></tr>
<tr><td>Kenny NOLAN ► 1874 Pk:78 [0|0|1]</td><td>421</td></tr>
<tr><td>Kenny Nolan (77) 78(1) [0|0|16]</td><td>421</td></tr>
<tr><td>NORMA JEAN ► 2423 Pk:134 [0|0|1]</td><td>181</td></tr>
<tr><td>Norma Jean (78) 134(1) [0|0|11]</td><td>181</td></tr>
<tr><td>Freddie NORTH ► 3203 Pk:179 [0|0|1]</td><td>39</td></tr>
<tr><td>Friend (72) 179(2) [0|0|5]</td><td>39.4</td></tr>
<tr><td>Aldo NOVA ► 704 Pk:8 [1|1|2]</td><td>3623</td></tr>
<tr><td>Aldo Nova (82) 8(6) [8|16|37]</td><td>3135</td></tr>
<tr><td>Subject: Aldo Nova (83) 56(2) [0|0|20]</td><td>488</td></tr>
<tr><td>NOVO COMBO ► 3015 Pk:167 [0|0|1]</td><td>64</td></tr>
<tr><td>Novo Combo (81) 167(1) [0|0|6]</td><td>63.5</td></tr>
<tr><td>NRBQ ► 3009 Pk:162 [0|0|2]</td><td>65</td></tr>
<tr><td>NRBQ (69) 162(1) [0|0|4]</td><td>52.0</td></tr>
<tr><td>Wild Weekend (89) 198(3) [0|0|3]</td><td>13.0</td></tr>
<tr><td>NUCLEAR ASSAULT ► 1870 Pk:126 [0|0|2]</td><td>426</td></tr>
<tr><td>Handle With Care (89) 126(1) [0|0|24]</td><td>309</td></tr>
<tr><td>Survive (88) 145(1) [0|0|11]</td><td>117</td></tr>
<tr><td>Ted NUGENT ► 248 Pk:13 [0|7|13]</td><td>14453</td></tr>
<tr><td>Cat Scratch Fever (77) 17(1) [0|19|39]</td><td>2820</td></tr>
<tr><td>Ted Nugent (75) 28(2) [0|6|62]</td><td>2458</td></tr>
<tr><td>Double Live Gonzo! (78) 13(1) [0|8|22]</td><td>1657</td></tr>
<tr><td>Free-For-All (76) 24(2) [0|8|32]</td><td>1648</td></tr>
<tr><td>Scream Dream (80) 13(2) [0|9|18]</td><td>1565</td></tr>
<tr><td>Weekend Warriors (78) 24(3) [0|10|20]</td><td>1390</td></tr>
<tr><td>State Of Shock (79) 18(2) [0|6|18]</td><td>1156</td></tr>
<tr><td>Penetrator (84) 56(2) [0|0|15]</td><td>426</td></tr>
<tr><td>Nugent (82) 51(2) [0|0|14]</td><td>409</td></tr>
<tr><td>Intensities In 10 Cities (81) 51(2) [0|0|10]</td><td>404</td></tr>
<tr><td>Little Miss Dangerous (86) 76(2) [0|0|14]</td><td>290</td></tr>
<tr><td>If You Can't Lick 'Em...Lick 'Em (88) 112(2) [0|0|7]</td><td>120</td></tr>
<tr><td>Great Gonzos! The Best Of Ted Nugent (81) 140(1) [0|0|8]</td><td>110</td></tr>
<tr><td>Gary NUMAN ► 840 Pk:16 [0|1|4]</td><td>2737</td></tr>
<tr><td>The Pleasure Principle (80) 16(2) [0|14|30]</td><td>2216</td></tr>
<tr><td>Telekon (80) 64(2) [0|0|10]</td><td>303</td></tr>
<tr><td>Replicas (79)-Gary Numan & Tubeway Army 124(1) [0|0|10]</td><td>177</td></tr>
<tr><td>Dance (81) 167(1) [0|0|4]</td><td>41.4</td></tr>
<tr><td>Bobby NUNN ► 2867 Pk:148 [0|0|1]</td><td>85</td></tr>
<tr><td>Second To Nunn (82) 148(1) [0|0|8]</td><td>85.2</td></tr>
<tr><td>NU SHOOZ ► 1098 Pk:27 [0|1|2]</td><td>1612</td></tr>
<tr><td>Poolside (86) 27(2) [0|8|32]</td><td>1359</td></tr>
<tr><td>Told U So (88) 93(2) [0|0|14]</td><td>253</td></tr>
<tr><td>N.W.A. ► 827 Pk:37 [0|1|1]</td><td>2777</td></tr>
<tr><td>Straight Outta Compton (89) 37(3) [0|9|81]</td><td>2777</td></tr>
<tr><td>The NYLONS ► 1368 Pk:43 [0|0|3]</td><td>1019</td></tr>
<tr><td>Happy Together (87) 43(1) [0|0|24]</td><td>752</td></tr>
<tr><td>Seamless (86) 133(1) [0|0|16]</td><td>174</td></tr>
<tr><td>Rockapella (89) 136(2) [0|0|10]</td><td>93.0</td></tr>
<tr><td>Laura NYRO ► 798 Pk:32 [0|1|8]</td><td>2953</td></tr>
<tr><td>New York Tendaberry (69) 32(1) [0|3|17]</td><td>825</td></tr>
<tr><td>Gonna Take A Miracle (71) 46(2) [0|0|17]</td><td>607</td></tr>
<tr><td>Christmas And The Beads Of Sweat (70) 51(1) [0|0|14]</td><td>588</td></tr>
<tr><td>Smile (76) 60(2) [0|0|14]</td><td>541</td></tr>
<tr><td>The First Songs (73) 97(1) [0|0|11]</td><td>222</td></tr>
<tr><td>Season Of Lights...Laura Nyro In Concert (77) 137(2) [0|0|5]</td><td>93.9</td></tr>
<tr><td>Eli And The Thirteenth Confession (68) 181(1) [0|0|7]</td><td>55.2</td></tr>
<tr><td>Mother's Spiritual (84) 182(1) [0|0|3]</td><td>20.5</td></tr>
</table>

▶ Highest Peak [Top10s|Top40s|Total]
Title (Yr) Peak(Wk) [T10 Wk|T40Wk|TotalWk] — Score

O

OAK RIDGE BOYS ▶ 489 Pk:14 [0|2|11] — 6346
- Fancy Free (81) 14(1) [0|10|48] — 3024
- Bobbie Sue (82) 20(3) [0|9|21] — 1175
- American Made (83) 51(3) [0|0|23] — 673
- Greatest Hits (80) 99(1) [0|0|21] — 355
- Greatest Hits, Vol. 2 (84) 71(2) [0|0|24] — 337
- Deliver (83) 121(1) [0|0|14] — 217
- Y'all Come Back Saloon (78) 120(2) [0|0|9] — 158
- Christmas (82) 73(2) [0|0|7] — 156
- Room Service (78) 164(5) [0|0|11] — 136
- Together (80) 154(1) [0|0|6] — 63.8
- Step On Out (85) 156(1) [0|0|5] — 51.9

OAKTOWN'S 3.5.7 ▶ 2320 Pk:126 [0|0|1] — 209
- Wild & Loose (89) 126(1) [0|0|16] — 209

John O'BANION ▶ 3116 Pk:164 [0|0|1] — 51
- John O'Banion (81) 164(1) [0|0|4] — 50.7

O'BRYAN ▶ 1287 Pk:64 [0|0|3] — 1172
- Be My Lover (84) 64(1) [0|0|21] — 535
- You And I (83) 87(1) [0|0|27] — 386
- Doin' Alright (82) 80(1) [0|0|12] — 251

Ric OCASEK ▶ 1050 Pk:28 [0|2|2] — 1743
- Beatitude (83) 28(5) [0|9|16] — 875
- This Side Of Paradise (86) 31(2) [0|5|23] — 868

OCEAN ▶ 1833 Pk:60 [0|0|1] — 455
- Put Your Hand In The Hand (71) 60(1) [0|0|13] — 455

Billy OCEAN ▶ 259 Pk:6 [2|3|5] — 13737
- Suddenly (84) 9(2) [2|57|86] — 6704
- Love Zone (86) 6(7) [12|30|48] — 4661
- Tear Down These Walls (88) 18(1) [0|11|31] — 2012
- Greatest Hits (89) 77(2) [0|0|16] — 314
- Nights (Feel Like Getting Down) (81) 152(1) [0|0|3] — 44.7

Phil OCHS ▶ 2416 Pk:149 [0|0|4] — 183
- Rehearsals For Retirement (69) 167(1) [0|0|7] — 94.0
- Pleasures Of The Harbor (67) 168(1) [0|0|5] — 48.8
- Phil Ochs In Concert (66) 149(1) [0|0|2] — 26.6
- Phil Ochs Greatest Hits (70) 194(2) [0|0|2] — 13.5

Carroll O'CONNOR ▶ 2217 Pk:118 [0|0|1] — 247
- Remembering You (72) 118(1) [0|0|13] — 247

Sinead O'CONNOR ▶ 1198 Pk:36 [0|1|1] — 1345
- The Lion And The Cobra (88) 36(3) [0|5|38] — 1345

Alan O'DAY ▶ 2337 Pk:109 [0|0|1] — 203
- Appetizers (77) 109(2) [0|0|9] — 203

ODETTA ▶ 2466 Pk:75 [0|0|1] — 169
- Odetta Sings Folk Songs (63) 75(1) [0|0|8] — 169

ODYSSEY ▶ 1085 Pk:36 [0|1|4] — 1646
- Odyssey (77) 36(2) [0|5|38] — 1458
- Hollywood Party Tonight (78) 123(2) [0|0|5] — 106
- I Got The Melody (81) 175(2) [0|0|5] — 48.5
- Hang Together (80) 181(1) [0|0|4] — 34.5

OFF BROADWAY USA ▶ 2246 Pk:101 [0|0|1] — 236
- On (80) 101(2) [0|0|11] — 236

OHIO EXPRESS ▶ 2471 Pk:126 [0|0|2] — 168
- Ohio Express (68) 126(2) [0|0|11] — 151
- Chewy, Chewy (69) 191(1) [0|0|2] — 16.8

OHIO PLAYERS ▶ 159 Pk:1 [2|5|16] — 21127
- Fire (74) 1(1) [10|19|29] — 5305
- Honey (75) 2(1) [8|24|36] — 5039
- Skin Tight (74) 11(3) [0|22|48] — 4072
- Contradiction (76) 12(2) [0|9|20] — 2029
- Ohio Players Gold (76) 31(2) [0|4|17] — 905
- Angel (77) 41(1) [0|0|27] — 861
- Pleasure (73) 63(1) [0|0|22] — 563
- Rattlesnake (75) 61(1) [0|0|14] — 488
- Ecstasy (73) 70(1) [0|0|19] — 415
- Everybody Up (79) 80(1) [0|0|14] — 367
- Jass-Ay-Lay-Dee (78) 69(3) [0|0|9] — 301
- Mr. Mean (77) 68(1) [0|0|10] — 265
- Climax (74) 102(1) [0|0|8] — 215
- Ohio Players Greatest Hits (75) 92(1) [0|0|7] — 199
- Pain (72) 177(1) [0|0|7] — 63.6
- Tenderness (81) 165(2) [0|0|3] — 39.0

OINGO BOINGO ▶ 1340 Pk:77 [0|0|8] — 1074
- Boi-ngo (87) 77(2) [0|0|16] — 293
- Dead Man's Party (85) 98(2) [0|0|16] — 258
- Boingo Alive (88) 90(3) [0|0|11] — 181
- Nothing To Fear (82) 148(1) [0|0|9] — 85.3
- Good For Your Soul (83) 144(1) [0|0|7] — 78.5
- Skeletons In The Closet: The Best Of Oingo Boingo (89) 150(2) [0|0|6] — 69.2
- Oingo Boingo (80) 163(2) [0|0|5] — 55.1
- Only A Lad (81) 172(1) [0|0|5] — 54.6

The O'JAYS ▶ 146 Pk:6 [3|10|17] — 22620
- Family Reunion (75) 7(1) [7|17|34] — 3525
- Ship Ahoy (73) 11(1) [0|19|48] — 3438
- So Full Of Love (78) 6(2) [3|13|28] — 2763
- Back Stabbers (72) 10(2) [2|11|44] — 2577
- Survival (75) 11(1) [0|14|24] — 2341
- Identify Yourself (79) 16(2) [0|8|30] — 1633
- Message In The Music (76) 20(1) [0|6|22] — 1623
- The O'Jays Live In London (74) 17(1) [0|7|24] — 1577
- Travelin' At The Speed Of Thought (77) 27(1) [0|5|16] — 907
- The Year 2000 (80) 36(2) [0|3|12] — 681
- Let Me Touch You (87) 66(1) [0|0|25] — 577
- My Favorite Person (82) 49(2) [0|0|13] — 343
- Serious (89) 114(1) [0|0|17] — 238
- Love Fever (85) 121(2) [0|0|12] — 148
- The O'Jays: Collectors' Items (78) 132(1) [0|0|6] — 102
- The O'Jays In Philadelphia (73) 156(1) [0|0|8] — 87.6
- When Will I See You Again (83) 142(1) [0|0|5] — 61.7

The O'KAYSIONS ▶ 2926 Pk:153 [0|0|1] — 76
- Girl Watcher (68) 153(2) [0|0|4] — 75.9

Danny O'KEEFE ▶ 1905 Pk:87 [0|0|2] — 404
- O'Keefe (72) 87(2) [0|0|16] — 331
- Breezy Stories (73) 172(1) [0|0|9] — 72.7

OLD & IN THE WAY ▶ 2323 Pk:99 [0|0|1] — 209
- Old & In The Way (75) 99(1) [0|0|8] — 209

Mike OLDFIELD ▶ 549 Pk:3 [1|1|6] — 5431
- Tubular Bells (73) 3(2) [12|23|45] — 4893
- Hergest Ridge (74) 87(2) [0|0|10] — 242
- Islands (88) 138(2) [0|0|8] — 116
- Ommadawn (75) 146(1) [0|0|7] — 108
- Five Miles Out (82) 164(2) [0|0|5] — 43.3
- QE 2 (81) 174(1) [0|0|3] — 30.1

OLIVER ▶ 823 Pk:19 [0|1|2] — 2803
- Good Morning Starshine (69) 19(1) [0|10|38] — 2471
- Oliver Again (70) 71(1) [0|0|13] — 332

David OLIVER ▶ 2538 Pk:128 [0|0|1] — 150
- David Oliver (78) 128(1) [0|0|8] — 150

Jane OLIVOR ▶ 1474 Pk:58 [0|0|4] — 854
- The Best Side Of Goodbye (80) 58(1) [0|0|12] — 382
- Stay The Night (78) 108(1) [0|0|12] — 208
- Chasing Rainbows (77) 86(1) [0|0|8] — 198
- In Concert (82) 144(2) [0|0|6] — 65.9

Nigel OLSSON ▶ 2933 Pk:140 [0|0|1] — 74
- Nigel (79) 140(1) [0|0|5] — 74.4

OMAR And The HOWLERS ▶ 2029 Pk:81 [0|0|1] — 338
- Hard Times In The Land Of Plenty (87) 81(2) [0|0|19] — 338

Alexander O'NEAL ▶ 1031 Pk:29 [0|1|4] — 1842
- Hearsay (87) 29(1) [0|8|40] — 1492
- Alexander O'Neal (85) 92(2) [0|0|18] — 260
- My Gift To You (88) 149(1) [0|0|5] — 54.8
- All Mixed Up (89) 185(2) [0|0|5] — 34.5

100 PROOF AGED IN SOUL ▶ 2878 Pk:151 [0|0|1] — 83
- Somebody's Been Sleeping In My Bed (70) 151(2) [0|0|7] — 82.9

ONE WAY ▶ 977 Pk:51 [0|0|8] — 2007
- Who's Foolin' Who (82) 51(1) [0|0|23] — 662
- Lady (84) 58(1) [0|0|20] — 481
- Fancy Dancer (81) 79(2) [0|0|19] — 383
- One Way Featuring Al Hudson(2) (80)-One Way Featuring Al Hudson 128(1) [0|0|12] — 226
- Love Is...One Way (81) 157(1) [0|0|8] — 91.7
- Wrap Your Body (85) 156(2) [0|0|9] — 68.1
- Shine On Me (83) 164(1) [0|0|6] — 53.0
- One Way Featuring Al Hudson (79)-One Way Featuring Al Hudson 181(2) [0|0|5] — 42.3

Yoko ONO ▶ 1649 Pk:49 [0|0|5] — 620
- Season Of Glass (81) 49(2) [0|0|9] — 358
- It's Alright (I See Rainbows) (82) 98(2) [0|0|13] — 202
- Yoko Ono/Plastic Ono Band (71) 182(1) [0|0|3] — 25.2
- Approximately Infinite Universe (73) 193(1) [0|0|4] — 23.1
- Fly (71) 199(2) [0|0|2] — 11.9

OPUS ▶ 1935 Pk:64 [0|0|1] — 385
- Up And Down (86) 64(2) [0|0|16] — 385

Roy ORBISON ▶ 440 Pk:5 [1|3|12] — 7260
- Mystery Girl (89) 5(2) [8|16|27] — 3024
- More Of Roy Orbison's Greatest Hits (64) 19(3) [0|16|30] — 1665
- In Dreams (63) 35(1) [0|2|23] — 882
- There Is Only One Roy Orbison (65) 55(1) [0|0|17] — 456
- In Dreams: The Greatest Hits (89) 95(1) [0|0|15] — 256
- For The Lonely: A Roy Orbison Anthology, 1956-1965 (89) 110(1) [0|0|13] — 200
- Early Orbison (64) 101(1) [0|0|11] — 185
- The Very Best Of Roy Orbison (66) 94(1) [0|0|9] — 179
- A Black & White Night: Live (Soundtrack) (89)-Roy Orbison and Friends 123(4) [0|0|12] — 168
- Orbisongs (65) 136(1) [0|0|11] — 144
- Class Of '55 (86)-Carl Perkins, Jerry Lee Lewis, Roy Orbison, & Johnny Cash [A] 87(2) [0|0|12] — 54.0
- The Orbison Way (66) 128(1) [0|0|3] — 45.2

ORCHESTRAL MANOEUVRES IN THE DARK ▶ 732 Pk:38 [0|1|6] — 3422
- Crush (85) 38(2) [0|5|53] — 1514
- In The Dark/The Best Of OMD (88 46(2) [0|0|29] — 1015
- The Pacific Age (86 47(2) [0|0|23] — 645
- Architecture And Morality (82) 144(4) [0|0|12] — 151
- Dazzle Ships (83 162(1) [0|0|6] — 56.2
- Junk Culture (84 182(3) [0|0|6] — 40.4

ORIGINAL CAST ▶ Pk:1 [3|15|78] — 72783
- Hair (68) 1(13) [28|59|151] — 18698
- Hello, Dolly! (64) 1(1) [35|58|90] — 10990
- Fiddler On The Roof (64) 7(2) [3|60|206] — 9072
- Man Of La Mancha (66) 31(3) [0|13|167] — 4961
- The Phantom Of The Opera (87)-Original London Cast 33(1) [0|5|255] — 4006
- Godspell (71) 34(1) [0|12|79] — 3506

▶ Highest Peak [Top10s|Top40s|Total]
Title (Yr) Peak(Wk) [T10 Wk|T40Wk|TotalWk] — **Score**

ORIGINAL CAST ▶ *Continued*

Mame (66) 23(2) [0|14|66] — 2733
Dreamgirls (82) 11(3) [0|15|29] — 2076
Cabaret (67) 37(1) [0|4|39] — 1286
On A Clear Day You Can See Forever (65) 59(1) [0|0|32] — 871
Annie (77) 81(1) [0|0|39] — 784
The Roar Of The Greasepaint-The Smell Of The Crowd (65) 54(1) [0|0|34] — 761
The Wiz (75) 43(1) [0|0|16] — 746
A Chorus Line (75) 98(1) [0|0|49] — 710
The Girl Who Came To Supper (64) 33(1) [0|3|14] — 570
No, No, Nanette (71) 61(1) [0|0|19] — 565
Golden Boy (64) 36(1) [0|3|16] — 564
Jesus Christ Superstar (72) 31(2) [0|4|10] — 560
Cats (83) 113(3) [0|0|64] — 536
110 In The Shade (64) 37(1) [0|2|15] — 511
Here's Love (63) 38(1) [0|1|16] — 503
What Makes Sammy Run? (64) 28(2) [0|3|14] — 453
Cats (82)-Original London Cast 86(2) [0|0|22] — 451
High Spirits (64) 76(2) [0|0|20] — 384
Promises, Promises (69) 95(1) [0|0|12] — 372
I Do! I Do! (67) 84(1) [0|0|16] — 362
La Cage Aux Folles (83) 52(1) [0|0|15] — 352
Evita (80) 105(2) [0|0|19] — 332
Sweet Charity (66) 92(1) [0|0|16] — 322
Sweeney Todd-The Demon Barber Of Fleet Street (79) 78(2) [0|0|11] — 288
Chicago (75) 73(1) [0|0|10] — 275
A Little Night Music (73) 94(1) [0|0|12] — 259
Half A Sixpence (65) 103(1) [0|0|14] — 220
Les Miserables (87)-Original London Cast 106(2) [0|0|15] — 211
42nd Street (81) 120(1) [0|0|11] — 195
Do I Hear A Waltz? (65) 81(1) [0|0|9] — 182
The Apple Tree (66) 113(1) [0|0|9] — 175
Dear World (69) 128(2) [0|0|8] — 172
Hamlet (64) 128(1) [0|0|13] — 171
Pippin (73) 129(1) [0|0|10] — 159
Cats (83)-Selections from Original Broadway Cast 131(2) [0|0|14] — 137
Flora, The Red Menace (65) 111(1) [0|0|8] — 136
Annie Get Your Gun (66) 113(1) [0|0|7] — 135
Fade Out-Fade In (64) 96(2) [0|0|8] — 133
Les Miserables (87) 117(2) [0|0|10] — 125
Sunday In The Park With George (84) 149(3) [0|0|11] — 122
Skyscraper (66) 128(2) [0|0|8] — 116
I Had A Ball (65) 126(2) [0|0|8] — 108
Ben Franklin In Paris (64) 132(1) [0|0|8] — 103
Jennie (64) 87(1) [0|0|5] — 95.9
Into The Woods (88) 126(2) [0|0|6] — 77.8
Zorba (69) 177(2) [0|0|7] — 72.8
1776 (69) 174(3) [0|0|6] — 69.0
Purlie (70) 138(2) [0|0|5] — 67.0
The Great Waltz (66) 118(1) [0|0|4] — 66.4
George M! (68) 161(1) [0|0|6] — 62.9
Applause (70) 168(1) [0|0|7] — 62.2
Illya Darling (67) 177(1) [0|0|8] — 60.6
They're Playing Our Song (79) 167(1) [0|0|6] — 58.0
Ain't Misbehavin' (78) 161(1) [0|0|5] — 56.7
Canterbury Tales (69) 171(2) [0|0|4] — 53.5
Baker Street (A Musical Adventure Of Sherlock Holmes) (65) 138(1) [0|0|4] — 53.5
The Mystery Of Edwin Drood (86) 150(2) [0|0|6] — 52.6
You're A Good Man, Charlie Brown (67) 165(2) [0|0|5] — 51.7
The Merry Widow (64) 137(1) [0|0|4] — 50.7

▶ Highest Peak [Top10s|Top40s|Total]
Title (Yr) Peak(Wk) [T10 Wk|T40Wk|TotalWk] — **Score**

Hair (69)-Original London Cast 186(1) [0|0|4] — 36.5
Follies In Concert (86) 181(2) [0|0|6] — 36.0
Follies (71) 172(1) [0|0|3] — 33.6
A Time For Singing (66) 145(2) [0|0|2] — 29.0
The Pirates Of Penzance (81) 178(1) [0|0|3] — 28.4
Bajour (65) 143(2) [0|0|2] — 26.4
Joy (70) 187(1) [0|0|4] — 25.4
The Boys In The Band (69) 195(2) [0|0|3] — 22.3
Company (70) 178(2) [0|0|2] — 20.9
Maggie Flynn (69) 185(2) [0|0|2] — 20.6
Dames At Sea (69) 195(1) [0|0|2] — 13.8
Woman Of The Year (81) 196(2) [0|0|2] — 12.4
Treemonisha (76) 200(2) [0|0|2] — 11.0

The ORIGINALS ▶ 3106 Pk:174 [0|0|2] — 52

Baby, I'm For Real (70) 174(1) [0|0|4] — 40.0
Portrait Of The Originals (70) 198(2) [0|0|2] — 11.5

ORION THE HUNTER ▶ 1933 Pk:57 [0|0|1] — 386

Orion The Hunter (84) 57(2) [0|0|14] — 386

ORLEANS ▶ 862 Pk:30 [0|2|3] — 2587

Let There Be Music (75) 33(1) [0|5|32] — 1317
Waking & Dreaming (76) 30(2) [0|5|16] — 926
Forever (79) 76(1) [0|0|13] — 345

ORPHEUS ▶ 1972 Pk:119 [0|0|3] — 365

Orpheus (68) 119(2) [0|0|14] — 206
Ascending (68) 159(1) [0|0|12] — 153
Joyful (69) 198(1) [0|0|1] — 6.4

Benjamin ORR ▶ 1908 Pk:86 [0|0|1] — 402

The Lace (86) 86(2) [0|0|22] — 402

Robert Ellis ORRALL ▶ 2794 Pk:146 [0|0|1] — 98

Special Pain (83) 146(2) [0|0|9] — 98.5

Jeffrey OSBORNE ▶ 429 Pk:25 [0|3|5] — 7415

Stay With Me Tonight (83) 25(1) [0|23|89] — 3485
Don't Stop (84) 39(4) [0|4|37] — 1412
Emotional (86) 26(1) [0|11|26] — 1155
Jeffrey Osborne (82) 49(3) [0|0|43] — 1048
One Love--One Dream (88) 86(1) [0|0|16] — 315

OSBORNE BROTHERS ▶ 3529 Pk:193 [0|0|1] — 7

Ru-beeeee (70) 193(1) [0|0|1] — 6.9

Ozzy OSBOURNE ▶ 199 Pk:6 [2|7|8] — 17459

Blizzard Of Ozz (81) 21(1) [0|16|104] — 4478
Diary Of A Madman (81) 16(4) [0|23|73] — 4170
The Ultimate Sin (86) 6(2) [8|17|39] — 2840
No Rest For The Wicked (88) 13(1) [0|13|27] — 1774
Bark At The Moon (83) 19(3) [0|11|29] — 1506
Speak Of The Devil (82) 14(4) [0|10|20] — 1334
Tribute (87)-Ozzy Osbourne/Randy Rhoads [A] 6(2) [6|14|23] — 1133
Mr. Crowley (82) 120(1) [0|0|18] — 224

OSIBISA ▶ 1142 Pk:55 [0|0|6] — 1494

Osibisa (71) 55(1) [0|0|19] — 692
Wcyaya (72) 66(1) [0|0|17] — 536
Heads (72) 125(1) [0|0|8] — 133
Super Fly T.N.T. (Soundtrack) (73) 159(1) [0|0|7] — 81.7
Osibirock (74) 175(1) [0|0|4] — 40.5
Welcome Home (76) 200(2) [0|0|2] — 10.6

Lee OSKAR ▶ 1157 Pk:29 [0|1|3] — 1445

Lee Oskar (76) 29(1) [0|4|24] — 1087
Before The Rain (78) 86(1) [0|0|12] — 290
My Road Our Road (81) 162(2) [0|0|6] — 68.4

K.T. OSLIN ▶ 1042 Pk:68 [0|0|2] — 1774

This Woman (88) 75(2) [0|0|52] — 951
80's Ladies (87) 68(4) [0|0|32] — 823

Donny OSMOND ▶ 226 Pk:6 [1|6|11] — 15478

The Donny Osmond Album (71) 13(1) [0|18|37] — 3214

▶ Highest Peak [Top10s|Top40s|Total]
Title (Yr) Peak(Wk) [T10 Wk|T40Wk|TotalWk] — **Score**

To You With Love, Donny (71) 12(3) [0|14|33] — 2927
Portrait Of Donny (72) 6(1) [4|10|36] — 2647
Too Young (72) 11(2) [0|14|30] — 2602
Alone Together (73) 26(2) [0|7|29] — 1132
My Best To You (72) 29(1) [0|6|20] — 1056
Donny (74) 57(1) [0|0|17] — 732
Donny Osmond (89) 54(3) [0|0|23] — 608
A Time For Us (73) 58(2) [0|0|13] — 394
Disco Train (76) 145(1) [0|0|8] — 113
Donald Clark Osmond (77) 169(1) [0|0|5] — 54.0

Donny & Marie OSMOND ▶ 755 Pk:35 [0|1|6] — 3215

I'm Leaving It All Up To You (74) 35(1) [0|4|30] — 1557
Donny & Marie - Featuring Songs From Their Television Show (76) 60(2) [0|0|38] — 830
Donny & Marie - New Season (76) 85(2) [0|0|14] — 343
Winning Combination (78) 99(2) [0|0|12] — 213
Goin' Coconuts (Soundtrack) (78) 98(1) [0|0|8] — 173
Make The World Go Away (75) 133(2) [0|0|6] — 98.5

Little Jimmy OSMOND ▶ 2096 Pk:105 [0|0|1] — 306

Killer Joe (72) 105(2) [0|0|14] — 306

Marie OSMOND ▶ 1470 Pk:59 [0|0|4] — 858

Paper Roses (73) 59(1) [0|0|23] — 583
In My Little Corner Of The World (74) 164(1) [0|0|9] — 92.9
This Is The Way That I Feel (77) 152(2) [0|0|6] — 92.2
Who's Sorry Now (75) 152(2) [0|0|6] — 89.7

The OSMONDS ▶ 263 Pk:10 [1|5|12] — 13441

Osmonds (71) 14(3) [0|10|43] — 3012
Phase-III (72) 10(1) [1|13|35] — 2523
The Osmonds "Live" (72) 13(2) [0|15|29] — 2368
Homemade (71) 22(2) [0|10|34] — 2172
Crazy Horses (72) 14(1) [0|11|22] — 1717
Love Me For A Reason (74) 47(1) [0|0|14] — 657
The Plan (73) 58(1) [0|0|20] — 648
Around The World - Live In Concert (75) 148(2) [0|0|8] — 103
Brainstorm (76) 145(2) [0|0|6] — 91.9
The Osmond Christmas Album (76) 127(2) [0|0|5] — 75.2
The Proud One (75) 160(1) [0|0|5] — 54.8
The Osmonds Greatest Hits (78) 192(1) [0|0|3] — 18.5

Gilbert O'SULLIVAN ▶ 719 Pk:9 [1|1|3] — 3507

Gilbert O'Sullivan-Himself (72) 9(2) [4|14|29] — 2604
Back To Front (73) 48(1) [0|0|19] — 713
I'm A Writer, Not A Fighter (73) 101(1) [0|0|10] — 190

OTHER ONES ▶ 2967 Pk:139 [0|0|1] — 70

The Other Ones (87) 139(2) [0|0|6] — 70.0

Shuggie OTIS ▶ 3050 Pk:181 [0|0|3] — 59

Inspiration Information (75) 181(2) [0|0|3] — 28.9
Kooper Session (70)-Al Kooper/Shuggie Otis [A] 182(1) [0|0|5] — 19.1
Here Comes Shuggie Otis (70) 199(2) [0|0|2] — 11.1

The OUTFIELD ▶ 510 Pk:9 [1|2|3] — 6062

Play Deep (85) 9(1) [6|29|66] — 4156
Bangin' (87) 18(1) [0|11|21] — 1345
Voices Of Babylon (89) 53(3) [0|0|23] — 562

The OUTLAWS ▶ 465 Pk:13 [0|4|10] — 6766

Outlaws (75) 13(1) [0|7|16] — 1506
Ghost Riders (80) 25(3) [0|7|26] — 1449
Bring It Back Alive (78) 29(1) [0|4|21] — 1068
Hurry Sundown (77) 51(2) [0|0|27] — 789
Lady In Waiting (76) 36(2) [0|2|12] — 594
In The Eye Of The Storm (79) 55(1) [0|0|18] — 538
Playin' To Win (78) 60(4) [0|0|18] — 467
Los Hombres Malo (82) 77(1) [0|0|9] — 168

<table>
<tr><th>► Highest Peak [Top10s|Top40s|Total]
Title (Yr) Peak(Wk) [T10 Wk|T40Wk|TotalWk]</th><th>Score</th></tr>
<tr><td>The OUTLAWS ► Continued</td><td></td></tr>
<tr><td>Greatest Hits Of The Outlaws/High Tides Forever (82) 136(2) [0|0|9]</td><td>107</td></tr>
<tr><td>Soldiers Of Fortune (86) 160(2) [0|0|10]</td><td>81.4</td></tr>
<tr><td>The OUTSIDERS ► 1363 Pk:37 [0|1|3]</td><td>1025</td></tr>
<tr><td>Time Won't Let Me (66) 37(2) [0|3|16]</td><td>651</td></tr>
<tr><td>The Outsiders Album #2 (66) 90(1) [0|0|10]</td><td>210</td></tr>
<tr><td>Happening 'Live!' (67) 103(2) [0|0|10]</td><td>164</td></tr>
<tr><td>OVERKILL ► 2277 Pk:142 [0|0|3]</td><td>222</td></tr>
<tr><td>Under The Influence (88) 142(1) [0|0|13]</td><td>154</td></tr>
<tr><td>The Years Of Decay (89) 155(1) [0|0|8]</td><td>62.9</td></tr>
<tr><td>Taking Over (87) 191(1) [0|0|1]</td><td>5.6</td></tr>
<tr><td>Buck OWENS ► 838 Pk:43 [0|0|16]</td><td>2743</td></tr>
<tr><td>The Best Of Buck Owens (64) 46(2) [0|0|31]</td><td>857</td></tr>
<tr><td>I've Got A Tiger By The Tail (65) 43(1) [0|0|22]</td><td>560</td></tr>
<tr><td>Together Again / My Heart Skips A Beat (64) 88(1) [0|0|18]</td><td>299</td></tr>
<tr><td>Tall Dark Stranger (69) 122(1) [0|0|10]</td><td>211</td></tr>
<tr><td>Carnegie Hall Concert (66) 114(1) [0|0|10]</td><td>192</td></tr>
<tr><td>Roll Out The Red Carpet For Buck Owens And His Buckaroos (66) 106(1) [0|0|10]</td><td>164</td></tr>
<tr><td>Buck Owens In London (69) 113(2) [0|0|5]</td><td>142</td></tr>
<tr><td>Big In Vegas (70) 141(1) [0|0|6]</td><td>69.4</td></tr>
<tr><td>I Don't Care (64) 135(1) [0|0|5]</td><td>63.6</td></tr>
<tr><td>Your Tender Loving Care (67) 177(1) [0|0|7]</td><td>54.2</td></tr>
<tr><td>Close-Up (69) 185(2) [0|0|5]</td><td>45.7</td></tr>
<tr><td>We're Gonna Get Together (70)-Buck Owens & Susan Raye [A] 154(1) [0|0|6]</td><td>35.8</td></tr>
<tr><td>I Wouldn't Live In New York City (70) 190(1) [0|0|2]</td><td>13.6</td></tr>
<tr><td>I've Got You On My Mind Again (69) 199(2) [0|0|2]</td><td>12.6</td></tr>
<tr><td>The Kansas City Song (70) 196(1) [0|0|2]</td><td>11.9</td></tr>
<tr><td>Your Mother's Prayer (70) 198(2) [0|0|2]</td><td>11.5</td></tr>
<tr><td>OXO ► 2780 Pk:117 [0|0|1]</td><td>100</td></tr>
<tr><td>Oxo (83) 117(1) [0|0|7]</td><td>100</td></tr>
<tr><td>OZARK MOUNTAIN DAREDEVILS ► 649 Pk:19 [0|2|7]</td><td>4267</td></tr>
<tr><td>It'll Shine When It Shines (74) 19(1) [0|7|31]</td><td>2033</td></tr>
<tr><td>The Ozark Mountain Daredevils (74) 26(1) [0|5|28]</td><td>1199</td></tr>
<tr><td>The Car Over The Lake Album (75) 57(1) [0|0|15]</td><td>477</td></tr>
<tr><td>Men From Earth (76) 74(1) [0|0|10]</td><td>332</td></tr>
<tr><td>Don't Look Down (77) 132(1) [0|0|10]</td><td>157</td></tr>
<tr><td>Ozark Mountain Daredevils (80) 170(1) [0|0|4]</td><td>38.5</td></tr>
<tr><td>It's Alive (78) 176(1) [0|0|3]</td><td>30.6</td></tr>
<tr><td>OZONE ► 3036 Pk:152 [0|0|1]</td><td>61</td></tr>
<tr><td>Li'l Suzy (82) 152(2) [0|0|6]</td><td>60.6</td></tr>
</table>

P

<table>
<tr><td>PABLO CRUISE ► 383 Pk:6 [1|4|6]</td><td>8695</td></tr>
<tr><td>Worlds Away (78) 6(3) [4|14|43]</td><td>3880</td></tr>
<tr><td>A Place In The Sun (77) 19(2) [0|17|46]</td><td>2997</td></tr>
<tr><td>Reflector (81) 34(2) [0|5|18]</td><td>949</td></tr>
<tr><td>Part Of The Game (79) 39(1) [0|2|17]</td><td>659</td></tr>
<tr><td>Lifeline (76) 139(2) [0|0|13]</td><td>169</td></tr>
<tr><td>Pablo Cruise (75) 174(2) [0|0|4]</td><td>42.5</td></tr>
<tr><td>PACIFIC GAS AND ELECTRIC ► 1619 Pk:91 [0|0|4]</td><td>654</td></tr>
<tr><td>Are You Ready (70) 101(2) [0|0|11]</td><td>225</td></tr>
<tr><td>Pacific Gas And Electric (69) 91(1) [0|0|8]</td><td>203</td></tr>
<tr><td>Get It On... (69) 159(1) [0|0|12]</td><td>162</td></tr>
<tr><td>PG&E (71) 182(1) [0|0|8]</td><td>63.7</td></tr>
<tr><td>Gene PAGE ► 3040 Pk:156 [0|0|1]</td><td>60</td></tr>
<tr><td>Hot City (75) 156(2) [0|0|4]</td><td>60.3</td></tr>
<tr><td>Jimmy PAGE ► 1162 Pk:26 [0|1|2]</td><td>1427</td></tr>
<tr><td>Outrider (88) 26(2) [0|6|20]</td><td>1052</td></tr>
</table>

<table>
<tr><th>► Highest Peak [Top10s|Top40s|Total]
Title (Yr) Peak(Wk) [T10 Wk|T40Wk|TotalWk]</th><th>Score</th></tr>
<tr><td>Death Wish II (Soundtrack) (82) 50(4) [0|0|10]</td><td>374</td></tr>
<tr><td>Patti PAGE ► 1266 Pk:27 [0|1|3]</td><td>1212</td></tr>
<tr><td>Hush, Hush, Sweet Charlotte (65) 27(1) [0|7|26]</td><td>1028</td></tr>
<tr><td>Say Wonderful Things (63) 83(1) [0|0|6]</td><td>128</td></tr>
<tr><td>Gentle On My Mind (68) 168(1) [0|0|6]</td><td>55.5</td></tr>
<tr><td>Tommy PAGE ► 3234 Pk:166 [0|0|1]</td><td>35</td></tr>
<tr><td>Tommy Page (89) 166(2) [0|0|5]</td><td>35.3</td></tr>
<tr><td>Kevin PAIGE ► 1810 Pk:107 [0|0|1]</td><td>476</td></tr>
<tr><td>Kevin Paige (89) 107(2) [0|0|31]</td><td>476</td></tr>
<tr><td>PALM BEACH BAND BOYS ► 3452 Pk:149 [0|0|1]</td><td>15</td></tr>
<tr><td>Winchester Cathedral (67) 149(1) [0|0|1]</td><td>14.5</td></tr>
<tr><td>Robert PALMER ► 275 Pk:8 [1|3|11]</td><td>12949</td></tr>
<tr><td>Riptide (85) 8(1) [4|35|90]</td><td>4955</td></tr>
<tr><td>Heavy Nova (88) 13(3) [0|20|44]</td><td>3027</td></tr>
<tr><td>Secrets (79) 19(1) [0|8|24]</td><td>1736</td></tr>
<tr><td>Double Fun (78) 45(2) [0|0|25]</td><td>1099</td></tr>
<tr><td>Clues (80) 59(2) [0|0|17]</td><td>506</td></tr>
<tr><td>Some People Can Do What They Like (76) 68(1) [0|0|16]</td><td>463</td></tr>
<tr><td>Addictions Vol. I (89) 79(2) [0|0|17]</td><td>373</td></tr>
<tr><td>Pride (83) 112(2) [0|0|19]</td><td>323</td></tr>
<tr><td>Sneakin' Sally Thru The Alley (75) 107(1) [0|0|15]</td><td>296</td></tr>
<tr><td>Pressure Drop (75) 136(1) [0|0|8]</td><td>122</td></tr>
<tr><td>Maybe It's Live (82) 148(1) [0|0|5]</td><td>50.6</td></tr>
<tr><td>PAPER LACE ► 2595 Pk:124 [0|0|1]</td><td>136</td></tr>
<tr><td>Paper Lace (74) 124(1) [0|0|8]</td><td>136</td></tr>
<tr><td>PARIS ► 2107 Pk:103 [0|0|2]</td><td>297</td></tr>
<tr><td>Paris (76) 103(1) [0|0|9]</td><td>212</td></tr>
<tr><td>Big Towne, 2061 (76) 152(2) [0|0|6]</td><td>85.0</td></tr>
<tr><td>Mica PARIS ► 1943 Pk:86 [0|0|1]</td><td>380</td></tr>
<tr><td>So Good (89) 86(2) [0|0|23]</td><td>380</td></tr>
<tr><td>Graham PARKER And The RUMOUR ► 709 Pk:40 [0|2|9]</td><td>3585</td></tr>
<tr><td>Squeezing Out Sparks (79) 40(2) [0|2|24]</td><td>974</td></tr>
<tr><td>The Up Escalator (80) 40(1) [0|1|15]</td><td>635</td></tr>
<tr><td>Steady Nerves (85)-Graham Parker & The Shot 57(3) [0|0|21]</td><td>573</td></tr>
<tr><td>Another Grey Area (82)-Graham Parker 51(2) [0|0|16]</td><td>467</td></tr>
<tr><td>The Mona Lisa's Sister (88)-Graham Parker 77(2) [0|0|19]</td><td>422</td></tr>
<tr><td>The Real Macaw (83)-Graham Parker 59(1) [0|0|14]</td><td>326</td></tr>
<tr><td>Stick To Me (77) 125(1) [0|0|5]</td><td>79.7</td></tr>
<tr><td>Heat Treatment (77)-Graham Parker 169(1) [0|0|7]</td><td>60.2</td></tr>
<tr><td>The Parkerilla (78) 149(1) [0|0|3]</td><td>49.4</td></tr>
<tr><td>Ray PARKER Jr./RAYDIO ► 325 Pk:11 [0|4|10]</td><td>10580</td></tr>
<tr><td>A Woman Needs Love (81)-Ray Parker Jr. & Raydio 13(2) [0|16|26]</td><td>2655</td></tr>
<tr><td>The Other Woman (82)-Ray Parker Jr. 11(2) [0|12|27]</td><td>1850</td></tr>
<tr><td>Rock On (79)-Raydio 45(2) [0|0|30]</td><td>1398</td></tr>
<tr><td>Raydio (78)-Raydio 27(1) [0|9|23]</td><td>1385</td></tr>
<tr><td>Two Places At The Same Time (80)-Ray Parker Jr. & Raydio 33(2) [0|5|21]</td><td>1077</td></tr>
<tr><td>Woman Out Of Control (83)-Ray Parker Jr. 45(2) [0|0|23]</td><td>805</td></tr>
<tr><td>Greatest Hits (82)-Ray Parker Jr. 51(3) [0|0|22]</td><td>583</td></tr>
<tr><td>Chartbusters (84)-Ray Parker Jr. 60(3) [0|0|15]</td><td>414</td></tr>
<tr><td>Sex And The Single Man (85)-Ray Parker Jr. 65(2) [0|0|13]</td><td>246</td></tr>
<tr><td>After Dark (87)-Ray Parker Jr. 86(2) [0|0|9]</td><td>168</td></tr>
<tr><td>Michael PARKS ► 678 Pk:24 [0|2|4]</td><td>3947</td></tr>
<tr><td>Closing The Gap (69) 35(1) [0|5|46]</td><td>2433</td></tr>
<tr><td>Long Lonesome Highway (70) 24(1) [0|6|21]</td><td>1232</td></tr>
<tr><td>Blue (70) 71(1) [0|0|8]</td><td>275</td></tr>
</table>

<table>
<tr><th>► Highest Peak [Top10s|Top40s|Total]
Title (Yr) Peak(Wk) [T10 Wk|T40Wk|TotalWk]</th><th>Score</th></tr>
<tr><td>Lost And Found (71) 195(1) [0|0|1]</td><td>7.0</td></tr>
<tr><td>PARLIAMENT ► 310 Pk:13 [0|5|8]</td><td>10992</td></tr>
<tr><td>Mothership Connection (76) 13(2) [0|17|37]</td><td>3129</td></tr>
<tr><td>Funkentelechy Vs. The Placebo Syndrome (77) 13(1) [0|19|34]</td><td>2705</td></tr>
<tr><td>Clones Of Dr. Funkenstein (76) 20(1) [0|8|22]</td><td>1598</td></tr>
<tr><td>Motor-Booty Affair (78) 23(2) [0|10|18]</td><td>1292</td></tr>
<tr><td>Parliament Live/P Funk Earth Tour (77) 29(2) [0|5|19]</td><td>991</td></tr>
<tr><td>Gloryhallastoopid (Or Pin The Tail On The Funky) (79) 44(2) [0|0|19]</td><td>661</td></tr>
<tr><td>Chocolate City (75) 91(2) [0|0|18]</td><td>378</td></tr>
<tr><td>Trombipulation (81) 61(2) [0|0|7]</td><td>238</td></tr>
<tr><td>John PARR ► 1585 Pk:48 [0|0|1]</td><td>693</td></tr>
<tr><td>John Parr (84) 48(2) [0|0|26]</td><td>693</td></tr>
<tr><td>Alan PARSONS PROJECT ► 161 Pk:7 [2|7|11]</td><td>20991</td></tr>
<tr><td>The Turn Of A Friendly Card (80) 13(2) [0|21|58]</td><td>4304</td></tr>
<tr><td>I Robot (77) 9(3) [4|19|54]</td><td>3902</td></tr>
<tr><td>Eye In The Sky (82) 7(6) [7|21|41]</td><td>3372</td></tr>
<tr><td>Eve (79) 13(2) [0|12|27]</td><td>2057</td></tr>
<tr><td>Tales Of Mystery & Imagination (76) 38(1) [0|4|46]</td><td>1902</td></tr>
<tr><td>Ammonia Avenue (84) 15(1) [0|13|26]</td><td>1684</td></tr>
<tr><td>Pyramid (78) 26(1) [0|9|25]</td><td>1491</td></tr>
<tr><td>The Best Of The Alan Parsons Project (83) 53(4) [0|0|29]</td><td>699</td></tr>
<tr><td>Vulture Culture (85) 46(3) [0|0|19]</td><td>625</td></tr>
<tr><td>Stereotomy (86) 43(2) [0|0|18]</td><td>586</td></tr>
<tr><td>Gaudi (87) 57(2) [0|0|14]</td><td>369</td></tr>
<tr><td>Gram PARSONS ► 3418 Pk:195 [0|0|1]</td><td>17</td></tr>
<tr><td>Grievous Angel (74) 195(1) [0|0|3]</td><td>17.4</td></tr>
<tr><td>PARTLAND BROTHERS ► 3078 Pk:146 [0|0|1]</td><td>55</td></tr>
<tr><td>Electric Honey (87) 146(2) [0|0|5]</td><td>55.2</td></tr>
<tr><td>Dolly PARTON ► 306 Pk:6 [1|6|17]</td><td>11130</td></tr>
<tr><td>9 To 5 And Odd Jobs (80) 11(2) [0|15|34]</td><td>2959</td></tr>
<tr><td>Here You Come Again (77) 20(2) [0|13|47]</td><td>2682</td></tr>
<tr><td>Heartbreaker (78) 27(2) [0|8|34]</td><td>1652</td></tr>
<tr><td>Trio (87)-Dolly Parton, Linda Ronstadt, Emmylou Harris [A] 6(1) [3|14|48]</td><td>848</td></tr>
<tr><td>Great Balls Of Fire (79) 40(1) [0|1|17]</td><td>598</td></tr>
<tr><td>New Harvest...First Gathering (77) 71(3) [0|0|21]</td><td>550</td></tr>
<tr><td>Greatest Hits (82) 77(2) [0|0|23]</td><td>442</td></tr>
<tr><td>Dolly Dolly Dolly (80) 71(1) [0|0|13]</td><td>385</td></tr>
<tr><td>The Great Pretender (84) 73(1) [0|0|14]</td><td>270</td></tr>
<tr><td>Once Upon A Christmas (84)-Kenny Rogers & Dolly Parton [A] 31(1) [0|4|8]</td><td>189</td></tr>
<tr><td>Heartbreak Express (82) 106(2) [0|0|12]</td><td>185</td></tr>
<tr><td>Burlap & Satin (83) 127(1) [0|0|11]</td><td>150</td></tr>
<tr><td>Rainbow (87) 153(1) [0|0|8]</td><td>89.9</td></tr>
<tr><td>A Real Live Dolly (70) 154(2) [0|0|2]</td><td>33.3</td></tr>
<tr><td>My Blue Ridge Mountain Boy (69) 194(2) [0|0|2]</td><td>14.7</td></tr>
<tr><td>Joshua (71) 198(1) [0|0|1]</td><td>6.5</td></tr>
<tr><td>Rhinestone (Soundtrack) (84) 135(2) [0|0|7]</td><td>76.5</td></tr>
<tr><td>PARTRIDGE FAMILY ► 152 Pk:3 [3|5|7]</td><td>22023</td></tr>
<tr><td>The Partridge Family Album (70) 4(2) [8|36|68]</td><td>7904</td></tr>
<tr><td>Up To Date (71) 3(3) [12|23|53]</td><td>6505</td></tr>
<tr><td>The Partridge Family Sound Magazine (71) 9(2) [3|22|35]</td><td>4266</td></tr>
<tr><td>The Partridge Family At Home With Their Greatest Hits (72) 21(2) [0|10|23]</td><td>1437</td></tr>
<tr><td>The Partridge Family Shopping Bag (72) 18(2) [0|7|17]</td><td>1205</td></tr>
<tr><td>The Partridge Family Notebook (72) 41(1) [0|0|16]</td><td>654</td></tr>
<tr><td>Crossword Puzzle (73) 167(2) [0|0|5]</td><td>52.0</td></tr>
</table>

▶ Highest Peak [Top10s|Top40s|Total]
Title (Yr) Peak(Wk) [T10 Wk|T40Wk|TotalWk] — **Score**

The PASADENAS ▶ 2265 Pk:89 [0|0|1] — **227**
To Whom It May Concern (89) 89(2) [0|0|12] — 227

PASSPORT ▶ 2063 Pk:137 [0|0|5] — **318**
Cross-Collateral (75) 137(2) [0|0|7] — 118
Sky Blue (78) 140(1) [0|0|7] — 105
Oceanliner (80) 163(1) [0|0|4] — 43.2
Blue Tattoo (81) 175(2) [0|0|3] — 29.7
Iguacu (77) 191(1) [0|0|3] — 21.7

Jaco PASTORIUS ▶ 3200 Pk:161 [0|0|1] — **40**
Word Of Mouth (81) 161(2) [0|0|3] — 39.7

Robbie PATTON ▶ 2997 Pk:162 [0|0|1] — **66**
Distant Shores (81) 162(1) [0|0|6] — 66.5

Billy PAUL ▶ 771 Pk:17 [0|1|9] — **3126**
360 Degrees Of Billy Paul (72) 17(1) [0|9|27] — 1761
War Of The Gods (73) 110(1) [0|0|26] — 439
Let 'Em In (77) 88(1) [0|0|18] — 405
When Love Is New (75) 139(1) [0|0|20] — 246
Got My Head On Straight (75) 140(2) [0|0|9] — 122
Ebony Woman (70) 183(1) [0|0|8] — 63.3
Only The Strong Survive (78) 152(1) [0|0|4] — 46.2
Live In Europe (74) 187(1) [0|0|4] — 30.0
Going East (71) 197(1) [0|0|2] — 13.0

Henry PAUL Band ▶ 1806 Pk:107 [0|0|3] — **480**
Grey Ghost (79) 107(2) [0|0|12] — 257
Feel The Heat (80) 120(1) [0|0|8] — 135
Anytime (81) 158(1) [0|0|8] — 87.8

Les PAUL ▶ 3322 Pk:172 [0|0|1] — **26**
Chester & Lester (76)-Chet Atkins And Les Paul [A] 172(2) [0|0|5] — 26.2

Pat PAULSEN ▶ 2022 Pk:71 [0|0|1] — **339**
Pat Paulsen For President (68) 71(1) [0|0|10] — 339

The PAUPERS ▶ 3417 Pk:178 [0|0|1] — **17**
Magic People (67) 178(1) [0|0|2] — 17.5

Luciano PAVAROTTI ▶ 1298 Pk:77 [0|0|5] — **1146**
O Sole Mio - Favorite Neapolitan Songs (79) 77(1) [0|0|21] — 434
Pavarotti's Greatest Hits (80) 94(2) [0|0|18] — 387
Mamma (84) 103(2) [0|0|14] — 210
Luciano (82) 141(1) [0|0|7] — 81.4
Yes, Giorgio (82) 158(2) [0|0|3] — 33.8

PAVLOV'S DOG ▶ 3093 Pk:181 [0|0|1] — **53**
Pampered Menial (75) 181(1) [0|0|6] — 52.6

Rita PAVONE ▶ 2021 Pk:60 [0|0|1] — **341**
Rita Pavone (64) 60(1) [0|0|14] — 341

Tom PAXTON ▶ 2376 Pk:120 [0|0|4] — **192**
How Come The Sun (71) 120(2) [0|0|3] — 67.7
The Things I Notice Now (69) 155(1) [0|0|4] — 67.2
Tom Paxton 6 (70) 184(1) [0|0|4] — 30.8
Peace Will Come (72) 191(2) [0|0|4] — 26.2

Johnny PAYCHECK ▶ 1911 Pk:72 [0|0|1] — **399**
Take This Job And Shove It (78) 72(1) [0|0|14] — 399

Freda PAYNE ▶ 1378 Pk:60 [0|0|3] — **1000**
Band Of Gold (70) 60(1) [0|0|13] — 465
Contact (71) 76(2) [0|0|18] — 448
The Best Of Freda Payne (72) 152(1) [0|0|8] — 86.8

PEACHES & HERB ▶ 384 Pk:2 [1|3|7] — **8645**
2-Hot! (78) 2(6) [13|23|46] — 6131
Let's Fall In Love (67) 30(1) [0|6|25] — 1183
Twice The Fire (79) 31(3) [0|5|30] — 1009
For Your Love (67) 135(1) [0|0|12] — 149
Worth The Wait (80) 120(1) [0|0|6] — 116
Sayin' Something! (81) 168(2) [0|0|3] — 34.2
Peaches & Herb's Greatest Hits (68) 187(1) [0|0|3] — 23.3

▶ Highest Peak [Top10s|Top40s|Total]
Title (Yr) Peak(Wk) [T10 Wk|T40Wk|TotalWk] — **Score**

PEANUT BUTTER CONSPIRACY ▶ 3450 Pk:196 [0|0|1] — **15**
The Peanut Butter Conspiracy Is Spreading (67) 196(1) [0|0|3] — 14.9

PEARL HARBOR And The EXPLOSIONS ▶ 2227 Pk:107 [0|0|2] — **243**
Pearl Harbor & The Explosions (80) 107(1) [0|0|11] — 210
Don't Follow Me, I'm Lost Too (81)-Pearl Harbor 170(2) [0|0|3] — 32.7

PEARLS BEFORE SWINE ▶ 3497 Pk:200 [0|0|1] — **12**
These Things Too (69) 200(2) [0|0|2] — 11.7

Duke PEARSON ▶ 3440 Pk:193 [0|0|1] — **16**
The Phantom (69) 193(2) [0|0|2] — 16.0

David PEASTON ▶ 2186 Pk:113 [0|0|1] — **264**
Introducing...David Peaston (89) 113(1) [0|0|18] — 264

PEBBLES ▶ 794 Pk:14 [0|1|1] — **2973**
Pebbles (88) 14(1) [0|19|38] — 2973

Ann PEEBLES ▶ 2769 Pk:155 [0|0|2] — **101**
I Can't Stand The Rain (74) 155(1) [0|0|7] — 81.4
Straight From The Heart (72) 188(2) [0|0|3] — 20.0

David PEEL & The LOWER EAST SIDE ▶ 3113 Pk:186 [0|0|2] — **51**
Have A Marijuana (69) 186(1) [0|0|3] — 30.2
The Pope Smokes Dope (72) 191(2) [0|0|3] — 20.6

Nia PEEPLES ▶ 1920 Pk:97 [0|0|1] — **393**
Nothin' But Trouble (88) 97(4) [0|0|21] — 393

Teddy PENDERGRASS ▶ 223 Pk:5 [1|7|11] — **15817**
Teddy (79) 5(2) [5|14|31] — 2994
TP (80) 14(3) [0|16|34] — 2966
Life Is A Song Worth Singing (78) 11(2) [0|15|35] — 2687
Teddy Pendergrass (77) 17(3) [0|11|35] — 2327
It's Time For Love (81) 19(2) [0|7|27] — 1462
Love Language (84) 38(4) [0|5|35] — 1095
Teddy Live! Coast To Coast (79) 33(3) [0|4|15] — 743
Joy (88) 54(2) [0|0|24] — 737
This One's For You (82) 59(1) [0|0|15] — 412
Workin' It Back (85) 96(2) [0|0|23] — 280
Heaven Only Knows (84) 123(1) [0|0|9] — 115

Michael PENN ▶ 1168 Pk:31 [0|1|1] — **1417**
March (89) 31(1) [0|8|34] — 1417

PENTANGLE ▶ 2768 Pk:183 [0|0|5] — **101**
Solomon's Seal (72) 184(2) [0|0|4] — 31.7
Reflection (71) 183(1) [0|0|3] — 27.1
The Pentangle (68) 192(2) [0|0|3] — 24.3
Basket Of Light (70) 200(2) [0|0|2] — 10.8
Cruel Sister (71) 193(1) [0|0|1] — 7.5

PEOPLE ▶ 2559 Pk:128 [0|0|1] — **147**
I Love You (68) 128(3) [0|0|8] — 147

PEOPLE'S CHOICE ▶ 1786 Pk:56 [0|0|2] — **494**
Boogie Down U.S.A. (75) 56(1) [0|0|15] — 462
We Got The Rhythm (76) 174(1) [0|0|3] — 32.1

PEPPERMINT RAINBOW ▶ 2231 Pk:106 [0|0|1] — **242**
Will You Be Staying After Sunday (69) 106(2) [0|0|9] — 242

PEPSI and SHIRLIE ▶ 2739 Pk:133 [0|0|1] — **107**
All Right Now (88)-Pepsi & Shirlie 133(1) [0|0|9] — 107

Carl PERKINS ▶ 3084 Pk:87 [0|0|1] — **54**
Class Of '55 (86)-Carl Perkins, Jerry Lee Lewis, Roy Orbison, & Johnny Cash [A] 87(2) [0|0|12] — 54.0

Itzhak PERLMAN ▶ 3037 Pk:149 [0|0|1] — **61**
A Different Kind Of Blues (81)-Itzhak Perlman & Andre Previn [A] 149(1) [0|0|9] — 60.6

▶ Highest Peak [Top10s|Top40s|Total]
Title (Yr) Peak(Wk) [T10 Wk|T40Wk|TotalWk] — **Score**

Joe PERRY PROJECT ▶ 1563 Pk:47 [0|0|2] — **719**
Let The Music Do The Talking (80) 47(2) [0|0|13] — 517
I've Got The Rock 'N' Rolls Again (81) 100(1) [0|0|10] — 202

Steve PERRY ▶ 756 Pk:12 [0|1|1] — **3214**
Street Talk (84) 12(4) [0|18|60] — 3214

The PERSUADERS ▶ 2648 Pk:141 [0|0|2] — **124**
Thin Line Between Love And Hate (72) 141(1) [0|0|7] — 93.1
The Persuaders (73) 178(1) [0|0|4] — 30.7

The PERSUASIONS ▶ 2016 Pk:88 [0|0|4] — **344**
Street Corner Symphony (72) 88(1) [0|0|12] — 276
We Still Ain't Got No Band (73) 178(1) [0|0|3] — 26.2
We Came To Play (71) 189(1) [0|0|3] — 24.6
Spread The Word (72) 195(2) [0|0|3] — 17.2

PETER And GORDON ▶ 885 Pk:21 [0|1|7] — **2456**
A World Without Love (64) 21(1) [0|5|14] — 598
Woman (66) 60(1) [0|0|14] — 366
True Love Ways (65) 49(1) [0|0|13] — 365
I Go To Pieces (65) 51(1) [0|0|15] — 360
The Best Of Peter And Gordon (66) 72(1) [0|0|12] — 301
Lady Godiva (67) 80(1) [0|0|13] — 270
I Don't Want To See You Again (65) 95(1) [0|0|11] — 196

PETER, PAUL & MARY ▶ 91 Pk:1 [3|9|11] — **31221**
In The Wind (63) 1(5) [28|58|80] — 10215
Peter, Paul And Mary In Concert (64) 4(3) [8|25|54] — 3909
Album 1700 (67) 15(2) [0|25|82] — 3755
A Song Will Rise (65) 8(3) [5|26|38] — 2954
10 Years Together/The Best Of Peter, Paul And Mary (70) 15(3) [0|11|40] — 2209
Late Again (68) 14(2) [0|12|22] — 2174
Peter, Paul And Mommy (69) 12(3) [0|9|25] — 2132
Peter, Paul And Mary Album (66) 22(1) [0|9|53] — 1924
See What Tomorrow Brings (65) 11(1) [0|8|39] — 1750
Reunion (78) 106(1) [0|0|7] — 160
No Easy Walk To Freedom (87) 173(2) [0|0|5] — 37.8

Bernadette PETERS ▶ 1945 Pk:114 [0|0|2] — **378**
Bernadette Peters (80) 114(1) [0|0|14] — 271
Now Playing (81) 151(1) [0|0|9] — 107

OSCAR PETERSON TRIO ▶ 2311 Pk:81 [0|0|1] — **212**
Oscar Peterson Trio + One (64) 81(1) [0|0|12] — 212

PET SHOP BOYS ▶ 479 Pk:7 [1|3|4] — **6535**
Please (86) 7(1) [6|21|31] — 3061
Actually (87) 25(1) [0|22|45] — 2421
Introspective (88) 34(2) [0|3|22] — 857
Disco (86) 95(2) [0|0|12] — 196

Tom PETTY And The HEARTBREAKERS ▶ 87 Pk:2 [5|8|9] — **32417**
Full Moon Fever (89)-Tom Petty 3(2) [34|51|71] — 9020
Damn The Torpedoes (79) 2(7) [20|29|66] — 8108
Hard Promises (81) 5(2) [11|17|31] — 4235
Long After Dark (82) 9(3) [4|22|32] — 3020
Southern Accents (85) 7(2) [6|18|32] — 2944
You're Gonna' Get It (78) 23(1) [0|8|24] — 1431
Let Me Up (I've Had Enough) (87) 20(2) [0|12|20] — 1401
Tom Petty And The Heartbreakers (77) 55(1) [0|0|42] — 1155
Pack Up The Plantation - Live! (85) 22(2) [0|9|26] — 1104

P.F.M. ▶ 2505 Pk:151 [0|0|2] — **158**
P.F.M. 'Cook' (74) 151(1) [0|0|8] — 115
Photos Of Ghosts (73)-Premiata Forneria Marconi 180(1) [0|0|6] — 43.6

▶ **Highest Peak [Top10s|Top40s|Total]**
Title (Yr) Peak(Wk) [T10 Wk|T40Wk|TotalWk] — **Score**

PHANTOM, ROCKER & SLICK ▶ 1722 Pk:61 [0|0|2] — 561
Phantom, Rocker & Slick (85) 61(2) [0|0|23] — 550
Cover Girl (86) 181(1) [0|0|2] — 10.9

PHILADELPHIA Orchestra ▶ 3008 Pk:136 [0|0|1] — 65
David Bowie Narrates Prokofiev's "Peter And The Wolf" (78)-David Bowie/ Philadephia Orchestra/Eugene Ormandy [A] 136(1) [0|0|8] — 65.2

Anthony PHILLIPS ▶ 3411 Pk:191 [0|0|1] — 18
The Geese & The Ghost (77) 191(1) [0|0|3] — 18.5

Esther PHILLIPS ▶ 1127 Pk:32 [0|1|6] — 1532
What A Diff'rence A Day Makes (75) 32(2) [0|6|17] — 969
From A Whisper To A Scream (72) ?137(1) [0|0|15] — 229
Burnin' (71) 115(1) [0|0|15] — 181
Alone Again, Naturally (72) 177(2) [0|0|8] — 63.2
Capricorn Princess (77) 150(1) [0|0|4] — 45.6
Confessin' The Blues (76) 170(1) [0|0|4] — 44.2

John PHILLIPS ▶ 2971 Pk:181 [0|0|1] — 70
John Phillips (John The Wolfking Of L.A.) (70) 181(1) [0|0|9] — 69.6

Shawn PHILLIPS ▶ 1074 Pk:50 [0|0|4] — 1666
Faces (72) 57(2) [0|0|20] — 583
Furthermore... (74) 50(2) [0|0|12] — 506
Bright White (73) 72(1) [0|0|13] — 351
Do You Wonder (75) 101(1) [0|0|9] — 227

PHOTOGLO ▶ 2317 Pk:119 [0|0|2] — 210
Fool In Love With You (81)-Jim Photoglo 119(1) [0|0|11] — 193
Photoglo (80) 194(1) [0|0|3] — 17.4

Bobby "Boris" PICKETT ▶ 3249 Pk:173 [0|0|1] — 33
The Original Monster Mash (73)-Bobby Pickett 173(1) [0|0|4] — 33.4

Wilson PICKETT ▶ 478 Pk:21 [0|2|14] — 6543
The Best Of Wilson Pickett (67) 35(2) [0|8|54] — 1510
The Exciting Wilson Pickett (66) 21(1) [0|7|29] — 1379
The Wicked Pickett (67) 42(2) [0|0|31] — 971
Wilson Pickett In Philadelphia (70) 64(1) [0|0|19] — 565
The Best Of Wilson Pickett, Vol. II (71) 73(1) [0|0|13] — 414
Hey Jude (69) 97(1) [0|0|14] — 377
I'm In Love (68) 70(2) [0|0|15] — 336
The Sound Of Wilson Pickett (67) 54(1) [0|0|11] — 300
The Midnight Mover (68) 91(1) [0|0|13] — 278
Don't Knock My Love (71) 132(2) [0|0|14] — 208
In The Midnight Hour (65) 107(1) [0|0|6] — 106
Wilson Pickett's Greatest Hits (73) 178(1) [0|0|8] — 61.5
Mr. Magic Man (73) 187(1) [0|0|3] — 19.1
Right On (70) 197(1) [0|0|3] — 17.0

PIECES OF A DREAM ▶ 1584 Pk:90 [0|0|4] — 694
Imagine This (84) 90(1) [0|0|15] — 255
We Are One (82) 114(3) [0|0|15] — 197
Joyride (86) 102(2) [0|0|12] — 182
Pieces Of A Dream (81) 170(2) [0|0|6] — 59.7

PILOT ▶ 2020 Pk:82 [0|0|1] — 342
Pilot (75) 82(1) [0|0|14] — 342

Michael PINDER ▶ 2606 Pk:133 [0|0|1] — 133
The Promise (76) 133(3) [0|0|8] — 133

PINK FLOYD ▶ 22 Pk:1 [6|9|17] — 59509
The Dark Side Of The Moon (73) 1(1) [27|63|741] — 23108
The Wall (79) 1(15) [27|35|123] — 13311
A Momentary Lapse Of Reason (87) 3(1) [15|26|56] — 5195
Wish You Were Here (75) 1(2) [9|15|39] — 5152
Animals (77) 3(3) [5|9|28] — 3108
The Final Cut (83) 6(2) [5|12|23] — 1966
Delicate Sound Of Thunder (88) 11(1) [0|10|21] — 1759
Meddle (71) 70(2) [0|0|73] — 1594
A Collection Of Great Dance Songs (81) 31(2) [0|7|16] — 892
Obscured By Clouds (Soundtrack) (72) 46(2) [0|0|25] — 839
A Nice Pair (73) 36(1) [0|4|17] — 810
Ummagumma (70) 74(1) [0|0|27] — 680
Atom Heart Mother (70) 55(2) [0|0|13] — 566
Works (83) 68(1) [0|0|9] — 211
The Piper At The Gates Of Dawn (67) 131(1) [0|0|11] — 144
More (Soundtrack) (73) 153(1) [0|0|7] — 89.3
Relics (71) 152(2) [0|0|7] — 85.3

The PIPKINS ▶ 2934 Pk:132 [0|0|1] — 74
Gimme Dat Ding! (70) 132(2) [0|0|4] — 74.4

Joe PISCOPO ▶ 3352 Pk:168 [0|0|1] — 24
New Jersey (85) 168(1) [0|0|3] — 24.1

Gene PITNEY ▶ 792 Pk:42 [0|0|9] — 2982
Greatest Hits Of All Times (66) 61(2) [0|0|51] — 1138
Looking Through The Eyes Of Love (65) 43(1) [0|0|24] — 785
It Hurts To Be In Love (64) 42(1) [0|0|17] — 472
Gene Pitney's Big Sixteen (64) 87(1) [0|0|9] — 172
I Must Be Seeing Things (65) 112(1) [0|0|9] — 142
Big Sixteen, Vol. 3 (66) 123(2) [0|0|8] — 129
Blue Gene (63) 105(1) [0|0|6] — 97.0
George Jones & Gene Pitney (65)-George Jones & Gene Pitney [A] 141(1) [0|0|4] — 24.8
She's A Heartbreaker (68) 193(1) [0|0|3] — 21.2

PIXIES ▶ 1824 Pk:98 [0|0|1] — 464
Doolittle (89) 98(1) [0|0|27] — 464

PLANET P ▶ 1494 Pk:42 [0|0|2] — 818
Planet P (83) 42(2) [0|0|23] — 633
Pink World (84)-Planet P Project 121(1) [0|0|14] — 185

Robert PLANT ▶ 297 Pk:5 [3|4|4] — 11787
Now And Zen (88) 6(1) [10|25|48] — 4702
The Principle Of Moments (83) 8(1) [5|18|40] — 3102
Pictures At Eleven (82) 5(6) [9|14|53] — 2950
Shaken 'N' Stirred (85) 20(2) [0|8|19] — 1032

The PLASMATICS ▶ 2128 Pk:134 [0|0|3] — 288
New Hope For The Wretched (81) 134(2) [0|0|10] — 145
Beyond The Valley Of 1984 (81) 142(1) [0|0|9] — 119
Metal Priestess (81) 177(1) [0|0|3] — 25.2

PLASTIC COW ▶ 3386 Pk:184 [0|0|1] — 20
The Plastic Cow Goes Moooooog (69) 184(2) [0|0|2] — 20.3

The PLATTERS ▶ 2653 Pk:100 [0|0|1] — 123
I Love You 1,000 Times (66) 100(2) [0|0|6] — 123

PLAYER ▶ 817 Pk:26 [0|2|3] — 2838
Player (77) 26(2) [0|6|34] — 1794
Danger Zone (78) 37(1) [0|2|23] — 970
Spies Of Life (82) 152(1) [0|0|7] — 74.5

PLEASURE ▶ 1057 Pk:67 [0|0|6] — 1727
Future Now (79) 67(1) [0|0|29] — 832
Special Things (80) 97(2) [0|0|14] — 282
Joyous (77) 113(2) [0|0|11] — 260
Get To The Feeling (78) 119(1) [0|0|13] — 235
Accept No Substitutes (76) 162(1) [0|0|5] — 67.0
Give It Up (82) 164(1) [0|0|6] — 51.1

The PLIMSOULS ▶ 2938 Pk:153 [0|0|2] — 74
The Plimsouls (81) 153(1) [0|0|4] — 52.9
Everywhere At Once (83) 186(1) [0|0|4] — 21.0

POCKETS ▶ 1396 Pk:57 [0|0|2] — 975
Come Go With Us (77) 57(2) [0|0|24] — 818
Take It On Up (78) 85(1) [0|0|6] — 157

POCO ▶ 291 Pk:14 [0|4|20] — 12029
Legend (78) 14(2) [0|10|52] — 2856
Deliverin' (71) 26(1) [0|6|21] — 1294
Legacy (89) 40(2) [0|2|28] — 1198
Crazy Eyes (73) 38(1) [0|2|23] — 865
Poco (70) 58(1) [0|0|19] — 653
Pickin' Up The Pieces (69) 63(1) [0|0|21] — 649
Under The Gun (80) 46(1) [0|0|16] — 608
Head Over Heels (75) 43(1) [0|0|18] — 604
Indian Summer (77) 57(1) [0|0|18] — 569
A Good Feelin' To Know (72) 69(2) [0|0|20] — 543
From The Inside (71) 52(3) [0|0|11] — 518
Seven (74) 68(1) [0|0|13] — 391
Cantamos (74) 76(1) [0|0|11] — 292
Blue And Gray (81) 76(2) [0|0|10] — 286
Rose Of Cimarron (76) 89(1) [0|0|15] — 259
The Very Best Of Poco (75) 90(2) [0|0|8] — 216
Cowboys & Englishmen (82) 131(2) [0|0|8] — 118
Inamorata (84) 167(2) [0|0|6] — 48.6
Live (76) 169(2) [0|0|4] — 47.5
Ghost Town (82) 195(2) [0|0|3] — 14.2

The POGUES ▶ 1843 Pk:88 [0|0|2] — 448
If I Should Fall From Grace With God (88) 88(3) [0|0|16] — 316
Peace & Love (89) 118(1) [0|0|9] — 131

POINT BLANK ▶ 1278 Pk:80 [0|0|5] — 1183
American Excess (81) 80(1) [0|0|24] — 637
On A Roll (82) 119(1) [0|0|17] — 231
The Hard Way (80) 110(1) [0|0|13] — 201
Airplay (79) 175(1) [0|0|9] — 77.4
Point Blank (76) 175(3) [0|0|3] — 36.3

Bonnie POINTER ▶ 1629 Pk:63 [0|0|2] — 644
Bonnie Pointer (II) (79) 63(2) [0|0|14] — 377
Bonnie Pointer (78) 96(1) [0|0|15] — 267

Noel POINTER ▶ 1773 Pk:95 [0|0|4] — 502
Hold On (78) 95(2) [0|0|13] — 227
Phantazia (77) 144(1) [0|0|8] — 118
Feel It (79) 138(4) [0|0|7] — 114
Calling (80) 167(1) [0|0|4] — 43.0

POINTER SISTERS ▶ 148 Pk:8 [1|7|16] — 22249
Break Out (83) 8(2) [6|65|105] — 9038
The Pointer Sisters (73) 13(1) [0|13|37] — 2503
Black & White (81) 12(2) [0|14|22] — 2271
Energy (78) 13(3) [0|10|32] — 2026
Contact (85) 24(1) [0|17|34] — 1809
Steppin' (75) 22(1) [0|7|22] — 1426
Special Things (80) 34(1) [0|5|24] — 1170
So Excited! (82) 59(1) [0|0|28] — 552
Hot Together (86) 48(3) [0|0|18] — 478
Live At The Opera House (74) 96(1) [0|0|15] — 313
That's A Plenty (74) 82(1) [0|0|10] — 250
Priority (79) 72(2) [0|0|8] — 222
The Best Of The Pointer Sisters (76) 164(3) [0|0|6] — 75.2
Serious Slammin' (88) 152(2) [0|0|6] — 64.7
Having A Party (77) 176(1) [0|0|3] — 27.3
Pointer Sisters' Greatest Hits (82) 178(2) [0|0|3] — 23.1

POISON ▶ 212 Pk:2 [2|2|2] — 16247
Open Up And Say...Ahh! (88) 2(1) [26|51|70] — 9336
Look What The Cat Dragged In (86) 3(2) [17|47|101] — 6911

▶ Highest Peak [Top10s | Top40s | Total]
Title (Yr) Peak(Wk) [T10 Wk | T40Wk | TotalWk] Score

The POLICE ▶ 68 Pk:1 [4|6|6] 38145
Synchronicity (83) 1(17) [40|50|75] 13507
Zenyatta Mondatta (80) 5(6) [21|31|153] 9097
Ghost In The Machine (81) 2(6) [24|30|109] 8836
Reggatta De Blanc (79) 25(2) [0|8|100] 2694
Outlandos D'Amour (79) 23(1) [0|11|63] 2233
Every Breath You Take-The Singles (86) 7(1) [4|13|26] 1778

Michel POLNAREFF ▶ 2276 Pk:117 [0|0|1] 223
Michel Polnareff (76) 117(2) [0|0|13] 223

Jean Luc PONTY ▶ 572 Pk:35 [0|2|12] 5091
Cosmic Messenger (78) 36(2) [0|3|28] 1114
Enigmatic Ocean (77) 35(1) [0|3|16] 677
A Taste For Passion (79) 54(1) [0|0|21] 666
Imaginary Voyage (76) 67(2) [0|0|23] 617
Mystical Adventure (82) 44(1) [0|0|14] 497
Civilized Evil (80) 73(1) [0|0|18] 496
Individual Choice (83) 85(1) [0|0|15] 292
Aurora (76) 123(1) [0|0|13] 274
Jean-Luc Ponty: Live (79) 68(1) [0|0|10] 270
Open Mind (84) 171(3) [0|0|13] 89.7
Upon The Wings Of Music (75) 158(2) [0|0|5] 61.6
Fables (85) 166(2) [0|0|4] 36.4

Iggy POP ▶ 1177 Pk:72 [0|0|7] 1394
Blah-Blah-Blah (86) 75(2) [0|0|27] 518
Idiot (77) 72(3) [0|0|13] 377
Instinct (88) 110(2) [0|0|12] 174
Soldier (80) 125(1) [0|0|7] 123
Lust For Life (77) 120(1) [0|0|6] 115
Party (81) 166(2) [0|0|5] 50.4
New Values (79) 180(2) [0|0|4] 34.8

Pope JOHN PAUL II ▶ 2927 Pk:126 [0|0|1] 76
Pope John Paul II Sings At The Festival Of Sacroso (79) 126(2) [0|0|4] 75.7

POPPY FAMILY ▶ 2045 Pk:76 [0|0|1] 330
Which Way You Goin' Billy? (70) 76(2) [0|0|11] 330

POP WILL EAT ITSELF ▶ 3131 Pk:169 [0|0|1] 49
This Is The Day...This Is The Hour...This Is This! (89) 169(2) [0|0|6] 48.7

David PORTER ▶ 2199 Pk:104 [0|0|2] 255
David Porter...Into A Real Thing (71) 104(1) [0|0|9] 161
Gritty, Groovy, & Gettin' It (70) 163(1) [0|0|10] 93.6

Sandy POSEY ▶ 2656 Pk:129 [0|0|2] 123
Born A Woman (66) 129(1) [0|0|7] 92.1
I Take It Back (67) 182(1) [0|0|4] 30.4

Mike POST ▶ 1863 Pk:70 [0|0|2] 434
Television Theme Songs (82) 70(2) [0|0|17] 415
Railhead Overture (75) 195(1) [0|0|3] 18.5

POTLIQUOR ▶ 3001 Pk:168 [0|0|1] 66
Levee Blues (72) 168(1) [0|0|7] 65.9

POUSETTE-DART BAND ▶ 2521 Pk:143 [0|0|2] 153
Amnesia (77) 143(1) [0|0|7] 93.0
3 (78) 161(1) [0|0|5] 60.2

Adam Clayton POWELL ▶ 2454 Pk:112 [0|0|1] 173
Keep The Faith, Baby! (67) 112(1) [0|0|9] 173

POWER STATION ▶ 677 Pk:6 [1|1|1] 3972
The Power Station (85) 6(2) [11|25|44] 3972

POZO-SECO SINGERS ▶ 2044 Pk:81 [0|0|2] 331
I Can Make It With You (67) 81(1) [0|0|10] 228
Time (66) 127(1) [0|0|6] 103

Andy PRATT ▶ 1854 Pk:90 [0|0|3] 440
Resolution (76) 104(1) [0|0|10] 230
Shiver In The Night (77) 90(2) [0|0|9] 187
Andy Pratt (73) 192(1) [0|0|4] 22.8

▶ Highest Peak [Top10s | Top40s | Total]
Title (Yr) Peak(Wk) [T10 Wk | T40Wk | TotalWk] Score

PRATT & McCLAIN ▶ 3439 Pk:190 [0|0|1] 16
Pratt & McClain Featuring "Happy Days" (76) 190(2) [0|0|2] 16.0

PREFAB SPROUT ▶ 3239 Pk:178 [0|0|1] 35
Two Wheels Good (85) 178(1) [0|0|5] 34.5

PRELUDE ▶ 1893 Pk:94 [0|0|2] 411
Owlcreek Incident (75) 111(2) [0|0|14] 233
After The Gold Rush (74) 94(2) [0|0|7] 178

The PRESIDENTS ▶ 2887 Pk:158 [0|0|1] 82
5-10-15-20 (25-30 Years Of Love) (71) 158(2) [0|0|6] 81.7

Elvis PRESLEY ▶ 10 Pk:1 [11|27|71] 71798
Elvis' Golden Records Volume 3 (63) 3(2) [13|20|63] 4515
Aloha From Hawaii Via Satellite (73) 1(1) [7|19|52] 4378
Moody Blue (77) 3(3) [8|17|31] 3887
Roustabout (Soundtrack) (64) 1(1) [12|20|27] 3337
From Elvis In Memphis (69) 13(2) [0|15|34] 3133
Elvis As Recorded At Madison Square Garden (72) 11(2) [0|18|34] 3063
Elvis - TV Special (68) 8(3) [3|14|32] 3062
Fun In Acapulco (Soundtrack) (63) 3(3) [7|16|24] 2835
Girl Happy (Soundtrack) (65) 8(2) [6|17|31] 2361
From Memphis To Vegas/ From Vegas To Memphis (69) 12(3) [0|12|24] 2345
Kissin' Cousins (Soundtrack) (64) 6(3) [5|15|30] 2182
On Stage-February, 1970 (70) 13(1) [0|11|20] 2088
Elvis Country ("I'm 10,000 Years Old") (71) 12(1) [0|10|21] 1982
Burning Love And Hits From His Movies, Volume 2 (72) 22(3) [0|11|25] 1789
Spinout (Soundtrack) (66) 18(3) [0|10|32] 1755
Elvis For Everyone! (65) 10(1) [1|11|27] 1740
Elvis In Concert (77) 5(2) [4|7|18] 1640
Harum Scarum (Soundtrack) (65) 8(2) [4|11|23] 1634
How Great Thou Art (67) 18(1) [0|9|29] 1505
Elvis-That's The Way It Is (70) 21(2) [0|6|23] 1454
Paradise, Hawaiian Style (Soundtrack) (66) 15(2) [0|9|19] 1246
Elvis-World Wide 50 Gold Award Hits, Vol. 1 (70) 45(1) [0|0|36] 1117
Frankie And Johnny (Soundtrack) (66) 20(1) [0|9|19] 1086
Elvis-A Legendary Performer, Volume 1 (74) 43(1) [0|0|28] 975
Elvis' Gold Records, Volume 4 (68) 33(1) [0|4|22] 954
Love Letters From Elvis (71) 33(2) [0|5|15] 953
Welcome To My World (77) 44(1) [0|0|25] 901
Elvis Aron Presley (80) 27(2) [0|5|14] 845
Elvis: Recorded Live On Stage In Memphis (74) 33(1) [0|4|13] 744
Elvis Now (72) 43(1) [0|0|19] 703
Clambake (Soundtrack) (67) 40(1) [0|1|14] 687
Elvis-A Legendary Performer, Volume 2 (76) 46(2) [0|0|17] 662
From Elvis Presley Boulevard, Memphis, Tennessee (76) 41(1) [0|0|17] 658
Separate Ways (73) 46(1) [0|0|18] 636
Double Trouble (Soundtrack) (67) 47(2) [0|0|20] 579
Promised Land (75) 47(1) [0|0|12] 547
Almost In Love (70) 65(1) [0|0|18] 516

▶ Highest Peak [Top10s | Top40s | Total]
Title (Yr) Peak(Wk) [T10 Wk | T40Wk | TotalWk] Score

Elvis (73) 52(1) [0|0|13] 490
Today (75) 57(1) [0|0|13] 487
Guitar Man (81) 49(1) [0|0|12] 480
Raised On Rock/For Ol' Times Sake (73) 50(1) [0|0|13] 451
You'll Never Walk Alone (71) 69(2) [0|0|12] 374
Elvis: A Golden Celebration (84) 80(2) [0|0|19] 356
Elvis Sings Hits From His Movies, Volume 1 (72) 87(1) [0|0|15] 355
C'mon Everybody (71) 70(1) [0|0|11] 351
Elvis Sings Flaming Star (69) 96(1) [0|0|16] 340
Speedway (Soundtrack) (68) 82(1) [0|0|13] 327
The Sun Sessions (76) 76(1) [0|0|11] 282
Let's Be Friends (70) 105(2) [0|0|11] 275
He Touched Me (72) 79(1) [0|0|10] 270
Good Times (74) 90(1) [0|0|8] 197
This Is Elvis (Soundtrack) (81) 115(3) [0|0|10] 194
Elvis Sings For Children And Grownups Too (78) 130(1) [0|0|11] 192
Elvis: A Canadian Tribute (78) 86(1) [0|0|7] 192
Elvis-A Legendary Performer, Volume 3 (79) 113(2) [0|0|11] 183
He Walks Beside Me (Favorite Songs Of Faith And Inspiration) (78) 113(2) [0|0|8] 175
I Got Lucky (71) 104(1) [0|0|8] 165
Elvis-The Other Sides - Worldwide Gold Award Hits, Vol. 2 (71) 120(2) [0|0|7] 136
Having Fun With Elvis On Stage (74) 130(2) [0|0|7] 126
Rocker (84) 154(1) [0|0|13] 123
Our Memories Of Elvis (79) 132(2) [0|0|7] 111
The Elvis Medley (82) 133(2) [0|0|9] 110
I Was The One (83) 103(1) [0|0|6] 99.2
The Top Ten Hits (87) 117(2) [0|0|8] 98.8
Greatest Hits Volume One (81) 142(2) [0|0|7] 96.1
The Number One Hits (87) 143(1) [0|0|9] 90.9
Our Memories Of Elvis Volume 2 (79) 157(2) [0|0|5] 66.0
Elvis: The First Live Recordings (84) 163(1) [0|0|4] 41.0
A Valentine Gift For You (85) 154(1) [0|0|3] 31.6
Elvis Back In Memphis (70) 183(1) [0|0|3] 25.2
The Christmas Album (85) 178(2) [0|0|2] 15.1

Billy PRESTON ▶ 493 Pk:17 [0|3|10] 6260
I Wrote A Simple Song (72) 32(1) [0|8|38] 1666
Music Is My Life (72) 32(1) [0|6|35] 1282
The Kids & Me (74) 17(2) [0|6|14] 1119
Late At Night (80) 49(2) [0|0|18] 627
It's My Pleasure (75) 43(1) [0|0|14] 588
Everybody Likes Some Kind Of Music (73) 52(1) [0|0|18] 541
That's The Way God Planned It (72) 127(2) [0|0|12] 216
Wildest Organ In Town! (66) 118(1) [0|0|6] 106
The Most Exciting Organ Ever (65) 143(2) [0|0|3] 37.0
Billy Preston & Syreeta (81)-Billy Preston & Syreeta [A] 127(4) [0|0|9] 77.6

The PRETENDERS ▶ 279 Pk:5 [3|5|6] 12453
Pretenders (80) 9(2) [4|17|78] 4145
Learning To Crawl (84) 5(4) [10|22|42] 3545
Pretenders II (81) 10(3) [3|9|19] 1727
Get Close (86) 25(3) [0|14|29] 1457
Extended Play (81) 27(2) [0|4|29] 1225
The Singles (87) 69(3) [0|0|15] 353

PRETTY MAIDS ▶ 3025 Pk:165 [0|0|1] 62
Future World (87) 165(2) [0|0|8] 62.4

PRETTY POISON ▶ 2561 Pk:104 [0|0|1] 146
Catch Me, I'm Falling (88) 104(2) [0|0|8] 146

► Highest Peak [Top10s|Top40s|Total]
Title (Yr) Peak(Wk) [T10 Wk|T40Wk|TotalWk] — **Score**

- **PRETTY THINGS ► 2139 Pk:104 [0|0|2] — 284**
- Silk Torpedo (75) 104(2) [0|0|9] — 208
- Savage Eye (76) 163(1) [0|0|6] — 75.8
- **Andre PREVIN ► 2487 Pk:130 [0|0|3] — 164**
- A Different Kind Of Blues (81)-Itzhak Perlman & Andre Previn [A] 149(1) [0|0|9] — 60.6
- Andre Previn in Hollywood (63) 130(2) [0|0|4] — 57.9
- My Fair Lady (64) 147(2) [0|0|4] — 45.1
- **Alan PRICE ► 2221 Pk:117 [0|0|2] — 245**
- O Lucky Man! (73) 117(1) [0|0|14] — 221
- Alan Price (77) 187(2) [0|0|3] — 23.7
- **Leontyne PRICE ► 1781 Pk:66 [0|0|3] — 496**
- Great Scenes From Gershwin's "Porgy And Bess" (63) 66(1) [0|0|16] — 325
- Giacomo Puccini: Tosca (63) 79(2) [0|0|6] — 138
- Georges Bizet: Carmen (64) 147(1) [0|0|3] — 33.0
- **Ray PRICE ► 552 Pk:28 [0|1|9] — 5359**
- For The Good Times (70) 28(3) [0|16|59] — 3115
- I Won't Mention It Again (71) 49(1) [0|0|24] — 985
- San Antonio Rose (80)-Willie Nelson & Ray Price [A] 70(2) [0|0|25] — 319
- Danny Boy (67) 106(2) [0|0|17] — 314
- Touch My Heart (67) 129(1) [0|0|12] — 185
- The Lonesomest Lonesome (72) 145(1) [0|0|12] — 180
- Ray Price's All-Time Greatest Hits (72) 165(1) [0|0|10] — 104
- Welcome To My World (71) 146(1) [0|0|5] — 82.7
- She's Got To Be A Saint (73) 161(1) [0|0|7] — 74.0
- **Charley PRIDE ► 234 Pk:22 [0|4|17] — 14897**
- The Best Of Charley Pride (69) 24(1) [0|16|65] — 4079
- Just Plain Charley (70) 22(2) [0|7|27] — 1606
- The Sensational Charley Pride (69) 44(1) [0|0|39] — 1596
- Charley Pride's 10th Album (70) 30(2) [0|2|38] — 1554
- Charley Pride Sings Heart Songs (71) 38(1) [0|2|26] — 1401
- Charley Pride: In Person (69) 62(2) [0|0|43] — 1331
- From Me To You (71) 42(1) [0|0|26] — 1020
- I'm Just Me (71) 50(2) [0|0|19] — 717
- The Best Of Charley Pride, Volume 2 (72) 50(1) [0|0|15] — 584
- Did You Think To Pray (71) 76(1) [0|0|15] — 455
- A Sunshiny Day With Charley Pride (72) 115(2) [0|0|15] — 283
- Songs Of Love By Charley Pride (73) 149(2) [0|0|8] — 94.6
- Sweet Country (73) 166(1) [0|0|6] — 56.8
- Greatest Hits (81) 185(1) [0|0|7] — 48.5
- The Incomparable Charley Pride (73) 189(1) [0|0|8] — 46.0
- The Best Of Charley Pride, Vol. III (77) 188(2) [0|0|2] — 16.1
- The Country Way (68) 199(1) [0|0|2] — 9.8
- **Maxi PRIEST ► 2204 Pk:108 [0|0|1] — 253**
- Maxi Priest (88) 108(1) [0|0|17] — 253
- **The PRIMITIVES ► 1997 Pk:106 [0|0|2] — 352**
- Pure (89) 113(1) [0|0|15] — 205
- Lovely (88) 106(2) [0|0|9] — 147
- **PRINCE ► 45 Pk:1 [6|9|11] — 45278**
- Purple Rain (Soundtrack) (84)-Prince And The Revolution 1(24) [32|42|72] — 13717
- 1999 (82) 9(7) [11|57|153] — 8588
- Around The World In A Day (85)-Prince And The Revolution 1(3) [14|27|40] — 5561
- Batman (Soundtrack) (89) 1(6) [10|17|34] — 4618
- Sign 'O' The Times (87) 6(2) [4|12|54] — 3322
- Parade: Music From The Motion Picture Under The Cherry Moon (Soundtrack) (86)-Prince And The Revolution 3(3) [9|17|28] — 3097
- Controversy (81) 21(3) [0|5|64] — 2142

► Highest Peak [Top10s|Top40s|Total]
Title (Yr) Peak(Wk) [T10 Wk|T40Wk|TotalWk] — **Score**

- Prince (79) 22(2) [0|10|28] — 1850
- Lovesexy (88) 11(1) [0|9|21] — 1341
- Dirty Mind (80) 45(1) [0|0|52] — 986
- For You (78) 163(1) [0|0|5] — 57.3
- **John PRINE ► 1320 Pk:66 [0|0|8] — 1101**
- Common Sense (75) 66(2) [0|0|10] — 321
- Bruised Orange (78) 116(1) [0|0|13] — 236
- Sweet Revenge (73) 135(1) [0|0|11] — 162
- Diamonds In The Rough (72) 148(1) [0|0|10] — 142
- Storm Windows (80) 144(1) [0|0|7] — 94.1
- Pink Cadillac (79) 152(1) [0|0|7] — 94.0
- John Prine (72) 154(1) [0|0|3] — 40.2
- Prime Prine - Best John Prine (77) 196(1) [0|0|2] — 11.9
- **PRISM ► 1456 Pk:53 [0|0|3] — 883**
- Small Change (82) 53(1) [0|0|20] — 640
- Prism (77) 137(1) [0|0|10] — 141
- See Forever Eyes (78) 158(2) [0|0|8] — 102
- **The PROCLAIMERS ► 1328 Pk:31 [0|1|1] — 1089**
- Sunshine On Leith (89) 31(1) [0|3|37] — 1089
- **PROCOL HARUM ► 322 Pk:5 [1|6|11] — 10625**
- Procol Harum Live In Concert with the Edmonton Symphony Orchestra (72) 5(1) [5|19|28] — 3272
- Shine On Brightly (68) 24(2) [0|7|20] — 1363
- Grand Hotel (73) 21(1) [0|7|22] — 1329
- A Salty Dog (69) 32(1) [0|5|20] — 1235
- Broken Barricades (71) 32(2) [0|5|20] — 1029
- Home (70) 34(1) [0|6|15] — 967
- Procol Harum (67) 47(1) [0|0|16] — 649
- Procol's Ninth (75) 52(1) [0|0|8] — 321
- Exotic Birds And Fruit (74) 86(1) [0|0|9] — 232
- The Best Of Procol Harum (73) 131(1) [0|0|10] — 145
- Something Magic (77) 147(1) [0|0|6] — 84.0
- **The PRODUCERS ► 3317 Pk:163 [0|0|1] — 27**
- The Producers (81) 163(1) [0|0|2] — 26.5
- **PROPHET ► 2840 Pk:137 [0|0|1] — 89**
- Cycle Of The Moon (88) 137(1) [0|0|7] — 88.8
- **Jeanne PRUETT ► 2478 Pk:122 [0|0|1] — 166**
- Satin Sheets (73) 122(1) [0|0|9] — 166
- **Richard PRYOR ► 395 Pk:12 [0|5|10] — 8377**
- That Ni*ger's Crazy (74) 29(1) [0|8|53] — 2290
- Is It Something I Said? (75) 12(2) [0|8|25] — 1914
- Bicentennial Ni*ger (76) 22(2) [0|7|19] — 1217
- Wanted (78) 32(2) [0|3|20] — 1002
- Richard Pryor Live On The Sunset Strip (Soundtrack) (82) 21(3) [0|7|17] — 956
- Richard Pryor's Greatest Hits (77) 68(1) [0|0|12] — 314
- Are You Serious??? (77) 58(1) [0|0|9] — 282
- Richard Pryor: Here And Now (Soundtrack) (83) 71(1) [0|0|13] — 267
- L.A. Jail (77) 114(1) [0|0|5] — 97.0
- Outrageous (79) 176(2) [0|0|4] — 38.0
- **Arthur PRYSOCK ► 1766 Pk:97 [0|0|5] — 505**
- A Portrait Of Arthur Prysock (63) 97(1) [0|0|7] — 118
- Arthur Prysock/Count Basie (66)-Arthur Prysock/Count Basie [A] 107(1) [0|0|13] — 116
- A Double Header With Arthur Prysock (65) 116(1) [0|0|7] — 115
- Everlasting Songs For Everlasting Lovers (64) 131(2) [0|0|8] — 103
- All My Life (77) 153(1) [0|0|4] — 54.3
- **PSEUDO ECHO ► 1520 Pk:54 [0|0|1] — 769**
- Love An Adventure (87) 54(3) [0|0|27] — 769
- **PSYCHEDELIC FURS ► 723 Pk:29 [0|1|7] — 3498**
- Midnight To Midnight (87) 29(2) [0|11|27] — 1246
- Forever Now (82) 61(4) [0|0|32] — 902

► Highest Peak [Top10s|Top40s|Total]
Title (Yr) Peak(Wk) [T10 Wk|T40Wk|TotalWk] — **Score**

- Mirror Moves (84) 43(2) [0|0|27] — 792
- Talk Talk Talk (81) 89(2) [0|0|14] — 292
- All Of This And Nothing (88) 102(2) [0|0|8] — 123
- The Psychedelic Furs (80) 140(1) [0|0|7] — 97.5
- Book Of Days (89) 138(2) [0|0|4] — 45.7
- **PUBLIC ENEMY ► 1208 Pk:42 [0|0|2] — 1326**
- It Takes A Nation Of Millions To Hold Us Back (88) 42(2) [0|0|51] — 1159
- Yo! Bum Rush The Show (88) 125(1) [0|0|12] — 167
- **PUBLIC IMAGE LIMITED ► 1590 Pk:106 [0|0|5] — 691**
- 9 (89) 106(2) [0|0|23] — 318
- Album (86) 115(2) [0|0|16] — 194
- Happy? (87) 169(1) [0|0|10] — 74.0
- The Flowers Of Romance (81) 114(2) [0|0|4] — 74.0
- Second Edition (80) 171(2) [0|0|3] — 31.5
- **Gary PUCKETT And The UNION GAP ► 436 Pk:20 [0|3|6] — 7325**
- Young Girl (68) 21(2) [0|11|39] — 2196
- Incredible (68) 20(1) [0|10|20] — 1854
- Woman, Woman (68)-The Union Gap Featuring Gary Puckett 22(2) [0|8|45] — 1662
- Gary Puckett & The Union Gap's Greatest Hits (70) 50(2) [0|0|33] — 1094
- The New Gary Puckett And The Union Gap Album (69) 50(1) [0|0|14] — 505
- The Gary Puckett Album (71)-Gary Puckett 196(1) [0|0|2] — 13.5
- **PURE LOVE & PLEASURE ► 3468 Pk:195 [0|0|1] — 13**
- A Record Of Pure Love & Pleasure (70) 195(1) [0|0|2] — 12.7
- **PURE PRAIRIE LEAGUE ► 560 Pk:24 [0|4|9] — 5203**
- Bustin' Out (75) 34(1) [0|3|24] — 1144
- Two Lane Highway (75) 24(1) [0|6|14] — 957
- Firin' Up (80) 37(2) [0|3|24] — 890
- If The Shoe Fits (76) 33(2) [0|3|16] — 788
- Something In The Night (81) 72(1) [0|0|15] — 386
- Dance (76) 99(2) [0|0|14] — 330
- Live, Takin' The Stage (77) 68(1) [0|0|11] — 320
- Just Fly (78) 79(1) [0|0|11] — 290
- Can't Hold Back (79) 124(1) [0|0|6] — 97.3
- **Flora PURIM ► 1577 Pk:59 [0|0|6] — 704**
- Open Your Eyes You Can Fly (76) 59(2) [0|0|15] — 470
- 500 Miles High (76) 146(1) [0|0|5] — 73.7
- Nothing Will Be As It Was...Tomorrow (77) 163(1) [0|0|4] — 50.7
- Stories To Tell (75) 172(2) [0|0|5] — 46.9
- Everyday, Everynight (78) 174(2) [0|0|4] — 44.4
- Encounter (77) 194(1) [0|0|3] — 17.9
- **PURSUIT OF HAPPINESS ► 1967 Pk:93 [0|0|1] — 368**
- Love Junk (88) 93(1) [0|0|21] — 368
- **The PYRAMIDS ► 2822 Pk:119 [0|0|1] — 91**
- The Original Penetration! And Other Favorites (64) 119(1) [0|0|6] — 91.3
- **PYTHON LEE JACKSON ► 3152 Pk:182 [0|0|1] — 46**
- In A Broken Dream (72) 182(2) [0|0|6] — 46.2

Q

- **Q ► 3196 Pk:140 [0|0|1] — 41**
- Dancin' Man (77) 140(2) [0|0|2] — 40.6
- **QUARTERFLASH ► 589 Pk:8 [1|2|3] — 4884**
- Quarterflash (81) 8(3) [4|21|52] — 3953
- Take Another Picture (83) 34(1) [0|4|21] — 878
- Back Into Blue (85) 150(2) [0|0|5] — 53.0
- **Bill QUATEMAN ► 2622 Pk:129 [0|0|1] — 128**
- Night After Night (77) 129(1) [0|0|8] — 128

<table>
<tr><th>▶ Highest Peak [Top10s | Top40s | Total]
Title (Yr) Peak(Wk) [T10 Wk | T40Wk | TotalWk]</th><th>Score</th></tr>
<tr><td>Suzi QUATRO ▶ 1078 Pk:37 [0 | 1 | 6]</td><td>1657</td></tr>
<tr><td>If You Knew Suzi... (79) 37(1) [0 | 5 | 20]</td><td>943</td></tr>
<tr><td>Suzi...And Other Four Letter Words (79) 117(1) [0 | 0 | 14]</td><td>255</td></tr>
<tr><td>Quatro (74) 126(1) [0 | 0 | 10]</td><td>169</td></tr>
<tr><td>Suzi Quatro (74) 142(1) [0 | 0 | 13]</td><td>156</td></tr>
<tr><td>Your Mama Won't Like Me (75) 146(2) [0 | 0 | 6]</td><td>85.3</td></tr>
<tr><td>Rock Hard (80) 165(1) [0 | 0 | 5]</td><td>48.5</td></tr>
<tr><td>QUAZAR ▶ 2719 Pk:121 [0 | 0 | 1]</td><td>111</td></tr>
<tr><td>Quazar (78) 121(2) [0 | 0 | 5]</td><td>111</td></tr>
<tr><td>QUEEN ▶ 78 Pk:1 [5 | 12 | 15]</td><td>34591</td></tr>
<tr><td>The Game (80) 1(5) [21 | 31 | 43]</td><td>9015</td></tr>
<tr><td>A Night At The Opera (75) 4(3) [7 | 28 | 56]</td><td>5738</td></tr>
<tr><td>News Of The World (77) 3(2) [13 | 21 | 37]</td><td>5213</td></tr>
<tr><td>Sheer Heart Attack (74) 12(2) [0 | 10 | 32]</td><td>2420</td></tr>
<tr><td>Jazz (78) 6(2) [5 | 11 | 18]</td><td>2182</td></tr>
<tr><td>Greatest Hits (81) 14(6) [0 | 13 | 26]</td><td>2106</td></tr>
<tr><td>A Day At The Races (77) 5(1) [4 | 8 | 19]</td><td>1797</td></tr>
<tr><td>Queen Live Killers (79) 16(2) [0 | 7 | 14]</td><td>1183</td></tr>
<tr><td>The Works (84) 23(1) [0 | 9 | 20]</td><td>1088</td></tr>
<tr><td>Flash Gordon (Soundtrack) (80) 23(2) [0 | 7 | 15]</td><td>1073</td></tr>
<tr><td>Hot Space (82) 22(3) [0 | 5 | 21]</td><td>846</td></tr>
<tr><td>The Miracle (89) 24(1) [0 | 4 | 14]</td><td>619</td></tr>
<tr><td>Queen II (74) 49(1) [0 | 0 | 13]</td><td>514</td></tr>
<tr><td>Queen (73) 83(1) [0 | 0 | 22]</td><td>408</td></tr>
<tr><td>A Kind Of Magic (86) 46(3) [0 | 0 | 13]</td><td>387</td></tr>
<tr><td>Queen LATIFAH ▶ 2335 Pk:124 [0 | 0 | 1]</td><td>204</td></tr>
<tr><td>All Hail The Queen (89) 124(2) [0 | 0 | 17]</td><td>204</td></tr>
<tr><td>QUEENSRYCHE ▶ 818 Pk:47 [0 | 0 | 4]</td><td>2832</td></tr>
<tr><td>Operation: Mindcrime (88) 50(2) [0 | 0 | 52]</td><td>1266</td></tr>
<tr><td>Rage For Order (86) 47(5) [0 | 0 | 21]</td><td>630</td></tr>
<tr><td>The Warning (84) 61(3) [0 | 0 | 23]</td><td>502</td></tr>
<tr><td>Queensryche (83) 81(1) [0 | 0 | 22]</td><td>435</td></tr>
<tr><td>QUESTION MARK & The MYSTERIANS ▶ 1862 Pk:66 [0 | 0 | 1]</td><td>434</td></tr>
<tr><td>96 Tears (66)-? (Question Mark) & The Mysterians 66(2) [0 | 0 | 15]</td><td>434</td></tr>
<tr><td>QUICKSILVER MESSENGER SERVICE ▶ 472 Pk:25 [0 | 4 | 9]</td><td>6702</td></tr>
<tr><td>Happy Trails (69) 27(2) [0 | 6 | 30]</td><td>1713</td></tr>
<tr><td>Just For Love (70) 27(2) [0 | 8 | 24]</td><td>1359</td></tr>
<tr><td>What About Me (71) 26(1) [0 | 4 | 20]</td><td>1101</td></tr>
<tr><td>Shady Grove (70) 25(1) [0 | 5 | 24]</td><td>1062</td></tr>
<tr><td>Quicksilver Messenger Service (68) 63(1) [0 | 0 | 25]</td><td>679</td></tr>
<tr><td>Solid Silver (75) 89(1) [0 | 0 | 12]</td><td>231</td></tr>
<tr><td>Quicksilver (71) 114(1) [0 | 0 | 9]</td><td>201</td></tr>
<tr><td>Anthology (73) 108(1) [0 | 0 | 10]</td><td>185</td></tr>
<tr><td>Comin' Thru (72) 134(1) [0 | 0 | 10]</td><td>171</td></tr>
<tr><td>QUIET RIOT ▶ 346 Pk:1 [1 | 3 | 4]</td><td>9745</td></tr>
<tr><td>Metal Health (83) 1(1) [17 | 36 | 81]</td><td>7033</td></tr>
<tr><td>Condition Critical (84) 15(3) [0 | 10 | 28]</td><td>1402</td></tr>
<tr><td>QR III (86) 31(2) [0 | 9 | 27]</td><td>1142</td></tr>
<tr><td>Quiet Riot (88) 119(2) [0 | 0 | 11]</td><td>168</td></tr>
<tr><td><h1>R</h1></td><td></td></tr>
<tr><td>Eddie RABBITT ▶ 463 Pk:19 [0 | 3 | 7]</td><td>6832</td></tr>
<tr><td>Horizon (80) 19(2) [0 | 15 | 54]</td><td>3151</td></tr>
<tr><td>Step By Step (81) 23(1) [0 | 8 | 34]</td><td>1720</td></tr>
<tr><td>Radio Romance (82) 31(2) [0 | 7 | 25]</td><td>1143</td></tr>
<tr><td>Loveline (79) 91(1) [0 | 0 | 20]</td><td>432</td></tr>
<tr><td>The Best Of Eddie Rabbitt (79) 151(1) [0 | 0 | 12]</td><td>160</td></tr>
<tr><td>Greatest Hits - Vol. II (83) 131(3) [0 | 0 | 11]</td><td>126</td></tr>
<tr><td>Variations (78) 143(2) [0 | 0 | 7]</td><td>99.4</td></tr>
<tr><td>Trevor RABIN ▶ 2351 Pk:111 [0 | 0 | 2]</td><td>199</td></tr>
<tr><td>Can't Look Away (89) 111(3) [0 | 0 | 10]</td><td>174</td></tr>
</table>

<table>
<tr><th>▶ Highest Peak [Top10s | Top40s | Total]
Title (Yr) Peak(Wk) [T10 Wk | T40Wk | TotalWk]</th><th>Score</th></tr>
<tr><td>Trevor Rabin (78) 192(2) [0 | 0 | 4]</td><td>25.3</td></tr>
<tr><td>RACING CARS ▶ 3428 Pk:198 [0 | 0 | 1]</td><td>17</td></tr>
<tr><td>Downtown Tonight (77) 198(1) [0 | 0 | 3]</td><td>16.9</td></tr>
<tr><td>The RADIATORS ▶ 2150 Pk:122 [0 | 0 | 2]</td><td>281</td></tr>
<tr><td>Zigzagging Through Ghostland (89) 122(2) [0 | 0 | 11]</td><td>142</td></tr>
<tr><td>Law Of The Fish (87) 139(2) [0 | 0 | 16]</td><td>139</td></tr>
<tr><td>Gilda RADNER ▶ 1941 Pk:69 [0 | 0 | 1]</td><td>380</td></tr>
<tr><td>Live From New York (79) 69(2) [0 | 0 | 12]</td><td>380</td></tr>
<tr><td>The RAES ▶ 3041 Pk:161 [0 | 0 | 1]</td><td>60</td></tr>
<tr><td>Dancin' Up A Storm (79) 161(1) [0 | 0 | 5]</td><td>60.2</td></tr>
<tr><td>Gerry RAFFERTY ▶ 476 Pk:1 [1 | 2 | 3]</td><td>6588</td></tr>
<tr><td>City To City (78) 1(1) [8 | 23 | 49]</td><td>5110</td></tr>
<tr><td>Night Owl (79) 29(2) [0 | 6 | 21]</td><td>1168</td></tr>
<tr><td>Snakes And Ladders (80) 61(1) [0 | 0 | 9]</td><td>310</td></tr>
<tr><td>RAGING SLAB ▶ 2442 Pk:113 [0 | 0 | 1]</td><td>174</td></tr>
<tr><td>Raging Slab (89) 113(1) [0 | 0 | 15]</td><td>174</td></tr>
<tr><td>--Raiders see: Paul Revere and the Raiders</td><td></td></tr>
<tr><td>RAIL ▶ 2790 Pk:143 [0 | 0 | 1]</td><td>99</td></tr>
<tr><td>Rail (84) 143(1) [0 | 0 | 10]</td><td>98.9</td></tr>
<tr><td>RAINBOW ▶ 565 Pk:30 [0 | 3 | 10]</td><td>5147</td></tr>
<tr><td>Straight Between The Eyes (82) 30(3) [0 | 5 | 23]</td><td>891</td></tr>
<tr><td>Ritchie Blackmore's R-A-I-N-B-O-W (75) 30(1) [0 | 4 | 15]</td><td>851</td></tr>
<tr><td>Bent Out Of Shape (83) 34(1) [0 | 4 | 21]</td><td>848</td></tr>
<tr><td>Rainbow Rising (76)-Blackmore's Rainbow 48(2) [0 | 0 | 17]</td><td>676</td></tr>
<tr><td>Difficult To Cure (81) 50(2) [0 | 0 | 16]</td><td>650</td></tr>
<tr><td>Down To Earth (79) 66(1) [0 | 0 | 15]</td><td>413</td></tr>
<tr><td>On Stage (77) 65(1) [0 | 0 | 9]</td><td>305</td></tr>
<tr><td>Long Live Rock 'N' Roll (78) 89(2) [0 | 0 | 11]</td><td>282</td></tr>
<tr><td>Finyl Vinyl (86) 87(2) [0 | 0 | 10]</td><td>179</td></tr>
<tr><td>Jealous Lover (81) 147(1) [0 | 0 | 4]</td><td>51.1</td></tr>
<tr><td>The RAINMAKERS ▶ 1681 Pk:85 [0 | 0 | 2]</td><td>599</td></tr>
<tr><td>The Rainmakers (86) 85(1) [0 | 0 | 22]</td><td>342</td></tr>
<tr><td>Tornado (87) 116(2) [0 | 0 | 19]</td><td>257</td></tr>
<tr><td>Bonnie RAITT ▶ 264 Pk:1 [1 | 4 | 9]</td><td>13284</td></tr>
<tr><td>Nick Of Time (89) 1(3) [11 | 40 | 185]</td><td>8820</td></tr>
<tr><td>Sweet Forgiveness (77) 25(2) [0 | 4 | 22]</td><td>1224</td></tr>
<tr><td>The Glow (79) 30(1) [0 | 5 | 21]</td><td>1017</td></tr>
<tr><td>Green Light (82) 38(1) [0 | 3 | 18]</td><td>682</td></tr>
<tr><td>Home Plate (75) 43(2) [0 | 0 | 12]</td><td>541</td></tr>
<tr><td>Takin My Time (73) 87(1) [0 | 0 | 20]</td><td>390</td></tr>
<tr><td>Streetlights (74) 80(1) [0 | 0 | 8]</td><td>232</td></tr>
<tr><td>Give It Up (72) 138(1) [0 | 0 | 15]</td><td>216</td></tr>
<tr><td>Nine Lives (86) 115(1) [0 | 0 | 11]</td><td>162</td></tr>
<tr><td>RAMATAM ▶ 3095 Pk:182 [0 | 0 | 1]</td><td>52</td></tr>
<tr><td>Ramatam (72) 182(1) [0 | 0 | 7]</td><td>52.5</td></tr>
<tr><td>Eddie RAMBEAU ▶ 3347 Pk:148 [0 | 0 | 1]</td><td>24</td></tr>
<tr><td>Concrete And Clay (65) 148(2) [0 | 0 | 2]</td><td>24.5</td></tr>
<tr><td>RAM JAM ▶ 1599 Pk:34 [0 | 1 | 1]</td><td>680</td></tr>
<tr><td>Ram Jam (77) 34(1) [0 | 4 | 12]</td><td>680</td></tr>
<tr><td>The RAMONES ▶ 788 Pk:44 [0 | 0 | 12]</td><td>3030</td></tr>
<tr><td>Rocket To Russia (77) 49(3) [0 | 0 | 25]</td><td>921</td></tr>
<tr><td>End Of The Century (80) 44(1) [0 | 0 | 14]</td><td>575</td></tr>
<tr><td>Pleasant Dreams (81) 58(2) [0 | 0 | 11]</td><td>372</td></tr>
<tr><td>Ramones (76) 111(1) [0 | 0 | 18]</td><td>362</td></tr>
<tr><td>Road To Ruin (78) 103(1) [0 | 0 | 11]</td><td>201</td></tr>
<tr><td>Subterranean Jungle (83) 83(3) [0 | 0 | 9]</td><td>183</td></tr>
<tr><td>Leave Home (77) 148(1) [0 | 0 | 10]</td><td>150</td></tr>
<tr><td>Brain Drain (89) 122(2) [0 | 0 | 6]</td><td>96.2</td></tr>
<tr><td>Animal Boy (86) 143(2) [0 | 0 | 6]</td><td>60.2</td></tr>
<tr><td>Too Tough To Die (84) 171(1) [0 | 0 | 6]</td><td>44.6</td></tr>
<tr><td>Ramones Mania (88) 168(2) [0 | 0 | 5]</td><td>42.2</td></tr>
<tr><td>Halfway To Sanity (87) 172(1) [0 | 0 | 3]</td><td>21.9</td></tr>
</table>

<table>
<tr><th>▶ Highest Peak [Top10s | Top40s | Total]
Title (Yr) Peak(Wk) [T10 Wk | T40Wk | TotalWk]</th><th>Score</th></tr>
<tr><td>Jean-Pierre RAMPAL & Claude BOLLING ▶ 3180 Pk:173 [0 | 0 | 1]</td><td>43</td></tr>
<tr><td>Suite Flute & Jazz Piano (76) 173(1) [0 | 0 | 4]</td><td>43.2</td></tr>
<tr><td>Boots RANDOLPH ▶ 670 Pk:36 [0 | 1 | 12]</td><td>4040</td></tr>
<tr><td>Boots With Strings (67) 36(2) [0 | 4 | 47]</td><td>1533</td></tr>
<tr><td>The Sound Of Boots (68) 60(1) [0 | 0 | 24]</td><td>777</td></tr>
<tr><td>...With Love/The Seductive Sax Of Boots Randolph (69) 82(2) [0 | 0 | 17]</td><td>566</td></tr>
<tr><td>Yakety Revisited (70) 113(1) [0 | 0 | 18]</td><td>343</td></tr>
<tr><td>Sunday Sax (68) 76(1) [0 | 0 | 12]</td><td>277</td></tr>
<tr><td>Homer Louis Randolph, III (71) 141(1) [0 | 0 | 11]</td><td>151</td></tr>
<tr><td>Hit Boots 1970 (70) 157(2) [0 | 0 | 9]</td><td>118</td></tr>
<tr><td>The World Of Boots Randolph (71) 144(2) [0 | 0 | 8]</td><td>104</td></tr>
<tr><td>Boots Randolph Plays More Yakety Sax! (65) 118(1) [0 | 0 | 5]</td><td>81.4</td></tr>
<tr><td>Boots With Brass (71) 168(1) [0 | 0 | 3]</td><td>38.8</td></tr>
<tr><td>Boots Randolph With The Knightsbridge Strings & Voices (68) 189(2) [0 | 0 | 5]</td><td>31.6</td></tr>
<tr><td>Boots Randolph Plays The Great Hits Of Today (72) 192(2) [0 | 0 | 3]</td><td>19.9</td></tr>
<tr><td>RANK AND FILE ▶ 3204 Pk:165 [0 | 0 | 1]</td><td>39</td></tr>
<tr><td>Sundown (83) 165(1) [0 | 0 | 5]</td><td>39.3</td></tr>
<tr><td>Billy RANKIN ▶ 2527 Pk:119 [0 | 0 | 1]</td><td>152</td></tr>
<tr><td>Growin' Up Too Fast (84) 119(1) [0 | 0 | 11]</td><td>152</td></tr>
<tr><td>Kenny RANKIN ▶ 1158 Pk:63 [0 | 0 | 5]</td><td>1445</td></tr>
<tr><td>Silver Morning (74) 63(1) [0 | 0 | 25]</td><td>581</td></tr>
<tr><td>Kenny Rankin Album (77) 99(2) [0 | 0 | 23]</td><td>394</td></tr>
<tr><td>Inside (75) 81(1) [0 | 0 | 15]</td><td>358</td></tr>
<tr><td>After The Roses (80) 171(1) [0 | 0 | 6]</td><td>57.7</td></tr>
<tr><td>Like A Seed (72) 184(1) [0 | 0 | 8]</td><td>54.6</td></tr>
<tr><td>RANKING ROGER ▶ 2953 Pk:151 [0 | 0 | 1]</td><td>72</td></tr>
<tr><td>Radical Departure (88) 151(2) [0 | 0 | 7]</td><td>71.8</td></tr>
<tr><td>RARE BIRD ▶ 2219 Pk:117 [0 | 0 | 2]</td><td>246</td></tr>
<tr><td>Rare Bird (70) 117(1) [0 | 0 | 13]</td><td>233</td></tr>
<tr><td>Epic Forest (73) 194(2) [0 | 0 | 2]</td><td>12.6</td></tr>
<tr><td>RARE EARTH ▶ 250 Pk:12 [0 | 4 | 9]</td><td>14173</td></tr>
<tr><td>Get Ready (69) 12(3) [0 | 28 | 77]</td><td>5848</td></tr>
<tr><td>Ecology (70) 15(5) [0 | 18 | 49]</td><td>3565</td></tr>
<tr><td>One World (71) 28(1) [0 | 11 | 25]</td><td>1962</td></tr>
<tr><td>Rare Earth In Concert (72) 29(1) [0 | 4 | 21]</td><td>1137</td></tr>
<tr><td>Ma (73) 65(2) [0 | 0 | 23]</td><td>650</td></tr>
<tr><td>Back To Earth (75) 59(2) [0 | 0 | 11]</td><td>450</td></tr>
<tr><td>Willie Remembers.. (72) 90(1) [0 | 0 | 20]</td><td>445</td></tr>
<tr><td>Band Together (78) 156(1) [0 | 0 | 6]</td><td>70.3</td></tr>
<tr><td>Rare Earth (77) 187(1) [0 | 0 | 6]</td><td>45.7</td></tr>
<tr><td>RASCALS/YOUNG RASCALS ▶ 130 Pk:1 [3 | 6 | 10]</td><td>24629</td></tr>
<tr><td>Time Peace/The Rascals' Greatest Hits (68)-The Rascals 1(1) [25 | 32 | 58]</td><td>9593</td></tr>
<tr><td>Groovin' (67)-The Young Rascals 5(1) [13 | 21 | 59]</td><td>4184</td></tr>
<tr><td>Collections (67)-The Young Rascals 14(1) [0 | 24 | 74]</td><td>3678</td></tr>
<tr><td>The Young Rascals (66)-The Young Rascals 15(1) [0 | 14 | 84]</td><td>2658</td></tr>
<tr><td>Once Upon A Dream (68)-The Rascals 9(2) [3 | 12 | 30]</td><td>2202</td></tr>
<tr><td>Freedom Suite (69)-The Rascals 17(2) [0 | 6 | 16]</td><td>1363</td></tr>
<tr><td>See (70)-The Rascals 45(3) [0 | 0 | 16]</td><td>663</td></tr>
<tr><td>Peaceful World (71)-The Rascals 122(2) [0 | 0 | 12]</td><td>256</td></tr>
<tr><td>The Island Of Real (72)-The Rascals 180(2) [0 | 0 | 3]</td><td>27.7</td></tr>
<tr><td>Search And Nearness (71)-The Rascals 198(1) [0 | 0 | 1]</td><td>6.2</td></tr>
<tr><td>RASPBERRIES ▶ 1003 Pk:36 [0 | 1 | 5]</td><td>1932</td></tr>
<tr><td>Raspberries (72) 51(1) [0 | 0 | 30]</td><td>859</td></tr>
<tr><td>Fresh (72) 36(3) [0 | 4 | 16]</td><td>782</td></tr>
<tr><td>Side 3 (73) 128(1) [0 | 0 | 7]</td><td>115</td></tr>
</table>

▶ Highest Peak [Top10s | Top40s | Total]
Title (Yr) Peak(Wk) [T10 Wk | T40Wk | TotalWk] — Score

RASPBERRIES ▶ *Continued*
- Starting Over (74) 143(1) [0|0|6] — 100
- Raspberries' Best Featuring Eric Carmen (76) 138(1) [0|0|4] — 77.3

RATCHELL ▶ 3277 Pk:176 [0|0|1] — 31
- Ratchell (72) 176(1) [0|0|3] — 30.9

RATT ▶ 332 Pk:7 [2|4|5] — 10425
- Out Of The Cellar (84) 7(4) [9|26|56] — 4307
- Invasion Of Your Privacy (85) 7(1) [6|18|42] — 2750
- Reach For The Sky (88) 17(1) [0|13|27] — 1768
- Dancing Undercover (86) 26(2) [0|7|40] — 1372
- Ratt (84) 133(3) [0|0|19] — 228

Genya RAVAN ▶ 2340 Pk:106 [0|0|2] — 202
- ...And I Mean It! (79) 106(1) [0|0|6] — 124
- Urban Desire (78) 147(1) [0|0|6] — 78.3

RAVEN ▶ 1879 Pk:81 [0|0|2] — 419
- Stay Hard (85) 81(3) [0|0|15] — 292
- The Pack Is Back (86) 121(2) [0|0|10] — 127

Lou RAWLS ▶ 144 Pk:4 [3|6|22] — 22767
- Lou Rawls Live (66) 4(1) [6|38|74] — 5676
- Lou Rawls Soulin' (66) 7(1) [6|22|51] — 3955
- All Things In Time (76) 7(2) [4|12|35] — 2947
- Too Much! (67) 18(2) [0|14|22] — 1724
- Lou Rawls Carryin' On! (67) 20(2) [0|11|31] — 1676
- When You Hear Lou, You've Heard It All (77) 41(1) [0|0|34] — 1512
- Unmistakably Lou (77) 41(2) [0|0|29] — 891
- That's Lou (67) 29(1) [0|2|20] — 797
- Natural Man (71) 68(1) [0|0|24] — 745
- The Way It Was - The Way It Is (69) 71(1) [0|0|23] — 689
- Let Me Be Good To You (79) 49(1) [0|0|15] — 569
- Sit Down And Talk To Me (80) 81(1) [0|0|18] — 446
- Feelin' Good (68) 103(1) [0|0|22] — 386
- The Best Of Lou Rawls (68) 103(2) [0|0|16] — 304
- Lou Rawls Live(2) (78) 108(1) [0|0|8] — 134
- Shades Of Blue (81) 110(2) [0|0|6] — 133
- You're Good For Me (68) 165(2) [0|0|6] — 53.1
- When The Night Comes (83) 163(1) [0|0|4] — 40.0
- Silk & Soul (72) 186(1) [0|0|4] — 29.6
- You've Made Me So Very Happy (70) 172(2) [0|0|3] — 29.2
- Close-Up (69) 191(1) [0|0|3] — 22.9
- Your Good Thing (69) 200(2) [0|0|2] — 11.2

Don RAY ▶ 2336 Pk:113 [0|0|1] — 203
- The Garden Of Love (78) 113(2) [0|0|11] — 203

Susan RAYE ▶ 3103 Pk:154 [0|0|2] — 52
- We're Gonna Get Together (70)-Buck Owens & Susan Raye [A] 154(1) [0|0|6] — 35.8
- One Night Stand (70) 190(2) [0|0|2] — 15.9

RAY, GOODMAN & BROWN ▶ 935 Pk:17 [0|1|3] — 2198
- Ray, Goodman & Brown (80) 17(2) [0|11|23] — 1827
- Ray, Goodman & Brown II (80) 84(2) [0|0|12] — 286
- Stay (82) 151(1) [0|0|7] — 85.2

Chris REA ▶ 1530 Pk:49 [0|0|2] — 755
- What Ever Happened To Benny Santini (78) 49(1) [0|0|12] — 511
- New Light Through Old Windows (89) 92(4) [0|0|13] — 243

READY FOR THE WORLD ▶ 648 Pk:17 [0|2|3] — 4267
- Ready For the World (85) 17(5) [0|30|48] — 3043
- Long Time Coming (86) 32(2) [0|5|26] — 980
- Ruff 'N' Ready (88) 65(2) [0|0|10] — 244

REAL LIFE ▶ 1754 Pk:58 [0|0|2] — 518
- Heart Land (84) 58(1) [0|0|24] — 503
- Send Me An Angel '89 (89) 191(1) [0|0|3] — 15.5

The RECORDS ▶ 1640 Pk:41 [0|0|1] — 629
- The Records (79) 41(2) [0|0|14] — 629

REDBONE ▶ 1365 Pk:66 [0|0|4] — 1021
- Wovoka (74) 66(1) [0|0|16] — 424
- Potlatch (70) 99(1) [0|0|17] — 301
- Message From A Drum (72) 75(2) [0|0|9] — 264
- Beaded Dreams Through Turquoise Eyes (74) 174(1) [0|0|3] — 31.6

Leon REDBONE ▶ 1216 Pk:38 [0|1|4] — 1313
- Double Time (77) 38(2) [0|4|13] — 713
- On The Track (76) 87(1) [0|0|15] — 396
- From Branch To Branch (81) 152(1) [0|0|11] — 155
- Champagne Charlie (78) 163(1) [0|0|4] — 50.3

Otis REDDING ▶ 253 Pk:4 [2|5|15] — 14072
- The Dock Of The Bay (68) 4(3) [7|20|42] — 3733
- History Of Otis Redding (67) 9(2) [3|19|50] — 3564
- Otis Redding Live In Europe (67) 32(2) [0|4|42] — 1113
- The Immortal Otis Redding (68) 58(1) [0|0|21] — 759
- Monterey International Pop Festival (70)-Otis Redding/The Jimi Hendrix Experience [A] 16(2) [0|8|20] — 751
- The Soul Album (66) 54(1) [0|0|29] — 725
- Otis Blue/Otis Redding Sings Soul (65) 75(1) [0|0|34] — 721
- Love Man (69) 46(2) [0|0|14] — 663
- Otis Redding In Person At The Whisky A Go Go (68) 82(2) [0|0|17] — 528
- The Best Of Otis Redding (72) 76(2) [0|0|15] — 389
- Complete & Unbelievable....The Otis Redding Dictionary Of Soul (66) 73(1) [0|0|15] — 388
- Pain In My Heart (64) 103(1) [0|0|8] — 129
- The Great Otis Redding Sings Soul Ballads (65) 147(1) [0|0|3] — 35.3
- Tell The Truth (70) 200(2) [0|0|2] — 10.6
- King & Queen (67)-Otis Redding & Carla Thomas [A] 36(2) [0|3|31] — 563

The REDDINGS ▶ 2054 Pk:106 [0|0|3] — 327
- Steamin' Hot (82) 153(3) [0|0|12] — 121
- The Awakening (80) 174(3) [0|0|12] — 105
- Class (81) 106(2) [0|0|5] — 101

Helen REDDY ▶ 154 Pk:5 [3|7|10] — 21797
- I Am Woman (72) 14(4) [0|17|62] — 4068
- Long Hard Climb (73) 8(3) [4|15|43] — 3510
- Helen Reddy's Greatest Hits (75) 5(3) [7|11|51] — 3481
- Free And Easy (74) 8(1) [3|16|28] — 3045
- Love Song For Jeffrey (74) 11(1) [0|14|35] — 2630
- No Way To Treat A Lady (75) 11(1) [0|10|34] — 2270
- Music, Music (76) 16(1) [0|8|13] — 1285
- I Don't Know How To Love Him (71) 100(1) [0|0|37] — 896
- Ear Candy (77) 75(2) [0|0|19] — 532
- Helen Reddy (71) 167(1) [0|0|7] — 79.7

REDEYE ▶ 2322 Pk:113 [0|0|1] — 209
- Redeye (70) 113(2) [0|0|12] — 209

RED FLAG ▶ 3286 Pk:178 [0|0|1] — 29
- Naive Art (89) 178(2) [0|0|4] — 29.4

RED HOT CHILI PEPPERS ▶ 1144 Pk:52 [0|0|2] — 1485
- Mother's Milk (89) 52(1) [0|0|42] — 1311
- Uplift Mofo Party Plan (87) 148(1) [0|0|18] — 174

RED ROCKERS ▶ 2018 Pk:71 [0|0|1] — 343
- Good As Gold (83) 71(2) [0|0|16] — 343

RED 7 ▶ 2461 Pk:105 [0|0|2] — 171
- Red 7 (85) 105(2) [0|0|10] — 147
- When The Sun Goes Down (87) 175(2) [0|0|3] — 23.3

RED SIREN ▶ 2529 Pk:124 [0|0|1] — 152
- All Is Forgiven (89) 124(1) [0|0|12] — 152

Dan REED Network ▶ 1907 Pk:95 [0|0|2] — 403
- Dan Reed Network (88) 95(2) [0|0|19] — 351
- Slam (89) 160(1) [0|0|6] — 52.6

Jerry REED ▶ 1124 Pk:45 [0|0|7] — 1537
- When You're Hot, You're Hot (71) 45(1) [0|0|20] — 916
- Georgia Sunshine (71) 102(1) [0|0|11] — 254
- The Best Of Jerry Reed (72) 116(2) [0|0|12] — 240
- Ko-Ko Joe (71) 153(2) [0|0|5] — 74.7
- Lord, Mr. Ford (73) 183(1) [0|0|4] — 27.9
- Cookin' (70) 194(1) [0|0|2] — 13.1
- Smell The Flowers (72) 196(1) [0|0|2] — 11.8

Lou REED ▶ 382 Pk:10 [1|3|18] — 8712
- Transformer (72) 29(2) [0|9|31] — 1506
- Sally Can't Dance (74) 10(2) [2|7|14] — 1504
- Rock N Roll Animal (74) 45(1) [0|0|27] — 1104
- New York (89) 40(1) [0|1|22] — 942
- New Sensations (84) 56(1) [0|0|32] — 889
- Mistrial (86) 47(2) [0|0|21] — 684
- Coney Island Baby (76) 41(1) [0|0|14] — 665
- Lou Reed Live (75) 62(2) [0|0|10] — 363
- Rock And Roll Heart (76) 64(1) [0|0|8] — 271
- Street Hassle (78) 89(1) [0|0|9] — 220
- Berlin (73) 98(1) [0|0|11] — 208
- Walk On The Wild Side-The Best Of Lou Reed (77) 156(1) [0|0|6] — 77.5
- The Bells (79) 130(1) [0|0|4] — 74.3
- Legendary Hearts (83) 159(1) [0|0|7] — 60.6
- Growing Up In Public (80) 158(2) [0|0|5] — 56.6
- Rock And Roll Diary 1967-1980 (80) 178(3) [0|0|4] — 37.4
- The Blue Mask (82) 169(1) [0|0|4] — 34.6
- Lou Reed (72) 189(1) [0|0|2] — 14.6

Della REESE ▶ 3292 Pk:149 [0|0|1] — 29
- Della Reese Live (66) 149(1) [0|0|2] — 28.8

Dianne REEVES ▶ 2837 Pk:172 [0|0|1] — 90
- Dianne Reeves (88) 172(1) [0|0|12] — 89.5

Jim REEVES ▶ 536 Pk:9 [1|3|6] — 5560
- The Best Of Jim Reeves (64) 9(1) [3|18|43] — 2545
- Distant Drums (66) 21(1) [0|10|29] — 1514
- Moonlight And Roses (64) 30(2) [0|2|30] — 922
- The Jim Reeves Way (65) 45(1) [0|0|13] — 439
- The Best Of Jim Reeves Volume II (66) 100(1) [0|0|6] — 107
- Blue Side Of Lonesome (67) 185(1) [0|0|5] — 32.2

RE-FLEX ▶ 1669 Pk:53 [0|0|1] — 604
- The Politics Of Dancing (83) 53(1) [0|0|28] — 604

REGINA ▶ 2700 Pk:102 [0|0|1] — 114
- Curiosity (86) 102(2) [0|0|8] — 114

Terry REID ▶ 2207 Pk:147 [0|0|3] — 252
- Bang, Bang You're Terry Reid (68) 153(2) [0|0|8] — 104
- Terry Reid (69) 147(2) [0|0|5] — 82.8
- River (73) 172(1) [0|0|8] — 65.6

Carl REINER & Mel BROOKS ▶ 2549 Pk:150 [0|0|1] — 149
- 2000 And Thirteen (73) 150(1) [0|0|12] — 149

R.E.M. ▶ 269 Pk:10 [1|6|8] — 13110
- Green (88) 12(3) [0|27|40] — 3841
- R.E.M. No. 5: Document (87) 10(1) [1|20|33] — 2688
- Fables Of The Reconstruction (85) 28(2) [0|14|42] — 1668
- Reckoning (84) 27(5) [0|6|53] — 1613
- Lifes Rich Pageant (86) 21(2) [0|12|32] — 1563
- Murmur (83) 36(1) [0|3|30] — 913
- Eponymous (88) 44(2) [0|0|19] — 432
- Dead Letter Office (87) 52(1) [0|0|14] — 393

► Highest Peak [Top10s|Top40s|Total]
Title (Yr) Peak(Wk) [T10 Wk|T40Wk|TotalWk] — Score

RENAISSANCE ► 763 Pk:46 [0|0|8] — 3192
Live At Carnegie Hall (76) 55(2) [0|0|20] — 844
Novella (77) 46(1) [0|0|16] — 640
A Song For All Seasons (78) 58(1) [0|0|14] — 529
Scheherazade And Other Stories (75) 48(1) [0|0|13] — 512
Turn Of The Cards (74) 94(2) [0|0|21] — 465
Azure D'or (79) 125(2) [0|0|9] — 141
Ashes Are Burning (73) 171(1) [0|0|4] — 40.6
Camera Camera (81) 196(3) [0|0|4] — 21.3

The RENAISSANCE ► 3489 Pk:198 [0|0|1] — 12
Bacharach Baroque (71) 198(1) [0|0|2] — 12.0

Diane RENAY ► 2154 Pk:54 [0|0|1] — 277
Navy Blue (64) 54(1) [0|0|11] — 277

RENÉ & ANGELA ► 1049 Pk:64 [0|0|2] — 1749
Street Called Desire (85) 64(4) [0|0|70] — 1585
Wall To Wall (81) 100(1) [0|0|8] — 164

RENÉ & RENÉ ► 2353 Pk:129 [0|0|1] — 197
Lo Mucho Que Te Quiero (69) 129(1) [0|0|9] — 197

REO SPEEDWAGON ► 97 Pk:1 [3|6|13] — 29876
Hi Infidelity (80) 1(15) [30|50|101] — 16076
Wheels Are Turnin' (84) 7(1) [7|21|49] — 3592
Good Trouble (82) 7(9) [10|16|24] — 2702
You Can Tune A Piano But You Can't Tuna Fish (78) 29(1) [0|5|48] — 1679
Life As We Know It (87) 28(2) [0|7|48] — 1504
REO Speedwagon Live/You Get What You Play For (77) 72(1) [0|0|50] — 1014
Nine Lives (79) 33(1) [0|5|23] — 1007
A Decade Of Rock And Roll 1970 To 1980 (80) 55(1) [0|0|34] — 835
The Hits (88) 56(1) [0|0|22] — 745
This Time We Mean It (75) 74(2) [0|0|10] — 312
Lost In A Dream (74) 98(2) [0|0|14] — 278
Ridin' The Storm Out (74) 171(2) [0|0|8] — 66.7
R.E.O. (76) 159(1) [0|0|5] — 65.8

The REPLACEMENTS ► 1466 Pk:57 [0|0|3] — 869
Don't Tell A Soul (89) 57(2) [0|0|19] — 602
Pleased To Meet Me (87) 131(1) [0|0|19] — 229
Tim (86) 183(1) [0|0|7] — 37.3

RESTLESS HEART ► 1659 Pk:73 [0|0|2] — 614
Wheels (87) 73(2) [0|0|25] — 456
Big Dreams In A Small Town (88) 114(2) [0|0|11] — 158

RETURN TO FOREVER ► 746 Pk:32 [0|4|6] — 3297
Where Have I Known You Before (74) 32(2) [0|4|23] — 1018
Romantic Warrior (76) 35(2) [0|3|15] — 715
Musicmagic (77) 38(1) [0|2|17] — 642
No Mystery (75) 39(2) [0|2|13] — 601
Hymn Of The Seventh Galaxy (73) 124(1) [0|0|15] — 268
Return To Forever Live (79) 155(1) [0|0|4] — 53.2

REVERBERI ► 2968 Pk:169 [0|0|1] — 70
Reverberi & Schumann, Chopin, Liszt (76) 169(2) [0|0|7] — 69.8

Paul REVERE And The RAIDERS ► 196 Pk:5 [4|6|14] — 17747
Greatest Hits (67) 9(2) [2|19|47] — 3215
Just Like Us! (66) 5(1) [4|19|43] — 2924
The Spirit Of '67 (66) 9(3) [7|17|33] — 2863
Midnight Ride (66) 9(1) [4|15|43] — 2770
Indian Reservation (71)-Raiders 19(1) [0|11|20] — 1744
Revolution! (67) 25(1) [0|7|21] — 919
Here They Come! (65) 71(1) [0|0|45] — 838
Hard 'N' Heavy (With Marshmallow) (69) 51(2) [0|0|19] — 752
Alias Pink Puzz (69) 48(2) [0|0|12] — 605
Goin' To Memphis (68) 61(2) [0|0|23] — 547
Something Happening (68) 122(1) [0|0|14] — 287
Collage (70)-Raiders 154(2) [0|0|9] — 122
All-Time Greatest Hits (72) 143(1) [0|0|8] — 107
Two All-Time Great Selling LP's (69)-Raiders 166(2) [0|0|4] — 53.7

Debbie REYNOLDS ► 1332 Pk:23 [0|1|2] — 1088
The Singing Nun (66) 23(1) [0|4|25] — 1067
Do It Debbie's Way (84) 182(1) [0|0|3] — 20.4

RHINOCEROS ► 1513 Pk:105 [0|0|3] — 779
Rhinoceros (68) 115(1) [0|0|22] — 524
Satin Chickens (69) 105(1) [0|0|9] — 202
Better Times Are Coming (70) 178(2) [0|0|6] — 52.6

Randy RHOADS ► 1304 Pk:6 [1|1|1] — 1133
Tribute (87)-Ozzy Osbourne/Randy Rhoads [A] 6(2) [6|14|23] — 1133

Emitt RHODES ► 1152 Pk:29 [0|1|3] — 1458
Emitt Rhodes (70) 29(1) [0|7|20] — 1413
Mirror (71) 182(1) [0|0|4] — 37.4
The American Dream (71) 194(1) [0|0|1] — 7.4

RHYTHM CORPS ► 2356 Pk:104 [0|0|1] — 197
Common Ground (88) 104(2) [0|0|14] — 197

RHYTHM HERITAGE ► 1480 Pk:40 [0|1|2] — 848
Disco-Fied (76) 40(2) [0|2|17] — 737
Last Night On Earth (77) 138(2) [0|0|6] — 111

Buddy RICH ► 1430 Pk:91 [0|0|5] — 924
Swingin' New Big Band (66) 91(1) [0|0|27] — 532
Big Swing Face (67) 97(1) [0|0|21] — 283
Mercy, Mercy (68) 186(1) [0|0|6] — 46.8
Rich In London (72) 180(1) [0|0|5] — 37.1
Buddy & Soul (69) 186(1) [0|0|3] — 24.1

Charlie RICH ► 296 Pk:8 [1|4|12] — 11834
Behind Closed Doors (73) 8(1) [6|32|105] — 6008
Very Special Love Songs (74) 24(2) [0|11|31] — 1830
The Silver Fox (74) 25(2) [0|9|17] — 1371
There Won't Be Anymore (74) 36(1) [0|2|27] — 1100
Every Time You Touch Me (I Get High) (75) 54(1) [0|0|20] — 540
The Best Of Charlie Rich (74) 89(1) [0|0|19] — 372
She Called Me Baby (74) 84(2) [0|0|15] — 333
Greatest Hits(2) (76) 148(1) [0|0|6] — 91.9
Silver Linings (76) 160(1) [0|0|6] — 73.7
Greatest Hits (75) 162(2) [0|0|4] — 50.7
Charlie Rich Sings The Songs Of Hank Williams & Others (74) 177(1) [0|0|4] — 38.5
Rollin' With The Flow (77) 180(1) [0|0|3] — 25.2

Cliff RICHARD ► 1117 Pk:76 [0|0|5] — 1554
I'm No Hero (80) 80(2) [0|0|34] — 723
I'm Nearly Famous (76) 76(2) [0|0|15] — 366
We Don't Talk Anymore (79) 93(2) [0|0|15] — 290
It's All In The Game (64) 115(1) [0|0|7] — 104
Wired For Sound (81) 132(2) [0|0|4] — 70.4

Keith RICHARDS ► 1351 Pk:24 [0|1|1] — 1040
Talk Is Cheap (88) 24(1) [0|7|23] — 1040

Lionel RICHIE ► 82 Pk:1 [3|3|3] — 33853
Can't Slow Down (83) 1(3) [59|78|160] — 17509
Lionel Richie (82) 3(7) [21|39|140] — 9861
Dancing On The Ceiling (86) 1(2) [20|38|58] — 6483

Don RICKLES ► 1415 Pk:54 [0|0|2] — 947
Hello Dummy! (68) 54(2) [0|0|29] — 906
Don Rickles Speaks! (69) 180(1) [0|0|4] — 40.7

Stan RIDGWAY ► 2775 Pk:131 [0|0|1] — 101
The Big Heat (86) 131(2) [0|0|9] — 101

Joshua RIFKIN ► 1446 Pk:75 [0|0|3] — 895
Piano Rags By Scott Joplin, Volumes I & II (74) 75(1) [0|0|15] — 455
The Baroque Beatles Book (65) 83(1) [0|0|17] — 336
Piano Rags By Scott Joplin, Volume III (74) 126(2) [0|0|5] — 105

RIGHTEOUS BROTHERS ► 198 Pk:4 [3|10|15] — 17573
You've Lost That Lovin' Feelin' (65) 4(4) [10|19|67] — 3910
Soul & Inspiration (66) 7(2) [5|19|32] — 2668
Just Once In My Life... (65) 9(3) [3|18|41] — 2570
Back To Back (65) 16(1) [0|11|26] — 1425
Right Now! (65) 11(2) [0|9|21] — 1264
Some Blue-Eyed Soul (65) 14(2) [0|10|20] — 1260
Greatest Hits (67) 21(1) [0|5|50] — 1203
Give It To The People (74) 27(2) [0|8|18] — 1183
Go Ahead And Cry (66) 32(1) [0|6|20] — 974
This Is New! (65) 39(1) [0|1|20] — 645
The Best Of The Righteous Brothers (66) 130(2) [0|0|11] — 163
Sayin' Somethin' (67) 155(2) [0|0|15] — 154
Greatest Hits, Vol. 2 (69) 126(2) [0|0|5] — 127
One For The Road (68) 187(1) [0|0|2] — 19.2
Souled Out (67) 198(2) [0|0|2] — 9.7

Cheryl Pepsii RILEY ► 2484 Pk:128 [0|0|1] — 164
Me, Myself And I (88) 128(2) [0|0|11] — 164

Jeannie C. RILEY ► 889 Pk:12 [0|1|3] — 2440
Harper Valley P.T.A. (68) 12(2) [0|12|27] — 2265
Things Go Better With Love (69) 142(1) [0|0|7] — 132
Yearbooks And Yesterdays (69) 187(2) [0|0|5] — 43.1

The RINGS ► 3029 Pk:164 [0|0|1] — 62
The Rings (81) 164(2) [0|0|6] — 61.8

Miguel RIOS ► 2998 Pk:140 [0|0|1] — 66
A Song Of Joy (70) 140(1) [0|0|4] — 66.1

Waldo DE LOS RIOS ► 1615 Pk:53 [0|0|1] — 659
Sinfonias (71) 53(2) [0|0|16] — 659

RIOT ► 2012 Pk:99 [0|0|3] — 345
Fire Down Under (81) 99(1) [0|0|11] — 198
Thundersteel (88) 150(2) [0|0|10] — 106
Born In America (84) 175(1) [0|0|6] — 41.4

RIP CHORDS ► 1942 Pk:56 [0|0|1] — 380
Hey Little Cobra And Other Hot Rod Hits (64) 56(2) [0|0|17] — 380

Minnie RIPERTON ► 402 Pk:4 [1|4|6] — 8198
Perfect Angel (74) 4(1) [6|18|47] — 4299
Adventures In Paradise (75) 18(1) [0|8|23] — 1579
Minnie (79) 29(1) [0|4|27] — 1155
Love Lives Forever (80) 35(2) [0|4|15] — 790
Stay In Love (77) 71(2) [0|0|10] — 323
Come To My Garden (74) 160(1) [0|0|4] — 51.7

The RIPPINGTONS ► 1747 Pk:85 [0|0|2] — 522
Kilimanjaro (88)-The Rippingtons Featuring Russ Freeman 110(2) [0|0|15] — 283
Tourist In Paradise (89)-The Rippingtons Featuring Russ Freeman 85(2) [0|0|12] — 239

RITCHIE FAMILY ► 936 Pk:30 [0|1|5] — 2196
Arabian Nights (76) 30(1) [0|7|25] — 1244
Brazil (75) 53(1) [0|0|12] — 500
Life Is Music (77) 100(1) [0|0|10] — 226
African Queens (77) 164(2) [0|0|12] — 137
American Generation (78) 148(1) [0|0|6] — 90.3

Lee RITENOUR ► 954 Pk:26 [0|1|9] — 2128
Rit (81) 26(1) [0|7|23] — 1396
Rit/2 (82) 99(3) [0|0|14] — 223
The Captain's Journey (78) 121(2) [0|0|7] — 136
Feel The Night (79) 136(1) [0|0|6] — 97.1
Banded Together (84) 145(2) [0|0|8] — 89.7
Festival (89) 156(2) [0|0|8] — 77.9
Rio (82) 163(3) [0|0|6] — 60.5
Captain Fingers (77) 178(1) [0|0|5] — 43.2
Harlequin (85)-Dave Grusin & Lee Ritenour [A] 192(1) [0|0|2] — 4.7

► Highest Peak [Top10s|Top40s|Total] Title (Yr) Peak(Wk) [T10 Wk|T40Wk|TotalWk]	Score
Joan RIVERS ► 1457 Pk:22 [0|1|1]	**880**
What Becomes A Semi-Legend Most? (83) 22(2) [0|6|21]	880
Johnny RIVERS ► 216 Pk:5 [1|8|16]	**16072**
Realization (68) 5(5) [9|16|41]	4252
Johnny Rivers At The Whisky A Go Go (64) 12(1) [0|20|45]	2271
A Touch Of Gold (69) 26(1) [0|10|25]	1863
Johnny Rivers' Golden Hits (66) 29(2) [0|9|36]	1388
Rewind (67) 14(2) [0|8|21]	1352
Changes (66) 33(2) [0|5|46]	1137
Meanwhile Back At The Whisky A Go Go (65) 21(2) [0|6|19]	885
Here We A Go Go Again! (64) 38(1) [0|1|23]	609
...And I Know You Wanna Dance (66) 52(1) [0|0|21]	583
Johnny Rivers In Action! (65) 42(2) [0|0|14]	499
L.A. Reggae (72) 78(1) [0|0|20]	409
Johnny Rivers Rocks The Folk (65) 91(1) [0|0|18]	345
Slim Slo Slider (70) 100(1) [0|0|9]	202
Outside Help (78) 142(2) [0|0|8]	110
New Lovers And Old Friends (75) 147(1) [0|0|6]	100
Home Grown (71) 148(1) [0|0|4]	67.8
The RIVIERAS ► 2929 Pk:115 [0|0|1]	**75**
Let's Have A Party (64)-The Rivieras 115(2) [0|0|5]	75.4
ROACHFORD ► 2492 Pk:109 [0|0|1]	**162**
Roachford (89) 109(2) [0|0|12]	162
The ROAD ► 3499 Pk:199 [0|0|1]	**11**
The Road (70) 199(2) [0|0|2]	11.3
Rob BASE ► 695 Pk:31 [0|1|2]	**3771**
It Takes Two (88)-Rob Base & D.J. E-Z Rock 31(1) [0|8|81]	2923
The Incredible Base (89) 50(2) [0|0|26]	848
Marty ROBBINS ► 1623 Pk:117 [0|0|6]	**650**
My Woman, My Woman, My Wife (70) 117(1) [0|0|16]	271
Marty Robbins Greatest Hits, Vol. III (71) 143(2) [0|0|10]	142
I Walk Alone (68) 160(2) [0|0|7]	85.9
Biggest Hits (83) 170(1) [0|0|9]	70.5
Today (71) 175(1) [0|0|6]	52.1
It's A Sin (69) 194(1) [0|0|4]	29.0
Rockie ROBBINS ► 1774 Pk:71 [0|0|2]	**501**
You And Me (80) 71(2) [0|0|16]	419
I Believe In Love (81) 147(2) [0|0|6]	82.1
The ROBBS ► 3540 Pk:200 [0|0|1]	**5**
The Robbs (68) 200(1) [0|0|1]	4.5
Robbie ROBERTSON ► 1279 Pk:38 [0|1|1]	**1181**
Robbie Robertson (87) 38(2) [0|4|34]	1181
Freddy ROBINSON ► 2721 Pk:133 [0|0|1]	**111**
The Coming Atlantis (70) 133(2) [0|0|7]	111
Smokey ROBINSON ► 229 Pk:10 [1|6|16]	**15341**
Being With You (81) 10(2) [2|17|28]	3208
One Heartbeat (87) 26(2) [0|17|58]	2397
Where There's Smoke (79) 17(2) [0|11|47]	2370
Warm Thoughts (80) 14(2) [0|12|21]	1895
A Quiet Storm (75) 36(3) [0|3|42]	1552
Yes It's You Lady (82) 33(3) [0|4|17]	722
Deep In My Soul (77) 47(1) [0|0|14]	555
Smokey's Family Robinson (76) 57(1) [0|0|15]	531
Smokey (73) 70(1) [0|0|19]	499
Touch The Sky (83) 50(3) [0|0|17]	423
Love Breeze (78) 75(1) [0|0|19]	415
Pure Smokey (74) 99(1) [0|0|17]	311
Smoke Signals (86) 104(2) [0|0|13]	188
Essar (84) 141(2) [0|0|11]	116
Blame It On Love And All The Great Hits (83) 124(1) [0|0|7]	97.0
Smokin' (79) 165(1) [0|0|6]	62.6
Tom ROBINSON Band ► 2329 Pk:144 [0|0|2]	**206**
Power In The Darkness (78) 144(2) [0|0|8]	132
TRB Two (79) 163(1) [0|0|7]	73.9
Vicki Sue ROBINSON ► 957 Pk:45 [0|0|3]	**2107**
Never Gonna Let You Go (76) 49(2) [0|0|39]	1365
Vicki Sue Robinson (76) 45(1) [0|0|16]	568
Half And Half (78) 110(1) [0|0|9]	174
Wanda ROBINSON ► 2783 Pk:186 [0|0|1]	**100**
Black Ivory (71) 186(1) [0|0|13]	100
The ROCHES ► 1795 Pk:58 [0|0|3]	**488**
The Roches (79) 58(2) [0|0|11]	357
Nurds (80) 130(1) [0|0|7]	111
Keep On Doing (82) 183(1) [0|0|3]	20.1
ROCK And HYDE ► 2177 Pk:94 [0|0|1]	**267**
Under The Volcano (87) 94(1) [0|0|15]	267
The ROCKETS ► 1196 Pk:53 [0|0|3]	**1348**
Rockets (79)-Rockets 56(2) [0|0|26]	800
No Ballads (80)-Rockets 53(2) [0|0|15]	489
Back Talk (81)-Rockets 165(1) [0|0|5]	58.6
ROCKIN' SIDNEY ► 3233 Pk:166 [0|0|1]	**36**
My Toot-Toot (85) 166(3) [0|0|4]	35.7
ROCKPILE ► 1188 Pk:27 [0|1|1]	**1371**
Seconds Of Pleasure (80) 27(3) [0|10|19]	1371
ROCKWELL ► 1046 Pk:15 [0|1|2]	**1753**
Somebody's Watching Me (84) 15(2) [0|12|30]	1634
Captured (85) 120(2) [0|0|9]	120
Jimmie RODGERS ► 2613 Pk:145 [0|0|3]	**132**
It's Over (66) 145(1) [0|0|4]	56.2
Windmills Of Your Mind (69) 183(2) [0|0|4]	39.0
Child Of Clay (68) 162(1) [0|0|4]	36.3
Paul RODGERS ► 2665 Pk:135 [0|0|1]	**120**
Cut Loose (83) 135(1) [0|0|10]	120
RODNEY O & Joe COOLEY ► 3455 Pk:187 [0|0|1]	**14**
Me And Joe (89) 187(2) [0|0|2]	13.8
Johnny RODRIGUEZ ► 2430 Pk:156 [0|0|2]	**179**
Introducing Johnny Rodriguez (73) 156(1) [0|0|14]	144
All I Ever Meant To Do Was Sing (73) 174(1) [0|0|4]	35.5
Tommy ROE ► 674 Pk:21 [0|2|5]	**4009**
12 In A Roe/A Collection Of Tommy Roe's Greatest Hits (69) 21(1) [0|13|29]	2145
Dizzy (69) 25(2) [0|8|18]	1461
Sweet Pea (66) 94(1) [0|0|13]	258
We Can Make Music (70) 134(1) [0|0|6]	108
It's Now Winters Day (67) 159(2) [0|0|3]	36.7
ROGER ► 858 Pk:26 [0|2|3]	**2610**
The Many Facets Of Roger (81) 26(1) [0|6|25]	1271
Unlimited! (87) 35(1) [0|5|24]	1000
The Saga Continues... (84) 64(2) [0|0|14]	339
D.J. ROGERS ► 3075 Pk:175 [0|0|1]	**56**
On The Road Again (76) 175(2) [0|0|5]	56.0
Eric ROGERS & His Orchestra ► 3034 Pk:114 [0|0|1]	**61**
Vaudeville! (66) 114(1) [0|0|3]	61.2
Kenny ROGERS ► 44 Pk:1 [4|15|23]	**45527**
Kenny Rogers' Greatest Hits (80) 1(2) [20|36|181]	12108
The Gambler (78) 12(3) [0|21|112]	6142
Kenny (79) 5(2) [10|26|53]	5370
Share Your Love (81) 6(2) [5|13|50]	3955
Eyes That See In The Dark (83) 6(4) [8|24|38]	3792
Ten Years Of Gold (78) 33(2) [0|4|104]	2566
Gideon (80) 12(2) [0|11|34]	2123
Twenty Greatest Hits (83) 22(2) [0|11|30]	1524
We've Got Tonight (83) 18(1) [0|12|27]	1326
What About Me? (84) 31(3) [0|8|31]	1199
Kenny Rogers (77) 30(2) [0|4|25]	1088
Love Will Turn You Around (82) 34(2) [0|7|24]	905
The Heart Of The Matter (85) 51(3) [0|0|28]	827
Daytime Friends (77) 39(1) [0|2|21]	597
Christmas (81) 34(2) [0|4|13]	589
Love Or Something Like It (78) 53(2) [0|0|12]	544
Duets (84) 85(2) [0|0|11]	220
Once Upon A Christmas (84)-Kenny Rogers & Dolly Parton [A] 31(1) [0|4|8]	189
They Don't Make Them Like They Used To (86) 137(1) [0|0|15]	169
Something Inside So Strong (89) 141(2) [0|0|8]	96.9
Christmas In America (89) 119(2) [0|0|6]	89.7
Love Is What We Make It (85) 145(1) [0|0|7]	74.9
I Prefer The Moonlight (87) 163(2) [0|0|4]	31.7
Kenny ROGERS & Dottie WEST ► 1752 Pk:82 [0|0|2]	**520**
Classics (79) 82(1) [0|0|23]	498
Everytime Two Fools Collide (80) 186(2) [0|0|3]	21.5
Kenny ROGERS & The FIRST EDITION ► 690 Pk:26 [0|1|8]	**3818**
Something's Burning (70) 26(3) [0|6|24]	1344
Ruby, Don't Take Your Love To Town (69) 48(1) [0|0|18]	735
Greatest Hits (71) 57(1) [0|0|16]	697
Tell It All Brother (70) 61(1) [0|0|16]	560
The First Edition (68)-The First Edition 118(1) [0|0|15]	207
The Ballad Of Calico (72) 118(2) [0|0|14]	178
The First Edition 69 (69)-The First Edition 164(2) [0|0|4]	55.6
Transition (71) 155(1) [0|0|3]	43.0
ROLLING STONES ► 2 Pk:1 [31|33|35]	**145643**
Some Girls (78) 1(2) [23|32|82]	10361
Tattoo You (81) 1(9) [22|30|58]	9921
Hot Rocks 1964-1971 (72) 4(2) [8|30|243]	9918
Sticky Fingers (71) 1(4) [15|26|62]	8853
Emotional Rescue (80) 1(7) [14|20|51]	7106
Out Of Our Heads (65) 1(3) [16|35|65]	5973
Big Hits (High Tide And Green Grass) (66) 3(3) [9|35|99]	5844
Exile On Main St. (72) 1(4) [11|17|43]	5537
Goats Head Soup (73) 1(4) [11|19|37]	5266
Let It Bleed (69) 3(2) [10|19|44]	5094
Through The Past, Darkly (Big Hits Vol. 2) (69) 2(2) [9|16|32]	4827
Steel Wheels (89) 3(4) [13|27|36]	4806
Black And Blue (76) 1(4) [9|14|24]	4733
Aftermath (66) 2(2) [11|26|50]	4649
The Rolling Stones, Now! (65) 5(2) [9|29|53]	4325
Between The Buttons (67) 2(4) [10|19|47]	4292
Flowers (67) 3(6) [10|18|35]	4192
It's Only Rock 'N Roll (74) 1(1) [7|11|20]	3928
Their Satanic Majesties Request (67) 2(6) [10|13|30]	3838
December's Children (And Everybody's) (65) 4(3) [8|22|33]	3215
Beggars Banquet (68) 5(3) [4|13|32]	3171
12 x 5 (64) 3(4) [8|20|38]	2795
'Get Yer Ya-Ya's Out!' (70) 6(2) [7|10|23]	2715
Got Live If You Want It! (66) 6(2) [5|11|48]	2455
Dirty Work (86) 4(2) [6|15|25]	2422
More Hot Rocks (Big Hits & Fazed Cookies) (72) 9(3) [5|12|29]	2367
Made In The Shade (75) 6(2) [4|9|17]	2123

<table>
<tr><th>▶ Highest Peak [Top10s | Top40s | Total]
Title (Yr) Peak(Wk) [T10 Wk | T40Wk | TotalWk]</th><th>Score</th></tr>
<tr><td>ROLLING STONES ▶ Continued</td><td></td></tr>
<tr><td>Undercover (83) 4(2) [4|12|23]</td><td>2032</td></tr>
<tr><td>Still Life (American Concert 1981) (82) 5(4) [5|10|23]</td><td>1847</td></tr>
<tr><td>Love You Live (77) 5(3) [4|7|17]</td><td>1840</td></tr>
<tr><td>England's Newest Hit Makers/The Rolling Stones (64) 11(1) [0|12|35]</td><td>1808</td></tr>
<tr><td>Metamorphosis (75) 8(2) [3|8|13]</td><td>1693</td></tr>
<tr><td>Sucking In The Seventies (81) 15(2) [0|6|12]</td><td>1065</td></tr>
<tr><td>Singles Collection - The London Years (89) 91(1) [0|0|22]</td><td>436</td></tr>
<tr><td>Rewind (1971-1984) (84) 86(1) [0|0|11]</td><td>196</td></tr>
<tr><td>ROMAN HOLLIDAY ▶ 2325 Pk:116 [0|0|2]</td><td>209</td></tr>
<tr><td>Roman Holliday (83) 142(1) [0|0|11]</td><td>116</td></tr>
<tr><td>Cookin' On The Roof (83) 116(1) [0|0|6]</td><td>93.1</td></tr>
<tr><td>The ROMANTICS ▶ 804 Pk:14 [0|1|5]</td><td>2930</td></tr>
<tr><td>In Heat (83) 14(1) [0|15|36]</td><td>2167</td></tr>
<tr><td>The Romantics (80) 61(1) [0|0|15]</td><td>468</td></tr>
<tr><td>Rhythm Romance (85) 72(2) [0|0|11]</td><td>229</td></tr>
<tr><td>National Breakout (80) 176(2) [0|0|7]</td><td>48.1</td></tr>
<tr><td>Strictly Personal (81) 182(1) [0|0|2]</td><td>16.8</td></tr>
<tr><td>ROMEO'S DAUGHTER ▶ 3491 Pk:191 [0|0|1]</td><td>12</td></tr>
<tr><td>Romeo's Daughter (88) 191(2) [0|0|2]</td><td>11.9</td></tr>
<tr><td>ROMEO VOID ▶ 1654 Pk:68 [0|0|3]</td><td>617</td></tr>
<tr><td>Instincts (84) 68(4) [0|0|19]</td><td>398</td></tr>
<tr><td>Benefactor (82) 119(3) [0|0|13]</td><td>148</td></tr>
<tr><td>Never Say Never (82) 147(1) [0|0|6]</td><td>70.4</td></tr>
<tr><td>The RONETTES ▶ 2584 Pk:96 [0|0|1]</td><td>139</td></tr>
<tr><td>...Presenting The Fabulous Ronettes Featuring Veronica (64) 96(1) [0|0|8]</td><td>139</td></tr>
<tr><td>RONNY And The DAYTONAS ▶ 2872 Pk:122 [0|0|1]</td><td>84</td></tr>
<tr><td>G.T.O. (64) 122(1) [0|0|6]</td><td>84.4</td></tr>
<tr><td>Mick RONSON ▶ 1964 Pk:103 [0|0|3]</td><td>369</td></tr>
<tr><td>Play Don't Worry (75) 103(2) [0|0|9]</td><td>208</td></tr>
<tr><td>Y U I Orta (89)-Ian Hunter/Mick Ronson [A] 157(3) [0|0|20]</td><td>98.7</td></tr>
<tr><td>Slaughter On 10th Avenue (74) 156(1) [0|0|5]</td><td>63.0</td></tr>
<tr><td>Linda RONSTADT ▶ 25 Pk:1 [10|13|23]</td><td>57697</td></tr>
<tr><td>Simple Dreams (77) 1(5) [16|23|47]</td><td>8545</td></tr>
<tr><td>Heart Like A Wheel (74) 1(1) [11|19|51]</td><td>5903</td></tr>
<tr><td>What's New (83)-Linda Ronstadt & The Nelson Riddle Orchestra 3(5) [15|25|81]</td><td>5736</td></tr>
<tr><td>Greatest Hits (76) 6(1) [7|15|80]</td><td>5314</td></tr>
<tr><td>Mad Love (80) 3(4) [12|17|36]</td><td>4864</td></tr>
<tr><td>Living In The U.S.A. (78) 1(1) [9|17|32]</td><td>4804</td></tr>
<tr><td>Cry Like A Rainstorm, Howl Like The Wind (89)-Linda Ronstadt (Featuring Aaron Neville) 7(1) [7|37|58]</td><td>4767</td></tr>
<tr><td>Hasten Down The Wind (76) 3(3) [8|15|36]</td><td>4346</td></tr>
<tr><td>Prisoner In Disguise (75) 4(3) [8|10|28]</td><td>3251</td></tr>
<tr><td>Don't Cry Now (73) 45(1) [0|0|56]</td><td>1894</td></tr>
<tr><td>Lush Life (84) 13(2) [0|11|26]</td><td>1541</td></tr>
<tr><td>Greatest Hits, Volume 2 (80) 26(3) [0|10|21]</td><td>1391</td></tr>
<tr><td>Get Closer (82) 31(4) [0|6|28]</td><td>1075</td></tr>
<tr><td>Canciones de Mi Padre (87) 42(1) [0|0|35]</td><td>1069</td></tr>
<tr><td>Trio (87)-Dolly Parton, Linda Ronstadt, Emmylou Harris [A] 6(1) [3|14|48]</td><td>848</td></tr>
<tr><td>For Sentimental Reasons (86) 46(1) [0|0|27]</td><td>755</td></tr>
<tr><td>A Retrospective (77) 46(1) [0|0|9]</td><td>410</td></tr>
<tr><td>Different Drum (74) 92(1) [0|0|15]</td><td>311</td></tr>
<tr><td>Evergreen, Vol. 2 (67)-The Stone Poneys 100(1) [0|0|15]</td><td>266</td></tr>
<tr><td>Silk Purse (70) 103(1) [0|0|10]</td><td>250</td></tr>
<tr><td>'Round Midnight (86) 124(2) [0|0|17]</td><td>202</td></tr>
<tr><td>Linda Ronstadt (72) 163(1) [0|0|10]</td><td>111</td></tr>
<tr><td>The Stone Poneys Featuring Linda Ronstadt (75) 172(2) [0|0|4]</td><td>43.6</td></tr>
</table>

<table>
<tr><th>▶ Highest Peak [Top10s | Top40s | Total]
Title (Yr) Peak(Wk) [T10 Wk | T40Wk | TotalWk]</th><th>Score</th></tr>
<tr><td>Franklin D. ROOSEVELT ▶ 3187 Pk:109 [0|0|1]</td><td>43</td></tr>
<tr><td>Actual Speeches Of Franklin D. Roosevelt And John F. Kennedy (64)-Franklin D. Roosevelt And John F. Kennedy [A] 109(1) [0|0|5]</td><td>42.8</td></tr>
<tr><td>Biff ROSE ▶ 1748 Pk:75 [0|0|2]</td><td>521</td></tr>
<tr><td>The Thorn In Mrs. Rose's Side (69) 75(1) [0|0|14]</td><td>460</td></tr>
<tr><td>Children Of Light (69) 181(1) [0|0|7]</td><td>61.8</td></tr>
<tr><td>ROSE GARDEN ▶ 3408 Pk:176 [0|0|1]</td><td>19</td></tr>
<tr><td>The Rose Garden (68) 176(1) [0|0|2]</td><td>18.8</td></tr>
<tr><td>Jimmy ROSELLI ▶ 2187 Pk:96 [0|0|4]</td><td>264</td></tr>
<tr><td>Life & Love Italian Style (65) 96(1) [0|0|11]</td><td>193</td></tr>
<tr><td>Core Spezzato (69) 184(1) [0|0|3]</td><td>28.9</td></tr>
<tr><td>The Great Ones! (65) 145(1) [0|0|2]</td><td>26.0</td></tr>
<tr><td>There Must Be A Way (67) 191(1) [0|0|3]</td><td>16.2</td></tr>
<tr><td>ROSE ROYCE ▶ 433 Pk:9 [1|3|5]</td><td>7384</td></tr>
<tr><td>Rose Royce II/In Full Bloom (77) 9(2) [3|14|33]</td><td>2948</td></tr>
<tr><td>Car Wash (76) 14(2) [0|13|40]</td><td>2828</td></tr>
<tr><td>Rose Royce III/Strikes Again! (78) 28(3) [0|6|24]</td><td>1341</td></tr>
<tr><td>Rose Royce IV/Rainbow Connection (79) 74(1) [0|0|8]</td><td>195</td></tr>
<tr><td>Golden Touch (81) 160(2) [0|0|7]</td><td>71.0</td></tr>
<tr><td>ROSE TATTOO ▶ 3438 Pk:197 [0|0|1]</td><td>16</td></tr>
<tr><td>Rock 'N' Roll Outlaw (80) 197(1) [0|0|3]</td><td>16.1</td></tr>
<tr><td>Diana ROSS ▶ 48 Pk:1 [4|16|26]</td><td>44648</td></tr>
<tr><td>Diana (80) 2(2) [18|34|52]</td><td>7266</td></tr>
<tr><td>Lady Sings The Blues (Soundtrack) (72) 1(2) [13|24|54]</td><td>6201</td></tr>
<tr><td>Diana Ross (II) (76) 5(1) [7|18|32]</td><td>3743</td></tr>
<tr><td>Touch Me In The Morning (73) 5(2) [6|15|28]</td><td>2899</td></tr>
<tr><td>Why Do Fools Fall In Love (81) 15(6) [0|20|33]</td><td>2846</td></tr>
<tr><td>The Boss (79) 14(2) [0|17|37]</td><td>2825</td></tr>
<tr><td>Swept Away (84) 26(1) [0|18|45]</td><td>2303</td></tr>
<tr><td>Diana Ross (70) 19(2) [0|14|28]</td><td>2261</td></tr>
<tr><td>Diana Ross' Greatest Hits (76) 13(2) [0|14|23]</td><td>2188</td></tr>
<tr><td>Baby It's Me (77) 18(2) [0|13|19]</td><td>1845</td></tr>
<tr><td>Silk Electric (82) 27(2) [0|7|24]</td><td>1176</td></tr>
<tr><td>All The Great Hits (81) 37(2) [0|3|32]</td><td>1126</td></tr>
<tr><td>Everything Is Everything (70) 42(2) [0|0|16]</td><td>804</td></tr>
<tr><td>To Love Again (81) 32(2) [0|4|14]</td><td>791</td></tr>
<tr><td>Diana & Marvin (73)-Diana Ross & Marvin Gaye [A] 26(1) [0|5|47]</td><td>759</td></tr>
<tr><td>An Evening With Diana Ross (77) 29(1) [0|3|14]</td><td>739</td></tr>
<tr><td>Diana Ross Live At Caesars Palace (74) 64(2) [0|0|17]</td><td>640</td></tr>
<tr><td>Ross (II) (83) 32(1) [0|4|17]</td><td>630</td></tr>
<tr><td>Diana! (71) 46(2) [0|0|15]</td><td>624</td></tr>
<tr><td>Ross (78) 49(2) [0|0|17]</td><td>618</td></tr>
<tr><td>Surrender (71) 56(1) [0|0|14]</td><td>609</td></tr>
<tr><td>Last Time I Saw Him (73) 52(1) [0|0|17]</td><td>584</td></tr>
<tr><td>Eaten Alive (85) 45(2) [0|0|20]</td><td>498</td></tr>
<tr><td>Diana Ross Anthology (83) 63(1) [0|0|12]</td><td>298</td></tr>
<tr><td>Red Hot Rhythm & Blues (87) 73(2) [0|0|14]</td><td>278</td></tr>
<tr><td>Workin' Overtime (89) 116(2) [0|0|6]</td><td>96.0</td></tr>
<tr><td>ROSSINGTON COLLINS BAND ▶ 724 Pk:13 [0|2|3]</td><td>3494</td></tr>
<tr><td>Anytime, Anyplace, Anywhere (80) 13(3) [0|13|29]</td><td>2669</td></tr>
<tr><td>This Is The Way (81) 24(1) [0|5|16]</td><td>780</td></tr>
<tr><td>Love Your Man (88)-The Rossington Band 140(1) [0|0|4]</td><td>45.1</td></tr>
<tr><td>ROTARY CONNECTION ▶ 1478 Pk:37 [0|1|2]</td><td>849</td></tr>
<tr><td>Rotary Connection (68) 37(2) [0|4|31]</td><td>798</td></tr>
<tr><td>Aladdin (68) 176(2) [0|0|5]</td><td>51.7</td></tr>
</table>

<table>
<tr><th>▶ Highest Peak [Top10s | Top40s | Total]
Title (Yr) Peak(Wk) [T10 Wk | T40Wk | TotalWk]</th><th>Score</th></tr>
<tr><td>David Lee ROTH ▶ 366 Pk:4 [2|3|3]</td><td>9025</td></tr>
<tr><td>Eat 'Em And Smile (86) 4(2) [8|21|36]</td><td>3485</td></tr>
<tr><td>Skyscraper (88) 6(6) [8|16|27]</td><td>3013</td></tr>
<tr><td>Crazy From The Heat (85) 15(4) [0|20|33]</td><td>2528</td></tr>
<tr><td>ROUGH DIAMOND ▶ 2483 Pk:103 [0|0|1]</td><td>164</td></tr>
<tr><td>Rough Diamond (77) 103(2) [0|0|8]</td><td>164</td></tr>
<tr><td>Demis ROUSSOS ▶ 3149 Pk:184 [0|0|1]</td><td>46</td></tr>
<tr><td>Demis Roussos (78) 184(1) [0|0|6]</td><td>46.3</td></tr>
<tr><td>John ROWLES ▶ 3532 Pk:197 [0|0|1]</td><td>6</td></tr>
<tr><td>Cheryl Moana Marie (71) 197(1) [0|0|1]</td><td>6.5</td></tr>
<tr><td>ROXETTE ▶ 710 Pk:23 [0|1|1]</td><td>3575</td></tr>
<tr><td>Look Sharp! (89) 23(2) [0|21|71]</td><td>3575</td></tr>
<tr><td>ROXY MUSIC ▶ 563 Pk:23 [0|3|11]</td><td>5188</td></tr>
<tr><td>Manifesto (79) 23(1) [0|8|16]</td><td>1194</td></tr>
<tr><td>Flesh + Blood (80) 35(2) [0|3|19]</td><td>901</td></tr>
<tr><td>Siren (75) 50(1) [0|0|20]</td><td>863</td></tr>
<tr><td>Country Life (75) 37(1) [0|3|15]</td><td>719</td></tr>
<tr><td>Avalon (82) 53(3) [0|0|27]</td><td>613</td></tr>
<tr><td>Musique/The High Road (83) 67(1) [0|0|22]</td><td>443</td></tr>
<tr><td>Viva! Roxy Music (76) 81(1) [0|0|7]</td><td>204</td></tr>
<tr><td>Street Life-20 Great Hits (89)-Bryan Ferry/Roxy Music 100(1) [0|0|11]</td><td>169</td></tr>
<tr><td>The Atlantic Years (84) 183(2) [0|0|6]</td><td>37.6</td></tr>
<tr><td>Stranded (74) 186(1) [0|0|4]</td><td>30.1</td></tr>
<tr><td>For Your Pleasure (73) 193(2) [0|0|2]</td><td>13.3</td></tr>
<tr><td>Billy Joe ROYAL ▶ 2113 Pk:96 [0|0|2]</td><td>295</td></tr>
<tr><td>Cherry Hill Park (70) 100(1) [0|0|9]</td><td>173</td></tr>
<tr><td>Down In The Boondocks (65) 96(1) [0|0|7]</td><td>122</td></tr>
<tr><td>ROYAL GUARDSMEN ▶ 1343 Pk:44 [0|0|3]</td><td>1052</td></tr>
<tr><td>Snoopy vs. The Red Baron (67) 44(1) [0|0|22]</td><td>582</td></tr>
<tr><td>Snoopy And His Friends (67) 46(3) [0|0|11]</td><td>453</td></tr>
<tr><td>Snoopy For President (68) 189(1) [0|0|2]</td><td>16.3</td></tr>
<tr><td>ROYAL PHILHARMONIC Orchestra ▶ 461 Pk:4 [1|2|4]</td><td>6873</td></tr>
<tr><td>Hooked On Classics (81)-Royal Philharmonic Orchestra Conducted By Louis Clark 4(6) [9|22|68]</td><td>5342</td></tr>
<tr><td>Hooked On Classics II (Can't Stop The Classics) (82) 33(4) [0|7|41]</td><td>1225</td></tr>
<tr><td>Hooked On Classics III (Journey Through The Classics) (83) 89(1) [0|0|14]</td><td>252</td></tr>
<tr><td>Concerto For Group And Orchestra (70)-Deep Purple/The Royal Philharmonic Orchestra [A] 149(2) [0|0|8]</td><td>54.8</td></tr>
<tr><td>ROYAL SCOTS DRAGOON GUARDS ▶ 1502 Pk:34 [0|1|1]</td><td>804</td></tr>
<tr><td>Amazing Grace (72) 34(1) [0|5|15]</td><td>804</td></tr>
<tr><td>The RUBBERBANDITS ▶ 2088 Pk:116 [0|0|2]</td><td>308</td></tr>
<tr><td>Hendrix Songbook (69)-The Rubber Band 116(1) [0|0|8]</td><td>183</td></tr>
<tr><td>Cream Songbook (69)-The Rubber Band 135(2) [0|0|6]</td><td>125</td></tr>
<tr><td>RUBICON ▶ 2809 Pk:147 [0|0|1]</td><td>95</td></tr>
<tr><td>Rubicon (78) 147(2) [0|0|7]</td><td>95.3</td></tr>
<tr><td>David RUFFIN ▶ 721 Pk:31 [0|2|6]</td><td>3506</td></tr>
<tr><td>Who I Am (75) 31(1) [0|6|27]</td><td>1641</td></tr>
<tr><td>My Whole World Ended (69) 31(1) [0|7|17]</td><td>1192</td></tr>
<tr><td>Everything's Coming Up Love (76) 51(1) [0|0|12]</td><td>504</td></tr>
<tr><td>David Ruffin (73) 160(1) [0|0|7]</td><td>78.5</td></tr>
<tr><td>Feelin' Good (69) 148(1) [0|0|7]</td><td>76.7</td></tr>
<tr><td>I Am My Brother's Keeper (70)-The Ruffin Brothers (Jimmy & David) [A] 178(1) [0|0|3]</td><td>13.6</td></tr>
<tr><td>Jimmy RUFFIN ▶ 2241 Pk:133 [0|0|4]</td><td>238</td></tr>
<tr><td>Top Ten (67) 133(1) [0|0|11]</td><td>140</td></tr>
<tr><td>Sunrise (80) 152(2) [0|0|6]</td><td>70.8</td></tr>
<tr><td>Ruff'N Ready (69) 196(1) [0|0|2]</td><td>14.0</td></tr>
<tr><td>I Am My Brother's Keeper (70)-The Ruffin Brothers (Jimmy & David) [A] 178(1) [0|0|3]</td><td>13.6</td></tr>
</table>

<table>
<tr><th>► Highest Peak [Top10s | Top40s | Total]
Title (Yr) Peak(Wk) [T10 Wk | T40Wk | TotalWk]</th><th>Score</th></tr>
<tr><td>Mason RUFFNER ► 2052 Pk:80 [0 | 0 | 1]</td><td>327</td></tr>
<tr><td>Gypsy Blood (87) 80(2) [0 | 0 | 16]</td><td>327</td></tr>
<tr><td>RUFUS ► 189 Pk:4 [3 | 6 | 11]</td><td>18333</td></tr>
<tr><td>Rufus Featuring Chaka Khan (75)-Rufus And Chaka Khan 7(1) [5 | 24 | 32]</td><td>4562</td></tr>
<tr><td>Rufusized (75)-Rufus And Chaka Khan 7(1) [4 | 12 | 24]</td><td>2759</td></tr>
<tr><td>Rags To Rufus (74) 4(1) [4 | 11 | 30]</td><td>2614</td></tr>
<tr><td>Masterjam (79)-Rufus And Chaka Khan 14(3) [0 | 16 | 26]</td><td>2405</td></tr>
<tr><td>Street Player (78)-Rufus And Chaka Khan 14(2) [0 | 14 | 26]</td><td>2079</td></tr>
<tr><td>Ask Rufus (77)-Rufus And Chaka Khan 12(2) [0 | 10 | 25]</td><td>2013</td></tr>
<tr><td>Live-Stompin' At The Savoy (83)-Rufus And Chaka Khan 50(1) [0 | 0 | 33]</td><td>1003</td></tr>
<tr><td>Party 'Til You're Broke (81) 73(1) [0 | 0 | 11]</td><td>304</td></tr>
<tr><td>Camouflage (81)-Rufus And Chaka Khan 98(1) [0 | 0 | 14]</td><td>301</td></tr>
<tr><td>Numbers (79) 81(1) [0 | 0 | 9]</td><td>242</td></tr>
<tr><td>Rufus (73) 175(2) [0 | 0 | 6]</td><td>50.9</td></tr>
<tr><td>The RUMOUR ► 2273 Pk:124 [0 | 0 | 2]</td><td>225</td></tr>
<tr><td>Max (77) 124(1) [0 | 0 | 10]</td><td>184</td></tr>
<tr><td>Frogs Sprouts Clogs And Krauts (79) 160(2) [0 | 0 | 3]</td><td>40.3</td></tr>
<tr><td>The RUNAWAYS ► 3105 Pk:172 [0 | 0 | 2]</td><td>52</td></tr>
<tr><td>Queens Of Noise (77) 172(1) [0 | 0 | 4]</td><td>38.7</td></tr>
<tr><td>The Runaways (76) 194(1) [0 | 0 | 2]</td><td>12.9</td></tr>
<tr><td>Todd RUNDGREN ► 483 Pk:29 [0 | 2 | 12]</td><td>6505</td></tr>
<tr><td>Something/Anything? (72) 29(2) [0 | 8 | 48]</td><td>2116</td></tr>
<tr><td>Hermit Of Mink Hollow (78) 36(1) [0 | 2 | 26]</td><td>1256</td></tr>
<tr><td>Todd (74) 54(1) [0 | 0 | 17]</td><td>593</td></tr>
<tr><td>Healing (81) 48(2) [0 | 0 | 13]</td><td>503</td></tr>
<tr><td>Faithful (76) 54(1) [0 | 0 | 15]</td><td>463</td></tr>
<tr><td>Back To The Bars (78) 75(2) [0 | 0 | 15]</td><td>409</td></tr>
<tr><td>A Wizard/A True Star (73) 86(1) [0 | 0 | 15]</td><td>351</td></tr>
<tr><td>The Ever Popular Tortured Artist Effect (83) 66(3) [0 | 0 | 13]</td><td>286</td></tr>
<tr><td>Nearly Human (89) 102(2) [0 | 0 | 11]</td><td>200</td></tr>
<tr><td>Initiation (75) 86(2) [0 | 0 | 7]</td><td>197</td></tr>
<tr><td>A Cappella (85) 128(2) [0 | 0 | 8]</td><td>84.4</td></tr>
<tr><td>Runt (71) 185(1) [0 | 0 | 6]</td><td>47.7</td></tr>
<tr><td>RUN-D.M.C. ► 282 Pk:3 [2 | 2 | 4]</td><td>12371</td></tr>
<tr><td>Raising Hell (86) 3(3) [14 | 49 | 71]</td><td>7388</td></tr>
<tr><td>Tougher Than Leather (88) 9(1) [2 | 14 | 28]</td><td>2081</td></tr>
<tr><td>King Of Rock (85) 52(3) [0 | 0 | 56]</td><td>1556</td></tr>
<tr><td>Run D.M.C. (84) 53(2) [0 | 0 | 65]</td><td>1346</td></tr>
<tr><td>RUNNER ► 3173 Pk:167 [0 | 0 | 1]</td><td>44</td></tr>
<tr><td>Runner (79) 167(2) [0 | 0 | 4]</td><td>43.8</td></tr>
<tr><td>RUSH ► 125 Pk:3 [6 | 11 | 17]</td><td>25584</td></tr>
<tr><td>Moving Pictures (81) 3(3) [14 | 29 | 68]</td><td>6817</td></tr>
<tr><td>Permanent Waves (80) 4(3) [5 | 15 | 36]</td><td>3066</td></tr>
<tr><td>Power Windows (85) 10(2) [2 | 14 | 28]</td><td>2056</td></tr>
<tr><td>Exit...Stage Left (81) 10(3) [3 | 14 | 21]</td><td>2016</td></tr>
<tr><td>Signals (82) 10(1) [1 | 11 | 33]</td><td>1996</td></tr>
<tr><td>Grace Under Pressure (84) 10(4) [4 | 12 | 27]</td><td>1905</td></tr>
<tr><td>Hold Your Fire (87) 13(2) [0 | 14 | 30]</td><td>1873</td></tr>
<tr><td>Presto (89) 16(2) [0 | 11 | 27]</td><td>1481</td></tr>
<tr><td>A Farewell To Kings (77) 33(2) [0 | 5 | 17]</td><td>922</td></tr>
<tr><td>A Show Of Hands (89) 21(1) [0 | 5 | 15]</td><td>820</td></tr>
<tr><td>Hemispheres (78) 47(3) [0 | 0 | 21]</td><td>737</td></tr>
<tr><td>All The World's A Stage: Recorded Live (76) 40(2) [0 | 2 | 23]</td><td>698</td></tr>
<tr><td>2112 (76) 61(2) [0 | 0 | 34]</td><td>574</td></tr>
<tr><td>Rush (74) 105(1) [0 | 0 | 13]</td><td>234</td></tr>
<tr><td>Fly By Night (75) 113(1) [0 | 0 | 8]</td><td>182</td></tr>
<tr><td>Archives (78) 121(1) [0 | 0 | 6]</td><td>119</td></tr>
<tr><td>Caress Of Steel (75) 148(1) [0 | 0 | 6]</td><td>88.6</td></tr>
</table>

<table>
<tr><th>► Highest Peak [Top10s | Top40s | Total]
Title (Yr) Peak(Wk) [T10 Wk | T40Wk | TotalWk]</th><th>Score</th></tr>
<tr><td>Jennifer RUSH ► 2591 Pk:118 [0 | 0 | 1]</td><td>137</td></tr>
<tr><td>Heart Over Mind (87) 118(3) [0 | 0 | 10]</td><td>137</td></tr>
<tr><td>Merrilee RUSH ► 3329 Pk:196 [0 | 0 | 1]</td><td>26</td></tr>
<tr><td>Angel Of The Morning (68) 196(2) [0 | 0 | 4]</td><td>25.7</td></tr>
<tr><td>Tom RUSH ► 1118 Pk:68 [0 | 0 | 8]</td><td>1554</td></tr>
<tr><td>Tom Rush (70) 76(1) [0 | 0 | 16]</td><td>500</td></tr>
<tr><td>The Circle Game (68) 68(2) [0 | 0 | 14]</td><td>399</td></tr>
<tr><td>Wrong End Of The Rainbow (70) 110(1) [0 | 0 | 9]</td><td>186</td></tr>
<tr><td>Merrimack County (72) 128(1) [0 | 0 | 10]</td><td>163</td></tr>
<tr><td>Ladies Love Outlaws (74) 124(2) [0 | 0 | 9]</td><td>159</td></tr>
<tr><td>Take A Little Walk With Me (66) 122(1) [0 | 0 | 7]</td><td>114</td></tr>
<tr><td>The Best Of Tom Rush (76) 184(1) [0 | 0 | 3]</td><td>27.4</td></tr>
<tr><td>Classic Rush (71) 198(1) [0 | 0 | 1]</td><td>6.2</td></tr>
<tr><td>Patrice RUSHEN ► 684 Pk:14 [0 | 3 | 7]</td><td>3852</td></tr>
<tr><td>Straight From The Heart (82) 14(2) [0 | 8 | 28]</td><td>1343</td></tr>
<tr><td>Pizzazz (79) 39(2) [0 | 2 | 22]</td><td>807</td></tr>
<tr><td>Now (84) 40(3) [0 | 3 | 25]</td><td>714</td></tr>
<tr><td>Posh (80) 71(1) [0 | 0 | 18]</td><td>472</td></tr>
<tr><td>Watch Out! (87) 77(2) [0 | 0 | 19]</td><td>342</td></tr>
<tr><td>Patrice (79) 98(2) [0 | 0 | 6]</td><td>130</td></tr>
<tr><td>Shout It Out (77) 164(1) [0 | 0 | 4]</td><td>45.3</td></tr>
<tr><td>Bobby RUSSELL ► 3278 Pk:183 [0 | 0 | 1]</td><td>31</td></tr>
<tr><td>Saturday Morning Confusion (71) 183(2) [0 | 0 | 3]</td><td>30.6</td></tr>
<tr><td>Brenda RUSSELL ► 1090 Pk:49 [0 | 0 | 3]</td><td>1635</td></tr>
<tr><td>Get Here (88) 49(2) [0 | 0 | 28]</td><td>926</td></tr>
<tr><td>Brenda Russell (79) 65(1) [0 | 0 | 20]</td><td>542</td></tr>
<tr><td>Love Life (81) 107(2) [0 | 0 | 8]</td><td>166</td></tr>
<tr><td>Leon RUSSELL ► 232 Pk:2 [2 | 8 | 12]</td><td>15035</td></tr>
<tr><td>Carney (72) 2(4) [10 | 20 | 35]</td><td>4705</td></tr>
<tr><td>Leon Live (73) 9(1) [4 | 12 | 26]</td><td>2331</td></tr>
<tr><td>Leon Russell & The Shelter People (71) 17(1) [0 | 10 | 29]</td><td>2296</td></tr>
<tr><td>Will O' The Wisp (75) 30(2) [0 | 7 | 40]</td><td>1823</td></tr>
<tr><td>Stop All That Jazz (74) 34(2) [0 | 3 | 16]</td><td>901</td></tr>
<tr><td>Hank Wilson's Back, Vol. I (73) 28(1) [0 | 6 | 15]</td><td>855</td></tr>
<tr><td>Leon Russell (70) 60(2) [0 | 0 | 19]</td><td>591</td></tr>
<tr><td>Best Of Leon (76) 40(1) [0 | 1 | 16]</td><td>587</td></tr>
<tr><td>One For The Road (79)-Willie Nelson And Leon Russell [A] 25(1) [0 | 5 | 18]</td><td>450</td></tr>
<tr><td>Asylum Choir II (71)-Leon Russell & Marc Benno [A] 70(2) [0 | 0 | 20]</td><td>288</td></tr>
<tr><td>Americana (78) 115(2) [0 | 0 | 10]</td><td>192</td></tr>
<tr><td>The Live Album (81)-Leon Russell And The New Grass Revival 187(1) [0 | 0 | 2]</td><td>16.7</td></tr>
<tr><td>Leon & Mary RUSSELL ► 1249 Pk:34 [0 | 1 | 2]</td><td>1235</td></tr>
<tr><td>Wedding Album (76) 34(1) [0 | 4 | 28]</td><td>1162</td></tr>
<tr><td>Make Love To The Music (77) 142(1) [0 | 0 | 5]</td><td>73.2</td></tr>
<tr><td>The RUSTIX ► 3495 Pk:200 [0 | 0 | 1]</td><td>12</td></tr>
<tr><td>Bedlam (69) 200(2) [0 | 0 | 2]</td><td>11.8</td></tr>
<tr><td>Mike RUTHERFORD ► 2395 Pk:145 [0 | 0 | 2]</td><td>187</td></tr>
<tr><td>Smallcreep's Day (80) 163(2) [0 | 0 | 11]</td><td>117</td></tr>
<tr><td>Acting Very Strange (82) 145(2) [0 | 0 | 6]</td><td>70.1</td></tr>
<tr><td>The RUTLES ► 2074 Pk:63 [0 | 0 | 1]</td><td>313</td></tr>
<tr><td>The Rutles (78) 63(2) [0 | 0 | 9]</td><td>313</td></tr>
<tr><td>Bobby RYDELL ► 2142 Pk:67 [0 | 0 | 2]</td><td>283</td></tr>
<tr><td>The Top Hits Of 1963 (64) 67(1) [0 | 0 | 9]</td><td>214</td></tr>
<tr><td>Forget Him (64) 98(1) [0 | 0 | 4]</td><td>69.3</td></tr>
<tr><td>Mitch RYDER And The DETROIT WHEELS ► 742 Pk:23 [0 | 3 | 5]</td><td>3346</td></tr>
<tr><td>Breakout...!!! (66) 23(1) [0 | 7 | 34]</td><td>1345</td></tr>
<tr><td>All Mitch Ryder Hits! (67) 37(1) [0 | 4 | 26]</td><td>949</td></tr>
<tr><td>Sock It To Me! (67) 34(2) [0 | 3 | 16]</td><td>770</td></tr>
<tr><td>Take A Ride............ (66) 78(1) [0 | 0 | 7]</td><td>164</td></tr>
<tr><td>Never Kick A Sleeping Dog (83)-Mitch Ryder 120(1) [0 | 0 | 9]</td><td>119</td></tr>
</table>

<table>
<tr><th>► Highest Peak [Top10s | Top40s | Total]
Title (Yr) Peak(Wk) [T10 Wk | T40Wk | TotalWk]</th><th>Score</th></tr>
</table>

S

<table>
<tr><td>Sue SAAD And The NEXT ► 2467 Pk:131 [0 | 0 | 1]</td><td>169</td></tr>
<tr><td>Sue Saad And The Next (80) 131(1) [0 | 0 | 12]</td><td>169</td></tr>
<tr><td>SAD CAFÉ ► 1820 Pk:94 [0 | 0 | 3]</td><td>468</td></tr>
<tr><td>Misplaced Ideals (79) 94(1) [0 | 0 | 14]</td><td>343</td></tr>
<tr><td>Sad Café (81) 160(2) [0 | 0 | 6]</td><td>66.7</td></tr>
<tr><td>Facades (79) 146(1) [0 | 0 | 5]</td><td>58.3</td></tr>
<tr><td>SADE ► 255 Pk:1 [3 | 3 | 3]</td><td>14002</td></tr>
<tr><td>Promise (85) 1(2) [16 | 27 | 46]</td><td>5873</td></tr>
<tr><td>Diamond Life (85) 5(2) [10 | 27 | 81]</td><td>4672</td></tr>
<tr><td>Stronger Than Pride (88) 7(2) [6 | 21 | 45]</td><td>3456</td></tr>
<tr><td>SSgt Barry SADLER ► 616 Pk:1 [1 | 1 | 2]</td><td>4592</td></tr>
<tr><td>Ballads Of The Green Berets (66) 1(5) [10 | 20 | 32]</td><td>4543</td></tr>
<tr><td>The "A" Team (66) 130(1) [0 | 0 | 3]</td><td>49.1</td></tr>
<tr><td>SA-FIRE ► 1515 Pk:79 [0 | 0 | 1]</td><td>773</td></tr>
<tr><td>Sa-Fire (88)-SaFire 79(1) [0 | 0 | 46]</td><td>773</td></tr>
<tr><td>SAGA ► 976 Pk:29 [0 | 1 | 3]</td><td>2008</td></tr>
<tr><td>Worlds Apart (82) 29(5) [0 | 13 | 36]</td><td>1669</td></tr>
<tr><td>Behaviour (85) 87(2) [0 | 0 | 10]</td><td>181</td></tr>
<tr><td>Heads Or Tales (83) 92(1) [0 | 0 | 9]</td><td>158</td></tr>
<tr><td>Carole Bayer SAGER ► 1691 Pk:60 [0 | 0 | 1]</td><td>590</td></tr>
<tr><td>Sometimes Late At Night (81) 60(1) [0 | 0 | 22]</td><td>590</td></tr>
<tr><td>Mort SAHL ► 2843 Pk:149 [0 | 0 | 1]</td><td>88</td></tr>
<tr><td>Sing A Song Of Watergate... (73) 149(1) [0 | 0 | 7]</td><td>88.5</td></tr>
<tr><td>Doug SAHM And Band ► 2562 Pk:125 [0 | 0 | 1]</td><td>146</td></tr>
<tr><td>Doug Sahm And Band (73) 125(1) [0 | 0 | 10]</td><td>146</td></tr>
<tr><td>SAILCAT ► 1578 Pk:38 [0 | 1 | 1]</td><td>704</td></tr>
<tr><td>Motorcycle Mama (72) 38(2) [0 | 2 | 14]</td><td>704</td></tr>
<tr><td>Buffy SAINTE-MARIE ► 1647 Pk:97 [0 | 0 | 6]</td><td>622</td></tr>
<tr><td>Little Wheel Spin And Spin (66) 97(1) [0 | 0 | 10]</td><td>187</td></tr>
<tr><td>Moonshot (72) 134(1) [0 | 0 | 8]</td><td>126</td></tr>
<tr><td>Fire & Fleet & Candlelight (67) 126(1) [0 | 0 | 6]</td><td>97.8</td></tr>
<tr><td>The Best Of Buffy Sainte-Marie (70) 142(1) [0 | 0 | 7]</td><td>83.1</td></tr>
<tr><td>I'm Gonna Be A Country Girl Again (68) 171(2) [0 | 0 | 7]</td><td>74.1</td></tr>
<tr><td>She Used To Wanna Be A Ballerina (71) 182(1) [0 | 0 | 6]</td><td>53.3</td></tr>
<tr><td>SAINT TROPEZ ► 1768 Pk:65 [0 | 0 | 2]</td><td>504</td></tr>
<tr><td>Belle De Jour (79) 65(1) [0 | 0 | 11]</td><td>319</td></tr>
<tr><td>Je T'aime (77) 131(4) [0 | 0 | 10]</td><td>185</td></tr>
<tr><td>Soupy SALES ► 2168 Pk:80 [0 | 0 | 2]</td><td>269</td></tr>
<tr><td>Soupy Sales Sez Do The Mouse And Other Teen Hits (65) 80(1) [0 | 0 | 7]</td><td>148</td></tr>
<tr><td>Spy With A Pie (65) 102(2) [0 | 0 | 7]</td><td>122</td></tr>
<tr><td>SALSOUL Orchestra ► 566 Pk:14 [0 | 1 | 8]</td><td>5134</td></tr>
<tr><td>The Salsoul Orchestra (75) 14(2) [0 | 14 | 45]</td><td>2820</td></tr>
<tr><td>Magic Journey (77) 61(1) [0 | 0 | 20]</td><td>633</td></tr>
<tr><td>Christmas Jollies (76) 48(1) [0 | 0 | 13]</td><td>438</td></tr>
<tr><td>Nice 'N' Naasty (76) 61(2) [0 | 0 | 14]</td><td>424</td></tr>
<tr><td>Cuchi-Cuchi (77)-Charo And The Salsoul Orchestra 100(2) [0 | 0 | 15]</td><td>355</td></tr>
<tr><td>Greatest Disco Hits/Music For Non-Stop Dancing (78) 97(1) [0 | 0 | 13]</td><td>265</td></tr>
<tr><td>Up The Yellow Brick Road (78) 117(1) [0 | 0 | 8]</td><td>152</td></tr>
<tr><td>Christmas Jollies II (81) 170(2) [0 | 0 | 5]</td><td>47.3</td></tr>
<tr><td>SALT-N-PEPA ► 795 Pk:26 [0 | 2 | 2]</td><td>2970</td></tr>
<tr><td>Hot, Cool And Vicious (87) 26(4) [0 | 14 | 53]</td><td>1947</td></tr>
<tr><td>A Salt With A Deadly Pepa (88) 38(1) [0 | 4 | 31]</td><td>1023</td></tr>
<tr><td>SAM & DAVE ► 1063 Pk:45 [0 | 0 | 4]</td><td>1712</td></tr>
<tr><td>Hold On, I'm Comin' (66) 45(2) [0 | 0 | 15]</td><td>620</td></tr>
<tr><td>The Best Of Sam & Dave (69) 87(1) [0 | 0 | 17]</td><td>459</td></tr>
<tr><td>Soul Men (67) 62(1) [0 | 0 | 13]</td><td>389</td></tr>
<tr><td>Double Dynamite (67) 118(1) [0 | 0 | 13]</td><td>244</td></tr>
</table>

<table>
<tr><th>► Highest Peak [Top10s | Top40s | Total]
Title (Yr) Peak(Wk) [T10 Wk | T40Wk | TotalWk]</th><th>Score</th></tr>
<tr><td>Joe SAMPLE ► 881 Pk:56 [0|0|5]</td><td>2487</td></tr>
<tr><td>Rainbow Seeker (78) 62(1) [0|0|25]</td><td>870</td></tr>
<tr><td>Carmel (79) 56(2) [0|0|26]</td><td>717</td></tr>
<tr><td>Voices In The Rain (81) 65(3) [0|0|20]</td><td>603</td></tr>
<tr><td>Spellbound (89) 129(1) [0|0|14]</td><td>154</td></tr>
<tr><td>The Hunter (83) 125(1) [0|0|14]</td><td>143</td></tr>
<tr><td>SAM THE SHAM And The PHARAOHS ► 1261 Pk:26 [0|1|3]</td><td>1219</td></tr>
<tr><td>Wooly Bully (65) 26(2) [0|5|18]</td><td>739</td></tr>
<tr><td>The Best Of Sam The Sham And The Pharaohs (67) 98(1) [0|0|17]</td><td>301</td></tr>
<tr><td>Li'l Red Riding Hood (66) 82(1) [0|0|7]</td><td>179</td></tr>
<tr><td>David SANBORN ► 546 Pk:45 [0|0|10]</td><td>5444</td></tr>
<tr><td>Voyeur (81) 45(2) [0|0|22]</td><td>953</td></tr>
<tr><td>Backstreet (83) 81(1) [0|0|33]</td><td>744</td></tr>
<tr><td>A Change Of Heart (87) 74(2) [0|0|37]</td><td>692</td></tr>
<tr><td>Close-Up (88) 59(4) [0|0|28]</td><td>638</td></tr>
<tr><td>Double Vision (86)-Bob James/David Sanborn [A] 50(2) [0|0|64]</td><td>608</td></tr>
<tr><td>Hideaway (80) 63(1) [0|0|19]</td><td>561</td></tr>
<tr><td>Straight To The Heart (85) 64(2) [0|0|32]</td><td>542</td></tr>
<tr><td>As We Speak (82) 70(4) [0|0|23]</td><td>481</td></tr>
<tr><td>Sanborn (76) 125(1) [0|0|8]</td><td>143</td></tr>
<tr><td>Heart To Heart (78) 151(1) [0|0|6]</td><td>82.4</td></tr>
<tr><td>The SANDALS ► 2215 Pk:110 [0|0|1]</td><td>247</td></tr>
<tr><td>The Endless Summer (67) 110(1) [0|0|13]</td><td>247</td></tr>
<tr><td>Pharoah SANDERS ► 2666 Pk:163 [0|0|3]</td><td>120</td></tr>
<tr><td>Love Will Find A Way (78) 163(1) [0|0|5]</td><td>55.9</td></tr>
<tr><td>Thembi (71) 175(1) [0|0|3]</td><td>34.9</td></tr>
<tr><td>Karma (69) 188(1) [0|0|4]</td><td>29.4</td></tr>
<tr><td>Tony SANDLER And Ralph YOUNG ► 1777 Pk:85 [0|0|4]</td><td>499</td></tr>
<tr><td>Side By Side (66) 85(1) [0|0|19]</td><td>420</td></tr>
<tr><td>Pretty Things Come In Twos (69) 188(1) [0|0|4]</td><td>34.3</td></tr>
<tr><td>On The Move (67) 166(2) [0|0|3]</td><td>33.5</td></tr>
<tr><td>Honey Come Back (70) 199(2) [0|0|2]</td><td>11.1</td></tr>
<tr><td>The SANDPIPERS ► 783 Pk:13 [0|1|7]</td><td>3060</td></tr>
<tr><td>Guantanamera (66) 13(1) [0|10|37]</td><td>1942</td></tr>
<tr><td>The Sandpipers (67) 53(1) [0|0|28]</td><td>566</td></tr>
<tr><td>Come Saturday Morning (70) 96(1) [0|0|11]</td><td>287</td></tr>
<tr><td>Greatest Hits (70) 160(1) [0|0|10]</td><td>110</td></tr>
<tr><td>Misty Roses (68) 135(1) [0|0|5]</td><td>78.6</td></tr>
<tr><td>Softly (68) 180(1) [0|0|5]</td><td>40.2</td></tr>
<tr><td>The Wonder Of You (69) 194(2) [0|0|5]</td><td>36.3</td></tr>
<tr><td>SANFORD/TOWNSEND Band ► 1633 Pk:57 [0|0|2]</td><td>639</td></tr>
<tr><td>The Sanford/Townsend Band (77) 57(1) [0|0|15]</td><td>433</td></tr>
<tr><td>Duo-Glide (78) 92(2) [0|0|8]</td><td>205</td></tr>
<tr><td>SAN FRANCISCO Symphony ► 2609 Pk:105 [0|0|1]</td><td>132</td></tr>
<tr><td>William Russo: Three Pieces For Blues Band And Symphony Orchestra (73)- San Francisco Symphony/Siegel-Schwall Band [A] 105(1) [0|0|15]</td><td>132</td></tr>
<tr><td>Samantha SANG ► 1587 Pk:29 [0|1|1]</td><td>692</td></tr>
<tr><td>Emotion (78) 29(1) [0|3|14]</td><td>692</td></tr>
<tr><td>SAN SEBASTIAN Strings ► 508 Pk:20 [0|1|7]</td><td>6092</td></tr>
<tr><td>The Sea (67) 52(1) [0|0|143]</td><td>3867</td></tr>
<tr><td>Home To The Sea (69) 20(1) [0|4|20]</td><td>992</td></tr>
<tr><td>The Sky (68) 68(1) [0|0|25]</td><td>488</td></tr>
<tr><td>For Lovers (69) 84(2) [0|0|17]</td><td>475</td></tr>
<tr><td>The Earth (67) 115(1) [0|0|13]</td><td>167</td></tr>
<tr><td>The Complete Sea (70) 162(1) [0|0|5]</td><td>55.0</td></tr>
<tr><td>The Soft Sea (70) 171(1) [0|0|5]</td><td>47.6</td></tr>
<tr><td>SANTA ESMERALDA ► 940 Pk:25 [0|1|3]</td><td>2178</td></tr>
<tr><td>Don't Let Me Be Misunderstood (77) 25(2) [0|8|23]</td><td>1462</td></tr>
</table>

<table>
<tr><th>► Highest Peak [Top10s | Top40s | Total]
Title (Yr) Peak(Wk) [T10 Wk | T40Wk | TotalWk]</th><th>Score</th></tr>
<tr><td>The House Of The Rising Sun (78) 41(2) [0|0|14]</td><td>606</td></tr>
<tr><td>Beauty (78) 141(1) [0|0|6]</td><td>111</td></tr>
<tr><td>Mongo SANTAMARIA ► 1115 Pk:62 [0|0|8]</td><td>1561</td></tr>
<tr><td>Stone Soul (69) 62(1) [0|0|24]</td><td>756</td></tr>
<tr><td>La Bamba (65) 79(1) [0|0|15]</td><td>353</td></tr>
<tr><td>Soul Bag (68) 171(2) [0|0|18]</td><td>167</td></tr>
<tr><td>El Pussy Cat (65) 112(2) [0|0|10]</td><td>144</td></tr>
<tr><td>Hey! Let's Party (66) 135(2) [0|0|5]</td><td>77.6</td></tr>
<tr><td>Feelin' Alright (70) 171(2) [0|0|3]</td><td>35.8</td></tr>
<tr><td>Workin' On A Groovy Thing (69) 193(1) [0|0|2]</td><td>13.9</td></tr>
<tr><td>Mongo '70 (70) 195(2) [0|0|2]</td><td>13.4</td></tr>
<tr><td>SANTANA ► 26 Pk:1 [7|14|17]</td><td>56859</td></tr>
<tr><td>Abraxas (70) 1(6) [30|40|88]</td><td>14731</td></tr>
<tr><td>Santana (69) 4(6) [28|42|108]</td><td>12586</td></tr>
<tr><td>Santana III (71) 1(5) [11|22|39]</td><td>7577</td></tr>
<tr><td>Zebop! (81) 9(4) [7|21|32]</td><td>4051</td></tr>
<tr><td>Caravanserai (72) 8(2) [6|17|32]</td><td>3161</td></tr>
<tr><td>Amigos (76) 10(2) [2|11|26]</td><td>2247</td></tr>
<tr><td>Moonflower (77) 10(4) [4|9|24]</td><td>2061</td></tr>
<tr><td>Santana's Greatest Hits (74) 17(1) [0|11|21]</td><td>1831</td></tr>
<tr><td>Inner Secrets (78) 27(2) [0|5|33]</td><td>1716</td></tr>
<tr><td>Shango (82) 22(3) [0|10|23]</td><td>1288</td></tr>
<tr><td>Welcome (73) 25(1) [0|9|21]</td><td>1273</td></tr>
<tr><td>Marathon (79) 25(1) [0|6|22]</td><td>1206</td></tr>
<tr><td>Borboletta (74) 20(1) [0|5|19]</td><td>1170</td></tr>
<tr><td>Festival (77) 27(2) [0|4|19]</td><td>1094</td></tr>
<tr><td>Beyond Appearances (85) 50(2) [0|0|21]</td><td>605</td></tr>
<tr><td>Freedom (87) 95(2) [0|0|11]</td><td>191</td></tr>
<tr><td>Viva Santana (88) 142(2) [0|0|6]</td><td>70.2</td></tr>
<tr><td>Carlos SANTANA ► 705 Pk:8 [1|3|7]</td><td>3621</td></tr>
<tr><td>Love Devotion Surrender (73)-Carlos Santana & Mahavishnu John McLaughlin [A] 14(1) [0|7|24]</td><td>747</td></tr>
<tr><td>Havana Moon (83) 31(2) [0|4|17]</td><td>611</td></tr>
<tr><td>The Swing Of Delight (80)-Devadip Carlos Santana 65(2) [0|0|10]</td><td>321</td></tr>
<tr><td>Oneness/Silver Dreams-Golden Reality (79)- Devadip 87(2) [0|0|9]</td><td>234</td></tr>
<tr><td>Illuminations (74)-Devadip Carlos Santana & Turiya Alice Coltrane [A] 79(2) [0|0|8]</td><td>124</td></tr>
<tr><td>Blues For Salvador (87) 195(1) [0|0|1]</td><td>4.8</td></tr>
<tr><td>Carlos Santana & Buddy Miles! Live! (72)-Carlos Santana & Buddy Miles [A] 8(3) [8|14|33]</td><td>1579</td></tr>
<tr><td>SARAYA ► 1712 Pk:79 [0|0|1]</td><td>574</td></tr>
<tr><td>Saraya (89) 79(3) [0|0|39]</td><td>574</td></tr>
<tr><td>Father Guido SARDUCCI ► 3405 Pk:179 [0|0|1]</td><td>19</td></tr>
<tr><td>Live At St. Douglas Convent (80) 179(2) [0|0|2]</td><td>18.9</td></tr>
<tr><td>Joe SATRIANI ► 553 Pk:23 [0|2|3]</td><td>5352</td></tr>
<tr><td>Surfing With The Alien (87) 29(4) [0|9|75]</td><td>2477</td></tr>
<tr><td>Flying In A Blue Dream (89) 23(3) [0|14|39]</td><td>1863</td></tr>
<tr><td>Dreaming #11 (88) 42(1) [0|0|26]</td><td>1012</td></tr>
<tr><td>Esther SATTERFIELD ► 3212 Pk:180 [0|0|1]</td><td>38</td></tr>
<tr><td>The Need To Be (76) 180(1) [0|0|4]</td><td>38.5</td></tr>
<tr><td>SATURDAY NIGHT BAND ► 2105 Pk:125 [0|0|1]</td><td>299</td></tr>
<tr><td>Come On Dance, Dance (78) 125(4) [0|0|17]</td><td>299</td></tr>
<tr><td>Merl SAUNDERS ► 3328 Pk:197 [0|0|1]</td><td>26</td></tr>
<tr><td>Fire Up (73) 197(2) [0|0|5]</td><td>25.8</td></tr>
<tr><td>SAVAGE GRACE ► 2981 Pk:182 [0|0|1]</td><td>68</td></tr>
<tr><td>Savage Grace (70) 182(1) [0|0|8]</td><td>67.8</td></tr>
<tr><td>Telly SAVALAS ► 2400 Pk:117 [0|0|1]</td><td>187</td></tr>
<tr><td>Telly (75) 117(1) [0|0|8]</td><td>187</td></tr>
<tr><td>SAVATAGE ► 2078 Pk:116 [0|0|2]</td><td>311</td></tr>
<tr><td>Hall Of The Mountain King (87) 116(1) [0|0|23]</td><td>242</td></tr>
<tr><td>Fight For The Rock (86) 158(2) [0|0|7]</td><td>68.7</td></tr>
</table>

<table>
<tr><th>► Highest Peak [Top10s | Top40s | Total]
Title (Yr) Peak(Wk) [T10 Wk | T40Wk | TotalWk]</th><th>Score</th></tr>
<tr><td>SAVOY BROWN ► 669 Pk:34 [0|2|11]</td><td>4086</td></tr>
<tr><td>Hellbound Train (72) 34(1) [0|7|21]</td><td>1172</td></tr>
<tr><td>Looking In (70) 39(1) [0|1|19]</td><td>847</td></tr>
<tr><td>Street Corner Talking (71) 75(1) [0|0|17]</td><td>535</td></tr>
<tr><td>A Step Further (69) 71(1) [0|0|14]</td><td>439</td></tr>
<tr><td>Jack The Toad (73) 84(1) [0|0|14]</td><td>336</td></tr>
<tr><td>Raw Sienna (70) 121(2) [0|0|18]</td><td>308</td></tr>
<tr><td>Boogie Brothers (74) 101(1) [0|0|8]</td><td>185</td></tr>
<tr><td>Lion's Share (72) 151(2) [0|0|10]</td><td>119</td></tr>
<tr><td>Wire Fire (75) 153(2) [0|0|7]</td><td>92.6</td></tr>
<tr><td>Rock 'N' Roll Warriors (81) 185(1) [0|0|4]</td><td>31.6</td></tr>
<tr><td>Blue Matter (69) 182(1) [0|0|2]</td><td>21.6</td></tr>
<tr><td>SAWYER BROWN ► 2698 Pk:140 [0|0|1]</td><td>114</td></tr>
<tr><td>Sawyer Brown (85) 140(2) [0|0|11]</td><td>114</td></tr>
<tr><td>SAXON ► 2166 Pk:130 [0|0|4]</td><td>271</td></tr>
<tr><td>Power & The Glory (83) 155(1) [0|0|10]</td><td>91.7</td></tr>
<tr><td>Innocence Is No Excuse (85) 130(2) [0|0|8]</td><td>91.0</td></tr>
<tr><td>Rock The Nations (87) 149(2) [0|0|6]</td><td>51.8</td></tr>
<tr><td>Crusader (84) 174(2) [0|0|5]</td><td>36.3</td></tr>
<tr><td>Leo SAYER ► 466 Pk:10 [1|4|6]</td><td>6752</td></tr>
<tr><td>Endless Flight (76) 10(2) [2|14|51]</td><td>3371</td></tr>
<tr><td>Just A Boy (75) 16(1) [0|7|22]</td><td>1483</td></tr>
<tr><td>Living In A Fantasy (80) 36(2) [0|6|23]</td><td>1070</td></tr>
<tr><td>Thunder In My Heart (77) 37(1) [0|2|15]</td><td>427</td></tr>
<tr><td>Leo Sayer (78) 101(1) [0|0|14]</td><td>267</td></tr>
<tr><td>Another Year (75) 125(1) [0|0|7]</td><td>134</td></tr>
<tr><td>Boz SCAGGS ► 157 Pk:2 [2|4|10]</td><td>21311</td></tr>
<tr><td>Silk Degrees (76) 2(5) [10|53|115]</td><td>11882</td></tr>
<tr><td>Middle Man (80) 8(2) [4|21|33]</td><td>3683</td></tr>
<tr><td>Down Two Then Left (77) 11(2) [0|14|23]</td><td>2430</td></tr>
<tr><td>Hits! (80) 24(6) [0|14|26]</td><td>1868</td></tr>
<tr><td>Other Roads (88) 47(4) [0|0|18]</td><td>628</td></tr>
<tr><td>Slow Dancer (74) 81(1) [0|0|20]</td><td>459</td></tr>
<tr><td>Moments (71) 124(2) [0|0|9]</td><td>163</td></tr>
<tr><td>My Time (72) 138(1) [0|0|9]</td><td>135</td></tr>
<tr><td>Boz Scaggs (74) 171(1) [0|0|5]</td><td>50.6</td></tr>
<tr><td>Boz Scaggs & Band (71) 198(1) [0|0|2]</td><td>11.4</td></tr>
<tr><td>SCANDAL ► 789 Pk:17 [0|2|2]</td><td>3024</td></tr>
<tr><td>Warrior (84)-Scandal Featuring Patty Smyth 17(3) [0|14|41]</td><td>2050</td></tr>
<tr><td>Scandal (83) 39(1) [0|3|32]</td><td>974</td></tr>
<tr><td>Joey SCARBURY ► 2459 Pk:104 [0|0|1]</td><td>172</td></tr>
<tr><td>America's Greatest Hero (81) 104(2) [0|0|9]</td><td>172</td></tr>
<tr><td>SCARLETT & BLACK ► 2453 Pk:107 [0|0|1]</td><td>173</td></tr>
<tr><td>Scarlett & Black (88) 107(2) [0|0|11]</td><td>173</td></tr>
<tr><td>Michael SCHENKER Group ► 1418 Pk:81 [0|0|4]</td><td>940</td></tr>
<tr><td>Perfect Timing (87)-McAuley Schenker Group 95(2) [0|0|24]</td><td>413</td></tr>
<tr><td>The Michael Schenker Group (80) 100(1) [0|0|14]</td><td>263</td></tr>
<tr><td>MSG (81) 81(1) [0|0|8]</td><td>195</td></tr>
<tr><td>Assault Attack (83) 151(1) [0|0|7]</td><td>68.4</td></tr>
<tr><td>Lalo SCHIFRIN ► 1412 Pk:47 [0|0|1]</td><td>953</td></tr>
<tr><td>Music From Mission: Impossible (Soundtrack) (67) 47(2) [0|0|31]</td><td>953</td></tr>
<tr><td>Peter SCHILLING ► 1702 Pk:61 [0|0|1]</td><td>582</td></tr>
<tr><td>Error In The System (83) 61(1) [0|0|23]</td><td>582</td></tr>
<tr><td>Timothy B. SCHMIT ► 2306 Pk:106 [0|0|2]</td><td>213</td></tr>
<tr><td>Timothy B. (87) 106(2) [0|0|11]</td><td>167</td></tr>
<tr><td>Playin' It Cool (84) 160(2) [0|0|5]</td><td>46.9</td></tr>
<tr><td>John SCHNEIDER ► 1176 Pk:37 [0|1|3]</td><td>1401</td></tr>
<tr><td>Now Or Never (81) 37(1) [0|3|22]</td><td>1167</td></tr>
<tr><td>Too Good To Stop Now (84) 111(2) [0|0|12]</td><td>159</td></tr>
<tr><td>White Christmas (81) 155(1) [0|0|7]</td><td>74.9</td></tr>
<tr><td>Neal SCHON ► 2536 Pk:42 [0|0|1]</td><td>151</td></tr>
<tr><td>Through The Fire (84)-Hagar, Schon, Aaronson, Shrieve [A] 42(2) [0|0|18]</td><td>151</td></tr>
</table>

► Highest Peak [Top10s|Top40s|Total]
Title (Yr) Peak(Wk) [T10 Wk|T40Wk|TotalWk] Score

Neal SCHON & Jan HAMMER ► 2070 Pk:115 [0|0|2] 316
Here To Stay (83) 122(4) [0|0|12] 170
Untold Passion (81) 115(2) [0|0|8] 145
SCHOOLLY D ► 3373 Pk:180 [0|0|1] 22
Smoke Some Kill (88) 180(1) [0|0|3] 21.6
Diane SCHUUR ► 2881 Pk:170 [0|0|1] 82
Talkin' 'Bout You (88) 170(3) [0|0|10] 82.2
Eddie SCHWARTZ ► 3276 Pk:195 [0|0|1] 31
No Refuge (82) 195(2) [0|0|6] 30.9
SCORPIONS ► 221 Pk:5 [3|4|9] 15852
Love At First Sting (84) 6(2) [13|27|63] 4637
Savage Amusement (88) 5(1) [7|22|43] 3456
Blackout (82) 10(2) [2|17|74] 3091
World Wide Live (85) 14(1) [0|16|43] 2451
Best Of Rockers N' Ballads (89) 43(2) [0|0|23] 834
Animal Magnetism (80) 52(1) [0|0|21] 690
Lovedrive (79) 55(2) [0|0|23] 632
Best Of Scorpions (79) 180(3) [0|0|4] 35.3
Best Of Scorpions Vol. 2 (84) 175(1) [0|0|4] 25.8
Christopher SCOTT ► 3226 Pk:175 [0|0|1] 37
Switched-On Bacharach (69) 175(1) [0|0|3] 36.7
Marilyn SCOTT ► 3285 Pk:189 [0|0|1] 30
Dreams Of Tomorrow (79) 189(2) [0|0|4] 29.5
Peggy SCOTT & Jo Jo BENSON ► 3257 Pk:196 [0|0|1] 33
Soulshake (69) 196(1) [0|0|5] 32.6
Tom SCOTT & The L.A. EXPRESS ► 706 Pk:18 [0|1|9] 3615
Tom Cat (75) 18(2) [0|8|27] 1598
New York Connection (75)-Tom Scott 42(1) [0|0|25] 870
Blow It Out (77)-Tom Scott 87(1) [0|0|14] 287
Tom Scott & The L.A. Express (74) 141(3) [0|0|16] 244
Intimate Strangers (78)-Tom Scott 123(1) [0|0|13] 209
Apple Juice (81)-Tom Scott 123(1) [0|0|11] 199
L.A. Express (76)-L.A. Express 167(1) [0|0|8] 82.5
Street Beat (79)-Tom Scott 162(3) [0|0|6] 63.7
Desire (82)-Tom Scott 164(1) [0|0|7] 62.4
Gil SCOTT-HERON ► 1642 Pk:106 [0|0|3] 625
Reflections (81) 106(1) [0|0|27] 440
Moving Target (82) 123(1) [0|0|9] 115
Real Eyes (80) 159(2) [0|0|6] 70.8
Gil SCOTT-HERON & Brian JACKSON ► 953 Pk:30 [0|1|6] 2128
The First Minute Of A New Day (75) 30(1) [0|3|17] 912
Secrets (78) 61(1) [0|0|21] 667
1980 (80) 82(1) [0|0|12] 298
From South Africa To South Carolina (75) 103(1) [0|0|5] 101
Bridges (77) 130(2) [0|0|5] 93.4
It's Your World (76) 168(2) [0|0|5] 55.6
SCREAMING BLUE MESSIAHS ► 2841 Pk:172 [0|0|1] 89
Bikini Red (88) 172(1) [0|0|11] 88.8
SCRITTI POLITTI ► 1443 Pk:50 [0|0|2] 900
Cupid And Psyche 85 (85) 50(2) [0|0|28] 767
Provision (88) 113(2) [0|0|8] 133
SCRUFFY THE CAT ► 3122 Pk:177 [0|0|1] 50
Moons Of Jupiter (88) 177(1) [0|0|8] 49.6
Earl SCRUGGS Revue ► 2082 Pk:104 [0|0|3] 310
Anniversary Special Volume One (75) 104(2) [0|0|10] 206
The Earl Scruggs Revue (73) 169(1) [0|0|5] 52.7

► Highest Peak [Top10s|Top40s|Total]
Title (Yr) Peak(Wk) [T10 Wk|T40Wk|TotalWk] Score

The Earl Scruggs Revue, Volume II (76) 161(2) [0|0|4] 50.9
Johnny SEA ► 3302 Pk:147 [0|0|1] 28
Day For Decision (66) 147(1) [0|0|2] 28.0
SEA HAGS ► 3048 Pk:163 [0|0|1] 59
Sea Hags (89) 163(2) [0|0|7] 59.3
SEA LEVEL ► 1079 Pk:31 [0|1|4] 1657
Cats On The Coast (78) 31(1) [0|3|16] 833
Sea Level (77) 43(2) [0|0|15] 548
On The Edge (78) 137(3) [0|0|16] 196
Ball Room (80) 152(1) [0|0|6] 79.9
Dan SEALS ► 2027 Pk:59 [0|0|1] 338
Won't Be Blue Anymore (86) 59(2) [0|0|15] 338
SEALS & CROFTS ► 136 Pk:4 [2|6|12] 23363
Summer Breeze (72) 7(3) [5|33|109] 6716
Diamond Girl (73) 4(1) [12|31|77] 6512
Unborn Child (74) 14(2) [0|16|34] 2815
Greatest Hits (75) 11(2) [0|11|54] 2708
Get Closer (76) 37(1) [0|10|29] 1828
I'll Play For You (75) 30(2) [0|5|23] 1186
Seals & Crofts I And II (74) 81(1) [0|0|12] 351
Takin' It Easy (78) 78(1) [0|0|13] 329
Sudan Village (76) 73(2) [0|0|10] 305
Year Of Sunday (71) 133(1) [0|0|20] 301
Down Home (70) 122(1) [0|0|10] 179
One On One (Soundtrack) (77) 118(2) [0|0|7] 133
The SEARCHERS ► 1149 Pk:22 [0|1|6] 1472
Meet The Searchers/Needles & Pins (64) 22(2) [0|8|21] 999
This Is Us (64) 97(1) [0|0|14] 210
The New Searchers LP (65) 112(2) [0|0|7] 114
Hear! Hear! (64) 120(2) [0|0|8] 112
The Searchers No. 4 (65) 149(1) [0|0|2] 23.5
The Searchers (80) 191(2) [0|0|2] 14.2
Marvin SEASE ► 2256 Pk:114 [0|0|1] 231
Marvin Sease (87) 114(2) [0|0|17] 231
SEATRAIN ► 1293 Pk:48 [0|0|3] 1160
Seatrain (71) 48(1) [0|0|23] 883
The Marblehead Messenger (71) 91(1) [0|0|9] 224
Sea Train (69) 168(2) [0|0|4] 53.6
SEAWIND ► 1683 Pk:83 [0|0|4] 596
Seawind(2) (80) 83(1) [0|0|11] 266
Light The Light (79) 143(1) [0|0|14] 199
Window Of A Child (78) 122(2) [0|0|7] 114
Seawind (77) 188(2) [0|0|2] 16.9
John SEBASTIAN ► 831 Pk:20 [0|1|5] 2761
John B. Sebastian (70) 20(2) [0|7|31] 1865
Cheapo-Cheapo Productions Presents Real Live John Sebastian (71) 75(1) [0|0|13] 324
Welcome Back (76) 79(1) [0|0|10] 275
The Four Of Us (71) 93(2) [0|0|9] 244
John Sebastian Live (70) 129(1) [0|0|3] 53.4
Neil SEDAKA ► 462 Pk:16 [0|3|8] 6870
Sedaka's Back (74) 23(1) [0|8|62] 2755
The Hungry Years (75) 16(2) [0|10|32] 2358
Steppin' Out (76) 26(1) [0|5|22] 1098
A Song (77) 59(1) [0|0|7] 268
In The Pocket (80) 135(1) [0|0|13] 202
Neil Sedaka's Greatest Hits (77) 143(2) [0|0|5] 77.9
Solitaire (76) 159(1) [0|0|4] 58.0
Neil Sedaka Sings His Greatest Hits (75) 161(2) [0|0|4] 54.1
SEDUCTION ► 1146 Pk:36 [0|1|1] 1477
Nothing Matters Without Love (89) 36(1) [0|7|47] 1477
The SEEDS ► 2124 Pk:87 [0|0|2] 290
Future (67) 87(1) [0|0|8] 180

► Highest Peak [Top10s|Top40s|Total]
Title (Yr) Peak(Wk) [T10 Wk|T40Wk|TotalWk] Score

The Seeds (67) 132(1) [0|0|7] 110
Pete SEEGER ► 1314 Pk:42 [0|0|2] 1116
We Shall Overcome (63) 42(1) [0|0|36] 1099
Together In Concert (75)-Pete Seeger/Arlo Guthrie [A] 181(1) [0|0|4] 17.7
The SEEKERS ► 828 Pk:10 [1|1|5] 2767
Georgy Girl (67) 10(2) [2|12|28] 2096
The New Seekers (65) 62(1) [0|0|16] 353
The Best Of The Seekers (67) 97(1) [0|0|10] 189
A World Of Our Own (65) 123(1) [0|0|6] 93.1
The Seekers (65) 145(1) [0|0|3] 36.0
George SEGAL ► 3526 Pk:199 [0|0|1] 9
The Yama Yama Man (67) 199(1) [0|0|2] 8.7
Bob SEGER ► 51 Pk:1 [6|7|12] 43818
Against The Wind (80)-Bob Seger & The Silver Bullet Band 1(6) [22|43|110] 11583
Stranger In Town (78)-Bob Seger & The Silver Bullet Band 4(2) [12|33|110] 8305
Night Moves (76)-Bob Seger & The Silver Bullet Band 8(1) [4|23|88] 5606
Like A Rock (86)-Bob Seger & The Silver Bullet Band 3(4) [15|28|62] 5287
Nine Tonight (81)-Bob Seger & The Silver Bullet Band 3(4) [10|21|70] 4899
The Distance (83)-Bob Seger & The Silver Bullet Band 5(6) [14|23|39] 3858
'Live' Bullet (76)-Bob Seger & The Silver Bullet Band 34(1) [0|2|154] 3359
Ramblin' Gamblin' Man (69)-Bob Seger System 62(2) [0|0|10] 467
Beautiful Loser (75) 131(1) [0|0|18] 290
Smokin' O.P.'s (72) 180(1) [0|0|11] 85.3
Mongrel (70)-Bob Seger System 171(1) [0|0|4] 40.6
Back In '72 (73) 188(2) [0|0|6] 38.5
The SELECTER ► 3205 Pk:175 [0|0|1] 39
Too Much Pressure (80) 175(1) [0|0|4] 39.0
Michael SEMBELLO ► 2432 Pk:80 [0|0|1] 178
Bossa Nova Hotel (83) 80(1) [0|0|10] 178
SERENDIPITY SINGERS ► 919 Pk:11 [0|1|3] 2264
The Serendipity Singers (64) 11(1) [0|18|29] 1915
The Many Sides Of The Serendipity Singers (64) 68(1) [0|0|15] 326
Take Your Shoes Off With The Serendipity Singers (65) 149(2) [0|0|2] 24.0
Brian SETZER ► 1546 Pk:45 [0|0|2] 733
The Knife Feels Like Justice (86) 45(3) [0|0|18] 633
Live Nude Guitars (88) 140(2) [0|0|8] 100
707 ► 2428 Pk:129 [0|0|2] 180
Mega Force (82) 129(2) [0|0|9] 107
The Second Album (81) 159(1) [0|0|6] 73.2
7 SECONDS ► 2362 Pk:153 [0|0|1] 194
Soulforce Revolution (89) 153(2) [0|0|19] 194
Doc SEVERINSEN ► 2456 Pk:133 [0|0|4] 172
Command Performances (66) 133(1) [0|0|6] 96.6
Fever! (66) 147(1) [0|0|2] 29.2
Night Journey (76) 189(1) [0|0|4] 26.8
Brass Roots (71) 185(2) [0|0|2] 19.5
Doc SEVERINSEN And The TONIGHT SHOW Orchestra ► 1719 Pk:65 [0|0|1] 563
The Tonight Show Band (86)-The Tonight Show Band with Doc Severinsen 65(4) [0|0|26] 563
--Doc Severinsen see also Mancini, Henry
SEX PISTOLS ► 2175 Pk:106 [0|0|1] 268
Never Mind The Bollocks Here's The Sex Pistols (77) 106(2) [0|0|12] 268
Charlie SEXTON ► 1005 Pk:15 [0|1|2] 1926
Pictures For Pleasure (85) 15(3) [0|13|34] 1753
Charlie Sexton (89) 104(1) [0|0|9] 173
Phil SEYMOUR ► 1953 Pk:64 [0|0|1] 376
Phil Seymour (81) 64(1) [0|0|16] 376

► Highest Peak [Top10s | Top40s | Total] Title (Yr) Peak(Wk) [T10 Wk | T40Wk | TotalWk]	Score
SHADOWFAX ► 1618 Pk:114 [0|0|4]	**655**
The Dreams Of Children (84) 126(2) [0|0|20]	220
Too Far To Whisper (86) 114(1) [0|0|16]	213
Shadowdance (83) 145(1) [0|0|19]	180
Folksongs For A Nuclear Village (88) 168(2) [0|0|5]	42.3
SHADOWS OF KNIGHT ► 1708 Pk:46 [0|0|1]	**576**
Gloria (66) 46(1) [0|0|18]	576
SHAKTI With John MCLAUGHLIN ► 3035 Pk:168 [0|0|2]	**61**
A Handful Of Beauty (77) 168(1) [0|0|4]	46.6
Shakti With John McLaughlin (76) 194(2) [0|0|2]	14.1
SHALAMAR ► 488 Pk:23 [0|4|8]	**6358**
Big Fun (79) 23(2) [0|11|36]	1879
Three For Love (81) 40(2) [0|2|36]	1577
Friends (82) 35(1) [0|3|25]	943
The Look (83) 38(1) [0|2|23]	746
Uptown Festival (77) 48(1) [0|0|14]	541
Heart Break (84) 90(4) [0|0|24]	409
Go For It (81) 115(2) [0|0|15]	225
Disco Gardens (78) 171(1) [0|0|4]	38.7
SHA NA NA ► 1139 Pk:38 [0|1|7]	**1504**
The Golden Age Of Rock 'N' Roll (73) 38(1) [0|2|24]	861
Sha Na Na (71) 122(1) [0|0|9]	177
The Night Is Still Young (72) 156(1) [0|0|14]	151
From The Streets Of New York (73) 140(1) [0|0|11]	140
Hot Sox (74) 165(2) [0|0|6]	65.4
Rock & Roll Is Here To Stay! (69) 183(1) [0|0|7]	57.3
Sha Na Now (75) 162(2) [0|0|4]	52.5
The SHANGRI-LAS ► 2772 Pk:109 [0|0|1]	**101**
Leader Of The Pack (65) 109(1) [0|0|6]	101
SHANICE ► 2417 Pk:149 [0|0|1]	**183**
Discovery (87)-Shanice Wilson 149(2) [0|0|18]	183
Bud SHANK ► 1684 Pk:56 [0|0|1]	**596**
Michelle (66) 56(1) [0|0|21]	596
Ravi SHANKAR ► 1366 Pk:43 [0|0|5]	**1020**
Ravi Shankar At The Monterey International Pop Festival (67) 43(2) [0|0|19]	808
Ravi Shankar In New York (67) 148(2) [0|0|7]	74.9
Ravi Shankar In San Francisco (68) 140(1) [0|0|4]	71.7
West Meets East (67)-Yehudi Menuhin & Ravi Shankar [A] 161(1) [0|0|7]	34.2
Shankar Family & Friends (75) 176(1) [0|0|3]	31.0
SHANNON ► 1135 Pk:32 [0|1|2]	**1511**
Let The Music Play (84) 32(2) [0|4|37]	1253
Do You Wanna Get Away (85) 92(2) [0|0|16]	257
Del SHANNON ► 2422 Pk:123 [0|0|1]	**182**
Drop Down And Get Me (81) 123(1) [0|0|14]	182
Feargal SHARKEY ► 2236 Pk:75 [0|0|1]	**240**
Feargal Sharkey (86) 75(2) [0|0|11]	240
SHARKS ► 3323 Pk:189 [0|0|1]	**26**
First Water (73) 189(1) [0|0|4]	26.0
Marlena SHAW ► 1650 Pk:62 [0|0|3]	**620**
Sweet Beginnings (77) 62(1) [0|0|14]	514
Who Is This Bitch, Anyway? (75) 159(1) [0|0|5]	63.7
Acting Up (78) 171(1) [0|0|4]	42.2
Roland SHAW Orchestra ► 1509 Pk:38 [0|1|2]	**790**
Themes From The James Bond Thrillers (65) 38(1) [0|1|25]	708
More Themes From The James Bond Thrillers (66) 119(1) [0|0|5]	82.2
Sandie SHAW ► 2944 Pk:100 [0|0|1]	**73**
Sandie Shaw (65) 100(1) [0|0|4]	72.8

► Highest Peak [Top10s | Top40s | Total] Title (Yr) Peak(Wk) [T10 Wk | T40Wk | TotalWk]	Score
Tommy SHAW ► 1449 Pk:50 [0|0|2]	**892**
Girls With Guns (84) 50(3) [0|0|25]	725
What If (85) 87(2) [0|0|9]	167
SHEILA E. ► 768 Pk:28 [0|1|3]	**3150**
The Glamorous Life (84) 28(2) [0|9|46]	1845
Romance 1600 (85) 50(1) [0|0|33]	1028
Sheila E. (87) 56(2) [0|0|12]	278
Pete SHELLEY ► 2398 Pk:121 [0|0|2]	**187**
Homosapien (82) 121(1) [0|0|10]	136
XL-1 (83) 151(1) [0|0|5]	50.6
Ricky Van SHELTON ► 1268 Pk:76 [0|0|2]	**1208**
Wild-Eyed Dream (87) 76(1) [0|0|41]	720
Loving Proof (88) 78(2) [0|0|24]	487
T.G. SHEPPARD ► 1928 Pk:119 [0|0|3]	**388**
I Love 'Em All (81) 119(1) [0|0|12]	234
Finally! (82) 152(2) [0|0|13]	136
T.G. Sheppard's Greatest Hits (83) 189(2) [0|0|3]	17.8
The SHERBS ► 2037 Pk:100 [0|0|1]	**334**
The Skill (81) 100(2) [0|0|16]	334
SHERIFF ► 1939 Pk:60 [0|0|1]	**381**
Sheriff (89) 60(2) [0|0|14]	381
Allan SHERMAN ► 445 Pk:1 [1|3|5]	**7160**
My Son, The Nut (63) 1(8) [12|24|32]	5346
Allan In Wonderland (64) 25(2) [0|6|19]	743
For Swingin' Livers Only! (64) 32(2) [0|5|17]	652
My Name Is Allan (65) 88(2) [0|0|11]	234
Peter And The Commissar (64)-Allan Sherman/ Boston Pops Orchestra/Arthur Fiedler [A] 53(1) [0|0|14]	185
Bobby SHERMAN ► 359 Pk:10 [1|3|6]	**9243**
Here Comes Bobby (70) 10(2) [2|12|48]	3180
Bobby Sherman (69) 11(1) [0|15|35]	3166
With Love, Bobby (70) 20(2) [0|8|26]	1837
Portrait Of Bobby (71) 48(1) [0|0|14]	590
Getting Together (71) 71(1) [0|0|8]	244
Bobby Sherman's Greatest Hits (72) 83(1) [0|0|9]	225
SHINEHEAD ► 3354 Pk:185 [0|0|1]	**24**
Unity (88) 185(1) [0|0|4]	23.8
SHIRLEY (& COMPANY) ► 3224 Pk:169 [0|0|1]	**37**
Shame Shame Shame (75) 169(2) [0|0|3]	37.1
Michelle SHOCKED ► 1244 Pk:73 [0|0|2]	**1238**
Short Sharp Shocked (88) 73(1) [0|0|35]	790
Captain Swing (89) 95(2) [0|0|26]	448
SHOCKING BLUE ► 1543 Pk:31 [0|1|1]	**737**
The Shocking Blue (70) 31(1) [0|3|17]	737
SHOES ► 1803 Pk:50 [0|0|2]	**482**
Present Tense (79) 50(1) [0|0|12]	373
Tongue Twister (81) 140(3) [0|0|7]	109
SHOOTING STAR ► 1312 Pk:82 [0|0|5]	**1119**
Hang On For Your Life (81) 92(1) [0|0|30]	686
Ill Wishes (82) 82(2) [0|0|9]	165
Shooting Star (80) 147(1) [0|0|14]	147
Touch Me Tonight-The Best Of Shooting Star (89) 151(2) [0|0|7]	65.5
Burning (83) 162(1) [0|0|6]	55.0
Bobby SHORT ► 2958 Pk:169 [0|0|1]	**71**
Bobby Short Loves Cole Porter (72) 169(1) [0|0|8]	71.0
Wayne SHORTER ► 3307 Pk:183 [0|0|1]	**28**
Native Dancer (75) 183(2) [0|0|3]	27.5
SHOTGUN ► 2803 Pk:163 [0|0|2]	**97**
Shotgun III (79) 163(2) [0|0|4]	48.6
Good Bad & Funky (78) 172(1) [0|0|5]	48.1

► Highest Peak [Top10s | Top40s | Total] Title (Yr) Peak(Wk) [T10 Wk | T40Wk | TotalWk]	Score
SHOTGUN MESSIAH ► 1985 Pk:99 [0|0|1]	**358**
Shotgun Messiah (89) 99(1) [0|0|23]	358
SHRIEKBACK ► 2385 Pk:145 [0|0|3]	**190**
Go Bang! (88) 169(2) [0|0|12]	107
Big Night Music (87) 145(2) [0|0|6]	65.2
Care (83) 188(1) [0|0|3]	17.5
Michael SHRIEVE ► 2110 Pk:42 [0|0|2]	**296**
Through The Fire (84)-Hagar, Schon, Aaronson, Shrieve [A] 42(2) [0|0|18]	151
Go (76)-Stomu Yamashta/Steve Winwood/Michael Shrieve [A] 60(3) [0|0|12]	145
SHY ► 3522 Pk:193 [0|0|1]	**10**
Excess All Areas (87) 193(1) [0|0|2]	9.5
Jane SIBERRY ► 2866 Pk:149 [0|0|1]	**85**
The Speckless Sky (86) 149(2) [0|0|8]	85.4
SIDE EFFECT ► 1591 Pk:86 [0|0|3]	**690**
Goin' Bananas (78) 86(1) [0|0|15]	303
What You Need (77) 115(1) [0|0|13]	242
Rainbow Visions (79) 135(2) [0|0|8]	146
SIDEWINDERS ► 3199 Pk:169 [0|0|1]	**40**
Witchdoctor (89) 169(1) [0|0|5]	39.8
SIEGEL-SCHWALL Band ► 2610 Pk:105 [0|0|1]	**132**
William Russo: Three Pieces For Blues Band And Symphony Orchestra (73)-San Francisco Symphony/Siegel-Schwall Band [A] 105(1) [0|0|15]	132
Bunny SIGLER ► 1808 Pk:77 [0|0|2]	**479**
Let Me Party With You (78) 77(2) [0|0|13]	320
I've Always Wanted To Sing...Not Just Write Songs (79) 119(1) [0|0|9]	159
SIGUE SIGUE SPUTNIK ► 2513 Pk:96 [0|0|1]	**156**
Flaunt It (86) 96(2) [0|0|10]	156
The SILENCERS ► 2748 Pk:147 [0|0|1]	**105**
A Letter From St. Paul (87) 147(2) [0|0|11]	105
SILK ► 3434 Pk:191 [0|0|1]	**17**
Smooth As Raw Silk (69) 191(2) [0|0|2]	16.6
Beverly SILLS ► 2681 Pk:113 [0|0|1]	**118**
Music Of Victor Herbert (76) 113(2) [0|0|6]	118
SILVER ► 2823 Pk:142 [0|0|1]	**91**
Silver (76) 142(1) [0|0|6]	91.3
Horace SILVER Quintet ► 2403 Pk:95 [0|0|2]	**185**
Song For My Father (Cantiga Para Meu Pai) (65) 95(1) [0|0|10]	153
The Cape Verdean Blues (66)-Horace Silver Quintet Plus J.J. Johnson 130(1) [0|0|2]	32.0
SILVER APPLES ► 3406 Pk:193 [0|0|1]	**19**
Silver Apples (68) 193(2) [0|0|3]	18.9
SILVER CONDOR ► 2378 Pk:141 [0|0|1]	**191**
Silver Condor (81) 141(4) [0|0|12]	191
SILVER CONVENTION ► 609 Pk:10 [1|2|4]	**4658**
Save Me (75) 10(1) [1|10|25]	2031
Silver Convention (76) 13(1) [0|10|24]	1891
Madhouse (76) 65(2) [0|0|12]	393
Golden Girls (77) 71(2) [0|0|10]	344
Shel SILVERSTEIN ► 2810 Pk:155 [0|0|1]	**95**
Freakin' At The Freakers Ball (73) 155(1) [0|0|8]	95.2
Gene SIMMONS ► 1038 Pk:22 [0|1|1]	**1803**
Gene Simmons (78)-Gene Simmons(2) 22(2) [0|12|22]	1803
Jumpin' Gene SIMMONS ► 3005 Pk:132 [0|0|1]	**66**
Jumpin' Gene Simmons (64) 132(1) [0|0|5]	65.6
Patrick SIMMONS ► 2134 Pk:52 [0|0|1]	**286**
Arcade (83) 52(1) [0|0|11]	286
Richard SIMMONS ► 1410 Pk:44 [0|0|1]	**954**
Reach (82) 44(2) [0|0|40]	954

▶ Highest Peak [Top10s I Top40s I Total] Title (Yr) Peak(Wk) [T10 Wk I T40Wk I TotalWk]	Score
Carly SIMON ▶ 113 Pk:1 [4 I 10 I 15]	**27298**
No Secrets (72) 1(5) [14 I 23 I 71]	7375
Hotcakes (74) 3(1) [7 I 16 I 35]	3664
Boys In The Trees (78) 10(3) [3 I 17 I 29]	3027
Coming Around Again (87) 25(2) [0 I 10 I 60]	2616
Anticipation (71) 30(2) [0 I 5 I 31]	1699
Playing Possum (75) 10(2) [2 I 9 I 17]	1696
The Best Of Carly Simon (75) 17(2) [0 I 9 I 19]	1571
Carly Simon (71) 30(1) [0 I 7 I 25]	1399
Come Upstairs (80) 36(2) [0 I 4 I 32]	1356
Another Passenger (76) 29(1) [0 I 4 I 13]	808
Torch (81) 50(1) [0 I 0 I 24]	753
Spy (79) 45(2) [0 I 0 I 13]	511
Hello Big Man (83) 69(2) [0 I 0 I 17]	355
Greatest Hits Live (88) 87(3) [0 I 0 I 13]	258
Spoiled Girl (85) 88(2) [0 I 0 I 11]	209
Joe SIMON ▶ 1107 Pk:71 [0 I 0 I 7]	**1585**
The Chokin' Kind (69) 81(1) [0 I 0 I 17]	587
Drowning In The Sea Of Love (72) 71(1) [0 I 0 I 12]	347
The Power Of Joe Simon (73) 97(1) [0 I 0 I 12]	219
Get Down (75) 129(2) [0 I 0 I 12]	199
The Sounds Of Simon (71) 153(1) [0 I 0 I 12]	118
The Best Of Joe Simon (72) 147(1) [0 I 0 I 8]	101
Joe Simon...Better Than Ever (69) 192(1) [0 I 0 I 2]	14.6
Paul SIMON ▶ 92 Pk:1 [4 I 8 I 9]	**31217**
Graceland (86) 3(1) [24 I 52 I 97]	8543
Still Crazy After All These Years (75) 1(1) [22 I 29 I 40]	8118
There Goes Rhymin' Simon (73) 2(2) [8 I 24 I 48]	4781
Paul Simon (72) 4(2) [11 I 18 I 36]	4225
One-Trick Pony (80) 12(2) [0 I 13 I 26]	2214
Greatest Hits, Etc. (77) 18(1) [0 I 9 I 23]	1544
Paul Simon In Concert/Live Rhymin' (74) 33(1) [0 I 3 I 17]	776
Hearts And Bones (83) 35(2) [0 I 8 I 18]	766
Negotiations And Love Songs (1971-1986) (88) 110(1) [0 I 0 I 14]	251
SIMON & GARFUNKEL ▶ 24 Pk:1 [6 I 8 I 8]	**58590**
The Graduate (Soundtrack) (68) 1(9) [26 I 47 I 69]	11898
Bridge Over Troubled Water (70) 1(10) [17 I 24 I 85]	11307
Parsley, Sage, Rosemary And Thyme (66) 4(2) [17 I 60 I 145]	10665
Bookends (68) 1(7) [20 I 40 I 66]	10281
Simon And Garfunkel's Greatest Hits (72) 5(4) [7 I 22 I 127]	5831
Sounds Of Silence (66) 21(2) [0 I 34 I 141]	5415
The Concert In Central Park (82) 6(2) [5 I 11 I 34]	2249
Wednesday Morning, 3 AM (66) 30(1) [0 I 4 I 31]	943
Nina SIMONE ▶ 1475 Pk:99 [0 I 0 I 9]	**854**
Wild Is The Wind (66) 110(1) [0 I 0 I 9]	173
Nina Simone In Concert (64) 102(1) [0 I 0 I 11]	168
Black Gold (70) 149(2) [0 I 0 I 12]	156
I Put A Spell On You (65) 99(2) [0 I 0 I 8]	147
Pastel Blues (65) 139(1) [0 I 0 I 7]	87.7
Silk & Soul (67) 158(1) [0 I 0 I 4]	43.6
Here Comes The Sun (71) 190(2) [0 I 0 I 4]	30.2
The Best Of Nina Simone (69) 187(1) [0 I 0 I 3]	26.8
The Best Of Nina Simone(2) (70) 189(1) [0 I 0 I 3]	20.9
SIMPLE MINDS ▶ 602 Pk:10 [1 I 1 I 5]	**4711**
Once Upon A Time (85) 10(5) [5 I 27 I 42]	3400
Sparkle In The Rain (84) 64(2) [0 I 0 I 24]	481
New Gold Dream (81-82-83-84) (83) 69(2) [0 I 0 I 19]	413
Street Fighting Years (89) 70(2) [0 I 0 I 12]	246

▶ Highest Peak [Top10s I Top40s I Total] Title (Yr) Peak(Wk) [T10 Wk I T40Wk I TotalWk]	Score
Simple Minds Live: In The City Of Light (87) 96(2) [0 I 0 I 10]	171
SIMPLY RED ▶ 521 Pk:16 [0 I 3 I 3]	**5859**
Picture Book (86) 16(3) [0 I 18 I 60]	2549
A New Flame (89) 22(1) [0 I 14 I 39]	2305
Men And Women (87) 31(2) [0 I 5 I 26]	1006
Valerie SIMPSON ▶ 2525 Pk:159 [0 I 0 I 2]	**152**
Valerie Simpson (72) 162(3) [0 I 0 I 6]	76.8
Valerie Simpson Exposed (71) 159(2) [0 I 0 I 6]	75.7
Frank SINATRA ▶ 49 Pk:1 [7 I 18 I 31]	**44458**
Strangers In The Night (66) 1(1) [14 I 43 I 73]	6964
September Of My Years (65) 5(2) [11 I 46 I 69]	6107
That's Life (66) 6(3) [9 I 22 I 61]	4016
Sinatra '65 (65) 9(1) [3 I 32 I 44]	3267
Sinatra's Sinatra (63) 8(2) [2 I 17 I 43]	2630
A Man And His Music (65) 9(2) [3 I 20 I 32]	2377
Cycles (68) 18(1) [0 I 7 I 28]	2141
My Way (69) 11(2) [0 I 8 I 19]	1986
Trilogy: Past, Present And Future (80) 17(2) [0 I 12 I 24]	1804
Ol' Blue Eyes Is Back (73) 13(1) [0 I 10 I 22]	1676
Days Of Wine And Roses, Moon River, And Other Academy Award Winners (64) 10(2) [2 I 16 I 24]	1588
Softly, As I Leave You (64) 19(1) [0 I 12 I 28]	1352
Frank Sinatra (67) 24(1) [0 I 9 I 23]	1161
A Man Alone & Other Songs Of Rod McKuen (69) 30(2) [0 I 5 I 16]	1098
Frank Sinatra's Greatest Hits! (68) 55(1) [0 I 0 I 25]	1062
My Kind Of Broadway (65) 30(1) [0 I 3 I 16]	656
Sinatra - The Main Event Live (74) 37(1) [0 I 2 I 12]	620
Francis Albert Sinatra & Antonio Carlos Jobim (67)-Frank Sinatra & Antonio Carlos Jobim [A] 19(2) [0 I 6 I 28]	611
Some Nice Things I've Missed (74) 48(1) [0 I 0 I 12]	586
Moonlight Sinatra (66) 34(1) [0 I 2 I 14]	567
She Shot Me Down (81) 52(2) [0 I 0 I 13]	476
Frank Sinatra's Greatest Hits, Vol. 2 (72) 88(2) [0 I 0 I 17]	430
Sinatra & Company (71) 73(1) [0 I 0 I 15]	430
L.A. Is My Lady (84) 58(2) [0 I 0 I 13]	294
Watertown (70) 101(1) [0 I 0 I 10]	225
Francis A. & Edward K. (68)-Frank Sinatra & Duke Ellington [A] 78(2) [0 I 0 I 13]	163
Tell Her You Love Her (63) 129(1) [0 I 0 I 4]	62.9
America, I Hear You Singing (64)-Frank Sinatra/Bing Crosby/Frank Waring [A] 116(1) [0 I 0 I 7]	36.1
Round #1 (75) 170(1) [0 I 0 I 3]	34.9
Close-Up (69) 186(2) [0 I 0 I 3]	28.7
The Movie Songs (67) 195(1) [0 I 0 I 2]	10.3
Frank SINATRA & Count BASIE ▶ 613 Pk:9 [1 I 2 I 2]	**4616**
It Might As Well Be Swing (64) 13(1) [0 I 15 I 31]	1904
Sinatra At The Sands (66)-Frank Sinatra With Count Basie And The Orchestra 9(1) [2 I 15 I 44]	2712
Nancy SINATRA ▶ 378 Pk:5 [1 I 4 I 9]	**8806**
Boots (66) 5(3) [8 I 24 I 42]	3329
Nancy & Lee (68)-Nancy Sinatra & Lee Hazlewood [A] 13(1) [0 I 18 I 44]	1303
Movin' With Nancy (68) 37(2) [0 I 4 I 32]	1226
Sugar (67) 18(1) [0 I 6 I 24]	1188
Country, My Way (67) 43(1) [0 I 0 I 26]	707
How Does That Grab You? (66) 41(1) [0 I 0 I 15]	537
Nancy (69) 91(1) [0 I 0 I 8]	241
Nancy's Greatest Hits (70) 99(1) [0 I 0 I 7]	156
Nancy In London (66) 122(1) [0 I 0 I 7]	119

▶ Highest Peak [Top10s I Top40s I Total] Title (Yr) Peak(Wk) [T10 Wk I T40Wk I TotalWk]	Score
Pete SINFIELD ▶ 3284 Pk:190 [0 I 0 I 1]	**30**
Still (73) 190(1) [0 I 0 I 5]	29.7
SINGING NUN ▶ 471 Pk:1 [1 I 1 I 2]	**6724**
The Singing Nun (63)-The Singing Nun (Soeur Sourire) 1(10) [18 I 22 I 39]	6488
Her Joy, Her Songs (64)-The Singing Nun (Soeur Sourire) 90(2) [0 I 0 I 14]	236
SIOUXSIE & The BANSHEES ▶ 1481 Pk:68 [0 I 0 I 4]	**845**
Peepshow (88) 68(1) [0 I 0 I 20]	501
Tinderbox (86) 88(1) [0 I 0 I 15]	261
Hyaena (84) 157(1) [0 I 0 I 7]	65.1
Through The Looking Glass (87) 188(1) [0 I 0 I 3]	18.1
SIR DOUGLAS Quintet ▶ 1900 Pk:81 [0 I 0 I 2]	**408**
Mendocino (69) 81(1) [0 I 0 I 11]	377
Border Wave (81) 184(2) [0 I 0 I 4]	30.9
Sir Lord BALTIMORE ▶ 3486 Pk:198 [0 I 0 I 1]	**12**
Kingdom Come (71) 198(2) [0 I 0 I 2]	12.1
Sir MIX-A-LOT ▶ 1020 Pk:67 [0 I 0 I 2]	**1866**
Swass (88) 82(1) [0 I 0 I 58]	973
Seminar (89) 67(2) [0 I 0 I 41]	893
SISTER SLEDGE ▶ 504 Pk:3 [1 I 2 I 5]	**6121**
We Are Family (79) 3(2) [9 I 19 I 33]	4071
Love Somebody Today (80) 31(2) [0 I 5 I 15]	849
All American Girls (81) 42(1) [0 I 0 I 29]	817
The Sisters (82) 69(2) [0 I 0 I 14]	322
Bet Cha Say That To All The Girls (83) 169(1) [0 I 0 I 8]	62.8
SISTERS OF MERCY ▶ 2065 Pk:101 [0 I 0 I 1]	**317**
Floodland (88) 101(2) [0 I 0 I 16]	317
Ricky SKAGGS ▶ 1436 Pk:61 [0 I 0 I 4]	**918**
Waitin' For The Sun To Shine (82) 77(2) [0 I 0 I 30]	551
Highways And Heartaches (82) 61(3) [0 I 0 I 12]	310
Country Boy (84) 180(1) [0 I 0 I 5]	30.2
Favorite Country Hits (85) 181(2) [0 I 0 I 4]	26.4
SKID ROW ▶ 389 Pk:6 [1 I 1 I 1]	**8481**
Skid Row (89) 6(1) [11 I 57 I 78]	8481
SKY ▶ 2192 Pk:125 [0 I 0 I 2]	**262**
Sky (80) 125(1) [0 I 0 I 15]	232
Sky 3 (81) 181(1) [0 I 0 I 3]	29.2
SKY (2) ▶ 2976 Pk:160 [0 I 0 I 1]	**69**
Sky (70) 160(1) [0 I 0 I 6]	68.6
SKYLARK ▶ 2119 Pk:102 [0 I 0 I 1]	**292**
Skylark (73) 102(1) [0 I 0 I 16]	292
SKYY ▶ 702 Pk:18 [0 I 1 I 7]	**3643**
Skyy Line (81) 18(2) [0 I 11 I 33]	1892
Skyway (80) 61(1) [0 I 0 I 23]	798
Skyyport (80) 85(1) [0 I 0 I 20]	446
Skyyjammer (82) 81(2) [0 I 0 I 13]	287
Skyy (79) 117(2) [0 I 0 I 9]	147
Start Of A Romance (89) 155(1) [0 I 0 I 5]	51.5
Skyylight (83) 183(1) [0 I 0 I 3]	20.4
SLADE ▶ 909 Pk:33 [0 I 1 I 7]	**2312**
Keep Your Hands Off My Power Supply (84) 33(2) [0 I 4 I 23]	937
Slayed? (73) 69(1) [0 I 0 I 26]	649
Slade In Flame (Soundtrack) (75) 93(1) [0 I 0 I 14]	357
Sladest (73) 129(1) [0 I 0 I 7]	115
Slade Alive! (72) 158(1) [0 I 0 I 11]	114
Rogues Gallery (85) 132(2) [0 I 0 I 6]	87.0
Stomp Your Hands, Clap Your Feet (74) 168(1) [0 I 0 I 5]	52.0
SLAVE ▶ 604 Pk:22 [0 I 1 I 8]	**4710**
Slave (77) 22(1) [0 I 12 I 28]	1934
Stone Jam (80) 53(2) [0 I 0 I 34]	943

► Highest Peak [Top10s | Top40s | Total] Title (Yr) Peak(Wk) [T10 Wk | T40Wk | TotalWk]	Score
SLAVE ► *Continued*	
Show Time (81) 46(1) [0|0|23]	712
The Hardness Of The World (77) 67(1) [0|0|15]	418
Just A Touch Of Love (79) 92(2) [0|0|15]	350
The Concept (78) 78(1) [0|0|10]	274
Visions Of The Lite (83) 177(1) [0|0|6]	39.9
Bad Enuff (83) 168(1) [0|0|5]	39.2
SLAYER ► 1532 Pk:57 [0|0|2]	**752**
South Of Heaven (88) 57(2) [0|0|19]	452
Reign In Blood (86) 94(3) [0|0|18]	301
Percy SLEDGE ► 1310 Pk:37 [0|1|5]	**1124**
When A Man Loves A Woman (66) 37(1) [0|2|21]	794
The Best Of Percy Sledge (69) 133(1) [0|0|11]	174
Take Time To Know Her (68) 148(1) [0|0|6]	85.1
Warm & Tender Soul (66) 136(2) [0|0|3]	49.5
The Percy Sledge Way (67) 178(2) [0|0|3]	21.7
Grace SLICK ► 1053 Pk:32 [0|1|6]	**1737**
Dreams (80) 32(2) [0|4|16]	884
Welcome To The Wrecking Ball (81) 48(1) [0|0|14]	516
Manhole (74) 127(1) [0|0|7]	117
Sunfighter (71)-Grace Slick and Paul Kantner [A] 89(1) [0|0|9]	110
Baron Von Tollbooth & The Chrome Nun (73)-Paul Kantner, Grace Slick & David Freiberg [A] 120(1) [0|0|12]	66.5
Conspicuous Only In Its Absence (68)-The Great Society With Grace Slick 166(1) [0|0|4]	43.4
SLICK RICK ► 1099 Pk:31 [0|1|1]	**1609**
The Great Adventures Of Slick Rick (89) 31(3) [0|5|40]	1609
SLY & THE FAMILY STONE ► 127 Pk:1 [3|5|9]	**24976**
Greatest Hits (70) 2(1) [15|27|79]	8278
Stand! (69) 13(1) [0|24|102]	6820
There's A Riot Goin' On (71) 1(2) [10|18|31]	5000
Fresh (73) 7(1) [6|16|33]	2971
Small Talk (74) 15(1) [0|7|15]	1344
High On You (75)-Sly Stone 45(1) [0|0|10]	396
Dance To The Music (68) 142(2) [0|0|7]	88.3
Back On The Right Track (79) 152(1) [0|0|3]	42.6
Life (68) 195(2) [0|0|5]	35.6
SLY FOX ► 1427 Pk:31 [0|1|1]	**928**
Let's Go All The Way (86) 31(2) [0|4|22]	928
Millie SMALL ► 3004 Pk:132 [0|0|1]	**66**
My Boy Lollipop (64) 132(1) [0|0|5]	65.7
SMALL FACES/FACES ► 527 Pk:6 [1|3|8]	**5746**
A Nod Is As Good As A Wink...To A Blind Horse (71)-Faces 6(4) [6|14|24]	3065
Ooh La La (73)-Faces 21(2) [0|7|16]	1060
Long Player (71)-Faces 29(1) [0|5|19]	1022
First Step (70)-Small Faces 119(1) [0|0|12]	185
Rod Stewart/Faces Live - Coast To Coast Overture And Beginners (74)-Rod Stewart/Faces [A] 63(1) [0|0|11]	154
Ogdens' Nut Gone Flake (68)-Small Faces 159(1) [0|0|15]	149
Early Faces (72)-Small Faces 176(1) [0|0|10]	85.8
There Are But Four Small Faces (68)-Small Faces 178(1) [0|0|3]	24.9
SMITH ► 896 Pk:17 [0|1|2]	**2410**
A Group Called Smith (69) 17(2) [0|11|28]	2072
Minus-Plus (70) 74(1) [0|0|12]	338
Cal SMITH ► 3164 Pk:170 [0|0|2]	**45**
Cal Smith Sings (69) 170(2) [0|0|2]	27.9
I've Found Someone Of My Own (73) 191(1) [0|0|3]	17.0
Connie SMITH ► 2876 Pk:105 [0|0|1]	**83**
Connie Smith (65) 105(1) [0|0|5]	83.3

► Highest Peak [Top10s | Top40s | Total] Title (Yr) Peak(Wk) [T10 Wk | T40Wk | TotalWk]	Score
Frankie SMITH ► 1876 Pk:54 [0|0|1]	**420**
Children Of Tomorrow (81) 54(2) [0|0|10]	420
Hurricane SMITH ► 1703 Pk:53 [0|0|1]	**582**
Hurricane Smith (73) 53(2) [0|0|18]	582
Jerry SMITH ► 3493 Pk:200 [0|0|1]	**12**
Truck Stop (69)-Jerry Smith and his Pianos 200(2) [0|0|2]	11.8
Jimmy SMITH ► 335 Pk:12 [0|6|18]	**10320**
Who's Afraid Of Virginia Woolf? (64) 16(2) [0|15|31]	1774
Organ Grinder Swing (65) 15(1) [0|10|31]	1532
The Cat (64) 12(2) [0|13|32]	1520
Any Number Can Win (63) 25(2) [0|7|33]	1278
Got My Mojo Workin' (66) 28(2) [0|10|27]	1222
Monster (65) 35(1) [0|4|24]	865
Respect (67) 60(1) [0|0|20]	586
Prayer Meetin' (64) 86(1) [0|0|20]	373
Hoochie Cooche Man (66) 77(2) [0|0|14]	349
Rockin' The Boat (63) 64(1) [0|0|8]	184
Bucket (66) 121(1) [0|0|9]	166
Jimmy & Wes The Dynamic Duo (67)-Jimmy Smith & Wes Montgomery [A] 129(2) [0|0|23]	133
Livin' It Up! (68) 169(1) [0|0|10]	119
Jimmy Smith's Greatest Hits! (68) 128(1) [0|0|4]	80.4
The Boss (69) 144(2) [0|0|3]	60.4
Blue Bash! (63)-Kenny Burrell/Jimmy Smith [A] 108(1) [0|0|4]	35.8
The Best Of Jimmy Smith (67) 185(1) [0|0|4]	27.7
Groove Drops (70) 197(1) [0|0|3]	16.8
Kate SMITH ► 1159 Pk:36 [0|1|5]	**1441**
How Great Thou Art (66) 36(3) [0|5|24]	962
Kate Smith At Carnegie Hall (63) 83(1) [0|0|18]	378
The Kate Smith Anniversary Album (66) 130(1) [0|0|3]	50.2
Kate Smith Today (66) 148(1) [0|0|2]	28.3
The Sweetest Sounds (64) 145(1) [0|0|2]	22.9
Kathy SMITH ► 2678 Pk:144 [0|0|1]	**118**
Kathy Smith's Aerobic Fitness (82) 144(2) [0|0|13]	118
Lonnie SMITH ► 3426 Pk:186 [0|0|1]	**17**
Move Your Hand (70) 186(2) [0|0|2]	17.0
Lonnie Liston SMITH ► 910 Pk:58 [0|0|8]	**2311**
Renaissance (76)-Lonnie Liston Smith & The Cosmic Echoes 73(2) [0|0|20]	513
Visions Of A New World (75)-Lonnie Liston Smith & The Cosmic Echoes 74(1) [0|0|15]	378
Reflections Of A Golden Dream (76)-Lonnie Liston Smith & The Cosmic Echoes 75(2) [0|0|14]	359
Live! (77) 58(2) [0|0|11]	346
Expansions (75)-Lonnie Liston Smith & The Cosmic Echoes 85(1) [0|0|13]	329
Loveland (78) 120(2) [0|0|13]	250
Exotic Mysteries (79) 123(2) [0|0|8]	126
Dreams Of Tomorrow (83) 193(1) [0|0|2]	10.3
O.C. SMITH ► 722 Pk:19 [0|1|5]	**3498**
Hickory Holler Revisited (68) 19(2) [0|10|42]	2145
For Once In My Life (69) 50(1) [0|0|15]	678
O.C. Smith At Home (69) 58(1) [0|0|16]	540
Help Me Make It Through The Night (71) 159(1) [0|0|7]	90.4
O.C. Smith's Greatest Hits (70) 177(2) [0|0|5]	44.5
Patti SMITH ► 668 Pk:18 [0|2|5]	**4089**
Easter (78)-Patti Smith Group 20(1) [0|8|23]	1463
Wave (79)-Patti Smith Group 18(2) [0|7|19]	1349
Horses (75) 47(2) [0|0|17]	750
Dream Of Life (88) 65(4) [0|0|15]	365
Radio Ethiopia (76)-Patti Smith Group 122(1) [0|0|8]	162

► Highest Peak [Top10s | Top40s | Total] Title (Yr) Peak(Wk) [T10 Wk | T40Wk | TotalWk]	Score
Rex SMITH ► 1113 Pk:19 [0|1|3]	**1564**
Sooner Or Later (79) 19(2) [0|8|19]	1488
Everlasting Love (81) 167(2) [0|0|4]	43.0
Forever, Rex Smith (80) 165(1) [0|0|3]	32.5
Sammi SMITH ► 1313 Pk:33 [0|1|2]	**1119**
Help Me Make It Through The Night (71) 33(2) [0|4|21]	1102
Lonesome (71) 191(2) [0|0|2]	16.2
The SMITHEREENS ► 713 Pk:41 [0|0|3]	**3547**
Especially For You (86) 51(1) [0|0|50]	1438
11 (89) 41(1) [0|0|38]	1219
Green Thoughts (88) 60(3) [0|0|31]	890
The SMITHS ► 887 Pk:55 [0|0|6]	**2442**
Strangeways, Here We Come (87) 55(2) [0|0|27]	656
The Queen Is Dead (86) 70(1) [0|0|37]	611
Louder Than Bombs (87) 62(2) [0|0|25]	463
Meat Is Murder (85) 110(2) [0|0|32]	450
Rank (88) 77(2) [0|0|8]	166
The Smiths (84) 150(2) [0|0|11]	97.0
SMOKESTACK LIGHTNIN' ► 3488 Pk:200 [0|0|1]	**12**
Off The Wall (69) 200(2) [0|0|2]	12.1
SMOKIE ► 3043 Pk:173 [0|0|1]	**60**
Midnight Cafe (77) 173(2) [0|0|6]	60.1
SMOTHERS BROTHERS ► 636 Pk:13 [0|3|7]	**4351**
Curb Your Tongue, Knave! (63) 13(2) [0|10|33]	1511
It Must Have Been Something I Said! (64) 23(2) [0|7|28]	1022
Mom Always Liked You Best! (65) 39(2) [0|2|28]	1004
Tour De Farce American History And Other Unrelated Subjects (64) 58(1) [0|0|20]	402
Aesop's Fables The Smothers Brothers Way (65) 57(1) [0|0|10]	249
Golden Hits Of The Smothers Brothers, Vol. 2 (66) 119(1) [0|0|6]	106
Smothers Comedy Brothers Hour (68) 164(2) [0|0|4]	56.2
Patty SMYTH ► 1868 Pk:66 [0|0|1]	**428**
Never Enough (87) 66(2) [0|0|20]	428
SNAIL ► 2344 Pk:135 [0|0|2]	**202**
Snail (78) 135(2) [0|0|12]	186
Flow (79) 186(1) [0|0|2]	15.2
SNEAKER ► 2313 Pk:149 [0|0|1]	**211**
Sneaker (81) 149(2) [0|0|17]	211
SNIFF 'N' The TEARS ► 1464 Pk:35 [0|1|2]	**870**
Fickle Heart (79) 35(1) [0|3|17]	856
Love Action (81) 192(2) [0|0|2]	13.7
Phoebe SNOW ► 356 Pk:4 [1|3|7]	**9372**
Phoebe Snow (74) 4(1) [5|22|58]	4909
Second Childhood (76) 13(2) [0|10|22]	1755
It Looks Like Snow (76) 29(3) [0|7|21]	1229
Rock Away (81) 51(2) [0|0|18]	579
Never Letting Go (77) 73(2) [0|0|15]	372
Something Real (89) 75(1) [0|0|20]	352
Against The Grain (78) 100(1) [0|0|7]	175
SO ► 2554 Pk:124 [0|0|1]	**148**
Horseshoe In The Glove (88) 124(3) [0|0|9]	148
Gino SOCCIO ► 1651 Pk:79 [0|0|2]	**619**
Outline (79) 79(2) [0|0|13]	356
Closer (81) 96(2) [0|0|14]	263
SOFT CELL ► 808 Pk:22 [0|1|3]	**2899**
Non-Stop Erotic Cabaret (82) 22(1) [0|18|41]	2367
Non-Stop Ecstatic Dancing (82) 57(2) [0|0|14]	348
The Art Of Falling Apart (83) 84(4) [0|0|8]	184
SOFT MACHINE ► 2685 Pk:160 [0|0|1]	**117**
The Soft Machine (68) 160(1) [0|0|9]	117

<table>
<tr><th>► Highest Peak [Top10s | Top40s | Total]
Title (Yr) Peak(Wk) [T10 Wk | T40Wk | TotalWk]</th><th>Score</th></tr>
<tr><td>SONNY & CHER ► 243 Pk:2 [1 | 5 | 12]</td><td>14615</td></tr>
<tr><td>Look At Us (65) 2(8) [14 | 25 | 44]</td><td>5119</td></tr>
<tr><td>All I Ever Need Is You (72) 14(2) [0 | 15 | 29]</td><td>2618</td></tr>
<tr><td>The Best Of Sonny & Cher (67) 23(1) [0 | 10 | 64]</td><td>2144</td></tr>
<tr><td>Sonny & Cher Live (71) 35(1) [0 | 2 | 40]</td><td>1756</td></tr>
<tr><td>The Wondrous World Of Sonny & Cher (66) 34(2) [0 | 6 | 20]</td><td>890</td></tr>
<tr><td>In Case You're In Love (67) 45(2) [0 | 0 | 29]</td><td>850</td></tr>
<tr><td>Good Times (Soundtrack) (67) 73(1) [0 | 0 | 18]</td><td>401</td></tr>
<tr><td>Baby Don't Go (65)-Sonny & Cher & Friends 69(1) [0 | 0 | 16]</td><td>369</td></tr>
<tr><td>The Two Of Us (72) 122(2) [0 | 0 | 12]</td><td>224</td></tr>
<tr><td>Mama Was A Rock And Roll Singer Papa Used To Write All Her Songs (73) 132(2) [0 | 0 | 6]</td><td>96.6</td></tr>
<tr><td>Greatest Hits (74) 146(2) [0 | 0 | 6]</td><td>86.2</td></tr>
<tr><td>Sonny & Cher Live In Las Vegas, Vol. 2 (73) 175(1) [0 | 0 | 7]</td><td>61.2</td></tr>
<tr><td>SONS OF CHAMPLIN ► 1840 Pk:117 [0 | 0 | 5]</td><td>449</td></tr>
<tr><td>A Circle Filled With Love (76) 117(1) [0 | 0 | 10]</td><td>172</td></tr>
<tr><td>Loosen Up Naturally (69) 137(1) [0 | 0 | 9]</td><td>154</td></tr>
<tr><td>The Sons (69) 171(2) [0 | 0 | 6]</td><td>63.2</td></tr>
<tr><td>Welcome To The Dance (73) 186(1) [0 | 0 | 5]</td><td>32.3</td></tr>
<tr><td>Loving Is Why (77) 188(1) [0 | 0 | 4]</td><td>28.1</td></tr>
<tr><td>SOPWITH "CAMEL" ► 3496 Pk:191 [0 | 0 | 1]</td><td>12</td></tr>
<tr><td>Sopwith Camel (67) 191(1) [0 | 0 | 2]</td><td>11.8</td></tr>
<tr><td>S.O.S. BAND ► 660 Pk:12 [0 | 1 | 7]</td><td>4170</td></tr>
<tr><td>S.O.S. (80) 12(3) [0 | 11 | 20]</td><td>1865</td></tr>
<tr><td>On The Rise (83) 47(1) [0 | 0 | 29]</td><td>900</td></tr>
<tr><td>Sands Of Time (86) 44(2) [0 | 0 | 20]</td><td>674</td></tr>
<tr><td>Just The Way You Like It (84) 60(2) [0 | 0 | 27]</td><td>558</td></tr>
<tr><td>Too (81) 117(2) [0 | 0 | 6]</td><td>103</td></tr>
<tr><td>S.O.S. III (82) 172(1) [0 | 0 | 8]</td><td>60.5</td></tr>
<tr><td>Diamonds In The Raw (89) 194(2) [0 | 0 | 2]</td><td>10.2</td></tr>
<tr><td>David SOUL ► 1383 Pk:40 [0 | 1 | 2]</td><td>989</td></tr>
<tr><td>David Soul (77) 40(1) [0 | 1 | 22]</td><td>813</td></tr>
<tr><td>Playing To An Audience Of One (77) 86(2) [0 | 0 | 7]</td><td>176</td></tr>
<tr><td>SOUL CHILDREN ► 2552 Pk:154 [0 | 0 | 2]</td><td>148</td></tr>
<tr><td>Soul Children (69) 154(1) [0 | 0 | 6]</td><td>81.6</td></tr>
<tr><td>Genesis (72) 159(1) [0 | 0 | 6]</td><td>66.7</td></tr>
<tr><td>SOULFUL STRINGS ► 1311 Pk:59 [0 | 0 | 5]</td><td>1121</td></tr>
<tr><td>Groovin' With The Soulful Strings (67) 59(1) [0 | 0 | 34]</td><td>802</td></tr>
<tr><td>In Concert/Back By Demand (69) 125(1) [0 | 0 | 6]</td><td>140</td></tr>
<tr><td>Paint It Black (67) 166(1) [0 | 0 | 15]</td><td>121</td></tr>
<tr><td>Spring Fever (69) 183(1) [0 | 0 | 4]</td><td>31.4</td></tr>
<tr><td>Another Exposure (68) 189(1) [0 | 0 | 4]</td><td>27.1</td></tr>
<tr><td>SOUL SURVIVORS ► 2399 Pk:123 [0 | 0 | 1]</td><td>187</td></tr>
<tr><td>When The Whistle Blows Anything Goes (67) 123(1) [0 | 0 | 13]</td><td>187</td></tr>
<tr><td>SOUL II SOUL ► 620 Pk:14 [0 | 1 | 1]</td><td>4558</td></tr>
<tr><td>Keep On Movin' (89) 14(4) [0 | 36 | 51]</td><td>4558</td></tr>
<tr><td>SOUNDS OF SUNSHINE ► 3054 Pk:187 [0 | 0 | 1]</td><td>59</td></tr>
<tr><td>Love Means You Never Have To Say You're Sorry (71) 187(1) [0 | 0 | 8]</td><td>58.8</td></tr>
<tr><td>SOUNDS ORCHESTRAL ► 1145 Pk:11 [0 | 1 | 1]</td><td>1484</td></tr>
<tr><td>Cast Your Fate To The Wind (65) 11(2) [0 | 9 | 28]</td><td>1484</td></tr>
<tr><td>SOUNDTRACK-MOVIE ► Pk:1 [39 | 111 | 371]</td><td>442594</td></tr>
<tr><td>The Sound Of Music (65) 1(2) [109 | 161 | 233]</td><td>29435</td></tr>
<tr><td>Doctor Zhivago (66) 1(1) [71 | 115 | 157]</td><td>21854</td></tr>
<tr><td>Dirty Dancing (87) 1(18) [48 | 68 | 96]</td><td>16684</td></tr>
<tr><td>Mary Poppins (64) 1(14) [48 | 78 | 114]</td><td>14811</td></tr>
<tr><td>Grease (78) 1(12) [29 | 39 | 77]</td><td>13745</td></tr>
<tr><td>Woodstock (70) 1(4) [24 | 36 | 68]</td><td>11782</td></tr>
<tr><td>My Fair Lady (64) 4(2) [30 | 77 | 111]</td><td>9912</td></tr>
</table>

<table>
<tr><th>► Highest Peak [Top10s | Top40s | Total]
Title (Yr) Peak(Wk) [T10 Wk | T40Wk | TotalWk]</th><th>Score</th></tr>
<tr><td>Flashdance (83) 1(2) [25 | 54 | 78]</td><td>9902</td></tr>
<tr><td>Romeo & Juliet (69) 2(2) [17 | 31 | 74]</td><td>9730</td></tr>
<tr><td>Easy Rider (69) 6(1) [6 | 41 | 72]</td><td>8708</td></tr>
<tr><td>Top Gun (86) 1(5) [20 | 33 | 93]</td><td>8187</td></tr>
<tr><td>Footloose (84) 1(10) [20 | 27 | 61]</td><td>7852</td></tr>
<tr><td>A Man And A Woman (66) 10(2) [2 | 44 | 93]</td><td>6866</td></tr>
<tr><td>Goldfinger (64) 1(3) [22 | 36 | 70]</td><td>6654</td></tr>
<tr><td>Beverly Hills Cop (85) 1(2) [22 | 32 | 62]</td><td>6652</td></tr>
<tr><td>Love Story (71) 2(6) [13 | 22 | 39]</td><td>6436</td></tr>
<tr><td>American Graffiti (73) 10(1) [1 | 41 | 60]</td><td>6407</td></tr>
<tr><td>Cocktail (88) 2(1) [19 | 28 | 61]</td><td>6310</td></tr>
<tr><td>Star Wars (77) 2(3) [10 | 22 | 53]</td><td>6071</td></tr>
<tr><td>More Dirty Dancing (88) 3(5) [13 | 27 | 52]</td><td>5578</td></tr>
<tr><td>Urban Cowboy (80) 3(2) [14 | 23 | 47]</td><td>5546</td></tr>
<tr><td>The Big Chill (83) 17(2) [0 | 19 | 161]</td><td>5525</td></tr>
<tr><td>Tommy (75) 2(1) [11 | 19 | 35]</td><td>5315</td></tr>
<tr><td>Butch Cassidy And The Sundance Kid (69) 16(2) [0 | 26 | 74]</td><td>4935</td></tr>
<tr><td>2001: A Space Odyssey (68) 24(1) [0 | 11 | 120]</td><td>4561</td></tr>
<tr><td>Camelot (67) 11(4) [0 | 23 | 87]</td><td>4487</td></tr>
<tr><td>The Good, The Bad And The Ugly (68) 4(2) [10 | 21 | 52]</td><td>4465</td></tr>
<tr><td>Fame (80) 7(2) [5 | 16 | 82]</td><td>4319</td></tr>
<tr><td>Oliver! (68) 20(2) [0 | 8 | 91]</td><td>4128</td></tr>
<tr><td>Rocky (77) 4(6) [9 | 14 | 34]</td><td>4092</td></tr>
<tr><td>Midnight Cowboy (69) 19(2) [0 | 19 | 57]</td><td>3978</td></tr>
<tr><td>Fiddler On The Roof (71) 30(2) [0 | 4 | 90]</td><td>3657</td></tr>
<tr><td>The Empire Strikes Back (80) 4(4) [9 | 17 | 28]</td><td>3643</td></tr>
<tr><td>Zorba The Greek (65) 26(2) [0 | 23 | 79]</td><td>3295</td></tr>
<tr><td>Sgt. Pepper's Lonely Hearts Club Band (78) 5(6) [9 | 12 | 28]</td><td>3219</td></tr>
<tr><td>Cabaret (72) 25(1) [0 | 9 | 72]</td><td>3000</td></tr>
<tr><td>FM (78) 5(2) [4 | 12 | 24]</td><td>2902</td></tr>
<tr><td>Pretty In Pink (86) 5(4) [9 | 17 | 27]</td><td>2899</td></tr>
<tr><td>Thank God It's Friday (78) 10(3) [3 | 15 | 27]</td><td>2815</td></tr>
<tr><td>Ghostbusters (84) 6(3) [8 | 17 | 34]</td><td>2711</td></tr>
<tr><td>Thoroughly Modern Millie (67) 16(2) [0 | 12 | 48]</td><td>2607</td></tr>
<tr><td>American Gigolo (80) 7(3) [5 | 15 | 25]</td><td>2595</td></tr>
<tr><td>Beverly Hills Cop II (87) 8(1) [6 | 17 | 26]</td><td>2457</td></tr>
<tr><td>Paint Your Wagon (69) 28(2) [0 | 4 | 56]</td><td>2453</td></tr>
<tr><td>Wild In The Streets (68) 12(2) [0 | 12 | 32]</td><td>2424</td></tr>
<tr><td>The Godfather (72) 21(2) [0 | 14 | 35]</td><td>2381</td></tr>
<tr><td>Good Morning, Vietnam (88) 10(2) [2 | 14 | 35]</td><td>2363</td></tr>
<tr><td>Endless Love (81) 9(2) [2 | 14 | 20]</td><td>2231</td></tr>
<tr><td>Heavy Metal (81) 12(2) [0 | 13 | 28]</td><td>2195</td></tr>
<tr><td>Rocky IV (85) 10(1) [1 | 16 | 30]</td><td>2167</td></tr>
<tr><td>Breakin' (84) 8(2) [4 | 14 | 23]</td><td>2129</td></tr>
<tr><td>Jungle Book (68) 19(2) [0 | 11 | 34]</td><td>2083</td></tr>
<tr><td>Thunderball (65) 10(1) [1 | 13 | 28]</td><td>1962</td></tr>
<tr><td>Bonnie And Clyde (68) 12(3) [0 | 13 | 21]</td><td>1955</td></tr>
<tr><td>Woodstock Two (71) 7(1) [2 | 9 | 17]</td><td>1948</td></tr>
<tr><td>The Unsinkable Molly Brown (64) 11(2) [0 | 16 | 33]</td><td>1870</td></tr>
<tr><td>The Little Mermaid (89) 32(2) [0 | 6 | 48]</td><td>1861</td></tr>
<tr><td>Mahogany (75) 19(2) [0 | 10 | 26]</td><td>1828</td></tr>
<tr><td>Jesus Christ Superstar (73) 21(1) [0 | 8 | 39]</td><td>1818</td></tr>
<tr><td>St. Elmo's Fire (85) 21(2) [0 | 11 | 37]</td><td>1793</td></tr>
<tr><td>Back To The Future (85) 12(2) [0 | 14 | 32]</td><td>1783</td></tr>
<tr><td>Valley Of The Dolls (68) 11(2) [0 | 9 | 27]</td><td>1769</td></tr>
<tr><td>Against All Odds (84) 12(4) [0 | 12 | 22]</td><td>1684</td></tr>
<tr><td>To Sir, With Love (67) 16(4) [0 | 11 | 22]</td><td>1569</td></tr>
<tr><td>The Muppet Movie: Original Soundtrack Recording (79) 32(2) [0 | 5 | 34]</td><td>1544</td></tr>
<tr><td>Vision Quest (85) 11(1) [0 | 12 | 23]</td><td>1542</td></tr>
<tr><td>Stand By Me (86) 31(6) [0 | 10 | 45]</td><td>1541</td></tr>
<tr><td>Godspell (73) 50(2) [0 | 0 | 51]</td><td>1518</td></tr>
<tr><td>White Nights (85) 17(2) [0 | 12 | 26]</td><td>1513</td></tr>
</table>

<table>
<tr><th>► Highest Peak [Top10s | Top40s | Total]
Title (Yr) Peak(Wk) [T10 Wk | T40Wk | TotalWk]</th><th>Score</th></tr>
<tr><td>The Breakfast Club (85) 17(2) [0 | 13 | 26]</td><td>1501</td></tr>
<tr><td>A Clockwork Orange (72) 34(1) [0 | 5 | 31]</td><td>1470</td></tr>
<tr><td>Gone With The Wind (67) 24(1) [0 | 9 | 36]</td><td>1418</td></tr>
<tr><td>Summer Of '42 (71) 52(1) [0 | 0 | 34]</td><td>1406</td></tr>
<tr><td>Ghostbusters II (89) 14(1) [0 | 10 | 19]</td><td>1340</td></tr>
<tr><td>Rocky III (82) 15(5) [0 | 10 | 19]</td><td>1334</td></tr>
<tr><td>Born Free (66) 42(1) [0 | 0 | 48]</td><td>1322</td></tr>
<tr><td>Beat Street (84) 14(2) [0 | 9 | 21]</td><td>1313</td></tr>
<tr><td>Lost Boys (87) 15(1) [0 | 9 | 39]</td><td>1302</td></tr>
<tr><td>Close Encounters Of The Third Kind (78) 17(2) [0 | 8 | 16]</td><td>1256</td></tr>
<tr><td>What's New Pussycat? (65) 14(1) [0 | 10 | 22]</td><td>1253</td></tr>
<tr><td>The Rocky Horror Picture Show (78) 49(2) [0 | 0 | 58]</td><td>1220</td></tr>
<tr><td>Doctor Dolittle (67) 55(2) [0 | 0 | 44]</td><td>1165</td></tr>
<tr><td>Live And Let Die (73) 17(1) [0 | 7 | 15]</td><td>1146</td></tr>
<tr><td>Casino Royale (67) 22(2) [0 | 9 | 21]</td><td>1140</td></tr>
<tr><td>Annie (82) 35(2) [0 | 7 | 31]</td><td>1104</td></tr>
<tr><td>Less Than Zero (87) 31(2) [0 | 7 | 23]</td><td>1080</td></tr>
<tr><td>The Way We Were (74) 20(1) [0 | 5 | 15]</td><td>1079</td></tr>
<tr><td>You Only Live Twice (67) 27(1) [0 | 6 | 26]</td><td>1077</td></tr>
<tr><td>Arthur (The Album) (81) 32(3) [0 | 7 | 22]</td><td>1071</td></tr>
<tr><td>Two Of A Kind (Soundtrack) (83) 26(1) [0 | 8 | 20]</td><td>1055</td></tr>
<tr><td>E.T. - The Extra-Terrestrial (82) 37(2) [0 | 5 | 33]</td><td>1043</td></tr>
<tr><td>From Russia With Love (64) 27(1) [0 | 6 | 34]</td><td>1036</td></tr>
<tr><td>All That Jazz (80) 36(2) [0 | 3 | 23]</td><td>995</td></tr>
<tr><td>You Light Up My Life (77) 17(2) [0 | 5 | 15]</td><td>988</td></tr>
<tr><td>Ruthless People (86) 20(1) [0 | 9 | 16]</td><td>988</td></tr>
<tr><td>Jaws (75) 30(1) [0 | 4 | 17]</td><td>922</td></tr>
<tr><td>Return Of The Jedi (83) 20(2) [0 | 6 | 17]</td><td>913</td></tr>
<tr><td>Wattstax: The Living Word (73) 28(1) [0 | 6 | 17]</td><td>886</td></tr>
<tr><td>Candy (69) 49(2) [0 | 0 | 16]</td><td>881</td></tr>
<tr><td>Chitty Chitty Bang Bang (68) 58(2) [0 | 0 | 28]</td><td>881</td></tr>
<tr><td>Streets Of Fire (84) 32(2) [0 | 6 | 21]</td><td>871</td></tr>
<tr><td>Tom Jones (64) 38(1) [0 | 3 | 23]</td><td>857</td></tr>
<tr><td>Colors (88) 31(2) [0 | 5 | 19]</td><td>822</td></tr>
<tr><td>The Karate Kid Part II (86) 30(2) [0 | 9 | 17]</td><td>808</td></tr>
<tr><td>The Wiz (78) 40(1) [0 | 1 | 17]</td><td>795</td></tr>
<tr><td>Out Of Africa (86) 38(2) [0 | 2 | 22]</td><td>773</td></tr>
<tr><td>Rain Man (89) 31(2) [0 | 5 | 16]</td><td>760</td></tr>
<tr><td>Times Square (80) 37(2) [0 | 4 | 17]</td><td>751</td></tr>
<tr><td>The Big Chill: More Songs From (84) 85(1) [0 | 0 | 49]</td><td>740</td></tr>
<tr><td>Coal Miner's Daughter (80) 40(1) [0 | 1 | 20]</td><td>733</td></tr>
<tr><td>An Officer And A Gentleman (82) 38(2) [0 | 3 | 23]</td><td>732</td></tr>
<tr><td>American Hot Wax (78) 31(1) [0 | 4 | 11]</td><td>718</td></tr>
<tr><td>Buster (88) 54(2) [0 | 0 | 23]</td><td>717</td></tr>
<tr><td>Midnight Express (78) 59(1) [0 | 0 | 26]</td><td>715</td></tr>
<tr><td>Teachers (84) 34(3) [0 | 4 | 16]</td><td>714</td></tr>
<tr><td>Finian's Rainbow (68) 90(1) [0 | 0 | 26]</td><td>680</td></tr>
<tr><td>Sweet Charity (69) 72(2) [0 | 0 | 22]</td><td>673</td></tr>
<tr><td>The Lord Of The Rings (78) 39(1) [0 | 2 | 12]</td><td>664</td></tr>
<tr><td>An American Tail (87) 42(2) [0 | 0 | 19]</td><td>629</td></tr>
<tr><td>Grand Prix (67) 76(3) [0 | 0 | 28]</td><td>624</td></tr>
<tr><td>New York, New York (77) 50(3) [0 | 0 | 14]</td><td>579</td></tr>
<tr><td>The Spy Who Loved Me (77) 40(2) [0 | 2 | 16]</td><td>565</td></tr>
<tr><td>Fast Times At Ridgemont High (82) 54(3) [0 | 0 | 20]</td><td>559</td></tr>
<tr><td>Lost Horizon (73) 58(1) [0 | 0 | 21]</td><td>550</td></tr>
<tr><td>The Great Escape (63) 50(1) [0 | 0 | 21]</td><td>542</td></tr>
<tr><td>Superman - The Movie (79) 44(1) [0 | 0 | 13]</td><td>533</td></tr>
<tr><td>A View To A Kill (85) 38(2) [0 | 4 | 15]</td><td>533</td></tr>
<tr><td>Running Scared (86) 43(2) [0 | 0 | 15]</td><td>529</td></tr>
<tr><td>Batman Original Motion Picture Score (89) 30(1) [0 | 4 | 12]</td><td>528</td></tr>
<tr><td>Star! (68) 98(1) [0 | 0 | 20]</td><td>506</td></tr>
<tr><td>Mad Max Beyond Thunderdome (85) 39(2) [0 | 2 | 13]</td><td>503</td></tr>
</table>

▶ Highest Peak [Top10s | Top40s | Total] Title (Yr) Peak(Wk) [T10 Wk | T40Wk | TotalWk]	Score
SOUNDTRACK-MOVIE ▶ *Continued*	
Little Shop Of Horrors (87) 47(2) [0|0|17]	502
Working Girl (89) 45(1) [0|0|14]	501
Cat People (82) 47(2) [0|0|14]	461
For Your Eyes Only (81) 84(2) [0|0|19]	460
Star Trek - The Motion Picture (80) 50(1) [0|0|11]	460
The Story Of Star Wars (77) 36(2) [0|2|10]	457
Man Of La Mancha (72) 76(1) [0|0|17]	446
All This And World War II (76) 48(2) [0|0|9]	438
Hair (79) 65(2) [0|0|16]	428
True Grit (69) 77(2) [0|0|12]	419
Indiana Jones And The Temple Of Doom (John Williams) (84) 42(2) [0|0|10]	416
Krush Groove (85) 79(2) [0|0|20]	411
Berry Gordy's The Last Dragon (85) 58(2) [0|0|15]	404
Animal House (78) 71(1) [0|0|18]	399
Jewel Of The Nile (85) 55(2) [0|0|17]	395
Perfect (85) 45(2) [0|0|12]	390
School Daze (88) 81(2) [0|0|17]	374
Robin And The 7 Hoods (64) 56(1) [0|0|14]	374
Breakin' 2 Electric Boogaloo (85) 52(2) [0|0|13]	363
Say Anything (89) 62(2) [0|0|14]	361
Hawaii (66) 85(1) [0|0|16]	360
A Fistful Of Dollars (67) 107(1) [0|0|28]	359
Every Which Way But Loose (79) 78(3) [0|0|15]	359
The Best Little Whorehouse In Texas (82) 63(1) [0|0|15]	357
Nashville (75) 80(1) [0|0|13]	348
Shaft's Big Score! (72) 100(1) [0|0|16]	346
Do The Right Thing (89) 68(2) [0|0|14]	343
9 1/2 Weeks (86) 59(2) [0|0|15]	339
9 To 5 (80) 77(1) [0|0|15]	338
The Great Muppet Caper (81) 66(2) [0|0|11]	332
Sweet Sweetback's Baadasssss Song (71) 139(1) [0|0|19]	329
Diamonds Are Forever (72) 74(2) [0|0|12]	327
Some Kind Of Wonderful (87) 57(2) [0|0|13]	310
The Deep (77) 70(1) [0|0|10]	308
The Great Gatsby (74) 85(1) [0|0|16]	307
About Last Night... (86) 72(1) [0|0|14]	307
Iron Eagle (86) 54(2) [0|0|11]	303
Caddyshack (80) 78(2) [0|0|12]	303
Absolute Beginners (86) 62(2) [0|0|13]	295
The Sandpiper (65) 89(1) [0|0|15]	294
On Her Majesty's Secret Service (70) 103(1) [0|0|13]	291
The Buddy Holly Story (78) 86(2) [0|0|13]	290
Grease 2 (82) 71(2) [0|0|13]	260
Platoon (87) 75(2) [0|0|13]	258
The Bible (66) 102(1) [0|0|13]	254
The Color Purple (86) 79(2) [0|0|13]	254
The Color Of Money (86) 81(2) [0|0|15]	251
M*A*S*H (70) 120(1) [0|0|16]	250
The Greatest Story Ever Told (65) 82(1) [0|0|13]	249
Bright Lights, Big City (88) 67(2) [0|0|11]	247
Airport (70) 104(1) [0|0|19]	247
Manhattan (79) 94(1) [0|0|11]	246
Star Trek II: The Wrath Of Khan (82) 61(2) [0|0|9]	243
The Magic Christian (70) 106(1) [0|0|12]	243
Irma La Douce (63) 69(1) [0|0|11]	242
Barry Lyndon (76) 132(1) [0|0|15]	241
More American Graffiti (Soundtrack) (79) 84(2) [0|0|12]	240
Smokey And The Bandit 2 (80) 103(2) [0|0|11]	238
The Strawberry Statement (70) 91(1) [0|0|9]	232
That's Entertainment (74) 128(1) [0|0|14]	231
Road House (89) 67(2) [0|0|10]	220
American Anthem (86) 91(3) [0|0|12]	218
A Chorus Line-The Movie (85) 77(2) [0|0|12]	217
Soul To Soul (71) 112(1) [0|0|10]	215
Tequila Sunrise (89) 101(1) [0|0|13]	214
Scrooge (70) 95(2) [0|0|8]	212
"10" (80) 80(1) [0|0|9]	212
Country (84) 120(2) [0|0|15]	207
The Yellow Rolls-Royce (65) 82(1) [0|0|10]	200
Light Of Day (87) 82(2) [0|0|10]	192
Song Of Norway (71) 95(2) [0|0|8]	191
Dream A Little Dream (89) 94(2) [0|0|10]	191
Metropolis (84) 110(2) [0|0|13]	187
Popeye (80) 115(1) [0|0|10]	184
Down And Out In Beverly Hills (86) 68(2) [0|0|7]	183
It's A Mad, Mad, Mad, Mad World (63) 101(1) [0|0|11]	183
Cotton Club (85) 93(1) [0|0|10]	180
Cleopatra Jones (73) 109(2) [0|0|10]	179
She's Having A Baby (88) 92(1) [0|0|8]	175
Star Trek III - The Search For Spock (84) 82(2) [0|0|8]	175
Patton (71) 117(2) [0|0|8]	174
Foul Play (78) 102(2) [0|0|7]	169
Shocker (89) 97(2) [0|0|12]	168
Young Frankenstein (75) 128(3) [0|0|8]	166
Electric Dreams (84) 94(2) [0|0|9]	164
Weird Science (85) 105(2) [0|0|11]	162
The Karate Kid (84) 114(2) [0|0|12]	159
Scrooged (88) 93(1) [0|0|9]	159
Pete's Dragon (77) 131(2) [0|0|10]	157
Hiding Out (87) 146(2) [0|0|13]	156
The Trial Of Billy Jack (74) 130(1) [0|0|8]	155
The Warriors (79) 125(1) [0|0|8]	154
Eyes Of Laura Mars (78) 124(2) [0|0|9]	152
King Kong (77) 123(2) [0|0|8]	149
Terms Of Endearment (84) 111(1) [0|0|10]	147
Alien (79) 113(2) [0|0|8]	147
The Idolmaker (80) 130(1) [0|0|9]	145
Let The Good Times Roll (73) 117(1) [0|0|9]	145
The Cardinal (64) 100(1) [0|0|9]	143
The Mission (87) 132(1) [0|0|13]	143
Superman II (81) 133(1) [0|0|9]	142
Z (70) 128(2) [0|0|8]	137
Paper Moon (73) 154(1) [0|0|12]	136
The Big Easy (87) 107(2) [0|0|9]	134
It's My Turn (80) 137(2) [0|0|11]	134
Darling Lili (70) 113(2) [0|0|7]	134
Roadie (80) 125(2) [0|0|8]	133
Looking For Mr. Goodbar (77) 134(2) [0|0|8]	132
Billy Jack (71) 135(1) [0|0|7]	131
The Aristocats (71) 137(2) [0|0|10]	131
Disorderlies (87) 99(2) [0|0|8]	131
Shaft In Africa (73) 147(1) [0|0|9]	130
Any Which Way You Can (81) 141(1) [0|0|9]	123
On Golden Pond (82) 147(1) [0|0|11]	118
Ragtime (82) 134(2) [0|0|9]	118
Over The Top (87) 120(2) [0|0|8]	117
Mary Poppins(2) (73) 141(1) [0|0|8]	114
1776 (72) 163(1) [0|0|11]	112
Into The Night (85) 118(2) [0|0|8]	112
Interlude (68) 136(1) [0|0|5]	110
Porky's Revenge (85) 122(2) [0|0|8]	110
Tootsie (83) 144(3) [0|0|12]	109
2001: A Space Odyssey (Volume Two) (70) 147(1) [0|0|7]	108
Twins (89) 162(3) [0|0|12]	108
Urban Cowboy II (81) 134(1) [0|0|6]	107
The Last Emperor (88) 152(1) [0|0|10]	107
Cobra (86) 100(2) [0|0|6]	105
Salsa (88) 112(2) [0|0|6]	105
Rock 'N' Roll High School (79) 118(2) [0|0|6]	104
Beat Street II (84) 137(2) [0|0|9]	104
The Flamingo Kid (85) 130(2) [0|0|8]	101
Lisztomania (75) 145(2) [0|0|6]	101
Bronco Billy (80) 123(1) [0|0|6]	100
In The Heat Of The Night (67) 153(1) [0|0|11]	99.1
Hairspray (88) 114(1) [0|0|6]	95.5
Soul Man (86) 138(2) [0|0|9]	93.5
Lilies Of The Field (64) 110(1) [0|0|6]	92.6
The Happiest Millionaire (68) 166(1) [0|0|9]	92.2
The Secret Of My Success (87) 131(2) [0|0|8]	91.6
Who's Afraid Of Virginia Woolf? (66) 119(1) [0|0|5]	90.4
Bless The Beasts & Children (71) 176(1) [0|0|10]	89.5
Beetlejuice (88) 118(1) [0|0|6]	88.5
Rollerball (75) 156(1) [0|0|6]	87.8
Our Man Flint (66) 118(2) [0|0|5]	86.4
The Golden Child (87) 126(2) [0|0|7]	84.8
Gremlins (84) 143(1) [0|0|7]	77.8
Soup For One (82) 168(1) [0|0|12]	77.1
R.P.M. (70) 148(2) [0|0|6]	76.6
The Greatest (77) 166(2) [0|0|8]	74.1
One Flew Over The Cuckoo's Nest (76) 158(2) [0|0|7]	73.8
Lord Jim (65) 123(1) [0|0|5]	71.8
Rocky II (79) 147(1) [0|0|5]	71.6
Dragnet (87) 137(2) [0|0|6]	70.8
Summer Lovers (82) 152(1) [0|0|7]	65.7
The Lion In Winter (69) 182(1) [0|0|7]	65.7
Octopussy (83) 137(1) [0|0|5]	63.3
Oliver & Company (89) 170(1) [0|0|7]	63.3
Sharky's Machine (82) 171(1) [0|0|8]	62.2
The Love Machine (71) 172(1) [0|0|6]	62.0
Quest For Fire (82) 154(2) [0|0|6]	61.6
Wattstax 2: The Living Word (73) 157(2) [0|0|5]	60.4
Goodbye, Mr. Chips (69) 164(1) [0|0|5]	59.6
How To Succeed In Business Without Really Trying (67) 146(1) [0|0|4]	59.5
All The Right Moves (83) 165(1) [0|0|7]	58.2
Quicksilver (86) 140(2) [0|0|5]	57.7
Empire Of The Sun (88) 150(2) [0|0|5]	57.2
Billy Jack(2) (74) 167(1) [0|0|5]	55.3
Party Party (83) 169(4) [0|0|6]	52.3
The Thomas Crown Affair (68) 182(1) [0|0|6]	52.2
Tron (82) 135(2) [0|0|5]	52.0
Bull Durham (88) 157(1) [0|0|6]	51.2
Moonraker (79) 159(1) [0|0|4]	51.0
Barbarella (68) 183(1) [0|0|5]	50.6
Ice Castles (79) 174(1) [0|0|5]	50.2
The King Of Comedy (83) 162(1) [0|0|6]	49.4
$ (Dollars) (72) 173(2) [0|0|5]	48.7
Those Glorious MGM Musicals: Singin' In The Rain/Easter Parade (73) 185(1) [0|0|7]	48.1
Meatballs (79) 170(1) [0|0|5]	46.7
The Pirate Movie (82) 166(2) [0|0|6]	46.5
The Towering Inferno (75) 158(1) [0|0|3]	45.5
Live For Life (68) 188(3) [0|0|7]	44.7
Youngblood (86) 166(2) [0|0|6]	43.7
Poltergeist (82) 168(1) [0|0|5]	41.1

► Highest Peak [Top10s|Top40s|Total]
Title (Yr) Peak(Wk) [T10 Wk|T40Wk|TotalWk] — Score

SOUNDTRACK-MOVIE ► *Continued*

Conan The Barbarian (82) 162(2) [0|0|5] — 39.9
Those Glorious MGM Musicals: Show Boat/ Annie Get Your Gun (73) 184(1) [0|0|6] — 39.4
The Victors (64) 145(1) [0|0|3] — 39.1
Bill & Ted's Excellent Adventure (89) 170(2) [0|0|4] — 38.9
Tap (89) 166(2) [0|0|4] — 38.8
The Empire Strikes Back/The Adventures Of Luke Skywalker (80) 178(2) [0|0|4] — 36.5
2010 (85) 173(2) [0|0|5] — 36.0
Christine (84) 177(1) [0|0|5] — 35.6
The Carpetbaggers (64) 141(1) [0|0|3] — 35.6
Jumpin' Jack Flash (86) 159(2) [0|0|4] — 35.3
Fletch (85) 160(1) [0|0|4] — 35.2
Becket (64) 147(2) [0|0|3] — 35.1
1969 (88) 186(1) [0|0|6] — 34.0
The 7th Dawn (64) 148(1) [0|0|3] — 33.7
The Night The Lights Went Out In Georgia (81) 189(1) [0|0|5] — 32.7
Bird (88) 169(1) [0|0|3] — 29.3
The Ipcress File (65) 133(1) [0|0|2] — 29.0
Victor/Victoria (82) 174(2) [0|0|4] — 28.8
Guess Who's Coming To Dinner (68) 177(1) [0|0|3] — 28.4
Hell's Angels '69 (69) 184(1) [0|0|3] — 28.3
Lenny (75) 180(1) [0|0|3] — 28.2
Gandhi (83) 168(1) [0|0|3] — 27.5
Hurry Sundown (67) 153(1) [0|0|2] — 27.2
Lethal Weapon 2 (89) 164(2) [0|0|3] — 27.0
Superman III (83) 163(1) [0|0|3] — 26.5
D.C. Cab (84) 181(1) [0|0|4] — 26.3
Hang 'Em High (68) 193(1) [0|0|4] — 25.4
Thief Of Hearts (84) 179(1) [0|0|4] — 25.4
Shenandoah (65) 147(1) [0|0|2] — 24.8
Hells Angels On Wheels (67) 165(2) [0|0|2] — 23.4
War And Peace (68) 189(2) [0|0|3] — 23.2
Topkapi (65) 150(2) [0|0|2] — 23.1
The Fall Of The Roman Empire (64) 147(1) [0|0|2] — 22.9
Ryan's Daughter (70) 199(2) [0|0|4] — 22.3
Cocoon (85) 188(1) [0|0|4] — 21.0
Up The Creek (84) 185(1) [0|0|3] — 19.9
A Fine Mess (86) 183(1) [0|0|3] — 19.6
Planet Of The Apes (68) 195(1) [0|0|3] — 18.4
The Godfather, Part II (75) 184(1) [0|0|2] — 18.3
Heartbreak Hotel (88) 176(2) [0|0|2] — 17.6
Mame (74) 196(1) [0|0|3] — 17.6
The Wild Bunch (69) 192(2) [0|0|2] — 16.0
Somewhere In Time (80) 187(2) [0|0|2] — 15.7
Nothing In Common (86) 190(2) [0|0|3] — 15.7
Coming To America (88) 177(1) [0|0|2] — 15.5
For Love Of Ivy (68) 192(1) [0|0|2] — 14.9
Married To The Mob (88) 197(2) [0|0|3] — 13.7
Round Midnight (87) 196(1) [0|0|3] — 13.6
Pennies From Heaven (82) 188(1) [0|0|2] — 13.0
The Odd Couple (68) 190(1) [0|0|2] — 12.8
Back To The Beach (87) 188(1) [0|0|2] — 11.8
Electra Glide In Blue (73) 194(1) [0|0|2] — 11.8
The Sterile Cuckoo (70) 200(2) [0|0|2] — 10.7
Come Back Charleston Blue (72) 198(2) [0|0|2] — 10.4
Phantom Of The Paradise (75) 194(1) [0|0|1] — 7.2
Sing (89) 196(1) [0|0|1] — 4.7
Blind Date (87) 198(1) [0|0|1] — 4.4

SOUNDTRACK-TV ► Pk:1 [2|7|25] — 18674

Miami Vice (85) 1(11) [18|22|34] — 6180
All In The Family (71) 8(1) [3|12|22] — 2564
The Sesame Street Book & Record (70) 23(1) [0|9|54] — 2333
Dark Shadows (The Score) (69) 18(2) [0|8|19] — 1589
Sunshine (73) 34(1) [0|7|23] — 1135
Here's Johnny--Magic Moments From The Tonight Show (74) 30(2) [0|3|11] — 652
NBC's Saturday Night Live (76) 38(2) [0|3|13] — 606
Mickey Mouse Club (75) 51(2) [0|0|13] — 470
Moonlighting (87) 50(2) [0|0|14] — 442
Laugh-In (68) 105(1) [0|0|17] — 410
Laugh-In '69 (69) 88(2) [0|0|10] — 322
Sesame Street 2 (71) 78(1) [0|0|10] — 290
Mickie Finn's - America's No.1 Speakeasy (66) 120(1) [0|0|15] — 238
The Dukes Of Hazzard (82) 93(2) [0|0|14] — 234
Miami Vice II (86) 82(1) [0|0|12] — 211
The Music Of Cosmos (81) 136(2) [0|0|13] — 201
Batman (66) 112(1) [0|0|8] — 137
All In The Family - 2nd Album (72) 129(1) [0|0|8] — 132
Shogun (80) 115(2) [0|0|6] — 122
Music From The Bill Cosby Show-- A House Full Of Love (86) 125(1) [0|0|7] — 103
Battlestar Galacticia (78) 144(1) [0|0|6] — 86.2
Beauty & The Beast: Of Love And Hope (89) 157(1) [0|0|10] — 85.1
The Muppet Show (78) 153(2) [0|0|5] — 60.5
The Waltons' Christmas Album (74) 125(1) [0|0|2] — 47.6
The Stars Of Hee Haw (70) 196(2) [0|0|4] — 24.4

Joe SOUTH ► 1305 Pk:60 [0|0|3] — 1131

Don't It Make You Want To Go Home? (70) 60(2) [0|0|23] — 655
Introspect (69) 117(1) [0|0|14] — 283
Joe South's Greatest Hits (70) 125(1) [0|0|11] — 193

J.D. SOUTHER ► 1344 Pk:41 [0|0|2] — 1051

You're Only Lonely (79)-John David Souther 41(3) [0|0|22] — 773
Black Rose (76)-John David Souther 85(1) [0|0|11] — 278

SOUTHER, HILLMAN, FURAY Band ► 883 Pk:11 [0|2|2] — 2483

The Souther, Hillman, Furay Band (74) 11(1) [0|11|22] — 1884
Trouble In Paradise (75) 39(1) [0|1|11] — 599

SOUTHERN COMFORT ► 3462 Pk:196 [0|0|1] — 13

Frog City (71) 196(1) [0|0|2] — 13.3

SOUTHSIDE JOHNNY & The ASBURY JUKES ► 907 Pk:48 [0|0|10] — 2348

The Jukes (79) 48(1) [0|0|14] — 578
Love Is A Sacrifice (80) 67(2) [0|0|15] — 452
Hearts Of Stone (78) 112(1) [0|0|20] — 414
Reach Up And Touch The Sky (81) 80(4) [0|0|12] — 364
This Time It's For Real (77) 85(1) [0|0|9] — 246
I Don't Want To Go Home (76) 125(2) [0|0|9] — 142
In The Heat (84)-Southside Johnny & The Jukes 164(2) [0|0|8] — 66.7
Trash It Up (83)-Southside Johnny & The Jukes 154(2) [0|0|6] — 59.3
At Least We Got Shoes (86)-Southside Johnny & The Jukes 189(1) [0|0|4] — 20.7
Slow Dance (88)-Southside Johnny 198(1) [0|0|1] — 4.7

Red SOVINE ► 2600 Pk:119 [0|0|1] — 134

Teddy Bear (76) 119(2) [0|0|6] — 134

SPANDAU BALLET ► 985 Pk:19 [0|1|2] — 1980

True (83) 19(1) [0|8|37] — 1516
Parade (84) 50(3) [0|0|16] — 464

SPANKY And OUR GANG ► 1034 Pk:56 [0|0|4] — 1816

Like To Get To Know You (68) 56(2) [0|0|25] — 819
Spanky's Greatest Hit(s) (69) 91(1) [0|0|17] — 418
Spanky And Our Gang (67) 77(2) [0|0|15] — 375
Anything You Choose/Without Rhyme Or Reason (69) 101(1) [0|0|7] — 204

SPARKS ► 1353 Pk:63 [0|0|6] — 1038

Propaganda (75) 63(1) [0|0|13] — 404
Kimono My House (74) 101(1) [0|0|14] — 264
In Outer Space (83) 88(1) [0|0|17] — 246
Indiscreet (75) 169(1) [0|0|6] — 60.7
Angst In My Pants (82) 173(2) [0|0|6] — 45.7
Whomp That Sucker (81) 182(2) [0|0|2] — 18.3

SPECIAL ED ► 1699 Pk:73 [0|0|1] — 583

Youngest In Charge (89) 73(1) [0|0|28] — 583

The SPECIALS ► 1637 Pk:84 [0|0|2] — 632

The Specials (80) 84(1) [0|0|21] — 516
More Specials (80) 98(1) [0|0|5] — 116

Paul SPEER ► 2827 Pk:125 [0|0|1] — 91

Natural States (88)-David Lanz & Paul Speer [A] 125(1) [0|0|12] — 91.0

Judson SPENCE ► 2815 Pk:168 [0|0|1] — 94

Judson Spence (88) 168(4) [0|0|13] — 94.3

Tracie SPENCER ► 2289 Pk:146 [0|0|1] — 220

Tracie Spencer (88) 146(1) [0|0|21] — 220

Jimmie SPHEERIS ► 2727 Pk:135 [0|0|1] — 109

The Dragon Is Dancing (75) 135(1) [0|0|6] — 109

SPIDER ► 2458 Pk:130 [0|0|2] — 172

Spider (80) 130(1) [0|0|10] — 156
Between The Lines (81) 185(1) [0|0|2] — 16.3

SPIDERS FROM MARS ► 3498 Pk:197 [0|0|1] — 12

Spiders From Mars (76) 197(1) [0|0|2] — 11.5

SPINAL TAP ► 2646 Pk:121 [0|0|1] — 124

This Is Spinal Tap (Soundtrack) (84) 121(2) [0|0|10] — 124

SPINNERS ► 209 Pk:8 [2|8|17] — 16544

Pick Of The Litter (75) 8(3) [5|16|26] — 3195
Mighty Love (74) 16(1) [0|14|35] — 2520
New And Improved (74) 9(1) [2|14|26] — 2351
Happiness Is Being With The Spinners (76) 25(2) [0|9|30] — 1974
Spinners (73) 14(1) [0|11|28] — 1782
Spinners Live! (75) 20(2) [0|9|21] — 1636
Dancin' And Lovin' (80) 32(1) [0|4|20] — 910
Yesterday, Today & Tomorrow (77) 26(1) [0|4|13] — 695
Spinners/8 (77) 57(1) [0|0|13] — 480
Love Trippin' (80) 53(2) [0|0|13] — 439
The Best Of The Spinners(2) (78) 115(2) [0|0|9] — 180
The Best Of The Spinners (73) 124(1) [0|0|10] — 151
Labor Of Love (81) 128(2) [0|0|6] — 110
From Here To Eternally (79) 165(1) [0|0|4] — 44.4
Grand Slam (83) 167(2) [0|0|6] — 43.8
Can't Shake This Feelin' (82) 196(2) [0|0|4] — 19.7
2nd Time Around (70) 199(2) [0|0|2] — 11.9

SPIRAL STARECASE ► 1769 Pk:79 [0|0|1] — 503

More Today Than Yesterday (69) 79(1) [0|0|16] — 503

SPIRIT ► 567 Pk:22 [0|2|9] — 5128

The Family That Plays Together (69) 22(2) [0|12|28] — 2156
Spirit (68) 31(1) [0|3|32] — 1101
Clear Spirit (69) 55(2) [0|0|15] — 702
Twelve Dreams Of Dr. Sardonicus (70) 63(1) [0|0|14] — 417
Feedback (72) 63(1) [0|0|14] — 372
The Best Of Spirit (73) 119(1) [0|0|12] — 213

▶ Highest Peak [Top10s | Top40s | Total] Title (Yr) Peak(Wk) [T10 Wk | T40Wk | TotalWk]	Score
SPIRIT ▶ *Continued*	
Spirit Of '76 (75) 147(2) [0|0|9]	106
Farther Along (76) 179(1) [0|0|4]	37.1
Spirit(2) (73) 191(1) [0|0|4]	22.6
SPLINTER ▶ 1995 Pk:81 [0|0|1]	**352**
The Place I Love (74) 81(1) [0|0|14]	352
SPLIT ENZ ▶ 871 Pk:40 [0|1|4]	**2526**
True Colours (80) 40(2) [0|2|25]	1146
Waiata (81) 45(2) [0|0|19]	824
Time And Tide (82) 58(1) [0|0|20]	445
Conflicting Emotions (84) 137(1) [0|0|10]	111
SPOOKY TOOTH ▶ 892 Pk:44 [0|0|8]	**2418**
Spooky Two (69) 44(2) [0|0|19]	907
The Last Puff (70) 84(1) [0|0|13]	343
You Broke My Heart So I Busted Your Jaw (73) 84(1) [0|0|14]	335
Ceremony (70) 92(1) [0|0|14]	327
Witness (73) 99(1) [0|0|10]	216
The Mirror (74) 130(1) [0|0|8]	139
Tobacco Road (71) 152(1) [0|0|7]	107
That Was Only Yesterday (76)-Gary Wright And Spooky Tooth 172(2) [0|0|4]	43.5
The SPORTS ▶ 3481 Pk:194 [0|0|1]	**12**
Don't Throw Stones (79) 194(2) [0|0|2]	12.3
Dusty SPRINGFIELD ▶ 1228 Pk:62 [0|0|7]	**1283**
Dusty In Memphis (69) 99(2) [0|0|14]	304
Stay Awhile/I Only Want To Be With You (64) 62(1) [0|0|13]	289
A Brand New Me (70) 107(2) [0|0|13]	257
You Don't Have To Say You Love Me (66) 77(1) [0|0|10]	233
The Look Of Love (67) 135(1) [0|0|7]	116
Dusty Springfield's Golden Hits (66) 137(1) [0|0|3]	46.6
Dusty (64) 136(1) [0|0|3]	37.4
Rick SPRINGFIELD ▶ 184 Pk:2 [2|6|9]	**18828**
Working Class Dog (81) 7(2) [5|38|73]	6754
Success Hasn't Spoiled Me Yet (82) 2(3) [12|15|35]	3922
Living In Oz (83) 12(3) [0|24|57]	3368
Hard To Hold (Soundtrack) (84) 16(3) [0|9|36]	1538
Tao (85) 21(2) [0|11|27]	1524
Beginnings (72) 35(2) [0|4|17]	828
Rock Of Life (88) 55(1) [0|0|16]	545
Beautiful Feelings (84) 78(2) [0|0|13]	275
Wait For Night (82) 159(2) [0|0|8]	74.1
Bruce SPRINGSTEEN ▶ 27 Pk:1 [7|7|9]	**54719**
Born In The U.S.A. (84) 1(7) [84|96|139]	23827
The River (80) 1(4) [8|22|107]	6583
Born To Run (75) 3(2) [11|12|110]	5889
Tunnel Of Love (87) 1(1) [10|33|45]	5349
Darkness On The Edge Of Town (78) 5(3) [8|17|97]	4951
Bruce Springsteen & The E Street Band Live 1975-1985 (86) 1(7) [11|15|26]	3897
Nebraska (82) 3(4) [7|11|29]	2563
Greetings From Asbury Park, N.J. (75) 60(1) [0|0|43]	845
The Wild, The Innocent And The E Street Shuffle (75) 59(1) [0|0|34]	814
SPYRO GYRA ▶ 365 Pk:19 [0|2|13]	**9067**
Morning Dance (79) 27(3) [0|11|41]	2545
Catching The Sun (80) 19(1) [0|8|29]	1533
Carnaval (80) 49(1) [0|0|30]	959
Freetime (81) 41(2) [0|0|27]	930
Incognito (82) 46(2) [0|0|24]	669
Access All Areas (84) 59(1) [0|0|19]	531
Alternating Currents (85) 66(2) [0|0|23]	457
Breakout (86) 71(1) [0|0|19]	421

▶ Highest Peak [Top10s | Top40s | Total] Title (Yr) Peak(Wk) [T10 Wk | T40Wk | TotalWk]	Score
City Kids (83) 66(1) [0|0|16]	363
Spyro Gyra (78) 99(2) [0|0|12]	262
Stories Without Words (87) 84(1) [0|0|9]	176
Rites Of Summer (88) 104(2) [0|0|8]	133
Point Of View (89) 120(2) [0|0|6]	87.8
SPYS ▶ 2731 Pk:138 [0|0|1]	**109**
S.P.Y.S. (82) 138(3) [0|0|10]	109
SQUEEZE ▶ 586 Pk:32 [0|2|7]	**4918**
Babylon And On (87) 36(2) [0|7|29]	1284
East Side Story (81) 44(1) [0|0|25]	1091
Sweets From A Stranger (82) 32(2) [0|4|30]	822
Argybargy (80) 71(1) [0|0|24]	584
Singles 45's And Under (83) 47(3) [0|0|21]	543
Cosi Fan Tutti Frutti (85) 57(2) [0|0|20]	447
Frank (89) 113(3) [0|0|10]	147
Billy SQUIER ▶ 224 Pk:5 [2|3|6]	**15757**
Don't Say No (81) 5(3) [7|38|111]	8125
Emotions In Motion (82) 5(8) [9|29|50]	4779
Signs Of Life (84) 11(4) [0|14|29]	2034
Hear & Now (89) 64(1) [0|0|17]	394
Enough Is Enough (86) 61(2) [0|0|16]	322
The Tale Of The Tape (80) 169(1) [0|0|12]	103
Chris SQUIRE ▶ 1940 Pk:69 [0|0|1]	**380**
Fish Out Of Water (76) 69(2) [0|0|12]	380
SRC ▶ 2262 Pk:134 [0|0|2]	**228**
Milestones (69) 134(1) [0|0|9]	161
SRC (68) 147(2) [0|0|4]	67.2
STACEY Q ▶ 1479 Pk:59 [0|0|2]	**848**
Better Than Heaven (86) 59(2) [0|0|39]	649
Hard Machine (88) 115(1) [0|0|11]	199
STACKRIDGE ▶ 3063 Pk:191 [0|0|1]	**57**
Pinafore Days (74) 191(1) [0|0|9]	57.5
Jim STAFFORD ▶ 1406 Pk:55 [0|0|1]	**961**
Jim Stafford (74) 55(1) [0|0|33]	961
Terry STAFFORD ▶ 2349 Pk:81 [0|0|1]	**199**
Suspicion! (64) 81(1) [0|0|11]	199
STAGE DOLLS ▶ 2473 Pk:118 [0|0|1]	**167**
Stage Dolls (89) 118(1) [0|0|12]	167
STALLION ▶ 3077 Pk:191 [0|0|1]	**56**
Stallion (77) 191(1) [0|0|9]	55.6
STAMPEDERS ▶ 2993 Pk:172 [0|0|1]	**67**
Sweet City Woman (71) 172(1) [0|0|6]	66.8
Joe STAMPLEY ▶ 3392 Pk:170 [0|0|1]	**20**
Hey Joe, Hey Moe (81)-Moe Bandy & Joe Stampley [A] 170(1) [0|0|4]	20.0
The STANDELLS ▶ 1767 Pk:52 [0|0|1]	**505**
Dirty Water (66) 52(2) [0|0|16]	505
STANKY BROWN Group ▶ 2973 Pk:192 [0|0|3]	**69**
Stanky Brown (78) 192(2) [0|0|5]	33.9
Our Pleasure To Serve You (76) 192(2) [0|0|3]	22.2
If The Lights Don't Get You The Helots Will (77) 195(1) [0|0|2]	12.7
Michael STANLEY Band ▶ 968 Pk:64 [0|0|7]	**2047**
Heartland (80) 86(2) [0|0|32]	664
North Coast (81) 79(2) [0|0|15]	414
Cabin Fever (78) 99(1) [0|0|18]	406
You Can't Fight Fashion (83) 64(2) [0|0|17]	399
MSB (82) 136(2) [0|0|6]	76.1
Greatest Hints (79) 148(1) [0|0|5]	61.4
You Break It...You Bought It! (75) 184(1) [0|0|3]	26.0
Paul STANLEY ▶ 1296 Pk:40 [0|1|1]	**1149**
Paul Stanley (78) 40(3) [0|3|18]	1149
Mavis STAPLES ▶ 3288 Pk:188 [0|0|1]	**29**
Only For The Lonely (70) 188(1) [0|0|4]	29.1

▶ Highest Peak [Top10s | Top40s | Total] Title (Yr) Peak(Wk) [T10 Wk | T40Wk | TotalWk]	Score
Pop STAPLES ▶ 3382 Pk:171 [0|0|1]	**21**
Jammed Together (69)-Albert King, Steve Cropper, Pop Staples [A] 171(2) [0|0|5]	20.7
STAPLE SINGERS ▶ 630 Pk:19 [0|2|6]	**4439**
Bealtitude: Respect Yourself (72) 19(1) [0|12|37]	2328
Let's Do It Again (Soundtrack) (75) 20(2) [0|8|18]	1324
Be What You Are (73) 102(1) [0|0|21]	348
The Staple Swingers (71) 117(1) [0|0|11]	199
City In The Sky (74) 125(1) [0|0|9]	169
Pass It On (76)-The Staples 155(2) [0|0|5]	70.1
STARBUCK ▶ 1916 Pk:78 [0|0|2]	**396**
Moonlight Feels Right (76) 78(1) [0|0|14]	376
Rock 'N' Roll Rocket (77) 182(2) [0|0|2]	20.0
STARCASTLE ▶ 1661 Pk:95 [0|0|3]	**610**
Starcastle (76) 95(2) [0|0|15]	333
Fountains Of Light (77) 101(2) [0|0|11]	235
Citadel (77) 156(2) [0|0|3]	42.0
STARGARD ▶ 1434 Pk:26 [0|1|2]	**922**
Stargard (78) 26(1) [0|6|13]	905
Back 2 Back (81) 186(2) [0|0|2]	17.1
STARLAND VOCAL BAND ▶ 979 Pk:20 [0|1|2]	**2006**
Starland Vocal Band (76) 20(2) [0|10|25]	1758
Rear View Mirror (77) 104(2) [0|0|13]	248
STARPOINT ▶ 1178 Pk:60 [0|0|3]	**1392**
Restless (85) 60(3) [0|0|47]	1039
Sensational (87) 95(2) [0|0|14]	244
Keep On It (81) 138(2) [0|0|8]	109
Brenda K. STARR ▶ 1580 Pk:58 [0|0|1]	**700**
Brenda K. Starr (88) 58(1) [0|0|24]	700
Edwin STARR ▶ 1126 Pk:52 [0|0|5]	**1533**
War & Peace (70) 52(2) [0|0|13]	513
25 Miles (69) 73(1) [0|0|13]	452
Clean (79) 80(1) [0|0|14]	345
H.A.P.P.Y. Radio (79) 115(2) [0|0|8]	160
Involved (71) 178(1) [0|0|7]	63.6
Ringo STARR ▶ 329 Pk:2 [2|5|9]	**10520**
Ringo (73) 2(2) [8|19|37]	4551
Goodnight Vienna (74) 8(2) [5|12|25]	2581
Sentimental Journey (70) 22(1) [0|6|14]	955
Ringo's Rotogravure (76) 28(3) [0|6|9]	798
Blast From Your Past (75) 30(2) [0|5|11]	762
Beaucoups of Blues (70) 65(1) [0|0|15]	444
Stop And Smell The Roses (81) 98(1) [0|0|12]	251
Bad Boy (78) 129(2) [0|0|6]	106
Ringo The 4th (77) 163(1) [0|0|6]	73.4
STARS ON ▶ 898 Pk:9 [1|1|3]	**2396**
Stars On Long Play (81) 9(4) [5|8|24]	2230
Stars On Long Play II (81) 120(3) [0|0|6]	116
Stars On Long Play III (82) 163(2) [0|0|6]	50.5
STARZ ▶ 1693 Pk:89 [0|0|3]	**589**
Starz (76) 123(2) [0|0|13]	213
Violation (77) 89(1) [0|0|8]	211
Attention Shoppers! (78) 105(1) [0|0|9]	166
STATLER BROTHERS ▶ 1271 Pk:103 [0|0|13]	**1196**
The Best Of The Statler Brothers (75) 121(2) [0|0|20]	348
Years Ago (81) 103(1) [0|0|9]	201
Bed Of Rose's (71) 126(1) [0|0|11]	171
The Best Of The Statler Bros. Rides Again, Vol. II (80) 153(2) [0|0|11]	130
Entertainers...On And Off The Record (78) 155(1) [0|0|9]	111
Flowers On The Wall (66) 125(2) [0|0|3]	49.5
10th Anniversary (80) 169(1) [0|0|5]	45.6

▶ **Highest Peak [Top10s|Top40s|Total]**
Title (Yr) Peak(Wk) [T10 Wk|T40Wk|TotalWk] — **Score**

STATLER BROTHERS ▶ *Continued*

The Statler Brothers Christmas Card (78) 183(3) [0|0|4] — 33.6
Atlanta Blue (84) 177(2) [0|0|4] — 28.8
Today (83) 193(1) [0|0|5] — 24.8
Pictures Of Moments To Remember (71) 181(1) [0|0|2] — 19.5
The Originals (79) 183(2) [0|0|2] — 18.9
Four For The Show (86) 183(2) [0|0|2] — 13.7

Candi STATON ▶ 1890 Pk:129 [0|0|3] — 413

Young Hearts Run Free (76) 129(1) [0|0|14] — 281
Chance (79) 129(1) [0|0|6] — 117
Stand By Your Man (71) 188(1) [0|0|2] — 14.7

STATUS QUO ▶ 2812 Pk:148 [0|0|1] — 95

Status Quo (76) 148(2) [0|0|7] — 94.5

STEADY B ▶ 2964 Pk:149 [0|0|2] — 70

What's My Name (87) 149(2) [0|0|7] — 64.9
Let The Hustlers Play (88) 193(1) [0|0|1] — 5.3

STEALERS WHEEL ▶ 1551 Pk:50 [0|0|2] — 725

Stealers Wheel (73) 50(1) [0|0|22] — 699
Ferguslie Park (74) 181(1) [0|0|3] — 25.6

STEALIN HORSES ▶ 2615 Pk:146 [0|0|1] — 131

Stealin Horses (88) 146(2) [0|0|12] — 131

STEAM ▶ 2032 Pk:84 [0|0|1] — 335

Steam (70) 84(2) [0|0|13] — 335

STEEL BREEZE ▶ 1562 Pk:50 [0|0|1] — 719

Steel Breeze (82) 50(4) [0|0|28] — 719

STEELEYE SPAN ▶ 2817 Pk:143 [0|0|2] — 93

All Around My Hat (75) 143(1) [0|0|6] — 73.9
Storm Force Ten (78) 191(1) [0|0|3] — 19.4

STEEL PULSE ▶ 2009 Pk:120 [0|0|3] — 347

True Democracy (82) 120(2) [0|0|13] — 154
Earth Crisis (84) 154(1) [0|0|12] — 100
State Of...Emergency (88) 127(2) [0|0|7] — 93.2

STEELY DAN ▶ 117 Pk:3 [3|8|9] — 26790

Aja (77) 3(7) [20|52|60] — 9774
Gaucho (80) 9(3) [6|19|36] — 3629
Pretzel Logic (74) 8(1) [3|19|36] — 3468
Can't Buy A Thrill (72) 17(1) [0|17|59] — 3203
The Royal Scam (76) 15(2) [0|9|29] — 2133
Katy Lied (75) 13(1) [0|9|26] — 1776
Greatest Hits (78) 30(1) [0|9|22] — 1375
Countdown To Ecstasy (73) 35(1) [0|3|34] — 1301
Gold (82) 115(1) [0|0|9] — 131

David STEINBERG ▶ 3159 Pk:182 [0|0|1] — 45

Disguised As A Normal Person (71) 182(1) [0|0|6] — 45.5

Jim STEINMAN ▶ 1602 Pk:63 [0|0|1] — 676

Bad For Good (81) 63(1) [0|0|17] — 676

Van STEPHENSON ▶ 1742 Pk:54 [0|0|1] — 533

Righteous Anger (84) 54(2) [0|0|20] — 533

STEPPENWOLF ▶ 110 Pk:3 [4|8|14] — 27952

The Second (68) 3(1) [14|24|52] — 6505
Steppenwolf (68) 6(3) [7|25|87] — 4857
Steppenwolf 'Live' (70) 7(2) [5|15|53] — 4000
At Your Birthday Party (69) 7(2) [2|11|29] — 2980
Monster (69) 17(2) [0|16|46] — 2957
Steppenwolf Gold/Their Great Hits (71) 24(2) [0|9|36] — 2035
Steppenwolf 7 (70) 19(2) [0|7|17] — 1589
Early Steppenwolf (69) 29(2) [0|6|19] — 1339
Slow Flux (74) 47(2) [0|0|12] — 538
For Ladies Only (71) 54(1) [0|0|11] — 528
Rest In Peace (72) 62(2) [0|0|13] — 431
16 Greatest Hits (73) 152(2) [0|0|9] — 103
Hour Of The Wolf (75) 155(1) [0|0|4] — 56.7

▶ **Highest Peak [Top10s|Top40s|Total]**
Title (Yr) Peak(Wk) [T10 Wk|T40Wk|TotalWk] — **Score**

Rock & Roll Rebels (87)-John Kay & Steppenwolf 171(1) [0|0|4] — 32.9

Cat STEVENS ▶ 57 Pk:1 [7|9|13] — 42184

Teaser And The Firecat (71) 2(1) [17|37|67] — 8980
Tea For The Tillerman (71) 8(3) [6|44|79] — 7879
Catch Bull At Four (72) 1(3) [12|26|48] — 6321
Buddha And The Chocolate Box (74) 2(3) [13|25|36] — 6219
Foreigner (73) 3(1) [6|15|43] — 3640
Cat Stevens Greatest Hits (75) 6(2) [8|12|45] — 3509
Izitso (77) 7(2) [4|12|23] — 2460
Numbers (75) 13(2) [0|13|19] — 1931
Back To Earth (78) 33(1) [0|4|15] — 653
Very Young And Early Songs (72) 94(1) [0|0|10] — 235
Mona Bone Jakon (71) 164(1) [0|0|16] — 171
Matthew & Son/New Masters (71) 173(1) [0|0|12] — 120
Footsteps In The Dark: Greatest Hits Volume 2 (84) 165(3) [0|0|8] — 66.0

Ray STEVENS ▶ 841 Pk:35 [0|1|10] — 2737

Everything Is Beautiful (70) 35(1) [0|3|19] — 937
Gitarzan (69) 57(1) [0|0|13] — 628
Misty (75) 106(2) [0|0|14] — 317
He Thinks He's Ray Stevens (85) 118(2) [0|0|19] — 204
Ray Stevens' Greatest Hits (71) 95(1) [0|0|8] — 197
Shriner's Convention (80) 132(1) [0|0|8] — 120
Boogity Boogity (74) 159(1) [0|0|11] — 117
Ray Stevens...Unreal!!! (70) 141(2) [0|0|8] — 101
Turn Your Radio On (72) 175(1) [0|0|9] — 76.3
The Very Best Of Ray Stevens (75) 173(1) [0|0|4] — 38.9

Steve STEVENS ATOMIC PLAYBOYS ▶ 2509 Pk:119 [0|0|1] — 157

Atomic Playboys (89) 119(1) [0|0|12] — 157

B.W. STEVENSON ▶ 1713 Pk:45 [0|0|1] — 569

My Maria (73) 45(1) [0|0|14] — 569

Stevie B ▶ 1194 Pk:75 [0|0|2] — 1356

In My Eyes (89) 75(1) [0|0|46] — 933
Party Your Body (88) 78(1) [0|0|21] — 424

Al STEWART ▶ 347 Pk:5 [2|4|6] — 9727

Year Of The Cat (76) 5(3) [5|21|48] — 4916
Time Passages (78) 10(1) [1|14|31] — 2841
Modern Times (75) 30(2) [0|3|23] — 964
24 Carrots (80) 37(2) [0|4|13] — 637
Live/Indian Summer (81) 110(2) [0|0|11] — 208
Past, Present And Future (74) 133(2) [0|0|14] — 160

Amii STEWART ▶ 1125 Pk:19 [0|1|1] — 1535

Knock On Wood (79) 19(1) [0|9|23] — 1535

Billy STEWART ▶ 2191 Pk:97 [0|0|2] — 262

I Do Love You (65) 97(2) [0|0|10] — 178
Unbelievable (66) 138(1) [0|0|6] — 83.9

Gary STEWART ▶ 3268 Pk:165 [0|0|1] — 31

Cactus And A Rose (80) 165(1) [0|0|3] — 31.3

Jermaine STEWART ▶ 1186 Pk:32 [0|1|3] — 1373

Frantic Romantic (86) 32(2) [0|5|25] — 939
Say It Again (88) 98(2) [0|0|12] — 218
The Word Is Out (85) 90(2) [0|0|11] — 216

John STEWART ▶ 761 Pk:10 [1|1|7] — 3199

Bombs Away Dream Babies (79) 10(1) [1|14|28] — 2711
Dream Babies Go To Hollywood (80) 85(2) [0|0|10] — 222
Fire In The Wind (77) 126(2) [0|0|8] — 135
Wingless Angels (75) 150(2) [0|0|6] — 82.3
California Bloodlines (69) 193(2) [0|0|3] — 23.1
The Lonesome Picker Rides Again (72) 195(2) [0|0|2] — 12.8
The Phoenix Concerts-Live (74) 195(1) [0|0|2] — 12.7

▶ **Highest Peak [Top10s|Top40s|Total]**
Title (Yr) Peak(Wk) [T10 Wk|T40Wk|TotalWk] — **Score**

Rod STEWART ▶ 19 Pk:1 [6|16|21] — 61323

Every Picture Tells A Story (71) 1(4) [20|35|52] — 10659
A Night On The Town (76) 2(5) [11|30|57] — 7129
Foot Loose & Fancy Free (77) 2(6) [15|27|47] — 7013
Blondes Have More Fun (78) 1(3) [14|24|37] — 6671
Out Of Order (88) 20(2) [0|46|72] — 5537
Never A Dull Moment (72) 2(3) [14|21|36] — 5459
Tonight I'm Yours (81) 11(4) [0|20|31] — 3006
Atlantic Crossing (75) 9(1) [2|10|29] — 2387
Foolish Behaviour (80) 12(5) [0|15|21] — 2330
Camouflage (84) 18(2) [0|19|35] — 2113
Gasoline Alley (70) 27(1) [0|7|57] — 1802
Smiler (74) 13(1) [0|5|14] — 1129
Rod Stewart Greatest Hits (79) 22(2) [0|7|19] — 1118
Sing It Again Rod (73) 31(1) [0|3|25] — 1094
Body Wishes (83) 30(1) [0|4|22] — 979
Rod Stewart (86) 28(2) [0|7|19] — 846
Storyteller/Complete Anthology: 1964-1990 (89) 54(1) [0|0|18] — 550
The Best Of Rod Stewart (76) 90(1) [0|0|26] — 532
Absolutely Live (82) 46(3) [0|0|13] — 427
The Rod Stewart Album (69) 139(1) [0|0|27] — 389
Rod Stewart/Faces Live - Coast To Coast Overture And Beginners (74)-Rod Stewart/Faces [A] 63(1) [0|0|11] — 154

Wynn STEWART ▶ 2951 Pk:158 [0|0|1] — 72

It's Such A Pretty World Today (67) 158(1) [0|0|8] — 72.0

Stephen STILLS ▶ 315 Pk:3 [2|6|10] — 10877

Stephen Stills (70) 3(3) [10|16|39] — 4358
Stephen Stills 2 (71) 8(2) [3|9|20] — 2174
Stills (75) 19(2) [0|6|17] — 1239
Super Session (68)-Mike Bloomfield/Al Kooper/Steve Stills [A] 12(1) [0|10|37] — 799
Illegal Stills (76) 31(1) [0|3|15] — 766
Long May You Run (76)-Stills-Young Band [A] 26(1) [0|6|18] — 573
Stephen Stills Live (75) 42(2) [0|0|11] — 492
Right By You (84) 75(2) [0|0|12] — 245
Thoroughfare Gap (78) 83(3) [0|0|4] — 137
Still Stills-The Best Of Stephen Stills (77) 127(1) [0|0|5] — 93.6

Stephen STILLS & MANASSAS ▶ 652 Pk:4 [1|2|2] — 4240

Manassas (72)-Stephen Stills/Manassas 4(2) [7|15|30] — 3270
Down The Road (73)-Stephen Stills/Manassas 26(2) [0|6|18] — 969

STING ▶ 312 Pk:2 [2|2|2] — 10962

The Dream Of The Blue Turtles (85) 2(6) [19|37|58] — 7101
...Nothing Like The Sun (87) 9(4) [4|26|52] — 3861

Sonny STITT ▶ 3385 Pk:172 [0|0|1] — 20

What's New!!! (67) 172(2) [0|0|2] — 20.4

STONE CITY BAND ▶ 2616 Pk:122 [0|0|1] — 130

In 'N' Out (80) 122(2) [0|0|8] — 130

STONE FURY ▶ 2632 Pk:144 [0|0|1] — 127

Burns Like A Star (84) 144(2) [0|0|12] — 127

--Stone Poneys See Ronstadt, Linda

The STOOGES ▶ 2060 Pk:106 [0|0|2] — 320

The Stooges (69) 106(1) [0|0|11] — 297
Raw Power (73)-Iggy And The Stooges 182(1) [0|0|3] — 22.5

Paul STOOKEY ▶ 1573 Pk:42 [0|0|1] — 706

Paul And.. (71) 42(2) [0|0|15] — 706

STORIES ▶ 1333 Pk:29 [0|1|2] — 1087

About Us (73) 29(1) [0|6|19] — 1018
Stories (72) 182(2) [0|0|9] — 69.0

▶ **Highest Peak [Top10s | Top40s | Total]**
Title (Yr) Peak(Wk) [T10 Wk | T40Wk | TotalWk] — Score

George STRAIT ▶ 966 Pk:68 [0|0|8] — 2051
Greatest Hits, Volume Two (87) 68(2) [0|0|31] — 631
Beyond The Blue Neon (89) 92(2) [0|0|24] — 391
Ocean Front Property (87) 117(1) [0|0|28] — 365
If You Ain't Lovin' (You Ain't Livin') (88) 87(2) [0|0|14] — 262
Does Fort Worth Ever Cross Your Mind (84) 139(2) [0|0|16] — 148
#7 (86) 126(1) [0|0|11] — 121
Greatest Hits (85) 157(1) [0|0|8] — 76.2
Right Or Wrong (84) 163(1) [0|0|7] — 56.5

Billy STRANGE ▶ 2771 Pk:135 [0|0|2] — 101
The James Bond Theme (64) 135(1) [0|0|5] — 63.7
English Hits Of '65 (65) 146(2) [0|0|3] — 37.5

The STRANGELOVES ▶ 3315 Pk:141 [0|0|1] — 27
I Want Candy (65) 141(2) [0|0|2] — 26.9

The STRANGLERS ▶ 3272 Pk:172 [0|0|1] — 31
Dreamtime (87) 172(2) [0|0|4] — 30.9

STRAWBERRY ALARM CLOCK ▶ 1024 Pk:11 [0|1|1] — 1854
Incense And Peppermints (67) 11(3) [0|13|24] — 1854

STRAWBS ▶ 1246 Pk:47 [0|0|7] — 1236
Ghosts (75) 47(2) [0|0|13] — 552
Hero And Heroine (74) 94(1) [0|0|17] — 292
Bursting At The Seams (73) 121(1) [0|0|9] — 157
Nomadness (75) 147(1) [0|0|6] — 91.0
Deep Cuts (76) 144(1) [0|0|5] — 75.1
Burning For You (77) 175(1) [0|0|4] — 38.6
Grave New World (72) 191(2) [0|0|5] — 30.2

STRAY CATS ▶ 349 Pk:2 [1|2|4] — 9692
Built For Speed (82) 2(15) [18|37|74] — 7957
Rant 'N' Rave With The Stray Cats (83) 14(2) [0|10|29] — 1548
Blast Off (89) 111(2) [0|0|9] — 118
Rock Therapy (86) 122(2) [0|0|5] — 69.0

Meryl STREEP ▶ 3487 Pk:180 [0|0|1] — 12
The Velveteen Rabbit (85)-Meryl Streep & George Winston [A] 180(1) [0|0|4] — 12.1

Janey STREET ▶ 2950 Pk:145 [0|0|1] — 72
Heroes, Angels & Friends (84) 145(2) [0|0|6] — 72.0

STREETS ▶ 2856 Pk:166 [0|0|1] — 87
1st (83) 166(1) [0|0|11] — 86.8

Barbra STREISAND ▶ 3 Pk:1 [21|34|40] — 126028
Guilty (80) 1(3) [18|33|49] — 9281
The Second Barbra Streisand Album (63) 2(3) [18|47|74] — 8127
People (64) 1(5) [21|48|84] — 7751
Funny Girl (Soundtrack) (68) 12(1) [0|31|108] — 7627
The Third Album (64) 5(8) [22|42|74] — 6437
Funny Girl (Original Cast) (64) 2(3) [22|40|51] — 6318
My Name Is Barbra (Soundtrack) (65) 2(3) [17|46|68] — 6304
The Broadway Album (85) 1(3) [18|24|50] — 5422
Barbra Streisand's Greatest Hits, Volume 2 (78) 1(3) [11|17|46] — 5226
My Name Is Barbra, Two... (65) 2(3) [19|31|48] — 5109
Memories (81) 10(6) [6|15|104] — 3838
The Way We Were (74) 1(2) [6|12|31] — 3692
Streisand Superman (77) 3(4) [7|14|25] — 3602
Color Me Barbra (Soundtrack) (66) 3(2) [9|22|36] — 3524
Wet (79) 7(4) [8|14|26] — 3155
Stoney End (71) 10(4) [4|11|29] — 2716
Barbra Joan Streisand (71) 11(2) [0|15|26] — 2697
Funny Lady (Soundtrack) (75) 6(1) [4|9|25] — 2399
Je M'appelle Barbra (66) 5(2) [6|13|29] — 2334
Songbird (78) 12(2) [0|13|27] — 2155
Till I Loved You (88) 10(1) [1|14|26] — 2133
ButterFly (74) 13(1) [0|11|24] — 2119
Yentl (Soundtrack) (83) 9(2) [2|13|26] — 1871
One Voice (87) 9(2) [3|12|28] — 1848
Simply Streisand (67) 12(3) [0|12|23] — 1808
Lazy Afternoon (75) 12(2) [0|10|20] — 1783
Live Concert At The Forum (72) 19(2) [0|8|27] — 1749
A Happening In Central Park (68) 30(2) [0|13|20] — 1678
Emotion (84) 19(3) [0|11|28] — 1464
The Main Event (Soundtrack) (79) 20(1) [0|9|18] — 1408
Hello, Dolly! (Soundtrack) (69) 49(1) [0|0|33] — 1382
A Collection: Greatest Hits...And More (89) 26(3) [0|12|25] — 1234
Barbra Streisand's Greatest Hits (70) 32(1) [0|2|30] — 1001
What About Today? (69) 31(1) [0|4|17] — 891
Classical Barbra (76) 46(2) [0|0|14] — 511
Barbra Streisand...And Other Musical Instruments (Soundtrack) (73) 64(1) [0|0|16] — 437
On A Clear Day You Can See Forever (Soundtrack) (70) 108(1) [0|0|24] — 377
A Christmas Album (81) 108(2) [0|0|9] — 154
The Owl And The Pussycat (Soundtrack) (71) 186(1) [0|0|6] — 41.8
A Star Is Born (Soundtrack) (76)-Barbra Streisand & Kris Kristofferson [A] 1(6) [18|28|51] — 4426

The STRIKERS ▶ 3294 Pk:174 [0|0|1] — 29
The Strikers (81)-Strikers 174(1) [0|0|3] — 28.8

Jud STRUNK ▶ 2634 Pk:138 [0|0|1] — 126
Daisy A Day (73) 138(1) [0|0|9] — 126

STRYPER ▶ 653 Pk:32 [0|2|4] — 4229
To Hell With The Devil (86) 32(2) [0|12|74] — 2270
In God We Trust (88) 32(3) [0|5|25] — 935
Soldiers Under Command (85) 84(2) [0|0|64] — 684
The Yellow And Black Attack (86) 103(3) [0|0|30] — 339

STUFF ▶ 1926 Pk:61 [0|0|2] — 390
More Stuff (77) 61(1) [0|0|13] — 349
Stuff (76) 163(1) [0|0|3] — 40.2

STYLE COUNCIL ▶ 1420 Pk:56 [0|0|5] — 938
My Ever Changing Moods (84) 56(2) [0|0|22] — 576
Internationalists (85) 123(1) [0|0|11] — 140
The Cost Of Loving (87) 122(2) [0|0|10] — 138
Introducing The Style Council (83) 172(1) [0|0|5] — 42.1
Confessions Of A Pop Group (88) 174(1) [0|0|6] — 41.5

The STYLISTICS ▶ 328 Pk:14 [0|3|10] — 10541
The Stylistics (71) 23(1) [0|18|38] — 2783
Round 2: The Stylistics (72) 32(2) [0|9|38] — 2006
Let's Put It All Together (74) 14(2) [0|8|31] — 1986
The Best Of The Stylistics (75) 41(1) [0|0|30] — 1097
Rockin' Roll Baby (73) 66(1) [0|0|44] — 1094
Heavy (74) 43(2) [0|0|16] — 620
Thank You Baby (75) 72(2) [0|0|13] — 398
You Are Beautiful (75) 99(2) [0|0|11] — 254
Hurry Up This Way Again (80) 127(1) [0|0|12] — 179
Fabulous (76) 117(2) [0|0|6] — 124

STYX ▶ 60 Pk:1 [5|7|11] — 40950
Paradise Theater (81) 1(3) [27|35|61] — 10999
The Grand Illusion (77) 6(2) [12|37|127] — 8016
Pieces Of Eight (78) 6(1) [8|28|92] — 7036
Cornerstone (79) 2(1) [18|26|60] — 6989
Kilroy Was Here (83) 3(2) [16|22|34] — 3996
Equinox (75) 58(1) [0|0|50] — 1352
Styx II (75) 20(2) [0|6|19] — 1258
Caught In The Act - Live (84) 31(2) [0|6|15] — 662
Crystal Ball (76) 66(1) [0|0|18] — 510
Man Of Miracles (74) 154(1) [0|0|12] — 121
The Serpent Is Rising (74) 192(1) [0|0|2] — 12.1

SUAVE ▶ 2301 Pk:101 [0|0|1] — 215
I'm Your Playmate (88) 101(1) [0|0|12] — 215

The SUGARCUBES ▶ 1385 Pk:54 [0|0|2] — 988
Life's Too Good (88) 54(2) [0|0|29] — 813
Here Today, Tomorrow Next Week! (89) 70(2) [0|0|9] — 175

SUGARHILL GANG ▶ 1676 Pk:50 [0|0|1] — 601
8th Wonder (82) 50(1) [0|0|18] — 601

SUGARLOAF ▶ 963 Pk:24 [0|1|3] — 2070
Sugarloaf (70) 24(2) [0|10|29] — 1782
Spaceship Earth (71) 111(2) [0|0|9] — 206
Don't Call Us-We'll Call You (75)-Sugarloaf/Jerry Corbetta 152(1) [0|0|6] — 82.6

SUICIDAL TENDENCIES ▶ 1855 Pk:100 [0|0|3] — 440
Join The Army (87) 100(2) [0|0|13] — 199
How Will I Laugh Tomorrow When I Can't Even Smile Today (88) 111(2) [0|0|12] — 189
Controlled By Hatred/Feel Like Shit...Deja Vu (89) 150(2) [0|0|5] — 52.0

Kasim SULTON ▶ 3518 Pk:197 [0|0|1] — 10
Kasim (82) 197(2) [0|0|2] — 10.0

Donna SUMMER ▶ 59 Pk:1 [4|12|15] — 41664
Bad Girls (79) 1(6) [16|26|49] — 8577
Live And More (78) 1(1) [12|32|75] — 8386
On The Radio: Greatest Hits: Volumes I & II (79) 1(1) [18|23|39] — 6739
I Remember Yesterday (77) 18(1) [0|18|40] — 3051
Love To Love You Baby (75) 11(2) [0|13|30] — 2422
Once Upon A Time... (77) 26(2) [0|10|58] — 2318
She Works Hard For The Money (83) 9(1) [1|15|32] — 2220
Four Seasons Of Love (76) 29(1) [0|5|26] — 1707
A Love Trilogy (76) 21(1) [0|9|27] — 1681
Donna Summer (82) 20(5) [0|9|37] — 1550
The Wanderer (80) 13(3) [0|9|18] — 1445
Another Place And Time (89) 53(2) [0|0|20] — 512
Cats Without Claws (84) 40(2) [0|2|17] — 500
Walk Away - Collector's Edition (The Best Of 1977-1980) (80) 50(2) [0|0|15] — 470
All Systems Go (87) 122(2) [0|0|6] — 86.7

Henry LEE SUMMER ▶ 1318 Pk:56 [0|0|2] — 1104
Henry Lee Summer (88) 56(2) [0|0|23] — 744
I've Got Everything (89) 78(1) [0|0|17] — 361

Andy SUMMERS & Robert FRIPP ▶ 2002 Pk:60 [0|0|2] — 350
I Advance Masked (82) 60(3) [0|0|11] — 297
Bewitched (84) 155(2) [0|0|5] — 53.7

Bill SUMMERS & SUMMERS HEAT ▶ 1709 Pk:92 [0|0|2] — 576
Jam The Box! (81) 92(1) [0|0|16] — 301
Call It What You Want (81) 129(1) [0|0|15] — 275

SUN ▶ 1438 Pk:69 [0|0|2] — 910
Sunburn (78) 69(1) [0|0|22] — 691
Destination: Sun (79) 85(1) [0|0|10] — 219

SUNNY & The SUNLINERS ▶ 3110 Pk:142 [0|0|2] — 51
Talk To Me (63) 142(1) [0|0|2] — 26.7
The Original Peanuts (65)-The Sunglows 148(1) [0|0|2] — 24.3

SUNSHINE COMPANY ▶ 2570 Pk:126 [0|0|1] — 143
Happy Is The Sunshine Company (67) 126(1) [0|0|10] — 143

SUPERSAX ▶ 2845 Pk:169 [0|0|2] — 88
Supersax Plays Bird (73) 169(1) [0|0|7] — 63.1
Supersax Plays Bird, Volume 2/Salt Peanuts (74) 182(1) [0|0|3] — 25.0

▶ Highest Peak [Top10s|Top40s|Total]
Title (Yr) Peak(Wk) [T10 Wk|T40Wk|TotalWk] — Score

SUPERTRAMP ▶ 121 Pk:1 [3|6|9] — 26526
Breakfast In America (79) 1(6) [26|48|88] — 13764
Even In The Quietest Moments... (77) 16(2) [0|17|49] — 3418
"...Famous Last Words..." (82) 5(7) [7|17|28] — 2901
Paris (80) 8(2) [3|11|26] — 2219
Crime Of The Century (74) 38(2) [0|3|76] — 1891
Brother Where You Bound (85) 21(2) [0|10|22] — 1176
Crisis? What Crisis? (75) 44(1) [0|0|28] — 935
Free As A Bird (87) 101(2) [0|0|11] — 155
Supertramp (78) 158(1) [0|0|5] — 65.0

Diana ROSS & The SUPREMES And The TEMPTATIONS ▶ 287 Pk:1 [2|4|4] — 12112
TCB (Soundtrack) (68) 1(1) [11|19|34] — 6057
Diana Ross & The Supremes Join The Temptations (68) 2(1) [8|14|32] — 4480
Together (69) 28(1) [0|3|18] — 1020
On Broadway (Soundtrack) (69) 38(1) [0|2|12] — 555

The SUPREMES & FOUR TOPS ▶ 1792 Pk:113 [0|0|3] — 490
The Magnificent 7 (70) 113(2) [0|0|16] — 348
The Return Of The Magnificent Seven (71) 154(1) [0|0|6] — 83.5
Dynamite (72) 160(1) [0|0|6] — 58.6

The SUPREMES/Diana ROSS And The SUPREMES ▶ 32 Pk:1 [6|14|21] — 49628
Diana Ross And The Supremes Greatest Hits (67)-Diana Ross & The Supremes 1(5) [24|49|89] — 11993
Where Did Our Love Go (64)-The Supremes 2(4) [19|48|89] — 7153
The Supremes A' Go-Go (66)-The Supremes 1(2) [15|31|60] — 6652
The Supremes At The Copa (65)-The Supremes 11(1) [0|24|54] — 3076
The Supremes Sing Holland-Dozier-Holland (67)-The Supremes 6(2) [5|17|29] — 2805
More Hits By The Supremes (65)-The Supremes 6(2) [4|17|37] — 2713
I Hear A Symphony (66)-The Supremes 8(3) [6|14|55] — 2599
Reflections (68)-Diana Ross & The Supremes 18(2) [0|9|29] — 1832
Love Child (68)-Diana Ross & The Supremes 14(1) [0|7|21] — 1803
The Supremes Sing Rodgers & Hart (67)-The Supremes 20(3) [0|7|19] — 1262
Let The Sunshine In (69)-Diana Ross & The Supremes 24(2) [0|6|18] — 1255
Cream Of The Crop (69)-Diana Ross & The Supremes 33(2) [0|7|20] — 1222
Diana Ross & The Supremes Greatest Hits, Volume 3 (70)-Diana Ross & The Supremes 31(1) [0|6|25] — 1218
A Bit Of Liverpool (64)-The Supremes 21(3) [0|8|21] — 1016
Live At London's Talk Of The Town (68)-Diana Ross & The Supremes 57(2) [0|0|18] — 869
Farewell (70)-Diana Ross & The Supremes 46(1) [0|0|18] — 705
Anthology (1962-1969) (74)-Diana Ross & The Supremes 66(1) [0|0|15] — 464
We Remember Sam Cooke (65)-The Supremes 75(2) [0|0|19] — 427
25th Anniversary (86)-Diana Ross & The Supremes 112(2) [0|0|17] — 237
The Supremes Sing Country Western & Pop (65)-The Supremes 79(2) [0|0|8] — 179
Funny Girl (68)-Diana Ross & The Supremes 150(1) [0|0|12] — 148

The SUPREMES ▶ 711 Pk:25 [0|1|7] — 3572
Right On (70) 25(1) [0|6|19] — 1100
High Energy (76) 42(2) [0|0|15] — 700
New Ways But Love Stays (70) 68(2) [0|0|17] — 645
Floy Joy (72) 54(2) [0|0|15] — 509
Touch (71) 85(1) [0|0|10] — 301
The Supremes (72) 129(1) [0|0|13] — 217
The Supremes(2) (75) 152(1) [0|0|8] — 100

SURFACE ▶ 1094 Pk:55 [0|0|2] — 1623
2nd Wave (88) 56(2) [0|0|39] — 1080
Surface (87) 55(1) [0|0|19] — 542

The SURFARIS ▶ 2162 Pk:94 [0|0|2] — 273
The Surfaris Play Wipe Out And Others (63) 94(1) [0|0|11] — 199
Hit City 64 (64) 120(1) [0|0|5] — 74.5

SURVIVOR ▶ 369 Pk:2 [1|2|7] — 8985
Eye Of The Tiger (82) 2(4) [12|19|41] — 4056
Vital Signs (84) 16(3) [0|27|61] — 3378
When Seconds Count (86) 49(5) [0|0|24] — 750
Premonition (81) 82(3) [0|0|25] — 583
Caught In The Game (83) 82(1) [0|0|9] — 139
Survivor (80) 169(1) [0|0|7] — 64.9
Too Hot To Sleep (88) 187(2) [0|0|2] — 13.5

SUSAN ▶ 3109 Pk:169 [0|0|1] — 51
Falling In Love Again (79) 169(1) [0|0|5] — 51.0

SUSAN of SESAME STREET ▶ 2084 Pk:86 [0|0|1] — 309
Susan Sings Songs From Sesame Street (70) 86(1) [0|0|13] — 309

SUTHERLAND BROTHERS And QUIVER ▶ 1954 Pk:77 [0|0|3] — 376
Lifeboat (73) 77(1) [0|0|17] — 343
Dream Kid (74) 193(1) [0|0|3] — 19.4
Reach For The Sky (76) 195(1) [0|0|2] — 13.1

Billy SWAN ▶ 1235 Pk:21 [0|1|1] — 1265
I Can Help (74) 21(2) [0|7|16] — 1265

Brad SWANSON ▶ 3404 Pk:185 [0|0|1] — 19
Quentin's Theme (69)-Brad Swanson & His Whispering Organ Sound 185(1) [0|0|2] — 19.0

Keith SWEAT ▶ 633 Pk:15 [0|1|1] — 4409
Make It Last Forever (88) 15(1) [0|27|67] — 4409

SWEAT BAND ▶ 2788 Pk:150 [0|0|1] — 99
Sweat Band (80) 150(2) [0|0|8] — 99.1

The SWEET ▶ 645 Pk:25 [0|2|6] — 4273
Desolation Boulevard (75) 25(2) [0|6|44] — 2306
Give Us A Wink (76) 27(2) [0|7|13] — 1008
Level Headed (78) 52(1) [0|0|28] — 808
Cut Above The Rest (79) 151(1) [0|0|5] — 70.2
Off The Record (77) 151(1) [0|0|4] — 56.9
The Sweet (73) 191(1) [0|0|4] — 24.4

Rachel SWEET ▶ 1771 Pk:97 [0|0|3] — 502
Fool Around (79) 97(2) [0|0|9] — 206
Protect The Innocent (80) 123(1) [0|0|11] — 175
...And Then He Kissed Me (81) 124(2) [0|0|7] — 121

SWEET INSPIRATIONS ▶ 2688 Pk:90 [0|0|1] — 117
The Sweet Inspirations (68) 90(1) [0|0|6] — 117

SWEET SENSATION ▶ 2885 Pk:163 [0|0|1] — 82
Sad Sweet Dreamer (75) 163(1) [0|0|7] — 82.0

SWEET SENSATION (2) ▶ 1504 Pk:63 [0|0|1] — 799
Take It While It's Hot (88)-Sweet Sensation(2) 63(1) [0|0|32] — 799

SWEET TEE ▶ 2705 Pk:169 [0|0|1] — 113
It's Tee Time (89) 169(3) [0|0|13] — 113

SWEET THUNDER ▶ 2383 Pk:125 [0|0|1] — 190
Sweet Thunder (78) 125(2) [0|0|11] — 190

SWEETWATER ▶ 3490 Pk:200 [0|0|1] — 12
Sweetwater (69) 200(2) [0|0|2] — 11.9

SWINGING BLUE JEANS ▶ 2563 Pk:90 [0|0|1] — 146
Hippy Hippy Shake (64) 90(1) [0|0|9] — 146

SWINGIN' MEDALLIONS ▶ 2202 Pk:88 [0|0|1] — 253
Double Shot (Of My Baby's Love) (66) 88(1) [0|0|12] — 253

SWINGLE SINGERS ▶ 661 Pk:15 [0|1|3] — 4147
Bach's Greatest Hits (63) 15(2) [0|24|74] — 3751
Going Baroque (64) 65(2) [0|0|17] — 320
Anyone For Mozart? (65) 140(1) [0|0|6] — 76.7

SWING OUT SISTER ▶ 948 Pk:40 [0|1|2] — 2136
It's Better To Travel (87) 40(1) [0|1|43] — 1716
Kaleidoscope World (89) 61(2) [0|0|19] — 420

SWITCH ▶ 733 Pk:37 [0|2|5] — 3404
Switch II (79) 37(1) [0|4|36] — 1396
Switch (78) 37(2) [0|4|33] — 1220
Reaching For Tomorrow (80) 57(1) [0|0|14] — 398
This Is My Dream (80) 85(1) [0|0|17] — 353
Switch V (81) 174(2) [0|0|4] — 37.9

SYBIL ▶ 1849 Pk:75 [0|0|1] — 445
Sybil (89) 75(2) [0|0|24] — 445

Keith SYKES ▶ 2593 Pk:147 [0|0|1] — 137
I'm Not Strange I'm Just Like You (80) 147(3) [0|0|11] — 137

Sylvain SYLVAIN ▶ 2516 Pk:123 [0|0|1] — 156
Sylvain Sylvain (80) 123(2) [0|0|8] — 156

Foster SYLVERS ▶ 2965 Pk:159 [0|0|1] — 70
Foster Sylvers (73) 159(1) [0|0|7] — 70.1

The SYLVERS ▶ 1092 Pk:58 [0|0|6] — 1624
Showcase (76) 58(3) [0|0|25] — 697
Something Special (76) 80(3) [0|0|18] — 469
New Horizons (77) 134(2) [0|0|13] — 231
Forever Yours (78) 132(1) [0|0|8] — 123
The Sylvers (73) 180(1) [0|0|7] — 53.3
The Sylvers II (73) 164(1) [0|0|5] — 49.5

SYLVESTER ▶ 861 Pk:28 [0|1|7] — 2595
Step II (78) 28(1) [0|6|42] — 1651
Stars (79) 63(2) [0|0|15] — 508
Living Proof (79) 123(1) [0|0|12] — 200
Sell My Soul (80) 147(3) [0|0|8] — 103
Too Hot To Sleep (81) 156(1) [0|0|4] — 53.1
Mutual Attraction (87) 164(2) [0|0|5] — 40.7
All I Need (83) 168(2) [0|0|5] — 39.2

SYLVIA ▶ 2106 Pk:70 [0|0|1] — 298
Pillow Talk (73) 70(1) [0|0|12] — 298

SYLVIA (2) ▶ 1273 Pk:56 [0|0|4] — 1192
Just Sylvia (82) 56(1) [0|0|33] — 782
Snapshot (83) 77(1) [0|0|11] — 227
Drifter (81) 139(1) [0|0|11] — 154
Surprise (84) 178(1) [0|0|4] — 28.9

SYNDICATE OF SOUND ▶ 3293 Pk:148 [0|0|1] — 29
Little Girl (66) 148(1) [0|0|2] — 28.8

SYNERGY ▶ 1597 Pk:66 [0|0|3] — 685
Electronic Realizations For Rock Orchestra (75) 66(1) [0|0|18] — 422
Sequencer (76) 144(4) [0|0|11] — 178
Cords (78) 146(1) [0|0|6] — 85.0

SYREETA ▶ 1519 Pk:73 [0|0|5] — 769
Syreeta(2) (80) 73(2) [0|0|15] — 313
Stevie Wonder Presents Syreeta (74) 116(2) [0|0|17] — 302
Billy Preston & Syreeta (81)-Billy Preston & Syreeta [A] 127(4) [0|0|9] — 77.6
Syreeta (72) 185(2) [0|0|8] — 56.3
Set My Love In Motion (82) 189(3) [0|0|3] — 19.9

The SYSTEM ▶ 1364 Pk:62 [0|0|3] — 1024
Don't Disturb This Groove (87) 62(5) [0|0|25] — 692
Sweat (83) 94(1) [0|0|23] — 300
X-Periment (84) 182(1) [0|0|5] — 31.4

► Highest Peak [Top10s | Top40s | Total]
Title (Yr) Peak(Wk) [T10 Wk | T40Wk | TotalWk] — Score

Gabor SZABO ► 2120 Pk:140 [0|0|5] — 291
Gabor Szabo 1969 (69) 143(2) [0|0|7] — 130
Spellbinder (67) 140(1) [0|0|4] — 62.3
Lena & Gabor (70)-Lena Horne & Gabor Szabo [A] 162(1) [0|0|10] — 44.1
Bacchanal (68) 157(1) [0|0|3] — 43.0
The Sorcerer (68) 194(2) [0|0|2] — 11.5

T

TACO ► 1218 Pk:23 [0|1|1] — 1311
After Eight (83) 23(2) [0|11|24] — 1311

TAKE 6 ► 1818 Pk:71 [0|0|1] — 470
Take 6 (89) 71(2) [0|0|19] — 470

TALKING HEADS ► 181 Pk:15 [0|8|10] — 19104
Speaking In Tongues (83) 15(2) [0|25|51] — 3554
Little Creatures (85) 20(3) [0|24|77] — 3390
Stop Making Sense (84) 41(4) [0|0|118] — 2336
More Songs About Buildings And Food (78) 29(1) [0|5|42] — 2250
Remain In Light (80) 19(2) [0|9|27] — 1717
True Stories: A Film By David Byrne, The Complete Soundtrack (86) 17(3) [0|15|29] — 1713
Fear Of Music (79) 21(1) [0|10|30] — 1626
Naked (88) 19(1) [0|10|21] — 1340
Talking Heads: 77 (77) 97(2) [0|0|29] — 598
The Name Of This Band Is Talking Heads (82) 31(2) [0|4|14] — 579

TALK TALK ► 1233 Pk:42 [0|0|3] — 1268
It's My Life (84) 42(3) [0|0|22] — 690
The Colour Of Spring (86) 58(2) [0|0|17] — 460
The Party's Over (82) 132(2) [0|0|16] — 118

TA MARA & The SEEN ► 1582 Pk:54 [0|0|1] — 695
Ta Mara & The Seen (85) 54(3) [0|0|25] — 695

TANGERINE DREAM ► 1741 Pk:96 [0|0|7] — 533
Thief (Soundtrack) (81) 115(1) [0|0|10] — 213
Legend (Soundtrack) (86) 96(2) [0|0|7] — 114
Stratosfear (77) 158(1) [0|0|7] — 88.8
Sorcerer (Soundtrack) (77) 153(2) [0|0|6] — 74.1
Encore (77) 178(1) [0|0|2] — 20.0
Phaedra (74) 196(1) [0|0|2] — 12.2
Exit (81) 195(2) [0|0|2] — 11.6

TANGIER ► 2030 Pk:91 [0|0|1] — 338
Four Winds (89) 91(1) [0|0|17] — 338

Marc TANNER BAND ► 2725 Pk:140 [0|0|1] — 109
No Escape (79) 140(2) [0|0|8] — 109

TANTRUM ► 3448 Pk:199 [0|0|1] — 15
Rather Be Rockin' (80) 199(2) [0|0|3] — 15.1

TARNEY/SPENCER Band ► 2954 Pk:174 [0|0|2] — 72
Three's A Crowd (78) 174(1) [0|0|4] — 37.9
Run For Your Life (79) 181(1) [0|0|4] — 33.9

TASTE ► 2390 Pk:133 [0|0|1] — 189
Taste (69) 133(2) [0|0|9] — 189

A TASTE OF HONEY ► 571 Pk:6 [1|2|4] — 5093
A Taste Of Honey (78) 6(2) [5|14|27] — 3180
Twice As Sweet (80) 36(2) [0|4|32] — 1161
Another Taste (79) 59(1) [0|0|13] — 457
Ladies Of The Eighties (82) 73(4) [0|0|12] — 294

TAVARES ► 583 Pk:24 [0|2|10] — 4955
Sky High! (76) 24(2) [0|11|31] — 1862
In The City (75) 26(2) [0|5|17] — 1056
Love Storm (77) 59(2) [0|0|22] — 655
Hard Core Poetry (74) 121(2) [0|0|23] — 349
Best Of Tavares (77) 72(2) [0|0|10] — 269
Madame Butterfly (79) 92(2) [0|0|11] — 223
Supercharged (80) 75(2) [0|0|7] — 196

► Highest Peak [Top10s | Top40s | Total]
Title (Yr) Peak(Wk) [T10 Wk | T40Wk | TotalWk] — Score

Future Bound (78) 115(2) [0|0|8] — 162
New Directions (82) 137(1) [0|0|11] — 98.2
Check It Out (74) 160(1) [0|0|8] — 84.3

TAXXI ► 2826 Pk:161 [0|0|1] — 91
States Of Emergency (82) 161(1) [0|0|11] — 91.1

Alex TAYLOR ► 3436 Pk:190 [0|0|1] — 16
With Friends And Neighbors (71) 190(1) [0|0|2] — 16.2

Andy TAYLOR ► 1731 Pk:46 [0|0|1] — 549
Thunder (87) 46(4) [0|0|17] — 549

James TAYLOR ► 43 Pk:2 [7|12|14] — 45567
Sweet Baby James (70) 3(4) [12|54|102] — 11267
Mud Slide Slim And The Blue Horizon (71) 2(4) [20|31|45] — 8844
JT (77) 4(5) [12|24|39] — 5169
Gorilla (75) 6(1) [6|15|27] — 3257
One Man Dog (72) 4(2) [7|12|25] — 2862
Dad Loves His Work (81) 10(3) [3|12|23] — 2592
Flag (79) 10(1) [1|10|23] — 2110
In The Pocket (76) 16(1) [0|14|24] — 2054
Walking Man (74) 13(2) [0|10|18] — 1857
Greatest Hits (76) 23(2) [0|7|41] — 1710
Never Die Young (88) 25(2) [0|11|34] — 1606
That's Why I'm Here (85) 34(3) [0|8|30] — 1103
James Taylor (70) 62(1) [0|0|28] — 892
James Taylor And The Original Flying Machine-1967 (71) 74(1) [0|0|8] — 245

Johnnie TAYLOR ► 542 Pk:5 [1|1|10] — 5485
Eargasm (76) 5(2) [6|11|28] — 2713
Who's Making Love... (69) 42(1) [0|0|18] — 866
Taylored In Silk (73) 54(1) [0|0|20] — 638
Rated Extraordinaire (77) 51(1) [0|0|11] — 399
One Step Beyond (71) 112(2) [0|0|11] — 253
Raw Blues (69) 126(1) [0|0|9] — 208
The Johnnie Taylor Philosophy Continues (69) 109(1) [0|0|6] — 176
Johnnie Taylor's Greatest Hits (70) 141(1) [0|0|5] — 92.7
Ever Ready (78) 164(1) [0|0|6] — 72.4
Super Taylor (74) 182(1) [0|0|8] — 67.1

Kate TAYLOR ► 2436 Pk:88 [0|0|1] — 177
Sister Kate (71) 88(2) [0|0|8] — 177

Little Johnny TAYLOR ► 3325 Pk:140 [0|0|1] — 26
Little Johnny Taylor (63) 140(1) [0|0|2] — 25.9

Livingston TAYLOR ► 1724 Pk:82 [0|0|3] — 560
Livingston Taylor (70) 82(2) [0|0|20] — 391
Liv (71) 147(1) [0|0|10] — 139
Over The Rainbow (73) 189(1) [0|0|5] — 30.5

Mick TAYLOR ► 2830 Pk:119 [0|0|1] — 91
Mick Taylor (79) 119(1) [0|0|5] — 90.8

R. Dean TAYLOR ► 3533 Pk:198 [0|0|1] — 6
I Think, Therefore I Am (71) 198(1) [0|0|1] — 6.1

Roger TAYLOR ► 2267 Pk:121 [0|0|1] — 226
Fun In Space (81) 121(1) [0|0|10] — 226

The T-BONES ► 2183 Pk:75 [0|0|1] — 265
No Matter What Shape (Your Stomach's In) (66) 75(1) [0|0|12] — 265

T-CONNECTION ► 1254 Pk:51 [0|0|6] — 1225
T-Connection (79) 51(2) [0|0|19] — 560
Magic (77) 109(1) [0|0|11] — 218
On Fire (78) 139(1) [0|0|11] — 150
Pure & Natural (82) 123(1) [0|0|10] — 138
Everything Is Cool (81) 138(1) [0|0|8] — 137
Totally Connected (79) 188(3) [0|0|3] — 22.5

TEARDROP EXPLODES ► 2712 Pk:156 [0|0|2] — 112
Kilimanjaro (81) 156(2) [0|0|6] — 77.1
Wilder (82) 176(3) [0|0|4] — 34.9

► Highest Peak [Top10s | Top40s | Total]
Title (Yr) Peak(Wk) [T10 Wk | T40Wk | TotalWk] — Score

TEARS FOR FEARS ► 238 Pk:1 [2|2|3] — 14793
Songs From The Big Chair (85) 1(5) [32|55|82] — 11182
The Seeds Of Love (89) 8(3) [3|17|34] — 2355
The Hurting (83) 73(1) [0|0|69] — 1256

TECHNOTRONIC ► 776 Pk:10 [1|1|1] — 3107
Pump Up The Jam - The Album (89) 10(1) [1|22|55] — 3107

TEE SET ► 2916 Pk:158 [0|0|1] — 78
Ma Belle Amie (70) 158(2) [0|0|6] — 78.2

Kiri TE KANAWA ► 2414 Pk:136 [0|0|1] — 183
Blue Skies (85)-Kiri Te Kanawa/Nelson Riddle And His Orchestra 136(1) [0|0|16] — 183

Nino TEMPO & April STEVENS ► 1975 Pk:48 [0|0|1] — 364
Deep Purple (63) 48(1) [0|0|14] — 364

The TEMPTATIONS ► 8 Pk:2 [8|24|37] — 72959
The Temptations Greatest Hits (66) 5(2) [14|65|120] — 10179
Cloud Nine (69) 4(1) [9|26|40] — 5561
All Directions (72) 2(2) [11|25|44] — 5346
Puzzle People (69) 5(2) [11|19|41] — 5097
Temptations Greatest Hits II (70) 15(2) [0|12|70] — 3633
Psychedelic Shack (70) 9(2) [4|18|30] — 3327
A Song For You (75) 13(1) [0|16|36] — 3279
Sky's The Limit (71) 16(1) [0|15|35] — 2951
Wish It Would Rain (68) 13(2) [0|14|41] — 2761
With A Lot O' Soul (67) 7(1) [5|18|36] — 2677
Masterpiece (73) 7(2) [5|14|28] — 2636
Temptations Live! (67) 10(1) [1|18|51] — 2619
Temptin' Temptations (65) 11(1) [0|19|37] — 2552
The Temptations In A Mellow Mood (67) 13(1) [0|14|44] — 2492
Gettin' Ready (66) 12(2) [0|18|35] — 2397
Live At The Copa (69) 15(1) [0|9|24] — 2337
Solid Rock (72) 24(2) [0|8|22] — 1379
1990 (73) 19(1) [0|8|22] — 1377
The Temptations Show (69) 24(1) [0|9|16] — 1318
Live At London's Talk Of The Town (70) 21(2) [0|6|18] — 1188
Wings Of Love (76) 29(1) [0|6|20] — 1161
The Temptations Sing Smokey (65) 35(1) [0|3|26] — 892
Truly For You (84) 55(4) [0|0|34] — 835
House Party (75) 40(2) [0|2|20] — 730
The Temptations Do The Temptations (76) 53(2) [0|0|14] — 619
Anthology (73) 65(1) [0|0|26] — 608
To Be Continued... (86) 74(2) [0|0|33] — 607
Power (80) 45(1) [0|0|14] — 601
Reunion (82) 37(2) [0|2|18] — 557
Together Again (87) 112(2) [0|0|21] — 288
Meet The Temptations (64) 95(1) [0|0|11] — 193
Hear To Tempt You (77) 113(1) [0|0|13] — 190
25th Anniversary (86) 140(2) [0|0|16] — 171
The Temptations (81) 119(1) [0|0|9] — 143
Touch Me (86) 146(2) [0|0|10] — 97.7
Back To Basics (84) 152(1) [0|0|9] — 82.6
Surface Thrills (83) 159(3) [0|0|9] — 77.8

10cc ► 627 Pk:15 [0|2|9] — 4465
The Original Soundtrack (75) 15(2) [0|10|25] — 1986
Deceptive Bends (77) 31(1) [0|5|20] — 884
Bloody Tourists (78) 69(1) [0|0|17] — 563
How Dare You! (76) 47(1) [0|0|13] — 513
Sheet Music (74) 81(1) [0|0|14] — 333
Live And Let Live (77) 146(1) [0|0|6] — 88.8
100cc (75) 161(1) [0|0|5] — 53.9
Greatest Hits 1972-1978 (79) 188(1) [0|0|4] — 25.9
Look Hear? (80) 180(1) [0|0|2] — 18.1

► Highest Peak [Top10s | Top40s | Total]
Title (Yr) Peak(Wk) [T10 Wk | T40Wk | TotalWk] — Score

Toni TENNILLE ► 2575 Pk:142 [0|0|2] — 142
More Than You Know (84) 142(1) [0|0|11] — 132
All Of Me (87) 198(2) [0|0|2] — 9.6

10,000 MANIACS ► 624 Pk:13 [0|2|2] — 4531
Blind Man's Zoo (89) 13(1) [0|19|28] — 2375
In My Tribe (87) 37(1) [0|2|77] — 2156

TEN WHEEL DRIVE With Genya RAVAN ► 2069 Pk:151 [0|0|3] — 316
Construction #1 (70) 151(2) [0|0|16] — 192
Brief Replies (70) 161(1) [0|0|8] — 87.4
Peculiar Friends (71) 190(1) [0|0|5] — 36.9

TEN YEARS AFTER ► 305 Pk:14 [0|5|12] — 11163
Cricklewood Green (70) 14(2) [0|8|30] — 2062
A Space In Time (71) 17(1) [0|10|26] — 2003
SSSSH (69) 20(1) [0|7|23] — 1688
Watt (70) 21(1) [0|8|16] — 1340
Rock & Roll Music To The World (72) 43(1) [0|0|25] — 1038
Recorded Live (73) 39(1) [0|2|21] — 815
Stonedhenge (69) 61(1) [0|0|18] — 684
Alvin Lee & Company (72) 55(2) [0|0|18] — 677
Positive Vibrations (74) 81(1) [0|0|14] — 379
Undead (68) 115(1) [0|0|14] — 273
About Time (89) 120(2) [0|0|10] — 156
Goin' Home! Their Greatest Hits (75) 174(1) [0|0|5] — 47.1

Robert TEPPER ► 2890 Pk:144 [0|0|1] — 81
No Easy Way Out (86) 144(2) [0|0|8] — 81.5

Sonny TERRY & Brownie McGHEE ► 3280 Pk:185 [0|0|1] — 30
Sonny & Brownie (73) 185(1) [0|0|5] — 30.1

Tony TERRY ► 2339 Pk:151 [0|0|1] — 203
Forever Yours (88) 151(1) [0|0|20] — 203

TESLA ► 588 Pk:18 [0|2|2] — 4905
The Great Radio Controversy (89) 18(1) [0|16|67] — 3201
Mechanical Resonance (87) 32(2) [0|8|61] — 1704

TESTAMENT ► 1815 Pk:77 [0|0|2] — 473
Practice What You Preach (89) 77(2) [0|0|12] — 267
The New Order (88) 136(1) [0|0|14] — 206

Joe TEX ► 872 Pk:17 [0|1|9] — 2525
I Gotcha (72) 17(1) [0|11|21] — 1501
Live And Lively (68) 84(2) [0|0|17] — 316
Bumps And Bruises (77) 108(1) [0|0|9] — 214
The Love You Save (66) 108(1) [0|0|8] — 138
Hold What You've Got (65) 124(2) [0|0|7] — 102
The New Boss (65) 142(1) [0|0|7] — 90.2
Soul Country (68) 154(1) [0|0|7] — 86.7
Buying A Book (69) 190(1) [0|0|5] — 39.1
The Best Of Joe Tex (67) 168(1) [0|0|4] — 37.4

TEXAS ► 2087 Pk:88 [0|0|1] — 308
Southside (89) 88(2) [0|0|16] — 308

TEXTONES ► 3094 Pk:176 [0|0|1] — 53
Midnight Mission (84) 176(1) [0|0|8] — 52.5

The THE ► 1886 Pk:89 [0|0|2] — 414
Infected (87) 89(2) [0|0|18] — 281
Mind Bomb (89) 138(2) [0|0|12] — 133

THEE PROPHETS ► 3140 Pk:163 [0|0|1] — 47
Playgirl (69) 163(1) [0|0|3] — 47.1

THEM ► 1517 Pk:54 [0|0|3] — 771
Them (65) 54(1) [0|0|23] — 554
Them Featuring Van Morrison (72) 154(3) [0|0|11] — 135
Them Again (66) 138(2) [0|0|6] — 82.2

Mike THEODORE Orchestra ► 3388 Pk:178 [0|0|1] — 20
Cosmic Wind (77) 178(1) [0|0|2] — 20.1

THEY MIGHT BE GIANTS ► 2010 Pk:89 [0|0|1] — 346
Lincoln (88) 89(2) [0|0|19] — 346

THIN LIZZY ► 714 Pk:18 [0|2|9] — 3532
Jailbreak (76) 18(2) [0|10|28] — 1839
Bad Reputation (77) 39(2) [0|2|11] — 532
Johnny The Fox (76) 52(1) [0|0|11] — 298
Black Rose/A Rock Legend (79) 81(1) [0|0|12] — 267
Live And Dangerous (78) 84(1) [0|0|12] — 240
Chinatown (80) 120(1) [0|0|10] — 177
Renegade (82) 157(1) [0|0|11] — 106
Thunder And Lightning (83) 159(2) [0|0|5] — 55.4
'Life' Live (84) 185(1) [0|0|3] — 18.6

3rd BASS ► 1445 Pk:55 [0|0|1] — 897
The Cactus Album (89) 55(1) [0|0|30] — 897

THIRD POWER ► 3475 Pk:194 [0|0|1] — 13
Believe (70) 194(1) [0|0|2] — 12.5

THIRD WORLD ► 1030 Pk:55 [0|0|8] — 1842
Journey To Addis (78) 55(2) [0|0|24] — 697
You've Got The Power (82) 63(1) [0|0|27] — 555
Serious Business (89) 107(1) [0|0|14] — 236
Sense Of Purpose (85) 119(3) [0|0|11] — 163
All The Way Strong (83) 137(2) [0|0|7] — 89.4
The Story's Been Told (79) 157(1) [0|0|5] — 61.0
Rock The World (81) 186(1) [0|0|3] — 23.8
Third World, Prisoner in The Street (Soundtrack) (80) 186(2) [0|0|2] — 16.4

.38 SPECIAL ► 285 Pk:10 [1|5|8] — 12291
Wild-Eyed Southern Boys (81) 18(2) [0|18|57] — 3509
Special Forces (82)-38 Special 10(3) [3|11|42] — 2351
Strength In Numbers (86)-38 Special 17(1) [0|20|31] — 2220
Tour De Force (83)-38 Special 22(2) [0|20|39] — 2197
Rock & Roll Strategy (88)-Thirty Eight Special 61(1) [0|0|41] — 821
Flashback (87)-38 Special 35(2) [0|3|17] — 591
Rockin' Into The Night (80)-38-Special 57(1) [0|0|19] — 531
.38 Special (77)-38 Special 148(1) [0|0|5] — 71.3

B.J. THOMAS ► 424 Pk:12 [0|1|10] — 7507
Raindrops Keep Fallin' On My Head (70) 12(2) [0|23|41] — 4324
Greatest Hits, Volume 1 (69) 90(2) [0|0|28] — 735
Most Of All (70) 67(1) [0|0|24] — 612
Everybody's Out Of Town (70) 72(1) [0|0|20] — 495
Reunion (75) 59(1) [0|0|14] — 449
Greatest Hits, Volume Two (71) 92(1) [0|0|13] — 347
On My Way (69) 133(1) [0|0|12] — 239
B.J. Thomas (77) 114(1) [0|0|12] — 174
Billy Joe Thomas (72) 145(1) [0|0|9] — 120
New Looks (83) 193(1) [0|0|3] — 14.5

Carla THOMAS ► 1373 Pk:36 [0|1|6] — 1005
King & Queen (67)-Otis Redding & Carla Thomas [A] 36(2) [0|3|31] — 563
Comfort Me (66) 134(1) [0|0|10] — 140
The Queen Alone (67) 133(1) [0|0|6] — 93.7
Memphis Queen (69) 151(1) [0|0|5] — 92.9
Carla (66) 130(1) [0|0|5] — 82.5
The Best Of Carla Thomas (69) 190(1) [0|0|4] — 32.8

Irma THOMAS ► 2608 Pk:104 [0|0|1] — 132
Wish Someone Would Care (64) 104(1) [0|0|8] — 132

Lillo THOMAS ► 3435 Pk:186 [0|0|1] — 17
All Of You (84) 186(1) [0|0|3] — 16.5

Ray THOMAS ► 1919 Pk:68 [0|0|2] — 393
From Mighty Oaks (75) 68(1) [0|0|11] — 318
Hopes Wishes & Dreams (76) 147(2) [0|0|5] — 75.0

Rufus THOMAS ► 2644 Pk:138 [0|0|2] — 124
Rufus Thomas Live/Doing The Push & Pull At P.J.'s (71) 147(2) [0|0|5] — 84.2
Walking The Dog (63) 138(1) [0|0|3] — 40.1

Timmy THOMAS ► 1764 Pk:53 [0|0|1] — 506
Why Can't We Live Together (73) 53(1) [0|0|15] — 506

Richard THOMPSON ► 2050 Pk:102 [0|0|4] — 328
Across A Crowded Room (85) 102(2) [0|0|13] — 203
Daring Adventures (86) 142(2) [0|0|6] — 65.8
Amnesia (88) 182(2) [0|0|5] — 33.2
Hand Of Kindness (83) 186(1) [0|0|5] — 26.3

Robbin THOMPSON Band ► 2891 Pk:168 [0|0|1] — 81
Two B's Please (80) 168(1) [0|0|11] — 81.5

Sue THOMPSON ► 3194 Pk:134 [0|0|1] — 41
Paper Tiger (65) 134(1) [0|0|3] — 41.3

THOMPSON TWINS ► 446 Pk:10 [1|3|7] — 7153
Into The Gap (84) 10(2) [2|24|53] — 3487
Here's To Future Days (85) 20(1) [0|24|35] — 2347
Side Kicks (83) 34(3) [0|4|25] — 843
Close To The Bone (87) 76(1) [0|0|14] — 274
In The Name Of Love (82) 148(2) [0|0|8] — 81.0
Big Trash (89) 143(2) [0|0|6] — 79.3
The Best Of The Thompson Twins/Greatest Mixes (88) 175(2) [0|0|6] — 41.3

Ali THOMSON ► 2086 Pk:99 [0|0|1] — 308
Take A Little Rhythm (80) 99(1) [0|0|15] — 308

Big Mama THORNTON ► 3467 Pk:198 [0|0|1] — 13
Stronger Than Dirt (69) 198(2) [0|0|2] — 12.8

George THOROGOOD & The DESTROYERS ► 411 Pk:32 [0|4|7] — 7915
Maverick (85) 32(1) [0|15|42] — 1995
Move It On Over (78) 33(1) [0|7|47] — 1895
Live (86) 33(3) [0|4|42] — 1273
Born To Be Bad (88) 32(3) [0|10|24] — 1214
Bad To The Bone (82) 43(4) [0|0|48] — 965
More George Thorogood And The Destroyers (80) 68(2) [0|0|12] — 327
Better Than The Rest (79) 78(1) [0|0|10] — 246

Billy THORPE ► 1398 Pk:39 [0|1|2] — 972
Children Of The Sun (79) 39(1) [0|1|23] — 906
21st Century Man (80) 151(2) [0|0|5] — 66.5

THP ORCHESTRA ► 1772 Pk:65 [0|0|1] — 502
Two Hot For Love! (78) 65(1) [0|0|19] — 502

3 ► 2441 Pk:97 [0|0|1] — 175
To The Power Of Three (88) 97(2) [0|0|10] — 175

3° DEGREES ► 1206 Pk:28 [0|1|5] — 1329
The Three Degrees (74) 28(1) [0|5|15] — 960
International (75) 99(1) [0|0|8] — 185
Maybe (70) 139(2) [0|0|7] — 100
New Dimensions (78) 169(1) [0|0|8] — 78.3
Three Degrees Live (76) 199(1) [0|0|1] — 5.6

THREE DOG NIGHT ► 40 Pk:5 [5|12|14] — 47366
Golden Bisquits (71) 5(4) [9|30|61] — 6926
Was Captured Live At The Forum (69) 6(7) [11|24|72] — 6338
Suitable For Framing (69) 16(4) [0|27|74] — 5812
Three Dog Night (69) 11(1) [0|26|62] — 5552
Naturally (70) 14(2) [0|23|64] — 4797
It Ain't Easy (70) 8(2) [5|20|48] — 4535
Seven Separate Fools (72) 6(2) [6|19|40] — 3787
Harmony (71) 8(2) [4|21|34] — 3761
Joy To The World-Their Greatest Hits (74) 15(1) [0|8|17] — 1638
Around The World With Three Dog Night (73) 18(1) [0|9|27] — 1513

► Highest Peak [Top10s|Top40s|Total]
Title (Yr) Peak(Wk) [T10 Wk|T40Wk|TotalWk] Score

THREE DOG NIGHT ► *Continued*

Hard Labor (74) 20(1) [0|8|22] 1312

Cyan (73) 26(1) [0|6|17] 934

Coming Down Your Way (75) 70(1) [0|0|12] 349

American Pastime (76) 123(2) [0|0|6] 112

The THREE O'CLOCK ► 2696 Pk:125 [0|0|1] 114

Arrive Without Travelling (85) 125(2) [0|0|10] 114

THREE TIMES DOPE ► 2367 Pk:122 [0|0|1] 194

Original Stylin' (89) 122(2) [0|0|18] 194

THRILLS ► 3375 Pk:199 [0|0|1] 22

First Thrills (81) 199(2) [0|0|4] 21.6

THUNDERCLAP NEWMAN ► 2766 Pk:161 [0|0|1] 102

Hollywood Dream (70) 161(1) [0|0|10] 102

TIERRA ► 1435 Pk:38 [0|1|1] 919

City Nights (80) 38(3) [0|4|21] 919

TIFFANY ► 352 Pk:1 [1|2|2] 9580

Tiffany (87)-Tiffany 1(2) [22|35|69] 7298

Hold An Old Friend's Hand (88)-Tiffany 17(4) [0|19|29] 2282

Tanita TIKARAM ► 1656 Pk:59 [0|0|1] 616

Ancient Heart (89) 59(1) [0|0|23] 616

Johnny TILLOTSON ► 1864 Pk:48 [0|0|2] 434

Talk Back Trembling Lips (64) 48(1) [0|0|14] 398

She Understands Me (65) 148(1) [0|0|3] 35.8

'TIL TUESDAY ► 847 Pk:19 [0|1|3] 2702

Voices Carry (85) 19(1) [0|12|31] 1712

Welcome Home (86) 49(3) [0|0|26] 755

Everything's Different Now (88) 124(3) [0|0|19] 234

TIMBUK 3 ► 1347 Pk:50 [0|0|2] 1045

Greetings From Timbuk 3 (86) 50(1) [0|0|30] 822

Eden Alley (88) 107(5) [0|0|13] 223

The TIME ► 541 Pk:24 [0|2|3] 5509

Ice Cream Castle (84) 24(3) [0|34|57] 3275

What Time Is It? (82) 26(3) [0|8|33] 1120

The Time (81) 50(1) [0|0|32] 1115

TIMES TWO ► 2607 Pk:137 [0|0|1] 133

X2 (88) 137(1) [0|0|11] 133

TIN MACHINE ► 1603 Pk:28 [0|1|1] 676

Tin Machine (89) 28(1) [0|5|17] 676

TIN TIN ► 3530 Pk:197 [0|0|1] 7

Tin Tin (71) 197(1) [0|0|1] 6.8

TINY TIM ► 1015 Pk:7 [1|1|1] 1886

God Bless Tiny Tim (68) 7(2) [2|10|32] 1886

Cal TJADER ► 1461 Pk:52 [0|0|2] 876

Soul Sauce (65) 52(1) [0|0|22] 620

Several Shades Of Jade (63) 79(1) [0|0|14] 256

TKA ► 2601 Pk:135 [0|0|1] 134

Scars Of Love (88) 135(2) [0|0|11] 134

TKO ► 3393 Pk:181 [0|0|1] 20

Let It Roll (79) 181(2) [0|0|2] 20.0

TNT ► 1746 Pk:100 [0|0|2] 524

Tell No Tales (87) 100(1) [0|0|21] 335

Intuition (89) 115(1) [0|0|12] 188

TOBY BEAU ► 1512 Pk:40 [0|1|1] 781

Toby Beau (78) 40(1) [0|1|23] 781

TODAY ► 1873 Pk:86 [0|0|1] 421

Today (89) 86(2) [0|0|22] 421

The TOKENS ► 2957 Pk:134 [0|0|2] 71

Back To Back (67)-The Tokens/The Happenings [A] 134(1) [0|0|6] 45.4

I Hear Trumpets Blow (66) 148(1) [0|0|2] 25.9

Isao TOMITA ► 899 Pk:49 [0|0|7] 2395

Snowflakes Are Dancing (74)-Tomita 57(1) [0|0|25] 780

► Highest Peak [Top10s|Top40s|Total]
Title (Yr) Peak(Wk) [T10 Wk|T40Wk|TotalWk] Score

Moussorgsky: Pictures At An Exhibition (75) 49(1) [0|0|12] 493

Holst: The Planets (77)-Tomita 67(2) [0|0|13] 423

Firebird (76) 71(1) [0|0|12] 380

Kosmos (78)-Tomita 115(1) [0|0|10] 188

The Bermuda Triangle (79) 152(1) [0|0|6] 83.2

Ravel Bolero (80)-Tomita 174(1) [0|0|5] 48.2

Lily TOMLIN ► 781 Pk:15 [0|1|3] 3085

This Is A Recording (71) 15(1) [0|11|25] 2097

And That's The Truth (72) 41(2) [0|0|22] 895

On Stage (77) 120(2) [0|0|6] 93.2

TOMMY TUTONE ► 1026 Pk:20 [0|1|3] 1852

Tommy Tutone-2 (82) 20(3) [0|8|30] 1453

Tommy Tutone (80) 68(2) [0|0|13] 377

National Emotion (83) 179(1) [0|0|3] 21.9

Gary TOMS Empire ► 3270 Pk:178 [0|0|1] 31

7-6-5-4-3-2-1 Blow Your Whistle (75) 178(1) [0|0|3] 31.2

TOM TOM CLUB ► 971 Pk:23 [0|1|3] 2038

Tom Tom Club (81) 23(1) [0|10|33] 1635

Close To The Bone (83) 73(1) [0|0|13] 257

Boom Boom Chi Boom Boom (89) 114(2) [0|0|11] 146

TONE-LOC ► 575 Pk:1 [1|1|1] 5062

Loc-ed After Dark (89) 1(1) [12|23|42] 5062

Oscar TONEY, Jr. ► 3318 Pk:192 [0|0|1] 27

For Your Precious Love (67) 192(1) [0|0|5] 26.5

TONY! TONI! TONE! ► 1484 Pk:69 [0|0|1] 844

Who? (88) 69(2) [0|0|46] 844

TOO SHORT ► 894 Pk:37 [0|1|1] 2412

Life Is...Too Short (89) 37(2) [0|8|78] 2412

TOOTS And The MAYTALS ► 2354 Pk:157 [0|0|2] 197

Funky Kingston (75) 164(1) [0|0|13] 132

Reggae Got Soul (76) 157(1) [0|0|5] 65.4

TORA TORA ► 1537 Pk:47 [0|0|1] 746

Surprise Attack (89) 47(1) [0|0|33] 746

TORONTO ► 2787 Pk:162 [0|0|2] 99

Get It On Credit (82) 162(2) [0|0|10] 70.8

Lookin' For Trouble (80) 185(1) [0|0|4] 28.4

Richard TORRANCE And EUREKA ► 2043 Pk:107 [0|0|1] 331

Belle Of The Ball (75) 107(1) [0|0|17] 331

Peter TOSH ► 1195 Pk:59 [0|0|6] 1355

Mama Africa (83) 59(1) [0|0|17] 465

Bush Doctor (78) 104(2) [0|0|20] 346

Wanted Dread & Alive (81) 91(1) [0|0|13] 288

Mystic Man (79) 123(1) [0|0|10] 165

Captured Live (84) 152(2) [0|0|8] 78.1

Legalize It (76) 199(1) [0|0|2] 11.4

TOTO ► 217 Pk:4 [2|4|8] 15986

Toto IV (82) 4(4) [22|42|82] 7593

Toto (78) 9(2) [2|20|48] 4137

Hydra (79) 37(3) [0|3|29] 1408

Fahrenheit (86) 40(2) [0|2|36] 1052

Isolation (84) 42(4) [0|0|21] 663

The Seventh One (88) 64(3) [0|0|18] 562

Turn Back (81) 41(2) [0|0|10] 516

Dune (Soundtrack) (84) 168(2) [0|0|8] 54.6

Wayne TOUPS & ZYDECAJUN ► 3334 Pk:183 [0|0|1] 25

Blast From The Bayou (89) 183(2) [0|0|4] 25.4

TOWER OF POWER ► 453 Pk:15 [0|3|10] 7063

Back To Oakland (74) 26(1) [0|5|35] 1748

Tower of Power (73) 15(1) [0|8|31] 1596

Urban Renewal (75) 22(2) [0|5|16] 1149

Ain't Nothin' Stoppin' Us Now (76) 42(4) [0|0|17] 805

► Highest Peak [Top10s|Top40s|Total]
Title (Yr) Peak(Wk) [T10 Wk|T40Wk|TotalWk] Score

Bump City (72) 85(1) [0|0|20] 514

In The Slot (75) 67(2) [0|0|11] 328

East Bay Grease (71) 106(2) [0|0|12] 311

Back On The Streets (79) 106(1) [0|0|12] 230

We Came To Play (78) 89(2) [0|0|8] 195

Live And In Living Color (76) 99(1) [0|0|8] 188

Pete TOWNSHEND ► 398 Pk:5 [1|4|9] 8239

Empty Glass (80) 5(3) [9|19|30] 3960

White City - A Novel (85) 26(3) [0|11|29] 1391

All The Best Cowboys Have Chinese Eyes (82) 26(1) [0|9|26] 1124

Scoop (83) 35(2) [0|4|13] 516

Who Came First (72) 69(1) [0|0|17] 508

The Iron Man (The Musical By Pete Townshend) (89) 58(4) [0|0|13] 355

Rough Mix (77)-Pete Townshend & Ronnie Lane [A] 45(1) [0|0|12] 244

Pete Townshend's Deep End Live! (86) 98(2) [0|0|9] 138

Another Scoop (87) 198(1) [0|0|1] 4.3

Simon TOWNSHEND ► 3091 Pk:169 [0|0|1] 53

Sweet Sound (83) 169(1) [0|0|7] 53.0

The TOYS ► 2510 Pk:92 [0|0|1] 157

The Toys sing "A Lover's Concerto" and "Attack!" (66) 92(1) [0|0|8] 157

T'PAU ► 1490 Pk:31 [0|1|1] 831

T'Pau (87) 31(1) [0|3|24] 831

TRAFFIC ► 186 Pk:5 [4|8|12] 18515

John Barleycorn Must Die (70) 5(2) [5|16|38] 3781

The Low Spark Of High Heeled Boys (71) 7(2) [2|20|30] 3342

Shoot Out At The Fantasy Factory (73) 6(1) [6|12|29] 2471

When The Eagle Flies (74) 9(1) [2|10|27] 2051

Traffic (68) 17(2) [0|8|26] 1909

Last Exit (69) 19(1) [0|7|22] 1637

Welcome To The Canteen (71)-Traffic, Etc. 26(3) [0|7|19] 1188

Traffic-On The Road (73) 29(2) [0|5|24] 958

Best Of Traffic (70) 48(3) [0|0|14] 649

Mr. Fantasy (68) 88(2) [0|0|22] 459

Heavy Traffic (75) 155(1) [0|0|3] 43.6

More Heavy Traffic (75) 193(1) [0|0|4] 26.2

The TRAMMPS ► 830 Pk:46 [0|0|6] 2761

Disco Inferno (77) 46(1) [0|0|49] 1394

Where The Happy People Go (76) 50(1) [0|0|24] 946

Trammps III (77) 85(1) [0|0|13] 258

The Best Of The Trammps (78) 139(2) [0|0|6] 95.1

Trammps (75) 159(2) [0|0|4] 51.2

The Whole World's Dancing (79) 184(1) [0|0|2] 16.6

TRANSVISION VAMP ► 2629 Pk:115 [0|0|1] 127

Pop Art (88) 115(1) [0|0|8] 127

TRAPEZE ► 2565 Pk:146 [0|0|2] 145

Hot Wire (75) 146(1) [0|0|6] 83.5

The Final Swing (74) 172(2) [0|0|6] 61.6

The TRASHMEN ► 1966 Pk:48 [0|0|1] 369

Surfin' Bird (64) 48(1) [0|0|15] 369

TRAVELING WILBURYS ► 487 Pk:3 [1|1|1] 6396

Volume 1 (88) 3(6) [22|32|53] 6396

Mary TRAVERS ► 1362 Pk:71 [0|0|5] 1027

Mary (71) 71(1) [0|0|29] 882

Morning Glory (72) 157(1) [0|0|5] 52.5

All My Choices (73) 169(1) [0|0|6] 48.6

It's In Everyone Of Us (78) 186(1) [0|0|5] 38.2

Circles (74) 200(1) [0|0|1] 5.5

Pat TRAVERS ► 607 Pk:20 [0|3|7] 4672

Crash And Burn (80)-Pat Travers Band 20(1) [0|12|25] 1651

▶ Highest Peak [Top10s|Top40s|Total]
Title (Yr) Peak(Wk) [T10 Wk|T40Wk|TotalWk] — **Score**

Pat TRAVERS ▶ *Continued*
- Pat Travers Band Live! Go For What You Know (79)-Pat Travers Band 29(1) [0|4|22] 1151
- Radio Active (81) 37(2) [0|2|15] 679
- Putting It Straight (77) 70(1) [0|0|22] 481
- Heat In The Street (78) 99(2) [0|0|16] 327
- Pat Travers' Black Pearl (82) 74(3) [0|0|13] 252
- Hot Shot (84) 108(2) [0|0|8] 131

Randy TRAVIS ▶ 403 Pk:19 [0|3|5] 8181
- Always & Forever (87) 19(1) [0|21|103] 3934
- Storms Of Life (86) 85(2) [0|0|100] 1430
- Old 8 x 10 (88) 35(1) [0|6|43] 1338
- No Holdin' Back (89) 33(1) [0|3|47] 1311
- An Old Time Christmas (89) 70(1) [0|0|7] 169

John TRAVOLTA ▶ 1217 Pk:39 [0|1|3] 1311
- John Travolta (76) 39(2) [0|4|22] 995
- Can't Let You Go (77) 66(1) [0|0|9] 228
- Travolta Fever (78) 161(3) [0|0|7] 88.3

TREAT HER RIGHT ▶ 2245 Pk:127 [0|0|1] 236
- Treat Her Right (88) 127(2) [0|0|18] 236

The TREMELOES ▶ 2703 Pk:119 [0|0|1] 113
- Here Comes My Baby (67) 119(2) [0|0|8] 113

T. REX ▶ 682 Pk:17 [0|2|5] 3869
- The Slider (72) 17(2) [0|11|24] 1758
- Electric Warrior (71) 32(1) [0|5|34] 1648
- Tyrannosaurus Rex (A Beginning) (72) 113(3) [0|0|12] 242
- Tanx (73) 102(1) [0|0|10] 186
- T-Rex (71) 188(1) [0|0|5] 36.1

TRINERE & FRIENDS ▶ 3520 Pk:196 [0|0|1] 10
- Greatest Hits (89) 196(2) [0|0|2] 9.6

TRIUMPH ▶ 387 Pk:23 [0|5|9] 8542
- Allied Forces (81) 23(1) [0|9|59] 2287
- Never Surrender (83) 26(2) [0|12|27] 1416
- Thunder Seven (84) 35(2) [0|7|30] 1173
- Just A Game (79) 48(1) [0|0|28] 1073
- Progressions Of Power (80) 32(1) [0|6|18] 951
- The Sport Of Kings (86) 33(2) [0|5|27] 890
- Stages (85) 50(2) [0|0|18] 506
- Surveillance (87) 82(2) [0|0|13] 227
- Rock & Roll Machine (79) 185(2) [0|0|2] 17.8

TRIUMVIRAT ▶ 1001 Pk:27 [0|1|3] 1937
- Spartacus (75) 27(1) [0|5|17] 1010
- Illusions On A Double Dimple (74) 55(1) [0|0|17] 716
- Old Loves Die Hard (76) 85(2) [0|0|8] 211

The TROGGS ▶ 1536 Pk:52 [0|0|2] 747
- Wild Thing (66) 52(1) [0|0|16] 563
- Love Is All Around (68) 109(1) [0|0|9] 184

TROOP ▶ 2702 Pk:133 [0|0|1] 114
- Troop (88) 133(2) [0|0|9] 114

TROOPER ▶ 3230 Pk:182 [0|0|1] 36
- Thick As Thieves (78) 182(2) [0|0|4] 36.2

TROPEA ▶ 2370 Pk:138 [0|0|2] 193
- Tropea (76) 138(1) [0|0|7] 102
- Short Trip To Space (77) 149(1) [0|0|7] 91.7

TROUBADOURS Du ROI BAUDOUIN ▶ 3165 Pk:184 [0|0|1] 45
- Missa Luba (69)-Les Troubadours Du Roi Baudouin 184(2) [0|0|5] 44.8

TROUBLE FUNK ▶ 2508 Pk:121 [0|0|1] 157
- Drop The Bomb (82) 121(2) [0|0|14] 157

Robin TROWER ▶ 265 Pk:5 [3|8|13] 13240
- Truce (82)-Jack Bruce & Robin Trower [A] 109(2) [0|0|6] 60.1
- Bridge Of Sighs (74) 7(1) [3|21|31] 3733
- For Earth Below (75) 5(2) [6|9|17] 2314
- Robin Trower Live! (76) 10(2) [2|8|20] 1702
- Long Misty Days (76) 24(1) [0|6|19] 1487
- In City Dreams (77) 25(1) [0|6|19] 1202
- Caravan To Midnight (78) 37(2) [0|4|17] 817
- Victims Of The Fury (80) 34(2) [0|3|15] 772
- Passion (86) 100(2) [0|0|25] 383
- Twice Removed From Yesterday (73) 106(1) [0|0|24] 349
- B.L.T. (81)-Jack Bruce/Bill Lordan/Robin Trower [A] 37(1) [0|3|16] 281
- Take What You Need (88) 133(2) [0|0|10] 130
- Back It Up (83) 191(1) [0|0|2] 10.8

Andrea TRUE Connection ▶ 1522 Pk:47 [0|0|1] 764
- More, More, More (76) 47(2) [0|0|17] 764

The TRUTH ▶ 2692 Pk:115 [0|0|1] 115
- Weapons Of Love (87) 115(2) [0|0|8] 115

Gil TRYTHALL ▶ 2940 Pk:157 [0|0|1] 73
- Switched On Nashville: Country Moog (70) 157(2) [0|0|6] 73.4

TSOL ▶ 3456 Pk:184 [0|0|1] 14
- Hit And Run (87) 184(1) [0|0|2] 13.7

The TUBES ▶ 569 Pk:18 [0|2|9] 5104
- Outside Inside (83) 18(1) [0|14|34] 1846
- The Completion Backward Principle (81) 36(3) [0|4|27] 1117
- Young And Rich (76) 46(1) [0|0|15] 621
- Remote Control (79) 46(1) [0|0|18] 603
- The Tubes (75) 113(1) [0|0|18] 311
- What Do You Want From Live (78) 82(1) [0|0|8] 223
- Love Bomb (85) 87(2) [0|0|10] 192
- Now (77) 122(2) [0|0|6] 107
- T.R.A.S.H. (Tubes Rarities And Smash Hits) (81) 148(1) [0|0|6] 83.2

TUCK & PATTI ▶ 2831 Pk:162 [0|0|1] 90
- Love Warriors (89) 162(3) [0|0|11] 90.5

Louise TUCKER ▶ 2611 Pk:127 [0|0|1] 132
- Midnight Blue (83) 127(1) [0|0|10] 132

Tanya TUCKER ▶ 1339 Pk:54 [0|0|5] 1076
- TNT (78) 54(1) [0|0|22] 686
- Tanya Tucker (75) 113(2) [0|0|7] 149
- Tear Me Apart (79) 121(3) [0|0|8] 149
- Would You Lay With Me (In A Field Of Stone) (74) 159(1) [0|0|6] 65.3
- Should I Do It (81) 180(1) [0|0|3] 25.9

TUFF DARTS ▶ 2924 Pk:156 [0|0|1] 76
- Tuff Darts! (78) 156(1) [0|0|6] 76.5

Ike & Tina TURNER ▶ 578 Pk:25 [0|2|12] 5053
- Workin' Together (70) 25(1) [0|8|38] 1877
- Live At Carnegie Hall/What You Hear Is What You Get (71) 25(2) [0|11|22] 1685
- Come Together (70) 130(1) [0|0|19] 324
- Outta Season (69) 91(1) [0|0|12] 324
- 'Nuff Said (71) 108(2) [0|0|10] 220
- River Deep-Mountain High (69) 102(1) [0|0|8] 194
- In Person (69) 142(1) [0|0|9] 128
- Feel Good (72) 160(1) [0|0|9] 106
- Live! The Ike & Tina Turner Show (65) 126(1) [0|0|6] 87.6
- Nutbush City Limits (73) 163(1) [0|0|6] 64.3
- The Hunter (69) 176(1) [0|0|3] 32.3
- Get Back! (85) 189(1) [0|0|2] 11.8

Joe Lynn TURNER ▶ 2764 Pk:143 [0|0|1] 102
- Rescue You (85) 143(2) [0|0|12] 102

Spyder TURNER ▶ 3220 Pk:158 [0|0|1] 37
- Stand By Me (67) 158(2) [0|0|3] 37.4

Tina TURNER ▶ 218 Pk:3 [2|3|5] 15981
- Private Dancer (84) 3(11) [39|62|106] 11671
- Break Every Rule (86) 4(1) [6|17|52] 3207
- Foreign Affair (89) 31(2) [0|5|21] 847
- Tina Live In Europe (88) 86(2) [0|0|9] 183
- Acid Queen (75) 155(1) [0|0|5] 71.3

Stanley TURRENTINE ▶ 748 Pk:63 [0|0|14] 3278
- Pieces Of Dreams (74) 69(1) [0|0|21] 478
- In The Pocket (75) 65(2) [0|0|14] 426
- West Side Highway (78) 63(1) [0|0|12] 394
- Have You Ever Seen The Rain (75) 76(1) [0|0|16] 366
- The Man With The Sad Face (76) 96(2) [0|0|14] 356
- Everybody Come On Out (76) 100(3) [0|0|14] 352
- The Sugar Man (75) 110(1) [0|0|13] 256
- What About You! (78) 106(2) [0|0|13] 253
- Nightwings (77) 84(1) [0|0|9] 234
- The Baddest Turrentine (74) 185(1) [0|0|7] 53.4
- Tender Togetherness (81) 162(2) [0|0|3] 37.1
- Rough 'N Tumble (67) 149(1) [0|0|2] 27.6
- The Look Of Love (68) 193(1) [0|0|3] 21.9
- Sugar (71) 182(1) [0|0|3] 21.6

The TURTLES ▶ 581 Pk:7 [1|2|7] 4987
- The Turtles! Golden Hits (67) 7(3) [6|16|39] 2929
- Happy Together (67) 25(2) [0|7|22] 1203
- It Ain't Me Babe (65) 98(1) [0|0|19] 322
- Turtle Soup (69) 117(2) [0|0|9] 197
- The Turtles Present The Battle Of The Bands (68) 128(2) [0|0|12] 177
- The Turtles! More Golden Hits (70) 146(1) [0|0|9] 116
- The Turtles' Greatest Hits/Happy Together Again (74) 194(2) [0|0|7] 44.1

TUXEDO JUNCTION ▶ 1441 Pk:56 [0|0|1] 905
- Tuxedo Junction (78) 56(2) [0|0|32] 905

TWENNYNINE ▶ 1572 Pk:54 [0|0|3] 706
- Best Of Friends (79)-Twennynine Featuring Lenny White 54(2) [0|0|16] 513
- Twennynine With Lenny White (80)-Twennynine Featuring Lenny White 106(2) [0|0|8] 137
- Just Like Dreamin' (81)-Twennynine Featuring Lenny White 162(3) [0|0|5] 55.9

24-7 SPYZ ▶ 2244 Pk:113 [0|0|1] 236
- Harder Than You (89) 113(2) [0|0|16] 236

20/20 ▶ 1961 Pk:127 [0|0|2] 371
- Look Out (81) 127(2) [0|0|12] 191
- 20/20 (79) 138(1) [0|0|13] 180

Dwight TWILLEY ▶ 1082 Pk:39 [0|1|5] 1652
- Jungle (84) 39(1) [0|3|21] 753
- Twilley Don't Mind (77)-Dwight Twilley Band 70(2) [0|0|13] 347
- Sincerely (76)-Dwight Twilley Band 138(1) [0|0|14] 215
- Scuba Divers (82) 109(2) [0|0|11] 177
- Twilley (79) 113(2) [0|0|9] 161

TWIN HYPE ▶ 2693 Pk:140 [0|0|1] 115
- Twin Hype (89) 140(2) [0|0|11] 115

TWISTED SISTER ▶ 637 Pk:15 [0|1|5] 4349
- Stay Hungry (84) 15(3) [0|26|51] 3275
- Come Out And Play (85) 53(2) [0|0|17] 518
- Love Is For Suckers (87) 74(2) [0|0|11] 245
- You Can't Stop Rock 'N' Roll (83) 130(1) [0|0|14] 169
- Under The Blade (85) 125(2) [0|0|11] 142

Conway TWITTY ▶ 1093 Pk:65 [0|0|8] 1623
- Hello Darlin' (70) 65(1) [0|0|26] 701
- How Much More Can She Stand (71) 91(1) [0|0|9] 199
- Southern Comfort (82) 144(1) [0|0|15] 156
- You've Never Been This Far Before/Baby's Gone (73) 134(1) [0|0|9] 143

▶ Highest Peak [Top10s|Top40s|Total]
Title (Yr) Peak(Wk) [T10 Wk|T40Wk|TotalWk] **Score**

Conway TWITTY ▶ *Continued* 1623
I Wonder What She'll Think About Me Leaving (71) 142(1) [0|0|8] 137
Fifteen Years Ago (71) 140(1) [0|0|7] 125
I Can't See Me Without You (72) 130(1) [0|0|9] 118
I Love You More Today (69) 161(1) [0|0|3] 45.1

Conway TWITTY & Loretta LYNN ▶ 1542 Pk:78 [0|0|3] 741
We Only Make Believe (71) 78(1) [0|0|15] 380
Lead Me On (72) 106(1) [0|0|13] 254
Louisiana Woman, Mississippi Man (73) 153(1) [0|0|9] 107

2 LIVE CREW ▶ 574 Pk:29 [0|1|3] 5065
As Nasty As They Wanna Be (89) 29(1) [0|31|81] 3974
Move Somethin' (88) 68(2) [0|0|42] 798
2 Live Crew Is What We Are (87) 128(1) [0|0|33] 293

TYCOON ▶ 1625 Pk:41 [0|0|1] 648
Tycoon (79) 41(1) [0|0|17] 648

Bonnie TYLER ▶ 619 Pk:4 [1|2|4] 4566
Faster Than The Speed Of Night (83) 4(1) [7|18|32] 2933
It's A Heartache (78) 16(1) [0|8|17] 1428
Secret Dreams & Forbidden Fire (86) 106(2) [0|0|8] 128
Diamond Cut (79) 145(1) [0|0|5] 77.0

The TYMES ▶ 2330 Pk:117 [0|0|2] 205
The Sound Of The Wonderful Tymes (63) 117(1) [0|0|10] 150
Somewhere (64) 122(1) [0|0|4] 55.6

McCoy TYNER ▶ 1533 Pk:66 [0|0|8] 749
Together (79) 66(2) [0|0|11] 295
Fly With The Wind (76) 128(1) [0|0|11] 188
Inner Voices (78) 171(1) [0|0|8] 79.3
Atlantis (75) 161(1) [0|0|5] 57.9
Supertrios (77) 167(2) [0|0|5] 57.3
The Greeting (78) 170(1) [0|0|3] 35.6
Focal Point (77) 187(2) [0|0|3] 24.5
Trident (76) 198(2) [0|0|2] 11.5

TYZIK ▶ 3142 Pk:172 [0|0|1] 47
Jammin' In Manhattan (84) 172(1) [0|0|6] 47.0

U

UB40 ▶ 539 Pk:14 [0|2|6] 5531
Labour Of Love (83) 14(1) [0|15|63] 2783
UB40 (88) 44(2) [0|0|27] 832
Little Baggariddim (85) 40(3) [0|3|25] 811
Geffrey Morgan... (84) 60(1) [0|0|26] 566
Rat In The Kitchen (86) 53(2) [0|0|17] 427
CCCP - Live In Moscow (87) 121(2) [0|0|8] 112

--Ubiquity see Ayers, Roy Ubiquity

UFO ▶ 573 Pk:23 [0|1|10] 5089
Lights Out (77) 23(2) [0|12|24] 1861
Obsession (78) 41(2) [0|0|18] 863
Strangers In The Night (79) 42(1) [0|0|15] 650
No Place To Run (80) 51(1) [0|0|13] 427
Force It (75) 71(1) [0|0|13] 334
Mechanix (82) 82(1) [0|0|14] 298
Misdemeanor (86) 106(2) [0|0|19] 293
The Wild The Willing And The Innocent (81) 77(2) [0|0|11] 269
Making Contact (83) 153(1) [0|0|5] 49.4
No Heavy Petting (76) 169(1) [0|0|4] 45.0

U.K. ▶ 1316 Pk:45 [0|0|3] 1109
Danger Money (79) 45(1) [0|0|11] 524
U.K. (78) 65(1) [0|0|15] 453
Night After Night (79) 109(1) [0|0|6] 132

▶ Highest Peak [Top10s|Top40s|Total]
Title (Yr) Peak(Wk) [T10 Wk|T40Wk|TotalWk] **Score**

Tracey ULLMAN ▶ 1503 Pk:34 [0|1|1] 803
You Broke My Heart In 17 Places (84) 34(2) [0|5|20] 803

ULTIMATE ▶ 2590 Pk:157 [0|0|1] 138
Ultimate (79) 157(1) [0|0|11] 138

ULTIMATE SPINACH ▶ 1323 Pk:34 [0|1|2] 1098
Ultimate Spinach (68) 34(1) [0|4|24] 1084
Behold & See (68) 198(2) [0|0|2] 13.7

ULTRAVOX ▶ 1541 Pk:61 [0|0|4] 742
Quartet (83) 61(1) [0|0|17] 433
Lament (84) 115(2) [0|0|9] 125
Vienna (80) 164(1) [0|0|9] 102
Rage In Eden (81) 144(2) [0|0|6] 81.9

UNDERGROUND SUNSHINE ▶ 3188 Pk:161 [0|0|1] 43
Let There Be Light (69) 161(1) [0|0|3] 42.6

The UNDERTONES ▶ 2879 Pk:154 [0|0|1] 83
The Undertones (80) 154(1) [0|0|7] 82.6

UNDERWORLD ▶ 2242 Pk:139 [0|0|1] 237
Underneath The Radar (88) 139(2) [0|0|19] 237

UNDISPUTED TRUTH ▶ 1123 Pk:43 [0|0|6] 1539
The Undisputed Truth (71) 43(1) [0|0|18] 809
Method To The Madness (77) 66(2) [0|0|17] 430
Face To Face With The Truth (72) 114(1) [0|0|12] 226
Higher Than High (75) 173(1) [0|0|4] 42.3
Cosmic Truth (75) 186(2) [0|0|2] 17.8
Law Of The Land (73) 191(2) [0|0|2] 14.0

The UNFORGIVEN ▶ 3463 Pk:185 [0|0|1] 13
The Unforgiven (86) 185(2) [0|0|2] 13.0

UNICORN ▶ 2756 Pk:129 [0|0|1] 103
Blue Pine Trees (74) 129(1) [0|0|5] 103

UNITED STATES OF AMERICA ▶ 3000 Pk:181 [0|0|1] 66
The United States Of America (68) 181(1) [0|0|9] 66.1

UNLIMITED TOUCH ▶ 2797 Pk:142 [0|0|1] 98
Unlimited Touch (81) 142(1) [0|0|7] 97.8

The UNTOUCHABLES ▶ 2931 Pk:162 [0|0|1] 75
Agent Double O Soul (89) 162(2) [0|0|9] 74.8

UP WITH PEOPLE ▶ 1984 Pk:61 [0|0|1] 360
Up With People! (66) 61(2) [0|0|14] 360

Midge URE ▶ 2083 Pk:88 [0|0|1] 310
Answers To Nothing (89) 88(1) [0|0|16] 310

URIAH HEEP ▶ 413 Pk:23 [0|5|15] 7871
Demons And Wizards (72) 23(2) [0|13|38] 2202
The Magician's Birthday (72) 31(1) [0|8|22] 1222
Uriah Heep Live (73) 37(1) [0|5|30] 1071
Sweet Freedom (73) 33(1) [0|3|23] 942
Wonderworld (74) 38(2) [0|2|15] 735
Look At Yourself (71) 93(2) [0|0|20] 448
Abominog (82) 56(3) [0|0|16] 430
Return To Fantasy (75) 85(2) [0|0|10] 281
Salisbury (71) 103(2) [0|0|9] 211
Head First (83) 159(1) [0|0|10] 96.9
The Best Of Uriah Heep (76) 145(2) [0|0|6] 89.0
High And Mighty (76) 161(1) [0|0|3] 40.0
Fallen Angel (78) 186(2) [0|0|5] 39.7
Firefly (77) 166(1) [0|0|3] 35.8
Uriah Heep (70) 186(1) [0|0|4] 27.3

USA-EUROPEAN CONNECTION ▶ 1762 Pk:66 [0|0|1] 510
Come Into My Heart (78) 66(2) [0|0|19] 510

USA For AFRICA ▶ 826 Pk:1 [1|1|1] 2778
We Are The World (85) 1(3) [7|11|22] 2778

▶ Highest Peak [Top10s|Top40s|Total]
Title (Yr) Peak(Wk) [T10 Wk|T40Wk|TotalWk] **Score**

UTFO ▶ 1381 Pk:67 [0|0|4] 994
Lethal (87) 67(2) [0|0|20] 462
UTFO (85) 80(2) [0|0|20] 399
Skeezer Pleezer (86) 142(2) [0|0|8] 79.6
Doin' It! (89) 143(2) [0|0|4] 52.8

UTOPIA ▶ 707 Pk:32 [0|2|10] 3612
Adventures In Utopia (80) 32(2) [0|5|21] 1025
Todd Rundgren's Utopia (74) 34(2) [0|2|15] 783
Utopia (82) 84(2) [0|0|19] 343
Todd Rundgren's Utopia/Another Live (75) 66(1) [0|0|9] 299
Deface The Music (80) 65(2) [0|0|9] 264
Oblivion (84) 74(2) [0|0|12] 263
Oops! Wrong Planet (77) 73(1) [0|0|8] 242
Ra (77) 79(1) [0|0|7] 187
Swing To The Right (82) 102(1) [0|0|10] 156
POV (85) 161(2) [0|0|6] 50.1

U2 ▶ 84 Pk:1 [2|6|8] 32944
The Joshua Tree (87) 1(9) [35|58|103] 12139
Rattle And Hum (Soundtrack) (88) 1(6) [14|23|38] 5894
The Unforgettable Fire (84) 12(3) [0|22|132] 4535
War (83) 12(1) [0|16|179] 4509
Under A Blood Red Sky (83) 28(3) [0|13|180] 3718
Boy (81) 63(2) [0|0|47] 1154
October (81) 104(2) [0|0|38] 583
Wide Awake In America (85) 37(1) [0|1|23] 413

V

VAIN ▶ 2888 Pk:154 [0|0|1] 82
No Respect (89) 154(2) [0|0|8] 81.5

Jerry VALE ▶ 473 Pk:22 [0|5|18] 6646
The Language Of Love (63) 22(1) [0|6|35] 1249
Be My Love (64) 26(2) [0|6|22] 911
Till The End Of Time (64) 28(1) [0|6|18] 797
Have You Looked Into Your Heart (65) 30(2) [0|5|23] 761
It's Magic (66) 38(1) [0|1|17] 576
There Goes My Heart (65) 42(1) [0|0|17] 521
Standing Ovation! (65) 55(1) [0|0|18] 500
The Impossible Dream (67) 117(1) [0|0|23] 360
Till (69) 90(1) [0|0|12] 339
This Guy's In Love With You (68) 135(1) [0|0|20] 308
Great Moments On Broadway (66) 111(1) [0|0|4] 76.4
Time Alone Will Tell (67) 128(2) [0|0|6] 75.7
You Don't Have To Say You Love Me (68) 163(1) [0|0|7] 65.6
Where's The Playground Susie? (69) 180(1) [0|0|4] 43.9
Let It Be (70) 189(1) [0|0|4] 25.1
With Love, Jerry Vale (69) 193(2) [0|0|2] 15.5
Jerry Vale Sings 16 Greatest Hits Of The 60's (70) 196(2) [0|0|2] 12.5
Jerry Vale Sings The Great Hits Of Nat King Cole (72) 200(2) [0|0|2] 10.3

Ritchie VALENS ▶ 2596 Pk:100 [0|0|1] 136
The Best Of Ritchie Valens (87) 100(2) [0|0|10] 136

Dave VALENTIN ▶ 3156 Pk:184 [0|0|2] 46
Pied Piper (81) 184(3) [0|0|4] 32.8
Land Of The Third Eye (80) 194(2) [0|0|2] 13.0

Frankie VALLI ▶ 901 Pk:34 [0|1|7] 2384
Closeup (75) 51(2) [0|0|28] 1095
Solo (67) 34(1) [0|2|23] 849
Our Day Will Come (75) 107(2) [0|0|8] 171
Frankie Valli Gold (75) 132(2) [0|0|8] 132
Frankie Valli...Is The Word (78) 160(2) [0|0|7] 85.1

▶ Highest Peak [Top10s | Top40s | Total]
Title (Yr) Peak(Wk) [T10 Wk | T40Wk | TotalWk] Score

Frankie VALLI ▶ *Continued*
Timeless (68) 176(2) [0|0|5] 45.6
Half & Half (70)-Frankie Valli & The 4 Seasons [A] 190(2) [0|0|2] 7.6
--Van Beethoven, Camper see: Camper Van Beethoven
VANDENBERG ▶ 1895 Pk:65 [0|0|2] 410
Vandenberg (83) 65(4) [0|0|18] 355
Heading For A Storm (84) 169(2) [0|0|7] 55.4
Luther VANDROSS ▶ 205 Pk:9 [1|7|7] 16919
Give Me The Reason (86) 14(1) [0|32|53] 3534
The Best Of Luther Vandross...The Best Of Love (89) 26(2) [0|22|51] 2564
Any Love (88) 9(1) [3|15|33] 2513
The Night I Fell In Love (85) 19(3) [0|15|56] 2435
Never Too Much (81) 19(2) [0|10|36] 2394
Forever, For Always, For Love (82) 20(5) [0|12|36] 1945
Busy Body (83) 32(4) [0|9|41] 1534
Theo VANESS ▶ 2842 Pk:145 [0|0|1] 89
Bad, Bad Boy (79) 145(2) [0|0|6] 88.8
VANGELIS ▶ 456 Pk:1 [1|1|2] 7000
Chariots Of Fire (Soundtrack) (81) 1(4) [14|20|57] 6161
Opera Sauvage (86) 42(1) [0|0|39] 839
VAN HALEN ▶ 56 Pk:1 [7|8|8] 42406
1984 (MCMLXXXIV) (84) 2(5) [27|52|77] 9001
OU812 (88) 1(4) [16|35|48] 6971
5150 (86) 1(3) [14|32|64] 6636
Van Halen (78) 19(2) [0|12|169] 6065
Van Halen II (79) 6(3) [9|18|47] 4482
Diver Down (82) 3(3) [9|16|65] 3394
Women And Children First (80) 6(5) [9|13|31] 3216
Fair Warning (81) 5(3) [5|12|23] 2642
VANILLA FUDGE ▶ 273 Pk:6 [1|5|5] 12984
Vanilla Fudge (67) 6(4) [11|39|80] 6459
Near The Beginning (69) 16(2) [0|9|27] 2128
Renaissance (68) 20(2) [0|9|33] 1979
The Beat Goes On (68) 17(4) [0|9|33] 1677
Rock & Roll (69) 34(1) [0|4|13] 741
VANITY ▶ 1071 Pk:45 [0|0|3] 1680
Vanity 6 - Vanity 6 (82) 45(2) [0|0|31] 805
Wild Animal (84) 62(2) [0|0|23] 460
Skin On Skin (86) 66(2) [0|0|20] 415
Gino VANNELLI ▶ 380 Pk:13 [0|4|9] 8771
Brother To Brother (78) 13(3) [0|11|35] 2750
Nightwalker (81) 15(4) [0|15|26] 2311
The Gist Of The Gemini (76) 32(2) [0|5|22] 1043
A Pauper In Paridise (77) 33(2) [0|4|16] 879
Storm At Sunup (75) 66(1) [0|0|23] 656
Powerful People (74) 60(2) [0|0|30] 597
Black Cars (85) 62(2) [0|0|25] 449
Big Dreamers Never Sleep (87) 160(2) [0|0|7] 63.4
The Best Of Gino Vannelli (81) 172(2) [0|0|2] 22.7
Randy VANWARMER ▶ 2254 Pk:81 [0|0|1] 232
Warmer (79) 81(2) [0|0|10] 232
Johnny Van ZANT Band ▶ 1476 Pk:48 [0|0|4] 853
No More Dirty Deals (80) 48(1) [0|0|15] 540
Round Two (81) 119(2) [0|0|10] 191
Van-Zant (85)-Van-Zant 170(1) [0|0|8] 65.9
Last Of The Wild Ones (82) 159(1) [0|0|6] 55.8
The VAPORS ▶ 1458 Pk:62 [0|0|2] 879
New Clear Days (80) 62(1) [0|0|28] 689
Magnets (81) 109(1) [0|0|9] 191
VARIOUS ARTISTS ▶ Pk:1 [4|19|188] 69190
Jesus Christ Superstar (70) 1(3) [41|65|101] 18456
Tommy (72) 5(3) [6|13|38] 2970
The Super Hits (67) 12(2) [0|14|60] 2829
Welcome To The LBJ Ranch! (65) 3(3) [6|14|25] 2345
You Don't Have To Be Jewish (65) 9(1) [2|14|34] 1942
A Very Special Christmas (87) 20(3) [0|7|31] 1351
No Nukes/The MUSE Concerts For A Non-Nuclear Future (79) 19(2) [0|9|18] 1322
A Night At Studio 54 (79) 21(1) [0|6|25] 1295
Themes Like Old Times (69) 31(2) [0|7|17] 1158
Dick Clark/20 Years Of Rock N' Roll (73) 27(2) [0|7|18] 1028
Free To Be...You And Me (73) 68(1) [0|0|58] 929
The Super Hits, Vol. 2 (68) 76(1) [0|0|33] 861
When You're In Love The Whole World Is Jewish (66) 22(2) [0|5|18] 841
Mickey Mouse Disco (80) 35(2) [0|4|27] 815
Nadia's Theme (The Young And The Restless) (76) 42(1) [0|0|19] 794
Fillmore: The Last Days (72) 40(2) [0|2|16] 752
Opening Nights At The Met (66) 49(1) [0|0|21] 745
The Secret Policeman's Other Ball (82) 29(1) [0|5|16] 710
1988 Summer Olympics-One Moment In Time (88) 31(2) [0|3|17] 676
The Big Sounds Of The Drags! (63) 27(1) [0|2|18] 655
25 #1 Hits From 25 Years (83) 42(2) [0|0|28] 641
Concerts For The People Of Kampuchea (81) 36(2) [0|3|12] 610
Chess (85) 47(2) [0|0|21] 589
The Super Hits, Vol. 3 (68) 68(1) [0|0|19] 583
Our Wedding Album or The Great Society Affair (66) 40(2) [0|2|14] 565
Happy Anniversary, Charlie Brown (89) 65(3) [0|0|21] 534
16 Original Big Hits, Volume 5 (66) 57(1) [0|0|19] 522
20 Original Winners Of 1964 (65) 44(1) [0|0|18] 514
The War Of The Worlds (78) 98(1) [0|0|25] 513
Apollo Saturday Night (64) 43(2) [0|0|17] 480
Oldies But Goodies, Vol. 6 (64) 31(1) [0|3|11] 478
Casino Lights (82) 63(5) [0|0|19] 457
Greenpeace/Rainbow Warriors (89) 68(2) [0|0|24] 443
Music To Read James Bond By (65) 72(2) [0|0|27] 430
Television's Greatest Hits (85) 82(2) [0|0|34] 429
First Great Rock Festivals Of The Seventies: Isle Of Wight/Atlanta Pop Fest (71) 47(2) [0|0|9] 427
The Watergate Comedy Hour (73) 62(1) [0|0|15] 419
Hot Rod Rally (63) 62(1) [0|0|15] 409
16 Original Big Hits, Volume 6 (67) 95(1) [0|0|25] 377
Exposed/A Cheap Peek At Today's Provocative New Rock (81) 51(2) [0|0|9] 376
Joseph And The Amazing Technicolor Dreamcoat (71) 84(1) [0|0|12] 370
Windham Hill Records Sampler '84 (84) 108(4) [0|0|25] 361
The Greatest Hits From England (67) 87(2) [0|0|18] 349
The Wrestling Album (85) 84(2) [0|0|19] 343
16 Original Big Hits, Volume 7 (67) 79(1) [0|0|18] 336
Great Voices Of The Century (64) 70(1) [0|0|15] 315
Requiem (85) 77(2) [0|0|14] 311
Windham Hill Records Sampler '86 (86) 102(2) [0|0|18] 306
Solid Gold Soul (66) 107(1) [0|0|19] 302
The New First Family, 1968 (66) 72(1) [0|0|10] 288
A Winter's Solstice (85) 77(1) [0|0|19] 278
Sesame Street Fever (78) 75(1) [0|0|10] 278
More American Graffiti (75) 84(2) [0|0|10] 276
Make A Difference Foundation: Stairway To Heaven/Highway To Hell (89) 87(1) [0|0|15] 269
The Secret Policeman's Ball (81) 106(1) [0|0|12] 268
DisinHAIRited (70) 95(1) [0|0|13] 252
Bubble Gum Music Is The Naked Truth (69) 105(1) [0|0|9] 244
Stay Awake (88) 119(4) [0|0|15] 237
This Is Soul (68) 146(1) [0|0|22] 236
Folkways: A Vision Shared - A Tribute To Woody Guthrie And Leadbelly (88) 70(2) [0|0|10] 235
California Jam 2 (78) 84(1) [0|0|10] 234
Rap's Greatest Hits (86) 114(2) [0|0|17] 228
The First Nine Months Are The Hardest! (64) 96(1) [0|0|14] 227
Different Strokes (71) 85(2) [0|0|7] 222
Piledriver -- The Wrestling Album II (87) 123(2) [0|0|20] 221
Disco Party (78) 115(2) [0|0|12] 220
Winners (80) 69(2) [0|0|7] 216
Windham Hill Records Sampler '88 (88) 134(1) [0|0|16] 216
16 Original Big Hits (64) 84(1) [0|0|11] 215
Every Man Has A Woman (84) 75(2) [0|0|10] 213
Signs Of The Zodiac (69) 147(2) [0|0|15] 208
MTV's Rock 'N Roll To Go (85) 91(2) [0|0|12] 204
Echoes Of An Era (82) 105(1) [0|0|11] 195
The Winning Hand (83) 109(1) [0|0|14] 194
Fool Britannia (63) 87(1) [0|0|10] 192
The Official Music Of The XXIIIrd Olympiad-Los Angeles 1984 (84) 92(2) [0|0|13] 192
Volunteer Jam VI (80) 104(2) [0|0|9] 191
James Blonde, Secret Agent 006.95, "The Man From T.A.N.T.E." (65) 93(1) [0|0|9] 180
Super Oldies/Vol. 3 (68) 130(1) [0|0|9] 173
Pick Hits Of The Radio Good Guys (64) 80(2) [0|0|8] 172
Disco Boogie (77) 115(2) [0|0|11] 164
The South's Greatest Hits (77) 142(2) [0|0|11] 152
History Of British Rock, Volume 3 (75) 145(3) [0|0|10] 151
TeeVee Toons - The Commercials (89) 159(1) [0|0|18] 150
Rock For Amnesty (87) 121(2) [0|0|11] 148
25 Years Of Grammy Greats (83) 107(1) [0|0|9] 145
Television's Greatest Hits Volume II (86) 149(2) [0|0|16] 142
The Legend Of Jesse James (80) 154(4) [0|0|13] 141
History Of British Rock, Volume 2 (74) 141(1) [0|0|11] 141
Let's Clean Up The Ghetto (77) 121(2) [0|0|9] 140
The Super Hits, Vol. 4 (69) 164(2) [0|0|10] 140
A Child's Garden Of Grass (A Pre-Legalization Comedy) (71) 148(1) [0|0|9] 139
A Treasury Of Great Contemporary Hits (69) 144(1) [0|0|7] 137
Milestone Jazzstars In Concert (79) 122(2) [0|0|8] 135
Saturday Night At The Uptown (64) 95(1) [0|0|8] 134
Zodiac: Cosmic Sounds, The (67) 118(1) [0|0|9] 133
Oldies But Goodies, Vol. 7 (65) 121(2) [0|0|9] 133
The Motown Story: The First 25 Years (83) 114(1) [0|0|9] 127
A Winter's Solstice II (88) 108(1) [0|0|7] 125
Motortown Review In Paris (65) 111(1) [0|0|7] 117
World Of Country Music (65) 107(2) [0|0|7] 115

▶ Highest Peak [Top10s | Top40s | Total]
Title (Yr) Peak(Wk) [T10 Wk | T40Wk | TotalWk] — Score

VARIOUS ARTISTS ▶ *Continued* — **69190**

In Harmony 2 (81) 129(1) [0|0|10] — 105
Dance Discotheque (64) 102(1) [0|0|6] — 104
Live! For Life (86) 105(2) [0|0|7] — 104
Motown Winners' Circle/No. 1 Hits, Vol. 2 (69) 135(2) [0|0|5] — 103
16 Original Big Hits, Volume 9 (68) 173(1) [0|0|9] — 96.4
Electric Breakdance (84) 147(2) [0|0|9] — 94.3
A Live Mutherforya (78) 151(3) [0|0|6] — 91.0
Motown At The Hollywood Palace (70) 105(2) [0|0|4] — 90.6
The Motor-Town Review, Vol. 2 (64) 102(2) [0|0|5] — 89.2
Songs Of The Humpback Whale (71) 176(1) [0|0|8] — 83.8
Volunteer Jam (76) 153(1) [0|0|6] — 82.8
20/20 Twenty No.1 Hits From Twenty Years At Motown (80) 150(2) [0|0|6] — 81.5
Exposed II (81) 124(2) [0|0|5] — 80.7
Christmas Rap (87) 130(1) [0|0|8] — 80.3
16 Original Big Hits, Volume 4 (66) 108(1) [0|0|5] — 80.0
History Of British Blues, Volume One (73) 160(1) [0|0|8] — 78.7
Windham Hill Piano Sampler (85) 167(2) [0|0|12] — 73.5
Rock's Greatest Hits (69) 182(1) [0|0|7] — 69.8
Disco Gold (75) 153(2) [0|0|5] — 69.3
Music People, The (72) 165(2) [0|0|6] — 66.4
In Harmony - A Sesame Street Record (81) 156(1) [0|0|5] — 65.0
Motown Winners' Circle/No. 1 Hits, Vol. 1 (69) 159(1) [0|0|4] — 63.9
Volunteer Jam VII (81) 149(2) [0|0|4] — 63.0
Disco Spectacular Inspired By The Film "Hair" (79) 159(1) [0|0|5] — 61.3
16 Original Big Hits, Volume 8 (67) 163(2) [0|0|7] — 60.8
Metropolitan Opera Gala Honoring Sir Rudolf Bing (72) 176(2) [0|0|7] — 60.8
The Original Hits Of Right Now (69) 166(1) [0|0|5] — 60.4
The Original Hootenanny (63) 128(1) [0|0|4] — 60.3
Guitar Speak (88) 171(3) [0|0|8] — 60.0
The Jewish American Princess (71) 183(2) [0|0|7] — 59.6
Heavy Sounds (70) 128(1) [0|0|3] — 57.8
The Super Groups (69) 178(1) [0|0|5] — 51.8
The Stax/Volt Revue - Live In London (67) 145(1) [0|0|4] — 51.3
A GRP Christmas Collection (89) 140(1) [0|0|4] — 50.7
Truth Of Truths - A Contemporary Rock Opera (71) 185(1) [0|0|7] — 50.0
Mar Y Sol (72) 186(2) [0|0|7] — 49.9
Everything You Always Wanted To Know About The Godfather - But Don't Ask (72) 178(2) [0|0|6] — 49.0
Empire Jazz (80) 168(1) [0|0|5] — 45.8
The Yiddish Are Coming! The Yiddish Are Coming! (67) 165(1) [0|0|5] — 45.1
Motortown Review Live (69) 177(1) [0|0|5] — 45.0
Beware Of Greeks Bearing Gifts (69) 190(1) [0|0|6] — 44.9
Live At Yankee Stadium (69) 169(1) [0|0|4] — 44.8
Apollo 11: Flight To The Moon (69) 185(1) [0|0|5] — 43.4
The Music For UNICEF Concert/A Gift Of Song (79) 171(2) [0|0|4] — 41.5
The Island Story, 1962-1987: The 25th Anniversary (87) 180(2) [0|0|6] — 41.4
Dracula's Greatest Hits (64) 129(1) [0|0|3] — 41.4
The Way To Become The Sensuous Woman By "J" (71) 181(1) [0|0|4] — 39.8
History Of Rhythm & Blues, Volume 2/The Golden Years 1953-55 (68) 173(1) [0|0|5] — 39.3
Hot Rod Hootenanny (64) 138(1) [0|0|3] — 38.7
White Mansions (78) 181(3) [0|0|4] — 38.3
The Core Of Rock (70) 175(2) [0|0|4] — 38.1
Heavy Hits! (69) 151(1) [0|0|2] — 37.1
Rap's Greatest Hits, Volume 2 (87) 167(1) [0|0|4] — 36.6
Soul Explosion (69) 172(1) [0|0|3] — 35.7
History Of Rhythm & Blues, Volume 4/The Big Beat 1958-60 (68) 180(1) [0|0|4] — 33.8
Lyndon Johnson's Lonely Hearts Club Band (68) 176(2) [0|0|5] — 33.6
A Country Christmas (82) 172(2) [0|0|4] — 32.3
Windham Hill Records Sampler '89 (89) 176(2) [0|0|4] — 31.0
Urgh! A Music War (81) 173(2) [0|0|3] — 30.5
Golden Instrumentals (67) 177(2) [0|0|4] — 29.9
The Muppet Alphabet Album (71) 189(1) [0|0|4] — 28.4
Brazil Classics 1: Beleza Tropical (89) 178(2) [0|0|4] — 27.8
Earle Doud Presents Spiro T. Agnew Is A Riot! (71) 185(1) [0|0|3] — 26.7
The Astromusical House Of... (70) 180(2) [0|0|3] — 25.5
Big Sur Festival/One Hand Clapping (72) 191(1) [0|0|4] — 25.4
Murray The K - Live From The Brooklyn Fox (63) 148(1) [0|0|2] — 24.6
History Of Rhythm & Blues, Volume 1/The Roots 1947-52 (68) 187(1) [0|0|3] — 22.5
Hustle Hits (76) 177(2) [0|0|2] — 21.7
History Of Rhythm & Blues, Volume 3/Rock & Roll 1956-57 (68) 189(3) [0|0|3] — 21.6
Family Portrait (68) 194(1) [0|0|4] — 19.8
Threads Of Glory - 200 Years Of America In Words & Music (75) 192(1) [0|0|3] — 19.6
A Tribute To Woody Guthrie - Part One (72) 183(2) [0|0|2] — 17.3
The Greatest Hits From Memphis (69) 189(1) [0|0|2] — 16.8
The Prince's Trust 10th Anniversary Birthday Party (87) 194(1) [0|0|3] — 15.0
A Tribute To Woody Guthrie - Part Two (72) 189(2) [0|0|2] — 14.7
Super Oldies/Vol. 5 (69) 196(2) [0|0|2] — 14.3
Underground Gold (69) 196(1) [0|0|2] — 13.6
Best Of The Soundtracks (69) 198(2) [0|0|2] — 13.2
Super Rock (70) 197(2) [0|0|2] — 12.9
The Big Hits Now (70) 197(2) [0|0|2] — 12.1
An Anthology Of British Blues Vol. 2 (68) 200(2) [0|0|2] — 12.1
Live At Bill Graham's Fillmore West (69) 200(2) [0|0|2] — 11.8
Dr. Demento's Delights (75) 198(1) [0|0|2] — 11.7
History Of British Rock (74) 198(1) [0|0|2] — 11.5
The Amazing Mets (69) 197(1) [0|0|1] — 6.6
The New Spirit Of Capitol (70) 200(1) [0|0|1] — 5.3
England's Greatest Hits (67) 197(1) [0|0|1] — 4.9

Sarah VAUGHAN ▶ 3124 Pk:173 [0|0|1] — **49**

Sarah Vaughan/Michel Legrand (72)- Sarah Vaughan/Michel Legrand [A] 173(1) [0|0|12] — 49.3

Stevie Ray VAUGHAN And DOUBLE TROUBLE ▶ 523 Pk:31 [0|4|5] — **5856**

In Step (89) 33(1) [0|6|47] — 1544
Couldn't Stand The Weather (84) 31(3) [0|8|38] — 1443
Soul To Soul (85) 34(2) [0|6|39] — 1106
Texas Flood (83) 38(1) [0|3|33] — 1049
Live Alive (86) 52(2) [0|0|25] — 713

Billy VAUGHN and His Orchestra ▶ 550 Pk:18 [0|2|17] — **5387**

Pearly Shells (65) 18(1) [0|9|29] — 1224
Moon Over Naples (65) 31(2) [0|6|29] — 1130
Alfie (66) 44(1) [0|0|35] — 821
The Windmills Of Your Mind (69) 95(1) [0|0|16] — 448
Blue Velvet & 1963's Great Hits (64) 51(2) [0|0|17] — 446
Mexican Pearls (65) 45(1) [0|0|15] — 406
Michelle (66) 56(1) [0|0|14] — 393
Number 1 Hits, Vol. #1 (63) 94(1) [0|0|8] — 153
That's Life & Pineapple Market (67) 130(1) [0|0|7] — 101
Golden Hits/The Best Of Billy Vaughn (67) 159(2) [0|0|8] — 84.1
Forever (64) 144(2) [0|0|4] — 48.0
Another Hit Album! (64) 141(2) [0|0|3] — 36.5
Josephine (67) 147(1) [0|0|2] — 28.7
Great Country Hits (66) 149(1) [0|0|2] — 27.3
A Current Set Of Standards (68) 198(2) [0|0|3] — 17.9
Winter World Of Love (70) 188(1) [0|0|2] — 15.2
Ode To Billy Joe (67) 200(2) [0|0|2] — 8.9

Billy VAUGHN Singers ▶ 2100 Pk:114 [0|0|2] — **302**

Sweet Maria (67) 114(2) [0|0|20] — 262
I Love You (67) 161(1) [0|0|5] — 40.6

Bobby VEE ▶ 1921 Pk:66 [0|0|3] — **392**

Come Back When You Grow Up (67) 66(2) [0|0|12] — 322
Just Today (68) 187(2) [0|0|7] — 46.8
Bobby Vee Sings The New Sound From England! (64) 146(1) [0|0|2] — 23.4

Suzanne VEGA ▶ 832 Pk:11 [0|1|2] — **2760**

Solitude Standing (87) 11(2) [0|16|32] — 2315
Suzanne Vega (85) 91(2) [0|0|31] — 445

Tata VEGA ▶ 2903 Pk:170 [0|0|1] — **80**

Try My Love (79) 170(2) [0|0|8] — 79.8

Martha VELEZ ▶ 2310 Pk:153 [0|0|1] — **212**

Escape From Babylon (76) 153(1) [0|0|17] — 212

VELVET UNDERGROUND ▶ 1991 Pk:85 [0|0|4] — **353**

VU (85) 85(2) [0|0|13] — 249
The Velvet Underground & Nico (67)- The Velvet Underground & Nico 171(1) [0|0|13] — 86.0
White Light/White Heat (68) 199(1) [0|0|2] — 9.4
The Velvet Underground (85)- The Velvet Underground & Nico 197(1) [0|0|2] — 8.9

The VENTURES ▶ 191 Pk:11 [0|11|25] — **18179**

Hawaii Five-O (69) 11(3) [0|14|24] — 2935
The Ventures A Go-Go (65) 16(1) [0|20|35] — 1996
The Ventures On Stage (65) 27(1) [0|9|30] — 1192
Walk, Don't Run, Vol. 2 (64) 17(2) [0|10|24] — 1134
Let's Go! (63) 30(1) [0|2|33] — 1075
Wild Things! (66) 33(1) [0|6|26] — 1001
Golden Greats By The Ventures (67) 50(2) [0|0|44] — 976
The Ventures Knock Me Out! (65) 31(1) [0|5|24] — 969
(The) Ventures In Space (64) 27(1) [0|7|18] — 872
Where The Action Is (66) 33(1) [0|3|22] — 866
Go With The Ventures! (66) 39(2) [0|2|25] — 723
$1,000,000.00 Weekend (67) 55(2) [0|0|21] — 682
The Ventures/Batman Theme (66) 42(2) [0|0|21] — 646
Guitar Freakout (67) 57(1) [0|0|26] — 639
The Fabulous Ventures (64) 32(1) [0|4|19] — 594
The Ventures 10th Anniversary Album (70) 91(2) [0|0|21] — 539
Super Psychedelics (67) 67(1) [0|0|15] — 321

▶ Highest Peak [Top10s|Top40s|Total] Title (Yr) Peak(Wk) [T10 Wk|T40Wk|TotalWk]	Score
The VENTURES ▶ *Continued*	**18179**
Play Guitar With The Ventures (65) 96(1) [0|0|13]	237
Swamp Rock (69) 81(1) [0|0|12]	229
Underground Fire (69) 157(2) [0|0|14]	206
The Horse (68) 128(2) [0|0|9]	159
More Golden Greats (70) 154(2) [0|0|5]	64.8
Joy/The Ventures Play The Classics (72) 146(1) [0|0|3]	53.7
Flights Of Fantasy (68) 169(1) [0|0|6]	50.9
Theme From Shaft (72) 195(1) [0|0|3]	18.3
Billy VERA & The BEATERS ▶ 1172 Pk:15 [0|1|2]	**1411**
By Request (The Best of Billy Vera & The Beaters) (86) 15(1) [0|10|26]	1239
Billy & The Beaters (81) 118(1) [0|0|10]	172
Tom VERLAINE ▶ 3338 Pk:177 [0|0|1]	**25**
Dreamtime (81) 177(1) [0|0|3]	25.1
VESTA ▶ 2619 Pk:131 [0|0|1]	**129**
Vesta 4 U - Vesta Williams (89) 131(1) [0|0|10]	129
VICTORY ▶ 3337 Pk:182 [0|0|1]	**25**
Culture Killed The Native (89) 182(1) [0|0|5]	25.2
VILLAGE PEOPLE ▶ 210 Pk:3 [2|4|7]	**16445**
Cruisin' (78) 3(4) [9|26|45]	6026
Macho Man (78) 24(2) [0|8|69]	3831
Go West (79) 8(3) [5|13|21]	2579
Village People (77) 54(2) [0|0|86]	2422
Live And Sleazy (79) 32(2) [0|5|20]	1074
Can't Stop The Music (Soundtrack) (80) 47(2) [0|0|12]	445
Renaissance (81) 138(2) [0|0|4]	66.7
VILLAGE STOMPERS ▶ 917 Pk:5 [1|1|2]	**2281**
Washington Square (63) 5(1) [2|14|30]	2244
More Sounds of Washington Square (64) 139(1) [0|0|3]	36.4
Vinnie VINCENT INVASION ▶ 1284 Pk:64 [0|0|2]	**1179**
Vinnie Vincent Invasion (86) 64(2) [0|0|29]	781
All Systems Go (88) 64(2) [0|0|15]	397
Bobby VINTON ▶ 292 Pk:8 [1|6|21]	**11983**
There! I've Said It Again (64) 8(2) [5|12|28]	1993
Bobby Vinton's Greatest Hits (64) 12(1) [0|14|38]	1869
Melodies Of Love (74) 16(1) [0|7|22]	1610
I Love How You Love Me (69) 21(1) [0|6|24]	1563
Please Love Me Forever (67) 41(1) [0|0|33]	1135
Mr. Lonely (65) 18(3) [0|7|13]	832
Tell Me Why (64) 31(1) [0|4|12]	472
Vinton (69) 69(1) [0|0|12]	465
Ev'ry Day Of My Life (72) 72(1) [0|0|15]	423
Sealed With A Kiss (72) 77(1) [0|0|14]	394
Bobby Vinton's All-Time Greatest Hits (72) 119(1) [0|0|16]	259
My Elusive Dreams (70) 90(2) [0|0|6]	172
Bobby Vinton's Greatest Hits Of Love (70) 138(1) [0|0|8]	130
With Love (74) 109(2) [0|0|5]	122
Heart Of Hearts (75) 108(2) [0|0|5]	120
Take Good Care Of My Baby (68) 164(1) [0|0|8]	92.6
Satin Pillows And Careless (66) 110(2) [0|0|5]	86.7
Bobby Vinton Sings For Lonely Nights (65) 116(1) [0|0|5]	82.0
The Bobby Vinton Show (75) 161(2) [0|0|7]	77.7
Bobby Vinton Sings The Golden Decade Of Love (75) 154(2) [0|0|5]	66.1
The Name Is Love (77) 183(1) [0|0|2]	18.1
VIO-LENCE ▶ 3114 Pk:154 [0|0|1]	**51**
Eternal Nightmare (88) 154(2) [0|0|6]	50.7

▶ Highest Peak [Top10s|Top40s|Total] Title (Yr) Peak(Wk) [T10 Wk|T40Wk|TotalWk]	Score
VIOLENT FEMMES ▶ 1662 Pk:84 [0|0|2]	**610**
The Blind Leading The Naked (86) 84(2) [0|0|24]	389
3 (89) 93(3) [0|0|13]	221
VISAGE ▶ 3225 Pk:178 [0|0|1]	**37**
Visage (81) 178(2) [0|0|4]	36.9
The VISCOUNTS ▶ 3320 Pk:144 [0|0|1]	**26**
Harlem Nocturne (66) 144(1) [0|0|2]	26.3
Joe VITALE ▶ 3305 Pk:181 [0|0|1]	**28**
Plantation Harbor (81) 181(1) [0|0|3]	27.8
VITAMIN Z ▶ 3398 Pk:183 [0|0|1]	**19**
Rites Of Passage (85) 183(1) [0|0|3]	19.5
VIXEN ▶ 1154 Pk:41 [0|0|1]	**1452**
Vixen (88) 41(1) [0|0|40]	1452
The VOGUES ▶ 739 Pk:29 [0|2|5]	**3376**
Turn Around, Look At Me (68) 29(1) [0|4|30]	1536
Till (69) 30(2) [0|6|23]	1450
Memories (69) 115(1) [0|0|9]	189
The Vogues' Greatest Hits (70) 148(1) [0|0|9]	107
Five O'Clock World (66) 137(1) [0|0|7]	94.5
VOICES OF EAST HARLEM ▶ 3362 Pk:191 [0|0|1]	**23**
Right On Be Free (70) 191(2) [0|0|3]	22.6
VOIVOD ▶ 2268 Pk:114 [0|0|1]	**226**
Nothingface (89) 114(2) [0|0|16]	226
Andreas VOLLENWEIDER ▶ 897 Pk:52 [0|0|5]	**2399**
Down To The Moon (86) 60(1) [0|0|39]	859
White Winds (85) 76(2) [0|0|39]	665
Dancing With The Lion (89) 52(2) [0|0|19]	488
...Behind The Gardens-Behind The Wall-Under The Tree... (84) 121(2) [0|0|18]	246
Caverna Magica (...Under The Tree-In The Cave...) (84) 149(1) [0|0|15]	141
Roger VOUDOURIS ▶ 3240 Pk:171 [0|0|1]	**34**
Radio Dream (79) 171(2) [0|0|3]	34.4
VOYAGE ▶ 1075 Pk:40 [0|1|2]	**1664**
Fly Away (78) 47(2) [0|0|27]	918
Voyage (78) 40(2) [0|2|21]	745
V.S.O.P ▶ 2792 Pk:123 [0|0|1]	**99**
The Quintet (77) 123(2) [0|0|5]	98.6

W

▶ Highest Peak [Top10s|Top40s|Total] Title (Yr) Peak(Wk) [T10 Wk|T40Wk|TotalWk]	Score
Jack WAGNER ▶ 1329 Pk:44 [0|0|3]	**1089**
All I Need (84) 44(2) [0|0|29]	884
Lighting Up The Night (85) 150(2) [0|0|15]	129
Don't Give Up Your Day Job (87) 151(2) [0|0|8]	76.5
Porter WAGONER ▶ 2737 Pk:161 [0|0|3]	**107**
The Carroll County Accident (69) 161(1) [0|0|8]	87.0
You Got-ta Have A License (70) 190(2) [0|0|2]	15.2
The Cold Hard Facts Of Life (67) 199(1) [0|0|1]	4.8
Porter WAGONER and Dolly PARTON ▶ 2097 Pk:137 [0|0|5]	**306**
Porter Wayne And Dolly Rebecca (70) 137(2) [0|0|7]	135
Always, Always (69) 162(1) [0|0|5]	71.9
Two Of A Kind (71) 142(1) [0|0|3]	46.3
Just The Two Of Us (69) 184(1) [0|0|4]	37.8
Once More (70) 191(1) [0|0|2]	15.2
The WAIKIKIS ▶ 2488 Pk:93 [0|0|1]	**163**
Hawaii Tattoo (65) 93(1) [0|0|9]	163
The WAILERS ▶ 2902 Pk:127 [0|0|1]	**80**
Tall Cool One (64) 127(1) [0|0|6]	79.9
Loudon WAINWRIGHT III ▶ 2005 Pk:102 [0|0|3]	**349**
Album III (73) 102(1) [0|0|13]	248
Unrequited (75) 156(1) [0|0|5]	72.3

▶ Highest Peak [Top10s|Top40s|Total] Title (Yr) Peak(Wk) [T10 Wk|T40Wk|TotalWk]	Score
T Shirt (76) 188(1) [0|0|4]	28.7
John WAITE ▶ 657 Pk:10 [1|2|4]	**4189**
No Brakes (84) 10(1) [1|17|43]	2827
Mask Of Smiles (85) 36(2) [0|3|16]	672
Ignition (82) 68(3) [0|0|23]	426
Rover's Return (87) 77(1) [0|0|12]	263
The WAITRESSES ▶ 1392 Pk:41 [0|0|3]	**979**
Wasn't Tomorrow Wonderful? (82) 41(1) [0|0|24]	787
I Could Rule The World If I Could Only Get The Parts (82) 128(2) [0|0|10]	139
Bruiseology (83) 155(2) [0|0|5]	52.7
Tom WAITS ▶ 1419 Pk:89 [0|0|9]	**938**
Heartattack And Vine (80) 96(2) [0|0|10]	238
Franks Wild Years (87) 115(2) [0|0|10]	159
Small Change (76) 89(1) [0|0|5]	137
Foreign Affairs (77) 113(1) [0|0|8]	134
Nighthawks At The Diner (75) 164(2) [0|0|6]	77.1
Big Time (88) 152(2) [0|0|6]	58.8
Swordfishtrombones (83) 167(1) [0|0|7]	56.8
Rain Dogs (85) 181(2) [0|0|7]	39.5
Blue Valentine (78) 181(2) [0|0|4]	37.3
Rick WAKEMAN ▶ 434 Pk:3 [1|3|7]	**7357**
Journey To The Centre Of The Earth (74)- Rick Wakeman With The London Symphony Orchestra & The English Chamber Choir 3(2) [6|16|27]	3498
The Six Wives Of Henry VIII (73) 30(1) [0|13|45]	2130
The Myths And Legends Of King Arthur And The Knights Of The Round Table (75) 21(1) [0|6|15]	1164
No Earthly Connection (76) 67(1) [0|0|8]	269
Rick Wakeman's Criminal Record (77) 128(1) [0|0|8]	132
White Rock (Soundtrack) (77) 126(1) [0|0|7]	114
Rhapsodies (79) 170(1) [0|0|5]	50.2
Narada Michael WALDEN ▶ 1335 Pk:74 [0|0|4]	**1082**
The Dance Of Life (80) 74(2) [0|0|19]	491
Awakening (79) 103(2) [0|0|16]	340
Victory (80) 103(1) [0|0|8]	182
Confidence (82) 135(1) [0|0|6]	68.6
David T. WALKER ▶ 2729 Pk:166 [0|0|2]	**109**
On Love (76) 166(1) [0|0|5]	58.0
Press On (74) 187(1) [0|0|8]	50.9
Jerry Jeff WALKER ▶ 1141 Pk:60 [0|0|8]	**1494**
A Man Must Carry On (77) 60(2) [0|0|21]	610
It's A Good Night For Singin' (76) 84(1) [0|0|10]	282
Contrary To Ordinary (78) 111(1) [0|0|9]	174
Walker's Collectibles (75) 141(1) [0|0|8]	139
Ridin' High (75) 119(1) [0|0|7]	132
Viva Terlingua! (73) 160(1) [0|0|11]	110
The Best Of Jerry Jeff Walker (80) 185(1) [0|0|3]	23.8
Reunion (81) 188(2) [0|0|3]	22.8
Jimmie WALKER ▶ 2372 Pk:130 [0|0|1]	**193**
Dyn-O-Mite (75) 130(2) [0|0|12]	193
Jr. WALKER & The ALL STARS ▶ 743 Pk:43 [0|0|10]	**3316**
Greatest Hits (69) 43(2) [0|0|18]	915
Shotgun (65) 108(1) [0|0|35]	527
What Does It Take To Win Your Love (70) 92(1) [0|0|22]	497
Road Runner (66) 64(2) [0|0|13]	388
Rainbow Funk (71) 91(1) [0|0|14]	321
Moody Jr. (72) 142(2) [0|0|16]	235
Live! (67) 119(2) [0|0|11]	173
A Gassssss (70) 110(1) [0|0|5]	107

▶ Highest Peak [Top10s | Top40s | Total] Title (Yr) Peak(Wk) [T10 Wk | T40Wk | TotalWk]	Score
Jr. WALKER & The ALL STARS ▶ *Continued*	**3316**
Soul Session (66) 130(1) [0|0|7]	102
Home Cookin' (69) 172(1) [0|0|4]	50.9
Jerry WALLACE ▶ 2439 Pk:96 [0|0|2]	**176**
In The Misty Moonlight (64) 96(1) [0|0|7]	115
Do You Know What It's Like To Be Lonesome? (73) 179(1) [0|0|8]	60.6
WALL OF VOODOO ▶ 1624 Pk:45 [0|0|2]	**650**
Call Of The West (83) 45(2) [0|0|23]	631
Dark Continent (81) 177(1) [0|0|2]	18.9
Joe WALSH ▶ 251 Pk:6 [2|5|10]	**14162**
The Smoker You Drink, The Player You Get (73) 6(2) [6|20|54]	4294
"But Seriously Folks..." (78) 8(2) [4|14|27]	3226
So What (75) 11(1) [0|10|22]	2050
There Goes The Neighborhood (81) 20(1) [0|9|18]	1499
You Can't Argue With A Sick Mind (76) 20(2) [0|9|18]	1384
Barnstorm (72) 79(1) [0|0|29]	506
You Bought It-You Name It (83) 48(1) [0|0|14]	438
The Confessor (85) 65(2) [0|0|19]	436
The Best Of Joe Walsh (78) 71(1) [0|0|7]	211
Got Any Gum? (87) 113(2) [0|0|8]	117
Steve WALSH ▶ 2777 Pk:124 [0|0|1]	**100**
Schemer-Dreamer (80) 124(1) [0|0|6]	100
Walter WANDERLEY ▶ 1069 Pk:22 [0|1|1]	**1682**
Rain Forest (66) 22(1) [0|9|41]	1682
WANG CHUNG ▶ 803 Pk:30 [0|1|4]	**2930**
Points On The Curve (84) 30(3) [0|6|37]	1405
Mosaic (86) 41(2) [0|0|36]	1118
To Live And Die In L.A. (Soundtrack) (85) 85(2) [0|0|18]	311
The Warmer Side Of Cool (89) 123(1) [0|0|6]	96.7
Dexter WANSEL ▶ 2555 Pk:139 [0|0|2]	**148**
Voyager (78) 139(1) [0|0|6]	110
What The World Is Comin' To (77) 168(1) [0|0|3]	37.5
WAR ▶ 107 Pk:1 [4|8|15]	**28429**
The World Is A Ghetto (72) 1(2) [16|25|68]	7568
All Day Music (71) 16(3) [0|20|49]	3774
Deliver The Word (73) 6(2) [7|14|36]	3392
Why Can't We Be Friends? (75) 8(1) [3|19|31]	3374
War Live! (74) 13(1) [0|11|35]	2702
Greatest Hits (76) 6(3) [4|13|21]	2664
Galaxy (77) 15(2) [0|12|23]	1878
Platinum Jazz (77) 23(1) [0|7|14]	1029
The Music Band (79) 41(2) [0|0|16]	784
Outlaw (82) 48(2) [0|0|27]	677
The Music Band 2 (79) 111(3) [0|0|13]	242
Youngblood (78) 69(1) [0|0|6]	185
The Best Of War...And More (87) 156(2) [0|0|10]	84.5
War (71) 190(2) [0|0|6]	44.7
Life (Is So Strange) (83) 164(1) [0|0|4]	32.3
--See also Burdon, Eric and War	
Anita WARD ▶ 943 Pk:8 [1|1|1]	**2164**
Songs Of Love (79) 8(2) [4|10|19]	2164
Steve WARINER ▶ 3473 Pk:187 [0|0|1]	**13**
Greatest Hits (87) 187(2) [0|0|2]	12.6
Frank WARING ▶ 3231 Pk:116 [0|0|1]	**36**
America, I Hear You Singing (64)-Frank Sinatra/Bing Crosby/Frank Waring [A] 116(1) [0|0|7]	36.1
WARLOCK ▶ 1739 Pk:80 [0|0|1]	**534**
Triumph And Agony (87) 80(1) [0|0|27]	534
Jennifer WARNES ▶ 1121 Pk:43 [0|0|3]	**1550**
Jennifer Warnes (77) 43(1) [0|0|18]	623

▶ Highest Peak [Top10s | Top40s | Total] Title (Yr) Peak(Wk) [T10 Wk | T40Wk | TotalWk]	Score
Shot Through The Heart (79) 94(1) [0|0|23]	467
Famous Blue Raincoat (87) 72(2) [0|0|21]	460
WARRANT ▶ 587 Pk:10 [1|1|1]	**4909**
Dirty Rotten Filthy Stinking Rich (89) 10(3) [3|33|65]	4909
Rusty WARREN ▶ 1641 Pk:52 [0|0|2]	**627**
Banned In Boston? (63) 52(1) [0|0|18]	522
More Knockers Up! (66) 124(1) [0|0|7]	105
Dionne WARWICK ▶ 72 Pk:6 [2|14|33]	**36632**
Dionne Warwick's Golden Hits, Part One (67) 10(2) [2|23|69]	4514
Dionne(2) (79) 12(1) [0|13|54]	3593
Valley Of The Dolls (68) 6(2) [5|18|48]	3381
Promises, Promises (68) 18(1) [0|11|39]	2942
Here Where There Is Love (67) 18(2) [0|15|66]	2757
Soulful (69) 11(2) [0|9|28]	2188
I'll Never Fall In Love Again (70) 23(2) [0|14|39]	2099
Friends (85) 12(2) [0|13|26]	1836
Dionne Warwick's Golden Hits, Part 2 (69) 28(1) [0|4|28]	1504
Heartbreaker (82) 25(3) [0|10|28]	1452
No Night So Long (80) 23(2) [0|6|25]	1396
Dionne Warwick's Greatest Motion Picture Hits (69) 31(2) [0|5|24]	1296
The Windows Of The World (67) 22(2) [0|6|31]	1218
Very Dionne (70) 37(2) [0|4|24]	1139
Here I Am (66) 45(1) [0|0|29]	810
The Dionne Warwicke Story (71)-Dionne Warwicke 48(1) [0|0|17]	695
Reservations For Two (87) 56(2) [0|0|27]	540
Dionne (72)-Dionne Warwicke 54(1) [0|0|14]	511
Make Way For Dionne Warwick (64) 68(2) [0|0|20]	423
How Many Times Can We Say Goodbye (83) 57(2) [0|0|17]	404
Hot! Live And Otherwise (81) 72(1) [0|0|14]	359
A Man And A Woman (77)-Isaac Hayes & Dionne Warwick [A] 49(1) [0|0|13]	253
Track Of The Cat (75) 137(2) [0|0|15]	231
Dionne Warwick In Paris (66) 76(1) [0|0|11]	230
Friends In Love (82) 83(2) [0|0|12]	196
Finder Of Lost Loves (85) 106(2) [0|0|11]	161
The Sensitive Sound Of Dionne Warwick (65) 107(1) [0|0|9]	149
On Stage and in The Movies (67) 169(3) [0|0|9]	90.2
Then Came You (75) 167(1) [0|0|6]	64.9
Just Being Myself (73)-Dionne Warwicke 178(1) [0|0|8]	59.8
Only Love Can Break A Heart (77) 188(1) [0|0|7]	50.6
From Within (72) 169(1) [0|0|5]	50.1
Greatest Hits 1979-1990 (89) 177(1) [0|0|7]	39.2
Dinah WASHINGTON ▶ 2897 Pk:130 [0|0|1]	**80**
A Stranger On Earth (64) 130(2) [0|0|6]	80.4
Grover WASHINGTON Jr. ▶ 156 Pk:5 [3|9|17]	**21353**
Winelight (80) 5(7) [8|27|52]	5367
Mister Magic (75) 10(1) [1|17|34]	3167
Live At The Bijou (78) 11(2) [0|9|32]	2135
Feels So Good (75) 10(1) [1|7|30]	2039
Come Morning (81) 28(2) [0|5|27]	1388
Skylarkin' (80) 24(2) [0|6|22]	1170
Paradise (79) 24(2) [0|6|19]	1148
Reed Seed (78) 35(2) [0|5|23]	1025
A Secret Place (77) 31(2) [0|6|16]	940
The Best Is Yet To Come (82) 50(3) [0|0|25]	712
Inner City Blues (72) 62(2) [0|0|25]	690
Inside Moves (84) 79(1) [0|0|23]	414
Strawberry Moon (87) 66(2) [0|0|16]	311

▶ Highest Peak [Top10s | Top40s | Total] Title (Yr) Peak(Wk) [T10 Wk | T40Wk | TotalWk]	Score
Soul Box (73) 100(1) [0|0|14]	286
All The King's Horses (72) 111(1) [0|0|17]	275
Baddest (80) 96(1) [0|0|10]	198
Anthology (81) 149(1) [0|0|7]	87.9
WAS (NOT WAS) ▶ 1286 Pk:43 [0|0|2]	**1174**
What Up, Dog? (88) 43(2) [0|0|37]	1057
Born To Laugh At Tornadoes (83) 134(2) [0|0|9]	118
W.A.S.P. ▶ 932 Pk:48 [0|0|5]	**2209**
The Last Command (85) 49(2) [0|0|23]	639
W.A.S.P. (84) 74(2) [0|0|31]	490
Inside The Electric Circus (86) 60(2) [0|0|19]	418
The Headless Children (89) 48(3) [0|0|13]	409
Live...In The Raw (87) 77(2) [0|0|14]	253
The WATERBOYS ▶ 1732 Pk:76 [0|0|1]	**548**
Fisherman's Blues (88) 76(2) [0|0|26]	548
WATERFRONT ▶ 2397 Pk:103 [0|0|1]	**187**
Waterfront (89) 103(1) [0|0|13]	187
Muddy WATERS ▶ 1552 Pk:70 [0|0|5]	**724**
Fathers And Sons (69) 70(1) [0|0|10]	329
Electric Mud (68) 127(2) [0|0|8]	196
Hard Again (77) 143(1) [0|0|7]	114
I'm Ready (78) 157(1) [0|0|6]	70.5
King Bee (81) 192(2) [0|0|2]	14.5
Roger WATERS ▶ 1167 Pk:31 [0|1|2]	**1417**
The Pros & Cons Of Hitchhiking (84) 31(3) [0|7|18]	796
Radio K.A.O.S. (87) 50(2) [0|0|19]	622
Jody WATLEY ▶ 441 Pk:10 [1|2|3]	**7245**
Jody Watley (87) 10(1) [1|44|74]	4882
Larger Than Life (89) 16(2) [0|17|40]	2129
You Wanna Dance With Me? (89) 86(3) [0|0|13]	234
Doc WATSON ▶ 3377 Pk:193 [0|0|1]	**21**
Memories (75) 193(2) [0|0|3]	21.3
Johnny Guitar WATSON ▶ 694 Pk:20 [0|1|7]	**3778**
A Real Mother For Ya (77) 20(2) [0|13|27]	2149
Ain't That A Bitch (76) 52(2) [0|0|22]	892
Love Jones (80) 115(2) [0|0|14]	305
Funk Beyond The Call Of Duty (77) 84(1) [0|0|14]	254
Giant (78) 157(1) [0|0|7]	93.5
Master Funk (78)-Watsonian Institute 154(1) [0|0|4]	54.5
Johnny "Guitar" Watson And The Family Clone (81) 177(2) [0|0|3]	30.1
Ernie WATTS ▶ 2669 Pk:161 [0|0|1]	**120**
Chariots Of Fire (82) 161(2) [0|0|12]	120
WA WA NEE ▶ 2261 Pk:123 [0|0|1]	**228**
Wa Wa Nee (87) 123(1) [0|0|17]	228
WAX ▶ 2486 Pk:101 [0|0|1]	**164**
Magnetic Heaven (86) 101(2) [0|0|11]	164
Fee WAYBILL ▶ 3002 Pk:146 [0|0|1]	**66**
Read My Lips (84) 146(2) [0|0|6]	65.9
John WAYNE ▶ 1936 Pk:66 [0|0|1]	**383**
America, Why I Love Her (73) 66(1) [0|0|16]	383
WAYSTED ▶ 3466 Pk:185 [0|0|1]	**13**
Save Your Prayers (87) 185(1) [0|0|2]	12.9
WEATHER GIRLS ▶ 2295 Pk:91 [0|0|1]	**219**
Two Tons O' Fun (80)-Two Tons Of Fun 91(2) [0|0|11]	219
Jim WEATHERLY ▶ 2137 Pk:94 [0|0|1]	**285**
The Songs Of Jim Weatherly (74) 94(2) [0|0|14]	285
WEATHER REPORT ▶ 498 Pk:30 [0|2|15]	**6193**
Heavy Weather (77) 30(2) [0|5|22]	1268
Mysterious Traveller (74) 46(3) [0|0|23]	1067
Tale Spinnin' (75) 31(2) [0|4|14]	765
Mr. Gone (78) 52(3) [0|0|14]	617

► Highest Peak [Top10s | Top40s | Total] Title (Yr) Peak(Wk) [T10 Wk | T40Wk | TotalWk]	Score
WEATHER REPORT ► *Continued*	
Black Market (76) 42(1) [0 | 0 | 12]	483
8:30 (79) 47(2) [0 | 0 | 11]	464
Night Passage (80) 57(1) [0 | 0 | 14]	447
Sweetnighter (73) 85(1) [0 | 0 | 17]	357
Weather Report(2) (82) 68(1) [0 | 0 | 11]	298
Procession (83) 96(2) [0 | 0 | 10]	171
Domino Theory (84) 136(1) [0 | 0 | 8]	111
I Sing The Body Electric (72) 147(1) [0 | 0 | 6]	90.6
Weather Report (71) 191(2) [0 | 0 | 4]	29.4
Sportin' Life (85) 191(1) [0 | 0 | 3]	15.5
This Is This (86) 195(2) [0 | 0 | 2]	9.7
Dennis WEAVER ► 3454 Pk:191 [0 | 0 | 1]	**14**
Dennis Weaver (72) 191(2) [0 | 0 | 2]	13.9
WE FIVE ► 1345 Pk:32 [0 | 1 | 2]	**1051**
You Were On My Mind (65) 32(3) [0 | 6 | 30]	997
Make Someone Happy (68) 172(1) [0 | 0 | 6]	53.6
Bob WEIR ► 1450 Pk:68 [0 | 0 | 2]	**891**
Heaven Help The Fool (78) 69(1) [0 | 0 | 16]	448
Ace (72) 68(1) [0 | 0 | 15]	444
Tim WEISBERG ► 854 Pk:8 [1 | 1 | 8]	**878**
Twin Sons Of Different Mothers (78)-Dan Fogelberg/Tim Weisberg [A] 8(3) [5 | 13 | 35]	1752
Night-Rider! (79) 114(1) [0 | 0 | 11]	245
Tim Weisberg 4 (74) 100(2) [0 | 0 | 13]	219
Listen To The City (75) 105(1) [0 | 0 | 7]	141
Live At Last! (76) 148(1) [0 | 0 | 7]	111
Party Of One (80) 171(2) [0 | 0 | 7]	70.1
Dreamspeaker (73) 160(1) [0 | 0 | 4]	48.2
Smile!/The Best Of Tim Weisberg (79) 169(2) [0 | 0 | 4]	43.1
Tim WEISBERG Band ► 2017 Pk:108 [0 | 0 | 2]	**344**
Tim Weisberg Band (77) 108(2) [0 | 0 | 12]	266
Rotations (78) 159(2) [0 | 0 | 6]	78.3
Eric WEISSBERG ► 1008 Pk:1 [1 | 1 | 2]	**1908**
Dueling Banjos (73)-Eric Weissberg & Steve Mandell [A] 1(3) [9 | 14 | 25]	1902
Rural Free Delivery (73)-Eric Weissberg & Deliverance [A] 196(2) [0 | 0 | 2]	5.8
Bob WELCH ► 525 Pk:12 [0 | 2 | 4]	**5780**
French Kiss (77) 12(2) [0 | 29 | 46]	4546
Three Hearts (79) 20(2) [0 | 5 | 17]	1007
The Other One (79) 105(3) [0 | 0 | 8]	168
Man Overboard (80) 162(2) [0 | 0 | 5]	59.5
Lenny WELCH ► 2272 Pk:73 [0 | 0 | 2]	**225**
Since I Fell For You (64) 73(1) [0 | 0 | 10]	200
Since I Fell For You(2) (66) 147(1) [0 | 0 | 2]	24.8
Lawrence WELK ► 427 Pk:12 [0 | 3 | 19]	**7461**
Winchester Cathedral (66) 12(2) [0 | 18 | 41]	2716
Galveston (69) 55(1) [0 | 0 | 20]	825
Wonderful! Wonderful! (63) 29(1) [0 | 3 | 26]	777
Early Hits Of 1964 (64) 37(2) [0 | 3 | 19]	719
Lawrence Welk's "Hits Of Our Time" (67) 72(2) [0 | 0 | 18]	336
The Lawrence Welk Television Show 10th Anniversary (64) 73(1) [0 | 0 | 16]	308
Apples & Bananas (65) 57(1) [0 | 0 | 12]	286
Candida (70) 133(1) [0 | 0 | 17]	227
My First Of 1965 (65) 108(1) [0 | 0 | 12]	182
Golden Hits/The Best Of Lawrence Welk (67) 130(1) [0 | 0 | 12]	172
Love Is Blue (68) 130(1) [0 | 0 | 12]	167
Reminiscing (72) 149(2) [0 | 0 | 10]	127
Today's Great Hits (66) 93(1) [0 | 0 | 6]	118
Jean (69) 145(1) [0 | 0 | 7]	113

► Highest Peak [Top10s | Top40s | Total] Title (Yr) Peak(Wk) [T10 Wk | T40Wk | TotalWk]	Score
The Golden Millions (65) 115(2) [0 | 0 | 6]	96.0
Memories (69)-Lawrence Welk And His Orchestra 173(1) [0 | 0 | 8]	92.3
Champagne On Broadway (66)-Lawrence Welk And His Orchestra 106(1) [0 | 0 | 5]	86.5
A Tribute To The All-Time Greats (64) 127(1) [0 | 0 | 5]	68.3
Lawrence Welk Plays I Love You Truly And Other Songs Of Love (69)176(2) [0 | 0 | 4]	45.6
Freddy WELLER ► 2659 Pk:144 [0 | 0 | 1]	**122**
Games People Play / These Are Not My People (69) 144(1) [0 | 0 | 7]	122
Orson WELLES ► 1776 Pk:66 [0 | 0 | 1]	**499**
The Begatting Of The President (70) 66(1) [0 | 0 | 16]	499
Mary WELLS ► 974 Pk:18 [0 | 1 | 4]	**2022**
Greatest Hits (64) 18(2) [0 | 12 | 37]	1555
Together (64)-Marvin Gaye & Mary Wells [A] 42(1) [0 | 0 | 16]	244
Mary Wells Sings My Guy (64) 111(1) [0 | 0 | 12]	174
Mary Wells (65) 145(2) [0 | 0 | 4]	49.7
WENDY and LISA ► 1971 Pk:88 [0 | 0 | 2]	**365**
Wendy And Lisa (87) 88(1) [0 | 0 | 13]	245
Fruit At The Bottom (89) 119(2) [0 | 0 | 8]	120
David WERNER ► 2121 Pk:65 [0 | 0 | 1]	**290**
David Werner (79) 65(1) [0 | 0 | 11]	290
Fred WESLEY & The HORNY HORNS ► 3195 Pk:181 [0 | 0 | 1]	**41**
A Blow For Me A Toot To You (77) 181(1) [0 | 0 | 5]	40.7
Dottie WEST ► 2290 Pk:126 [0 | 0 | 1]	**220**
Wild West (81) 126(1) [0 | 0 | 15]	220
Leslie WEST ► 1782 Pk:72 [0 | 0 | 2]	**496**
Mountain (69) 72(2) [0 | 0 | 14]	427
The Great Fatsby (75) 168(2) [0 | 0 | 6]	69.4
Mae WEST ► 2851 Pk:116 [0 | 0 | 1]	**88**
Way Out West (66) 116(2) [0 | 0 | 5]	87.7
WEST, BRUCE & LAING ► 1174 Pk:26 [0 | 1 | 3]	**1406**
Why Dontcha (72) 26(1) [0 | 6 | 20]	1100
Whatever Turns You On (73) 87(1) [0 | 0 | 10]	247
Live 'N' Kickin' (74) 165(2) [0 | 0 | 6]	59.5
WET WET WET ► 2761 Pk:123 [0 | 0 | 1]	**103**
Popped In Souled Out (88) 123(3) [0 | 0 | 7]	103
WET WILLIE ► 1072 Pk:41 [0 | 0 | 8]	**1678**
Keep On Smilin' (74) 41(1) [0 | 0 | 24]	1033
Dixie Rock (75) 114(1) [0 | 0 | 7]	157
Manorisms (78) 118(1) [0 | 0 | 8]	153
The Wetter The Better (76) 133(1) [0 | 0 | 7]	120
Which One's Willie (79) 172(1) [0 | 0 | 11]	100
Greatest Hits (78) 158(1) [0 | 0 | 6]	73.8
Drippin' Wet!/Live (73) 189(2) [0 | 0 | 4]	26.2
Left Coast Live (77) 191(2) [0 | 0 | 2]	15.4
Kirk WHALUM ► 2657 Pk:142 [0 | 0 | 1]	**122**
And You Know That! (88) 142(1) [0 | 0 | 10]	122
WHAM! ► 286 Pk:1 [2 | 2 | 3]	**12152**
Make It Big (84) 1(3) [25 | 56 | 80]	9851
Music From The Edge Of Heaven (86) 10(2) [2 | 11 | 28]	1761
Fantastic (83) 83(1) [0 | 0 | 44]	540
WHAT IS THIS ► 3364 Pk:187 [0 | 0 | 1]	**23**
What Is This (85) 187(1) [0 | 0 | 4]	22.5
Billy Edd WHEELER ► 3182 Pk:132 [0 | 0 | 1]	**43**
Memories Of America / Ode To The Little Brown Shack Out Back (65) 132(1) [0 | 0 | 3]	43.1
WHEN IN ROME ► 1812 Pk:84 [0 | 0 | 1]	**475**
When In Rome (88) 84(1) [0 | 0 | 24]	475
The WHISPERS ► 327 Pk:6 [1 | 5 | 13]	**10547**
The Whispers (80) 6(2) [9 | 17 | 35]	3555
Just Gets Better With Time (87) 22(2) [0 | 12 | 37]	1710

► Highest Peak [Top10s | Top40s | Total] Title (Yr) Peak(Wk) [T10 Wk | T40Wk | TotalWk]	Score
Imagination (81) 23(2) [0 | 11 | 27]	1662
Love For Love (83) 37(1) [0 | 3 | 29]	964
Love Is Where You Find It (82) 35(3) [0 | 4 | 25]	952
Headlights (78) 77(2) [0 | 0 | 28]	536
So Good (84) 88(1) [0 | 0 | 26]	462
Open Up Your Love (77) 65(2) [0 | 0 | 10]	301
This Kind Of Lovin' (81) 100(3) [0 | 0 | 9]	191
Whisper In Your Ear (79) 146(1) [0 | 0 | 9]	121
One For The Money (76) 189(1) [0 | 0 | 6]	45.2
The Best Of The Whispers (82) 180(1) [0 | 0 | 5]	33.1
The Whispers' Love Story (72) 186(2) [0 | 0 | 2]	16.1
Ian WHITCOMB ► 2386 Pk:125 [0 | 0 | 1]	**189**
You Turn Me On! (65) 125(1) [0 | 0 | 13]	189
Barry WHITE ► 201 Pk:1 [2 | 7 | 14]	**17306**
Can't Get Enough (74) 1(1) [7 | 13 | 38]	3956
I've Got So Much To Give (73) 16(2) [0 | 10 | 63]	2762
Stone Gon' (73) 20(1) [0 | 16 | 37]	2562
Barry White Sings For Someone You Love (77) 8(2) [3 | 13 | 33]	2402
Just Another Way To Say I Love You (75) 17(1) [0 | 8 | 17]	1555
Barry White's Greatest Hits (75) 23(2) [0 | 5 | 25]	1277
Barry White The Man (78) 36(3) [0 | 3 | 28]	1191
Let The Music Play (76) 42(1) [0 | 0 | 15]	626
The Message Is Love (79) 67(2) [0 | 0 | 9]	274
Barry White's Sheet Music (80) 85(1) [0 | 0 | 11]	262
The Right Night & Barry White (87) 159(2) [0 | 0 | 17]	136
Is This Whatcha Wont? (76) 125(1) [0 | 0 | 9]	120
I Love To Sing The Songs I Sing (79) 132(2) [0 | 0 | 6]	110
Change (82) 148(1) [0 | 0 | 6]	73.0
Karyn WHITE ► 807 Pk:19 [0 | 1 | 1]	**2905**
Karyn White (88) 19(1) [0 | 17 | 54]	2905
Lenny WHITE ► 3265 Pk:177 [0 | 0 | 1]	**32**
Venusian Summer (76) 177(2) [0 | 0 | 3]	31.6
Maurice WHITE ► 1978 Pk:61 [0 | 0 | 1]	**363**
Maurice White (85) 61(2) [0 | 0 | 19]	363
Tony Joe WHITE ► 1511 Pk:51 [0 | 0 | 3]	**786**
Black And White (69) 51(1) [0 | 0 | 16]	722
Tony Joe White (71) 167(1) [0 | 0 | 4]	38.1
...Continued (69) 183(1) [0 | 0 | 3]	25.8
WHITE LION ► 486 Pk:11 [0 | 2 | 3]	**6411**
Pride (87) 11(1) [0 | 31 | 86]	4513
Big Game (89) 19(2) [0 | 13 | 26]	1730
Fight To Survive (88) 151(1) [0 | 0 | 14]	168
WHITE PLAINS ► 3128 Pk:166 [0 | 0 | 1]	**49**
My Baby Loves Lovin' (70) 166(1) [0 | 0 | 4]	48.9
WHITESNAKE ► 207 Pk:2 [2 | 3 | 6]	**16712**
Whitesnake (87) 2(10) [41 | 54 | 76]	11814
Slip Of The Tongue (89) 10(1) [1 | 20 | 34]	2611
Slide It In (84) 40(2) [0 | 2 | 85]	1759
Ready An' Willing (80) 90(1) [0 | 0 | 16]	319
Live In The Heart Of The City (80) 146(1) [0 | 0 | 12]	131
Come An' Get It (81) 151(2) [0 | 0 | 6]	78.1
WHITE WOLF ► 2564 Pk:137 [0 | 0 | 2]	**145**
Endangered Species (86) 137(2) [0 | 0 | 8]	88.5
Standing Alone (85) 162(2) [0 | 0 | 7]	56.8
Margaret WHITING ► 2517 Pk:109 [0 | 0 | 1]	**154**
The Wheel Of Hurt (67) 109(1) [0 | 0 | 8]	154
Keith WHITLEY ► 2189 Pk:115 [0 | 0 | 2]	**262**
Don't Close Your Eyes (89) 121(2) [0 | 0 | 14]	158
I Wonder Do You Think Of Me (89) 115(2) [0 | 0 | 7]	104
Bobby WHITLOCK ► 2491 Pk:140 [0 | 0 | 2]	**162**
Bobby Whitlock (72) 140(1) [0 | 0 | 10]	142
Raw Velvet (72) 190(1) [0 | 0 | 3]	20.8

► Highest Peak [Top10s|Top40s|Total]
Title (Yr) Peak(Wk) [T10 Wk|T40Wk|TotalWk] Score

Slim WHITMAN ► 3026 Pk:175 [0|0|2] 62
Christmas With Slim Whitman (80) 184(2) [0|0|4] 33.1
Songs I Love To Sing (80) 175(1) [0|0|3] 29.3

Roger WHITTAKER ► 1058 Pk:31 [0|1|6] 1722
The Last Farewell And Other Hits (75) 31(2) [0|5|24] 1323
Voyager (80) 154(3) [0|0|12] 140
When I Need You (79) 115(2) [0|0|5] 115
Mirrors Of My Mind (79) 157(2) [0|0|10] 93.5
Live In Concert (81) 177(1) [0|0|3] 30.1
With Love (80) 175(2) [0|0|2] 21.3

The WHO ► 39 Pk:2 [9|12|20] 47372
Tommy (69) 4(2) [14|47|126] 12174
Live At Leeds (70) 4(3) [14|24|44] 5677
Who's Next (71) 4(2) [11|20|41] 5051
Quadrophenia (73) 2(1) [9|18|40] 3945
Who Are You (78) 2(2) [10|13|30] 3916
Face Dances (81) 4(4) [8|14|20] 3313
The Who By Numbers (75) 8(2) [4|14|25] 2563
The Kids Are Alright (Soundtrack) (79) 8(2) [3|11|25] 2320
It's Hard (82) 8(5) [7|10|32] 2131
Meaty Beaty Big And Bouncy (71) 11(1) [0|8|21] 1680
Odds & Sods (74) 15(2) [0|8|15] 1359
The Who Sell Out (68) 48(1) [0|0|23] 574
Hooligans (81) 52(2) [0|0|19] 561
Magic Bus-The Who On Tour (68) 39(1) [0|2|10] 547
Quadrophenia (Soundtrack) (79) 46(1) [0|0|16] 542
Happy Jack (67) 67(1) [0|0|22] 417
Who's Last (84) 81(2) [0|0|14] 292
Who's Greatest Hits (83) 94(1) [0|0|13] 186
Who's Missing (85) 116(2) [0|0|8] 92.6
Magic Bus (74) 185(1) [0|0|4] 29.5

WHODINI ► 696 Pk:30 [0|3|3] 3761
Escape (84) 35(1) [0|5|48] 1624
Back In Black (86) 35(2) [0|4|39] 1272
Open Sesame (87) 30(2) [0|6|22] 865

WICHITA TRAIN WHISTLE ► 2724 Pk:144 [0|0|1] 110
Mike Nesmith Presents/The Wichita Train Whistle Sings (68) 144(2) [0|0|7] 110

WIDOWMAKER ► 2687 Pk:150 [0|0|1] 117
Too Late To Cry (77) 150(1) [0|0|9] 117

Jane WIEDLIN ► 1829 Pk:105 [0|0|2] 459
Fur (88) 105(2) [0|0|21] 379
Jane Wiedlin (85) 127(2) [0|0|6] 80.3

Rusty WIER ► 1918 Pk:103 [0|0|2] 395
Don't It Make You Wanna Dance (75) 103(1) [0|0|14] 264
Rusty Wier (76) 131(1) [0|0|9] 131

WILBURN BROTHERS ► 3208 Pk:143 [0|0|1] 39
Little Johnny From Down The Street (70) 143(2) [0|0|2] 38.7

WILD CHERRY ► 676 Pk:5 [1|1|3] 3979
Wild Cherry (76) 5(2) [8|15|29] 3397
Electrified Funk (77) 51(1) [0|0|9] 380
I Love My Music (78) 84(1) [0|0|9] 202

Danny WILDE ► 2991 Pk:176 [0|0|1] 67
Any Man's Hunger (88) 176(1) [0|0|9] 67.0

Eugene WILDE ► 2271 Pk:97 [0|0|1] 225
Eugene Wilde (85) 97(2) [0|0|15] 225

Kim WILDE ► 1133 Pk:40 [0|1|4] 1516
Another Step (87) 40(2) [0|2|26] 887
Kim Wilde (82) 86(2) [0|0|22] 352

► Highest Peak [Top10s|Top40s|Total]
Title (Yr) Peak(Wk) [T10 Wk|T40Wk|TotalWk] Score

Teases And Dares (85) 84(2) [0|0|10] 186
Close (88) 114(1) [0|0|6] 91.2

Matthew WILDER ► 1852 Pk:49 [0|0|1] 443
I Don't Speak The Language (84) 49(2) [0|0|16] 443

WILD MAN STEVE ► 2978 Pk:179 [0|0|2] 68
My Man! Wild Man! (69) 185(1) [0|0|6] 47.5
Wild! Wild! Wild! Wild! (70) 179(2) [0|0|2] 20.8

WILD ONES ► 3351 Pk:149 [0|0|1] 24
The Arthur Sound (65) 149(1) [0|0|2] 24.1

WILD TURKEY ► 3412 Pk:193 [0|0|1] 18
Battle Hymn (72) 193(2) [0|0|3] 18.2

WILL And The KILL ► 2730 Pk:129 [0|0|1] 109
Will And The Kill (88) 129(2) [0|0|8] 109

Andy WILLIAMS ► 46 Pk:3 [10|14|26] 45079
Born Free (67) 5(2) [12|35|79] 6101
Dear Heart (65) 4(3) [15|45|65] 5727
Love Story (71) 3(1) [9|16|33] 4207
The Academy Award Winning "Call Me Irresponsible" (64) 5(3) [8|27|63] 3722
Honey (68) 9(2) [5|24|40] 3600
The Shadow Of Your Smile (66) 6(2) [4|18|54] 3103
The Great Songs From "My Fair Lady" And Other Broadway Hits (64) 5(2) [8|20|33] 2848
Happy Heart (69) 9(2) [3|10|23] 2702
Love, Andy (67) 8(2) [4|11|36] 2267
The Wonderful World Of Andy Williams (64) 9(3) [4|16|24] 1973
Love Theme From "The Godfather" (72) 29(1) [0|8|26] 1342
In The Arms Of Love (67) 21(1) [0|11|22] 1306
Andy Williams' Newest Hits (66) 23(1) [0|8|23] 1185
Get Together With Andy Williams (69) 27(1) [0|6|21] 1087
Andy Williams' Greatest Hits (70) 42(1) [0|0|20] 798
Raindrops Keep Fallin' On My Head (70) 43(1) [0|0|19] 740
The Andy Williams Show (70) 81(1) [0|0|17] 537
You've Got A Friend (71) 54(1) [0|0|12] 497
Hawaiian Wedding Song (65) 61(2) [0|0|18] 435
Alone Again (Naturally) (72) 86(2) [0|0|18] 416
The Andy Williams Sound Of Music (69) 139(1) [0|0|7] 147
Canadian Sunset (65) 112(2) [0|0|6] 100
The Impossible Dream (72) 123(2) [0|0|5] 88.4
You Lay So Easy On My Mind (74) 150(1) [0|0|4] 63.0
Andy Williams' Greatest Hits, Vol. 2 (73) 174(1) [0|0|5] 48.7
Solitaire (73) 185(1) [0|0|6] 40.8

Danny WILLIAMS ► 2986 Pk:122 [0|0|1] 67
White On White (64) 122(1) [0|0|5] 67.4

Deniece WILLIAMS ► 484 Pk:19 [0|4|8] 6497
This Is Niecy (76) 33(2) [0|6|36] 1691
Niecy (82) 20(3) [0|7|22] 1107
My Melody (81) 74(1) [0|0|32] 955
Let's Hear It For The Boy (84) 26(1) [0|6|19] 786
Song Bird (77) 66(1) [0|0|20] 670
That's What Friends Are For (78)-Johnny Mathis & Deniece Williams [A] 19(2) [0|8|16] 614
I'm So Proud (83) 54(2) [0|0|19] 477
When Love Comes Calling (79) 96(2) [0|0|8] 199

Don WILLIAMS ► 1189 Pk:57 [0|0|4] 1366
I Believe In You (80) 57(1) [0|0|31] 981
Especially For You (81) 109(1) [0|0|11] 227
Expressions (79) 161(1) [0|0|7] 83.4
Listen To The Radio (82) 166(3) [0|0|8] 74.4

► Highest Peak [Top10s|Top40s|Total]
Title (Yr) Peak(Wk) [T10 Wk|T40Wk|TotalWk] Score

Hank WILLIAMS Jr. ► 386 Pk:16 [0|2|20] 8574
Your Cheatin' Heart (Soundtrack) (65) 16(1) [0|13|37] 1666
Born To Boogie (87) 28(1) [0|3|47] 1235
Hank Williams, Jr.'s Greatest Hits (82) 107(2) [0|0|70] 915
Greatest Hits III (89) 61(1) [0|0|35] 726
Wild Streak (88) 55(1) [0|0|19] 617
The Pressure Is On (81) 76(2) [0|0|23] 500
Rowdy (81) 82(2) [0|0|15] 402
Hank "Live" (87) 71(1) [0|0|24] 392
Five-O (85) 72(2) [0|0|22] 374
Strong Stuff (83) 64(2) [0|0|16] 327
Major Moves (84) 100(1) [0|0|19] 322
Montana Cafe (86) 93(2) [0|0|18] 296
High Notes (82) 123(1) [0|0|20] 225
Habits Old And New (80) 154(1) [0|0|17] 213
Man Of Steel (83) 116(2) [0|0|13] 195
Songs My Father Left Me (69) 164(1) [0|0|4] 60.9
Greatest Hits, Vol. II (86) 183(1) [0|0|8] 42.9
A Time To Sing (Soundtrack) (68) 189(2) [0|0|3] 25.7
Live At Cobo Hall, Detroit (69) 187(2) [0|0|2] 18.7
Father & Son (65)-Hank Williams Sr. & Hank Williams Jr. [A] 139(1) [0|0|3] 19.8

Hank WILLIAMS Sr. ► 3395 Pk:139 [0|0|1] 20
Father & Son (65)-Hank Williams Sr. & Hank Williams Jr. [A] 139(1) [0|0|3] 19.8

--John Williams see: Boston Pops; London Symphony Orchestra; Soundtracks

Lenny WILLIAMS ► 1324 Pk:87 [0|0|4] 1094
Spark Of Love (78) 87(1) [0|0|25] 463
Choosing You (77) 99(1) [0|0|26] 406
Love Current (79) 108(1) [0|0|9] 208
Let's Do It Today (80) 185(2) [0|0|2] 16.9

Mason WILLIAMS ► 790 Pk:14 [0|1|4] 2989
The Mason Williams Phonograph Record (68) 14(2) [0|8|34] 1993
Music By Mason Williams (69) 44(2) [0|0|17] 745
Classical Gas (87)-Mason Williams & Mannheim Steamroller [A] 118(1) [0|0|19] 136
The Mason Williams Ear Show (68) 164(2) [0|0|8] 114

Paul WILLIAMS ► 1414 Pk:95 [0|0|6] 950
Just An Old Fashioned Love Song (71) 141(1) [0|0|21] 288
A Little Bit Of Love (74) 95(2) [0|0|9] 231
Life Goes On (72) 159(1) [0|0|14] 155
Here Comes Inspiration (74) 165(1) [0|0|10] 109
Classics (77) 155(1) [0|0|8] 85.3
Ordinary Fool (75) 146(1) [0|0|6] 81.6

Robin WILLIAMS ► 925 Pk:10 [1|1|2] 2239
Reality... What A Concept (79) 10(2) [2|12|22] 2118
Throbbing Python Of Love (83) 119(1) [0|0|9] 121

Roger WILLIAMS ► 326 Pk:7 [1|3|18] 10549
Born Free (66) 7(2) [4|23|69] 4216
I'll Remember You (66) 24(2) [0|11|67] 2126
The Solid Gold Steinway (64) 27(1) [0|4|19] 661
Roger! (67) 51(1) [0|0|27] 618
Happy Heart (69) 60(1) [0|0|11] 560
Golden Hits (67) 87(2) [0|0|29] 473
Summer Wind (65) 63(1) [0|0|18] 460
For You (63) 59(1) [0|0|12] 287
Love Story (71) 112(1) [0|0|13] 234
Only For Lovers (69) 131(2) [0|0|10] 202
Love Theme From "Romeo & Juliet" (69) 145(1) [0|0|10] 162
10th Anniversary/Limited Edition (64) 108(1) [0|0|8] 120

► Highest Peak [Top10s | Top40s | Total] Title (Yr) Peak(Wk) [T10 Wk | T40Wk | TotalWk]	Score
Roger WILLIAMS ► *Continued*	
Academy Award Winners (64) 126(1) [0|0|9]	118
Autumn Leaves-1965 (65) 130(1) [0|0|7]	95.5
Roger Williams Plays The Hits (65) 118(1) [0|0|6]	89.4
Love Theme From The Godfather (72) 187(2) [0|0|8]	51.4
More Than A Miracle (68) 164(1) [0|0|5]	48.9
Summer Of '42 (71) 187(1) [0|0|3]	26.1
Tony WILLIAMS ► 2597 Pk:113 [0|0|1]	**135**
Joy Of Flying (79) 113(1) [0|0|7]	135
Vanessa WILLIAMS ► 1147 Pk:38 [0|1|1]	**1476**
The Right Stuff (88) 38(1) [0|4|55]	1476
Williams, Vesta see VESTA	
WILLIE & The POOR BOYS ► 2364 Pk:96 [0|0|1]	**194**
Willie & The Poor Boys (85) 96(2) [0|0|12]	194
WILLIE, WAYLON, JOHNNY & KRIS ► 1723 Pk:92 [0|0|1]	**561**
Highwayman (85) 92(1) [0|0|35]	561
Bruce WILLIS ► 1105 Pk:14 [0|1|1]	**1592**
The Return Of Bruno (87) 14(3) [0|11|29]	1592
WILL TO POWER ► 1665 Pk:68 [0|0|1]	**609**
Will To Power (88) 68(1) [0|0|29]	609
WILMER And The DUKES ► 3232 Pk:173 [0|0|1]	**36**
Wilmer & The Dukes (69)-Wilmer & The Dukes 173(1) [0|0|3]	36.1
Al WILSON ► 1783 Pk:70 [0|0|3]	**495**
Show And Tell (73) 70(1) [0|0|17]	409
La La Peace Song (74) 171(1) [0|0|7]	67.9
I've Got A Feeling (76) 185(2) [0|0|2]	18.6
Brian WILSON ► 1884 Pk:54 [0|0|1]	**415**
Brian Wilson (88) 54(3) [0|0|13]	415
Carl WILSON ► 3419 Pk:185 [0|0|1]	**17**
Carl Wilson (81) 185(1) [0|0|2]	17.4
Dennis WILSON ► 2426 Pk:96 [0|0|1]	**181**
Pacific Ocean Blue (77) 96(2) [0|0|8]	181
Flip WILSON ► 564 Pk:17 [0|2|5]	**5155**
"The Devil Made Me Buy This Dress" (70) 17(1) [0|9|54]	2590
Cowboys & Colored People (67) 34(2) [0|5|63]	1514
"Flip" - The Flip Wilson Show (71) 45(1) [0|0|15]	503
Geraldine/Don't Fight The Feeling (72) 63(2) [0|0|15]	441
You Devil You (68) 147(1) [0|0|7]	106
Jackie WILSON ► 2420 Pk:108 [0|0|3]	**182**
Whispers (67) 108(1) [0|0|7]	127
Higher And Higher (67) 163(1) [0|0|4]	46.1
Manufacturers Of Soul (68)-Jackie Wilson And Count Basie [A] 195(2) [0|0|3]	9.0
J. Frank WILSON and The CAVALIERS ► 2079 Pk:54 [0|0|1]	**311**
Last Kiss (64) 54(1) [0|0|14]	311
Nancy WILSON ► 120 Pk:4 [4|11|31]	**26555**
Hollywood-My Way (63) 11(3) [0|20|58]	3710
Yesterday's Love Songs/Today's Blues (64) 4(1) [6|26|42]	3448
How Glad I Am (64) 4(2) [10|18|31]	2768
Today, Tomorrow, Forever (64) 10(3) [3|24|30]	2325
A Touch Of Today (66) 15(1) [0|12|33]	1697
The Nancy Wilson Show! (65) 24(2) [0|18|29]	1643
Today-My Way (65) 7(1) [2|11|21]	1472
Gentle Is My Love (65) 17(1) [0|8|24]	1261
Now I'm A Woman (70) 54(1) [0|0|21]	927
Tender Loving Care (66) 35(1) [0|3|23]	901
Nancy-Naturally (67) 35(2) [0|3|21]	876
Easy (68) 51(1) [0|0|24]	852
Lush Life (67) 46(1) [0|0|19]	751

► Highest Peak [Top10s | Top40s | Total] Title (Yr) Peak(Wk) [T10 Wk | T40Wk | TotalWk]	Score
From Broadway With Love (66) 44(2) [0|0|18]	553
Just For Now (67) 40(1) [0|1|15]	527
Hurt So Bad (69) 92(1) [0|0|18]	437
All In Love Is Fair (74) 97(2) [0|0|18]	359
Nancy (69) 117(1) [0|0|14]	339
Son Of A Preacher Man (69) 122(2) [0|0|15]	338
Welcome To My Love (68) 115(1) [0|0|17]	272
Come Get To This (75) 119(1) [0|0|10]	226
This Mother's Daughter (76) 126(1) [0|0|13]	223
The Best Of Nancy Wilson (68) 145(1) [0|0|14]	215
The Sound Of Nancy Wilson (68) 122(1) [0|0|7]	134
Kaleidoscope (71) 151(2) [0|0|6]	96.0
Can't Take My Eyes Off You (70) 155(1) [0|0|6]	71.4
The Two Of Us (84)-Ramsey Lewis & Nancy Wilson [A] 144(1) [0|0|9]	46.5
But Beautiful (71) 185(1) [0|0|5]	39.8
The Right To Love (71) 185(1) [0|0|3]	25.9
Close-Up (69) 193(2) [0|0|2]	15.6
I've Never Been To Me (77) 198(1) [0|0|1]	5.7
The WINANS ► 2495 Pk:109 [0|0|1]	**161**
Decisions (87) 109(1) [0|0|11]	161
BeBe & CeCe WINANS ► 1835 Pk:95 [0|0|1]	**453**
Heaven (89) 95(1) [0|0|25]	453
Angela WINBUSH ► 1613 Pk:81 [0|0|2]	**662**
Sharp (87) 81(1) [0|0|28]	464
The Real Thing (89) 113(2) [0|0|17]	199
Jesse WINCHESTER ► 1915 Pk:115 [0|0|4]	**396**
Nothing But A Breeze (77) 115(1) [0|0|16]	252
A Touch On The Rainy Side (78) 156(2) [0|0|7]	100
Third Down, 110 To Go (72) 193(2) [0|0|5]	28.6
Talk Memphis (81) 188(1) [0|0|2]	15.7
WIND IN THE WILLOWS ► 3397 Pk:195 [0|0|1]	**20**
The Wind In The Willows (68) 195(3) [0|0|3]	19.6
WING And A PRAYER FIFE And DRUM CORPS. ► 1617 Pk:47 [0|0|1]	**655**
Babyface (76)-The Wing And A Prayer Fife And Drum Corps 47(1) [0|0|16]	655
WINGER ► 654 Pk:21 [0|1|1]	**4224**
Winger (88) 21(3) [0|35|64]	4224
Pete WINGFIELD ► 3134 Pk:165 [0|0|1]	**49**
Breakfast Special (75) 165(1) [0|0|5]	48.5
George WINSTON ► 671 Pk:54 [0|0|4]	**4037**
December (83) 54(1) [0|0|178]	3285
Autumn (84) 139(1) [0|0|44]	449
Winter Into Spring (84) 127(2) [0|0|32]	291
The Velveteen Rabbit (85)-Meryl Streep & George Winston [A] 180(1) [0|0|4]	12.1
The WINSTONS ► 1927 Pk:78 [0|0|1]	**388**
Color Him Father (69) 78(2) [0|0|12]	388
Edgar WINTER ► 316 Pk:3 [1|3|8]	**10742**
They Only Come Out At Night (72)-The Edgar Winter Group 3(1) [9|25|80]	6108
Shock Treatment (74)-The Edgar Winter Group 13(1) [0|13|23]	2159
Roadwork (72)-Edgar Winter's White Trash 23(1) [0|9|25]	1487
Edgar Winter's White Trash (71)-Edgar Winter's White Trash 111(1) [0|0|19]	392
Jasmine Nightdreams (75) 69(2) [0|0|10]	312
Together (76)-Johnny & Edgar Winter [A] 89(1) [0|0|9]	138
The Edgar Winter Group With Rick Derringer (75)-Edgar Winter Group With Rick Derringer 124(1) [0|0|8]	134
Entrance (70) 196(2) [0|0|2]	12.3
Johnny WINTER ► 408 Pk:22 [0|4|15]	**8027**
Johnny Winter (69) 24(2) [0|8|23]	1679

► Highest Peak [Top10s | Top40s | Total] Title (Yr) Peak(Wk) [T10 Wk | T40Wk | TotalWk]	Score
Still Alive And Well (73) 22(1) [0|11|24]	1571
Live/Johnny Winter And (71) 40(2) [0|2|27]	1240
The Progressive Blues Experiment (69) 40(1) [0|1|20]	1012
Saints & Sinners (74) 42(1) [0|0|16]	637
Second Winter (69) 55(1) [0|0|17]	598
John Dawson Winter III (74) 78(2) [0|0|12]	389
Captured Live (76) 93(1) [0|0|12]	265
The Johnny Winter Story (69) 111(2) [0|0|6]	158
Together (76)-Johnny & Edgar Winter [A] 89(1) [0|0|9]	138
Nothin' But The Blues (77) 146(2) [0|0|8]	112
Serious Business (85) 156(2) [0|0|10]	83.9
White Hot & Blue (78) 141(2) [0|0|4]	71.4
Johnny Winter And (70) 154(1) [0|0|4]	49.2
Guitar Slinger (84) 183(1) [0|0|4]	23.3
Paul WINTER ► 2638 Pk:138 [0|0|1]	**125**
Canyon (86) 138(1) [0|0|11]	125
Jonathan WINTERS ► 3137 Pk:145 [0|0|2]	**48**
Jonathan Winters' Mad, Mad, Mad, Mad World (64) 145(1) [0|0|2]	25.3
Whistle Stopping With Jonathan Winters (64) 148(2) [0|0|2]	22.4
Robert WINTERS and FALL ► 2200 Pk:71 [0|0|1]	**255**
Magic Man (81) 71(2) [0|0|8]	255
Steve WINWOOD ► 138 Pk:1 [3|6|8]	**23159**
Back In The High Life (86) 3(2) [14|60|86]	7480
Arc Of A Diver (81) 3(6) [13|26|43]	5990
Roll With It (88) 1(1) [14|31|45]	5737
Steve Winwood (77) 22(1) [0|10|17]	1352
Chronicles (87) 26(1) [0|10|26]	1238
Talking Back To The Night (82) 28(4) [0|6|25]	988
Winwood (71) 93(2) [0|0|8]	229
Go (76)-Stomu Yamashta/Steve Winwood/ Michael Shrieve [A] 60(3) [0|0|12]	145
WIRE ► 2781 Pk:135 [0|0|1]	**100**
It's Beginning To And Back Again (89) 135(2) [0|0|10]	100
WIRE TRAIN ► 2699 Pk:150 [0|0|2]	**114**
...In A Chamber (84) 150(1) [0|0|9]	88.8
Ten Women (87) 181(1) [0|0|4]	25.0
WISHBONE ASH ► 1018 Pk:44 [0|0|10]	**1881**
Wishbone Four (73) 44(1) [0|0|15]	591
Live Dates (73) 82(1) [0|0|18]	398
There's The Rub (74) 88(1) [0|0|13]	379
Locked In (76) 136(1) [0|0|9]	153
Argus (72) 169(2) [0|0|13]	118
New England (76) 154(1) [0|0|9]	93.2
Pilgrimage (71) 174(2) [0|0|7]	66.5
Front Page News (77) 166(2) [0|0|4]	40.4
Hot Ash (82) 192(1) [0|0|4]	21.7
Just Testing (80) 179(1) [0|0|2]	19.2
WITCH QUEEN ► 2985 Pk:158 [0|0|1]	**68**
Witch Queen (79) 158(2) [0|0|6]	67.5
Bill WITHERS ► 391 Pk:4 [1|3|11]	**8442**
Still Bill (72) 4(3) [4|25|43]	4281
Just As I Am (71) 39(1) [0|1|33]	1160
Menagerie (77) 39(1) [0|2|26]	1085
Bill Withers Live At Carnegie Hall (73) 63(2) [0|0|21]	629
+'Justments (74) 67(1) [0|0|21]	619
Making Music (75) 81(1) [0|0|15]	367
'Bout Love (79) 134(1) [0|0|9]	134
Watching You, Watching Me (85) 143(2) [0|0|8]	80.9
Naked & Warm (76) 169(1) [0|0|4]	41.4
Bill Withers Greatest Hits (81) 183(1) [0|0|3]	25.1
The Best Of Bill Withers (75) 182(1) [0|0|2]	18.6

▶ **Highest Peak [Top10s|Top40s|Total]**
Title (Yr) Peak(Wk) [T10 Wk|T40Wk|TotalWk] **Score**

Jimmy WITHERSPOON ▶ 3365 Pk:176 [0|0|1] 22
Love Is A Five Letter Word (75) 176(1) [0|0|2] 22.4
Peter WOLF ▶ 1104 Pk:24 [0|1|2] 1593
Lights Out (84) 24(2) [0|8|26] 1151
Come As You Are (87) 53(2) [0|0|15] 443
Bobby WOMACK ▶ 464 Pk:29 [0|2|13] 6777
Understanding (72) 43(2) [0|0|48] 2180
The Poet (81) 29(2) [0|6|23] 1109
Facts Of Life (73) 37(1) [0|1|21] 828
Across 110th Street (Soundtrack) (73) 50(1) [0|0|20] 667
Lookin' For A Love Again (74) 85(1) [0|0|19] 447
Communication (71) 83(2) [0|0|17] 426
The Poet II (84) 60(1) [0|0|14] 368
So Many Rivers (85) 66(2) [0|0|19] 358
Safety Zone (76) 147(1) [0|0|11] 152
Bobby Womack's Greatest Hits (74) 142(1) [0|0|7] 99.5
I Don't Know What The World Is Coming To (75) 126(1) [0|0|4] 80.2
The Womack "Live" (71) 188(1) [0|0|5] 36.3
Fly Me To The Moon (68) 174(2) [0|0|2] 26.3
The WOMENFOLK ▶ 2883 Pk:118 [0|0|1] 82
The Womenfolk (64) 118(2) [0|0|6] 82.1
Stevie WONDER ▶ 11 Pk:1 [9|16|22] 71559
Songs In The Key Of Life (76) 1(14) [35|44|80] 16923
Innervisions (73) 4(1) [10|58|89] 9362
Talking Book (72) 3(3) [9|30|109] 8080
Hotter Than July (80) 3(7) [16|25|40] 6054
Fullfillingness First Finale (74) 1(2) [7|11|65] 5002
In Square Circle (85) 5(2) [13|29|50] 4553
The Woman In Red (Soundtrack) (84) 4(3) [11|21|40] 3577
Journey Through The Secret Life Of Plants (79) 4(5) [9|15|22] 3272
Music Of My Mind (72) 21(1) [0|11|35] 2134
Stevie Wonder's Original Musiquarium I (82) 4(3) [6|8|28] 2112
Characters (87) 17(3) [0|13|31] 1959
Greatest Hits (68) 37(2) [0|4|29] 1317
My Cherie Amour (69) 34(1) [0|4|20] 1073
Signed Sealed & Delivered (70) 25(1) [0|5|16] 1054
Up-Tight Everything's Alright (66) 33(1) [0|3|25] 1029
Where I'm Coming From (71) 62(1) [0|0|27] 981
For Once In My Life (69) 50(3) [0|0|18] 799
Looking Back (77) 34(1) [0|3|13] 701
I Was Made To Love Her (67) 45(2) [0|0|13] 589
Stevie Wonder's Greatest Hits, Vol. 2 (71) 69(1) [0|0|12] 425
Stevie Wonder Live (70) 81(1) [0|0|15] 410
Down To Earth (67) 92(1) [0|0|7] 155
Brenton WOOD ▶ 3447 Pk:184 [0|0|1] 15
Oogum Boogum (67) 184(2) [0|0|2] 15.2
Ronnie WOOD ▶ 1607 Pk:45 [0|0|3] 670
Gimmie Some Neck (79)-Ron Wood 45(2) [0|0|13] 470
Now Look (75) 118(2) [0|0|6] 141
1234 (81) 164(2) [0|0|5] 58.9
Roy WOOD ▶ 3135 Pk:176 [0|0|1] 48
Boulders (73) 176(1) [0|0|6] 47.8
The WOODENTOPS ▶ 3250 Pk:185 [0|0|1] 33
Giant (86)-Woodentops 185(1) [0|0|6] 33.4
Stevie WOODS ▶ 2377 Pk:153 [0|0|1] 192
Take Me To Your Heaven (81) 153(2) [0|0|25] 192
Bruce WOOLLEY & The CAMERA CLUB ▶ 3423 Pk:184 [0|0|1] 17
Bruce Woolley & The Camera Club (80) 184(1) [0|0|2] 17.2

▶ **Highest Peak [Top10s|Top40s|Total]**
Title (Yr) Peak(Wk) [T10 Wk|T40Wk|TotalWk] **Score**

WORLD PARTY ▶ 1432 Pk:39 [0|1|1] 923
Private Revolution (86) 39(3) [0|3|31] 923
WRABIT ▶ 2855 Pk:157 [0|0|1] 87
Wrabit (82) 157(1) [0|0|8] 86.9
WRATHCHILD AMERICA ▶ 3287 Pk:190 [0|0|1] 29
Climbing The Walls (89) 190(2) [0|0|6] 29.2
Link WRAY & His RAY MEN ▶ 3279 Pk:186 [0|0|1] 30
Link Wray (71) 186(1) [0|0|4] 30.1
Bernard WRIGHT ▶ 2108 Pk:116 [0|0|1] 297
'Nard (81) 116(2) [0|0|14] 297
Betty WRIGHT ▶ 981 Pk:26 [0|1|4] 1995
Betty Wright Live (78) 26(2) [0|7|36] 1624
Mother Wit (88) 127(2) [0|0|13] 167
I Love The Way You Love (72) 123(1) [0|0|6] 111
Betty Travelin' In The Wright Circle (79) 138(2) [0|0|6] 92.4
Charles WRIGHT And The WATTS 103rd STREET Band ▶ 1851 Pk:140 [0|0|4] 445
You're So Beautiful (71) 147(2) [0|0|11] 189
Together (69)-The Watts 103rd Street Band 140(1) [0|0|5] 108
Express Yourself (70) 182(2) [0|0|10] 78.7
In The Jungle, Babe (69)-The Watts 103rd Street Rhythm Band 145(2) [0|0|4] 68.6
Gary WRIGHT ▶ 381 Pk:7 [1|2|5] 8756
The Dream Weaver (75) 7(3) [8|35|75] 6852
Light Of Smiles (77) 23(1) [0|9|15] 1205
The Right Place (81) 79(1) [0|0|19] 460
Touch And Gone (77) 117(2) [0|0|9] 166
Headin' Home (79) 147(1) [0|0|5] 73.0
Steven WRIGHT ▶ 3516 Pk:192 [0|0|1] 10
I Have A Pony (85) 192(1) [0|0|2] 10.0
Bill WYMAN ▶ 2093 Pk:99 [0|0|2] 307
Monkey Grip (74) 99(1) [0|0|11] 249
Stone Alone (76) 166(1) [0|0|5] 57.9
Tammy WYNETTE ▶ 592 Pk:37 [0|1|12] 4799
Tammy's Greatest Hits (69) 37(1) [0|2|61] 1964
Stand By Your Man (69) 43(1) [0|0|21] 1059
Tammy's Touch (70) 85(2) [0|0|17] 403
The Ways To Love A Man (70) 83(1) [0|0|11] 295
The First Lady (70) 119(1) [0|0|14] 271
We Sure Can Love Each Other (71) 115(2) [0|0|10] 204
D-I-V-O-R-C-E (68) 147(1) [0|0|15] 188
Tammy's Greatest Hits, Volume II (71) 118(1) [0|0|8] 183
Bedtime Story (72) 133(1) [0|0|9] 133
The World Of Tammy Wynette (70) 145(1) [0|0|2] 37.0
We Go Together (71)-Tammy Wynette & George Jones [A] 169(1) [0|0|6] 36.3
Inspiration (69) 189(1) [0|0|3] 25.1

X

X ▶ 1274 Pk:76 [0|0|6] 1192
More Fun In The New World (83) 86(2) [0|0|23] 351
Under The Big Black Sun (82) 76(3) [0|0|15] 297
Ain't Love Grand (85) 89(3) [0|0|14] 262
See How We Are (87) 107(2) [0|0|11] 179
Wild Gift (81) 165(1) [0|0|5] 62.7
Live At The Whisky A Go-Go On The Fabulous Sunset Strip (88) 175(2) [0|0|5] 40.6
XAVIER ▶ 2755 Pk:129 [0|0|1] 104
Point Of Pleasure (82) 129(1) [0|0|7] 104
XTC ▶ 779 Pk:41 [0|0|7] 3095
Black Sea (80) 41(1) [0|0|24] 1114

▶ **Highest Peak [Top10s|Top40s|Total]**
Title (Yr) Peak(Wk) [T10 Wk|T40Wk|TotalWk] **Score**

Oranges And Lemons (89) 44(3) [0|0|21] 731
English Settlement (82) 48(1) [0|0|20] 559
Skylarking (87) 70(2) [0|0|29] 531
Drums And Wires (80) 176(2) [0|0|8] 67.4
Mummer (84) 145(2) [0|0|5] 59.2
The Big Express (84) 178(1) [0|0|5] 34.4
XYMOX ▶ 2994 Pk:165 [0|0|1] 67
Twist Of Shadows (89) 165(1) [0|0|10] 66.8
XYZ ▶ 2003 Pk:99 [0|0|1] 350
XYZ (89) 99(2) [0|0|24] 350

Y

YACHTS ▶ 3308 Pk:179 [0|0|1] 28
S.O.S. (79) 179(2) [0|0|3] 27.5
Stomu YAMASHTA ▶ 2324 Pk:60 [0|0|2] 209
Go (76)-Stomu Yamashta/ Steve Winwood/Michael Shrieve [A] 60(3) [0|0|12] 145
Go Too (77) 156(2) [0|0|6] 64.2
Y&T ▶ 1084 Pk:46 [0|0|5] 1646
In Rock We Trust (84) 46(2) [0|0|17] 533
Open Fire (85) 70(3) [0|0|17] 442
Contagious (87) 78(2) [0|0|13] 299
Down For The Count (85) 91(2) [0|0|12] 187
Mean Streak (83) 103(1) [0|0|12] 186
"Weird Al" YANKOVIC ▶ 744 Pk:17 [0|2|6] 3313
"Weird Al" Yankovic In 3-D (84) 17(3) [0|11|23] 1444
Even Worse (88) 27(1) [0|9|26] 1209
Dare To Be Stupid (85) 50(2) [0|0|16] 490
"Weird Al" Yankovic (83) 139(1) [0|0|8] 93.9
UHF/Original Motion Picture Soundtrack And Other Stuff (89) 146(2) [0|0|4] 47.7
Polka Party! (86) 177(2) [0|0|4] 27.6
Glenn YARBROUGH ▶ 913 Pk:35 [0|1|10] 2297
Baby The Rain Must Fall (65) 35(1) [0|3|24] 652
The Lonely Things (66) 61(1) [0|0|24] 573
It's Gonna Be Fine (65) 75(1) [0|0|12] 251
Live At The Hungry i (66) 85(2) [0|0|9] 240
Honey & Wine (67) 141(1) [0|0|18] 211
For Emily, Whenever I May Find Her (67) 159(2) [0|0|14] 137
Come Share My Life (65) 112(1) [0|0|8] 122
One More Round (64) 142(1) [0|0|4] 46.5
Glenn Yarbrough Sings The Rod McKuen Songbook (69) 189(2) [0|0|5] 45.0
Each Of Us Alone (The Words And Music Of Rod McKuen) (68) 188(2) [0|0|2] 19.3
YARBROUGH & PEOPLES ▶ 975 Pk:16 [0|1|2] 2020
The Two Of Us (80) 16(2) [0|11|24] 1775
Be A Winner (84) 90(2) [0|0|16] 245
The YARDBIRDS ▶ 752 Pk:28 [0|1|6] 3246
Yardbirds Greatest Hits (67) 28(1) [0|8|37] 1513
Having A Rave Up With The Yardbirds (65) 53(2) [0|0|33] 777
Over Under Sideways Down (66) 52(1) [0|0|16] 503
For Your Love (65) 96(1) [0|0|11] 198
Little Games (67) 80(1) [0|0|8] 187
The Yardbirds/Featuring Performances By Jeff Beck, Eric Clapton, Jimmy Page (70) 155(1) [0|0|6] 67.9
Peter YARROW ▶ 2811 Pk:163 [0|0|1] 95
Peter (72) 163(2) [0|0|8] 94.5
YAZ ▶ 1595 Pk:69 [0|0|2] 686
Upstairs At Eric's (82)-Yazoo 92(1) [0|0|32] 411
You And Me Both (83) 69(1) [0|0|13] 275

► Highest Peak [Top10s | Top40s | Total] Title (Yr) Peak(Wk) [T10 Wk | T40Wk | TotalWk]	Score
YELLO ► 2146 Pk:92 [0|0|3]	**282**
One Second (87) 92(2) [0|0|10]	184
Flag (89) 152(2) [0|0|9]	73.1
You Gotta Say Yes To Another Excess (83) 184(2) [0|0|4]	24.3
YELLOWJACKETS ► 2568 Pk:145 [0|0|3]	**144**
Mirage A Trois (83) 145(1) [0|0|10]	106
Samurai Samba (85) 179(1) [0|0|4]	28.3
Shades (86) 195(1) [0|0|2]	9.0
YELLOW MAGIC ORCHESTRA ► 1845 Pk:81 [0|0|2]	**447**
Yellow Magic Orchestra (80) 81(1) [0|0|21]	427
X-Multiplies (80) 177(2) [0|0|2]	20.6
YES ► 88 Pk:3 [7|13|16]	**31781**
Fragile (72) 4(7) [15|21|46]	5692
90125 (83) 5(4) [12|28|53]	4449
Close To The Edge (72) 3(1) [7|15|32]	3249
Tales From Topographic Oceans (74) 6(2) [6|11|27]	2614
Going For The One (77) 8(2) [4|11|21]	2421
Yessongs (73) 12(1) [0|10|32]	2009
Big Generator (87) 15(3) [0|18|30]	2009
Relayer (74) 5(1) [4|9|16]	2003
The Yes Album (71) 40(1) [0|1|50]	1807
Tormato (78) 10(2) [2|7|14]	1480
Drama (80) 18(2) [0|7|19]	1330
Yesterdays (75) 17(2) [0|5|12]	1075
Anderson, Bruford, Wakeman, Howe (89)-Anderson, Bruford, Wakeman, Howe 30(1) [0|7|16]	867
Yesshows (80) 43(2) [0|0|12]	488
9012Live - The Solos (85) 81(3) [0|0|11]	217
Classic Yes (82) 142(2) [0|0|5]	71.1
YIPES!! ► 3221 Pk:177 [0|0|1]	**37**
Yipes!! (79) 177(1) [0|0|4]	37.3
Dwight YOAKAM ► 921 Pk:55 [0|0|4]	**2260**
Guitars, Cadillacs, Etc., Etc. (86) 61(2) [0|0|65]	993
Hillbilly Deluxe (87) 55(2) [0|0|28]	679
Buenas Noches From A Lonely Room (88) 68(1) [0|0|15]	384
Just Lookin' For A Hit (89) 68(2) [0|0|10]	204
Barry YOUNG ► 2116 Pk:67 [0|0|1]	**294**
One Has My Name (66) 67(2) [0|0|12]	294
Jesse Colin YOUNG ► 597 Pk:26 [0|3|8]	**4771**
Light Shine (74) 37(2) [0|3|29]	1446
Song For Juli (73) 51(1) [0|0|44]	1183
Songbird (75) 26(2) [0|4|14]	887
On The Road (76) 34(2) [0|3|15]	799
Love On The Wing (77) 64(1) [0|0|9]	299
Together (72) 157(1) [0|0|6]	76.7
The Soul Of A City Boy (74) 172(1) [0|0|6]	54.2
American Dreams (78) 165(2) [0|0|2]	26.4
John Paul YOUNG ► 2058 Pk:119 [0|0|1]	**322**
Love Is In The Air (78) 119(1) [0|0|18]	322
Neil YOUNG ► 63 Pk:1 [4|16|23]	**39694**
Harvest (72) 1(2) [16|25|41]	7962
After The Gold Rush (70) 8(5) [9|21|66]	5639
Rust Never Sleeps (79)-Neil Young & Crazy Horse 8(2) [5|17|39]	3716
Everybody Knows This Is Nowhere (69)-Neil Young & Crazy Horse 34(2) [0|5|98]	3638
Comes A Time (78) 7(2) [4|11|30]	2660
Live Rust (79)-Neil Young With Crazy Horse 15(2) [0|13|24]	1985
On The Beach (74) 16(1) [0|9|18]	1502
Zuma (75)-Neil Young With Crazy Horse 25(2) [0|7|21]	1307
American Stars 'N Bars (77)-Neil Young, Crazy Horse & The Bullets 21(1) [0|9|15]	1261

► Highest Peak [Top10s | Top40s | Total] Title (Yr) Peak(Wk) [T10 Wk | T40Wk | TotalWk]	Score
Freedom (89) 35(2) [0|4|28]	1127
Re-ac-tor (81)-Neil Young & Crazy Horse 27(3) [0|9|17]	1078
Trans (83) 19(6) [0|7|17]	981
Time Fades Away (73) 22(1) [0|6|18]	939
Journey Through The Past (Soundtrack) (72) 45(1) [0|0|21]	858
Tonight's The Night (75) 25(2) [0|5|12]	851
Hawks & Doves (80) 30(3) [0|6|16]	800
Decade (77) 43(3) [0|0|18]	731
Landing On Water (86) 46(2) [0|0|16]	586
Long May You Run (76)-Stills-Young Band [A] 26(1) [0|6|18]	573
This Note's For You (88)-Neil Young & The Bluenotes 61(2) [0|0|18]	490
Everybody's Rockin' (83)-Neil and the Shocking Pinks 46(2) [0|0|15]	486
Old Ways (85) 75(2) [0|0|12]	264
Life (87)-Neil Young With Crazy Horse 75(2) [0|0|11]	259
--See also: Crazy Horse	
Paul YOUNG ► 728 Pk:19 [0|1|3]	**3453**
The Secret Of Association (85) 19(6) [0|24|43]	2699
No Parlez (84) 79(1) [0|0|23]	432
Between Two Fires (86) 77(2) [0|0|17]	321
YOUNG AMERICANS ► 3251 Pk:178 [0|0|1]	**33**
Time For Livin' (69) 178(1) [0|0|3]	33.3
Lonnie YOUNGBLOOD ► 3207 Pk:127 [0|0|1]	**39**
Two Great Experiences Together! (71)-Jimi Hendrix & Lonnie Youngblood [A] 127(1) [0|0|4]	38.8
The YOUNGBLOODS ► 1164 Pk:80 [0|0|8]	**1419**
Elephant Mountain (69) 118(2) [0|0|29]	548
Rock Festival (70) 80(3) [0|0|13]	389
The Best Of The Youngbloods (70) 144(1) [0|0|10]	131
Ride The Wind (71) 157(3) [0|0|8]	109
The Youngbloods (67) 131(1) [0|0|8]	95.8
High On A Ridge Top (72) 185(1) [0|0|10]	67.1
Good And Dusty (71) 160(1) [0|0|5]	56.9
Sunlight (71) 186(1) [0|0|3]	23.8
YOUNG-HOLT UNLIMITED ► 821 Pk:9 [1|1|3]	**2816**
Soulful Strut (69) 9(2) [2|14|30]	2672
Wack Wack (67)-The Young-Holt Trio 132(1) [0|0|6]	96.2
Just A Melody (69) 185(1) [0|0|6]	48.4
YOUNG M.C. ► 629 Pk:9 [1|1|1]	**4442**
Stone Cold Rhymin' (89) 9(1) [4|30|48]	4442
YUTAKA ► 3198 Pk:174 [0|0|1]	**40**
Love Light (81) 174(1) [0|0|4]	39.8

Z

► Highest Peak [Top10s | Top40s | Total] Title (Yr) Peak(Wk) [T10 Wk | T40Wk | TotalWk]	Score
Pia ZADORA ► 2214 Pk:113 [0|0|1]	**247**
Pia & Phil (86) 113(2) [0|0|20]	247
Michael ZAGER Band ► 2212 Pk:120 [0|0|1]	**248**
Lets All Chant (78) 120(1) [0|0|13]	248
ZAGER & EVANS ► 1382 Pk:30 [0|1|1]	**992**
2525 (Exordium & Terminus) (69) 30(2) [0|5|13]	992
ZAPP ► 802 Pk:19 [0|3|5]	**2936**
Zapp (80) 19(2) [0|7|19]	1180
Zapp II (82) 25(3) [0|6|19]	845
Zapp III (83) 39(1) [0|2|22]	565
The New Zapp IV U (85) 110(2) [0|0|26]	308
V (89) 154(2) [0|0|4]	38.5
Frank ZAPPA ► 204 Pk:10 [1|9|33]	**17113**
Apostrophe (') (74) 10(1) [1|15|43]	3152

► Highest Peak [Top10s | Top40s | Total] Title (Yr) Peak(Wk) [T10 Wk | T40Wk | TotalWk]	Score
Over-Nite Sensation (73)-The Mothers 32(1) [0|4|50]	1629
Sheik Yerbouti (79) 21(1) [0|8|23]	1539
A Ship Arriving Too Late To Save A Drowning Witch (82) 23(2) [0|7|22]	1044
Joe's Garage Act I (79) 27(2) [0|5|25]	1031
Absolutely Free (67)-Mothers Of Invention 41(2) [0|0|22]	890
Roxy & Elsewhere (74)-Zappa/Mothers 27(1) [0|3|18]	874
We're Only In It For The Money (68)-Mothers Of Invention 30(1) [0|4|19]	842
One Size Fits All (75)-Frank Zappa And The Mothers Of Invention 26(1) [0|5|12]	775
The Mothers/Fillmore East-June 1971 (71)-The Mothers 38(1) [0|3|15]	666
Uncle Meat (69)-Mothers Of Invention 43(2) [0|0|11]	592
Joe's Garage Acts II + III (79) 53(1) [0|0|12]	446
Zoot Allures (76) 61(3) [0|0|13]	431
Frank Zappa's 200 Motels (Soundtrack) (71) 59(1) [0|0|13]	420
Tinsel Town Rebellion (81) 66(2) [0|0|11]	364
Cruising With Ruben & The Jets (68)-Mothers Of Invention 110(1) [0|0|12]	318
Zappa In New York (78) 57(1) [0|0|8]	294
Freak Out! (67)-Mothers Of Invention 130(2) [0|0|23]	254
Burnt Weeny Sandwich (70)-Mothers Of Invention 94(1) [0|0|8]	216
Chunga's Revenge (70) 119(1) [0|0|14]	209
Just Another Band From L.A. (72)-The Mothers 85(1) [0|0|9]	208
You Are What You Is (81) 93(1) [0|0|7]	161
Bongo Fury (75)-Frank Zappa/Captain Beefheart/The Mothers [A] 66(1) [0|0|8]	133
Mothermania/The Best Of The Mothers (69)-Mothers Of Invention 151(2) [0|0|9]	129
Waka/Jawaka - Hot Rats (72) 152(1) [0|0|7]	86.2
Studio Tan (78) 147(1) [0|0|6]	79.3
Hot Rats (69) 173(1) [0|0|6]	66.0
Frank Zappa Meets The Mothers Of Prevention (86) 153(2) [0|0|6]	55.4
Lumpy Gravy (68)-The Abnuceals Emuukha Electric Symphony Orchestra And Chorus 159(1) [0|0|5]	55.1
The Man From Utopia (83) 153(1) [0|0|5]	51.7
Orchestral Favorites (79) 168(1) [0|0|4]	42.8
Sleep Dirt (79) 175(2) [0|0|4]	39.8
Weasels Ripped My Flesh (70)-Mothers Of Invention 189(2) [0|0|3]	22.4
ZEBRA ► 1270 Pk:29 [0|1|2]	**1202**
Zebra (83) 29(2) [0|7|28]	1010
No Tellin' Lies (84) 84(2) [0|0|11]	192
ZENO ► 2470 Pk:107 [0|0|1]	**168**
Zeno (86) 107(2) [0|0|10]	168
ZEPHYR ► 1346 Pk:48 [0|0|1]	**1050**
Zephyr (69) 48(2) [0|0|26]	1050
Warren ZEVON ► 599 Pk:8 [1|2|6]	**4725**
Excitable Boy (78) 8(2) [4|13|28]	2546
Bad Luck Streak In Dancing School (80) 20(1) [0|8|16]	1220
Sentimental Hygiene (87) 63(4) [0|0|18]	469
Stand In The Fire (81) 80(3) [0|0|10]	277
The Envoy (82) 93(1) [0|0|13]	195
Warren Zevon (76) 189(2) [0|0|2]	16.7
ZODIAC MINDWARP & The LOVE REACTION ► 2321 Pk:132 [0|0|1]	**209**
Tattooed Beat Messiah (88) 132(2) [0|0|15]	209
The ZOMBIES ► 1394 Pk:39 [0|1|2]	**977**
The Zombies (65) 39(1) [0|1|17]	655
Odessey & Oracle (69) 95(1) [0|0|13]	322

Act ▶ Highest Peak [Top10s | Top40s | Total] Title (Yr) Peak(Wk) [T10 Wk | T40Wk | TotalWk]	Score
ZZ TOP ▶ 86 Pk:4 [4 | 7 | 9]	**32519**
Eliminator (83) 9(1) [4 | 82 | 183]	11592
Afterburner (85) 4(3) [15 | 36 | 70]	5557
Tres Hombres (73) 8(1) [2 | 24 | 81]	4957
Fandango! (75) 10(1) [1 | 21 | 47]	4374
Deguello (79) 24(3) [0 | 14 | 43]	2062
El Loco (81) 17(2) [0 | 12 | 22]	1836
Tejas (77) 17(2) [0 | 8 | 24]	1636
The Best Of ZZ Top (77) 94(2) [0 | 0 | 19]	276
Rio Grande Mud (72) 104(2) [0 | 0 | 10]	227

Ranking The Albums

For Albums 1-6000

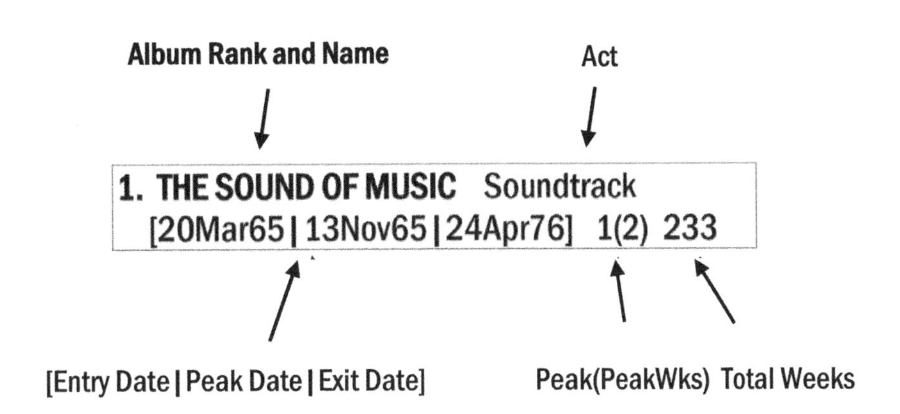

For Albums 6001-13843

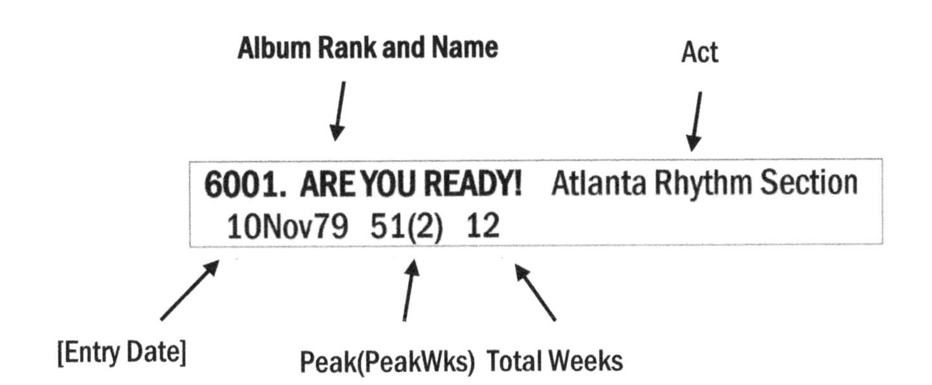

Ranking the Albums: 1-3500

Albums 1-3500 are albums with average score or better

Rank.	Title	Act	Enter	Peak	Exit	Peak(Wks)	TotWks	Score
1.	THE SOUND OF MUSIC	Soundtrack	20Mar65	13Nov65	24Apr76	1(2)	233	29435
2.	RUMOURS	Fleetwood Mac	26Feb77	02Apr77	19Apr80	1(31)	134	27526
3.	THRILLER	Michael Jackson	25Dec82	26Feb83	20Apr85	1(37)	122	25933
4.	TAPESTRY	Carole King	10Apr71	19Jun71	15Jan77	1(15)	302	25830
5.	BORN IN THE U.S.A.	Bruce Springsteen	23Jun84	07Jul84	14Feb87	1(7)	139	23827
6.	BLOOD, SWEAT & TEARS	Blood, Sweat & Tears	01Feb69	29Mar69	27Feb71	1(7)	109	23126
7.	THE DARK SIDE OF THE MOON	Pink Floyd	17Mar73	28Apr73	08Oct88	1(1)	741	23108
8.	WHIPPED CREAM & OTHER DELIGHTS	Herb Alpert's Tijuana Brass	15May65	27Nov65	07Dec68	1(8)	185	22164
9.	DOCTOR ZHIVAGO	Soundtrack	19Mar66	05Nov66	15Mar69	1(1)	157	21854
10.	FRAMPTON COMES ALIVE!	Peter Frampton	31Jan76	10Apr76	03Dec77	1(10)	97	20521
11.	HYSTERIA	Def Leppard	22Aug87	23Jul88	03Mar90	1(6)	133	19758
12.	FOREVER YOUR GIRL	Paula Abdul	23Jul88	07Oct89	22Feb92	1(10)	175	19418
13.	SATURDAY NIGHT FEVER (SOUNDTRACK)	Bee Gees	26Nov77	21Jan78	08Mar80	1(24)	120	19144
14.	HAIR	Original Cast Recording	03Aug68	26Apr69	19Jun71	1(13)	151	18698
15.	IN-A-GADDA-DA-VIDA	Iron Butterfly	20Jul68	09Aug69	20Mar71	4(1)	140	18683
16.	JESUS CHRIST SUPERSTAR	Various Artists	21Nov70	20Feb71	21Oct72	1(3)	101	18456
17.	WHITNEY HOUSTON	Whitney Houston	30Mar85	08Mar86	14May88	1(14)	162	18282
18.	FLEETWOOD MAC	Fleetwood Mac	02Aug75	04Sep76	02Feb80	1(1)	148	18198
19.	SGT. PEPPER'S LONELY HEARTS CLUB BAND	The Beatles	24Jun67	01Jul67	10Oct87	1(15)	175	17889
20.	APPETITE FOR DESTRUCTION	Guns N' Roses	29Aug87	06Aug88	30Jun90	1(5)	147	17811
21.	CAN'T SLOW DOWN	Lionel Richie	12Nov83	03Dec83	14Feb87	1(3)	160	17509
22.	!!GOING PLACES!!	Herb Alpert & The Tijuana Brass	16Oct65	05Mar66	01Feb69	1(6)	164	17192
23.	ESCAPE	Journey	08Aug81	12Sep81	09Jun84	1(1)	146	17166
24.	SONGS IN THE KEY OF LIFE	Stevie Wonder	16Oct76	16Oct76	21Feb81	1(14)	80	16923
25.	DIRTY DANCING	Soundtrack	19Sep87	14Nov87	15Jul89	1(18)	96	16684
26.	FAITH	George Michael	21Nov87	16Jan88	15Jul89	1(12)	87	16081
27.	HI INFIDELITY	REO Speedwagon	13Dec80	21Feb81	13Nov82	1(15)	101	16076
28.	ABBEY ROAD	The Beatles	18Oct69	01Nov69	06Feb88	1(11)	129	15679
29.	4	Foreigner	25Jul81	22Aug81	19Mar83	1(10)	81	15590
30.	DON'T BE CRUEL	Bobby Brown	23Jul88	21Jan89	26May90	1(6)	97	15398
31.	SPORTS	Huey Lewis & The News	08Oct83	30Jun84	16May87	1(1)	158	15377
32.	JOHN DENVER'S GREATEST HITS	John Denver	08Dec73	30Mar74	09Apr77	1(3)	175	15297
33.	MARY POPPINS	Soundtrack	03Oct64	13Mar65	03Dec66	1(14)	114	14811
34.	SLIPPERY WHEN WET	Bon Jovi	13Sep86	25Oct86	25Jun88	1(8)	94	14801
35.	ABRAXAS	Santana	10Oct70	24Oct70	10Jun72	1(6)	88	14731
36.	GIRL YOU KNOW IT'S TRUE	Milli Vanilli	25Mar89	23Sep89	15Sep90	1(7)	78	14650
37.	THE STRANGER	Billy Joel	08Oct77	18Feb78	14Nov81	2(6)	137	14610
38.	HANGIN' TOUGH	New Kids On The Block	27Aug88	09Sep89	02Mar91	1(2)	132	14550
39.	CHICAGO	Chicago	14Feb70	23May70	31May75	4(5)	134	14299
40.	BOSTON	Boston	25Sep76	04Dec76	13Jun87	3(6)	132	14152
41.	NO JACKET REQUIRED	Phil Collins	09Mar85	30Mar85	11Jul87	1(7)	123	14141
42.	LED ZEPPELIN II	Led Zeppelin	08Nov69	27Dec69	24Nov79	1(7)	98	13989
43.	LED ZEPPELIN IV	Led Zeppelin	27Nov71	18Dec71	25Jul87	2(4)	259	13899
44.	BREAKFAST IN AMERICA	Supertramp	31Mar79	19May79	05Mar83	1(6)	88	13764
45.	JANET JACKSON'S RHYTHM NATION 1814	Janet Jackson	07Oct89	28Oct89	11Jan92	1(4)	108	13746
46.	GREASE	Soundtrack	20May78	29Jul78	09Feb80	1(12)	77	13745
47.	PURPLE RAIN (SOUNDTRACK)	Prince And The Revolution	14Jul84	04Aug84	23Nov85	1(24)	72	13717
48.	THE BEATLES [WHITE ALBUM]	The Beatles	14Dec68	28Dec68	21Nov87	1(9)	155	13693
49.	SYNCHRONICITY	The Police	02Jul83	23Jul83	01Dec84	1(17)	75	13507
50.	THE MONKEES	The Monkees	08Oct66	12Nov66	24Jan87	1(13)	102	13494
51.	OFF THE WALL	Michael Jackson	01Sep79	16Feb80	06Oct84	3(3)	169	13427
52.	THE WALL	Pink Floyd	15Dec79	19Jan80	29Sep90	1(15)	123	13311
53.	BAD	Michael Jackson	26Sep87	26Sep87	20May89	1(6)	87	13217
54.	WHAT NOW MY LOVE	Herb Alpert & The Tijuana Brass	14May66	28May66	26Oct68	1(9)	129	12888
55.	SOUL PROVIDER	Michael Bolton	22Jul89	14Apr90	29May93	3(3)	202	12887
56.	HOTEL CALIFORNIA	Eagles	25Dec76	15Jan77	09Feb80	1(8)	107	12868
57.	GOODBYE YELLOW BRICK ROAD	Elton John	20Oct73	10Nov73	27Feb88	1(8)	103	12843
58.	BUSINESS AS USUAL	Men At Work	03Jul82	13Nov82	17Mar84	1(15)	90	12719
59.	CHRISTOPHER CROSS	Christopher Cross	16Feb80	06Sep80	01May82	6(3)	116	12682
60.	SANTANA	Santana	13Sep69	15Nov69	02Oct71	4(6)	108	12586
61.	MORE OF THE MONKEES	The Monkees	04Feb67	11Feb67	07Feb87	1(18)	96	12541
62.	BELLA DONNA	Stevie Nicks	15Aug81	05Sep81	15Feb86	1(1)	143	12532
63.	CONTROL	Janet Jackson	08Mar86	05Jul86	12Mar88	1(2)	106	12415
64.	TOMMY	The Who	07Jun69	19Sep70	26Jul75	4(2)	126	12174
65.	ARE YOU EXPERIENCED?	The Jimi Hendrix Experience	26Aug67	05Oct68	30Aug69	5(1)	106	12140
66.	THE JOSHUA TREE	U2	04Apr87	25Apr87	18Mar89	1(9)	103	12139
67.	KENNY ROGERS' GREATEST HITS	Kenny Rogers	18Oct80	13Dec80	14Apr84	1(2)	181	12108
68.	THEIR GREATEST HITS 1971-1975	Eagles	06Mar76	13Mar76	08Mar80	1(5)	133	12106
69.	DIANA ROSS AND THE SUPREMES GREATEST HITS	Diana Ross & The Supremes	30Sep67	28Oct67	07Jun69	1(5)	89	11993
70.	FLY LIKE AN EAGLE	The Steve Miller Band	29May76	23Oct76	01Apr78	3(2)	97	11974
71.	BROTHERS IN ARMS	Dire Straits	08Jun85	31Aug85	11Apr87	1(9)	97	11915
72.	THE GRADUATE (SOUNDTRACK)	Simon & Garfunkel	16Mar68	06Apr68	02Sep72	1(9)	69	11898
73.	SILK DEGREES	Boz Scaggs	20Mar76	18Sep76	27May78	2(5)	115	11882
74.	WHITESNAKE	Whitesnake	18Apr87	13Jun87	24Sep88	2(10)	76	11814
75.	WOODSTOCK	Soundtrack	06Jun70	11Jul70	18Sep71	1(4)	68	11782
76.	PRIVATE DANCER	Tina Turner	16Jun84	29Sep84	21Jun86	3(11)	106	11671
77.	GLASS HOUSES	Billy Joel	22Mar80	14Jun80	14Nov81	1(6)	73	11662
78.	WHITNEY	Whitney Houston	27Jun87	27Jun87	04Feb89	1(11)	85	11594
79.	ELIMINATOR	ZZ Top	23Apr83	12Nov83	18Oct86	9(1)	183	11592
80.	AGAINST THE WIND	Bob Seger & The Silver Bullet Band	15Mar80	03May80	09Apr83	1(6)	110	11583
81.	HEART	Heart	13Jul85	21Dec85	19Sep87	1(1)	92	11541
82.	JOHNNY CASH AT SAN QUENTIN	Johnny Cash	05Jul69	23Aug69	31Oct70	1(4)	70	11537
83.	RECKLESS	Bryan Adams	24Nov84	10Aug85	30May87	1(2)	83	11440
84.	CHICAGO TRANSIT AUTHORITY	Chicago	17May69	19Jul69	07Jun75	17(2)	171	11343
85.	BRIDGE OVER TROUBLED WATER	Simon & Garfunkel	14Feb70	07Mar70	25Sep71	1(10)	85	11307
86.	SWEET BABY JAMES	James Taylor	14Mar70	07Nov70	19Feb72	3(4)	102	11267
87.	WICHITA LINEMAN	Glen Campbell	16Nov68	21Dec68	27Sep69	1(5)	46	11245
88.	THE DOORS	The Doors	25Mar67	16Sep67	10Jan81	2(2)	121	11218
89.	THE LONG RUN	Eagles	20Oct79	03Nov79	15Nov80	1(9)	57	11205
90.	DEJA VU	Crosby, Stills, Nash & Young	04Apr70	16May70	15Oct77	1(1)	97	11184
91.	SONGS FROM THE BIG CHAIR	Tears For Fears	06Apr85	13Jul85	25Oct86	1(5)	82	11182
92.	PYROMANIA	Def Leppard	05Feb83	14May83	25Feb89	2(2)	116	11178
93.	BAND ON THE RUN	Paul McCartney And Wings	22Dec73	13Apr74	05Mar77	1(4)	116	11152
94.	BACK HOME AGAIN	John Denver	29Jun74	10Aug74	08May76	1(1)	96	11102
95.	CRIMES OF PASSION	Pat Benatar	23Aug80	17Jan81	29May82	2(5)	93	11064
96.	AN INNOCENT MAN	Billy Joel	20Aug83	08Oct83	28Sep85	4(5)	111	11007

Rank. Title	Act	Enter	Peak	Exit	Peak(Wks)	TotWks	Score
97. PARADISE THEATER	Styx	31Jan81	04Apr81	27Mar82	1(3)	61	10999
98. HELLO, DOLLY!	Original Cast	22Feb64	06Jun64	06Nov65	1(1)	90	10990
99. CLOSE TO YOU	Carpenters	19Sep70	05Dec70	13May72	2(1)	87	10928
100. RED OCTOPUS	Jefferson Starship	19Jul75	06Sep75	12Mar77	1(4)	87	10755
101. 52ND STREET	Billy Joel	28Oct78	18Nov78	14Nov81	1(8)	76	10703
102. ONE OF THESE NIGHTS	Eagles	28Jun75	26Jul75	17Jul76	1(5)	56	10702
103. PARSLEY, SAGE, ROSEMARY AND THYME	Simon & Garfunkel	12Nov66	24Dec66	18Jul70	4(2)	145	10665
104. EVERY PICTURE TELLS A STORY	Rod Stewart	19Jun71	02Oct71	10Jun72	1(4)	52	10659
105. CROSBY, STILLS & NASH	Crosby, Stills & Nash	28Jun69	15Nov69	15Oct77	6(3)	107	10638
106. LIKE A VIRGIN	Madonna	01Dec84	09Feb85	19Sep87	1(3)	108	10496
107. COSMO'S FACTORY	Creedence Clearwater Revival	25Jul70	22Aug70	13Nov71	1(9)	69	10485
108. CHEAP THRILLS	Big Brother And The Holding Company	31Aug68	12Oct68	29Nov69	1(8)	66	10453
109. CARPENTERS	Carpenters	05Jun71	03Jul71	15Jul72	2(2)	59	10448
110. BACK IN BLACK	AC/DC	23Aug80	20Dec80	23Mar91	4(3)	131	10402
111. SOME GIRLS	The Rolling Stones	24Jun78	15Jul78	05Dec81	1(2)	82	10361
112. HONEY IN THE HORN	Al Hirt	21Sep63	07Mar64	11Sep65	3(8)	104	10337
113. BOOKENDS	Simon & Garfunkel	27Apr68	25May68	26Jul69	1(7)	66	10281
114. THE RAW & THE COOKED	Fine Young Cannibals	11Mar89	03Jun89	19May90	1(7)	63	10227
115. IN THE WIND	Peter, Paul & Mary	26Oct63	02Nov63	01May65	1(5)	80	10215
116. THE TEMPTATIONS GREATEST HITS	The Temptations	17Dec66	11Feb67	29Mar69	5(2)	120	10179
117. YOU DON'T MESS AROUND WITH JIM	Jim Croce	01Jul72	12Jan74	30Nov74	1(5)	93	10154
118. LED ZEPPELIN	Led Zeppelin	15Feb69	17May69	01Dec79	10(1)	95	10151
119. KICK	INXS	14Nov87	27Feb88	27May89	3(4)	81	10126
120. DOUBLE VISION	Foreigner	08Jul78	09Sep78	05Dec81	3(8)	88	10010
121. TATTOO YOU	The Rolling Stones	12Sep81	19Sep81	16Oct82	1(9)	58	9921
122. HOT ROCKS 1964-1971	The Rolling Stones	08Jan72	12Feb72	20Jan90	4(2)	243	9918
123. MY FAIR LADY	Soundtrack	10Oct64	06Feb65	19Nov66	4(2)	111	9912
124. FLASHDANCE	Soundtrack	30Apr83	25Jun83	20Oct84	1(2)	78	9902
125. FOREIGNER	Foreigner	26Mar77	22Oct77	19Sep81	4(5)	113	9882
126. GET LUCKY	Loverboy	14Nov81	01May82	10Mar84	7(2)	122	9866
127. LIONEL RICHIE	Lionel Richie	23Oct82	27Nov82	22Jun85	3(7)	140	9861
128. BAYOU COUNTRY	Creedence Clearwater Revival	08Feb69	07Jun69	10Oct70	7(1)	88	9860
129. BEAUTY AND THE BEAT	Go-Go's	01Aug81	06Mar82	11Dec82	1(6)	72	9856
130. MAKE IT BIG	Wham!	10Nov84	02Mar85	17May86	1(3)	80	9851
131. DISRAELI GEARS	Cream	09Dec67	29Jun68	26Mar77	4(2)	83	9811
132. ASIA	Asia	03Apr82	15May82	29Oct83	1(9)	64	9795
133. THAT'S THE WAY OF THE WORLD (SOUNDTRACK)	Earth, Wind & Fire	15Mar75	17May75	27Mar76	1(3)	55	9789
134. AJA	Steely Dan	15Oct77	22Oct77	02Dec78	3(7)	60	9774
135. NEW JERSEY	Bon Jovi	08Oct88	15Oct88	17Mar90	1(4)	76	9744
136. ...BUT SERIOUSLY	Phil Collins	02Dec89	30Dec89	07Sep91	1(4)	90	9734
137. ROMEO & JULIET	Soundtrack	08Feb69	12Jul69	04Jul70	2(2)	74	9730
138. WINGS AT THE SPEED OF SOUND	Wings	10Apr76	24Apr76	26Mar77	1(7)	51	9726
139. TIME PEACE/THE RASCALS' GREATEST HITS	The Rascals	13Jul68	28Sep68	11Oct69	1(1)	58	9593
140. AMERICAN FOOL	John Cougar	08May82	11Sep82	10May86	1(9)	106	9588
141. H2O	Daryl Hall & John Oates	30Oct82	15Jan83	11Feb84	3(15)	68	9556
142. GREEN RIVER	Creedence Clearwater Revival	13Sep69	04Oct69	15May71	1(4)	88	9555
143. RAPTURE	Anita Baker	19Apr86	21Mar87	15Apr89	11(2)	157	9452
144. DOUBLE FANTASY	John Lennon & Yoko Ono	06Dec80	27Dec80	01May82	1(8)	74	9397
145. ELTON JOHN'S GREATEST HITS	Elton John	23Nov74	30Nov74	26Mar77	1(10)	104	9369
146. INNERVISIONS	Stevie Wonder	18Aug73	22Sep73	14Feb81	4(1)	89	9362
147. OPEN UP AND SAY...AHH!	Poison	21May88	18Jun88	16Sep89	2(1)	70	9336
148. SHE'S SO UNUSUAL	Cyndi Lauper	24Dec83	02Jun84	19Oct85	4(4)	96	9304
149. MINUTE BY MINUTE	The Doobie Brothers	23Dec78	07Apr79	16Aug80	1(5)	87	9288
150. HOUSES OF THE HOLY	Led Zeppelin	14Apr73	12May73	01Dec79	1(2)	99	9285
151. GUILTY	Barbra Streisand	11Oct80	25Oct80	12Sep81	1(3)	49	9281
152. SCARECROW	John Mellencamp	14Sep85	16Nov85	14Feb87	2(3)	75	9110
153. ZENYATTA MONDATTA	The Police	25Oct80	07Feb81	12May84	5(6)	153	9097
154. FIDDLER ON THE ROOF	Original Cast	31Oct64	30Jan65	03May69	7(2)	206	9072
155. INVISIBLE TOUCH	Genesis	28Jun86	02Aug86	06Feb88	3(2)	85	9040
156. BREAK OUT	The Pointer Sisters	26Nov83	06Oct84	23Nov85	8(2)	105	9038
157. FULL MOON FEVER	Tom Petty	13May89	08Jul89	15Sep90	3(2)	71	9020
158. THE GAME	Queen	19Jul80	20Sep80	09May81	1(5)	43	9015
159. A HARD DAY'S NIGHT (SOUNDTRACK)	The Beatles	18Jul64	25Jul64	03Jul65	1(14)	51	9013
160. AMERICAN PIE	Don McLean	13Nov71	22Jan72	07Oct72	1(7)	48	9002
161. 1984 (MCMLXXXIV)	Van Halen	28Jan84	17Mar84	13Jul85	2(5)	77	9001
162. TRUE BLUE	Madonna	19Jul86	16Aug86	06Feb88	1(5)	82	8991
163. TEASER AND THE FIRECAT	Cat Stevens	09Oct71	04Dec71	09Jul77	2(1)	67	8980
164. THE AGE OF AQUARIUS	The 5th Dimension	31May69	28Jun69	10Oct70	2(2)	72	8929
165. PEARL	Janis Joplin	30Jan71	27Feb71	13Nov71	1(9)	42	8905
166. STICKY FINGERS	The Rolling Stones	15May71	22May71	14Nov81	1(4)	62	8853
167. A STAR IS BORN (SOUNDTRACK)	Barbra Streisand & Kris Kristofferson	11Dec76	12Feb77	26Nov77	1(6)	51	8852
168. MUD SLIDE SLIM AND THE BLUE HORIZON	James Taylor	08May71	24Jul71	11Mar72	2(4)	45	8844
169. GHOST IN THE MACHINE	The Police	24Oct81	05Dec81	12May84	2(6)	109	8836
170. NICK OF TIME	Bonnie Raitt	15Apr89	07Apr90	09Jan93	1(3)	185	8820
171. RAM	Paul & Linda McCartney	05Jun71	21Aug71	12Feb72	2(2)	37	8807
172. HEARTBEAT CITY	The Cars	07Apr84	14Jul84	27Jul85	3(1)	69	8802
173. EASY RIDER	Soundtrack	06Sep69	09May70	16Jan71	6(1)	72	8708
174. HEADQUARTERS	The Monkees	10Jun67	24Jun67	06Dec86	1(1)	68	8689
175. PUMP	Aerosmith	30Sep89	04Nov89	18Jan92	5(3)	110	8649
176. DR. FEELGOOD	Mötley Crüe	23Sep89	14Oct89	19Oct91	1(2)	109	8619
177. 1999	Prince	20Nov82	28May83	19Oct85	9(7)	153	8588
178. SHAFT (SOUNDTRACK)	Isaac Hayes	21Aug71	06Nov71	07Oct72	1(1)	60	8587
179. S.R.O.	Herb Alpert & The Tijuana Brass	10Dec66	31Dec66	20Jul68	2(6)	85	8579
180. BAD GIRLS	Donna Summer	12May79	16Jun79	12Apr80	1(6)	49	8577
181. IN THROUGH THE OUT DOOR	Led Zeppelin	08Sep79	15Sep79	14Jun80	1(7)	41	8553
182. SIMPLE DREAMS	Linda Ronstadt	24Sep77	03Dec77	12Aug78	1(5)	47	8545
183. GRACELAND	Paul Simon	13Sep86	04Apr87	16Jul88	3(1)	97	8543
184. SKID ROW	Skid Row	11Feb89	23Sep89	04Aug90	6(1)	78	8481
185. CAPTAIN FANTASTIC AND THE BROWN DIRT COWBOY	Elton John	07Jun75	07Jun75	27Mar76	1(7)	43	8391
186. THE END OF THE INNOCENCE	Don Henley	15Jul89	23Sep89	16May92	8(1)	148	8388
187. LIVE AND MORE	Donna Summer	16Sep78	11Nov78	16Feb80	1(1)	75	8386
188. WHEELS OF FIRE	Cream	13Jul68	10Aug68	12Mar77	1(4)	50	8375
189. BREEZIN'	George Benson	17Apr76	31Jul76	08Oct77	1(2)	78	8344
190. STRANGER IN TOWN	Bob Seger & The Silver Bullet Band	27May78	22Jul78	22Oct83	4(2)	110	8305
191. MEET THE BEATLES!	The Beatles	01Feb64	15Feb64	05Jun65	1(11)	71	8283
192. GREATEST HITS	Sly & The Family Stone	07Nov70	19Dec70	06May72	2(1)	79	8278
193. THE JAZZ SINGER (SOUNDTRACK)	Neil Diamond	29Nov80	07Feb81	23Apr83	3(7)	115	8275
194. FREEZE-FRAME	The J. Geils Band	14Nov81	06Feb82	12Mar83	1(4)	70	8234
195. SPIRITS HAVING FLOWN	Bee Gees	17Feb79	03Mar79	01Mar80	1(6)	55	8229
196. THE BEATLES 1967-1970	The Beatles	14Apr73	26May73	21Apr84	1(1)	169	8202
197. TOP GUN	Soundtrack	07Jun86	26Jul86	12Mar88	1(5)	93	8187
198. MAGICAL MYSTERY TOUR (SOUNDTRACK)	The Beatles	23Dec67	06Jan68	07Nov87	1(8)	91	8172
199. FACE VALUE	Phil Collins	14Mar81	04Jul81	25Apr87	7(4)	164	8163
200. FEELS SO RIGHT	Alabama	28Mar81	05Sep81	21Apr84	16(2)	161	8135
201. A NEW WORLD RECORD	Electric Light Orchestra	30Oct76	08Jan77	18Feb78	5(2)	69	8133

Rank. Title Act
[Enter | Peak | Exit] Peak(Wks) TotWks — Score

202. LIKE A PRAYER Madonna
[08Apr89 | 22Apr89 | 22Sep90] 1(6) 77 — 8128

203. THE SECOND BARBRA STREISAND ALBUM
Barbra Streisand
[14Sep63 | 09Nov63 | 06Feb65] 2(3) 74 — 8127

204. DON'T SAY NO Billy Squier
[02May81 | 05Sep81 | 03Nov84] 5(3) 111 — 8125

205. STILL CRAZY AFTER ALL THESE YEARS
Paul Simon
[25Oct75 | 06Dec75 | 24Jul76] 1(1) 40 — 8118

206. DAMN THE TORPEDOES
Tom Petty And The Heartbreakers
[10Nov79 | 09Feb80 | 07Nov81] 2(7) 66 — 8108

207. AQUALUNG Jethro Tull
[15May71 | 05Jun71 | 14May77] 7(7) 76 — 8099

208. WONDERFULNESS Bill Cosby
[28May66 | 30Jul66 | 01Jun68] 7(1) 106 — 8093

209. TALKING BOOK Stevie Wonder
[18Nov72 | 03Feb73 | 14Dec74] 3(3) 109 — 8080

210. BEACHES (SOUNDTRACK) Bette Midler
[21Jan89 | 10Jun89 | 04Jul92] 2(3) 176 — 8076

211. HELLO DOLLY! Louis Armstrong
[16May64 | 13Jun64 | 09Oct65] 1(6) 74 — 8075

212. FRONTIERS Journey
[19Feb83 | 12Mar83 | 29Sep84] 2(9) 85 — 8070

213. NASHVILLE SKYLINE Bob Dylan
[03May69 | 24May69 | 21Mar70] 3(4) 47 — 8062

214. COLOUR BY NUMBERS Culture Club
[05Nov83 | 04Feb84 | 15Dec84] 2(6) 59 — 8038

215. THE GRAND ILLUSION Styx
[30Jul77 | 25Feb78 | 02May81] 6(2) 127 — 8016

216. IF YOU CAN BELIEVE YOUR EYES AND EARS
The Mamas & The Papas
[12Mar66 | 21May66 | 09Mar68] 1(1) 105 — 7986

217. CHICAGO VII Chicago
[30Mar74 | 27Apr74 | 19Jul75] 1(1) 69 — 7973

218. HARVEST Neil Young
[04Mar72 | 11Mar72 | 09Dec72] 1(2) 41 — 7962

219. BUILT FOR SPEED Stray Cats
[03Jul82 | 27Nov82 | 26Nov83] 2(15) 74 — 7957

220. TRACY CHAPMAN Tracy Chapman
[30Apr88 | 27Aug88 | 24Jun89] 1(1) 61 — 7949

221. SLOWHAND Eric Clapton
[26Nov77 | 01Apr78 | 21Apr79] 2(5) 74 — 7923

222. THE PARTRIDGE FAMILY ALBUM
The Partridge Family
[31Oct70 | 02Jan71 | 12Feb72] 4(2) 68 — 7904

223. TEA FOR THE TILLERMAN Cat Stevens
[06Feb71 | 17Apr71 | 16Jul77] 8(3) 79 — 7879

224. FIRST TAKE Roberta Flack
[31Jan70 | 29Apr72 | 17Feb73] 1(5) 54 — 7872

225. FOOTLOOSE Soundtrack
[18Feb84 | 21Apr84 | 18May85] 1(10) 61 — 7852

226. TOM JONES LIVE IN LAS VEGAS
Tom Jones
[15Nov69 | 06Dec69 | 31Oct70] 3(5) 51 — 7828

227. HONKY CHÂTEAU Elton John
[17Jun72 | 15Jul72 | 11Aug73] 1(5) 61 — 7808

228. DONOVAN'S GREATEST HITS Donovan
[22Feb69 | 12Apr69 | 14Mar70] 4(4) 56 — 7771

229. PEOPLE Barbra Streisand
[03Oct64 | 31Oct64 | 07May66] 1(5) 84 — 7751

230. FELICIANO! Jose Feliciano
[20Jul68 | 02Nov68 | 01Nov69] 2(3) 59 — 7730

231. JOHNNY CASH AT FOLSOM PRISON
Johnny Cash
[15Jun68 | 31Aug68 | 10Oct70] 13(2) 122 — 7728

232. LICENSED TO ILL Beastie Boys
[29Nov86 | 07Mar87 | 12Mar88] 1(7) 68 — 7721

233. CHICAGO IX: CHICAGO'S GREATEST HITS
Chicago
[29Nov75 | 13Dec75 | 31Dec77] 1(5) 72 — 7717

234. THE CARS The Cars
[01Jul78 | 24Mar79 | 09Jun84] 18(2) 139 — 7689

235. REPEAT OFFENDER Richard Marx
[20May89 | 02Sep89 | 18Aug90] 1(1) 66 — 7671

236. WINDSONG John Denver
[04Oct75 | 18Oct75 | 30Oct76] 1(2) 45 — 7642

Rank. Title Act
[Enter | Peak | Exit] Peak(Wks) TotWks — Score

237. FUNNY GIRL (SOUNDTRACK)
Barbra Streisand
[28Sep68 | 25Jan69 | 17Oct70] 12(1) 108 — 7627

238. SOUTH OF THE BORDER
Herb Alpert & The Tijuana Brass
[16Jan65 | 16Apr66 | 25Jan69] 6(1) 163 — 7622

239. TOTO IV Toto
[24Apr82 | 10Jul82 | 12Nov83] 4(4) 82 — 7593

240. TOYS IN THE ATTIC Aerosmith
[26Apr75 | 13Sep75 | 15Oct77] 11(1) 128 — 7586

241. SANTANA III Santana
[16Oct71 | 13Nov71 | 08Jul72] 1(5) 39 — 7577

242. THE WORLD IS A GHETTO War
[18Nov72 | 17Feb73 | 02Mar74] 1(2) 68 — 7568

243. GET THE KNACK The Knack
[30Jun79 | 11Aug79 | 29Mar80] 1(5) 40 — 7540

244. THE WAY IT IS Bruce Hornsby & The Range
[21Jun86 | 07Mar87 | 07Nov87] 3(4) 73 — 7530

245. BACK IN THE HIGH LIFE Steve Winwood
[19Jul86 | 06Sep86 | 05Mar88] 3(2) 86 — 7480

246. BIG BAMBU Cheech & Chong
[01Jul72 | 30Sep72 | 21Dec74] 2(1) 111 — 7459

247. COMMODORES Commodores
[02Apr77 | 18Jun77 | 01Apr78] 3(3) 53 — 7441

248. FORE! Huey Lewis & The News
[13Sep86 | 18Oct86 | 07Nov87] 1(1) 61 — 7433

249. COURT AND SPARK Joni Mitchell
[09Feb74 | 02Mar74 | 26Apr75] 2(4) 64 — 7427

250. ALL THINGS MUST PASS
George Harrison
[19Dec70 | 02Jan71 | 04Sep71] 1(7) 38 — 7410

251. BEAT OF THE BRASS
Herb Alpert & The Tijuana Brass
[11May68 | 27Jul68 | 17May69] 1(2) 54 — 7403

252. CHICAGO V Chicago
[29Jul72 | 19Aug72 | 10May75] 1(9) 51 — 7391

253. RAISING HELL Run-D.M.C.
[14Jun86 | 20Sep86 | 17Oct87] 3(3) 71 — 7388

254. NO SECRETS Carly Simon
[09Dec72 | 13Jan73 | 13Apr74] 1(5) 71 — 7375

255. WHY IS THERE AIR? Bill Cosby
[28Aug65 | 13Aug66 | 20Jul68] 19(1) 152 — 7355

256. MUSIC Carole King
[11Dec71 | 01Jan72 | 07Oct72] 1(3) 44 — 7352

257. THE STING (SOUNDTRACK)
Marvin Hamlisch
[26Jan74 | 04May74 | 02Nov74] 1(5) 41 — 7349

258. THE BEST OF THE ANIMALS The Animals
[12Feb66 | 26Mar66 | 06Apr68] 6(3) 113 — 7333

259. HOT BUTTERED SOUL Isaac Hayes
[12Jul69 | 25Oct69 | 23Jan71] 8(3) 81 — 7331

260. TIFFANY Tiffany
[26Sep87 | 23Jan88 | 11Feb89] 1(2) 69 — 7298

261. BROTHERS AND SISTERS
The Allman Brothers Band
[25Aug73 | 08Sep73 | 14Sep74] 1(5) 56 — 7279

262. SOMEWHERE MY LOVE
Ray Conniff & His Orchestra & Chorus
[16Jul66 | 24Sep66 | 06Jul68] 3(4) 90 — 7273

263. DIANA Diana Ross
[14Jun80 | 04Oct80 | 06Jun81] 2(2) 52 — 7266

264. FEELS SO GOOD Chuck Mangione
[29Oct77 | 17Jun78 | 10May80] 2(2) 88 — 7254

265. BLOOMING HITS
Paul Mauriat And His Orchestra
[16Dec67 | 02Mar68 | 07Dec68] 1(5) 50 — 7252

266. McCARTNEY Paul McCartney
[09May70 | 23May70 | 27Mar71] 1(3) 47 — 7209

267. COSMIC THING The B-52s
[22Jul89 | 10Mar90 | 13Oct90] 4(1) 65 — 7172

268. CARIBOU Elton John
[06Jul74 | 13Jul74 | 12Jul75] 1(4) 54 — 7168

269. WHERE DID OUR LOVE GO The Supremes
[19Sep64 | 16Jan65 | 28May66] 2(4) 89 — 7153

270. STREET SONGS Rick James
[02May81 | 01Aug81 | 25Sep82] 3(2) 74 — 7134

271. A NIGHT ON THE TOWN Rod Stewart
[17Jul76 | 04Dec76 | 13Aug77] 2(5) 57 — 7129

Rank. Title Act
[Enter | Peak | Exit] Peak(Wks) TotWks — Score

272. SO Peter Gabriel
[14Jun86 | 26Jul86 | 07Oct89] 2(3) 93 — 7120

273. EMOTIONAL RESCUE The Rolling Stones
[19Jul80 | 26Jul80 | 28Nov81] 1(7) 51 — 7106

274. THE DREAM OF THE BLUE TURTLES Sting
[13Jul85 | 07Sep85 | 16Aug86] 2(6) 58 — 7101

275. GETZ/GILBERTO Stan Getz And
Joao Gilberto Featuring Antonio Carlos Jobim
[06Jun64 | 08Aug64 | 02Apr66] 2(2) 96 — 7098

276. BLIND FAITH Blind Faith
[16Aug69 | 20Sep69 | 16Apr77] 1(2) 45 — 7080

**277. DON'T SHOOT ME
I'M ONLY THE PIANO PLAYER** Elton John
[10Feb73 | 03Mar73 | 19Oct74] 1(2) 89 — 7076

278. THE CAPTAIN AND ME The Doobie Brothers
[31Mar73 | 21Jul73 | 19Jul75] 7(2) 102 — 7061

279. WILLY AND THE POORBOYS
Creedence Clearwater Revival
[13Dec69 | 10Jan70 | 30Jan71] 3(6) 60 — 7040

280. PIECES OF EIGHT Styx
[30Sep78 | 02Dec78 | 02May81] 6(1) 92 — 7036

281. METAL HEALTH Quiet Riot
[23Apr83 | 26Nov83 | 03Nov84] 1(1) 81 — 7033

282. NOT FRAGILE Bachman-Turner Overdrive
[31Aug74 | 19Oct74 | 06Sep75] 1(1) 50 — 7020

283. FOOT LOOSE & FANCY FREE Rod Stewart
[26Nov77 | 07Jan78 | 14Oct78] 2(6) 47 — 7013

284. CORNERSTONE Styx
[13Oct79 | 24Nov79 | 02May81] 2(1) 60 — 6989

285. HELP! (SOUNDTRACK) The Beatles
[28Aug65 | 11Sep65 | 25Jun66] 1(9) 44 — 6986

286. I NEVER LOVED A MAN THE WAY I LOVE YOU
Aretha Franklin
[08Apr67 | 27May67 | 05Oct68] 2(3) 79 — 6978

287. THIS IS TOM JONES Tom Jones
[14Jun69 | 12Jul69 | 04Apr70] 4(3) 43 — 6974

288. OU812 Van Halen
[18Jun88 | 25Jun88 | 13May89] 1(4) 48 — 6971

289. STRANGERS IN THE NIGHT Frank Sinatra
[18Jun66 | 23Jul66 | 04Nov67] 1(1) 73 — 6964

290. MISTAKEN IDENITY Kim Carnes
[02May81 | 27Jun81 | 24Apr82] 1(4) 52 — 6959

291. CHICAGO VI Chicago
[14Jul73 | 28Jul73 | 07Jun75] 1(5) 73 — 6934

292. GOLDEN BISQUITS Three Dog Night
[27Feb71 | 24Apr71 | 22Apr72] 5(4) 61 — 6926

293. LOOK WHAT THE CAT DRAGGED IN Poison
[02Aug86 | 23May87 | 02Jul88] 3(2) 101 — 6911

294. 4 WAY STREET
Crosby, Stills, Nash & Young
[24Apr71 | 15May71 | 05Feb72] 1(1) 42 — 6910

295. ENDLESS SUMMER The Beach Boys
[20Jul74 | 05Oct74 | 14Nov81] 1(1) 156 — 6903

296. THE BEST OF BREAD Bread
[31Mar73 | 12May73 | 02Apr77] 2(1) 119 — 6903

297. LET IT LOOSE
Gloria Estefan & Miami Sound Machine
[20Jun87 | 28May88 | 22Apr89] 6(2) 97 — 6903

298. LED ZEPPELIN III Led Zeppelin
[24Oct70 | 31Oct70 | 01Dec79] 1(4) 42 — 6898

299. MADONNA Madonna
[03Sep83 | 20Oct84 | 05Sep87] 8(3) 168 — 6893

300. BACHMAN-TURNER OVERDRIVE II
Bachman-Turner Overdrive
[19Jan74 | 31Aug74 | 13Sep75] 4(2) 75 — 6892

301. LET IT BE (SOUNDTRACK) The Beatles
[30May70 | 13Jun70 | 05Dec87] 1(4) 59 — 6889

302. BEATLES '65 The Beatles
[02Jan65 | 09Jan65 | 07May66] 1(9) 71 — 6884

303. GREATEST HITS The Association
[28Dec68 | 08Feb69 | 05Sep70] 4(3) 75 — 6883

304. NIGHT SONGS Cinderella
[19Jul86 | 07Feb87 | 14Nov87] 3(3) 70 — 6880

305. LONG DISTANCE VOYAGER
The Moody Blues
[13Jun81 | 25Jul81 | 06Mar82] 1(3) 39 — 6873

306. A MAN AND A WOMAN Soundtrack
[19Nov66 | 06May67 | 24Aug68] 10(2) 93 — 6866

Rank. Title Act
[Enter | Peak | Exit] Peak(Wks) TotWks — Score

307. THE DREAM WEAVER Gary Wright
[23Aug75 | 10Apr76 | 05Feb77] 7(3) 75 — 6852

308. WHAT WERE ONCE VICES ARE NOW HABITS
The Doobie Brothers
[16Mar74 | 22Mar75 | 19Jul75] 4(1) 62 — 6848

309. CHICAGO III Chicago
[30Jan71 | 20Feb71 | 03May75] 2(2) 63 — 6848

310. GRATITUDE Earth, Wind & Fire
[06Dec75 | 17Jan76 | 11Dec76] 1(3) 54 — 6844

311. GENTLE ON MY MIND Glen Campbell
[02Dec67 | 12Oct68 | 09Aug69] 5(1) 76 — 6843

312. THE BEATLES 1962-1966 The Beatles
[14Apr73 | 19May73 | 14Apr84] 3(2) 164 — 6830

313. STAND! Sly & The Family Stone
[26Apr69 | 07Jun69 | 03Apr71] 13(1) 102 — 6820

314. MOVING PICTURES Rush
[07Mar81 | 28Mar81 | 19Mar83] 3(3) 68 — 6817

315. POINT OF KNOW RETURN Kansas
[15Oct77 | 06May78 | 30Sep78] 4(2) 51 — 6810

316. REVOLVER The Beatles
[03Sep66 | 10Sep66 | 17Feb68] 1(6) 77 — 6808

317. BETWEEN THE LINES Janis Ian
[22Mar75 | 20Sep75 | 05Jun76] 1(1) 64 — 6807

318. HERE AT LAST...BEE GEES...LIVE Bee Gees
[04Jun77 | 30Jul77 | 16Jun79] 8(1) 90 — 6803

319. RICHARD MARX Richard Marx
[20Jun87 | 03Sep88 | 04Feb89] 8(2) 86 — 6799

320. ARETHA: LADY SOUL Aretha Franklin
[24Feb68 | 16Mar68 | 15Feb69] 2(2) 52 — 6779

321. WORKING CLASS DOG Rick Springfield
[14Mar81 | 05Sep81 | 31Jul82] 7(2) 73 — 6754

322. RUBBER SOUL The Beatles
[25Dec65 | 08Jan66 | 07Mar81] 1(6) 59 — 6749

323. AMERICA America
[19Feb72 | 25Mar72 | 18Nov72] 1(5) 40 — 6744

324. ON THE RADIO: GREATEST HITS: VOLUMES I & II Donna Summer
[03Nov79 | 05Jan80 | 26Jul80] 1(1) 39 — 6739

325. BARRY MANILOW LIVE Barry Manilow
[28May77 | 16Jul77 | 02Sep78] 1(1) 67 — 6736

326. CHICAGO X Chicago
[03Jul76 | 07Aug76 | 07May77] 3(1) 44 — 6723

327. SUMMER BREEZE Seals & Crofts
[02Sep72 | 23Dec72 | 28Sep74] 7(3) 109 — 6716

328. SUDDENLY Billy Ocean
[25Aug84 | 24Nov84 | 12Apr86] 9(2) 86 — 6704

329. BOOK OF DREAMS The Steve Miller Band
[21May77 | 25Jun77 | 02Sep78] 2(2) 68 — 6696

330. MIRAGE Fleetwood Mac
[17Jul82 | 07Aug82 | 21May83] 1(5) 45 — 6695

331. SOUNDS LIKE...
Herb Alpert & The Tijuana Brass
[03Jun67 | 17Jun67 | 01Jun68] 1(1) 53 — 6677

332. OUT OF THE BLUE Debbie Gibson
[05Sep87 | 27Feb88 | 13May89] 7(2) 89 — 6673

333. BLONDES HAVE MORE FUN Rod Stewart
[23Dec78 | 10Feb79 | 01Sep79] 1(3) 37 — 6671

334. GOLDFINGER Soundtrack
[12Dec64 | 20Mar65 | 09Apr66] 1(3) 70 — 6654

335. THE SUPREMES A' GO-GO The Supremes
[24Sep66 | 22Oct66 | 11Nov67] 1(2) 60 — 6652

336. BEVERLY HILLS COP Soundtrack
[12Jan85 | 22Jun85 | 15Mar86] 1(2) 62 — 6652

337. 5150 Van Halen
[12Apr86 | 26Apr86 | 27Jun87] 1(3) 64 — 6636

338. PRECIOUS TIME Pat Benatar
[25Jul81 | 15Aug81 | 31Jul82] 1(1) 54 — 6605

339. THE RIVER Bruce Springsteen
[01Nov80 | 08Nov80 | 15Feb86] 1(4) 107 — 6583

340. CHICAGO 17 Chicago
[02Jun84 | 26Jan85 | 12Oct85] 4(1) 72 — 6572

341. DIFFERENT LIGHT The Bangles
[01Feb86 | 31Jan87 | 22Aug87] 2(2) 82 — 6569

342. SUPERFLY (SOUNDTRACK) Curtis Mayfield
[26Aug72 | 21Oct72 | 07Jul73] 1(4) 46 — 6533

343. RUNNING ON EMPTY Jackson Browne
[07Jan78 | 04Mar78 | 31Mar79] 3(2) 65 — 6523

344. DIAMOND GIRL Seals & Crofts
[21Apr73 | 18Aug73 | 05Oct74] 4(1) 77 — 6512

Rank. Title Act
[Enter | Peak | Exit] Peak(Wks) TotWks — Score

345. THE SECOND Steppenwolf
[05Oct68 | 04Jan69 | 01Nov69] 3(1) 52 — 6505

346. UP TO DATE The Partridge Family
[03Apr71 | 24Apr71 | 01Apr72] 3(3) 53 — 6505

347. LOVE WILL KEEP US TOGETHER
Captain & Tennille
[14Jun75 | 02Aug75 | 04Jun77] 2(1) 104 — 6501

348. THE SINGING NUN
The Singing Nun (Soeur Sourire)
[09Nov63 | 07Dec63 | 01Aug64] 1(10) 39 — 6488

349. DANCING ON THE CEILING
Lionel Richie
[30Aug86 | 27Sep86 | 03Oct87] 1(2) 58 — 6483

350. CHEAP TRICK AT BUDOKAN Cheap Trick
[24Feb79 | 14Jul79 | 23Feb80] 4(4) 53 — 6482

351. POEMS, PRAYERS & PROMISES
John Denver
[17Apr71 | 14Aug71 | 19Oct74] 15(5) 80 — 6479

352. HISTORY/AMERICA'S GREATEST HITS
America
[22Nov75 | 20Dec75 | 29Jan77] 3(6) 63 — 6466

353. VANILLA FUDGE Vanilla Fudge
[16Sep67 | 18Nov67 | 22Mar69] 6(4) 80 — 6459

354. ALWAYS ON MY MIND Willie Nelson
[20Mar82 | 10Jul82 | 04Feb84] 2(4) 99 — 6455

355. MACHINE HEAD Deep Purple
[15Apr72 | 11Aug73 | 31Aug74] 7(2) 118 — 6452

356. STORM FRONT Billy Joel
[04Nov89 | 16Dec89 | 25May91] 1(1) 69 — 6443

357. THE THIRD ALBUM Barbra Streisand
[29Feb64 | 21Mar64 | 11Sep65] 5(8) 74 — 6437

358. LOVE STORY Soundtrack
[02Jan71 | 06Mar71 | 25Sep71] 2(6) 39 — 6436

359. PHYSICAL GRAFFITI Led Zeppelin
[15Mar75 | 22Mar75 | 08Dec79] 1(6) 41 — 6436

360. G N' R LIES Guns N' Roses
[17Dec88 | 13May89 | 27Jan90] 2(1) 53 — 6434

361. HOLD OUT Jackson Browne
[19Jul80 | 13Sep80 | 04Apr81] 1(1) 38 — 6411

362. HELP YOURSELF Tom Jones
[01Feb69 | 12Apr69 | 04Apr70] 5(2) 54 — 6408

363. AMERICAN GRAFFITI Soundtrack
[01Sep73 | 09Feb74 | 19Oct74] 10(1) 60 — 6407

364. REVENGE Bill Cosby
[13May67 | 17Jun67 | 28Sep68] 2(1) 73 — 6405

365. DAYS OF FUTURE PASSED Moody Blues
With The London Festival Orchestra
[04May68 | 21Oct72 | 19Sep87] 3(5) 106 — 6396

366. VOLUME 1 Traveling Wilburys
[12Nov88 | 28Jan89 | 24Mar90] 3(6) 53 — 6396

367. MIDNIGHT MAGIC Commodores
[18Aug79 | 27Oct79 | 24May80] 3(2) 41 — 6387

368. PRIVATE EYES Daryl Hall & John Oates
[26Sep81 | 13Feb82 | 20Nov82] 5(3) 61 — 6383

369. WAS CAPTURED LIVE AT THE FORUM
Three Dog Night
[29Nov69 | 27Dec69 | 10Apr71] 6(7) 72 — 6338

370. GIVING YOU THE BEST THAT I GOT
Anita Baker
[05Nov88 | 24Dec88 | 19Aug89] 1(4) 42 — 6333

371. SURREALISTIC PILLOW Jefferson Airplane
[25Mar67 | 05Aug67 | 13Apr68] 3(1) 56 — 6325

372. CATCH BULL AT FOUR Cat Stevens
[14Oct72 | 18Nov72 | 08Sep73] 1(3) 48 — 6321

373. FUNNY GIRL (ORIGINAL CAST)
Barbra Streisand
[02May64 | 06Jun64 | 17Apr65] 2(3) 51 — 6318

374. LOS COCHINOS Cheech & Chong
[08Sep73 | 06Oct73 | 18Jan75] 2(1) 69 — 6317

375. THE MAMAS & THE PAPAS
The Mamas & The Papas
[01Oct66 | 22Oct66 | 09Mar68] 4(7) 76 — 6311

376. COCKTAIL Soundtrack
[13Aug88 | 07Jan89 | 07Oct89] 2(1) 61 — 6310

377. BEACH BOYS CONCERT The Beach Boys
[07Nov64 | 05Dec64 | 08Jan66] 1(4) 62 — 6309

378. MY NAME IS BARBRA (SOUNDTRACK)
Barbra Streisand
[22May65 | 19Jun65 | 03Sep66] 2(3) 68 — 6304

Rank. Title Act
[Enter | Peak | Exit] Peak(Wks) TotWks — Score

379. SEVENTH SOJOURN The Moody Blues
[18Nov72 | 09Dec72 | 15Sep73] 1(5) 44 — 6301

380. VOICES Daryl Hall & John Oates
[16Aug80 | 13Jun81 | 10Jul82] 17(1) 100 — 6297

381. ELECTRIC YOUTH Debbie Gibson
[11Feb89 | 11Mar89 | 27Jan90] 1(5) 51 — 6295

382. NATURAL HIGH Commodores
[27May78 | 08Jul78 | 06Jan79] 3(8) 33 — 6240

383. THE DUDE Quincy Jones
[04Apr81 | 24Apr82 | 09Oct82] 10(1) 80 — 6231

384. BUDDHA AND THE CHOCOLATE BOX
Cat Stevens
[13Apr74 | 11May74 | 14Dec74] 2(3) 36 — 6219

385. THE LONESOME JUBILEE
John Mellencamp
[19Sep87 | 03Oct87 | 17Sep88] 6(7) 53 — 6213

386. DUOTONES Kenny G
[06Sep86 | 18Jul87 | 13Aug88] 6(2) 102 — 6209

387. LADY SINGS THE BLUES (SOUNDTRACK)
Diana Ross
[25Nov72 | 07Apr73 | 01Dec73] 1(2) 54 — 6201

388. WHAT'S GOING ON Marvin Gaye
[12Jun71 | 31Jul71 | 09Jun84] 6(3) 53 — 6199

389. MIAMI VICE TV Soundtrack
[12Oct85 | 02Nov85 | 31May86] 1(11) 34 — 6180

390. BAD ANIMALS Heart
[13Jun87 | 01Aug87 | 21May88] 2(3) 50 — 6177

391. WAR CHILD Jethro Tull
[26Oct74 | 28Dec74 | 24May75] 2(3) 31 — 6168

392. THE CONCERT FOR BANGLA DESH
George Harrison and Friends
[08Jan72 | 22Jan72 | 14Oct72] 2(6) 41 — 6165

393. CHARIOTS OF FIRE (SOUNDTRACK)
Vangelis
[17Oct81 | 17Apr82 | 13Nov82] 1(4) 57 — 6161

394. THIRD STAGE Boston
[18Oct86 | 01Nov86 | 26Sep87] 1(4) 50 — 6153

395. THE GAMBLER Kenny Rogers
[16Dec78 | 07Jul79 | 21Feb81] 12(3) 112 — 6142

396. LET'S DANCE David Bowie
[30Apr83 | 25Jun83 | 26Jan85] 4(1) 68 — 6138

397. 2-HOT! Peaches & Herb
[25Nov78 | 05May79 | 06Oct79] 2(6) 46 — 6131

398. THEY ONLY COME OUT AT NIGHT
The Edgar Winter Group
[09Dec72 | 09Jun73 | 15Jun74] 3(1) 80 — 6108

399. SEPTEMBER OF MY YEARS Frank Sinatra
[21Aug65 | 26Feb66 | 10Dec66] 5(2) 69 — 6107

400. ALL 'N ALL Earth, Wind & Fire
[03Dec77 | 07Jan78 | 21Oct78] 3(6) 47 — 6106

401. BORN FREE Andy Williams
[13May67 | 17Jun67 | 09Nov68] 5(2) 79 — 6101

402. THIRD ALBUM The Jackson 5
[26Sep70 | 24Oct70 | 04Sep71] 4(3) 50 — 6084

403. STAR WARS Soundtrack
[18Jun77 | 10Sep77 | 17Jun78] 2(3) 53 — 6071

404. CANDY-O The Cars
[30Jun79 | 25Aug79 | 02Jun84] 3(4) 62 — 6067

405. THE MAMAS & THE PAPAS DELIVER
The Mamas & The Papas
[18Mar67 | 08Apr67 | 30Mar68] 2(7) 55 — 6067

406. VAN HALEN Van Halen
[11Mar78 | 20May78 | 01Dec84] 19(2) 169 — 6065

407. EVERY GOOD BOY DESERVES FAVOUR
The Moody Blues
[21Aug71 | 04Sep71 | 10Jun72] 2(3) 43 — 6059

408. TCB (SOUNDTRACK) Diana Ross & The Supremes And The Temptations
[28Dec68 | 08Feb69 | 16Aug69] 1(1) 34 — 6057

409. HOTTER THAN JULY Stevie Wonder
[15Nov80 | 06Dec80 | 15Aug81] 3(7) 40 — 6054

410. RELEASE ME Engelbert Humperdinck
[17Jun67 | 02Sep67 | 04Jul70] 7(3) 118 — 6029

411. CRUISIN' Village People
[21Oct78 | 17Feb79 | 25Aug79] 3(4) 45 — 6026

412. DREAMBOAT ANNIE Heart
[10Apr76 | 30Oct76 | 21Jun80] 7(2) 100 — 6018

413. BEHIND CLOSED DOORS Charlie Rich
[19May73 | 09Feb74 | 17May75] 8(1) 105 — 6008

Rank. Title Act
[Enter | Peak | Exit] Peak(Wks) TotWks Score

414. BIGGER THAN BOTH OF US
Daryl Hall & John Oates
[28Aug76 | 06Nov76 | 24Sep77] 13(1) 57 5998

415. THE BEST OF HERMAN'S HERMITS
Herman's Hermits
[20Nov65 | 25Dec65 | 18Nov67] 5(3) 105 5995

416. ARC OF A DIVER Steve Winwood
[17Jan81 | 18Apr81 | 07Nov81] 3(6) 43 5990

417. TANGO IN THE NIGHT Fleetwood Mac
[02May87 | 23May87 | 28May88] 7(3) 57 5973

418. OUT OF OUR HEADS The Rolling Stones
[07Aug65 | 21Aug65 | 05Nov66] 1(3) 65 5973

419. VENUS AND MARS Wings
[14Jun75 | 19Jul75 | 05Mar77] 1(1) 77 5972

420. BEST OF CREAM Cream
[19Jul69 | 13Sep69 | 16May70] 3(1) 44 5962

421. DESIRE Bob Dylan
[24Jan76 | 07Feb76 | 18Sep76] 1(5) 35 5953

422. CLOSER TO HOME Grand Funk Railroad
[11Jul70 | 29Aug70 | 18Sep71] 6(4) 63 5948

423. THICK AS A BRICK Jethro Tull
[20May72 | 03Jun72 | 31Mar73] 1(2) 46 5915

424. THE ISAAC HAYES MOVEMENT Isaac Hayes
[18Apr70 | 13Jun70 | 18Sep71] 8(1) 75 5908

425. HEART LIKE A WHEEL Linda Ronstadt
[07Dec74 | 15Feb75 | 13Dec75] 1(1) 51 5903

426. PERMANENT VACATION Aerosmith
[19Sep87 | 21Nov87 | 31Dec88] 11(4) 67 5898

427. SERGIO MENDES & BRASIL '66
Sergio Mendes & Brasil '66
[10Sep66 | 10Dec66 | 01Feb69] 7(1) 126 5896

428. SEVEN AND THE RAGGED TIGER
Duran Duran
[10Dec83 | 11Feb84 | 23Feb85] 8(5) 64 5895

429. RATTLE AND HUM (SOUNDTRACK) U2
[29Oct88 | 12Nov88 | 15Jul89] 1(6) 38 5894

430. BORN TO RUN Bruce Springsteen
[13Sep75 | 11Oct75 | 17Jan87] 3(2) 110 5889

431. THIS ONE'S FOR YOU Barry Manilow
[21Aug76 | 16Apr77 | 08Oct77] 6(2) 60 5876

432. PROMISE Sade
[21Dec85 | 15Feb86 | 01Nov86] 1(2) 46 5873

433. THE HEAT IS ON The Isley Brothers
[14Jun75 | 13Sep75 | 13Mar76] 1(1) 40 5866

434. PARANOID Black Sabbath
[20Feb71 | 20Mar71 | 08Nov75] 12(3) 70 5864

435. GET READY Rare Earth
[06Dec69 | 27Jun70 | 29May71] 12(3) 77 5848

436. BIG HITS (HIGH TIDE AND GREEN GRASS)
The Rolling Stones
[16Apr66 | 14May66 | 02Mar68] 3(3) 99 5844

437. PART 3 KC And The Sunshine Band
[23Oct76 | 27Nov76 | 08Apr78] 13(1) 77 5842

438. SIMON AND GARFUNKEL'S GREATEST HITS
Simon & Garfunkel
[01Jul72 | 29Jul72 | 10Apr76] 5(4) 127 5831

439. DIRTY DEEDS DONE DIRT CHEAP AC/DC
[18Apr81 | 30May81 | 01May82] 3(6) 55 5829

440. SHAUN CASSIDY Shaun Cassidy
[25Jun77 | 08Oct77 | 14Oct78] 3(2) 57 5827

441. SUITABLE FOR FRAMING Three Dog Night
[12Jul69 | 23Aug69 | 05Dec70] 16(4) 74 5812

442. LOOK AROUND
Sergio Mendes & Brasil '66
[09Mar68 | 13Jul68 | 22Feb69] 5(2) 51 5796

443. THE INNOCENT AGE Dan Fogelberg
[12Sep81 | 10Oct81 | 13Nov82] 6(6) 62 5782

444. WAITING FOR THE SUN The Doors
[10Aug68 | 07Sep68 | 20Sep69] 1(4) 41 5773

445. WELCOME TO THE REAL WORLD Mr. Mister
[31Aug85 | 01Mar86 | 04Oct86] 1(1) 58 5753

446. ROCKS Aerosmith
[29May76 | 26Jun76 | 28May77] 3(3) 53 5740

447. EVERYBODY LOVES SOMEBODY
Dean Martin
[15Aug64 | 31Oct64 | 17Jul65] 2(4) 49 5739

448. A NIGHT AT THE OPERA Queen
[27Dec75 | 17Apr76 | 19Mar77] 4(3) 56 5738

449. PISCES, AQUARIUS, CAPRICORN, AND JONES LTD. The Monkees
[25Nov67 | 02Dec67 | 06Dec86] 1(5) 64 5738

450. ROLL WITH IT Steve Winwood
[09Jul88 | 20Aug88 | 13May89] 1(1) 45 5737

451. WHAT'S NEW
Linda Ronstadt & The Nelson Riddle Orchestra
[01Oct83 | 24Dec83 | 13Apr85] 3(5) 81 5736

452. DEAR HEART Andy Williams
[10Apr65 | 29May65 | 02Jul66] 4(3) 65 5727

453. PARALLEL LINES Blondie
[23Sep78 | 28Apr79 | 06Sep80] 6(3) 103 5717

454. IMAGINE John Lennon/Plastic Ono Band
[18Sep71 | 30Oct71 | 25Apr81] 1(1) 45 5713

455. LONG COLD WINTER Cinderella
[23Jul88 | 10Sep88 | 21Oct89] 10(5) 66 5711

456. HAVE YOU NEVER BEEN MELLOW
Olivia Newton-John
[22Feb75 | 15Mar75 | 20Sep75] 1(1) 31 5700

457. FRAGILE Yes
[22Jan72 | 26Feb72 | 21Apr84] 4(7) 46 5692

458. EAT A PEACH The Allman Brothers Band
[18Mar72 | 29Apr72 | 29Nov75] 4(2) 48 5683

459. LIVE AT LEEDS The Who
[30May70 | 15Aug70 | 27Mar71] 4(3) 44 5677

460. LOU RAWLS LIVE Lou Rawls
[07May66 | 23Jul66 | 30Sep67] 4(1) 74 5676

461. THE FINAL COUNTDOWN Europe
[01Nov86 | 28Mar87 | 23Apr88] 8(2) 78 5668

462. GALVESTON Glen Campbell
[12Apr69 | 03May69 | 31Jan70] 2(1) 42 5663

463. THE FOUR TOPS GREATEST HITS Four Tops
[30Sep67 | 25Nov67 | 15Feb69] 4(1) 73 5647

464. AFTER THE GOLD RUSH Neil Young
[19Sep70 | 17Oct70 | 18Dec71] 8(5) 66 5639

465. ELECTRIC LADYLAND
The Jimi Hendrix Experience
[19Oct68 | 16Nov68 | 28Jun69] 1(2) 37 5633

466. JOE COCKER! Joe Cocker
[22Nov69 | 07Feb70 | 21Nov70] 11(3) 53 5627

467. I LOVE ROCK 'N ROLL
Joan Jett & the Blackhearts
[19Dec81 | 10Apr82 | 29Jan83] 2(3) 59 5608

468. NIGHT MOVES
Bob Seger & The Silver Bullet Band
[13Nov76 | 12Mar77 | 30Aug80] 8(1) 88 5606

469. DESOLATION ANGELS Bad Company
[31Mar79 | 19May79 | 08Dec79] 3(2) 37 5595

470. SPITFIRE Jefferson Starship
[10Jul76 | 14Aug76 | 26Mar77] 3(6) 38 5588

471. RHYMES & REASONS Carole King
[04Nov72 | 16Dec72 | 02Jun73] 2(5) 31 5586

472. MORE DIRTY DANCING Soundtrack
[19Mar88 | 23Apr88 | 11Mar89] 3(5) 52 5578

473. BLOOD, SWEAT & TEARS 3
Blood, Sweat & Tears
[18Jul70 | 08Aug70 | 24Apr71] 1(2) 41 5566

474. CLOUD NINE The Temptations
[15Mar69 | 03May69 | 13Dec69] 4(1) 40 5561

475. AROUND THE WORLD IN A DAY
Prince And The Revolution
[11May85 | 01Jun85 | 08Feb86] 1(3) 40 5561

476. AFTERBURNER ZZ Top
[16Nov85 | 07Dec85 | 28Mar87] 4(3) 70 5557

477. THREE DOG NIGHT Three Dog Night
[25Jan69 | 21Jun69 | 11Apr70] 11(1) 62 5552

478. IN THE HEAT OF THE NIGHT Pat Benatar
[20Oct79 | 15Mar80 | 27Mar82] 12(2) 122 5547

479. URBAN COWBOY Soundtrack
[17May80 | 06Sep80 | 04Apr81] 3(2) 47 5546

480. OUT OF ORDER Rod Stewart
[04Jun88 | 01Apr89 | 14Oct89] 20(2) 72 5537

481. EXILE ON MAIN ST. The Rolling Stones
[10Jun72 | 17Jun72 | 31Mar73] 1(4) 43 5537

482. PHYSICAL Olivia Newton-John
[31Oct81 | 12Dec81 | 27Nov82] 6(7) 57 5534

483. THE BIG CHILL Soundtrack
[22Oct83 | 21Jan84 | 15Nov86] 17(2) 161 5525

484. LIFE AND TIMES Jim Croce
[17Feb73 | 08Dec73 | 21Sep74] 7(2) 84 5513

485. JUICE Juice Newton
[07Mar81 | 20Feb82 | 27Nov82] 22(3) 86 5505

486. KISSING TO BE CLEVER Culture Club
[08Jan83 | 19Mar83 | 08Sep84] 14(10) 88 5493

487. COMBAT ROCK The Clash
[12Jun82 | 22Jan83 | 06Aug83] 7(5) 61 5485

488. EVEN NOW Barry Manilow
[25Feb78 | 08Apr78 | 31Mar79] 3(3) 58 5474

489. THE BAND The Band
[18Oct69 | 07Feb70 | 19Sep70] 9(1) 49 5473

490. BY THE TIME I GET TO PHOENIX
Glen Campbell
[30Dec67 | 07Sep68 | 26Jul69] 15(4) 80 5471

491. NEVER A DULL MOMENT Rod Stewart
[12Aug72 | 09Sep72 | 14Apr73] 2(3) 36 5459

492. ELTON JOHN Elton John
[03Oct70 | 06Feb71 | 18Sep71] 4(1) 51 5452

493. CENTERFIELD John Fogerty
[26Jan85 | 23Mar85 | 11Jan86] 1(1) 51 5442

494. SOMETHING NEW The Beatles
[08Aug64 | 22Aug64 | 15May65] 2(9) 41 5426

495. THE BROADWAY ALBUM Barbra Streisand
[23Nov85 | 25Jan86 | 11Jul87] 1(3) 50 5422

496. PHOENIX Dan Fogelberg
[08Dec79 | 08Mar80 | 30Aug80] 3(2) 39 5420

497. DON'T LOOK BACK Boston
[02Sep78 | 16Sep78 | 21Mar87] 1(2) 45 5419

498. DIRE STRAITS Dire Straits
[06Jan79 | 14Apr79 | 13Oct79] 2(1) 41 5417

499. SOUNDS OF SILENCE Simon & Garfunkel
[19Feb66 | 01Jun68 | 26Sep70] 21(2) 141 5415

500. I AM Earth, Wind & Fire
[16Jun79 | 14Jul79 | 01Mar80] 3(3) 38 5406

501. LIVE ALBUM Grand Funk Railroad
[05Dec70 | 26Dec70 | 05Feb72] 5(2) 62 5403

502. EMERGENCY Kool & The Gang
[15Dec84 | 12Oct85 | 10May86] 13(1) 74 5376

503. KENNY Kenny Rogers
[29Sep79 | 02Feb80 | 06Dec80] 5(2) 53 5370

504. WINELIGHT Grover Washington Jr.
[15Nov80 | 11Apr81 | 07Nov81] 5(7) 52 5367

505. CHILDREN OF THE WORLD Bee Gees
[02Oct76 | 13Nov76 | 13May78] 8(3) 63 5355

506. TUNNEL OF LOVE Bruce Springsteen
[24Oct87 | 07Nov87 | 27Aug88] 1(1) 45 5349

507. ALL DIRECTIONS The Temptations
[19Aug72 | 02Dec72 | 16Jun73] 2(2) 44 5346

508. MY SON, THE NUT Allan Sherman
[17Aug63 | 31Aug63 | 21Mar64] 1(8) 32 5346

509. HOOKED ON CLASSICS
Royal Philharmonic Orchestra
Conducted By Louis Clark
[14Nov81 | 16Jan82 | 26Feb83] 4(6) 68 5342

510. THE PINK PANTHER (SOUNDTRACK) Henry Mancini And His Orchestra
[11Apr64 | 15Aug64 | 11Dec65] 8(2) 88 5336

511. ON THE THRESHOLD OF A DREAM The Moody Blues
[31May69 | 26Jul69 | 01Jan72] 20(1) 136 5328

512. UH-HUH John Mellencamp
[05Nov83 | 28Jan84 | 24May86] 9(1) 66 5328

513. SUNDOWN Gordon Lightfoot
[02Feb74 | 22Jun74 | 16Nov74] 1(2) 42 5326

514. MARIA MULDAUR Maria Muldaur
[22Sep73 | 18May74 | 12Oct74] 3(3) 56 5319

515. JANE FONDA'S WORKOUT RECORD
Jane Fonda
[29May82 | 26Mar83 | 08Sep84] 15(4) 120 5318

516. ON THE BORDER Eagles
[20Apr74 | 01Jun74 | 15May76] 17(1) 87 5317

517. TOMMY Soundtrack
[29Mar75 | 31May75 | 22Nov75] 2(1) 35 5315

518. GREATEST HITS Linda Ronstadt
[18Dec76 | 29Jan77 | 24Jun78] 6(1) 80 5314

519. FIRE Ohio Players
[23Nov74 | 08Feb75 | 07Jun75] 1(1) 29 5305

Rank. Title Act
[Enter | Peak | Exit] Peak(Wks) TotWks — Score

520. ABACAB Genesis
[17Oct81 | 14Nov81 | 16Aug86] 7(1) 64 — 5305

521. REBEL YELL Billy Idol
[03Dec83 | 14Jul84 | 22Jun85] 6(3) 82 — 5290

522. LIKE A ROCK
Bob Seger & The Silver Bullet Band
[19Apr86 | 24May86 | 20Jun87] 3(4) 62 — 5287

523. INTRODUCING...THE BEATLES The Beatles
[08Feb64 | 29Feb64 | 09Jan65] 2(9) 49 — 5276

524. ANYTIME...ANYWHERE Rita Coolidge
[02Apr77 | 15Oct77 | 08Apr78] 6(4) 54 — 5275

525. ALIVE! KISS
[11Oct75 | 13Dec75 | 12Nov77] 9(4) 110 — 5270

526. GOATS HEAD SOUP
The Rolling Stones
[29Sep73 | 13Oct73 | 08Jun74] 1(4) 37 — 5266

527. BAND OF GYPSYS Jimi Hendrix
[02May70 | 16May70 | 26Jun71] 5(4) 61 — 5259

528. WINGS OVER AMERICA
Paul McCartney And Wings
[25Dec76 | 22Jan77 | 02Sep78] 1(1) 86 — 5248

529. BAT OUT OF HELL Meat Loaf
[29Oct77 | 16Sep78 | 27Oct79] 14(1) 82 — 5240

530. CUTS BOTH WAYS Gloria Estefan
[29Jul89 | 09Sep89 | 17Nov90] 8(2) 69 — 5235

531. NILSSON SCHMILSSON Nilsson
[04Dec71 | 01Apr72 | 14Oct72] 3(3) 46 — 5228

532. BARBRA STREISAND'S GREATEST HITS, VOLUME 2 Barbra Streisand
[02Dec78 | 06Jan79 | 13Oct79] 1(3) 46 — 5226

533. RICKIE LEE JONES Rickie Lee Jones
[07Apr79 | 30Jun79 | 08Dec79] 3(2) 36 — 5217

534. NEWS OF THE WORLD Queen
[26Nov77 | 18Feb78 | 05Aug78] 3(2) 37 — 5213

535. INDTRODUCING THE HARDLINE ACCORDING TO TERENCE TRENT D'ARBY
Terence Trent D'Arby
[24Oct87 | 07May88 | 10Dec88] 4(2) 60 — 5202

536. CHICAGO AT CARNEGIE HALL Chicago
[13Nov71 | 15Jan72 | 24May75] 3(1) 46 — 5202

537. A MOMENTARY LAPSE OF REASON
Pink Floyd
[26Sep87 | 24Oct87 | 15Oct88] 3(1) 56 — 5195

538. AN EVENING WITH JOHN DENVER
John Denver
[08Mar75 | 12Apr75 | 14Feb76] 2(2) 50 — 5194

539. THE BEATLES' SECOND ALBUM
The Beatles
[25Apr64 | 02May64 | 08May65] 1(5) 55 — 5191

540. JT James Taylor
[09Jul77 | 27Aug77 | 01Apr78] 4(5) 39 — 5169

541. RIO Duran Duran
[05Jun82 | 12Mar83 | 02Feb85] 6(7) 129 — 5168

542. WHENEVER YOU NEED SOMEBODY
Rick Astley
[23Jan88 | 12Mar88 | 11Mar89] 10(2) 60 — 5157

543. WISH YOU WERE HERE Pink Floyd
[27Sep75 | 04Oct75 | 19Jun76] 1(2) 39 — 5152

544. THE KINGSMEN IN PERSON The Kingsmen
[18Jan64 | 06Jun64 | 17Sep66] 20(1) 131 — 5152

545. JUST ONE NIGHT Eric Clapton
[03May80 | 21Jun80 | 29Nov80] 2(6) 31 — 5135

546. THE JOKER The Steve Miller Band
[20Oct73 | 22Dec73 | 06Jul74] 2(1) 38 — 5132

547. BREAKIN' AWAY Al Jarreau
[22Aug81 | 10Oct81 | 06Aug83] 9(3) 103 — 5128

548. TRYIN' TO GET THE FEELIN' Barry Manilow
[08Nov75 | 07Feb76 | 05Nov77] 5(2) 87 — 5128

549. LOOK AT US Sonny & Cher
[21Aug65 | 11Sep65 | 18Jun66] 2(8) 44 — 5119

550. BABY I'M-A WANT YOU Bread
[05Feb72 | 25Mar72 | 24Feb73] 3(1) 56 — 5112

551. CITY TO CITY Gerry Rafferty
[06May78 | 08Jul78 | 07Apr79] 1(1) 49 — 5110

552. AWB Average White Band
[21Sep74 | 22Feb75 | 12Jul75] 1(1) 43 — 5109

553. MY NAME IS BARBRA, TWO...
Barbra Streisand
[06Nov65 | 27Nov65 | 01Oct66] 2(3) 48 — 5109

554. EARTH Jefferson Starship
[18Mar78 | 06May78 | 04Nov78] 5(7) 34 — 5106

555. PUZZLE PEOPLE The Temptations
[11Oct69 | 29Nov69 | 18Jul70] 5(2) 41 — 5097

556. LET IT BLEED The Rolling Stones
[06Dec69 | 27Dec69 | 25Oct80] 3(2) 44 — 5094

557. ROCKY MOUNTAIN HIGH John Denver
[16Sep72 | 10Mar73 | 15Sep73] 4(3) 53 — 5091

558. BAD COMPANY Bad Company
[27Jul74 | 28Sep74 | 08Sep79] 1(1) 64 — 5083

559. BALL Iron Butterfly
[15Feb69 | 05Apr69 | 13Dec69] 3(1) 44 — 5063

560. LOC-ED AFTER DARK Tone-Loc
[18Feb89 | 15Apr89 | 24Feb90] 1(1) 42 — 5062

561. IF YOU LOVE ME LET ME KNOW
Olivia Newton-John
[08Jun74 | 12Oct74 | 02Aug75] 1(1) 61 — 5055

562. WHO'S NEXT The Who
[14Aug71 | 11Sep71 | 20May72] 4(2) 41 — 5051

563. CHICAGO VIII Chicago
[12Apr75 | 03May75 | 25Oct75] 1(2) 29 — 5049

564. OUT OF THE BLUE Electric Light Orchestra
[26Nov77 | 07Jan78 | 30Dec78] 4(4) 58 — 5045

565. THE ONE THAT YOU LOVE Air Supply
[13Jun81 | 01Aug81 | 31Jul82] 10(4) 60 — 5042

566. I GOT A NAME Jim Croce
[15Dec73 | 26Jan74 | 14Dec74] 2(2) 53 — 5040

567. HONEY Ohio Players
[23Aug75 | 27Sep75 | 24Apr76] 2(1) 36 — 5039

568. THE DIVINE MISS M Bette Midler
[09Dec72 | 24Mar73 | 18May74] 9(2) 76 — 5034

569. BILL COSBY IS A VERY FUNNY FELLOW, RIGHT! Bill Cosby
[27Jun64 | 06Aug66 | 03Aug68] 21(1) 128 — 5024

570. HOT AUGUST NIGHT Neil Diamond
[09Dec72 | 17Feb73 | 23Apr77] 5(3) 78 — 5024

571. I'M STILL IN LOVE WITH YOU Al Green
[21Oct72 | 30Dec72 | 26Jan74] 4(2) 67 — 5005

572. FULLFILLINGNESS FIRST FINALE
Stevie Wonder
[10Aug74 | 14Sep74 | 29Jan77] 1(2) 65 — 5002

573. THERE'S A RIOT GOIN' ON
Sly & The Family Stone
[13Nov71 | 18Dec71 | 10Jun72] 1(2) 31 — 5000

574. HEY JUDE The Beatles
[21Mar70 | 28Mar70 | 31Oct70] 2(4) 33 — 4999

575. MAD DOGS & ENGLISHMEN (SOUNDTRACK)
Joe Cocker
[05Sep70 | 10Oct70 | 04Sep71] 2(1) 53 — 4992

576. CSN Crosby, Stills & Nash
[09Jul77 | 13Aug77 | 18Feb78] 2(4) 33 — 4989

577. ...AND JUSTICE FOR ALL Metallica
[24Sep88 | 08Oct88 | 21Apr90] 6(2) 83 — 4977

578. TUMBLEWEED CONNECTION Elton John
[23Jan71 | 13Feb71 | 02Oct71] 5(4) 37 — 4966

579. LET'S STAY TOGETHER Al Green
[12Feb72 | 01Apr72 | 03Mar73] 8(2) 56 — 4963

580. MAN OF LA MANCHA Original Cast
[22Jan66 | 18Mar67 | 29Mar69] 31(3) 167 — 4961

581. TRES HOMBRES ZZ Top
[04Aug73 | 10Aug74 | 20Sep75] 8(1) 81 — 4957

582. RIPTIDE Robert Palmer
[23Nov85 | 17May86 | 08Aug87] 8(1) 90 — 4955

583. WILDFLOWERS Judy Collins
[06Jan68 | 28Dec68 | 07Jun69] 5(1) 75 — 4954

584. SPIRIT Earth, Wind & Fire
[16Oct76 | 30Oct76 | 07May77] 2(2) 30 — 4953

585. DARKNESS ON THE EDGE OF TOWN
Bruce Springsteen
[17Jun78 | 29Jul78 | 26Oct85] 5(3) 97 — 4951

586. VIVID Living Colour
[03Sep88 | 06May89 | 10Feb90] 6(2) 76 — 4950

587. A WILD AND CRAZY GUY Steve Martin
[04Nov78 | 09Dec78 | 28Apr79] 2(6) 26 — 4946

588. BUTCH CASSIDY AND THE SUNDANCE KID
Soundtrack
[29Nov69 | 07Feb70 | 24Apr71] 16(2) 74 — 4935

589. C'EST CHIC Chic
[02Dec78 | 23Dec78 | 27Oct79] 4(4) 48 — 4931

590. YEAR OF THE CAT Al Stewart
[09Oct76 | 19Feb77 | 03Sep77] 5(3) 48 — 4916

591. TUSK Fleetwood Mac
[03Nov79 | 17Nov79 | 12Jul80] 4(3) 37 — 4913

592. PHOEBE SNOW Phoebe Snow
[07Sep74 | 15Mar75 | 15Jan77] 4(1) 58 — 4909

593. DIRTY ROTTEN FILTHY STINKING RICH
Warrant
[04Mar89 | 16Sep89 | 26May90] 10(3) 65 — 4909

594. THE BEST OF THE LOVIN' SPOONFUL
The Lovin' Spoonful
[18Mar67 | 06May67 | 09Mar68] 3(2) 52 — 4907

595. ALL SUMMER LONG The Beach Boys
[01Aug64 | 22Aug64 | 03Jul65] 4(5) 49 — 4899

596. NINE TONIGHT
Bob Seger & The Silver Bullet Band
[26Sep81 | 17Oct81 | 27Sep86] 3(4) 70 — 4899

597. BILLION DOLLAR BABIES Alice Cooper
[17Mar73 | 21Apr73 | 23Feb74] 1(1) 50 — 4898

598. BEATLES VI The Beatles
[26Jun65 | 10Jul65 | 02Apr66] 1(6) 41 — 4898

599. TUBULAR BELLS Mike Oldfield
[10Nov73 | 30Mar74 | 14Sep74] 3(2) 45 — 4893

600. JODY WATLEY Jody Watley
[21Mar87 | 23May87 | 13Aug88] 10(1) 74 — 4882

601. THE IN CROWD Ramsey Lewis Trio
[14Aug65 | 06Nov65 | 20Aug66] 2(1) 47 — 4876

602. PENDULUM
Creedence Clearwater Revival
[26Dec70 | 30Jan71 | 09Oct71] 5(1) 42 — 4865

603. MAD LOVE Linda Ronstadt
[15Mar80 | 22Mar80 | 15Nov80] 3(4) 36 — 4864

604. STEPPENWOLF Steppenwolf
[09Mar68 | 07Sep68 | 21Feb70] 6(3) 87 — 4857

605. BIG BAM BOOM Daryl Hall & John Oates
[27Oct84 | 01Dec84 | 12Oct85] 5(2) 51 — 4851

606. IMAGINATION Gladys Knight & The Pips
[27Oct73 | 29Dec73 | 10May75] 9(1) 61 — 4850

607. LONDON TOWN Wings
[15Apr78 | 06May78 | 21Oct78] 2(6) 28 — 4850

608. EXPOSURE Exposé
[21Feb87 | 20Feb88 | 16Jul88] 16(2) 74 — 4850

609. THROUGH THE PAST, DARKLY (BIG HITS VOL. 2) The Rolling Stones
[13Sep69 | 11Oct69 | 18Apr70] 2(2) 32 — 4827

610. ABC The Jackson 5
[06Jun70 | 11Jul70 | 15May71] 4(2) 50 — 4817

611. TOM JONES LIVE! Tom Jones
[15Mar69 | 10May69 | 18Apr70] 13(4) 58 — 4814

612. JOHN WESLEY HARDING Bob Dylan
[27Jan68 | 17Feb68 | 18Jan69] 2(4) 52 — 4807

613. STEEL WHEELS The Rolling Stones
[16Sep89 | 07Oct89 | 19May90] 3(4) 36 — 4806

614. LIVING IN THE U.S.A. Linda Ronstadt
[07Oct78 | 04Nov78 | 12May79] 1(1) 32 — 4804

615. LEFTOVERTURE Kansas
[06Nov76 | 02Apr77 | 20Aug77] 5(4) 42 — 4802

616. NATURALLY Three Dog Night
[12Dec70 | 29May71 | 26Feb72] 14(2) 64 — 4797

617. THERE GOES RHYMIN' SIMON Paul Simon
[26May73 | 07Jul73 | 20Apr74] 2(2) 48 — 4781

618. EMOTIONS IN MOTION Billy Squier
[07Aug82 | 18Sep82 | 20Oct84] 5(8) 50 — 4779

619. STRANGE DAYS The Doors
[04Nov67 | 18Nov67 | 11Jan69] 3(4) 63 — 4773

620. CRY LIKE A RAINSTORM, HOWL LIKE THE WIND
Linda Ronstadt (Featuring Aaron Neville)
[21Oct89 | 17Mar90 | 24Nov90] 7(1) 58 — 4767

621. BRIEFCASE FULL OF BLUES Blues Brothers
[23Dec78 | 03Feb79 | 07Jul79] 1(1) 29 — 4763

622. MADE IN JAPAN Deep Purple
[21Apr73 | 11Aug73 | 13Apr74] 6(2) 52 — 4753

623. CARGO Men At Work
[07May83 | 21May83 | 07Apr84] 3(5) 49 — 4751

624. MIDNIGHT MADNESS Night Ranger
[19Nov83 | 16Jun84 | 09Mar85] 15(10) 69 — 4751

625. BLOOD ON THE TRACKS Bob Dylan
[08Feb75 | 01Mar75 | 19Jul75] 1(2) 24 — 4750

Rank. Title Act
[Enter|Peak|Exit] Peak(Wks) TotWks Score

626. INTRODUCING HERMAN'S HERMITS Herman's Hermits
[20Feb65|24Apr65|20Nov65] 2(4) 40 4748

627. LAYLA AND OTHER ASSORTED LOVE SONGS Derek & The Dominos
[21Nov70|19Dec70|26Feb77] 16(1) 77 4748

628. TENDER LOVER Babyface
[05Aug89|03Mar90|29Sep90] 14(1) 61 4740

629. BLACK AND BLUE The Rolling Stones
[08May76|15May76|16Oct76] 1(4) 24 4733

630. CHAPTER TWO Roberta Flack
[29Aug70|24Oct70|18Mar72] 33(1) 82 4728

631. MY CUP RUNNETH OVER Ed Ames
[04Mar67|22Apr67|14Sep68] 4(3) 81 4722

632. 461 OCEAN BOULEVARD Eric Clapton
[20Jul74|17Aug74|04Jan75] 1(4) 25 4705

633. CARNEY Leon Russell
[15Jul72|07Oct72|10Mar73] 2(4) 35 4705

634. GIRLS, GIRLS, GIRLS Mötley Crüe
[13Jun87|27Jun87|23Apr88] 2(1) 46 4702

635. NOW AND ZEN Robert Plant
[12Mar88|21May88|04Feb89] 6(1) 48 4702

636. MADMAN ACROSS THE WATER Elton John
[27Nov71|05Feb72|11Nov72] 8(2) 51 4698

637. SHOUT AT THE DEVIL Mötley Crüe
[15Oct83|31Mar84|15Aug87] 17(2) 111 4698

638. MOUNTAIN MUSIC Alabama
[13Mar82|08May82|12May84] 14(2) 114 4690

639. THE SINGLES 1969-1973 Carpenters
[01Dec73|05Jan74|23Apr83] 1(1) 49 4680

640. DIAMOND LIFE Sade
[23Feb85|01Jun85|06Sep86] 5(2) 81 4672

641. I'M IN YOU Peter Frampton
[25Jun77|16Jul77|28Jan78] 2(4) 32 4671

642. SOMETHING SPECIAL Kool & The Gang
[17Oct81|28Nov81|22Jan83] 12(2) 67 4669

643. A QUESTION OF BALANCE The Moody Blues
[12Sep70|10Oct70|05Feb72] 3(1) 74 4666

644. FAREWELL TO THE FIRST GOLDEN ERA The Mamas & The Papas
[11Nov67|09Dec67|01Feb69] 5(3) 65 4665

645. LOVE ZONE Billy Ocean
[17May86|28Jun86|11Apr87] 6(7) 48 4661

646. HE'S THE D.J., I'M THE RAPPER D.J. Jazzy Jeff & The Fresh Prince
[23Apr88|24Sep88|06May89] 4(1) 55 4651

647. AFTERMATH The Rolling Stones
[09Jul66|13Aug66|17Jun67] 2(2) 50 4649

648. HERMAN'S HERMITS ON TOUR Herman's Hermits
[19Jun65|10Jul65|12Mar66] 2(6) 39 4648

649. LET'S GET IT ON Marvin Gaye
[15Sep73|20Oct73|02Jun84] 2(1) 61 4642

650. LOVE AT FIRST STING Scorpions
[17Mar84|16Jun84|28Sep85] 6(2) 63 4637

651. MOODS Neil Diamond
[15Jul72|09Sep72|21Apr73] 5(3) 41 4630

652. SHOOTING RUBBERBANDS AT THE STARS Edie Brickell & New Bohemians
[24Sep88|18Feb89|30Sep89] 4(2) 54 4620

653. BATMAN (SOUNDTRACK) Prince
[08Jul89|22Jul89|24Feb90] 1(6) 34 4618

654. RAISED ON RADIO Journey
[10May86|31May86|15Aug87] 4(2) 67 4605

655. KC AND THE SUNSHINE BAND KC And The Sunshine Band
[02Aug75|20Dec75|19Jun76] 4(2) 47 4590

656. SURVIVAL Grand Funk Railroad
[01May71|29May71|29Jan72] 6(1) 40 4577

657. BRINGING IT ALL BACK HOME Bob Dylan
[01May65|09Oct65|19Feb66] 6(1) 43 4566

658. BEST OF THE DOOBIES The Doobie Brothers
[20Nov76|22Jan77|24Jan81] 5(1) 93 4564

659. RUFUS FEATURING CHAKA KHAN Rufus And Chaka Khan
[06Dec75|06Mar76|10Jul76] 7(1) 32 4562

Rank. Title Act
[Enter|Peak|Exit] Peak(Wks) TotWks Score

660. 2001: A SPACE ODYSSEY Soundtrack
[13Jul68|09Nov68|24Oct70] 24(1) 120 4561

661. KEEP ON MOVIN' Soul II Soul
[08Jul89|16Sep89|23Jun90] 14(4) 51 4558

662. IN SQUARE CIRCLE Stevie Wonder
[19Oct85|23Nov85|27Sep86] 5(2) 50 4553

663. RINGO Ringo Starr
[17Nov73|01Dec73|27Jul74] 2(2) 37 4551

664. ALICE'S RESTAURANT Arlo Guthrie
[18Nov67|15Nov69|25Apr70] 17(2) 99 4547

665. FRENCH KISS Bob Welch
[08Oct77|14Jan78|19Aug78] 12(2) 46 4546

666. BALLADS OF THE GREEN BERETS SSgt Barry Sadler
[26Feb66|12Mar66|01Oct66] 1(5) 32 4543

667. AMERICAN WOMAN The Guess Who
[14Feb70|16May70|27Feb71] 9(4) 55 4539

668. BIGGER AND DEFFER LL Cool J
[20Jun87|29Aug87|18Jun88] 3(1) 53 4537

669. IT AIN'T EASY Three Dog Night
[02May70|16May70|27Mar71] 8(2) 48 4535

670. THE UNFORGETTABLE FIRE U2
[20Oct84|24Nov84|19Sep87] 12(3) 132 4535

671. AUTOAMERICAN Blondie
[13Dec80|21Feb81|01Aug81] 7(5) 34 4533

672. FACE THE MUSIC Electric Light Orchestra
[25Oct75|21Feb76|18Sep76] 8(1) 48 4530

673. A MAN WITHOUT LOVE Engelbert Humperdinck
[24Aug68|09Nov68|04Jul70] 12(2) 78 4524

674. DIANA ROSS PRESENTS THE JACKSON 5 The Jackson 5
[17Jan70|25Apr70|22Aug70] 5(1) 32 4519

675. ELVIS' GOLDEN RECORDS VOLUME 3 Elvis Presley
[14Sep63|16Nov63|11Feb78] 3(2) 63 4515

676. DIONNE WARWICK'S GOLDEN HITS, PART ONE Dionne Warwick
[18Nov67|23Dec67|08Mar69] 10(2) 69 4514

677. PRIDE White Lion
[26Sep87|07May88|13May89] 11(1) 86 4513

678. WAR U2
[19Mar83|07May83|19Sep87] 12(1) 179 4509

679. THE DOORS GREATEST HITS The Doors
[01Nov80|06Dec80|03Aug91] 17(2) 99 4507

680. EVOLUTION Journey
[14Apr79|05May79|13Mar82] 20(2) 96 4507

681. LITTLE QUEEN Heart
[28May77|09Jul77|04Mar78] 9(2) 41 4503

682. NIGHT AND DAY Joe Jackson
[17Jul82|27Nov82|13Aug83] 4(6) 57 4503

683. HELLO, I MUST BE GOING! Phil Collins
[27Nov82|05Feb83|11Apr87] 8(5) 141 4492

684. CAMELOT Soundtrack
[11Nov67|03Feb68|05Jul69] 11(4) 87 4487

685. LOOK OUT FOR #1 The Brothers Johnson
[06Mar76|05Jun76|10Sep77] 9(2) 49 4485

686. VAN HALEN II Van Halen
[14Apr79|19May79|01Mar80] 6(3) 47 4482

687. THE BEACH BOYS TODAY! The Beach Boys
[27Mar65|01May65|05Mar66] 4(6) 50 4482

688. DIANA ROSS & THE SUPREMES JOIN THE TEMPTATIONS Diana Ross & The Supremes And The Temptations
[30Nov68|11Jan69|05Jul69] 2(1) 32 4480

689. BLIZZARD OF OZZ Ozzy Osbourne
[18Apr81|08Aug81|09Apr83] 21(1) 104 4478

690. THE GOOD, THE BAD AND THE UGLY Soundtrack
[10Feb68|11May68|01Feb69] 4(2) 52 4465

691. MAIN COURSE Bee Gees
[21Jun75|20Mar76|20Nov76] 14(1) 75 4461

692. REACH THE BEACH The Fixx
[28May83|15Oct83|20Oct84] 8(2) 54 4454

693. MARVIN GAYE LIVE AT THE LONDON PALLADIUM Marvin Gaye
[02Apr77|14May77|24Sep77] 3(3) 26 4450

694. 90125 Yes
[03Dec83|21Jan84|01Dec84] 5(4) 53 4449

Rank. Title Act
[Enter|Peak|Exit] Peak(Wks) TotWks Score

695. A WARM SHADE OF IVORY Henry Mancini And His Orchestra
[03May69|02Aug69|14Feb70] 5(1) 42 4446

696. HOLIDAY America
[13Jul74|23Nov74|12Jul75] 3(1) 53 4445

697. STONE COLD RHYMIN' Young M.C.
[23Sep89|09Dec89|18Aug90] 9(1) 48 4442

698. GIVE ME THE NIGHT George Benson
[09Aug80|04Oct80|25Apr81] 3(2) 38 4441

699. KNEE DEEP IN THE HOOPLA Starship
[05Oct85|01Mar86|13Sep86] 7(3) 50 4436

700. COTTON CANDY Al Hirt
[23May64|27Jun64|22May65] 6(2) 53 4430

701. HONEY Bobby Goldsboro
[20Apr68|15Jun68|15Mar69] 5(3) 48 4427

702. WEEKEND IN L.A. George Benson
[11Feb78|15Apr78|28Oct78] 5(3) 38 4426

703. ROBERTA FLACK & DONNY HATHAWAY Roberta Flack & Donny Hathaway
[13May72|15Jul72|03Feb73] 3(2) 39 4421

704. MAKE IT LAST FOREVER Keith Sweat
[09Jan88|30Apr88|15Apr89] 15(1) 67 4409

705. BEE GEES GREATEST Bee Gees
[17Nov79|12Jan80|21Jun80] 1(1) 32 4406

706. THE WILD HEART Stevie Nicks
[02Jul83|23Jul83|23Jun84] 5(7) 52 4401

707. HOT ON THE TRACKS Commodores
[10Jul76|02Oct76|02Apr77] 12(3) 39 4400

708. HEART OF STONE Cher
[22Jul89|14Oct89|21Jul90] 10(2) 53 4398

709. ENGELBERT HUMPERDINCK Engelbert Humperdinck
[03Jan70|14Feb70|10Oct70] 5(2) 41 4394

710. THE BEST OF THE GUESS WHO The Guess Who
[17Apr71|22May71|19Feb72] 12(2) 45 4389

711. ALOHA FROM HAWAII VIA SATELLITE Elvis Presley
[24Feb73|05May73|20Apr74] 1(1) 52 4378

712. FOR THOSE ABOUT TO ROCK (WE SALUTE YOU) AC/DC
[12Dec81|26Dec81|03Jul82] 1(3) 30 4377

713. RED ROSE SPEEDWAY Paul McCartney And Wings
[12May73|02Jun73|08Dec73] 1(3) 31 4375

714. FANDANGO! ZZ Top
[17May75|13Sep75|27Nov76] 10(1) 47 4374

715. ARETHA LIVE AT FILLMORE WEST Aretha Franklin
[05Jun71|26Jun71|22Jan72] 7(2) 34 4367

716. GOODBYE Cream
[15Feb69|15Mar69|09Aug69] 2(2) 26 4361

717. THE TOM JONES FEVER ZONE Tom Jones
[15Jun68|17May69|07Mar70] 14(1) 82 4358

718. STEPHEN STILLS Stephen Stills
[28Nov70|02Jan71|21Aug71] 3(3) 39 4358

719. LOST IN LOVE Air Supply
[17May80|27Sep80|05Jun82] 22(3) 104 4355

720. NEIL DIAMOND/GOLD Neil Diamond
[22Aug70|19Sep70|11Sep71] 10(2) 56 4353

721. THE BRIDGE Billy Joel
[16Aug86|20Sep86|04Jul87] 7(4) 47 4352

722. THE CRY OF LOVE Jimi Hendrix
[06Mar71|27Mar71|27Nov71] 3(2) 39 4351

723. PHOTOGRAPHS & MEMORIES/ HIS GREATEST HITS Jim Croce
[05Oct74|16Nov74|28Feb76] 2(2) 46 4349

724. HASTEN DOWN THE WIND Linda Ronstadt
[28Aug76|25Sep76|30Apr77] 3(3) 36 4346

725. LOVERBOY Loverboy
[31Jan81|23May81|26Mar83] 13(2) 105 4338

726. THE 5TH DIMENSION/GREATEST HITS The 5th Dimension
[16May70|20Jun70|29May71] 5(2) 55 4338

727. THE ROLLING STONES, NOW! The Rolling Stones
[20Mar65|24Apr65|19Mar66] 5(2) 53 4325

Rank. Title Act
[Enter | Peak | Exit] Peak(Wks) TotWks Score

728. RAINDROPS KEEP FALLIN' ON MY HEAD B.J. Thomas
[03Jan70 | 21Mar70 | 10Oct70] 12(2) 41 4324

729. DISCOVERY Electric Light Orchestra
[23Jun79 | 21Jul79 | 16Feb80] 5(2) 35 4323

730. FAME Soundtrack
[07Jun80 | 06Sep80 | 31Jul82] 7(2) 82 4319

731. BODY HEAT Quincy Jones
[25May74 | 02Nov74 | 15Mar75] 6(1) 43 4311

732. OUT OF THE CELLAR Ratt
[24Mar84 | 04Aug84 | 13Apr85] 7(4) 56 4307

733. HEART BREAK New Edition
[09Jul88 | 29Oct88 | 17Jun89] 12(1) 50 4305

734. THE TURN OF A FRIENDLY CARD The Alan Parsons Project
[15Nov80 | 21Feb81 | 19Dec81] 13(2) 58 4304

735. TELL IT TO MY HEART Taylor Dayne
[30Jan88 | 29Oct88 | 20May89] 21(1) 69 4302

736. LIVING IN THE PAST Jethro Tull
[11Nov72 | 23Dec72 | 09Jun73] 3(3) 31 4299

737. PERFECT ANGEL Minnie Riperton
[17Aug74 | 29Mar75 | 05Jul75] 4(1) 47 4299

738. THE SMOKER YOU DRINK, THE PLAYER YOU GET Joe Walsh
[23Jun73 | 10Nov73 | 19Apr75] 6(2) 54 4294

739. BETWEEN THE BUTTONS The Rolling Stones
[18Feb67 | 11Mar67 | 06Jan68] 2(4) 47 4292

740. THE TIME HAS COME The Chambers Brothers
[17Feb68 | 26Oct68 | 22Mar69] 4(2) 58 4290

741. STILL BILL Bill Withers
[20May72 | 22Jul72 | 10Mar73] 4(3) 43 4281

742. SILHOUETTE Kenny G
[22Oct88 | 03Dec88 | 18Nov89] 8(1) 57 4280

743. LA BAMBA (SOUNDTRACK) Los Lobos
[25Jul87 | 12Sep87 | 21May88] 1(2) 44 4269

744. THE PARTRIDGE FAMILY SOUND MAGAZINE The Partridge Family
[28Aug71 | 25Sep71 | 22Apr72] 9(2) 35 4266

745. ROCK AND ROLL OVER KISS
[20Nov76 | 25Dec76 | 24Sep77] 11(2) 45 4256

746. HEAD GAMES Foreigner
[29Sep79 | 27Oct79 | 03Oct81] 5(3) 41 4255

747. INSIGHT OUT The Association
[22Jul67 | 02Sep67 | 02Nov68] 8(1) 68 4254

748. WELCOME TO MY NIGHTMARE Alice Cooper
[22Mar75 | 21Jun75 | 29Nov75] 5(1) 37 4253

749. REALIZATION Johnny Rivers
[29Jun68 | 31Aug68 | 05Apr69] 5(5) 41 4252

750. ROCK ME TONIGHT Freddie Jackson
[25May85 | 07Dec85 | 26Jul86] 10(1) 62 4250

751. SHININ' ON Grand Funk
[30Mar74 | 04May74 | 12Oct74] 5(2) 29 4246

752. WE'RE AN AMERICAN BAND Grand Funk
[18Aug73 | 22Sep73 | 13Apr74] 2(2) 35 4245

753. BEST OF BEE GEES Bee Gees
[26Jul69 | 06Sep69 | 27Jun70] 9(1) 49 4241

754. BUILDING THE PERFECT BEAST Don Henley
[15Dec84 | 16Mar85 | 22Feb86] 13(5) 63 4238

755. TO BE CONTINUED Isaac Hayes
[05Dec70 | 26Dec70 | 25Dec71] 11(2) 56 4236

756. HARD PROMISES Tom Petty And The Heartbreakers
[23May81 | 25Jul81 | 19Dec81] 5(2) 31 4235

757. PAUL SIMON Paul Simon
[12Feb72 | 01Apr72 | 14Oct72] 4(2) 36 4225

758. WINGER Winger
[17Sep88 | 11Feb89 | 02Dec89] 21(3) 64 4224

759. PRESENCE Led Zeppelin
[24Apr76 | 01May76 | 03Nov79] 1(2) 30 4218

760. BORN FREE Roger Williams
[10Dec66 | 14Jan67 | 30Mar68] 7(2) 69 4216

761. LOVE STORY Andy Williams
[20Feb71 | 17Apr71 | 02Oct71] 3(1) 33 4207

762. SPANISH FLY Lisa Lisa And Cult Jam
[09May87 | 20Jun87 | 02Apr88] 7(3) 48 4194

Rank. Title Act
[Enter | Peak | Exit] Peak(Wks) TotWks Score

763. FLOWERS The Rolling Stones
[22Jul67 | 12Aug67 | 16Mar68] 3(6) 35 4192

764. BOB DYLAN'S GREATEST HITS Bob Dylan
[06May67 | 17Jun67 | 12Apr75] 10(1) 94 4188

765. GROOVIN' The Young Rascals
[12Aug67 | 23Sep67 | 21Sep68] 5(1) 59 4184

766. L.A. WOMAN The Doors
[08May71 | 05Jun71 | 25Dec71] 9(1) 34 4180

767. NOW & THEN Carpenters
[02Jun73 | 21Jul73 | 09Mar74] 2(1) 41 4176

768. LIVING IN THE MATERIAL WORLD George Harrison
[16Jun73 | 23Jun73 | 08Dec73] 1(5) 26 4174

769. DIARY OF A MADMAN Ozzy Osbourne
[21Nov81 | 19Dec81 | 09Apr83] 16(4) 73 4170

770. CELEBRATE! Kool & The Gang
[18Oct80 | 07Mar81 | 15Aug81] 10(2) 44 4159

771. PLAY DEEP The Outfield
[02Nov85 | 14Jun86 | 14Mar87] 9(1) 66 4156

772. INGREDIENTS IN A RECIPE FOR SOUL Ray Charles
[31Aug63 | 12Oct63 | 02May64] 2(2) 36 4154

773. KILLER Alice Cooper
[04Dec71 | 22Jan72 | 09Dec72] 21(2) 54 4153

774. PRETENDERS The Pretenders
[26Jan80 | 07Jun80 | 18Jul81] 9(2) 78 4145

775. GRAND FUNK Grand Funk Railroad
[31Jan70 | 21Mar70 | 08May71] 11(2) 67 4140

776. TOTO Toto
[21Oct78 | 17Feb79 | 15Sep79] 9(2) 48 4137

777. BEAUTIFUL NOISE Neil Diamond
[03Jul76 | 14Aug76 | 12Feb77] 4(3) 33 4132

778. SERENADE Neil Diamond
[26Oct74 | 28Dec74 | 26Apr75] 3(2) 27 4131

779. ARETHA NOW Aretha Franklin
[13Jul68 | 17Aug68 | 08Mar69] 3(2) 35 4130

780. OLIVER! Soundtrack
[28Dec68 | 24May69 | 19Sep70] 20(2) 91 4128

781. GET NERVOUS Pat Benatar
[20Nov82 | 15Jan83 | 01Oct83] 4(5) 46 4128

782. SUMMERTIME DREAM Gordon Lightfoot
[26Jun76 | 04Dec76 | 02Apr77] 12(2) 41 4127

783. FOOL ON THE HILL Sergio Mendes & Brasil '66
[07Dec68 | 11Jan69 | 28Jun69] 3(1) 30 4126

784. GREATEST HITS VOL. I & II Billy Joel
[20Jul85 | 28Sep85 | 09Feb91] 6(2) 65 4119

785. HERB ALPERT'S NINTH Herb Alpert & The Tijuana Brass
[23Dec67 | 10Feb68 | 21Dec68] 4(2) 49 4113

786. SONG OF JOY Captain & Tennille
[20Mar76 | 01May76 | 14May77] 9(2) 61 4113

787. THE BIRDS, THE BEES & THE MONKEES The Monkees
[11May68 | 18May68 | 22Nov86] 3(4) 50 4110

788. CUTS LIKE A KNIFE Bryan Adams
[19Feb83 | 25Jun83 | 30Nov85] 8(3) 89 4109

789. MASTER OF REALITY Black Sabbath
[04Sep71 | 25Sep71 | 24Jun72] 8(2) 43 4105

790. "YESTERDAY" AND TODAY The Beatles
[09Jul66 | 30Jul66 | 04Feb67] 1(5) 31 4104

791. ROCKY Soundtrack
[05Mar77 | 14May77 | 22Oct77] 4(6) 34 4092

792. LADIES' NIGHT Kool & The Gang
[22Sep79 | 15Dec79 | 26Jul80] 13(4) 45 4088

793. XANADU (SOUNDTRACK) Olivia Newton-John/Electric Light Orchestra
[12Jul80 | 04Oct80 | 14Mar81] 4(3) 36 4087

794. SWITCHED-ON BACH Walter Carlos
[18Jan69 | 26Apr69 | 25Apr70] 10(1) 56 4085

795. DARE The Human League
[27Feb82 | 10Jul82 | 13Nov82] 3(3) 38 4081

796. THE BEST OF CHARLEY PRIDE Charley Pride
[01Nov69 | 27Dec69 | 23Jan71] 24(1) 65 4079

797. HEAVEN ON EARTH Belinda Carlisle
[24Oct87 | 27Feb88 | 08Oct88] 13(2) 51 4078

798. SKIN TIGHT Ohio Players
[27Apr74 | 06Jul74 | 22Mar75] 11(3) 48 4072

Rank. Title Act
[Enter | Peak | Exit] Peak(Wks) TotWks Score

799. WE ARE FAMILY Sister Sledge
[24Feb79 | 16Jun79 | 06Oct79] 3(2) 33 4071

800. MILES OF AISLES Joni Mitchell
[14Dec74 | 08Feb75 | 10May75] 2(1) 22 4070

801. SHADOW DANCING Andy Gibb
[17Jun78 | 08Jul78 | 07Apr79] 7(5) 43 4069

802. I AM WOMAN Helen Reddy
[09Dec72 | 17Feb73 | 09Feb74] 14(4) 62 4068

803. NERVOUS NIGHT Hooters
[25May85 | 22Mar86 | 18Oct86] 12(1) 74 4059

804. EYE OF THE TIGER Survivor
[26Jun82 | 14Aug82 | 02Apr83] 2(4) 41 4056

805. RAMBLIN' FEATURING GREEN, GREEN The New Christy Minstrels
[24Aug63 | 12Oct63 | 06Feb65] 15(1) 77 4052

806. ZEBOP! Santana
[18Apr81 | 13Jun81 | 21Nov81] 9(4) 32 4051

807. PRIMITIVE LOVE Miami Sound Machine
[23Nov85 | 04Oct86 | 25Apr87] 21(1) 75 4048

808. THE BEST OF EARTH, WIND & FIRE, VOL. I Earth, Wind & Fire
[02Dec78 | 27Jan79 | 19Jan80] 6(1) 60 4044

809. MY WORLD Eddy Arnold
[16Oct65 | 08Jan66 | 19Nov66] 7(3) 58 4040

810. NEW EDITION New Edition
[13Oct84 | 23Feb85 | 19Oct85] 6(2) 54 4038

811. A DAY IN THE LIFE Wes Montgomery
[07Oct67 | 30Dec67 | 11Jan69] 13(2) 67 4035

812. THE LONDON CHUCK BERRY SESSIONS Chuck Berry
[10Jun72 | 28Oct72 | 28Apr73] 8(3) 47 4034

813. AXIS: BOLD AS LOVE The Jimi Hendrix Experience
[10Feb68 | 09Mar68 | 08Feb69] 3(3) 53 4033

814. OLIVIA'S GREATEST HITS, VOL. 2 Olivia Newton-John
[09Oct82 | 13Nov82 | 26May84] 16(4) 86 4032

815. THAT'S LIFE Frank Sinatra
[31Dec66 | 25Feb67 | 24Feb68] 6(3) 61 4016

816. SMASH HITS The Jimi Hendrix Experience
[02Aug69 | 06Sep69 | 21Nov70] 6(2) 35 4007

817. THE PHANTOM OF THE OPERA Original London Cast Recording
[23May87 | 19Mar88 | 03Jul93] 33(1) 255 4006

818. HISTORY OF ERIC CLAPTON Eric Clapton
[15Apr72 | 01Jul72 | 27Jan73] 6(2) 42 4002

819. WINNER IN YOU Patti LaBelle
[24May86 | 19Jul86 | 13Dec86] 1(1) 30 4001

820. STEPPENWOLF 'LIVE' Steppenwolf
[18Apr70 | 16May70 | 17Apr71] 7(2) 53 4000

821. KILROY WAS HERE Styx
[19Mar83 | 30Apr83 | 05Nov83] 3(2) 34 3996

822. NO PARKING ON THE DANCE FLOOR Midnight Star
[30Jul83 | 14Jan84 | 25May85] 27(2) 96 3986

823. GREATEST HITS Waylon Jennings
[05May79 | 07Jul79 | 11Jul81] 28(1) 115 3978

824. MIDNIGHT COWBOY Soundtrack
[09Aug69 | 25Oct69 | 05Sep70] 19(2) 57 3978

825. YOUNG AMERICANS David Bowie
[22Mar75 | 12Apr75 | 08May76] 9(2) 51 3974

826. AS NASTY AS THEY WANNA BE The 2 Live Crew
[29Jul89 | 20Jan90 | 09Feb91] 29(1) 81 3974

827. SHAKE IT UP The Cars
[28Nov81 | 19Dec81 | 04Sep82] 9(4) 41 3973

828. THE POWER STATION The Power Station
[13Apr85 | 27Jul85 | 08Feb86] 6(2) 44 3972

829. EMPTY GLASS Pete Townshend
[17May80 | 12Jul80 | 06Dec80] 5(3) 30 3960

830. INFINITY Journey
[11Feb78 | 06May78 | 20Mar82] 21(1) 123 3957

831. CAN'T GET ENOUGH Barry White
[07Sep74 | 26Oct74 | 24May75] 1(1) 38 3956

832. LOU RAWLS SOULIN' Lou Rawls
[10Sep66 | 12Nov66 | 26Aug67] 7(1) 51 3955

833. SHARE YOUR LOVE Kenny Rogers
[11Jul81 | 15Aug81 | 19Jun82] 6(2) 50 3955

Rank. Title Act
[Enter|Peak|Exit] Peak(Wks) TotWks Score

834. QUARTERFLASH Quarterflash
[31Oct81|27Feb82|23Oct82] 8(3) 52 3953

835. WHO'S ZOOMIN' WHO? Aretha Franklin
[27Jul85|30Nov85|12Jul86] 13(1) 51 3951

836. TUG OF WAR Paul McCartney
[15May82|29May82|27Nov82] 1(3) 29 3951

837. ROCK OF THE WESTIES Elton John
[08Nov75|08Nov75|01May76] 1(3) 26 3949

838. AGENT PROVOCATEUR Foreigner
[05Jan85|02Feb85|09Nov85] 4(3) 45 3946

839. QUADROPHENIA The Who
[10Nov73|24Nov73|10Aug74] 2(1) 40 3945

840. RISE Herb Alpert
[13Oct79|01Dec79|05Jul80] 6(1) 39 3939

841. TRILOGY Emerson, Lake & Palmer
[29Jul72|30Sep72|07Apr73] 5(1) 37 3937

842. BLUE MIDNIGHT
Bert Kaempfert And His Orchestra
[23Jan65|17Apr65|05Feb66] 5(1) 55 3936

843. ALWAYS & FOREVER Randy Travis
[30May87|11Jul87|13May89] 19(1) 103 3934

844. IT'S ONLY ROCK 'N ROLL
The Rolling Stones
[02Nov74|23Nov74|15Mar75] 1(1) 20 3928

845. SUCCESS HASN'T SPOILED ME YET
Rick Springfield
[27Mar82|22May82|20Nov82] 2(3) 35 3922

846. WHO ARE YOU The Who
[09Sep78|21Oct78|31Mar79] 2(2) 30 3916

847. ...TWICE SHY Great White
[06May89|08Jul89|14Apr90] 9(1) 50 3912

848. YOU'VE LOST THAT LOVIN' FEELIN'
The Righteous Brothers
[23Jan65|27Feb65|30Apr66] 4(4) 67 3910

849. PETER, PAUL AND MARY IN CONCERT
Peter, Paul & Mary
[15Aug64|26Sep64|21Aug65] 4(3) 54 3909

850. I ROBOT The Alan Parsons Project
[16Jul77|15Oct77|20Jun81] 9(3) 54 3902

851. BRUCE SPRINGSTEEN & THE E STREET BAND LIVE 1975-1985 Bruce Springsteen
[29Nov86|29Nov86|23May87] 1(7) 26 3897

852. THEATRE OF PAIN Mötley Crüe
[13Jul85|17Aug85|29Aug87] 6(1) 72 3895

853. MOODY BLUE Elvis Presley
[23Jul77|17Sep77|18Feb78] 3(3) 31 3887

854. THE RETURN OF ROGER MILLER
Roger Miller
[06Feb65|17Apr65|25Dec65] 4(2) 47 3884

855. WORLDS AWAY Pablo Cruise
[17Jun78|26Aug78|07Apr79] 6(3) 43 3880

856. HEART SHAPED WORLD Chris Isaak
[15Jul89|06Apr91|21Mar92] 7(4) 74 3876

857. JONATHAN LIVINGSTON SEAGULL (SOUNDTRACK) Neil Diamond
[03Nov73|15Dec73|21Aug76] 2(1) 34 3874

858. HEARTS America
[05Apr75|14Jun75|31Jan76] 4(1) 44 3874

859. THE SEA The San Sebastian Strings
[25Mar67|03Aug68|11Apr70] 52(1) 143 3867

860. ...NOTHING LIKE THE SUN Sting
[31Oct87|21Nov87|22Oct88] 9(4) 52 3861

861. THE PRETENDER Jackson Browne
[20Nov76|18Dec76|16Jul77] 5(3) 35 3859

862. UNDER THE INFLUENCE OF...
Love Unlimited
[08Sep73|16Feb74|06Jul74] 3(2) 44 3858

863. THE DISTANCE
Bob Seger & The Silver Bullet Band
[15Jan83|19Feb83|08Oct83] 5(6) 39 3858

864. GREATEST HITS Barry Manilow
[02Dec78|10Feb79|13Mar82] 7(1) 75 3851

865. THE SONG REMAINS THE SAME (SOUNDTRACK) Led Zeppelin
[06Nov76|13Nov76|17Nov79] 2(3) 48 3843

866. GENESIS Genesis
[29Oct83|03Dec83|28Mar87] 9(1) 50 3843

867. GREEN R.E.M.
[26Nov88|18Feb89|26Aug89] 12(3) 40 3841

868. MILLION MILE REFLECTIONS
The Charlie Daniels Band
[12May79|01Sep79|01Mar80] 5(3) 43 3838

869. MEMORIES Barbra Streisand
[12Dec81|26Dec81|05Apr86] 10(6) 104 3838

870. THEIR SATANIC MAJESTIES REQUEST
The Rolling Stones
[23Dec67|06Jan68|13Jul68] 2(6) 30 3838

871. ON STAGE Loggins & Messina
[11May74|10Aug74|08Nov75] 5(2) 37 3837

872. PLANET WAVES Bob Dylan with The Band
[09Feb74|16Feb74|29Jun74] 1(4) 21 3836

873. VERITIES & BALDERDASH Harry Chapin
[07Sep74|28Dec74|19Apr75] 4(1) 33 3835

874. FLOWING RIVERS Andy Gibb
[02Jul77|08Oct77|14Oct78] 19(4) 68 3832

875. MACHO MAN Village People
[25Mar78|09Sep78|14Jul79] 24(2) 69 3831

876. KILLING ME SOFTLY Roberta Flack
[01Sep73|22Sep73|31Aug74] 3(2) 53 3825

877. LAP OF LUXURY Cheap Trick
[07May88|24Sep88|25Mar89] 16(1) 47 3824

878. REJOICE The Emotions
[25Jun77|27Aug77|04Feb78] 7(3) 33 3823

879. TO RUSSELL, MY BROTHER, WHOM I SLEPT WITH Bill Cosby
[06Apr68|04May68|15Feb69] 7(2) 46 3821

880. GREATEST HITS Air Supply
[20Aug83|19Nov83|31Aug85] 7(1) 51 3820

881. THE ROSE (SOUNDTRACK) Bette Midler
[22Dec79|23Feb80|25Oct80] 12(3) 45 3819

882. ABRACADABRA The Steve Miller Band
[26Jun82|18Sep82|05Feb83] 3(6) 33 3819

883. GOLDEN HITS Roger Miller
[13Nov65|26Feb66|10Dec66] 6(2) 57 3805

884. THE SOFT PARADE The Doors
[09Aug69|23Aug69|14Feb70] 6(2) 28 3805

885. DUELING BANJOS
Eric Weissberg & Steve Mandell
[27Jan73|17Mar73|14Jul73] 1(3) 25 3805

886. DIAMONDS & RUST Joan Baez
[17May75|26Jul75|27Mar76] 11(1) 46 3801

887. EYES THAT SEE IN THE DARK
Kenny Rogers
[24Sep83|12Nov83|09Jun84] 6(4) 38 3792

888. LOVE TRACKS Gloria Gaynor
[06Jan79|31Mar79|25Aug79] 4(2) 34 3789

889. SEVEN SEPARATE FOOLS Three Dog Night
[29Jul72|30Sep72|28Apr73] 6(2) 40 3787

890. A SONG FOR YOU Carpenters
[08Jul72|12Aug72|14Apr73] 4(3) 41 3786

891. JOHN BARLEYCORN MUST DIE Traffic
[11Jul70|15Aug70|27Mar71] 5(2) 38 3781

892. KEEP THE FIRE Kenny Loggins
[20Oct79|08Mar80|25Oct80] 16(2) 43 3776

893. ALL DAY MUSIC War
[20Nov71|03Jun72|21Oct72] 16(3) 49 3774

894. THE NYLON CURTAIN Billy Joel
[16Oct82|20Nov82|11Jun83] 7(4) 35 3773

895. DESTROYER KISS
[03Apr76|15May76|05Nov77] 11(1) 78 3772

896. DOG AND BUTTERFLY Heart
[07Oct78|20Jan79|09Jun79] 17(1) 36 3764

897. HARMONY Three Dog Night
[23Oct71|20Nov71|10Jun72] 8(2) 34 3761

898. ARETHA ARRIVES Aretha Franklin
[26Aug67|07Oct67|01Jun68] 5(5) 41 3756

899. YELLOW SUBMARINE (SOUNDTRACK)
The Beatles
[08Feb69|01Mar69|26Sep87] 2(2) 25 3755

900. ALBUM 1700 Peter, Paul & Mary
[02Sep67|21Oct67|22Aug70] 15(2) 82 3755

901. ODE TO BILLIE JOE Bobbie Gentry
[16Sep67|14Oct67|06Apr68] 1(2) 30 3754

902. BACH'S GREATEST HITS Swingle Singers
[26Oct63|11Jan64|20Mar65] 15(2) 74 3751

903. ROCK 'N SOUL PART 1
Daryl Hall & John Oates
[19Nov83|28Jan84|15Sep84] 7(2) 44 3750

904. CHANGES IN LATITUDES, CHANGES IN ATTITUDES Jimmy Buffett
[12Feb77|23Jul77|26Nov77] 12(2) 42 3750

905. DIANA ROSS (II) Diana Ross
[06Mar76|26Jun76|09Oct76] 5(1) 32 3743

906. SPANISH EYES Al Martino
[19Feb66|16Apr66|08Jul67] 8(2) 73 3743

907. THE 4 SEASONS' GOLD VAULT OF HITS
The 4 Seasons
[11Dec65|19Feb66|02Dec67] 10(2) 88 3741

908. SCHOOL'S OUT Alice Cooper
[01Jul72|29Jul72|03Feb73] 2(3) 32 3734

909. THE DOCK OF THE BAY Otis Redding
[23Mar68|13Apr68|04Jan69] 4(3) 42 3733

910. BRIDGE OF SIGHS Robin Trower
[20Apr74|31Aug74|16Nov74] 7(1) 31 3733

911. CHAMPAGNE JAM Atlanta Rhythm Section
[01Apr78|03Jun78|30Dec78] 7(2) 40 3722

912. THE ACADEMY AWARD WINNING "CALL ME IRRESPONSIBLE" Andy Williams
[09May64|06Jun64|17Jul65] 5(3) 63 3722

913. DO IT ('TIL YOU'RE SATISFIED) B.T. Express
[23Nov74|01Mar75|21Jun75] 5(1) 31 3720

914. KILLIN' TIME Clint Black
[10Jun89|19May90|29Feb92] 31(1) 143 3718

915. UNDER A BLOOD RED SKY U2
[10Dec83|28Jan84|19Sep87] 28(3) 180 3718

916. RUST NEVER SLEEPS
Neil Young & Crazy Horse
[21Jul79|01Sep79|12Apr80] 8(2) 39 3716

917. DAYLIGHT AGAIN Crosby, Stills & Nash
[17Jul82|14Aug82|23Apr83] 8(5) 41 3714

918. HOLLYWOOD-MY WAY Nancy Wilson
[17Aug63|14Sep63|19Sep64] 11(3) 58 3710

919. BOBBIE GENTRY & GLEN CAMPBELL
Bobbie Gentry & Glen Campbell
[12Oct68|23Nov68|30Aug69] 11(2) 47 3701

920. RIGHT ON TIME The Brothers Johnson
[21May77|09Jul77|17Dec77] 13(3) 31 3695

921. THE WAY WE WERE Barbra Streisand
[16Feb74|16Mar74|14Sep74] 1(2) 31 3692

922. MIDDLE MAN Boz Scaggs
[19Apr80|14Jun80|29Nov80] 8(2) 33 3683

923. COLLECTIONS The Young Rascals
[21Jan67|29Apr67|07Sep68] 14(1) 74 3678

924. WALLS AND BRIDGES John Lennon
[12Oct74|16Nov74|21Mar81] 1(1) 35 3671

925. 7 WISHES Night Ranger
[08Jun85|27Jul85|12Apr86] 10(3) 45 3665

926. HOTCAKES Carly Simon
[02Feb74|09Mar74|28Sep74] 3(1) 35 3664

927. WORD UP! Cameo
[27Sep86|20Dec86|03Oct87] 8(1) 54 3662

928. FIDDLER ON THE ROOF Soundtrack
[30Oct71|08Jan72|14Jul73] 30(2) 90 3657

929. DISINTEGRATION The Cure
[20May89|10Jun89|21Jul90] 12(3) 55 3656

930. RAISE! Earth, Wind & Fire
[14Nov81|28Nov81|01May82] 5(8) 25 3652

931. E PLURIBUS FUNK Grand Funk Railroad
[04Dec71|01Jan72|24Jun72] 5(2) 30 3651

932. THE EMPIRE STRIKES BACK Soundtrack
[17May80|12Jul80|22Nov80] 4(4) 28 3643

933. LIVE Kenny G
[09Dec89|24Mar90|18Apr92] 16(1) 122 3642

934. FOREIGNER Cat Stevens
[28Jul73|01Sep73|18May74] 3(1) 43 3640

935. EVERYBODY KNOWS THIS IS NOWHERE
Neil Young & Crazy Horse
[21Jun69|29Aug70|18Sep71] 34(2) 98 3638

936. TEMPTATIONS GREATEST HITS II
The Temptations
[26Sep70|31Oct70|22Jan72] 15(2) 70 3633

937. GAUCHO Steely Dan
[06Dec80|17Jan81|08Aug81] 9(3) 36 3629

938. I STARTED OUT AS A CHILD Bill Cosby
[21Nov64|27Feb65|08Jun68] 32(1) 140 3629

939. TOULOUSE STREET The Doobie Brothers
[26Aug72|02Dec72|05Jul75] 21(2) 119 3618

Rank. Title Act
[Enter|Peak|Exit] Peak(Wks) TotWks Score

940. STREISAND SUPERMAN Barbra Streisand
[02Jul77|30Jul77|17Dec77] 3(4) 25 3602

941. HEAD HUNTERS Herbie Hancock
[12Jan74|23Mar74|30Nov74] 13(1) 47 3602

942. HONEY Andy Williams
[08Jun68|10Aug68|08Mar69] 9(2) 40 3600

943. DIONNE(2) Dionne Warwick
[09Jun79|20Oct79|14Jun80] 12(1) 54 3593

944. WHEELS ARE TURNIN' REO Speedwagon
[24Nov84|16Mar85|26Oct85] 7(1) 49 3592

945. HIGHWAY 61 REVISITED Bob Dylan
[02Oct65|06Nov65|20Aug66] 3(1) 47 3582

946. ONE STEP CLOSER The Doobie Brothers
[11Oct80|25Oct80|18Apr81] 3(3) 28 3578

947. THE WOMAN IN RED (SOUNDTRACK)
Stevie Wonder
[22Sep84|10Nov84|22Jun85] 4(3) 40 3577

948. LOOK SHARP! Roxette
[22Apr89|24Feb90|25Aug90] 23(2) 71 3575

949. EAT TO THE BEAT Blondie
[20Oct79|24Nov79|04Oct80] 17(3) 51 3570

950. ECOLOGY Rare Earth
[11Jul70|15Aug70|12Jun71] 15(5) 49 3565

951. ROCK 'N' ROLL MUSIC The Beatles
[26Jun76|10Jul76|15Jan77] 2(2) 30 3564

952. HISTORY OF OTIS REDDING Otis Redding
[02Dec67|16Mar68|09Nov68] 9(2) 50 3564

953. SIMPLE PLEASURES Bobby McFerrin
[23Apr88|08Oct88|06May89] 5(3) 55 3562

954. THE WHISPERS The Whispers
[05Jan80|12Apr80|30Aug80] 6(2) 35 3555

955. SPEAKING IN TONGUES Talking Heads
[25Jun83|29Oct83|09Jun84] 15(2) 51 3554

956. EDDIE & THE CRUISERS (SOUNDTRACK)
John Cafferty & The Beaver Brown Band
[15Oct83|06Oct84|13Jul85] 9(5) 62 3552

957. LEARNING TO CRAWL The Pretenders
[04Feb84|25Feb84|17Nov84] 5(4) 42 3545

958. CLAUDINE Claudine Longet
[15Apr67|15Jul67|20Apr68] 11(3) 54 3541

959. IN THE POCKET Commodores
[11Jul81|29Aug81|10Apr82] 13(2) 40 3539

960. GIVE ME THE REASON Luther Vandross
[18Oct86|21Feb87|17Oct87] 14(1) 53 3534

961. BEST OF THE BEACH BOYS The Beach Boys
[23Jul66|24Sep66|17Feb68] 8(1) 78 3529

962. MAYBE TOMORROW The Jackson 5
[01May71|22May71|05Feb72] 11(2) 41 3527

963. FAMILY REUNION The O'Jays
[29Nov75|24Jan76|17Jul76] 7(1) 34 3525

964. STATION TO STATION David Bowie
[07Feb76|28Feb76|11Sep76] 3(2) 32 3525

965. FANTASY LOVE AFFAIR Peter Brown
[14Jan78|01Jul78|11Nov78] 11(2) 44 3524

966. COLOR ME BARBRA (SOUNDTRACK)
Barbra Streisand
[09Apr66|30Apr66|10Dec66] 3(2) 36 3524

967. COMMODORES LIVE! Commodores
[12Nov77|10Dec77|20May78] 3(2) 28 3522

968. BRAIN SALAD SURGERY
Emerson, Lake & Palmer
[15Dec73|26Jan74|02Nov74] 11(1) 47 3512

969. LONG HARD CLIMB Helen Reddy
[11Aug73|22Sep73|01Jun74] 8(3) 43 3510

970. WILD-EYED SOUTHERN BOYS .38 Special
[21Feb81|23May81|25Sep82] 18(2) 57 3509

971. CAT STEVENS GREATEST HITS Cat Stevens
[12Jul75|23Aug75|03Sep77] 6(2) 45 3509

972. GODSPELL Original Cast Recording
[07Aug71|26Aug72|15Mar75] 34(1) 79 3506

973. TWIN SONS OF DIFFERENT MOTHERS
Dan Fogelberg/Tim Weisberg
[16Sep78|14Oct78|12May79] 8(3) 35 3504

974. WRAP AROUND JOY Carole King
[28Sep74|09Nov74|12Apr75] 1(1) 29 3499

975. JOURNEY TO THE CENTRE OF THE EARTH
Rick Wakeman With The London Symphony Orchestra & The English Chamber Choir
[15Jun74|20Jul74|14Dec74] 3(2) 27 3498

Rank. Title Act
[Enter|Peak|Exit] Peak(Wks) TotWks Score

976. BACKLESS Eric Clapton
[02Dec78|13Jan79|11Aug79] 8(3) 37 3494

977. TRUE COLORS Cyndi Lauper
[04Oct86|15Nov86|01Aug87] 4(2) 44 3490

978. STARDUST Willie Nelson
[13May78|01Jul78|04Jul81] 30(1) 117 3488

979. INTO THE GAP Thompson Twins
[17Mar84|05May84|16Mar85] 10(2) 53 3487

980. STAY WITH ME TONIGHT Jeffrey Osborne
[06Aug83|17Mar84|13Apr85] 25(1) 89 3485

981. EAT 'EM AND SMILE David Lee Roth
[26Jul86|30Aug86|28Mar87] 4(2) 36 3485

982. NIGHTWATCH Kenny Loggins
[22Jul78|07Oct78|17Feb79] 7(5) 31 3483

983. HELEN REDDY'S GREATEST HITS
Helen Reddy
[06Dec75|17Jan76|15Jan77] 5(3) 51 3481

984. IN FLIGHT George Benson
[12Feb77|19Mar77|08Oct77] 9(2) 35 3477

985. BREAKAWAY Art Garfunkel
[25Oct75|29Nov75|01May76] 7(2) 28 3474

986. DARYL HALL & JOHN OATES
Daryl Hall & John Oates
[13Sep75|26Jun76|26Mar77] 17(1) 76 3473

987. JOURNEYMAN Eric Clapton
[25Nov89|27Jan90|10Nov90] 16(1) 51 3472

988. GO FOR YOUR GUNS The Isley Brothers
[16Apr77|21May77|03Dec77] 6(2) 34 3468

989. PRETZEL LOGIC Steely Dan
[30Mar74|17Aug74|30Nov74] 8(1) 36 3468

990. ONE MORE FROM THE ROAD
Lynyrd Skynyrd
[02Oct76|13Nov76|27Sep80] 9(3) 43 3462

991. STRONGER THAN PRIDE Sade
[04Jun88|02Jul88|08Apr89] 7(2) 45 3456

992. SAVAGE AMUSEMENT Scorpions
[07May88|04Jun88|25Feb89] 5(1) 43 3456

993. DEPARTURE Journey
[22Mar80|26Apr80|12Dec81] 8(2) 57 3453

994. YESTERDAY'S LOVE SONGS/ TODAY'S BLUES Nancy Wilson
[25Jan64|14Mar64|07Nov64] 4(1) 42 3448

995. DIESEL AND DUST Midnight Oil
[13Feb88|04Jun88|25Feb89] 21(3) 55 3447

996. FIREFALL Firefall
[08May76|02Oct76|03Dec77] 28(2) 67 3446

997. STREET SURVIVORS Lynyrd Skynyrd
[05Nov77|10Dec77|06Sep80] 5(2) 34 3443

998. JOPLIN IN CONCERT Janis Joplin
[13May72|24Jun72|11Nov72] 4(2) 27 3439

999. SHIP AHOY The O'Jays
[10Nov73|23Feb74|05Oct74] 11(1) 48 3438

1000. NEW KIDS ON THE BLOCK
New Kids On The Block
[05Aug89|30Dec89|09Feb91] 25(3) 80 3437

1001. I GOT DEM OL' KOZMIC BLUES AGAIN MAMA! Janis Joplin
[11Oct69|08Nov69|18Apr70] 5(3) 28 3427

1002. A TRAMP SHINING Richard Harris
[18May68|13Jul68|09Aug69] 4(3) 42 3427

1003. DUKE Genesis
[26Apr80|12Jul80|22Nov80] 11(2) 31 3426

1004. EVEN IN THE QUIETEST MOMENTS...
Supertramp
[23Apr77|23Jul77|02Feb80] 16(2) 49 3418

1005. A FLOCK OF SEAGULLS
A Flock Of Seagulls
[22May82|23Oct82|30Apr83] 10(3) 50 3417

1006. CRIMSON & CLOVER
Tommy James And The Shondells
[01Feb69|01Mar69|27Sep69] 8(4) 35 3415

1007. CRUSHIN' Fat Boys
[13Jun87|12Sep87|14May88] 8(3) 49 3405

1008. ONCE UPON A TIME Simple Minds
[09Nov85|01Mar86|23Aug86] 10(5) 42 3400

1009. TUFF ENUFF The Fabulous Thunderbirds
[15Mar86|05Jul86|14Mar87] 13(3) 53 3398

1010. WILD CHERRY Wild Cherry
[24Jul76|25Sep76|05Feb77] 5(2) 29 3397

Rank. Title Act
[Enter|Peak|Exit] Peak(Wks) TotWks Score

1011. DIVER DOWN Van Halen
[08May82|12Jun82|09Jun84] 3(3) 65 3394

1012. MOVING WAVES Focus
[20Jan73|02Jun73|06Oct73] 8(2) 38 3393

1013. DELIVER THE WORD War
[01Sep73|06Oct73|04May74] 6(2) 36 3392

1014. LITTLE CREATURES Talking Heads
[06Jul85|27Jul85|20Dec86] 20(3) 77 3390

1015. TOTALLY HOT Olivia Newton-John
[09Dec78|24Feb79|22Sep79] 7(2) 39 3388

1016. MEMPHIS UNDERGROUND Herbie Mann
[24May69|19Jul69|21Mar70] 20(1) 44 3383

1017. VALLEY OF THE DOLLS Dionne Warwick
[09Mar68|13Apr68|01Feb69] 6(2) 48 3381

1018. VITAL SIGNS Survivor
[29Sep84|13Jul85|23Nov85] 16(3) 61 3378

1019. PIRATES Rickie Lee Jones
[08Aug81|26Sep81|20Feb82] 5(2) 29 3376

1020. QUIET FIRE Roberta Flack
[11Dec71|08Jan72|04Nov72] 18(2) 48 3375

1021. WHY CAN'T WE BE FRIENDS? War
[05Jul75|30Aug75|31Jan76] 8(1) 31 3374

1022. EYE IN THE SKY The Alan Parsons Project
[19Jun82|09Oct82|26Mar83] 7(6) 41 3372

1023. ENDLESS FLIGHT Leo Sayer
[27Nov76|04Jun77|12Nov77] 10(2) 51 3371

1024. LIVING IN OZ Rick Springfield
[30Apr83|18Jun83|26May84] 12(3) 57 3368

1025. EMERSON, LAKE & PALMER
Emerson, Lake & Palmer
[06Feb71|01May71|20Nov71] 18(2) 42 3365

1026. I WANT YOU Marvin Gaye
[03Apr76|05Jun76|19May84] 4(1) 28 3363

1027. IN EFFECT MODE Al B. Sure!
[14May88|10Sep88|20May89] 20(1) 54 3363

1028. CAN'T FIGHT FATE Taylor Dayne
[18Nov89|07Apr90|01Dec90] 25(1) 55 3361

1029. THOROUGHBRED Carole King
[07Feb76|27Mar76|26Jun76] 3(3) 21 3360

1030. 'LIVE' BULLET
Bob Seger & The Silver Bullet Band
[01May76|19Jun76|06Sep86] 34(1) 154 3359

1031. BE YOURSELF TONIGHT Eurythmics
[25May85|20Jul85|29Mar86] 9(1) 45 3357

1032. CURTIS Curtis Mayfield
[03Oct70|28Nov70|04Sep71] 19(1) 49 3351

1033. KEEP IT UP Loverboy
[02Jul83|23Jul83|24Mar84] 7(5) 39 3349

1034. A LONELY MAN The Chi-Lites
[29Apr72|24Jun72|30Dec72] 5(1) 36 3349

1035. THE LOW SPARK OF HIGH HEELED BOYS
Traffic
[11Dec71|19Feb72|01Jul72] 7(2) 30 3342

1036. VALOTTE Julian Lennon
[10Nov84|23Feb85|21Sep85] 17(2) 46 3339

1037. 1100 BEL AIR PLACE Julio Iglesias
[01Sep84|27Oct84|20Apr85] 5(2) 34 3337

1038. ROUSTABOUT (SOUNDTRACK)
Elvis Presley
[14Nov64|02Jan65|15May65] 1(1) 27 3337

1039. JOAN BAEZ/5 Joan Baez
[21Nov64|26Dec64|19Feb66] 12(2) 66 3336

1040. BOOTS Nancy Sinatra
[12Mar66|09Apr66|24Dec66] 5(3) 42 3329

1041. PSYCHEDELIC SHACK The Temptations
[04Apr70|02May70|24Oct70] 9(2) 30 3327

1042. SIGN 'O' THE TIMES Prince
[18Apr87|09May87|23Apr88] 6(2) 54 3322

1043. DONNY HATHAWAY LIVE Donny Hathaway
[04Mar72|08Jul72|18Nov72] 18(2) 38 3318

1044. SUMMER DAYS (AND SUMMER NIGHTS!!)
The Beach Boys
[24Jul65|04Sep65|05Mar66] 2(1) 33 3318

1045. TOUCH Eurythmics
[04Feb84|07Apr84|13Oct84] 7(3) 37 3314

1046. FACE DANCES The Who
[04Apr81|25Apr81|15Aug81] 4(4) 20 3313

1047. BEN Michael Jackson
[26Aug72|11Nov72|31Mar73] 5(3) 32 3309

Rank. Title Act
[Enter|Peak|Exit] Peak(Wks) TotWks — Score

1048. AND THEN...ALONG COMES THE ASSOCIATION The Association
[20Aug66|19Nov66|30Sep67] 5(1) 59 — 3303

1049. A PASSION PLAY Jethro Tull
[21Jul73|18Aug73|23Feb74] 1(1) 32 — 3303

1050. CALL ME Al Green
[19May73|23Jun73|23Feb74] 10(2) 41 — 3301

1051. ZORBA THE GREEK Soundtrack
[01May65|18Sep65|29Oct66] 26(2) 79 — 3295

1052. LIGHT UP THE NIGHT The Brothers Johnson
[08Mar80|03May80|27Sep80] 5(2) 30 — 3294

1053. BLUE MOVES Elton John
[13Nov76|13Nov76|09Apr77] 3(3) 22 — 3289

1054. MOUNTAIN CLIMBING! Mountain
[14Mar70|02May70|05Dec70] 17(2) 39 — 3285

1055. DECEMBER George Winston
[12Mar83|21Jan84|19Jan91] 54(1) 178 — 3285

1056. LITA Lita Ford
[20Feb88|28May88|16Sep89] 29(4) 62 — 3280

1057. A SONG FOR YOU The Temptations
[08Feb75|26Apr75|11Oct75] 13(1) 36 — 3279

1058. STAY HUNGRY Twisted Sister
[07Jul84|15Sep84|10Aug85] 15(3) 51 — 3275

1059. ICE CREAM CASTLE The Time
[28Jul84|13Oct84|24Aug85] 24(3) 57 — 3275

1060. JOURNEY THROUGH THE SECRET LIFE OF PLANTS Stevie Wonder
[24Nov79|08Dec79|19Apr80] 4(5) 22 — 3272

1061. PROCOL HARUM LIVE IN CONCERT WITH THE EDMONTON SYMPHONY ORCHESTRA Procol Harum
[13May72|22Jul72|18Nov72] 5(1) 28 — 3272

1062. L-O-V-E Nat King Cole
[06Feb65|27Mar65|23Oct65] 4(3) 38 — 3271

1063. MANASSAS Stephen Stills/Manassas
[29Apr72|10Jun72|18Nov72] 4(2) 30 — 3270

1064. THE CLOSER YOU GET Alabama
[26Mar83|30Apr83|21Jul84] 10(1) 70 — 3270

1065. SINATRA '65 Frank Sinatra
[03Jul65|11Sep65|30Apr66] 9(1) 44 — 3267

1066. GORILLA James Taylor
[31May75|16Aug75|29Nov75] 6(1) 27 — 3257

1067. HIGHWAY TO HELL AC/DC
[25Aug79|10Nov79|03Apr82] 17(2) 83 — 3255

1068. THE JETS The Jets
[05Apr86|19Jul86|05Sep87] 21(2) 70 — 3252

1069. JOURNEY'S GREATEST HITS Journey
[03Dec88|11Feb89|27Oct90] 10(2) 92 — 3252

1070. PRISONER IN DISGUISE Linda Ronstadt
[04Oct75|08Nov75|10Apr76] 4(3) 28 — 3251

1071. SO FAR Crosby, Stills, Nash & Young
[07Sep74|02Nov74|08Mar75] 1(1) 27 — 3250

1072. CLOSE TO THE EDGE Yes
[07Oct72|02Dec72|12May73] 3(1) 32 — 3249

1073. FULL SAIL Loggins & Messina
[10Nov73|05Jan74|12Oct74] 10(1) 49 — 3243

1074. CATCH A RISING STAR John Gary
[09Nov63|22Feb64|16Jan65] 19(2) 63 — 3242

1075. DR. BUZZARD'S ORIGINAL SAVANNAH BAND Dr. Buzzard's Original Savannah Band
[21Aug76|05Feb77|23Jul77] 22(2) 49 — 3237

1076. CHARADE (SOUNDTRACK) Henry Mancini And His Orchestra
[28Dec63|22Feb64|10Oct64] 6(3) 42 — 3236

1077. "BUT SERIOUSLY FOLKS..." Joe Walsh
[10Jun78|26Aug78|09Dec78] 8(2) 27 — 3226

1078. OPEN OUR EYES Earth, Wind & Fire
[30Mar74|18May74|07Dec74] 15(2) 37 — 3222

1079. SGT. PEPPER'S LONELY HEARTS CLUB BAND Soundtrack
[12Aug78|19Aug78|17Feb79] 5(6) 28 — 3219

1080. CUT THE CAKE Average White Band
[28Jun75|16Aug75|06Dec75] 4(1) 24 — 3219

1081. SPIRIT John Denver
[04Sep76|25Sep76|26Mar77] 7(2) 30 — 3216

1082. WOMEN AND CHILDREN FIRST Van Halen
[19Apr80|17May80|15Nov80] 6(5) 31 — 3216

1083. DECEMBER'S CHILDREN (AND EVERYBODY'S) The Rolling Stones
[11Dec65|08Jan66|23Jul66] 4(3) 33 — 3215

1084. GREATEST HITS Paul Revere & The Raiders
[13May67|10Jun67|30Mar68] 9(2) 47 — 3215

1085. TAP ROOT MANUSCRIPT Neil Diamond
[21Nov70|19Dec70|25Sep71] 13(2) 45 — 3215

1086. THE DONNY OSMOND ALBUM Donny Osmond
[10Jul71|25Sep71|18Mar72] 13(1) 37 — 3214

1087. STREET TALK Steve Perry
[28Apr84|09Jun84|15Jun85] 12(4) 60 — 3214

1088. SWEET SENSATION Stephanie Mills
[03May80|21Jun80|28Feb81] 16(2) 44 — 3213

1089. HELLO, I'M JOHNNY CASH Johnny Cash
[14Feb70|14Mar70|05Sep70] 6(1) 30 — 3209

1090. BEING WITH YOU Smokey Robinson
[14Mar81|06Jun81|19Sep81] 10(2) 28 — 3208

1091. BREAK EVERY RULE Tina Turner
[27Sep86|08Nov86|19Sep87] 4(1) 52 — 3207

1092. SECOND HELPING Lynyrd Skynyrd
[04May74|12Oct74|08Mar75] 12(2) 45 — 3205

1093. CAN'T BUY A THRILL Steely Dan
[02Dec72|24Mar73|12Jan74] 17(1) 59 — 3203

1094. THE GREAT RADIO CONTROVERSY Tesla
[18Feb89|11Mar89|30Jun90] 18(1) 67 — 3201

1095. CAPTURED Journey
[21Feb81|14Mar81|12Jun82] 9(4) 69 — 3197

1096. MORRISON HOTEL The Doors
[07Mar70|21Mar70|05Sep70] 4(4) 27 — 3197

1097. PICK OF THE LITTER Spinners
[09Aug75|04Oct75|31Jan76] 8(3) 26 — 3195

1098. VOLUME ONE The Honeydrippers
[20Oct84|01Dec84|18May85] 4(2) 31 — 3186

1099. BACK ON THE BLOCK Quincy Jones
[09Dec89|03Feb90|13Apr91] 9(2) 40 — 3185

1100. LOOKIN' THROUGH THE WINDOWS The Jackson 5
[03Jun72|05Aug72|13Jan73] 7(1) 33 — 3181

1101. DESTINY The Jacksons
[16Dec78|14Apr79|22Sep79] 11(2) 41 — 3181

1102. SPRING SESSION M Missing Persons
[30Oct82|26Feb83|19May84] 17(6) 40 — 3181

1103. HERE COMES BOBBY Bobby Sherman
[11Apr70|16May70|06Mar71] 10(2) 48 — 3180

1104. A TASTE OF HONEY A Taste Of Honey
[17Jun78|07Oct78|16Dec78] 6(2) 27 — 3180

1105. MUSIC FROM "A FISTFUL OF DOLLARS" & "FOR A FEW DOLLARS MORE" & "THE GOOD, THE BAD AND THE UGLY" Hugo Montenegro, His Orchestra And Chorus
[17Feb68|29Jun68|09Nov68] 9(1) 39 — 3176

1106. STRONG PERSUADER The Robert Cray Band
[20Dec86|04Apr87|21Nov87] 13(3) 49 — 3174

1107. EAGLES LIVE Eagles
[29Nov80|20Dec80|23May81] 6(4) 26 — 3172

1108. BEGGARS BANQUET The Rolling Stones
[14Dec68|11Jan69|01Nov80] 5(3) 32 — 3171

1109. MISTER MAGIC Grover Washington Jr.
[08Mar75|28Jun75|25Oct75] 10(1) 34 — 3167

1110. THE DAVE CLARK FIVE'S GREATEST HITS The Dave Clark Five
[26Feb66|30Apr66|19Aug67] 9(1) 62 — 3166

1111. BOBBY SHERMAN Bobby Sherman
[08Nov69|31Jan70|04Jul70] 11(1) 35 — 3166

1112. THE WILD ANGELS (SOUNDTRACK) Davie Allan And The Arrows
[15Oct66|28Jan67|17Feb68] 17(2) 71 — 3165

1113. UP, UP AND AWAY The 5th Dimension
[17Jun67|12Aug67|11Jan69] 8(2) 83 — 3162

1114. CARAVANSERAI Santana
[04Nov72|02Dec72|09Jun73] 8(2) 32 — 3161

1115. GLAD ALL OVER The Dave Clark Five
[11Apr64|23May64|13Mar65] 3(1) 32 — 3158

1116. GYPSYS, TRAMPS & THIEVES Cher
[25Sep71|04Dec71|29Jul72] 16(1) 45 — 3158

1117. CARLOS SANTANA & BUDDY MILES! LIVE! Carlos Santana & Buddy Miles
[08Jul72|02Sep72|17Feb73] 8(3) 33 — 3157

1118. FANTASY Carole King
[23Jun73|21Jul73|02Mar74] 6(3) 37 — 3155

1119. WET Barbra Streisand
[03Nov79|08Dec79|26Apr80] 7(4) 26 — 3155

1120. APOSTROPHE (') Frank Zappa
[20Apr74|29Jun74|08Feb75] 10(1) 43 — 3152

1121. HORIZON Eddie Rabbitt
[12Jul80|21Mar81|18Jul81] 19(2) 54 — 3151

1122. ANN MURRAY'S GREATEST HITS Anne Murray
[04Oct80|06Dec80|21Jan84] 16(5) 64 — 3147

1123. DISCO NIGHTS GQ
[07Apr79|09Jun79|01Dec79] 13(1) 35 — 3146

1124. THE LETTERMEN!!!...AND "LIVE!" The Lettermen
[25Nov67|09Mar68|19Oct68] 10(5) 48 — 3145

1125. STOP AND SMELL THE ROSES Mac Davis
[04May74|21Sep74|08Mar75] 13(2) 45 — 3144

1126. AT FILLMORE EAST The Allman Brothers Band
[24Jul71|04Sep71|10Jun72] 13(1) 47 — 3136

1127. ALDO NOVA Aldo Nova
[20Feb82|22May82|30Oct82] 8(6) 37 — 3135

1128. FROM ELVIS IN MEMPHIS Elvis Presley
[14Jun69|19Jul69|31Jan70] 13(2) 34 — 3133

1129. LET'S GET SERIOUS Jermaine Jackson
[12Apr80|12Jul80|25Oct80] 6(3) 29 — 3133

1130. MOTHERSHIP CONNECTION Parliament
[21Feb76|05Jun76|30Oct76] 13(2) 37 — 3129

1131. SLOW TRAIN COMING Bob Dylan
[08Sep79|22Sep79|01Mar80] 3(4) 26 — 3127

1132. LITTLE DEUCE COUPE The Beach Boys
[09Nov63|08Feb64|31Oct64] 4(2) 46 — 3127

1133. LITTLE CRIMINALS Randy Newman
[22Oct77|18Feb78|06May78] 9(2) 29 — 3124

1134. FOR THE GOOD TIMES Ray Price
[12Sep70|30Jan71|23Oct71] 28(3) 59 — 3115

1135. DREAM INTO ACTION Howard Jones
[20Apr85|29Jun85|22Feb86] 10(1) 45 — 3115

1136. LET'S GET IT STARTED MC Hammer
[03Dec88|22Jul89|09Jun90] 30(1) 80 — 3114

1137. SCENES FROM THE SOUTHSIDE Bruce Hornsby & The Range
[21May88|09Jul88|19Nov88] 5(1) 27 — 3112

1138. GUY Guy
[30Jul88|20May89|25Nov89] 27(5) 70 — 3108

1139. ANIMALS Pink Floyd
[19Feb77|05Mar77|27Aug77] 3(3) 28 — 3108

1140. JOAN BAEZ IN CONCERT, PART 2 Joan Baez
[07Dec63|18Jan64|08Aug64] 7(3) 36 — 3108

1141. PUMP UP THE JAM - THE ALBUM Technotronic
[23Dec89|07Apr90|19Dec92] 10(1) 55 — 3107

1142. MOUTH TO MOUTH Lipps Inc.
[19Apr80|31May80|11Oct80] 5(5) 26 — 3106

1143. THE SHADOW OF YOUR SMILE Andy Williams
[14May66|25Jun66|20May67] 6(2) 54 — 3103

1144. THE PRINCIPLE OF MOMENTS Robert Plant
[30Jul83|08Oct83|28Apr84] 8(1) 40 — 3102

1145. PARADE: MUSIC FROM THE MOTION PICTURE UNDER THE CHERRY MOON (SOUNDTRACK) Prince And The Revolution
[19Apr86|03May86|25Oct86] 3(3) 28 — 3097

1146. HIGH 'N' DRY Def Leppard
[08Aug81|17Oct81|17Mar84] 38(1) 106 — 3096

1147. BLACKOUT Scorpions
[27Mar82|29May82|06Oct84] 10(2) 74 — 3091

1148. INTO THE FIRE Bryan Adams
[18Apr87|16May87|28Nov87] 7(1) 33 — 3091

1149. BARRY MANILOW II Barry Manilow
[23Nov74|22Feb75|20Aug77] 9(1) 58 — 3088

Rank. Title Act [Enter | Peak | Exit] Peak(Wks) TotWks	Score
1150. THE OTHER SIDE OF LIFE The Moody Blues [17May86 | 28Jun86 | 19Sep87] 9(4) 42	3087
1151. "5TH" Lee Michaels [05Jun71 | 09Oct71 | 05Feb72] 16(1) 36	3084
1152. CLOUD NINE George Harrison [21Nov87 | 23Jan88 | 18Jun88] 8(1) 31	3080
1153. SLEEPER CATCHER Little River Band [17Jun78 | 28Oct78 | 11Aug79] 16(2) 61	3077
1154. THE SUPREMES AT THE COPA The Supremes [13Nov65 | 01Jan66 | 19Nov66] 11(1) 54	3076
1155. LIFE, LOVE & PAIN Club Nouveau [20Dec86 | 25Apr87 | 17Oct87] 6(1) 44	3075
1156. CROWDED HOUSE Crowded House [30Aug86 | 16May87 | 16Jan88] 12(1) 58	3074
1157. BLACK MOSES Isaac Hayes [11Dec71 | 08Jan72 | 29Jul72] 10(2) 34	3071
1158. RUN WITH THE PACK Bad Company [14Feb76 | 10Apr76 | 21Aug76] 5(2) 28	3069
1159. LOVE IS THE MESSAGE MFSB [19Jan74 | 20Apr74 | 14Sep74] 4(1) 35	3069
1160. PERMANENT WAVES Rush [02Feb80 | 08Mar80 | 23May81] 4(3) 36	3066
1161. A NOD IS AS GOOD AS A WINK... TO A BLIND HORSE Faces [18Dec71 | 05Feb72 | 27May72] 6(4) 24	3065
1162. ELVIS AS RECORDED AT MADISON SQUARE GARDEN Elvis Presley [08Jul72 | 09Sep72 | 24Feb73] 11(2) 34	3063
1163. ELVIS - TV SPECIAL Elvis Presley [21Dec68 | 08Feb69 | 26Jul69] 8(3) 32	3062
1164. PLEASE Pet Shop Boys [19Apr86 | 21Jun86 | 15Nov86] 7(1) 31	3061
1165. FREEDOM AT POINT ZERO Jefferson Starship [01Dec79 | 02Feb80 | 07Jun80] 10(1) 28	3057
1166. SWEET DREAMS (ARE MADE OF THIS) Eurythmics [28May83 | 27Aug83 | 07Jul84] 15(3) 59	3056
1167. I REMEMBER YESTERDAY Donna Summer [04Jun77 | 05Nov77 | 04Mar78] 18(1) 40	3051
1168. BEE GEES' 1ST Bee Gees [26Aug67 | 02Dec67 | 17Aug68] 7(1) 52	3047
1169. HEROES Commodores [28Jun80 | 12Jul80 | 07Feb81] 7(3) 33	3045
1170. FREE AND EASY Helen Reddy [02Nov74 | 04Jan75 | 10May75] 8(1) 28	3045
1171. READY FOR THE WORLD Ready For The World [22Jun85 | 12Oct85 | 17May86] 17(5) 48	3043
1172. I'M GLAD YOU'RE HERE WITH ME TONIGHT Neil Diamond [03Dec77 | 11Feb78 | 13May78] 6(2) 24	3041
1173. CHEECH AND CHONG Cheech & Chong [25Sep71 | 04Mar72 | 09Dec72] 28(3) 64	3041
1174. LET'S GET SMALL Steve Martin [08Oct77 | 26Nov77 | 20Jan79] 10(2) 68	3035
1175. CAN'T HOLD BACK Eddie Money [30Aug86 | 06Dec86 | 03Oct87] 20(3) 58	3034
1176. SURFER GIRL The Beach Boys [12Oct63 | 23Nov63 | 13Mar65] 7(2) 56	3030
1177. HEAVY NOVA Robert Palmer [16Jul88 | 27Aug88 | 13May89] 13(3) 44	3027
1178. BOYS IN THE TREES Carly Simon [22Apr78 | 01Jul78 | 04Nov78] 10(3) 29	3027
1179. ANKA Paul Anka [31Aug74 | 26Oct74 | 08Mar75] 9(2) 28	3025
1180. MYSTERY GIRL Roy Orbison [18Feb89 | 08Apr89 | 19Aug89] 5(2) 27	3024
1181. TRIUMPH The Jacksons [18Oct80 | 08Nov80 | 02May81] 10(4) 29	3024
1182. FANCY FREE The Oak Ridge Boys [13Jun81 | 15Aug81 | 08May82] 14(1) 48	3024
1183. ALIVE II KISS [26Nov77 | 07Jan78 | 02Sep78] 7(2) 33	3023
1184. FREEDOM OF CHOICE Devo [14Jun80 | 29Nov80 | 30May81] 22(2) 51	3023

Rank. Title Act [Enter | Peak | Exit] Peak(Wks) TotWks	Score
1185. ANYWAY YOU LIKE IT Thelma Houston [25Dec76 | 07May77 | 03Sep77] 11(2) 37	3022
1186. LISTEN LIKE THIEVES INXS [02Nov85 | 12Apr86 | 15Nov86] 11(1) 55	3022
1187. BOB DYLAN'S GREATEST HITS, VOL. II Bob Dylan [11Dec71 | 22Jan72 | 22Mar75] 14(1) 36	3021
1188. LONG AFTER DARK Tom Petty And The Heartbreakers [20Nov82 | 22Jan83 | 25Jun83] 9(3) 32	3020
1189. (FOR GOD'S SAKE) GIVE MORE POWER TO THE PEOPLE The Chi-Lites [21Aug71 | 20Nov71 | 25Mar72] 12(1) 32	3014
1190. SKYSCRAPER David Lee Roth [13Feb88 | 27Feb88 | 13Aug88] 6(6) 27	3013
1191. OSMONDS The Osmonds [30Jan71 | 27Feb71 | 20Nov71] 14(3) 43	3012
1192. LOVIN' EVERY MINUTE OF IT Loverboy [14Sep85 | 19Oct85 | 12Jul86] 13(5) 44	3011
1193. SMOKIN' Humble Pie [01Apr72 | 13May72 | 18Nov72] 6(1) 34	3010
1194. DURAN DURAN Duran Duran [19Feb83 | 20Aug83 | 13Oct84] 10(1) 87	3007
1195. STRAIGHT SHOOTER Bad Company [19Apr75 | 31May75 | 29Nov75] 3(1) 33	3006
1196. TONIGHT I'M YOURS Rod Stewart [21Nov81 | 19Dec81 | 19Jun82] 11(4) 31	3006
1197. VOLUNTEERS Jefferson Airplane [22Nov69 | 13Dec69 | 19Sep70] 13(2) 44	3005
1198. BRASS CONSTRUCTION Brass Construction [07Feb76 | 15May76 | 02Oct76] 10(1) 35	3002
1199. CABARET Soundtrack [18Mar72 | 09Jun73 | 01Dec73] 25(1) 72	3000
1200. A PLACE IN THE SUN Pablo Cruise [05Mar77 | 06Aug77 | 14Jan78] 19(2) 46	2997
1201. TEDDY Teddy Pendergrass [23Jun79 | 11Aug79 | 19Jan80] 5(2) 31	2994
1202. TAKIN' IT TO THE STREETS The Doobie Brothers [03Apr76 | 22May76 | 29Jan77] 8(1) 44	2991
1203. PANORAMA The Cars [06Sep80 | 20Sep80 | 14Mar81] 5(4) 28	2985
1204. SUGAR LIPS Al Hirt [22Aug64 | 21Nov64 | 17Jul65] 9(2) 48	2984
1205. AT YOUR BIRTHDAY PARTY Steppenwolf [15Mar69 | 12Apr69 | 27Sep69] 7(2) 29	2980
1206. THE KINKS GREATEST HITS! The Kinks [27Aug66 | 19Nov66 | 11Nov67] 9(1) 64	2978
1207. PEBBLES Pebbles [13Feb88 | 11Jun88 | 29Oct88] 14(1) 38	2973
1208. FRESH Sly & The Family Stone [30Jun73 | 18Aug73 | 09Feb74] 7(1) 33	2971
1209. LOGGINS AND MESSINA Loggins & Messina [11Nov72 | 03Feb73 | 05Jan74] 16(1) 61	2971
1210. MELISSA Melissa Manchester [01Mar75 | 13Sep75 | 06Dec75] 12(1) 41	2971
1211. TOMMY Various Artists [09Dec72 | 27Jan73 | 05Jul75] 5(3) 38	2970
1212. ELDORADO Electric Light Orchestra [19Oct74 | 07Dec74 | 24May75] 16(2) 32	2969
1213. WHIPLASH SMILE Billy Idol [08Nov86 | 13Dec86 | 26Sep87] 6(1) 47	2968
1214. PORTRAIT The 5th Dimension [09May70 | 30Jan71 | 05Jun71] 20(2) 50	2967
1215. TP Teddy Pendergrass [23Aug80 | 04Oct80 | 11Apr81] 14(3) 34	2966
1216. SCREAMING FOR VENGEANCE Judas Priest [24Jul82 | 30Oct82 | 23Jul83] 17(8) 53	2965
1217. YOU DON'T BRING ME FLOWERS Neil Diamond [16Dec78 | 27Jan79 | 30Jun79] 4(3) 29	2963
1218. 9 TO 5 AND ODD JOBS Dolly Parton [06Dec80 | 21Mar81 | 25Jul81] 11(2) 34	2959
1219. MONSTER Steppenwolf [15Nov69 | 03Jan70 | 26Sep70] 17(2) 46	2957

Rank. Title Act [Enter | Peak | Exit] Peak(Wks) TotWks	Score
1220. A SONG WILL RISE Peter, Paul & Mary [10Apr65 | 22May65 | 25Dec65] 8(3) 38	2954
1221. SKY'S THE LIMIT The Temptations [08May71 | 26Jun71 | 01Jan72] 16(1) 35	2951
1222. PICTURES AT ELEVEN Robert Plant [17Jul82 | 07Aug82 | 17Mar84] 5(6) 53	2950
1223. WINCHESTER CATHEDRAL The New Vaudeville Band [10Dec66 | 21Jan67 | 08Jul67] 5(3) 31	2950
1224. ROSE ROYCE II/IN FULL BLOOM Rose Royce [27Aug77 | 26Nov77 | 08Apr78] 9(2) 33	2948
1225. ALL THINGS IN TIME Lou Rawls [05Jun76 | 11Sep76 | 05Mar77] 7(2) 35	2947
1226. THE ALBUM ABBA [18Feb78 | 22Jul78 | 25Nov78] 14(2) 41	2946
1227. SOUTHERN ACCENTS Tom Petty And The Heartbreakers [13Apr85 | 11May85 | 16Nov85] 7(2) 32	2944
1228. PROMISES, PROMISES Dionne Warwick [14Dec68 | 01Mar69 | 06Sep69] 18(1) 39	2942
1229. STILL WATERS RUN DEEP Four Tops [11Apr70 | 07Nov70 | 23Jan71] 21(1) 42	2937
1230. GLEN CAMPBELL - "LIVE" Glen Campbell [20Sep69 | 01Nov69 | 04Apr70] 13(1) 29	2936
1231. HAWAII FIVE-O The Ventures [10May69 | 12Jul69 | 18Oct69] 11(3) 24	2935
1232. WHALES & NIGHTINGALES Judy Collins [05Dec70 | 06Feb71 | 31Jul71] 17(1) 35	2934
1233. LAID BACK Gregg Allman [24Nov73 | 02Feb74 | 17Aug74] 13(1) 39	2934
1234. FASTER THAN THE SPEED OF NIGHT Bonnie Tyler [06Aug83 | 05Nov83 | 10Mar84] 4(1) 32	2933
1235. THE TURTLES! GOLDEN HITS The Turtles [18Nov67 | 03Feb68 | 01Mar69] 7(3) 39	2929
1236. ROCK OF AGES The Band [09Sep72 | 11Nov72 | 17Mar73] 6(2) 28	2929
1237. HUNTING HIGH AND LOW a-ha [20Jul85 | 02Nov85 | 07Jun86] 15(2) 47	2928
1238. THANKFUL Natalie Cole [10Dec77 | 08Apr78 | 02Sep78] 16(1) 39	2927
1239. TO YOU WITH LOVE, DONNY Donny Osmond [06Nov71 | 27Nov71 | 17Jun72] 12(3) 33	2927
1240. A ROCK AND ROLL ALTERNATIVE Atlanta Rhythm Section [15Jan77 | 21May77 | 08Oct77] 11(1) 39	2926
1241. JUST LIKE US! Paul Revere & The Raiders [05Feb66 | 02Apr66 | 26Nov66] 5(1) 43	2924
1242. IT TAKES TWO Rob Base & D.J. E-Z Rock [08Oct88 | 26Nov88 | 21Apr90] 31(1) 81	2923
1243. WILLIE NELSON'S GREATEST HITS (& SOME THAT WILL BE) Willie Nelson [19Sep81 | 31Oct81 | 25Jun83] 27(1) 93	2922
1244. GRAHAM NASH/DAVID CROSBY Graham Nash/David Crosby [22Apr72 | 20May72 | 14Oct72] 4(3) 26	2912
1245. KARYN WHITE Karyn White [15Oct88 | 11Mar89 | 21Oct89] 19(1) 54	2905
1246. COME GET IT! Rick James [24Jun78 | 16Sep78 | 24Feb79] 13(1) 36	2904
1247. FM Soundtrack [06May78 | 24Jun78 | 14Oct78] 5(2) 24	2902
1248. "...FAMOUS LAST WORDS..." Supertramp [13Nov82 | 27Nov82 | 21May83] 5(7) 28	2901
1249. FM & AM George Carlin [19Feb72 | 15Apr72 | 14Oct72] 13(3) 35	2901
1250. PRETTY IN PINK Soundtrack [01Mar86 | 03May86 | 30Aug86] 5(4) 27	2899
1251. TOUCH ME IN THE MORNING Diana Ross [14Jul73 | 01Sep73 | 19Jan74] 5(2) 28	2899
1252. 7800 DEGREES FAHRENHEIT Bon Jovi [18May85 | 08Jun85 | 03Oct87] 37(3) 104	2896
1253. TOO HOT TO HANDLE Heatwave [06Aug77 | 19Nov77 | 10Jun78] 11(1) 45	2892

Rank. Title Act
[Enter|Peak|Exit] Peak(Wks) TotWks Score

1254. WANTED! THE OUTLAWS
Waylon Jennings, Willie Nelson, Jessi Colter, Tompall Glaser
[07Feb76|03Apr76|26Mar77] 10(2) 51 2890

1255. HOMECOMING America
[02Dec72|06Jan73|07Jul73] 9(4) 32 2887

1256. JOHN LENNON/PLASTIC ONO BAND
John Lennon/Plastic Ono Band
[26Dec70|30Jan71|07Mar81] 6(1) 33 2885

1257. HEAD TO THE SKY Earth, Wind & Fire
[09Jun73|18Aug73|12Oct74] 27(1) 71 2882

1258. YOUNG, GIFTED AND BLACK
Aretha Franklin
[19Feb72|15Apr72|16Sep72] 11(2) 31 2870

1259. THE SPIRIT OF '67
Paul Revere & The Raiders
[31Dec66|11Feb67|12Aug67] 9(3) 33 2863

1260. ONE MAN DOG James Taylor
[25Nov72|13Jan73|12May73] 4(2) 25 2862

1261. THE GAP BAND III The Gap Band
[27Dec80|14Mar81|05Sep81] 16(2) 37 2856

1262. LEGEND Poco
[25Nov78|07Apr79|17Nov79] 14(2) 52 2856

1263. BLUE LIGHTS IN THE BASEMENT
Roberta Flack
[07Jan78|29Apr78|12Aug78] 8(1) 32 2852

1264. JUST LIKE THE FIRST TIME
Freddie Jackson
[15Nov86|14Mar87|31Oct87] 23(2) 51 2850

1265. CROWN OF CREATION
Jefferson Airplane
[07Sep68|02Nov68|22Feb69] 6(2) 25 2849

1266. NETHER LANDS Dan Fogelberg
[04Jun77|23Jul77|25Feb78] 13(1) 39 2848

1267. THE GREAT SONGS FROM "MY FAIR LADY" AND OTHER BROADWAY HITS Andy Williams
[26Sep64|12Dec64|08May65] 5(2) 33 2848

1268. WHY DO FOOLS FALL IN LOVE Diana Ross
[07Nov81|05Dec81|19Jun82] 15(6) 33 2846

1269. TIME PASSAGES Al Stewart
[07Oct78|16Dec78|05May79] 10(1) 31 2841

1270. 3 + 3 The Isley Brothers
[08Sep73|10Nov73|18May74] 8(1) 37 2841

1271. THE ULTIMATE SIN Ozzy Osbourne
[15Feb86|05Apr86|08Nov86] 6(2) 39 2840

1272. WHO DO WE THINK WE ARE! Deep Purple
[20Jan73|17Mar73|22Dec73] 15(3) 49 2840

1273. SHOWDOWN The Isley Brothers
[22Apr78|03Jun78|09Sep78] 4(3) 21 2838

1274. FLIRTIN' WITH DISASTER Molly Hatchet
[29Sep79|01Dec79|20Dec80] 19(2) 48 2838

1275. BIG TYME Heavy D & The Boyz
[01Jul89|09Sep89|16Jun90] 19(3) 51 2838

1276. WIND ON THE WATER
David Crosby/Graham Nash
[11Oct75|29Nov75|02Oct76] 6(2) 31 2837

1277. GAP BAND IV The Gap Band
[12Jun82|11Sep82|04Jun83] 14(5) 52 2837

1278. FUN IN ACAPULCO (SOUNDTRACK)
Elvis Presley
[21Dec63|18Jan64|30May64] 3(3) 24 2835

1279. UP YOUR ALLEY
Joan Jett & the Blackhearts
[28May88|22Oct88|08Apr89] 19(1) 46 2833

1280. KEEP ON PUSHING The Impressions
[08Aug64|10Oct64|27Mar65] 8(2) 34 2831

1281. THE WORST OF JEFFERSON AIRPLANE
Jefferson Airplane
[12Dec70|30Jan71|11Sep71] 12(1) 40 2830

1282. THE SUPER HITS Various Artists
[05Aug67|28Oct67|21Sep68] 12(2) 60 2829

1283. CAR WASH Rose Royce
[09Oct76|05Feb77|09Jul77] 14(2) 40 2828

1284. WIVES AND LOVERS Jack Jones
[28Dec63|25Apr64|26Dec64] 18(2) 53 2827

1285. NO BRAKES John Waite
[14Jul84|29Sep84|11May85] 10(1) 43 2827

1286. THE BOSS Diana Ross
[16Jun79|29Sep79|23Feb80] 14(2) 37 2825

Rank. Title Act
[Enter|Peak|Exit] Peak(Wks) TotWks Score

1287. MCCARTNEY II Paul McCartney
[14Jun80|21Jun80|18Oct80] 3(5) 19 2823

1288. THEM CHANGES Buddy Miles
[04Jul70|19Sep70|27Nov71] 35(2) 74 2822

1289. WHO WILL ANSWER? AND OTHER SONGS OF OUR TIME Ed Ames
[24Feb68|01Jun68|01Feb69] 13(1) 50 2821

1290. STAMPEDE The Doobie Brothers
[17May75|28Jun75|01Nov75] 4(2) 25 2821

1291. CAT SCRATCH FEVER Ted Nugent
[25Jun77|13Aug77|18Mar78] 17(1) 39 2820

1292. THE SALSOUL ORCHESTRA
The Salsoul Orchestra
[29Nov75|10Apr76|02Oct76] 14(2) 45 2820

1293. EVERYTHING The Bangles
[05Nov88|22Apr89|19Aug89] 15(2) 42 2818

1294. HEARTLIGHT Neil Diamond
[16Oct82|27Nov82|04Jun83] 9(3) 34 2817

1295. ANOTHER TICKET
Eric Clapton And His Band
[21Mar81|25Apr81|08Aug81] 7(2) 21 2816

1296. ONE FOR THE ROAD The Kinks
[28Jun80|30Aug80|07Feb81] 14(4) 33 2816

1297. THANK GOD IT'S FRIDAY Soundtrack
[13May78|22Jul78|11Nov78] 10(3) 27 2815

1298. UNBORN CHILD Seals & Crofts
[02Mar74|20Apr74|19Oct74] 14(2) 34 2815

1299. PET SOUNDS The Beach Boys
[28May66|02Jul66|14Jul90] 10(1) 44 2810

1300. PICTURE THIS Huey Lewis & The News
[27Feb82|12Jun82|23Feb85] 13(4) 59 2810

1301. BAD ENGLISH Bad English
[15Jul89|25Nov89|11Aug90] 21(2) 52 2809

1302. SPIRIT OF AMERICA The Beach Boys
[03May75|28Jun75|16Oct76] 8(2) 43 2808

1303. IN THE DARK Grateful Dead
[25Jul87|22Aug87|12Mar88] 6(2) 34 2807

1304. THE SUPREMES SING HOLLAND-DOZIER-HOLLAND The Supremes
[18Feb67|18Mar67|02Sep67] 6(2) 29 2805

1305. THE IMPOSSIBLE DREAM Jack Jones
[16Jul66|29Oct66|20Jan68] 9(1) 64 2802

1306. GOING TO A GO-GO
Smokey Robinson & The Miracles
[27Nov65|26Feb66|27Aug66] 8(2) 40 2801

1307. MEETING IN THE LADIES ROOM Klymaxx
[02Feb85|22Feb86|10May86] 18(3) 67 2800

1308. 12 X 5 The Rolling Stones
[14Nov64|12Dec64|13Nov65] 3(4) 38 2795

1309. CHICAGO 16 Chicago
[26Jun82|18Sep82|12Mar83] 9(5) 38 2792

1310. SONIC TEMPLE The Cult
[29Apr89|27May89|09Dec89] 10(6) 33 2792

1311. HARVEST FOR THE WORLD
The Isley Brothers
[29May76|03Jul76|20Nov76] 9(2) 26 2792

1312. PAINTED, TAINTED ROSE Al Martino
[12Oct63|30Nov63|08Aug64] 9(1) 44 2792

1313. JAMES GANG RIDES AGAIN
The James Gang
[25Jul70|31Oct70|20Nov71] 20(1) 66 2788

1314. LOVE GUN KISS
[09Jul77|30Jul77|31Dec77] 4(2) 26 2788

1315. UNPREDICTABLE Natalie Cole
[05Mar77|23Apr77|10Sep77] 8(2) 28 2786

1316. ONE VOICE Barry Manilow
[20Oct79|17Nov79|05Apr80] 9(3) 25 2784

1317. LIVIN' INSIDE YOUR LOVE George Benson
[17Mar79|21Apr79|08Sep79] 7(2) 26 2783

1318. THE STYLISTICS The Stylistics
[18Dec71|18Mar72|02Sep72] 23(1) 38 2783

1319. LABOUR OF LOVE UB40
[26Nov83|05Nov88|18Feb89] 14(1) 63 2783

1320. PRELUDE Deodato
[20Jan73|07Apr73|14Jul73] 3(1) 26 2782

1321. MELISSA ETHERIDGE Melissa Etheridge
[18Jun88|13May89|09Sep89] 22(1) 65 2781

1322. WE ARE THE WORLD USA For Africa
[20Apr85|27Apr85|14Sep85] 1(3) 22 2778

Rank. Title Act
[Enter|Peak|Exit] Peak(Wks) TotWks Score

1323. STRAIGHT OUTTA COMPTON N.W.A.
[04Mar89|15Apr89|15Sep90] 37(3) 81 2777

1324. STREET LIFE The Crusaders
[09Jun79|22Sep79|01Mar80] 18(1) 39 2774

1325. SITTIN' IN
Kenny Loggins With Jim Messina
[18Mar72|14Apr73|28Sep74] 70(1) 113 2771

1326. MIDNIGHT RIDE
Paul Revere & The Raiders
[11Jun66|06Aug66|01Apr67] 9(1) 43 2770

1327. ONCE BITTEN Great White
[18Jul87|10Oct87|16Jul88] 23(2) 53 2769

1328. HOW GLAD I AM Nancy Wilson
[05Sep64|14Nov64|03Apr65] 4(2) 31 2768

1329. FALCO 3 Falco
[01Mar86|26Apr86|30Aug86] 3(1) 27 2764

1330. SUPER TROUPER ABBA
[13Dec80|28Feb81|29Aug81] 17(3) 38 2763

1331. SO FULL OF LOVE The O'Jays
[29Apr78|24Jun78|04Nov78] 6(2) 28 2763

1332. I'VE GOT SO MUCH TO GIVE Barry White
[21Apr73|16Jun73|29Jun74] 16(2) 63 2762

1333. TO OUR CHILDREN'S CHILDREN'S CHILDREN The Moody Blues
[10Jan70|07Feb70|07Nov70] 14(3) 44 2762

1334. JUDITH Judy Collins
[12Apr75|14Jun75|29Nov75] 17(1) 34 2761

1335. WISH IT WOULD RAIN The Temptations
[25May68|17Aug68|01Mar69] 13(2) 41 2761

1336. RUFUSIZED Rufus And Chaka Khan
[04Jan75|01Mar75|14Jun75] 7(1) 24 2759

1337. AL GREEN EXPLORES YOUR MIND
Al Green
[23Nov74|04Jan75|05Jul75] 15(1) 33 2759

1338. HERE WHERE THERE IS LOVE
Dionne Warwick
[07Jan67|12Aug67|06Apr68] 18(2) 66 2757

1339. IT MUST BE HIM Vikki Carr
[21Oct67|03Feb68|07Sep68] 12(2) 47 2756

1340. SEDAKA'S BACK Neil Sedaka
[07Dec74|08Mar75|06Mar76] 23(1) 62 2755

1341. GEORGIA SATELLITES
The Georgia Satellites
[01Nov86|28Feb87|15Aug87] 5(1) 42 2752

1342. TARKUS Emerson, Lake & Palmer
[03Jul71|17Jul71|25Dec71] 9(2) 26 2751

1343. I FEEL A SONG
Gladys Knight & The Pips
[16Nov74|28Dec74|11Oct75] 17(3) 41 2750

1344. INVASION OF YOUR PRIVACY Ratt
[29Jun85|27Jul85|12Apr86] 7(1) 42 2750

1345. BROTHER TO BROTHER Gino Vannelli
[30Sep78|16Dec78|26May79] 13(3) 35 2750

1346. BLUE SKY-NIGHT THUNDER
Michael Murphey
[22Feb75|19Jul75|08Nov75] 18(1) 38 2744

1347. LOVE STINKS The J. Geils Band
[09Feb80|19Apr80|27Mar82] 18(2) 42 2737

1348. HONEYSUCKLE ROSE (SOUNDTRACK)
Willie Nelson & Family
[06Sep80|04Oct80|09May81] 11(3) 36 2735

1349. TRASH Alice Cooper
[12Aug89|18Nov89|02Jun90] 20(2) 43 2735

1350. BENEFIT Jethro Tull
[09May70|06Jun70|13Feb71] 11(2) 41 2733

1351. TOM Tom Jones
[09May70|30May70|31Oct70] 6(2) 26 2733

1352. MAME Original Cast
[02Jul66|24Sep66|30Sep67] 23(2) 66 2733

1353. GOLDEN GREATS
Gary Lewis And The Playboys
[22Oct66|31Dec66|02Sep67] 10(4) 46 2733

1354. INSEPARABLE Natalie Cole
[30Aug75|29Nov75|18Sep76] 18(1) 56 2731

1355. BLOW BY BLOW Jeff Beck
[12Apr75|07Jun75|27Sep75] 4(1) 25 2731

1356. SMOOTH TALK
Evelyn "Champagne" King
[27May78|23Sep78|16Jun79] 14(2) 45 2726

Rank. Title Act
[Enter|Peak|Exit] Peak(Wks) TotWks Score

1357. GOIN' OUT OF MY HEAD The Lettermen
[13Apr68|22Jun68|08Feb69] 13(1) 44 2723

1358. THE BEST OF AL HIRT Al Hirt
[30Jan65|10Apr65|20Nov65] 13(1) 43 2719

1359. WINCHESTER CATHEDRAL Lawrence Welk
[03Dec66|25Feb67|09Sep67] 12(2) 41 2716

1360. STONEY END Barbra Streisand
[20Feb71|13Mar71|04Sep71] 10(4) 29 2716

1361. 'GET YER YA-YA'S OUT!'
The Rolling Stones
[17Oct70|24Oct70|20Mar71] 6(2) 23 2715

1362. ENLIGHTENED ROGUES
The Allman Brothers Band
[17Mar79|14Apr79|25Aug79] 9(4) 24 2714

1363. MORE HITS BY THE SUPREMES
The Supremes
[21Aug65|16Oct65|30Apr66] 6(2) 37 2713

1364. EARGASM Johnnie Taylor
[13Mar76|24Apr76|18Sep76] 5(2) 28 2713

1365. SINATRA AT THE SANDS Frank Sinatra
With Count Basie And The Orchestra
[20Aug66|15Oct66|17Jun67] 9(1) 44 2712

1366. BOMBS AWAY DREAM BABIES
John Stewart
[19May79|25Aug79|24Nov79] 10(1) 28 2711

1367. FOOL FOR THE CITY Foghat
[11Oct75|03Apr76|02Oct76] 23(2) 52 2711

1368. GHOSTBUSTERS Soundtrack
[07Jul84|18Aug84|23Feb85] 6(3) 34 2711

1369. GREATEST HITS Seals & Crofts
[15Nov75|03Jan76|20Nov76] 11(2) 54 2708

1370. DANCE!...YA KNOW IT! Bobby Brown
[02Dec89|17Feb90|14Jul90] 9(3) 33 2707

1371. MOTHER LODE Loggins & Messina
[09Nov74|28Dec74|24May75] 8(1) 29 2707

1372. FUNKENTELECHY VS. THE PLACEBO SYNDROME Parliament
[24Dec77|18Mar78|12Aug78] 13(1) 34 2705

1373. THE CRAZY WORLD OF ARTHUR BROWN
The Crazy World Of Arthur Brown
[07Sep68|16Nov68|15Feb69] 7(2) 24 2702

1374. HAPPY HEART Andy Williams
[17May69|14Jun69|18Oct69] 9(2) 23 2702

1375. GOOD TROUBLE REO Speedwagon
[10Jul82|07Aug82|18Dec82] 7(9) 24 2702

1376. WAR LIVE! War
[23Mar74|11May74|16Nov74] 13(1) 35 2702

1377. THE SECRET OF ASSOCIATION
Paul Young
[25May85|17Aug85|15Mar86] 19(6) 43 2699

1378. BEFORE THE FLOOD Bob Dylan/The Band
[13Jul74|03Aug74|16Nov74] 3(2) 19 2697

1379. BARBRA JOAN STREISAND
Barbra Streisand
[18Sep71|06Nov71|11Mar72] 11(2) 26 2697

1380. REGGATTA DE BLANC The Police
[03Nov79|22Dec79|07Apr84] 25(2) 100 2694

1381. MIDNIGHT LOVE Marvin Gaye
[20Nov82|18Dec82|09Jun84] 7(5) 41 2691

1382. THE PLASTIC ONO BAND - LIVE PEACE IN TORONTO 1969 The Plastic Ono Band
[10Jan70|07Feb70|15Aug70] 10(2) 32 2690

1383. TRUTH Jeff Beck
[24Aug68|16Nov68|14Jun69] 15(1) 33 2689

1384. R.E.M. NO. 5: DOCUMENT R.E.M.
[26Sep87|07Nov87|07May88] 10(1) 33 2688

1385. FIRST UNDER THE WIRE Little River Band
[04Aug79|29Sep79|15Mar80] 10(3) 33 2687

1386. LIFE IS A SONG WORTH SINGING
Teddy Pendergrass
[01Jul78|19Aug78|24Feb79] 11(2) 35 2687

1387. HERE YOU COME AGAIN Dolly Parton
[29Oct77|21Jan78|16Sep78] 20(2) 47 2682

1388. A PRIVATE HEAVEN Sheena Easton
[20Oct84|02Feb85|15Jun85] 15(2) 35 2682

1389. AUTOBAHN Kraftwerk
[08Feb75|03May75|05Jul75] 5(1) 22 2679

1390. GOLD & PLATINUM Lynyrd Skynyrd
[15Dec79|09Feb80|07Mar81] 12(2) 65 2678

Rank. Title Act
[Enter|Peak|Exit] Peak(Wks) TotWks Score

1391. WITH A LOT O' SOUL The Temptations
[12Aug67|30Sep67|13Apr68] 7(1) 36 2677

1392. SOULFUL STRUT Young-Holt Unlimited
[04Jan69|08Feb69|26Jul69] 9(2) 30 2672

1393. ANYTIME, ANYPLACE, ANYWHERE
The Rossington Collins Band
[12Jul80|20Sep80|24Jan81] 13(3) 29 2669

1394. SOUL & INSPIRATION
The Righteous Brothers
[30Apr66|21May66|03Dec66] 7(2) 32 2668

1395. EAZY-DUZ-IT Eazy-E
[10Dec88|20May89|25Aug90] 41(1) 90 2665

1396. GREATEST HITS War
[04Sep76|25Sep76|22Jan77] 6(3) 21 2664

1397. MARVIN GAYE LIVE! Marvin Gaye
[13Jul74|07Sep74|18Jan75] 8(2) 28 2663

1398. COMES A TIME Neil Young
[21Oct78|09Dec78|12May79] 7(2) 30 2660

1399. THE YOUNG RASCALS The Young Rascals
[07May66|23Jul66|27Jul68] 15(1) 84 2658

1400. A WOMAN NEEDS LOVE
Ray Parker Jr. & Raydio
[18Apr81|20Jun81|10Oct81] 13(2) 26 2655

1401. FELICIANO/10 TO 23 Jose Feliciano
[05Jul69|02Aug69|07Mar70] 16(2) 36 2654

1402. FRESH CREAM Cream
[13May67|31Aug68|08Feb69] 39(1) 92 2650

1403. PORTRAIT OF DONNY Donny Osmond
[27May72|22Jul72|27Jan73] 6(1) 36 2647

1404. NATALIE Natalie Cole
[29May76|17Jul76|18Dec76] 13(1) 30 2646

1405. BLACK SABBATH Black Sabbath
[29Aug70|26Dec70|20Nov71] 23(2) 65 2645

1406. FAIR WARNING Van Halen
[30May81|13Jun81|31Oct81] 5(3) 23 2642

1407. NIGHTS ARE FOREVER
England Dan & John Ford Coley
[21Aug76|13Nov76|19Mar77] 17(1) 31 2640

1408. GATHER ME Melanie
[13Nov71|12Feb72|13May72] 15(1) 27 2640

1409. ANGEL CLARE Art Garfunkel
[29Sep73|10Nov73|16Mar74] 5(1) 25 2638

1410. ARENA Duran Duran
[01Dec84|05Jan85|08Jun85] 4(3) 28 2637

1411. MASTERPIECE The Temptations
[10Mar73|21Apr73|15Sep73] 7(2) 28 2636

1412. STAGE FRIGHT The Band
[05Sep70|03Oct70|30Jan71] 5(1) 22 2635

1413. BORN LATE Shaun Cassidy
[26Nov77|14Jan78|16Sep78] 6(3) 37 2635

1414. THE ALLNIGHTER Glenn Frey
[14Jul84|29Jun85|25Jan86] 22(2) 65 2635

1415. JACKSON 5 GREATEST HITS The Jacksons
[01Jan72|05Feb72|07Oct72] 12(1) 41 2634

1416. LOVE SONG FOR JEFFREY Helen Reddy
[20Apr74|21Sep74|14Dec74] 11(1) 35 2630

1417. SHUT DOWN, VOLUME 2 The Beach Boys
[11Apr64|23May64|26Dec64] 13(2) 38 2630

1418. SINATRA'S SINATRA Frank Sinatra
[05Oct63|30Nov63|25Jul64] 8(2) 43 2630

1419. RHYTHM OF THE NIGHT DeBarge
[23Mar85|01Jun85|15Feb86] 19(2) 48 2623

1420. TEMPTATIONS LIVE! The Temptations
[01Apr67|20May67|16Mar68] 10(1) 51 2619

1421. ALL I EVER NEED IS YOU Sonny & Cher
[26Feb72|29Apr72|09Sep72] 14(2) 29 2618

1422. COMING AROUND AGAIN Carly Simon
[25Apr87|19Sep87|11Jun88] 25(2) 60 2616

1423. SIT DOWN YOUNG STRANGER
Gordon Lightfoot
[30May70|06Mar71|21Aug71] 12(2) 37 2614

1424. RAGS TO RUFUS Rufus
[29Jun74|21Sep74|18Jan75] 4(1) 30 2614

1425. TALES FROM TOPOGRAPHIC OCEANS Yes
[02Feb74|09Mar74|03Aug74] 6(2) 27 2614

1426. SLIP OF THE TONGUE Whitesnake
[25Nov89|16Dec89|14Jul90] 10(1) 34 2611

1427. THE BYRDS' GREATEST HITS The Byrds
[02Sep67|14Oct67|16Mar68] 6(3) 29 2607

Rank. Title Act
[Enter|Peak|Exit] Peak(Wks) TotWks Score

1428. THOROUGHLY MODERN MILLIE
Soundtrack
[15Apr67|03Jun67|09Mar68] 16(2) 48 2607

1429. NANCY & LEE
Nancy Sinatra & Lee Hazlewood
[13Apr68|15Jun68|08Feb69] 13(1) 44 2606

1430. FOUR TOPS LIVE! Four Tops
[17Dec66|11Mar67|07Oct67] 17(1) 43 2605

1431. NIGHTBIRDS Labelle
[21Dec74|22Mar75|28Jun75] 7(3) 28 2605

1432. GILBERT O'SULLIVAN-HIMSELF
Gilbert O'Sullivan
[12Aug72|30Sep72|24Feb73] 9(2) 29 2604

1433. TOO YOUNG Donny Osmond
[22Jul72|23Sep72|10Feb73] 11(2) 30 2602

1434. DEAN MARTIN'S GREATEST HITS! VOL. 1
Dean Martin
[01Jun68|17Aug68|22Feb69] 26(1) 39 2602

1435. SELF PORTRAIT Bob Dylan
[04Jul70|25Jul70|28Nov70] 4(2) 22 2600

1436. I HEAR A SYMPHONY The Supremes
[19Mar66|30Apr66|26Aug67] 8(3) 55 2599

1437. FRUID PINK Frijid Pink
[24Jan70|04Apr70|15Aug70] 11(4) 30 2597

1438. AMERICAN GIGOLO Soundtrack
[01Mar80|26Apr80|16Aug80] 7(3) 25 2595

1439. BABY DON'T GET HOOKED ON ME
Mac Davis
[16Sep72|25Nov72|22Feb75] 11(2) 44 2594

1440. ARETHA FRANKLIN: SOUL '69
Aretha Franklin
[15Feb69|08Mar69|04Oct69] 15(2) 32 2593

1441. SUN GODDESS Ramsey Lewis
[28Dec74|29Mar75|19Jul75] 12(1) 30 2592

1442. DAD LOVES HIS WORK James Taylor
[21Mar81|02May81|22Aug81] 10(3) 23 2592

1443. "THE DEVIL MADE ME BUY THIS DRESS"
Flip Wilson
[28Feb70|27Jun70|06Mar71] 17(1) 54 2590

1444. LET'S KEEP IT THAT WAY Anne Murray
[04Mar78|25Nov78|26May79] 12(1) 52 2589

1445. MIKE + THE MECHANICS
Mike + The Mechanics
[23Nov85|15Mar86|22Nov86] 26(6) 53 2589

1446. GOODNIGHT VIENNA Ringo Starr
[30Nov74|11Jan75|17May75] 8(2) 25 2581

1447. ON TIME Grand Funk Railroad
[11Oct69|06Dec69|24Oct70] 27(1) 55 2581

1448. GO WEST Village People
[14Apr79|19May79|01Sep79] 8(3) 21 2579

1449. BACK STABBERS The O'Jays
[09Sep72|04Nov72|07Jul73] 10(2) 44 2577

1450. PICKIN' ON NASHVILLE
The Kentucky Headhunters
[16Dec89|19May90|26Oct91] 41(1) 96 2571

1451. VICTORY The Jacksons
[21Jul84|04Aug84|09Feb85] 4(3) 30 2571

1452. JUST ONCE IN MY LIFE...
The Righteous Brothers
[29May65|14Aug65|05Mar66] 9(3) 41 2570

1453. JERMAINE JACKSON Jermaine Jackson
[19May84|16Jun84|20Apr85] 19(3) 49 2569

1454. TEN YEARS OF GOLD Kenny Rogers
[04Feb78|01Apr78|21Feb81] 33(2) 104 2566

1455. CAROLINA DREAMS
The Marshall Tucker Band
[26Feb77|28May77|29Oct77] 23(1) 36 2565

1456. ALL IN THE FAMILY TV Soundtrack
[20Nov71|15Jan72|15Apr72] 8(1) 22 2564

1457. THE BEST OF LUTHER VANDROSS...THE BEST OF LOVE Luther Vandross
[04Nov89|27Jan90|20Oct90] 26(2) 51 2564

1458. IT'S A BEAUTIFUL DAY
It's A Beautiful Day
[14Jun69|15Nov69|10Oct70] 47(2) 70 2563

1459. THE WHO BY NUMBERS The Who
[25Oct75|29Nov75|10Apr76] 8(2) 25 2563

1460. NEBRASKA Bruce Springsteen
[09Oct82|30Oct82|16Feb85] 3(4) 29 2563

Rank. Title Act
[Enter|Peak|Exit] Peak(Wks) TotWks Score

1461. PHOENIX Grand Funk Railroad
[14Oct72|02Dec72|14Apr73] 7(2) 27 2563

1462. CHILDREN OF SANCHEZ Chuck Mangione
[23Sep78|25Nov78|21Jul79] 14(2) 44 2562

1463. STONE GON' Barry White
[17Nov73|09Feb74|27Jul74] 20(1) 37 2562

1464. YOU LIGHT UP MY LIFE Debby Boone
[29Oct77|24Dec77|08Jul78] 6(3) 37 2560

1465. SONGS IN THE ATTIC Billy Joel
[03Oct81|17Oct81|03Apr82] 8(3) 27 2554

1466. MAKING MOVIES Dire Straits
[15Nov80|27Dec80|13Jun81] 19(3) 31 2553

1467. TEMPTIN' TEMPTATIONS The Temptations
[27Nov65|05Feb66|06Aug66] 11(1) 37 2552

1468. BOOGIE WITH CANNED HEAT
Canned Heat
[24Feb68|26Oct68|15Feb69] 16(2) 52 2552

1469. PICTURE BOOK Simply Red
[19Apr86|12Jul86|06Jun87] 16(3) 60 2549

1470. ENGELBERT Engelbert Humperdinck
[22Mar69|10May69|04Apr70] 12(2) 33 2547

1471. EXCITABLE BOY Warren Zevon
[25Feb78|13May78|02Sep78] 8(2) 28 2546

1472. BLOODSHOT The J. Geils Band
[28Apr73|16Jun73|23Feb74] 10(1) 44 2546

1473. MORNING DANCE Spyro Gyra
[07Apr79|15Sep79|12Jan80] 27(3) 41 2545

1474. JULIO Julio Iglesias
[02Apr83|21May83|08Dec84] 32(1) 89 2545

1475. THE BEST OF JIM REEVES Jim Reeves
[08Aug64|14Nov64|29May65] 9(1) 43 2545

1476. TRIO
Dolly Parton, Linda Ronstadt, Emmylou Harris
[28Mar87|02May87|05Mar88] 6(1) 48 2543

1477. ROCK A LITTLE Stevie Nicks
[14Dec85|08Feb86|09Aug86] 12(1) 35 2539

1478. RASTAMAN VIBRATION
Bob Marley And The Wailers
[15May76|03Jul76|09Oct76] 8(2) 22 2535

1479. WELCOME BACK, MY FRIENDS, TO THE SHOW THAT NEVER ENDS - LADIES AND GENTLEMEN Emerson, Lake & Palmer
[07Sep74|26Oct74|15Feb75] 4(1) 24 2531

1480. CREEDENCE GOLD
Creedence Clearwater Revival
[02Dec72|17Feb73|11Aug73] 15(1) 37 2531

1481. THE THIN RED LINE Glass Tiger
[19Jul86|07Feb87|04Jul87] 27(2) 51 2531

1482. THE SHADOW OF YOUR SMILE
Johnny Mathis
[02Apr66|25Jun66|18Feb67] 9(1) 45 2530

1483. FOUR TOPS REACH OUT Four Tops
[12Aug67|16Sep67|21Sep68] 11(4) 59 2530

1484. DREAM POLICE Cheap Trick
[06Oct79|27Oct79|22Mar80] 6(2) 25 2528

1485. CRAZY FROM THE HEAT David Lee Roth
[23Feb85|16Mar85|05Oct85] 15(4) 33 2528

1486. GREATEST HITS, VOL. 2
Smokey Robinson & The Miracles
[24Feb68|23Mar68|28Dec68] 7(2) 44 2524

1487. PHASE-III The Osmonds
[29Jan72|11Mar72|23Sep72] 10(1) 35 2523

1488. MIGHTY LOVE Spinners
[16Mar74|25May74|09Nov74] 16(1) 35 2520

1489. SONGS FROM THE WOOD Jethro Tull
[05Mar77|14May77|30Jul77] 8(2) 22 2518

1490. ANY LOVE Luther Vandross
[22Oct88|19Nov88|03Jun89] 9(1) 33 2513

1491. THE HISSING OF SUMMER LAWNS
Joni Mitchell
[06Dec75|03Jan76|27Mar76] 4(3) 17 2504

1492. THE BEATLES AT THE HOLLYWOOD BOWL
The Beatles
[21May77|11Jun77|10Sep77] 2(2) 17 2503

1493. THE POINTER SISTERS The Pointer Sisters
[23Jun73|27Oct73|02Mar74] 13(1) 37 2503

1494. THAT WAS THE YEAR THAT WAS
Tom Lehrer
[06Nov65|08Jan66|22Oct66] 18(1) 51 2499

Rank. Title Act
[Enter|Peak|Exit] Peak(Wks) TotWks Score

1495. TIME AND TIDE Basia
[20Feb88|26Nov88|05Aug89] 36(1) 77 2498

1496. THE TEMPTATIONS IN A MELLOW MOOD
The Temptations
[23Dec67|16Mar68|19Oct68] 13(1) 44 2492

1497. ARETHA'S GOLD Aretha Franklin
[19Jul69|16Aug69|28Feb70] 18(1) 33 2486

1498. ROSE GARDEN Lynn Anderson
[09Jan71|27Feb71|21Aug71] 19(3) 33 2483

1499. CURTIS/LIVE! Curtis Mayfield
[29May71|03Jul71|12Feb72] 21(1) 38 2481

1500. DARK HORSE George Harrison
[28Dec74|25Jan75|19Apr75] 4(1) 17 2480

1501. SOUL SEARCHING Average White Band
[17Jul76|28Aug76|19Feb77] 9(1) 32 2478

1502. THE LAST WALTZ Engelbert Humperdinck
[23Dec67|03Feb68|07Feb70] 10(2) 60 2478

1503. SURFING WITH THE ALIEN Joe Satriani
[21Nov87|30Apr88|22Apr89] 29(4) 75 2477

1504. DIAMOND DOGS David Bowie
[15Jun74|20Jul74|30Nov74] 5(2) 25 2476

1505. THE LEXICON OF LOVE ABC
[25Sep82|29Jan83|18Jun83] 24(10) 39 2473

1506. SOMETHING TO LOVE L.T.D.
[13Aug77|14Jan78|01Apr78] 21(2) 34 2471

1507. GOOD MORNING STARSHINE Oliver
[02Aug69|04Oct69|18Apr70] 19(1) 38 2471

1508. SHOOT OUT AT THE FANTASY FACTORY
Traffic
[03Feb73|31Mar73|18Aug73] 6(1) 29 2471

1509. CHANGESONEBOWIE David Bowie
[19Jun76|17Jul76|12Mar77] 10(1) 39 2467

1510. WELCOME TO MY WORLD Dean Martin
[02Sep67|25Nov67|27Jul68] 20(1) 48 2465

1511. THIRDS The James Gang
[17Apr71|12Jun71|06Nov71] 27(2) 30 2465

1512. IZITSO Cat Stevens
[21May77|02Jul77|22Oct77] 7(2) 23 2460

1513. BLUE Joni Mitchell
[03Jul71|31Jul71|08Jan72] 15(2) 28 2459

1514. TED NUGENT Ted Nugent
[22Nov75|10Apr76|26Feb77] 28(2) 62 2458

1515. HIGH ADVENTURE Kenny Loggins
[25Sep82|23Oct82|23Jul83] 13(3) 44 2457

1516. BEVERLY HILLS COP II Soundtrack
[13Jun87|08Aug87|05Dec87] 8(1) 26 2457

1517. AS THE BAND TURNS Atlantic Starr
[18May85|29Mar86|30Aug86] 17(2) 68 2457

1518. GOT LIVE IF YOU WANT IT!
The Rolling Stones
[17Dec66|21Jan67|11Nov67] 6(2) 48 2455

1519. THE ICE MAN COMETH Jerry Butler
[04Jan69|17May69|22Nov69] 29(1) 47 2455

1520. ALL FOUR ONE The Motels
[24Apr82|14Aug82|29Jan83] 16(2) 41 2453

1521. PAINT YOUR WAGON Soundtrack
[25Oct69|13Dec69|28Nov70] 28(2) 56 2453

1522. WORLD WIDE LIVE Scorpions
[13Jul85|28Sep85|03May86] 14(1) 43 2451

1523. ROLL ON Alabama
[11Feb84|31Mar84|13Apr85] 21(2) 62 2447

1524. THE CROSSING Big Country
[24Sep83|05Nov83|07Jul84] 18(2) 42 2443

1525. NEW MORNING Bob Dylan
[14Nov70|05Dec70|17Apr71] 7(1) 23 2443

1526. MY LOVE FORGIVE ME Robert Goulet
[26Dec64|27Feb65|10Jul65] 5(2) 29 2442

1527. WORKS, VOLUME 1
Emerson, Lake & Palmer
[09Apr77|21May77|01Oct77] 12(2) 26 2442

1528. 15 BIG ONES The Beach Boys
[17Jul76|28Aug76|15Jan77] 8(1) 27 2437

1529. THE NIGHT I FELL IN LOVE
Luther Vandross
[06Apr85|15Jun85|26Apr86] 19(3) 56 2435

1530. GENTLE ON MY MIND Dean Martin
[04Jan69|01Mar69|21Jun69] 14(1) 25 2434

1531. CLOSING THE GAP Michael Parks
[08Nov69|14Mar70|19Sep70] 35(1) 46 2433

Rank. Title Act
[Enter|Peak|Exit] Peak(Wks) TotWks Score

1532. SON OF SCHMILSSON Nilsson
[22Jul72|23Sep72|17Feb73] 12(2) 31 2432

1533. DOWN TWO THEN LEFT Boz Scaggs
[10Dec77|14Jan78|13May78] 11(2) 23 2430

1534. BUSTIN' OUT OF L SEVEN Rick James
[10Feb79|24Mar79|11Aug79] 16(3) 27 2430

1535. STONES Neil Diamond
[13Nov71|11Dec71|29Apr72] 11(2) 25 2428

1536. BEBE LE STRANGE Heart
[08Mar80|22Mar80|02Aug80] 5(2) 22 2426

1537. MAKE IT EASY ON YOURSELF
Burt Bacharach
[28Jun69|02Aug69|01May71] 51(2) 87 2425

1538. WILD IN THE STREETS Soundtrack
[06Jul68|26Oct68|08Feb69] 12(2) 32 2424

1539. THE ROARING SILENCE
Manfred Mann's Earth Band
[25Sep76|12Mar77|04Jun77] 10(2) 37 2423

1540. LOVE TO LOVE YOU BABY Donna Summer
[01Nov75|14Feb76|22May76] 11(2) 30 2422

1541. VILLAGE PEOPLE Village People
[01Oct77|29Apr78|19May79] 54(2) 86 2422

1542. DIRTY WORK The Rolling Stones
[12Apr86|03May86|27Sep86] 4(2) 25 2422

1543. ACTUALLY Pet Shop Boys
[03Oct87|21Nov87|06Aug88] 25(1) 45 2421

1544. GOING FOR THE ONE Yes
[30Jul77|01Oct77|17Dec77] 8(2) 21 2421

1545. SHEER HEART ATTACK Queen
[14Dec74|10May75|19Jul75] 12(2) 32 2420

1546. CANDLES IN THE RAIN Melanie
[09May70|04Jul70|16Jan71] 17(3) 37 2416

1547. RISQUE Chic
[25Aug79|22Sep79|15Dec79] 5(2) 17 2414

1548. B, S & T; 4 Blood, Sweat & Tears
[10Jul71|21Aug71|11Dec71] 10(2) 23 2413

1549. LIFE IS...TOO SHORT Too Short
[25Feb89|20May89|18Aug90] 37(2) 78 2412

1550. RHINESTONE COWBOY Glen Campbell
[09Aug75|18Oct75|28Feb76] 17(2) 30 2409

1551. DYNASTY KISS
[23Jun79|21Jul79|08Dec79] 9(3) 25 2407

1552. MOONTAN Golden Earring
[04May74|10Aug74|16Nov74] 12(2) 29 2405

1553. MASTERJAM Rufus And Chaka Khan
[17Nov79|22Dec79|10May80] 14(3) 26 2405

1554. FLOATERS The Floaters
[25Jun77|24Sep77|10Dec77] 10(2) 25 2403

1555. KENNY LOGGINS ALIVE Kenny Loggins
[04Oct80|15Nov80|02May81] 11(2) 31 2402

1556. BARRY WHITE SINGS FOR SOMEONE YOU LOVE Barry White
[17Sep77|12Nov77|01Jul78] 8(2) 33 2402

1557. LATE FOR THE SKY Jackson Browne
[12Oct74|30Nov74|26Apr75] 14(2) 29 2401

1558. FUNNY LADY (SOUNDTRACK)
Barbra Streisand
[29Mar75|10May75|13Sep75] 6(1) 25 2399

1559. GIVE THE PEOPLE WHAT THEY WANT
The Kinks
[12Sep81|17Oct81|15May82] 15(2) 36 2399

1560. THE TURNING POINT John Mayall
[20Sep69|08Nov69|03Oct70] 32(2) 55 2398

1561. GETTIN' READY The Temptations
[09Jul66|24Sep66|04Mar67] 12(2) 35 2397

1562. ONE HEARTBEAT Smokey Robinson
[28Mar87|20Jun87|30Apr88] 26(2) 58 2397

1563. SUPER SESSION
Mike Bloomfield/Al Kooper/Steve Stills
[31Aug68|07Dec68|17May69] 12(1) 37 2396

1564. NEVER TOO MUCH Luther Vandross
[19Sep81|14Nov81|22May82] 19(2) 36 2394

1565. BURN Deep Purple
[02Mar74|20Apr74|21Sep74] 9(1) 30 2392

1566. JIM NABORS SINGS LOVE ME WITH ALL YOUR HEART Jim Nabors
[15Oct66|31Dec66|07Feb70] 24(2) 56 2391

1567. I CAN STAND A LITTLE RAIN Joe Cocker
[24Aug74|26Oct74|14Jun75] 11(1) 36 2387

Rank. Title Act
[Enter|Peak|Exit] Peak(Wks) TotWks Score

1568. ATLANTIC CROSSING Rod Stewart
[06Sep75|01Nov75|08Jan77] 9(1) 29 2387

1569. BLESSED ARE... Joan Baez
[18Sep71|23Oct71|19Feb72] 11(2) 23 2387

1570. STAND UP Jethro Tull
[11Oct69|15Nov69|11Jul70] 20(1) 40 2387

1571. YOU LIGHT UP MY LIFE Johnny Mathis
[01Apr78|03Jun78|09Sep78] 9(3) 24 2385

1572. BLACK SABBATH, VOL. 4 Black Sabbath
[21Oct72|23Dec72|19May73] 13(1) 31 2382

1573. BARK Jefferson Airplane
[18Sep71|09Oct71|05Feb72] 11(2) 21 2382

1574. THE GODFATHER Soundtrack
[08Apr72|01Jul72|02Dec72] 21(2) 35 2381

1575. A MAN AND HIS MUSIC Frank Sinatra
[25Dec65|19Feb66|30Jul66] 9(2) 32 2377

1576. CITY LIFE The Blackbyrds
[22Nov75|22May76|21Aug76] 16(1) 40 2376

1577. BLIND MAN'S ZOO 10,000 Maniacs
[03Jun89|29Jul89|09Dec89] 13(1) 28 2375

1578. 11/17/1970 Elton John
[29May71|10Jul71|30Oct71] 11(1) 23 2371

1579. DRAGON FLY Jefferson Starship
[26Oct74|21Dec74|17Jan76] 11(1) 37 2371

1580. MALO Malo
[12Feb72|13May72|09Sep72] 14(1) 31 2371

1581. WHERE THERE'S SMOKE
Smokey Robinson
[30Jun79|01Mar80|17May80] 17(2) 47 2370

1582. GO ALL THE WAY The Isley Brothers
[19Apr80|17May80|13Sep80] 8(4) 22 2369

1583. BETTE MIDLER Bette Midler
[08Dec73|19Jan74|08Jun74] 6(1) 27 2369

1584. THE OSMONDS "LIVE" The Osmonds
[17Jun72|29Jul72|30Dec72] 13(2) 29 2368

1585. LYNYRD SKYNYRD (PRONOUNCED LEH-NERD SKIN-NERD) Lynyrd Skynyrd
[22Sep73|22Feb75|06Sep80] 27(2) 79 2368

1586. NON-STOP EROTIC CABARET Soft Cell
[30Jan82|07Aug82|06Nov82] 22(1) 41 2367

1587. MORE HOT ROCKS (BIG HITS & FAZED COOKIES) The Rolling Stones
[30Dec72|17Feb73|14Jul73] 9(3) 29 2367

1588. GOOD MORNING, VIETNAM Soundtrack
[06Feb88|26Mar88|01Oct88] 10(2) 35 2363

1589. (REMEMBER ME) I'M THE ONE WHO LOVES YOU Dean Martin
[28Aug65|13Nov65|21May66] 12(1) 39 2362

1590. ERIC CARMEN Eric Carmen
[15Nov75|20Mar76|30Oct76] 21(2) 51 2361

1591. GIRL HAPPY (SOUNDTRACK) Elvis Presley
[17Apr65|12Jun65|13Nov65] 8(2) 31 2361

1592. THE HUNGRY YEARS Neil Sedaka
[11Oct75|27Dec75|15May76] 16(2) 32 2358

1593. THE SEEDS OF LOVE Tears For Fears
[07Oct89|28Oct89|26May90] 8(3) 34 2355

1594. WE MUST BELIEVE IN MAGIC
Crystal Gayle
[03Sep77|10Dec77|29Apr78] 12(2) 35 2354

1595. NEW AND IMPROVED Spinners
[14Dec74|08Feb75|07Jun75] 9(1) 26 2351

1596. SPECIAL FORCES 38 Special
[29May82|17Jul82|12Mar83] 10(3) 42 2351

1597. ALL THAT JAZZ Breathe
[04Jun88|24Dec88|20May89] 34(3) 51 2350

1598. HOUSTON Dean Martin
[20Nov65|15Jan66|09Jul66] 11(1) 34 2347

1599. HERE'S TO FUTURE DAYS
Thompson Twins
[19Oct85|22Feb86|14Jun86] 20(1) 35 2347

1600. FROM MEMPHIS TO VEGAS / FROM VEGAS TO MEMPHIS Elvis Presley
[29Nov69|27Dec69|09May70] 12(3) 24 2345

1601. WELCOME TO THE LBJ RANCH!
Various Artists
[27Nov65|18Dec65|14May66] 3(3) 25 2345

1602. CENTRAL HEATING Heatwave
[22Apr78|03Jun78|14Oct78] 10(2) 26 2341

Rank. Title Act
[Enter|Peak|Exit] Peak(Wks) TotWks Score

1603. SURVIVAL The O'Jays
[26Apr75|28Jun75|04Oct75] 11(1) 24 2341

1604. FOUR WHEEL DRIVE
Bachman-Turner Overdrive
[31May75|28Jun75|25Oct75] 5(2) 22 2340

1605. VITAL IDOL Billy Idol
[10Oct87|14Nov87|23Apr88] 10(1) 29 2338

1606. HOT STREETS Chicago
[21Oct78|02Dec78|05May79] 12(1) 29 2337

1607. SLEEPING WITH THE PAST Elton John
[16Sep89|07Oct89|15Sep90] 23(1) 53 2337

1608. LIVE AT THE COPA The Temptations
[04Jan69|01Mar69|14Jun69] 15(1) 24 2337

1609. STOP MAKING SENSE Talking Heads
[22Sep84|13Oct84|20Dec86] 41(4) 118 2336

1610. BLOODROCK 2 Bloodrock
[07Nov70|13Feb71|17Jul71] 21(3) 37 2334

1611. JE M'APPELLE BARBRA Barbra Streisand
[19Nov66|07Jan67|03Jun67] 5(2) 29 2334

1612. THE SESAME STREET BOOK & RECORD
TV Soundtrack
[25Jul70|03Oct70|22Jan72] 23(1) 54 2333

1613. I FEEL FOR YOU Chaka Khan
[20Oct84|01Dec84|21Sep85] 14(3) 49 2332

1614. LEON LIVE Leon Russell
[07Jul73|11Aug73|29Dec73] 9(1) 26 2331

1615. FOOLISH BEHAVIOUR Rod Stewart
[06Dec80|27Dec80|25Apr81] 12(5) 21 2330

1616. BEALTITUDE: RESPECT YOURSELF
The Staple Singers
[26Feb72|03Jun72|04Nov72] 19(1) 37 2328

1617. TEDDY PENDERGRASS
Teddy Pendergrass
[19Mar77|28May77|12Nov77] 17(3) 35 2327

1618. NEITHER ONE OF US
Gladys Knight & The Pips
[10Mar73|19May73|29Sep73] 9(1) 30 2326

1619. TODAY, TOMORROW, FOREVER
Nancy Wilson
[30May64|27Jun64|19Dec64] 10(3) 30 2325

1620. OL' WAYLON Waylon Jennings
[21May77|30Jul77|31Dec77] 15(2) 33 2323

1621. MIND GAMES John Lennon
[24Nov73|08Dec73|11Apr81] 9(3) 31 2321

1622. THE KIDS ARE ALRIGHT (SOUNDTRACK)
The Who
[30Jun79|18Aug79|15Dec79] 8(2) 25 2320

1623. ONCE UPON A TIME... Donna Summer
[26Nov77|14Jan78|30Dec78] 26(2) 58 2318

1624. SOLITUDE STANDING Suzanne Vega
[16May87|15Aug87|19Dec87] 11(2) 32 2315

1625. THE SILVER TONGUED DEVIL AND I
Kris Kristofferson
[31Jul71|25Sep71|05Feb72] 21(2) 28 2314

1626. FOR EARTH BELOW Robin Trower
[01Mar75|12Apr75|21Jun75] 5(2) 17 2314

1627. THERE'S A KIND OF HUSH ALL OVER THE WORLD Herman's Hermits
[18Mar67|29Apr67|11Nov67] 13(2) 35 2311

1628. NIGHTWALKER Gino Vannelli
[11Apr81|30May81|03Oct81] 15(4) 26 2311

1629. HURT SO BAD The Lettermen
[06Sep69|18Oct69|28Mar70] 17(1) 30 2311

1630. ARMED FORCES
Elvis Costello And The Attractions
[27Jan79|10Mar79|14Jul79] 10(2) 25 2310

1631. PIECE OF MIND Iron Maiden
[11Jun83|20Aug83|17Nov84] 14(1) 45 2309

1632. WAKE UP EVERYBODY
Harold Melvin And The Blue Notes
[13Dec75|28Feb76|22May76] 9(1) 24 2307

1633. INSIDE INFORMATION Foreigner
[26Dec87|27Feb88|03Sep88] 15(1) 37 2306

1634. DESOLATION BOULEVARD The Sweet
[26Jul75|25Oct75|22May76] 25(2) 44 2306

1635. THIS GIRL'S IN LOVE WITH YOU
Aretha Franklin
[14Feb70|04Apr70|05Sep70] 17(2) 30 2306

Rank. Title Act
[Enter|Peak|Exit] Peak(Wks) TotWks Score

1636. A NEW FLAME Simply Red
[11Mar89|12Aug89|02Dec89] 22(1) 39 2305

1637. REG STRIKES BACK Elton John
[09Jul88|03Sep88|21Jan89] 16(1) 29 2304

1638. SWEPT AWAY Diana Ross
[29Sep84|10Nov84|03Aug85] 26(1) 45 2303

1639. LEON RUSSELL & THE SHELTER PEOPLE
Leon Russell
[29May71|17Jul71|11Dec71] 17(1) 29 2296

1640. GOLDEN GRASS The Grass Roots
[23Nov68|15Feb69|13Dec69] 25(2) 43 2292

1641. THAT NI*GER'S CRAZY Richard Pryor
[15Jun74|28Sep74|31Jan76] 29(1) 53 2290

1642. TIME EXPOSURE Little River Band
[19Sep81|14Nov81|28Aug82] 21(1) 50 2288

1643. ALLIED FORCES Triumph
[19Sep81|21Nov81|20Apr85] 23(1) 59 2287

1644. GET OFF Foxy
[22Jul78|04Nov78|20Jan79] 12(1) 27 2286

1645. TODAY The New Christy Minstrels
[18Apr64|06Jun64|05Dec64] 9(2) 34 2283

1646. BLAM!! The Brothers Johnson
[12Aug78|16Sep78|20Jan79] 7(3) 24 2283

1647. HOLD AN OLD FRIEND'S HAND Tiffany
[10Dec88|21Jan89|24Jun89] 17(4) 29 2282

1648. WILD AND PEACEFUL Kool & The Gang
[13Oct73|02Mar74|30Nov74] 33(1) 60 2282

1649. FULL MOON The Charlie Daniels Band
[09Aug80|06Sep80|21Mar81] 11(2) 33 2276

1650. HERE AND THERE Elton John
[22May76|12Jun76|02Oct76] 4(2) 20 2275

1651. RHAPSODIES FOR YOUNG LOVERS
Midnight String Quartet
[19Nov66|18Mar67|30Dec67] 17(1) 59 2273

1652. JOHNNY RIVERS AT THE WHISKY A GO GO
Johnny Rivers
[20Jun64|01Aug64|24Apr65] 12(1) 45 2271

1653. BLACK & WHITE The Pointer Sisters
[11Jul81|05Sep81|05Dec81] 12(2) 22 2271

1654. NO WAY TO TREAT A LADY Helen Reddy
[12Jul75|27Sep75|28Feb76] 11(1) 34 2270

1655. TO HELL WITH THE DEVIL Stryper
[22Nov86|07Feb87|16Apr88] 32(2) 74 2270

1656. SELF CONTROL Laura Branigan
[28Apr84|11Aug84|02Mar85] 23(2) 45 2270

1657. LOVE, ANDY Andy Williams
[18Nov67|20Jan68|20Jul68] 8(2) 36 2267

1658. TRIBUTE Ozzy Osbourne/Randy Rhoads
[09May87|13Jun87|10Oct87] 6(2) 23 2266

1659. HERB ALPERT'S TIJUANA BRASS, VOLUME 2 Herb Alpert's Tijuana Brass
[15Jan66|16Apr66|04Feb67] 17(1) 56 2265

1660. BON JOVI Bon Jovi
[25Feb84|28Apr84|03Oct87] 43(2) 86 2265

1661. HARPER VALLEY P.T.A. Jeannie C. Riley
[12Oct68|23Nov68|12Apr69] 12(2) 27 2265

1662. 200 M.P.H. Bill Cosby
[26Oct68|04Jan69|12Apr69] 16(1) 25 2263

1663. DIANA ROSS Diana Ross
[11Jul70|03Oct70|16Jan71] 19(2) 28 2261

1664. NUTHIN' FANCY Lynyrd Skynyrd
[12Apr75|31May75|23Aug75] 9(2) 20 2261

1665. CRASH LANDING Jimi Hendrix
[22Mar75|10May75|02Aug75] 5(1) 20 2260

1666. BACK TO THE EGG Wings
[30Jun79|21Jul79|08Dec79] 8(2) 24 2258

1667. MODERN TIMES Jefferson Starship
[18Apr81|06Jun81|28Nov81] 26(3) 33 2256

1668. HEY, LITTLE ONE Glen Campbell
[06Apr68|15Jun68|29Mar69] 26(1) 51 2254

1669. BOY IN THE BOX Corey Hart
[20Jul85|24Aug85|29Mar86] 20(7) 37 2253

1670. BLONDE ON BLONDE Bob Dylan
[23Jul66|01Oct66|15Mar75] 9(1) 34 2252

1671. CHICAGO XI Chicago
[01Oct77|12Nov77|11Feb78] 6(2) 20 2251

1672. CRYING TIME Ray Charles
[12Mar66|09Jul66|12Nov66] 15(1) 36 2251

Rank. Title Act	[Enter|Peak|Exit] Peak(Wks) TotWks	Score
1673. **MORE SONGS ABOUT BUILDINGS AND FOOD** Talking Heads	[12Aug78|25Nov78|26May79] 29(1) 42	2250
1674. **THE CONCERT IN CENTRAL PARK** Simon & Garfunkel	[13Mar82|17Apr82|01Oct83] 6(2) 34	2249
1675. **AMIGOS** Santana	[10Apr76|05Jun76|02Oct76] 10(2) 26	2247
1676. **WASHINGTON SQUARE** The Village Stompers	[02Nov63|28Dec63|23May64] 5(1) 30	2244
1677. **GREATEST HITS** The Cars	[23Nov85|21Dec85|16Aug86] 12(4) 39	2244
1678. **THE HOLLIES' GREATEST HITS** The Hollies	[03Jun67|12Aug67|02Mar68] 11(3) 40	2243
1679. **FANTASTIC VOYAGE** Lakeside	[29Nov80|21Feb81|25Jul81] 16(2) 35	2242
1680. **BRICK** Brick	[10Sep77|26Nov77|15Apr78] 15(1) 32	2241
1681. **ARRIVAL** ABBA	[22Jan77|16Apr77|26Aug78] 20(2) 50	2238
1682. **OUTLANDOS D'AMOUR** The Police	[03Mar79|05May79|21Apr84] 23(1) 63	2233
1683. **WALKING WITH A PANTHER** LL Cool J	[01Jul89|22Jul89|18Nov89] 6(1) 21	2231
1684. **RHAPSODY IN WHITE** Love Unlimited Orchestra	[09Feb74|30Mar74|27Jul74] 8(2) 25	2231
1685. **ENDLESS LOVE** Soundtrack	[01Aug81|26Sep81|12Dec81] 9(2) 20	2231
1686. **STARS ON LONG PLAY** Stars On	[09May81|11Jul81|17Oct81] 9(4) 24	2230
1687. **AEROSMITH** Aerosmith	[13Oct73|03Apr76|18Sep76] 21(2) 59	2229
1688. **FUTURE SHOCK** Herbie Hancock	[03Sep83|15Oct83|24Nov84] 43(2) 65	2229
1689. **SON OF A SON OF A SAILOR** Jimmy Buffett	[08Apr78|20May78|21Oct78] 10(2) 29	2228
1690. **FOR THE ROSES** Joni Mitchell	[02Dec72|03Feb73|09Jun73] 11(2) 28	2227
1691. **LIVE! BOOTLEG** Aerosmith	[11Nov78|13Jan79|07Apr79] 13(2) 22	2223
1692. **CHEECH & CHONG'S WEDDING ALBUM** Cheech & Chong	[19Oct74|23Nov74|05Apr75] 5(1) 25	2222
1693. **CONSCIOUS PARTY** Ziggy Marley And The Melody Makers	[23Apr88|02Jul88|04Feb89] 23(1) 42	2220
1694. **SHE WORKS HARD FOR THE MONEY** Donna Summer	[16Jul83|27Aug83|18Feb84] 9(1) 32	2220
1695. **STRENGTH IN NUMBERS** 38 Special	[17May86|28Jun86|13Dec86] 17(1) 31	2220
1696. **WHEN HARRY MET SALLY (SOUNDTRACK)** Harry Connick Jr.	[19Aug89|23Sep89|11Apr92] 42(2) 122	2220
1697. **PARIS** Supertramp	[11Oct80|01Nov80|04Apr81] 8(2) 26	2219
1698. **GOLDEN HITS OF THE 4 SEASONS** The 4 Seasons	[07Sep63|19Oct63|24Oct64] 15(1) 56	2218
1699. **TO BE TRUE** Harold Melvin And The Blue Notes	[01Mar75|31May75|04Oct75] 26(1) 32	2217
1700. **LAWYERS IN LOVE** Jackson Browne	[20Aug83|10Sep83|31Mar84] 8(3) 33	2216
1701. **THE PLEASURE PRINCIPLE** Gary Numan	[02Feb80|24May80|23Aug80] 16(2) 30	2216
1702. **ONE-TRICK PONY** Paul Simon	[06Sep80|18Oct80|28Feb81] 12(2) 26	2214
1703. **BEFORE THE NEXT TEARDROP FALLS** Freddy Fender	[19Apr75|28Jun75|07Feb76] 20(1) 43	2213
1704. **LEGEND** Bob Marley And The Wailers	[18Aug84|27Oct84|03Aug91] 54(2) 113	2209
1705. **10 YEARS TOGETHER/THE BEST OF PETER, PAUL AND MARY** Peter, Paul & Mary	[20Jun70|11Jul70|20Mar71] 15(3) 40	2209

Rank. Title Act	[Enter|Peak|Exit] Peak(Wks) TotWks	Score
1706. **THE GEORGE BENSON COLLECTION** George Benson	[21Nov81|30Jan82|15May82] 14(2) 26	2205
1707. **SAINT DOMINIC'S PREVIEW** Van Morrison	[05Aug72|23Sep72|10Feb73] 15(3) 28	2203
1708. **ONCE UPON A DREAM** The Rascals	[02Mar68|30Mar68|21Sep68] 9(2) 30	2202
1709. **SHARE THE LAND** The Guess Who	[17Oct70|28Nov70|03Apr71] 14(2) 25	2202
1710. **DEMONS AND WIZARDS** Uriah Heep	[17Jun72|28Oct72|03Mar73] 23(2) 38	2202
1711. **...AND THEN THERE WERE THREE...** Genesis	[15Apr78|03Jun78|09Aug80] 14(1) 33	2200
1712. **INSTANT FUNK** Instant Funk	[17Feb79|19May79|14Jul79] 12(1) 22	2198
1713. **TOUR DE FORCE** 38 Special	[03Dec83|04Feb84|25Aug84] 22(2) 39	2197
1714. **YOUNG GIRL** Gary Puckett And The Union Gap	[18May68|20Jul68|08Feb69] 21(2) 39	2196
1715. **SABBATH BLOODY SABBATH** Black Sabbath	[26Jan74|16Mar74|31Aug74] 11(1) 32	2195
1716. **HEAVY METAL** Soundtrack	[08Aug81|03Oct81|13Feb82] 12(2) 28	2195
1717. **GUITAR MAN** Bread	[18Nov72|23Dec72|02Jun73] 18(1) 29	2192
1718. **TONY'S GREATEST HITS, VOLUME III** Tony Bennett	[21Aug65|30Oct65|04Jun66] 20(1) 42	2192
1719. **SOULFUL** Dionne Warwick	[05Apr69|17May69|11Oct69] 11(2) 28	2188
1720. **DIANA ROSS' GREATEST HITS** Diana Ross	[07Aug76|02Oct76|08Jan77] 13(2) 23	2188
1721. **BACK FOR THE ATTACK** Dokken	[05Dec87|19Dec87|16Jul88] 13(1) 33	2188
1722. **WADE IN THE WATER** Ramsey Lewis	[10Sep66|22Oct66|15Jul67] 16(2) 34	2188
1723. **KILLER ON THE RAMPAGE** Eddy Grant	[23Apr83|16Jul83|12Nov83] 10(3) 30	2188
1724. **AGENTS OF FORTUNE** Blue Öyster Cult	[19Jun76|20Nov76|12Feb77] 29(1) 35	2186
1725. **GOT TO BE THERE** Michael Jackson	[19Feb72|01Apr72|22Jul72] 14(2) 23	2185
1726. **THE COWSILLS IN CONCERT** The Cowsills	[10May69|31May69|18Oct69] 16(2) 24	2183
1727. **ABSOLUTELY LIVE** The Doors	[08Aug70|05Sep70|19Dec70] 8(1) 20	2183
1728. **KISSIN' COUSINS (SOUNDTRACK)** Elvis Presley	[11Apr64|02May64|31Oct64] 6(3) 30	2182
1729. **JAZZ** Queen	[09Dec78|06Jan79|07Apr79] 6(2) 18	2182
1730. **ROCK 'N' ROLL** John Lennon	[08Mar75|19Apr75|14Jun75] 6(1) 15	2182
1731. **UNDERSTANDING** Bobby Womack	[24Jun72|04Nov72|19May73] 43(2) 48	2180
1732. **CLASS CLOWN** George Carlin	[14Oct72|02Dec72|09Jun73] 22(2) 35	2176
1733. **STEPHEN STILLS 2** Stephen Stills	[17Jul71|07Aug71|27Nov71] 8(2) 20	2174
1734. **LATE AGAIN** Peter, Paul & Mary	[14Sep68|07Dec68|08Feb69] 14(2) 22	2174
1735. **NO REASON TO CRY** Eric Clapton	[16Oct76|13Nov76|05Mar77] 15(3) 21	2173
1736. **ERIC BURDON DECLARES "WAR"** Eric Burdon And War	[16May70|22Aug70|14Nov70] 18(3) 27	2173
1737. **HOMEMADE** The Osmonds	[26Jun71|07Aug71|12Feb72] 22(2) 34	2172
1738. **ROCKY IV** Soundtrack	[16Nov85|22Feb86|07Jun86] 10(1) 30	2167
1739. **IN HEAT** The Romantics	[22Oct83|18Feb84|23Jun84] 14(1) 36	2167
1740. **SONGS OF LOVE** Anita Ward	[26May79|07Jul79|29Sep79] 8(2) 19	2164

Rank. Title Act	[Enter|Peak|Exit] Peak(Wks) TotWks	Score
1741. **THE BEST OF TOMMY JAMES & THE SHONDELLS** Tommy James And The Shondells	[13Dec69|24Jan70|10Oct70] 21(1) 41	2162
1742. **DONOVAN IN CONCERT** Donovan	[27Jul68|21Sep68|22Feb69] 18(2) 31	2162
1743. **IF THAT'S WHAT IT TAKES** Michael McDonald	[28Aug82|02Oct82|02Apr83] 6(6) 32	2160
1744. **FRIEND OR FOE** Adam Ant	[06Nov82|05Mar83|09Jul83] 16(3) 36	2159
1745. **SHOCK TREATMENT** The Edgar Winter Group	[25May74|17Aug74|26Oct74] 13(1) 23	2159
1746. **KINGDOM COME** Kingdom Come	[19Mar88|30Apr88|01Oct88] 12(1) 29	2156
1747. **SOLITUDE/SOLITAIRE** Peter Cetera	[12Jul86|23Aug86|02May87] 23(1) 43	2156
1748. **THE FAMILY THAT PLAYS TOGETHER** Spirit	[18Jan69|01Mar69|02Sep72] 22(2) 28	2156
1749. **FIVE-A-SIDE (AN ACE ALBUM)** Ace	[15Mar75|31May75|09Aug75] 11(1) 22	2156
1750. **IN MY TRIBE** 10,000 Maniacs	[19Sep87|21May88|04Mar89] 37(1) 77	2156
1751. **SONGBIRD** Barbra Streisand	[17Jun78|22Jul78|16Dec78] 12(2) 27	2155
1752. **THE B-52'S** The B-52s	[11Aug79|10May80|14Feb81] 59(2) 74	2154
1753. **A REAL MOTHER FOR YA** Johnny Guitar Watson	[16Apr77|25Jun77|15Oct77] 20(2) 27	2149
1754. **IS IT STILL GOOD TO YA** Ashford & Simpson	[09Sep78|28Oct78|17Mar79] 20(1) 28	2148
1755. **LIVE FROM EARTH** Pat Benatar	[15Oct83|19Nov83|09Mar85] 13(2) 34	2147
1756. **MANHATTANS** The Manhattans	[01May76|14Aug76|30Oct76] 16(1) 27	2147
1757. **HICKORY HOLLER REVISITED** O.C. Smith	[15Jun68|28Dec68|29Mar69] 19(2) 42	2145
1758. **12 IN A ROE/A COLLECTION OF TOMMY ROE'S GREATEST HITS** Tommy Roe	[27Dec69|07Mar70|11Jul70] 21(1) 29	2145
1759. **AMAZING GRACE** Aretha Franklin	[17Jun72|22Jul72|18Nov72] 7(1) 23	2145
1760. **JARREAU** Al Jarreau	[16Apr83|28May83|04Feb84] 13(2) 43	2144
1761. **THE BEST OF SONNY & CHER** Sonny & Cher	[12Aug67|23Sep67|18Mar72] 23(1) 64	2144
1762. **CONTROVERSY** Prince	[07Nov81|21Nov81|04May85] 21(3) 64	2142
1763. **CYCLES** Frank Sinatra	[28Dec68|15Feb69|01Nov69] 18(1) 28	2141
1764. **SOMEWHERE IN TIME** Iron Maiden	[11Oct86|22Nov86|04Jul87] 11(1) 39	2136
1765. **LIVE AT THE BIJOU** Grover Washington Jr.	[07Jan78|18Mar78|12Aug78] 11(2) 32	2135
1766. **HONEY** Ray Conniff & His Orchestra & Chorus	[01Jun68|31Aug68|22Feb69] 22(1) 39	2135
1767. **PETER GABRIEL (III)** Peter Gabriel	[21Jun80|23Aug80|03Jan81] 22(2) 29	2135
1768. **MUSIC OF MY MIND** Stevie Wonder	[25Mar72|15Jul72|18Nov72] 21(1) 35	2134
1769. **TILL I LOVED YOU** Barbra Streisand	[12Nov88|10Dec88|06May89] 10(1) 26	2133
1770. **THE ROYAL SCAM** Steely Dan	[22May76|10Jul76|31Jan81] 15(2) 29	2133
1771. **DESPERADO** Eagles	[05May73|30Jun73|15May76] 41(1) 70	2133
1772. **PETER, PAUL AND MOMMY** Peter, Paul & Mary	[14Jun69|12Jul69|13Dec69] 12(3) 25	2132
1773. **I CAN'T STAND STILL** Don Henley	[04Sep82|04Dec82|30Apr83] 24(7) 35	2131
1774. **THE PAPAS & THE MAMAS** The Mamas & The Papas	[25May68|03Aug68|11Jan69] 15(1) 34	2131

Rank. Title Act
[Enter|Peak|Exit] Peak(Wks) TotWks Score

1775. IT'S HARD The Who
[25Sep82|23Oct82|30Apr83] 8(5) 32 2131

1776. TALK SHOW Go-Go's
[07Apr84|26May84|10Nov84] 18(3) 32 2131

1777. PAT GARRETT & BILLY THE KID (SOUNDTRACK) Bob Dylan
[04Aug73|27Oct73|23Feb74] 16(2) 30 2130

1778. THE SIX WIVES OF HENRY VIII Rick Wakeman
[24Mar73|30Jun73|26Jan74] 30(1) 45 2130

1779. BREAKIN' Soundtrack
[02Jun84|21Jul84|03Nov84] 8(2) 23 2129

1780. LARGER THAN LIFE Jody Watley
[15Apr89|20May89|13Jan90] 16(2) 40 2129

1781. BIRDS OF FIRE The Mahavishnu Orchestra
[10Feb73|07Apr73|20Oct73] 15(2) 37 2128

1782. NEAR THE BEGINNING Vanilla Fudge
[01Mar69|12Apr69|30Aug69] 16(2) 27 2128

1783. 2ND VAULT OF GOLDEN HITS The 4 Seasons
[03Dec66|11Mar67|02Dec67] 22(2) 53 2127

1784. LIVING YEARS Mike + The Mechanics
[19Nov88|08Apr89|29Jul89] 13(2) 37 2127

1785. I'LL REMEMBER YOU Roger Williams
[26Mar66|03Sep66|05Aug67] 24(2) 67 2126

1786. GIDEON Kenny Rogers
[12Apr80|31May80|20Dec80] 12(2) 34 2123

1787. MADE IN THE SHADE The Rolling Stones
[21Jun75|19Jul75|11Oct75] 6(2) 17 2123

1788. NICOLETTE Nicolette Larson
[18Nov78|03Mar79|28Jul79] 15(2) 37 2121

1789. THE NATURE OF THE BEAST April Wine
[31Jan81|18Apr81|19Sep81] 26(1) 34 2119

1790. BUTTERFLY Barbra Streisand
[16Nov74|04Jan75|26Apr75] 13(1) 24 2119

1791. REALITY... WHAT A CONCEPT Robin Williams
[21Jul79|15Sep79|15Dec79] 10(2) 22 2118

1792. SCARY MONSTERS David Bowie
[04Oct80|15Nov80|04Apr81] 12(2) 27 2118

1793. SOMETHING/ANYTHING? Todd Rundgren
[25Mar72|05Jan74|11May74] 29(2) 48 2116

1794. SOUVENIRS Dan Fogelberg
[07Dec74|01Mar75|07Jun75] 17(2) 27 2116

1795. LADIES OF THE CANYON Joni Mitchell
[11Apr70|25Apr70|21Nov70] 27(3) 33 2113

1796. CAMOUFLAGE Rod Stewart
[30Jun84|11Aug84|23Feb85] 18(2) 35 2113

1797. GREATEST HITS/LIVE Heart
[06Dec80|20Dec80|23May81] 13(3) 25 2112

1798. STEVIE WONDER'S ORIGINAL MUSIQUARIUM I Stevie Wonder
[29May82|12Jun82|04Dec82] 4(3) 28 2112

1799. WHO KNOWS WHERE THE TIME GOES Judy Collins
[21Dec68|01Mar69|02Aug69] 29(2) 33 2111

1800. FLAG James Taylor
[12May79|16Jun79|13Oct79] 10(1) 23 2110

1801. AHH... THE NAME IS BOOTSY, BABY Bootsy's Rubber Band
[05Feb77|23Apr77|09Jul77] 16(4) 23 2108

1802. BAY CITY ROLLERS Bay City Rollers
[27Sep75|24Jan76|22May76] 20(2) 35 2107

1803. TOO LOW FOR ZERO Elton John
[11Jun83|25Feb84|01Sep84] 25(1) 54 2107

1804. GREATEST HITS Queen
[14Nov81|05Dec81|08May82] 14(6) 26 2106

1805. SUNNY SIDE! The Kingston Trio
[17Aug63|21Sep63|01Feb64] 7(2) 25 2104

1806. KEEP IT LIVE Dazz Band
[03Apr82|10Jul82|20Nov82] 14(4) 34 2100

1807. STAYING ALIVE (SOUNDTRACK) Bee Gees
[16Jul83|27Aug83|14Jan84] 6(2) 27 2100

1808. EDDIE MONEY Eddie Money
[07Jan78|22Apr78|09Dec78] 37(2) 49 2099

1809. I'LL NEVER FALL IN LOVE AGAIN Dionne Warwick
[02May70|04Jul70|23Jan71] 23(2) 39 2099

1810. ON THE WATERS Bread
[08Aug70|05Sep70|13Mar71] 12(2) 32 2097

1811. THIS IS A RECORDING Lily Tomlin
[27Mar71|01May71|11Sep71] 15(1) 25 2097

1812. GEORGY GIRL The Seekers
[25Feb67|08Apr67|02Sep67] 10(2) 28 2096

1813. FUN AND GAMES Chuck Mangione
[23Feb80|15Mar80|26Jul80] 8(4) 23 2095

1814. THE UNICORN The Irish Rovers
[06Apr68|22Jun68|25Jan69] 24(2) 43 2090

1815. REVENGE Eurythmics
[09Aug86|04Oct86|21Mar87] 12(1) 33 2090

1816. ON STAGE-FEBRUARY, 1970 Elvis Presley
[20Jun70|25Jul70|31Oct70] 13(1) 20 2088

1817. THE ORIGINAL VOICE TRACKS FROM HIS GREATEST MOVIES W.C. Fields
[04Jan69|05Apr69|19Jul69] 30(1) 29 2088

1818. BURT BACHARACH Burt Bacharach
[19Jun71|17Jul71|27Nov71] 18(2) 24 2088

1819. SONGS FOR BEGINNERS Graham Nash
[19Jun71|10Jul71|27Nov71] 15(3) 24 2087

1820. PICTURES AT AN EXHIBITION Emerson, Lake & Palmer
[22Jan72|19Feb72|24Jun72] 10(2) 23 2084

1821. JUNGLE BOOK Soundtrack
[03Feb68|30Mar68|21Sep68] 19(2) 34 2083

1822. FAREWELL ANDROMEDA John Denver
[16Jun73|25Aug73|09Feb74] 16(2) 35 2083

1823. ALICE COOPER'S GREATEST HITS Alice Cooper
[31Aug74|16Nov74|01Feb75] 8(1) 23 2081

1824. TOUGHER THAN LEATHER Run-D.M.C.
[04Jun88|02Jul88|10Dec88] 9(1) 28 2081

1825. STREET PLAYER Rufus And Chaka Khan
[11Feb78|15Apr78|05Aug78] 14(2) 26 2079

1826. ALICE COOPER GOES TO HELL Alice Cooper
[17Jul76|18Dec76|19Feb77] 27(1) 32 2077

1827. WIN, LOSE OR DRAW The Allman Brothers Band
[13Sep75|11Oct75|13Dec75] 5(2) 14 2076

1828. ANIMALIZE KISS
[06Oct84|01Dec84|22Jun85] 19(1) 38 2076

1829. DREAMGIRLS Original Cast
[22May82|21Aug82|04Dec82] 11(3) 29 2076

1830. WAYLON & WILLIE Waylon Jennings & Willie Nelson
[04Feb78|01Apr78|19Aug78] 12(1) 29 2075

1831. A GROUP CALLED SMITH Smith
[23Aug69|29Nov69|28Mar70] 17(2) 28 2072

1832. NIGHTSHIFT Commodores
[16Feb85|27Apr85|26Oct85] 12(3) 37 2071

1833. GTR GTR
[17May86|12Jul86|08Nov86] 11(2) 26 2069

1834. KISS ME, KISS ME, KISS ME The Cure
[20Jun87|04Jul87|11Jun88] 35(4) 52 2063

1835. DEGUELLO ZZ Top
[24Nov79|16Feb80|10Mar84] 24(3) 43 2062

1836. CRICKLEWOOD GREEN Ten Years After
[18Apr70|16May70|07Nov70] 14(2) 30 2062

1837. BILLY IDOL Billy Idol
[31Jul82|16Jul83|08Dec84] 45(1) 104 2061

1838. MOONFLOWER Santana
[05Nov77|10Dec77|15Apr78] 10(4) 24 2061

1839. CRAZY NIGHTS KISS
[10Oct87|31Oct87|28May88] 18(1) 34 2060

1840. IF I SHOULD LOVE AGAIN Barry Manilow
[17Oct81|14Nov81|03Apr82] 14(3) 25 2058

1841. LOOK SHARP! Joe Jackson
[07Apr79|30Jun79|29Dec79] 20(2) 39 2057

1842. EVE The Alan Parsons Project
[15Sep79|20Oct79|15Mar80] 13(2) 27 2057

1843. DAN FOGELBERG/GREATEST HITS Dan Fogelberg
[13Nov82|18Dec82|09Jul83] 15(4) 35 2056

1844. POWER WINDOWS Rush
[09Nov85|14Dec85|17May86] 10(2) 28 2056

1845. ALL THE GIRLS IN THE WORLD BEWARE!!! Grand Funk
[21Dec74|22Feb75|31May75] 10(1) 24 2054

1846. IN THE POCKET James Taylor
[03Jul76|21Aug76|11Dec76] 16(1) 24 2054

1847. ARETHA IN PARIS Aretha Franklin
[23Nov68|04Jan69|05Apr69] 13(2) 20 2053

1848. GOIN' BACK TO INDIANA The Jackson 5
[09Oct71|20Nov71|01Apr72] 16(1) 26 2052

1849. TRY A LITTLE KINDNESS Glen Campbell
[07Feb70|28Feb70|15Aug70] 12(2) 28 2051

1850. WHEN THE EAGLE FLIES Traffic
[28Sep74|16Nov74|29Mar75] 9(1) 27 2051

1851. SO WHAT Joe Walsh
[04Jan75|22Mar75|31May75] 11(1) 22 2050

1852. WARRIOR Scandal Featuring Patty Smyth
[04Aug84|06Oct84|11May85] 17(3) 41 2050

1853. BIG DADDY John Mellencamp
[27May89|17Jun89|28Oct89] 7(1) 23 2048

1854. ARETHA'S GREATEST HITS Aretha Franklin
[25Sep71|23Oct71|13May72] 19(2) 34 2043

1855. SEE THE LIGHT The Jeff Healey Band
[08Oct88|23Sep89|27Jan90] 22(3) 69 2041

1856. MARTIKA Martika
[04Feb89|19Aug89|02Dec89] 15(1) 39 2041

1857. FEELS SO GOOD Grover Washington Jr.
[15Nov75|20Dec75|05Jun76] 10(1) 30 2039

1858. WHO'S THAT GIRL (SOUNDTRACK) Madonna
[15Aug87|12Sep87|20Feb88] 7(2) 28 2038

1859. STEPPENWOLF GOLD/THEIR GREAT HITS Steppenwolf
[06Mar71|27Mar71|06Nov71] 24(2) 36 2035

1860. SIGNS OF LIFE Billy Squier
[04Aug84|01Sep84|16Feb85] 11(4) 29 2034

1861. IT'LL SHINE WHEN IT SHINES Ozark Mountain Daredevils
[14Dec74|08Mar75|12Jul75] 19(1) 31 2033

1862. UNDERCOVER The Rolling Stones
[26Nov83|10Dec83|28Apr84] 4(2) 23 2032

1863. NOTHIN' MATTERS AND WHAT IF IT DID John Cougar
[04Oct80|23May81|05Mar83] 37(2) 55 2032

1864. SAVE ME Silver Convention
[13Sep75|13Dec75|28Feb76] 10(1) 25 2031

1865. FIRE AND WATER Free
[05Sep70|31Oct70|06Mar71] 17(2) 27 2029

1866. CONTRADICTION Ohio Players
[12Jun76|24Jul76|23Oct76] 12(2) 20 2029

1867. ENERGY The Pointer Sisters
[02Dec78|03Mar79|07Jul79] 13(3) 32 2026

1868. PERFECT STRANGERS Deep Purple
[01Dec84|09Feb85|06Jul85] 17(2) 32 2024

1869. TINY BUBBLES Don Ho
[17Dec66|01Apr67|25Nov67] 15(1) 50 2021

1870. ENCORE John Gary
[22Feb64|28Mar64|02Jan65] 16(3) 46 2020

1871. CROSSROADS Tracy Chapman
[21Oct89|11Nov89|14Apr90] 9(2) 26 2020

1872. JEFF BECK, TIM BOGERT, CARMINE APPICE Beck, Bogert & Appice
[07Apr73|09Jun73|06Oct73] 12(1) 27 2019

1873. MELLOW MADNESS Quincy Jones
[23Aug75|18Oct75|13Mar76] 16(2) 30 2019

1874. FLYING START The Blackbyrds
[07Dec74|31May75|30Aug75] 30(1) 39 2018

1875. EXIT...STAGE LEFT Rush
[14Nov81|05Dec81|03Apr82] 10(3) 21 2016

1876. MR. TAMBOURINE MAN The Byrds
[26Jun65|07Aug65|12Mar66] 6(3) 38 2014

1877. SPACE ODDITY David Bowie
[18Nov72|07Apr73|21Jul73] 16(1) 36 2014

1878. THE RISE AND FALL OF ZIGGY STARDUST AND THE SPIDERS FROM MARS David Bowie
[17Jun72|07Apr73|01Sep90] 75(1) 81 2014

1879. NO CONTROL Eddie Money
[10Jul82|23Oct82|07May83] 20(3) 44 2013

Rank. Title Act
[Enter|Peak|Exit] Peak(Wks) TotWks Score

1880. ASK RUFUS Rufus And Chaka Khan
[05Feb77|05Mar77|23Jul77] 12(2) 25 2013

1881. TEAR DOWN THESE WALLS Billy Ocean
[19Mar88|07May88|15Oct88] 18(1) 31 2012

1882. PERFORMANCE-ROCKIN' THE FILLMORE
Humble Pie
[06Nov71|18Dec71|10Jun72] 21(1) 32 2010

1883. MECCA FOR MODERNS
The Manhattan Transfer
[13Jun81|22Aug81|12Dec81] 22(4) 27 2009

1884. YESSONGS Yes
[26May73|23Jun73|29Dec73] 12(1) 32 2009

1885. BIG GENERATOR Yes
[17Oct87|07Nov87|07May88] 15(3) 30 2009

1886. MOVIN' ON Commodores
[08Nov75|27Dec75|12Jun76] 29(1) 32 2007

1887. ROUND 2: THE STYLISTICS The Stylistics
[11Nov72|10Mar73|28Jul73] 32(2) 38 2006

1888. OCTAVE The Moody Blues
[01Jul78|19Aug78|20Jan79] 13(1) 30 2006

1889. HAIR OF THE DOG Nazareth
[26Apr75|27Mar76|14Nov81] 17(2) 40 2005

1890. RELAYER Yes
[28Dec74|01Feb75|12Apr75] 5(1) 16 2003

1891. A SPACE IN TIME Ten Years After
[28Aug71|09Oct71|19Feb72] 17(1) 26 2003

1892. OLIVIA NEWTON-JOHN'S GREATEST HITS
Olivia Newton-John
[12Nov77|14Jan78|18Mar78] 13(2) 19 2002

1893. MERRY, MERRY CHRISTMAS
New Kids On The Block
[14Oct89|23Dec89|19Jan91] 9(1) 28 2001

1894. SUNSHINE SUPERMAN Donovan
[24Sep66|26Nov66|09Sep67] 11(1) 29 2000

1895. THIS IS THE MOODY BLUES
The Moody Blues
[23Nov74|04Jan75|10May75] 11(1) 25 2000

1896. LOVE IT TO DEATH Alice Cooper
[20Mar71|15May71|04Dec71] 35(2) 38 1999

1897. NOTORIOUS Duran Duran
[20Dec86|31Jan87|08Aug87] 12(1) 34 1997

1898. SIGNALS Rush
[02Oct82|27Nov82|30Jun84] 10(1) 33 1996

1899. THE VENTURES A GO-GO The Ventures
[25Sep65|11Dec65|21May66] 16(1) 35 1996

1900. MAVERICK
George Thorogood & The Destroyers
[02Mar85|06Jul85|14Dec85] 32(1) 42 1995

1901. WILD LIFE Wings
[25Dec71|22Jan72|22Apr72] 10(2) 18 1994

1902. THERE! I'VE SAID IT AGAIN Bobby Vinton
[01Feb64|28Mar64|08Aug64] 8(2) 28 1993

1903. THE MASON WILLIAMS PHONOGRAPH RECORD Mason Williams
[29Jun68|14Sep68|15Feb69] 14(2) 34 1993

1904. DAVID LIVE David Bowie
[26Oct74|30Nov74|15Mar75] 8(1) 21 1991

1905. SPECTRUM Billy Cobham
[17Nov73|02Mar74|07Sep74] 26(1) 43 1990

1906. FRAMPTON Peter Frampton
[29Mar75|17May75|20Nov76] 32(2) 64 1990

1907. THE ORIGINAL SOUNDTRACK 10cc
[19Apr75|02Aug75|04Oct75] 15(2) 25 1986

1908. THE DAVE CLARK FIVE RETURN!
The Dave Clark Five
[20Jun64|18Jul64|14Nov64] 5(1) 22 1986

1909. MY WAY Frank Sinatra
[10May69|31May69|13Sep69] 11(2) 19 1986

1910. LET'S PUT IT ALL TOGETHER The Stylistics
[25May74|13Jul74|21Dec74] 14(2) 31 1986

1911. LIVE RUST Neil Young With Crazy Horse
[08Dec79|02Feb80|17May80] 15(2) 24 1985

1912. GREAT WHITE NORTH
Bob & Doug McKenzie
[09Jan82|03Apr82|29May82] 8(2) 21 1984

1913. LOVE AND ROCKETS Love And Rockets
[20May89|12Aug89|11Nov89] 14(1) 26 1984

Rank. Title Act
[Enter|Peak|Exit] Peak(Wks) TotWks Score

1914. ELVIS COUNTRY ("I'M 10,000 YEARS OLD") Elvis Presley
[23Jan71|27Feb71|12Jun71] 12(1) 21 1982

1915. THREE LOCK BOX Sammy Hagar
[25Dec82|09Apr83|13Aug83] 17(2) 34 1980

1916. RENAISSANCE Vanilla Fudge
[13Jul68|14Sep68|22Feb69] 20(2) 33 1979

1917. FOR ONCE IN MY LIFE Vikki Carr
[29Mar69|21Jun69|06Dec69] 29(2) 34 1978

1918. RAINBOW BRIDGE (SOUNDTRACK)
Jimi Hendrix
[09Oct71|20Nov71|26Feb72] 15(1) 21 1976

1919. HAPPINESS IS BEING WITH THE SPINNERS
Spinners
[31Jul76|04Sep76|19Feb77] 25(2) 30 1974

1920. THE WONDERFUL WORLD OF ANDY WILLIAMS Andy Williams
[25Jan64|29Feb64|04Jul64] 9(3) 24 1973

1921. ODESSA Bee Gees
[22Feb69|29Mar69|09Aug69] 20(3) 25 1972

1922. BELINDA Belinda Carlisle
[07Jun86|20Sep86|24Jan87] 13(1) 34 1971

1923. ALL FOR LOVE New Edition
[07Dec85|19Apr86|01Nov86] 32(1) 48 1967

1924. ONE ON ONE Bob James/Earl Klugh
[03Nov79|15Dec79|14Jun80] 23(3) 33 1967

1925. THE FINAL CUT Pink Floyd
[09Apr83|07May83|10Sep83] 6(2) 23 1966

1926. COLD ON THE SHOULDER
Gordon Lightfoot
[01Mar75|26Apr75|12Jul75] 10(1) 20 1965

1927. THIRTY THREE & 1/3 George Harrison
[11Dec76|15Jan77|30Apr77] 11(2) 21 1965

1928. TAMMY'S GREATEST HITS
Tammy Wynette
[06Sep69|08Nov69|31Oct70] 37(1) 61 1964

1929. THE BASEMENT TAPES
Bob Dylan And The Band
[26Jul75|06Sep75|25Oct75] 7(2) 14 1964

1930. MANNA Bread
[27Mar71|22May71|11Sep71] 21(3) 25 1963

1931. BEACH BOYS' PARTY! The Beach Boys
[27Nov65|01Jan66|07May66] 6(1) 24 1962

1932. ONE WORLD Rare Earth
[17Jul71|18Sep71|01Jan72] 28(1) 25 1962

1933. THUNDERBALL Soundtrack
[11Dec65|05Mar66|18Jun66] 10(1) 28 1962

1934. TENDER IS THE NIGHT Johnny Mathis
[15Feb64|14Mar64|22Aug64] 13(3) 28 1962

1935. CHARACTERS Stevie Wonder
[05Dec87|19Dec87|02Jul88] 17(3) 31 1959

1936. VACATION Go-Go's
[14Aug82|18Sep82|19Feb83] 8(5) 28 1956

1937. EMPTY SKY Elton John
[01Feb75|01Mar75|31May75] 6(1) 18 1955

1938. BONNIE AND CLYDE Soundtrack
[06Apr68|27Apr68|24Aug68] 12(3) 21 1955

1939. KEEP YOUR EYE ON ME Herb Alpert
[21Mar87|13Jun87|17Oct87] 18(3) 31 1954

1940. HORIZON Carpenters
[28Jun75|26Jul75|25Oct75] 13(3) 18 1952

1941. WOODSTOCK TWO Soundtrack
[10Apr71|08May71|31Jul71] 7(1) 17 1948

1942. MONOLITH Kansas
[09Jun79|30Jun79|17Nov79] 10(2) 24 1948

1943. SWISS MOVEMENT
Les McCann & Eddie Harris
[13Dec69|28Feb70|29Aug70] 29(1) 38 1948

1944. HOT, COOL AND VICIOUS Salt-N-Pepa
[01Aug87|27Feb88|20Aug88] 26(4) 53 1947

1945. WAITING FOR COLUMBUS Little Feat
[11Mar78|29Apr78|26Aug78] 18(2) 25 1946

1946. FOREVER, FOR ALWAYS, FOR LOVE
Luther Vandross
[16Oct82|11Dec82|18Jun83] 20(5) 36 1945

1947. BEGINNINGS The Allman Brothers Band
[10Mar73|28Apr73|23Mar74] 25(1) 55 1945

Rank. Title Act
[Enter|Peak|Exit] Peak(Wks) TotWks Score

1948. YOU DON'T HAVE TO BE JEWISH
Various Artists
[18Sep65|27Nov65|07May66] 9(1) 34 1942

1949. GUANTANAMERA The Sandpipers
[29Oct66|07Jan67|08Jul67] 13(1) 37 1942

1950. FACES Earth, Wind & Fire
[22Nov80|06Dec80|11Apr81] 10(2) 21 1942

1951. GETZ AU GO GO The New Stan Getz Quartet Featuring Astrud Gilberto
[19Dec64|03Jul65|30Oct65] 24(2) 46 1938

1952. SLAVE Slave
[09Apr77|30Jul77|15Oct77] 22(1) 28 1934

1953. CELEBRATE ME HOME Kenny Loggins
[07May77|23Jul77|17Dec77] 27(1) 33 1932

1954. HENDRIX IN THE WEST Jimi Hendrix
[04Mar72|25Mar72|08Jul72] 12(3) 19 1932

1955. NUMBERS Cat Stevens
[13Dec75|24Jan76|17Apr76] 13(2) 19 1931

1956. WIRED Jeff Beck
[26Jun76|07Aug76|11Dec76] 16(1) 25 1931

1957. ALL IN THE NAME OF LOVE Atlantic Starr
[25Apr87|25Jul87|21Nov87] 18(1) 31 1929

1958. TOGETHERNESS L.T.D.
[17Jun78|23Sep78|09Dec78] 18(1) 26 1929

1959. FOGHAT LIVE Foghat
[10Sep77|05Nov77|25Mar78] 11(1) 29 1928

1960. MIXED EMOTIONS Exile
[19Aug78|28Oct78|10Feb79] 14(2) 26 1927

1961. VOULEZ-VOUS ABBA
[07Jul79|01Sep79|05Jan80] 19(2) 27 1925

1962. PETER, PAUL AND MARY ALBUM
Peter, Paul & Mary
[27Aug66|15Oct66|26Aug67] 22(1) 53 1924

1963. FIRE OF UNKNOWN ORIGIN
Blue Öyster Cult
[11Jul81|19Sep81|06Feb82] 24(2) 31 1923

1964. MUSCLE OF LOVE Alice Cooper
[08Dec73|12Jan74|27Apr74] 10(2) 21 1921

1965. LET ME IN YOUR LIFE Aretha Franklin
[16Mar74|11May74|31Aug74] 14(1) 25 1918

1966. THE LIVE ADVENTURES OF MIKE BLOOMFIELD AND AL KOOPER
Mike Bloomfield/Al Kooper
[08Feb69|08Mar69|21Jun69] 18(2) 20 1918

1967. THE SERENDIPITY SINGERS
The Serendipity Singers
[07Mar64|23May64|19Sep64] 11(1) 29 1915

1968. LIVE AT THE SAHARA TAHOE Isaac Hayes
[19May73|30Jun73|10Nov73] 14(2) 26 1914

1969. LIVE IT UP The Isley Brothers
[07Sep74|26Oct74|15Mar75] 14(2) 28 1914

1970. IS IT SOMETHING I SAID? Richard Pryor
[23Aug75|04Oct75|07Feb76] 12(2) 25 1914

1971. THE EAGLES Eagles
[24Jun72|05Aug72|01Nov75] 22(1) 49 1912

1972. ONE EIGHTY Ambrosia
[19Apr80|12Jul80|29Nov80] 25(1) 33 1910

1973. AFTERTONES Janis Ian
[24Jan76|28Feb76|29May76] 12(2) 19 1910

1974. EXODUS Bob Marley And The Wailers
[11Jun77|20Aug77|19Nov77] 20(5) 24 1910

1975. TRAFFIC Traffic
[30Nov68|25Jan69|05Jul69] 17(2) 26 1909

1976. IT'S IMPOSSIBLE Perry Como
[16Jan71|20Mar71|17Jul71] 22(2) 27 1909

1977. LIVE IN COOK COUNTY JAIL B.B. King
[20Feb71|27Mar71|02Oct71] 25(3) 33 1908

1978. OLE ELO Electric Light Orchestra
[03Jul76|07Aug76|23Apr77] 32(1) 43 1908

1979. GRACE UNDER PRESSURE Rush
[05May84|19May84|03Nov84] 10(4) 27 1905

1980. JESUS WAS A CAPRICORN
Kris Kristofferson
[25Nov72|13Oct73|16Mar74] 31(1) 54 1905

1981. IT MIGHT AS WELL BE SWING
Frank Sinatra & Count Basie
[22Aug64|24Oct64|20Mar65] 13(1) 31 1904

Rank.	Title	Act	Enter	Peak	Exit	Peak(Wks)	TotWks	Score
1982.	**TALES OF MYSTERY & IMAGINATION**	The Alan Parsons Project	15May76	10Jul76	12Nov77	38(1)	46	1902
1983.	**DAYDREAM**	The Lovin' Spoonful	02Apr66	11Jun66	29Oct66	10(1)	31	1900
1984.	**SPARKLE (SOUNDTRACK)**	Aretha Franklin	19Jun76	07Aug76	27Nov76	18(3)	24	1899
1985.	**WATERMARK**	Enya	04Feb89	22Apr89	28Oct89	25(4)	39	1899
1986.	**STAR WARS & OTHER GALACTIC FUNK**	Meco	06Aug77	15Oct77	11Feb78	13(2)	28	1899
1987.	**MAGIC**	The Jets	07Nov87	09Jul88	15Oct88	35(1)	50	1898
1988.	**VINCEBUS ERUPTUM**	Blue Cheer	09Mar68	20Apr68	07Sep68	11(3)	27	1897
1989.	**WARM THOUGHTS**	Smokey Robinson	15Mar80	24May80	02Aug80	14(2)	21	1895
1990.	**MOVE IT ON OVER**	George Thorogood & The Destroyers	09Dec78	28Apr79	27Oct79	33(1)	47	1895
1991.	**DON'T CRY NOW**	Linda Ronstadt	20Oct73	02Mar74	24May75	45(1)	56	1894
1992.	**RAG DOLL**	The 4 Seasons	08Aug64	19Sep64	30Jan65	7(1)	26	1894
1993.	**SKYY LINE**	Skyy	21Nov81	03Apr82	03Jul82	18(2)	33	1892
1994.	**CRIME OF THE CENTURY**	Supertramp	07Dec74	24May75	23Feb80	38(2)	76	1891
1995.	**SILVER CONVENTION**	Silver Convention	10Apr76	26Jun76	18Sep76	13(1)	24	1891
1996.	**JOY**	Isaac Hayes	27Oct73	22Dec73	27Apr74	16(1)	27	1890
1997.	**RHYTHM OF YOUTH**	Men Without Hats	06Aug83	24Sep83	28Jan84	13(3)	26	1887
1998.	**GOD BLESS TINY TIM**	Tiny Tim	04May68	13Jul68	07Dec68	7(2)	32	1886
1999.	**IDEA**	Bee Gees	31Aug68	19Oct68	01Mar69	17(3)	27	1886
2000.	**THE FIRM**	The Firm	02Mar85	13Apr85	12Oct85	17(2)	33	1884
2001.	**THE SOUTHER, HILLMAN, FURAY BAND**	The Souther, Hillman, Furay Band	20Jul74	07Sep74	14Dec74	11(1)	22	1884
2002.	**THE DOOR IS STILL OPEN TO MY HEART**	Dean Martin	14Nov64	19Dec64	05Jun65	9(3)	30	1884
2003.	**ALPHA**	Asia	27Aug83	10Sep83	11Feb84	6(4)	25	1881
2004.	**SEVEN YEAR ACHE**	Rosanne Cash	28Mar81	01Aug81	31Oct81	26(1)	32	1880
2005.	**BIG FUN**	Shalamar	10Nov79	22Mar80	02Aug80	23(2)	36	1879
2006.	**GALAXY**	War	03Dec77	18Feb78	06May78	15(2)	23	1878
2007.	**CAUGHT UP**	Millie Jackson	02Nov74	28Dec74	22Mar75	21(1)	21	1877
2008.	**WORKIN' TOGETHER**	Ike & Tina Turner	05Dec70	24Apr71	21Aug71	25(1)	38	1877
2009.	**DEODATO 2**	Deodato	11Aug73	29Sep73	06Apr74	19(1)	35	1875
2010.	**QUIET LIES**	Juice Newton	29May82	17Jul82	09Apr83	20(2)	46	1875
2011.	**I HOPE WE GET TO LOVE IN TIME**	Marilyn McCoo & Billy Davis Jr.	18Sep76	22Jan77	04Jun77	30(1)	38	1875
2012.	**THE BLUES BROTHERS (SOUNDTRACK)**	Blues Brothers	28Jun80	09Aug80	01Nov80	13(2)	19	1874
2013.	**HOLD YOUR FIRE**	Rush	26Sep87	17Oct87	16Apr88	13(2)	30	1873
2014.	**HOW TO BE A...ZILLIONAIRE!**	ABC	05Oct85	16Nov85	12Jul86	30(2)	41	1871
2015.	**YENTL (SOUNDTRACK)**	Barbra Streisand	26Nov83	07Jan84	19May84	9(2)	26	1871
2016.	**SOMETHING SPECIAL FOR YOUNG LOVERS**	Ray Charles Singers	04Apr64	01Aug64	14Nov64	11(1)	33	1871
2017.	**THE UNSINKABLE MOLLY BROWN**	Soundtrack	18Jul64	12Sep64	27Feb65	11(2)	33	1870
2018.	**COME ON OVER**	Olivia Newton-John	20Mar76	15May76	28Aug76	13(1)	24	1869
2019.	**BOBBY VINTON'S GREATEST HITS**	Bobby Vinton	03Oct64	30Jan65	19Jun65	12(1)	38	1869
2020.	**BODY AND SOUL**	Joe Jackson	07Apr84	26May84	20Oct84	20(4)	29	1868
2021.	**HITS!**	Boz Scaggs	29Nov80	10Jan81	23May81	24(6)	26	1868
2022.	**JOHN B. SEBASTIAN**	John Sebastian	28Mar70	25Apr70	24Oct70	20(2)	31	1865
2023.	**S.O.S.**	The S.O.S. Band	28Jun80	09Aug80	08Nov80	12(3)	20	1865
2024.	**MINSTREL IN THE GALLERY**	Jethro Tull	27Sep75	25Oct75	27Dec75	7(3)	14	1864
2025.	**SUBSTANCE**	New Order	05Sep87	30Jan88	11Feb89	36(1)	60	1864
2026.	**AFTER 7**	After 7	14Oct89	28Jul90	02Mar91	35(1)	72	1864
2027.	**A TOUCH OF GOLD**	Johnny Rivers	14Jun69	16Aug69	29Nov69	26(1)	25	1863
2028.	**FLYING IN A BLUE DREAM**	Joe Satriani	18Nov89	02Dec89	11Aug90	23(3)	39	1863
2029.	**TIMES OF YOUR LIFE**	Paul Anka	13Dec75	28Feb76	29May76	22(2)	25	1862
2030.	**EVERY HOME SHOULD HAVE ONE**	Patti Austin	03Oct81	19Feb83	28May83	36(8)	44	1862
2031.	**SKY HIGH!**	Tavares	12Jun76	18Sep76	08Jan77	24(2)	31	1862
2032.	**THE LITTLE MERMAID**	Soundtrack	16Dec89	24Feb90	10Nov90	32(2)	48	1861
2033.	**LIGHTS OUT**	UFO	11Jun77	01Oct77	19Nov77	23(2)	24	1861
2034.	**WALKING MAN**	James Taylor	13Jul74	24Aug74	09Nov74	13(2)	18	1857
2035.	**VOLCANO**	Jimmy Buffett	15Sep79	27Oct79	22Mar80	14(1)	28	1857
2036.	**INCREDIBLE**	Gary Puckett And The Union Gap	02Nov68	04Jan69	15Mar69	20(1)	20	1854
2037.	**INCENSE AND PEPPERMINTS**	Strawberry Alarm Clock	04Nov67	06Jan68	13Apr68	11(3)	24	1854
2038.	**DAWN'S NEW RAGTIME FOLLIES**	Dawn Featuring Tony Orlando	20Oct73	01Feb75	22Mar75	43(1)	58	1852
2039.	**SMALL WORLD**	Huey Lewis & The News	20Aug88	10Sep88	11Mar89	11(2)	30	1851
2040.	**AFTER THE LOVIN'**	Engelbert Humperdinck	27Nov76	05Feb77	04Jun77	17(2)	28	1851
2041.	**PRINCE**	Prince	17Nov79	19Jan80	24May80	22(2)	28	1850
2042.	**THE OTHER WOMAN**	Ray Parker Jr.	24Apr82	12Jun82	23Oct82	11(2)	27	1850
2043.	**ONE VOICE**	Barbra Streisand	09May87	06Jun87	14Nov87	9(2)	28	1848
2044.	**ERIC CLAPTON**	Eric Clapton	25Jul70	29Aug70	12Mar77	13(2)	32	1847
2045.	**STILL LIFE (AMERICAN CONCERT 1981)**	The Rolling Stones	26Jun82	10Jul82	27Nov82	5(4)	23	1847
2046.	**LOW BUDGET**	The Kinks	28Jul79	01Sep79	24Nov79	11(2)	18	1846
2047.	**SOUNDS...AND STUFF LIKE THAT!!**	Quincy Jones	24Jun78	12Aug78	04Nov78	15(1)	20	1846
2048.	**OUTSIDE INSIDE**	The Tubes	02Apr83	02Jul83	19Nov83	18(1)	34	1846
2049.	**CHICAGO 19**	Chicago	09Jul88	14Jan89	22Apr89	37(2)	42	1846
2050.	**THE GLAMOROUS LIFE**	Sheila E.	07Jul84	06Oct84	18May85	28(2)	46	1845
2051.	**BABY IT'S ME**	Diana Ross	08Oct77	03Dec77	11Feb78	18(2)	19	1845
2052.	**WE MADE IT HAPPEN**	Engelbert Humperdinck	11Jul70	01Aug70	10Apr71	19(2)	40	1843
2053.	**CHIC**	Chic	17Dec77	04Mar78	16Sep78	27(1)	40	1842
2054.	**WHAT CHA GONNA DO...WITH MY LOVIN'?**	Stephanie Mills	19May79	29Sep79	05Jan80	22(2)	34	1842
2055.	**LIFE FOR THE TAKING**	Eddie Money	27Jan79	10Mar79	21Jul79	17(2)	26	1842
2056.	**WELCOME TO THE PLEASURE DOME**	Frankie Goes To Hollywood	24Nov84	15Dec84	31Aug85	33(5)	41	1841
2057.	**WORLD MACHINE**	Level 42	22Mar86	21Jun86	22Nov86	18(2)	36	1841
2058.	**ONLY FOUR YOU**	Mary Jane Girls	16Mar85	22Jun85	30Nov85	18(2)	38	1841
2059.	**BECK-OLA**	Jeff Beck Group	12Jul69	02Aug69	29Nov69	15(3)	21	1841
2060.	**LOVE YOU LIVE**	The Rolling Stones	08Oct77	29Oct77	28Jan78	5(3)	17	1840
2061.	**LIFE BEYOND L.A.**	Ambrosia	12Aug78	02Dec78	24Feb79	19(2)	29	1840
2062.	**HIDEAWAY**	America	01May76	05Jun76	25Sep76	11(3)	22	1839
2063.	**JAILBREAK**	Thin Lizzy	17Apr76	24Jul76	23Oct76	18(2)	28	1839
2064.	**SHAKE YOU DOWN**	Gregory Abbott	01Nov86	14Feb87	04Jul87	22(1)	36	1838
2065.	**WITH LOVE, BOBBY**	Bobby Sherman	24Oct70	14Nov70	17Apr71	20(2)	26	1837
2066.	**IN SEARCH OF THE LOST CHORD**	The Moody Blues	14Sep68	07Dec68	16Aug69	23(1)	29	1837
2067.	**EL LOCO**	ZZ Top	08Aug81	26Sep81	02Jan82	17(2)	22	1836
2068.	**FRIENDS**	Dionne Warwick	21Dec85	01Mar86	14Jun86	12(2)	26	1836
2069.	**STANDING HAMPTON**	Sammy Hagar	30Jan82	12Jun82	04Sep82	28(2)	32	1836
2070.	**EQUINOX**	Sergio Mendes & Brasil '66	29Apr67	03Jun67	09Mar68	24(2)	46	1836
2071.	**LET US GO INTO THE HOUSE OF THE LORD**	The Edwin Hawkins Singers	03May69	14Jun69	04Oct69	15(1)	23	1835
2072.	**AMBROSIA**	Ambrosia	03May75	06Sep75	13Dec75	22(1)	33	1835
2073.	**THE HURDY GURDY MAN**	Donovan	19Oct68	21Dec68	01Mar69	20(1)	20	1832
2074.	**REFLECTIONS**	Diana Ross & The Supremes	27Apr68	15Jun68	09Nov68	18(2)	29	1832
2075.	**SANTANA'S GREATEST HITS**	Santana	27Jul74	28Sep74	14Dec74	17(1)	21	1831
2076.	**VERY SPECIAL LOVE SONGS**	Charlie Rich	23Mar74	04May74	19Oct74	24(2)	31	1830
2077.	**ALONE TOGETHER**	Dave Mason	04Jul70	01Aug70	19Dec70	22(2)	25	1830
2078.	**SUMMER OF '42**	Peter Nero	27Nov71	15Jan72	27May72	23(2)	27	1829
2079.	**SHEENA EASTON**	Sheena Easton	14Mar81	13Jun81	26Nov83	24(1)	38	1828
2080.	**MAHOGANY**	Soundtrack	08Nov75	24Jan76	01May76	19(2)	26	1828
2081.	**GET CLOSER**	Seals & Crofts	01May76	25Sep76	13Nov76	37(1)	29	1828
2082.	**RAY, GOODMAN & BROWN**	Ray, Goodman & Brown	26Jan80	05Apr80	28Jun80	17(2)	23	1827
2083.	**WILL O' THE WISP**	Leon Russell	03May75	07Jun75	31Jan76	30(2)	40	1823
2084.	**CHASE**	Chase	08May71	21Aug71	30Oct71	22(1)	26	1820
2085.	**SHAVED FISH**	John Lennon/Plastic Ono Band	08Nov75	13Dec75	16May81	12(1)	32	1819
2086.	**THE POINT!**	Nilsson	06Mar71	08May71	15Feb75	25(1)	32	1819

Rank	Title	Act	Enter	Peak	Exit	Peak(Wks)	TotWks	Score
2087	THRUST	Herbie Hancock	05Oct74	09Nov74	08Mar75	13(1)	23	1819
2088	JESUS CHRIST SUPERSTAR	Soundtrack	30Jun73	15Sep73	23Mar74	21(1)	39	1818
2089	NANTUCKET SLEIGHRIDE	Mountain	06Feb71	27Feb71	21Aug71	16(1)	29	1818
2090	GREATEST HITS	Tony Orlando & Dawn	28Jun75	30Aug75	31Jan76	16(1)	32	1816
2091	TROUBLE MAN	Marvin Gaye	30Dec72	03Mar73	19May73	14(2)	21	1815
2092	STRUTTIN' MY STUFF	Elvin Bishop	24Jan76	22May76	11Sep76	18(2)	34	1815
2093	BLOW UP YOUR VIDEO	AC/DC	05Mar88	26Mar88	13Aug88	12(1)	24	1815
2094	GREATEST HITS	ABBA	18Sep76	27Nov76	17Nov79	48(1)	61	1814
2095	THEN & NOW...THE BEST OF THE MONKEES	The Monkees	26Jul86	13Sep86	14Mar87	21(2)	34	1814
2096	TURBO	Judas Priest	12Apr86	26Apr86	31Jan87	17(2)	36	1811
2097	SAMMY DAVIS JR. NOW	Sammy Davis Jr.	29Apr72	15Jul72	21Oct72	11(1)	26	1810
2098	LIVE AT THE APOLLO, VOLUME II	James Brown	07Sep68	28Dec68	31May69	32(1)	39	1809
2099	CONTACT	The Pointer Sisters	10Aug85	09Nov85	29Mar86	24(1)	34	1809
2100	NIGHT IN THE RUTS	Aerosmith	01Dec79	19Jan80	05Apr80	14(2)	19	1808
2101	SIMPLY STREISAND	Barbra Streisand	11Nov67	06Jan68	13Apr68	12(3)	23	1808
2102	ENGLAND'S NEWEST HIT MAKERS/THE ROLLING STONES	The Rolling Stones	27Jun64	22Aug64	20Feb65	11(1)	35	1808
2103	THE YES ALBUM	Yes	08May71	22Jan72	10Jun72	40(1)	50	1807
2104	THE MOVIE SONG ALBUM	Tony Bennett	12Mar66	18Jun66	24Sep66	18(2)	29	1804
2105	TRILOGY: PAST, PRESENT AND FUTURE	Frank Sinatra	12Apr80	05Jul80	20Sep80	17(2)	24	1804
2106	DOWNTOWN	Petula Clark	13Feb65	01May65	16Oct65	21(2)	36	1803
2107	LOVE CHILD	Diana Ross & The Supremes	14Dec68	25Jan69	03May69	14(1)	21	1803
2108	GENE SIMMONS	Gene Simmons	14Oct78	06Jan79	10Mar79	22(2)	22	1803
2109	GASOLINE ALLEY	Rod Stewart	20Jun70	08Aug70	04Dec71	27(1)	57	1802
2110	CHAKA	Chaka Khan	04Nov78	16Dec78	24Mar79	12(3)	21	1800
2111	THE GOLDEN AGE OF WIRELESS	Thomas Dolby	19Mar83	18Jun83	24Sep83	13(2)	28	1799
2112	A DAY AT THE RACES	Queen	15Jan77	12Feb77	21May77	5(1)	19	1797
2113	BROADCAST	Cutting Crew	21Mar87	23May87	23Jan88	16(2)	45	1795
2114	LOVE APPROACH	Tom Browne	26Jul80	01Nov80	17Jan81	18(2)	26	1795
2115	PLAYER	Player	05Nov77	25Feb78	24Jun78	26(2)	34	1794
2116	SEPTEMBER MORN	Neil Diamond	12Jan80	16Feb80	24May80	10(3)	20	1793
2117	ST. ELMO'S FIRE	Soundtrack	13Jul85	07Sep85	22Mar86	21(2)	37	1793
2118	JOHN DENVER'S GREATEST HITS, VOLUME 2	John Denver	05Mar77	02Apr77	02Jul77	6(1)	18	1792
2119	EVERLASTING	Natalie Cole	08Aug87	30Apr88	10Sep88	42(2)	58	1792
2120	IF I COULD ONLY REMEMBER MY NAME	David Crosby	20Mar71	03Apr71	17Jul71	12(2)	18	1792
2121	LIVIN' ON THE FAULT LINE	The Doobie Brothers	10Sep77	15Oct77	28Jan78	10(3)	21	1792
2122	MY CHERIE	Al Martino	11Sep65	12Mar66	30Jul66	19(1)	47	1791
2123	ALL THIS LOVE	DeBarge	11Sep82	18Jun83	25May85	24(2)	48	1789
2124	BURNING LOVE AND HITS FROM HIS MOVIES, VOLUME 2	Elvis Presley	11Nov72	06Jan73	28Apr73	22(3)	25	1789
2125	CREEDENCE CLEARWATER REVIVAL	Creedence Clearwater Revival	20Jul68	07Dec68	04Jul70	52(1)	73	1789
2126	MARIANNE FAITHFULL	Marianne Faithfull	05Jun65	25Sep65	01Jan66	12(1)	31	1789
2127	COMMUNIQUE	Dire Straits	30Jun79	04Aug79	03Nov79	11(2)	19	1787
2128	RECORDS	Foreigner	25Dec82	12Feb83	11Jun83	10(4)	25	1785
2129	DEFENDERS OF THE FAITH	Judas Priest	04Feb84	25Feb84	13Oct84	18(4)	37	1785
2130	BURNIN' SKY	Bad Company	26Mar77	23Apr77	03Sep77	15(2)	24	1784
2131	LAZY AFTERNOON	Barbra Streisand	01Nov75	20Dec75	13Mar76	12(2)	20	1783
2132	BACK TO THE FUTURE	Soundtrack	27Jul85	05Oct85	01Mar86	12(2)	32	1783
2133	SPINNERS	Spinners	21Apr73	09Jun73	27Oct73	14(1)	28	1782
2134	SUGARLOAF	Sugarloaf	15Aug70	17Oct70	27Feb71	24(2)	29	1782
2135	LOVE AT THE GREEK	Neil Diamond	26Feb77	09Apr77	16Jul77	8(2)	21	1780
2136	TROPICO	Pat Benatar	24Nov84	22Dec84	20Apr85	14(4)	22	1780
2137	BREAKING HEARTS	Elton John	21Jul84	11Aug84	09Mar85	20(5)	34	1779
2138	EVERY BREATH YOU TAKE-THE SINGLES	The Police	22Nov86	20Dec86	16May87	7(1)	26	1778
2139	KATY LIED	Steely Dan	12Apr75	31May75	31Jan81	13(1)	26	1776
2140	THE TWO OF US	Yarbrough & Peoples	27Dec80	28Mar81	06Jun81	16(2)	24	1775
2141	WHO'S AFRAID OF VIRGINIA WOOLF?	Jimmy Smith	18Apr64	13Jun64	14Nov64	16(2)	31	1774
2142	NO REST FOR THE WICKED	Ozzy Osbourne	22Oct88	19Nov88	22Apr89	13(1)	27	1774
2143	COAST TO COAST	The Dave Clark Five	02Jan65	27Feb65	22May65	6(1)	21	1773
2144	ANGEL OF THE NIGHT	Angela Bofill	03Nov79	08Mar80	14Jun80	34(1)	33	1773
2145	ON THE WAY TO THE SKY	Neil Diamond	28Nov81	16Jan82	29May82	17(2)	27	1772
2146	EDDIE KENDRICKS	Eddie Kendricks	16Jun73	03Nov73	16Mar74	18(1)	40	1772
2147	BLUE JAYS	Justin Hayward & John Lodge	29Mar75	17May75	30Aug75	16(1)	23	1772
2148	BARRY MANILOW I	Barry Manilow	02Aug75	25Oct75	16Jul77	28(2)	51	1772
2149	PIANO MAN	Billy Joel	05Jan74	30Mar74	05Oct74	27(2)	40	1770
2150	LONDON CALLING	The Clash	09Feb80	22Mar80	20Sep80	27(3)	33	1770
2151	VALLEY OF THE DOLLS	Soundtrack	03Feb68	30Mar68	03Aug68	11(2)	27	1769
2152	TOUCHING YOU TOUCHING ME	Neil Diamond	13Dec69	24Jan70	31Oct70	30(1)	47	1768
2153	REACH FOR THE SKY	Ratt	19Nov88	17Dec88	20May89	17(1)	27	1768
2154	M.U. THE BEST OF JETHRO TULL	Jethro Tull	24Jan76	06Mar76	26Jun76	13(2)	23	1768
2155	SEARCHIN' FOR A RAINBOW	The Marshall Tucker Band	13Sep75	08Nov75	01May76	15(2)	34	1767
2156	ANOTHER PAGE	Christopher Cross	19Feb83	12Mar83	31Mar84	11(5)	31	1765
2157	THE NIGHTFLY	Donald Fagen	30Oct82	27Nov82	30Apr83	11(4)	27	1763
2158	MARDI GRAS	Creedence Clearwater Revival	29Apr72	20May72	07Oct72	12(1)	24	1763
2159	MUSIC FROM THE EDGE OF HEAVEN	Wham!	19Jul86	23Aug86	24Jan87	10(2)	28	1761
2160	360 DEGREES OF BILLY PAUL	Billy Paul	25Nov72	03Feb73	26May73	17(1)	27	1761
2161	CAROL HENSEL'S EXERCISE AND DANCE PROGRAM	Carol Hensel	21Mar81	23May81	19Jun82	56(1)	55	1759
2162	DELICATE SOUND OF THUNDER	Pink Floyd	10Dec88	14Jan89	29Apr89	11(1)	21	1759
2163	LIVE CREAM	Cream	02May70	06Jun70	19Sep70	15(1)	21	1759
2164	SLIDE IT IN	Whitesnake	19May84	25Aug84	12Mar88	40(2)	85	1759
2165	STARLAND VOCAL BAND	Starland Vocal Band	29May76	21Aug76	13Nov76	20(2)	25	1758
2166	THREE SIDES LIVE	Genesis	26Jun82	21Aug82	11Dec82	10(3)	25	1758
2167	BOBBY CALDWELL	Bobby Caldwell	18Nov78	10Mar79	16Jun79	21(2)	31	1758
2168	THE SLIDER	T. Rex	26Aug72	11Nov72	03Feb73	17(2)	24	1758
2169	BLOW MY FUSE	Kix	15Oct88	02Dec89	24Mar90	46(1)	60	1757
2170	SONNY & CHER LIVE	Sonny & Cher	02Oct71	11Dec71	01Jul72	35(1)	40	1756
2171	SECOND CHILDHOOD	Phoebe Snow	14Feb76	27Mar76	10Jul76	13(2)	22	1755
2172	SPINOUT (SOUNDTRACK)	Elvis Presley	29Oct66	17Dec66	03Jun67	18(3)	32	1755
2173	NEIL DIAMOND/HIS 12 GREATEST HITS	Neil Diamond	08Jun74	13Jul74	11Feb78	29(1)	42	1754
2174	PICTURES FOR PLEASURE	Charlie Sexton	30Nov85	22Mar86	19Jul86	15(3)	34	1753
2175	GREATEST HITS ON EARTH	The 5th Dimension	30Sep72	11Nov72	10Mar73	14(2)	24	1753
2176	WHAT YOU DON'T KNOW	Exposé	01Jul89	05Aug89	09Jun90	33(2)	50	1752
2177	COLD BLOOD	Cold Blood	27Dec69	04Apr70	11Jul70	23(1)	29	1750
2178	SEE WHAT TOMORROW BRINGS	Peter, Paul & Mary	30Oct65	18Dec65	23Jul66	11(1)	39	1750
2179	ACE FREHLEY	Ace Frehley	14Oct78	13Jan79	17Mar79	26(3)	23	1749
2180	LIVE CONCERT AT THE FORUM	Barbra Streisand	18Nov72	06Jan73	19May73	19(2)	27	1749
2181	CITY OF ANGELS	The Miracles	25Oct75	07Feb76	15May76	33(1)	30	1749
2182	BORN TO LOVE	Peabo Bryson & Roberta Flack	13Aug83	19Nov83	26May84	25(1)	42	1749
2183	BACK TO OAKLAND	Tower Of Power	09Mar74	20Apr74	02Nov74	26(1)	35	1748
2184	WITH A LITTLE HELP FROM MY FRIENDS	Joe Cocker	31May69	26Jul69	11Apr70	35(2)	37	1745
2185	BACK TO THE WORLD	Curtis Mayfield	09Jun73	28Jul73	01Dec73	16(2)	26	1745
2186	INDIAN RESERVATION	Raiders	19Jun71	31Jul71	30Oct71	19(1)	20	1744
2187	LOVE'S LINES, ANGLES AND RHYMES	The 5th Dimension	13Mar71	01May71	14Aug71	17(1)	23	1742
2188	GREATEST HITS	Alabama	01Mar86	05Apr86	15Nov86	24(3)	38	1740
2189	A FIFTH OF BEETHOVEN	Walter Murphy & The Big Apple Band	04Sep76	30Oct76	14May77	15(1)	29	1740

Rank. Title Act
[Enter|Peak|Exit] Peak(Wks) TotWks Score

2190. ELVIS FOR EVERYONE! Elvis Presley
[14Aug65|23Oct65|12Feb66] 10(1) 27 1740
2191. STATE OF CONFUSION The Kinks
[11Jun83|06Aug83|26Nov83] 12(1) 25 1739
2192. BRAVE NEW WORLD
The Steve Miller Band
[28Jun69|26Jul69|20Dec69] 22(2) 26 1738
2193. JESSE JOHNSON'S REVUE
Jesse Johnson's Revue
[16Mar85|20Apr85|04Jan86] 43(5) 43 1738
2194. TURN! TURN! TURN! The Byrds
[01Jan66|05Mar66|01Oct66] 17(1) 40 1737
2195. SECRETS Robert Palmer
[21Jul79|06Oct79|29Dec79] 19(1) 24 1736
2196. HANG ON RAMSEY! Ramsey Lewis Trio
[19Feb66|16Apr66|20Aug66] 15(2) 27 1732
2197. BIG GAME White Lion
[01Jul89|05Aug89|23Dec89] 19(2) 26 1730
2198. HOOKED ON SWING Larry Elgart And His Manhattan Swing Orchestra
[19Jun82|14Aug82|26Mar83] 24(5) 41 1729
2199. PRETENDERS II The Pretenders
[29Aug81|12Sep81|02Jan82] 10(3) 19 1727
2200. CHER(2) Cher
[05Dec87|07May88|10Sep88] 32(3) 41 1727
2201. SWEETHEART Engelbert Humperdinck
[20Feb71|03Apr71|31Jul71] 22(2) 24 1726
2202. WILLIE NELSON AND FAMILY LIVE
Willie Nelson
[02Dec78|27Jan79|29Nov80] 32(2) 55 1726
2203. TOO MUCH! Lou Rawls
[06May67|01Jul67|30Sep67] 18(2) 22 1724
2204. STEP BY STEP Eddie Rabbitt
[22Aug81|17Oct81|10Apr82] 23(1) 34 1720
2205. THE FREEWHEELIN' BOB DYLAN
Bob Dylan
[07Sep63|05Oct63|11Apr64] 22(1) 32 1720
2206. COLD BLOODED Rick James
[27Aug83|29Oct83|10Mar84] 16(1) 29 1717
2207. REMAIN IN LIGHT Talking Heads
[01Nov80|06Dec80|02May81] 19(2) 27 1717
2208. CRAZY HORSES The Osmonds
[14Oct72|23Dec72|10Mar73] 14(1) 22 1717
2209. PARTNERS IN CRIME Rupert Holmes
[10Nov79|15Mar80|07Jun80] 33(2) 31 1717
2210. INNER SECRETS Santana
[04Nov78|02Dec78|16Jun79] 27(2) 33 1716
2211. WILD, WILD WEST The Escape Club
[27Aug88|26Nov88|13May89] 27(3) 38 1716
2212. IT'S BETTER TO TRAVEL Swing Out Sister
[29Aug87|27Feb88|18Jun88] 40(1) 43 1716
2213. BLOWS AGAINST THE EMPIRE
Paul Kantner/Jefferson Starship
[19Dec70|09Jan71|22May71] 20(3) 23 1714
2214. HAPPY TRAILS 3
Quicksilver Messenger Service
[29Mar69|10May69|01Nov69] 27(2) 30 1713
2215. TRUE STORIES: A FILM BY DAVID BYRNE, THE COMPLETE SOUNDTRACK Talking Heads
[04Oct86|08Nov86|18Apr87] 17(3) 29 1713
2216. VOICES CARRY 'Til Tuesday
[20Apr85|27Jul85|16Nov85] 19(1) 31 1712
2217. ...ALL THE RAGE General Public
[27Oct84|16Feb85|20Jul85] 26(2) 39 1712
2218. IN YOUR EYES George Benson
[18Jun83|23Jul83|11Feb84] 27(1) 35 1711
2219. JUST GETS BETTER WITH TIME
The Whispers
[30May87|15Aug87|06Feb88] 22(2) 37 1710
2220. GREATEST HITS James Taylor
[04Dec76|15Jan77|01Apr78] 23(2) 41 1710
2221. UNDER LOCK AND KEY Dokken
[21Dec85|15Feb86|28Mar87] 32(3) 67 1710
2222. IT MUST BE HIM
Ray Conniff & His Orchestra & Chorus
[17Feb68|04May68|18Jan69] 25(1) 41 1710
2223. I (WHO HAVE NOTHING) Tom Jones
[14Nov70|12Dec70|14Aug71] 23(1) 40 1710

Rank. Title Act
[Enter|Peak|Exit] Peak(Wks) TotWks Score

2224. MARIA ELENA Los Indios Tabajaras
[16Nov63|04Jan64|13Jun64] 7(2) 31 1708
2225. GEORGE HARRISON George Harrison
[17Mar79|28Apr79|14Jul79] 14(1) 18 1708
2226. SHE'S THE BOSS Mick Jagger
[16Mar85|20Apr85|28Sep85] 13(1) 29 1708
2227. GREEN IS BLUES Al Green
[06Jan73|17Mar73|14Jul73] 19(1) 28 1707
2228. FOUR SEASONS OF LOVE Donna Summer
[06Nov76|11Dec76|30Apr77] 29(1) 26 1707
2229. MERCY, MERCY, MERCY!
"Cannonball" Adderley Quintet
[25Feb67|08Apr67|26Aug67] 13(2) 27 1705
2230. INDIGO GIRLS Indigo Girls
[15Apr89|02Sep89|09Dec89] 22(3) 35 1704
2231. MECHANICAL RESONANCE Tesla
[31Jan87|04Apr87|26Mar88] 32(2) 61 1704
2232. ROBIN TROWER LIVE! Robin Trower
[27Mar76|01May76|07Aug76] 10(2) 20 1702
2233. DISCO BABY
Van McCoy & The Soul City Symphony
[26Apr75|26Jul75|27Sep75] 12(1) 23 1701
2234. LOVE IS BLUE Johnny Mathis
[13Apr68|22Jun68|11Jan69] 26(1) 40 1700
2235. ANTICIPATION Carly Simon
[27Nov71|04Mar72|24Jun72] 30(2) 31 1699
2236. MAGAZINE Heart
[22Apr78|03Jun78|07Oct78] 17(1) 25 1698
2237. 21 AT 33 Elton John
[31May80|19Jul80|18Oct80] 13(2) 21 1698
2238. PIPES OF PEACE Paul McCartney
[19Nov83|17Dec83|28Apr84] 15(1) 24 1698
2239. A TOUCH OF TODAY Nancy Wilson
[28May66|30Jul66|07Jan67] 15(1) 33 1697
2240. PLAYING POSSUM Carly Simon
[03May75|31May75|23Aug75] 10(2) 17 1696
2241. NO FUN ALOUD Glenn Frey
[26Jun82|14Aug82|12Mar83] 32(3) 38 1696
2242. JEFF BECK GROUP Jeff Beck Group
[13May72|01Jul72|04Nov72] 19(2) 26 1694
2243. DRAW THE LINE Aerosmith
[24Dec77|28Jan78|06May78] 11(3) 20 1694
2244. FLOWERS IN THE DIRT Paul McCartney
[24Jun89|01Jul89|26May90] 21(3) 49 1694
2245. METAMORPHOSIS The Rolling Stones
[21Jun75|12Jul75|13Sep75] 8(2) 13 1693
2246. DIAMANTINA COCKTAIL Little River Band
[25Jun77|13Aug77|20May78] 49(1) 48 1693
2247. THIS IS NIECY Deniece Williams
[30Oct76|19Mar77|02Jul77] 33(2) 36 1691
2248. BILL COSBY SINGS/SILVER THROAT
Bill Cosby
[02Sep67|18Nov67|24Feb68] 18(2) 26 1688
2249. SSSSH Ten Years After
[30Aug69|04Oct69|29Aug70] 20(1) 23 1688
2250. SHE'S A LADY Tom Jones
[22May71|12Jun71|02Oct71] 17(3) 20 1686
2251. LIVE IN AUSTRALIA (WITH THE MELBOURNE SYMPHONY ORCHESTRA)
Elton John
[25Jul87|06Feb88|30Apr88] 24(2) 41 1685
2252. LIVE AT CARNEGIE HALL/WHAT YOU HEAR IS WHAT YOU GET Ike & Tina Turner
[10Jul71|21Aug71|04Dec71] 25(2) 22 1685
2253. AGAINST ALL ODDS Soundtrack
[31Mar84|28Apr84|25Aug84] 12(4) 22 1684
2254. AMMONIA AVENUE
The Alan Parsons Project
[17Mar84|28Apr84|08Sep84] 15(1) 26 1684
2255. BRAVE AND CRAZY Melissa Etheridge
[07Oct89|11Nov89|10Nov90] 22(1) 58 1683
2256. BLUES FOR ALLAH Grateful Dead
[06Sep75|25Oct75|29Nov75] 12(2) 13 1682
2257. RAIN FOREST Walter Wanderley
[03Sep66|10Dec66|10Jun67] 22(1) 41 1682
2258. THE PROMISE OF A FUTURE
Hugh Masekela
[08Jun68|24Aug68|02Nov68] 17(1) 22 1681

Rank. Title Act
[Enter|Peak|Exit] Peak(Wks) TotWks Score

2259. GREATEST HITS Fleetwood Mac
[10Dec88|11Feb89|03Jun89] 14(1) 26 1681
2260. A LOVE TRILOGY Donna Summer
[27Mar76|05Jun76|25Sep76] 21(1) 27 1681
2261. IT MUST BE MAGIC Teena Marie
[13Jun81|22Aug81|28Nov81] 23(1) 25 1680
2262. MEATY BEATY BIG AND BOUNCY
The Who
[20Nov71|04Dec71|08Apr72] 11(1) 21 1680
2263. DAWN (GO AWAY) AND 11 OTHER GREAT SONGS The 4 Seasons
[28Mar64|18Apr64|12Sep64] 6(2) 25 1679
2264. STREET-LEGAL Bob Dylan
[08Jul78|12Aug78|09Dec78] 11(1) 23 1679
2265. YOU CAN TUNE A PIANO BUT YOU CAN'T TUNA FISH REO Speedwagon
[22Apr78|17Jun78|27Jun81] 29(1) 48 1679
2266. JOHNNY WINTER Johnny Winter
[10May69|07Jun69|11Oct69] 24(2) 23 1679
2267. HEJIRA Joni Mitchell
[11Dec76|15Jan77|09Apr77] 13(2) 18 1679
2268. A HAPPENING IN CENTRAL PARK
Barbra Streisand
[12Oct68|14Dec68|22Feb69] 30(2) 20 1678
2269. BLESS ITS POINTED LITTLE HEAD
Jefferson Airplane
[01Mar69|15Mar69|12Jul69] 17(2) 20 1678
2270. THE BEAT GOES ON Vanilla Fudge
[02Mar68|06Apr68|12Oct68] 17(4) 33 1677
2271. OL' BLUE EYES IS BACK Frank Sinatra
[27Oct73|22Dec73|23Mar74] 13(1) 22 1676
2272. IN THE HEART Kool & The Gang
[10Dec83|03Mar84|18Aug84] 29(2) 37 1676
2273. LOU RAWLS CARRYIN' ON! Lou Rawls
[21Jan67|01Apr67|19Aug67] 20(2) 31 1676
2274. JUMP UP! Elton John
[08May82|12Jun82|18Dec82] 17(3) 33 1675
2275. LOVE SONG Anne Murray
[09Mar74|27Jul74|19Oct74] 24(2) 33 1675
2276. JERMAINE Jermaine Jackson
[12Aug72|07Oct72|14Apr73] 27(1) 36 1673
2277. ANIMALIZATION The Animals
[20Aug66|08Oct66|11Mar67] 20(2) 30 1672
2278. WHATCHA SEE IS WHATCHA GET
The Dramatics
[22Jan72|25Mar72|01Jul72] 20(1) 24 1670
2279. I'LL TAKE CARE OF YOUR CARES
Frankie Laine
[13May67|22Jul67|25Nov67] 16(2) 29 1670
2280. WORLDS APART Saga
[23Oct82|19Feb83|25Jun83] 29(5) 36 1669
2281. STRAIGHT UP Badfinger
[25Dec71|04Mar72|29Jul72] 31(1) 32 1669
2282. FABLES OF THE RECONSTRUCTION
R.E.M.
[29Jun85|03Aug85|12Apr86] 28(2) 42 1668
2283. THE ANIMALS The Animals
[05Sep64|31Oct64|06Mar65] 7(3) 27 1667
2284. AMERICAN DREAM
Crosby, Stills, Nash & Young
[03Dec88|07Jan89|29Apr89] 16(1) 22 1667
2285. YOUR CHEATIN' HEART (SOUNDTRACK)
Hank Williams Jr.
[02Jan65|17Apr65|11Sep65] 16(1) 37 1666
2286. I WROTE A SIMPLE SONG Billy Preston
[22Jan72|29Jul72|04Nov72] 32(1) 38 1666
2287. ROSES IN THE SNOW Emmylou Harris
[24May80|12Jul80|10Jan81] 26(2) 34 1665
2288. TIME Electric Light Orchestra
[22Aug81|19Sep81|02Jan82] 16(3) 20 1665
2289. MORE OF ROY ORBISON'S GREATEST HITS
Roy Orbison
[22Aug64|24Oct64|13Mar65] 19(3) 30 1665
2290. IMAGINATION The Whispers
[17Jan81|28Mar81|18Jul81] 23(2) 27 1662
2291. WOMAN, WOMAN
The Union Gap Featuring Gary Puckett
[17Feb68|04May68|21Dec68] 22(2) 45 1662

Rank. Title Act
[Enter|Peak|Exit] Peak(Wks) TotWks Score

2292. BOOTSY? PLAYER OF THE YEAR Bootsy's Rubber Band
[25Feb78|15Apr78|05Aug78] 16(2) 24 1658

2293. CONQUISTADOR Maynard Ferguson
[02Apr77|25Jun77|24Sep77] 22(2) 26 1657

2294. DOUBLE LIVE GONZO! Ted Nugent
[11Feb78|15Apr78|08Jul78] 13(1) 22 1657

2295. LIZA WITH A "Z" (SOUNDTRACK) Liza Minnelli
[30Sep72|25Nov72|03Mar73] 19(3) 23 1653

2296. WORKINGMAN'S DEAD Grateful Dead
[27Jun70|18Jul70|19Dec70] 27(2) 26 1652

2297. HEARTBREAKER Dolly Parton
[12Aug78|07Oct78|31Mar79] 27(2) 34 1652

2298. CRASH AND BURN Pat Travers Band
[05Apr80|17May80|20Sep80] 20(1) 25 1651

2299. FOREVER Kool & The Gang
[06Dec86|24Jan87|19Sep87] 25(1) 42 1651

2300. LOW David Bowie
[29Jan77|19Feb77|04Jun77] 11(2) 19 1651

2301. STEP II Sylvester
[05Aug78|28Oct78|19May79] 28(1) 42 1651

2302. THE LAST POETS The Last Poets
[20Jun70|19Sep70|09Jan71] 29(1) 30 1649

2303. FREE-FOR-ALL Ted Nugent
[02Oct76|20Nov76|19Nov77] 24(2) 32 1648

2304. ELECTRIC WARRIOR T. Rex
[06Nov71|08Apr72|24Jun72] 32(1) 34 1648

2305. THE NANCY WILSON SHOW! Nancy Wilson
[06Feb65|08May65|21Aug65] 24(2) 29 1643

2306. DEAR HEART Jack Jones
[09Jan65|20Mar65|26Jun65] 11(1) 25 1642

2307. BROTHER, BROTHER, BROTHER The Isley Brothers
[01Jul72|14Oct72|10Feb73] 29(2) 33 1642

2308. WHO I AM David Ruffin
[15Nov75|14Feb76|15May76] 31(1) 27 1641

2309. ELVIS IN CONCERT Elvis Presley
[29Oct77|19Nov77|25Feb78] 5(2) 18 1640

2310. ASYLUM KISS
[05Oct85|16Nov85|19Apr86] 20(1) 29 1639

2311. AL GREEN/GREATEST HITS Al Green
[22Mar75|03May75|09Aug75] 17(1) 21 1639

2312. JOY TO THE WORLD-THEIR GREATEST HITS Three Dog Night
[21Dec74|22Feb75|12Apr75] 15(1) 17 1638

2313. THE INNOCENTS Erasure
[18Jun88|22Oct88|27May89] 49(1) 50 1638

2314. BLACK BEAR ROAD C.W. McCall
[29Nov75|14Feb76|03Apr76] 12(2) 19 1637

2315. LAST EXIT Traffic
[17May69|21Jun69|11Oct69] 19(1) 22 1637

2316. I NEVER SAID GOODBYE Sammy Hagar
[11Jul87|15Aug87|12Dec87] 14(1) 23 1636

2317. TEJAS ZZ Top
[22Jan77|26Feb77|02Jul77] 17(2) 24 1636

2318. SPINNERS LIVE! Spinners
[13Dec75|06Mar76|01May76] 20(2) 21 1636

2319. ROCKIHNROLL Greg Kihn Band
[11Apr81|29Aug81|14Nov81] 32(1) 32 1636

2320. LET IT FLOW Dave Mason
[30Apr77|04Jun77|15Apr78] 37(1) 49 1636

2321. THIS TIME Al Jarreau
[21Jun80|16Aug80|14Feb81] 27(2) 35 1635

2322. TOM TOM CLUB Tom Tom Club
[24Oct81|03Apr82|10Jul82] 23(1) 33 1635

2323. INFORMATION SOCIETY Information Society
[20Aug88|12Nov88|06May89] 25(1) 38 1635

2324. CHOCOLATE CHIP Isaac Hayes
[21Jun75|02Aug75|25Oct75] 18(2) 19 1634

2325. HARUM SCARUM (SOUNDTRACK) Elvis Presley
[13Nov65|01Jan66|16Apr66] 8(2) 23 1634

2326. GET YOUR WINGS Aerosmith
[06Apr74|18Oct75|07Aug76] 74(1) 86 1634

2327. SOMEBODY'S WATCHING ME Rockwell
[11Feb84|31Mar84|01Sep84] 15(2) 30 1634

Rank. Title Act
[Enter|Peak|Exit] Peak(Wks) TotWks Score

2328. GOLD PLATED The Climax Blues Band
[23Oct76|02Jul77|01Oct77] 27(1) 44 1633

2329. IDENTIFY YOURSELF The O'Jays
[15Sep79|20Oct79|05Apr80] 16(2) 30 1633

2330. MOOG - THE ELECTRIC ECLECTICS OF DICK HYMAN Dick Hyman
[19Apr69|19Jul69|06Dec69] 30(3) 30 1633

2331. CHINESE WALL Philip Bailey
[10Nov84|23Feb85|06Jul85] 22(3) 35 1633

2332. CAUGHT IN THE ACT Commodores
[22Mar75|26Jul75|01Nov75] 26(1) 33 1632

2333. SEVENTH SON OF A SEVENTH SON Iron Maiden
[30Apr88|28May88|01Oct88] 12(1) 23 1631

2334. ONE NATION UNDER A GROOVE Funkadelic
[07Oct78|25Nov78|03Mar79] 16(1) 22 1631

2335. WARM Herb Alpert & The Tijuana Brass
[05Jul69|02Aug69|27Dec69] 28(3) 26 1630

2336. OVER-NITE SENSATION The Mothers
[06Oct73|01Dec73|14Sep74] 32(1) 50 1629

2337. MELTING POT Booker T. & The MG's
[13Feb71|27Mar71|30Oct71] 43(1) 38 1626

2338. FEAR OF MUSIC Talking Heads
[01Sep79|03Nov79|22Mar80] 21(1) 30 1626

2339. MARK, DON & MEL 1969-71 Grand Funk Railroad
[13May72|17Jun72|11Nov72] 17(2) 27 1625

2340. I CAN SEE CLEARLY NOW Johnny Nash
[07Oct72|09Dec72|05May73] 23(2) 31 1624

2341. BETTY WRIGHT LIVE Betty Wright
[17Jun78|14Oct78|17Feb79] 26(2) 36 1624

2342. ESCAPE Whodini
[24Nov84|16Feb85|19Oct85] 35(1) 48 1624

2343. OKIE FROM MUSKOGEE Merle Haggard And The Strangers
[24Jan70|07Mar70|27Feb71] 46(1) 52 1623

2344. MESSAGE IN THE MUSIC The O'Jays
[02Oct76|06Nov76|26Feb77] 20(1) 22 1623

2345. CAMEOSIS Cameo
[24May80|16Aug80|15Nov80] 25(3) 26 1618

2346. LIVING A LIE Al Martino
[08Feb64|04Apr64|15Aug64] 13(1) 28 1616

2347. WINDS OF CHANGE Jefferson Starship
[30Oct82|11Dec82|28May83] 26(6) 31 1616

2348. HEAD FIRST The Babys
[27Jan79|14Apr79|14Jul79] 22(2) 25 1615

2349. RED HEADED STRANGER Willie Nelson
[26Jul75|29Nov75|15May76] 28(2) 43 1615

2350. HEY RICKY Melissa Manchester
[15May82|18Sep82|05Feb83] 19(5) 39 1614

2351. RECKONING R.E.M.
[05May84|02Jun84|04May85] 27(5) 53 1613

2352. LIVING THE BLUES Canned Heat
[07Dec68|25Jan69|29Mar69] 18(2) 17 1612

2353. MELODIES OF LOVE Bobby Vinton
[30Nov74|18Jan75|26Apr75] 16(1) 22 1610

2354. THE MANHATTAN TRANSFER The Manhattan Transfer
[03May75|19Jul75|17Jan76] 33(1) 38 1609

2355. THE GREAT ADVENTURES OF SLICK RICK Slick Rick
[21Jan89|10Jun89|21Oct89] 31(3) 40 1609

2356. JUST PLAIN CHARLEY Charley Pride
[28Feb70|28Mar70|29Aug70] 22(2) 27 1606

2357. NEVER DIE YOUNG James Taylor
[13Feb88|12Mar88|01Oct88] 25(2) 34 1606

2358. IN THE RIGHT PLACE Dr. John
[24Mar73|23Jun73|03Nov73] 24(2) 33 1606

2359. THE MARSHALL TUCKER BAND The Marshall Tucker Band
[07Jul73|17Nov73|06Apr74] 29(1) 40 1606

2360. I'VE GOTTA BE ME Sammy Davis Jr.
[11Jan69|05Apr69|28Jun69] 24(3) 25 1606

2361. THE ELECTRIFYING EDDIE HARRIS Eddie Harris
[13Apr68|07Sep68|18Jan69] 36(1) 41 1604

2362. ARETHA (II) Aretha Franklin
[15Nov86|24Jan87|08Aug87] 32(2) 39 1604

Rank. Title Act
[Enter|Peak|Exit] Peak(Wks) TotWks Score

2363. HOW YA LIKE ME NOW Kool Moe Dee
[28Nov87|21May88|05Nov88] 35(1) 50 1604

2364. THE NEARNESS OF YOU John Gary
[24Jul65|18Sep65|05Feb66] 11(2) 29 1604

2365. BACHMAN-TURNER OVERDRIVE Bachman-Turner Overdrive
[18Aug73|15Jun74|30Nov74] 70(1) 68 1602

2366. AFTER MIDNIGHT The Manhattans
[19Apr80|12Jul80|11Oct80] 24(2) 26 1600

2367. BARRY Barry Manilow
[13Dec80|24Jan81|25Apr81] 15(2) 20 1599

2368. WAITRESS IN THE DONUT SHOP Maria Muldaur
[09Nov74|04Jan75|03May75] 23(1) 26 1598

2369. TOM CAT Tom Scott & The L.A. Express
[15Mar75|14Jun75|06Mar76] 18(2) 27 1598

2370. CLONES OF DR. FUNKENSTEIN Parliament
[16Oct76|04Dec76|12Mar77] 20(1) 22 1598

2371. PETER GABRIEL (SECURITY) Peter Gabriel
[02Oct82|06Nov82|30Apr83] 28(9) 31 1598

2372. ARE YOU READY FOR THE COUNTRY Waylon Jennings
[17Jul76|28Aug76|19Mar77] 34(1) 35 1598

2373. TOWER OF POWER Tower Of Power
[02Jun73|01Sep73|29Dec73] 15(1) 31 1596

2374. THE SENSATIONAL CHARLEY PRIDE Charley Pride
[28Jun69|16Aug69|21Mar70] 44(1) 39 1596

2375. MEDDLE Pink Floyd
[06Nov71|27Nov71|23Feb80] 70(2) 73 1594

2376. WINDOWS AND WALLS Dan Fogelberg
[18Feb84|10Mar84|18Aug84] 15(3) 27 1593

2377. THE RETURN OF BRUNO Bruce Willis
[14Feb87|07Mar87|29Aug87] 14(3) 29 1592

2378. TOO-RYE-AY Dexys Midnight Runners
[12Feb83|30Apr83|23Jul83] 14(2) 24 1589

2379. STEPPENWOLF 7 Steppenwolf
[21Nov70|19Dec70|13Mar71] 19(2) 17 1589

2380. DARK SHADOWS (THE SCORE) TV Soundtrack
[02Aug69|13Sep69|06Dec69] 18(2) 19 1589

2381. DAYS OF WINE AND ROSES, MOON RIVER, AND OTHER ACADEMY AWARD WINNERS Frank Sinatra
[11Apr64|09May64|19Sep64] 10(2) 24 1588

2382. EXTRA TEXTURE (READ ALL ABOUT IT) George Harrison
[11Oct75|25Oct75|20Dec75] 8(3) 11 1587

2383. MASTER OF PUPPETS Metallica
[29Mar86|10May86|08Aug87] 29(2) 72 1587

2384. ALL AMERICAN BOY Rick Derringer
[01Dec73|23Mar74|29Jun74] 25(1) 31 1586

2385. WILD PLANET The B-52s
[20Sep80|18Oct80|21Mar81] 18(1) 27 1586

2386. YOU CAN DANCE Madonna
[05Dec87|23Jan88|30Apr88] 14(1) 22 1585

2387. STREET CALLED DESIRE René & Angela
[06Jul85|15Mar86|01Nov86] 64(4) 70 1585

2388. LIVES IN THE BALANCE Jackson Browne
[22Mar86|05Apr86|18Oct86] 23(3) 31 1582

2389. THIS IS MY SONG Ray Conniff & His Orchestra & Chorus
[03Jun67|29Jul67|13Apr68] 30(2) 46 1582

2390. ADVENTURES IN PARADISE Minnie Riperton
[31May75|26Jul75|01Nov75] 18(1) 23 1579

2391. HANGING IN THERE Hudson and Landry
[10Apr71|19Jun71|02Oct71] 30(2) 26 1579

2392. IT'S A MOTHER James Brown
[06Sep69|04Oct69|14Feb70] 26(1) 24 1579

2393. TOO OLD TO ROCK 'N' ROLL: TOO YOUNG TO DIE! Jethro Tull
[29May76|03Jul76|16Oct76] 14(1) 21 1579

2394. CHERYL LYNN Cheryl Lynn
[18Nov78|03Mar79|09Jun79] 23(1) 30 1578

2395. THREE FOR LOVE Shalamar
[10Jan81|28Mar81|12Sep81] 40(2) 36 1577

Rank. Title Act
[Enter|Peak|Exit] Peak(Wks) TotWks — Score

2396. THE O'JAYS LIVE IN LONDON The O'Jays
[29Jun74|14Sep74|07Dec74] 17(1) 24 — 1577

2397. THE BEST OF THE LETTERMEN The Lettermen
[08Oct66|14Jan67|08Apr67] 17(1) 27 — 1573

2398. STILL ALIVE AND WELL Johnny Winter
[07Apr73|09Jun73|15Sep73] 22(1) 24 — 1571

2399. THE BEST OF CARLY SIMON Carly Simon
[06Dec75|17Jan76|10Apr76] 17(2) 19 — 1571

2400. VOA Sammy Hagar
[11Aug84|15Dec84|13Apr85] 32(3) 36 — 1571

2401. TO SIR, WITH LOVE Soundtrack
[23Sep67|02Dec67|17Feb68] 16(4) 22 — 1569

2402. A NEW PLACE IN THE SUN Glen Campbell
[22Jun68|12Oct68|01Feb69] 24(1) 33 — 1569

2403. CLEARLY LOVE Olivia Newton-John
[11Oct75|08Nov75|06Mar76] 12(2) 22 — 1569

2404. 24/7 Dino
[25Mar89|02Sep89|17Feb90] 34(3) 48 — 1569

2405. SCREAM DREAM Ted Nugent
[31May80|05Jul80|27Sep80] 13(2) 18 — 1565

2406. LIFES RICH PAGEANT R.E.M.
[23Aug86|11Oct86|28Mar87] 21(2) 32 — 1563

2407. I LOVE HOW YOU LOVE ME Bobby Vinton
[04Jan69|22Feb69|14Jun69] 21(1) 24 — 1563

2408. TOOTH AND NAIL Dokken
[13Oct84|29Jun85|08Mar86] 49(2) 74 — 1562

2409. THE OTHER SIDE OF THE MIRROR Stevie Nicks
[10Jun89|08Jul89|28Oct89] 10(1) 21 — 1562

2410. MINGUS Joni Mitchell
[07Jul79|01Sep79|03Nov79] 17(1) 18 — 1561

2411. GRATEFUL DEAD FROM THE MARS HOTEL Grateful Dead
[13Jul74|24Aug74|23Nov74] 16(1) 20 — 1560

2412. BLINDED BY SCIENCE Thomas Dolby
[05Feb83|02Apr83|03Sep83] 20(4) 31 — 1559

2413. SMASHES, THRASHES & HITS KISS
[03Dec88|21Jan89|03Jun89] 21(2) 27 — 1558

2414. I'M LEAVING IT ALL UP TO YOU Donny & Marie Osmond
[07Sep74|09Nov74|29Mar75] 35(1) 30 — 1557

2415. KING OF ROCK Run-D.M.C.
[23Feb85|02Mar85|15Mar86] 52(3) 56 — 1556

2416. NON-STOP B.T. Express
[02Aug75|04Oct75|06Dec75] 19(1) 19 — 1555

2417. SHADES OF DEEP PURPLE Deep Purple
[07Sep68|16Nov68|08Feb69] 24(1) 23 — 1555

2418. JUST ANOTHER WAY TO SAY I LOVE YOU Barry White
[12Apr75|07Jun75|02Aug75] 17(1) 17 — 1555

2419. GREATEST HITS Mary Wells
[30May64|08Aug64|06Feb65] 18(2) 37 — 1555

2420. CHARLEY PRIDE'S 10TH ALBUM Charley Pride
[18Jul70|12Sep70|03Apr71] 30(2) 38 — 1554

2421. A QUIET STORM Smokey Robinson
[19Apr75|14Jun75|31Jan76] 36(3) 42 — 1552

2422. FIRST OFFENSE Corey Hart
[14Jul84|15Sep84|16Mar85] 31(3) 36 — 1550

2423. DONNA SUMMER Donna Summer
[14Aug82|18Sep82|23Apr83] 20(5) 37 — 1550

2424. RANT 'N' RAVE WITH THE STRAY CATS Stray Cats
[10Sep83|15Oct83|24Mar84] 14(2) 29 — 1548

2425. METAMORPHOSIS Iron Butterfly
[29Aug70|03Oct70|30Jan71] 16(1) 23 — 1547

2426. TONIGHT David Bowie
[20Oct84|24Nov84|30Mar85] 11(2) 24 — 1546

2427. BERT KAEMPFERT'S GREATEST HITS Bert Kaempfert And His Orchestra
[08Oct66|31Dec66|08Jul67] 30(1) 40 — 1545

2428. GREATEST HITS, ETC. Paul Simon
[03Dec77|04Feb78|06May78] 18(1) 23 — 1544

2429. THE MUPPET MOVIE: ORIGINAL SOUNDTRACK RECORDING Soundtrack
[21Jul79|10Nov79|08Mar80] 32(2) 34 — 1544

Rank. Title Act
[Enter|Peak|Exit] Peak(Wks) TotWks — Score

2430. IN STEP Stevie Ray Vaughan And Double Trouble
[01Jul89|26Aug89|10Nov90] 33(1) 47 — 1544

2431. VISION QUEST Soundtrack
[02Mar85|04May85|03Aug85] 11(1) 23 — 1542

2432. KINKS-SIZE The Kinks
[03Apr65|19Jun65|16Oct65] 13(1) 29 — 1542

2433. LUSH LIFE Linda Ronstadt
[08Dec84|05Jan85|01Jun85] 13(2) 26 — 1541

2434. STAND BY ME Soundtrack
[20Sep86|06Dec86|25Jul87] 31(6) 45 — 1541

2435. SHEIK YERBOUTI Frank Zappa
[24Mar79|02Jun79|25Aug79] 21(1) 23 — 1539

2436. HARD TO HOLD (SOUNDTRACK) Rick Springfield
[07Apr84|05May84|12Jan85] 16(3) 36 — 1538

2437. SEX MACHINE James Brown
[12Sep70|28Nov70|10Apr71] 29(1) 31 — 1538

2438. TURN AROUND, LOOK AT ME The Vogues
[07Sep68|21Dec68|29Mar69] 29(1) 30 — 1536

2439. KNOCK ON WOOD Amii Stewart
[17Mar79|05May79|18Aug79] 19(1) 23 — 1535

2440. BUSY BODY Luther Vandross
[24Dec83|11Feb84|29Sep84] 32(4) 41 — 1534

2441. ALARM CLOCK Richie Havens
[09Jan71|19Jun71|28Aug71] 29(1) 34 — 1533

2442. BOOTS WITH STRINGS Boots Randolph
[14Jan67|06May67|02Dec67] 36(2) 47 — 1533

2443. CATCHING THE SUN Spyro Gyra
[22Mar80|03May80|04Oct80] 19(1) 29 — 1533

2444. ORGAN GRINDER SWING Jimmy Smith
[18Sep65|27Nov65|16Apr66] 15(1) 31 — 1532

2445. COMPLETELY WELL B.B. King
[27Dec69|04Apr70|18Jul70] 38(2) 30 — 1531

2446. NO ONE CAN DO IT BETTER The D.O.C.
[19Aug89|23Sep89|07Apr90] 20(2) 34 — 1531

2447. GOOD HIGH Brick
[13Nov76|05Feb77|23Apr77] 19(2) 24 — 1530

2448. BIG THING Duran Duran
[05Nov88|26Nov88|29Apr89] 24(2) 26 — 1528

2449. IT'S OUR THING The Isley Brothers
[03May69|31May69|30Aug69] 22(3) 18 — 1527

2450. RUNNING IN THE FAMILY Level 42
[11Apr87|01Aug87|28Nov87] 23(1) 34 — 1525

2451. KATRINA AND THE WAVES Katrina & The Waves
[13Apr85|15Jun85|16Nov85] 25(2) 32 — 1525

2452. HUMS OF THE LOVIN' SPOONFUL The Lovin' Spoonful
[17Dec66|25Feb67|10Jun67] 14(2) 26 — 1525

2453. PURE DYNAMITE! LIVE AT THE ROYAL James Brown
[29Feb64|18Apr64|25Jul64] 10(1) 22 — 1525

2454. FLEETWOOD MAC LIVE Fleetwood Mac
[27Dec80|17Jan81|25Apr81] 14(3) 18 — 1524

2455. TAO Rick Springfield
[27Apr85|01Jun85|26Oct85] 21(2) 27 — 1524

2456. TWENTY GREATEST HITS Kenny Rogers
[12Nov83|07Jan84|02Jun84] 22(2) 30 — 1524

2457. I'M THE MAN Joe Jackson
[27Oct79|15Dec79|12Apr80] 22(1) 25 — 1521

2458. THE CAT Jimmy Smith
[19Sep64|12Dec64|24Apr65] 12(2) 32 — 1520

2459. GAP BAND V- JAMMIN' The Gap Band
[10Sep83|15Oct83|30Jun84] 28(1) 43 — 1519

2460. UNFORGETTABLE Nat King Cole
[20Mar65|17Jul65|11Dec65] 30(1) 39 — 1519

2461. GODSPELL Soundtrack
[14Apr73|09Jun73|22Feb75] 50(2) 51 — 1518

2462. FRANKE & THE KNOCKOUTS Franke & The Knockouts
[28Mar81|20Jun81|26Sep81] 31(1) 27 — 1518

2463. DIANA & MARVIN Diana Ross & Marvin Gaye
[17Nov73|15Dec73|05Oct74] 26(1) 47 — 1518

2464. POWERLIGHT Earth, Wind & Fire
[12Mar83|26Mar83|30Jul83] 12(4) 21 — 1518

2465. SAM COOKE AT THE COPA Sam Cooke
[31Oct64|13Mar65|21May66] 29(1) 55 — 1517

Rank. Title Act
[Enter|Peak|Exit] Peak(Wks) TotWks — Score

2466. GREATEST HITS Ronnie Milsap
[25Oct80|28Feb81|01Aug81] 36(1) 41 — 1516

2467. TRUE Spandau Ballet
[14May83|29Oct83|31Mar84] 19(1) 37 — 1516

2468. CRUSH Orchestral Manoeuvres In The Dark
[27Jul85|23Nov85|26Jul86] 38(2) 53 — 1514

2469. JONATHAN LIVINGSTON SEAGULL Richard Harris
[08Sep73|15Dec73|09Mar74] 25(1) 27 — 1514

2470. DISTANT DRUMS Jim Reeves
[04Jun66|03Sep66|17Dec66] 21(1) 29 — 1514

2471. COWBOYS & COLORED PEOPLE Flip Wilson
[26Aug67|24Feb68|02Nov68] 34(2) 63 — 1514

2472. WHITE NIGHTS Soundtrack
[02Nov85|01Feb86|26Apr86] 17(2) 26 — 1513

2473. AROUND THE WORLD WITH THREE DOG NIGHT Three Dog Night
[17Mar73|12May73|15Sep73] 18(1) 27 — 1513

2474. YARDBIRDS GREATEST HITS The Yardbirds
[29Apr67|17Jun67|06Jan68] 28(1) 37 — 1513

2475. MOBY GRAPE Moby Grape
[01Jul67|02Sep67|30Dec67] 24(1) 27 — 1512

2476. WHEN YOU HEAR LOU, YOU'VE HEARD IT ALL Lou Rawls
[10Dec77|29Apr78|29Jul78] 41(1) 34 — 1512

2477. CURB YOUR TONGUE, KNAVE! The Smothers Brothers
[14Dec63|01Feb64|25Jul64] 13(2) 33 — 1511

2478. LONG JOHN SILVER Jefferson Airplane
[19Aug72|30Sep72|06Jan73] 20(2) 21 — 1511

2479. THE BEST OF WILSON PICKETT Wilson Pickett
[11Nov67|17Feb68|16Nov68] 35(2) 54 — 1510

2480. THE NUMBER OF THE BEAST Iron Maiden
[10Apr82|12Jun82|10Nov84] 33(2) 65 — 1510

2481. PONCHO & LEFTY Merle Haggard/Willie Nelson
[12Feb83|20Aug83|11Feb84] 37(1) 53 — 1509

2482. TRANSFORMER Lou Reed
[16Dec72|28Apr73|14Jul73] 29(2) 31 — 1506

2483. BARK AT THE MOON Ozzy Osbourne
[10Dec83|28Jan84|23Jun84] 19(3) 29 — 1506

2484. OUTLAWS The Outlaws
[09Aug75|11Oct75|22Nov75] 13(1) 16 — 1506

2485. HOW GREAT THOU ART Elvis Presley
[25Mar67|20May67|07Oct67] 18(1) 29 — 1505

2486. DEAR HEART AND OTHER SONGS ABOUT LOVE Henry Mancini And His Orchestra And Chorus
[30Jan65|03Apr65|17Jul65] 11(1) 25 — 1504

2487. SALLY CAN'T DANCE Lou Reed
[05Oct74|23Nov74|04Jan75] 10(2) 14 — 1504

2488. LIFE AS WE KNOW IT REO Speedwagon
[28Feb87|04Apr87|23Jan88] 28(2) 48 — 1504

2489. BULLETBOYS BulletBoys
[29Oct88|11Feb89|16Sep89] 34(3) 47 — 1504

2490. DIONNE WARWICK'S GOLDEN HITS, PART 2 Dionne Warwick
[01Nov69|06Dec69|09May70] 28(1) 28 — 1504

2491. GREATEST HITS The Judds
[27Aug88|10Sep88|23Jan93] 76(2) 97 — 1503

2492. ON THE BEACH Neil Young
[03Aug74|14Sep74|30Nov74] 16(1) 18 — 1502

2493. MONTEREY INTERNATIONAL POP FESTIVAL Otis Redding/The Jimi Hendrix Experience
[19Sep70|17Oct70|30Jan71] 16(2) 20 — 1502

2494. THE BREAKFAST CLUB Soundtrack
[09Mar85|18May85|31Aug85] 17(2) 26 — 1501

2495. I GOTCHA Joe Tex
[22Apr72|01Jul72|09Sep72] 17(1) 21 — 1501

2496. SWEET & SOUR TEARS Ray Charles
[21Mar64|18Apr64|22Aug64] 9(2) 23 — 1499

2497. YESTERDAY'S GONE Chad & Jeremy
[26Sep64|27Feb65|19Jun65] 22(1) 39 — 1499

Rank. Title Act
[Enter | Peak | Exit] Peak(Wks) TotWks — Score

2498. THERE GOES THE NEIGHBORHOOD Joe Walsh
[23May81 | 18Jul81 | 19Sep81] 20(1) 18 — 1499

2499. CLOUDS Joni Mitchell
[14Jun69 | 19Jul69 | 28Feb70] 31(1) 36 — 1498

2500. BITCHES BREW Miles Davis
[16May70 | 04Jul70 | 28Nov70] 35(2) 29 — 1497

2501. TRUE CONFESSIONS Bananarama
[16Aug86 | 20Sep86 | 21Feb87] 15(2) 28 — 1497

2502. BOB DYLAN AT BUDOKAN Bob Dylan
[12May79 | 16Jun79 | 27Oct79] 13(2) 25 — 1495

2503. CODA Led Zeppelin
[18Dec82 | 15Jan83 | 02Apr83] 6(3) 16 — 1495

2504. SENSE OF DIRECTION The Climax Blues Band
[15Jun74 | 05Oct74 | 28Dec74] 37(2) 29 — 1495

2505. LOVE DEVOTION SURRENDER Carlos Santana & Mahavishnu John McLaughlin
[07Jul73 | 18Aug73 | 15Dec73] 14(1) 24 — 1493

2506. EAT IT Humble Pie
[24Mar73 | 05May73 | 11Aug73] 13(3) 21 — 1493

2507. THE BEST OF EDDY ARNOLD Eddy Arnold
[06May67 | 24Jun67 | 01Feb69] 34(2) 57 — 1493

2508. MUSIC MAN Waylon Jennings
[07Jun80 | 12Jul80 | 28Mar81] 36(2) 43 — 1492

2509. HEARSAY Alexander O'Neal
[22Aug87 | 26Sep87 | 21May88] 29(1) 40 — 1492

2510. PYRAMID The Alan Parsons Project
[01Jul78 | 19Aug78 | 16Dec78] 26(1) 25 — 1491

2511. THE CLARKE/DUKE PROJECT Stanley Clarke & George Duke
[09May81 | 04Jul81 | 10Oct81] 33(4) 23 — 1491

2512. THE KINGSMEN, VOLUME II The Kingsmen
[26Sep64 | 28Nov64 | 05Jun65] 15(1) 37 — 1490

2513. INDIANOLA MISSISSIPPI SEEDS B.B. King
[17Oct70 | 28Nov70 | 24Apr71] 26(1) 28 — 1489

2514. SOONER OR LATER Rex Smith
[28Apr79 | 23Jun79 | 01Sep79] 19(2) 19 — 1488

2515. PHANTOMS The Fixx
[08Sep84 | 20Oct84 | 23Mar85] 19(3) 29 — 1488

2516. RICK NELSON SINGS "FOR YOU" Rick Nelson
[04Jan64 | 29Feb64 | 30May64] 14(2) 22 — 1487

2517. LONG MISTY DAYS Robin Trower
[09Oct76 | 13Nov76 | 12Feb77] 24(1) 19 — 1487

2518. ROADWORK Edgar Winter's White Trash
[25Mar72 | 20May72 | 09Sep72] 23(1) 25 — 1487

2519. I'LL ALWAYS LOVE YOU Anne Murray
[03Nov79 | 19Jan80 | 05Apr80] 24(2) 23 — 1486

2520. CAST YOUR FATE TO THE WIND Sounds Orchestral
[29May65 | 10Jul65 | 04Dec65] 11(2) 28 — 1484

2521. JUST A BOY Leo Sayer
[08Feb75 | 24May75 | 05Jul75] 16(1) 22 — 1483

2522. WHAT CHA' GONNA DO FOR ME Chaka Khan
[09May81 | 20Jun81 | 05Sep81] 17(2) 18 — 1482

2523. PRESTO Rush
[02Dec89 | 16Dec89 | 02Jun90] 16(2) 27 — 1481

2524. CHERISH David Cassidy
[12Feb72 | 04Mar72 | 15Jul72] 15(2) 23 — 1480

2525. EVANGELINE Emmylou Harris
[21Feb81 | 28Mar81 | 01Aug81] 22(3) 24 — 1480

2526. FORTUOSITY The Mills Brothers
[16Mar68 | 04May68 | 07Sep68] 21(3) 26 — 1480

2527. TORMATO Yes
[14Oct78 | 18Nov78 | 13Jan79] 10(2) 14 — 1480

2528. OF A SIMPLE MAN Lobo
[14Oct72 | 06Jan73 | 12May73] 37(1) 31 — 1478

2529. NOTHING MATTERS WITHOUT LOVE Seduction
[28Oct89 | 17Mar90 | 15Sep90] 36(1) 47 — 1477

2530. TIME OUT FOR SMOKEY ROBINSON & THE MIRACLES Smokey Robinson & The Miracles
[09Aug69 | 13Sep69 | 13Dec69] 25(2) 19 — 1477

2531. SPECIAL BEAT SERVICE The English Beat
[13Nov82 | 09Apr83 | 10Sep83] 39(3) 44 — 1477

Rank. Title Act
[Enter | Peak | Exit] Peak(Wks) TotWks — Score

2532. THE RIGHT STUFF Vanessa Williams
[09Jul88 | 15Apr89 | 22Jul89] 38(1) 55 — 1476

2533. MAKE YOUR MOVE Captain & Tennille
[17Nov79 | 09Feb80 | 26Apr80] 23(2) 24 — 1476

2534. THE LAST IN LINE Dio
[21Jul84 | 25Aug84 | 16Mar85] 23(2) 35 — 1475

2535. ONE IN A MILLION YOU Larry Graham
[21Jun80 | 16Aug80 | 29Nov80] 26(3) 24 — 1475

2536. WORD OF MOUTH Toni Basil
[23Oct82 | 11Dec82 | 14May83] 22(7) 30 — 1472

2537. TODAY-MY WAY Nancy Wilson
[05Jun65 | 31Jul65 | 23Oct65] 7(1) 21 — 1472

2538. THE 3RD TIME AROUND Roger Miller
[24Jul65 | 04Sep65 | 01Jan66] 13(2) 24 — 1472

2539. DON'T GO TO STRANGERS Eydie Gorme
[04Jun66 | 06Aug66 | 15Jul67] 22(2) 37 — 1472

2540. WHITE GOLD Love Unlimited Orchestra
[09Nov74 | 04Jan75 | 10May75] 28(1) 27 — 1472

2541. HOLD ON! (SOUNDTRACK) Herman's Hermits
[26Mar66 | 28May66 | 17Sep66] 14(2) 26 — 1471

2542. A CLOCKWORK ORANGE Soundtrack
[05Feb72 | 22Apr72 | 02Sep72] 34(1) 31 — 1470

2543. THE TIME OF MY LIFE! John Davidson
[08Oct66 | 10Dec66 | 18Mar67] 19(2) 24 — 1469

2544. GREATEST HITS 1974-78 The Steve Miller Band
[09Dec78 | 03Feb79 | 07Apr79] 18(2) 18 — 1469

2545. HEADHUNTER Krokus
[16Apr83 | 09Jul83 | 21Jan84] 25(2) 41 — 1468

2546. TUPELO HONEY Van Morrison
[30Oct71 | 27Nov71 | 08Apr72] 27(3) 24 — 1468

2547. FLICK OF THE SWITCH AC/DC
[10Sep83 | 15Oct83 | 11Feb84] 15(2) 23 — 1466

2548. WINNER TAKES ALL The Isley Brothers
[16Jun79 | 07Jul79 | 27Oct79] 14(2) 20 — 1464

2549. EMOTION Barbra Streisand
[27Oct84 | 10Nov84 | 04May85] 19(3) 28 — 1464

2550. EASTER Patti Smith Group
[08Apr78 | 24Jun78 | 09Sep78] 20(1) 23 — 1463

2551. GET HAPPY!! Elvis Costello And The Attractions
[22Mar80 | 12Apr80 | 28Jun80] 11(2) 15 — 1463

2552. IT'S TIME FOR LOVE Teddy Pendergrass
[03Oct81 | 31Oct81 | 03Apr82] 19(2) 27 — 1462

2553. DON'T LET ME BE MISUNDERSTOOD Santa Esmeralda
[12Nov77 | 18Feb78 | 15Apr78] 25(2) 23 — 1462

2554. MUSIC FOR THE MASSES Depeche Mode
[24Oct87 | 21Nov87 | 03Dec88] 35(2) 59 — 1461

2555. DIZZY Tommy Roe
[12Apr69 | 17May69 | 09Aug69] 25(2) 18 — 1461

2556. THE GENIUS OF JANKOWSKI! Horst Jankowski
[22May65 | 28Aug65 | 18Dec65] 18(1) 31 — 1460

2557. ELITE HOTEL Emmylou Harris
[24Jan76 | 20Mar76 | 26Jun76] 25(1) 23 — 1460

2558. ROBBIE NEVIL Robbie Nevil
[29Nov86 | 07Feb87 | 10Oct87] 37(2) 46 — 1460

2559. COCKED & LOADED L.A. Guns
[16Sep89 | 07Jul90 | 06Oct90] 38(1) 56 — 1459

2560. SOLID Ashford & Simpson
[10Nov84 | 02Mar85 | 13Jul85] 29(2) 36 — 1459

2561. ELTON JOHN'S GREATEST HITS, VOLUME II Elton John
[22Oct77 | 03Dec77 | 04Mar78] 21(3) 20 — 1459

2562. THROWIN' DOWN Rick James
[05Jun82 | 10Jul82 | 06Nov82] 13(4) 23 — 1459

2563. DAWN PATROL Night Ranger
[25Dec82 | 02Apr83 | 03Nov84] 38(4) 69 — 1458

2564. ODYSSEY Odyssey
[08Oct77 | 24Dec77 | 24Jun78] 36(2) 38 — 1458

2565. GET CLOSE The Pretenders
[15Nov86 | 20Dec86 | 30May87] 25(3) 29 — 1457

2566. JOHNNY Johnny Mathis
[24Aug63 | 12Oct63 | 22Feb64] 20(2) 27 — 1457

2567. BLOODROCK 3 Bloodrock
[10Apr71 | 01May71 | 11Sep71] 27(5) 23 — 1457

Rank. Title Act
[Enter | Peak | Exit] Peak(Wks) TotWks — Score

2568. KEEPER OF THE CASTLE Four Tops
[11Nov72 | 13Jan73 | 09Jun73] 33(1) 31 — 1457

2569. ELVIS-THAT'S THE WAY IT IS Elvis Presley
[12Dec70 | 02Jan71 | 15May71] 21(2) 23 — 1454

2570. TOMMY TUTONE-2 Tommy Tutone
[06Feb82 | 22May82 | 28Aug82] 20(3) 30 — 1453

2571. MUSIC FROM BIG PINK The Band
[10Aug68 | 16Nov68 | 21Mar70] 30(1) 40 — 1452

2572. THE LAST WALTZ (SOUNDTRACK) The Band
[29Apr78 | 24Jun78 | 09Sep78] 16(2) 20 — 1452

2573. REMEMBER THE FUTURE Nektar
[20Jul74 | 16Nov74 | 25Jan75] 19(2) 28 — 1452

2574. VIXEN Vixen
[01Oct88 | 15Apr89 | 01Jul89] 41(1) 40 — 1452

2575. HEARTBREAKER Dionne Warwick
[30Oct82 | 15Jan83 | 07May83] 25(3) 28 — 1452

2576. THE PAYBACK James Brown
[05Jan74 | 20Apr74 | 07Sep74] 34(1) 36 — 1451

2577. ALICIA BRIDGES Alicia Bridges
[30Sep78 | 13Jan79 | 05May79] 33(2) 32 — 1450

2578. TILL The Vogues
[15Feb69 | 26Apr69 | 19Jul69] 30(2) 23 — 1450

2579. LIVIN' FOR YOU Al Green
[29Dec73 | 09Feb74 | 20Jul74] 24(1) 30 — 1449

2580. GHOST RIDERS The Outlaws
[13Dec80 | 21Feb81 | 06Jun81] 25(3) 26 — 1449

2581. DANCING MACHINE The Jackson 5ive
[05Oct74 | 23Nov74 | 22Feb75] 16(2) 21 — 1448

2582. IN A SPECIAL WAY DeBarge
[22Oct83 | 18Feb84 | 11May85] 36(1) 40 — 1448

2583. LIGHT SHINE Jesse Colin Young
[20Apr74 | 27Jul74 | 02Nov74] 37(2) 29 — 1446

2584. THE WANDERER Donna Summer
[08Nov80 | 22Nov80 | 07Mar81] 13(3) 18 — 1445

2585. LICK IT UP KISS
[15Oct83 | 12Nov83 | 05May84] 24(2) 30 — 1444

2586. "WEIRD AL" YANKOVIC IN 3-D "Weird Al" Yankovic
[17Mar84 | 28Apr84 | 18Aug84] 17(3) 23 — 1444

2587. COULDN'T STAND THE WEATHER Stevie Ray Vaughan And Double Trouble
[23Jun84 | 14Jul84 | 09Mar85] 31(3) 38 — 1443

2588. YOU COULD HAVE BEEN WITH ME Sheena Easton
[28Nov81 | 03Apr82 | 26Nov83] 47(1) 53 — 1443

2589. NOW AND FOREVER Air Supply
[19Jun82 | 21Aug82 | 05Mar83] 25(3) 38 — 1443

2590. NO PROTECTION Starship
[25Jul87 | 15Aug87 | 09Jan88] 12(1) 25 — 1442

2591. THE TRINITY SESSION Cowboy Junkies
[28Jan89 | 01Apr89 | 12Aug89] 26(1) 29 — 1441

2592. BRITNY FOX Britny Fox
[23Jul88 | 08Oct88 | 01Apr89] 39(2) 37 — 1441

2593. ESPECIALLY FOR YOU The Smithereens
[16Aug86 | 28Feb87 | 25Jul87] 51(1) 50 — 1438

2594. THE PARTRIDGE FAMILY AT HOME WITH THEIR GREATEST HITS The Partridge Family
[16Sep72 | 04Nov72 | 17Feb73] 21(2) 23 — 1437

2595. SEND IT Ashford & Simpson
[15Oct77 | 03Dec77 | 26Aug78] 52(1) 46 — 1434

2596. MY AIM IS TRUE Elvis Costello
[03Dec77 | 18Mar78 | 05Aug78] 32(2) 36 — 1432

2597. YOU'RE GONNA' GET IT Tom Petty And The Heartbreakers
[10Jun78 | 12Aug78 | 18Nov78] 23(1) 24 — 1431

2598. GRAZIN' The Friends Of Distinction
[03May69 | 19Jul69 | 18Oct69] 35(1) 25 — 1430

2599. STORMS OF LIFE Randy Travis
[19Jul86 | 30Aug86 | 11Jun88] 85(2) 100 — 1430

2600. FIRE ON THE MOUNTAIN The Charlie Daniels Band
[28Dec74 | 15Mar75 | 16Aug75] 38(1) 34 — 1429

2601. IT'S A HEARTACHE Bonnie Tyler
[03Jun78 | 08Jul78 | 23Sep78] 16(1) 17 — 1428

2602. HEARTBEAT Don Johnson
[13Sep86 | 18Oct86 | 14Mar87] 17(2) 27 — 1426

2603. STEPPIN' The Pointer Sisters
[14Jun75 | 13Sep75 | 08Nov75] 22(1) 22 — 1426

Rank. Title Act
[Enter|Peak|Exit] Peak(Wks) TotWks Score

2604. STARFISH The Church
[12Mar88|25Jun88|12Nov88] 41(2) 36 1426

2605. DEAN MARTIN HITS AGAIN Dean Martin
[13Feb65|17Apr65|28Aug65] 13(1) 29 1425

2606. BACK TO BACK The Righteous Brothers
[25Dec65|05Mar66|18Jun66] 16(1) 26 1425

2607. KIHNSPIRACY Greg Kihn Band
[12Mar83|30Apr83|20Aug83] 15(2) 24 1424

2608. PRIME TIME Tony Orlando & Dawn
[07Dec74|22Feb75|29Mar75] 16(1) 17 1423

2609. DON'T LET GO Isaac Hayes
[29Sep79|19Jan80|19Apr80] 39(1) 30 1423

2610. DON'T STOP BELIEVIN'
Olivia Newton-John
[06Nov76|11Dec76|14May77] 30(2) 28 1423

2611. STRIKES Blackfoot
[12May79|18Aug79|16Feb80] 42(2) 41 1420

2612. WHO MADE WHO (SOUNDTRACK) AC/DC
[21Jun86|23Aug86|04Apr87] 33(4) 42 1419

2613. EMERSON, LAKE, & POWELL
Emerson, Lake & Powell
[14Jun86|26Jul86|06Dec86] 23(3) 26 1419

2614. ROBERTA FLACK FEATURING DONNY HATHAWAY
Roberta Flack Featuring Donny Hathaway
[29Mar80|31May80|06Sep80] 25(2) 24 1419

2615. HOROWITZ AT CARNEGIE HALL - AN HISTORIC RETURN Vladimir Horowitz
[24Jul65|18Sep65|26Feb66] 22(2) 32 1418

2616. GONE WITH THE WIND Soundtrack
[14Oct67|10Feb68|01Feb69] 24(1) 36 1418

2617. MARCH Michael Penn
[25Nov89|07Apr90|14Jul90] 31(1) 34 1417

2618. NEVER SURRENDER Triumph
[29Jan83|09Apr83|30Jul83] 26(2) 27 1416

2619. CYCLES The Doobie Brothers
[10Jun89|01Jul89|21Oct89] 17(1) 20 1414

2620. LUXURY LINER Emmylou Harris
[22Jan77|05Mar77|11Jun77] 21(2) 21 1413

2621. SPIRIT IN THE DARK Aretha Franklin
[12Sep70|03Oct70|06Feb71] 25(2) 22 1413

2622. MISTY BLUE Dorothy Moore
[29May76|17Jul76|30Oct76] 29(1) 23 1413

2623. BLOOD, SWEAT & TEARS GREATEST HITS
Blood, Sweat & Tears
[11Mar72|08Apr72|09Sep72] 19(2) 27 1413

2624. EMITT RHODES Emitt Rhodes
[12Dec70|23Jan71|24Apr71] 29(1) 20 1413

2625. BOOMTOWN David & David
[16Aug86|06Dec86|02May87] 39(2) 38 1413

2626. DON'T STOP Jeffrey Osborne
[20Oct84|24Nov84|29Jun85] 39(4) 37 1412

2627. AIN'T NO 'BOUT-A-DOUBT IT
Graham Central Station
[02Aug75|04Oct75|10Jan76] 22(1) 24 1412

2628. JACKRABBIT SLIM Steve Forbert
[10Nov79|01Mar80|03May80] 20(1) 26 1412

2629. SHINE ON L.T.D.
[06Sep80|01Nov80|14Mar81] 28(1) 28 1409

2630. THE MAIN EVENT (SOUNDTRACK)
Barbra Streisand
[07Jul79|01Sep79|03Nov79] 20(1) 18 1408

2631. HYDRA Toto
[17Nov79|15Dec79|31May80] 37(3) 29 1408

2632. A NEW TIME-A NEW DAY
The Chambers Brothers
[12Oct68|21Dec68|01Mar69] 16(1) 21 1408

2633. WHO LOVES YOU The 4 Seasons
[29Nov75|24Jan76|26Jun76] 38(2) 31 1408

2634. 3 FEET HIGH AND RISING De La Soul
[01Apr89|10Jun89|14Oct89] 24(2) 29 1407

2635. SUMMER OF '42 Soundtrack
[11Sep71|20Nov71|29Apr72] 52(1) 34 1406

2636. POINTS ON THE CURVE Wang Chung
[25Feb84|14Jul84|03Nov84] 30(3) 37 1405

2637. WOW Moby Grape
[04May68|15Jun68|09Nov68] 20(1) 28 1405

2638. ALL TOGETHER NOW Argent
[01Jul72|23Sep72|02Dec72] 23(3) 23 1403

2639. CONDITION CRITICAL Quiet Riot
[04Aug84|18Aug84|09Feb85] 15(3) 28 1402

2640. CHICAGO 18 Chicago
[18Oct86|07Mar87|22Aug87] 35(2) 45 1402

2641. CHARLEY PRIDE SINGS HEART SONGS
Charley Pride
[04Dec71|22Jan72|27May72] 38(1) 26 1401

2642. LET ME UP (I'VE HAD ENOUGH)
Tom Petty And The Heartbreakers
[09May87|20Jun87|19Sep87] 20(2) 20 1401

2643. FASCINATION! The Human League
[18Jun83|20Aug83|31Dec83] 22(1) 29 1400

2644. CARLY SIMON Carly Simon
[24Apr71|31Jul71|09Oct71] 30(1) 25 1399

2645. NATIVE SONS Loggins & Messina
[31Jan76|28Feb76|22May76] 16(1) 17 1399

2646. ROCK ON Raydio
[14Apr79|18Aug79|03Nov79] 45(2) 30 1398

2647. MAZE FEATURING FRANKIE BEVERLY
Maze Featuring Frankie Beverly
[26Feb77|17Sep77|31Dec77] 52(2) 45 1398

2648. OUT OF THIS WORLD Europe
[27Aug88|08Oct88|11Feb89] 19(1) 25 1396

2649. RIT Lee Ritenour
[09May81|18Jul81|10Oct81] 26(1) 23 1396

2650. NO NIGHT SO LONG Dionne Warwick
[09Aug80|20Sep80|24Jan81] 23(2) 25 1396

2651. SWITCH II Switch
[02Jun79|01Sep79|02Feb80] 37(1) 36 1396

2652. MR. MUSIC...MANTOVANI
Mantovani
[08Oct66|17Dec66|03Jun67] 27(2) 35 1396

2653. BIRTHDAY The Association
[04May68|15Jun68|26Oct68] 23(1) 26 1395

2654. CLAUDINE (SOUNDTRACK)
Gladys Knight & The Pips
[23Mar74|13Jul74|09Nov74] 35(2) 34 1395

2655. FOR EVERYMAN Jackson Browne
[10Nov73|22Dec73|27Jul74] 43(1) 38 1395

2656. DISCO INFERNO The Trammps
[22Jan77|23Apr77|05Aug78] 46(1) 49 1394

2657. COMPOSITE TRUTH Mandrill
[17Feb73|16Jun73|08Sep73] 28(1) 30 1394

2658. BRASS CONSTRUCTION II
Brass Construction
[20Nov76|25Dec76|16Apr77] 26(3) 22 1394

2659. WALKING IN SPACE Quincy Jones
[22Nov69|04Apr70|15Aug70] 56(1) 39 1393

2660. BROKEN HEART The Babys
[08Oct77|24Dec77|01Apr78] 34(3) 26 1392

2661. WHITE CITY - A NOVEL Pete Townshend
[30Nov85|08Feb86|14Jun86] 26(3) 29 1391

2662. GREATEST HITS, VOLUME 2
Linda Ronstadt
[08Nov80|06Dec80|28Mar81] 26(3) 21 1391

2663. UNGUARDED Amy Grant
[15Jun85|07Sep85|01Mar86] 35(1) 38 1391

2664. WEEKEND WARRIORS Ted Nugent
[11Nov78|16Dec78|24Mar79] 24(3) 20 1390

2665. OPEN ROAD Donovan
[18Jul70|15Aug70|21Nov70] 16(2) 19 1389

2666. FLASH Flash
[20May72|09Sep72|02Dec72] 33(2) 29 1389

2667. JOHNNY RIVERS' GOLDEN HITS
Johnny Rivers
[24Sep66|26Nov66|09Sep67] 29(2) 36 1388

2668. COME MORNING Grover Washington Jr.
[12Dec81|13Feb82|12Jun82] 28(2) 27 1388

2669. I AM THE PRESIDENT David Frye
[27Dec69|14Feb70|25Apr70] 19(1) 18 1388

2670. RAYDIO Raydio
[11Feb78|22Apr78|15Jul78] 27(1) 23 1385

2671. YOU CAN'T ARGUE WITH A SICK MIND
Joe Walsh
[10Apr76|29May76|07Aug76] 20(2) 18 1384

2672. DREAM WITH DEAN Dean Martin
[29Aug64|14Nov64|27Mar65] 15(2) 31 1384

2673. FOUR TOPS SECOND ALBUM Four Tops
[13Nov65|29Jan66|09Jul66] 20(2) 35 1384

2674. MANCINI PLAYS THE THEME FROM LOVE STORY
Henry Mancini And His Orchestra And Chorus
[23Jan71|20Mar71|19Jun71] 26(2) 22 1384

2675. "POPS" GOES THE TRUMPET Al Hirt & Boston Pops Orchestra
[26Sep64|05Dec64|24Apr65] 18(1) 31 1383

2676. LISTEN A Flock Of Seagulls
[28May83|16Jul83|29Oct83] 16(2) 23 1383

2677. HELLO, DOLLY! (SOUNDTRACK)
Barbra Streisand
[15Nov69|07Feb70|27Jun70] 49(1) 33 1382

2678. WIND & WUTHERING Genesis
[22Jan77|02Apr77|11Jun77] 26(2) 21 1382

2679. THE HIT SOUNDS OF THE LETTERMEN
The Lettermen
[21Aug65|16Oct65|29Jan66] 13(1) 24 1382

2680. LOSING THEIR HEADS
Hudson and Landry
[27Nov71|22Jan72|29Apr72] 33(1) 23 1381

2681. MILK AND HONEY
John Lennon & Yoko Ono
[11Feb84|10Mar84|16Jun84] 11(1) 19 1381

2682. GREATEST HITS FROM THE BEGINNING
The Miracles
[17Apr65|10Jul65|02Oct65] 21(1) 25 1381

2683. SPIKE Elvis Costello
[25Feb89|22Apr89|12Aug89] 32(1) 25 1380

2684. STAY FREE Ashford & Simpson
[01Sep79|29Sep79|02Feb80] 23(3) 23 1380

2685. HEAVY HORSES Jethro Tull
[29Apr78|10Jun78|19Aug78] 19(2) 17 1379

2686. SOLID ROCK The Temptations
[29Jan72|25Mar72|24Jun72] 24(2) 22 1379

2687. THE EXCITING WILSON PICKETT
Wilson Pickett
[27Aug66|05Nov66|11Mar67] 21(1) 29 1379

2688. 1990 The Temptations
[29Dec73|23Feb74|25May74] 19(1) 22 1377

2689. I DON'T WANT TO BE HURT ANYMORE
Nat King Cole
[01Aug64|22Aug64|05Jun65] 18(2) 45 1375

2690. GREATEST HITS Steely Dan
[18Nov78|03Feb79|14Apr79] 30(1) 22 1375

2691. PERHAPS LOVE Placido Domingo
[07Nov81|30Jan82|08May82] 18(2) 27 1375

2692. TARKIO Brewer And Shipley
[06Mar71|01May71|28Aug71] 34(2) 26 1374

2693. A SINGLE MAN Elton John
[11Nov78|09Dec78|10Mar79] 15(2) 18 1374

2694. RED ROSES FOR A BLUE LADY Vic Dana
[10Apr65|29May65|28Aug65] 13(1) 21 1373

2695. POST CARD Mary Hopkin
[29Mar69|19Apr69|09Aug69] 28(2) 20 1373

2696. DANCING UNDERCOVER Ratt
[25Oct86|15Nov86|25Jul87] 26(2) 40 1372

2697. THE SILVER FOX Charlie Rich
[07Dec74|01Feb75|29Mar75] 25(2) 17 1371

2698. SECONDS OF PLEASURE Rockpile
[15Nov80|27Dec80|21Mar81] 27(3) 19 1371

2699. THE DREAM ACADEMY
The Dream Academy
[09Nov85|08Mar86|19Jul86] 20(1) 37 1369

2700. SOME DAYS ARE DIAMONDS John Denver
[04Jul81|19Sep81|23Jan82] 32(2) 30 1369

2701. HEAVEN AND HELL Black Sabbath
[14Jun80|19Jul80|22Nov80] 28(3) 24 1367

2702. AMADEUS (SOUNDTRACK)
Neville Marriner
[24Nov84|20Apr85|17May86] 56(2) 78 1365

2703. NEVER GONNA LET YOU GO Vicki Sue Robinson
[10Apr76|26Jun76|12Feb77] 49(2) 39 1365

2704. HOLD ME IN YOUR ARMS Rick Astley
[28Jan89|18Feb89|01Jul89] 19(3) 23 1365

2705. ALADDIN SANE David Bowie
[12May73|16Jun73|06Oct73] 17(2) 22 1365

2706. LONGER FUSE Dan Hill
[10Dec77|11Mar78|20May78] 21(2) 24 1364

Rank. Title Act
[Enter|Peak|Exit] Peak(Wks) TotWks Score

2707. CUT Golden Earring
[11Dec82|09Apr83|02Jul83] 24(2) 30 1364

2708. FREEDOM SUITE The Rascals
[29Mar69|19Apr69|12Jul69] 17(2) 16 1363

2709. DEDICATION Bay City Rollers
[18Sep76|13Nov76|05Mar77] 26(1) 25 1363

2710. SHINE ON BRIGHTLY Procol Harum
[12Oct68|21Dec68|22Feb69] 24(2) 20 1363

2711. PELICAN WEST Haircut One Hundred
[24Apr82|07Aug82|01Jan83] 31(3) 37 1363

2712. LOVE OVER GOLD Dire Straits
[16Oct82|13Nov82|21May83] 19(3) 32 1361

2713. TOLEDO WINDOW BOX George Carlin
[07Dec74|01Feb75|29Mar75] 19(2) 17 1359

2714. ODDS & SODS The Who
[26Oct74|30Nov74|01Feb75] 15(2) 15 1359

2715. POOLSIDE Nu Shooz
[31May86|12Jul86|03Jan87] 27(2) 32 1359

2716. JUST FOR LOVE
Quicksilver Messenger Service
[22Aug70|12Sep70|30Jan71] 27(2) 24 1359

2717. MAN OF COLOURS Icehouse
[17Oct87|14May88|13Aug88] 43(1) 44 1358

2718. THERE AND BACK Jeff Beck
[12Jul80|09Aug80|22Nov80] 21(2) 20 1358

2719. NATURAL HIGH Bloodstone
[14Apr73|14Jul73|15Dec73] 30(1) 36 1357

2720. FERRY CROSS THE MERSEY (SOUNDTRACK) Gerry And The Pacemakers
[27Feb65|15May65|10Jul65] 13(1) 20 1357

2721. COME UPSTAIRS Carly Simon
[12Jul80|15Nov80|14Feb81] 36(2) 32 1356

2722. THE HOOPLE Mott The Hoople
[27Apr74|08Jun74|28Sep74] 28(1) 23 1356

2723. IF I WERE YOUR WOMAN Stephanie Mills
[27Jun87|29Aug87|27Feb88] 30(1) 36 1353

2724. AS ONE Kool & The Gang
[09Oct82|18Dec82|19Mar83] 29(4) 24 1353

2725. STEVE WINWOOD Steve Winwood
[16Jul77|01Oct77|05Nov77] 22(1) 17 1352

2726. REWIND Johnny Rivers
[24Jun67|29Jul67|11Nov67] 14(2) 21 1352

2727. DO YOU WANNA GO PARTY
KC And The Sunshine Band
[07Jul79|04Aug79|15Mar80] 50(1) 37 1352

2728. SOFTLY, AS I LEAVE YOU Frank Sinatra
[19Dec64|06Mar65|26Jun65] 19(1) 28 1352

2729. EQUINOX Styx
[20Dec75|27Mar76|23Feb80] 58(1) 50 1352

2730. A VERY SPECIAL CHRISTMAS
Various Artists
[14Nov87|26Dec87|12Jan91] 20(3) 31 1351

2731. SAILOR The Steve Miller Band
[02Nov68|14Dec68|22Feb69] 24(1) 17 1350

2732. DEREK & THE DOMINOS IN CONCERT
Derek & The Dominos
[27Jan73|24Mar73|16Jun73] 20(1) 21 1350

2733. WAVE Patti Smith Group
[19May79|16Jun79|22Sep79] 18(2) 19 1349

2734. HORIZONTAL Bee Gees
[10Feb68|16Mar68|06Jul68] 12(1) 22 1349

2735. BANANARAMA Bananarama
[02Jun84|29Sep84|02Feb85] 30(5) 36 1349

2736. ELAN Firefall
[28Oct78|06Jan79|07Apr79] 27(2) 24 1347

2737. RUN D.M.C. Run-D.M.C.
[23Jun84|28Jul84|14Sep85] 53(2) 65 1346

2738. THE LION AND THE COBRA
Sinead O'Connor
[06Feb88|23Apr88|16Jun90] 36(3) 38 1345

2739. MAGIC TOUCH Stanley Jordan
[25May85|27Jul85|23Aug86] 64(2) 66 1345

2740. BANGIN' The Outfield
[04Jul87|15Aug87|21Nov87] 18(1) 21 1345

2741. BREAKOUT...!!!
Mitch Ryder And The Detroit Wheels
[06Aug66|18Mar67|01Jul67] 23(1) 34 1345

2742. HOT IN THE SHADE KISS
[04Nov89|25Nov89|07Jul90] 29(1) 36 1344

Rank. Title Act
[Enter|Peak|Exit] Peak(Wks) TotWks Score

2743. BUT THE LITTLE GIRLS UNDERSTAND
The Knack
[01Mar80|29Mar80|31May80] 15(1) 14 1344

2744. SMALL TALK Sly & The Family Stone
[27Jul74|21Sep74|02Nov74] 15(1) 15 1344

2745. SOMETHING'S BURNING
Kenny Rogers & The First Edition
[18Apr70|02May70|26Sep70] 26(3) 24 1344

2746. SNOWBIRD Anne Murray
[03Oct70|31Oct70|01May71] 41(2) 31 1344

2747. STONED SOUL PICNIC The 5th Dimension
[24Aug68|19Oct68|08Feb69] 21(2) 21 1343

2748. STRAIGHT FROM THE HEART
Patrice Rushen
[01May82|26Jun82|06Nov82] 14(2) 28 1343

2749. LOVE THEME FROM "THE GODFATHER"
Andy Williams
[08Apr72|24Jun72|30Sep72] 29(1) 26 1342

2750. ROSE ROYCE III/STRIKES AGAIN!
Rose Royce
[09Sep78|30Sep78|17Feb79] 28(3) 24 1341

2751. LOVESEXY Prince
[28May88|11Jun88|22Oct88] 11(1) 21 1341

2752. NAKED Talking Heads
[02Apr88|07May88|20Aug88] 19(1) 21 1340

2753. EUROPE '72 Grateful Dead
[02Dec72|27Jan73|12May73] 24(1) 24 1340

2754. WATT Ten Years After
[12Dec70|30Jan71|27Mar71] 21(1) 16 1340

2755. GHOSTBUSTERS II Soundtrack
[01Jul89|29Jul89|04Nov89] 14(1) 19 1340

2756. YOU'RE NEVER ALONE WITH A SCHIZOPHRENIC Ian Hunter
[28Apr79|23Jun79|06Oct79] 35(1) 24 1340

2757. EARLY STEPPENWOLF Steppenwolf
[05Jul69|23Aug69|08Nov69] 29(2) 19 1339

2758. THE BEST OF HERMAN'S HERMITS, VOLUME 2 Herman's Hermits
[03Dec66|04Feb67|08Jul67] 20(2) 32 1339

2759. NAKED EYES Naked Eyes
[16Apr83|18Jun83|28Jan84] 32(2) 42 1339

2760. OLD 8 X 10 Randy Travis
[30Jul88|03Sep88|20May89] 35(1) 43 1338

2761. AL GREEN IS LOVE Al Green
[13Sep75|15Nov75|14Feb76] 28(1) 23 1338

2762. DEDICATION Gary U.S. Bonds
[02May81|13Jun81|12Sep81] 27(2) 20 1338

2763. HEADED FOR THE FUTURE Neil Diamond
[24May86|19Jul86|25Oct86] 20(1) 23 1336

2764. IRONS IN THE FIRE Teena Marie
[13Sep80|22Nov80|28Mar81] 38(3) 29 1335

2765. THE BEATLES' STORY The Beatles
[12Dec64|02Jan65|03Apr65] 7(4) 17 1335

2766. BARABAJAGAL Donovan
[13Sep69|18Oct69|21Feb70] 23(2) 24 1335

2767. MESSAGES FROM THE BOYS The Boys
[26Nov88|11Feb89|29Jul89] 33(2) 36 1335

2768. ROCKY III Soundtrack
[10Jul82|21Aug82|13Nov82] 15(5) 19 1334

2769. SPEAK OF THE DEVIL Ozzy Osbourne
[11Dec82|15Jan83|23Apr83] 14(4) 20 1334

2770. PUNCH THE CLOCK
Elvis Costello And The Attractions
[13Aug83|01Oct83|21Jan84] 24(1) 24 1334

2771. THE HAPPIEST GIRL IN THE WHOLE U.S.A.
Donna Fargo
[15Jul72|09Sep72|05May73] 47(2) 43 1333

2772. HAVING A WILD WEEKEND
The Dave Clark Five
[14Aug65|16Oct65|01Jan66] 15(1) 21 1332

2773. INFIDELS Bob Dylan
[19Nov83|03Dec83|28Apr84] 20(5) 24 1332

2774. CHARLEY PRIDE: IN PERSON
Charley Pride
[15Feb69|31May69|06Dec69] 62(2) 43 1331

2775. DRAMA Yes
[13Sep80|04Oct80|17Jan81] 18(2) 19 1330

2776. GRAND HOTEL Procol Harum
[31Mar73|26May73|25Aug73] 21(1) 22 1329

Rank. Title Act
[Enter|Peak|Exit] Peak(Wks) TotWks Score

2777. JUMP TO IT Aretha Franklin
[14Aug82|09Oct82|05Mar83] 23(4) 30 1328

2778. NEW KIND OF FEELING Anne Murray
[17Feb79|07Apr79|01Sep79] 23(2) 29 1327

2779. WE'VE GOT TONIGHT Kenny Rogers
[12Mar83|30Apr83|08Oct83] 18(1) 27 1326

2780. LET'S DO IT AGAIN (SOUNDTRACK)
The Staple Singers
[01Nov75|03Jan76|28Feb76] 20(2) 18 1324

2781. EDDIE MURPHY: COMEDIAN
Eddie Murphy
[19Nov83|28Jan84|01Jun85] 35(1) 44 1323

2782. THE LAST FAREWELL AND OTHER HITS
Roger Whittaker
[03May75|14Jun75|11Oct75] 31(2) 24 1323

2783. NO NUKES/THE MUSE CONCERTS FOR A NON-NUCLEAR FUTURE Various Artists
[22Dec79|09Feb80|19Apr80] 19(2) 18 1322

2784. BORN FREE Soundtrack
[30Jul66|24Dec66|02Sep67] 42(1) 48 1322

2785. REACH FOR IT George Duke
[29Oct77|07Jan78|08Apr78] 25(2) 24 1322

2786. CROSSWINDS Billy Cobham
[04May74|15Jun74|21Sep74] 23(2) 21 1322

2787. LABOUR OF LUST Nick Lowe
[14Jul79|22Sep79|08Dec79] 31(3) 22 1321

2788. LOVE SONGS The Beatles
[12Nov77|10Dec77|14Mar81] 24(2) 31 1319

2789. AN EVENING OF MAGIC - CHUCK MANGIONE LIVE AT THE HOLLYWOOD BOWL
Chuck Mangione
[30Jun79|01Sep79|01Dec79] 27(1) 23 1318

2790. THE BEST OF BLONDIE Blondie
[31Oct81|12Dec81|03Apr82] 30(2) 23 1318

2791. THE TEMPTATIONS SHOW
The Temptations
[09Aug69|13Sep69|22Nov69] 24(1) 16 1318

2792. GREATEST HITS Stevie Wonder
[27Apr68|13Jul68|09Nov68] 37(2) 29 1317

2793. LET THERE BE MUSIC Orleans
[29Mar75|01Nov75|22Nov75] 33(1) 32 1317

2794. TORN BETWEEN TWO LOVERS
Mary MacGregor
[15Jan77|26Mar77|21May77] 17(1) 19 1316

2795. UNDERDOG Atlanta Rhythm Section
[23Jun79|04Aug79|10Nov79] 26(3) 21 1315

2796. STARCHILD Teena Marie
[15Dec84|06Apr85|10Aug85] 31(2) 35 1315

2797. MISS THE MISSISSIPPI Crystal Gayle
[29Sep79|08Dec79|05Apr80] 36(2) 28 1314

2798. HEAD ON Bachman-Turner Overdrive
[03Jan76|06Mar76|22May76] 23(2) 21 1314

2799. HERE, MY DEAR Marvin Gaye
[06Jan79|17Feb79|26May79] 26(2) 21 1313

2800. BEAT STREET Soundtrack
[02Jun84|21Jul84|20Oct84] 14(2) 21 1313

2801. EVOLUTION Dennis Coffey
[13Nov71|29Jan72|29Apr72] 36(1) 25 1313

2802. POWERSLAVE Iron Maiden
[29Sep84|13Oct84|18May85] 21(3) 34 1313

2803. HARD LABOR Three Dog Night
[06Apr74|25May74|31Aug74] 20(1) 22 1312

2804. SKYNYRD'S FIRST AND...LAST
Lynyrd Skynyrd
[23Sep78|28Oct78|20Jan79] 15(2) 18 1312

2805. MOTHER'S MILK Red Hot Chili Peppers
[16Sep89|02Dec89|30Jun90] 52(1) 42 1311

2806. AFTER EIGHT Taco
[23Jul83|10Sep83|31Dec83] 23(2) 24 1311

2807. NO HOLDIN' BACK Randy Travis
[14Oct89|04Nov89|01Sep90] 33(1) 47 1311

2808. A LITTLE BIT OF HEAVEN John Gary
[23Jan65|17Apr65|04Sep65] 17(2) 33 1308

2809. ZUMA Neil Young With Crazy Horse
[29Nov75|10Jan76|17Apr76] 25(2) 21 1307

2810. IN THE ARMS OF LOVE Andy Williams
[21Jan67|22Apr67|17Jun67] 21(1) 22 1306

2811. STRENGTH The Alarm
[09Nov85|15Feb86|12Jul86] 39(3) 36 1304

Rank. Title Act
[Enter|Peak|Exit] Peak(Wks) TotWks Score

2812. VISIONS Gladys Knight & The Pips
[21May83|25Jun83|04Feb84] 34(2) 33 1303

2813. LOST BOYS Soundtrack
[01Aug87|03Oct87|02Jul88] 15(1) 39 1302

2814. COUNTDOWN TO ECSTASY Steely Dan
[21Jul73|22Sep73|08Jun74] 35(1) 34 1301

2815. SECOND MOVEMENT
Les McCann & Eddie Harris
[29May71|10Jul71|27Nov71] 41(1) 27 1301

2816. THE BEATLES SONG BOOK
The Hollyridge Strings
[20Jun64|05Sep64|05Dec64] 15(1) 25 1300

2817. CORNELIUS BROTHERS & SISTER ROSE
Cornelius Brothers & Sister Rose
[29Jul72|28Oct72|13Jan73] 29(1) 25 1299

2818. IRON BUTTERFLY LIVE Iron Butterfly
[23May70|06Jun70|24Oct70] 20(2) 23 1298

2819. FAREWELL, ANGELINA Joan Baez
[23Oct65|11Dec65|23Apr66] 10(1) 27 1298

2820. IF I WERE YOUR WOMAN
Gladys Knight & The Pips
[15May71|14Aug71|06Nov71] 35(1) 26 1297

2821. WATERMARK Art Garfunkel
[04Feb78|18Mar78|20May78] 19(1) 16 1296

2822. DIONNE WARWICK'S GREATEST MOTION PICTURE HITS Dionne Warwick
[16Aug69|18Oct69|24Jan70] 31(2) 24 1296

2823. SOMEWHERE IN ENGLAND
George Harrison
[20Jun81|11Jul81|12Sep81] 11(2) 13 1295

2824. A NIGHT AT STUDIO 54 Various Artists
[28Jul79|01Sep79|12Jan80] 21(1) 25 1295

2825. OOH YEAH! Daryl Hall & John Oates
[21May88|04Jun88|12Nov88] 24(2) 26 1295

2826. DELIVERIN' Poco
[06Feb71|27Feb71|26Jun71] 26(1) 21 1294

2827. TURNIN' ON High Inergy
[05Nov77|07Jan78|22Apr78] 28(3) 25 1294

2828. ROBERT GOULET IN PERSON
Robert Goulet
[19Oct63|30Nov63|21Mar64] 16(2) 23 1292

2829. AUDIO-VISIONS Kansas
[04Oct80|08Nov80|21Feb81] 26(1) 21 1292

2830. MOTOR-BOOTY AFFAIR Parliament
[16Dec78|10Feb79|14Apr79] 23(2) 18 1292

2831. HOT PANTS James Brown
[04Sep71|02Oct71|01Jan72] 22(2) 18 1291

2832. SOUTHERN NIGHTS Glen Campbell
[19Mar77|21May77|13Aug77] 22(2) 22 1291

2833. MONEY AND CIGARETTES Eric Clapton
[19Feb83|26Mar83|25Jun83] 16(4) 19 1289

2834. DON'T STOP Billy Idol
[24Oct81|29Oct83|17Nov84] 71(1) 68 1288

2835. ABOUT FACE David Gilmour
[17Mar84|09Jun84|22Sep84] 32(3) 28 1288

2836. THIS IS ALL I ASK Tony Bennett
[24Aug63|16Nov63|14Mar64] 24(1) 30 1288

2837. SHANGO Santana
[04Sep82|23Oct82|05Feb83] 22(3) 23 1288

2838. FIFTH DIMENSION The Byrds
[27Aug66|08Oct66|04Mar67] 24(2) 28 1288

2839. FULL MOON
Kris Kristofferson & Rita Coolidge
[22Sep73|27Oct73|03Sep77] 26(2) 33 1287

2840. STANDING ON A BEACH -- THE SINGLES
The Cure
[14Jun86|23Aug86|11Jul87] 48(2) 57 1287

2841. CABARET Original Cast
[07Jan67|08Apr67|30Sep67] 37(1) 39 1286

2842. MUSIC, MUSIC Helen Reddy
[14Aug76|11Sep76|06Nov76] 16(1) 13 1285

2843. HOW COULD IT BE Eddie Murphy
[12Oct85|25Jan86|05Apr86] 26(1) 26 1285

2844. BABYLON AND ON Squeeze
[03Oct87|05Dec87|16Apr88] 36(2) 29 1284

2845. BEST KEPT SECRET Sheena Easton
[17Sep83|15Oct83|02Jun84] 33(2) 38 1284

2846. MUSIC IS MY LIFE Billy Preston
[23Dec72|21Jul73|06Oct73] 32(1) 35 1282

Rank. Title Act
[Enter|Peak|Exit] Peak(Wks) TotWks Score

2847. LAW AND ORDER
Lindsey Buckingham
[07Nov81|12Dec81|17Apr82] 32(1) 24 1282

2848. NUMBER 5 The Steve Miller Band
[25Jul70|12Sep70|16Jan71] 23(1) 26 1282

2849. LISA LISA & CULT JAM WITH FULL FORCE
Lisa Lisa And Cult Jam With Full Force
[31Aug85|05Oct85|14Mar87] 52(2) 66 1280

2850. EL DEBARGE El DeBarge
[14Jun86|05Jul86|15Nov86] 24(3) 23 1280

2851. ALL I REALLY WANT TO DO Cher
[18Sep65|06Nov65|26Feb66] 16(2) 24 1280

2852. MAN-CHILD Herbie Hancock
[18Oct75|29Nov75|27Mar76] 21(1) 24 1279

2853. DAVE MASON Dave Mason
[02Nov74|07Dec74|19Apr75] 25(2) 25 1279

2854. SIGN IN PLEASE Autograph
[05Jan85|30Mar85|20Jul85] 29(2) 29 1278

2855. ANY NUMBER CAN WIN Jimmy Smith
[09Nov63|14Dec63|20Jun64] 25(2) 33 1278

2856. ELECTRIC The Cult
[25Apr87|16May87|28Nov87] 38(3) 32 1278

2857. ON THE MOVE Trini Lopez
[11Apr64|18Jul64|21Nov64] 32(1) 33 1277

2858. WHEN THE SNOW IS ON THE ROSES
Ed Ames
[16Dec67|02Mar68|01Jun68] 24(1) 25 1277

2859. BARRY WHITE'S GREATEST HITS
Barry White
[15Nov75|13Dec75|01May76] 23(2) 25 1277

2860. IN THE COURT OF THE CRIMSON KING - AN OBSERVATION BY KING CRIMSON
King Crimson
[13Dec69|21Mar70|30May70] 28(2) 25 1277

2861. SPIRIT IN THE SKY Norman Greenbaum
[28Feb70|18Apr70|15Aug70] 23(2) 25 1276

2862. EDDIE MURPHY Eddie Murphy
[14Aug82|09Oct82|21Apr84] 52(5) 53 1275

2863. LUNA SEA Firefall
[20Aug77|01Oct77|25Feb78] 27(1) 28 1275

2864. WELCOME Santana
[01Dec73|29Dec73|20Apr74] 25(1) 21 1273

2865. RECOLLECTIONS Judy Collins
[20Sep69|18Oct69|04Apr70] 29(1) 29 1273

2866. FEELINGS Morris Albert
[06Sep75|29Nov75|03Apr76] 37(2) 31 1273

2867. LIVE George Thorogood & The Destroyers
[23Aug86|20Sep86|06Jun87] 33(3) 42 1273

2868. BACK IN BLACK Whodini
[17May86|12Jul86|07Feb87] 35(2) 39 1272

2869. GIUFFRIA Giuffria
[08Dec84|02Mar85|22Jun85] 26(2) 29 1272

2870. WIDE AWAKE IN DREAMLAND
Pat Benatar
[23Jul88|10Sep88|04Feb89] 28(2) 29 1272

2871. THE MANY FACETS OF ROGER Roger
[03Oct81|21Nov81|20Mar82] 26(1) 25 1271

2872. THE GLOW OF LOVE Change
[10May80|19Jul80|25Oct80] 29(2) 25 1270

2873. TUNEWEAVING
Dawn Featuring Tony Orlando
[24Mar73|16Jun73|10Nov73] 30(1) 34 1269

2874. GO TO HEAVEN Grateful Dead
[17May80|28Jun80|04Oct80] 23(2) 21 1269

2875. HEAVY WEATHER Weather Report
[02Apr77|21May77|27Aug77] 30(2) 22 1268

2876. QUENTIN'S THEME
The Charles Randolph Grean Sounde
[26Jul69|30Aug69|01Nov69] 23(2) 15 1266

2877. BOWIE PIN UPS David Bowie
[10Nov73|22Dec73|30Mar74] 23(1) 21 1266

2878. OPERATION: MINDCRIME Queensryche
[21May88|04Jun88|07Oct89] 50(2) 52 1266

2879. HIGHWAY CALL Richard Betts
[31Aug74|19Oct74|14Dec74] 19(2) 16 1266

2880. RESTLESS NIGHTS Karla Bonoff
[29Sep79|17Nov79|22Mar80] 31(2) 26 1266

2881. LODGER David Bowie
[16Jun79|14Jul79|22Sep79] 20(2) 15 1265

Rank. Title Act
[Enter|Peak|Exit] Peak(Wks) TotWks Score

2882. IF MY FRIENDS COULD SEE ME NOW
Linda Clifford
[20May78|22Jul78|14Oct78] 22(2) 22 1265

2883. I CAN HELP Billy Swan
[07Dec74|01Feb75|22Mar75] 21(2) 16 1265

2884. RIGHT NOW!
The Righteous Brothers
[02Jan65|06Mar65|22May65] 11(2) 21 1264

2885. AFTER BATHING AT BAXTER'S
Jefferson Airplane
[23Dec67|27Jan68|25May68] 17(2) 23 1263

2886. AN ANTHOLOGY Duane Allman
[09Dec72|03Feb73|02Jun73] 28(1) 26 1263

2887. THE SUPREMES SING RODGERS & HART
The Supremes
[17Jun67|22Jul67|21Oct67] 20(3) 19 1262

2888. IT'S YOUR NIGHT James Ingram
[12Nov83|17Mar84|25Aug84] 46(1) 42 1262

2889. FREEDOM FOR THE STALLION
The Hues Corporation
[29Jun74|03Aug74|26Oct74] 20(2) 18 1261

2890. AMERICAN STARS 'N BARS
Neil Young, Crazy Horse & The Bullets
[02Jul77|27Aug77|08Oct77] 21(1) 15 1261

2891. GENTLE IS MY LOVE Nancy Wilson
[28Aug65|06Nov65|05Feb66] 17(1) 24 1261

2892. SOME BLUE-EYED SOUL
The Righteous Brothers
[16Jan65|06Mar65|29May65] 14(2) 20 1260

2893. LICORICE STICK Pete Fountain
[22Aug64|24Oct64|19Jun65] 48(1) 44 1260

2894. BRANIGAN Laura Branigan
[25Sep82|25Dec82|28May83] 34(5) 36 1260

2895. STYX II Styx
[25Jan75|08Mar75|31May75] 20(2) 19 1258

2896. THE HURTING Tears For Fears
[07May83|16Jul83|08Mar86] 73(1) 69 1256

2897. CLOSE ENCOUNTERS OF THE THIRD KIND
Soundtrack
[07Jan78|18Feb78|22Apr78] 17(2) 16 1256

2898. HERMIT OF MINK HOLLOW
Todd Rundgren
[06May78|24Jun78|28Oct78] 36(1) 26 1256

2899. LET THE SUNSHINE IN
Diana Ross & The Supremes
[21Jun69|19Jul69|18Oct69] 24(2) 18 1255

2900. X-STATIC Daryl Hall & John Oates
[27Oct79|15Dec79|05Apr80] 33(1) 24 1254

2901. LITTLE ROBBERS The Motels
[15Oct83|05Nov83|24Mar84] 22(4) 24 1254

2902. LET THE MUSIC PLAY Shannon
[11Feb84|24Mar84|20Oct84] 32(2) 37 1253

2903. WHAT'S NEW PUSSYCAT? Soundtrack
[07Aug65|25Sep65|01Jan66] 14(1) 22 1253

2904. WE TOO ARE ONE Eurythmics
[30Sep89|18Nov89|07Apr90] 34(2) 28 1252

2905. PLEASURE VICTIM Berlin
[19Feb83|07May83|08Oct83] 30(1) 34 1250

2906. THE LANGUAGE OF LOVE Jerry Vale
[07Sep63|16Nov63|02May64] 22(1) 35 1249

2907. PAPA'S GOT A BRAND NEW BAG
James Brown
[11Sep65|08Jan66|12Mar66] 26(2) 27 1247

2908. PARADISE, HAWAIIAN STYLE (SOUNDTRACK) Elvis Presley
[16Jul66|03Sep66|19Nov66] 15(2) 19 1246

2909. MIDNIGHT TO MIDNIGHT
Psychedelic Furs
[07Mar87|02May87|05Sep87] 29(2) 27 1246

2910. CANDIDA Dawn
[19Dec70|30Jan71|22May71] 35(2) 23 1245

2911. ONE ON ONE Cheap Trick
[29May82|09Oct82|27Nov82] 39(1) 27 1245

2912. SERGIO MENDES(2) Sergio Mendes
[07May83|30Jul83|05Nov83] 27(2) 27 1245

2913. THESE ARE MY SONGS Petula Clark
[02Sep67|04Nov67|02Mar68] 27(2) 27 1245

2914. LIVE AFTER DEATH Iron Maiden
[16Nov85|14Dec85|12Apr86] 19(1) 22 1244

Rank. Title Act	Enter	Peak	Exit	Peak(Wks)	TotWks	Score
2915. ARABIAN NIGHTS The Ritchie Family	24Jul76	13Nov76	08Jan77	30(1)	25	1244
2916. CHAIN LIGHTNING Don McLean	14Feb81	11Apr81	04Jul81	28(2)	21	1243
2917. STREET LADY Donald Byrd	30Mar74	18May74	05Oct74	33(1)	28	1243
2918. A LONG TIME COMIN' Electric Flag	20Apr68	01Jun68	28Dec68	31(1)	35	1243
2919. SLEEPWALKER The Kinks	26Feb77	23Apr77	11Jun77	21(2)	16	1242
2920. FEEL LIKE MAKIN' LOVE Roberta Flack	29Mar75	10May75	20Sep75	24(2)	26	1242
2921. STONE BLUE Foghat	20May78	01Jul78	21Oct78	25(2)	23	1242
2922. LIVE/JOHNNY WINTER AND Johnny Winter	13Mar71	29May71	11Sep71	40(2)	27	1240
2923. EUPHRATES RIVER The Main Ingredient	09Mar74	13Jul74	05Oct74	52(1)	31	1240
2924. STILLS Stephen Stills	05Jul75	02Aug75	25Oct75	19(2)	17	1239
2925. BY REQUEST (THE BEST OF BILLY VERA & THE BEATERS) Billy Vera & The Beaters	06Dec86	28Feb87	30May87	15(1)	26	1239
2926. BRILLIANCE Atlantic Starr	27Mar82	22May82	09Oct82	18(2)	29	1239
2927. SOULED Jose Feliciano	07Dec68	25Jan69	12Apr69	24(1)	19	1238
2928. CHRONICLES Steve Winwood	21Nov87	16Jan88	14May88	26(1)	26	1238
2929. GREATEST HITS Little River Band	04Dec82	12Feb83	25Jun83	33(6)	30	1237
2930. A1A Jimmy Buffett	08Feb75	05Apr75	15Oct77	25(2)	27	1237
2931. AL GREEN GETS NEXT TO YOU Al Green	28Aug71	12Feb72	17Jun72	58(1)	43	1237
2932. CRASH The Human League	04Oct86	22Nov86	21Mar87	24(2)	25	1236
2933. A SALTY DOG Procol Harum	10May69	14Jun69	20Sep69	32(1)	20	1235
2934. BORN TO BOOGIE Hank Williams Jr.	01Aug87	19Sep87	18Jun88	28(1)	47	1235
2935. ENERGIZED Foghat	02Feb74	23Mar74	24Aug74	34(1)	30	1235
2936. DISTANT LIGHT The Hollies	15Jul72	23Sep72	02Dec72	21(1)	21	1234
2937. BLUE MAGIC Blue Magic	16Mar74	31Aug74	30Nov74	45(1)	34	1234
2938. A COLLECTION: GREATEST HITS... AND MORE Barbra Streisand	21Oct89	18Nov89	07Apr90	26(3)	25	1234
2939. BURTON CUMMINGS Burton Cummings	06Nov76	29Jan77	19Mar77	30(1)	20	1233
2940. AMERICAN TOUR The Dave Clark Five	29Aug64	26Sep64	06Mar65	11(1)	28	1233
2941. THERE'S NO GETTIN' OVER ME Ronnie Milsap	05Sep81	17Oct81	03Apr82	31(1)	31	1232
2942. LONG LONESOME HIGHWAY Michael Parks	23May70	20Jun70	10Oct70	24(1)	21	1232
2943. SURF'S UP The Beach Boys	11Sep71	30Oct71	01Jan72	29(1)	17	1232
2944. I WANNA HAVE SOME FUN Samantha Fox	26Nov88	18Feb89	15Jul89	37(1)	34	1231
2945. JOHNNY CASH'S GREATEST HITS, VOLUME I Johnny Cash	22Jul67	29Nov69	05Sep70	82(1)	71	1231
2946. BLACK BYRD Donald Byrd	28Apr73	21Jul73	15Dec73	36(1)	34	1230
2947. THE LATIN ALBUM Trini Lopez	22Aug64	31Oct64	30Jan65	18(2)	24	1229
2948. IT LOOKS LIKE SNOW Phoebe Snow	06Nov76	18Dec76	09Apr77	29(3)	21	1229
2949. POINT OF ENTRY Judas Priest	04Apr81	23May81	19Sep81	39(2)	25	1229
2950. JETHRO TULL LIVE - BURSTING OUT Jethro Tull	21Oct78	02Dec78	27Jan79	21(1)	15	1229
2951. THAT'S WHAT FRIENDS ARE FOR Johnny Mathis & Deniece Williams	29Jul78	02Sep78	11Nov78	19(2)	16	1227
2952. SHANGRI-LA Robert Maxwell His Harp And Orchestra	18Apr64	13Jun64	26Sep64	17(1)	24	1227
2953. MOVIN' WITH NANCY Nancy Sinatra	13Jan68	16Mar68	17Aug68	37(2)	32	1226
2954. EXTENDED PLAY The Pretenders	18Apr81	16May81	31Oct81	27(2)	29	1225
2955. HOOKED ON CLASSICS II (CAN'T STOP THE CLASSICS) Royal Philharmonic Orchestra	28Aug82	09Oct82	04Jun83	33(4)	41	1225
2956. LOVE IS BLUE Claudine Longet	13Apr68	22Jun68	31Aug68	29(2)	21	1225
2957. PEARLY SHELLS Billy Vaughn And His Orchestra	02Jan65	17Apr65	17Jul65	18(1)	29	1224
2958. SWEET FORGIVENESS Bonnie Raitt	23Apr77	28May77	17Sep77	25(2)	22	1224
2959. GOT MY MOJO WORKIN' Jimmy Smith	12Mar66	02Jul66	10Sep66	28(2)	27	1222
2960. CREAM OF THE CROP Diana Ross & The Supremes	29Nov69	17Jan70	11Apr70	33(2)	20	1222
2961. FRANCIS ALBERT SINATRA & ANTONIO CARLOS JOBIM Frank Sinatra & Antonio Carlos Jobim	15Apr67	20May67	21Oct67	19(2)	28	1222
2962. THE MAGICIAN'S BIRTHDAY Uriah Heep	02Dec72	03Feb73	28Apr73	31(1)	22	1222
2963. THE ROCKY HORROR PICTURE SHOW Soundtrack	15Apr78	03Jun78	19May79	49(2)	58	1220
2964. BAD LUCK STREAK IN DANCING SCHOOL Warren Zevon	08Mar80	05Apr80	21Jun80	20(1)	16	1220
2965. WAVELENGTH Van Morrison	14Oct78	16Dec78	17Mar79	28(1)	23	1220
2966. COMMODORES' GREATEST HITS Commodores	25Nov78	13Jan79	07Apr79	23(2)	20	1220
2967. SWITCH Switch	02Sep78	25Nov78	14Apr79	37(2)	33	1220
2968. I WANT TO GO WITH YOU Eddy Arnold	26Mar66	04Jun66	01Oct66	26(1)	28	1219
2969. PSYCHEDELIC LOLLIPOP Blues Magoos	03Dec66	11Mar67	08Jul67	21(1)	32	1219
2970. CREST OF A KNAVE Jethro Tull	10Oct87	12Dec87	16Apr88	32(1)	28	1219
2971. 11 The Smithereens	18Nov89	31Mar90	04Aug90	41(1)	38	1219
2972. TOUCHDOWN Bob James	16Dec78	03Mar79	30Jun79	37(1)	29	1218
2973. THE WINDOWS OF THE WORLD Dionne Warwick	16Sep67	25Nov67	13Apr68	22(2)	31	1218
2974. DIANA ROSS & THE SUPREMES GREATEST HITS, VOLUME 3 Diana Ross & The Supremes	10Jan70	14Feb70	27Jun70	31(1)	25	1218
2975. THE INCOMPARABLE MANTOVANI Mantovani	07Nov64	26Dec64	28Aug65	37(1)	43	1218
2976. MRS. MILLER'S GREATEST HITS Mrs. Miller	07May66	16Jul66	27Aug66	15(1)	17	1217
2977. BICENTENNIAL NI*GER Richard Pryor	09Oct76	06Nov76	12Feb77	22(2)	19	1217
2978. DOUBLE VISION Bob James/David Sanborn	14Jun86	19Jul86	29Aug87	50(2)	64	1216
2979. BETTER DAYS & HAPPY ENDINGS Melissa Manchester	21Feb76	27Mar76	12Jun76	24(2)	17	1216
2980. BRANIGAN 2 Laura Branigan	09Apr83	11Jun83	17Nov84	29(1)	37	1216
2981. STARS & STRIPES FOREVER Nitty Gritty Dirt Band	13Jul74	21Sep74	30Nov74	28(2)	21	1215
2982. BORN TO BE BAD George Thorogood & The Destroyers	06Feb88	05Mar88	16Jul88	32(3)	24	1214
2983. BETWEEN THE SHEETS The Isley Brothers	04Jun83	09Jul83	05Nov83	19(1)	23	1214
2984. FASTWAY Fastway	28May83	10Sep83	31Dec83	31(1)	32	1213
2985. DISCO TEX AND HIS SEX-O-LETTES Disco Tex & The Sex-O-Lettes Review Starring Sir Monti Rock III	03May75	06Sep75	27Sep75	36(1)	22	1210
2986. ELECTRIC MUSIC FOR THE MIND AND BODY Country Joe & The Fish	10Jun67	23Sep67	24Feb68	39(3)	38	1210
2987. EVEN WORSE "Weird Al" Yankovic	07May88	02Jul88	29Oct88	27(1)	26	1209
2988. A NEW LIFE The Marshall Tucker Band	09Mar74	06Apr74	14Sep74	37(1)	28	1208
2989. MCFADDEN & WHITEHEAD McFadden & Whitehead	02Jun79	14Jul79	22Sep79	23(3)	17	1208
2990. STORMBRINGER Deep Purple	07Dec74	28Dec74	15Mar75	20(2)	15	1207
2991. MARATHON Santana	20Oct79	08Dec79	15Mar80	25(1)	22	1206
2992. TAKE ME HOME Cher	24Feb79	12May79	14Jul79	25(2)	21	1205
2993. LIGHT OF SMILES Gary Wright	22Jan77	05Mar77	30Apr77	23(1)	15	1205
2994. THE PARTRIDGE FAMILY SHOPPING BAG The Partridge Family	25Mar72	22Apr72	15Jul72	18(2)	17	1205
2995. 13 The Doors	19Dec70	16Jan71	08May71	25(1)	21	1204
2996. 40 HOUR WEEK Alabama	23Feb85	30Mar85	23Nov85	28(3)	40	1203
2997. HAPPY TOGETHER The Turtles	29Apr67	10Jun67	23Sep67	25(2)	22	1203
2998. BEST OF B.T.O. (SO FAR) Bachman-Turner Overdrive	14Aug76	09Oct76	20Nov76	19(2)	15	1203
2999. ABSOLUTE TORCH AND TWANG k.d. lang & The Reclines	17Jun89	24Mar90	07Jul90	69(1)	56	1203
3000. GREATEST HITS The Righteous Brothers	16Sep67	25Nov67	24Aug68	21(1)	50	1203
3001. IN CITY DREAMS Robin Trower	01Oct77	26Nov77	04Feb78	25(1)	19	1202
3002. TOUCH ME Samantha Fox	29Nov86	28Feb87	06Jun87	24(2)	28	1202
3003. COME IN FROM THE RAIN Captain & Tennille	23Apr77	28May77	30Jul77	18(1)	15	1201
3004. ANIMOTION Animotion	23Feb85	25May85	14Sep85	28(1)	30	1200
3005. THE OZARK MOUNTAIN DAREDEVILS Ozark Mountain Daredevils	16Feb74	13Jul74	12Oct74	26(1)	28	1199
3006. WHAT ABOUT ME? Kenny Rogers	22Sep84	17Nov84	20Apr85	31(3)	31	1199
3007. LIVE & WELL B.B. King	14Jun69	06Sep69	31Jan70	56(2)	34	1199
3008. LEGACY Poco	23Sep89	11Nov89	31Mar90	40(2)	28	1198
3009. WHISTLING DOWN THE WIRE David Crosby/Graham Nash	24Jul76	18Sep76	30Oct76	26(2)	15	1198
3010. ALBUM Joan Jett & the Blackhearts	16Jul83	13Aug83	26Nov83	20(2)	20	1196
3011. THE JACKSONS The Jacksons	04Dec76	05Feb77	04Jun77	36(2)	27	1195
3012. WHERE I SHOULD BE Peter Frampton	23Jun79	21Jul79	06Oct79	19(2)	16	1195
3013. MANIFESTO Roxy Music	31Mar79	26May79	14Jul79	23(1)	16	1194
3014. AUGUST Eric Clapton	27Dec86	21Mar87	15Aug87	37(2)	34	1193

Rank. Title Act
[Enter|Peak|Exit] Peak(Wks) TotWks Score

3015. SOMEWHERE OVER THE RAINBOW Willie Nelson
[21Mar81|11Apr81|22Aug81] 31(3) 23 1192

3016. THAT WAS THE WEEK THAT WAS (BBC TELECAST TRIBUTE ON 11/23/1963) No Artist
[28Dec63|08Feb64|04Apr64] 5(1) 15 1192

3017. MY WHOLE WORLD ENDED David Ruffin
[21Jun69|02Aug69|11Oct69] 31(1) 17 1192

3018. THE VENTURES ON STAGE The Ventures
[19Jun65|09Oct65|08Jan66] 27(1) 30 1192

3019. M.P.G. Marvin Gaye
[14Jun69|19Jul69|11Oct69] 33(1) 18 1191

3020. PLANETARY INVASION Midnight Star
[08Dec84|16Feb85|13Jul85] 32(2) 32 1191

3021. BARRY WHITE THE MAN Barry White
[28Oct78|16Dec78|05May79] 36(3) 28 1191

3022. BROOKLYN BRIDGE Brooklyn Bridge
[29Mar69|10May69|18Oct69] 54(2) 30 1190

3023. THE PRESIDENTIAL YEARS 1960-1963 (NARRATED BY DAVID TEIG) John Fitzgerald Kennedy
[28Dec63|01Feb64|28Mar64] 8(2) 14 1189

3024. FEELINGS Paul Anka
[05Apr75|31May75|18Oct75] 36(2) 29 1189

3025. WELCOME TO THE CANTEEN Traffic, Etc.
[02Oct71|30Oct71|05Feb72] 26(3) 19 1188

3026. SUGAR Nancy Sinatra
[18Feb67|15Apr67|29Jul67] 18(1) 24 1188

3027. LIVE AT LONDON'S TALK OF THE TOWN The Temptations
[22Aug70|19Sep70|19Dec70] 21(2) 18 1188

3028. HOBO'S LULLABY Arlo Guthrie
[10Jun72|28Oct72|24Feb73] 52(2) 38 1186

3029. THERE IS The Dells
[25May68|31Aug68|11Jan69] 29(1) 29 1186

3030. I'LL PLAY FOR YOU Seals & Crofts
[05Apr75|17May75|06Sep75] 30(2) 23 1186

3031. LOVE LIFE Berlin
[31Mar84|09Jun84|20Oct84] 28(2) 30 1186

3032. ABANDONED LUNCHEONETTE Daryl Hall & John Oates
[23Feb74|20Nov76|05Feb77] 33(1) 38 1186

3033. SPECIAL OCCASION Smokey Robinson & The Miracles
[05Oct68|18Jan69|08Mar69] 42(2) 23 1185

3034. ANDY WILLIAMS' NEWEST HITS Andy Williams
[05Feb66|02Apr66|09Jul66] 23(1) 23 1185

3035. THAT HONEY HORN SOUND Al Hirt
[13Mar65|08May65|11Sep65] 28(3) 27 1185

3036. QUEEN LIVE KILLERS Queen
[07Jul79|04Aug79|06Oct79] 16(2) 14 1183

3037. SONG FOR JULI Jesse Colin Young
[06Oct73|24Nov73|03Aug74] 51(1) 44 1183

3038. I'M NO ANGEL The Gregg Allman Band
[07Mar87|09May87|12Sep87] 30(3) 28 1183

3039. GIVE IT TO THE PEOPLE The Righteous Brothers
[31Aug74|02Nov74|28Dec74] 27(2) 18 1183

3040. LET'S FALL IN LOVE Peaches & Herb
[25Mar67|01Jul67|09Sep67] 30(1) 25 1183

3041. ENDLESS WIRE Gordon Lightfoot
[04Feb78|18Mar78|17Jun78] 22(2) 20 1183

3042. GALLANT MEN Senator Everett McKinley Dirksen
[07Jan67|18Feb67|22Apr67] 16(2) 16 1182

3043. MELLOW YELLOW Donovan
[18Feb67|25Mar67|08Jul67] 14(2) 21 1182

3044. ROBBIE ROBERTSON Robbie Robertson
[14Nov87|26Dec87|02Jul88] 38(2) 34 1181

3045. LIVE IN NEW ORLEANS Maze Featuring Frankie Beverly
[04Jul81|15Aug81|02Jan82] 34(2) 27 1181

3046. A GIFT FROM A FLOWER TO A GARDEN Donovan
[06Jan68|02Mar68|01Jun68] 19(1) 22 1181

3047. ZAPP Zapp
[27Sep80|01Nov80|31Jan81] 19(2) 19 1180

Rank. Title Act
[Enter|Peak|Exit] Peak(Wks) TotWks Score

3048. THE FOLK ALBUM Trini Lopez
[30Jan65|03Apr65|03Jul65] 18(1) 23 1177

3049. THE GLEN CAMPBELL GOODTIME ALBUM Glen Campbell
[03Oct70|07Nov70|20Feb71] 27(2) 21 1176

3050. BROTHER WHERE YOU BOUND Supertramp
[01Jun85|13Jul85|26Oct85] 21(2) 22 1176

3051. SILK ELECTRIC Diana Ross
[23Oct82|04Dec82|02Apr83] 27(2) 24 1176

3052. MOTT Mott The Hoople
[25Aug73|20Oct73|09Mar74] 35(2) 29 1175

3053. BOBBIE SUE The Oak Ridge Boys
[20Feb82|03Apr82|10Jul82] 20(3) 21 1175

3054. COSMIC WHEELS Donovan
[31Mar73|26May73|11Aug73] 25(2) 20 1174

3055. THUNDER SEVEN Triumph
[08Dec84|02Mar85|29Jun85] 35(2) 30 1173

3056. DON MCLEAN Don McLean
[23Dec72|03Mar73|28Apr73] 23(2) 19 1173

3057. HELLBOUND TRAIN Savoy Brown
[18Mar72|27May72|05Aug72] 34(1) 21 1172

3058. MANTOVANI MAGIC Mantovani
[05Mar66|28May66|27Aug66] 23(1) 26 1172

3059. STEPHANIE Stephanie Mills
[16May81|27Jun81|17Oct81] 30(2) 23 1171

3060. BORBOLETTA Santana
[02Nov74|14Dec74|08Mar75] 20(1) 19 1170

3061. SPECIAL THINGS The Pointer Sisters
[30Aug80|29Nov80|07Feb81] 34(1) 24 1170

3062. IT'S JUST BEGUN The Jimmy Castor Bunch
[22Apr72|15Jul72|23Sep72] 27(1) 23 1170

3063. SKYLARKIN' Grover Washington Jr.
[08Mar80|19Apr80|02Aug80] 24(2) 22 1170

3064. DO YOU BELIEVE IN MAGIC The Lovin' Spoonful
[04Dec65|06Aug66|24Sep66] 32(1) 35 1170

3065. NIGHT OWL Gerry Rafferty
[16Jun79|07Jul79|03Nov79] 29(2) 21 1168

3066. NOW OR NEVER John Schneider
[27Jun81|22Aug81|21Nov81] 37(1) 22 1167

3067. USA UNION John Mayall
[24Oct70|14Nov70|20Mar71] 22(1) 22 1167

3068. THE BYRDS (UNTITLED) The Byrds
[17Oct70|28Nov70|06Mar71] 40(2) 21 1166

3069. GLEN CAMPBELL'S GREATEST HITS Glen Campbell
[17Apr71|29May71|01Nov75] 39(1) 27 1166

3070. MORE TRINI LOPEZ AT PJ'S Trini Lopez
[07Dec63|04Jan64|11Apr64] 11(2) 19 1165

3071. LOVESHINE Con Funk Shun
[01Jul78|16Sep78|04Nov78] 32(1) 19 1165

3072. TECHNIQUE New Order
[11Feb89|11Mar89|26Aug89] 32(1) 28 1165

3073. DOCTOR DOLITTLE Soundtrack
[14Oct67|24Feb68|10Aug68] 55(2) 44 1165

3074. THE MYTHS AND LEGENDS OF KING ARTHUR AND THE KNIGHTS OF THE ROUND TABLE Rick Wakeman
[19Apr75|31May75|26Jul75] 21(1) 15 1164

3075. SO FINE Loggins & Messina
[13Sep75|01Nov75|06Dec75] 21(1) 13 1163

3076. ANY DAY NOW Joan Baez
[25Jan69|22Feb69|07Jun69] 30(3) 20 1163

3077. WEDDING ALBUM Leon & Mary Russell
[01May76|03Jul76|06Nov76] 34(1) 28 1162

3078. TWICE AS SWEET A Taste Of Honey
[02Aug80|30May81|01Aug81] 36(2) 32 1161

3079. WINGS OF LOVE The Temptations
[03Apr76|05Jun76|14Aug76] 29(1) 20 1161

3080. FRANK SINATRA Frank Sinatra
[16Sep67|04Nov67|17Feb68] 24(1) 23 1161

3081. MAKE IT HAPPEN Smokey Robinson & The Miracles
[30Sep67|18Nov67|02Mar68] 28(2) 23 1160

3082. JUST AS I AM Bill Withers
[26Jun71|25Sep71|05Feb72] 39(1) 33 1160

Rank. Title Act
[Enter|Peak|Exit] Peak(Wks) TotWks Score

3083. SMACKWATER JACK Quincy Jones
[16Oct71|11Dec71|27May72] 56(2) 33 1160

3084. DEVOTION L.T.D.
[21Jul79|25Aug79|29Dec79] 29(2) 24 1159

3085. IT TAKES A NATION OF MILLIONS TO HOLD US BACK Public Enemy
[23Jul88|13Aug88|19Aug89] 42(2) 51 1159

3086. E.C. WAS HERE Eric Clapton
[06Sep75|18Oct75|29Nov75] 20(2) 13 1158

3087. CHILD IS FATHER TO THE MAN Blood, Sweat & Tears
[13Apr68|01Jun68|07Feb70] 47(2) 55 1158

3088. THEMES LIKE OLD TIMES Various Artists
[01Mar69|05Apr69|21Jun69] 31(2) 17 1158

3089. THE YARD WENT ON FOREVER... Richard Harris
[16Nov68|11Jan69|22Feb69] 27(1) 15 1158

3090. THE BEST OF THE DOORS(2) The Doors
[08Aug87|13Apr91|03Aug91] 32(1) 43 1157

3091. STATE OF SHOCK Ted Nugent
[02Jun79|30Jun79|29Sep79] 18(2) 18 1156

3092. TOUGH ALL OVER John Cafferty & The Beaver Brown Band
[08Jun85|06Jul85|11Jan86] 40(3) 32 1156

3093. MINNIE Minnie Riperton
[19May79|15Sep79|17Nov79] 29(1) 27 1155

3094. EMOTIONAL Jeffrey Osborne
[28Jun86|23Aug86|20Dec86] 26(1) 26 1155

3095. TOM PETTY AND THE HEARTBREAKERS Tom Petty And The Heartbreakers
[24Sep77|04Mar78|22Mar80] 55(1) 42 1155

3096. BOY U2
[14Mar81|11Apr81|19Sep87] 63(2) 47 1154

3097. THE SIDEWINDER Lee Morgan
[10Oct64|09Jan65|01May65] 25(3) 30 1153

3098. JOE COCKER Joe Cocker
[02Dec72|13Jan73|21Apr73] 30(2) 21 1153

3099. SUMMER SIDE OF LIFE Gordon Lightfoot
[29May71|03Jul71|09Oct71] 38(2) 20 1152

3100. UNFINISHED BUSINESS The Blackbyrds
[27Nov76|19Feb77|07May77] 34(1) 24 1152

3101. PAT TRAVERS BAND LIVE! GO FOR WHAT YOU KNOW Pat Travers Band
[21Jul79|22Sep79|15Dec79] 29(1) 22 1151

3102. LIGHTS OUT Peter Wolf
[11Aug84|15Sep84|02Feb85] 24(2) 26 1151

3103. URBAN RENEWAL Tower Of Power
[25Jan75|08Mar75|10May75] 22(2) 16 1149

3104. BELAFONTE AT THE GREEK THEATRE Harry Belafonte
[18Apr64|06Jun64|29Aug64] 17(1) 20 1149

3105. PAUL STANLEY Paul Stanley
[14Oct78|16Dec78|10Feb79] 40(3) 18 1149

3106. PARADISE Grover Washington Jr.
[28Apr79|16Jun79|01Sep79] 24(2) 19 1148

3107. AMERICAN BEAUTY Grateful Dead
[12Dec70|30Jan71|17Apr71] 30(1) 19 1148

3108. LONG MAY YOU RUN Stills-Young Band
[09Oct76|27Nov76|05Feb77] 26(1) 18 1147

3109. ANDY KIM Andy Kim
[14Sep74|23Nov74|04Jan75] 21(1) 17 1147

3110. TRUE COLOURS Split Enz
[30Aug80|15Nov80|14Feb81] 40(2) 25 1146

3111. LIVE AND LET DIE Soundtrack
[28Jul73|01Sep73|03Nov73] 17(1) 15 1146

3112. ROMANTICALLY Johnny Mathis
[28Dec63|08Feb64|27Jun64] 23(1) 27 1146

3113. ROCKY MOUNTAIN CHRISTMAS John Denver
[08Nov75|27Dec75|15Jan77] 14(2) 16 1146

3114. THE HUNGER Michael Bolton
[10Oct87|02Apr88|16Jul88] 46(1) 41 1145

3115. KICK OUT THE JAMS MC5
[08Mar69|10May69|09Aug69] 30(2) 23 1145

3116. ME MYSELF I Joan Armatrading
[07Jun80|09Aug80|08Nov80] 28(2) 23 1145

3117. BUSTIN' OUT Pure Prairie League
[08Feb75|31May75|19Jul75] 34(1) 24 1144

Rank.	Title	Act	Enter	Peak	Exit	Peak(Wks)	TotWks	Score
3118.	NEW TRADITIONALISTS	Devo	10Oct81	07Nov81	27Mar82	23(2)	25	1144
3119.	THE FOX	Elton John	06Jun81	27Jun81	10Oct81	21(2)	19	1144
3120.	BROOK BENTON TODAY	Brook Benton	21Feb70	04Apr70	25Jul70	27(1)	23	1144
3121.	COMPUTER-WORLD	Kraftwerk	06Jun81	22Aug81	20Mar82	72(1)	42	1144
3122.	RADIO ROMANCE	Eddie Rabbitt	06Nov82	26Feb83	23Apr83	31(2)	25	1143
3123.	KNOWLEDGE IS KING	Kool Moe Dee	17Jun89	15Jul89	18Nov89	25(2)	23	1142
3124.	QR III	Quiet Riot	02Aug86	20Sep86	31Jan87	31(2)	27	1142
3125.	EDIZIONE D'ORO (THE 4 SEASONS GOLD EDITION-29 GOLD HITS)	The 4 Seasons	28Dec68	08Mar69	17May69	37(1)	21	1140
3126.	CASINO ROYALE	Soundtrack	13May67	15Jul67	30Sep67	22(2)	21	1140
3127.	NUCLEAR FURNITURE	Jefferson Starship	16Jun84	28Jul84	17Nov84	28(4)	23	1140
3128.	THE MANY MOODS OF TONY	Tony Bennett	22Feb64	28Mar64	01Aug64	20(2)	24	1139
3129.	CITY NIGHTS	Nick Gilder	23Sep78	09Dec78	03Feb79	33(1)	20	1139
3130.	VERY DIONNE	Dionne Warwick	12Dec70	23Jan71	22May71	37(2)	24	1139
3131.	GREATEST HITS OF ALL TIMES	Gene Pitney	17Dec66	25Mar67	02Dec67	61(2)	51	1138
3132.	FRIENDS AND STRANGERS	Ronnie Laws	07May77	18Jun77	12Nov77	37(2)	28	1138
3133.	NIGHTMARES...AND OTHER TALES FROM THE VINYL JUNGLE	The J. Geils Band	19Oct74	30Nov74	15Mar75	26(2)	22	1138
3134.	RARE EARTH IN CONCERT	Rare Earth	01Jan72	05Feb72	20May72	29(1)	21	1137
3135.	CHANGES	Johnny Rivers	17Dec66	18Feb67	28Oct67	33(2)	46	1137
3136.	PLEASE LOVE ME FOREVER	Bobby Vinton	16Dec67	02Mar68	27Jul68	41(1)	33	1135
3137.	SUNSHINE	TV Soundtrack	01Dec73	09Feb74	04May74	34(1)	23	1135
3138.	THE BLASTERS	The Blasters	09Jan82	08May82	31Jul82	36(3)	30	1135
3139.	ALIVE SHE CRIED	The Doors	05Nov83	03Dec83	17Mar84	23(2)	20	1135
3140.	ON THROUGH THE NIGHT	Def Leppard	03May80	05Jul80	10Mar84	51(1)	51	1134
3141.	LET ME BE YOUR WOMAN	Linda Clifford	07Apr79	19May79	28Jul79	26(2)	17	1134
3142.	WALK, DON'T RUN, VOL. 2	The Ventures	10Oct64	12Dec64	20Mar65	17(2)	24	1134
3143.	MY WAY	Major Harris	29Mar75	05Jul75	23Aug75	28(2)	22	1132
3144.	ALONE TOGETHER	Donny Osmond	24Mar73	12May73	06Oct73	26(2)	29	1132
3145.	THE DISREGARD OF TIMEKEEPING	Bonham	07Oct89	16Dec89	21Apr90	38(1)	29	1131
3146.	MOON OVER NAPLES	Billy Vaughn And His Orchestra	09Oct65	11Dec65	23Apr66	31(2)	29	1130
3147.	SMILER	Rod Stewart	26Oct74	30Nov74	25Jan75	13(1)	14	1129
3148.	LONG HARD RIDE	The Marshall Tucker Band	26Jun76	14Aug76	06Nov76	32(2)	20	1128
3149.	CAPTURED ANGEL	Dan Fogelberg	04Oct75	22Nov75	07Feb76	23(1)	19	1128
3150.	FLOWERS	The Emotions	28Aug76	27Nov76	26Feb77	45(1)	27	1128
3151.	ARETHA	Aretha Franklin	25Oct80	06Dec80	16May81	47(3)	30	1128
3152.	INVISIBLE TEARS	Ray Conniff & His Orchestra & Chorus	03Oct64	19Dec64	03Apr65	23(1)	27	1127
3153.	INTO THE LIGHT	Chris de Burgh	20Sep86	20Jun87	19Sep87	25(2)	32	1127
3154.	FREEDOM	Neil Young	21Oct89	25Nov89	28Apr90	35(2)	28	1127
3155.	KING & QUEEN	Otis Redding & Carla Thomas	22Apr67	29Jul67	18Nov67	36(2)	31	1126
3156.	ALL THE GREAT HITS	Diana Ross	24Oct81	28Nov81	29May82	37(2)	32	1126
3157.	DOUBLE PLATINUM	KISS	20May78	01Jul78	28Oct78	22(2)	24	1125
3158.	HEY NOW HEY (THE OTHER SIDE OF THE SKY)	Aretha Franklin	14Jul73	18Aug73	24Nov73	30(2)	20	1124
3159.	BIRTH DAY	The New Birth	10Mar73	09Jun73	22Sep73	31(1)	29	1124
3160.	ALL THE BEST COWBOYS HAVE CHINESE EYES	Pete Townshend	10Jul82	11Sep82	01Jan83	26(1)	26	1124
3161.	MISSING PERSONS	Missing Persons	15May82	25Sep82	02Apr83	46(2)	47	1124
3162.	CHIM CHIM CHER-EE	The New Christy Minstrels	26Jun65	04Sep65	20Nov65	22(1)	22	1123
3163.	KINGS OF THE WILD FRONTIER	Adam And The Ants	28Feb81	13Jun81	24Oct81	44(2)	35	1122
3164.	JUICY FRUIT	Mtume	28May83	09Jul83	22Oct83	26(2)	22	1121
3165.	WHAT TIME IS IT?	The Time	25Sep82	30Oct82	07May83	26(3)	33	1120
3166.	THE KIDS & ME	Billy Preston	21Sep74	02Nov74	21Dec74	17(2)	14	1119
3167.	WE'RE A WINNER	The Impressions	02Mar68	22Jun68	31Aug68	35(1)	27	1118
3168.	ROD STEWART GREATEST HITS	Rod Stewart	24Nov79	05Jan80	29Mar80	22(2)	19	1118
3169.	PAUL'S BOUTIQUE	Beastie Boys	12Aug89	02Sep89	18Nov89	14(2)	15	1118
3170.	MOSAIC	Wang Chung	01Nov86	06Dec86	04Jul87	41(2)	36	1118
3171.	THE $5.98 E.P.: GARAGE DAYS RE-REVISITED	Metallica	12Sep87	10Oct87	02Apr88	28(2)	30	1117
3172.	THE COMPLETION BACKWARD PRINCIPLE	The Tubes	30May81	25Jul81	28Nov81	36(3)	27	1117
3173.	ELVIS-WORLD WIDE 50 GOLD AWARD HITS, VOL. 1	Elvis Presley	22Aug70	10Oct70	17Dec77	45(1)	36	1117
3174.	SACRED HEART	Dio	31Aug85	21Sep85	15Mar86	29(4)	29	1116
3175.	KARLA BONOFF	Karla Bonoff	01Oct77	26Nov77	01Jul78	52(1)	40	1115
3176.	THE TIME	The Time	12Sep81	31Oct81	17Apr82	50(1)	32	1115
3177.	REVOLUTION OF THE MIND - LIVE AT THE APOLLO, VOLUME III	James Brown	25Dec71	29Jan72	13May72	39(2)	21	1114
3178.	COSMIC MESSENGER	Jean-Luc Ponty	02Sep78	04Nov78	10Mar79	36(2)	28	1114
3179.	FIREBALL	Deep Purple	21Aug71	18Sep71	18Dec71	32(1)	18	1114
3180.	REACHING FOR THE SKY	Peabo Bryson	11Mar78	06May78	23Sep78	49(2)	29	1114
3181.	ONE MORE SONG	Randy Meisner	01Nov80	28Mar81	13Jun81	50(1)	33	1114
3182.	BLACK SEA	XTC	22Nov80	21Feb81	02May81	41(1)	24	1114
3183.	ROCKIN' WITH THE RHYTHM	The Judds	16Nov85	07Jun86	25Apr87	66(1)	57	1113
3184.	GOOD VIBRATIONS/BEST OF THE BEACH BOYS	The Beach Boys	19Jul75	30Aug75	11Sep76	25(2)	23	1113
3185.	OTIS REDDING LIVE IN EUROPE	Otis Redding	19Aug67	16Sep67	29Jun68	32(2)	42	1113
3186.	THE POET	Bobby Womack	26Dec81	13Mar82	29May82	29(2)	23	1109
3187.	A MAN AND HIS SOUL	Ray Charles	25Mar67	13May67	25May68	77(1)	62	1109
3188.	NIECY	Deniece Williams	17Apr82	12Jun82	11Sep82	20(3)	22	1107
3189.	SOUL TO SOUL	Stevie Ray Vaughan And Double Trouble	12Oct85	23Nov85	05Jul86	34(2)	39	1106
3190.	STAY WITH ME	Regina Belle	16Sep89	18Nov89	04Aug90	63(2)	44	1106
3191.	CAHOOTS	The Band	16Oct71	30Oct71	15Jan72	21(2)	14	1105
3192.	ROCK N ROLL ANIMAL	Lou Reed	02Mar74	06Apr74	31Aug74	45(1)	27	1104
3193.	THE BEACH BOYS IN CONCERT	The Beach Boys	08Dec73	26Jan74	28Aug76	25(1)	24	1104
3194.	PACK UP THE PLANTATION - LIVE!	Tom Petty And The Heartbreakers	14Dec85	01Mar86	07Jun86	22(2)	26	1104
3195.	ANNIE	Soundtrack	29May82	14Aug82	29Jan83	35(2)	31	1104
3196.	COMEDY IS NOT PRETTY!	Steve Martin	06Oct79	03Nov79	01Mar80	25(3)	22	1104
3197.	THAT'S WHY I'M HERE	James Taylor	23Nov85	21Dec85	14Jun86	34(3)	30	1103
3198.	PLUG ME INTO SOMETHING	Henry Gross	08Feb75	26Apr75	12Jul75	26(1)	23	1103
3199.	WATCH OUT!	Baja Marimba Band	19Nov66	18Mar67	09Sep67	54(1)	43	1103
3200.	HELP ME MAKE IT THROUGH THE NIGHT	Sammi Smith	13Feb71	10Apr71	03Jul71	33(2)	21	1102
3201.	DAVID GILMOUR	David Gilmour	01Jul78	26Aug78	28Oct78	29(2)	18	1102
3202.	WHAT ABOUT ME	Quicksilver Messenger Service	23Jan71	20Feb71	05Jun71	26(1)	20	1101
3203.	SPIRIT	Spirit	20Apr68	07Sep68	23Nov68	31(1)	32	1101
3204.	CLOSE ENOUGH FOR ROCK 'N' ROLL	Nazareth	08May76	22May76	07Aug76	24(3)	14	1101
3205.	WHY DONTCHA	West, Bruce & Laing	04Nov72	06Jan73	17Mar73	26(1)	20	1100
3206.	RIGHT ON	The Supremes	06Jun70	27Jun70	10Oct70	25(1)	19	1100
3207.	THERE WON'T BE ANYMORE	Charlie Rich	23Feb74	06Apr74	24Aug74	36(1)	27	1100
3208.	DOUBLE FUN	Robert Palmer	01Apr78	29Apr78	16Sep78	45(2)	25	1099
3209.	CROSSWINDS	Peabo Bryson	09Dec78	03Mar79	02Jun79	35(1)	26	1099
3210.	AFTER DARK	Andy Gibb	01Mar80	12Apr80	07Jun80	21(1)	15	1099
3211.	WE SHALL OVERCOME	Pete Seeger	14Dec63	11Apr64	15Aug64	42(1)	36	1099
3212.	THE MAGIC MUSIC OF FAR AWAY PLACES	Bert Kaempfert And His Orchestra	04Sep65	06Nov65	05Feb66	27(1)	23	1099
3213.	WAKE ME WHEN IT'S OVER	Faster Pussycat	23Sep89	19May90	11Aug90	48(1)	41	1099
3214.	THE 2ND CRUSADE	The Crusaders	10Mar73	02Jun73	22Sep73	45(1)	29	1098
3215.	A MAN ALONE & OTHER SONGS OF ROD MCKUEN	Frank Sinatra	06Sep69	11Oct69	20Dec69	30(2)	16	1098
3216.	OCCUPATION: FOOLE	George Carlin	10Nov73	08Dec73	30Mar74	35(1)	21	1098
3217.	STEPPIN' OUT	Neil Sedaka	01May76	12Jun76	25Sep76	26(1)	22	1098
3218.	THE BEST OF THE STYLISTICS	The Stylistics	22Feb75	12Apr75	13Sep75	41(1)	30	1097
3219.	SOUTHERN COMFORT	The Crusaders	26Oct74	28Dec74	29Mar75	31(2)	23	1097
3220.	LOVE LANGUAGE	Teddy Pendergrass	16Jun84	28Jul84	16Feb85	38(4)	35	1095

Rank. Title Act	[Enter|Peak|Exit] Peak(Wks) TotWks	Score
3221. **CLOSEUP** Frankie Valli	[29Mar75|02Aug75|04Oct75] 51(2) 28	1095
3222. **MUSIC - A PART OF ME** David McCallum	[26Feb66|21May66|06Aug66] 27(1) 24	1095
3223. **HEADS** Bob James	[26Nov77|25Feb78|24Jun78] 47(1) 31	1095
3224. **READY OR NOT** Lou Gramm	[28Feb87|25Apr87|22Aug87] 27(1) 26	1094
3225. **ROCKIN' ROLL BABY** The Stylistics	[24Nov73|12Jan74|21Sep74] 66(1) 44	1094
3226. **GARY PUCKETT & THE UNION GAP'S GREATEST HITS** Gary Puckett And The Union Gap	[11Jul70|05Sep70|20Feb71] 50(2) 33	1094
3227. **FESTIVAL** Santana	[22Jan77|12Feb77|28May77] 27(2) 19	1094
3228. **SING IT AGAIN ROD** Rod Stewart	[07Jul73|18Aug73|22Dec73] 31(1) 25	1094
3229. **HE DON'T LOVE YOU (LIKE I LOVE YOU)** Tony Orlando & Dawn	[26Apr75|14Jun75|16Aug75] 20(2) 17	1093
3230. **PROJECTIONS** The Blues Project	[17Dec66|13May67|07Oct67] 52(2) 36	1092
3231. **UNION** Toni Childs	[25Jun88|15Oct88|29Apr89] 63(1) 45	1092
3232. **CHAIN REACTION** The Crusaders	[23Aug75|04Oct75|13Dec75] 26(2) 17	1091
3233. **PLACES AND SPACES** Donald Byrd	[15Nov75|24Jan76|29May76] 49(2) 29	1091
3234. **THE CHIPMUNKS SING THE BEATLES HITS** The Chipmunks	[05Sep64|10Oct64|06Feb65] 14(1) 23	1091
3235. **DADDY DON'T YOU WALK SO FAST** Wayne Newton	[17Jun72|02Sep72|04Nov72] 34(2) 21	1091
3236. **RARITIES** The Beatles	[12Apr80|31May80|19Jul80] 21(1) 15	1091
3237. **THE IMPRESSIONS** The Impressions	[31Aug63|04Jan64|11Apr64] 43(1) 33	1091
3238. **EAST SIDE STORY** Squeeze	[30May81|22Aug81|14Nov81] 44(1) 25	1091
3239. **JANIS IAN** Janis Ian	[17Jun67|02Sep67|23Dec67] 29(1) 28	1090
3240. **DOWN HERE ON THE GROUND** Wes Montgomery	[04May68|31Aug68|23Nov68] 38(1) 30	1090
3241. **SUNSHINE ON LEITH** The Proclaimers	[08Apr89|07Aug93|27Nov93] 31(1) 37	1089
3242. **SO EARLY IN THE SPRING - THE FIRST 15 YEARS** Judy Collins	[06Aug77|22Oct77|04Feb78] 42(2) 27	1088
3243. **KENNY ROGERS** Kenny Rogers	[07May77|25Jun77|24May80] 30(2) 25	1088
3244. **HOUNDS OF LOVE** Kate Bush	[26Oct85|14Dec85|26Apr86] 30(1) 27	1088
3245. **THE WORKS** Queen	[17Mar84|28Apr84|28Jul84] 23(1) 20	1088
3246. **ACTION** The Blackbyrds	[08Oct77|26Nov77|29Apr78] 43(1) 30	1087
3247. **LEE OSKAR** Lee Oskar	[03Apr76|10Jul76|11Sep76] 29(1) 24	1087
3248. **THE BRASS ARE COMIN'** Herb Alpert & The Tijuana Brass	[22Nov69|03Jan70|04Apr70] 30(1) 20	1087
3249. **GET TOGETHER WITH ANDY WILLIAMS** Andy Williams	[08Nov69|13Dec69|28Mar70] 27(1) 21	1087
3250. **GIMME BACK MY BULLETS** Lynyrd Skynyrd	[21Feb76|27Mar76|05Jun76] 20(2) 16	1086
3251. **CRYSTAL ILLUSIONS** Sergio Mendes & Brasil '66	[16Aug69|04Oct69|06Dec69] 33(1) 17	1086
3252. **FRANKIE AND JOHNNY (SOUNDTRACK)** Elvis Presley	[23Apr66|28May66|27Aug66] 20(1) 19	1086
3253. **MENAGERIE** Bill Withers	[29Oct77|11Feb78|22Apr78] 39(1) 26	1085
3254. **ULTIMATE SPINACH** Ultimate Spinach	[24Feb68|08Jun68|03Aug68] 34(1) 24	1084
3255. **LEAVING IT ALL BEHIND** The Grass Roots	[06Dec69|27Dec69|25Apr70] 36(3) 21	1084
3256. **A TRICK OF THE TAIL** Genesis	[20Mar76|15May76|24Jul76] 31(2) 19	1084
3257. **SHE'S STRANGE** Cameo	[17Mar84|05May84|25Aug84] 27(1) 24	1083
3258. **TOUCH THE WORLD** Earth, Wind & Fire	[21Nov87|19Dec87|28May88] 33(1) 28	1083
3259. **FEELIN' BITCHY** Millie Jackson	[22Oct77|28Jan78|25Mar78] 34(1) 23	1083
3260. **RAW LIKE SUSHI** Neneh Cherry	[24Jun89|16Sep89|17Feb90] 40(1) 35	1083
3261. **BYRDS** The Byrds	[24Mar73|12May73|14Jul73] 20(1) 17	1081
3262. **ROOTS (SOUNDTRACK)** Quincy Jones	[19Feb77|02Apr77|21May77] 21(1) 14	1081
3263. **2ND WAVE** Surface	[26Nov88|09Sep89|02Dec89] 56(2) 39	1080
3264. **EVERYTHING'S ARCHIE** The Archies	[06Sep69|20Dec69|16May70] 66(1) 36	1080
3265. **LESS THAN ZERO** Soundtrack	[05Dec87|16Jan88|07May88] 31(2) 23	1080
3266. **THE WAY WE WERE** Soundtrack	[16Feb74|16Mar74|25May74] 20(1) 15	1079
3267. **THE GAP BAND II** The Gap Band	[22Dec79|29Mar80|28Jun80] 42(1) 28	1079
3268. **RE-AC-TOR** Neil Young & Crazy Horse	[21Nov81|19Dec81|13Mar82] 27(3) 17	1078
3269. **THREE** Bob James	[03Jul76|18Sep76|01Jan77] 49(2) 27	1077
3270. **YOU ONLY LIVE TWICE** Soundtrack	[15Jul67|16Sep67|06Jan68] 27(1) 26	1077
3271. **TWO PLACES AT THE SAME TIME** Ray Parker Jr. & Raydio	[12Apr80|24May80|30Aug80] 33(2) 21	1077
3272. **PETER CRISS** Peter Criss	[14Oct78|25Nov78|24Feb79] 43(2) 20	1076
3273. **GOLDEN TIME OF DAY** Maze Featuring Frankie Beverly	[04Feb78|01Apr78|01Jul78] 27(1) 22	1075
3274. **YESTERDAYS** Yes	[22Mar75|12Apr75|07Jun75] 17(2) 12	1075
3275. **ALL THE LOVE IN THE WORLD** Mac Davis	[08Feb75|22Mar75|10May75] 21(2) 14	1075
3276. **GET CLOSER** Linda Ronstadt	[16Oct82|13Nov82|23Apr83] 31(4) 28	1075
3277. **LET'S GO!** The Ventures	[31Aug63|12Oct63|11Apr64] 30(1) 33	1075
3278. **LIVE AND SLEAZY** Village People	[20Oct79|08Dec79|01Mar80] 32(2) 20	1074
3279. **PERSON TO PERSON** Average White Band	[22Jan77|05Mar77|21May77] 28(1) 18	1074
3280. **MY CHERIE AMOUR** Stevie Wonder	[11Oct69|15Nov69|21Feb70] 34(1) 20	1073
3281. **FLASH GORDON (SOUNDTRACK)** Queen	[27Dec80|07Feb81|04Apr81] 23(2) 15	1073
3282. **JUST A GAME** Triumph	[05May79|07Jul79|10Nov79] 48(1) 28	1073
3283. **URIAH HEEP LIVE** Uriah Heep	[05May73|16Jun73|24Nov73] 37(1) 30	1071
3284. **BEE GEES GOLD, VOLUME ONE** Bee Gees	[13Nov76|22Jan77|20May78] 50(1) 33	1071
3285. **SECRETS** Con Funk Shun	[15Oct77|03Dec77|22Apr78] 51(2) 28	1071
3286. **ARTHUR (THE ALBUM)** Soundtrack	[05Sep81|31Oct81|30Jan82] 32(3) 22	1071
3287. **LIVING IN A FANTASY** Leo Sayer	[18Oct80|10Jan81|21Mar81] 36(2) 23	1070
3288. **CANCIONES DE MI PADRE** Linda Ronstadt	[12Dec87|06Feb88|06Aug88] 42(1) 35	1069
3289. **BRING IT BACK ALIVE** The Outlaws	[25Mar78|06May78|12Aug78] 29(1) 21	1068
3290. **THE LOVER IN ME** Sheena Easton	[03Dec88|18Feb89|27May89] 44(4) 26	1067
3291. **THE SINGING NUN** Debbie Reynolds	[30Apr66|25Jun66|15Oct66] 23(1) 25	1067
3292. **MYSTERIOUS TRAVELLER** Weather Report	[22Jun74|20Jul74|23Nov74] 46(3) 23	1067
3293. **TOGETHER FOREVER** The Marshall Tucker Band	[13May78|24Jun78|26Aug78] 22(1) 16	1067
3294. **THERE'S ONE IN EVERY CROWD** Eric Clapton	[12Apr75|24May75|12Jul75] 21(1) 14	1066
3295. **I'M THE MAN** Anthrax	[19Dec87|30Jan88|17Sep88] 53(1) 40	1066
3296. **BEHIND THE SUN** Eric Clapton	[06Apr85|25May85|12Oct85] 34(1) 28	1065
3297. **SUCKING IN THE SEVENTIES** The Rolling Stones	[04Apr81|18Apr81|20Jun81] 15(2) 12	1065
3298. **BEATIN' THE ODDS** Molly Hatchet	[20Sep80|11Oct80|07Feb81] 25(2) 21	1065
3299. **RETROSPECTIVE/ THE BEST OF BUFFALO SPRINGFIELD** The Buffalo Springfield	[01Mar69|15Mar69|19Jun71] 42(3) 24	1065
3300. **WAKING UP WITH THE HOUSE ON FIRE** Culture Club	[24Nov84|01Dec84|06Apr85] 26(5) 20	1065
3301. **LET ME BE YOUR ANGEL** Stacy Lattisaw	[05Jul80|18Oct80|10Jan81] 44(1) 28	1063
3302. **BALIN** Marty Balin	[06Jun81|22Aug81|07Nov81] 35(2) 23	1063
3303. **SHADY GROVE** Quicksilver Messenger Service	[24Jan70|28Feb70|04Jul70] 25(1) 24	1062
3304. **MOONDOG MATINEE** The Band	[17Nov73|05Jan74|30Mar74] 28(1) 20	1062
3305. **FRANK SINATRA'S GREATEST HITS!** Frank Sinatra	[07Sep68|16Nov68|22Feb69] 55(1) 25	1062
3306. **JOY AND PAIN** Maze Featuring Frankie Beverly	[02Aug80|04Oct80|24Jan81] 31(1) 23	1061
3307. **WILLIE NELSON SINGS KRISTOFFERSON** Willie Nelson	[17Nov79|12Jan80|03May80] 42(2) 25	1061
3308. **JAMES GANG LIVE IN CONCERT** The James Gang	[11Sep71|09Oct71|25Dec71] 24(1) 16	1060
3309. **OOH LA LA** Faces	[21Apr73|02Jun73|04Aug73] 21(2) 16	1060
3310. **STAND BY YOUR MAN** Tammy Wynette	[08Feb69|22Mar69|28Jun69] 43(1) 21	1059
3311. **IMAGES** The Crusaders	[15Jul78|09Sep78|11Nov78] 34(3) 18	1059
3312. **WHAT UP, DOG?** Was (Not Was)	[15Oct88|08Apr89|24Jun89] 43(2) 37	1057
3313. **IN THE CITY** Tavares	[09Aug75|18Oct75|29Nov75] 26(2) 17	1056
3314. **MY BEST TO YOU** Donny Osmond	[16Dec72|03Feb73|28Apr73] 29(1) 20	1056
3315. **TWO OF A KIND (SOUNDTRACK)** Soundtrack	[03Dec83|04Feb84|14Apr84] 26(1) 20	1055
3316. **INJOY** Bar-Kays	[10Nov79|22Dec79|19Apr80] 35(3) 24	1054
3317. **SIGNED SEALED & DELIVERED** Stevie Wonder	[29Aug70|26Sep70|12Dec70] 25(1) 16	1054
3318. **BIG WORLD** Joe Jackson	[19Apr86|24May86|04Oct86] 34(2) 25	1053
3319. **OUTRIDER** Jimmy Page	[09Jul88|30Jul88|19Nov88] 26(2) 20	1052
3320. **WHEN I DREAM** Crystal Gayle	[15Jul78|12Aug78|07Apr79] 52(1) 39	1052
3321. **FAHRENHEIT** Toto	[13Sep86|29Nov86|16May87] 40(2) 36	1052
3322. **HOLLAND** The Beach Boys	[27Jan73|24Mar73|28Jun75] 36(1) 30	1051
3323. **ZEPHYR** Zephyr	[20Dec69|14Mar70|13Jun70] 48(2) 26	1050
3324. **HARD RAIN** Bob Dylan	[02Oct76|30Oct76|18Dec76] 17(2) 12	1050

Rank. Title Act	[Enter|Peak|Exit] Peak(Wks) TotWks	Score
3325. **WAKE OF THE FLOOD** Grateful Dead	[27Oct73|08Dec73|02Mar74] 18(1) 19	1050
3326. **MUSIC BOX DANCER** Frank Mills	[17Mar79|05May79|30Jun79] 21(1) 16	1050
3327. **TOGETHER** Country Joe & The Fish	[13Jul68|24Aug68|26Oct68] 23(2) 16	1050
3328. **TEXAS FLOOD** Stevie Ray Vaughan And Double Trouble	[23Jul83|01Oct83|03Mar84] 38(1) 33	1049
3329. **RADIO** LL Cool J	[11Jan86|15Mar86|27Sep86] 46(3) 38	1049
3330. **LUXURY OF LIFE** Five Star	[21Sep85|08Mar86|09Aug86] 57(2) 47	1049
3331. **LIGHT OF WORLDS** Kool & The Gang	[05Oct74|23Nov74|24May75] 63(3) 34	1049
3332. **EVERY GENERATION** Ronnie Laws	[16Feb80|22Mar80|21Jun80] 24(3) 19	1049
3333. **HIS BAND AND THE STREET CHOIR** Van Morrison	[26Dec70|09Jan71|17Apr71] 32(2) 17	1048
3334. **JEFFREY OSBORNE** Jeffrey Osborne	[19Jun82|14Aug82|09Apr83] 49(3) 43	1048
3335. **WILD HEART OF THE YOUNG** Karla Bonoff	[03Apr82|19Jun82|27Nov82] 49(1) 35	1046
3336. **ALONG THE RED LEDGE** Daryl Hall & John Oates	[09Sep78|04Nov78|03Feb79] 27(2) 22	1046
3337. **DYLAN** Bob Dylan	[22Dec73|02Feb74|30Mar74] 17(1) 15	1045
3338. **GET LOOSE** Evelyn King	[11Sep82|06Nov82|16Apr83] 27(3) 32	1044
3339. **A SHIP ARRIVING TOO LATE TO SAVE A DROWNING WITCH** Frank Zappa	[12Jun82|21Aug82|06Nov82] 23(2) 22	1044
3340. **IN THE NIGHT-TIME** Michael Henderson	[08Jul78|30Sep78|13Jan79] 38(1) 28	1044
3341. **E.T. - THE EXTRA-TERRESTRIAL** Soundtrack	[03Jul82|28Aug82|12Feb83] 37(2) 33	1043
3342. **THE GIST OF THE GEMINI** Gino Vannelli	[14Aug76|02Oct76|15Jan77] 32(2) 22	1043
3343. **STATE OF EUPHORIA** Anthrax	[08Oct88|22Oct88|10Jun89] 30(2) 36	1043
3344. **NORTHERN LIGHTS-SOUTHERN CROSS** The Band	[13Dec75|31Jan76|17Apr76] 26(1) 19	1042
3345. **MISFITS** The Kinks	[03Jun78|15Jul78|21Oct78] 40(1) 21	1041
3346. **ANOTHER TIME, ANOTHER PLACE** Engelbert Humperdinck	[11Sep71|09Oct71|18Dec71] 25(1) 15	1041
3347. **BREAD & ROSES** Judy Collins	[11Sep76|16Oct76|22Jan77] 25(1) 20	1041
3348. **IDLEWILD SOUTH** The Allman Brothers Band	[24Oct70|12Dec70|20Mar71] 38(1) 22	1041
3349. **THE BOX TOPS SUPER HITS** The Box Tops	[07Dec68|22Feb69|12Jul69] 45(1) 26	1041
3350. **FLY ON THE WALL** AC/DC	[20Jul85|07Sep85|08Feb86] 32(2) 30	1041
3351. **TALK IS CHEAP** Keith Richards	[22Oct88|19Nov88|25Mar89] 24(1) 23	1040
3352. **LEIF GARRETT** Leif Garrett	[17Dec77|11Feb78|27May78] 37(2) 24	1040
3353. **HARD NOSE THE HIGHWAY** Van Morrison	[11Aug73|08Sep73|15Dec73] 27(2) 19	1039
3354. **RESTLESS** Starpoint	[05Oct85|01Feb86|23Aug86] 60(3) 47	1039
3355. **SO RED THE ROSE** Arcadia	[21Dec85|18Jan86|12Apr86] 23(2) 17	1039
3356. **THE MANTOVANI SOUND - BIG HITS FROM BROADWAY AND HOLLYWOOD** Mantovani	[20Mar65|22May65|16Oct65] 26(1) 31	1039
3357. **ROCK & ROLL MUSIC TO THE WORLD** Ten Years After	[14Oct72|23Dec72|31Mar73] 43(1) 25	1038
3358. **DOOR TO DOOR** The Cars	[12Sep87|26Sep87|13Feb88] 26(3) 23	1037
3359. **RUNNING LIKE THE WIND** The Marshall Tucker Band	[05May79|16Jun79|29Sep79] 30(1) 22	1037
3360. **ME AND BOBBY MCGEE** Kris Kristofferson	[11Sep71|09Oct71|05Feb72] 43(1) 22	1036
3361. **FROM RUSSIA WITH LOVE** Soundtrack	[02May64|22Aug64|14Aug65] 27(1) 34	1036
3362. **DOWN ON THE FARM** Little Feat	[08Dec79|05Jan80|26Apr80] 29(1) 21	1036
3363. **SAY IT LOUD-I'M BLACK AND I'M PROUD** James Brown	[12Apr69|31May69|06Sep69] 53(2) 22	1035
3364. **NEVER LET ME DOWN** David Bowie	[23May87|30May87|14Nov87] 34(1) 26	1035
3365. **ATF** After The Fire	[12Mar83|30Apr83|23Jul83] 25(3) 20	1034
3366. **EMPTY ROOMS** John Mayall	[14Mar70|25Apr70|18Jul70] 33(1) 19	1034
3367. **DON'T BE AFRAID OF THE DARK** The Robert Cray Band	[27Aug88|24Sep88|01Apr89] 32(2) 32	1034
3368. **TO SIR WITH LOVE** Lulu	[11Nov67|16Dec67|23Mar68] 24(2) 20	1033
3369. **SHOWTIME** The J. Geils Band	[04Dec82|29Jan83|09Apr83] 23(3) 19	1033
3370. **DON'T CRY OUT LOUD** Melissa Manchester	[09Dec78|31Mar79|09Jun79] 33(1) 27	1033
3371. **GLORIA, MARTY & STRINGS** Gloria Lynne	[21Sep63|20Jun64|18Jul64] 27(1) 22	1033
3372. **SIMPLE THINGS** Carole King	[06Aug77|24Sep77|05Nov77] 17(1) 14	1033
3373. **KEEP ON SMILIN'** Wet Willie	[01Jun74|21Sep74|09Nov74] 41(1) 24	1033
3374. **SHAKEN 'N' STIRRED** Robert Plant	[15Jun85|13Jul85|19Oct85] 20(2) 19	1032
3375. **FOCUS 3** Focus	[14Apr73|23Jun73|08Sep73] 35(1) 22	1031
3376. **JOE'S GARAGE ACT I** Frank Zappa	[22Sep79|20Oct79|08Mar80] 27(2) 25	1031
3377. **BROKEN BARRICADES** Procol Harum	[08May71|29May71|18Sep71] 32(2) 20	1029
3378. **PLATINUM JAZZ** War	[23Jul77|17Sep77|22Oct77] 23(1) 14	1029
3379. **UP-TIGHT EVERYTHING'S ALRIGHT** Stevie Wonder	[18Jun66|01Oct66|03Dec66] 33(1) 25	1029
3380. **GIVE MY REGARDS TO BROAD STREET** Paul McCartney	[10Nov84|24Nov84|09Mar85] 21(2) 18	1029
3381. **POWER** Ice-T	[01Oct88|12Nov88|13May89] 35(1) 33	1029
3382. **LOVE ME AGAIN** Rita Coolidge	[17Jun78|05Aug78|11Nov78] 32(1) 22	1028
3383. **HUSH, HUSH, SWEET CHARLOTTE** Patti Page	[22May65|17Jul65|13Nov65] 27(1) 26	1028
3384. **ROMANCE 1600** Sheila E.	[21Sep85|08Mar86|03May86] 50(1) 33	1028
3385. **RED ROSES FOR A BLUE LADY** Wayne Newton	[01May65|19Jun65|11Sep65] 17(1) 20	1028
3386. **DICK CLARK/20 YEARS OF ROCK N' ROLL** Various Artists	[14Jul73|25Aug73|10Nov73] 27(2) 18	1028
3387. **ALL OUR LOVE** Gladys Knight & The Pips	[12Dec87|19Mar88|11Jun88] 39(1) 27	1027
3388. **SO FAR, SO GOOD... SO WHAT!** Megadeth	[06Feb88|27Feb88|09Jul88] 28(1) 23	1027
3389. **COME FROM THE SHADOWS** Joan Baez	[27May72|08Jul72|04Nov72] 48(2) 24	1027
3390. **RIDE A ROCK HORSE** Roger Daltrey	[09Aug75|13Sep75|10Jan76] 28(2) 23	1027
3391. **WE ARE ONE** Maze Featuring Frankie Beverly	[28May83|18Jun83|19Nov83] 25(3) 26	1026
3392. **HOLY DIVER** Dio	[25Jun83|22Oct83|10Mar84] 56(1) 38	1026
3393. **THE DEAN MARTIN TV SHOW** Dean Martin	[03Dec66|04Feb67|01Jul67] 34(1) 31	1026
3394. **REED SEED** Grover Washington Jr.	[21Oct78|09Dec78|24Mar79] 35(2) 23	1025
3395. **ADVENTURES IN UTOPIA** Utopia	[26Jan80|23Feb80|14Jun80] 32(2) 21	1025
3396. **LOST WITHOUT YOUR LOVE** Bread	[15Jan77|26Feb77|30Apr77] 26(2) 16	1024
3397. **CHIPMUNK PUNK** The Chipmunks	[09Aug80|20Sep80|31Jan81] 34(2) 26	1024
3398. **GREATEST HITS** Herb Alpert & The Tijuana Brass	[21Mar70|11Apr70|24Oct70] 43(1) 32	1024
3399. **THE SENSUAL WORLD** Kate Bush	[04Nov89|25Nov89|28Apr90] 43(2) 26	1024
3400. **A SALT WITH A DEADLY PEPA** Salt-N-Pepa	[13Aug88|24Sep88|11Mar89] 38(1) 31	1023
3401. **LONG PLAYER** Faces	[13Mar71|01May71|17Jul71] 29(1) 19	1022
3402. **JACKSONS LIVE** The Jacksons	[28Nov81|23Jan82|22Sep84] 30(2) 19	1022
3403. **FOXY LADY** Cher	[29Jul72|30Sep72|23Dec72] 43(2) 22	1022
3404. **IT MUST HAVE BEEN SOMETHING I SAID!** The Smothers Brothers	[23May64|04Jul64|28Nov64] 23(2) 28	1022
3405. **TIME TO THINK** The Kingston Trio	[01Feb64|07Mar64|20Jun64] 18(2) 21	1022
3406. **SANDINISTA!** The Clash	[07Feb81|07Mar81|20Jun81] 24(2) 20	1021
3407. **TEQUILA** Wes Montgomery	[03Sep66|12Nov66|08Apr67] 51(1) 32	1021
3408. **PUT YOUR HEAD ON MY SHOULDER** The Lettermen	[14Dec68|22Feb69|03May69] 43(2) 21	1020
3409. **VIEW FROM THE GROUND** America	[28Aug82|30Oct82|05Mar83] 41(8) 28	1020
3410. **WARMER COMMUNICATIONS** Average White Band	[01Apr78|06May78|22Jul78] 28(2) 17	1020
3411. **FROM ME TO YOU** Charley Pride	[06Feb71|20Mar71|31Jul71] 42(1) 26	1020
3412. **URBAN CHIPMUNK** The Chipmunks	[06Jun81|15Aug81|30Jan82] 56(1) 35	1020
3413. **TOGETHER** Diana Ross & The Supremes And The Temptations	[25Oct69|22Nov69|21Feb70] 28(1) 18	1020
3414. **THE MONKEES GREATEST HITS(2)** The Monkees	[07Aug76|02Oct76|02Aug86] 58(1) 30	1019
3415. **WHERE HAVE I KNOWN YOU BEFORE** Return To Forever	[28Sep74|30Nov74|01Mar75] 32(2) 23	1018
3416. **ABOUT US** Stories	[28Jul73|15Sep73|01Dec73] 29(1) 19	1018
3417. **STORMWATCH** Jethro Tull	[06Oct79|10Nov79|26Jan80] 22(1) 17	1018
3418. **CHRISTINE McVIE** Christine McVie	[18Feb84|17Mar84|21Jul84] 26(3) 23	1017
3419. **AWAY WE A GO-GO** Smokey Robinson & The Miracles	[17Dec66|25Feb67|17Jun67] 41(1) 27	1017
3420. **THE GLOW** Bonnie Raitt	[13Oct79|08Dec79|01Mar80] 30(1) 21	1017
3421. **A BIT OF LIVERPOOL** The Supremes	[28Nov64|06Feb65|17Apr65] 21(3) 21	1016
3422. **SHOW ME** The Cover Girls	[15Aug87|27Feb88|05Nov88] 64(1) 61	1016
3423. **4 TOPS ON TOP** Four Tops	[27Aug66|19Nov66|21Jan67] 32(2) 22	1015
3424. **IN THE DARK/THE BEST OF OMD** Orchestral Manoeuvres In The Dark	[26Mar88|14May88|08Oct88] 46(2) 29	1015
3425. **VINYL CONFESSIONS** Kansas	[12Jun82|17Jul82|23Oct82] 16(2) 20	1015
3426. **ROGER AND OUT** Roger Miller	[27Jun64|12Dec64|17Jul65] 37(2) 46	1015

Rank. Title Act
[Enter|Peak|Exit] Peak(Wks) TotWks Score

3427. SHAKEDOWN STREET Grateful Dead
[09Dec78|17Feb79|14Apr79] 41(1) 19 1015

3428. WE GOT TO LIVE TOGETHER Buddy Miles
[14Nov70|05Dec70|08May71] 53(2) 26 1014

3429. MARRYING MAIDEN It's A Beautiful Day
[04Jul70|01Aug70|21Nov70] 28(1) 21 1014

3430. REO SPEEDWAGON LIVE/ YOU GET WHAT YOU PLAY FOR
REO Speedwagon
[19Mar77|23Apr77|23May81] 72(1) 50 1014

3431. CAUGHT LIVE + 5 The Moody Blues
[04Jun77|23Jul77|10Sep77] 26(2) 15 1013

3432. HIP HUG-HER Booker T. & The MG's
[24Jun67|30Sep67|06Jan68] 35(1) 29 1013

3433. THE PROGRESSIVE BLUES EXPERIMENT
Johnny Winter
[12Apr69|17May69|23Aug69] 40(1) 20 1012

3434. HEAVY Iron Butterfly
[09Mar68|08Jun68|22Feb69] 78(1) 49 1012

3435. DREAMING #11 Joe Satriani
[26Nov88|04Feb89|20May89] 42(1) 26 1012

3436. NAJEE'S THEME Najee
[28Feb87|02May87|02Jan88] 56(2) 45 1012

3437. NO DICE Badfinger
[28Nov70|19Dec70|06Mar71] 28(2) 15 1012

3438. THE JEALOUS KIND Delbert McClinton
[22Nov80|07Mar81|30May81] 34(1) 28 1011

3439. SPARTACUS Triumvirat
[07Jun75|23Aug75|27Sep75] 27(1) 17 1010

3440. ZEBRA Zebra
[14May83|13Aug83|19Nov83] 29(2) 28 1010

3441. THE PRESENT The Moody Blues
[10Sep83|08Oct83|04Feb84] 26(3) 22 1010

3442. LEE MICHAELS Lee Michaels
[30Aug69|15Nov69|21Feb70] 53(2) 26 1009

3443. EASY LOVING Freddie Hart
[09Oct71|18Dec71|19Feb72] 37(1) 20 1009

3444. TWICE THE FIRE Peaches & Herb
[10Nov79|15Dec79|31May80] 31(3) 30 1009

3445. GIVE US A WINK The Sweet
[06Mar76|17Apr76|29May76] 27(2) 13 1008

3446. THE BEST OF MANCINI
Henry Mancini And His Orchestra
[08Aug64|17Oct64|03Apr65] 42(1) 35 1007

3447. THREE HEARTS Bob Welch
[10Mar79|07Apr79|30Jun79] 20(2) 17 1007

3448. TWO FOR THE SHOW Kansas
[18Nov78|13Jan79|24Mar79] 32(1) 19 1007

3449. NINE LIVES REO Speedwagon
[11Aug79|29Sep79|28Mar81] 33(1) 23 1007

3450. BELL & JAMES Bell & James
[03Feb79|28Apr79|09Jun79] 31(1) 19 1006

3451. FEVER Ronnie Laws
[12Jun76|10Jul76|30Oct76] 46(2) 21 1006

3452. MEN AND WOMEN Simply Red
[28Mar87|02May87|19Sep87] 31(2) 26 1006

3453. LADY Jack Jones
[25Mar67|13May67|09Sep67] 23(2) 25 1006

Rank. Title Act
[Enter|Peak|Exit] Peak(Wks) TotWks Score

3454. A FRESH AIRE CHRISTMAS
Mannheim Steamroller
[26Nov88|24Dec88|19Jan91] 36(3) 24 1006

3455. CARELESS Stephen Bishop
[08Jan77|15Oct77|03Dec77] 34(2) 32 1005

3456. DESERT MOON Dennis DeYoung
[06Oct84|17Nov84|23Mar85] 29(3) 25 1005

3457. MOM ALWAYS LIKED YOU BEST!
The Smothers Brothers
[16Oct65|29Jan66|23Apr66] 39(2) 28 1004

3458. SEVEN THE HARD WAY Pat Benatar
[14Dec85|28Dec85|26Apr86] 26(4) 20 1004

3459. TOO FAST FOR LOVE Mötley Crüe
[17Dec83|31Mar84|11Jul87] 77(1) 62 1004

3460. COLORS OF THE DAY/ THE BEST OF JUDY COLLINS Judy Collins
[27May72|08Jul72|04Nov72] 37(2) 24 1004

3461. FOR A FEW DOLLARS MORE AND OTHER MOTION PICTURE THEMES
Leroy Holmes And His Orchestra
[09Sep67|23Dec67|23Mar68] 42(2) 29 1003

3462. LIVE-STOMPIN' AT THE SAVOY
Rufus And Chaka Khan
[03Sep83|29Oct83|14Apr84] 50(1) 33 1003

3463. WANTED Richard Pryor
[16Dec78|17Feb79|28Apr79] 32(2) 20 1002

3464. WILD THINGS! The Ventures
[17Sep66|26Nov66|11Mar67] 33(1) 26 1001

3465. BARBRA STREISAND'S GREATEST HITS
Barbra Streisand
[28Feb70|28Mar70|19Sep70] 32(1) 30 1001

3466. UNLIMITED! Roger
[28Nov87|30Jan88|07May88] 35(1) 24 1000

3467. MEET THE SEARCHERS/NEEDLES & PINS
The Searchers
[11Apr64|27Jun64|29Aug64] 22(2) 21 999

3468. THE YOUTH OF TODAY Musical Youth
[08Jan83|26Feb83|04Jun83] 23(4) 22 999

3469. DANA DANE WITH FAME Dana Dane
[12Sep87|17Oct87|16Apr88] 46(2) 32 998

3470. HERE COMES THE NIGHT Barry Manilow
[18Dec82|22Jan83|18Jun83] 32(4) 27 998

3471. AIR SUPPLY Air Supply
[29Jun85|20Jul85|16Nov85] 26(4) 21 997

3472. DISCOTHEQUE Herbie Mann
[19Apr75|14Jun75|16Aug75] 27(2) 18 997

3473. YOU WERE ON MY MIND We Five
[16Oct65|25Dec65|10Sep66] 32(3) 30 997

3474. NEW BLOOD Blood, Sweat & Tears
[04Nov72|30Dec72|24Feb73] 32(1) 17 997

3475. DOUBLE GOLD Neil Diamond
[20Jan73|31Mar73|09Jun73] 36(1) 21 996

3476. SOMEBODY LIKE ME Eddy Arnold
[24Dec66|18Mar67|15Jul67] 36(1) 30 996

3477. LIVE CREAM - VOLUME II Cream
[01Apr72|13May72|15Jul72] 27(1) 16 995

3478. RADIANT Atlantic Starr
[14Mar81|16May81|03Oct81] 47(1) 30 995

Rank. Title Act
[Enter|Peak|Exit] Peak(Wks) TotWks Score

3479. JOHN TRAVOLTA John Travolta
[22May76|31Jul76|16Oct76] 39(2) 22 995

3480. ALL THAT JAZZ Soundtrack
[22Mar80|19Apr80|23Aug80] 36(2) 23 995

3481. I'M IN LOVE Evelyn King
[25Jul81|19Sep81|21Nov81] 28(1) 18 995

3482. LET IT ROLL Little Feat
[20Aug88|08Oct88|01Apr89] 36(1) 33 994

3483. JEFF BECK WITH THE JAN HAMMER GROUP LIVE Jeff Beck With The Jan Hammer Group
[02Apr77|14May77|09Jul77] 23(1) 15 994

3484. CIRCLE OF LOVE The Steve Miller Band
[14Nov81|05Dec81|06Mar82] 26(2) 17 994

3485. GUITARS, CADILLACS, ETC., ETC.
Dwight Yoakam
[19Apr86|07Jun86|11Jul87] 61(2) 65 993

3486. HOT TUNA Hot Tuna
[18Jul70|05Sep70|21Nov70] 30(1) 19 993

3487. THE 5TH DIMENSION/LIVE!!
The 5th Dimension
[23Oct71|27Nov71|19Feb72] 32(2) 18 993

3488. 2525 (EXORDIUM & TERMINUS)
Zager & Evans
[02Aug69|30Aug69|25Oct69] 30(2) 13 992

3489. HOME TO THE SEA
The San Sebastian Strings
[18Jan69|15Feb69|07Jun69] 20(1) 20 992

3490. DELANEY & BONNIE & FRIENDS ON TOUR WITH ERIC CLAPTON
Delaney & Bonnie & Friends
[18Apr70|09May70|08Aug70] 29(1) 17 991

3491. PARLIAMENT LIVE/P FUNK EARTH TOUR
Parliament
[21May77|25Jun77|24Sep77] 29(2) 19 991

3492. WILD HONEY The Beach Boys
[30Dec67|09Mar68|06Apr68] 24(2) 15 991

3493. SATIN DOLL Bobbi Humphrey
[07Dec74|01Mar75|05Apr75] 30(2) 18 991

3494. SAM HARRIS Sam Harris
[29Sep84|24Nov84|13Apr85] 35(2) 29 989

3495. THE MORE I SEE YOU/CALL ME
Chris Montez
[02Jul66|10Sep66|10Dec66] 33(1) 24 989

3496. YOUR ALL-TIME FAVORITE SONGS
John Gary
[30Oct65|18Dec65|16Apr66] 21(2) 25 989

3497. DRESSED TO KILL KISS
[19Apr75|14Jun75|26Feb77] 32(2) 29 989

3498. COMING BACK HARD AGAIN Fat Boys
[09Jul88|06Aug88|17Dec88] 33(2) 24 988

3499. TALKING BACK TO THE NIGHT
Steve Winwood
[21Aug82|18Sep82|05Feb83] 28(4) 25 988

3500. YOU LIGHT UP MY LIFE Soundtrack
[29Oct77|19Nov77|04Feb78] 17(2) 15 988

Ranking the Albums: 3501-6000

Rank.	Title	Act	Entry	Peak	Exit	Peak(Wks)	TotWks	Score
3501.	HALF-BREED	Cher	22Sep73	10Nov73	09Mar74	28(1)	25	988
3502.	RUTHLESS PEOPLE	Soundtrack	05Jul86	30Aug86	18Oct86	20(1)	16	988
3503.	ALLIGATOR WOMAN	Cameo	10Apr82	15May82	18Sep82	23(3)	24	987
3504.	REALLY ROSIE (SOUNDTRACK)	Carole King	08Mar75	12Apr75	14Jun75	20(2)	15	987
3505.	UNCLE JAM WANTS YOU	Funkadelic	13Oct79	10Nov79	02Feb80	18(1)	17	986
3506.	DIRTY MIND	Prince	08Nov80	06Dec80	02Mar85	45(1)	52	986
3507.	ALL SHOOK UP	Cheap Trick	15Nov80	06Dec80	21Feb81	24(2)	15	985
3508.	I WON'T MENTION IT AGAIN	Ray Price	12Jun71	10Jul71	20Nov71	49(1)	24	985
3509.	ANOTHER SIDE OF BOB DYLAN	Bob Dylan	19Sep64	05Dec64	05Feb66	43(1)	41	985
3510.	TOO TOUGH	Angela Bofill	12Feb83	02Apr83	17Sep83	40(3)	32	984
3511.	SLOPPY SECONDS	Dr. Hook & The Medicine Show	02Dec72	07Apr73	30Jun73	41(1)	31	984
3512.	GRATEFUL DEAD	Grateful Dead	16Oct71	13Nov71	01Jan72	25(1)	12	983
3513.	STRETCHIN' OUT IN BOOTSY'S RUBBER BAND	Bootsy's Rubber Band	01May76	17Jul76	30Oct76	59(1)	27	982
3514.	THE PROPHET BY KAHLIL GIBRAN	Richard Harris	28Dec74	15Feb75	05Apr75	29(1)	15	981
3515.	I BELIEVE IN YOU	Don Williams	04Oct80	20Dec80	02May81	57(1)	31	981
3516.	TRANS	Neil Young	22Jan83	05Feb83	14May83	19(6)	17	981
3517.	IT'S TRUE! IT'S TRUE!	Bill Cosby	08Feb69	22Mar69	14Jun69	37(1)	19	981
3518.	WHERE I'M COMING FROM	Stevie Wonder	08May71	14Aug71	06Nov71	62(1)	27	981
3519.	LONG TIME COMING	Ready For The World	06Dec86	21Feb87	30May87	32(2)	26	980
3520.	DO ME BABY	Meli'sa Morgan	08Feb86	29Mar86	11Oct86	41(1)	36	980
3521.	SHILO	Neil Diamond	12Sep70	28Nov70	27Feb71	52(1)	25	980
3522.	ERIC CLAPTON'S RAINBOW CONCERT	Eric Clapton	22Sep73	20Oct73	22Dec73	18(2)	14	980
3523.	SLEEPING BEAUTY	Cheech & Chong	26Jun76	07Aug76	18Sep76	25(2)	13	980
3524.	THE LOOK OF LOVE	Claudine Longet	14Oct67	23Dec67	27Apr68	33(1)	29	979
3525.	BODY WISHES	Rod Stewart	25Jun83	30Jul83	19Nov83	30(1)	22	979
3526.	THE BREAKFAST CLUB	The Breakfast Club	28Mar87	06Jun87	17Oct87	43(2)	30	978
3527.	HOLLIES	The Hollies	11May74	17Aug74	12Oct74	28(1)	23	978
3528.	THE HEAD ON THE DOOR	The Cure	05Oct85	07Dec85	06Sep86	59(2)	49	978
3529.	THE FIGHTIN' SIDE OF ME	Merle Haggard	25Jul70	05Sep70	06Mar71	68(2)	33	977
3530.	NIGHTCLUBBING	Grace Jones	23May81	25Jul81	03Oct81	32(2)	20	977
3531.	IN VISIBLE SILENCE	The Art Of Noise	03May86	28Jun86	22Nov86	53(2)	30	977
3532.	GOLDEN GREATS BY THE VENTURES	The Ventures	02Sep67	11Nov67	12Oct68	50(2)	44	976
3533.	A KIND OF HUSH	Carpenters	10Jul76	14Aug76	23Oct76	33(2)	16	976
3534.	ELVIS-A LEGENDARY PERFORMER, VOLUME 1	Elvis Presley	02Feb74	02Mar74	17Dec77	43(1)	28	975
3535.	GO AHEAD AND CRY	The Righteous Brothers	03Sep66	12Nov66	14Jan67	32(1)	20	974
3536.	SCANDAL	Scandal	29Jan83	11Jun83	03Sep83	39(1)	32	974
3537.	THE COWSILLS	The Cowsills	04Nov67	13Jan68	24Feb68	31(1)	17	974
3538.	SQUEEZING OUT SPARKS	Graham Parker And The Rumour	14Apr79	26May79	22Sep79	40(2)	24	974
3539.	UNITED	Marvin Gaye & Tammi Terrell	07Oct67	25Nov67	03Aug68	69(1)	44	973
3540.	SPRING!	The Lettermen	08Jul67	19Aug67	30Dec67	31(1)	26	973
3541.	SWASS	Sir Mix-A-Lot	22Oct88	21Jan89	25Nov89	82(1)	58	973
3542.	THE BROADSWORD AND THE BEAST	Jethro Tull	01May82	19Jun82	21Aug82	19(3)	17	973
3543.	THE WICKED PICKETT	Wilson Pickett	21Jan67	25Mar67	19Aug67	42(2)	31	971
3544.	IT'S A GAME	Bay City Rollers	23Jul77	27Aug77	01Oct77	23(2)	11	971
3545.	CHANSON	Chanson	14Oct78	06Jan79	03Mar79	41(1)	21	970
3546.	DANGER ZONE	Player	09Sep78	11Nov78	10Feb79	37(1)	23	970
3547.	DOWN THE ROAD	Stephen Stills/Manassas	12May73	16Jun73	08Sep73	26(2)	18	969
3548.	THE VENTURES KNOCK ME OUT!	The Ventures	13Feb65	01May65	24Jul65	31(1)	24	969
3549.	WHAT A DIFF'RENCE A DAY MAKES	Esther Phillips	02Aug75	18Oct75	22Nov75	32(2)	17	969
3550.	RAINDROPS KEEP FALLIN' ON MY HEAD	Johnny Mathis	04Apr70	16May70	26Sep70	38(1)	26	968
3551.	WHEATFIELD SOUL	The Guess Who	26Apr69	05Jul69	30Aug69	45(2)	19	968
3552.	THE BLITZ	Krokus	08Sep84	03Nov84	09Mar85	31(1)	27	967
3553.	HOME	Procol Harum	11Jul70	15Aug70	17Oct70	34(1)	15	967
3554.	LOVE THEME FROM "ROMEO AND JULIET"	Johnny Mathis	20Sep69	25Oct69	28Feb70	52(3)	24	967
3555.	TRAFALGAR	Bee Gees	25Sep71	16Oct71	25Dec71	34(1)	14	966
3556.	JUST ANOTHER DAY IN PARADISE	Bertie Higgins	27Feb82	19Jun82	14Aug82	38(2)	25	966
3557.	BAD TO THE BONE	George Thorogood & The Destroyers	28Aug82	25Sep82	16Nov85	43(4)	48	965
3558.	I'M IN LOVE AGAIN	Patti LaBelle	07Jan84	03Mar84	01Sep84	40(2)	35	965
3559.	GIPSY KINGS	Gipsy Kings	17Dec88	15Apr89	30Sep89	57(2)	42	965
3560.	POWERGLIDE	New Riders Of The Purple Sage	06May72	24Jun72	02Sep72	33(2)	18	964
3561.	MODERN TIMES	Al Stewart	01Mar75	19Apr75	08Jan77	30(2)	23	964
3562.	LOVE FOR LOVE	The Whispers	02Apr83	21May83	15Oct83	37(1)	29	964
3563.	LEFTOVER WINE	Melanie	26Sep70	17Oct70	30Jan71	33(1)	19	962
3564.	McVICAR (SOUNDTRACK)	Roger Daltrey	16Aug80	13Sep80	22Nov80	22(2)	15	962
3565.	HOW GREAT THOU ART	Kate Smith	15Jan66	16Apr66	25Jun66	36(3)	24	962
3566.	BRIDGE OVER TROUBLED WATER	Ray Conniff & His Orchestra & Chorus	25Apr70	30May70	31Oct70	47(3)	28	962
3567.	UPRISING	Bob Marley And The Wailers	09Aug80	04Oct80	10Jan81	45(1)	23	962
3568.	WHAMMY!	The B-52s	21May83	18Jun83	12Nov83	29(2)	26	962
3569.	ICE ON ICE	Jerry Butler	04Oct69	22Nov69	07Mar70	41(1)	23	961
3570.	I'VE GOT THE MUSIC IN ME	The Kiki Dee Band	16Nov74	21Dec74	15Mar75	28(1)	18	961
3571.	JIM STAFFORD	Jim Stafford	16Mar74	12Oct74	26Oct74	55(1)	33	961
3572.	BISH	Stephen Bishop	16Sep78	18Nov78	20Jan79	35(2)	19	960
3573.	THE THREE DEGREES	The Three Degrees	14Dec74	08Feb75	22Mar75	28(1)	15	960
3574.	CARNAVAL	Spyro Gyra	01Nov80	13Dec80	23May81	49(1)	30	959
3575.	"FRIENDS" (SOUNDTRACK)	Elton John	27Mar71	01May71	31Jul71	36(1)	19	958
3576.	TRAFFIC-ON THE ROAD	Traffic	03Nov73	01Dec73	20Sep75	29(2)	24	958
3577.	NATALIE...LIVE	Natalie Cole	15Jul78	09Sep78	28Oct78	31(2)	16	957
3578.	WILD THINGS RUN FAST	Joni Mitchell	20Nov82	11Dec82	09Apr83	25(4)	21	957
3579.	TWO LANE HIGHWAY	Pure Prairie League	07Jun75	19Jul75	06Sep75	24(1)	14	957
3580.	MEAN BUSINESS	The Firm	22Feb86	15Mar86	28Jun86	22(3)	19	957
3581.	TURN THE WORLD AROUND	Eddy Arnold	07Oct67	16Dec67	08Jun68	34(1)	36	957
3582.	PEOPLE GET READY	The Impressions	06Mar65	22May65	10Jul65	23(2)	19	957
3583.	DONE WITH MIRRORS	Aerosmith	30Nov85	28Dec85	07Jun86	36(3)	28	956
3584.	RICHARD PRYOR LIVE ON THE SUNSET STRIP (SOUNDTRACK)	Richard Pryor	17Apr82	29May82	07Aug82	21(3)	17	956
3585.	MY MELODY	Deniece Williams	04Apr81	29Aug81	07Nov81	74(1)	32	955
3586.	SENTIMENTAL JOURNEY	Ringo Starr	16May70	20Jun70	15Aug70	22(1)	14	955
3587.	THE LADY'S NOT FOR SALE	Rita Coolidge	11Nov72	24Feb73	21Apr73	46(1)	24	954
3588.	REACH	Richard Simmons	05Jun82	17Jul82	05Mar83	44(2)	40	954
3589.	THIS YEARS MODEL	Elvis Costello And The Attractions	15Apr78	20May78	05Aug78	30(2)	17	954
3590.	ELVIS' GOLD RECORDS, VOLUME 4	Elvis Presley	02Mar68	01Jun68	27Jul68	33(1)	22	954
3591.	HOT NUMBERS	Foxy	14Apr79	19May79	28Jul79	29(1)	16	954
3592.	LOVE LETTERS FROM ELVIS	Elvis Presley	26Jun71	10Jul71	02Oct71	33(2)	15	953
3593.	MUSIC FROM MISSION: IMPOSSIBLE (SOUNDTRACK)	Lalo Schifrin	30Dec67	13Apr68	27Jul68	47(2)	31	953

Rank. Title Act
[Entry | Peak | Exit] Peak(Wks) TotWks Score

3594. ON YOUR FEET OR ON YOUR KNEES Blue Öyster Cult
[15Mar75 | 19Apr75 | 07Jun75] 22(2) 13 953

3595. SUPERSONIC--THE ALBUM J.J. Fad
[23Jul88 | 13Aug88 | 11Feb89] 49(2) 30 953

3596. VOYEUR David Sanborn
[18Apr81 | 23May81 | 12Sep81] 45(2) 22 953

3597. LIVE AT THE PARAMOUNT (SEATTLE) The Guess Who
[19Aug72 | 14Oct72 | 06Jan73] 39(1) 21 952

3598. LOVE IS BLUE The Dells
[23Aug69 | 25Oct69 | 07Feb70] 54(1) 24 952

3599. LOVE IS WHERE YOU FIND IT The Whispers
[23Jan82 | 10Apr82 | 10Jul82] 35(3) 25 952

3600. PROGRESSIONS OF POWER Triumph
[29Mar80 | 24May80 | 26Jul80] 32(1) 18 951

3601. L.A. GUNS L.A. Guns
[06Feb88 | 09Apr88 | 03Dec88] 50(1) 33 951

3602. HUMAN'S LIB Howard Jones
[24Mar84 | 30Jun84 | 05Oct85] 59(2) 43 951

3603. MOONDANCE Van Morrison
[14Mar70 | 30May70 | 08Aug70] 29(2) 22 951

3604. THIS WOMAN K.T. Oslin
[24Sep88 | 05Nov88 | 16Sep89] 75(2) 52 951

3605. INTRODUCING THE BEAU BRUMMELS The Beau Brummels
[08May65 | 24Jul65 | 25Sep65] 24(1) 21 950

3606. TRACES Classics IV
[26Apr69 | 07Jun69 | 06Sep69] 45(2) 20 950

3607. THE BEST OF WES MONTGOMERY Wes Montgomery
[09Dec67 | 23Mar68 | 24Aug68] 56(2) 38 950

3608. ALL MITCH RYDER HITS! Mitch Ryder And The Detroit Wheels
[14Oct67 | 27Jan68 | 06Apr68] 37(1) 26 949

3609. REFLECTOR Pablo Cruise
[18Jul81 | 12Sep81 | 14Nov81] 34(2) 18 949

3610. POWER Kansas
[15Nov86 | 24Jan87 | 16May87] 35(2) 27 949

3611. TIME LOVES A HERO Little Feat
[14May77 | 18Jun77 | 10Sep77] 34(2) 18 948

3612. YOU ARE MY STARSHIP Norman Connors
[24Jul76 | 09Oct76 | 01Jan77] 39(1) 24 947

3613. THE JOHNNY CASH SHOW Johnny Cash
[14Nov70 | 26Dec70 | 13Mar71] 44(1) 18 947

3614. HOT BOX Fatback
[19Apr80 | 14Jun80 | 18Oct80] 44(1) 27 946

3615. GRAND SLAM The Isley Brothers
[21Mar81 | 25Apr81 | 11Jul81] 28(3) 17 946

3616. WHERE THE HAPPY PEOPLE GO The Trammps
[15May76 | 26Jun76 | 23Oct76] 50(1) 24 946

3617. WINGS GREATEST Wings
[09Dec78 | 20Jan79 | 07Apr79] 29(1) 18 946

3618. SO TENDERLY John Gary
[15Aug64 | 21Nov64 | 20Feb65] 42(1) 28 945

3619. NATURALLY J.J. Cale
[22Jan72 | 08Apr72 | 16Sep72] 51(2) 32 944

3620. STONE JAM Slave
[01Nov80 | 21Mar81 | 20Jun81] 53(2) 34 943

3621. RUNAWAY HORSES Belinda Carlisle
[21Oct89 | 16Dec89 | 07Apr90] 37(1) 25 943

3622. THE BIG THROWDOWN Levert
[05Sep87 | 17Oct87 | 13Feb88] 32(2) 24 943

3623. HOW WILL THE WOLF SURVIVE Los Lobos
[15Dec84 | 09Mar85 | 03Aug85] 47(3) 34 943

3624. IMPERIAL BEDROOM Elvis Costello And The Attractions
[24Jul82 | 25Sep82 | 01Jan83] 30(3) 24 943

3625. IF YOU KNEW SUZI... Suzi Quatro
[24Mar79 | 09Jun79 | 04Aug79] 37(1) 20 943

3626. WALKABOUT The Fixx
[14Jun86 | 02Aug86 | 01Nov86] 30(2) 21 943

3627. FRIENDS Shalamar
[20Feb82 | 22May82 | 07Aug82] 35(1) 25 943

3628. WEDNESDAY MORNING, 3 AM Simon & Garfunkel
[22Jan66 | 26Feb66 | 01Feb69] 30(1) 31 943

Rank. Title Act
[Entry | Peak | Exit] Peak(Wks) TotWks Score

3629. SWEET FREEDOM Uriah Heep
[06Oct73 | 10Nov73 | 09Mar74] 33(1) 23 942

3630. NEW YORK Lou Reed
[28Jan89 | 08Apr89 | 24Jun89] 40(1) 22 942

3631. JOHN DENVER John Denver
[27Jan79 | 03Mar79 | 05May79] 25(2) 15 942

3632. ONE WAY HOME Hooters
[08Aug87 | 29Aug87 | 30Jan88] 27(3) 26 942

3633. CARL CARLTON Carl Carlton
[08Aug81 | 10Oct81 | 12Dec81] 34(2) 19 941

3634. A SECRET PLACE Grover Washington Jr.
[15Jan77 | 05Mar77 | 30Apr77] 31(2) 16 940

3635. LOVE TO THE WORLD L.T.D.
[21Aug76 | 11Dec76 | 12Mar77] 52(2) 30 940

3636. REACH FOR THE SKY The Allman Brothers Band
[23Aug80 | 04Oct80 | 15Nov80] 27(2) 13 940

3637. VOX HUMANA Kenny Loggins
[20Apr85 | 11May85 | 16Nov85] 41(1) 31 940

3638. HEROES ARE HARD TO FIND Fleetwood Mac
[05Oct74 | 23Nov74 | 11Oct75] 34(1) 26 940

3639. TIME FADES AWAY Neil Young
[27Oct73 | 24Nov73 | 23Feb74] 22(1) 18 939

3640. FRANTIC ROMANTIC Jermaine Stewart
[14Jun86 | 06Sep86 | 29Nov86] 32(2) 25 939

3641. GORD'S GOLD Gordon Lightfoot
[22Nov75 | 17Jan76 | 22Jan77] 34(1) 24 938

3642. EVERYTHING IS BEAUTIFUL Ray Stevens
[13Jun70 | 18Jul70 | 17Oct70] 35(1) 19 937

3643. KEEP YOUR HANDS OFF MY POWER SUPPLY Slade
[05May84 | 30Jun84 | 06Oct84] 33(2) 23 937

3644. INSPIRATION Maze Featuring Frankie Beverly
[07Apr79 | 26May79 | 01Sep79] 33(1) 22 937

3645. GARDEN PARTY Rick Nelson And The Stone Canyon Band
[09Dec72 | 10Feb73 | 07Apr73] 32(1) 18 936

3646. CRISIS? WHAT CRISIS? Supertramp
[13Dec75 | 31Jan76 | 03Sep77] 44(1) 28 935

3647. IN GOD WE TRUST Stryper
[16Jul88 | 23Jul88 | 31Dec88] 32(3) 25 935

3648. NIGHT SHIFT Foghat
[20Nov76 | 11Dec76 | 09Apr77] 36(2) 21 935

3649. PLAYING FOR KEEPS Eddie Money
[09Aug80 | 04Oct80 | 29Nov80] 35(1) 17 934

3650. CYAN Three Dog Night
[20Oct73 | 08Dec73 | 09Feb74] 26(1) 17 934

3651. 2ND ANNIVERSARY Gladys Knight & The Pips
[18Oct75 | 06Dec75 | 31Jan76] 24(2) 16 933

3652. STRAIGHT AHEAD Brian Auger's Oblivion Express
[06Apr74 | 04May74 | 17Aug74] 45(2) 20 933

3653. BOOGIE DOWN! Eddie Kendricks
[16Mar74 | 13Apr74 | 06Jul74] 30(1) 17 933

3654. IN MY EYES Stevie B
[11Mar89 | 24Jun89 | 14Apr90] 75(1) 46 933

3655. ROCK N' ROLL LOVE LETTER Bay City Rollers
[20Mar76 | 08May76 | 03Jul76] 31(1) 16 932

3656. THE DRAMATIC JACKPOT Ron Banks And The Dramatics
[22Mar75 | 31May75 | 19Jul75] 31(1) 18 931

3657. GOLD Jefferson Starship
[17Feb79 | 10Mar79 | 19May79] 20(2) 14 931

3658. ROOTS Curtis Mayfield
[06Nov71 | 11Dec71 | 11Mar72] 40(1) 19 931

3659. STREETLIFE SERENADE Billy Joel
[02Nov74 | 28Dec74 | 01Mar75] 35(1) 18 931

3660. FREETIME Spyro Gyra
[29Aug81 | 03Oct81 | 27Feb82] 41(2) 27 930

3661. MAGIC Tom Browne
[21Feb81 | 21Mar81 | 27Jun81] 37(2) 19 929

3662. FREE TO BE...YOU AND ME Various Artists
[06Jan73 | 20Apr74 | 17Jan76] 68(1) 58 929

3663. FEEL THE NEED Leif Garrett
[25Nov78 | 10Feb79 | 31Mar79] 34(2) 19 929

3664. THE JIM NABORS HOUR Jim Nabors
[27Jun70 | 11Jul70 | 27Feb71] 34(2) 23 929

Rank. Title Act
[Entry | Peak | Exit] Peak(Wks) TotWks Score

3665. SPIRIT OF LOVE Con Funk Shun
[12Apr80 | 17May80 | 23Aug80] 30(3) 20 929

3666. LET'S GO ALL THE WAY Sly Fox
[01Mar86 | 10May86 | 26Jul86] 31(2) 22 928

3667. REFLECTING The Chad Mitchell Trio
[07Mar64 | 25Apr64 | 26Sep64] 29(1) 30 928

3668. NOW I'M A WOMAN Nancy Wilson
[28Nov70 | 06Feb71 | 17Apr71] 54(1) 21 927

3669. INSTANT REPLAY The Monkees
[01Mar69 | 12Apr69 | 07Jun69] 32(1) 15 927

3670. GET HERE Brenda Russell
[19Mar88 | 25Jun88 | 24Sep88] 49(2) 28 926

3671. WAKING & DREAMING Orleans
[28Aug76 | 16Oct76 | 11Dec76] 30(2) 16 926

3672. ELO'S GREATEST HITS Electric Light Orchestra
[08Dec79 | 05Jan80 | 15Mar80] 30(3) 15 925

3673. MARY JANE GIRLS Mary Jane Girls
[14May83 | 17Sep83 | 18Feb84] 56(1) 41 924

3674. COPPERHEAD ROAD Steve Earle
[12Nov88 | 28Jan89 | 20May89] 56(1) 28 924

3675. QUARTER MOON IN A TEN CENT TOWN Emmylou Harris
[04Feb78 | 18Mar78 | 03Jun78] 29(1) 18 924

3676. YOUNGER THAN YESTERDAY The Byrds
[18Mar67 | 13May67 | 26Aug67] 24(1) 24 923

3677. TWO OF A KIND Earl Klugh & Bob James
[06Nov82 | 11Dec82 | 21May83] 44(4) 29 923

3678. SCOTT JOPLIN: THE RED BACK BOOK New England Conservatory Chorus
[19May73 | 31Aug74 | 26Oct74] 65(1) 36 923

3679. PRIVATE REVOLUTION World Party
[27Dec86 | 28Mar87 | 25Jul87] 39(3) 31 923

3680. KYLIE Kylie Minogue
[10Sep88 | 07Jan89 | 18Mar89] 53(2) 28 922

3681. SCHOOL DAYS Stanley Clarke
[25Sep76 | 13Nov76 | 19Feb77] 34(1) 22 922

3682. MOB RULES Black Sabbath
[28Nov81 | 19Dec81 | 27Mar82] 29(3) 18 922

3683. MOONLIGHT AND ROSES Jim Reeves
[13Jun64 | 05Sep64 | 02Jan65] 30(2) 30 922

3684. JAWS Soundtrack
[26Jul75 | 20Sep75 | 15Nov75] 30(1) 17 922

3685. A FAREWELL TO KINGS Rush
[24Sep77 | 29Oct77 | 14Jan78] 33(2) 17 922

3686. ARIZONA Mark Lindsay
[07Mar70 | 04Apr70 | 11Jul70] 36(1) 19 921

3687. ROCKET TO RUSSIA The Ramones
[26Nov77 | 18Feb78 | 13May78] 49(3) 25 921

3688. THE LAMB LIES DOWN ON BROADWAY Genesis
[14Dec74 | 01Feb75 | 29Mar75] 41(1) 16 920

3689. ONE BRIGHT DAY Ziggy Marley And The Melody Makers
[12Aug89 | 16Sep89 | 09Dec89] 26(2) 18 920

3690. ANGIE Angela Bofill
[17Feb79 | 21Apr79 | 11Aug79] 47(1) 26 920

3691. GREEN, GREEN GRASS OF HOME Tom Jones
[04Mar67 | 07Jun69 | 15Nov69] 65(1) 45 920

3692. ROUGH DIAMONDS Bad Company
[04Sep82 | 09Oct82 | 01Jan83] 26(3) 18 920

3693. HAT TRICK America
[17Nov73 | 08Dec73 | 16Mar74] 28(1) 18 920

3694. CITY NIGHTS Tierra
[27Dec80 | 14Mar81 | 16May81] 38(3) 21 919

3695. WHAT GOES AROUND COMES AROUND Waylon Jennings
[10Nov79 | 15Dec79 | 17May80] 49(1) 28 919

3696. REVOLUTION! Paul Revere & The Raiders
[02Sep67 | 21Oct67 | 20Jan68] 25(1) 21 919

3697. DENNIS YOST & THE CLASSICS IV/GOLDEN GREATS-VOLUME I Classics IV
[06Dec69 | 31Jan70 | 18Apr70] 50(1) 20 919

3698. BARRY MANILOW/GREATEST HITS-VOL. II Barry Manilow
[03Dec83 | 14Jan84 | 07Apr84] 30(2) 19 919

3699. THIS DIAMOND RING Gary Lewis And The Playboys
[27Mar65 | 29May65 | 11Sep65] 26(1) 25 919

Rank. Title Act
[Entry | Peak | Exit] Peak(Wks) TotWks — Score

3700. FLY AWAY Voyage
[16Dec78 | 24Mar79 | 16Jun79] 47(2) 27 — 918

3701. MADNESS Madness
[30Apr83 | 16Jul83 | 12Nov83] 41(1) 29 — 918

3702. JAMES BROWN PLAYS & DIRECTS THE POPCORN James Brown
[23Aug69 | 27Sep69 | 17Jan70] 40(1) 22 — 918

3703. BEAUTY ON A BACK STREET Daryl Hall & John Oates
[17Sep77 | 22Oct77 | 07Jan78] 30(1) 17 — 917

3704. PORTRAIT OF MY LOVE The Lettermen
[13Mar65 | 01May65 | 14Aug65] 27(2) 23 — 916

3705. JONATHAN BUTLER Jonathan Butler
[30May87 | 08Aug87 | 09Jan88] 50(2) 33 — 916

3706. UNION JACKS The Babys
[19Jan80 | 15Mar80 | 14Jun80] 42(1) 22 — 916

3707. WHEN YOU'RE HOT, YOU'RE HOT Jerry Reed
[01May71 | 31Jul71 | 11Sep71] 45(1) 20 — 916

3708. FREDDIE & THE DREAMERS Freddie And The Dreamers
[17Apr65 | 19Jun65 | 21Aug65] 19(2) 19 — 916

3709. THE WORLD OF JOHNNY CASH Johnny Cash
[06Jun70 | 20Jun70 | 23Jan71] 54(1) 34 — 915

3710. GREATEST HITS Jr. Walker & The All Stars
[28Jun69 | 02Aug69 | 18Apr70] 43(2) 18 — 915

3711. HANK WILLIAMS, JR.'S GREATEST HITS Hank Williams Jr.
[13Nov82 | 22Jan83 | 10Mar84] 107(2) 70 — 915

3712. FLOWERS OF EVIL Mountain
[18Dec71 | 22Jan72 | 01Apr72] 35(2) 16 — 915

3713. MURMUR R.E.M.
[14May83 | 13Aug83 | 29Dec84] 36(1) 30 — 913

3714. RETURN OF THE JEDI Soundtrack
[11Jun83 | 09Jul83 | 01Oct83] 20(2) 17 — 913

3715. BENNY AND US Average White Band & Ben E. King
[23Jul77 | 10Sep77 | 10Dec77] 33(2) 21 — 912

3716. THE FIRST MINUTE OF A NEW DAY Gil Scott-Heron & Brian Jackson
[01Feb75 | 05Apr75 | 24May75] 30(1) 17 — 912

3717. NIGHTCRUISING Bar-Kays
[14Nov81 | 16Jan82 | 29May82] 55(2) 29 — 912

3718. BE MY LOVE Jerry Vale
[29Aug64 | 07Nov64 | 23Jan65] 26(2) 22 — 911

3719. DANCIN' AND LOVIN' Spinners
[19Jan80 | 05Apr80 | 31May80] 32(1) 20 — 910

3720. HEAVEN TONIGHT Cheap Trick
[10Jun78 | 08Jul78 | 04Nov78] 48(1) 22 — 909

3721. COCONUT TELEGRAPH Jimmy Buffett
[21Feb81 | 04Apr81 | 20Jun81] 30(1) 18 — 909

3722. ACTION REPLAY Howard Jones
[03May86 | 12Jul86 | 11Oct86] 34(1) 24 — 909

3723. JOURNEY TO LOVE Stanley Clarke
[01Nov75 | 06Dec75 | 06Mar76] 34(2) 19 — 909

3724. MAKING A GOOD THING BETTER Olivia Newton-John
[09Jul77 | 17Sep77 | 22Oct77] 34(1) 16 — 908

3725. BETE NOIRE Bryan Ferry
[21Nov87 | 23Apr88 | 18Jun88] 63(2) 31 — 907

3726. TRAVELIN' AT THE SPEED OF THOUGHT The O'Jays
[04Jun77 | 09Jul77 | 17Sep77] 27(1) 16 — 907

3727. SPOOKY TWO Spooky Tooth
[16Aug69 | 11Oct69 | 20Dec69] 44(2) 19 — 907

3728. OUR HERO...PAT COOPER Pat Cooper
[28May66 | 23Jul66 | 22Apr67] 82(1) 42 — 906

3729. DAVID'S ALBUM Joan Baez
[07Jun69 | 26Jul69 | 06Sep69] 36(2) 14 — 906

3730. HELLO DUMMY! Don Rickles
[15Jun68 | 28Sep68 | 18Jan69] 54(2) 29 — 906

3731. CHILDREN OF THE SUN Billy Thorpe
[05May79 | 29Sep79 | 03Nov79] 39(1) 23 — 906

3732. SPLIT COCONUT Dave Mason
[18Oct75 | 22Nov75 | 07Feb76] 27(2) 17 — 906

3733. LOVE WILL TURN YOU AROUND Kenny Rogers
[24Jul82 | 18Sep82 | 01Jan83] 34(2) 24 — 905

3734. CANDY Con Funk Shun
[02Jun79 | 07Jul79 | 27Oct79] 46(2) 22 — 905

Rank. Title Act
[Entry | Peak | Exit] Peak(Wks) TotWks — Score

3735. FRANCE JOLI France Joli
[08Sep79 | 17Nov79 | 29Dec79] 26(1) 17 — 905

3736. COLOR OF SUCCESS Morris Day
[19Oct85 | 23Nov85 | 17May86] 37(2) 31 — 905

3737. STARGARD Stargard
[04Mar78 | 22Apr78 | 27May78] 26(1) 13 — 905

3738. TUXEDO JUNCTION Tuxedo Junction
[18Feb78 | 03Jun78 | 23Sep78] 56(2) 32 — 905

3739. OHIO PLAYERS GOLD Ohio Players
[13Nov76 | 11Dec76 | 05Mar77] 31(2) 17 — 905

3740. CAUGHT IN THE ACT Grand Funk Railroad
[13Sep75 | 18Oct75 | 15Nov75] 21(2) 10 — 905

3741. DANGEROUS AGE Bad Company
[17Sep88 | 19Nov88 | 17Jun89] 58(2) 40 — 904

3742. GYPSY Gypsy
[10Oct70 | 21Nov70 | 20Feb71] 44(1) 20 — 904

3743. I CAN'T STAND MYSELF (WHEN YOU TOUCH ME) James Brown
[23Mar68 | 04May68 | 22Jun68] 17(1) 14 — 903

3744. FOREVER NOW Psychedelic Furs
[13Nov82 | 02Apr83 | 18Jun83] 61(4) 32 — 902

3745. THE BIG PRIZE Honeymoon Suite
[15Mar86 | 03May86 | 08Nov86] 61(2) 35 — 902

3746. I LOVE YOU MORE AND MORE EVERY DAY/ TEARS AND ROSES Al Martino
[27Jun64 | 29Aug64 | 12Dec64] 31(1) 25 — 902

3747. WELCOME TO MY WORLD Elvis Presley
[16Apr77 | 28May77 | 17Dec77] 44(1) 25 — 901

3748. TENDER LOVING CARE Nancy Wilson
[27Aug66 | 12Nov66 | 28Jan67] 35(1) 23 — 901

3749. HARBOR America
[12Mar77 | 09Apr77 | 11Jun77] 21(2) 14 — 901

3750. FLESH + BLOOD Roxy Music
[28Jun80 | 16Aug80 | 01Nov80] 35(2) 19 — 901

3751. ONE FOR THE ROAD Willie Nelson And Leon Russell
[30Jun79 | 28Jul79 | 27Oct79] 25(1) 18 — 901

3752. HIGH CRIME Al Jarreau
[24Nov84 | 08Dec84 | 20Jul85] 49(2) 35 — 901

3753. STOP ALL THAT JAZZ Leon Russell
[22Jun74 | 13Jul74 | 05Oct74] 34(2) 16 — 901

3754. TONIGHT! Four Tops
[12Sep81 | 21Nov81 | 30Jan82] 37(1) 21 — 900

3755. GOOD OLD BOYS Randy Newman
[05Oct74 | 30Nov74 | 08Mar75] 36(2) 23 — 900

3756. DOWN TO EARTH Nektar
[15Feb75 | 19Apr75 | 28Jun75] 32(1) 20 — 900

3757. ON THE RISE The S.O.S. Band
[27Aug83 | 05Nov83 | 10Mar84] 47(1) 29 — 900

3758. KUNG FU FIGHTING AND OTHER GREAT LOVE SONGS Carl Douglas
[14Dec74 | 01Feb75 | 05Apr75] 37(1) 17 — 900

3759. LAST TIME AROUND The Buffalo Springfield
[17Aug68 | 26Oct68 | 21Dec68] 42(1) 19 — 900

3760. SONGS FOR THE NEW DEPRESSION Bette Midler
[31Jan76 | 28Feb76 | 08May76] 27(1) 15 — 899

3761. DANNY'S SONG Anne Murray
[28Apr73 | 02Jun73 | 06Oct73] 39(2) 24 — 898

3762. BLACK CAESAR (SOUNDTRACK) James Brown
[03Mar73 | 14Apr73 | 21Jul73] 31(2) 21 — 898

3763. YOUTHQUAKE Dead Or Alive
[13Jul85 | 31Aug85 | 23Nov85] 31(3) 20 — 898

3764. THOSE SOUTHERN KNIGHTS The Crusaders
[22May76 | 17Jul76 | 18Sep76] 38(2) 18 — 897

3765. THE SONNY SIDE OF CHER Cher
[23Apr66 | 09Jul66 | 27Aug66] 26(2) 19 — 897

3766. NEVER CAN SAY GOODBYE Gloria Gaynor
[01Feb75 | 08Mar75 | 10May75] 25(2) 15 — 897

3767. THE CACTUS ALBUM 3rd Bass
[02Dec89 | 17Feb90 | 23Jun90] 55(1) 30 — 897

3768. SOME GREAT REWARD Depeche Mode
[19Jan85 | 17Aug85 | 30Nov85] 51(2) 42 — 896

3769. I DON'T KNOW HOW TO LOVE HIM Helen Reddy
[05Jun71 | 20Oct73 | 29Dec73] 100(1) 37 — 896

3770. AND THAT'S THE TRUTH Lily Tomlin
[25Mar72 | 06May72 | 19Aug72] 41(2) 22 — 895

Rank. Title Act
[Entry | Peak | Exit] Peak(Wks) TotWks — Score

3771. EXTENSIONS The Manhattan Transfer
[08Dec79 | 07Jun80 | 16Aug80] 55(1) 37 — 895

3772. UNCLE CHARLIE & HIS DOG TEDDY Nitty Gritty Dirt Band
[05Dec70 | 27Mar71 | 17Jul71] 66(1) 32 — 894

3773. SEMINAR Sir Mix-A-Lot
[18Nov89 | 25Nov89 | 25Aug90] 67(2) 41 — 893

3774. JAMES TAYLOR James Taylor
[03Oct70 | 28Nov70 | 10Apr71] 62(1) 28 — 892

3775. THE TEMPTATIONS SING SMOKEY The Temptations
[03Apr65 | 05Jun65 | 25Sep65] 35(1) 26 — 892

3776. AIN'T THAT A BITCH Johnny Guitar Watson
[07Aug76 | 16Oct76 | 01Jan77] 52(2) 22 — 892

3777. A COLLECTION OF GREAT DANCE SONGS Pink Floyd
[12Dec81 | 09Jan82 | 27Mar82] 31(2) 16 — 892

3778. A LITTLE BIT MORE Dr. Hook
[15May76 | 30Oct76 | 22Jan77] 62(1) 31 — 891

3779. WHAT ABOUT TODAY? Barbra Streisand
[06Sep69 | 04Oct69 | 27Dec69] 31(1) 17 — 891

3780. TRUE STORIES AND OTHER DREAMS Judy Collins
[10Feb73 | 07Apr73 | 23Jun73] 27(1) 20 — 891

3781. UNMISTAKABLY LOU Lou Rawls
[16Apr77 | 21May77 | 29Oct77] 41(2) 29 — 891

3782. STRAIGHT BETWEEN THE EYES Rainbow
[08May82 | 12Jun82 | 09Oct82] 30(3) 23 — 891

3783. FIRIN' UP Pure Prairie League
[17May80 | 19Jul80 | 25Oct80] 37(2) 24 — 890

3784. THE SPORT OF KINGS Triumph
[06Sep86 | 08Nov86 | 07Mar87] 33(2) 27 — 890

3785. ABSOLUTELY FREE Mothers Of Invention
[08Jul67 | 23Sep67 | 02Dec67] 41(2) 22 — 890

3786. THE WONDROUS WORLD OF SONNY & CHER Sonny & Cher
[16Apr66 | 02Jul66 | 27Aug66] 34(2) 20 — 890

3787. GREEN THOUGHTS The Smithereens
[09Apr88 | 07May88 | 05Nov88] 60(3) 31 — 890

3788. NEW SENSATIONS Lou Reed
[16Jun84 | 20Oct84 | 19Jan85] 56(1) 32 — 889

3789. THE MERCY & LOVE (CAN MAKE YOU HAPPY) Mercy
[21Jun69 | 26Jul69 | 27Sep69] 38(1) 15 — 889

3790. ADVENTURES IN THE LAND OF MUSIC Dynasty
[02Aug80 | 04Oct80 | 20Dec80] 43(1) 21 — 888

3791. WILL THE CIRCLE BE UNBROKEN Nitty Gritty Dirt Band
[30Dec72 | 17Mar73 | 04Aug73] 68(1) 32 — 888

3792. SONGBIRD Jesse Colin Young
[22Mar75 | 03May75 | 21Jun75] 26(2) 14 — 887

3793. FOLLOW THE LEADER Eric B. & Rakim
[13Aug88 | 03Sep88 | 26Nov88] 22(2) 16 — 887

3794. ANOTHER STEP Kim Wilde
[04Apr87 | 13Jun87 | 26Sep87] 40(2) 26 — 887

3795. IT'S BEEN A LONG TIME The New Birth
[17Nov73 | 06Apr74 | 03Aug74] 50(1) 31 — 887

3796. THE KINGSMEN, VOLUME 3 The Kingsmen
[20Feb65 | 01May65 | 19Jun65] 22(2) 18 — 887

3797. WATTSTAX: THE LIVING WORD Soundtrack
[17Feb73 | 21Apr73 | 09Jun73] 28(1) 17 — 886

3798. MANNHEIM STEAMROLLER CHRISTMAS Mannheim Steamroller
[22Dec84 | 07Jan89 | 12Jan91] 50(1) 39 — 886

3799. JAY & THE AMERICANS GREATEST HITS! Jay & The Americans
[20Nov65 | 29Jan66 | 02Apr66] 21(1) 20 — 885

3800. MOTT THE HOOPLE LIVE Mott The Hoople
[30Nov74 | 18Jan75 | 22Feb75] 23(1) 13 — 885

3801. MEANWHILE BACK AT THE WHISKY A GO GO Johnny Rivers
[26Jun65 | 21Aug65 | 30Oct65] 21(2) 19 — 885

3802. A SESSION WITH GARY LEWIS AND THE PLAYBOYS Gary Lewis And The Playboys
[18Sep65 | 13Nov65 | 29Jan66] 18(2) 20 — 884

3803. DECEPTIVE BENDS 10cc
[14May77 | 25Jun77 | 24Sep77] 31(1) 20 — 884

Rank. Title Act
[Entry|Peak|Exit] Peak(Wks) TotWks Score

3804. DREAMS Grace Slick
[05Apr80|03May80|19Jul80] 32(2) 16 884

3805. ALL I NEED Jack Wagner
[22Sep84|09Feb85|06Apr85] 44(2) 29 884

3806. RHAPSODY AND BLUES
The Crusaders
[12Jul80|16Aug80|25Oct80] 29(2) 16 883

3807. SEATRAIN Seatrain
[30Jan71|10Apr71|03Jul71] 48(1) 23 883

3808. THE CONCERT SOUND OF HENRY MANCINI
Henry Mancini And His Orchestra
[01Aug64|12Sep64|05Dec64] 15(2) 19 882

3809. GO WEST Go West
[23Mar85|01Jun85|16Nov85] 60(1) 35 882

3810. MARY Mary Travers
[17Apr71|24Jul71|30Oct71] 71(1) 29 882

3811. IN DREAMS Roy Orbison
[17Aug63|02Nov63|18Jan64] 35(1) 23 882

3812. CANDY Soundtrack
[01Feb69|15Mar69|17May69] 49(2) 16 881

3813. IT'S LIKE YOU NEVER LEFT Dave Mason
[10Nov73|15Dec73|18May74] 50(2) 28 881

3814. CHITTY CHITTY BANG BANG Soundtrack
[09Nov68|22Feb69|17May69] 58(2) 28 881

3815. WHAT BECOMES A SEMI-LEGEND MOST?
Joan Rivers
[23Apr83|28May83|10Sep83] 22(2) 21 880

3816. THREE HEARTS IN THE HAPPY ENDING MACHINE Daryl Hall
[06Sep86|27Sep86|28Feb87] 29(3) 26 879

3817. A PAUPER IN PARIDISE Gino Vannelli
[19Nov77|21Jan78|04Mar78] 33(2) 16 879

3818. TAKE ANOTHER PICTURE Quarterflash
[09Jul83|27Aug83|26Nov83] 34(1) 21 878

3819. YOU REALLY GOT ME The Kinks
[12Dec64|06Mar65|05Jun65] 29(1) 26 877

3820. OH HAPPY DAY Glen Campbell
[23May70|27Jun70|26Sep70] 38(2) 19 877

3821. DREAMING MY DREAMS Waylon Jennings
[05Jul75|23Aug75|22Nov75] 49(1) 21 876

3822. NANCY-NATURALLY Nancy Wilson
[28Jan67|08Apr67|17Jun67] 35(2) 21 876

3823. RAM IT DOWN Judas Priest
[04Jun88|18Jun88|08Oct88] 31(3) 19 876

3824. BEATITUDE Ric Ocasek
[29Jan83|05Mar83|14May83] 28(5) 16 875

3825. WINDOWS The Charlie Daniels Band
[03Apr82|15May82|07Aug82] 26(3) 19 875

3826. HIGH PRIORITY Cherrelle
[01Feb86|12Apr86|23Aug86] 36(2) 30 874

3827. ROXY & ELSEWHERE Zappa/Mothers
[05Oct74|23Nov74|01Feb75] 27(1) 18 874

3828. HALL & OATES LIVE AT THE APOLLO WITH DAVID RUFFIN & EDDIE KENDRICK
Daryl Hall & John Oates
[28Sep85|26Oct85|25Jan86] 21(2) 18 873

3829. SADDLE TRAMP The Charlie Daniels Band
[15May76|03Jul76|11Sep76] 35(1) 18 873

3830. (THE) VENTURES IN SPACE The Ventures
[25Jan64|29Feb64|23May64] 27(1) 18 872

3831. OTHER VOICES The Doors
[06Nov71|11Dec71|12Feb72] 31(1) 15 872

3832. ON A CLEAR DAY YOU CAN SEE FOREVER
Original Cast
[11Dec65|16Apr66|16Jul66] 59(1) 32 871

3833. STREETS OF FIRE Soundtrack
[16Jun84|04Aug84|03Nov84] 32(2) 21 871

3834. NEW YORK CONNECTION Tom Scott
[20Dec75|13Mar76|05Jun76] 42(1) 25 870

3835. RAINBOW SEEKER Joe Sample
[25Feb78|29Apr78|12Aug78] 62(1) 25 870

3836. WHO DO YA (LOVE)
KC And The Sunshine Band
[19Aug78|16Sep78|11Nov78] 36(4) 13 870

3837. LIVE AT LONDON'S TALK OF THE TOWN
Diana Ross & The Supremes
[05Oct68|04Jan69|01Feb69] 57(2) 18 869

3838. JONATHAN EDWARDS Jonathan Edwards
[20Nov71|29Jan72|01Apr72] 42(2) 20 869

Rank. Title Act
[Entry|Peak|Exit] Peak(Wks) TotWks Score

3839. REEL MUSIC The Beatles
[10Apr82|08May82|26Jun82] 19(3) 12 869

3840. I AM LOVE Peabo Bryson
[28Nov81|27Feb82|08May82] 40(2) 24 868

3841. FLYING COWBOYS Rickie Lee Jones
[14Oct89|18Nov89|31Mar90] 39(2) 25 868

3842. THIS SIDE OF PARADISE Ric Ocasek
[11Oct86|15Nov86|14Mar87] 31(2) 23 868

3843. LOVE, PEACE AND HAPPINESS
The Chambers Brothers
[27Dec69|17Jan70|08Aug70] 58(1) 33 868

3844. ANTHOLOGY The Steve Miller Band
[18Nov72|10Feb73|04Dec76] 56(2) 39 868

3845. ANDERSON, BRUFORD, WAKEMAN, HOWE
Anderson, Bruford, Wakeman, Howe
[01Jul89|29Jul89|14Oct89] 30(1) 16 867

3846. WHO'S MAKING LOVE... Johnnie Taylor
[25Jan69|01Mar69|24May69] 42(1) 18 866

3847. WHERE THE ACTION IS The Ventures
[12Feb66|30Apr66|09Jul66] 33(1) 22 866

3848. WASHINGTON COUNTY Arlo Guthrie
[07Nov70|05Dec70|27Feb71] 33(1) 17 865

3849. OPEN SESAME Whodini
[17Oct87|21Nov87|12Mar88] 30(2) 22 865

3850. CRAZY EYES Poco
[15Sep73|27Oct73|16Feb74] 38(1) 23 865

3851. HARDER...FASTER April Wine
[10Nov79|15Dec79|01Aug81] 64(3) 40 865

3852. 2 HYPE Kid 'N Play
[17Dec88|21Jan89|04Nov89] 96(1) 47 865

3853. MONSTER Jimmy Smith
[08May65|24Jul65|16Oct65] 35(1) 24 865

3854. SOMEWHERE THERE'S A SOMEONE
Dean Martin
[12Mar66|14May66|10Sep66] 40(2) 27 864

3855. OBSESSION UFO
[29Jul78|23Sep78|25Nov78] 41(2) 18 863

3856. SIREN Roxy Music
[29Nov75|14Feb76|10Apr76] 50(1) 20 863

3857. DANGEROUS TOYS Dangerous Toys
[17Jun89|16Sep89|17Feb90] 65(3) 36 863

3858. SOUL SEARCHING Glenn Frey
[03Sep88|05Nov88|07Jan89] 36(2) 19 862

3859. THE SUPER HITS, VOL. 2 Various Artists
[20Jul68|09Nov68|01Mar69] 76(1) 33 861

3860. ANGEL Ohio Players
[09Apr77|14May77|08Oct77] 41(1) 27 861

3861. HAROLD MELVIN & THE BLUE NOTES
Harold Melvin And The Blue Notes
[02Sep72|09Dec72|31Mar73] 53(3) 31 861

3862. THE GOLDEN AGE OF ROCK 'N' ROLL
Sha Na Na
[21Apr73|16Jun73|29Sep73] 38(1) 24 861

3863. TRUST Elvis Costello And The Attractions
[14Feb81|07Mar81|23May81] 28(2) 15 860

3864. SUMMER SOUNDS Robert Goulet
[14Aug65|30Oct65|18Dec65] 31(2) 19 860

3865. DOWN TO THE MOON Andreas Vollenweider
[02Aug86|27Sep86|25Apr87] 60(1) 39 859

3866. ICE ON FIRE Elton John
[30Nov85|05Apr86|07Jun86] 48(2) 28 859

3867. RASPBERRIES Raspberries
[20May72|28Oct72|09Dec72] 51(1) 30 859

3868. HIGH COUNTRY SNOWS Dan Fogelberg
[11May85|15Jun85|12Oct85] 30(2) 23 858

3869. MCGUINN, CLARK & HILLMAN
McGuinn, Clark & Hillman
[24Feb79|05May79|30Jun79] 39(1) 19 858

3870. JOURNEY THROUGH THE PAST (SOUNDTRACK) Neil Young
[25Nov72|03Feb73|14Apr73] 45(1) 21 858

3871. DADDY'S LITTLE GIRL Al Martino
[24Jun67|19Aug67|11Nov67] 23(1) 21 858

3872. TOM JONES Soundtrack
[21Mar64|11Jul64|22Aug64] 38(1) 23 857

3873. INTROSPECTIVE Pet Shop Boys
[05Nov88|03Dec88|01Apr89] 34(2) 22 857

3874. THE BEST OF BUCK OWENS Buck Owens
[18Jul64|12Sep64|13Feb65] 46(2) 31 857

Rank. Title Act
[Entry|Peak|Exit] Peak(Wks) TotWks Score

3875. MANDRILL Mandrill
[24Apr71|19Jun71|18Sep71] 48(1) 22 857

3876. HELL James Brown
[27Jul74|07Sep74|30Nov74] 35(2) 19 857

3877. 2 YEARS ON Bee Gees
[30Jan71|13Feb71|01May71] 32(2) 14 857

3878. GRAHAM CENTRAL STATION
Graham Central Station
[09Feb74|04May74|03Aug74] 48(1) 26 856

3879. FICKLE HEART Sniff 'N' The Tears
[28Jul79|20Oct79|17Nov79] 35(1) 17 856

3880. HANK WILSON'S BACK, VOL. I
Leon Russell
[22Sep73|27Oct73|29Dec73] 28(1) 15 855

3881. IN THE WAKE OF POSEIDON King Crimson
[12Sep70|26Sep70|05Dec70] 31(2) 13 854

3882. CALIFORNIA DREAMING Wes Montgomery
[25Mar67|03Jun67|28Oct67] 65(1) 32 854

3883. ALL THE GREAT HITS Commodores
[04Dec82|22Jan83|14May83] 37(3) 24 854

3884. SUR LA MER The Moody Blues
[25Jun88|23Jul88|29Oct88] 38(2) 19 852

3885. GREATEST HITS The Marshall Tucker Band
[21Oct78|16Dec78|05Dec81] 67(3) 32 852

3886. EASY Nancy Wilson
[01Jun68|10Aug68|09Nov68] 51(1) 24 852

3887. RITCHIE BLACKMORE'S R-A-I-N-B-O-W
Rainbow
[06Sep75|25Oct75|13Dec75] 30(1) 15 851

3888. 2:00 A.M. PARADISE CAFE Barry Manilow
[15Dec84|26Jan85|27Apr85] 28(2) 20 851

3889. TONIGHT'S THE NIGHT Neil Young
[12Jul75|09Aug75|27Sep75] 25(2) 12 851

3890. I WANT TO LIVE John Denver
[03Dec77|14Jan78|10Jun78] 45(1) 25 850

3891. IN CASE YOU'RE IN LOVE Sonny & Cher
[25Mar67|13May67|07Oct67] 45(2) 29 850

3892. STRANGE MAN, CHANGED MAN
Bram Tchaikovsky
[30Jun79|01Sep79|27Oct79] 36(1) 18 850

3893. DON'T IT FEEL GOOD Ramsey Lewis
[04Oct75|22Nov75|28Feb76] 46(1) 22 849

3894. FREHLEY'S COMET Ace Frehley
[23May87|20Jun87|07Nov87] 43(2) 25 849

3895. REACH OUT Burt Bacharach
[28Oct67|21Sep68|15May71] 96(1) 65 849

3896. LOVE SOMEBODY TODAY Sister Sledge
[08Mar80|19Apr80|14Jun80] 31(2) 15 849

3897. WIDE RECEIVER Michael Henderson
[30Aug80|01Nov80|10Jan81] 35(1) 18 849

3898. SOLO Frankie Valli
[22Jul67|02Sep67|23Dec67] 34(1) 23 849

3899. BENT OUT OF SHAPE Rainbow
[01Oct83|19Nov83|18Feb84] 34(1) 21 848

3900. THE INCREDIBLE BASE Rob Base
[09Dec89|20Jan90|02Jun90] 50(2) 26 848

3901. THE BEST OF BREAD, VOLUME TWO Bread
[01Jun74|13Jul74|28Sep74] 32(2) 18 848

3902. THE BEST OF RONNIE DOVE Ronnie Dove
[02Apr66|11Jun66|20Aug66] 35(3) 21 848

3903. INDIVIDUALLY & COLLECTIVELY
The 5th Dimension
[01Apr72|24Jun72|04Nov72] 58(2) 32 848

3904. FOREIGN AFFAIR Tina Turner
[07Oct89|28Oct89|24Feb90] 31(2) 21 847

3905. STRAIGHT FROM THE HEART Peabo Bryson
[16Jun84|11Aug84|08Dec84] 44(2) 26 847

3906. THE AGE OF CONSENT Bronski Beat
[19Jan85|09Mar85|06Jul85] 36(2) 25 847

3907. LOOKING IN Savoy Brown
[17Oct70|21Nov70|20Feb71] 39(1) 19 847

3908. FLYING HIGH TOGETHER
Smokey Robinson & The Miracles
[19Aug72|21Oct72|13Jan73] 46(2) 22 847

3909. BYE BYE BLUES
Bert Kaempfert And His Orchestra
[12Mar66|30Apr66|17Sep66] 46(1) 28 846

3910. HOT SPACE Queen
[29May82|19Jun82|16Oct82] 22(3) 21 846

Rank. Title Act	[Entry|Peak|Exit] Peak(Wks) TotWks	Score
3911. ROD STEWART Rod Stewart	[12Jul86|16Aug86|15Nov86] 28(2) 19	846
3912. GREETINGS FROM ASBURY PARK, N.J. Bruce Springsteen	[26Jul75|18Oct75|15Feb86] 60(1) 43	845
3913. ELVIS ARON PRESLEY Elvis Presley	[23Aug80|20Sep80|22Nov80] 27(2) 14	845
3914. ZAPP II Zapp	[14Aug82|18Sep82|18Dec82] 25(3) 19	845
3915. DON'T LOOK ANY FURTHER Dennis Edwards	[03Mar84|02Jun84|01Sep84] 48(2) 27	845
3916. THE ROMANTIC WORLD OF EDDY ARNOLD Eddy Arnold	[15Jun68|10Aug68|18Jan69] 56(2) 32	844
3917. A LETTERMEN KIND OF LOVE The Lettermen	[08Feb64|21Mar64|12Sep64] 31(1) 32	844
3918. BRITISH STEEL Judas Priest	[31May80|12Jul80|27Sep80] 34(2) 18	844
3919. PAC-MAN FEVER Buckner & Garcia	[13Mar82|29May82|26Jun82] 24(2) 16	844
3920. THE VISITORS ABBA	[09Jan82|13Feb82|01May82] 29(2) 17	844
3921. LIVE AT CARNEGIE HALL Renaissance	[05Jun76|14Aug76|16Oct76] 55(2) 20	844
3922. MUSIC FROM MARY POPPINS, THE SOUND OF MUSIC, MY FAIR LADY, & OTHER GREAT MOVIE THEMES Ray Conniff & His Orchestra & Chorus	[05Jun65|21Aug65|09Oct65] 34(2) 19	844
3923. SWEET EXORCIST Curtis Mayfield	[25May74|06Jul74|09Nov74] 39(1) 22	844
3924. WHO? Tony! Toni! Tone!	[28May88|02Jul88|08Apr89] 69(2) 46	844
3925. SIDE KICKS Thompson Twins	[26Feb83|02Apr83|13Aug83] 34(3) 25	843
3926. B.L.T. Jack Bruce/Bill Lordan/Robin Trower	[21Mar81|09May81|04Jul81] 37(1) 16	843
3927. HARD WORK John Handy	[05Jun76|18Sep76|23Oct76] 43(2) 21	843
3928. PEACE SELLS...BUT WHO'S BUYING? Megadeth	[25Oct86|29Nov86|12Sep87] 76(1) 47	843
3929. ROBERT GOULET ON BROADWAY Robert Goulet	[11Dec65|05Feb66|07May66] 33(2) 22	842
3930. BUDDY MILES LIVE Buddy Miles	[02Oct71|13Nov71|11Mar72] 50(1) 24	842
3931. CROSSROADS Eric Clapton	[07May88|21May88|29Oct88] 34(2) 26	842
3932. WEEKEND IN LONDON The Dave Clark Five	[03Apr65|05Jun65|04Sep65] 24(1) 23	842
3933. WE'RE ONLY IN IT FOR THE MONEY Mothers Of Invention	[16Mar68|04May68|20Jul68] 30(1) 19	842
3934. WHEN YOU'RE IN LOVE THE WHOLE WORLD IS JEWISH Various Artists	[02Apr66|21May66|30Jul66] 22(2) 18	841
3935. IF LOVING YOU IS WRONG I DON'T WANT TO BE RIGHT Luther Ingram	[30Sep72|16Dec72|17Feb73] 39(1) 21	840
3936. OPERA SAUVAGE Vangelis	[13Dec86|11Apr87|05Sep87] 42(1) 39	839
3937. SOMETHING'S GOING ON Frida	[13Nov82|09Apr83|21May83] 41(2) 28	839
3938. OBSCURED BY CLOUDS (SOUNDTRACK) Pink Floyd	[24Jun72|19Aug72|05Jul75] 46(2) 25	839
3939. THE TIMES THEY ARE A-CHANGIN' Bob Dylan	[07Mar64|18Apr64|25Jul64] 20(1) 21	839
3940. HERE THEY COME! Paul Revere & The Raiders	[03Jul65|09Apr66|09Jul66] 71(1) 45	838
3941. COMPUTER GAMES George Clinton	[18Dec82|30Apr83|30Jul83] 40(1) 33	838
3942. IN THE GROOVE Marvin Gaye	[02Nov68|15Feb69|03May69] 63(2) 27	838
3943. SABOTAGE Black Sabbath	[23Aug75|27Sep75|22Nov75] 28(2) 14	837
3944. IN MY LIFE Judy Collins	[07Jan67|08Apr67|25Jan69] 46(1) 34	836
3945. TRULY FOR YOU The Temptations	[17Nov84|09Mar85|06Jul85] 55(4) 34	835
3946. SEASONS OF THE HEART John Denver	[20Mar82|22May82|30Oct82] 39(2) 33	835
3947. AEROSMITH'S GREATEST HITS Aerosmith	[29Nov80|20Dec80|30Apr88] 53(3) 40	835
3948. A DECADE OF ROCK AND ROLL 1970 TO 1980 REO Speedwagon	[19Apr80|31May80|20Jun81] 55(1) 34	835
3949. BEST OF ROCKERS N' BALLADS Scorpions	[02Dec89|03Feb90|05May90] 43(2) 23	834
3950. THE FLOCK The Flock	[20Sep69|08Nov69|31Jan70] 48(2) 20	833
3951. LOST AND FOUND Humble Pie	[30Sep72|25Nov72|10Feb73] 37(1) 20	833
3952. JIM NABORS BY REQUEST Jim Nabors	[20May67|08Jul67|17Feb68] 50(1) 40	833
3953. CATS ON THE COAST Sea Level	[04Feb78|18Mar78|20May78] 31(1) 16	833
3954. UB40 UB40	[20Aug88|08Oct88|18Feb89] 44(2) 27	832
3955. MR. LONELY Bobby Vinton	[16Jan65|13Feb65|10Apr65] 18(3) 13	832
3956. FUTURE NOW Pleasure	[11Aug79|24Nov79|23Feb80] 67(1) 29	832
3957. AND I LOVE YOU SO Perry Como	[26May73|21Jul73|29Sep73] 34(1) 19	831
3958. T'PAU T'Pau	[06Jun87|29Aug87|14Nov87] 31(1) 24	831
3959. DONNY & MARIE - FEATURING SONGS FROM THEIR TELEVISION SHOW Donny & Marie Osmond	[03Apr76|29May76|12Feb77] 60(2) 38	830
3960. PETULA Petula Clark	[07Sep68|12Oct68|25Jan69] 51(2) 21	829
3961. FACTS OF LIFE Bobby Womack	[07Jul73|25Aug73|24Nov73] 37(1) 21	828
3962. BEGINNINGS Rick Springfield	[12Aug72|14Oct72|02Dec72] 35(2) 17	828
3963. THE HEART OF THE MATTER Kenny Rogers	[19Oct85|28Dec85|26Apr86] 51(3) 28	827
3964. UP POPS RAMSEY LEWIS Ramsey Lewis	[09Mar68|29Jun68|05Oct68] 52(2) 31	827
3965. BARE WIRES John Mayall's Bluesbreakers	[14Sep68|16Nov68|18Jan69] 59(2) 19	826
3966. SWEET PASSION Aretha Franklin	[18Jun77|16Jul77|22Oct77] 49(4) 19	826
3967. CATCH THE WIND Donovan	[17Jul65|20Nov65|18Dec65] 30(1) 23	826
3968. AMERICAN GARAGE Pat Metheny Group	[24Nov79|02Feb80|03May80] 53(1) 24	826
3969. MUSIC BOX Evelyn "Champagne" King	[14Apr79|19May79|04Aug79] 35(2) 17	826
3970. THOSE WERE THE DAYS Johnny Mathis	[14Dec68|01Mar69|03May69] 60(1) 21	825
3971. NEW YORK TENDABERRY Laura Nyro	[01Nov69|29Nov69|21Feb70] 32(1) 17	825
3972. GALVESTON Lawrence Welk	[19Apr69|14Jun69|30Aug69] 55(1) 20	825
3973. THE SESSION Jerry Lee Lewis	[17Mar73|26May73|21Jul73] 37(1) 19	825
3974. FEEL MY SOUL Jennifer Holliday	[22Oct83|05Nov83|17Mar84] 31(2) 22	825
3975. FAT BOYS Fat Boys	[05Jan85|09Feb85|05Oct85] 48(2) 40	824
3976. MY KIND OF TOWN Jack Jones	[08May65|07Aug65|25Sep65] 29(1) 21	824
3977. HE'S A FRIEND Eddie Kendricks	[31Jan76|24Apr76|05Jun76] 38(1) 19	824
3978. REEL LIFE Boy Meets Girl	[22Oct88|14Jan89|15Apr89] 50(2) 26	824
3979. WAIATA Split Enz	[23May81|20Jun81|26Sep81] 45(2) 19	824
3980. ANIMALISM The Animals	[03Dec66|21Jan67|29Apr67] 33(2) 22	823
3981. 80'S LADIES K.T. Oslin	[12Dec87|26Mar88|16Jul88] 68(4) 32	823
3982. NATURE PLANNED IT Four Tops	[27May72|21Oct72|20Jan73] 50(2) 28	823
3983. GREETINGS FROM TIMBUK 3 Timbuk 3	[04Oct86|10Jan87|25Apr87] 50(1) 30	822
3984. COLORS Soundtrack	[14May88|04Jun88|17Sep88] 31(2) 19	822
3985. SWEETS FROM A STRANGER Squeeze	[29May82|10Jul82|18Dec82] 32(2) 30	822
3986. THE CALIFORNIA RAISINS The California Raisins	[05Dec87|23Jan88|06Aug88] 60(2) 36	822
3987. SOMEBODY'S KNOCKIN' Terri Gibbs	[14Feb81|11Apr81|01Aug81] 53(3) 25	822
3988. ROCK & ROLL STRATEGY Thirty Eight Special	[22Oct88|20May89|29Jul89] 61(1) 41	821
3989. ALFIE Billy Vaughn And His Orchestra	[22Oct66|07Jan67|17Jun67] 44(1) 35	821
3990. A SHOW OF HANDS Rush	[28Jan89|18Feb89|06May89] 21(1) 15	820
3991. LIKE TO GET TO KNOW YOU Spanky And Our Gang	[27Apr68|20Jul68|12Oct68] 56(2) 25	819
3992. FEETS DON'T FAIL ME NOW Herbie Hancock	[17Mar79|05May79|11Aug79] 38(1) 22	819
3993. JIVE BUNNY - THE ALBUM Jive Bunny & The Mastermixers	[30Dec89|10Feb90|05May90] 26(1) 19	818
3994. ON THE THIRD DAY Electric Light Orchestra	[29Dec73|09Mar74|08Jun74] 52(1) 24	818
3995. JUKE JOINT JUMP Elvin Bishop	[10May75|14Jun75|30Aug75] 46(2) 17	818
3996. GREATEST HITS 1982-1989 Chicago	[09Dec89|10Feb90|26May90] 37(1) 25	818
3997. THE AMERICAN TOUR WITH ED RUDY The Beatles	[06Jun64|25Jul64|29Aug64] 20(2) 13	818
3998. COME GO WITH US Pockets	[22Oct77|24Dec77|01Apr78] 57(2) 24	818
3999. ALL AMERICAN GIRLS Sister Sledge	[28Feb81|04Apr81|12Sep81] 42(1) 29	817
4000. ROCK & ROLL OUTLAWS Foghat	[09Nov74|30Nov74|20Mar76] 40(2) 19	817
4001. CARAVAN TO MIDNIGHT Robin Trower	[26Aug78|21Oct78|16Dec78] 37(2) 17	817
4002. MARIPOSA DO ORA Dave Mason	[01Jul78|19Aug78|04Nov78] 41(1) 19	815
4003. RECORDED LIVE Ten Years After	[23Jun73|04Aug73|10Nov73] 39(1) 21	815
4004. MICKEY MOUSE DISCO Various Artists	[12Apr80|07Jun80|11Oct80] 35(2) 27	815
4005. HOT CHOCOLATE Hot Chocolate	[22Nov75|14Feb76|10Apr76] 41(2) 21	815
4006. THE WILD, THE INNOCENT AND THE E STREET SHUFFLE Bruce Springsteen	[26Jul75|18Oct75|20Dec80] 59(1) 34	814
4007. FEEL ME Cameo	[06Dec80|17Jan81|28Mar81] 44(1) 17	814
4008. EYE OF THE ZOMBIE John Fogerty	[11Oct86|01Nov86|14Feb87] 26(2) 19	814
4009. LIFE'S TOO GOOD The Sugarcubes	[18Jun88|01Oct88|31Dec88] 54(2) 29	813
4010. DAVID SOUL David Soul	[22Jan77|23Apr77|18Jun77] 40(1) 22	813
4011. EYES OF A STRANGER The Deele	[27Feb88|30Apr88|13Aug88] 54(2) 25	813
4012. PSYCHO CAFE Bang Tango	[01Jul89|28Oct89|24Mar90] 58(2) 39	813
4013. ROCK ON David Essex	[05Jan74|16Mar74|25May74] 32(1) 21	812
4014. CALIENTE! Gato Barbieri	[02Oct76|02Apr77|07May77] 75(1) 32	811
4015. LITTLE BAGGARIDDIM UB40	[17Aug85|05Oct85|01Feb86] 40(3) 25	811
4016. HEART STRING Earl Klugh	[19May79|16Jun79|06Oct79] 49(1) 21	811
4017. JERMAINE(2) Jermaine Jackson	[06Dec80|21Feb81|06Jun81] 44(1) 23	810
4018. HERE I AM Dionne Warwick	[01Jan66|26Mar66|16Jul66] 45(1) 29	810

Rank. Title Act
[Entry|Peak|Exit] Peak(Wks) TotWks Score

4019. A NICE PAIR Pink Floyd
[22Dec73|09Feb74|13Apr74] 36(1) 17 810

4020. JO JO GUNNE Jo Jo Gunne
[26Feb72|27May72|22Jul72] 57(2) 22 809

4021. IN OUR LIFETIME Marvin Gaye
[07Feb81|14Mar81|30May81] 32(2) 17 809

4022. BLUE Double
[26Jul86|27Sep86|13Dec86] 30(1) 21 809

4023. THE UNDISPUTED TRUTH
The Undisputed Truth
[24Jul71|25Sep71|20Nov71] 43(1) 18 809

4024. 20/20 George Benson
[26Jan85|16Feb85|31Aug85] 45(3) 32 809

4025. THE KARATE KID PART II Soundtrack
[12Jul86|06Sep86|01Nov86] 30(2) 17 808

4026. ANOTHER PASSENGER Carly Simon
[26Jun76|24Jul76|18Sep76] 29(1) 13 808

4027. ONE NIGHT OF SIN Joe Cocker
[16Sep89|03Feb90|07Apr90] 52(1) 30 808

4028. RAVI SHANKAR AT THE MONTEREY INTERNATIONAL POP FESTIVAL Ravi Shankar
[18Nov67|10Feb68|23Mar68] 43(2) 19 808

4029. LEVEL HEADED The Sweet
[18Feb78|08Jul78|26Aug78] 52(1) 28 808

4030. COUNTRY Anne Murray
[31Aug74|26Oct74|14Dec74] 32(1) 16 808

4031. THE EARLY BEATLES The Beatles
[24Apr65|12Jun65|11Oct86] 43(1) 35 807

4032. PIZZAZZ Patrice Rushen
[24Nov79|01Mar80|19Apr80] 39(2) 22 807

4033. WE'RE THE BEST OF FRIENDS
Natalie Cole & Peabo Bryson
[15Dec79|01Mar80|19Apr80] 44(1) 19 806

4034. FROM EVERY STAGE Joan Baez
[07Feb76|20Mar76|29May76] 34(1) 17 806

4035. IT'S NOT UNUSUAL Tom Jones
[03Jul65|28Aug65|18Oct69] 54(2) 42 806

4036. VANITY 6 Vanity 6
[02Oct82|11Dec82|30Apr83] 45(2) 31 805

4037. HEADS & TALES Harry Chapin
[18Mar72|01Jul72|16Sep72] 60(1) 27 805

4038. THERE IT IS James Brown
[08Jul72|04Nov72|25Nov72] 60(1) 21 805

4039. HOW 'BOUT US Champaign
[21Mar81|16May81|01Aug81] 53(1) 20 805

4040. AIN'T NOTHIN' STOPPIN' US NOW
Tower Of Power
[11Sep76|09Oct76|01Jan77] 42(4) 17 805

4041. WOMAN OUT OF CONTROL Ray Parker Jr.
[26Nov83|11Feb84|28Apr84] 45(2) 23 805

4042. EVERYTHING IS EVERYTHING Diana Ross
[21Nov70|26Dec70|06Mar71] 42(2) 16 804

4043. AMAZING GRACE
Royal Scots Dragoon Guards
[24Jun72|29Jul72|30Sep72] 34(1) 15 804

4044. SANDS OF TIME Jay & The Americans
[15Mar69|26Apr69|02Aug69] 51(2) 21 804

4045. RELEASE Henry Gross
[14Feb76|19Jun76|21Aug76] 64(1) 28 804

4046. KOOKOO Debbie Harry
[29Aug81|26Sep81|14Nov81] 25(1) 12 803

4047. YOU BROKE MY HEART IN 17 PLACES
Tracey Ullman
[24Mar84|12May84|04Aug84] 34(2) 20 803

4048. THE HIT SOUND OF DEAN MARTIN
Dean Martin
[27Aug66|05Nov66|11Feb67] 50(1) 25 802

4049. GROOVIN' WITH THE SOULFUL STRINGS
The Soulful Strings
[11Nov67|06Apr68|29Jun68] 59(1) 34 802

4050. BY THE LIGHT OF THE MOON Los Lobos
[14Feb87|14Mar87|19Sep87] 47(2) 32 802

4051. HAWKS & DOVES Neil Young
[22Nov80|20Dec80|07Mar81] 30(3) 16 800

4052. ROCKETS Rockets
[14Apr79|16Jun79|06Oct79] 56(2) 26 800

4053. DR. HOOK & THE MEDICINE SHOW
Dr. Hook & The Medicine Show
[29Apr72|08Jul72|30Sep72] 45(1) 23 800

Rank. Title Act
[Entry|Peak|Exit] Peak(Wks) TotWks Score

4054. MANHATTAN TOWER/THE MAN WHO LOVES MANHATTAN Robert Goulet
[02May64|11Jul64|26Sep64] 31(1) 22 800

4055. JOAN ARMATRADING Joan Armatrading
[09Oct76|18Jun77|23Jul77] 67(2) 27 799

4056. FOR ONCE IN MY LIFE Stevie Wonder
[11Jan69|15Feb69|10May69] 50(3) 18 799

4057. THE HOLY LAND Johnny Cash
[15Feb69|05Apr69|28Jun69] 54(2) 20 799

4058. TAKE IT WHILE IT'S HOT Sweet Sensation(2)
[08Oct88|13May89|16Sep89] 63(1) 32 799

4059. ON THE ROAD Jesse Colin Young
[27Mar76|15May76|03Jul76] 34(2) 15 799

4060. ANDY WILLIAMS' GREATEST HITS
Andy Williams
[07Mar70|11Apr70|18Jul70] 42(1) 20 798

4061. SKYWAY Skyy
[15Mar80|31May80|16Aug80] 61(1) 23 798

4062. MOVE SOMETHIN' The 2 Live Crew
[04Jun88|02Jul88|18Mar89] 68(2) 42 798

4063. WHAT A FEELIN' Irene Cara
[10Dec83|25Feb84|18Aug84] 77(1) 37 798

4064. ROTARY CONNECTION Rotary Connection
[16Mar68|18May68|02Nov68] 37(2) 31 798

4065. RINGO'S ROTOGRAVURE Ringo Starr
[16Oct76|13Nov76|11Dec76] 28(3) 9 798

4066. TILL THE END OF TIME Jerry Vale
[22Feb64|18Apr64|20Jun64] 28(1) 18 797

4067. AND IN THIS CORNER...
D.J. Jazzy Jeff & The Fresh Prince
[18Nov89|02Dec89|31Mar90] 39(4) 20 797

4068. BEST OF GEORGE HARRISON
George Harrison
[27Nov76|25Dec76|05Mar77] 31(2) 15 797

4069. SHUTTERED ROOM The Fixx
[13Nov82|09Apr83|22Sep84] 106(1) 51 797

4070. THAT'S LOU Lou Rawls
[26Aug67|16Sep67|06Jan68] 29(1) 20 797

4071. IT'S A BIG DADDY THING Big Daddy Kane
[07Oct89|21Oct89|28Apr90] 33(1) 30 796

4072. YOUR SAVING GRACE The Steve Miller Band
[29Nov69|17Jan70|28Feb70] 38(2) 14 796

4073. THE PROS & CONS OF HITCHHIKING
Roger Waters
[19May84|09Jun84|15Sep84] 31(3) 18 796

4074. LIVE - FULL HOUSE The J. Geils Band
[21Oct72|02Dec72|14Apr73] 54(2) 26 795

4075. ALF Alison Moyet
[06Apr85|01Jun85|21Sep85] 45(2) 25 795

4076. THE WIZ Soundtrack
[21Oct78|25Nov78|10Feb79] 40(1) 17 795

4077. AMONG THE LIVING Anthrax
[11Apr87|30May87|12Dec87] 62(2) 36 795

4078. WHEN A MAN LOVES A WOMAN
Percy Sledge
[04Jun66|13Aug66|22Oct66] 37(1) 21 794

4079. FLYING HIGH ON YOUR LOVE Bar-Kays
[10Dec77|21Jan78|13May78] 47(2) 23 794

4080. BUSTIN' LOOSE
Chuck Brown & The Soul Searchers
[17Feb79|24Mar79|19May79] 31(1) 14 794

4081. LIZA MINNELLI THE SINGER Liza Minnelli
[24Mar73|12May73|04Aug73] 38(1) 20 794

4082. LOVE STORY Johnny Mathis
[13Mar71|17Apr71|10Jul71] 47(1) 18 794

4083. NADIA'S THEME (THE YOUNG AND THE RESTLESS) Various Artists
[06Nov76|15Jan77|12Mar77] 42(1) 19 794

4084. MIRACLES Change
[18Apr81|13Jun81|12Sep81] 46(1) 22 793

4085. CLOSER TO IT!
Brian Auger's Oblivion Express
[04Aug73|27Oct73|02Mar74] 64(2) 31 793

4086. JANIS JOPLIN'S GREATEST HITS Janis Joplin
[14Jul73|18Aug73|08Dec73] 37(1) 22 793

4087. THE ILLUSION The Illusion
[10May69|11Oct69|08Nov69] 69(1) 27 792

4088. OH MERCY Bob Dylan
[07Oct89|28Oct89|10Mar90] 30(2) 23 792

Rank. Title Act
[Entry|Peak|Exit] Peak(Wks) TotWks Score

4089. ALL FLY HOME Al Jarreau
[14Oct78|09Dec78|21Apr79] 78(2) 28 792

4090. MIRROR MOVES Psychedelic Furs
[26May84|07Jul84|24Nov84] 43(2) 27 792

4091. SINGS LIKE CRAZY Frank Fontaine
[24Aug63|12Oct63|08Feb64] 44(2) 25 792

4092. TO LOVE AGAIN Diana Ross
[14Mar81|04Apr81|13Jun81] 32(2) 14 791

4093. A PORTRAIT OF RAY Ray Charles
[13Apr68|22Jun68|21Sep68] 51(1) 24 791

4094. AUTOGRAPH John Denver
[01Mar80|19Apr80|21Jun80] 39(2) 17 791

4095. STEPPING INTO TOMORROW
Donald Byrd
[29Mar75|10May75|02Aug75] 42(1) 19 791

4096. NOTHING TO LOSE Eddie Money
[22Oct88|03Dec88|06May89] 49(1) 29 791

4097. MOLLY HATCHET Molly Hatchet
[11Nov78|09Jun79|09Feb80] 64(1) 42 790

4098. LOVE LIVES FOREVER Minnie Riperton
[06Sep80|11Oct80|13Dec80] 35(2) 15 790

4099. SHORT SHARP SHOCKED
Michelle Shocked
[17Sep88|04Feb89|13May89] 73(1) 35 790

4100. JACKSON BROWNE Jackson Browne
[18Mar72|27May72|19Aug72] 53(2) 23 790

4101. PETER NERO IN PERSON Peter Nero
[07Sep63|23Nov63|08Feb64] 31(1) 23 789

4102. HURRY SUNDOWN The Outlaws
[28May77|09Jul77|26Nov77] 51(2) 27 789

4103. A NIGHT TO REMEMBER Cyndi Lauper
[27May89|24Jun89|14Oct89] 37(4) 21 788

4104. IF THE SHOE FITS Pure Prairie League
[07Feb76|27Mar76|22May76] 33(2) 16 788

4105. EVERYTHING IS EVERYTHING
Donny Hathaway
[29May71|21Aug71|13Nov71] 73(1) 25 788

4106. HE AIN'T HEAVY, HE'S MY BROTHER
The Hollies
[04Apr70|18Apr70|04Jul70] 32(2) 14 787

4107. WASN'T TOMORROW WONDERFUL?
The Waitresses
[06Feb82|08May82|17Jul82] 41(1) 24 787

4108. FREE AS THE WIND The Crusaders
[18Jun77|09Jul77|24Sep77] 41(3) 15 787

4109. LET'S HEAR IT FOR THE BOY
Deniece Williams
[09Jun84|14Jul84|13Oct84] 26(1) 19 786

4110. SMILEY SMILE The Beach Boys
[30Sep67|16Dec67|17Feb68] 41(1) 21 786

4111. LOOKING THROUGH THE EYES OF LOVE
Gene Pitney
[18Sep65|04Dec65|26Feb66] 43(1) 24 785

4112. RAINBOW Neil Diamond
[01Sep73|06Oct73|22Dec73] 35(2) 17 785

4113. DO IT BABY The Miracles
[14Sep74|23Nov74|01Feb75] 41(1) 21 784

4114. REAL PEOPLE Chic
[26Jul80|30Aug80|01Nov80] 30(2) 15 784

4115. ANNIE Original Cast
[18Jun77|30Jul77|22May82] 81(1) 39 784

4116. ROAD FOOD The Guess Who
[11May74|15Jun74|02Nov74] 60(1) 26 784

4117. LIVE AT BASIN ST. EAST Trini Lopez
[24Oct64|12Dec64|20Mar65] 30(1) 22 784

4118. THE MUSIC BAND War
[14Apr79|19May79|28Jul79] 41(2) 16 784

4119. TODD RUNDGREN'S UTOPIA Utopia
[09Nov74|14Dec74|15Feb75] 34(2) 15 783

4120. RAPPIN' RODNEY Rodney Dangerfield
[12Nov83|24Dec83|24Mar84] 36(3) 20 783

4121. BLUE KENTUCKY GIRL Emmylou Harris
[05May79|16Jun79|29Sep79] 43(2) 22 783

4122. JUST SYLVIA Sylvia (2)
[07Aug82|27Nov82|19Mar83] 56(1) 33 782

4123. FRESH Raspberries
[09Dec72|27Jan73|24Mar73] 36(3) 16 782

4124. THE ASSOCIATION The Association
[04Oct69|01Nov69|24Jan70] 32(1) 17 782

Rank. Title Act
[Entry | Peak | Exit] Peak(Wks) TotWks — Score

4125. VINNIE VINCENT INVASION Vinnie Vincent Invasion
[20Sep86 | 15Nov86 | 04Apr87] 64(2) 29 — 781

4126. TOBY BEAU Toby Beau
[10Jun78 | 02Sep78 | 11Nov78] 40(1) 23 — 781

4127. SANCTUARY The J. Geils Band
[16Dec78 | 03Feb79 | 12May79] 49(1) 22 — 781

4128. FIRE IT UP Rick James
[03Nov79 | 15Dec79 | 15Mar80] 34(1) 20 — 781

4129. PAID IN FULL Eric B. & Rakim
[12Sep87 | 24Oct87 | 28May88] 58(1) 38 — 780

4130. TOUCH Con Funk Shun
[13Dec80 | 14Feb81 | 18Apr81] 51(1) 19 — 780

4131. THE NASHVILLE SOUND Danny Davis And The Nashville Brass
[15Feb69 | 07Jun69 | 26Jul69] 78(1) 24 — 780

4132. SNOWFLAKES ARE DANCING Tomita
[31Aug74 | 07Dec74 | 15Feb75] 57(1) 25 — 780

4133. THIS IS THE WAY The Rossington Collins Band
[10Oct81 | 07Nov81 | 23Jan82] 24(1) 16 — 780

4134. SHAKE Sam Cooke
[13Feb65 | 27Mar65 | 17Jul65] 44(1) 23 — 780

4135. MISPLACED CHILDHOOD Marillion
[24Aug85 | 09Nov85 | 19Apr86] 47(2) 35 — 780

4136. A MESSAGE TO THE PEOPLE Buddy Miles
[10Apr71 | 12Jun71 | 18Sep71] 60(1) 24 — 779

4137. COLLABORATION George Benson/Earl Klugh
[11Jul87 | 29Aug87 | 06Feb88] 59(2) 31 — 779

4138. STANDING OVATION Gladys Knight & The Pips
[08Jan72 | 26Feb72 | 17Jun72] 60(1) 24 — 779

4139. THE BEST OF BILL COSBY Bill Cosby
[06Sep69 | 04Oct69 | 21Feb70] 51(2) 25 — 778

4140. NEW RIDERS OF THE PURPLE SAGE New Riders Of The Purple Sage
[11Sep71 | 30Oct71 | 18Dec71] 39(2) 15 — 778

4141. SECRET OMEN Cameo
[28Jul79 | 29Sep79 | 15Dec79] 46(1) 21 — 778

4142. SHIRLEY MURDOCK! Shirley Murdock
[14Feb87 | 28Mar87 | 08Aug87] 44(2) 26 — 777

4143. WONDERFUL! WONDERFUL! Lawrence Welk
[07Dec63 | 22Feb64 | 30May64] 29(1) 26 — 777

4144. THE SOUND OF BOOTS Boots Randolph
[31Aug68 | 30Nov68 | 08Feb69] 60(1) 24 — 777

4145. UNDER A RAGING MOON Roger Daltrey
[12Oct85 | 23Nov85 | 05Apr86] 42(2) 26 — 777

4146. HAVING A RAVE UP WITH THE YARDBIRDS The Yardbirds
[18Dec65 | 12Feb66 | 20Aug66] 53(2) 33 — 777

4147. BORDER LORD Kris Kristofferson
[18Mar72 | 15Apr72 | 01Jul72] 41(2) 16 — 777

4148. PAUL SIMON IN CONCERT/LIVE RHYMIN' Paul Simon
[23Mar74 | 20Apr74 | 13Jul74] 33(1) 17 — 776

4149. DON'T LET GO George Duke
[03Jun78 | 08Jul78 | 02Sep78] 39(1) 14 — 776

4150. MARSHALL CRENSHAW Marshall Crenshaw
[29May82 | 31Jul82 | 27Nov82] 50(2) 27 — 776

4151. ALIVE ALIVE-O! Jose Feliciano
[20Dec69 | 17Jan70 | 21Mar70] 29(1) 14 — 775

4152. CULTOSAURUS ERECTUS Blue Öyster Cult
[12Jul80 | 23Aug80 | 25Oct80] 34(2) 16 — 775

4153. ONE SIZE FITS ALL Frank Zappa And The Mothers Of Invention
[19Jul75 | 23Aug75 | 04Oct75] 26(1) 12 — 775

4154. BEST OF GLADYS KNIGHT & THE PIPS Gladys Knight & The Pips
[07Feb76 | 27Mar76 | 15May76] 36(3) 15 — 774

4155. OUT OF AFRICA Soundtrack
[01Feb86 | 26Apr86 | 28Jun86] 38(2) 22 — 773

4156. TEMPLE OF LOW MEN Crowded House
[23Jul88 | 13Aug88 | 26Nov88] 40(2) 19 — 773

4157. YOU'RE ONLY LONELY John David Souther
[22Sep79 | 15Dec79 | 16Feb80] 41(3) 22 — 773

4158. SA-FIRE SaFire
[08Oct88 | 13May89 | 19Aug89] 79(1) 46 — 773

Rank. Title Act
[Entry | Peak | Exit] Peak(Wks) TotWks — Score

4159. EAST-WEST The Butterfield Blues Band
[08Oct66 | 11Mar67 | 22Apr67] 65(2) 29 — 773

4160. VICTIMS OF THE FURY Robin Trower
[01Mar80 | 12Apr80 | 07Jun80] 34(2) 15 — 772

4161. ECHO & THE BUNNYMEN(2) Echo & The Bunnymen
[08Aug87 | 17Oct87 | 16Apr88] 51(1) 37 — 771

4162. PET SOUNDS/CARL AND THE PASSIONS - SO TOUGH The Beach Boys
[03Jun72 | 15Jul72 | 14Oct72] 50(2) 20 — 771

4163. TERRAPIN STATION Grateful Dead
[20Aug77 | 01Oct77 | 03Dec77] 28(1) 16 — 771

4164. THE FRIENDS OF MR. CAIRO Jon And Vangelis
[08Aug81 | 24Oct81 | 07Aug82] 64(1) 34 — 771

4165. NIGHT FLIGHT Yvonne Elliman
[11Mar78 | 29Apr78 | 01Jul78] 40(2) 17 — 770

4166. SOCK IT TO ME! Mitch Ryder And The Detroit Wheels
[08Apr67 | 13May67 | 22Jul67] 34(2) 16 — 770

4167. SHOW SOME EMOTION Joan Armatrading
[22Oct77 | 24Dec77 | 11Mar78] 52(2) 21 — 770

4168. ANIMAL MAGIC The Blow Monkeys
[21Jun86 | 09Aug86 | 18Oct86] 35(2) 18 — 769

4169. JOAN Joan Baez
[02Sep67 | 14Oct67 | 13Jan68] 38(2) 20 — 769

4170. LOVE AN ADVENTURE Pseudo Echo
[21Mar87 | 11Jul87 | 19Sep87] 54(3) 27 — 769

4171. HIROSHIMA Hiroshima
[22Dec79 | 08Mar80 | 21Jun80] 51(2) 27 — 768

4172. RUNNING DOWN THE ROAD Arlo Guthrie
[25Oct69 | 06Dec69 | 28Feb70] 54(1) 19 — 768

4173. PRIMITIVE Neil Diamond
[18Aug84 | 15Sep84 | 02Feb85] 35(3) 25 — 767

4174. DICE Andrew Dice Clay
[29Apr89 | 21Oct89 | 17Mar90] 94(1) 47 — 767

4175. CUPID AND PSYCHE 85 Scritti Politti
[03Aug85 | 18Jan86 | 12Apr86] 50(2) 28 — 767

4176. TRACES/MEMORIES The Lettermen
[07Feb70 | 21Feb70 | 11Jul70] 42(2) 23 — 766

4177. MALICE IN WONDERLAND Nazareth
[16Feb80 | 15Mar80 | 21Jun80] 41(3) 19 — 766

4178. ILLEGAL STILLS Stephen Stills
[15May76 | 03Jul76 | 21Aug76] 31(1) 15 — 766

4179. COLD SWEAT James Brown
[16Sep67 | 28Oct67 | 06Jan68] 35(2) 17 — 766

4180. HEARTS AND BONES Paul Simon
[19Nov83 | 07Jan84 | 17Mar84] 35(2) 18 — 766

4181. LOLA VERSUS POWERMAN AND THE MONEYGOROUND, PART ONE The Kinks
[26Dec70 | 23Jan71 | 13Mar71] 35(1) 12 — 766

4182. TALE SPINNIN' Weather Report
[07Jun75 | 28Jun75 | 06Sep75] 31(2) 14 — 765

4183. NOT SHY Walter Egan
[15Apr78 | 07Oct78 | 02Dec78] 44(1) 31 — 765

4184. MORE, MORE, MORE Andrea True Connection
[19Jun76 | 07Aug76 | 09Oct76] 47(2) 17 — 764

4185. FLAME Ronnie Laws
[04Nov78 | 16Dec78 | 31Mar79] 51(4) 22 — 764

4186. HALLELUJAH Canned Heat
[09Aug69 | 30Aug69 | 15Nov69] 37(2) 15 — 763

4187. BOOGIE MOTEL Foghat
[13Oct79 | 03Nov79 | 01Mar80] 35(1) 21 — 763

4188. DON'T LET LOVE SLIP AWAY Freddie Jackson
[13Aug88 | 27Aug88 | 04Mar89] 48(2) 30 — 762

4189. ESCAPE ARTIST Garland Jeffreys
[21Mar81 | 09May81 | 18Jul81] 59(4) 18 — 762

4190. BROTHER LOVE'S TRAVELLING SALVATION SHOW Neil Diamond
[17May69 | 05Jul69 | 22Nov69] 82(2) 25 — 762

4191. 12 GREATEST HITS VOL. II Neil Diamond
[29May82 | 10Jul82 | 12Mar83] 48(2) 42 — 762

4192. YESTERDAY, WHEN I WAS YOUNG Roy Clark
[05Jul69 | 13Sep69 | 15Nov69] 50(1) 20 — 762

4193. BLAST FROM YOUR PAST Ringo Starr
[06Dec75 | 17Jan76 | 14Feb76] 30(2) 11 — 762

Rank. Title Act
[Entry | Peak | Exit] Peak(Wks) TotWks — Score

4194. BACK IN TOWN The Kingston Trio
[30May64 | 11Jul64 | 10Oct64] 22(2) 20 — 761

4195. THE ROAR OF THE GREASEPAINT-THE SMELL OF THE CROWD Original Cast
[10Apr65 | 31Jul65 | 27Nov65] 54(1) 34 — 761

4196. I'VE ALWAYS BEEN CRAZY Waylon Jennings
[21Oct78 | 25Nov78 | 31Mar79] 48(1) 24 — 761

4197. HAVE YOU LOOKED INTO YOUR HEART Jerry Vale
[06Mar65 | 08May65 | 07Aug65] 30(2) 23 — 761

4198. SHABOOH SHOOBAH INXS
[19Mar83 | 28May83 | 15Oct83] 46(3) 31 — 761

4199. RAIN MAN Soundtrack
[11Mar89 | 29Apr89 | 24Jun89] 31(2) 16 — 760

4200. THE JOHN LENNON COLLECTION John Lennon
[04Dec82 | 08Jan83 | 19Mar83] 33(4) 16 — 760

4201. GLOW Rick James
[11May85 | 15Jun85 | 02Nov85] 50(2) 26 — 759

4202. THE IMMORTAL OTIS REDDING Otis Redding
[20Jul68 | 05Oct68 | 07Dec68] 58(1) 21 — 759

4203. AN EVENING WITH WALLY LONDO FEATURING BILL SLASZO George Carlin
[08Nov75 | 03Jan76 | 14Feb76] 34(2) 15 — 758

4204. DALTREY Roger Daltrey
[26May73 | 14Jul73 | 06Oct73] 45(1) 20 — 757

4205. IN THE EYE OF THE STORM Roger Hodgson
[27Oct84 | 01Dec84 | 23Mar85] 46(5) 22 — 757

4206. SEPTEMBER SONG Jimmy Durante
[21Sep63 | 16Nov63 | 25Jan64] 30(1) 19 — 756

4207. STONE SOUL Mongo Santamaria
[01Mar69 | 03May69 | 09Aug69] 62(1) 24 — 756

4208. THE HOUSE OF BLUE LIGHT Deep Purple
[31Jan87 | 21Feb87 | 27Jun87] 34(3) 22 — 756

4209. WELCOME HOME 'Til Tuesday
[25Oct86 | 22Nov86 | 18Apr87] 49(3) 26 — 755

4210. ROBBIE DUPREE Robbie Dupree
[14Jun80 | 23Aug80 | 22Nov80] 51(1) 24 — 755

4211. SOMEWHERE OVER CHINA Jimmy Buffett
[23Jan82 | 13Feb82 | 01May82] 31(3) 15 — 755

4212. FOR SENTIMENTAL REASONS Linda Ronstadt
[11Oct86 | 22Nov86 | 11Apr87] 46(1) 27 — 755

4213. AS FALLS WICHITA, SO FALLS WICHITA FALLS Pat Metheny & Lyle Mays
[20Jun81 | 22Aug81 | 07Nov81] 50(1) 21 — 754

4214. THE CHICAGO THEME Hubert Laws
[21Jun75 | 13Sep75 | 18Oct75] 42(2) 18 — 753

4215. JUNGLE Dwight Twilley
[18Feb84 | 28Apr84 | 07Jul84] 39(1) 21 — 753

4216. TORCH Carly Simon
[17Oct81 | 21Nov81 | 27Mar82] 50(1) 24 — 753

4217. CREATURES OF THE NIGHT KISS
[20Nov82 | 29Jan83 | 26Mar83] 45(6) 19 — 752

4218. THE SHELTER OF YOUR ARMS Sammy Davis Jr.
[04Apr64 | 13Jun64 | 01Aug64] 26(2) 18 — 752

4219. HEADS UP! Baja Marimba Band
[27May67 | 02Sep67 | 13Jul68] 77(1) 44 — 752

4220. HARD 'N' HEAVY (WITH MARSHMALLOW) Paul Revere & The Raiders
[05Apr69 | 10May69 | 09Aug69] 51(2) 19 — 752

4221. CHUCK BERRY'S GREATEST HITS Chuck Berry
[06Jun64 | 29Aug64 | 24Oct64] 34(2) 21 — 752

4222. FILLMORE: THE LAST DAYS Various Artists
[15Jul72 | 26Aug72 | 28Oct72] 40(2) 16 — 752

4223. HAPPY TOGETHER The Nylons
[23May87 | 15Aug87 | 31Oct87] 43(1) 24 — 752

4224. ROCK ME BABY David Cassidy
[11Nov72 | 23Dec72 | 03Mar73] 41(1) 17 — 751

4225. BALLAD OF EASY RIDER The Byrds
[13Dec69 | 17Jan70 | 04Apr70] 36(1) 17 — 751

4226. TIMES SQUARE Soundtrack
[27Sep80 | 29Nov80 | 17Jan81] 37(2) 17 — 751

4227. FLIGHT LOG (1966-1976) Jefferson Starship
[29Jan77 | 05Mar77 | 07May77] 37(1) 15 — 751

Rank. Title Act
[Entry|Peak|Exit] Peak(Wks) TotWks Score

4228. LUSH LIFE Nancy Wilson
[02Sep67|14Oct67|06Jan68] 46(1) 19 751

4229. WONDERWALL MUSIC George Harrison
[11Jan69|01Mar69|26Apr69] 49(2) 16 750

4230. WHEN SECONDS COUNT Survivor
[08Nov86|27Dec86|18Apr87] 49(5) 24 750

4231. HORSES Patti Smith
[13Dec75|07Feb76|03Apr76] 47(2) 17 750

4232. CHICAGO 13 Chicago
[01Sep79|29Sep79|03Nov79] 21(2) 10 750

4233. ROUGH AND READY Jeff Beck Group
[06Nov71|11Dec71|19Feb72] 46(2) 16 750

4234. PLEASURE & PAIN Dr. Hook
[18Nov78|01Sep79|06Oct79] 66(1) 34 749

4235. SAVED Bob Dylan
[12Jul80|02Aug80|20Sep80] 24(2) 11 749

4236. TOGETHER FOR THE FIRST TIME...LIVE
B.B. King & Bobby Bland
[26Oct74|11Jan75|08Mar75] 43(1) 20 749

4237. TENTH The Marshall Tucker Band
[22Mar80|26Apr80|28Jun80] 32(1) 15 749

4238. SONGWRITER Justin Hayward
[12Mar77|21May77|25Jun77] 37(1) 16 749

4239. FROM LUXURY TO HEARTACHE Culture Club
[26Apr86|07Jun86|16Aug86] 32(2) 17 748

4240. DIMPLES Richard "Dimples" Fields
[25Jul81|12Sep81|14Nov81] 33(2) 17 748

4241. I'M JESSI COLTER Jessi Colter
[03May75|05Jul75|01Nov75] 50(2) 27 748

4242. JUST US Alabama
[17Oct87|14Nov87|23Apr88] 55(1) 28 748

4243. MIDNIGHT COWBOY Ferrante & Teicher
[22Nov69|14Feb70|16May70] 61(1) 26 748

4244. DEVIL'S GUN C.J. & Co.
[09Jul77|22Oct77|10Dec77] 60(1) 23 747

4245. MANTOVANI'S GOLDEN HITS Mantovani
[11Mar67|22Apr67|24Feb68] 53(2) 33 747

4246. 99 LUFTBALLONS Nena
[24Mar84|14Apr84|23Jun84] 27(3) 14 747

4247. LOST IN THE OZONE
Commander Cody & His Lost Planet Airmen
[27Nov71|10Jun72|08Jul72] 82(2) 33 747

4248. THE BOOKER T. SET Booker T. & The MG's
[14Jun69|19Jul69|11Oct69] 53(1) 18 747

4249. MANDRILL IS Mandrill
[29Apr72|08Jul72|07Oct72] 56(2) 24 747

4250. CAREFUL The Motels
[12Jul80|16Aug80|22Nov80] 45(2) 20 746

4251. SURPRISE ATTACK Tora Tora
[15Jul89|23Sep89|24Feb90] 47(1) 33 746

4252. BAD REPUTATION
Joan Jett & the Blackhearts
[14Mar81|09Oct82|08Jan83] 51(4) 21 746

4253. THE WIZ Original Cast
[03May75|19Jul75|16Aug75] 43(1) 16 746

4254. THE LOOK Shalamar
[06Aug83|24Sep83|07Jan84] 38(1) 23 746

4255. OPENING NIGHTS AT THE MET
Various Artists
[08Oct66|24Dec66|25Feb67] 49(1) 21 745

4256. VOYAGE Voyage
[08Apr78|01Jul78|26Aug78] 40(2) 21 745

4257. THE HITS REO Speedwagon
[25Jun88|10Sep88|19Nov88] 56(1) 22 745

4258. YOU KNOW HOW TO LOVE ME Phyllis Hyman
[08Dec79|09Feb80|26Apr80] 50(1) 21 745

4259. MUSIC BY MASON WILLIAMS
Mason Williams
[10May69|07Jun69|30Aug69] 44(2) 17 745

4260. NATURAL MAN Lou Rawls
[04Sep71|08Jan72|12Feb72] 68(1) 24 745

4261. DIVINE MADNESS (SOUNDTRACK)
Bette Midler
[29Nov80|20Dec80|28Feb81] 34(3) 14 745

4262. GINGER BAKER'S AIR FORCE
Ginger Baker's Air Force
[23May70|06Jun70|29Aug70] 33(2) 15 745

4263. MOVING VIOLATION The Jackson 5
[14Jun75|16Aug75|20Sep75] 36(1) 15 744

Rank. Title Act
[Entry|Peak|Exit] Peak(Wks) TotWks Score

4264. BACKSTREET David Sanborn
[26Nov83|28Jan84|07Jul84] 81(1) 33 744

4265. HENRY LEE SUMMER Henry Lee Summer
[12Mar88|07May88|13Aug88] 56(2) 23 744

4266. ELVIS: RECORDED LIVE ON STAGE IN MEMPHIS Elvis Presley
[27Jul74|24Aug74|19Oct74] 33(1) 13 744

4267. DON QUIXOTE Gordon Lightfoot
[25Mar72|22Apr72|15Jul72] 42(1) 17 744

4268. DON JUAN'S RECKLESS DAUGHTER
Joni Mitchell
[07Jan78|28Jan78|01Apr78] 25(2) 13 744

4269. ALLAN IN WONDERLAND
Allan Sherman
[11Apr64|13Jun64|15Aug64] 25(2) 19 743

4270. STREETNOISE
Julie Driscoll/Brian Auger & The Trinity
[14Jun69|12Jul69|27Sep69] 41(1) 16 743

4271. THE FLAT EARTH Thomas Dolby
[17Mar84|14Apr84|14Jul84] 35(2) 18 743

4272. HOME Stephanie Mills
[22Jul89|26Aug89|21Apr90] 82(3) 38 743

4273. TEDDY LIVE! COAST TO COAST
Teddy Pendergrass
[22Dec79|02Feb80|29Mar80] 33(3) 15 743

4274. PETER GABRIEL Peter Gabriel
[12Mar77|30Apr77|02Jul77] 38(2) 17 742

4275. TOTAL ECLIPSE Billy Cobham
[21Dec74|25Jan75|15Mar75] 36(1) 13 742

4276. LEATHER AND LACE
Waylon Jennings & Jessi Colter
[21Mar81|18Apr81|25Jul81] 43(2) 19 742

4277. 16 OF THEIR GREATEST HITS
The Mamas & The Papas
[27Sep69|08Nov69|04Apr70] 61(1) 26 742

4278. FEATS DON'T FAIL ME NOW Little Feat
[07Sep74|23Nov74|21Dec74] 36(1) 16 742

4279. TWO GQ
[05Apr80|03May80|16Aug80] 46(2) 20 741

4280. ROCK & ROLL Vanilla Fudge
[25Oct69|08Nov69|17Jan70] 34(1) 13 741

4281. I LIKE IT LIKE THAT The Dave Clark Five
[11Dec65|05Feb66|26Mar66] 32(2) 16 741

4282. WITHOUT A SONG Willie Nelson
[26Nov83|14Jan84|14Jul84] 54(1) 34 740

4283. SAME TRAIN, A DIFFERENT TIME
Merle Haggard
[14Jun69|26Jul69|11Oct69] 67(1) 18 740

4284. RAINDROPS KEEP FALLIN' ON MY HEAD
Andy Williams
[13Jun70|04Jul70|17Oct70] 43(1) 19 740

4285. THE BIG CHILL: MORE SONGS FROM
Soundtrack
[28Apr84|09Jun84|18May85] 85(1) 49 740

4286. GIVIN' IT BACK The Isley Brothers
[25Sep71|04Dec71|11Mar72] 71(1) 25 739

4287. STRANGERS IN THE NIGHT
Bert Kaempfert And His Orchestra
[09Jul66|03Sep66|26Nov66] 39(2) 21 739

4288. NEW CHAUTAUQUA Pat Metheny
[05May79|16Jun79|29Sep79] 44(1) 22 739

4289. AN EVENING WITH DIANA ROSS Diana Ross
[12Feb77|02Apr77|14May77] 29(1) 14 739

4290. WOOLY BULLY
Sam The Sham and the Pharaohs
[12Jun65|28Aug65|09Oct65] 26(2) 18 739

4291. THE ELECTRIC HORSEMAN (SOUNDTRACK)
Willie Nelson/Dave Grusin
[12Jan80|08Mar80|28Jun80] 52(2) 25 738

4292. LACE AND WHISKEY Alice Cooper
[28May77|02Jul77|10Sep77] 42(2) 16 737

4293. JOY Teddy Pendergrass
[28May88|16Jul88|05Nov88] 54(2) 24 737

4294. THE SHOCKING BLUE The Shocking Blue
[14Feb70|14Mar70|06Jun70] 31(1) 17 737

4295. HEMISPHERES Rush
[18Nov78|23Dec78|07Apr79] 47(3) 21 737

4296. SO LONG, BANNATYNE The Guess Who
[21Aug71|25Sep71|04Dec71] 52(1) 16 737

Rank. Title Act
[Entry|Peak|Exit] Peak(Wks) TotWks Score

4297. NO RESPECT Rodney Dangerfield
[02Aug80|20Sep80|06Dec80] 48(1) 19 737

4298. DISCO-FIED Rhythm Heritage
[06Mar76|24Apr76|26Jun76] 40(2) 17 737

4299. CIMARRON Emmylou Harris
[12Dec81|30Jan82|24Apr82] 46(1) 20 737

4300. ANOTHER PLACE Hiroshima
[30Nov85|01Mar86|04Oct86] 79(2) 45 736

4301. THE LOVE ALBUM Trini Lopez
[12Jun65|07Aug65|16Oct65] 32(1) 19 736

4302. BEYOND Herb Alpert
[26Jul80|23Aug80|11Oct80] 28(2) 12 735

4303. GREATEST HITS, VOLUME 1 B.J. Thomas
[08Nov69|14Feb70|16May70] 90(2) 28 735

4304. WONDERWORLD Uriah Heep
[06Jul74|24Aug74|12Oct74] 38(2) 15 735

4305. THE SWING INXS
[26May84|14Jul84|01Dec84] 52(2) 28 735

4306. POWER PLAY April Wine
[10Jul82|14Aug82|20Nov82] 37(2) 20 735

4307. RUBY, DON'T TAKE YOUR LOVE TO TOWN
Kenny Rogers & The First Edition
[11Oct69|29Nov69|07Feb70] 48(1) 18 735

4308. ROCK IN A HARD PLACE Aerosmith
[25Sep82|16Oct82|29Jan83] 32(4) 19 734

4309. THE TOUCH Alabama
[25Oct86|22Nov86|16May87] 42(1) 30 734

4310. RISING FORCE Yngwie Malmsteen
[04May85|22Jun85|22Feb86] 60(3) 43 734

4311. WHITE FEATHERS Kajagoogoo
[11Jun83|09Jul83|22Oct83] 38(2) 20 734

4312. COAL MINER'S DAUGHTER Soundtrack
[29Mar80|17May80|09Aug80] 40(1) 20 733

4313. LOW RIDE Earl Klugh
[07May83|11Jun83|15Oct83] 38(3) 24 733

4314. EVERYBODY LOVES THE SUNSHINE
Roy Ayers Ubiquity
[14Aug76|30Oct76|04Dec76] 51(1) 17 733

4315. THEIR 16 GREATEST HITS
The Grass Roots
[02Oct71|20Nov71|12Feb72] 58(1) 20 733

4316. CRY TOUGH Nils Lofgren
[17Apr76|05Jun76|31Jul76] 32(1) 16 732

4317. AN OFFICER AND A GENTLEMAN
Soundtrack
[30Oct82|11Dec82|02Apr83] 38(2) 23 732

4318. DONNY Donny Osmond
[07Dec74|01Mar75|29Mar75] 57(1) 17 732

4319. EVERY 1'S A WINNER Hot Chocolate
[06Jan79|03Mar79|21Apr79] 31(2) 16 731

4320. DECADE Neil Young
[26Nov77|24Dec77|25Mar78] 43(3) 18 731

4321. ORANGES AND LEMONS XTC
[18Mar89|22Apr89|05Aug89] 44(3) 21 731

4322. HOUSE PARTY The Temptations
[29Nov75|20Dec75|10Apr76] 40(2) 20 730

4323. MIRRORS Blue Öyster Cult
[07Jul79|25Aug79|27Oct79] 44(2) 17 730

4324. LIVE AT THE GARDEN James Brown
[10Jun67|12Aug67|30Sep67] 41(2) 17 730

4325. BORDERLINE Ry Cooder
[24Jan81|14Mar81|09May81] 43(2) 16 729

4326. IMAGINE: JOHN LENNON (SOUNDTRACK)
John Lennon
[22Oct88|19Nov88|18Feb89] 31(1) 18 729

4327. LOVE ALL THE HURT AWAY Aretha Franklin
[29Aug81|03Oct81|19Dec81] 36(2) 17 729

4328. UNDER THE BOARDWALK The Drifters
[15Aug64|07Nov64|09Jan65] 40(2) 22 728

4329. WOW! Bananarama
[26Sep87|17Oct87|19Mar88] 44(2) 26 727

4330. AFL1-3603 Dave Davies
[26Jul80|30Aug80|25Oct80] 42(2) 14 727

4331. PRESSURE SENSITIVE Ronnie Laws
[27Sep75|06Dec75|10Apr76] 73(1) 29 727

4332. A MESSAGE FROM THE PEOPLE Ray Charles
[29Apr72|01Jul72|23Sep72] 52(2) 22 726

4333. ANIMAL TRACKS The Animals
[18Sep65|27Nov65|05Mar66] 57(1) 25 726

Rank	Title	Act	Entry	Peak	Exit	Peak(Wks)	TotWks	Score
4334.	FEARLESS	Tim Curry	08Sep79	17Nov79	16Feb80	53(2)	24	726
4335.	TURN AROUND LOOK AT ME	Ray Conniff & His Orchestra & Chorus	26Oct68	18Jan69	22Mar69	70(1)	22	726
4336.	SUN CITY	Artists United Against Apartheid	23Nov85	14Dec85	22Mar86	31(2)	18	726
4337.	GREATEST HITS III	Hank Williams Jr.	25Feb89	06May89	11Nov89	61(1)	35	726
4338.	VERY SPECIAL	Debra Laws	11Apr81	29Aug81	10Oct81	70(1)	27	726
4339.	THE SECRET VALUE OF DAYDREAMING	Julian Lennon	12Apr86	03May86	09Aug86	32(2)	18	725
4340.	THE SOUL ALBUM	Otis Redding	30Apr66	02Jul66	12Nov66	54(1)	29	725
4341.	I CAN DREAM ABOUT YOU	Dan Hartman	03Nov84	22Dec84	11May85	55(3)	28	725
4342.	BURGERS	Hot Tuna	18Mar72	13May72	19Aug72	68(2)	23	725
4343.	GIRLS WITH GUNS	Tommy Shaw	20Oct84	24Nov84	06Apr85	50(3)	25	725
4344.	CLASSIC CRYSTAL	Crystal Gayle	17Nov79	05Jan80	12Apr80	62(3)	22	725
4345.	BILL COSBY	Bill Cosby	18Oct69	17Jan70	28Mar70	70(1)	24	724
4346.	I'M NO HERO	Cliff Richard	11Oct80	13Dec80	30May81	80(2)	34	723
4347.	GO WITH THE VENTURES!	The Ventures	11Jun66	20Aug66	26Nov66	39(2)	25	723
4348.	TURN BACK THE CLOCK	Johnny Hates Jazz	16Apr88	11Jun88	01Oct88	56(1)	25	723
4349.	THE FIRST FAMILY RIDES AGAIN	Rich Little	13Feb82	27Mar82	08May82	29(2)	13	723
4350.	THE HEALER	John Lee Hooker	07Oct89	31Mar90	23Jun90	62(1)	38	722
4351.	TOMCATTIN'	Blackfoot	21Jun80	23Aug80	01Nov80	50(1)	20	722
4352.	YES IT'S YOU LADY	Smokey Robinson	20Feb82	20Mar82	12Jun82	33(3)	17	722
4353.	CHASE THE CLOUDS AWAY	Chuck Mangione	26Apr75	28Jun75	30Aug75	47(1)	19	722
4354.	BLACK AND WHITE	Tony Joe White	26Jul69	30Aug69	08Nov69	51(1)	16	722
4355.	FIELDS OF FIRE	Corey Hart	18Oct86	15Nov86	18Apr87	55(2)	27	722
4356.	MARCHING OUT	Yngwie J. Malmsteen's Rising Force	07Sep85	26Oct85	15Mar86	52(2)	28	721
4357.	OTIS BLUE/OTIS REDDING SINGS SOUL	Otis Redding	16Oct65	05Feb66	02Jul66	75(1)	34	721
4358.	WILD-EYED DREAM	Ricky Van Shelton	26Dec87	09Apr88	01Oct88	76(1)	41	720
4359.	THEY'RE PLAYING OUR SONG	Al Hirt	12Feb66	23Apr66	11Jun66	39(2)	18	720
4360.	BADLANDS	Badlands	10Jun89	19Aug89	02Dec89	57(2)	26	720
4361.	KASHIF	Kashif	09Apr83	11Jun83	19Nov83	54(2)	33	720
4362.	RECKONING	Grateful Dead	18Apr81	23May81	01Aug81	43(1)	16	720
4363.	DANCING IN THE DRAGON'S JAWS	Bruce Cockburn	23Feb80	28Jun80	02Aug80	45(2)	24	720
4364.	ARE YOU READY FOR FREDDY	Freddy Fender	18Oct75	06Dec75	14Feb76	41(2)	18	720
4365.	THE CHI-LITES GREATEST HITS	The Chi-Lites	21Oct72	09Dec72	31Mar73	55(2)	24	719
4366.	STEEL BREEZE	Steel Breeze	18Sep82	06Nov82	26Mar83	50(4)	28	719
4367.	EARLY HITS OF 1964	Lawrence Welk	11Apr64	23May64	15Aug64	37(2)	19	719
4368.	COUNTRY LIFE	Roxy Music	25Jan75	22Mar75	03May75	37(1)	15	719
4369.	AMERICAN HOT WAX	Soundtrack	08Apr78	20May78	17Jun78	31(1)	11	718
4370.	I'M JUST ME	Charley Pride	24Jul71	21Aug71	27Nov71	50(2)	19	717
4371.	BUSTER	Soundtrack	15Oct88	14Jan89	18Mar89	54(2)	23	717
4372.	CARMEL	Joe Sample	10Feb79	10Mar79	04Aug79	56(2)	26	717
4373.	KISS UNMASKED	KISS	21Jun80	26Jul80	20Sep80	35(2)	14	717
4374.	AVALON SUNSET	Van Morrison	01Jul89	05Aug89	24Mar90	91(2)	39	716
4375.	THE TWAIN SHALL MEET	Eric Burdon & The Animals	06Apr68	22Jun68	19Oct68	79(1)	29	716
4376.	ILLUSIONS ON A DOUBLE DIMPLE	Triumvirat	10Aug74	21Sep74	30Nov74	55(1)	17	716
4377.	LET LOVE RULE	Lenny Kravitz	25Nov89	10Feb90	02Jun90	61(1)	28	715
4378.	ROMANTIC WARRIOR	Return To Forever	03Apr76	29May76	10Jul76	35(2)	15	715
4379.	MIDNIGHT EXPRESS	Soundtrack	25Nov78	10Mar79	19May79	59(1)	26	715
4380.	GOODBYE CRUEL WORLD	Elvis Costello And The Attractions	07Jul84	28Jul84	24Nov84	35(2)	21	715
4381.	BEAST FROM THE EAST	Dokken	03Dec88	17Dec88	25Mar89	33(3)	17	715
4382.	EXTRATERRESTRIAL LIVE	Blue Öyster Cult	15May82	03Jul82	18Sep82	29(2)	19	714
4383.	NOW	Patrice Rushen	16Jun84	28Jul84	01Dec84	40(3)	25	714
4384.	TEACHERS	Soundtrack	27Oct84	01Dec84	09Feb85	34(3)	16	714
4385.	BACK TO FRONT	Gilbert O'Sullivan	06Jan73	17Mar73	12May73	48(1)	19	713
4386.	LIVE ALIVE	Stevie Ray Vaughan And Double Trouble	20Dec86	24Jan87	06Jun87	52(2)	25	713
4387.	GET DOWN	Gene Chandler	25Nov78	17Feb79	07Apr79	47(3)	20	713
4388.	STRAIGHT SHOOTER	The James Gang	18Mar72	13May72	22Jul72	58(1)	19	713
4389.	SINGIN' OUR MIND	The Chad Mitchell Trio	09Nov63	21Dec63	04Apr64	39(1)	22	713
4390.	DOUBLE TIME	Leon Redbone	22Jan77	05Mar77	16Apr77	38(2)	13	713
4391.	ONCE UPON A DREAM	Enchantment	21Jan78	04Mar78	10Jun78	46(2)	21	712
4392.	SHOW TIME	Slave	10Oct81	21Nov81	13Mar82	46(1)	23	712
4393.	SELLING ENGLAND BY THE POUND	Genesis	15Dec73	13Apr74	29Jun74	70(1)	29	712
4394.	THE BEST IS YET TO COME	Grover Washington Jr.	11Dec82	29Jan83	28May83	50(3)	25	712
4395.	EVITA	Festival	09Feb80	29Mar80	07Jun80	50(1)	18	711
4396.	ABOUT LOVE	Gladys Knight & The Pips	31May80	19Jul80	27Sep80	48(1)	18	711
4397.	A CHORUS LINE	Original Cast	16Aug75	27Sep75	20Aug77	98(1)	49	710
4398.	THE SECRET POLICEMAN'S OTHER BALL	Various Artists	20Mar82	15May82	03Jul82	29(1)	16	710
4399.	UNDER WRAPS	Shaun Cassidy	19Aug78	16Sep78	11Nov78	33(2)	13	710
4400.	PRESS TO PLAY	Paul McCartney	13Sep86	11Oct86	07Feb87	30(2)	22	710
4401.	ROCK THE HOUSE	D.J. Jazzy Jeff & The Fresh Prince	25Apr87	17Dec88	25Mar89	83(3)	35	709
4402.	AMY GRANT - THE COLLECTION	Amy Grant	20Sep86	07Feb87	02May87	66(2)	33	709
4403.	DECLARATION	The Alarm	10Mar84	14Apr84	04Aug84	50(2)	22	709
4404.	NAUGHTY	Chaka Khan	21Jun80	12Jul80	04Oct80	43(4)	16	709
4405.	MIRROR	Graham Central Station	26Jun76	14Aug76	09Oct76	46(1)	16	708
4406.	THEMES FROM THE JAMES BOND THRILLERS	The Roland Shaw Orchestra	27Feb65	19Jun65	14Aug65	38(1)	25	708
4407.	EMPIRE BURLESQUE	Bob Dylan	22Jun85	13Jul85	12Oct85	33(3)	17	708
4408.	COUNTRY, MY WAY	Nancy Sinatra	02Sep67	14Oct67	24Feb68	43(1)	26	707
4409.	LADY T	Teena Marie	15Mar80	21Jun80	16Aug80	45(1)	23	706
4410.	THE MESSAGE	Grandmaster Flash & The Furious Five	16Oct82	20Nov82	26Mar83	53(4)	24	706
4411.	PAUL AND..	Paul Stookey	21Aug71	04Sep71	27Nov71	42(2)	15	706
4412.	SKY HIGH	Jigsaw	13Dec75	14Feb76	17Apr76	55(2)	19	705
4413.	FAREWELL	Diana Ross & The Supremes	16May70	30May70	12Sep70	46(1)	18	705
4414.	BIOGRAPH	Bob Dylan	07Dec85	11Jan86	03May86	33(2)	22	705
4415.	ONE GOOD REASON	Paul Carrack	21Nov87	27Feb88	18Jun88	67(1)	31	704
4416.	HITS AGAIN!	Gary Lewis And The Playboys	28May66	06Aug66	05Nov66	47(1)	24	704
4417.	THE PEOPLE'S CHOICE	Ferrante & Teicher	28Nov64	09Jan65	10Apr65	35(3)	20	704
4418.	BLACK ON BLACK	Waylon Jennings	06Mar82	24Apr82	07Aug82	39(2)	23	704
4419.	STANDING ON THE EDGE	Cheap Trick	17Aug85	12Oct85	14Dec85	35(2)	18	704
4420.	THE MANTOVANI TOUCH	Mantovani	02Mar68	20Apr68	17Aug68	64(3)	25	704
4421.	MOTORCYCLE MAMA	Sailcat	12Aug72	07Oct72	11Nov72	38(2)	14	704
4422.	TOO HOT TO STOP	Bar-Kays	13Nov76	26Feb77	09Apr77	69(1)	22	703
4423.	ELVIS NOW	Elvis Presley	12Feb72	18Mar72	17Jun72	43(1)	19	703
4424.	LONE JUSTICE	Lone Justice	11May85	20Jul85	26Oct85	56(1)	25	703
4425.	CLEAR SPIRIT	Spirit	23Aug69	04Oct69	29Nov69	55(2)	15	702
4426.	LOOKING BACK	Stevie Wonder	24Dec77	18Feb78	18Mar78	34(1)	13	701
4427.	HELLO DARLIN'	Conway Twitty	04Jul70	25Jul70	26Dec70	65(1)	26	701
4428.	BRENDA K. STARR	Brenda K. Starr	21May88	16Jul88	29Oct88	58(1)	24	700
4429.	HAPPINESS IS DEAN MARTIN	Dean Martin	13May67	29Jul67	28Oct67	46(1)	25	700
4430.	HIGH ENERGY	The Supremes	22May76	19Jun76	28Aug76	42(2)	15	700
4431.	THE BEST OF THE ALAN PARSONS PROJECT	The Alan Parsons Project	19Nov83	17Dec83	02Jun84	53(4)	29	699
4432.	I GOT YOU (I FEEL GOOD)	James Brown	22Jan66	05Mar66	14May66	36(1)	17	699
4433.	STEALERS WHEEL	Stealers Wheel	24Feb73	26May73	21Jul73	50(1)	22	699
4434.	I HEARD THAT!!	Quincy Jones	02Oct76	06Nov76	08Jan77	43(2)	15	699
4435.	ALL THE WORLD'S A STAGE: RECORDED LIVE	Rush	02Oct76	20Nov76	19Apr80	40(2)	23	698
4436.	THE THOM BELL SESSIONS	Elton John	30Jun79	01Sep79	27Oct79	51(1)	18	698
4437.	JOURNEY TO ADDIS	Third World	25Nov78	17Mar79	05May79	55(2)	24	697
4438.	SHOWCASE	The Sylvers	14Feb76	29May76	31Jul76	58(3)	25	697
4439.	TO WHOM IT MAY CONCERN	Bee Gees	11Nov72	23Dec72	10Feb73	35(1)	14	697
4440.	BARREL	Lee Michaels	01Aug70	05Sep70	05Dec70	51(2)	19	697
4441.	GREATEST HITS	Kenny Rogers & The First Edition	20Feb71	13Mar71	05Jun71	57(1)	16	697

Rank. Title Act	[Entry | Peak | Exit] Peak(Wks) TotWks	Score
4442. **SWEET DREAMS: THE LIFE AND TIMES OF PATSY CLINE (SOUNDTRACK)** Patsy Cline	[16Nov85 | 14Dec85 | 15Mar86] 29(2) 18	696
4443. **BEST OF THE DOOBIES VOL. II** The Doobie Brothers	[21Nov81 | 19Dec81 | 27Feb82] 39(1) 15	696
4444. **OUT WHERE THE BRIGHT LIGHTS ARE GLOWING** Ronnie Milsap	[18Apr81 | 23May81 | 31Oct81] 89(2) 29	696
4445. **THE KEY** Joan Armatrading	[30Apr83 | 11Jun83 | 24Sep83] 32(1) 22	696
4446. **TA MARA & THE SEEN** Ta Mara & The Seen	[02Nov85 | 01Feb86 | 19Apr86] 54(3) 25	695
4447. **THE DIONNE WARWICKE STORY** Dionne Warwicke	[30Oct71 | 18Dec71 | 19Feb72] 48(1) 17	695
4448. **CAN'T STOP THE LOVE** Maze Featuring Frankie Beverly	[30Mar85 | 04May85 | 19Oct85] 45(2) 30	695
4449. **YESTERDAY, TODAY & TOMORROW** Spinners	[02Apr77 | 30Apr77 | 25Jun77] 26(1) 13	695
4450. **MEASURE FOR MEASURE** Icehouse	[24May86 | 09Aug86 | 01Nov86] 55(3) 24	694
4451. **20 GREATEST HITS** The Beatles	[13Nov82 | 15Jan83 | 12May84] 50(2) 28	693
4452. **FIREWORKS** Jose Feliciano	[30May70 | 08Aug70 | 10Oct70] 57(1) 20	693
4453. **GHETTO MUSIC: THE BLUEPRINT OF HIP HOP** Boogie Down Productions	[22Jul89 | 12Aug89 | 11Nov89] 36(2) 17	693
4454. **PRECIOUS MOMENTS** Jermaine Jackson	[22Mar86 | 03May86 | 16Aug86] 46(2) 22	693
4455. **JOHN PARR** John Parr	[15Dec84 | 23Mar85 | 08Jun85] 48(2) 26	693
4456. **ENUFF Z'NUFF** Enuff Z'Nuff	[30Sep89 | 25Nov89 | 19May90] 74(1) 34	693
4457. **THE ORIGINALS** KISS	[21Aug76 | 25Sep76 | 25Jun77] 36(2) 17	692
4458. **APOCALYPSE** The Mahavishnu Orchestra	[01Jun74 | 13Jul74 | 31Aug74] 43(2) 14	692
4459. **A CHANGE OF HEART** David Sanborn	[14Feb87 | 28Mar87 | 16Jan88] 74(2) 37	692
4460. **DON'T DISTURB THIS GROOVE** The System	[18Apr87 | 04Jul87 | 03Oct87] 62(5) 25	692
4461. **OSIBISA** Osibisa	[03Jul71 | 14Aug71 | 06Nov71] 55(1) 19	692
4462. **EMOTION** Samantha Sang	[11Mar78 | 22Apr78 | 10Jun78] 29(1) 14	692
4463. **PETULA CLARK'S GREATEST HITS, VOL. 1** Petula Clark	[28Dec68 | 15Feb69 | 19Apr69] 57(1) 17	692
4464. **SUNBURN** Sun	[06May78 | 02Sep78 | 30Sep78] 69(1) 22	691
4465. **JUST COOLIN'** Levert	[26Nov88 | 22Apr89 | 24Jun89] 79(1) 31	691
4466. **PASSAGE** Carpenters	[22Oct77 | 03Dec77 | 18Feb78] 49(1) 18	691
4467. **KOHUEPT (LIVE IN LENINGRAD)** Billy Joel	[07Nov87 | 05Dec87 | 05Mar88] 38(1) 18	691
4468. **LET'S DO IT** Roy Ayers	[11Mar78 | 29Apr78 | 03Jun78] 33(1) 13	690
4469. **IT'S MY LIFE** Talk Talk	[07Apr84 | 16Jun84 | 01Sep84] 42(3) 22	690
4470. **ANIMAL MAGNETISM** Scorpions	[17May80 | 05Jul80 | 04Oct80] 52(1) 21	690
4471. **SONGS FROM A ROOM** Leonard Cohen	[12Apr69 | 10May69 | 02Aug69] 63(2) 17	690
4472. **SUN SECRETS** The Eric Burdon Band	[21Dec74 | 08Mar75 | 05Apr75] 51(1) 16	690
4473. **INNER CITY BLUES** Grover Washington Jr.	[01Jan72 | 26Feb72 | 17Jun72] 62(2) 25	690
4474. **THE WAY IT WAS - THE WAY IT IS** Lou Rawls	[14Jun69 | 06Sep69 | 15Nov69] 71(1) 23	689
4475. **NEW GOLD HITS** The 4 Seasons	[24Jun67 | 29Jul67 | 09Dec67] 37(1) 25	689
4476. **NEW CLEAR DAYS** The Vapors	[16Aug80 | 06Dec80 | 21Feb81] 62(1) 28	689
4477. **GARCIA** Jerry Garcia	[29Jan72 | 19Feb72 | 29Apr72] 35(2) 14	689
4478. **I'VE NEVER BEEN TO ME** Charlene	[10Apr82 | 12Jun82 | 21Aug82] 36(2) 20	688
4479. **CLAMBAKE (SOUNDTRACK)** Elvis Presley	[02Dec67 | 10Feb68 | 02Mar68] 40(1) 14	687
4480. **NEIL DIAMOND'S GREATEST HITS** Neil Diamond	[03Aug68 | 05Dec70 | 29May71] 100(1) 40	687
4481. **JOHN COUGAR** John Cougar	[18Aug79 | 05Jan80 | 01Mar80] 64(2) 29	687
4482. **ALL BY MYSELF** Eddie Kendricks	[22May71 | 19Jun71 | 26Feb72] 80(2) 32	686
4483. **HANG ON FOR YOUR LIFE** Shooting Star	[19Sep81 | 05Dec81 | 10Apr82] 92(1) 30	686
4484. **TNT** Tanya Tucker	[02Dec78 | 24Feb79 | 28Apr79] 54(1) 22	686
4485. **FIRST PULL UP THEN PULL DOWN** Hot Tuna	[26Jun71 | 24Jul71 | 18Sep71] 43(1) 13	685
4486. **SOUL KISS** Olivia Newton-John	[02Nov85 | 23Nov85 | 15Feb86] 29(3) 16	685
4487. **MISTRIAL** Lou Reed	[24May86 | 05Jul86 | 11Oct86] 47(2) 21	684
4488. **STONEDHENGE** Ten Years After	[22Feb69 | 12Apr69 | 21Jun69] 61(1) 18	684
4489. **SOLDIERS UNDER COMMAND** Stryper	[28Sep85 | 30Nov85 | 04Apr87] 84(2) 64	684
4490. **CRAZY FOR YOU** Earl Klugh	[14Nov81 | 05Dec81 | 15May82] 53(2) 27	683
4491. **SWANS AGAINST THE SUN** Michael Murphey	[06Dec75 | 17Jan76 | 28Feb76] 44(2) 13	683
4492. **PROPOSITIONS** Bar-Kays	[20Nov82 | 25Dec82 | 04Jun83] 51(3) 29	683
4493. **$1,000,000.00 WEEKEND** The Ventures	[23Dec67 | 16Mar68 | 11May68] 55(2) 21	682
4494. **GREEN LIGHT** Bonnie Raitt	[06Mar82 | 17Apr82 | 03Jul82] 38(1) 18	682
4495. **FINE YOUNG CANNIBALS** Fine Young Cannibals	[25Jan86 | 24May86 | 02Aug86] 49(1) 28	682
4496. **SOMETHING ABOUT YOU** Angela Bofill	[21Nov81 | 19Dec81 | 17Apr82] 61(4) 22	681
4497. **WRITER: CAROLE KING** Carole King	[01May71 | 21Aug71 | 30Oct71] 84(1) 27	681
4498. **THE YEAR 2000** The O'Jays	[30Aug80 | 04Oct80 | 15Nov80] 36(2) 12	681
4499. **DESIDERATA** Les Crane	[04Dec71 | 08Jan72 | 12Feb72] 32(2) 11	680
4500. **RAM JAM** Ram Jam	[10Sep77 | 05Nov77 | 26Nov77] 34(1) 12	680
4501. **FINIAN'S RAINBOW** Soundtrack	[05Oct68 | 15Feb69 | 29Mar69] 90(1) 26	680
4502. **THE KING FAMILY SHOW!** King Family	[10Jul65 | 14Aug65 | 23Oct65] 34(1) 16	680
4503. **THE ICEBERG (FREEDOM OF SPEECH... JUST WATCH WHAT YOU SAY)** Ice-T	[28Oct89 | 11Nov89 | 05May90] 37(2) 28	680
4504. **UMMAGUMMA** Pink Floyd	[03Jan70 | 21Mar70 | 04Jul70] 74(1) 27	680
4505. **RADIO ACTIVE** Pat Travers	[28Mar81 | 25Apr81 | 04Jul81] 37(2) 15	679
4506. **HILLBILLY DELUXE** Dwight Yoakam	[16May87 | 13Jun87 | 21Nov87] 55(2) 28	679
4507. **QUICKSILVER MESSENGER SERVICE** Quicksilver Messenger Service	[22Jun68 | 12Oct68 | 07Dec68] 63(1) 25	679
4508. **WILD TALES** Graham Nash	[26Jan74 | 02Mar74 | 27Apr74] 34(1) 14	678
4509. **FOR ONCE IN MY LIFE** O.C. Smith	[01Mar69 | 12Apr69 | 07Jun69] 50(1) 15	678
4510. **ALVIN LEE & COMPANY** Ten Years After	[08Apr72 | 27May72 | 05Aug72] 55(2) 18	677
4511. **OUTLAW** War	[20Mar82 | 08May82 | 18Sep82] 48(2) 27	677
4512. **ENIGMATIC OCEAN** Jean-Luc Ponty	[01Oct77 | 12Nov77 | 14Jan78] 35(1) 16	677
4513. **BAD FOR GOOD** Jim Steinman	[16May81 | 11Jul81 | 05Sep81] 63(1) 17	676
4514. **RENAISSANCE** The Association	[07Jan67 | 18Mar67 | 15Apr67] 34(1) 15	676
4515. **TIN MACHINE** Tin Machine	[10Jun89 | 01Jul89 | 30Sep89] 28(1) 17	676
4516. **COOL NIGHT** Paul Davis	[19Dec81 | 22May82 | 03Jul82] 52(1) 29	676
4517. **SECONDS OUT** Genesis	[03Dec77 | 24Dec77 | 18Mar78] 47(2) 16	676
4518. **RAINBOW RISING** Blackmore's Rainbow	[05Jun76 | 10Jul76 | 25Sep76] 48(2) 17	676
4519. **1988 SUMMER OLYMPICS-ONE MOMENT IN TIME** Various Artists	[24Sep88 | 22Oct88 | 14Jan89] 31(2) 17	676
4520. **FUTURE BLUES** Canned Heat	[12Sep70 | 17Oct70 | 16Jan71] 59(2) 19	675
4521. **CLOSE UP** Tom Jones	[17Jun72 | 05Aug72 | 28Oct72] 64(1) 20	675
4522. **(IF YOU LET ME MAKE LOVE TO YOU THEN) WHY CAN'T I TOUCH YOU?** Ronnie Dyson	[05Sep70 | 24Oct70 | 02Jan71] 55(1) 18	675
4523. **PEARLS-SONGS OF GOFFIN AND KING** Carole King	[07Jun80 | 26Jul80 | 27Sep80] 44(1) 17	674
4524. **SANDS OF TIME** The S.O.S. Band	[24May86 | 05Jul86 | 04Oct86] 44(2) 20	674
4525. **ODYSSEY** Yngwie J. Malmsteen's Rising Force	[23Apr88 | 14May88 | 20Aug88] 40(2) 18	674
4526. **AMERICAN MADE** The Oak Ridge Boys	[26Feb83 | 09Apr83 | 30Jul83] 51(3) 23	673
4527. **SWEET CHARITY** Soundtrack	[08Mar69 | 10May69 | 02Aug69] 72(2) 22	673
4528. **MASK OF SMILES** John Waite	[31Aug85 | 12Oct85 | 14Dec85] 36(2) 16	672
4529. **KEYED UP** Ronnie Milsap	[30Apr83 | 25Jun83 | 03Sep83] 36(1) 19	672
4530. **LEPRECHAUN** Chick Corea	[06Mar76 | 01May76 | 12Jun76] 42(1) 15	672
4531. **ELECTRIC LIGHT ORCHESTRA II** Electric Light Orchestra	[21Apr73 | 23Jun73 | 15Sep73] 62(2) 22	672
4532. **SINGLE LIFE** Cameo	[13Jul85 | 17Aug85 | 11Jan86] 58(2) 27	671
4533. **PASSIONWORKS** Heart	[17Sep83 | 22Oct83 | 04Feb84] 39(1) 21	671
4534. **MANILOW** Barry Manilow	[30Nov85 | 28Dec85 | 09Aug86] 42(3) 24	671
4535. **DRASTIC MEASURES** Kansas	[13Aug83 | 24Sep83 | 31Dec83] 41(2) 21	670
4536. **SONG BIRD** Deniece Williams	[19Nov77 | 07Jan78 | 01Apr78] 66(1) 20	670
4537. **BEFORE AND AFTER** Chad & Jeremy	[26Jun65 | 28Aug65 | 23Oct65] 37(2) 18	670
4538. **ANDY GIBB'S GREATEST HITS** Andy Gibb	[06Dec80 | 31Jan81 | 04Apr81] 46(1) 18	670
4539. **THREE O'CLOCK IN THE MORNING** Bert Kaempfert And His Orchestra	[10Jul65 | 11Sep65 | 04Dec65] 42(1) 22	670
4540. **SILKY SOUL** Maze Featuring Frankie Beverly	[23Sep89 | 14Oct89 | 17Feb90] 37(2) 22	670
4541. **INCOGNITO** Spyro Gyra	[23Oct82 | 20Nov82 | 02Apr83] 46(2) 24	669
4542. **GIMME SOME LOVIN'** The Spencer Davis Group	[25Mar67 | 27May67 | 09Sep67] 54(3) 25	668
4543. **BAPTISM** Joan Baez	[10Aug68 | 19Oct68 | 25Jan69] 84(2) 25	668
4544. **PRIMITIVE COOL** Mick Jagger	[03Oct87 | 17Oct87 | 13Feb88] 41(2) 20	668
4545. **SECRETS** Gil Scott-Heron & Brian Jackson	[09Sep78 | 25Nov78 | 27Jan79] 61(1) 21	667
4546. **ACROSS 110TH STREET (SOUNDTRACK)** Bobby Womack	[13Jan73 | 14Apr73 | 26May73] 50(1) 20	667
4547. **THE BEST OF CHAD MITCHELL TRIO** The Chad Mitchell Trio	[28Sep63 | 09Nov63 | 04Apr64] 63(1) 28	667
4548. **IN HEAT** Love Unlimited	[12Oct74 | 07Dec74 | 12Apr75] 85(1) 27	667
4549. **"A"** Jethro Tull	[13Sep80 | 11Oct80 | 29Nov80] 30(2) 12	667

Rank. Title Act
[Entry | Peak | Exit] Peak(Wks) TotWks Score

4550. A TASTE FOR PASSION Jean-Luc Ponty
[27Oct79 | 08Dec79 | 15Mar80] 54(1) 21 666

4551. THE MOTHERS/FILLMORE EAST-JUNE 1971 The Mothers
[21Aug71 | 18Sep71 | 27Nov71] 38(1) 15 666

4552. TOUGHER THAN LEATHER Willie Nelson
[19Mar83 | 21May83 | 30Jul83] 39(1) 20 666

4553. WHITE WINDS Andreas Vollenweider
[02Mar85 | 22Jun85 | 23Nov85] 76(2) 39 665

4554. SOME TIME IN NEW YORK CITY John Lennon & Yoko Ono
[01Jul72 | 12Aug72 | 21Oct72] 48(2) 17 665

4555. CONEY ISLAND BABY Lou Reed
[07Feb76 | 06Mar76 | 08May76] 41(1) 14 665

4556. HEARTLAND Michael Stanley Band
[27Sep80 | 28Feb81 | 02May81] 86(2) 32 664

4557. FEEL NO FRET Average White Band
[07Apr79 | 19May79 | 14Jul79] 32(1) 15 664

4558. BOTH SIDES OF HERMAN'S HERMITS Herman's Hermits
[20Aug66 | 15Oct66 | 07Jan67] 48(1) 21 664

4559. THE LORD OF THE RINGS Soundtrack
[09Dec78 | 10Feb79 | 24Feb79] 39(1) 12 664

4560. OUT ON A LIMB Moms Mabley
[29Feb64 | 25Apr64 | 08Aug64] 48(1) 24 663

4561. UNDER THE BLUE MOON New Edition
[20Dec86 | 07Feb87 | 23May87] 43(2) 23 663

4562. LOVE MAN Otis Redding
[19Jul69 | 23Aug69 | 18Oct69] 46(2) 14 663

4563. ROCK YOUR BABY George McCrae
[03Aug74 | 07Sep74 | 09Nov74] 38(2) 15 663

4564. ISOLATION Toto
[24Nov84 | 15Dec84 | 13Apr85] 42(4) 21 663

4565. THIS WAS Jethro Tull
[01Mar69 | 12Apr69 | 21Jun69] 62(2) 17 663

4566. SEE The Rascals
[10Jan70 | 07Feb70 | 25Apr70] 45(3) 16 663

4567. GREATEST STORIES-LIVE Harry Chapin
[01May76 | 29May76 | 04Sep76] 48(2) 19 662

4568. THE HIT MAN Eddie Kendricks
[12Jul75 | 30Aug75 | 27Dec75] 63(1) 25 662

4569. ALPHABET CITY ABC
[22Aug87 | 19Sep87 | 06Feb88] 48(3) 25 662

4570. ELVIS-A LEGENDARY PERFORMER, VOLUME 2 Elvis Presley
[07Feb76 | 06Mar76 | 29May76] 46(2) 17 662

4571. RAY CHARLES INVITES YOU TO LISTEN Ray Charles
[08Jul67 | 02Sep67 | 24Feb68] 76(2) 34 662

4572. CAUGHT IN THE ACT - LIVE Styx
[21Apr84 | 19May84 | 28Jul84] 31(2) 15 662

4573. WHO'S FOOLIN' WHO One Way
[03Apr82 | 12Jun82 | 04Sep82] 51(1) 23 662

4574. HIGH ON THE HOG Black Oak Arkansas
[24Nov73 | 16Feb74 | 20Apr74] 52(1) 22 661

4575. LEAD ME ON Maxine Nightingale
[21Jul79 | 29Sep79 | 17Nov79] 45(2) 18 661

4576. GLORYHALLASTOOPID (OR PIN THE TAIL ON THE FUNKY) Parliament
[22Dec79 | 09Feb80 | 26Apr80] 44(2) 19 661

4577. THE SOLID GOLD STEINWAY Roger Williams
[08Feb64 | 21Mar64 | 13Jun64] 27(1) 19 661

4578. BLOODROCK LIVE Bloodrock
[03Jun72 | 26Aug72 | 28Oct72] 67(1) 22 661

4579. LIFELINE Roy Ayers Ubiquity
[02Jul77 | 13Aug77 | 17Dec77] 72(2) 25 660

4580. WALK UNDER LADDERS Joan Armatrading
[17Oct81 | 27Mar82 | 22May82] 88(2) 32 660

4581. MESOPOTAMIA The B-52s
[20Feb82 | 13Mar82 | 19Jun82] 35(2) 18 660

4582. THE MAGAZINE Rickie Lee Jones
[13Oct84 | 10Nov84 | 02Mar85] 44(2) 21 659

4583. SINFONIAS Waldo De Los Rios
[05Jun71 | 17Jul71 | 18Sep71] 53(2) 16 659

4584. THE BEST OF CHAD & JEREMY Chad & Jeremy
[23Apr66 | 02Jul66 | 24Sep66] 49(1) 23 659

4585. IN THE PUREST FORM Mass Production
[21Jul79 | 29Sep79 | 10Nov79] 43(1) 17 659

Rank. Title Act
[Entry | Peak | Exit] Peak(Wks) TotWks Score

4586. INTO THE MUSIC Van Morrison
[08Sep79 | 13Oct79 | 01Dec79] 43(2) 13 659

4587. PART OF THE GAME Pablo Cruise
[17Nov79 | 15Dec79 | 08Mar80] 39(1) 17 659

4588. FROM ELVIS PRESLEY BOULEVARD, MEMPHIS, TENNESSEE Elvis Presley
[05Jun76 | 17Jul76 | 25Sep76] 41(1) 17 658

4589. AS FAR AS SIAM Red Rider
[12Sep81 | 05Dec81 | 20Feb82] 65(2) 24 658

4590. SHADOWS AND LIGHT Joni Mitchell
[04Oct80 | 25Oct80 | 17Jan81] 38(2) 16 657

4591. LOVE ME FOR A REASON The Osmonds
[02Nov74 | 28Dec74 | 01Feb75] 47(1) 14 657

4592. WILDSIDE Loverboy
[12Sep87 | 17Oct87 | 30Jan88] 42(1) 21 657

4593. WORKS, VOLUME 2 Emerson, Lake & Palmer
[10Dec77 | 21Jan78 | 11Mar78] 37(1) 14 657

4594. EVE OF DESTRUCTION Barry McGuire
[25Sep65 | 04Dec65 | 12Feb66] 37(1) 21 656

4595. H Bob James
[12Jul80 | 16Aug80 | 08Nov80] 47(3) 18 656

4596. STRANGEWAYS, HERE WE COME The Smiths
[10Oct87 | 31Oct87 | 09Apr88] 55(2) 27 656

4597. MY KIND OF BROADWAY Frank Sinatra
[25Dec65 | 05Mar66 | 09Apr66] 30(1) 16 656

4598. STORM AT SUNUP Gino Vannelli
[19Jul75 | 27Sep75 | 20Dec75] 66(1) 23 656

4599. DEAD SET Grateful Dead
[19Sep81 | 10Oct81 | 28Nov81] 29(2) 11 656

4600. LADIES INVITED The J. Geils Band
[01Dec73 | 05Jan74 | 30Mar74] 51(1) 18 655

4601. THE BIG SOUNDS OF THE DRAGS! Various Artists
[14Dec63 | 07Mar64 | 11Apr64] 27(1) 18 655

4602. BABYFACE The Wing And A Prayer Fife And Drum Corps
[14Feb76 | 17Apr76 | 29May76] 47(1) 16 655

4603. RICK NELSON IN CONCERT Rick Nelson
[21Feb70 | 18Apr70 | 27Jun70] 54(1) 19 655

4604. DON'T IT MAKE YOU WANT TO GO HOME? Joe South
[17Jan70 | 07Mar70 | 20Jun70] 60(2) 23 655

4605. THE ZOMBIES The Zombies
[27Feb65 | 01May65 | 19Jun65] 39(1) 17 655

4606. LOVE STORM Tavares
[30Apr77 | 28May77 | 24Sep77] 59(2) 22 655

4607. THE PARTRIDGE FAMILY NOTEBOOK The Partridge Family
[16Dec72 | 27Jan73 | 31Mar73] 41(1) 16 654

4608. GERRY & THE PACEMAKERS GREATEST HITS Gerry And The Pacemakers
[15May65 | 24Jul65 | 09Oct65] 44(2) 22 654

4609. (PURPLE PASSAGES) Deep Purple
[21Oct72 | 02Dec72 | 03Mar73] 57(1) 20 654

4610. TAKING LIBERTIES Elvis Costello
[11Oct80 | 08Nov80 | 10Jan81] 28(1) 14 654

4611. HOT HOUSE FLOWERS Wynton Marsalis
[13Oct84 | 10Nov84 | 06Jul85] 90(2) 39 654

4612. EARTH - SUN - MOON Love And Rockets
[31Oct87 | 30Jan88 | 07May88] 64(2) 28 653

4613. SAVAGE Eurythmics
[26Dec87 | 06Feb88 | 30Apr88] 41(2) 19 653

4614. BACK TO EARTH Cat Stevens
[23Dec78 | 10Feb79 | 31Mar79] 33(1) 15 653

4615. WAYLON "LIVE" Waylon Jennings
[18Dec76 | 05Feb77 | 09Apr77] 46(1) 17 653

4616. BIG BROTHER & THE HOLDING COMPANY Big Brother And The Holding Company
[02Sep67 | 14Oct67 | 04Jan69] 60(2) 30 653

4617. POCO Poco
[06Jun70 | 08Aug70 | 10Oct70] 58(1) 19 653

4618. IT FEELS SO GOOD The Manhattans
[26Feb77 | 28May77 | 09Jul77] 68(1) 20 652

4619. BATMAN THEME Neal Hefti
[12Mar66 | 28May66 | 30Jul66] 41(2) 21 652

4620. JOYSTICK Dazz Band
[17Dec83 | 25Feb84 | 28Jul84] 73(2) 33 652

Rank. Title Act
[Entry | Peak | Exit] Peak(Wks) TotWks Score

4621. FLASH Jeff Beck
[20Jul85 | 17Aug85 | 16Nov85] 39(2) 18 652

4622. HERE'S JOHNNY--MAGIC MOMENTS FROM THE TONIGHT SHOW TV Soundtrack
[21Dec74 | 25Jan75 | 01Mar75] 30(2) 11 652

4623. FOR SWINGIN' LIVERS ONLY! Allan Sherman
[28Nov64 | 16Jan65 | 20Mar65] 32(2) 17 652

4624. BABY THE RAIN MUST FALL Glenn Yarbrough
[12Jun65 | 17Jul65 | 20Nov65] 35(1) 24 652

4625. FLUSH THE FASHION Alice Cooper
[24May80 | 05Jul80 | 13Sep80] 44(2) 17 651

4626. TIME WON'T LET ME The Outsiders
[28May66 | 23Jul66 | 10Sep66] 37(2) 16 651

4627. JUICE Oran 'Juice' Jones
[20Sep86 | 15Nov86 | 14Feb87] 44(1) 22 651

4628. DIFFICULT TO CURE Rainbow
[07Mar81 | 18Apr81 | 20Jun81] 50(2) 16 650

4629. REAL FRIENDS The Friends Of Distinction
[28Mar70 | 25Apr70 | 15Aug70] 68(1) 21 650

4630. MA Rare Earth
[16Jun73 | 18Aug73 | 17Nov73] 65(2) 23 650

4631. STRANGERS IN THE NIGHT UFO
[03Feb79 | 24Mar79 | 12May79] 42(1) 15 650

4632. GOOD KING BAD George Benson
[26Jun76 | 21Aug76 | 09Oct76] 51(2) 16 649

4633. SOME TOUGH CITY Tony Carey
[31Mar84 | 19May84 | 08Sep84] 60(2) 24 649

4634. SLAYED? Slade
[17Feb73 | 07Jul73 | 11Aug73] 69(1) 26 649

4635. BETTER THAN HEAVEN Stacey Q
[27Sep86 | 25Oct86 | 20Jun87] 59(2) 39 649

4636. BEST OF TRAFFIC Traffic
[03Jan70 | 07Feb70 | 04Apr70] 48(3) 14 649

4637. PICKIN' UP THE PIECES Poco
[28Jun69 | 20Sep69 | 15Nov69] 63(1) 21 649

4638. PROCOL HARUM Procol Harum
[23Sep67 | 02Dec67 | 06Jan68] 47(1) 16 649

4639. THOSE OF YOU WITH OR WITHOUT CHILDREN, YOU'LL UNDERSTAND Bill Cosby
[21Jun86 | 19Jul86 | 27Sep86] 26(2) 15 648

4640. DO WHAT YOU WANNA DO The Dramatics
[13May78 | 01Jul78 | 19Aug78] 44(1) 15 648

4641. TYCOON Tycoon
[31Mar79 | 16Jun79 | 21Jul79] 41(1) 17 648

4642. THE PLAN The Osmonds
[07Jul73 | 04Aug73 | 17Nov73] 58(1) 20 648

4643. AIN'T THAT GOOD NEWS Sam Cooke
[04Apr64 | 11Jul64 | 08Aug64] 34(1) 19 648

4644. SKYWRITER The Jackson 5ive
[14Apr73 | 16Jun73 | 28Jul73] 44(1) 16 647

4645. VIVA HATE Morrissey
[09Apr88 | 30Apr88 | 20Aug88] 48(2) 20 647

4646. BLACK & BLUE Harold Melvin And The Blue Notes
[10Nov73 | 12Jan74 | 23Mar74] 57(1) 20 647

4647. THE VENTURES/BATMAN THEME The Ventures
[05Mar66 | 21May66 | 23Jul66] 42(2) 21 646

4648. TAKE NO PRISONERS Molly Hatchet
[05Dec81 | 16Jan82 | 06Mar82] 36(1) 14 645

4649. NEW WAYS BUT LOVE STAYS The Supremes
[24Oct70 | 02Jan71 | 13Feb71] 68(2) 17 645

4650. THE PACIFIC AGE Orchestral Manoeuvres In The Dark
[18Oct86 | 29Nov86 | 21Mar87] 47(2) 23 645

4651. WE'D LIKE TO TEACH THE WORLD TO SING The New Seekers
[25Dec71 | 29Jan72 | 25Mar72] 37(2) 14 645

4652. THIS IS NEW! The Righteous Brothers
[19Jun65 | 07Aug65 | 30Oct65] 39(1) 20 645

4653. WE ALL KNOW WHO WE ARE Cameo
[18Feb78 | 22Apr78 | 22Jul78] 58(2) 23 644

4654. DON'T SUPPOSE Limahl
[27Apr85 | 22Jun85 | 07Sep85] 41(1) 20 642

4655. IF I RULED THE WORLD - SONGS FOR THE JET SET Tony Bennett
[22May65 | 31Jul65 | 16Oct65] 47(2) 22 642

Rank	Title	Act	Entry	Peak	Exit	Peak(Wks)	TotWks	Score
4656	8:15 12:15	Bill Cosby	12Jul69	30Aug69	25Oct69	62(2)	16	642
4657	CACTUS	Cactus	25Jul70	10Oct70	21Nov70	54(2)	18	642
4658	MUSICMAGIC	Return To Forever	02Apr77	21May77	23Jul77	38(1)	17	642
4659	PORTRAIT OF PETULA	Petula Clark	17May69	31May69	26Jul69	37(2)	11	642
4660	VOCALESE	The Manhattan Transfer	10Aug85	12Oct85	10May86	74(2)	40	641
4661	STREET OPERA	Ashford & Simpson	29May82	03Jul82	09Oct82	45(3)	20	641
4662	25 #1 HITS FROM 25 YEARS	Various Artists	04Jun83	02Jul83	10Dec83	42(2)	28	641
4663	THE LAST RECORD ALBUM	Little Feat	15Nov75	13Dec75	21Feb76	36(2)	15	641
4664	THE BIZ NEVER SLEEPS	The Diabolical Biz Markie	28Oct89	04Nov89	19May90	66(2)	30	640
4665	NOVELLA	Renaissance	05Feb77	02Apr77	21May77	46(1)	16	640
4666	VOLCANIC ACTION OF MY SOUL	Ray Charles	29May71	26Jun71	11Sep71	52(1)	16	640
4667	SMALL CHANGE	Prism	06Feb82	03Apr82	19Jun82	53(1)	20	640
4668	DIANA ROSS LIVE AT CAESARS PALACE	Diana Ross	15Jun74	17Aug74	05Oct74	64(2)	17	640
4669	WAR HEROES	Jimi Hendrix	09Dec72	10Feb73	07Apr73	48(1)	18	640
4670	WINDS OF CHANGE	Eric Burdon & The Animals	23Sep67	25Nov67	03Feb68	42(2)	20	639
4671	REFLECTIONS	Jerry Garcia	14Feb76	10Apr76	15May76	42(1)	14	639
4672	THE LAST COMMAND	W.A.S.P.	23Nov85	14Dec85	26Apr86	49(2)	23	639
4673	GUITAR FREAKOUT	The Ventures	18Feb67	15Apr67	12Aug67	57(1)	26	639
4674	I HAVE DREAMED	The Lettermen	05Apr69	07Jun69	02Aug69	74(1)	18	638
4675	CLOSE-UP	David Sanborn	16Jul88	23Jul88	21Jan89	59(4)	28	638
4676	TAYLORED IN SILK	Johnnie Taylor	14Jul73	01Sep73	24Nov73	54(1)	20	638
4677	WANNA BE A STAR	Chilliwack	03Oct81	19Dec81	24Apr82	78(1)	30	638
4678	ELECTRIC UNIVERSE	Earth, Wind & Fire	03Dec83	07Jan84	17Mar84	40(2)	16	638
4679	JAMES BROWN PLAYS JAMES BROWN - TODAY & YESTERDAY	James Brown	20Nov65	22Jan66	26Mar66	42(1)	19	637
4680	SAINTS & SINNERS	Johnny Winter	23Feb74	06Apr74	08Jun74	42(1)	16	637
4681	SAN ANTONIO ROSE	Willie Nelson & Ray Price	14Jun80	19Jul80	29Nov80	70(2)	25	637
4682	YOU'RE ALL I NEED	Marvin Gaye & Tammi Terrell	21Sep68	07Dec68	08Feb69	60(2)	21	637
4683	AMERICAN EXCESS	Point Blank	25Apr81	12Sep81	03Oct81	80(1)	24	637
4684	24 CARROTS	Al Stewart	13Sep80	11Oct80	06Dec80	37(2)	13	637
4685	OFFRAMP	Pat Metheny Group	22May82	19Jun82	27Nov82	50(2)	28	637
4686	SEPARATE WAYS	Elvis Presley	27Jan73	17Mar73	26May73	46(1)	18	636
4687	SOMETIMES YOU WIN	Dr. Hook	24Nov79	12Jan80	05Jul80	71(2)	32	635
4688	THE UP ESCALATOR	Graham Parker And The Rumour	31May80	05Jul80	06Sep80	40(1)	15	635
4689	OLIAS OF SUNHILLOW	Jon Anderson	24Jul76	11Sep76	16Oct76	47(1)	13	634
4690	THE LAST WORD IN LONESOME	Eddy Arnold	30Jul66	17Sep66	02Sep67	46(1)	22	634
4691	COME TASTE THE BAND	Deep Purple	06Dec75	10Jan76	06Mar76	43(2)	14	634
4692	SUPER BAD	James Brown	30Jan71	03Apr71	08May71	61(1)	15	634
4693	MAGIC JOURNEY	The Salsoul Orchestra	25Jun77	01Oct77	05Nov77	61(1)	20	633
4694	ORIGINAL MUSIC FROM THE MAN FROM U.N.C.L.E.	Hugo Montenegro, His Orchestra And Chorus	29Jan66	28May66	11Jun66	52(1)	20	633
4695	THE KNIFE FEELS LIKE JUSTICE	Brian Setzer	22Mar86	26Apr86	19Jul86	45(3)	18	633
4696	PLANET P	Planet P	26Mar83	28May83	27Aug83	42(2)	23	633
4697	LOVEDRIVE	Scorpions	28Jul79	29Sep79	29Dec79	55(2)	23	632
4698	HEARTLAND	The Judds	04Apr87	25Apr87	14Nov87	52(2)	31	632
4699	CALL OF THE WEST	Wall Of Voodoo	15Jan83	09Apr83	18Jun83	45(2)	23	631
4700	THE GETAWAY	Chris de Burgh	09Apr83	18Jun83	03Sep83	43(2)	22	631
4701	GREATEST HITS, VOLUME TWO	George Strait	26Sep87	07Nov87	23Apr88	68(2)	31	631
4702	YER' ALBUM	The James Gang	01Nov69	07Feb70	11Apr70	83(1)	24	631
4703	ROSS (II)	Diana Ross	16Jul83	20Aug83	05Nov83	32(1)	17	630
4704	RAGE FOR ORDER	Queensryche	26Jul86	09Aug86	07Feb87	47(5)	21	630
4705	B.B. KING IN LONDON	B.B. King	16Oct71	13Nov71	05Feb72	57(1)	17	629
4706	AN AMERICAN TAIL	Soundtrack	31Jan87	28Mar87	06Jun87	42(2)	19	629
4707	MYSTERY TO ME	Fleetwood Mac	17Nov73	22Dec73	27Sep75	67(1)	26	629
4708	BILL WITHERS LIVE AT CARNEGIE HALL	Bill Withers	21Apr73	16Jun73	08Sep73	63(2)	21	629
4709	THE RECORDS	The Records	25Aug79	20Oct79	24Nov79	41(2)	14	629
4710	BJ4	Bob James	09Apr77	14May77	30Jul77	38(1)	17	629
4711	ONE OF THE BOYS	Roger Daltrey	09Jul77	17Sep77	12Nov77	46(1)	19	629
4712	CAROL HENSEL'S EXERCISE AND DANCE PROGRAM, VOLUME 2	Carol Hensel	19Dec81	06Mar82	26Jun82	70(1)	28	628
4713	HER GREATEST HITS	Carole King	01Apr78	06May78	24Jun78	47(2)	13	628
4714	THE LITTLE OLD LADY FROM PASADENA	Jan & Dean	10Oct64	16Jan65	20Feb65	40(1)	20	628
4715	BIG LIFE	Night Ranger	11Apr87	02May87	08Aug87	28(2)	18	628
4716	KAYA	Bob Marley And The Wailers	22Apr78	27May78	12Aug78	50(2)	17	628
4717	GITARZAN	Ray Stevens	21Jun69	19Jul69	13Sep69	57(1)	13	628
4718	OTHER ROADS	Boz Scaggs	04Jun88	25Jun88	01Oct88	47(4)	18	628
4719	LATE AT NIGHT	Billy Preston	08Mar80	10May80	05Jul80	49(2)	18	627
4720	CATHOLIC BOY	The Jim Carroll Band	15Nov80	07Mar81	18Apr81	73(2)	23	627
4721	AMOR	Eydie Gorme	12Sep64	14Nov64	06Feb65	54(2)	22	627
4722	SOMEWHERE IN AFRIKA	Manfred Mann's Earth Band	28Jan84	24Mar84	16Jun84	40(2)	21	627
4723	BUILT TO LAST	Grateful Dead	18Nov89	02Dec89	24Feb90	27(1)	15	626
4724	THE KINGS ARE HERE	The Kings	16Aug80	11Oct80	07Feb81	74(2)	26	626
4725	LET THE MUSIC PLAY	Barry White	14Feb76	03Apr76	22May76	42(1)	15	626
4726	LIVE & MORE	Roberta Flack & Peabo Bryson	20Dec80	14Feb81	25Apr81	52(1)	19	626
4727	VULTURE CULTURE	The Alan Parsons Project	09Mar85	06Apr85	13Jul85	46(3)	19	625
4728	GULF WINDS	Joan Baez	06Nov76	11Dec76	26Feb77	62(1)	17	625
4729	SHELTER	Lone Justice	29Nov86	28Mar87	20Jun87	65(2)	30	625
4730	GO	Hiroshima	15Aug87	12Sep87	19Mar88	75(2)	32	624
4731	DIANA!	Diana Ross	24Apr71	22May71	31Jul71	46(2)	15	624
4732	WE CAN FLY! UP-UP AND AWAY	The Johnny Mann Singers	15Jul67	02Sep67	16Dec67	51(2)	23	624
4733	GRAND PRIX	Soundtrack	18Mar67	27May67	23Sep67	76(3)	28	624
4734	THE GRATEFUL DEAD	Grateful Dead	06May67	29Jul67	11Nov67	73(1)	28	623
4735	JENNIFER WARNES	Jennifer Warnes	26Feb77	21May77	25Jun77	43(1)	18	623
4736	CRUSADERS 1	The Crusaders	04Mar72	24Jun72	16Sep72	96(1)	29	623
4737	I-FEEL-LIKE-I'M-FIXIN'-TO-DIE	Country Joe & The Fish	23Dec67	03Feb68	29Jun68	67(1)	28	623
4738	I THINK WE'RE ALL BOZOS ON THIS BUS	Firesign Theatre	25Sep71	30Oct71	25Dec71	50(1)	14	623
4739	PATCHES	Clarence Carter	26Sep70	24Oct70	12Dec70	44(2)	12	622
4740	JANET JACKSON	Janet Jackson	20Nov82	22Jan83	07May83	63(1)	25	622
4741	RADIO K.A.O.S.	Roger Waters	04Jul87	25Jul87	07Nov87	50(2)	19	622
4742	MY BOYFRIEND'S BACK	The Angels	28Sep63	23Nov63	28Dec63	33(2)	14	621
4743	MANTOVANI/MANHATTAN	Mantovani	09Nov63	04Jan64	04Apr64	51(1)	22	621
4744	SHE CRIED	The Lettermen	14Nov64	26Dec64	27Mar65	41(2)	20	621
4745	BACK ON THE STREETS	Donnie Iris	13Dec80	04Apr81	16May81	57(1)	23	621
4746	YOUNG AND RICH	The Tubes	15May76	03Jul76	21Aug76	46(1)	15	621
4747	GET IT RIGHT	Aretha Franklin	30Jul83	03Sep83	26Nov83	36(1)	18	621
4748	DEAN MARTIN'S GREATEST HITS! VOL. 2	Dean Martin	07Sep68	12Oct68	25Jan69	83(1)	21	621
4749	PUT IT WHERE YOU WANT IT	Average White Band	05Apr75	17May75	28Jun75	39(2)	13	620
4750	MAGIC CHRISTIAN MUSIC	Badfinger	28Mar70	25Apr70	18Jul70	55(1)	17	620
4751	SOUL SAUCE	Cal Tjader	17Apr65	17Jul65	02Oct65	52(1)	22	620
4752	DICKEY BETTS & GREAT SOUTHERN	Dickey Betts & Great Southern	30Apr77	28May77	16Jul77	31(1)	12	620
4753	HEAVY	The Stylistics	02Nov74	14Dec74	15Feb75	43(2)	16	620
4754	GREATEST HITS	Melissa Manchester	26Feb83	16Apr83	16Jul83	43(3)	21	620
4755	HOLD ON, I'M COMIN'	Sam & Dave	06Aug66	08Oct66	12Nov66	45(2)	15	620
4756	SINATRA - THE MAIN EVENT LIVE	Frank Sinatra	07Dec74	11Jan75	22Feb75	37(1)	12	620
4757	THE TEMPTATIONS DO THE TEMPTATIONS	The Temptations	11Sep76	23Oct76	11Dec76	53(2)	14	619
4758	THE MIRACLE	Queen	24Jun89	08Jul89	23Sep89	24(1)	14	619
4759	HEAVY!	Victor Buono	18Sep71	23Oct71	08Jan72	66(2)	17	619
4760	+'JUSTMENTS	Bill Withers	06Apr74	18May74	24Aug74	67(1)	21	619
4761	10TH ANNIVERSARY - GOLDEN PIANO HITS	Ferrante & Teicher	11Oct69	06Dec69	11Apr70	93(1)	27	619
4762	A LITTLE LOVE	Aurra	27Feb82	24Apr82	05Jun82	38(2)	15	619

Rank	Title	Act	Entry	Peak	Exit	Peak(Wks)	TotWks	Score
4763.	ROGER!	Roger Williams	13May67	08Jul67	11Nov67	51(1)	27	618
4764.	ONE TO ONE	Howard Jones	01Nov86	15Nov86	21Mar87	56(4)	21	618
4765.	A LITTLE TOUCH OF SCHMILSSON IN THE NIGHT	Nilsson	23Jun73	04Aug73	13Oct73	46(1)	17	618
4766.	ROSS	Diana Ross	21Oct78	02Dec78	10Feb79	49(2)	17	618
4767.	MR. BIG	Mr. Big	22Jul89	26Aug89	18Nov89	46(2)	18	618
4768.	MR. GONE	Weather Report	28Oct78	25Nov78	27Jan79	52(3)	14	617
4769.	WILD STREAK	Hank Williams Jr.	16Jul88	13Aug88	19Nov88	55(1)	19	617
4770.	THE BOOK OF TALIESYN	Deep Purple	11Jan69	22Feb69	12Apr69	54(2)	14	617
4771.	IMAGINARY VOYAGE	Jean-Luc Ponty	04Dec76	19Feb77	07May77	67(2)	23	617
4772.	HEADKEEPER	Dave Mason	26Feb72	29Apr72	27May72	51(1)	14	617
4773.	SUGAR SHACK	Jimmy Gilmer And The Fireballs	16Nov63	21Dec63	15Feb64	26(1)	14	617
4774.	ANCIENT HEART	Tanita Tikaram	11Feb89	13May89	15Jul89	59(1)	23	616
4775.	WHO CAN I TURN TO	Tony Bennett	19Dec64	13Feb65	24Apr65	42(2)	19	616
4776.	THE JONES GIRLS	The Jones Girls	09Jun79	21Jul79	22Sep79	50(1)	16	616
4777.	SONGS OF KRISTOFFERSON	Kris Kristofferson	07May77	11Jun77	03Sep77	45(2)	18	616
4778.	CROW MUSIC	Crow	13Sep69	24Jan70	28Feb70	69(1)	24	616
4779.	PHILADELPHIA FREEDOM	MFSB	06Dec75	17Jan76	21Feb76	39(1)	12	616
4780.	DANGER DANGER	Danger Danger	19Aug89	11Nov89	15Sep90	88(1)	42	615
4781.	KLAATU	Klaatu	02Apr77	14May77	11Jun77	32(1)	11	615
4782.	HEARTBEAT	Curtis Mayfield	11Aug79	20Oct79	24Nov79	42(2)	16	615
4783.	INFORMATION	Dave Edmunds	21May83	16Jul83	01Oct83	51(2)	20	615
4784.	REFLECTIONS	Peter Nero	06Jun64	04Jul64	28Nov64	38(1)	26	614
4785.	HOT PROPERTY	Heatwave	12May79	16Jun79	11Aug79	38(2)	14	614
4786.	MY HOME'S IN ALABAMA	Alabama	19Jul80	30Aug80	06Dec80	71(1)	21	614
4787.	YOUR WISH IS MY COMMAND	Lakeside	09Jan82	06Mar82	12Jun82	58(1)	23	613
4788.	BOX OF FROGS	Box Of Frogs	07Jul84	25Aug84	17Nov84	45(3)	20	613
4789.	AVALON	Roxy Music	19Jun82	17Jul82	18Dec82	53(3)	27	613
4790.	MANTOVANI/HOLLYWOOD	Mantovani	23Sep67	09Dec67	17Feb68	49(1)	22	613
4791.	MODERN HEART	Champaign	02Apr83	23Jul83	10Sep83	64(1)	24	612
4792.	SOLID GROUND	Ronnie Laws	10Oct81	21Nov81	13Feb82	51(2)	19	612
4793.	EGO TRIP	Kurtis Blow	13Oct84	16Mar85	22Jun85	83(2)	37	612
4794.	KIHNTINUED	Greg Kihn	10Apr82	22May82	31Jul82	33(3)	17	612
4795.	MOST OF ALL	B.J. Thomas	12Dec70	06Feb71	22May71	67(1)	24	612
4796.	THE ASTRUD GILBERTO ALBUM	Astrud Gilberto	15May65	17Jul65	11Sep65	41(2)	18	612
4797.	KOOL & THE GANG GREATEST HITS!	Kool & The Gang	08Mar75	12Apr75	09Aug75	81(1)	23	611
4798.	HAVANA MOON	Carlos Santana	23Apr83	28May83	13Aug83	31(2)	17	611
4799.	SAMANTHA FOX	Samantha Fox	24Oct87	25Jun88	27Aug88	51(1)	25	611
4800.	COLOR MY WORLD/WHO AM I	Petula Clark	18Feb67	08Apr67	19Aug67	49(1)	27	611
4801.	ALICE'S RESTAURANT (SOUNDTRACK)	Arlo Guthrie	18Oct69	27Dec69	07Feb70	63(1)	17	611
4802.	THE QUEEN IS DEAD	The Smiths	19Jul86	23Aug86	28Mar87	70(1)	37	611
4803.	OVER THE EDGE	Hurricane	30Apr88	15Oct88	31Dec88	92(2)	36	611
4804.	HEAD (SOUNDTRACK)	The Monkees	21Dec68	08Feb69	29Mar69	45(2)	15	611
4805.	I STAND ALONE	Al Kooper	08Feb69	15Mar69	03May69	54(1)	13	610
4806.	THIS IS LOVE	Johnny Mathis	17Oct64	26Dec64	27Feb65	40(1)	20	610
4807.	A MAN MUST CARRY ON	Jerry Jeff Walker	28May77	09Jul77	15Oct77	60(2)	21	610
4808.	CONCERTS FOR THE PEOPLE OF KAMPUCHEA	Various Artists	18Apr81	09May81	04Jul81	36(2)	12	610
4809.	HERE WE A GO GO AGAIN!	Johnny Rivers	17Oct64	12Dec64	20Mar65	38(1)	23	609
4810.	HERE WE ARE AGAIN	Country Joe & The Fish	21Jun69	05Jul69	30Aug69	48(2)	11	609
4811.	RHYME & REASON	Missing Persons	31Mar84	12May84	14Jul84	43(2)	16	609
4812.	SURRENDER	Diana Ross	07Aug71	28Aug71	06Nov71	56(1)	14	609
4813.	WILL TO POWER	Will To Power	10Sep88	10Dec88	25Mar89	68(1)	29	609
4814.	UNDER THE GUN	Poco	26Jul80	13Sep80	08Nov80	46(1)	16	608
4815.	ANTHOLOGY	The Temptations	15Sep73	27Oct73	06Apr74	65(1)	26	608
4816.	DONNY OSMOND	Donny Osmond	13May89	10Jun89	14Oct89	54(3)	23	608
4817.	GONNA TAKE A MIRACLE	Laura Nyro	25Dec71	29Jan72	15Apr72	46(2)	17	607
4818.	THE PATH	Ralph MacDonald	04Mar78	20May78	24Jun78	57(1)	17	607
4819.	THE FAT BOYS ARE BACK!	Fat Boys	31Aug85	21Sep85	12Apr86	63(2)	33	607
4820.	DREAM COME TRUE	Earl Klugh	19Apr80	17May80	23Aug80	42(1)	19	607
4821.	MAD, BAD AND DANGEROUS TO KNOW	Dead Or Alive	27Dec86	14Mar87	13Jun87	52(2)	25	607
4822.	SUPERNATURAL	Ben E. King	03May75	28Jun75	02Aug75	39(1)	14	607
4823.	STEPHANIE MILLS	Stephanie Mills	29Mar86	07Jun86	23Aug86	47(2)	22	607
4824.	TO BE CONTINUED...	The Temptations	02Aug86	01Nov86	14Mar87	74(2)	33	607
4825.	NBC'S SATURDAY NIGHT LIVE	Soundtrack	25Dec76	12Feb77	19Mar77	38(2)	13	606
4826.	PIECES OF THE SKY	Emmylou Harris	15Mar75	03May75	21Jun75	45(2)	15	606
4827.	THE HOUSE OF THE RISING SUN	Santa Esmeralda	25Feb78	08Apr78	27May78	41(2)	14	606
4828.	FOUR TOPS	Four Tops	27Feb65	14Aug65	06Nov65	63(2)	27	606
4829.	AIN'T IT FUNKY	James Brown	14Feb70	14Mar70	02May70	43(3)	12	606
4830.	KEEP ON JUMPIN'	Musique	30Sep78	25Nov78	20Jan79	62(3)	17	605
4831.	BEYOND APPEARANCES	Santana	23Mar85	20Apr85	10Aug85	50(2)	21	605
4832.	ALIAS PINK PUZZ	Paul Revere & The Raiders	23Aug69	04Oct69	08Nov69	48(2)	12	605
4833.	BEAT CRAZY	Joe Jackson	08Nov80	13Dec80	21Feb81	41(1)	16	605
4834.	HAVE A SMILE WITH ME	Ray Charles	29Aug64	03Oct64	12Dec64	36(2)	16	605
4835.	THROUGH THE FIRE	Hagar, Schon, Aaronson, Shrieve	31Mar84	12May84	28Jul84	42(2)	18	605
4836.	THE POLITICS OF DANCING	Re-Flex	24Dec83	24Mar84	30Jun84	53(1)	28	604
4837.	MASS (FROM THE LITURGY OF THE ROMAN MASS)	Leonard Bernstein	25Dec71	22Jan72	26Aug72	53(1)	20	604
4838.	HEADLINES	Midnight Star	14Jun86	05Jul86	13Dec86	56(2)	27	604
4839.	ICICLE WORKS	Icicle Works	21Apr84	30Jun84	18Aug84	40(2)	18	604
4840.	HOY-HOY!	Little Feat	22Aug81	26Sep81	14Nov81	39(1)	13	604
4841.	WELCOME TO THE PONDEROSA	Lorne Greene	28Nov64	30Jan65	03Apr65	35(1)	19	604
4842.	HEAD OVER HEELS	Poco	19Jul75	23Aug75	15Nov75	43(1)	18	604
4843.	BACK TO THE ROOTS	John Mayall	17Apr71	22May71	24Jul71	52(1)	15	604
4844.	VOICES IN THE RAIN	Joe Sample	31Jan81	14Mar81	13Jun81	65(3)	20	603
4845.	SEXAPPEAL	Georgio	25Apr87	09Jan88	16Apr88	117(1)	52	603
4846.	JOY	Apollo 100	19Feb72	25Mar72	03Jun72	47(2)	16	603
4847.	REMOTE CONTROL	The Tubes	31Mar79	19May79	28Jul79	46(1)	18	603
4848.	THE DELFONICS	The Delfonics	15Aug70	10Oct70	12Dec70	61(1)	18	603
4849.	DON'T TELL A SOUL	The Replacements	18Feb89	11Mar89	24Jun89	57(2)	19	602
4850.	8TH WONDER	Sugarhill Gang	30Jan82	13Mar82	29May82	50(1)	18	601
4851.	SUMMERTIME GROOVE	Hamilton Bohannon	12Aug78	02Dec78	16Dec78	58(1)	19	601
4852.	BARE TREES	Fleetwood Mac	22Apr72	03Jun72	04Oct75	70(2)	27	601
4853.	KING OF AMERICA	Elvis Costello And The Attractions	22Mar86	12Apr86	19Jul86	39(2)	18	601
4854.	DON'T LOOK BACK	Natalie Cole	14Jun80	26Jul80	08Nov80	77(1)	22	601
4855.	WITH YOU	Stacy Lattisaw	25Jul81	05Sep81	31Oct81	46(1)	15	601
4856.	POWER	The Temptations	17May80	12Jul80	16Aug80	45(1)	14	601
4857.	NO MYSTERY	Return To Forever	15Mar75	05Apr75	07Jun75	39(2)	13	601
4858.	SCHOOLBOYS IN DISGRACE	The Kinks	06Dec75	24Jan76	06Mar76	45(3)	14	600
4859.	A CHRISTMAS TOGETHER	John Denver & The Muppets	10Nov79	05Jan80	26Jan80	26(2)	12	600
4860.	LOOK TO THE RAINBOW: LIVE IN EUROPE	Al Jarreau	25Jun77	17Sep77	01Oct77	49(1)	15	599
4861.	TROUBLE IN PARADISE	The Souther, Hillman, Furay Band	21Jun75	26Jul75	30Aug75	39(1)	11	599
4862.	IS THAT ALL THERE IS?	Peggy Lee	13Dec69	07Feb70	11Apr70	55(1)	18	598
4863.	TANTALIZINGLY HOT	Stephanie Mills	07Aug82	04Sep82	11Dec82	48(6)	19	598
4864.	GREAT BALLS OF FIRE	Dolly Parton	23Jun79	21Jul79	13Oct79	40(1)	17	598
4865.	THE MANFRED MANN ALBUM	Manfred Mann	21Nov64	06Feb65	20Mar65	35(1)	18	598
4866.	A WORLD WITHOUT LOVE	Peter And Gordon	04Jul64	08Aug64	03Oct64	21(1)	14	598
4867.	SECOND WINTER	Johnny Winter	06Dec69	27Dec69	28Mar70	55(1)	17	598
4868.	TALKING HEADS: 77	Talking Heads	08Oct77	04Mar78	22Apr78	97(2)	29	598
4869.	LIVING EYES	Bee Gees	21Nov81	19Dec81	06Feb82	41(3)	12	598
4870.	POWERFUL PEOPLE	Gino Vannelli	28Sep74	30Nov74	19Apr75	60(2)	30	597
4871.	LONELY AGAIN	Eddy Arnold	18Mar67	13May67	26Aug67	57(1)	24	597
4872.	DAYTIME FRIENDS	Kenny Rogers	20Aug77	01Oct77	10May80	39(1)	21	597

Rank. Title Act
[Entry|Peak|Exit] Peak(Wks) TotWks Score

4873. RICHARD NIXON: A FANTASY David Frye
[11Aug73|15Sep73|17Nov73] 45(1) 15 597

4874. DAYDREAMING Morris Day
[12Mar88|09Apr88|18Jun88] 41(2) 15 596

4875. MICHELLE Bud Shank
[12Feb66|02Apr66|02Jul66] 56(1) 21 596

4876. LAST OF THE RUNAWAYS Giant
[14Oct89|16Jun90|28Jul90] 80(1) 36 595

4877. NOTHING'S SHOCKING Jane's Addiction
[17Sep88|25Feb89|13May89] 103(2) 35 595

4878. MAIDEN VOYAGE Ramsey Lewis
[20Jul68|26Oct68|30Nov68] 55(2) 20 595

4879. EVERYBODY NEEDS LOVE Gladys Knight & The Pips
[14Oct67|16Dec67|23Mar68] 60(2) 24 595

4880. BLIND BABY The New Birth
[24May75|09Aug75|13Sep75] 57(1) 17 595

4881. LAND OF GIANTS The New Christy Minstrels
[29Aug64|26Sep64|30Jan65] 48(1) 23 594

4882. THE FABULOUS VENTURES The Ventures
[18Jul64|05Sep64|05Dec64] 32(1) 19 594

4883. HAVE YOU SEEN ME LATELY? Sam Kinison
[26Nov88|24Dec88|18Mar89] 43(3) 17 594

4884. LADY IN WAITING The Outlaws
[10Apr76|15May76|26Jun76] 36(2) 12 594

4885. MANTOVANI OLE Mantovani
[23Oct65|04Dec65|12Mar66] 41(1) 21 593

4886. SONGS YOU WON'T FORGET Peter Nero
[10Oct64|05Dec64|27Feb65] 42(1) 21 593

4887. LET ME BE THERE Olivia Newton-John
[29Dec73|09Mar74|11May74] 54(1) 20 593

4888. STONEGROUND WORDS Melanie
[11Nov72|23Dec72|24Mar73] 70(3) 20 593

4889. RUBY, RUBY Gato Barbieri
[29Oct77|10Dec77|11Mar78] 66(1) 20 593

4890. TODD Todd Rundgren
[16Mar74|20Apr74|06Jul74] 54(1) 17 593

4891. MARY IN THE MORNING Al Martino
[14Oct67|27Jan68|02Mar68] 63(1) 21 593

4892. THE GREAT RACE (SOUNDTRACK) Henry Mancini And His Orchestra
[02Oct65|11Dec65|26Feb66] 63(2) 22 592

4893. UNCLE MEAT Mothers Of Invention
[03May69|31May69|12Jul69] 43(2) 11 592

4894. SHORT STORIES Harry Chapin
[29Dec73|16Mar74|01Jun74] 61(1) 23 591

4895. WISHBONE FOUR Wishbone Ash
[28Apr73|09Jun73|04Aug73] 44(1) 15 591

4896. LEON RUSSELL Leon Russell
[11Apr70|02May70|15Aug70] 60(2) 19 591

4897. FLASHBACK 38 Special
[22Aug87|26Sep87|12Dec87] 35(2) 17 591

4898. LIVING IN THE 20TH CENTURY The Steve Miller Band
[15Nov86|07Feb87|18Apr87] 65(1) 23 590

4899. SECRET MESSAGES Electric Light Orchestra
[16Jul83|20Aug83|29Oct83] 36(1) 16 590

4900. SOMETIMES LATE AT NIGHT Carole Bayer Sager
[16May81|11Jul81|10Oct81] 60(1) 22 590

4901. PORTRAIT OF BOBBY Bobby Sherman
[24Apr71|29May71|24Jul71] 48(1) 14 590

4902. SHAKE IT WELL The Dramatics
[13Aug77|01Oct77|17Dec77] 60(1) 19 590

4903. CHRISTMAS Kenny Rogers
[21Nov81|09Jan82|15Jan83] 34(2) 13 589

4904. CHESS Various Artists
[16Mar85|25May85|03Aug85] 47(2) 21 589

4905. SO NICE Johnny Mathis
[08Oct66|07Jan67|04Feb67] 50(1) 18 589

4906. BETWEEN NOTHINGNESS & ETERNITY The Mahavishnu Orchestra
[22Dec73|26Jan74|23Mar74] 41(2) 14 589

4907. I WAS MADE TO LOVE HER Stevie Wonder
[30Sep67|25Nov67|23Dec67] 45(2) 13 589

4908. ONE NIGHT WITH A STRANGER Martin Briley
[07May83|30Jul83|01Oct83] 55(1) 22 589

4909. THE HISTORY MIX VOL. I Godley & Creme
[17Aug85|05Oct85|23Nov85] 37(2) 15 589

Rank. Title Act
[Entry|Peak|Exit] Peak(Wks) TotWks Score

4910. COMMAND PERFORMANCE/LIVE IN PERSON Jan & Dean
[27Feb65|15May65|12Jun65] 33(1) 16 588

4911. IT'S MY PLEASURE Billy Preston
[19Jul75|13Sep75|18Oct75] 43(1) 14 588

4912. CHUCK BERRY ON STAGE Chuck Berry
[24Aug63|12Oct63|14Dec63] 29(1) 17 588

4913. CHRISTMAS AND THE BEADS OF SWEAT Laura Nyro
[26Dec70|30Jan71|27Mar71] 51(1) 14 588

4914. SHOCK The Motels
[17Aug85|28Sep85|30Nov85] 36(1) 16 588

4915. LYLE LOVETT AND HIS LARGE BAND Lyle Lovett
[18Feb89|22Apr89|08Jul89] 62(1) 21 588

4916. COCKER Joe Cocker
[12Apr86|07Jun86|09Aug86] 50(2) 18 588

4917. TRILOGY Yngwie Malmsteen
[11Oct86|01Nov86|14Mar87] 44(2) 23 587

4918. BEST OF LEON Leon Russell
[23Oct76|04Dec76|05Feb77] 40(1) 16 587

4919. THE CHOKIN' KIND Joe Simon
[21Jun69|09Aug69|11Oct69] 81(1) 17 587

4920. KING COOL Donnie Iris
[26Sep81|07Nov81|26Jun82] 84(2) 31 587

4921. EB 84 The Everly Brothers
[13Oct84|03Nov84|02Feb85] 38(2) 17 587

4922. KEEP YOUR DISTANCE Curiosity Killed The Cat
[22Aug87|26Sep87|05Mar88] 55(1) 29 587

4923. UPENDO NI PAMOJA Ramsey Lewis Trio
[24Jun72|30Sep72|11Nov72] 79(1) 21 587

4924. SOUND IN YOUR MIND Willie Nelson
[20Mar76|08May76|26Jun76] 48(1) 15 587

4925. WHERE DO YOU GO WHEN YOU DREAM Anne Murray
[02May81|30May81|08Aug81] 55(2) 15 587

4926. STEREOTOMY The Alan Parsons Project
[01Feb86|01Mar86|31May86] 43(2) 18 586

4927. SOME NICE THINGS I'VE MISSED Frank Sinatra
[03Aug74|31Aug74|19Oct74] 48(1) 12 586

4928. LANDING ON WATER Neil Young
[16Aug86|27Sep86|29Nov86] 46(2) 16 586

4929. RESPECT Jimmy Smith
[07Oct67|09Dec67|17Feb68] 60(1) 20 586

4930. SECRETS Herbie Hancock
[11Sep76|09Oct76|01Jan77] 49(2) 17 584

4931. LAST TIME I SAW HIM Diana Ross
[29Dec73|23Feb74|20Apr74] 52(1) 17 584

4932. ARGYBARGY Squeeze
[26Apr80|05Jul80|04Oct80] 71(1) 24 584

4933. MOUNTAIN LIVE (THE ROAD GOES EVER ON) Mountain
[13May72|22Jul72|09Sep72] 63(1) 18 584

4934. THE MANTOVANI SCENE Mantovani
[05Apr69|31May69|26Jul69] 73(1) 17 584

4935. BREAKING ALL THE RULES Peter Frampton
[13Jun81|01Aug81|05Sep81] 43(1) 13 584

4936. THE BEST OF CHARLEY PRIDE, VOLUME 2 Charley Pride
[18Mar72|06May72|24Jun72] 50(1) 15 584

4937. DO YOU Sheena Easton
[23Nov85|14Dec85|29Mar86] 40(2) 19 584

4938. YELLOW MOON The Neville Brothers
[08Apr89|03Jun89|16Sep89] 66(3) 24 583

4939. THE SUPER HITS, VOL. 3 Various Artists
[23Nov68|15Feb69|29Mar69] 68(1) 19 583

4940. PAPER ROSES Marie Osmond
[22Sep73|24Nov73|23Feb74] 59(1) 23 583

4941. PREMONITION Survivor
[24Oct81|19Dec81|10Apr82] 82(3) 25 583

4942. YOUNGEST IN CHARGE Special Ed
[03Jun89|22Jul89|09Dec89] 73(1) 28 583

4943. OCTOBER U2
[07Nov81|28Nov81|19Sep87] 104(2) 38 583

4944. GAP BAND VI The Gap Band
[19Jan85|09Feb85|22Jun85] 58(2) 23 583

Rank. Title Act
[Entry|Peak|Exit] Peak(Wks) TotWks Score

4945. TOUCH John Klemmer
[27Dec75|08May76|16Oct76] 90(1) 40 583

4946. ...AND I KNOW YOU WANNA DANCE Johnny Rivers
[16Apr66|18Jun66|03Sep66] 52(1) 21 583

4947. VOYEUR Kim Carnes
[25Sep82|09Oct82|19Feb83] 49(3) 22 583

4948. GREATEST HITS Ray Parker Jr.
[18Dec82|29Jan83|14May83] 51(3) 22 583

4949. VIVA TIRADO El Chicano
[13Jun70|01Aug70|03Oct70] 51(1) 17 583

4950. FACES Shawn Phillips
[02Dec72|27Jan73|14Apr73] 57(2) 20 583

4951. ERROR IN THE SYSTEM Peter Schilling
[08Oct83|21Jan84|10Mar84] 61(1) 23 582

4952. CICERO PARK Hot Chocolate
[01Mar75|03May75|21Jun75] 55(1) 17 582

4953. SNOOPY VS. THE RED BARON The Royal Guardsmen
[11Feb67|15Apr67|08Jul67] 44(1) 22 582

4954. HURRICANE SMITH Hurricane Smith
[06Jan73|24Mar73|05May73] 53(2) 18 582

4955. UPTIGHT (SOUNDTRACK) Booker T. & The MG's
[08Feb69|24May69|09Aug69] 98(1) 27 581

4956. IN THE NICK OF TIME Nicolette Larson
[03Nov79|08Dec79|22Mar80] 47(1) 21 581

4957. EXILES Dan Fogelberg
[20Jun87|25Jul87|24Oct87] 48(3) 19 581

4958. HOUSE OF MUSIC T.S. Monk
[31Jan81|11Apr81|27Jun81] 64(1) 22 581

4959. BLUES FROM LAUREL CANYON John Mayall
[22Feb69|19Apr69|14Jun69] 68(1) 17 581

4960. I CAME TO DANCE Nils Lofgren
[19Mar77|30Apr77|04Jun77] 36(1) 12 581

4961. THE VISITOR Mick Fleetwood
[18Jul81|29Aug81|17Oct81] 43(2) 14 581

4962. SILVER MORNING Kenny Rankin
[16Nov74|29Mar75|14Jun75] 63(1) 25 581

4963. EXTREME Extreme
[08Apr89|17Jun89|11Nov89] 80(1) 32 580

4964. MODERN MAN Stanley Clarke
[29Apr78|03Jun78|02Sep78] 57(2) 19 580

4965. RAY'S MOODS Ray Charles
[17Sep66|03Dec66|07Jan67] 52(1) 17 580

4966. THE NAME OF THIS BAND IS TALKING HEADS Talking Heads
[17Apr82|22May82|17Jul82] 31(2) 14 579

4967. DOUBLE TROUBLE (SOUNDTRACK) Elvis Presley
[24Jun67|19Aug67|04Nov67] 47(2) 20 579

4968. JOE JACKSON'S JUMPIN' JIVE Joe Jackson
[01Aug81|05Sep81|24Oct81] 42(1) 13 579

4969. ROCK AWAY Phoebe Snow
[04Apr81|23May81|01Aug81] 51(2) 18 579

4970. PLAYING UP A STORM The Gregg Allman Band
[11Jun77|23Jul77|27Aug77] 42(1) 12 579

4971. NEW YORK, NEW YORK Soundtrack
[16Jul77|13Aug77|15Oct77] 50(3) 14 579

4972. CASINO Al Di Meola
[29Apr78|17Jun78|19Aug78] 52(1) 17 578

4973. THE JUKES Southside Johnny & The Asbury Jukes
[18Aug79|29Sep79|17Nov79] 48(1) 14 578

4974. THERE GOES MY EVERYTHING Jack Greene
[25Feb67|15Apr67|15Jul67] 66(1) 21 577

4975. LET ME TOUCH YOU The O'Jays
[10Oct87|05Dec87|26Mar88] 66(1) 25 577

4976. WORD OF MOUTH The Kinks
[15Dec84|09Feb85|27Apr85] 57(3) 20 577

4977. THE STREET GIVETH... AND THE STREET TAKETH AWAY Cat Mother & the All Night News Boys
[05Jul69|09Aug69|11Oct69] 55(1) 15 577

4978. TO KNOW YOU IS TO LOVE YOU B.B. King
[08Sep73|20Oct73|13Apr74] 71(2) 25 576

4979. GLORIA The Shadows Of Knight
[14May66|23Jul66|10Sep66] 46(1) 18 576

Rank. Title Act
[Entry|Peak|Exit] Peak(Wks) TotWks — Score

4980. BARBARA MANDRELL LIVE Barbara Mandrell
[05Sep81|07Nov81|13Feb82] 86(2) 24 — 576

4981. GOOD TO BE BACK Natalie Cole
[27May89|17Jun89|28Oct89] 59(2) 23 — 576

4982. SHADOWLAND k.d. lang
[28May88|20Aug88|12Nov88] 73(2) 25 — 576

4983. MY EVER CHANGING MOODS The Style Council
[07Apr84|30Jun84|01Sep84] 56(2) 22 — 576

4984. HANG ON SLOOPY The McCoys
[20Nov65|19Feb66|26Mar66] 44(1) 19 — 576

4985. IT'S MAGIC Jerry Vale
[12Feb66|30Apr66|04Jun66] 38(1) 17 — 576

4986. END OF THE CENTURY The Ramones
[23Feb80|29Mar80|24May80] 44(1) 14 — 575

4987. HEARTBREAKER Free
[03Feb73|07Apr73|19May73] 47(1) 16 — 575

4988. ASYLUM CHOIR II Leon Russell & Marc Benno
[04Dec71|15Jan72|15Apr72] 70(2) 20 — 575

4989. RAISIN' HELL Elvin Bishop
[27Aug77|08Oct77|12Nov77] 38(2) 12 — 575

4990. 2112 Rush
[10Apr76|29May76|27Feb82] 61(2) 34 — 574

4991. EYE OF THE HURRICANE The Alarm
[07Nov87|28Nov87|28May88] 77(2) 30 — 574

4992. BOYS AND GIRLS Bryan Ferry
[29Jun85|20Jul85|14Dec85] 63(2) 25 — 574

4993. VICTIM OF LOVE Elton John
[27Oct79|24Nov79|29Dec79] 35(2) 10 — 574

4994. I LOVE YOU SO Natalie Cole
[07Apr79|05May79|14Jul79] 52(2) 15 — 574

4995. THE WHO SELL OUT The Who
[06Jan68|02Mar68|08Jun68] 48(1) 23 — 574

4996. SARAYA Saraya
[29Apr89|24Jun89|27Jan90] 79(3) 39 — 574

4997. CHOICE John Gary
[12Mar66|21May66|23Jul66] 51(1) 20 — 573

4998. LOVE The Cult
[28Dec85|26Apr86|16Aug86] 87(2) 34 — 573

4999. THE RESURRECTION OF PIGBOY CRABSHAW The Butterfield Blues Band
[13Jan68|30Mar68|27Apr68] 52(2) 16 — 573

5000. STEADY NERVES Graham Parker & The Shot
[20Apr85|15Jun85|07Sep85] 57(3) 21 — 573

5001. JAZZ BLUES FUSION John Mayall
[17Jun72|22Jul72|14Oct72] 64(2) 18 — 573

5002. ANTHOLOGY Gladys Knight & The Pips
[16Feb74|06Apr74|20Jul74] 77(1) 23 — 573

5003. THE LONELY THINGS Glenn Yarbrough
[25Jun66|10Sep66|03Dec66] 61(1) 24 — 573

5004. EXPERIENCE GLORIA GAYNOR Gloria Gaynor
[11Oct75|13Dec75|28Feb76] 64(1) 21 — 572

5005. MADE IN AMERICA Carpenters
[04Jul81|15Aug81|10Oct81] 52(1) 15 — 572

5006. BROKEN BLOSSOM Bette Midler
[17Dec77|18Feb78|18Mar78] 51(2) 14 — 571

5007. CHANGE OF ADDRESS Krokus
[03May86|28Jun86|23Aug86] 45(2) 17 — 571

5008. ELECTRIC LADY Con Funk Shun
[18May85|22Jun85|09Nov85] 62(3) 26 — 571

5009. STILL TOGETHER Gladys Knight & The Pips
[23Apr77|28May77|10Sep77] 51(2) 21 — 570

5010. I'M A FOOL Dino, Desi & Billy
[25Sep65|20Nov65|05Mar66] 51(1) 24 — 570

5011. LIVE AT CARNEGIE HALL Al Hirt
[24Jul65|18Sep65|18Dec65] 47(1) 22 — 570

5012. THE GIRL WHO CAME TO SUPPER Original Cast
[25Jan64|22Feb64|25Apr64] 33(1) 14 — 570

5013. SOULFUL TAPESTRY The Honey Cone
[11Dec71|04Mar72|22Apr72] 72(1) 20 — 570

5014. MY MARIA B.W. Stevenson
[15Sep73|27Oct73|15Dec73] 45(1) 14 — 569

5015. CRY LIKE A BABY The Box Tops
[27Apr68|29Jun68|31Aug68] 59(2) 19 — 569

5016. RELEASE YOURSELF Graham Central Station
[05Oct74|23Nov74|01Feb75] 51(2) 18 — 569

5017. INDIAN SUMMER Poco
[14May77|09Jul77|10Sep77] 57(1) 18 — 569

5018. THE ROAD GOES ON FOREVER, A COLLECTION OF THEIR GREATEST RECORDINGS The Allman Brothers Band
[13Dec75|24Jan76|13Mar76] 43(1) 14 — 569

5019. THE DELLS GREATEST HITS The Dells
[14Jun69|13Sep69|08Nov69] 102(2) 22 — 569

5020. THE REAL MCCOY Charlie McCoy
[06May72|16Sep72|21Oct72] 98(2) 25 — 569

5021. LET ME BE GOOD TO YOU Lou Rawls
[02Jun79|07Jul79|08Sep79] 49(1) 15 — 569

5022. NILS Nils Lofgren
[21Jul79|01Sep79|20Oct79] 54(1) 14 — 568

5023. VICKI SUE ROBINSON Vicki Sue Robinson
[23Oct76|04Dec76|12Feb77] 45(1) 16 — 568

5024. LAST MANGO IN PARIS Jimmy Buffett
[06Jul85|24Aug85|16Nov85] 53(3) 20 — 568

5025. MOONLIGHT SINATRA Frank Sinatra
[23Apr66|25Jun66|23Jul66] 34(1) 14 — 567

5026. ATOM HEART MOTHER Pink Floyd
[07Nov70|26Dec70|30Jan71] 55(2) 13 — 566

5027. ...WITH LOVE/THE SEDUCTIVE SAX OF BOOTS RANDOLPH Boots Randolph
[10May69|21Jun69|30Aug69] 82(2) 17 — 566

5028. GEFFREY MORGAN... UB40
[10Nov84|15Dec84|04May85] 60(1) 26 — 566

5029. THE SANDPIPERS The Sandpipers
[27May67|05Aug67|02Dec67] 53(1) 28 — 566

5030. RICHIE HAVENS ON STAGE Richie Havens
[23Sep72|25Nov72|20Jan73] 55(2) 18 — 565

5031. WILSON PICKETT IN PHILADELPHIA Wilson Pickett
[03Oct70|21Nov70|06Feb71] 64(1) 19 — 565

5032. OUR WEDDING ALBUM OR THE GREAT SOCIETY AFFAIR Various Artists
[10Sep66|12Nov66|10Dec66] 40(2) 14 — 565

5033. PRIVATE AUDITION Heart
[12Jun82|03Jul82|11Sep82] 25(2) 14 — 565

5034. THE SPY WHO LOVED ME Soundtrack
[27Aug77|05Nov77|10Dec77] 40(2) 16 — 565

5035. I COULDN'T LIVE WITHOUT YOUR LOVE Petula Clark
[03Sep66|05Nov66|17Dec66] 43(1) 16 — 565

5036. MASQUE Kansas
[27Dec75|20Mar76|08May76] 70(1) 20 — 565

5037. SOME ENCHANTED EVENING Blue Öyster Cult
[30Sep78|18Nov78|16Dec78] 44(1) 12 — 565

5038. ZAPP III Zapp
[03Sep83|01Oct83|28Jan84] 39(1) 22 — 565

5039. YOU ASKED FOR IT! Ferrante & Teicher
[24Sep66|10Dec66|11Feb67] 57(1) 21 — 565

5040. NO, NO, NANETTE Original Cast
[13Mar71|10Apr71|17Jul71] 61(1) 19 — 565

5041. BAREFOOT BALLET John Klemmer
[18Sep76|30Oct76|01Jan77] 66(1) 16 — 564

5042. JAMMING WITH EDWARD! Nicky Hopkins
[12Feb72|26Feb72|22Apr72] 33(2) 11 — 564

5043. RIDE THE LIGHTNING Metallica
[29Sep84|09Mar85|28Jun86] 100(2) 50 — 564

5044. KNIGHTS OF THE SOUND TABLE Cameo
[20Jun81|11Jul81|12Sep81] 44(2) 13 — 564

5045. GOLDEN BOY Original Cast
[19Dec64|20Feb65|03Apr65] 36(1) 16 — 564

5046. WILD THING The Troggs
[03Sep66|05Nov66|17Dec66] 52(1) 16 — 563

5047. THE TONIGHT SHOW BAND The Tonight Show Band with Doc Severinsen
[01Nov86|27Dec86|25Apr87] 65(4) 26 — 563

5048. PLEASURE Ohio Players
[24Feb73|19May73|21Jul73] 63(1) 22 — 563

5049. BLOODY TOURISTS 10cc
[14Oct78|25Nov78|03Feb79] 69(1) 17 — 563

5050. THE SEVENTH ONE Toto
[19Mar88|30Apr88|16Jul88] 64(3) 18 — 562

5051. VOICES OF BABYLON The Outfield
[15Apr89|06May89|16Sep89] 53(3) 23 — 562

5052. SUNBEAM The Emotions
[26Aug78|09Sep78|11Nov78] 40(3) 12 — 562

5053. LIVE AT THE RIVIERA, LAS VEGAS Engelbert Humperdinck
[01Jan72|29Jan72|25Mar72] 45(2) 13 — 562

5054. "HEROES" David Bowie
[12Nov77|10Dec77|18Mar78] 35(1) 19 — 561

5055. HERB ALPERT/HUGH MASEKELA Herb Alpert/Hugh Masekela
[11Feb78|25Mar78|17Jun78] 65(1) 19 — 561

5056. SOAP OPERA The Kinks
[17May75|12Jul75|09Aug75] 51(1) 13 — 561

5057. HIDEAWAY David Sanborn
[08Mar80|17May80|12Jul80] 63(1) 19 — 561

5058. HOOLIGANS The Who
[17Oct81|14Nov81|20Feb82] 52(2) 19 — 561

5059. WWII Waylon Jennings & Willie Nelson
[30Oct82|20Nov82|26Mar83] 57(3) 22 — 561

5060. HIGHWAYMAN Willie, Waylon, Johnny & Kris
[01Jun85|17Aug85|25Jan86] 92(1) 35 — 561

5061. HAPPY HEART Roger Williams
[31May69|28Jun69|09Aug69] 60(1) 11 — 560

5062. I'VE GOT A TIGER BY THE TAIL Buck Owens
[03Apr65|26Jun65|28Aug65] 43(1) 22 — 560

5063. T-CONNECTION T-Connection
[27Jan79|07Apr79|02Jun79] 51(2) 19 — 560

5064. TELL IT ALL BROTHER Kenny Rogers & The First Edition
[31Oct70|21Nov70|13Feb71] 61(1) 16 — 560

5065. GUESS WHO B.B. King
[09Sep72|25Nov72|20Jan73] 65(1) 20 — 560

5066. CHALK MARK IN A RAIN STORM Joni Mitchell
[09Apr88|30Apr88|23Jul88] 45(2) 16 — 560

5067. JESUS CHRIST SUPERSTAR Original Broadway Cast Recording
[08Jan72|15Jan72|11Mar72] 31(2) 10 — 560

5068. TOM JONES LIVE AT CAESARS PALACE Tom Jones
[06Nov71|04Dec71|05Feb72] 43(1) 14 — 560

5069. THE MORNING AFTER The J. Geils Band
[06Nov71|11Dec71|26Feb72] 64(1) 17 — 559

5070. FAST TIMES AT RIDGEMONT HIGH Soundtrack
[28Aug82|25Sep82|08Jan83] 54(3) 20 — 559

5071. POP GOES THE WORLD Men Without Hats
[14Nov87|20Feb88|30Apr88] 73(2) 25 — 559

5072. ENGLISH SETTLEMENT XTC
[20Mar82|22May82|31Jul82] 48(1) 20 — 559

5073. GARCIA (II) Jerry Garcia
[22Jun74|13Jul74|28Sep74] 49(2) 15 — 559

5074. MAIN SQUEEZE Chuck Mangione
[20Nov76|12Feb77|30Apr77] 86(1) 24 — 558

5075. WHERE WE ALL BELONG The Marshall Tucker Band
[21Dec74|18Jan75|22Mar75] 54(2) 14 — 558

5076. EXPRESS Love And Rockets
[01Nov86|07Mar87|23May87] 72(2) 30 — 558

5077. JUST THE WAY YOU LIKE IT The S.O.S. Band
[01Sep84|13Oct84|02Mar85] 60(2) 27 — 558

5078. THE NOTORIOUS BYRD BROTHERS The Byrds
[03Feb68|30Mar68|08Jun68] 47(2) 19 — 558

5079. STRICTLY BUSINESS EPMD
[09Jul88|13Aug88|10Dec88] 80(1) 23 — 558

5080. SOUTHERN STAR Alabama
[18Feb89|18Mar89|08Jul89] 62(2) 21 — 558

5081. BOP TILL YOU DROP Ry Cooder
[11Aug79|13Oct79|17Nov79] 62(2) 15 — 557

5082. REUNION The Temptations
[01May82|05Jun82|28Aug82] 37(2) 18 — 557

5083. BEST OF THE BEACH BOYS, VOL. 2 The Beach Boys
[12Aug67|23Sep67|06Jan68] 50(2) 22 — 557

5084. ALL I NEED IS TIME Gladys Knight & The Pips
[14Jul73|01Sep73|01Dec73] 70(1) 21 — 557

Rank. Title Act
[Entry | Peak | Exit] Peak(Wks) TotWks Score

5085. BOATS AGAINST THE CURRENT Eric Carmen
[10Sep77 | 08Oct77 | 03Dec77] 45(1) 13 556

5086. STILL CRUISIN' The Beach Boys
[16Sep89 | 07Oct89 | 10Feb90] 46(1) 22 556

5087. OH NO! IT'S DEVO Devo
[20Nov82 | 18Dec82 | 02Apr83] 47(3) 20 556

5088. TIME, TIME Ed Ames
[08Jul67 | 19Aug67 | 23Mar68] 77(2) 38 556

5089. LAST SAFE PLACE Le Roux
[06Feb82 | 01May82 | 26Jun82] 64(2) 21 556

5090. I KNOW A PLACE Petula Clark
[29May65 | 03Jul65 | 18Sep65] 42(2) 17 555

5091. ON BROADWAY (SOUNDTRACK)
Diana Ross & The Supremes And The Temptations
[06Dec69 | 27Dec69 | 21Feb70] 38(1) 12 555

5092. NEW ENGLAND New England
[19May79 | 23Jun79 | 08Sep79] 50(2) 17 555

5093. DEEP IN MY SOUL Smokey Robinson
[19Feb77 | 02Apr77 | 21May77] 47(1) 14 555

5094. YOU'VE GOT THE POWER Third World
[20Mar82 | 05Jun82 | 18Sep82] 63(1) 27 555

5095. DRAG CITY Jan & Dean
[18Jan64 | 22Feb64 | 18Apr64] 22(1) 14 555

5096. ON THE LINE Gary U.S. Bonds
[26Jun82 | 14Aug82 | 16Oct82] 52(2) 17 555

5097. CHER Cher
[01Oct66 | 12Nov66 | 14Jan67] 59(1) 16 555

5098. DANGEROUS Bar-Kays
[21Apr84 | 16Jun84 | 15Sep84] 52(1) 22 555

5099. THEM Them
[24Jul65 | 06Nov65 | 28May66] 54(1) 23 554

5100. ALMOST PERSUADED David Houston
[06Aug66 | 05Nov66 | 14Jan67] 57(1) 20 554

5101. FROM BROADWAY WITH LOVE Nancy Wilson
[05Feb66 | 23Apr66 | 04Jun66] 44(2) 18 553

5102. THE MAN WITH THE HORN Miles Davis
[25Jul81 | 12Sep81 | 21Nov81] 53(2) 18 553

5103. ROMANCE DANCE Kim Carnes
[05Jul80 | 16Aug80 | 25Oct80] 57(2) 17 553

5104. RENDEZ-VOUS Jean Michel Jarre
[03May86 | 31May86 | 13Sep86] 52(4) 20 553

5105. GHOSTS Strawbs
[08Mar75 | 05Apr75 | 31May75] 47(2) 13 552

5106. SO EXCITED! The Pointer Sisters
[17Jul82 | 04Sep82 | 22Jan83] 59(1) 28 552

5107. MOTEL SHOT Delaney & Bonnie
[03Apr71 | 31Jul71 | 04Sep71] 65(1) 23 552

5108. 101 Depeche Mode
[01Apr89 | 15Apr89 | 05Aug89] 45(2) 19 551

5109. HAMILTON, JOE FRANK & REYNOLDS
Hamilton, Joe Frank & Reynolds
[19Jun71 | 24Jul71 | 25Sep71] 59(2) 15 551

5110. HEAVEN 17 Heaven 17
[12Feb83 | 26Mar83 | 20Aug83] 68(3) 28 551

5111. PRIEST...LIVE Judas Priest
[20Jun87 | 11Jul87 | 26Sep87] 38(2) 15 551

5112. WAITIN' FOR THE SUN TO SHINE
Ricky Skaggs
[12Jun82 | 10Jul82 | 01Jan83] 77(2) 30 551

5113. DRIFT AWAY Dobie Gray
[10Mar73 | 09Jun73 | 28Jul73] 64(1) 21 551

5114. THE SPICE OF LIFE Jerry Butler
[17Jun72 | 23Sep72 | 25Nov72] 92(2) 24 551

5115. LET ME TICKLE YOUR FANCY
Jermaine Jackson
[21Aug82 | 09Oct82 | 04Dec82] 46(3) 16 551

5116. RAIN FOREST Paul Hardcastle
[23Mar85 | 20Apr85 | 07Sep85] 63(2) 25 551

5117. LOST HORIZON Soundtrack
[03Feb73 | 14Apr73 | 23Jun73] 58(1) 21 550

5118. STORYTELLER/COMPLETE ANTHOLOGY: 1964-1990 Rod Stewart
[02Dec89 | 13Jan90 | 31Mar90] 54(1) 18 550

5119. PHANTOM, ROCKER & SLICK
Phantom, Rocker & Slick
[26Oct85 | 07Dec85 | 29Mar86] 61(2) 23 550

5120. NEW HARVEST...FIRST GATHERING
Dolly Parton
[02Apr77 | 02Jul77 | 20Aug77] 71(3) 21 550

Rank. Title Act
[Entry | Peak | Exit] Peak(Wks) TotWks Score

5121. THE NEVER ENDING IMPRESSIONS
The Impressions
[28Mar64 | 20Jun64 | 22Aug64] 52(1) 22 550

5122. STAGE David Bowie
[21Oct78 | 02Dec78 | 13Jan79] 44(1) 13 549

5123. YOU SEND ME Roy Ayers
[19Aug78 | 07Oct78 | 25Nov78] 48(2) 15 549

5124. THUNDER Andy Taylor
[28Mar87 | 09May87 | 18Jul87] 46(4) 17 549

5125. TIME & CHARGES The Buckinghams
[10Jun67 | 19Aug67 | 11Nov67] 58(1) 23 548

5126. GROOVE-A-THON Isaac Hayes
[21Feb76 | 03Apr76 | 08May76] 45(1) 12 548

5127. LOVE IS BLUE Al Martino
[20Apr68 | 29Jun68 | 10Aug68] 56(1) 17 548

5128. SEA LEVEL Sea Level
[05Mar77 | 23Apr77 | 11Jun77] 43(2) 15 548

5129. VOICES OF THE HEART Carpenters
[19Nov83 | 07Jan84 | 24Mar84] 46(2) 19 548

5130. NEVER, NEVER, NEVER Shirley Bassey
[26May73 | 28Jul73 | 29Sep73] 60(1) 19 548

5131. FISHERMAN'S BLUES The Waterboys
[10Dec88 | 11Feb89 | 03Jun89] 76(2) 26 548

5132. ELEPHANT MOUNTAIN The Youngbloods
[10May69 | 21Jun69 | 13Dec69] 118(2) 29 548

5133. HAWAIIAN ALBUM
Ray Conniff & His Orchestra & Chorus
[28Oct67 | 13Jan68 | 03Feb68] 39(1) 15 547

5134. GOIN' TO MEMPHIS
Paul Revere & The Raiders
[02Mar68 | 20Apr68 | 03Aug68] 61(2) 23 547

5135. MAGIC BUS-THE WHO ON TOUR The Who
[26Oct68 | 07Dec68 | 28Dec68] 39(1) 10 547

5136. PROMISED LAND Elvis Presley
[01Feb75 | 15Mar75 | 19Apr75] 47(1) 12 547

5137. THE BLUE RIDGE RANGERS
The Blue Ridge Rangers
[05May73 | 16Jun73 | 11Aug73] 47(1) 15 546

5138. PAPER MONEY Montrose
[16Nov74 | 21Dec74 | 15Feb75] 65(1) 14 546

5139. DONNY HATHAWAY Donny Hathaway
[15May71 | 24Jul71 | 02Oct71] 89(1) 21 546

5140. THIRTY SECONDS OVER WINTERLAND
Jefferson Airplane
[14Apr73 | 02Jun73 | 28Jul73] 52(1) 16 546

5141. ROCK OF LIFE Rick Springfield
[20Feb88 | 02Apr88 | 04Jun88] 55(1) 16 545

5142. IT'S TOO LATE TO STOP NOW Van Morrison
[16Mar74 | 20Apr74 | 06Jul74] 53(1) 17 545

5143. THE ADVENTURES OF PANAMA RED
New Riders Of The Purple Sage
[20Oct73 | 24Nov73 | 16Feb74] 55(1) 18 545

5144. SEND ME YOUR LOVE Kashif
[21Jul84 | 08Sep84 | 08Dec84] 51(2) 21 545

5145. ONE PARTICULAR HARBOUR Jimmy Buffett
[08Oct83 | 29Oct83 | 17Mar84] 59(3) 24 545

5146. MY KIND OF FOLK SONGS Gale Garnett
[26Sep64 | 12Dec64 | 20Feb65] 43(1) 22 544

5147. AL-DI-LA AND OTHER EXTRA-SPECIAL SONGS FOR YOUNG LOVERS Ray Charles Singers
[05Sep64 | 14Nov64 | 30Jan65] 45(1) 22 544

5148. LOVE OR SOMETHING LIKE IT Kenny Rogers
[29Jul78 | 16Sep78 | 14Oct78] 53(2) 12 544

5149. MONKEY ISLAND The J. Geils Band
[09Jul77 | 27Aug77 | 29Oct77] 51(1) 17 544

5150. THE BEST OF ERIC CARMEN Eric Carmen
[11Jun88 | 27Aug88 | 22Oct88] 59(1) 20 543

5151. A GOOD FEELIN' TO KNOW Poco
[25Nov72 | 24Feb73 | 07Apr73] 69(2) 20 543

5152. SINGLES 45'S AND UNDER Squeeze
[08Jan83 | 26Feb83 | 28May83] 47(3) 21 543

5153. HARD TIMES FOR LOVERS Judy Collins
[17Mar79 | 28Apr79 | 30Jun79] 54(2) 16 543

5154. SURFACE Surface
[30May87 | 04Jul87 | 03Oct87] 55(1) 19 542

5155. BRENDA RUSSELL Brenda Russell
[22Sep79 | 17Nov79 | 02Feb80] 65(1) 20 542

5156. TODAY Bobby Goldsboro
[07Jun69 | 26Jul69 | 30Aug69] 60(1) 13 542

Rank. Title Act
[Entry | Peak | Exit] Peak(Wks) TotWks Score

5157. QUADROPHENIA (SOUNDTRACK) The Who
[13Oct79 | 17Nov79 | 26Jan80] 46(1) 16 542

5158. STRAIGHT TO THE HEART David Sanborn
[09Feb85 | 02Mar85 | 14Sep85] 64(2) 32 542

5159. THE GREAT ESCAPE Soundtrack
[21Sep63 | 16Nov63 | 08Feb64] 50(1) 21 542

5160. DOING MY THING
Paul Mauriat And His Orchestra
[01Mar69 | 12Apr69 | 28Jun69] 77(1) 18 542

5161. AN ANTHOLOGY, VOL. II Duane Allman
[31Aug74 | 19Oct74 | 14Dec74] 49(1) 16 541

5162. UPTOWN FESTIVAL Shalamar
[21May77 | 18Jun77 | 20Aug77] 48(1) 14 541

5163. EVERYBODY LIKES SOME KIND OF MUSIC
Billy Preston
[27Oct73 | 08Dec73 | 23Feb74] 52(1) 18 541

5164. HOME PLATE Bonnie Raitt
[11Oct75 | 15Nov75 | 27Dec75] 43(2) 12 541

5165. RED RUBBER BALL The Cyrkle
[06Aug66 | 22Oct66 | 12Nov66] 47(2) 15 541

5166. I WISH YOU LOVE Gloria Lynne
[06Jun64 | 08Aug64 | 10Oct64] 43(1) 19 541

5167. SMILE Laura Nyro
[13Mar76 | 10Apr76 | 12Jun76] 60(2) 14 541

5168. THE NET Little River Band
[18Jun83 | 16Jul83 | 05Nov83] 61(1) 21 541

5169. NO MORE DIRTY DEALS
Johnny Van Zant Band
[06Sep80 | 08Nov80 | 13Dec80] 48(1) 15 540

5170. SWING STREET Barry Manilow
[12Dec87 | 30Jan88 | 30Apr88] 70(1) 21 540

5171. RESERVATIONS FOR TWO Dionne Warwick
[22Aug87 | 19Sep87 | 20Feb88] 56(2) 27 540

5172. O.C. SMITH AT HOME O.C. Smith
[18Oct69 | 08Nov69 | 31Jan70] 58(1) 16 540

5173. FANTASTIC Wham!
[20Aug83 | 08Oct83 | 16Nov85] 83(1) 44 540

5174. EVERY TIME YOU TOUCH ME (I GET HIGH)
Charlie Rich
[21Jun75 | 09Aug75 | 01Nov75] 54(1) 20 540

5175. STANLEY CLARKE Stanley Clarke
[18Jan75 | 22Mar75 | 03May75] 59(2) 16 539

5176. THE VENTURES 10TH ANNIVERSARY ALBUM
The Ventures
[10Oct70 | 14Nov70 | 27Feb71] 91(2) 21 539

5177. SLOW FLUX Steppenwolf
[21Sep74 | 26Oct74 | 07Dec74] 47(2) 12 538

5178. IN THE EYE OF THE STORM The Outlaws
[03Nov79 | 15Dec79 | 01Mar80] 55(1) 18 538

5179. LIVING ALL ALONE Phyllis Hyman
[11Oct86 | 11Apr87 | 25Jul87] 78(2) 41 537

5180. HOW DOES THAT GRAB YOU? Nancy Sinatra
[04Jun66 | 23Jul66 | 10Sep66] 41(1) 15 537

5181. CROSS THAT LINE Howard Jones
[15Apr89 | 06May89 | 09Sep89] 65(1) 22 537

5182. THE ANDY WILLIAMS SHOW Andy Williams
[14Nov70 | 19Dec70 | 06Mar71] 81(1) 17 537

5183. CATS Original Broadway Cast Recording
[26Feb83 | 02Apr83 | 22Mar86] 113(3) 64 536

5184. WCYAYA Osibisa
[12Feb72 | 11Mar72 | 03Jun72] 66(1) 17 536

5185. HEADLIGHTS The Whispers
[27May78 | 22Jul78 | 27Jan79] 77(2) 28 536

5186. WORLD IN MOTION Jackson Browne
[24Jun89 | 08Jul89 | 07Oct89] 45(2) 16 536

5187. JOURNEY TO THE CENTER OF THE MIND
The Amboy Dukes
[15Jun68 | 21Sep68 | 16Nov68] 74(2) 23 535

5188. I'M THE ONE Roberta Flack
[19Jun82 | 07Aug82 | 06Nov82] 59(2) 21 535

5189. BE MY LOVER O'Bryan
[26May84 | 28Jul84 | 13Oct84] 64(1) 21 535

5190. STREET CORNER TALKING Savoy Brown
[18Sep71 | 20Nov71 | 08Jan72] 75(1) 17 535

5191. I'LL SEARCH MY HEART AND OTHER GREAT HITS Johnny Mathis
[09May64 | 04Jul64 | 22Aug64] 35(1) 16 535

5192. GO INSANE Lindsey Buckingham
[01Sep84 | 29Sep84 | 15Dec84] 45(4) 16 534

Rank. Title Act
[Entry | Peak | Exit] Peak(Wks) TotWks Score

5193. DISCIPLINE King Crimson
[31Oct81 | 28Nov81 | 20Feb82] 45(2) 17 534

5194. TRIUMPH AND AGONY Warlock
[19Dec87 | 09Apr88 | 18Jun88] 80(1) 27 534

5195. HAPPY ANNIVERSARY, CHARLIE BROWN
Various Artists
[11Nov89 | 23Dec89 | 31Mar90] 65(3) 21 534

5196. GULA MATARI Quincy Jones
[05Sep70 | 17Oct70 | 19Dec70] 63(2) 16 534

5197. FOUND ALL THE PARTS Cheap Trick
[05Jul80 | 19Jul80 | 20Sep80] 39(2) 12 533

5198. RIGHTEOUS ANGER Van Stephenson
[02Jun84 | 11Aug84 | 13Oct84] 54(2) 20 533

5199. WHITE HOT Angel
[04Feb78 | 01Apr78 | 29Apr78] 55(1) 13 533

5200. IN ROCK WE TRUST Y&T
[18Aug84 | 15Sep84 | 08Dec84] 46(2) 17 533

5201. THE SWEETHEART TREE Johnny Mathis
[16Oct65 | 27Nov65 | 09Apr66] 71(1) 26 533

5202. SUPERMAN - THE MOVIE Soundtrack
[13Jan79 | 24Feb79 | 07Apr79] 44(1) 13 533

5203. GREG LAKE Greg Lake
[31Oct81 | 19Dec81 | 20Feb82] 62(4) 17 533

5204. A VIEW TO A KILL Soundtrack
[29Jun85 | 27Jul85 | 05Oct85] 38(2) 15 533

5205. EAR CANDY Helen Reddy
[21May77 | 09Jul77 | 24Sep77] 75(2) 19 532

5206. WISHES Jon Butcher
[04Apr87 | 06Jun87 | 03Oct87] 77(2) 27 532

5207. SWINGIN' NEW BIG BAND Buddy Rich
[31Dec66 | 18Mar67 | 01Jul67] 91(1) 27 532

5208. VIKKI! Vikki Carr
[23Mar68 | 18May68 | 06Jul68] 63(2) 16 532

5209. BAD REPUTATION Thin Lizzy
[24Sep77 | 29Oct77 | 03Dec77] 39(2) 11 532

5210. THE BEST OF ROD STEWART Rod Stewart
[15May76 | 19Jun76 | 26Mar77] 90(1) 26 532

5211. FIRST CIRCLE Pat Metheny Group
[13Oct84 | 03Nov84 | 08Jun85] 91(2) 35 532

5212. SECRET COMBINATION Randy Crawford
[23May81 | 08Aug81 | 26Sep81] 71(1) 19 532

5213. ROCKIN' INTO THE NIGHT 38-Special
[05Jan80 | 29Mar80 | 10May80] 57(1) 19 531

5214. TWANGIN... Dave Edmunds
[16May81 | 20Jun81 | 15Aug81] 48(2) 14 531

5215. SHOT OF LOVE Bob Dylan
[05Sep81 | 26Sep81 | 31Oct81] 33(2) 9 531

5216. GIRL AT HER VOLCANO Rickie Lee Jones
[02Jul83 | 06Aug83 | 15Oct83] 39(1) 16 531

5217. ACCESS ALL AREAS Spyro Gyra
[14Jul84 | 25Aug84 | 17Nov84] 59(1) 19 531

5218. SMOKEY'S FAMILY ROBINSON
Smokey Robinson
[06Mar76 | 24Apr76 | 12Jun76] 57(1) 15 531

5219. SKYLARKING XTC
[24Jan87 | 06Jun87 | 08Aug87] 70(2) 29 531

5220. STEPPIN' OUT High Inergy
[22Jul78 | 23Sep78 | 14Oct78] 42(2) 13 530

5221. ALL THEIR GREATEST HITS!
Harold Melvin And The Blue Notes
[03Jul76 | 31Jul76 | 02Oct76] 51(2) 14 530

5222. A MUSICAL AFFAIR Ashford & Simpson
[23Aug80 | 13Sep80 | 08Nov80] 38(2) 12 530

5223. RUNNING SCARED Soundtrack
[05Jul86 | 23Aug86 | 11Oct86] 43(2) 15 529

5224. FOUR SEASONS STORY The 4 Seasons
[13Dec75 | 17Jan76 | 03Apr76] 51(1) 17 529

5225. YOU GAVE ME A MOUNTAIN Frankie Laine
[19Apr69 | 24May69 | 28Jun69] 55(1) 11 529

5226. UP, UP AND AWAY Johnny Mathis
[23Dec67 | 09Mar68 | 04May68] 60(2) 20 529

5227. A SONG FOR ALL SEASONS Renaissance
[25Mar78 | 03Jun78 | 24Jun78] 58(1) 14 529

5228. FOR LADIES ONLY Steppenwolf
[02Oct71 | 13Nov71 | 11Dec71] 54(1) 11 528

5229. BATMAN ORIGINAL MOTION PICTURE SCORE
Soundtrack
[26Aug89 | 16Sep89 | 11Nov89] 30(1) 12 528

Rank. Title Act
[Entry | Peak | Exit] Peak(Wks) TotWks Score

5230. JOY RIDE The Dramatics
[30Oct76 | 19Mar77 | 21May77] 103(1) 25 528

5231. OTIS REDDING IN PERSON AT THE WHISKY A GO GO Otis Redding
[30Nov68 | 25Jan69 | 22Mar69] 82(2) 17 528

5232. I'M EASY Keith Carradine
[26Jun76 | 18Sep76 | 16Oct76] 61(1) 17 528

5233. SOUL MESSAGE Richard "Groove" Holmes
[14May66 | 17Sep66 | 05Nov66] 89(2) 26 528

5234. SNEAKIN' OUT Stacy Lattisaw
[28Aug82 | 23Oct82 | 11Dec82] 55(4) 16 528

5235. ROOTS AND BRANCHES The Dillards
[10Jun72 | 29Jul72 | 07Oct72] 79(2) 18 528

5236. EVERYBODY LOVES A CLOWN
Gary Lewis And The Playboys
[04Dec65 | 05Feb66 | 19Mar66] 44(2) 16 528

5237. UNCHAIN MY HEART Joe Cocker
[14Nov87 | 16Jan88 | 14May88] 89(2) 27 528

5238. BRASS ON IVORY Henry Mancini & Doc Severinsen With Orchestra and Chorus
[29Apr72 | 01Jul72 | 02Sep72] 74(2) 19 527

5239. JUST FOR NOW Nancy Wilson
[03Jun67 | 05Aug67 | 09Sep67] 40(1) 15 527

5240. STRIP Adam Ant
[10Dec83 | 24Dec83 | 02Jun84] 65(3) 26 527

5241. SHOTGUN Jr. Walker & The All Stars
[10Jul65 | 14Aug65 | 22Oct66] 108(1) 35 527

5242. FM/LIVE The Climax Blues Band
[01Dec73 | 02Feb74 | 22Jun74] 107(1) 30 526

5243. LOVE & UNDERSTANDING Kool & The Gang
[20Mar76 | 29May76 | 31Jul76] 68(2) 20 526

5244. MIRACLE ROW Janis Ian
[29Jan77 | 05Mar77 | 16Apr77] 45(1) 12 526

5245. MIRROR STARS The Fabulous Poodles
[10Feb79 | 14Apr79 | 02Jun79] 61(4) 17 526

5246. BITTER SWEET The Main Ingredient
[24Jun72 | 11Nov72 | 20Jan73] 79(2) 27 526

5247. MAKE A LITTLE MAGIC The Dirt Band
[19Jul80 | 23Aug80 | 01Nov80] 62(2) 16 525

5248. HAMBURGER CONCERTO Focus
[03Aug74 | 19Oct74 | 07Dec74] 66(2) 19 525

5249. BROTHERS OF THE ROAD
The Allman Brothers Band
[22Aug81 | 26Sep81 | 07Nov81] 44(1) 12 524

5250. PRIVATE PASSION Jeff Lorber
[15Nov86 | 21Feb87 | 09May87] 68(2) 26 524

5251. MARAUDER Blackfoot
[25Jul81 | 29Aug81 | 10Oct81] 48(2) 12 524

5252. GOLDEN ERA, VOL. 2
The Mamas & The Papas
[28Sep68 | 16Nov68 | 21Dec68] 53(1) 13 524

5253. DANGER MONEY U.K.
[24Mar79 | 05May79 | 02Jun79] 45(1) 11 524

5254. RHINOCEROS Rhinoceros
[28Dec68 | 15Feb69 | 31May69] 115(1) 22 524

5255. LUCKY SEVEN Bob James
[25Aug79 | 15Sep79 | 24Nov79] 42(2) 14 523

5256. ENERGY TO BURN B.T. Express
[29May76 | 19Jun76 | 14Aug76] 43(2) 12 523

5257. BANNED IN BOSTON? Rusty Warren
[19Oct63 | 21Dec63 | 15Feb64] 52(1) 18 522

5258. LIVE AT THE LONDON PALLADIUM
Judy Garland & Liza Minelli
[04Sep65 | 30Oct65 | 04Dec65] 41(2) 14 522

5259. BEWITCHED Jack Jones
[20Jun64 | 29Aug64 | 24Oct64] 43(1) 19 522

5260. HOTLINE The J. Geils Band
[27Sep75 | 25Oct75 | 22Nov75] 36(2) 9 522

5261. THE LATIN SOUND OF HENRY MANCINI
Henry Mancini And His Orchestra
[26Jun65 | 04Sep65 | 16Oct65] 46(1) 17 522

5262. 16 ORIGINAL BIG HITS, VOLUME 5
Various Artists
[05Nov66 | 24Dec66 | 11Mar67] 57(1) 19 522

5263. THERE GOES MY HEART Jerry Vale
[16Oct65 | 25Dec65 | 05Feb66] 42(1) 17 521

5264. SECRETS OF FLYING Johnny Kemp
[11Jun88 | 30Jul88 | 15Oct88] 68(1) 19 521

Rank. Title Act
[Entry | Peak | Exit] Peak(Wks) TotWks Score

5265. PEOPLE ARE PEOPLE Depeche Mode
[28Jul84 | 24Aug85 | 26Oct85] 71(1) 30 521

5266. BOYS DON'T CRY Boys Don't Cry
[21Jun86 | 12Jul86 | 25Oct86] 55(3) 19 520

5267. THIGHS AND WHISPERS Bette Midler
[22Sep79 | 27Oct79 | 12Jan80] 65(1) 17 520

5268. WHERE DO WE GO FROM HERE
Michael Damian
[17Jun89 | 15Jul89 | 03Mar90] 61(2) 27 520

5269. THE RANGERS WALTZ The Mom & Dads
[13Nov71 | 19Feb72 | 22Apr72] 85(1) 23 519

5270. TARANTELLA Chuck Mangione
[16May81 | 06Jun81 | 22Aug81] 55(2) 15 519

5271. SONG FOR AMERICA Kansas
[22Mar75 | 17May75 | 28Jun75] 57(2) 15 519

5272. TOO MANY RIVERS Brenda Lee
[25Sep65 | 13Nov65 | 25Dec65] 36(2) 14 519

5273. BLAH-BLAH-BLAH Iggy Pop
[18Oct86 | 15Nov86 | 18Apr87] 75(2) 27 518

5274. FROM THE INSIDE Poco
[25Sep71 | 23Oct71 | 04Dec71] 52(3) 11 518

5275. A MEMORIAL ALBUM
John Fitzgerald Kennedy
[18Jan64 | 01Feb64 | 14Mar64] 18(2) 9 518

5276. GET IT TOGETHER The Jackson 5ive
[06Oct73 | 01Dec73 | 03Aug74] 100(1) 29 518

5277. COME OUT AND PLAY Twisted Sister
[21Dec85 | 01Feb86 | 12Apr86] 53(2) 17 518

5278. NEW CITY Blood, Sweat & Tears
[31May75 | 19Jul75 | 23Aug75] 47(2) 13 518

5279. ONE VICE AT A TIME Krokus
[10Apr82 | 05Jun82 | 21Aug82] 53(2) 20 517

5280. EAGLES GREATEST HITS: VOLUME 2 Eagles
[13Nov82 | 08Jan83 | 19Feb83] 52(3) 15 517

5281. STEALING FIRE Bruce Cockburn
[25Aug84 | 23Feb85 | 13Apr85] 74(2) 31 517

5282. LET THE MUSIC DO THE TALKING
The Joe Perry Project
[12Apr80 | 24May80 | 05Jul80] 47(2) 13 517

5283. CERTIFIED LIVE Dave Mason
[27Nov76 | 08Jan77 | 19Mar77] 78(1) 17 517

5284. RECONCILED The Call
[08Mar86 | 24May86 | 27Sep86] 82(2) 30 517

5285. THE SPECIALS The Specials
[26Jan80 | 15Mar80 | 14Jun80] 84(1) 21 516

5286. WELCOME TO THE WRECKING BALL
Grace Slick
[14Feb81 | 21Mar81 | 16May81] 48(1) 14 516

5287. TURN BACK Toto
[07Feb81 | 07Mar81 | 11Apr81] 41(2) 10 516

5288. LET THE DAY BEGIN The Call
[01Jul89 | 23Sep89 | 25Nov89] 64(1) 22 516

5289. ALMOST IN LOVE Elvis Presley
[21Nov70 | 12Dec70 | 20Mar71] 65(1) 18 516

5290. BOYS IN HEAT Britny Fox
[25Nov89 | 02Dec89 | 28Apr90] 79(3) 23 516

5291. SCOOP Pete Townshend
[26Mar83 | 23Apr83 | 18Jun83] 35(2) 13 516

5292. L.A. MIDNIGHT B.B. King
[26Feb72 | 01Apr72 | 17Jun72] 53(2) 17 516

5293. BE YOURSELF Patti LaBelle
[22Jul89 | 12Aug89 | 13Jan90] 86(1) 26 515

5294. MOUNTAIN DANCE Dave Grusin
[21Mar81 | 23May81 | 18Jul81] 74(1) 18 515

5295. BAD BENSON George Benson
[28Dec74 | 15Feb75 | 03May75] 78(1) 19 515

5296. PUSH PUSH Herbie Mann
[30Oct71 | 04Dec71 | 01Apr72] 119(1) 23 515

5297. THE BEST OF THE BAND The Band
[04Sep76 | 16Oct76 | 04Dec76] 51(2) 14 515

5298. QUEEN II Queen
[11May74 | 15Jun74 | 03Aug74] 49(1) 13 514

5299. 20 ORIGINAL WINNERS OF 1964
Various Artists
[20Mar65 | 08May65 | 17Jul65] 44(1) 18 514

5300. MY LIFE IN THE BUSH OF GHOSTS
Brian Eno - David Byrne
[21Mar81 | 11Apr81 | 13Jun81] 44(2) 13 514

Rank. Title Act
[Entry | Peak | Exit] Peak(Wks) TotWks Score

5301. SWEET BEGINNINGS Marlena Shaw
[02Apr77 | 14May77 | 02Jul77] 62(1) 14 514

5302. LIFESTYLE (LIVING & LOVING) John Klemmer
[18Jun77 | 06Aug77 | 08Oct77] 51(1) 17 514

5303. BUMP CITY Tower Of Power
[17Jun72 | 19Aug72 | 28Oct72] 85(1) 20 514

5304. THE WAR OF THE WORLDS Various Artists
[12Aug78 | 16Sep78 | 27Jan79] 98(1) 25 513

5305. VIKKI CARR'S LOVE STORY Vikki Carr
[10Jul71 | 28Aug71 | 09Oct71] 60(1) 14 513

5306. GREATEST HITS SOUND OF MONEY
Eddie Money
[02Dec89 | 10Feb90 | 31Mar90] 53(1) 18 513

5307. BEST OF FRIENDS
Twennynine Featuring Lenny White
[08Dec79 | 23Feb80 | 22Mar80] 54(2) 16 513

5308. RENAISSANCE
Lonnie Liston Smith & The Cosmic Echoes
[11Dec76 | 12Mar77 | 23Apr77] 73(2) 20 513

5309. HOW DARE YOU! 10cc
[14Feb76 | 27Mar76 | 08May76] 47(1) 13 513

5310. WAR & PEACE Edwin Starr
[05Sep70 | 10Oct70 | 28Nov70] 52(2) 13 513

5311. DON'T LET THE SUN CATCH YOU CRYING
Gerry And The Pacemakers
[11Jul64 | 29Aug64 | 26Sep64] 29(2) 12 513

5312. THE CONCERT
Creedence Clearwater Revival
[20Dec80 | 14Mar81 | 02May81] 62(1) 20 512

5313. WISHFUL THINKING Earl Klugh
[31Mar84 | 12May84 | 01Sep84] 69(2) 23 512

5314. A TIME FOR LOVE Tony Bennett
[08Oct66 | 07Jan67 | 04Feb67] 68(1) 18 512

5315. SCHEHERAZADE AND OTHER STORIES
Renaissance
[30Aug75 | 25Oct75 | 22Nov75] 48(1) 13 512

5316. ANOTHER PLACE AND TIME Donna Summer
[20May89 | 24Jun89 | 30Sep89] 53(2) 20 512

5317. MARVIN GAYE ANTHOLOGY Marvin Gaye
[20Apr74 | 25May74 | 07Sep74] 61(1) 21 512

5318. WHAT EVER HAPPENED TO BENNY SANTINI
Chris Rea
[12Aug78 | 30Sep78 | 28Oct78] 49(1) 12 511

5319. SAY IT WITH SILENCE Hubert Laws
[08Apr78 | 27May78 | 05Aug78] 71(2) 18 511

5320. CLASSICAL BARBRA Barbra Streisand
[06Mar76 | 03Apr76 | 05Jun76] 46(2) 14 511

5321. TIGER IN THE RAIN Michael Franks
[17Mar79 | 26May79 | 30Jun79] 68(1) 16 511

5322. NEVER RUN NEVER HIDE Benny Mardones
[07Jun80 | 27Sep80 | 08Jul89] 65(1) 24 511

5323. MANTOVANI TODAY Mantovani
[04Apr70 | 18Apr70 | 12Sep70] 77(1) 24 511

5324. SPY Carly Simon
[30Jun79 | 21Jul79 | 22Sep79] 45(2) 13 511

5325. 110 IN THE SHADE Original Cast
[04Jan64 | 22Feb64 | 11Apr64] 37(1) 15 511

5326. DIONNE Dionne Warwicke
[29Jan72 | 11Mar72 | 29Apr72] 54(1) 14 511

5327. PETER GABRIEL/PLAYS LIVE Peter Gabriel
[25Jun83 | 30Jul83 | 08Oct83] 44(1) 16 510

5328. THE ARCHIES The Archies
[02Nov68 | 22Feb69 | 22Mar69] 88(1) 21 510

5329. IT AIN'T EASY Long John Baldry
[03Jul71 | 28Aug71 | 30Oct71] 83(1) 18 510

5330. CANDY GIRL New Edition
[03Sep83 | 08Oct83 | 14Apr84] 90(2) 33 510

5331. NAZZ NAZZ Nazz
[10May69 | 28Jun69 | 16Aug69] 80(2) 15 510

5332. CRYSTAL BALL Styx
[30Oct76 | 27Nov76 | 26Feb77] 66(1) 18 510

5333. COME INTO MY HEART
USA-European Connection
[08Apr78 | 24Jun78 | 12Aug78] 66(2) 19 510

5334. YOU HAD TO BE THERE Jimmy Buffett
[11Nov78 | 16Dec78 | 10Mar79] 72(1) 18 510

5335. MR. LOOK SO GOOD!
Richard "Dimples" Fields
[06Mar82 | 22May82 | 17Jul82] 63(1) 20 510

Rank. Title Act
[Entry | Peak | Exit] Peak(Wks) TotWks Score

5336. CHILLIN' Force M.D.'s
[22Feb86 | 03May86 | 09Aug86] 69(1) 25 509

5337. FLOY JOY The Supremes
[27May72 | 01Jul72 | 02Sep72] 54(2) 15 509

5338. WHY NOT ME The Judds
[01Dec84 | 02Mar85 | 25May85] 71(1) 26 509

5339. STARS Sylvester
[28Apr79 | 19May79 | 04Aug79] 63(2) 15 508

5340. SCRATCH The Crusaders
[13Apr74 | 25May74 | 24Aug74] 73(2) 20 508

5341. NATTY DREAD Bob Marley And The Wailers
[10May75 | 20Sep75 | 22Nov75] 92(2) 28 508

5342. WHO CAME FIRST Pete Townshend
[18Nov72 | 03Feb73 | 10Mar73] 69(1) 17 508

5343. THIS IS YOUR LIFE Norman Connors
[27May78 | 02Sep78 | 16Sep78] 68(1) 17 507

5344. THIS IS BIG AUDIO DYNAMITE
Big Audio Dynamite
[23Nov85 | 15Feb86 | 23Aug86] 103(2) 35 507

5345. WITH EVERYTHING I FEEL IN ME
Aretha Franklin
[21Dec74 | 08Feb75 | 15Mar75] 57(1) 13 507

5346. PEOPLE Hothouse Flowers
[27Aug88 | 29Oct88 | 08Apr89] 88(2) 33 507

5347. THE "POPS" GOES COUNTRY
Chet Atkins/Boston Pops/Arthur Fiedler
[18Jun66 | 27Aug66 | 19Nov66] 62(2) 23 507

5348. STAGES Triumph
[02Nov85 | 30Nov85 | 01Mar86] 50(2) 18 506

5349. BARNSTORM Joe Walsh
[21Oct72 | 17Nov73 | 16Feb74] 79(1) 29 506

5350. WHY CAN'T WE LIVE TOGETHER
Timmy Thomas
[20Jan73 | 10Mar73 | 28Apr73] 53(1) 15 506

5351. FURTHERMORE...
Shawn Phillips
[30Nov74 | 04Jan75 | 15Feb75] 50(2) 12 506

5352. KBC BAND KBC Band
[08Nov86 | 14Feb87 | 18Apr87] 75(2) 24 506

5353. FOGHAT (II) Foghat
[31Mar73 | 19May73 | 04Aug73] 67(1) 19 506

5354. BLOWIN' AWAY Joan Baez
[25Jun77 | 06Aug77 | 24Sep77] 54(1) 14 506

5355. A MAN AND A WOMAN
Isaac Hayes & Dionne Warwick
[19Feb77 | 02Apr77 | 14May77] 49(1) 13 506

5356. STAR! Soundtrack
[26Oct68 | 18Jan69 | 08Mar69] 98(1) 20 506

5357. CLUES Robert Palmer
[11Oct80 | 01Nov80 | 31Jan81] 59(2) 17 506

5358. UNIVERSAL LOVE MFSB
[14Jun75 | 26Jul75 | 06Sep75] 44(2) 13 505

5359. GLADYS KNIGHT & THE PIPS GREATEST HITS
Gladys Knight & The Pips
[04Apr70 | 09May70 | 01Aug70] 55(1) 16 505

5360. THE NEW GARY PUCKETT AND THE UNION GAP ALBUM Gary Puckett And The Union Gap
[06Dec69 | 10Jan70 | 07Mar70] 50(1) 14 505

5361. CARAVAN OF LOVE Isley Jasper Isley
[02Nov85 | 14Dec85 | 26Apr86] 77(2) 26 505

5362. DR. BUZZARD'S ORIGINAL SAVANNAH BAND MEETS KING PENETT
Dr. Buzzard's Original Savannah Band
[11Feb78 | 18Mar78 | 08Apr78] 36(2) 9 505

5363. DIRTY WATER The Standells
[02Jul66 | 24Sep66 | 15Oct66] 52(2) 16 505

5364. EVERYTHING'S COMING UP LOVE
David Ruffin
[12Jun76 | 17Jul76 | 28Aug76] 51(1) 12 504

5365. "FLIP" - THE FLIP WILSON SHOW
Flip Wilson
[02Jan71 | 23Jan71 | 10Apr71] 45(1) 15 503

5366. MORE TODAY THAN YESTERDAY
Spiral Starecase
[14Jun69 | 26Jul69 | 27Sep69] 79(1) 16 503

5367. BORN AGAIN Black Sabbath
[22Oct83 | 12Nov83 | 04Feb84] 39(1) 16 503

5368. EN ESPANOL Vikki Carr
[09Sep72 | 02Dec72 | 24Feb73] 106(2) 25 503

Rank. Title Act
[Entry | Peak | Exit] Peak(Wks) TotWks Score

5369. CANNED HEAT COOK BOOK (THE BEST OF CANNED HEAT) Canned Heat
[06Dec69 | 03Jan70 | 11Apr70] 86(1) 19 503

5370. A PERIOD OF TRANSITION Van Morrison
[07May77 | 11Jun77 | 16Jul77] 43(2) 11 503

5371. REFLECTIONS Rick James
[25Aug84 | 22Sep84 | 29Dec84] 41(2) 19 503

5372. HEALING Todd Rundgren
[21Feb81 | 07Mar81 | 16May81] 48(2) 13 503

5373. COUNT THREE AND PRAY Berlin
[08Nov86 | 29Nov86 | 21Mar87] 61(2) 20 503

5374. HERE'S LOVE Original Cast
[16Nov63 | 18Jan64 | 29Feb64] 38(1) 16 503

5375. HEART LAND Real Life
[07Jan84 | 03Mar84 | 16Jun84] 58(1) 24 503

5376. OVER UNDER SIDEWAYS DOWN
The Yardbirds
[27Aug66 | 22Oct66 | 10Dec66] 52(1) 16 503

5377. FREEDOM MEANS The Dells
[28Aug71 | 02Oct71 | 11Dec71] 81(1) 16 503

5378. MAD MAX BEYOND THUNDERDOME
Soundtrack
[24Aug85 | 21Sep85 | 16Nov85] 39(2) 13 503

5379. LIVE AT FILLMORE WEST King Curtis
[21Aug71 | 02Oct71 | 27Nov71] 54(2) 15 502

5380. TWO HOT FOR LOVE! THP Orchestra
[04Feb78 | 06May78 | 10Jun78] 65(1) 19 502

5381. LITTLE SHOP OF HORRORS Soundtrack
[17Jan87 | 28Feb87 | 09May87] 47(2) 17 502

5382. FULL CIRCLE The Doors
[05Aug72 | 16Sep72 | 11Nov72] 68(3) 15 502

5383. GAMMA 2 Gamma
[13Sep80 | 29Nov80 | 17Jan81] 65(1) 19 502

5384. THE WARNING Queensryche
[13Oct84 | 10Nov84 | 16Mar85] 61(3) 23 502

5385. REPEAT WHEN NECESSARY
Dave Edmunds
[04Aug79 | 29Sep79 | 10Nov79] 54(2) 15 501

5386. PEEPSHOW Siouxsie & The Banshees
[01Oct88 | 03Dec88 | 11Feb89] 68(1) 20 501

5387. WORKING GIRL Soundtrack
[11Mar89 | 29Apr89 | 10Jun89] 45(1) 14 501

5388. 'FRISCO MABEL JOY Mickey Newbury
[13Nov71 | 29Jan72 | 19Feb72] 58(1) 15 501

5389. BYRDMANIAX The Byrds
[24Jul71 | 14Aug71 | 25Sep71] 46(1) 10 501

5390. CATS WITHOUT CLAWS Donna Summer
[22Sep84 | 13Oct84 | 12Jan85] 40(2) 17 500

5391. THE MONTY PYTHON MATCHING TIE & HANDKERCHIEF Monty Python
[24May75 | 12Jul75 | 16Aug75] 48(2) 13 500

5392. THE PRESSURE IS ON Hank Williams Jr.
[05Sep81 | 10Oct81 | 06Feb82] 76(2) 23 500

5393. STANDING OVATION! Jerry Vale
[30Jan65 | 03Apr65 | 29May65] 55(1) 18 500

5394. A LITTLE SPICE Loose Ends
[06Jul85 | 07Sep85 | 09Nov85] 46(2) 19 500

5395. BRAZIL The Ritchie Family
[04Oct75 | 22Nov75 | 20Dec75] 53(1) 12 500

5396. EVOLUTION The Hollies
[05Aug67 | 02Sep67 | 04Nov67] 43(2) 14 500

5397. TOM RUSH Tom Rush
[14Mar70 | 23May70 | 27Jun70] 76(1) 16 500

5398. THE BEGATTING OF THE PRESIDENT
Orson Welles
[22Aug70 | 17Oct70 | 05Dec70] 66(1) 16 499

5399. DOG EAT DOG Joni Mitchell
[23Nov85 | 14Dec85 | 29Mar86] 63(5) 19 499

5400. ALCHEMY-DIRE STRAITS LIVE Dire Straits
[21Apr84 | 19May84 | 18Aug84] 46(2) 18 499

5401. LOVE Love
[14May66 | 30Jul66 | 10Sep66] 57(1) 18 499

5402. JOHNNY RIVERS IN ACTION! Johnny Rivers
[20Feb65 | 17Apr65 | 22May65] 42(2) 14 499

5403. HANKY PANKY
Tommy James And The Shondells
[30Jul66 | 08Oct66 | 05Nov66] 46(1) 15 499

5404. SMOKEY Smokey Robinson
[14Jul73 | 22Sep73 | 17Nov73] 70(1) 19 499

Rank. Title Act [Entry|Peak|Exit] Peak(Wks) TotWks	Score
5405. FAREWELL MY SUMMER LOVE Michael Jackson [02Jun84|07Jul84|08Sep84] 46(2) 15	498
5406. SEQUEL Harry Chapin [01Nov80|20Dec80|07Feb81] 58(1) 15	498
5407. CLASSICS Kenny Rogers & Dottie West [14Apr79|09Jun79|12Jan80] 82(1) 23	498
5408. BORN TO BE ALIVE Patrick Hernandez [28Jul79|22Sep79|03Nov79] 61(2) 15	498
5409. WHIRLWINDS Deodato [04May74|08Jun74|17Aug74] 63(1) 16	498
5410. EATEN ALIVE Diana Ross [12Oct85|16Nov85|22Feb86] 45(2) 20	498
5411. YOU'VE GOT A FRIEND Andy Williams [28Aug71|11Sep71|13Nov71] 54(1) 12	497
5412. MYSTICAL ADVENTURE Jean-Luc Ponty [13Feb82|17Apr82|15May82] 44(1) 14	497
5413. DON'T PLAY WITH FIRE Peabo Bryson [04Dec82|22Jan83|23Apr83] 55(3) 21	497
5414. WHAT DOES IT TAKE TO WIN YOUR LOVE Jr. Walker & The All Stars [17Jan70|07Mar70|13Jun70] 92(1) 22	497
5415. LIVE - BLOW YOUR FACE OUT The J. Geils Band [22May76|26Jun76|31Jul76] 40(1) 11	496
5416. THE SINGLES (THE FIRST TEN YEARS) ABBA [18Dec82|05Feb83|16Apr83] 62(6) 18	496
5417. CIVILIZED EVIL Jean-Luc Ponty [18Oct80|06Dec80|14Feb81] 73(1) 18	496
5418. LIVE! IN THE AIR AGE Be Bop Deluxe [20Aug77|17Sep77|26Nov77] 65(1) 15	495
5419. CITY OF NEW ORLEANS Willie Nelson [04Aug84|15Sep84|26Jan85] 69(1) 26	495
5420. THE BEST YEARS OF OUR LIVES Neil Diamond [07Jan89|28Jan89|22Apr89] 46(2) 16	495
5421. EVERYBODY'S OUT OF TOWN B.J. Thomas [02May70|16May70|12Sep70] 72(1) 20	495
5422. JUST BE MY LADY Larry Graham [08Aug81|19Sep81|31Oct81] 46(1) 13	495
5423. FIRST OFFENCE The Inmates [01Dec79|09Feb80|22Mar80] 49(2) 17	495
5424. BORN AGAIN Randy Newman [01Sep79|06Oct79|10Nov79] 41(2) 11	495
5425. VEHICLE The Ides Of March [27Jun70|01Aug70|12Sep70] 55(1) 12	494
5426. ROCK ON Humble Pie [08May71|12Jun71|06Nov71] 118(1) 23	494
5427. HEART'S HORIZON Al Jarreau [03Dec88|28Jan89|06May89] 75(2) 23	494
5428. APPRENTICE (IN A MUSICAL WORKSHOP) Dave Loggins [02Nov74|30Nov74|15Feb75] 54(1) 16	493
5429. MOUSSORGSKY: PICTURES AT AN EXHIBITION Isao Tomita [24May75|05Jul75|09Aug75] 49(1) 12	493
5430. THUNDERBOX Humble Pie [09Mar74|13Apr74|08Jun74] 52(1) 14	493
5431. STEPHEN STILLS LIVE Stephen Stills [27Dec75|14Feb76|06Mar76] 42(2) 11	492
5432. A LETTER TO MYSELF The Chi-Lites [24Mar73|28Apr73|16Jun73] 50(1) 13	492
5433. THE DANCE OF LIFE Narada Michael Walden [05Jan80|01Mar80|10May80] 74(2) 19	491
5434. THE SONGS I LOVE Perry Como [21Sep63|16Nov63|18Jan64] 59(2) 18	491
5435. PETER GABRIEL (II) Peter Gabriel [22Jul78|26Aug78|23Sep78] 45(2) 10	491
5436. OASIS Jimmy Messina [20Oct79|15Dec79|19Jan80] 58(1) 14	491
5437. SPECTRES Blue Öyster Cult [12Nov77|03Dec77|11Feb78] 43(2) 14	491
5438. THE SON OF ROCK AND ROLL Rocky Burnette [21Jun80|23Aug80|20Sep80] 53(1) 14	491
5439. AERIE John Denver [04Dec71|15Jan72|18Mar72] 75(3) 16	491
5440. GET ON THE GOOD FOOT James Brown [09Dec72|27Jan73|31Mar73] 68(2) 17	490
5441. ELVIS Elvis Presley [21Jul73|18Aug73|13Oct73] 52(1) 13	490
5442. W.A.S.P. W.A.S.P. [06Oct84|03Nov84|04May85] 74(2) 31	490
5443. UNTOUCHABLES Lakeside [28May83|18Jun83|24Sep83] 42(2) 18	490
5444. DARE TO BE STUPID "Weird Al" Yankovic [13Jul85|10Aug85|26Oct85] 50(2) 16	490
5445. CHOICE! THE BEST OF THE RAMSEY LEWIS TRIO Ramsey Lewis Trio [06Nov65|22Jan66|12Mar66] 54(1) 19	490
5446. THIS NOTE'S FOR YOU Neil Young & The Bluenotes [30Apr88|21May88|27Aug88] 61(2) 18	490
5447. LOVIN' THINGS The Grass Roots [29Mar69|26Apr69|12Jul69] 73(1) 16	490
5448. ONE FINE MORNING Lighthouse [24Jul71|06Nov71|11Dec71] 80(2) 21	490
5449. BODIES AND SOULS The Manhattan Transfer [08Oct83|05Nov83|14Jul84] 52(2) 27	490
5450. FULL OF FIRE Al Green [20Mar76|01May76|03Jul76] 59(1) 16	489
5451. NAZZ Nazz [19Oct68|07Mar70|04Apr70] 118(1) 26	489
5452. SHOT OF LOVE Lakeside [06Jan79|31Mar79|12May79] 74(1) 19	489
5453. CASUAL GODS Jerry Harrison: Casual Gods [06Feb88|30Apr88|18Jun88] 78(1) 20	489
5454. NIGHTRIDER The Charlie Daniels Band [04Oct75|15Nov75|20Dec75] 57(1) 12	489
5455. NO BALLADS Rockets [02Feb80|08Mar80|10May80] 53(2) 15	489
5456. GOIN' PLACES Michael Henderson [27Aug77|01Oct77|19Nov77] 49(1) 13	489
5457. HOUSE OF LORDS House Of Lords [19Nov88|25Feb89|20May89] 78(1) 27	489
5458. AFTER THE SNOW Modern English [19Mar83|30Apr83|26May84] 70(1) 28	488
5459. YOU'VE GOT IT BAD GIRL Quincy Jones [02Jun73|21Jul73|10Nov73] 94(1) 24	488
5460. RATTLESNAKE Ohio Players [20Dec75|06Mar76|20Mar76] 61(1) 14	488
5461. ROUGH MIX Pete Townshend & Ronnie Lane [15Oct77|05Nov77|31Dec77] 45(1) 12	488
5462. THE SKY The San Sebastian Strings [17Feb68|27Apr68|24Aug68] 68(1) 25	488
5463. OBJECTS OF DESIRE Michael Franks [30Jan82|27Feb82|01May82] 45(3) 14	488
5464. FIELD DAY Marshall Crenshaw [18Jun83|06Aug83|17Sep83] 52(1) 14	488
5465. SUBJECT: ALDO NOVA Aldo Nova [15Oct83|19Nov83|25Feb84] 56(2) 20	488
5466. DANCING WITH THE LION Andreas Vollenweider [15Apr89|06May89|19Aug89] 52(2) 19	488
5467. I TAKE A LOT OF PRIDE IN WHAT I AM Dean Martin [04Oct69|29Nov69|24Jan70] 90(2) 17	488
5468. TOGETHER Marvin Gaye & Mary Wells [16May64|01Aug64|29Aug64] 42(1) 16	488
5469. YESSHOWS Yes [20Dec80|31Jan81|07Mar81] 43(2) 12	488
5470. SOUL ZODIAC Nat Adderley Sextet and Rick Holmes [01Jul72|30Sep72|11Nov72] 75(1) 20	488
5471. TODAY Elvis Presley [07Jun75|02Aug75|30Aug75] 57(1) 13	487
5472. LOVING PROOF Ricky Van Shelton [29Oct88|12Nov88|08Apr89] 78(2) 24	487
5473. HOT WATER Jimmy Buffett [09Jul88|13Aug88|08Oct88] 46(2) 14	487
5474. PATTI Patti LaBelle [10Aug85|07Sep85|22Feb86] 72(3) 29	486
5475. LAST TRAIN TO HICKSVILLE...THE HOME OF HAPPY FEET Dan Hicks & His Hot Licks [09Jun73|28Jul73|06Oct73] 67(1) 18	486
5476. WATTS IN A TANK Diesel [08Aug81|14Nov81|30Jan82] 68(2) 24	486
5477. EVERYBODY'S ROCKIN' Neil and the Shocking Pinks [20Aug83|24Sep83|26Nov83] 46(2) 15	486
5478. SONGS FOR A TAILOR Jack Bruce [25Oct69|15Nov69|03Jan70] 55(2) 11	485
5479. THE FINAL FRONTIER Keel [19Apr86|07Jun86|16Aug86] 53(2) 18	485
5480. LETTER FROM HOME Pat Metheny Group [22Jul89|26Aug89|18Nov89] 66(2) 18	485
5481. THE NIGHT THE LIGHTS WENT OUT IN GEORGIA Vicki Lawrence [28Apr73|09Jun73|28Jul73] 51(1) 14	485
5482. BALANCE OF POWER Electric Light Orchestra [01Mar86|05Apr86|07Jun86] 49(3) 15	484
5483. THE WHOLE STORY Kate Bush [20Dec86|07Feb87|20Jun87] 76(1) 27	484
5484. NON STOP Julio Iglesias [04Jun88|09Jul88|24Sep88] 52(2) 17	484
5485. KILLERS Iron Maiden [06Jun81|15Aug81|07Nov81] 78(1) 23	484
5486. BLACK MARKET Weather Report [17Apr76|29May76|03Jul76] 42(1) 12	483
5487. GET IT OUT'CHA SYSTEM Millie Jackson [22Jul78|19Aug78|21Oct78] 55(3) 14	483
5488. LIVE EVIL Black Sabbath [05Feb83|19Feb83|23Apr83] 37(4) 12	483
5489. BEST SHOTS Pat Benatar [25Nov89|16Dec89|07Apr90] 67(1) 20	483
5490. I ONLY HAVE EYES FOR YOU Johnny Mathis [26Jun76|21Aug76|02Oct76] 79(1) 15	483
5491. THE VERY BEST OF CONNIE FRANCIS Connie Francis [02Nov63|18Jan64|04Apr64] 68(1) 23	482
5492. WILD HONEY & 20/20 The Beach Boys [03Aug74|28Sep74|12Oct74] 50(1) 11	482
5493. ONE MORE STORY Peter Cetera [20Aug88|10Sep88|10Dec88] 58(3) 17	482
5494. THE SEER Big Country [19Jul86|09Aug86|08Nov86] 59(2) 17	482
5495. SPARKLE IN THE RAIN Simple Minds [18Feb84|07Apr84|28Jul84] 64(2) 24	481
5496. WINNERS The Brothers Johnson [18Jul81|15Aug81|10Oct81] 48(2) 13	481
5497. LADY One Way [26May84|07Jul84|06Oct84] 58(1) 20	481
5498. WILD! Erasure [11Nov89|25Nov89|14Apr90] 57(2) 23	481
5499. AS WE SPEAK David Sanborn [10Jul82|21Aug82|11Dec82] 70(4) 23	481
5500. PUTTING IT STRAIGHT Pat Travers [17Dec77|25Mar78|13May78] 70(1) 22	481
5501. SPINNERS/8 Spinners [24Dec77|25Feb78|18Mar78] 57(1) 13	480
5502. PATTI LA BELLE Patti LaBelle [24Sep77|05Nov77|07Jan78] 62(1) 16	480
5503. LIVING Judy Collins [04Dec71|29Jan72|26Feb72] 64(1) 13	480
5504. APOLLO SATURDAY NIGHT Various Artists [22Feb64|04Apr64|13Jun64] 43(2) 17	480
5505. BUFFALO SPRINGFIELD AGAIN The Buffalo Springfield [18Nov67|06Jan68|17Feb68] 44(1) 14	480
5506. GUITAR MAN Elvis Presley [14Feb81|28Mar81|02May81] 49(1) 12	480
5507. SOMETHING TO TALK ABOUT Anne Murray [15Feb86|29Mar86|19Jul86] 68(2) 23	479
5508. SOME THINGS DON'T COME EASY England Dan & John Ford Coley [08Apr78|13May78|08Jul78] 61(2) 14	479
5509. PIECES OF DREAMS Stanley Turrentine [19Oct74|21Dec74|08Mar75] 69(1) 21	478
5510. MISTER HEARTBREAK Laurie Anderson [17Mar84|21Apr84|21Jul84] 60(2) 19	478
5511. OLDIES BUT GOODIES, VOL. 6 Various Artists [25Jan64|29Feb64|04Apr64] 31(1) 11	478

Rank. Title Act
[Entry | Peak | Exit] Peak(Wks) TotWks Score

5512. ARTHUR (OR THE DECLINE AND FALL OF THE BRITISH EMPIRE) The Kinks
[22Nov69 | 20Dec69 | 04Apr70] 105(2) 20 478

5513. HOT TOGETHER The Pointer Sisters
[29Nov86 | 20Dec86 | 28Mar87] 48(3) 18 478

5514. CHAKA KHAN Chaka Khan
[18Dec82 | 12Feb83 | 16Apr83] 52(1) 18 477

5515. I'M SO PROUD Deniece Williams
[04Jun83 | 25Jun83 | 08Oct83] 54(2) 19 477

5516. BY ALL MEANS NECESSARY
Boogie Down Productions
[30Apr88 | 28May88 | 01Oct88] 75(1) 23 477

5517. THE CAR OVER THE LAKE ALBUM
Ozark Mountain Daredevils
[08Nov75 | 20Dec75 | 14Feb76] 57(1) 15 477

5518. LATER THAT SAME YEAR
Matthews' Southern Comfort
[17Apr71 | 05Jun71 | 24Jul71] 72(1) 15 477

5519. DREAMS AND ALL THAT STUFF Leo Kottke
[09Nov74 | 07Dec74 | 25Jan75] 45(2) 12 477

5520. AS ONE Bar-Kays
[13Dec80 | 24Jan81 | 28Mar81] 57(1) 16 476

5521. THE INNER MOUNTING FLAME
Mahavishnu Orchestra With John McLaughlin
[29Jan72 | 03Jun72 | 29Jul72] 89(1) 26 476

5522. LIVE/DEAD Grateful Dead
[03Jan70 | 21Feb70 | 11Apr70] 64(1) 15 476

5523. LITTLE ARROWS Leapy Lee
[18Jan69 | 15Feb69 | 05Apr69] 71(1) 12 476

5524. KEVIN PAIGE Kevin Paige
[23Sep89 | 02Dec89 | 21Apr90] 107(2) 31 476

5525. SHE SHOT ME DOWN Frank Sinatra
[05Dec81 | 09Jan82 | 27Feb82] 52(2) 13 476

5526. THUNDER IN THE EAST Loudness
[02Mar85 | 04May85 | 10Aug85] 74(2) 24 475

5527. SPIRIT OF THE BOOGIE
Kool & The Gang
[30Aug75 | 27Sep75 | 29Nov75] 48(2) 14 475

5528. WHEN IN ROME When In Rome
[15Oct88 | 28Jan89 | 25Mar89] 84(1) 24 475

5529. STREET PARTY Black Oak Arkansas
[27Jul74 | 14Sep74 | 12Oct74] 56(1) 12 475

5530. DANCING IN THE STREET Ramsey Lewis
[28Oct67 | 27Jan68 | 10Feb68] 59(1) 16 475

5531. COCOMOTION El Coco
[15Oct77 | 25Feb78 | 18Mar78] 82(1) 23 475

5532. FOR LOVERS The San Sebastian Strings
[22Nov69 | 27Dec69 | 14Mar70] 84(2) 17 475

5533. A NEW SONG FOR YOUNG LOVE
The Lettermen
[25Jun66 | 20Aug66 | 01Oct66] 52(2) 15 474

5534. LIVE AT THE CAFE AU GO GO
The Blues Project
[21May66 | 16Jul66 | 08Oct66] 77(1) 21 474

5535. HELP IS ON THE WAY Melissa Manchester
[20Nov76 | 08Jan77 | 12Feb77] 60(2) 13 474

5536. BELLAVIA Chuck Mangione
[29Nov75 | 03Jan76 | 06Mar76] 68(1) 15 474

5537. DEAD RINGER Meat Loaf
[19Sep81 | 10Oct81 | 28Nov81] 45(2) 11 474

5538. THIRTEEN BLUE MAGIC LANE Blue Magic
[04Oct75 | 08Nov75 | 20Dec75] 50(1) 12 474

5539. MORE HIT SOUNDS OF THE LETTERMEN!
The Lettermen
[19Feb66 | 07May66 | 11Jun66] 57(1) 17 474

5540. WITH LOVE - CHER Cher
[18Nov67 | 20Jan68 | 17Feb68] 47(2) 14 473

5541. GOLDEN HITS Roger Williams
[09Sep67 | 21Oct67 | 23Mar68] 87(2) 29 473

5542. IAN HUNTER Ian Hunter
[17May75 | 28Jun75 | 16Aug75] 50(1) 14 473

5543. PHOENIX Labelle
[20Sep75 | 18Oct75 | 13Dec75] 44(2) 13 473

5544. LOVE AMONG THE CANNIBALS Starship
[19Aug89 | 30Sep89 | 16Dec89] 64(2) 18 473

5545. JUKEBOX Dazz Band
[20Oct84 | 08Dec84 | 04May85] 83(1) 29 473

5546. A LITTLE GOOD NEWS Anne Murray
[15Oct83 | 07Jan84 | 25Aug84] 72(1) 24 473

Rank. Title Act
[Entry | Peak | Exit] Peak(Wks) TotWks Score

5547. VOICE OF AMERICA Little Steven
[09Jun84 | 21Jul84 | 29Sep84] 55(2) 17 472

5548. TELL ME WHY Bobby Vinton
[25Jul64 | 05Sep64 | 10Oct64] 31(1) 12 472

5549. POSH Patrice Rushen
[29Nov80 | 07Feb81 | 28Mar81] 71(1) 18 472

5550. IT HURTS TO BE IN LOVE Gene Pitney
[14Nov64 | 26Dec64 | 06Mar65] 42(1) 17 472

5551. KINKS KINKDOM The Kinks
[25Dec65 | 05Mar66 | 16Apr66] 47(1) 17 472

5552. NO LOOKIN' BACK Michael McDonald
[07Sep85 | 05Oct85 | 14Dec85] 45(2) 15 472

5553. LITTLE RIVER BAND Little River Band
[02Oct76 | 11Dec76 | 12Mar77] 80(1) 24 472

5554. WARM The Lettermen
[04Feb67 | 25Mar67 | 27May67] 58(1) 17 471

5555. PENGUIN Fleetwood Mac
[28Apr73 | 02Jun73 | 21Jul73] 49(1) 13 470

5556. WALK AWAY - COLLECTOR'S EDITION (THE BEST OF 1977-1980) Donna Summer
[11Oct80 | 15Nov80 | 17Jan81] 50(2) 15 470

5557. OPEN YOUR EYES YOU CAN FLY Flora Purim
[13Mar76 | 08May76 | 19Jun76] 59(2) 15 470

5558. WAYNE NEWTON - NOW! Wayne Newton
[04Jun66 | 06Aug66 | 22Oct66] 80(2) 21 470

5559. GIMMIE SOME NECK Ron Wood
[12May79 | 09Jun79 | 04Aug79] 45(2) 13 470

5560. MICKEY MOUSE CLUB TV Soundtrack
[03May75 | 14Jun75 | 26Jul75] 51(2) 13 470

5561. HAG Merle Haggard And The Strangers
[17Apr71 | 22May71 | 24Jul71] 66(1) 15 470

5562. THE SCENE CHANGES Perry Como
[29May65 | 10Jul65 | 18Sep65] 47(2) 17 470

5563. TAKE 6 Take 6
[11Mar89 | 13May89 | 15Jul89] 71(2) 19 470

5564. SENTIMENTAL HYGIENE Warren Zevon
[27Jun87 | 25Jul87 | 24Oct87] 63(4) 18 469

5565. THE FUGS Fugs
[02Jul66 | 20Aug66 | 31Dec66] 95(2) 26 469

5566. SOMETHING SPECIAL The Sylvers
[20Nov76 | 25Dec76 | 19Mar77] 80(3) 18 469

5567. THE LONDON HOWLIN' WOLF SESSIONS
Howlin' Wolf
[21Aug71 | 11Sep71 | 27Nov71] 79(1) 15 468

5568. THE ROMANTICS The Romantics
[02Feb80 | 29Mar80 | 10May80] 61(1) 15 468

5569. COMIN' FROM ALL ENDS The New Birth
[17Aug74 | 19Oct74 | 23Nov74] 56(1) 15 468

5570. INVITATION TO THE MOVIES/BORN FREE
Matt Monro
[13May67 | 24Jun67 | 07Oct67] 86(1) 22 467

5571. LOST IN SPACE The Jonzun Crew
[14May83 | 23Jul83 | 24Sep83] 66(1) 20 467

5572. RAMBLIN' GAMBLIN' MAN
Bob Seger System
[08Feb69 | 22Feb69 | 12Apr69] 62(2) 10 467

5573. PLAYIN' TO WIN The Outlaws
[25Nov78 | 16Dec78 | 24Mar79] 60(4) 18 467

5574. ALL AROUND THE TOWN Bob James
[21Feb81 | 21Mar81 | 06Jun81] 66(1) 16 467

5575. PATA PATA Miriam Makeba
[09Dec67 | 27Jan68 | 04May68] 74(1) 22 467

5576. ANOTHER GREY AREA Graham Parker
[10Apr82 | 08May82 | 24Jul82] 51(2) 16 467

5577. SHOT THROUGH THE HEART Jennifer Warnes
[09Jun79 | 10Nov79 | 15Dec79] 94(1) 23 467

5578. CAN'T WE FALL IN LOVE AGAIN
Phyllis Hyman
[01Aug81 | 12Sep81 | 24Oct81] 57(1) 13 467

5579. STEALIN' HOME Ian Matthews
[11Nov78 | 17Feb79 | 21Apr79] 80(1) 24 467

5580. KISS KISS
[20Apr74 | 08Jun74 | 15May76] 87(1) 23 466

5581. FOR THE SAKE OF LOVE Isaac Hayes
[18Nov78 | 03Feb79 | 17Mar79] 75(2) 18 466

5582. EVERYTHING IS BEAUTIFUL Jim Nabors
[05Sep70 | 19Sep70 | 27Feb71] 124(1) 26 466

5583. BORN TO DIE Grand Funk Railroad
[31Jan76 | 06Mar76 | 10Apr76] 47(1) 11 465

Rank. Title Act
[Entry | Peak | Exit] Peak(Wks) TotWks Score

5584. MAMA AFRICA Peter Tosh
[18Jun83 | 13Aug83 | 08Oct83] 59(1) 17 465

5585. BAND OF GOLD Freda Payne
[22Aug70 | 10Oct70 | 14Nov70] 60(1) 13 465

5586. TURN OF THE CARDS Renaissance
[03Aug74 | 02Nov74 | 21Dec74] 94(2) 21 465

5587. VINTON Bobby Vinton
[14Jun69 | 19Jul69 | 30Aug69] 69(1) 12 465

5588. THE BLACKBYRDS The Blackbyrds
[22Jun74 | 19Oct74 | 23Nov74] 96(1) 23 465

5589. PARADE Spandau Ballet
[18Aug84 | 29Sep84 | 01Dec84] 50(3) 16 464

5590. 8:30 Weather Report
[06Oct79 | 17Nov79 | 15Dec79] 47(2) 11 464

5591. SLOW TURNING John Hiatt
[24Sep88 | 15Oct88 | 22Apr89] 98(3) 31 464

5592. ANTHOLOGY (1962-1969)
Diana Ross & The Supremes
[29Jun74 | 31Aug74 | 05Oct74] 66(1) 15 464

5593. CAMERON Rafael Cameron
[02Aug80 | 04Oct80 | 29Nov80] 67(1) 18 464

5594. SHARP Angela Winbush
[07Nov87 | 12Dec87 | 14May88] 81(1) 28 464

5595. LIVE OBLIVION, VOL. 1
Brian Auger's Oblivion Express
[07Dec74 | 18Jan75 | 01Mar75] 51(1) 13 464

5596. DOOLITTLE Pixies
[06May89 | 02Sep89 | 04Nov89] 98(1) 27 464

5597. LATE NIGHT GUITAR Earl Klugh
[06Dec80 | 17Jan81 | 09May81] 98(3) 23 463

5598. LOUDER THAN BOMBS The Smiths
[25Apr87 | 09May87 | 10Oct87] 62(2) 25 463

5599. SPARK OF LOVE Lenny Williams
[22Jul78 | 09Sep78 | 06Jan79] 87(1) 25 463

5600. SOME PEOPLE CAN DO WHAT THEY LIKE
Robert Palmer
[23Oct76 | 04Dec76 | 05Feb77] 68(1) 16 463

5601. FASTER PUSSYCAT Faster Pussycat
[29Aug87 | 10Oct87 | 23Apr88] 97(2) 35 463

5602. FAITHFUL Todd Rundgren
[15May76 | 26Jun76 | 21Aug76] 54(1) 15 463

5603. HIPSWAY Hipsway
[21Feb87 | 18Apr87 | 20Jun87] 55(2) 18 462

5604. WE COULD Al Martino
[06Feb65 | 03Apr65 | 15May65] 41(1) 15 462

5605. BOOGIE DOWN U.S.A. People's Choice
[06Sep75 | 25Oct75 | 13Dec75] 56(1) 15 462

5606. LETHAL UTFO
[03Oct87 | 14Nov87 | 13Feb88] 67(2) 20 462

5607. GREATEST HITS VOL.2 ABBA
[22Dec79 | 19Jan80 | 22Mar80] 46(2) 14 462

5608. TOUCH Laura Branigan
[01Aug87 | 26Dec87 | 05Mar88] 87(3) 28 462

5609. FALL INTO SPRING Rita Coolidge
[25May74 | 06Jul74 | 31Aug74] 55(1) 15 462

5610. SO GOOD The Whispers
[01Dec84 | 09Mar85 | 25May85] 88(1) 26 462

5611. SOMEWHERE IN MY LIFETIME Phyllis Hyman
[03Feb79 | 17Mar79 | 26May79] 70(1) 17 461

5612. LIVE! Smokey Robinson & The Miracles
[15Feb69 | 15Mar69 | 17May69] 71(1) 14 461

5613. THE FACES I'VE BEEN Jim Croce
[01Nov75 | 24Jan76 | 28Feb76] 87(1) 18 461

5614. CAT PEOPLE Soundtrack
[17Apr82 | 05Jun82 | 17Jul82] 47(2) 14 461

5615. THE BILLIE HOLIDAY STORY Billie Holiday
[23Dec72 | 31Mar73 | 12May73] 85(1) 21 460

5616. JAM ON REVENGE Newcleus
[08Sep84 | 29Sep84 | 16Mar85] 74(2) 28 460

5617. FOR YOUR EYES ONLY Soundtrack
[25Jul81 | 17Oct81 | 28Nov81] 84(2) 19 460

5618. FAMOUS BLUE RAINCOAT
Jennifer Warnes
[14Feb87 | 21Mar87 | 04Jul87] 72(2) 21 460

5619. WILD ANIMAL Vanity
[22Sep84 | 03Nov84 | 23Feb85] 62(2) 23 460

5620. STAR TREK - THE MOTION PICTURE
Soundtrack
[05Jan80 | 16Feb80 | 15Mar80] 50(1) 11 460

Rank. Title Act
[Entry|Peak|Exit] Peak(Wks) TotWks Score

5621. SUMMER WIND Roger Williams
[09Oct65|25Dec65|05Feb66] 63(1) 18 460

5622. THE COLOUR OF SPRING Talk Talk
[22Mar86|03May86|12Jul86] 58(2) 17 460

5623. CONSTRICTOR Alice Cooper
[18Oct86|22Nov86|07Mar87] 59(1) 21 460

5624. THE THORN IN MRS. ROSE'S SIDE Biff Rose
[08Feb69|05Apr69|10May69] 75(1) 14 460

5625. BACKSTAGE PASS Little River Band
[19Apr80|31May80|21Jun80] 44(1) 10 460

5626. THE RIGHT PLACE Gary Wright
[27Jun81|19Sep81|31Oct81] 79(1) 19 460

5627. THE BIG FOLK HITS The Brothers Four
[12Oct63|30Nov63|22Feb64] 56(1) 20 459

5628. THE BEST OF SAM & DAVE Sam & Dave
[15Feb69|26Apr69|07Jun69] 87(1) 17 459

5629. SLOW DANCER Boz Scaggs
[23Mar74|27Apr74|04Jun77] 81(1) 20 459

5630. BALLS TO THE WALL Accept
[04Feb84|17Mar84|28Jul84] 74(1) 26 459

5631. FREE AT LAST Free
[27May72|08Jul72|09Sep72] 69(1) 16 459

5632. MR. FANTASY Traffic
[27Apr68|29Jun68|21Dec68] 88(2) 22 459

5633. A HEART FILLED WITH SONG John Gary
[08Oct66|26Nov66|28Jan67] 73(1) 17 458

5634. THE GREGG ALLMAN TOUR
Gregg Allman
[16Nov74|21Dec74|01Feb75] 50(1) 12 458

5635. THE BEST OF JOAN BAEZ Joan Baez
[23Nov63|28Dec63|21Mar64] 45(1) 18 458

5636. ALTERNATING CURRENTS
Spyro Gyra
[29Jun85|31Aug85|30Nov85] 66(2) 23 457

5637. ANOTHER TASTE A Taste Of Honey
[14Jul79|18Aug79|06Oct79] 59(1) 13 457

5638. I WALK THE LINE Johnny Cash
[25Jul64|19Sep64|14Nov64] 53(2) 17 457

5639. CASINO LIGHTS Various Artists
[13Nov82|11Dec82|19Mar83] 63(5) 19 457

5640. THE STORY OF STAR WARS Soundtrack
[17Dec77|21Jan78|18Feb78] 36(2) 10 457

5641. COCK ROBIN Cock Robin
[13Jul85|05Oct85|16Nov85] 61(2) 19 457

5642. WORKING MY WAY BACK TO YOU
The 4 Seasons
[29Jan66|02Apr66|07May66] 50(1) 15 457

5643. THERE IS ONLY ONE ROY ORBISON
Roy Orbison
[04Sep65|27Nov65|25Dec65] 55(1) 17 456

5644. MORE CREEDENCE GOLD
Creedence Clearwater Revival
[21Jul73|18Aug73|17Nov73] 61(1) 18 456

5645. ICE WATER Leo Kottke
[02Feb74|09Mar74|01Jun74] 69(1) 18 456

5646. WHEELS Restless Heart
[11Apr87|06Jun87|26Sep87] 73(2) 25 456

5647. LEGEND Lynyrd Skynyrd
[10Oct87|31Oct87|30Jan88] 41(2) 17 456

5648. ALL THE BEST! Paul McCartney
[19Dec87|09Jan88|09Apr88] 62(3) 17 456

5649. WILD AND PEACEFUL Teena Marie
[05May79|07Jul79|15Sep79] 94(2) 20 455

5650. PUT YOUR HAND IN THE HAND Ocean
[29May71|26Jun71|21Aug71] 60(1) 13 455

5651. LITTLE CHILDREN
Billy J. Kramer With The Dakotas
[20Jun64|05Sep64|26Sep64] 48(1) 15 455

5652. JEFF BECK'S GUITAR SHOP
Jeff Beck With Terry Bozzio & Tony Hymas
[21Oct89|28Oct89|17Feb90] 49(2) 18 455

5653. PIANO RAGS BY SCOTT JOPLIN, VOLUMES I & II Joshua Rifkin
[22Jun74|17Aug74|28Sep74] 75(1) 15 455

5654. DID YOU THINK TO PRAY Charley Pride
[17Apr71|12Jun71|24Jul71] 76(1) 15 455

5655. GLORIOUS RESULTS OF A MISSPENT YOUTH
Joan Jett & the Blackhearts
[27Oct84|15Dec84|16Mar85] 67(1) 21 454

5656. SIMPLE MAN The Charlie Daniels Band
[25Nov89|20Jan90|19May90] 82(1) 25 454

5657. THE MICHAEL JOHNSON ALBUM
Michael Johnson
[15Jul78|16Sep78|04Nov78] 81(1) 17 454

5658. HEAVEN BeBe & CeCe Winans
[04Mar89|03Jun89|19Aug89] 95(1) 25 453

5659. U.K. U.K.
[20May78|24Jun78|26Aug78] 65(1) 15 453

5660. SNOOPY AND HIS FRIENDS
The Royal Guardsmen
[23Dec67|27Jan68|02Mar68] 46(3) 11 453

5661. WHAT MAKES SAMMY RUN? Original Cast
[04Apr64|16May64|04Jul64] 28(2) 14 453

5662. MR. SPOCK'S MUSIC FROM OUTER SPACE
Leonard Nimoy
[10Jun67|05Aug67|25Nov67] 83(1) 25 453

5663. LOVE IS A SACRIFICE
Southside Johnny & The Asbury Jukes
[14Jun80|12Jul80|20Sep80] 67(2) 15 452

5664. THE FAMILY The Family
[07Sep85|12Oct85|01Feb86] 62(2) 22 452

5665. ALL OVER THE PLACE The Bangles
[04Aug84|03Nov84|23Feb85] 80(2) 30 452

5666. WHERE LOVE HAS GONE Jack Jones
[29Aug64|17Oct64|30Jan65] 62(1) 23 452

5667. I AM THE GREATEST! Cassius Clay
[12Oct63|23Nov63|16May64] 61(1) 20 452

5668. SPEAK TO ME OF LOVE
Ray Conniff & His Orchestra & Chorus
[30May64|01Aug64|03Oct64] 50(1) 19 452

5669. SOUTH OF HEAVEN Slayer
[06Aug88|20Aug88|10Dec88] 57(2) 19 452

5670. 25 MILES Edwin Starr
[17May69|28Jun69|09Aug69] 73(1) 13 452

5671. G FORCE Kenny G
[24Mar84|12May84|11Aug84] 62(1) 21 451

5672. CONFETTI Sergio Mendes
[19May84|18Aug84|13Oct84] 70(2) 22 451

5673. I THINK WE'RE ALONE NOW
Tommy James And The Shondells
[29Apr67|10Jun67|26Aug67] 74(2) 18 451

5674. FEVER Roy Ayers
[26May79|07Jul79|01Sep79] 67(1) 15 451

5675. OUT OF LIMITS! The Marketts
[08Feb64|21Mar64|09May64] 37(1) 14 451

5676. CATS Original London Cast
[06Nov82|05Feb83|02Apr83] 86(2) 22 451

5677. RAISED ON ROCK/FOR OL' TIMES SAKE
Elvis Presley
[24Nov73|05Jan74|16Feb74] 50(1) 13 451

5678. BACK TO EARTH Rare Earth
[12Jul75|02Aug75|20Sep75] 59(2) 11 450

5679. MAN IN BLACK Johnny Cash
[26Jun71|17Jul71|11Sep71] 56(1) 12 450

5680. HOT AUGUST NIGHT II Neil Diamond
[21Nov87|09Jan88|12Mar88] 59(2) 17 450

5681. BABYLON A.D. Babylon A.D.
[02Dec89|31Mar90|04Aug90] 88(1) 28 450

5682. THE BEST OF ERIC BURDON AND THE ANIMALS, VOL. II Eric Burdon & The Animals
[10Jun67|08Jul67|18Nov67] 71(1) 24 450

5683. MEAT IS MURDER The Smiths
[02Mar85|11May85|05Oct85] 110(2) 32 450

5684. BELOW THE BELT Franke & The Knockouts
[10Apr82|12Jun82|07Aug82] 48(2) 18 449

5685. BLACK CARS Gino Vannelli
[29Jun85|20Jul85|14Dec85] 62(2) 25 449

5686. EL RAYO-X David Lindley
[16May81|18Jul81|12Sep81] 83(1) 18 449

5687. INSTANT REPLAY Dan Hartman
[16Dec78|03Mar79|21Apr79] 80(2) 19 449

5688. AUTUMN George Winston
[02Jun84|11Jan86|10Jan87] 139(1) 44 449

5689. DYLAN AND THE DEAD
Bob Dylan & The Grateful Dead
[18Feb89|04Mar89|29Apr89] 37(2) 11 449

5690. REUNION B.J. Thomas
[29Mar75|07Jun75|28Jun75] 59(1) 14 449

5691. THE MEN IN MY LITTLE GIRL'S LIFE
Mike Douglas
[29Jan66|12Mar66|07May66] 46(1) 15 448

5692. CONTACT Freda Payne
[12Jun71|14Aug71|09Oct71] 76(2) 18 448

5693. CITY LIFE Boogie Boys
[31Aug85|02Nov85|21Dec85] 53(2) 17 448

5694. HEAVEN HELP THE FOOL Bob Weir
[11Feb78|15Apr78|27May78] 69(1) 16 448

5695. CAPTAIN SWING Michelle Shocked
[11Nov89|18Nov89|05May90] 95(2) 26 448

5696. LOOK AT YOURSELF Uriah Heep
[25Sep71|06Nov71|15Apr72] 93(2) 20 448

5697. THE WINDMILLS OF YOUR MIND
Billy Vaughn And His Orchestra
[17May69|21Jun69|30Aug69] 95(1) 16 448

5698. AND ONCE AGAIN Isaac Hayes
[17May80|19Jul80|23Aug80] 59(1) 15 447

5699. FEELINGS Johnny Mathis
[08Nov75|24Jan76|27Mar76] 97(2) 21 447

5700. COSI FAN TUTTI FRUTTI Squeeze
[21Sep85|02Nov85|01Feb86] 57(2) 20 447

5701. THE GAP BAND The Gap Band
[19May79|07Jul79|15Sep79] 77(2) 18 447

5702. LICENSE TO DREAM Kleeer
[07Mar81|09May81|20Jun81] 81(2) 16 447

5703. LOOKIN' FOR A LOVE AGAIN Bobby Womack
[09Feb74|06Apr74|15Jun74] 85(1) 19 447

5704. NIGHT PASSAGE Weather Report
[13Dec80|17Jan81|14Mar81] 57(1) 14 447

5705. SLAVE TO THE RHYTHM Grace Jones
[23Nov85|21Dec85|05Apr86] 73(4) 20 447

5706. JOE'S GARAGE ACTS II + III Frank Zappa
[15Dec79|26Jan80|01Mar80] 53(1) 12 446

5707. SKYYPORT Skyy
[06Dec80|21Feb81|18Apr81] 85(1) 20 446

5708. BLUE VELVET & 1963'S GREAT HITS
Billy Vaughn And His Orchestra
[01Feb64|14Mar64|23May64] 51(2) 17 446

5709. MAN OF LA MANCHA Soundtrack
[09Dec72|24Feb73|31Mar73] 76(1) 17 446

5710. DREAM OF A LIFETIME Marvin Gaye
[08Jun85|29Jun85|14Sep85] 41(2) 15 446

5711. LIVING IN THE BACKGROUND
Baltimora
[18Jan86|15Mar86|10May86] 49(2) 17 446

5712. CALM ANIMALS The Fixx
[11Feb89|01Apr89|10Jun89] 72(2) 18 446

5713. SIT DOWN AND TALK TO ME Lou Rawls
[12Jan80|09Feb80|10May80] 81(1) 18 446

5714. CAN'T STOP THE MUSIC (SOUNDTRACK)
Village People
[21Jun80|26Jul80|06Sep80] 47(2) 12 445

5715. CENTIPEDE Rebbie Jackson
[27Oct84|22Dec84|23Feb85] 63(3) 18 445

5716. MADE IN AMERICA Blues Brothers
[27Dec80|14Feb81|14Mar81] 49(1) 12 445

5717. SYBIL Sybil
[21Oct89|02Dec89|31Mar90] 75(2) 24 445

5718. BLIND TO REASON Grayson Hugh
[15Oct88|16Sep89|25Nov89] 71(2) 24 445

5719. SUZANNE VEGA Suzanne Vega
[15Jun85|31Aug85|14Jun86] 91(2) 31 445

5720. TIME AND TIDE Split Enz
[08May82|26Jun82|18Sep82] 58(1) 20 445

5721. WAVES Katrina & The Waves
[12Apr86|10May86|26Jul86] 49(2) 16 445

5722. WILLIE REMEMBERS.. Rare Earth
[25Nov72|20Jan73|07Apr73] 90(1) 20 445

5723. HOOKER 'N HEAT
Canned Heat And John Lee Hooker
[27Feb71|03Apr71|26Jun71] 73(1) 16 444

5724. A SENSE OF WONDER Van Morrison
[09Mar85|06Apr85|29Jun85] 61(3) 17 444

5725. FREE HAND Gentle Giant
[16Aug75|20Sep75|25Oct75] 48(1) 11 444

5726. TOGETHER AGAIN...LIVE
B.B. King & Bobby Bland
[17Jul76|28Aug76|16Oct76] 73(1) 14 444

Rank. Title Act
[Entry|Peak|Exit] Peak(Wks) TotWks Score

5727. BEAUCOUPS OF BLUES Ringo Starr
[17Oct70|21Nov70|23Jan71] 65(1) 15 444

5728. SECRET TREATIES Blue Öyster Cult
[27Apr74|01Jun74|27Jul74] 53(1) 14 444

5729. ACE Bob Weir
[17Jun72|05Aug72|23Sep72] 68(1) 15 444

5730. MUSIQUE/THE HIGH ROAD
Roxy Music
[09Apr83|11Jun83|03Sep83] 67(1) 22 443

5731. GREENPEACE/RAINBOW WARRIORS
Various Artists
[15Jul89|19Aug89|13Jan90] 68(2) 24 443

5732. I DON'T SPEAK THE LANGUAGE
Matthew Wilder
[07Jan84|03Mar84|21Apr84] 49(2) 16 443

5733. THE MAGIC OF THE BLUE Blue Magic
[28Dec74|08Feb75|22Mar75] 71(1) 13 443

5734. COME AS YOU ARE Peter Wolf
[18Apr87|09May87|25Jul87] 53(2) 15 443

5735. MOONLIGHTING TV Soundtrack
[08Aug87|29Aug87|07Nov87] 50(2) 14 442

5736. ROCK ISLAND Jethro Tull
[30Sep89|14Oct89|27Jan90] 56(2) 18 442

5737. DREAM ON George Duke
[06Mar82|10Apr82|22May82] 48(2) 12 442

5738. SUNLIGHT Herbie Hancock
[08Jul78|02Sep78|30Sep78] 58(1) 13 442

5739. OPEN FIRE Y&T
[20Jul85|07Sep85|09Nov85] 70(3) 17 442

5740. DEVO-LIVE Devo
[18Apr81|09May81|04Jul81] 50(1) 12 442

5741. GREATEST HITS Dolly Parton
[16Oct82|04Dec82|19Mar83] 77(2) 23 442

5742. KILN HOUSE Fleetwood Mac
[31Oct70|05Dec70|30Jan71] 69(2) 14 442

5743. CHANGESTWOBOWIE David Bowie
[12Dec81|16Jan82|10Apr82] 68(1) 18 441

5744. DISTANT SHORES Chad & Jeremy
[24Sep66|26Nov66|24Dec66] 61(1) 14 441

5745. GERALDINE/DON'T FIGHT THE FEELING
Flip Wilson
[13May72|24Jun72|19Aug72] 63(2) 15 441

5746. HERO Clarence Clemons
[23Nov85|18Jan86|22Mar86] 62(2) 18 441

5747. ELEGANT GYPSY Al Di Meola
[07May77|04Jun77|23Jul77] 58(2) 12 441

5748. IN MY OWN DREAM
The Butterfield Blues Band
[24Aug68|28Sep68|14Dec68] 79(1) 17 440

5749. INSIDE YOU The Isley Brothers
[31Oct81|21Nov81|23Jan82] 45(1) 13 440

5750. CARICATURES Donald Byrd
[12Feb77|12Mar77|14May77] 60(1) 14 440

5751. ALIENS ATE MY BUICK Thomas Dolby
[07May88|02Jul88|10Sep88] 70(1) 19 440

5752. KEEP ON DANCIN' Gary's Gang
[31Mar79|14Apr79|02Jun79] 42(2) 10 440

5753. BIG & BEAUTIFUL Fat Boys
[24May86|21Jun86|27Sep86] 62(2) 19 440

5754. WHILE THE CITY SLEEPS... George Benson
[20Sep86|11Oct86|28Feb87] 77(1) 24 440

5755. REFLECTIONS Gil Scott-Heron
[26Sep81|20Feb82|27Mar82] 106(1) 27 440

5756. WAR OF THE GODS Billy Paul
[17Nov73|02Mar74|11May74] 110(1) 26 439

5757. THE JIM REEVES WAY Jim Reeves
[06Mar65|24Apr65|29May65] 45(1) 13 439

5758. A STEP FURTHER Savoy Brown
[13Sep69|11Oct69|27Dec69] 71(1) 14 439

5759. BRASS CONSTRUCTION 5
Brass Construction
[15Dec79|01Mar80|26Apr80] 89(1) 20 439

5760. HOT NUMBER The Fabulous Thunderbirds
[18Jul87|15Aug87|24Oct87] 49(1) 15 439

5761. LOVE TRIPPIN' Spinners
[21Jun80|26Jul80|13Sep80] 53(2) 13 439

5762. IF AN ANGEL CAME TO SEE YOU, WOULD YOU MAKE HER FEEL AT HOME? Black Oak Arkansas
[08Jul72|07Oct72|11Nov72] 93(2) 19 439

5763. SIGN OF THE TIMES Bob James
[12Sep81|10Oct81|12Dec81] 56(1) 14 439

5764. RICHARD NIXON SUPERSTAR David Frye
[11Dec71|15Jan72|04Mar72] 60(2) 13 438

5765. YOU BOUGHT IT-YOU NAME IT Joe Walsh
[09Jul83|20Aug83|08Oct83] 48(1) 14 438

5766. CHRISTMAS JOLLIES The Salsoul Orchestra
[11Dec76|14Jan78|04Feb78] 48(1) 13 438

5767. NICK THE KNIFE Nick Lowe
[20Feb82|20Mar82|22May82] 50(2) 14 438

5768. ALL THIS AND WORLD WAR II Soundtrack
[27Nov76|25Dec76|22Jan77] 48(2) 9 438

5769. LAST DAYS AND TIME Earth, Wind & Fire
[25Nov72|14Apr73|12May73] 87(1) 25 438

5770. IT'S HARD TO BE HUMBLE Mac Davis
[24May80|12Jul80|30Aug80] 69(2) 15 437

5771. SONG SUNG BLUE Johnny Mathis
[21Oct72|09Dec72|17Feb73] 83(2) 18 437

5772. HURT SO BAD Nancy Wilson
[08Nov69|17Jan70|07Mar70] 92(1) 18 437

5773. DAY BY DAY Najee
[09Jul88|13Aug88|26Nov88] 76(2) 21 437

5774. THE BEST OF FRIENDS Loggins & Messina
[11Dec76|08Jan77|26Feb77] 61(1) 12 437

5775. BARBRA STREISAND...AND OTHER MUSICAL INSTRUMENTS (SOUNDTRACK) Barbra Streisand
[24Nov73|22Dec73|09Mar74] 64(1) 16 437

5776. WE SOLD OUR SOULS FOR ROCK 'N' ROLL
Black Sabbath
[28Feb76|10Apr76|01May76] 48(1) 10 437

5777. DEEP SEA SKIVING Bananarama
[16Apr83|11Jun83|20Aug83] 63(1) 19 437

5778. SINGLES COLLECTION - THE LONDON YEARS
The Rolling Stones
[09Sep89|28Oct89|03Feb90] 91(1) 22 436

5779. AT PEACE WITH WOMAN The Jones Girls
[18Oct80|29Nov80|28Mar81] 96(1) 24 436

5780. THE CONFESSOR Joe Walsh
[01Jun85|29Jun85|05Oct85] 65(2) 19 436

5781. QUEENSRYCHE Queensryche
[17Sep83|05Nov83|11Feb84] 81(1) 22 435

5782. HAWAIIAN WEDDING SONG Andy Williams
[22May65|10Jul65|18Sep65] 61(2) 18 435

5783. UNREAL Bloodstone
[05Jan74|13Apr74|01Jun74] 110(1) 22 435

5784. HOW DO YOU DO? Mouth & MacNeal
[01Jul72|02Sep72|14Oct72] 77(1) 16 434

5785. GO Stomu Yamashta/Steve Winwood/ Michael Shrieve
[21Aug76|02Oct76|06Nov76] 60(3) 12 434

5786. RUMBLE
Tommy Conwell And The Young Rumblers
[03Sep88|29Oct88|11Mar89] 103(1) 28 434

5787. 96 TEARS
? (Question Mark) & The Mysterians
[19Nov66|31Dec66|25Feb67] 66(2) 15 434

5788. PORTRAITS The Buckinghams
[10Feb68|30Mar68|25May68] 53(1) 16 434

5789. O SOLE MIO - FAVORITE NEAPOLITAN SONGS
Luciano Pavarotti
[24Nov79|02Feb80|12Apr80] 77(1) 21 434

5790. WHERE'S THE PARTY? Eddie Money
[05Nov83|03Dec83|10Mar84] 67(1) 19 434

5791. RIVER OF TIME The Judds
[22Apr89|13May89|02Sep89] 51(2) 20 434

5792. CANNED HEAT Canned Heat
[12Aug67|18Nov67|13Jan68] 76(1) 23 433

5793. THE SANFORD/TOWNSEND BAND The Sanford/Townsend Band
[13Aug77|01Oct77|19Nov77] 57(1) 15 433

5794. BREAD & BUTTER The Newbeats
[03Oct64|26Dec64|06Feb65] 56(2) 19 433

5795. QUARTET Ultravox
[12Mar83|30Apr83|02Jul83] 61(1) 17 433

5796. READY OR NOT...HERE'S GODFREY CAMBRIDGE Godfrey Cambridge
[11Jul64|19Sep64|03Oct64] 42(1) 13 432

5797. LOVELINE Eddie Rabbitt
[09Jun79|15Sep79|20Oct79] 91(1) 20 432

5798. JUST FOR YOU Neil Diamond
[16Sep67|21Oct67|20Jan68] 80(1) 19 432

5799. NO PARLEZ Paul Young
[14Apr84|09Jun84|05Oct85] 79(1) 23 432

5800. BUTT OF COURSE The Jimmy Castor Bunch
[01Mar75|17May75|21Jun75] 74(1) 17 432

5801. THE FIRST TIME EVER (I SAW YOUR FACE)
Johnny Mathis
[10Jun72|22Jul72|16Sep72] 71(1) 15 432

5802. EPONYMOUS R.E.M.
[22Oct88|12Nov88|25Feb89] 44(2) 19 432

5803. LIVETIME Daryl Hall & John Oates
[27May78|01Jul78|29Jul78] 42(1) 10 431

5804. THE BUCKINGHAMS' GREATEST HITS
The Buckinghams
[24May69|19Jul69|09Aug69] 73(1) 12 431

5805. THE MAD HATTER Chick Corea
[11Mar78|29Apr78|10Jun78] 61(2) 14 431

5806. ZOOT ALLURES Frank Zappa
[27Nov76|18Dec76|19Feb77] 61(3) 13 431

5807. REST IN PEACE
Steppenwolf
[17Jun72|22Jul72|09Sep72] 62(2) 13 431

5808. NICE TO BE WITH YOU Gallery
[05Aug72|16Sep72|11Nov72] 75(1) 15 431

5809. Q: ARE WE NOT MEN? A: WE ARE DEVO!
Devo
[28Oct78|23Dec78|24Feb79] 78(2) 18 430

5810. THE HUNTER Blondie
[19Jun82|10Jul82|04Sep82] 33(2) 12 430

5811. FRANK SINATRA'S GREATEST HITS, VOL. 2
Frank Sinatra
[10Jun72|08Jul72|30Sep72] 88(2) 17 430

5812. SINATRA & COMPANY Frank Sinatra
[24Apr71|05Jun71|31Jul71] 73(1) 15 430

5813. SHOWTIME James Brown
[09May64|20Jun64|05Sep64] 61(1) 18 430

5814. MIDNIGHT LIGHTNING
Jimi Hendrix
[29Nov75|20Dec75|07Feb76] 43(1) 11 430

5815. MUSIC TO READ JAMES BOND BY
Various Artists
[13Mar65|22May65|11Sep65] 72(2) 27 430

5816. COMING OUT
The Manhattan Transfer
[18Sep76|16Oct76|13Nov76] 48(2) 9 430

5817. METHOD TO THE MADNESS
Undisputed Truth
[29Jan77|26Feb77|21May77] 66(2) 17 430

5818. MONEY TALKS Bar-Kays
[11Nov78|06Jan79|17Feb79] 72(2) 15 430

5819. ABOMINOG Uriah Heep
[07Aug82|25Sep82|20Nov82] 56(3) 16 430

5820. THE BEACH BOYS The Beach Boys
[29Jun85|20Jul85|28Sep85] 52(3) 14 429

5821. THE EYES OF THE BEACON STREET UNION
Beacon Street Union
[09Mar68|27Apr68|22Jun68] 75(3) 16 429

5822. HAVANA DAYDREAMIN' Jimmy Buffett
[14Feb76|27Mar76|15May76] 65(1) 14 429

5823. JAMAICA SAY YOU WILL Joe Cocker
[30Aug75|04Oct75|01Nov75] 42(1) 10 429

5824. TELEVISION'S GREATEST HITS
Various Artists
[09Nov85|08Feb86|28Jun86] 82(2) 34 429

5825. HAIR Soundtrack
[07Apr79|19May79|21Jul79] 65(2) 16 428

5826. ROYAL RAPPIN'S
Millie Jackson & Isaac Hayes
[20Oct79|22Dec79|23Feb80] 80(2) 19 428

5827. NEVER ENOUGH Patty Smyth
[21Mar87|18Apr87|01Aug87] 66(2) 20 428

5828. THUNDER IN MY HEART Leo Sayer
[22Oct77|12Nov77|28Jan78] 37(1) 15 427

5829. ABSOLUTELY LIVE Rod Stewart
[20Nov82|18Dec82|12Feb83] 46(3) 13 427

5830. 1957-1972
Smokey Robinson & The Miracles
[06Jan73|24Feb73|21Apr73] 75(2) 16 427

Rank. Title Act
[Entry | Peak | Exit] Peak(Wks) TotWks Score

5831. FIRST GREAT ROCK FESTIVALS OF THE SEVENTIES: ISLE OF WIGHT/ATLANTA POP FEST Various Artists
[18Sep71 | 09Oct71 | 13Nov71] 47(2) 9 427

5832. BLACKS AND BLUES Bobbi Humphrey
[30Mar74 | 25May74 | 17Aug74] 84(1) 21 427

5833. MOUNTAIN Leslie West
[06Sep69 | 18Oct69 | 06Dec69] 72(2) 14 427

5834. NO PLACE TO RUN UFO
[19Jan80 | 16Feb80 | 12Apr80] 51(1) 13 427

5835. YELLOW MAGIC ORCHESTRA Yellow Magic Orchestra
[26Jan80 | 22Mar80 | 14Jun80] 81(1) 21 427

5836. DOS Malo
[11Nov72 | 16Dec72 | 10Feb73] 62(1) 14 427

5837. RAT IN THE KITCHEN UB40
[30Aug86 | 04Oct86 | 20Dec86] 53(2) 17 427

5838. WE REMEMBER SAM COOKE The Supremes
[08May65 | 12Jun65 | 11Sep65] 75(2) 19 427

5839. BITE DOWN HARD Jo Jo Gunne
[17Mar73 | 19May73 | 07Jul73] 75(1) 17 426

5840. CONCERT FOR LOVERS Ferrante & Teicher
[14Dec63 | 14Mar64 | 04Apr64] 63(1) 17 426

5841. GETTIN' DOWN TO IT James Brown
[31May69 | 19Jul69 | 30Aug69] 99(2) 14 426

5842. BLACK CELEBRATION Depeche Mode
[26Apr86 | 17May86 | 18Oct86] 90(2) 26 426

5843. DEDICATED The Marshall Tucker Band
[23May81 | 06Jun81 | 08Aug81] 53(2) 12 426

5844. IGNITION John Waite
[17Jul82 | 18Sep82 | 20Apr85] 68(3) 23 426

5845. PENETRATOR Ted Nugent
[18Feb84 | 07Apr84 | 26May84] 56(2) 15 426

5846. COMMUNICATION Bobby Womack
[04Dec71 | 29Jan72 | 25Mar72] 83(2) 17 426

5847. IN THE POCKET Stanley Turrentine
[10May75 | 14Jun75 | 09Aug75] 65(2) 14 426

5848. SPOOKY LADY'S SIDESHOW Kris Kristofferson
[25May74 | 27Jul74 | 24Aug74] 78(1) 14 426

5849. BLUE MURDER Blue Murder
[13May89 | 24Jun89 | 30Sep89] 69(2) 21 425

5850. LONG HARD LOOK Lou Gramm
[11Nov89 | 17Feb90 | 14Apr90] 85(1) 23 425

5851. STEVIE WONDER'S GREATEST HITS, VOL. 2 Stevie Wonder
[20Nov71 | 08Jan72 | 05Feb72] 69(1) 12 425

5852. FOUR DAYS THAT SHOCKED THE WORLD (NARRATED BY REID COLLINS) No Artist
[08Feb64 | 29Feb64 | 11Apr64] 29(2) 10 424

5853. BABY I LOVE YOU Andy Kim
[02Aug69 | 30Aug69 | 01Nov69] 82(2) 14 424

5854. WOVOKA Redbone
[16Mar74 | 11May74 | 29Jun74] 66(1) 16 424

5855. NIGHT BEAT Sam Cooke
[14Sep63 | 12Oct63 | 18Jan64] 62(1) 19 424

5856. UNFINISHED BUSINESS EPMD
[19Aug89 | 09Sep89 | 18Nov89] 53(3) 14 424

5857. NICE 'N' NAASTY The Salsoul Orchestra
[23Oct76 | 13Nov76 | 22Jan77] 61(2) 14 424

5858. NEW! IMPROVED! BLUE CHEER Blue Cheer
[03May69 | 14Jun69 | 02Aug69] 84(2) 14 424

5859. MY SPANISH HEART Chick Corea
[15Jan77 | 12Feb77 | 02Apr77] 55(1) 12 424

5860. PARTY YOUR BODY Stevie B
[23Jul88 | 24Sep88 | 10Dec88] 78(1) 21 424

5861. ELLA AND BASIE! Ella & Basie
[19Oct63 | 14Dec63 | 29Feb64] 69(1) 20 424

5862. WELCOME TO THE CLUB Ian Hunter
[26Apr80 | 24May80 | 16Aug80] 69(1) 17 423

5863. MAKE WAY FOR DIONNE WARWICK Dionne Warwick
[12Sep64 | 28Nov64 | 23Jan65] 68(2) 20 423

5864. TOUCH THE SKY Smokey Robinson
[29Jan83 | 26Feb83 | 21May83] 50(3) 17 423

5865. ROMANTIC JOURNEY Norman Connors
[09Apr77 | 21May77 | 23Jul77] 94(2) 16 423

5866. JUJU MUSIC King Sunny Ade & His African Beats
[09Apr83 | 17Sep83 | 22Oct83] 111(1) 29 423

5867. THE YOUNG MODS' FORGOTTEN STORY The Impressions
[24May69 | 06Sep69 | 27Sep69] 104(1) 18 423

5868. HOLST: THE PLANETS Tomita
[08Jan77 | 05Feb77 | 02Apr77] 67(2) 13 423

5869. EV'RY DAY OF MY LIFE Bobby Vinton
[08Apr72 | 20May72 | 15Jul72] 72(1) 15 423

5870. ELECTRONIC REALIZATIONS FOR ROCK ORCHESTRA Synergy
[21Jun75 | 06Sep75 | 18Oct75] 66(1) 18 422

5871. UNSUNG HEROES The Dregs
[18Apr81 | 23May81 | 18Jul81] 67(2) 14 422

5872. HIGHLY PRIZED POSSESSION Anne Murray
[14Dec74 | 08Feb75 | 08Mar75] 70(1) 13 422

5873. LET IT FLOW Elvin Bishop
[27Jul74 | 07Sep74 | 16Nov74] 100(1) 17 422

5874. THE MONA LISA'S SISTER Graham Parker
[28May88 | 02Jul88 | 01Oct88] 77(2) 19 422

5875. I WANNA PLAY FOR YOU Stanley Clarke
[21Jul79 | 25Aug79 | 20Oct79] 62(1) 14 422

5876. THINK OF ONE Wynton Marsalis
[09Jul83 | 02Jun84 | 21Jul84] 102(1) 29 422

5877. BREAKOUT Spyro Gyra
[12Jul86 | 27Sep86 | 15Nov86] 71(1) 19 421

5878. TODAY Today
[14Jan89 | 11Feb89 | 10Jun89] 86(2) 22 421

5879. CITIZEN KIHN Greg Kihn
[23Mar85 | 27Apr85 | 15Jun85] 51(2) 13 421

5880. KENNY NOLAN Kenny Nolan
[26Mar77 | 21May77 | 09Jul77] 78(1) 16 421

5881. SOMEBODY ELSE IS TAKING MY PLACE Al Martino
[19Jun65 | 17Jul65 | 04Sep65] 42(1) 12 421

5882. GREATEST HITS! Trini Lopez
[26Nov66 | 07Jan67 | 04Feb67] 47(2) 11 421

5883. THIS IS LOVE Al Martino
[29Oct66 | 07Jan67 | 21Jan67] 57(1) 13 421

5884. SIDE BY SIDE Tony Sandler And Ralph Young
[17Dec66 | 01Apr67 | 22Apr67] 85(1) 19 420

5885. CHILDREN OF TOMORROW Frankie Smith
[08Aug81 | 05Sep81 | 10Oct81] 54(2) 10 420

5886. JAMES BROWN SOUL CLASSICS James Brown
[17Jun72 | 05Aug72 | 30Sep72] 83(2) 16 420

5887. SEE YOU IN HELL Grim Reaper
[25Aug84 | 27Oct84 | 23Feb85] 73(2) 27 420

5888. KALEIDOSCOPE WORLD Swing Out Sister
[27May89 | 17Jun89 | 30Sep89] 61(2) 19 420

5889. FRANK ZAPPA'S 200 MOTELS (SOUNDTRACK) Frank Zappa
[30Oct71 | 04Dec71 | 22Jan72] 59(1) 13 420

5890. BARKING AT AIRPLANES Kim Carnes
[29Jun85 | 27Jul85 | 28Sep85] 48(2) 14 419

5891. FLASH AND THE PAN Flash And The Pan
[26May79 | 18Aug79 | 08Sep79] 80(2) 16 419

5892. YOU AND ME Rockie Robbins
[07Jun80 | 02Aug80 | 20Sep80] 71(2) 16 419

5893. TRUE GRIT Soundtrack
[02Aug69 | 13Sep69 | 18Oct69] 77(2) 12 419

5894. THE WATERGATE COMEDY HOUR Various Artists
[23Jun73 | 21Jul73 | 29Sep73] 62(1) 15 419

5895. COAL MINER'S DAUGHTER Loretta Lynn
[13Feb71 | 03Apr71 | 05Jun71] 81(1) 17 419

5896. ENCOUNTERS OF EVERY KIND Meco
[14Jan78 | 18Feb78 | 08Apr78] 62(2) 13 419

5897. ASTRA Asia
[07Dec85 | 28Dec85 | 29Mar86] 67(3) 17 418

5898. INSIDE THE ELECTRIC CIRCUS W.A.S.P.
[08Nov86 | 22Nov86 | 14Mar87] 60(2) 19 418

5899. GREATEST HITS Martha & The Vandellas
[11Jun66 | 30Jul66 | 17Sep66] 50(1) 15 418

5900. SPANKY'S GREATEST HIT(S) Spanky And Our Gang
[01Nov69 | 24Jan70 | 21Feb70] 91(1) 17 418

5901. DIFFORD & TILBROOK Difford & Tilbrook
[14Jul84 | 04Aug84 | 20Oct84] 55(3) 15 418

5902. THE DARK Metal Church
[08Nov86 | 24Jan87 | 11Apr87] 92(1) 23 418

5903. MELISSA MANCHESTER Melissa Manchester
[03Nov79 | 15Dec79 | 24May80] 63(1) 21 418

5904. THE HARDNESS OF THE WORLD Slave
[17Dec77 | 25Feb78 | 25Mar78] 67(1) 15 418

5905. TWELVE DREAMS OF DR. SARDONICUS Spirit
[26Dec70 | 13Feb71 | 27Mar71] 63(1) 14 417

5906. DEATH WALKS BEHIND YOU Atomic Rooster
[03Jul71 | 11Sep71 | 09Oct71] 90(2) 15 417

5907. HAPPY JACK The Who
[20May67 | 22Jul67 | 14Oct67] 67(1) 22 417

5908. TRINI Trini Lopez
[07May66 | 25Jun66 | 20Aug66] 54(1) 16 417

5909. INDIANA JONES AND THE TEMPLE OF DOOM (JOHN WILLIAMS) Soundtrack
[16Jun84 | 14Jul84 | 18Aug84] 42(2) 10 416

5910. LARKS' TONGUES IN ASPIC King Crimson
[05May73 | 16Jun73 | 04Aug73] 61(1) 14 416

5911. LOVE ME Yvonne Elliman
[12Mar77 | 04Jun77 | 25Jun77] 68(1) 16 416

5912. TEASER Angela Bofill
[26Nov83 | 11Feb84 | 14Apr84] 81(1) 21 416

5913. NO GUTS...NO GLORY Molly Hatchet
[26Mar83 | 30Apr83 | 06Aug83] 59(1) 20 416

5914. ONE DAY AT A TIME Joan Baez
[21Mar70 | 02May70 | 20Jun70] 80(1) 14 416

5915. CHICO DEBARGE Chico DeBarge
[15Nov86 | 07Feb87 | 06Jun87] 90(2) 30 416

5916. THREE OF A PERFECT PAIR King Crimson
[07Apr84 | 28Apr84 | 28Jul84] 58(2) 17 416

5917. ALONE AGAIN (NATURALLY) Andy Williams
[30Sep72 | 02Dec72 | 27Jan73] 86(2) 18 416

5918. TELEVISION THEME SONGS Mike Post
[27Feb82 | 08May82 | 19Jun82] 70(2) 17 415

5919. ANYONE CAN SEE Irene Cara
[30Jan82 | 13Mar82 | 22May82] 76(2) 17 415

5920. ECSTASY Ohio Players
[29Sep73 | 10Nov73 | 02Feb74] 70(1) 19 415

5921. THE BEST OF MOUNTAIN Mountain
[24Feb73 | 14Apr73 | 09Jun73] 72(1) 16 415

5922. LOVE BREEZE Smokey Robinson
[15Apr78 | 24Jun78 | 19Aug78] 75(1) 19 415

5923. CANNED WHEAT PACKED BY THE GUESS WHO The Guess Who
[04Oct69 | 29Nov69 | 28Mar70] 91(1) 17 415

5924. BRIAN WILSON Brian Wilson
[30Jul88 | 13Aug88 | 22Oct88] 54(3) 13 415

5925. BEFORE HIS TIME Willie Nelson
[21May77 | 25Jun77 | 27Aug77] 78(2) 15 415

5926. THROUGH THE STORM Aretha Franklin
[20May89 | 10Jun89 | 16Sep89] 55(2) 18 415

5927. TO BONNIE FROM DELANEY Delaney & Bonnie & Friends
[10Oct70 | 31Oct70 | 12Dec70] 58(1) 10 415

5928. SKIN ON SKIN Vanity
[22Mar86 | 10May86 | 02Aug86] 66(2) 20 415

5929. THE PAINTER Paul Anka
[23Oct76 | 08Jan77 | 29Jan77] 85(1) 15 415

5930. CHARTBUSTERS Ray Parker Jr.
[15Dec84 | 26Jan85 | 23Mar85] 60(3) 15 414

5931. NORTH COAST Michael Stanley Band
[01Aug81 | 10Oct81 | 07Nov81] 79(2) 15 414

5932. THE BEST OF WILSON PICKETT, VOL. II Wilson Pickett
[22May71 | 26Jun71 | 14Aug71] 73(1) 13 414

5933. MACHISMO Cameo
[12Nov88 | 26Nov88 | 18Mar89] 56(1) 19 414

5934. INSIDE MOVES Grover Washington Jr.
[10Nov84 | 15Dec84 | 13Apr85] 79(1) 23 414

5935. LIVE Alabama
[25Jun88 | 09Jul88 | 29Oct88] 76(3) 19 414

5936. FANDANGO Herb Alpert
[29May82 | 04Sep82 | 20Nov82] 100(2) 26 414

Rank. Title	Act	Entry	Peak	Exit	Peak(Wks)	TotWks	Score
5937. HEARTS OF STONE	Southside Johnny & The Asbury Jukes	04Nov78	13Jan79	17Mar79	112(1)	20	414
5938. ALL THE YOUNG DUDES	Mott The Hoople	11Nov72	24Feb73	17Mar73	89(1)	19	414
5939. LET THE MUSIC PLAY	Arpeggio	10Feb79	31Mar79	26May79	75(3)	16	413
5940. PERFECT TIMING	McAuley Schenker Group	24Oct87	21Nov87	02Apr88	95(2)	24	413
5941. DOWN TO EARTH	Rainbow	25Aug79	06Oct79	01Dec79	66(1)	15	413
5942. TWISTING BY THE POOL	Dire Straits	12Mar83	30Apr83	18Jun83	53(1)	15	413
5943. IN YOUR FACE	Kingdom Come	13May89	27May89	19Aug89	49(2)	15	413
5944. KLYMAXX	Klymaxx	06Dec86	01Aug87	19Sep87	98(2)	31	413
5945. NEW GOLD DREAM (81-82-83-84)	Simple Minds	19Feb83	09Apr83	25Jun83	69(2)	19	413
5946. MY BOY	Richard Harris	18Dec71	29Jan72	18Mar72	71(1)	14	413
5947. GENE CHANDLER '80	Gene Chandler	07Jun80	02Aug80	04Oct80	87(1)	18	413
5948. ODORI	Hiroshima	15Nov80	13Dec80	14Mar81	72(1)	18	413
5949. WIDE AWAKE IN AMERICA	U2	29Jun85	29Jun85	19Sep87	37(1)	23	413
5950. NERUDA	Red Rider	05Feb83	19Mar83	21May83	66(4)	16	413
5951. RIDING HIGH	Faze-O	04Mar78	06May78	24Jun78	98(1)	17	412
5952. THIS ONE'S FOR YOU	Teddy Pendergrass	21Aug82	09Oct82	27Nov82	59(1)	15	412
5953. BUDDY HOLLY & THE CRICKETS 20 GOLDEN GREATS	Buddy Holly	05Aug78	23Sep78	21Oct78	55(1)	12	412
5954. DON'T COME HOME A DRINKIN'	Loretta Lynn	08Apr67	17Jun67	19Aug67	80(1)	20	412
5955. LONG LIVE THE NEW FLESH	Flesh For Lulu	12Dec87	12Mar88	21May88	89(1)	24	412
5956. THE ELECTRIC FLAG	Electric Flag	18Jan69	01Mar69	05Apr69	76(1)	12	412
5957. THIS BOOT IS MADE FOR FONK-N	Bootsy's Rubber Band	21Jul79	18Aug79	15Sep79	52(1)	9	411
5958. UPSTAIRS AT ERIC'S	Yazoo	02Oct82	20Nov82	07May83	92(1)	32	411
5959. KRUSH GROOVE	Soundtrack	26Oct85	14Dec85	08Mar86	79(2)	20	411
5960. LIVING MY LIFE	Grace Jones	11Dec82	25Dec82	23Apr83	86(4)	20	411
5961. BACK TO BACK	The Brecker Brothers	28Feb76	24Apr76	12Jun76	82(2)	16	411
5962. A RETROSPECTIVE	Linda Ronstadt	21May77	02Jul77	16Jul77	46(1)	9	410
5963. SOMEBODY'S GONNA LOVE YOU	Lee Greenwood	28May83	23Jul83	15Oct83	73(1)	21	410
5964. LOVE AFFAIR	Ray Conniff & His Orchestra & Chorus	18Sep65	13Nov65	01Jan66	54(1)	16	410
5965. STEVIE WONDER LIVE	Stevie Wonder	11Apr70	30May70	18Jul70	81(1)	15	410
5966. LAUGH-IN	TV Soundtrack	19Oct68	25Jan69	08Feb69	105(1)	17	410
5967. NUGENT	Ted Nugent	17Jul82	28Aug82	16Oct82	51(2)	14	409
5968. ALLIES	Crosby, Stills & Nash	02Jul83	06Aug83	17Sep83	43(2)	12	409
5969. PREFLYTE	The Byrds	06Sep69	18Oct69	22Sep73	84(2)	15	409
5970. HOT ROD RALLY	Various Artists	14Dec63	11Jan64	21Mar64	62(1)	15	409
5971. BACK TO THE BARS	Todd Rundgren	02Dec78	20Jan79	10Mar79	75(2)	15	409
5972. L.A. REGGAE	Johnny Rivers	04Nov72	10Feb73	17Mar73	78(1)	20	409
5973. THE HEADLESS CHILDREN	W.A.S.P.	22Apr89	29Apr89	15Jul89	48(3)	13	409
5974. LOVE IS SUCH A FUNNY GAME	Michael Cooper	16Jan88	12Mar88	02Jul88	98(3)	25	409
5975. HEART BREAK	Shalamar	08Dec84	05Jan85	18May85	90(4)	24	409
5976. SHOW AND TELL	Al Wilson	22Dec73	09Mar74	13Apr74	70(1)	17	409
5977. WE WENT TO DIFFERENT SCHOOLS TOGETHER	The Jaggerz	11Apr70	16May70	20Jun70	62(1)	11	408
5978. ANNETTE'S BEACH PARTY	Annette	19Oct63	14Dec63	11Jan64	39(1)	13	408
5979. SOMEBODY'S WAITING	Anne Murray	03May80	21Jun80	09Aug80	88(4)	15	408
5980. ONLY THE BEST	Ferrante & Teicher	11Sep65	06Nov65	04Dec65	49(1)	13	408
5981. QUEEN	Queen	03Nov73	02Feb74	30Mar74	83(1)	22	408
5982. FOR THE GOOD TIMES/ THE JIM NABORS HOUR	Jim Nabors	27Mar71	08May71	19Jun71	75(1)	13	407
5983. PASSIN' THRU	The James Gang	07Oct72	02Dec72	13Jan73	72(1)	15	407
5984. THE MAN WHO SOLD THE WORLD	David Bowie	18Nov72	06Jan73	21Apr73	105(1)	23	407
5985. MY FAIR LADY	Nat King Cole	26Sep64	07Nov64	05Jun65	74(2)	23	407
5986. BLACK TALK!	Charles Earland	11Jul70	12Sep70	14Nov70	108(1)	19	406
5987. CABIN FEVER	Michael Stanley Band	08Jul78	30Sep78	04Nov78	99(1)	18	406
5988. HUMAN RACING	Nik Kershaw	05May84	21Jul84	15Sep84	70(2)	20	406
5989. CHOOSING YOU	Lenny Williams	06Aug77	22Oct77	18Feb78	99(1)	26	406
5990. MEXICAN PEARLS	Billy Vaughn And His Orchestra	24Apr65	26Jun65	31Jul65	45(1)	15	406
5991. WEAR YOUR LOVE LIKE HEAVEN	Donovan	30Dec67	24Feb68	06Apr68	60(2)	15	405
5992. NIGHT AFTER NIGHT	Nils Lofgren	29Oct77	26Nov77	31Dec77	44(2)	10	405
5993. LET 'EM IN	Billy Paul	22Jan77	02Apr77	21May77	88(1)	18	405
5994. MAURIAT MAGIC	Paul Mauriat And His Orchestra	08Jun68	07Sep68	05Oct68	71(1)	18	405
5995. REALITY	James Brown	25Jan75	01Mar75	29Mar75	56(1)	10	404
5996. STANDING TALL	The Crusaders	10Oct81	31Oct81	23Jan82	59(2)	16	404
5997. INTENSITIES IN 10 CITIES	Ted Nugent	21Mar81	11Apr81	23May81	51(2)	10	404
5998. LIGHT OF LIFE	Bar-Kays	23Dec78	10Feb79	14Apr79	86(1)	17	404
5999. PROPAGANDA	Sparks	08Feb75	05Apr75	03May75	63(1)	13	404
6000. HOW MANY TIMES CAN WE SAY GOODBYE	Dionne Warwick	29Oct83	26Nov83	18Feb84	57(2)	17	404

Ranking the Albums: 6001-13843

Rank. Title Act	Entry Peak(Pk Wks) TotWks	Scr
6001. **ARE YOU READY!** Atlanta Rhythm Section	10Nov79 51(2) 12	404
6002. **BERRY GORDY'S THE LAST DRAGON** Soundtrack	30Mar85 58(2) 15	404
6003. **WEIRD SCENES INSIDE THE GOLD MINE** The Doors	12Feb72 55(1) 11	404
6004. **STAND IN LINE** Impellitteri	25Jun88 91(2) 20	404
6005. **THE RHYTHM & BLUES ALBUM** Trini Lopez	28Aug65 46(1) 12	403
6006. **IN TIME** Engelbert Humperdinck	19Aug72 72(1) 14	403
6007. **WHAT IS BEAT?** English Beat	17Dec83 87(1) 22	403
6008. **STEELTOWN** Big Country	24Nov84 70(4) 17	403
6009. **SMOOTH SAILIN'** Isley Brothers	20Jun87 64(2) 17	403
6010. **YE-ME-LE** Sergio Mendes & Brasil '66	13Dec69 71(1) 16	403
6011. **TAMMY'S TOUCH** Tammy Wynette	16May70 85(2) 17	403
6012. **THE LACE** Benjamin Orr	08Nov86 86(2) 22	402
6013. **EVERYBODY'S IN SHOW-BIZ** The Kinks	23Sep72 70(2) 14	402
6014. **TOUR DE FARCE AMERICAN HISTORY AND OTHER UNRELATED SUBJECTS** Smothers Brothers	19Dec64 58(1) 20	402
6015. **THE GOLDEN HITS OF LESLEY GORE** Lesley Gore	17Jul65 95(1) 24	402
6016. **HEAD EAST LIVE!** Head East	03Feb79 65(1) 14	402
6017. **LAST DATE** Emmylou Harris	13Nov82 65(4) 17	402
6018. **ROAD SONG** Wes Montgomery	16Nov68 94(1) 16	402
6019. **ROWDY** Hank Williams Jr.	21Feb81 82(2) 15	402
6020. **FLAVOURS** Guess Who	01Feb75 48(1) 9	401
6021. **BLOWFLY'S PARTY [X-RATED]** Blowfly	24May80 82(2) 20	401
6022. **DISCO CONNECTION** Isaac Hayes Movement	17Jan76 85(1) 17	401
6023. **GOOD TIMES** Sonny & Cher	27May67 73(1) 18	401
6024. **PARTY MIX!** The B-52s	08Aug81 55(2) 11	401
6025. **D.E. 7TH** Dave Edmunds	01May82 46(2) 14	401
6026. **LINES** Charlie	15Apr78 75(1) 14	400
6027. **MARVIN GAYE'S GREATEST HITS (2)** Marvin Gaye	02Oct76 44(2) 8	400
6028. **THE MORNING AFTER** Maureen McGovern	28Jul73 77(1) 16	400
6029. **RATED EXTRAORDINAIRE** Johnnie Taylor	19Mar77 51(1) 11	399
6030. **UTFO** UTFO	15Jun85 80(2) 20	399
6031. **YOU CAN'T FIGHT FASHION** Michael Stanley Band	24Sep83 64(2) 17	399
6032. **THE CIRCLE GAME** Tom Rush	20Apr68 68(2) 14	399
6033. **SONGS OF THE YOUNG WORLD** Eddy Arnold	08Mar69 77(1) 13	399
6034. **BEAUTIFUL VISION** Van Morrison	06Mar82 44(2) 11	399
6035. **ANIMAL HOUSE** Soundtrack	02Sep78 71(1) 18	399
6036. **TAKE THIS JOB AND SHOVE IT** Johnny Paycheck	8Feb78 72(1) 14	399
6037. **REACHING FOR TOMORROW** Switch	12Apr80 57(1) 14	398
6038. **BLACK MARKET CLASH** The Clash	22Nov80 74(2) 16	398
6039. **HOOKED ON A FEELING** Blue Swede	06Apr74 80(1) 17	398
6040. **INSTINCTS** Romeo Void	25Aug84 68(4) 19	398
6041. **LIVE DATES** Wishbone Ash	01Dec73 82(1) 18	398
6042. **THELMA & JERRY** Thelma Houston & Jerry Butler	18Jun77 53(1) 12	398
6043. **TRAVELS** Pat Metheny Group	25Jun83 62(1) 17	398
6044. **TALK BACK TREMBLING LIPS** Johnny Tillotson	22Feb64 48(1) 14	398
6045. **THANK YOU BABY** The Stylistics	14Jun75 72(2) 13	398
6046. **ALL SYSTEMS GO** Vinnie Vincent Invasion	21May88 64(2) 15	397
6047. **SWEET HARMONY** Maria Muldaur	13Mar76 53(2) 12	397
6048. **SHOCKADELICA** Jesse Johnson	18Oct86 70(2) 20	397
6049. **THE BLUE ALBUM** Harold Melvin And The Blue Notes	22Mar80 95(2) 20	397
6050. **TECHNICAL ECSTASY** Black Sabbath	30Oct76 51(1) 12	397
6051. **SOMETHING ELSE** Shirley Bassey	12Jun71 123(1) 24	397
6052. **ALL FIRED UP** Fastway	21Jul84 59(2) 14	396
6053. **ON THE TRACK** Leon Redbone	31Jul76 87(1) 15	396
6054. **ON TO VICTORY** Humble Pie	12Apr80 60(1) 14	396
6055. **HIGH ON YOU** Sly Stone	08Nov75 45(1) 10	396
6056. **THE SHADOW OF YOUR SMILE** Astrud Gilberto	09Oct65 66(1) 18	395
6057. **JEWEL OF THE NILE** Soundtrack	28Dec85 55(2) 17	395
6058. **JOY OF COOKING** Joy Of Cooking	06Mar71 100(2) 17	395
6059. **20/20** Beach Boys	01Mar69 68(1) 11	395
6060. **DIRT, SILVER & GOLD** Nitty Gritty Dirt Band	18Dec76 77(2) 13	395
6061. **CHUCK BERRY'S GOLDEN DECADE** Chuck Berry	20May67 72(1) 20	395
6062. **CAPTAIN & TENNILLE'S GREATEST HITS** Captain & Tennille	10Dec77 55(1) 12	395
6063. **FLYING THE FLAG** Climax Blues Band	25Apr81 75(1) 16	395
6064. **FEELING GOOD** Walter Jackson	09Oct76 113(5) 18	395
6065. **KENNY RANKIN ALBUM** Kenny Rankin	12Mar77 99(2) 23	394
6066. **TO THE MAX** Con Funk Shun	04Dec82 115(1) 29	394
6067. **WEST SIDE HIGHWAY** Stanley Turrentine	18Mar78 63(1) 12	394
6068. **HEAR & NOW** Billy Squier	15Jul89 64(1) 17	394
6069. **SEALED WITH A KISS** Bobby Vinton	29Jul72 77(1) 14	394
6070. **CONFRONTATION** Bob Marley And The Wailers	02Jul83 55(1) 15	394
6071. **A TIME FOR US** Donny Osmond	08Dec73 58(2) 13	394
6072. **SIX HOURS PAST SUNSET** Henry Mancini And His Orchestra	01Nov69 91(1) 16	394
6073. **PLASTIC LETTERS** Blondie	25Feb78 72(1) 17	393
6074. **MICHELLE** Billy Vaughn And His Orchestra	12Feb66 56(1) 14	393
6075. **NOTHIN' BUT TROUBLE** Nia Peeples	14May88 97(4) 21	393
6076. **DEAD LETTER OFFICE** R.E.M.	16May87 52(1) 14	393
6077. **MADHOUSE** Silver Convention	13Nov76 65(2) 12	393
6078. **EDGAR WINTER'S WHITE TRASH** Edgar Winter's White Trash	01May71 111(1) 19	392
6079. **HANK "LIVE"** Hank Williams Jr.	14Feb87 71(1) 24	392
6080. **PRISONER OF LOVE** James Brown	28Sep63 73(2) 17	392
6081. **FRIENDSHIP** Ray Charles	23Feb85 75(1) 20	392
6082. **ONE BAD HABIT** Michael Franks	10May80 83(1) 21	392
6083. **THE DELFONICS SUPER HITS** The Delfonics	29Nov69 111(1) 19	392
6084. **SECRET SECRETS** Joan Armatrading	30Mar85 73(1) 19	392
6085. **CHANCE** Manfred Mann's Earth Band	24Jan81 87(2) 16	391
6086. **LIVE AT LAST** Bette Midler	28May77 49(1) 11	391
6087. **OXYGENE** Jean Michel Jarre	15Oct77 78(1) 19	391
6088. **SEVEN** Poco	11May74 68(1) 13	391
6089. **BEYOND THE BLUE NEON** George Strait	04Mar89 92(2) 24	391
6090. **LUXURY YOU CAN AFFORD** Joe Cocker	16Sep78 76(2) 13	391
6091. **GOING FOR BROKE** Eddy Grant	23Jun84 64(2) 17	391
6092. **LIVINGSTON TAYLOR** Livingston Taylor	25Jul70 82(2) 20	391
6093. **THE MAGIC GARDEN** 5th Dimension	13Jan68 105(2) 31	390
6094. **TAKIN MY TIME** Bonnie Raitt	27Oct73 87(1) 20	390
6095. **GALAXIAN** Jeff Lorber Fusion	18Apr81 77(1) 15	390
6096. **PERFECT** Soundtrack	29Jun85 45(2) 12	390
6097. **MUNGO JERRY** Mungo Jerry	12Sep70 64(1) 11	390
6098. **RICHARD P. HAVENS, 1983** Richie Havens	11Jan69 80(2) 11	390
6099. **DANCE YOUR TROUBLES AWAY** Archie Bell & The Drells	10Jan76 95(1) 20	390
6100. **SUNSHINE** The Emotions	03Dec77 88(2) 15	390
6101. **OUTSIDEINSIDE** Blue Cheer	28Sep68 90(1) 16	389
6102. **AN AMERICAN PRAYER -JIM MORRISON** Jim Morrison / The Doors	16Dec78 54(2) 13	389
6103. **SOUL MEN** Sam & Dave	18Nov67 62(1) 13	389
6104. **JOHN DAWSON WINTER III** Johnny Winter	07Dec74 78(2) 12	389

Rank. Title Act Entry Peak(Pk Wks) TotWks	Scr
6105. THE BEST OF OTIS REDDING Otis Redding 16Sep72 76(2) 15	389
6106. SISYPHUS Cold Blood 23Jan71 60(1) 13	389
6107. DREGS OF THE EARTH Dixie Dregs 10May80 81(1) 17	389
6108. ROCK FESTIVAL The Youngbloods 31Oct70 80(3) 13	389
6109. THE ROD STEWART ALBUM Rod Stewart 13Dec69 139(1) 27	389
6110. THE BLIND LEADING THE NAKED Violent Femmes 15Feb86 84(2) 24	389
6111. GO ON... Mr. Mister 26Sep87 55(2) 17	389
6112. COLOR HIM FATHER The Winstons 02Aug69 78(2) 12	388
6113. MYSTIC VOYAGE Roy Ayers Ubiquity 21Feb76 90(1) 18	388
6114. COMPLETE & UNBELIEVABLE....THE OTIS REDDING DICTIONARY OF SOUL Otis Redding 26Nov66 73(1) 15	388
6115. ELECTRIC RENDEZVOUS Al Di Meola 06Feb82 55(2) 13	388
6116. RHYME PAYS Ice-T 15Aug87 93(2) 27	388
6117. ROAD RUNNER Jr. Walker & The All Stars 03Sep66 64(2) 13	388
6118. THE ALARM The Alarm 30Jul83 126(1) 37	388
6119. ON THE ONE Dazz Band 12Feb83 59(3) 16	387
6120. A KIND OF MAGIC Queen 19Jul86 46(3) 13	387
6121. PAVAROTTI'S GREATEST HITS Luciano Pavarotti 07Jun80 94(2) 18	387
6122. 9.9 9.9 14Sep85 79(1) 22	387
6123. ANYTHING GOES Harpers Bizarre 09Dec67 76(1) 13	386
6124. SOMEWHERE I'VE NEVER TRAVELLED Ambrosia 18Sep76 79(1) 17	386
6125. L IS FOR LOVER Al Jarreau 04Oct86 81(2) 28	386
6126. STREET MACHINE Sammy Hagar 08Sep79 71(1) 13	386
6127. SOMETHING IN THE NIGHT Pure Prairie League 02May81 72(1) 15	386
6128. PLEASURES OF THE FLESH Exodus 28Nov87 82(2) 20	386
6129. YOU AND I O'Bryan 12Mar83 87(1) 27	386
6130. ORION THE HUNTER Orion The Hunter 19May84 57(2) 14	386
6131. FEELIN' GOOD Lou Rawls 09Mar68 103(1) 22	386
6132. MAIN STREET PEOPLE Four Tops 22Sep73 66(2) 14	385
6133. LET ME SING Brenda Lee 21Dec63 39(1) 13	385
6134. UP AND DOWN Opus 01Mar86 64(2) 16	385
6135. HEAD EAST Head East 11Mar78 78(1) 14	385
6136. ROCK 'N' COUNTRY Freddy Fender 28Feb76 59(1) 11	385
6137. DOLLY DOLLY DOLLY Dolly Parton 03May80 71(1) 13	385
6138. THEN PLAY ON Fleetwood Mac 13Dec69 109(1) 22	385
6139. BUENAS NOCHES FROM A LONELY ROOM Dwight Yoakam 20Aug88 68(1) 15	384
6140. YOYO Bourgeois Tagg 24Oct87 84(1) 21	384
6141. SINGIN' Melissa Manchester 23Jul77 60(3) 11	384
6142. THE BEST OF LITTLE ANTHONY & THE IMPERIALS Little Anthony And The Imperials 05Mar66 97(2) 23	384
6143. DREAM EVIL Dio 15Aug87 43(2) 11	384
6144. LAND OF DREAMS Randy Newman 15Oct88 80(1) 19	384
6145. JEAN Ray Conniff & His Orchestra & Chorus 20Dec69 103(1) 21	384
6146. HIGH SPIRITS Original Cast 16May64 76(2) 20	384
6147. AMERICA, WHY I LOVE HER John Wayne 03Mar73 66(1) 16	383
6148. FANCY DANCER One Way 26Sep81 79(2) 19	383
6149. PASSION Robin Trower 27Dec86 100(2) 25	383
6150. IT NEVER RAINS IN SOUTHERN CALIFORNIA Albert Hammond 09Dec72 77(2) 15	383
6151. A NICE PLACE TO BE George Howard 27Dec86 109(3) 26	383
6152. VEEDON FLEECE Van Morrison 09Nov74 53(2) 10	383
6153. SACRED SONGS Daryl Hall 29Mar80 58(2) 12	383
6154. PROMISE OF LOVE Delegation 17Feb79 84(2) 16	382
6155. THE BEST SIDE OF GOODBYE Jane Olivor 23Feb80 58(1) 12	382
6156. ANTHEM OF THE SUN Grateful Dead 31Aug68 87(1) 17	382
6157. THE SAGITTARIUS MOVEMENT Jerry Butler 02Oct71 123(1) 22	381
6158. GOODBYE, COLUMBUS The Association 10May69 99(2) 18	381
6159. WEST SIDE STORY Leonard Bernstein 25May85 70(2) 20	381
6160. HIGH 'N' DRY(2) Def Leppard 02Jun84 72(2) 18	381
6161. YOURS FOREVER Atlantic Starr 19Nov83 91(1) 28	381
6162. THE ITALIAN VOICE OF AL MARTINO Al Martino 18Apr64 57(1) 15	381
6163. SHERIFF Sheriff 07Jan89 60(2) 14	381
6164. ROCK YOU TO HELL Grim Reaper 01Aug87 93(1) 21	381
6165. FISH OUT OF WATER Chris Squire 24Jan76 69(2) 12	380
6166. LIVE FROM NEW YORK Gilda Radner 01Dec79 69(2) 12	380
6167. ELECTRIFIED FUNK Wild Cherry 02Apr77 51(1) 9	380
6168. KINGFISH Kingfish 27Mar76 50(1) 9	380
6169. INDUSTRY STANDARD The Dregs 27Mar82 56(2) 15	380
6170. HEY LITTLE COBRA AND OTHER HOT ROD HITS Rip Chords 22Feb64 56(2) 17	380
6171. THE KINGSMEN ON CAMPUS The Kingsmen 30Oct65 68(2) 17	380
6172. WE ONLY MAKE BELIEVE Conway Twitty & Loretta Lynn 13Mar71 78(1) 15	380
6173. ATLANTIC STARR Atlantic Starr 26Aug78 67(1) 13	380
6174. FIREBIRD Isao Tomita 14Feb76 71(1) 12	380
6175. SO GOOD Mica Paris 13May89 86(2) 23	380
6176. DECADE Duran Duran 09Dec89 67(1) 16	379
6177. POSITIVE VIBRATIONS Ten Years After 18May74 81(1) 14	379
6178. FUR Jane Wiedlin 28May88 105(2) 21	379
6179. THERE'S THE RUB Wishbone Ash 30Nov74 88(1) 13	379
6180. CHEAT THE NIGHT Deborah Allen 03Dec83 67(1) 20	379
6181. A DRAMATIC EXPERIENCE The Dramatics 13Oct73 86(1) 18	379
6182. RAUNCH 'N' ROLL Black Oak Arkansas 17Mar73 90(1) 16	379
6183. ERIC CLAPTON AT HIS BEST Eric Clapton 14Oct72 87(1) 17	379
6184. LOOKING BACK John Mayall 13Sep69 79(2) 12	378
6185. HONEYMOON SUITE Honeymoon Suite 25Aug84 60(2) 17	378
6186. DAN HILL Dan Hill 06Dec75 104(2) 17	378
6187. VISIONS OF A NEW WORLD Lonnie Liston Smith & The Cosmic Echoes 18Oct75 74(1) 15	378
6188. ONCE UPON A CHRISTMAS Kenny Rogers & Dolly Parton 08Dec84 31(1) 8	378
6189. NO STRANGER TO LOVE Roy Ayers 15Dec79 82(1) 18	378
6190. WALKIN' IN LOVE LAND Eddy Arnold 09Nov68 70(1) 13	378
6191. CHOCOLATE CITY Parliament 03May75 91(2) 18	378
6192. DARK LADY Cher 01Jun74 69(1) 14	378
6193. KATE SMITH AT CARNEGIE HALL Kate Smith 21Dec63 83(1) 18	378
6194. BONNIE POINTER (II) Bonnie Pointer 22Dec79 63(2) 14	377
6195. SOUND TRACK RECORDINGS FROM THE FILM JIMI HENDRIX Jimi Hendrix 14Jul73 89(1) 18	377
6196. 16 ORIGINAL BIG HITS, VOLUME 6 Various Artists 25Feb67 95(1) 25	377
6197. HEY JUDE Wilson Pickett 01Mar69 97(1) 14	377
6198. I LOVE YOU Eddie Holman 21Feb70 75(1) 13	377
6199. IDIOT Iggy Pop 09Apr77 72(3) 13	377
6200. ALMOST BLUE Elvis Costello And The Attractions 14Nov81 50(2) 13	377
6201. THE BEST OF THE JAMES GANG FEATURING JOE WALSH James Gang 10Feb73 79(1) 16	377
6202. TOMMY TUTONE Tommy Tutone 24May80 68(2) 13	377
6203. MORE GENIUS OF JANKOWSKI Horst Jankowski 04Dec65 65(1) 13	377
6204. MENDOCINO Sir Douglas Quintet 19Apr69 81(1) 11	377
6205. MAN ON THE LINE Chris de Burgh 30Jun84 69(1) 19	377
6206. ON A CLEAR DAY YOU CAN SEE FOREVER Barbra Streisand 25Jul70 108(1) 24	377
6207. PRINCE CHARMING Adam And The Ants 12Dec81 94(2) 21	377
6208. HOW MUCH, HOW MUCH I LOVE YOU Love And Kisses 13May78 85(4) 17	377
6209. TERENCE TRENT D'ARBY'S NEITHER FISH NOR FLESH Terence Trent D'Arby 25Nov89 61(2) 15	377
6210. EXPOSED/A CHEAP PEEK AT TODAY'S PROVOCATIVE NEW ROCK Various Artists 27Jun81 51(2) 9	376
6211. TRUE TO LIFE Ray Charles 12Nov77 78(1) 20	376
6212. PHIL SEYMOUR Phil Seymour 21Feb81 64(1) 16	376
6213. LIVE IN NEW YORK CITY John Lennon 22Mar86 41(2) 11	376
6214. MOONLIGHT FEELS RIGHT Starbuck 24Jul76 78(1) 14	376
6215. SEVEN STEPS TO HEAVEN Miles Davis 14Sep63 62(1) 15	376
6216. PUSSY CATS Nilsson 07Sep74 60(1) 12	375
6217. GHETTO BLASTER The Crusaders 21Apr84 79(2) 22	375
6218. THIS IS MADNESS Last Poets 03Apr71 104(1) 15	375

Rank. Title Act Entry Peak(Pk Wks) TotWks	Scr
6219. EXPECT NO MERCY Nazareth 19Nov77 82(1) 16	375
6220. KOOL MOE DEE Kool Moe Dee 18Apr87 83(2) 21	375
6221. THE POWER AND THE GLORY Gentle Giant 12Oct74 78(2) 13	375
6222. MARGIE JOSEPH MAKES A NEW IMPRESSION Margie Joseph 06Feb71 67(2) 14	375
6223. SPANKY AND OUR GANG Spanky And Our Gang 09Sep67 77(2) 15	375
6224. FIVE-O Hank Williams Jr. 18May85 72(2) 22	374
6225. SINGER OF SONGS - TELLER OF TALES Paul Davis 21Jan78 82(2) 18	374
6226. TWO HEARTS Men At Work 22Jun85 50(2) 13	374
6227. BLESSING IN DISGUISE Metal Church 11Mar89 75(1) 15	374
6228. DEATH WISH II Jimmy Page 03Apr82 50(4) 10	374
6229. SCHOOL DAZE Soundtrack 19Mar88 81(2) 17	374
6230. YESTERDAY'S DREAMS Four Tops 28Sep68 91(1) 16	374
6231. SURVIVAL Bob Marley And The Wailers 17Nov79 70(1) 14	374
6232. ROBIN AND THE 7 HOODS Soundtrack 18Jul64 56(1) 14	374
6233. BUFFALO SPRINGFIELD Buffalo Springfield 25Mar67 80(2) 16	374
6234. THE JOHN GARY CARNEGIE HALL CONCERT John Gary 07Oct67 76(2) 19	374
6235. YOU'LL NEVER WALK ALONE Elvis Presley 20Mar71 69(2) 12	374
6236. COMING BACK FOR MORE William Bell 02Apr77 63(2) 12	373
6237. AOXOMOXOA Grateful Dead 21Jun69 73(1) 11	373
6238. ADDICTIONS VOL. I Robert Palmer 25Nov89 79(2) 17	373
6239. PERRY COMO IN ITALY Perry Como 22Oct66 81(1) 16	373
6240. ON THE EDGE The Babys 15Nov80 71(2) 15	373
6241. PRAYER MEETIN' Jimmy Smith 01Aug64 86(1) 20	373
6242. RED King Crimson 23Nov74 66(2) 11	373
6243. PRESENT TENSE Shoes 13Oct79 50(1) 12	373
6244. NEVER LETTING GO Phoebe Snow 22Oct77 73(2) 15	372
6245. PLEASANT DREAMS The Ramones 08Aug81 58(2) 11	372
6246. A LOT OF LOVE Melba Moore 23Aug86 91(2) 29	372
6247. JANIS Janis Joplin 17May75 54(2) 9	372
6248. THE BEST OF CHARLIE RICH Charlie Rich 27Apr74 89(1) 19	372
6249. TWO Bob James 12Apr75 75(1) 14	372
6250. FEEDBACK Spirit 18Mar72 63(1) 14	372
6251. I LOVE HOW YOU LOVE ME Ray Conniff & His Orchestra & Chorus 08Mar69 101(1) 14	372
6252. PROMISES, PROMISES Original Cast 25Jan69 95(1) 12	372
6253. THE RAMBLIN' MAN Waylon Jennings 05Oct74 105(1) 17	372
6254. DREAM Captain & Tennille 22Jul78 131(2) 30	372
6255. "JI" Junior 08May82 71(3) 16	371
6256. NEW ORLEANS AT MIDNIGHT Pete Fountain 13Jun64 53(1) 14	371
6257. EDWARD BEAR Edward Bear 10Feb73 63(1) 16	371
6258. BEAUTY STAB ABC 17Dec83 69(2) 14	371
6259. MANDRE Mandre 17Sep77 64(1) 13	371
6260. PORTFOLIO Grace Jones 22Oct77 109(2) 20	371
6261. FOR THE WORKING GIRL Melissa Manchester 13Sep80 68(3) 11	371
6262. GOOD SINGIN' GOOD PLAYIN' Grand Funk Railroad 28Aug76 52(1) 9	370
6263. ICEHOUSE Icehouse 25Jul81 82(2) 15	370
6264. UNDERTOW Firefall 12Apr80 68(2) 15	370
6265. HAPPY SAD Tim Buckley 19Apr69 81(1) 12	370
6266. PETER AND THE COMMISSAR Allan Sherman/Boston Pops Orchestra/Arthur Fiedler 21Nov64 53(1) 14	370
6267. MAIDEN JAPAN Iron Maiden 31Oct81 89(2) 30	370
6268. HEART OVER MIND Anne Murray 27Oct84 92(1) 25	370
6269. JOSEPH AND THE AMAZING TECHNICOLOR DREAMCOAT Various Artists 03Apr71 84(1) 12	370
6270. SILK AND STEEL Five Star 04Oct86 80(2) 25	369
6271. GAUDI Alan Parsons Project 07Feb87 57(2) 14	369
6272. FOLLOW THE RAINBOW George Duke 17Mar79 56(2) 11	369
6273. TROUBADOUR J.J. Cale 25Sep76 84(2) 18	369
6274. BABY DON'T GO Sonny & Cher & Friends 23Oct65 69(1) 16	369
6275. FANCY Bobbie Gentry 09May70 96(1) 17	369
6276. BRASS CONSTRUCTION III Brass Construction 19Nov77 66(2) 14	369
6277. SURFIN' BIRD The Trashmen 15Feb64 48(1) 15	369
6278. MR. BIG STUFF Jean Knight 21Aug71 60(1) 11	369
6279. LOVE STORY Tony Bennett 06Mar71 67(2) 13	369
6280. BABYLON BY BUS Bob Marley And The Wailers 16Dec78 102(2) 16	368
6281. LOVE JUNK Pursuit Of Happiness 17Dec88 93(1) 21	368
6282. ALTON McCLAIN & DESTINY Alton McClain & Destiny 31Mar79 88(2) 16	368
6283. OUT OF MIND OUT OF SIGHT Models 03May86 84(1) 18	368
6284. THE POET II Bobby Womack 07Apr84 60(1) 14	368
6285. MONEY FOR NOTHING Dire Straits 12Nov88 62(2) 17	368
6286. TAKE IT TO THE LIMIT Willie Nelson With Waylon Jennings 21May83 60(1) 16	368
6287. BRASIL Manhattan Transfer 05Dec87 96(1) 19	368
6288. MAKING MUSIC Bill Withers 08Nov75 81(1) 15	367
6289. DIRTY LOOKS Juice Newton 10Sep83 52(1) 15	367
6290. EVERYBODY UP Ohio Players 14Apr79 80(1) 14	367
6291. DEAD MAN'S CURVE/THE NEW GIRL IN SCHOOL Jan & Dean 23May64 80(2) 21	367
6292. THE KINGSTON TRIO (NICK-BOB-JOHN) Kingston Trio 16Jan65 53(1) 13	367
6293. IN FLIGHT Alvin Lee 04Jan75 65(2) 12	367
6294. HAVE YOU EVER SEEN THE RAIN Stanley Turrentine 01Nov75 76(1) 16	366
6295. THE ASSOCIATION "LIVE" The Association 18Jul70 79(1) 12	366
6296. I'M NEARLY FAMOUS Cliff Richard 07Aug76 76(2) 15	366
6297. WOMAN Peter And Gordon 16Apr66 60(1) 14	366
6298. THE WIZARD OF OZ Meco 23Sep78 68(2) 12	366
6299. BORN YESTERDAY Everly Brothers 08Feb86 83(4) 19	366
6300. THE LAST OF THE MOHICANS Bow Wow Wow 15May82 67(1) 22	366
6301. TRUE LOVE WAYS Peter And Gordon 14Aug65 49(1) 13	365
6302. PORTRAIT GALLERY Harry Chapin 04Oct75 53(1) 8	365
6303. OCEAN FRONT PROPERTY George Strait 14Feb87 117(1) 28	365
6304. FIRED UP 'N' KICKIN' Fatback 12Aug78 73(1) 12	365
6305. PROFILE: BEST OF EMMYLOU HARRIS Emmylou Harris 02Dec78 81(1) 17	365
6306. DREAM OF LIFE Patti Smith 30Jul88 65(4) 15	365
6307. REACH UP AND TOUCH THE SKY Southside Johnny & The Asbury Jukes 09May81 80(4) 12	364
6308. (TURN ON) THE MUSIC MACHINE Music Machine 21Jan67 76(1) 16	364
6309. JAZZERCISE Judi Sheppard Missett 05Dec81 117(3) 20	364
6310. TINSEL TOWN REBELLION Frank Zappa 30May81 66(2) 11	364
6311. DEEP PURPLE Nino Tempo & April Stevens 23Nov63 48(1) 14	364
6312. BREAKIN' 2 ELECTRIC BOOGALOO Soundtrack 12Jan85 52(2) 13	363
6313. UNLEASHED IN THE EAST (LIVE IN JAPAN) Judas Priest 06Oct79 70(2) 11	363
6314. MAURICE WHITE Maurice White 05Oct85 61(2) 19	363
6315. BLAZE OF GLORY Joe Jackson 06May89 61(2) 21	363
6316. YOU'RE MY MAN Lynn Anderson 24Jul71 99(1) 14	363
6317. LOU REED LIVE Lou Reed 05Apr75 62(2) 10	363
6318. CITY KIDS Spyro Gyra 13Aug83 66(1) 16	363
6319. ROBERT JOHN Robert John 25Aug79 68(1) 14	363
6320. RAMONES The Ramones 05Jun76 111(1) 18	362
6321. MAGIC MAN Herb Alpert 22Aug81 61(1) 10	362
6322. RAIDERS OF THE LOST ARK London Symphony Orchestra/John Williams 04Jul81 62(1) 13	362
6323. THOSE WERE THE DAYS Percy Faith 15Feb69 88(1) 14	362
6324. NEVER SAY DIE! Black Sabbath 28Oct78 69(2) 14	362
6325. I DO! I DO! Original Cast 14Jan67 84(1) 16	362
6326. DANCIN' ON THE EDGE Lita Ford 04Aug84 66(2) 16	361
6327. THE WONDERFUL WORLD OF ANTONIO CARLOS JOBIM Antonio Carlos Jobim 11Sep65 57(1) 14	361
6328. SAY ANYTHING Soundtrack 06May89 62(2) 14	361
6329. CYMANDE Cymande 13Jan73 85(1) 17	361
6330. BEGIN TO LOVE Robert Goulet 05Jun65 69(1) 16	361
6331. PUT A LITTLE LOVE IN YOUR HEART Jackie DeShannon 01Nov69 81(1) 15	361
6332. HOTTER THAN HELL KISS 16Nov74 100(1) 15	361
6333. WINDHAM HILL RECORDS SAMPLER '84 Various Artists 20Oct84 108(4) 25	361

Rank. Title Act	Entry Peak(Pk Wks) TotWks	Scr
6334. MONSTER Herbie Hancock	19Apr80 94(1) 18	361
6335. I'VE GOT EVERYTHING Henry Lee Summer	27May89 78(1) 17	361
6336. CRUZADOS Cruzados	02Nov85 76(2) 18	360
6337. LIVE AND UNCENSORED Millie Jackson	22Dec79 94(2) 18	360
6338. I GO TO PIECES Peter And Gordon	22May65 51(1) 15	360
6339. YOU SMILE-THE SONG BEGINS Herb Alpert & The Tijuana Brass	01Jun74 66(1) 11	360
6340. HAWAII Soundtrack	19Nov66 85(1) 16	360
6341. GREATEST HITS Sergio Mendes & Brasil '66	04Jul70 101(2) 20	360
6342. THE IMPOSSIBLE DREAM Jerry Vale	18Mar67 117(1) 23	360
6343. UP WITH PEOPLE! Up With People	23Jul66 61(2) 14	360
6344. STARLESS AND BIBLE BLACK King Crimson	04May74 64(1) 11	360
6345. SHE'S JUST MY STYLE	Gary Lewis And The Playboys 12Mar66 71(1) 17	360
6346. SAY YOU'LL STAY UNTIL TOMORROW	Tom Jones 05Mar77 76(2) 16	359
6347. LOVE BOOK The Lettermen	09Oct71 88(1) 13	359
6348. THE WORLD OF MANTOVANI Mantovani	01Nov69 92(1) 17	359
6349. A FISTFUL OF DOLLARS Soundtrack	24Jun67 107(1) 28	359
6350. CHILD OF THE NOVELTY Mahogany Rush	24Aug74 74(2) 15	359
6351. LIVE AT THE SEX MACHINE Kool & The Gang	27Feb71 122(1) 19	359
6352. MAGGOT BRAIN Funkadelic	14Aug71 108(1) 16	359
6353. ALL IN LOVE IS FAIR Nancy Wilson	28Sep74 97(2) 18	359
6354. EVERY WHICH WAY BUT LOOSE Soundtrack	20Jan79 78(3) 15	359
6355. BEGINNINGS Steve Howe	20Dec75 63(1) 11	359
6356. LOOKING BACK Nat King Cole	04Sep65 60(1) 14	359
6357. HOT! LIVE AND OTHERWISE Dionne Warwick	13Jun81 72(1) 14	359
6358. REFLECTIONS OF A GOLDEN DREAM Lonnie Liston Smith & The Cosmic Echoes	10Apr76 75(2) 14	359
6359. HISTORY OF THE GRATEFUL DEAD, VOL. 1 (BEAR'S CHOICE) Grateful Dead	28Jul73 60(1) 11	359
6360. SO MANY RIVERS Bobby Womack	21Sep85 66(2) 19	358
6361. ELECTRIC COMIC BOOK Blues Magoos	22Apr67 74(1) 16	358
6362. OFFERING Axe	26Jun82 81(3) 20	358
6363. SEASON OF GLASS Yoko Ono	27Jun81 49(2) 9	358
6364. COMMANDER CODY & HIS LOST PLANET AIRMEN Commander Cody &	His Lost Planet Airmen 01Mar75 58(2) 10	358
6365. I HAVE A RIGHT Gloria Gaynor	20Oct79 58(1) 11	358
6366. SHOTGUN MESSIAH Shotgun Messiah	21Oct89 99(1) 23	358
6367. VISIONS OF THE EMERALD BEYOND	Mahavishnu Orchestra 22Mar75 68(1) 11	358
6368. STEAL YOUR FACE Grateful Dead	03Jul76 56(1) 9	358
6369. OFF TO SEE THE LIZARD Jimmy Buffett	15Jul89 57(2) 13	358
6370. INSIDE Kenny Rankin	13Dec75 81(1) 15	358
6371. MARK-ALMOND 73 Mark-Almond	25Aug73 73(1) 14	358
6372. YOU WANT IT, YOU GOT IT Detroit Emeralds	05Feb72 78(2) 13	358
6373. SLADE IN FLAME Slade	05Jul75 93(1) 14	357
6374. DOING IT TO DEATH The JB's	28Jul73 77(1) 13	357
6375. 10 1/2 The Dramatics	08Mar80 61(2) 12	357
6376. THE BEST LITTLE WHOREHOUSE IN TEXAS	Soundtrack 07Aug82 63(1) 15	357
6377. THE ROCHES The Roches	16Jun79 58(2) 11	357
6378. MORE MILES PER GALLON Buddy Miles	23Aug75 68(1) 11	357
6379. A TRIBUTE TO THE BEST DAMN FIDDLE PLAYER IN THE WORLD (OR, MY SALUTE TO BOB WILLS)	Merle Haggard 19Dec70 58(2) 9	357
6380. MIDNIGHT BELIEVER B.B. King	20May78 124(1) 24	357
6381. NO FRILLS Bette Midler	27Aug83 60(1) 13	357
6382. EXTENSION OF A MAN Donny Hathaway	21Jul73 69(1) 13	357
6383. SWEETNIGHTER Weather Report	26May73 85(1) 17	357
6384. RADIOLAND Nicolette Larson	24Jan81 62(1) 12	357
6385. MOTHER FACTOR Mother's Finest	30Sep78 123(1) 21	357
6386. OUTLINE Gino Soccio	21Apr79 79(2) 13	356
6387. THE MAN WITH THE SAD FACE	Stanley Turrentine 7Nov76 96(2) 14	356
6388. ELVIS: A GOLDEN CELEBRATION	Elvis Presley 17Nov84 80(2) 19	356
6389. THE HAPPENINGS The Happenings	15Oct66 61(2) 12	356
6390. SHEFFIELD STEEL Joe Cocker	10Jul82 105(2) 23	356
6391. A POCKET FULL OF MIRACLES Smokey	Robinson & The Miracles 24Oct70 56(1) 11	356
6392. HELLO BIG MAN Carly Simon	08Oct83 69(2) 17	355
6393. SHIPWRECKED Gonzalez	20Jan79 67(2) 14	355
6394. CUCHI-CUCHI Charo And The Salsoul Orchestra	26Nov77 100(2) 15	355
6395. ELVIS SINGS HITS FROM HIS MOVIES, VOLUME 1 Elvis Presley	08Jul72 87(1) 15	355
6396. THE IRON MAN (THE MUSICAL BY PETE TOWNSHEND)	Pete Townshend 15Jul89 58(4) 13	355
6397. GREATEST HITS Oak Ridge Boys	22Nov80 99(1) 21	355
6398. MORE MAURIAT Paul Mauriat	30Mar68 122(1) 22	355
6399. BUBBLE GUM, LEMONADE &....SOMETHING FOR MAMA	Mama Cass 05Jul69 91(2) 14	355
6400. BEAT King Crimson	03Jul82 52(2) 14	355
6401. VANDENBERG Vandenberg	08Jan83 65(4) 18	355
6402. FLEETWOOD MAC IN CHICAGO	Fleetwood Mac 03Jul71 118(3) 22	355
6403. LEAVING ON A JET PLANE Percy Faith	14Feb70 88(1) 14	355
6404. SONGS FOR LONESOME LOVERS	Ray Charles Singers 05Dec64 88(1) 20	354
6405. THE BOYS FROM DORAVILLE	Atlanta Rhythm Section 16Aug80 65(2) 11	354
6406. ONE Bob James	02Nov74 85(1) 14	354
6407. SPECIAL REQUEST The Lettermen	14Sep68 82(2) 14	354
6408. ENNEA Chase	08Apr72 71(2) 12	354
6409. FIONA Fiona	30Mar85 71(1) 18	354
6410. KNOCKED OUT LOADED Bob Dylan	02Aug86 53(1) 13	353
6411. THE SINGLES The Pretenders	05Dec87 69(3) 15	353
6412. LA BAMBA Mongo Santamaria	28Aug65 79(1) 15	353
6413. DO IT ALL Michael Henderson	04Aug79 64(1) 12	353
6414. THE NEW SEEKERS The Seekers	12Jun65 62(1) 16	353
6415. SLEIGHT OF HAND Joan Armatrading	05Jul86 68(1) 16	353
6416. THIS IS MY DREAM Switch	15Nov80 85(1) 17	353
6417. KIM WILDE Kim Wilde	05Jun82 86(2) 22	352
6418. SOMETHING REAL Phoebe Snow	15Apr89 75(1) 20	352
6419. THE PLACE I LOVE Splinter	26Oct74 81(1) 14	352
6420. LA CAGE AUX FOLLES Original Cast	24Sep83 52(1) 15	352
6421. SHORT BACK 'N' SIDES Ian Hunter	29Aug81 62(1) 11	352
6422. EVERYBODY COME ON OUT	Stanley Turrentine 12Jun76 100(3) 14	352
6423. HOLD ME Laura Branigan	10Aug85 71(3) 15	351
6424. C'MON EVERYBODY Elvis Presley	24Jul71 70(1) 11	351
6425. GREEN TAMBOURINE Lemon Pipers	17Feb68 90(1) 18	351
6426. QUINELLA Atlanta Rhythm Section	19Sep81 70(1) 16	351
6427. MORE FUN IN THE NEW WORLD X	08Oct83 86(2) 23	351
6428. HANG ON IN THERE BABY Johnny Bristol	31Aug74 82(1) 17	351
6429. A WIZARD/A TRUE STAR Todd Rundgren	31Mar73 86(1) 15	351
6430. RIDE THE WILD SURF Jan & Dean	17Oct64 66(1) 19	351
6431. BO DONALDSON AND THE HEYWOODS Bo Donaldson And The Heywoods	06Jul74 97(1) 16	351
6432. FABULOUS DISASTER Exodus	25Feb89 82(1) 17	351
6433. DAN REED NETWORK Dan Reed Network	02Apr88 95(2) 19	351
6434. SEALS & CROFTS I AND II Seals & Crofts	10Aug74 81(1) 12	351
6435. BRIGHT WHITE Shawn Phillips	15Dec73 72(1) 13	351
6436. THE MONKEES GREATEST HITS	The Monkees 28Jun69 89(1) 12	350
6437. GORKY PARK Gorky Park	09Sep89 80(2) 21	350
6438. HARD LINE The Blasters	23Mar85 86(2) 19	350
6439. GREATEST HITS New Christy Minstrels	18Jun66 76(1) 16	350
6440. XYZ XYZ	16Dec89 99(2) 24	350
6441. JUST A TOUCH OF LOVE Slave	08Dec79 92(2) 15	350
6442. FLY, LITTLE WHITE DOVE, FLY The Bells	01May71 90(1) 14	350
6443. ORIGINAL GOLDEN HITS, VOLUME I	Johnny Cash 27Sep69 95(2) 13	350
6444. MORE STUFF Stuff	30Jul77 61(1) 13	349
6445. LOOK INTO THE FUTURE Journey	14Feb76 100(1) 15	349
6446. TWICE REMOVED FROM YESTERDAY	Robin Trower 12May73 106(1) 24	349
6447. SILK + STEEL Giuffria	24May86 60(2) 14	349

Rank. Title Act Entry Peak(Pk Wks) TotWks	Scr
6448. CHANGE. The Alarm 14Oct89 75(1) 23	349
6449. HOOCHIE COOCHE MAN Jimmy Smith 10Sep66 77(2) 14	349
6450. MANCINI COUNTRY Henry Mancini And His Orchestra And Chorus 19Dec70 91(1) 17	349
6451. DIMENSIONS Box Tops 06Sep69 77(2) 11	349
6452. THE GENUINE IMITATION LIFE GAZETTE 4 Seasons 15Feb69 85(1) 11	349
6453. THE GREATEST HITS FROM ENGLAND Various Artists 13May67 87(2) 18	349
6454. COMING DOWN YOUR WAY Three Dog Night 21Jun75 70(1) 12	349
6455. THE FINE ART OF SURFACING Boomtown Rats 01Dec79 103(2) 16	349
6456. HARD CORE POETRY Tavares 21Sep74 121(2) 23	349
6457. BE WHAT YOU ARE Staple Singers 25Aug73 102(1) 21	348
6458. 4 TOPS ON BROADWAY Four Tops 08Apr67 79(2) 15	348
6459. THE BEST OF THE STATLER BROTHERS Statler Brothers 13Sep75 121(2) 20	348
6460. THE MAGNIFICENT 7 The Supremes & Four Tops 17Oct70 113(2) 16	348
6461. THE FIRST 10 YEARS Joan Baez 21Nov70 73(2) 11	348
6462. NASHVILLE Soundtrack 19Jul75 80(1) 13	348
6463. POETIC CHAMPIONS COMPOSE Van Morrison 10Oct87 90(2) 22	348
6464. NON-STOP ECSTATIC DANCING Soft Cell 14Aug82 57(2) 14	348
6465. APOLLONIA 6 Apollonia 6 27Oct84 62(2) 17	348
6466. BURNIN' THING Mac Davis 05Jul75 64(2) 10	347
6467. DROWNING IN THE SEA OF LOVE Joe Simon 25Mar72 71(1) 12	347
6468. THE BEST OF ED AMES Ed Ames 18Oct69 119(1) 16	347
6469. TWILLEY DON'T MIND Dwight Twilley Band 08Oct77 70(2) 13	347
6470. GREATEST HITS, VOLUME TWO B.J. Thomas 20Nov71 92(1) 13	347
6471. LINCOLN They Might Be Giants 24Dec88 89(2) 19	346
6472. THE INVISIBLE MAN'S BAND Invisible Man's Band 31May80 90(1) 14	346
6473. LIVE! Lonnie Liston Smith 30Jul77 58(2) 11	346
6474. FOR THOSE IN LOVE Percy Faith 23Mar68 121(1) 22	346
6475. SHAFT'S BIG SCORE! Soundtrack 26Aug72 100(1) 16	346
6476. BUSH DOCTOR Peter Tosh 09Dec78 104(2) 20	346
6477. RARE PRECIOUS & BEAUTIFUL Bee Gees 07Dec68 99(1) 12	346
6478. LOVE STORY Ray Conniff & His Orchestra & Chorus 27Mar71 98(1) 15	346
6479. LOVE BEACH Emerson, Lake & Palmer 09Dec78 55(3) 9	346
6480. ENCHANTMENT Enchantment 05Mar77 104(1) 19	346
6481. BARRY MANILOW Barry Manilow 20May89 64(2) 16	345
6482. CLEAN Edwin Starr 20Jan79 80(1) 14	345
6483. HYSTERIA Human League 16Jun84 62(1) 13	345
6484. IF MY ANCESTORS COULD SEE ME NOW Ivan Neville 12Nov88 107(1) 23	345
6485. OUTSIDE LOOKING IN BoDeans 10Oct87 86(2) 20	345
6486. THE REAL THING Taj Mahal 12Jun71 84(2) 13	345
6487. FOR YOU Eddie Kendricks 07Dec74 108(1) 14	345
6488. JOHNNY RIVERS ROCKS THE FOLK Johnny Rivers 25Sep65 91(1) 18	345
6489. FOREVER Orleans 05May79 76(1) 13	345
6490. PASSION: MUSIC FOR THE LAST TEMPTATION OF CHRIST Peter Gabriel 01Jul89 60(2) 14	344
6491. LIFE IN A TIN CAN Bee Gees 03Feb73 69(2) 13	344
6492. THE FOOL CIRCLE Nazareth 14Feb81 70(2) 13	344
6493. WILD & BLUE John Anderson 09Apr83 58(1) 12	344
6494. GOIN' PLACES Jacksons 29Oct77 63(1) 11	344
6495. SUNBURST FINISH Be Bop Deluxe 07Feb76 96(2) 17	344
6496. PARADISE Peabo Bryson 03May80 79(2) 16	344
6497. GOLDEN GIRLS Silver Convention 16Jul77 71(2) 10	344
6498. ANOTHER TIME, ANOTHER PLACE Fever Tree 28Dec68 83(3) 13	344
6499. DO THE RIGHT THING Soundtrack 22Jul89 68(2) 14	343
6500. GOOD AS GOLD Red Rockers 14May83 71(2) 16	343
6501. THE WRESTLING ALBUM Various Artists 30Nov85 84(2) 19	343
6502. DONNY & MARIE - NEW SEASON Donny & Marie Osmond 27Nov76 85(2) 14	343
6503. THE LAST PUFF Spooky Tooth 15Aug70 84(1) 13	343
6504. LIFEBOAT Sutherland Brothers And Quiver 18Aug73 77(1) 17	343
6505. MISPLACED IDEALS Sad Café 27Jan79 94(1) 14	343
6506. UTOPIA Utopia 16Oct82 84(2) 19	343
6507. TOUCH AND GO Force M.D.'s 15Aug87 67(2) 16	343
6508. MY FAVORITE PERSON The O'Jays 15May82 49(2) 13	343
6509. YAKETY REVISITED Boots Randolph 10Jan70 113(1) 18	343
6510. (YOU DON'T HAVE TO) PAINT ME A PICTURE Gary Lewis And The Playboys 11Feb67 79(1) 16	343
6511. GREATEST HITS The Marvelettes 19Mar66 84(2) 16	342
6512. I'M COMING HOME Johnny Mathis 17Nov73 115(1) 22	342
6513. ORANGE BLOSSOM SPECIAL Johnny Cash 20Mar65 49(2) 13	342
6514. THE ASTRODOME PRESENTS IN PERSON SONNY JAMES Sonny James 18Oct69 83(1) 13	342
6515. DOWDY FERRY ROAD England Dan & John Ford Coley 23Apr77 80(2) 15	342
6516. STARS Janis Ian 01Jun74 83(2) 20	342
6517. PILOT Pilot 31May75 82(1) 14	342
6518. THE RAINMAKERS The Rainmakers 13Sep86 85(1) 22	342
6519. BILL COSBY "HIMSELF" SOUNDTRACK) Bill Cosby 18Dec82 64(2) 14	342
6520. OLD SOCKS, NEW SHOES...NEW SOCKS, OLD SHOES The Jazz Crusaders 17Oct70 90(1) 16	342
6521. LOW-LIFE New Order 08Jun85 94(2) 22	342
6522. WATCH OUT! Patrice Rushen 28Mar87 77(2) 19	342
6523. RITA PAVONE Rita Pavone 20Jun64 60(1) 14	341
6524. MARK-ALMOND II Mark-Almond 15Jan72 87(2) 16	341
6525. ALMIGHTY FIRE Aretha Franklin 13May78 63(1) 11	341
6526. JAM/1980'S James Brown 06May78 121(1) 22	341
6527. MOVE ALONG Grass Roots 24Jun72 86(1) 14	341
6528. REACHING FOR THE WORLD Harold Melvin And The Blue Notes 05Feb77 56(1) 10	341
6529. AWAKENING Narada Michael Walden 10Mar79 103(2) 16	340
6530. ELVIS SINGS FLAMING STAR Elvis Presley 19Apr69 96(1) 16	340
6531. ALONG THE AXIS Jon Butcher Axis 12Oct85 66(1) 17	340
6532. ONE STORMY NIGHT Mystic Moods Orchestra 30Apr66 63(1) 14	340
6533. PAT PAULSEN FOR PRESIDENT Pat Paulsen 19Oct68 71(1) 10	339
6534. TILL Jerry Vale 15Feb69 90(1) 12	339
6535. THE YELLOW AND BLACK ATTACK Stryper 23Aug86 103(3) 30	339
6536. THE SAGA CONTINUES... Roger 02Jun84 64(2) 14	339
6537. BIONIC BOOGIE Bionic Boogie 28Jan78 88(1) 16	339
6538. NANCY Nancy Wilson 08Feb69 117(1) 14	339
6539. PAPA JOHN CREACH Papa John Creach 01Jan72 94(2) 14	339
6540. THE REAL CHUCKEEBOO Loose Ends 23Jul88 80(3) 15	339
6541. 9 1/2 WEEKS Soundtrack 29Mar86 59(2) 15	339
6542. NO SWEAT Blood, Sweat & Tears 25Aug73 72(2) 12	338
6543. 9 TO 5 Soundtrack 27Dec80 77(1) 15	338
6544. SEATTLE Perry Como 21Jun69 93(1) 11	338
6545. FOUR IN BLUE Smokey Robinson & The Miracles 06Dec69 78(1) 12	338
6546. WON'T BE BLUE ANYMORE Dan Seals 08Feb86 59(2) 15	338
6547. MINUS-PLUS Smith 04Jul70 74(1) 12	338
6548. CRAWLER Crawler 10Sep77 85(1) 13	338
6549. ...KEEP SMILING Laid Back 31Mar84 67(1) 15	338
6550. SON OF A PREACHER MAN Nancy Wilson 05Jul69 122(2) 15	338
6551. HARD TIMES IN THE LAND OF PLENTY Omar And The Howlers 27Jun87 81(2) 19	338
6552. THE RIGHT TO ROCK Keel 09Mar85 99(1) 21	338
6553. THUNDER ISLAND Jay Ferguson 25Mar78 72(1) 12	338
6554. FOUR WINDS Tangier 29Jul89 91(1) 17	338
6555. SOUND AFFECTS The Jam 07Feb81 72(1) 11	337
6556. IT'S ABOUT TIME John Denver 15Oct83 61(2) 15	337
6557. GREATEST HITS, VOL. 2 Oak Ridge Boys 08Sep84 71(2) 24	337
6558. CLUB NINJA Blue Öyster Cult 22Feb86 63(2) 14	337
6559. RAY CHARLES LIVE IN CONCERT Ray Charles 20Feb65 80(1) 18	337
6560. 16 ORIGINAL BIG HITS, VOLUME 7 Various Artists 14Oct67 79(1) 18	336
6561. LAWRENCE WELK'S "HITS OF OUR TIME" Lawrence Welk 15Apr67 72(2) 18	336
6562. I'M IN LOVE Wilson Pickett 24Feb68 70(2) 15	336
6563. FREESTYLE Bobbi Humphrey 01Jul78 89(1) 14	336
6564. FIGHT DIRTY Charlie 01Sep79 60(2) 10	336

Rank. Title Act
Entry Peak(Pk Wks) TotWks Scr

6565. LOVE IS EVERYTHING Johnny Mathis
20Mar65 52(1) 11 336

6566. THE BAROQUE BEATLES BOOK
Joshua Rifkin 11Dec65 83(1) 17 336

6567. JACK THE TOAD Savoy Brown
30Jun73 84(1) 14 336

6568. SUPER MANN Herbie Mann
24Feb79 77(1) 13 336

6569. STEAM Steam
10Jan70 84(2) 13 335

6570. TELL NO TALES TNT
23May87 100(1) 21 335

6571. FOUR TOPS NOW! Four Tops
05Jul69 74(1) 10 335

6572. STREET BEAT The Deele
04Feb84 78(2) 19 335

6573. MELBA(2) Melba Moore
18Nov78 114(1) 18 335

6574. MEET THE BRADY BUNCH Brady Bunch
13May72 108(1) 19 335

6575. MORE GOLDEN GRASS Grass Roots
24Oct70 152(1) 27 335

6576. YOU BROKE MY HEART SO I BUSTED YOUR JAW Spooky Tooth 19May73 84(1) 14 335

6577. LORD SUTCH AND HEAVY FRIENDS
Lord Sutch And Heavy Friends 21Feb70 84(2) 13 335

6578. THE SKILL The Sherbs
28Feb81 100(2) 16 334

6579. I'D LIKE TO TEACH THE WORLD TO SING
Hillside Singers 08Jan72 71(1) 16 334

6580. FORCE IT UFO
09Aug75 71(1) 13 334

6581. A DIFFERENT KIND OF CRAZY Head East
17Nov79 96(1) 16 334

6582. MORE OF THE BEST OF BILL COSBY
Bill Cosby 14Mar70 80(1) 16 334

6583. DREAM STREET ROSE Gordon Lightfoot
05Apr80 60(1) 11 334

6584. THE BUTTERFIELD BLUES BAND/LIVE
Butterfield Blues Band 16Jan71 72(1) 12 334

6585. SHE CALLED ME BABY Charlie Rich
26Oct74 84(2) 15 333

6586. ALVIN STONE (THE BIRTH & DEATH OF A GANGSTER) Fantastic Four 21Jun75 99(2) 16 333

6587. STARCASTLE Starcastle
13Mar76 95(2) 15 333

6588. SHEET MUSIC 10cc
10Aug74 81(1) 14 333

6589. ALL THIS AND HEAVEN TOO Andrew Gold
25Feb78 81(4) 14 333

6590. THE GREATEST LIVE SHOW ON EARTH
Jerry Lee Lewis 05Dec64 71(2) 17 332

6591. MONTY PYTHON'S FLYING CIRCUS
Monty Python 02Aug75 83(2) 15 332

6592. THE GREAT MUPPET CAPER Soundtrack
11Jul81 66(2) 11 332

6593. MEN FROM EARTH
Ozark Mountain Daredevils 02Oct76 74(1) 10 332

6594. THINK VISUAL The Kinks
20Dec86 81(2) 16 332

6595. SOFTLY, AS I LEAVE YOU Eydie Gorme
18Feb67 85(2) 18 332

6596. OLIVER AGAIN Oliver
16May70 71(1) 13 332

6597. REFLECTIONS OF MY LIFE The Marmalade
20Jun70 71(2) 13 332

6598. EVITA Original Cast
23Aug80 105(2) 19 332

6599. THIS IS MY COUNTRY The Impressions
07Dec68 107(1) 13 331

6600. BELLE OF THE BALL Richard Torrance And Eureka 08Mar75 107(1) 17 331

6601. VIBRATIONS Roy Ayers Ubiquity
15Jan77 74(2) 12 331

6602. CHRONICLE (THE 20 GREATEST HITS)
Creedence Clearwater Revival 06Mar76 100(1) 14 331

6603. RHAPSODIES FOR YOUNG LOVERS, VOLUME TWO Midnight String Quartet 29Jul67 67(1) 16 331

Rank. Title Act
Entry Peak(Pk Wks) TotWks Scr

6604. O'KEEFE Danny O'Keefe
02Sep72 87(2) 16 331

6605. MORE AMOR Eydie Gorme
28Aug65 53(2) 11 331

6606. ONE Bee Gees
19Aug89 68(2) 13 331

6607. REAL LOVE Ashford & Simpson
06Sep86 74(2) 18 331

6608. LIGHTNING STRIKES Loudness
31May86 64(2) 16 331

6609. SWEET SIXTEEN Reba McEntire
03Jun89 78(1) 18 331

6610. WHICH WAY YOU GOIN' BILLY?
Poppy Family 20Jun70 76(2) 11 330

6611. FRAMPTON'S CAMEL Peter Frampton
09Jun73 110(1) 22 330

6612. JUST OUTSIDE OF TOWN Mandrill
13Oct73 82(1) 15 330

6613. LIKE GANGBUSTERS JoBoxers
15Oct83 70(2) 15 330

6614. BONK Big Pig
26Mar88 93(2) 17 330

6615. DANCE Pure Prairie League
20Nov76 99(2) 14 330

6616. ONE WAY...OR ANOTHER Cactus
20Mar71 88(1) 13 330

6617. FALLIN' IN LOVE Hamilton, Joe Frank & Reynolds 13Dec75 82(1) 14 330

6618. DREAMLAND EXPRESS John Denver
06Jul85 90(2) 19 330

6619. SOLID Mandrill
26Apr75 92(1) 14 330

6620. MINIMUM WAGE ROCK & ROLL Bus Boys
29Nov80 85(1) 15 330

6621. SILK N' SOUL Gladys Knight And The Pips
11Jan69 136(1) 16 329

6622. TAKIN' IT EASY Seals & Crofts
13May78 78(1) 13 329

6623. SWEET SWEETBACK'S BAADASSSSS SONG
Soundtrack 03Jul71 139(1) 19 329

6624. FATHERS AND SONS Muddy Waters
27Sep69 70(1) 10 329

6625. SPACE & FIRST TAKES Lee Michaels
25Mar72 78(1) 13 329

6626. OPEN SESAME Kool & The Gang
20Nov76 110(1) 18 329

6627. EXPANSIONS Lonnie Liston Smith & The Cosmic Echoes 24May75 85(1) 13 329

6628. THE DEVIL IN ME Thelma Houston
12Nov77 64(2) 11 328

6629. STRANGER IN THE CITY John Miles
19Mar77 93(1) 15 328

6630. SHOUT! B.T. Express
25Feb78 67(2) 11 328

6631. GOIN' FOR MYSELF Dennis Coffey
25Mar72 90(2) 14 328

6632. EARLY MORNING RAIN Ian & Sylvia
19Jun65 77(1) 18 328

6633. MOSAIQUE Gipsy Kings
16Dec89 95(2) 19 328

6634. PRIMAL SCREAM Maynard Ferguson
17Apr76 75(1) 14 328

6635. TRY TO REMEMBER Brothers Four
13Nov65 76(1) 15 328

6636. THE WILD ANGELS, VOL. II
Davie Allan And The Arrows 22Apr67 94(1) 18 328

6637. IN THE SLOT Tower Of Power
11Oct75 67(2) 11 328

6638. STILL STANDING Jason & The Scorchers
22Nov86 91(4) 19 328

6639. GYPSY BLOOD Mason Ruffner
13Jun87 80(2) 16 327

6640. NEW ROUTES Lulu
21Feb70 88(1) 14 327

6641. EAST Hiroshima
25Mar89 105(2) 19 327

6642. STRONG STUFF Hank Williams Jr.
23Apr83 64(2) 16 327

Rank. Title Act
Entry Peak(Pk Wks) TotWks Scr

6643. HEAT IN THE STREET Pat Travers
21Oct78 99(2) 16 327

6644. THE ZAGORA Loose Ends
04Apr87 59(2) 14 327

6645. DIAMONDS ARE FOREVER Soundtrack
08Jan72 74(2) 12 327

6646. FRANCIS A. & EDWARD K. Frank Sinatra & Duke Ellington 24Feb68 78(2) 13 327

6647. CEREMONY Spooky Tooth
21Mar70 92(1) 14 327

6648. MORE GEORGE THOROGOOD AND THE DESTROYERS George Thorogood & The Destroyers
08Nov80 68(2) 12 327

6649. SPEEDWAY Elvis Presley
06Jul68 82(1) 13 327

6650. FLORIDAYS Jimmy Buffett
28Jun86 66(1) 16 326

6651. THE REAL MACAW Graham Parker
20Aug83 59(1) 14 326

6652. THE MANY SIDES OF THE SERENDIPITY SINGERS Serendipity Singers
27Jun64 68(1) 15 326

6653. GREAT SCENES FROM GERSHWIN'S "PORGY AND BESS" Leontyne Price 05Oct63 66(1) 16 325

6654. RHYTHM AND ROMANCE Rosanne Cash
22Jun85 101(1) 21 325

6655. ANGEL OF THE MORNING (HIT THEMES FOR YOUNG LOVERS) Percy Faith 21Sep68 95(1) 11 325

6656. THIRD ANNUAL PIPE DREAM
Atlanta Rhythm Section 14Sep74 74(1) 12 325

6657. I'VE GOT YOU Gloria Gaynor
14Aug76 107(1) 14 325

6658. ALIVE ON ARRIVAL Steve Forbert
10Feb79 82(2) 15 325

6659. REI MOMO David Byrne
21Oct89 71(2) 18 324

6660. COME TOGETHER Ike & Tina Turner
16May70 130(1) 19 324

6661. OUTTA SEASON Ike & Tina Turner
19Apr69 91(1) 12 324

6662. ELTON JOHN'S GREATEST HITS, VOLUME III 1979-1987 Elton John
03Oct87 84(2) 23 324

6663. FATE FOR BREAKFAST Art Garfunkel
07Apr79 67(2) 14 324

6664. THE EVERLOVIN' WORLD OF EDDY ARNOLD
Eddy Arnold 24Feb68 122(2) 21 324

6665. CHEAPO-CHEAPO PRODUCTIONS PRESENTS REAL LIVE JOHN SEBASTIAN John Sebastian
24Apr71 75(1) 13 324

6666. BROKEN ENGLISH Marianne Faithfull
02Feb80 82(1) 15 323

6667. STAY IN LOVE Minnie Riperton
19Mar77 71(2) 10 323

6668. BITTER TEARS (BALLADS OF THE AMERICAN INDIAN) Johnny Cash 07Nov64 47(1) 13 323

6669. LET'S TAKE IT TO THE STAGE Funkadelic
19Jul75 102(1) 16 323

6670. WALKIN' THE RAZOR'S EDGE Helix
18Aug84 69(2) 16 323

6671. LET'S LIVE FOR TODAY Grass Roots
19Aug67 75(2) 15 323

6672. PRIDE Robert Palmer
30Apr83 112(2) 19 323

6673. CROSBY/NASH - LIVE
David Crosby/Graham Nash 19Nov77 52(1) 8 323

6674. LOVE ISLAND Deodato
29Apr78 98(1) 17 323

6675. THERE'S NO GOOD IN GOODBYE
The Manhattans 04Mar78 78(2) 12 323

6676. ROD McKUEN AT CARNEGIE HALL
Rod McKuen 11Oct69 96(2) 16 323

6677. MAJOR MOVES Hank Williams Jr.
09Jun84 100(1) 19 322

6678. ENOUGH IS ENOUGH Billy Squier
18Oct86 61(2) 16 322

6679. STAMP ALBUM Climax Blues Band
13Sep75 69(1) 11 322

Rank. Title Act	Entry Peak(Pk Wks) TotWks	Scr
6680. THE GOOD BOOK Melanie	27Feb71 80(1) 10	322
6681. LOVE IS IN THE AIR John Paul Young	11Nov78 119(1) 18	322
6682. EXPOSURE Robert Fripp	26May79 79(2) 14	322
6683. FOUR SAIL Love	06Sep69 102(1) 12	322
6684. COME BACK WHEN YOU GROW UP Bobby Vee	07Oct67 66(2) 12	322
6685. LAUGH-IN '69 TV Soundtrack	05Apr69 88(2) 10	322
6686. ODESSEY & ORACLE The Zombies	15Mar69 95(1) 13	322
6687. THE SISTERS Sister Sledge	13Feb82 69(2) 14	322
6688. IT AIN'T ME BABE The Turtles	23Oct65 98(1) 19	322
6689. SWEET CHARITY Original Cast	12Mar66 92(1) 16	322
6690. COMMON SENSE John Prine	26Apr75 66(2) 10	321
6691. THE SWING OF DELIGHT Devadip Carlos Santana	06Sep80 65(2) 10	321
6692. RAINBOW FUNK Jr. Walker & The All Stars	24Jul71 91(1) 14	321
6693. RORY GALLAGHER/LIVE! Rory Gallagher	26Aug72 101(1) 15	321
6694. BETWEEN TWO FIRES Paul Young	22Nov86 77(2) 17	321
6695. HOME, HOME ON THE ROAD New Riders Of The Purple Sage	27Apr74 68(1) 12	321
6696. I CAPRICORN Shirley Bassey	18Mar72 94(2) 13	321
6697. SUPER PSYCHEDELICS The Ventures	03Jun67 67(1) 15	321
6698. PROCOL'S NINTH Procol Harum	23Aug75 52(1) 8	321
6699. LIVE, TAKIN' THE STAGE Pure Prairie League	10Sep77 68(1) 11	320
6700. LET ME PARTY WITH YOU Bunny Sigler	25Feb78 77(2) 13	320
6701. SHINE ON Climax Blues Band	29Apr78 71(2) 11	320
6702. GOING BAROQUE Swingle Singers	30May64 65(2) 17	320
6703. X-RATED Black Oak Arkansas	18Oct75 99(2) 17	320
6704. FROM THE INSIDE Alice Cooper	16Dec78 60(1) 11	320
6705. BELLAMY BROTHERS Bellamy Brothers	15May76 69(2) 12	320
6706. SMOKEY ROBINSON & THE MIRACLES' ANTHOLOGY Smokey Robinson & The Miracles	16Feb74 97(1) 17	320
6707. BEST OF BEE GEES, VOL. 2 Bee Gees	04Aug73 98(1) 16	320
6708. THE GIFT The Jam	27Mar82 82(1) 16	320
6709. FOREVER GOLD Isley Brothers	27Aug77 58(1) 11	319
6710. DAVE MASON & CASS ELLIOT Dave Mason & Cass Elliot	13Mar71 49(2) 7	319
6711. LEAD ME ON Amy Grant	23Jul88 71(2) 13	319
6712. GOIN' OFF Biz Markie	19Mar88 90(2) 18	319
6713. BELLE DE JOUR Saint Tropez	05May79 65(1) 11	319
6714. 2300 JACKSON ST. Jacksons	17Jun89 59(2) 11	319
6715. READY AN' WILLING Whitesnake	16Aug80 90(1) 16	319
6716. BEFORE WE WERE SO RUDELY INTERRUPTED The Animals	27Aug77 70(2) 11	319
6717. AN AMERICAN DREAM Dirt Band	26Jan80 76(1) 14	319
6718. NOBODY BUT ME Human Beinz	09Mar68 65(1) 10	319
6719. NONA Nona Hendryx	23Apr83 83(1) 19	319
6720. THE MONKEES PRESENT The Monkees	01Nov69 100(1) 14	318
6721. 9 Public Image Limited	03Jun89 106(2) 23	318
6722. TODAY'S BEST Glen Gray &The Casa Loma Orchestra	19Oct63 69(1) 15	318
6723. MY LOVE Petula Clark	09Apr66 68(1) 12	318
6724. FROM MIGHTY OAKS Ray Thomas	09Aug75 68(1) 11	318
6725. CRUISING WITH RUBEN & THE JETS Mothers Of Invention	21Dec68 110(1) 12	318
6726. SWEETHEART OF THE RODEO The Byrds	31Aug68 77(2) 10	317
6727. MISTY Ray Stevens	28Jun75 106(2) 14	317
6728. FLOODLAND Sisters Of Mercy	06Feb88 101(2) 16	317
6729. GREATEST HITS Bay City Rollers	03Dec77 77(1) 11	317
6730. THE LETTER/NEON RAINBOW Box Tops	18Nov67 87(1) 15	317
6731. SOUL MAKOSSA Manu Dibango	30Jun73 79(1) 13	317
6732. FLAT AS A PANCAKE Head East	30Aug75 126(2) 17	317
6733. SOMETHIN' STUPID Lennon Sisters	27May67 77(1) 18	317
6734. ROBBERY Teena Marie	26Nov83 119(1) 24	317
6735. THE OTHER MAN'S GRASS IS ALWAYS GREENER Petula Clark	17Feb68 93(2) 23	317
6736. IF I SHOULD FALL FROM GRACE WITH GOD The Pogues	27Feb88 88(3) 16	316
6737. LIVE AND LIVELY Joe Tex	24Feb68 84(2) 17	316
6738. THE KENNEDY WIT (NARRATED BY DAVID BRINKLEY) John Fitzgerald Kennedy	26Dec64 49(1) 11	316
6739. TROUBLE IN PARADISE Randy Newman	12Feb83 64(4) 13	316
6740. SECRETS Wilton Felder	09Mar85 81(1) 16	316
6741. THE KINK KRONIKLES The Kinks	15Apr72 94(2) 13	316
6742. DEAR FRIENDS Firesign Theatre	26Feb72 75(2) 11	316
6743. FOR THE GOOD TIMES Dean Martin	27Feb71 113(1) 15	316
6744. ONE LOVE--ONE DREAM Jeffrey Osborne	27Aug88 86(1) 16	315
6745. THE FALCON & THE SNOWMAN Pat Metheny Group	09Mar85 54(2) 10	315
6746. STRANGE UNIVERSE Mahogany Rush	21Jun75 84(1) 13	315
6747. REAL LIFE AIN'T THIS WAY Jay Ferguson	21Apr79 86(2) 16	315
6748. DAN HILL(2) Dan Hill	08Aug87 90(1) 19	315
6749. ISLANDS The Band	26Mar77 64(2) 10	315
6750. CLOSER TO THE FLAME Rob Jungklas	14Jun86 102(1) 22	315
6751. HERMAN BROOD & HIS WILD ROMANCE Herman Brood	26May79 122(2) 19	315
6752. MANCINI '67 Henry Mancini And His Orchestra	18Mar67 65(1) 13	315
6753. GREAT VOICES OF THE CENTURY Various Artists	25Apr64 70(1) 15	315
6754. JULIA FORDHAM Julia Fordham	03Dec88 118(2) 25	315
6755. MR. STICK MAN Pete Fountain	08May65 64(1) 14	314
6756. BACK TO AVALON Kenny Loggins	20Aug88 69(2) 14	314
6757. SPAGHETTI SAUCE & OTHER DELIGHTS Pat Cooper	17Dec66 84(1) 14	314
6758. GREATEST HITS Billy Ocean	04Nov89 77(2) 16	314
6759. FUNK OR WALK Brides Of Funkenstein	04Nov78 70(1) 13	314
6760. COUNTRY PREACHER "Cannonball" Adderley Quintet	14Mar70 136(1) 22	314
6761. RICHARD PRYOR'S GREATEST HITS Richard Pryor	25Jun77 68(1) 12	314
6762. THE ACADEMY AWARD SONGS Henry Mancini And His Orchestra And Chorus	12Mar66 74(2) 13	314
6763. DANNY BOY Ray Price	10Jun67 106(2) 17	314
6764. PATTI AUSTIN Patti Austin	31Mar84 87(1) 18	314
6765. THE REVOLUTION BY NIGHT Blue Öyster Cult	26Nov83 93(1) 16	313
6766. THE RUTLES The Rutles	25Mar78 63(2) 9	313
6767. YOUR ALL-TIME COUNTRY FAVORITES John Gary	9Jul66 65(1) 12	313
6768. LOVE MAGIC L.T.D.	28Nov81 83(1) 12	313
6769. ROMEO & JULIET Alec R. Costandinos And The Synconic Orchestra	25Mar78 92(2) 17	313
6770. BRITISH LIONS British Lions	29Apr78 83(1) 15	313
6771. BIRTH, SCHOOL, WORK, DEATH The Godfathers	20Feb88 91(2) 16	313
6772. LIVE AT THE OPERA HOUSE Pointer Sisters	14Sep74 96(1) 15	313
6773. SYREETA(2) Syreeta	17May80 73(2) 15	313
6774. THE METERS The Meters	21Jun69 108(1) 15	313
6775. JASMINE NIGHTDREAMS Edgar Winter	21Jun75 69(2) 10	312
6776. ROCKIN' Guess Who	18Mar72 79(1) 10	312
6777. THIS TIME WE MEAN IT REO Speedwagon	02Aug75 74(2) 10	312
6778. WITHOUT YOU Robert Goulet	17Oct64 72(1) 16	312
6779. THESE DAYS Crystal Gayle	27Sep80 79(1) 11	312
6780. BLESS YOUR HEART Freddie Hart	01Jul72 93(2) 14	311
6781. DIAMOND SUN Glass Tiger	07May88 82(2) 15	311
6782. DREAM Nitty Gritty Dirt Band	04Oct75 66(1) 9	311
6783. STRAWBERRY MOON Grover Washington Jr.	29Aug87 66(2) 16	311
6784. THE TUBES The Tubes	02Aug75 113(1) 18	311
6785. WHEN WILL I SEE YOU AGAIN Johnny Mathis	19Apr75 99(1) 13	311
6786. EAST BAY GREASE Tower Of Power	10Apr71 106(2) 12	311
6787. REQUIEM Various Artists	06Apr85 77(2) 14	311
6788. 80/81 Pat Metheny	01Nov80 89(1) 14	311
6789. DIFFERENT DRUM Linda Ronstadt	02Feb74 92(1) 15	311
6790. PURE SMOKEY Smokey Robinson	13Apr74 99(1) 17	311
6791. YOU MAKE ME FEEL SO YOUNG Ray Conniff & His Orchestra & Chorus	15Feb64 73(1) 17	311
6792. LAST KISS J. Frank Wilson and The Cavaliers	14Nov64 54(1) 14	311
6793. NAKED TO THE WORLD Teena Marie	16Apr88 65(2) 13	311

Rank. Title Act Entry Peak(Pk Wks) TotWks	Scr
6794. TO LIVE AND DIE IN L.A. Wang Chung 02Nov85 85(2) 18	311
6795. HIGHWAYS AND HEARTACHES Ricky Skaggs 16Oct82 61(3) 12	310
6796. LOOKING GLASS Looking Glass 01Jul72 113(2) 18	310
6797. SNAKES AND LADDERS Gerry Rafferty 14Jun80 61(1) 9	310
6798. SOME KIND OF WONDERFUL Soundtrack 21Mar87 57(2) 13	310
6799. PHONE CALL FROM GOD Jerry Jordan 31May75 79(2) 12	310
6800. ANSWERS TO NOTHING Midge Ure 11Feb89 88(1) 16	310
6801. RECYCLED Nektar 03Apr76 89(1) 14	309
6802. SUSAN SINGS SONGS FROM SESAME STREET Susan of Sesame Street 01Aug70 86(1) 13	309
6803. HANDLE WITH CARE Nuclear Assault 18Nov89 126(1) 24	309
6804. ISLANDS King Crimson 05Feb72 76(1) 12	309
6805. LAST OF THE BROOKLYN COWBOYS Arlo Guthrie 28Apr73 87(1) 14	309
6806. YOU Aretha Franklin 15Nov75 83(1) 11	309
6807. THE DEEP Soundtrack 02Jul77 70(1) 10	308
6808. SCOUNDREL DAYS a-ha 01Nov86 74(2) 20	308
6809. THE NEW ZAPP IV U Zapp 23Nov85 110(2) 26	308
6810. ROD STEWART/FACES LIVE - COAST TO COAST OVERTURE AND BEGINNERS Rod Stewart/Faces 05Jan74 63(1) 11	308
6811. TAKE A LITTLE RHYTHM Ali Thomson 05Jul80 99(1) 15	308
6812. SOUTHSIDE Texas 19Aug89 88(2) 16	308
6813. CALL ME IRRESPONSIBLE Jack Jones 09May64 98(1) 20	308
6814. HARRY Nilsson 23Aug69 120(1) 15	308
6815. DESTINY Chaka Khan 23Aug86 67(2) 12	308
6816. RAW SIENNA Savoy Brown 25Apr70 121(2) 18	308
6817. THE LAWRENCE WELK TELEVISION SHOW 10TH ANNIVERSARY Lawrence Welk 08Aug64 73(1) 16	308
6818. THIS GUY'S IN LOVE WITH YOU Jerry Vale 10Aug68 135(1) 20	308
6819. HAVE A GOOD TIME Al Green 27Nov76 93(2) 14	307
6820. THE GREAT GATSBY Soundtrack 20Apr74 85(1) 16	307
6821. GUITAR TOWN Steve Earle 25Oct86 89(2) 20	307
6822. WHEN I DIE Motherlode 04Oct69 93(1) 12	307
6823. ABOUT LAST NIGHT... Soundtrack 26Jul86 72(1) 14	307
6824. R.B. GREAVES R.B. Greaves 03Jan70 85(2) 14	307
6825. OUTRAGEOUS Lakeside 28Jul84 68(2) 15	307
6826. PEARLY SHELLS Burl Ives 05Dec64 65(1) 15	307
6827. WINDHAM HILL RECORDS SAMPLER '86 Various Artists 29Mar86 102(2) 18	306
6828. KILLER JOE Little Jimmy Osmond 02Dec72 105(2) 14	306
6829. SAM-I-AM Sam Harris 15Feb86 69(1) 14	305
6830. GYPSY COWBOY New Riders Of The Purple Sage 09Dec72 85(1) 13	305
6831. LOVE JONES Johnny Guitar Watson 05Jul80 115(2) 14	305
6832. MANCINI CONCERT Henry Mancini And His Orchestra 31Jul71 85(1) 11	305
6833. CONNIE FRANCIS SINGS FOR MAMA Connie Francis 01May65 78(1) 15	305
6834. ON STAGE Rainbow 16Jul77 65(1) 9	305
6835. BEACH BOYS '69 (THE BEACH BOYS LIVE IN LONDON) Beach Boys 11Dec76 75(2) 10	305
6836. MICHAEL MARTIN MURPHEY Michael Murphey 04Sep82 69(1) 16	305
6837. SUDAN VILLAGE Seals & Crofts 11Dec76 73(2) 10	305
6838. DUSTY IN MEMPHIS Dusty Springfield 15Mar69 99(2) 14	304
6839. CLOSE TO YOU Johnny Mathis 10Oct70 61(1) 9	304
6840. PARTY 'TIL YOU'RE BROKE Rufus 28Mar81 73(1) 11	304
6841. IT WAS ALMOST LIKE A SONG Ronnie Milsap 10Sep77 97(2) 15	304
6842. THE NEED OF LOVE Earth, Wind & Fire 15Jan72 89(1) 13	304
6843. GET THAT FEELING Jimi Hendrix and Curtis Knight 30Dec67 75(2) 12	304
6844. PRESENTING: THE BACHELORS The Bachelors 20Jun64 70(1) 16	304
6845. GOOD LOVE Meli'sa Morgan 19Dec87 108(1) 19	304
6846. THE BEST OF LOU RAWLS Lou Rawls 31Aug68 103(2) 16	304
6847. BOSTON, MASS. Del Fuegos 26Oct85 132(1) 34	304
6848. HOLD ON Dan Hill 21Jan78 79(3) 14	304
6849. THEME FROM "Z" AND OTHER FILM MUSIC Henry Mancini And His Orchestra 25Apr70 111(2) 17	303
6850. IRON EAGLE Soundtrack 15Feb86 54(2) 11	303
6851. STINGRAY Joe Cocker 15May76 70(1) 10	303
6852. GO AWAY FROM MY WORLD Marianne Faithfull 25Dec65 81(1) 16	303
6853. REAL McCOY Van McCoy 08May76 106(1) 17	303
6854. AUTOMATIC Jesus And Mary Chain 25Nov89 105(1) 25	303
6855. GOIN' BANANAS Side Effect 07Jan78 86(1) 15	303
6856. TELEKON Gary Numan 04Oct80 64(2) 10	303
6857. CADDYSHACK Soundtrack 23Aug80 78(2) 12	303
6858. SOLID GOLD SOUL Various Artists 19Mar66 107(1) 19	302
6859. KISS ME GOODBYE Jim Nabors 13Jul68 153(1) 26	302
6860. STEVIE WONDER PRESENTS SYREETA Syreeta 20Jul74 116(2) 17	302
6861. DANCE BAND ON THE TITANIC Harry Chapin 17Sep77 58(1) 10	302
6862. BUSTER POINDEXTER Buster Poindexter And His Banshees Of Blue 09Jan88 90(1) 15	302
6863. YOU, ME AND HE Mtume 15Sep84 77(2) 19	302
6864. SLEEPWALK Larry Carlton 30Jan82 99(1) 16	302
6865. CON FUNK SHUN 7 Con Funk Shun 12Dec81 82(1) 13	302
6866. HOW SWEET IT IS FOR LOVERS Jackie Gleason 26Nov66 71(2) 11	302
6867. STYLE Cameo 07May83 53(1) 12	301
6868. POTLATCH Redbone 07Nov70 99(1) 17	301
6869. THE BEST OF SAM THE SHAM AND THE PHARAOHS Sam The Sham and the Pharaohs 11Mar67 98(1) 17	301
6870. JAM THE BOX! Bill Summers & Summers Heat 12Dec81 92(1) 16	301
6871. YEAR OF SUNDAY Seals & Crofts 04Dec71 133(1) 20	301
6872. ARE YOU GONNA BE THE ONE Robert Gordon 18Apr81 117(4) 15	301
6873. CAMOUFLAGE Rufus And Chaka Khan 31Oct81 98(1) 14	301
6874. TOUCH The Supremes 26Jun71 85(1) 10	301
6875. CHRISTMAS WISHES Anne Murray 28Nov81 54(2) 8	301
6876. THE BEST OF PETER AND GORDON Peter And Gordon 30Jul66 72(1) 12	301
6877. JASS-AY-LAY-DEE Ohio Players 09Sep78 69(3) 9	301
6878. REIGN IN BLOOD Slayer 15Nov86 94(3) 18	301
6879. PIPE DREAMS Gladys Knight And The Pips 27Nov76 94(2) 12	301
6880. OPEN UP YOUR LOVE The Whispers 16Jul77 65(2) 10	301
6881. NO SECOND CHANCE Charlie 04Jun77 111(1) 15	301
6882. 10 GOLDEN YEARS Brenda Lee 25Jun66 70(1) 14	300
6883. GLORIA LORING Gloria Loring 06Sep86 61(2) 14	300
6884. DOWN IN THE GROOVE Bob Dylan 18Jun88 61(3) 10	300
6885. SWEAT The System 12Mar83 94(1) 23	300
6886. THE SOUND OF WILSON PICKETT Wilson Pickett 12Aug67 54(1) 11	300
6887. SKIN DIVE Michael Franks 15Jun85 137(2) 27	300
6888. HIS GREATEST HITS Engelbert Humperdinck 21Dec74 103(2) 14	300
6889. TOGETHER AGAIN / MY HEART SKIPS A BEAT Buck Owens 05Sep64 88(1) 18	299
6890. CONTAGIOUS Y&T 11Jul87 78(2) 13	299
6891. TODD RUNDGREN'S UTOPIA/ANOTHER LIVE Utopia 15Nov75 66(1) 9	299
6892. INSIDE RONNIE MILSAP Ronnie Milsap 03Jul82 66(2) 14	299
6893. COME ON DANCE, DANCE Saturday Night Band 27May78 125(4) 17	299
6894. LOVE ON THE WING Jesse Colin Young 02Apr77 64(1) 9	299
6895. EVERY SHADE OF LOVE Jesse Johnson 16Apr88 79(2) 13	299
6896. THE TROUBLEMAKER Willie Nelson 16Oct76 60(1) 7	298
6897. MECHANIX UFO 20Feb82 82(1) 14	298
6898. 1980 Gil Scott-Heron & Brian Jackson 08Mar80 82(1) 12	298
6899. PILLOW TALK Sylvia 02Jun73 70(1) 12	298
6900. JOHNNY THE FOX Thin Lizzy 13Nov76 52(1) 11	298
6901. WEATHER REPORT(2) Weather Report 20Feb82 68(1) 11	298
6902. PLAYING TO WIN LRB 09Feb85 75(3) 14	298
6903. SERGIO MENDES AND THE NEW BRASIL '77 Sergio Mendes And The New Brasil '77 20Aug77 81(2) 12	298
6904. DIANA ROSS ANTHOLOGY Diana Ross 11Jun83 63(1) 12	298
6905. THE HOUSE OF DOLLS Gene Loves Jezebel 14Nov87 108(1) 22	298
6906. UNDER THE BIG BLACK SUN X 17Jul82 76(3) 15	297
6907. RIGHT BACK WHERE WE STARTED FROM Maxine Nightingale 29May76 65(1) 9	297

Rank. Title Act Entry Peak(Pk Wks) TotWks	Scr
6908. PUCKER UP Lipps Inc. 11Oct80 63(1) 9	297
6909. THE LUXURY GAP Heaven 17 04Jun83 72(2) 13	297
6910. THE STOOGES The Stooges 23Aug69 106(1) 11	297
6911. SING A SONG WITH THE KINGSTON TRIO Kingston Trio 11Jan64 69(1) 14	297
6912. 'NARD Bernard Wright 14Mar81 116(2) 14	297
6913. CHI-LITES The Chi-Lites 15Sep73 89(1) 14	297
6914. I ADVANCE MASKED Andy Summers & Robert Fripp 06Nov82 60(3) 11	297
6915. MONTANA CAFE Hank Williams Jr. 19Jul86 93(2) 18	296
6916. 22B3 Device 12Jul86 73(2) 16	296
6917. SNEAKIN' SALLY THRU THE ALLEY Robert Palmer 14Jun75 107(1) 15	296
6918. EDDIE FISHER TODAY! Eddie Fisher 24Jul65 52(1) 10	296
6919. BLACK ROCK Bar-Kays 27Feb71 90(2) 12	296
6920. THE WAYS TO LOVE A MAN Tammy Wynette 21Feb70 83(1) 11	295
6921. WHAT'S WRONG WITH THIS PICTURE? Andrew Gold 07May77 95(1) 16	295
6922. LONG LIVE THE KANE Big Daddy Kane 16Jul88 116(1) 19	295
6923. ABSOLUTE BEGINNERS Soundtrack 12Apr86 62(2) 13	295
6924. TOGETHER McCoy Tyner 26May79 66(2) 11	295
6925. ARABESQUE John Klemmer 17Jun78 83(1) 10	295
6926. THE BEATLES WITH TONY SHERIDAN AND THEIR GUESTS The Beatles 15Feb64 68(2) 14	295
6927. THE BEST OF AL MARTINO Al Martino 31Aug68 108(2) 16	295
6928. LADIES OF THE EIGHTIES A Taste Of Honey 24Apr82 73(4) 12	294
6929. SPANISH RHAPSODIES FOR YOUNG LOVERS Midnight String Quartet 08Apr67 76(1) 12	294
6930. CHICAGO XIV Chicago 09Aug80 71(2) 9	294
6931. THE SANDPIPER Soundtrack 23Oct65 89(1) 15	294
6932. ZAPPA IN NEW YORK Frank Zappa 15Apr78 57(1) 8	294
6933. INVISIBLE TEARS Johnny Mann Singers 03Oct64 77(2) 15	294
6934. ONE HAS MY NAME Barry Young 01Jan66 67(2) 12	294
6935. GOIN' LATIN Ramsey Lewis 25Mar67 95(1) 16	294
6936. NERO GOES "POPS" Peter Nero/Boston Pops Orchestra 23Oct65 86(1) 16	294
6937. L.A. IS MY LADY Frank Sinatra 25Aug84 58(2) 13	294
6938. FROM MONTY, WITH LOVE Mantovani 27Mar71 105(1) 15	294
6939. EINZELHAFT Falco 07May83 64(1) 13	293
6940. MUSIC OF HAWAII Henry Mancini And His Orchestra And Chorus 17Dec66 121(2) 19	293
6941. UGLY EGO Cameo 04Nov78 83(1) 15	293
6942. MISDEMEANOR UFO 05Apr86 106(2) 19	293
6943. GREATEST AMERICAN WALTZES Connie Francis 05Oct63 94(1) 17	293
6944. HOMETOWN BOY MAKES GOOD Elvin Bishop 20Nov76 70(1) 12	293
6945. AMERICA'S CHOICE Hot Tuna 10May75 75(1) 11	293
6946. 2 LIVE CREW IS WHAT WE ARE 2 Live Crew 11Apr87 128(1) 33	293
6947. WONDERLAND Big Country 05May84 65(2) 12	293
6948. BOI-NGO Oingo Boingo 21Mar87 77(2) 16	293
6949. PASTICHE Manhattan Transfer 18Feb78 66(2) 10	293
6950. DREAMING A DREAM Crown Heights Affair 04Oct75 121(1) 17	292
6951. STILL CAUGHT UP Millie Jackson 26Jul75 112(2) 16	292
6952. CANTAMOS Poco 30Nov74 76(1) 11	292
6953. WHO'S LAST The Who 01Dec84 81(2) 14	292
6954. MOONLIGHT MADNESS Teri DeSario 19Jan80 80(1) 13	292
6955. ANIMAL LOGIC Animal Logic 09Dec89 106(1) 21	292
6956. HERO AND HEROINE Strawbs 02Mar74 94(1) 17	292
6957. MIKE'S MURDER Joe Jackson 24Sep83 64(1) 13	292
6958. SKYLARK Skylark 07Apr73 102(1) 16	292
6959. INDIVIDUAL CHOICE Jean-Luc Ponty 27Aug83 85(1) 15	292
6960. DRAMA V Ron Banks And The Dramatics 15Nov75 93(1) 12	292
6961. STAY HARD Raven 23Mar85 81(3) 15	292
6962. TALK TALK TALK Psychedelic Furs 27Jun81 89(2) 14	292
6963. NORWOOD Glen Campbell 27Jun70 90(1) 13	291
6964. WINTER INTO SPRING George Winston 12May84 127(2) 32	291
6965. NASTY, NASTY Black 'N Blue 25Oct86 110(1) 20	291
6966. ANIMAL GRACE April Wine 17Mar84 62(1) 12	291
6967. YOURS TRULY Tom Browne 12Dec81 97(1) 14	291
6968. TEXAS IN MY REAR VIEW MIRROR Mac Davis 18Oct80 67(1) 9	291
6969. ON HER MAJESTY'S SECRET SERVICE Soundtrack 07Feb70 103(1) 13	291
6970. CHAD & JEREMY SING FOR YOU Chad & Jeremy 27Mar65 69(1) 14	290
6971. JUDY COLLINS' FIFTH ALBUM Judy Collins 02Oct65 69(1) 13	290
6972. BEAUTIFUL LOSER Bob Seger 12Apr75 131(1) 18	290
6973. THE BUDDY HOLLY STORY Soundtrack 22Jul78 86(2) 13	290
6974. CONTINUATION Philip Bailey 10Sep83 71(1) 14	290
6975. LITTLE MISS DANGEROUS Ted Nugent 22Mar86 76(2) 14	290
6976. DAVID WERNER David Werner 01Sep79 65(1) 11	290
6977. A TONIC FOR THE TROOPS Boomtown Rats 03Mar79 112(1) 13	290
6978. INTERMISSION Dio 28Jun86 70(2) 16	290
6979. MUSIC FROM THE ELDER KISS 05Dec81 75(1) 11	290
6980. BEFORE THE RAIN Lee Oskar 16Sep78 86(1) 12	290
6981. JUST FLY Pure Prairie League 13May78 79(1) 11	290
6982. WE DON'T TALK ANYMORE Cliff Richard 08Dec79 93(2) 15	290
6983. SESAME STREET 2 TV Soundtrack 11Dec71 78(1) 10	290
6984. NO MEAN CITY Nazareth 03Feb79 88(2) 14	290
6985. STAY AWHILE/I ONLY WANT TO BE WITH YOU Dusty Springfield 27Jun64 62(1) 13	289
6986. IN COLOR Cheap Trick 24Sep77 73(1) 12	289
6987. AMERICA EATS ITS YOUNG Funkadelic 17Jun72 123(2) 15	289
6988. HANDS DOWN Bob James 17Jul82 72(2) 17	289
6989. PETER McCANN Peter McCann 30Jul77 82(2) 12	289
6990. HOT LICKS, COLD STEEL & TRUCKERS FAVORITES Commander Cody & His Lost Planet Airmen 09Sep72 94(1) 13	289
6991. TURN THE HANDS OF TIME Peabo Bryson 28Feb81 82(1) 11	289
6992. PLUG ME IN Eddie Harris 03Aug68 120(2) 16	289
6993. ROCK BILLY BOOGIE Robert Gordon 24Mar79 106(3) 12	288
6994. WANTED DREAD & ALIVE Peter Tosh 18Jul81 91(1) 13	288
6995. FAITH, HOPE AND CHARITY Faith, Hope And Charity 30Aug75 100(1) 14	288
6996. THE LAST ONE TO KNOW Reba McEntire 10Oct87 102(2) 20	288
6997. OPEN ALL NIGHT Georgia Satellites 02Jul88 77(2) 13	288
6998. BRUJO New Riders Of The Purple Sage 02Nov74 68(1) 9	288
6999. LARGE AND IN CHARGE Chunky A 16Dec89 71(1) 13	288
7000. JUST AN OLD FASHIONED LOVE SONG Paul Williams 25Dec71 141(1) 21	288
7001. PHYLLIS HYMAN Phyllis Hyman 30Apr77 107(1) 14	288
7002. SALONGO Ramsey Lewis 22May76 77(1) 11	288
7003. TOGETHER AGAIN The Temptations 24Oct87 112(2) 21	288
7004. SWEENEY TODD-THE DEMON BARBER OF FLEET STREET Original Cast 09Jun79 78(2) 11	288
7005. L.A. (LIGHT ALBUM) Beach Boys 07Apr79 100(1) 13	288
7006. YOU'VE GOT A FRIEND Johnny Mathis 04Sep71 80(1) 10	288
7007. IN THE NIGHT Cheryl Lynn 11Jul81 104(3) 13	288
7008. THE NEW FIRST FAMILY, 1968 Various Artists 17Dec66 72(1) 10	288
7009. GAMMA 3 Gamma 20Mar82 72(1) 12	288
7010. MENUDO Menudo 25May85 100(2) 19	287
7011. COME SATURDAY MORNING The Sandpipers 15Aug70 96(1) 11	287
7012. STRANGE BEHAVIOR Animotion 15Mar86 71(2) 14	287
7013. STEADY ON Shawn Colvin 16Dec89 111(1) 24	287
7014. SKYYJAMMER Skyy 20Nov82 81(2) 13	287
7015. SOMETHING HAPPENING Paul Revere & The Raiders 14Sep68 122(1) 14	287
7016. WORD PICTURES FEATURING AUTUMN OF MY LIFE Bobby Goldsboro 21Sep68 116(1) 13	287
7017. FOR YOU Roger Williams 12Oct63 59(1) 12	287
7018. HARDCORE JOLLIES Funkadelic 27Nov76 96(4) 12	287
7019. BLOW IT OUT Tom Scott 10Sep77 87(1) 14	287
7020. KEEPER OF THE SEVEN KEYS - PART I Helloween 04Jul87 104(1) 21	286
7021. SOUL BOX Grover Washington Jr. 14Jul73 100(1) 14	286
7022. BLUE AND GRAY Poco 25Jul81 76(2) 10	286
7023. POWERAGE AC/DC 24Jun78 133(2) 17	286

Rank. Title Act Entry Peak(Pk Wks) TotWks	Scr
7024. RAY, GOODMAN & BROWN II Ray, Goodman & Brown 04Oct80 84(2) 12	286
7025. THE EVER POPULAR TORTURED ARTIST EFFECT Todd Rundgren 22Jan83 66(3) 13	286
7026. MAHVELOUS Billy Crystal 21Sep85 65(2) 13	286
7027. KID BLUE Louise Goffin 04Aug79 87(1) 13	286
7028. APPLES & BANANAS Lawrence Welk 17Apr65 57(1) 12	286
7029. ARCADE Patrick Simmons 07May83 52(1) 11	286
7030. CLAPTON Eric Clapton 17Feb73 67(1) 11	286
7031. JACK JONES SINGS Jack Jones 26Nov66 75(2) 12	286
7032. LITTLE STEVIE ORBIT Steve Forbert 11Oct80 70(1) 9	285
7033. TRY IT OUT Klique 08Oct83 70(2) 14	285
7034. SAME GOES FOR YOU Leif Garrett 15Dec79 129(1) 22	285
7035. LAKE Lake 20Aug77 92(1) 15	285
7036. LOVE CHANGES Kashif 05Dec87 118(3) 19	285
7037. BIG SCREEN - LITTLE SCREEN Henry Mancini And His Orchestra 29Jan72 109(1) 15	285
7038. TEASER Tommy Bolin 20Dec75 96(2) 14	285
7039. THE SONGS OF JIM WEATHERLY Jim Weatherly 28Sep74 94(2) 14	285
7040. THE FABULOUS BAKER BOYS Dave Grusin 18Nov89 74(2) 13	285
7041. NITTY GRITTY Gladys Knight And The Pips 25Oct69 81(1) 10	285
7042. HOLD ME, THRILL ME, KISS ME Mel Carter 18Sep65 62(1) 12	285
7043. CRAZY HORSE Crazy Horse 27Mar71 84(1) 11	285
7044. RARE HENDRIX Jimi Hendrix 02Sep72 82(2) 11	285
7045. FEVER Con Funk Shun 03Dec83 105(1) 21	285
7046. OH HOW WE DANCED Jim Capaldi 04Mar72 82(1) 11	284
7047. DANGER ZONE Sammy Hagar 21Jun80 85(1) 12	284
7048. GLENN JONES Glenn Jones 10Oct87 94(1) 17	284
7049. JFK THE MAN, THE PRESIDENT (NARRATED BY BARRY GRAY) John Fitzgerald Kennedy 11Jan64 42(1) 8	284
7050. RAINDANCING Alison Moyet 20Jun87 94(5) 17	284
7051. SPELL Deon Estus 01Apr89 89(1) 15	284
7052. SPONTANEOUS INVENTIONS Bobby McFerrin 21Mar87 103(1) 19	284
7053. YEAH! Brownsville Station 15Sep73 98(1) 19	284
7054. TODAY'S THEMES FOR YOUNG LOVERS Percy Faith 16Sep67 111(1) 17	284
7055. MR. JORDAN Julian Lennon 01Apr89 87(1) 15	284
7056. THE ARCHIES GREATEST HITS The Archies 28Nov70 114(2) 12	283
7057. RISING Mark-Almond 21Oct72 103(1) 14	283
7058. BIG SWING FACE Buddy Rich 15Jul67 97(1) 21	283
7059. HIS CALIFORNIA ALBUM Bobby Blue Bland 03Nov73 136(1) 19	283
7060. KURTIS BLOW Kurtis Blow 18Oct80 71(1) 10	283
7061. IN SESSION Chairmen Of The Board 28Nov70 117(1) 16	283
7062. MOZART: PIANO CONCERTOS NOS. 17 & 21 Géza Anda 29Jun68 115(1) 17	283
7063. KILIMANJARO The Rippingtons Featuring Russ Freeman 07May88 110(2) 15	283
7064. INTROSPECT Joe South 08Feb69 117(1) 14	283
7065. A SUNSHINY DAY WITH CHARLEY PRIDE Charley Pride 19Aug72 115(2) 15	283
7066. IT'S A FACT Jeff Lorber 27Mar82 73(2) 13	283
7067. STRAIGHT AHEAD Larry Gatlin & The Gatlin Brothers Band 17Nov79 102(1) 16	282
7068. WAR BABIES Daryl Hall & John Oates 26Oct74 86(2) 10	282
7069. MIRACLE Kane Gang 21Nov87 115(2) 20	282
7070. LONG LIVE ROCK 'N' ROLL Rainbow 06May78 89(2) 11	282
7071. IT'S A GOOD NIGHT FOR SINGIN' Jerry Jeff Walker 03Jul76 84(1) 10	282
7072. SPECIAL THINGS Pleasure 12Jul80 97(2) 14	282
7073. ARE YOU SERIOUS??? Richard Pryor 28May77 58(1) 9	282
7074. JUST KIDDIN' AROUND Ray Conniff & Billy Butterfield 14Sep63 85(1) 13	282
7075. ONE DOZEN ROSES Smokey Robinson & The Miracles 25Sep71 92(2) 10	282
7076. HOLD ME TIGHT Johnny Nash 23Nov68 109(1) 12	282
7077. THE SUN SESSIONS Elvis Presley 17Apr76 76(1) 11	282
7078. ULTRA WAVE Bootsy 06Dec80 70(3) 9	281
7079. SOLAR FIRE Manfred Mann's Earth Band 02Mar74 96(2) 15	281
7080. THE IMPRESSIONS GREATEST HITS The Impressions 20Mar65 83(2) 15	281
7081. RETURN TO FANTASY Uriah Heep 02Aug75 85(2) 10	281
7082. HIGH LONESOME Charlie Daniels Band 04Dec76 83(2) 10	281
7083. YOUNG HEARTS RUN FREE Candi Staton 26Jun76 129(1) 14	281
7084. COMMON ONE Van Morrison 20Sep80 73(1) 10	281
7085. L.A. BOPPERS L.A. Boppers 15Mar80 85(1) 11	281
7086. ROLLING DOWN A MOUNTAINSIDE Main Ingredient 10May75 90(2) 12	281
7087. LOVE THEME FROM "THE GODFATHER" Ray Conniff & His Orchestra & Chorus 03Jun72 114(2) 14	281
7088. SOUND-SYSTEM Herbie Hancock 01Sep84 71(2) 14	281
7089. INFECTED The The 14Feb87 89(2) 18	281
7090. SONGS YOU KNOW BY HEART: JIMMY BUFFETT'S GREATEST HIT(S) Jimmy Buffett 16Nov85 100(2) 24	280
7091. DEEP PURPLE IN ROCK Deep Purple 12Sep70 143(1) 21	280
7092. SPLENDIDO HOTEL Al Di Meola 12Jul80 119(2) 14	280
7093. MEET DANNY WILSON Danny Wilson 18Jul87 79(1) 16	280
7094. EYES ON THIS MC Lyte 21Oct89 86(2) 20	280
7095. FACE TO FACE Evelyn "Champagne" King 24Dec83 91(1) 20	280
7096. WORKIN' IT BACK Teddy Pendergrass 07Dec85 96(2) 23	280
7097. WHAT LOVE HAS...JOINED TOGETHER Smokey Robinson & The Miracles 30May70 97(1) 11	279
7098. A PORTRAIT OF MERLE HAGGARD Merle Haggard 18Oct69 99(1) 11	279
7099. ME AND MRS. JONES Johnny Mathis 17Feb73 83(1) 14	279
7100. THE BLUES PROJECT LIVE AT TOWN HALL Blues Project 07Oct67 71(1) 11	279
7101. ALL BY MYSELF Regina Belle 11Jul87 85(1) 15	278
7102. ONE STEP CLOSER Gavin Christopher 05Jul86 74(3) 15	278
7103. NEXT POSITION PLEASE Cheap Trick 10Sep83 61(1) 11	278
7104. THE MIDNIGHT MOVER Wilson Pickett 13Jul68 91(1) 13	278
7105. RED HOT RHYTHM & BLUES Diana Ross 30May87 73(2) 14	278
7106. BREAKAWAY Kris Kristofferson & Rita Coolidge 21Dec74 103(1) 12	278
7107. PLEASE DON'T TOUCH Steve Hackett 29Apr78 103(2) 14	278
7108. BLACK ROSE John David Souther 08May76 85(1) 11	278
7109. LOST IN A DREAM REO Speedwagon 16Nov74 98(2) 14	278
7110. HOW CRUEL Joan Armatrading 08Dec79 136(1) 18	278
7111. SHEILA E. Sheila E. 21Mar87 56(2) 12	278
7112. A WINTER'S SOLSTICE Various Artists 07Dec85 77(1) 19	278
7113. SESAME STREET FEVER Various Artists 09Sep78 75(1) 10	278
7114. GLOBE OF FROGS Robyn Hitchcock And The Egyptians 05Mar88 111(1) 15	278
7115. NAVY BLUE Diane Renay 04Apr64 54(1) 11	277
7116. HEARTBEAT, IT'S A LOVEBEAT DeFranco Family 13Oct73 109(1) 16	277
7117. ON EARTH AS IT IS IN HEAVEN Angel 05Mar77 76(1) 12	277
7118. SUNDAY SAX Boots Randolph 23Mar68 76(1) 12	277
7119. SHIRLEY BASSEY IS REALLY "SOMETHING" Shirley Bassey 17Oct70 105(1) 13	277
7120. WHAT A LIFE! Divinyls 07Dec85 91(2) 18	277
7121. STAND IN THE FIRE Warren Zevon 17Jan81 80(3) 10	277
7122. DR. HECKLE AND MR. JIVE England Dan & John Ford Coley 14Apr79 106(2) 12	277
7123. YOU AIN'T HEARD NOTHIN' YET Danny Davis And The Nashville Brass 30May70 102(1) 12	277
7124. TOGETHER Johnny & Edgar Winter 19Jun76 89(1) 9	276
7125. COWBOYS AND INDIANS New Christy Minstrels 13Feb65 62(1) 11	276
7126. THE BEST OF ZZ TOP ZZ Top 17Dec77 94(2) 19	276
7127. GREAT BALLS OF FIRE Jerry Lee Lewis 22Jul89 62(1) 10	276
7128. A PLACE LIKE THIS Robbie Nevil 26Nov88 118(2) 21	276
7129. STREET CORNER SYMPHONY The Persuasions 12Feb72 88(1) 12	276
7130. TURN THIS MUTHA OUT Idris Muhammad 18Jun77 127(2) 19	276
7131. MORE AMERICAN GRAFFITI Various Artists 05Apr75 84(2) 10	276
7132. BILL COSBY IS NOT HIMSELF THESE DAYS-(RAT OWN, RAT OWN, RAT OWN) Bill Cosby 05Jun76 100(2) 12	276
7133. AFTER DARK Cruzados 01Aug87 106(2) 21	276
7134. BLUE Michael Parks 10Oct70 71(1) 8	275
7135. STRANGE FRUIT Billie Holiday 13Jan73 108(1) 16	275
7136. CALL IT WHAT YOU WANT Bill Summers & Summers Heat 04Apr81 129(1) 15	275
7137. ALL THE KING'S HORSES Grover Washington Jr. 09Sep72 111(1) 17	275
7138. SOUND OF A DRUM Ralph MacDonald 25Sep76 114(1) 16	275
7139. LET'S BE FRIENDS Elvis Presley 09May70 105(2) 11	275

Rank. Title Act Entry Peak(Pk Wks) TotWks	Scr
7140. **COUNTRY JOE & THE FISH/GREATEST HITS** Country Joe & The Fish 03Jan70 74(2) 9	275
7141. **YOU AND ME BOTH** Yaz 13Aug83 69(1) 13	275
7142. **FOGHAT** Foghat 15Jul72 127(2) 22	275
7143. **CHICAGO** Original Cast 23Aug75 73(1) 10	275
7144. **SOUL COAXING (AME CALINE)** Raymond Lefevre and His Orchestra 30Mar68 117(1) 16	275
7145. **WELCOME BACK** John Sebastian 15May76 79(1) 10	275
7146. **BEAUTIFUL FEELINGS** Rick Springfield 08Dec84 78(2) 13	275
7147. **SEND YOUR LOVE** Aurra 13Jun81 103(1) 13	274
7148. **FOOLS GOLD** Fools Gold 24Apr76 100(1) 13	274
7149. **A TIME FOR LIVING, A TIME FOR HOPE** Ed Ames 08Mar69 114(2) 14	274
7150. **AURORA** Jean-Luc Ponty 10Apr76 123(1) 13	274
7151. **PREMONITION** Peter Frampton 08Feb86 80(2) 14	274
7152. **RAISE YOUR FIST AND YELL** Alice Cooper 24Oct87 73(2) 15	274
7153. **SECOND SIGHTING** Frehley's Comet 11Jun88 81(3) 13	274
7154. **CLOSE TO THE BONE** Thompson Twins 25Apr87 76(1) 14	274
7155. **THE MESSAGE IS LOVE** Barry White 28Apr79 67(2) 9	274
7156. **THE CONCEPT** Slave 19Aug78 78(1) 10	274
7157. **ARLO** Arlo Guthrie 26Oct68 100(2) 12	274
7158. **UNDEAD** Ten Years After 10Aug68 115(1) 14	273
7159. **MY OWN WAY TO ROCK** Burton Cummings 09Jul77 51(2) 6	273
7160. **MUSIC MAESTRO PLEASE** Love Unlimited Orchestra 10Jan76 92(1) 15	273
7161. **RAW SOUL** James Brown 08Apr67 88(1) 14	273
7162. **TURN BACK THE HANDS OF TIME** Tyrone Davis 11Jul70 90(1) 11	273
7163. **SILVERBIRD** Mark Lindsay 05Sep70 82(1) 10	273
7164. **CLASSICAL GAS** Mason Williams & Mannheim Steamroller 19Dec87 118(1) 19	272
7165. **WELCOME TO MY LOVE** Nancy Wilson 03Feb68 115(1) 17	272
7166. **KINDA KINKS** The Kinks 28Aug65 60(2) 9	272
7167. **CANDLES** Heatwave 13Dec80 71(2) 10	272
7168. **MEN WITHOUT WOMEN** Little Steven And The Disciples Of Soul 04Dec82 118(3) 18	272
7169. **MAGNETIC FIELDS** Jean Michel Jarre 11Jul81 98(2) 12	272
7170. **FOTOMAKER** Fotomaker 25Mar78 88(2) 13	272
7171. **NO GURU, NO METHOD, NO TEACHER** Van Morrison 16Aug86 70(2) 13	272
7172. **BUS STOP** The Hollies 22Oct66 75(1) 11	272
7173. **THE FIRST LADY** Tammy Wynette 31Oct70 119(1) 14	271
7174. **SATISFIED** Rita Coolidge 22Sep79 95(3) 16	271
7175. **THE BEST OF THE ART OF NOISE** Art Of Noise 17Dec88 83(1) 14	271
7176. **BERNADETTE PETERS** Bernadette Peters 03May80 114(1) 14	271
7177. **MY WOMAN, MY WOMAN, MY WIFE** Marty Robbins 23May70 117(1) 16	271
7178. **BOYS CLUB** Boys Club 26Nov88 93(2) 16	271
7179. **THE ALBUM OF THE SOUNDTRACK OF THE TRAILER OF THE FILM OF "MONTY PYTHON AND THE HOLY GRAIL"** Monty Python 23Aug75 87(2) 11	271
7180. **STEP BY STEP** Jeff Lorber 09Mar85 90(2) 16	271
7181. **GOIN' OUT OF MY HEAD** Little Anthony And The Imperials 20Feb65 74(1) 13	271
7182. **TONIGHT I'LL SAY A PRAYER** Eydie Gorme 07Mar70 105(1) 12	271
7183. **JOHN EDDIE** John Eddie 21Jun86 83(2) 15	271
7184. **ROCK AND ROLL HEART** Lou Reed 13Nov76 64(1) 8	271
7185. **A CHIPMUNK CHRISTMAS** The Chipmunks 21Nov81 72(2) 9	271
7186. **JEAN-LUC PONTY: LIVE** Jean-Luc Ponty 19May79 68(1) 10	270
7187. **INSIDE STORY** Grace Jones 13Dec86 81(2) 16	270
7188. **IN PERSON AT CARNEGIE HALL** Clancy Brothers And Tommy Makem 16Nov63 60(1) 12	270
7189. **THE GREAT PRETENDER** Dolly Parton 18Feb84 73(1) 14	270
7190. **LADY GODIVA** Peter And Gordon 04Feb67 80(1) 13	270
7191. **HE TOUCHED ME** Elvis Presley 22Apr72 79(1) 10	270
7192. **SECOND ALBUM** Roy Buchanan 10Mar73 86(1) 13	270
7193. **THRILLER!** Cold Blood 28Apr73 97(1) 14	270
7194. **OBSESSION** Bob James 22Nov86 142(1) 27	270
7195. **FUTURE GAMES** Fleetwood Mac 30Oct71 91(2) 12	270
7196. **ROCK LOVE** Steve Miller Band 09Oct71 82(2) 9	269
7197. **CAPTAIN SAD AND HIS SHIP OF FOOLS** The Cowsills 07Sep68 105(2) 12	269
7198. **GALVESTON** Jim Nabors 14Jun69 145(2) 19	269
7199. **8TH DAY** 8th Day 07Aug71 131(1) 16	269
7200. **HOOKED ON BIG BANDS** Frank Barber Orchestra 05Jun82 94(3) 16	269
7201. **BEST OF TAVARES** Tavares 15Oct77 72(2) 10	269
7202. **ESPECIALLY FOR YOU** John Gary 11Feb67 117(2) 14	269
7203. **MAKE A DIFFERENCE FOUNDATION: STAIRWAY TO HEAVEN/HIGHWAY TO HELL** Various Artists 16Dec89 87(1) 15	269
7204. **GLENN MEDEIROS** Glenn Medeiros 13Jun87 83(2) 17	269
7205. **THE WILD THE WILLING AND THE INNOCENT** UFO 31Jan81 77(2) 11	269
7206. **NO EARTHLY CONNECTION** Rick Wakeman 15May76 67(1) 8	269
7207. **BLOODLINE** Glen Campbell 01May76 63(2) 9	269
7208. **MODERN ROMANS** The Call 26Mar83 84(1) 15	268
7209. **STAIRSTEPS** Stairsteps 13Jun70 83(1) 12	268
7210. **ARK** The Animals 10Sep83 66(1) 10	268
7211. **DREAM A LITTLE DREAM** Mama Cass 19Oct68 87(1) 10	268
7212. **SUBURBAN VOODOO** Paul Carrack 11Sep82 78(1) 14	268
7213. **NEW HORIZON** Isaac Hayes 17Dec77 78(1) 12	268
7214. **LIVING LARGE...** Heavy D & The Boyz 14Nov87 92(2) 16	268
7215. **IMAGES** Ronnie Milsap 16Jun79 98(2) 15	268
7216. **NEVER MIND THE BOLLOCKS HERE'S THE SEX PISTOLS** Sex Pistols 10Dec77 106(2) 12	268
7217. **ONE LORD, ONE FAITH, ONE BAPTISM** Aretha Franklin 26Dec87 106(3) 16	268
7218. **LIVE!** Brother Jack McDuff 09Nov63 81(1) 14	268
7219. **'74 JAILBREAK** AC/DC 17Nov84 76(2) 14	268
7220. **A SONG** Neil Sedaka 28May77 59(1) 7	268
7221. **THE SECRET POLICEMAN'S BALL** Various Artists 23May81 106(1) 12	268
7222. **HYMN OF THE SEVENTH GALAXY** Return To Forever 08Dec73 124(1) 15	268
7223. **MESSINA** Jim Messina 20Jun81 95(3) 11	267
7224. **YOU GOTTA WASH YOUR ASS** Redd Foxx 03Jan76 87(1) 13	267
7225. **PRACTICE WHAT YOU PREACH** Testament 02Sep89 77(2) 12	267
7226. **RICHARD PRYOR: HERE AND NOW** Richard Pryor 12Nov83 71(1) 13	267
7227. **KC TEN** KC 04Feb84 93(1) 18	267
7228. **I'VE GOT THE CURE** Stephanie Mills 13Oct84 73(2) 15	267
7229. **UNDER THE VOLCANO** Rock And Hyde 02May87 94(1) 15	267
7230. **BONNIE POINTER** Bonnie Pointer 16Dec78 96(1) 15	267
7231. **BEELZEBUBBA** Dead Milkmen 24Dec88 101(2) 23	267
7232. **LOVE YOU** Beach Boys 30Apr77 53(1) 7	267
7233. **BLACK ROSE/A ROCK LEGEND** Thin Lizzy 02Jun79 81(1) 12	267
7234. **LOOKIN' FOR LOVE** Johnny Lee 15Nov80 132(1) 21	267
7235. **COMING ON STRONG** Brenda Lee 24Dec66 94(1) 12	267
7236. **LEO SAYER** Leo Sayer 19Aug78 101(1) 14	267
7237. **I'M A MAN** Macho 07Oct78 101(1) 14	266
7238. **MARVIN GAYE'S GREATEST HITS** Marvin Gaye 30May64 72(1) 14	266
7239. **MERCILESS** Stephanie Mills 17Sep83 104(1) 19	266
7240. **WALK AWAY RENEE/PRETTY BALLERINA** Left Banke 25Mar67 67(1) 11	266
7241. **ROMANY** The Hollies 27Jan73 84(1) 12	266
7242. **SEAWIND(2)** Seawind 25Oct80 83(1) 11	266
7243. **BONGO FURY** Frank Zappa/Captain Beefheart/The Mothers 01Nov75 66(1) 8	266
7244. **FUNKADELIC** Funkadelic 21Mar70 126(1) 17	266
7245. **FRIENDS** Chick Corea 19Aug78 86(2) 10	266
7246. **TOO LATE THE HERO** John Entwistle 10Oct81 71(2) 9	266
7247. **DA CAPO** Love 11Feb67 80(1) 11	266
7248. **EVERGREEN, VOL. 2** Stone Poneys 02Dec67 100(1) 15	266
7249. **TIM WEISBERG BAND** Tim Weisberg Band 20Aug77 108(2) 12	266
7250. **KEEL** Keel 27Jun87 79(1) 13	265
7251. **ELECTRIC GUITARIST** Johnny McLaughlin 27May78 105(1) 14	265
7252. **WIPE THE WINDOWS-CHECK THE OIL-DOLLAR GAS** Allman Brothers Band 04Dec76 75(2) 10	265
7253. **NO MATTER WHAT SHAPE (YOUR STOMACH'S IN)** The T-Bones 12Feb66 75(1) 12	265
7254. **METAL HEART** Accept 30Mar85 94(2) 14	265
7255. **GREATEST DISCO HITS/MUSIC FOR NON-STOP DANCING** Salsoul Orchestra 09Sep78 97(1) 13	265

Rank. Title Act Entry Peak(Pk Wks) TotWks	Scr
7256. THERE'S LOVE & THERE'S LOVE & THERE'S LOVE Jack Jones 18Sep65 86(1) 13	265
7257. JIMMY & WES THE DYNAMIC DUO Jimmy Smith & Wes Montgomery 20May67 129(2) 23	265
7258. HOT Hot 28May77 125(1) 15	265
7259. MY HANG-UP IS YOU Freddie Hart 18Mar72 89(1) 11	265
7260. NOW DO-U-WANTA DANCE Graham Central Station 23Apr77 67(1) 10	265
7261. DRUMS ALONG THE MOHAWK Jean Beauvoir 28Jun86 93(2) 15	265
7262. NO. 10, UPPING STREET Big Audio Dynamite 01Nov86 119(2) 23	265
7263. CAPTURED LIVE Johnny Winter 06Mar76 93(1) 12	265
7264. MR. MEAN Ohio Players 24Dec77 68(1) 10	265
7265. A KIND OF HUSH John Davidson 02Dec67 79(2) 12	265
7266. OLD WAYS Neil Young 07Sep85 75(2) 12	264
7267. WHEN THE GOING GETS TOUGH, THE TOUGH GET GOING Bow Wow Wow 26Mar83 82(1) 13	264
7268. ONLY ONE LOVE IN MY LIFE Ronnie Milsap 24Jun78 109(2) 12	264
7269. DEFACE THE MUSIC Utopia 25Oct80 65(2) 9	264
7270. KIMONO MY HOUSE Sparks 24Aug74 101(1) 14	264
7271. TO LEFTY FROM WILLIE Willie Nelson 09Jul77 91(1) 12	264
7272. LONG WAY TO HEAVEN Helix 29Jun85 103(1) 17	264
7273. DON'T IT MAKE YOU WANNA DANCE Rusty Wier 19Jul75 103(1) 14	264
7274. INTRODUCING...DAVID PEASTON David Peaston 05Aug89 113(1) 18	264
7275. ARETHA FRANKLIN'S GREATEST HITS Aretha Franklin 10Jun67 94(1) 14	264
7276. MOVIN' ON Danny Davis And The Nashville Brass 27Dec69 141(1) 20	264
7277. PHOTO-FINISH Rory Gallagher 04Nov78 116(1) 15	264
7278. WILLIAM RUSSO: THREE PIECES FOR BLUES BAND AND SYMPHONY ORCHESTRA San Francisco Symphony/Siegel-Schwall Band 07Apr73 105(1) 15	264
7279. (WHO'S AFRAID OF?) THE ART OF NOISE! Art Of Noise14Jul84 85(3) 13	264
7280. THE BEST OF MARIO LANZA Mario Lanza 08Aug64 87(1) 15	264
7281. MESSAGE FROM A DRUM Redbone 05Feb72 75(2) 9	264
7282. NORTHERN JOURNEY Ian & Sylvia 05Sep64 70(2) 12	263
7283. ROVER'S RETURN John Waite 11Jul87 77(1) 12	263
7284. HARDWARE Krokus 04Apr81 103(1) 12	263
7285. ZIGGY STARDUST-THE MOTION PICTURE David Bowie 12Nov83 89(1) 15	263
7286. HIGH VOLTAGE AC/DC 18Jul81 146(1) 19	263
7287. THE MICHAEL SCHENKER GROUP Michael Schenker Group 20Sep80 100(1) 14	263
7288. CLOSER Gino Soccio 23May81 96(2) 14	263
7289. SIOGO Blackfoot 11Jun83 82(1) 13	263
7290. BILL COSBY SINGS/HOORAY FOR THE SALVATION ARMY BAND! Bill Cosby 24Feb68 74(2) 11	263
7291. SONGS OF LEONARD COHEN Leonard Cohen 02Mar68 83(2) 14	263
7292. OBLIVION Utopia 11Feb84 74(2) 12	263
7293. BARRY WHITE'S SHEET MUSIC Barry White 26Jul80 85(1) 11	262
7294. IF YOU AIN'T LOVIN' (YOU AIN'T LIVIN') George Strait 19Mar88 87(2) 14	262
7295. THE BEST OF CLARENCE CARTER Clarence Carter 22May71 103(1) 10	262
7296. THE JULY 5TH ALBUM 5th Dimension 15Aug70 63(1) 8	262
7297. IN THE BEGINNING Isaac Hayes 26Feb72 102(1) 12	262
7298. EASY LISTENING Mel Carter 01Oct66 81(1) 11	262
7299. THE MACK Willie Hutch 02Jun73 114(1) 16	262
7300. GARDEN IN THE CITY Melanie 04Dec71 115(1) 12	262
7301. TWO SIDES OF LEONARD NIMOY Leonard Nimoy 24Feb68 97(2) 13	262
7302. LOVE SONGS - MEXICO/S.A. Tony Mottola 11Dec65 85(1) 13	262
7303. CHAMELEON Labelle 25Sep76 94(1) 10	262
7304. AIN'T LOVE GRAND X 17Aug85 89(3) 14	262
7305. SWEET MARIA Billy Vaughn Singers 18Mar67 114(2) 20	262
7306. SPYRO GYRA Spyro Gyra 20May78 99(2) 12	262
7307. GOLDEN JUBILEE CONCERT - RACHMANINOFF CONCERTO NO. 3 Vladimir Horowitz 29Apr78 102(2) 14	262
7308. I HAVE A DREAM Rev. Martin Luther King, Jr. 04May68 69(1) 8	261
7309. VERY TOGETHER Eumir Deodato 09Oct76 86(1) 11	261
7310. REALLY J.J. Cale 30Dec72 92(2) 11	261
7311. THE BLACK-MAN'S BURDON Eric Burdon And War 26Dec70 82(1) 9	261
7312. TINDERBOX Siouxsie & The Banshees 24May86 88(1) 15	261
7313. YOU SHOULDN'T-NUF BIT FISH George Clinton 07Jan84 102(1) 18	261
7314. HUNKY DORY David Bowie 15Apr72 93(2) 16	261
7315. AMERICAN FLYER American Flyer 04Sep76 87(1) 10	260
7316. WINDJAMMER Freddie Hubbard 04Sep76 85(2) 9	260
7317. ALEXANDER O'NEAL Alexander O'Neal 27Apr85 92(2) 18	260
7318. THE PATSY CLINE STORY Patsy Cline 31Aug63 74(1) 12	260
7319. BI-COASTAL Peter Allen 29Nov80 123(1) 20	260
7320. JOYOUS Pleasure 23Apr77 113(2) 11	260
7321. JOHNNY ONE TIME Brenda Lee 24May69 98(1) 9	260
7322. THANKS I'LL EAT IT HERE Lowell George 14Apr79 71(2) 9	260
7323. SAVE THE CHILDREN The Intruders 19May73 133(1) 18	260
7324. TRY TOO HARD Dave Clark Five 25Jun66 77(1) 11	260
7325. GREASE 2 Soundtrack 19Jun82 71(2) 13	260
7326. SOMEDAY WE'LL LOOK BACK Merle Haggard 18Sep71 108(2) 10	260
7327. A LITTLE NIGHT MUSIC Original Cast 05May73 94(1) 12	259
7328. LIVE FROM DEEP IN THE HEART OF TEXAS Commander Cody & His Lost Planet Airmen 16Feb74 105(2) 14	259
7329. MEGATOP PHOENIX Big Audio Dynamite 23Sep89 85(1) 13	259
7330. BOBBY VINTON'S ALL-TIME GREATEST HITS Bobby Vinton 25Nov72 119(1) 16	259
7331. ROSE OF CIMARRON Poco 29May76 89(1) 15	259
7332. LIFE Neil Young With Crazy Horse 25Jul87 75(2) 11	259
7333. BRING THE FAMILY John Hiatt 04Jul87 107(2) 17	259
7334. EXIT 0 Steve Earle And The Dukes 13Jun87 90(1) 14	259
7335. FREEWAYS Bachman-Turner Overdrive 19Mar77 70(1) 9	259
7336. SHABAZZ (RECORDED LIVE IN EUROPE) Billy Cobham 28Jun75 74(2) 8	259
7337. FERVOR Jason & The Scorchers 10Mar84 116(1) 23	258
7338. PLATOON Soundtrack 04Apr87 75(2) 13	258
7339. TRAMMPS III The Trammps 17Dec77 85(1) 13	258
7340. THE BEST OF/SKELETONS FROM THE CLOSET Grateful Dead 09Mar74 75(1) 10	258
7341. DEAD MAN'S PARTY Oingo Boingo 16Nov85 98(2) 16	258
7342. YOU'LL NEVER WALK ALONE The Lettermen 30Oct65 73(1) 13	258
7343. SWEET PEA Tommy Roe 05Nov66 94(1) 13	258
7344. KING OF STAGE Bobby Brown 13Dec86 88(2) 17	258
7345. HONOR AMONG THIEVES The Brandos 26Sep87 108(2) 19	258
7346. GREATEST HITS LIVE Carly Simon 27Aug88 87(3) 13	258
7347. THE TWO OF US Marilyn McCoo & Billy Davis Jr. 20Aug77 57(1) 8	257
7348. GRETCHEN GOES TO NEBRASKA King's X 05Aug89 123(1) 18	257
7349. EMERSON, LAKE & PALMER IN CONCERT Emerson, Lake & Palmer 01Dec79 73(3) 10	257
7350. GREY GHOST Henry Paul Band 02Jun79 107(2) 12	257
7351. DO YOU WANNA GET AWAY Shannon 25May85 92(2) 16	257
7352. LIVE AT THE REGAL B.B. King 25Sep71 78(1) 8	257
7353. CLOSE TO THE BONE Tom Tom Club 20Aug83 73(1) 13	257
7354. WATERBED Herbie Mann 27Sep75 75(2) 7	257
7355. TORNADO The Rainmakers 28Nov87 116(2) 19	257
7356. A BRAND NEW ME Dusty Springfield 28Feb70 107(2) 13	257
7357. THE SUGAR MAN Stanley Turrentine 08Mar75 110(1) 13	256
7358. ANOTHER VOYAGE Ramsey Lewis Trio 06Sep69 139(2) 14	256
7359. STILL LIFE (TALKING) Pat Metheny Group 22Aug87 86(2) 15	256
7360. FOR ANIMALS ONLY Baja Marimba Band 08Jan66 102(1) 16	256
7361. JACKSON 5 ANTHOLOGY Jackson 5 17Jul76 84(1) 9	256
7362. THE BEST OF THE BYRDS (GREATEST HITS, VOLUME II) The Byrds 16Dec72 114(1) 13	256
7363. PEACEFUL WORLD The Rascals 05Jun71 122(2) 12	256
7364. SEVERAL SHADES OF JADE Cal Tjader 28Sep63 79(1) 14	256
7365. IN DREAMS: THE GREATEST HITS Roy Orbison 07Jan89 95(1) 15	256
7366. SUZI...AND OTHER FOUR LETTER WORDS Suzi Quatro 06Oct79 117(1) 14	255
7367. I REMEMBER YOU Robert Goulet 30Apr66 73(1) 12	255
7368. GENESIS LIVE Genesis 18May74 105(1) 14	255
7369. BUILD ME UP BUTTERCUP The Foundations 08Mar69 92(1) 11	255
7370. BLOODROCK PASSAGE Bloodrock 30Sep72 104(2) 14	255

Rank. Title Act Entry Peak(Pk Wks) TotWks	Scr
7371. THE BEST OF DEAN MARTIN Dean Martin 17Dec66 95(2) 13	255
7372. BLACK TIE The Manhattans 08Aug81 86(3) 10	255
7373. WE CAN'T GO WRONG Cover Girls 07Oct89 108(1) 19	255
7374. IMAGINE THIS Pieces Of A Dream 25Feb84 90(1) 15	255
7375. IN DEEP Argent 07Apr73 90(2) 11	255
7376. LOVE MUSIC Sergio Mendes & Brasil '77 02Jun73 116(1) 15	255
7377. MUSIC & ME Michael Jackson 05May73 92(1) 12	255
7378. LOST & FOUND Jason & The Scorchers 30Mar85 96(1) 15	255
7379. MAGIC MAN Robert Winters And Fall 09May81 71(2) 8	255
7380. PRETTY PAPER Willie Nelson 01Dec79 73(1) 8	255
7381. FOUR TOPS GREATEST HITS, VOL. 2 Four Tops 25Sep71 106(1) 10	255
7382. TELL MAMA Etta James 09Mar68 82(2) 13	255
7383. THE BRECKER BROTHERS Brecker Brothers 07Jun75 102(1) 13	255
7384. SODA FOUNTAIN SHUFFLE Earl Klugh 11May85 110(1) 17	255
7385. THE BATMAN THEME The Marketts 12Mar66 82(1) 12	255
7386. COSMIC SLOP Funkadelic 21Jul73 112(1) 13	255
7387. THE BIBLE Soundtrack 12Nov66 102(1) 13	254
7388. YOU ARE BEAUTIFUL The Stylistics 08Nov75 99(2) 11	254
7389. DUTY NOW FOR THE FUTURE Devo 30Jun79 73(2) 10	254
7390. SWEET SOUL MUSIC Arthur Conley 13May67 93(1) 13	254
7391. THE COLOR PURPLE Soundtrack 08Mar86 79(2) 13	254
7392. FRIDAY NIGHT IN SAN FRANCISCO Al Di Meola/John McLaughlin/Paco De Lucia 30May81 97(1) 13	254
7393. FUNK BEYOND THE CALL OF DUTY Johnny Guitar Watson 24Dec77 84(1) 14	254
7394. A COUNTRY COLLECTION Anne Murray 09Feb80 73(1) 9	254
7395. LEAD ME ON Conway Twitty & Loretta Lynn 04Mar72 106(1) 13	254
7396. FREAK OUT! Mothers Of Invention 11Feb67 130(2) 23	254
7397. GEORGIA SUNSHINE Jerry Reed 06Mar71 102(1) 11	254
7398. MISTRESS Mistress 15Sep79 100(2) 14	254
7399. LOVE & HOPE & SEX & DREAMS BoDeans 07Jun86 115(2) 19	254
7400. YO FRANKIE Dion 20May89 130(1) 19	253
7401. MUSWELL HILLBILLIES The Kinks 18Dec71 100(2) 14	253
7402. DOUBLE SHOT (OF MY BABY'S LOVE) Swingin' Medallions 30Jul66 88(1) 12	253
7403. HAVANA CANDY Patti Austin 03Dec77 116(3) 13	253
7404. SLINGSHOT Michael Henderson 19Sep81 86(2) 11	253
7405. WOODY ALLEN Woody Allen 15Aug64 63(2) 11	253
7406. GIANT STEP/DE OLE FOLKS AT HOME Taj Mahal 11Oct69 85(2) 9	253
7407. KEEP ON MOVING Butterfield Blues Band 01Nov69 102(1) 10	253
7408. MAXI PRIEST Maxi Priest 03Dec88 108(1) 17	253
7409. WHAT ABOUT YOU! Stanley Turrentine 16Sep78 106(2) 13	253
7410. LIVE...IN THE RAW W.A.S.P. 10Oct87 77(2) 14	253
7411. TOLD U SO Nu Shooz 23Apr88 93(2) 14	253
7412. ONE STEP BEYOND Johnnie Taylor 17Apr71 112(2) 11	253
7413. MICHAEL MORALES Michael Morales 17Jun89 113(3) 20	253
7414. GOMM WITH THE WIND Ian Gomm 22Sep79 104(2) 12	253
7415. GAMMA 1 Gamma 22Sep79 131(1) 17	253
7416. WOULD YOU TAKE ANOTHER CHANCE ON ME? Jerry Lee Lewis 27Nov71 115(3) 12	252
7417. CONEY ISLAND Herb Alpert & The Tijuana Brass 26Apr75 88(1) 10	252
7418. ZIG ZAG The Hooters 02Dec89 115(1) 16	252
7419. HOOKED ON CLASSICS III (JOURNEY THROUGH THE CLASSICS) Royal Philharmonic Orchestra 23Apr83 89(1) 14	252
7420. NOTHING BUT A BREEZE Jesse Winchester 28May77 115(1) 16	252
7421. PAT TRAVERS' BLACK PEARL Pat Travers 06Nov82 74(3) 13	252
7422. STRAIGHT TO THE SKY Lisa Lisa And Cult Jam 13May89 77(3) 13	252
7423. NEXT Journey 19Feb77 85(1) 10	252
7424. DISINHAIRITED Various Artists 14Feb70 95(1) 13	252
7425. SHANGRI-LA! Percy Faith 19Oct63 80(2) 15	252
7426. MALA FEMMENA & CONNIE'S BIG HITS FROM ITALY Connie Francis 19Oct63 70(1) 13	251
7427. MOONMADNESS Camel 22May76 118(2) 13	251
7428. HAND TO MOUTH General Public 25Oct86 83(1) 16	251
7429. PARADISE WITH AN OCEAN VIEW Country Joe McDonald 01Nov75 124(1) 14	251
7430. IT'S GONNA BE FINE Glenn Yarbrough 06Nov65 75(1) 12	251
7431. DOIN' ALRIGHT O'Bryan 10Apr82 80(1) 12	251
7432. MAGNUM CUM LOUDER Hoodoo Gurus 12Aug89 101(1) 15	251
7433. THE LAST TIME I SAW HER Glen Campbell 07Aug71 87(1) 9	251
7434. THE COLOR OF MONEY Soundtrack 15Nov86 81(2) 15	251
7435. THE 4 SEASONS ENTERTAIN YOU 4 Seasons 10Apr65 77(1) 13	251
7436. NEGOTIATIONS AND LOVE SONGS (1971-1986) Paul Simon 12Nov88 110(1) 14	251
7437. STOP AND SMELL THE ROSES Ringo Starr 14Nov81 98(1) 12	251
7438. ROY BUCHANAN Roy Buchanan 09Sep72 107(1) 12	250
7439. CLOUDS ACROSS THE SUN Firefall 10Jan81 102(2) 13	250
7440. SILK PURSE Linda Ronstadt 24Oct70 103(1) 10	250
7441. BOTH SIDES NOW Robert Goulet 12Apr69 135(1) 13	250
7442. THAT'S A PLENTY Pointer Sisters 09Mar74 82(1) 10	250
7443. THE "KILLER" ROCKS ON Jerry Lee Lewis 22Apr72 105(1) 12	250
7444. BANG James Gang 05Jan74 122(1) 18	250
7445. LOVELAND Lonnie Liston Smith 22Apr78 120(2) 13	250
7446. M*A*S*H Soundtrack 11Jul70 120(1) 16	250
7447. GHOST TOWN PARADE Les Dudek 06May78 100(2) 11	250
7448. GOODNIGHT MY LOVE Paul Anka 15Mar69 101(2) 11	250
7449. HOLLYWOOD, TENNESSEE Crystal Gayle 19Sep81 99(2) 16	249
7450. BLOCKBUSTERS Jay & The Americans 12Jun65 113(2) 17	249
7451. BREAKOUT Johnny Hammond 11Sep71 125(1) 14	249
7452. WHEN I WAS A KID Bill Cosby 06Mar71 72(1) 8	249
7453. MUSIC: A BIT MORE OF ME David McCallum 11Jun66 79(1) 12	249
7454. MONKEY GRIP Bill Wyman 15Jun74 99(1) 11	249
7455. AESOP'S FABLES THE SMOTHERS BROTHERS WAY Smothers Brothers 05Jun65 57(1) 10	249
7456. VU Velvet Underground 09Mar85 85(2) 13	249
7457. THE GREATEST STORY EVER TOLD Soundtrack 17Apr65 82(1) 13	249
7458. DISCOTHEQUE DANCE...DANCE...DANCE Enoch Light & The Light Brigade 07Nov64 84(1) 15	248
7459. ALBUM III Loudon Wainwright III 03Mar73 102(1) 13	248
7460. LIVE--EVIL Miles Davis 25Dec71 125(2) 13	248
7461. LETS ALL CHANT Michael Zager Band 22Apr78 120(1) 13	248
7462. OLD CREST ON A NEW WAVE Dave Mason 14Jun80 74(2) 10	248
7463. REAR VIEW MIRROR Starland Vocal Band 11Jun77 104(2) 13	248
7464. ILLUMINATIONS Devadip Carlos Santana & Turiya Alice Coltrane 12Oct74 79(2) 8	248
7465. FREIGHT TRAIN HEART Jimmy Barnes 11Jun88 104(3) 15	248
7466. 'SNAZ Nazareth 10Oct81 83(1) 9	248
7467. HIGH-RISE Ashford & Simpson 17Sep83 84(1) 12	247
7468. FOREVER Pete Drake And His Talking Steel Guitar 02May64 85(1) 14	247
7469. BRIGHT LIGHTS, BIG CITY Soundtrack 02Apr88 67(2) 11	247
7470. PIA & PHIL Pia Zadora 08Mar86 113(2) 20	247
7471. THE BELLE ALBUM Al Green 24Dec77 103(2) 12	247
7472. THE WORM Jimmy McGriff 28Dec68 161(1) 19	247
7473. STEVE ARRINGTON'S HALL OF FAME: I Steve Arrington's Hall Of Fame 12Mar83 101(1) 17	247
7474. THE ENDLESS SUMMER The Sandals 04Feb67 110(1) 13	247
7475. K-9 POSSE K-9 Posse 04Mar89 98(3) 14	247
7476. REMEMBERING YOU Carroll O'Connor 17Jun72 118(1) 13	247
7477. IT'S ONLY LOVE Rita Coolidge 06Dec75 85(1) 10	247
7478. WHATEVER TURNS YOU ON West, Bruce & Laing 28Jul73 87(1) 10	247
7479. AIRPORT Soundtrack 18Apr70 104(1) 19	247
7480. PLAY 'N' THE GAME Nazareth 04Dec76 75(1) 9	247
7481. THE MASKED MARAUDERS Masked Marauders 03Jan70 114(2) 12	247
7482. CHILDREN OF THE FUTURE Steve Miller Band 15Jun68 134(1) 18	246
7483. WHEN LOVE IS NEW Billy Paul 27Dec75 139(1) 20	246
7484. SMOKING IN THE FIELDS Del Fuegos 28Oct89 139(1) 22	246
7485. THIS TIME IT'S FOR REAL Southside Johnny & The Asbury Jukes 07May77 85(1) 9	246
7486. LIGHTNIN' STRIKES Lou Christie 05Mar66 103(1) 14	246
7487. BETTER THAN THE REST George Thorogood & The Destroyers 01Sep79 78(1) 10	246

Rank. Title Act Entry Peak(Pk Wks) TotWks	Scr
7488. SOUTHERN BY THE GRACE OF GOD/ LYNYRD SKYNYRD TRIBUTE TOUR 1987 Lynyrd Skynyrd 16Apr88 68(2) 11	246
7489. ...BEHIND THE GARDENS-BEHIND THE WALL-UNDER THE TREE... Andreas Vollenweider 01Dec84 121(2) 18	246
7490. SEX AND THE SINGLE MAN Ray Parker Jr. 26Oct85 65(2) 13	246
7491. YOUR MOVE America 02Jul83 81(1) 14	246
7492. STREET FIGHTING YEARS Simple Minds 20May89 70(2) 12	246
7493. IN OUTER SPACE Sparks 30Apr83 88(1) 17	246
7494. AIRPORT LOVE THEME Vincent Bell 20Jun70 75(2) 8	246
7495. IS IT IN Eddie Harris 12Oct74 100(1) 11	246
7496. MANHATTAN Soundtrack 28Jul79 94(1) 11	246
7497. FAIRYTALE Donovan 18Dec65 85(1) 13	246
7498. ROY CLARK COUNTRY! Roy Clark 29Jul72 112(1) 12	246
7499. NIGHT-RIDER! Tim Weisberg 14Apr79 114(1) 11	245
7500. FATBACK XII Fatback 29Sep79 89(1) 12	245
7501. GREATEST HITS VOL. 2 Ronnie Milsap 31Aug85 102(2) 20	245
7502. BE A WINNER Yarbrough & Peoples 14Apr84 90(2) 16	245
7503. WENDY AND LISA Wendy And Lisa 19Sep87 88(1) 13	245
7504. LOVE IS FOR SUCKERS Twisted Sister 01Aug87 74(2) 11	245
7505. JAMES TAYLOR AND THE ORIGINAL FLYING MACHINE-1967 James Taylor 06Feb71 74(1) 8	245
7506. RIGHT BY YOU Stephen Stills 01Sep84 75(2) 12	245
7507. CARDIAC ARREST Cameo 20Aug77 116(1) 15	244
7508. LIVE! Bob Marley And The Wailers 23Oct76 90(1) 9	244
7509. GETTING TOGETHER Bobby Sherman 09Oct71 71(1) 8	244
7510. SOMEWHERE IN THE STARS Rosanne Cash 10Jul82 76(2) 12	244
7511. TAKE IT HOME B.B. King 25Aug79 112(1) 12	244
7512. MOZART: REQUIEM MASS Boston Symphony Orchestra 28Mar64 82(2) 12	244
7513. OLD DAN'S RECORDS Gordon Lightfoot 18Nov72 95(1) 12	244
7514. RUFF 'N' READY Ready For The World 15Oct88 65(2) 10	244
7515. SHOT IN THE DARK Great White 16Aug86 82(1) 13	244
7516. HOW LATE'LL YA PLAY 'TIL David Bromberg 09Oct76 104(2) 11	244
7517. THAT'S THE STUFF Autograph 16Nov85 92(2) 15	244
7518. BUBBLE GUM MUSIC IS THE NAKED TRUTH Various Artists 22Mar69 105(1) 9	244
7519. ENCORE! JOSE FELICIANO'S FINEST PERFORMANCES Jose Feliciano 17Apr71 92(2) 10	244
7520. DOUBLE DYNAMITE Sam & Dave 21Jan67 118(1) 13	244
7521. TOM SCOTT & THE L.A. EXPRESS Tom Scott & The L.A. Express 27Apr74 141(3) 16	244
7522. SENSATIONAL Starpoint 21Mar87 95(2) 14	244
7523. THE FOUR OF US John Sebastian 18Sep71 93(2) 9	244
7524. 1-2-3 Len Barry 20Nov65 90(1) 13	244
7525. THE HEADBOYS The Headboys 10Nov79 113(1) 15	244
7526. THE REAL DEAL Isley Brothers 21Aug82 87(3) 12	244
7527. YOU'LL NEVER KNOW Rodney Franklin 19Apr80 104(1) 13	243
7528. LOVE AND TOUCH Tyrone Davis 02Oct76 89(1) 9	243
7529. A DECADE OF HITS Charlie Daniels Band 23Jul83 84(1) 12	243
7530. NEW LIGHT THROUGH OLD WINDOWS Chris Rea 04Mar89 92(4) 13	243
7531. GAMES THAT LOVERS PLAY Eddie Fisher 26Nov66 72(1) 10	243
7532. STAR TREK II: THE WRATH OF KHAN Soundtrack 17Jul82 61(2) 9	243
7533. RACING AFTER MIDNIGHT Honeymoon Suite 14May88 86(2) 10	243
7534. EVERYTHING YOU'VE HEARD IS TRUE Tom Johnston 20Oct79 100(2) 13	243
7535. SUNNY Bobby Hebb 10Sep66 103(1) 12	243
7536. THE MAGIC CHRISTIAN Soundtrack 21Mar70 106(1) 12	243
7537. MAKE A JOYFUL NOISE Mother Earth 23Aug69 95(2) 9	243
7538. IN THE MOOD WITH TYRONE DAVIS Tyrone Davis 07Apr79 115(2) 12	243
7539. IRMA LA DOUCE Soundtrack 14Sep63 69(1) 11	242
7540. THE MUSIC BAND 2 War 08Dec79 111(3) 13	242
7541. WHAT YOU NEED Side Effect 19Mar77 115(1) 13	242
7542. OOPS! WRONG PLANET Utopia 24Sep77 73(1) 8	242
7543. HALL OF THE MOUNTAIN KING Savatage 10Oct87 116(1) 23	242
7544. WE'VE ONLY JUST BEGUN Ray Conniff & His Orchestra & Chorus 26Dec70 120(1) 13	242
7545. FREEDOM NO COMPROMISE Little Steven 13Jun87 80(2) 12	242
7546. BABE RUTH Babe Ruth 22Feb75 75(1) 7	242
7547. NUMBERS Rufus 10Feb79 81(1) 9	242
7548. NIGHT OF THE LIVING DREGS Dixie Dregs 19May79 111(1) 13	242
7549. INSTANT LOVE Cheryl Lynn 17Jul82 133(2) 20	242
7550. THE STORY OF A YOUNG HEART A Flock Of Seagulls 25Aug84 66(1) 10	242
7551. TYRANNOSAURUS REX (A BEGINNING) T. Rex 07Oct72 113(3) 12	242
7552. CONCRETE BLONDE Concrete Blonde 21Feb87 96(2) 16	242
7553. HERGEST RIDGE Mike Oldfield 21Sep74 87(2) 10	242
7554. WILL YOU BE STAYING AFTER SUNDAY Peppermint Rainbow 02Aug69 106(2) 9	242
7555. DOWNTOWN Marshall Crenshaw 12Oct85 110(2) 18	242
7556. STORMS Nanci Griffith 16Sep89 99(1) 14	242
7557. HISTORICAL FIGURES AND ANCIENT HEADS Canned Heat 04Mar72 87(1) 12	242
7558. NANCY Nancy Sinatra 03May69 91(1) 8	241
7559. BARRY LYNDON Soundtrack 14Feb76 132(1) 15	241
7560. THE WORLD'S GREATEST ENTERTAINER Doug E. Fresh & The Get Fresh Crew 18Jun88 88(1) 13	241
7561. BRASS IMPACT Brass Choir Conducted By Warren Kime 15Apr67 89(1) 12	241
7562. TICKET TO RIDE Carpenters 06Mar71 150(2) 16	241
7563. SEASONS IN THE SUN Terry Jacks 16Mar74 81(1) 9	241
7564. THE BEST OF JERRY REED Jerry Reed 15Jul72 116(2) 12	240
7565. HOME BoDeans 22Jul89 94(2) 13	240
7566. LIVE AT THE HUNGRY I Glenn Yarbrough 05Nov66 85(2) 9	240
7567. CARNIVAL Duran Duran 02Oct82 98(3) 15	240
7568. EVERYTHING Climie Fisher 28May88 120(1) 16	240
7569. BUFFALO SPRINGFIELD(2) Buffalo Springfield 08Dec73 104(1) 13	240
7570. MORE AMERICAN GRAFFITI Soundtrack 11Aug79 84(2) 12	240
7571. FEARGAL SHARKEY Feargal Sharkey 08Mar86 75(2) 11	240
7572. LOOKIN' FOR TROUBLE Joyce Kennedy 08Sep84 79(2) 13	240
7573. CATCHING UP WITH DEPECHE MODE Depeche Mode 07Dec85 113(1) 18	240
7574. LIVE AND DANGEROUS Thin Lizzy 22Jul78 84(1) 12	240
7575. CAT IN THE HAT Bobby Caldwell 29Mar80 113(2) 15	239
7576. POP GOES THE MOVIES Meco 03Apr82 68(2) 9	239
7577. EVERYBODY GOTTA BE SOMEPLACE Myron Cohen 02Apr66 102(1) 13	239
7578. THE GENIE (THEMES & VARIATIONS FROM THE TV SERIES "TAXI") Bob James 04Jun83 77(1) 11	239
7579. TOURIST IN PARADISE The Rippingtons Featuring Russ Freeman 10Jun89 85(2) 12	239
7580. ON MY WAY B.J. Thomas 18Jan69 133(1) 12	239
7581. MY WOMAN, MY WOMAN, MY WIFE Dean Martin 12Sep70 97(2) 12	239
7582. OUR BELOVED REVOLUTIONARY SWEETHEART Camper van Beethoven 18Jun88 124(1) 17	238
7583. RIDDLES IN THE SAND Jimmy Buffett 29Sep84 87(1) 14	238
7584. HEARTATTACK AND VINE Tom Waits 04Oct80 96(2) 10	238
7585. NAT KING COLE AT THE SANDS Nat King Cole 19Feb66 74(1) 11	238
7586. TROMBIPULATION Parliament 10Jan81 61(2) 7	238
7587. SMOKEY AND THE BANDIT 2 Soundtrack 06Sep80 103(2) 11	238
7588. LIVE & IN CONCERT Four Tops 26Oct74 92(1) 9	238
7589. LOVE NOTES Ramsey Lewis 28May77 79(2) 10	238
7590. SERIOUS The O'Jays 27May89 114(1) 17	238
7591. MICKIE FINN'S - AMERICA'S NO.1 SPEAKEASY TV Soundtrack 23Jul66 120(1) 15	238
7592. IF YOU WANT BLOOD YOU'VE GOT IT AC/DC 23Dec78 113(1) 14	237
7593. STAY AWAKE Various Artists 12Nov88 119(4) 15	237
7594. THE BEACH BOYS SONG BOOK Hollyridge Strings 10Oct64 82(2) 12	237
7595. LEMMINGS National Lampoon 23Jun73 107(1) 13	237
7596. ENDLESS BOOGIE John Lee Hooker 27Mar71 126(2) 13	237
7597. UNDERNEATH THE RADAR Underworld 19Mar88 139(2) 19	237
7598. PLAY GUITAR WITH THE VENTURES The Ventures 07Aug65 96(1) 13	237
7599. THEM King Diamond 23Jul88 89(2) 12	237
7600. THE CATHERINE WHEEL (ORIGINAL CAST) David Byrne 19Dec81 104(1) 12	237
7601. 25TH ANNIVERSARY Diana Ross & The Supremes 17May86 112(2) 17	237
7602. THE GAME OF LOVE Wayne Fontana & The Mindbenders 01May65 58(1) 9	237

Rank. Title Act	Entry Peak(Pk Wks) TotWks	Scr
7603. WAX MUSEUM Jay & The Americans	28Feb70 105(1) 11	236
7604. STREET FEVER Moon Martin	15Nov80 138(3) 15	236
7605. BLUE BELL KNOLL Cocteau Twins	15Oct88 109(2) 18	236
7606. HARDER THAN YOU 24-7 SPYZ	17Jun89 113(2) 16	236
7607. THOSE WERE THE DAYS Julius Wechter and the Baja Marimba Band	08Mar69 117(1) 10	236
7608. SAY NO MORE Les Dudek	23Apr77 107(1) 12	236
7609. BOBBY GOLDSBORO'S GREATEST HITS	Bobby Goldsboro 04Jul70 103(1) 10	236
7610. CHARLIE McCOY Charlie McCoy	25Nov72 120(1) 13	236
7611. TREAT HER RIGHT Treat Her Right	09Apr88 127(2) 18	236
7612. CLASSICS LIVE Aerosmith	26Apr86 84(1) 12	236
7613. SERIOUS BUSINESS Third World	15Jul89 107(1) 14	236
7614. HER JOY, HER SONGS	Singing Nun (Soeur Sourire) 11Apr64 90(2) 14	236
7615. BRUISED ORANGE John Prine	08Jul78 116(1) 13	236
7616. ON Off Broadway USA	16Feb80 101(2) 11	236
7617. FEAR NO EVIL Grim Reaper	06Jul85 108(1) 14	236
7618. THIS IS SOUL Various Artists	16Mar68 146(1) 22	236
7619. ROBERTA FLACK Roberta Flack	30Sep78 74(1) 10	235
7620. FOUNTAINS OF LIGHT Starcastle	05Feb77 101(2) 11	235
7621. SEVENTH STAR Black Sabbath Featuring	Tony Iommi 15Feb86 78(2) 11	235
7622. MOODY JR. Jr. Walker & The All Stars	08Jan72 142(2) 16	235
7623. MORE THAN FRIENDS Jonathan Butler	05Nov88 113(2) 22	235
7624. CARL ANDERSON Carl Anderson	23Aug86 87(2) 12	235
7625. TURNSTILES Billy Joel	05Jun76 122(2) 12	235
7626. FOLKWAYS: A VISION SHARED - A TRIBUTE TO WOODY GUTHRIE AND LEADBELLY Various Artists	17Sep88 70(2) 10	235
7627. LOUISIANA'S LE ROUX Louisiana's Le Roux	08Jul78 135(1) 15	235
7628. VERY YOUNG AND EARLY SONGS	Cat Stevens 08Jan72 94(1) 10	235
7629. GET TO THE FEELING Pleasure	13May78 119(1) 13	235
7630. THE HOMECOMING Hagood Hardy	03Jan76 112(3) 14	235
7631. UNITED Commodores	22Nov86 101(3) 15	235
7632. VOICES & IMAGES Camouflage	14Jan89 100(3) 14	235
7633. RUSH Rush	21Sep74 105(1) 13	234
7634. LOVE STORY Roger Williams	06Mar71 112(1) 13	234
7635. EVERYTHING'S DIFFERENT NOW	'Til Tuesday 19Nov88 124(3) 19	234
7636. THE DUKES OF HAZZARD TV Soundtrack	17Apr82 93(2) 14	234
7637. RUNNIN' OUT OF FOOLS Aretha Franklin	19Dec64 84(2) 13	234
7638. YOU WANNA DANCE WITH ME? Jody Watley	02Dec89 86(3) 13	234
7639. INTRODUCING JONATHAN BUTLER	Jonathan Butler 24May86 101(2) 16	234
7640. ONENESS/SILVER DREAMS-GOLDEN REALITY	Devadip 31Mar79 87(2) 9	234
7641. ESCAPE FROM DOMINATION Moon Martin	08Sep79 80(1) 11	234
7642. I LOVE 'EM ALL T.G. Sheppard	25Apr81 119(1) 12	234
7643. RECOVERY: LIVE! Great White	13Feb88 99(2) 12	234
7644. CALIFORNIA JAM 2 Various Artists	22Jul78 84(1) 10	234
7645. THIS LOVE FOR YOU Al Martino	25Mar67 99(1) 12	234
7646. TO THE HEART Mark-Almond	31Jul76 112(2) 14	234
7647. MY NAME IS ALLAN Allan Sherman	18Dec65 88(2) 11	234
7648. NIGHTWINGS Stanley Turrentine	10Sep77 84(1) 9	234
7649. RADIO ONE Jimi Hendrix Experience	03Dec88 119(2) 17	234
7650. GOD'S OWN MEDICINE Mission U.K.	07Mar87 108(1) 18	233
7651. DIAMOND IN THE ROUGH Jessi Colter	07Aug76 79(1) 8	233
7652. RARE BIRD Rare Bird	07Mar70 117(1) 13	233
7653. SPEND THE NIGHT Isley Brothers Featuring	Ronald Isley 02Sep89 89(1) 13	233
7654. ROCKS, PEBBLES AND SAND	Stanley Clarke 28Jun80 95(2) 11	233
7655. YOU DON'T HAVE TO SAY YOU LOVE ME	Dusty Springfield 16Jul66 77(1) 10	233
7656. UNDER WRAPS Jethro Tull	27Oct84 76(2) 12	233
7657. MANHATTANS GREATEST HITS	The Manhattans 13Dec80 87(2) 10	233
7658. 20 YEARS OF JETHRO TULL Jethro Tull	13Aug88 97(2) 15	233
7659. OWLCREEK INCIDENT Prelude	22Nov75 111(2) 14	233
7660. SONGS, PICTURES AND STORIES OF THE FABULOUS BEATLES The Beatles	31Oct64 63(1) 11	233
7661. MEANT FOR EACH OTHER Barbara Mandrell & Lee Greenwood	08Sep84 89(1) 13	232
7662. STREETLIGHTS Bonnie Raitt	02Nov74 80(1) 8	232
7663. SKY Sky	01Nov80 125(1) 15	232
7664. SHINE Average White Band	31May80 116(2) 12	232
7665. HEART ATTACK Krokus	07May88 87(1) 11	232
7666. ANIMOTION(2) Animotion	25Mar89 110(1) 17	232
7667. MIDNIGHT STAR Midnight Star	05Nov88 96(2) 15	232
7668. BIG CITY Merle Haggard	07Nov81 161(1) 28	232
7669. WORDS AND MUSIC Roger Miller	19Nov66 108(1) 13	232
7670. EXOTIC BIRDS AND FRUIT Procol Harum	20Apr74 86(1) 9	232
7671. THE STRAWBERRY STATEMENT Soundtrack	12Sep70 91(1) 9	232
7672. MARILYN MARTIN Marilyn Martin	22Feb86 72(2) 11	232
7673. DELIRIOUS NOMAD Armored Saint	07Dec85 108(2) 19	232
7674. WARMER Randy VanWarmer	02Jun79 81(2) 10	232
7675. ARTHUR PRYSOCK/COUNT BASIE	Arthur Prysock/Count Basie 26Mar66 107(1) 13	232
7676. CHOICE QUALITY STUFF/ANYTIME	It's A Beautiful Day 11Dec71 130(1) 16	232
7677. EVERY GREAT MOTOWN HIT OF MARVIN GAYE	Marvin Gaye 22Oct83 80(1) 16	232
7678. SOLID SILVER	Quicksilver Messenger Service 15Nov75 89(1) 12	231
7679. STANDARDS, VOLUME 1 Stanley Jordan	14Feb87 116(2) 18	231
7680. TRACK OF THE CAT Dionne Warwick	06Dec75 137(2) 15	231
7681. NEW HORIZONS The Sylvers	26Nov77 134(2) 13	231
7682. GAP GOLD/BEST OF THE GAP BAND	Gap Band 09Mar85 103(2) 16	231
7683. BLAZE Herman's Hermits	07Oct67 75(1) 9	231
7684. ISLE OF MAN Isle Of Man	19Jul86 110(2) 18	231
7685. WITH A TASTE OF HONEY Morgana King	22Aug64 118(2) 15	231
7686. CERRONE IV - THE GOLDEN TOUCH Cerrone	18Nov78 118(1) 13	231
7687. TWICE THE LOVE George Benson	24Sep88 76(2) 10	231
7688. SLAUGHTER'S BIG RIP-OFF James Brown	28Jul73 92(1) 11	231
7689. MARVIN SEASE Marvin Sease	18Jul87 114(2) 17	231
7690. THAT'S ENTERTAINMENT Soundtrack	22Jun74 128(1) 14	231
7691. MY SECOND ALBUM Donna Fargo	17Mar73 104(2) 11	231
7692. TIME AFTER TIME Chris Montez	14Jan67 106(2) 11	231
7693. ON A ROLL Point Blank	17Apr82 119(1) 17	231
7694. RAY CONNIFF'S WORLD OF HITS Ray Conniff & His Orchestra & Chorus	18Mar67 78(1) 10	231
7695. A LITTLE BIT OF LOVE Paul Williams	23Nov74 95(2) 9	231
7696. LOUD AND CLEAR Autograph	11Apr87 108(2) 15	231
7697. ROUGH RIDERS Lakeside	03Nov79 141(3) 18	231
7698. HUMANS Bruce Cockburn	18Oct80 81(2) 9	231
7699. AVALANCHE Mountain	10Aug74 102(1) 9	230
7700. RESOLUTION Andy Pratt	10Jul76 104(1) 10	230
7701. DIONNE WARWICK IN PARIS	Dionne Warwick 16Apr66 76(1) 11	230
7702. LATOYA JACKSON LaToya Jackson	18Oct80 116(2) 13	230
7703. DION Dion	21Dec68 128(1) 11	230
7704. BACK ON THE STREETS Tower Of Power	11Aug79 106(1) 12	230
7705. FAMILY Hubert Laws	08Nov80 133(1) 13	230
7706. WHEN THE BOYS MEET THE GIRLS	Connie Francis 29Jan66 61(1) 9	230
7707. DOROTHY MOORE Dorothy Moore	06Aug77 120(1) 13	230
7708. McLEMORE AVENUE Booker T. & The MG's	02May70 107(1) 15	229
7709. THE BOY GENIUS Kwamé Featuring A New	Beginning 27May89 114(2) 18	229
7710. WINWOOD Steve Winwood	29May71 93(2) 8	229
7711. ARTIFICIAL PARADISE Guess Who	20Jan73 110(1) 12	229
7712. FROM A WHISPER TO A SCREAM	Esther Phillips 18Mar72 137(1) 15	229
7713. NEW BALLADS Rod McKuen	14Mar70 126(1) 13	229
7714. PLEASED TO MEET ME The Replacements	30May87 131(1) 19	229
7715. SWAMP ROCK The Ventures	13Dec69 81(1) 12	229
7716. RHYTHM ROMANCE The Romantics	21Sep85 72(2) 11	229

Rank.	Title	Act	Entry	Peak(Pk Wks)	TotWks	Scr
7717.	BYE BYE BLUES	Brenda Lee	09Apr66	94(1)	13	229
7718.	LIVE + 1	Frehley's Comet	27Feb88	84(2)	10	229
7719.	DANCE THE COOL JERK	The Capitols	23Jul66	95(1)	12	229
7720.	DOUBLE DOSE	Hot Tuna	15Apr78	92(1)	10	229
7721.	I'M REAL	James Brown	18Jun88	96(1)	14	229
7722.	JON BUTCHER AXIS	Jon Butcher Axis	26Mar83	91(1)	13	228
7723.	HALL OF THE MOUNTAIN GRILL	Hawkwind	05Oct74	110(1)	12	228
7724.	RAP'S GREATEST HITS	Various Artists	08Nov86	114(2)	17	228
7725.	FLASH IN THE CAN	Flash	09Dec72	121(1)	13	228
7726.	I AM WHAT I AM	George Jones	13Jun81	132(1)	14	228
7727.	A FUNKY THIDE OF SINGS	Billy Cobham	15Nov75	79(1)	7	228
7728.	PORTRAIT OF SAMMY DAVIS, JR.	Sammy Davis Jr.	14Oct72	128(1)	15	228
7729.	CITY STREETS	Carole King	06May89	111(1)	16	228
7730.	RATT	Ratt	30Jun84	133(3)	19	228
7731.	WA WA NEE	Wa Wa Nee	07Nov87	123(1)	17	228
7732.	I CAN MAKE IT WITH YOU	Pozo-Seco Singers	04Feb67	81(1)	10	228
7733.	CAN'T LET YOU GO	John Travolta	12Mar77	66(1)	9	228
7734.	EYE TO EYE	Eye To Eye	19Jun82	99(2)	15	228
7735.	SURVEILLANCE	Triumph	28Nov87	82(2)	13	227
7736.	THE FIRST NINE MONTHS ARE THE HARDEST!	Various Artists	11Jul64	96(1)	14	227
7737.	HOLD ON	Noel Pointer	18Mar78	95(2)	13	227
7738.	1984 (FOR THE LOVE OF BIG BROTHER)	Eurythmics	05Jan85	93(1)	14	227
7739.	RIO GRANDE MUD	ZZ Top	06May72	104(2)	10	227
7740.	MARIA McKEE	Maria McKee	01Jul89	120(2)	15	227
7741.	BRIEF ENCOUNTER	Marillion	22Mar86	67(2)	10	227
7742.	TO WHOM IT MAY CONCERN	The Pasadenas	18Mar89	89(2)	12	227
7743.	SNAPSHOT	Sylvia (2)	18Jun83	77(1)	11	227
7744.	STILL THE SAME OLE ME	George Jones	28Nov81	115(2)	14	227
7745.	GOOD TO GO LOVER	Gwen Guthrie	30Aug86	89(2)	13	227
7746.	CANDIDA	Lawrence Welk	12Dec70	133(1)	17	227
7747.	DO YOU WONDER	Shawn Phillips	13Sep75	101(1)	9	227
7748.	ESPECIALLY FOR YOU	Don Williams	25Jul81	109(1)	11	227
7749.	DANKE SCHOEN	Wayne Newton	12Oct63	55(1)	9	226
7750.	ONE WAY FEATURING AL HUDSON(2)	One Way Featuring Al Hudson	02Aug80	128(1)	12	226
7751.	COME GET TO THIS	Nancy Wilson	26Jul75	119(1)	10	226
7752.	ROCKBIRD	Debbie Harry	13Dec86	97(2)	13	226
7753.	WE'RE GONNA MAKE IT	Little Milton	05Jun65	101(2)	14	226
7754.	LIFE IS MUSIC	Ritchie Family	12Feb77	100(1)	10	226
7755.	THE GREAT BLIND DEGREE	Richie Havens	13Nov71	126(1)	11	226
7756.	FUN IN SPACE	Roger Taylor	09May81	121(1)	10	226
7757.	AN EVENING WITH BELAFONTE/MAKEBA	Harry Belafonte & Miriam Makeba	10Jul65	85(1)	11	226
7758.	NOTHINGFACE	Voivod	16Dec89	114(2)	16	226
7759.	FACE TO FACE WITH THE TRUTH	Undisputed Truth	05Feb72	114(1)	12	226
7760.	BROTHERHOOD	New Order	25Oct86	117(1)	21	226
7761.	GIRLS TO CHAT & BOYS TO BOUNCE	Foghat	25Jul81	92(1)	9	226
7762.	LOVE HYSTERIA	Peter Murphy	14May88	135(2)	19	226
7763.	BOBBY SHERMAN'S GREATEST HITS	Bobby Sherman	25Mar72	83(1)	9	225
7764.	HIGH NOTES	Hank Williams Jr.	08May82	123(1)	20	225
7765.	WATERTOWN	Frank Sinatra	11Apr70	101(1)	10	225
7766.	AL HIRT PLAYS BERT KAEMPFERT	Al Hirt	10Feb68	116(1)	13	225
7767.	GARDEN OF LOVE	Rick James	23Aug80	83(2)	10	225
7768.	ARE YOU READY	Pacific Gas And Electric	04Jul70	101(2)	11	225
7769.	GO FOR IT	Shalamar	24Oct81	115(2)	15	225
7770.	THE COMMUNARDS	The Communards	20Dec86	90(2)	16	225
7771.	FEMALE TROUBLE	Nona Hendryx	23May87	96(2)	13	225
7772.	EUGENE WILDE	Eugene Wilde	26Jan85	97(2)	15	225
7773.	MR. CROWLEY	Ozzy Osbourne	08May82	120(1)	18	224
7774.	GETTING TOGETHER	Ferrante & Teicher	30May70	97(1)	10	224
7775.	MUSIC TO WATCH GIRLS BY	Bob Crewe Generation	25Feb67	100(1)	11	224
7776.	THE TWO OF US	Sonny & Cher	09Sep72	122(2)	12	224
7777.	CALUMET	Lobo	30Jun73	128(1)	14	224
7778.	SHADOWS	Gordon Lightfoot	20Feb82	87(2)	12	224
7779.	THE DIARY OF A BAND (VOLUME 1 & 2)	John Mayall	28Feb70	93(2)	11	224
7780.	BELIEVE	Mass Production	27Aug77	83(1)	9	224
7781.	JOHNNY MATHIS' ALL-TIME GREATEST HITS	Johnny Mathis	24Jun72	141(1)	15	224
7782.	BEST OF ELVIS COSTELLO/THE ATTRACTIONS	Elvis Costello And The Attractions	30Nov85	116(2)	16	224
7783.	ONE-EYED JACK	Garland Jeffreys	15Apr78	99(1)	10	224
7784.	WITCH DOCTOR	Instant Funk	08Dec79	129(1)	13	224
7785.	I LIKE YOUR STYLE	Jermaine Jackson	26Sep81	86(1)	10	224
7786.	EVOLUTION	Malo	28Apr73	101(1)	11	224
7787.	THE MARBLEHEAD MESSENGER	Seatrain	09Oct71	91(1)	9	224
7788.	MADAME BUTTERFLY	Tavares	03Feb79	92(2)	11	223
7789.	RIT/2	Lee Ritenour	04Dec82	99(3)	14	223
7790.	CAFE RACERS	Kim Carnes	19Nov83	97(1)	16	223
7791.	THE KINK KONTROVERSY	The Kinks	30Apr66	95(2)	12	223
7792.	THE BEST OF MANHATTAN TRANSFER	Manhattan Transfer	12Dec81	103(2)	11	223
7793.	WHAT DO YOU WANT FROM LIVE	The Tubes	11Mar78	82(1)	8	223
7794.	WHO'S TO BLESS...AND WHO'S TO BLAME	Kris Kristofferson	06Dec75	105(2)	11	223
7795.	EDEN ALLEY	Timbuk 3	07May88	107(5)	13	223
7796.	THIS MOTHER'S DAUGHTER	Nancy Wilson	01May76	126(1)	13	223
7797.	SPANISH MOONLIGHT	John Gary	13May67	90(1)	11	223
7798.	MICHEL POLNAREFF	Michel Polnareff	21Feb76	117(2)	13	223
7799.	SO HAPPY	Eddie Murphy	26Aug89	70(2)	9	223
7800.	PRIORITY	Pointer Sisters	22Sep79	72(2)	8	222
7801.	SUMMER HEAT	Brick	05Sep81	89(2)	10	222
7802.	YOU'RE GETTIN' EVEN WHILE I'M GETTIN' ODD	J. Geils Band	24Nov84	80(3)	10	222
7803.	LOVE RHAPSODIES	Midnight String Quartet	30Mar68	129(2)	17	222
7804.	THE FIRST SONGS	Laura Nyro	03Feb73	97(1)	11	222
7805.	DIFFERENT STROKES	Various Artists	13Mar71	85(2)	7	222
7806.	IT'S ALRIGHT WITH ME	Patti LaBelle	31Mar79	145(1)	16	222
7807.	THE LETTERMEN IN CONCERT	The Lettermen	31Aug63	76(1)	10	222
7808.	URBAN DAYDREAMS	David Benoit	13May89	101(2)	14	222
7809.	KEEM-O-SABE	Electric Indian	04Oct69	104(2)	9	222
7810.	DRASTIC PLASTIC	Be Bop Deluxe	11Mar78	95(2)	9	222
7811.	DAYS OF INNOCENCE	Moving Pictures	04Dec82	101(3)	16	222
7812.	THE AURA WILL PREVAIL	George Duke	31May75	111(2)	10	222
7813.	COWBOYS TO GIRLS	The Intruders	27Jul68	112(2)	9	222
7814.	DREAM BABIES GO TO HOLLYWOOD	John Stewart	12Apr80	85(2)	10	222
7815.	O LUCKY MAN!	Alan Price	11Aug73	117(1)	14	221
7816.	SPREADING THE DISEASE	Anthrax	21Dec85	113(1)	18	221
7817.	RITA COOLIDGE	Rita Coolidge	03Apr71	105(1)	10	221
7818.	MAMA	Heintje	05Dec70	108(1)	11	221
7819.	RIDIN' HIGH	The Impressions	05Mar66	79(1)	10	221
7820.	PEOPLE...HOLD ON	Eddie Kendricks	03Jun72	131(2)	14	221
7821.	SUMMERTIME	MFSB	10Jul76	106(1)	9	221
7822.	3	Violent Femmes	04Feb89	93(3)	13	221
7823.	SONGS FROM LIQUID DAYS	Philip Glass	12Apr86	91(2)	13	221
7824.	I JUST CAN'T STOP IT	English Beat	09Aug80	142(1)	14	221
7825.	PILEDRIVER -- THE WRESTLING ALBUM II	Various Artists	17Oct87	123(2)	20	221
7826.	BARRY GOUDREAU	Barry Goudreau	20Sep80	88(3)	8	220
7827.	YOU DON'T STAND A CHANCE IF YOU CAN'T DANCE	Jimmy James & The Vagabonds	29Nov75	139(1)	16	220
7828.	WOMAN TO WOMAN	Shirley Brown	25Jan75	98(2)	11	220
7829.	SUNFIGHTER	Grace Slick and Paul Kantner	25Dec71	89(1)	9	220
7830.	KICK OFF YOUR MUDDY BOOTS	Graeme Edge Band	11Oct75	107(2)	9	220
7831.	BURCHFIELD NINES	Michael Franks	08Apr78	90(1)	10	220
7832.	THE DREAMS OF CHILDREN	Shadowfax	17Nov84	126(2)	20	220

Rank. Title Act Entry Peak(Pk Wks) TotWks	Scr
7833. THE BEST OF JERRY LEE LEWIS Jerry Lee Lewis 09May70 114(2) 14	220
7834. TRACIE SPENCER Tracie Spencer 25Jun88 146(1) 21	220
7835. WILD WEST Dottie West 11Apr81 126(1) 15	220
7836. ROAD HOUSE Soundtrack 03Jun89 67(2) 10	220
7837. STREET HASSLE Lou Reed 08Apr78 89(1) 9	220
7838. HALF A SIXPENCE Original Cast 12Jun65 103(1) 14	220
7839. IN MY QUIET ROOM Harry Belafonte 16Jul66 82(1) 10	220
7840. DUETS Kenny Rogers 05May84 85(2) 11	220
7841. SUMMERTIME Herb Alpert & The Tijuana Brass 24Jul71 111(1) 10	220
7842. AFFAIR Cherrelle 19Nov88 106(3) 15	220
7843. DISCO PARTY Various Artists 15Jul78 115(2) 12	220
7844. 'NUFF SAID Ike & Tina Turner 20Nov71 108(2) 10	220
7845. LOVE BYRD Donald Byrd And 125th Street N.Y.C. 03Oct81 93(1) 10	220
7846. DON'T JUST STAND THERE Patty Duke 18Sep65 90(1) 12	220
7847. IT TAKES ONE TO KNOW ONE Detective 14Jan78 103(2) 12	219
7848. JOHN FOGERTY John Fogerty 04Oct75 78(1) 7	219
7849. CUT THE CRAP The Clash 07Dec85 88(2) 12	219
7850. THE POWER OF JOE SIMON Joe Simon 17Feb73 97(1) 12	219
7851. BOOGIE WOOGIE DANCIN' SHOES Claudja Barry 02Jun79 101(1) 10	219
7852. NIGHT FADES AWAY Nils Lofgren 26Sep81 99(1) 11	219
7853. BOTTOMS UP The Chi-Lites 04Jun83 98(1) 12	219
7854. DO THE FREDDIE Freddie And The Dreamers 19Jun65 85(1) 12	219
7855. DESTINATION: SUN Sun 21Jul79 85(1) 10	219
7856. TIM WEISBERG 4 Tim Weisberg 23Nov74 100(2) 13	219
7857. TWO TONS O' FUN Two Tons Of Fun 17May80 91(2) 11	219
7858. JIMMY BARNES Jimmy Barnes 08Mar86 109(2) 16	219
7859. LOVE AND KISSES Love And Kisses 30Jul77 135(2) 14	218
7860. CUCUMBER CASTLE Bee Gees 09May70 94(2) 8	218
7861. MY RADIO SURE SOUNDS GOOD TO ME Larry Graham And Graham Central Station 01Jul78 105(1) 11	218
7862. AKIMBO ALOGO Kim Mitchell 18May85 106(2) 15	218
7863. SAY IT AGAIN Jermaine Stewart 23Apr88 98(2) 12	218
7864. I DON'T WANT TO LOSE YOU BABY Chad & Jeremy 06Nov65 77(1) 11	218
7865. FINGER PAINTINGS Earl Klugh 09Jul77 84(1) 8	218
7866. DR. JOHN'S GUMBO Dr. John 13May72 112(3) 11	218
7867. MAGIC T-Connection 14May77 109(1) 11	218
7868. AMERICAN ANTHEM Soundtrack 05Jul86 91(3) 12	218
7869. TRAVELIN' Tommy James And The Shondells 11Apr70 91(2) 9	217
7870. RICCOCHET DAYS Modern English 24Mar84 93(1) 12	217
7871. THE SUPREMES The Supremes 25Nov72 129(1) 13	217
7872. PONTIAC Lyle Lovett 20Feb88 117(1) 14	217
7873. PEOPLE LIKE US Mamas & The Papas 06Nov71 84(2) 8	217
7874. DELIVER Oak Ridge Boys 19Nov83 121(1) 14	217
7875. A CHORUS LINE-THE MOVIE Soundtrack 28Dec85 77(2) 12	217
7876. 9012LIVE - THE SOLOS Yes 30Nov85 81(3) 11	217
7877. ORIGINAL GOLDEN HITS, VOLUME II Johnny Cash 27Sep69 98(1) 8	217
7878. CAMERON'S IN LOVE Rafael Cameron 18Jul81 101(1) 12	217
7879. I'M A MAN Spencer Davis Group 15Jul67 83(1) 9	216
7880. LITTLE AMERICA Little America 25Apr87 102(2) 14	216
7881. WINNERS Various Artists 06Sep80 69(2) 7	216
7882. R&B SKELETONS IN THE CLOSET George Clinton 24May86 81(2) 12	216
7883. THAT'S THE WAY GOD PLANNED IT Billy Preston 10Jun72 127(2) 12	216
7884. GIVE ME YOUR LOVE Barbara Mason 03Feb73 95(1) 12	216
7885. BURNT WEENY SANDWICH Mothers Of Invention 14Mar70 94(1) 8	216
7886. GIVE IT UP Bonnie Raitt 21Oct72 138(1) 15	216
7887. THE VERY BEST OF POCO Poco 02Aug75 90(2) 8	216
7888. CLASS OF '55 Carl Perkins, Jerry Lee Lewis, Roy Orbison, & Johnny Cash 21Jun86 87(2) 12	216
7889. WITNESS Spooky Tooth 10Nov73 99(1) 10	216
7890. THE RUMOUR Olivia Newton-John 03Sep88 67(2) 9	216
7891. WINDHAM HILL RECORDS SAMPLER '88 Various Artists 27Feb88 134(1) 16	216
7892. THE WORD IS OUT Jermaine Stewart 02Mar85 90(2) 11	216
7893. TERRY KNIGHT AND THE PACK Terry Knight and The Pack 26Nov66 127(1) 13	216
7894. SINCERELY Dwight Twilley Band 31Jul76 138(1) 14	215
7895. 16 ORIGINAL BIG HITS Various Artists 11Apr64 84(1) 11	215
7896. SOUL TO SOUL Soundtrack 25Sep71 112(1) 10	215
7897. ANOTHER TIME Earth, Wind & Fire 07Sep74 97(1) 10	215
7898. THE HOTTEST NIGHT OF THE YEAR Anne Murray 28Aug82 90(3) 12	215
7899. LIVING TOGETHER, GROWING TOGETHER 5th Dimension 24Mar73 108(1) 11	215
7900. CLIMAX Ohio Players 02Nov74 102(1) 8	215
7901. 4 OF A KIND D.R.I. 23Jul88 116(2) 14	215
7902. THE BEST OF NANCY WILSON Nancy Wilson 31Aug68 145(1) 14	215
7903. ADDRISI BROTHERS Addrisi Brothers 02Jul77 118(1) 14	215
7904. LIVERPOOL Frankie Goes To Hollywood 15Nov86 88(2) 13	215
7905. I'M YOUR PLAYMATE Suave 23Apr88 101(1) 12	215
7906. THE TEA DANCE D.C. LaRue 08Jan77 115(1) 11	214
7907. STORMIN' Brainstorm 26Mar77 145(2) 16	214
7908. BUMPS AND BRUISES Joe Tex 07May77 108(1) 9	214
7909. TEQUILA SUNRISE Soundtrack 21Jan89 101(1) 13	214
7910. NEW YORK DOLLS New York Dolls 01Sep73 116(2) 12	214
7911. THE TOP HITS OF 1963 Bobby Rydell 18Jan64 67(1) 9	214
7912. COLONEL ABRAMS Colonel Abrams 19Apr86 75(2) 11	214
7913. BOUNCING OFF THE SATELLITES The B-52s 04Oct86 85(2) 15	214
7914. CHER SUPERPAK Cher 08Jan72 92(1) 10	213
7915. THE ESSENTIAL JIMI HENDRIX Jimi Hendrix 12Aug78 114(2) 15	213
7916. THE BEST OF SPIRIT Spirit 21Jul73 119(1) 12	213
7917. MEMORY IN THE MAKING John Kilzer 11Jun88 110(2) 15	213
7918. EVERY MAN HAS A WOMAN Various Artists 13Oct84 75(2) 10	213
7919. LEATHERWOLF Leatherwolf 05Mar88 105(1) 12	213
7920. STRIKE LIKE LIGHTNING Lonnie Mack 15Jun85 130(2) 21	213
7921. WINNING COMBINATION Donny & Marie Osmond 07Jan78 99(2) 12	213
7922. TOO FAR TO WHISPER Shadowfax 12Jul86 114(1) 16	213
7923. ROCK AND ROLL QUEEN Mott The Hoople 15Jun74 112(1) 11	213
7924. INSIDE OUT Philip Bailey 24May86 84(2) 11	213
7925. STARZ Starz 11Sep76 123(2) 13	213
7926. THIEF Tangerine Dream 09May81 115(1) 10	213
7927. SUFFICIENTLY BREATHLESS Captain Beyond 01Sep73 90(2) 10	213
7928. WHAT'S NEXT Frank Marino And Mahogany Rush 08Mar80 88(1) 9	213
7929. HABITS OLD AND NEW Hank Williams Jr. 21Jun80 154(1) 17	213
7930. SCROOGE Soundtrack 26Dec70 95(2) 8	212
7931. HOW SWEET IT IS Frank Fontaine 07Mar64 92(1) 12	212
7932. ESCAPE FROM BABYLON Martha Velez 15May76 153(1) 17	212
7933. MIAMI James Gang 14Sep74 97(1) 10	212
7934. PARIS Paris 07Feb76 103(1) 9	212
7935. ALL NIGHT LONG Sammy Hagar 19Aug78 89(1) 9	212
7936. EMERALD CITY Teena Marie 05Jul86 81(2) 11	212
7937. OSCAR PETERSON TRIO + ONE Oscar Peterson Trio 31Oct64 81(1) 12	212
7938. "10" Soundtrack 05Jan80 80(1) 9	212
7939. RED TAPE Atlanta Rhythm Section 05Jun76 146(2) 15	212
7940. JANIS IAN (II) Janis Ian 16Sep78 120(2) 11	212
7941. TIME PIECES -- THE BEST OF ERIC CLAPTON Eric Clapton 22May82 101(2) 14	212
7942. HONEY & WINE Glenn Yarbrough 16Sep67 141(1) 18	211
7943. ROCKET FUEL Alvin Lee 03Jun78 115(1) 11	211
7944. SNEAKER Sneaker 12Dec81 149(2) 17	211
7945. MONTROSE Montrose 11May74 133(1) 12	211
7946. LIKE IT IS, LIKE IT WAS The Dells 14Mar70 126(2) 12	211
7947. FOREVER, MICHAEL Michael Jackson 15Feb75 101(2) 9	211
7948. SALISBURY Uriah Heep 30Jan71 103(2) 9	211

Rank. Title Act Entry Peak(Pk Wks) TotWks	Scr
7949. I WISH I WAS EIGHTEEN AGAIN George Burns 09Feb80 93(2) 10	211
7950. GREATEST HITS Moody Blues 09Dec89 113(1) 16	211
7951. MIAMI VICE II TV Soundtrack 06Dec86 82(1) 12	211
7952. THE BEST OF JOE WALSH Joe Walsh 28Oct78 71(1) 7	211
7953. I GOT THE FEELIN' James Brown 18May68 135(1) 14	211
7954. NO MUSS...NO FUSS Donnie Iris 16Mar85 115(1) 15	211
7955. CHANGING TIMES Four Tops 17Oct70 109(1) 12	211
7956. VIOLATION Starz 16Apr77 89(1) 8	211
7957. LES MISERABLES Original London Cast 11Apr87 106(2) 15	211
7958. WORKS Pink Floyd 18Jun83 68(1) 9	211
7959. OLD LOVES DIE HARD Triumvirat 07Aug76 85(2) 8	211
7960. KEEPER OF THE SEVEN KEYS - PART II Helloween 29Oct88 108(2) 16	211
7961. TALL DARK STRANGER Buck Owens 08Nov69 122(1) 10	211
7962. THE ELECTRIC PRUNES Electric Prunes 15Apr67 113(1) 12	211
7963. CLOSE-UP The Lettermen 23Aug69 90(1) 8	210
7964. PEARL HARBOR & THE EXPLOSIONS Pearl Harbor And The Explosions 26Jan80 107(1) 11	210
7965. THE COMPLETE STORY OF ROXANNE... THE ALBUM Dr. J.R. Kool & The Other Roxannes 20Jul85 113(1) 13	210
7966. FULL HOUSE Frankie Miller 18Jun77 124(1) 12	210
7967. GREATEST HITS Reba McEntire 06Jun87 139(2) 23	210
7968. THIS IS US The Searchers 29Aug64 97(1) 14	210
7969. FALSE ACCUSATIONS Robert Cray Band 05Apr86 141(3) 21	210
7970. BOY MEETS GIRL Boy Meets Girl 04May85 76(2) 11	210
7971. MAMMA Luciano Pavarotti 08Sep84 103(2) 14	210
7972. HOOTENANNY WITH THE HIGHWAYMEN The Highwaymen 07Sep63 79(1) 9	210
7973. IRISH TOUR '74 Rory Gallagher 14Sep74 110(1) 11	210
7974. THE OUTSIDERS ALBUM #2 The Outsiders 17Sep66 90(1) 10	210
7975. WILD & LOOSE Oaktown's 3.5.7 13May89 126(1) 16	209
7976. HUSH John Klemmer 13Jun81 99(1) 9	209
7977. CHET ATKINS PICKS ON THE BEATLES Chet Atkins 09Apr66 112(1) 13	209
7978. INTIMATE STRANGERS Tom Scott 18Nov78 123(1) 13	209
7979. WILL THE CIRCLE BE UNBROKEN, VOL.II Nitty Gritty Dirt Band 27May89 95(2) 12	209
7980. TATTOOED BEAT MESSIAH Zodiac Mindwarp & The Love Reaction 26Mar88 132(2) 15	209
7981. SPOILED GIRL Carly Simon 20Jul85 88(2) 11	209
7982. REDEYE Redeye 12Dec70 113(2) 12	209
7983. THE BODY AND SOUL OF TOM JONES Tom Jones 16Jun73 93(2) 10	209
7984. ONE KISS FOR OLD TIMES' SAKE Ronnie Dove 24Jul65 119(1) 14	209
7985. OLD & IN THE WAY Old & In The Way 29Mar75 99(1) 8	209
7986. WITH SYMPATHY Ministry 25Jun83 96(1) 14	209
7987. NO EXIT Fates Warning 23Apr88 111(3) 13	209
7988. TRIUMVIRATE Mike Bloomfield/ John Paul Hammond/Dr. John 16Jun73 105(1) 12	209
7989. CHUNGA'S REVENGE Frank Zappa 21Nov70 119(1) 14	209
7990. THE RAMSEY LEWIS TRIO AT THE BOHEMIAN CAVERNS Ramsey Lewis Trio 17Oct64 103(1) 13	208
7991. SILK TORPEDO Pretty Things 01Mar75 104(2) 9	208
7992. JUST ANOTHER BAND FROM L.A. The Mothers 22Apr72 85(1) 9	208
7993. FAREWELL SONG Janis Joplin 13Feb82 104(1) 11	208
7994. LOVE CURRENT Lenny Williams 07Jul79 108(1) 9	208
7995. DON'T CHA LOVE IT The Miracles 08Feb75 96(2) 9	208
7996. RAW BLUES Johnnie Taylor 26Apr69 126(1) 9	208
7997. STAY THE NIGHT Jane Olivor 08Jul78 108(1) 12	208
7998. BAD ATTITUDE Meat Loaf 18May85 74(1) 10	208
7999. LIVE/INDIAN SUMMER Al Stewart 14Nov81 110(2) 11	208
8000. BERLIN Lou Reed 20Oct73 98(1) 11	208
8001. BANKRUPT Dr. Hook 05Jul75 141(1) 16	208
8002. SERGIO MENDES Sergio Mendes 15Feb75 105(2) 10	208
8003. SIGNS OF THE ZODIAC Various Artists 06Dec69 147(2) 15	208
8004. DON'T KNOCK MY LOVE Wilson Pickett 25Dec71 132(2) 14	208
8005. PLAY DON'T WORRY Mick Ronson 08Feb75 103(2) 9	208
8006. COME INTO OUR WORLD The Emotions 08Dec79 96(3) 10	207
8007. NEVER LET HER GO David Gates 15Feb75 102(2) 9	207
8008. TOGETHER BROTHERS Love Unlimited Orchestra 06Jul74 96(1) 10	207
8009. GROOVE APPROVED Paul Carrack 11Nov89 120(2) 18	207
8010. MORNING Jim Ed Brown 06Feb71 81(2) 9	207
8011. RECALL THE BEGINNING...A JOURNEY FROM EDEN Steve Miller Band 01Apr72 109(1) 10	207
8012. ALL DRESSED UP & NO PLACE TO GO Nicolette Larson 14Aug82 75(1) 10	207
8013. IRISH HEARTBEAT Van Morrison & The Chieftains 23Jul88 102(2) 13	207
8014. THE FIRST EDITION First Edition 13Jan68 118(1) 15	207
8015. COUNTRY Soundtrack 01Dec84 120(2) 15	207
8016. WE CAN FLY The Cowsills 09Mar68 89(2) 14	207
8017. ON THE ROAD George Carlin 21May77 90(1) 9	207
8018. UNDERGROUND FIRE The Ventures 18Jan69 157(2) 14	206
8019. ANNIVERSARY SPECIAL VOLUME ONE Earl Scruggs Revue 21Jun75 104(2) 10	206
8020. THE BABYS The Babys 05Mar77 133(2) 13	206
8021. FOOL AROUND Rachel Sweet 04Aug79 97(2) 9	206
8022. AGAINST THE GRAIN Rory Gallagher 29Nov75 121(1) 13	206
8023. THE NEW ORDER Testament 25Jun88 136(1) 14	206
8024. OPEN FIRE Ronnie Montrose 11Feb78 98(2) 10	206
8025. MADE IN U.S.A. Beach Boys 26Jul86 96(1) 12	206
8026. THE LEGENDARY CHRISTINE PERFECT ALBUM Christine McVie 14Aug76 104(2) 10	206
8027. MOBY GRAPE '69 Moby Grape 01Mar69 113(1) 10	206
8028. HOOKED ON SWING 2 Larry Elgart And His Manhattan Swing Orchestra 12Feb83 89(2) 14	206
8029. QUEEN OF THE NIGHT Maggie Bell 20Apr74 122(1) 13	206
8030. ORPHEUS Orpheus 09Mar68 119(2) 14	206
8031. SPACESHIP EARTH Sugarloaf 13Feb71 111(2) 9	206
8032. OKIE J.J. Cale 15Jun74 128(1) 11	206
8033. THE BEST OF THE COWSILLS The Cowsills 18Jan69 127(1) 9	205
8034. CARNIVAL Maynard Ferguson 07Oct78 113(1) 9	205
8035. THE COUNTRY MUSIC HALL OF FAME HITS, VOL. 1 Jerry Lee Lewis 10May69 127(2) 10	205
8036. FREE YOUR MIND...AND YOUR ASS WILL FOLLOW Funkadelic 31Oct70 92(2) 10	205
8037. DUO-GLIDE Sanford/Townsend Band 11Feb78 92(2) 8	205
8038. FIRST GLANCE April Wine 21Apr79 114(2) 11	205
8039. WHEN LIGHTS ARE LOW Tony Bennett 23May64 79(1) 12	205
8040. PURE The Primitives 23Dec89 113(1) 15	205
8041. YOU FOOLED ME Grey And Hanks 03Feb79 97(2) 11	205
8042. THE AGE OF ELECTRONICUS Dick Hyman 27Sep69 110(1) 11	205
8043. BUMPIN' Wes Montgomery 11Dec65 116(2) 13	205
8044. YOU WERE ONLY FOOLING Vic Damone 10Jul65 86(2) 10	205
8045. LIBRA Julio Iglesias 24Aug85 92(2) 12	204
8046. IT'S A MAN'S MAN'S MAN'S WORLD James Brown 10Sep66 90(1) 9	204
8047. MTV'S ROCK 'N ROLL TO GO Various Artists 02Mar85 91(2) 12	204
8048. TIGHT SHOES Foghat 21Jun80 106(1) 10	204
8049. ANYTHING YOU CHOOSE/WITHOUT RHYME OR REASON Spanky And Our Gang 15Feb69 101(1) 7	204
8050. VIVA! ROXY MUSIC Roxy Music 07Aug76 81(1) 7	204
8051. WE SURE CAN LOVE EACH OTHER Tammy Wynette 22May71 115(2) 10	204
8052. TYRANNY AND MUTATION Blue Öyster Cult 17Mar73 122(1) 13	204
8053. YOU WANT IT, YOU GOT IT Bryan Adams 30Jan82 118(1) 13	204
8054. APOLOGIZE Ed Ames 10Aug68 135(2) 14	204
8055. THE DISCO KID Van McCoy 18Oct75 80(1) 7	204
8056. JUST LOOKIN' FOR A HIT Dwight Yoakam 14Oct89 68(2) 10	204
8057. ALL HAIL THE QUEEN Queen Latifah 16Dec89 124(2) 17	204
8058. HE THINKS HE'S RAY STEVENS Ray Stevens 19Jan85 118(2) 19	204
8059. THE OTHER SIDE OF THE RAINBOW Melba Moore 13Nov82 152(1) 19	204
8060. MUSICAL CHAIRS Sammy Hagar 21Jan78 100(1) 11	203
8061. THE GARDEN OF LOVE Don Ray 23Sep78 113(2) 11	203
8062. WATER SIGN Jeff Lorber Fusion 08Sep79 119(1) 14	203
8063. APPETIZERS Alan O'Day 03Sep77 109(2) 9	203
8064. V.S.O.P. Herbie Hancock 07May77 79(1) 7	203

Rank. Title Act	Entry Peak(Pk Wks) TotWks	Scr
8065. **THE BEST** Quincy Jones	17Jul82 122(2) 17	203
8066. **HIGH VOLTAGE** Eddie Harris	16Aug69 122(1) 9	203
8067. **LIVE 'N' KICKIN'** Kingfish	21May77 103(1) 10	203
8068. **TASTY JAM** Fatback	20Jun81 102(1) 8	203
8069. **FOREVER YOURS** Tony Terry	09Jan88 151(1) 20	203
8070. **ACROSS A CROWDED ROOM**	Richard Thompson 09Mar85 102(2) 13	203
8071. **ALL HUNG UP** Irish Rovers	09Nov68 119(1) 8	203
8072. **PACIFIC GAS AND ELECTRIC**	Pacific Gas And Electric 13Sep69 91(1) 8	203
8073. **SATIN CHICKENS** Rhinoceros	27Sep69 105(1) 9	202
8074. **KNNILLSSON** Nilsson	06Aug77 108(2) 10	202
8075. **I'VE GOT THE ROCK 'N' ROLLS AGAIN**	Joe Perry Project 04Jul81 100(1) 10	202
8076. **MAC DAVIS** Mac Davis	21Apr73 120(1) 13	202
8077. **VICES** Kick Axe	30Jun84 126(2) 15	202
8078. **IN THE POCKET** Neil Sedaka	17May80 135(1) 13	202
8079. **ONLY FOR LOVERS** Roger Williams	25Jan69 131(2) 10	202
8080. **SLIM SLO SLIDER** Johnny Rivers	08Aug70 100(1) 9	202
8081. **THE BEST OF B.B. KING** B.B. King	24Feb73 101(1) 11	202
8082. **'ROUND MIDNIGHT** Linda Ronstadt	11Oct86 124(2) 17	202
8083. **I LOVE MY MUSIC** Wild Cherry	18Feb78 84(1) 9	202
8084. **IT'S ALRIGHT (I SEE RAINBOWS)** Yoko Ono	25Dec82 98(2) 13	202
8085. **MELANIE AT CARNEGIE HALL** Melanie	12May73 109(2) 11	202
8086. **CHANGE OF HEART** Change	28Apr84 102(1) 15	202
8087. **JOHNNY MATHIS SINGS** Johnny Mathis	01Apr67 103(1) 11	201
8088. **THE SHOUTING STAGE** Joan Armatrading	20Aug88 100(1) 13	201
8089. **THE HARD WAY** Point Blank	31May80 110(1) 13	201
8090. **DON'T TAKE IT PERSONAL** Jermaine Jackson	02Dec89 115(2) 16	201
8091. **KEEP THE FAITH** Black Oak Arkansas	12Feb72 103(1) 10	201
8092. **CHER SUPERPAK, VOL. II** Cher	07Oct72 95(1) 9	201
8093. **YEARS AGO** Statler Brothers	11Jul81 103(1) 9	201
8094. **ROAD TO RUIN** The Ramones	21Oct78 103(1) 11	201
8095. **SHOWDOWN!** Albert Collins, Robert Cray,	Johnny Copeland 15Feb86 124(1) 18	201
8096. **QUICKSILVER**	Quicksilver Messenger Service 04Dec71 114(1) 9	201
8097. **FIVE SPECIAL** 5 Special	11Aug79 118(3) 11	201
8098. **GOT TO FIND A WAY** Curtis Mayfield	16Nov74 76(2) 7	201
8099. **BULLISH** Herb Alpert & The Tijuana Brass	25Aug84 75(1) 10	201
8100. **THE GOONIES** Dave Grusin	29Jun85 73(2) 10	201
8101. **THE MUSIC OF COSMOS** TV Soundtrack	09May81 136(2) 13	201
8102. **TODAY'S ROMANTIC HITS/FOR LOVERS ONLY, VOL. 2**	Jackie Gleason 06Jun64 82(1) 10	201
8103. **DINOSAUR SWAMPS** The Flock	17Oct70 96(2) 9	200
8104. **KING OF HEARTS** Engelbert Humperdinck	11Aug73 113(1) 10	200
8105. **FOR THE LONELY: A ROY ORBISON ANTHOLOGY, 1956-1965** Roy Orbison	07Jan89 110(1) 13	200
8106. **NIGHTTIDE** Mystic Moods Orchestra	08Oct66 110(1) 10	200
8107. **THE YELLOW ROLLS-ROYCE** Soundtrack	07Aug65 82(1) 10	200
8108. **BOLD AS LOVE** Bardeux	30Apr88 104(2) 12	200
8109. **ACT A FOOL** King Tee	21Jan89 125(1) 15	200
8110. **SAIL AWAY** Randy Newman	17Jun72 163(1) 18	200
8111. **BLUES IMAGE** Blues Image	16Aug69 112(1) 9	200
8112. **LYNN ANDERSON'S GREATEST HITS**	Lynn Anderson 11Nov72 129(1) 14	200
8113. **LIVING PROOF** Sylvester	24Nov79 123(1) 12	200
8114. **LONDON UNDERGROUND** Herbie Mann	30Mar74 109(1) 10	200
8115. **SINCE I FELL FOR YOU** Lenny Welch	01Feb64 73(1) 10	200
8116. **CHRISTMAS IN THE STARS/STAR WARS CHRISTMAS ALBUM**	Meco 13Dec80 61(3) 6	200
8117. **NEARLY HUMAN** Todd Rundgren	17Jun89 102(2) 11	200
8118. **OCEAN RAIN** Echo & The Bunnymen	09Jun84 87(1) 11	199
8119. **DAVE MASON IS ALIVE!** Dave Mason	21Apr73 116(1) 11	199
8120. **HARD MACHINE** Stacey Q	05Mar88 115(1) 11	199
8121. **LIGHT THE LIGHT** Seawind	24Mar79 143(1) 14	199
8122. **BARON VON TOLLBOOTH & THE CHROME NUN** Paul Kantner, Grace Slick & David Freiberg	23Jun73 120(1) 12	199
8123. **SUSPICION!** Terry Stafford	16May64 81(1) 11	199
8124. **THE STAPLE SWINGERS** Staple Singers	20Mar71 117(1) 11	199
8125. **OHIO PLAYERS GREATEST HITS** Ohio Players	22Feb75 92(1) 7	199
8126. **JOIN THE ARMY** Suicidal Tendencies	23May87 100(2) 13	199
8127. **ENCORE/THE CHUCK MANGIONE CONCERTS**	Chuck Mangione 06Dec75 102(1) 10	199
8128. **APPLE JUICE** Tom Scott	11Jul81 123(1) 11	199
8129. **SWITCH** Golden Earring	12Apr75 108(2) 8	199
8130. **I THINK OF YOU** Perry Como	26Jun71 101(1) 9	199
8131. **TOUCAN DO IT TOO** Amazing Rhythm Aces	16Apr77 114(1) 11	199
8132. **GLOW** Al Jarreau	28Aug76 132(1) 11	199
8133. **THE SURFARIS PLAY WIPE OUT AND OTHERS**	The Surfaris 30Nov63 94(1) 11	199
8134. **FOR MEN ONLY** Millie Jackson	21Jun80 100(1) 10	199
8135. **WHEN LOVE COMES CALLING**	Deniece Williams 18Aug79 96(2) 8	199
8136. **NATURALLY** Leon Haywood	17May80 92(2) 10	199
8137. **KEEP ON MOVING STRAIGHT AHEAD**	Lakeside 12Dec81 109(4) 10	199
8138. **THE REAL THING** Angela Winbush	11Nov89 113(2) 17	199
8139. **HOW MUCH MORE CAN SHE STAND**	Conway Twitty 22May71 91(1) 9	199
8140. **FIERCE HEART** Jim Capaldi	21May83 91(1) 12	199
8141. **GET DOWN** Joe Simon	19Jul75 129(2) 12	199
8142. **GREAT FOLK THEMES** Percy Faith	15Feb64 103(1) 12	198
8143. **THE FLAG** Rick James	05Jul86 95(2) 12	198
8144. **LIVE 1980/86** Joe Jackson	21May88 91(3) 12	198
8145. **TOGETHER AGAIN!** Benny Goodman Quartet	07Mar64 90(1) 10	198
8146. **LOVE IS** Eric Burdon & The Animals	11Jan69 123(2) 10	198
8147. **BADDEST** Grover Washington Jr.	13Sep80 96(1) 10	198
8148. **CRACKERS INTERNATIONAL** Erasure	13May89 73(3) 10	198
8149. **EVERYBODY KNOWS** Steve Lawrence	12Sep64 73(1) 9	198
8150. **FIRE DOWN UNDER** Riot	12Sep81 99(1) 11	198
8151. **A THING CALLED LOVE** Johnny Cash	29Apr72 112(1) 9	198
8152. **THE BEST OF THE CRUSADERS**	The Crusaders 18Dec76 122(2) 10	198
8153. **CHASING RAINBOWS** Jane Olivor	22Oct77 86(1) 8	198
8154. **LES PLUS GRANDS SUCCES DE CHIC - CHIC'S GREATEST HITS** Chic	22Dec79 88(2) 9	198
8155. **FOR YOUR LOVE** The Yardbirds	31Jul65 96(1) 11	198
8156. **MICHAEL BOLTON** Michael Bolton	07May83 89(1) 13	198
8157. **HOPPKORV** Hot Tuna	20Nov76 116(2) 10	198
8158. **BLOOD & CHOCOLATE** Elvis Costello And	The Attractions 11Oct86 84(2) 11	197
8159. **Y U I ORTA** Ian Hunter/Mick Ronson	28Oct89 157(3) 20	197
8160. **WITH THE NAKED EYE** Greg Kihn Band	11Aug79 114(1) 10	197
8161. **WE ARE ONE** Pieces Of A Dream	28Aug82 114(3) 15	197
8162. **RAY STEVENS' GREATEST HITS** Ray Stevens	04Sep71 95(1) 8	197
8163. **THE COUNTRY MUSIC HALL OF FAME HITS, VOL. 2** Jerry Lee Lewis	10May69 124(1) 10	197
8164. **RELEASED** Patti LaBelle	12Apr80 114(1) 13	197
8165. **GOOD TIMES** Elvis Presley	06Apr74 90(1) 8	197
8166. **WOMEN'S LOVE RIGHTS** Laura Lee	29Jan72 117(1) 11	197
8167. **TURTLE SOUP** The Turtles	01Nov69 117(2) 9	197
8168. **WE GOTTA START LOVIN'** Bobby Goldsboro	23Jan71 120(1) 13	197
8169. **LO MUCHO QUE TE QUIERO** René & René	11Jan69 129(1) 9	197
8170. **INITIATION** Todd Rundgren	14Jun75 86(2) 7	197
8171. **DUMB WAITERS** The Korgis	08Nov80 113(2) 12	197
8172. **COMMON GROUND** Rhythm Corps	13Aug88 104(2) 14	197
8173. **WHITE SHOES** Emmylou Harris	19Nov83 116(1) 13	197
8174. **GOT A FEELING** Patrick Juvet	01Jul78 125(1) 14	197
8175. **FREE LIVE!** Free	11Sep71 89(1) 8	197
8176. **GOTTA TRAVEL ON** Ray Bryant Trio	25Jun66 111(1) 12	196
8177. **ELECTRIC MUD** Muddy Waters	09Nov68 127(2) 8	196
8178. **TAKE NO PRISONERS** Peabo Bryson	06Jul85 102(2) 13	196
8179. **LOVE THEME FROM "ROMEO & JULIET"**	Percy Faith 27Sep69 134(1) 11	196

Rank. Title Act Entry Peak(Pk Wks) TotWks	Scr
8180. ON THE EDGE Sea Level 28Oct78 137(3) 16	196
8181. REWIND (1971-1984) Rolling Stones 28Jul84 86(1) 11	196
8182. A LEGENDARY PERFORMER Glenn Miller Orchestra 25Jan75 115(1) 9	196
8183. I DON'T WANT TO SEE YOU AGAIN Peter And Gordon 02Jan65 95(1) 11	196
8184. STAN KENTON TODAY Stan Kenton 01Jul72 146(1) 14	196
8185. SUPERCHARGED Tavares 08Mar80 75(2) 7	196
8186. FRIENDS IN LOVE Dionne Warwick 22May82 83(2) 12	196
8187. NEWBORN James Gang 31May75 109(2) 9	196
8188. BLOODROCK U.S.A. Bloodrock 06Nov71 88(1) 7	196
8189. LIZARD King Crimson 20Mar71 113(2) 10	196
8190. DISCO Pet Shop Boys 27Dec86 95(2) 12	196
8191. OH, JULIE! Barry Manilow 25Sep82 69(2) 9	196
8192. THERE'S NO PLACE LIKE AMERICA TODAY Curtis Mayfield 07Jun75 120(1) 11	196
8193. TIGHTEN UP VOL. '88 Big Audio Dynamite 13Aug88 102(1) 12	196
8194. LIGHT OF THE STABLE: THE CHRISTMAS ALBUM Emmylou Harris 29Nov80 102(3) 9	196
8195. AFRODISIAC Main Ingredient 05May73 132(1) 13	195
8196. THE ENVOY Warren Zevon 14Aug82 93(1) 13	195
8197. NIGHTSONGS Earl Klugh 27Oct84 107(2) 17	195
8198. MAN OF STEEL Hank Williams Jr. 19Nov83 116(2) 13	195
8199. ROSE ROYCE IV/RAINBOW CONNECTION Rose Royce 08Sep79 74(1) 8	195
8200. MSG Michael Schenker Group 24Oct81 81(1) 8	195
8201. ECHOES OF AN ERA Various Artists 06Feb82 105(1) 11	195
8202. WE CAME TO PLAY Tower Of Power 22Apr78 89(2) 8	195
8203. SOUND + VISION David Bowie 14Oct89 97(1) 16	195
8204. I'M TELLING YOU NOW Freddie And The Dreamers 08May65 86(2) 10	195
8205. LIVE AND OUTRAGEOUS (RATED XXX) Millie Jackson 13Mar82 113(1) 13	195
8206. 42ND STREET Original Cast 17Jan81 120(1) 11	195
8207. DREAMS, DREAMS, DREAMS Chilliwack 26Mar77 142(1) 13	194
8208. SOULFORCE REVOLUTION 7 Seconds 04Nov89 153(2) 19	194
8209. HERE COME THE JUDGE Pigmeat Markham 20Jul68 109(1) 9	194
8210. WILLIE & THE POOR BOYS Willie & The Poor Boys 25May85 96(2) 12	194
8211. SONGS FROM "CAT BALLOU" AND OTHER MOTION PICTURES Nat King Cole 03Jul65 77(1) 9	194
8212. DON'T CRUSH THAT DWARF, HAND ME THE PLIERS Firesign Theatre 19Sep70 106(2) 10	194
8213. BING CROSBY'S GREATEST HITS Bing Crosby 10Dec77 98(2) 9	194
8214. JOHN HARTFORD John Hartford 14Jun69 137(1) 9	194
8215. RIVER DEEP-MOUNTAIN HIGH Ike & Tina Turner 27Sep69 102(1) 8	194
8216. THE WINNING HAND Various Artists 15Jan83 109(1) 14	194
8217. COUNTERPOINT Ralph MacDonald 14Jul79 110(2) 10	194
8218. C.J. FISH Country Joe & The Fish 02May70 111(1) 9	194

Rank. Title Act Entry Peak(Pk Wks) TotWks	Scr
8219. THIS IS ELVIS Elvis Presley 25Apr81 115(3) 10	194
8220. ORIGINAL STYLIN' Three Times Dope 22Apr89 122(2) 18	194
8221. 5 TO 1 Tom Kimmel 04Jul87 104(2) 15	194
8222. ALBUM Public Image Limited 08Mar86 115(2) 16	194
8223. CHANGE OF HEART Eric Carmen 28Oct78 137(1) 12	193
8224. DAVE GRUSIN COLLECTION Dave Grusin 25Feb89 110(3) 12	193
8225. ERIC IS HERE Eric Burdon And The Animals 25Mar67 121(1) 13	193
8226. STRAIGHT AHEAD Amy Grant 20Apr85 133(2) 20	193
8227. MEET THE TEMPTATIONS The Temptations 09May64 95(1) 11	193
8228. LIVING IN A BOX Living In A Box 08Aug87 89(2) 13	193
8229. MODERN MUSIC Be Bop Deluxe 16Oct76 88(1) 8	193
8230. FOOL IN LOVE WITH YOU Jim Photoglo 06Jun81 119(1) 11	193
8231. STREET RATS Humble Pie 26Apr75 100(2) 8	193
8232. JOE SOUTH'S GREATEST HITS Joe South 12Sep70 125(1) 11	193
8233. SON OF DRACULA Nilsson 04May74 106(1) 9	193
8234. DYN-O-MITE Jimmie Walker 31May75 130(2) 12	193
8235. LIFE & LOVE ITALIAN STYLE Jimmy Roselli 26Jun65 96(1) 11	193
8236. PLAYGROUND IN MY MIND Clint Holmes 26May73 122(1) 12	192
8237. FOOL BRITANNIA Various Artists 19Oct63 87(1) 10	192
8238. THE OFFICIAL MUSIC OF THE XXIIRD OLYMPIAD-LOS ANGELES 1984 Various Artists 14Jul84 92(2) 13	192
8239. LOVE BOMB The Tubes 23Mar85 87(2) 10	192
8240. LOVE NOTES Chuck Mangione 17Jul82 83(2) 10	192
8241. CLASS OF '65 Floyd Cramer 23Oct65 107(1) 13	192
8242. WE GO A LONG WAY BACK Bloodstone 17Jul82 95(2) 11	192
8243. THE BEST OF THE LETTERMEN, VOL. 2 The Lettermen 22Feb69 128(1) 10	192
8244. FINALE Loggins & Messina 12Nov77 83(1) 8	192
8245. KEEP ON DANCING The Gentrys 18Dec65 99(1) 10	192
8246. FIFTH ANGEL Fifth Angel 16Apr88 117(2) 13	192
8247. NO TELLIN' LIES Zebra 22Sep84 84(2) 11	192
8248. ELVIS SINGS FOR CHILDREN AND GROWNUPS TOO Elvis Presley 05Aug78 130(1) 11	192
8249. AMERICANA Leon Russell 12Aug78 115(2) 10	192
8250. ELVIS: A CANADIAN TRIBUTE Elvis Presley 04Nov78 86(1) 7	192
8251. LIGHT OF DAY Soundtrack 14Mar87 82(2) 10	192
8252. GUITAR COUNTRY Chet Atkins 29Feb64 64(1) 8	192
8253. CARNEGIE HALL CONCERT Buck Owens 24Sep66 114(1) 10	192
8254. TAKE ME TO YOUR HEAVEN Stevie Woods 05Dec81 153(2) 25	192
8255. CONSTRUCTION #1 Ten Wheel Drive With Genya Ravan 10Jan70 151(2) 16	192
8256. SILVER CONDOR Silver Condor 04Jul81 141(4) 12	191

Rank. Title Act Entry Peak(Pk Wks) TotWks	Scr
8257. ROCKIN' CHAIR Gwen McCrae 28Jun75 121(2) 10	191
8258. CHRISTMAS Alabama 23Nov85 75(2) 9	191
8259. POWER IN THE MUSIC Guess Who 26Jul75 87(1) 7	191
8260. ROUND TWO Johnny Van Zant Band 13Jun81 119(2) 10	191
8261. EVERY STEP OF THE WAY David Benoit 04Jun88 129(2) 14	191
8262. A CLASSIC CASE: THE MUSIC OF JETHRO TULL London Symphony Orchestra/Ian Anderson 11Jan86 93(2) 13	191
8263. SONG OF NORWAY Soundtrack 23Jan71 95(2) 8	191
8264. DREAM A LITTLE DREAM Soundtrack 08Apr89 94(2) 10	191
8265. SHORT STORIES Jon And Vangelis 31May80 125(1) 15	191
8266. VOLUNTEER JAM VI Various Artists 19Jul80 104(2) 9	191
8267. THIS KIND OF LOVIN' The Whispers 03Oct81 100(3) 9	191
8268. GODDESS OF LOVE Phyllis Hyman 18Jun83 112(1) 12	191
8269. NIGHTINGALES & BOMBERS Manfred Mann's Earth Band 13Sep75 120(1) 10	191
8270. FREEDOM Santana 07Mar87 95(2) 11	191
8271. MAGNETS The Vapors 04Apr81 109(1) 9	191
8272. LOOK OUT 20/20 20Jun81 127(2) 12	191
8273. MEETING OF THE MINDS Four Tops 27Apr74 118(1) 11	190
8274. CATHEDRALS D.C. LaRue 26Jun76 139(2) 13	190
8275. HEAR TO TEMPT YOU The Temptations 10Dec77 113(1) 13	190
8276. TELL ME THIS IS A DREAM The Delfonics 24Jun72 123(1) 11	190
8277. SWEET THUNDER Sweet Thunder 15Jul78 125(2) 11	190
8278. IT'S ONLY THE GOOD TIMES Wayne Newton 04Feb67 131(1) 13	190
8279. BRITTEN: WAR REQUIEM Benjamin Britten 07Sep63 68(1) 8	190
8280. EASTER ISLAND Kris Kristofferson 01Apr78 86(2) 7	190
8281. I'M A WRITER, NOT A FIGHTER Gilbert O'Sullivan 13Oct73 101(1) 10	190
8282. MIDNIGHT WIND Charlie Daniels Band 12Nov77 105(1) 11	190
8283. HOT SPOT Dazz Band 17Aug85 98(2) 12	190
8284. THE BAND PLAYS ON Back Street Crawler 15Nov75 111(2) 10	190
8285. DERRINGER LIVE Rick Derringer 16Jul77 123(2) 10	190
8286. FRIENDS & LOVE... A CHUCK MANGIONE CONCERT Chuck Mangione 03Jul71 116(1) 11	190
8287. MASTER OF THE GAME George Duke 24Nov79 125(1) 11	189
8288. FOREVER AND EVER Howard Hewett 16Apr88 110(2) 12	189
8289. FAME Grace Jones 05Aug78 97(1) 8	189
8290. YOU'RE SO BEAUTIFUL Charles Wright And The Watts 103rd Street Band 15May71 147(2) 11	189
8291. YOU TURN ME ON! Ian Whitcomb 10Jul65 125(1) 13	189
8292. THE BEST OF THE SEEKERS The Seekers 19Aug67 97(1) 10	189
8293. JAMES BROWN PLAYS NEW BREED James Brown 16Apr66 101(1) 11	189
8294. TOUCH THE SKY Carole King 23Jun79 104(2) 9	189

Rank. Title Act Entry Peak(Pk Wks) TotWks	Scr
8295. **PRIVATE EYES** Tommy Bolin 02Oct76 98(1) 8	189
8296. **NIGHT** Night 11Aug79 113(2) 10	189
8297. **THE TIN MAN WAS A DREAMER** Nicky Hopkins 05May73 108(1) 10	189
8298. **HOW WILL I LAUGH TOMORROW WHEN I CAN'T EVEN SMILE TODAY** Suicidal Tendencies 01Oct88 111(2) 12	189
8299. **TASTE** Taste 16Aug69 133(2) 9	189
8300. **MEMORIES** The Vogues 27Sep69 115(1) 9	189
8301. **BEAUTY AND THE BEARD** Al Hirt & Ann-Margret 29Feb64 83(2) 9	189
8302. **RED** The Communards 06Feb88 93(1) 9	189
8303. **ART OF TEA** Michael Franks 31Jul76 131(2) 13	189
8304. **TAKE ME ALL THE WAY** Stacy Lattisaw 11Oct86 131(2) 22	189
8305. **BAJA MARIMBA BAND** Baja Marimba Band 25Apr64 88(2) 12	189
8306. **MR. NICE GUY** Ronnie Laws 13Aug83 98(1) 11	189
8307. **KOSMOS** Tomita 18Feb78 115(1) 10	188
8308. **TEN PERCENT** Double Exposure 21Aug76 129(1) 11	188
8309. **COOL FROM THE WIRE** Dirty Looks 21May88 134(2) 14	188
8310. **PURE POP FOR NOW PEOPLE** Nick Lowe 29Apr78 127(1) 10	188
8311. **LIVE AND IN LIVING COLOR** Tower Of Power 22May76 99(1) 8	188
8312. **DANGEROUS MOMENTS** Martin Briley 09Feb85 85(2) 10	188
8313. **BLACK OAK ARKANSAS** Black Oak Arkansas 28Aug71 127(1) 12	188
8314. **JUNKYARD** Junkyard 12Aug89 105(2) 11	188
8315. **MARK-ALMOND** Mark-Almond 05Jun71 154(2) 15	188
8316. **INTUITION** TNT 18Mar89 115(1) 12	188
8317. **FEVER TREE** Fever Tree 18May68 156(1) 21	188
8318. **ARTISTRY** Deodato 16Nov74 102(2) 9	188
8319. **FLY WITH THE WIND** McCoy Tyner 12Jun76 128(1) 11	188
8320. **BY REQUEST** Brenda Lee 13Jun64 90(1) 11	188
8321. **CHANGE NO CHANGE** Elliot Easton 09Mar85 99(2) 11	188
8322. **ALWAYS IN MY HEART** Los Indios Tabajaras 16May64 85(1) 10	188
8323. **PRESSURE** Bram Tchaikovsky 17May80 108(1) 10	188
8324. **SMOKE SIGNALS** Smokey Robinson 15Feb86 104(2) 13	188
8325. **GRAVITY** Kenny G 01Jun85 97(2) 12	188
8326. **POOL IT!** The Monkees 19Sep87 72(2) 9	188
8327. **JUNGLE FEVER** Chakachas 08Apr72 117(1) 11	188
8328. **D-I-V-O-R-C-E** Tammy Wynette 07Sep68 147(1) 15	188
8329. **JEALOUSY** Dirt Band 05Sep81 102(1) 9	187
8330. **RA** Utopia 26Feb77 79(1) 7	187
8331. **RANDY MEISNER** Randy Meisner 21Aug82 94(3) 11	187
8332. **MADNESS, MONEY AND MUSIC** Sheena Easton 16Oct82 85(3) 12	187
8333. **JUST VISITING THIS PLANET** Jellybean 05Sep87 101(2) 11	187
8334. **WATERFRONT** Waterfront 20May89 103(1) 13	187
8335. **BOOK EARLY** City Boy 16Sep78 115(2) 9	187
8336. **METROPOLIS** Soundtrack 25Aug84 110(2) 13	187
8337. **LITTLE GAMES** The Yardbirds 12Aug67 80(1) 8	187
8338. **LITTLE WHEEL SPIN AND SPIN** Buffy Sainte-Marie 21May66 97(1) 10	187
8339. **SHIVER IN THE NIGHT** Andy Pratt 27Aug77 90(2) 9	187
8340. **WHEN THE WHISTLE BLOWS ANYTHING GOES** Soul Survivors 18Nov67 123(1) 13	187
8341. **TELLY** Telly Savalas 04Jan75 117(1) 8	187
8342. **SOUL SERENADE** King Curtis 13Jun64 103(1) 12	187
8343. **DOWN FOR THE COUNT** Y&T 23Nov85 91(2) 12	187
8344. **SNAIL** Snail 08Jul78 135(2) 12	186
8345. **WRONG END OF THE RAINBOW** Tom Rush 26Dec70 110(1) 9	186
8346. **TALES OF KIDD FUNKADELIC** Funkadelic 09Oct76 103(1) 10	186
8347. **CAPTAIN BEYOND** Captain Beyond 19Aug72 134(2) 12	186
8348. **TEASES AND DARES** Kim Wilde 09Feb85 84(2) 10	186
8349. **WHO'S GREATEST HITS** The Who 21May83 94(1) 13	186
8350. **I HEAR YOU ROCKIN'** Dave Edmunds Band 31Jan87 106(1) 12	186
8351. **SERENADE FOR ELISABETH** Gunter Kallmann Chorus 01May65 97(2) 10	186
8352. **JESSI** Jessi Colter 07Feb76 109(3) 8	186
8353. **THE MISSING PIECE** Gentle Giant 15Oct77 81(1) 7	186
8354. **TAPESTRY** Don McLean 12Feb72 111(1) 10	186
8355. **TANX** T. Rex 28Apr73 102(1) 10	186
8356. **MEAN STREAK** Y&T 10Sep83 103(1) 12	186
8357. **BE TRUE TO YOU** Eric Andersen 19Apr75 113(1) 9	186
8358. **TOUCH MY HEART** Ray Price 04Mar67 129(1) 12	185
8359. **A GROOVY KIND OF LOVE** The Mindbenders 16Jul66 92(1) 9	185
8360. **NADIA'S THEME (THE YOUNG AND THE RESTLESS)** Barry De Vorzon 06Nov76 133(2) 12	185
8361. **HEARTBREAK EXPRESS** Dolly Parton 24Apr82 106(2) 12	185
8362. **EARLY ORBISON** Roy Orbison 17Oct64 101(1) 11	185
8363. **MOVING ON** John Mayall 28Oct72 116(1) 11	185
8364. **OUT OF CONTROL** Brothers Johnson 04Aug84 91(1) 11	185
8365. **INTERNATIONAL** Three Degrees 21Jun75 99(1) 8	185
8366. **JE T'AIME** Saint Tropez 26Nov77 131(4) 10	185
8367. **YOUNGBLOOD** War 19Aug78 69(1) 6	185
8368. **THE WORLD OF MIRIAM MAKEBA** Miriam Makeba 16Nov63 86(1) 10	185
8369. **FAT MATTRESS** Fat Mattress 15Nov69 134(2) 10	185
8370. **THE WONDERFUL WORLD OF MAKE BELIEVE** Johnny Mathis 25Jul64 75(1) 10	185
8371. **SHARING YOUR LOVE** Change 15May82 66(2) 9	185
8372. **FROZEN GHOST** Frozen Ghost 11Apr87 107(2) 13	185
8373. **IN THE BEGINNING** Nature's Divine 10Nov79 91(1) 8	185
8374. **PINK WORLD** Planet P Project 01Dec84 121(1) 14	185
8375. **BOOGIE BROTHERS** Savoy Brown 20Apr74 101(1) 8	185
8376. **ANTHOLOGY** Quicksilver Messenger Service 19May73 108(1) 10	185
8377. **CRUSADE** John Mayall's Bluesbreakers 17Feb68 135(1) 14	185
8378. **FIRST STEP** Small Faces 18Apr70 119(1) 12	185
8379. **COLOR IN YOUR LIFE** Missing Persons 09Aug86 86(1) 11	184
8380. **WARNER BROTHERS PRESENTS MONTROSE!** Montrose 18Oct75 79(1) 7	184
8381. **THE TEARS OF A CLOWN** Smokey Robinson & The Miracles 26Dec70 143(2) 12	184
8382. **GRAB IT!** L'Trimm 05Nov88 132(2) 16	184
8383. **LE SPANK** Le Pamplemousse 21Jan78 116(1) 11	184
8384. **POPEYE** Soundtrack 27Dec80 115(1) 10	184
8385. **MAX** The Rumour 13Aug77 124(1) 10	184
8386. **ONE SECOND** Yello 26Sep87 92(2) 10	184
8387. **UNFINISHED MUSIC NO. 1: TWO VIRGINS** John Lennon & Yoko Ono 08Feb69 124(1) 8	184
8388. **MAC BAND** Mac Band Featuring The McCampbell Brothers 23Jul88 109(2) 14	184
8389. **INTO THE WOODS** The Call 04Jul87 123(2) 13	184
8390. **FUEL FOR THE FIRE** Naked Eyes 08Sep84 83(3) 10	184
8391. **MUSTA NOTTA GOTTA LOTTA** Joe Ely 11Apr81 135(1) 11	184
8392. **THE ART OF FALLING APART** Soft Cell 26Feb83 84(4) 8	184
8393. **WHISTLE RYMES** John Entwistle 18Nov72 138(2) 13	184
8394. **SOUL SERENADE** Gloria Lynne 05Jun65 82(1) 10	184
8395. **LOVE IS ALL AROUND** The Troggs 18May68 109(1) 9	184
8396. **FIRST** David Gates 27Oct73 107(1) 10	184
8397. **ROCKIN' THE BOAT** Jimmy Smith 09Nov63 64(1) 8	184
8398. **CLEAR LIGHT** Clear Light 25Nov67 126(1) 13	184
8399. **AN IMITATION OF LOVE** Millie Jackson 27Dec86 119(2) 17	184
8400. **LAND OF PASSION** Hubert Laws 28Apr79 93(1) 8	184
8401. **ELVIS-A LEGENDARY PERFORMER, VOLUME 3** Elvis Presley 06Jan79 113(2) 11	183
8402. **TINA LIVE IN EUROPE** Tina Turner 09Apr88 86(2) 9	183
8403. **GIVE YOUR BABY A STANDING OVATION** The Dells 23Jun73 99(1) 9	183
8404. **SOUL ON TOP** James Brown 16May70 125(1) 10	183
8405. **BURNING BRIDGES AND OTHER GREAT MOTION PICTURE THEMES** Mike Curb Congregation 13Mar71 117(2) 8	183
8406. **DOWN AND OUT IN BEVERLY HILLS** Soundtrack 05Apr86 68(2) 7	183
8407. **YELLOW RIVER** Christie 12Dec70 115(1) 10	183
8408. **IT'S A MAD, MAD, MAD, MAD WORLD** Soundtrack 21Dec63 101(1) 11	183
8409. **BLUE SKIES** Kiri Te Kanawa/Nelson Riddle And His Orchestra 07Dec85 136(1) 16	183
8410. **DISCOVERY** Shanice Wilson 28Nov87 149(2) 18	183
8411. **SUBTERRANEAN JUNGLE** The Ramones 26Mar83 83(3) 9	183

Rank. Title Act Entry Peak(Pk Wks) TotWks	Scr
8412. TAMMY'S GREATEST HITS, VOLUME II Tammy Wynette 18Sep71 118(1) 8	183
8413. HENDRIX SONGBOOK The Rubber Band 06Sep69 116(1) 8	183
8414. ANNE MURRAY Anne Murray 03Apr71 121(2) 9	182
8415. DO I HEAR A WALTZ? Original Cast 22May65 81(1) 9	182
8416. ENCORE! MORE OF THE CONCERT SOUND OF HENRY MANCINI Henry Mancini And His Orchestra 09Dec67 126(1) 12	182
8417. FIRST TASTE OF SIN Cold Blood 22Apr72 133(1) 11	182
8418. VICTORY Narada Michael Walden 18Oct80 103(1) 8	182
8419. JOYRIDE Pieces Of A Dream 02Aug86 102(2) 12	182
8420. FLY BY NIGHT Rush 15Mar75 113(1) 8	182
8421. ALIENS Horslips 25Feb78 98(2) 9	182
8422. NATURAL STATES David Lanz & Paul Speer 30Jan88 125(1) 12	182
8423. GOOD MUSIC Joan Jett & the Blackhearts 25Oct86 105(1) 16	182
8424. IT'S A BEAUTIFUL DAY...TODAY It's A Beautiful Day 07Apr73 114(1) 10	182
8425. COUNTRY CASANOVA Commander Cody & His Lost Planet Airmen 16Jun73 104(1) 9	182
8426. TALK TO YOUR DAUGHTER Robben Ford 06Aug88 120(2) 13	182
8427. MY FIRST OF 1965 Lawrence Welk 03Apr65 108(1) 12	182
8428. DROP DOWN AND GET ME Del Shannon 12Dec81 123(1) 14	182
8429. FORGOTTEN SONGS & UNSUNG HEROES John Kay 29Apr72 113(1) 11	182
8430. THE JOHNNY CASH COLLECTION (HIS GREATEST HITS, VOLUME II) Johnny Cash 23Oct71 94(1) 8	181
8431. NORMA JEAN Norma Jean 26Aug78 134(1) 11	181
8432. OH YES I CAN David Crosby 18Feb89 104(2) 10	181
8433. TO THE LIMIT Joan Armatrading 11Nov78 125(2) 12	181
8434. ROBERT HAZARD Robert Hazard 26Mar83 102(1) 11	181
8435. ETTA JAMES ROCKS THE HOUSE Etta James 01Feb64 96(1) 10	181
8436. THE JIMI HENDRIX CONCERTS Jimi Hendrix 25Sep82 79(2) 8	181
8437. NOW VOYAGER Barry Gibb 20Oct84 72(2) 8	181
8438. PRESERVATION ACT 2 The Kinks 15Jun74 114(1) 11	181
8439. BOINGO ALIVE Oingo Boingo 22Oct88 90(3) 11	181
8440. BEHAVIOUR Saga 21Sep85 87(2) 10	181
8441. PACIFIC OCEAN BLUE Dennis Wilson 10Sep77 96(2) 8	181
8442. SEX MACHINE TODAY James Brown 24May75 103(2) 8	181
8443. BURNIN' Esther Phillips 02Jan71 115(1) 15	181
8444. 20/20 20/20 03Nov79 138(1) 13	180
8445. THE BEST OF THE SPINNERS(2) Spinners 20May78 115(2) 9	180
8446. THERE MUST BE A BETTER WORLD SOMEWHERE B.B. King 28Feb81 131(1) 10	180
8447. THE LONESOMEST LONESOME Ray Price 29Jul72 145(1) 12	180
8448. FUTURE The Seeds 12Aug67 87(1) 8	180
8449. THE MANILOW COLLECTION/TWENTY CLASSIC HITS Barry Manilow 29Jun85 100(2) 12	180
8450. HEARTS IN MOTION Air Supply 06Sep86 84(2) 9	180
8451. WILD AND FREE Dazz Band 30Aug86 100(2) 11	180
8452. YOU'VE GOT A GOOD LOVE COMIN' Lee Greenwood 09Jun84 150(1) 20	180
8453. SURVIVAL OF THE FITTEST Headhunters 19Apr75 126(1) 10	180
8454. THE INTRODUCTION Steve Morse Band 01Sep84 101(1) 12	180
8455. JAMES BLONDE, SECRET AGENT 006.95, "THE MAN FROM T.A.N.T.E." Various Artists 18Dec65 93(1) 9	180
8456. WRAP YOUR ARMS AROUND ME Agnetha Faltskog 17Sep83 102(1) 11	180
8457. COTTON CLUB Soundtrack 19Jan85 93(1) 10	180
8458. FOUR SIDES OF MELANIE Melanie 01Apr72 103(1) 9	180
8459. YELLOW FEVER Hot Tuna 29Nov75 97(1) 9	180
8460. SHADOWDANCE Shadowfax 19Nov83 145(1) 19	180
8461. DELICIOUS TOGETHER Betty Everett & Jerry Butler 03Oct64 102(1) 11	180
8462. HEART PLAY John Lennon & Yoko Ono 14Jan84 94(1) 12	179
8463. THE VERY BEST OF ROY ORBISON Roy Orbison 13Aug66 94(1) 9	179
8464. LI'L RED RIDING HOOD Sam The Sham and the Pharaohs 24Sep66 82(1) 7	179
8465. HURRY UP THIS WAY AGAIN The Stylistics 08Nov80 127(1) 12	179
8466. HUGH MASEKELA IS ALIVE AND WELL AT THE WHISKY Hugh Masekela 06Jan68 90(2) 10	179
8467. DOWN HOME Seals & Crofts 31Oct70 122(1) 10	179
8468. MY FEET ARE SMILING Leo Kottke 07Apr73 108(1) 11	179
8469. LIVE Stephane Grappelli/David Grisman 06Jun81 108(1) 10	179
8470. LABYRINTH David Bowie 19Jul86 68(2) 8	179
8471. EVERYBODY LOVES A NUT Johnny Cash 09Jul66 88(1) 9	179
8472. CLEOPATRA JONES Soundtrack 18Aug73 109(2) 10	179
8473. STONEHEART Brick 19May79 100(1) 8	179
8474. RADIO DINNER National Lampoon 02Sep72 132(2) 12	179
8475. WELCOME HOME Carole King 17Jun78 104(1) 8	179
8476. THE SUPREMES SING COUNTRY WESTERN & POP The Supremes 20Mar65 79(2) 8	179
8477. FACE TO FACE Face To Face 16Jun84 126(1) 16	179
8478. FOURTEEN 14K FOLK SONGS The Limeliters 28Sep63 73(1) 8	179
8479. FINYL VINYL Rainbow 15Mar86 87(2) 10	179
8480. EUPHORIA Gato Barbieri 11Aug79 116(1) 9	179
8481. LIGHTLY LATIN Perry Como 11Jun66 86(1) 9	179
8482. HAPPINESS IS Ray Conniff & His Orchestra & Chorus 02Apr66 80(1) 9	179
8483. SEE HOW WE ARE X 11Jul87 107(2) 11	179
8484. BOSSA NOVA HOTEL Michael Sembello 08Oct83 80(1) 10	178
8485. TOM COCHRANE & RED RIDER Tom Cochrane & Red Rider 02Aug86 112(1) 12	178
8486. QUESTIONNAIRE Chaz Jankel 06Mar82 126(1) 14	178
8487. AFTER THE GOLD RUSH Prelude 07Dec74 94(2) 7	178
8488. THE BALLAD OF CALICO Kenny Rogers & The First Edition 05Feb72 118(2) 14	178
8489. VINTAGE DEAD Grateful Dead 31Oct70 127(1) 10	178
8490. SEQUENCER Synergy 26Jun76 144(4) 11	178
8491. STOP! STOP! STOP! The Hollies 25Feb67 91(2) 8	178
8492. ANOTHER NIGHT The Hollies 29Mar75 123(2) 10	178
8493. I DO LOVE YOU Billy Stewart 03Jul65 97(2) 10	178
8494. TOUCH DANCE Eurythmics 07Jul84 115(1) 11	177
8495. CHINATOWN Thin Lizzy 29Nov80 120(1) 10	177
8496. MOODS OF MARVIN GAYE Marvin Gaye 16Jul66 118(1) 10	177
8497. ABILENE George Hamilton IV 05Oct63 77(1) 8	177
8498. RARE PRECIOUS & BEAUTIFUL, VOLUME 2 Bee Gees 28Mar70 100(1) 8	177
8499. REPLICAS Gary Numan & Tubeway Army 15Sep79 124(1) 10	177
8500. SCUBA DIVERS Dwight Twilley 13Mar82 109(2) 11	177
8501. SHA NA NA Sha Na Na 07Aug71 122(1) 9	177
8502. FOXIE Bob James 08Oct83 106(1) 13	177
8503. REFLECTIONS The Lettermen 05Sep70 134(2) 11	177
8504. SAY YOU LOVE ME Jennifer Holliday 14Sep85 110(2) 14	177
8505. THE TURTLES PRESENT THE BATTLE OF THE BANDS The Turtles 16Nov68 128(2) 12	177
8506. BEND ME, SHAPE ME American Breed 24Feb68 99(1) 10	177
8507. RAISING FEAR Armored Saint 26Sep87 114(2) 12	177
8508. MUDDY MISSISSIPPI LINE Bobby Goldsboro 17Jan70 139(2) 11	177
8509. SISTER KATE Kate Taylor 27Mar71 88(2) 8	177
8510. KING'S RECORD SHOP Rosanne Cash 15Aug87 138(1) 20	176
8511. PLAYING TO AN AUDIENCE OF ONE David Soul 10Sep77 86(2) 7	176
8512. BORN TO WANDER 4 Seasons 29Feb64 84(1) 9	176
8513. BLOW YOUR COOL! Hoodoo Gurus 02May87 120(4) 13	176
8514. IN CONCERT Deodato/Airto 23Mar74 114(1) 9	176
8515. MIREILLE MATHIEU Mireille Mathieu 04Oct69 118(1) 8	176
8516. DOG DAYS Atlanta Rhythm Section 06Sep75 113(2) 9	176
8517. STORIES WITHOUT WORDS Spyro Gyra 26Sep87 84(1) 9	176
8518. FRIENDS Beach Boys 06Jul68 126(1) 10	176
8519. MILES DAVIS AT FILLMORE Miles Davis 12Dec70 123(2) 12	176
8520. THE JOHNNIE TAYLOR PHILOSOPHY CONTINUES Johnnie Taylor 05Jul69 109(1) 6	176
8521. IN AND OUT OF FOCUS Focus 30Jun73 104(1) 9	176
8522. THE DUCK Jackie Lee 05Feb66 85(1) 9	176
8523. SHE'S HAVING A BABY Soundtrack 12Mar88 92(1) 8	175
8524. WHAT GOES AROUND The Hollies 09Jul83 90(1) 9	175
8525. PROTECT THE INNOCENT Rachel Sweet 22Mar80 123(1) 11	175
8526. DELUSIONS First Choice 01Oct77 103(2) 8	175
8527. CAROL HENSEL'S EXERCISE AND DANCE PROGRAM, VOLUME 3 Carol Hensel 22Jan83 104(2) 12	175

Rank. Title Act Entry Peak(Pk Wks) TotWks	Scr
8528. HE WALKS BESIDE ME (FAVORITE SONGS OF FAITH AND INSPIRATION) Elvis Presley 13May78 113(2) 8	175
8529. THE WARMTH OF EDDY Eddy Arnold 01Nov69 116(1) 8	175
8530. SYNCHRO SYSTEM King Sunny Ade & His African Beats 20Aug83 91(1) 10	175
8531. I LOVE DIXIE BLUES...SO I RECORDED "LIVE" IN NEW ORLEANS Merle Haggard And The Strangers 25Aug73 126(1) 11	175
8532. TO THE POWER OF THREE 3 19Mar88 97(2) 10	175
8533. LIVE - ON TOUR IN EUROPE Billy Cobham/ George Duke Band 23Oct76 99(1) 9	175
8534. ST. JULIAN Julian Cope 04Apr87 105(2) 12	175
8535. HERE TODAY, TOMORROW NEXT WEEK! The Sugarcubes 14Oct89 70(2) 9	175
8536. STAR TREK III - THE SEARCH FOR SPOCK Soundtrack 23Jun84 82(2) 8	175
8537. CROSSROADS Ry Cooder 10May86 85(3) 9	175
8538. THE APPLE TREE Original Cast 17Dec66 113(1) 9	175
8539. KEEPING IN TOUCH Anne Murray 02Oct76 96(4) 6	175
8540. BURNT LIPS Leo Kottke 02Sep78 143(2) 12	175
8541. AGAINST THE GRAIN Phoebe Snow 28Oct78 100(1) 7	175
8542. RAGING SLAB Raging Slab 28Oct89 113(1) 15	174
8543. INSTINCT Iggy Pop 23Jul88 110(2) 12	174
8544. APPLES, PEACHES, PUMPKIN PIE Jay And The Techniques 28Oct67 129(1) 13	174
8545. SEAMLESS The Nylons 29Mar86 133(1) 16	174
8546. LEO KOTTKE Leo Kottke 29Jan77 107(1) 9	174
8547. ROMEO'S ESCAPE Dave Alvin 26Sep87 116(1) 13	174
8548. PATTON Soundtrack 22May71 117(2) 8	174
8549. CONTRARY TO ORDINARY Jerry Jeff Walker 01Jul78 111(1) 9	174
8550. HOW TO BE A JEWISH MOTHER Gertrude Berg 17Jul65 131(1) 12	174
8551. HALF AND HALF Vicki Sue Robinson 11Feb78 110(1) 9	174
8552. DR. HOOK/GREATEST HITS Dr. Hook 20Dec80 142(3) 12	174
8553. TRUE LOVE Crystal Gayle 04Dec82 120(1) 12	174
8554. ANNIE'S CHRISTMAS No Artist 20Nov82 96(4) 9	174
8555. MARY WELLS SINGS MY GUY Mary Wells 25Jul64 111(1) 12	174
8556. NO PAROLE FROM ROCK 'N' ROLL Alcatrazz 07Jan84 128(1) 18	174
8557. CHECKERED FLAG Dick Dale and The Del-Tones 14Dec63 106(1) 11	174
8558. I TOUCHED A DREAM The Dells 30Aug80 137(1) 12	174
8559. THE BEST OF PERCY SLEDGE Percy Sledge 01Mar69 133(1) 11	174
8560. UPLIFT MOFO PARTY PLAN Red Hot Chili Peppers 21Nov87 148(1) 18	174
8561. PAT METHENY GROUP Pat Metheny Group 26Aug78 123(1) 12	174
8562. CAN'T LOOK AWAY Trevor Rabin 19Aug89 111(3) 10	174
8563. B.J. THOMAS B.J. Thomas 27Aug77 114(1) 12	174
8564. THE SING-ALONG WORLD OF TRINI LOPEZ Trini Lopez 18Dec65 101(1) 10	174
8565. NIGHTFLIGHT TO VENUS Boney M 02Sep78 134(2) 10	174

Rank. Title Act Entry Peak(Pk Wks) TotWks	Scr
8566. THE HANDSOME DEVILS Hello People 30Nov74 145(2) 13	174
8567. COMMODORES 13 Commodores 01Oct83 103(1) 11	173
8568. WHITE KNUCKLE RIDE Duke Jupiter 02Jun84 122(1) 12	173
8569. TIME CHANGES Dave Brubeck Quartet 18Apr64 81(1) 9	173
8570. DIMENSION "3" Enoch Light & The Light Brigade 30May64 78(1) 9	173
8571. SONGS FROM THE FILM Tommy Keene 29Mar86 148(2) 17	173
8572. MASK Roger Glover 16Jun84 101(1) 12	173
8573. SOUL LIMBO Booker T. & The MG's 19Oct68 127(1) 9	173
8574. NICK LOWE AND HIS COWBOY OUTFIT Nick Lowe And His Cowboy Outfit 23Jun84 113(1) 12	173
8575. GOIN' COCONUTS Donny & Marie Osmond 11Nov78 98(1) 8	173
8576. WARM LEATHERETTE Grace Jones 21Jun80 132(1) 10	173
8577. HOLD YOUR HORSES First Choice 31Mar79 135(1) 12	173
8578. LIVE! Jr. Walker & The All Stars 07Oct67 119(2) 11	173
8579. FLEX Lene Lovich 08Mar80 94(1) 8	173
8580. MY SWEET SUMMER SUITE Love Unlimited Orchestra 30Oct76 123(2) 8	173
8581. CHARLIE SEXTON Charlie Sexton 18Feb89 104(1) 9	173
8582. SCARLETT & BLACK Scarlett & Black 19Mar88 107(2) 11	173
8583. WESTERN UNION Five Americans 08Jul67 121(1) 10	173
8584. CHERRY HILL PARK Billy Joe Royal 03Jan70 100(1) 9	173
8585. MR. MUSIC HEAD Adrian Belew 22Jul89 114(1) 11	173
8586. WILD IS THE WIND Nina Simone 05Nov66 110(1) 9	173
8587. KEEP THE FAITH, BABY! Adam Clayton Powell 25Feb67 112(1) 9	173
8588. HOPE Klaatu 15Oct77 83(1) 7	173
8589. SUPER OLDIES/VOL. 3 Various Artists 29Jun68 130(1) 9	173
8590. MORE I CANNOT WISH YOU Ed Ames 05Nov66 90(1) 7	172
8591. JINGLE JANGLE The Archies 03Jan70 125(2) 10	172
8592. DANGEROUS ACQUAINTANCES Marianne Faithfull 17Oct81 104(1) 9	172
8593. PICK HITS OF THE RADIO GOOD GUYS Various Artists 18Jan64 80(2) 8	172
8594. MY ELUSIVE DREAMS Bobby Vinton 11Apr70 90(2) 6	172
8595. GENE PITNEY'S BIG SIXTEEN Gene Pitney 04Apr64 87(1) 9	172
8596. FLIP-FLOP Guadalcanal Diary 25Mar89 132(2) 13	172
8597. BILLY & THE BEATERS Billy Vera & The Beaters 16May81 118(1) 10	172
8598. DOWN HOMERS Danny Davis And The Nashville Brass 31Oct70 140(1) 12	172
8599. THE KIDS FROM "FAME" LIVE! Kids From Fame 26Mar83 98(1) 11	172
8600. KINGS OF THE SUN Kings Of The Sun 30Apr88 136(1) 16	172
8601. DEAR WORLD Original Cast 05Apr69 128(2) 8	172
8602. A CIRCLE FILLED WITH LOVE Sons Of Champlin 05Jun76 117(1) 10	172
8603. GOLDEN HITS/THE BEST OF LAWRENCE WELK Lawrence Welk 14Oct67 130(1) 12	172

Rank. Title Act Entry Peak(Pk Wks) TotWks	Scr
8604. AMERICA'S GREATEST HERO Joey Scarbury 22Aug81 104(2) 9	172
8605. HERE'S MY LOVE Linda Clifford 01Dec79 117(2) 9	172
8606. LONE RHINO Adrian Belew 24Jul82 82(2) 9	172
8607. LOADING ZONE Roy Buchanan 18Jun77 105(2) 8	172
8608. ANGEL STATION Manfred Mann's Earth Band 12May79 144(1) 13	172
8609. WHAT PRICE PARADISE China Crisis 07Mar87 114(2) 12	172
8610. GET OUT OF MY ROOM Cheech & Chong 12Oct85 71(2) 11	171
8611. THE DELTA SWEETE Bobbie Gentry 23Mar68 132(1) 12	171
8612. WOMAN, WOMAN Robert Goulet 14Sep68 162(2) 15	171
8613. MONA BONE JAKON Cat Stevens 20Mar71 164(1) 16	171
8614. SMASH YOUR HEAD AGAINST THE WALL John Entwistle 23Oct71 126(2) 9	171
8615. BRIAN'S SONG THEMES & VARIATIONS Michel Legrand 11Mar72 127(2) 10	171
8616. SIMPLE MINDS LIVE: IN THE CITY OF LIGHT Simple Minds 18Jul87 96(2) 10	171
8617. BED OF ROSE'S Statler Brothers 30Jan71 126(1) 11	171
8618. 14 KARAT Fatback 01Nov80 91(1) 7	171
8619. 25TH ANNIVERSARY The Temptations 17May86 140(2) 16	171
8620. OUR DAY WILL COME Frankie Valli 13Dec75 107(2) 8	171
8621. 15 GREAT HITS The Kingsmen 20Aug66 87(1) 8	171
8622. HAMLET Original Cast 15Aug64 128(1) 13	171
8623. CLUTCHING AT STRAWS Marillion 11Jul87 103(2) 11	171
8624. CRY Ronnie Dove 04Mar67 121(1) 12	171
8625. SOUL SURVIVOR Al Green 02May87 131(1) 14	171
8626. COMIN' THRU Quicksilver Messenger Service 06May72 134(1) 10	171
8627. SCISSORS CUT Art Garfunkel 12Sep81 113(1) 8	171
8628. PROCESSION Weather Report 19Mar83 96(2) 10	171
8629. STAIRCASE/HOURGLASS/SUNDIAL/SAND Keith Jarrett 06Aug77 141(1) 12	170
8630. OPEN Blues Image 25Apr70 147(2) 13	170
8631. HERE TO STAY Neal Schon & Jan Hammer 05Feb83 122(4) 12	170
8632. TOGETHER Anne Murray 06Dec75 142(1) 11	170
8633. ERUPTION Eruption 01Apr78 133(1) 13	170
8634. DUTCH MASTERS - A SELECTION OF THEIR FINEST RECORDINGS 1969-1973 Focus 01Mar75 120(2) 9	170
8635. THE FLYING LIZARDS Flying Lizards 23Feb80 99(1) 8	170
8636. POLICY Martha Davis 14Nov87 127(1) 13	170
8637. THE BEST OF THE 4 TOPS Four Tops 12May73 103(1) 9	170
8638. FIRST CUCKOO Eumir Deodato 06Sep75 110(1) 9	170
8639. BURNING THE BALLROOM DOWN Amazing Rhythm Aces 15Apr78 116(2) 9	170
8640. CITY IN THE SKY Staple Singers 14Sep74 125(1) 9	169
8641. TEQUILA MOCKINGBIRD Ramsey Lewis 24Dec77 111(2) 9	169

Rank. Title Act Entry Peak(Pk Wks) TotWks	Scr
8642. **STREET LIFE-20 GREAT HITS** Bryan Ferry/Roxy Music 26Aug89 100(1) 11	169
8643. **LIFELINE** Pablo Cruise 17Apr76 139(2) 13	169
8644. **FOUL PLAY** Soundtrack 02Sep78 102(2) 7	169
8645. **BREAD** Bread 18Oct69 127(1) 9	169
8646. **ODETTA SINGS FOLK SONGS** Odetta 28Sep63 75(1) 8	169
8647. **MAGNIFICENT MOVIE THEMES** Enoch Light & The Light Brigade 11Sep65 105(1) 10	169
8648. **YOU CAN'T STOP ROCK 'N' ROLL** Twisted Sister 27Aug83 130(1) 14	169
8649. **THE BEST OF THE 50 GUITARS OF TOMMY GARRETT** 50 Guitars of Tommy Garrett 03May69 147(1) 9	169
8650. **TO BE WITH YOU** Tony Orlando & Dawn 20Mar76 94(1) 6	169
8651. **THE LEAGUE OF GENTLEMEN** Robert Fripp 04Apr81 90(2) 7	169
8652. **QUATRO** Suzi Quatro 05Oct74 126(1) 10	169
8653. **SUE SAAD AND THE NEXT** Sue Saad And The Next 01Mar80 131(1) 12	169
8654. **PORGY & BESS** Ray Charles And Cleo Laine 04Dec76 138(3) 11	169
8655. **SAMMY JOHNS** Sammy Johns 29Mar75 148(1) 12	169
8656. **ROUGH NIGHT IN JERICHO** Dreams So Real 26Nov88 150(1) 18	169
8657. **AN OLD TIME CHRISTMAS** Randy Travis 02Dec89 70(1) 7	169
8658. **AN EVENING WITH HERBIE HANCOCK AND CHICK COREA** Herbie Hancock And Chick Corea 31Mar79 100(1) 8	169
8659. **TALES OF THE UNEXPECTED** Frank Marino And Mahogany Rush 12May79 129(1) 10	169
8660. **THEY DON'T MAKE THEM LIKE THEY USED TO** Kenny Rogers 13Dec86 137(1) 15	169
8661. **NINA SIMONE IN CONCERT** Nina Simone 19Sep64 102(1) 11	168
8662. **NASHVILLE BY CARR** Vikki Carr 09May70 111(1) 8	168
8663. **ZENO** Zeno 10May86 107(2) 10	168
8664. **LOVE CONFESSIONS** Miki Howard 20Feb88 145(2) 16	168
8665. **WIZARD ISLAND** Jeff Lorber Fusion 31May80 123(1) 12	168
8666. **A BLACK & WHITE NIGHT: LIVE** Roy Orbison and Friends 02Dec89 123(4) 12	168
8667. **FIGHT TO SURVIVE** White Lion 16Apr88 151(1) 14	168
8668. **SHOCKER** Soundtrack 18Nov89 97(2) 12	168
8669. **LOOKIN' BACK** 4 Seasons 17Dec66 107(1) 9	168
8670. **THE OTHER ONE** Bob Welch 01Dec79 105(3) 8	168
8671. **QUIET RIOT** Quiet Riot 19Nov88 119(2) 11	168
8672. **LOS HOMBRES MALO** The Outlaws 01May82 77(1) 9	168
8673. **INTRODUCING LOBO** Lobo 05Jun71 163(1) 15	168
8674. **AFTER DARK** Ray Parker Jr. 10Oct87 86(2) 9	168
8675. **THIN RED LINE** The Cretones 29Mar80 125(1) 10	167
8676. **SOUL BAG** Mongo Santamaria 10Aug68 171(2) 18	167
8677. **STAGE DOLLS** Stage Dolls 19Aug89 118(1) 12	167
8678. **REINFORCEMENTS** Brian Auger's Oblivion Express 11Oct75 115(1) 8	167
8679. **DANCE ACROSS THE FLOOR** Jimmy 'Bo' Horne 01Jul78 122(1) 10	167
8680. **THE EARTH** San Sebastian Strings 23Sep67 115(1) 13	167
8681. **YO! BUM RUSH THE SHOW** Public Enemy 23Jan88 125(1) 12	167
8682. **WHAT IF** Tommy Shaw 26Oct85 87(2) 9	167
8683. **TURN OF THE SCREW** Dirty Looks 19Aug89 118(1) 11	167
8684. **TRANS-EUROPE EXPRESS** Kraftwerk 16Apr77 119(1) 10	167
8685. **MOTHER WIT** Betty Wright 23Apr88 127(2) 13	167
8686. **LOVE IS BLUE** Lawrence Welk 06Apr68 130(1) 12	167
8687. **WORKBOOK** Bob Mould 27May89 127(1) 14	167
8688. **WE ARE ONE** Mandrill 12Nov77 124(1) 10	167
8689. **NO FUEL LEFT FOR THE PILGRIMS** Disneyland After Dark 30Sep89 116(1) 11	167
8690. **TIMOTHY B.** Timothy B. Schmit 03Oct87 106(2) 11	167
8691. **MASS IN F MINOR** Electric Prunes 06Jan68 135(2) 13	166
8692. **THE BEST OF HERMAN'S HERMITS, VOLUME III** Herman's Hermits 13Jan68 102(1) 8	166
8693. **LENA HORNE: THE LADY AND HER MUSIC (ORIGINAL CAST)** Lena Horne 26Sep81 112(2) 9	166
8694. **FUNKY SERENITY** Ramsey Lewis 03Mar73 117(1) 10	166
8695. **QUIET NIGHTS** Miles Davis 11Apr64 93(2) 9	166
8696. **THE FIRST TIME EVER (I SAW YOUR FACE)** Vikki Carr 24Jun72 146(1) 12	166
8697. **GREATEST HITS** KC And The Sunshine Band 22Mar80 132(2) 11	166
8698. **THE NATCH'L BLUES** Taj Mahal 22Feb69 160(1) 14	166
8699. **TOUCH AND GONE** Gary Wright 10Dec77 117(2) 9	166
8700. **SATIN SHEETS** Jeanne Pruett 07Jul73 122(1) 9	166
8701. **BIZET: CARMEN** Maria Callas 27Feb65 87(2) 8	166
8702. **LOVE LIFE** Brenda Russell 11Apr81 107(2) 8	166
8703. **BIG HITS BY BURT BACHARACH... HAL DAVID...BOB DYLAN...** 4 Seasons 18Dec65 106(1) 10	166
8704. **I WANNA BE FREE** Loretta Lynn 26Jun71 110(1) 7	166
8705. **ATTENTION SHOPPERS!** Starz 11Feb78 105(1) 9	166
8706. **STARLIGHT DANCER** Kayak 04Mar78 117(1) 9	166
8707. **YOUNG FRANKENSTEIN** Soundtrack 22Mar75 128(3) 8	166
8708. **ALIVE AND SCREAMIN'** Krokus 22Nov86 97(2) 12	166
8709. **BUCKET** Jimmy Smith 12Nov66 121(1) 9	166
8710. **EARLY FLIGHT** Jefferson Airplane 04May74 110(1) 8	166
8711. **INDECENT EXPOSURE (SOME OF THE BEST OF GEORGE CARLIN)** George Carlin 06Jan79 112(1) 8	166
8712. **RANK** The Smiths 01Oct88 77(2) 8	166
8713. **I GOT LUCKY** Elvis Presley 27Nov71 104(1) 8	165
8714. **III WISHES** Shooting Star 07Aug82 82(2) 9	165
8715. **AMY HOLLAND** Amy Holland 30Aug80 146(1) 14	165
8716. **MYSTIC MAN** Peter Tosh 04Aug79 123(1) 10	165
8717. **GLEN TRAVIS CAMPBELL** Glen Campbell 25Nov72 148(3) 13	165
8718. **RODNEY CROWELL** Rodney Crowell 03Oct81 105(1) 8	165
8719. **HEART LIKE A GUN** Fiona 25Nov89 150(1) 16	165
8720. **JOHN FITZGERALD KENNEDY...AS WE REMEMBER HIM (NARRATED BY CHARTLES KURALT)** John Fitzgerald Kennedy 11Dec65 93(1) 8	165
8721. **DREAMS** Allman Brothers Band 15Jul89 103(2) 11	165
8722. **AEROBIC DANCING** Barbara Ann Auer 20Jun81 145(2) 15	165
8723. **THE DEED IS DONE** Molly Hatchet 24Nov84 117(2) 13	165
8724. **HAPPENING 'LIVE!'** The Outsiders 26Aug67 103(2) 10	164
8725. **DISCO BOOGIE** Various Artists 24Dec77 115(2) 11	164
8726. **WALL TO WALL** René & Angela 22Aug81 100(1) 8	164
8727. **ROMEO KNIGHT** Boogie Boys 19Mar88 117(2) 11	164
8728. **ROUGH DIAMOND** Rough Diamond 07May77 103(2) 8	164
8729. **THE DOOBIE BROTHERS FAREWELL TOUR** Doobie Brothers 23Jul83 79(1) 9	164
8730. **ME, MYSELF AND I** Cheryl Pepsii Riley 12Nov88 128(2) 11	164
8731. **NATURAL ACT** Kris Kristofferson & Rita Coolidge 03Feb79 106(2) 9	164
8732. **ROLL OUT THE RED CARPET FOR BUCK OWENS AND HIS BUCKAROOS** Buck Owens 12Mar66 106(1) 10	164
8733. **THE BROOKLYN, BRONX & QUEENS BAND** Brooklyn, Bronx & Queens Band 29Aug81 109(1) 9	164
8734. **AN EVENING WITH GROUCHO** Groucho Marx 25Nov72 160(1) 15	164
8735. **ELECTRIC DREAMS** Soundtrack 01Sep84 94(2) 9	164
8736. **MAGNETIC HEAVEN** Wax 26Apr86 101(2) 11	164
8737. **TAKE A RIDE...........** Mitch Ryder And The Detroit Wheels 05Mar66 78(1) 7	164
8738. **MOMENTS** Boz Scaggs 17Apr71 124(2) 9	163
8739. **SENSE OF PURPOSE** Third World 13Apr85 119(3) 11	163
8740. **SIMPLICITY** Tim Curry 29Aug81 112(2) 8	163
8741. **CRY** Lynn Anderson 08Apr72 114(1) 9	163
8742. **HAWAII TATTOO** The Waikikis 16Jan65 93(1) 9	163
8743. **BOB McGRATH FROM SESAME STREET** Bob McGrath 15Aug70 126(1) 11	163
8744. **SUITE FOR SUSAN MOORE AND DAMION-WE ARE-ONE, ONE, ALL IN ONE** Tim Hardin 26Apr69 129(1) 8	163
8745. **MERRIMACK COUNTY** Tom Rush 29Apr72 128(1) 10	163
8746. **VISITORS** Automatic Man 08Oct77 109(1) 8	163
8747. **WAVE** Antonio Carlos Jobim 13Jan68 114(1) 11	163
8748. **BREAKING THE CHAINS** Dokken 15Oct83 136(1) 13	163
8749. **CONTAGIOUS** Bar-Kays 07Nov87 110(2) 14	163
8750. **INTO THE PURPLE VALLEY** Ry Cooder 12Feb72 113(1) 8	163
8751. **THE BEST OF THE RIGHTEOUS BROTHERS** Righteous Brothers 21May66 130(2) 11	163
8752. **REFLECTIONS** 5th Dimension 06Nov71 112(2) 7	163

Rank. Title Act Entry Peak(Pk Wks) TotWks	Scr
8753. DESITIVELY BONNAROO Dr. John 04May74 105(1) 8	163
8754. PEACE ON YOU Roger McGuinn 28Sep74 92(2) 6	163
8755. BENSON & FARRELL George Benson & Joe Farrell 30Oct76 100(1) 8	162
8756. SOMETHIN'S HAPPENING Peter Frampton 30Mar74 125(1) 9	162
8757. LIFE Gladys Knight And The Pips 23Mar85 126(2) 12	162
8758. THE MAGNIFICENT MEN "LIVE!" Magnificent Men 29Jul67 89(1) 9	162
8759. GET IT ON... Pacific Gas And Electric 01Feb69 159(1) 12	162
8760. JEAN CARN Jean Carn 19Feb77 122(1) 10	162
8761. FUTURE BOUND Tavares 13May78 115(2) 8	162
8762. RADIO ETHIOPIA Patti Smith Group 27Nov76 122(1) 8	162
8763. LOVE THEME FROM "ROMEO & JULIET" Roger Williams 09Aug69 145(1) 10	162
8764. SWEET REVENGE John Prine 24Nov73 135(1) 11	162
8765. STILLNESS Sergio Mendes & Brasil '66 09Jan71 130(1) 9	162
8766. TIM MOORE Tim Moore 12Oct74 119(2) 9	162
8767. SONGS OF LOVE AND HATE Leonard Cohen 01May71 145(1) 11	162
8768. RITA COOLIDGE/GREATEST HITS Rita Coolidge 14Feb81 107(2) 8	162
8769. ROACHFORD Roachford 20May89 109(2) 12	162
8770. THE LETTERMEN LOOK AT LOVE The Lettermen 20Jun64 94(2) 10	162
8771. NEW YORK-LONDON-PARIS-MUNICH M 22Dec79 79(2) 8	162
8772. EL CHICANO El Chicano 04Aug73 162(1) 16	162
8773. A TASTE OF YESTERDAY'S WINE Merle Haggard/George Jones 25Sep82 123(4) 12	162
8774. MOTHER NATURE'S SON Ramsey Lewis 29Mar69 156(2) 14	162
8775. NINE LIVES Bonnie Raitt 30Aug86 115(1) 11	162
8776. WEIRD SCIENCE Soundtrack 31Aug85 105(2) 11	162
8777. SHIRLEY BASSEY BELTS THE BEST! Shirley Bassey 24Apr65 85(1) 9	161
8778. DAVID PORTER...INTO A REAL THING David Porter 30Jan71 104(1) 9	161
8779. LAND OF THE MIDNIGHT SUN Al Di Meola 27Mar76 129(2) 10	161
8780. FINDER OF LOST LOVES Dionne Warwick 02Mar85 106(2) 11	161
8781. PAUL ANKA GOLD Paul Anka 14Dec74 125(1) 9	161
8782. HELP ME MAKE IT THROUGH THE NIGHT Jim Nabors 24Jul71 122(1) 10	161
8783. THE ISLEYS LIVE Isley Brothers 17Mar73 139(1) 13	161
8784. I BELIEVE IN MUSIC Mac Davis 25Dec71 160(1) 17	161
8785. KNIGHT TIME Gladys Knight And The Pips 16Mar74 139(1) 11	161
8786. TWILLEY Dwight Twilley 24Mar79 113(2) 9	161
8787. DECISIONS The Winans 26Sep87 109(1) 11	161
8788. LYDIA Cold Blood 10Aug74 126(1) 8	161
8789. CHERYL LADD Cheryl Ladd 12Aug78 129(2) 11	161
8790. YOU ARE WHAT YOU IS Frank Zappa 03Oct81 93(1) 7	161
8791. TOUCH Gladys Knight And The Pips 05Sep81 109(1) 8	161
8792. MILESTONES SRC 14Jun69 134(1) 9	161
8793. CUNNING STUNTS Caravan 23Aug75 124(1) 10	161
8794. THE OFFICIAL "LIVE" GENTLE GIANT - PLAYING THE FOOL Gentle Giant 19Feb77 89(1) 6	160
8795. REUNION Peter, Paul & Mary 21Oct78 106(1) 7	160
8796. LIVE WIRE/BLUES POWER Albert King 16Nov68 150(1) 10	160
8797. EVERYTHING IS A-OK! The Astronauts 08Feb64 100(1) 9	160
8798. MAGNIFICENT MADNESS John Klemmer 09Aug80 146(1) 11	160
8799. BETTER DAYS The Blackbyrds 17Jan81 133(1) 11	160
8800. THE BEST OF EDDIE RABBITT Eddie Rabbitt 24Nov79 151(1) 12	160
8801. REACHING OUT Menudo 10Mar84 108(2) 12	160
8802. PAST, PRESENT AND FUTURE Al Stewart 01Jun74 133(2) 14	160
8803. LEVON HELM & THE RCO ALL-STARS Levon Helm 19Nov77 142(1) 10	160
8804. NOBODY'S PERFECT Deep Purple 23Jul88 105(2) 9	160
8805. THE NEW LOOK Fontella Bass 26Feb66 93(1) 8	160
8806. H.A.P.P.Y. RADIO Edwin Starr 28Jul79 115(2) 8	160
8807. THE GREAT YEARS Johnny Mathis 01Aug64 88(1) 10	160
8808. GET ME TO THE COUNTRY McKendree Spring 03May75 118(2) 8	160
8809. UNIVERSAL RHYTHM Ralph MacDonald 13Oct84 108(2) 10	160
8810. FRANKS WILD YEARS Tom Waits 26Sep87 115(2) 10	159
8811. TROPICO Gato Barbieri 29Jul78 96(1) 7	159
8812. OUT HERE ON MY OWN Lamont Dozier 26Jan74 136(1) 13	159
8813. THE KARATE KID Soundtrack 21Jul84 114(2) 12	159
8814. KIND OF A DRAG The Buckinghams 25Mar67 109(1) 8	159
8815. DRUMS A GO-GO Sandy Nelson 02Oct65 118(1) 11	159
8816. MACHINE GUN Commodores 24Aug74 138(1) 9	159
8817. SCROOGED Soundtrack 03Dec88 93(1) 9	159
8818. I'VE GOT A REASON Richie Furay Band 07Aug76 130(1) 8	159
8819. TOO GOOD TO STOP NOW John Schneider 17Nov84 111(2) 12	159
8820. JOHN W. ANDERSON PRESENTS KASANDRA KaSandra 23Nov68 142(2) 8	159
8821. MAN IN MOTION Night Ranger 22Oct88 81(2) 8	159
8822. A 25TH ANNIVERSARY IN SHOW BUSINESS SALUTE TO RAY CHARLES Ray Charles 20Nov71 152(1) 10	159
8823. BODYHEAT James Brown 15Jan77 126(2) 10	159
8824. C.K. Chaka Khan 17Dec88 125(3) 12	159
8825. I'VE ALWAYS WANTED TO SING...NOT JUST WRITE SONGS Bunny Sigler 07Apr79 119(1) 9	159
8826. OUT OF THE SHADOWS Dave Grusin 07Aug82 88(2) 9	159
8827. 8 Madhouse 21Feb87 107(2) 11	159
8828. THE HORSE The Ventures 24Aug68 128(2) 9	159
8829. LOVE THEME FROM "THE GODFATHER" Al Martino 03Jun72 138(2) 10	159
8830. PIPPIN Original Cast 13Jan73 129(1) 10	159
8831. LADIES LOVE OUTLAWS Tom Rush 19Oct74 124(2) 9	159
8832. AFTER THE WAR Gary Moore 25Mar89 114(2) 9	158
8833. SOUTH RAMPART STREET PARADE Pete Fountain 07Sep63 91(1) 9	158
8834. BOB NEWHART FACES BOB NEWHART (FACES BOB NEWHART) Bob Newhart 29Feb64 113(1) 11	158
8835. TAKE IT OFF Chic 19Dec81 124(1) 9	158
8836. DON'T CLOSE YOUR EYES Keith Whitley 03Jun89 121(2) 14	158
8837. HEADS OR TALES Saga 22Oct83 92(1) 9	158
8838. THE JOEY HEATHERTON ALBUM Joey Heatherton 21Oct72 154(1) 13	158
8839. BLACK IS BLACK Los Bravos 12Nov66 93(1) 7	158
8840. THE JOHNNY WINTER STORY Johnny Winter 27Sep69 111(2) 6	158
8841. NATURAL AVENUE John Lodge 23Apr77 121(1) 9	158
8842. CARRIE LUCAS IN DANCELAND Carrie Lucas 19May79 119(2) 10	158
8843. BIG DREAMS IN A SMALL TOWN Restless Heart 27Aug88 114(2) 11	158
8844. EASY DOES IT Al Kooper 19Sep70 105(1) 8	158
8845. Y'ALL COME BACK SALOON Oak Ridge Boys 18Feb78 120(2) 9	158
8846. ON THE ROAD TO KINGDOM COME Harry Chapin 30Oct76 87(1) 6	157
8847. PETE'S DRAGON Soundtrack 24Dec77 131(2) 10	157
8848. KEEPIN' THE SUMMER ALIVE Beach Boys 12Apr80 75(1) 6	157
8849. DIXIE ROCK Wet Willie 08Mar75 114(1) 7	157
8850. WATCHOUT! Martha & The Vandellas 21Jan67 116(1) 8	157
8851. TAKE IT ON UP Pockets 28Oct78 85(1) 6	157
8852. BURSTING AT THE SEAMS Strawbs 28Apr73 121(1) 9	157
8853. DROP THE BOMB Trouble Funk 08May82 121(2) 14	157
8854. ATOMIC PLAYBOYS Steve Stevens Atomic Playboys 02Sep89 119(1) 12	157
8855. DON'T LOOK DOWN Ozark Mountain Daredevils 9Nov77 132(1) 10	157
8856. ONE'S ON THE WAY Loretta Lynn 08Apr72 109(1) 9	157
8857. JUST BEFORE THE BULLETS FLY Gregg Allman Band 06Aug88 117(2) 11	157
8858. BREATHLESS Camel 10Feb79 134(1) 10	157
8859. LIFE IS YOU Batdorf And Rodney 12Jul75 140(2) 10	157
8860. THE TOYS SING "A LOVER'S CONCERTO" AND "ATTACK!" The Toys 05Feb66 92(1) 8	157
8861. MACALLA Clannad 22Mar86 131(2) 12	157
8862. MILES Miles Jaye 12Dec87 125(2) 12	157
8863. COME AND GET YOURSELF SOME Leon Haywood 16Aug75 140(1) 13	156
8864. TRACY Cuff Links 06Dec69 138(1) 11	156
8865. INCREDIBLE KALEIDOSCOPE Kaleidoscope 14Jun69 139(1) 8	156
8866. FLAUNT IT Sigue Sigue Sputnik 23Aug86 96(2) 10	156
8867. A SPECIAL PART OF ME Johnny Mathis 10Mar84 157(1) 19	156

Rank. Title Act Entry Peak(Pk Wks) TotWks	Scr
8868. MARCH OF THE SAINT Armored Saint 22Dec84 138(2) 16	156
8869. PERFECT TIMING Donna Allen 04Apr87 133(1) 13	156
8870. NATURAL PROGRESSIONS Bernie Leadon-Michel Georgiades Band 20Aug77 91(1) 6	156
8871. SOUTHERN COMFORT Conway Twitty 13Feb82 144(1) 15	156
8872. SUZI QUATRO Suzi Quatro 30Mar74 142(1) 13	156
8873. SYLVAIN SYLVAIN Sylvain Sylvain 16Feb80 123(2) 8	156
8874. REGGAE Herbie Mann 17Aug74 141(2) 11	156
8875. SOMETHING TO BELIEVE IN Curtis Mayfield 26Jul80 128(2) 10	156
8876. SWING TO THE RIGHT Utopia 20Mar82 102(1) 10	156
8877. CHRISTMAS Oak Ridge Boys 04Dec82 73(2) 7	156
8878. NANCY'S GREATEST HITS Nancy Sinatra 03Oct70 99(1) 7	156
8879. BLACK GOLD Nina Simone 14Mar70 149(2) 12	156
8880. SPIDER Spider 17May80 130(1) 10	156
8881. HIDING OUT Soundtrack 05Dec87 146(2) 13	156
8882. ABOUT TIME Ten Years After 16Sep89 120(2) 10	156
8883. ONE BY ONE The Impressions 18Sep65 104(1) 9	156
8884. LIVE IN LOS ANGELES Maze Featuring Frankie Beverly 20Sep86 92(2) 11	155
8885. ANNE MURRAY / GLEN CAMPBELL Anne Murray & Glen Campbell 11Dec71 128(1) 8	155
8886. DOWN TO EARTH Stevie Wonder 28Jan67 92(1) 7	155
8887. FULL BLOOM Carol Douglas 16Jul77 139(1) 10	155
8888. GINSENG WOMAN Eric Gale 09Apr77 148(1) 12	155
8889. ABIGAIL King Diamond 11Jul87 123(1) 13	155
8890. BILLY PRESTON & SYREETA Billy Preston & Syreeta 08Aug81 127(4) 9	155
8891. LIFE GOES ON Paul Williams 02Dec72 159(1) 14	155
8892. MIRAGE Camel 30Nov74 149(2) 13	155
8893. FREE AS A BIRD Supertramp 31Oct87 101(2) 11	155
8894. THE ROSE OF ENGLAND Nick Lowe And His Cowboy Outfit 21Sep85 119(3) 12	155
8895. THE TRIAL OF BILLY JACK Soundtrack 21Dec74 130(1) 8	155
8896. MILSAP MAGIC Ronnie Milsap 05Apr80 137(2) 13	155
8897. FROM BRANCH TO BRANCH Leon Redbone 11Apr81 152(1) 11	155
8898. SUITE FOR THE SINGLE GIRL Jerry Butler 12Mar77 146(1) 11	155
8899. REPEAT-THE BEST OF JETHRO TULL, VOL. II Jethro Tull 03Dec77 94(2) 6	154
8900. "TWANGIN'" UP A STORM! Duane Eddy 05Oct63 93(1) 8	154
8901. DRIFTER Sylvia (2) 09May81 139(1) 11	154
8902. THE SECOND BROOKLYN BRIDGE Brooklyn Bridge 11Oct69 145(1) 8	154
8903. WATCH Manfred Mann's Earth Band 11Mar78 83(1) 6	154
8904. LIVE IT UP David Johansen 03Jul82 148(2) 15	154
8905. WARM AND TENDER Olivia Newton-John 02Dec89 124(2) 13	154
8906. SWEET, DELICIOUS & MARVELOUS California Raisins 08Oct88 140(1) 15	154
8907. DISTURBING THE PEACE Alcatrazz 20Apr85 145(2) 16	154
8908. THE WARRIORS Soundtrack 05May79 125(1) 8	154
8909. THE WHEEL OF HURT Margaret Whiting 18Feb67 109(1) 8	154
8910. TRUTH IS ON ITS WAY Nikki Giovanni 21Aug71 165(2) 13	154
8911. HIGH HAT Boy George 25Mar89 126(1) 11	154
8912. GREENHOUSE Leo Kottke 12Feb72 127(2) 9	154
8913. UNDER THE INFLUENCE Overkill 30Jul88 142(1) 13	154
8914. SAYIN' SOMETHIN' Righteous Brothers 08Apr67 155(2) 15	154
8915. 8 FOR THE 80'S Webster Lewis 15Mar80 114(1) 9	154
8916. N.E.W.S. Golden Earring 17Mar84 107(1) 9	154
8917. LOOSEN UP NATURALLY Sons Of Champlin 14Jun69 137(1) 9	154
8918. SPELLBOUND Joe Sample 15Apr89 129(1) 14	154
8919. A CHRISTMAS ALBUM Barbra Streisand 19Dec81 108(2) 9	154
8920. TRUE DEMOCRACY Steel Pulse 17Jul82 120(2) 13	154
8921. TRAPPED BY A THING CALLED LOVE Denise LaSalle 05Feb72 120(1) 9	154
8922. LONDON 0 HULL 4 The Housemartins 07Feb87 124(2) 14	153
8923. LOCKED IN Wishbone Ash 27Mar76 136(1) 9	153
8924. HEAVY CREAM Cream 28Oct72 135(1) 10	153
8925. LULU Lulu 26Sep81 126(1) 10	153
8926. SKYBIRD Tony Orlando & Dawn 01Nov75 93(2) 6	153
8927. NEVER BUY TEXAS FROM A COWBOY Brides Of Funkenstein 16Feb80 93(2) 7	153
8928. OFF THE BEATLE TRACK George Martin 05Sep64 111(2) 10	153
8929. AIRWAVES Badfinger 24Mar79 125(1) 8	153
8930. NUMBER 1 HITS, VOL. #1 Billy Vaughn And His Orchestra 09Nov63 94(1) 8	153
8931. SONG FOR MY FATHER (CANTIGA PARA MEU PAI) Horace Silver Quintet 12Jun65 95(1) 10	153
8932. ONE TO ONE Carole King 03Apr82 119(3) 11	153
8933. WILD FRONTIER Gary Moore 16May87 139(1) 15	153
8934. MANORISMS Wet Willie 21Jan78 118(1) 8	153
8935. LIVING WITH THE ANIMALS Mother Earth 22Feb69 144(1) 8	153
8936. WHISPER TAMES THE LION Drivin' N' Cryin' 02Apr88 130(2) 12	153
8937. THE ANIMALS ON TOUR The Animals 20Mar65 99(1) 9	153
8938. ASCENDING Orpheus 28Sep68 159(1) 12	153
8939. NILS LOFGREN Nils Lofgren 22Mar75 141(1) 9	152
8940. E-S-P Bee Gees 17Oct87 96(2) 9	152
8941. PURE PLEASURE Dynamic Superiors 09Aug75 130(1) 10	152
8942. GROWIN' UP TOO FAST Billy Rankin 24Mar84 119(1) 11	152
8943. NOT INSANE OR ANYTHING YOU WANT TO Firesign Theatre 25Nov72 115(2) 8	152
8944. PARTING SHOULD BE PAINLESS Roger Daltrey 17Mar84 102(2) 9	152
8945. GIVE 'EM ENOUGH ROPE The Clash 24Feb79 128(1) 10	152
8946. SLEEPING GYPSY Michael Franks 19Feb77 119(1) 9	152
8947. ALL IS FORGIVEN Red Siren 08Apr89 124(1) 12	152
8948. EYES OF LAURA MARS Soundtrack 12Aug78 124(2) 9	152
8949. MONDO BONGO Boomtown Rats 21Feb81 116(2) 8	152
8950. THE SOUTH'S GREATEST HITS Various Artists 30Jul77 142(2) 11	152
8951. MISSING WHITE HOUSE TAPES National Lampoon 16Mar74 118(1) 8	152
8952. EARTHBOUND 5th Dimension 23Aug75 136(1) 8	152
8953. GOLDEN YEARS David Bowie 27Aug83 99(1) 9	152
8954. CARRY ON Bobby Caldwell 17Apr82 133(1) 13	152
8955. HOMELESS BROTHER Don McLean 23Nov74 120(2) 8	152
8956. UP THE YELLOW BRICK ROAD Salsoul Orchestra 25Mar78 117(1) 8	152
8957. THE REAL DONOVAN Donovan 01Oct66 96(1) 7	152
8958. LIVE! IN LAS VEGAS Sandy Nelson 21Nov64 122(2) 11	152
8959. THE BEST OF JOAN C. BAEZ Joan Baez 17Dec77 121(2) 8	152
8960. SAFETY ZONE Bobby Womack 17Jan76 147(1) 11	152
8961. IN FULL EFFECT Mantronix 09Apr88 108(2) 8	152
8962. SOLID BRASS Herb Alpert & The Tijuana Brass 17Jun72 135(1) 9	151
8963. THE NIGHT IS STILL YOUNG Sha Na Na 01Jul72 156(1) 14	151
8964. LONG STROKE ADC Band 16Dec78 139(2) 9	151
8965. HISTORY OF BRITISH ROCK, VOLUME 3 Various Artists 22Nov75 145(3) 10	151
8966. FORTUNE 410 Donnie Iris 02Jul83 127(1) 12	151
8967. OHIO EXPRESS Ohio Express 06Jul68 126(2) 11	151
8968. ARCHITECTURE AND MORALITY Orchestral Manoeuvres In The Dark 06Feb82 144(4) 12	151
8969. THE BEST OF THE SPINNERS Spinners 12May73 124(1) 10	151
8970. ITALIAN X RAYS Steve Miller Band 10Nov84 101(2) 10	151
8971. LONEWOLF Michael Martin Murphey 01Apr78 99(2) 6	151
8972. THE BEST OF THE ANDREWS SISTERS Andrews Sisters 06Oct73 126(1) 9	151
8973. HOMER LOUIS RANDOLPH, III Boots Randolph 12Jun71 141(1) 11	151
8974. BANDIT IN A BATHING SUIT David Bromberg 17Jun78 130(1) 9	151
8975. OTHER SIDE OF ABBEY ROAD George Benson 24Jul76 125(1) 8	151
8976. MAGIC IN YOUR EYES Earl Klugh 01Jul78 139(2) 9	151
8977. CHUCK BERRY'S GOLDEN DECADE, VOL. 2 Chuck Berry 24Feb73 110(1) 8	151
8978. I'D LIKE TO TEACH THE WORLD TO SING Ray Conniff & His Orchestra & Chorus 12Feb72 138(1) 11	151
8979. NOEL Noel 22Oct88 126(1) 13	151
8980. LIVE AT THE WHISKY A GO GO Herbie Mann 22Nov69 139(1) 10	150
8981. TEEVEE TOONS - THE COMMERCIALS Various Artists 10Jun89 159(1) 18	150
8982. A WOMAN'S POINT OF VIEW Shirley Murdock 23Jul88 137(1) 15	150
8983. JOE COCKER'S GREATEST HITS Joe Cocker 10Dec77 114(2) 8	150
8984. DAVID OLIVER David Oliver 27May78 128(1) 8	150

Rank. Title Act	Entry Peak(Pk Wks) TotWks	Scr
8985. E-MAN GROOVIN' Jimmy Castor Bunch	25Sep76 132(1) 9	150
8986. THE BEST OF THE BEST OF MERLE HAGGARD Merle Haggard	07Oct72 137(1) 9	150
8987. BURLAP & SATIN Dolly Parton	04Jun83 127(1) 11	150
8988. FREE Concrete Blonde	13May89 148(1) 18	150
8989. STONEHENGE Richie Havens	10Jan70 155(1) 14	150
8990. WHERE CAN YOU GO FOR A BROKEN HEART? George Maharis	14Sep63 77(1) 7	150
8991. PHENIX Cannonball Adderley	20Sep75 121(2) 8	150
8992. THE SOUND OF THE WONDERFUL TYMES The Tymes	21Dec63 117(1) 10	150
8993. LEAVE HOME The Ramones	12Feb77 148(1) 10	150
8994. A BRAZILIAN LOVE AFFAIR George Duke	31May80 119(1) 9	150
8995. ON FIRE T-Connection	21Jan78 139(1) 11	150
8996. SHADES J.J. Cale	28Feb81 110(1) 7	150
8997. THE SECOND LATIN ALBUM Trini Lopez	27Aug66 110(1) 8	150
8998. TONY SINGS THE GREAT HITS OF TODAY! Tony Bennett	28Feb70 144(1) 11	150
8999. THE SENSITIVE SOUND OF DIONNE WARWICK Dionne Warwick	06Mar65 107(1) 9	149
9000. SONG OF SEVEN Jon Anderson	06Dec80 143(1) 11	149
9001. AFRICANISM Kongas	18Mar78 120(2) 8	149
9002. OGDENS' NUT GONE FLAKE Small Faces	21Sep68 159(1) 15	149
9003. I'M DOIN' FINE NOW New York City	16Jun73 122(1) 10	149
9004. KING KONG Soundtrack	08Jan77 123(2) 8	149
9005. TANYA TUCKER Tanya Tucker	17May75 113(2) 7	149
9006. THE BITTEREST PILL (I EVER HAD TO SWALLOW) The Jam	27Nov82 135(2) 14	149
9007. FOR YOUR LOVE Peaches & Herb	02Sep67 135(1) 12	149
9008. THE EVERLOVIN' SOUL OF ROY CLARK Roy Clark	03Jan70 129(1) 9	149
9009. DISCOVER Gene Loves Jezebel	18Oct86 155(2) 19	149
9010. LOST IN THE FIFTIES TONIGHT Ronnie Milsap	03May86 121(2) 12	149
9011. TEAR ME APART Tanya Tucker	01Dec79 121(3) 8	149
9012. L Steve Hillage	15Jan77 130(1) 9	149
9013. TANE CAIN Tane Cain	11Sep82 121(2) 10	149
9014. COME DANCE TO THE HITS Sammy Kaye And His Orchestra	30May64 97(1) 9	149
9015. BORN 2B BLUE Steve Miller	08Oct88 108(2) 10	149
9016. 2000 AND THIRTEEN Carl Reiner & Mel Brooks	24Nov73 150(1) 12	149
9017. THE KAEMPFERT TOUCH Bert Kaempfert And His Orchestra	28Mar70 87(1) 7	149
9018. WHAT'S UP, TIGER LILY? Lovin' Spoonful	24Sep66 126(2) 9	148
9019. UM, UM, UM, UM, UM, UM/THE BEST OF MAJOR LANCE Major Lance	28Mar64 100(1) 9	148
9020. CHUCKII Chuckii Booker	22Jul89 116(1) 10	148
9021. REBA Reba McEntire	21May88 118(2) 10	148
9022. BENEFACTOR Romeo Void	04Sep82 119(3) 13	148
9023. SWEET REPLIES Honey Cone	19Jun71 137(2) 8	148
9024. FUNNY GIRL Diana Ross & The Supremes	05Oct68 150(1) 12	148
9025. IT'S ONLY ROCK AND ROLL Waylon Jennings	30Apr83 109(1) 11	148
9026. GEMS Aerosmith	10Dec88 133(1) 11	148
9027. DOES FORT WORTH EVER CROSS YOUR MIND George Strait	10Nov84 139(2) 16	148
9028. KEEP MOVIN' ON Merle Haggard	28Jun75 129(2) 9	148
9029. THE WHAM OF THAT MEMPHIS MAN! Lonnie Mack	30Nov63 103(1) 9	148
9030. MY LIFE FOR A SONG Placido Domingo	09Apr83 117(1) 11	148
9031. EVERYTHING'S KOOL & THE GANG: GREATEST HITS & MORE Kool & The Gang	20Aug88 109(2) 11	148
9032. IS THIS WHAT YOU WANT? Jackie Lomax	21Jun69 145(2) 9	148
9033. HORSESHOE IN THE GLOVE So	19Mar88 124(3) 9	148
9034. CANNED HEAT CONCERT (RECORDED LIVE IN EUROPE) Canned Heat	17Jul71 133(1) 9	148
9035. GEORGE BENSON IN CONCERT-CARNEGIE HALL George Benson	29Jan77 122(1) 8	148
9036. 5 J.J. Cale	08Sep79 136(1) 9	148
9037. LEATHER JACKETS Elton John	06Dec86 91(3) 9	148
9038. NEXT OF KIHN Greg Kihn Band	16Sep78 145(1) 12	148
9039. SOUPY SALES SEZ DO THE MOUSE AND OTHER TEEN HITS Soupy Sales	15May65 80(1) 7	148
9040. DO IT! Neil Diamond	27Feb71 100(1) 6	148
9041. NO GOODBYES Daryl Hall & John Oates	26Mar77 92(1) 6	148
9042. ROCK FOR AMNESTY Various Artists	24Jan87 121(2) 11	148
9043. LOVE FEVER The O'Jays	19Oct85 121(2) 12	148
9044. BETTER DAYS Paul Butterfield's Better Days	03Feb73 145(1) 13	148
9045. A TASTE OF HONEY Pete Fountain	23Apr66 100(1) 8	148
9046. SKYY Skyy	19May79 117(2) 9	147
9047. TERMS OF ENDEARMENT Soundtrack	21Apr84 111(1) 10	147
9048. THE ANDY WILLIAMS SOUND OF MUSIC Andy Williams	01Feb69 139(1) 7	147
9049. I PUT A SPELL ON YOU Nina Simone	26Jun65 99(2) 8	147
9050. THE BEST OF FERRANTE & TEICHER Ferrante & Teicher	06Mar71 134(1) 9	147
9051. ALIEN Soundtrack	07Jul79 113(2) 8	147
9052. RED 7 Red 7	25May85 105(2) 10	147
9053. DUANE & GREGG ALLMAN Allman Brothers Band	13May72 129(1) 8	147
9054. LOVE UNLIMITED Love Unlimited	29Apr72 151(1) 12	147
9055. GREATEST HITS OF ROD McKUEN Rod McKuen	01Mar69 149(1) 10	147
9056. FRANK Squeeze	07Oct89 113(3) 10	147
9057. THE DELLS MUSICAL MENU/ALWAYS TOGETHER The Dells	08Mar69 146(2) 10	147
9058. SHOOTING STAR Shooting Star	15Mar80 147(1) 14	147
9059. THE SEX LIFE OF THE PRIMATE (AND OTHER BITS OF GOSSIP) Shelley Berman	26Sep64 88(1) 8	147
9060. WINGS UPON YOUR HORNS Loretta Lynn	28Feb70 146(2) 11	147
9061. AL GREEN'S GREATEST HITS VOLUME II Al Green	02Jul77 134(2) 9	147
9062. LOVELY The Primitives	10Sep88 106(2) 9	147
9063. MILES DAVIS IN EUROPE Miles Davis	26Sep64 116(1) 10	147
9064. I LOVE YOU People	27Jul68 128(3) 8	147
9065. LOVING IS LIVING The McCrarys	09Sep78 138(2) 9	147
9066. DETECTIVE Detective	14May77 135(2) 9	146
9067. BIG SCIENCE Laurie Anderson	29May82 124(1) 12	146
9068. CATCH ME, I'M FALLING Pretty Poison	30Apr88 104(2) 8	146
9069. DOUG SAHM AND BAND Doug Sahm And Band	17Feb73 125(1) 10	146
9070. BOOM BOOM CHI BOOM BOOM Tom Tom Club	15Apr89 114(2) 11	146
9071. HIPPY HIPPY SHAKE Swinging Blue Jeans	30May64 90(1) 9	146
9072. ODYSSEY Charles Earland	03Apr76 155(1) 11	146
9073. RAZAMANAZ Nazareth	18Aug73 157(2) 13	146
9074. RAINBOW VISIONS Side Effect	20Jan79 135(2) 8	146
9075. UNTOLD PASSION Neal Schon & Jan Hammer	17Oct81 115(2) 8	145
9076. LOVE THEME FROM THE FLIGHT OF THE PHOENIX Brass Ring featuring Phil Bodner	25Jun66 109(1) 8	145
9077. M.F. HORN/3 Maynard Ferguson	28Jul73 128(1) 8	145
9078. SANDMAN Nilsson	07Feb76 111(2) 7	145
9079. THIS DAY AND AGE D.L. Byron	16Feb80 133(1) 10	145
9080. THE BEST OF PROCOL HARUM Procol Harum	20Oct73 131(1) 10	145
9081. THE LORD'S PRAYER AND OTHER SACRED SONGS Jim Nabors	16Nov68 173(2) 12	145
9082. 25 YEARS OF GRAMMY GREATS Various Artists	11Jun83 107(1) 9	145
9083. WOLF CREEK PASS C.W. McCall	12Apr75 143(2) 9	145
9084. MORE Vic Dana	16Nov63 111(1) 9	145
9085. HERBIE MANN LIVE AT NEWPORT Herbie Mann	21Dec63 104(1) 8	145
9086. THE IDOLMAKER Soundtrack	20Dec80 130(1) 9	145
9087. MASSTERPIECE Mass Production	29Mar80 133(1) 9	145
9088. NEW HOPE FOR THE WRETCHED The Plasmatics	21Feb81 134(2) 10	145
9089. THE ADVENTURES OF CAPTAIN SKY Captain Sky	27Jan79 157(2) 12	145
9090. LET THE GOOD TIMES ROLL Soundtrack	28Jul73 117(1) 9	145
9091. EL PUSSY CAT Mongo Santamaria	27Mar65 112(2) 10	144
9092. THE PIPER AT THE GATES OF DAWN Pink Floyd	02Dec67 131(1) 11	144
9093. YOU'RE NOT ALONE Roy Buchanan	20May78 119(2) 7	144
9094. CORRIDORS OF POWER Gary Moore	23Apr83 149(1) 13	144
9095. ORBISONGS Roy Orbison	06Nov65 136(1) 11	144
9096. ANOTHER MOTHER FURTHER Mother's Finest	17Sep77 134(1) 8	144
9097. WHAT A LONG STRANGE TRIP IT'S BEEN Grateful Dead	12Nov77 121(2) 8	144
9098. JEFFERSON AIRPLANE TAKES OFF Jefferson Airplane	17Sep66 128(2) 11	144
9099. CLAUDJA Claudja Barry	25Feb78 131(2) 10	144
9100. FRANK MARINO & MAHOGANY RUSH LIVE Mahogany Rush	11Mar78 129(1) 11	144

Rank. Title Act	Entry Peak(Pk Wks) TotWks	Scr
9101. INTRODUCING JOHNNY RODRIGUEZ	Johnny Rodriguez 07Apr73 156(1) 14	144
9102. THE JUDDS The Judds	08Dec84 153(1) 15	144
9103. BLACK DROPS Charles Earland	21Nov70 131(2) 10	144
9104. THE TEMPTATIONS The Temptations	29Aug81 119(1) 9	143
9105. TEXAS GOLD Asleep At The Wheel	20Sep75 136(1) 8	143
9106. THE CARDINAL Soundtrack	08Feb64 100(1) 9	143
9107. SANBORN David Sanborn	28Aug76 125(1) 8	143
9108. VICTORY DAY Tom Cochrane & Red Rider	12Nov88 144(2) 13	143
9109. THE MAN-MACHINE Kraftwerk	13May78 130(1) 9	143
9110. CREATION Fever Tree	07Feb70 97(2) 6	143
9111. MARIA ELENA 50 Guitars of Tommy Garrett	14Dec63 94(1) 8	143
9112. HAPPY IS THE SUNSHINE COMPANY	Sunshine Company 21Oct67 126(1) 10	143
9113. FEELIN' BLUESY Gladys Knight And The Pips	08Jun68 158(1) 13	143
9114. BLACK 'N' BLUE Black 'N Blue	15Sep84 116(2) 11	143
9115. THE HUNTER Joe Sample	16Apr83 125(1) 14	143
9116. LOVE HIM! Doris Day	14Mar64 102(1) 8	143
9117. HOW SWEET IT IS TO BE LOVED BY YOU	Marvin Gaye 27Feb65 128(2) 10	143
9118. ALL OF THE ABOVE John Hall Band	05Dec81 158(3) 13	143
9119. YEAH!!! Aretha Franklin	10Jul65 101(1) 8	143
9120. YOU'VE NEVER BEEN THIS FAR BEFORE / BABY'S GONE Conway Twitty	15Sep73 134(1) 9	143
9121. THE MISSION Soundtrack	21Feb87 132(1) 13	143
9122. BIG PLANS FOR EVERYBODY Let's Active	26Apr86 111(2) 10	142
9123. I MUST BE SEEING THINGS Gene Pitney	17Jul65 112(1) 9	142
9124. A BEATLES' SONGBOOK (THE BROTHERS FOUR SING LENNON/McCARTNEY) Brothers Four	30Jul66 97(1) 7	142
9125. I DON'T WANT TO GO HOME Southside	Johnny & The Asbury Jukes 10Jul76 125(2) 9	142
9126. MOODS Barbara Mandrell	26May79 132(1) 9	142
9127. A PLACE FOR MY STUFF! George Carlin	19Dec81 145(1) 13	142
9128. NEVER SAY NEVER Melba Moore	24Dec83 147(1) 14	142
9129. EVERYTHING'S GOOD ABOUT YOU	The Lettermen 06Feb71 119(1) 10	142
9130. LOVE SEASON Alex Bugnon	01Apr89 127(3) 11	142
9131. TELEVISION'S GREATEST HITS VOLUME II	Various Artists 15Nov86 149(2) 16	142
9132. UNDER THE BLADE Twisted Sister	06Jul85 125(2) 11	142
9133. THE DRIFTERS' GOLDEN HITS The Drifters	16Mar68 122(2) 8	142
9134. DIAMONDS IN THE ROUGH John Prine	28Oct72 148(1) 10	142
9135. CONDITION OF THE HEART Kashif	21Dec85 144(2) 14	142
9136. BUCK OWENS IN LONDON Buck Owens	05Jul69 113(2) 5	142
9137. MARTY ROBBINS GREATEST HITS, VOL. III	Marty Robbins 08May71 143(2) 10	142
9138. ZIGZAGGING THROUGH GHOSTLAND	The Radiators 01Apr89 122(2) 11	142
9139. BOBBY WHITLOCK Bobby Whitlock	01Apr72 140(1) 10	142
9140. SUPERMAN II Soundtrack	04Jul81 133(1) 9	142
9141. PRISM Prism	01Oct77 137(1) 10	141
9142. LISTEN TO THE CITY Tim Weisberg	11Oct75 105(1) 7	141
9143. KEEP MOVING Madness	17Mar84 109(1) 8	141
9144. NUDE Dead Or Alive	22Jul89 106(2) 9	141
9145. NOW LOOK Ronnie Wood	19Jul75 118(2) 6	141
9146. RICK DANKO Rick Danko	24Dec77 119(1) 8	141
9147. GIMME SOMETHING REAL	Ashford & Simpson 10Nov73 156(1) 13	141
9148. WELCOME TO OUR WORLD Mass Production	08Jan77 142(1) 10	141
9149. THE LEGEND OF JESSE JAMES	Various Artists 06Dec80 154(4) 13	141
9150. NEW YORK WONDERLAND Andre	Kostelanetz And His Orchestra 23May64 68(1) 7	141
9151. THE DAVE CLARK FIVE/MORE GREATEST HITS	Dave Clark Five 10Dec66 103(1) 7	141
9152. DEFROSTED Frijid Pink	31Oct70 149(1) 12	141
9153. HISTORY OF BRITISH ROCK, VOLUME 2	Various Artists 21Dec74 141(1) 11	141
9154. REAL LIVE Bob Dylan	05Jan85 115(2) 9	141
9155. ONE STEP BEYOND Madness	08Mar80 128(1) 9	141
9156. RECKLESS ABANDON David Bromberg	19Nov77 132(2) 9	141
9157. CAVERNA MAGICA (...UNDER THE TREE-IN THE CAVE...) Andreas Vollenweider	15Dec84 149(1) 15	141
9158. CHAPTER VII Buddy MILES Band	10Mar73 123(1) 9	141
9159. THE SLIGHTLY IRREVERENT MITCHELL TRIO	Mitchell Trio 14Nov64 128(1) 11	141
9160. AZURE D'OR Renaissance	16Jun79 125(2) 9	141
9161. SAFETY IN NUMBERS Crack The Sky	11Mar78 124(1) 8	141
9162. INTERNATIONALISTS Style Council	29Jun85 123(1) 11	140
9163. YOU'RE UNDER ARREST Miles Davis	01Jun85 111(2) 12	140
9164. HEAR 'N AID Hear 'N Aid	05Jul86 80(2) 7	140
9165. FAME AND FORTUNE Bad Company	25Oct86 106(2) 9	140
9166. COMFORT ME Carla Thomas	05Mar66 134(1) 10	140
9167. THE PAUL BUTTERFIELD BLUES BAND	Paul Butterfield Blues Band 04Dec65 123(1) 9	140
9168. WITH LOVE Tony Bennett	01Jul72 167(2) 14	140
9169. CAN'T WAIT ALL NIGHT Juice Newton	14Jul84 128(2) 10	140
9170. AUTOMATIC MAN Automatic Man	02Oct76 120(1) 7	140
9171. LET'S CLEAN UP THE GHETTO Various Artists	06Aug77 121(2) 9	140
9172. CHEWING PINE Leo Kottke	25Oct75 114(2) 7	140
9173. VOYAGER Roger Whittaker	09Feb80 154(3) 12	140
9174. FROM THE STREETS OF NEW YORK	Sha Na Na 01Dec73 140(1) 11	140
9175. IN CONCERT/BACK BY DEMAND	Soulful Strings 03May69 125(1) 6	140
9176. GIVE ME JUST A LITTLE MORE TIME	Chairmen Of The Board 02May70 133(2) 10	140
9177. TOP TEN Jimmy Ruffin	13May67 133(1) 11	140
9178. THE BEST OF THE IMPRESSIONS	The Impressions 21Sep68 172(1) 15	140
9179. WALKIN' IN THE SUNSHINE Roger Miller	01Jul67 118(2) 8	140
9180. MFSB MFSB	21Apr73 131(1) 10	140
9181. JEFFERSON AIRPLANE Jefferson Airplane	23Sep89 85(2) 7	140
9182. THE SUPER HITS, VOL. 4 Various Artists	19Jul69 164(2) 10	140
9183. GUESS WHO'S COMIN' TO THE CRIB?	Full Force 05Dec87 126(3) 11	140
9184. STORMY WEEKEND Mystic Moods Orchestra	23May70 165(1) 15	140
9185. MYSTERY STREET John Brannen	12Mar88 156(1) 14	140
9186. MOMS WOWS Moms Mabley	18Jul64 118(1) 10	139
9187. A CHILD'S GARDEN OF GRASS (A PRE-LEGALIZATION COMEDY) Various Artists	05Jun71 148(1) 9	139
9188. THE MIRROR Spooky Tooth	21Sep74 130(1) 8	139
9189. LAW OF THE FISH The Radiators	19Dec87 139(2) 16	139
9190. CAUGHT IN THE GAME Survivor	22Oct83 82(1) 9	139
9191. WALKER'S COLLECTIBLES Jerry Jeff Walker	11Jan75 141(1) 8	139
9192. JOURNEY Journey	03May75 138(1) 9	139
9193. LIV Livingston Taylor	18Dec71 147(1) 10	139
9194. ...PRESENTING THE FABULOUS RONETTES FEATURING VERONICA The Ronettes	26Dec64 96(1) 8	139
9195. MASTER OF DISGUISE Lizzy Borden	26Aug89 133(1) 10	139
9196. I COULD RULE THE WORLD IF I COULD ONLY GET THE PARTS The Waitresses	18Dec82 128(2) 10	139
9197. SKITCH...TONIGHT! Skitch Henderson	09Oct65 103(1) 8	139
9198. RUSS BALLARD Russ Ballard	09Jun84 147(2) 13	139
9199. MORNING, NOON & THE NITE-LITERS	The Nite-Liters 24Jul71 167(1) 13	139
9200. THE BEATLES FEATURING TONY SHERIDAN - IN THE BEGINNING (CIRCA 1960) The Beatles	16May70 117(2) 7	139
9201. SUICIDE SAL Maggie Bell	05Apr75 130(2) 8	139
9202. EXTENSIONS Mystic Moods Orchestra	03May69 155(1) 9	139
9203. ONE DAY IN YOUR LIFE Michael Jackson	25Apr81 144(1) 10	139
9204. HERE COMES THAT RAINY DAY FEELING AGAIN The Fortunes	10Jul71 134(2) 10	138
9205. NON FICTION The Blasters	14May83 95(1) 8	138
9206. NICE FEELIN' Rita Coolidge	18Dec71 135(1) 8	138
9207. SURE SHOT Crown Heights Affair	29Mar80 148(2) 12	138
9208. BEST OF FREE Free	24May75 120(2) 7	138
9209. FOREVER BY YOUR SIDE The Manhattans	06Aug83 104(1) 8	138
9210. INHERIT THE WIND Wilton Felder	08Nov80 142(1) 13	138
9211. NEW VINTAGE Maynard Ferguson	26Nov77 124(2) 8	138
9212. LIVE AT THE RAINBOW Focus	17Nov73 132(2) 10	138
9213. GIACOMO PUCCINI: TOSCA Leontyne Price	07Sep63 79(2) 6	138
9214. THE COST OF LOVING Style Council	18Apr87 122(2) 10	138
9215. FULL FORCE GET BUSY 1 TIME! Full Force	30Aug86 141(3) 13	138

Rank. Title Act Entry Peak(Pk Wks) TotWks	Scr
9216. 10 FROM 6 Bad Company 18Jan86 137(1) 14	138
9217. PURE & NATURAL T-Connection 20Mar82 123(1) 10	138
9218. PETE TOWNSHEND'S DEEP END LIVE! Pete Townshend 25Oct86 98(2) 9	138
9219. FRIENDS Larry Carlton 18Jun83 126(1) 11	138
9220. HERE I AM Sharon Bryant 09Sep89 139(1) 13	138
9221. LET THE MUSIC PLAY Dazz Band 27Jun81 154(2) 11	138
9222. ULTIMATE Ultimate 03Mar79 157(1) 11	138
9223. THE LOVE YOU SAVE Joe Tex 07May66 108(1) 8	138
9224. WE SHOULD BE TOGETHER Crystal Gayle 11Aug79 128(3) 8	138
9225. THOROUGHFARE GAP Stephen Stills 11Nov78 83(3) 4	137
9226. STACKED DECK Amazing Rhythm Aces 18Oct75 120(1) 8	137
9227. THE BOY'S DOIN' IT Hugh Masekela 09Aug75 132(1) 9	137
9228. Z Soundtrack 11Apr70 128(2) 8	137
9229. CATS Selections from Original Broadway Cast 26Feb83 131(2) 14	137
9230. JUMP ON IT Montrose 25Sep76 118(2) 7	137
9231. TWENNYNINE WITH LENNY WHITE Twennynine Featuring Lenny White 01Nov80 106(2) 8	137
9232. HEART OVER MIND Jennifer Rush 27Jun87 118(3) 10	137
9233. SMALL CHANGE Tom Waits 06Nov76 89(1) 5	137
9234. EVERYTHING IS COOL T-Connection 21Mar81 138(1) 8	137
9235. RUSSIAN ROULETTE Accept 17May86 114(2) 9	137
9236. THE HARDER THEY COME Jimmy Cliff 22Mar75 140(2) 8	137
9237. A TREASURY OF GREAT CONTEMPORARY HITS Various Artists 26Jul69 144(1) 7	137
9238. THE WHITE KNIGHT Cledus Maggard And The Citizen's Band 13Mar76 135(2) 8	137
9239. FOR EMILY, WHENEVER I MAY FIND HER Glenn Yarbrough 27May67 159(2) 14	137
9240. I WONDER WHAT SHE'LL THINK ABOUT ME LEAVING Conway Twitty 18Sep71 142(1) 8	137
9241. BATMAN TV Soundtrack 23Apr66 112(1) 8	137
9242. THRASH ZONE D.R.I. 23Dec89 140(1) 13	137
9243. HONEST LULLABY Joan Baez 04Aug79 113(2) 7	137
9244. I'M NOT STRANGE I'M JUST LIKE YOU Keith Sykes 22Nov80 147(3) 11	137
9245. AFRICAN QUEENS Ritchie Family 30Jul77 164(2) 12	137
9246. PAPER MOON Soundtrack 04Aug73 154(1) 12	136
9247. MAGIC The Floaters 22Apr78 131(2) 8	136
9248. HOMOSAPIEN Pete Shelley 26Jun82 121(1) 10	136
9249. ROOM SERVICE Oak Ridge Boys 17Jun78 164(5) 11	136
9250. THE BEST PART OF THE FAT BOYS Fat Boys 03Oct87 108(2) 10	136
9251. EVERY MOTHERS' SON Every Mothers' Son 10Jun67 117(1) 10	136
9252. PAPER LACE Paper Lace 07Sep74 124(1) 8	136
9253. FINALLY! T.G. Sheppard 30Jan82 152(2) 13	136
9254. THE CAPTAIN'S JOURNEY Lee Ritenour 24Jun78 121(2) 7	136
9255. FOR THE PEOPLE IN THE LAST HARD TOWN Tom T. Hall 26Jan74 149(1) 11	136
9256. THE BEST OF RITCHIE VALENS Ritchie Valens 29Aug87 100(2) 10	136
9257. ANNUNZIO PAOLO MANTOVANI Mantovani 27May72 156(2) 12	136
9258. FLORA, THE RED MENACE Original Cast 03Jul65 111(1) 8	136
9259. MANCINI'S ANGELS Henry Mancini 11Jun77 126(1) 8	136
9260. THE RIGHT NIGHT & BARRY WHITE Barry White 21Nov87 159(2) 17	136
9261. KILL 'EM ALL(2) Metallica 13Feb88 120(2) 8	136
9262. PERRY Perry Como 17Aug74 138(2) 10	136
9263. LIFE & TIMES Billy Cobham 10Apr76 128(1) 8	136
9264. ROUND TRIP The Knack 07Nov81 93(2) 6	136
9265. ELVIS-THE OTHER SIDES - WORLDWIDE GOLD AWARD HITS, VOL. 2 Elvis Presley 28Aug71 120(2) 7	136
9266. CYPRESS Let's Active 10Nov84 138(1) 16	136
9267. LIVING ROOM SUITE Harry Chapin 01Jul78 133(3) 8	136
9268. WE ALL HAVE A STAR Wilton Felder 09Dec78 173(2) 14	136
9269. AMERICA Kurtis Blow 02Nov85 153(3) 15	136
9270. THE BEST OF CHUCK MANGIONE Chuck Mangione 16Sep78 105(1) 6	135
9271. LOVE IN C MINOR Cerrone 26Feb77 153(1) 10	135
9272. JOY OF FLYING Tony Williams 12May79 113(1) 7	135
9273. MILESTONE JAZZSTARS IN CONCERT Various Artists 27Jan79 122(2) 8	135
9274. ALLIGATOR BOGALOO Lou Donaldson 07Oct67 141(1) 11	135
9275. STAY AWHILE Kingston Trio 19Jun65 126(1) 10	135
9276. THE HEART OF A WOMAN Johnny Mathis 28Dec74 139(2) 7	135
9277. KEY LIME PIE Camper van Beethoven 07Oct89 141(3) 12	135
9278. FIRE IN THE WIND John Stewart 26Nov77 126(2) 8	135
9279. THE ORIGINAL RECORDINGS Billie Holiday 24Feb73 135(1) 9	135
9280. TRACK RECORD Joan Armatrading 21Jan84 113(1) 10	135
9281. MY TIME Boz Scaggs 23Sep72 138(1) 9	135
9282. ANNIE GET YOUR GUN Original Cast 06Aug66 113(1) 7	135
9283. FEEL THE HEAT Henry Paul Band 02Aug80 120(1) 8	135
9284. EARTH, WIND & FIRE Earth, Wind & Fire 15May71 172(1) 13	135
9285. THEM FEATURING VAN MORRISON Them 22Jul72 154(3) 11	135
9286. THE SOUND OF SUNSHINE Sunshine Band 04Oct75 131(1) 8	135
9287. I NEED SOME MONEY Eddie Harris 19Apr75 125(1) 9	135
9288. 2XS Nazareth 10Jul82 122(2) 10	135
9289. PORTER WAYNE AND DOLLY REBECCA Porter Wagoner and Dolly Parton 04Apr70 137(2) 7	135
9290. OUT OF THE SILENT PLANET King's X 07May88 144(1) 11	134
9291. THE BIG EASY Soundtrack 24Oct87 107(2) 9	134
9292. IT'S MY TURN Soundtrack 22Nov80 137(2) 11	134
9293. GOIN' PLACES John Davidson 29Jun68 151(1) 10	134
9294. TEDDY BEAR Red Sovine 11Sep76 119(2) 6	134
9295. SCARS OF LOVE TKA 30Jan88 135(2) 11	134
9296. SATURDAY NIGHT AT THE UPTOWN Various Artists 07Nov64 95(1) 8	134
9297. JUICY FRUIT (DISCO FREAK) Isaac Hayes 24Jul76 124(1) 7	134
9298. BELIEVERS Don McLean 28Nov81 156(1) 11	134
9299. 'BOUT LOVE Bill Withers 17Mar79 134(1) 9	134
9300. THE SYMPHONY SESSIONS David Foster 20Feb88 111(2) 8	134
9301. BALANCE Balance 29Aug81 133(1) 12	134
9302. LOU RAWLS LIVE(2) Lou Rawls 11Nov78 108(1) 8	134
9303. I'LL MAKE YOU MUSIC Beverly Bremers 16Sep72 124(1) 8	134
9304. THE EDGAR WINTER GROUP WITH RICK DERRINGER Edgar Winter Group With Rick Derringer 18Oct75 124(1) 8	134
9305. DARLING LILI Soundtrack 01Aug70 113(2) 7	134
9306. ANOTHER YEAR Leo Sayer 11Oct75 125(1) 7	134
9307. THE SOUND OF NANCY WILSON Nancy Wilson 12Oct68 122(1) 7	134
9308. FOREIGN AFFAIRS Tom Waits 22Oct77 113(1) 8	134
9309. BOOKER T. & PRISCILLA Booker T. & Priscilla 14Aug71 106(1) 6	134
9310. BEDTIME STORY Tammy Wynette 08Apr72 133(1) 9	133
9311. BLACKJACK Blackjack 21Jul79 127(1) 7	133
9312. PROVISION Scritti Politti 16Jul88 113(2) 8	133
9313. FADE OUT-FADE IN Original Cast 25Jul64 96(2) 8	133
9314. RITES OF SUMMER Spyro Gyra 16Jul88 104(2) 8	133
9315. HEADS Osibisa 28Oct72 125(1) 8	133
9316. HE'S SO FINE Jody Miller 28Aug71 117(1) 8	133
9317. SHADES OF BLUE Lou Rawls 10Jan81 110(2) 6	133
9318. THE PROMISE Michael Pinder 01May76 133(3) 8	133
9319. TO EACH HIS OWN Frankie Laine 23Mar68 127(1) 9	133
9320. THE BEST OF DONOVAN Donovan 08Nov69 135(1) 7	133
9321. ONE ON ONE Seals & Crofts 08Oct77 118(2) 7	133
9322. MIND BOMB The The 22Jul89 138(2) 12	133
9323. THE RIDDLE Nik Kershaw 27Apr85 113(2) 10	133
9324. ROADIE Soundtrack 21Jun80 125(2) 8	133
9325. INNER WORLDS Mahavishnu Orchestra John McLaughlin 21Feb76 118(2) 7	133
9326. BORN ON A FRIDAY Cleo Laine 07Feb76 158(2) 10	133
9327. ZODIAC: COSMIC SOUNDS, THE Various Artists 15Jul67 118(1) 9	133
9328. OLDIES BUT GOODIES, VOL. 7 Various Artists 09Jan65 121(2) 9	133
9329. X2 Times Two 30Apr88 137(1) 11	133
9330. WHY AM I TREATED SO BAD! "Cannonball" Adderley Quintet 10Jun67 154(1) 12	133
9331. GHOST WRITER Garland Jeffreys 26Mar77 140(2) 10	133

Rank. Title Act / Entry Peak(Pk Wks) TotWks	Scr
9332. FROM HELLO DOLLY TO GOODBYE CHARLIE Bobby Darin 26Dec64 107(2) 8	132
9333. STATELESS Lene Lovich 04Aug79 137(2) 10	132
9334. WISH SOMEONE WOULD CARE Irma Thomas 27Jun64 104(1) 8	132
9335. NIGHT AFTER NIGHT U.K. 20Oct79 109(1) 6	132
9336. THE BEST OF BOOKER T. & THE MG'S Booker T. & The MG's 23Nov68 167(2) 11	132
9337. MORE THAN YOU KNOW Toni Tennille 09Jun84 142(1) 11	132
9338. RIDIN' HIGH Jerry Jeff Walker 04Oct75 119(1) 7	132
9339. THINGS GO BETTER WITH LOVE Jeannie C. Riley 13Sep69 142(1) 7	132
9340. TO THE DOOR OF THE SUN Al Martino 08Feb75 129(2) 8	132
9341. RICK WAKEMAN'S CRIMINAL RECORD Rick Wakeman 17Dec77 128(1) 8	132
9342. POWER IN THE DARKNESS Tom Robinson Band 15Jul78 144(2) 8	132
9343. LOOKING FOR MR. GOODBAR Soundtrack 26Nov77 134(2) 8	132
9344. FRANKIE VALLI GOLD Frankie Valli 20Dec75 132(2) 8	132
9345. ALL IN THE FAMILY - 2ND ALBUM TV Soundtrack 30Dec72 129(1) 8	132
9346. MIDNIGHT BLUE Louise Tucker 06Aug83 127(1) 10	132
9347. LATIN PULSE Nancy Ames 29Oct66 133(1) 8	132
9348. WHAT THE WORLD NEEDS NOW IS LOVE Tom Clay 28Aug71 92(1) 5	132
9349. EQUINOXE Jean Michel Jarre 03Feb79 126(1) 8	132
9350. FUNKY KINGSTON Toots And The Maytals 01Nov75 164(1) 13	132
9351. HELL BENT FOR LEATHER Judas Priest 31Mar79 128(1) 7	131
9352. FROZEN IN THE NIGHT Dan Hill 23Sep78 118(2) 6	131
9353. PEACE & LOVE The Pogues 12Aug89 118(1) 9	131
9354. RUSTY WIER Rusty Wier 17Jan76 131(1) 9	131
9355. BILLY JACK Soundtrack 09Oct71 135(1) 7	131
9356. STEALIN HORSES Stealin Horses 25Jun88 146(2) 12	131
9357. TEN YEARS OF GOLD Aretha Franklin 25Dec76 135(1) 8	131
9358. HOT SHOT Pat Travers 05May84 108(2) 8	131
9359. DONOVAN P. LEITCH Donovan 14Nov70 128(1) 8	131
9360. GOLD Steely Dan 03Jul82 115(1) 9	131
9361. CLOSER TO THE GROUND Joy Of Cooking 09Oct71 136(1) 7	131
9362. LOVING YOU JUST CROSSED MY MIND Sam Neely 16Sep72 147(2) 11	131
9363. LIVE IN THE HEART OF THE CITY Whitesnake 27Dec80 146(1) 12	131
9364. THE BEST OF THE YOUNGBLOODS The Youngbloods 05Sep70 144(1) 10	131
9365. GRITS & SOUL James Brown 10Apr65 124(1) 10	131
9366. THE ARISTOCATS Soundtrack 23Jan71 137(2) 10	131
9367. DISORDERLIES Soundtrack 12Sep87 99(2) 8	131
9368. BOBBY VINTON'S GREATEST HITS OF LOVE Bobby Vinton 17Jan70 138(1) 8	130
9369. THE BEST OF THE STATLER BROS. RIDES AGAIN, VOL. II Statler Brothers 02Feb80 153(2) 11	130
9370. DAVID BOWIE NARRATES PROKOFIEV'S "PETER AND THE WOLF" David Bowie/ Philadephia Orchestra/Eugene Ormandy 06May78 136(1) 8	130
9371. CATFISH Four Tops 13Nov76 124(2) 8	130
9372. THOSE WERE THE DAYS Exotic Guitars 04Jan69 167(1) 11	130
9373. GABOR SZABO 1969 Gabor Szabo 16Aug69 143(2) 7	130
9374. FREQUENCY Nick Gilder 07Jul79 127(2) 8	130
9375. IN 'N' OUT Stone City Band 22Mar80 122(2) 8	130
9376. PATRICE Patrice Rushen 17Feb79 98(2) 6	130
9377. SHAFT IN AFRICA Soundtrack 21Jul73 147(1) 9	130
9378. SHOUT Devo 03Nov84 83(2) 6	130
9379. TAKING IT HOME Buckwheat Zydeco 17Sep88 104(1) 7	130
9380. MUCH LES Les McCann 29Mar69 169(1) 10	130
9381. HELLUVA BAND Angel 19Jun76 155(1) 10	130
9382. TAKE WHAT YOU NEED Robin Trower 21May88 133(2) 10	130
9383. JUST OUT OF REACH Perry Como 20Dec75 142(1) 9	129
9384. LOOK AT ME The Moments 12Jul75 132(1) 8	129
9385. LIVE AT CARNEGIE HALL Shirley Bassey 22Sep73 136(1) 8	129
9386. DEEP IN THE HEART OF NOWHERE Bob Geldof 13Dec86 130(1) 12	129
9387. VESTA 4 U Vesta 02Sep89 131(1) 10	129
9388. PICTURES FROM THE FRONT Jon Butcher 18Feb89 121(3) 8	129
9389. MY NATION UNDERGROUND Julian Cope 10Dec88 155(1) 13	129
9390. LIGHTING UP THE NIGHT Jack Wagner 19Oct85 150(2) 15	129
9391. MOTHERMANIA/THE BEST OF THE MOTHERS Mothers Of Invention 05Apr69 151(2) 9	129
9392. THE SPOTLIGHT KID Captain Beefheart 19Feb72 131(1) 9	129
9393. MY BEST TO YOU John Davidson 08Apr67 125(1) 8	129
9394. LITTLE GREEN BAG George Baker Selection 04Jul70 107(1) 6	129
9395. THE NEW EBB TIDE Frank Chacksfield And His Orch. 28Nov64 120(2) 9	129
9396. BOP DOO-WOP Manhattan Transfer 05Jan85 127(2) 11	129
9397. THE MIGHTY MIGHTY DELLS The Dells 21Sep74 114(2) 8	129
9398. TIGHTEN UP Archie Bell & The Drells 25May68 142(1) 8	129
9399. BIG SIXTEEN, VOL. 3 Gene Pitney 19Mar66 123(2) 8	129
9400. PAIN IN MY HEART Otis Redding 02May64 103(1) 8	129
9401. TRACES OF LOVE Bert Kaempfert And His Orchestra 01Nov69 153(1) 10	129
9402. AIN'T LIFE GRAND Black Oak Arkansas 31May75 145(2) 8	128
9403. SAY WONDERFUL THINGS Patti Page 21Sep63 83(1) 6	128
9404. BEST OF GLEN CAMPBELL Glen Campbell 27Nov76 116(1) 6	128
9405. NIGHT AFTER NIGHT Bill Quateman 12Feb77 129(1) 8	128
9406. FRIENDS & SMILEY SMILE Beach Boys 09Nov74 125(2) 6	128
9407. VINTAGE YEARS Fleetwood Mac 01Mar75 138(2) 9	128
9408. THE WANDERING MINSTRELS New Christy Minstrels 16Oct65 125(1) 9	128
9409. MUSIC FUH YA (MUSICA PARA TU) Taj Mahal 29Jan77 134(1) 8	128
9410. ALL THE TIME Jack Greene 22Jul67 151(2) 12	128
9411. BLACK CODES (FROM THE UNDERGROUND) Wynton Marsalis 19Oct85 118(2) 10	128
9412. ORIGINAL GOLDEN HITS - VOLUME 2 Jerry Lee Lewis 27Sep69 122(2) 5	128
9413. AND THE SINGER SINGS HIS SONGS Neil Diamond 09Oct76 102(1) 5	128
9414. THE BEATLES LIVE! AT THE STAR-CLUB IN HAMBURG, GERMANY; 1962 The Beatles 02Jul77 111(1) 7	128
9415. SECRET DREAMS & FORBIDDEN FIRE Bonnie Tyler 26Apr86 106(2) 8	128
9416. CURTIS IN CHICAGO Curtis Mayfield 17Nov73 135(1) 10	128
9417. LARSEN-FEITEN BAND Larsen-Feiten Band 13Sep80 142(1) 10	128
9418. ALWAYS IN THE MOOD Shirley Jones 23Aug86 128(1) 10	128
9419. GET AS MUCH LOVE AS YOU CAN Jones Girls 05Dec81 155(1) 15	128
9420. CHILDREN Mission U.K. 30Apr88 126(2) 10	128
9421. DANCING IN THE MOONLIGHT King Harvest 27Jan73 136(1) 10	128
9422. ON THE CORNER Miles Davis 18Nov72 156(1) 11	128
9423. IN PERSON Ike & Tina Turner 19Jul69 142(1) 9	128
9424. LA LA MEANS I LOVE YOU The Delfonics 08Jun68 100(1) 6	128
9425. JUDY COLLINS #3 Judy Collins 28Mar64 126(1) 10	128
9426. LOOKING FOR LOVE Connie Francis 01Aug64 122(1) 9	127
9427. RESTRICTIONS Cactus 27Nov71 155(1) 10	127
9428. BOOKER T. & THE M.G.'S GREATEST HITS Booker T. & The MG's 14Nov70 132(1) 8	127
9429. GREATEST HITS, VOL. 2 Righteous Brothers 05Apr69 126(2) 5	127
9430. THE KINGBEES The Kingbees 31May80 160(2) 12	127
9431. TROUBLEMAKER Ian McLagan 19Jan80 125(1) 9	127
9432. KILLING ME SOFTLY WITH HER SONG Johnny Mathis 30Jun73 120(2) 7	127
9433. WHISPERS Jackie Wilson 14Jan67 108(1) 7	127
9434. POP ART Transvision Vamp 24Sep88 115(1) 8	127
9435. TO LOVERS EVERYWHERE U.S.A. Mantovani 30Oct71 150(1) 9	127
9436. HUMANESQUE Jack Green 18Oct80 121(1) 8	127
9437. THE PACK IS BACK Raven 08Mar86 121(2) 10	127
9438. ROGER McGUINN Roger McGuinn 14Jul73 137(1) 9	127
9439. REMINISCING Lawrence Welk 23Dec72 149(2) 10	127
9440. THE MOTOWN STORY: THE FIRST 25 YEARS Various Artists 09Jul83 114(1) 9	127
9441. THE FIRST TIME WE MET The Independents 19May73 127(1) 9	127
9442. WAREHOUSE: SONGS AND STORIES Husker Du 14Feb87 117(2) 10	127
9443. BURNS LIKE A STAR Stone Fury 24Nov84 144(2) 12	127
9444. MOONSHOT Buffy Sainte-Marie 06May72 134(1) 8	126
9445. OVER THERE (LIVE AT THE VENUE, LONDON) The Blasters 30Oct82 117(4) 8	126

Rank. Title Act Entry Peak(Pk Wks) TotWks	Scr
9446. OUT OF OUR HANDS Flash 01Sep73 135(1) 8	126
9447. GREATEST HITS - VOL. II Eddie Rabbitt 01Oct83 131(3) 11	126
9448. DAISY A DAY Jud Strunk 05May73 138(1) 9	126
9449. DIALOGUE Michael Johnson 15Sep79 157(1) 12	126
9450. THE GOOD, THE BAD AND THE UGLY AND OTHER MOTION PICTURE THEMES Leroy Holmes And His Orchestra 01Jun68 138(2) 8	126
9451. HAVING FUN WITH ELVIS ON STAGE Elvis Presley 02Nov74 130(2) 7	126
9452. MY NAME IS JERMAINE Jermaine Jackson 25Sep76 164(2) 11	126
9453. REJOICING Pat Metheny 12May84 116(2) 9	126
9454. RISING FOR THE MOON Fairport Convention 16Aug75 143(1) 8	126
9455. BLACK MAGIC WOMAN Fleetwood Mac 16Oct71 143(2) 7	126
9456. EXOTIC MYSTERIES Lonnie Liston Smith 17Feb79 123(2) 8	126
9457. EVERLASTING LOVE Carl Carlton 18Jan75 132(2) 7	126
9458. MOROCCAN ROLL Brand X 21May77 125(1) 8	126
9459. FEEL THE SHAKE Jetboy 12Nov88 135(1) 10	126
9460. THE BEST OF DEAN MARTIN, VOL. 2 Dean Martin 22Feb69 145(1) 7	126
9461. THE MAN WHO BUILT AMERICA Horslips 10Mar79 155(1) 9	126
9462. HEADLESS CROSS Black Sabbath 13May89 115(1) 8	126
9463. DANZIG Danzig 08Oct88 125(2) 9	126
9464. CREAM SONGBOOK The Rubber Band 02Aug69 135(2) 6	125
9465. WISH ME A RAINBOW Gunter Kallmann Chorus 24Dec66 126(1) 8	125
9466. CANYON Paul Winter 03May86 138(1) 11	125
9467. GREAT WHITE Great White 24Mar84 144(1) 12	125
9468. A WINTER'S SOLSTICE II Various Artists 10Dec88 108(1) 7	125
9469. LAMENT Ultravox 19May84 115(2) 9	125
9470. THE GOLDDIGGERS Golddiggers 02Aug69 142(1) 7	125
9471. FIFTEEN YEARS AGO Conway Twitty 23Jan71 140(1) 7	125
9472. BYABLUE Keith Jarrett 01Oct77 117(1) 6	125
9473. SHE STILL COMES AROUND (TO LOVE WHAT'S LEFT OF ME) Jerry Lee Lewis 08Feb69 149(1) 7	125
9474. EDDIE HARRIS LIVE AT NEWPORT Eddie Harris 27Nov71 164(1) 10	125
9475. LES MISERABLES Original Cast 20Jun87 117(2) 10	125
9476. COLLAGE Noel Harrison 09Dec67 135(1) 9	125
9477. WALTER CARLOS' CLOCKWORK ORANGE Walter Carlos 08Jul72 146(1) 9	125
9478. THE CLARKE/DUKE PROJECT II Stanley Clarke & George Duke 26Nov83 146(1) 10	125
9479. CLOSE-UP Beach Boys 16Aug69 136(2) 6	125
9480. FRESH FISH SPECIAL Robert Gordon 18Mar78 124(1) 7	125
9481. SHADAY Ofra Haza 21Jan89 130(2) 9	124
9482. STAR FLEET PROJECT Brian May And Friends 19Nov83 125(1) 9	124
9483. FABULOUS The Stylistics 19Jun76 117(2) 6	124
9484. THIS IS SPINAL TAP Spinal Tap 28Apr84 121(2) 10	124
9485. ASS Badfinger 15Dec73 122(1) 8	124
9486. PREVAILING AIRS Paul Mauriat And His Orchestra 12Oct68 142(2) 7	124
9487. ANTHOLOGY Marvin Gaye 21Apr84 109(1) 8	124
9488. HIGH LAND, HARD RAIN Aztec Camera 10Sep83 129(1) 10	124
9489. ...AND I MEAN IT! Genya Ravan 29Sep79 106(1) 6	124
9490. WAITING Fun Boy Three 30Jul83 104(1) 7	124
9491. OPUS X Chilliwack 27Nov82 112(2) 10	124
9492. GOOD-BYES & BUTTERFLIES Five Man Electrical Band 31Jul71 148(1) 9	124
9493. MARIE The Bachelors 04Sep65 89(1) 6	124
9494. STRIKES TWICE Larry Carlton 06Sep80 138(1) 8	124
9495. FEELIN' GROOVY Harpers Bizarre 06May67 108(1) 7	124
9496. TREAT ME RIGHT Roy Head 04Dec65 122(1) 8	124
9497. CONSPIRACY King Diamond 30Sep89 111(2) 8	124
9498. THE SONGSTRESS Anita Baker 29Oct83 139(2) 11	123
9499. FOREVER YOURS The Sylvers 16Sep78 132(1) 8	123
9500. ALL OF THIS AND NOTHING Psychedelic Furs 24Sep88 102(2) 8	123
9501. SUITES FROM STAR WARS AND CLOSE ENCOUNTERS OF THE THIRD KIND Zubin Mehta, Los Angeles Philharmonic Orchestra 04Mar78 130(1) 8	123
9502. ROCKER Elvis Presley 08Dec84 154(1) 13	123
9503. BLOW YOUR OWN HORN Herb Alpert 24Sep83 120(1) 8	123
9504. SOLDIER Iggy Pop 08Mar80 125(1) 7	123
9505. IN THE HEAT OF THE NIGHT Jeff Lorber 05May84 106(1) 7	123
9506. RUN FOR THE ROSES Jerry Garcia 20Nov82 100(2) 8	123
9507. HOME TO MYSELF Melissa Manchester 23Jun73 156(2) 13	123
9508. LAND OF MAKE BELIEVE Chuck Mangione 08Dec73 157(1) 12	123
9509. I'LL PROVE IT TO YOU Gregory Abbott 04Jun88 132(2) 9	123
9510. DANNY JOE BROWN AND THE DANNY JOE BROWN BAND Danny Joe Brown And The Danny Joe Brown Band 04Jul81 120(2) 7	123
9511. WHA'PPEN English Beat 27Jun81 126(1) 6	123
9512. WINNERS Kleeer 26Apr80 140(2) 10	123
9513. THE INTRUDERS GREATEST HITS The Intruders 25Jan69 144(2) 6	123
9514. ANY WHICH WAY YOU CAN Soundtrack 17Jan81 141(1) 9	123
9515. EMERGENCY Melissa Manchester 03Dec83 135(3) 9	123
9516. CHUBBY CHECKER'S GREATEST HITS Chubby Checker 23Dec72 152(2) 10	123
9517. I LOVE YOU 1,000 TIMES The Platters 09Jul66 100(2) 6	123
9518. GLASS MOON Glass Moon 10May80 148(1) 9	123
9519. BLACK PEARL Black Pearl 03May69 130(1) 5	123
9520. BACK TO THE WORLD Dennis DeYoung 29Mar86 108(2) 8	123
9521. THE ROAD The Kinks 06Feb88 110(2) 7	123
9522. ANNIE IN WONDERLAND Annie Haslem 24Dec77 167(1) 13	123
9523. NEW RIDERS New Riders Of The Purple Sage 12Jun76 145(1) 8	123
9524. THE BADDEST HUBBARD Freddie Hubbard 11Jan75 127(2) 7	122
9525. DOWN IN THE BOONDOCKS Billy Joe Royal 18Sep65 96(1) 7	122
9526. AND YOU KNOW THAT! Kirk Whalum 19Mar88 142(1) 10	122
9527. IN HEAT Black 'N Blue 23Apr88 133(2) 9	122
9528. GERRY & THE PACEMAKERS SECOND ALBUM Gerry And The Pacemakers 21Nov64 129(2) 9	122
9529. SUMMER (THE FIRST TIME) Bobby Goldsboro 29Sep73 150(1) 11	122
9530. COLLAGE Raiders 11Apr70 154(2) 9	122
9531. LIZA! LIZA! Liza Minnelli 21Nov64 115(1) 8	122
9532. A NEW PERSPECTIVE Donald Byrd 11Jul64 110(1) 8	122
9533. COME TOGETHER Mike Curb Congregation 04Jul70 105(1) 5	122
9534. GAMES PEOPLE PLAY / THESE ARE NOT MY PEOPLE Freddy Weller 16Aug69 144(1) 7	122
9535. GOT MY HEAD ON STRAIGHT Billy Paul 15Mar75 140(2) 9	122
9536. SHOGUN TV Soundtrack 04Oct80 115(2) 6	122
9537. UNSUNG HEROES The Crusaders 24Nov73 173(1) 14	122
9538. LET THERE BE ROCK AC/DC 13Aug77 154(1) 11	122
9539. I'M ALL YOURS-BABY! Ray Charles 05Apr69 167(1) 11	122
9540. WITH LOVE Bobby Vinton 07Dec74 109(2) 5	122
9541. COME SHARE MY LIFE Glenn Yarbrough 08May65 112(1) 8	122
9542. SPY WITH A PIE Soupy Sales 24Apr65 102(2) 7	122
9543. INVITATION Norman Connors 21Jul79 137(1) 7	122
9544. SUNDAY IN THE PARK WITH GEORGE Original Cast 25Aug84 149(3) 11	122
9545. STREET FAIR Magic Organ 06May72 135(2) 7	122
9546. PRESSURE DROP Robert Palmer 22Nov75 136(1) 8	122
9547. HOT TRACKS Nazareth 02Jul77 120(2) 6	122
9548. GET UP OFFA THAT THING James Brown 14Aug76 147(2) 8	121
9549. 5 BY 5 Dave Clark Five 25Mar67 119(1) 7	121
9550. BEAUTIFUL SUNDAY Daniel Boone 07Oct72 142(2) 9	121
9551. LEE MICHAELS LIVE Lee Michaels 07Apr73 135(1) 8	121
9552. MASTERPIECE Isley Brothers 07Dec85 140(2) 12	121
9553. LOVE WILL FOLLOW George Howard 19Apr86 142(2) 11	121
9554. THE FIRST OF A MILLION KISSES Fairground Attraction 21Jan89 137(2) 11	121
9555. A DIFFERENT KIND OF BLUES Itzhak Perlman & Andre Previn 14Mar81 149(1) 9	121
9556. MARIANNE FAITHFULL'S GREATEST HITS Marianne Faithfull 05Apr69 171(2) 10	121
9557. IT'S A NEW DAY SO LET A MAN COME IN James Brown 04Jul70 121(2) 6	121
9558. MAN OF MIRACLES Styx 09Nov74 154(1) 12	121
9559. THROBBING PYTHON OF LOVE Robin Williams 02Apr83 119(1) 9	121
9560. THE CLASH The Clash 08Sep79 126(2) 6	121

Rank. Title Act	Entry Peak(Pk Wks) TotWks	Scr
9561. #7 George Strait	05Jul86 126(1) 11	121
9562. FROST MUSIC The Frost	21Jun69 168(1) 10	121
9563. THE DREAM DUET	Anna Moffo & Sergio Franchi 25Jan64 97(1) 7	121
9564. WHISPER IN YOUR EAR The Whispers	14Apr79 146(1) 9	121
9565. THE WORLD'S GREATEST INTERNATIONAL	HITS! Petula Clark 23Oct65 129(2) 9	121
9566. PAINT IT BLACK Soulful Strings	26Aug67 166(1) 15	121
9567. CERRONE 3 - SUPERNATURE Cerrone	21Jan78 129(2) 8	121
9568. TASTY Patti LaBelle	24Jun78 129(1) 7	121
9569. TWIN PEAKS Mountain	09Mar74 142(2) 8	121
9570. ...AND THEN HE KISSED ME Rachel Sweet	05Sep81 124(2) 7	121
9571. JOURNEY TO THE LAND OF...ENCHANTMENT	Enchantment 17Mar79 145(1) 8	121
9572. STEAMIN' HOT The Reddings	29May82 153(3) 12	121
9573. INDIAN GIVER 1910 Fruitgum Co.	05Apr69 147(2) 8	121
9574. I'LL PLAY THE BLUES FOR YOU Albert King	07Oct72 140(2) 8	121
9575. SETTING SONS The Jam	16Feb80 137(2) 8	121
9576. LIGHTS OUT, SWEET DREAMS Bert	Kaempfert And His Orchestra 30Nov63 79(1) 6	121
9577. 10TH ANNIVERSARY/LIMITED EDITION	Roger Williams 04Apr64 108(1) 8	120
9578. HEART OF HEARTS Bobby Vinton	19Jul75 108(2) 5	120
9579. THE BEST DAYS OF MY LIFE Johnny Mathis	24Feb79 122(2) 7	120
9580. PLAYERS IN THE DARK Dr. Hook	03Apr82 118(3) 7	120
9581. TRUCE Jack Bruce & Robin Trower	30Jan82 109(2) 6	120
9582. IT CRAWLED INTO MY HAND, HONEST	The Fugs 19Oct68 167(1) 10	120
9583. GAP BAND VII Gap Band	01Feb86 159(1) 15	120
9584. CUT LOOSE Paul Rodgers	26Nov83 135(1) 10	120
9585. SHRINER'S CONVENTION Ray Stevens	15Mar80 132(1) 8	120
9586. MATTHEW & SON/NEW MASTERS	Cat Stevens 03Apr71 173(1) 12	120
9587. BILLY JOE THOMAS B.J. Thomas	20May72 145(1) 9	120
9588. RADIO FREE NIXON David Frye	27Mar71 123(1) 6	120
9589. CHARIOTS OF FIRE Ernie Watts	20Feb82 161(2) 12	120
9590. DRUM DISCOTHEQUE Sandy Nelson	10Jul65 120(2) 8	120
9591. BEAUTIFUL PEOPLE New Seekers	03Apr71 136(1) 6	120
9592. CAPTURED Rockwell	23Feb85 120(2) 9	120
9593. SPRING FEVER Rick Derringer	26Apr75 141(1) 8	120
9594. IS THIS WHATCHA WONT? Barry White	27Nov76 125(1) 9	120
9595. IF YOU CAN'T LICK 'EM...LICK 'EM	Ted Nugent 05Mar88 112(2) 7	120
9596. FRUIT AT THE BOTTOM Wendy And Lisa	08Apr89 119(2) 8	120
9597. KINKY FRIEDMAN Kinky Friedman	01Feb75 132(1) 6	120
9598. THE WETTER THE BETTER Wet Willie	03Apr76 133(1) 7	120
9599. THE BEST OF EMERSON, LAKE AND PALMER	Emerson, Lake & Palmer 29Nov80 108(2) 7	119
9600. E.H. IN THE U.K. Eddie Harris	16Feb74 150(1) 11	119
9601. ARCHIVES Rush	15Apr78 121(1) 6	119
9602. I WANT CANDY Bow Wow Wow	18Sep82 123(1) 9	119
9603. CALL ON ME Evelyn "Champagne" King	11Oct80 124(3) 7	119
9604. LIVIN' IT UP! Jimmy Smith	26Oct68 169(1) 10	119
9605. LION'S SHARE Savoy Brown	04Nov72 151(2) 10	119
9606. BRIDGE OVER TROUBLED WATER Peggy Lee	06Jun70 142(2) 9	119
9607. LINE OF FIRE The Headpins	21Jan84 114(1) 9	119
9608. CARLIN ON CAMPUS George Carlin	04Aug84 136(1) 11	119
9609. NANCY IN LONDON Nancy Sinatra	03Sep66 122(1) 7	119
9610. CALLING CARD Rory Gallagher	30Oct76 163(1) 11	119
9611. NEVER KICK A SLEEPING DOG Mitch Ryder	09Jul83 120(1) 9	119
9612. BUSTIN' LOOSE Roberta Flack	27Jun81 161(1) 11	119
9613. AND THE FEELING'S GOOD Jose Feliciano	21Dec74 136(2) 7	119
9614. SEDUCTION James Last Band	28Jun80 148(1) 8	119
9615. BEYOND THE VALLEY OF 1984	The Plasmatics 06Jun81 142(1) 9	119
9616. AIN'T NOTHING YOU CAN DO Bobby Bland	01Aug64 119(1) 8	118
9617. READ MY LIPS Melba Moore	27Apr85 130(2) 10	118
9618. CROSS-COLLATERAL Passport	15Mar75 137(2) 7	118
9619. HERBIE MANN & FIRE ISLAND Herbie Mann	01Oct77 122(1) 7	118
9620. TUCKERIZED Marshall Tucker Band	12Jun82 95(2) 7	118
9621. BANGING THE WALL Bar-Kays	21Sep85 115(2) 9	118
9622. MR. JAWS AND OTHER FABLES	Dickie Goodman 06Dec75 144(1) 8	118
9623. PASSIONFRUIT Michael Franks	29Oct83 141(1) 11	118
9624. BE THANKFUL FOR WHAT YOU GOT	William DeVaughn 03Aug74 165(1) 11	118
9625. KATHY SMITH'S AEROBIC FITNESS	Kathy Smith 13Mar82 144(2) 13	118
9626. THE VOICE OF SCOTT McKENZIE	Scott McKenzie 09Dec67 127(2) 7	118
9627. I NEED TIME Bloodstone	10Aug74 141(1) 8	118
9628. CHANCES ARE Bob Marley	31Oct81 117(1) 6	118
9629. GARY LEWIS NOW!	Gary Lewis And The Playboys 17Aug68 150(1) 9	118
9630. BLAST OFF Stray Cats	29Apr89 111(2) 9	118
9631. YOUNG MAN RUNNING Corey Hart	09Jul88 121(2) 8	118
9632. PHANTAZIA Noel Pointer	18Jun77 144(1) 8	118
9633. CLASS OF '66 Floyd Cramer	17Sep66 123(2) 7	118
9634. THE SOUL OF PAUL MAURIAT Paul Mauriat	03May69 157(1) 8	118
9635. TODAY'S GREAT HITS Lawrence Welk	29Jan66 93(1) 6	118
9636. TODAY'S ROMANTIC HITS/FOR LOVERS ONLY	Jackie Gleason 07Dec63 115(1) 8	118
9637. DERRINGER Derringer	31Jul76 154(1) 9	118
9638. MUSIC OF VICTOR HERBERT Beverly Sills	03Jan76 113(2) 6	118
9639. ARGUS Wishbone Ash	24Jun72 169(2) 13	118
9640. VISIONS Grant Green	16Oct71 151(1) 9	118
9641. I CAN'T SEE ME WITHOUT YOU	Conway Twitty 08Apr72 130(1) 9	118
9642. ON GOLDEN POND Soundtrack	27Feb82 147(1) 11	118
9643. HIT BOOTS 1970 Boots Randolph	10Oct70 157(2) 9	118
9644. RAGTIME Soundtrack	23Jan82 134(2) 9	118
9645. ACADEMY AWARD WINNERS Roger Williams	05Sep64 126(1) 9	118
9646. THAT'S WHAT I AM HERE FOR	Roy Buchanan 23Feb74 152(1) 10	118
9647. THE PARTY'S OVER Talk Talk	18Sep82 132(2) 16	118
9648. LIVE IN EUROPE Creedence Clearwater	Revival 24Nov73 143(1) 10	118
9649. INARTICULATE SPEECH OF THE HEART	Van Morrison 09Apr83 116(1) 8	118
9650. ROCK AND ROLL MUSIC The Frost	29Nov69 148(1) 8	118
9651. POPCORN Hot Butter	21Oct72 137(1) 7	118
9652. THE SOUNDS OF SIMON Joe Simon	03Apr71 153(1) 12	118
9653. COWBOYS & ENGLISHMEN Poco	20Feb82 131(2) 8	118
9654. TIME EXPOSURE Stanley Clarke	28Apr84 149(1) 12	118
9655. A PORTRAIT OF ARTHUR PRYSOCK	Arthur Prysock 28Dec63 97(1) 7	118
9656. THE STARS WE ARE Marc Almond	28Jan89 144(2) 11	118
9657. INTRODUCING THE ELEVENTH HOUSE WITH LARRY CORYELL Eleventh House	13Apr74 163(1) 11	118
9658. BORN TO LAUGH AT TORNADOES Was (Not	Was) 15Oct83 134(2) 9	118
9659. AN EVENING WITH BELAFONTE/MOUSKOURI Harry Belafonte & Nana Mouskouri	09Apr66 124(1) 8	118
9660. THE SOFT MACHINE Soft Machine	21Dec68 160(1) 9	117
9661. OVER THE TOP Soundtrack	07Mar87 120(2) 8	117
9662. GOT ANY GUM? Joe Walsh	01Aug87 113(2) 8	117
9663. MOTORTOWN REVIEW IN PARIS	Various Artists 18Dec65 111(1) 7	117
9664. MARVIN GAYE SUPER HITS Marvin Gaye	07Nov70 117(2) 6	117
9665. MANHOLE Grace Slick	09Feb74 127(1) 7	117
9666. TEEN SCENE Chet Atkins	21Sep63 93(1) 6	117
9667. BIRD IN A SILVER CAGE Herbie Mann	12Feb77 132(2) 7	117
9668. DON'T TURN AROUND Black Ivory	22Apr72 158(2) 9	117
9669. THE BEST OF KOOL AND THE GANG	Kool & The Gang 25Sep71 157(1) 8	117
9670. SMALLCREEP'S DAY Mike Rutherford	05Apr80 163(2) 11	117
9671. CHANCE Candi Staton	28Jul79 129(1) 6	117
9672. YOU'RE THE ONE FOR ME "D" Train	26Jun82 128(2) 9	117
9673. TOO LATE TO CRY Widowmaker	11Jun77 150(1) 9	117
9674. SUNDAY MORNING SUITE Frank Mills	24Nov79 149(1) 9	117
9675. REFLECTIONS George Howard	18Jun88 109(1) 8	117
9676. GROOVIN' YOU Harvey Mason	28Apr79 149(1) 8	117

Rank. Title Act	Entry Peak(Pk Wks) TotWks	Scr
9677. **BOOGITY BOOGITY** Ray Stevens	15Jun74 159(1) 11	117
9678. **GET UP WITH IT** Miles Davis	04Jan75 141(1) 8	117
9679. **THE BUTTERFLY BALL AND THE GRASSHOPPER'S FEAST** Roger Glover	24Jan76 142(2) 8	117
9680. **SURVIVE** Nuclear Assault	13Aug88 145(1) 11	117
9681. **I COMMIT TO LOVE** Howard Hewett	01Nov86 159(2) 16	117
9682. **STRANGE FIRE** Indigo Girls	25Nov89 159(1) 14	117
9683. **WHAT IT WAS, WAS LOVE** Steve Lawrence & Eydie Gorme	08Mar69 141(1) 6	117
9684. **THE SWEET INSPIRATIONS** Sweet Inspirations	06Apr68 90(1) 6	117
9685. **HEYDEY** The Church	21Jun86 146(1) 11	116
9686. **JOHNNY MATHIS IN PERSON** Johnny Mathis	05Feb72 128(1) 7	116
9687. **WHERE ARE YOU NOW, MY SON?** Joan Baez	19May73 138(1) 9	116
9688. **MORRIS ALBERT** Morris Albert	12Jun76 135(1) 7	116
9689. **ALL OF THE GOOD ONES ARE TAKEN** Ian Hunter	06Aug83 125(1) 8	116
9690. **TROUBLE WALKIN'** Ace Frehley	11Nov89 102(2) 9	116
9691. **THE LOOK OF LOVE** Dusty Springfield	23Dec67 135(1) 7	116
9692. **ESSAR** Smokey Robinson	30Jun84 141(2) 11	116
9693. **DETROIT DIESEL** Alvin Lee	23Aug86 124(2) 9	116
9694. **MAUREEN McGOVERN** Maureen McGovern	08Sep79 162(1) 10	116
9695. **WORTH THE WAIT** Peaches & Herb	11Oct80 120(1) 6	116
9696. **SKYSCRAPER** Original Cast	08Jan66 128(2) 8	116
9697. **I WONDER WHAT SHE'S DOING TONITE?** Tommy Boyce & Bobby Hart	20Apr68 109(1) 5	116
9698. **IN THE LAND OF SALVATION AND SIN** Georgia Satellites	11Nov89 130(2) 13	116
9699. **PURE MUSIC** Chase	27Apr74 155(1) 10	116
9700. **ISLANDS** Mike Oldfield	27Feb88 138(2) 8	116
9701. **AN EVENING WASTED WITH TOM LEHRER** Tom Lehrer	26Mar66 133(1) 8	116
9702. **COUNTRY & WESTERN MEETS RHYTHM & BLUES** Ray Charles	11Sep65 116(1) 7	116
9703. **THE TURTLES! MORE GOLDEN HITS** The Turtles	11Apr70 146(1) 9	116
9704. **MORE SPECIALS** The Specials	08Nov80 98(1) 5	116
9705. **IRONHORSE** Ironhorse	07Apr79 153(1) 10	116
9706. **STARS ON LONG PLAY II** Stars On	31Oct81 120(3) 6	116
9707. **ON SOLID GROUND** Larry Carlton	10Jun89 126(2) 8	116
9708. **ROMAN HOLLIDAY** Roman Holliday	03Sep83 142(1) 11	116
9709. **I'M LEAVING IT UP TO YOU** Dale & Grace	01Feb64 100(1) 7	116
9710. **LESLEY GORE SINGS OF MIXED-UP HEARTS** Lesley Gore	25Jan64 125(2) 8	115
9711. **LUST FOR LIFE** Iggy Pop	17Sep77 120(1) 6	115
9712. **WISE GUY** Kid Creole & The Coconuts	03Jul82 145(2) 12	115
9713. **IN LONDON** Al Jarreau	21Sep85 125(1) 9	115
9714. **SLADEST** Slade	20Oct73 129(1) 7	115
9715. **WEAPONS OF LOVE** The Truth	30May87 115(2) 8	115
9716. **RAMPANT** Nazareth	13Jul74 157(1) 9	115
9717. **TWIN HYPE** Twin Hype	26Aug89 140(2) 11	115
9718. **BURNIN' LOVE** Con Funk Shun	19Jul86 121(2) 11	115
9719. **ELECTRIC CAFE** Kraftwerk	29Nov86 156(2) 14	115
9720. **CIVILIZED MAN** Joe Cocker	19May84 133(1) 9	115
9721. **CHRONICLE II** Creedence Clearwater Revival	01Nov86 165(2) 16	115
9722. **IN THE MISTY MOONLIGHT** Jerry Wallace	07Nov64 96(1) 7	115
9723. **YES, I'M READY** Barbara Mason	02Oct65 129(1) 8	115
9724. **MOVING TARGET** Gil Scott-Heron	02Oct82 123(1) 9	115
9725. **GLORY OF LOVE** Herbie Mann	03Feb68 151(1) 12	115
9726. **GOING THROUGH THE MOTIONS** Hot Chocolate	28Jul79 112(2) 6	115
9727. **WHEN I NEED YOU** Roger Whittaker	05May79 115(2) 5	115
9728. **SIDE 3** Raspberries	06Oct73 128(1) 7	115
9729. **A DOUBLE HEADER WITH ARTHUR PRYSOCK** Arthur Prysock	17Jul65 116(1) 7	115
9730. **HEAVEN ONLY KNOWS** Teddy Pendergrass	07Jan84 123(1) 9	115
9731. **FUNCTION AT THE JUNCTION** B.T. Express	28May77 111(2) 5	115
9732. **TOUCH** Sarah McLachlan	29Apr89 132(1) 12	115
9733. **CELLOPHANE SYMPHONY** Tommy James And The Shondells	25Oct69 141(1) 6	115
9734. **P.F.M. 'COOK'** P.F.M.	28Dec74 151(1) 8	115
9735. **WORLD OF COUNTRY MUSIC** Various Artists	10Jul65 107(2) 7	115
9736. **INFINITE RIDER ON THE BIG DOGMA** Michael Nesmith	04Aug79 151(2) 9	115
9737. **THE MASON WILLIAMS EAR SHOW** Mason Williams	28Dec68 164(2) 8	114
9738. **WHITE ROCK** Rick Wakeman	26Feb77 126(1) 7	114
9739. **HARD AGAIN** Muddy Waters	19Feb77 143(1) 7	114
9740. **ARRIVE WITHOUT TRAVELLING** The Three O'Clock	25May85 125(2) 10	114
9741. **IN SEARCH OF A SONG** Tom T. Hall	09Oct71 137(2) 6	114
9742. **TURTLE BAY** Herbie Mann	22Sep73 146(1) 8	114
9743. **IT'S A BEAUTIFUL DAY AT CARNEGIE HALL** It's A Beautiful Day	11Nov72 144(2) 9	114
9744. **THERE'S A MEETIN' HERE TONITE** Joe & Eddie	18Jan64 119(1) 7	114
9745. **WINDOW OF A CHILD** Seawind	21Jan78 122(2) 7	114
9746. **MARY POPPINS(2)** Soundtrack	04Aug73 141(1) 8	114
9747. **TAKE A LITTLE WALK WITH ME** Tom Rush	11Jun66 122(1) 7	114
9748. **LEGEND** Tangerine Dream	17May86 96(2) 7	114
9749. **NEVER GET OUT OF THESE BLUES ALIVE** John Lee Hooker	18Mar72 130(1) 6	114
9750. **A STREET CALLED STRAIGHT** Roy Buchanan	15May76 148(3) 7	114
9751. **SAWYER BROWN** Sawyer Brown	23Feb85 140(2) 11	114
9752. **THE MARVELETTES** The Marvelettes	08Apr67 129(1) 8	114
9753. **MY FUNNY VALENTINE** Miles Davis	24Apr65 138(1) 9	114
9754. **LISTEN TO THE MESSAGE** Club Nouveau	18Jun88 98(2) 6	114
9755. **CURIOSITY** Regina	04Oct86 102(2) 8	114
9756. **FOREVER LOVERS** Mac Davis	10Apr76 156(1) 9	114
9757. **TROOP** Troop	03Sep88 133(2) 9	114
9758. **VOICES IN THE SKY-BEST OF THE MOODY BLUES** Moody Blues	23Mar85 132(2) 9	114
9759. **IMAGES 1966-1967** David Bowie	17Mar73 144(1) 9	114
9760. **THE NEW SEARCHERS LP** The Searchers	20Mar65 112(2) 7	114
9761. **STREET READY** Leatherwolf	29Apr89 123(1) 8	114
9762. **HUGH MASEKELA'S LATEST** Hugh Masekela	05Aug67 151(2) 10	114
9763. **SLADE ALIVE!** Slade	07Oct72 158(1) 11	114
9764. **FEEL IT** Noel Pointer	01Sep79 138(4) 7	114
9765. **COLOURS** Claudine Longet	01Feb69 155(1) 7	113
9766. **HERE COMES MY BABY** The Tremeloes	24Jun67 119(2) 8	113
9767. **KIHNTAGIOUS** Greg Kihn Band	16Jun84 121(1) 9	113
9768. **BORN TO GET DOWN** Muscle Shoals Horns	03Jul76 154(3) 8	113
9769. **RICH MAN** Climax Blues Band	17Feb73 150(1) 10	113
9770. **DISCO TRAIN** Donny Osmond	21Aug76 145(1) 8	113
9771. **DR. BYRDS & MR. HYDE** The Byrds	15Mar69 153(1) 7	113
9772. **IT'S TEE TIME** Sweet Tee	25Feb89 169(3) 13	113
9773. **CLOSE-UP** Merle Haggard	23Aug69 140(1) 6	113
9774. **MANTOVANI...MEMORIES** Mantovani	09Nov68 143(2) 7	113
9775. **AGNES ENGLISH** John Fred And His Playboy Band	03Feb68 154(1) 10	113
9776. **CHI COLTRANE** Chi Coltrane	23Sep72 148(1) 10	113
9777. **THE CAMERA NEVER LIES** Michael Franks	01Aug87 147(1) 11	113
9778. **OH! BROTHER** Larry Gatlin	22Jul78 140(2) 8	113
9779. **ON THE ROAD TO FREEDOM** Alvin Lee & Myron LeFevre	12Jan74 138(1) 8	113
9780. **JEAN** Lawrence Welk	15Nov69 145(1) 7	113
9781. **WATERLOO** ABBA	17Aug74 145(1) 8	113
9782. **BELIEVE** The Jets	02Sep89 107(1) 7	113
9783. **ROAD ISLAND** Ambrosia	29May82 115(2) 7	113
9784. **RIGHT-OFF!** Hudson and Landry	06Jan73 147(1) 9	112
9785. **BREAK OF HEARTS** Katrina And The Waves	02Sep89 122(2) 8	112
9786. **POWERFUL STUFF** Fabulous Thunderbirds	06May89 118(3) 7	112
9787. **WHERE DID OUR LOVE GO** Donnie Elbert	01Jan72 153(1) 9	112
9788. **IT'S A GUITAR WORLD** Chet Atkins	06May67 148(2) 9	112
9789. **MR. HANDS** Herbie Hancock	29Nov80 117(1) 6	112
9790. **1776** Soundtrack	30Dec72 163(1) 11	112
9791. **THREE TIMES IN LOVE** Tommy James	22Mar80 134(1) 7	112
9792. **ELECTRODYNAMICS** Dick Hyman	09Nov63 117(1) 7	112
9793. **LIFE STORIES** Earl Klugh	30Aug86 143(2) 11	112

Rank. Title Act Entry Peak(Pk Wks) TotWks	Scr
9794. **GOD SAVE THE QUEEN/UNDER HEAVY MANNERS** Robert Fripp 26Apr80 110(2) 6	112
9795. **LIVE** Sensational Alex Harvey Band 01Nov75 100(2) 4	112
9796. **HEAR! HEAR!** The Searchers 20Jun64 120(2) 8	112
9797. **SPANISH GREASE** Willie Bobo 26Feb66 137(1) 8	112
9798. **THE GOLDEN HITS OF JERRY LEE LEWIS** Jerry Lee Lewis 28Mar64 116(1) 8	112
9799. **BAD BOY** Robert Gordon 02Feb80 150(1) 9	112
9800. **CITY** McGuinn & Chris Hillman Featuring Gene Clark 16Feb80 136(2) 7	112
9801. **IMAGINOS** Blue Öyster Cult 20Aug88 122(1) 8	112
9802. **INTO THE NIGHT** Soundtrack 13Apr85 118(2) 8	112
9803. **LOW RENT RENDEZVOUS** Ace Spectrum 23Aug75 138(1) 7	112
9804. **CCCP - LIVE IN MOSCOW** UB40 29Aug87 121(2) 8	112
9805. **CATS UNDER THE STARS** Jerry Garcia Band 15Apr78 114(1) 5	112
9806. **SPOOKY** Classics IV 09Mar68 140(3) 7	112
9807. **AMERICAN PASTIME** Three Dog Night 24Apr76 123(2) 6	112
9808. **NOTHIN' BUT THE BLUES** Johnny Winter 23Jul77 146(2) 8	112
9809. **CONFLICTING EMOTIONS** Split Enz 21Jul84 137(1) 10	111
9810. **RADIO-ACTIVITY** Kraftwerk 13Dec75 140(1) 8	111
9811. **GETTING TO THIS** Blodwyn Pig 27Jun70 96(1) 5	111
9812. **CREATIVE SOURCE** Creative Source 19Jan74 152(1) 10	111
9813. **MIRABAI** Mirabai 30Aug75 128(1) 6	111
9814. **LINDA RONSTADT** Linda Ronstadt 12Feb72 163(1) 10	111
9815. **LIVE AT LAST!** Tim Weisberg 02Oct76 148(1) 7	111
9816. **I LOVE THE WAY YOU LOVE** Betty Wright 26Feb72 123(1) 6	111
9817. **BEAST FROM THE EAST** Mandrill 07Feb76 143(2) 8	111
9818. **AMERICA/LIVE** America 17Dec77 129(2) 7	111
9819. **ROCKIN' RADIO** Tom Browne 03Dec83 147(1) 12	111
9820. **ENTERTAINERS...ON AND OFF THE RECORD** Statler Brothers 10Jun78 155(1) 9	111
9821. **DOMINO THEORY** Weather Report 24Mar84 136(1) 8	111
9822. **FROM HERE TO ETERNITY** Giorgio 29Oct77 130(2) 7	111
9823. **O.F.R.** Nitro 12Aug89 140(1) 9	111
9824. **LAST NIGHT ON EARTH** Rhythm Heritage 19Feb77 138(2) 6	111
9825. **OUR MEMORIES OF ELVIS** Elvis Presley 10Mar79 132(2) 7	111
9826. **NURDS** The Roches 22Nov80 130(1) 7	111
9827. **QUAZAR** Quazar 11Nov78 121(2) 5	111
9828. **INSANE ASYLUM** Kathi McDonald 06Apr74 156(1) 11	111
9829. **BEAUTY** Santa Esmeralda 02Sep78 141(1) 6	111
9830. **THE COMING ATLANTIS** Freddy Robinson 19Sep70 133(2) 7	111
9831. **JOHN DAVIDSON** John Davidson 17May69 153(1) 7	110
9832. **NEVER FELT SO GOOD** James Ingram 13Sep86 123(2) 9	110
9833. **REDWING** Grinder Switch 19Nov77 144(3) 8	110
9834. **THE DOCTOR** Cheap Trick 18Oct86 115(2) 9	110
9835. **WHEN A GUITAR PLAYS THE BLUES** Roy Buchanan 03Aug85 161(1) 13	110
9836. **VIVA TERLINGUA!** Jerry Jeff Walker 15Dec73 160(1) 11	110
9837. **MADE IN ENGLAND** Atomic Rooster 07Oct72 149(1) 8	110
9838. **OUTSIDE HELP** Johnny Rivers 14Jan78 142(2) 8	110
9839. **LABOR OF LOVE** Spinners 04Apr81 128(2) 6	110
9840. **IN A SENTIMENTAL MOOD** Dr. John 27May89 142(2) 11	110
9841. **VOYAGER** Dexter Wansel 01Apr78 139(1) 6	110
9842. **MOTHER'S FINEST** Mother's Finest 11Sep76 148(2) 8	110
9843. **7-TEASE** Donovan 14Dec74 135(1) 6	110
9844. **BAD LUCK IS ALL I HAVE** Eddie Harris 27Sep75 133(1) 6	110
9845. **RIGHT ON!** Original Last Poets 06Mar71 106(1) 6	110
9846. **BITTERSWEET WHITE LIGHT** Cher 14Apr73 140(2) 8	110
9847. **QUEEN ELVIS** Robyn Hitchcock And The Egyptians 01Apr89 139(1) 9	110
9848. **GREAT GONZOS! THE BEST OF TED NUGENT** Ted Nugent 28Nov81 140(1) 8	110
9849. **I LOVE TO SING THE SONGS I SING** Barry White 18Aug79 132(2) 6	110
9850. **THE MONROES** The Monroes 19Jun82 109(2) 9	110
9851. **THE BEST OF SAM COOKE, VOLUME 2** Sam Cooke 24Jul65 128(2) 8	110
9852. **ON TARGET** Fastway 22Apr89 135(2) 10	110
9853. **INTERLUDE** Soundtrack 19Oct68 136(1) 5	110
9854. **CAN'T YOU HEAR THE SONG?** Wayne Newton 18Nov72 164(1) 11	110
9855. **CONCERTO FOR GROUP AND ORCHESTRA** Deep Purple/The Royal Philharmonic Orchestra 16May70 149(2) 8	110
9856. **GREATEST HITS** The Sandpipers 18Apr70 160(1) 10	110
9857. **THE SEEDS** The Seeds 14Jan67 132(1) 7	110
9858. **PORKY'S REVENGE** Soundtrack 13Apr85 122(2) 8	110
9859. **THE ELVIS MEDLEY** Elvis Presley 27Nov82 133(2) 9	110
9860. **MIKE NESMITH PRESENTS/THE WICHITA TRAIN WHISTLE SINGS** Wichita Train Whistle 03Aug68 144(2) 7	110
9861. **FUNDAMENTAL ROLL** Walter Egan 14May77 137(1) 6	109
9862. **TONGUE TWISTER** Shoes 07Feb81 140(3) 7	109
9863. **UP UP AND AWAY** Boston Pops Orchestra 26Oct68 157(1) 7	109
9864. **BACK IN THE USA** MC5 21Feb70 137(2) 7	109
9865. **LOVE, LIFE & FEELINGS** Shirley Bassey 09Oct76 149(1) 8	109
9866. **ROBERT GORDON WITH LINK WRAY** Robert Gordon With Link Wray 01Oct77 142(1) 8	109
9867. **STAY TUNED** Chet Atkins 27Apr85 145(2) 13	109
9868. **THIRD GENERATION** Hiroshima 20Aug83 142(1) 9	109
9869. **NO ESCAPE** Marc Tanner Band 03Mar79 140(2) 8	109
9870. **OLD ENOUGH** Lou Ann Barton 24Apr82 133(1) 9	109
9871. **HOME OF THE BRAVE** Laurie Anderson 26Apr86 145(2) 12	109
9872. **THEM COTTON PICKIN' DAYS IS OVER** Godfrey Cambridge 03Apr65 142(1) 9	109
9873. **SILENT LETTER** America 07Jul79 110(1) 6	109
9874. **THE SLIDE AREA** Ry Cooder 12Jun82 105(1) 7	109
9875. **KEEP ON IT** Starpoint 09May81 138(2) 8	109
9876. **EVERY ONE OF US** Eric Burdon & The Animals 24Aug68 152(2) 8	109
9877. **HOLD ME** Bert Kaempfert And His Orchestra 13May67 122(1) 7	109
9878. **TOOTSIE** Soundtrack 26Feb83 144(3) 12	109
9879. **THE DRAGON IS DANCING** Jimmie Spheeris 20Sep75 135(1) 6	109
9880. **TOO LONG IN THE WASTELAND** James McMurtry 14Oct89 125(1) 9	109
9881. **HERE COMES INSPIRATION** Paul Williams 02Mar74 165(1) 10	109
9882. **DIFFERENT STYLE!** Musical Youth 17Dec83 144(1) 12	109
9883. **BLUE RIVER** Eric Andersen 15Jul72 169(1) 11	109
9884. **DEF, DUMB & BLONDE** Deborah Harry 14Oct89 123(2) 8	109
9885. **WILL AND THE KILL** Will And The Kill 09Apr88 129(2) 8	109
9886. **S.P.Y.S.** Spys 14Aug82 138(3) 10	109
9887. **RIDE THE WIND** The Youngbloods 24Jul71 157(3) 8	109
9888. **BET YOUR HEART ON ME** Johnny Lee 24Oct81 147(1) 8	109
9889. **AMERICA, I HEAR YOU SINGING** Frank Sinatra/Bing Crosby/Frank Waring 30May64 116(1) 7	108
9890. **FLYING HOME** Stanley Jordan 15Oct88 131(2) 9	108
9891. **I HAD A BALL** Original Cast 30Jan65 126(2) 8	108
9892. **THE WORLD WE KNEW** Bert Kaempfert And His Orchestra 07Oct67 136(1) 7	108
9893. **CAN I CHANGE MY MIND** Tyrone Davis 29Mar69 146(1) 6	108
9894. **HEY JUDE/HEY BING!** Bing Crosby 29Mar69 162(2) 8	108
9895. **TOUGH GUYS** Isaac Hayes 15Jun74 146(1) 8	108
9896. **DAVE GRUSIN AND THE GRP ALL-STARS/LIVE IN JAPAN** Dave Grusin and the GRP All-Stars 18Jul81 140(2) 7	108
9897. **BRISTOL'S CREME** Johnny Bristol 11Dec76 154(1) 11	108
9898. **2001: A SPACE ODYSSEY (VOLUME TWO)** Soundtrack 10Oct70 147(1) 7	108
9899. **MORE THEMES FOR YOUNG LOVERS** Percy Faith 30May64 110(1) 7	108
9900. **OMMADAWN** Mike Oldfield 20Dec75 146(1) 7	108
9901. **BLACK MAGIC** Martha Reeves & The Vandellas 01Apr72 146(2) 7	108
9902. **TOGETHER** Watts 103rd Street Band 19Apr69 140(1) 5	108
9903. **MY BEST** Kitaro 10May86 141(2) 10	108
9904. **THE PLAYER** First Choice 26Oct74 143(2) 7	108
9905. **THE BEST OF RAMSEY LEWIS** Ramsey Lewis 14Mar70 172(1) 12	108
9906. **YOU NEVER KNOW WHO YOUR FRIENDS ARE** Al Kooper 11Oct69 125(1) 6	108
9907. **MANTOVANI/TANGO** Mantovani 15Jun68 148(2) 7	108

Rank. Title Act Entry Peak(Pk Wks) TotWks	Scr
9908. I'LL BE THERE! Gerry And The Pacemakers 27Feb65 120(1) 7	108
9909. THE FUNK IS ON Instant Funk 18Oct80 130(2) 6	108
9910. LOVE OR PHYSICAL Ashford & Simpson 18Mar89 135(2) 8	108
9911. WE CAN MAKE MUSIC Tommy Roe 31Oct70 134(1) 6	108
9912. A TIME TO KEEP: 1963 Chet Huntley & David Brinkley 14Mar64 115(1) 7	108
9913. TWINS Soundtrack 21Jan89 162(3) 12	108
9914. SHAME ON THE WORLD Main Ingredient 13Dec75 158(1) 8	108
9915. MAXIMUM SECURITY Tony MacAlpine 04Jul87 146(2) 11	108
9916. TOBACCO ROAD Spooky Tooth 05Jun71 152(1) 7	107
9917. FROLIC THROUGH THE PARK Death Angel 06Aug88 143(1) 11	107
9918. A LEGEND IN MY TIME Ronnie Milsap 15Feb75 138(2) 7	107
9919. EARL KLUGH Earl Klugh 10Jul76 124(1) 6	107
9920. THE BEST OF JIM REEVES VOLUME II Jim Reeves 12Feb66 100(1) 6	107
9921. GREATEST HITS OF THE OUTLAWS/HIGH TIDES FOREVER The Outlaws 27Nov82 136(2) 9	107
9922. THE WAY OF LOVE Jim Nabors 17Jun72 157(1) 8	107
9923. GO BANG! Shriekback 23Jul88 169(2) 12	107
9924. LOUISIANA WOMAN, MISSISSIPPI MAN Conway Twitty & Loretta Lynn 25Aug73 153(1) 9	107
9925. LAST NIGHT I HAD THE STRANGEST DREAM Mason Proffit 06Nov71 186(1) 14	107
9926. EAT THE HEAT Accept 24Jun89 139(2) 9	107
9927. URBAN COWBOY II Soundtrack 10Jan81 134(1) 6	107
9928. A GASSSSS Jr. Walker & The All Stars 03Oct70 110(1) 5	107
9929. SHE WAS ONLY A GROCER'S DAUGHTER Blow Monkeys 25Apr87 134(2) 8	107
9930. CELEBRATION El Chicano 06May72 173(1) 13	107
9931. ETTA JAMES Etta James 15Sep73 154(1) 9	107
9932. RICH AND POOR Randy Crawford 18Nov89 159(3) 13	107
9933. NOW PLAYING Bernadette Peters 03Oct81 151(1) 9	107
9934. FIRST IMPRESSIONS The Impressions 09Aug75 115(1) 5	107
9935. NOW The Tubes 28May77 122(2) 6	107
9936. 100% COTTON James Cotton Band 18Jan75 146(1) 9	107
9937. MEGA FORCE 707 03Jul82 129(2) 9	107
9938. ALL RIGHT NOW Pepsi & Shirlie 27Feb88 133(1) 9	107
9939. MORE NASHVILLE SOUNDS Danny Davis And The Nashville Brass 12Jul69 143(1) 6	107
9940. GOLDEN BUTTER/ THE BEST OF THE PAUL BUTTERFIELD BLUES BAND Butterfield Blues Band 20May72 136(2) 6	107
9941. SOONER OR LATER Larry Graham 26Jun82 142(1) 9	107
9942. 1,2,3 RED LIGHT 1910 Fruitgum Co. 05Oct68 163(1) 12	107
9943. THE VOGUES' GREATEST HITS The Vogues 10Jan70 148(1) 9	107
9944. ALL-TIME GREATEST HITS Paul Revere & The Raiders 08Jul72 143(1) 8	107
9945. KICK THE WALL Jimmy Davis & Junction 31Oct87 122(2) 8	107
9946. THE LAST EMPEROR Soundtrack 27Feb88 152(1) 10	107
9947. LIVING AND DYING IN 3/4 TIME Jimmy Buffett 02Mar74 176(2) 13	106
9948. MILLIE JACKSON Millie Jackson 16Sep72 166(1) 11	106
9949. YOU DEVIL YOU Flip Wilson 01Jun68 147(1) 7	106
9950. RESULTS Liza Minnelli 11Nov89 128(1) 10	106
9951. LIVE SENTENCE Alcatrazz 09Jun84 133(1) 10	106
9952. KEEP YOUR EYE ON THE SPARROW Merry Clayton 06Sep75 146(2) 8	106
9953. MIRAGE A TROIS Yellowjackets 28May83 145(1) 10	106
9954. 50 GUITARS IN LOVE 50 Guitars of Tommy Garrett 26Nov66 99(2) 5	106
9955. IN THE MIDNIGHT HOUR Wilson Pickett 30Oct65 107(1) 6	106
9956. U.S. 1 Head East 08Nov80 137(1) 6	106
9957. KEEPIN' LOVE NEW Howard Johnson 11Sep82 122(2) 9	106
9958. MIDNIGHT LIGHT LeBlanc & Carr 18Mar78 145(1) 7	106
9959. RENEGADE Thin Lizzy 20Feb82 157(1) 11	106
9960. THE CLOWN DIED IN MARVIN GARDENS Beacon Street Union 14Sep68 173(1) 10	106
9961. SPIRIT OF '76 Spirit 07Jun75 147(2) 9	106
9962. GOLDEN HITS OF THE SMOTHERS BROTHERS, VOL. 2 Smothers Brothers 13Aug66 119(1) 6	106
9963. WILDEST ORGAN IN TOWN! Billy Preston 09Jul66 118(1) 6	106
9964. FEEL GOOD Ike & Tina Turner 22Jul72 160(1) 9	106
9965. THUNDERSTEEL Riot 14May88 150(2) 10	106
9966. THE FIRST HURRAH! Clancy Brothers And Tommy Makem 02May64 91(1) 6	106
9967. BABY, I'M YOURS Barbara Lewis 25Sep65 118(1) 7	106
9968. AMIGO Arlo Guthrie 02Oct76 133(1) 6	106
9969. BLUE JEANS Chocolate Milk 12Dec81 162(1) 10	106
9970. HOLLYWOOD PARTY TONIGHT Odyssey 11Nov78 123(2) 5	106
9971. BAD BOY Ringo Starr 20May78 129(2) 6	106
9972. CHRISTIAN OF THE WORLD Tommy James And The Shondells 11Sep71 131(2) 8	105
9973. LET ME KNOW YOU Stanley Clarke 21Aug82 114(2) 8	105
9974. LOOKING FOR JACK Colin James Hay 21Feb87 126(2) 9	105
9975. SKY BLUE Passport 03Jun78 140(1) 7	105
9976. JOHN MAYALL-LIVE IN EUROPE John Mayall 01May71 146(1) 8	105
9977. PETER CETERA Peter Cetera 23Jan82 143(2) 10	105
9978. TRY A LITTLE LOVE Sam Cooke 30Oct65 120(1) 7	105
9979. THE AWAKENING The Reddings 20Dec80 174(3) 12	105
9980. PIANO RAGS BY SCOTT JOPLIN, VOLUME III Joshua Rifkin 14Dec74 126(2) 5	105
9981. AZTECA Azteca 13Jan73 151(2) 9	105
9982. AFOOT Let's Active 18Feb84 154(1) 11	105
9983. A LETTER FROM ST. PAUL The Silencers 22Aug87 147(2) 11	105
9984. MORE KNOCKERS UP! Rusty Warren 01Jan66 124(1) 7	105
9985. THINK I'LL GO SOMEWHERE AND CRY MYSELF TO SLEEP Al Martino 18Jun66 116(1) 6	105
9986. HIGH GEAR Neil Larsen 01Sep79 139(1) 7	105
9987. COBRA Soundtrack 28Jun86 100(2) 6	105
9988. IN HARMONY 2 Various Artists 21Nov81 129(1) 10	105
9989. SALSA Soundtrack 25Jun88 112(2) 6	105
9990. LOVIN' SOUND Ian & Sylvia 08Jul67 148(1) 10	105
9991. GETTIN' LUCKY Head East 02Apr77 136(1) 7	105
9992. THE BLACK MOTION PICTURE EXPERIENCE Cecil Holmes Soulful Sounds 28Apr73 141(1) 10	105
9993. DANCE DISCOTHEQUE Various Artists 27Jun64 102(1) 6	104
9994. STRAIGHT TO THE POINT Atlantic Starr 02Jun79 142(2) 7	104
9995. GLAMOUR Dave Davies 18Jul81 152(1) 8	104
9996. BANG Bang 08Apr72 164(1) 10	104
9997. ROMEO & JULIET Hubert Laws 06Nov76 139(1) 6	104
9998. SUNDAY CONCERT Gordon Lightfoot 15Nov69 143(1) 6	104
9999. IT'S ALL IN THE GAME Cliff Richard 18Apr64 115(1) 7	104
10000. WINDSONG Randy Crawford 26Jun82 148(1) 10	104
10001. ANGEL EYES Willie Nelson 16Jun84 116(2) 7	104
10002. CANDY APPLE GREY Husker Du 12Apr86 140(2) 10	104
10003. IN CONCERT Miles Davis 05May73 152(1) 8	104
10004. SAY IT LOUD! Lou Donaldson 05Apr69 153(1) 7	104
10005. CHARITY BALL Fanny 23Oct71 150(1) 7	104
10006. IN THE BEGINNING/ THE WORLD OF ARETHA FRANKLIN 1960-1967 Aretha Franklin 24Jun72 160(2) 9	104
10007. BE A BROTHER Big Brother And The Holding Company 28Nov70 134(2) 6	104
10008. LOVE CRAZY The Miracles 19Mar77 117(2) 5	104
10009. CA$HFLOW Ca$hflow 03May86 144(2) 11	104
10010. JAN & DEAN GOLDEN HITS, VOLUME 2 Jan & Dean 02Oct65 107(1) 6	104
10011. ROCK 'N' ROLL HIGH SCHOOL Soundtrack 02Jun79 118(2) 6	104
10012. RAY PRICE'S ALL-TIME GREATEST HITS Ray Price 09Sep72 165(1) 10	104
10013. THE WORLD OF BOOTS RANDOLPH Boots Randolph 27Nov71 144(2) 8	104
10014. ROD McKUEN'S GREATEST HITS-2 Rod McKuen 19Sep70 148(1) 8	104
10015. FORCE MAJEURE Doro 29Apr89 154(2) 11	104
10016. BEAT STREET II Soundtrack 29Sep84 137(2) 9	104
10017. RAISING HELL Fatback Band 28Feb76 158(1) 8	104
10018. BANG, BANG YOU'RE TERRY REID Terry Reid 21Dec68 153(2) 8	104
10019. I WONDER DO YOU THINK OF ME Keith Whitley 02Sep89 115(2) 7	104
10020. PAST MASTERS - VOLUME 2 The Beatles 02Apr88 121(2) 7	104
10021. NINE TO THE UNIVERSE Jimi Hendrix 26Apr80 127(1) 7	104
10022. A.C. Andre Cymone 21Sep85 121(2) 8	104
10023. POINT OF PLEASURE Xavier 24Apr82 129(1) 7	104

Rank. Title Act Entry Peak(Pk Wks) TotWks	Scr
10024. PERFECT COMBINATION Stacy Lattisaw & Johnny Gill 31Mar84 139(1) 8	104
10025. GRITS AIN'T GROCERIES Little Milton 14Jun69 159(1) 7	104
10026. LIVE! FOR LIFE Various Artists 07Jun86 105(2) 7	104
10027. BALLADS, BLUES AND BOASTERS Harry Belafonte 17Oct64 103(1) 7	104
10028. MUSIC FROM THE BILL COSBY SHOW--A HOUSE FULL OF LOVE TV Soundtrack 01Mar86 125(1) 7	103
10029. BEN FRANKLIN IN PARIS Original Cast 26Dec64 132(1) 8	103
10030. BLUE PINE TREES Unicorn 26Oct74 129(1) 5	103
10031. SOUND OF SEXY SOUL The Delfonics 08Mar69 155(2) 6	103
10032. YOU WON'T BELIEVE YOUR EARS Wes Harrison 02Nov63 83(1) 5	103
10033. THE GOOD LIFE WITH THE DRIFTERS The Drifters 06Feb65 103(1) 6	103
10034. YOU AIN'T WOMAN ENOUGH Loretta Lynn 04Mar67 140(1) 9	103
10035. EVERYBODY LOVES THE PILOT (EXCEPT THE CREW) Jon Astley 01Aug87 135(2) 10	103
10036. ANOTHER PLACE ANOTHER TIME Jerry Lee Lewis 29Jun68 160(1) 12	103
10037. SELL MY SOUL Sylvester 27Sep80 147(3) 8	103
10038. IN YOUR MIND Bryan Ferry 23Apr77 126(1) 5	103
10039. CATE BROS. Cate Bros. 07Feb76 158(1) 9	103
10040. CIRCLES New Seekers 15Jul72 166(3) 10	103
10041. DO IT YOURSELF Ian Dury And The Blockheads 21Jul79 126(1) 6	103
10042. TIME Pozo-Seco Singers 30Jul66 127(1) 6	103
10043. EVERLASTING SONGS FOR EVERLASTING LOVERS Arthur Prysock 15Aug64 131(2) 8	103
10044. HERE'S THE WORLD FOR YA Paul Hyde And The Payolas 08Jun85 144(2) 10	103
10045. 16 GREATEST HITS Steppenwolf 24Feb73 152(2) 9	103
10046. SURVIVAL OF THE FITTEST/LIVE Ted Nugent And The Amboy Dukes 06Mar71 129(2) 5	103
10047. REACT The Fixx 18Jul87 110(2) 7	103
10048. PERFECT SYMMETRY Fates Warning 16Sep89 141(1) 9	103
10049. BACK TO THE ROOTS Ramsey Lewis 19Jun71 163(1) 9	103
10050. AROUND THE WORLD - LIVE IN CONCERT The Osmonds 20Dec75 148(2) 8	103
10051. TOO S.O.S. Band 22Aug81 117(2) 6	103
10052. THERE'S NO ME WITHOUT YOU The Manhattans 11Aug73 150(1) 8	103
10053. POPPED IN SOULED OUT Wet Wet Wet 16Jul88 123(3) 7	103
10054. MANFRED MANN'S EARTH BAND Manfred Mann's Earth Band 26Feb72 138(2) 6	103
10055. MOTOWN WINNERS' CIRCLE/NO. 1 HITS, VOL. 2 Various Artists 22Feb69 135(2) 5	103
10056. FANCY DANCER Bobbi Humphrey 29Nov75 133(2) 5	103
10057. THE TALE OF THE TAPE Billy Squier 07Jun80 169(1) 12	103
10058. JULIAN COPE Julian Cope 21Feb87 109(2) 6	102
10059. ORIGINAL GOLDEN HITS - VOLUME 1 Jerry Lee Lewis 27Sep69 119(2) 4	102
10060. SO MUCH FOR DREAMING Ian & Sylvia 01Apr67 130(2) 7	102
10061. A COWBOY AFRAID OF HORSES Lobo 05Apr75 151(2) 7	102
10062. KGB KGB 06Mar76 124(1) 6	102
10063. SOUL SESSION Jr. Walker & The All Stars 09Apr66 130(1) 7	102
10064. MY FAIR LADY Ferrante & Teicher 14Nov64 145(2) 9	102
10065. HOLD WHAT YOU'VE GOT Joe Tex 06Feb65 124(2) 7	102
10066. POSITIVE POWER Steve Arrington's Hall Of Fame 25Feb84 141(1) 9	102
10067. VIENNA Ultravox 13Sep80 164(1) 9	102
10068. 50 FABULOUS PIANO FAVORITES Ferrante & Teicher 21Mar64 128(2) 7	102
10069. RESCUE YOU Joe Lynn Turner 02Nov85 143(2) 12	102
10070. HOLLYWOOD DREAM Thunderclap Newman 10Oct70 161(1) 10	102
10071. DOUBLE TROUBLE LIVE Molly Hatchet 07Dec85 130(3) 9	102
10072. #10 Guess Who 14Jul73 155(1) 8	102
10073. DUIT ON MON DEI Nilsson 05Apr75 141(2) 7	102
10074. TRUCK TURNER Isaac Hayes 03Aug74 156(1) 9	102
10075. A CHILD'S ADVENTURE Marianne Faithfull 26Mar83 107(2) 7	102
10076. SEE FOREVER EYES Prism 29Jul78 158(2) 8	102
10077. THE O'JAYS: COLLECTORS' ITEMS The O'Jays 07Jan78 132(1) 6	102
10078. TROPEA Tropea 20Mar76 138(1) 7	102
10079. USA King Crimson 24May75 125(1) 5	102
10080. NEVER GONNA BE ANOTHER ONE Thelma Houston 30May81 144(1) 6	102
10081. SO CLOSE, SO VERY FAR TO GO Jake Holmes 14Nov70 135(1) 6	102
10082. IN HEARING OF ATOMIC ROOSTER Atomic Rooster 11Dec71 167(1) 9	102
10083. CHIPMUNK ROCK The Chipmunks 05Jun82 109(1) 6	102
10084. 2400 FULTON ST. Jefferson Airplane 18Apr87 138(2) 9	101
10085. JOLLY WHAT! THE BEATLES & FRANK IFIELD The Beatles/Frank Ifield 04Apr64 104(1) 6	101
10086. SOMETIMES I JUST FEEL LIKE SMILIN' Butterfield Blues Band 04Sep71 124(2) 6	101
10087. SATISFIED WITH YOU Dave Clark Five 01Oct66 127(1) 6	101
10088. RAY STEVENS...UNREAL!!! Ray Stevens 12Dec70 141(2) 8	101
10089. THAT'S LIFE & PINEAPPLE MARKET Billy Vaughn And His Orchestra 13May67 130(1) 7	101
10090. FROM SOUTH AFRICA TO SOUTH CAROLINA Gil Scott-Heron & Brian Jackson 08Nov75 103(1) 5	101
10091. LEADER OF THE PACK The Shangri-Las 13Mar65 109(1) 6	101
10092. THE FLAMINGO KID Soundtrack 16Feb85 130(2) 8	101
10093. CLASS The Reddings 01Aug81 106(2) 5	101
10094. THE KIDS FROM "FAME" Kids From Fame 03Apr82 146(2) 8	101
10095. DARKROOM Angel City 08Nov80 133(1) 6	101
10096. SILK Fuse One 13Feb82 139(1) 8	101
10097. ARLO GUTHRIE Arlo Guthrie 08Jun74 165(1) 10	101
10098. HEART OF THE CITY Barrabas 23Aug75 149(1) 7	101
10099. EARTH & SKY Graham Nash 08Mar80 117(1) 5	101
10100. ERIC CARMEN (II) Eric Carmen 09Feb85 128(2) 10	101
10101. JANE FONDA'S WORKOUT RECORD FOR PREGNANCY, BIRTH AND RECOVERY Jane Fonda 21May83 115(1) 7	101
10102. THE HANGMAN'S BEAUTIFUL DAUGHTER Incredible String Band 20Jul68 161(1) 9	101
10103. KING SIZE B.B. King 12Feb77 154(1) 7	101
10104. PETE'S PLACE Pete Fountain 02Jan65 121(1) 7	101
10105. PUMP IRON! Alvin Lee 06Sep75 131(2) 5	101
10106. THE BEST OF JOE SIMON Joe Simon 30Dec72 147(1) 8	101
10107. STANDING ON THE EDGE Frankie Miller 26Jun82 135(2) 9	101
10108. THE BIG HEAT Stan Ridgway 12Apr86 131(2) 9	101
10109. CRY BABY AND 11 OTHER HITS Garnet Mimms & The Enchanters 23Nov63 91(1) 5	101
10110. LISZTOMANIA Soundtrack 08Nov75 145(2) 6	101
10111. GONE TROPPO George Harrison 27Nov82 108(2) 7	100
10112. LIVE NUDE GUITARS Brian Setzer 28May88 140(2) 8	100
10113. BOSS BEAT Sandy Nelson 08Jan66 126(1) 7	100
10114. GERONIMO'S CADILLAC Michael Murphey 23Sep72 160(1) 9	100
10115. THE SUPREMES(2) The Supremes 28Jun75 152(1) 8	100
10116. SCHEMER-DREAMER Steve Walsh 16Feb80 124(1) 6	100
10117. LIVE Reba McEntire 14Oct89 124(3) 8	100
10118. STARTING OVER Raspberries 19Oct74 143(1) 6	100
10119. MAYBE Three Degrees 08Aug70 139(2) 7	100
10120. WHICH ONE'S WILLIE Wet Willie 09Jun79 172(1) 11	100
10121. A TOUCH ON THE RAINY SIDE Jesse Winchester 26Aug78 156(2) 7	100
10122. IN THE SPIRIT OF THINGS Kansas 05Nov88 114(2) 6	100
10123. BRONCO BILLY Soundtrack 05Jul80 123(1) 6	99.9
10124. CONVERTIBLE MUSIC Josie Cotton 07Aug82 147(2) 12	99.9
10125. CANADIAN SUNSET Andy Williams 03Jul65 112(2) 6	99.9
10126. THIS ISLAND Eurogliders 22Dec84 140(2) 11	99.9
10127. RETURN TO MAGENTA Mink De Ville 10Jun78 126(2) 5	99.9
10128. CHRISTMAS PORTRAIT Carpenters 09Dec78 145(1) 7	99.9
10129. OXO Oxo 30Apr83 117(1) 7	99.8
10130. FUNLAND Bram Tchaikovsky 23May81 158(1) 8	99.8
10131. THE ALICE COOPER SHOW Alice Cooper 17Dec77 131(1) 6	99.8
10132. IT'S BEGINNING TO AND BACK AGAIN Wire 08Jul89 135(2) 10	99.8
10133. TASTEFUL SOUL Main Ingredient 13Mar71 146(1) 9	99.8
10134. PSYCHOTIC REACTION Count Five 03Dec66 122(1) 6	99.8
10135. EARTH CRISIS Steel Pulse 31Mar84 154(1) 12	99.7
10136. NEW LOVERS AND OLD FRIENDS Johnny Rivers 20Sep75 147(1) 6	99.7
10137. BLACK IVORY Wanda Robinson 16Oct71 186(1) 13	99.6

Rank. Title Act Entry Peak(Pk Wks) TotWks	Scr
10138. GOOD TIMES Kool & The Gang 17Mar73 142(1) 7	99.6
10139. I Patrick Moraz 05Jun76 132(1) 5	99.6
10140. KING FLOYD King Floyd 29May71 130(1) 5	99.6
10141. SHAKE SOME ACTION Flamin' Groovies 21Aug76 142(1) 7	99.5
10142. GOIN' UP IN SMOKE Eddie Kendricks 09Oct76 144(1) 7	99.5
10143. BOBBY WOMACK'S GREATEST HITS Bobby Womack 14Dec74 142(1) 7	99.5
10144. VARIATIONS Eddie Rabbitt 24Jun78 143(2) 7	99.4
10145. LOVE TALK The Manhattans 14Apr79 141(2) 7	99.4
10146. HAPPINESS HEARTACHES Brian Auger's Oblivion Express 19Feb77 127(2) 5	99.2
10147. I WAS THE ONE Elvis Presley 21May83 103(1) 6	99.2
10148. IN THE HEAT OF THE NIGHT Soundtrack 30Sep67 153(1) 11	99.1
10149. SWEAT BAND Sweat Band 13Dec80 150(2) 8	99.1
10150. HAWAII TATTOO Martin Denny and His Orchestra 16Jan65 123(1) 7	99.0
10151. UK JIVE The Kinks 25Nov89 122(2) 8	99.0
10152. RAIL Rail 25Aug84 143(1) 10	98.9
10153. IN A SILENT WAY Miles Davis 06Sep69 134(2) 6	98.9
10154. IT ALL COMES BACK Paul Butterfield's Better Days 03Nov73 156(1) 8	98.9
10155. MAJOR'S GREATEST HITS Major Lance 04Sep65 109(1) 6	98.8
10156. THE TOP TEN HITS Elvis Presley 15Aug87 117(2) 8	98.8
10157. THE DREAMING Kate Bush 13Nov82 157(2) 11	98.8
10158. SOMETIMES Facts Of Life 09Apr77 146(1) 7	98.8
10159. DENVER CHRISTMAS GIFT PAK John Denver 20Dec75 138(1) 6	98.7
10160. SARAH VAUGHAN/MICHEL LEGRAND Sarah Vaughan/Michel Legrand 01Jul72 173(1) 12	98.7
10161. THE ELECTRIC SPANKING OF WAR BABIES Funkadelic 29Aug81 105(2) 4	98.7
10162. THE QUINTET V.S.O.P 12Nov77 123(2) 5	98.6
10163. DON'T STOP THE MUSIC Brecker Brothers 07May77 135(1) 6	98.6
10164. MAKE THE WORLD GO AWAY Donny & Marie Osmond 28Jun75 133(2) 6	98.5
10165. REUNION-LIVE AT MADISON SQUARE GARDEN 1972 Dion 24Feb73 144(1) 8	98.5
10166. SPECIAL PAIN Robert Ellis Orrall 16Apr83 146(2) 9	98.5
10167. HIGH ENERGY Freddie Hubbard 14Sep74 153(1) 7	98.4
10168. THE BAKER GURVITZ ARMY Baker Gurvitz Army 15Feb75 140(1) 7	98.4
10169. ANNIE Anne Murray 20May72 143(1) 8	98.4
10170. LARRY CARLTON Larry Carlton 26Aug78 174(2) 10	98.4
10171. ALONE/BUT NEVER ALONE Larry Carlton 28Jun86 141(2) 11	98.4
10172. ...MILLIONS LIKE US Millions Like Us 19Dec87 171(1) 12	98.4
10173. THE WORLD ACCORDING TO ME Jackie Mason 09Jan88 146(1) 9	98.4
10174. THE NITTY GRITTY DIRT BAND Nitty Gritty Dirt Band 08Apr67 151(1) 8	98.4
10175. ANTHOLOGY The Babys 07Nov81 138(1) 7	98.3
10176. THE GREATEST HITS OF ERIC BURDON AND THE ANIMALS Eric Burdon & The Animals 15Mar69 153(1) 6	98.2
10177. STARING AT THE SUN Level 42 29Oct88 128(1) 7	98.2
10178. NEW DIRECTIONS Tavares 11Dec82 137(1) 11	98.2
10179. THE STORY OF THE CLASH, VOLUME I The Clash 28May88 142(2) 8	98.0
10180. UNLIMITED TOUCH Unlimited Touch 20Jun81 142(1) 7	97.8
10181. SPECIAL FORCES Alice Cooper 19Sep81 125(2) 5	97.8
10182. FIRE & FLEET & CANDLELIGHT Buffy Sainte-Marie 08Jul67 126(1) 6	97.8
10183. MAGIC Four Tops 29Jun85 140(2) 9	97.8
10184. TOUCH ME The Temptations 25Jan86 146(2) 10	97.7
10185. WILL POWER Joe Jackson 02May87 131(2) 8	97.6
10186. ON THE NILE Egyptian Lover 09Feb85 146(2) 10	97.6
10187. TRINI LOPEZ IN LONDON Trini Lopez 04Mar67 114(1) 6	97.5
10188. BULLDOG Bulldog 18Nov72 176(1) 12	97.5
10189. THE PSYCHEDELIC FURS Psychedelic Furs 22Nov80 140(1) 7	97.5
10190. SURVIVAL OF THE FRESHEST Boogie Boys 09Aug86 124(2) 9	97.4
10191. CAN'T HOLD BACK Pure Prairie League 23Jun79 124(1) 6	97.3
10192. IN THE NAME OF LOVE Peggy Lee 26Sep64 97(1) 6	97.3
10193. MORNING STAR Hubert Laws 24Feb73 148(1) 9	97.3
10194. I'VE GOTTA BE ME Tony Bennett 06Sep69 137(2) 5	97.2
10195. RIDE 'EM COWBOY Paul Davis 11Jan75 148(1) 6	97.2
10196. FARTHER ALONG The Byrds 25Dec71 152(1) 7	97.2
10197. FEEL THE NIGHT Lee Ritenour 16Jun79 136(1) 6	97.1
10198. NIGHT ON BALD MOUNTAIN Fireballet 06Sep75 151(1) 8	97.1
10199. L.A. JAIL Richard Pryor 04Jun77 114(1) 5	97.0
10200. BLUE GENE Gene Pitney 23Nov63 105(1) 6	97.0
10201. THE SMITHS The Smiths 05May84 150(2) 11	97.0
10202. BLAME IT ON LOVE AND ALL THE GREAT HITS Smokey Robinson 03Sep83 124(1) 7	97.0
10203. DAVID GRISMAN - QUINTET "80" David Grisman 13Sep80 152(1) 8	96.9
10204. HEAD FIRST Uriah Heep 04Jun83 159(1) 10	96.9
10205. MENACE TO SOCIETY Lizzy Borden 01Nov86 144(2) 10	96.9
10206. SOMETHING INSIDE SO STRONG Kenny Rogers 27May89 141(2) 8	96.9
10207. I'VE BEEN HERE ALL THE TIME Luther Ingram 15Jan72 175(1) 11	96.9
10208. A MOMENT'S PLEASURE Millie Jackson 21Apr79 144(3) 6	96.8
10209. TANTILLA House Of Freaks 06May89 154(1) 10	96.8
10210. THE WARMER SIDE OF COOL Wang Chung 10Jun89 123(1) 6	96.7
10211. THE PURSUIT OF HAPPINESS Beat Farmers 05Sep87 131(1) 8	96.7
10212. CENTRAL LINE Central Line 09Jan82 145(2) 9	96.6
10213. COMMAND PERFORMANCES Doc Severinsen 26Nov66 133(1) 6	96.6
10214. MAMA WAS A ROCK AND ROLL SINGER PAPA USED TO WRITE ALL HER SONGS Sonny & Cher 30Jun73 132(2) 6	96.6
10215. THE HAPPY TRUMPET Al Hirt 30Jul66 125(1) 6	96.6
10216. ALL THE GOOD TIMES Nitty Gritty Dirt Band 05Feb72 162(1) 10	96.5
10217. PERFORMANCE Ashford & Simpson 17Oct81 125(1) 6	96.5
10218. 16 ORIGINAL BIG HITS, VOLUME 9 Various Artists 16Nov68 173(1) 9	96.4
10219. LETTERMEN 1 The Lettermen 18Mar72 136(1) 6	96.3
10220. THE AMAZING RHYTHM ACES Amazing Rhythm Aces 17Feb79 144(1) 7	96.3
10221. THE MOMENTS LIVE AT THE NEW YORK STATE WOMANS PRISON The Moments 15May71 147(2) 8	96.3
10222. BRAIN DRAIN The Ramones 17Jun89 122(2) 6	96.2
10223. WACK WACK Young-Holt Trio 14Jan67 132(1) 6	96.2
10224. JANE FONDA'S WORKOUT RECORD NEW AND IMPROVED Jane Fonda 18Aug84 135(2) 10	96.1
10225. TASTE THE MUSIC Kleeer 20Feb82 139(1) 8	96.1
10226. ROME 35/MM Enoch Light & The Light Brigade 04Apr64 121(2) 7	96.1
10227. PORCUPINE Echo & The Bunnymen 26Mar83 137(1) 9	96.1
10228. GREATEST HITS VOLUME ONE Elvis Presley 19Dec81 142(2) 7	96.1
10229. DISTANT LOVER Alphonse Mouzon 04Dec82 146(3) 11	96.0
10230. THE ONE GIVETH, THE COUNT TAKETH AWAY William "Bootsy" Collins 29May82 120(1) 8	96.0
10231. WORKIN' OVERTIME Diana Ross 24Jun89 116(2) 6	96.0
10232. THE GOLDEN MILLIONS Lawrence Welk 09Jan65 115(2) 6	96.0
10233. KALEIDOSCOPE Nancy Wilson 25Dec71 151(2) 6	96.0
10234. SUBSTANCE Joy Division 27Aug88 146(2) 8	95.9
10235. INTERVIEW Gentle Giant 29May76 137(3) 5	95.9
10236. WASN'T THAT A PARTY The Rovers 25Apr81 157(1) 8	95.9
10237. WANTED DEAD OR ALIVE (BANG! BANG! PUSH, PUSH, PUSH) Joe Cuba Sextet 07Jan67 131(1) 6	95.9
10238. JENNIE Original Cast 04Jan64 87(1) 5	95.9
10239. THE YOUNGBLOODS The Youngbloods 25Mar67 131(1) 8	95.8
10240. KING SWAMP King Swamp 03Jun89 159(1) 14	95.8
10241. FANNY HILL Fanny 01Apr72 135(1) 6	95.8
10242. TWO SIDES OF PETER BANKS Peter Banks 08Sep73 152(1) 8	95.8
10243. LOVIN' THE NIGHT AWAY Dillman Band 16May81 145(2) 7	95.6
10244. BROADWAY'S CLOSER TO SUNSET BLVD. Isley, Jasper, Isley 09Feb85 135(2) 10	95.5
10245. ST. LOUIS TO LIVERPOOL Chuck Berry 12Dec64 124(1) 7	95.5
10246. AUTUMN LEAVES-1965 Roger Williams 25Dec65 130(1) 7	95.5
10247. HAIRSPRAY Soundtrack 02Apr88 114(1) 6	95.5
10248. 12 Bob James 27Oct84 136(2) 10	95.4
10249. ROGER MILLER Roger Miller 30Aug69 163(1) 7	95.4
10250. RUBICON Rubicon 25Mar78 147(2) 7	95.3

Rank. Title Act	Entry Peak(Pk Wks) TotWks	Scr
10251. **HISTORIC DEAD** Grateful Dead	26Jun71 154(1) 7	95.3
10252. **MONTY PYTHON'S CONTRACTUAL OBLIGATION ALBUM** Monty Python	15Nov80 164(1) 9	95.3
10253. **EVERYTHING PLAYING** Lovin' Spoonful	20Jan68 118(2) 7	95.3
10254. **FREAKIN' AT THE FREAKERS BALL** Shel Silverstein	20Jan73 155(1) 8	95.2
10255. **STARS** Cher	10May75 153(2) 7	95.1
10256. **THE BEST OF THE TRAMMPS** The Trammps	09Sep78 139(2) 6	95.1
10257. **THE BEST OF IRON BUTTERFLY/EVOLUTION** Iron Butterfly	25Dec71 137(1) 6	95.0
10258. **LIGHTHOUSE** Kim Carnes	14Jun86 116(2) 7	94.9
10259. **RUNNING FOR MY LIFE** Judy Collins	03May80 142(3) 6	94.9
10260. **FOREVER CHANGES** Love	06Jan68 154(2) 10	94.9
10261. **IT'S NOT KILLING ME** Michael Bloomfield	11Oct69 127(1) 5	94.9
10262. **THE FORCE** Kool & The Gang	28Jan78 142(1) 7	94.8
10263. **FINGER LICKIN GOOD** Dennis Coffey	17Jan76 147(2) 7	94.8
10264. **ONE MAN BAND** Ronnie Dyson	07Apr73 142(1) 7	94.7
10265. **UNDERCOVER LOVER** Debbie Jacobs-Rock	01Sep79 153(1) 8	94.7
10266. **THAT THE SPIRIT NEEDS** Jose Feliciano	13Nov71 173(1) 9	94.7
10267. **FACE TO FACE** GQ	14Nov81 140(2) 8	94.6
10268. **SONGS OF LOVE BY CHARLEY PRIDE** Charley Pride	17Feb73 149(2) 8	94.6
10269. **PETER** Peter Yarrow	04Mar72 163(2) 8	94.5
10270. **STATUS QUO** Status Quo	17Apr76 148(2) 7	94.5
10271. **FIVE O'CLOCK WORLD** The Vogues	12Feb66 137(1) 7	94.5
10272. **NIGHTOUT** Ellen Foley	29Sep79 137(1) 6	94.5
10273. **MAMA LET HIM PLAY** Doucette	25Mar78 159(1) 8	94.5
10274. **MISTY** Richard "Groove" Holmes	24Dec66 134(1) 6	94.4
10275. **ELECTRIC BREAKDANCE** Various Artists	08Sep84 147(2) 9	94.3
10276. **AL GREEN** Al Green	16Sep72 162(1) 9	94.3
10277. **JUDSON SPENCE** Judson Spence	10Dec88 168(4) 13	94.3
10278. **PHANTOM OF THE NIGHT** Kayak	03Mar79 145(1) 7	94.3
10279. **THE BEST OF THE DOORS** The Doors	29Sep73 158(1) 8	94.2
10280. **TRULY FINE CITIZEN** Moby Grape	20Sep69 157(1) 6	94.2
10281. **ATTITUDES** Brass Construction	22May82 114(3) 8	94.2
10282. **RONNIE DOVE SINGS THE HITS FOR YOU** Ronnie Dove	22Oct66 122(2) 5	94.1
10283. **HOW CAN I UNLOVE YOU** Lynn Anderson	04Dec71 132(2) 5	94.1
10284. **FRESH AIRE VI** Mannheim Steamroller	13Dec86 155(1) 14	94.1
10285. **STORM WINDOWS** John Prine	30Aug80 144(1) 7	94.1
10286. **REHEARSALS FOR RETIREMENT** Phil Ochs	14Jun69 167(1) 7	94.0
10287. **PINK CADILLAC** John Prine	08Sep79 152(1) 7	94.0
10288. **"WEIRD AL" YANKOVIC** "Weird Al" Yankovic	21May83 139(1) 8	93.9
10289. **HONEY IN THE ROCK** Charlie Daniels Band	28Jul73 164(1) 9	93.9
10290. **SEASON OF LIGHTS...LAURA NYRO IN CONCERT** Laura Nyro	02Jul77 137(2) 5	93.9
10291. **EVERYTHING YOU KNOW IS WRONG** Firesign Theatre	02Nov74 147(1) 6	93.8
10292. **MS. AMERICA** Vikki Carr	23Jun73 142(1) 7	93.8
10293. **GOLDEN DOWN** Willie Nile	02May81 158(1) 8	93.8
10294. **THE QUEEN ALONE** Carla Thomas	01Jul67 133(1) 6	93.7
10295. **GENE & JERRY - ONE & ONE** Gene Chandler & Jerry Butler	27Mar71 143(2) 5	93.7
10296. **GRITTY, GROOVY, & GETTIN' IT** David Porter	28Mar70 163(1) 10	93.6
10297. **STILL STILLS-THE BEST OF STEPHEN STILLS** Stephen Stills	08Jan77 127(1) 5	93.6
10298. **EYDIE GORME'S GREATEST HITS** Eydie Gorme	02Dec67 148(1) 9	93.5
10299. **GIANT** Johnny Guitar Watson	28Oct78 157(1) 7	93.5
10300. **SANFORD AND SON** Redd Foxx	29Jul72 155(2) 8	93.5
10301. **SOUL MAN** Soundtrack	15Nov86 138(2) 9	93.5
10302. **MIRRORS OF MY MIND** Roger Whittaker	08Dec79 157(2) 10	93.5
10303. **BRIDGES** Gil Scott-Heron & Brian Jackson	22Oct77 130(2) 5	93.4
10304. **BREAKING CURFEW** Red Rider	23Jun84 137(2) 8	93.3
10305. **WILD ROMANCE** Herb Alpert	24Aug85 151(2) 10	93.3
10306. **NEW ENGLAND** Wishbone Ash	18Dec76 154(1) 9	93.2
10307. **SOLD OUT** The Fools	05Apr80 151(1) 8	93.2
10308. **ON STAGE** Lily Tomlin	12Nov77 120(2) 6	93.2
10309. **BEST OF THE J. GEILS BAND** J. Geils Band	21Jul79 129(2) 5	93.2
10310. **STATE OF...EMERGENCY** Steel Pulse	23Jul88 127(2) 7	93.2
10311. **PERSONAL ATTENTION** Stacy Lattisaw	05Mar88 153(2) 10	93.2
10312. **McGUINNESS FLINT** McGuinness Flint	30Jan71 155(2) 8	93.2
10313. **BUT WHAT WILL THE NEIGHORS THINK** Rodney Crowell	26Apr80 155(1) 10	93.2
10314. **COOKIN' ON THE ROOF** Roman Holliday	22Oct83 116(1) 6	93.1
10315. **THIN LINE BETWEEN LOVE AND HATE** The Persuaders	11Mar72 141(1) 7	93.1
10316. **A WORLD OF OUR OWN** The Seekers	25Sep65 123(1) 6	93.1
10317. **D&B TOGETHER** Delaney & Bonnie	15Apr72 133(2) 6	93.0
10318. **AMNESIA** Pousette-Dart Band	19Mar77 143(1) 7	93.0
10319. **ROCKAPELLA** The Nylons	10Jun89 136(2) 10	93.0
10320. **BROADWAY BOUQUET** Percy Faith	04Dec65 101(1) 5	93.0
10321. **MEMPHIS QUEEN** Carla Thomas	05Jul69 151(1) 5	92.9
10322. **THE TWO OF US** Ramsey Lewis & Nancy Wilson	08Sep84 144(1) 9	92.9
10323. **OUR SONG** Jack Jones	14Oct67 148(1) 7	92.9
10324. **GRASSHOPPER** J.J. Cale	03Apr82 149(1) 8	92.9
10325. **IN MY LITTLE CORNER OF THE WORLD** Marie Osmond	20Jul74 164(1) 9	92.9
10326. **BACK TO BACK** The Mar-Keys/Booker T. & The MG's	26Aug67 98(2) 4	92.8
10327. **FOR LOVERS OF ALL AGES** Ferrante & Teicher	25Jun66 119(2) 5	92.8
10328. **IN NO SENSE? NONSENSE!** Art Of Noise	17Oct87 134(1) 9	92.8
10329. **IRON AGE** Mother's Finest	23May81 168(1) 8	92.8
10330. **SUMMER WIND** Wayne Newton	23Oct65 114(2) 6	92.7
10331. **JOHNNIE TAYLOR'S GREATEST HITS** Johnnie Taylor	19Dec70 141(1) 5	92.7
10332. **GROSS MISCONDUCT** M.O.D.	11Mar89 151(1) 8	92.7
10333. **WITHOUT HER** Jack Jones	16Dec67 146(1) 7	92.7
10334. **WIRE FIRE** Savoy Brown	22Nov75 153(2) 7	92.6
10335. **LILIES OF THE FIELD** Soundtrack	30May64 110(1) 6	92.6
10336. **AORTA** Aorta	12Apr69 167(1) 8	92.6
10337. **WHO'S MISSING** The Who	28Dec85 116(2) 8	92.6
10338. **TAKE GOOD CARE OF MY BABY** Bobby Vinton	15Jun68 164(1) 8	92.6
10339. **TOO STUFFED TO JUMP** Amazing Rhythm Aces	05Jun76 157(1) 7	92.6
10340. **THE GREAT MARCH TO FREEDOM** Rev. Martin Luther King, Jr.	26Oct63 141(1) 9	92.6
10341. **ORGASMATRON** Motorhead	29Nov86 157(3) 11	92.4
10342. **LARRY GATLIN'S GREATEST HITS VOL.1** Larry Gatlin	23Dec78 171(1) 9	92.4
10343. **LOVE TOKEN** Mystic Moods Orchestra	22Nov69 165(1) 8	92.4
10344. **BETTY TRAVELIN' IN THE WRIGHT CIRCLE** Betty Wright	02Jun79 138(2) 6	92.4
10345. **BAD INFLUENCE** Robert Cray Band	07Mar87 143(1) 11	92.4
10346. **18 YELLOW ROSES** Bobby Darin	24Aug63 98(1) 5	92.3
10347. **MEMORIES** Lawrence Welk	08Feb69 173(1) 8	92.3
10348. **FRIENDS IN LOVE** Johnny Mathis	08May82 147(1) 9	92.2
10349. **THIS IS THE WAY THAT I FEEL** Marie Osmond	30Apr77 152(2) 6	92.2
10350. **LIVE AT THE INTERNATIONAL, LAS VEGAS** Jerry Lee Lewis	10Oct70 149(1) 6	92.2
10351. **THE HAPPIEST MILLIONAIRE** Soundtrack	23Mar68 166(1) 9	92.2
10352. **BORN A WOMAN** Sandy Posey	17Dec66 129(1) 7	92.1
10353. **THE BAD C.C.** Carl Carlton	23Oct82 133(2) 7	92.1
10354. **THE BEST OF FREDDY FENDER** Freddy Fender	21May77 155(2) 7	92.1
10355. **FOUR STRONG WINDS** Ian & Sylvia	28Sep63 115(1) 6	92.1
10356. **KINKS' GREATEST-CELLULOID HEROES** The Kinks	26Jun76 144(2) 5	92.1
10357. **FEEL** George Duke	01Feb75 141(2) 6	92.0
10358. **MAZARATI** Mazarati	19Apr86 133(1) 8	92.0
10359. **OUR MANN FLUTE** Herbie Mann	08Oct66 139(1) 6	91.9
10360. **GREATEST HITS(2)** Charlie Rich	03Jul76 148(1) 6	91.9
10361. **BRAINSTORM** The Osmonds	23Oct76 145(2) 6	91.9
10362. **CLASSICS** The Doors	08Jun85 124(2) 7	91.9
10363. **LOUD 'N' PROUD** Nazareth	09Mar74 150(1) 8	91.8
10364. **LEFTY** Art Garfunkel	16Apr88 134(2) 8	91.8
10365. **THE GILDED PALACE OF SIN** Flying Burrito Brothers	03May69 164(1) 7	91.7
10366. **LOVE IS...ONE WAY** One Way	07Mar81 157(1) 8	91.7

Rank.	Title	Act	Entry	Peak(Pk Wks)	TotWks	Scr
10367.	SHORT TRIP TO SPACE	Tropea	14May77	149(1)	7	91.7
10368.	POWER & THE GLORY	Saxon	18Jun83	155(1)	10	91.7
10369.	KEITH EMERSON WITH THE NICE	The Nice	26Feb72	152(1)	8	91.7
10370.	THE SCREEN SCENE	Peter Nero	19Feb66	114(1)	6	91.6
10371.	THE SECRET OF MY SUCCESS	Soundtrack	13Jun87	131(2)	8	91.6
10372.	THE ONE AND ONLY...	Gladys Knight And The Pips	16Sep78	145(1)	6	91.6
10373.	LIVE AT THE HOLLYWOOD BOWL	The Doors	11Jul87	154(2)	11	91.5
10374.	WISH YOU WERE HERE	Badfinger	09Nov74	148(1)	6	91.4
10375.	CHARLIE	Charlie	23Jul83	145(1)	9	91.4
10376.	LUCILLE TALKS BACK	B.B. King	08Nov75	140(1)	5	91.4
10377.	THE ORIGINAL PENETRATION! AND OTHER FAVORITES	The Pyramids	14Mar64	119(1)	6	91.3
10378.	SILVER	Silver	25Sep76	142(1)	6	91.3
10379.	ERES TU "TOUCH THE WIND"	Mocedades	16Mar74	152(2)	7	91.2
10380.	CLOSE	Kim Wilde	01Oct88	114(1)	6	91.2
10381.	HONKY-TONK STARDUST COWBOY	Jonathan Edwards	18Nov72	167(2)	9	91.2
10382.	AMERICAN GOTHIC	David Ackles	12Aug72	167(1)	10	91.2
10383.	STATES OF EMERGENCY	Taxxi	25Dec82	161(1)	11	91.1
10384.	THE BLUES ALONE	John Mayall	15Jun68	128(1)	5	91.1
10385.	INNOCENCE IS NO EXCUSE	Saxon	02Nov85	130(2)	8	91.0
10386.	NOMADNESS	Strawbs	11Oct75	147(1)	6	91.0
10387.	A LIVE MUTHERFORYA	Various Artists	05Aug78	151(3)	6	91.0
10388.	BACH TO THE BLUES	Ramsey Lewis Trio	04Jul64	125(1)	7	90.9
10389.	SOUL MAKOSSA	Afrique	16Jun73	152(1)	8	90.9
10390.	THE NUMBER ONE HITS	Elvis Presley	08Aug87	143(1)	9	90.9
10391.	SOLID GOLD '69	Chet Atkins	13Dec69	150(1)	7	90.9
10392.	FRAGILE	Cherrelle	08Sep84	144(1)	8	90.8
10393.	THE MEMPHIS HORNS BAND II	Memphis Horns	10Jun78	163(1)	9	90.8
10394.	MICK TAYLOR	Mick Taylor	21Jul79	119(1)	5	90.8
10395.	BACK TO BACK	The Tokens/The Happenings	22Jul67	134(1)	6	90.8
10396.	OUR TIME'S COMING	Dino, Desi & Billy	12Feb66	119(1)	6	90.7
10397.	SONGS FOR LATIN LOVERS	Ray Charles Singers	21Aug65	125(1)	6	90.7
10398.	KING SIZE SOUL	King Curtis	09Dec67	168(4)	9	90.7
10399.	MOTOWN AT THE HOLLYWOOD PALACE	Various Artists	11Apr70	105(2)	4	90.6
10400.	I SING THE BODY ELECTRIC	Weather Report	15Jul72	147(1)	6	90.6
10401.	I'M A LONESOME FUGITIVE	Merle Haggard	13May67	165(2)	10	90.6
10402.	PALOMA BLANCA	George Baker Selection	31Jan76	153(2)	7	90.6
10403.	ONE OF A KIND	Bill Bruford	07Jul79	123(1)	5	90.5
10404.	LOVE WARRIORS	Tuck & Patti	24Jun89	162(3)	11	90.5
10405.	HELP ME MAKE IT THROUGH THE NIGHT	O.C. Smith	31Jul71	159(1)	7	90.4
10406.	WHO'S AFRAID OF VIRGINIA WOOLF?	Soundtrack	03Sep66	119(1)	5	90.4
10407.	THE PHOSPHORESCENT RAT	Hot Tuna	09Feb74	148(1)	7	90.3
10408.	ODE TO MY LADY	Willie Hutch	15Nov75	150(2)	6	90.3
10409.	AMERICAN GENERATION	Ritchie Family	02Sep78	148(1)	6	90.3
10410.	FOWL PLAY	Julius Wechter and the Baja Marimba Band	20Jan68	168(1)	9	90.3
10411.	WORLD OF WONDERS	Bruce Cockburn	26Jul86	143(3)	8	90.3
10412.	THE WHOLE THING STARTED WITH ROCK & ROLL AND NOW IT'S OUT OF CONTROL	Ray Manzarek	08Feb75	150(1)	6	90.2
10413.	THEATER OF THE MIND	Mtume	05Jul86	135(2)	8	90.2
10414.	BRASS CONSTRUCTION 6	Brass Construction	20Sep80	121(2)	5	90.2
10415.	ON STAGE AND IN THE MOVIES	Dionne Warwick	13May67	169(3)	9	90.2
10416.	THE NEW BOSS	Joe Tex	27Nov65	142(1)	7	90.2
10417.	PICTURES	Atlanta	26May84	140(2)	7	90.1
10418.	UP	Le Roux	23Aug80	145(2)	6	90.0
10419.	RAINBOW	Dolly Parton	19Dec87	153(1)	8	89.9
10420.	WOMAN ACROSS THE RIVER	Freddie King	21Jul73	158(1)	8	89.8
10421.	MARILYN & BILLY	Marilyn McCoo & Billy Davis Jr.	07Oct78	146(1)	6	89.8
10422.	OPEN MIND	Jean-Luc Ponty	08Dec84	171(3)	13	89.7
10423.	CHRISTMAS IN AMERICA	Kenny Rogers	16Dec89	119(2)	6	89.7
10424.	WHO'S SORRY NOW	Marie Osmond	08Mar75	152(2)	6	89.7
10425.	BANDED TOGETHER	Lee Ritenour	23Jun84	145(2)	8	89.7
10426.	SHAKE OFF THE DEMON	Brewer And Shipley	25Dec71	164(2)	8	89.6
10427.	IN SEARCH OF THE RAINBOW SEEKERS	Mtume	18Oct80	119(1)	4	89.6
10428.	DIANNE REEVES	Dianne Reeves	23Apr88	172(1)	12	89.5
10429.	STEPS IN TIME	King	17Aug85	140(2)	9	89.5
10430.	BLESS THE BEASTS & CHILDREN	Soundtrack	27Nov71	176(1)	10	89.5
10431.	IN THE BEGINNING	Journey	05Jan80	152(1)	8	89.5
10432.	DAVID CLAYTON-THOMAS!	David Clayton-Thomas	27Sep69	159(2)	8	89.5
10433.	KOKOMO	Kokomo	07Jun75	159(1)	9	89.5
10434.	BEST OF THE BEACH BOYS, VOL. 3	Beach Boys	07Sep68	153(1)	6	89.4
10435.	SUNSHINE	The Archies	12Sep70	137(1)	6	89.4
10436.	ALL THE WAY STRONG	Third World	01Oct83	137(2)	7	89.4
10437.	ROGER WILLIAMS PLAYS THE HITS	Roger Williams	10Apr65	118(1)	6	89.4
10438.	MORE	Pink Floyd	01Sep73	153(1)	7	89.3
10439.	LET IT ROCK	Johnny And The Distractions	20Feb82	152(1)	9	89.2
10440.	THE MOTOR-TOWN REVIEW, VOL. 2	Various Artists	30May64	102(2)	5	89.2
10441.	DEUCE	Kurtis Blow	18Jul81	137(1)	5	89.2
10442.	JESSIE'S JIG & OTHER FAVORITES	Steve Goodman	23Aug75	144(1)	6	89.1
10443.	GREATEST HITS	Cher	16Nov74	152(2)	7	89.1
10444.	ANIMAL NOTES	Crack The Sky	30Oct76	142(1)	5	89.1
10445.	THE BEST OF URIAH HEEP	Uriah Heep	20Mar76	145(2)	6	89.0
10446.	LIQUID LOVE	Freddie Hubbard	19Jul75	149(2)	6	89.0
10447.	GRAND FUNK HITS	Grand Funk	20Nov76	126(1)	5	88.9
10448.	I WANT OUT-LIVE	Helloween	22Apr89	123(2)	7	88.9
10449.	KANSAS	Kansas	15Jun74	174(2)	10	88.9
10450.	CYCLE OF THE MOON	Prophet	12Mar88	137(1)	7	88.8
10451.	BIKINI RED	Screaming Blue Messiahs	16Jan88	172(1)	11	88.8
10452.	...IN A CHAMBER	Wire Train	18Feb84	150(1)	9	88.8
10453.	STRATOSFEAR	Tangerine Dream	02Apr77	158(1)	7	88.8
10454.	LIVE AND LET LIVE	10cc	24Dec77	146(1)	6	88.8
10455.	DINO	Dean Martin	05Feb72	117(2)	4	88.8
10456.	REPLAY	Crosby, Stills & Nash	10Jan81	122(2)	5	88.8
10457.	BAD, BAD BOY	Theo Vaness	16Jun79	145(2)	6	88.8
10458.	DAVID	David Houston	13Sep69	143(1)	5	88.7
10459.	LOVE IS ALL AROUND	War Featuring Eric Burdon	25Dec76	140(2)	5	88.7
10460.	LA DIVA	Aretha Franklin	13Oct79	146(1)	6	88.6
10461.	CARESS OF STEEL	Rush	18Oct75	148(1)	6	88.6
10462.	DECOY	Miles Davis	30Jun84	169(2)	11	88.6
10463.	BEETLEJUICE	Soundtrack	25Jun88	118(1)	6	88.5
10464.	QUEEN OF THE HOUSE	Jody Miller	26Jun65	124(1)	6	88.5
10465.	ENDANGERED SPECIES	White Wolf	21Jun86	137(2)	8	88.5
10466.	ONCE UPON A TIME	Kingston Trio	12Jul69	163(1)	6	88.5
10467.	SING A SONG OF WATERGATE...	Mort Sahl	30Jun73	149(1)	7	88.5
10468.	WILLIE NILE	Willie Nile	12Apr80	145(2)	6	88.5
10469.	THE IMPOSSIBLE DREAM	Andy Williams	08Jan72	123(2)	5	88.4
10470.	SOMETIMES WHEN WE TOUCH	Cleo Laine & James Galway	26Jul80	150(1)	6	88.4
10471.	KILL 'EM ALL	Metallica	05Apr86	155(2)	10	88.4
10472.	LOU CHRISTIE	Lou Christie	24Aug63	124(1)	6	88.4
10473.	DANCE TO THE MUSIC	Sly & The Family Stone	04May68	142(2)	7	88.3
10474.	TRAVOLTA FEVER	John Travolta	23Dec78	161(3)	7	88.3
10475.	LENA & GABOR	Lena Horne & Gabor Szabo	16May70	162(1)	10	88.1
10476.	WHERE TO NOW	Charlie Dore	26Apr80	145(1)	7	88.0
10477.	GLASSWORKS	Philip Glass	10Apr82	121(2)	6	88.0
10478.	ANTHOLOGY	Grover Washington Jr.	24Oct81	149(1)	7	87.9
10479.	98.6/AIN'T GONNA LIE	Keith	25Mar67	124(1)	5	87.9
10480.	ANYTIME	Henry Paul Band	26Dec81	158(1)	8	87.8
10481.	POINT OF VIEW	Spyro Gyra	08Jul89	120(2)	6	87.8
10482.	LAUGHING AT THE PIECES	Doctor And The Medics	13Sep86	125(1)	8	87.8
10483.	ROLLERBALL	Soundtrack	23Aug75	156(1)	6	87.8

Rank. Title Act	Entry Peak(Pk Wks) TotWks	Scr
10484. **WAY OUT WEST** Mae West	23Jul66 116(2) 5	87.7
10485. **PASTEL BLUES** Nina Simone	16Oct65 139(1) 7	87.7
10486. **THE O'JAYS IN PHILADELPHIA** The O'Jays	28Apr73 156(1) 8	87.6
10487. **STAY & OTHER GREAT HITS** 4 Seasons	06Jun64 100(2) 5	87.6
10488. **STEVE MILLER BAND - LIVE** Steve Miller Band	30Apr83 125(1) 7	87.6
10489. **LIVE! THE IKE & TINA TURNER SHOW** Ike & Tina Turner	06Feb65 126(1) 6	87.6
10490. **MUSE** Grace Jones	01Sep79 156(2) 7	87.5
10491. **BRIEF REPLIES** Ten Wheel Drive With Genya Ravan	01Aug70 161(1) 8	87.4
10492. **FAMOUS AT NIGHT** John Hunter	09Feb85 148(2) 9	87.4
10493. **MERRY CLAYTON** Merry Clayton	20Nov71 180(1) 11	87.4
10494. **MUSIC TO WATCH GIRLS BY** Al Hirt	18Mar67 127(1) 5	87.4
10495. **LULLABY** Book Of Love	23Jul88 156(2) 10	87.3
10496. **DO YOU KNOW THE WAY TO SAN JOSE?** Julius Wechter and the Baja Marimba Band	31Aug68 171(1) 8	87.3
10497. **WORDS OF EARNEST** Goose Creek Symphony	03Jun72 167(2) 8	87.3
10498. **MATHIS IS...** Johnny Mathis	19Mar77 139(2) 5	87.2
10499. **ENGLISH MUFFINS** Mystic Moods Orch.	28Nov70 174(2) 9	87.2
10500. **SNIPER AND OTHER LOVE SONGS** Harry Chapin	28Oct72 160(1) 8	87.2
10501. **INVITATION TO OPENNESS** Les McCann	08Apr72 141(1) 6	87.1
10502. **THE MARCH ON WASHINGTON** Rev. Martin Luther King, Jr.	02Nov63 102(1) 5	87.1
10503. **TRICK OR TREAT** Fastway	22Nov86 156(1) 12	87.1
10504. **TUTU** Miles Davis	25Oct86 141(2) 10	87.1
10505. **RIDDLE OF THE SPHINX** Bloodstone	22Feb75 147(2) 6	87.0
10506. **PROUD MARY** Solomon Burke	05Jul69 140(2) 4	87.0
10507. **ROGUES GALLERY** Slade	04May85 132(2) 6	87.0
10508. **DANGEROUS** Natalie Cole	29Jun85 140(2) 9	87.0
10509. **THE CARROLL COUNTY ACCIDENT** Porter Wagoner	15Mar69 161(1) 8	87.0
10510. **GREATEST HITS** Nilsson	17Jun78 140(1) 5	87.0
10511. **WRABIT** Wrabit	06Feb82 157(1) 8	86.9
10512. **FLOWING FREE FOREVER** Michael Murphey	20Nov76 130(1) 5	86.8
10513. **1ST** Streets	03Dec83 166(1) 11	86.8
10514. **THE BEST OF FREDA PAYNE** Freda Payne	15Apr72 152(1) 8	86.8
10515. **MYSTERY OF BULGARIAN VOICES** Bulgarian State Radio & T.V. Female Choir	17Dec88 165(1) 10	86.8
10516. **SATIN PILLOWS AND CARELESS** Bobby Vinton	12Feb66 110(2) 5	86.7
10517. **SOUL COUNTRY** Joe Tex	27Jul68 154(1) 7	86.7
10518. **ALL SYSTEMS GO** Donna Summer	10Oct87 122(2) 6	86.7
10519. **NOBODY DOES IT LIKE ME** Shirley Bassey	21Sep74 142(1) 6	86.6
10520. **DREAMBOY** Dreamboy	14Jan84 168(1) 11	86.6
10521. **SWITCHED-ON ROCK** Moog Machine	27Sep69 170(1) 8	86.6
10522. **SLEEPLESS NIGHTS** Brooklyn Dreams	24Mar79 151(1) 7	86.6
10523. **THE MINSTREL MAN** Willie Nelson	01Aug81 148(1) 7	86.5
10524. **SAMMY HAGAR** Sammy Hagar	26Feb77 167(1) 9	86.5
10525. **CHAMPAGNE ON BROADWAY** Lawrence Welk	26Mar66 106(1) 5	86.5
10526. **LET GO** Charlie Byrd Quartet	06Sep69 129(1) 4	86.5
10527. **MECO PLAYS MUSIC FROM THE EMPIRE STRIKES BACK** Meco	02Aug80 140(1) 8	86.5
10528. **DOUBLE TROUBLE** Frankie Miller	13May78 177(1) 10	86.5
10529. **STRANGERS IN THE WIND** Bay City Rollers	14Oct78 129(1) 4	86.5
10530. **OUR MAN FLINT** Soundtrack	19Mar66 118(2) 5	86.4
10531. **YEARS GONE BY** Albert King	24May69 133(1) 4	86.3
10532. **AMERICAN WORKER** Bus Boys	21Aug82 139(3) 7	86.3
10533. **THE NEW LEE DORSEY** Lee Dorsey	12Nov66 129(1) 5	86.3
10534. **SUPERSTAR** Vikki Carr	08Jan72 118(1) 4	86.2
10535. **SAVE THE LAST DANCE FOR ME** DeFranco Family	29Jun74 163(1) 7	86.2
10536. **GREATEST HITS** Sonny & Cher	28Sep74 146(2) 6	86.2
10537. **NEW GENERATION** Chambers Brothers	27Feb71 145(1) 7	86.2
10538. **BATTLESTAR GALACTICIA** TV Soundtrack	21Oct78 144(1) 6	86.2
10539. **WAKA/JAWAKA - HOT RATS** Frank Zappa	09Sep72 152(1) 7	86.2
10540. **LOVE AND DANCING** League Unlimited Orchestra	18Sep82 135(2) 7	86.1
10541. **NO PLACE FOR DISGRACE** Flotsam And Jetsam	18Jun88 143(2) 8	86.1
10542. **THE VELVET UNDERGROUND & NICO** Velvet Underground & Nico	13May67 171(1) 13	86.0
10543. **VAN GO** Beat Farmers	12Jul86 135(2) 9	85.9
10544. **I WALK ALONE** Marty Robbins	14Dec68 160(2) 7	85.9
10545. **FLATT AND SCRUGGS AT CARNEGIE HALL!** Flatt & Scruggs	28Sep63 134(1) 6	85.9
10546. **BUNDLE OF JOY** Freddie Hubbard	29Oct77 146(1) 6	85.8
10547. **STILL FEELS GOOD** Tom Johnston	16May81 158(1) 7	85.8
10548. **STAR PEOPLE** Miles Davis	21May83 136(1) 7	85.8
10549. **EARLY FACES** Small Faces	05Aug72 176(1) 10	85.8
10550. **SHANGRI-LA** Bardeux	14Oct89 133(2) 7	85.8
10551. **RAMSEY LEWIS, THE PIANO PLAYER** Ramsey Lewis	21Mar70 157(2) 8	85.7
10552. **MUSICAL SHAPES** Carlene Carter	04Oct80 139(2) 6	85.7
10553. **GIVE, GET, TAKE AND HAVE** Curtis Mayfield	03Jul76 171(1) 8	85.6
10554. **SOUTHERN WINDS** Maria Muldaur	08Apr78 143(3) 5	85.6
10555. **ACTUAL SPEECHES OF FRANKLIN D. ROOSEVELT AND JOHN F. KENNEDY** Franklin D. Roosevelt And John F. Kennedy	18Jan64 109(1) 5	85.6
10556. **THE DELLS VS. THE DRAMATICS** The Dells/The Dramatics	04May74 156(1) 6	85.5
10557. **SAM COOKE LIVE AT THE HARLEM SQUARE CLUB** Sam Cooke	22Jun85 134(1) 8	85.5
10558. **JEALOUSY** Major Harris	28Feb76 153(2) 6	85.5
10559. **BAD LUCK** Atlanta Disco Band	17Jan76 172(1) 9	85.4
10560. **CLUB PARADISE** Jimmy Cliff	26Jul86 122(2) 6	85.4
10561. **GO FOR THE THROAT** Humble Pie	09May81 154(1) 6	85.4
10562. **BLUEPRINT** Rory Gallagher	21Apr73 147(1) 7	85.4
10563. **THE SPECKLESS SKY** Jane Siberry	14Jun86 149(2) 8	85.4
10564. **CLASSICS** Paul Williams	06Aug77 155(1) 8	85.3
10565. **MOTHER FOCUS** Focus	27Sep75 152(2) 6	85.3
10566. **YOUR MAMA WON'T LIKE ME** Suzi Quatro	10May75 146(2) 6	85.3
10567. **NOTHING TO FEAR** Oingo Boingo	04Sep82 148(1) 9	85.3
10568. **WHAT'S NEW PUSSYCAT?** Tom Jones	18Sep65 114(2) 5	85.3
10569. **HERE COME THE WARM JETS** Brian Eno	24Aug74 151(1) 6	85.3
10570. **SMOKIN' O.P.'S** Bob Seger	22Jul72 180(1) 11	85.3
10571. **IRRESISTIBLE** Miles Jaye	10Jun89 160(2) 9	85.3
10572. **RELICS** Pink Floyd	31Jul71 152(2) 7	85.3
10573. **SECOND TO NUNN** Bobby Nunn	23Oct82 148(1) 8	85.2
10574. **STAY** Ray, Goodman & Brown	09Jan82 151(1) 7	85.2
10575. **HEY JOE** The Leaves	30Jul66 127(1) 5	85.2
10576. **BELLY UP!** Dr. Hook & The Medicine Show	27Oct73 141(1) 6	85.2
10577. **MAGIC WINDOWS** Herbie Hancock	03Oct81 140(1) 6	85.2
10578. **DEFECTOR** Steve Hackett	30Aug80 144(1) 6	85.1
10579. **TAKE TIME TO KNOW HER** Percy Sledge	25May68 148(1) 6	85.1
10580. **BEAUTY & THE BEAST: OF LOVE AND HOPE** TV Soundtrack	17Jun89 157(1) 10	85.1
10581. **PRIMITIVE MAN** Icehouse	09Oct82 129(2) 6	85.1
10582. **SUPER BLUE** Freddie Hubbard	15Jul78 131(2) 5	85.1
10583. **FRANKIE VALLI...IS THE WORD** Frankie Valli	26Aug78 160(2) 7	85.1
10584. **...THAT'S THE WAY IT IS** Nilsson	10Jul76 158(1) 6	85.0
10585. **CORDS** Synergy	16Sep78 146(1) 6	85.0
10586. **BIG TOWNE, 2061** Paris	11Sep76 152(2) 6	85.0
10587. **GREATEST HITS COLLECTION** Bananarama	03Dec88 151(2) 9	84.8
10588. **THE GOLDEN CHILD** Soundtrack	24Jan87 126(2) 7	84.8
10589. **UNFINISHED MUSIC NO. 2: LIFE WITH THE LIONS** John Lennon & Yoko Ono	28Jun69 174(2) 8	84.7
10590. **THE CHAMBERS BROTHERS' GREATEST HITS** Chambers Brothers	04Dec71 166(1) 7	84.7
10591. **COMMODORES ANTHOLOGY** Commodores	11Jun83 141(1) 7	84.5
10592. **THE ILLINOIS SPEED PRESS** Illinois Speed Press	24May69 144(2) 4	84.5
10593. **WE'RE MOVIN' UP** Atlantic Starr	20May89 125(2) 6	84.5
10594. **THE BEST OF WAR...AND MORE** War	30May87 156(2) 10	84.5
10595. **PERFECT VIEW** The Graces	09Sep89 147(1) 9	84.5
10596. **COMPARTMENTS** Jose Feliciano	19May73 156(1) 8	84.5

Rank. Title Act Entry Peak(Pk Wks) TotWks	Scr
10597. PLAYING TO WIN Rick Nelson 21Feb81 153(2) 6	84.4
10598. A CAPPELLA Todd Rundgren 12Oct85 128(2) 8	84.4
10599. G.T.O. Ronny And The Daytonas 05Dec64 122(1) 6	84.4
10600. REFLECTIONS Stan Getz 11Apr64 122(1) 6	84.4
10601. I HEAR A SYMPHONY Hank Crawford 17Apr76 159(1) 7	84.3
10602. CHECK IT OUT Tavares 09Feb74 160(1) 8	84.3
10603. RUFUS THOMAS LIVE/ DOING THE PUSH & PULL AT P.J.'S Rufus Thomas 03Apr71 147(2) 5	84.2
10604. DIG THE NEW BREED The Jam 15Jan83 131(1) 9	84.2
10605. TONY BENNETT'S GREATEST HITS, VOLUME IV Tony Bennett 10May69 174(1) 8	84.2
10606. GUSTAV HOLST: THE PLANETS Zubin Mehta, Los Angeles Philharmonic Orchestra 10Jun72 175(1) 10	84.1
10607. SLIPPIN' AWAY Chris Hillman 19Jun76 152(2) 6	84.1
10608. GOLDEN HITS/THE BEST OF BILLY VAUGHN Billy Vaughn And His Orchestra 23Sep67 159(2) 8	84.1
10609. AEROBIC DANCE HITS, VOLUME ONE Carla Capuano 13Mar82 152(3) 8	84.0
10610. EXTRAPOLATION John McLaughlin 21Oct72 152(2) 6	84.0
10611. GOLDEN FOLK SONG HITS, VOLUME TWO Johnny Mann Singers 12Oct63 90(1) 4	84.0
10612. SOUL SERENADE Willie Mitchell 11May68 151(1) 7	84.0
10613. YESTERDAY ONCE MORE Carpenters 25May85 144(2) 8	84.0
10614. SOMETHING MAGIC Procol Harum 26Mar77 147(1) 6	84.0
10615. THE BEST OF JOHNNY MATHIS 1975-1980 Johnny Mathis 27Dec80 140(2) 7	83.9
10616. SERIOUS BUSINESS Johnny Winter 19Oct85 156(2) 10	83.9
10617. UNBELIEVABLE Billy Stewart 07May66 138(1) 6	83.9
10618. ELLINGTON '65: HITS OF THE 60'S/ THIS TIME BY ELLINGTON Duke Ellington 03Oct64 133(1) 7	83.8
10619. SONGS OF THE HUMPBACK WHALE Various Artists 27Mar71 176(1) 8	83.8
10620. MUSIC KEEPS ME TOGETHER Taj Mahal 18Oct75 155(1) 7	83.6
10621. MY FAREWELL TO ELVIS Merle Haggard 19Nov77 133(1) 5	83.5
10622. HOT WIRE Trapeze 04Jan75 146(1) 6	83.5
10623. NORMAN CONNORS PRESENTS AQUARIAN DREAM Aquarian Dream 09Oct76 154(1) 6	83.5
10624. THE RETURN OF THE MAGNIFICENT SEVEN The Supremes & Four Tops 26Jun71 154(1) 6	83.5
10625. THIS IS IT Melba Moore 08May76 145(2) 5	83.5
10626. A MAN AND A WOMAN & OTHER MOTION PICTURE THEMES Ferrante & Teicher 18Feb67 133(2) 5	83.5
10627. THE SECOND ADVENTURE Dynasty 10Oct81 119(2) 4	83.4
10628. ONLY MAKE BELIEVE Bell & James 03Nov79 125(2) 4	83.4
10629. EXPRESSIONS Don Williams 27Jan79 161(1) 7	83.4
10630. ELECTRIC CHURCH Buddy Miles Express 07Jun69 145(2) 4	83.4
10631. CONNIE SMITH Connie Smith 22May65 105(1) 5	83.3
10632. THE ANITA KERR SINGERS REFLECT ON THE HITS OF BURT BACHARACH & HAL DAVID Anita Kerr Singers 22Mar69 162(1) 6	83.3
10633. T.R.A.S.H. (TUBES RARITIES AND SMASH HITS) The Tubes 29Aug81 148(1) 6	83.2
10634. THE BERMUDA TRIANGLE Isao Tomita 03Mar79 152(1) 6	83.2
10635. VIVE LE ROCK Adam Ant 19Oct85 131(2) 7	83.1
10636. THE BEST OF BUFFY SAINTE-MARIE Buffy Sainte-Marie 24Oct70 142(1) 7	83.1
10637. BLUES FOR MISTER JIMMY Jimmy McGriff 29May65 130(1) 6	83.1
10638. GET RHYTHM Ry Cooder 28Nov87 177(1) 12	83.1
10639. MADE IN EUROPE Deep Purple 27Nov76 148(1) 6	83.0
10640. FOOLISH PLEASURES Heartsfield 16Aug75 159(1) 7	83.0
10641. SOMEBODY'S BEEN SLEEPING IN MY BED 100 Proof Aged in Soul 12Dec70 151(2) 7	82.9
10642. THE ABOMINABLE SHOWMAN Nick Lowe 02Apr83 129(2) 7	82.8
10643. VOLUNTEER JAM Various Artists 24Jul76 153(1) 6	82.8
10644. SATURDAY NIGHT FIEDLER Boston Pops Orchestra 08Sep79 147(1) 6	82.8
10645. TERRY REID Terry Reid 18Oct69 147(2) 5	82.8
10646. WELCOME TO MY WORLD Ray Price 04Dec71 146(1) 5	82.7
10647. GREATEST HITS Wes Montgomery 04Apr70 175(1) 9	82.7
10648. DON'T CALL US-WE'LL CALL YOU Sugarloaf/Jerry Corbetta 12Apr75 152(1) 6	82.6
10649. THE UNDERTONES The Undertones 26Jan80 154(1) 7	82.6
10650. RAIN DANCES Camel 12Nov77 136(2) 5	82.6
10651. THE ESSENTIAL JIMI HENDRIX VOL.II Jimi Hendrix 18Aug79 156(2) 7	82.6
10652. BACK TO BASICS The Temptations 21Apr84 152(1) 9	82.6
10653. CARLA Carla Thomas 15Oct66 130(1) 5	82.5
10654. L.A. EXPRESS L.A. Express 06Mar76 167(1) 8	82.5
10655. FRIENDS B.B. King 17Aug74 153(1) 6	82.5
10656. IN CONCERT Julio Iglesias 25Aug84 159(2) 9	82.5
10657. HEART TO HEART David Sanborn 03Jun78 151(1) 6	82.4
10658. I'VE FOUND SOMEONE OF MY OWN Free Movement 29Jan72 167(1) 8	82.3
10659. WINGLESS ANGELS John Stewart 17May75 150(2) 6	82.3
10660. I CAN SEE CLEARLY NOW Ray Conniff & His Orchestra & Chorus 10Feb73 165(1) 10	82.3
10661. THE FIRST TIME EVER (I SAW YOUR FACE) Peter Nero 08Jul72 172(2) 9	82.3
10662. MORE THEMES FROM THE JAMES BOND THRILLERS Roland Shaw Orchestra 05Feb66 119(1) 5	82.2
10663. TALKIN' 'BOUT YOU Diane Schuur 12Nov88 170(3) 10	82.2
10664. THEM AGAIN Them 16Apr66 138(2) 6	82.2
10665. McKENDREE SPRING 3 McKendree Spring 20May72 163(1) 7	82.2
10666. THE SEA OF LOVE The Adventures 16Apr88 144(1) 9	82.1
10667. I BELIEVE IN LOVE Rockie Robbins 12Sep81 147(2) 6	82.1
10668. THE WOMENFOLK The Womenfolk 02May64 118(2) 6	82.1
10669. FOREVER YOUNG Alphaville 22Dec84 180(1) 15	82.1
10670. BALLS OF FIRE Black Oak Arkansas 12Jun76 173(3) 7	82.1
10671. IN CONTROL The Controllers 17Dec77 146(1) 6	82.1
10672. BOBBY VINTON SINGS FOR LONELY NIGHTS Bobby Vinton 03Jul65 116(1) 5	82.0
10673. MIRROR IMAGE Blood, Sweat & Tears 07Sep74 149(1) 6	82.0
10674. SAD SWEET DREAMER Sweet Sensation 03May75 163(1) 7	82.0
10675. LET ME TELL YOU ABOUT A SONG Merle Haggard 08Apr72 166(1) 8	81.9
10676. SPRINGTIME Ferrante & Teicher 24Apr65 130(1) 6	81.9
10677. RAGE IN EDEN Ultravox 24Oct81 144(2) 6	81.9
10678. EZO EZO 13Jun87 150(2) 9	81.9
10679. TEN YEARS ARE GONE John Mayall 06Oct73 157(1) 7	81.9
10680. DON HO-AGAIN! Don Ho and the Aliis 05Mar66 117(1) 5	81.8
10681. 5-10-15-20 (25-30 YEARS OF LOVE) The Presidents 30Jan71 158(2) 6	81.7
10682. SUPER FLY T.N.T. Osibisa 21Jul73 159(1) 7	81.7
10683. ORDINARY FOOL Paul Williams 13Dec75 146(1) 6	81.6
10684. BRAZILIA John Klemmer 02Jun79 172(1) 9	81.6
10685. SOUL CHILDREN Soul Children 06Sep69 154(1) 6	81.6
10686. 2ND STREET Back Street Crawler 14Aug76 140(1) 5	81.5
10687. NO RESPECT Vain 26Aug89 154(2) 8	81.5
10688. 20/20 TWENTY NO.1 HITS FROM TWENTY YEARS AT MOTOWN Various Artists 12Apr80 150(2) 6	81.5
10689. NO EASY WAY OUT Robert Tepper 19Apr86 144(2) 8	81.5
10690. TWO B'S PLEASE Robbin Thompson Band 25Oct80 168(1) 11	81.5
10691. BOOTS RANDOLPH PLAYS MORE YAKETY SAX! Boots Randolph 13Nov65 118(1) 5	81.4
10692. SOLDIERS OF FORTUNE The Outlaws 08Nov86 160(2) 10	81.4
10693. LUCIANO Luciano Pavarotti 24Apr82 141(1) 7	81.4
10694. I CAN'T STAND THE RAIN Ann Peebles 09Mar74 155(1) 7	81.4
10695. PERSPECTIVE ON BUD & TRAVIS Bud & Travis 28Mar64 129(1) 6	81.3
10696. PLAY ONE MORE Ian & Sylvia 28May66 142(1) 6	81.3
10697. FILET OF SOUL Jan & Dean 14May66 127(2) 5	81.2
10698. LOVE CORPORATION Hues Corporation 05Jul75 147(1) 5	81.1
10699. AMBUSH Marc Benno 23Sep72 171(2) 8	81.1
10700. REBEL MUSIC Bob Marley And The Wailers 06Sep86 140(1) 9	81.1
10701. INNOCENT EYES Graham Nash 26Apr86 136(2) 7	81.1
10702. IN THE NAME OF LOVE Thompson Twins 26Jun82 148(2) 8	81.0
10703. A WOMAN'S GOT THE POWER The A's 11Jul81 146(1) 7	80.9
10704. DISGUISE Chuck Mangione 15Sep84 148(2) 8	80.9
10705. WATCHING YOU, WATCHING ME Bill Withers 25May85 143(2) 8	80.9
10706. ROUTES Ramsey Lewis 23Aug80 173(1) 8	80.8
10707. EXPOSED II Various Artists 05Dec81 124(2) 5	80.7
10708. BOYS, BOYS, BOYS Lesley Gore 18Jul64 127(1) 6	80.5

Rank. Title Act	Entry Peak(Pk Wks) TotWks	Scr
10709. THE VERY BEST OF GORDON LIGHTFOOT Gordon Lightfoot	27Jul74 155(1) 9	80.5
10710. LORD OF THE RINGS Bo Hansson	05May73 154(1) 8	80.5
10711. FEEL THE SPIRIT Leroy Hutson	06Mar76 170(1) 8	80.5
10712. ANGEL Angel	20Dec75 156(2) 6	80.5
10713. THE HOLLIES' GREATEST HITS(2) The Hollies	20Oct73 157(1) 7	80.5
10714. JIMMY SMITH'S GREATEST HITS! Jimmy Smith	08Jun68 128(1) 4	80.4
10715. ARMAGEDDON Armageddon	07Jun75 151(1) 6	80.4
10716. HELP YOURSELF Larry Gatlin & The Gatlin Brothers Band	01Nov80 118(1) 4	80.4
10717. A STRANGER ON EARTH Dinah Washington	04Apr64 130(2) 6	80.4
10718. HOT DOG Lou Donaldson	04Oct69 158(1) 6	80.3
10719. PERSUASIVE PERCUSSION 1966 Enoch Light & The Light Brigade	21May66 144(2) 6	80.3
10720. SATURDAY NIGHT SPECIAL Norman Connors	11Oct75 150(2) 5	80.3
10721. SHO IS FUNKY DOWN HERE James Brown	01May71 137(2) 4	80.3
10722. CHRISTMAS RAP Various Artists	12Dec87 130(1) 8	80.3
10723. JANE WIEDLIN Jane Wiedlin	26Oct85 127(2) 6	80.3
10724. RUB IT IN Billy "Crash" Craddock	24Aug74 142(2) 5	80.2
10725. I DON'T KNOW WHAT THE WORLD IS COMING TO Bobby Womack	24May75 126(1) 4	80.2
10726. RAY CONNIFF'S GREATEST HITS Ray Conniff & His Orchestra & Chorus	12Jul69 158(1) 5	80.2
10727. AMOUR Richard Clayderman	24Nov84 160(3) 9	80.1
10728. QUEEN OF THE NEIGHBORHOOD The Flame	14May77 147(1) 5	80.0
10729. EMOTION DFX2	20Aug83 143(1) 8	80.0
10730. 16 ORIGINAL BIG HITS, VOLUME 4 Various Artists	15Jan66 108(1) 5	80.0
10731. TALL COOL ONE The Wailers	27Jun64 127(1) 6	79.9
10732. BALL ROOM Sea Level	23Aug80 152(1) 6	79.9
10733. TIME FOR ANOTHER Ace	27Dec75 153(1) 6	79.8
10734. I WANT TO COME BACK AS A SONG Walter Jackson	30Apr77 141(1) 5	79.8
10735. CORNBREAD, EARL AND ME The Blackbyrds	05Jul75 150(2) 6	79.8
10736. TRY MY LOVE Tata Vega	21Apr79 170(2) 8	79.8
10737. ROYAL JAM The Crusaders With B.B.King And The Royal Philharmonic Orchestra	17Jul82 144(1) 7	79.8
10738. NO OTHER Gene Clark	02Nov74 144(2) 5	79.8
10739. HELEN REDDY Helen Reddy	04Dec71 167(1) 7	79.7
10740. SCORCHING BEAUTY Iron Butterfly	15Feb75 138(2) 6	79.7
10741. STICK TO ME Graham Parker And The Rumour	05Nov77 125(1) 5	79.7
10742. SKEEZER PLEEZER UTFO	09Aug86 142(2) 8	79.6
10743. NITZINGER Nitzinger	02Sep72 170(1) 8	79.5
10744. SIXTEEN Stacy Lattisaw	27Aug83 160(1) 8	79.4
10745. INNER VOICES McCoy Tyner	28Jan78 171(1) 8	79.3
10746. UPTOWN Neville Brothers	02May87 155(1) 9	79.3
10747. NEXUS Argent	04May74 149(1) 6	79.3
10748. STUDIO TAN Frank Zappa	21Oct78 147(1) 6	79.3
10749. BIG TRASH Thompson Twins	21Oct89 143(2) 6	79.3
10750. CLEO LAINE LIVE!!! AT CARNEGIE HALL Cleo Laine	06Apr74 157(1) 8	79.1
10751. GET YOURSELF UP Head East	22May76 161(1) 6	79.0
10752. EBONEE WEBB Ebonee Webb	12Sep81 157(2) 7	79.0
10753. THE GENE CHANDLER SITUATION Gene Chandler	31Oct70 178(1) 9	79.0
10754. YESTERGROOVIN' Chet Atkins	25Apr70 139(1) 5	78.9
10755. LI'L OL' GROOVEMAKER...BASIE! Count Basie	07Sep63 123(1) 5	78.9
10756. REVELATIONS New Colony Six	20Jul68 157(2) 6	78.8
10757. GET RHYTHM Johnny Cash	29Nov69 164(2) 6	78.8
10758. THRU THE YEARS John Mayall	13Nov71 164(1) 7	78.7
10759. THE WINDMILLS OF YOUR MIND Ed Ames	05Jul69 157(2) 6	78.7
10760. HISTORY OF BRITISH BLUES, VOLUME ONE Various Artists	28Apr73 160(1) 8	78.7
10761. DON HARRISON BAND Don Harrison Band	01May76 159(1) 6	78.7
10762. EXPRESS YOURSELF Charles Wright And The Watts 103rd Street Band	08Aug70 182(2) 10	78.7
10763. LIVIN' LARGE E.U.	22Apr89 158(1) 9	78.6
10764. SWING, SWING, SWING Boston Pops Orchestra/John Williams	17May86 155(2) 8	78.6
10765. MISTY ROSES The Sandpipers	13Jan68 135(1) 5	78.6
10766. DAVID RUFFIN David Ruffin	17Mar73 160(1) 7	78.5
10767. GOOD FOR YOUR SOUL Oingo Boingo	10Sep83 144(1) 7	78.5
10768. DREAMS Dreams	28Nov70 146(2) 6	78.5
10769. MR. DREAM MERCHANT Jerry Butler	20Jan68 154(1) 7	78.5
10770. LOVE MAKES A WOMAN Barbara Acklin	05Oct68 146(2) 5	78.5
10771. THE GREAT MEMPHIS HITS King Curtis	03Jun67 185(2) 12	78.4
10772. I HEARD IT IN A LOVE SONG McFadden & Whitehead	04Oct80 153(1) 6	78.4
10773. THE RHYTHMATIST Stewart Copeland	07Sep85 148(2) 8	78.4
10774. TRIAL BY FIRE: LIVE IN LENINGRAD Yngwie Malmsteen	11Nov89 128(2) 8	78.4
10775. BROWNE SUGAR Tom Browne	11Aug79 147(2) 6	78.4
10776. THE PASSENGER Melvin James	03Oct87 146(2) 8	78.4
10777. URBAN DESIRE Genya Ravan	02Sep78 147(1) 6	78.3
10778. NEW DIMENSIONS Three Degrees	23Dec78 169(1) 8	78.3
10779. AND I LOVE YOU SO Shirley Bassey	25Nov72 171(1) 8	78.3
10780. ROTATIONS Tim Weisberg Band	06May78 159(2) 6	78.3
10781. ME & PAUL Willie Nelson	30Mar85 152(1) 7	78.3
10782. MA BELLE AMIE Tee Set	16May70 158(2) 6	78.2
10783. NDEDA Quincy Jones	04Mar72 173(2) 9	78.2
10784. CAPTURED LIVE Peter Tosh	22Sep84 152(2) 8	78.1
10785. PAIS TROPICAL Sergio Mendes & Brasil '77	16Oct71 166(1) 6	78.1
10786. COME AN' GET IT Whitesnake	30May81 151(2) 6	78.1
10787. A TRIBUTE TO JACK JOHNSON Miles Davis	24Apr71 159(2) 8	78.0
10788. BURNIN' The Wailers(2)	11Oct75 151(2) 6	78.0
10789. NEIL SEDAKA'S GREATEST HITS Neil Sedaka	22Oct77 143(2) 5	77.9
10790. FESTIVAL Lee Ritenour	21Jan89 156(2) 8	77.9
10791. THE BEST OF SAM COOKE Sam Cooke	30Jan65 136(1) 6	77.9
10792. KEEPER OF THE FLAME Delbert McClinton	30Jun79 146(2) 6	77.8
10793. INTO THE WOODS Original Cast	26Mar88 126(2) 6	77.8
10794. SURFACE THRILLS The Temptations	19Mar83 159(3) 9	77.8
10795. GREMLINS Soundtrack	07Jul84 143(1) 7	77.8
10796. PERFECT FIT Jerry Knight	11Apr81 146(1) 6	77.8
10797. LOOK OUT FOR THE CHEATER Bob Kuban And The In-Men	23Apr66 129(2) 5	77.8
10798. THE BOBBY VINTON SHOW Bobby Vinton	27Dec75 161(2) 7	77.7
10799. INDIAN LOVE CALL Exotic Guitars	31May69 162(2) 6	77.7
10800. CHILL OUT Black Uhuru	24Jul82 146(1) 7	77.7
10801. SYMPHONIC SOUL Henry Mancini And His Orchestra	14Feb76 159(2) 6	77.7
10802. CHAPEL OF LOVE Dixie Cups	29Aug64 112(1) 5	77.6
10803. KINGS OF WEST COAST L.A. Dream Team	13Sep86 138(1) 7	77.6
10804. ALIBI America	06Sep80 142(2) 6	77.6
10805. HEY! LET'S PARTY Mongo Santamaria	04Jun66 135(2) 5	77.6
10806. TWO GREAT EXPERIENCES TOGETHER! Jimi Hendrix & Lonnie Youngblood	20Mar71 127(1) 4	77.5
10807. WALK ON THE WILD SIDE-THE BEST OF LOU REED Lou Reed	16Apr77 156(1) 6	77.5
10808. COME BACK HOME Bobby Goldsboro	28Aug71 142(2) 5	77.5
10809. NIGHT GROOVES The Blackbyrds	06Jan79 159(1) 7	77.4
10810. AIRPLAY Point Blank	18Aug79 175(1) 9	77.4
10811. SAY NO MORE Badfinger	28Mar81 155(1) 6	77.3
10812. TOGETHER ON BROADWAY Steve Lawrence & Eydie Gorme	20May67 136(1) 6	77.3
10813. TAKE IT TO THE LIMIT Norman Connors	27Sep80 145(1) 6	77.3
10814. FREEDOM MARCH ON WASHINGTON Rev. Martin Luther King, Jr.	09Nov63 119(1) 5	77.3
10815. RASPBERRIES' BEST FEATURING ERIC CARMEN Raspberries	12Jun76 138(1) 4	77.3
10816. STRANGE ANGELS Laurie Anderson	18Nov89 171(1) 12	77.3
10817. SIMON SAYS 1910 Fruitgum Co.	20Apr68 162(1) 8	77.2
10818. SOUP FOR ONE Soundtrack	12Jun82 168(1) 12	77.1
10819. KILIMANJARO Teardrop Explodes	28Feb81 156(2) 6	77.1
10820. NIGHTHAWKS AT THE DINER Tom Waits	29Nov75 164(2) 6	77.1
10821. DIAMOND CUT Bonnie Tyler	17Feb79 145(1) 5	77.0
10822. MORE GOLDEN HITS BY THE FOUR SEASONS 4 Seasons	05Sep64 105(1) 5	77.0
10823. SHOULDA GONE DANCIN' High Inergy	26May79 147(2) 5	77.0
10824. FIDDLER ON THE ROOF Herschel Bernardi	12Nov66 138(1) 5	77.0

Rank. Title Act Entry Peak(Pk Wks) TotWks	Scr
10825. ELLA FITZGERALD SINGS THE GEORGE AND IRA GERSHWIN SONG BOOKS Ella Fitzgerald 28Mar64 111(2) 5	76.9
10826. FRIENDS & PEOPLE Friends Of Distinction 07Aug71 166(1) 7	76.9
10827. FAVORITES Crystal Gayle 03May80 149(1) 6	76.9
10828. WILLIE NELSON LIVE Willie Nelson 08May76 149(1) 7	76.8
10829. SAMMY'S BACK ON BROADWAY Sammy Davis Jr. 04Sep65 104(1) 4	76.8
10830. VALERIE SIMPSON Valerie Simpson 26Aug72 162(3) 6	76.8
10831. TOGETHER Jesse Colin Young 25Mar72 157(1) 6	76.7
10832. FEELIN' GOOD David Ruffin 13Dec69 148(1) 7	76.7
10833. HITS/GREATEST & OTHERS Joan Baez 07Jul73 163(1) 8	76.7
10834. ANYONE FOR MOZART? Swingle Singers 20Feb65 140(1) 6	76.7
10835. UP IN SMOKE Cheech & Chong 02Dec78 162(1) 7	76.7
10836. R.P.M. Soundtrack 31Oct70 148(2) 6	76.6
10837. THE FLYING BURRITO BROS. Flying Burrito Brothers 12Jun71 176(1) 9	76.5
10838. TRACY NELSON Tracy Nelson 19Oct74 145(1) 5	76.5
10839. OCTOPUS Gentle Giant 31Mar73 170(1) 9	76.5
10840. TUFF DARTS! Tuff Darts 18Mar78 156(1) 6	76.5
10841. RHINESTONE Dolly Parton 21Jul84 135(2) 7	76.5
10842. DON'T GIVE UP YOUR DAY JOB Jack Wagner 02May87 151(2) 8	76.5
10843. GREAT MOMENTS ON BROADWAY Jerry Vale 02Jul66 111(1) 4	76.4
10844. TURN YOUR RADIO ON Ray Stevens 05Feb72 175(1) 9	76.3
10845. LOOKS SO FINE Instant Funk 10Apr82 147(2) 7	76.3
10846. GREATEST HITS George Strait 20Apr85 157(1) 8	76.2
10847. SHANGRI-LA Vic Dana 16May64 116(1) 5	76.2
10848. DEEP PURPLE Deep Purple 12Jul69 162(1) 6	76.2
10849. UNITED WE STAND Brotherhood Of Man 08Aug70 168(2) 8	76.1
10850. MSB Michael Stanley Band 04Sep82 136(2) 6	76.1
10851. TEN YEARS OF HARMONY (1970-1980) Beach Boys 26Dec81 156(1) 8	76.0
10852. GIRL WATCHER The O'Kaysions 09Nov68 153(2) 4	75.9
10853. SAVAGE EYE Pretty Things 21Feb76 163(1) 6	75.8
10854. TIME ALONE WILL TELL Jerry Vale 16Sep67 128(2) 6	75.7
10855. POPE JOHN PAUL II SINGS AT THE FESTIVAL OF SACROSO Pope John Paul II 03Nov79 126(2) 4	75.7
10856. IF I WERE A CARPENTER Bobby Darin 11Feb67 142(1) 5	75.7
10857. VALERIE SIMPSON EXPOSED Valerie Simpson 31Jul71 159(2) 6	75.7
10858. A SONG OR TWO Cashman & West 14Oct72 168(2) 8	75.7
10859. THE EXOTIC GUITARS Exotic Guitars 03Aug68 155(1) 5	75.5
10860. THE HONEY WIND BLOWS Brothers Four 01May65 118(1) 5	75.5
10861. MIGRATION Dave Grusin 21Oct89 145(1) 8	75.4
10862. TWANG BAR KING Adrian Belew 01Oct83 146(2) 7	75.4
10863. LET'S HAVE A PARTY The Rivieras 13Jun64 115(2) 5	75.4
10864. REVISITED Love 05Sep70 142(1) 7	75.3
10865. SO GOOD Don And The Goodtimes 05Aug67 109(1) 4	75.3
10866. THE OSMOND CHRISTMAS ALBUM The Osmonds 18Dec76 127(2) 5	75.2
10867. THE BEST OF THE POINTER SISTERS Pointer Sisters 04Dec76 164(3) 6	75.2
10868. TRAGEDY/A MILLION TO ONE Brian Hyland 19Apr69 160(1) 5	75.1
10869. DEEP CUTS Strawbs 30Oct76 144(1) 5	75.1
10870. HOPES WISHES & DREAMS Ray Thomas 14Aug76 147(2) 5	75.0
10871. COME INTO MY LIFE Jermaine Jackson 16Jun73 152(1) 6	75.0
10872. BEHOLD THE MIGHTY ARMY New Birth 10Dec77 164(1) 6	75.0
10873. RAVI SHANKAR IN NEW YORK Ravi Shankar 29Jul67 148(2) 7	74.9
10874. LOVE IS WHAT WE MAKE IT Kenny Rogers 20Apr85 145(1) 7	74.9
10875. WHITE CHRISTMAS John Schneider 05Dec81 155(1) 7	74.9
10876. WALK A FINE LINE Paul Anka 13Aug83 156(1) 8	74.9
10877. THE PEABO BRYSON COLLECTION Peabo Bryson 14Jul84 168(1) 10	74.9
10878. AGENT DOUBLE O SOUL The Untouchables 01Apr89 162(2) 9	74.8
10879. TIME ODYSSEY Vinnie Moore 18Jun88 147(2) 7	74.7
10880. RIDIN' HIGH Martha Reeves & The Vandellas 01Jun68 167(1) 8	74.7
10881. KO-KO JOE Jerry Reed 18Sep71 153(2) 5	74.7
10882. STREET ACTION BTO 18Mar78 130(1) 4	74.6
10883. LISTEN TO A COUNTRY SONG Lynn Anderson 09Sep72 160(2) 7	74.6
10884. SPIES OF LIFE Player 06Feb82 152(1) 7	74.5
10885. SONIC SEASONINGS Walter Carlos 08Jul72 168(2) 7	74.5
10886. HIT CITY 64 The Surfaris 07Mar64 120(1) 5	74.5
10887. FEARLESS Nina Hagen 28Jan84 151(2) 8	74.5
10888. EDDIE & THE CRUISERS II John Cafferty & The Beaver Brown Band 26Aug89 121(2) 6	74.5
10889. MATERIAL THANGZ The Deele 06Jul85 155(1) 8	74.5
10890. HEAT WAVE Martha & The Vandellas 23Nov63 125(1) 5	74.4
10891. CHRISTIANE F. David Bowie 03Apr82 135(2) 7	74.4
10892. NIGEL Nigel Olsson 24Mar79 140(1) 5	74.4
10893. GIMME DAT DING! The Pipkins 08Aug70 132(2) 4	74.4
10894. LISTEN TO THE RADIO Don Williams 01May82 166(3) 8	74.4
10895. AHEAD RINGS OUT Blodwyn Pig 13Dec69 149(1) 5	74.4
10896. JUMPIN' THE GUNNE Jo Jo Gunne 22Dec73 169(1) 7	74.3
10897. SPLASHDOWN Breakwater 07Jun80 141(1) 5	74.3
10898. THE BELLS Lou Reed 02Jun79 130(1) 4	74.3
10899. ALONE AGAIN (NATURALLY) Ray Conniff & His Orchestra & Chorus 07Oct72 180(1) 10	74.2
10900. REVOLUCION El Chicano 17Apr71 178(2) 9	74.1
10901. SORCERER Tangerine Dream 23Jul77 153(2) 6	74.1
10902. WAIT FOR NIGHT Rick Springfield 18Dec82 159(2) 8	74.1
10903. BA-FA Hudson Brothers 13Dec75 165(2) 6	74.1
10904. THE CHRISTIANS The Christians 12Mar88 158(2) 8	74.1
10905. I'M GONNA BE A COUNTRY GIRL AGAIN Buffy Sainte-Marie 03Aug68 171(2) 7	74.1
10906. THE GREATEST Soundtrack 25Jun77 166(2) 8	74.1
10907. HAPPY? Public Image Limited 24Oct87 169(1) 10	74.0
10908. SHE'S GOT TO BE A SAINT Ray Price 21Apr73 161(1) 7	74.0
10909. THE FLOWERS OF ROMANCE Public Image Limited 30May81 114(2) 4	74.0
10910. DUNE David Matthews 03Sep77 169(1) 7	73.9
10911. TRB TWO Tom Robinson Band 12May79 163(1) 7	73.9
10912. ALL AROUND MY HAT Steeleye Span 06Dec75 143(1) 6	73.9
10913. GUARDIAN OF THE LIGHT George Duke 30Apr83 147(1) 7	73.8
10914. GREATEST HITS Wet Willie 18Mar78 158(1) 6	73.8
10915. ONE FLEW OVER THE CUCKOO'S NEST Soundtrack 17Apr76 158(2) 7	73.8
10916. EAST COAST/WEST COAST Don Ho and the Aliis 27May67 115(1) 5	73.7
10917. THE FABULOUS IMPRESSIONS The Impressions 15Jul67 184(2) 11	73.7
10918. 500 MILES HIGH Flora Purim 16Oct76 146(1) 5	73.7
10919. SILVER LININGS Charlie Rich 03Apr76 160(1) 6	73.7
10920. FACE TO FACE Angel City 10May80 152(2) 7	73.6
10921. FOLK SONGS AROUND THE WORLD Mantovani 18Apr64 135(1) 6	73.6
10922. WINDHAM HILL PIANO SAMPLER Various Artists 21Dec85 167(2) 12	73.5
10923. THE SUN STILL SHINES Sonny Charles 25Dec82 136(2) 7	73.4
10924. RINGO THE 4TH Ringo Starr 15Oct77 163(1) 6	73.4
10925. SWITCHED ON NASHVILLE: COUNTRY MOOG Gil Trythall 07Feb70 157(2) 6	73.4
10926. BECK Joe Beck 28Jun75 140(1) 5	73.4
10927. THE WINDMILLS ARE WEAKENING Bob Newhart 24Apr65 126(2) 5	73.4
10928. OUT OF THE MIST Illusion 02Jul77 163(1) 7	73.3
10929. A TENDER LOOK AT LOVE Roger Miller 24Aug68 173(1) 8	73.3
10930. MAKE LOVE TO THE MUSIC Leon & Mary Russell 25Jun77 142(1) 5	73.2
10931. THE SECOND ALBUM 707 07Feb81 159(1) 6	73.2
10932. THE ORIGINAL DISCO MAN James Brown 11Aug79 152(1) 6	73.2
10933. FLAG Yello 15Apr89 152(2) 9	73.1
10934. RUN FOR COVER Gary Moore 15Mar86 146(2) 7	73.1
10935. THE RETURN OF ROCK Jerry Lee Lewis 05Jun65 121(1) 5	73.1
10936. TENDERLY George Benson 05Aug89 140(2) 6	73.1
10937. SCHOOL PUNKS Brownsville Station 15Jun74 170(1) 8	73.1
10938. PRIVATE COLLECTION Jon And Vangelis 13Aug83 148(1) 7	73.1
10939. HEADIN' HOME Gary Wright 17Mar79 147(1) 5	73.0
10940. CHANGE Barry White 02Oct82 148(1) 6	73.0

Rank. Title Act	Entry Peak(Pk Wks) TotWks	Scr
10941. DESMOND CHILD AND ROUGE	Desmond Child And Rouge 24Mar79 157(1) 6	73.0
10942. MILKY WAY Chocolate Milk	14Apr79 161(1) 6	72.9
10943. SANDIE SHAW Sandie Shaw	12Jun65 100(1) 4	72.8
10944. ZORBA Original Cast	25Jan69 177(2) 7	72.8
10945. BOBBY & THE MIDNITES	Bobby And The Midnites 21Nov81 158(2) 7	72.8
10946. MASTER JACK Four Jacks And A Jill	22Jun68 155(2) 6	72.8
10947. WONDERFUL Rick James	23Jul88 148(2) 8	72.8
10948. DREAMER Bobby Bland	03Aug74 172(1) 7	72.7
10949. BREEZY STORIES Danny O'Keefe	11Aug73 172(1) 9	72.7
10950. THE BEST OF DAVE MASON Dave Mason	29Jun74 183(1) 9	72.6
10951. FAME AND FASHION - DAVID BOWIE'S ALL TIME GREATEST HITS David Bowie	21Apr84 147(1) 6	72.6
10952. WE GO TOGETHER Tammy Wynette & George Jones	13Nov71 169(1) 6	72.6
10953. JOHN F. KENNEDY - A MEMORIAL ALBUM	John Fitzgerald Kennedy 25Jan64 101(1) 4	72.5
10954. BOURGEOIS TAGG Bourgeois Tagg	31May86 139(2) 7	72.5
10955. EARLY ALLMAN Allman Joys	03Nov73 171(1) 8	72.5
10956. EVER READY Johnnie Taylor	06May78 164(1) 6	72.4
10957. OVER THE LINE Greg Guidry	17Apr82 147(1) 7	72.4
10958. MY FAVORITE THINGS	Dave Brubeck Quartet 26Mar66 133(1) 5	72.4
10959. UNREQUITED Loudon Wainwright III	15Mar75 156(1) 5	72.3
10960. LIES The Knickerbockers	12Feb66 134(2) 5	72.2
10961. DON HO-GREATEST HITS!	Don Ho and the Aliis 23Aug69 162(1) 6	72.1
10962. JAMES BROWN PLAYS NOTHING BUT SOUL	James Brown 24Aug68 150(1) 5	72.0
10963. HEROES, ANGELS & FRIENDS Janey Street	03Nov84 145(2) 6	72.0
10964. IT'S SUCH A PRETTY WORLD TODAY	Wynn Stewart 22Jul67 158(1) 8	72.0
10965. PASSION CRIMES Darling Cruel	09Sep89 160(2) 8	72.0
10966. ALWAYS, ALWAYS Porter Wagoner and Dolly Parton	16Aug69 162(1) 5	71.9
10967. RADICAL DEPARTURE Ranking Roger	13Aug88 151(2) 7	71.8
10968. THE MIND IS A TERRIBLE THING TO TASTE	Ministry 09Dec89 163(3) 10	71.8
10969. CLOSE PERSONAL FRIEND	Robert Johnson(2) 13Jan79 174(1) 8	71.8
10970. LORD JIM Soundtrack	27Mar65 123(1) 5	71.8
10971. RAVI SHANKAR IN SAN FRANCISCO	Ravi Shankar 03Aug68 140(1) 4	71.7
10972. I KNEW JESUS (BEFORE HE WAS A STAR)	Glen Campbell 09Jun73 154(1) 6	71.7
10973. SECOND GENERATION Gaylord & Holiday	21Feb76 180(1) 8	71.7
10974. BLUE BASH! Kenny Burrell/Jimmy Smith	30Nov63 108(1) 4	71.6
10975. WE'RE GONNA GET TOGETHER	Buck Owens & Susan Raye 16May70 154(1) 6	71.6
10976. THE MOVIE ALBUM Ramsey Lewis	22Jul67 124(1) 4	71.6
10977. ROCKY II Soundtrack	25Aug79 147(1) 5	71.6
10978. SYNTHESIS Cryan' Shames	15Feb69 184(1) 9	71.6
10979. ORANGE COLORED SKY Bert Kaempfert And His Orchestra	13Feb71 140(1) 6	71.5
10980. LEGACY Ramsey Lewis	28Oct78 149(1) 5	71.4
10981. WHITE HOT & BLUE Johnny Winter	26Aug78 141(2) 4	71.4
10982. THE EVOLUTION OF MANN Herbie Mann	03Feb73 172(1) 8	71.4
10983. CAN'T TAKE MY EYES OFF YOU	Nancy Wilson 28Mar70 155(1) 6	71.4
10984. INDESTRUCTIBLE Four Tops	24Sep88 149(2) 7	71.3
10985. .38 SPECIAL 38 Special	28May77 148(1) 5	71.3
10986. ETTA JAMES TOP TEN Etta James	24Aug63 117(1) 4	71.3
10987. COLD SPRING HARBOR Billy Joel	14Jan84 158(1) 8	71.3
10988. ACID QUEEN Tina Turner	20Sep75 155(1) 5	71.3
10989. SIMPLICITY OF EXPRESSION-DEPTH OF THOUGHT Billy Cobham	14Oct78 166(1) 6	71.1
10990. CLASSIC YES Yes	09Jan82 142(2) 5	71.1
10991. GOLDEN TOUCH Rose Royce	24Jan81 160(2) 7	71.0
10992. BOBBY SHORT LOVES COLE PORTER	Bobby Short 04Mar72 169(1) 8	71.0
10993. SKY DIVE Freddie Hubbard	10Mar73 165(1) 7	70.9
10994. DRAGNET Soundtrack	18Jul87 137(2) 6	70.8
10995. REAL EYES Gil Scott-Heron	20Dec80 159(2) 6	70.8
10996. MORE OF EVERYTHING! The Limeliters	09May64 118(1) 5	70.8
10997. SUNRISE Jimmy Ruffin	31May80 152(2) 6	70.8
10998. GET IT ON CREDIT Toronto	04Sep82 162(2) 10	70.8
10999. HAPPY HEART Nick DeCaro	19Apr69 165(1) 5	70.6
11000. ELECTRIC DREAMS John McLaughlin With The One Truth Band	28Apr79 147(1) 5	70.6
11001. MARS NEEDS GUITARS! Hoodoo Gurus	10May86 140(2) 7	70.5
11002. I'M READY Muddy Waters	25Feb78 157(1) 6	70.5
11003. BIGGEST HITS Marty Robbins	22Jan83 170(1) 9	70.5
11004. STAR WALK Larry Graham And Graham Central Station	14Jul79 136(2) 4	70.5
11005. A GATHERING OF PROMISES	Bubble Puppy 17May69 176(1) 6	70.5
11006. JOURNEY TO A RAINBOW Chuck Mangione	25Jun83 154(1) 7	70.5
11007. HONI SOIT (O NEE SWA) John Cale	11Apr81 154(2) 5	70.4
11008. WIRED FOR SOUND Cliff Richard	17Oct81 132(2) 4	70.4
11009. ONE LIVE BADGER Badger	11Aug73 167(1) 8	70.4
11010. NEVER SAY NEVER Romeo Void	06Mar82 147(1) 6	70.4
11011. THIS OLD HEART OF MINE Isley Brothers	18Jun66 140(1) 5	70.4
11012. THE BEST OF DARK HORSE	George Harrison 04Nov89 132(2) 6	70.3
11013. BILLY SATELLITE Billy Satellite	01Sep84 139(2) 6	70.3
11014. BAND TOGETHER Rare Earth	03Jun78 156(1) 6	70.3
11015. SONGS TO LEARN & SING	Echo & The Bunnymen 11Jan86 158(1) 9	70.3
11016. TONY CAREY [I WON'T BE HOME TONIGHT] Tony Carey	02Apr83 167(1) 9	70.2
11017. VIVA SANTANA Santana	29Oct88 142(2) 6	70.2
11018. CUT ABOVE THE REST The Sweet	12May79 151(1) 5	70.2
11019. PARTY OF ONE Tim Weisberg	02Aug80 171(2) 7	70.1
11020. ACTING VERY STRANGE Mike Rutherford	09Oct82 145(2) 6	70.1
11021. FOSTER SYLVERS Foster Sylvers	21Jul73 159(1) 7	70.1
11022. PASS IT ON The Staples	25Sep76 155(2) 5	70.1
11023. EVERY TURN OF THE WORLD	Christopher Cross 30Nov85 127(1) 6	70.1
11024. SHADOW MAN Johnny Clegg & Savuka	10Sep88 155(2) 7	70.0
11025. MOVIN' TOWARD HAPPINESS	Mason Proffit 17Apr71 177(1) 8	70.0
11026. NEW YEAR, NEW BAND, NEW COMPANY	John Mayall 15Mar75 140(1) 4	70.0
11027. THE OTHER ONES Other Ones	16May87 139(2) 6	70.0
11028. CRACK THE SKY Crack The Sky	24Jan76 161(1) 6	69.9
11029. DON'T FORGET I STILL LOVE YOU	Bobbi Martin 06Mar65 127(1) 5	69.9
11030. HOW'S TRICKS Jack Bruce Band	07May77 153(1) 5	69.9
11031. YOUR SQUAW IS ON THE WARPATH	Loretta Lynn 05Apr69 168(1) 5	69.9
11032. THE MIRACLES ON STAGE The Miracles	05Oct63 139(1) 5	69.9
11033. ROCK'S GREATEST HITS Various Artists	05Jul69 182(1) 7	69.8
11034. REVERBERI & SCHUMANN, CHOPIN, LISZT	Reverberi 21Feb76 169(2) 7	69.8
11035. I HAD TO SAY IT Millie Jackson	07Feb81 137(1) 4	69.8
11036. ENCORE-LIVE IN CONCERT Argent	11Jan75 151(2) 4	69.8
11037. SPLIT ENDS The Move	03Mar73 172(1) 8	69.8
11038. JOHNNY MATHIS SINGS THE MUSIC OF BACHARACH & KAEMPFERT Johnny Mathis	23Jan71 169(1) 7	69.8
11039. TIGHTROPE Steve Khan	04Feb78 157(1) 5	69.7
11040. CHUBBY CHECKER IN PERSON	Chubby Checker 12Oct63 104(1) 4	69.7
11041. JOHN PHILLIPS (JOHN THE WOLFKING OF L.A.) John Phillips	02May70 181(1) 9	69.6
11042. THE FERRANTE AND TEICHER CONCERT	Ferrante & Teicher 01Jan66 134(2) 5	69.6
11043. COMPETITION COUPE The Astronauts	28Mar64 123(1) 5	69.6
11044. I'M A BLUES MAN Z.Z. Hill	07Jan84 170(2) 9	69.5
11045. I SEE THE LIGHT Five Americans	30Apr66 136(1) 5	69.5
11046. SHIP OF MEMORIES Focus	04Jun77 163(1) 7	69.4
11047. THOUGHTS OF MOVIN' ON Lighthouse	29Jan72 157(1) 7	69.4
11048. THE GREAT FATSBY Leslie West	19Apr75 168(2) 6	69.4
11049. BIG IN VEGAS Buck Owens	07Feb70 141(1) 6	69.4
11050. FORGET HIM Bobby Rydell	07Mar64 98(1) 4	69.3
11051. DISCO GOLD Various Artists	26Jul75 153(2) 5	69.3
11052. NEW WORLDS Mandrill	13Jan79 154(2) 5	69.2
11053. OASIS Roberta Flack	14Jan89 159(1) 8	69.2
11054. SKELETONS IN THE CLOSET: THE BEST OF OINGO BOINGO Oingo Boingo	11Feb89 150(2) 6	69.2
11055. LIVE AT THE LONDON PALLADIUM (CONDENSED) Judy Garland & Liza Minelli	09Jun73 164(1) 8	69.2
11056. THREE PIECE SUITE Ramsey Lewis	20Jun81 152(2) 5	69.2

Rank. Title Act Entry Peak(Pk Wks) TotWks	Scr
11057. NIGHT LIGHTS HARMONY Four Tops 14Jun75 148(1) 5	69.2
11058. HITS 1979-1989 Rosanne Cash 01Apr89 152(1) 7	69.1
11059. ALL AMERICAN ALIEN BOY Ian Hunter 22May76 177(1) 7	69.1
11060. 1776 Original Cast 17May69 174(3) 6	69.0
11061. ROCK THERAPY Stray Cats 27Sep86 122(2) 5	69.0
11062. STORIES Stories 01Jul72 182(2) 9	69.0
11063. LIVE MADISON SQUARE GARDEN CENTER Bill Cosby 12Sep70 165(2) 6	68.9
11064. FUN & GAMES The Connells 06May89 163(1) 10	68.9
11065. LOVE STORY Ronnie Aldrich 22May71 169(1) 6	68.9
11066. MIDSTREAM Debby Boone 12Aug78 147(1) 5	68.7
11067. THE BEST OF MICHAEL JACKSON Michael Jackson 27Sep75 156(2) 5	68.7
11068. FIGHT FOR THE ROCK Savatage 21Jun86 158(2) 7	68.7
11069. IN THE JUNGLE, BABE Watts 103rd Street Rhythm Band 18Oct69 145(2) 4	68.6
11070. CONFIDENCE Narada Michael Walden 05Jun82 135(1) 6	68.6
11071. 500 MILES AWAY FROM HOME Bobby Bare 01Feb64 133(1) 5	68.6
11072. SKY Sky (2) 19Dec70 160(1) 6	68.6
11073. OH, WHAT A MIGHTY TIME New Riders Of The Purple Sage 08Nov75 144(1) 4	68.6
11074. ANOTHER PERFECT DAY Motorhead 23Jul83 153(1) 7	68.5
11075. TIPPY TOEING Harden Trio 25Jun66 146(1) 5	68.5
11076. WEST MEETS EAST Yehudi Menuhin & Ravi Shankar 15Jul67 161(1) 7	68.4
11077. ASSAULT ATTACK Michael Schenker Group 09Apr83 151(1) 7	68.4
11078. CATTLE CALL Eddy Arnold 26Oct63 131(1) 5	68.4
11079. RALF AND FLORIAN Kraftwerk 20Sep75 160(1) 5	68.4
11080. MY ROAD OUR ROAD Lee Oskar 01Aug81 162(2) 6	68.4
11081. FULL FORCE Full Force 15Feb86 160(2) 8	68.4
11082. A TRIBUTE TO THE ALL-TIME GREATS Lawrence Welk 25Apr64 127(1) 5	68.3
11083. THE BOARD OF DIRECTORS Count Basie & The Mills Brothers 06Apr68 145(1) 6	68.3
11084. THE SILENCE (IL SILENZIO) Roy Etzel 18Dec65 140(1) 5	68.3
11085. TOP PRIORITY Rory Gallagher 06Oct79 140(2) 4	68.3
11086. THE BEST OF ROY CLARK Roy Clark 03Apr71 178(1) 8	68.2
11087. IN THE BEGINNING Roy Buchanan 28Dec74 160(1) 6	68.2
11088. SOUL SPIN Four Tops 13Dec69 163(1) 6	68.2
11089. THE JOYS OF LIFE Karen Beth 06Sep69 171(2) 6	68.2
11090. THE FUNNY SIDES OF MOMS MABLEY Moms Mabley 04Jan64 134(1) 5	68.1
11091. WRAP YOUR BODY One Way 10Aug85 156(2) 9	68.1
11092. COMMAND PERFORMANCE! LES & LARRY ELGART PLAY THE GREAT DANCE HITS Les & Larry Elgart 10Oct64 128(1) 5	68.1
11093. M.I.U. ALBUM Beach Boys 21Oct78 151(3) 4	68.1

Rank. Title Act Entry Peak(Pk Wks) TotWks	Scr
11094. THE YARDBIRDS/ FEATURING PERFORMANCES BY JEFF BECK, ERIC CLAPTON, JIMMY PAGE The Yardbirds 03Oct70 155(1) 6	67.9
11095. LA LA PEACE SONG Al Wilson 19Oct74 171(1) 7	67.9
11096. SCENARIO Al Di Meola 29Oct83 128(1) 6	67.9
11097. SAVAGE GRACE Savage Grace 06Jun70 182(1) 8	67.8
11098. HOME GROWN Johnny Rivers 11Sep71 148(1) 4	67.8
11099. AMERICAN BOY & GIRL Garland Jeffreys 22Sep79 151(1) 5	67.8
11100. POWER AND LOVE Manchild 15Oct77 154(1) 6	67.7
11101. WILDERNESS C.W. McCall 08May76 143(2) 4	67.7
11102. HOW COME THE SUN Tom Paxton 14Aug71 120(2) 3	67.7
11103. TRUCKLOAD OF LOVIN' Albert King 20Mar76 166(1) 6	67.6
11104. TENEMENT STEPS The Motors 12Apr80 174(1) 8	67.6
11105. 4 BY FOUR 4 By Four 27Jun87 141(2) 7	67.6
11106. IN THE GARDEN Gypsy 07Aug71 173(1) 8	67.5
11107. IN ONE EAR AND GONE TOMORROW The Buckinghams 21Sep68 161(1) 5	67.5
11108. WITCH QUEEN Witch Queen 28Apr79 158(2) 6	67.5
11109. MARVIN GAYE AND HIS GIRLS Marvin Gaye 14Jun69 183(1) 7	67.5
11110. WHITE ON WHITE Danny Williams 13Jun64 122(1) 5	67.4
11111. DRUMS AND WIRES XTC 26Jan80 176(2) 8	67.4
11112. FOR ONCE IN MY LIFE Tony Bennett 13Jan68 164(1) 7	67.3
11113. A TASTE OF TEQUILA Mariachi Brass Feat. Chet Baker 26Feb66 120(1) 4	67.3
11114. SRC SRC 28Sep68 147(2) 4	67.2
11115. DURELL COLEMAN Durell Coleman 28Sep85 155(2) 7	67.2
11116. THE THINGS I NOTICE NOW Tom Paxton 16Aug69 155(1) 4	67.2
11117. SUPER TAYLOR Johnnie Taylor 08Jun74 182(1) 8	67.1
11118. FLY ME TO THE MOON Earl Grant 04Jan64 139(1) 5	67.1
11119. HIGH ON A RIDGE TOP The Youngbloods 09Dec72 185(1) 10	67.1
11120. VISUAL LIES Lizzy Borden 26Sep87 146(1) 7	67.1
11121. MUDLARK Leo Kottke 19Jun71 168(2) 7	67.0
11122. PURLIE Original Cast 13Jun70 138(2) 5	67.0
11123. FRESH FLAVOR Jane Morgan 26Nov66 134(1) 4	67.0
11124. ACCEPT NO SUBSTITUTES Pleasure 28Aug76 162(1) 5	67.0
11125. ANY MAN'S HUNGER Danny Wilde 26Mar88 176(1) 9	67.0
11126. ROOT HOG OR DIE Mojo Nixon & Skid Roper 06May89 151(1) 7	66.9
11127. MAN TO MAN Hot Chocolate 18Sep76 172(2) 6	66.9
11128. THE DIRT BAND Dirt Band 08Jul78 163(1) 6	66.9
11129. HAPPY LOVE Natalie Cole 26Sep81 132(2) 4	66.8
11130. WARRIOR ON THE EDGE OF TIME Hawkwind 14Jun75 150(1) 5	66.8
11131. FEELING GOOD Roy Ayers 20Mar82 160(1) 7	66.8

Rank. Title Act Entry Peak(Pk Wks) TotWks	Scr
11132. SWEET CITY WOMAN Stampeders 23Oct71 172(1) 6	66.8
11133. TWIST OF SHADOWS Xymox 03Jun89 165(1) 10	66.8
11134. RIDIN' THE STORM OUT REO Speedwagon 12Jan74 171(2) 8	66.7
11135. RENAISSANCE Village People 01Aug81 138(2) 4	66.7
11136. MUSIC FOR THE KNEE PLAYS David Byrne 01Jun85 141(2) 6	66.7
11137. COMPANY B Company B 18Jul87 143(2) 6	66.7
11138. LOOSE Crazy Horse 05Feb72 170(1) 6	66.7
11139. IN THE HEAT Southside Johnny & The Jukes 08Sep84 164(2) 8	66.7
11140. GENESIS Soul Children 29Apr72 159(1) 6	66.7
11141. SAD CAFÉ Sad Café 15Aug81 160(2) 6	66.7
11142. DREAM STREET Janet Jackson 27Oct84 147(2) 6	66.6
11143. TONY BENNETT'S ALL-TIME GREATEST HITS Tony Bennett 21Oct72 175(2) 7	66.6
11144. THE STEVE MARTIN BROTHERS Steve Martin 14Nov81 135(2) 4	66.6
11145. THIS IS AL MARTINO Al Martino 30Mar68 129(1) 4	66.5
11146. 21ST CENTURY MAN Billy Thorpe 08Nov80 151(2) 5	66.5
11147. DISTANT SHORES Robbie Patton 15Aug81 162(1) 6	66.5
11148. PILGRIMAGE Wishbone Ash 11Sep71 174(2) 7	66.5
11149. MUSIC PEOPLE, THE Various Artists 18Mar72 165(2) 6	66.4
11150. THE GREAT WALTZ Original Cast 01Jan66 118(1) 4	66.4
11151. SPECTRAL MORNINGS Steve Hackett 07Jul79 138(2) 4	66.4
11152. A TAB IN THE OCEAN Nektar 18Sep76 141(2) 4	66.4
11153. TURN UP THE MUSIC Mass Production 16May81 166(2) 6	66.3
11154. LAST TANGO IN PARIS Gato Barbieri 05May73 166(1) 7	66.3
11155. CHILDREN (GET TOGETHER) Edwin Hawkins Singers 02Oct71 180(1) 8	66.3
11156. TEEN BEAT '65 Sandy Nelson 06Mar65 135(2) 5	66.2
11157. A SONG OF JOY Miguel Rios 22Aug70 140(1) 4	66.1
11158. STOP START Modern English 05Apr86 154(2) 7	66.1
11159. BOBBY VINTON SINGS THE GOLDEN DECADE OF LOVE Bobby Vinton 28Jun75 154(2) 5	66.1
11160. THE UNITED STATES OF AMERICA United States Of America 04May68 181(1) 9	66.1
11161. HOT RATS Frank Zappa 29Nov69 173(1) 6	66.0
11162. OUR MEMORIES OF ELVIS VOLUME 2 Elvis Presley 25Aug79 157(2) 5	66.0
11163. SINNER...AND SAINT Rory Gallagher 22Feb75 156(2) 5	66.0
11164. STAY ON THESE ROADS a-ha 04Jun88 148(2) 6	66.0
11165. DANCING ON THE EDGE Roy Buchanan 28Jun86 153(2) 8	66.0
11166. FOOTSTEPS IN THE DARK: GREATEST HITS VOLUME 2 Cat Stevens 15Dec84 165(3) 8	66.0
11167. LEVEE BLUES Potliquor 19Feb72 168(1) 7	65.9
11168. IN CONCERT Jane Olivor 29May82 144(2) 6	65.9
11169. READ MY LIPS Fee Waybill 10Nov84 146(2) 6	65.9
11170. IN THE BLUE CANADIAN ROCKIES Mom & Dads 06May72 165(2) 6	65.9

Rank. Title Act / Entry Peak(Pk Wks) TotWks	Scr
11171. **HEROES & ZEROS** Glen Burtnick 24Oct87 147(2) 6	65.9
11172. **VAN-ZANT** Van-Zant 04May85 170(1) 8	65.9
11173. **JUST FAMILY** Dee Dee Bridgewater 06May78 170(1) 7	65.9
11174. **SOLID** Michael Henderson 04Dec76 173(1) 7	65.8
11175. **R.E.O.** REO Speedwagon 19Jun76 159(1) 5	65.8
11176. **MAKE YOUR OWN KIND OF MUSIC** Mama Cass 06Dec69 169(1) 6	65.8
11177. **MY TOWN, MY GUY & ME** Lesley Gore 04Dec65 120(1) 4	65.8
11178. **DARING ADVENTURES** Richard Thompson 25Oct86 142(2) 6	65.8
11179. **MY BOY LOLLIPOP** Millie Small 08Aug64 132(1) 5	65.7
11180. **JERRY KNIGHT** Jerry Knight 24May80 165(1) 7	65.7
11181. **DON'T FIGHT IT** Red Rider 26Apr80 146(1) 5	65.7
11182. **SUMMER LOVERS** Soundtrack 28Aug82 152(1) 7	65.7
11183. **ACADEMY AWARD LOSERS** Steve Lawrence 15Feb64 135(1) 5	65.7
11184. **THE LION IN WINTER** Soundtrack 03May69 182(1) 7	65.7
11185. **JUMPIN' GENE SIMMONS** Jumpin' Gene Simmons 14Nov64 132(1) 5	65.6
11186. **MARTHA & THE VANDELLAS LIVE!** Martha & The Vandellas 07Oct67 140(1) 5	65.6
11187. **RIVER** Terry Reid 07Apr73 172(1) 8	65.6
11188. **YOU DON'T HAVE TO SAY YOU LOVE ME** Jerry Vale 16Mar68 163(1) 7	65.6
11189. **KIKI DEE** Kiki Dee 14May77 159(1) 5	65.6
11190. **WHITE BIRD** David Laflamme 25Dec76 159(1) 6	65.6
11191. **LIZA MINNELLI AT CARNEGIE HALL** Liza Minnelli 14Nov87 156(2) 8	65.5
11192. **TOUCH ME TONIGHT- THE BEST OF SHOOTING STAR** Shooting Star 04Nov89 151(2) 7	65.5
11193. **BARBEQUE KING** Jorma Kaukonen & Vital Parts 14Feb81 163(2) 6	65.5
11194. **FABULOUS** Dick Hyman 04Apr64 132(1) 5	65.4
11195. **THE GLORY OF LOVE** Eddy Arnold 05Jul69 167(1) 5	65.4
11196. **GET ON DOWN WITH BOBBY BLAND** Bobby Bland 13Sep75 154(2) 5	65.4
11197. **REGGAE GOT SOUL** Toots And The Maytals 17Jul76 157(1) 5	65.4
11198. **HOT SOX** Sha Na Na 01Jun74 165(2) 6	65.4
11199. **REAL TO REEL** Climax Blues Band 16Jun79 170(2) 6	65.3
11200. **WOULD YOU LAY WITH ME (IN A FIELD OF STONE)** Tanya Tucker 30Mar74 159(1) 6	65.3
11201. **BIG NIGHT MUSIC** Shriekback 21Feb87 145(2) 6	65.2
11202. **THE FEEL OF NEIL DIAMOND** Neil Diamond 29Oct66 137(1) 4	65.2
11203. **HYAENA** Siouxsie & The Banshees 07Jul84 157(1) 7	65.1
11204. **THE ENCHANTED WORLD OF FERRANTE & TEICHER** Ferrante & Teicher 18Jul64 128(1) 5	65.1
11205. **CLOSE UP THE HONKY TONKS** Flying Burrito Brothers 13Jul74 158(1) 5	65.1
11206. **SUPERTRAMP** Supertramp 04Mar78 158(1) 5	65.0
11207. **IN HARMONY - A SESAME STREET RECORD** Various Artists 10Jan81 156(1) 5	65.0
11208. **STARBOOTY** Ubiquity 08Apr78 146(1) 4	65.0
11209. **THE BEST OF PETER NERO** Peter Nero 20Feb65 123(2) 4	65.0
11210. **LEONARD COHEN: LIVE SONGS** Leonard Cohen 26May73 156(1) 5	64.9
11211. **SURVIVOR** Survivor 29Mar80 169(1) 7	64.9
11212. **THEN CAME YOU** Dionne Warwick 08Mar75 167(1) 6	64.9
11213. **SHOW TIME** Ry Cooder 10Sep77 158(1) 5	64.9
11214. **WHAT'S MY NAME** Steady B 31Oct87 149(2) 7	64.9
11215. **MY MERRY-GO-ROUND** Johnny Nash 14Jul73 169(1) 6	64.8
11216. **EMPTY ARMS** Sonny James 24Apr71 150(1) 5	64.8
11217. **MIDNIGHT CREEPER** Lou Donaldson 26Oct68 182(3) 6	64.8
11218. **MORE GOLDEN GREATS** The Ventures 14Mar70 154(2) 5	64.8
11219. **GRAND FUNK LIVES** Grand Funk Railroad 17Oct81 149(2) 5	64.8
11220. **WE WANT MILES** Miles Davis 29May82 159(2) 7	64.8
11221. **ME AND YOU** The Chi-Lites 10Apr82 162(2) 7	64.7
11222. **SERIOUS SLAMMIN'** Pointer Sisters 19Mar88 152(2) 6	64.7
11223. **KRISTY & JIMMY McNICHOL** Kristy And Jimmy McNichol 19Aug78 116(1) 4	64.7
11224. **PART OF YOU** Eric Gale 21Jul79 154(1) 5	64.6
11225. **DAVE BRUBECK'S GREATEST HITS** Dave Brubeck 30Jul66 134(1) 4	64.5
11226. **SUNFLOWER** Beach Boys 26Sep70 151(1) 4	64.5
11227. **YOU DON'T KNOW ME** Mickey Gilley 22Aug81 170(2) 6	64.5
11228. **LIGHTS IN THE NIGHT** Flash And The Pan 31May80 159(2) 6	64.4
11229. **LAST OF THE RED HOT BURRITOS** Flying Burrito Brothers 03Jun72 171(1) 7	64.4
11230. **POWER & PASSION** Mama's Boys 15Jun85 151(2) 6	64.3
11231. **SECOND WIND** Brian Auger's Oblivion Express 03Jun72 170(2) 7	64.3
11232. **NUTBUSH CITY LIMITS** Ike & Tina Turner 22Dec73 163(1) 6	64.3
11233. **I AM NOT AFRAID** Hugh Masekela 28Sep74 149(1) 4	64.3
11234. **WASHINGTON SQUARE** New Band Of Spike Jones 23Nov63 113(1) 4	64.3
11235. **TESTIFYIN'** Clarence Carter 16Aug69 138(1) 3	64.2
11236. **GOOD TIME CHARLIE** Charlie McCoy 21Jul73 155(1) 6	64.2
11237. **GO TOO** Stomu Yamashta 15Oct77 156(2) 6	64.2
11238. **HIGH ON YOUR LOVE** Debbie Jacobs 09Feb80 178(4) 7	64.2
11239. **DOIN' MICKEY'S MONKEY** The Miracles 04Jan64 113(1) 4	64.2
11240. **BUTT ROCKIN'** Fabulous Thunderbirds 28Mar81 176(1) 7	64.1
11241. **JUST PET** Petula Clark 27Dec69 176(1) 7	64.1
11242. **SOFT AND SOULFUL** Bill Medley 05Apr69 152(1) 4	64.0
11243. **EAST** Cold Chisel 13Jun81 171(2) 6	64.0
11244. **THE LIGHT SIDE: THE DARK SIDE** Dick Gregory 16Aug69 182(1) 8	64.0
11245. **THE GREAT LOST KINKS ALBUM** The Kinks 24Feb73 145(1) 5	63.9
11246. **THE BEST OF WES MONTGOMERY, VOL. 2** Wes Montgomery 07Sep68 187(1) 8	63.9
11247. **MOTOWN WINNERS' CIRCLE/NO. 1 HITS, VOL. 1** Various Artists 22Feb69 159(1) 4	63.9
11248. **TYRONE DAVIS** Tyrone Davis 08Jan83 137(2) 6	63.9
11249. **SPIRIT OF ST. LOUIS** Ellen Foley 04Apr81 152(2) 4	63.8
11250. **RISING** Dr. Hook 06Dec80 175(3) 8	63.8
11251. **PARADISE AND LUNCH** Ry Cooder 08Jun74 167(1) 6	63.8
11252. **HOW TO BEAT THE HIGH COST OF LIVING** Hubert Laws And Earl Klugh 27Sep80 134(2) 4	63.8
11253. **TOGETHER** Oak Ridge Boys 29Mar80 154(1) 6	63.8
11254. **SHOW ME TO THE STAGE** Henry Gross 12Mar77 176(2) 7	63.8
11255. **ATLANTA'S BURNING DOWN** Dickey Betts 29Apr78 157(2) 5	63.7
11256. **ELISA FIORILLO** Elisa Fiorillo 20Feb88 163(2) 8	63.7
11257. **PG&E** Pacific Gas And Electric 28Aug71 182(1) 8	63.7
11258. **STREET BEAT** Tom Scott 15Dec79 162(3) 6	63.7
11259. **THE JAMES BOND THEME** Billy Strange 24Oct64 135(1) 5	63.7
11260. **WHO IS THIS BITCH, ANYWAY?** Marlena Shaw 05Jul75 159(1) 5	63.7
11261. **HEART DON'T LIE** LaToya Jackson 09Jun84 149(2) 6	63.7
11262. **BLUE ÖYSTER CULT** Blue Öyster Cult 20May72 172(1) 8	63.7
11263. **PAIN** Ohio Players 04Mar72 177(1) 7	63.6
11264. **INVOLVED** Edwin Starr 31Jul71 178(1) 7	63.6
11265. **I DON'T CARE** Buck Owens 12Dec64 135(1) 5	63.6
11266. **LOVE OF THE COMMON PEOPLE** Ed Ames 03Jan70 172(1) 6	63.6
11267. **NOVO COMBO** Novo Combo 10Oct81 167(1) 6	63.5
11268. **MONSTER** Fetchin Bones 18Nov89 175(1) 8	63.4
11269. **THE ORIGINAL DISCO DUCK** Rick Dees And His Cast Of Idiots 05Mar77 157(2) 5	63.4
11270. **BIG DREAMERS NEVER SLEEP** Gino Vannelli 23May87 160(2) 7	63.4
11271. **OCTOPUSSY** Soundtrack 16Jul83 137(1) 5	63.3
11272. **OLIVER & COMPANY** Soundtrack 07Jan89 170(1) 7	63.3
11273. **EBONY WOMAN** Billy Paul 22Aug70 183(1) 8	63.3
11274. **BADFINGER** Badfinger 09Mar74 161(1) 5	63.3
11275. **LIVING BLACK!** Charles Earland 15May71 176(1) 7	63.3
11276. **TRUTH AND SOUL** Fishbone 01Oct88 153(1) 9	63.3
11277. **THE SONS** Sons Of Champlin 08Nov69 171(2) 6	63.2
11278. **ALONE AGAIN, NATURALLY** Esther Phillips 30Dec72 177(2) 8	63.2
11279. **SOUL SISTER** Aretha Franklin 06Aug66 132(1) 4	63.2
11280. **SUPERSAX PLAYS BIRD** Supersax 14Jul73 169(1) 7	63.1
11281. **LIVE AT P.J.'S** Kool & The Gang 01Jan72 171(1) 7	63.1
11282. **ELOISE LAWS** Eloise Laws 14Feb81 175(1) 7	63.1
11283. **RIGOR MORTIS SETS IN** John Entwistle 07Jul73 174(2) 7	63.0
11284. **VOLUNTEER JAM VII** Various Artists 25Jul81 149(2) 4	63.0
11285. **YOU LAY SO EASY ON MY MIND** Andy Williams 28Dec74 150(1) 4	63.0
11286. **SLAUGHTER ON 10TH AVENUE** Mick Ronson 06Apr74 156(1) 5	63.0

Rank. Title Act Entry Peak(Pk Wks) TotWks	Scr
11287. LET'S STICK TOGETHER Bryan Ferry 16Oct76 160(1) 5	63.0
11288. FEMME FATALE Femme Fatale 28Jan89 141(2) 5	63.0
11289. THE FLYING MACHINE Flying Machine 27Dec69 179(2) 7	63.0
11290. ELYSIAN ENCOUNTER Baker Gurvitz Army 15Nov75 165(2) 5	62.9
11291. THE YEARS OF DECAY Overkill 18Nov89 155(1) 8	62.9
11292. GEORGE M! Original Cast 25May68 161(1) 6	62.9
11293. THE PRESIDENTIAL YEARS (1960-1963) John Fitzgerald Kennedy 25Jan64 119(2) 4	62.9
11294. ROGER McGUINN & BAND Roger McGuinn 05Jul75 165(2) 5	62.9
11295. SWING YOUR DADDY Jim Gilstrap 30Aug75 179(1) 7	62.9
11296. TELL HER YOU LOVE HER Frank Sinatra 28Sep63 129(1) 4	62.9
11297. 8.5 Earth Quake 04Sep76 151(1) 4	62.8
11298. THE FUGS FIRST ALBUM The Fugs 29Oct66 142(2) 4	62.8
11299. BET CHA SAY THAT TO ALL THE GIRLS Sister Sledge 04Jun83 169(1) 8	62.8
11300. LONESOME CITIES Rod McKuen 16Nov68 175(1) 5	62.7
11301. STANDING ON THE VERGE OF GETTING IT ON Funkadelic 07Sep74 163(2) 5	62.7
11302. CONNECTIONS AND DISCONNECTIONS Funkadelic(2) 11Apr81 151(2) 4	62.7
11303. WILD GIFT X 06Jun81 165(1) 5	62.7
11304. MATHEMATICS Melissa Manchester 18May85 144(2) 6	62.7
11305. THE FIVE STAIRSTEPS Five Stairsteps 25Mar67 139(1) 4	62.7
11306. DANNY DAVIS & WILLIE NELSON WITH THE NASHVILLE BRASS Danny Davis And Willie Nelson With The Nashville Brass 15Mar80 150(1) 5	62.6
11307. MUSIC FROM ACROSS THE WAY James Last 19Feb72 160(1) 5	62.6
11308. SMOKIN' Smokey Robinson 20Jan79 165(1) 6	62.6
11309. THE SOURCE Grandmaster Flash 17May86 145(2) 6	62.5
11310. ONE HELL OF A WOMAN Vikki Carr 28Sep74 155(1) 5	62.5
11311. LIVE AT THE COCOANUT GROVE Sergio Franchi 27Mar65 114(1) 4	62.5
11312. DESIRE Tom Scott 25Sep82 164(1) 7	62.4
11313. FUTURE WORLD Pretty Maids 20Jun87 165(2) 8	62.4
11314. NEMESIS Axe 10Sep83 156(1) 6	62.4
11315. SPELLBINDER Gabor Szabo 28Jan67 140(1) 4	62.3
11316. APPLAUSE Original Cast 23May70 168(1) 7	62.2
11317. SHARKY'S MACHINE Soundtrack 23Jan82 171(1) 8	62.2
11318. PRIMAL ROOTS Sergio Mendes & Brasil '77 15Jul72 164(2) 5	62.2
11319. JAMMED TOGETHER Albert King, Steve Cropper, Pop Staples 12Jul69 171(2) 5	62.2
11320. THE ART OF EXCELLENCE Tony Bennett 21Jun86 160(2) 8	62.2
11321. LIVE WITHOUT A NET Angel 23Feb80 149(1) 4	62.2
11322. DRIVE ON Mott 01Nov75 160(1) 5	62.2
11323. DANCING ON THE COUCH Go West 22Aug87 172(1) 9	62.2
11324. BLAST! (THE LATEST AND THE GREATEST) Brothers Johnson 22Jan83 138(2) 5	62.2
11325. WOMAN OF THE WORLD / TO MAKE A MAN Loretta Lynn 09Aug69 148(1) 4	62.1
11326. THE THINGS I LOVE Jim Nabors 16Sep67 147(1) 6	62.0
11327. THE LOVE MACHINE Soundtrack 28Aug71 172(1) 6	62.0
11328. CRYSTAL GAYLE'S GREATEST HITS Crystal Gayle 10Sep83 169(1) 8	62.0
11329. MY CHERIE AMOUR John Davidson 22Nov69 165(1) 5	62.0
11330. CLIMAX Climax 24Jun72 177(1) 7	61.9
11331. MOST OF THE GIRLS LIKE TO DANCE BUT ONLY SOME OF THE BOYS LIKE TO Don Dixon 07Mar87 162(1) 8	61.9
11332. CONCERT IN THE PARK Boston Pops Orchestra 19Oct63 116(2) 4	61.9
11333. LIVE AT THE GREEK THEATRE Vikki Carr 24Nov73 172(1) 7	61.9
11334. THE RINGS The Rings 21Feb81 164(2) 6	61.8
11335. DOWN THE LINE John Mayall 10Feb73 158(1) 7	61.8
11336. DISCOVERY! Vikki Carr 18Jul64 114(1) 4	61.8
11337. LOOK WHAT YOU'RE DOING TO THE MAN Melba Moore 20Feb71 157(2) 5	61.8
11338. CHILDREN OF LIGHT Biff Rose 12Jul69 181(1) 7	61.8
11339. ROCK 'N ROLL AGAIN Commander Cody Band 03Sep77 163(1) 5	61.8
11340. WHEN WILL I SEE YOU AGAIN The O'Jays 13Aug83 142(1) 5	61.7
11341. THE FINAL SWING Trapeze 02Nov74 172(2) 6	61.6
11342. QUEST FOR FIRE Soundtrack 17Apr82 154(2) 6	61.6
11343. UPON THE WINGS OF MUSIC Jean-Luc Ponty 26Jul75 158(2) 5	61.6
11344. 'OT 'N' SWEATY Cactus 28Oct72 162(2) 5	61.6
11345. MEMPHIS TWO-STEP Herbie Mann 17Apr71 137(1) 3	61.5
11346. PROUD WORDS ON A DUSTY SHELF Ken Hensley 07Apr73 173(1) 7	61.5
11347. YOU DON'T HAVE TO BE A BABY TO CRY The Caravelles 15Feb64 127(1) 4	61.5
11348. WILSON PICKETT'S GREATEST HITS Wilson Pickett 10Feb73 178(1) 8	61.5
11349. TONIGHT YOU'RE MINE Eric Carmen 28Jun80 160(1) 5	61.5
11350. LITE ME UP Herbie Hancock 29May82 151(2) 6	61.5
11351. LEAVE SCARS Dark Angel 01Apr89 159(1) 6	61.5
11352. ISLAND LIFE Grace Jones 18Jan86 161(2) 7	61.5
11353. ROCK 'N' ROLL Motorhead 24Oct87 150(2) 6	61.4
11354. GREATEST HINTS Michael Stanley Band 04Aug79 148(1) 5	61.4
11355. MO' ROOTS Taj Mahal 12Oct74 165(1) 6	61.4
11356. DISCO SPECTACULAR INSPIRED BY THE FILM "HAIR" Various Artists 28Apr79 159(1) 5	61.3
11357. FROM NASHVILLE WITH LOVE Chet Atkins 17Dec66 140(1) 4	61.3
11358. CARL ORFF: CARMINA BURANA Cleveland Orchestra 29Mar75 152(1) 4	61.3
11359. VAUDEVILLE! Eric Rogers & His Orchestra 12Nov66 114(1) 3	61.2
11360. SONNY & CHER LIVE IN LAS VEGAS, VOL. 2 Sonny & Cher 22Dec73 175(1) 7	61.2
11361. DEKADANCE INXS 01Oct83 148(2) 6	61.2
11362. FRIENDLY PERSUASION Ray Conniff & His Orchestra & Chorus 03Apr65 141(1) 5	61.1
11363. TRUTHDARE DOUBLEDARE Bronski Beat 02Aug86 147(2) 6	61.1
11364. THE SNOW GOOSE Camel 19Jul75 162(2) 5	61.1
11365. THE STORY'S BEEN TOLD Third World 21Jul79 157(1) 5	61.0
11366. CHET PICKS ON THE POPS Chet Atkins/Boston Pops/Arthur Fiedler 11Oct69 160(1) 4	61.0
11367. SWEET MEMORIES Willie Nelson 03Mar79 154(2) 5	60.9
11368. SONGS MY FATHER LEFT ME Hank Williams Jr. 21Jun69 164(1) 4	60.9
11369. RUN BABY RUN The Newbeats 22Jan66 131(1) 4	60.8
11370. 16 ORIGINAL BIG HITS, VOLUME 8 Various Artists 30Dec67 163(2) 7	60.8
11371. METROPOLITAN OPERA GALA HONORING SIR RUDOLF BING Various Artists 15Jul72 176(2) 7	60.8
11372. PAST MASTERS - VOLUME 1 The Beatles 02Apr88 149(2) 6	60.8
11373. A BEAUTIFUL THING Cleo Laine 28Dec74 168(2) 5	60.7
11374. INDISCREET Sparks 29Nov75 169(1) 6	60.7
11375. TONY ORLANDO & DAWN II Tony Orlando & Dawn 11Jan75 165(2) 5	60.7
11376. LEO KOTTKE 1971-76 DID YOU HEAR ME? Leo Kottke 27Nov76 153(2) 4	60.7
11377. GEORGE McCRAE George McCrae 05Jul75 152(1) 5	60.6
11378. LI'L SUZY Ozone 04Sep82 152(2) 6	60.6
11379. LIGHTHOUSE LIVE! Lighthouse 29Jul72 178(1) 7	60.6
11380. ILLYA DARLING Original Cast 17Jun67 177(1) 8	60.6
11381. LEGENDARY HEARTS Lou Reed 09Apr83 159(1) 7	60.6
11382. DO YOU KNOW WHAT IT'S LIKE TO BE LONESOME? Jerry Wallace 03Mar73 179(1) 8	60.6
11383. DRY DREAMS Jim Carroll Band 22May82 156(2) 7	60.6
11384. RIO Lee Ritenour 17Apr82 163(3) 6	60.5
11385. THE MUPPET SHOW TV Soundtrack 21Jan78 153(2) 5	60.5
11386. THE WALK The Cure 13Aug83 177(1) 9	60.5
11387. S.O.S. III S.O.S. Band 25Dec82 172(1) 8	60.5
11388. DAVE MASON AT HIS BEST Dave Mason 22Mar75 133(2) 3	60.5
11389. THE BRIDE STRIPPED BARE Bryan Ferry 04Nov78 159(2) 5	60.5
11390. THE BOSS Jimmy Smith 26Jul69 144(2) 3	60.4
11391. WATTSTAX 2: THE LIVING WORD Soundtrack 15Sep73 157(2) 5	60.4
11392. THE ORIGINAL HITS OF RIGHT NOW Various Artists 13Dec69 166(1) 5	60.4
11393. 12 STRING GUITAR! The Folkswingers 28Sep63 132(1) 4	60.4
11394. WHEN ALL THE PIECES FIT Peter Frampton 14Oct89 152(2) 6	60.4
11395. THE ORIGINAL HOOTENANNY Various Artists 31Aug63 128(1) 4	60.3
11396. HOT CITY Gene Page 01Feb75 156(2) 4	60.3
11397. IT'S TIME Mighty Clouds Of Joy 26Oct74 165(1) 5	60.3
11398. HEAT TREATMENT Graham Parker 29Jan77 169(1) 7	60.2
11399. DANCIN' UP A STORM The Raes 24Mar79 161(1) 5	60.2
11400. ANIMAL BOY The Ramones 21Jun86 143(2) 6	60.2
11401. I LOVE THE BLUES, SHE HEARD MY CRY George Duke 24Jan76 169(2) 6	60.2
11402. 3 Pousette-Dart Band 10Jun78 161(1) 5	60.2

Rank. Title Act Entry Peak(Pk Wks) TotWks	Scr
11403. THE HOUSE OF LOVE House Of Love 17Sep88 156(1) 7	60.2
11404. TOGETHER AGAIN! Willis Jackson & Jack McDuff 23Jul66 137(1) 4	60.1
11405. TAKE A LOOK Aretha Franklin 21Oct67 173(2) 8	60.1
11406. MIDNIGHT CAFE Smokie 22Jan77 173(2) 6	60.1
11407. ARABESQUE Henry Mancini And His Orchestra 10Sep66 142(2) 4	60.1
11408. THE BEST OF SONNY JAMES Sonny James 24Dec66 141(2) 4	60.1
11409. FASTER & LLOUDER Foster & Lloyd 13May89 142(1) 6	60.0
11410. GUITAR SPEAK Various Artists 17Dec88 171(3) 8	60.0
11411. STARTING ALL OVER AGAIN Mel And Tim 06Jan73 175(1) 7	59.9
11412. ENCORE: WOODY HERMAN - 1963 Woody Herman 17Aug63 136(2) 4	59.9
11413. CRY YOUNG Ahmad Jamal 30Dec67 168(1) 8	59.8
11414. JUST BEING MYSELF Dionne Warwicke 03Feb73 178(1) 8	59.8
11415. CONCERT IN BLUES Willie Hutch 03Apr76 163(2) 6	59.7
11416. PIECES OF A DREAM Pieces Of A Dream 31Oct81 170(2) 6	59.7
11417. BUD & TRAVIS...IN CONCERT Bud & Travis 09Nov63 126(1) 4	59.6
11418. JOHNNY CASH: AMERICA (A 200-YEAR SALUTE IN STORY AND SONG) Johnny Cash 16Sep72 176(2) 7	59.6
11419. FITS LIKE A GLOVE Howie Mandel 21Jun86 148(2) 6	59.6
11420. GOODBYE, MR. CHIPS Soundtrack 06Dec69 164(1) 5	59.6
11421. THE JEWISH AMERICAN PRINCESS Various Artists 06Nov71 183(2) 7	59.6
11422. POSITIVE Peabo Bryson 13Feb88 157(1) 6	59.6
11423. JONI MITCHELL Joni Mitchell 18May68 189(1) 9	59.6
11424. GO LITTLE HONDA The Hondells 28Nov64 119(2) 4	59.5
11425. MORE CHAD & JEREMY Chad & Jeremy 20Aug66 144(1) 4	59.5
11426. LIVE 'N' KICKIN' West, Bruce & Laing 11May74 165(2) 6	59.5
11427. KATE BUSH Kate Bush 09Jul83 148(1) 6	59.5
11428. THE BEST OF THE REST Lynyrd Skynyrd 20Nov82 171(5) 7	59.5
11429. WE'RE ALL IN THIS TOGETHER Chocolate Milk 24Jun78 171(3) 5	59.5
11430. HERE COMES...FATS DOMINO Fats Domino 05Oct63 130(1) 4	59.5
11431. HOW TO SUCCEED IN BUSINESS WITHOUT REALLY TRYING Soundtrack 22Apr67 146(1) 4	59.5
11432. MAN OVERBOARD Bob Welch 11Oct80 162(2) 5	59.5
11433. LISTEN TO YOUR HEART Paul Anka 25Nov78 179(1) 7	59.5
11434. THE SILENCERS Dean Martin 02Jul66 108(1) 3	59.4
11435. TRASH IT UP Southside Johnny & The Jukes 01Oct83 154(2) 6	59.3
11436. THE JAM The Jam 19Dec81 176(3) 7	59.3
11437. THIS IS YOUR TIME Change 02Apr83 161(1) 7	59.3
11438. FOR ADULTS ONLY Bill Cosby 11Dec71 181(1) 7	59.3
11439. SEA HAGS Sea Hags 24Jun89 163(2) 7	59.3
11440. BALLIN' JACK Ballin' Jack 02Jan71 180(1) 8	59.3

Rank. Title Act Entry Peak(Pk Wks) TotWks	Scr
11441. THE IMPOSSIBLE DREAM Johnny Mathis 16Aug69 163(1) 4	59.2
11442. THE BEST OF THE LOVIN' SPOONFUL, VOLUME 2 Lovin' Spoonful 30Mar68 156(1) 5	59.2
11443. BASIC Glen Campbell 16Dec78 164(3) 5	59.2
11444. HOLD ON, I'M COMIN' Herbie Mann 16Jun73 163(1) 6	59.2
11445. MUMMER XTC 25Feb84 145(2) 5	59.2
11446. HELICON 4 Seasons 14May77 168(1) 5	59.1
11447. ANNIE'S SONG AND OTHER GALWAY FAVORITES James Galway 03Mar79 153(1) 5	59.1
11448. LOVINGLY YOURS Millie Jackson 19Feb77 175(1) 6	59.1
11449. OVER HERE! (ORIGINAL CAST) Andrews Sisters 13Jul74 137(1) 3	59.1
11450. DEEPEST PURPLE: THE VERY BEST OF DEEP PURPLE Deep Purple 01Nov80 148(1) 4	59.0
11451. DIFFERENT MOODS OF ME Lonnie Jordan 25Feb78 158(2) 5	59.0
11452. PORTRAIT OF MY WOMAN Eddy Arnold 13Mar71 141(2) 4	59.0
11453. I WALK THE LINE Johnny Cash 12Dec70 176(2) 6	58.9
11454. MINE EYES HAVE SEEN THE GLORY Anita Bryant 21Jan67 146(1) 4	58.9
11455. JOSE JIMENEZ IN JOLLYWOOD Jose Jimenez 14Dec63 128(1) 4	58.9
11456. 1234 Ronnie Wood 19Sep81 164(2) 5	58.9
11457. ABSOLUTELY Madness 22Nov80 146(2) 4	58.9
11458. LOVE MEANS YOU NEVER HAVE TO SAY YOU'RE SORRY Sounds Of Sunshine 14Aug71 187(1) 8	58.8
11459. TAKE IT TO THE MAX AKA The Max Demian Band 03Mar79 159(2) 5	58.8
11460. THE ETERNAL IDOL Black Sabbath 26Dec87 168(1) 6	58.8
11461. BOTH SIDES OF LOVE Paul Anka 09May81 171(2) 6	58.8
11462. HARMONY Anne Murray 20Jun87 149(2) 6	58.8
11463. BIG TIME Tom Waits 08Oct88 152(2) 6	58.8
11464. RIDE ON Alvin Lee 26May79 158(1) 5	58.8
11465. PAUL HUMPHREY & THE COOL AID CHEMISTS Paul Humphrey & The Cool Aid Chemists 12Jun71 170(1) 6	58.8
11466. DYNAMITE The Supremes & Four Tops 08Jan72 160(1) 6	58.6
11467. BACK TALK Rockets 08Aug81 165(1) 5	58.6
11468. THE EVERLY BROTHERS' ORIGINAL GREATEST HITS Everly Brothers 18Jul70 180(1) 8	58.6
11469. IF NOT FOR YOU Olivia Newton-John 27Nov71 158(1) 4	58.6
11470. CHEQUERED PAST Chequered Past 15Sep84 151(2) 6	58.5
11471. IN BLACK AND WHITE Barbara Mandrell 29May82 153(2) 6	58.5
11472. BY POPULAR DEMAND Ferrante & Teicher 12Jun65 120(1) 4	58.4
11473. AGHARTA Miles Davis 13Mar76 168(2) 5	58.4
11474. THE BEST OF MARK-ALMOND Mark-Almond 26May73 177(2) 7	58.4
11475. BRIGHT EYES Melissa Manchester 04May74 159(1) 5	58.4
11476. KICKIN' Mighty Clouds Of Joy 24Jan76 168(1) 6	58.3
11477. FACADES Sad Café 15Sep79 146(1) 5	58.3

Rank. Title Act Entry Peak(Pk Wks) TotWks	Scr
11478. BOOGIE WOOGIE BUGLE GIRLS Andrews Sisters 13Oct73 167(1) 7	58.2
11479. ALL THE RIGHT MOVES Soundtrack 03Dec83 165(1) 7	58.2
11480. THE METHOD TO OUR MADNESS Lords Of The New Church 27Apr85 158(1) 7	58.2
11481. VALLEY HI Ian Matthews 22Sep73 181(2) 7	58.1
11482. PLAYS THE ACADEMY AWARD WINNER BORN FREE AND OTHER GREAT MOVIE THEMES Percy Faith 27May67 152(2) 5	58.1
11483. WILD HORSES/ROCK STEADY Johnny Hammond 20May72 174(1) 6	58.0
11484. STREET CORNER HEROES Robbie Dupree 13Jun81 169(1) 5	58.0
11485. SOLITAIRE Neil Sedaka 18Sep76 159(1) 4	58.0
11486. THIS IS DAMITA JO Damita Jo 27Mar65 121(1) 4	58.0
11487. THEY'RE PLAYING OUR SONG Original Cast 24Mar79 167(1) 6	58.0
11488. ON LOVE David T. Walker 04Sep76 166(1) 5	58.0
11489. STONE ALONE Bill Wyman 27Mar76 166(1) 5	57.9
11490. ATLANTIS McCoy Tyner 14Jun75 161(1) 5	57.9
11491. ANDRE PREVIN IN HOLLYWOOD Andre Previn 30Nov63 130(2) 4	57.9
11492. THE BEST OF CROSBY/NASH David Crosby/Graham Nash 28Oct78 150(1) 4	57.9
11493. FOLKS OF THE 80'S (PART III) Men Without Hats 06Oct84 127(2) 4	57.9
11494. HEAVY SOUNDS Various Artists 28Feb70 128(1) 3	57.8
11495. QUICKSILVER Soundtrack 01Mar86 140(2) 5	57.7
11496. AFTER THE ROSES Kenny Rankin 28Jun80 171(1) 6	57.7
11497. THE VOICE OF AFRICA Miriam Makeba 30May64 122(1) 4	57.7
11498. TELL IT LIKE IT IS George Benson 23Aug69 145(2) 3	57.7
11499. STATE OF THE HEART Mary Chapin Carpenter 09Dec89 183(1) 10	57.7
11500. BIRDY Peter Gabriel 20Apr85 162(1) 7	57.6
11501. THEM CHANGES Ramsey Lewis 24Oct70 177(1) 7	57.5
11502. FLYING AGAIN Flying Burrito Brothers 25Oct75 138(1) 3	57.5
11503. SPACE RITUAL/ALIVE IN LIVERPOOL AND LONDON Hawkwind 24Nov73 179(1) 8	57.5
11504. USED TO BE Charlene 27Nov82 162(1) 7	57.5
11505. NEW BOOTS & PANTIES!!! Ian Dury 06May78 168(2) 5	57.5
11506. PINAFORE DAYS Stackridge 28Dec74 191(1) 9	57.5
11507. STORE AT THE SUN Jon Butcher Axis 31Mar84 160(1) 6	57.5
11508. THE ART OF DEFENSE Nona Hendryx 05May84 167(1) 7	57.4
11509. YOU'RE A BIG BOY NOW Lovin' Spoonful 15Apr67 160(1) 5	57.4
11510. REMATCH Sammy Hagar 08Jan83 171(2) 9	57.4
11511. MIRACLES BY ENGELBERT HUMPERDINCK Engelbert Humperdinck 16Jul77 167(1) 5	57.4
11512. VENICE BLUE Bobby Darin 10Jul65 132(2) 4	57.4
11513. ATLANTA RHYTHM SECTION Atlanta Rhythm Section 09Apr77 154(1) 4	57.4
11514. BRAZIL-ONCE AGAIN Herbie Mann 27May78 165(1) 5	57.3
11515. HERE'S WHAT'S HAPPENING! Floyd Cramer 06May67 166(1) 6	57.3

Rank. Title Act Entry Peak(Pk Wks) TotWks	Scr
11516. ROCK & ROLL IS HERE TO STAY! Sha Na Na 13Dec69 183(1) 7	57.3
11517. HANG 'EM HIGH Hugo Montenegro, His Orchestra And Chorus 21Sep68 166(2) 5	57.3
11518. SUPERTRIOS McCoy Tyner 09Jul77 167(2) 5	57.3
11519. FOR YOU Prince 28Oct78 163(1) 5	57.3
11520. JUST FOR THE RECORD Barbara Mandrell 13Oct79 166(2) 5	57.3
11521. THE DYNAMIC CLARENCE CARTER Clarence Carter 05Apr69 169(2) 4	57.3
11522. EMPIRE OF THE SUN Soundtrack 13Feb88 150(2) 5	57.2
11523. TRINI LOPEZ - NOW! Trini Lopez 02Sep67 162(1) 7	57.1
11524. I'M YOURS Linda Clifford 04Oct80 160(1) 6	57.1
11525. THE SCATTERING Cutting Crew 03Jun89 150(2) 6	57.1
11526. CASTLES Joy Of Cooking 10Jun72 174(2) 6	57.0
11527. THE HAPPENINGS GOLDEN HITS! The Happenings 10Aug68 156(2) 4	56.9
11528. OFF THE RECORD The Sweet 14May77 151(1) 4	56.9
11529. GOOD AND DUSTY The Youngbloods 04Dec71 160(1) 5	56.9
11530. STANDING ALONE White Wolf 16Feb85 162(2) 7	56.8
11531. SWEET COUNTRY Charley Pride 28Jul73 166(1) 6	56.8
11532. NOT FAKIN' IT Michael Monroe 07Oct89 161(1) 8	56.8
11533. FLIP Nils Lofgren 22Jun85 150(2) 5	56.8
11534. SWORDFISHTROMBONES Tom Waits 29Oct83 167(1) 7	56.8
11535. CARRY IT ON Joan Baez 01Jan72 164(2) 5	56.8
11536. AIN'T MISBEHAVIN' Original Cast 23Sep78 161(1) 5	56.7
11537. HOUR OF THE WOLF Steppenwolf 20Sep75 155(1) 4	56.7
11538. MAGNETIC SOUTH Michael Nesmith & The First National Band 17Oct70 143(1) 3	56.7
11539. GROWING UP IN PUBLIC Lou Reed 10May80 158(2) 5	56.6
11540. DIFFERENT KINDA DIFFERENT Johnny Mathis 09Aug80 164(1) 5	56.6
11541. MELBA Melba Moore 25Dec76 177(1) 7	56.6
11542. ARTHUR FIEDLER "SUPERSTAR" Boston Pops Orchestra Arthur Fiedler 04Dec71 174(1) 5	56.6
11543. GIGOLO Fatback 09Jan82 148(1) 4	56.6
11544. ECHO PARK Keith Barbour 01Nov69 163(2) 4	56.6
11545. GLITTER Gary Glitter 28Oct72 186(2) 8	56.5
11546. RIGHT OR WRONG George Strait 03Mar84 163(1) 7	56.5
11547. TALES FROM THE OZONE Commander Cody & His Lost Planet Airmen 11Oct75 168(1) 6	56.5
11548. PLAIN FROM THE HEART Delbert McClinton 05Dec81 181(1) 9	56.5
11549. ALIVE 'N KICKIN' Alive 'N Kickin'+D1393 17Oct70 129(1) 3	56.5
11550. THROUGH THE EYES OF LOVE Ray Charles 25Nov72 186(1) 8	56.4
11551. SOLD Boy George 01Aug87 145(2) 5	56.4
11552. GRAVITY James Brown 18Oct86 156(2) 6	56.4
11553. THE SOUND OF MUSIC The dB's 28Nov87 171(2) 8	56.4
11554. WE MUST BE DOING SOMETHING RIGHT! Joe Cuba Sextet 17Sep66 119(1) 3	56.4
11555. SARAH DASH Sarah Dash 20Jan79 182(1) 7	56.4
11556. FEARLESS Family 05Feb72 177(1) 7	56.3
11557. CRABBY APPLETON Crabby Appleton 27Jun70 175(2) 6	56.3
11558. SYREETA Syreeta 12Aug72 185(2) 8	56.3
11559. SINFUL Angel 03Mar79 159(1) 5	56.3
11560. SMOTHERS COMEDY BROTHERS HOUR Smothers Brothers 16Nov68 164(2) 4	56.2
11561. DAZZLE SHIPS Orchestral Manoeuvres In The Dark 23Apr83 162(1) 6	56.2
11562. IT'S OVER Jimmie Rodgers 30Jul66 145(1) 4	56.2
11563. VINTAGE-CANNED HEAT Canned Heat 17Jan70 173(2) 5	56.2
11564. THE MAN & HIS MUSIC Sam Cooke 05Apr86 175(1) 8	56.1
11565. MY HEART SINGS Al Martino 28Nov70 172(2) 6	56.1
11566. THE BOBBY BLOOM ALBUM Bobby Bloom 28Nov70 126(1) 3	56.1
11567. STEALIN' HOME Babe Ruth 25Oct75 169(2) 6	56.0
11568. I'M ON THE OUTSIDE (LOOKING IN) Little Anthony And The Imperials 16Jan65 135(1) 4	56.0
11569. ON THE ROAD AGAIN D.J. Rogers 18Sep76 175(2) 5	56.0
11570. MOMENTS GREATEST HITS The Moments 27Mar71 184(2) 7	56.0
11571. JUST LIKE DREAMIN' Twennynine Featuring Lenny White 05Dec81 162(3) 5	55.9
11572. LOVE WILL FIND A WAY Pharoah Sanders 20May78 163(1) 5	55.9
11573. SPIRIT OF A WOMAN American Flyer 02Jul77 171(1) 5	55.9
11574. LAST OF THE WILD ONES Johnny Van Zant Band 18Sep82 159(1) 6	55.8
11575. HEAVENLY BODY The Chi-Lites 29Nov80 179(3) 6	55.8
11576. TOUCH 'EM WITH LOVE Bobbie Gentry 09Aug69 164(1) 4	55.7
11577. EL JUICIO (THE JUDGEMENT) Keith Jarrett 02Aug75 160(1) 5	55.7
11578. DANCE & EXERCISE WITH THE HITS Linda Fratianne 20Feb82 174(1) 7	55.7
11579. IT'S YOUR WORLD Gil Scott-Heron & Brian Jackson 13Nov76 168(2) 5	55.6
11580. TOUR DE FORCE - "LIVE" Al Di Meola 25Dec82 165(1) 7	55.6
11581. STALLION Stallion 26Mar77 191(1) 9	55.6
11582. BEFORE AND AFTER SCIENCE Brian Eno 27May78 171(2) 5	55.6
11583. SOMEWHERE The Tymes 07Mar64 122(1) 4	55.6
11584. THE FIRST EDITION 69 First Edition 22Mar69 164(2) 4	55.6
11585. GENTLE ON MY MIND Patti Page 27Jul68 168(1) 6	55.5
11586. MYSTIC DRAGONS Blue Magic 25Sep76 170(1) 5	55.5
11587. HEADING FOR A STORM Vandenberg 28Jan84 169(2) 7	55.4
11588. THUNDER AND LIGHTNING Thin Lizzy 28May83 159(2) 5	55.4
11589. FRANK ZAPPA MEETS THE MOTHERS OF PREVENTION Frank Zappa 18Jan86 153(2) 6	55.4
11590. SUNDAY AND ME Jay & The Americans 19Mar66 141(1) 4	55.4
11591. BILLY JACK(2) Soundtrack 05Jan74 167(1) 5	55.3
11592. IT'S TOO LATE Ferrante & Teicher 09Oct71 172(1) 5	55.2
11593. END OF THE BEGINNING Richie Havens 02Oct76 157(1) 4	55.2
11594. ELI AND THE THIRTEENTH CONFESSION Laura Nyro 10Aug68 181(1) 7	55.2
11595. MY OWN HOUSE David Bromberg 24Feb79 152(2) 4	55.2
11596. MUSIC FROM SONGWRITER Willie Nelson & Kris Kristofferson 10Nov84 152(2) 5	55.2
11597. ELECTRIC HONEY Partland Brothers 27Jun87 146(2) 5	55.2
11598. CRISTO REDENTOR Harvey Mandel 20Sep69 169(2) 4	55.2
11599. GLASS HOUSE ROCK Greg Kihn Band 26Apr80 167(1) 5	55.2
11600. OINGO BOINGO Oingo Boingo 25Oct80 163(2) 5	55.1
11601. LUMPY GRAVY Abnuceals Emuukha Electric Symphony Orchestra And Chorus 08Jun68 159(1) 5	55.1
11602. BABY, WON'T YOU CHANGE YOUR MIND Black Ivory 20Jan73 188(2) 9	55.1
11603. SCENES IN THE CITY Branford Marsalis 19May84 164(2) 7	55.1
11604. BURNING Shooting Star 30Jul83 162(1) 6	55.0
11605. CURRENT Heatwave 10Jul82 156(2) 6	55.0
11606. COOL KIDS Kix 28May83 177(1) 8	55.0
11607. THE COMPLETE SEA San Sebastian Strings 17Jan70 162(1) 5	55.0
11608. NIGHT FLIGHT Justin Hayward 09Aug80 166(2) 5	55.0
11609. A LEGENDARY PERFORMER Henry Mancini And His Orchestra And Chorus 18Sep76 161(2) 4	54.9
11610. HIGHLY DISTINCT Friends Of Distinction 25Oct69 173(1) 6	54.9
11611. THE WONDERFUL WORLD OF JULIE LONDON Julie London 23Nov63 136(1) 4	54.9
11612. THE PROUD ONE The Osmonds 30Aug75 160(1) 5	54.8
11613. SUNDAY IN NEW YORK Peter Nero 29Feb64 133(1) 4	54.8
11614. MY GIFT TO YOU Alexander O'Neal 17Dec88 149(1) 5	54.8
11615. PRODUCT Brand X 03Nov79 165(2) 6	54.8
11616. DETROIT Detroit 29Jan72 176(1) 6	54.7
11617. LIKE A SEED Kenny Rankin 09Sep72 184(1) 8	54.6
11618. DUNE Toto 22Dec84 168(2) 8	54.6
11619. ONLY A LAD Oingo Boingo 15Aug81 172(1) 5	54.6
11620. BREAKWATER Breakwater 21Apr79 173(3) 5	54.5
11621. 1975: THE DUETS Dave Brubeck And Paul Desmond 10Jan76 167(1) 5	54.5
11622. COME A LITTLE BIT CLOSER Jay & The Americans 12Dec64 131(1) 4	54.5
11623. MASTER FUNK Watsonian Institute 15Apr78 154(1) 4	54.5
11624. GODDESS IN PROGRESS Julie Brown 02Feb85 168(1) 7	54.4
11625. THE MONKEY TIME Major Lance 05Oct63 113(1) 3	54.3
11626. PRIDE IN WHAT I AM Merle Haggard 15Mar69 189(1) 7	54.3
11627. COMMAND PERFORMANCES Enoch Light & The Light Brigade 13Jun64 129(1) 4	54.3
11628. ALL MY LIFE Arthur Prysock 29Jan77 153(1) 4	54.3
11629. WHY LADY WHY Gary Morris 15Oct83 174(1) 8	54.3

Rank. Title Act Entry Peak(Pk Wks) TotWks	Scr
11630. THE SOUL OF A CITY BOY Jesse Colin Young 09Feb74 172(1) 6	54.2
11631. YOUR TENDER LOVING CARE Buck Owens 30Sep67 177(1) 7	54.2
11632. DOMINGO-CON AMORE Placido Domingo 13Mar82 164(2) 6	54.2
11633. TO THE HILT Golden Earring 28Feb76 156(1) 4	54.1
11634. LOOSE SALUTE Michael Nesmith & The First National Band 02Jan71 159(1) 4	54.1
11635. NEIL SEDAKA SINGS HIS GREATEST HITS Neil Sedaka 01Mar75 161(2) 4	54.1
11636. YVONNE Yvonne Elliman 10Nov79 174(2) 6	54.1
11637. THE ART OF CONTROL Peter Frampton 28Aug82 174(2) 8	54.1
11638. ENGLISH ROSE Fleetwood Mac 08Feb69 184(1) 6	54.0
11639. JAMES BROWN PLAYS THE REAL THING James Brown 15Jul67 164(2) 5	54.0
11640. CHANGE UP THE GROOVE Roy Ayers Ubiquity 05Oct74 156(1) 4	54.0
11641. THOSE WERE THE DAYS Pete Fountain 22Mar69 186(2) 6	54.0
11642. I WEAR THE FACE Mr. Mister 14Apr84 170(1) 7	54.0
11643. DONALD CLARK OSMOND Donny Osmond 03Sep77 169(1) 5	54.0
11644. GREATEST HITS Lee Greenwood 18May85 163(2) 8	54.0
11645. REUNION (THE SONGS OF JIMMY WEBB) Glen Campbell 16Nov74 166(2) 5	53.9
11646. 100CC 10cc 13Sep75 161(1) 5	53.9
11647. THE DELLS SING DIONNE WARWICKE'S GREATEST HITS The Dells 24Jun72 162(1) 5	53.8
11648. TWO ALL-TIME GREAT SELLING LP'S Raiders 08Nov69 166(2) 4	53.7
11649. JOY/THE VENTURES PLAY THE CLASSICS The Ventures 18Mar72 146(1) 3	53.7
11650. BEWITCHED Andy Summers & Robert Fripp 20Oct84 155(2) 5	53.7
11651. MAKE SOMEONE HAPPY We Five 27Jan68 172(1) 6	53.6
11652. THE WORLD WITHIN Stix Hooper 10Nov79 166(1) 5	53.6
11653. NOTHING BUT THE TRUTH Ruben Blades 07May88 156(2) 6	53.6
11654. SEEN ONE EARTH Pete Bardens 17Oct87 148(2) 5	53.6
11655. SEA TRAIN Seatrain 17May69 168(2) 4	53.6
11656. CANTERBURY TALES Original Cast 19Apr69 171(2) 4	53.5
11657. SUNNY DAYS Lighthouse 13Jan73 190(1) 9	53.5
11658. BAKER STREET (A MUSICAL ADVENTURE OF SHERLOCK HOLMES) Original Cast 08May65 138(1) 4	53.5
11659. DIFFERENT KIND OF TENSION Buzzcocks 23Feb80 163(1) 6	53.4
11660. THE BADDEST TURRENTINE Stanley Turrentine 16Nov74 185(1) 7	53.4
11661. JOHN SEBASTIAN LIVE John Sebastian 10Oct70 129(1) 3	53.4
11662. 20 GRANITE CREEK Moby Grape 18Sep71 177(1) 5	53.4
11663. JOHN CONLEE'S GREATEST HITS John Conlee 11Jun83 166(1) 6	53.4
11664. OUT OF SIGHT, OUT OF MIND Little Anthony And The Imperials 04Oct69 172(2) 5	53.4
11665. TALES TO WARM YOUR MIND Irish Rovers 10May69 182(1) 5	53.3
11666. THE SYLVERS The Sylvers 03Mar73 180(1) 7	53.3
11667. RHYMES & REASONS John Denver 25Oct69 148(2) 3	53.3
11668. SHE USED TO WANNA BE A BALLERINA Buffy Sainte-Marie 10Apr71 182(1) 6	53.3

Rank. Title Act Entry Peak(Pk Wks) TotWks	Scr
11669. BLOODROCK Bloodrock 25Apr70 160(2) 5	53.2
11670. RETURN TO FOREVER LIVE Return To Forever 03Mar79 155(1) 4	53.2
11671. MOMS THE WORD Moms Mabley 19Sep64 128(2) 4	53.2
11672. TOO HOT TO SLEEP Sylvester 11Jul81 156(1) 4	53.1
11673. YOU'RE GOOD FOR ME Lou Rawls 20Jul68 165(2) 6	53.1
11674. COAST TO COAST Joe & Eddie 15Feb64 140(1) 4	53.0
11675. WIND OF CHANGE Peter Frampton 07Oct72 177(2) 6	53.0
11676. SWEET SOUND Simon Townshend 03Dec83 169(1) 7	53.0
11677. BLOWIN' GOLD John Klemmer 13Sep69 176(1) 5	53.0
11678. SHINE ON ME One Way 20Aug83 164(1) 6	53.0
11679. BACK INTO BLUE Quarterflash 05Oct85 150(2) 5	53.0
11680. I NEVER PICKED COTTON Roy Clark 29Aug70 176(1) 6	53.0
11681. SOLID AND RAUNCHY THE 3RD Bill Black's Combo 13Sep69 168(1) 4	52.9
11682. PEACE IN OUR TIME Big Country 29Oct88 160(2) 6	52.9
11683. THE PLIMSOULS The Plimsouls 04Apr81 153(1) 4	52.9
11684. GREATEST HITS Julius Wechter and the Baja Marimba Band 04Apr70 180(1) 6	52.9
11685. SILK 'N' BRASS Jackie Gleason 05Feb66 141(1) 4	52.8
11686. DOIN' IT! UTFO 10Jun89 143(2) 4	52.8
11687. MR. BAD GUY Freddie Mercury 18May85 159(1) 6	52.8
11688. RURAL SPACE Brewer And Shipley 27Jan73 174(1) 7	52.8
11689. BRUISEOLOGY The Waitresses 04Jun83 155(2) 5	52.7
11690. THE EARL SCRUGGS REVUE Earl Scruggs Revue 22Sep73 169(1) 5	52.7
11691. NOW WE MAY BEGIN Randy Crawford 31May80 180(1) 7	52.6
11692. PEACING IT ALL TOGETHER Lighthouse 09May70 133(2) 3	52.6
11693. BUCKY FELLINI Dead Milkmen 01Aug87 163(1) 7	52.6
11694. SLAM Dan Reed Network 21Oct89 160(1) 6	52.6
11695. THE ENTERTAINER Marvin Hamlisch 31Aug74 170(2) 5	52.6
11696. THE MYSTERY OF EDWIN DROOD Original Cast 28Jun86 150(2) 6	52.6
11697. BETTER TIMES ARE COMING Rhinoceros 11Jul70 178(2) 6	52.6
11698. PAMPERED MENIAL Pavlov's Dog 05Apr75 181(1) 6	52.6
11699. SHA NA NOW Sha Na Na 09Aug75 162(2) 4	52.5
11700. STOP YOUR MOTOR The Association 14Aug71 158(1) 4	52.5
11701. IN TOO MUCH TOO SOON New York Dolls 01Jun74 167(1) 5	52.5
11702. MIDNIGHT MISSION Textones 24Nov84 176(1) 8	52.5
11703. MORNING GLORY Mary Travers 29Apr72 157(1) 5	52.5
11704. RAMATAM Ramatam 02Sep72 182(1) 7	52.5
11705. ELOISE Eloise Laws 04Feb78 156(1) 5	52.5
11706. CATCH A FIRE The Wailers(2) 08Nov75 171(1) 5	52.4
11707. THE BEST OF ISAAC HAYES Isaac Hayes 23Aug75 165(1) 4	52.4

Rank. Title Act Entry Peak(Pk Wks) TotWks	Scr
11708. CERRONE'S PARADISE Cerrone 06Aug77 162(2) 5	52.3
11709. BENNY GOODMAN TODAY Benny Goodman And His Orchestra 03Apr71 189(1) 7	52.3
11710. CHESTER & LESTER Chet Atkins And Les Paul 29May76 172(2) 5	52.3
11711. PARTY PARTY Soundtrack 05Feb83 169(4) 6	52.3
11712. STEVE FORBERT Steve Forbert 24Jul82 159(2) 6	52.3
11713. THE THOMAS CROWN AFFAIR Soundtrack 31Aug68 182(1) 6	52.2
11714. THE FIVE FACES OF MANFRED MANN Manfred Mann 06Mar65 141(2) 4	52.2
11715. THE WHEEL Asleep At The Wheel 16Apr77 162(1) 4	52.2
11716. LAND OF 1000 DANCES Cannibal And The Headhunters 08May65 141(2) 4	52.2
11717. KISS THE SKY Jimi Hendrix 17Nov84 148(1) 5	52.2
11718. BURT BACHARACH'S GREATEST HITS Burt Bacharach 14Dec74 173(2) 5	52.2
11719. IT'S TIME Bonnie Bramlett 22Feb75 168(2) 5	52.1
11720. TODAY Marty Robbins 18Sep71 175(1) 6	52.1
11721. STOMP YOUR HANDS, CLAP YOUR FEET Slade 09Mar74 168(1) 5	52.0
11722. TRON Soundtrack 31Jul82 135(2) 5	52.0
11723. CONTROLLED BY HATRED/ FEEL LIKE SHIT...DEJA VU Suicidal Tendencies 28Oct89 150(2) 5	52.0
11724. CROSSWORD PUZZLE Partridge Family 07Jul73 167(2) 5	52.0
11725. AIRBORNE Don Felder 03Dec83 178(1) 8	52.0
11726. THAT'S HOW MUCH I LOVE YOU The Manhattans 01Mar75 160(1) 4	52.0
11727. NRBQ NRBQ 19Jul69 162(1) 4	52.0
11728. SAM NEELY-2 Sam Neely 10Feb73 175(1) 6	51.9
11729. THE WILD PLACES Duncan Browne 19May79 174(2) 5	51.9
11730. STEP ON OUT Oak Ridge Boys 20Apr85 156(1) 5	51.9
11731. MORE BIG FOLK HITS Brothers Four 31Oct64 134(1) 4	51.9
11732. ROCK THE NATIONS Saxon 14Feb87 149(2) 6	51.8
11733. THE SUPER GROUPS Various Artists 01Mar69 178(1) 5	51.8
11734. THIS IS THE GIRL THAT IS Nancy Ames 26Sep64 133(1) 4	51.8
11735. YOU'RE A GOOD MAN, CHARLIE BROWN Original Cast 01Jul67 165(2) 5	51.7
11736. THE MAN FROM UTOPIA Frank Zappa 16Apr83 153(1) 5	51.7
11737. ISRAELITES Desmond Dekker And The Aces 06Sep69 153(1) 3	51.7
11738. ALADDIN Rotary Connection 19Oct68 176(2) 5	51.7
11739. COME TO MY GARDEN Minnie Riperton 16Nov74 160(1) 4	51.7
11740. COLONIZATION New Colony Six 02Sep67 172(2) 7	51.6
11741. BIG DEAL Killer Dwarfs 28May88 165(1) 6	51.6
11742. WHERE'S THE MONEY? Dan Hicks & His Hot Licks 02Oct71 195(2) 8	51.5
11743. LIVE AT THE ROYAL FESTIVAL HALL Glen Campbell 07Jan78 171(3) 5	51.5
11744. RIFF RAFF Dave Edmunds 13Oct84 140(2) 4	51.5
11745. NO ARMS CAN EVER HOLD YOU The Bachelors 03Apr65 136(1) 4	51.5
11746. OUT AMONG 'EM Love Childs Afro Cuban Blues Band 12Jul75 168(2) 5	51.5

Rank. Title Act Entry Peak(Pk Wks) TotWks	Scr
11747. **EAST OF MIDNIGHT** Gordon Lightfoot 09Aug86 165(1) 6	51.5
11748. **START OF A ROMANCE** Skyy 27May89 155(1) 5	51.5
11749. **LOVE THEME FROM "THE GODFATHER"** Roger Williams 08Apr72 187(2) 8	51.4
11750. **AERIAL PANDEMONIUM BALLET** Nilsson 17Jul71 149(1) 3	51.4
11751. **HAPPY JUST TO BE LIKE I AM** Taj Mahal 15Jan72 181(1) 6	51.3
11752. **THE STAX/VOLT REVUE - LIVE IN LONDON** Various Artists 02Sep67 145(1) 4	51.3
11753. **MAXOOM** Mahogany Rush 01Mar75 159(1) 4	51.3
11754. **SEARCHPARTY** John Hall Band 05Mar83 147(2) 5	51.3
11755. **LUCKY** Marty Balin 12Mar83 156(2) 6	51.2
11756. **LIVE AT THE WINTER GARDEN** Liza Minnelli 18May74 150(1) 4	51.2
11757. **STRANGE KIND OF LOVE** Love And Money 25Mar89 175(2) 7	51.2
11758. **BULL DURHAM** Soundtrack 06Aug88 157(1) 6	51.2
11759. **SCRIPT FOR A JESTER'S TEAR** Marillion 25Jun83 175(1) 7	51.2
11760. **WHAT THE WORLD NEEDS NOW IS LOVE!** Jack Jones 24Feb68 167(2) 6	51.2
11761. **COUNTRY-FOLK** Waylon Jennings & The Kimberlys 04Oct69 169(1) 4	51.2
11762. **TRAMMPS** The Trammps 05Jul75 159(2) 4	51.2
11763. **JEALOUS LOVER** Rainbow 14Nov81 147(1) 4	51.1
11764. **SPEAK & SPELL** Depeche Mode 26Dec81 192(1) 9	51.1
11765. **GIVE IT UP** Pleasure 15May82 164(1) 6	51.1
11766. **FALLING IN LOVE AGAIN** Susan 05May79 169(1) 5	51.0
11767. **MOONRAKER** Soundtrack 18Aug79 159(1) 4	51.0
11768. **14 GREATEST HITS** Michael Jackson & The Jackson 5 23Jun84 168(1) 7	51.0
11769. **CELI BEE & THE BUZZY BUNCH** Celi Bee And The Buzzy Bunch 23Jul77 169(2) 5	51.0
11770. **GO FOR YOUR LIFE** Mountain 27Apr85 166(2) 6	51.0
11771. **THE EARL SCRUGGS REVUE, VOLUME II** Earl Scruggs Revue 17Apr76 161(2) 4	50.9
11772. **HOME COOKIN'** Jr. Walker & The All Stars 08Feb69 172(1) 4	50.9
11773. **RUFUS** Rufus 04Aug73 175(2) 6	50.9
11774. **REUNION CONCERT** Everly Brothers 10Mar84 162(2) 5	50.9
11775. **FLIGHTS OF FANTASY** The Ventures 25May68 169(1) 6	50.9
11776. **THE MADCAP LAUGHS** Syd Barrett 17Aug74 163(2) 4	50.9
11777. **IT HURTS SO GOOD** Millie Jackson 29Sep73 175(1) 6	50.9
11778. **WE'VE GOT TO GET IT ON AGAIN** Addrisi Brothers 08Apr72 137(1) 3	50.9
11779. **PRESS ON** David T. Walker 09Feb74 187(1) 8	50.9
11780. **CLASSICS THE EARLY YEARS** Neil Diamond 25Jun83 171(1) 7	50.8
11781. **THAT'S THE WAY LOVE SHOULD BE** Dave Rowland And Sugar 17Sep77 157(1) 4	50.8
11782. **JAZZ IMPRESSIONS OF NEW YORK** Dave Brubeck Quartet 27Feb65 142(1) 4	50.8
11783. **A GRP CHRISTMAS COLLECTION** Various Artists 07Jan89 140(1) 4	50.7
11784. **THE MERRY WIDOW** Original Cast 17Oct64 137(1) 4	50.7
11785. **ETERNAL NIGHTMARE** Vio-Lence 20Aug88 154(2) 6	50.7
11786. **NOTHING WILL BE AS IT WAS...TOMORROW** Flora Purim 26Mar77 163(1) 4	50.7
11787. **GREATEST HITS** Charlie Rich 21Jun75 162(2) 4	50.7
11788. **JOHN O'BANION** John O'Banion 16May81 164(1) 4	50.7
11789. **BIG BAND HITS OF THE 30'S & 40'S!** Enoch Light & The Light Brigade 24Jul71 176(1) 5	50.7
11790. **BIO** Chuck Berry 08Sep73 175(1) 6	50.6
11791. **ONLY LOVE CAN BREAK A HEART** Dionne Warwick 02Jul77 188(1) 7	50.6
11792. **FIRST BASE** Babe Ruth 11Aug73 178(2) 6	50.6
11793. **MAYBE IT'S LIVE** Robert Palmer 15May82 148(1) 5	50.6
11794. **GOOD THANG** Faze-O 11Nov78 145(1) 3	50.6
11795. **BOZ SCAGGS** Boz Scaggs 13Jul74 171(1) 5	50.6
11796. **XL-1** Pete Shelley 23Jul83 151(1) 5	50.6
11797. **BARBARELLA** Soundtrack 07Dec68 183(1) 5	50.6
11798. **HAI HAI** Roger Hodgson 31Oct87 163(2) 6	50.6
11799. **THE SPIRIT'S IN IT** Patti LaBelle 03Oct81 156(3) 4	50.5
11800. **FACE TO FACE** The Kinks 11Feb67 135(1) 3	50.5
11801. **STARS ON LONG PLAY III** Stars On 08May82 163(2) 6	50.5
11802. **SPUN GOLD** Barbara Mandrell 03Sep83 140(1) 4	50.5
11803. **PARTY** Iggy Pop 19Sep81 166(2) 5	50.4
11804. **THIRTEEN** Emmylou Harris 08Mar86 157(2) 6	50.4
11805. **WHISPERS AND PROMISES** Earl Klugh 20May89 150(2) 5	50.4
11806. **LAURA (WHAT'S HE GOT THAT I AIN'T GOT)** Brook Benton 28Oct67 156(1) 4	50.3
11807. **CHICKEN SKIN MUSIC** Ry Cooder 23Oct76 177(2) 5	50.3
11808. **CHAMPAGNE CHARLIE** Leon Redbone 16Sep78 163(1) 4	50.3
11809. **MEAN** Montrose 30May87 165(2) 7	50.2
11810. **SOME OF MY BEST JOKES ARE FRIENDS** George Clinton 10Aug85 163(2) 6	50.2
11811. **THE KATE SMITH ANNIVERSARY ALBUM** Kate Smith 25Jun66 130(1) 3	50.2
11812. **ICE CASTLES** Soundtrack 21Apr79 174(1) 5	50.2
11813. **COUP DE GRACE** Mink De Ville 24Oct81 161(2) 5	50.2
11814. **RHAPSODIES** Rick Wakeman 21Jul79 170(1) 5	50.2
11815. **MOVIN' ON** Buckwheat 01Apr72 179(1) 6	50.2
11816. **FROM WITHIN** Dionne Warwick 08Apr72 169(1) 5	50.1
11817. **SKY ISLANDS** Caldera 01Oct77 159(1) 4	50.1
11818. **POV** Utopia 16Mar85 161(2) 6	50.1
11819. **TRUTH OF TRUTHS - A CONTEMPORARY ROCK OPERA** Various Artists 18Dec71 185(1) 7	50.0
11820. **BEST OF BRIAN AUGER** Brian Auger 23Apr77 151(2) 3	50.0
11821. **ROY CLARK / SUPERPICKER** Roy Clark 05May73 172(1) 6	50.0
11822. **PASS THE PLATE** The Crusaders 26Jun71 168(2) 4	50.0
11823. **LOVE IS JUST A GAME** Larry Gatlin 01Apr78 175(2) 5	50.0
11824. **MARY SOL** Various Artists 07Oct72 186(2) 7	49.9
11825. **FOR THE LOVE OF HIM** Bobbi Martin 30May70 176(1) 5	49.9
11826. **16 GREATEST HITS** The Impressions 20Mar71 180(1) 6	49.9
11827. **REAL LIFE STORY** Terri Lyne Carrington 29Apr89 169(1) 7	49.9
11828. **CAGE THE SONGBIRD** Crystal Gayle 12Nov83 171(1) 6	49.9
11829. **SWING THE HEARTACHE - THE BBC SESSIONS** Bauhaus 12Aug89 169(1) 6	49.8
11830. **WANTED DEAD OR ALIVE** David Bromberg 23Feb74 167(1) 5	49.8
11831. **AL TIJUANA AND HIS JEWISH BRASS** Lou Jacobi 12Nov66 134(2) 3	49.7
11832. **GEORGE JONES & GENE PITNEY** George Jones & Gene Pitney 20Mar65 141(1) 4	49.7
11833. **MARY WELLS** Mary Wells 01May65 145(2) 4	49.7
11834. **TRADE WINDS** Earl Grant 15May65 143(1) 4	49.7
11835. **ANOTHER BEGINNING** Les McCann 18Jan75 166(2) 4	49.6
11836. **MOONS OF JUPITER** Scruffy The Cat 17Dec88 177(1) 8	49.6
11837. **MAMA'S BOYS** Mama's Boys 11Aug84 172(1) 8	49.6
11838. **INSTANT DEATH** Eddie Harris 22Jul72 185(1) 7	49.6
11839. **THE SYLVERS II** The Sylvers 04Aug73 164(1) 5	49.5
11840. **WARM & TENDER SOUL** Percy Sledge 26Nov66 136(2) 3	49.5
11841. **TALK TO THE PEOPLE** Les McCann 07Oct72 181(2) 6	49.5
11842. **FLOWERS ON THE WALL** Statler Brothers 26Feb66 125(2) 3	49.5
11843. **HEAVY MENTAL** The Fools 28Mar81 158(1) 4	49.5
11844. **MAKING CONTACT** UFO 30Apr83 153(1) 5	49.4
11845. **THE PARKERILLA** Graham Parker And The Rumour 01Jul78 149(1) 3	49.4
11846. **THE KING OF COMEDY** Soundtrack 16Apr83 162(1) 6	49.4
11847. **BRUCE COCKBURN/RESUME** Bruce Cockburn 23May81 174(2) 5	49.4
11848. **LOVE POTION** New Birth 28Aug76 168(2) 4	49.3
11849. **LOVE-IN** Charles Lloyd Quartet 19Aug67 171(1) 7	49.3
11850. **JOHNNY WINTER AND** Johnny Winter 26Sep70 154(1) 4	49.2
11851. **A LITTLE KNIGHT MUSIC** Gladys Knight And The Pips 26Apr75 164(2) 4	49.1
11852. **THE "A" TEAM** SSgt Barry Sadler 09Jul66 130(1) 3	49.1
11853. **A SCRATCH IN THE SKY** Cryan' Shames 13Jan68 156(2) 5	49.1
11854. **THE CHUCK MANGIONE QUARTET** Chuck Mangione 15Jul72 180(2) 6	49.1
11855. **DISTANT THUNDER** Aswad 13Aug88 173(3) 7	49.1
11856. **JUST WANNA ROCK 'N' ROLL** Jose Feliciano 06Sep75 165(1) 4	49.1
11857. **IN CONTROL VOLUME I** Marley Marl 08Oct88 163(2) 5	49.0
11858. **VINTAGE 74** Sergio Mendes & Brasil '77 18May74 176(1) 5	49.0
11859. **EVERYTHING YOU ALWAYS WANTED TO KNOW ABOUT THE GODFATHER - BUT DON'T ASK** Various Artists 22Jul72 178(2) 6	49.0
11860. **ADVENTURES IN MODERN RECORDING** The Buggles 27Mar82 161(2) 5	48.9
11861. **BEST OF NORMAN CONNORS & FRIENDS** Norman Connors 13Jan79 175(1) 5	48.9
11862. **MY BABY LOVES LOVIN'** White Plains 22Aug70 166(1) 4	48.9

Rank. Title Act Entry Peak(Pk Wks) TotWks	Scr
11863. MORE THAN A MIRACLE Roger Williams 02Mar68 164(1) 5	48.9
11864. SLIDES Richard Harris 16Dec72 181(1) 6	48.9
11865. THE JERK The Larks 23Jan65 143(1) 4	48.9
11866. MORE OF THE GOOD LIFE T.S. Monk 09Jan82 176(1) 8	48.8
11867. PLEASURES OF THE HARBOR Phil Ochs 09Dec67 168(1) 5	48.8
11868. LIKE CHILDREN Jerry Goodman & Jan Hammer 08Feb75 150(1) 3	48.7
11869. PARADISE BALLROOM Graeme Edge Band 09Jul77 164(2) 4	48.7
11870. $ (DOLLARS) Soundtrack 19Feb72 173(2) 5	48.7
11871. THIS IS THE DAY...THIS IS THE HOUR...THIS IS THIS! Pop Will Eat Itself 26Aug89 169(2) 6	48.7
11872. SEXTANT Herbie Hancock 02Jun73 176(1) 6	48.7
11873. EVERYTHING STOPS FOR TEA Long John Baldry 06May72 180(1) 6	48.7
11874. RESURRECTION SHUFFLE Ashton, Gardner & Dyke 07Aug71 178(1) 6	48.7
11875. MEMORIES John Mayall 13Nov71 179(2) 5	48.7
11876. ANDY WILLIAMS' GREATEST HITS, VOL. 2 Andy Williams 07Jul73 174(1) 5	48.7
11877. THE BEST OF DAVE EDMUNDS Dave Edmunds 09Jan82 163(1) 5	48.6
11878. SHOTGUN III Shotgun 05May79 163(2) 4	48.6
11879. RISE AND SHINE The Bears 30Apr88 159(1) 5	48.6
11880. INAMORATA Poco 19May84 167(2) 6	48.6
11881. ALL MY CHOICES Mary Travers 24Feb73 169(1) 6	48.6
11882. ST. LOUIE TO FRISCO TO MEMPHIS Chuck Berry 04Nov72 185(2) 7	48.6
11883. GREATEST HITS Charley Pride 21Nov81 185(1) 7	48.5
11884. ROCK HARD Suzi Quatro 01Nov80 165(1) 5	48.5
11885. BREAKFAST SPECIAL Pete Wingfield 06Dec75 165(1) 5	48.5
11886. I GOT THE MELODY Odyssey 18Jul81 175(2) 5	48.5
11887. COME SHARE MY LOVE Miki Howard 14Mar87 171(2) 6	48.5
11888. ENOCH LIGHT & THE BRASS MENAGERIE Enoch Light & The Light Brigade 26Apr69 192(2) 7	48.4
11889. THE HITS OF BROADWAY AND HOLLYWOOD Ed Ames 21Dec68 186(2) 6	48.4
11890. JUST A MELODY Young-Holt Unlimited 16Aug69 185(1) 6	48.4
11891. WYNTON MARSALIS Wynton Marsalis 06Mar82 165(1) 5	48.4
11892. 1 + 1 Grin 05Feb72 180(1) 6	48.4
11893. STRIKING IT RICH! Dan Hicks & His Hot Licks 20May72 170(1) 5	48.3
11894. OUR SHINING HOUR Sammy Davis-Count Basie 27Mar65 141(1) 4	48.3
11895. PRESERVATION ACT 1 The Kinks 15Dec73 177(1) 6	48.2
11896. RAVEL BOLERO Tomita 09Feb80 174(1) 5	48.2
11897. DREAMSPEAKER Tim Weisberg 29Dec73 160(1) 4	48.2
11898. KEEP THE FIRE BURNING Louisiana's Le Roux 09Jun79 162(2) 4	48.1
11899. THOSE GLORIOUS MGM MUSICALS: SINGIN' IN THE RAIN/EASTER PARADE Soundtrack 15Sep73 185(1) 7	48.1
11900. NATIONAL BREAKOUT The Romantics 06Dec80 176(2) 7	48.1
11901. GOOD BAD & FUNKY Shotgun 29Apr78 172(1) 5	48.1
11902. PASS ME BY Peggy Lee 22May65 145(1) 4	48.1
11903. FOREVER Billy Vaughn And His Orchestra 20Jun64 144(2) 4	48.0
11904. POPS IN SPACE Boston Pops Orchestra/John Williams 20Dec80 181(1) 6	48.0
11905. DAVID MERRICK PRESENTS HITS FROM HIS BROADWAY HITS John Gary/Ann-Margret 14Nov64 141(1) 4	48.0
11906. CHRISTMAS TYME Engelbert Humperdinck 24Dec77 156(1) 4	47.9
11907. IN SEARCH OF FREEDOM Rev. Dr. Martin Luther King, Jr. 08Jun68 150(1) 3	47.9
11908. CARNEGIE HALL Hubert Laws 30Jun73 175(1) 6	47.8
11909. RUMBLE FISH Stewart Copeland 17Dec83 157(1) 5	47.8
11910. INSTANT GROOVE King Curtis 19Jul69 160(2) 3	47.8
11911. BOULDERS Roy Wood 03Nov73 176(1) 6	47.8
11912. TWO SIDES OF THE MOON Keith Moon 05Apr75 155(2) 3	47.8
11913. HANDFUL OF SOUL James Brown 03Dec66 135(1) 3	47.8
11914. ROCK N' ROLL NIGHTS BTO 07Apr79 165(2) 4	47.7
11915. THE MARX BROS. (THE ORIGINAL VOICE TRACKS FROM THEIR GREATEST MOVIES) Groucho Marx 11Oct69 155(1) 3	47.7
11916. UHF/ORIGINAL MOTION PICTURE SOUNDTRACK AND OTHER STUFF "Weird Al" Yankovic 19Aug89 146(2) 4	47.7
11917. BLACK SEEDS Main Ingredient 02Oct71 176(1) 5	47.7
11918. RUNT Todd Rundgren 09Jan71 185(1) 6	47.7
11919. CLOSER THAN CLOSE Jean Carne 06Sep86 162(2) 6	47.6
11920. THE SOFT SEA San Sebastian Strings 26Sep70 171(1) 5	47.6
11921. GREAT THEMES FROM HIT FILMS Enoch Light & The Light Brigade 03Oct64 143(2) 4	47.6
11922. THE WALTONS' CHRISTMAS ALBUM TV Soundtrack 21Dec74 125(1) 2	47.6
11923. WILLIE MITCHELL LIVE Willie Mitchell 16Mar68 172(2) 5	47.6
11924. BATDORF & RODNEY Batdorf & Rodney 28Oct72 185(1) 7	47.6
11925. TOM FOGERTY Tom Fogerty 03Jun72 180(2) 6	47.6
11926. CALIFORNIA NIGHTS Lesley Gore 13May67 169(1) 5	47.5
11927. LIVE Poco 03Apr76 169(2) 4	47.5
11928. MY MAN! WILD MAN! Wild Man Steve 01Nov69 185(1) 6	47.5
11929. HUSTLE TO SURVIVE Les McCann 22Nov75 161(1) 4	47.4
11930. THE BEST OF JERRY BUTLER Jerry Butler 27Jun70 167(2) 5	47.4
11931. THE TALE OF THE GIANT RAT OF SUMATRA Firesign Theatre 02Mar74 172(1) 5	47.4
11932. CHRISTMAS JOLLIES II Salsoul Orchestra 19Dec81 170(2) 5	47.3
11933. HEAVEN HELP THE CHILD Mickey Newbury 10Mar73 173(1) 5	47.3
11934. BIG SPENDER Peggy Lee 30Jul66 130(1) 3	47.2
11935. CLASSIC LIGHTFOOT (THE BEST OF LIGHTFOOT/VOLUME 2) Gordon Lightfoot 26Jun71 178(2) 5	47.2
11936. DONALD BYRD'S BEST Donald Byrd 18Dec76 167(1) 4	47.2
11937. TONY MAKES IT HAPPEN! Tony Bennett 13May67 178(1) 6	47.2
11938. GENETIC WALK Ahmad Jamal 15Mar80 173(1) 5	47.1
11939. PLAYGIRL Thee Prophets 28Jun69 163(1) 3	47.1
11940. SOMETHING ELSE AGAIN Richie Havens 24Feb68 184(1) 7	47.1
11941. DO ME RIGHT Detroit Emeralds 19Jun71 151(1) 3	47.1
11942. REBEL John Miles 22May76 171(1) 4	47.1
11943. GOIN' HOME! THEIR GREATEST HITS Ten Years After 19Jul75 174(1) 5	47.1
11944. BIG FUN Miles Davis 08Jun74 179(1) 5	47.1
11945. POLAR AC Freddie Hubbard 17May75 167(1) 4	47.1
11946. HOW GREAT THOU ART Jim Nabors 23Oct71 166(1) 4	47.0
11947. IN THE MOOD FOR SOMETHING RUDE Foghat 13Nov82 162(1) 5	47.0
11948. JAMMIN' IN MANHATTAN Tyzik 08Sep84 172(1) 6	47.0
11949. JUST A STONE'S THROW AWAY Valerie Carter 02Apr77 182(1) 5	47.0
11950. STORIES TO TELL Flora Purim 15Feb75 172(2) 5	46.9
11951. LEVEL ONE Eleventh House 09Aug75 163(1) 4	46.9
11952. PLAYIN' IT COOL Timothy B. Schmit 10Nov84 160(2) 5	46.9
11953. SOMETHING HEAVY GOING DOWN - LIVE FROM THE TWILIGHT ZONE Golden Earring 24Nov84 158(2) 6	46.8
11954. JUST TODAY Bobby Vee 27Apr68 187(2) 7	46.8
11955. MERCY, MERCY Buddy Rich 30Nov68 186(1) 6	46.8
11956. RICH AND FAMOUS Blue Mercedes 14May88 165(2) 5	46.8
11957. CORY AND ME Cory Daye 13Oct79 171(2) 5	46.8
11958. ANGEL EYES Dave Brubeck Quartet 09Oct65 122(1) 3	46.7
11959. TOUCHING HOME Jerry Lee Lewis 24Jul71 152(1) 3	46.7
11960. MEATBALLS Soundtrack 18Aug79 170(1) 5	46.7
11961. ORIGINAL THEME FROM BONNIE & CLYDE Flatt & Scruggs 08Jun68 161(1) 4	46.6
11962. A HANDFUL OF BEAUTY Shakti With John McLaughlin 02Apr77 168(1) 4	46.6
11963. LAUGHTER Ian Dury And The Blockheads 07Feb81 159(1) 4	46.6
11964. DUSTY SPRINGFIELD'S GOLDEN HITS Dusty Springfield 24Dec66 137(1) 3	46.6
11965. HEARTBREAK RADIO Rita Coolidge 12Sep81 160(1) 4	46.5
11966. BLOWIN' YOUR MIND! Van Morrison 07Oct67 182(1) 7	46.5
11967. THE HORSE Cliff Nobles & Co. 21Sep68 159(1) 3	46.5
11968. THE PIRATE MOVIE Soundtrack 28Aug82 166(2) 6	46.5
11969. ONE MORE ROUND Glenn Yarbrough 19Sep64 142(1) 4	46.5
11970. THE GOOD EARTH Manfred Mann's Earth Band 30Nov74 157(2) 3	46.5
11971. TATTOO Rory Gallagher 01Dec73 186(1) 7	46.5
11972. MAX Q Max Q 07Oct89 182(2) 8	46.4
11973. GENE CHANDLER - LIVE ON STAGE IN '65 Gene Chandler 08Jan66 124(1) 3	46.4
11974. SOME COME RUNNING Jim Capaldi 17Dec88 183(2) 8	46.4
11975. ONLY THE LONELY Sonny James 12Apr69 161(1) 3	46.3
11976. TWO OF A KIND Porter Wagoner and Dolly Parton 13Mar71 142(1) 3	46.3

Rank. Title Act Entry Peak(Pk Wks) TotWks	Scr
11977. CANDIDA & KNOCK THREE TIMES Tony Orlando & Dawn 18Jan75 170(2) 4	46.3
11978. DREAM Mills Brothers 24May69 184(2) 5	46.3
11979. DEMIS ROUSSOS Demis Roussos 17Jun78 184(1) 6	46.3
11980. MAN FROM TWO WORLDS Chico Hamilton 19Dec64 145(2) 4	46.3
11981. TOUGH Kurtis Blow 09Oct82 167(2) 5	46.3
11982. SCOTCH ON THE ROCKS Band Of The Black Watch 20Mar76 164(1) 4	46.2
11983. IRON FIST Motorhead 22May82 174(1) 6	46.2
11984. PLAYS TUNES BY CHUCK BERRY Bill Black's Combo 11Jul64 143(1) 4	46.2
11985. IN A BROKEN DREAM Python Lee Jackson 07Oct72 182(2) 6	46.2
11986. ONLY THE STRONG SURVIVE Billy Paul 28Jan78 152(1) 4	46.2
11987. LUNCH Audience 24Jun72 175(2) 5	46.1
11988. HIGHER AND HIGHER Jackie Wilson 25Nov67 163(1) 4	46.1
11989. BABY TONIGHT Marlon Jackson 28Nov87 175(2) 7	46.1
11990. LOVE IS FAIR Barbara Mandrell 27Sep80 175(1) 6	46.0
11991. TOO HOT TO STOP IT The Manhattans 13Apr85 171(2) 6	46.0
11992. THE INCOMPARABLE CHARLEY PRIDE Charley Pride 06Jan73 189(1) 8	46.0
11993. "DETROIT CITY" AND OTHER HITS Bobby Bare 26Oct63 119(1) 3	46.0
11994. SEX & VIOLINS Martin Mull 17Jun78 157(2) 3	45.9
11995. LIVING SOUL Richard "Groove" Holmes 29Oct66 143(1) 3	45.9
11996. CURTIS MAYFIELD/HIS EARLY YEARS WITH THE IMPRESSIONS Curtis Mayfield 03Mar73 180(2) 6	45.9
11997. EXPLOSIVE BRASS IMPACT Warren Kime & His Brass Impact Orchestra 11Nov67 177(2) 7	45.8
11998. CONVERSATIONS Brass Construction 11Jun83 176(1) 6	45.8
11999. ESCAPADE Tim Finn 17Sep83 161(1) 5	45.8
12000. WHEN YOU'RE # 1 Gene Chandler 25Aug79 153(2) 3	45.8
12001. STAND UP Del Fuegos 18Apr87 167(2) 6	45.8
12002. EMPIRE JAZZ Various Artists 02Aug80 168(1) 5	45.8
12003. CLOSE-UP Buck Owens 16Aug69 185(2) 5	45.7
12004. YUSEF LATEEF'S DETROIT Yusef Lateef 16Aug69 183(1) 5	45.7
12005. LIVING TOGETHER Burt Bacharach 05Jan74 181(1) 6	45.7
12006. ANGST IN MY PANTS Sparks 22May82 173(2) 6	45.7
12007. NOT THE BOY NEXT DOOR Peter Allen 12Mar83 170(2) 6	45.7
12008. THIS MOMENT IN TIME Engelbert Humperdinck 19May79 164(1) 4	45.7
12009. BOOK OF DAYS Psychedelic Furs 25Nov89 138(2) 4	45.7
12010. JAMES BROWN...LIVE/HOT ON THE ONE James Brown 16Aug80 170(2) 5	45.7
12011. RARE EARTH Rare Earth 01Oct77 187(1) 6	45.7
12012. LAWRENCE WELK PLAYS I LOVE YOU TRULY AND OTHER SONGS OF LOVE Lawrence Welk 13Sep69 176(2) 4	45.6
12013. A CURIOUS FEELING Tony Banks 15Dec79 171(1) 5	45.6
12014. 10TH ANNIVERSARY Statler Brothers 06Sep80 169(1) 5	45.6

Rank. Title Act Entry Peak(Pk Wks) TotWks	Scr
12015. TIMELESS Frankie Valli 10Aug68 176(2) 5	45.6
12016. CAPRICORN PRINCESS Esther Phillips 08Jan77 150(1) 4	45.6
12017. JUDY GARLAND'S GREATEST HITS Judy Garland 16Aug69 161(1) 3	45.5
12018. 2 X 4 Guadalcanal Diary 16Jan88 183(1) 7	45.5
12019. DISGUISED AS A NORMAL PERSON David Steinberg 23Jan71 182(1) 6	45.5
12020. THE TOWERING INFERNO Soundtrack 01Feb75 158(1) 3	45.5
12021. COUCHOIS Couchois 21Apr79 170(1) 4	45.4
12022. MARSALIS STANDARD TIME: VOL. 1 Wynton Marsalis 26Sep87 153(1) 5	45.4
12023. ONE BIG DAY Face To Face 18Jun88 176(1) 7	45.4
12024. MY MOVIE OF YOU Leif Garrett 12Dec81 185(1) 7	45.4
12025. CLOSE YOUR EYES Edward Bear 07Jul73 183(2) 6	45.4
12026. THE BEST OF THE BLUES BROTHERS Blues Brothers 09Jan82 143(2) 3	45.4
12027. I HAD IT ALL THE TIME Tyrone Davis 01Jul72 182(1) 6	45.4
12028. MIDNIGHT LOVE AFFAIR Carol Douglas 06Nov76 188(1) 6	45.4
12029. TAKE TEN Paul Desmond 28Dec63 129(1) 3	45.4
12030. SEARCH FOR THE NEW LAND Lee Morgan 26Nov66 143(2) 3	45.3
12031. "NOW APPEARING" AT OLE' MISS B.B. King 26Apr80 162(2) 4	45.3
12032. EVERYBODY WANTS SOME Gucci Crew II 23Sep89 173(1) 6	45.3
12033. WALK AWAY Matt Monro 13Mar65 126(1) 3	45.3
12034. MR. NATURAL Bee Gees 15Jun74 178(1) 5	45.3
12035. SHOUT IT OUT Patrice Rushen 16Apr77 164(1) 4	45.3
12036. ONE FOR THE MONEY The Whispers 28Aug76 189(1) 6	45.2
12037. LOVEJOY Albert King 03Jul71 188(1) 6	45.2
12038. THE ORBISON WAY Roy Orbison 05Mar66 128(1) 3	45.2
12039. BAJA MARIMBA BAND RIDES AGAIN Baja Marimba Band 24Apr65 123(1) 3	45.1
12040. THE YIDDISH ARE COMING! THE YIDDISH ARE COMING! Various Artists 14Oct67 165(1) 5	45.1
12041. LOVE YOUR MAN Rossington Band 16Jul88 140(1) 4	45.1
12042. 1980 B.T. Express 31May80 164(1) 4	45.1
12043. MY FAIR LADY Andre Previn 19Dec64 147(2) 4	45.1
12044. I LOVE YOU MORE TODAY Conway Twitty 16Aug69 161(1) 3	45.1
12045. U.S.A. FOR M.O.D. M.O.D. 07Nov87 153(2) 5	45.1
12046. DINNER AT THE RITZ City Boy 12Feb77 170(1) 4	45.1
12047. D'YA LIKE SCRATCHIN' Malcolm McLaren 18Feb84 173(2) 6	45.1
12048. MOTORTOWN REVIEW LIVE Various Artists 23Aug69 177(1) 5	45.0
12049. NO HEAVY PETTING UFO 19Jun76 169(1) 4	45.0
12050. THE BEST OF KANSAS Kansas 08Sep84 154(2) 5	45.0
12051. GLENN YARBROUGH SINGS THE ROD McKUEN SONGBOOK Glenn Yarbrough 10May69 189(2) 5	45.0
12052. GOODBYE GIRL David Gates 12Aug78 165(1) 4	44.9

Rank. Title Act Entry Peak(Pk Wks) TotWks	Scr
12053. BEWARE OF GREEKS BEARING GIFTS Various Artists 11Jan69 190(1) 6	44.9
12054. COUNTERFEIT Martin L. Gore 12Aug89 156(2) 5	44.9
12055. LISTEN TO THE WARM Rod McKuen 27Jan68 178(1) 6	44.8
12056. PRETTIES FOR YOU Alice Cooper 28Jun69 193(2) 6	44.8
12057. MISSA LUBA Les Troubadours Du Roi Baudouin 02Aug69 184(2) 5	44.8
12058. YOU & ME Jerry Butler 11Jul70 172(1) 4	44.8
12059. LIVE AT YANKEE STADIUM Various Artists 18Oct69 169(1) 4	44.8
12060. LOVE IS ALL WE HAVE TO GIVE Checkmates, LTD. 18Oct69 178(2) 4	44.8
12061. HOLLYWOOD SITUATION Hudson Brothers 07Dec74 176(2) 4	44.7
12062. WAR War 24Apr71 190(2) 6	44.7
12063. IN THE STRUGGLE FOR FREEDOM AND HUMAN DIGNITY Rev. Martin Luther King, Jr. 08Jun68 154(1) 3	44.7
12064. LIVE FOR LIFE Soundtrack 27Jan68 188(3) 7	44.7
12065. SON OF CACTUS New Cactus Band 12May73 183(1) 6	44.7
12066. NIGHTS (FEEL LIKE GETTING DOWN) Billy Ocean 25Jul81 152(1) 3	44.7
12067. LIVE OBLIVION, VOL. 2 Brian Auger's Oblivion Express 13Mar76 169(1) 4	44.6
12068. SOMETHIN' ELSE Danny Davis And The Nashville Brass 03Apr71 161(1) 3	44.6
12069. TOO TOUGH TO DIE The Ramones 03Nov84 171(1) 6	44.6
12070. O.C. SMITH'S GREATEST HITS O.C. Smith 19Sep70 177(2) 5	44.5
12071. CAN'T HELP FALLING IN LOVE Al Martino 11Apr70 184(1) 5	44.5
12072. MENLOVE AVENUE John Lennon 22Nov86 127(2) 4	44.5
12073. CRISS-CROSS Thelonious Monk 30Nov63 127(1) 3	44.5
12074. EVERYDAY, EVERYNIGHT Flora Purim 03Jun78 174(2) 4	44.4
12075. NIGHT FEVER Fatback Band 28Aug76 182(1) 5	44.4
12076. VERY GREASY David Lindley & El Rayo-X 24Sep88 174(1) 6	44.4
12077. THE LIVE KINKS The Kinks 09Sep67 162(1) 4	44.4
12078. FROM HERE TO ETERNALLY Spinners 26May79 165(1) 4	44.4
12079. I WROTE A SONG... Don Gibson 02Nov63 134(1) 3	44.4
12080. SO WHAT'S NEW? Horst Jankowski 03Dec66 107(2) 2	44.3
12081. ROBERT GOULET ON BROADWAY, VOLUME 2 Robert Goulet 11Mar67 145(1) 3	44.2
12082. CONFESSIN' THE BLUES Esther Phillips 31Jan76 170(1) 4	44.2
12083. DALLAS Floyd Cramer 24May80 170(1) 5	44.1
12084. ANCIENT DREAMS Candlemass 21Jan89 174(2) 6	44.1
12085. ESSENCE TO ESSENCE Donovan 02Feb74 174(1) 5	44.1
12086. NICE DAY FOR SOMETHING Lee Michaels 02Jun73 172(1) 5	44.1
12087. THE TURTLES' GREATEST HITS/HAPPY TOGETHER AGAIN The Turtles 21Dec74 194(2) 7	44.1
12088. THE MIGHTY QUINN Manfred Mann 01Jun68 176(1) 5	44.1
12089. PETER NERO-UP CLOSE Peter Nero 16Jul66 141(1) 3	44.0
12090. THERE'S GONNA BE A SHOWDOWN Archie Bell & The Drells 16Aug69 163(1) 3	44.0

Rank. Title Act Entry Peak(Pk Wks) TotWks	Scr
12091. WHERE'S THE PLAYGROUND SUSIE? Jerry Vale 05Jul69 180(1) 4	43.9
12092. JOY Percy Faith 01Apr72 176(1) 6	43.9
12093. EMERGE Litter 16Aug69 175(2) 5	43.9
12094. TOBY The Chi-Lites 13Jul74 181(1) 5	43.9
12095. INNER CONFLICTS Billy Cobham 03Jun78 172(2) 4	43.9
12096. FOR THE CHILDREN OF THE WORLD, ART LINKLETTER NARRATES "THE BIBLE..IN THE BEGINNING" Art Linkletter 31Dec66 143(2) 3	43.8
12097. THE GREAT SONGS! Nat King Cole 26Nov66 145(1) 3	43.8
12098. RUNNER Runner 23Jun79 167(2) 4	43.8
12099. FARRENHEIT Farrenheit 09May87 179(1) 7	43.8
12100. GRAND SLAM Spinners 08Jan83 167(2) 6	43.8
12101. ROMAN GODS The Fleshtones 06Mar82 174(3) 5	43.8
12102. YOUNGBLOOD Soundtrack 01Mar86 166(2) 6	43.7
12103. 3614 JACKSON HIGHWAY Cher 16Aug69 160(1) 3	43.7
12104. TYPICAL AMERICAN BOYS Mitchell Trio 01May65 130(1) 3	43.7
12105. I'LL SHARE MY WORLD WITH YOU George Jones 02Aug69 185(1) 5	43.7
12106. CHICAGO - GREATEST HITS, VOLUME II Chicago 12Dec81 171(2) 5	43.7
12107. PHOTOS OF GHOSTS Premiata Forneria Marconi 20Oct73 180(1) 6	43.6
12108. SILK & SOUL Nina Simone 25Nov67 158(1) 4	43.6
12109. FULLY EXPOSED Willie Hutch 13Oct73 183(2) 6	43.6
12110. HEAVY TRAFFIC Traffic 03May75 155(1) 3	43.6
12111. THE STONE PONEYS FEATURING LINDA RONSTADT Linda Ronstadt 14Jun75 172(2) 4	43.6
12112. SOMETHING SPECIAL! THE BEST OF TOMMY JAMES & THE SHONDELLS Tommy James And The Shondells 24Feb68 174(2) 5	43.6
12113. RESTLESS EYES Janis Ian 04Jul81 156(1) 3	43.5
12114. WHY NOT ME Fred Knoblock 04Oct80 179(1) 5	43.5
12115. PROFILES Nick Mason & Rick Fenn 31Aug85 154(2) 5	43.5
12116. THAT WAS ONLY YESTERDAY Gary Wright And Spooky Tooth 24Apr76 172(2) 4	43.5
12117. STOP Eric Burdon Band 09Aug75 171(1) 5	43.5
12118. CONSPICUOUS ONLY IN ITS ABSENCE Great Society With Grace Slick 04May68 166(1) 4	43.4
12119. APOLLO 11: FLIGHT TO THE MOON Various Artists 06Sep69 185(1) 5	43.4
12120. ROCK & ROLL ADULT Garland Jeffreys 31Oct81 163(2) 4	43.4
12121. GOODBYE AND HELLO Tim Buckley 04Nov67 171(2) 5	43.3
12122. TAKA BOOM Taka Boom 09Jun79 171(2) 4	43.3
12123. THE MUSIC LOVERS Ferrante & Teicher 08May71 172(1) 4	43.3
12124. WAITING ON YOU Brick 12Jul80 179(2) 5	43.3
12125. GHOST ON THE BEACH Insiders 10Oct87 167(1) 5	43.3
12126. FIVE MILES OUT Mike Oldfield 08May82 164(2) 5	43.3
12127. OCEANLINER Passport 05Apr80 163(1) 4	43.2
12128. SUITE FLUTE & JAZZ PIANO Jean-Pierre Rampal & Claude Bolling 31Jan76 173(1) 4	43.2
12129. CAPTAIN FINGERS Lee Ritenour 04Jun77 178(1) 5	43.2
12130. A BROKEN FRAME Depeche Mode 04Dec82 177(1) 8	43.2
12131. SMILE!/THE BEST OF TIM WEISBERG Tim Weisberg 09Jun79 169(2) 4	43.1
12132. IT AIN'T WHERE YOU BEEN Latimore 26Mar77 181(1) 5	43.1
12133. YEARBOOKS AND YESTERDAYS Jeannie C. Riley 15Mar69 187(2) 5	43.1
12134. MEMORIES OF AMERICA / ODE TO THE LITTLE BROWN SHACK OUT BACK Billy Edd Wheeler 13Feb65 132(1) 3	43.1
12135. EVERLASTING LOVE Rex Smith 22Aug81 167(2) 4	43.0
12136. GREAT CONTEMPORARY INSTRUMENTAL HITS Ray Conniff & His Orchestra & Chorus 11Sep71 185(1) 5	43.0
12137. BACCHANAL Gabor Szabo 15Jun68 157(1) 3	43.0
12138. CALLING Noel Pointer 16Aug80 167(1) 4	43.0
12139. TRANSITION Kenny Rogers & The First Edition 25Sep71 155(1) 3	43.0
12140. I WILL FOLLOW HIM Little Peggy March 17Aug63 139(1) 3	43.0
12141. NIGHTHAWKS The Nighthawks 26Jul80 166(1) 4	42.9
12142. DEAN FRIEDMAN Dean Friedman 04Jun77 192(2) 6	42.9
12143. GREATEST HITS, VOL. II Hank Williams Jr. 11Jan86 183(1) 8	42.9
12144. MADAME X Madame X 10Oct87 162(2) 5	42.9
12145. NOTHING SAYS I LOVE YOU LIKE I LOVE YOU Jerry Butler 13Jan79 160(1) 4	42.9
12146. ORCHESTRAL FAVORITES Frank Zappa 02Jun79 168(1) 4	42.8
12147. BRANDENBURG GATE: REVISITED Dave Brubeck Quartet 21Dec63 137(1) 3	42.8
12148. ALL THE PEOPLE ARE TALKIN' John Anderson 29Oct83 163(1) 5	42.8
12149. NOW HEAR THIS Moms Mabley 13Nov65 133(1) 3	42.7
12150. FEELINGS The Lettermen 26Jun71 192(2) 6	42.7
12151. OUT HERE Love 27Dec69 176(1) 5	42.7
12152. WITHOUT YOU IN MY LIFE Tyrone Davis 11Aug73 174(1) 6	42.7
12153. CONCERT IN STEREO/ LIVE AT THE SAHARA/TAHOE Ray Conniff & His Orchestra & Chorus 26Sep70 177(1) 5	42.6
12154. LET THERE BE LIGHT Underground Sunshine 08Nov69 161(1) 3	42.6
12155. BACK ON THE RIGHT TRACK Sly & The Family Stone 10Nov79 152(1) 3	42.6
12156. ANDY KIM'S GREATEST HITS Andy Kim 21Dec74 190(2) 6	42.5
12157. THERE MUST BE MORE TO LOVE THAN THIS Jerry Lee Lewis 30Jan71 190(1) 6	42.5
12158. PABLO CRUISE Pablo Cruise 16Aug75 174(2) 4	42.5
12159. LOVE FANTASY Roy Ayers 01Nov80 157(1) 3	42.4
12160. KISMET Mantovani 14Mar64 134(1) 3	42.4
12161. WORDS WE CAN DANCE TO Steve Goodman 15May76 175(1) 4	42.4
12162. MORE THAN EVER Blood, Sweat & Tears 31Jul76 165(2) 3	42.4
12163. FOLKSONGS FOR A NUCLEAR VILLAGE Shadowfax 14May88 168(2) 5	42.3
12164. HIGHER THAN HIGH Undisputed Truth 22Nov75 173(1) 4	42.3
12165. TREASURE CHEST Herbie Hancock 12Oct74 158(1) 3	42.3
12166. ONE WAY FEATURING AL HUDSON One Way Featuring Al Hudson 17Nov79 181(2) 5	42.3
12167. ALL OUT Grin 10Mar73 186(1) 7	42.3
12168. ACTING UP Marlena Shaw 08Apr78 171(1) 4	42.2
12169. SWEET TALKIN' GUY The Chiffons 20Aug66 149(1) 3	42.2
12170. RAMONES MANIA The Ramones 25Jun88 168(2) 5	42.2
12171. THE JOAN BAEZ BALLAD BOOK Joan Baez 16Dec72 188(1) 7	42.2
12172. NIGHTLINE Randy Crawford 05Nov83 164(1) 5	42.1
12173. INTRODUCING THE STYLE COUNCIL Style Council 22Oct83 172(1) 5	42.1
12174. THE NEW BEATLES SONG BOOK Hollyridge Strings 04Jun66 142(1) 3	42.1
12175. HOW HARD IT IS Big Brother And The Holding Company 04Sep71 157(1) 3	42.0
12176. THE STEVE HOWE ALBUM Steve Howe 16Feb80 164(1) 4	42.0
12177. THE McCARTNEY INTERVIEW Paul McCartney 31Jan81 158(2) 3	42.0
12178. CITADEL Starcastle 19Nov77 156(2) 3	42.0
12179. IMITATION LIFE Robin Lane & The Chartbusters 25Apr81 172(1) 4	41.9
12180. FEARLESS Hoyt Axton 10Apr76 171(1) 4	41.9
12181. THE OWL AND THE PUSSYCAT Barbra Streisand 06Feb71 186(1) 6	41.8
12182. THE SUN, MOON & HERBS Dr. John 09Oct71 184(1) 5	41.8
12183. CHAPTER THREE - VIVA EMILIANO ZAPATA Gato Barbieri 26Oct74 160(2) 3	41.8
12184. CLEAR SPOT Captain Beefheart & The Magic Band 23Dec72 191(2) 7	41.7
12185. THE FIRST 25 YEARS-THE SILVER ANNIVERSARY ALBUM Johnny Mathis 25Jul81 173(2) 4	41.6
12186. APPALOOSA Appaloosa 16Aug69 178(2) 4	41.6
12187. AMERICA IS 200 YEARS OLD...AND THERE'S STILL HOPE! Bob Hope 03Jul76 175(1) 4	41.6
12188. THE MUSIC FOR UNICEF CONCERT/ A GIFT OF SONG Various Artists 18Aug79 171(2) 4	41.5
12189. CONFESSIONS OF A POP GROUP Style Council 13Aug88 174(1) 6	41.5
12190. SIMPLY CARRIE Carrie Lucas 23Apr77 183(1) 5	41.4
12191. SPANISH STRINGS Enoch Light & The Light Brigade 22Apr67 163(1) 4	41.4
12192. THE RHYTHM & THE BLUES Z.Z. Hill 05Feb83 165(1) 5	41.4
12193. SUNSHINE DREAM Beach Boys 03Jul82 180(3) 6	41.4
12194. BORN IN AMERICA Riot 14Jan84 175(1) 6	41.4
12195. DANCE Gary Numan 24Oct81 167(1) 4	41.4
12196. THE ISLAND STORY, 1962-1987: THE 25TH ANNIVERSARY Various Artists 26Dec87 180(2) 6	41.4
12197. NAKED & WARM Bill Withers 06Nov76 169(1) 4	41.4
12198. DRACULA'S GREATEST HITS Various Artists 05Dec64 129(1) 3	41.4
12199. PAPER TIGER Sue Thompson 20Mar65 134(1) 3	41.3
12200. 1963-THE YEAR'S MOST POPULAR THEMES Enoch Light & The Light Brigade 02Nov63 133(1) 3	41.3
12201. THE BEST OF THE THOMPSON TWINS/GREATEST MIXES Thompson Twins 27Aug88 175(2) 6	41.3

Rank. Title Act Entry Peak(Pk Wks) TotWks	Scr
12202. MORE THAN MUSIC Mystic Moods Orch. 25Mar67 157(1) 4	41.3
12203. THE GREATEST OF THE GUESS WHO Guess Who 30Apr77 173(1) 4	41.3
12204. THE BEST OF BARBARA MANDRELL Barbara Mandrell 24Feb79 170(2) 4	41.3
12205. YOU ARE THE SUNSHINE OF MY LIFE Ray Conniff & His Orchestra & Chorus 07Jul73 176(2) 5	41.2
12206. PASSION, GRACE & FIRE Al Di Meola/ John McLaughlin/Paco De Lucia 20Aug83 171(2) 5	41.2
12207. FROM GENESIS TO REVELATION Genesis 12Oct74 170(1) 4	41.1
12208. DOWN HOME STYLE Brother Jack McDuff 13Dec69 192(1) 6	41.1
12209. SAMMY DAVIS JR. SALUTES THE STARS OF THE LONDON PALLADIUM Sammy Davis Jr. 14Mar64 139(1) 3	41.1
12210. POLTERGEIST Soundtrack 17Jul82 168(1) 5	41.1
12211. ELVIS: THE FIRST LIVE RECORDINGS Elvis Presley 17Mar84 163(1) 4	41.0
12212. SHADES Keith Jarrett 12Feb77 174(1) 4	40.9
12213. THE BEST OF NAT KING COLE Nat King Cole 14Sep68 187(2) 5	40.8
12214. ELECTRIC FOLKLORE LIVE The Alarm 29Oct88 167(2) 5	40.8
12215. FICKLE Michael Henderson 04Jun83 169(1) 5	40.8
12216. SOLITAIRE Andy Williams 17Nov73 185(1) 6	40.8
12217. MUTUAL ATTRACTION Sylvester 14Feb87 164(2) 5	40.7
12218. JESUS CHRIST, SUPERSTAR Percy Faith 18Dec71 186(1) 6	40.7
12219. MAN IS NOT ALONE Senator Everett McKinley Dirksen 05Aug67 148(1) 3	40.7
12220. DON RICKLES SPEAKS! Don Rickles 12Apr69 180(1) 4	40.7
12221. A BLOW FOR ME A TOOT TO YOU Fred Wesley & The Horny Horns 30Apr77 181(1) 5	40.7
12222. I LOVE YOU Billy Vaughn Singers 12Aug67 161(1) 5	40.6
12223. DANCIN' MAN Q 18Jun77 140(2) 2	40.6
12224. LIVE AT THE WHISKY A GO-GO ON THE FABULOUS SUNSET STRIP X 14May88 175(2) 5	40.6
12225. MONGREL Bob Seger System 31Oct70 171(1) 4	40.6
12226. ASHES ARE BURNING Renaissance 22Sep73 171(1) 4	40.6
12227. CHANGING HORSES Incredible String Band 06Dec69 166(1) 3	40.6
12228. YEH YEH Georgie Fame 01May65 137(1) 3	40.5
12229. OSIBIROCK Osibisa 28Sep74 175(1) 4	40.5
12230. INSIDE STRAIGHT "Cannonball" Adderley Quintet 29Sep73 179(1) 5	40.5
12231. THE NAT KING COLE SONG BOOK Hollyridge Strings 24Apr65 136(1) 3	40.5
12232. JUNK CULTURE Orchestral Manoeuvres In The Dark 24Nov84 182(3) 6	40.4
12233. "ALIVE" AGAIN...NATURALLY The Lettermen 23Jun73 193(2) 7	40.4
12234. FRONT PAGE NEWS Wishbone Ash 05Nov77 166(2) 4	40.4
12235. FROGS SPROUTS CLOGS AND KRAUTS The Rumour 04Aug79 160(2) 3	40.3
12236. TALK IT OVER IN THE MORNING Anne Murray 09Oct71 179(1) 4	40.3
12237. VICTIMS OF THE FUTURE Gary Moore 09Jun84 172(1) 5	40.3
12238. SOFTLY The Sandpipers 07Sep68 180(1) 5	40.2

Rank. Title Act Entry Peak(Pk Wks) TotWks	Scr
12239. FOR ALL THE SEASONS OF YOUR MIND Janis Ian 30Dec67 179(2) 5	40.2
12240. JOHN PRINE John Prine 26Feb72 154(1) 3	40.2
12241. THE BEST OF ROD McKUEN Rod McKuen 16Aug69 175(2) 4	40.2
12242. STUFF Stuff 27Nov76 163(1) 3	40.2
12243. THE PEOPLE WHO GRINNED THEMSELVES TO DEATH The Housemartins 16Jan88 177(1) 6	40.1
12244. BEAT & SOUL Everly Brothers 25Sep65 141(1) 3	40.1
12245. WALKING THE DOG Rufus Thomas 28Dec63 138(1) 3	40.1
12246. IT'S JUST A MATTER OF TIME Sonny James 11Apr70 177(1) 4	40.1
12247. WHEN THE NIGHT COMES Lou Rawls 14May83 163(1) 4	40.0
12248. BABY, I'M FOR REAL The Originals 17Jan70 174(1) 4	40.0
12249. TRIP TO HEAVEN Freddie Hart 22Sep73 188(1) 6	40.0
12250. HEY JOE, HEY MOE Moe Bandy & Joe Stampley 11Apr81 170(1) 4	40.0
12251. HIGH AND MIGHTY Uriah Heep 26Jun76 161(1) 3	40.0
12252. PUSH Bros 23Jul88 171(1) 5	40.0
12253. CONAN THE BARBARIAN Soundtrack 12Jun82 162(2) 5	39.9
12254. NEW AFFAIR The Emotions 26Sep81 168(2) 4	39.9
12255. VISIONS OF THE LITE Slave 15Jan83 177(1) 6	39.9
12256. BUT BEAUTIFUL Nancy Wilson 17Jul71 185(1) 5	39.8
12257. SLEEP DIRT Frank Zappa 17Feb79 175(2) 4	39.8
12258. MORE SONGS ABOUT LOVE & HATE The Godfathers 20May89 174(1) 6	39.8
12259. LOVE LIGHT Yutaka 11Jul81 174(1) 4	39.8
12260. WITCHDOCTOR Sidewinders 13May89 169(1) 5	39.8
12261. THE WAY TO BECOME THE SENSUOUS WOMAN BY "J" Various Artists 16Oct71 181(1) 4	39.8
12262. KNIFE Aztec Camera 13Oct84 175(2) 6	39.8
12263. WORD OF MOUTH Jaco Pastorius 15Aug81 161(2) 3	39.7
12264. FALLEN ANGEL Uriah Heep 04Nov78 186(2) 5	39.7
12265. THE WORLD OF LYNN ANDERSON Lynn Anderson 30Oct71 174(1) 4	39.7
12266. STANDING OVATION AT NEWPORT Herbie Mann 27Nov65 143(2) 3	39.6
12267. OUT OF THE STORM Jack Bruce 07Dec74 160(1) 3	39.6
12268. THE LAND OF RAPE AND HONEY Ministry 05Nov88 164(2) 4	39.6
12269. FATHER & SON Hank Williams Sr. & Hank Williams Jr. 07Aug65 139(1) 3	39.6
12270. FROM A CHILD TO A WOMAN Julio Iglesias 01Sep84 181(1) 6	39.6
12271. BELO HORIZONTE John McLaughlin 12Dec81 172(3) 4	39.6
12272. RAIN DOGS Tom Waits 16Nov85 181(2) 7	39.5
12273. INTUITION Linx 20Jun81 175(1) 4	39.5
12274. BIRDS OF A FEATHER Jack Blanchard & Misty Morgan 04Jul70 185(1) 5	39.5
12275. THOSE GLORIOUS MGM MUSICALS: SHOW BOAT/ANNIE GET YOUR GUN Soundtrack 15Sep73 184(1) 6	39.4

Rank. Title Act Entry Peak(Pk Wks) TotWks	Scr
12276. THE DUKE AT TANGLEWOOD Duke Ellington/Boston Pops Orchestra/Arthur Fiedler 14May66 145(1) 3	39.4
12277. FRIEND Freddie North 01Jan72 179(2) 5	39.4
12278. ATTACKING A STRAW MAN New Colony Six 01Nov69 179(1) 4	39.4
12279. DANCE PARTY Martha & The Vandellas 29May65 139(1) 3	39.3
12280. SUNDOWN Rank And File 07May83 165(1) 5	39.3
12281. INSIDE LOOKIN' OUT Junior 23Jul83 177(1) 6	39.3
12282. HERE COMES THE NIGHT David Johansen 11Jul81 160(1) 3	39.3
12283. HISTORY OF RHYTHM & BLUES, VOLUME 2/THE GOLDEN YEARS 1953-55 Various Artists 30Mar68 173(1) 5	39.3
12284. RAY CHARLES LIVE Ray Charles 19May73 182(2) 5	39.3
12285. BIG CIRCUMSTANCE Bruce Cockburn 25Feb89 182(1) 7	39.3
12286. IN LOVE Cheryl Lynn 19Jan80 167(1) 4	39.3
12287. MEMPHIS BEAT Jerry Lee Lewis 14May66 145(1) 3	39.2
12288. GREATEST HITS 1979-1990 Dionne Warwick 23Dec89 177(1) 7	39.2
12289. YOU GOT WHAT IT TAKES Dave Clark Five 12Aug67 149(1) 3	39.2
12290. ALL I NEED Sylvester 19Mar83 168(2) 5	39.2
12291. BAD ENUFF Slave 22Oct83 168(1) 5	39.2
12292. THE VICTORS Soundtrack 04Jan64 145(1) 3	39.1
12293. BUYING A BOOK Joe Tex 19Jul69 190(1) 5	39.1
12294. FOXY BROWN Willie Hutch 18May74 179(1) 4	39.1
12295. MUD WILL BE FLUNG TONIGHT! Bette Midler 21Dec85 183(1) 6	39.1
12296. 3 SHIPS Jon Anderson 28Dec85 166(2) 5	39.1
12297. TENDERNESS Ohio Players 11Apr81 165(2) 3	39.0
12298. WINDMILLS OF YOUR MIND Jimmie Rodgers 30Aug69 183(2) 4	39.0
12299. ELECTRIC COFFEY Dennis Coffey 20Jan73 189(2) 6	39.0
12300. HOROWITZ ON TELEVISION Vladimir Horowitz 16Nov68 185(1) 4	39.0
12301. SWEET SURRENDER Margie Joseph 17Aug74 165(1) 3	39.0
12302. TOO MUCH PRESSURE The Selecter 03May80 175(1) 4	39.0
12303. THE VERY BEST OF RAY STEVENS Ray Stevens 27Dec75 173(1) 4	38.9
12304. BILL & TED'S EXCELLENT ADVENTURE Soundtrack 08Apr89 170(2) 4	38.9
12305. COME DANCING WITH THE KINKS/THE BEST OF THE KINKS 1977-1986 The Kinks 19Jul86 159(1) 4	38.8
12306. BOOTS WITH BRASS Boots Randolph 09Jan71 168(1) 3	38.8
12307. IN LOVE Bunny Debarge 14Mar87 172(2) 5	38.8
12308. AMAZON BEACH The Kings 26Sep81 170(1) 4	38.8
12309. TAP Soundtrack 11Mar89 166(2) 4	38.8
12310. WHITE NOISE Jay Ferguson 17Apr82 178(3) 5	38.8
12311. 16 GREATEST HITS James Gang 08Dec73 181(1) 5	38.7
12312. QUEENS OF NOISE The Runaways 05Feb77 172(1) 4	38.7

Rank. Title Act Entry Peak(Pk Wks) TotWks	Scr
12313. **HOT ROD HOOTENANNY** Various Artists 15Feb64 138(1) 3	38.7
12314. **THE KING FAMILY ALBUM** King Family 02Oct65 142(1) 3	38.7
12315. **LITTLE JOHNNY FROM DOWN THE STREET** Wilburn Brothers 28Mar70 143(2) 2	38.7
12316. **THE GREAT AMERICAN EAGLE TRAGEDY** Earth Opera 22Mar69 181(1) 4	38.7
12317. **DISCO GARDENS** Shalamar 04Nov78 171(1) 4	38.7
12318. **DAVID JONES** Davy Jones 27May67 185(1) 6	38.6
12319. **BURNING FOR YOU** Strawbs 06Aug77 175(1) 4	38.6
12320. **RESCUE** Clarence Clemons 05Nov83 174(1) 5	38.6
12321. **CRISTOFORI'S DREAM** David Lanz 05Nov88 180(1) 6	38.6
12322. **ACT LIKE NOTHING'S WRONG** Al Kooper 08Jan77 182(2) 5	38.6
12323. **BRIAN HYLAND** Brian Hyland 30Jan71 171(1) 4	38.6
12324. **SASSY SOUL STRUT** Lou Donaldson 22Sep73 176(2) 4	38.6
12325. **V** Zapp 07Oct89 154(2) 4	38.5
12326. **WELCOME TWO MISSOURI** Missouri 23Jun79 174(1) 4	38.5
12327. **CHARLIE RICH SINGS THE SONGS OF HANK WILLIAMS & OTHERS** Charlie Rich 19Oct74 177(1) 4	38.5
12328. **OZARK MOUNTAIN DAREDEVILS** Ozark Mountain Daredevils 24May80 170(1) 4	38.5
12329. **BACK IN '72** Bob Seger 03Mar73 188(2) 6	38.5
12330. **THE NEED TO BE** Esther Satterfield 24Jul76 180(1) 4	38.5
12331. **LITTLE DREAMER** Peter Green 25Oct80 186(1) 5	38.4
12332. **AFTERNOONS IN UTOPIA** Alphaville 30Aug86 174(1) 6	38.4
12333. **VERTICAL SMILES** Blackfoot 27Oct84 176(3) 5	38.4
12334. **WHY YOU BEEN GONE SO LONG** Johnny Darrell 06Sep69 172(1) 3	38.4
12335. **WHITE MANSIONS** Various Artists 22Jul78 181(3) 4	38.3
12336. **IF 3** If 25Sep71 171(2) 3	38.3
12337. **MANTOVANI IN CONCERT** Mantovani 07Nov70 167(1) 3	38.3
12338. **HEAR! HERE!** The Hollies 12Feb66 145(1) 3	38.3
12339. **DAVE GRUSIN AND THE NY/LA DREAM BAND** Dave Grusin 16Apr83 181(1) 6	38.2
12340. **KOOPER SESSION** Al Kooper/Shuggie Otis 24Jan70 182(1) 5	38.2
12341. **LE CHAT BLEU** Mink De Ville 13Sep80 163(2) 3	38.2
12342. **NIGHT ATTACK** Angel City 20Mar82 174(1) 5	38.2
12343. **BRASS CONSTRUCTION IV** Brass Construction 18Nov78 174(1) 4	38.2
12344. **IT'S IN EVERYONE OF US** Mary Travers 11Mar78 186(1) 5	38.2
12345. **THREE QUARTETS** Chick Corea 01Aug81 179(2) 4	38.2
12346. **TONY JOE WHITE** Tony Joe White 06Mar71 167(1) 4	38.1
12347. **THE CORE OF ROCK** Various Artists 13Jun70 175(2) 4	38.1
12348. **THE ORIGINAL HUMAN BEING** Blue Cheer 07Nov70 188(1) 5	38.1
12349. **IN STYLE** David Johansen 29Sep79 177(2) 4	38.0
12350. **GORME COUNTRY STYLE** Eydie Gorme 15Feb64 143(1) 3	38.0
12351. **SIRIUS** Clannad 05Mar88 183(2) 5	38.0
12352. **LIVE SHOTS** Joe Ely 24Oct81 159(2) 3	38.0
12353. **SALUTE** Gordon Lightfoot 13Aug83 175(1) 5	38.0
12354. **OUTRAGEOUS** Richard Pryor 08Sep79 176(2) 4	38.0
12355. **THE BEST OF SOLOMON BURKE** Solomon Burke 31Jul65 141(1) 3	38.0
12356. **I'D LIKE TO TEACH THE WORLD TO SING** Edwin Hawkins Singers 27May72 171(1) 4	38.0
12357. **HITS MADE FAMOUS BY ELVIS PRESLEY** Hollyridge Strings 13Feb65 144(2) 3	38.0
12358. **SWITCH V** Switch 21Nov81 174(2) 4	37.9
12359. **THREE'S A CROWD** The Tarney/Spencer Band 29Jul78 174(1) 4	37.9
12360. **LEGENDS OF THE LOST AND FOUND - NEW GREATEST STORIES LIVE** Harry Chapin 27Oct79 163(1) 3	37.8
12361. **BIG FUN** Inner City 24Jun89 162(2) 4	37.8
12362. **RECYCLING THE BLUES & OTHER RELATED STUFF** Taj Mahal 04Nov72 177(2) 4	37.8
12363. **AMANDLA** Miles Davis 17Jun89 177(2) 5	37.8
12364. **JUST THE TWO OF US** Porter Wagoner and Dolly Parton 22Mar69 184(1) 4	37.8
12365. **WAYNE COCHRAN!** Wayne Cochran 30Mar68 167(1) 4	37.8
12366. **SUNDAY NIGHT AT THE MOVIES** Brass Ring featuring Phil Bodner 15Apr67 157(1) 3	37.8
12367. **NO EASY WALK TO FREEDOM** Peter, Paul & Mary 14Mar87 173(2) 5	37.8
12368. **IT HAPPENED ONE BITE** Dan Hicks 25Mar78 165(2) 3	37.8
12369. **THE FLYING NUN** Sally Field 23Dec67 172(1) 4	37.7
12370. **FOLK 'N ROLL** Jan & Dean 15Jan66 145(2) 3	37.7
12371. **NEW FEELIN'** Liza Minnelli 28Nov70 158(1) 3	37.7
12372. **PEACH MELBA** Melba Moore 05Jul75 176(2) 4	37.6
12373. **PAUL DAVIS** Paul Davis 26Apr80 173(2) 4	37.6
12374. **THE ATLANTIC YEARS** Roxy Music 21Jan84 183(2) 6	37.6
12375. **ENGLISH HITS OF '65** Billy Strange 03Jul65 146(2) 3	37.5
12376. **ONLY LIFE** The Feelies 19Nov88 173(2) 5	37.5
12377. **WHAT THE WORLD IS COMIN' TO** Dexter Wansel 30Apr77 168(1) 3	37.5
12378. **MIRROR** Emitt Rhodes 27Nov71 182(1) 4	37.4
12379. **DUSTY** Dusty Springfield 05Dec64 136(1) 3	37.4
12380. **ROCK AND ROLL DIARY 1967-1980** Lou Reed 20Dec80 178(3) 4	37.4
12381. **GREATEST HITS** Dave Dee, Dozy, Beaky, Mick And Tich 05Aug67 155(2) 3	37.4
12382. **STAND BY ME** Spyder Turner 25Mar67 158(2) 3	37.4
12383. **HEY!** Julio Iglesias 01Sep84 179(1) 6	37.4
12384. **THE BEST OF JOE TEX** Joe Tex 02Sep67 168(1) 4	37.4
12385. **BILL BLACK'S COMBO GOES BIG BAND** Bill Black's Combo 28Nov64 139(2) 3	37.3
12386. **BLUE VALENTINE** Tom Waits 18Nov78 181(2) 4	37.3
12387. **TIM** The Replacements 01Feb86 183(1) 7	37.3
12388. **BLACK MAGIC WOMAN** Percy Faith 31Jul71 184(1) 5	37.3
12389. **YIPES!!** Yipes!! 06Oct79 177(1) 4	37.3
12390. **TEN LITTLE BOTTLES** Johnny Bond 29May65 142(1) 3	37.2
12391. **MARVIN GAYE/GREATEST HITS, VOL. 2** Marvin Gaye 30Sep67 178(1) 5	37.2
12392. **KALYAN** Kalyan 16Apr77 173(1) 4	37.1
12393. **HEAVY HITS!** Various Artists 09Aug69 151(1) 2	37.1
12394. **FARTHER ALONG** Spirit 31Jul76 179(1) 4	37.1
12395. **GREATEST HITS** Dave & Sugar 07Mar81 179(2) 4	37.1
12396. **RICH IN LONDON** Buddy Rich 20May72 180(1) 5	37.1
12397. **TENDER TOGETHERNESS** Stanley Turrentine 10Oct81 162(2) 3	37.1
12398. **SHAME SHAME SHAME** Shirley (And Company) 02Aug75 169(2) 3	37.1
12399. **LIKE IT IS, WAS AND EVERMORE SHALL BE** Donovan 06Apr68 177(2) 4	37.0
12400. **PREPPIE** Cheryl Lynn 28Apr84 161(1) 5	37.0
12401. **THE WORLD OF TAMMY WYNETTE** Tammy Wynette 15Aug70 145(1) 2	37.0
12402. **ST-11261** Brewer And Shipley 11May74 185(1) 5	37.0
12403. **THE MOST EXCITING ORGAN EVER** Billy Preston 12Jun65 143(2) 3	37.0
12404. **TONGUE IN CHIC** Chic 04Dec82 173(2) 6	36.9
12405. **PECULIAR FRIENDS** Ten Wheel Drive With Genya Ravan 19Jun71 190(1) 5	36.9
12406. **NEW BEGINNINGS** The Dells 23Sep78 169(2) 3	36.9
12407. **VISAGE** Visage 08Aug81 178(2) 4	36.9
12408. **IF YOU'RE EVER IN TEXAS** Freddy Fender 06Nov76 170(2) 3	36.9
12409. **THE BEST OF EDDY ARNOLD, VOLUME II** Eddy Arnold 30May70 146(2) 2	36.8
12410. **LIVE AND LOWDOWN AT THE APOLLO VOL 1** James Brown 22Nov80 163(2) 3	36.8
12411. **PROFILE II: THE BEST OF EMMYLOU HARRIS** Emmylou Harris 06Oct84 176(1) 6	36.8
12412. **VELVET VOICES AND BOLD BRASS** Anita Kerr Singers 20Sep69 172(1) 3	36.8
12413. **THE BLACK MESSIAH** Cannonball Adderley 26Feb72 167(1) 3	36.8
12414. **IT'S NOW WINTERS DAY** Tommy Roe 22Apr67 159(2) 3	36.7
12415. **SWITCHED-ON BACHARACH** Christopher Scott 04Oct69 175(1) 3	36.7
12416. **MYSTERY WALK** M + M 28Jul84 163(2) 4	36.7
12417. **WHAT IF** Dixie Dregs 27May78 182(2) 4	36.6
12418. **NO FREE LUNCH** Green On Red 03May86 177(1) 6	36.6
12419. **RAP'S GREATEST HITS, VOLUME 2** Various Artists 02May87 167(1) 4	36.6
12420. **RED SAILS IN THE SUNSET** Midnight Oil 03Aug85 177(2) 6	36.6
12421. **THE ALLMAN BROTHERS BAND** Allman Brothers Band 24Jan70 188(1) 5	36.5
12422. **HAIR** Original London Cast 10May69 186(1) 4	36.5
12423. **THE YOUNGEST TEENAGER** Moms Mabley 06Sep69 173(1) 3	36.5
12424. **THE EMPIRE STRIKES BACK/ THE ADVENTURES OF LUKE SKYWALKER** Soundtrack 06Sep80 178(2) 4	36.5
12425. **ANOTHER HIT ALBUM!** Billy Vaughn And His Orchestra 29Aug64 141(2) 3	36.5
12426. **UNDERGROUND** Electric Prunes 02Sep67 172(2) 4	36.4
12427. **THE BEATLES ALBUM** Percy Faith 17Oct70 179(1) 4	36.4
12428. **FABLES** Jean-Luc Ponty 02Nov85 166(2) 4	36.4
12429. **MORE SOUNDS OF WASHINGTON SQUARE** Village Stompers 25Apr64 139(1) 3	36.4

Rank. Title Act	Entry Peak(Pk Wks) TotWks	Scr
12430. **THE WOMACK "LIVE"** Bobby Womack	17Apr71 188(1) 5	36.3
12431. **CHILD OF CLAY** Jimmie Rodgers	06Jan68 162(1) 4	36.3
12432. **CRUSADER** Saxon	14Apr84 174(2) 5	36.3
12433. **DISCOVERY** Larry Carlton	01Aug87 180(1) 6	36.3
12434. **THE WONDER OF YOU** The Sandpipers	10May69 194(2) 5	36.3
12435. **POINT BLANK** Point Blank	11Sep76 175(3) 3	36.3
12436. **BRANDED MAN** Merle Haggard And The Strangers	21Oct67 167(1) 4	36.3
12437. **DOING HIS THING** Ray Charles	26Jul69 172(1) 3	36.3
12438. **SOUVENIR D'ITALIE** Robert Goulet	06Sep69 174(2) 3	36.2
12439. **SWEET EVIL** Derringer	19Feb77 169(1) 3	36.2
12440. **THICK AS THIEVES** Trooper	26Aug78 182(2) 4	36.2
12441. **THE AMERICAN DREAM** Rev. Martin Luther King, Jr.	18May68 173(1) 4	36.2
12442. **T-REX** T. Rex	01May71 188(1) 5	36.1
12443. **WALKING WILD** New England	18Jul81 176(2) 4	36.1
12444. **WILMER & THE DUKES** Wilmer & The Dukes	16Aug69 173(1) 3	36.1
12445. **NEW BEGINNINGS...** Morgana King	27Oct73 184(1) 5	36.0
12446. **FOLLIES IN CONCERT** Original Cast	25Jan86 181(2) 6	36.0
12447. **THE SEEKERS** The Seekers	05Jun65 145(1) 3	36.0
12448. **2010** Soundtrack	02Feb85 173(2) 5	36.0
12449. **CIRCUS** Argent	29Mar75 171(2) 3	35.9
12450. **FEELIN' ALRIGHT** Mongo Santamaria	11Apr70 171(2) 3	35.8
12451. **SHE UNDERSTANDS ME** Johnny Tillotson	06Feb65 148(1) 3	35.8
12452. **FIREFLY** Uriah Heep	30Apr77 166(1) 3	35.8
12453. **BANDSTAND** Family	28Oct72 183(1) 5	35.7
12454. **A TIME FOR US** Jack Jones	16Aug69 183(2) 4	35.7
12455. **MY TOOT-TOOT** Rockin' Sidney	24Aug85 166(3) 4	35.7
12456. **BACK AGAIN** The Bachelors	07Nov64 142(2) 3	35.7
12457. **HOOKED ON ROCK CLASSICS** London Symphony Orchestra	05Mar83 145(2) 3	35.7
12458. **SOUL EXPLOSION** Various Artists	05Apr69 172(1) 3	35.7
12459. **LIFE** Sly & The Family Stone	07Dec68 195(2) 5	35.6
12460. **CAREER GIRLS** Peter Nero	29May65 147(1) 3	35.6
12461. **THE GREETING** McCoy Tyner	14Oct78 170(1) 3	35.6
12462. **CHRISTINE** Soundtrack	21Jan84 177(1) 5	35.6
12463. **THE BEATLES VS. THE FOUR SEASONS** The Beatles/Four Seasons	10Oct64 142(1) 3	35.6
12464. **SUPER COUNTRY** Danny Davis And The Nashville Brass	18Sep71 184(1) 4	35.6
12465. **THE CARPETBAGGERS** Soundtrack	05Sep64 141(1) 3	35.6
12466. **ACCEPT NO SUBSTITUTE - THE ORIGINAL DELANEY & BONNIE & FRIENDS** Delaney & Bonnie & Friends	26Jul69 175(1) 3	35.6
12467. **ALL I EVER MEANT TO DO WAS SING** Johnny Rodriguez	27Oct73 174(1) 4	35.5
12468. **SONG PAINTER** Mac Davis	19Oct74 182(1) 4	35.5
12469. **TOGETHER IN CONCERT** Pete Seeger/Arlo Guthrie	17May75 181(1) 4	35.4
12470. **THE GREAT OTIS REDDING SINGS SOUL BALLADS** Otis Redding	10Apr65 147(1) 3	35.3
12471. **THE GODZ** The Godz	08Apr78 191(2) 5	35.3
12472. **THE FABULOUS RHINESTONES** Fabulous Rhinestones	29Jul72 193(1) 6	35.3
12473. **JUMPIN' JACK FLASH** Soundtrack	22Nov86 159(2) 4	35.3
12474. **TOMMY PAGE** Tommy Page	06May89 166(2) 5	35.3
12475. **DARKLANDS** Jesus And Mary Chain	17Oct87 161(2) 4	35.3
12476. **BEST OF SCORPIONS** Scorpions	17Nov79 180(3) 4	35.3
12477. **LICENSE TO KILL** Malice	11Apr87 177(2) 6	35.3
12478. **FLETCH** Soundtrack	27Jul85 160(1) 4	35.2
12479. **THE FIRE STILL BURNS** Russ Ballard	03Aug85 166(2) 4	35.2
12480. **SECOND TIME AROUND** The Kinks	20Sep80 177(1) 4	35.2
12481. **ANIMATION** Jon Anderson	03Jul82 176(1) 5	35.2
12482. **LOVERS** Mickey Newbury	05Apr75 172(2) 3	35.2
12483. **SURFIN' M.O.D.** M.O.D.	17Sep88 186(2) 6	35.1
12484. **BECKET** Soundtrack	09May64 147(2) 3	35.1
12485. **KING OF THE BLUES GUITAR** Albert King	01Mar69 194(1) 5	35.0
12486. **BIG BROTHER & THE HOLDING COMPANY(2)** Big Brother And The Holding Company	15May71 185(1) 4	35.0
12487. **CHANGES** The Monkees	08Nov86 152(1) 4	34.9
12488. **ROUND TRIP** Gap Band	09Dec89 189(2) 7	34.9
12489. **WILDER** Teardrop Explodes	06Feb82 176(3) 4	34.9
12490. **HARD** Gang Of Four	08Oct83 168(1) 4	34.9
12491. **ROUND #1** Frank Sinatra	04Jan75 170(1) 3	34.9
12492. **WONDERS OF THE WINE** David Houston	26Sep70 170(2) 3	34.9
12493. **BECOMING** Lori Lieberman	18Aug73 192(2) 6	34.9
12494. **SPIRIT OF PLACE** Goanna	25Jun83 179(1) 5	34.9
12495. **THEMBI** Pharoah Sanders	31Jul71 175(1) 3	34.9
12496. **NEW VALUES** Iggy Pop	06Oct79 180(2) 4	34.8
12497. **FIYO ON THE BAYOU** Neville Brothers	29Aug81 166(1) 3	34.8
12498. **WEE TAM** Incredible String Band	22Mar69 174(1) 3	34.8
12499. **WE'VE GOT A LIVE ONE HERE** Commander Cody & His Lost Planet Airmen	31Jul76 170(1) 3	34.8
12500. **JERRY BUTLER SINGS ASSORTED SOUNDS** Jerry Butler	06Feb71 186(1) 4	34.8
12501. **THE STORY OF BONNIE & CLYDE** Flatt & Scruggs	06Jul68 187(1) 5	34.8
12502. **DOIN' OUR THING** Booker T. & The MG's	18May68 176(1) 4	34.8
12503. **DANCING IN THE SUN** George Howard	27Jul85 169(2) 4	34.7
12504. **JUST A SINGER** Lobo	10Aug74 183(1) 4	34.7
12505. **RENAISSANCE** The Miracles	02Jun73 174(1) 4	34.7
12506. **PASTORALE** Rod McKuen	20Mar71 182(1) 4	34.7
12507. **THE BLUE MASK** Lou Reed	27Feb82 169(1) 4	34.6
12508. **HONKY TONK HEROES** Waylon Jennings	11Aug73 185(1) 5	34.6
12509. **NICK MASON'S FICTITIOUS SPORTS** Nick Mason	04Jul81 170(2) 3	34.6
12510. **MUSIC OF A PEOPLE** Stanley Black With The London Festival Orchestra And Chorus	12Jun65 148(2) 3	34.5
12511. **TWO WHEELS GOOD** Prefab Sprout	02Nov85 178(1) 5	34.5
12512. **ALL MIXED UP** Alexander O'Neal	25Feb89 185(2) 5	34.5
12513. **HANG TOGETHER** Odyssey	14Jun80 181(1) 4	34.5
12514. **THE BIG EXPRESS** XTC	10Nov84 178(1) 5	34.4
12515. **RADIO DREAM** Roger Voudouris	07Jul79 171(2) 3	34.4
12516. **BIDDU ORCHESTRA** Biddu Orchestra	21Feb76 170(1) 3	34.4
12517. **FRESH AIR** Julius Wechter and the Baja Marimba Band	18Oct69 176(1) 3	34.4
12518. **PRETTY THINGS COME IN TWOS** Tony Sandler And Ralph Young	05Jul69 188(1) 4	34.3
12519. **TOTALLY OUT OF CONTROL** Hudson Brothers	30Nov74 179(1) 4	34.3
12520. **WARM AND WONDERFUL** Bert Kaempfert And His Orchestra	29Mar69 194(1) 5	34.2
12521. **SAYIN' SOMETHING!** Peaches & Herb	12Sep81 168(2) 3	34.2
12522. **FROM DISCO TO LOVE** Van McCoy	16Aug75 181(1) 4	34.1
12523. **MEXICAN TRIP** Mystic Moods Orchestra	25Nov67 164(1) 3	34.1
12524. **1969** Soundtrack	17Dec88 186(1) 6	34.0
12525. **THE VERY BEST OF DAVE MASON** Dave Mason	28Oct78 179(1) 4	34.0
12526. **STANKY BROWN** Stanky Brown Group	29Apr78 192(2) 5	33.9
12527. **RUN FOR YOUR LIFE** The Tarney/Spencer Band	12May79 181(1) 4	33.9
12528. **YES, GIORGIO** Luciano Pavarotti	06Nov82 158(2) 3	33.8
12529. **HISTORY OF RHYTHM & BLUES, VOLUME 4/THE BIG BEAT 1958-60** Various Artists	06Apr68 180(1) 4	33.8
12530. **SERIOUS** Deja	05Dec87 186(1) 6	33.7
12531. **THE 7TH DAWN** Soundtrack	17Oct64 148(1) 3	33.7
12532. **SHADDAP YOU FACE** Joe Dolce	27Jun81 181(2) 4	33.7
12533. **FLAUNT THE IMPERFECTION** China Crisis	01Jun85 171(1) 4	33.7
12534. **THE STATLER BROTHERS CHRISTMAS CARD** Statler Brothers	16Dec78 183(3) 4	33.6
12535. **LYNDON JOHNSON'S LONELY HEARTS CLUB BAND** Various Artists	20Jan68 176(2) 5	33.6
12536. **FOLLIES** Original Cast	05Jun71 172(1) 3	33.6
12537. **GLORIOUS** Gloria Gaynor	19Mar77 183(1) 4	33.5
12538. **RUNAWAY** Bill Champlin	06Feb82 178(3) 4	33.5
12539. **MIDNIGHT DIAMOND** Dobie Gray	17Feb79 174(1) 4	33.5
12540. **WELL KEPT SECRET** James Last	16Aug75 172(1) 3	33.5
12541. **ON THE MOVE** Tony Sandler And Ralph Young	15Apr67 166(2) 3	33.5
12542. **TWO'S COMPANY** Aztec Two Step	25Dec76 181(2) 4	33.5
12543. **THE BEST OF KING CURTIS** King Curtis	21Dec68 190(1) 4	33.4

Rank. Title Act	Entry Peak(Pk Wks) TotWks	Scr
12544. THE GOOD THINGS IN LIFE Tony Bennett	09Dec72 196(3) 6	33.4
12545. THE ORIGINAL MONSTER MASH Bobby Pickett	29Sep73 173(1) 4	33.4
12546. GIANT The Woodentops	20Sep86 185(1) 6	33.4
12547. TIME IN A BOTTLE/JIM CROCE'S GREATEST LOVE SONGS Jim Croce	26Feb77 170(1) 3	33.4
12548. A REAL LIVE DOLLY Dolly Parton	15Aug70 154(2) 2	33.3
12549. THE BALLAD OF SALLY ROSE Emmylou Harris	25May85 171(2) 4	33.3
12550. THE RIGHT COMBINATION Linda Clifford & Curtis Mayfield	19Jul80 180(2) 4	33.3
12551. TIME FOR LIVIN' Young Americans	19Apr69 178(1) 3	33.3
12552. AMNESIA Richard Thompson	05Nov88 182(2) 5	33.2
12553. SUMMER OF '42 Tony Bennett	19Feb72 182(2) 4	33.2
12554. MIDNIGHT ON THE WATER David Bromberg	12Jul75 173(2) 3	33.2
12555. BEST BITS Roger Daltrey	27Mar82 185(2) 5	33.1
12556. THE BEST OF THE WHISPERS The Whispers	13Mar82 180(1) 5	33.1
12557. LYDIA PENSE & COLD BLOOD Cold Blood	13Mar76 179(1) 4	33.1
12558. CHRISTMAS WITH SLIM WHITMAN Slim Whitman	13Dec80 184(2) 4	33.1
12559. INCREDIBLE! LIVE! Country Joe McDonald	19Feb72 179(2) 4	33.1
12560. HANK CRAWFORD'S BACK Hank Crawford	29Jan77 167(1) 3	33.0
12561. GEORGES BIZET: CARMEN Leontyne Price	31Oct64 147(1) 3	33.0
12562. I'M IN LOVE WITH YOU Detroit Emeralds	21Apr73 181(1) 4	33.0
12563. MORE 50 GUITARS IN LOVE 50 Guitars of Tommy Garrett	08Jul67 168(2) 3	33.0
12564. ONE MORE TIME Wayne Newton	01Jun68 186(1) 5	33.0
12565. URBAN BEACHES Cactus World News	09Aug86 179(1) 5	33.0
12566. VICTORY Larry Graham	30Jul83 173(1) 4	33.0
12567. ROCK & ROLL REBELS John Kay & Steppenwolf	26Sep87 171(1) 4	32.9
12568. THE BIG HUGE Incredible String Band	22Mar69 180(1) 3	32.9
12569. MEDICINE SHOW Dream Syndicate	04Aug84 171(1) 4	32.8
12570. THE BEST OF CARLA THOMAS Carla Thomas	19Jul69 190(1) 4	32.8
12571. PIED PIPER Dave Valentin	08Aug81 184(3) 4	32.8
12572. ON A NIGHT LIKE THIS Buckwheat Zydeco	14Nov87 172(1) 5	32.7
12573. JUST BETWEEN US Gerald Albright	27Feb88 181(2) 5	32.7
12574. CASTLES IN THE SAND David Allan Coe	09Jul83 179(1) 5	32.7
12575. DON'T FOLLOW ME, I'M LOST TOO Pearl Harbor	21Feb81 170(2) 3	32.7
12576. THE NIGHT THE LIGHTS WENT OUT IN GEORGIA Soundtrack	22Aug81 189(1) 5	32.7
12577. MELLOW YELLOW Odell Brown & The Organ-Izers	09Sep67 173(1) 4	32.7
12578. SOULSHAKE Peggy Scott & Jo Jo Benson	01Mar69 196(1) 5	32.6
12579. GREATEST HITS Juice Newton	21Jul84 178(2) 5	32.6
12580. FRIDAY ON MY MIND The Easybeats	10Jun67 180(1) 5	32.6
12581. THE CAROL DOUGLAS ALBUM Carol Douglas	29Mar75 177(1) 3	32.6
12582. FOREVER, REX SMITH Rex Smith	12Jan80 165(1) 3	32.5
12583. A COUNTRY CHRISTMAS Various Artists	25Dec82 172(2) 4	32.3
12584. LIFE (IS SO STRANGE) War	23Jul83 164(1) 4	32.3
12585. ESQUIRE Esquire	28Mar87 165(2) 4	32.3
12586. SLOW DOWN WORLD Donovan	05Jun76 174(1) 3	32.3
12587. WELCOME TO THE DANCE Sons Of Champlin	09Jun73 186(1) 5	32.3
12588. THE HUNTER Ike & Tina Turner	22Nov69 176(1) 3	32.3
12589. SOLID GOLDSBORO - BOBBY GOLDSBORO'S GREATEST HITS Bobby Goldsboro	06May67 165(2) 3	32.3
12590. LET'S FALL IN LOVE Hugo & Luigi	26Oct63 125(1) 2	32.2
12591. BLUE SIDE OF LONESOME Jim Reeves	15Jul67 185(1) 5	32.2
12592. OCTOBERON Barclay James Harvest	19Feb77 174(1) 3	32.2
12593. WE GOT THE RHYTHM People's Choice	26Jun76 174(1) 3	32.1
12594. ROD McKUEN GRAND TOUR Rod McKuen	06Nov71 177(2) 3	32.1
12595. A MEMORIAL Robert Francis Kennedy	11Jan69 187(2) 4	32.1
12596. THE BEST OF LYNN ANDERSON Lynn Anderson	03May69 180(1) 3	32.1
12597. TAP STEP Chick Corea	10May80 170(2) 3	32.1
12598. CROW BY CROW Crow	06Jun70 181(2) 4	32.1
12599. THE BROTHERS: ISLEY Isley Brothers	18Oct69 180(1) 3	32.0
12600. CHIEFTAINS 5 The Chieftains	28Feb76 187(1) 4	32.0
12601. THE CAPE VERDEAN BLUES Horace Silver Quintet Plus J.J. Johnson	26Feb66 130(1) 2	32.0
12602. STORIES Gloria Gaynor	24May80 178(1) 4	31.9
12603. SHADES OF LACE Lace	23Jan88 187(2) 5	31.9
12604. MY KIND OF JAZZ Ray Charles	11Jul70 155(2) 2	31.9
12605. COME AS YOU ARE Ashford & Simpson	08May76 189(2) 4	31.8
12606. SOLOMON'S SEAL Pentangle	28Oct72 184(2) 4	31.7
12607. NEVER SAY YOU CAN'T SURVIVE Curtis Mayfield	26Mar77 173(1) 3	31.7
12608. CURED Steve Hackett	24Oct81 169(2) 3	31.7
12609. MAHOGANY RUSH IV Mahogany Rush	05Jun76 175(1) 3	31.7
12610. I PREFER THE MOONLIGHT Kenny Rogers	26Sep87 163(2) 4	31.7
12611. OPEN ALL NIGHT Leroi Bros.	28Mar87 181(2) 5	31.7
12612. THE BALLAD OF BONNIE AND CLYDE Georgie Fame	11May68 185(1) 4	31.6
12613. A VALENTINE GIFT FOR YOU Elvis Presley	02Mar85 154(1) 3	31.6
12614. BOOTS RANDOLPH WITH THE KNIGHTSBRIDGE STRINGS & VOICES Boots Randolph	03Feb68 189(2) 5	31.6
12615. RHAPSODY IN BLUE Walter Murphy	16Jul77 175(1) 3	31.6
12616. STREET LANGUAGE Rodney Crowell	23Aug86 177(1) 5	31.6
12617. ROCK 'N' ROLL WARRIORS Savoy Brown	25Jul81 185(1) 4	31.6
12618. BEADED DREAMS THROUGH TURQUOISE EYES Redbone	26Oct74 174(1) 3	31.6
12619. VENUSIAN SUMMER Lenny White	31Jan76 177(2) 3	31.6
12620. WAR, WAR, WAR Country Joe McDonald	07Aug71 185(1) 4	31.5
12621. LA PISTOLA Y EL CORAZON Los Lobos	05Nov88 179(2) 4	31.5
12622. FINALLY GOT MYSELF TOGETHER The Impressions	06Jul74 176(1) 3	31.5
12623. SECOND EDITION Public Image Limited	10May80 171(2) 3	31.5
12624. SAUSALITO Al Martino	19Jul69 189(2) 4	31.5
12625. WEDDING ALBUM John Lennon & Yoko Ono	13Dec69 178(1) 3	31.4
12626. EL CONDOR PASA Paul Mauriat	29May71 180(2) 3	31.4
12627. X-PERIMENT The System	31Mar84 182(1) 5	31.4
12628. SPRING FEVER Soulful Strings	29Nov69 183(1) 4	31.4
12629. LANA! Lana Cantrell	16Nov68 166(2) 2	31.3
12630. CACTUS AND A ROSE Gary Stewart	16Aug80 165(1) 3	31.3
12631. THE BOOK OF PRIDE Giant Steps	12Nov88 184(1) 5	31.3
12632. ABBA ABBA	15Nov75 174(1) 3	31.3
12633. 7-6-5-4-3-2-1 BLOW YOUR WHISTLE Gary Toms Empire	27Sep75 178(1) 3	31.2
12634. SLEEPLESS NIGHTS Gram Parsons And The Flying Burrito Brothers	22May76 185(1) 4	31.2
12635. BOBBY GOLDSBORO'S 10TH ANNIVERSARY ALBUM Bobby Goldsboro	16Nov74 174(1) 3	31.2
12636. PETER NERO PLAYS LOVE IS BLUE AND TEN OTHER GREAT SONGS Peter Nero	20Apr68 180(2) 4	31.2
12637. LOUDER THAN HELL Sam Kinison	08Nov86 175(1) 5	31.2
12638. BAD FOR ME Dee Dee Bridgewater	26May79 182(1) 4	31.1
12639. LOVE ME TENDER B.B. King	15May82 179(1) 5	31.1
12640. WINDHAM HILL RECORDS SAMPLER '89 Various Artists	15Apr89 176(2) 4	31.0
12641. SHANKAR FAMILY & FRIENDS Ravi Shankar	11Jan75 176(1) 3	31.0
12642. HIT AND RUN Girlschool	22May82 182(2) 5	31.0
12643. THE STEVE LAWRENCE SHOW Steve Lawrence	11Dec65 133(1) 2	30.9
12644. DREAMTIME The Stranglers	02May87 172(2) 4	30.9
12645. LET'S MAKE A NEW DOPE DEAL Cheech & Chong	19Jul80 173(1) 3	30.9
12646. THE CLIQUE The Clique	17Jan70 177(1) 3	30.9
12647. BORDER WAVE Sir Douglas Quintet	14Feb81 184(2) 4	30.9
12648. AQUA DREAM McGuffey Lane	23Jan82 193(1) 6	30.9
12649. A SYMPHONY FOR SUSAN The Arbors	11Feb67 144(2) 2	30.9
12650. NO REFUGE Eddie Schwartz	06Feb82 195(2) 6	30.9
12651. SHOWTIME Johnny Cash And The Tennessee Two	27Dec69 181(1) 4	30.9
12652. MIRIAM MAKEBA IN CONCERT! Miriam Makeba	18Nov67 182(2) 4	30.9
12653. RATCHELL Ratchell	15Apr72 176(1) 3	30.9
12654. T.B. SHEETS Van Morrison	26Jan74 181(1) 4	30.8
12655. WHATEVER Friends Of Distinction	31Oct70 179(1) 3	30.8
12656. KEEP YOUR SOUL TOGETHER Freddie Hubbard	19Jan74 186(1) 5	30.8

Rank. Title Act Entry Peak(Pk Wks) TotWks	Scr
12657. **WINDMILLS OF YOUR MIND** Percy Faith 31May69 194(1) 4	30.8
12658. **TOM PAXTON 6** Tom Paxton 06Jun70 184(1) 4	30.8
12659. **BAD TO THE BONE** L.A. Dream Team 14Nov87 162(2) 4	30.7
12660. **THE PERSUADERS** The Persuaders 07Apr73 178(1) 4	30.7
12661. **FROM THE GREENHOUSE** Crack The Sky 24Jun89 186(1) 5	30.6
12662. **BEAT SURRENDER** The Jam 09Apr83 171(1) 4	30.6
12663. **IT'S ALIVE** Ozark Mountain Daredevils 30Sep78 176(1) 3	30.6
12664. **WHEELIN' AND DEALIN'** Asleep At The Wheel 18Sep76 179(2) 3	30.6
12665. **STRAPHANGIN'** Brecker Brothers 20Jun81 176(2) 3	30.6
12666. **SATURDAY MORNING CONFUSION** Bobby Russell 16Oct71 183(2) 3	30.6
12667. **URGH! A MUSIC WAR** Various Artists 26Sep81 173(2) 3	30.5
12668. **MOOG POWER** Hugo Montenegro, His Orchestra And Chorus 30Aug69 182(1) 4	30.5
12669. **OVER THE RAINBOW** Livingston Taylor 03Nov73 189(1) 5	30.5
12670. **FANS** Malcolm McLaren 02Feb85 190(2) 6	30.5
12671. **WHEN THE SNOW IS ON THE ROSES** Sonny James 23Sep72 190(1) 5	30.4
12672. **BILL MEDLEY 100%** Bill Medley 12Oct68 188(2) 4	30.4
12673. **STAINED CLASS** Judas Priest 08Apr78 173(1) 3	30.4
12674. **I TAKE IT BACK** Sandy Posey 30Sep67 182(1) 4	30.4
12675. **SECOND TIME ROUND** Cymande 30Jun73 180(1) 4	30.4
12676. **THIEF IN THE NIGHT** George Duke 20Apr85 183(1) 5	30.4
12677. **SIMPLE THINGS** Richie Havens 03Oct87 173(1) 4	30.4
12678. **COUNTRY BOY** Ricky Skaggs 10Nov84 180(1) 5	30.2
12679. **HAVE A MARIJUANA** David Peel & The Lower East Side 24May69 186(1) 3	30.2
12680. **I COULD HAVE BEEN A SAILOR** Peter Allen 21Apr79 171(2) 3	30.2
12681. **HERE COMES THE SUN** Nina Simone 21Aug71 190(2) 4	30.2
12682. **THE BIGGEST PRIZE IN SPORT** 999 23Feb80 177(2) 3	30.2
12683. **GRAVE NEW WORLD** Strawbs 15Jul72 191(2) 5	30.2
12684. **QE 2** Mike Oldfield 04Jul81 174(1) 3	30.1
12685. **STRANDED** Roxy Music 18May74 186(1) 4	30.1
12686. **LINK WRAY** Link Wray & His Ray Men 24Jul71 186(1) 4	30.1
12687. **JAPANESE WHISPERS** The Cure 25Feb84 181(1) 5	30.1
12688. **ARBOUR ZENA** Keith Jarrett 10Jul76 179(1) 3	30.1
12689. **ANGEL BAND** Emmylou Harris 01Aug87 166(2) 4	30.1
12690. **JOHNNY "GUITAR" WATSON AND THE FAMILY CLONE** Johnny Guitar Watson 27Jun81 177(2) 3	30.1
12691. **LIVE IN CONCERT** Roger Whittaker 13Jun81 177(1) 3	30.1
12692. **SONNY & BROWNIE** Sonny Terry & Brownie McGhee 07Apr73 185(1) 5	30.1
12693. **LIVE IN EUROPE** Billy Paul 06Jul74 187(1) 4	30.0
12694. **IN THE SUMMER OF HIS YEARS** Connie Francis 01Feb64 126(1) 2	30.0
12695. **AEROBIC SHAPE UP II** Joanie Greggains 18Jun83 177(1) 4	30.0
12696. **CLOSE-UP** Sonny James 23Aug69 184(2) 3	30.0
12697. **BURNING SENSATIONS** Burning Sensations 30Jul83 175(1) 4	29.9
12698. **KOOL JAZZ** Kool & The Gang 12Jan74 187(2) 4	29.9
12699. **GOLDEN INSTRUMENTALS** Various Artists 14Oct67 177(2) 4	29.9
12700. **FIRE AND GASOLINE** Steve Jones 21Oct89 169(2) 4	29.9
12701. **THE POWER OF MUSIC** The Miracles 16Oct76 178(1) 3	29.9
12702. **BLUES 'N JAZZ** B.B. King 02Jul83 172(1) 4	29.9
12703. **TERROR RISING** Lizzy Borden 02May87 188(1) 6	29.8
12704. **BLUE TATTOO** Passport 29Aug81 175(2) 3	29.7
12705. **STILL** Pete Sinfield 06Oct73 190(1) 5	29.7
12706. **GIVE IT AWAY** The Chi-Lites 13Sep69 180(2) 3	29.7
12707. **THE RHYMER AND OTHER FIVE AND DIMERS** Tom T. Hall 09Jun73 181(1) 4	29.7
12708. **STEPPIN' OUT** George Howard 01Sep84 178(1) 4	29.7
12709. **LIFE OF BRIAN** Monty Python 10Nov79 155(1) 2	29.7
12710. **DANCE FOREVER** Cheryl Ladd 28Apr79 179(2) 3	29.6
12711. **ABSTRACT EMOTIONS** Randy Crawford 26Jul86 178(2) 4	29.6
12712. **SILK & SOUL** Lou Rawls 26Feb72 186(1) 4	29.6
12713. **DARLIN'** Tom Jones 23May81 179(1) 3	29.6
12714. **HOW THE HELL DO YOU SPELL RYTHUM** Amazing Rhythm Aces 04Oct80 175(1) 3	29.6
12715. **DREAMS OF TOMORROW** Marilyn Scott 21Apr79 189(2) 4	29.5
12716. **MY SPECIAL LOVE** LaToya Jackson 12Sep81 175(2) 3	29.5
12717. **MAGIC BUS** The Who 21Dec74 185(1) 4	29.5
12718. **NAIVE ART** Red Flag 23Sep89 178(2) 4	29.4
12719. **TURN ON SOME HAPPY!** Danny Davis And The Nashville Brass 25Nov72 193(1) 5	29.4
12720. **WEATHER REPORT** Weather Report 24Jul71 191(2) 4	29.4
12721. **KARMA** Pharoah Sanders 16Aug69 188(1) 4	29.4
12722. **MARVIN GAYE & TAMMI TERRELL GREATEST HITS** Marvin Gaye & Tammi Terrell 13Jun70 171(1) 3	29.3
12723. **WHERE THE BEAT MEETS THE STREET** Bobby And The Midnites 25Aug84 166(1) 4	29.3
12724. **BIRD** Soundtrack 12Nov88 169(1) 3	29.3
12725. **SONGS I LOVE TO SING** Slim Whitman 25Oct80 175(1) 3	29.3
12726. **REFLECTIONS IN BLUE** Bobby Bland 14May77 185(1) 4	29.3
12727. **MAGIC IS A CHILD** Nektar 05Nov77 172(1) 3	29.3
12728. **PORTFOLIO** Richie Havens 09Jun73 182(1) 4	29.3
12729. **A SONG FOR YOU** Ron Carter 21Oct78 178(1) 3	29.3
12730. **SKY 3** Sky 02May81 181(1) 3	29.2
12731. **YOU'VE MADE ME SO VERY HAPPY** Lou Rawls 18Apr70 172(2) 3	29.2
12732. **CLIMBING THE WALLS** Wrathchild America 30Sep89 190(2) 6	29.2
12733. **FEVER!** Doc Severinsen 27Aug66 147(1) 2	29.2
12734. **WARM AND TENDER** Petula Clark 10Apr71 178(1) 3	29.2
12735. **BROADWAY - BASIE'S WAY** Count Basie 10Dec66 143(1) 2	29.2
12736. **ONLY FOR THE LONELY** Mavis Staples 12Sep70 188(1) 4	29.1
12737. **FAITHFULL FOREVER...** Marianne Faithfull 19Nov66 147(2) 2	29.1
12738. **THE BEAU BRUMMELS** Beau Brummels 05Jul75 180(2) 3	29.1
12739. **MRS. BROWN, YOU'VE GOT A LOVELY DAUGHTER** Herman's Hermits 28Sep68 182(1) 3	29.0
12740. **A TIME FOR SINGING** Original Cast 06Aug66 145(2) 2	29.0
12741. **YOUNGER GIRL** The Critters 24Sep66 147(1) 2	29.0
12742. **THE RIGHT TO BE ITALIAN** Holly And The Italians 11Jul81 177(2) 3	29.0
12743. **IT'S A SIN** Marty Robbins 19Jul69 194(1) 4	29.0
12744. **CITY BOY** City Boy 28Aug76 177(1) 3	29.0
12745. **THE IPCRESS FILE** Soundtrack 13Nov65 133(1) 2	29.0
12746. **MUSIC MAXIMUS** Main Ingredient 05Mar77 177(1) 3	29.0
12747. **CORE SPEZZATO** Jimmy Roselli 21Jun69 184(1) 3	28.9
12748. **YOUNG, LOUD AND SNOTTY** Dead Boys 22Oct77 189(2) 4	28.9
12749. **INSPIRATION INFORMATION** Shuggie Otis 22Mar75 181(2) 3	28.9
12750. **SURPRISE** Sylvia (2) 28Apr84 178(1) 4	28.9
12751. **SWEET AND WONDERFUL** Jean Carn 15Aug81 176(1) 3	28.8
12752. **OOOH SO GOOD 'N BLUES** Taj Mahal 01Dec73 190(1) 5	28.8
12753. **OF CABBAGES AND KINGS** Chad & Jeremy 11Nov67 186(2) 5	28.8
12754. **DELLA REESE LIVE** Della Reese 22Oct66 149(1) 2	28.8
12755. **ATLANTA BLUE** Statler Brothers 26May84 177(2) 4	28.8
12756. **VICTOR/VICTORIA** Soundtrack 05Jun82 174(2) 4	28.8
12757. **THE TENDER GENDER** Kenny Burrell 17Dec66 146(1) 2	28.8
12758. **FEEL THE FIRE** Jermaine Jackson 27Aug77 174(1) 3	28.8
12759. **LITTLE GIRL** Syndicate Of Sound 27Aug66 148(1) 2	28.8
12760. **THE STRIKERS** The Strikers 29Aug81 174(1) 3	28.8
12761. **WHAT DID YOU DO IN THE WAR, DADDY?** Henry Mancini And His Orchestra 10Sep66 148(2) 2	28.8
12762. **FEELIN' RIGHT** Razzy Bailey 27Feb82 176(1) 4	28.7
12763. **T SHIRT** Loudon Wainwright III 19Jun76 188(1) 4	28.7
12764. **#1** Sonny James 28Nov70 187(1) 4	28.7
12765. **TIMES OF OUR LIVES** Judy Collins 13Mar82 190(1) 5	28.7
12766. **JOSEPHINE** Billy Vaughn And His Orchestra 29Jul67 147(1) 2	28.7
12767. **FIVE BRIDGES** The Nice 29Aug70 197(3) 5	28.7
12768. **A NIGHT ON THE TOWN** Brownsville Station 07Oct72 190(1) 5	28.7
12769. **AREA CODE 615** Area Code 615 18Oct69 191(2) 4	28.7
12770. **CLOSE-UP** Frank Sinatra 23Aug69 186(2) 3	28.7

Rank. Title Act Entry Peak(Pk Wks) TotWks	Scr
12771. IN BLACK AND WHITE Jenny Burton 24Mar84 181(2) 4	28.7
12772. CHRIS JAGGER Chris Jagger 03Nov73 186(1) 4	28.6
12773. THIRD DOWN, 110 TO GO Jesse Winchester 30Dec72 193(2) 5	28.6
12774. THAT'S ALL THAT MATTERS TO ME Mickey Gilley 30Aug80 177(2) 3	28.5
12775. RENAISSANCE Ray Charles 28Jun75 175(1) 3	28.5
12776. TONIGHT France Joli 28Jun80 175(1) 3	28.5
12777. THE PIRATES OF PENZANCE Original Cast 06Jun81 178(1) 3	28.4
12778. LOOKIN' FOR TROUBLE Toronto 30Aug80 185(1) 4	28.4
12779. SCATTERLINGS Juluka 13Aug83 186(1) 5	28.4
12780. BACHMAN-TURNER-BACHMAN AS BRAVE BELT Bachman-Turner Overdrive 08Mar75 180(1) 3	28.4
12781. GUESS WHO'S COMING TO DINNER Soundtrack 27Apr68 177(1) 3	28.4
12782. THE MUPPET ALPHABET ALBUM Various Artists 25Dec71 189(1) 4	28.4
12783. THE VILLAGE CALLER! Johnny Lytle 26Feb66 141(2) 2	28.3
12784. THE BEST OF JUDY GARLAND Judy Garland 04Jan64 136(1) 2	28.3
12785. KATE SMITH TODAY Kate Smith 03Dec66 148(1) 2	28.3
12786. IT'S A BEAUTIFUL THING Maxine Nightingale 08Jan83 176(2) 4	28.3
12787. HELL'S ANGELS '69 Soundtrack 11Oct69 184(1) 3	28.3
12788. ARMED AND EXTREMELY DANGEROUS First Choice 27Oct73 184(1) 4	28.3
12789. DION'S GREATEST HITS Dion 24Mar73 194(1) 5	28.3
12790. SAMURAI SAMBA Yellowjackets 13Apr85 179(1) 4	28.3
12791. LENNY Soundtrack 18Jan75 180(1) 3	28.2
12792. SONGS Kids From Fame 15Jan83 181(4) 4	28.2
12793. LOVING IS WHY Sons Of Champlin 28May77 188(1) 4	28.1
12794. MY OWN WAY Willie Nelson 03Dec83 182(1) 5	28.1
12795. I APPRECIATE Alicia Myers 08Dec84 186(2) 5	28.1
12796. IT'S THE WORLD GONE CRAZY Glen Campbell 28Feb81 178(1) 3	28.1
12797. THE FANATIC Felony 26Mar83 185(2) 5	28.1
12798. DAY FOR DECISION Johnny Sea 06Aug66 147(1) 2	28.0
12799. PAUL ANKA Paul Anka 15Jan72 188(1) 4	28.0
12800. TOM JONES' GREATEST HITS Tom Jones 05Jan74 185(1) 4	27.9
12801. DANCIN' IN THE KEY OF LIFE Steve Arrington 18May85 185(2) 5	27.9
12802. ALFIE Carmen McRae 14Jan67 150(2) 2	27.9
12803. ALL-TIME GREATEST HITS The Lettermen 23Feb74 186(1) 4	27.9
12804. NORTH OF A MIRACLE Nick Heyward 14Jan84 178(2) 4	27.9
12805. CAL SMITH SINGS Cal Smith 06Sep69 170(2) 2	27.9
12806. LORD, MR. FORD Jerry Reed 11Aug73 183(1) 4	27.9
12807. PLANTATION HARBOR Joe Vitale 04Jul81 181(1) 3	27.8
12808. THE MYSTIC MOODS OF LOVE Mystic Moods Orch. 24Feb68 182(1) 4	27.8
12809. BRAZIL CLASSICS 1: BELEZA TROPICAL Various Artists 22Apr89 178(2) 4	27.8
12810. NIGHTHAWKS Keith Emerson 02May81 183(1) 3	27.8
12811. NEW DIRECTIONS Gary Lewis And The Playboys 08Jul67 185(1) 4	27.7
12812. WATERBEDS IN TRINIDAD! The Association 20May72 194(2) 5	27.7
12813. THE BEST OF JIMMY SMITH Jimmy Smith 09Dec67 185(1) 4	27.7
12814. THE ISLAND OF REAL The Rascals 13May72 180(2) 3	27.7
12815. POLKA PARTY! "Weird Al" Yankovic 15Nov86 177(2) 4	27.6
12816. ROUGH 'N TUMBLE Stanley Turrentine 07Jan67 149(1) 2	27.6
12817. GUTS FOR LOVE Garland Jeffreys 26Feb83 176(2) 4	27.6
12818. RIGHTEOUS Harvey Mandel 10May69 187(1) 3	27.6
12819. SOMETHING ELSE BY THE KINKS The Kinks 02Mar68 153(2) 2	27.5
12820. NATIVE DANCER Wayne Shorter 12Jul75 183(2) 3	27.5
12821. GANDHI Soundtrack 30Apr83 168(1) 3	27.5
12822. S.O.S. Yachts 20Oct79 179(2) 3	27.5
12823. THE BEST OF TOM RUSH Tom Rush 07Feb76 184(1) 3	27.4
12824. TERENCE BOYLAN Terence Boylan 05Nov77 181(2) 3	27.4
12825. JUDY GARLAND AT HOME AT THE PALACE - OPENING NIGHT Judy Garland 16Sep67 174(1) 3	27.4
12826. SO SO SATISFIED Ashford & Simpson 05Feb77 180(1) 3	27.4
12827. CAROLYNE MAS Carolyne Mas 22Sep79 172(1) 3	27.4
12828. SPACED OUT Enoch Light & The Light Brigade 21Mar70 191(1) 4	27.3
12829. HAVING A PARTY Pointer Sisters 24Dec77 176(1) 3	27.3
12830. I AM MY BROTHER'S KEEPER Ruffin Brothers (Jimmy & David) 07Nov70 178(1) 3	27.3
12831. PROOF THROUGH THE NIGHT T-Bone Burnett 01Oct83 188(2) 5	27.3
12832. URIAH HEEP Uriah Heep 03Oct70 186(1) 4	27.3
12833. GREAT COUNTRY HITS Billy Vaughn And His Orchestra 23Jul66 149(1) 2	27.3
12834. HURRY SUNDOWN Soundtrack 22Apr67 153(1) 2	27.2
12835. THE MANCINI GENERATION Henry Mancini And His Orchestra 23Sep72 195(1) 5	27.2
12836. BEHIND THE EYES Tim Moore 02Aug75 181(1) 3	27.2
12837. CRY John Klemmer 18Nov78 178(1) 3	27.2
12838. THE PRICE YOU GOT TO PAY TO BE FREE "Cannonball" Adderley Quintet 06Mar71 169(2) 2	27.1
12839. L.O.V.E. Paul Mauriat And His Orchestra 01Nov69 186(2) 3	27.1
12840. ANOTHER EXPOSURE Soulful Strings 03Aug68 189(1) 4	27.1
12841. REFLECTION Pentangle 04Dec71 183(1) 3	27.1
12842. LET IT OUT (LET IT ALL HANG OUT) The Hombres 09Dec67 180(2) 4	27.1
12843. THE BOBBY FULLER FOUR Bobby Fuller Four 02Apr66 144(2) 2	27.0
12844. INXS INXS 18Aug84 164(1) 3	27.0
12845. MONDO MANDO David Grisman 24Oct81 174(1) 3	27.0
12846. 20 GOLDEN HITS Mamas & The Papas 03Mar73 186(2) 4	27.0
12847. LETHAL WEAPON 2 Soundtrack 02Sep89 164(2) 3	27.0
12848. THE BEST OF FIREFALL Firefall 26Dec81 186(1) 4	26.9
12849. TOGETHER: A NEW CHUCK MANGIONE CONCERT Chuck Mangione 20Nov71 194(1) 4	26.9
12850. 10,9,8,7,6,5,4,3,2,1 Midnight Oil 04Feb84 178(1) 5	26.9
12851. ANY OLD WIND THAT BLOWS Johnny Cash 24Feb73 188(1) 4	26.9
12852. I WANT CANDY The Strangeloves 13Nov65 141(2) 2	26.9
12853. THE BEST OF NINA SIMONE Nina Simone 19Apr69 187(1) 3	26.8
12854. NIGHT JOURNEY Doc Severinsen 17Apr76 189(1) 4	26.8
12855. ALBERT LIVE Albert King 12Mar77 182(1) 3	26.8
12856. FIRE ON THE BAYOU The Meters 06Sep75 179(1) 3	26.7
12857. THE WAY WE WERE Willis Jackson 30Aug75 182(1) 3	26.7
12858. TALK TO ME Sunny & The Sunliners 02Nov63 142(1) 2	26.7
12859. THE AMBOY DUKES Amboy Dukes 10Feb68 183(1) 4	26.7
12860. EARLE DOUD PRESENTS SPIRO T. AGNEW IS A RIOT! Various Artists 16Jan71 185(1) 3	26.7
12861. THE BEST...LOVIN' SPOONFUL Lovin' Spoonful 24Apr76 183(1) 3	26.6
12862. LOVE COUNTRY STYLE Ray Charles 22Aug70 192(1) 4	26.6
12863. FEELING CAVALIER Ebn-Ozn 31Mar84 185(2) 4	26.6
12864. PHIL OCHS IN CONCERT Phil Ochs 09Jul66 149(1) 2	26.6
12865. SHORT CUT DRAW BLOOD Jim Capaldi 14Feb76 193(1) 4	26.6
12866. MY TOOT TOOT Jean Knight 03Aug85 180(1) 4	26.6
12867. SUPERMAN III Soundtrack 02Jul83 163(1) 3	26.5
12868. THE PRODUCERS The Producers 06Jun81 163(1) 2	26.5
12869. FOR YOUR PRECIOUS LOVE Oscar Toney, Jr. 29Jul67 192(1) 5	26.5
12870. LOVE, PEACE & SOUL Honey Cone 23Sep72 189(1) 4	26.5
12871. AMERICAN DREAMS Jesse Colin Young 09Dec78 165(2) 2	26.4
12872. FAVORITE COUNTRY HITS Ricky Skaggs 09Mar85 181(2) 4	26.4
12873. SUN SHIP John Coltrane 13Nov71 186(2) 3	26.4
12874. BAJOUR Original Cast 20Feb65 143(2) 2	26.4
12875. THE BEST OF THE GUESS WHO, VOLUME II Guess Who 12Jan74 186(1) 4	26.4
12876. HAND OF KINDNESS Richard Thompson 30Jul83 186(1) 5	26.3
12877. VOYAGE OF THE ACOLYTE Steve Hackett 17Apr76 191(1) 4	26.3
12878. THREE FRIENDS Gentle Giant 21Oct72 197(2) 5	26.3
12879. D.C. CAB Soundtrack 11Feb84 181(1) 4	26.3
12880. WINDFALL Rick Nelson And The Stone Canyon Band 23Feb74 190(1) 4	26.3
12881. MACKINTOSH & T.J. Waylon Jennings 17Apr76 189(1) 4	26.3
12882. K-SCOPE Phil Manzanera 10Feb79 176(1) 3	26.3
12883. FLY ME TO THE MOON Bobby Womack 28Dec68 174(2) 2	26.3
12884. HARLEM NOCTURNE The Viscounts 29Jan66 144(1) 2	26.3
12885. DRIPPIN' WET!/LIVE Wet Willie 12May73 189(2) 4	26.2
12886. PEACE WILL COME Tom Paxton 26Aug72 191(2) 4	26.2

Rank. Title Act Entry Peak(Pk Wks) TotWks	Scr
12887. MORE HEAVY TRAFFIC Traffic 27Sep75 193(1) 4	26.2
12888. AQUARIUS Charlie Byrd 28Jun69 197(2) 4	26.2
12889. GOOD, BAD BUT BEAUTIFUL Shirley Bassey 29Nov75 186(1) 3	26.2
12890. WE STILL AIN'T GOT NO BAND The Persuasions 09Jun73 178(1) 3	26.2
12891. LIGHTS FROM THE VALLEY Chilliwack 12Aug78 191(1) 4	26.2
12892. WHAT MORE CAN I SAY? Audio Two 25Jun88 185(2) 4	26.2
12893. SPEAK HER NAME Walter Jackson 24Jun67 194(1) 5	26.2
12894. THANK YOU...FOR F.U.M.L. (FUNKING UP MY LIFE) Donald Byrd 18Nov78 191(1) 4	26.1
12895. SUMMER OF '42 Roger Williams 18Sep71 187(1) 3	26.1
12896. HOLLYWOOD Maynard Ferguson 22May82 185(1) 4	26.1
12897. AEREO-PLAIN John Hartford 27Nov71 193(1) 4	26.1
12898. FIRST WATER Sharks 25Aug73 189(1) 4	26.0
12899. THE GREAT ONES! Jimmy Roselli 11Sep65 145(1) 2	26.0
12900. ROLLING THUNDER Mickey Hart 21Oct72 190(1) 4	26.0
12901. HOME GROWN Booker T. & Priscilla 22Jul72 190(1) 4	26.0
12902. FALSE START Love 26Dec70 184(2) 3	26.0
12903. YOU BREAK IT...YOU BOUGHT IT! Michael Stanley Band 13Sep75 184(1) 3	26.0
12904. KING OF ROCK AND ROLL Little Richard 13Nov71 193(1) 4	26.0
12905. THE TOP The Cure 23Jun84 180(1) 4	26.0
12906. THE RIGHT TO LOVE Nancy Wilson 12Jun71 185(1) 3	25.9
12907. GREATEST HITS 1972-1978 10cc 22Dec79 188(1) 4	25.9
12908. I HEAR TRUMPETS BLOW The Tokens 21May66 148(1) 2	25.9
12909. SHOULD I DO IT Tanya Tucker 01Aug81 180(1) 3	25.9
12910. LITTLE JOHNNY TAYLOR Little Johnny Taylor 09Nov63 140(1) 2	25.9
12911. HALLWAY SYMPHONY Hamilton, Joe Frank & Reynolds 19Feb72 191(1) 4	25.9
12912. BEST OF SCORPIONS VOL. 2 Scorpions 04Aug84 175(1) 4	25.8
12913. PINBALL WIZARDS New Seekers 19May73 190(1) 4	25.8
12914. BITTERSWEET Chairmen Of The Board 06May72 178(2) 3	25.8
12915. FOR THE "IN" CROWD Jack Jones 26Mar66 147(1) 2	25.8
12916. ...CONTINUED Tony Joe White 22Nov69 183(1) 3	25.8
12917. TRUTH IN DISGUISE Denise Lopez 26Nov88 184(1) 4	25.8
12918. THEN YOU CAN TELL ME GOODBYE The Casinos 13May67 187(1) 4	25.8
12919. FIRE UP Merl Saunders 02Jun73 197(2) 5	25.8
12920. VINTAGE '78 Eddie Kendricks 22Apr78 180(1) 3	25.8
12921. AWAKENING Mystic Moods Orchestra 05May73 190(1) 4	25.7
12922. WALKING THROUGH FIRE April Wine 05Oct85 174(2) 4	25.7
12923. A TIME TO SING Hank Williams Jr. 02Nov68 189(2) 3	25.7
12924. ANGEL OF THE MORNING Merrilee Rush 19Oct68 196(2) 4	25.7
12925. 'U' Incredible String Band 23Jan71 183(1) 3	25.6
12926. FERGUSLIE PARK Stealers Wheel 13Apr74 181(1) 3	25.6
12927. A BOUQUET OF HITS Ferrante & Teicher 21Dec68 198(1) 4	25.5
12928. THE FUNKY BROADWAY Dyke And The Blazers 04Nov67 186(1) 4	25.5
12929. MADRUGADA Melanie 11May74 192(1) 4	25.5
12930. HOLE IN THE WALL Billy Larkin & The Delegates 02Apr66 148(1) 2	25.5
12931. LAPLAND Baltimore And Ohio Marching Band 20Jan68 177(1) 3	25.5
12932. THE ASTROMUSICAL HOUSE OF... Various Artists 28Feb70 180(2) 3	25.5
12933. HANG 'EM HIGH Soundtrack 17Aug68 193(1) 4	25.4
12934. GONE IS LOVE Paul Mauriat 19Sep70 184(2) 3	25.4
12935. THIEF OF HEARTS Soundtrack 22Dec84 179(1) 4	25.4
12936. BIG SUR FESTIVAL/ONE HAND CLAPPING Various Artists 08Apr72 191(1) 4	25.4
12937. JOY Original Cast 14Mar70 187(1) 4	25.4
12938. BLAST FROM THE BAYOU Wayne Toups & Zydecajun 18Mar89 183(2) 4	25.4
12939. DON'T BE CONCERNED Bob Lind 16Apr66 148(1) 2	25.4
12940. "IN" BEAT Sandy Nelson 23Apr66 148(1) 2	25.3
12941. TREVOR RABIN Trevor Rabin 09Dec78 192(2) 4	25.3
12942. JONATHAN WINTERS' MAD, MAD, MAD, MAD WORLD Jonathan Winters 21Mar64 145(1) 2	25.3
12943. THE HIGH AND THE MIGHTY Donnie Iris 27Nov82 180(2) 4	25.2
12944. YOKO ONO/PLASTIC ONO BAND Yoko Ono 06Feb71 182(1) 3	25.2
12945. SCOTT BAIO Scott Baio 04Sep82 181(2) 4	25.2
12946. ROLLIN' WITH THE FLOW Charlie Rich 29Oct77 180(1) 3	25.2
12947. ELVIS BACK IN MEMPHIS Elvis Presley 21Nov70 183(1) 3	25.2
12948. METAL PRIESTESS The Plasmatics 05Dec81 177(1) 3	25.2
12949. CULTURE KILLED THE NATIVE Victory 06May89 182(1) 5	25.2
12950. DREAMTIME Tom Verlaine 10Oct81 177(1) 3	25.1
12951. TOP OF THE WORLD Lynn Anderson 11Aug73 179(1) 3	25.1
12952. INSPIRATION Tammy Wynette 24May69 189(1) 3	25.1
12953. DANSEPARC Martha And The Muffins 21May83 184(1) 4	25.1
12954. BILL WITHERS GREATEST HITS Bill Withers 16May81 183(1) 3	25.1
12955. LET IT BE Jerry Vale 27Jun70 189(1) 4	25.1
12956. THAT'S THE WAY LOVE IS Marvin Gaye 01Nov69 189(1) 3	25.0
12957. BAREBACK RIDER Mason Proffit 19May73 198(2) 5	25.0
12958. SUPERSAX PLAYS BIRD, VOLUME 2/SALT PEANUTS Supersax 06Apr74 182(1) 3	25.0
12959. TEN WOMEN Wire Train 02May87 181(1) 4	25.0
12960. GREASE BAND Grease Band 17Apr71 190(2) 3	25.0
12961. FAT ALBERT Bill Cosby 16Jun73 187(1) 4	25.0
12962. THE CORPORATION The Corporation 01Mar69 197(2) 4	25.0
12963. AMERICA THE BEAUTIFUL Gary McFarland 19Apr69 189(2) 3	24.9
12964. FOREST FLOWER Charles Lloyd Quartet 15Jul67 188(2) 4	24.9
12965. YOURS FOREVER MORE Forever More 07Mar70 180(1) 3	24.9
12966. LOVE LETTERS Force M.D.'s 15Dec84 185(3) 4	24.9
12967. THERE ARE BUT FOUR SMALL FACES Small Faces 16Mar68 178(1) 3	24.9
12968. HEAVEN RIGHT HERE ON EARTH Natural Four 05Jul75 182(1) 3	24.9
12969. JERRY LEE LEWIS Jerry Lee Lewis 28Apr79 186(1) 3	24.8
12970. SHENANDOAH Soundtrack 09Oct65 147(1) 2	24.8
12971. SINCE I FELL FOR YOU(2) Lenny Welch 01Jan66 147(1) 2	24.8
12972. TODAY Statler Brothers 25Jun83 193(1) 5	24.8
12973. LIVE FREE OR DIE Balaam And The Angel 30Apr88 174(1) 3	24.6
12974. DAVID COURTNEY'S FIRST DAY David Courtney 21Feb76 194(1) 4	24.6
12975. WE CAME TO PLAY The Persuasions 18Sep71 189(1) 3	24.6
12976. MURRAY THE K - LIVE FROM THE BROOKLYN FOX Various Artists 30Nov63 148(1) 2	24.6
12977. WOODY HERMAN: 1964 Woody Herman 21Mar64 148(2) 2	24.6
12978. ELECTRIC LOVE Electronic Concept Orchestra 18Oct69 175(1) 2	24.5
12979. FOCAL POINT McCoy Tyner 22Jan77 187(2) 3	24.5
12980. BLUE RABBIT Johnny Hodges/ Wild Bill Davis 20Feb65 148(1) 2	24.5
12981. CONCRETE AND CLAY Eddie Rambeau 24Jul65 148(2) 2	24.5
12982. UNCONDITIONALLY GUARANTEED Captain Beefheart & The Magic Band 27Apr74 192(1) 4	24.5
12983. THE BIG ONES, VOLUME II Floyd Cramer 25Apr70 183(1) 3	24.4
12984. JUBILATION Paul Anka 03Jun72 192(2) 4	24.4
12985. THIS IS ETHEL ENNIS Ethel Ennis 21Mar64 147(1) 2	24.4
12986. M.V.P. Harvey Mason 30May81 186(1) 3	24.4
12987. WHERE DOES LOVE GO Charles Boyer 08Jan66 148(1) 2	24.4
12988. THE SWEET The Sweet 28Jul73 191(1) 4	24.4
12989. THE STARS OF HEE HAW TV Soundtrack 23May70 196(2) 4	24.4
12990. MIDNIGHT CRAZY Mac Davis 16Jan82 174(1) 3	24.3
12991. CARAMBA! Lee Morgan 01Mar69 190(1) 3	24.3
12992. THE PENTANGLE Pentangle 21Dec68 192(2) 3	24.3
12993. NO STRINGS Ace 12Feb77 170(1) 2	24.3
12994. THE ORIGINAL PEANUTS The Sunglows 14Aug65 148(1) 2	24.3
12995. YOU GOTTA SAY YES TO ANOTHER EXCESS Yello 16Jul83 184(2) 4	24.3
12996. GLORY ROAD Gillan 06Dec80 183(1) 3	24.3
12997. SURVIVIN' IN THE 80'S Andre Cymone 15Oct83 185(1) 4	24.2
12998. REAL TRUE LOVIN' Steve Lawrence & Eydie Gorme 10May69 188(1) 3	24.2
12999. I'VE GOTTA BE ME Peter Nero 10May69 193(2) 3	24.2
13000. AFTER HERE THROUGH MIDLAND Cock Robin 05Sep87 166(2) 3	24.2
13001. THE VELVETEEN RABBIT Meryl Streep & George Winston 20Apr85 180(1) 4	24.2

Rank. Title Act / Entry Peak(Pk Wks) TotWks	Scr
13002. I WANTED SOMEONE TO LOVE Frankie Laine 14Oct67 162(2) 2	24.1
13003. ROY CLARK / THE ENTERTAINER Roy Clark 13Apr74 186(1) 3	24.1
13004. THE BEST OF EARTH, WIND & FIRE, VOL. II Earth, Wind & Fire 10Dec88 190(2) 4	24.1
13005. BUDDY & SOUL Buddy Rich 13Sep69 186(1) 3	24.1
13006. THE ARTHUR SOUND Wild Ones 20Nov65 149(1) 2	24.1
13007. 50 GUITARS GO ITALIANO 50 Guitars of Tommy Garrett 13Jun64 142(1) 2	24.1
13008. NEW JERSEY Joe Piscopo 27Jul85 168(1) 3	24.1
13009. TRUE BLUE Hank Crawford 08Aug64 143(1) 2	24.0
13010. INSIDE THE MIND OF BILL COSBY Bill Cosby 30Sep72 191(1) 4	24.0
13011. RINGS Cymarron 02Oct71 187(1) 3	24.0
13012. LONELY GUITAR Duane Eddy 16May64 144(1) 2	24.0
13013. TAKE YOUR SHOES OFF WITH THE SERENDIPITY SINGERS Serendipity Singers 16Jan65 149(2) 2	24.0
13014. MY GOAL'S BEYOND Mahavishnu John McLaughlin 01Jul72 194(2) 4	23.9
13015. I WANNA BE SELFISH Ashford & Simpson 20Jul74 195(1) 4	23.9
13016. POWER OF LOVE Arlo Guthrie 27Jun81 184(2) 3	23.9
13017. THE BEST OF JERRY JEFF WALKER Jerry Jeff Walker 19Jul80 185(1) 3	23.8
13018. UNITY Shinehead 05Nov88 185(1) 4	23.8
13019. THE RACE IS ON George Jones 26Jun65 149(1) 2	23.8
13020. ROCK THE WORLD Third World 25Jul81 186(1) 3	23.8
13021. METRO MUSIC Martha And The Muffins 13Sep80 186(1) 3	23.8
13022. PROFILE Jan Akkerman 13Oct73 192(2) 4	23.8
13023. SUNLIGHT The Youngbloods 07Aug71 186(1) 3	23.8
13024. COME FLY WITH ME Bobby Bland 01Jul78 185(1) 3	23.8
13025. PHASES AND STAGES Willie Nelson 05Jun76 187(2) 3	23.8
13026. STONE FLUTE Herbie Mann 07Mar70 184(1) 3	23.7
13027. PATTERN DISRUPTIVE Dickey Betts Band 12Nov88 187(2) 4	23.7
13028. ALAN PRICE Alan Price 19Nov77 187(2) 3	23.7
13029. MONTY PYTHON LIVE! AT CITY CENTER Monty Python 05Jun76 186(1) 3	23.7
13030. PHASE TWO Jimmy Castor Bunch 23Sep72 192(1) 4	23.7
13031. PRESENTING RUBIN MITCHELL Rubin Mitchell 15Apr67 164(2) 2	23.7
13032. THE SEARCHERS NO. 4 The Searchers 23Oct65 149(1) 2	23.5
13033. SOLO FLIGHTS Chet Atkins 30Mar68 184(1) 3	23.5
13034. SONGS OF THE FREE Gang Of Four 26Jun82 175(1) 3	23.5
13035. BOBBY VEE SINGS THE NEW SOUND FROM ENGLAND! Bobby Vee 27Jun64 146(1) 2	23.4
13036. THE BEST OF THE NEW BIRTH New Birth 19Jul75 175(2) 2	23.4
13037. EMOTIONS Mystic Moods Orchestra 09Nov68 194(1) 3	23.4
13038. HELLS ANGELS ON WHEELS Soundtrack 30Sep67 165(2) 2	23.4
13039. HARMONY Ray Conniff & His Orchestra & Chorus 13Oct73 194(1) 4	23.4
13040. CHANGIN' TIMES FEATURING FOGGY MOUNTAIN BREAKDOWN Flatt & Scruggs 30Mar68 194(2) 4	23.3
13041. PEACHES & HERB'S GREATEST HITS Peaches & Herb 21Sep68 187(1) 3	23.3
13042. HELLO, DOLLY! Ella Fitzgerald 22Aug64 146(1) 2	23.3
13043. PORTRAIT OF CARRIE Carrie Lucas 31Jan81 185(1) 3	23.3
13044. NEW YORK CAKE Kano 09Jan82 189(1) 4	23.3
13045. THINK PINK Fabulous Poodles 01Dec79 185(1) 3	23.3
13046. RANDY NEWMAN/LIVE Randy Newman 02Oct71 191(1) 3	23.3
13047. LOVE OF A GENTLE WOMAN John Gary 19Apr69 192(1) 3	23.3
13048. GUITAR SLINGER Johnny Winter 04Aug84 183(1) 4	23.3
13049. WHEN THE SUN GOES DOWN Red 7 30May87 175(2) 3	23.3
13050. WAR AND PEACE Soundtrack 17Aug68 189(2) 3	23.2
13051. EGG CREAM Egg Cream Feat. Andy Adams 28May77 197(2) 4	23.2
13052. TOPKAPI Soundtrack 09Jan65 150(2) 2	23.1
13053. CALIFORNIA BLOODLINES John Stewart 21Jun69 193(2) 3	23.1
13054. APPROXIMATELY INFINITE UNIVERSE Yoko Ono 24Feb73 193(1) 4	23.1
13055. TOPKAPI Jimmy McGriff 21Nov64 146(1) 2	23.1
13056. POINTER SISTERS' GREATEST HITS Pointer Sisters 13Nov82 178(2) 3	23.1
13057. NIGHT CRUISER Eumir Deodato 27Sep80 186(1) 3	23.0
13058. JUGGERNAUT Frank Marino 14Aug82 185(1) 4	23.0
13059. THE SWEETEST SOUNDS Kate Smith 31Oct64 145(1) 2	22.9
13060. THE RETURN OF THE MOONGLOWS The Moonglows 05Aug72 193(1) 4	22.9
13061. NEON The Cyrkle 01Apr67 164(1) 2	22.9
13062. MY SONG Keith Jarrett 02Sep78 174(1) 2	22.9
13063. HERE ARE THE HONEYCOMBS The Honeycombs 02Jan65 147(1) 2	22.9
13064. CLOSE-UP Lou Rawls 23Aug69 191(1) 3	22.9
13065. THE FALL OF THE ROMAN EMPIRE Soundtrack 13Jun64 147(1) 2	22.9
13066. WATERFALL If 28Oct72 195(2) 4	22.8
13067. COMIN' AT YA! Coke Escovedo 29May76 190(2) 3	22.8
13068. RALLY 'ROUND THE FLAGG Fannie Flagg 23Sep67 183(1) 3	22.8
13069. ANDY PRATT Andy Pratt 12May73 192(1) 4	22.8
13070. REUNION Jerry Jeff Walker 20Jun81 188(2) 3	22.8
13071. MIXED BAG II Richie Havens 12Oct74 186(1) 3	22.7
13072. IN THE LONG GRASS Boomtown Rats 25May85 188(1) 4	22.7
13073. THE BEST OF GINO VANNELLI Gino Vannelli 19Sep81 172(2) 2	22.7
13074. THE BOSS IS BACK! Gene Ammons 06Jun70 174(1) 2	22.7
13075. GETTIN' AWAY WITH MURDER Patti Austin 09Nov85 182(1) 4	22.7
13076. SPIRIT(2) Spirit 25Aug73 191(1) 4	22.6
13077. RIGHT ON BE FREE Voices Of East Harlem 10Oct70 191(2) 3	22.6
13078. WESTBOUND #9 Flaming Ember 29Aug70 188(2) 3	22.5
13079. RAW POWER Iggy And The Stooges 28Apr73 182(1) 3	22.5
13080. WHAT IS THIS What Is This 14Sep85 187(1) 4	22.5
13081. GIRL TALK Lesley Gore 12Dec64 146(1) 2	22.5
13082. LET'S BURN Clarence Carter 28Feb81 189(1) 3	22.5
13083. HISTORY OF RHYTHM & BLUES, VOLUME 1/THE ROOTS 1947-52 Various Artists 06Apr68 187(1) 3	22.5
13084. TOTALLY CONNECTED T-Connection 24Nov79 188(3) 3	22.5
13085. WHISTLE STOPPING WITH JONATHAN WINTERS Jonathan Winters 19Dec64 148(2) 2	22.4
13086. UNITED STATES LIVE Laurie Anderson 26Jan85 192(1) 5	22.4
13087. SPINNING WHEEL Lenny Dee 03Jan70 189(1) 3	22.4
13088. LOVE IS A FIVE LETTER WORD Jimmy Witherspoon 08Mar75 176(1) 2	22.4
13089. BRASS, IVORY & STRINGS Henry Mancini & Doc Severinsen With Orchestra and Chorus 09Jun73 185(1) 3	22.4
13090. WEASELS RIPPED MY FLESH Mothers Of Invention 26Sep70 189(2) 3	22.4
13091. RYAN'S DAUGHTER Soundtrack 19Dec70 199(2) 4	22.3
13092. LIQUID ACROBAT AS REGARDS THE AIR Incredible String Band 19Feb72 189(1) 3	22.3
13093. THE BOYS IN THE BAND Original Cast 14Jun69 195(2) 3	22.3
13094. JUST FOR A THRILL Earl Grant 11Jul64 149(2) 2	22.3
13095. THE MAD, MAD, MAD, MAD, MAD LADS Mad Lads 09Aug69 180(2) 2	22.3
13096. SWEET LOU Lou Donaldson 28Sep74 185(1) 3	22.3
13097. OUR PLEASURE TO SERVE YOU Stanky Brown Group 15May76 192(2) 3	22.2
13098. UNORTHODOX BEHAVIOUR Brand X 13Nov76 191(2) 3	22.2
13099. LUCILLE B.B. King 12Oct68 192(2) 3	22.1
13100. DAVID CLAYTON-THOMAS David Clayton-Thomas 15Apr72 184(1) 3	22.1
13101. HOT Maynard Ferguson 01Sep79 188(2) 3	22.1
13102. TOM JONES GREATEST HITS(2) Tom Jones 05Mar77 191(2) 3	22.1
13103. NO REST FOR THE WICKED Helix 22Oct83 186(1) 4	22.1
13104. PIECE OF MIND The Happenings 06Sep69 181(2) 2	22.1
13105. STRANGE LAND Box Of Frogs 14Jun86 177(2) 3	22.0
13106. PLEASURE ONE Heaven 17 04Apr87 177(2) 3	22.0
13107. SUPERBAD Chris Jasper 05Mar88 182(2) 3	22.0
13108. GRIN Grin 07Aug71 192(1) 3	22.0
13109. A NEW KIND OF CONNIE... Connie Francis 05Dec64 149(1) 2	22.0
13110. LOVE & GUITARS Eddy Arnold 02May70 191(2) 3	22.0
13111. SERGIO MENDES' FAVORITE THINGS Sergio Mendes 08Jun68 197(1) 4	21.9
13112. HALFWAY TO SANITY The Ramones 10Oct87 172(1) 3	21.9
13113. SUGAR & SPICE Cryan' Shames 13May67 192(1) 4	21.9
13114. BOOGIE BANDS & ONE NIGHT STANDS Kathy Dalton 16Nov74 190(1) 3	21.9
13115. THE LOOK OF LOVE Stanley Turrentine 02Nov68 193(1) 3	21.9
13116. FIDDLER ON THE ROOF Ferrante & Teicher 01Jan72 186(1) 3	21.9

Rank. Title Act Entry Peak(Pk Wks) TotWks	Scr
13117. **NATIONAL EMOTION** Tommy Tutone 29Oct83 179(1) 3	21.9
13118. **NO MAN'S LAND** Lene Lovich 15Jan83 188(1) 4	21.8
13119. **COLOSSEUM LIVE** Colosseum 20Nov71 192(2) 3	21.8
13120. **LADY CORYELL** Larry Coryell 31May69 196(1) 3	21.8
13121. **YOU'VE GOT A FRIEND** Mark Lindsay 09Oct71 180(2) 2	21.8
13122. **ASCENCION** Malo 23Mar74 188(1) 3	21.7
13123. **IF WE MAKE IT THROUGH DECEMBER** Merle Haggard 23Mar74 190(1) 3	21.7
13124. **IGUACU** Passport 23Apr77 191(1) 3	21.7
13125. **HUSTLE HITS** Various Artists 10Apr76 177(2) 2	21.7
13126. **THE TIME IS NEAR** Keef Hartley Band 28Nov70 191(2) 3	21.7
13127. **THE PERCY SLEDGE WAY** Percy Sledge 05Aug67 178(2) 3	21.7
13128. **HOT ASH** Wishbone Ash 23Jan82 192(1) 4	21.7
13129. **HISTORY OF RHYTHM & BLUES, VOLUME 3/ROCK & ROLL 1956-57** Various Artists 06Apr68 189(3) 3	21.6
13130. **THE FREE ELECTRIC BAND** Albert Hammond 01Sep73 193(1) 4	21.6
13131. **SMOKE SOME KILL** Schoolly D 06Aug88 180(1) 3	21.6
13132. **DRY YOUR EYES** Brenda & The Tabulations 01Jul67 191(1) 4	21.6
13133. **SUGAR** Stanley Turrentine 20Mar71 182(1) 3	21.6
13134. **DEVIL'S ANGELS** Davie Allan And The Arrows 19Aug67 165(1) 2	21.6
13135. **FIRST THRILLS** Thrills 27Jun81 199(2) 4	21.6
13136. **AZTEC CAMERA** Aztec Camera 13Apr85 181(2) 3	21.6
13137. **BLUE MATTER** Savoy Brown 12Apr69 182(1) 2	21.6
13138. **PSYCHOCANDY** Jesus And Mary Chain 22Feb86 188(2) 4	21.5
13139. **A WHITER SHADE OF PALE** Munich Machine 01Jul78 190(1) 3	21.5
13140. **EVERYTIME TWO FOOLS COLLIDE** Kenny Rogers & Dottie West 05Jan80 186(2) 3	21.5
13141. **LOVING ARMS** Dobie Gray 10Nov73 188(2) 3	21.5
13142. **TREACHEROUS: A HISTORY OF THE NEVILLE BROTHERS 1955-1985** Neville Brothers 11Apr87 178(2) 3	21.5
13143. **ELECTRIC HAVENS** Richie Havens 30Nov68 192(1) 3	21.4
13144. **REMEMBRANCE DAYS** Dream Academy 14Nov87 181(2) 3	21.4
13145. **EXTRA PLAY** Kaja 27Apr85 185(1) 4	21.3
13146. **CAMERA CAMERA** Renaissance 12Dec81 196(3) 4	21.3
13147. **MEMORIES** Doc Watson 30Aug75 193(2) 3	21.3
13148. **WITH LOVE** Roger Whittaker 29Nov80 175(2) 2	21.3
13149. **ON AND ON** Fat Boys 28Oct89 175(1) 3	21.2
13150. **MERRY CHRISTMAS/HAPPY NEW YEAR'S** Montana Orchestra 19Dec81 195(1) 4	21.2
13151. **SHE'S A HEARTBREAKER** Gene Pitney 14Sep68 193(1) 3	21.2
13152. **CHER'S GOLDEN GREATS** Cher 30Nov68 195(1) 3	21.2
13153. **ACTION SPEAKS LOUDER THAN WORDS** Chocolate Milk 25Oct75 191(2) 3	21.2
13154. **FREE FALL** Alvin Lee 20Dec80 198(1) 4	21.1
13155. **HE'S ALL I'VE GOT** Love Unlimited 26Feb77 192(1) 3	21.1
13156. **AWAKEN THE GUARDIAN** Fates Warning 07Feb87 191(3) 4	21.1
13157. **EVERYWHERE AT ONCE** The Plimsouls 23Jul83 186(1) 4	21.0
13158. **IF YOU GO AWAY** Damita Jo 06May67 169(1) 2	21.0
13159. **CLEAR SAILIN'** Chris Hillman 17Sep77 188(1) 3	21.0
13160. **POWERHOUSE** The Jazz Crusaders 04Jan69 184(2) 2	21.0
13161. **COCOON** Soundtrack 27Jul85 188(1) 4	21.0
13162. **HALF NELSON** Willie Nelson 12Oct85 178(2) 3	20.9
13163. **SURPRISES** Herbie Mann 08May76 178(1) 2	20.9
13164. **FOR LITTLE ONES** Donovan 13Jan68 185(1) 3	20.9
13165. **MAMAS AND PAPAS/SOUL TRAIN** Classics IV 01Feb69 196(2) 3	20.9
13166. **BONDAGE** Angelo Bond 02Aug75 179(1) 2	20.9
13167. **THE BEST OF NINA SIMONE(2)** Nina Simone 25Jul70 189(1) 3	20.9
13168. **COMPANY** Original Cast 20Jun70 178(2) 2	20.9
13169. **BASIC MILES - THE CLASSIC PERFORMANCES OF MILES DAVIS** Miles Davis 13Oct73 189(1) 3	20.9
13170. **DIRECTIONS** Miles Davis 11Apr81 179(2) 2	20.9
13171. **DAWN FEATURING TONY ORLANDO** Dawn Featuring Tony Orlando 18Dec71 178(2) 2	20.9
13172. **ART IN AMERICA** Art In America 26Mar83 176(1) 3	20.9
13173. **SUITE FOR LATE SUMMER** Dion 02Dec72 197(1) 4	20.9
13174. **STILL IN LOVE** Carrie Lucas 11Sep82 180(1) 3	20.9
13175. **RAW VELVET** Bobby Whitlock 04Nov72 190(1) 3	20.8
13176. **WILD! WILD! WILD! WILD!** Wild Man Steve 06Jun70 179(2) 2	20.8
13177. **FROM ME TO YOU** George Duke 14May77 192(1) 3	20.8
13178. **FOURSIDER** Herb Alpert & The Tijuana Brass 08Dec73 196(1) 4	20.8
13179. **AT LEAST WE GOT SHOES** Southside Johnny & The Jukes 21Jun86 189(1) 4	20.7
13180. **THE CINDERELLA THEORY** George Clinton 02Sep89 192(1) 4	20.7
13181. **LENNY BRUCE/CARNEGIE HALL** Lenny Bruce 15Mar75 178(1) 2	20.7
13182. **I'M READY** Natalie Cole 17Sep83 182(1) 3	20.6
13183. **HIGH TENSION WIRES** Steve Morse 24Jun89 182(2) 3	20.6
13184. **THE POPE SMOKES DOPE** David Peel & The Lower East Side 27May72 191(2) 3	20.6
13185. **MAGGIE FLYNN** Original Cast 11Jan69 185(2) 2	20.6
13186. **TWO FOR THE ROAD** Henry Mancini And His Orchestra 28Oct67 183(1) 3	20.6
13187. **X-MULTIPLIES** Yellow Magic Orchestra 20Sep80 177(2) 2	20.6
13188. **DAWN EXPLOSION** Captain Beyond 11Jun77 181(2) 2	20.5
13189. **HURRICANE EYES** Loudness 15Aug87 190(1) 4	20.5
13190. **MY SHY VIOLET** Mills Brothers 10Aug68 190(1) 3	20.5
13191. **ONE MORE TRY FOR LOVE** Ronnie Milsap 02Jun84 180(1) 3	20.5
13192. **THE BEST OF EDDIE HARRIS** Eddie Harris 18Apr70 191(1) 3	20.5
13193. **MOTHER'S SPIRITUAL** Laura Nyro 10Mar84 182(1) 3	20.5
13194. **FANTASY** Fantasy 15Aug70 194(2) 3	20.4
13195. **SKYYLIGHT** Skyy 06Aug83 183(1) 3	20.4
13196. **THE CANDYMEN** The Candymen 11Nov67 195(2) 4	20.4
13197. **DO IT DEBBIE'S WAY** Debbie Reynolds 26May84 182(1) 3	20.4
13198. **WHAT'S NEW!!!** Sonny Stitt 08Apr67 172(2) 2	20.4
13199. **J MOOD** Wynton Marsalis 01Nov86 185(2) 4	20.3
13200. **THE PLASTIC COW GOES MOOOOOOG** Plastic Cow 08Nov69 184(2) 2	20.3
13201. **LOVE THE ONE YOU'RE WITH** Mystic Moods Orchestra 29Apr72 184(1) 3	20.2
13202. **WOMAN IN FLAMES** Champaign 10Nov84 184(2) 3	20.2
13203. **THE DAMNATION OF ADAM BLESSING** Damnation Of Adam Blessing 28Mar70 181(2) 2	20.2
13204. **SURREAL THING** Kris Kristofferson 21Aug76 180(1) 2	20.1
13205. **COSMIC WIND** Mike Theodore Orchestra 01Oct77 178(1) 2	20.1
13206. **KEEP ON DOING** The Roches 13Nov82 183(1) 3	20.1
13207. **CALYPSO IN BRASS** Harry Belafonte 29Apr67 172(1) 2	20.0
13208. **ENCORE** Tangerine Dream 03Dec77 178(1) 2	20.0
13209. **JAMES DARREN/ALL** James Darren 03Jun67 187(1) 3	20.0
13210. **SYNERGY** Glass Harp 27Nov71 192(1) 3	20.0
13211. **THE BEST OF WAYNE NEWTON** Wayne Newton 07Oct67 194(1) 4	20.0
13212. **THE MAGNIFICENT MEN** Magnificent Men 08Apr67 171(1) 2	20.0
13213. **ROCK 'N' ROLL ROCKET** Starbuck 11Jun77 182(2) 2	20.0
13214. **STRAIGHT FROM THE HEART** Ann Peebles 22Apr72 188(2) 3	20.0
13215. **LET IT ROLL** TKO 21Apr79 181(2) 2	20.0
13216. **THE MUSIC MAN** Paul Anka 18Jun77 195(2) 3	20.0
13217. **THE SINGING STORY TELLER** Johnny Cash And The Tennessee Two 16May70 186(1) 3	20.0
13218. **EVERYBODY'S TALKIN'** King Curtis 25Mar72 189(1) 3	20.0
13219. **SET MY LOVE IN MOTION** Syreeta 30Jan82 189(3) 3	19.9
13220. **WHALE MEAT AGAIN** Jim Capaldi 07Sep74 191(1) 3	19.9
13221. **BOOTS RANDOLPH PLAYS THE GREAT HITS OF TODAY** Boots Randolph 02Dec72 192(2) 3	19.9
13222. **WHERE IS LOVE?** Jack Jones 21Sep68 195(2) 3	19.9
13223. **THE FUZZ** The Fuzz 02Oct71 196(1) 3	19.9
13224. **UP THE CREEK** Soundtrack 12May84 185(1) 3	19.9
13225. **LIVING THE BLUES(2)** Canned Heat 30Oct71 182(1) 2	19.9
13226. **FILM ON FILM - GREAT MOVIE THEMES** Enoch Light & The Light Brigade 15Apr67 173(1) 2	19.8
13227. **TOO YOUNG TO FEEL THIS OLD** McKendree Spring 27Mar76 193(1) 3	19.8
13228. **AN EVENING WITH CHICK COREA & HERBIE HANCOCK** Chick Corea & Herbie Hancock 24Nov79 175(1) 2	19.8
13229. **MOVING FINGER** The Hollies 13Feb71 183(2) 2	19.8
13230. **MY WAY OF LIFE** Bert Kaempfert And His Orchestra 02Nov68 186(2) 2	19.8

Rank.	Title	Act	Entry	Peak(Pk Wks)	TotWks	Scr
13231.	**FAMILY PORTRAIT**	Various Artists	17Feb68	194(1)	4	19.8
13232.	**DA'KRASH**	da'Krash	16Apr88	184(2)	3	19.7
13233.	**HOMEWARD BOUND**	Harry Belafonte	10Jan70	192(1)	3	19.7
13234.	**CAN'T SHAKE THIS FEELIN'**	Spinners	16Jan82	196(2)	4	19.7
13235.	**THE WIND IN THE WILLOWS**	Wind In The Willows	17Aug68	195(3)	3	19.6
13236.	**A FINE MESS**	Soundtrack	23Aug86	183(1)	3	19.6
13237.	**RIP IT TO SHREDS-THE ANIMALS GREATEST HITS LIVE**	The Animals	15Sep84	193(2)	4	19.6
13238.	**THREADS OF GLORY - 200 YEARS OF AMERICA IN WORDS & MUSIC**	Various Artists	27Dec75	192(1)	3	19.6
13239.	**BRASS ROOTS**	Doc Severinsen	16Oct71	185(2)	2	19.5
13240.	**PICTURES OF MOMENTS TO REMEMBER**	Statler Brothers	16Oct71	181(1)	2	19.5
13241.	**MOTELS**	The Motels	01Dec79	175(1)	2	19.5
13242.	**LITTLE RICHARD'S GREATEST HITS**	Little Richard	19Aug67	184(1)	3	19.5
13243.	**RITES OF PASSAGE**	Vitamin Z	10Aug85	183(1)	3	19.5
13244.	**BEFOUR**	Brian Auger & The Trinity	01Aug70	184(1)	3	19.5
13245.	**PERSPECTIVE**	America	10Nov84	185(1)	3	19.5
13246.	**MOMENTS**	Julio Iglesias	15Sep84	191(1)	4	19.5
13247.	**BOBBIE GENTRY'S GREATEST!**	Bobbie Gentry	27Dec69	180(1)	2	19.4
13248.	**MICK JONES**	Mick Jones	23Sep89	184(1)	3	19.4
13249.	**MAD LOVE**	Golden Earring	28May77	182(2)	2	19.4
13250.	**STORM FORCE TEN**	Steeleye Span	25Mar78	191(1)	3	19.4
13251.	**DREAM KID**	Sutherland Brothers And Quiver	11May74	193(1)	3	19.4
13252.	**EACH OF US ALONE (THE WORDS AND MUSIC OF ROD Mc KUEN)**	Glenn Yarbrough	09Nov68	188(2)	2	19.3
13253.	**FARQUAHR**	Farquahr	05Dec70	195(1)	3	19.3
13254.	**SONGS OF FOX HOLLOW**	Tom T. Hall	19Apr75	180(1)	2	19.3
13255.	**MIRRORS - REFLECTIONS OF TODAY**	Dick Hyman and The Group	27Apr68	179(2)	2	19.2
13256.	**TONY MOTTOLA'S GUITAR FACTORY**	Tony Mottola	16May70	189(1)	3	19.2
13257.	**CINCO**	El Chicano	06Apr74	194(1)	3	19.2
13258.	**JUST TESTING**	Wishbone Ash	29Mar80	179(1)	2	19.2
13259.	**OUTRAGEOUS**	Kim Fowley	19Apr69	198(1)	3	19.2
13260.	**JOHNNY CASH**	Johnny Cash	11Oct69	186(2)	2	19.2
13261.	**ONE FOR THE ROAD**	Righteous Brothers	14Dec68	187(1)	2	19.2
13262.	**WALKING ON NEW GRASS**	Wayne Newton	31Aug68	196(1)	3	19.2
13263.	**MR. MAGIC MAN**	Wilson Pickett	28Apr73	187(1)	3	19.1
13264.	**THERE'S MUSIC IN THE AIR**	Letta Mbulu	19Mar77	192(1)	3	19.1
13265.	**BRIGHTEN THE CORNER**	Ella Fitzgerald	19Aug67	172(1)	2	19.1
13266.	**IN ONE EYE AND OUT THE OTHER**	Cate Bros.	30Oct76	182(1)	2	19.0
13267.	**HOMECOOKING**	Sergio Mendes And Brazil '77	27Mar76	180(1)	2	19.0
13268.	**THE KLOWNS**	The Klowns	12Dec70	184(2)	2	19.0
13269.	**QUENTIN'S THEME**	Brad Swanson & His Whispering Organ Sound	18Oct69	185(1)	2	19.0
13270.	**LIVE AT ST. DOUGLAS CONVENT**	Father Guido Sarducci	10May80	179(2)	2	18.9
13271.	**THE ORIGINALS**	Statler Brothers	14Jul79	183(2)	2	18.9
13272.	**NUNSEXMONKROCK**	Nina Hagen	05Jun82	184(1)	3	18.9
13273.	**SILVER APPLES**	Silver Apples	03Aug68	193(2)	3	18.9
13274.	**DARK CONTINENT**	Wall Of Voodoo	17Oct81	177(1)	2	18.9
13275.	**BACH LIVE AT FILLMORE EAST**	Virgil Fox	29May71	183(1)	2	18.8
13276.	**MARK, DON & TERRY 1966-67**	Terry Knight and The Pack	04Nov72	192(2)	3	18.8
13277.	**THE ROSE GARDEN**	Rose Garden	16Mar68	176(1)	2	18.8
13278.	**GAYLE McCORMICK**	Gayle McCormick	16Oct71	198(2)	3	18.8
13279.	**FRESH FRUIT IN FOREIGN PLACES**	Kid Creole & The Coconuts	18Jul81	180(1)	2	18.7
13280.	**WHAT CAN YOU DO TO ME NOW**	Willie Nelson	08Nov75	196(1)	3	18.7
13281.	**LIVE AT COBO HALL, DETROIT**	Hank Williams Jr.	18Oct69	187(2)	2	18.7
13282.	**OUR GOLDEN FAVORITES**	Ferrante & Teicher	02Dec67	177(2)	2	18.7
13283.	**MAKIN' FRIENDS**	Razzy Bailey	20Jun81	183(2)	2	18.7
13284.	**LIVING BY THE DAYS**	Don Nix	11Sep71	197(2)	3	18.6
13285.	**THE BEST OF BILL WITHERS**	Bill Withers	17May75	182(1)	2	18.6
13286.	**'LIFE' LIVE**	Thin Lizzy	28Jan84	185(1)	3	18.6
13287.	**FREEWHEELIN'**	Fabulous Rhinestones	22Sep73	193(2)	3	18.6
13288.	**I'VE GOT A FEELING**	Al Wilson	10Jul76	185(2)	2	18.6
13289.	**THE TWO RING CIRCUS**	Erasure	16Jan88	186(1)	3	18.6
13290.	**CLOSE-UP**	Nat King Cole	23Aug69	197(1)	3	18.5
13291.	**BACK TO THE COUNTRY**	Loretta Lynn	19Apr75	182(1)	2	18.5
13292.	**THE BEST OF THE ALLMAN BROTHERS BAND**	Allman Brothers Band	21Nov81	189(1)	3	18.5
13293.	**SUCK 'EM UP**	Don Ho and the Aliis	22Mar69	199(2)	3	18.5
13294.	**TOTAL DEVO**	Devo	02Jul88	189(2)	3	18.5
13295.	**THE OSMONDS GREATEST HITS**	The Osmonds	14Jan78	192(1)	3	18.5
13296.	**THE GEESE & THE GHOST**	Anthony Phillips	26Mar77	191(1)	3	18.5
13297.	**RAILHEAD OVERTURE**	Mike Post	08Nov75	195(1)	3	18.5
13298.	**WORLD ANTHEM**	Mahogany Rush	28May77	184(2)	2	18.4
13299.	**PLANET OF THE APES**	Soundtrack	27Jul68	195(1)	3	18.4
13300.	**THE LOOK OF LOVE AND OTHER RHAPSODIES FOR YOUNG LOVERS**	Midnight String Quartet	17Aug68	194(1)	3	18.4
13301.	**LOVING POWER**	The Impressions	13Mar76	195(1)	3	18.3
13302.	**THEME FROM SHAFT**	The Ventures	15Jan72	195(1)	3	18.3
13303.	**THE GODFATHER, PART II**	Soundtrack	08Mar75	184(1)	2	18.3
13304.	**WHOMP THAT SUCKER**	Sparks	15Aug81	182(2)	2	18.3
13305.	**NEW YORK CITY (YOU'RE A WOMAN)**	Al Kooper	03Jul71	198(2)	3	18.2
13306.	**MARATHON**	Rodney Franklin	25Feb84	187(1)	3	18.2
13307.	**JERRY BUTLER'S GOLDEN HITS LIVE**	Jerry Butler	16Mar68	178(2)	2	18.2
13308.	**BATTLE HYMN**	Wild Turkey	06May72	193(2)	3	18.2
13309.	**MIXED BAG**	Richie Havens	06Jul68	182(1)	2	18.1
13310.	**LOOK HEAR?**	10cc	17May80	180(1)	2	18.1
13311.	**THROUGH THE LOOKING GLASS**	Siouxsie & The Banshees	11Apr87	188(1)	3	18.1
13312.	**THE NAME IS LOVE**	Bobby Vinton	11Jun77	183(1)	2	18.1
13313.	**VOLUME VIII**	Average White Band	20Sep80	182(1)	2	18.1
13314.	**THE BEST OF BILL DEAL & THE RHONDELS**	Bill Deal & The Rhondels	11Apr70	185(1)	2	18.0
13315.	**THE MUSIC OF PAUL SIMON**	Boston Pops Orchestra	26Feb72	196(2)	3	18.0
13316.	**MANUFACTURERS OF SOUL**	Jackie Wilson And Count Basie	01Jun68	195(2)	3	18.0
13317.	**MYSTERIES**	Keith Jarrett	17Jul76	184(1)	2	18.0
13318.	**ONE PIECE AT A TIME**	Johnny Cash And The Tennessee Three	17Jul76	185(1)	2	18.0
13319.	**NOT JUST THE GIRL NEXT DOOR**	Nancy Martinez	21Feb87	178(1)	3	17.9
13320.	**ENCOUNTER**	Flora Purim	13Aug77	194(1)	3	17.9
13321.	**THE MANHATTAN TRANSFER LIVE**	Manhattan Transfer	30May87	187(2)	3	17.9
13322.	**A CURRENT SET OF STANDARDS**	Billy Vaughn And His Orchestra	28Sep68	198(2)	3	17.9
13323.	**T.G. SHEPPARD'S GREATEST HITS**	T.G. Sheppard	11Jun83	189(2)	3	17.8
13324.	**TIGERS WILL SURVIVE**	Ian Matthews	12Feb72	196(1)	3	17.8
13325.	**ROCK & ROLL MACHINE**	Triumph	19May79	185(2)	2	17.8
13326.	**LUIS GASCA**	Luis Gasca	27May72	195(2)	3	17.8
13327.	**COSMIC TRUTH**	Undisputed Truth	21Jun75	186(2)	2	17.8
13328.	**DO YOUR OWN THING**	Brook Benton	19Jul69	189(1)	2	17.7
13329.	**THE HEART NEVER LIES**	Michael Martin Murphey	29Oct83	187(1)	3	17.7
13330.	**PEOPLE LIKE YOU**	Eddie Fisher	01Jul67	193(2)	3	17.7
13331.	**A CHILD OF THE 50'S**	Robert Klein	28Apr73	191(1)	3	17.7
13332.	**FATS IS BACK**	Fats Domino	19Oct68	189(2)	2	17.7
13333.	**I'VE ALWAYS WANTED TO DO THIS**	Jack Bruce And Friends	13Dec80	182(1)	2	17.7
13334.	**SWEET GINGERBREAD MAN**	Mike Curb Congregation	21Nov70	185(1)	2	17.6
13335.	**BARBED WIRE KISSES**	Jesus And Mary Chain	18Jun88	192(1)	3	17.6
13336.	**ON THE STRENGTH**	Grandmaster Flash & The Furious Five	30Apr88	189(2)	3	17.6
13337.	**EASY**	Marvin Gaye & Tammi Terrell	18Oct69	184(1)	2	17.6
13338.	**HEARTBREAK HOTEL**	Soundtrack	29Oct88	176(2)	2	17.6
13339.	**MAME**	Soundtrack	13Apr74	196(1)	3	17.6
13340.	**CARE**	Shriekback	25Jun83	188(1)	3	17.5
13341.	**LOVE'S THE THING**	Barbara Mason	22Feb75	187(2)	2	17.5
13342.	**MAGIC PEOPLE**	The Paupers	11Nov67	178(1)	2	17.5
13343.	**GRIEVOUS ANGEL**	Gram Parsons	16Feb74	195(1)	3	17.4
13344.	**CARL WILSON**	Carl Wilson	02May81	185(1)	2	17.4
13345.	**LANGUAGE**	Gary Myrick	06Aug83	186(1)	3	17.4
13346.	**PHOTOGLO**	Photoglo	24May80	194(1)	3	17.4

Rank. Title Act / Entry Peak(Pk Wks) TotWks	Scr
13347. **A TRIBUTE TO WOODY GUTHRIE - PART ONE** Various Artists 29Apr72 183(2) 2	17.3
13348. **DAMN RIGHT I AM SOMEBODY** Fred Wesley & The JB's 29Jun74 197(1) 3	17.3
13349. **GENTLE ON MY MIND** Lenny Dee 08Jun68 196(2) 3	17.3
13350. **BLACK BACH** Lamont Dozier 25Jan75 186(1) 2	17.3
13351. **SKIP A ROPE** Henson Cargill 23Mar68 179(1) 2	17.3
13352. **CUBA** Gibson Brothers 28Jul79 185(2) 2	17.3
13353. **BRUCE WOOLLEY & THE CAMERA CLUB** Bruce Woolley & The Camera Club 08Mar80 184(1) 2	17.2
13354. **ROBBIN'S NEST** Willie Mitchell 07Nov70 188(1) 2	17.2
13355. **SPREAD THE WORD** The Persuasions 18Nov72 195(2) 3	17.2
13356. **TO YOU HONEY, HONEY WITH LOVE** David Hudson 23Aug80 184(1) 2	17.2
13357. **I'M EVERYONE I'VE EVER LOVED** Martin Mull 26Mar77 184(1) 2	17.2
13358. **SPENCER DAVIS' GREATEST HITS** Spencer Davis Group 30Mar68 195(2) 3	17.2
13359. **FLIRT** Evelyn "Champagne" King 25Jun88 192(1) 3	17.1
13360. **TOUCH YOU** Jimmy Hall 22Nov80 183(1) 2	17.1
13361. **BACK 2 BACK** Stargard 04Jul81 186(2) 2	17.1
13362. **AIN'T NO BIG THING, BUT IT'S GROWING** New Birth 30Oct71 189(2) 2	17.1
13363. **BOOGER BEAR** Buddy Miles Express 19Jan74 194(1) 3	17.1
13364. **RIGHT ON** Wilson Pickett 04Apr70 197(1) 3	17.0
13365. **MOVE YOUR HAND** Lonnie Smith 16May70 186(2) 2	17.0
13366. **SOUL DIRECTIONS** Arthur Conley 06Jul68 185(2) 2	17.0
13367. **JUST FOLKS...A FIRESIGN CHAT** Firesign Theatre 11Jun77 184(1) 2	17.0
13368. **EXPRESSION** John Coltrane 18Nov67 194(2) 3	17.0
13369. **ELECTRONIC SOUND** George Harrison 05Jul69 191(1) 2	17.0
13370. **LOVE IS THE FOUNDATION** Loretta Lynn 22Sep73 183(1) 2	17.0
13371. **FLEETWOOD MAC (1968)** Fleetwood Mac 17Aug68 198(1) 3	17.0
13372. **I'VE FOUND SOMEONE OF MY OWN** Cal Smith 14Apr73 191(1) 3	17.0
13373. **VELVET KISS, LICK OF THE LIME** Lions And Ghosts 24Oct87 187(2) 3	17.0
13374. **LET'S DO IT TODAY** Lenny Williams 15Nov80 185(2) 2	16.9
13375. **DOWNTOWN TONIGHT** Racing Cars 02Apr77 198(1) 3	16.9
13376. **WAITING FOR SPRING** David Benoit 11Nov89 187(1) 3	16.9
13377. **HEAVEN UP HERE** Echo & The Bunnymen 25Jul81 184(1) 2	16.9
13378. **LOVE IS A SOFT TOUCH** Ferrante & Teicher 05Dec70 188(2) 2	16.9
13379. **SEAWIND** Seawind 07May77 188(2) 2	16.9
13380. **LITTLE BIT O' SOUL** Music Explosion 26Aug67 178(1) 2	16.9
13381. **GROOVE DROPS** Jimmy Smith 23May70 197(1) 3	16.8
13382. **CLASSIC ROCK - VOLUME ONE** London Symphony Orchestra 21Apr79 185(1) 2	16.8
13383. **STRICTLY PERSONAL** The Romantics 14Nov81 182(1) 2	16.8
13384. **CARRYIN' ON WITH JOHNNY CASH & JUNE CARTER** Johnny Cash & June Carter 07Oct67 194(1) 3	16.8
13385. **THE GREATEST HITS FROM MEMPHIS** Various Artists 27Sep69 189(1) 2	16.8
13386. **CHEWY, CHEWY** Ohio Express 08Feb69 191(1) 2	16.8
13387. **MOTT THE HOOPLE** Mott The Hoople 04Jul70 185(1) 2	16.7
13388. **THE LIVE ALBUM** Leon Russell And The New Grass Revival 04Apr81 187(1) 2	16.7
13389. **THE NEW BORN FREE** The Hesitations 24Feb68 193(1) 3	16.7
13390. **WARREN ZEVON** Warren Zevon 28Aug76 189(2) 2	16.7
13391. **"BABBACOMBE" LEE** Fairport Convention 25Mar72 195(1) 3	16.7
13392. **THE LAST FIVE YEARS** Rick Grech 29Sep73 195(1) 3	16.6
13393. **LOVE** Aztec Camera 19Dec87 193(3) 3	16.6
13394. **JUNKFOOD JUNKIE** Larry Groce 27Mar76 187(1) 2	16.6
13395. **THE WHOLE WORLD'S DANCING** The Trammps 26May79 184(1) 2	16.6
13396. **SMOOTH AS RAW SILK** Silk 08Nov69 191(2) 2	16.6
13397. **ALL OF YOU** Lillo Thomas 06Oct84 186(1) 3	16.5
13398. **ISLEYS' GREATEST HITS** Isley Brothers 22Dec73 195(1) 3	16.5
13399. **TALES OF THE NEW WEST** Beat Farmers 08Jun85 186(1) 3	16.5
13400. **THIRD WORLD, PRISONER IN THE STREET** Third World 30Aug80 186(2) 2	16.4
13401. **PRIME TIME** Grey And Hanks 23Feb80 195(1) 3	16.4
13402. **EN ESPANOL!** Ray Conniff & His Orchestra & Chorus 13May67 180(1) 2	16.4
13403. **DAY BY DAY** Percy Faith 23Sep72 197(3) 3	16.4
13404. **SNOOPY FOR PRESIDENT** Royal Guardsmen 31Aug68 189(1) 2	16.3
13405. **THE DON HO TV SHOW** Don Ho 18Oct69 188(1) 2	16.3
13406. **SLOW FREIGHT** Ray Bryant 13May67 193(1) 3	16.3
13407. **BETWEEN THE LINES** Spider 11Jul81 185(1) 2	16.3
13408. **THE BEST OF HERBIE MANN** Herbie Mann 28Mar70 189(2) 2	16.3
13409. **MINK DEVILLE** Mink De Ville 13Aug77 186(1) 2	16.3
13410. **MIXED BAG(2)** Richie Havens 07Nov70 190(1) 2	16.2
13411. **LOVE STORY** Andre Kostelanetz And His Orchestra 10Apr71 183(1) 2	16.2
13412. **WITH FRIENDS AND NEIGHBORS** Alex Taylor 20Mar71 190(1) 2	16.2
13413. **THERE MUST BE A WAY** Jimmy Roselli 18Nov67 191(1) 3	16.2
13414. **FOR THE FIRST TIME** Brenda & Pete 15Jun68 187(2) 2	16.2
13415. **LONESOME** Sammi Smith 21Aug71 191(2) 2	16.2
13416. **SOUTHBOUND** Hoyt Axton 12Apr75 188(1) 2	16.2
13417. **BANGOR FLYING CIRCUS** Bangor Flying Circus 27Dec69 190(2) 2	16.2
13418. **ROCK 'N' ROLL OUTLAW** Rose Tattoo 29Nov80 197(1) 3	16.1
13419. **THE BEST OF CHARLEY PRIDE, VOL. III** Charley Pride 22Jan77 188(2) 2	16.1
13420. **THE WHISPERS' LOVE STORY** The Whispers 13May72 186(2) 2	16.1
13421. **PRATT & McCLAIN FEATURING "HAPPY DAYS"** Pratt & McClain 10Jul76 190(2) 2	16.0
13422. **NOT GUILTY...** Larry Gatlin & The Gatlin Brothers Band 17Oct81 184(1) 2	16.0
13423. **I FEEL GOOD, I FEEL FINE** Bobby Bland 27Oct79 187(2) 2	16.0
13424. **THE WILD BUNCH** Soundtrack 18Oct69 192(2) 2	16.0
13425. **ECHO & THE BUNNYMEN** Echo & The Bunnymen 11Feb84 188(1) 3	16.0
13426. **THE PHANTOM** Duke Pearson 05Apr69 193(2) 2	16.0
13427. **HIGHWAY** Free 27Feb71 190(1) 2	16.0
13428. **PARADISE BAR AND GRILL** Mad River 09Aug69 192(2) 2	16.0
13429. **WATER BABIES** Miles Davis 07May77 190(2) 2	15.9
13430. **ONE NIGHT STAND** Susan Raye 26Sep70 190(2) 2	15.9
13431. **THE CARNIVAL** The Carnival 06Dec69 191(2) 2	15.8
13432. **THE SNAKE** Harvey Mandel 22Jul72 198(2) 3	15.8
13433. **SANFORD & FOXX** Redd Foxx 03Jun72 198(2) 3	15.8
13434. **THE REAL LENNY BRUCE** Lenny Bruce 05Apr75 191(2) 2	15.8
13435. **QUEEN OF THE NIGHT** Loleatta Holloway 02Dec78 187(1) 2	15.8
13436. **TALK MEMPHIS** Jesse Winchester 27Jun81 188(1) 2	15.7
13437. **SOMEWHERE IN TIME** Soundtrack 06Dec80 187(2) 2	15.7
13438. **NOTHING IN COMMON** Soundtrack 20Sep86 190(2) 3	15.7
13439. **MORE SAUCY STORIES FROM... PAT COOPER** Pat Cooper 22Mar69 193(2) 2	15.7
13440. **PEOPLE** Johnny Mathis 13Sep69 192(1) 2	15.7
13441. **IF** If 31Oct70 187(1) 2	15.7
13442. **LET'S WORK TOGETHER** Wilbert Harrison 24Jan70 190(2) 2	15.7
13443. **CLOSE-UP** Nancy Wilson 23Aug69 193(2) 2	15.6
13444. **COMING TO AMERICA** Soundtrack 30Jul88 177(1) 2	15.5
13445. **SPORTIN' LIFE** Weather Report 27Apr85 191(1) 3	15.5
13446. **SEND ME AN ANGEL '89** Real Life 01Jul89 191(1) 3	15.5
13447. **CLOSE-UP** Jackie Gleason 23Aug69 192(1) 2	15.5
13448. **HOMESICK HEROS** Charlie Daniels Band 12Nov88 181(2) 2	15.5
13449. **BACK STREET CRAWLER** Paul Kossoff 06Sep75 191(2) 2	15.5
13450. **IF YOU EVER LEAVE ME** Jack Jones 27Apr68 198(1) 3	15.5
13451. **WITH LOVE, JERRY VALE** Jerry Vale 01Nov69 193(2) 2	15.5
13452. **JOOLS & BRIAN** Julie Driscoll/Brian Auger & The Trinity 10May69 194(1) 2	15.5
13453. **IT'S MY TIME** Maynard Ferguson 27Sep80 188(2) 2	15.5
13454. **THE BEST OF JOHN KLEMMER-VOLUME ONE/MOSAIC** John Klemmer 24Nov79 187(2) 2	15.5
13455. **JUNGLE GRASS** The Aquarians 01Nov69 192(1) 2	15.4
13456. **LEFT COAST LIVE** Wet Willie 04Jun77 191(2) 2	15.4
13457. **GLENN MILLER'S BIGGEST HITS** Boston Pops Orchestra 05Apr69 192(1) 2	15.4
13458. **ANDREW GOLD** Andrew Gold 10Jan76 190(2) 2	15.4
13459. **JIMI PLAYS MONTEREY** Jimi Hendrix 08Mar86 192(2) 3	15.3
13460. **THE BEST OF THE ANIMALS(2)** The Animals 25Aug73 188(2) 2	15.3
13461. **WILD IN THE STREETS** Helix 07Nov87 179(2) 2	15.3

Rank. Title Act	Entry Peak(Pk Wks) TotWks	Scr
13462. THE CIRCUS Erasure	18Jul87 190(1) 3	15.3
13463. BLACK PEARL-LIVE! Black Pearl	17Oct70 189(1) 2	15.2
13464. WINTER WORLD OF LOVE Billy Vaughn And His Orchestra	14Mar70 188(1) 2	15.2
13465. RAMSEY LEWIS' NEWLY RECORDED ALL-TIME, NON-STOP GOLDEN HITS Ramsey Lewis	13Oct73 198(1) 3	15.2
13466. FLOW Snail	10Nov79 186(1) 2	15.2
13467. OOGUM BOOGUM Brenton Wood	22Jul67 184(2) 2	15.2
13468. YOU GOT-TA HAVE A LICENSE Porter Wagoner	16May70 190(2) 2	15.2
13469. ONCE MORE Porter Wagoner and Dolly Parton	10Oct70 191(1) 2	15.2
13470. LIVING INSIDE YOUR LOVE Earl Klugh	11Dec76 188(1) 2	15.1
13471. HALF & HALF Frankie Valli & The 4 Seasons	13Jun70 190(2) 2	15.1
13472. BLUES-THE COMMON GROUND Kenny Burrell	31Aug68 191(1) 2	15.1
13473. RATHER BE ROCKIN' Tantrum	19Jan80 199(2) 3	15.1
13474. SECOND THOUGHTS McKendree Spring	28Nov70 192(2) 2	15.1
13475. THE CHRISTMAS ALBUM Elvis Presley	28Dec85 178(2) 2	15.1
13476. SOLID GOLD Gang Of Four	06Jun81 190(2) 2	15.1
13477. FABULOUS BROADWAY Boston Pops Orchestra	09Jan71 190(1) 2	15.0
13478. SHE EVEN WOKE ME UP TO SAY GOODBYE Jerry Lee Lewis	28Feb70 186(1) 2	15.0
13479. LIBERATED FANTASIES George Duke	04Dec76 190(2) 2	15.0
13480. MADURA Madura	30Oct71 186(1) 2	15.0
13481. THE PRINCE'S TRUST 10TH ANNIVERSARY BIRTHDAY PARTY Various Artists	06Jun87 194(1) 3	15.0
13482. THE PEANUT BUTTER CONSPIRACY IS SPREADING Peanut Butter Conspiracy	20May67 196(1) 3	14.9
13483. LEARNING TO LOVE Rodney Franklin	22Jan83 190(2) 3	14.9
13484. OUR FAMILY PORTRAIT Five Stairsteps & Cubie	27Jan68 195(1) 3	14.9
13485. BARNET DOGS Russ Ballard	16Aug80 187(1) 2	14.9
13486. FOR LOVE OF IVY Soundtrack	14Sep68 192(1) 2	14.9
13487. NIGHT THINGS Ronnie Milsap	29Nov75 191(1) 2	14.9
13488. BERT KAEMPFERT NOW! Bert Kaempfert And His Orchestra	25Sep71 188(1) 2	14.8
13489. A LATIN LOVE-IN Tony Mottola	02Dec67 198(2) 3	14.8
13490. RELIGHT MY FIRE Dan Hartman	15Mar80 189(1) 2	14.8
13491. EVERYTHING I PLAY IS FUNKY Lou Donaldson	11Jul70 190(1) 2	14.8
13492. 74 MILES AWAY - WALK TALL "Cannonball" Adderley Quintet	09Dec67 186(1) 2	14.8
13493. MY BLUE RIDGE MOUNTAIN BOY Dolly Parton	22Nov69 194(2) 2	14.7
13494. STAND BY YOUR MAN Candi Staton	27Feb71 188(1) 2	14.7
13495. A TRIBUTE TO WOODY GUTHRIE - PART TWO Various Artists	29Apr72 189(2) 2	14.7
13496. BEAST Beast	13Sep69 195(2) 2	14.7
13497. MARRIAGE ON THE ROCKS/ROCK BOTTOM Amboy Dukes	21Mar70 191(1) 2	14.7
13498. JOE SIMON...BETTER THAN EVER Joe Simon	29Nov69 192(1) 2	14.6
13499. LOU REED Lou Reed	24Jun72 189(1) 2	14.6
13500. MASEKELA Hugh Masekela	29Mar69 195(2) 2	14.6
13501. WINCHESTER CATHEDRAL Palm Beach Band Boys	28Jan67 149(1) 1	14.5
13502. NEW LOOKS B.J. Thomas	21May83 193(1) 3	14.5
13503. BLOODLINE Levert	25Oct86 192(1) 3	14.5
13504. KING BEE Muddy Waters	16May81 192(2) 2	14.5
13505. UNIVERSAL CONSCIOUSNESS Alice Coltrane	13Nov71 190(1) 2	14.3
13506. SUPER OLDIES/VOL. 5 Various Artists	12Jul69 196(2) 2	14.3
13507. CONCRETE 999	27Jun81 192(2) 2	14.3
13508. TWITCH Ministry	05Apr86 194(2) 3	14.3
13509. GHOST TOWN Poco	04Dec82 195(2) 3	14.2
13510. NOTHING IS SACRED The Godz	17Feb79 189(1) 2	14.2
13511. WAYLON Waylon	16May70 192(2) 2	14.2
13512. TONY BENNETT'S "SOMETHING" Tony Bennett	14Nov70 193(1) 2	14.2
13513. THE SEARCHERS The Searchers	15Mar80 191(2) 2	14.2
13514. LIZ DAMON'S ORIENT EXPRESS Liz Damon's Orient Express	06Mar71 190(1) 2	14.1
13515. SHAKTI WITH JOHN McLAUGHLIN Shakti With John McLaughlin	12Jun76 194(2) 2	14.1
13516. BLUE AFTERNOON Tim Buckley	07Feb70 192(1) 2	14.1
13517. THE CHAMBERS BROTHERS GREATEST HITS Chambers Brothers	05Dec70 193(1) 2	14.0
13518. RUFF'N READY Jimmy Ruffin	19Apr69 196(1) 2	14.0
13519. LAW OF THE LAND Undisputed Truth	18Aug73 191(2) 2	14.0
13520. FRAMED Asleep At The Wheel	06Sep80 191(1) 2	13.9
13521. LIFE GOES ON Paul Anka	27Dec69 194(1) 2	13.9
13522. WORKIN' ON A GROOVY THING Mongo Santamaria	29Nov69 193(1) 2	13.9
13523. DENNIS WEAVER Dennis Weaver	13May72 191(2) 2	13.9
13524. EVERYBODY'S DOIN' THE HUSTLE & DEAD ON THE DOUBLE BUMP James Brown	04Oct75 193(1) 2	13.9
13525. ELLA Ella Fitzgerald	18Oct69 196(2) 2	13.9
13526. EXPERIENCE IN E, TENSITY, DIALOGUES "Cannonball" Adderley Quintet	26Sep70 194(2) 2	13.9
13527. SOUNDS OF LOVE Andre Kostelanetz And His Orchestra	01Nov69 194(1) 2	13.8
13528. MAKE IT WITH YOU Peggy Lee	19Dec70 194(2) 2	13.8
13529. ME AND JOE Rodney O & Joe Cooley	04Mar89 187(2) 2	13.8
13530. DAMES AT SEA Original Cast	02Aug69 195(1) 2	13.8
13531. THE CHANGE HAS COME Chubby Checker	06Mar82 186(1) 2	13.8
13532. WITH LOVE, FROM LYNN Lynn Anderson	12Apr69 197(2) 2	13.7
13533. LIVE! MUTHA Black Oak Arkansas	28Feb76 194(1) 2	13.7
13534. FOUR FOR THE SHOW Statler Brothers	09Aug86 183(2) 2	13.7
13535. THE J. GEILS BAND J. Geils Band	30Jan71 195(2) 2	13.7
13536. HIT AND RUN TSOL	04Jul87 184(1) 2	13.7
13537. MARRIED TO THE MOB Soundtrack	01Oct88 197(2) 3	13.7
13538. BEHOLD & SEE Ultimate Spinach	09Nov68 198(2) 2	13.7
13539. LOVE ACTION Sniff 'N' The Tears	19Sep81 192(2) 2	13.7
13540. MANIFEST DESTINY The Dictators	30Jul77 193(1) 2	13.6
13541. TONS OF SOBS Free	13Sep69 197(2) 2	13.6
13542. CLASS GUITAR Chet Atkins	20Jan68 189(2) 2	13.6
13543. UNDERGROUND GOLD Various Artists	27Sep69 196(1) 2	13.6
13544. I WOULDN'T LIVE IN NEW YORK CITY Buck Owens	28Nov70 190(1) 2	13.6
13545. ROUND MIDNIGHT Soundtrack	24Jan87 196(1) 3	13.6
13546. MONY MONY Tommy James And The Shondells	27Jul68 193(2) 2	13.5
13547. PHIL OCHS GREATEST HITS Phil Ochs	14Mar70 194(2) 2	13.5
13548. THE GARY PUCKETT ALBUM Gary Puckett	16Oct71 196(1) 2	13.5
13549. TOO HOT TO SLEEP Survivor	05Nov88 187(2) 2	13.5
13550. GET HAPPY WITH THE LONDON PHILHARMONIC ORCHESTRA Tony Bennett	20Nov71 195(1) 2	13.5
13551. MONGO '70 Mongo Santamaria	03Oct70 195(2) 2	13.4
13552. W. C. FIELDS ON RADIO W.C. Fields	18Oct69 197(2) 2	13.4
13553. THE INCREDIBLE SOUL OF B.B. KING B.B. King	11Apr70 193(1) 2	13.4
13554. WE'LL CRY TOGETHER Maxine Brown	29Nov69 195(1) 2	13.4
13555. AMERICA THE BEAUTIFUL Tennessee Ernie Ford	25Apr70 192(1) 2	13.4
13556. RICK SINGS NELSON Rick Nelson And The Stone Canyon Band	07Nov70 196(2) 2	13.4
13557. YOU NEED SOMEONE TO LOVE New Christy Minstrels	28Nov70 195(1) 2	13.4
13558. FOR YOUR PLEASURE Roxy Music	28Jul73 193(2) 2	13.3
13559. MELANIE Melanie	15Nov69 196(1) 2	13.3
13560. THE BEST OF MANDRILL Mandrill	26Jul75 194(1) 2	13.3
13561. THE AMERICAN DREAM American Dream	28Feb70 194(2) 2	13.3
13562. TIMES HAVE CHANGED The Impressions	29Apr72 192(2) 2	13.3
13563. OFFICIAL MUSIC King Biscuit Boy with Crowbar	26Dec70 194(1) 2	13.3
13564. FROG CITY Southern Comfort	14Aug71 196(1) 2	13.3
13565. STONE FLOWER Antonio Carlos Jobim	09Jan71 196(2) 2	13.2
13566. THE HUSTLE AND BEST OF VAN McCOY Van McCoy	08Jan77 193(1) 2	13.2
13567. SPECIAL Jimmy Cliff	14Aug82 186(2) 2	13.2
13568. BEST OF THE SOUNDTRACKS Various Artists	08Feb69 198(2) 2	13.2
13569. GRADUALLY GOING TORNADO Bill Bruford	29Mar80 191(1) 2	13.2
13570. MY BABE Roy Buchanan	24Jan81 193(1) 2	13.2
13571. DAVID FOSTER David Foster	19Jul86 195(2) 3	13.2
13572. HOW CAN YOU BE IN TWO PLACES AT ONCE WHEN YOU'RE NOT ANYWHERE AT ALL Firesign Theatre	18Oct69 195(1) 2	13.1
13573. DAVID BROMBERG David Bromberg	25Mar72 194(2) 2	13.1
13574. COOKIN' Jerry Reed	16May70 194(1) 2	13.1

Rank. Title Act Entry Peak(Pk Wks) TotWks	Scr
13575. REACH FOR THE SKY Sutherland Brothers And Quiver 08May76 195(1) 2	13.1
13576. LOVE'S HAPPENING Five Stairsteps & Cubie 26Apr69 198(2) 2	13.1
13577. LAND OF THE THIRD EYE Dave Valentin 25Oct80 194(2) 2	13.0
13578. WILD WEEKEND NRBQ 30Dec89 198(3) 3	13.0
13579. PENNIES FROM HEAVEN Soundtrack 23Jan82 188(1) 2	13.0
13580. THE UNFORGIVEN The Unforgiven 09Aug86 185(2) 2	13.0
13581. BELAFONTE ON CAMPUS Harry Belafonte 29Jul67 199(1) 3	13.0
13582. RISE AND SHINE! Kokomo 17Apr76 194(1) 2	13.0
13583. WHOLE LOTTA LOVE C.C.S. 03Apr71 197(2) 2	13.0
13584. THE LIFE AND TIMES OF COUNTRY JOE & THE FISH FROM HAIGHT-ASHBURY TO WOODSTOCK Country Joe & The Fish 30Oct71 197(2) 2	13.0
13585. GOING EAST Billy Paul 16Oct71 197(1) 2	13.0
13586. WILD EXHIBITIONS Walter Egan 28May83 187(1) 2	12.9
13587. FOLLOW MY MIND Jimmy Cliff 01Nov75 195(1) 2	12.9
13588. SUPER ROCK Various Artists 14Nov70 197(2) 2	12.9
13589. CIRCUS OF POWER Circus Of Power 12Nov88 185(1) 2	12.9
13590. THE RUNAWAYS The Runaways 21Aug76 194(1) 2	12.9
13591. SAVE YOUR PRAYERS Waysted 21Mar87 185(1) 2	12.9
13592. SEE JUNGLE! SEE JUNGLE! GO JOIN YOUR GANG YEAH! CITY ALL OVER, GO APE CRAZY Bow Wow Wow 21Nov81 192(2) 2	12.9
13593. THE LONESOME PICKER RIDES AGAIN John Stewart 15Jan72 195(2) 2	12.8
13594. STRONGER THAN DIRT Big Mama Thornton 30Aug69 198(2) 2	12.8
13595. THE ODD COUPLE Soundtrack 27Jul68 190(1) 2	12.8
13596. IF THE LIGHTS DON'T GET YOU THE HELOTS WILL Stanky Brown Group 05Mar77 195(1) 2	12.7
13597. A RECORD OF PURE LOVE & PLEASURE Pure Love & Pleasure 25Apr70 195(1) 2	12.7
13598. STORY SONGS OF THE TRAINS AND RIVERS Johnny Cash And The Tennessee Two 27Dec69 197(2) 2	12.7
13599. COKE Coke Escovedo 13Mar76 195(1) 2	12.7
13600. THE PHOENIX CONCERTS-LIVE John Stewart 06Jul74 195(1) 2	12.7
13601. THE MERRY-GO-ROUND The Merry-Go-Round 18Nov67 190(1) 2	12.7
13602. THE ARMADA ORCHESTRA Armada Orchestra 17Jan76 196(2) 2	12.6
13603. I'VE GOT YOU ON MY MIND AGAIN Buck Owens 15Feb69 199(2) 2	12.6
13604. OUTA HAND Coney Hatch 17Sep83 186(1) 2	12.6
13605. BABY I WANT YOU Funky Communication Committee 08Sep79 192(1) 2	12.6
13606. GREATEST HITS Steve Wariner 17Oct87 187(2) 2	12.6
13607. MOONDOG SERENADE Cashman & West 11Aug73 192(1) 2	12.6
13608. EPIC FOREST Rare Bird 18Aug73 194(2) 2	12.6
13609. WHAT'S UP FRONT THAT-COUNTS The Counts 01Jul72 193(1) 2	12.6
13610. BELIEVE Third Power 04Jul70 194(1) 2	12.5
13611. TRACES Andre Kostelanetz And His Orchestra 07Jun69 200(2) 2	12.5
13612. RELEASED Jade Warrior 06May72 194(2) 2	12.5
13613. JE T'AIME (BEAUTIFUL LOVE) Jane Birkin Serge Gainsbourg 07Mar70 196(2) 2	12.5
13614. JEAN Al Martino 20Dec69 196(1) 2	12.5
13615. BRING ME HOME Mother Earth 15May71 199(2) 2	12.5
13616. JERRY VALE SINGS 16 GREATEST HITS OF THE 60'S Jerry Vale 14Feb70 196(2) 2	12.5
13617. THE SENSATIONAL SONNY JAMES Sonny James 11Sep71 197(1) 2	12.4
13618. WOMAN OF THE YEAR Original Cast 27Jun81 196(2) 2	12.4
13619. WORD OF MOUTH Merryweather & Friends 04Oct69 199(2) 2	12.4
13620. MY LOVE / DON'T KEEP ME HANGIN' ON Sonny James 19Sep70 197(2) 2	12.4
13621. HAPPY BIRTHDAY, RUTHY BABY McGuinness Flint 11Sep71 198(2) 2	12.4
13622. ELEPHANT'S MEMORY Elephant's Memory 10May69 200(2) 2	12.4
13623. SOUL SISTER Erma Franklin 18Oct69 199(2) 2	12.4
13624. IF WALLS COULD TALK Little Milton 28Mar70 197(2) 2	12.4
13625. I WISH YOU LOVE Robert Goulet 14Nov70 198(2) 2	12.3
13626. DON'T THROW STONES The Sports 24Nov79 194(2) 2	12.3
13627. HERE COME THE HARDY BOYS Hardy Boys 15Nov69 199(2) 2	12.3
13628. I LOOKED UP Incredible String Band 25Jul70 196(2) 2	12.3
13629. TURN AROUND, LOOK AT ME Lenny Dee 08Mar69 199(2) 2	12.3
13630. THE BEST OF ENGLAND DAN & JOHN FORD COLEY England Dan & John Ford Coley 05Jan80 194(2) 2	12.3
13631. MINOR DETAIL Minor Detail 01Oct83 187(1) 2	12.3
13632. ENTRANCE Edgar Winter 27Jun70 196(2) 2	12.3
13633. BABY, BABY David Houston 18Apr70 194(1) 2	12.3
13634. THIS IS CLARENCE CARTER Clarence Carter 07Dec68 200(2) 2	12.2
13635. THE INCREDIBLE ROY CLARK Roy Clark 14Aug71 197(1) 2	12.2
13636. PHAEDRA Tangerine Dream 06Jul74 196(1) 2	12.2
13637. THIS IS HENRY MANCINI Henry Mancini And His Orchestra And Chorus 26Sep70 196(1) 2	12.2
13638. THE SOUL GOES ON Jerry Butler 27Jul68 195(1) 2	12.2
13639. BLOW-UP Herbie Hancock 13May67 192(2) 2	12.2
13640. THE BIG HITS NOW Various Artists 08Aug70 197(2) 2	12.1
13641. THERE'S GOTTA BE A CHANGE Albert Collins 12Feb72 196(2) 2	12.1
13642. KINGDOM COME Sir Lord Baltimore 06Feb71 198(2) 2	12.1
13643. AN ANTHOLOGY OF BRITISH BLUES VOL. 2 Various Artists 28Dec68 200(2) 2	12.1
13644. THE SERPENT IS RISING Styx 09Feb74 192(1) 2	12.1
13645. OFF THE WALL Smokestack Lightnin' 12Apr69 200(2) 2	12.1
13646. BEST OF THE BLUES PROJECT Blues Project 09Aug69 199(1) 2	12.0
13647. BACHARACH BAROQUE The Renaissance 09Jan71 198(1) 2	12.0
13648. MORE HITS OF THE 50'S AND 60'S Count Basie 22Feb64 150(1) 1	12.0
13649. SING AWAY THE WORLD Ed Ames 11Jul70 194(1) 2	12.0
13650. SWEETWATER Sweetwater 13Sep69 200(2) 2	11.9
13651. TABERNAKEL Jan Akkerman 02Mar74 195(1) 2	11.9
13652. SILVER CYCLES Eddie Harris 22Feb69 199(1) 2	11.9
13653. PRIME PRINE - BEST JOHN PRINE John Prine 15Jan77 196(1) 2	11.9
13654. ROMEO'S DAUGHTER Romeo's Daughter 19Nov88 191(2) 2	11.9
13655. 2ND TIME AROUND Spinners 14Nov70 199(2) 2	11.9
13656. I THINK I LOVE YOU Percy Faith 27Feb71 198(1) 2	11.9
13657. THE KANSAS CITY SONG Buck Owens 19Sep70 196(1) 2	11.9
13658. FLY Yoko Ono 13Nov71 199(2) 2	11.9
13659. THE BRAND NEW Z.Z. HILL Z.Z. Hill 22Jan72 194(1) 2	11.8
13660. SMELL THE FLOWERS Jerry Reed 01Apr72 196(1) 2	11.8
13661. BATTLE AXE Billion Dollar Babies 11Jun77 198(1) 2	11.8
13662. LIVE AT BILL GRAHAM'S FILLMORE WEST Various Artists 25Oct69 200(2) 2	11.8
13663. TRUCK STOP Jerry Smith and his Pianos 26Jul69 200(2) 2	11.8
13664. LIKE AN OLD FASHIONED WALTZ Sandy Denny 20Jul74 197(1) 2	11.8
13665. BACK TO THE BEACH Soundtrack 05Sep87 188(1) 2	11.8
13666. THROUGH THE EYES OF LOVE The Frost 17Oct70 197(1) 2	11.8
13667. GET BACK! Ike & Tina Turner 11May85 189(1) 2	11.8
13668. ELECTRA GLIDE IN BLUE Soundtrack 20Oct73 194(1) 2	11.8
13669. LOOK-KA PY PY The Meters 24Jan70 198(2) 2	11.8
13670. BEDLAM The Rustix 15Nov69 200(2) 2	11.8
13671. BREAK OF DAWN Firefall 12Mar83 199(1) 3	11.8
13672. SOPWITH CAMEL Sopwith "Camel" 28Oct67 191(1) 2	11.8
13673. BO-DAY-SHUS!!! Mojo Nixon & Skid Roper 10Oct87 189(1) 2	11.7
13674. THE DAISY DILLMAN BAND Dillman Band 01Apr78 198(2) 2	11.7
13675. TAKE ME TO TOMORROW John Denver 02May70 197(1) 2	11.7
13676. THESE THINGS TOO Pearls Before Swine 27Sep69 200(2) 2	11.7
13677. DR. DEMENTO'S DELIGHTS Various Artists 29Nov75 198(1) 2	11.7
13678. EXIT Tangerine Dream 21Nov81 195(2) 2	11.6
13679. THE DIS-ADVANTAGES OF YOU Brass Ring featuring Phil Bodner 24Jun67 193(1) 2	11.6
13680. HELD OVER! TODAY'S GREAT MOVIE THEMES Percy Faith 13Jun70 196(1) 2	11.6
13681. SWEET SOUL King Curtis 17Aug68 198(2) 2	11.6
13682. MEMPHIS Petula Clark 08Aug70 198(2) 2	11.6
13683. STEP BY STEP BY STEP Stairsteps 12Dec70 199(2) 2	11.6
13684. PETER NERO PLAYS BORN FREE AND OTHERS Peter Nero 13May67 193(1) 2	11.6
13685. JACKIE Jackie DeShannon 22Jul72 196(2) 2	11.6
13686. TRIDENT McCoy Tyner 03Jan76 198(2) 2	11.5
13687. HISTORY OF BRITISH ROCK Various Artists 01Jun74 198(1) 2	11.5
13688. GET READY King Curtis 29Aug70 198(2) 2	11.5
13689. NO ANSWER Electric Light Orchestra 03Jun72 196(2) 2	11.5

Rank. Title Act Entry Peak(Pk Wks) TotWks	Scr
13690. RURAL FREE DELIVERY Eric Weissberg & Deliverance 20Oct73 196(2) 2	11.5
13691. AFRICA, CENTER OF THE WORLD Roy Ayers 15Aug81 197(2) 2	11.5
13692. SPIDERS FROM MARS Spiders From Mars 03Apr76 197(1) 2	11.5
13693. YOUR MOTHER'S PRAYER Buck Owens 25Apr70 198(2) 2	11.5
13694. PORTRAIT OF THE ORIGINALS The Originals 11Jul70 198(2) 2	11.5
13695. THE SORCERER Gabor Szabo 13Jan68 194(2) 2	11.5
13696. LEGALIZE IT Peter Tosh 31Jul76 199(1) 2	11.4
13697. THE JAMES COTTON BLUES BAND James Cotton Band 16Dec67 194(1) 2	11.4
13698. GET YOUR ROCKS OFF Manfred Mann's Earth Band 23Jun73 196(1) 2	11.4
13699. BOZ SCAGGS & BAND Boz Scaggs 11Dec71 198(1) 2	11.4
13700. JAN AKKERMAN Jan Akkerman 08Apr78 198(1) 2	11.3
13701. THE ROAD The Road 31Jan70 199(2) 2	11.3
13702. HOME STYLE Brook Benton 22Aug70 199(2) 2	11.3
13703. BONGO ROCK Incredible Bongo Band 18Aug73 197(2) 2	11.3
13704. SONGS FROM THE STAGE AND SCREEN Michael Crawford 30Jul88 192(2) 2	11.2
13705. THE WELL-TEMPERED SYNTHESIZER Walter Carlos 03Jan70 199(1) 2	11.2
13706. THE BELLE STARS Belle Stars 28May83 191(1) 2	11.2
13707. A TIME FOR LOVE Percy Faith 23Jan71 200(2) 2	11.2
13708. COSMIC COWBOY SOUVENIR Michael Murphey 16Jun73 196(2) 2	11.2
13709. YOUR GOOD THING Lou Rawls 20Dec69 200(2) 2	11.2
13710. ICON Icon 09Jun84 190(1) 2	11.2
13711. THE VINTAGE YEARS The Impressions Featuring Jerry Butler & Curtis Mayfield 05Feb77 199(2) 2	11.1
13712. HERE COMES SHUGGIE OTIS Shuggie Otis 07Mar70 199(2) 2	11.1
13713. HONEY COME BACK Tony Sandler And Ralph Young 11Jul70 199(2) 2	11.1
13714. TREEMONISHA Original Cast 08May76 200(2) 2	11.0
13715. ZIG-ZAG WALK Foghat 25Jun83 192(1) 2	11.0
13716. CARNIVAL John Handy 16Apr77 200(2) 2	11.0
13717. ROYAL BED BOUNCER Kayak 17Jan76 199(1) 2	11.0
13718. LOVE IS BLUE Manny Kellem - His Orchestra And Voices 13Apr68 197(1) 2	11.0
13719. KWICK Kwick 07Jun80 197(1) 2	10.9
13720. CAROL BURNETT FEATURING IF I COULD WRITE A SONG Carol Burnett 29Jan72 199(2) 2	10.9
13721. COVER GIRL Phantom, Rocker & Slick 18Oct86 181(1) 2	10.9
13722. GENTLY SWINGIN' Earl Grant 23Mar68 192(1) 2	10.9
13723. BACK IT UP Robin Trower 01Oct83 191(1) 2	10.8
13724. SUCKER FOR A PRETTY FACE Eric Martin Band 24Sep83 191(1) 2	10.8
13725. COMING OF AGE Five Man Electrical Band 12Feb72 199(2) 2	10.8
13726. EVERLASTING LOVE Robert Knight 16Dec67 196(2) 2	10.8
13727. BASKET OF LIGHT Pentangle 31Jan70 200(2) 2	10.8
13728. ANOTHER DAY/ANOTHER DOLLAR Gang Of Four 13Feb82 195(2) 2	10.8
13729. INSTRUMENTAL DIRECTIONS The Nite-Liters 20May72 198(2) 2	10.7
13730. THE STERILE CUCKOO Soundtrack 06Jun70 200(2) 2	10.7
13731. BACHMAN TURNER OVERDRIVE(2) Bachman-Turner Overdrive 29Sep84 191(1) 2	10.6
13732. HARD CORE Paul Dean 25Feb89 195(2) 2	10.6
13733. TELL THE TRUTH Otis Redding 29Aug70 200(2) 2	10.6
13734. WELCOME HOME Osibisa 24Apr76 200(2) 2	10.6
13735. ROGER MILLER 1970 Roger Miller 14Feb70 200(2) 2	10.6
13736. BILL BLACK'S GREATEST HITS Bill Black's Combo 19Aug67 195(2) 2	10.5
13737. SANCTUARY Dion 01Jan72 200(2) 2	10.5
13738. EDEN'S CHILDREN Eden's Children 09Mar68 196(1) 2	10.5
13739. COME BACK CHARLESTON BLUE Soundtrack 23Sep72 198(2) 2	10.4
13740. STRUTTIN' The Meters 18Jul70 200(2) 2	10.4
13741. LET'S MAKE UP AND BE FRIENDLY Bonzo Dog Band 10Jun72 199(2) 2	10.3
13742. SOUND ALARM Michael Anderson 13Aug88 194(2) 2	10.3
13743. THE MOVIE SONGS Frank Sinatra 29Jul67 195(1) 2	10.3
13744. JERRY VALE SINGS THE GREAT HITS OF NAT KING COLE Jerry Vale 12Feb72 200(2) 2	10.3
13745. DREAMS OF TOMORROW Lonnie Liston Smith 30Jul83 193(1) 2	10.3
13746. SHAKE, RATTLE & ROLL Arthur Conley 19Aug67 193(1) 2	10.3
13747. STRENGTH OF STEEL Anvil 18Jul87 191(1) 2	10.2
13748. DIAMONDS IN THE RAW S.O.S. Band 04Nov89 194(2) 2	10.2
13749. RIP IT UP Dead Or Alive 30Jul88 195(2) 2	10.2
13750. CROSS COUNTRY Cross Country 13Oct73 198(1) 2	10.1
13751. MY GIRL JOSEPHINE Jerry Jaye 29Jul67 195(1) 2	10.1
13752. MOTOWN REMEMBERS MARVIN GAYE Marvin Gaye 03May86 193(1) 2	10.1
13753. ASIA Kitaro 30Nov85 191(1) 2	10.1
13754. SWEET RAIN Stan Getz 02Sep67 195(1) 2	10.0
13755. MR. C. Norman Connors 05Dec81 197(1) 2	10.0
13756. I HAVE A PONY Steven Wright 23Nov85 192(1) 2	10.0
13757. DANGEROUS DREAMS The Nails 23Aug86 194(2) 2	10.0
13758. IVORY COAST Bob James 10Sep88 196(2) 2	10.0
13759. KASIM Kasim Sulton 27Feb82 197(2) 2	10.0
13760. CHRIS ISAAK Chris Isaak 11Apr87 194(1) 2	10.0
13761. TRIANGLE Beau Brummels 30Sep67 197(1) 2	9.9
13762. SOMETHING SUPER! King Richard's Fluegel Knights 27Jan68 198(2) 2	9.9
13763. A POSSIBLE PROJECTION OF THE FUTURE/CHILDHOOD'S END Al Kooper 06May72 200(2) 2	9.8
13764. MY SPORTIN' LIFE John Kay 14Jul73 200(2) 2	9.8
13765. THE COUNTRY WAY Charley Pride 30Mar68 199(1) 2	9.8
13766. SOULED OUT Righteous Brothers 28Oct67 198(2) 2	9.7
13767. THIS IS THIS Weather Report 23Aug86 195(2) 2	9.7
13768. GREATEST HITS Trinere & Friends 23Sep89 196(2) 2	9.6
13769. ALL OF ME Toni Tennille 26Dec87 198(2) 2	9.6
13770. BROTHER ARAB Arabian Prince 16Dec89 193(1) 2	9.6
13771. EXCESS ALL AREAS Shy 27Jun87 193(1) 2	9.5
13772. HARLEQUIN Dave Grusin & Lee Ritenour 05Oct85 192(1) 2	9.5
13773. NO BLUE THING Ray Lynch 24Jun89 197(2) 2	9.4
13774. WHITE LIGHT/WHITE HEAT Velvet Underground 16Mar68 199(1) 2	9.4
13775. RADIO SILENCE Boris Grebenshikov 26Aug89 198(2) 2	9.2
13776. A TASTE OF BRASS FOR LOVERS ONLY Jackie Gleason 24Jun67 200(2) 2	9.0
13777. SHADES Yellowjackets 06Sep86 195(1) 2	9.0
13778. THE VELVET UNDERGROUND Velvet Underground & Nico 20Apr85 197(1) 2	8.9
13779. ODE TO BILLY JOE Billy Vaughn And His Orchestra 28Oct67 200(2) 2	8.9
13780. THE HOLLYWOOD MUSICALS Johnny Mathis & Henry Mancini 10Jan87 197(2) 2	8.9
13781. THE HOLE Golden Earring 12Jul86 196(2) 2	8.8
13782. THE MONKEES SONG BOOK Golden Gate Strings 27May67 200(2) 2	8.8
13783. THE YAMA YAMA MAN George Segal 02Sep67 199(1) 2	8.7
13784. BIRD ON A WIRE Tim Hardin 31Jul71 189(1) 1	8.6
13785. KINGDOM BLOW Kurtis Blow 13Dec86 196(2) 2	8.6
13786. CAPTAIN MARVEL Stan Getz 01Mar75 191(1) 1	8.0
13787. CANDLELAND Ian McCulloch 25Nov89 179(1) 1	8.0
13788. MAD DOG John Entwistle's Ox 01Mar75 192(1) 1	7.7
13789. THE PRINCESS BRIDE Mark Knopfler 31Oct87 180(1) 1	7.5
13790. CRUEL SISTER Pentangle 13Mar71 193(1) 1	7.5
13791. THE AMERICAN DREAM Emitt Rhodes 17Apr71 194(1) 1	7.4
13792. MAMA'S BIG ONES Mama Cass 13Mar71 194(1) 1	7.2
13793. PHANTOM OF THE PARADISE Soundtrack 01Mar75 194(1) 1	7.2
13794. TENKU Kitaro 04Apr87 183(1) 1	7.0
13795. LOST AND FOUND Michael Parks 13Mar71 195(1) 1	7.0
13796. PASTELS Ron Carter 12Mar77 193(1) 1	7.0
13797. RU-BEEEEE Osborne Brothers 04Jul70 193(1) 1	6.9
13798. TIN TIN Tin Tin 05Jun71 197(1) 1	6.8
13799. HOLD ME Johnny & Jonie Mosby 11Oct69 197(1) 1	6.7
13800. THE AMAZING METS Various Artists 22Nov69 197(1) 1	6.6
13801. IN THE LIGHT Keith Jarrett 13Mar76 195(1) 1	6.6
13802. TIRAMI SU Al Di Meola Project 23Jan88 190(1) 1	6.6
13803. DISCO FANTASY Coke Escovedo 12Feb77 195(1) 1	6.5
13804. JOSHUA Dolly Parton 12Jun71 198(1) 1	6.5
13805. CHERYL MOANA MARIE John Rowles 20Mar71 197(1) 1	6.5
13806. THE IMPOSSIBLE DREAM Sensational Alex Harvey Band 01Mar75 197(1) 1	6.5

Rank. Title Act Entry Peak(Pk Wks) TotWks	Scr
13807. JOYFUL Orpheus 11Oct69 198(1) 1	6.4
13808. THE CLIMAX CHICAGO BLUES BAND PLAYS ON Climax Blues Band 28Nov70 197(1) 1	6.3
13809. CLASSIC RUSH Tom Rush 27Mar71 198(1) 1	6.2
13810. SEARCH AND NEARNESS The Rascals 20Mar71 198(1) 1	6.2
13811. SO...WHERE'S THE SHOW? Jo Jo Gunne 28Dec74 198(1) 1	6.2
13812. I THINK, THEREFORE I AM R. Dean Taylor 20Feb71 198(1) 1	6.1
13813. IN THE MOOD Andrews Sisters 20Jul74 198(1) 1	6.0
13814. KEEP ON BUMPIN' & MASTERPLAN The Kay-Gees 01Mar75 199(1) 1	5.9
13815. BIG ONES Loverboy 23Dec89 189(1) 1	5.9
13816. THE SONGS OF BACHARACH AND DAVID Ed Ames 20Feb71 199(1) 1	5.8
13817. ON MY SIDE The Cowsills 08May71 200(1) 1	5.8
13818. DAY BY DAY Cleo Laine 20Jul74 199(1) 1	5.8
13819. I'VE NEVER BEEN TO ME Nancy Wilson 30Jul77 198(1) 1	5.7

Rank. Title Act Entry Peak(Pk Wks) TotWks	Scr
13820. THREE DEGREES LIVE Three Degrees 17Jan76 199(1) 1	5.6
13821. TAKING OVER Overkill 11Apr87 191(1) 1	5.6
13822. OLD FASHION CHRISTMAS Carpenters 05Jan85 190(1) 1	5.5
13823. ALBERT FINNEY'S ALBUM Albert Finney 03Sep77 199(1) 1	5.5
13824. CIRCLES Mary Travers 20Jul74 200(1) 1	5.5
13825. ANGEL DELIGHT Fairport Convention 04Dec71 200(1) 1	5.5
13826. PAT McLAUGHLIN Pat McLaughlin 16Apr88 195(1) 1	5.4
13827. THE MAIN INGREDIENT L.T.D. Main Ingredient 22Aug70 200(1) 1	5.4
13828. LET THE HUSTLERS PLAY Steady B 22Oct88 193(1) 1	5.3
13829. THE NEW SPIRIT OF CAPITOL Various Artists 07Mar70 200(1) 1	5.3
13830. BRIGHTER THAN A THOUSAND SUNS Killing Joke 11Apr87 194(1) 1	5.1
13831. ENGLAND'S GREATEST HITS Various Artists 09Sep67 197(1) 1	4.9
13832. BLUES FOR SALVADOR Carlos Santana 07Nov87 195(1) 1	4.8

Rank. Title Act Entry Peak(Pk Wks) TotWks	Scr
13833. THE COLD HARD FACTS OF LIFE Porter Wagoner 01Jul67 199(1) 1	4.8
13834. SLOW DANCE Southside Johnny 03Dec88 198(1) 1	4.7
13835. SING Soundtrack 29Apr89 196(1) 1	4.7
13836. BA-DOP-BOOM-BANG Grandmaster Flash 25Apr87 197(1) 1	4.6
13837. WORKERS PLAYTIME Billy Bragg 05Nov88 198(1) 1	4.6
13838. THE ROBBS The Robbs 13Jan68 200(1) 1	4.5
13839. GOT TO BE TOUGH M.C. Shy D 27Jun87 197(1) 1	4.5
13840. BLIND DATE Soundtrack 02May87 198(1) 1	4.4
13841. ANOTHER SCOOP Pete Townshend 04Apr87 198(1) 1	4.3
13842. TEST PATTERNS Tommy Boyce & Bobby Hart 09Sep67 200(1) 1	4.3
13843. ROACHES: THE BEGINNING Bobby Jimmy & The Critters 29Nov86 200(1) 1	3.6

The Albums Alphabetically

In order to make the title information fit on one line, abbreviations may be used for both Title and Act. An abbreviation is shown by an ellipsis (...). Between the Title and the Act and the Rank, there is sufficient information to find that album in other lists.

Where an album has allocated credit to the underlying artists in a collaboration, designated by [A], all the underlying artists will appear with the title of the record.

A

Title	Act	Rank
"A"	JETHRO TULL	4549
Abacab	GENESIS	520
Abandoned Luncheonet...	Daryl HALL & John OA...	3032
Abba	ABBA	12632
Abbey Road	The BEATLES	28
ABC	JACKSON 5	610
Abigail	KING DIAMOND	8889
Abilene	George HAMILTON IV	8497
The Abominable Showman	Nick LOWE	10642
Abominog	URIAH HEEP	5819
About Face	David GILMOUR	2835
About Last Night...	SOUNDTRACK-MOVIE	6823
About Love	Gladys KNIGHT & The ...	4396
About Time	TEN YEARS AFTER	8882
About Us	STORIES	3416
Abracadabra	Steve MILLER Band	882
Abraxas	SANTANA	35
Absolute Beginners	SOUNDTRACK-MOVIE	6923
Absolutely	MADNESS	11457
Absolutely Free	Frank ZAPPA	3785
Absolutely Live	Rod STEWART	5829
Absolutely Live	The DOORS	1727
Absolute Torch And Twang	K.D. LANG	2999
Abstract Emotions	Randy CRAWFORD	12711
A.C.	Andre CYMONE	10022
Academy Award Losers	Steve LAWRENCE	11183
The Academy Award So...	Henry MANCINI and hi...	6762
Academy Award Winners	Roger WILLIAMS	9645
The Academy Award Winning "...	Andy WILLIAMS	912
Accept No Substitutes	PLEASURE	11124
Accept No Substitute...	DELANEY & BONNIE & F...	12466
Access All Areas	SPYRO GYRA	5217
Ace	Bob WEIR	5729
Ace Frehley	Ace FREHLEY	2179
Acid Queen	Tina TURNER	10988
Across A Crowded Room	Richard THOMPSON	8070
Across 110th Street (Soundtr...	Bobby WOMACK	4546
Act A Fool	KING TEE	8109
Acting Up	Marlena SHAW	12168
Acting Very Strange	Mike RUTHERFORD	11020
Action	The BLACKBYRDS	3246
Action Replay	Howard JONES	3722
Action Speaks Louder Than ...	CHOCOLATE MILK	13153
Act Like Nothing's Wrong	Al KOOPER	12322
Actually	PET SHOP BOYS	1543
Actual Speeches Of F... [A]	Franklin D. ROOSEVEL...	10555
Actual Speeches Of F... [A]	John Fitzgerald KENN...	10555
Addictions Vol. I	Robert PALMER	6238
Addrisi Brothers	ADDRISI BROTHERS	7903
Adventures In Modern Recordin...	The BUGGLES	11860
Adventures In Paradise	Minnie RIPERTON	2390
Adventures In The Land Of Music	DYNASTY	3790
Adventures In Utopia	UTOPIA	3395
The Adventures Of Captain Sky	CAPTAIN SKY	9089
The Adventures Of Pa...	NEW RIDERS Of The PU...	5143
Aereo-Plain	John HARTFORD	12897
Aerial Pandemonium Ballet	NILSSON	11750
Aerie	John DENVER	5439
Aerobic Dance Hits, Volume ...	Carla CAPUANO	10609
Aerobic Dancing	Barbara Ann AUER	8722
Aerobic Shape Up II	Joanie GREGGAINS	12695
Aerosmith	AEROSMITH	1687
Aerosmith's Greatest Hits	AEROSMITH	3947
Aesop's Fables The Smot...	SMOTHERS BROTHERS	7455

Title	Act	Rank
Affair	CHERRELLE	7842
AFL1-3603	Dave DAVIES	4330
Afoot	LET'S ACTIVE	9982
Africa, Center Of The World	Roy AYERS	13691
Africanism	KONGAS	9001
African Queens	RITCHIE FAMILY	9245
Afrodisiac	MAIN INGREDIENT	8195
After Bathing At Bax...	JEFFERSON AIRPLANE/S...	2885
Afterburner	ZZ TOP	476
After Dark	Andy GIBB	3210
After Dark	CRUZADOS	7133
After Dark	Ray PARKER Jr./RAYDI...	8674
After Eight	TACO	2806
After Here Through Midland	COCK ROBIN	13000
Aftermath	ROLLING STONES	647
After Midnight	The MANHATTANS	2366
Afternoons In Utopia	ALPHAVILLE	12332
After 7	AFTER 7	2026
After The Gold Rush	Neil YOUNG	464
After The Gold Rush	PRELUDE	8487
After The Lovin'	Engelbert HUMPERDINC...	2040
After The Roses	Kenny RANKIN	11496
After The Snow	MODERN ENGLISH	5458
After The War	Gary MOORE	8832
Aftertones	Janis IAN	1973
Against All Odds	SOUNDTRACK-MOVIE	2253
Against The Grain	Phoebe SNOW	8541
Against The Grain	Rory GALLAGHER	8022
Against The Wind	Bob SEGER	80
Agent Double O Soul	The UNTOUCHABLES	10878
Agent Provocateur	FOREIGNER	838
Agents Of Fortune	BLUE ÖYSTER CULT	1724
The Age Of Aquarius	5TH DIMENSION	164
The Age Of Consent	BRONSKI BEAT	3906
The Age Of Electronicus	Dick HYMAN	8042
Agharta	Miles DAVIS	11473
Agnes English	John FRED & His PLAY...	9775
Ahead Rings Out	BLODWYN PIG	10895
Ahh... The Name Is B...	BOOTSY'S RUBBER BAND	1801
Ain't It Funky	James BROWN	4829
Ain't Life Grand	BLACK OAK ARKANSAS	9402
Ain't Love Grand	X	7304
Ain't Misbehavin'	ORIGINAL CAST	11536
Ain't No Big Thing, But It's Gr...	NEW BIRTH	13362
Ain't No 'Bout-A-Dou...	Larry GRAHAM/GRAHA ...	2627
Ain't Nothing You Can Do	Bobby BLAND	9616
Ain't Nothin' Stoppin' Us ...	TOWER OF POWER	4040
Ain't That A Bitch	Johnny Guitar WATSON	3776
Ain't That Good News	Sam COOKE	4643
Airborne	Don FELDER	11725
Airplay	POINT BLANK	10810
Airport	SOUNDTRACK-MOVIE	7479
Airport Love Theme	Vincent BELL	7494
Air Supply	AIR SUPPLY	3471
Airwaves	BADFINGER	8929
Aja	STEELY DAN	134
Akimbo Alogo	Kim MITCHELL	7862
Aladdin	ROTARY CONNECTION	11738
Aladdin Sane	David BOWIE	2705
Alan Price	Alan PRICE	13028
The Alarm	The ALARM	6118
Alarm Clock	Richie HAVENS	2441
Albert Finney's Album	Albert FINNEY	13823
Albert Live	Albert KING	12855
Album	Joan JETT & The BLAC...	3010
Album	PUBLIC IMAGE LIMITED	8222

Title	Act	Rank
The Album	ABBA	1226
The Album Of The Soundtrack ...	MONTY PYTHON	7179
Album 1700	PETER, PAUL & MARY	900
Album III	Loudon WAINWRIGHT II...	7459
Alchemy-Dire Straits Live	DIRE STRAITS	5400
Al-Di-La And Other Ex...	Ray CHARLES Singers	5147
Aldo Nova	Aldo NOVA	1127
Alexander O'Neal	Alexander O'NEAL	7317
Alf	Alison MOYET	4075
Alfie	Billy VAUGHN and His...	3989
Alfie	Carmen McRAE	12802
Al Green	Al GREEN	10276
Al Green Explores Your Mind	Al GREEN	1337
Al Green Gets Next To You	Al GREEN	2931
Al Green/Greatest Hits	Al GREEN	2311
Al Green Is Love	Al GREEN	2761
Al Green's Greatest Hits Volume ...	Al GREEN	9061
Al Hirt Plays Bert Kaempfert	Al HIRT	7766
Alias Pink Puzz	Paul REVERE And The ...	4832
Alibi	AMERICA	10804
Alice Cooper Goes To ...	ALICE COOPER (Solo)	1826
Alice Cooper's Greates...	ALICE COOPER (Grp)	1823
The Alice Cooper Show	ALICE COOPER (Solo)	10131
Alice's Restaurant	Arlo GUTHRIE	664
Alice's Restaurant (Soundtra...	Arlo GUTHRIE	4801
Alicia Bridges	Alicia BRIDGES	2577
Alien	SOUNDTRACK-MOVIE	9051
Aliens	HORSLIPS	8421
Aliens Ate My Buick	Thomas DOLBY	5751
Alive!	KISS	525
"Alive" Again...Naturally	The LETTERMEN	12233
Alive Alive-O!	José FELICIANO	4151
Alive And Screamin'	KROKUS	8708
Alive 'N Kickin'	ALIVE 'N KICKIN'	11549
Alive On Arrival	Steve FORBERT	6658
Alive She Cried	The DOORS	3139
Alive II	KISS	1183
All American Alien Boy	Ian HUNTER	11059
All American Boy	Rick DERRINGER	2384
All American Girls	SISTER SLEDGE	3999
Allan In Wonderland	Allan SHERMAN	4269
All Around My Hat	STEELEYE SPAN	10912
All Around The Town	Bob JAMES	5574
All By Myself	Eddie KENDRICKS	4482
All By Myself	Regina BELLE	7101
All Day Music	WAR	893
All Directions	The TEMPTATIONS	507
All Dressed Up & No Plac...	Nicolette LARSON	8012
All Fired Up	FASTWAY	6052
All Fly Home	Al JARREAU	4089
All For Love	NEW EDITION	1923
All Four One	The MOTELS	1520
All Hail The Queen	Queen LATIFAH	8057
All Hung Up	IRISH ROVERS	8071
Allied Forces	TRIUMPH	1643
Allies	CROSBY, STILLS & NAS...	5968
All I Ever Meant To Do W...	Johnny RODRIGUEZ	12467
All I Ever Need Is You	SONNY & CHER	1421
Alligator Bogaloo	Lou DONALDSON	9274
Alligator Woman	CAMEO	3503
All I Need	Jack WAGNER	3805
All I Need	SYLVESTER	12290
All I Need Is Time	Gladys KNIGHT & The ...	5084
All In Love Is Fair	Nancy WILSON	6353
All In The Family	SOUNDTRACK-TV	1456
All In The Family - 2nd Alb...	SOUNDTRACK-TV	9345

Title	Act	Rank
All In The Name Of Love	ATLANTIC STARR	1957
All I Really Want To Do	CHER	2851
All Is Forgiven	RED SIREN	8947
The Allman Brothers ...	ALLMAN BROTHERS Band	12421
All Mitch Ryder Hits...	Mitch RYDER And The ...	3608
All Mixed Up	Alexander O'NEAL	12512
All My Choices	Mary TRAVERS	11881
All My Life	Arthur PRYSOCK	11628
All 'N All	EARTH, WIND & FIRE	400
The Allnighter	Glenn FREY	1414
All Night Long	Sammy HAGAR	7935
All Of Me	Toni TENNILLE	13769
All Of The Above	John HALL Band	9118
All Of This And Nothing	PSYCHEDELIC FURS	9500
All Of You	Lillo THOMAS	13397
All Our Love	Gladys KNIGHT & The ...	3387
All Out	GRIN	12167
All Over the Place	The BANGLES	5665
All Right Now	PEPSI and SHIRLIE	9938
All Shook Up	CHEAP TRICK	3507
All Summer Long	BEACH BOYS	595
All Systems Go	Donna SUMMER	10518
All Systems Go	Vinnie VINCENT INVAS...	6046
All That Jazz	BREATHE	1597
All That Jazz	SOUNDTRACK-MOVIE	3480
All The Best!	Paul McCARTNEY	5648
All The Best Cowboys Have ...	Pete TOWNSHEND	3160
All The Girls In The ...	GRAND FUNK RAILROAD	1845
All Of The Good Ones Are Taken	Ian HUNTER	9689
All The Good Times	NITTY GRITTY DIRT BA...	10216
All The Great Hits	Diana ROSS	3156
All The Great Hits	The COMMODORES	3883
All Their Greatest H...	Harold MELVIN And Th...	5221
All The King's Horse...	Grover WASHINGTON Jr...	7137
All The Love In The World	Mac DAVIS	3275
All The People Are Talkin'	John ANDERSON	12148
...All The Rage	GENERAL PUBLIC	2217
All The Right Moves	SOUNDTRACK-MOVIE	11479
All The Time	Jack GREENE	9410
All The Way Strong	THIRD WORLD	10436
All The World's A Stage: Recorded Li...	RUSH	4435
All The Young Dudes	MOTT THE HOOPLE	5938
All Things In Time	Lou RAWLS	1225
All Things Must Pass	George HARRISON	250
All This And Heaven Too	Andrew GOLD	6589
All This And World War I...	SOUNDTRACK-MOVIE	5768
All This Love	DeBARGE	2123
All-Time Greatest Hi...	Paul REVERE And The ...	9944
All-Time Greatest Hits	The LETTERMEN	12803
All Together Now	ARGENT	2638
Almighty Fire	Aretha FRANKLIN	6525
Almost Blue	Elvis COSTELLO & The...	6200
Almost In Love	Elvis PRESLEY	5289
Almost Persuaded	David HOUSTON	5100
Aloha From Hawaii Via Satel...	Elvis PRESLEY	711
Alone Again (Natural...	Ray CONNIFF & His Or...	10899
Alone Again (Naturally)	Andy WILLIAMS	5917
Alone Again, Naturally	Esther PHILLIPS	11278
Alone/But Never Alone	Larry CARLTON	10171
Alone Together	Dave MASON	2077
Alone Together	Donny OSMOND	3144
Along The Axis	Jon BUTCHER AXIS	6531
Along The Red Ledge	Daryl HALL & John OA...	3336
Alpha	ASIA	2003
Alphabet City	ABC	4569
Alternating Currents	SPYRO GYRA	5636

Title	Act	Rank
Al Tijuana And His Jewish Bras...	Lou JACOBI	11831
Alton McClain & Dest...	Alton McCLAIN & DEST...	6282
Alvin Lee & Company	TEN YEARS AFTER	4510
Alvin Stone (The Birth & D...	FANTASTIC FOUR	6586
Always, Always	Porter WAGONER and D...	10966
Always & Forever	Randy TRAVIS	843
Always In My Heart	Los INDIOS TABAJARAS	8322
Always In The Mood	Shirley JONES	9418
Always On My Mind	Willie NELSON	354
Amadeus (Soundtrack)	Neville MARRINER	2702
Amandla	Miles DAVIS	12363
Amazing Grace	Aretha FRANKLIN	1759
Amazing Grace	ROYAL SCOTS DRAGOON ...	4043
The Amazing Mets	VARIOUS ARTISTS	13800
The Amazing Rhythm Ac...	AMAZING RHYTHM ACES	10220
Amazon Beach	The KINGS	12308
The Amboy Dukes	AMBOY DUKES	12859
Ambrosia	AMBROSIA	2072
Ambush	Marc BENNO	10699
America	AMERICA	323
America	Kurtis BLOW	9269
America Eats Its Young	FUNKADELIC	6987
America, I Hear You Singing [A]	Bing CROSBY	9889
America, I Hear You Singing [A]	Frank SINATRA	9889
America, I Hear You Singing [A]	Frank WARING	9889
America Is 200 Years Old...And T...	Bob HOPE	12187
America/Live	AMERICA	9818
Americana	Leon RUSSELL	8249
American Anthem	SOUNDTRACK-MOVIE	7868
American Beauty	GRATEFUL DEAD	3107
American Boy & Girl	Garland JEFFREYS	11099
American Dream	CROSBY, STILLS, NASH...	2284
An American Dream	NITTY GRITTY DIRT BA...	6717
The American Dream	AMERICAN DREAM	13561
The American Dream	Emitt RHODES	13791
The American Dream	Rev. Martin Luther K...	12441
American Dreams	Jesse Colin YOUNG	12871
American Excess	POINT BLANK	4683
American Flyer	AMERICAN FLYER	7315
American Fool	John MELLENCAMP	140
American Garage	PAT METHENY GROUP	3968
American Generation	RITCHIE FAMILY	10409
American Gigolo	SOUNDTRACK-MOVIE	1438
American Gothic	David ACKLES	10382
American Graffiti	SOUNDTRACK-MOVIE	363
American Hot Wax	SOUNDTRACK-MOVIE	4369
American Made	OAK RIDGE BOYS	4526
American Pastime	THREE DOG NIGHT	9807
American Pie	Don McLEAN	160
An American Prayer -Jim Morriso...	The DOORS	6102
American Stars 'N Bars	Neil YOUNG	2890
An American Tail	SOUNDTRACK-MOVIE	4706
American Tour	Dave CLARK Five	2940
The American Tour With Ed Rud...	The BEATLES	3997
American Woman	GUESS WHO	667
American Worker	BUS BOYS	10532
America's Choice	HOT TUNA	6945
America's Greatest Hero	Joey SCARBURY	8604
America The Beautifu...	"Tennessee" Ernie FO...	13555
America The Beautiful	Gary McFARLAND	12963
America, Why I Love Her	John WAYNE	6147
Amigo	Arlo GUTHRIE	9968
Amigos	SANTANA	1675
Ammonia Avenue	Alan PARSONS PROJECT	2254
Amnesia	POUSETTE-DART BAND	10318
Amnesia	Richard THOMPSON	12552

Title	Act	Rank
Among The Living	ANTHRAX	4077
Amor	Eydie GORME	4721
Amour	Richard CLAYDERMAN	10727
Amy Holland	Amy HOLLAND	8715
Ancient Dreams	CANDLEMASS	12084
Ancient Heart	Tanita TIKARAM	4774
Anderson, Bruford, Wakeman, Howe	YES	3845
...And I Know You Wanna Dan...	Johnny RIVERS	4946
And I Love You So	Perry COMO	3957
And I Love You So	Shirley BASSEY	10779
...And I Mean It!	Genya RAVAN	9489
And In This Corner...	D.J. JAZZY JEFF & TH...	4067
...And Justice For All	METALLICA	577
And Once Again	Isaac HAYES	5698
Andre Previn in Hollywood	Andre PREVIN	11491
Andrew Gold	Andrew GOLD	13458
And That's The Truth	Lily TOMLIN	3770
And The Feeling's Good	José FELICIANO	9613
And Then...Along Comes Th...	The ASSOCIATION	1048
...And Then He Kissed Me	Rachel SWEET	9570
...And Then There Were Three...	GENESIS	1711
And The Singer Sings His Son...	Neil DIAMOND	9413
Andy Gibb's Greatest Hits	Andy GIBB	4538
Andy Kim	Andy KIM	3109
Andy Kim's Greatest Hits	Andy KIM	12156
And You Know That!	Kirk WHALUM	9526
Andy Pratt	Andy PRATT	13069
Andy Williams' Greatest Hits	Andy WILLIAMS	4060
Andy Williams' Greatest Hits Vol. 2	Andy WILLIAMS	11876
Andy Williams' Newest Hits	Andy WILLIAMS	3034
The Andy Williams Show	Andy WILLIAMS	5182
The Andy Williams Sound Of ...	Andy WILLIAMS	9048
Angel	ANGEL	10712
Angel	OHIO PLAYERS	3860
Angel Band	Emmylou HARRIS	12689
Angel Clare	Art GARFUNKEL	1409
Angel Delight	FAIRPORT CONVENTION	13825
Angel Eyes	Dave BRUBECK Quartet	11958
Angel Eyes	Willie NELSON	10001
Angel Of The Morning	Merrilee RUSH	12924
Angel Of The Morning...	Percy FAITH His Orch...	6655
Angel Of The Night	Angela BOFILL	2144
Angel Station	MANFRED MANN'S EARTH...	8608
Angie	Angela BOFILL	3690
Angst In My Pants	SPARKS	12006
Animal Boy	The RAMONES	11400
Animal Grace	APRIL WINE	6966
Animal House	SOUNDTRACK-MOVIE	6035
Animalism	The ANIMALS/Eric BUR...	3980
Animalization	The ANIMALS/Eric BUR...	2277
Animalize	KISS	1828
Animal Logic	ANIMAL LOGIC	6955
Animal Magic	BLOW MONKEYS	4168
Animal Magnetism	SCORPIONS	4470
Animal Notes	CRACK THE SKY	10444
Animals	PINK FLOYD	1139
The Animals	The ANIMALS/Eric BUR...	2283
The Animals On Tour	The ANIMALS/Eric BUR...	8937
Animal Tracks	The ANIMALS/Eric BUR...	4333
Animation	Jon ANDERSON	12481
Animotion	ANIMOTION	3004
Animotion(2)	ANIMOTION	7666
The Anita Kerr Singers...	Anita KERR Singers	10632
Anka	Paul ANKA	1179
Anne Murray	Anne MURRAY	8414
Anne Murray / Glen Campbell [A]	Anne MURRAY	8885

Title	Act	Rank
Anne Murray / Glen Campbell [A]	Glen CAMPBELL	8885
Annette's Beach Party	ANNETTE	5978
Annie	Anne MURRAY	10169
Annie	ORIGINAL CAST	4115
Annie	SOUNDTRACK-MOVIE	3195
Annie Get Your Gun	ORIGINAL CAST	9282
Annie In Wonderland	Annie HASLEM	9522
Annie's Christmas	No Artist	8554
Annie's Song And Other Galwa...	James GALWAY	11447
Anniversary Special Vo...	Earl SCRUGGS Revue	8019
Ann Murray's Greatest Hits	Anne MURRAY	1122
Annunzio Paolo Mantovani	MANTOVANI	9257
Old Fashion Christmas	CARPENTERS	13822
Another Beginning	Les McCANN	11835
Another Day/Another Dollar	GANG OF FOUR	13728
Another Exposure	SOULFUL STRINGS	12840
Another Grey Area	Graham PARKER And Th...	5576
Another Hit Album!	Billy VAUGHN and His...	12425
Another Mother Further	MOTHER'S FINEST	9096
Another Night	The HOLLIES	8492
Another Page	Christopher CROSS	2156
Another Passenger	Carly SIMON	4026
Another Perfect Day	MOTORHEAD	11074
Another Place	HIROSHIMA	4300
Another Place And Time	Donna SUMMER	5316
Another Place Another Tim...	Jerry Lee LEWIS	10036
Another Scoop	Pete TOWNSHEND	13841
Another Side Of Bob Dylan	Bob DYLAN	3509
Another Step	Kim WILDE	3794
Another Taste	A TASTE OF HONEY	5637
Another Ticket	Eric CLAPTON	1295
Another Time	EARTH, WIND & FIRE	7897
Another Time, Anothe...	Engelbert HUMPERDINC...	3346
Another Time, Another Place	FEVER TREE	6498
Another Voyage	Ramsey LEWIS Trio	7358
Another Year	Leo SAYER	9306
Answers To Nothing	Midge URE	6800
Anthem Of The Sun	GRATEFUL DEAD	6156
An Anthology	Duane ALLMAN	2886
Anthology	Gladys KNIGHT & The ...	5002
Anthology	Grover WASHINGTON Jr...	10478
Anthology	Marvin GAYE	9487
Anthology	QUICKSILVER MESSENGE...	8376
Anthology	Steve MILLER Band	3844
Anthology	The BABYS	10175
Anthology	The TEMPTATIONS	4815
Anthology (1962-1969...	The SUPREMES/Diana ...	5592
An Anthology Of British B...	VARIOUS ARTISTS	13643
An Anthology, Vol. II	Duane ALLMAN	5161
Anticipation	Carly SIMON	2235
Any Day Now	Joan BAEZ	3076
Any Love	Luther VANDROSS	1490
Any Man's Hunger	Danny WILDE	11125
Any Number Can Win	Jimmy SMITH	2855
Any Old Wind That Blows	Johnny CASH	12851
Anyone Can See	Irene CARA	5919
Anyone For Mozart?	SWINGLE SINGERS	10834
Anything Goes	HARPERS BIZARRE	6123
Anything You Choose/W...	SPANKY And OUR GANG	8049
Anytime	Henry PAUL Band	10480
Anytime...Anywhere	Rita COOLIDGE	524
Anytime, Anyplace, A...	ROSSINGTON COLLINS B...	1393
Anyway You Like It	Thelma HOUSTON	1185
Any Which Way You Can	SOUNDTRACK-MOVIE	9514
A1A	Jimmy BUFFETT	2930
Aorta	AORTA	10336

Title	Act	Rank
Aoxomoxoa	GRATEFUL DEAD	6237
Apocalypse	John McLAUGHLIN/MAHA...	4458
Apollo 11: Flight To The ...	VARIOUS ARTISTS	12119
Apollonia 6	APOLLONIA 6	6465
Apollo Saturday Night	VARIOUS ARTISTS	5504
Apologize	Ed AMES	8054
Apostrophe (')	Frank ZAPPA	1120
Appaloosa	APPALOOSA	12186
Appetite For Destruction	GUNS N' ROSES	20
Appetizers	Alan O'DAY	8063
Applause	ORIGINAL CAST	11316
Apple Juice	Tom SCOTT & The L.A....	8128
Apples & Bananas	Lawrence WELK	7028
Apples, Peaches, Pum...	JAY And The TECHNIQU...	8544
The Apple Tree	ORIGINAL CAST	8538
Apprentice (In A Musical Wor...	Dave LOGGINS	5428
Approximately Infinite Universe	Yoko ONO	13054
Aqua Dream	McGUFFEY LANE	12648
Aqualung	JETHRO TULL	207
Aquarius	Charlie BYRD	12888
Arabesque (Soundtrac...	Henry MANCINI and hi...	11407
Arabesque	John KLEMMER	6925
Arabian Nights	RITCHIE FAMILY	2915
Arbour Zena	Keith JARRETT	12688
Arcade	Patrick SIMMONS	7029
The Archies	The ARCHIES	5328
The Archies Greatest Hits	The ARCHIES	7056
Architecture And Mor...	ORCHESTRAL MANOEUV...	8968
Archives	RUSH	9601
Arc Of A Diver	Steve WINWOOD	416
Area Code 615	AREA CODE 615	12769
Arena	DURAN DURAN	1410
Aretha	Aretha FRANKLIN	3151
Aretha (II)	Aretha FRANKLIN	2362
Aretha Arrives	Aretha FRANKLIN	898
Aretha Franklin's Greates...	Aretha FRANKLIN	7275
Aretha Franklin: Soul '69	Aretha FRANKLIN	1440
Aretha In Paris	Aretha FRANKLIN	1847
Aretha: Lady Soul	Aretha FRANKLIN	320
Aretha Live At Fillmore W...	Aretha FRANKLIN	715
Aretha Now	Aretha FRANKLIN	779
Aretha's Gold	Aretha FRANKLIN	1497
Aretha's Greatest Hits	Aretha FRANKLIN	1854
Are You Experienced?	Jimi HENDRIX EXPERIE...	65
Are You Gonna Be The One	Robert GORDON	6872
Are You Ready!	ATLANTA RHYTHM SECTI...	6001
Are You Ready	PACIFIC GAS AND ELEC...	7768
Are You Ready For Freddy	Freddy FENDER	4364
Are You Ready For The Cou...	Waylon JENNINGS	2372
Are You Serious???	Richard PRYOR	7073
Argus	WISHBONE ASH	9639
Argybargy	SQUEEZE	4932
The Aristocats	SOUNDTRACK-MOVIE	9366
Arizona	Mark LINDSAY	3686
Ark	The ANIMALS/Eric BUR...	7210
Arlo	Arlo GUTHRIE	7157
Arlo Guthrie	Arlo GUTHRIE	10097
Armageddon	ARMAGEDDON	10715
Armed And Extremely Dangerou...	FIRST CHOICE	12788
Armed Forces	Elvis COSTELLO & The...	1630
Around The World In A Day	PRINCE	475
Around The World - Live In Co...	The OSMONDS	10050
Around The World With Thr...	THREE DOG NIGHT	2473
Arrival	ABBA	1681
Arrive Without Travelli...	The THREE O'CLOCK	9740
Arthur (Or The Decline And Fall...	The KINKS	5512

Title	Act	Rank
Arthur Fiedler "Supe...	BOSTON POPS Orchestr...	11542
Arthur Prysock/Count Basie [A]	Arthur PRYSOCK	7675
Arthur Prysock/Count Basie [A]	Count BASIE	7675
The Arthur Sound	WILD ONES	13006
Arthur (The Album)	SOUNDTRACK-MOVIE	3286
Artificial Paradise	GUESS WHO	7711
Art In America	ART IN AMERICA	13172
Artistry	DEODATO	8318
The Art Of Control	Peter FRAMPTON	11637
The Art Of Defense	Nona HENDRYX	11508
The Art Of Excellence	Tony BENNETT	11320
The Art Of Falling Apart	SOFT CELL	8392
Art Of Tea	Michael FRANKS	8303
Ascencion	MALO	13122
Ascending	ORPHEUS	8938
As Falls Wichita, So Falls Wi... [A]	Pat METHENY	4213
As Falls Wichita, So Falls Wich... [A]	Lyle MAYS	4213
As Far As Siam	Tom COCHRANE/RED RID...	4589
Ashes Are Burning	RENAISSANCE	12226
Asia	ASIA	132
Asia	KITARO	13753
Ask Rufus	RUFUS	1880
As Nasty As They Wanna Be	2 LIVE CREW	826
As One	KOOL & The GANG	2724
As One	The BAR-KAYS	5520
Ass	BADFINGER	9485
Assault Attack	Michael SCHENKER Gro...	11077
The Association	The ASSOCIATION	4124
The Association "Live"	The ASSOCIATION	6295
As The Band Turns	ATLANTIC STARR	1517
Astra	ASIA	5897
The Astrodome Presents In Per...	Sonny JAMES	6514
The Astromusical House Of...	VARIOUS ARTISTS	12932
The Astrud Gilberto Album	Astrud GILBERTO	4796
Azure D'or	RENAISSANCE	9160
As We Speak	David SANBORN	5499
Asylum	KISS	2310
Asylum Choir II [A]	Leon RUSSELL	4988
Asylum Choir II [A]	Marc BENNO	4988
The "A" Team	SSgt Barry SADLER	11852
ATF	AFTER THE FIRE	3365
At Fillmore East	ALLMAN BROTHERS Band	1126
A Time To Sing (Soundtr...	Hank WILLIAMS Jr.	12923
Atlanta Blue	STATLER BROTHERS	12755
Atlanta Rhythm Secti...	ATLANTA RHYTHM SECTI...	11513
Atlanta's Burning Down	Dickey BETTS	11255
Atlantic Crossing	Rod STEWART	1568
Atlantic Starr	ATLANTIC STARR	6173
The Atlantic Years	ROXY MUSIC	12374
Atlantis	McCoy TYNER	11490
At Least We Got Shoe...	SOUTHSIDE JOHNNY & T...	13179
Atom Heart Mother	PINK FLOYD	5026
Atomic Playboys	Steve STEVENS ATOMIC...	8854
At Peace With Woman	JONES GIRLS	5779
Attacking A Straw Man	NEW COLONY SIX	12278
Attention Shoppers!	STARZ	8705
Attitudes	BRASS CONSTRUCTION	10281
At Your Birthday Party	STEPPENWOLF	1205
Audio-Visions	KANSAS	2829
August	Eric CLAPTON	3014
The Aura Will Prevail	George DUKE	7812
Aurora	Jean-Luc PONTY	7150
Autoamerican	BLONDIE	671
Autobahn	KRAFTWERK	1389
Autograph	John DENVER	4094
Automatic	JESUS AND MARY CHAIN	6854

Title	Act	Rank
Automatic Man	AUTOMATIC MAN	9170
Autumn	George WINSTON	5688
Autumn Leaves-1965	Roger WILLIAMS	10246
Avalanche	MOUNTAIN	7699
Avalon	ROXY MUSIC	4789
Avalon Sunset	Van MORRISON	4374
Awakening	MYSTIC MOODS Orchestra	12921
Awakening	Narada Michael WALDE...	6529
The Awakening	The REDDINGS	9979
Awaken The Guardian	FATES WARNING	13156
Away We A Go-Go	The MIRACLES/Smokey ...	3419
AWB	AVERAGE WHITE BAND/A...	552
Axis: Bold As Love	Jimi HENDRIX EXPERIE...	813
Azteca	AZTECA	9981
Aztec Camera	AZTEC CAMERA	13136

B

Title	Act	Rank
"Babbacombe" Lee	FAIRPORT CONVENTION	13391
Babe Ruth	BABE RUTH	7546
Baby, Baby	David HOUSTON	13633
Baby Don't Get Hooked On Me	Mac DAVIS	1439
Baby Don't Go	SONNY & CHER	6274
Babyface	WING And A PRAYER FI...	4602
Baby I Love You	Andy KIM	5853
Baby I'm-A Want You	BREAD	550
Baby, I'm For Real	The ORIGINALS	12248
Baby, I'm Yours	Barbara LEWIS	9967
Baby It's Me	Diana ROSS	2051
Baby I Want You	FUNKY COMMUNICATION ...	13605
Babylon A.D.	BABYLON A.D.	5681
Babylon And On	SQUEEZE	2844
Babylon By Bus	Bob MARLEY And The W...	6280
The Babys	The BABYS	8020
Baby The Rain Must Fall	Glenn YARBROUGH	4624
Baby Tonight	Marlon JACKSON	11989
Baby, Won't You Change Your M...	BLACK IVORY	11602
Bacchanal	Gabor SZABO	12137
Bacharach Baroque	The RENAISSANCE	13647
Bach Live At Fillmore East	Virgil FOX	13275
Bachman-Turner-Bachm...	BACHMAN-TURNER O...	12780
Bachman-Turner Overdrive	BACHMAN-TURNER O...	2365
Bachman Turner Overdrive(2)...	BACHMAN-TURN...	13731
Bachman-Turner Overdrive II	BACHMAN-TURNER ...	300
Bach's Greatest Hits	SWINGLE SINGERS	902
Bach To The Blues	Ramsey LEWIS Trio	10388
Back Again	The BACHELORS	12456
Back For The Attack	DOKKEN	1721
Back Home Again	John DENVER	94
Back In Black	AC/DC	110
Back In Black	WHODINI	2868
Back In '72	Bob SEGER	12329
Back In The High Life	Steve WINWOOD	245
Back In The USA	MC5	9864
Back Into Blue	QUARTERFLASH	11679
Back In Town	KINGSTON TRIO	4194
Back It Up	Robin TROWER	13723
Backless	Eric CLAPTON	976
Back On The Block	Quincy JONES	1099
Back On The Right Tr...	SLY & THE FAMILY STO...	12155
Back On The Streets	Donnie IRIS	4745
Back On The Streets	TOWER OF POWER	7704
Back Stabbers	The O'JAYS	1449
Backstage Pass	LITTLE RIVER BAND	5625
Backstreet	David SANBORN	4264
Back Street Crawler	Paul KOSSOFF	13449
Back Talk	The ROCKETS	11467

Title	Act	Rank
Back To Avalon	Kenny LOGGINS	6756
Back 2 Back	STARGARD	13361
Back To Back [A]	BOOKER T. & The M.G....	10326
Back To Back [A]	The HAPPENINGS	10395
Back To Back [A]	The MAR-KEYS	10326
Back To Back [A]	The TOKENS	10395
Back To Back	BRECKER BROTHERS	5961
Back To Back	RIGHTEOUS BROTHERS	2606
Back To Basics	The TEMPTATIONS	10652
Back To Earth	Cat STEVENS	4614
Back To Earth	RARE EARTH	5678
Back To Front	Gilbert O'SULLIVAN	4385
Back To Oakland	TOWER OF POWER	2183
Back To The Bars	Todd RUNDGREN	5971
Back To The Beach	SOUNDTRACK-MOVIE	13665
Back To The Country	Loretta LYNN	13291
Back To The Egg	Paul McCARTNEY & WIN...	1666
Back To The Future	SOUNDTRACK-MOVIE	2132
Back To The Roots	John MAYALL	4843
Back To The Roots	Ramsey LEWIS	10049
Back To The World	Curtis MAYFIELD	2185
Back To The World	Dennis DeYOUNG	9520
Bad	Michael JACKSON	53
Bad Animals	HEART	390
Bad Attitude	MEAT LOAF	7998
Bad, Bad Boy	Theo VANESS	10457
Bad Benson	George BENSON	5295
Bad Boy	Ringo STARR	9971
Bad Boy	Robert GORDON	9799
Bad Company	BAD COMPANY	558
Baddest	Grover WASHINGTON Jr...	8147
The Baddest Hubbard	Freddie HUBBARD	9524
The Baddest Turrentine	Stanley TURRENTINE	11660
Bad English	BAD ENGLISH	1301
Bad Enuff	SLAVE	12291
Badfinger	BADFINGER	11274
Bad For Good	Jim STEINMAN	4513
Bad For Me	Dee Dee BRIDGEWATER	12638
Bad Girls	Donna SUMMER	180
Bad Influence	Robert CRAY Band	10345
Badlands	BADLANDS	4360
Bad Luck	ATLANTA DISCO BAND	10559
Bad Luck Is All I Have	Eddie HARRIS	9844
Bad Luck Streak In Dancing S...	Warren ZEVON	2964
Ba-Dop-Boom-Bang	GRANDMASTER FLASH	13836
Bad Reputation	Joan JETT & The BLAC...	4252
Bad Reputation	THIN LIZZY	5209
Bad To The Bone	George THOROGOOD & T...	3557
Bad To The Bone	L.A. DREAM TEAM	12659
Ba-Fa	HUDSON BROTHERS	10903
Baja Marimba Band	BAJA MARIMBA BAND	8305
Baja Marimba Band Rides...	BAJA MARIMBA BAND	12039
Bajour	ORIGINAL CAST	12874
The Baker Gurvitz Army	BAKER GURVITZ ARMY	10168
Baker Street (A Musical Adv...	ORIGINAL CAST	11658
Balance	BALANCE	9301
Balance Of Power	ELECTRIC LIGHT ORCHE...	5482
Balin	Marty BALIN	3302
Ball	IRON BUTTERFLY	559
The Ballad Of Bonnie And Cly...	Georgie FAME	12612
The Ballad Of Calico	Kenny ROGERS & The F...	8488
Ballad Of Easy Rider	The BYRDS	4225
The Ballad Of Sally Rose	Emmylou HARRIS	12549
Ballads, Blues And Boaste...	Harry BELAFONTE	10027
Ballads Of The Green Be...	SSgt Barry SADLER	666
Ballin' Jack	BALLIN' JACK	11440

Title	Act	Rank
Ball Room	SEA LEVEL	10732
Balls Of Fire	BLACK OAK ARKANSAS	10670
Balls To The Wall	ACCEPT	5630
Bananarama	BANANARAMA	2735
The Band	The BAND	489
Banded Together	Lee RITENOUR	10425
Bandit In A Bathing Suit	David BROMBERG	8974
Band Of Gold	Freda PAYNE	5585
Band Of Gypsys	Jimi HENDRIX	527
Band On The Run	Paul McCARTNEY & WIN...	93
The Band Plays On	BACK STREET CRAWLER	8284
Bandstand	FAMILY	12453
Band Together	RARE EARTH	11014
Bang	BANG	9996
Bang	JAMES GANG	7444
Bang, Bang You're Terry Reid	Terry REID	10018
Bangin'	The OUTFIELD	2740
Banging The Wall	The BAR-KAYS	9621
Bangor Flying Circus	BANGOR FLYING CIRCUS	13417
Bankrupt	DR. HOOK	8001
Banned In Boston?	Rusty WARREN	5257
Baptism	Joan BAEZ	4543
Barabajagal	DONOVAN	2766
Barbara Mandrell Live	Barbara MANDRELL	4980
Barbarella	SOUNDTRACK-MOVIE	11797
Barbed Wire Kisses	JESUS AND MARY CHAIN	13335
Barbeque King	Jorma KAUKONEN & VIT...	11193
Barbra Joan Streisand	Barbra STREISAND	1379
Barbra Streisand...And O...	Barbra STREISAND	5775
Barbra Streisand's Great...	Barbra STREISAND	3465
Barbra Streisand's Great...Vol. 2	Barbra STREISA...	532
Bareback Rider	MASON PROFFIT	12957
Barefoot Ballet	John KLEMMER	5041
Bare Trees	FLEETWOOD MAC	4852
Bare Wires	John MAYALL'S BLUESB...	3965
Bark	JEFFERSON AIRPLANE/S...	1573
Bark At The Moon	Ozzy OSBOURNE	2483
Barking At Airplanes	Kim CARNES	5890
Barnet Dogs	Russ BALLARD	13485
Barnstorm	Joe WALSH	5349
Baron Von Tollbooth & The ... [A]	David FREIBERG	8122
Baron Von Tollbooth & The Ch... [A]	Paul KANTNER	8122
Baron Von Tollbooth & The Chr... [A]	Grace SLICK	8122
The Baroque Beatles Book	Joshua RIFKIN	6566
Barrel	Lee MICHAELS	4440
Barry	Barry MANILOW	2367
Barry Goudreau	Barry GOUDREAU	7826
Barry Lyndon	SOUNDTRACK-MOVIE	7559
Barry Manilow	Barry MANILOW	6481
Barry Manilow Live	Barry MANILOW	325
Barry Manilow I	Barry MANILOW	2148
Barry Manilow II	Barry MANILOW	1149
Barry White's Greatest Hits	Barry WHITE	2859
Barry White Sings For Someone...	Barry WHITE	1556
Barry White's Sheet Music	Barry WHITE	7293
Barry White The Man	Barry WHITE	3021
The Basement Tapes	Bob DYLAN And The BA...	1929
Basic	Glen CAMPBELL	11443
Basic Miles - The Classic Per...	Miles DAVIS	13169
Basket Of Light	PENTANGLE	13727
Batdorf & Rodney	BATDORF & RODNEY	11924
Batman	SOUNDTRACK-TV	9241
Batman (Soundtrack)	PRINCE	653
Batman Original Motion P...	SOUNDTRACK-MOVIE	5229
Batman Theme	Neal HEFTI	4619
The Batman Theme	The MARKETTS	7385

Title | Act	Rank
Bat Out Of Hell | MEAT LOAF	529
Battle Axe | BILLION DOLLAR BABIE...	13661
Battle Hymn | WILD TURKEY	13308
Battlestar Galacticia | SOUNDTRACK-TV	10538
Bay City Rollers | BAY CITY ROLLERS	1802
Bayou Country | CREEDENCE CLEARWATER...	128
B.B. King In London | B.B. KING	4705
Be A Brother | BIG BROTHER And The ...	10007
The Beach Boys | BEACH BOYS	5820
Beach Boys Concert | BEACH BOYS	377
The Beach Boys In Concert | BEACH BOYS	3193
Beach Boys' Party! | BEACH BOYS	1931
Beach Boys '69 (The Beach Boys... | BEACH BOYS	6835
The Beach Boys Song Bo... | HOLLYRIDGE STRINGS	7594
The Beach Boys Today! | BEACH BOYS	687
Beaches (Soundtrack) | Bette MIDLER	210
Beaded Dreams Through Turquoise E... | REDBONE	12618
Bealtitude: Respect Yourse... | STAPLE SINGERS	1616
Beast | BEAST	13496
Beast From The East | DOKKEN	4381
Beast From The East | MANDRILL	9817
Beat | KING CRIMSON	6400
Beat & Soul | EVERLY BROTHERS	12244
Beat Crazy | Joe JACKSON	4833
The Beat Goes On | VANILLA FUDGE	2270
Beatin' The Odds | MOLLY HATCHET	3298
Beatitude | Ric OCASEK	3824
The Beatles [White Album] | The BEATLES	48
The Beatles Album | Percy FAITH His Orch...	12427
The Beatles At The Hollywood ... | The BEATLES	1492
The Beatles Featuring Tony Sh... | The BEATLES	9200
The Beatles Live! At The Star... | The BEATLES	9414
The Beatles 1967-1970 | The BEATLES	196
The Beatles 1962-1966 | The BEATLES	312
The Beatles' Second Album | The BEATLES	539
Beatles '65 | The BEATLES	302
The Beatles Song Book | HOLLYRIDGE STRINGS	2816
A Beatles' Songbook (The Br... | BROTHERS FOUR	9124
The Beatles' Story | The BEATLES	2765
Beatles VI | The BEATLES	598
The Beatles vs. The Four Seas... [A] | The BEATLES	12463
The Beatles vs. The Four Season... [A] | 4 SEASONS	12463
The Beatles With Tony Sherida... | The BEATLES	6926
Beat Of The Brass | Herb ALPERT & The TI...	251
Beat Street | SOUNDTRACK-MOVIE	2800
Beat Street II | SOUNDTRACK-MOVIE	10016
Beat Surrender | The JAM	12662
The Beau Brummels | BEAU BRUMMELS	12738
Beaucoups of Blues | Ringo STARR	5727
Beautiful Feelings | Rick SPRINGFIELD	7146
Beautiful Loser | Bob SEGER	6972
Beautiful Noise | Neil DIAMOND	777
Beautiful People | NEW SEEKERS	9591
Beautiful Sunday | Daniel BOONE	9550
A Beautiful Thing | Cleo LAINE	11373
Beautiful Vision | Van MORRISON	6034
Beauty | SANTA ESMERALDA	9829
Beauty And The Beard [A] | Al HIRT	8301
Beauty And The Beard [A] | ANN-MARGRET	8301
Beauty & The Beast: Of Love... | SOUNDTRACK-TV	10580
Beauty And The Beat | The GO-GO'S	129
Beauty On A Back Str... | Daryl HALL & John OA...	3703
Beauty Stab | ABC	6258
Be A Winner | YARBROUGH & PEOPLES	7502
Bebe Le Strange | HEART	1536
Beck | Joe BECK	10926

Title | Act	Rank
Becket | SOUNDTRACK-MOVIE	12484
Beck-Ola | Jeff BECK Group	2059
Becoming | Lori LIEBERMAN	12493
Bedlam | The RUSTIX	13670
Bed Of Rose's | STATLER BROTHERS	8617
Bedtime Story | Tammy WYNETTE	9310
Bee Gees' 1st | BEE GEES	1168
Bee Gees Gold, Volume One | BEE GEES	3284
Bee Gees Greatest | BEE GEES	705
Beelzebubba | DEAD MILKMEN	7231
Beetlejuice | SOUNDTRACK-MOVIE	10463
Before And After | CHAD & JEREMY	4537
Before And After Science | Brian ENO	11582
Before His Time | Willie NELSON	5925
Before The Flood | Bob DYLAN And The BA...	1378
Before The Next Teardrop Fa... | Freddy FENDER	1703
Before The Rain | Lee OSKAR	6980
Before We Were So Ru... | The ANIMALS/Eric BUR...	6716
Befour | Brian AUGER	13244
The Begatting Of The Preside... | Orson WELLES	5398
Beggars Banquet | ROLLING STONES	1108
Beginnings | ALLMAN BROTHERS Band	1947
Beginnings | Rick SPRINGFIELD	3962
Beginnings | Steve HOWE	6355
Begin To Love | Robert GOULET	6330
Behaviour | SAGA	8440
Behind Closed Doors | Charlie RICH	413
Behind The Eyes | Tim MOORE	12836
...Behind The Garden... | Andreas VOLLENWEIDER	7489
Behind The Sun | Eric CLAPTON	3296
Behold & See | ULTIMATE SPINACH	13538
Behold The Mighty Army | NEW BIRTH	10872
Being With You | Smokey ROBINSON	1090
Belafonte At The Greek Th... | Harry BELAFONTE	3104
Belafonte On Campus | Harry BELAFONTE	13581
Believe | MASS PRODUCTION	7780
Believe | The JETS	9782
Believe | THIRD POWER	13610
Believers | Don McLEAN	9298
Belinda | Belinda CARLISLE	1922
Bella Donna | Stevie NICKS	62
Bellamy Brothers | BELLAMY BROTHERS	6705
Bell & James | BELL And JAMES	3450
Bellavia | Chuck MANGIONE	5536
The Belle Album | Al GREEN	7471
Belle De Jour | SAINT TROPEZ	6713
Belle Of The Ball | Richard TORRANCE And...	6600
The Belle Stars | BELLE STARS	13706
The Bells | Lou REED	10898
Belly Up! | DR. HOOK	10576
Belo Horizonte | John McLAUGHLIN	12271
Below The Belt | FRANKE AND THE KNOCK...	5684
Be My Love | Jerry VALE	3718
Be My Lover | O'BRYAN	5189
Ben | Michael JACKSON	1047
Bend Me, Shape Me | AMERICAN BREED	8506
Benefactor | ROMEO VOID	9022
Benefit | JETHRO TULL	1350
Ben Franklin In Paris | ORIGINAL CAST	10029
Benny And Us [A] | AVERAGE WHITE BAND/A...	3715
Benny And Us [A] | Ben E. KING	3715
Benny Goodman Today | Benny GOODMAN	11709
Benson & Farrell [A] | George BENSON	8755
Benson & Farrell [A] | Joe FARRELL	8755
Bent Out Of Shape | RAINBOW	3899
Berlin | Lou REED	8000

Title | Act	Rank
The Bermuda Triangle | Isao TOMITA	10634
Bernadette Peters | Bernadette PETERS	7176
Berry Gordy's The Last D... | SOUNDTRACK-MOVIE	6002
Bert Kaempfert Now! | Bert KAEMPFERT And H...	13488
Bert Kaempfert's Gre... | Bert KAEMPFERT And H...	2427
The Best | Quincy JONES	8065
The Best...Lovin' Spoonful | LOVIN' SPOONFUL	12861
Best Bits | Roger DALTREY	12555
The Best Days Of My Life | Johnny MATHIS	9579
The Best Is Yet To C... | Grover WASHINGTON Jr...	4394
Best Kept Secret | Sheena EASTON	2845
The Best Little Whorehou... | SOUNDTRACK-MOVIE	6376
The Best Of Al Hirt | Al HIRT	1358
The Best Of The Allm... | ALLMAN BROTHERS Band	13292
The Best Of Al Martino | Al MARTINO	6927
The Best Of Barbara Mand... | Barbara MANDRELL	12204
The Best Of B.B. King | B.B. KING	8081
Best Of Bee Gees | BEE GEES	753
Best Of Bee Gees, Vol. 2 | BEE GEES	6707
The Best Of Bill Cosby | Bill COSBY	4139
The Best Of Bill Dea... | Bill DEAL & The RHON...	13314
The Best Of Bill Withers | Bill WITHERS	13285
The Best Of Blondie | BLONDIE	2790
The Best Of Booker T... | BOOKER T. & The M.G....	9336
The Best Of Bread | BREAD	296
The Best Of Bread, Volume Two | BREAD	3901
Best Of Brian Auger | Brian AUGER	11820
Best Of B.T.O. (So F... | BACHMAN-TURNER OVERD...	2998
The Best Of Buck Owens | Buck OWENS	3874
The Best Of Buffy Sain... | Buffy SAINTE-MARIE	10636
The Best Of Carla Thomas | Carla THOMAS	12570
The Best Of Carly Simon | Carly SIMON	2399
The Best Of Chad & Jeremy | CHAD & JEREMY	4584
The Best Of Chad Mitch... | Chad MITCHELL Trio	4547
The Best Of Charley Pride | Charley PRIDE	796
The Best Of Charley Pride, Vol. 3 | Charley PRIDE	13419
The Best Of Charley Pride, Vol. 2 | Charley PRIDE	4936
The Best Of Charlie Rich | Charlie RICH	6248
The Best Of Chuck Mangione | Chuck MANGIONE	9270
The Best Of Clarence Cart... | Clarence CARTER	7295
Best Of Cream | CREAM	420
The Best Of Crosby/N... | David CROSBY/Graham ...	11492
The Best Of Dark Horse | George HARRISON	11012
The Best Of Dave Edmunds | Dave EDMUNDS	11877
The Best Of Dave Mason | Dave MASON	10950
The Best Of Dean Martin | Dean MARTIN	7371
The Best Of Dean Martin, Vol.... | Dean MARTIN	9460
The Best Of Donovan | DONOVAN	9320
The Best Of Earth, Win...Vol. 1 | EARTH, WIND & FIRE	808
The Best Of Earth, Win...Vol. 2 | EARTH, WIND & FIRE	13004
The Best Of Ed Ames | Ed AMES	6468
The Best Of Eddie Harris | Eddie HARRIS	13192
The Best Of Eddie Rabbitt | Eddie RABBITT	8800
The Best Of Eddy Arnold | Eddy ARNOLD	2507
The Best Of Eddy Arnold, Volu... | Eddy ARNOLD	12409
Best Of Elvis Costel... | Elvis COSTELLO & The...	7782
The Best Of Emerson,... | EMERSON, LAKE & PALM...	9599
The Best Of England ... | ENGLAND DAN & John F...	13630
The Best Of Eric Bur... | The ANIMALS/Eric BUR...	5682
The Best Of Eric Carmen | Eric CARMEN	5150
The Best Of Ferrante &... | FERRANTE & TEICHER	9050
The Best Of Firefall | FIREFALL	12848
The Best Of Freda Payne | Freda PAYNE	10514
The Best Of Freddy Fender | Freddy FENDER	10354
Best Of Free | FREE	9208
Best Of Friends | TWENNYNINE	5307

Title | Act	Rank
The Best Of Friends | LOGGINS & MESSINA	5774
Best Of George Harrison | George HARRISON	4068
The Best Of Gino Vannelli | Gino VANNELLI	13073
Best Of Gladys Knigh... | Gladys KNIGHT & The ...	4154
Best Of Glen Campbell | Glen CAMPBELL	9404
The Best Of Herbie Mann | Herbie MANN	13408
The Best Of Herman's Her... | HERMAN'S HERMITS	415
The Best Of Herman's Hermits, Vol. 3 | HERMAN' ...	8692
The Best Of Herman's Hermits, Vol. 2 | HERMAN' ...	2758
The Best Of Iron Butterfly... | IRON BUTTERFLY	10257
The Best Of Isaac Hayes | Isaac HAYES	11707
The Best Of Jerry Butler | Jerry BUTLER	11930
The Best Of Jerry Jeff ... | Jerry Jeff WALKER	13017
The Best Of Jerry Lee Lew... | Jerry Lee LEWIS	7833
The Best Of Jerry Reed | Jerry REED	7564
The Best Of Jimmy Smith | Jimmy SMITH	12813
The Best Of Jim Reeves | Jim REEVES	1475
The Best Of Jim Reeves Volume ... | Jim REEVES	9920
The Best Of Joan Baez | Joan BAEZ	5635
The Best Of Joan C. Baez | Joan BAEZ	8959
The Best Of Joe Simon | Joe SIMON	10106
The Best Of Joe Tex | Joe TEX	12384
The Best Of Joe Walsh | Joe WALSH	7952
The Best Of John Klemmer-Vol... | John KLEMMER	13454
The Best Of Johnny Mathis 1... | Johnny MATHIS	10615
The Best Of Judy Garland | Judy GARLAND	12784
The Best Of Kansas | KANSAS	12050
The Best of King Curtis | KING CURTIS	12543
The Best Of Kool And The ... | KOOL & The GANG	9669
Best Of Leon | Leon RUSSELL	4918
The Best Of Little A... | LITTLE ANTHONY And T...	6142
The Best Of Lou Rawls | Lou RAWLS	6846
The Best Of Luther Vandro... | Luther VANDROSS	1457
The Best Of Lynn Anderson | Lynn ANDERSON	12596
The Best Of Mancini | Henry MANCINI and hi...	3446
The Best Of Mandrill | MANDRILL	13560
The Best Of Manhattan ... | MANHATTAN TRANSFER	7792
The Best Of Mario Lanza | Mario LANZA	7280
The Best Of Mark-Almond | MARK-ALMOND	11474
The Best Of Michael Jacks... | Michael JACKSON	11067
The Best Of Mountain | MOUNTAIN	5921
The Best Of Nancy Wilson | Nancy WILSON	7902
The Best Of Nat King Cole | Nat King COLE	12213
The Best Of Nina Simone(2) | Nina SIMONE	13167
The Best Of Nina Simone | Nina SIMONE	12853
Best Of Norman Connors & F... | Norman CONNORS	11861
Skeletons In The Closet: The... | OINGO BOINGO	11054
In The Dark/The Best... | ORCHESTRAL MANOEUV...	3424
The Best Of Otis Redding | Otis REDDING	6105
The Best Of Percy Sledge | Percy SLEDGE	8559
The Best Of Peter And Go... | PETER And GORDON	6876
The Best Of Peter Nero | Peter NERO	11209
The Best Of Procol Harum | PROCOL HARUM	9080
The Best Of Ramsey Lewis | Ramsey LEWIS	9905
The Best Of Ritchie Valens | Ritchie VALENS	9256
Best Of Rockers N' Ballads | SCORPIONS	3949
The Best Of Rod McKuen | Rod McKUEN	12241
The Best Of Rod Stewart | Rod STEWART	5210
The Best Of Ronnie Dove | Ronnie DOVE	3902
The Best Of Roy Clark | Roy CLARK	11086
The Best Of Sam & Dave | SAM & DAVE	5628
The Best Of Sam Cooke | Sam COOKE	10791
The Best Of Sam Cooke, Volume 2 | Sam COOKE	9851
The Best Of Sam The ... | SAM THE SHAM And The...	6869
Best Of Scorpions | SCORPIONS	12476
Best Of Scorpions Vol. 2 | SCORPIONS	12912

Title | Act	Rank
The Best Of/Skeletons From ... | GRATEFUL DEAD	7340
The Best Of Solomon Burke | Solomon BURKE	12355
The Best Of Sonny & Cher | SONNY & CHER	1761
The Best Of Sonny James | Sonny JAMES	11408
The Best Of The Spinners(2) | SPINNERS	8445
The Best Of Spirit | SPIRIT	7916
Best Of Tavares | TAVARES	7201
The Best Of The Alan... | Alan PARSONS PROJECT	4431
The Best Of The Andrews S... | ANDREWS SISTERS	8972
The Best Of The Animals(2) | The ANIMALS/Eric BU...	13460
The Best Of The Animals | The ANIMALS/Eric BUR...	258
The Best Of The Art Of Noise | ART OF NOISE	7175
The Best Of The Band | The BAND	5297
Best Of The Beach Boys | BEACH BOYS	961
Best Of The Beach Boys, Vol. 3 | BEACH BOYS	10434
Best Of The Beach Boys, Vol. 2 | BEACH BOYS	5083
The Best Of The Best Of Mer... | Merle HAGGARD	8986
The Best Of The Blues Brot... | BLUES BROTHERS	12026
Best Of The Blues Project | BLUES PROJECT	13646
The Best Of The Byrds (Greatest... | The BYRDS	7362
The Best Of The Cowsills | The COWSILLS	8033
The Best Of The Crusaders | The CRUSADERS	8152
Best Of The Doobies | DOOBIE BROTHERS	658
Best Of The Doobies Vol. ... | DOOBIE BROTHERS	4443
The Best Of The Doors | The DOORS	10279
The Best Of The Doors(2) | The DOORS	3090
The Best Of The 50 Guitars ... | Tommy GARRETT	8649
The Best Of The 4 Tops | FOUR TOPS	8637
The Best Of The Guess Who | GUESS WHO	710
The Best Of The Guess Who, Volu... | GUESS WHO	12875
The Best Of The Impressio... | The IMPRESSIONS	9178
The Best Of The James Gang Fea... | JAMES GANG	6201
Best Of The J. Geils Band | J. GEILS Band	10309
The Best Of The Lettermen | The LETTERMEN	2397
The Best Of The Lettermen, ... | The LETTERMEN	8243
The Best Of The Lovin' Spoonful | LOVIN' SPOONFUL	594
The Best Of The Lovin' Spoonful Vol. 2 | LOVIN' SP...	11442
The Best Of The New Birth | NEW BIRTH	13036
The Best Of The Pointer S... | POINTER SISTERS	10867
The Best Of The Rest | LYNYRD SKYNYRD	11428
The Best Of The Righte... | RIGHTEOUS BROTHERS	8751
The Best Of The Seekers | The SEEKERS	8292
Best Of The Soundtracks | VARIOUS ARTISTS	13568
The Best Of The Spinners | SPINNERS	8969
The Best Of The Statle ...Vol 2. | STATLER BROTHERS	9369
The Best Of The Statler ... | STATLER BROTHERS	6459
The Best Of The Stylistics | The STYLISTICS	3218
The Best Of The Whispers | The WHISPERS	12556
The Best Of The Youngbloo... | The YOUNGBLOODS	9364
The Best Of Tommy Ja... | Tommy JAMES And The ...	1741
The Best Of Tom Rush | Tom RUSH	12823
Best Of Traffic | TRAFFIC	4636
The Best Of The Trammps | The TRAMMPS	10256
The Best Of War...And More | WAR	10594
The Best Of Wayne Newton | Wayne NEWTON	13211
The Best Of Wes Montgomery | Wes MONTGOMERY	3607
The Best Of Wes Montgomery... | Wes MONTGOMERY	11246
The Best Of Wilson Pickett | Wilson PICKETT	2479
The Best Of Wilson Pickett... | Wilson PICKETT	5932
The Best Of ZZ Top | ZZ TOP	7126
The Best Part Of The Fat Boys | FAT BOYS	9250
Best Shots | Pat BENATAR	5489
The Best Side Of Goodbye | Jane OLIVOR	6155
The Best Of Uriah Heep | URIAH HEEP	10445
The Best Years Of Our Lives | Neil DIAMOND	5420
Bet Cha Say That To All The... | SISTER SLEDGE	11299

Title | Act	Rank
Bete Noire | Bryan FERRY	3725
Be Thankful For What You... | William DeVAUGHN	9624
Be True To You | Eric ANDERSEN	8357
Bette Midler | Bette MIDLER	1583
Better Days | Paul BUTTERFIELD Blu...	9044
Better Days | The BLACKBYRDS	8799
Better Days & Happy En... | Melissa MANCHESTER	2979
Better Than Heaven | STACEY Q	4635
Better Than The Rest | George THOROGOOD & T...	7487
Better Times Are Coming | RHINOCEROS	11697
Betty Travelin' In The Wrigh... | Betty WRIGHT	10344
Betty Wright Live | Betty WRIGHT	2341
Between Nothingness ... | John McLAUGHLIN/MA...	4906
Between The Buttons | ROLLING STONES	739
Between The Lines | Janis IAN	317
Between The Lines | SPIDER	13407
Between The Sheets | ISLEY BROTHERS	2983
Between Two Fires | Paul YOUNG	6694
Bet Your Heart On Me | Johnny LEE	9888
Beverly Hills Cop | SOUNDTRACK-MOVIE	336
Beverly Hills Cop II | SOUNDTRACK-MOVIE	1516
Beware Of Greeks Bearing ... | VARIOUS ARTISTS	12053
Be What You Are | STAPLE SINGERS	6457
Bewitched | Andy SUMMERS & Rober...	11650
Bewitched | Jack JONES	5259
Beyond | Herb ALPERT	4302
Beyond Appearances | SANTANA	4831
Beyond The Blue Neon | George STRAIT	6089
Beyond The Valley Of 1984 | The PLASMATICS	9615
Be Yourself | Patti LaBELLE	5293
Be Yourself Tonight | EURYTHMICS	1031
The B-52's | The B-52s	1752
The Bible | SOUNDTRACK-MOVIE	7387
Bicentennial Ni*ger | Richard PRYOR	2977
Bi-Coastal | Peter ALLEN	7319
Biddu Orchestra | BIDDU Orchestra	12516
Big & Beautiful | FAT BOYS	5753
Big Bam Boom | Daryl HALL & John OA...	605
Big Bambu | CHEECH & CHONG	246
Big Band Hits Of The... | Enoch LIGHT & The LI...	11789
Big Brother & The Holding Company | BIG BROTHE...	4616
Big Brother & The Holding Company(2) | BIG BROT...	12486
The Big Chill | SOUNDTRACK-MOVIE	483
The Big Chill: More Song... | SOUNDTRACK-MOVIE	4285
Big Circumstance | Bruce COCKBURN	12285
Big City | Merle HAGGARD	7668
Big Daddy | John MELLENCAMP	1853
Big Deal | KILLER DWARFS	11741
Big Dreamers Never Sleep | Gino VANNELLI	11270
Big Dreams In A Small Town | RESTLESS HEART	8843
The Big Easy | SOUNDTRACK-MOVIE	9291
The Big Express | XTC	12514
The Big Folk Hits | BROTHERS FOUR	5627
Big Fun | INNER CITY	12361
Big Fun | Miles DAVIS	11944
Big Fun | SHALAMAR	2005
Big Game | WHITE LION	2197
Big Generator | YES	1885
Bigger And Deffer | LL COOL J	668
Bigger Than Both Of ... | Daryl HALL & John OA...	414
Biggest Hits | Marty ROBBINS	11003
The Biggest Prize In Sport | 999	12682
The Big Heat | Stan RIDGWAY	10108
Big Hits (High Tide And Gr... | ROLLING STONES	436
Big Hits By Burt Bacharach...Ha... | 4 SEASONS	8703
The Big Hits Now | VARIOUS ARTISTS	13640

Title | Act	Rank
The Big Huge | INCREDIBLE STRING BA...	12568
Big In Vegas | Buck OWENS	11049
Big Life | NIGHT RANGER	4715
Big Night Music | SHRIEKBACK	11201
Big Ones | LOVERBOY	13815
The Big Ones, Volume II | Floyd CRAMER	12983
Big Plans For Everybody | LET'S ACTIVE	9122
The Big Prize | HONEYMOON SUITE	3745
Big Science | Laurie ANDERSON	9067
Big Screen - Little ... | Henry MANCINI and hi...	7037
Big Sixteen, Vol. 3 | Gene PITNEY	9399
The Big Sounds Of The Dra... | VARIOUS ARTISTS	4601
Big Spender | Peggy LEE	11934
Big Sur Festival/One Hand... | VARIOUS ARTISTS	12936
Big Swing Face | Buddy RICH	7058
Big Thing | DURAN DURAN	2448
The Big Throwdown | LEVERT	3622
Big Time | Tom WAITS	11463
Big Towne, 2061 | PARIS	10586
Big Trash | THOMPSON TWINS	10749
Big Tyme | HEAVY D & The BOYZ	1275
Big World | Joe JACKSON	3318
Bikini Red | SCREAMING BLUE MESSI...	10451
Bill & Ted's Excellent A... | SOUNDTRACK-MOVIE	12304
Bill Black's Combo Goe... | Bill BLACK'S Combo	12385
Bill Black's Greatest ... | Bill BLACK'S Combo	13736
Bill Cosby | Bill COSBY	4345
Bill Cosby "Himself" Soundtrac... | Bill COSBY	6519
Bill Cosby Is A Very Funny Fel... | Bill COSBY	569
Bill Cosby Is Not Himself Thes... | Bill COSBY	7132
Bill Cosby Sings/Hooray For Th... | Bill COSBY	7290
Bill Cosby Sings/Silver Throat | Bill COSBY	2248
The Billie Holiday Story | Billie HOLIDAY	5615
Billion Dollar Babies | ALICE COOPER (Grp)	597
Bill Medley 100% | Bill MEDLEY	12672
Bill Withers Greatest Hits | Bill WITHERS	12954
Bill Withers Live At Carnegi... | Bill WITHERS	4708
Billy & The Beaters | Billy VERA & The BEA...	8597
Billy Idol | Billy IDOL	1837
Billy Jack(2) | SOUNDTRACK-MOVIE	11591
Billy Jack | SOUNDTRACK-MOVIE	9355
Billy Joe Thomas | B.J. THOMAS	9587
Greatest Hits | Billy OCEAN	6758
Billy Preston & Syreeta [A] | Billy PRESTON	8890
Billy Preston & Syreeta [A] | SYREETA	8890
Billy Satellite | BILLY SATELLITE	11013
Bing Crosby's Greatest Hits | Bing CROSBY	8213
Bio | Chuck BERRY	11790
Biograph | Bob DYLAN	4414
Bionic Boogie | BIONIC BOOGIE	6537
Bird | SOUNDTRACK-MOVIE	12724
Bird In A Silver Cage | Herbie MANN	9667
Bird On A Wire | Tim HARDIN	13784
Birds Of A Feather | Jack BLANCHARD & Mis...	12274
Birds Of Fire | John McLAUGHLIN/MAHA...	1781
The Birds, The Bees & The Mon... | The MONKEES	787
Birdy (Soundtrack) | Peter GABRIEL	11500
Birth Day | NEW BIRTH	3159
Birthday | The ASSOCIATION	2653
Birth, School, Work, Death | The GODFATHERS	6771
Bish | Stephen BISHOP	3572
Bitches Brew | Miles DAVIS	2500
Bite Down Hard | JO JO GUNNE	5839
A Bit Of Liverpool | The SUPREMES/Diana R...	3421
The Bitterest Pill (I Ever Had To... | The JAM	9006
Bitter Sweet | MAIN INGREDIENT	5246

Title | Act	Rank
Bittersweet | CHAIRMEN OF THE BOAR...	12914
Bittersweet White Light | CHER	9846
Bitter Tears (Ballads Of The ... | Johnny CASH	6668
Bizet: Carmen | Maria CALLAS	8701
The Biz Never Sleeps | Biz MARKIE	4664
BJ4 | Bob JAMES	4710
B.J. Thomas | B.J. THOMAS	8563
Black & Blue | Harold MELVIN And Th...	4646
Black And Blue | ROLLING STONES	629
Black & White | POINTER SISTERS	1653
Black And White | Tony Joe WHITE	4354
A Black & White Night: Live (... | Roy ORBISON	8666
Black Bach | Lamont DOZIER	13350
Black Bear Road | C.W. McCALL	2314
Black Byrd | Donald BYRD	2946
The Blackbyrds | The BLACKBYRDS	5588
Black Caesar (Soundtrack) | James BROWN	3762
Black Cars | Gino VANNELLI	5685
Black Celebration | DEPECHE MODE	5842
Black Codes (From The Und... | Wynton MARSALIS	9411
Black Drops | Charles EARLAND	9103
Black Gold | Nina SIMONE	8879
Black Is Black | Los BRAVOS	8839
Black Ivory | Wanda ROBINSON	10137
Blackjack | BLACKJACK	9311
Black Magic | MARTHA & The VANDELL...	9901
Black Magic Woman | FLEETWOOD MAC	9455
Black Magic Woman | Percy FAITH His Orch...	12388
The Black-Man's Burdon | Eric BURDON & WAR	7311
Black Market | WEATHER REPORT	5486
Black Market Clash | The CLASH	6038
The Black Messiah | "Cannonball" ADDERLE...	12413
Black Moses | Isaac HAYES	1157
The Black Motion Pic... | Cecil HOLMES SOULFUL...	9992
Black 'N' Blue | BLACK 'N BLUE	9114
Black Oak Arkansas | BLACK OAK ARKANSAS	8313
Black On Black | Waylon JENNINGS	4418
Blackout | SCORPIONS	1147
Black Pearl | BLACK PEARL	9519
Black Pearl-Live! | BLACK PEARL	13463
Black Rock | The BAR-KAYS	6919
Black Rose | J.D. SOUTHER	7108
Black Rose/A Rock Legend | THIN LIZZY	7233
Black Sabbath | BLACK SABBATH	1405
Black Sabbath, Vol. 4 | BLACK SABBATH	1572
Blacks and Blues | Bobbi HUMPHREY	5832
Black Sea | XTC	3182
Black Seeds | MAIN INGREDIENT	11917
Black Talk! | Charles EARLAND	5986
Black Tie | The MANHATTANS	7372
Blah-Blah-Blah | Iggy POP	5273
Blam!! | BROTHERS JOHNSON	1646
Blame It On Love And All ... | Smokey ROBINSON	10202
Blast! (The Latest And T... | BROTHERS JOHNSON	11324
The Blasters | The BLASTERS	3138
Blast From The Bayou | Wayne TOUPS & ZYDECA...	12938
Blast From Your Past | Ringo STARR	4193
Blast Off | STRAY CATS	9630
Blaze | HERMAN'S HERMITS	7683
Blaze Of Glory | Joe JACKSON	6315
Blessed Are ... | Joan BAEZ	1569
Blessing In Disguise | METAL CHURCH	6227
Bless Its Pointed Li... | JEFFERSON AIRPLANE/S...	2269
Bless The Beasts & Child... | SOUNDTRACK-MOVIE	10430
Bless Your Heart | Freddie HART	6780
Blind Baby | NEW BIRTH	4880

Title | Act	Rank
Blind Date | SOUNDTRACK-MOVIE	13840
Blinded By Science | Thomas DOLBY	2412
Blind Faith | BLIND FAITH	276
The Blind Leading The Nake... | VIOLENT FEMMES	6110
Blind Man's Zoo | 10,000 MANIACS	1577
Blind To Reason | Grayson HUGH	5718
The Blitz | KROKUS	3552
Blizzard Of Ozz | Ozzy OSBOURNE	689
Blockbusters | JAY & The AMERICANS	7450
Blonde On Blonde | Bob DYLAN	1670
Blondes Have More Fun | Rod STEWART	333
Blood & Chocolate | Elvis COSTELLO & The...	8158
Bloodline | Glen CAMPBELL	7207
Bloodline | LEVERT	13503
Blood On The Tracks | Bob DYLAN	625
Bloodrock | BLOODROCK	11669
Bloodrock Live | BLOODROCK	4578
Bloodrock Passage | BLOODROCK	7370
Bloodrock 3 | BLOODROCK	2567
Bloodrock 2 | BLOODROCK	1610
Bloodrock U.S.A. | BLOODROCK	8188
Bloodshot | J. GEILS Band	1472
Blood, Sweat & Tears | BLOOD, SWEAT & TEARS	6
Blood, Sweat & Tears Greatest... | BLOOD, SWEAT ...	2623
Blood, Sweat & Tears 3 | BLOOD, SWEAT & TEARS	473
Bloody Tourists | 10cc	5049
Blooming Hits | Paul MAURIAT And His...	265
Blow By Blow | Jeff BECK	1355
Blowfly's Party [X-Rated] | BLOWFLY	6021
A Blow For Me A Toot... | Fred WESLEY & The HO...	12221
Blowin' Away | Joan BAEZ	5354
Blowin' Gold | John KLEMMER	11677
Blowin' Your Mind! | Van MORRISON	11966
Blow It Out | Tom SCOTT & The L.A....	7019
Blow My Fuse | KIX	2169
Blows Against The E... [A] | JEFFERSON AIRPLANE...	2213
Blows Against The Empire [A] | Paul KANTNER	2213
Blow-Up (Soundtrack) | Herbie HANCOCK	13639
Blow Up Your Video | AC/DC	2093
Blow Your Cool! | HOODOO GURUS	8513
Blow Your Own Horn | Herb ALPERT	9503
B.L.T. [A] | Jack BRUCE	3926
B.L.T. [A] | LORDAN	3926
B.L.T. [A] | Robin TROWER	3926
Blue | DOUBLE	4022
Blue | Joni MITCHELL	1513
Blue | Michael PARKS	7134
Blue Afternoon | Tim BUCKLEY	13516
The Blue Album | Harold MELVIN And Th...	6049
Blue And Gray | POCO	7022
Blue Bash! [A] | Jimmy SMITH	10974
Blue Bash! [A] | Kenny BURRELL	10974
Blue Bell Knoll | COCTEAU TWINS	7605
Blue Gene | Gene PITNEY	10200
Blue Jays [A] | John LODGE	2147
Blue Jays [A] | Justin HAYWARD	2147
Blue Jeans | CHOCOLATE MILK	9969
Blue Kentucky Girl | Emmylou HARRIS	4121
Blue Lights In The Basement | Roberta FLACK	1263
Blue Magic | BLUE MAGIC	2937
The Blue Mask | Lou REED	12507
Blue Matter | SAVOY BROWN	13137
Blue Midnight | Bert KAEMPFERT And H...	842
Blue Moves | Elton JOHN	1053
Blue Murder | BLUE MURDER	5849
Blue Öyster Cult | BLUE ÖYSTER CULT	11262

Title	Act	Rank
Blue Pine Trees	UNICORN	10030
Blueprint	Rory GALLAGHER	10562
Blue Rabbit [A]	Johnny HODGES	12980
Blue Rabbit [A]	Wild Bill DAVIS	12980
The Blue Ridge Rangers	John FOGERTY	5137
Blue River	Eric ANDERSEN	9883
The Blues Alone	John MAYALL	10384
The Blues Brothers (Soundt...	BLUES BROTHERS	2012
Blues For Allah	GRATEFUL DEAD	2256
Blues For Mister Jimmy	Jimmy McGRIFF	10637
Blues For Salvador	Carlos SANTANA	13832
Blues From Laurel Canyon	John MAYALL	4959
Blue Side Of Lonesome	Jim REEVES	12591
Blues Image	BLUES IMAGE	8111
Blue Skies	Kiri TE KANAWA	8409
Blue Sky-Night Thunder	Michael MURPHEY	1346
Blues 'N Jazz	B.B. KING	12702
The Blues Project Live At T...	BLUES PROJECT	7100
Blues-The Common Ground	Kenny BURRELL	13472
Blue Tattoo	PASSPORT	12704
Blue Valentine	Tom WAITS	12386
Blue Velvet & 1963's...	Billy VAUGHN and His...	5708
The Board Of Directors [A]	Count BASIE	11083
The Board Of Directors [A]	MILLS BROTHERS	11083
Boats Against The Current	Eric CARMEN	5085
Bobbie Gentry & Glen Campb... [A]	Bobbie GENTRY	919
Bobbie Gentry & Glen Camp... [A]	Glen CAMPBELL	919
Bobbie Gentry's Greatest!	Bobbie GENTRY	13247
Bobbie Sue	OAK RIDGE BOYS	3053
Bobby & The Midnites	BOBBY And The MIDNIT...	10945
The Bobby Bloom Album	Bobby BLOOM	11566
Bobby Caldwell	Bobby CALDWELL	2167
The Bobby Fuller Four	Bobby FULLER Four	12843
Bobby Goldsboro's Greates...	Bobby GOLDSBORO	7609
Bobby Goldsboro's 10th An...	Bobby GOLDSBORO	12635
Bobby Sherman	Bobby SHERMAN	1111
Bobby Sherman's Greatest Hi...	Bobby SHERMAN	7763
Bobby Short Loves Cole Porter	Bobby SHORT	10992
Bobby Vee Sings The New Sound F...	Bobby VEE	13035
Bobby Vinton's All-Time Grea...	Bobby VINTON	7330
Bobby Vinton's Greatest Hits	Bobby VINTON	2019
Bobby Vinton's Greatest Hits...	Bobby VINTON	9368
The Bobby Vinton Show	Bobby VINTON	10798
Bobby Vinton Sings For Lonel...	Bobby VINTON	10672
Bobby Vinton Sings The Golde...	Bobby VINTON	11159
Bobby Whitlock	Bobby WHITLOCK	9139
Bobby Womack's Greatest Hits	Bobby WOMACK	10143
Bob Dylan At Budokan	Bob DYLAN	2502
Bob Dylan's Greatest Hits	Bob DYLAN	764
Bob Dylan's Greatest Hits, Vol....	Bob DYLAN	1187
Bob McGrath From Sesame Stree...	Bob McGRATH	8743
Bob Newhart Faces Bob Newhart...	Bob NEWHART	8834
Bo-Day-Shus!!!	Mojo NIXON & Skid RO...	13673
Bodies And Souls	MANHATTAN TRANSFER	5449
Bo Donaldson And The Heywoods...	Bo DONALDS...	6431
Body And Soul	Joe JACKSON	2020
The Body And Soul Of Tom Jones	Tom JONES	7983
Body Heat	Quincy JONES	731
Bodyheat	James BROWN	8823
Body Wishes	Rod STEWART	3525
Boi-ngo	OINGO BOINGO	6948
Boingo Alive	OINGO BOINGO	8439
Bold As Love	BARDEUX	8108
Bombs Away Dream Babies	John STEWART	1366
Bondage	Angelo BOND	13166
Bongo Fury [A]	CAPTAIN BEEFHEART	7243

Title	Act	Rank
Bongo Fury [A]	Frank ZAPPA	7243
Bongo Rock	INCREDIBLE BONGO BAN...	13703
Bon Jovi	BON JOVI	1660
Bonk	BIG PIG	6614
Bonnie And Clyde	SOUNDTRACK-MOVIE	1938
Bonnie Pointer	Bonnie POINTER	7230
Bonnie Pointer (II)	Bonnie POINTER	6194
Booger Bear	Buddy MILES	13363
Boogie Bands & One Night Sta...	Kathy DALTON	13114
Boogie Brothers	SAVOY BROWN	8375
Boogie Down!	Eddie KENDRICKS	3653
Boogie Down U.S.A.	PEOPLE'S CHOICE	5605
Boogie Motel	FOGHAT	4187
Boogie With Canned Heat	CANNED HEAT	1468
Boogie Woogie Bugle Girls	ANDREWS SISTERS	11478
Boogie Woogie Dancin' Shoes	Claudja BARRY	7851
Boogity Boogity	Ray STEVENS	9677
Book Early	CITY BOY	8335
Bookends	SIMON & GARFUNKEL	113
Booker T. & Priscill...	BOOKER T. & PRISCILL...	9309
Home Grown	BOOKER T. & PRISCILL...	12901
Booker T. & The M.G....	BOOKER T. & The M.G....	9428
The Booker T. Set	BOOKER T. & The M.G....	4248
Book Of Days	PSYCHEDELIC FURS	12009
Book Of Dreams	Steve MILLER Band	329
The Book Of Pride	GIANT STEPS	12631
The Book Of Taliesyn	DEEP PURPLE	4770
Boom Boom Chi Boom Boom	TOM TOM CLUB	9070
Boomtown	DAVID & DAVID	2625
Boots	Nancy SINATRA	1040
Boots Randolph Plays More ...	Boots RANDOLPH	10691
Boots Randolph Plays The G...	Boots RANDOLPH	13221
Boots Randolph With The Kn...	Boots RANDOLPH	12614
Boots With Brass	Boots RANDOLPH	12306
Boots With Strings	Boots RANDOLPH	2442
Bootsy? Player Of Th...	BOOTSY'S RUBBER BAND	2292
Bop Doo-Wop	MANHATTAN TRANSFER	9396
Bop Till You Drop	Ry COODER	5081
Borboletta	SANTANA	3060
Borderline	Ry COODER	4325
Border Lord	Kris KRISTOFFERSON	4147
Border Wave	SIR DOUGLAS Quintet	12647
Born Again	BLACK SABBATH	5367
Born Again	Randy NEWMAN	5424
Born A Woman	Sandy POSEY	10352
Born Free	Andy WILLIAMS	401
Born Free	Roger WILLIAMS	760
Born Free	SOUNDTRACK-MOVIE	2784
Born In America	RIOT	12194
Born In The U.S.A.	Bruce SPRINGSTEEN	5
Born Late	Shaun CASSIDY	1413
Born On A Friday	Cleo LAINE	9326
Born To Be Alive	Patrick HERNANDEZ	5408
Born To Be Bad	George THOROGOOD & T...	2982
Born 2B Blue	Steve MILLER Band	9015
Born To Boogie	Hank WILLIAMS Jr.	2934
Born To Die	GRAND FUNK RAILROAD	5583
Born To Get Down	MUSCLE SHOALS HORNS	9768
Born To Laugh At Tornadoes	WAS (NOT WAS)	9658
Born To Love	Roberta FLACK & Peab...	2182
Born To Run	Bruce SPRINGSTEEN	430
Born To Wander	4 SEASONS	8512
Born Yesterday	EVERLY BROTHERS	6299
The Boss	Diana ROSS	1286
The Boss	Jimmy SMITH	11390
Bossa Nova Hotel	Michael SEMBELLO	8484

Title	Act	Rank
Boss Beat	Sandy NELSON	10113
The Boss Is Back!	Gene AMMONS	13074
Boston	BOSTON	40
Boston, Mass.	DEL FUEGOS	6847
Both Sides Now	Robert GOULET	7441
Both Sides Of Herman's H...	HERMAN'S HERMITS	4558
Both Sides Of Love	Paul ANKA	11461
Bottoms Up	The CHI-LITES	7853
Boulders	Roy WOOD	11911
Bouncing Off The Satellites	The B-52s	7913
A Bouquet Of Hits	FERRANTE & TEICHER	12927
Bourgeois Tagg	BOURGEOIS TAGG	10954
'Bout Love	Bill WITHERS	9299
Bowie Pin Ups	David BOWIE	2877
Box Of Frogs	BOX OF FROGS	4788
The Box Tops Super Hits	BOX TOPS	3349
Boy	U2	3096
Boy In The Box	Corey HART	1669
Boy Meets Girl	BOY MEETS GIRL	7970
Boys And Girls	Bryan FERRY	4992
Boys, Boys, Boys	Lesley GORE	10708
Boys Club	BOYS CLUB	7178
The Boy's Doin' It	Hugh MASEKELA	9227
Boys Don't Cry	BOYS DON'T CRY	5266
The Boys From Doravi...	ATLANTA RHYTHM SECTI...	6405
Boys In Heat	BRITNY FOX	5290
The Boys In The Band	ORIGINAL CAST	13093
Boys In The Trees	Carly SIMON	1178
Boz Scaggs	Boz SCAGGS	11795
Boz Scaggs & Band	Boz SCAGGS	13699
Brain Drain	The RAMONES	10222
Brain Salad Surgery	EMERSON, LAKE & PALM...	968
Brainstorm	The OSMONDS	10361
Branded Man	Merle HAGGARD	12436
Brandenburg Gate: Re...	Dave BRUBECK Quartet	12147
A Brand New Me	Dusty SPRINGFIELD	7356
The Brand New Z.Z. Hill	Z.Z. HILL	13659
Branigan	Laura BRANIGAN	2894
Branigan 2	Laura BRANIGAN	2980
Brasil	MANHATTAN TRANSFER	6287
The Brass Are Comin'	Herb ALPERT & The Ti...	3248
Brass Construction	BRASS CONSTRUCTION	1198
Brass Construction 5	BRASS CONSTRUCTION	5759
Brass Construction IV	BRASS CONSTRUCTION	12343
Brass Construction 6	BRASS CONSTRUCTION	10414
Brass Construction III	BRASS CONSTRUCTION	6276
Brass Construction II	BRASS CONSTRUCTION	2658
Brass Impact	Warren KIME	7561
Brass, Ivory & Strin...	Henry MANCINI & Doc ...	13089
Brass On Ivory	Henry MANCINI & Doc ...	5238
Brass Roots	Doc SEVERINSEN	13239
Brave And Crazy	Melissa ETHERIDGE	2255
Brave New World	Steve MILLER Band	2192
Brazil	RITCHIE FAMILY	5395
Brazil Classics 1: Beleza...	VARIOUS ARTISTS	12809
Brazilia	John KLEMMER	10684
A Brazilian Love Affair	George DUKE	8994
Brazil-Once Again	Herbie MANN	11514
Bread	BREAD	8645
Bread & Butter	The NEWBEATS	5794
Bread & Roses	Judy COLLINS	3347
Breakaway	Art GARFUNKEL	985
Breakaway	Kris KRISTOFFERSON &...	7106
Break Every Rule	Tina TURNER	1091
The Breakfast Club	BREAKFAST CLUB	3526
The Breakfast Club	SOUNDTRACK-MOVIE	2494

Title	Act	Rank
Breakfast In America	SUPERTRAMP	44
Breakfast Special	Pete WINGFIELD	11885
Breakin'	SOUNDTRACK-MOVIE	1779
Breakin' Away	Al JARREAU	547
Breaking All The Rules	Peter FRAMPTON	4935
Breaking Curfew	Tom COCHRANE/RED RIDER	10304
Breaking Hearts	Elton JOHN	2137
Breaking The Chains	DOKKEN	8748
Breakin' 2 Electric Boog...	SOUNDTRACK-MOVIE	6312
Break Of Dawn	FIREFALL	13671
Break Of Hearts	KATRINA & The WAVES	9785
Break Out	POINTER SISTERS	156
Breakout	Johnny HAMMOND	7451
Breakout	SPYRO GYRA	5877
Breakout...!!!	Mitch RYDER And The DETROIT...	2741
Breakwater	BREAKWATER	11620
Breathless	CAMEL	8858
The Brecker Brothers	BRECKER BROTHERS	7383
Breezin'	George BENSON	189
Breezy Stories	Danny O'KEEFE	10949
Brenda K. Starr	Brenda K. STARR	4428
Brenda Russell	Brenda RUSSELL	5155
Brian Hyland	Brian HYLAND	12323
Brian's Song Themes & Vari...	Michel LEGRAND	8615
Brian Wilson	Brian WILSON	5924
Brick	BRICK	1680
The Bride Stripped Bare	Bryan FERRY	11389
The Bridge	Billy JOEL	721
Bridge Of Sighs	Robin TROWER	910
Bridge Over Troubled Wa...	SIMON & GARFUNKEL	85
Bridge Over Troubled Water	Peggy LEE	9606
Bridge Over Troubled...	Ray CONNIFF & His Or...	3566
Bridges	Gil SCOTT-HERON & Br...	10303
Briefcase Full Of Blues	BLUES BROTHERS	621
Brief Encounter	MARILLION	7741
Brief Replies	TEN WHEEL DRIVE With...	10491
Brighten The Corner	Ella FITZGERALD	13265
Brighter Than A Thousand Sun...	KILLING JOKE	13830
Bright Eyes	Melissa MANCHESTER	11475
Bright Lights, Big City	SOUNDTRACK-MOVIE	7469
Bright White	Shawn PHILLIPS	6435
Brilliance	ATLANTIC STARR	2926
Bringing It All Back Home	Bob DYLAN	657
Bring It Back Alive	The OUTLAWS	3289
Bring Me Home	MOTHER EARTH	13615
Bring The Family	John HIATT	7333
Bristol's Creme	Johnny BRISTOL	9897
British Lions	BRITISH LIONS	6770
British Steel	JUDAS PRIEST	3918
Britny Fox	BRITNY FOX	2592
Britten: War Requiem	Benjamin BRITTEN	8279
Broadcast	CUTTING CREW	2113
The Broadsword And The Beast	JETHRO TULL	3542
The Broadway Album	Barbra STREISAND	495
Broadway - Basie's Way	Count BASIE	12735
Broadway Bouquet	Percy FAITH His Orch...	10320
Broadway's Closer To S...	ISLEY JASPER ISLEY	10244
Broken Barricades	PROCOL HARUM	3377
Broken Blossom	Bette MIDLER	5006
Broken English	Marianne FAITHFULL	6666
A Broken Frame	DEPECHE MODE	12130
Broken Heart	The BABYS	2660
Bronco Billy	SOUNDTRACK-MOVIE	10123
Brook Benton Today	Brook BENTON	3120
Brooklyn Bridge	BROOKLYN BRIDGE	3022
The Brooklyn, Bronx ...	BROOKLYN, BRONX & QU...	8733

Title	Act	Rank
Brother Arab	ARABIAN PRINCE	13770
Brother, Brother, Brother	ISLEY BROTHERS	2307
Brotherhood	NEW ORDER	7760
Brother Love's Travelling Sa...	Neil DIAMOND	4190
Brothers And Sisters	ALLMAN BROTHERS Band	261
Brothers In Arms	DIRE STRAITS	71
The Brothers: Isley	ISLEY BROTHERS	12599
Brothers Of The Road	ALLMAN BROTHERS Band	5249
Brother To Brother	Gino VANNELLI	1345
Brother Where You Bound	SUPERTRAMP	3050
Browne Sugar	Tom BROWNE	10775
Bruce Cockburn Resume	Bruce COCKBURN	11847
Bruce Springsteen & The...	Bruce SPRINGSTEEN	851
Bruce Woolley & The ...	Bruce WOOLLEY & The ...	13353
Bruised Orange	John PRINE	7615
Bruiseology	The WAITRESSES	11689
Brujo	NEW RIDERS Of The PU...	6998
B, S & T; 4	BLOOD, SWEAT & TEARS	1548
Bubble Gum, Lemonade &....Somet...	MAMA CASS	6399
Bubble Gum Music Is The N...	VARIOUS ARTISTS	7518
Bucket	Jimmy SMITH	8709
The Buckinghams' Greatest...	The BUCKINGHAMS	5804
Buck Owens In London	Buck OWENS	9136
Bucky Fellini	DEAD MILKMEN	11693
Bud & Travis...In Concert	BUD And TRAVIS	11417
Buddha And The Chocolate Box	Cat STEVENS	384
Buddy & Soul	Buddy RICH	13005
Buddy Holly & The Crickets 20...	Buddy HOLLY	5953
The Buddy Holly Story	SOUNDTRACK-MOVIE	6973
Buddy Miles Live	Buddy MILES	3930
Buenas Noches From A Lonely...	Dwight YOAKAM	6139
Buffalo Springfield(2...	BUFFALO SPRINGFIELD	7569
Buffalo Springfield	BUFFALO SPRINGFIELD	6233
Buffalo Springfield A...	BUFFALO SPRINGFIELD	5505
Building The Perfect Beast	Don HENLEY	754
Build Me Up Buttercup	The FOUNDATIONS	7369
Built For Speed	STRAY CATS	219
Built To Last	GRATEFUL DEAD	4723
Bulldog	BULLDOG	10188
Bull Durham	SOUNDTRACK-MOVIE	11758
Bulletboys	BULLETBOYS	2489
Bullish	Herb ALPERT & The TI...	8099
Bump City	TOWER OF POWER	5303
Bumpin'	Wes MONTGOMERY	8043
Bumps And Bruises	Joe TEX	7908
Bundle Of Joy	Freddie HUBBARD	10546
Burchfield Nines	Michael FRANKS	7831
Burgers	HOT TUNA	4342
Burlap & Satin	Dolly PARTON	8987
Burn	DEEP PURPLE	1565
Burnin'	Bob MARLEY And The W...	10788
Burnin'	Esther PHILLIPS	8443
Burning	SHOOTING STAR	11604
Burning Bridges And ...	MIKE CURB CONGREGATI...	8405
Burning For You	STRAWBS	12319
Burning Love And Hits From ...	Elvis PRESLEY	2124
Burning Sensations	BURNING SENSATIONS	12697
Burning The Ballroom ...	AMAZING RHYTHM ACES	8639
Burnin' Love	CON FUNK SHUN	9718
Burnin' Sky	BAD COMPANY	2130
Burnin' Thing	Mac DAVIS	6466
Burns Like A Star	STONE FURY	9443
Burnt Lips	Leo KOTTKE	8540
Burnt Weeny Sandwich	Frank ZAPPA	7885
Bursting At The Seams	STRAWBS	8852
Burt Bacharach	Burt BACHARACH	1818

Title	Act	Rank
Burt Bacharach's Greatest ...	Burt BACHARACH	11718
Burton Cummings	Burton CUMMINGS	2939
Bush Doctor	Peter TOSH	6476
Business As Usual	MEN AT WORK	58
Bus Stop	The HOLLIES	7172
Buster	SOUNDTRACK-MOVIE	4371
Buster Poindexter	David JOHANSEN	6862
Bustin' Loose	Chuck BROWN & The SO...	4080
Bustin' Loose	Roberta FLACK	9612
Bustin' Out	PURE PRAIRIE LEAGUE	3117
Bustin' Out Of L Seven	Rick JAMES	1534
Busy Body	Luther VANDROSS	2440
But Beautiful	Nancy WILSON	12256
Butch Cassidy And The Su...	SOUNDTRACK-MOVIE	588
...But Seriously	Phil COLLINS	136
"But Seriously Folks..."	Joe WALSH	1077
The Butterfield Blue...	Paul BUTTERFIELD Blu...	6584
ButterFly	Barbra STREISAND	1790
The Butterfly Ball And The G...	Roger GLOVER	9679
But The Little Girls Understand	The KNACK	2743
Butt Of Course	Jimmy CASTOR Bunch	5800
Butt Rockin'	FABULOUS THUNDERBIRD...	11240
But What Will The Neighbor...	Rodney CROWELL	10313
Buying A Book	Joe TEX	12293
Byablue	Keith JARRETT	9472
By All Means Necessa...	BOOGIE DOWN PRODUC...	5516
Bye Bye Blues	Bert KAEMPFERT And H...	3909
Bye Bye Blues	Brenda LEE	7717
By Popular Demand	FERRANTE & TEICHER	11472
Byrdmaniax	The BYRDS	5389
Byrds	The BYRDS	3261
The Byrds (Untitled)	The BYRDS	3068
The Byrds' Greatest Hits	The BYRDS	1427
By Request	Brenda LEE	8320
By Request (The Best...	Billy VERA & The BEA...	2925
By The Light Of The Moon	Los LOBOS	4050
By The Time I Get To Phoenix	Glen CAMPBELL	490

C

Title	Act	Rank
Ca$hflow	CASHFLOW	10009
Cabaret	ORIGINAL CAST	2841
Cabaret	SOUNDTRACK-MOVIE	1199
Cabin Fever	Michael STANLEY Band	5987
Cactus	CACTUS	4657
The Cactus Album	3rd BASS	3767
Cactus And A Rose	Gary STEWART	12630
Caddyshack	SOUNDTRACK-MOVIE	6857
Cafe Racers	Kim CARNES	7790
Cage The Songbird	Crystal GAYLE	11828
Cahoots	The BAND	3191
Caliente!	Gato BARBIERI	4014
California Bloodlines	John STEWART	13053
California Dreaming	Wes MONTGOMERY	3882
California Jam 2	VARIOUS ARTISTS	7644
California Nights	Lesley GORE	11926
The California Raisins	CALIFORNIA RAISINS	3986
Calling	Noel POINTER	12138
Calling Card	Rory GALLAGHER	9610
Call It What You Wan...	Bill SUMMERS & SUMME...	7136
Call Me	Al GREEN	1050
Call Me Irresponsible	Jack JONES	6813
Call Of The West	WALL OF VOODOO	4699
Call On Me	Evelyn "Champagne" KING	9603
Calm Animals	The FIXX	5712
Cal Smith Sings	Cal SMITH	12805
Calumet	LOBO	7777

Title | Act	Rank
Calypso In Brass | Harry BELAFONTE	13207
Camelot | SOUNDTRACK-MOVIE	684
Cameosis | CAMEO	2345
Camera Camera | RENAISSANCE	13146
The Camera Never Lies | Michael FRANKS	9777
Cameron | Rafael CAMERON	5593
Cameron's In Love | Rafael CAMERON	7878
Camouflage | Rod STEWART	1796
Camouflage | RUFUS	6873
Canadian Sunset | Andy WILLIAMS	10125
Canciones de Mi Padre | Linda RONSTADT	3288
Candida | DAWN/Tony ORLANDO	2910
Candida | Lawrence WELK	7746
Candida & Knock Three T... | DAWN/Tony ORLANDO	11977
Candleland | Ian McCULLOCH	13787
Candles | HEATWAVE	7167
Candles In The Rain | MELANIE	1546
Candy | CON FUNK SHUN	3734
Candy | SOUNDTRACK-MOVIE	3812
Candy Apple Grey | HUSKER DU	10002
Candy Girl | NEW EDITION	5330
The Candymen | The CANDYMEN	13196
Candy-O | The CARS	404
Can I Change My Mind | Tyrone DAVIS	9893
Canned Heat | CANNED HEAT	5792
Canned Heat Concert (Recorded... | CANNED HEAT	9034
Canned Heat Cook Book (The Be... | CANNED HEAT	5369
Canned Wheat Packed by The Gues... | GUESS WHO	5923
Cantamos | POCO	6952
Can't Buy A Thrill | STEELY DAN	1093
Canterbury Tales | ORIGINAL CAST	11656
Can't Fight Fate | Taylor DAYNE	1028
Can't Get Enough | Barry WHITE	831
Can't Help Falling In Love | Al MARTINO	12071
Can't Hold Back | Eddie MONEY	1175
Can't Hold Back | PURE PRAIRIE LEAGUE	10191
Can't Let You Go | John TRAVOLTA	7733
Can't Look Away | Trevor RABIN	8562
Can't Shake This Feelin' | SPINNERS	13234
Can't Slow Down | Lionel RICHIE	21
Can't Stop The Love | MAZE Featuring Frank...	4448
Can't Stop The Music (Soun... | VILLAGE PEOPLE	5714
Can't Take My Eyes Off You | Nancy WILSON	10983
Can't Wait All Night | Juice NEWTON	9169
Can't We Fall In Love Again | Phyllis HYMAN	5578
Can't You Hear The Song? | Wayne NEWTON	9854
Canyon | Paul WINTER	9466
The Cape Verdean Blu... | Horace SILVER Quinte...	12601
A Cappella | Todd RUNDGREN	10598
Capricorn Princess | Esther PHILLIPS	12016
The Captain And Me | DOOBIE BROTHERS	278
Captain & Tennille's G... | CAPTAIN & TENNILLE	6062
Captain Beyond | CAPTAIN BEYOND	8347
Captain Fantastic And The Brow... | Elton JOHN	185
Captain Fingers | Lee RITENOUR	12129
Captain Marvel | Stan GETZ	13786
Captain Sad And His Ship Of ... | The COWSILLS	7197
The Captain's Journey | Lee RITENOUR	9254
Captain Swing | Michelle SHOCKED	5695
Captured | JOURNEY	1095
Captured | ROCKWELL	9592
Captured Angel | Dan FOGELBERG	3149
Captured Live | Johnny WINTER	7263
Captured Live | Peter TOSH	10784
Caramba! | Lee MORGAN	12991
Caravan Of Love | ISLEY JASPER ISLEY	5361

Title | Act	Rank
Caravanserai | SANTANA	1114
Caravan To Midnight | Robin TROWER	4001
Cardiac Arrest | CAMEO	7507
The Cardinal | SOUNDTRACK-MOVIE	9106
Care | SHRIEKBACK	13340
Career Girls | Peter NERO	12460
Careful | The MOTELS	4250
Careless | Stephen BISHOP	3455
Caress Of Steel | RUSH	10461
Cargo | MEN AT WORK	623
Caribou | Elton JOHN	268
Caricatures | Donald BYRD	5750
Carla | Carla THOMAS	10653
Carl Anderson | Carl ANDERSON	7624
Carl Carlton | Carl CARLTON	3633
Carlin on Campus | George CARLIN	9608
Carl Orff: Carmina Bu... | CLEVELAND Orchestra	11358
Carlos Santana & Buddy Mil... [A] | Carlos SANTANA	1117
Carlos Santana & Buddy Miles!... [A] | Buddy MILES	1117
Carl Wilson | Carl WILSON	13344
Carly Simon | Carly SIMON	2644
Carmel | Joe SAMPLE	4372
Carnaval | SPYRO GYRA	3574
Carnegie Hall | Hubert LAWS	11908
Carnegie Hall Concert | Buck OWENS	8253
Carney | Leon RUSSELL	633
Carnival | DURAN DURAN	7567
Carnival | John HANDY	13716
Carnival | Maynard FERGUSON	8034
The Carnival | The CARNIVAL	13431
Carol Burnett Featuring If ... | Carol BURNETT	13720
The Carol Douglas Album | Carol DOUGLAS	12581
Carol Hensel's Exercise... | Carol HENSEL	2161
Carol Hensel's Exercise...Vol. 3 | Carol HENSEL	8527
Carol Hensel's Exercise...Vol. 2 | Carol HENSEL	4712
Carolina Dreams | MARSHALL TUCKER Band	1455
Carolyne Mas | Carolyne MAS	12827
The Car Over The Lak... | OZARK MOUNTAIN DARED...	5517
Carpenters | CARPENTERS	109
The Carpetbaggers | SOUNDTRACK-MOVIE	12465
Carrie Lucas In Danceland | Carrie LUCAS	8842
The Carroll County Acciden... | Porter WAGONER	10509
Carryin' On With Joh... | Johnny CASH & June C...	13384
Carry It On (Soundtrack) | Joan BAEZ	11535
Carry On | Bobby CALDWELL	8954
The Cars | The CARS	234
Car Wash | ROSE ROYCE	1283
Casino | Al Di MEOLA	4972
Casino Lights | VARIOUS ARTISTS	5639
Casino Royale | SOUNDTRACK-MOVIE	3126
Castles | JOY OF COOKING	11526
Castles In The Sand | David Allan COE	12574
Cast Your Fate To The W... | SOUNDS ORCHESTRAL	2520
Casual Gods | Jerry HARRISON: CASU...	5453
The Cat | Jimmy SMITH	2458
Catch A Fire | Bob MARLEY And The W...	11706
Catch A Rising Star | John GARY	1074
Catch Bull At Four | Cat STEVENS	372
Catching The Sun | SPYRO GYRA	2443
Catching Up With Depeche Mod... | DEPECHE MODE	7573
Catch Me, I'm Falling | PRETTY POISON	9068
Catch The Wind | DONOVAN	3967
Cate Bros. | CATE BROS.	10039
Catfish | FOUR TOPS	9371
Cathedrals | D.C. LaRUE	8274
The Catherine Wheel (Original... | David BYRNE	7600

Title | Act	Rank
Catholic Boy | Jim CARROLL Band	4720
Cat In The Hat | Bobby CALDWELL	7575
Cat People | SOUNDTRACK-MOVIE	5614
Cats (Original London Cast) | ORIGINAL CAST	5676
Cats (Original Broadway Cast) | ORIGINAL CAST	5183
Cats Selections From Original Br... | ORIGINAL CAST	9229
Cat Scratch Fever | Ted NUGENT	1291
Cats On The Coast | SEA LEVEL	3953
Cat Stevens Greatest Hits | Cat STEVENS	971
Cats Under The Stars | Jerry GARCIA	9805
Cats Without Claws | Donna SUMMER	5390
Cattle Call | Eddy ARNOLD	11078
Caught In The Act | GRAND FUNK RAILROAD	3740
Caught In The Act | The COMMODORES	2332
Caught In The Act - Live | STYX	4572
Caught In The Game | SURVIVOR	9190
Caught Live + 5 | MOODY BLUES	3431
Caught Up | Millie JACKSON	2007
Caverna Magica (...Und... | Andreas VOLLENWEIDER	9157
Celebrate! | KOOL & The GANG	770
Celebrate Me Home | Kenny LOGGINS	1953
Celebration | EL CHICANO	9930
Celi Bee & The Buzzy... | CELI BEE And The BUZ...	11769
Cellophane Symphony | Tommy JAMES And The ...	9733
Centerfield | John FOGERTY	493
Centipede | Rebbie JACKSON	5715
Central Heating | HEATWAVE	1602
Central Line | CENTRAL LINE	10212
Ceremony | SPOOKY TOOTH	6647
Cerrone IV - The Golden Touch | CERRONE	7686
Cerrone's Paradise | CERRONE	11708
Cerrone 3 - Supernature | CERRONE	9567
Certified Live | Dave MASON	5283
C'est Chic | CHIC	589
Chad & Jeremy Sing For You | CHAD & JEREMY	6970
Chain Lightning | Don McLEAN	2916
Chain Reaction | The CRUSADERS	3232
Chaka | Chaka KHAN	2110
Chaka Khan | Chaka KHAN	5514
Chalk Mark In A Rain Storm | Joni MITCHELL	5066
The Chambers Brothers Gre... | CHAMBERS BROTH...	13517
The Chambers Brothers' ... | CHAMBERS BROTHERS	10590
Chameleon | Patti LaBELLE	7303
Champagne Charlie | Leon REDBONE	11808
Champagne Jam | ATLANTA RHYTHM SECTI...	911
Champagne On Broadway | Lawrence WELK	10525
Chance | Candi STATON	9671
Chance | MANFRED MANN'S EARTH...	6085
Chances Are | Bob MARLEY And The W...	9628
Change. | The ALARM	6448
Change | Barry WHITE	10940
The Change Has Come | Chubby CHECKER	13531
Change No Change | Elliot EASTON	8321
Change Of Address | KROKUS	5007
A Change Of Heart | David SANBORN	4459
Change Of Heart | CHANGE	8086
Change Of Heart | Eric CARMEN	8223
Changes | Johnny RIVERS	3135
Changes | The MONKEES	12487
Changes In Latitudes, Chang... | Jimmy BUFFETT	904
Changesonebowie | David BOWIE	1509
Changestwobowie | David BOWIE	5743
Change Up The Groove | Roy AYERS UBIQUITY	11640
Changing Horses | INCREDIBLE STRING BA...	12227
Changing Times | FOUR TOPS	7955
Changin' Times Featuring ... | FLATT & SCRUGGS	13040

Title | Act	Rank
Chanson | CHANSON	3545
Chapel Of Love | DIXIE CUPS	10802
Chapter VII | Buddy MILES	9158
Chapter Three - Viva Emilia... | Gato BARBIERI	12183
Chapter Two | Roberta FLACK	630
Characters | Stevie WONDER	1935
Charade (Soundtrack) | Henry MANCINI and hi...	1076
Chariots Of Fire | Ernie WATTS	9589
Chariots Of Fire (Soundtrack) | VANGELIS	393
Charity Ball | FANNY	10005
Charley Pride: In Person | Charley PRIDE	2774
Charley Pride Sings Heart S... | Charley PRIDE	2641
Charley Pride's 10th Album | Charley PRIDE	2420
Charlie | CHARLIE	10375
Charlie McCoy | Charlie McCOY	7610
Charlie Rich Sings The Songs... | Charlie RICH	12327
Charlie Sexton | Charlie SEXTON	8581
Chartbusters | Ray PARKER Jr./RAYDI...	5930
Chase | CHASE	2084
Chase The Clouds Away | Chuck MANGIONE	4353
Chasing Rainbows | Jane OLIVOR	8153
Cheapo-Cheapo Productions ... | John SEBASTIAN	6665
Cheap Thrills | BIG BROTHER And The ...	108
Cheap Trick At Budokan | CHEAP TRICK	350
Cheat The Night | Deborah ALLEN	6180
Checkered Flag | Dick DALE and The DE...	8557
Check It Out | TAVARES	10602
Cheech And Chong | CHEECH & CHONG	1173
Cheech & Chong's Wedding A... | CHEECH & CHONG	1692
Chequered Past | CHEQUERED PAST	11470
Cher(2) | CHER	2200
Cher | CHER	5097
Cherish | David CASSIDY	2524
Cherry Hill Park | Billy Joe ROYAL	8584
Cher's Golden Greats | CHER	13152
Cher Superpak | CHER	7914
Cher Superpak, Vol. II | CHER	8092
Cheryl Ladd | Cheryl LADD	8789
Cheryl Lynn | Cheryl LYNN	2394
Cheryl Moana Marie | John ROWLES	13805
Chess | VARIOUS ARTISTS	4904
Chester & Lester [A] | Chet ATKINS	11710
Chester & Lester [A] | Les PAUL	11710
Chet Atkins Picks On The Beat... | Chet ATKINS	7977
Chet Picks On The Po... | Chet ATKINS/BOSTON P...	11366
Chewing Pine | Leo KOTTKE	9172
Chewy, Chewy | OHIO EXPRESS	13386
Chic | CHIC	2053
Chicago | ORIGINAL CAST	7143
Chicago | CHICAGO	39
Chicago III | CHICAGO	309
Chicago V | CHICAGO	252
Chicago VI | CHICAGO	291
Chicago VII | CHICAGO	217
Chicago VIII | CHICAGO	563
Chicago IX: Chicago's Greatest Hi... | CHICAGO	233
Chicago X | CHICAGO	326
Chicago XI | CHICAGO	1671
Chicago 13 | CHICAGO	4232
Chicago XIV | CHICAGO	6930
Chicago 16 | CHICAGO	1309
Chicago 17 | CHICAGO	340
Chicago 18 | CHICAGO	2640
Chicago At Carnegie Hall | CHICAGO	536
Chicago - Greatest Hits, Volume II | CHICAGO	12106
The Chicago Theme | Hubert LAWS	4214

Title | Act	Rank
Chicago Transit Authority | CHICAGO	84
Chicken Skin Music | Ry COODER	11807
Chico DeBarge | Chico DeBARGE	5915
Chi Coltrane | Chi COLTRANE	9776
Chieftains 5 | The CHIEFTAINS	12600
Child Is Father To The M... | BLOOD, SWEAT & TEARS	3087
Child Of Clay | Jimmie RODGERS	12431
A Child Of The 50's | Robert KLEIN	13331
Child Of The Novelty | MAHOGANY RUSH	6350
Children | MISSION U.K.	9420
Children (Get Togeth... | Edwin HAWKINS Singer...	11155
Children Of Light | Biff ROSE	11338
Children Of Sanchez | Chuck MANGIONE	1462
Children Of The Future | Steve MILLER Band	7482
Children Of The Sun | Billy THORPE	3731
Children Of The World | BEE GEES	505
Children Of Tomorrow | Frankie SMITH	5885
A Child's Adventure | Marianne FAITHFULL	10075
A Child's Garden Of Grass... | VARIOUS ARTISTS	9187
Chi-Lites | The CHI-LITES	6913
The Chi-Lites Greatest Hits | The CHI-LITES	4365
Chillin' | FORCE M.D.'S	5336
Chill Out | BLACK UHURU	10800
Chim Chim Cher-ee | NEW CHRISTY MINSTREL...	3162
Chinatown | THIN LIZZY	8495
Chinese Wall | Philip BAILEY	2331
A Chipmunk Christmas | The CHIPMUNKS	7185
Chipmunk Punk | The CHIPMUNKS	3397
Chipmunk Rock | The CHIPMUNKS	10083
The Chipmunks Sing The Beat... | The CHIPMUNKS	3234
Chitty Chitty Bang Bang | SOUNDTRACK-MOVIE	3814
Chocolate Chip | Isaac HAYES	2324
Chocolate City | PARLIAMENT	6191
Choice | John GARY	4997
Choice! The Best Of The... | Ramsey LEWIS Trio	5445
Choice Quality Stuff... | IT'S A BEAUTIFUL DAY	7676
The Chokin' Kind | Joe SIMON	4919
Choosing You | Lenny WILLIAMS	5989
A Chorus Line | ORIGINAL CAST	4397
A Chorus Line-The Movie | SOUNDTRACK-MOVIE	7875
Chris Isaak | Chris ISAAK	13760
Chris Jagger | Chris JAGGER	12772
Christiane F. (Soundtrack) | David BOWIE	10891
Christian Of The Wor... | Tommy JAMES And The ...	9972
The Christians | The CHRISTIANS	10904
Christine | SOUNDTRACK-MOVIE	12462
Christine McVie | Christine McVIE	3418
Christmas | ALABAMA	8258
Christmas | Kenny ROGERS	4903
Christmas | OAK RIDGE BOYS	8877
A Christmas Album | Barbra STREISAND	8919
The Christmas Album | Elvis PRESLEY	13475
Christmas And The Beads Of Swe... | Laura NYRO	4913
Christmas In America | Kenny ROGERS	10423
Christmas In The Stars/Star Wars Chr... | MECO	8116
Christmas Jollies | SALSOUL Orchestra	5766
Christmas Jollies II | SALSOUL Orchestra	11932
Christmas Portrait | CARPENTERS	10128
Christmas Rap | VARIOUS ARTISTS	10722
A Christmas Together | John DENVER & The MU...	4859
Christmas Tyme | Engelbert HUMPERDINC...	11906
Christmas Wishes | Anne MURRAY	6875
Christmas With Slim Whitman | Slim WHITMAN	12558
Christopher Cross | Christopher CROSS	59
Chronicle (The 20 Gr... | CREEDENCE CLEARWAT...	6602
Chronicles | Steve WINWOOD	2928

Title | Act	Rank
Chronicle II | CREEDENCE CLEARWATER...	9721
Chubby Checker In Person | Chubby CHECKER	11040
Chubby Checker's Greatest ... | Chubby CHECKER	9516
Chuck Berry On Stage | Chuck BERRY	4912
Chuck Berry's Golden Decade | Chuck BERRY	6061
Chuck Berry's Golden Decade, ... | Chuck BERRY	8977
Chuck Berry's Greatest Hits | Chuck BERRY	4221
Chuckii | Chuckii BOOKER	9020
The Chuck Mangione Quartet | Chuck MANGIONE	11854
Chunga's Revenge | Frank ZAPPA	7989
Cicero Park | HOT CHOCOLATE	4952
Cimarron | Emmylou HARRIS	4299
Cinco | EL CHICANO	13257
The Cinderella Theory | George CLINTON	13180
A Circle Filled With Lov... | SONS OF CHAMPLIN	8602
The Circle Game | Tom RUSH	6032
Circle Of Love | Steve MILLER Band	3484
Circles | Mary TRAVERS	13824
Circles | NEW SEEKERS	10040
Circus | ARGENT	12449
The Circus | ERASURE	13462
Circus Of Power | CIRCUS OF POWER	13589
Citadel | STARCASTLE	12178
Citizen Kihn | Greg KIHN Band	5879
City | McGUINN, CLARK & HIL...	9800
City Boy | CITY BOY	12744
City In The Sky | STAPLE SINGERS	8640
City Kids | SPYRO GYRA	6318
City Life | BOOGIE BOYS	5693
City Life | The BLACKBYRDS	1576
City Nights | Nick GILDER	3129
City Nights | TIERRA	3694
City Of Angels | The MIRACLES	2181
City of New Orleans | Willie NELSON	5419
City Streets | Carole KING	7729
City To City | Gerry RAFFERTY	551
Civilized Evil | Jean-Luc PONTY	5417
Civilized Man | Joe COCKER	9720
C.J. Fish | COUNTRY JOE & The FI...	8218
C.K. | Chaka KHAN	8824
Clambake (Soundtrack) | Elvis PRESLEY	4479
Clapton | Eric CLAPTON	7030
The Clarke/Duke Project | Stanley CLARKE & Geo...	2511
The Clarke/Duke Project II | Stanley CLARKE & Ge...	9478
The Clash | The CLASH	9560
Class | The REDDINGS	10093
Class Clown | George CARLIN	1732
Class Guitar | Chet ATKINS	13542
Classical Barbra | Barbra STREISAND	5320
Classical Gas [A] | MANNHEIM STEAMROLLER	7164
Classical Gas [A] | Mason WILLIAMS	7164
A Classic Case: The ... | LONDON SYMPHONY Orch...	8262
Classic Crystal | Crystal GAYLE	4344
Classic Lightfoot (The B... | Gordon LIGHTFOOT	11935
Classic Rock - Volum... | LONDON SYMPHONY Orc...	13382
Classic Rush | Tom RUSH	13809
Classics | Kenny ROGERS & Dotti...	5407
Classics | Paul WILLIAMS	10564
Classics | The DOORS	10362
Classics Live | AEROSMITH	7612
Classics The Early Years | Neil DIAMOND	11780
Classic Yes | YES	10990
Class Of '55 [A] | Carl PERKINS	7888
Class Of '55 [A] | Jerry Lee LEWIS	7888
Class Of '55 [A] | Johnny CASH	7888
Class Of '55 [A] | Roy ORBISON	7888

Title | Act	Rank
Class Of '66 | Floyd CRAMER	9633
Class Of '65 | Floyd CRAMER	8241
Claudine | Claudine LONGET	958
Claudine (Soundtrack... | Gladys KNIGHT & The ...	2654
Claudja | Claudja BARRY	9099
Clean | Edwin STARR	6482
Clear Light | CLEAR LIGHT	8398
Clearly Love | Olivia NEWTON-JOHN	2403
Clear Sailin' | Chris HILLMAN	13159
Clear Spirit | SPIRIT	4425
Clear Spot | CAPTAIN BEEFHEART & ...	12184
Cleo Laine Live!!! At Carnegie... | Cleo LAINE	10750
Cleopatra Jones | SOUNDTRACK-MOVIE	8472
Climax | CLIMAX	11330
Climax | OHIO PLAYERS	7900
The Climax Chicago Blue... | CLIMAX BLUES BAND	13808
Climbing The Walls | WRATHCHILD AMERICA	12732
The Clique | The CLIQUE	12646
A Clockwork Orange | SOUNDTRACK-MOVIE	2542
Clones Of Dr. Funkenstein | PARLIAMENT	2370
Close | Kim WILDE	10380
Close Encounters Of A Th... | SOUNDTRACK-MOVIE	2897
Close Enough For Rock 'N' Roll | NAZARETH	3204
Close Personal Friend | Robert JOHNSON	10969
Closer | Gino SOCCIO	7288
Closer Than Close | Jean CARN	11919
Closer To Home | GRAND FUNK RAILROAD	422
Closer To It! | Brian AUGER	4085
Closer To The Flame | Rob JUNGKLAS	6750
Closer To The Ground | JOY OF COOKING	9361
The Closer You Get | ALABAMA	1064
Close To The Bone | THOMPSON TWINS	7154
Close To The Bone | TOM TOM CLUB	7353
Close To The Edge | YES	1072
Close To You | CARPENTERS	99
Close To You | Johnny MATHIS	6839
Close Up | Tom JONES	4521
Closeup | Frankie VALLI	3221
Close-Up | BEACH BOYS	9479
Close-Up | Buck OWENS	12003
Close-Up | David SANBORN	4675
Close-Up | Frank SINATRA	12770
Close-Up | Jackie GLEASON	13447
Close-Up | Lou RAWLS	13064
Close-Up | Merle HAGGARD	9773
Close-Up | Nancy WILSON	13443
Close-Up | Nat King COLE	13290
Close-Up | Sonny JAMES	12696
Close-Up | The LETTERMEN	7963
Close Up The Honky T... | FLYING BURRITO BROTH...	11205
Close Your Eyes | Edward BEAR	12025
Closing The Gap | Michael PARKS	1531
Cloud Nine | George HARRISON	1152
Cloud Nine | The TEMPTATIONS	474
Clouds | Joni MITCHELL	2499
Clouds Across The Sun | FIREFALL	7439
The Clown Died In Mar... | BEACON STREET UNION	9960
Club Ninja | BLUE ÖYSTER CULT	6558
Club Paradise (Soundtrack) | Jimmy CLIFF	10560
Clues | Robert PALMER	5357
Clutching At Straws | MARILLION	8623
C'mon Everybody | Elvis PRESLEY	6424
Coal Miner's Daughter | Loretta LYNN	5895
Coal Miner's Daughter | SOUNDTRACK-MOVIE	4312
Coast To Coast | Dave CLARK Five	2143
Coast To Coast | JOE & EDDIE	11674

Title | Act	Rank
Cobra | SOUNDTRACK-MOVIE	9987
Cocked & Loaded | L.A. GUNS	2559
Cocker | Joe COCKER	4916
Cock Robin | COCK ROBIN	5641
Cocktail | SOUNDTRACK-MOVIE	376
Cocomotion | EL COCO	5531
Coconut Telegraph | Jimmy BUFFETT	3721
Cocoon | SOUNDTRACK-MOVIE	13161
Coda | LED ZEPPELIN	2503
Coke | Coke ESCOVEDO	13599
Cold Blood | COLD BLOOD	2177
Cold Blooded | Rick JAMES	2206
The Cold Hard Facts Of Lif... | Porter WAGONER	13833
Cold On The Shoulder | Gordon LIGHTFOOT	1926
Cold Spring Harbor | Billy JOEL	10987
Cold Sweat | James BROWN	4179
Collaboration [A] | Earl KLUGH	4137
Collaboration [A] | George BENSON	4137
Collage | Noel HARRISON	9476
Collage | Paul REVERE And The ...	9530
Amy Grant - The Collection | Amy GRANT	4402
A Collection: Greatest H... | Barbra STREISAND	2938
A Collection Of Great Dance So... | PINK FLOYD	3777
Collections | RASCALS/YOUNG RASCAL...	923
Colonel Abrams | Colonel ABRAMS	7912
Colonization | NEW COLONY SIX	11740
Color Him Father | The WINSTONS	6112
Color In Your Life | MISSING PERSONS	8379
Color Me Barbra (Soundtr... | Barbra STREISAND	966
Color My World/Who Am I | Petula CLARK	4800
The Color Of Money | SOUNDTRACK-MOVIE	7434
Color Of Success | Morris DAY	3736
The Color Purple | SOUNDTRACK-MOVIE	7391
Colors | SOUNDTRACK-MOVIE	3984
Colors Of The Day/The Best O... | Judy COLLINS	3460
Colosseum Live | COLOSSEUM	13119
Colour By Numbers | CULTURE CLUB	214
The Colour Of Spring | TALK TALK	5622
Colours | Claudine LONGET	9765
Combat Rock | The CLASH	487
Come A Little Bit Clo... | JAY & The AMERICANS	11622
Come And Get Yourself Some | Leon HAYWOOD	8863
Come An' Get It | WHITESNAKE	10786
Come As You Are | ASHFORD & SIMPSON	12605
Come As You Are | Peter WOLF	5734
Come Back Charleston Blu... | SOUNDTRACK-MOVIE	13739
Come Back Home | Bobby GOLDSBORO	10808
Come Back When You Grow Up | Bobby VEE	6684
Come Dance To The Hi... | Sammy KAYE & His Orc...	9014
Come Dancing With The Kinks/The... | The KINKS	12305
Comedy Is Not Pretty! | Steve MARTIN	3196
Come Fly With Me | Bobby BLAND	13024
Come From The Shadows | Joan BAEZ	3389
Come Get It! | Rick JAMES	1246
Come Get To This | Nancy WILSON	7751
Come Go With Us | POCKETS	3998
Come In From The Rain | CAPTAIN & TENNILLE	3003
Come Into My Heart | USA-EUROPEAN CONNECT...	5333
Come Into My Life | Jermaine JACKSON	10871
Come Into Our World | The EMOTIONS	8006
Come Morning | Grover WASHINGTON Jr...	2668
Come On Dance, Dance | SATURDAY NIGHT BAND	6893
Come On Over | Olivia NEWTON-JOHN	2018
Come Out And Play | TWISTED SISTER	5277
Comes A Time | Neil YOUNG	1398
Come Saturday Morning | The SANDPIPERS	7011

Title | Act	Rank
Come Share My Life | Glenn YARBROUGH	9541
Come Share My Love | Miki HOWARD	11887
Come Taste The Band | DEEP PURPLE	4691
Come Together | Ike & Tina TURNER	6660
Come Together | MIKE CURB CONGREGATI...	9533
Come To My Garden | Minnie RIPERTON	11739
Come Upstairs | Carly SIMON	2721
Comfort Me | Carla THOMAS	9166
Comin' At Ya! | Coke ESCOVEDO	13067
Comin' From All Ends | NEW BIRTH	5569
Coming Around Again | Carly SIMON	1422
The Coming Atlantis | Freddy ROBINSON	9830
Coming Back For More | William BELL	6236
Coming Back Hard Again | FAT BOYS	3498
Coming Down Your Way | THREE DOG NIGHT	6454
Coming Of Age | FIVE MAN ELECTRICAL ...	13725
Coming On Strong | Brenda LEE	7235
Coming Out | MANHATTAN TRANSFER	5816
Coming To America | SOUNDTRACK-MOVIE	13444
Comin' Thru | QUICKSILVER MESSENGE...	8626
Commander Cody & His Lost... | COMMANDER CO...	6364
Command Performance! Les & ... [A] | Larry ELGART	11092
Command Performance! Les & La... [A] | Les ELGART	11092
Command Performance/Live In Pe... | JAN & DEAN	4910
Command Performances | Doc SEVERINSEN	10213
Command Performances | Enoch LIGHT & The Li...	11627
Commodores | The COMMODORES	247
Commodores Anthology | The COMMODORES	10591
Commodores' Greatest Hits | The COMMODORES	2966
Commodores Live! | The COMMODORES	967
Commodores 13 | The COMMODORES	8567
Common Ground | RHYTHM CORPS	8172
Common One | Van MORRISON	7084
Common Sense | John PRINE	6690
The Communards | The COMMUNARDS	7770
Communication | Bobby WOMACK	5846
Communique | DIRE STRAITS	2127
Company | ORIGINAL CAST	13168
Company B | COMPANY B	11137
Compartments | José FELICIANO	10596
Competition Coupe | The ASTRONAUTS	11043
Complete & Unbelievable....T... | Otis REDDING	6114
Completely Well | B.B. KING	2445
The Complete Sea | SAN SEBASTIAN String...	11607
The Completion Backward Princip... | The TUBES	3172
Composite Truth | MANDRILL	2657
Computer Games | George CLINTON	3941
Computer-World | KRAFTWERK	3121
Conan The Barbarian | SOUNDTRACK-MOVIE	12253
The Concept | SLAVE	7156
The Concert | CREEDENCE CLEARWATER...	5312
The Concert For Bangla De... | George HARRISON	392
Concert For Lovers | FERRANTE & TEICHER	5840
Concert In Blues | Willie HUTCH	11415
The Concert In Central ... | SIMON & GARFUNKEL	1674
Concert In Stereo/Li... | Ray CONNIFF & His Or...	12153
Concert In The Park | BOSTON POPS Orchestr...	11332
Concerto For Group A... [A] | ROYAL PHILHARMONI...	9855
Concerto For Group And Orches... [A] | DEEP PURPLE	9855
Concerts For The People O... | VARIOUS ARTISTS	4808
The Concert Sound Of... | Henry MANCINI and hi...	3808
Concrete | 999	13507
Concrete And Clay | Eddie RAMBEAU	12981
Concrete Blonde | CONCRETE BLONDE	7552
Condition Critical | QUIET RIOT	2639
Condition Of The Heart | KASHIF	9135

Title | Act	Rank
Coney Island | Herb ALPERT & The Ti...	7417
Coney Island Baby | Lou REED	4555
Confessin' The Blues | Esther PHILLIPS	12082
Confessions Of A Pop Group | STYLE COUNCIL	12189
The Confessor | Joe WALSH	5780
Confetti | Sergio MENDES	5672
Confidence | Narada Michael WALDE...	11070
Conflicting Emotions | SPLIT ENZ	9809
Confrontation | Bob MARLEY And The W...	6070
Con Funk Shun 7 | CON FUNK SHUN	6865
Connections And Disconnecti... | FUNKADELIC(2)	11302
Connie Francis Sings For M... | Connie FRANCIS	6833
Connie Smith | Connie SMITH	10631
Conquistador | Maynard FERGUSON	2293
Conscious Party | Ziggy MARLEY & The M...	1693
Conspicuous Only In Its Absen... | Grace SLICK	12118
Conspiracy | KING DIAMOND	9497
Constrictor | ALICE COOPER (Solo)	5623
Construction #1 | TEN WHEEL DRIVE With...	8255
Contact | Freda PAYNE	5692
Contact | POINTER SISTERS	2099
Contagious | The BAR-KAYS	8749
Contagious | Y&T	6890
Continuation | Philip BAILEY	6974
...Continued | Tony Joe WHITE	12916
Contradiction | OHIO PLAYERS	1866
Contrary To Ordinary | Jerry Jeff WALKER	8549
Control | Janet JACKSON	63
Controlled By Hatred/... | SUICIDAL TENDENCIES	11723
Controversy | PRINCE	1762
Conversations | BRASS CONSTRUCTION	11998
Convertible Music | Josie COTTON	10124
Cookin' | Jerry REED	13574
Cookin' On The Roof | ROMAN HOLLIDAY	10314
Cool From The Wire | DIRTY LOOKS	8309
Cool Kids | KIX	11606
Cool Night | Paul DAVIS	4516
Copperhead Road | Steve EARLE	3674
Cords | SYNERGY	10585
The Core Of Rock | VARIOUS ARTISTS	12347
Core Spezzato | Jimmy ROSELLI	12747
Cornbread, Earl And Me (So... | The BLACKBYRDS	10735
Cornelius Brothers &... | CORNELIUS BROTHERS &...	2817
Cornerstone | STYX	284
The Corporation | The CORPORATION	12962
Corridors Of Power | Gary MOORE	9094
Cory And Me | Cory DAYE	11957
Cosi Fan Tutti Frutti | SQUEEZE	5700
Cosmic Cowboy Souvenir | Michael MURPHEY	13708
Cosmic Messenger | Jean-Luc PONTY	3178
Cosmic Slop | FUNKADELIC	7386
Cosmic Thing | The B-52s	267
Cosmic Truth | UNDISPUTED TRUTH	13327
Cosmic Wheels | DONOVAN	3054
Cosmic Wind | Mike THEODORE Orches...	13205
Cosmo's Factory | CREEDENCE CLEARWATER...	107
The Cost Of Loving | STYLE COUNCIL	9214
Cotton Candy | Al HIRT	700
Cotton Club | SOUNDTRACK-MOVIE	8457
Couchois | COUCHOIS	12021
Couldn't Stand The W... | Stevie Ray VAUGHAN A...	2587
Countdown To Ecstasy | STEELY DAN	2814
Counterfeit | Martin L. GORE	12054
Counterpoint | Ralph MacDONALD	8217
Country | Anne MURRAY	4030
Country | SOUNDTRACK-MOVIE	8015

Title | Act	Rank
Country & Western Meets Rhyth... | Ray CHARLES	9702
Country Boy | Ricky SKAGGS	12678
Country Casanova | COMMANDER CODY & His...	8425
A Country Christmas | VARIOUS ARTISTS	12583
A Country Collection | Anne MURRAY	7394
Country-Folk [A] | The KIMBERLYS	11761
Country-Folk [A] | Waylon JENNINGS	11761
Country Joe & The Fi... | COUNTRY JOE & The Fl...	7140
Country Life | ROXY MUSIC	4368
The Country Music Hall...Vol. 1 | Jerry Lee LEWIS	8035
The Country Music Hall...Vol. 2 | Jerry Lee LEWIS	8163
Country, My Way | Nancy SINATRA	4408
Country Preacher | "Cannonball" ADDERLE...	6760
The Country Way | Charley PRIDE	13765
Count Three And Pray | BERLIN	5373
Coup De Grace | MINK DE VILLE	11813
Court And Spark | Joni MITCHELL	249
Cover Girl | PHANTOM, ROCKER & SL...	13721
A Cowboy Afraid Of Horses | LOBO	10061
Cowboys & Colored People | Flip WILSON	2471
Cowboys & Englishmen | POCO	9653
Cowboys And Indians | NEW CHRISTY MINSTREL...	7125
Cowboys To Girls | The INTRUDERS	7813
The Cowsills | The COWSILLS	3537
The Cowsills In Concert | The COWSILLS	1726
Crabby Appleton | CRABBY APPLETON	11557
Crackers International | ERASURE	8148
Crack The Sky | CRACK THE SKY	11028
Crash | HUMAN LEAGUE	2932
Crash And Burn | Pat TRAVERS	2298
Crash Landing | Jimi HENDRIX	1665
Crawler | BACK STREET CRAWLER	6548
Crazy Eyes | POCO	3850
Crazy For You | Earl KLUGH	4490
Crazy From The Heat | David Lee ROTH	1485
Crazy Horse | CRAZY HORSE	7043
Crazy Horses | The OSMONDS	2208
Crazy Nights | KISS	1839
The Crazy World Of A... | Crazy World Of Arthu...	1373
Cream Of The Crop | The SUPREMES/Diana R...	2960
Cream Songbook | The RUBBERBANDITS	9464
Creation | FEVER TREE	9110
Creative Source | CREATIVE SOURCE	9812
Creatures Of The Night | KISS	4217
Creedence Clearwater Revival... | CREEDENCE CL...	2125
Creedence Gold | CREEDENCE CLEARWATER...	1480
Crest Of A Knave | JETHRO TULL	2970
Cricklewood Green | TEN YEARS AFTER	1836
Crime Of The Century | SUPERTRAMP	1994
Crimes Of Passion | Pat BENATAR	95
Crimson & Clover | Tommy JAMES And The ...	1006
Crisis? What Crisis? | SUPERTRAMP	3646
Criss-Cross | Thelonious MONK	12073
Cristofori's Dream | David LANZ	12321
Cristo Redentor | Harvey MANDEL	11598
Crosby/Nash - Live | David CROSBY/Graham ...	6673
Crosby, Stills & Nas... | CROSBY, STILLS & NAS...	105
Cross-Collateral | PASSPORT	9618
Cross Country | CROSS COUNTRY	13750
The Crossing | BIG COUNTRY	1524
Crossroads (Soundtrack) | Ry COODER	8537
Crossroads | Eric CLAPTON	3931
Crossroads | Tracy CHAPMAN	1871
Cross That Line | Howard JONES	5181
Crosswinds | Billy COBHAM	2786
Crosswinds | Peabo BRYSON	3209

Title | Act	Rank
Crossword Puzzle | PARTRIDGE FAMILY	11724
Crow By Crow | CROW	12598
Crowded House | CROWDED HOUSE	1156
Crow Music | CROW	4778
Crown Of Creation | JEFFERSON AIRPLANE/S...	1265
Cruel Sister | PENTANGLE	13790
Cruisin' | VILLAGE PEOPLE	411
Cruising With Ruben & The Jet... | Frank ZAPPA	6725
Crusade | John MAYALL'S BLUESB...	8377
Crusader | SAXON	12432
Crusaders 1 | The CRUSADERS	4736
Crush | ORCHESTRAL MANOEUVRE...	2468
Crushin' | FAT BOYS	1007
Cruzados | CRUZADOS	6336
Cry | John KLEMMER	12837
Cry | Lynn ANDERSON	8741
Cry | Ronnie DOVE	8624
Cry Baby And 11 Othe... | Garnet MIMMS & The E...	10109
Crying Time | Ray CHARLES	1672
Cry Like A Baby | BOX TOPS	5015
Cry Like A Rainstorm, Howl... | Linda RONSTADT	620
The Cry Of Love | Jimi HENDRIX	722
Crystal Ball | STYX	5332
Crystal Gayle's Greatest Hi... | Crystal GAYLE	11328
Crystal Illusions | Sergio MENDES And BR...	3251
Cry Tough | Nils LOFGREN	4316
Cry Young | Ahmad JAMAL Trio	11413
CSN | CROSBY, STILLS & NAS...	576
Cuba | GIBSON BROTHERS	13352
Cuchi-Cuchi | SALSOUL Orchestra	6394
Cucumber Castle | BEE GEES	7860
Cultosaurus Erectus | BLUE ÖYSTER CULT	4152
Culture Killed The Native | VICTORY	12949
Cunning Stunts | CARAVAN	8793
Cupid And Psyche 85 | SCRITTI POLITTI	4175
Curb Your Tongue, Knave... | SMOTHERS BROTHERS	2477
Cured | Steve HACKETT	12608
Curiosity | REGINA	9755
A Curious Feeling | Tony BANKS	12013
Current | HEATWAVE	11605
A Current Set Of Sta... | Billy VAUGHN and His...	13322
Curtis | Curtis MAYFIELD	1032
Curtis In Chicago | Curtis MAYFIELD	9416
Curtis/Live! | Curtis MAYFIELD	1499
Curtis Mayfield/His Early... | Curtis MAYFIELD	11996
Cut | GOLDEN EARRING	2707
Cut Above The Rest | The SWEET	11018
Cut Loose | Paul RODGERS	9584
Cuts Both Ways | Gloria ESTEFAN/MIAMI...	530
Cuts Like A Knife | Bryan ADAMS	788
Cut The Cake | AVERAGE WHITE BAND/A...	1080
Cut The Crap | The CLASH	7849
Cyan | THREE DOG NIGHT	3650
Cycle Of The Moon | PROPHET	10450
Cycles | DOOBIE BROTHERS	2619
Cycles | Frank SINATRA	1763
Cymande | CYMANDE	6329
Cypress | LET'S ACTIVE	9266
D	
Da Capo | LOVE	7247
Daddy Don't You Walk So Fast | Wayne NEWTON	3235
Daddy's Little Girl | Al MARTINO	3871
Dad Loves His Work | James TAYLOR	1442
Daisy A Day | Jud STRUNK	9448
The Daisy Dillman Band | DILLMAN Band	13674

Title	Act	Rank
Da'Krash	DA'KRASH	13232
Dallas	Floyd CRAMER	12083
Daltrey	Roger DALTREY	4204
Dames At Sea	ORIGINAL CAST	13530
The Damnation Of...	DAMNATION OF ADAM BLES...	13203
Damn Right I Am Somebody	The JB'S	13348
Damn The Torpedoes	Tom PETTY And The HE...	206
Dana Dane With Fame	Dana DANE	3469
Dance	Gary NUMAN	12195
Dance	PURE PRAIRIE LEAGUE	6615
Dance!...Ya Know It!	Bobby BROWN	1370
Dance Across The Floor	Jimmy 'Bo' HORNE	8679
Dance & Exercise With The...	Linda FRATIANNE	11578
Dance Band On The Titanic	Harry CHAPIN	6861
Dance Discotheque	VARIOUS ARTISTS	9993
Dance Forever	Cheryl LADD	12710
The Dance Of Life	Narada Michael WALDE...	5433
Dance Party	MARTHA & The VANDELL...	12279
Dance The Cool Jerk	The CAPITOLS	7719
Dance To The Music	SLY & THE FAMILY STO...	10473
Dance Your Troubles ...	Archie BELL & The DR...	6099
Dancin' And Lovin'	SPINNERS	3719
Dancing In The Dragon's Ja...	Bruce COCKBURN	4363
Dancing In The Moonlight	KING HARVEST	9421
Dancing In The Street	Ramsey LEWIS	5530
Dancing In The Sun	George HOWARD	12503
Dancing Machine	JACKSON 5	2581
Dancing On The Ceiling	Lionel RICHIE	349
Dancing On The Couch	GO WEST	11323
Dancing On The Edge	Roy BUCHANAN	11165
Dancing Undercover	RATT	2696
Dancing With The Lio...	Andreas VOLLENWEIDER	5466
Dancin' In The Key O...	Steve ARRINGTON'S HA...	12801
Dancin' Man	Q	12223
Dancin' On The Edge	Lita FORD	6326
Dancin' Up A Storm	The RAES	11399
D&B Together	DELANEY & BONNIE & F...	10317
Dan Fogelberg/Greatest Hits	Dan FOGELBERG	1843
Danger Danger	DANGER DANGER	4780
Danger Money	U.K.	5253
Dangerous	Natalie COLE	10508
Dangerous	The BAR-KAYS	5098
Dangerous Acquaintance...	Marianne FAITHFULL	8592
Dangerous Age	BAD COMPANY	3741
Dangerous Dreams	The NAILS	13757
Dangerous Moments	Martin BRILEY	8312
Dangerous Toys	DANGEROUS TOYS	3857
Danger Zone	PLAYER	3546
Danger Zone	Sammy HAGAR	7047
Dan Hill	Dan HILL	6186
Dan Hill(2)	Dan HILL	6748
Danke Schoen	Wayne NEWTON	7749
Danny Boy	Ray PRICE	6763
Danny Davis & Willie Nelson W... [A]	Danny DAVIS	11306
Danny Davis & Willie Nelson... [A]	Willie NELSON	11306
Danny Joe Brown And The D...	Danny Joe BROWN	9510
Danny's Song	Anne MURRAY	3761
Dan Reed Network	Dan REED Network	6433
Danseparc	M + M	12953
Danzig	DANZIG	9463
Dare	HUMAN LEAGUE	795
Dare To Be Stupid	"Weird Al" YANKOVIC	5444
Daring Adventures	Richard THOMPSON	11178
The Dark	METAL CHURCH	5902
Dark Continent	WALL OF VOODOO	13274
Dark Horse	George HARRISON	1500

Title	Act	Rank
Dark Lady	CHER	6192
Darklands	JESUS AND MARY CHAIN	12475
Darkness On The Edge Of...	Bruce SPRINGSTEEN	585
Darkroom	ANGEL CITY	10095
Dark Shadows (The Score)	SOUNDTRACK-TV	2380
The Dark Side Of The Moon	PINK FLOYD	7
Darlin'	Tom JONES	12713
Darling Lili	SOUNDTRACK-MOVIE	9305
Daryl Hall & John Oa...	Daryl HALL & John OA...	986
Dave Brubeck's Great...	Dave BRUBECK Quartet	11225
The Dave Clark Five/More ...	Dave CLARK Five	9151
The Dave Clark Five Retur...	Dave CLARK Five	1908
The Dave Clark Five's Gre...	Dave CLARK Five	1110
Dave Grusin and the GRP All-S...	Dave GRUSIN	9896
Dave Grusin and the NY/LA Dre...	Dave GRUSIN	12339
Dave Grusin Collection	Dave GRUSIN	8224
Dave Mason	Dave MASON	2853
Dave Mason & Cass Elliot [A]	Dave MASON	6710
Dave Mason & Cass Elliot [A]	MAMA CASS	6710
Dave Mason At His Best	Dave MASON	11388
Dave Mason Is Alive!	Dave MASON	8119
David	David HOUSTON	10458
David Bowie Narrates Prokofie... [A]	David BOWIE	9370
David Bowie Narrates... [A]	PHILADELPHIA Orche...	9370
David Bromberg	David BROMBERG	13573
David Clayton-Thomas	David CLAYTON-THOMAS	13100
David Clayton-Thomas...	David CLAYTON-THOMAS	10432
David Courtney's First Day	David COURTNEY	12974
David Foster	David FOSTER	13571
David Gilmour	David GILMOUR	3201
David Grisman - Quintet "80...	David GRISMAN	10203
David Jones	David JONES	12318
David Live	David BOWIE	1904
David Merrick Presents Hits F... [A]	ANN-MARGRET	11905
David Merrick Presents Hits Fro... [A]	John GARY	11905
David Oliver	David OLIVER	8984
David Porter...Into A Real T...	David PORTER	8778
David Ruffin	David RUFFIN	10766
David's Album	Joan BAEZ	3729
David Soul	David SOUL	4010
David Werner	David WERNER	6976
Dawn (Go Away) And 11 Other Gre...	4 SEASONS	2263
Dawn Explosion	CAPTAIN BEYOND	13188
Dawn Featuring Tony Orl...	DAWN/Tony ORLANDO	13171
Dawn Patrol	NIGHT RANGER	2563
Dawn's New Ragtime Foll...	DAWN/Tony ORLANDO	2038
A Day At The Races	QUEEN	2112
Day By Day	Cleo LAINE	13818
Day By Day	NAJEE	5773
Day By Day	Percy FAITH His Orch...	13403
Daydream	LOVIN' SPOONFUL	1983
Daydreaming	Morris DAY	4874
Day For Decision	Johnny SEA	12798
A Day In The Life	Wes MONTGOMERY	811
Daylight Again	CROSBY, STILLS & NAS...	917
Days Of Future Passed	MOODY BLUES	365
Days Of Innocence	MOVING PICTURES	7811
Days Of Wine And Roses, Moo...	Frank SINATRA	2381
Daytime Friends	Kenny ROGERS	4872
Dazzle Ships	ORCHESTRAL MANOEUVRE...	11561
D.C. Cab	SOUNDTRACK-MOVIE	12879
D.E. 7th	Dave EDMUNDS	6025
Dead Letter Office	R.E.M.	6076
Dead Man's Curve/The New Girl ...	JAN & DEAN	6291
Dead Man's Party	OINGO BOINGO	7341
Dead Ringer	MEAT LOAF	5537

Title	Act	Rank
Dead Set	GRATEFUL DEAD	4599
Dean Friedman	Dean FRIEDMAN	12142
Dean Martin Hits Again	Dean MARTIN	2605
Dean Martin's Greatest Hits! Vol. 1	Dean MARTIN	1434
Dean Martin's Greatest Hits! Vol. 2	Dean MARTIN	4748
The Dean Martin TV Show	Dean MARTIN	3393
Dear Friends	FIRESIGN THEATRE	6742
Dear Heart	Andy WILLIAMS	452
Dear Heart	Jack JONES	2306
Dear Heart And Other...	Henry MANCINI and hi...	2486
Dear World	ORIGINAL CAST	8601
Death Walks Behind You	ATOMIC ROOSTER	5906
Death Wish II (Soundtrack)	Jimmy PAGE	6228
Decade	DURAN DURAN	6176
Decade	Neil YOUNG	4320
A Decade Of Hits	Charlie DANIELS Band	7529
A Decade Of Rock And Roll ...	REO SPEEDWAGON	3948
December	George WINSTON	1055
December's Children (And E...	ROLLING STONES	1083
Deceptive Bends	10cc	3803
Decisions	The WINANS	8787
Declaration	The ALARM	4403
Decoy	Miles DAVIS	10462
Dedicated	MARSHALL TUCKER Band	5843
Dedication	BAY CITY ROLLERS	2709
Dedication	Gary (U.S.) BONDS	2762
The Deed Is Done	MOLLY HATCHET	8723
The Deep	SOUNDTRACK-MOVIE	6807
Deep Cuts	STRAWBS	10869
Pete Townshend's Deep End ...	Pete TOWNSHEND	9218
Deepest Purple: The Very Best...	DEEP PURPLE	11450
Deep In My Soul	Smokey ROBINSON	5093
Deep In The Heart Of Nowhere	Bob GELDOF	9386
Deep Purple	DEEP PURPLE	10848
Deep Purple	Nino TEMPO & April S...	6311
Deep Purple In Rock	DEEP PURPLE	7091
Deep Sea Skiving	BANANARAMA	5777
Deface The Music	UTOPIA	7269
Def, Dumb & Blonde	Debbie HARRY	9884
Defector	Steve HACKETT	10578
Defenders Of The Faith	JUDAS PRIEST	2129
Defrosted	FRIJID PINK	9152
Deguello	ZZ TOP	1835
Deja Vu	CROSBY, STILLS, NASH...	90
Dekadance	INXS	11361
Delaney & Bonnie & F...	DELANEY & BONNIE & F...	3490
The Delfonics	The DELFONICS	4848
The Delfonics Super Hits	The DELFONICS	6083
Delicate Sound Of Thunder	PINK FLOYD	2162
Delicious Together [A]	Betty EVERETT	8461
Delicious Together [A]	Jerry BUTLER	8461
Delirious Nomad	ARMORED SAINT	7673
Deliver	OAK RIDGE BOYS	7874
Deliverin'	POCO	2826
Deliver The Word	WAR	1013
Della Reese Live	Della REESE	12754
The Dells Greatest Hits	The DELLS	5019
The Dells Musical Menu/Always T...	The DELLS	9057
The Dells Sing Dionne Warwicke'...	The DELLS	11647
The Dells vs. The Dramatics [A]	The DELLS	10556
The Dells vs. The Dramatics [A]	The DRAMATICS	10556
The Delta Sweete	Bobbie GENTRY	8611
Delusions	FIRST CHOICE	8526
Demis Roussos	Demis ROUSSOS	11979
Demons And Wizards	URIAH HEEP	1710
Dennis Weaver	Dennis WEAVER	13523

Title | Act	Rank
Dennis Yost & The Classics IV... | CLASSICS IV	3697
Denver Christmas Gift Pak | John DENVER	10159
Deodato 2 | DEODATO	2009
Departure | JOURNEY	993
Derek & The Dominos ... | DEREK And The DOMINO...	2732
Derringer | Rick DERRINGER	9637
Derringer Live | Rick DERRINGER	8285
Desert Moon | Dennis DeYOUNG	3456
Desiderata | Les CRANE	4499
Desire | Bob DYLAN	421
Desire | Tom SCOTT & The L.A....	11312
Desitively Bonnaroo | DR. JOHN	8753
Desmond Child And Rouge... | Desmond CHILD an...	10941
Desolation Angels | BAD COMPANY	469
Desolation Boulevard | The SWEET	1634
Desperado | EAGLES	1771
Destination: Sun | SUN	7855
Destiny | Chaka KHAN	6815
Destiny | JACKSON 5	1101
Destroyer | KISS	895
Detective | DETECTIVE	9066
Detroit | DETROIT	11616
"Detroit City" And Other Hits | Bobby BARE	11993
Detroit Diesel | Alvin LEE	9693
Deuce | Kurtis BLOW	10441
The Devil In Me | Thelma HOUSTON	6628
"The Devil Made Me Buy This D... | Flip WILSON	1443
Devil's Angels (Soun... | Davie ALLAN And The ...	13134
Devil's Gun | C.J. & CO.	4244
Devo-Live | DEVO	5740
Devotion | L.T.D.	3084
Dialogue | Michael JOHNSON	9449
Diamantina Cocktail | LITTLE RIVER BAND	2246
Diamond Cut | Bonnie TYLER	10821
Diamond Dogs | David BOWIE	1504
Diamond Girl | SEALS & CROFTS	344
Diamond In The Rough | Jessi COLTER	7651
Diamond Life | SADE	640
Diamonds & Rust | Joan BAEZ	886
Diamonds Are Forever | SOUNDTRACK-MOVIE	6645
Diamonds In The Raw | S.O.S. BAND	13748
Diamonds In The Rough | John PRINE	9134
Diamond Sun | GLASS TIGER	6781
Diana | Diana ROSS	263
Diana! | Diana ROSS	4731
Diana & Marvin [A] | Diana ROSS	2463
Diana & Marvin [A] | Marvin GAYE	2463
Diana Ross | Diana ROSS	1663
Diana Ross (II) | Diana ROSS	905
Diana Ross And The S... | The SUPREMES/Diana R...	69
Diana Ross & The Sup... | The SUPREMES/Diana ...	2974
Diana Ross & The Supremes Join The Temp... | Diana ROSS & The SUPREMES And The TEMPTATIONS...	688
Diana Ross Anthology | Diana ROSS	6904
Diana Ross' Greatest Hits | Diana ROSS	1720
Diana Ross Live At Caesars Pal... | Diana ROSS	4668
Diana Ross Presents The Jackson... | JACKSON 5	674
Dianne Reeves | Dianne REEVES	10428
Diary Of A Madman | Ozzy OSBOURNE	769
Dice | Andrew Dice CLAY	4174
Dick Clark/20 Years Of Ro... | VARIOUS ARTISTS	3386
Dickey Betts & Great Souther... | Dickey BETTS	4752
Did You Think To Pray | Charley PRIDE	5654
Diesel And Dust | MIDNIGHT OIL	995
Different Drum | Linda RONSTADT	6789
Different Kinda Different | Johnny MATHIS	11540
A Different Kind Of Blues [A] | Andre PREVIN	9555

Title | Act	Rank
A Different Kind Of Blues [A] | Itzhak PERLMAN	9555
A Different Kind Of Crazy | HEAD EAST	6581
Different Kind Of Tension | BUZZCOCKS	11659
Different Light | The BANGLES	341
Different Moods Of Me | Lonnie JORDAN	11451
Different Strokes | VARIOUS ARTISTS	7805
Different Style! | MUSICAL YOUTH	9882
Difficult To Cure | RAINBOW	4628
Difford & Tilbrook | DIFFORD & TILBROOK	5901
Dig The New Breed | The JAM	10604
Dimensions | BOX TOPS	6451
Dimension "3" | Enoch LIGHT & The LI...	8570
Dimples | Richard "Dimples" FI...	4240
Dinner At The Ritz | CITY BOY	12046
Dino | Dean MARTIN	10455
Dinosaur Swamps | The FLOCK	8103
Dion | DION	7703
Dionne | Dionne WARWICK	5326
Dionne(2) | Dionne WARWICK	943
The Dionne Warwicke Story | Dionne WARWICK	4447
Dionne Warwick In Paris | Dionne WARWICK	7701
Dionne Warwick's Golde...Part 1 | Dionne WARWICK	676
Dionne Warwick's Golde...Part 2 | Dionne WARWICK	2490
Dionne Warwick's Greatest Mot... | Dionne WARWICK	2822
Dion's Greatest Hits | DION	12789
Directions | Miles DAVIS	13170
Dire Straits | DIRE STRAITS	498
The Dirt Band | NITTY GRITTY DIRT BA...	11128
Dirt, Silver & Gold | NITTY GRITTY DIRT BA...	6060
Dirty Dancing | SOUNDTRACK-MOVIE	25
Dirty Deeds Done Dirt Cheap | AC/DC	439
Dirty Looks | Juice NEWTON	6289
Dirty Mind | PRINCE	3506
Dirty Rotten Filthy Stinking Rich | WARRANT	593
Dirty Water | The STANDELLS	5363
Dirty Work | ROLLING STONES	1542
The Dis-Advantages Of You | BRASS RING	13679
Discipline | KING CRIMSON	5193
Disco | PET SHOP BOYS	8190
Disco Baby | Van McCOY	2233
Disco Boogie | VARIOUS ARTISTS	8725
Disco Connection | Isaac HAYES	6022
Disco Fantasy | Coke ESCOVEDO	13803
Disco-Fied | RHYTHM HERITAGE	4298
Disco Gardens | SHALAMAR	12317
Disco Gold | VARIOUS ARTISTS	11051
Disco Inferno | The TRAMMPS	2656
The Disco Kid | Van McCOY	8055
Disco Nights | GQ	1123
Disco Party | VARIOUS ARTISTS	7843
Disco Spectacular Inspire... | VARIOUS ARTISTS	11356
Disco Tex And His Se... | DISCO TEX & The SEX-...	2985
Discotheque | Herbie MANN	3472
Discotheque Dance...... | Enoch LIGHT & The LIGHT...	7458
Disco Train | Donny OSMOND	9770
Discover | GENE LOVES JEZEBEL	9009
Discovery | ELECTRIC LIGHT ORCHE...	729
Discovery | Larry CARLTON	12433
Discovery | SHANICE	8410
Discovery! | Vikki CARR	11336
Disguise | Chuck MANGIONE	10704
Disguised As A Normal Per... | David STEINBERG	12019
DisinHAIRited | VARIOUS ARTISTS	7424
Disintegration | The CURE	929
Disorderlies | SOUNDTRACK-MOVIE	9367
Disraeli Gears | CREAM	131

Title | Act	Rank
The Disregard Of Timekeeping | BONHAM	3145
The Distance | Bob SEGER	863
Distant Drums | Jim REEVES	2470
Distant Light | The HOLLIES	2936
Distant Lover | Alphonse MOUZON	10229
Distant Shores | CHAD & JEREMY	5744
Distant Shores | Robbie PATTON	11147
Distant Thunder | ASWAD	11855
Disturbing The Peace | ALCATRAZZ	8907
Diver Down | VAN HALEN	1011
Divine Madness (Soundtrack) | Bette MIDLER	4261
The Divine Miss M | Bette MIDLER	568
D-I-V-O-R-C-E | Tammy WYNETTE	8328
Dixie Rock | WET WILLIE	8849
Dizzy | Tommy ROE	2555
The Dock Of The Bay | Otis REDDING	909
The Doctor | CHEAP TRICK	9834
Doctor Dolittle | SOUNDTRACK-MOVIE	3073
Doctor Zhivago | SOUNDTRACK-MOVIE	9
R.E.M. No. 5: Document | R.E.M.	1384
Does Fort Worth Ever Cross ... | George STRAIT	9027
Dog And Butterfly | HEART	896
Dog Days | ATLANTA RHYTHM SECTION	8516
Dog Eat Dog | Joni MITCHELL	5399
Do I Hear A Waltz? | ORIGINAL CAST	8415
Doin' Alright | O'BRYAN	7431
Doing His Thing | Ray CHARLES	12437
Doing It To Death | The JB'S	6374
Doing My Thing | Paul MAURIAT And His Orchestra	5160
Doin' It! | UTFO	11686
Doin' Mickey's Monkey | The MIRACLES/Smokey ROBINSON And The MIRACLES	11239
Doin' Our Thing | BOOKER T. & The M.Gs	12502
Do It! | Neil DIAMOND	9040
Do It All | Michael HENDERSON	6413
Do It Baby | The MIRACLES	4113
Do It Debbie's Way | Debbie REYNOLDS	13197
Do It ('Til You're Satisfied) | B.T. EXPRESS	913
Do It Yourself | Ian DURY And The BLOCKHEADS	10041
$ (Dollars) | SOUNDTRACK-MOVIE	11870
Dolly Dolly Dolly | Dolly PARTON	6137
Do Me Baby | Meli'sa MORGAN	3520
Do Me Right | DETROIT EMERALDS	11941
Domingo-Con Amore | Placido DOMINGO	11632
Domino Theory | WEATHER REPORT	9821
Donald Byrd's Best | Donald BYRD	11936
Donald Clark Osmond | Donny OSMOND	11643
Done With Mirrors | AEROSMITH	3583
Don Harrison Band | Don HARRISON Band	10761
Don Ho-Again! | Don HO and the ALIIS	10680
Don Ho-Greatest Hits... | Don HO and the ALIIS	10961
The Don Ho TV Show | Don HO and the ALIIS	13405
Don Juan's Reckless Daughter | Joni MITCHELL	4268
Don McLean | Don McLEAN	3056
Donna Summer | Donna SUMMER	2423
Donny | Donny OSMOND	4318
Donny & Marie - Feat... | Donny & Marie OSMOND	3959
Donny & Marie - New ... | Donny & Marie OSMOND	6502
Donny Hathaway | Donny HATHAWAY	5139
Donny Hathaway Live | Donny HATHAWAY	1043
Donny Osmond | Donny OSMOND	4816
The Donny Osmond Album | Donny OSMOND	1086
Donovan In Concert | DONOVAN	1742
Donovan P. Leitch | DONOVAN	9359
Donovan's Greatest Hits | DONOVAN	228
Don Quixote | Gordon LIGHTFOOT	4267
Don Rickles Speaks! | Don RICKLES	12220

Title | Act	Rank
Don't Be Afraid Of The D... | Robert CRAY Band	3367
Don't Be Concerned | Bob LIND	12939
Don't Be Cruel | Bobby BROWN	30
Don't Call Us-We'll Call You | SUGARLOAF	10648
Don't Cha Love It | The MIRACLES	7995
Don't Close Your Eyes | Keith WHITLEY	8836
Don't Come Home A Drinkin' | Loretta LYNN	5954
Don't Crush That Dwarf, ... | FIRESIGN THEATRE	8212
Don't Cry Now | Linda RONSTADT	1991
Don't Cry Out Loud | Melissa MANCHESTER	3370
Don't Disturb This Groove | The SYSTEM	4460
Don't Fight It | Tom COCHRANE/RED RID...	11181
Don't Follow Me, I'm... | PEARL HARBOR And The...	12575
Don't Forget I Still Love Yo... | Bobbi MARTIN	11029
Don't Give Up Your Day Job | Jack WAGNER	10842
Don't Go To Strangers | Eydie GORME	2539
Don't It Feel Good | Ramsey LEWIS	3893
Don't It Make You Wanna Dance | Rusty WIER	7273
Don't It Make You Want To Go Ho... | Joe SOUTH	4604
Don't Just Stand There | Patty DUKE	7846
Don't Knock My Love | Wilson PICKETT	8004
Don't Let Go | George DUKE	4149
Don't Let Go | Isaac HAYES	2609
Don't Let Love Slip Away | Freddie JACKSON	4188
Don't Let Me Be Misunders... | SANTA ESMERALDA	2553
Don't Let The Sun Ca... | GERRY And The PACEMA...	5311
Don't Look Any Further | Dennis EDWARDS	3915
Don't Look Back | BOSTON	497
Don't Look Back | Natalie COLE	4854
Don't Look Down | OZARK MOUNTAIN DARED...	8855
Don't Play With Fire | Peabo BRYSON	5413
Don't Say No | Billy SQUIER	204
Don't Shoot Me I'm Only The Piano... | Elton JOHN	277
Don't Stop | Billy IDOL	2834
Don't Stop | Jeffrey OSBORNE	2626
Don't Stop Believin' | Olivia NEWTON-JOHN	2610
Don't Stop The Music | BRECKER BROTHERS	10163
Don't Suppose | LIMAHL	4654
Don't Take It Personal | Jermaine JACKSON	8090
Don't Tell A Soul | The REPLACEMENTS	4849
Don't Throw Stones | The SPORTS	13626
Don't Turn Around | BLACK IVORY	9668
The Doobie Brothers Farew... | DOOBIE BROTHERS	8729
Doolittle | PIXIES	5596
The Door Is Still Open To My ... | Dean MARTIN	2002
The Doors | The DOORS	88
The Doors Greatest Hits | The DOORS	679
Door To Door | The CARS	3358
Dorothy Moore | Dorothy MOORE	7707
Dos | MALO	5836
Do The Freddie | FREDDIE And The DREA...	7854
Do The Right Thing | SOUNDTRACK-MOVIE	6499
Double Dose | HOT TUNA	7720
Double Dynamite | SAM & DAVE	7520
Double Fantasy | John LENNON & Yoko O...	144
Double Fun | Robert PALMER	3208
Double Gold | Neil DIAMOND	3475
A Double Header With Arthu... | Arthur PRYSOCK	9729
Double Live Gonzo! | Ted NUGENT	2294
Double Platinum | KISS	3157
Double Shot (Of My Ba... | SWINGIN' MEDALLIONS	7402
Double Time | Leon REDBONE	4390
Double Trouble (Soundtrack) | Elvis PRESLEY	4967
Double Trouble | Frankie MILLER(1)	10528
Double Trouble Live | MOLLY HATCHET	10071
Double Vision [A] | Bob JAMES	2978

Title | Act	Rank
Double Vision [A] | David SANBORN	2978
Double Vision | FOREIGNER	120
Doug Sahm And Band | Doug SAHM And Band	9069
Dowdy Ferry Road | ENGLAND DAN & John F...	6515
Do What You Wanna Do | The DRAMATICS	4640
Down And Out In Beverly ... | SOUNDTRACK-MOVIE	8406
Down For The Count | Y&T	8343
Down Here On The Ground | Wes MONTGOMERY	3240
Down Home | SEALS & CROFTS	8467
Down Homers | Danny DAVIS And The ...	8598
Down Home Style | Brother Jack McDUFF	12208
Down In The Boondocks | Billy Joe ROYAL	9525
Down In The Groove | Bob DYLAN	6884
Down On The Farm | LITTLE FEAT	3362
Down The Line | John MAYALL	11335
Down The Road | Stephen STILLS & MAN...	3547
Down To Earth | NEKTAR	3756
Down To Earth | RAINBOW	5941
Down To Earth | Stevie WONDER	8886
Down To The Moon | Andreas VOLLENWEIDER	3865
Downtown | Marshall CRENSHAW	7555
Downtown | Petula CLARK	2106
Downtown Tonight | RACING CARS	13375
Down Two Then Left | Boz SCAGGS	1533
Do You | Sheena EASTON	4937
Do You Believe In Magic | LOVIN' SPOONFUL	3064
Do You Know The Way To ... | BAJA MARIMBA BAND	10496
Do You Know What It's Like ... | Jerry WALLACE	11382
Do Your Own Thing | Brook BENTON	13328
Do You Wanna Get Away | SHANNON	7351
Do You Wanna Go Part... | KC And The SUNSHINE ...	2727
Do You Wonder | Shawn PHILLIPS	7747
Dracula's Greatest Hits | VARIOUS ARTISTS	12198
Drag City | JAN & DEAN	5095
Dragnet | SOUNDTRACK-MOVIE	10994
Dragon Fly | JEFFERSON AIRPLANE/S...	1579
The Dragon Is Dancing | Jimmie SPHEERIS	9879
Drama | YES	2775
A Dramatic Experience | The DRAMATICS	6181
The Dramatic Jackpot | The DRAMATICS	3656
Drama V | The DRAMATICS	6960
Drastic Measures | KANSAS	4535
Drastic Plastic | BE BOP DELUXE	7810
Draw The Line | AEROSMITH	2243
Dr. Buzzard's Original Savannah... | DR. BUZZARD...	1075
Dr. Buzzard's...Meets King Pen | DR. BUZZARD'S ...	5362
Dr. Byrds & Mr. Hyde | The BYRDS	9771
Dr. Demento's Delights | VARIOUS ARTISTS	13677
Dream | CAPTAIN & TENNILLE	6254
Dream | MILLS BROTHERS	11978
Dream | NITTY GRITTY DIRT BA...	6782
The Dream Academy | DREAM ACADEMY	2699
Dream A Little Dream | MAMA CASS	7211
Dream A Little Dream | SOUNDTRACK-MOVIE	8264
Dream Babies Go To Hollywood | John STEWART	7814
Dreamboat Annie | HEART	412
Dreamboy | DREAMBOY	10520
Dream Come True | Earl KLUGH	4820
The Dream Duet [A] | Anna MOFFO	9563
The Dream Duet [A] | Sergio FRANCHI	9563
Dreamer | Bobby BLAND	10948
Dream Evil | DIO	6143
Dreamgirls | ORIGINAL CAST	1829
The Dreaming | Kate BUSH	10157
Dreaming A Dream | CROWN HEIGHTS AFFAIR	6950
Dreaming My Dreams | Waylon JENNINGS	3821

Title | Act	Rank
Dreaming #11 | Joe SATRIANI	3435
Dream Into Action | Howard JONES	1135
Dream Kid | SUTHERLAND BROTHERS ...	13251
Dreamland Express | John DENVER	6618
Dream Of A Lifetime | Marvin GAYE	5710
Dream Of Life | Patti SMITH	6306
The Dream Of The Blue Turtles | STING	274
Dream On | George DUKE	5737
Dream Police | CHEAP TRICK	1484
Dreams | ALLMAN BROTHERS Band	8721
Dreams | DREAMS	10768
Dreams | Grace SLICK	3804
Dreams And All That Stuff | Leo KOTTKE	5519
Dreams, Dreams, Dreams | CHILLIWACK	8207
The Dreams Of Children | SHADOWFAX	7832
Dreams Of Tomorrow | Lonnie Liston SMITH	13745
Dreams Of Tomorrow | Marilyn SCOTT	12715
Dreamspeaker | Tim WEISBERG	11897
Dream Street | Janet JACKSON	11142
Dream Street Rose | Gordon LIGHTFOOT	6583
Dreamtime | The STRANGLERS	12644
Dreamtime | Tom VERLAINE	12950
The Dream Weaver | Gary WRIGHT	307
Dream With Dean | Dean MARTIN	2672
Dregs Of The Earth | DIXIE DREGS	6107
Dressed To Kill | KISS	3497
Dr. Feelgood | MÖTLEY CRÜE	176
Dr. Heckle And Mr. J... | ENGLAND DAN & John F...	7122
Dr. Hook & The Medicine Show | DR. HOOK	4053
Dr. Hook/Greatest Hits | DR. HOOK	8552
Drift Away | Dobie GRAY	5113
Drifter | SYLVIA (2)	8901
The Drifters' Golden Hits | The DRIFTERS	9133
Drippin' Wet!/Live | WET WILLIE	12885
Drive On | MOTT THE HOOPLE	11322
Dr. John's Gumbo | DR. JOHN	7866
The Sun, Moon & Herbs | DR. JOHN	12182
Drop Down And Get Me | Del SHANNON	8428
Drop The Bomb | TROUBLE FUNK	8853
Drowning In The Sea Of Love | Joe SIMON	6467
Drum Discotheque | Sandy NELSON	9590
Drums A Go-Go | Sandy NELSON	8815
Drums Along The Mohawk | Jean BEAUVOIR	7261
Drums And Wires | XTC	11111
Dry Dreams | Jim CARROLL Band	11383
Dry Your Eyes | BRENDA & The TABULAT...	13132
Duane & Gregg Allman | ALLMAN BROTHERS Band	9053
The Duck | Jackie LEE	8522
The Dude | Quincy JONES	383
Dueling Banjos [A] | Eric WEISSBERG	885
Dueling Banjos [A] | Steve MANDELL	885
Duets | Kenny ROGERS	7840
Duit On Mon Dei | NILSSON	10073
Duke | GENESIS	1003
The Duke At Tanglewood [A] | BOSTON POPS Orche...	12276
The Duke At Tanglewood [A] | Duke ELLINGTON	12276
The Dukes Of Hazzard | SOUNDTRACK-TV	7636
Dumb Waiters | The KORGIS	8171
Dune | David MATTHEWS	10910
Dune (Soundtrack) | TOTO	11618
Duo-Glide | SANFORD/TOWNSEND Ban...	8037
Duotones | KENNY G	386
Duran Duran | DURAN DURAN	1194
Durell Coleman | Durell COLEMAN	11115
Dusty | Dusty SPRINGFIELD	12379
Dusty In Memphis | Dusty SPRINGFIELD	6838

Title | Act	Rank
Dusty Springfield's Gol... | Dusty SPRINGFIELD	11964
Dutch Masters - A Selection Of Thei... | FOCUS	8634
Duty Now For The Future | DEVO	7389
D'ya Like Scratchin' | Malcolm McLAREN	12047
Dylan | Bob DYLAN	3337
Dylan And The Dead [A] | Bob DYLAN	5689
Dylan And The Dead [A] | GRATEFUL DEAD	5689
The Dynamic Clarence Cart... | Clarence CARTER	11521
Dynamite | The SUPREMES & FOUR ...	11466
Dynasty | KISS	1551
Dyn-O-Mite | Jimmie WALKER	8234

E

Title | Act	Rank
Each Of Us Alone (The Wor... | Glenn YARBROUGH	13252
The Eagles | EAGLES	1971
Eagles Greatest Hits: Volume 2 | EAGLES	5280
Eagles Live | EAGLES	1107
Ear Candy | Helen REDDY	5205
Eargasm | Johnnie TAYLOR	1364
Earle Doud Presents Spiro... | VARIOUS ARTISTS	12860
Earl Klugh | Earl KLUGH	9919
The Earl Scruggs Revue | Earl SCRUGGS Revue	11690
The Earl Scruggs Revue... | Earl SCRUGGS Revue	11771
Early Allman | ALLMAN BROTHERS Band	10955
The Early Beatles | The BEATLES	4031
Early Faces | SMALL FACES/FACES	10549
Early Flight | JEFFERSON AIRPLANE/S...	8710
Early Hits Of 1964 | Lawrence WELK	4367
Early Morning Rain | IAN & SYLVIA	6632
Early Orbison | Roy ORBISON	8362
Early Steppenwolf | STEPPENWOLF	2757
Earth | JEFFERSON AIRPLANE/S...	554
The Earth | SAN SEBASTIAN String...	8680
Earth & Sky | Graham NASH	10099
Earthbound | 5TH DIMENSION	8952
Earth Crisis | STEEL PULSE	10135
Earth - Sun - Moon | LOVE AND ROCKETS	4612
Earth, Wind & Fire | EARTH, WIND & FIRE	9284
East | COLD CHISEL	11243
East | HIROSHIMA	6641
East Bay Grease | TOWER OF POWER	6786
East Coast/West Coas... | Don HO and the ALIIS	10916
Easter | Patti SMITH	2550
Easter Island | Kris KRISTOFFERSON	8280
East Of Midnight | Gordon LIGHTFOOT	11747
East Side Story | SQUEEZE	3238
East-West | Paul BUTTERFIELD Blu...	4159
Easy | Marvin GAYE & Tammi ...	13337
Easy | Nancy WILSON	3886
Easy Does It | Al KOOPER	8844
Easy Listening | Mel CARTER	7298
Easy Loving | Freddie HART	3443
Easy Rider | SOUNDTRACK-MOVIE	173
Eat A Peach | ALLMAN BROTHERS Band	458
Eat 'Em And Smile | David Lee ROTH	981
Eaten Alive | Diana ROSS	5410
Eat It | HUMBLE PIE	2506
Eat The Heat | ACCEPT	9926
Eat To The Beat | BLONDIE	949
Eazy-Duz-It | EAZY-E	1395
EB 84 | EVERLY BROTHERS	4921
Ebónee Webb | EBONEE WEBB	10752
Ebony Woman | Billy PAUL	11273
Echo & The Bunnymen | ECHO & The BUNNYMEN	13425
Echo & The Bunnymen(2) | ECHO & The BUNNYMEN	4161
Echoes Of An Era | VARIOUS ARTISTS	8201

Title | Act	Rank
Echo Park | Keith BARBOUR	11544
Ecology | RARE EARTH	950
Ecstasy | OHIO PLAYERS	5920
E.C. Was Here | Eric CLAPTON	3086
Eddie & The Cruisers | John CAFFERTY & The ...	956
Eddie & The Cruisers II | John CAFFERTY & The ...	10888
Eddie Fisher Today! | Eddie FISHER	6918
Eddie Harris Live At Newport | Eddie HARRIS	9474
Eddie Kendricks | Eddie KENDRICKS	2146
Eddie Money | Eddie MONEY	1808
Eddie Murphy | Eddie MURPHY	2862
Eddie Murphy: Comedian | Eddie MURPHY	2781
Eden Alley | TIMBUK 3	7795
Eden's Children | EDEN'S CHILDREN	13738
The Edgar Winter Group With ... | Edgar WINTER	9304
Edgar Winter's White Trash | Edgar WINTER	6078
Edizione D'Oro (The 4 Seasons G... | 4 SEASONS	3125
Edward Bear | Edward BEAR	6257
Egg Cream | EGG CREAM	13051
Ego Trip | Kurtis BLOW	4793
E.H. in the U.K. | Eddie HARRIS	9600
8 | MADHOUSE	8827
18 Yellow Roses | Bobby DARIN	10346
8:15 12:15 | Bill COSBY	4656
8 For The 80's | Webster LEWIS	8915
8th Day | 8TH DAY	7199
8th Wonder | SUGARHILL GANG	4850
80's Ladies | K.T. OSLIN	3981
8.5 | EARTH QUAKE	11297
8:30 | WEATHER REPORT	5590
80/81 | PAT METHENY GROUP	6788
Einzelhaft | FALCO	6939
Elan | FIREFALL	2736
El Chicano | EL CHICANO	8772
El Condor Pasa | Paul MAURIAT And His...	12626
El DeBarge | El DeBARGE	2850
Eldorado | ELECTRIC LIGHT ORCHE...	1212
Electra Glide In Blue | SOUNDTRACK-MOVIE	13668
Electric | The CULT	2856
Electric Breakdance | VARIOUS ARTISTS	10275
Electric Cafe | KRAFTWERK	9719
Electric Church | Buddy MILES	10630
Electric Coffey | Dennis COFFEY	12299
Electric Comic Book | BLUES MAGOOS	6361
Electric Dreams | John McLAUGHLIN/MAHA...	11000
Electric Dreams | SOUNDTRACK-MOVIE	8735
The Electric Flag | ELECTRIC FLAG	5956
Electric Folklore Live | The ALARM	12214
Electric Guitarist | John McLAUGHLIN	7251
Electric Havens | Richie HAVENS	13143
Electric Honey | PARTLAND BROTHERS	11597
The Electric Horseman (Soun... [A] | Willie NELSON	4291
The Electric Horseman (Soundt... [A] | Dave GRUSIN	4291
Electric Lady | CON FUNK SHUN	5008
Electric Ladyland | Jimi HENDRIX EXPERIE...	465
Electric Light Orche... | ELECTRIC LIGHT ORCHE...	4531
Electric Love | ELECTRONIC CONCEPT O...	12978
Electric Mud | Muddy WATERS	8177
Electric Music For T... | COUNTRY JOE & The FISH	2986
The Electric Prunes | ELECTRIC PRUNES	7962
Electric Rendezvous | Al Di MEOLA	6115
The Electric Spanking Of War B... | FUNKADELIC	10161
Electric Universe | EARTH, WIND & FIRE	4678
Electric Warrior | T. REX	2304
Electric Youth | Debbie GIBSON	381
Electrified Funk | WILD CHERRY	6167

Title | Act	Rank
The Electrifying Eddie Harri... | Eddie HARRIS	2361
Electrodynamics | Dick HYMAN	9792
Electronic Realizations For Rock ... | SYNERGY	5870
Electronic Sound | George HARRISON	13369
Elegant Gypsy | Al Di MEOLA	5747
Elephant Mountain | The YOUNGBLOODS	5132
Elephant's Memory | ELEPHANT'S MEMORY	13622
11 | The SMITHEREENS	2971
1100 Bel Air Place | Julio IGLESIAS	1037
11/17/1970 | Elton JOHN	1578
Eli And The Thirteenth Confess... | Laura NYRO	11594
Eliminator | ZZ TOP	79
Elisa Fiorillo | Elisa FIORILLO	11256
Elite Hotel | Emmylou HARRIS	2557
El Juicio (The Judgement) | Keith JARRETT	11577
Ella | Ella FITZGERALD	13525
Ella And Basie! [A] | Count BASIE	5861
Ella And Basie! [A] | Ella FITZGERALD	5861
Ella Fitzgerald Sings The... | Ella FITZGERALD	10825
Ellington '65: Hits Of The... | Duke ELLINGTON	10618
El Loco | ZZ TOP	2067
Eloise | Eloise LAWS	11705
Eloise Laws | Eloise LAWS	11282
ELO's Greatest Hits | ELECTRIC LIGHT ORCHE...	3672
El Pussy Cat | Mongo SANTAMARIA	9091
El Rayo-X | David LINDLEY	5686
Elton John | Elton JOHN	492
Elton John's Greatest Hits | Elton JOHN	145
Elton John's Greatest Hits, Vol. 3 | Elton JOHN	6662
Elton John's Greatest Hits, Vol.2 | Elton JOHN	2561
Elvis | Elvis PRESLEY	5441
Elvis - TV Special | Elvis PRESLEY	1163
Elvis: A Canadian Tribute | Elvis PRESLEY	8250
Elvis Aron Presley | Elvis PRESLEY	3913
Elvis As Recorded At Madiso... | Elvis PRESLEY	1162
Elvis Back In Memphis | Elvis PRESLEY	12947
Elvis Country ("I'm 10,000 ... | Elvis PRESLEY	1914
Elvis For Everyone! | Elvis PRESLEY	2190
Elvis' Gold Records, Volume... | Elvis PRESLEY	3590
Elvis In Concert | Elvis PRESLEY	2309
The Elvis Medley | Elvis PRESLEY	9859
Elvis Now | Elvis PRESLEY	4423
Elvis: Recorded Live On Sta... | Elvis PRESLEY	4266
Elvis Sings Flaming Star | Elvis PRESLEY	6530
Elvis Sings For Children An... | Elvis PRESLEY	8248
Elvis Sings Hits From His M... | Elvis PRESLEY	6395
Elvis-That's The Way It Is | Elvis PRESLEY	2569
Elvis: The First Live Recor... | Elvis PRESLEY	12211
Elvis-The Other Sides - Wor... | Elvis PRESLEY	9265
Elysian Encounter | BAKER GURVITZ ARMY	11290
E-Man Groovin' | Jimmy CASTOR Bunch	8985
Emerald City | Teena MARIE	7936
Emerge | The LITTER	12093
Emergency | KOOL & The GANG	502
Emergency | Melissa MANCHESTER	9515
Emerson, Lake & Palmer | EMERSON, LAKE & PAL...	1025
Emerson, Lake & Palmer In Concert... | EMERSON,...	7349
Emerson, Lake, & Powell | EMERSON, LAKE & PO...	2613
Emitt Rhodes | Emitt RHODES	2624
Emotion | Barbra STREISAND	2549
Emotion | DFX2	10729
Emotion | Samantha SANG	4462
Emotional | Jeffrey OSBORNE	3094
Emotional Rescue | ROLLING STONES	273
Emotions | MYSTIC MOODS Orchestra	13037
Emotions In Motion | Billy SQUIER	618

Title	Act	Rank
Empire Burlesque	Bob DYLAN	4407
Empire Jazz	VARIOUS ARTISTS	12002
Empire Of The Sun	SOUNDTRACK-MOVIE	11522
The Empire Strikes Back	SOUNDTRACK-MOVIE	932
The Empire Strikes Back/...	SOUNDTRACK-MOVIE	12424
Empty Arms	Sonny JAMES	11216
Empty Glass	Pete TOWNSHEND	829
Empty Rooms	John MAYALL	3366
Empty Sky	Elton JOHN	1937
The Enchanted World Of...	FERRANTE & TEICHER	11204
Enchantment	ENCHANTMENT	6480
Encore	John GARY	1870
Encore	TANGERINE DREAM	13208
Encore! Jose Feliciano's F...	José FELICIANO	7519
Encore! More Of The ...	Henry MANCINI and hi...	8416
Encore-Live In Concert	ARGENT	11036
Encore/The Chuck Mangione ...	Chuck MANGIONE	8127
Encore: Woody Herman - 1963	Woody HERMAN	11412
Encounter	Flora PURIM	13320
Encounters Of Every Kind	MECO	5896
Endangered Species	WHITE WOLF	10465
Endless Boogie	John Lee HOOKER	7596
Endless Flight	Leo SAYER	1023
Endless Love	SOUNDTRACK-MOVIE	1685
Endless Summer	BEACH BOYS	295
The Endless Summer	The SANDALS	7474
Endless Wire	Gordon LIGHTFOOT	3041
End Of The Beginning	Richie HAVENS	11593
End Of The Century	The RAMONES	4986
The End Of The Innocence	Don HENLEY	186
Energized	FOGHAT	2935
Energy	POINTER SISTERS	1867
Energy To Burn	B.T. EXPRESS	5256
En Espanol	Vikki CARR	5368
En Espanol!	Ray CONNIFF & His Or...	13402
Engelbert	Engelbert HUMPERDINC...	1470
Engelbert Humperdinc...	Engelbert HUMPERDINC...	709
England's Greatest Hits	VARIOUS ARTISTS	13831
England's Newest Hit Maker...	ROLLING STONES	2102
English Hits Of '65	Billy STRANGE	12375
English Muffins	MYSTIC MOODS Orchestra	10499
English Rose	FLEETWOOD MAC	11638
English Settlement	XTC	5072
Enigmatic Ocean	Jean-Luc PONTY	4512
Enlightened Rogues	ALLMAN BROTHERS Band	1362
Ennea	CHASE	6408
Enoch Light & The Br...	Enoch LIGHT & The LI...	11888
Enough Is Enough	Billy SQUIER	6678
The Entertainer	Marvin HAMLISCH	11695
Entertainers...On And Of...	STATLER BROTHERS	9820
Entrance	Edgar WINTER	13632
Enuff Z'Nuff	ENUFF Z'NUFF	4456
The Envoy	Warren ZEVON	8196
Epic Forest	RARE BIRD	13608
E Pluribus Funk	GRAND FUNK RAILROAD	931
Eponymous	R.E.M.	5802
Equinox	Sergio MENDES And BR...	2070
Equinox	STYX	2729
Equinoxe	Jean Michel JARRE	9349
Eres Tu "Touch The Wind"	MOCEDADES	10379
Eric Burdon Declares "W...	Eric BURDON & WAR	1736
Eric Carmen	Eric CARMEN	1590
Eric Carmen (II)	Eric CARMEN	10100
Eric Clapton	Eric CLAPTON	2044
Eric Clapton At His Best	Eric CLAPTON	6183
Eric Clapton's Rainbow Conce...	Eric CLAPTON	3522

Title	Act	Rank
Eric Is Here	The ANIMALS/Eric BUR...	8225
Error In The System	Peter SCHILLING	4951
Eruption	ERUPTION	8633
Escapade	Tim FINN	11999
Escape	JOURNEY	23
Escape	WHODINI	2342
Escape Artist	Garland JEFFREYS	4189
Escape From Babylon	Martha VELEZ	7932
Escape From Domination	Moon MARTIN	7641
E-S-P	BEE GEES	8940
Especially For You	Don WILLIAMS	7748
Especially For You	John GARY	7202
Especially For You	The SMITHEREENS	2593
Esquire	ESQUIRE	12585
Essar	Smokey ROBINSON	9692
Essence To Essence	DONOVAN	12085
The Essential Jimi Hendrix	Jimi HENDRIX	7915
The Essential Jimi Hendrix V...	Jimi HENDRIX	10651
The Eternal Idol	BLACK SABBATH	11460
Eternal Nightmare	VIO-LENCE	11785
Etta James	Etta JAMES	9931
Etta James Rocks The House	Etta JAMES	8435
Etta James Top Ten	Etta JAMES	10986
E.T. - The Extra-Terrest...	SOUNDTRACK-MOVIE	3341
Eugene Wilde	Eugene WILDE	7772
Euphoria	Gato BARBIERI	8480
Euphrates River	MAIN INGREDIENT	2923
Europe '72	GRATEFUL DEAD	2753
Evangeline	Emmylou HARRIS	2525
Eve	Alan PARSONS PROJECT	1842
An Evening Of Magic - Chuc...	Chuck MANGIONE	2789
An Evening Wasted With Tom Leh...	Tom LEHRER	9701
An Evening With Belafont/M... [A]	Miriam MAKEBA	7757
An Evening With Belafonte/Makeba [A]	Harry BEL...	7757
An Evening With Belafont/... [A]	Nana MOUSKOURI	9659
An Evening With Belafonte/Mouskouri [A]	Harry B...	9659
An Evening With Chick Core... [A]	Herbie HANCOCK	13228
An Evening With Chick Corea &... [A]	Chick COREA	13228
An Evening With Diana Ross	Diana ROSS	4289
An Evening With Groucho	Groucho MARX	8734
An Evening With Herbie Han... [A]	Herbie HANCOCK	8658
An Evening With Herbie Hancoc... [A]	Chick COREA	8658
An Evening With John Denver	John DENVER	538
An Evening With Wally Londo...	George CARLIN	4203
Even In The Quietest Moments...	SUPERTRAMP	1004
Even Now	Barry MANILOW	488
Even Worse	"Weird Al" YANKOVIC	2987
Eve Of Destruction	Barry McGUIRE	4594
Evergreen, Vol. 2	Linda RONSTADT	7248
Everlasting	Natalie COLE	2119
Everlasting Love	Carl CARLTON	9457
Everlasting Love	Rex SMITH	12135
Everlasting Love	Robert KNIGHT	13726
Everlasting Songs For Ever...	Arthur PRYSOCK	10043
The Everlovin' Soul Of Roy Clar...	Roy CLARK	9008
The Everlovin' World Of Eddy ...	Eddy ARNOLD	6664
The Everly Brothers' Orig...	EVERLY BROTHERS	11468
The Ever Popular Tortured A...	Todd RUNDGREN	7025
Ever Ready	Johnnie TAYLOR	10956
Everybody Come On Out	Stanley TURRENTINE	6422
Everybody Gotta Be Someplace	Myron COHEN	7577
Everybody Knows	Steve LAWRENCE	8149
Everybody Knows This Is Nowher...	Neil YOUNG	935
Everybody Likes Some Kind O...	Billy PRESTON	5163
Everybody Loves A Cl...	Gary LEWIS And The P...	5236
Everybody Loves A Nut	Johnny CASH	8471

Title	Act	Rank
Everybody Loves Somebody	Dean MARTIN	447
Everybody Loves The Pilot (Exc...	Jon ASTLEY	10035
Everybody Loves The Su...	Roy AYERS UBIQUITY	4314
Everybody Needs Love	Gladys KNIGHT & The ...	4879
Everybody's Doin' The Hustle ...	James BROWN	13524
Everybody's In Show-Biz	The KINKS	6013
Everybody's Out Of Town	B.J. THOMAS	5421
Everybody's Rockin'	Neil YOUNG	5477
Everybody's Talkin'	KING CURTIS	13218
Everybody Up	OHIO PLAYERS	6290
Everybody Wants Some	GUCCI CREW II	12032
Every Breath You Take-The Sing...	The POLICE	2138
Everyday, Everynight	Flora PURIM	12074
Every Generation	Ronnie LAWS	3332
Every Good Boy Deserves Favou...	MOODY BLUES	407
Every Great Motown Hit Of Mar...	Marvin GAYE	7677
Every Home Should Have One	Patti AUSTIN	2030
Every Man Has A Woman	VARIOUS ARTISTS	7918
Every Mothers' Son	EVERY MOTHERS' SON	9251
Every One Of Us	The ANIMALS/Eric BUR...	9876
Every 1's A Winner	HOT CHOCOLATE	4319
Every Picture Tells A Story	Rod STEWART	104
Every Shade Of Love	Jesse JOHNSON	6895
Every Step Of The Way	David BENOIT	8261
Everything	CLIMIE FISHER	7568
Everything	The BANGLES	1293
Everything I Play Is Funky	Lou DONALDSON	13491
Everything Is A-OK!	The ASTRONAUTS	8797
Everything Is Beautiful	Jim NABORS	5582
Everything Is Beautiful	Ray STEVENS	3642
Everything Is Cool	T-CONNECTION	9234
Everything Is Everything	Diana ROSS	4042
Everything Is Everything	Donny HATHAWAY	4105
Everything Playing	LOVIN' SPOONFUL	10253
Everything's Archie	The ARCHIES	3264
Everything's Coming Up Love	David RUFFIN	5364
Everything's Different Now	'TIL TUESDAY	7635
Everything's Good About You	The LETTERMEN	9129
Everything's Kool & The G...	KOOL & The GANG	9031
Everything Stops For Tea	Long John BALDRY	11873
Everything You Always Wan...	VARIOUS ARTISTS	11859
Everything You Know Is W...	FIRESIGN THEATRE	10291
Everything You've Heard Is T...	Tom JOHNSTON	7534
Everytime Two Fools ...	Kenny ROGERS & Dotti...	13140
Every Time You Touch Me (I G...	Charlie RICH	5174
Every Turn Of The World	Christopher CROSS	11023
Everywhere At Once	The PLIMSOULS	13157
Every Which Way But Loos...	SOUNDTRACK-MOVIE	6354
Evita	FESTIVAL	4395
Evita	ORIGINAL CAST	6598
Evolution	Dennis COFFEY	2801
Evolution	JOURNEY	680
Evolution	MALO	7786
Evolution	The HOLLIES	5396
The Evolution Of Mann	Herbie MANN	10982
Ev'ry Day Of My Life	Bobby VINTON	5869
Excess All Areas	SHY	13771
Excitable Boy	Warren ZEVON	1471
The Exciting Wilson Picket...	Wilson PICKETT	2687
Exile On Main St.	ROLLING STONES	481
Exiles	Dan FOGELBERG	4957
Exit	TANGERINE DREAM	13678
Exit...Stage Left	RUSH	1875
Exit 0	Steve EARLE And The ...	7334
Exodus	Bob MARLEY And The W...	1974
Exotic Birds And Fruit	PROCOL HARUM	7670

Title	Act	Rank
The Exotic Guitars	EXOTIC GUITARS	10859
Exotic Mysteries	Lonnie Liston SMITH	9456
Expansions	Lonnie Liston SMITH	6627
Expect No Mercy	NAZARETH	6219
Experience Gloria Gaynor	Gloria GAYNOR	5004
Experience In E, Ten...	"Cannonball" ADDERLE...	13526
Explosive Brass Impact	Warren KIME	11997
Exposed/A Cheap Peek At T...	VARIOUS ARTISTS	6210
Exposed II	VARIOUS ARTISTS	10707
Exposure	EXPOSÉ	608
Exposure	Robert FRIPP	6682
Express	LOVE AND ROCKETS	5076
Expression	John COLTRANE	13368
Expressions	Don WILLIAMS	10629
Express Yourself	Charles WRIGHT And T...	10762
Extended Play	The PRETENDERS	2954
Extension Of A Man	Donny HATHAWAY	6382
Extensions	MANHATTAN TRANSFER	3771
Extensions	MYSTIC MOODS Orchestra	9202
Extra Play	KAJAGOOGOO	13145
Extrapolation	John McLAUGHLIN	10610
Extraterrestrial Live	BLUE ÖYSTER CULT	4382
Extra Texture (Read All A...	George HARRISON	2382
Extreme	EXTREME	4963
Eydie Gorme's Greatest Hits	Eydie GORME	10298
Eye In The Sky	Alan PARSONS PROJECT	1022
Eye Of The Hurricane	The ALARM	4991
Eye Of The Tiger	SURVIVOR	804
Eye Of The Zombie	John FOGERTY	4008
Eyes Of A Stranger	The DEELE	4011
Eyes Of Laura Mars	SOUNDTRACK-MOVIE	8948
The Eyes Of The Beaco...	BEACON STREET UNION	5821
Eyes On This	MC LYTE	7094
Eyes That See In The Dark	Kenny ROGERS	887
Eye To Eye	EYE TO EYE	7734
EZO	EZO	10678

F

Title	Act	Rank
Fables	Jean-Luc PONTY	12428
Fables Of The Reconstruction	R.E.M.	2282
Fabulous	Dick HYMAN	11194
Fabulous	The STYLISTICS	9483
The Fabulous Baker Boys (Soun...	Dave GRUSIN	7040
Fabulous Broadway	BOSTON POPS Orchestra	13477
Fabulous Disaster	EXODUS	6432
The Fabulous Impressions	The IMPRESSIONS	10917
The Fabulous Rhinest...	FABULOUS RHINESTONES	12472
The Fabulous Ventures	The VENTURES	4882
Facades	SAD CAFÉ	11477
Face Dances	The WHO	1046
Faces	EARTH, WIND & FIRE	1950
Faces	Shawn PHILLIPS	4950
The Faces I've Been	Jim CROCE	5613
Face The Music	ELECTRIC LIGHT ORCHE...	672
Face To Face	ANGEL CITY	10920
Face To Face	Evelyn "Champagne" K...	7095
Face To Face	FACE TO FACE	8477
Face To Face	GQ	10267
Face To Face	The KINKS	11800
Face To Face With The Truth	UNDISPUTED TRUTH	7759
Face Value	Phil COLLINS	199
Facts Of Life	Bobby WOMACK	3961
Fade Out-Fade In	ORIGINAL CAST	9313
Fahrenheit	TOTO	3321
Fair Warning	VAN HALEN	1406
Fairytale	DONOVAN	7497
Faith	George MICHAEL	26
Faithful	Todd RUNDGREN	5602
Faithfull Forever...	Marianne FAITHFULL	12737
Faith, Hope And Charity	FAITH, HOPE AND CHAR...	6995
The Falcon & The Snowman	Pat METHENY Group	6745
Falco 3	FALCO	1329
Fallen Angel	URIAH HEEP	12264
Falling In Love Again	SUSAN	11766
Fallin' In Love	HAMILTON, JOE FRANK ...	6617
Fall Into Spring	Rita COOLIDGE	5609
The Fall Of The Roman Em...	SOUNDTRACK-MOVIE	13065
False Accusations	Robert CRAY Band	7969
False Start	LOVE	12902
Fame	Grace JONES	8289
Fame	SOUNDTRACK-MOVIE	730
Fame And Fashion - David Bowi...	David BOWIE	10951
Fame And Fortune	BAD COMPANY	9165
Family	Hubert LAWS	7705
The Family	The FAMILY	5664
Family Portrait	VARIOUS ARTISTS	13231
Family Reunion	The O'JAYS	963
The Family That Plays Together	SPIRIT	1748
Famous At Night	John HUNTER	10492
Famous Blue Raincoat	Jennifer WARNES	5618
"...Famous Last Words..."	SUPERTRAMP	1248
The Fanatic	FELONY	12797
Fancy	Bobbie GENTRY	6275
Fancy Dancer	Bobbi HUMPHREY	10056
Fancy Dancer	ONE WAY	6148
Fancy Free	OAK RIDGE BOYS	1182
Fandango	Herb ALPERT	5936
Fandango!	ZZ TOP	714
Fanny Hill	FANNY	10241
Fans	Malcolm McLAREN	12670
Fantastic	WHAM!	5173
Fantastic Voyage	LAKESIDE	1679
Fantasy	Carole KING	1118
Fantasy	FANTASY	13194
Fantasy Love Affair	Peter BROWN	965
Farewell	The SUPREMES/Diana R...	4413
Farewell Andromeda	John DENVER	1822
Farewell, Angelina	Joan BAEZ	2819
Farewell My Summer Love	Michael JACKSON	5405
Farewell Song	Janis JOPLIN	7993
A Farewell To Kings	RUSH	3685
Farewell To The First G...	MAMAS & The PAPAS	644
Farquahr	FARQUAHR	13253
Farrenheit	FARRENHEIT	12099
Farther Along	SPIRIT	12394
Farther Along	The BYRDS	10196
Fascination!	HUMAN LEAGUE	2643
Faster & Llouder	FOSTER & LLOYD	11409
Faster Pussycat	FASTER PUSSYCAT	5601
Faster Than The Speed Of Night	Bonnie TYLER	1234
Fast Times At Ridgemont H...	SOUNDTRACK-MOVIE	5070
Fastway	FASTWAY	2984
Fat Albert	Bill COSBY	12961
Fatback XII	FATBACK	7500
Fat Boys	FAT BOYS	3975
The Fat Boys Are Back!	FAT BOYS	4819
Fate For Breakfast	Art GARFUNKEL	6663
Father & Son [A]	Hank WILLIAMS Jr.	12269
Father & Son [A]	Hank WILLIAMS Sr.	12269
Fathers And Sons	Muddy WATERS	6624
Fat Mattress	FAT MATTRESS	8369
Fats Is Back	Fats DOMINO	13332
Favorite Country Hits	Ricky SKAGGS	12872
Favorites	Crystal GAYLE	10827
Feargal Sharkey	Feargal SHARKEY	7571
Fearless	FAMILY	11556
Fearless	Hoyt AXTON	12180
Fearless	Nina HAGEN	10887
Fearless	Tim CURRY	4334
Fear No Evil	GRIM REAPER	7617
Fear Of Music	TALKING HEADS	2338
Feats Don't Fail Me Now	LITTLE FEAT	4278
Feedback	SPIRIT	6250
Feel	George DUKE	10357
Feel Good	Ike & Tina TURNER	9964
Feelin' Alright	Mongo SANTAMARIA	12450
Feelin' Bitchy	Millie JACKSON	3259
Feelin' Bluesy	Gladys KNIGHT & The ...	9113
Feeling Cavalier	EBN-OZN	12863
Feeling Good	Roy AYERS	11131
Feeling Good	Walter JACKSON	6064
Feelin' Good	David RUFFIN	10832
Feelin' Good	Lou RAWLS	6131
Feelin' Groovy	HARPERS BIZARRE	9495
Feelings	Johnny MATHIS	5699
Feelings	Morris ALBERT	2866
Feelings	Paul ANKA	3024
Feelings	The LETTERMEN	12150
Feelin' Right	Razzy BAILEY	12762
Feel It	Noel POINTER	9764
Feel Like Makin' Love	Roberta FLACK	2920
Feel Me	CAMEO	4007
Feel My Soul	Jennifer HOLLIDAY	3974
Feel No Fret	AVERAGE WHITE BAND/AWB	4557
The Feel Of Neil Diamond	Neil DIAMOND	11202
Feels So Good	Chuck MANGIONE	264
Feels So Good	Grover WASHINGTON Jr...	1857
Feels So Right	ALABAMA	200
Feel The Fire	Jermaine JACKSON	12758
Feel The Heat	Henry PAUL Band	9283
Feel The Need	Leif GARRETT	3663
Feel The Night	Lee RITENOUR	10197
Feel The Shake	JETBOY	9459
Feel The Spirit	Leroy HUTSON	10711
Feets Don't Fail Me Now	Herbie HANCOCK	3992
Feliciano!	José FELICIANO	230
Feliciano/10 To 23	José FELICIANO	1401
Female Trouble	Nona HENDRYX	7771
Femme Fatale	FEMME FATALE	11288
Ferguslie Park	STEALERS WHEEL	12926
The Ferrante And Teich...	FERRANTE & TEICHER	11042
Ferry Cross The Mers...	GERRY And The PACEMA...	2720
Fervor	JASON & The SCORCHER...	7337
Festival	Lee RITENOUR	10790
Festival	SANTANA	3227
Fever	CON FUNK SHUN	7045
Fever	Ronnie LAWS	3451
Fever	Roy AYERS	5674
Fever!	Doc SEVERINSEN	12733
Fever Tree	FEVER TREE	8317
Fickle	Michael HENDERSON	12215
Fickle Heart	SNIFF 'N' The TEARS	3879
Fiddler On The Roof	FERRANTE & TEICHER	13116
Fiddler On The Roof	Herschel BERNARDI	10824
Fiddler On The Roof	ORIGINAL CAST	154
Fiddler On The Roof	SOUNDTRACK-MOVIE	928
Field Day	Marshall CRENSHAW	5464
Fields Of Fire	Corey HART	4355

Title	Act	Rank
Fierce Heart	Jim CAPALDI	8140
15 Big Ones	BEACH BOYS	1528
15 Great Hits	The KINGSMEN	8621
Fifteen Years Ago	Conway TWITTY	9471
"5th"	Lee MICHAELS	1151
Fifth Angel	FIFTH ANGEL	8246
Fifth Dimension	The BYRDS	2838
The 5th Dimension/Greatest ...	5TH DIMENSION	726
The 5th Dimension/Live!!	5TH DIMENSION	3487
A Fifth Of Beethoven	Walter MURPHY	2189
50 Fabulous Piano Favo...	FERRANTE & TEICHER	10068
50 Guitars Go Italiano	Tommy GARRETT	13007
50 Guitars In Love	Tommy GARRETT	9954
5150	VAN HALEN	337
52nd Street	Billy JOEL	101
Fight Dirty	CHARLIE	6564
Fight For The Rock	SAVATAGE	11068
The Fightin' Side Of Me	Merle HAGGARD	3529
Fight To Survive	WHITE LION	8667
Filet Of Soul	JAN & DEAN	10697
Fillmore: The Last Days	VARIOUS ARTISTS	4222
Film On Film - Great...	Enoch LIGHT & The Li...	13226
The Final Countdown	EUROPE	461
The Final Cut	PINK FLOYD	1925
Finale	LOGGINS & MESSINA	8244
The Final Frontier	KEEL	5479
Finally!	T.G. SHEPPARD	9253
Finally Got Myself Togeth...	The IMPRESSIONS	12622
The Final Swing	TRAPEZE	11341
Finder Of Lost Loves	Dionne WARWICK	8780
The Fine Art Of Surfacing	BOOMTOWN RATS	6455
A Fine Mess	SOUNDTRACK-MOVIE	13236
Fine Young Cannibals	FINE YOUNG CANNIBALS	4495
Finger Lickin Good	Dennis COFFEY	10263
Finger Paintings	Earl KLUGH	7865
Finian's Rainbow	SOUNDTRACK-MOVIE	4501
Finyl Vinyl	RAINBOW	8479
Fiona	FIONA	6409
Fire	OHIO PLAYERS	519
Fire & Fleet & Candlel...	Buffy SAINTE-MARIE	10182
Fire And Gasoline	Steve JONES	12700
Fire And Water	FREE	1865
Fireball	DEEP PURPLE	3179
Firebird	Isao TOMITA	6174
Fire Down Under	RIOT	8150
Fired Up 'N' Kickin'	FATBACK	6304
Firefall	FIREFALL	996
Firefly	URIAH HEEP	12452
Fire In The Wind	John STEWART	9278
Fire It Up	Rick JAMES	4128
Fire Of Unknown Origin	BLUE ÖYSTER CULT	1963
Fire On The Bayou	The METERS	12856
Fire On The Mountain	Charlie DANIELS Band	2600
The Fire Still Burns	Russ BALLARD	12479
Fire Up	Merl SAUNDERS	12919
Fireworks	José FELICIANO	4452
Firin' Up	PURE PRAIRIE LEAGUE	3783
The Firm	The FIRM	2000
1st	STREETS	10513
First	David GATES	8396
First Base	BABE RUTH	11792
First Circle	PAT METHENY GROUP	5211
First Cuckoo	DEODATO	8638
The First Edition	Kenny ROGERS & The F...	8014
The First Edition 69	Kenny ROGERS & The F...	11584
The First Family Rides Again	Rich LITTLE	4349

Title	Act	Rank
First Glance	APRIL WINE	8038
First Great Rock Festival...	VARIOUS ARTISTS	5831
The First Hurrah!	CLANCY BROTHERS AND ...	9966
First Impressions	The IMPRESSIONS	9934
The First Lady	Tammy WYNETTE	7173
The First Minute Of ...	Gil SCOTT-HERON & Br...	3716
The First Nine Months Are...	VARIOUS ARTISTS	7736
The First Of A Milli...	FAIRGROUND ATTRACTIO...	9554
First Offence	The INMATES	5423
First Offense	Corey HART	2422
First Pull Up Then Pull Down	HOT TUNA	4485
The First Songs	Laura NYRO	7804
First Step	SMALL FACES/FACES	8378
First Take	Roberta FLACK	224
First Taste Of Sin	COLD BLOOD	8417
The First 10 Years	Joan BAEZ	6461
First Thrills	THRILLS	13135
The First Time Ever (I Saw ...	Johnny MATHIS	5801
The First Time Ever (I Saw You...	Peter NERO	10661
The First Time Ever (I Saw You...	Vikki CARR	8696
The First Time We Met	The INDEPENDENTS	9441
The First 25 Years-The Silv...	Johnny MATHIS	12185
First Under The Wire	LITTLE RIVER BAND	1385
First Water	SHARKS	12898
Fisherman's Blues	The WATERBOYS	5131
Fish Out Of Water	Chris SQUIRE	6165
A Fistful Of Dollars	SOUNDTRACK-MOVIE	6349
Fits Like A Glove	Howie MANDEL	11419
5	J.J. CALE	9036
Five-A-Side (An Ace Album)	ACE	1749
Five Bridges	The NICE	12767
5 By 5	Dave CLARK Five	9549
The Five Faces Of Manfred Ma...	MANFRED MANN	11714
500 Miles Away From Home	Bobby BARE	11071
500 Miles High	Flora PURIM	10918
Five Miles Out	Mike OLDFIELD	12126
The $5.98 E.P.: Garage Days Re-...	METALLICA	3171
Five-O	Hank WILLIAMS Jr.	6224
Five O'Clock World	The VOGUES	10271
Five Special	5 SPECIAL	8097
The Five Stairsteps	FIVE STAIRSTEPS	11305
5-10-15-20 (25-30 Years Of...	The PRESIDENTS	10681
5 To 1	Tom KIMMEL	8221
Fiyo On The Bayou	NEVILLE BROTHERS	12497
Flag	James TAYLOR	1800
Flag	YELLO	10933
The Flag	Rick JAMES	8143
Flame	Ronnie LAWS	4185
The Flamingo Kid	SOUNDTRACK-MOVIE	10092
Flash	FLASH	2666
Flash	Jeff BECK	4621
Flash And The Pan	FLASH & THE PAN	5891
Flashback	.38 SPECIAL	4897
Flashdance	SOUNDTRACK-MOVIE	124
Flash Gordon (Soundtrack)	QUEEN	3281
Flash In The Can	FLASH	7725
Flat As A Pancake	HEAD EAST	6732
The Flat Earth	Thomas DOLBY	4271
Flatt And Scruggs At Carn...	FLATT & SCRUGGS	10545
Flaunt It	SIGUE SIGUE SPUTNIK	8866
Flaunt The Imperfection	CHINA CRISIS	12533
Flavours	GUESS WHO	6020
Fleetwood Mac Live	FLEETWOOD MAC	2454
Fleetwood Mac	FLEETWOOD MAC	18
Fleetwood Mac (1968)	FLEETWOOD MAC	13371
Fleetwood Mac In Chicago	FLEETWOOD MAC	6402

Title	Act	Rank
Flesh + Blood	ROXY MUSIC	3750
Fletch	SOUNDTRACK-MOVIE	12478
Flex	Lene LOVICH	8579
Flick Of The Switch	AC/DC	2547
Flight Log (1966-197...	JEFFERSON AIRPLANE/S...	4227
Flights Of Fantasy	The VENTURES	11775
Flip	Nils LOFGREN	11533
Flip-Flop	GUADALCANAL DIARY	8596
"Flip" - The Flip Wilson Show	Flip WILSON	5365
Flirt	Evelyn "Champagne" K...	13359
Flirtin' With Disaster	MOLLY HATCHET	1274
Floaters	The FLOATERS	1554
The Flock	The FLOCK	3950
A Flock Of Seagulls	A FLOCK OF SEAGULLS	1005
Floodland	SISTERS OF MERCY	6728
Flora, The Red Menace	ORIGINAL CAST	9258
Floridays	Jimmy BUFFETT	6650
Flow	SNAIL	13466
Flowers	ROLLING STONES	763
Flowers	The EMOTIONS	3150
Flowers In The Dirt	Paul McCARTNEY	2244
Flowers Of Evil	MOUNTAIN	3712
The Flowers Of Roman...	PUBLIC IMAGE LIMITED	10909
Flowers On The Wall	STATLER BROTHERS	11842
Flowing Free Forever	Michael MURPHEY	10512
Flowing Rivers	Andy GIBB	874
Floy Joy	The SUPREMES	5337
Flush The Fashion	ALICE COOPER (Solo)	4625
Fly	Yoko ONO	13658
Fly Away	VOYAGE	3700
Fly By Night	RUSH	8420
Flying Again	FLYING BURRITO BROTH...	11502
The Flying Burrito B...	FLYING BURRITO BROTH...	10837
Flying Cowboys	Rickie Lee JONES	3841
Flying High On Your Love	The BAR-KAYS	4079
Flying High Together	The MIRACLES/Smokey ...	3908
Flying Home	Stanley JORDAN	9890
Flying In A Blue Dream	Joe SATRIANI	2028
The Flying Lizards	FLYING LIZARDS	8635
The Flying Machine	FLYING MACHINE	11289
The Flying Nun	Sally FIELD	12369
Flying Start	The BLACKBYRDS	1874
Flying The Flag	CLIMAX BLUES Band	6063
Fly Like An Eagle	Steve MILLER Band	70
Fly, Little White Dove, Fly	The BELLS	6442
Fly Me To The Moon	Bobby WOMACK	12883
Fly Me To The Moon	Earl GRANT	11118
Fly On The Wall	AC/DC	3350
Fly With The Wind	McCoy TYNER	8319
FM	SOUNDTRACK-MOVIE	1247
FM & AM	George CARLIN	1249
FM/Live	CLIMAX BLUES BAND	5242
Focal Point	McCoy TYNER	12979
Focus 3	FOCUS	3375
Foghat	FOGHAT	7142
Foghat (II)	FOGHAT	5353
Foghat Live	FOGHAT	1959
The Folk Album	Trini LOPEZ	3048
Folk 'N Roll	JAN & DEAN	12370
Folks Of The 80's (Part ...	MEN WITHOUT HATS	11493
Folk Songs Around The World	MANTOVANI	10921
Folksongs For A Nuclear Village	SHADOWFAX	12163
Folkways: A Vision Shared...	VARIOUS ARTISTS	7626
Follies	ORIGINAL CAST	12536
Follies In Concert	ORIGINAL CAST	12446
Follow My Mind	Jimmy CLIFF	13587

Title | Act	Rank
Follow The Leader | ERIC B. & RAKIM	3793
Follow The Rainbow | George DUKE	6272
Fool Around | Rachel SWEET	8021
Fool Britannia | VARIOUS ARTISTS	8237
The Fool Circle | NAZARETH	6492
Fool For The City | FOGHAT	1367
Fool In Love With You | PHOTOGLO	8230
Foolish Behaviour | Rod STEWART	1615
Foolish Pleasures | HEARTSFIELD	10640
Fool On The Hill | Sergio MENDES And BR...	783
Fools Gold | FOOLS GOLD	7148
Footloose | SOUNDTRACK-MOVIE	225
Foot Loose & Fancy Free | Rod STEWART	283
Footsteps In The Dark: Greate... | Cat STEVENS	11166
For Adults Only | Bill COSBY	11438
For A Few Dollars Mo... | LeRoy HOLMES and His...	3461
For All The Seasons Of Your Min... | Janis IAN	12239
For Animals Only | BAJA MARIMBA BAND	7360
The Force | KOOL & The GANG	10262
Force It | UFO	6580
Force Majeure | DORO	10015
Fore! | Huey LEWIS And The N...	248
For Earth Below | Robin TROWER	1626
Foreign Affair | Tina TURNER	3904
Foreign Affairs | Tom WAITS	9308
Foreigner | Cat STEVENS	934
Foreigner | FOREIGNER	125
For Emily, Whenever I May... | Glenn YARBROUGH	9239
Forest Flower | Charles LLOYD Quarte...	12964
Forever | Billy VAUGHN and His...	11903
Forever | KOOL & The GANG	2299
Forever | ORLEANS	6489
Forever | Pete DRAKE	7468
Forever And Ever | Howard HEWETT	8288
Forever By Your Side | The MANHATTANS	9209
Forever Changes | LOVE	10260
Forever, For Always, For ... | Luther VANDROSS	1946
Forever Gold | ISLEY BROTHERS	6709
Forever Lovers | Mac DAVIS	9756
Forever, Michael | Michael JACKSON	7947
Forever Now | PSYCHEDELIC FURS	3744
Forever, Rex Smith | Rex SMITH	12582
For Everyman | Jackson BROWNE	2655
Forever Young | ALPHAVILLE	10669
Forever Your Girl | Paula ABDUL	12
Forever Yours | The SYLVERS	9499
Forever Yours | Tony TERRY	8069
Forget Him | Bobby RYDELL	11050
(For God's Sake) Give More ... | The CHI-LITES	1189
Forgotten Songs & Unsung Heroes | John KAY	8429
For Ladies Only | STEPPENWOLF	5228
For Little Ones | DONOVAN	13164
For Love Of Ivy | SOUNDTRACK-MOVIE	13486
For Lovers | SAN SEBASTIAN String...	5532
For Lovers Of All Ages | FERRANTE & TEICHER	10327
For Men Only | Millie JACKSON	8134
For Once In My Life | O.C. SMITH	4509
For Once In My Life | Stevie WONDER	4056
For Once In My Life | Tony BENNETT	11112
For Once In My Life | Vikki CARR	1917
For Sentimental Reasons | Linda RONSTADT	4212
For Swingin' Livers Only! | Allan SHERMAN	4623
For The Children Of The Wo... | Art LINKLETTER	12096
For The First Time [A] | Brenda LEE	13414
For The First Time [A] | Pete FOUNTAIN	13414
For The Good Times | Dean MARTIN	6743
For The Good Times | Ray PRICE	1134
For The Good Times/The Jim Nab... | Jim NABORS	5982
For The "In" Crowd | Jack JONES	12915
For The Lonely: A Roy Orbison... | Roy ORBISON	8105
For The Love Of Him | Bobbi MARTIN	11825
For The People In The Last Ha... | Tom T. HALL	9255
For The Roses | Joni MITCHELL	1690
For The Sake Of Love | Isaac HAYES	5581
For The Working Girl | Melissa MANCHESTER	6261
For Those About To Rock (We Salute ... | AC/DC	712
For Those In Love | Percy FAITH His Orch...	6474
Fortune 410 | Donnie IRIS	8966
Fortuosity | MILLS BROTHERS	2526
40 Hour Week | ALABAMA	2996
42nd Street | ORIGINAL CAST	8206
For You | Eddie KENDRICKS	6487
For You | PRINCE	11519
For You | Roger WILLIAMS	7017
For Your Eyes Only | SOUNDTRACK-MOVIE	5617
For Your Love | PEACHES & HERB	9007
For Your Love | The YARDBIRDS	8155
For Your Pleasure | ROXY MUSIC	13558
For Your Precious Love | Oscar TONEY, Jr.	12869
Foster Sylvers | Foster SYLVERS	11021
Fotomaker | FOTOMAKER	7170
Foul Play | SOUNDTRACK-MOVIE	8644
Found All The Parts | CHEAP TRICK	5197
Fountains Of Light | STARCASTLE	7620
4 | FOREIGNER	29
4 By Four | 4 BY FOUR	11105
Four Days That Shock... | John Fitzgerald KENN...	5852
Four For The Show | STATLER BROTHERS	13534
Four In Blue | The MIRACLES/Smokey ...	6545
4 Of A Kind | D.R.I.	7901
The Four Of Us | John SEBASTIAN	7523
Four Sail | LOVE	6683
The 4 Seasons Entertain You | 4 SEASONS	7435
The 4 Seasons' Gold Vault of Hi... | 4 SEASONS	907
Four Seasons Of Love | Donna SUMMER	2228
Four Seasons Story | 4 SEASONS	5224
Foursider | Herb ALPERT & The Tl...	13178
Four Sides Of Melanie | MELANIE	8458
461 Ocean Boulevard | Eric CLAPTON	632
Four Strong Winds | IAN & SYLVIA	10355
Fourteen 14K Folk Songs | The LIMELITERS	8478
14 Greatest Hits [A] | JACKSON 5	11768
14 Greatest Hits [A] | Michael JACKSON	11768
14 Karat | FATBACK	8618
Four Tops | FOUR TOPS	4828
The Four Tops Greatest Hits | FOUR TOPS	463
Four Tops Greatest Hits, Vol. 2 | FOUR TOPS	7381
Four Tops Live! | FOUR TOPS	1430
Four Tops Now! | FOUR TOPS	6571
4 Tops On Broadway | FOUR TOPS	6458
4 Tops On Top | FOUR TOPS	3423
Four Tops Reach Out | FOUR TOPS	1483
Four Tops Second Album | FOUR TOPS	2673
4 Way Street | CROSBY, STILLS, NASH...	294
Four Wheel Drive | BACHMAN-TURNER OVERD...	1604
Four Winds | TANGIER	6554
Fowl Play | BAJA MARIMBA BAND	10410
The Fox | Elton JOHN	3119
Foxie | Bob JAMES	8502
Foxy Brown (Soundtrack) | Willie HUTCH	12294
Foxy Lady | CHER	3403
Fragile | CHERRELLE	10392
Fragile | YES	457
Framed | ASLEEP AT THE WHEEL	13520
Frampton | Peter FRAMPTON	1906
Frampton Comes Alive! | Peter FRAMPTON	10
Frampton's Camel | Peter FRAMPTON	6611
France Joli | France JOLI	3735
Francis A. & Edward K. [A] | Duke ELLINGTON	6646
Francis A. & Edward K. [A] | Frank SINATRA	6646
Francis Albert Sinat... [A] | Antonio Carlos JOBIM	2961
Francis Albert Sinatra & An... [A] | Frank SINATRA	2961
Frank | SQUEEZE	9056
Franke & The Knockouts | FRANKE AND THE KNOC...	2462
Frankie And Johnny (Soundtr... | Elvis PRESLEY	3252
Frankie Valli Gold | Frankie VALLI	9344
Frankie Valli...Is The Word | Frankie VALLI	10583
Frank Marino & Mahogany Ru... | MAHOGANY RUSH	9100
Frank Sinatra | Frank SINATRA	3080
Frank Sinatra's Greatest Hits... | Frank SINATRA	3305
Frank Sinatra's Greatest Hits Vol. 2 | Frank SINATRA	5811
Franks Wild Years | Tom WAITS	8810
Frank Zappa's 200 Motels (Sou... | Frank ZAPPA	5889
Frantic Romantic | Jermaine STEWART	3640
Freakin' At The Freakers... | Shel SILVERSTEIN	10254
Freak Out! | Frank ZAPPA	7396
Freddie & The Dreame... | FREDDIE And The DREA...	3708
Free | CONCRETE BLONDE	8988
Free And Easy | Helen REDDY	1170
Free As A Bird | SUPERTRAMP	8893
Free As The Wind | The CRUSADERS	4108
Free At Last | FREE	5631
Freedom | Neil YOUNG	3154
Freedom | SANTANA	8270
Freedom At Point Zer... | JEFFERSON AIRPLANE/S...	1165
Freedom For The Stallion | HUES CORPORATION	2889
Freedom March On Was... | Rev. Martin Luther K...	10814
Freedom Means | The DELLS	5377
Freedom No Compromise | LITTLE STEVEN	7545
Freedom Of Choice | DEVO	1184
Freedom Suite | RASCALS/YOUNG RASCAL...	2708
The Free Electric Band | Albert HAMMOND	13130
Free Fall | Alvin LEE	13154
Free-For-All | Ted NUGENT	2303
Free Hand | GENTLE GIANT	5725
Free Live! | FREE	8175
Freestyle | Bobbi HUMPHREY	6563
Freetime | SPYRO GYRA	3660
Free To Be...You And Me | VARIOUS ARTISTS	3662
Freeways | BACHMAN-TURNER OVERD...	7335
Freewheelin' | FABULOUS RHINESTONES	13287
The Freewheelin' Bob Dylan | Bob DYLAN	2205
Free Your Mind...And Your Ass ... | FUNKADELIC	8036
Freeze-Frame | J. GEILS Band	194
Frehley's Comet | Ace FREHLEY	3894
Freight Train Heart | Jimmy BARNES	7465
French Kiss | Bob WELCH	665
Frequency | Nick GILDER	9374
Fresh | RASPBERRIES	4123
Fresh | SLY & THE FAMILY STO...	1208
Fresh Air | BAJA MARIMBA BAND	12517
A Fresh Aire Christm... | MANNHEIM STEAMROLLER	3454
Fresh Aire VI | MANNHEIM STEAMROLLER	10284
Fresh Cream | CREAM	1402
Fresh Fish Special | Robert GORDON	9480
Fresh Flavor | Jane MORGAN	11123
Fresh Fruit In Forei... | KID CREOLE & The COC...	13279
Friday Night In San ... | Al Di MEOLA/John McL...	7392

Title | Act	Rank
Friday On My Mind | The EASYBEATS	12580
Friend | Freddie NORTH	12277
Friendly Persuasion | Ray CONNIFF & His Or...	11362
Friend Or Foe | Adam ANT	1744
"Friends" (Soundtrack) | Elton JOHN	3575
Friends | B.B. KING	10655
Friends | BEACH BOYS	8518
Friends | Chick COREA	7245
Friends | Dionne WARWICK	2068
Friends | Larry CARLTON	9219
Friends | SHALAMAR	3627
Friends & Love...A Chuck M... | Chuck MANGIONE	8286
Friends & People | FRIENDS OF DISTINCTI...	10826
Friends & Smiley Smile | BEACH BOYS	9406
Friends And Strangers | Ronnie LAWS	3132
Friendship | Ray CHARLES	6081
Friends In Love | Dionne WARWICK	8186
Friends In Love | Johnny MATHIS	10348
The Friends Of Mr. Cairo | JON And VANGELIS	4164
Frijid Pink | FRIJID PINK	1437
'Frisco Mabel Joy | Mickey NEWBURY	5388
Frog City | SOUTHERN COMFORT	13564
Frogs Sprouts Clogs And Krauts | The RUMOUR	12235
Frolic Through The Park | DEATH ANGEL	9917
From A Child To A Woman | Julio IGLESIAS	12270
From A Whisper To A Screa... | Esther PHILLIPS	7712
From Branch To Branch | Leon REDBONE	8897
From Broadway With Love | Nancy WILSON	5101
From Disco To Love | Van McCOY	12522
From Elvis In Memphis | Elvis PRESLEY	1128
From Elvis Presley Boulevar... | Elvis PRESLEY	4588
From Every Stage | Joan BAEZ	4034
From Genesis To Revelation | GENESIS	12207
From Hello Dolly To Goodbye C... | Bobby DARIN	9332
From Here To Eternally | SPINNERS	12078
From Here To Eternity | Giorgio MORODER	9822
From Luxury To Heartache | CULTURE CLUB	4239
From Memphis To Vegas / Fro... | Elvis PRESLEY	1600
From Me To You | Charley PRIDE	3411
From Me To You | George DUKE	13177
From Mighty Oaks | Ray THOMAS	6724
From Monty, With Love | MANTOVANI	6938
From Nashville With Love | Chet ATKINS	11357
From Russia With Love | SOUNDTRACK-MOVIE	3361
From South Africa To... | Gil SCOTT-HERON & Br...	10090
From The Greenhouse | CRACK THE SKY	12661
From The Inside | ALICE COOPER (Solo)	6704
From The Inside | POCO	5274
From The Streets Of New York | SHA NA NA	9174
From Within | Dionne WARWICK	11816
Frontiers | JOURNEY	212
Front Page News | WISHBONE ASH	12234
Frost Music | The FROST	9562
Frozen Ghost | FROZEN GHOST	8372
Frozen In The Night | Dan HILL	9352
Fruit At The Bottom | WENDY and LISA	9596
Fuel For The Fire | NAKED EYES	8390
The Fugs | The FUGS	5565
The Fugs First Album | The FUGS	11298
Full Bloom | Carol DOUGLAS	8887
Full Circle | The DOORS	5382
Fulfillingness First Final... | Stevie WONDER	572
Full Force | FULL FORCE	11081
Full Force Get Busy 1 Time! | FULL FORCE	9215
Full House | Frankie MILLER(1)	7966
Full Moon | Charlie DANIELS Band	1649

Title | Act	Rank
Full Moon | Kris KRISTOFFERSON &...	2839
Full Moon Fever | Tom PETTY And The HE...	157
Full Of Fire | Al GREEN	5450
Full Sail | LOGGINS & MESSINA	1073
Fully Exposed | Willie HUTCH	12109
Fun & Games | The CONNELLS	11064
Fun And Games | Chuck MANGIONE	1813
Function At The Junction | B.T. EXPRESS	9731
Fundamental Roll | Walter EGAN	9861
Fun In Acapulco (Soundtrack... | Elvis PRESLEY	1278
Fun In Space | Roger TAYLOR	7756
Funkadelic | FUNKADELIC	7244
Funk Beyond The Call... | Johnny Guitar WATSON	7393
Funkentelechy Vs. The Placebo ... | PARLIAMENT	1372
The Funk Is On | INSTANT FUNK	9909
Funk Or Walk | BRIDES OF FUNKENSTEI...	6759
The Funky Broadway | DYKE And The BLAZERS	12928
Funky Kingston | TOOTS And The MAYTAL...	9350
Funky Serenity | Ramsey LEWIS	8694
A Funky Thide Of Sings | Billy COBHAM	7727
Funland | BRAM TCHAIKOVSKY	10130
Funny Girl (Original Cas... | Barbra STREISAND	373
Funny Girl | The SUPREMES/Diana R...	9024
Funny Girl (Soundtrack) | Barbra STREISAND	237
Funny Lady (Soundtrack) | Barbra STREISAND	1558
The Funny Sides Of Moms Mable... | Moms MABLEY	11090
Fur | Jane WIEDLIN	6178
Furthermore... | Shawn PHILLIPS	5351
Future | The SEEDS	8448
Future Blues | CANNED HEAT	4520
Future Bound | TAVARES	8761
Future Games | FLEETWOOD MAC	7195
Future Now | PLEASURE	3956
Future Shock | Herbie HANCOCK	1688
Future World | PRETTY MAIDS	11313
The Fuzz | The FUZZ	13223
Frank Zappa Meets The Mothers... | Frank ZAPPA	11589
G	
Gabor Szabo 1969 | Gabor SZABO	9373
Galaxian | Jeff LORBER	6095
Galaxy | WAR	2006
Gallant Men | Senator Everett McKi...	3042
Galveston | Glen CAMPBELL	462
Galveston | Jim NABORS	7198
Galveston | Lawrence WELK	3972
The Gambler | Kenny ROGERS	395
The Game | QUEEN	158
The Game Of Love | The MINDBENDERS	7602
Games People Play / These A... | Freddy WELLER	9534
Games That Lovers Play | Eddie FISHER	7531
Gamma 1 | GAMMA	7415
Gamma 3 | GAMMA	7009
Gamma 2 | GAMMA	5383
Gandhi | SOUNDTRACK-MOVIE	12821
The Gap Band | GAP BAND	5701
Gap Band V- Jammin' | GAP BAND	2459
Gap Band IV | GAP BAND	1277
Gap Band VII | GAP BAND	9583
Gap Band VI | GAP BAND	4944
The Gap Band III | GAP BAND	1261
The Gap Band II | GAP BAND	3267
Gap Gold/Best Of The Gap Band | GAP BAND	7682
Garcia | Jerry GARCIA	4477
Garcia (II) | Jerry GARCIA	5073
Garden In The City | MELANIE	7300

Title | Act	Rank
Garden Of Love | Rick JAMES	7767
The Garden Of Love | Don RAY	8061
Garden Party | Rick NELSON	3645
Gary Lewis Now! | Gary LEWIS And The P...	9629
The Gary Puckett Alb... | Gary PUCKETT And The...	13548
Gary Puckett & The U... | Gary PUCKETT And The...	3226
Gasoline Alley | Rod STEWART	2109
A Gasssss | Jr. WALKER & The ALL...	9928
A Gathering Of Promises | BUBBLE PUPPY	11005
Gather Me | MELANIE	1408
Gaucho | STEELY DAN	937
Gaudi | Alan PARSONS PROJECT	6271
Gayle McCormick | Gayle McCORMICK	13278
The Geese & The Ghost | Anthony PHILLIPS	13296
Geffrey Morgan... | UB40	5028
Gems | AEROSMITH	9026
Gene & Jerry - One & One [A] | Gene CHANDLER	10295
Gene & Jerry - One & One [A] | Jerry BUTLER	10295
Gene Chandler '80 | Gene CHANDLER	5947
Gene Chandler - Live On Sta... | Gene CHANDLER	11973
The Gene Chandler Situation | Gene CHANDLER	10753
Gene Pitney's Big Sixteen | Gene PITNEY	8595
Gene Simmons | Gene SIMMONS	2108
Genesis | GENESIS	866
Genesis | SOUL CHILDREN	11140
Genesis Live | GENESIS	7368
Genetic Walk | Ahmad JAMAL Trio	11938
The Genie (Themes & Variations ... | Bob JAMES	7578
The Genius Of Jankowski! | Horst JANKOWSKI	2556
Gentle Is My Love | Nancy WILSON	2891
Gentle On My Mind | Dean MARTIN	1530
Gentle On My Mind | Glen CAMPBELL	311
Gentle On My Mind | Lenny DEE	13349
Gentle On My Mind | Patti PAGE	11585
Gently Swingin' | Earl GRANT	13722
The Genuine Imitation Life Gaze... | 4 SEASONS	6452
The George Benson Collectio... | George BENSON	1706
George Benson In Concert-Ca... | George BENSON	9035
George Harrison | George HARRISON	2225
George Jones & Gene Pitney [A] | Gene PITNEY	11832
George Jones & Gene Pitney [A] | George JONES	11832
George M! | ORIGINAL CAST	11292
George McCrae | George McCRAE	11377
Georges Bizet: Carmen | Leontyne PRICE	12561
Georgia Satellites | GEORGIA SATELLITES	1341
Georgia Sunshine | Jerry REED	7397
Georgy Girl | The SEEKERS	1812
Geraldine/Don't Fight The Fee... | Flip WILSON	5745
Geronimo's Cadillac | Michael MURPHEY	10114
Gerry & The Pacemakers Great... | GERRY And The ...	4608
Gerry & The Pacemakers Second... | GERRY And Th...	9528
Get As Much Love As You Can | JONES GIRLS	9419
The Getaway | Chris De BURGH	4700
Get Back! | Ike & Tina TURNER	13667
Get Close | The PRETENDERS	2565
Get Closer | Linda RONSTADT	3276
Get Closer | SEALS & CROFTS	2081
Get Down | Gene CHANDLER	4387
Get Down | Joe SIMON	8141
Get Happy!! | Elvis COSTELLO & The...	2551
Get Happy with the London Ph... | Tony BENNETT	13550
Get Here | Brenda RUSSELL	3670
Get It On... | PACIFIC GAS AND ELEC...	8759
Get It On Credit | TORONTO	10998
Get It Out'cha System | Millie JACKSON	5487
Get It Right | Aretha FRANKLIN	4747

Title | Act	Rank
Get It Together | JACKSON 5	5276
Get Loose | Evelyn "Champagne" K...	3338
Get Lucky | LOVERBOY	126
Get Me To The Country | McKENDREE SPRING	8808
Get Nervous | Pat BENATAR	781
Get Off | FOXY	1644
Get On Down With Bobby Bland | Bobby BLAND	11196
Get On The Good Foot | James BROWN	5440
Get Out Of My Room | CHEECH & CHONG	8610
Get Ready | KING CURTIS	13688
Get Ready | RARE EARTH	435
Get Rhythm | Johnny CASH	10757
Get Rhythm | Ry COODER	10638
Get That Feeling [A] | Curtis KNIGHT	6843
Get That Feeling [A] | Jimi HENDRIX	6843
Get The Knack | The KNACK	243
Gettin' Away With Murder | Patti AUSTIN	13075
Gettin' Down To It | James BROWN	5841
Getting Together | Bobby SHERMAN	7509
Getting Together | FERRANTE & TEICHER	7774
Getting To This | BLODWYN PIG	9811
Gettin' Lucky | HEAD EAST	9991
Gettin' Ready | The TEMPTATIONS	1561
Get Together With Andy Will... | Andy WILLIAMS	3249
Get To The Feeling | PLEASURE	7629
Get Up Offa That Thing | James BROWN	9548
Get Up With It | Miles DAVIS	9678
'Get Yer Ya-Ya's Out!' | ROLLING STONES	1361
Get Your Rocks Off | MANFRED MANN'S EARTH...	13698
Get Yourself Up | HEAD EAST	10751
Get Your Wings | AEROSMITH	2326
Getz Au Go Go | Stan GETZ	1951
Getz/Gilberto [A] | Joao GILBERTO	275
Getz/Gilberto [A] | Stan GETZ	275
G Force | KENNY G	5671
Ghetto Blaster | The CRUSADERS	6217
Ghetto Music: The Bl... | BOOGIE DOWN PRODUCTI...	4453
Ghostbusters | SOUNDTRACK-MOVIE	1368
Ghostbusters II | SOUNDTRACK-MOVIE	2755
Ghost In The Machine | The POLICE	169
Ghost On The Beach | INSIDERS	12125
Ghost Riders | The OUTLAWS	2580
Ghosts | STRAWBS	5105
Ghost Town | POCO	13509
Ghost Town Parade | Les DUDEK	7447
Ghost Writer | Garland JEFFREYS	9331
Giacomo Puccini: Tosca | Leontyne PRICE	9213
Giant | Johnny Guitar WATSON	10299
Giant | The WOODENTOPS	12546
Giant Step/De Ole Folks At Home | Taj MAHAL	7406
Gideon | Kenny ROGERS	1786
The Gift | The JAM	6708
A Gift From A Flower To A Garden | DONOVAN	3046
Gigolo | FATBACK	11543
Gilbert O'Sullivan-Him... | Gilbert O'SULLIVAN	1432
The Gilded Palace Of... | FLYING BURRITO BROTH...	10365
Gimme Back My Bullets | LYNYRD SKYNYRD	3250
Gimme Dat Ding! | The PIPKINS	10893
Gimme Some Lovin' | Spencer DAVIS Group	4542
Gimme Something Real | ASHFORD & SIMPSON	9147
Gimmie Some Neck | Ronnie WOOD	5559
Ginger Baker's Air F... | Ginger BAKER's Air F...	4262
Ginseng Woman | Eric GALE	8888
Gipsy Kings | GIPSY KINGS	3559
Girl At Her Volcano | Rickie Lee JONES	5216
Girl Happy (Soundtrack) | Elvis PRESLEY	1591

Title | Act	Rank
Girls, Girls, Girls | MÖTLEY CRÜE	634
Girls To Chat & Boys To Bounce | FOGHAT	7761
Girls With Guns | Tommy SHAW	4343
Girl Talk | Lesley GORE	13081
Girl Watcher | The O'KAYSIONS	10852
The Girl Who Came To Supper | ORIGINAL CAST	5012
Girl You Know It's True | MILLI VANILLI	36
The Gist Of The Gemini | Gino VANNELLI	3342
Gitarzan | Ray STEVENS	4717
Giuffria | GIUFFRIA	2869
Give 'Em Enough Rope | The CLASH	8945
Give, Get, Take And Have | Curtis MAYFIELD	10553
Give It Away | The CHI-LITES	12706
Give It To The People | RIGHTEOUS BROTHERS	3039
Give It Up | Bonnie RAITT	7886
Give It Up | PLEASURE	11765
Give Me Just A Littl... | CHAIRMEN OF THE BOAR...	9176
Give Me The Night | George BENSON	698
Give Me The Reason | Luther VANDROSS	960
Give Me Your Love | Barbara MASON	7884
Give My Regards To Broad S... | Paul McCARTNEY	3380
Give The People What They Want | The KINKS	1559
Give Us A Wink | The SWEET	3445
Give Your Baby A Standing Ovati... | The DELLS	8403
Giving You The Best That I Go... | Anita BAKER	370
Givin' It Back | ISLEY BROTHERS	4286
Glad All Over | Dave CLARK Five	1115
Gladys Knight & The ... | Gladys KNIGHT & The ...	5359
The Glamorous Life | SHEILA E.	2050
Glamour | Dave DAVIES	9995
Glass House Rock | Greg KIHN Band	11599
Glass Houses | Billy JOEL	77
Glass Moon | GLASS MOON	9518
Glassworks | Philip GLASS	10477
The Glen Campbell Goodtime ... | Glen CAMPBELL	3049
Glen Campbell - "Live" | Glen CAMPBELL	1230
Glen Campbell's Greatest Hits | Glen CAMPBELL	3069
Glenn Jones | Glenn JONES	7048
Glenn Medeiros | Glenn MEDEIROS	7204
Glenn Miller's Bigge... | BOSTON POPS Orchestr...	13457
Glenn Yarbrough Sings The... | Glenn YARBROUGH	12051
Glen Travis Campbell | Glen CAMPBELL	8717
Glitter | Gary GLITTER	11545
Globe Of Frogs | Robyn HITCHCOCK And ...	7114
Gloria | SHADOWS OF KNIGHT	4979
Gloria Loring | Gloria LORING	6883
Gloria, Marty & Strings | Gloria LYNNE	3371
Glorious | Gloria GAYNOR	12537
Glorious Results Of ... | Joan JETT & The BLAC...	5655
Gloryhallastoopid (Or Pin The ... | PARLIAMENT	4576
Glory Of Love | Herbie MANN	9725
The Glory Of Love | Eddy ARNOLD	11195
Glory Road | GILLAN	12996
Glow | Al JARREAU	8132
Glow | Rick JAMES	4201
The Glow | Bonnie RAITT	3420
The Glow Of Love | CHANGE	2872
G N' R Lies | GUNS N' ROSES	360
Go [A] | Michael SHRIEVE	5785
Go [A] | Steve WINWOOD	5785
Go [A] | Stomu YAMASHTA	5785
Go | HIROSHIMA	4730
Go Ahead And Cry | RIGHTEOUS BROTHERS	3535
Go All The Way | ISLEY BROTHERS	1582
Goats Head Soup | ROLLING STONES	526
Go Away From My World | Marianne FAITHFULL	6852

Title | Act	Rank
Go Bang! | SHRIEKBACK	9923
God Bless Tiny Tim | TINY TIM	1998
Goddess In Progress | Julie BROWN	11624
Goddess Of Love | Phyllis HYMAN	8268
The Godfather | SOUNDTRACK-MOVIE	1574
The Godfather, Part II | SOUNDTRACK-MOVIE	13303
God Save The Queen/Under Hea... | Robert FRIPP	9794
God's Own Medicine | MISSION U.K.	7650
Godspell | ORIGINAL CAST	972
Godspell | SOUNDTRACK-MOVIE	2461
The Godz | The GODZ	12471
Go For It | SHALAMAR	7769
Go For The Throat | HUMBLE PIE	10561
Go For Your Guns | ISLEY BROTHERS	988
Go For Your Life | MOUNTAIN	11770
Goin' Back To Indiana | JACKSON 5	1848
Goin' Bananas | SIDE EFFECT	6855
Goin' Coconuts (Soun... | Donny & Marie OSMOND	8575
Goin' For Myself | Dennis COFFEY	6631
Going Baroque | SWINGLE SINGERS	6702
Going East | Billy PAUL	13585
Going For Broke | Eddy GRANT	6091
Going For The One | YES	1544
!!Going Places!! | Herb ALPERT & The TI...	22
Going Through The Motions | HOT CHOCOLATE	9726
Going To A Go-Go | The MIRACLES/Smokey ...	1306
Goin' Home! Their Greates... | TEN YEARS AFTER	11943
Goin' Latin | Ramsey LEWIS	6935
Goin' Off | Biz MARKIE	6712
Goin' Out Of My Head | LITTLE ANTHONY And T...	7181
Goin' Out Of My Head | The LETTERMEN	1357
Goin' Places | JACKSON 5	6494
Goin' Places | John DAVIDSON	9293
Goin' Places | Michael HENDERSON	5456
Go Insane | Lindsey BUCKINGHAM	5192
Goin' To Memphis | Paul REVERE And The ...	5134
Goin' Up In Smoke | Eddie KENDRICKS	10142
Gold | JEFFERSON AIRPLANE/S...	3657
Gold | STEELY DAN	9360
Gold & Platinum | LYNYRD SKYNYRD	1390
The Golddiggers | GOLDDIGGERS	9470
The Golden Age Of Rock 'N' Roll | SHA NA NA	3862
The Golden Age Of Wireless | Thomas DOLBY	2111
Golden Bisquits | THREE DOG NIGHT	292
Golden Boy | ORIGINAL CAST	5045
Golden Butter/The Be... | Paul BUTTERFIELD Blu...	9940
Elvis: A Golden Celebration | Elvis PRESLEY	6388
The Golden Child | SOUNDTRACK-MOVIE	10588
Golden Down | Willie NILE	10293
Golden Era, Vol. 2 | MAMAS & The PAPAS	5252
Golden Folk Song Hits... | Johnny MANN Singers	10611
Golden Girls | SILVER CONVENTION	6497
Golden Grass | GRASS ROOTS	1640
Golden Greats | Gary LEWIS And The P...	1353
Golden Greats By The Venture... | The VENTURES	3532
Golden Hits | Roger MILLER	883
Golden Hits | Roger WILLIAMS	5541
The Golden Hits Of Jerry ... | Jerry Lee LEWIS	9798
The Golden Hits Of Lesley Gore | Lesley GORE	6015
Golden Hits Of The 4 Seasons | 4 SEASONS	1698
Golden Hits Of The Smot... | SMOTHERS BROTHERS	9962
Golden Hits/The Best... | Billy VAUGHN and His...	10608
Golden Hits/The Best Of Law... | Lawrence WELK	8603
Golden Instrumentals | VARIOUS ARTISTS	12699
Golden Jubilee Concert ... | Vladimir HOROWITZ	7307
The Golden Millions | Lawrence WELK	10232

Title | Act	Rank
Elvis' Golden Records Volum... | Elvis PRESLEY	675
Golden Time Of Day | MAZE Featuring Frank...	3273
Golden Touch | ROSE ROYCE	10991
Golden Years | David BOWIE	8953
Goldfinger | SOUNDTRACK-MOVIE	334
Gold Plated | CLIMAX BLUES Band	2328
Go Little Honda | The HONDELLS	11424
Gomm With The Wind | Ian GOMM	7414
Gone Is Love | Paul MAURIAT And His...	12934
Gone Troppo | George HARRISON	10111
Gone With The Wind | SOUNDTRACK-MOVIE	2616
Gonna Take A Miracle | Laura NYRO	4817
Good And Dusty | The YOUNGBLOODS	11529
Good As Gold | RED ROCKERS	6500
Good Bad & Funky | SHOTGUN	11901
Good, Bad But Beautiful | Shirley BASSEY	12889
The Good Book | MELANIE	6680
Goodbye | CREAM	716
Goodbye And Hello | Tim BUCKLEY	12121
Goodbye, Columbus (Soundt... | The ASSOCIATION	6158
Goodbye Cruel World | Elvis COSTELLO & The...	4380
Goodbye Girl | David GATES	12052
Goodbye, Mr. Chips | SOUNDTRACK-MOVIE	11420
Good-Byes & Butterfl... | FIVE MAN ELECTRICAL ...	9492
Goodbye Yellow Brick Road | Elton JOHN	57
The Good Earth | MANFRED MANN'S EARTH...	11970
A Good Feelin' To Know | POCO	5151
Good For Your Soul | OINGO BOINGO	10767
Good High | BRICK	2447
Good King Bad | George BENSON	4632
The Good Life With The Drift... | The DRIFTERS	10033
Good Love | Meli'sa MORGAN	6845
Good Morning Starshine | OLIVER	1507
Good Morning, Vietnam | SOUNDTRACK-MOVIE	1588
Good Music | Joan JETT & The BLAC...	8423
Goodnight My Love | Paul ANKA	7448
Goodnight Vienna | Ringo STARR	1446
Good Old Boys | Randy NEWMAN	3755
Good Singin' Good Pla... | GRAND FUNK RAILROAD	6262
Good Thang | FAZE-O	11794
The Good, The Bad And Th... | SOUNDTRACK-MOVIE	690
The Good, The Bad An... | LeRoy HOLMES and His...	9450
The Good Things In Life | Tony BENNETT	12544
Good Time Charlie | Charlie McCOY	11236
Good Times (Soundtrack) | SONNY & CHER	6023
Good Times | Elvis PRESLEY	8165
Good Times | KOOL & The GANG	10138
Good To Be Back | Natalie COLE	4981
Good To Go Lover | Gwen GUTHRIE	7745
Good Trouble | REO SPEEDWAGON	1375
Good Vibrations/Best Of The Be... | BEACH BOYS	3184
Go On... | MR. MISTER	6111
The Goonies (Soundtrack) | Dave GRUSIN	8100
Gord's Gold | Gordon LIGHTFOOT	3641
Gorilla | James TAYLOR	1066
Gorky Park | GORKY PARK	6437
Gorme Country Style | Eydie GORME	12350
Got A Feeling | Patrick JUVET	8174
Got Any Gum? | Joe WALSH	9662
Got Live If You Want It! | ROLLING STONES	1518
Got My Head On Straight | Billy PAUL	9535
Got My Mojo Workin' | Jimmy SMITH	2959
Go To Heaven | GRATEFUL DEAD	2874
Go Too | Stomu YAMASHTA	11237

Title | Act	Rank
Gotta Travel On | Ray BRYANT	8176
Got To Be There | Michael JACKSON	1725
Got To Be Tough | MC SHY D	13839
Got To Find A Way | Curtis MAYFIELD	8098
Go West | GO WEST	3809
Go West | VILLAGE PEOPLE	1448
Go With The Ventures! | The VENTURES	4347
Grab It! | L'TRIMM	8382
Graceland | Paul SIMON	183
Grace Under Pressure | RUSH	1979
Gradually Going Tornado | Bill BRUFORD	13569
The Graduate (Soundtrac... | SIMON & GARFUNKEL	72
Graham Central Stati... | Larry GRAHAM/GRAHAM ...	3878
Graham Nash/David Crosby | David CROSBY/Grah...	1244
Grand Funk | GRAND FUNK RAILROAD	775
Grand Funk Hits | GRAND FUNK RAILROAD	10447
Grand Funk Lives | GRAND FUNK RAILROAD	11219
Grand Hotel | PROCOL HARUM	2776
The Grand Illusion | STYX	215
Grand Prix | SOUNDTRACK-MOVIE	4733
Grand Slam | ISLEY BROTHERS	3615
Grand Slam | SPINNERS	12100
Grasshopper | J.J. CALE	10324
Grateful Dead | GRATEFUL DEAD	3512
The Grateful Dead | GRATEFUL DEAD	4734
Grateful Dead From The Mars... | GRATEFUL DEAD	2411
Gratitude | EARTH, WIND & FIRE	310
Grave New World | STRAWBS	12683
Gravity | James BROWN	11552
Gravity | KENNY G	8325
Grazin' | FRIENDS OF DISTINCTI...	2598
Grease | SOUNDTRACK-MOVIE	46
Grease 2 | SOUNDTRACK-MOVIE	7325
Grease Band | GREASE BAND	12960
The Great Adventures Of Slick ... | SLICK RICK	2355
The Great American Eagle Trag... | EARTH OPERA	12316
Great Balls Of Fire (Soun... | Jerry Lee LEWIS	7127
Great Balls Of Fire | Dolly PARTON	4864
The Great Blind Degree | Richie HAVENS	7755
Great Contemporary I... | Ray CONNIFF & His Or...	12136
Great Country Hits | Billy VAUGHN and His...	12833
The Great Escape | SOUNDTRACK-MOVIE	5159
The Greatest | SOUNDTRACK-MOVIE	10906
Greatest American Waltzes | Connie FRANCIS	6943
Greatest Disco Hits/Mus... | SALSOUL Orchestra	7255
Greatest Hints | Michael STANLEY Band	11354
Greatest Hits(2) | Charlie RICH	10360
Greatest Hits | ABBA	2094
Greatest Hits | AIR SUPPLY	880
Greatest Hits | ALABAMA	2188
Greatest Hits | BAJA MARIMBA BAND	11684
Greatest Hits | Barry MANILOW	864
Greatest Hits | BAY CITY ROLLERS	6729
Greatest Hits | Charley PRIDE	11883
Greatest Hits | Charlie RICH	11787
Greatest Hits | CHER	10443
Greatest Hits | DAVE & SUGAR	12395
Greatest Hits | DAVE DEE, DOZY, BEAK...	12381
Greatest Hits | DAWN/Tony ORLANDO	2090
Greatest Hits | Dolly PARTON	5741
Greatest Hits | FLEETWOOD MAC	2259
Greatest Hits | George STRAIT	10846
Greatest Hits | Herb ALPERT & The TI...	3398
Greatest Hits | James TAYLOR	2220

Title | Act	Rank
Greatest Hits | Jr. WALKER & The ALL...	3710
Greatest Hits | Juice NEWTON	12579
Greatest Hits | KC And The SUNSHINE ...	8697
Greatest Hits | Kenny ROGERS & The F...	4441
Greatest Hits | Lee GREENWOOD	11644
Greatest Hits | Linda RONSTADT	518
Greatest Hits | LITTLE RIVER BAND	2929
Greatest Hits | MARSHALL TUCKER Band	3885
Greatest Hits | MARTHA & The VANDELL...	5899
Greatest Hits | Mary WELLS	2419
Greatest Hits | Melissa MANCHESTER	4754
Greatest Hits | MOODY BLUES	7950
Greatest Hits | NEW CHRISTY MINSTREL...	6439
Greatest Hits | NILSSON	10510
Greatest Hits | OAK RIDGE BOYS	6397
Greatest Hits | Paul REVERE And The ...	1084
Greatest Hits | QUEEN	1804
Greatest Hits | Ray PARKER Jr./RAYDI...	4948
Greatest Hits | Reba McENTIRE	7967
Greatest Hits | RIGHTEOUS BROTHERS	3000
Greatest Hits | Ronnie MILSAP	2466
Greatest Hits | SEALS & CROFTS	1369
Greatest Hits | Sergio MENDES And BR...	6341
Greatest Hits | SLY & THE FAMILY STO...	192
Greatest Hits | SONNY & CHER	10536
Greatest Hits | STEELY DAN	2690
Greatest Hits | Steve WARINER	13606
Greatest Hits | Stevie WONDER	2792
Greatest Hits | The ASSOCIATION	303
Greatest Hits | The CARS	1677
Greatest Hits | The JUDDS	2491
Greatest Hits | The MARVELETTES	6511
Greatest Hits | The SANDPIPERS	9856
Greatest Hits | WAR	1396
Greatest Hits | Waylon JENNINGS	823
Greatest Hits | Wes MONTGOMERY	10647
Greatest Hits | WET WILLIE	10914
Greatest Hits! | Trini LOPEZ	5882
Greatest Hits Collection | BANANARAMA	10587
Greatest Hits, Etc. | Paul SIMON	2428
The Greatest Hits From En... | VARIOUS ARTISTS	6453
The Greatest Hits From Me... | VARIOUS ARTISTS	13385
Greatest Hits From T... | The MIRACLES/Smokey ...	2682
Greatest Hits Live | Carly SIMON	7346
Greatest Hits/Live | HEART	1797
Greatest Hits 1982-1989 | CHICAGO	3996
Greatest Hits 1974-78 | Steve MILLER Band	2544
Greatest Hits 1979-1990 | Dionne WARWICK	12288
Greatest Hits 1972-1978 | 10cc	12907
Greatest Hits Of All Times | Gene PITNEY	3131
The Greatest Hits Of... | The ANIMALS/Eric BUR...	10176
Greatest Hits Of Rod McKuen | Rod McKUEN	9055
Greatest Hits Of The Outlaws/... | The OUTLAWS	9921
Greatest Hits On Earth | 5TH DIMENSION	2175
Greatest Hits Sound Of Money | Eddie MONEY	5306
Greatest Hits III | Hank WILLIAMS Jr.	4337
Greatest Hits Vol. I & II | Billy JOEL	784
Greatest Hits - Vol. II | Eddie RABBITT	9447
Greatest Hits Vol. 2 | Ronnie MILSAP	7501
Greatest Hits, Volume 2 | Linda RONSTADT	2662
Greatest Hits Vol.2 | ABBA	5607
Greatest Hits, Vol. ... | The MIRACLES/Smokey ...	1486
Greatest Hits, Vol. 2 | OAK RIDGE BOYS	6557
Greatest Hits, Vol. 2 | RIGHTEOUS BROTHERS	9429

Title | Act	Rank
Greatest Hits, Vol. II | Hank WILLIAMS Jr.	12143
Greatest Hits, Volume Two | George STRAIT	4701
Barry Manilow/Greatest Hits... | Barry MANILOW	3698
Greatest Hits Volume One | Elvis PRESLEY	10228
Greatest Hits, Volume 1 | B.J. THOMAS	4303
Greatest Hits, Volume Two | B.J. THOMAS	6470
The Greatest Live Show On... | Jerry Lee LEWIS	6590
The Greatest Of The Guess Who | GUESS WHO	12203
Greatest Stories-Live | Harry CHAPIN	4567
The Greatest Story Ever ... | SOUNDTRACK-MOVIE	7457
The Great Fatsby | Leslie WEST	11048
Great Folk Themes | Percy FAITH His Orch...	8142
The Great Gatsby | SOUNDTRACK-MOVIE	6820
Great Gonzos! The Best Of Ted ... | Ted NUGENT	9848
The Great Lost Kinks Album | The KINKS	11245
The Great March To F... | Rev. Martin Luther K...	10340
The Great Memphis Hits | KING CURTIS	10771
Great Moments On Broadway | Jerry VALE	10843
The Great Muppet Caper | SOUNDTRACK-MOVIE	6592
The Great Ones! | Jimmy ROSELLI	12899
The Great Otis Redding Sings... | Otis REDDING	12470
The Great Pretender | Dolly PARTON	7189
The Great Race (Soun... | Henry MANCINI and hi...	4892
The Great Radio Controversy | TESLA	1094
Great Scenes From Gershwin... | Leontyne PRICE	6653
The Great Songs! | Nat King COLE	12097
The Great Songs From "My Fa... | Andy WILLIAMS	1267
Great Themes From Hi... | Enoch LIGHT & The LI...	11921
Great Voices Of The Centu... | VARIOUS ARTISTS	6753
The Great Waltz | ORIGINAL CAST	11150
Great White | GREAT WHITE	9467
Great White North | Bob & Doug McKENZIE	1912
The Great Years | Johnny MATHIS	8807
Green | R.E.M.	867
Green, Green Grass Of Home | Tom JONES	3691
Greenhouse | Leo KOTTKE	8912
Green Is Blues | Al GREEN	2227
Green Light | Bonnie RAITT	4494
Greenpeace/Rainbow Warrio... | VARIOUS ARTISTS	5731
Green River | CREEDENCE CLEARWATER...	142
Green Tambourine | LEMON PIPERS	6425
Green Thoughts | The SMITHEREENS	3787
The Greeting | McCoy TYNER	12461
Greetings From Asbury P... | Bruce SPRINGSTEEN	3912
Greetings From Timbuk 3 | TIMBUK 3	3983
The Gregg Allman Tour | Gregg ALLMAN	5634
Greg Lake | Greg LAKE	5203
Gremlins | SOUNDTRACK-MOVIE	10795
Gretchen Goes To Nebraska | KING'S X	7348
Grey Ghost | Henry PAUL Band	7350
Grievous Angel | Gram PARSONS	13343
Grin | GRIN	13108
Grits Ain't Groceries | LITTLE MILTON	10025
Grits & Soul | James BROWN	9365
Gritty, Groovy, & Gettin' It | David PORTER	10296
Groove Approved | Paul CARRACK	8009
Groove-A-Thon | Isaac HAYES	5126
Groove Drops | Jimmy SMITH	13381
Groovin' | RASCALS/YOUNG RASCAL...	765
Groovin' With The Soulful... | SOULFUL STRINGS	4049
Groovin' You | Harvey MASON	9676
A Groovy Kind Of Love | The MINDBENDERS	8359
Gross Misconduct | M.O.D.	10332
a group called Smith | SMITH	1831
Growing Up In Public | Lou REED	11539
Growin' Up Too Fast | Billy RANKIN	8942

Title | Act	Rank
A GRP Christmas Collectio... | VARIOUS ARTISTS	11783
G.T.O. | RONNY And The DAYTON...	10599
GTR | GTR	1833
Guantanamera | The SANDPIPERS	1949
Guardian Of The Light | George DUKE	10913
Guess Who | B.B. KING	5065
Guess Who's Coming To Di... | SOUNDTRACK-MOVIE	12781
Guess Who's Comin' To The Crib... | FULL FORCE	9183
Guilty | Barbra STREISAND	151
Guitar Country | Chet ATKINS	8252
Guitar Freakout | The VENTURES	4673
Guitar Man | BREAD	1717
Guitar Man | Elvis PRESLEY	5506
Guitars, Cadillacs, Etc., E... | Dwight YOAKAM	3485
Guitar Slinger | Johnny WINTER	13048
Guitar Speak | VARIOUS ARTISTS	11410
Guitar Town | Steve EARLE	6821
Gula Matari | Quincy JONES	5196
Gulf Winds | Joan BAEZ	4728
Gustav Holst: The Pl... | Zubin MEHTA/LOS ANGE...	10606
Guts For Love | Garland JEFFREYS	12817
Guy | GUY	1138
Gypsy | GYPSY	3742
Gypsy Blood | Mason RUFFNER	6639
Gypsy Cowboy | NEW RIDERS Of The PU...	6830
Gypsys, Tramps & Thieves | CHER	1116

H

Title | Act	Rank
H | Bob JAMES	4595
H2O | Daryl HALL & John OA...	141
Habits Old And New | Hank WILLIAMS Jr.	7929
Hag | Merle HAGGARD	5561
Hai Hai | Roger HODGSON	11798
Hair (Original Broadway Cast) | ORIGINAL CAST	14
Hair (Original London Cast) | ORIGINAL CAST	12422
Hair | SOUNDTRACK-MOVIE	5825
Hair Of The Dog | NAZARETH	1889
Hairspray | SOUNDTRACK-MOVIE	10247
Half & Half [A] | 4 SEASONS	13471
Half & Half [A] | Frankie VALLI	13471
Half And Half | Vicki Sue ROBINSON	8551
Half A Sixpence | ORIGINAL CAST	7838
Half-Breed | CHER	3501
Half Nelson | Willie NELSON	13162
Halfway To Sanity | The RAMONES	13112
Hall & Oates Live At... | Daryl HALL & John OA...	3828
Hallelujah | CANNED HEAT	4186
Hall Of The Mountain Grill | HAWKWIND	7723
Hall Of The Mountain King | SAVATAGE	7543
Hallway Symphony | HAMILTON, JOE FRANK ...	12911
Hamburger Concerto | FOCUS	5248
Hamilton, Joe Frank ... | HAMILTON, JOE FRANK ...	5109
Hamlet | ORIGINAL CAST	8622
A Handful Of Beauty | SHAKTI With John McL...	11962
Handful Of Soul | James BROWN	11913
Handle With Care | NUCLEAR ASSAULT	6803
Hand Of Kindness | Richard THOMPSON	12876
Hands Down | Bob JAMES	6988
The Handsome Devils | HELLO PEOPLE	8566
Hand To Mouth | GENERAL PUBLIC	7428
Hang 'Em High | Hugo MONTENEGRO	11517
Hang 'Em High | SOUNDTRACK-MOVIE	12933
Hanging In There | HUDSON And LANDRY	2391
Hangin' Tough | NEW KIDS ON THE BLOC...	38
The Hangman's Beauti... | INCREDIBLE STRING BA...	10102

Title | Act	Rank
Hang On For Your Life | SHOOTING STAR	4483
Hang On In There Baby | Johnny BRISTOL	6428
Hang On Ramsey! | Ramsey LEWIS Trio	2196
Hang On Sloopy | The McCOYS	4984
Hang Together | ODYSSEY	12513
Hank Crawford's Back | Hank CRAWFORD	12560
Hank "Live" | Hank WILLIAMS Jr.	6079
Hank Williams, Jr.'s Gr... | Hank WILLIAMS Jr.	3711
Hank Wilson's Back, Vol. I | Leon RUSSELL	3880
Hanky Panky | Tommy JAMES And The ...	5403
A Happening In Central P... | Barbra STREISAND	2268
Happening 'Live!' | The OUTSIDERS	8724
The Happenings | The HAPPENINGS	6389
The Happenings Golden Hits... | The HAPPENINGS	11527
The Happiest Girl In The Whol... | Donna FARGO	2771
The Happiest Millionaire | SOUNDTRACK-MOVIE	10351
Happiness Heartaches | Brian AUGER	10146
Happiness Is | Ray CONNIFF & His Or...	8482
Happiness Is Being With The Spin... | SPINNERS	1919
Happiness Is Dean Martin | Dean MARTIN	4429
Happy? | PUBLIC IMAGE LIMITED	10907
Happy Anniversary, Charli... | VARIOUS ARTISTS	5195
Happy Birthday, Ruthy Ba... | McGUINNESS FLINT	13621
Happy Heart | Andy WILLIAMS	1374
Happy Heart | Nick DeCARO	10999
Happy Heart | Roger WILLIAMS	5061
Happy Is The Sunshine Co... | SUNSHINE COMPANY	9112
Happy Jack | The WHO	5907
Happy Just To Be Like I Am | Taj MAHAL	11751
Happy Love | Natalie COLE	11129
H.A.P.P.Y. Radio | Edwin STARR	8806
Happy Sad | Tim BUCKLEY	6265
Happy Together | The NYLONS	4223
Happy Together | The TURTLES	2997
Happy Trails | QUICKSILVER MESSENGE...	2214
The Happy Trumpet | Al HIRT	10215
Harbor | AMERICA	3749
Hard | GANG OF FOUR	12490
Hard Again | Muddy WATERS	9739
Hard Core | Paul DEAN	13732
Hardcore Jollies | FUNKADELIC	7018
Hard Core Poetry | TAVARES	6456
A Hard Day's Night (Soundtrac... | The BEATLES	159
Harder...Faster | APRIL WINE	3851
Harder Than You | 24-7 SPYZ	7606
The Harder They Come (Soundtr... | Jimmy CLIFF	9236
Hard Labor | THREE DOG NIGHT	2803
Hard Line | The BLASTERS	6438
Hard Machine | STACEY Q	8120
The Hardness Of The World | SLAVE	5904
Hard 'N' Heavy (With... | Paul REVERE And The ...	4220
Hard Nose The Highway | Van MORRISON	3353
Hard Promises | Tom PETTY And The HE...	756
Hard Rain | Bob DYLAN	3324
Hard Times For Lovers | Judy COLLINS	5153
Hard Times In The La... | OMAR And The HOWLERS	6551
Hard To Hold (Soundtrack... | Rick SPRINGFIELD	2436
Hardware | KROKUS	7284
The Hard Way | POINT BLANK	8089
Hard Work | John HANDY	3927
Harlem Nocturne | The VISCOUNTS	12884
Harlequin [A] | Dave GRUSIN	13772
Harlequin [A] | Lee RITENOUR	13772
Harmony | Anne MURRAY	11462
Harmony | Ray CONNIFF & His Or...	13039
Harmony | THREE DOG NIGHT	897

Title	Act	Rank
Harold Melvin & The ...	Harold MELVIN And Th...	3861
Harper Valley P.T.A.	Jeannie C. RILEY	1661
Harry	NILSSON	6814
Harum Scarum (Soundtrack)	Elvis PRESLEY	2325
Harvest	Neil YOUNG	218
Harvest For The World	ISLEY BROTHERS	1311
Hasten Down The Wind	Linda RONSTADT	724
Hat Trick	AMERICA	3693
Havana Candy	Patti AUSTIN	7403
Havana Daydreamin'	Jimmy BUFFETT	5822
Havana Moon	Carlos SANTANA	4798
Have A Good Time	Al GREEN	6819
Have A Marijuana	David PEEL & The LOW...	12679
Have A Smile With Me	Ray CHARLES	4834
Have You Ever Seen The...	Stanley TURRENTINE	6294
Have You Looked Into Your Hear...	Jerry VALE	4197
Have You Never Been Me...	Olivia NEWTON-JOHN	456
Have You Seen Me Lately?	Sam KINISON	4883
Having A Party	POINTER SISTERS	12829
Having A Rave Up With The Y...	The YARDBIRDS	4146
Having A Wild Weekend	Dave CLARK Five	2772
Having Fun With Elvis On St...	Elvis PRESLEY	9451
Hawaii	SOUNDTRACK-MOVIE	6340
Hawaiian Album	Ray CONNIFF & His Or...	5133
Hawaiian Wedding Song	Andy WILLIAMS	5782
Hawaii Five-O	The VENTURES	1231
Hawaii Tattoo	Martin DENNY	10150
Hawaii Tattoo	The WAIKIKIS	8742
Hawks & Doves	Neil YOUNG	4051
Head (Soundtrack)	The MONKEES	4804
The Headboys	The HEADBOYS	7525
Head East	HEAD EAST	6135
Head East Live!	HEAD EAST	6016
Headed For The Future	Neil DIAMOND	2763
Head First	The BABYS	2348
Head First	URIAH HEEP	10204
Head Games	FOREIGNER	746
Headhunter	KROKUS	2545
Head Hunters	Herbie HANCOCK	941
Heading For A Storm	VANDENBERG	11587
Headin' Home	Gary WRIGHT	10939
Headkeeper	Dave MASON	4772
The Headless Children	W.A.S.P.	5973
Headless Cross	BLACK SABBATH	9462
Headlights	The WHISPERS	5185
Headlines	MIDNIGHT STAR	4838
Head On	BACHMAN-TURNER OVERD...	2798
The Head On The Door	The CURE	3528
Head Over Heels	POCO	4842
Headquarters	The MONKEES	174
Heads	Bob JAMES	3223
Heads	OSIBISA	9315
Heads & Tales	Harry CHAPIN	4037
Heads Or Tales	SAGA	8837
Heads Up!	BAJA MARIMBA BAND	4219
Head To The Sky	EARTH, WIND & FIRE	1257
He Ain't Heavy, He's My Broth...	The HOLLIES	4106
The Healer	John Lee HOOKER	4350
Healing	Todd RUNDGREN	5372
Hear! Hear!	The SEARCHERS	9796
Hear! Here!	The HOLLIES	12338
Hear & Now	Billy SQUIER	6068
Hear 'N Aid	HEAR 'N AID	9164
Hearsay	Alexander O'NEAL	2509
Heart	HEART	81
Hearts And Bones	Paul SIMON	4180

Title	Act	Rank
Heart Attack	KROKUS	7665
Heartattack And Vine	Tom WAITS	7584
Heartbeat	Curtis MAYFIELD	4782
Heartbeat	Don JOHNSON	2602
Heartbeat City	The CARS	172
Heartbeat, It's A Lovebea...	DeFRANCO FAMILY	7116
Heart Break	NEW EDITION	733
Heart Break	SHALAMAR	5975
Heartbreaker	Dionne WARWICK	2575
Heartbreaker	Dolly PARTON	2297
Heartbreaker	FREE	4987
Heartbreak Express	Dolly PARTON	8361
Heartbreak Hotel	SOUNDTRACK-MOVIE	13338
Heartbreak Radio	Rita COOLIDGE	11965
Heart Don't Lie	LaToya JACKSON	11261
A Heart Filled With Song	John GARY	5633
Heart Land	REAL LIFE	5375
Heartland	Michael STANLEY Band	4556
Heartland	The JUDDS	4698
Heartlight	Neil DIAMOND	1294
Heart Like A Gun	FIONA	8719
Heart Like A Wheel	Linda RONSTADT	425
The Heart Never Lies	Michael MURPHEY	13329
The Heart Of A Woman	Johnny MATHIS	9276
Heart Of Hearts	Bobby VINTON	9578
Heart Of Stone	CHER	708
Heart Of The City	BARRABAS	10098
The Heart Of The Matter	Kenny ROGERS	3963
Hear To Tempt You	The TEMPTATIONS	8275
Heart Over Mind	Anne MURRAY	6268
Heart Over Mind	Jennifer RUSH	9232
Heart Play	John LENNON & Yoko O...	8462
Hearts	AMERICA	858
Heart Shaped World	Chris ISAAK	856
Heart's Horizon	Al JARREAU	5427
Hearts In Motion	AIR SUPPLY	8450
Hearts Of Stone	SOUTHSIDE JOHNNY & T...	5937
Heart String	Earl KLUGH	4016
Heart To Heart	David SANBORN	10657
Heat In The Street	Pat TRAVERS	6643
The Heat Is On	ISLEY BROTHERS	433
Heat Treatment	Graham PARKER And Th...	11398
Heat Wave	MARTHA & The VANDELL...	10890
Heaven	BeBe & CeCe WINANS	5658
Heaven And Hell	BLACK SABBATH	2701
Heaven Help The Child	Mickey NEWBURY	11933
Heaven Help The Fool	Bob WEIR	5694
Heavenly Body	The CHI-LITES	11575
Heaven On Earth	Belinda CARLISLE	797
Heaven Only Knows	Teddy PENDERGRASS	9730
Heaven Right Here On Earth	NATURAL FOUR	12968
Heaven 17	HEAVEN 17	5110
Heaven Tonight	CHEAP TRICK	3720
Heaven Up Here	ECHO & The BUNNYMEN	13377
Heavy	IRON BUTTERFLY	3434
Heavy	The STYLISTICS	4753
Heavy!	Victor BUONO	4759
Heavy Cream	CREAM	8924
Heavy Hits!	VARIOUS ARTISTS	12393
Heavy Horses	JETHRO TULL	2685
Heavy Mental	The FOOLS	11843
Heavy Metal	SOUNDTRACK-MOVIE	1716
Heavy Nova	Robert PALMER	1177
Heavy Sounds	VARIOUS ARTISTS	11494
Heavy Traffic	TRAFFIC	12110
Heavy Weather	WEATHER REPORT	2875

Title	Act	Rank
He Don't Love You (Like...	DAWN/Tony ORLANDO	3229
The Stars Of Hee Haw	SOUNDTRACK-TV	12989
Hejira	Joni MITCHELL	2267
Held Over! Today's G...	Percy FAITH His Orch...	13680
Helen Reddy	Helen REDDY	10739
Helen Reddy's Greatest Hits	Helen REDDY	983
Helicon	4 SEASONS	11446
Hell	James BROWN	3876
Hell Bent For Leather	JUDAS PRIEST	9351
Hellbound Train	SAVOY BROWN	3057
Hello Big Man	Carly SIMON	6392
Hello Darlin'	Conway TWITTY	4427
Hello Dolly!	Louis ARMSTRONG	211
Hello, Dolly! (Soundtrac...	Barbra STREISAND	2677
Hello, Dolly!	Ella FITZGERALD	13042
Hello, Dolly!	ORIGINAL CAST	98
Hello Dummy!	Don RICKLES	3730
Hello, I'm Johnny Cash	Johnny CASH	1089
Hello, I Must Be Going!	Phil COLLINS	683
Hells Angels On Wheels	SOUNDTRACK-MOVIE	13038
Hell's Angels '69	SOUNDTRACK-MOVIE	12787
Helluva Band	ANGEL	9381
Help! (Soundtrack)	The BEATLES	285
Help Is On The Way	Melissa MANCHESTER	5535
Help Me Make It Through The N...	Sammi SMITH	3200
Help Me Make It Through The Ni...	Jim NABORS	8782
Help Me Make It Through The Ni...	O.C. SMITH	10405
Help Yourself	Larry GATLIN/GATLIN ...	10716
Help Yourself	Tom JONES	362
Hemispheres	RUSH	4295
Hendrix In The West	Jimi HENDRIX	1954
Hendrix Songbook	The RUBBERBANDITS	8413
Henry Lee Summer	Henry LEE SUMMER	4265
Herb Alpert/Hugh Masekela [A]	Herb ALPERT	5055
Herb Alpert/Hugh Masekela [A]	Hugh MASEKELA	5055
Herb Alpert's Ninth	Herb ALPERT & The Ti...	785
Herb Alpert's Tijuan...	Herb ALPERT & The Ti...	1659
Herbie Mann & Fire Island	Herbie MANN	9619
Herbie Mann Live At Newport	Herbie MANN	9085
Here And There	Elton JOHN	1650
Here Are The Honeycombs	The HONEYCOMBS	13063
Here At Last...Bee Gees...Live	BEE GEES	318
Here Comes Bobby	Bobby SHERMAN	1103
Here Comes...Fats Domino	Fats DOMINO	11430
Here Comes Inspiration	Paul WILLIAMS	9881
Here Comes My Baby	The TREMELOES	9766
Here Comes Shuggie Otis	Shuggie OTIS	13712
Here Comes That Rainy Day Fe...	The FORTUNES	9204
Here Comes The Night	Barry MANILOW	3470
Here Comes The Night	David JOHANSEN	12282
Here Comes The Sun	Nina SIMONE	12681
Here Come The Hardy Boys	HARDY BOYS	13627
Here Come The Judge	Pigmeat MARKHAM	8209
Here Come The Warm Jets	Brian ENO	10569
Here I Am	Dionne WARWICK	4018
Here I Am	Sharon BRYANT	9220
Here, My Dear	Marvin GAYE	2799
Here's Love	ORIGINAL CAST	5374
Here's My Love	Linda CLIFFORD	8605
Here's The World For...	PAUL HYDE AND THE PA...	10044
Here's To Future Days	THOMPSON TWINS	1599
Here's What's Happening!	Floyd CRAMER	11515
Here They Come!	Paul REVERE And The ...	3940
Here Today, Tomorrow Next ...	The SUGARCUBES	8535
Here To Stay	Neal SCHON & Jan HAM...	8631
Here We A Go Go Again!	Johnny RIVERS	4809

Title | Act	Rank
Here We Are Again | COUNTRY JOE & The Fl...	4810
Here Where There Is Love | Dionne WARWICK	1338
Here You Come Again | Dolly PARTON	1387
Hergest Ridge | Mike OLDFIELD	7553
Her Greatest Hits | Carole KING	4713
Her Joy, Her Songs | SINGING NUN	7614
Herman Brood & His Wild Roma... | Herman BROOD	6751
Herman's Hermits On Tour | HERMAN'S HERMITS	648
Hermit Of Mink Hollow | Todd RUNDGREN	2898
Hero | Clarence CLEMONS	5746
Hero And Heroine | STRAWBS	6956
"Heroes" | David BOWIE	5054
Heroes | The COMMODORES	1169
Heroes & Zeros | Glen BURTNICK	11171
Heroes, Angels & Friends | Janey STREET	10963
Heroes Are Hard To Find | FLEETWOOD MAC	3638
He's A Friend | Eddie KENDRICKS	3977
He's All I've Got | LOVE UNLIMITED	13155
He's So Fine | Jody MILLER	9316
He's The D.J., I'm T... | D.J. JAZZY JEFF & TH...	646
He Thinks He's Ray Stevens | Ray STEVENS	8058
He Touched Me | Elvis PRESLEY	7191
He Walks Beside Me (Favorit... | Elvis PRESLEY	8528
Hey! | Julio IGLESIAS	12383
Hey! Let's Party | Mongo SANTAMARIA	10805
Heydey | The CHURCH	9685
Hey Joe | The LEAVES	10575
Hey Joe, Hey Moe [A] | Joe STAMPLEY	12250
Hey Joe, Hey Moe [A] | Moe BANDY	12250
Hey Jude | The BEATLES	574
Hey Jude | Wilson PICKETT	6197
Hey Jude/Hey Bing! | Bing CROSBY	9894
Hey Little Cobra And Other Hot... | RIP CHORDS	6170
Hey, Little One | Glen CAMPBELL	1668
Hey Now Hey (The Other Si... | Aretha FRANKLIN	3158
Hey Ricky | Melissa MANCHESTER	2350
Hickory Holler Revisited | O.C. SMITH	1757
Hideaway | AMERICA	2062
Hideaway | David SANBORN	5057
Hiding Out | SOUNDTRACK-MOVIE	8881
High Adventure | Kenny LOGGINS	1515
High And Mighty | URIAH HEEP	12251
The High And The Mighty | Donnie IRIS	12943
High Country Snows | Dan FOGELBERG	3868
High Crime | Al JARREAU	3752
High Energy | Freddie HUBBARD	10167
High Energy | The SUPREMES	4430
Higher And Higher | Jackie WILSON	11988
Higher Than High | UNDISPUTED TRUTH	12164
High Gear | Neil LARSEN	9986
High Hat | BOY GEORGE	8911
High Land, Hard Rain | AZTEC CAMERA	9488
High Lonesome | Charlie DANIELS Band	7082
Highly Distinct | FRIENDS OF DISTINCTI...	11610
Highly Prized Possession | Anne MURRAY	5872
High 'N' Dry | DEF LEPPARD	1146
High 'N' Dry(2) | DEF LEPPARD	6160
High Notes | Hank WILLIAMS Jr.	7764
High On A Ridge Top | The YOUNGBLOODS	11119
High On The Hog | BLACK OAK ARKANSAS	4574
High On You | SLY & THE FAMILY STO...	6055
High On Your Love | Debbie JACOBS	11238
High Priority | CHERRELLE	3826
High-Rise | ASHFORD & SIMPSON	7467
High Spirits | ORIGINAL CAST	6146
High Tension Wires | Steve MORSE Band	13183

Title | Act	Rank
High Voltage | AC/DC	7286
High Voltage | Eddie HARRIS	8066
Highway | FREE	13427
Highway Call | Dickey BETTS	2879
Highwayman | WILLIE, WAYLON, JOHN...	5060
Highways And Heartaches | Ricky SKAGGS	6795
Highway 61 Revisited | Bob DYLAN	945
Highway To Hell | AC/DC	1067
Hi Infidelity | REO SPEEDWAGON	27
Hillbilly Deluxe | Dwight YOAKAM	4506
Hip Hug-Her | BOOKER T. & The M.G....	3432
Hippy Hippy Shake | SWINGING BLUE JEANS	9071
Hipsway | HIPSWAY	5603
Hiroshima | HIROSHIMA	4171
His Band And The Street Choi... | Van MORRISON	3333
His California Album | Bobby BLAND	7059
His Greatest Hits | Engelbert HUMPERDINC...	6888
The Hissing Of Summer Lawns | Joni MITCHELL	1491
Historical Figures And Ancien... | CANNED HEAT	7557
Historic Dead | GRATEFUL DEAD	10251
History/America's Greatest Hits | AMERICA	352
The History Mix Vol. I | GODLEY & CREME	4909
History Of British Blues,... | VARIOUS ARTISTS	10760
History Of British Rock | VARIOUS ARTISTS	13687
History Of British Rock, Vol. 3 | VARIOUS ARTISTS	8965
History Of British Rock, Vol. 2 | VARIOUS ARTISTS	9153
History Of Eric Clapton | Eric CLAPTON	818
History Of Otis Redding | Otis REDDING	952
History Of Rhythm & Blues Vol. 4... | VARIOUS ARTISTS	12529
History Of Rhythm & Blues Vol. 1... | VARIOUS ARTISTS	13083
History Of Rhythm & Blues Vol. 3... | VARIOUS ARTISTS	13129
History Of Rhythm & Blues Vol. 2... | VARIOUS ARTISTS	12283
History Of The Grateful Dea... | GRATEFUL DEAD	6359
Hit And Run | GIRLSCHOOL	12642
Hit And Run | TSOL	13536
Hit Boots 1970 | Boots RANDOLPH	9643
Hit City 64 | The SURFARIS	10886
The Hit Man | Eddie KENDRICKS	4568
Hits! | Boz SCAGGS	2021
The Hits | REO SPEEDWAGON	4257
Hits Again! | Gary LEWIS And The P...	4416
Hits/Greatest & Others | Joan BAEZ	10833
Hits Made Famous By El... | HOLLYRIDGE STRINGS	12357
Hits 1979-1989 | Rosanne CASH	11058
The Hits Of Broadway And Hollywoo... | Ed AMES	11889
The Hit Sound Of Dean Martin | Dean MARTIN	4048
The Hit Sounds Of The Lette... | The LETTERMEN	2679
Hobo's Lullaby | Arlo GUTHRIE	3028
Hold An Old Friend's Hand | TIFFFANY	1647
Hold Me | Bert KAEMPFERT And H...	9877
Hold Me | Johnny & Jonie MOSBY	13799
Hold Me | Laura BRANIGAN	6423
Hold Me In Your Arms | Rick ASTLEY	2704
Hold Me, Thrill Me, Kiss Me | Mel CARTER	7042
Hold Me Tight | Johnny NASH	7076
Hold On | Dan HILL	6848
Hold On | Noel POINTER	7737
Hold On! (Soundtrack) | HERMAN'S HERMITS	2541
Hold On, I'm Comin' | Herbie MANN	11444
Hold On, I'm Comin' | SAM & DAVE	4755
Hold Out | Jackson BROWNE	361
Hold What You've Got | Joe TEX	10065
Hold Your Fire | RUSH	2013
Hold Your Horses | FIRST CHOICE	8577
The Hole | GOLDEN EARRING	13781
Hole In The Wall | Billy LARKIN & The D...	12930

Title | Act	Rank
Holiday | AMERICA	696
Holland | BEACH BOYS	3322
Hollies | The HOLLIES	3527
The Hollies' Greatest Hits | The HOLLIES	1678
Hollywood | Maynard FERGUSON	12896
Hollywood Dream | THUNDERCLAP NEWMAN	10070
The Hollywood Musica... [A] | Henry MANCINI and hi...	13780
The Hollywood Musicals [A] | Johnny MATHIS	13780
Hollywood-My Way | Nancy WILSON	918
Hollywood Party Tonight | ODYSSEY	9970
Hollywood Situation | HUDSON BROTHERS	12061
Hollywood, Tennessee | Crystal GAYLE	7449
Holst: The Planets | Isao TOMITA	5868
Holy Diver | DIO	3392
The Holy Land | Johnny CASH	4057
Home | BODEANS	7565
Home | PROCOL HARUM	3553
Home | Stephanie MILLS	4272
Homecoming | AMERICA	1255
The Homecoming | Hagood HARDY	7630
Home Cookin' | Jr. WALKER & The ALL...	11772
Homecooking | Sergio MENDES And BR...	13267
Home Grown | Johnny RIVERS	11098
Home, Home On The Ro... | NEW RIDERS Of The PU...	6695
Homeless Brother | Don McLEAN	8955
Homemade | The OSMONDS	1737
Home Of The Brave (Soundt... | Laurie ANDERSON	9871
Home Plate | Bonnie RAITT	5164
Homer Louis Randolph, III | Boots RANDOLPH	8973
Homesick Heros | Charlie DANIELS Band	13448
Home Style | Brook BENTON	13702
Home To Myself | Melissa MANCHESTER	9507
Home To The Sea | SAN SEBASTIAN String...	3489
Hometown Boy Makes Good | Elvin BISHOP	6944
Homeward Bound | Harry BELAFONTE	13233
Homosapien | Pete SHELLEY	9248
Honest Lullaby | Joan BAEZ	9243
Honey | Andy WILLIAMS	942
Honey | Bobby GOLDSBORO	701
Honey | OHIO PLAYERS	567
Honey | Ray CONNIFF & His Or...	1766
Honey & Wine | Glenn YARBROUGH	7942
Honey Come Back | Tony SANDLER And Ral...	13713
Honey In The Horn | Al HIRT	112
Honey In The Rock | Charlie DANIELS Band	10289
Honeymoon Suite | HONEYMOON SUITE	6185
Honeysuckle Rose (Soundtrac... | Willie NELSON	1348
The Honey Wind Blows | BROTHERS FOUR	10860
Honi Soit (o nee swa) | John CALE	11007
Honky Château | Elton JOHN	227
Honky Tonk Heroes | Waylon JENNINGS	12508
Honky-Tonk Stardust Cowb... | Jonathan EDWARDS	10381
Honor Among Thieves | The BRANDOS	7345
Hoochie Cooche Man | Jimmy SMITH	6449
Hooked On A Feeling | BLUE SWEDE	6039
Hooked On Big Bands | Frank BARBER Orchest...	7200
Hooked On Classics | ROYAL PHILHARMONIC O...	509
Hooked On Classics III... | ROYAL PHILHARMONIC O...	7419
Hooked On Classics II... | ROYAL PHILHARMONIC O...	2955
Hooked On Rock Class... | LONDON SYMPHONY Orch...	12457
Hooked On Swing | Larry ELGART And His...	2198
Hooked On Swing 2 | Larry ELGART And His...	8028
Hooker 'N Heat [A] | CANNED HEAT	5723
Hooker 'N Heat [A] | John Lee HOOKER	5723
Hooligans | The WHO	5058
The Hoople | MOTT THE HOOPLE	2722

Title	Act	Rank
Hootenanny With The Highwa...	The HIGHWAYMEN	7972
Hope	KLAATU	8588
Hopes Wishes & Dreams	Ray THOMAS	10870
Hoppkorv	HOT TUNA	8157
Horizon	CARPENTERS	1940
Horizon	Eddie RABBITT	1121
Horizontal	BEE GEES	2734
Horowitz at Carnegie Ha...	Vladimir HOROWITZ	2615
Horowitz On Television	Vladimir HOROWITZ	12300
The Horse	Cliff NOBLES & Co.	11967
The Horse	The VENTURES	8828
Horses	Patti SMITH	4231
Horseshoe In The Glove	SO	9033
Hot	HOT	7258
Hot	Maynard FERGUSON	13101
Hot! Live And Otherwise	Dionne WARWICK	6357
Hot Ash	WISHBONE ASH	13128
Hot August Night	Neil DIAMOND	570
Hot August Night II	Neil DIAMOND	5680
Hot Box	FATBACK	3614
Hot Buttered Soul	Isaac HAYES	259
Hotcakes	Carly SIMON	926
Hot Chocolate	HOT CHOCOLATE	4005
Hot City	Gene PAGE	11396
Hot, Cool And Vicious	SALT-N-PEPA	1944
Hot Dog	Lou DONALDSON	10718
Hotel California	EAGLES	56
Hot House Flowers	Wynton MARSALIS	4611
Hot In The Shade	KISS	2742
Hot Licks, Cold Stee...	COMMANDER CODY & His...	6990
Hotline	J. GEILS Band	5260
Hot Number	FABULOUS THUNDERBIRD...	5760
Hot Numbers	FOXY	3591
Hot On The Tracks	The COMMODORES	707
Hot Pants	James BROWN	2831
Hot Property	HEATWAVE	4785
Hot Rats	Frank ZAPPA	11161
Hot Rocks 1964-1971	ROLLING STONES	122
Hot Rod Hootenanny	VARIOUS ARTISTS	12313
Hot Rod Rally	VARIOUS ARTISTS	5970
Hot Shot	Pat TRAVERS	9358
Hot Sox	SHA NA NA	11198
Hot Space	QUEEN	3910
Hot Spot	DAZZ BAND	8283
Hot Streets	CHICAGO	1606
Hotter Than Hell	KISS	6332
Hotter Than July	Stevie WONDER	409
The Hottest Night Of The Year	Anne MURRAY	7898
Hot Together	POINTER SISTERS	5513
Hot Tracks	NAZARETH	9547
Hot Tuna	HOT TUNA	3486
Hot Water	Jimmy BUFFETT	5473
Hot Wire	TRAPEZE	10622
Hounds Of Love	Kate BUSH	3244
Hour Of The Wolf	STEPPENWOLF	11537
The House Of Blue Light	DEEP PURPLE	4208
The House Of Dolls	GENE LOVES JEZEBEL	6905
House Of Lords	HOUSE OF LORDS	5457
The House Of Love	HOUSE OF LOVE	11403
House Of Music	T.S. MONK	4958
The House Of The Rising S...	SANTA ESMERALDA	4827
House Party	The TEMPTATIONS	4322
Houses Of The Holy	LED ZEPPELIN	150
Houston	Dean MARTIN	1598
How 'Bout Us	CHAMPAIGN	4039
How Can I Unlove You	Lynn ANDERSON	10283

Title	Act	Rank
How Can You Be In Two Pl...	FIRESIGN THEATRE	13572
How Come The Sun	Tom PAXTON	11102
How Could It Be	Eddie MURPHY	2843
How Cruel	Joan ARMATRADING	7110
How Dare You!	10cc	5309
How Does That Grab You?	Nancy SINATRA	5180
How Do You Do?	MOUTH & MACNEAL	5784
How Glad I Am	Nancy WILSON	1328
How Great Thou Art	Elvis PRESLEY	2485
How Great Thou Art	Jim NABORS	11946
How Great Thou Art	Kate SMITH	3565
How Hard It Is	BIG BROTHER And The ...	12175
How Late'll Ya Play 'Til	David BROMBERG	7516
How Many Times Can We Say ...	Dionne WARWICK	6000
How Much, How Much I Love...	LOVE AND KISSES	6208
How Much More Can She Stand	Conway TWITTY	8139
How's Tricks	Jack BRUCE	11030
How Sweet It Is	Frank FONTAINE	7931
How Sweet It Is For Lovers	Jackie GLEASON	6866
How Sweet It Is To Be Loved B...	Marvin GAYE	9117
How The Hell Do You S...	AMAZING RHYTHM ACES	12714
How To Be A Jewish Mother	Gertrude BERG	8550
How To Beat The High Cost Of ... [A]	Hubert LAWS	11252
How To Beat The High Cost Of L... [A]	Earl KLUGH	11252
How To Be A...Zillionaire!	ABC	2014
How To Succeed In Busine...	SOUNDTRACK-MOVIE	11431
How Will I Laugh Tomo...	SUICIDAL TENDENCIES	8298
How Will The Wolf Survive	Los LOBOS	3623
How Ya Like Me Now	KOOL MOE DEE	2363
Hoy-Hoy!	LITTLE FEAT	4840
Hugh Masekela Is Alive And ...	Hugh MASEKELA	8466
Hugh Masekela's Latest	Hugh MASEKELA	9762
Humanesque	Jack GREEN	9436
Human Racing	Nik KERSHAW	5988
Humans	Bruce COCKBURN	7698
Human's Lib	Howard JONES	3602
Hums Of The Lovin' Spoonf...	LOVIN' SPOONFUL	2452
The Hunger	Michael BOLTON	3114
The Hungry Years	Neil SEDAKA	1592
Hunky Dory	David BOWIE	7314
The Hunter	BLONDIE	5810
The Hunter	Ike & Tina TURNER	12588
The Hunter	Joe SAMPLE	9115
Hunting High And Low	A-HA	1237
The Hurdy Gurdy Man	DONOVAN	2073
Hurricane Eyes	LOUDNESS	13189
Hurricane Smith	Hurricane SMITH	4954
Hurry Sundown	SOUNDTRACK-MOVIE	12834
Hurry Sundown	The OUTLAWS	4102
Hurry Up This Way Again	The STYLISTICS	8465
The Hurting	TEARS FOR FEARS	2896
Hurt So Bad	Nancy WILSON	5772
Hurt So Bad	The LETTERMEN	1629
Hush	John KLEMMER	7976
Hush, Hush, Sweet Charlotte	Patti PAGE	3383
The Hustle And Best Of Van McCo...	Van McCOY	13566
Hustle Hits	VARIOUS ARTISTS	13125
Hustle To Survive	Les McCANN	11929
Hyaena	SIOUXSIE & The BANSH...	11203
Hydra	TOTO	2631
Hymn Of The Seventh Gal...	RETURN TO FOREVER	7222
Hysteria	DEF LEPPARD	11
Hysteria	HUMAN LEAGUE	6483

I

Title	Act	Rank
I	Patrick MORAZ	10139
I (Who Have Nothing)	Tom JONES	2223
I Advance Masked	Andy SUMMERS & Rober...	6914
I Am	EARTH, WIND & FIRE	500
I Am Love	Peabo BRYSON	3840
I Am My Brother's Keeper [A]	David RUFFIN	12830
I Am My Brother's Keeper [A]	Jimmy RUFFIN	12830
I Am Not Afraid	Hugh MASEKELA	11233
I Am The Greatest!	Cassius CLAY	5667
I Am The President	David FRYE	2669
I Am What I Am	George JONES	7726
I Am Woman	Helen REDDY	802
Ian Hunter	Ian HUNTER	5542
I Appreciate	Alicia MYERS	12795
I Believe In Love	Rockie ROBBINS	10667
I Believe In Music	Mac DAVIS	8784
I Believe In You	Don WILLIAMS	3515
I Came To Dance	Nils LOFGREN	4960
I Can Dream About You	Dan HARTMAN	4341
I Can Help	Billy SWAN	2883
I Can Make It With You	POZO-SECO SINGERS	7732
I Can See Clearly No...	Ray CONNIFF & His Or...	10660
I Can See Clearly Now	Johnny NASH	2340
I Can Stand A Little Rain	Joe COCKER	1567
I Can't See Me Without You	Conway TWITTY	9641
I Can't Stand Myself (When Yo...	James BROWN	3743
I Can't Stand Still	Don HENLEY	1773
I Can't Stand The Rain	Ann PEEBLES	10694
I Capricorn	Shirley BASSEY	6696
The Iceberg (Freedom Of Speech...Just...	ICE-T	4503
Ice Castles	SOUNDTRACK-MOVIE	11812
Ice Cream Castle	The TIME	1059
Icehouse	ICEHOUSE	6263
The Ice Man Cometh	Jerry BUTLER	1519
Ice On Fire	Elton JOHN	3866
Ice On Ice	Jerry BUTLER	3569
Ice Water	Leo KOTTKE	5645
Icicle Works	ICICLE WORKS	4839
I Commit To Love	Howard HEWETT	9681
Icon	ICON	13710
I Could Have Been A Sailor	Peter ALLEN	12680
I Couldn't Live Without Your...	Petula CLARK	5035
I Could Rule The World If ...	The WAITRESSES	9196
Idea	BEE GEES	1999
Identify Yourself	The O'JAYS	2329
Idiot	Iggy POP	6199
Idlewild South	ALLMAN BROTHERS Band	3348
I'd Like To Teach Th...	Edwin HAWKINS Singer...	12356
I'd Like To Teach Th...	Ray CONNIFF & His Or...	8978
I'd Like To Teach The Wo...	HILLSIDE SINGERS	6579
I Do! I Do!	ORIGINAL CAST	6325
The Idolmaker	SOUNDTRACK-MOVIE	9086
I Do Love You	Billy STEWART	8493
I Don't Care	Buck OWENS	11265
I Don't Know How To Love Him	Helen REDDY	3769
I Don't Know What The World ...	Bobby WOMACK	10725
I Don't Speak The Language	Matthew WILDER	5732
I Don't Want To Be Hurt Any...	Nat King COLE	2689
I Don't Want To Go H...	SOUTHSIDE JOHNNY & T...	9125
I Don't Want To Lose You Ba...	CHAD & JEREMY	7864
I Don't Want To See You ...	PETER And GORDON	8183
If	IF	13441
If An Angel Came To Se...	BLACK OAK ARKANSAS	5762
I Feel A Song	Gladys KNIGHT & The ...	1343
I Feel For You	Chaka KHAN	1613
I Feel Good, I Feel Fine	Bobby BLAND	13423
I-Feel-Like-I'm-Fixi...	COUNTRY JOE & The Fl...	4737

Title | Act	Rank
If I Could Only Remember My ... | David CROSBY	2120
If I Ruled The World - Songs... | Tony BENNETT	4655
If I Should Fall From Grace Wi... | The POGUES	6736
If I Should Love Again | Barry MANILOW	1840
If I Were A Carpenter | Bobby DARIN	10856
If I Were Your Woman | Gladys KNIGHT & The ...	2820
If I Were Your Woman | Stephanie MILLS	2723
If Loving You Is Wrong I Do... | Luther INGRAM	3935
If My Ancestors Could See Me... | Ivan NEVILLE	6484
If My Friends Could See Me... | Linda CLIFFORD	2882
If Not For You | Olivia NEWTON-JOHN	11469
If That's What It Takes | Michael McDONALD	1743
If The Lights Don't Ge... | STANKY BROWN Group	13596
If The Shoe Fits | PURE PRAIRIE LEAGUE	4104
If 3 | IF	12336
If Walls Could Talk | LITTLE MILTON	13624
If We Make It Through Decem... | Merle HAGGARD	13123
If You Ain't Lovin' (You Ai... | George STRAIT	7294
If You Can Believe Your... | MAMAS & The PAPAS	216
If You Can't Lick 'Em...Lick '... | Ted NUGENT	9595
If You Ever Leave Me | Jack JONES	13450
If You Go Away | DAMITA JO	13158
If You Knew Suzi... | Suzi QUATRO	3625
(If You Let Me Make Love To ... | Ronnie DYSON	4522
If You Love Me Let Me ... | Olivia NEWTON-JOHN	561
If You're Ever In Texas | Freddy FENDER	12408
If You Want Blood You've Got It | AC/DC	7592
Ignition | John WAITE	5844
I Got A Name | Jim CROCE	566
I Gotcha | Joe TEX	2495
I Got Dem Ol' Kozmic Blues A... | Janis JOPLIN	1001
I Got Lucky | Elvis PRESLEY	8713
I Go To Pieces | PETER And GORDON	6338
I Got The Feelin' | James BROWN	7953
I Got The Melody | ODYSSEY	11886
I Got You (I Feel Good) | James BROWN	4432
Iguacu | PASSPORT	13124
I Had A Ball | ORIGINAL CAST	9891
I Had It All The Time | Tyrone DAVIS	12027
I Had To Say It | Millie JACKSON	11035
I Have A Dream | Rev. Martin Luther K...	7308
I Have A Pony | Steven WRIGHT	13756
I Have A Right | Gloria GAYNOR	6365
I Have Dreamed | The LETTERMEN	4674
I Hear A Symphony | Hank CRAWFORD	10601
I Hear A Symphony | The SUPREMES/Diana R...	1436
I Heard It In A Love... | McFADDEN & WHITEHEAD	10772
I Heard That!! | Quincy JONES	4434
I Hear Trumpets Blow | The TOKENS	12908
I Hear You Rockin' | Dave EDMUNDS	8350
I Hope We Get To Lov... | Marilyn McCOO & Bill...	2011
I Just Can't Stop It | ENGLISH BEAT	7824
I Knew Jesus (Before He Was... | Glen CAMPBELL	10972
I Know A Place | Petula CLARK	5090
I Like It Like That | Dave CLARK Five	4281
I Like Your Style | Jermaine JACKSON	7785
I'll Always Love You | Anne MURRAY	2519
I'll Be There! | GERRY And The PACEMA...	9908
Illegal Stills | Stephen STILLS	4178
The Illinois Speed P... | ILLINOIS SPEED PRESS	10592
I'll Make You Music | Beverly BREMERS	9303
I'll Never Fall In Love Ag... | Dionne WARWICK	1809
I'll Play For You | SEALS & CROFTS	3030
I'll Play The Blues For You | Albert KING	9574
I'll Prove It To You | Gregory ABBOTT	9509
I'll Remember You | Roger WILLIAMS	1785

Title | Act	Rank
I'll Search My Heart And Ot... | Johnny MATHIS	5191
I'll Share My World With You | George JONES	12105
I'll Take Care Of Your Care... | Frankie LAINE	2279
Illuminations [A] | Alice COLTRANE	7464
Illuminations [A] | Carlos SANTANA	7464
The Illusion | The ILLUSION	4087
Illusions On A Double Dimple | TRIUMVIRAT	4376
Illya Darling | ORIGINAL CAST	11380
I Looked Up | INCREDIBLE STRING BA...	13628
I Love Dixie Blues...So I R... | Merle HAGGARD	8531
I Love 'Em All | T.G. SHEPPARD	7642
I Love How You Love ... | Ray CONNIFF & His Or...	6251
I Love How You Love Me | Bobby VINTON	2407
I Love My Music | WILD CHERRY	8083
I Love Rock 'N Roll | Joan JETT & The BLAC...	467
I Love The Blues, She Heard M... | George DUKE	11401
I Love The Way You Love | Betty WRIGHT	9816
I Love To Sing The Songs I Si... | Barry WHITE	9849
I Love You | Billy VAUGHN Singers	12222
I Love You | Eddie HOLMAN	6198
I Love You | PEOPLE	9064
I Love You 1,000 Times | The PLATTERS	9517
I Love You More And More Every... | Al MARTINO	3746
I Love You More Today | Conway TWITTY	12044
I Love You So | Natalie COLE	4994
I'm A Blues Man | Z.Z. HILL	11044
I'm A Fool | DINO, DESI & BILLY	5010
Images | Ronnie MILSAP	7215
Images | The CRUSADERS	3311
Images 1966-1967 | David BOWIE	9759
Imaginary Voyage | Jean-Luc PONTY	4771
Imagination | Gladys KNIGHT & The ...	606
Imagination | The WHISPERS	2290
Imagine | John LENNON/PLASTIC ...	454
Imagine: John Lennon (Soundtr... | John LENNON	4326
Imagine This | PIECES OF A DREAM	7374
Imaginos | BLUE ÖYSTER CULT	9801
I'm All Yours-Baby! | Ray CHARLES	9539
I'm A Lonesome Fugitive | Merle HAGGARD	10401
I'm A Man | MACHO	7237
I'm A Man | Spencer DAVIS Group	7879
I'm A Writer, Not A Fi... | Gilbert O'SULLIVAN	8281
I'm Coming Home | Johnny MATHIS	6512
I'm Doin' Fine Now | NEW YORK CITY	9003
I'm Easy | Keith CARRADINE	5232
I'm Everyone I've Ever Loved | Martin MULL	13357
I'm Glad You're Here With Me... | Neil DIAMOND	1172
I'm Gonna Be A Country... | Buffy SAINTE-MARIE	10905
I'm In Love | Evelyn "Champagne" K...	3481
I'm In Love | Wilson PICKETT	6562
I'm In Love Again | Patti LaBELLE	3558
I'm In Love With You | DETROIT EMERALDS	12562
I'm In You | Peter FRAMPTON	641
Imitation Life | Robin LANE & The CHA...	12179
An Imitation Of Love | Millie JACKSON	8399
I'm Jessi Colter | Jessi COLTER	4241
I'm Just Me | Charley PRIDE	4370
I'm Leaving It All U... | Donny & Marie OSMOND	2414
I'm Leaving It Up To You | DALE & GRACE	9709
The Immortal Otis Redding | Otis REDDING	4202
I'm Nearly Famous | Cliff RICHARD	6296
I'm No Angel | Gregg ALLMAN Band	3038
I'm No Hero | Cliff RICHARD	4346
I'm Not Strange I'm Just Like... | Keith SYKES	9244
I'm On The Outside (... | LITTLE ANTHONY And T...	11568
Imperial Bedroom | Elvis COSTELLO & The...	3624

Title | Act	Rank
The Impossible Dream | Andy WILLIAMS	10469
The Impossible Dream | Jack JONES	1305
The Impossible Dream | Jerry VALE	6342
The Impossible Dream | Johnny MATHIS	11441
The Impossible Dream | Sensational Alex HAR...	13806
The Impressions | The IMPRESSIONS	3237
The Impressions Greatest ... | The IMPRESSIONS	7080
I'm Ready | Muddy WATERS	11002
I'm Ready | Natalie COLE	13182
I'm Real | James BROWN	7721
I'm So Proud | Deniece WILLIAMS	5515
I'm Still In Love With You | Al GREEN	571
I'm Telling You Now | FREDDIE And The DREA...	8204
I'm The Man | ANTHRAX	3295
I'm The Man | Joe JACKSON	2457
I'm The One | Roberta FLACK	5188
I Must Be Seeing Things | Gene PITNEY	9123
I'm Your Playmate | SUAVE	7905
I'm Yours | Linda CLIFFORD	11524
In A Broken Dream | PYTHON LEE JACKSON	11985
...In A Chamber | WIRE TRAIN	10452
In-A-Gadda-Da-Vida | IRON BUTTERFLY	15
Inamorata | POCO	11880
In And Out Of Focus | FOCUS	8521
Inarticulate Speech Of The H... | Van MORRISON	9649
In A Sentimental Mood | DR. JOHN	9840
In A Silent Way | Miles DAVIS	10153
In A Special Way | DeBARGE	2582
"In" Beat | Sandy NELSON	12940
In Black And White | Barbara MANDRELL	11471
In Black And White | Jenny BURTON	12771
In Case You're In Love | SONNY & CHER	3891
Incense And Peppermi... | STRAWBERRY ALARM CL...	2037
In City Dreams | Robin TROWER	3001
Incognito | SPYRO GYRA	4541
In Color | CHEAP TRICK	6986
The Incomparable Charley Pr... | Charley PRIDE	11992
The Incomparable Mantovani | MANTOVANI	2975
In Concert [A] | AIRTO	8514
In Concert [A] | DEODATO	8514
In Concert | Jane OLIVOR	11168
In Concert | Julio IGLESIAS	10656
In Concert | Miles DAVIS	10003
In Concert/Back By Demand | SOULFUL STRINGS	9175
In Control | The CONTROLLERS	10671
In Control Volume I | MARLEY MARL	11857
Incredible | Gary PUCKETT And The...	2036
Incredible! Live! | COUNTRY JOE & The Fl...	12559
The Incredible Base | Rob BASE	3900
Incredible Kaleidoscope | KALEIDOSCOPE	8865
The Incredible Roy Clark | Roy CLARK	13635
The Incredible Soul Of B.B. Kin... | B.B. KING	13553
The In Crowd | Ramsey LEWIS Trio	601
Indecent Exposure (Some Of ... | George CARLIN	8711
In Deep | ARGENT	7375
Indestructible | FOUR TOPS	10984
Indiana Jones And The Te... | SOUNDTRACK-MOVIE	5909
Indian Giver | 1910 FRUITGUM CO.	9573
Indian Love Call | EXOTIC GUITARS	10799
Indianola Mississippi Seeds | B.B. KING	2513
Indian Reservation | Paul REVERE And The ...	2186
Indian Summer | POCO	5017
Indigo Girls | INDIGO GIRLS	2230
Indiscreet | SPARKS	11374
Individual Choice | Jean-Luc PONTY	6959
Individually & Collectively | 5TH DIMENSION	3903

Title | Act	Rank
In Dreams | Roy ORBISON	3811
In Dreams: The Greatest Hits | Roy ORBISON	7365
Indtroducing The Har... | Terence Trent D'ARBY	535
Industry Standard | DIXIE DREGS	6169
I Need Some Money | Eddie HARRIS	9287
I Need Time | BLOODSTONE	9627
In Effect Mode | AL B. SURE!	1027
I Never Loved A Man The W... | Aretha FRANKLIN	286
I Never Picked Cotton | Roy CLARK	11680
I Never Said Goodbye | Sammy HAGAR	2316
Infected | The THE	7089
Infidels | Bob DYLAN	2773
Infinite Rider On The Big... | Michael NESMITH	9736
Infinity | JOURNEY	830
In Flight | Alvin LEE	6293
In Flight | George BENSON	984
Information | Dave EDMUNDS	4783
Information Society | INFORMATION SOCIETY	2323
In Full Effect | MANTRONIX	8961
In God We Trust | STRYPER	3647
Ingredients In A Recipe For S... | Ray CHARLES	772
In Harmony 2 | VARIOUS ARTISTS	9988
In Harmony - A Sesame Str... | VARIOUS ARTISTS	11207
In Hearing Of Atomic Roost... | ATOMIC ROOSTER	10082
In Heat | BLACK 'N BLUE	9527
In Heat | LOVE UNLIMITED	4548
In Heat | The ROMANTICS	1739
Inherit The Wind | Wilton FELDER	9210
Initiation | Todd RUNDGREN	8170
Injoy | The BAR-KAYS	3316
In London | Al JARREAU	9713
In Love | Bunny DeBARGE	12307
In Love | Cheryl LYNN	12286
In My Eyes | Stevie B	3654
In My Life | Judy COLLINS	3944
In My Little Corner Of The W... | Marie OSMOND	10325
In My Own Dream | Paul BUTTERFIELD Blu...	5748
In My Quiet Room | Harry BELAFONTE	7839
In My Tribe | 10,000 MANIACS	1750
Inner City Blues | Grover WASHINGTON Jr...	4473
Inner Conflicts | Billy COBHAM	12095
The Inner Mounting F... | John McLAUGHLIN/MAHA...	5521
Inner Secrets | SANTANA	2210
Innervisions | Stevie WONDER	146
Inner Voices | McCoy TYNER	10745
Inner Worlds | John McLAUGHLIN/MAHA...	9325
Innocence Is No Excuse | SAXON	10385
The Innocent Age | Dan FOGELBERG	443
Innocent Eyes | Graham NASH	10701
An Innocent Man | Billy JOEL	96
The Innocents | ERASURE	2313
In No Sense? Nonsense! | ART OF NOISE	10328
In 'N' Out | STONE CITY BAND	9375
In One Ear And Gone Tomor... | The BUCKINGHAMS	11107
In One Eye And Out The Other | CATE BROS.	13266
In Our Lifetime | Marvin GAYE	4021
In Outer Space | SPARKS	7493
In Person | Ike & Tina TURNER	9423
In Person At Carnegi... | CLANCY BROTHERS AND ...	7188
In Rock We Trust | Y&T	5200
Insane Asylum | Kathi McDONALD	9828
In Search Of A Song | Tom T. HALL	9741
In Search Of Freedom | Rev. Martin Luther K...	11907
In Search Of The Lost Chord | MOODY BLUES	2066
In Search Of The Rainbow Seekers | MTUME	10427
Inseparable | Natalie COLE	1354

Title | Act	Rank
In Session | CHAIRMEN OF THE BOAR...	7061
Inside | Kenny RANKIN	6370
Inside Information | FOREIGNER	1633
Inside Lookin' Out | JUNIOR	12281
Inside Moves | Grover WASHINGTON Jr...	5934
Inside Out | Philip BAILEY	7924
Inside Ronnie Milsap | Ronnie MILSAP	6892
Inside Story | Grace JONES	7187
Inside Straight | "Cannonball" ADDERLE...	12230
Inside The Electric Circus | W.A.S.P.	5898
Inside The Mind Of Bill Cosby | Bill COSBY	13010
Inside You | ISLEY BROTHERS	5749
Insight Out | The ASSOCIATION	747
Inspiration | MAZE Featuring Frank...	3644
Inspiration | Tammy WYNETTE	12952
Inspiration Information | Shuggie OTIS	12749
In Square Circle | Stevie WONDER	662
Instant Funk | INSTANT FUNK	1712
Instant Death | Eddie HARRIS	11838
Instant Groove | KING CURTIS	11910
Instant Love | Cheryl LYNN	7549
Instant Replay | Dan HARTMAN	5687
Instant Replay | The MONKEES	3669
In Step | Stevie Ray VAUGHAN A...	2430
Instinct | Iggy POP	8543
Instincts | ROMEO VOID	6040
Instrumental Directions | The NITE-LITERS	13729
In Style | David JOHANSEN	12349
Intensities In 10 Cities | Ted NUGENT	5997
Interlude | SOUNDTRACK-MOVIE	9853
Intermission | DIO	6978
International | 3° DEGREES	8365
Internationalists | STYLE COUNCIL	9162
Interview | GENTLE GIANT	10235
In The Arms Of Love | Andy WILLIAMS	2810
In The Beginning | Isaac HAYES	7297
In The Beginning | JOURNEY	10431
In The Beginning | NATURE'S DIVINE	8373
In The Beginning | Roy BUCHANAN	11087
In The Beginning/The Worl... | Aretha FRANKLIN	10006
In The Blue Canadian Rockies | MOM & DADS	11170
In The City | TAVARES	3313
Simple Minds Live: In The Ci... | SIMPLE MINDS	8616
In The Court Of The Crimson ... | KING CRIMSON	2860
In The Dark | GRATEFUL DEAD	1303
In The Eye Of The Storm | Roger HODGSON	4205
In The Eye Of The Storm | The OUTLAWS	5178
In The Garden | GYPSY	11106
In The Groove | Marvin GAYE	3942
In The Heart | KOOL & The GANG	2272
In The Heat | SOUTHSIDE JOHNNY & T...	11139
In The Heat Of The Night | Jeff LORBER	9505
In The Heat Of The Night | Pat BENATAR	478
In The Heat Of The Night | SOUNDTRACK-MOVIE	10148
In The Jungle, Babe | Charles WRIGHT And T...	11069
In The Land Of Salvati... | GEORGIA SATELLITES	9698
In The Light | Keith JARRETT	13801
In The Long Grass | BOOMTOWN RATS	13072
In The Midnight Hour | Wilson PICKETT	9955
In The Misty Moonlight | Jerry WALLACE	9722
In The Mood | ANDREWS SISTERS	13813
In The Mood For Something Rude | FOGHAT	11947
In The Mood With Tyrone Davi... | Tyrone DAVIS	7538
In The Name Of Love | Peggy LEE	10192
In The Name Of Love | THOMPSON TWINS	10702
In The Nick Of Time | Nicolette LARSON	4956

Title | Act	Rank
In The Night | Cheryl LYNN	7007
In The Night-Time | Michael HENDERSON	3340
In The Pocket | James TAYLOR	1846
In The Pocket | Neil SEDAKA	8078
In The Pocket | Stanley TURRENTINE	5847
In The Pocket | The COMMODORES	959
In The Purest Form | MASS PRODUCTION	4585
In The Right Place | DR. JOHN	2358
In The Slot | TOWER OF POWER	6637
In The Spirit Of Things | KANSAS	10122
In The Struggle For ... | Rev. Martin Luther K...	12063
In The Summer Of His Years | Connie FRANCIS	12694
In The Wake Of Poseidon | KING CRIMSON	3881
In The Wind | PETER, PAUL & MARY	115
In Through The Out Door | LED ZEPPELIN	181
Intimate Strangers | Tom SCOTT & The L.A....	7978
In Time | Engelbert HUMPERDINC...	6006
In Too Much Too Soon | NEW YORK DOLLS	11701
Into The Fire | Bryan ADAMS	1148
Into The Gap | THOMPSON TWINS	979
Into The Light | Chris De BURGH	3153
Into The Music | Van MORRISON	4586
Into The Night | SOUNDTRACK-MOVIE	9802
Into The Purple Valley | Ry COODER	8750
Into The Woods | ORIGINAL CAST	10793
Into The Woods | The CALL	8389
Introducing...David Peaston | David PEASTON	7274
Introducing Herman's Her... | HERMAN'S HERMITS	626
Introducing Johnny Rodri... | Johnny RODRIGUEZ	9101
Introducing Jonathan Buti... | Jonathan BUTLER	7639
Introducing Lobo | LOBO	8673
Introducing...The Beatles | The BEATLES	523
Introducing The Beau Brumme... | BEAU BRUMMELS	3605
Introducing The Eleventh H... | ELEVENTH HOUSE	9657
Introducing The Style Counc... | STYLE COUNCIL	12173
The Introduction | Steve MORSE Band	8454
Introspect | Joe SOUTH	7064
Introspective | PET SHOP BOYS	3873
The Intruders Greatest Hits | The INTRUDERS	9513
Intuition | LINX	12273
Intuition | TNT	8316
Invasion Of Your Privacy | RATT	1344
The Invisible Man's Band | FIVE STAIRSTEPS	6472
In Visible Silence | ART OF NOISE	3531
Invisible Tears | Johnny MANN Singers	6933
Invisible Tears | Ray CONNIFF & His Or...	3152
Invisible Touch | GENESIS	155
Invitation | Norman CONNORS	9543
Invitation To Openness | Les McCANN	10501
Invitation To The Movies/Born ... | Matt MONRO	5570
Involved | Edwin STARR	11264
INXS | INXS	12844
In Your Eyes | George BENSON	2218
In Your Face | KINGDOM COME	5943
In Your Mind | Bryan FERRY	10038
I Only Have Eyes For You | Johnny MATHIS	5490
The Ipcress File | SOUNDTRACK-MOVIE	12745
I Prefer The Moonlight | Kenny ROGERS	12610
I Put A Spell On You | Nina SIMONE	9049
I Remember Yesterday | Donna SUMMER	1167
I Remember You | Robert GOULET	7367
Irish Heartbeat [A] | The CHIEFTAINS	8013
Irish Heartbeat [A] | Van MORRISON	8013
Irish Tour '74 | Rory GALLAGHER	7973
Irma La Douce | SOUNDTRACK-MOVIE	7539
I Robot | Alan PARSONS PROJECT	850

Title	Act	Rank
Iron Age	MOTHER'S FINEST	10329
Iron Butterfly Live	IRON BUTTERFLY	2818
Iron Eagle	SOUNDTRACK-MOVIE	6850
Iron Fist	MOTORHEAD	11983
Ironhorse	IRONHORSE	9705
The Iron Man (The Musical ...	Pete TOWNSHEND	6396
Irons In The Fire	Teena MARIE	2764
Irresistible	Miles JAYE	10571
The Isaac Hayes Movement	Isaac HAYES	424
I See The Light	FIVE AMERICANS	11045
I Sing The Body Electric	WEATHER REPORT	10400
Is It In	Eddie HARRIS	7495
Is It Something I Said?	Richard PRYOR	1970
Is It Still Good To Ya	ASHFORD & SIMPSON	1754
Island Life	Grace JONES	11352
The Island Of Real	RASCALS/YOUNG RASCAL...	12814
Islands	KING CRIMSON	6804
Islands	Mike OLDFIELD	9700
Islands	The BAND	6749
The Island Story, 1962-19...	VARIOUS ARTISTS	12196
Isle Of Man	ISLE OF MAN	7684
Isleys' Greatest Hits	ISLEY BROTHERS	13398
The Isleys Live	ISLEY BROTHERS	8783
Isolation	TOTO	4564
Israelites	Desmond DEKKER And T...	11737
I Stand Alone	Al KOOPER	4805
I Started Out As A Child	Bill COSBY	938
Is That All There Is?	Peggy LEE	4862
Is This Whatcha Wont?	Barry WHITE	9594
Is This What You Want?	Jackie LOMAX	9032
It Ain't Easy	Long John BALDRY	5329
It Ain't Easy	THREE DOG NIGHT	669
It Ain't Me Babe	The TURTLES	6688
It Ain't Where You Been	LATIMORE	12132
I Take A Lot Of Pride In What...	Dean MARTIN	5467
I Take It Back	Sandy POSEY	12674
The Italian Voice Of Al Martin...	Al MARTINO	6162
Italian X Rays	Steve MILLER Band	8970
It All Comes Back	Paul BUTTERFIELD Blu...	10154
It Crawled Into My Hand, Honest	The FUGS	9582
It Feels So Good	The MANHATTANS	4618
It Happened One Bite	Dan HICKS & His HOT ...	12368
I Think I Love You	Percy FAITH His Orch...	13656
I Think Of You	Perry COMO	8130
I Think, Therefore I Am	R. Dean TAYLOR	13812
I Think We're All Bozos ...	FIRESIGN THEATRE	4738
I Think We're Alone ...	Tommy JAMES And The ...	5673
It Hurts So Good	Millie JACKSON	11777
It Hurts To Be In Love	Gene PITNEY	5550
It'll Shine When It ...	OZARK MOUNTAIN DARED...	1861
It Looks Like Snow	Phoebe SNOW	2948
It Might As Well Be ...	Frank SINATRA & Coun...	1981
It Must Be Him	Ray CONNIFF & His Or...	2222
It Must Be Him	Vikki CARR	1339
It Must Be Magic	Teena MARIE	2261
It Must Have Been Somet...	SMOTHERS BROTHERS	3404
It Never Rains In Southern...	Albert HAMMOND	6150
I Touched A Dream	The DELLS	8558
It's A Beautiful Day	IT'S A BEAUTIFUL DAY	1458
It's A Beautiful Day At C...	IT'S A BEAUTIFUL DAY	9743
It's A Beautiful Day...Today	IT'S A BEAUTIFUL DAY	8424
It's A Beautiful Thing	Maxine NIGHTINGALE	12786
It's A Big Daddy Thing	Big Daddy KANE	4071
It's About Time	John DENVER	6556
It's A Fact	Jeff LORBER	7066
It's A Game	BAY CITY ROLLERS	3544

Title	Act	Rank
It's A Good Night For S...	Jerry Jeff WALKER	7071
It's A Guitar World	Chet ATKINS	9788
It's A Heartache	Bonnie TYLER	2601
It's Alive	OZARK MOUNTAIN DARED...	12663
It's All In The Game	Cliff RICHARD	9999
It's Alright (I See Rainbows)	Yoko ONO	8084
It's Alright With Me	Patti LaBELLE	7806
It's A Mad, Mad, Mad, Ma...	SOUNDTRACK-MOVIE	8408
It's A Man's Man's Man's Worl...	James BROWN	8046
It's A Mother	James BROWN	2392
It's A New Day So Let A Man C...	James BROWN	9557
It's A Sin	Marty ROBBINS	12743
It's Been A Long Time	NEW BIRTH	3795
It's Beginning To And Back Again	WIRE	10132
It's Better To Travel	SWING OUT SISTER	2212
It's Gonna Be Fine	Glenn YARBROUGH	7430
It's Hard	The WHO	1775
It's Hard To Be Humble	Mac DAVIS	5770
It's Impossible	Perry COMO	1976
It's In Everyone Of Us	Mary TRAVERS	12344
It's Just A Matter Of Time	Sonny JAMES	12246
It's Just Begun	Jimmy CASTOR Bunch	3062
It's Like You Never Left	Dave MASON	3813
It's Magic	Jerry VALE	4985
It's My Life	TALK TALK	4469
It's My Pleasure	Billy PRESTON	4911
It's My Time	Maynard FERGUSON	13453
It's My Turn	SOUNDTRACK-MOVIE	9292
It's Not Killing Me	Mike BLOOMFIELD	10261
It's Not Unusual	Tom JONES	4035
It's Now Winters Day	Tommy ROE	12414
It's Only Love	Rita COOLIDGE	7477
It's Only Rock And Roll	Waylon JENNINGS	9025
It's Only Rock 'N Roll	ROLLING STONES	844
It's Only The Good Times	Wayne NEWTON	8278
It's Our Thing	ISLEY BROTHERS	2449
It's Over	Jimmie RODGERS	11562
It's Such A Pretty World Tod...	Wynn STEWART	10964
It's Tee Time	SWEET TEE	9772
It's The World Gone Crazy	Glen CAMPBELL	12796
It's Time	Bonnie BRAMLETT	11719
It's Time	MIGHTY CLOUDS OF JOY	11397
It's Time For Love	Teddy PENDERGRASS	2552
It's Too Late	FERRANTE & TEICHER	11592
It's Too Late To Stop Now	Van MORRISON	5142
It's True! It's True!	Bill COSBY	3517
It's Your Night	James INGRAM	2888
It's Your World	Gil SCOTT-HERON & Br...	11579
It Takes A Nation Of Million...	PUBLIC ENEMY	3085
It Takes One To Know One	DETECTIVE	7847
It Takes Two	Rob BASE	1242
It Was Almost Like A Song	Ronnie MILSAP	6841
I've Always Been Crazy	Waylon JENNINGS	4196
I've Always Wanted To Do This	Jack BRUCE	13333
I've Always Wanted To Sing.....	Bunny SIGLER	8825
I've Been Here All The Time	Luther INGRAM	10207
I've Found Someone Of My Ow...	FREE MOVEMENT	10658
I've Found Someone Of My Own	Cal SMITH	13372
I've Got A Feeling	Al WILSON	13288
I've Got A Reason	Richie FURAY Band	8818
I've Got A Tiger By The Tail	Buck OWENS	5062
I've Got Everything	Henry LEE SUMMER	6335
I've Got So Much To Give	Barry WHITE	1332
I've Gotta Be Me	Peter NERO	12999
I've Gotta Be Me	Sammy DAVIS Jr.	2360
I've Gotta Be Me	Tony BENNETT	10194

Title	Act	Rank
I've Got The Cure	Stephanie MILLS	7228
I've Got The Music In Me	Kiki DEE	3570
I've Got The Rock 'N' R...	Joe PERRY PROJECT	8075
I've Got You	Gloria GAYNOR	6657
I've Got You On My Mind Again	Buck OWENS	13603
I've Never Been To Me	CHARLENE	4478
I've Never Been To Me	Nancy WILSON	13819
Ivory Coast	Bob JAMES	13758
I Walk Alone	Marty ROBBINS	10544
I Walk The Line	Johnny CASH	5638
I Walk The Line (Soundtrack)	Johnny CASH	11453
I Wanna Be Free	Loretta LYNN	8704
I Wanna Be Selfish	ASHFORD & SIMPSON	13015
I Wanna Have Some Fun	Samantha FOX	2944
I Wanna Play For You	Stanley CLARKE	5875
I Want Candy	BOW WOW WOW	9602
I Want Candy	The STRANGELOVES	12852
I Wanted Someone To Love	Frankie LAINE	13002
I Want Out-Live	HELLOWEEN	10448
I Want To Come Back As A S...	Walter JACKSON	10734
I Want To Go With You	Eddy ARNOLD	2968
I Want To Live	John DENVER	3890
I Want You	Marvin GAYE	1026
I Was Made To Love Her	Stevie WONDER	4907
I Was The One	Elvis PRESLEY	10147
I Wear The Face	MR. MISTER	11642
I Will Follow Him	Little Peggy MARCH	12140
I Wish I Was Eighteen Again	George BURNS	7949
I Wish You Love	Gloria LYNNE	5166
I Wish You Love	Robert GOULET	13625
I Wonder Do You Think Of Me	Keith WHITLEY	10019
I Wonder What She'll Think ...	Conway TWITTY	9240
I Wonder What She's ...	Tommy BOYCE & Bobby ...	9697
I Won't Mention It Again	Ray PRICE	3508
I Wouldn't Live In New York Ci...	Buck OWENS	13544
I Wrote A Simple Song	Billy PRESTON	2286
I Wrote A Song...	Don GIBSON	12079
Izitso	Cat STEVENS	1512

J

Title	Act	Rank
Jackie	Jackie DeSHANNON	13685
Jack Jones Sings	Jack JONES	7031
Jackrabbit Slim	Steve FORBERT	2628
Jackson Browne	Jackson BROWNE	4100
Jackson 5 Anthology	JACKSON 5	7361
Jackson 5 Greatest Hits	JACKSON 5	1415
The Jacksons	JACKSON 5	3011
Jacksons Live	JACKSON 5	3402
Jack The Toad	SAVOY BROWN	6567
Jailbreak	THIN LIZZY	2063
The Jam	The JAM	11436
Jamaica Say You Will	Joe COCKER	5823
James Blonde, Secret Agen...	VARIOUS ARTISTS	8455
The James Bond Theme	Billy STRANGE	11259
James Brown...Live/Hot On The...	James BROWN	12010
James Brown Plays & Directs T...	James BROWN	3702
James Brown Plays James Brown...	James BROWN	4679
James Brown Plays New Breed	James BROWN	8293
James Brown Plays Nothing But...	James BROWN	10962
James Brown Plays The Real Th...	James BROWN	11639
James Brown Soul Classics	James BROWN	5886
The James Cotton Blues ...	James COTTON Band	13697
James Darren/All	James DARREN	13209
James Gang Live In Concert	JAMES GANG	3308
James Gang Rides Again	JAMES GANG	1313
James Taylor	James TAYLOR	3774

Title	Act	Rank
James Taylor And The Original Flying...	James TAYLOR	7505
Jammed Together [A]	Albert KING	11319
Jammed Together [A]	Pop STAPLES	11319
Jammed Together [A]	Steve CROPPER	11319
Jamming With Edward!	Nicky HOPKINS	5042
Jammin' In Manhattan	TYZIK	11948
Jam/1980's	James BROWN	6526
Jam On Revenge	NEWCLEUS	5616
Jam The Box!	Bill SUMMERS & SUMME...	6870
Jan Akkerman	Jan AKKERMAN	13700
Jan & Dean Golden Hits, Volume...	JAN & DEAN	10010
Jane Fonda's Workout Record	Jane FONDA	515
Jane Fonda's Workout Record Fo...	Jane FONDA	10101
Jane Fonda's Workout Record Ne...	Jane FONDA	10224
Janet Jackson	Janet JACKSON	4740
Janet Jackson's Rhythm Nati...	Janet JACKSON	45
Jane Wiedlin	Jane WIEDLIN	10723
Janis (Soundtrack)	Janis JOPLIN	6247
Janis Ian	Janis IAN	3239
Janis Ian (II)	Janis IAN	7940
Janis Joplin's Greatest Hits	Janis JOPLIN	4086
Japanese Whispers	The CURE	12687
Jarreau	Al JARREAU	1760
Jasmine Nightdreams	Edgar WINTER	6775
Jass-Ay-Lay-Dee	OHIO PLAYERS	6877
Jaws	SOUNDTRACK-MOVIE	3684
Jay & The Americans G...	JAY & The AMERICANS	3799
Jazz	QUEEN	1729
Jazz Blues Fusion	John MAYALL	5001
Jazzercise	Judi Sheppard MISSET...	6309
Jazz Impressions Of ...	Dave BRUBECK Quartet	11782
The Jazz Singer (Soundtrack)	Neil DIAMOND	193
The Jealous Kind	Delbert McCLINTON	3438
Jealous Lover	RAINBOW	11763
Jealousy	Major HARRIS	10558
Jealousy	NITTY GRITTY DIRT BA...	8329
Jean	Al MARTINO	13614
Jean	Lawrence WELK	9780
Jean	Ray CONNIFF & His Or...	6145
Jean Carn	Jean CARN	8760
Jean-Luc Ponty: Live	Jean-Luc PONTY	7186
Jeff Beck Group	Jeff BECK Group	2242
Jeff Beck's Guitar Shop [A]	Jeff BECK	5652
Jeff Beck's Guitar Shop [A]	Terry BOZZIO	5652
Jeff Beck's Guitar Shop [A]	Tony HYMAS	5652
Jeff Beck, Tim Bogert, Carm... [A]	Carmen APPICE	1872
Jeff Beck, Tim Bogert, Carmine ... [A]	Jeff BECK	1872
Jeff Beck, Tim Bogert, Carmine... [A]	Tim BOGERT	1872
Jeff Beck With The Jan H... [A]	Jan HAMMER Group	3483
Jeff Beck With The Jan Hammer G... [A]	Jeff BECK	3483
Jefferson Airplane	JEFFERSON AIRPLANE/S...	9181
Jefferson Airplane T...	JEFFERSON AIRPLANE/S...	9098
Jeffrey Osborne	Jeffrey OSBORNE	3334
Je M'appelle Barbra	Barbra STREISAND	1611
Jennie	ORIGINAL CAST	10238
Jennifer Warnes	Jennifer WARNES	4735
The Jerk	The LARKS	11865
Jermaine	Jermaine JACKSON	2276
Jermaine(2)	Jermaine JACKSON	4017
Jermaine Jackson	Jermaine JACKSON	1453
Jerry Butler's Golden Hits L...	Jerry BUTLER	13307
Jerry Butler Sings Assorted ...	Jerry BUTLER	12500
Jerry Knight	Jerry KNIGHT	11180
Jerry Lee Lewis	Jerry Lee LEWIS	12969
Jerry Vale Sings 16 Greatest H...	Jerry VALE	13616
Jerry Vale Sings The Great Hit...	Jerry VALE	13744

Title	Act	Rank
Jesse Johnson's Revue	Jesse JOHNSON	2193
Jessi	Jessi COLTER	8352
Jessie's Jig & Other Favori...	Steve GOODMAN	10442
Jesus Christ Superstar	ORIGINAL CAST	5067
Jesus Christ Superstar	SOUNDTRACK-MOVIE	2088
Jesus Christ Superstar	VARIOUS ARTISTS	16
Jesus Christ, Supers...	Percy FAITH His Orch...	12218
Jesus Was A Capricorn	Kris KRISTOFFERSON	1980
Je T'aime	SAINT TROPEZ	8366
Je T'Aime (Beautiful...	Jane BIRKIN & Serge ...	13613
Jethro Tull Live - Bursting O...	JETHRO TULL	2950
The Jets	The JETS	1068
Jewel Of The Nile	SOUNDTRACK-MOVIE	6057
The Jewish American Princ...	VARIOUS ARTISTS	11421
JFK The Man, The Pre...	John Fitzgerald KENN...	7049
The J. Geils Band	J. GEILS Band	13535
"Ji"	JUNIOR	6255
The Jimi Hendrix Concerts	Jimi HENDRIX	8436
Jimi Plays Monterey	Jimi HENDRIX	13459
Jimmy & Wes The Dynamic ... [A]	Wes MONTGOMERY	7257
Jimmy & Wes The Dynamic Duo [A]	Jimmy SMITH	7257
Jimmy Barnes	Jimmy BARNES	7858
Jimmy Smith's Greatest Hits!	Jimmy SMITH	10714
Jim Nabors By Request	Jim NABORS	3952
The Jim Nabors Hour	Jim NABORS	3664
Jim Nabors Sings Love Me With ...	Jim NABORS	1566
The Jim Reeves Way	Jim REEVES	5757
Jim Stafford	Jim STAFFORD	3571
Jingle Jangle	The ARCHIES	8591
Jive Bunny - The Alb...	JIVE BUNNY & The MAS...	3993
J Mood	Wynton MARSALIS	13199
Joan	Joan BAEZ	4169
Joan Armatrading	Joan ARMATRADING	4055
Joan Baez/5	Joan BAEZ	1039
The Joan Baez Ballad Book	Joan BAEZ	12171
Joan Baez In Concert, Part 2	Joan BAEZ	1140
Jody Watley	Jody WATLEY	600
Joe Cocker	Joe COCKER	3098
Joe Cocker!	Joe COCKER	466
Joe Cocker's Greatest Hits	Joe COCKER	8983
Joe Jackson's Jumpin' Jive	Joe JACKSON	4968
Joe's Garage Act I	Frank ZAPPA	3376
Joe's Garage Acts II + III	Frank ZAPPA	5706
Joe Simon...Better Than Ever	Joe SIMON	13498
Joe South's Greatest Hits	Joe SOUTH	8232
The Joey Heatherton Album	Joey HEATHERTON	8838
John Barleycorn Must Die	TRAFFIC	891
John B. Sebastian	John SEBASTIAN	2022
John Conlee's Greatest Hits	John CONLEE	11663
John Cougar	John MELLENCAMP	4481
John Davidson	John DAVIDSON	9831
John Dawson Winter III	Johnny WINTER	6104
John Denver	John DENVER	3631
John Denver's Greatest Hits	John DENVER	32
John Denver's Greatest Hits, ...	John DENVER	2118
John Eddie	John EDDIE	7183
John Fitzgerald Kenn...	John Fitzgerald KENN...	8720
John F. Kennedy - A ...	John Fitzgerald KENN...	10953
John Fogerty	John FOGERTY	7848
The John Gary Carnegie Hall Con...	John GARY	6234
John Hartford	John HARTFORD	8214
The John Lennon Collection	John LENNON	4200
John Lennon/Plastic ...	John LENNON/PLASTIC ...	1256
John Mayall-Live In Europe	John MAYALL	9976
The Johnnie Taylor Philoso...	Johnnie TAYLOR	8520
Johnnie Taylor's Greatest ...	Johnnie TAYLOR	10331

Title	Act	Rank
Johnny	Johnny MATHIS	2566
Johnny Cash	Johnny CASH	13260
Johnny Cash: America (A 200-Y...	Johnny CASH	11418
Johnny Cash At Folsom Prison	Johnny CASH	231
Johnny Cash At San Quentin	Johnny CASH	82
The Johnny Cash Collection (H...	Johnny CASH	8430
Johnny Cash's Greatest Hits, ...	Johnny CASH	2945
The Johnny Cash Show	Johnny CASH	3613
Johnny "Guitar" Wats...	Johnny Guitar WATSON	12690
Johnny Mathis' All-Time Gre...	Johnny MATHIS	7781
Johnny Mathis In Person	Johnny MATHIS	9686
Johnny Mathis Sings	Johnny MATHIS	8087
Johnny Mathis Sings The Mus...	Johnny MATHIS	11038
Johnny One Time	Brenda LEE	7321
Johnny Rivers At The Whisky...	Johnny RIVERS	1652
Johnny Rivers' Golden Hits	Johnny RIVERS	2667
Johnny Rivers In Action!	Johnny RIVERS	5402
Johnny Rivers Rocks The Fol...	Johnny RIVERS	6488
Johnny The Fox	THIN LIZZY	6900
Johnny Winter	Johnny WINTER	2266
Johnny Winter And	Johnny WINTER	11850
The Johnny Winter Story	Johnny WINTER	8840
John O'Banion	John O'BANION	11788
John Parr	John PARR	4455
John Phillips (John The Wol...	John PHILLIPS	11041
John Prine	John PRINE	12240
John Sebastian Live	John SEBASTIAN	11661
John Travolta	John TRAVOLTA	3479
John W. Anderson Presents KaSand...	KaSANDRA	8820
John Wesley Harding	Bob DYLAN	612
Join The Army	SUICIDAL TENDENCIES	8126
Jo Jo Gunne	JO JO GUNNE	4020
The Joker	Steve MILLER Band	546
Jolly What! The Beatles & Fr... [A]	Frank IFIELD	10085
Jolly What! The Beatles & Fra... [A]	The BEATLES	10085
Jonathan Butler	Jonathan BUTLER	3705
Jonathan Edwards	Jonathan EDWARDS	3838
Jonathan Livingston Seagul...	Richard HARRIS	2469
Jonathan Livingston Seagull ...	Neil DIAMOND	857
Jonathan Winters' Mad, M...	Jonathan WINTERS	12942
Jon Butcher Axis	Jon BUTCHER AXIS	7722
The Jones Girls	JONES GIRLS	4776
Joni Mitchell	Joni MITCHELL	11423
Jools & Brian	Brian AUGER	13452
Joplin In Concert	Janis JOPLIN	998
Jose Jimenez In Jollywood	Jose JIMENEZ	11455
Joseph And The Amazing Te...	VARIOUS ARTISTS	6269
Josephine	Billy VAUGHN and His...	12766
Joshua	Dolly PARTON	13804
The Joshua Tree	U2	66
Journey	JOURNEY	9192
Journeyman	Eric CLAPTON	987
Journey's Greatest Hits	JOURNEY	1069
Journey Through The Past (Soun...	Neil YOUNG	3870
Journey Through The Secret ...	Stevie WONDER	1060
Journey To Addis	THIRD WORLD	4437
Journey To A Rainbow	Chuck MANGIONE	11006
Journey To Love	Stanley CLARKE	3723
Journey To The Center Of The ...	AMBOY DUKES	5187
Journey To The Centre Of The...	Rick WAKEMAN	975
Journey To The Land Of...Ench...	ENCHANTMENT	9571
Joy	APOLLO 100	4846
Joy	Isaac HAYES	1996
Joy	ORIGINAL CAST	12937
Joy	Percy FAITH His Orch...	12092
Joy	Teddy PENDERGRASS	4293

Title | Act	Rank
Joy And Pain | MAZE Featuring Frank...	3306
Joyful | ORPHEUS	13807
Joy Of Cooking | JOY OF COOKING	6058
Joy Of Flying | Tony WILLIAMS	9272
Joyous | PLEASURE	7320
Joy Ride | The DRAMATICS	5230
Joyride | PIECES OF A DREAM	8419
The Joys Of Life | Karen BETH	11089
Joystick | DAZZ BAND	4620
Joy/The Ventures Play The Cl... | The VENTURES	11649
Joy To The World-Their Gr... | THREE DOG NIGHT	2312
JT | James TAYLOR	540
Jubilation | Paul ANKA	12984
The Judds | The JUDDS	9102
Judith | Judy COLLINS	1334
Judson Spence | Judson SPENCE	10277
Judy Collins' Fifth Album | Judy COLLINS	6971
Judy Collins #3 | Judy COLLINS	9425
Judy Garland At Home At The ... | Judy GARLAND	12825
Judy Garland's Greatest Hits | Judy GARLAND	12017
Juggernaut | MAHOGANY RUSH	13058
Juice | Juice NEWTON	485
Juice | Oran 'Juice' JONES	4627
Juicy Fruit | MTUME	3164
Juicy Fruit (Disco Freak) | Isaac HAYES	9297
JuJu Music | King Sunny ADE & His...	5866
Jukebox | DAZZ BAND	5545
Juke Joint Jump | Elvin BISHOP	3995
The Jukes | SOUTHSIDE JOHNNY & T...	4973
Julia Fordham | Julia FORDHAM	6754
Julian Cope | Julian COPE	10058
Julio | Julio IGLESIAS	1474
The July 5th Album | 5TH DIMENSION	7296
Jumpin' Gene Simmons | Jumpin' Gene SIMMONS	11185
Jumpin' Jack Flash | SOUNDTRACK-MOVIE	12473
Jumpin' The Gunne | JO JO GUNNE	10896
Jump On It | MONTROSE	9230
Jump To It | Aretha FRANKLIN	2777
Jump Up! | Elton JOHN	2274
Jungle | Dwight TWILLEY	4215
Jungle Book | SOUNDTRACK-MOVIE	1821
Jungle Fever | CHAKACHAS	8327
Jungle Grass | The AQUARIANS	13455
Junk Culture | ORCHESTRAL MANOEUVRE...	12232
Junkfood Junkie | Larry GROCE	13394
Junkyard | JUNKYARD	8314
Just A Boy | Leo SAYER	2521
Just A Game | TRIUMPH	3282
Just A Melody | YOUNG-HOLT UNLIMITED	11890
Just An Old Fashioned Love ... | Paul WILLIAMS	7000
Just Another Band From L.A. | Frank ZAPPA	7992
Just Another Day In Paradi... | Bertie HIGGINS	3556
Just Another Way To Say I Lov... | Barry WHITE	2418
Just As I Am | Bill WITHERS	3082
Just A Singer | LOBO	12504
Just A Stone's Throw Away | Valerie CARTER	11949
Just A Touch Of Love | SLAVE	6441
Just Before The Bullets... | Gregg ALLMAN Band	8857
Just Being Myself | Dionne WARWICK	11414
Just Be My Lady | Larry GRAHAM/GRAHAM ...	5422
Just Between Us | Gerald ALBRIGHT	12573
Just Coolin' | LEVERT	4465
Just Family | Dee Dee BRIDGEWATER	11173
Just Fly | PURE PRAIRIE LEAGUE	6981
Just Folks...a Firesign ... | FIRESIGN THEATRE	13367
Just For A Thrill | Earl GRANT	13094

Title | Act	Rank
Just For Love | QUICKSILVER MESSENGE...	2716
Just For Now | Nancy WILSON	5239
Just For The Record | Barbara MANDRELL	11520
Just For You | Neil DIAMOND	5798
Just Gets Better With Time | The WHISPERS	2219
Just Kiddin' Around [A] | Billy BUTTERFIELD	7074
Just Kiddin' Around [A] | Ray CONNIFF	7074
Just Like Dreamin' | TWENNYNINE	11571
Just Like The First Time | Freddie JACKSON	1264
Just Like Us! | Paul REVERE And The ...	1241
Just Lookin' For A Hit | Dwight YOAKAM	8056
+'Justments | Bill WITHERS	4760
Just Once In My Life..... | RIGHTEOUS BROTHERS	1452
Just One Night | Eric CLAPTON	545
Just Out Of Reach | Perry COMO	9383
Just Outside Of Town | MANDRILL	6612
Just Pet | Petula CLARK	11241
Just Plain Charley | Charley PRIDE	2356
Just Sylvia | SYLVIA (2)	4122
Just Testing | WISHBONE ASH	13258
Just The Two Of Us | Porter WAGONER and D...	12364
Just The Way You Like It | S.O.S. BAND	5077
Just Today | Bobby VEE	11954
Just Us | ALABAMA	4242
Just Visiting This Planet | JELLYBEAN	8333
Just Wanna Rock 'n' Roll | José FELICIANO	11856

K

Title | Act	Rank
The Kaempfert Touch | Bert KAEMPFERT And H...	9017
Kaleidoscope | Nancy WILSON	10233
Kaleidoscope World | SWING OUT SISTER	5888
Kalyan | KALYAN	12392
Kansas | KANSAS	10449
The Kansas City Song | Buck OWENS	13657
The Karate Kid | SOUNDTRACK-MOVIE	8813
The Karate Kid Part II | SOUNDTRACK-MOVIE	4025
Karla Bonoff | Karla BONOFF	3175
Karma | Pharoah SANDERS	12721
Karyn White | Karyn WHITE	1245
Kashif | KASHIF	4361
Kasim | Kasim SULTON	13759
Kate Bush | Kate BUSH	11427
The Kate Smith Anniversary Alb... | Kate SMITH	11811
Kate Smith At Carnegie Hall | Kate SMITH	6193
Kate Smith Today | Kate SMITH	12785
Kathy Smith's Aerobic Fitness | Kathy SMITH	9625
Katrina And The Waves | KATRINA & The WAVES	2451
Waves | KATRINA & The WAVES	5721
Katy Lied | STEELY DAN	2139
Kaya | Bob MARLEY And The W...	4716
KBC Band | KBC BAND	5352
KC And The Sunshine ... | KC And The SUNSHINE ...	655
KC Ten | KC And The SUNSHINE ...	7227
Keel | KEEL	7250
Keem-O-Sabe | ELECTRIC INDIAN	7809
Keeper Of The Castle | FOUR TOPS	2568
Keeper Of The Flame | Delbert McCLINTON	10792
Keeper Of The Seven Keys - Part I | HELLOWEEN	7020
Keeper Of The Seven Keys - Part II | HELLOWEEN	7960
Keeping In Touch | Anne MURRAY	8539
Keepin' Love New | Howard JOHNSON	9957
Keepin' The Summer Alive | BEACH BOYS	8848
Keep It Live | DAZZ BAND	1806
Keep It Up | LOVERBOY	1033
Keep Moving | MADNESS	9143
Keep Movin' On | Merle HAGGARD	9028

Title | Act	Rank
Keep On Bumpin' & Masterplan | The KAY-GEES	13814
Keep On Dancin' | GARY'S GANG	5752
Keep On Dancing | The GENTRYS	8245
Keep On Doing | The ROCHES	13206
Keep On It | STARPOINT	9875
Keep On Jumpin' | MUSIQUE	4830
Keep On Movin' | SOUL II SOUL	661
Keep On Moving | Paul BUTTERFIELD Blu...	7407
Keep On Moving Straight Ahead | LAKESIDE	8137
Keep On Pushing | The IMPRESSIONS	1280
Keep On Smilin' | WET WILLIE	3373
...Keep Smiling | LAID BACK	6549
Keep The Faith | BLACK OAK ARKANSAS	8091
Keep The Faith, Baby! | Adam Clayton POWELL	8587
Keep The Fire | Kenny LOGGINS	892
Keep The Fire Burning | Le ROUX	11898
Keep Your Distance | CURIOSITY KILLED THE...	4922
Keep Your Eye On Me | Herb ALPERT	1939
Keep Your Eye On The Sparro... | Merry CLAYTON	9952
Keep Your Hands Off My Power Supply | SLADE	3643
Keep Your Soul Together | Freddie HUBBARD	12656
Keith Emerson with The Nice | The NICE	10369
The Kennedy Wit (nar... | John Fitzgerald KENN...	6738
Kenny | Kenny ROGERS	503
Kenny Loggins Alive | Kenny LOGGINS	1555
Kenny Nolan | Kenny NOLAN	5880
Kenny Rankin Album | Kenny RANKIN	6065
Kenny Rogers | Kenny ROGERS	3243
Kenny Rogers' Greatest Hits | Kenny ROGERS	67
Kevin Paige | Kevin PAIGE	5524
The Key | Joan ARMATRADING	4445
Keyed Up | Ronnie MILSAP	4529
Key Lime Pie | CAMPER VAN BEETHOVEN	9277
KGB | KGB	10062
Kick | INXS	119
Kickin' | MIGHTY CLOUDS OF JOY	11476
Kick Off Your Muddy Boot... | Graeme EDGE Band	7830
Kick Out The Jams | MC5	3115
Kick The Wall | Jimmy DAVIS & JUNCTI...	9945
Kid Blue | Louise GOFFIN	7027
The Kids & Me | Billy PRESTON	3166
The Kids Are Alright (Soundtrack) | The WHO	1622
The Kids From "Fame" | KIDS FROM FAME	10094
The Kids From "Fame" Live! | KIDS FROM FAME	8599
Kihnspiracy | Greg KIHN Band	2607
Kihntagious | Greg KIHN Band	9767
Kihntinued | Greg KIHN Band	4794
Kiki Dee | Kiki DEE	11189
Kilimanjaro | TEARDROP EXPLODES	10819
Kilimanjaro | The RIPPINGTONS	7063
Kill 'Em All(2) | METALLICA	9261
Kill 'Em All | METALLICA	10471
Killer | ALICE COOPER (Grp)	773
Killer Joe | Little Jimmy OSMOND	6828
Killer On The Rampage | Eddy GRANT	1723
The "Killer" Rocks On | Jerry Lee LEWIS	7443
Killers | IRON MAIDEN	5485
Killing Me Softly | Roberta FLACK	876
Killing Me Softly With Her ... | Johnny MATHIS	9432
Killin' Time | Clint BLACK	914
Kiln House | FLEETWOOD MAC	5742
Kilroy Was Here | STYX	821
Kimono My House | SPARKS	7270
Kim Wilde | Kim WILDE	6417
Kinda Kinks | The KINKS	7166
Kind Of A Drag | The BUCKINGHAMS	8814

Title	Act	Rank
A Kind Of Hush	CARPENTERS	3533
A Kind Of Hush	John DAVIDSON	7265
A Kind Of Magic	QUEEN	6120
King & Queen [A]	Carla Thomas	3155
King & Queen [A]	Otis REDDING	3155
King Bee	Muddy WATERS	13504
The Kingbees	The KINGBEES	9430
King Cool	Donnie IRIS	4920
Kingdom Blow	Kurtis BLOW	13785
Kingdom Come	KINGDOM COME	1746
Kingdom Come	Sir Lord BALTIMORE	13642
The King Family Album	KING FAMILY	12314
The King Family Show!	KING FAMILY	4502
Kingfish	KINGFISH	6168
King Floyd	King FLOYD	10140
King Kong	SOUNDTRACK-MOVIE	9004
King Of America	Elvis COSTELLO & The...	4853
The King Of Comedy	SOUNDTRACK-MOVIE	11846
King Of Hearts	Engelbert HUMPERDINC...	8104
King Of Rock	RUN-D.M.C.	2415
King Of Rock And Roll	LITTLE RICHARD	12904
King Of Stage	Bobby BROWN	7344
King Of The Blues Guitar	Albert KING	12485
The Kings Are Here	The KINGS	4724
King Size	B.B. KING	10103
King Size Soul	KING CURTIS	10398
The Kingsmen In Person	The KINGSMEN	544
The Kingsmen On Campus	The KINGSMEN	6171
The Kingsmen, Volume 3	The KINGSMEN	3796
The Kingsmen, Volume II	The KINGSMEN	2512
Kings Of The Sun	KINGS OF THE SUN	8600
Kings Of The Wild Frontier	Adam ANT	3163
Kings Of West Coast	L.A. DREAM TEAM	10803
King's Record Shop	Rosanne CASH	8510
The Kingston Trio (Nick-Bob...	KINGSTON TRIO	6292
King Swamp	KING SWAMP	10240
The Kink Kontroversy	The KINKS	7791
The Kink Kronikles	The KINKS	6741
Kinks' Greatest-Celluloid Heroe...	The KINKS	10356
The Kinks Greatest Hits!	The KINKS	1206
Kinks Kinkdom	The KINKS	5551
Kinks-Size	The KINKS	2432
Kinky Friedman	Kinky FRIEDMAN	9597
Kismet	MANTOVANI	12160
KISS	KISS	5580
Kissin' Cousins (Soundtrack...	Elvis PRESLEY	1728
Kissing To Be Clever	CULTURE CLUB	486
Kiss Me Goodbye	Jim NABORS	6859
Kiss Me, Kiss Me, Kiss Me	The CURE	1834
Kiss The Sky	Jimi HENDRIX	11717
Kiss Unmasked	KISS	4373
Klaatu	KLAATU	4781
The Klowns	The KLOWNS	13268
Klymaxx	KLYMAXX	5944
Knee Deep In The Hoo...	JEFFERSON AIRPLANE/S...	699
Knife	AZTEC CAMERA	12262
The Knife Feels Like Justice	Brian SETZER	4695
Knights Of The Sound Table	CAMEO	5044
Knight Time	Gladys KNIGHT & The ...	8785
K-9 Posse	K-9 POSSE	7475
Knnillsson	NILSSON	8074
Knocked Out Loaded	Bob DYLAN	6410
Knock On Wood	Amii STEWART	2439
Knowledge Is King	KOOL MOE DEE	3123
Kohuept (Live In Leningrad)	Billy JOEL	4467
Ko-Ko Joe	Jerry REED	10881

Title	Act	Rank
Kokomo	KOKOMO	10433
KooKoo	Debbie HARRY	4046
Kool & The Gang Greatest ...	KOOL & The GANG	4797
Kool Jazz	KOOL & The GANG	12698
Kool Moe Dee	KOOL MOE DEE	6220
Kooper Session [A]	Al KOOPER	12340
Kooper Session [A]	Shuggie OTIS	12340
Kosmos	Isao TOMITA	8307
Kristy & Jimmy McNic...	Kristy And Jimmy McN...	11223
Krush Groove	SOUNDTRACK-MOVIE	5959
K-Scope	Phil MANZANERA	12882
Kung Fu Fighting And Other G...	Carl DOUGLAS	3758
Kurtis Blow	Kurtis BLOW	7060
Kwick	KWICK	13719
Kylie	Kylie MINOGUE	3680
L		
L	Steve HILLAGE	9012
La Bamba (Soundtrack)	Los LOBOS	743
La Bamba	Mongo SANTAMARIA	6412
L.A. Boppers	L.A. BOPPERS	7085
Labor Of Love	SPINNERS	9839
Labour Of Love	UB40	1319
Labour Of Lust	Nick LOWE	2787
Labyrinth (Soundtrack)	David BOWIE	8470
La Cage Aux Folles	ORIGINAL CAST	6420
The Lace	Benjamin ORR	6012
Lace And Whiskey	ALICE COOPER (Solo)	4292
Ladies Invited	J. GEILS Band	4600
Ladies Love Outlaws	Tom RUSH	8831
Ladies' Night	KOOL & The GANG	792
Ladies Of The Canyon	Joni MITCHELL	1795
Ladies Of The Eighties	A TASTE OF HONEY	6928
La Diva	Aretha FRANKLIN	10460
Lady	Jack JONES	3453
Lady	ONE WAY	5497
Lady Coryell	Larry CORYELL	13120
Lady Godiva	PETER And GORDON	7190
Lady In Waiting	The OUTLAWS	4884
Lady Sings The Blues (Soundtra...	Diana ROSS	387
The Lady's Not For Sale	Rita COOLIDGE	3587
Lady T	Teena MARIE	4409
L.A. Express	Tom SCOTT & The L.A....	10654
L.A. Guns	L.A. GUNS	3601
Laid Back	Gregg ALLMAN	1233
L.A. Is My Lady	Frank SINATRA	6937
L.A. Jail	Richard PRYOR	10199
Lake	LAKE	7035
La La Means I Love You	The DELFONICS	9424
La La Peace Song	Al WILSON	11095
L.A. (Light Album)	BEACH BOYS	7005
The Lamb Lies Down On Broadway	GENESIS	3688
Lament	ULTRAVOX	9469
L.A. Midnight	B.B. KING	5292
Lana!	Lana CANTRELL	12629
Landing On Water	Neil YOUNG	4928
Land Of 1000 Dances	CANNIBAL And The HEA...	11716
Land Of Dreams	Randy NEWMAN	6144
Land Of Giants	NEW CHRISTY MINSTREL...	4881
Land Of Make Believe	Chuck MANGIONE	9508
Land Of Passion	Hubert LAWS	8400
The Land Of Rape And Honey	MINISTRY	12268
Land Of The Midnight Sun	Al Di MEOLA	8779
Land Of The Third Eye	Dave VALENTIN	13577
Language	Gary MYRICK	13345
The Language Of Love	Jerry VALE	2906

Title	Act	Rank
La Pistola Y El Corazon	Los LOBOS	12621
Lapland	BALTIMORE And OHIO M...	12931
Lap Of Luxury	CHEAP TRICK	877
L.A. Reggae	Johnny RIVERS	5972
Large And In Charge	CHUNKY A	6999
Larger Than Life	Jody WATLEY	1780
Larks' Tongues In Aspic	KING CRIMSON	5910
Larry Carlton	Larry CARLTON	10170
Larry Gatlin's Great...	Larry GATLIN/GATLIN ...	10342
Larsen-Feiten Band	LARSEN-FEITEN BAND	9417
The Last Command	W.A.S.P.	4672
Last Date	Emmylou HARRIS	6017
Last Days And Time	EARTH, WIND & FIRE	5769
The Last Emperor	SOUNDTRACK-MOVIE	9946
Last Exit	TRAFFIC	2315
The Last Farewell And Oth...	Roger WHITTAKER	2782
The Last Five Years	Rick GRECH	13392
The Last In Line	DIO	2534
Last Kiss	J. Frank WILSON and ...	6792
Last Mango In Paris	Jimmy BUFFETT	5024
Last Night I Had The Strang...	MASON PROFFIT	9925
Last Night On Earth	RHYTHM HERITAGE	9824
Last Of The Brooklyn Cowboys	Arlo GUTHRIE	6805
The Last Of The Mohicans	BOW WOW WOW	6300
Last Of The Red Hot ...	FLYING BURRITO BROTH...	11229
Last Of The Runaways	GIANT	4876
Last Of The Wild One...	Johnny Van ZANT Band	11574
The Last One To Know	Reba McENTIRE	6996
The Last Poets	LAST POETS	2302
The Last Puff	SPOOKY TOOTH	6503
The Last Record Album	LITTLE FEAT	4663
Last Safe Place	Le ROUX	5089
Last Tango In Paris (Soundt...	Gato BARBIERI	11154
Last Time Around	BUFFALO SPRINGFIELD	3759
The Last Time I Saw Her	Glen CAMPBELL	7433
Last Time I Saw Him	Diana ROSS	4931
Last Train To Hicksv...	Dan HICKS & His HOT ...	5475
The Last Waltz	Engelbert HUMPERDINC...	1502
The Last Waltz (Soundtrack)	The BAND	2572
The Last Word In Lonesome	Eddy ARNOLD	4690
Late Again	PETER, PAUL & MARY	1734
Late At Night	Billy PRESTON	4719
Late For The Sky	Jackson BROWNE	1557
Late Night Guitar	Earl KLUGH	5597
Later That Same Year	Ian MATTHEWS	5518
The Latin Album	Trini LOPEZ	2947
A Latin Love-In	Tony MOTTOLA	13489
Latin Pulse	Nancy AMES	9347
The Latin Sound Of H...	Henry MANCINI and hi...	5261
LaToya Jackson	LaToya JACKSON	7702
Laugh-In	SOUNDTRACK-TV	5966
Laughing At The Piec...	DOCTOR And The MEDIC...	10482
Laugh-In '69	SOUNDTRACK-TV	6685
Laughter	Ian DURY And The BLO...	11963
Laura (What's He Got That I ...	Brook BENTON	11806
Law And Order	Lindsey BUCKINGHAM	2847
Law Of The Fish	The RADIATORS	9189
Law Of The Land	UNDISPUTED TRUTH	13519
L.A. Woman	The DOORS	766
Lawrence Welk Plays I Love ...	Lawrence WELK	12012
Lawrence Welk's "Hits Of Ou...	Lawrence WELK	6561
The Lawrence Welk Televisio...	Lawrence WELK	6817
Lawyers In Love	Jackson BROWNE	1700
Layla And Other Asso...	DEREK And The DOMINO...	627
Lazy Afternoon	Barbra STREISAND	2131
Leader Of The Pack	The SHANGRI-LAS	10091

Title | Act	Rank
Lead Me On | Amy GRANT	6711
Lead Me On | Conway TWITTY & Lore...	7395
Lead Me On | Maxine NIGHTINGALE	4575
The League Of Gentlemen | Robert FRIPP	8651
Learning To Crawl | The PRETENDERS	957
Learning To Love | Rodney FRANKLIN	13483
Leather And Lace [A] | Jessi COLTER	4276
Leather And Lace [A] | Waylon JENNINGS	4276
Leather Jackets | Elton JOHN	9037
Leatherwolf | LEATHERWOLF	7919
Leave Home | The RAMONES	8993
Leave Scars | DARK ANGEL	11351
Leaving It All Behind | GRASS ROOTS	3255
Leaving On A Jet Pla... | Percy FAITH His Orch...	6403
Le Chat Bleu | MINK DE VILLE	12341
Led Zeppelin | LED ZEPPELIN	118
Led Zeppelin IV | LED ZEPPELIN	43
Led Zeppelin III | LED ZEPPELIN	298
Led Zeppelin II | LED ZEPPELIN	42
Lee Michaels | Lee MICHAELS	3442
Lee Michaels Live | Lee MICHAELS	9551
Lee Oskar | Lee OSKAR	3247
Left Coast Live | WET WILLIE	13456
Leftoverture | KANSAS	615
Leftover Wine | MELANIE	3563
Lefty | Art GARFUNKEL	10364
Legacy | POCO	3008
Legacy | Ramsey LEWIS	10980
Legalize It | Peter TOSH	13696
Legend | Bob MARLEY And The W...	1704
Legend | LYNYRD SKYNYRD	5647
Legend | POCO	1262
Legend (Soundtrack) | TANGERINE DREAM	9748
The Legendary Christine P... | Christine McVIE	8026
Legendary Hearts | Lou REED	11381
A Legendary Performe... | Glenn MILLER Orchest...	8182
A Legendary Performe... | Henry MANCINI and hi...	11609
Elvis-A Legendary Performer, Vol. 1... | Elvis PRESLEY	3534
Elvis-A Legendary Performer, Vol. 3... | Elvis PRESLEY	8401
Elvis-A Legendary Performer, Vol. 2... | Elvis PRESLEY	4570
A Legend In My Time | Ronnie MILSAP	9918
The Legend Of Jesse James | VARIOUS ARTISTS	9149
Legends Of The Lost And Foun... | Harry CHAPIN	12360
Leif Garrett | Leif GARRETT	3352
Lemmings | NATIONAL LAMPOON	7595
Lena & Gabor [A] | Gabor SZABO	10475
Lena & Gabor [A] | Lena HORNE	10475
Lena Horne: The Lady And Her M... | Lena HORNE	8693
Lenny | SOUNDTRACK-MOVIE	12791
Lenny Bruce/Carnegie Hall | Lenny BRUCE	13181
Leo Kottke | Leo KOTTKE	8546
Leo Kottke 1971-76 Did You Hea... | Leo KOTTKE	11376
Leonard Cohen: Live Songs | Leonard COHEN	11210
Leon Live | Leon RUSSELL	1614
Leon Russell | Leon RUSSELL	4896
Leon Russell & The Shelter P... | Leon RUSSELL	1639
Leo Sayer | Leo SAYER	7236
Leprechaun | Chick COREA	4530
Lesley Gore Sings Of Mixed-Up... | Lesley GORE	9710
Les Miserables (Original Broadwa... | ORIGINAL CAST	9475
Les Miserables (Original London ... | ORIGINAL CAST	7957
Le Spank | Le PAMPLEMOUSSE	8383
Les Plus Grands Succes De Chic - Chi... | CHIC	8154
Less Than Zero | SOUNDTRACK-MOVIE	3265
Let 'Em In | Billy PAUL	5993
Let Go | Charlie BYRD	10526

Title | Act	Rank
Lethal | UTFO	5606
Lethal Weapon 2 | SOUNDTRACK-MOVIE	12847
Let It Be | Jerry VALE	12955
Let It Be (Soundtrack) | The BEATLES	301
Let It Bleed | ROLLING STONES	556
Let It Flow | Dave MASON	2320
Let It Flow | Elvin BISHOP	5873
Let It Loose | Gloria ESTEFAN/MIAMI...	297
Let It Out (Let It All Hang O... | The HOMBRES	12842
Let It Rock | JOHNNY And The DISTR...	10439
Let It Roll | LITTLE FEAT	3482
Let It Roll | TKO	13215
Let Love Rule | Lenny KRAVITZ	4377
Let Me Be Good To You | Lou RAWLS	5021
Let Me Be There | Olivia NEWTON-JOHN	4887
Let Me Be Your Angel | Stacy LATTISAW	3301
Let Me Be Your Woman | Linda CLIFFORD	3141
Let Me In Your Life | Aretha FRANKLIN	1965
Let Me Know You | Stanley CLARKE	9973
Let Me Party With You | Bunny SIGLER	6700
Let Me Sing | Brenda LEE	6133
Let Me Tell You About A Son... | Merle HAGGARD	10675
Let Me Tickle Your Fancy | Jermaine JACKSON	5115
Let Me Touch You | The O'JAYS	4975
Let Me Up (I've Had ... | Tom PETTY And The HE...	2642
Lets All Chant | Michael ZAGER Band	7461
Let's Be Friends | Elvis PRESLEY	7139
Let's Burn | Clarence CARTER	13082
Let's Clean Up The Ghetto | VARIOUS ARTISTS	9171
Let's Dance | David BOWIE	396
Let's Do It | Roy AYERS	4468
Let's Do It Again (Soundtr... | STAPLE SINGERS	2780
Let's Do It Today | Lenny WILLIAMS	13374
Let's Fall In Love | HUGO & LUIGI	12590
Let's Fall In Love | PEACHES & HERB	3040
Let's Get It On | Marvin GAYE	649
Let's Get It Started | MC HAMMER	1136
Let's Get Serious | Jermaine JACKSON	1129
Let's Get Small | Steve MARTIN	1174
Let's Go! | The VENTURES	3277
Let's Go All The Way | SLY FOX	3666
Let's Have A Party | The RIVIERAS	10863
Let's Hear It For The Bo... | Deniece WILLIAMS	4109
Let's Keep It That Way | Anne MURRAY	1444
Let's Live For Today | GRASS ROOTS	6671
Let's Make A New Dope Deal | CHEECH & CHONG	12645
Let's Make Up And Be Frien... | BONZO DOG BAND	13741
Let's Put It All Together | The STYLISTICS	1910
Let's Stay Together | Al GREEN	579
Let's Stick Together | Bryan FERRY	11287
Let's Take It To The Stage | FUNKADELIC	6669
Let's Work Together | Wilbert HARRISON	13442
Letter From Home | PAT METHENY GROUP	5480
A Letter From St. Paul | The SILENCERS	9983
The Lettermen!!!...And "Liv... | The LETTERMEN	1124
The Lettermen In Concert | The LETTERMEN	7807
A Lettermen Kind Of Love | The LETTERMEN	3917
The Lettermen Look At Love | The LETTERMEN	8770
Lettermen 1 | The LETTERMEN	10219
The Letter/Neon Rainbow | BOX TOPS	6730
A Letter To Myself | The CHI-LITES	5432
Let The Day Begin | The CALL	5288
Let The Good Times Roll | SOUNDTRACK-MOVIE	9090
Let The Hustlers Play | STEADY B	13828
Let The Music Do The Ta... | Joe PERRY PROJECT	5282
Let The Music Play | ARPEGGIO	5939

Title | Act	Rank
Let The Music Play | Barry WHITE	4725
Let The Music Play | DAZZ BAND	9221
Let The Music Play | SHANNON	2902
Let There Be Light | UNDERGROUND SUNSHINE	12154
Let There Be Music | ORLEANS	2793
Let There Be Rock | AC/DC	9538
Let The Sunshine In | The SUPREMES/Diana R...	2899
Let Us Go Into The H... | Edwin HAWKINS Singer...	2071
Levee Blues | POTLIQUOR	11167
Level Headed | The SWEET	4029
Level One | ELEVENTH HOUSE	11951
Levon Helm & The RCO All-Stars | Levon HELM	8803
The Lexicon Of Love | ABC	1505
Liberated Fantasies | George DUKE	13479
Libra | Julio IGLESIAS	8045
Licensed To Ill | BEASTIE BOYS	232
License To Dream | KLEEER	5702
License To Kill | MALICE	12477
Lick It Up | KISS	2585
Licorice Stick | Pete FOUNTAIN	2893
Lies | The KNICKERBOCKERS	10960
Life | Gladys KNIGHT & The ...	8757
Life | Neil YOUNG	7332
Life | SLY & THE FAMILY STO...	12459
Life & Love Italian Style | Jimmy ROSELLI	8235
Life & Times | Billy COBHAM	9263
Life And Times | Jim CROCE	484
The Life And Times O... | COUNTRY JOE & The Fl...	13584
Life As We Know It | REO SPEEDWAGON	2488
Life Beyond L.A. | AMBROSIA	2061
Lifeboat | SUTHERLAND BROTHERS ...	6504
Life For The Taking | Eddie MONEY	2055
Life Goes On | Paul ANKA	13521
Life Goes On | Paul WILLIAMS	8891
Life In A Tin Can | BEE GEES	6491
Life Is A Song Worth Si... | Teddy PENDERGRASS	1386
Life Is Music | RITCHIE FAMILY	7754
Life (Is So Strange) | WAR	12584
Life Is...Too Short | TOO SHORT	1549
Life Is You | BATDORF & RODNEY	8859
Lifeline | PABLO CRUISE	8643
Lifeline | Roy AYERS UBIQUITY	4579
'Life' Live | THIN LIZZY	13286
Life, Love & Pain | CLUB NOUVEAU	1155
Life Of Brian (Soundtrack) | MONTY PYTHON	12709
Lifes Rich Pageant | R.E.M.	2406
Life's Too Good | The SUGARCUBES	4009
Life Stories | Earl KLUGH	9793
Lifestyle (Living & Loving) | John KLEMMER	5302
Lighthouse | Kim CARNES	10258
Lighthouse Live! | LIGHTHOUSE	11379
Lighting Up The Night | Jack WAGNER	9390
Lightly Latin | Perry COMO	8481
Lightning Strikes | LOUDNESS	6608
Lightnin' Strikes | Lou CHRISTIE	7486
Light Of Day | SOUNDTRACK-MOVIE	8251
Light Of Life | The BAR-KAYS	5998
Light Of Smiles | Gary WRIGHT	2993
Light Of The Stable: The C... | Emmylou HARRIS	8194
Light Of Worlds | KOOL & The GANG	3331
Lights From The Valley | CHILLIWACK	12891
Light Shine | Jesse Colin YOUNG	2583
The Light Side: The Dark Sid... | Dick GREGORY	11244
Lights In The Night | FLASH & THE PAN	11228
Lights Out | Peter WOLF	3102
Lights Out | UFO	2033

Title | Act	Rank
Lights Out, Sweet Dr... | Bert KAEMPFERT And H...	9576
Light The Light | SEAWIND	8121
Light Up The Night | BROTHERS JOHNSON	1052
Like An Old Fashioned Waltz | Sandy DENNY	13664
Like A Prayer | MADONNA	202
Like A Rock | Bob SEGER	522
Like A Seed | Kenny RANKIN	11617
Like A Virgin | MADONNA	106
Like Children | Jerry GOODMAN & Jan ...	11868
Like Gangbusters | JOBOXERS	6613
Like It Is, Like It Was | The DELLS	7946
Like It Is, Was And Evermore Shal... | DONOVAN	12399
Like To Get To Know Y... | SPANKY And OUR GANG	3991
Lilies Of The Field | SOUNDTRACK-MOVIE	10335
Li'l Ol' Groovemaker...Basie! | Count BASIE	10755
Li'l Red Riding Hood | SAM THE SHAM And The...	8464
Li'l Suzy | OZONE	11378
Lincoln | THEY MIGHT BE GIANTS	6471
Linda Ronstadt | Linda RONSTADT	9814
Line Of Fire | The HEADPINS	9607
Lines | CHARLIE	6026
Link Wray | Link WRAY & His RAY ...	12686
The Lion And The Cobra | Sinead O'CONNOR	2738
Lionel Richie | Lionel RICHIE	127
The Lion In Winter | SOUNDTRACK-MOVIE	11184
Lion's Share | SAVOY BROWN	9605
Liquid Acrobat As Re... | INCREDIBLE STRING BA...	13092
Liquid Love | Freddie HUBBARD	10446
Lisa Lisa & Cult Jam... | LISA LISA And CULT J...	2849
L Is For Lover | Al JARREAU	6125
Listen | A FLOCK OF SEAGULLS	2676
Listen Like Thieves | INXS	1186
Listen To A Country Song | Lynn ANDERSON	10883
Listen To The City | Tim WEISBERG	9142
Listen To The Message | CLUB NOUVEAU	9754
Listen To The Radio | Don WILLIAMS	10894
Listen To The Warm | Rod McKUEN	12055
Listen To Your Heart | Paul ANKA	11433
Lisztomania | SOUNDTRACK-MOVIE	10110
Lita | Lita FORD	1056
Lite Me Up | Herbie HANCOCK	11350
Little America | LITTLE AMERICA	7880
Little Arrows | LEAPY LEE	5523
Little Baggariddim | UB40	4015
A Little Bit More | DR. HOOK	3778
A Little Bit Of Heaven | John GARY	2808
A Little Bit Of Love | Paul WILLIAMS	7695
Little Bit O' Soul | MUSIC EXPLOSION	13380
Little Children | Billy J. KRAMER with...	5651
Little Creatures | TALKING HEADS	1014
Little Criminals | Randy NEWMAN	1133
Little Deuce Coupe | BEACH BOYS	1132
Little Dreamer | Peter GREEN	12331
Little Games | The YARDBIRDS	8337
Little Girl | SYNDICATE OF SOUND	12759
A Little Good News | Anne MURRAY	5546
Little Green Bag | George BAKER Selecti...	9394
Little Johnny From Down ... | WILBURN BROTHERS	12315
Little Johnny Taylor | Little Johnny TAYLOR	12910
A Little Knight Musi... | Gladys KNIGHT & The ...	11851
A Little Love | AURRA	4762
The Little Mermaid | SOUNDTRACK-MOVIE	2032
Little Miss Dangerous | Ted NUGENT	6975
A Little Night Music | ORIGINAL CAST	7327
The Little Old Lady From Pasad... | JAN & DEAN	4714
Little Queen | HEART	681

Title | Act	Rank
Little Richard's Greatest ... | LITTLE RICHARD	13242
Little River Band | LITTLE RIVER BAND	5553
Little Robbers | The MOTELS	2901
Little Shop Of Horrors | SOUNDTRACK-MOVIE	5381
A Little Spice | LOOSE ENDS	5394
Little Stevie Orbit | Steve FORBERT	7032
A Little Touch Of Schmilsson In T... | NILSSON	4765
Little Wheel Spin And ... | Buffy SAINTE-MARIE	8338
Liv | Livingston TAYLOR	9193
Live [A] | David GRISMAN	8469
Live [A] | Stephane GRAPELLI	8469
Live | ALABAMA	5935
Live | George THOROGOOD & T...	2867
Live | KENNY G	933
Live | POCO	11927
Live | Reba McENTIRE	10117
Live | Sensational Alex HAR...	9795
Priest...Live | JUDAS PRIEST	5111
Live! | Bob MARLEY And The W...	7508
Live! | Brother Jack McDUFF	7218
Live! | Jr. WALKER & The ALL...	8578
Live! | Lonnie Liston SMITH	6473
Live! | The MIRACLES/Smokey ...	5612
Live! Bootleg | AEROSMITH	1691
Live! In Las Vegas | Sandy NELSON	8958
Live! Mutha | BLACK OAK ARKANSAS	13533
Live! The Ike & Tina Tu... | Ike & Tina TURNER	10489
The Live Adventures Of Mi... [A] | Mike BLOOMFIELD	1966
The Live Adventures Of Mike Blo... [A] | Al KOOPER	1966
Live After Death | IRON MAIDEN	2914
Live Album | GRAND FUNK RAILROAD	501
The Live Album | Leon RUSSELL	13388
Live Alive | Stevie Ray VAUGHAN A...	4386
Live And Dangerous | THIN LIZZY	7574
Live & In Concert | FOUR TOPS	7588
Live And In Living Color | TOWER OF POWER	8311
Live And Let Die | SOUNDTRACK-MOVIE	3111
Live And Let Live | 10cc	10454
Live And Lively | Joe TEX	6737
Live And Lowdown At The Apoll... | James BROWN	12410
Live & More | Roberta FLACK & Peab...	4726
Live And More | Donna SUMMER	187
Live And Outrageous (Rated... | Millie JACKSON	8205
Live And Sleazy | VILLAGE PEOPLE	3278
Live And Uncensored | Millie JACKSON	6337
Live & Well | B.B. KING	3007
Live At Basin St. East | Trini LOPEZ	4117
Live At Bill Graham's Fil... | VARIOUS ARTISTS	13662
Live At Carnegie Hall | Al HIRT	5011
Live At Carnegie Hall | RENAISSANCE	3921
Live At Carnegie Hall | Shirley BASSEY	9385
Liza Minnelli At Carnegie H... | Liza MINNELLI	11191
Live At Carnegie Hall/W... | Ike & Tina TURNER	2252
Live At Cobo Hall, Detr... | Hank WILLIAMS Jr.	13281
Live At Fillmore West | KING CURTIS	5379
Live At Last! | Tim WEISBERG	9815
Live At Last | Bette MIDLER	6086
Live At Leeds | The WHO	459
Live At London's Tal... | The SUPREMES/Diana R...	3837
Live At London's Talk Of ... | The TEMPTATIONS	3027
Live At P.J.'s | KOOL & The GANG	11281
Live At St. Douglas ... | Father Guido SARDUCC...	13270
Live At The Apollo, Volume II | James BROWN	2098
Live At The Bijou | Grover WASHINGTON Jr...	1765
Live At The Cafe Au Go Go | BLUES PROJECT	5534
Live At The Cocoanut Grove | Sergio FRANCHI	11311

Title | Act	Rank
Live At The Copa | The TEMPTATIONS	1608
Live At The Garden | James BROWN	4324
Live At The Greek Theatre | Vikki CARR	11333
Live At The Hollywood Bowl | The DOORS	10373
Live At The Hungry i | Glenn YARBROUGH	7566
Live At The International... | Jerry Lee LEWIS	10350
Live...London...(Condensed) | Judy GARLAND & Liza ...	11055
Live...London Palladium | Judy GARLAND & Liza ...	5258
Live At The Opera House | POINTER SISTERS	6772
Live At The Paramount (Seattle) | GUESS WHO	3597
Live At The Rainbow | FOCUS	9212
Live At The Regal | B.B. KING	7352
Live At The Riviera,... | Engelbert HUMPERDINC...	5053
Live At The Royal Festival ... | Glen CAMPBELL	11743
Live At The Sahara Tahoe | Isaac HAYES	1968
Live At The Sex Machine | KOOL & The GANG	6351
Live At The Whisky A Go Go | Herbie MANN	8980
Live At The Whisky A Go-Go On The Fabul... | X	12224
Live At The Winter Garden | Liza MINNELLI	11756
Live At Yankee Stadium | VARIOUS ARTISTS	12059
Live - Blow Your Face Out | J. GEILS Band	5415
'Live' Bullet | Bob SEGER	1030
Live Concert At The Foru... | Barbra STREISAND	2180
Live Cream | CREAM	2163
Live Cream - Volume II | CREAM	3477
Live Dates | WISHBONE ASH	6041
Live/Dead | GRATEFUL DEAD	5522
Live Evil | BLACK SABBATH	5488
Live--Evil | Miles DAVIS	7460
Live For Life | SOUNDTRACK-MOVIE	12064
Live! For Life | VARIOUS ARTISTS	10026
Live Free Or Die | BALAAM AND THE ANGEL	12973
Live From Deep In Th... | COMMANDER CODY & His...	7328
Live From Earth | Pat BENATAR	1755
Live From New York | Gilda RADNER	6166
Live - Full House | J. GEILS Band	4074
Live In Australia (With The Me... | Elton JOHN	2251
Live In Concert | Roger WHITTAKER	12691
Live In Cook County Jail | B.B. KING	1977
Live/Indian Summer | Al STEWART	7999
Live In Europe | Billy PAUL	12693
Live In Europe | CREEDENCE CLEARWATER...	9648
Live In Los Angeles | MAZE Featuring Frank...	8884
CCCP - Live In Moscow | UB40	9804
Live In New Orleans | MAZE Featuring Frank...	3045
Live In New York City | John LENNON	6213
Live! In The Air Age | BE BOP DELUXE	5418
Live In The Heart Of The City | WHITESNAKE	9363
Live...In The Raw | W.A.S.P.	7410
Live It Up | David JOHANSEN	8904
Live It Up | ISLEY BROTHERS	1969
Live/Johnny Winter And | Johnny WINTER	2922
The Live Kinks | The KINKS	12077
Live Madison Square Garden Cen... | Bill COSBY	11063
A Live Mutherforya | VARIOUS ARTISTS	10387
Live 1980/86 | Joe JACKSON	8144
Live 'N' Kickin' | KINGFISH	8067
Live 'N' Kickin' | WEST, BRUCE & LAING	11426
Live Nude Guitars | Brian SETZER	10112
Live Oblivion, Vol. 1 | Brian AUGER	5595
Live Oblivion, Vol. 2 | Brian AUGER	12067
Live - On Tour In Europe [A] | Billy COBHAM	8533
Live - On Tour In Europe [A] | George DUKE	8533
The Plastic Ono Band... | John LENNON/PLASTIC ...	1382
Live + 1 | FREHLEY'S COMET	7718
Liverpool | FRANKIE GOES TO HOLL...	7904

Title	Act	Rank
Live Rust	Neil YOUNG	1911
Live Sentence	ALCATRAZZ	9951
Live Shots	Joe ELY	12352
Lives In The Balance	Jackson BROWNE	2388
Live-Stompin' At The Savoy	RUFUS	3462
Live, Takin' The Stag...	PURE PRAIRIE LEAGUE	6699
Livetime	Daryl HALL & John OA...	5803
Live Wire/Blues Power	Albert KING	8796
Live Without A Net	ANGEL	11321
Livin' For You	Al GREEN	2579
Living	Judy COLLINS	5503
Living A Lie	Al MARTINO	2346
Living All Alone	Phyllis HYMAN	5179
Living And Dying In 3/4 Tim...	Jimmy BUFFETT	9947
Living Black!	Charles EARLAND	11275
Living By The Days	Don NIX	13284
Living Eyes	BEE GEES	4869
Living In A Box	LIVING IN A BOX	8228
Living In A Fantasy	Leo SAYER	3287
Living In Oz	Rick SPRINGFIELD	1024
Living Inside Your Love	Earl KLUGH	13470
Living In The Background	BALTIMORA	5711
Living In The Material Wo...	George HARRISON	768
Living In The Past	JETHRO TULL	736
Living In The 20th Cent...	Steve MILLER Band	4898
Living In The U.S.A.	Linda RONSTADT	614
Living Large...	HEAVY D & The BOYZ	7214
Living My Life	Grace JONES	5960
Living Proof	SYLVESTER	8113
Living Room Suite	Harry CHAPIN	9267
Living Soul	"Groove" HOLMES	11995
Livingston Taylor	Livingston TAYLOR	6092
Living The Blues(2)	CANNED HEAT	13225
Living The Blues	CANNED HEAT	2352
Living Together	Burt BACHARACH	12005
Living Together, Growing To...	5TH DIMENSION	7899
Living With The Animals	MOTHER EARTH	8935
Living Years	MIKE + THE MECHANICS	1784
Livin' Inside Your Love	George BENSON	1317
Livin' It Up!	Jimmy SMITH	9604
Livin' Large	E.U.	10763
Livin' On The Fault Line	DOOBIE BROTHERS	2121
Liza! Liza!	Liza MINNELLI	9531
Liza Minnelli The Singer	Liza MINNELLI	4081
Lizard	KING CRIMSON	8189
Liza With A "Z" (Soundtrack...	Liza MINNELLI	2295
Liz Damon's Orient E...	Liz DAMON'S ORIENT E...	13514
Loading Zone	Roy BUCHANAN	8607
Loc-ed After Dark	TONE-LOC	560
Locked In	WISHBONE ASH	8923
Lodger	David BOWIE	2881
Loggins And Messina	LOGGINS & MESSINA	1209
Lola Versus Powerman And The Mo...	The KINKS	4181
Lo Mucho Que Te Quiero	RENÉ & RENÉ	8169
London Calling	The CLASH	2150
The London Chuck Berry Sessio...	Chuck BERRY	812
The London Howlin' Wolf Sess...	HOWLIN' WOLF	5567
London 0 Hull 4	The HOUSEMARTINS	8922
London Town	Paul McCARTNEY & WIN...	607
London Underground	Herbie MANN	8114
Lone Justice	LONE JUSTICE	4424
Lonely Again	Eddy ARNOLD	4871
Lonely Guitar	Duane EDDY	13012
A Lonely Man	The CHI-LITES	1034
The Lonely Things	Glenn YARBROUGH	5003
Lone Rhino	Adrian BELEW	8606
Lonesome	Sammi SMITH	13415
Lonesome Cities	Rod McKUEN	11300
The Lonesome Jubilee	John MELLENCAMP	385
The Lonesome Picker Rides Ag...	John STEWART	13593
The Lonesomest Lonesome	Ray PRICE	8447
Lonewolf	Michael MURPHEY	8971
Long After Dark	Tom PETTY And The HE...	1188
Long Cold Winter	CINDERELLA	455
Long Distance Voyager	MOODY BLUES	305
Longer Fuse	Dan HILL	2706
Long Hard Climb	Helen REDDY	969
Long Hard Look	Lou GRAMM	5850
Long Hard Ride	MARSHALL TUCKER Band	3148
Long John Silver	JEFFERSON AIRPLANE/S...	2478
Long Live Rock 'N' Roll	RAINBOW	7070
Long Live The Kane	Big Daddy KANE	6922
Long Live The New Flesh	FLESH FOR LULU	5955
Long Lonesome Highway	Michael PARKS	2942
Long May You Run [A]	Neil YOUNG	3108
Long May You Run [A]	Stephen STILLS	3108
Long Misty Days	Robin TROWER	2517
Long Player	SMALL FACES/FACES	3401
The Long Run	EAGLES	89
Long Stroke	ADC BAND	8964
A Long Time Comin'	ELECTRIC FLAG	2918
Long Time Coming	READY FOR THE WORLD	3519
Long Way To Heaven	HELIX	7272
The Look	SHALAMAR	4254
Look Around	Sergio MENDES And BR...	442
Look At Me	The MOMENTS (2)	9384
Look At Us	SONNY & CHER	549
Look At Yourself	URIAH HEEP	5696
Look Hear?	10cc	13310
Lookin' Back	4 SEASONS	8669
Lookin' For A Love Again	Bobby WOMACK	5703
Lookin' For Love	Johnny LEE	7234
Lookin' For Trouble	Joyce KENNEDY	7572
Lookin' For Trouble	TORONTO	12778
Looking Back	John MAYALL	6184
Looking Back	Nat King COLE	6356
Looking Back	Stevie WONDER	4426
Looking For Jack	Colin James HAY	9974
Looking For Love (Soundtra...	Connie FRANCIS	9426
Looking For Mr. Goodbar	SOUNDTRACK-MOVIE	9343
Looking Glass	LOOKING GLASS	6796
Looking In	SAVOY BROWN	3907
Looking Through The Eyes Of L...	Gene PITNEY	4111
Lookin' Through The Windows	JACKSON 5	1100
Look Into The Future	JOURNEY	6445
Look-Ka Py Py	The METERS	13669
The Look Of Love	Claudine LONGET	3524
The Look Of Love	Dusty SPRINGFIELD	9691
The Look Of Love	Stanley TURRENTINE	13115
The Look Of Love And...	MIDNIGHT STRING QUAR...	13300
Look Out	20/20	8272
Look Out For #1	BROTHERS JOHNSON	685
Look Out For The Che...	Bob KUBAN And The IN...	10797
Look Sharp!	Joe JACKSON	1841
Look Sharp!	ROXETTE	948
Looks So Fine	INSTANT FUNK	10845
Look To The Rainbow: Live In E...	Al JARREAU	4860
Look What The Cat Dragged In	POISON	293
Look What You're Doing To The...	Melba MOORE	11337
Loose	CRAZY HORSE	11138
Loosen Up Naturally	SONS OF CHAMPLIN	8917
Loose Salute	Michael NESMITH	11634
Lord Jim	SOUNDTRACK-MOVIE	10970
Lord, Mr. Ford	Jerry REED	12806
Lord Of The Rings	Bo HANSSON	10710
The Lord Of The Rings	SOUNDTRACK-MOVIE	4559
The Lord's Prayer And Other Sa...	Jim NABORS	9081
Lord Sutch And Heavy...	LORD SUTCH And HEAVY...	6577
Los Cochinos	CHEECH & CHONG	374
Los Hombres Malo	The OUTLAWS	8672
Losing Their Heads	HUDSON And LANDRY	2680
Lost & Found	JASON & The SCORCHER...	7378
Lost And Found	HUMBLE PIE	3951
Lost And Found	Michael PARKS	13795
Lost Boys	SOUNDTRACK-MOVIE	2813
Lost Horizon	SOUNDTRACK-MOVIE	5117
Lost In A Dream	REO SPEEDWAGON	7109
Lost In Love	AIR SUPPLY	719
Lost In Space	JONZUN CREW	5571
Lost In The Fifties Tonight	Ronnie MILSAP	9010
Lost In The Ozone	COMMANDER CODY & His...	4247
Lost Without Your Love	BREAD	3396
A Lot Of Love	Melba MOORE	6246
Lou Christie	Lou CHRISTIE	10472
Loud And Clear	AUTOGRAPH	7696
Louder Than Bombs	The SMITHS	5598
Louder Than Hell	Sam KINISON	12637
Loud 'N' Proud	NAZARETH	10363
Louisiana's Le Roux	Le ROUX	7627
Louisiana Woman, Mis...	Conway TWITTY & Lore...	9924
Lou Rawls Carryin' On!	Lou RAWLS	2273
Lou Rawls Live(2)	Lou RAWLS	9302
Lou Rawls Live	Lou RAWLS	460
Lou Rawls Soulin'	Lou RAWLS	832
Lou Reed	Lou REED	13499
Lou Reed Live	Lou REED	6317
L.O.V.E.	Paul MAURIAT And His...	12839
Love	AZTEC CAMERA	13393
Love	LOVE	5401
Love	The CULT	4998
L-O-V-E	Nat King COLE	1062
Love Action	SNIFF 'N' The TEARS	13539
Love Affair	Ray CONNIFF & His Or...	5964
The Love Album	Trini LOPEZ	4301
Love All The Hurt Away	Aretha FRANKLIN	4327
Love Among The Canni...	JEFFERSON AIRPLANE/S...	5544
Love An Adventure	PSEUDO ECHO	4170
Love And Dancing	HUMAN LEAGUE	10540
Love & Guitars	Eddy ARNOLD	13110
Love & Hope & Sex & Dreams	BODEANS	7399
Love And Kisses	LOVE AND KISSES	7859
Love And Rockets	LOVE AND ROCKETS	1913
Love And Touch	Tyrone DAVIS	7528
Love & Understanding	KOOL & The GANG	5243
Love, Andy	Andy WILLIAMS	1657
Love Approach	Tom BROWNE	2114
Love At First Sting	SCORPIONS	650
Love At The Greek	Neil DIAMOND	2135
Love Beach	EMERSON, LAKE & PALM...	6479
Love Bomb	The TUBES	8239
Love Book	The LETTERMEN	6347
Love Breeze	Smokey ROBINSON	5922
Love Byrd	Donald BYRD And 125t...	7845
Love Changes	KASHIF	7036
Love Child	The SUPREMES/Diana R...	2107
Love Confessions	Miki HOWARD	8664
Love Corporation	HUES CORPORATION	10698
Love Country Style	Ray CHARLES	12862

Title	Act	Rank
Love Crazy	The MIRACLES	10008
Love Current	Lenny WILLIAMS	7994
Love Devotion Surrender [A]	Carlos SANTANA	2505
Love Devotion Surrender [A]	John McLAUGHLIN	2505
Lovedrive	SCORPIONS	4697
Love Fantasy	Roy AYERS	12159
Love Fever	The O'JAYS	9043
Love For Love	The WHISPERS	3562
Love Gun	KISS	1314
Love Him!	Doris DAY	9116
Love Hysteria	Peter MURPHY	7762
Love-In	Charles LLOYD Quarte...	11849
Love In C Minor	CERRONE	9271
Love Is	The ANIMALS/Eric BUR...	8146
Love Is A Five Letter W...	Jimmy WITHERSPOON	13088
Love Is All Around	Eric BURDON & WAR	10459
Love Is All Around	The TROGGS	8395
Love Is All We Have To G...	CHECKMATES, LTD.	12060
Love Is A Sacrifice	SOUTHSIDE JOHNNY & T...	5663
Love Is A Soft Touch	FERRANTE & TEICHER	13378
Love Is Blue	Al MARTINO	5127
Love Is Blue	Claudine LONGET	2956
Love Is Blue	Johnny MATHIS	2234
Love Is Blue	Lawrence WELK	8686
Love Is Blue	Manny KELLEM, His Or...	13718
Love Is Blue	The DELLS	3598
Love Is Everything	Johnny MATHIS	6565
Love Is Fair	Barbara MANDRELL	11990
Love Is For Suckers	TWISTED SISTER	7504
Love Is In The Air	John Paul YOUNG	6681
Love Is Just A Game	Larry GATLIN/GATLIN ...	11823
Love Island	DEODATO	6674
Love Is...One Way	ONE WAY	10366
Love Is Such A Funny Game	Michael COOPER	5974
Love Is The Foundation	Loretta LYNN	13370
Love Is The Message	MFSB	1159
Love Is What We Make It	Kenny ROGERS	10874
Love Is Where You Find It	The WHISPERS	3599
Love It To Death	ALICE COOPER (Grp)	1896
Love Jones	Johnny Guitar WATSON	6831
Lovejoy	Albert KING	12037
Love Junk	PURSUIT OF HAPPINESS	6281
Loveland	Lonnie Liston SMITH	7445
Love Language	Teddy PENDERGRASS	3220
Love Letters	FORCE M.D.'S	12966
Love Letters From Elvis	Elvis PRESLEY	3592
Love Life	BERLIN	3031
Love Life	Brenda RUSSELL	8702
Love, Life & Feelings	Shirley BASSEY	9865
Love Light	YUTAKA	12259
Loveline	Eddie RABBITT	5797
Love Lives Forever	Minnie RIPERTON	4098
Lovely	The PRIMITIVES	9062
The Love Machine	SOUNDTRACK-MOVIE	11327
Love Magic	L.T.D.	6768
Love Makes A Woman	Barbara ACKLIN	10770
Love Man	Otis REDDING	4562
Love Me	Yvonne ELLIMAN	5911
Love Me Again	Rita COOLIDGE	3382
Love Means You Never H...	SOUNDS OF SUNSHINE	11458
Love Me For A Reason	The OSMONDS	4591
Love Me Tender	B.B. KING	12639
Love Music	Sergio MENDES And BR...	7376
Love Notes	Chuck MANGIONE	8240
Love Notes	Ramsey LEWIS	7589
Love Of A Gentle Woman	John GARY	13047

Title	Act	Rank
Love Of The Common People	Ed AMES	11266
Love On The Wing	Jesse Colin YOUNG	6894
Love Or Physical	ASHFORD & SIMPSON	9910
Love Or Something Like It	Kenny ROGERS	5148
Love Over Gold	DIRE STRAITS	2712
Love, Peace And Happine...	CHAMBERS BROTHERS	3843
Love, Peace & Soul	HONEY CONE	12870
Love Potion	NEW BIRTH	11848
Loverboy	LOVERBOY	725
Love Rhapsodies	MIDNIGHT STRING QUAR...	7803
The Lover In Me	Sheena EASTON	3290
Lovers	Mickey NEWBURY	12482
Love Season	Alex BUGNON	9130
Lovesexy	PRINCE	2751
Love's Happening	FIVE STAIRSTEPS	13576
Loveshine	CON FUNK SHUN	3071
Love's Lines, Angles And Rh...	5TH DIMENSION	2187
Love Somebody Today	SISTER SLEDGE	3896
Love Song	Anne MURRAY	2275
Love Song For Jeffrey	Helen REDDY	1416
Love Songs	The BEATLES	2788
Love Songs - Mexico/S.A.	Tony MOTTOLA	7302
Love's The Thing	Barbara MASON	13341
Love Stinks	J. GEILS Band	1347
Love Storm	TAVARES	4606
Love Story	Andre KOSTELANETZ An...	13411
Love Story	Andy WILLIAMS	761
Love Story	Johnny MATHIS	4082
Love Story	Ray CONNIFF & His Or...	6478
Love Story	Roger WILLIAMS	7634
Love Story	Ronnie ALDRICH	11065
Love Story	SOUNDTRACK-MOVIE	358
Love Story	Tony BENNETT	6279
Love Talk	The MANHATTANS	10145
Love Theme From "Rom...	Percy FAITH His Orch...	8179
Love Theme From "Romeo & J...	Roger WILLIAMS	8763
Love Theme From "Romeo And ...	Johnny MATHIS	3554
Love Theme From The Flight Of ...	BRASS RING	9076
Love Theme From "The Godfa...	Roger WILLIAMS	11749
Love Theme From "The Godfat...	Andy WILLIAMS	2749
Love Theme From "The Godfather...	Al MARTINO	8829
Love Theme From "The...	Ray CONNIFF & His Or...	7087
Love The One You're With	MYSTIC MOODS Orchestra	13201
Love Token	MYSTIC MOODS Orchestra	10343
Love To Love You Baby	Donna SUMMER	1540
Love To The World	L.T.D.	3635
Love Tracks	Gloria GAYNOR	888
A Love Trilogy	Donna SUMMER	2260
Love Trippin'	SPINNERS	5761
Love Unlimited	LOVE UNLIMITED	9054
Love Warriors	TUCK & PATTI	10404
Love Will Find A Way	Pharoah SANDERS	11572
Love Will Follow	George HOWARD	9553
Love Will Keep Us Toge...	CAPTAIN & TENNILLE	347
Love Will Turn You Around	Kenny ROGERS	3733
Love You	BEACH BOYS	7232
Love You Live	ROLLING STONES	2060
Love Your Man	ROSSINGTON COLLINS B...	12041
The Love You Save	Joe TEX	9223
Love Zone	Billy OCEAN	645
Lovin' Every Minute Of It	LOVERBOY	1192
Loving Arms	Dobie GRAY	13141
Loving Is Living	McCRARYS	9065
Loving Is Why	SONS OF CHAMPLIN	12793
Lovingly Yours	Millie JACKSON	11448
Loving Power	The IMPRESSIONS	13301

Title	Act	Rank
Loving Proof	Ricky Van SHELTON	5472
Loving You Just Crossed My Mind	Sam NEELY	9362
Lovin' Sound	IAN & SYLVIA	9990
Lovin' The Night Away	DILLMAN Band	10243
Lovin' Things	GRASS ROOTS	5447
Low	David BOWIE	2300
Low Budget	The KINKS	2046
Low-Life	NEW ORDER	6521
Low Rent Rendezvous	ACE SPECTRUM	9803
Low Ride	Earl KLUGH	4313
The Low Spark Of High Heeled Boys	TRAFFIC	1035
Luciano	Luciano PAVAROTTI	10693
Lucille	B.B. KING	13099
Lucille Talks Back	B.B. KING	10376
Lucky	Marty BALIN	11755
Lucky Seven	Bob JAMES	5255
Luis Gasca	Luis GASCA	13326
Lullaby	BOOK OF LOVE	10495
Lulu	LULU	8925
Lumpy Gravy	Frank ZAPPA	11601
Luna Sea	FIREFALL	2863
Lunch	AUDIENCE	11987
Lush Life	Linda RONSTADT	2433
Lush Life	Nancy WILSON	4228
Lust For Life	Iggy POP	9711
The Luxury Gap	HEAVEN 17	6909
Luxury Liner	Emmylou HARRIS	2620
Luxury Of Life	FIVE STAR	3330
Luxury You Can Afford	Joe COCKER	6090
Lydia	COLD BLOOD	8788
Lydia Pense & Cold Blood	COLD BLOOD	12557
Lyle Lovett And His Large Ban...	Lyle LOVETT	4915
Lyndon Johnson's Lonely H...	VARIOUS ARTISTS	12535
Lynn Anderson's Greatest Hi...	Lynn ANDERSON	8112
Lynyrd Skynyrd (pronounced...	LYNYRD SKYNYRD	1585

M

Title	Act	Rank
Ma	RARE EARTH	4630
Ma Belle Amie	TEE SET	10782
Macalla	CLANNAD	8861
Mac Band	MAC Band	8388
Mac Davis	Mac DAVIS	8076
Machine Gun	The COMMODORES	8816
Machine Head	DEEP PURPLE	355
Machismo	CAMEO	5933
Macho Man	VILLAGE PEOPLE	875
The Mack (Soundtrack)	Willie HUTCH	7299
Mackintosh & T.J. (Soundt...	Waylon JENNINGS	12881
Madame Butterfly	TAVARES	7788
Madame X	MADAME X	12144
Mad, Bad And Dangerous To K...	DEAD OR ALIVE	4821
The Madcap Laughs	Syd BARRETT	11776
Mad Dog	John ENTWISTLE	13788
Mad Dogs & Englishmen (Soundtr...	Joe COCKER	575
Made In America	BLUES BROTHERS	5716
Made In America	CARPENTERS	5005
Made In England	ATOMIC ROOSTER	9837
Made In Europe	DEEP PURPLE	10639
Made In Japan	DEEP PURPLE	622
Made In The Shade	ROLLING STONES	1787
Made In U.S.A.	BEACH BOYS	8025
The Mad Hatter	Chick COREA	5805
Madhouse	SILVER CONVENTION	6077
Mad Love	GOLDEN EARRING	13249
Mad Love	Linda RONSTADT	603
The Mad, Mad, Mad, Mad, Mad Lads	MAD LADS	13095

Title | Act	Rank
Madman Across The Water | Elton JOHN	636
Mad Max Beyond Thunderdo... | SOUNDTRACK-MOVIE	5378
Madness | MADNESS	3701
Madness, Money And Music | Sheena EASTON	8332
Madonna | MADONNA	299
Madrugada | MELANIE	12929
Madura | MADURA	13480
Magazine | HEART	2236
The Magazine | Rickie Lee JONES	4582
Maggie Flynn | ORIGINAL CAST	13185
Maggot Brain | FUNKADELIC	6352
Magic | FOUR TOPS	10183
Magic | T-CONNECTION	7867
Magic | The FLOATERS	9247
Magic | The JETS	1987
Magic | Tom BROWNE	3661
Magical Mystery Tour (Soundtr... | The BEATLES	198
Magic Bus | The WHO	12717
Magic Bus-The Who On Tour | The WHO	5135
The Magic Christian | SOUNDTRACK-MOVIE	7536
Magic Christian Music | BADFINGER	4750
The Magic Garden | 5TH DIMENSION	6093
The Magician's Birthday | URIAH HEEP	2962
Magic In Your Eyes | Earl KLUGH	8976
Magic Is A Child | NEKTAR	12727
Magic Journey | SALSOUL Orchestra	4693
Magic Man | Herb ALPERT	6321
Magic Man | Robert WINTERS and F...	7379
The Magic Music Of F... | Bert KAEMPFERT And H...	3212
The Magic Of The Blue | BLUE MAGIC	5733
Magic People | The PAUPERS	13342
Magic Touch | Stanley JORDAN	2739
Magic Windows | Herbie HANCOCK	10577
Magnetic Fields | Jean Michel JARRE	7169
Magnetic Heaven | WAX	8736
Magnetic South | Michael NESMITH	11538
Magnets | The VAPORS	8271
Magnificent Madness | John KLEMMER	8798
The Magnificent Men | MAGNIFICENT MEN	13212
The Magnificent Men "Live... | MAGNIFICENT MEN	8758
Magnificent Movie Th... | Enoch LIGHT & The LI...	8647
The Magnificent 7 | The SUPREMES & FOUR ...	6460
Magnum Cum Louder | HOODOO GURUS	7432
Mahogany | SOUNDTRACK-MOVIE	2080
Mahogany Rush IV | MAHOGANY RUSH	12609
Mahvelous | Billy CRYSTAL	7026
Maiden Japan | IRON MAIDEN	6267
Maiden Voyage | Ramsey LEWIS	4878
Main Course | BEE GEES	691
The Main Event (Soundtra... | Barbra STREISAND	2630
The Main Ingredient L.T.D... | MAIN INGREDIENT	13827
Main Squeeze | Chuck MANGIONE	5074
Main Street People | FOUR TOPS	6132
Major Moves | Hank WILLIAMS Jr.	6677
Major's Greatest Hits | Major LANCE	10155
Make A Difference Foundat... | VARIOUS ARTISTS	7203
Make A Joyful Noise | MOTHER EARTH	7537
Make A Little Magic | NITTY GRITTY DIRT BA...	5247
Make It Big | WHAM!	130
Make It Easy On Yourself | Burt BACHARACH	1537
Make It Happen | The MIRACLES/Smokey ...	3081
Make It Last Forever | Keith SWEAT	704
Make It With You | Peggy LEE	13528
Make Love To The Musi... | Leon & Mary RUSSELL	10930
Make Someone Happy | WE FIVE	11651
Make The World Go Aw... | Donny & Marie OSMOND	10164

Title | Act	Rank
Make Way For Dionne Warwic... | Dionne WARWICK	5863
Make Your Move | CAPTAIN & TENNILLE	2533
Make Your Own Kind Of Music | MAMA CASS	11176
Makin' Friends | Razzy BAILEY	13283
Making A Good Thing Be... | Olivia NEWTON-JOHN	3724
Making Contact | UFO	11844
Making Music | Bill WITHERS	6288
Making Movies | DIRE STRAITS	1466
Mala Femmena & Connie's Bi... | Connie FRANCIS	7426
Malice In Wonderland | NAZARETH	4177
Malo | MALO	1580
Mama | HEINTJE	7818
Mama Africa | Peter TOSH	5584
Mama Let Him Play | DOUCETTE	10273
Mamas And Papas/Soul Train | CLASSICS IV	13165
The Mamas & The Papas | MAMAS & The PAPAS	375
The Mamas & The Papas D... | MAMAS & The PAPAS	405
Mama's Big Ones | MAMA CASS	13792
Mama's Boys | MAMA'S BOYS	11837
Mama Was A Rock And Roll Sin... | SONNY & CHER	10214
Mame | ORIGINAL CAST	1352
Mame | SOUNDTRACK-MOVIE	13339
Mamma | Luciano PAVAROTTI	7971
A Man Alone & Other Songs O... | Frank SINATRA	3215
A Man And A Woman [A] | Dionne WARWICK	5355
A Man And A Woman [A] | Isaac HAYES	5355
A Man And A Woman | SOUNDTRACK-MOVIE	306
A Man And A Woman & Ot... | FERRANTE & TEICHER	10626
The Man & His Music | Sam COOKE	11564
A Man And His Music | Frank SINATRA	1575
A Man And His Soul | Ray CHARLES	3187
Manassas | Stephen STILLS & MAN...	1063
Man-Child | Herbie HANCOCK	2852
Mancini Concert | Henry MANCINI and hi...	6832
Mancini Country | Henry MANCINI and hi...	6450
The Mancini Generati... | Henry MANCINI and hi...	12835
Mancini Plays The Th... | Henry MANCINI and hi...	2674
Mancini's Angels | Henry MANCINI and hi...	9259
Mancini '67 | Henry MANCINI and hi...	6752
Mandre | MANDRE	6259
Mandrill | MANDRILL	3875
Mandrill Is | MANDRILL	4249
The Manfred Mann Album | MANFRED MANN	4865
Manfred Mann's Earth... | MANFRED MANN'S EART...	10054
Man From Two Worlds | Chico HAMILTON	11980
The Man From Utopia | Frank ZAPPA	11736
Manhattan | SOUNDTRACK-MOVIE	7496
Manhattans | The MANHATTANS	1756
Manhattans Greatest Hits | The MANHATTANS	7657
Manhattan Tower/The Man Who... | Robert GOULET	4054
The Manhattan Transfer | MANHATTAN TRANSFER	2354
The Manhattan Transfer... | MANHATTAN TRANSFER	13321
Manhole | Grace SLICK	9665
Manifest Destiny | The DICTATORS	13540
Manifesto | ROXY MUSIC	3013
Manilow | Barry MANILOW	4534
Man In Black | Johnny CASH	5679
Man In Motion | NIGHT RANGER	8821
Man Is Not Alone | Senator Everett McKi...	12219
A Man Must Carry On | Jerry Jeff WALKER	4807
Manna | BREAD	1930
Mannheim Steamroller... | MANNHEIM STEAMROLLER	3798
Man Of Colours | ICEHOUSE	2717
Man Of La Mancha | ORIGINAL CAST	580
Man Of La Mancha | SOUNDTRACK-MOVIE	5709
Man Of Miracles | STYX	9558

Title | Act	Rank
Man Of Steel | Hank WILLIAMS Jr.	8198
Man On The Line | Chris De BURGH	6205
Manorisms | WET WILLIE	8934
Man Overboard | Bob WELCH	11432
Man To Man | HOT CHOCOLATE	11127
Mantovani/Hollywood | MANTOVANI	4790
Mantovani In Concert | MANTOVANI	12337
Mantovani Magic | MANTOVANI	3058
Mantovani/Manhattan | MANTOVANI	4743
Mantovani...Memories | MANTOVANI	9774
Mantovani Ole | MANTOVANI	4885
The Mantovani Scene | MANTOVANI	4934
Mantovani's Golden Hits | MANTOVANI	4245
The Mantovani Sound - Big Hits ... | MANTOVANI	3356
Mantovani/Tango | MANTOVANI	9907
Mantovani Today | MANTOVANI	5323
The Mantovani Touch | MANTOVANI	4420
Manufacturers Of Soul [A] | Count BASIE	13316
Manufacturers Of Soul [A] | Jackie WILSON	13316
The Man Who Built America | HORSLIPS	9461
The Man Who Sold The World | David BOWIE	5984
A Man Without Love | Engelbert HUMPERDINC...	673
The Man With The Sad F... | Stanley TURRENTINE	6387
The Man With The Horn | Miles DAVIS	5102
The Many Facets Of Roger | ROGER	2871
The Many Moods Of Tony | Tony BENNETT	3128
The Many Sides Of The... | SERENDIPITY SINGERS	6652
Marathon | Rodney FRANKLIN	13306
Marathon | SANTANA	2991
Marauder | BLACKFOOT	5251
The Marblehead Messenger | SEATRAIN	7787
March | Michael PENN	2617
Marching Out | Yngwie MALMSTEEN	4356
March Of The Saint | ARMORED SAINT	8868
The March On Washing... | Rev. Martin Luther K...	10502
Mardi Gras | CREEDENCE CLEARWATER...	2158
Margie Joseph Makes A New I... | Margie JOSEPH	6222
Maria Elena | Los INDIOS TABAJARAS	2224
Maria Elena | Tommy GARRETT	9111
Maria McKee | Maria McKEE	7740
Maria Muldaur | Maria MULDAUR	514
Marianne Faithfull | Marianne FAITHFULL	2126
Marianne Faithfull's G... | Marianne FAITHFULL	9556
Marie | The BACHELORS	9493
Marilyn & Billy | Marilyn McCOO & Bill...	10421
Marilyn Martin | Marilyn MARTIN	7672
Mariposa Do Ora | Dave MASON	4002
Mark-Almond | MARK-ALMOND	8315
Mark-Almond 73 | MARK-ALMOND	6371
Mark-Almond II | MARK-ALMOND	6524
Mark, Don & Mel 1969-... | GRAND FUNK RAILROAD	2339
Mark, Don & Terry 19... | Terry KNIGHT And The...	13276
Marriage On The Rocks/Rock Bo... | AMBOY DUKES	13497
Married To The Mob | SOUNDTRACK-MOVIE	13537
Marrying Maiden | IT'S A BEAUTIFUL DAY	3429
Marsalis Standard Time: V... | Wynton MARSALIS	12022
Marshall Crenshaw | Marshall CRENSHAW	4150
The Marshall Tucker ... | MARSHALL TUCKER Band	2359
Mars Needs Guitars! | HOODOO GURUS	11001
Martha & The Vandell... | MARTHA & The VANDELL...	11186
Martika | MARTIKA	1856
Marty Robbins Greatest Hits... | Marty ROBBINS	9137
The Marvelettes | The MARVELETTES	9752
Marvin Gaye And His Girls | Marvin GAYE	11109
Marvin Gaye & Tammi ... | Marvin GAYE & Tammi ...	12722
Marvin Gaye Anthology | Marvin GAYE	5317

Title	Act	Rank
Marvin Gaye/Greatest Hits, Vo...	Marvin GAYE	12391
Marvin Gaye Live!	Marvin GAYE	1397
Marvin Gaye Live At The Londo...	Marvin GAYE	693
Marvin Gaye's Greatest Hits	Marvin GAYE	7238
Marvin Gaye's Greatest Hits (2)	Marvin GAYE	6027
Marvin Gaye Super Hits	Marvin GAYE	9664
Marvin Sease	Marvin SEASE	7689
The Marx Bros. (The Original...	Groucho MARX	11915
Mary	Mary TRAVERS	3810
Mary In The Morning	Al MARTINO	4891
Mary Jane Girls	MARY JANE GIRLS	3673
Mary Poppins(2)	SOUNDTRACK-MOVIE	9746
Mary Poppins	SOUNDTRACK-MOVIE	33
Mar Y Sol	VARIOUS ARTISTS	11824
Mary Wells	Mary WELLS	11833
Mary Wells Sings My Guy	Mary WELLS	8555
Masekela	Hugh MASEKELA	13500
M*A*S*H	SOUNDTRACK-MOVIE	7446
Mask	Roger GLOVER	8572
The Masked Marauders	MASKED MARAUDERS	7481
Mask Of Smiles	John WAITE	4528
The Mason Williams Ear Sho...	Mason WILLIAMS	9737
The Mason Williams Phonogr...	Mason WILLIAMS	1903
Masque	KANSAS	5036
Mass (from the Liturgy ...	Leonard BERNSTEIN	4837
Mass In F Minor	ELECTRIC PRUNES	8691
Massterpiece	MASS PRODUCTION	9087
Master Funk	Johnny Guitar WATSON	11623
Master Jack	FOUR JACKS And A JIL...	10946
Masterjam	RUFUS	1553
Master Of Disguise	LIZZY BORDEN	9195
Master Of Puppets	METALLICA	2383
Master Of Reality	BLACK SABBATH	789
Master Of The Game	George DUKE	8287
Masterpiece	ISLEY BROTHERS	9552
Masterpiece	The TEMPTATIONS	1411
Material Thangz	The DEELE	10889
Mathematics	Melissa MANCHESTER	11304
Mathis Is...	Johnny MATHIS	10498
Matthew & Son/New Masters	Cat STEVENS	9586
Maureen McGovern	Maureen McGOVERN	9694
Mauriat Magic	Paul MAURIAT And His...	5994
Maurice White	Maurice WHITE	6314
Maverick	George THOROGOOD & T...	1900
Max	The RUMOUR	8385
Maximum Security	Tony MacALPINE	9915
Maxi Priest	Maxi PRIEST	7408
Maxoom	MAHOGANY RUSH	11753
Max Q	MAX Q	11972
Maybe	3° DEGREES	10119
Maybe It's Live	Robert PALMER	11793
Maybe Tomorrow	JACKSON 5	962
Mazarati	MAZARATI	10358
Maze Featuring Frank...	MAZE Featuring Frank...	2647
McCartney	Paul McCARTNEY	266
The McCartney Interview	Paul McCARTNEY	12177
McCartney II	Paul McCARTNEY	1287
McFadden & Whitehead	McFADDEN & WHITEHEAD	2989
McGuinn, Clark & Hil...	McGUINN, CLARK & HIL...	3869
McGuinness Flint	McGUINNESS FLINT	10312
McKendree Spring 3	McKENDREE SPRING	10665
McLemore Avenue	BOOKER T. & The M.G....	7708
McVicar (Soundtrack)	Roger DALTREY	3564
Mean	MONTROSE	11809
Mean Business	The FIRM	3580
Me And Bobby McGee	Kris KRISTOFFERSON	3360

Title	Act	Rank
Me And Joe	RODNEY O & Joe COOLE...	13529
Me And Mrs. Jones	Johnny MATHIS	7099
Me & Paul	Willie NELSON	10781
Me And You	The CHI-LITES	11221
Mean Streak	Y&T	8356
Meant For Each Other [A]	Barbara MANDRELL	7661
Meant For Each Other [A]	Lee GREENWOOD	7661
Meanwhile Back At The Whisk...	Johnny RIVERS	3801
Measure For Measure	ICEHOUSE	4450
Meatballs	SOUNDTRACK-MOVIE	11960
Meat Is Murder	The SMITHS	5683
Meaty Beaty Big And Bouncy	The WHO	2262
Mecca For Moderns	MANHATTAN TRANSFER	1883
Mechanical Resonance	TESLA	2231
Mechanix	UFO	6897
Meco Plays Music From The Empire Str...	MECO	10527
Meddle	PINK FLOYD	2375
Medicine Show	DREAM SYNDICATE	12569
Meet Danny Wilson	DANNY WILSON	7093
Meeting In The Ladies Room	KLYMAXX	1307
Meeting Of The Minds	FOUR TOPS	8273
Meet The Beatles!	The BEATLES	191
Meet The Brady Bunch	BRADY BUNCH	6574
Meet The Searchers/Needles ...	The SEARCHERS	3467
Meet The Temptations	The TEMPTATIONS	8227
Mega Force	707	9937
Megatop Phoenix	BIG AUDIO DYNAMITE	7329
Melanie	MELANIE	13559
Melanie At Carnegie Hall	MELANIE	8085
Melba(2)	Melba MOORE	6573
Melba	Melba MOORE	11541
Melissa	Melissa MANCHESTER	1210
Melissa Etheridge	Melissa ETHERIDGE	1321
Melissa Manchester	Melissa MANCHESTER	5903
Mellow Madness	Quincy JONES	1873
Mellow Yellow	DONOVAN	3043
Mellow Yellow	Odell BROWN & THE OR...	12577
Melodies Of Love	Bobby VINTON	2353
Melting Pot	BOOKER T. & The M.G....	2337
A Memorial	Robert Francis KENNE...	12595
A Memorial Album	John Fitzgerald KENN...	5275
Memories	Barbra STREISAND	869
Memories	Doc WATSON	13147
Memories	John MAYALL	11875
Memories	Lawrence WELK	10347
Memories	The VOGUES	8300
Memories Of America / O...	Billy Edd WHEELER	12134
Memory In The Making	John KILZER	7917
Memphis	Petula CLARK	13682
Memphis Beat	Jerry Lee LEWIS	12287
The Memphis Horns Band II	MEMPHIS HORNS	10393
Memphis Queen	Carla THOMAS	10321
Memphis Two-Step	Herbie MANN	11345
Memphis Underground	Herbie MANN	1016
Me, Myself And I	Cheryl Pepsii RILEY	8730
Me Myself I	Joan ARMATRADING	3116
Menace To Society	LIZZY BORDEN	10205
Menagerie	Bill WITHERS	3253
Men And Women	SIMPLY RED	3452
Mendocino	SIR DOUGLAS Quintet	6204
Men From Earth	OZARK MOUNTAIN DARED...	6593
The Men In My Little Girl's ...	Mike DOUGLAS	5691
Menlove Avenue	John LENNON	12072
Metal Priestess	The PLASMATICS	12948
Menudo	MENUDO	7010
Men Without Women	LITTLE STEVEN	7168

Title	Act	Rank
Merciless	Stephanie MILLS	7239
The Mercy & Love (Can Make You Happ...	MERCY	3789
Mercy, Mercy	Buddy RICH	11955
Mercy, Mercy, Mercy!	"Cannonball" ADDERLE...	2229
Merrimack County	Tom RUSH	8745
Merry Christmas/Happy N...	MONTANA Orchestra	13150
Merry Clayton	Merry CLAYTON	10493
The Merry-Go-Round	The MERRY-GO-ROUND	13601
Merry, Merry Christm...	NEW KIDS ON THE BLOC...	1893
The Merry Widow	ORIGINAL CAST	11784
Mesopotamia	The B-52s	4581
The Message	GRANDMASTER FLASH An...	4410
Message From A Drum	REDBONE	7281
A Message From The People	Ray CHARLES	4332
Message In The Music	The O'JAYS	2344
The Message Is Love	Barry WHITE	7155
Messages From The Boys	The BOYS	2767
A Message To The People	Buddy MILES	4136
Messina	Jim MESSINA	7223
Metal Health	QUIET RIOT	281
Metal Heart	ACCEPT	7254
Metamorphosis	IRON BUTTERFLY	2425
Metamorphosis	ROLLING STONES	2245
The Meters	The METERS	6774
The Method To Our Ma...	LORDS Of The NEW CHU...	11480
Method To The Madness	UNDISPUTED TRUTH	5817
Metro Music	M + M	13021
Metropolis	SOUNDTRACK-MOVIE	8336
Metropolitan Opera Gala H...	VARIOUS ARTISTS	11371
Mexican Pearls	Billy VAUGHN and His...	5990
Mexican Trip	MYSTIC MOODS Orchestra	12523
M.F. Horn/3	Maynard FERGUSON	9077
MFSB	MFSB	9180
Miami	JAMES GANG	7933
Miami Vice	SOUNDTRACK-TV	389
Miami Vice II	SOUNDTRACK-TV	7951
Michael Bolton	Michael BOLTON	8156
The Michael Johnson Album	Michael JOHNSON	5657
Michael Martin Murphey	Michael MURPHEY	6836
Michael Morales	Michael MORALES	7413
The Michael Schenker...	Michael SCHENKER Gro...	7287
Michelle	Billy VAUGHN and His...	6074
Michelle	Bud SHANK	4875
Michel Polnareff	Michel POLNAREFF	7798
Mickey Mouse Club	SOUNDTRACK-TV	5560
Mickey Mouse Disco	VARIOUS ARTISTS	4004
Mickie Finn's - America's N...	SOUNDTRACK-TV	7591
Mick Jones	Mick JONES	13248
Mick Taylor	Mick TAYLOR	10394
Middle Man	Boz SCAGGS	922
Midnight Believer	B.B. KING	6380
Midnight Blue	Louise TUCKER	9346
Midnight Cafe	SMOKIE	11406
Midnight Cowboy	FERRANTE & TEICHER	4243
Midnight Cowboy	SOUNDTRACK-MOVIE	824
Midnight Crazy	Mac DAVIS	12990
Midnight Creeper	Lou DONALDSON	11217
Midnight Diamond	Dobie GRAY	12539
Midnight Express	SOUNDTRACK-MOVIE	4379
Midnight Light	LEBLANC & CARR	9958
Midnight Lightning	Jimi HENDRIX	5814
Midnight Love	Marvin GAYE	1381
Midnight Love Affair	Carol DOUGLAS	12028
Midnight Madness	NIGHT RANGER	624
Midnight Magic	The COMMODORES	367
Midnight Mission	TEXTONES	11702

Title | Act	Rank
The Midnight Mover | Wilson PICKETT	7104
Midnight On The Water | David BROMBERG	12554
Midnight Ride | Paul REVERE And The ...	1326
Midnight Star | MIDNIGHT STAR	7667
Midnight To Midnight | PSYCHEDELIC FURS	2909
Midnight Wind | Charlie DANIELS Band	8282
Midstream | Debby BOONE	11066
Mighty Love | SPINNERS	1488
The Mighty Mighty Dells | The DELLS	9397
The Mighty Quinn | MANFRED MANN	12088
Migration | Dave GRUSIN	10861
Mike + The Mechanics | MIKE + THE MECHANICS	1445
Mike Nesmith Present... | WICHITA TRAIN WHISTL...	9860
Mike's Murder (Soundtrack) | Joe JACKSON	6957
Miles | Miles JAYE	8862
Miles Davis At Fillmore | Miles DAVIS	8519
Miles Davis In Europe | Miles DAVIS	9063
Miles Of Aisles | Joni MITCHELL	800
Milestone Jazzstars In Co... | VARIOUS ARTISTS	9273
Milestones | SRC	8792
Milk And Honey | John LENNON & Yoko O...	2681
Milky Way | CHOCOLATE MILK	10942
Millie Jackson | Millie JACKSON	9948
$1,000,000.00 Weekend | The VENTURES	4493
Million Mile Reflect... | Charlie DANIELS Band	868
...Millions Like Us | MILLIONS LIKE US	10172
Milsap Magic | Ronnie MILSAP	8896
Mind Bomb | The THE	9322
Mind Games | John LENNON	1621
The Mind Is A Terrible Thing To ... | MINISTRY	10968
Mine Eyes Have Seen The Glor... | Anita BRYANT	11454
Mingus | Joni MITCHELL	2410
Minimum Wage Rock & Roll | BUS BOYS	6620
Mink Deville | MINK DE VILLE	13409
Minnie | Minnie RIPERTON	3093
Minor Detail | MINOR DETAIL	13631
Minstrel In The Gallery | JETHRO TULL	2024
The Minstrel Man | Willie NELSON	10523
Minus-Plus | SMITH	6547
Minute By Minute | DOOBIE BROTHERS	149
Mirabai | MIRABAI	9813
Miracle | KANE GANG	7069
The Miracle | QUEEN	4758
Miracle Row | Janis IAN	5244
Miracles | CHANGE	4084
Miracles By Engelber... | Engelbert HUMPERDINC...	11511
The Miracles On Stag... | The MIRACLES/Smokey ...	11032
Mirage | CAMEL	8892
Mirage | FLEETWOOD MAC	330
Mirage A Trois | YELLOWJACKETS	9953
Mireille Mathieu | Mireille MATHIEU	8515
Miriam Makeba In Concert! | Miriam MAKEBA	12652
Mirror | Emitt RHODES	12378
Mirror | Larry GRAHAM/GRAHAM ...	4405
The Mirror | SPOOKY TOOTH	9188
Mirror Image | BLOOD, SWEAT & TEARS	10673
Mirror Moves | PSYCHEDELIC FURS	4090
Mirrors | BLUE ÖYSTER CULT	4323
Mirrors Of My Mind | Roger WHITTAKER	10302
Mirrors - Reflections Of Today | Dick HYMAN	13255
Mirror Stars | FABULOUS POODLES	5245
Misdemeanor | UFO	6942
Misfits | The KINKS	3345
Misplaced Childhood | MARILLION	4135
Misplaced Ideals | SAD CAFÉ	6505
Missa Luba | TROUBADOURS Du ROI B...	12057

Title | Act	Rank
Missing Persons | MISSING PERSONS	3161
The Missing Piece | GENTLE GIANT	8353
Missing White House Tape... | NATIONAL LAMPOON	8951
The Mission | SOUNDTRACK-MOVIE	9121
Miss The Mississippi | Crystal GAYLE	2797
Mistaken Idenity | Kim CARNES	290
Mister Heartbreak | Laurie ANDERSON	5510
Mister Magic | Grover WASHINGTON Jr...	1109
Mistress | MISTRESS	7398
Mistrial | Lou REED	4487
Misty | "Groove" HOLMES	10274
Misty | Ray STEVENS	6727
Misty Blue | Dorothy MOORE	2622
Misty Roses | The SANDPIPERS	10765
M.I.U. Album | BEACH BOYS	11093
Mixed Bag | Richie HAVENS	13309
Mixed Bag(2) | Richie HAVENS	13410
Mixed Bag II | Richie HAVENS	13071
Mixed Emotions | EXILE	1960
Mob Rules | BLACK SABBATH	3682
Moby Grape | MOBY GRAPE	2475
Moby Grape '69 | MOBY GRAPE	8027
Modern Heart | CHAMPAIGN	4791
Modern Man | Stanley CLARKE	4964
Modern Music | BE BOP DELUXE	8229
Modern Romans | The CALL	7208
Modern Times | Al STEWART	3561
Modern Times | JEFFERSON AIRPLANE/S...	1667
Molly Hatchet | MOLLY HATCHET	4097
Mom Always Liked You Be... | SMOTHERS BROTHERS	3457
A Momentary Lapse Of Reason | PINK FLOYD	537
Moments | Boz SCAGGS	8738
Moments | Julio IGLESIAS	13246
Moments Greatest Hits | The MOMENTS (2)	11570
The Moments Live at the N... | The MOMENTS (2)	10221
A Moment's Pleasure | Millie JACKSON	10208
Moms The Word | Moms MABLEY	11671
Moms Wows | Moms MABLEY	9186
Mona Bone Jakon | Cat STEVENS	8613
The Mona Lisa's Sist... | Graham PARKER And Th...	5874
Mondo Bongo | BOOMTOWN RATS	8949
Mondo Mando | David GRISMAN	12845
Money And Cigarettes | Eric CLAPTON	2833
Money For Nothing | DIRE STRAITS	6285
Money Talks | The BAR-KAYS	5818
Mongo '70 | Mongo SANTAMARIA	13551
Mongrel | Bob SEGER	12225
The Monkees | The MONKEES	50
The Monkees Greatest Hits(2) | The MONKEES	3414
The Monkees Greatest Hits | The MONKEES	6436
The Monkees Present | The MONKEES	6720
The Monkees Song Book | GOLDEN GATE Strings	13782
Monkey Grip | Bill WYMAN	7454
Monkey Island | J. GEILS Band	5149
The Monkey Time | Major LANCE	11625
Monolith | KANSAS	1942
The Monroes | The MONROES	9850
Monster | FETCHIN BONES	11268
Monster | Herbie HANCOCK	6334
Monster | Jimmy SMITH	3853
Monster | STEPPENWOLF	1219
Montana Cafe | Hank WILLIAMS Jr.	6915
Monterey Internation... [A] | Jimi HENDRIX EXPERIE...	2493
Monterey International Pop F... [A] | Otis REDDING	2493
Montrose | MONTROSE	7945
Monty Python Live! At City C... | MONTY PYTHON	13029

Title | Act	Rank
The Monty Python Matching Ti... | MONTY PYTHON	5391
Monty Python's Contractual O... | MONTY PYTHON	10252
Monty Python's Flying Circus | MONTY PYTHON	6591
Mony Mony | Tommy JAMES And The ...	13546
Moods | Barbara MANDRELL	9126
Moods | Neil DIAMOND	651
Moods Of Marvin Gaye | Marvin GAYE	8496
Moody Blue | Elvis PRESLEY	853
Moody Jr. | Jr. WALKER & The ALL...	7622
Moog Power | Hugo MONTENEGRO	12668
Moog - The Electric Eclectics ... | Dick HYMAN	2330
Moondance | Van MORRISON	3603
Moondog Matinee | The BAND	3304
Moondog Serenade | CASHMAN & WEST	13607
Moonflower | SANTANA	1838
Moonlight And Roses | Jim REEVES	3683
Moonlight Feels Right | STARBUCK	6214
Moonlighting | SOUNDTRACK-TV	5735
Moonlight Madness | Teri DeSARIO	6954
Moonlight Sinatra | Frank SINATRA	5025
Moonmadness | CAMEL	7427
Moon Over Naples | Billy VAUGHN and His...	3146
Moonraker | SOUNDTRACK-MOVIE	11767
Moonshot | Buffy SAINTE-MARIE	9444
Moons Of Jupiter | SCRUFFY THE CAT	11836
Moontan | GOLDEN EARRING	1552
More | Vic DANA	9084
More (Soundtrack) | PINK FLOYD	10438
More American Graffiti | SOUNDTRACK-MOVIE	7570
More American Graffiti | VARIOUS ARTISTS	7131
More Amor | Eydie GORME	6605
More Big Folk Hits | BROTHERS FOUR	11731
More Chad & Jeremy | CHAD & JEREMY	11425
More Creedence Gold | CREEDENCE CLEARWATER...	5644
More Dirty Dancing | SOUNDTRACK-MOVIE	472
More 50 Guitars In Love | Tommy GARRETT	12563
More Fun In The New World | X	6427
More Genius Of Jankowski | Horst JANKOWSKI	6203
More George Thorogoo... | George THOROGOOD & T...	6648
More Golden Grass | GRASS ROOTS	6575
More Golden Greats | The VENTURES	11218
More Golden Hits By The Four Se... | 4 SEASONS	10822
More Heavy Traffic | TRAFFIC	12887
More Hits By The Sup... | The SUPREMES/Diana R...	1363
More Hits Of The 50's And 60'... | Count BASIE	13648
More Hit Sounds Of The Lett... | The LETTERMEN	5539
More Hot Rocks (Big Hits &... | ROLLING STONES	1587
More I Cannot Wish You | Ed AMES	8590
The More I See You/Call Me | Chris MONTEZ	3495
More Knockers Up! | Rusty WARREN	9984
More Mauriat | Paul MAURIAT And His...	6398
More Miles Per Gallon | Buddy MILES	6378
More, More, More | Andrea TRUE Connecti...	4184
More Nashville Sound... | Danny DAVIS And The ...	9939
More Of Everything! | The LIMELITERS	10996
More Of Roy Orbison's Greates... | Roy ORBISON	2289
More Of The Best Of Bill Cosby | Bill COSBY	6582
More Of The Good Life | T.S. MONK	11866
More Of The Monkees | The MONKEES	61
More Saucy Stories From...Pat ... | Pat COOPER	13439
More Songs About Buildings ... | TALKING HEADS	1673
More Songs About Love & Ha... | The GODFATHERS	12258
More Sounds of Washingto... | VILLAGE STOMPERS	12429
More Specials | The SPECIALS	9704
More Stuff | STUFF	6444
More Than A Miracle | Roger WILLIAMS	11863

Title | Act	Rank
More Than Ever | BLOOD, SWEAT & TEARS	12162
More Than Friends | Jonathan BUTLER	7623
More Than Music | MYSTIC MOODS Orchestra	12202
More Than You Know | Toni TENNILLE	9337
More Themes For Youn... | Percy FAITH His Orch...	9899
More Themes From The... | Roland SHAW Orchestr...	10662
More Today Than Yesterda... | SPIRAL STARECASE	5366
More Trini Lopez At PJ's | Trini LOPEZ	3070
Morning | Jim Ed BROWN	8010
The Morning After | J. GEILS Band	5069
The Morning After | Maureen McGOVERN	6028
Morning Dance | SPYRO GYRA	1473
Morning Glory | Mary TRAVERS	11703
Morning, Noon & The Nite-... | The NITE-LITERS	9199
Morning Star | Hubert LAWS	10193
Moroccan Roll | BRAND X	9458
Mo' Roots | Taj MAHAL	11355
Morris Albert | Morris ALBERT	9688
Morrison Hotel | The DOORS	1096
Mosaic | WANG CHUNG	3170
Mosaique | GIPSY KINGS	6633
The Most Exciting Organ Eve... | Billy PRESTON	12403
Most Of All | B.J. THOMAS	4795
Most Of The Girls Like To Dance... | Don DIXON	11331
Motels | The MOTELS	13241
Motel Shot | DELANEY & BONNIE & F...	5107
Mother Factor | MOTHER'S FINEST	6385
Mother Focus | FOCUS	10565
Mother Lode | LOGGINS & MESSINA	1371
Mothermania/The Best Of The M... | Frank ZAPPA	9391
Mother Nature's Son | Ramsey LEWIS	8774
The Mothers/Fillmore East-Jun... | Frank ZAPPA	4551
Mother's Finest | MOTHER'S FINEST	9842
Mothership Connection | PARLIAMENT	1130
Mother's Milk | RED HOT CHILI PEPPER...	2805
Mother's Spiritual | Laura NYRO	13193
Mother Wit | Betty WRIGHT	8685
Motor-Booty Affair | PARLIAMENT	2830
Motorcycle Mama | SAILCAT	4421
Motortown Review In Paris | VARIOUS ARTISTS	9663
Motortown Review Live | VARIOUS ARTISTS	12048
The Motor-Town Review, Vo... | VARIOUS ARTISTS	10440
Motown At The Hollywood P... | VARIOUS ARTISTS	10399
Motown Remembers Marvin Gaye | Marvin GAYE	13752
The Motown Story: The Fir... | VARIOUS ARTISTS	9440
Motown Winners' Circle/No. 1...Vol. 1 | VARIOUS ARTISTS	11247
Motown Winners' Circle/No. 1...Vol. 2 | VARIOUS ARTISTS	10055
Mott | MOTT THE HOOPLE	3052
Mott The Hoople | MOTT THE HOOPLE	13387
Mott The Hoople Live | MOTT THE HOOPLE	3800
Mountain | Leslie WEST	5833
Mountain Climbing! | MOUNTAIN	1054
Mountain Dance | Dave GRUSIN	5294
Mountain Live (the road goes eve... | MOUNTAIN	4933
Mountain Music | ALABAMA	638
Moussorgsky: Pictures At An E... | Isao TOMITA	5429
Mouth To Mouth | LIPPS INC.	1142
Move Along | GRASS ROOTS	6527
Move It On Over | George THOROGOOD & T...	1990
Move Somethin' | 2 LIVE CREW	4062
Move Your Hand | Lonnie SMITH	13365
The Movie Album | Ramsey LEWIS	10976
The Movie Song Album | Tony BENNETT	2104
The Movie Songs | Frank SINATRA	13743
Moving Finger | The HOLLIES	13229

Title | Act	Rank
Moving On | John MAYALL	8363
Moving Pictures | RUSH	314
Moving Target | Gil SCOTT-HERON	9724
Moving Violation | JACKSON 5	4263
Moving Waves | FOCUS	1012
Movin' On | BUCKWHEAT	11815
Movin' On | Danny DAVIS And The ...	7276
Movin' On | The COMMODORES	1886
Movin' Toward Happiness | MASON PROFFIT	11025
Movin' With Nancy | Nancy SINATRA	2953
Mozart: Piano Concertos Nos. 17... | Géza ANDA	7062
Mozart: Requiem Mass | BOSTON SYMPHONY Orch...	7512
M.P.G. | Marvin GAYE	3019
Mr. Bad Guy | Freddie MERCURY	11687
Mr. Big | MR. BIG	4767
Mr. Big Stuff | Jean KNIGHT	6278
Mr. C. | Norman CONNORS	13755
Mr. Crowley | Ozzy OSBOURNE	7773
Mr. Dream Merchant | Jerry BUTLER	10769
Mr. Fantasy | TRAFFIC	5632
Mr. Gone | WEATHER REPORT	4768
Mr. Hands | Herbie HANCOCK	9789
Mr. Jaws And Other Fables | Dickie GOODMAN	9622
Mr. Jordan | Julian LENNON	7055
Mr. Lonely | Bobby VINTON	3955
Mr. Look So Good! | Richard "Dimples" Fields	5335
Mr. Magic Man | Wilson PICKETT	13263
Mr. Mean | OHIO PLAYERS	7264
Mr. Music Head | Adrian BELEW	8585
Mr. Music...Mantovani | MANTOVANI	2652
Mr. Natural | BEE GEES	12034
Mr. Nice Guy | Ronnie LAWS	8306
Mrs. Brown, You've Got A... | HERMAN'S HERMITS	12739
Mrs. Miller's Greatest Hits | Mrs. MILLER	2976
Mr. Spock's Music From Oute... | Leonard NIMOY	5662
Mr. Stick Man | Pete FOUNTAIN	6755
Mr. Tambourine Man | The BYRDS	1876
Ms. America | Vikki CARR	10292
MSB | Michael STANLEY Band	10850
MSG | Michael SCHENKER Gro...	8200
MTV's Rock 'N Roll To Go | VARIOUS ARTISTS	8047
Much Les | Les McCANN	9380
Muddy Mississippi Line | Bobby GOLDSBORO	8508
Mudlark | Leo KOTTKE	11121
Mud Slide Slim And The Blue ... | James TAYLOR	168
Mud Will Be Flung Tonight! | Bette MIDLER	12295
Mummer | XTC	11445
Mungo Jerry | MUNGO JERRY	6097
The Muppet Alphabet Album | VARIOUS ARTISTS	12782
The Muppet Movie: Origin... | SOUNDTRACK-MOVIE	2429
The Muppet Show | SOUNDTRACK-TV	11385
Murmur | R.E.M.	3713
Murray The K - Live From ... | VARIOUS ARTISTS	12976
Muscle Of Love | ALICE COOPER (Grp)	1964
Muse | Grace JONES	10490
Music | Carole KING	256
Music: A Bit More Of Me | David McCALLUM	7453
A Musical Affair | ASHFORD & SIMPSON	5222
Musical Chairs | Sammy HAGAR	8060
Musical Shapes | Carlene CARTER	10552
Music & Me | Michael JACKSON	7377
Music - A Part Of Me | David McCALLUM	3222
The Music Band | WAR	4118
The Music Band 2 | WAR	7540
Music Box | Evelyn "Champagne" K...	3969
Music Box Dancer | Frank MILLS	3326

Title | Act	Rank
Music By Mason Williams | Mason WILLIAMS	4259
Music For The Knee Plays | David BYRNE	11136
Music For The Masses | DEPECHE MODE	2554
The Music For UNICEF Conc... | VARIOUS ARTISTS	12188
Music From Across The Way | James LAST	11307
Music From "A Fistful Of ... | Hugo MONTENEGRO	1105
Music From Big Pink | The BAND	2571
Music From Mary Popp... | Ray CONNIFF & His Or...	3922
Music From Mission: Impossi... | Lalo SCHIFRIN	3593
Music From Songwriter (Soun... [A] | Willie NELSON	11596
Music From Songwriter ... [A] | Kris KRISTOFFERSON	11596
Music From The Bill Cosby S... | SOUNDTRACK-TV	10028
Music From The Edge Of Heaven | WHAM!	2159
Music From The Elder | KISS	6979
Music Fuh Ya (Musica Para Tu) | Taj MAHAL	9409
Music Is My Life | Billy PRESTON	2846
Music Keeps Me Together | Taj MAHAL	10620
The Music Lovers | FERRANTE & TEICHER	12123
Music Maestro Please | LOVE UNLIMITED ORCHE...	7160
Musicmagic | RETURN TO FOREVER	4658
Music Man | Waylon JENNINGS	2508
The Music Man | Paul ANKA	13216
Music Maximus | MAIN INGREDIENT	12746
Music, Music | Helen REDDY	2842
Music Of A People | Stanley BLACK	12510
The Music Of Cosmos | SOUNDTRACK-TV	8101
Music Of Hawaii | Henry MANCINI and hi...	6940
Music Of My Mind | Stevie WONDER	1768
The Music Of Paul Si... | BOSTON POPS Orchestr...	13315
Music Of Victor Herbert | Beverly SILLS	9638
Music People, The | VARIOUS ARTISTS	11149
Music To Read James Bond ... | VARIOUS ARTISTS	5815
Music To Watch Girls By | Al HIRT	10494
Music To Watch Girls... | Bob CREWE Generation	7775
Musique/The High Road | ROXY MUSIC	5730
Musta Notta Gotta Lotta | Joe ELY	8391
Muswell Hillbillies | The KINKS	7401
M.U. The Best Of Jethro Tull | JETHRO TULL	2154
Mutual Attraction | SYLVESTER	12217
M.V.P. | Harvey MASON	12986
My Aim Is True | Elvis COSTELLO	2596
My Babe | Roy BUCHANAN	13570
My Baby Loves Lovin' | WHITE PLAINS	11862
My Best | KITARO	9903
My Best To You | Donny OSMOND	3314
My Best To You | John DAVIDSON	9393
My Blue Ridge Mountain Boy | Dolly PARTON	13493
My Boy | Richard HARRIS	5946
My Boyfriend's Back | The ANGELS	4742
My Boy Lollipop | Millie SMALL	11179
My Cherie | Al MARTINO	2122
My Cherie Amour | John DAVIDSON	11329
My Cherie Amour | Stevie WONDER	3280
My Cup Runneth Over | Ed AMES	631
My Elusive Dreams | Bobby VINTON	8594
My Ever Changing Moods | STYLE COUNCIL	4983
My Fair Lady | Andre PREVIN	12043
My Fair Lady | FERRANTE & TEICHER	10064
My Fair Lady | Nat King COLE	5985
My Fair Lady | SOUNDTRACK-MOVIE	123
My Farewell To Elvis | Merle HAGGARD	10621
My Favorite Person | The O'JAYS	6508
My Favorite Things | Dave BRUBECK Quartet	10958
My Feet Are Smiling | Leo KOTTKE	8468
My First Of 1965 | Lawrence WELK	8427
My Funny Valentine | Miles DAVIS	9753

Title	Act	Rank
My Gift To You	Alexander O'NEAL	11614
My Girl Josephine	Jerry JAYE	13751
My Goal's Beyond	John McLAUGHLIN/MAHA...	13014
My Hang-Up Is You	Freddie HART	7259
My Heart Sings	Al MARTINO	11565
My Home's In Alabama	ALABAMA	4786
My Kind Of Broadway	Frank SINATRA	4597
My Kind Of Folk Songs	Gale GARNETT	5146
My Kind Of Jazz	Ray CHARLES	12604
My Kind Of Town	Jack JONES	3976
My Life For A Song	Placido DOMINGO	9030
My Life In The Bush Of Ghosts [A]	Brian ENO	5300
My Life In The Bush Of Ghosts [A]	David BYRNE	5300
My Love	Petula CLARK	6723
My Love / Don't Keep Me Hangi...	Sonny JAMES	13620
My Love Forgive Me	Robert GOULET	1526
My Man! Wild Man!	WILD MAN STEVE	11928
My Maria	B.W. STEVENSON	5014
My Melody	Deniece WILLIAMS	3585
My Merry-Go-Round	Johnny NASH	11215
My Movie Of You	Leif GARRETT	12024
My Name Is Allan	Allan SHERMAN	7647
My Name Is Barbra (Soundtrack)	Barbra STREISAND	378
My Name Is Barbra, Two.....	Barbra STREISAND	553
My Name Is Jermaine	Jermaine JACKSON	9452
My Nation Underground	Julian COPE	9389
My Own House	David BROMBERG	11595
My Own Way	Willie NELSON	12794
My Own Way To Rock	Burton CUMMINGS	7159
My Radio Sure Sounds...	Larry GRAHAM/GRAHAM CENTRAL STATION	7861
My Road Our Road	Lee OSKAR	11080
My Second Album	Donna FARGO	7691
My Shy Violet	MILLS BROTHERS	13190
My Song	Keith JARRETT	13062
My Son, The Nut	Allan SHERMAN	508
My Spanish Heart	Chick COREA	5859
My Special Love	LaToya JACKSON	12716
My Sportin' Life	John KAY	13764
Mysteries	Keith JARRETT	13317
Mysterious Traveller	WEATHER REPORT	3292
Mystery Girl	Roy ORBISON	1180
Mystery Of Bulgarian...	BULGARIAN STATE RADI...	10515
The Mystery Of Edwin Drood	ORIGINAL CAST	11696
Mystery Street	John BRANNEN	9185
Mystery To Me	FLEETWOOD MAC	4707
Mystery Walk	M + M	12416
Mystical Adventure	Jean-Luc PONTY	5412
Mystic Dragons	BLUE MAGIC	11586
Mystic Man	Peter TOSH	8716
The Mystic Moods Of Love	MYSTIC MOODS Orch...	12808
Mystic Voyage	Roy AYERS UBIQUITY	6113
My Sweet Summer Suit...	LOVE UNLIMITED ORCHESTRA	8580
The Myths And Legends Of Kin...	Rick WAKEMAN	3074
My Time	Boz SCAGGS	9281
My Toot Toot	Jean KNIGHT	12866
My Toot-Toot	ROCKIN' SIDNEY	12455
My Town, My Guy & Me	Lesley GORE	11177
My Way	Frank SINATRA	1909
My Way	Major HARRIS	3143
My Way Of Life	Bert KAEMPFERT And H...	13230
My Whole World Ended	David RUFFIN	3017
My Woman, My Woman, My Wife	Dean MARTIN	7581
My Woman, My Woman, My Wife	Marty ROBBINS	7177
My World	Eddy ARNOLD	809

N

Title	Act	Rank
Nadia's Theme (The Young ...	Barry De VORZON	8360
Nadia's Theme (The Young ...	VARIOUS ARTISTS	4083
Naive Art	RED FLAG	12718
Najee's Theme	NAJEE	3436
Naked	TALKING HEADS	2752
Naked & Warm	Bill WITHERS	12197
Naked Eyes	NAKED EYES	2759
Naked To The World	Teena MARIE	6793
The Name Is Love	Bobby VINTON	13312
The Name Of This Band Is Ta...	TALKING HEADS	4966
Nancy	Nancy SINATRA	7558
Nancy	Nancy WILSON	6538
Nancy & Lee [A]	Lee HAZLEWOOD	1429
Nancy & Lee [A]	Nancy SINATRA	1429
Nancy In London	Nancy SINATRA	9609
Nancy-Naturally	Nancy WILSON	3822
Nancy's Greatest Hits	Nancy SINATRA	8878
The Nancy Wilson Show!	Nancy WILSON	2305
Nantucket Sleighride	MOUNTAIN	2089
'Nard	Bernard WRIGHT	6912
Nashville	SOUNDTRACK-MOVIE	6462
Nashville by Carr	Vikki CARR	8662
Nashville Skyline	Bob DYLAN	213
The Nashville Sound	Danny DAVIS And The ...	4131
Nasty, Nasty	BLACK 'N BLUE	6965
Natalie	Natalie COLE	1404
Natalie...Live	Natalie COLE	3577
The Natch'l Blues	Taj MAHAL	8698
National Breakout	The ROMANTICS	11900
National Emotion	TOMMY TUTONE	13117
Native Dancer	Wayne SHORTER	12820
Native Sons	LOGGINS & MESSINA	2645
Nat King Cole At The Sands	Nat King COLE	7585
The Nat King Cole Song...	HOLLYRIDGE STRINGS	12231
Natty Dread	Bob MARLEY And The W...	5341
Natural Act	Kris KRISTOFFERSON &...	8731
Natural Avenue	John LODGE	8841
Natural High	BLOODSTONE	2719
Natural High	The COMMODORES	382
Naturally	J.J. CALE	3619
Naturally	Leon HAYWOOD	8136
Naturally	THREE DOG NIGHT	616
Natural Man	Lou RAWLS	4260
Natural Progressions	Bernie LEADON-Michel...	8870
Natural States [A]	David LANZ	8422
Natural States [A]	Paul SPEER	8422
The Nature Of The Beast	APRIL WINE	1789
Nature Planned It	FOUR TOPS	3982
Naughty	Chaka KHAN	4404
Navy Blue	Diane RENAY	7115
Nazz	NAZZ	5451
Nazz Nazz	NAZZ	5331
NBC's Saturday Night Live	SOUNDTRACK-TV	4825
Ndeda	Quincy JONES	10783
Nearly Human	Todd RUNDGREN	8117
The Nearness Of You	John GARY	2364
Near The Beginning	VANILLA FUDGE	1782
Nebraska	Bruce SPRINGSTEEN	1460
The Need Of Love	EARTH, WIND & FIRE	6842
The Need To Be	Esther SATTERFIELD	12330
Negotiations And Love Songs (1...	Paul SIMON	7436
Neil Diamond/Gold	Neil DIAMOND	720
Neil Diamond/His 12 Greatest...	Neil DIAMOND	2173
Neil Diamond's Greatest Hits	Neil DIAMOND	4480

Title	Act	Rank
Neil Sedaka's Greatest Hits	Neil SEDAKA	10789
Neil Sedaka Sings His Greates...	Neil SEDAKA	11635
Terence Trent D'Arby...	Terence Trent D'ARBY	6209
Neither One Of Us	Gladys KNIGHT & The ...	1618
Nemesis	AXE	11314
Neon	The CYRKLE	13061
Nero Goes "Pops" [A]	BOSTON POPS Orchestr...	6936
Nero Goes "Pops" [A]	Peter NERO	6936
Neruda	Tom COCHRANE/RED RID...	5950
Nervous Night	The HOOTERS	803
The Net	LITTLE RIVER BAND	5168
Nether Lands	Dan FOGELBERG	1266
Never A Dull Moment	Rod STEWART	491
Never Buy Texas From...	BRIDES OF FUNKENSTEI...	8927
Never Can Say Goodbye	Gloria GAYNOR	3766
Never Die Young	James TAYLOR	2357
The Never Ending Impressi...	The IMPRESSIONS	5121
Never Enough	Patty SMYTH	5827
Never Felt So Good	James INGRAM	9832
Never Get Out Of These Bl...	John Lee HOOKER	9749
Never Gonna Be Another One	Thelma HOUSTON	10080
Never Gonna Let You Go	Vicki Sue ROBINSON	2703
Never Kick A Sleepin...	Mitch RYDER And The ...	9611
Never Let Her Go	David GATES	8007
Never Let Me Down	David BOWIE	3364
Never Letting Go	Phoebe SNOW	6244
Never Mind The Bollocks Here'...	SEX PISTOLS	7216
Never, Never, Never	Shirley BASSEY	5130
Never Run Never Hide	Benny MARDONES	5322
Never Say Die!	BLACK SABBATH	6324
Never Say Never	Melba MOORE	9128
Never Say Never	ROMEO VOID	11010
Never Say You Can't Survi...	Curtis MAYFIELD	12607
Never Surrender	TRIUMPH	2618
Never Too Much	Luther VANDROSS	1564
New! Improved! Blue Cheer	BLUE CHEER	5858
New Affair	The EMOTIONS	12254
New And Improved	SPINNERS	1595
New Ballads	Rod McKUEN	7713
The New Beatles Song B...	HOLLYRIDGE STRINGS	12174
New Beginnings	The DELLS	12406
New Beginnings...	Morgana KING	12445
New Blood	BLOOD, SWEAT & TEARS	3474
New Boots & Panties!!!	Ian DURY	11505
Newborn	JAMES GANG	8187
The New Born Free	The HESITATIONS	13389
The New Boss	Joe TEX	10416
New Chautauqua	PAT METHENY GROUP	4288
New City	BLOOD, SWEAT & TEARS	5278
New Clear Days	The VAPORS	4476
New Dimensions	3° DEGREES	10778
New Directions	Gary LEWIS And The P...	12811
New Directions	TAVARES	10178
The New Ebb Tide	Frank CHACKSFIELD An...	9395
New Edition	NEW EDITION	810
New England	NEW ENGLAND	5092
New England	WISHBONE ASH	10306
New Feelin'	Liza MINNELLI	12371
The New First Family, 196...	VARIOUS ARTISTS	7008
A New Flame	SIMPLY RED	1636
The New Gary Puckett...	Gary PUCKETT And The...	5360
New Generation	CHAMBERS BROTHERS	10537
New Gold Dream (81-82-83-84)	SIMPLE MINDS	5945
New Gold Hits	4 SEASONS	4475
New Harvest...First Gathering	Dolly PARTON	5120
New Hope For The Wretched	The PLASMATICS	9088

Title	Act	Rank
New Horizon	Isaac HAYES	7213
New Horizons	The SYLVERS	7681
New Jersey	BON JOVI	135
New Jersey	Joe PISCOPO	13008
New Kids On The Bloc...	NEW KIDS ON THE BLOC...	1000
A New Kind Of Connie...	Connie FRANCIS	13109
New Kind Of Feeling	Anne MURRAY	2778
The New Lee Dorsey	Lee DORSEY	10533
A New Life	MARSHALL TUCKER Band	2988
New Light Through Old Windows	Chris REA	7530
The New Look	Fontella BASS	8805
New Looks	B.J. THOMAS	13502
New Lovers And Old Friends	Johnny RIVERS	10136
New Morning	Bob DYLAN	1525
The New Order	TESTAMENT	8023
New Orleans At Midnight	Pete FOUNTAIN	6256
A New Perspective	Donald BYRD	9532
A New Place In The Sun	Glen CAMPBELL	2402
New Riders	NEW RIDERS Of The PU...	9523
New Riders Of The Pu...	NEW RIDERS Of The PU...	4140
New Routes	LULU	6640
N.E.W.S.	GOLDEN EARRING	8916
The New Searchers LP	The SEARCHERS	9760
The New Seekers	The SEEKERS	6414
New Sensations	Lou REED	3788
News Of The World	QUEEN	534
A New Song For Young Love	The LETTERMEN	5533
The New Spirit Of Capitol	VARIOUS ARTISTS	13829
A New Time-A New Day	CHAMBERS BROTHERS	2632
New Traditionalists	DEVO	3118
New Values	Iggy POP	12496
New Vintage	Maynard FERGUSON	9211
New Ways But Love Stays	The SUPREMES	4649
A New World Record	ELECTRIC LIGHT ORCHE...	201
New Worlds	MANDRILL	11052
New Year, New Band, New Compa...	John MAYALL	11026
New York	Lou REED	3630
New York Cake	KANO	13044
New York City (You're A Woman)	Al KOOPER	13305
New York Connection	Tom SCOTT & The L.A....	3834
New York Dolls	NEW YORK DOLLS	7910
New York-London-Paris-Munich	M	8771
New York, New York	SOUNDTRACK-MOVIE	4971
New York Tendaberry	Laura NYRO	3971
New York Wonderland	Andre KOSTELANETZ An...	9150
The New Zapp IV U	ZAPP	6809
Next	JOURNEY	7423
Next Of Kihn	Greg KIHN Band	9038
Next Position Please	CHEAP TRICK	7103
Nexus	ARGENT	10747
Nice Day For Something	Lee MICHAELS	12086
Nice Feelin'	Rita COOLIDGE	9206
Nice 'N' Naasty	SALSOUL Orchestra	5857
A Nice Pair	PINK FLOYD	4019
A Nice Place To Be	George HOWARD	6151
Nice To Be With You	GALLERY	5808
Nick Lowe And His Co...	Nick LOWE And His CO...	8574
Nick Mason's Fictitious Sports	Nick MASON	12509
Nick Of Time	Bonnie RAITT	170
Nick The Knife	Nick LOWE	5767
Nicolette	Nicolette LARSON	1788
Niecy	Deniece WILLIAMS	3188
Nigel	Nigel OLSSON	10892
Night	NIGHT	8296
Night After Night	Bill QUATEMAN	9405
Night After Night	Nils LOFGREN	5992

Title	Act	Rank
Night After Night	U.K.	9335
Night And Day	Joe JACKSON	682
A Night At Studio 54	VARIOUS ARTISTS	2824
Night Attack	ANGEL CITY	12342
A Night At The Opera	QUEEN	448
Night Beat	Sam COOKE	5855
Nightbirds	Patti LaBELLE	1431
Nightclubbing	Grace JONES	3530
Night Cruiser	DEODATO	13057
Nightcruising	The BAR-KAYS	3717
Night Fades Away	Nils LOFGREN	7852
Night Fever	FATBACK	12075
Night Flight	Justin HAYWARD	11608
Night Flight	Yvonne ELLIMAN	4165
Nightflight To Venus	BONEY M	8565
The Nightfly	Donald FAGEN	2157
Night Grooves	The BLACKBYRDS	10809
Nighthawks	Keith EMERSON	12810
Nighthawks	The NIGHTHAWKS	12141
Nighthawks At The Diner	Tom WAITS	10820
The Night I Fell In Love	Luther VANDROSS	1529
Nightingales & Bomb...	MANFRED MANN'S EARTH...	8269
Night In The Ruts	AEROSMITH	2100
The Night Is Still Young	SHA NA NA	8963
Night Journey	Doc SEVERINSEN	12854
Night Lights Harmony	FOUR TOPS	11057
Nightline	Randy CRAWFORD	12172
Nightmares...And Other Tale...	J. GEILS Band	3133
Night Moves	Bob SEGER	468
Night Of The Living Dregs	DIXIE DREGS	7548
Night On Bald Mountain	FIREBALLET	10198
A Night On The Town	BROWNSVILLE STATION	12768
A Night On The Town	Rod STEWART	271
Nightout	Ellen FOLEY	10272
Night Owl	Gerry RAFFERTY	3065
Night Passage	WEATHER REPORT	5704
Night-Rider!	Tim WEISBERG	7499
Nightrider	Charlie DANIELS Band	5454
Nights (Feel Like Getting Dow...	Billy OCEAN	12066
Nights Are Forever	ENGLAND DAN & John F...	1407
Night Shift	FOGHAT	3648
Nightshift	The COMMODORES	1832
Night Songs	CINDERELLA	304
Nightsongs	Earl KLUGH	8197
The Night The Lights Wen...	SOUNDTRACK-MOVIE	12576
The Night The Lights Went ...	Vicki LAWRENCE	5481
Night Things	Ronnie MILSAP	13487
Nighttide	MYSTIC MOODS Orchestra	8106
A Night To Remember	Cyndi LAUPER	4103
Nightwalker	Gino VANNELLI	1628
Nightwatch	Kenny LOGGINS	982
Nightwings	Stanley TURRENTINE	7648
Nils	Nils LOFGREN	5022
Nils Lofgren	Nils LOFGREN	8939
Nilsson Schmilsson	NILSSON	531
Nina Simone In Concert	Nina SIMONE	8661
9	PUBLIC IMAGE LIMITED	6721
9 1/2 Weeks	SOUNDTRACK-MOVIE	6541
Nine Lives	Bonnie RAITT	8775
Nine Lives	REO SPEEDWAGON	3449
90125	YES	694
9012Live - The Solos	YES	7876
9.9	9.9	6122
Chicago 19	CHICAGO	2049
1980	B.T. EXPRESS	12042
1980	Gil SCOTT-HERON & Br...	6898

Title	Act	Rank
1988 Summer Olympics-One ...	VARIOUS ARTISTS	4519
1984 (For The Love Of Big Brot...	EURYTHMICS	7738
1984 (MCMLXXXIV)	VAN HALEN	161
1957-1972	The MIRACLES/Smokey ...	5830
1990	The TEMPTATIONS	2688
1999	PRINCE	177
1975: The Duets [A]	Dave BRUBECK	11621
1975: The Duets [A]	Paul DESMOND	11621
1969	SOUNDTRACK-MOVIE	12524
1963-The Year's Most...	Enoch LIGHT & The LI...	12200
9 To 5	SOUNDTRACK-MOVIE	6543
9 To 5 And Odd Jobs	Dolly PARTON	1218
Nine Tonight	Bob SEGER	596
Nine To The Universe	Jimi HENDRIX	10021
98.6/Ain't Gonna Lie	KEITH	10479
99 Luftballons	NENA	4246
96 Tears	QUESTION MARK & The ...	5787
Nitty Gritty	Gladys KNIGHT & The ...	7041
The Nitty Gritty Dir...	NITTY GRITTY DIRT BA...	10174
Nitzinger	NITZINGER	10743
No Answer	ELECTRIC LIGHT ORCHE...	13689
No Arms Can Ever Hold You	The BACHELORS	11745
No Ballads	The ROCKETS	5455
No Blue Thing	Ray LYNCH	13773
Nobody But Me	HUMAN BEINZ	6718
Nobody Does It Like Me	Shirley BASSEY	10519
Nobody's Perfect	DEEP PURPLE	8804
No Brakes	John WAITE	1285
No Control	Eddie MONEY	1879
No Dice	BADFINGER	3437
A Nod Is As Good As A W...	SMALL FACES/FACES	1161
No Earthly Connection	Rick WAKEMAN	7206
No Easy Walk To Freedo...	PETER, PAUL & MARY	12367
No Easy Way Out	Robert TEPPER	10689
Noel	NOEL	8979
No Escape	Marc TANNER BAND	9869
No Exit	FATES WARNING	7987
No Free Lunch	GREEN ON RED	12418
No Frills	Bette MIDLER	6381
No Fuel Left For The...	DISNEYLAND AFTER DAR...	8689
No Fun Aloud	Glenn FREY	2241
No Goodbyes	Daryl HALL & John OA...	9041
No Guru, No Method, No Teach...	Van MORRISON	7171
No Guts...No Glory	MOLLY HATCHET	5913
No Heavy Petting	UFO	12049
No Holdin' Back	Randy TRAVIS	2807
No Jacket Required	Phil COLLINS	41
No Lookin' Back	Michael McDONALD	5552
Nomadness	STRAWBS	10386
No Man's Land	Lene LOVICH	13118
No Matter What Shape (Your St...	The T-BONES	7253
No Mean City	NAZARETH	6984
No More Dirty Deals	Johnny Van ZANT Band	5169
No Muss...No Fuss	Donnie IRIS	7954
No Mystery	RETURN TO FOREVER	4857
Nona	Nona HENDRYX	6719
Non Fiction	The BLASTERS	9205
No Night So Long	Dionne WARWICK	2650
No, No, Nanette	ORIGINAL CAST	5040
Non Stop	Julio IGLESIAS	5484
Non-Stop	B.T. EXPRESS	2416
Non-Stop Ecstatic Dancing	SOFT CELL	6464
Non-Stop Erotic Cabaret	SOFT CELL	1586
No Nukes/The MUSE Concert...	VARIOUS ARTISTS	2783
No One Can Do It Better	THE D.O.C.	2446
No Other	Gene CLARK	10738

Title	Act	Rank
No Parking On The Dance Flo...	MIDNIGHT STAR	822
No Parlez	Paul YOUNG	5799
No Parole From Rock 'n' Roll	ALCATRAZZ	8556
No Place For Disgrace	FLOTSAM AND JETSAM	10541
No Place To Run	UFO	5834
No Protection	JEFFERSON AIRPLANE/S...	2590
No Reason To Cry	Eric CLAPTON	1735
No Refuge	Eddie SCHWARTZ	12650
No Respect	Rodney DANGERFIELD	4297
No Respect	VAIN	10687
No Rest For The Wicked	HELIX	13103
No Rest For The Wicked	Ozzy OSBOURNE	2142
Norma Jean	NORMA JEAN	8431
Norman Connors Presents Aq...	AQUARIAN DREAM	10623
North Coast	Michael STANLEY Band	5931
Northern Journey	IAN & SYLVIA	7282
Northern Lights-Southern Cross	The BAND	3344
North Of A Miracle	Nick HEYWARD	12804
Norwood (Soundtrack)	Glen CAMPBELL	6963
No Second Chance	CHARLIE	6881
No Secrets	Carly SIMON	254
No Stranger To Love	Roy AYERS	6189
No Strings	ACE	12993
No Sweat	BLOOD, SWEAT & TEARS	6542
No Tellin' Lies	ZEBRA	8247
Not Fakin' It	Michael MONROE	11532
Not Fragile	BACHMAN-TURNER OVERD...	282
Not Guilty...	Larry GATLIN/GATLIN ...	13422
Nothin' But The Blues	Johnny WINTER	9808
Nothin' But Trouble	Nia PEEPLES	6075
Nothing But A Breeze	Jesse WINCHESTER	7420
Nothing But The Truth	Ruben BLADES	11653
Nothingface	VOIVOD	7758
Nothing In Common	SOUNDTRACK-MOVIE	13438
Nothing Is Sacred	The GODZ	13510
...Nothing Like The Sun	STING	860
Nothing Matters Without Love	SEDUCTION	2529
Nothing Says I Love You Like...	Jerry BUTLER	12145
Nothing's Shocking	JANE'S ADDICTION	4877
Nothing To Fear	OINGO BOINGO	10567
Nothing To Lose	Eddie MONEY	4096
Nothing Will Be As It Was...Tom...	Flora PURIM	11786
Nothin' Matters And What ...	John MELLENCAMP	1863
Not Insane Or Anything Y...	FIRESIGN THEATRE	8943
Not Just The Girl Next Doo...	Nancy MARTINEZ	13319
Notorious	DURAN DURAN	1897
The Notorious Byrd Brothers	The BYRDS	5078
Not Shy	Walter EGAN	4183
Not The Boy Next Door	Peter ALLEN	12007
Novella	RENAISSANCE	4665
Novo Combo	NOVO COMBO	11267
Now	Patrice RUSHEN	4383
Now	The TUBES	9935
Now And Forever	AIR SUPPLY	2589
Now & Then	CARPENTERS	767
Now And Zen	Robert PLANT	635
"Now Appearing" At Ole' Miss	B.B. KING	12031
No Way To Treat A Lady	Helen REDDY	1654
Now Do-U-Wanta Dance	Larry GRAHAM/GRAHAM ...	7260
Now Hear This	Moms MABLEY	12149
Now I'm A Woman	Nancy WILSON	3668
Now Look	Ronnie WOOD	9145
Now Or Never	John SCHNEIDER	3066
Now Playing	Bernadette PETERS	9933
Now Voyager	Barry GIBB	8437
Now We May Begin	Randy CRAWFORD	11691

Title	Act	Rank
NRBQ	NRBQ	11727
Nuclear Furniture	JEFFERSON AIRPLANE/S...	3127
Nude	DEAD OR ALIVE	9144
'Nuff Said	Ike & Tina TURNER	7844
Nugent	Ted NUGENT	5967
Number 5	Steve MILLER Band	2848
The Number Of The Beast	IRON MAIDEN	2480
#1	Sonny JAMES	12764
The Number One Hits	Elvis PRESLEY	10390
Number 1 Hits, Vol. ...	Billy VAUGHN and His...	8930
Numbers	Cat STEVENS	1955
Numbers	RUFUS	7547
#7	George STRAIT	9561
#10	GUESS WHO	10072
No. 10, Upping Street	BIG AUDIO DYNAMITE	7262
Nunsexmonkrock	Nina HAGEN	13272
Nurds	The ROCHES	9826
Nutbush City Limits	Ike & Tina TURNER	11232
Nuthin' Fancy	LYNYRD SKYNYRD	1664
The Nylon Curtain	Billy JOEL	894

O

Title	Act	Rank
Oasis	Jim MESSINA	5436
Oasis	Roberta FLACK	11053
Objects Of Desire	Michael FRANKS	5463
Oblivion	UTOPIA	7292
Obscured By Clouds (Soundtrack...	PINK FLOYD	3938
Obsession	Bob JAMES	7194
Obsession	UFO	3855
Occupation: Foole	George CARLIN	3216
Ocean Front Property	George STRAIT	6303
Oceanliner	PASSPORT	12127
Ocean Rain	ECHO & The BUNNYMEN	8118
O.C. Smith At Home	O.C. SMITH	5172
O.C. Smith's Greatest Hits	O.C. SMITH	12070
Octave	MOODY BLUES	1888
October	U2	4943
Octoberon	BARCLAY JAMES HARVES...	12592
Octopus	GENTLE GIANT	10839
Octopussy	SOUNDTRACK-MOVIE	11271
The Odd Couple	SOUNDTRACK-MOVIE	13595
Odds & Sods	The WHO	2714
Odessa	BEE GEES	1921
Odessey & Oracle	The ZOMBIES	6686
Ode To Billie Joe	Bobbie GENTRY	901
Ode To Billy Joe	Billy VAUGHN and His...	13779
Ode To My Lady	Willie HUTCH	10408
Odetta Sings Folk Songs	ODETTA	8646
Odori	HIROSHIMA	5948
Odyssey	Charles EARLAND	9072
Odyssey	ODYSSEY	2564
Odyssey	Yngwie MALMSTEEN	4525
Of A Simple Man	LOBO	2528
Of Cabbages And Kings	CHAD & JEREMY	12753
Offering	AXE	6362
An Officer And A Gentlem...	SOUNDTRACK-MOVIE	4317
The Official "Live" Gentle G...	GENTLE GIANT	8794
Official Music	KING BISCUIT BOY	13563
The Official Music Of The...	VARIOUS ARTISTS	8238
Offramp	PAT METHENY GROUP	4685
Off The Beatle Track	George MARTIN & His ...	8928
Off The Record	The SWEET	11528
Off The Wall	Michael JACKSON	51
Off The Wall	SMOKESTACK LIGHTNIN'	13645
Off To See The Lizard	Jimmy BUFFETT	6369
O.F.R.	NITRO	9823

Title	Act	Rank
Ogdens' Nut Gone Flake	SMALL FACES/FACES	9002
Oh! Brother	Larry GATLIN/GATLIN ...	9778
Oh Happy Day	Glen CAMPBELL	3820
Oh How We Danced	Jim CAPALDI	7046
Ohio Express	OHIO EXPRESS	8967
Ohio Players Gold	OHIO PLAYERS	3739
Ohio Players Greatest Hits	OHIO PLAYERS	8125
Oh, Julie!	Barry MANILOW	8191
Oh Mercy	Bob DYLAN	4088
Oh No! It's Devo	DEVO	5087
Oh, What A Mighty Ti...	NEW RIDERS Of The PU...	11073
Oh Yes I Can	David CROSBY	8432
Oingo Boingo	OINGO BOINGO	11600
The O'Jays: Collectors' Items	The O'JAYS	10077
The O'Jays In Philadelphia	The O'JAYS	10486
The O'Jays Live In London	The O'JAYS	2396
O'Keefe	Danny O'KEEFE	6604
Okie	J.J. CALE	8032
Okie From Muskogee	Merle HAGGARD	2343
Ol' Blue Eyes Is Back	Frank SINATRA	2271
Old & In The Way	OLD & IN THE WAY	7985
Old Crest On A New Wave	Dave MASON	7462
Old Dan's Records	Gordon LIGHTFOOT	7513
Old 8 x 10	Randy TRAVIS	2760
Old Enough	Lou Ann BARTON	9870
Oldies But Goodies, Vol. 7	VARIOUS ARTISTS	9328
Oldies But Goodies, Vol. 6	VARIOUS ARTISTS	5511
Old Loves Die Hard	TRIUMVIRAT	7959
Old Socks, New Shoes...New ...	The CRUSADERS	6520
An Old Time Christmas	Randy TRAVIS	8657
Old Ways	Neil YOUNG	7266
Ole ELO	ELECTRIC LIGHT ORCHE...	1978
Olias Of Sunhillow	Jon ANDERSON	4689
Oliver!	SOUNDTRACK-MOVIE	780
Oliver Again	OLIVER	6596
Oliver & Company	SOUNDTRACK-MOVIE	11272
Olivia Newton-John's G...	Olivia NEWTON-JOHN	1892
Olivia's Greatest Hits...	Olivia NEWTON-JOHN	814
O Lucky Man!	Alan PRICE	7815
Ol' Waylon	Waylon JENNINGS	1620
Ommadawn	Mike OLDFIELD	9900
On	OFF BROADWAY USA	7616
On A Clear Day You Can S...	Barbra STREISAND	6206
On A Clear Day You Can See ...	ORIGINAL CAST	3832
On And On	FAT BOYS	13149
On A Night Like This	BUCKWHEAT ZYDECO	12572
On A Roll	POINT BLANK	7693
On Broadway (Soundtr...	Diana ROSS & The SUP...	5091
Once Bitten	GREAT WHITE	1327
Once More	Porter WAGONER and D...	13469
Once Upon A Christmas [A]	Dolly PARTON	6188
Once Upon A Christmas [A]	Kenny ROGERS	6188
Once Upon A Dream	ENCHANTMENT	4391
Once Upon A Dream	RASCALS/YOUNG RASCAL...	1708
Once Upon A Time	KINGSTON TRIO	10466
Once Upon A Time	SIMPLE MINDS	1008
Once Upon A Time...	Donna SUMMER	1623
One	BEE GEES	6606
One	Bob JAMES	6406
The One And Only...	Gladys KNIGHT & The ...	10372
On Earth As It Is In Heaven	ANGEL	7117
One Bad Habit	Michael FRANKS	6082
One Big Day	FACE TO FACE	12023
One Bright Day	Ziggy MARLEY & The M...	3689
One By One	The IMPRESSIONS	8883
One Day At A Time	Joan BAEZ	5914

Title	Act	Rank
One Day In Your Life	Michael JACKSON	9203
One Dozen Roses	The MIRACLES/Smokey ...	7075
One Eighty	AMBROSIA	1972
One-Eyed Jack	Garland JEFFREYS	7783
One Fine Morning	LIGHTHOUSE	5448
One Flew Over The Cuckoo...	SOUNDTRACK-MOVIE	10915
One For The Money	The WHISPERS	12036
One For The Road [A]	Leon RUSSELL	3751
One For The Road [A]	Willie NELSON	3751
One For The Road	RIGHTEOUS BROTHERS	13261
One For The Road	The KINKS	1296
The One Giveth, The ...	BOOTSY'S RUBBER BAND	10230
One Good Reason	Paul CARRACK	4415
One Has My Name	Barry YOUNG	6934
One Heartbeat	Smokey ROBINSON	1562
One Hell Of A Woman	Vikki CARR	11310
110 In The Shade	ORIGINAL CAST	5325
100cc	10cc	11646
100% Cotton	James COTTON Band	9936
One In A Million You	Larry GRAHAM/GRAHAM ...	2535
One Kiss For Old Times' Sake	Ronnie DOVE	7984
One Live Badger	BADGER	11009
One Lord, One Faith, One ...	Aretha FRANKLIN	7217
One Love--One Dream	Jeffrey OSBORNE	6744
One Man Band	Ronnie DYSON	10264
One Man Dog	James TAYLOR	1260
One More From The Road	LYNYRD SKYNYRD	990
One More Round	Glenn YARBROUGH	11969
One More Song	Randy MEISNER	3181
One More Story	Peter CETERA	5493
One More Time	Wayne NEWTON	12564
One More Try For Love	Ronnie MILSAP	13191
One Nation Under A Groove	FUNKADELIC	2334
Oneness/Silver Dreams-Gold...	Carlos SANTANA	7640
One Night Of Sin	Joe COCKER	4027
One Night Stand	Susan RAYE	13430
One Night With A Stranger	Martin BRILEY	4908
One Of A Kind	Bill BRUFORD	10403
One Of The Boys	Roger DALTREY	4711
One Of These Nights	EAGLES	102
101	DEPECHE MODE	5108
One On One (Soundtrack)	SEALS & CROFTS	9321
One On One	Bob JAMES & Earl KLU...	1924
One On One	CHEAP TRICK	2911
One Particular Harbour	Jimmy BUFFETT	5145
One Piece At A Time	Johnny CASH And The ...	13318
1 + 1	GRIN	11892
One Second	YELLO	8386
One Size Fits All	Frank ZAPPA	4153
One's On The Way	Loretta LYNN	8856
One Step Beyond	Johnnie TAYLOR	7412
One Step Beyond	MADNESS	9155
One Step Closer	DOOBIE BROTHERS	946
One Step Closer	Gavin CHRISTOPHER	7102
One Stormy Night	MYSTIC MOODS Orchestra	6532
The One That You Love	AIR SUPPLY	565
One To One	Carole KING	8932
One To One	Howard JONES	4764
One-Trick Pony	Paul SIMON	1702
1-2-3	Len BARRY	7524
1234	Ronnie WOOD	11456
1,2,3 Red Light	1910 FRUITGUM CO.	9942
One Vice At A Time	KROKUS	5279
One Voice	Barbra STREISAND	2043
One Voice	Barry MANILOW	1316
One Way Featuring Al Hudson(2)	ONE WAY	7750

Title	Act	Rank
One Way Featuring Al Hudson	ONE WAY	12166
One Way Home	The HOOTERS	3632
One Way...Or Another	CACTUS	6616
One World	RARE EARTH	1932
On Fire	T-CONNECTION	8995
On Golden Pond	SOUNDTRACK-MOVIE	9642
On Her Majesty's Secret ...	SOUNDTRACK-MOVIE	6969
On Love	David T. WALKER	11488
Only A Lad	OINGO BOINGO	11619
Only For Lovers	Roger WILLIAMS	8079
Only For The Lonely	Mavis STAPLES	12736
Only Four You	MARY JANE GIRLS	2058
Only Life	The FEELIES	12376
Only Love Can Break A Hear...	Dionne WARWICK	11791
Only Make Believe	BELL And JAMES	10628
Only One Love In My Life	Ronnie MILSAP	7268
Only The Best	FERRANTE & TEICHER	5980
Only The Lonely	Sonny JAMES	11975
Only The Strong Survive	Billy PAUL	11986
On My Side	The COWSILLS	13817
On My Way	B.J. THOMAS	7580
On Solid Ground	Larry CARLTON	9707
On Stage	Lily TOMLIN	10308
On Stage	LOGGINS & MESSINA	871
On Stage	RAINBOW	6834
On Stage and In The Movies	Dionne WARWICK	10415
On Stage-February, 1970	Elvis PRESLEY	1816
On Target	FASTWAY	9852
On The Beach	Neil YOUNG	2492
On The Border	EAGLES	516
On The Corner	Miles DAVIS	9422
On The Edge	SEA LEVEL	8180
On The Edge	The BABYS	6240
On The Line	Gary (U.S.) BONDS	5096
On The Move	Tony SANDLER And Ral...	12541
On The Move	Trini LOPEZ	2857
On The Nile	EGYPTIAN LOVER	10186
On The One	DAZZ BAND	6119
On The Radio: Greatest Hits:...	Donna SUMMER	324
On The Rise	S.O.S. BAND	3757
On The Road	George CARLIN	8017
On The Road	Jesse Colin YOUNG	4059
On The Road Again	D.J. ROGERS	11569
On The Road To Freedom [A]	Alvin LEE	9779
On The Road To Freedom [A]	Myron LeFEVRE	9779
On The Road To Kingdom Come	Harry CHAPIN	8846
On The Strength	GRANDMASTER FLASH An...	13336
On The Third Day	ELECTRIC LIGHT ORCHE...	3994
On The Threshold Of A Dream	MOODY BLUES	511
On The Track	Leon REDBONE	6053
On The Waters	BREAD	1810
On The Way To The Sky	Neil DIAMOND	2145
On Through The Night	DEF LEPPARD	3140
On Time	GRAND FUNK RAILROAD	1447
On To Victory	HUMBLE PIE	6054
On Your Feet Or On Your ...	BLUE ÖYSTER CULT	3594
Oogum Boogum	Brenton WOOD	13467
Ooh La La	SMALL FACES/FACES	3309
Ooh Yeah!	Daryl HALL & John OA...	2825
Oooh So Good 'N Blues	Taj MAHAL	12752
Oops! Wrong Planet	UTOPIA	7542
Open	BLUES IMAGE	8630
Open All Night	GEORGIA SATELLITES	6997
Open All Night	LEROI BROS.	12611
Open Fire	MONTROSE	8024
Open Fire	Y&T	5739

Title	Act	Rank
Opening Nights At The Met	VARIOUS ARTISTS	4255
Open Mind	Jean-Luc PONTY	10422
Open Our Eyes	EARTH, WIND & FIRE	1078
Open Road	DONOVAN	2665
Open Sesame	KOOL & The GANG	6626
Open Sesame	WHODINI	3849
Open Up And Say...Ahh!	POISON	147
Open Up Your Love	The WHISPERS	6880
Open Your Eyes You Can Fly	Flora PURIM	5557
Opera Sauvage	VANGELIS	3936
Operation: Mindcrime	QUEENSRYCHE	2878
Opus X	CHILLIWACK	9491
Orange Blossom Special	Johnny CASH	6513
Orange Colored Sky	Bert KAEMPFERT And H...	10979
Oranges And Lemons	XTC	4321
Orbisongs	Roy ORBISON	9095
The Orbison Way	Roy ORBISON	12038
Orchestral Favorites	Frank ZAPPA	12146
Ordinary Fool	Paul WILLIAMS	10683
Organ Grinder Swing	Jimmy SMITH	2444
Orgasmatron	MOTORHEAD	10341
The Original Disco Duck	Rick DEES	11269
The Original Disco Man	James BROWN	10932
Original Golden Hits - Vol. 1	Jerry Lee LEWIS	10059
Original Golden Hits, Volume I	Johnny CASH	6443
Original Golden Hits - Vol. 2	Jerry Lee LEWIS	9412
Original Golden Hits, Volume II	Johnny CASH	7877
The Original Hits Of Righ...	VARIOUS ARTISTS	11392
The Original Hootenanny	VARIOUS ARTISTS	11395
The Original Human Being	BLUE CHEER	12348
The Original Monster...	Bobby "Boris" PICKET...	12545
Original Music From The M...	Hugo MONTENEGRO	4694
The Original Peanuts	SUNNY & The SUNLINER...	12994
The Original Penetration! An...	The PYRAMIDS	10377
The Original Recordings	Billie HOLIDAY	9279
The Originals	KISS	4457
The Originals	STATLER BROTHERS	13271
The Original Soundtrack	10cc	1907
Original Stylin'	THREE TIMES DOPE	8220
Original Theme From Bonni...	FLATT & SCRUGGS	11961
The Original Voice Tracks Fro...	W.C. FIELDS	1817
Orion The Hunter	ORION THE HUNTER	6130
Orpheus	ORPHEUS	8030
Oscar Peterson Trio +...	OSCAR PETERSON TRIO	7937
Osibirock	OSIBISA	12229
Osibisa	OSIBISA	4461
The Osmond Christmas Album	The OSMONDS	10866
Osmonds	The OSMONDS	1191
The Osmonds Greatest Hits	The OSMONDS	13295
The Osmonds "Live"	The OSMONDS	1584
O Sole Mio - Favorite N...	Luciano PAVAROTTI	5789
The Other Man's Grass Is Alw...	Petula CLARK	6735
The Other One	Bob WELCH	8670
The Other Ones	OTHER ONES	11027
Other Roads	Boz SCAGGS	4718
Other Side Of Abbey Road	George BENSON	8975
The Other Side Of Life	MOODY BLUES	1150
The Other Side Of The Mirror	Stevie NICKS	2409
The Other Side Of The Rainbow	Melba MOORE	8059
Other Voices	The DOORS	3831
The Other Woman	Ray PARKER Jr./RAYDI...	2042
Otis Blue/Otis Redding Sings...	Otis REDDING	4357
Otis Redding In Person At Th...	Otis REDDING	5231
Otis Redding Live In Europe	Otis REDDING	3185
'Ot 'N' Sweaty	CACTUS	11344
OU812	VAN HALEN	288

Title	Act	Rank
Our Beloved Revoluti...	CAMPER VAN BEETHOVEN	7582
Our Day Will Come	Frankie VALLI	8620
Our Family Portrait	FIVE STAIRSTEPS	13484
Our Golden Favorites	FERRANTE & TEICHER	13282
Our Hero...Pat Cooper	Pat COOPER	3728
Our Man Flint	SOUNDTRACK-MOVIE	10530
Our Mann Flute	Herbie MANN	10359
Our Memories Of Elvis	Elvis PRESLEY	9825
Our Memories Of Elvis Volum...	Elvis PRESLEY	11162
Our Pleasure To Serve ...	STANKY BROWN Group	13097
Our Shining Hour [A]	Count BASIE	11894
Our Shining Hour [A]	Sammy DAVIS Jr.	11894
Our Song	Jack JONES	10323
Our Time's Coming	DINO, DESI & BILLY	10396
Our Wedding Album or The ...	VARIOUS ARTISTS	5032
Outa Hand	CONEY HATCH	13604
Out Among 'Em	LOVE CHILDS AFRO CUBAN BLUES BAND	11746
Out Here	LOVE	12151
Out Here On My Own	Lamont DOZIER	8812
Outlandos D'Amour	The POLICE	1682
Outlaw	WAR	4511
Outlaws	The OUTLAWS	2484
Outline	Gino SOCCIO	6386
Out Of Africa	SOUNDTRACK-MOVIE	4155
Out of Control	BROTHERS JOHNSON	8364
Out Of Limits!	The MARKETTS	5675
Out Of Mind Out Of Sight	MODELS	6283
Out Of Order	Rod STEWART	480
Out Of Our Hands	FLASH	9446
Out Of Our Heads	ROLLING STONES	418
Out Of Sight, Out Of...	LITTLE ANTHONY And The IMPERIALS	11664
Out Of The Blue	Debbie GIBSON	332
Out Of The Blue	ELECTRIC LIGHT ORCHESTRA	564
Out Of The Cellar	RATT	732
Out Of The Mist	ILLUSION	10928
Out Of The Shadows	Dave GRUSIN	8826
Out Of The Silent Planet	KING'S X	9290
Out Of The Storm	Jack BRUCE	12267
Out Of This World	EUROPE	2648
Out On A Limb	Moms MABLEY	4560
Outrageous	Kim FOWLEY	13259
Outrageous	LAKESIDE	6825
Outrageous	Richard PRYOR	12354
Outrider	Jimmy PAGE	3319
Outside Help	Johnny RIVERS	9838
Outside Inside	The TUBES	2048
Outsideinside	BLUE CHEER	6101
Outside Looking In	BODEANS	6485
The Outsiders Album #2	The OUTSIDERS	7974
Outta Season	Ike & Tina TURNER	6661
Out Where The Bright Lights...	Ronnie MILSAP	4444
Over Here! (Original Cast...	ANDREWS SISTERS	11449
Over-Nite Sensation	Frank ZAPPA	2336
Over The Edge	HURRICANE	4803
Over The Line	Greg GUIDRY	10957
Over The Rainbow	Livingston TAYLOR	12669
Over There (Live At The Venu...	The BLASTERS	9445
Over The Top	SOUNDTRACK-MOVIE	9661
Over Under Sideways Down	The YARDBIRDS	5376
The Owl And The Pussycat...	Barbra STREISAND	12181
Owlcreek Incident	PRELUDE	7659
Oxo	OXO	10129
Oxygene	Jean Michel JARRE	6087
Ozark Mountain Dared...	OZARK MOUNTAIN DARED...	12328
The Ozark Mountain D...	OZARK MOUNTAIN DARED...	3005

P

Title	Act	Rank
Pablo Cruise	PABLO CRUISE	12158
The Pacific Age	ORCHESTRAL MANOEUVRE...	4650
Pacific Gas And Elec...	PACIFIC GAS AND ELEC...	8072
Pacific Ocean Blue	Dennis WILSON	8441
The Pack Is Back	RAVEN	9437
Pack Up The Plantati...	Tom PETTY And The HE...	3194
Pac-Man Fever	BUCKNER And GARCIA	3919
Paid In Full	ERIC B. & RAKIM	4129
Pain	OHIO PLAYERS	11263
Pain In My Heart	Otis REDDING	9400
Painted, Tainted Rose	Al MARTINO	1312
The Painter	Paul ANKA	5929
Paint It Black	SOULFUL STRINGS	9566
Paint Your Wagon	SOUNDTRACK-MOVIE	1521
Pais Tropical	Sergio MENDES And BR...	10785
Paloma Blanca	George BAKER Selecti...	10402
Pampered Menial	PAVLOV'S DOG	11698
Panorama	The CARS	1203
Papa John Creach	Papa John CREACH	6539
The Papas & The Mamas	MAMAS & The PAPAS	1774
Papa's Got A Brand New Bag	James BROWN	2907
Paper Lace	PAPER LACE	9252
Paper Money	MONTROSE	5138
Paper Moon	SOUNDTRACK-MOVIE	9246
Paper Roses	Marie OSMOND	4940
Paper Tiger	Sue THOMPSON	12199
Parade	SPANDAU BALLET	5589
Parade: Music From The Motion Pict...	PRINCE	1145
Paradise	Grover WASHINGTON Jr...	3106
Paradise	Peabo BRYSON	6496
Paradise And Lunch	Ry COODER	11251
Paradise Ballroom	Graeme EDGE Band	11869
Paradise Bar And Grill	MAD RIVER	13428
Paradise, Hawaiian Style (S...	Elvis PRESLEY	2908
Paradise Theater	STYX	97
Paradise With An Oce...	COUNTRY JOE & The Fl...	7429
Parallel Lines	BLONDIE	453
Paranoid	BLACK SABBATH	434
Paris	PARIS	7934
Paris	SUPERTRAMP	1697
The Parkerilla	Graham PARKER And Th...	11845
Parliament Live/P Funk Earth T...	PARLIAMENT	3491
Parsley, Sage, Rosemary...	SIMON & GARFUNKEL	103
Parting Should Be Painless	Roger DALTREY	8944
Partners In Crime	Rupert HOLMES	2209
Part Of The Game	PABLO CRUISE	4587
Part Of You	Eric GALE	11224
The Partridge Family Alb...	PARTRIDGE FAMILY	222
The Partridge Family At ...	PARTRIDGE FAMILY	2594
The Partridge Family Not...	PARTRIDGE FAMILY	4607
The Partridge Family Sho...	PARTRIDGE FAMILY	2994
The Partridge Family Sou...	PARTRIDGE FAMILY	744
Part 3	KC And The SUNSHINE ...	437
Party	Iggy POP	11803
Party Mix!	The B-52s	6024
Party Of One	Tim WEISBERG	11019
Party Party	SOUNDTRACK-MOVIE	11711
The Party's Over	TALK TALK	9647
Party 'Til You're Broke	RUFUS	6840
Party Your Body	Stevie B	5860
Passage	CARPENTERS	4466
The Passenger	Melvin JAMES	10776
Passin' Thru	JAMES GANG	5983
Passion	Robin TROWER	6149

Title	Act	Rank
Passion Crimes	DARLING CRUEL	10965
Passionfruit	Michael FRANKS	9623
Passion, Grace & Fir...	Al Di MEOLA/John McL...	12206
A Passion Play	JETHRO TULL	1049
Passion: Music For The Last...	Peter GABRIEL	6490
Passionworks	HEART	4533
Pass It On	STAPLE SINGERS	11022
Pass Me By	Peggy LEE	11902
Pass The Plate	The CRUSADERS	11822
Pastel Blues	Nina SIMONE	10485
Pastels	Ron CARTER	13796
Pastiche	MANHATTAN TRANSFER	6949
Past Masters - Volume 1	The BEATLES	11372
Past Masters - Volume 2	The BEATLES	10020
Pastorale	Rod McKUEN	12506
Past, Present And Future	Al STEWART	8802
Pata Pata	Miriam MAKEBA	5575
Patches	Clarence CARTER	4739
Pat Garrett & Billy The Kid (So...	Bob DYLAN	1777
The Path	Ralph MacDONALD	4818
Pat McLaughlin	Pat McLAUGHLIN	13826
Pat Metheny Group	PAT METHENY GROUP	8561
Pat Paulsen For President	Pat PAULSEN	6533
Patrice	Patrice RUSHEN	9376
The Patsy Cline Story	Patsy CLINE	7318
Pattern Disruptive	Dickey BETTS	13027
Patti	Patti LaBELLE	5474
Patti Austin	Patti AUSTIN	6764
Patti La Belle	Patti LaBELLE	5502
Patton	SOUNDTRACK-MOVIE	8548
Pat Travers Band Live! Go For...	Pat TRAVERS	3101
Pat Travers' Black Pearl	Pat TRAVERS	7421
Paul And..	Paul STOOKEY	4411
Paul Anka	Paul ANKA	12799
Paul Anka Gold	Paul ANKA	8781
The Paul Butterfield...	Paul BUTTERFIELD Blu...	9167
Paul Davis	Paul DAVIS	12373
Paul Humphrey & The ...	Paul HUMPHREY & The ...	11465
Paul's Boutique	BEASTIE BOYS	3169
Paul Simon	Paul SIMON	757
Paul Simon In Concert/Live Rhy...	Paul SIMON	4148
Paul Stanley	Paul STANLEY	3105
A Pauper In Paridise	Gino VANNELLI	3817
Pavarotti's Greatest Hi...	Luciano PAVAROTTI	6121
The Payback	James BROWN	2576
The Peabo Bryson Collection	Peabo BRYSON	10877
Peace & Love	The POGUES	9353
Peaceful World	RASCALS/YOUNG RASCAL...	7363
Peace In Our Time	BIG COUNTRY	11682
Peace On You	Roger McGUINN	8754
Peace Sells...But Who's Buying?	MEGADETH	3928
Peace Will Come	Tom PAXTON	12886
Peaches & Herb's Greatest ...	PEACHES & HERB	13041
Peach Melba	Melba MOORE	12372
Peacing It All Together	LIGHTHOUSE	11692
The Peanut Butter Co...	PEANUT BUTTER CONSPI...	13482
Pearl	Janis JOPLIN	165
Pearl Harbor & The E...	PEARL HARBOR And The...	7964
Pearls-Songs Of Goffin And King	Carole KING	4523
Pearly Shells	Billy VAUGHN and His...	2957
Pearly Shells	Burl IVES	6826
Pebbles	PEBBLES	1207
Peculiar Friends	TEN WHEEL DRIVE With Genya RA...	12405
Peepshow	SIOUXSIE & The BANSHEES	5386
Pelican West	HAIRCUT ONE HUNDRED	2711
Pendulum	CREEDENCE CLEARWATER...	602

Title	Act	Rank
Penetrator	Ted NUGENT	5845
Penguin	FLEETWOOD MAC	5555
Pennies From Heaven	SOUNDTRACK-MOVIE	13579
The Pentangle	PENTANGLE	12992
People	Barbra STREISAND	229
People	HOTHOUSE FLOWERS	5346
People	Johnny MATHIS	13440
People Are People	DEPECHE MODE	5265
People Get Ready	The IMPRESSIONS	3582
People...Hold On	Eddie KENDRICKS	7820
People Like Us	MAMAS & The PAPAS	7873
People Like You	Eddie FISHER	13330
The People's Choice	FERRANTE & TEICHER	4417
The People Who Grinned T...	The HOUSEMARTINS	12243
The Percy Sledge Way	Percy SLEDGE	13127
Perfect	SOUNDTRACK-MOVIE	6096
Perfect Angel	Minnie RIPERTON	737
Perfect Combination [A]	Johnny GILL	10024
Perfect Combination [A]	Stacy LATTISAW	10024
Perfect Fit	Jerry KNIGHT	10796
Perfect Strangers	DEEP PURPLE	1868
Perfect Symmetry	FATES WARNING	10048
Perfect Timing	Donna ALLEN	8869
Perfect Timing	Michael SCHENKER Gro...	5940
Perfect View	The GRACES	10595
Performance	ASHFORD & SIMPSON	10217
Performance-Rockin' The Fillmo...	HUMBLE PIE	1882
Perhaps Love	Placido DOMINGO	2691
A Period Of Transition	Van MORRISON	5370
Permanent Vacation	AEROSMITH	426
Permanent Waves	RUSH	1160
Perry	Perry COMO	9262
Perry Como In Italy	Perry COMO	6239
Personal Attention	Stacy LATTISAW	10311
Person To Person	AVERAGE WHITE BAND/A...	3279
Perspective	AMERICA	13245
Perspective On Bud & Travi...	BUD And TRAVIS	10695
The Persuaders	The PERSUADERS	12660
Persuasive Percussio...	Enoch LIGHT & The LI...	10719
Peter	Peter YARROW	10269
Peter And The Commis... [A]	BOSTON POPS Orches...	6266
Peter And The Commissar [A]	Allan SHERMAN	6266
Peter Cetera	Peter CETERA	9977
Peter Criss	Peter CRISS	3272
Peter Gabriel	Peter GABRIEL	4274
Peter Gabriel (Security)	Peter GABRIEL	2371
Peter Gabriel (III)	Peter GABRIEL	1767
Peter Gabriel (II)	Peter GABRIEL	5435
Peter Gabriel/Plays Live	Peter GABRIEL	5327
Peter McCann	Peter McCANN	6989
Peter Nero In Person	Peter NERO	4101
Peter Nero Plays Born Free And...	Peter NERO	13684
Peter Nero Plays Love Is Blue ...	Peter NERO	12636
Peter Nero-Up Close	Peter NERO	12089
Peter, Paul And Mary A...	PETER, PAUL & MARY	1962
Peter, Paul And Mary I...	PETER, PAUL & MARY	849
Peter, Paul And Mommy	PETER, PAUL & MARY	1772
Pete's Dragon	SOUNDTRACK-MOVIE	8847
Pete's Place	Pete FOUNTAIN	10104
Pet Sounds	BEACH BOYS	1299
Pet Sounds/Carl And The Passio...	BEACH BOYS	4162
Petula	Petula CLARK	3960
Petula Clark's Greatest Hits...	Petula CLARK	4463
P.F.M. 'Cook'	P.F.M.	9734
PG&E	PACIFIC GAS AND ELEC...	11257
Phaedra	TANGERINE DREAM	13636

Title	Act	Rank
Phantazia	Noel POINTER	9632
The Phantom	Duke PEARSON	13426
Phantom Of The Night	KAYAK	10278
The Phantom Of The Opera	ORIGINAL CAST	817
Phantom Of The Paradise	SOUNDTRACK-MOVIE	13793
Phantom, Rocker & Sl...	PHANTOM, ROCKER & SL...	5119
Phantoms	The FIXX	2515
Phases And Stages	Willie NELSON	13025
Phase-III	The OSMONDS	1487
Phase Two	Jimmy CASTOR Bunch	13030
Phenix	"Cannonball" ADDERLE...	8991
Philadelphia Freedom	MFSB	4779
Phil Ochs Greatest Hits	Phil OCHS	13547
Phil Ochs In Concert	Phil OCHS	12864
Phil Seymour	Phil SEYMOUR	6212
Phoebe Snow	Phoebe SNOW	592
Phoenix	Dan FOGELBERG	496
Phoenix	GRAND FUNK RAILROAD	1461
Phoenix	Patti LaBELLE	5543
The Phoenix Concerts-Live	John STEWART	13600
Phone Call From God	Jerry JORDAN	6799
The Phosphorescent Rat	HOT TUNA	10407
Photo-Finish	Rory GALLAGHER	7277
Photoglo	PHOTOGLO	13346
Photographs & Memories/His Grea...	Jim CROCE	723
Photos Of Ghosts	P.F.M.	12107
Phyllis Hyman	Phyllis HYMAN	7001
Physical	Olivia NEWTON-JOHN	482
Physical Graffiti	LED ZEPPELIN	359
Pia & Phil	Pia ZADORA	7470
Piano Man	Billy JOEL	2149
Piano Rags By Scott Joplin, Vol. 1 & 2	Joshua RIFKIN	5653
Piano Rags By Scott Joplin, Vol. 3	Joshua RIFKIN	9980
Pick Hits Of The Radio Go...	VARIOUS ARTISTS	8593
Pickin' On Nashville	KENTUCKY HEADHUNTERS	1450
Pickin' Up The Pieces	POCO	4637
Pick Of The Litter	SPINNERS	1097
Picture Book	SIMPLY RED	1469
Pictures	ATLANTA	10417
Pictures At An Exhib...	EMERSON, LAKE & PALM...	1820
Pictures At Eleven	Robert PLANT	1222
Pictures For Pleasure	Charlie SEXTON	2174
Pictures From The Front	Jon BUTCHER AXIS	9388
Pictures Of Moments To R...	STATLER BROTHERS	13240
Picture This	Huey LEWIS And The N...	1300
Piece Of Mind	IRON MAIDEN	1631
Piece Of Mind	The HAPPENINGS	13104
Pieces Of A Dream	PIECES OF A DREAM	11416
Pieces Of Dreams	Stanley TURRENTINE	5509
Pieces Of Eight	STYX	280
Pieces Of The Sky	Emmylou HARRIS	4826
Pied Piper	Dave VALENTIN	12571
Piledriver -- The Wrestl...	VARIOUS ARTISTS	7825
Pilgrimage	WISHBONE ASH	11148
Pillow Talk	SYLVIA	6899
Pilot	PILOT	6517
Pinafore Days	STACKRIDGE	11506
Pinball Wizards	NEW SEEKERS	12913
Pink Cadillac	John PRINE	10287
The Pink Panther (So...	Henry MANCINI and hi...	510
Pink World	PLANET P	8374
Pipe Dreams	Gladys KNIGHT & The ...	6879
The Piper At The Gates Of Dawn	PINK FLOYD	9092
Pipes Of Peace	Paul McCARTNEY	2238
Pippin	ORIGINAL CAST	8830
The Pirate Movie	SOUNDTRACK-MOVIE	11968

Title	Act	Rank
Pirates	Rickie Lee JONES	1019
The Pirates Of Penzance	ORIGINAL CAST	12777
Pisces, Aquarius, Capricorn, ...	The MONKEES	449
Pizzazz	Patrice RUSHEN	4032
A Place For My Stuff!	George CARLIN	9127
The Place I Love	SPLINTER	6419
A Place In The Sun	PABLO CRUISE	1200
A Place Like This	Robbie NEVIL	7128
Places And Spaces	Donald BYRD	3233
Plain From The Heart	Delbert McCLINTON	11548
The Plan	The OSMONDS	4642
Planetary Invasion	MIDNIGHT STAR	3020
Planet Of The Apes	SOUNDTRACK-MOVIE	13299
Planet P	PLANET P	4696
Planet Waves	Bob DYLAN	872
Plantation Harbor	Joe VITALE	12807
The Plastic Cow Goes Moooooog	PLASTIC COW	13200
Plastic Letters	BLONDIE	6073
Platinum Jazz	WAR	3378
Platoon	SOUNDTRACK-MOVIE	7338
Play Deep	The OUTFIELD	771
Play Don't Worry	Mick RONSON	8005
Player	PLAYER	2115
The Player	FIRST CHOICE	9904
Players In The Dark	DR. HOOK	9580
Playgirl	THEE PROPHETS	11939
Playground In My Mind	Clint HOLMES	8236
Play Guitar With The Venture...	The VENTURES	7598
Playing For Keeps	Eddie MONEY	3649
Playing Possum	Carly SIMON	2240
Playing To An Audience Of One	David SOUL	8511
Playing To Win	LITTLE RIVER BAND	6902
Playing To Win	Rick NELSON	10597
Playing Up A Storm	Gregg ALLMAN Band	4970
Playin' It Cool	Timothy B. SCHMIT	11952
Playin' To Win	The OUTLAWS	5573
Play 'N' The Game	NAZARETH	7480
Play One More	IAN & SYLVIA	10696
The Academy Award Wi...	Percy FAITH His Orch...	11482
Plays Tunes By Chuck B...	Bill BLACK'S Combo	11984
Pleasant Dreams	The RAMONES	6245
Please	PET SHOP BOYS	1164
Please Don't Touch	Steve HACKETT	7107
Pleased To Meet Me	The REPLACEMENTS	7714
Please Love Me Forever	Bobby VINTON	3136
Pleasure	OHIO PLAYERS	5048
Pleasure & Pain	DR. HOOK	4234
Pleasure One	HEAVEN 17	13106
The Pleasure Principle	Gary NUMAN	1701
Pleasures Of The Flesh	EXODUS	6128
Pleasures Of The Harbor	Phil OCHS	11867
Pleasure Victim	BERLIN	2905
The Plimsouls	The PLIMSOULS	11683
Plug Me In	Eddie HARRIS	6992
Plug Me Into Something	Henry GROSS	3198
A Pocket Full Of Mir...	The MIRACLES/Smokey ...	6391
Poco	POCO	4617
Poems, Prayers & Promises	John DENVER	351
The Poet	Bobby WOMACK	3186
Poetic Champions Compose	Van MORRISON	6463
The Poet II	Bobby WOMACK	6284
The Point!	NILSSON	2086
Point Blank	POINT BLANK	12435
The Pointer Sisters	POINTER SISTERS	1493
Pointer Sisters' Greatest...	POINTER SISTERS	13056
Point Of Entry	JUDAS PRIEST	2949

Title | Act	Rank
Point Of Know Return | KANSAS	315
Point Of Pleasure | XAVIER	10023
Point Of View | SPYRO GYRA	10481
Points On The Curve | WANG CHUNG	2636
Polar AC | Freddie HUBBARD	11945
Policy | Martha DAVIS	8636
The Politics Of Dancing | RE-FLEX	4836
Polka Party! | "Weird Al" YANKOVIC	12815
Poltergeist | SOUNDTRACK-MOVIE	12210
Poncho & Lefty [A] | Merle HAGGARD	2481
Poncho & Lefty [A] | Willie NELSON	2481
Pontiac | Lyle LOVETT	7872
Pool It! | The MONKEES	8326
Poolside | NU SHOOZ	2715
Pop Art | TRANSVISION VAMP	9434
Popcorn | HOT BUTTER	9651
Pope John Paul II Sings... | Pope JOHN PAUL II	10855
The Pope Smokes Dope | David PEEL & The LOW...	13184
Popeye | SOUNDTRACK-MOVIE	8384
Pop Goes The Movies | MECO	7576
Pop Goes The World | MEN WITHOUT HATS	5071
Popped In Souled Out | WET WET WET	10053
The "Pops" Goes Coun... | Chet ATKINS/BOSTON P...	5347
"Pops" Goes The Trum... [A] | BOSTON POPS Orches...	2675
"Pops" Goes The Trumpet [A] | Al HIRT	2675
Pops In Space | BOSTON POPS Orchestr...	11904
Porcupine | ECHO & The BUNNYMEN	10227
Porgy & Bess [A] | Cleo LAINE	8654
Porgy & Bess [A] | Ray CHARLES	8654
Porky's Revenge | SOUNDTRACK-MOVIE	9858
Porter Wayne And Dol... | Porter WAGONER and D...	9289
Portfolio | Grace JONES	6260
Portfolio | Richie HAVENS	12728
Portrait | 5TH DIMENSION	1214
Portrait Gallery | Harry CHAPIN	6302
A Portrait Of Arthur Pryso... | Arthur PRYSOCK	9655
Portrait Of Bobby | Bobby SHERMAN	4901
Portrait Of Carrie | Carrie LUCAS	13043
Portrait Of Donny | Donny OSMOND	1403
A Portrait Of Merle Haggard | Merle HAGGARD	7098
Portrait Of My Love | The LETTERMEN	3704
Portrait Of My Woman | Eddy ARNOLD	11452
Portrait Of Petula | Petula CLARK	4659
A Portrait Of Ray | Ray CHARLES	4093
Portrait Of Sammy Davis, ... | Sammy DAVIS Jr.	7728
Portrait Of The Originals | The ORIGINALS	13694
Portraits | The BUCKINGHAMS	5788
Posh | Patrice RUSHEN	5549
Positive | Peabo BRYSON	11422
Positive Power | Steve ARRINGTON'S HA...	10066
Positive Vibrations | TEN YEARS AFTER	6177
A Possible Projection Of The Fu... | Al KOOPER	13763
Post Card | Mary HOPKIN	2695
Potlatch | REDBONE	6868
POV | UTOPIA	11818
Power | ICE-T	3381
Power | KANSAS	3610
Power | The TEMPTATIONS	4856
Powerage | AC/DC	7023
Power And Love | MANCHILD	11100
Power & Passion | MAMA'S BOYS	11230
Power & The Glory | SAXON	10368
The Power And The Glory | GENTLE GIANT	6221
Powerful People | Gino VANNELLI	4870
Powerful Stuff | FABULOUS THUNDERBIRD...	9786
Powerglide | NEW RIDERS Of The PU...	3560

Title | Act	Rank
Powerhouse | The CRUSADERS	13160
Power In The Darkness | Tom ROBINSON Band	9342
Power In The Music | GUESS WHO	8259
Powerlight | EARTH, WIND & FIRE	2464
The Power Of Joe Simon | Joe SIMON	7850
Power Of Love | Arlo GUTHRIE	13016
The Power Of Music | The MIRACLES	12701
Power Play | APRIL WINE	4306
Powerslave | IRON MAIDEN	2802
The Power Station | POWER STATION	828
Power Windows | RUSH	1844
Practice What You Preach | TESTAMENT	7225
Pratt & McClain Featuring... | PRATT & McCLAIN	13421
Prayer Meetin' | Jimmy SMITH	6241
Precious Moments | Jermaine JACKSON	4454
Precious Time | Pat BENATAR	338
Preflyte | The BYRDS	5969
Prelude | DEODATO	1320
Premonition | Peter FRAMPTON	7151
Premonition | SURVIVOR	4941
Preppie | Cheryl LYNN	12400
Presence | LED ZEPPELIN	759
The Present | MOODY BLUES	3441
Presenting Rubin Mitchell | Rubin MITCHELL	13031
Presenting: The Bachelors | The BACHELORS	6844
...Presenting The Fabulous R... | The RONETTES	9194
Present Tense | SHOES	6243
Preservation Act 1 | The KINKS	11895
Preservation Act 2 | The KINKS	8438
The Presidential Yea... | John Fitzgerald KENN...	11293
The Presidential Years (David Teig) | John Fitzgerald KENN...	3023
Press On | David T. WALKER	11779
Press To Play | Paul McCARTNEY	4400
Pressure | BRAM TCHAIKOVSKY	8323
Pressure Drop | Robert PALMER	9546
The Pressure Is On | Hank WILLIAMS Jr.	5392
Pressure Sensitive | Ronnie LAWS	4331
Presto | RUSH	2523
The Pretender | Jackson BROWNE	861
Pretenders | The PRETENDERS	774
Pretenders II | The PRETENDERS	2199
Pretties For You | ALICE COOPER (Grp)	12056
Pretty In Pink | SOUNDTRACK-MOVIE	1250
Pretty Paper | Willie NELSON	7380
Pretty Things Come I... | Tony SANDLER And Ral...	12518
Pretzel Logic | STEELY DAN	989
Prevailing Airs | Paul MAURIAT And His...	9486
The Price You Got To... | "Cannonball" ADDERLE...	12838
Pride | Robert PALMER	6672
Pride | WHITE LION	677
Pride In What I Am | Merle HAGGARD	11626
Primal Roots | Sergio MENDES And BR...	11318
Primal Scream | Maynard FERGUSON	6634
Prime Prine - Best John Prine | John PRINE	13653
Prime Time | DAWN/Tony ORLANDO	2608
Prime Time | GREY And HANKS	13401
Primitive | Neil DIAMOND	4173
Primitive Cool | Mick JAGGER	4544
Primitive Love | Gloria ESTEFAN/MIAMI...	807
Primitive Man | ICEHOUSE	10581
Prince | PRINCE	2041
Prince Charming | Adam ANT	6207
The Princess Bride (Soundtr... | Mark KNOPFLER	13789
The Prince's Trust 10th A... | VARIOUS ARTISTS	13481
The Principle Of Moments | Robert PLANT	1144
Priority | POINTER SISTERS	7800

Title | Act	Rank
Prism | PRISM	9141
Prisoner In Disguise | Linda RONSTADT	1070
Prisoner Of Love | James BROWN	6080
Private Audition | HEART	5033
Private Collection | JON And VANGELIS	10938
Private Dancer | Tina TURNER	76
Private Eyes | Daryl HALL & John OA...	368
Private Eyes | Tommy BOLIN	8295
A Private Heaven | Sheena EASTON	1388
Private Passion | Jeff LORBER	5250
Private Revolution | WORLD PARTY	3679
Procession | WEATHER REPORT	8628
Procol Harum | PROCOL HARUM	4638
Procol Harum Live In Concert... | PROCOL HARUM	1061
Procol's Ninth | PROCOL HARUM	6698
The Producers | The PRODUCERS	12868
Product | BRAND X	11615
Profile | Jan AKKERMAN	13022
Profile: Best Of Emmylou H... | Emmylou HARRIS	6305
Profiles [A] | Nick MASON	12115
Profiles [A] | Rick FENN	12115
Profile II: The Best Of Em... | Emmylou HARRIS	12411
Progressions Of Power | TRIUMPH	3600
The Progressive Blues Exper... | Johnny WINTER	3433
Projections | BLUES PROJECT	3230
Promise | SADE	432
The Promise | Michael PINDER	9318
Promised Land | Elvis PRESLEY	5136
The Promise Of A Future | Hugh MASEKELA	2258
Promise Of Love | DELEGATION	6154
Promises, Promises | Dionne WARWICK	1228
Promises, Promises | ORIGINAL CAST	6252
Proof Through The Night | T-Bone BURNETT	12831
Propaganda | SPARKS	5999
The Prophet By Kahlil Gibr... | Richard HARRIS	3514
Propositions | The BAR-KAYS	4492
The Pros & Cons Of Hitchhiki... | Roger WATERS	4073
Protect The Innocent | Rachel SWEET	8525
Proud Mary | Solomon BURKE	10506
The Proud One | The OSMONDS	11612
Proud Words On A Dusty Shelf | Ken HENSLEY	11346
Provision | SCRITTI POLITTI	9312
The Psychedelic Furs | PSYCHEDELIC FURS	10189
Psychedelic Lollipop | BLUES MAGOOS	2969
Psychedelic Shack | The TEMPTATIONS	1041
Psycho Cafe | BANG TANGO	4012
Psychocandy | JESUS AND MARY CHAIN	13138
Psychotic Reaction | COUNT FIVE	10134
Pucker Up | LIPPS INC.	6908
Pump | AEROSMITH	175
Pump Iron! | Alvin LEE	10105
Pump Up The Jam - The Album | TECHNOTRONIC	1141
Punch The Clock | Elvis COSTELLO & The...	2770
Pure | The PRIMITIVES	8040
Pure & Natural | T-CONNECTION	9217
Pure Dynamite! Live At The Ro... | James BROWN	2453
Pure Music | CHASE	9699
Pure Pleasure | DYNAMIC SUPERIORS	8941
Pure Pop For Now People | Nick LOWE	8310
Pure Smokey | Smokey ROBINSON	6790
Purlie | ORIGINAL CAST	11122
(Purple Passages) | DEEP PURPLE	4609
Purple Rain (Soundtrack) | PRINCE	47
The Pursuit Of Happiness | BEAT FARMERS	10211
Push | BROS	12252
Push Push | Herbie MANN	5296

Title | Act	Rank
Pussy Cats | NILSSON	6216
Put A Little Love In You... | Jackie DeSHANNON	6331
Put It Where You Wan... | AVERAGE WHITE BAND/A...	4749
Putting It Straight | Pat TRAVERS	5500
Put Your Hand In The Hand | OCEAN	5650
Put Your Head On My Shoulde... | The LETTERMEN	3408
Puzzle People | The TEMPTATIONS	555
Pyramid | Alan PARSONS PROJECT	2510
Pyromania | DEF LEPPARD	92

Q

Title | Act	Rank
Q: Are We Not Men? A: We Are Devo! | DEVO	5809
QE 2 | Mike OLDFIELD	12684
QR III | QUIET RIOT	3124
Quadrophenia | The WHO	839
Quadrophenia (Soundtrack) | The WHO	5157
Quarterflash | QUARTERFLASH	834
Quarter Moon In A Ten Cent... | Emmylou HARRIS	3675
Quartet | ULTRAVOX	5795
Quatro | Suzi QUATRO	8652
Quazar | QUAZAR	9827
Queen | QUEEN	5981
The Queen Alone | Carla THOMAS	10294
Queen Elvis | Robyn HITCHCOCK And ...	9847
The Queen Is Dead | The SMITHS	4802
Queen Live Killers | QUEEN	3036
Queen Of The House | Jody MILLER	10464
Queen Of The Neighborhood | The FLAME	10728
Queen Of The Night | Loleatta HOLLOWAY	13435
Queen Of The Night | Maggie BELL	8029
Queens Of Noise | The RUNAWAYS	12312
Queensryche | QUEENSRYCHE	5781
Queen II | QUEEN	5298
Quentin's Theme | Brad SWANSON	13269
Quentin's Theme | Charles Randolph GRE...	2876
Quest For Fire | SOUNDTRACK-MOVIE	11342
Questionnaire | Chaz JANKEL	8486
A Question Of Balance | MOODY BLUES	643
Quicksilver | QUICKSILVER MESSENGE...	8096
Quicksilver | SOUNDTRACK-MOVIE	11495
Quicksilver Messenge... | QUICKSILVER MESSENGE...	4507
Quiet Fire | Roberta FLACK	1020
Quiet Lies | Juice NEWTON	2010
Quiet Nights | Miles DAVIS	8695
Quiet Riot | QUIET RIOT	8671
A Quiet Storm | Smokey ROBINSON	2421
Quinella | ATLANTA RHYTHM SECTI...	6426
The Quintet | V.S.O.P	10162

R

Title | Act	Rank
Ra | UTOPIA	8330
The Race Is On | George JONES	13019
Racing After Midnight | HONEYMOON SUITE	7533
Radiant | ATLANTIC STARR	3478
Radical Departure | RANKING ROGER	10967
Radio | LL COOL J	3329
Radio Active | Pat TRAVERS	4505
Radio-Activity | KRAFTWERK	9810
Radio Dinner | NATIONAL LAMPOON	8474
Radio Dream | Roger VOUDOURIS	12515
Radio Ethiopia | Patti SMITH	8762
Radio Free Nixon | David FRYE	9588
Radio K.A.O.S. | Roger WATERS	4741
Radioland | Nicolette LARSON	6384
Radio One | Jimi HENDRIX EXPERIE...	7649
Radio Romance | Eddie RABBITT	3122

Title | Act	Rank
Radio Silence | Boris GREBENSHIKOV	13775
Rag Doll | 4 SEASONS	1992
Rage For Order | QUEENSRYCHE	4704
Rage In Eden | ULTRAVOX	10677
Raging Slab | RAGING SLAB	8542
Rags To Rufus | RUFUS	1424
Ragtime | SOUNDTRACK-MOVIE	9644
Raiders Of The Lost ... | LONDON SYMPHONY Orch...	6322
Rail | RAIL	10152
Railhead Overture | Mike POST	13297
Rainbow | Dolly PARTON	10419
Rainbow | Neil DIAMOND	4112
Rainbow Bridge (Soundtrack) | Jimi HENDRIX	1918
Rainbow Funk | Jr. WALKER & The ALL...	6692
Rainbow Rising | RAINBOW	4518
Rainbow Seeker | Joe SAMPLE	3835
Rainbow Visions | SIDE EFFECT	9074
Rain Dances | CAMEL	10650
Raindancing | Alison MOYET	7050
Rain Dogs | Tom WAITS	12272
Raindrops Keep Fallin' On M... | Andy WILLIAMS	4284
Raindrops Keep Fallin' On M... | Johnny MATHIS	3550
Raindrops Keep Fallin' On My ... | B.J. THOMAS	728
Rain Forest | Paul HARDCASTLE	5116
Rain Forest | Walter WANDERLEY	2257
The Rainmakers | The RAINMAKERS	6518
Rain Man | SOUNDTRACK-MOVIE	4199
Raise! | EARTH, WIND & FIRE	930
Raised On Radio | JOURNEY	654
Raised On Rock/For Ol' Time... | Elvis PRESLEY	5677
Raise Your Fist And Y... | ALICE COOPER (Solo)	7152
Raising Fear | ARMORED SAINT	8507
Raising Hell | FATBACK	10017
Raising Hell | RUN-D.M.C.	253
Raisin' Hell | Elvin BISHOP	4989
Ralf And Florian | KRAFTWERK	11079
Rally 'Round The Flagg | Fannie FLAGG	13068
Ram | Paul & Linda McCARTN...	171
Ramatam | RAMATAM	11704
Ramblin' Featuring G... | NEW CHRISTY MINSTREL...	805
Ramblin' Gamblin' Man | Bob SEGER	5572
The Ramblin' Man | Waylon JENNINGS	6253
Ram It Down | JUDAS PRIEST	3823
Ram Jam | RAM JAM	4500
Ramones | The RAMONES	6320
Ramones Mania | The RAMONES	12170
Rampant | NAZARETH	9716
Ramsey Lewis' Newly Recorded... | Ramsey LEWIS	13465
Ramsey Lewis, The Piano Play... | Ramsey LEWIS	10551
The Ramsey Lewis Trio A... | Ramsey LEWIS Trio	7990
R&B Skeletons In The Close... | George CLINTON	7882
Randy Meisner | Randy MEISNER	8331
Randy Newman/Live | Randy NEWMAN	13046
The Rangers Waltz | MOM & DADS	5269
Rank | The SMITHS	8712
Rant 'N' Rave With The Stray C... | STRAY CATS	2424
Rappin' Rodney | Rodney DANGERFIELD	4120
Rap's Greatest Hits | Various Artists	7724
Rap's Greatest Hits, Volu... | VARIOUS ARTISTS	12419
Rapture | Anita BAKER	143
Rare Bird | RARE BIRD	7652
Rare Earth | RARE EARTH	12011
Rare Earth In Concert | RARE EARTH	3134
Rare Hendrix | Jimi HENDRIX	7044
Rare Precious & Beautiful | BEE GEES	6477
Rare Precious & Beautiful, Volum... | BEE GEES	8498

Title | Act	Rank
Rarities | The BEATLES	3236
Raspberries | RASPBERRIES	3867
Raspberries' Best Featuring E... | RASPBERRIES	10815
Rastaman Vibration | Bob MARLEY And The W...	1478
Ratchell | RATCHELL	12653
Rated Extraordinaire | Johnnie TAYLOR	6029
Rather Be Rockin' | TANTRUM	13473
Rat In The Kitchen | UB40	5837
Ratt | RATT	7730
Rattle And Hum (Soundtrack) | U2	429
Rattlesnake | OHIO PLAYERS	5460
Raunch 'N' Roll | BLACK OAK ARKANSAS	6182
Ravel Bolero | Isao TOMITA	11896
Ravi Shankar At The Monterey... | Ravi SHANKAR	4028
Ravi Shankar In New York | Ravi SHANKAR	10873
Ravi Shankar In San Francisc... | Ravi SHANKAR	10971
The Raw & The Cooked | FINE YOUNG CANNIBALS	114
Raw Blues | Johnnie TAYLOR	7996
Raw Like Sushi | Neneh CHERRY	3260
Raw Power | The STOOGES	13079
Raw Sienna | SAVOY BROWN	6816
Raw Soul | James BROWN	7161
Raw Velvet | Bobby WHITLOCK	13175
Ray Charles Invites You To Li... | Ray CHARLES	4571
Ray Charles Live | Ray CHARLES	12284
Ray Charles Live In Concert | Ray CHARLES	6559
Ray Conniff's Greate... | Ray CONNIFF & His Or...	10726
Ray Conniff's World ... | Ray CONNIFF & His Or...	7694
Raydio | Ray PARKER Jr./RAYDI...	2670
Ray, Goodman & Brown | RAY, GOODMAN & BROWN	2082
Ray, Goodman & Brown... | RAY, GOODMAN & BROWN	7024
Ray Price's All-Time Greatest H... | Ray PRICE	10012
Ray's Moods | Ray CHARLES	4965
Ray Stevens' Greatest Hits | Ray STEVENS	8162
Ray Stevens...Unreal!!! | Ray STEVENS	10088
Razamanaz | NAZARETH	9073
R.B. Greaves | R.B. GREAVES	6824
Reach | Richard SIMMONS	3588
Reach For It | George DUKE	2785
Reach For The Sky | ALLMAN BROTHERS Band	3636
Reach For The Sky | RATT	2153
Reach For The Sky | SUTHERLAND BROTHERS ...	13575
Reaching For The Sky | Peabo BRYSON	3180
Reaching For The Wor... | Harold MELVIN And Th...	6528
Reaching For Tomorrow | SWITCH	6037
Reaching Out | MENUDO	8801
Reach Out | Burt BACHARACH	3895
Reach The Beach | The FIXX	692
Reach Up And Touch T... | SOUTHSIDE JOHNNY & T...	6307
React | The FIXX	10047
Re-ac-tor | Neil YOUNG	3268
Read My Lips | Fee WAYBILL	11169
Read My Lips | Melba MOORE	9617
Ready An' Willing | WHITESNAKE	6715
Ready For the World | READY FOR THE WORLD	1171
Ready Or Not | Lou GRAMM	3224
Ready Or Not...Here's G... | Godfrey CAMBRIDGE	5796
The Real Chuckeeboo | LOOSE ENDS	6540
The Real Deal | ISLEY BROTHERS	7526
The Real Donovan | DONOVAN	8957
Real Eyes | Gil SCOTT-HERON	10995
Real Friends | FRIENDS OF DISTINCTI...	4629
Reality | James BROWN	5995
Reality... What A Concept | Robin WILLIAMS	1791
Realization | Johnny RIVERS	749
The Real Lenny Bruce | Lenny BRUCE	13434

Title | Act	Rank
Real Life Ain't This Way | Jay FERGUSON	6747
Real Life Story | Terri Lyne CARRINGTO...	11827
Real Live | Bob DYLAN	9154
A Real Live Dolly | Dolly PARTON	12548
Real Love | ASHFORD & SIMPSON	6607
Really | J.J. CALE	7310
Really Rosie (Soundtrack) | Carole KING	3504
The Real Macaw | Graham PARKER And Th...	6651
Real McCoy | Van McCOY	6853
The Real McCoy | Charlie McCOY	5020
A Real Mother For Ya | Johnny Guitar WATSON	1753
Real People | CHIC	4114
The Real Thing | Angela WINBUSH	8138
The Real Thing | Taj MAHAL	6486
Real To Reel | CLIMAX BLUES Band	11199
Real True Lovin' | Steve LAWRENCE & Eyd...	12998
Rear View Mirror | STARLAND VOCAL BAND	7463
Reba | Reba McENTIRE	9021
Rebel | John MILES	11942
Rebel Music | Bob MARLEY And The W...	10700
Rebel Yell | Billy IDOL	521
Recall The Beginning...... | Steve MILLER Band	8011
Reckless | Bryan ADAMS	83
Reckless Abandon | David BROMBERG	9156
Reckoning | GRATEFUL DEAD	4362
Reckoning | R.E.M.	2351
Recollections | Judy COLLINS	2865
Reconciled | The CALL	5284
Recorded Live | TEN YEARS AFTER	4003
A Record Of Pure Lov... | PURE LOVE & PLEASURE	13597
Records | FOREIGNER	2128
The Records | The RECORDS	4709
Recovery: Live! | GREAT WHITE	7643
Recycled | NEKTAR	6801
Recycling The Blues & Other Rel... | Taj MAHAL	12362
Red | KING CRIMSON	6242
Red | The COMMUNARDS	8302
Redeye | REDEYE	7982
Red Headed Stranger | Willie NELSON	2349
Red Hot Rhythm & Blues | Diana ROSS	7105
Red Octopus | JEFFERSON AIRPLANE/S...	100
Red Roses For A Blue Lady | Vic DANA	2694
Red Roses For A Blue Lady | Wayne NEWTON	3385
Red Rose Speedway | Paul McCARTNEY & WIN...	713
Red Rubber Ball | The CYRKLE	5165
Red Sails In The Sunset | MIDNIGHT OIL	12420
Red 7 | RED 7	9052
Red Tape | ATLANTA RHYTHM SECTI...	7939
Redwing | GRINDER SWITCH	9833
Reed Seed | Grover WASHINGTON Jr...	3394
Reel Life | BOY MEETS GIRL	3978
Reel Music | The BEATLES	3839
Reflecting | Chad MITCHELL Trio	3667
Reflection | PENTANGLE	12841
Reflections | 5TH DIMENSION	8752
Reflections | George HOWARD	9675
Reflections | Gil SCOTT-HERON	5755
Reflections | Jerry GARCIA	4671
Reflections | Peter NERO	4784
Reflections | Rick JAMES	5371
Reflections | Stan GETZ	10600
Reflections | The LETTERMEN	8503
Reflections | The SUPREMES/Diana R...	2074
Reflections In Blue | Bobby BLAND	12726
Reflections Of A Gold... | Lonnie Liston SMITH	6358
Reflections Of My Life | The MARMALADE	6597

Title | Act	Rank
Reflector | PABLO CRUISE	3609
Reggae | Herbie MANN	8874
Reggae Got Soul | TOOTS And The MAYTAL...	11197
Reggatta De Blanc | The POLICE	1380
Reg Strikes Back | Elton JOHN	1637
Rehearsals For Retirement | Phil OCHS	10286
Reign In Blood | SLAYER	6878
Rei Momo | David BYRNE	6659
Reinforcements | Brian AUGER	8678
Rejoice | The EMOTIONS	878
Rejoicing | PAT METHENY GROUP	9453
Relayer | YES	1890
Release | Henry GROSS	4045
Released | JADE WARRIOR	13612
Released | Patti LaBELLE	8164
Release Me | Engelbert HUMPERDINC...	410
Release Yourself | Larry GRAHAM/GRAHAM ...	5016
Relics | PINK FLOYD	10572
Relight My Fire | Dan HARTMAN	13490
Remain In Light | TALKING HEADS	2207
Rematch | Sammy HAGAR	11510
Remembering You | Carroll O'CONNOR	7476
(Remember Me) I'm The One Who... | Dean MARTIN	1589
Remember The Future | NEKTAR	2573
Remembrance Days | DREAM ACADEMY	13144
Reminiscing | Lawrence WELK	9439
Remote Control | The TUBES	4847
Renaissance | Lonnie Liston SMITH	5308
Renaissance | Ray CHARLES	12775
Renaissance | The ASSOCIATION	4514
Renaissance | The MIRACLES	12505
Renaissance | VANILLA FUDGE	1916
Renaissance | VILLAGE PEOPLE	11135
Rendez-Vous | Jean Michel JARRE	5104
Renegade | THIN LIZZY	9959
R.E.O. | REO SPEEDWAGON	11175
REO Speedwagon Live/You Ge... | REO SPEEDWAGON	3430
Repeat Offender | Richard MARX	235
Repeat-The Best Of Jethro Tul... | JETHRO TULL	8899
Repeat When Necessary | Dave EDMUNDS	5385
Replay | CROSBY, STILLS & NAS...	10456
Replicas | Gary NUMAN	8499
Requiem | VARIOUS ARTISTS	6787
Rescue | Clarence CLEMONS	12320
Rescue You | Joe Lynn TURNER	10069
Reservations For Two | Dionne WARWICK	5171
Resolution | Andy PRATT	7700
Respect | Jimmy SMITH	4929
Rest In Peace | STEPPENWOLF	5807
Restless | STARPOINT	3354
Restless Eyes | Janis IAN	12113
Restless Nights | Karla BONOFF	2880
Restrictions | CACTUS	9427
Results | Liza MINNELLI	9950
The Resurrection Of ... | Paul BUTTERFIELD Blu...	4999
Resurrection Shuffle | ASHTON, GARDNER & DYKE	11874
A Retrospective | Linda RONSTADT	5962
Retrospective/The Bes... | BUFFALO SPRINGFIELD	3299
The Return Of Bruno | Bruce WILLIS	2377
The Return Of Rock | Jerry Lee LEWIS	10935
The Return Of Roger Miller | Roger MILLER	854
Return Of The Jedi | SOUNDTRACK-MOVIE	3714
The Return Of The Ma... | The SUPREMES & FOUR ...	10624
The Return Of The Moonglows | The MOONGLOWS	13060
Return To Fantasy | URIAH HEEP	7081
Return To Forever Live | RETURN TO FOREVER	11670

Title | Act	Rank
Return To Magenta | MINK DE VILLE	10127
Reunion | B.J. THOMAS	5690
Reunion | Jerry Jeff WALKER	13070
Reunion | PETER, PAUL & MARY	8795
Reunion | The TEMPTATIONS	5082
Reunion (The Songs Of Jimmy... | Glen CAMPBELL	11645
Reunion Concert | EVERLY BROTHERS	11774
Reunion-Live At Madison Square Garde... | DION	10165
Revelations | NEW COLONY SIX	10756
Revenge | Bill COSBY	364
Revenge | EURYTHMICS	1815
Reverberi & Schumann, Chopin, L... | REVERBERI	11034
Revisited | LOVE	10864
Revolucion | EL CHICANO	10900
Revolution! | Paul REVERE And The ...	3696
The Revolution By Night | BLUE ÖYSTER CULT	6765
Revolution Of The Mind - Live... | James BROWN	3177
Revolver | The BEATLES	316
Rewind (1971-1984) | ROLLING STONES	8181
Rewind | Johnny RIVERS	2726
Rhapsodies | Rick WAKEMAN	11814
Rhapsodies...Young Lovers | MIDNIGHT STRING QUARTET	1651
Rhapsodies...Young Lovers Vol. 2 | MIDNIGHT STRING QUARTET	6603
Rhapsody And Blues | The CRUSADERS	3806
Rhapsody In Blue | Walter MURPHY	12615
Rhapsody In White | LOVE UNLIMITED ORCHE...	1684
Rhinestone (Soundtrack) | Dolly PARTON	10841
Rhinestone Cowboy | Glen CAMPBELL	1550
Rhinoceros | RHINOCEROS	5254
Rhyme & Reason | MISSING PERSONS	4811
Rhyme Pays | ICE-T	6116
The Rhymer And Other Five And... | Tom T. HALL	12707
Rhymes & Reasons | Carole KING	471
Rhymes & Reasons | John DENVER	11667
The Rhythm & Blues Album | Trini LOPEZ	6005
Rhythm And Romance | Rosanne CASH	6654
The Rhythm & The Blues | Z.Z. HILL	12192
Rhythm Of The Night | DeBARGE	1419
Rhythm Of Youth | MEN WITHOUT HATS	1997
The Rhythmotist | Stewart COPELAND	10773
Rhythm Romance | The ROMANTICS	7716
Riccochet Days | MODERN ENGLISH	7870
Rich And Famous | BLUE MERCEDES	11956
Rich And Poor | Randy CRAWFORD	9932
Richard Marx | Richard MARX	319
Richard Nixon: A Fantasy | David FRYE	4873
Richard Nixon Superstar | David FRYE	5764
Richard P. Havens, 1983 | Richie HAVENS	6098
Richard Pryor: Here And Now... | Richard PRYOR	7226
Richard Pryor Live On The S... | Richard PRYOR	3584
Richard Pryor's Greatest Hi... | Richard PRYOR	6761
Richie Havens On Stage | Richie HAVENS	5030
Rich In London | Buddy RICH	12396
Rich Man | CLIMAX BLUES BAND	9769
Rick Danko | Rick DANKO	9146
Rickie Lee Jones | Rickie Lee JONES	533
Rick Nelson In Concert | Rick NELSON	4603
Rick Nelson Sings "For You" | Rick NELSON	2516
Rick Sings Nelson | Rick NELSON	13556
Rick Wakeman's Criminal Reco... | Rick WAKEMAN	9341
The Riddle | Nik KERSHAW	9323
Riddle Of The Sphinx | BLOODSTONE	10505
Riddles In The Sand | Jimmy BUFFETT	7583
Ride A Rock Horse | Roger DALTREY	3390
Ride 'Em Cowboy | Paul DAVIS	10195

Title	Act	Rank
Ride On	Alvin LEE	11464
Ride The Lightning	METALLICA	5043
Ride The Wild Surf (Soundtrack...	JAN & DEAN	6430
Ride The Wind	The YOUNGBLOODS	9887
Riding High	FAZE-O	5951
Ridin' High	Jerry Jeff WALKER	9338
Ridin' High	MARTHA & The VANDELL...	10880
Ridin' High	The IMPRESSIONS	7819
Ridin' The Storm Out	REO SPEEDWAGON	11134
Riff Raff	Dave EDMUNDS	11744
Right Back Where We St...	Maxine NIGHTINGALE	6907
Right By You	Stephen STILLS	7506
The Right Combination [A]	Curtis MAYFIELD	12550
The Right Combination [A]	Linda CLIFFORD	12550
Righteous	Harvey MANDEL	12818
Righteous Anger	Van STEPHENSON	5198
The Right Night & Barry White	Barry WHITE	9260
Right Now!	RIGHTEOUS BROTHERS	2884
Right-Off!	HUDSON And LANDRY	9784
Right On	The SUPREMES	3206
Right On	Wilson PICKETT	13364
Right On! (Soundtrack)	LAST POETS	9845
Right On Be Free	VOICES OF EAST HARLE...	13077
Right On Time	BROTHERS JOHNSON	920
Right Or Wrong	George STRAIT	11546
The Right Place	Gary WRIGHT	5626
The Right Stuff	Vanessa WILLIAMS	2532
The Right To Be Ital...	HOLLY And The ITALIA...	12742
The Right To Love	Nancy WILSON	12906
The Right To Rock	KEEL	6552
Rigor Mortis Sets In	John ENTWISTLE	11283
Ringo	Ringo STARR	663
Ringo's Rotogravure	Ringo STARR	4065
Ringo The 4th	Ringo STARR	10924
Rings	CYMARRON	13011
The Rings	The RINGS	11334
Rio	DURAN DURAN	541
Rio	Lee RITENOUR	11384
Rio Grande Mud	ZZ TOP	7739
Rip It To Shreds-The...	The ANIMALS/Eric BUR...	13237
Rip It Up	DEAD OR ALIVE	13749
Riptide	Robert PALMER	582
Rise	Herb ALPERT	840
The Rise And Fall Of Ziggy Stardust	David BOWIE	1878
Rise And Shine!	KOKOMO	13582
Rise And Shine	The BEARS	11879
Rising	DR. HOOK	11250
Rising	MARK-ALMOND	7057
Rising Force	Yngwie MALMSTEEN	4310
Rising For The Moon	FAIRPORT CONVENTION	9454
Risque	CHIC	1547
Rit	Lee RITENOUR	2649
Rit/2	Lee RITENOUR	7789
Rita Coolidge	Rita COOLIDGE	7817
Rita Coolidge/Greatest Hits	Rita COOLIDGE	8768
Rita Pavone	Rita PAVONE	6523
Ritchie Blackmore's R-A-I-N-B-O-W	RAINBOW	3887
Rites Of Passage	VITAMIN Z	13243
Rites Of Summer	SPYRO GYRA	9314
River	Terry REID	11187
The River	Bruce SPRINGSTEEN	339
River Deep-Mountain Hig...	Ike & Tina TURNER	8215
River Of Time	The JUDDS	5791
Roaches: The Beginni...	BOBBY JIMMY & The CR...	13843

Title	Act	Rank
Roachford	ROACHFORD	8769
The Road	The KINKS	9521
The Road	The ROAD	13701
Road Food	GUESS WHO	4116
The Road Goes On For...	ALLMAN BROTHERS Band	5018
Road House	SOUNDTRACK-MOVIE	7836
Roadie	SOUNDTRACK-MOVIE	9324
Road Island	AMBROSIA	9783
Road Runner	Jr. WALKER & The ALL...	6117
Road Song	Wes MONTGOMERY	6018
Road To Ruin	The RAMONES	8094
Roadwork	Edgar WINTER	2518
The Roaring Silence	MANFRED MANN'S EARTH...	1539
The Roar Of The Greasepaint...	ORIGINAL CAST	4195
Robbery	Teena MARIE	6734
Robbie Dupree	Robbie DUPREE	4210
Robbie Nevil	Robbie NEVIL	2558
Robbie Robertson	Robbie ROBERTSON	3044
Robbin's Nest	Willie MITCHELL	13354
The Robbs	The ROBBS	13838
Roberta Flack	Roberta FLACK	7619
Roberta Flack & Donny Hath... [A]	Donny HATHAWAY	703
Roberta Flack & Donny Hathaway [A]	Roberta FLACK	703
Roberta Flack Featuring Don...	Roberta FLACK	2614
Robert Gordon With Link Wra...	Robert GORDON	9866
Robert Goulet In Person	Robert GOULET	2828
Robert Goulet On Broadway	Robert GOULET	3929
Robert Goulet On Broadway, ...	Robert GOULET	12081
Robert Hazard	Robert HAZARD	8434
Robert John	Robert JOHN	6319
Robin And The 7 Hoods	SOUNDTRACK-MOVIE	6232
Robin Trower Live!	Robin TROWER	2232
The Roches	The ROCHES	6377
Rock N' Roll Nights	BACHMAN-TURNER OVERD...	11914
Rock A Little	Stevie NICKS	1477
Rock & Roll	VANILLA FUDGE	4280
Rock & Roll Adult	Garland JEFFREYS	12120
A Rock And Roll Alte...	ATLANTA RHYTHM SECTI...	1240
Rock And Roll Diary 1967-1980	Lou REED	12380
Rock And Roll Heart	Lou REED	7184
Rock & Roll Is Here To Stay!	SHA NA NA	11516
Rock & Roll Machine	TRIUMPH	13325
Rock And Roll Music	The FROST	9650
Rock & Roll Music To The ...	TEN YEARS AFTER	3357
Rock & Roll Outlaws	FOGHAT	4000
Rock And Roll Over	KISS	745
Rock And Roll Queen	MOTT THE HOOPLE	7923
Rock & Roll Rebels	STEPPENWOLF	12567
Rock & Roll Strategy	.38 SPECIAL	3988
Rockapella	The NYLONS	10319
Rock Away	Phoebe SNOW	4969
Rock Billy Boogie	Robert GORDON	6993
Rockbird	Debbie HARRY	7752
Rocker	Elvis PRESLEY	9502
Rocket Fuel	Alvin LEE	7943
Rockets	The ROCKETS	4052
Rocket To Russia	The RAMONES	3687
Rock Festival	The YOUNGBLOODS	6108
Rock For Amnesty	VARIOUS ARTISTS	9042
Rock Hard	Suzi QUATRO	11884
Rockihnroll	Greg KIHN Band	2319
Rockin'	GUESS WHO	6776
Rock In A Hard Place	AEROSMITH	4308
Rockin' Chair	Gwen McCRAE	8257

Title	Act	Rank
Rockin' Into The Night	.38 SPECIAL	5213
Rockin' Radio	Tom BROWNE	9819
Rockin' Roll Baby	The STYLISTICS	3225
Rockin' The Boat	Jimmy SMITH	8397
Rockin' With The Rhythm	The JUDDS	3183
Rock Island	JETHRO TULL	5736
Rock Love	Steve MILLER Band	7196
Rock Me Baby	David CASSIDY	4224
Rock Me Tonight	Freddie JACKSON	750
Rock 'N' Country	Freddy FENDER	6136
Rock 'N' Roll	John LENNON	1730
Rock 'N' Roll	MOTORHEAD	11353
Rock 'N Roll Again	COMMANDER CODY & His...	11339
Rock N Roll Animal	Lou REED	3192
Rock 'N' Roll High Schoo...	SOUNDTRACK-MOVIE	10011
Rock N' Roll Love Letter	BAY CITY ROLLERS	3655
Rock 'N' Roll Music	The BEATLES	951
Rock 'N' Roll Outlaw	ROSE TATTOO	13418
Rock 'N' Roll Rocket	STARBUCK	13213
Rock 'N' Roll Warriors	SAVOY BROWN	12617
Rock 'N Soul Part 1	Daryl HALL & John OA...	903
Rock Of Ages	The BAND	1236
Rock Of Life	Rick SPRINGFIELD	5141
Rock Of The Westies	Elton JOHN	837
Rock On	David ESSEX	4013
Rock On	HUMBLE PIE	5426
Rock On	Ray PARKER Jr./RAYDI...	2646
Rocks	AEROSMITH	446
Rock's Greatest Hits	VARIOUS ARTISTS	11033
Rocks, Pebbles And Sand	Stanley CLARKE	7654
Rock The House	D.J. JAZZY JEFF & TH...	4401
Rock The Nations	SAXON	11732
Rock Therapy	STRAY CATS	11061
Rock The World	THIRD WORLD	13020
Rocky	SOUNDTRACK-MOVIE	791
Rocky IV	SOUNDTRACK-MOVIE	1738
The Rocky Horror Picture...	SOUNDTRACK-MOVIE	2963
Rocky Mountain Christmas	John DENVER	3113
Rocky Mountain High	John DENVER	557
Rock Your Baby	George McCRAE	4563
Rock You To Hell	GRIM REAPER	6164
Rocky III	SOUNDTRACK-MOVIE	2768
Rocky II	SOUNDTRACK-MOVIE	10977
Rod McKuen At Carnegie Hall	Rod McKUEN	6676
Rod McKuen Grand Tour	Rod McKUEN	12594
Rod McKuen's Greatest Hits-2	Rod McKUEN	10014
Rodney Crowell	Rodney CROWELL	8718
Rod Stewart	Rod STEWART	3911
The Rod Stewart Album	Rod STEWART	6109
Rod Stewart/Faces Live - Coas... [A]	Rod STEWART	6810
Rod Stewart/Faces Live ... [A]	SMALL FACES/FACES	6810
Rod Stewart Greatest Hits	Rod STEWART	3168
Roger!	Roger WILLIAMS	4763
Roger And Out	Roger MILLER	3426
Roger McGuinn	Roger McGUINN	9438
Roger McGuinn & Band	Roger McGUINN	11294
Roger Miller	Roger MILLER	10249
Roger Miller 1970	Roger MILLER	13735
Roger Williams Plays The H...	Roger WILLIAMS	10437
Rogues Gallery	SLADE	10507
Rollerball	SOUNDTRACK-MOVIE	10483
Rolling Down A Mountainsi...	MAIN INGREDIENT	7086
The Rolling Stones, Now!	ROLLING STONES	727
Rolling Thunder	Mickey HART	12900

Title	Act	Rank
Rollin' With The Flow	Charlie RICH	12946
Roll On	ALABAMA	1523
Roll Out The Red Carpet For Bu...	Buck OWENS	8732
Roll With It	Steve WINWOOD	450
Romance Dance	Kim CARNES	5103
Romance 1600	SHEILA E.	3384
Roman Gods	The FLESHTONES	12101
Roman Holliday	ROMAN HOLLIDAY	9708
Romantically	Johnny MATHIS	3112
Romantic Journey	Norman CONNORS	5865
The Romantics	The ROMANTICS	5568
Romantic Warrior	RETURN TO FOREVER	4378
The Romantic World Of Eddy Ar...	Eddy ARNOLD	3916
Romany	The HOLLIES	7241
Romeo & Juliet	Alec R. COSTANDINOS	6769
Romeo & Juliet	Hubert LAWS	9997
Romeo & Juliet	SOUNDTRACK-MOVIE	137
Romeo Knight	BOOGIE BOYS	8727
Romeo's Daughter	ROMEO'S DAUGHTER	13654
Romeo's Escape	Dave ALVIN	8547
Rome 35/MM	Enoch LIGHT & The LI...	10226
Ronnie Dove Sings The Hits Fo...	Ronnie DOVE	10282
Room Service	OAK RIDGE BOYS	9249
Root Hog Or Die	Mojo NIXON & Skid RO...	11126
Roots (Soundtrack)	Quincy JONES	3262
Roots	Curtis MAYFIELD	3658
Roots And Branches	The DILLARDS	5235
Rory Gallagher/Live!	Rory GALLAGHER	6693
The Rose (Soundtrack)	Bette MIDLER	881
Rose Garden	Lynn ANDERSON	1498
The Rose Garden	ROSE GARDEN	13277
Rose Of Cimarron	POCO	7331
The Rose Of England	Nick LOWE And His CO...	8894
Rose Royce IV/Rainbow Connecti...	ROSE ROYCE	8199
Rose Royce III/Strikes Again!	ROSE ROYCE	2750
Rose Royce II/In Full Bloom	ROSE ROYCE	1224
Roses In The Snow	Emmylou HARRIS	2287
Ross	Diana ROSS	4766
Ross (II)	Diana ROSS	4703
Rotary Connection	ROTARY CONNECTION	4064
Rotations	Tim WEISBERG Band	10780
Rough And Ready	Jeff BECK Group	4233
Rough Diamond	ROUGH DIAMOND	8728
Rough Diamonds	BAD COMPANY	3692
Rough Mix [A]	Pete TOWNSHEND	5461
Rough Mix [A]	Ronnie LANE	5461
Rough Night In Jericho	DREAMS SO REAL	8656
Rough 'N Tumble	Stanley TURRENTINE	12816
Rough Riders	LAKESIDE	7697
Round Midnight	SOUNDTRACK-MOVIE	13545
'Round Midnight	Linda RONSTADT	8082
Round #1	Frank SINATRA	12491
Round Trip	GAP BAND	12488
Round Trip	The KNACK	9264
Round Two	Johnny Van ZANT Band	8260
Round 2: The Stylistics	The STYLISTICS	1887
Roustabout (Soundtrack)	Elvis PRESLEY	1038
Routes	Ramsey LEWIS	10706
Rover's Return	John WAITE	7283
Rowdy	Hank WILLIAMS Jr.	6019
Roxy & Elsewhere	Frank ZAPPA	3827
Royal Bed Bouncer	KAYAK	13717
Royal Jam	The CRUSADERS	10737
Royal Rappin's [A]	Isaac HAYES	5826
Royal Rappin's [A]	Millie JACKSON	5826
Roy Buchanan	Roy BUCHANAN	7438

Title	Act	Rank
Roy Clark Country!	Roy CLARK	7498
Roy Clark / Superpicker	Roy CLARK	11821
Roy Clark / The Entertainer	Roy CLARK	13003
R.P.M.	SOUNDTRACK-MOVIE	10836
Rubber Soul	The BEATLES	322
Ru-beeeee	OSBORNE BROTHERS	13797
Rubicon	RUBICON	10250
Rub It In	Billy "Crash" CRADDO...	10724
Ruby, Don't Take You...	Kenny ROGERS & The F...	4307
Ruby, Ruby	Gato BARBIERI	4889
Ruff 'N' Ready	READY FOR THE WORLD	7514
Ruff'N Ready	Jimmy RUFFIN	13518
Rufus	RUFUS	11773
Rufus Featuring Chaka Khan	RUFUS	659
Rufusized	RUFUS	1336
Rufus Thomas Live/Doing The ...	Rufus THOMAS	10603
Rumble	Tommy CONWELL And Th...	5786
Rumble Fish (Soundtrack)	Stewart COPELAND	11909
The Rumour	Olivia NEWTON-JOHN	7890
Rumours	FLEETWOOD MAC	2
Runaway	Bill CHAMPLIN	12538
Runaway Horses	Belinda CARLISLE	3621
The Runaways	The RUNAWAYS	13590
Run Baby Run	The NEWBEATS	11369
Run D.M.C.	RUN-D.M.C.	2737
Run For Cover	Gary MOORE	10934
Run For The Roses	Jerry GARCIA	9506
Run For Your Life	TARNEY/SPENCER Band	12527
Runner	RUNNER	12098
Running Down The Road	Arlo GUTHRIE	4172
Running For My Life	Judy COLLINS	10259
Running In The Family	LEVEL 42	2450
Running Like The Win...	MARSHALL TUCKER Band	3359
Running On Empty	Jackson BROWNE	343
Running Scared	SOUNDTRACK-MOVIE	5223
Runnin' Out Of Fools	Aretha FRANKLIN	7637
Runt	Todd RUNDGREN	11918
Run With The Pack	BAD COMPANY	1158
Rural Free Delivery [A]	DELIVERANCE	13690
Rural Free Delivery [A]	Eric WEISSBERG	13690
Rural Space	BREWER And SHIPLEY	11688
Rush	RUSH	7633
Russ Ballard	Russ BALLARD	9198
Russian Roulette	ACCEPT	9235
Rust Never Sleeps	Neil YOUNG	916
Rusty Wier	Rusty WIER	9354
Ruthless People	SOUNDTRACK-MOVIE	3502
The Rutles	The RUTLES	6766
Ryan's Daughter	SOUNDTRACK-MOVIE	13091

S

Title	Act	Rank
Sabbath Bloody Sabbath	BLACK SABBATH	1715
Sabotage	BLACK SABBATH	3943
Sacred Heart	DIO	3174
Sacred Songs	Daryl HALL	6153
Sad Café	SAD CAFÉ	11141
Saddle Tramp	Charlie DANIELS Band	3829
Sad Sweet Dreamer	SWEET SENSATION	10674
Safety In Numbers	CRACK THE SKY	9161
Safety Zone	Bobby WOMACK	8960
Sa-Fire	SA-FIRE	4158
The Saga Continues...	ROGER	6536
The Sagittarius Movement	Jerry BUTLER	6157
Sail Away	Randy NEWMAN	8110
Sailor	Steve MILLER Band	2731
Saint Dominic's Preview	Van MORRISON	1707

Title	Act	Rank
Saints & Sinners	Johnny WINTER	4680
Salisbury	URIAH HEEP	7948
Sally Can't Dance	Lou REED	2487
Salongo	Ramsey LEWIS	7002
Salsa	SOUNDTRACK-MOVIE	9989
The Salsoul Orchestra	SALSOUL Orchestra	1292
A Salt With A Deadly Pepa	SALT-N-PEPA	3400
A Salty Dog	PROCOL HARUM	2933
Salute	Gordon LIGHTFOOT	12353
Samantha Fox	Samantha FOX	4799
Sam Cooke At The Copa	Sam COOKE	2465
Sam Cooke Live At The Harlem Sq...	Sam COOKE	10557
Same Goes For You	Leif GARRETT	7034
Same Train, A Different Tim...	Merle HAGGARD	4283
Sam Harris	Sam HARRIS	3494
Sam-I-Am	Sam HARRIS	6829
Sammy Davis Jr. Now	Sammy DAVIS Jr.	2097
Sammy Davis Jr. Salutes T...	Sammy DAVIS Jr.	12209
Sammy Hagar	Sammy HAGAR	10524
Sammy Johns	Sammy JOHNS	8655
Sammy's Back On Broadway	Sammy DAVIS Jr.	10829
Sam Neely-2	Sam NEELY	11728
Samurai Samba	YELLOWJACKETS	12790
San Antonio Rose [A]	Ray PRICE	4681
San Antonio Rose [A]	Willie NELSON	4681
Sanborn	David SANBORN	9107
Sanctuary	DION	13737
Sanctuary	J. GEILS Band	4127
Sandie Shaw	Sandie SHAW	10943
Sandinista!	The CLASH	3406
Sandman	NILSSON	9078
The Sandpiper	SOUNDTRACK-MOVIE	6931
The Sandpipers	The SANDPIPERS	5029
Sands Of Time	JAY & The AMERICANS	4044
Sands Of Time	S.O.S. BAND	4524
Sanford & Foxx	Redd FOXX	13433
Sanford And Son	Redd FOXX	10300
The Sanford/Townsend Band	SANFORD/TOWNSEN...	5793
Santana	SANTANA	60
Santana's Greatest Hits	SANTANA	2075
Santana III	SANTANA	241
Sarah Dash	Sarah DASH	11555
Sarah Vaughan/Michel Legra... [A]	Michel LEGRAND	10160
Sarah Vaughan/Michel Legran... [A]	Sarah VAUGHAN	10160
Saraya	SARAYA	4996
Sassy Soul Strut	Lou DONALDSON	12324
Satin Chickens	RHINOCEROS	8073
Satin Doll	Bobbi HUMPHREY	3493
Satin Pillows And Careless	Bobby VINTON	10516
Satin Sheets	Jeanne PRUETT	8700
Satisfied	Rita COOLIDGE	7174
Satisfied With You	Dave CLARK Five	10087
Saturday Morning Confusion	Bobby RUSSELL	12666
Saturday Night At The Uptown	VARIOUS ARTISTS	9296
Saturday Night Fever (Soundtrack...	BEE GEES	13
Saturday Night Fiedler	BOSTON POPS Orchestra	10644
Saturday Night Special	Norman CONNORS	10720
Sausalito	Al MARTINO	12624
Savage	EURYTHMICS	4613
Savage Amusement	SCORPIONS	992
Savage Eye	PRETTY THINGS	10853
Savage Grace	SAVAGE GRACE	11097
Saved	Bob DYLAN	4235
Save Me	SILVER CONVENTION	1864
Save The Children	The INTRUDERS	7323
Save The Last Dance For Me	DeFRANCO FAMILY	10535

Title | Act	Rank
Save Your Prayers | WAYSTED	13591
Sawyer Brown | SAWYER BROWN	9751
Say Anything | SOUNDTRACK-MOVIE	6328
Sayin' Somethin' | RIGHTEOUS BROTHERS	8914
Sayin' Something! | PEACHES & HERB	12521
Say It Again | Jermaine STEWART	7863
Say It Loud! | Lou DONALDSON	10004
Say It Loud-I'm Black And I'm... | James BROWN	3363
Say It With Silence | Hubert LAWS	5319
Say No More | BADFINGER	10811
Say No More | Les DUDEK	7608
Say Wonderful Things | Patti PAGE	9403
Say You'll Stay Until Tomorrow | Tom JONES	6346
Say You Love Me | Jennifer HOLLIDAY	8504
Scandal | SCANDAL	3536
Scarecrow | John MELLENCAMP	152
Scarlett & Black | SCARLETT & BLACK	8582
Scars Of Love | TKA	9295
Scary Monsters | David BOWIE	1792
The Scattering | CUTTING CREW	11525
Scatterlings | JULUKA	12779
Scenario | Al Di MEOLA	11096
The Scene Changes | Perry COMO	5562
Scenes From The Sout... | Bruce HORNSBY And Th...	1137
Scenes In The City | Branford MARSALIS	11603
Scheherazade And Other Storie... | RENAISSANCE	5315
Schemer-Dreamer | Steve WALSH	10116
Schoolboys In Disgrace | The KINKS	4858
School Days | Stanley CLARKE	3681
School Daze | SOUNDTRACK-MOVIE	6229
School Punks | BROWNSVILLE STATION	10937
School's Out | ALICE COOPER (Grp)	908
Scissors Cut | Art GARFUNKEL	8627
Scoop | Pete TOWNSHEND	5291
Scorching Beauty | IRON BUTTERFLY	10740
Scotch On The Rocks | BAND Of The BLACK WA...	11982
Scott Baio | Scott BAIO	12945
Scott Joplin: The Re... | NEW ENGLAND CONSERVA...	3678
Scoundrel Days | A-HA	6808
Scratch | The CRUSADERS	5340
A Scratch In The Sky | CRYAN' SHAMES	11853
Scream Dream | Ted NUGENT	2405
Screaming For Vengeance | JUDAS PRIEST	1216
The Screen Scene | Peter NERO	10370
Script For A Jester's Tear | MARILLION	11759
Scrooge | SOUNDTRACK-MOVIE	7930
Scrooged | SOUNDTRACK-MOVIE	8817
Scuba Divers | Dwight TWILLEY	8500
The Sea | SAN SEBASTIAN String...	859
Sea Hags | SEA HAGS	11439
Sealed With A Kiss | Bobby VINTON	6069
Sea Level | SEA LEVEL	5128
Seals & Crofts I And II | SEALS & CROFTS	6434
Seamless | The NYLONS	8545
The Sea Of Love | The ADVENTURES	10666
Search And Nearness | RASCALS/YOUNG RASCAL...	13810
The Searchers | The SEARCHERS	13513
The Searchers No. 4 | The SEARCHERS	13032
Search For The New Land | Lee MORGAN	12030
Searchin' For A Rain... | MARSHALL TUCKER Band	2155
Searchparty | John HALL Band	11754
Season Of Glass | Yoko ONO	6363
Season Of Lights...Laura Nyro In... | Laura NYRO	10290
Seasons In The Sun | Terry JACKS	7563
Seasons Of The Heart | John DENVER	3946
Sea Train | SEATRAIN	11655

Title | Act	Rank
Seatrain | SEATRAIN	3807
Seattle | Perry COMO	6544
Seawind | SEAWIND	13379
Seawind(2) | SEAWIND	7242
The Second | STEPPENWOLF	345
The Second Adventure | DYNASTY	10627
Second Album | Roy BUCHANAN	7192
The Second Album | 707	10931
2nd Anniversary | Gladys KNIGHT & The ...	3651
The Second Barbra Streis... | Barbra STREISAND	203
The Second Brooklyn Bridg... | BROOKLYN BRIDGE	8902
Second Childhood | Phoebe SNOW	2171
The 2nd Crusade | The CRUSADERS	3214
Second Edition | PUBLIC IMAGE LIMITED	12623
Second Generation | GAYLORD & HOLIDAY	10973
Second Helping | LYNYRD SKYNYRD	1092
The Second Latin Album | Trini LOPEZ	8997
Second Movement | Les McCANN & Eddie H...	2815
Second Sighting | FREHLEY'S COMET	7153
Seconds Of Pleasure | ROCKPILE	2698
Seconds Out | GENESIS	4517
2nd Street | BACK STREET CRAWLER	10686
Second Thoughts | McKENDREE SPRING	13474
2nd Time Around | SPINNERS	13655
Second Time Around | The KINKS	12480
Second Time Round | CYMANDE	12675
Second To Nunn | Bobby NUNN	10573
2nd Vault Of Golden Hits | 4 SEASONS	1783
2nd Wave | SURFACE	3263
Second Wind | Brian AUGER	11231
Second Winter | Johnny WINTER	4867
Secret Combination | Randy CRAWFORD	5212
Secret Dreams & Forbidden Fi... | Bonnie TYLER	9415
Secret Messages | ELECTRIC LIGHT ORCHE...	4899
The Secret Of Association | Paul YOUNG	1377
The Secret Of My Success | SOUNDTRACK-MOVIE	10371
Secret Omen | CAMEO	4141
A Secret Place | Grover WASHINGTON Jr...	3634
The Secret Policeman's Ba... | VARIOUS ARTISTS	7221
The Secret Policeman's Ot... | VARIOUS ARTISTS	4398
Secrets | CON FUNK SHUN	3285
Secrets | Gil SCOTT-HERON & Br...	4545
Secrets | Herbie HANCOCK	4930
Secrets | Robert PALMER	2195
Secrets | Wilton FELDER	6740
Secret Secrets | Joan ARMATRADING	6084
Secrets Of Flying | Johnny KEMP	5264
Secret Treaties | BLUE ÖYSTER CULT	5728
The Secret Value Of DayDrea... | Julian LENNON	4339
Sedaka's Back | Neil SEDAKA	1340
Seduction | James LAST	9614
See | RASCALS/YOUNG RASCAL...	4566
The Seeds | The SEEDS	9857
The Seeds Of Love | TEARS FOR FEARS	1593
See Forever Eyes | PRISM	10076
See How We Are | X	8483
See Jungle! See Jungle! Go Jo... | BOW WOW WOW	13592
The Seekers | The SEEKERS	12447
Seen One Earth | Pete BARDENS	11654
The Seer | BIG COUNTRY	5494
See The Light | Jeff HEALEY Band	1855
See What Tomorrow Brin... | PETER, PAUL & MARY	2178
See You In Hell | GRIM REAPER	5887
Self Control | Laura BRANIGAN	1656
Self Portrait | Bob DYLAN	1435
Selling England By The Pound | GENESIS	4393

Title | Act	Rank
Sell My Soul | SYLVESTER	10037
Seminar | Sir MIX-A-LOT	3773
Send It | ASHFORD & SIMPSON	2595
Send Me An Angel '89 | REAL LIFE	13446
Send Me Your Love | KASHIF	5144
Send Your Love | AURRA	7147
Sensational | STARPOINT	7522
The Sensational Charley Pri... | Charley PRIDE	2374
The Sensational Sonny James | Sonny JAMES	13617
Sense Of Direction | CLIMAX BLUES BAND	2504
Sense Of Purpose | THIRD WORLD	8739
A Sense Of Wonder | Van MORRISON	5724
The Sensitive Sound Of Dio... | Dionne WARWICK	8999
The Sensual World | Kate BUSH	3399
Sentimental Hygiene | Warren ZEVON	5564
Sentimental Journey | Ringo STARR	3586
Separate Ways | Elvis PRESLEY	4686
September Morn | Neil DIAMOND	2116
September Of My Years | Frank SINATRA	399
September Song | Jimmy DURANTE	4206
Sequel | Harry CHAPIN	5406
Sequencer | SYNERGY	8490
Serenade | Neil DIAMOND	778
Serenade For Elisabe... | Gunter KALLMANN Chor...	8351
The Serendipity Singe... | SERENDIPITY SINGERS	1967
Sergio Mendes(2) | Sergio MENDES	2912
Sergio Mendes | Sergio MENDES	8002
Sergio Mendes & Bras... | Sergio MENDES And BR...	427
Sergio Mendes And Th... | Sergio MENDES And BR...	6903
Sergio Mendes' Favor... | Sergio MENDES And BR...	13111
Serious | DEJA	12530
Serious | The O'JAYS	7590
Serious Business | Johnny WINTER	10616
Serious Business | THIRD WORLD	7613
Serious Slammin' | POINTER SISTERS	11222
The Serpent Is Rising | STYX	13644
Sesame Street 2 | SOUNDTRACK-TV	6983
The Sesame Street Book & Re... | SOUNDTRACK-TV	1612
Sesame Street Fever | VARIOUS ARTISTS	7113
The Session | Jerry Lee LEWIS	3973
A Session With Gary ... | Gary LEWIS And The P...	3802
Set My Love In Motion | SYREETA	13219
Setting Sons | The JAM	9575
Seven | POCO	6088
Seven And The Ragged Tiger | DURAN DURAN	428
Seven Separate Fools | THREE DOG NIGHT	889
7-6-5-4-3-2-1 Blow Your ... | Gary TOMS Empire	12633
Seven Steps To Heaven | Miles DAVIS	6215
7-Tease | DONOVAN	9843
1776 | ORIGINAL CAST	11060
1776 | SOUNDTRACK-MOVIE	9790
The 7th Dawn | SOUNDTRACK-MOVIE	12531
Seven The Hard Way | Pat BENATAR	3458
The Seventh One | TOTO	5050
Seventh Sojourn | MOODY BLUES	379
Seventh Son Of A Seventh Son | IRON MAIDEN	2333
Seventh Star | BLACK SABBATH	7621
7800 Degrees Fahrenheit | BON JOVI	1252
'74 Jailbreak | AC/DC	7219
74 Miles Away - Walk... | "Cannonball" ADDERLE...	13492
7 Wishes | NIGHT RANGER	925
Seven Year Ache | Rosanne CASH	2004
Several Shades Of Jade | Cal TJADER	7364
Sex And The Single M... | Ray PARKER Jr./RAYDI...	7490
Sex & Violins | Martin MULL	11994
Sexappeal | GEORGIO	4845

Title | Act	Rank
The Sex Life Of The Primat... | Shelley BERMAN	9059
Sex Machine | James BROWN	2437
Sex Machine Today | James BROWN	8442
Sextant | Herbie HANCOCK	11872
Sgt. Pepper's Lonely Hea... | SOUNDTRACK-MOVIE	1079
Sgt. Pepper's Lonely Hearts C... | The BEATLES	19
Shabazz (Recorded Live In Eu... | Billy COBHAM	7336
Shabooh Shoobah | INXS	4198
Shaday | Ofra HAZA	9481
Shaddap You Face | Joe DOLCE	12532
Shades | J.J. CALE	8996
Shades | Keith JARRETT	12212
Shades | YELLOWJACKETS	13777
Shades Of Blue | Lou RAWLS	9317
Shades Of Deep Purple | DEEP PURPLE	2417
Shades of Lace | LACE	12603
Shadowdance | SHADOWFAX	8460
Shadow Dancing | Andy GIBB	801
Shadowland | K.D. LANG	4982
Shadow Man | Johnny CLEGG & SAVUK...	11024
The Shadow Of Your Smile | Andy WILLIAMS	1143
The Shadow Of Your Smile | Astrud GILBERTO	6056
The Shadow Of Your Smile | Johnny MATHIS	1482
Shadows | Gordon LIGHTFOOT	7778
Shadows And Light | Joni MITCHELL	4590
Shady Grove | QUICKSILVER MESSENGE...	3303
Shaft (Soundtrack) | Isaac HAYES	178
Shaft In Africa | SOUNDTRACK-MOVIE	9377
Shaft's Big Score! | SOUNDTRACK-MOVIE	6475
Shake | Sam COOKE	4134
Shakedown Street | GRATEFUL DEAD	3427
Shake It Up | The CARS	827
Shake It Well | The DRAMATICS	4902
Shaken 'N' Stirred | Robert PLANT	3374
Shake Off The Demon | BREWER And SHIPLEY	10426
Shake, Rattle & Roll | Arthur CONLEY	13746
Shake Some Action | FLAMIN' GROOVIES	10141
Shake You Down | Gregory ABBOTT	2064
Shakti With John McL... | SHAKTI With John McL...	13515
Shame On The World | MAIN INGREDIENT	9914
Shame Shame Shame | SHIRLEY (& COMPANY)	12398
Sha Na Na | SHA NA NA	8501
Sha Na Now | SHA NA NA	11699
Shango | SANTANA	2837
Shangri-La | BARDEUX	10550
Shangri-La | Robert MAXWELL	2952
Shangri-La | Vic DANA	10847
Shangri-La! | Percy FAITH His Orch...	7425
Shankar Family & Friends | Ravi SHANKAR	12641
Share The Land | GUESS WHO	1709
Share Your Love | Kenny ROGERS	833
Sharing Your Love | CHANGE	8371
Sharky's Machine | SOUNDTRACK-MOVIE	11317
Sharp | Angela WINBUSH	5594
Shaun Cassidy | Shaun CASSIDY	440
Shaved Fish | John LENNON/PLASTIC ...	2085
She Called Me Baby | Charlie RICH	6585
She Cried | The LETTERMEN	4744
Sheena Easton | Sheena EASTON	2079
Sheer Heart Attack | QUEEN	1545
Sheet Music | 10cc	6588
She Even Woke Me Up To Sa... | Jerry Lee LEWIS	13478
Sheffield Steel | Joe COCKER	6390
Sheik Yerbouti | Frank ZAPPA	2435
Sheila E. | SHEILA E.	7111
Shelter | LONE JUSTICE	4729

Title | Act	Rank
The Shelter Of Your Arms | Sammy DAVIS Jr.	4218
Shenandoah | SOUNDTRACK-MOVIE	12970
Sheriff | SHERIFF	6163
She's A Heartbreaker | Gene PITNEY	13151
She's A Lady | Tom JONES	2250
She's Got To Be A Saint | Ray PRICE	10908
She's Having A Baby | SOUNDTRACK-MOVIE	8523
She Shot Me Down | Frank SINATRA	5525
She's Just My Style | Gary LEWIS And The P...	6345
She's So Unusual | Cyndi LAUPER	148
She's Strange | CAMEO	3257
She's The Boss | Mick JAGGER	2226
She Still Comes Around (T... | Jerry Lee LEWIS	9473
She Understands Me | Johnny TILLOTSON	12451
She Used To Wanna Be A... | Buffy SAINTE-MARIE	11668
She Was Only A Grocer's Daug... | BLOW MONKEYS	9929
She Works Hard For The Money | Donna SUMMER	1694
Shilo | Neil DIAMOND	3521
Shine | AVERAGE WHITE BAND/A...	7664
Shine On | CLIMAX BLUES Band	6701
Shine On | L.T.D.	2629
Shine On Brightly | PROCOL HARUM	2710
Shine On Me | ONE WAY	11678
Shinin' On | GRAND FUNK RAILROAD	751
Ship Ahoy | The O'JAYS	999
A Ship Arriving Too Late To S... | Frank ZAPPA	3339
Ship Of Memories | FOCUS	11046
Shipwrecked | GONZALEZ	6393
Shirley Bassey Belts The B... | Shirley BASSEY	8777
Shirley Bassey Is Really "... | Shirley BASSEY	7119
Shirley Murdock! | Shirley MURDOCK	4142
Shiver In The Night | Andy PRATT	8339
Shock | The MOTELS	4914
Shockadelica | Jesse JOHNSON	6048
Shocker | SOUNDTRACK-MOVIE	8668
The Shocking Blue | SHOCKING BLUE	4294
Shock Treatment | Edgar WINTER	1745
Shogun | SOUNDTRACK-TV	9536
Sho Is Funky Down Here | James BROWN	10721
Shooting Rubberbands... | Edie BRICKELL & NEW ...	652
Shooting Star | SHOOTING STAR	9058
Shoot Out At The Fantasy Factory | TRAFFIC	1508
Short Back 'N' Sides | Ian HUNTER	6421
Short Cut Draw Blood | Jim CAPALDI	12865
Short Sharp Shocked | Michelle SHOCKED	4099
Short Stories | Harry CHAPIN	4894
Short Stories | JON And VANGELIS	8265
Short Trip To Space | TROPEA	10367
Shotgun | Jr. WALKER & The ALL...	5241
Shotgun Messiah | SHOTGUN MESSIAH	6366
Shotgun III | SHOTGUN	11878
Shot In The Dark | GREAT WHITE	7515
Shot Of Love | Bob DYLAN	5215
Shot Of Love | LAKESIDE	5452
Shot Through The Heart | Jennifer WARNES	5577
Shoulda Gone Dancin' | HIGH INERGY	10823
Should I Do It | Tanya TUCKER	12909
Shout | DEVO	9378
Shout! | B.T. EXPRESS	6630
Shout At The Devil | MÖTLEY CRÜE	637
The Shouting Stage | Joan ARMATRADING	8088
Shout It Out | Patrice RUSHEN	12035
Show And Tell | Al WILSON	5976
Showcase | The SYLVERS	4438
Showdown | ISLEY BROTHERS	1273
Showdown! [A] | Albert COLLINS	8095

Title | Act	Rank
Showdown! [A] | Johnny COPELAND	8095
Showdown! [A] | Robert CRAY Band	8095
Show Me | COVER GIRLS	3422
Show Me To The Stage | Henry GROSS	11254
A Show Of Hands | RUSH	3990
Show Some Emotion | Joan ARMATRADING	4167
Show Time | Ry COODER	11213
Show Time | SLAVE	4392
Showtime | James BROWN	5813
Showtime | Johnny CASH And The ...	12651
Showtime | J. GEILS Band	3369
Shriner's Convention | Ray STEVENS	9585
Shut Down, Volume 2 | BEACH BOYS	1417
Shuttered Room | The FIXX	4069
Side By Side | Tony SANDLER And Ral...	5884
Side Kicks | THOMPSON TWINS	3925
Side 3 | RASPBERRIES	9728
The Sidewinder | Lee MORGAN	3097
Signals | RUSH	1898
Signed Sealed & Delivered | Stevie WONDER	3317
Sign In Please | AUTOGRAPH	2854
Sign Of The Times | Bob JAMES	5763
Sign 'O' The Times | PRINCE	1042
Signs Of Life | Billy SQUIER	1860
Signs Of The Zodiac | VARIOUS ARTISTS	8003
The Silence (Il Silenzio) | Roy ETZEL	11084
The Silencers (Soundtrack) | Dean MARTIN	11434
Silent Letter | AMERICA	9873
Silhouette | KENNY G	742
Silk | FUSE ONE	10096
Silk & Soul | Lou RAWLS	12712
Silk & Soul | Nina SIMONE	12108
Silk + Steel | GIUFFRIA	6447
Silk And Steel | FIVE STAR	6270
Silk Degrees | Boz SCAGGS	73
Silk Electric | Diana ROSS	3051
Silk 'N' Brass | Jackie GLEASON	11685
Silk N' Soul | Gladys KNIGHT & The ...	6621
Silk Purse | Linda RONSTADT	7440
Silk Torpedo | PRETTY THINGS	7991
Silky Soul | MAZE Featuring Frank...	4540
Silver | SILVER	10378
Silver Apples | SILVER APPLES	13273
Silverbird | Mark LINDSAY	7163
Silver Condor | SILVER CONDOR	8256
Silver Convention | SILVER CONVENTION	1995
Silver Cycles | Eddie HARRIS	13652
The Silver Fox | Charlie RICH	2697
Silver Linings | Charlie RICH	10919
Silver Morning | Kenny RANKIN	4962
The Silver Tongued Dev... | Kris KRISTOFFERSON	1625
Simon And Garfunkel's G... | SIMON & GARFUNKEL	438
Simon Says | 1910 FRUITGUM CO.	10817
Simple Dreams | Linda RONSTADT	182
Simple Man | Charlie DANIELS Band	5656
Simple Pleasures | Bobby McFERRIN	953
Simple Things | Carole KING	3372
Simple Things | Richie HAVENS	12677
Simplicity | Tim CURRY	8740
Simplicity Of Expression-Dep... | Billy COBHAM	10989
Simply Carrie | Carrie LUCAS	12190
Simply Streisand | Barbra STREISAND	2101
Sinatra & Company | Frank SINATRA	5812
Sinatra At The Sands | Frank SINATRA & Coun...	1365
Sinatra '65 | Frank SINATRA	1065
Sinatra's Sinatra | Frank SINATRA	1418

Title | Act	Rank
Sinatra - The Main Event Li... | Frank SINATRA	4756
Since I Fell For You(2) | Lenny WELCH	12971
Since I Fell For You | Lenny WELCH	8115
Sincerely | Dwight TWILLEY	7894
Sinfonias | Waldo DE LOS RIOS	4583
Sinful | ANGEL	11559
Sing | SOUNDTRACK-MOVIE	13835
The Sing-Along World Of Trini... | Trini LOPEZ	8564
Sing A Song Of Watergate... | Mort SAHL	10467
Sing A Song with The Kingst... | KINGSTON TRIO	6911
Sing Away The World | Ed AMES	13649
Singer Of Songs - Teller Of Ta... | Paul DAVIS	6225
Singin' | Melissa MANCHESTER	6141
The Singing Nun | Debbie REYNOLDS	3291
The Singing Nun | SINGING NUN	348
The Singing Story Te... | Johnny CASH And The ...	13217
Singin' Our Mind | Chad MITCHELL Trio	4389
Sing It Again Rod | Rod STEWART	3228
Single Life | CAMEO	4532
A Single Man | Elton JOHN	2693
The Singles | The PRETENDERS	6411
The Singles (The First Ten Years) | ABBA	5416
Singles Collection - The L... | ROLLING STONES	5778
Singles 45's And Under | SQUEEZE	5152
The Singles 1969-1973 | CARPENTERS	639
Sings Like Crazy | Frank FONTAINE	4091
Sinner...And Saint | Rory GALLAGHER	11163
Siogo | BLACKFOOT	7289
Siren | ROXY MUSIC	3856
Sirius | CLANNAD	12351
Sister Kate | Kate TAYLOR	8509
The Sisters | SISTER SLEDGE	6687
Sisyphus | COLD BLOOD	6106
Sit Down And Talk To Me | Lou RAWLS	5713
Sit Down Young Stranger | Gordon LIGHTFOOT	1423
Sittin' In | LOGGINS & MESSINA	1325
Six Hours Past Sunse... | Henry MANCINI and hi...	6072
Sixteen | Stacy LATTISAW	10744
16 Greatest Hits | JAMES GANG	12311
16 Greatest Hits | STEPPENWOLF	10045
16 Greatest Hits | The IMPRESSIONS	11826
16 Of Their Greatest Hi... | MAMAS & The PAPAS	4277
16 Original Big Hits | VARIOUS ARTISTS	7895
16 Original Big Hits, Vol. 4 | VARIOUS ARTISTS	10730
16 Original Big Hits, Vol. 5 | VARIOUS ARTISTS	5262
16 Original Big Hits, Vol. 6 | VARIOUS ARTISTS	6196
16 Original Big Hits, Vol. 7 | VARIOUS ARTISTS	6560
16 Original Big Hits, Vol. 8 | VARIOUS ARTISTS	11370
16 Original Big Hits, Vol. 9 | VARIOUS ARTISTS	10218
The Six Wives Of Henry VIII | Rick WAKEMAN	1778
Skeezer Pleezer | UTFO	10742
Skid Row | SKID ROW	184
The Skill | The SHERBS	6578
Skin Dive | Michael FRANKS	6887
Skin On Skin | VANITY	5928
Skin Tight | OHIO PLAYERS	798
Skip A Rope | Henson CARGILL	13351
Skitch...Tonight! | Skitch HENDERSON	9197
Sky | SKY	7663
Sky | SKY (2)	11072
The Sky | SAN SEBASTIAN String...	5462
Skybird | DAWN/Tony ORLANDO	8926
Sky Blue | PASSPORT	9975
Sky Dive | Freddie HUBBARD	10993
Sky High | JIGSAW	4412
Sky High! | TAVARES	2031

Title | Act	Rank
Sky Islands | CALDERA	11817
Skylark | SKYLARK	6958
Skylarkin' | Grover WASHINGTON Jr...	3063
Skylarking | XTC	5219
Skynyrd's First And...Last | LYNYRD SKYNYRD	2804
Skyscraper | David Lee ROTH	1190
Skyscraper | ORIGINAL CAST	9696
Sky's The Limit | The TEMPTATIONS	1221
Sky 3 | SKY	12730
Skyway | SKYY	4061
Skywriter | JACKSON 5	4644
Skyy | SKYY	9046
Skyyjammer | SKYY	7014
Skyylight | SKYY	13195
Skyy Line | SKYY	1993
Skyyport | SKYY	5707
Slade Alive! | SLADE	9763
Slade In Flame (Soundtrack) | SLADE	6373
Sladest | SLADE	9714
Slam | Dan REED Network	11694
Slaughter On 10th Avenue | Mick RONSON	11286
Slaughter's Big Rip-Off (Soun... | James BROWN	7688
Slave | SLAVE	1952
Slave To The Rhythm | Grace JONES	5705
Slayed? | SLADE	4634
Sleep Dirt | Frank ZAPPA	12257
Sleeper Catcher | LITTLE RIVER BAND	1153
Sleeping Beauty | CHEECH & CHONG	3523
Sleeping Gypsy | Michael FRANKS	8946
Sleeping With The Past | Elton JOHN	1607
Sleepless Nights | BROOKLYN DREAMS	10522
Sleepless Nights | FLYING BURRITO BROTH...	12634
Sleepwalk | Larry CARLTON	6864
Sleepwalker | The KINKS	2919
Sleight Of Hand | Joan ARMATRADING	6415
The Slide Area | Ry COODER	9874
Slide It In | WHITESNAKE	2164
The Slider | T. REX	2168
Slides | Richard HARRIS	11864
The Slightly Irreveren... | Chad MITCHELL Trio	9159
Slim Slo Slider | Johnny RIVERS	8080
Slingshot | Michael HENDERSON	7404
Slip Of The Tongue | WHITESNAKE	1426
Slippery When Wet | BON JOVI	34
Slippin' Away | Chris HILLMAN	10607
Sloppy Seconds | DR. HOOK	3511
Slow Dance | SOUTHSIDE JOHNNY & T...	13834
Slow Dancer | Boz SCAGGS	5629
Slow Down World | DONOVAN	12586
Slow Flux | STEPPENWOLF	5177
Slow Freight | Ray BRYANT	13406
Slowhand | Eric CLAPTON	221
Slow Train Coming | Bob DYLAN	1131
Slow Turning | John HIATT	5591
Smackwater Jack | Quincy JONES	3083
Small Change | PRISM	4667
Small Change | Tom WAITS	9233
Smallcreep's Day | Mike RUTHERFORD	9670
Small Talk | SLY & THE FAMILY STO...	2744
Small World | Huey LEWIS And The N...	2039
Smashes, Thrashes & Hits | KISS	2413
Smash Hits | Jimi HENDRIX EXPERIE...	816
Smash Your Head Against Th... | John ENTWISTLE	8614
Smell The Flowers | Jerry REED	13660
Smile | Laura NYRO	5167
Smile!/The Best Of Tim Weisb... | Tim WEISBERG	12131

Title | Act	Rank
Smiler | Rod STEWART	3147
Smiley Smile | BEACH BOYS	4110
The Smiths | The SMITHS	10201
The Smoker You Drink, The Playe... | Joe WALSH	738
Smoke Signals | Smokey ROBINSON	8324
Smoke Some Kill | SCHOOLLY D	13131
Smokey | Smokey ROBINSON	5404
Smokey And The Bandit 2 | SOUNDTRACK-MOVIE	7587
Smokey Robinson & Th... | The MIRACLES/Smokey ...	6706
Smokey's Family Robinson | Smokey ROBINSON	5218
Smokin' | HUMBLE PIE	1193
Smokin' | Smokey ROBINSON	11308
Smoking In The Fields | DEL FUEGOS	7484
Smokin' O.P.'s | Bob SEGER	10570
Smooth As Raw Silk | SILK	13396
Smooth Sailin' | ISLEY BROTHERS	6009
Smooth Talk | Evelyn "Champagne" K...	1356
Smothers Comedy Brother... | SMOTHERS BROTHERS	11560
Snail | SNAIL	8344
The Snake | Harvey MANDEL	13432
Snakes And Ladders | Gerry RAFFERTY	6797
Snapshot | SYLVIA (2)	7743
'Snaz | NAZARETH	7466
Sneaker | SNEAKER	7944
Sneakin' Out | Stacy LATTISAW	5234
Sneakin' Sally Thru The All... | Robert PALMER	6917
Sniper and Other Love Songs | Harry CHAPIN	10500
Snoopy And His Friends | ROYAL GUARDSMEN	5660
Snoopy For President | ROYAL GUARDSMEN	13404
Snoopy vs. The Red Baron | ROYAL GUARDSMEN	4953
Snowbird | Anne MURRAY	2746
Snowflakes Are Dancing | Isao TOMITA	4132
The Snow Goose | CAMEL	11364
So | Peter GABRIEL	272
Soap Opera | The KINKS	5056
Sock It To Me! | Mitch RYDER And The ...	4166
So Close, So Very Far To Go | Jake HOLMES	10081
Soda Fountain Shuffle | Earl KLUGH	7384
So Early In The Spring - The... | Judy COLLINS	3242
So Excited! | POINTER SISTERS	5106
So Far | CROSBY, STILLS, NASH...	1071
So Far, So Good... So What! | MEGADETH	3388
So Fine | LOGGINS & MESSINA	3075
Soft And Soulful | Bill MEDLEY	11242
Softly | The SANDPIPERS	12238
Softly, As I Leave You | Eydie GORME	6595
Softly, As I Leave You | Frank SINATRA	2728
The Soft Machine | SOFT MACHINE	9660
The Soft Parade | The DOORS	884
The Soft Sea | SAN SEBASTIAN String...	11920
So Full Of Love | The O'JAYS	1331
So Good | DON And The GOODTIME...	10865
So Good | Mica PARIS	6175
So Good | The WHISPERS	5610
So Happy | Eddie MURPHY	7799
Solar Fire | MANFRED MANN'S EARTH...	7079
Sold | BOY GEORGE	11551
Soldier | Iggy POP	9504
Soldiers Of Fortune | The OUTLAWS	10692
Soldiers Under Command | STRYPER	4489
Sold Out | The FOOLS	10307
Solid | ASHFORD & SIMPSON	2560
Solid | MANDRILL	6619
Solid | Michael HENDERSON	11174
Solid And Raunchy The ... | Bill BLACK'S Combo	11681
Solid Brass | Herb ALPERT & The Ti...	8962

Title | Act	Rank
Solid Gold | GANG OF FOUR	13476
Solid Goldsboro - Bobby G... | Bobby GOLDSBORO	12589
Solid Gold '69 | Chet ATKINS	10391
Solid Gold Soul | VARIOUS ARTISTS	6858
The Solid Gold Steinway | Roger WILLIAMS	4577
Solid Ground | Ronnie LAWS	4792
Solid Rock | The TEMPTATIONS	2686
Solid Silver | QUICKSILVER MESSENGE...	7678
Solitaire | Andy WILLIAMS	12216
Solitaire | Neil SEDAKA	11485
Solitude/Solitaire | Peter CETERA	1747
Solitude Standing | Suzanne VEGA	1624
Solo | Frankie VALLI	3898
Solo Flights | Chet ATKINS	13033
Solomon's Seal | PENTANGLE	12606
So Long, Bannatyne | GUESS WHO	4296
So Many Rivers | Bobby WOMACK	6360
Some Blue-Eyed Soul | RIGHTEOUS BROTHERS	2892
Somebody Else Is Taking My Pla... | Al MARTINO	5881
Somebody Like Me | Eddy ARNOLD	3476
Somebody's Been Slee... | 100 PROOF AGED IN SO...	10641
Somebody's Gonna Love You | Lee GREENWOOD	5963
Somebody's Knockin' | Terri GIBBS	3987
Somebody's Waiting | Anne MURRAY	5979
Somebody's Watching Me | ROCKWELL	2327
Some Come Running | Jim CAPALDI	11974
Some Days Are Diamonds | John DENVER	2700
Someday We'll Look Back | Merle HAGGARD	7326
Some Enchanted Evening | BLUE ÖYSTER CULT	5037
Some Girls | ROLLING STONES	111
Some Great Reward | DEPECHE MODE	3768
Some Kind Of Wonderful | SOUNDTRACK-MOVIE	6798
Some Nice Things I've Misse... | Frank SINATRA	4927
Some Of My Best Jokes Are ... | George CLINTON	11810
Some People Can Do What The... | Robert PALMER	5600
Somethin' Else | Danny DAVIS And The ...	12068
Something About You | Angela BOFILL	4496
Something/Anything? | Todd RUNDGREN	1793
Something Else | Shirley BASSEY	6051
Something Else Again | Richie HAVENS	11940
Something Else By The Kinks | The KINKS	12819
Something Happening | Paul REVERE And The ...	7015
Something Heavy Going Down... | GOLDEN EARRING	11953
Something Inside So Strong | Kenny ROGERS	10206
Something In The Nigh... | PURE PRAIRIE LEAGUE	6127
Something Magic | PROCOL HARUM	10614
Something New | The BEATLES	494
Something Real | Phoebe SNOW	6418
Something's Burning | Kenny ROGERS & The F...	2745
Some Things Don't Co... | ENGLAND DAN & John F...	5508
Something's Going On | FRIDA	3937
Something Special | KOOL & The GANG	642
Something Special | The SYLVERS	5566
Something Special! T... | Tommy JAMES And The ...	12112
Something Special For... | Ray CHARLES Singers	2016
Something Super! | KING RICHARD'S FLUEG...	13762
Something To Believe In | Curtis MAYFIELD	8875
Something To Love | L.T.D.	1506
Something To Talk About | Anne MURRAY	5507
Somethin's Happening | Peter FRAMPTON	8756
Somethin' Stupid | LENNON SISTERS	6733
Some Time In New Yor... | John LENNON & Yoko O...	4554
Sometimes | FACTS OF LIFE	10158
Sometimes I Just Fee... | Paul BUTTERFIELD Blu...	10086
Sometimes Late At Nigh... | Carole Bayer SAGER	4900
Sometimes When We Touch [A] | Cleo LAINE	10470

Title | Act	Rank
Sometimes When We Touch [A] | James GALWAY	10470
Sometimes You Win | DR. HOOK	4687
Some Tough City | Tony CAREY	4633
Somewhere | The TYMES	11583
Somewhere In Afrika | MANFRED MANN'S EARTH...	4722
Somewhere In England | George HARRISON	2823
Somewhere In My Lifetime | Phyllis HYMAN	5611
Somewhere In The Stars | Rosanne CASH	7510
Somewhere In Time | IRON MAIDEN	1764
Somewhere In Time | SOUNDTRACK-MOVIE	13437
Somewhere I've Never Travelled | AMBROSIA	6124
Somewhere My Love | Ray CONNIFF & His Or...	262
Somewhere Over China | Jimmy BUFFETT	4211
Somewhere Over The Rainbow | Willie NELSON	3015
Somewhere There's A Someone | Dean MARTIN	3854
So Much For Dreaming | IAN & SYLVIA	10060
A Song | Neil SEDAKA	7220
Song Bird | Deniece WILLIAMS	4536
Songbird | Barbra STREISAND	1751
Songbird | Jesse Colin YOUNG	3792
A Song For All Seasons | RENAISSANCE	5227
Song For America | KANSAS	5271
Song For Juli | Jesse Colin YOUNG	3037
Song For My Father (... | Horace SILVER Quinte...	8931
A Song For You | CARPENTERS	890
A Song For You | Ron CARTER	12729
A Song For You | The TEMPTATIONS	1057
A Song Of Joy | Miguel RIOS	11157
Song Of Joy | CAPTAIN & TENNILLE	786
Song Of Norway | SOUNDTRACK-MOVIE	8263
Song Of Seven | Jon ANDERSON	9000
A Song Or Two | CASHMAN & WEST	10858
Song Painter | Mac DAVIS	12468
The Song Remains The Same (S... | LED ZEPPELIN	865
Songs | KIDS FROM FAME	12792
Songs For A Tailor | Jack BRUCE	5478
Songs For Beginners | Graham NASH	1819
Songs For Latin Lover... | Ray CHARLES Singers	10397
Songs For Lonesome Lo... | Ray CHARLES Singers	6404
Songs For The New Depression | Bette MIDLER	3760
Songs From A Room | Leonard COHEN	4471
Songs From "Cat Ballou" And... | Nat King COLE	8211
Songs From Liquid Days | Philip GLASS	7823
Songs From The Big Chair | TEARS FOR FEARS	91
Songs From The Film | Tommy KEENE	8571
Songs From The Stage And... | Michael CRAWFORD	13704
Songs From The Wood | JETHRO TULL	1489
The Songs I Love | Perry COMO	5434
Songs I Love To Sing | Slim WHITMAN	12725
Songs In The Attic | Billy JOEL	1465
Songs In The Key Of Life | Stevie WONDER	24
Songs My Father Left Me | Hank WILLIAMS Jr.	11368
The Songs Of Bacharach And David | Ed AMES	13816
Songs Of Fox Hollow | Tom T. HALL	13254
The Songs Of Jim Weatherly | Jim WEATHERLY	7039
Songs Of Kristofferson | Kris KRISTOFFERSON	4777
Songs Of Leonard Cohen | Leonard COHEN	7291
Songs Of Love | Anita WARD	1740
Songs Of Love And Hate | Leonard COHEN	8767
Songs Of Love By Charley Pr... | Charley PRIDE	10268
Songs Of The Free | GANG OF FOUR	13034
Songs Of The Humpback Wha... | VARIOUS ARTISTS	10619
Songs Of The Young World | Eddy ARNOLD	6033
Songs, Pictures And Stories O... | The BEATLES	7660
Songs To Learn & Sing | ECHO & The BUNNYMEN	11015
The Songstress | Anita BAKER	9498

Title | Act	Rank
Song Sung Blue | Johnny MATHIS	5771
Songs You Know By Heart: Ji... | Jimmy BUFFETT	7090
Songs You Won't Forget | Peter NERO	4886
A Song Will Rise | PETER, PAUL & MARY	1220
Songwriter | Justin HAYWARD	4238
So Nice | Johnny MATHIS	4905
Sonic Seasonings | Walter CARLOS	10885
Sonic Temple | The CULT	1310
Sonny & Brownie | Sonny TERRY & Browni...	12692
Sonny & Cher Live | SONNY & CHER	2170
Sonny & Cher Live In Las Veg... | SONNY & CHER	11360
The Sonny Side Of Cher | CHER	3765
Son Of A Preacher Man | Nancy WILSON	6550
Son Of A Son Of A Sailor | Jimmy BUFFETT	1689
Son Of Cactus | CACTUS	12065
Son Of Dracula (Soundtrack) | NILSSON	8233
The Son Of Rock And Roll | Rocky BURNETTE	5438
Son Of Schmilsson | NILSSON	1532
The Sons | SONS OF CHAMPLIN	11277
Sooner Or Later | Larry GRAHAM/GRAHAM ...	9941
Sooner Or Later | Rex SMITH	2514
Sopwith Camel | SOPWITH "CAMEL"	13672
Sorcerer (Soundtrack) | TANGERINE DREAM	10901
The Sorcerer | Gabor SZABO	13695
So Red The Rose | ARCADIA	3355
S.O.S. | S.O.S. BAND	2023
S.O.S. | YACHTS	12822
So So Satisfied | ASHFORD & SIMPSON	12826
S.O.S. III | S.O.S. BAND	11387
So Tenderly | John GARY	3618
The Soul Album | Otis REDDING	4340
Soul & Inspiration | RIGHTEOUS BROTHERS	1394
Soul Bag | Mongo SANTAMARIA	8676
Soul Box | Grover WASHINGTON Jr...	7021
Soul Children | SOUL CHILDREN	10685
Soul Coaxing (Ame Ca... | Raymond LEFEVRE And ...	7144
Soul Country | Joe TEX	10517
Soul Directions | Arthur CONLEY	13366
Souled | José FELICIANO	2927
Souled Out | RIGHTEOUS BROTHERS	13766
Soul Explosion | VARIOUS ARTISTS	12458
Soulforce Revolution | 7 SECONDS	8208
Soulful | Dionne WARWICK	1719
Soulful Strut | YOUNG-HOLT UNLIMITED	1392
Soulful Tapestry | HONEY CONE	5013
The Soul Goes On | Jerry BUTLER	13638
Soul Kiss | Olivia NEWTON-JOHN	4486
Soul Limbo | BOOKER T. & The M.G....	8573
Soul Makossa | AFRIQUE	10389
Soul Makossa | Manu DIBANGO	6731
Soul Man | SOUNDTRACK-MOVIE	10301
Soul Men | SAM & DAVE	6103
Soul Message | "Groove" HOLMES	5233
The Soul Of A City Boy | Jesse Colin YOUNG	11630
The Soul Of Paul Mau... | Paul MAURIAT And His...	9634
Soul On Top | James BROWN	8404
Soul Provider | Michael BOLTON	55
Soul Sauce | Cal TJADER	4751
Soul Searching | AVERAGE WHITE BAND/A...	1501
Soul Searching | Glenn FREY	3858
Soul Serenade | Gloria LYNNE	8394
Soul Serenade | KING CURTIS	8342
Soul Serenade | Willie MITCHELL	10612
Soul Session | Jr. WALKER & The ALL...	10063
Soulshake [A] | Peggy SCOTT & Jo Jo ...	12578
Soul Sister | Aretha FRANKLIN	11279

Title | Act	Rank
Soul Sister | Erma FRANKLIN	13623
Soul Spin | FOUR TOPS	11088
Soul Survivor | Al GREEN	8625
Soul To Soul | SOUNDTRACK-MOVIE	7896
Soul To Soul | Stevie Ray VAUGHAN A...	3189
Soul Zodiac | Nat ADDERLEY Sextet	5470
Sound + Vision | David BOWIE	8203
Sound Affects | The JAM	6555
Sound Alarm | Michael ANDERSON	13742
Sound In Your Mind | Willie NELSON	4924
The Sound Of Boots | Boots RANDOLPH	4144
The Sound Of Music | DB'S	11553
The Sound Of Music | SOUNDTRACK-MOVIE	1
The Sound Of Nancy Wilson | Nancy WILSON	9307
Sound Of Sexy Soul | The DELFONICS	10031
The Sound Of Sunshin... | KC And The SUNSHINE ...	9286
Sound Of A Drum | Ralph MacDONALD	7138
The Sound Of The Wonderful Tyme... | The TYMES	8992
The Sound Of Wilson Picket... | Wilson PICKETT	6886
Sounds...And Stuff Like That... | Quincy JONES	2047
Sounds Like... | Herb ALPERT & The TI...	331
Sounds Of Love | Andre KOSTELANETZ An...	13527
Sounds Of Silence | SIMON & GARFUNKEL	499
The Sounds Of Simon | Joe SIMON	9652
Sound-System | Herbie HANCOCK	7088
Sound Track Recordings From ... | Jimi HENDRIX	6195
Soup For One | SOUNDTRACK-MOVIE	10818
Soupy Sales Sez Do The Mouse ... | Soupy SALES	9039
The Source | GRANDMASTER FLASH	11309
Southbound | Hoyt AXTON	13416
The Souther, Hillman... | SOUTHER, HILLMAN, FU...	2001
Southern Accents | Tom PETTY And The HE...	1227
Southern By The Grace Of G... | LYNYRD SKYNYRD	7488
Southern Comfort | Conway TWITTY	8871
Southern Comfort | The CRUSADERS	3219
Southern Nights | Glen CAMPBELL	2832
Southern Star | ALABAMA	5080
Southern Winds | Maria MULDAUR	10554
South Of Heaven | SLAYER	5669
South Of The Border | Herb ALPERT & The TI...	238
South Rampart Street Parade | Pete FOUNTAIN	8833
The South's Greatest Hits | VARIOUS ARTISTS	8950
Southside | TEXAS	6812
Souvenir d'Italie | Robert GOULET	12438
Souvenirs | Dan FOGELBERG	1794
So What | Joe WALSH	1851
So What's New? | Horst JANKOWSKI	12080
So...Where's The Show? | JO JO GUNNE	13811
Space & First Takes | Lee MICHAELS	6625
Spaced Out | Enoch LIGHT & The LI...	12828
A Space In Time | TEN YEARS AFTER	1891
Space Oddity | David BOWIE	1877
Space Ritual/Alive In Liverpool ... | HAWKWIND	11503
Spaceship Earth | SUGARLOAF	8031
Spaghetti Sauce & Other Deligh... | Pat COOPER	6757
Spanish Eyes | Al MARTINO	906
Spanish Fly | LISA LISA And CULT J...	762
Spanish Grease | Willie BOBO	9797
Spanish Moonlight | John GARY	7797
Spanish Rhapsodies F... | MIDNIGHT STRING QUAR...	6929
Spanish Strings | Enoch LIGHT & The LI...	12191
Spanky And Our Gang | SPANKY And OUR GANG	6223
Spanky's Greatest Hit... | SPANKY And OUR GANG	5900
Sparkle (Soundtrack) | Aretha FRANKLIN	1984
Sparkle In The Rain | SIMPLE MINDS	5495
Spark Of Love | Lenny WILLIAMS	5599

Title | Act	Rank
Spartacus | TRIUMVIRAT	3439
Speak & Spell | DEPECHE MODE	11764
Speak Her Name | Walter JACKSON	12893
Speaking In Tongues | TALKING HEADS	955
Speak Of The Devil | Ozzy OSBOURNE	2769
Speak To Me Of Love | Ray CONNIFF & His Or...	5668
Special | Jimmy CLIFF	13567
Special Beat Service | ENGLISH BEAT	2531
Special Forces | .38 SPECIAL	1596
Special Forces | ALICE COOPER (Solo)	10181
Special Occasion | The MIRACLES/Smokey ...	3033
Special Pain | Robert Ellis ORRALL	10166
A Special Part Of Me | Johnny MATHIS	8867
Special Request | The LETTERMEN	6407
The Specials | The SPECIALS	5285
Special Things | PLEASURE	7072
Special Things | POINTER SISTERS	3061
The Speckless Sky | Jane SIBERRY	10563
Spectral Mornings | Steve HACKETT	11151
Spectres | BLUE ÖYSTER CULT	5437
Spectrum | Billy COBHAM	1905
Speedway (Soundtrack) | Elvis PRESLEY	6649
Spell | Deon ESTUS	7051
Spellbinder | Gabor SZABO	11315
Spellbound | Joe SAMPLE	8918
Spencer Davis' Greate... | Spencer DAVIS Group	13358
Spend The Night | ISLEY BROTHERS	7653
The Spice Of Life | Jerry BUTLER	5114
Spider | SPIDER	8880
Spiders From Mars | SPIDERS FROM MARS	13692
Spies Of Life | PLAYER	10884
Spike | Elvis COSTELLO	2683
Spinners | SPINNERS	2133
Spinners/8 | SPINNERS	5501
Spinners Live! | SPINNERS	2318
Spinning Wheel | Lenny DEE	13087
Spinout (Soundtrack) | Elvis PRESLEY	2172
Spirit | EARTH, WIND & FIRE	584
Spirit | John DENVER	1081
Spirit | SPIRIT	3203
Spirit(2) | SPIRIT	13076
Spirit In The Dark | Aretha FRANKLIN	2621
Spirit In The Sky | Norman GREENBAUM	2861
Spirit Of America | BEACH BOYS	1302
Spirit Of A Woman | AMERICAN FLYER	11573
Spirit Of Love | CON FUNK SHUN	3665
Spirit Of Place | GOANNA	12494
Spirit Of '76 | SPIRIT	9961
The Spirit Of '67 | Paul REVERE And The ...	1259
Spirit Of St. Louis | Ellen FOLEY	11249
Spirit Of The Boogie | KOOL & The GANG	5527
Spirits Having Flown | BEE GEES	195
The Spirit's In It | Patti LaBELLE	11799
Spitfire | JEFFERSON AIRPLANE/S...	470
Splashdown | BREAKWATER	10897
Splendido Hotel | Al Di MEOLA	7092
Split Coconut | Dave MASON	3732
Split Ends | The MOVE	11037
Spoiled Girl | Carly SIMON	7981
Spontaneous Inventions | Bobby McFERRIN	7052
Spooky | CLASSICS IV	9806
Spooky Lady's Sideshow | Kris KRISTOFFERSON	5848
Spooky Two | SPOOKY TOOTH	3727
Sportin' Life | WEATHER REPORT	13445
The Sport Of Kings | TRIUMPH	3784
Sports | Huey LEWIS And The N...	31

Title | Act	Rank
The Spotlight Kid | CAPTAIN BEEFHEART	9392
Spreading The Disease | ANTHRAX	7816
Spread The Word | The PERSUASIONS	13355
Spring! | The LETTERMEN	3540
Spring Fever | Rick DERRINGER	9593
Spring Fever | SOULFUL STRINGS	12628
Spring Session M | MISSING PERSONS	1102
Springtime | FERRANTE & TEICHER	10676
Spun Gold | Barbara MANDRELL	11802
Spy | Carly SIMON	5324
Spyro Gyra | SPYRO GYRA	7306
S.P.Y.S. | SPYS	9886
The Spy Who Loved Me | SOUNDTRACK-MOVIE	5034
Spy With A Pie | Soupy SALES	9542
Squeezing Out Sparks | Graham PARKER And Th...	3538
SRC | SRC	11114
S.R.O. | Herb ALPERT & The TI...	179
SSSSH | TEN YEARS AFTER	2249
Stacked Deck | AMAZING RHYTHM ACES	9226
Stage | David BOWIE	5122
Stage Dolls | STAGE DOLLS	8677
Stage Fright | The BAND	1412
Stages | TRIUMPH	5348
Stained Class | JUDAS PRIEST	12673
Staircase/Hourglass/Sundial... | Keith JARRETT	8629
Stairsteps | FIVE STAIRSTEPS	7209
Stallion | STALLION	11581
Stamp Album | CLIMAX BLUES Band	6679
Stampede | DOOBIE BROTHERS	1290
Stand! | SLY & THE FAMILY STO...	313
Standards, Volume 1 | Stanley JORDAN	7679
Stand By Me | SOUNDTRACK-MOVIE	2434
Stand By Me | Spyder TURNER	12382
Stand By Your Man | Candi STATON	13494
Stand By Your Man | Tammy WYNETTE	3310
Standing Alone | WHITE WOLF	11530
Standing Hampton | Sammy HAGAR	2069
Standing On A Beach -- The Singl... | The CURE	2840
Standing On The Edge | CHEAP TRICK	4419
Standing On The Edge | Frankie MILLER(1)	10107
Standing On The Verge Of Getti... | FUNKADELIC	11301
Standing Ovation | Gladys KNIGHT & The ...	4138
Standing Ovation! | Jerry VALE	5393
Standing Ovation At Newport | Herbie MANN	12266
Standing Tall | The CRUSADERS	5996
Stand In Line | IMPELLITTERI	6004
Stand In The Fire | Warren ZEVON	7121
Stand Up | DEL FUEGOS	12001
Stand Up | JETHRO TULL	1570
Stan Kenton Today | Stan KENTON	8184
Stanky Brown | STANKY BROWN Group	12526
Stanley Clarke | Stanley CLARKE	5175
The Staple Swingers | STAPLE SINGERS	8124
Star! | SOUNDTRACK-MOVIE	5356
Starbooty | Roy AYERS UBIQUITY	11208
Starcastle | STARCASTLE	6587
Starchild | Teena MARIE	2796
Stardust | Willie NELSON	978
Starfish | The CHURCH	2604
Star Fleet Project | Brian MAY	9482
Stargard | STARGARD	3737
Staring At The Sun | LEVEL 42	10177
A Star Is Born (Soundt... [A] | Kris KRISTOFFERSON	167
A Star Is Born (Soundtra... [A] | Barbra STREISAND	167
Starland Vocal Band | STARLAND VOCAL BAND	2165
Starless And Bible Black | KING CRIMSON	6344

Title | Act	Rank
Starlight Dancer | KAYAK	8706
Star People | Miles DAVIS	10548
Stars | CHER	10255
Stars | Janis IAN	6516
Stars | SYLVESTER	5339
Stars & Stripes Fore... | NITTY GRITTY DIRT BA...	2981
Stars On Long Play | STARS ON	1686
Stars On Long Play III | STARS ON	11801
Stars On Long Play II | STARS ON	9706
The Stars We Are | Marc ALMOND	9656
Starting All Over Again | MEL And TIM	11411
Starting Over | RASPBERRIES	10118
Start Of A Romance | SKYY	11748
Star Trek - The Motion P... | SOUNDTRACK-MOVIE	5620
Star Trek III - The Sear... | SOUNDTRACK-MOVIE	8536
Star Trek II: The Wrath ... | SOUNDTRACK-MOVIE	7532
Star Walk | Larry GRAHAM/GRAHAM ...	11004
Star Wars | SOUNDTRACK-MOVIE	403
Suites From Star War... | Zubin MEHTA/LOS ANGE...	9501
Star Wars & Other Galactic Funk | MECO	1986
The Story Of Star Wars | SOUNDTRACK-MOVIE	5640
Starz | STARZ	7925
Stateless | Lene LOVICH	9333
State Of Confusion | The KINKS	2191
State Of...Emergency | STEEL PULSE	10310
State Of Euphoria | ANTHRAX	3343
State Of Shock | Ted NUGENT	3091
State Of The Heart | Mary Chapin CARPENTE...	11499
States Of Emergency | TAXXI	10383
Station To Station | David BOWIE	964
The Statler Brothers Chr... | STATLER BROTHERS	12534
Status Quo | STATUS QUO	10270
The Stax/Volt Revue - Liv... | VARIOUS ARTISTS	11752
Stay | RAY, GOODMAN & BROWN	10574
Stay & Other Great Hits | 4 SEASONS	10487
Stay Awake | VARIOUS ARTISTS	7593
Stay Awhile | KINGSTON TRIO	9275
Stay Awhile/I Only Want... | Dusty SPRINGFIELD	6985
Stay Free | ASHFORD & SIMPSON	2684
Stay Hard | RAVEN	6961
Stay Hungry | TWISTED SISTER	1058
Staying Alive (Soundtrack) | BEE GEES	1807
Stay In Love | Minnie RIPERTON	6667
Stay On These Roads | A-HA	11164
Stay The Night | Jane OLIVOR	7997
Stay Tuned | Chet ATKINS	9867
Stay With Me | Regina BELLE	3190
Stay With Me Tonight | Jeffrey OSBORNE	980
Steady Nerves | Graham PARKER And Th...	5000
Steady On | Shawn COLVIN	7013
Stealers Wheel | STEALERS WHEEL	4433
Stealing Fire | Bruce COCKBURN	5281
Stealin' Home | BABE RUTH	11567
Stealin' Home | Ian MATTHEWS	5579
Stealin Horses | STEALIN HORSES	9356
Steal Your Face | GRATEFUL DEAD	6368
Steam | STEAM	6569
Steamin' Hot | The REDDINGS	9572
Steel Breeze | STEEL BREEZE	4366
Steeltown | BIG COUNTRY	6008
Steel Wheels | ROLLING STONES	613
St. Elmo's Fire | SOUNDTRACK-MOVIE	2117
Step By Step | Eddie RABBITT	2204
Step By Step | Jeff LORBER	7180
Step By Step By Step | FIVE STAIRSTEPS	13683
A Step Further | SAVOY BROWN	5758
Stephanie | Stephanie MILLS	3059
Stephanie Mills | Stephanie MILLS	4823
Stephen Stills | Stephen STILLS	718
Stephen Stills 2 | Stephen STILLS	1733
Stephen Stills Live | Stephen STILLS	5431
Step On Out | OAK RIDGE BOYS	11730
Steppenwolf | STEPPENWOLF	604
Steppenwolf Gold/Their Great ... | STEPPENWOLF	1859
Steppenwolf 'Live' | STEPPENWOLF	820
Steppenwolf 7 | STEPPENWOLF	2379
Steppin' | POINTER SISTERS	2603
Stepping Into Tomorrow | Donald BYRD	4095
Steppin' Out | George HOWARD	12708
Steppin' Out | HIGH INERGY	5220
Steppin' Out | Neil SEDAKA	3217
Steps In Time | KING	10429
Step II | SYLVESTER	2301
Stereotomy | Alan PARSONS PROJECT	4926
The Sterile Cuckoo | SOUNDTRACK-MOVIE	13730
Steve Arrington's Ha... | Steve ARRINGTON'S HA...	7473
Steve Forbert | Steve FORBERT	11712
The Steve Howe Album | Steve HOWE	12176
The Steve Lawrence Show | Steve LAWRENCE	12643
The Steve Martin Brothers | Steve MARTIN	11144
Steve Miller Band - Liv... | Steve MILLER Band	10488
Steve Winwood | Steve WINWOOD	2725
Stevie Wonder Live | Stevie WONDER	5965
Stevie Wonder Presents Syreeta | SYREETA	6860
Stevie Wonder's Greatest Hi... | Stevie WONDER	5851
Stevie Wonder's Original Mu... | Stevie WONDER	1798
Stick To Me | Graham PARKER And Th...	10741
Sticky Fingers | ROLLING STONES	166
Still | Pete SINFIELD	12705
Still Alive And Well | Johnny WINTER	2398
Still Bill | Bill WITHERS	741
Still Caught Up | Millie JACKSON	6951
Still Crazy After All These Ye... | Paul SIMON	205
Still Cruisin' | BEACH BOYS	5086
Still Feels Good | Tom JOHNSTON	10547
Still In Love | Carrie LUCAS	13174
Still Life (American Conce... | ROLLING STONES	2045
Still Life (Talking) | PAT METHENY GROUP	7359
Stillness | Sergio MENDES And BR...	8765
Stills | Stephen STILLS	2924
Still Standing | JASON & The SCORCHER...	6638
Still Stills-The Best Of S... | Stephen STILLS	10297
Still The Same Ole Me | George JONES	7744
Still Together | Gladys KNIGHT & The ...	5009
Still Waters Run Deep | FOUR TOPS	1229
The Sting (Soundtrack) | Marvin HAMLISCH	257
Stingray | Joe COCKER	6851
St. Julian | Julian COPE	8534
St. Louie To Frisco To Memphi... | Chuck BERRY	11882
St. Louis To Liverpool | Chuck BERRY	10245
Stomp Your Hands, Clap Your Feet | SLADE	11721
Stone Alone | Bill WYMAN	11489
Stone Blue | FOGHAT	2921
Stone Cold Rhymin' | YOUNG M.C.	697
Stonedhenge | TEN YEARS AFTER	4488
Stoned Soul Picnic | 5TH DIMENSION	2747
Stone Flower | Antonio Carlos JOBIM	13565
Stone Flute | Herbie MANN	13026
Stone Gon' | Barry WHITE	1463
Stoneground Words | MELANIE	4888
Stoneheart | BRICK	8473
Stonehenge | Richie HAVENS	8989
Stone Jam | SLAVE	3620
ST-11261 | BREWER And SHIPLEY	12402
The Stone Poneys Featuring... | Linda RONSTADT	12111
Stones | Neil DIAMOND	1535
Stone Soul | Mongo SANTAMARIA	4207
Stoney End | Barbra STREISAND	1360
The Stooges | The STOOGES	6910
Stop | Eric BURDON Band	12117
Stop! Stop! Stop! | The HOLLIES	8491
Stop All That Jazz | Leon RUSSELL	3753
Stop And Smell The Roses | Mac DAVIS	1125
Stop And Smell The Roses | Ringo STARR	7437
Stop Making Sense | TALKING HEADS	1609
Stop Start | MODERN ENGLISH	11158
Stop Your Motor | The ASSOCIATION	11700
Store At The Sun | Jon BUTCHER AXIS	11507
Stories | Gloria GAYNOR	12602
Stories | STORIES	11062
Stories To Tell | Flora PURIM	11950
Stories Without Words | SPYRO GYRA	8517
Storm At Sunup | Gino VANNELLI	4598
Stormbringer | DEEP PURPLE	2990
Storm Force Ten | STEELEYE SPAN	13250
Storm Front | Billy JOEL	356
Stormin' | BRAINSTORM	7907
Storms | Nanci GRIFFITH	7556
Storms Of Life | Randy TRAVIS	2599
Stormwatch | JETHRO TULL	3417
Storm Windows | John PRINE	10285
Stormy Weekend | MYSTIC MOODS Orchestra	9184
The Story Of A Young ... | A FLOCK OF SEAGULLS	7550
The Story Of Bonnie & Cly... | FLATT & SCRUGGS	12501
The Story Of The Clash, Volume ... | The CLASH	10179
The Story's Been Told | THIRD WORLD	11365
Story Songs Of The T... | Johnny CASH And The ...	13598
Storyteller/Complete Antholog... | Rod STEWART	5118
Straight Ahead | Amy GRANT	8226
Straight Ahead | Brian AUGER	3652
Straight Ahead | Larry GATLIN/GATLIN ...	7067
Straight Between The Eyes | RAINBOW	3782
Straight From The Heart | Ann PEEBLES	13214
Straight From The Heart | Patrice RUSHEN	2748
Straight From The Heart | Peabo BRYSON	3905
Straight Outta Compton | N.W.A.	1323
Straight Shooter | BAD COMPANY	1195
Straight Shooter | JAMES GANG	4388
Straight To The Heart | David SANBORN	5158
Straight To The Point | ATLANTIC STARR	9994
Straight To The Sky | LISA LISA And CULT J...	7422
Straight Up | BADFINGER	2281
Stranded | ROXY MUSIC	12685
Strange Angels | Laurie ANDERSON	10816
Strange Behavior | ANIMOTION	7012
Strange Days | The DOORS	619
Strange Fire | INDIGO GIRLS	9682
Strange Fruit | Billie HOLIDAY	7135
Strange Kind Of Love | LOVE AND MONEY	11757
Strange Land | BOX OF FROGS	13105
Strange Man, Changed Man | BRAM TCHAIKOVSKY	3892
The Stranger | Billy JOEL	37
Stranger In The City | John MILES	6629
Stranger In Town | Bob SEGER	190
A Stranger On Earth | Dinah WASHINGTON	10717
Strangers In The Night | Frank SINATRA	289
Strangers In The Nig... | Bert KAEMPFERT And H...	4287
Strangers In The Night | UFO	4631

Title | Act	Rank
Strangers In The Wind | BAY CITY ROLLERS	10529
Strange Universe | MAHOGANY RUSH	6746
Strangeways, Here We Come | The SMITHS	4596
Straphangin' | BRECKER BROTHERS	12665
Stratosfear | TANGERINE DREAM	10453
Strawberry Moon | Grover WASHINGTON Jr...	6783
The Strawberry Statement | SOUNDTRACK-MOVIE	7671
Street Action | BACHMAN-TURNER OVERD...	10882
Street Beat | The DEELE	6572
Street Beat | Tom SCOTT & The L.A....	11258
Street Called Desire | RENÉ & ANGELA	2387
A Street Called Straight | Roy BUCHANAN	9750
Street Corner Heroes | Robbie DUPREE	11484
Street Corner Symphony | The PERSUASIONS	7129
Street Corner Talking | SAVOY BROWN	5190
Street Fair | MAGIC ORGAN	9545
Street Fever | Moon MARTIN	7604
Street Fighting Years | SIMPLE MINDS	7492
The Street Giveth...... | CAT MOTHER & The ALL...	4977
Street Hassle | Lou REED	7837
Street Lady | Donald BYRD	2917
Street Language | Rodney CROWELL	12616
Street-Legal | Bob DYLAN	2264
Street Life | The CRUSADERS	1324
Streetlife Serenade | Billy JOEL	3659
Street Life-20 Great Hits | ROXY MUSIC	8642
Streetlights | Bonnie RAITT	7662
Street Machine | Sammy HAGAR	6126
Streetnoise | Brian AUGER	4270
Street Opera | ASHFORD & SIMPSON	4661
Street Party | BLACK OAK ARKANSAS	5529
Street Player | RUFUS	1825
Street Rats | HUMBLE PIE	8231
Street Ready | LEATHERWOLF	9761
Streets Of Fire | SOUNDTRACK-MOVIE	3833
Street Songs | Rick JAMES	270
Street Survivors | LYNYRD SKYNYRD	997
Street Talk | Steve PERRY	1087
Streisand Superman | Barbra STREISAND	940
Strength | The ALARM	2811
Strength In Numbers | .38 SPECIAL	1695
Strength Of Steel | ANVIL	13747
Stretchin' Out In Bo... | BOOTSY'S RUBBER BAND	3513
Strictly Business | EPMD	5079
Strictly Personal | The ROMANTICS	13383
Strike Like Lightning | Lonnie MACK	7920
The Strikers | The STRIKERS	12760
Strikes | BLACKFOOT	2611
Strikes Twice | Larry CARLTON	9494
Striking It Rich! | Dan HICKS & His HOT ...	11893
Strip | Adam ANT	5240
Stronger Than Dirt | Big Mama THORNTON	13594
Stronger Than Pride | SADE	991
Strong Persuader | Robert CRAY Band	1106
Strong Stuff | Hank WILLIAMS Jr.	6642
Struttin' | The METERS	13740
Struttin' My Stuff | Elvin BISHOP	2092
Studio Tan | Frank ZAPPA	10748
Stuff | STUFF	12242
Style | CAMEO	6867
The Stylistics | The STYLISTICS	1318
Styx II | STYX	2895
Subject: Aldo Nova | Aldo NOVA	5465
Substance | JOY DIVISION	10234
Substance | NEW ORDER	2025
Subterranean Jungle | The RAMONES	8411

Title | Act	Rank
Suburban Voodoo | Paul CARRACK	7212
Success Hasn't Spoiled M... | Rick SPRINGFIELD	845
Suck 'Em Up | Don HO and the ALIIS	13293
Sucker For A Pretty Face | Eric MARTIN Band	13724
Sucking In The Seventies | ROLLING STONES	3297
Sudan Village | SEALS & CROFTS	6837
Suddenly | Billy OCEAN	328
Sue Saad And The Nex... | Sue SAAD And The NEX...	8653
Sufficiently Breathless | CAPTAIN BEYOND	7927
Sugar | Nancy SINATRA	3026
Sugar | Stanley TURRENTINE	13133
Sugar & Spice | CRYAN' SHAMES	13113
Sugar Lips | Al HIRT	1204
Sugarloaf | SUGARLOAF	2134
The Sugar Man | Stanley TURRENTINE	7357
Sugar Shack | The FIREBALLS/Jimmy ...	4773
Suicide Sal | Maggie BELL	9201
Suitable For Framing | THREE DOG NIGHT	441
Suite Flute & Jazz P... [A] | Jean-Pierre RAMPAL &...	12128
Suite For Late Summer | DION	13173
Suite For Susan Moore And Dami... | Tim HARDIN	8744
Suite For The Single Girl | Jerry BUTLER	8898
Summer (The First Time) | Bobby GOLDSBORO	9529
Summer Breeze | SEALS & CROFTS	327
Summer Days (And Summer Nights... | BEACH BOYS	1044
Summer Heat | BRICK	7801
Summer Lovers | SOUNDTRACK-MOVIE	11182
Summer Of '42 | Peter NERO	2078
Summer Of '42 | Roger WILLIAMS	12895
Summer Of '42 | SOUNDTRACK-MOVIE	2635
Summer Of '42 | Tony BENNETT	12553
Summer Side Of Life | Gordon LIGHTFOOT	3099
Summer Sounds | Robert GOULET	3864
Summertime | Herb ALPERT & The TI...	7841
Summertime | MFSB	7821
Summertime Dream | Gordon LIGHTFOOT	782
Summertime Groove | Hamilton BOHANNON	4851
Summer Wind | Roger WILLIAMS	5621
Summer Wind | Wayne NEWTON	10330
Sunbeam | The EMOTIONS	5052
Sunburn | SUN	4464
Sunburst Finish | BE BOP DELUXE	6495
Sun City | ARTISTS UNITED AGAIN...	4336
Sunday And Me | JAY & The AMERICANS	11590
Sunday Concert | Gordon LIGHTFOOT	9998
Sunday In New York (Soundtrack... | Peter NERO	11613
Sunday In The Park With Geo... | ORIGINAL CAST	9544
Sunday Morning Suite | Frank MILLS	9674
Sunday Night At The Movies | BRASS RING	12366
Sunday Sax | Boots RANDOLPH	7118
Sundown | Gordon LIGHTFOOT	513
Sundown | RANK AND FILE	12280
Sunfighter [A] | Grace SLICK	7829
Sunfighter [A] | Paul KANTNER	7829
Sunflower | BEACH BOYS	11226
Sun Goddess | Ramsey LEWIS	1441
Sunlight | Herbie HANCOCK	5738
Sunlight | The YOUNGBLOODS	13023
Sunny | Bobby HEBB	7535
Sunny Days | LIGHTHOUSE	11657
Sunny Side! | KINGSTON TRIO	1805
Sunrise | Jimmy RUFFIN	10997
Sun Secrets | Eric BURDON Band	4472
The Sun Sessions | Elvis PRESLEY	7077
Sunshine | SOUNDTRACK-TV	3137
Sunshine | The ARCHIES	10435

Title | Act	Rank
Sunshine | The EMOTIONS	6100
Sunshine Dream | BEACH BOYS	12193
Sunshine On Leith | The PROCLAIMERS	3241
Sunshine Superman | DONOVAN	1894
A Sunshiny Day With Charley... | Charley PRIDE	7065
Sun Ship | John COLTRANE	12873
The Sun Still Shines | Sonny CHARLES	10923
Super Bad | James BROWN	4692
Superbad | Chris JASPER	13107
Super Blue | Freddie HUBBARD	10582
Supercharged | TAVARES	8185
Super Country | Danny DAVIS And The ...	12464
Superfly (Soundtrack) | Curtis MAYFIELD	342
Super Fly T.N.T. (Soundtrack) | OSIBISA	10682
The Super Groups | VARIOUS ARTISTS	11733
The Super Hits | VARIOUS ARTISTS	1282
The Super Hits, Vol. 4 | VARIOUS ARTISTS	9182
The Super Hits, Vol. 3 | VARIOUS ARTISTS	4939
The Super Hits, Vol. 2 | VARIOUS ARTISTS	3859
Super Mann | Herbie MANN	6568
Superman - The Movie | SOUNDTRACK-MOVIE	5202
Superman III | SOUNDTRACK-MOVIE	12867
Superman II | SOUNDTRACK-MOVIE	9140
Supernatural | Ben E. KING	4822
Super Oldies/Vol. 5 | VARIOUS ARTISTS	13506
Super Oldies/Vol. 3 | VARIOUS ARTISTS	8589
Super Psychedelics | The VENTURES	6697
Super Rock | VARIOUS ARTISTS	13588
Supersax Plays Bird | SUPERSAX	11280
Supersax Plays Bird, Volume 2/Sa... | SUPERSAX	12958
Super Session [A] | Al KOOPER	1563
Super Session [A] | Mike BLOOMFIELD	1563
Super Session [A] | Stephen STILLS	1563
Supersonic--The Album | J.J. FAD	3595
Superstar | Vikki CARR	10534
Super Taylor | Johnnie TAYLOR	11117
Supertramp | SUPERTRAMP	11206
Supertrios | McCoy TYNER	11518
Super Trouper | ABBA	1330
The Supremes(2) | The SUPREMES	10115
The Supremes | The SUPREMES	7871
The Supremes A' Go-G... | The SUPREMES/Diana R...	335
The Supremes At The ... | The SUPREMES/Diana R...	1154
The Supremes Sing Co... | The SUPREMES/Diana R...	8476
The Supremes Sing Ho... | The SUPREMES/Diana R...	1304
The Supremes Sing Ro... | The SUPREMES/Diana R...	2887
Sure Shot | CROWN HEIGHTS AFFAIR	9207
Surface | SURFACE	5154
Surface Thrills | The TEMPTATIONS	10794
The Surfaris Play Wipe Out A... | The SURFARIS	8133
Surfer Girl | BEACH BOYS	1176
Surfin' Bird | The TRASHMEN	6277
Surfing With The Alien | Joe SATRIANI	1503
Surfin' M.O.D. | M.O.D.	12483
Surf's Up | BEACH BOYS	2943
Sur La Mer | MOODY BLUES	3884
Surprise | SYLVIA (2)	12750
Surprise Attack | TORA TORA	4251
Surprises | Herbie MANN	13163
Surrealistic Pillow | JEFFERSON AIRPLANE/S...	371
Surreal Thing | Kris KRISTOFFERSON	13204
Surrender | Diana ROSS	4812
Surveillance | TRIUMPH	7735
Survival | Bob MARLEY And The W...	6231
Survival | GRAND FUNK RAILROAD	656
Survival | The O'JAYS	1603

Title	Act	Rank
Survival Of The Fittest	HEADHUNTERS	8453
Survival Of The Fittest/Live	AMBOY DUKES	10046
Survival Of The Freshest	BOOGIE BOYS	10190
Survive	NUCLEAR ASSAULT	9680
Survivin' In The 80's	Andre CYMONE	12997
Survivor	SURVIVOR	11211
Susan Sings Songs Fr...	SUSAN of SESAME STRE...	6802
Suspicion!	Terry STAFFORD	8123
Suzanne Vega	Suzanne VEGA	5719
Suzi...And Other Four Letter ...	Suzi QUATRO	7366
Suzi Quatro	Suzi QUATRO	8872
Swamp Rock	The VENTURES	7715
Swans Against The Sun	Michael MURPHEY	4491
Swass	Sir MIX-A-LOT	3541
Sweat	The SYSTEM	6885
Sweat Band	SWEAT BAND	10149
Sweeney Todd-The Demon Barb...	ORIGINAL CAST	7004
The Sweet	The SWEET	12988
Sweet & Sour Tears	Ray CHARLES	2496
Sweet And Wonderful	Jean CARN	12751
Sweet Baby James	James TAYLOR	86
Sweet Beginnings	Marlena SHAW	5301
Sweet Charity	ORIGINAL CAST	6689
Sweet Charity	SOUNDTRACK-MOVIE	4527
Sweet City Woman	STAMPEDERS	11132
Sweet Country	Charley PRIDE	11531
Sweet, Delicious & Mar...	CALIFORNIA RAISINS	8906
Sweet Dreams (Are Made Of This...	EURYTHMICS	1166
Sweet Dreams: The Life And Ti...	Patsy CLINE	4442
The Sweetest Sounds	Kate SMITH	13059
Sweet Evil	Rick DERRINGER	12439
Sweet Exorcist	Curtis MAYFIELD	3923
Sweet Forgiveness	Bonnie RAITT	2958
Sweet Freedom	URIAH HEEP	3629
Sweet Gingerbread Ma...	MIKE CURB CONGREGATI...	13334
Sweet Harmony	Maria MULDAUR	6047
Sweetheart	Engelbert HUMPERDINC...	2201
Sweetheart Of The Rodeo	The BYRDS	6726
The Sweetheart Tree	Johnny MATHIS	5201
The Sweet Inspirations	SWEET INSPIRATIONS	9684
Sweet Lou	Lou DONALDSON	13096
Sweet Maria	Billy VAUGHN Singers	7305
Sweet Memories	Willie NELSON	11367
Sweetnighter	WEATHER REPORT	6383
Sweet Passion	Aretha FRANKLIN	3966
Sweet Pea	Tommy ROE	7343
Sweet Rain	Stan GETZ	13754
Sweet Replies	HONEY CONE	9023
Sweet Revenge	John PRINE	8764
Sweet Sensation	Stephanie MILLS	1088
Sweets From A Stranger	SQUEEZE	3985
Sweet Sixteen	Reba McENTIRE	6609
Sweet Soul	KING CURTIS	13681
Sweet Soul Music	Arthur CONLEY	7390
Sweet Sound	Simon TOWNSHEND	11676
Sweet Surrender	Margie JOSEPH	12301
Sweet Sweetback's Baadas...	SOUNDTRACK-MOVIE	6623
Sweet Talkin' Guy	The CHIFFONS	12169
Sweet Thunder	SWEET THUNDER	8277
Sweetwater	SWEETWATER	13650
Swept Away	Diana ROSS	1638
The Swing	INXS	4305
Swingin' New Big Band	Buddy RICH	5207
The Swing Of Delight	Carlos SANTANA	6691
Swing Street	Barry MANILOW	5170
Swing, Swing, Swing	BOSTON POPS Orchestr...	10764

Title	Act	Rank
Swing The Heartache - The BBC Ses...	BAUHAUS	11829
Swing To The Right	UTOPIA	8876
Swing Your Daddy	Jim GILSTRAP	11295
Swiss Movement	Les McCANN & Eddie H...	1943
Switch	GOLDEN EARRING	8129
Switch	SWITCH	2967
Switched-On Bach	Walter CARLOS	794
Switched-On Bacharach	Christopher SCOTT	12415
Switched On Nashville: Count...	Gil TRYTHALL	10925
Switched-On Rock	MOOG MACHINE	10521
Switch V	SWITCH	12358
Switch II	SWITCH	2651
Swordfishtrombones	Tom WAITS	11534
Sybil	SYBIL	5717
Sylvain Sylvain	Sylvain SYLVAIN	8873
The Sylvers	The SYLVERS	11666
The Sylvers II	The SYLVERS	11839
Symphonic Soul	Henry MANCINI and hi...	10801
A Symphony For Susan	The ARBORS	12649
The Symphony Sessions	David FOSTER	9300
Synchronicity	The POLICE	49
Synchro System	King Sunny ADE & His...	8530
Synergy	GLASS HARP	13210
Synthesis	CRYAN' SHAMES	10978
Syreeta(2)	SYREETA	6773
Syreeta	SYREETA	11558

T

Title	Act	Rank
Tabernakel	Jan AKKERMAN	13651
A Tab In The Ocean	NEKTAR	11152
Taka Boom	Taka BOOM	12122
Take A Little Rhythm	Ali THOMSON	6811
Take A Little Walk With Me	Tom RUSH	9747
Take A Look	Aretha FRANKLIN	11405
Take Another Picture	QUARTERFLASH	3818
Take A Ride...........	Mitch RYDER And The ...	8737
Take Good Care Of My Baby	Bobby VINTON	10338
Take It Home	B.B. KING	7511
Take It Off	CHIC	8835
Take It On Up	POCKETS	8851
Take It To The Limit	Norman CONNORS	10813
Take It To The Limit	Willie NELSON	6286
Take It To The Max	AKA The MAX DEMIAN B...	11459
Take It While It's Ho...	SWEET SENSATION (2)	4058
Take Me All The Way	Stacy LATTISAW	8304
Take Me Home	CHER	2992
Take Me To Tomorrow	John DENVER	13675
Take Me To Your Heaven	Stevie WOODS	8254
Take No Prisoners	MOLLY HATCHET	4648
Take No Prisoners	Peabo BRYSON	8178
Take 6	TAKE 6	5563
Take Ten	Paul DESMOND	12029
Take This Job And Shove I...	Johnny PAYCHECK	6036
Take Time To Know Her	Percy SLEDGE	10579
Take What You Need	Robin TROWER	9382
Take Your Shoes Off W...	SERENDIPITY SINGERS	13013
Taking It Home	BUCKWHEAT ZYDECO	9379
Taking Liberties	Elvis COSTELLO	4610
Taking Over	OVERKILL	13821
Takin' It Easy	SEALS & CROFTS	6622
Takin' It To The Streets	DOOBIE BROTHERS	1202
Takin My Time	Bonnie RAITT	6094
The Tale Of The Giant Ra...	FIRESIGN THEATRE	11931
The Tale Of The Tape	Billy SQUIER	10057
Tales From The Ozone	COMMANDER CODY & His...	11547
Tales From Topographic Oceans	YES	1425

Title	Act	Rank
Tales Of Kidd Funkadelic	FUNKADELIC	8346
Tales Of Mystery & I...	Alan PARSONS PROJECT	1982
Tales Of The New West	BEAT FARMERS	13399
Tales Of The Unexpected	MAHOGANY RUSH	8659
Tale Spinnin'	WEATHER REPORT	4182
Tales To Warm Your Mind	IRISH ROVERS	11665
Talk Back Trembling Lips	Johnny TILLOTSON	6044
Talkin' 'Bout You	Diane SCHUUR	10663
Talking Back To The Night	Steve WINWOOD	3499
Talking Book	Stevie WONDER	209
Talking Heads: 77	TALKING HEADS	4868
Talk Is Cheap	Keith RICHARDS	3351
Talk It Over In The Morning	Anne MURRAY	12236
Talk Memphis	Jesse WINCHESTER	13436
Talk Show	The GO-GO'S	1776
Talk Talk Talk	PSYCHEDELIC FURS	6962
Talk To Me	SUNNY & The SUNLINER...	12858
Talk To The People	Les McCANN	11841
Talk To Your Daughter	Robben FORD	8426
Tall Cool One	The WAILERS	10731
Tall Dark Stranger	Buck OWENS	7961
Ta Mara & The Seen	TA MARA & The SEEN	4446
Tammy's Greatest Hits	Tammy WYNETTE	1928
Tammy's Greatest Hits, Volu...	Tammy WYNETTE	8412
Tammy's Touch	Tammy WYNETTE	6011
Tane Cain	Tané CAIN	9013
Tango In The Night	FLEETWOOD MAC	417
Tantalizingly Hot	Stephanie MILLS	4863
Tantilla	HOUSE OF FREAKS	10209
Tanx	T. REX	8355
Tanya Tucker	Tanya TUCKER	9005
Tao	Rick SPRINGFIELD	2455
Tap	SOUNDTRACK-MOVIE	12309
Tapestry	Carole KING	4
Tapestry	Don McLEAN	8354
Tap Root Manuscript	Neil DIAMOND	1085
Tap Step	Chick COREA	12597
Tarantella	Chuck MANGIONE	5270
Tarkio	BREWER And SHIPLEY	2692
Tarkus	EMERSON, LAKE & PALM...	1342
Taste	TASTE	8299
A Taste For Passion	Jean-Luc PONTY	4550
Tasteful Soul	MAIN INGREDIENT	10133
A Taste Of Brass For Lover...	Jackie GLEASON	13776
A Taste Of Honey	A TASTE OF HONEY	1104
A Taste Of Honey	Pete FOUNTAIN	9045
A Taste Of Tequila	MARIACHI BRASS	11113
A Taste Of Yesterday's Wine [A]	George JONES	8773
A Taste Of Yesterday's Wine [A]	Merle HAGGARD	8773
Taste The Music	KLEEER	10225
Tasty	Patti LaBELLE	9568
Tasty Jam	FATBACK	8068
Tattoo	Rory GALLAGHER	11971
Tattooed Beat Messia...	ZODIAC MINDWARP & Th...	7980
Tattoo You	ROLLING STONES	121
Taylored In Silk	Johnnie TAYLOR	4676
T.B. Sheets	Van MORRISON	12654
TCB (Soundtrack)	Diana ROSS & The SUP...	408
T-Connection	T-CONNECTION	5063
Teachers	SOUNDTRACK-MOVIE	4384
The Tea Dance	D.C. LaRUE	7906
Tea For The Tillerman	Cat STEVENS	223
Tear Down These Walls	Billy OCEAN	1881
Tear Me Apart	Tanya TUCKER	9011
The Tears Of A Clown	The MIRACLES/Smokey ...	8381
Teaser	Angela BOFILL	5912

Title	Act	Rank
Teaser	Tommy BOLIN	7038
Teaser And The Firecat	Cat STEVENS	163
Teases And Dares	Kim WILDE	8348
Technical Ecstasy	BLACK SABBATH	6050
Technique	NEW ORDER	3072
Teddy	Teddy PENDERGRASS	1201
Teddy Bear	Red SOVINE	9294
Teddy Live! Coast To Co...	Teddy PENDERGRASS	4273
Teddy Pendergrass	Teddy PENDERGRASS	1617
Ted Nugent	Ted NUGENT	1514
Teen Beat '65	Sandy NELSON	11156
Teen Scene	Chet ATKINS	9666
TeeVee Toons - The Commer...	VARIOUS ARTISTS	8981
Tejas	ZZ TOP	2317
Telekon	Gary NUMAN	6856
Television's Greatest Hits	VARIOUS ARTISTS	5824
Television's Greatest Hits Vol. II	VARIOUS ARTISTS	9131
Television Theme Songs	Mike POST	5918
Tell Her You Love Her	Frank SINATRA	11296
Tell It All Brother	Kenny ROGERS & The F...	5064
Tell It Like It Is	George BENSON	11498
Tell It To My Heart	Taylor DAYNE	735
Tell Mama	Etta JAMES	7382
Tell Me This Is A Dream	The DELFONICS	8276
Tell Me Why	Bobby VINTON	5548
Tell No Tales	TNT	6570
Tell The Truth	Otis REDDING	13733
Telly	Telly SAVALAS	8341
Temple Of Low Men	CROWDED HOUSE	4156
The Temptations	The TEMPTATIONS	9104
The Temptations Do The Te...	The TEMPTATIONS	4757
The Temptations Greatest ...	The TEMPTATIONS	116
Temptations Greatest Hits...	The TEMPTATIONS	936
The Temptations In A Mell...	The TEMPTATIONS	1496
Temptations Live!	The TEMPTATIONS	1420
The Temptations Show	The TEMPTATIONS	2791
The Temptations Sing Smok...	The TEMPTATIONS	3775
Temptin' Temptations	The TEMPTATIONS	1467
"10"	SOUNDTRACK-MOVIE	7938
10 1/2	The DRAMATICS	6375
The Tender Gender	Kenny BURRELL	12757
Tender Is The Night	Johnny MATHIS	1934
A Tender Look At Love	Roger MILLER	10929
Tender Lover	BABYFACE	628
Tender Loving Care	Nancy WILSON	3748
Tenderly	George BENSON	10936
Tenderness	OHIO PLAYERS	12297
Tender Togetherness	Stanley TURRENTINE	12397
Tenement Steps	The MOTORS	11104
10 From 6	BAD COMPANY	9216
10 Golden Years	Brenda LEE	6882
Tenku	KITARO	13794
Ten Little Bottles	Johnny BOND	12390
10,9,8,7,6,5,4,3,2,1	MIDNIGHT OIL	12850
Ten Percent	DOUBLE EXPOSURE	8308
Tenth	MARSHALL TUCKER Band	4237
10th Anniversary	STATLER BROTHERS	12014
10th Anniversary - Gol...	FERRANTE & TEICHER	4761
10th Anniversary/Limited E...	Roger WILLIAMS	9577
Ten Women	WIRE TRAIN	12959
Ten Years Are Gone	John MAYALL	10679
Ten Years Of Gold	Aretha FRANKLIN	9357
Ten Years Of Gold	Kenny ROGERS	1454
Ten Years Of Harmony (1970-198...	BEACH BOYS	10851
10 Years Together/The ...	PETER, PAUL & MARY	1705
Tequila	Wes MONTGOMERY	3407

Title	Act	Rank
Tequila Mockingbird	Ramsey LEWIS	8641
Tequila Sunrise	SOUNDTRACK-MOVIE	7909
Terence Boylan	Terence BOYLAN	12824
Terms Of Endearment	SOUNDTRACK-MOVIE	9047
Terrapin Station	GRATEFUL DEAD	4163
Terror Rising	LIZZY BORDEN	12703
Terry Knight And The Pack	Terry KNIGHT And The...	7893
Terry Reid	Terry REID	10645
Testifyin'	Clarence CARTER	11235
Test Patterns	Tommy BOYCE & Bobby ...	13842
Texas Flood	Stevie Ray VAUGHAN A...	3328
Texas Gold	ASLEEP AT THE WHEEL	9105
Texas In My Rear View Mirror	Mac DAVIS	6968
T.G. Sheppard's Greatest Hi...	T.G. SHEPPARD	13323
Thankful	Natalie COLE	1238
Thank God It's Friday	SOUNDTRACK-MOVIE	1297
Thanks I'll Eat It Here	Lowell GEORGE	7322
Thank You Baby	The STYLISTICS	6045
Thank You...For F.U.M.L. (Fun...	Donald BYRD	12894
That Honey Horn Sound	Al HIRT	3035
That Ni*ger's Crazy	Richard PRYOR	1641
That's All That Matters To ...	Mickey GILLEY	12774
That's A Plenty	POINTER SISTERS	7442
That's Entertainment	SOUNDTRACK-MOVIE	7690
That's How Much I Love You	The MANHATTANS	11726
That's Life	Frank SINATRA	815
That's Life & Pineap...	Billy VAUGHN and His...	10089
That's Lou	Lou RAWLS	4070
That's The Stuff	AUTOGRAPH	7517
That's The Way God Planned ...	Billy PRESTON	7883
...That's The Way It Is	NILSSON	10584
That's The Way Love Is	Marvin GAYE	12956
That's The Way Love Should B...	DAVE & SUGAR	11781
That's The Way Of The ...	EARTH, WIND & FIRE	133
That's What Friends Are ... [A]	Deniece WILLIAMS	2951
That's What Friends Are For [A]	Johnny MATHIS	2951
That's What I Am Here For	Roy BUCHANAN	9646
That's Why I'm Here	James TAYLOR	3197
That The Spirit Needs	José FELICIANO	10266
That Was Only Yesterday	SPOOKY TOOTH	12116
That Was The Week Th...	John Fitzgerald KENN...	3016
That Was The Year That Was	Tom LEHRER	1494
The Armada Orchestra	ARMADA Orchestra	13602
Theater Of The Mind	MTUME	10413
Theatre Of Pain	MÖTLEY CRÜE	852
The Bad C.C.	Carl CARLTON	10353
The Boy Genius	KWAMÉ & A NEW BEGINN...	7709
The Complete Story O...	DR. J.R. KOOL and Th...	7965
The Diary Of A Band (Volume 1...	John MAYALL	7779
The Hollies' Greatest Hits(2)	The HOLLIES	10713
Their Greatest Hits 1971-1975	EAGLES	68
Their Satanic Majesties Re...	ROLLING STONES	870
Their 16 Greatest Hits	GRASS ROOTS	4315
Thelma & Jerry [A]	Jerry BUTLER	6042
Thelma & Jerry [A]	Thelma HOUSTON	6042
Them	KING DIAMOND	7599
Them	THEM	5099
Them Again	THEM	10664
The Manilow Collection/Twen...	Barry MANILOW	8449
The Man-Machine	KRAFTWERK	9109
Thembi	Pharoah SANDERS	12495
Them Changes	Buddy MILES	1288
Them Changes	Ramsey LEWIS	11501
Them Cotton Pickin' Day...	Godfrey CAMBRIDGE	9872
Theme From Shaft	The VENTURES	13302
Theme From "Z" And O...	Henry MANCINI and Hi...	6849

Title	Act	Rank
Themes From The Jame...	Roland SHAW Orchestra	4406
Themes Like Old Times	VARIOUS ARTISTS	3088
Them Featuring Van Morrison	THEM	9285
Then & Now...The Best Of The ...	The MONKEES	2095
Then Came You	Dionne WARWICK	11212
Then Play On	FLEETWOOD MAC	6138
Then You Can Tell Me Goodbye	The CASINOS	12918
There! I've Said It Again	Bobby VINTON	1902
There And Back	Jeff BECK	2718
There Are But Four Smal...	SMALL FACES/FACES	12967
There Goes My Everything	Jack GREENE	4974
There Goes My Heart	Jerry VALE	5263
There Goes Rhymin' Simon	Paul SIMON	617
There Goes The Neighborhood	Joe WALSH	2498
There Is	The DELLS	3029
There Is Only One Roy Orbison	Roy ORBISON	5643
There It Is	James BROWN	4038
There Must Be A Better World So...	B.B. KING	8446
There Must Be A Way	Jimmy ROSELLI	13413
There Must Be More To Lov...	Jerry Lee LEWIS	12157
There's A Kind Of Hush A...	HERMAN'S HERMITS	1627
There's A Meetin' Here Tonite	JOE & EDDIE	9744
There's A Riot Goin'...	SLY & THE FAMILY STO...	573
There's Gonna Be A S...	Archie BELL & The DR...	12090
There's Gotta Be A Change	Albert COLLINS	13641
There's Love & There's Love & ...	Jack JONES	7256
There's Music In The Air	Letta MBULU	13264
There's No Gettin' Over Me	Ronnie MILSAP	2941
There's No Good In Goodbye	The MANHATTANS	6675
There's No Me Without You	The MANHATTANS	10052
There's No Place Like Ame...	Curtis MAYFIELD	8192
There's One In Every Crowd	Eric CLAPTON	3294
There's The Rub	WISHBONE ASH	6179
There Won't Be Anymore	Charlie RICH	3207
The Royal Scam	STEELY DAN	1770
These Are My Songs	Petula CLARK	2913
These Days	Crystal GAYLE	6779
These Things Too	PEARLS BEFORE SWINE	13676
(The) Ventures In Space	The VENTURES	3830
The Who By Numbers	The WHO	1459
They Don't Make Them Like Th...	Kenny ROGERS	8660
They Only Come Out At Night	Edgar WINTER	398
They're Playing Our Song	Al HIRT	4359
They're Playing Our Song	ORIGINAL CAST	11487
Thick As A Brick	JETHRO TULL	423
Thick As Thieves	TROOPER	12440
Thief (Soundtrack)	TANGERINE DREAM	7926
Thief In The Night	George DUKE	12676
Thief Of Hearts	SOUNDTRACK-MOVIE	12935
Thighs And Whispers	Bette MIDLER	5267
A Thing Called Love	Johnny CASH	8151
Things Go Better With Lo...	Jeannie C. RILEY	9339
The Things I Love	Jim NABORS	11326
The Things I Notice Now	Tom PAXTON	11116
Think I'll Go Somewhere And Cr...	Al MARTINO	9985
Think Of One	Wynton MARSALIS	5876
Think Pink	FABULOUS POODLES	13045
Think Visual	The KINKS	6594
Thin Line Between Love And...	The PERSUADERS	10315
The Thin Red Line	GLASS TIGER	1481
Thin Red Line	The CRETONES	8675
The Third Album	Barbra STREISAND	357
Third Album	JACKSON 5	402
Third Annual Pipe Dr...	ATLANTA RHYTHM SECTI...	6656
Third Down, 110 To Go	Jesse WINCHESTER	12773
Third Generation	HIROSHIMA	9868

Title | Act	Rank
Thirds | JAMES GANG	1511
Third Stage | BOSTON	394
The 3rd Time Around | Roger MILLER	2538
Third World, Prisoner In The ... | THIRD WORLD	13400
13 | The DOORS	2995
Thirteen | Emmylou HARRIS	11804
Thirteen Blue Magic Lane | BLUE MAGIC	5538
.38 Special | .38 SPECIAL	10985
Thirty Seconds Over ... | JEFFERSON AIRPLANE/S...	5140
3614 Jackson Highway | CHER	12103
Thirty Three & 1/3 | George HARRISON	1927
This Boot Is Made Fo... | BOOTSY'S RUBBER BAND	5957
This Day And Age | D.L. BYRON	9079
This Diamond Ring | Gary LEWIS And The P...	3699
This Girl's In Love With ... | Aretha FRANKLIN	1635
This Guy's In Love With You | Jerry VALE	6818
This Is All I Ask | Tony BENNETT	2836
This Is Al Martino | Al MARTINO	11145
This Is A Recording | Lily TOMLIN	1811
This Is Big Audio Dyna... | BIG AUDIO DYNAMITE	5344
This Is Clarence Carter | Clarence CARTER	13634
This Is Damita Jo | DAMITA JO	11486
This Is Elvis (Soundtrack) | Elvis PRESLEY	8219
This Is Ethel Ennis | Ethel ENNIS	12985
This Is Henry Mancin... | Henry MANCINI and hi...	13637
This Is It | Melba MOORE	10625
This Island | EUROGLIDERS	10126
This Is Love | Al MARTINO	5883
This Is Love | Johnny MATHIS	4806
This Is Madness | LAST POETS	6218
This Is My Country | The IMPRESSIONS	6599
This Is My Dream | SWITCH	6416
This Is My Song | Ray CONNIFF & His Or...	2389
This Is New! | RIGHTEOUS BROTHERS	4652
This Is Niecy | Deniece WILLIAMS	2247
This Is Soul | VARIOUS ARTISTS	7618
This Is Spinal Tap (Soundtrack... | SPINAL TAP	9484
This Is The Day...Thi... | POP WILL EAT ITSELF	11871
This Is The Girl That Is | Nancy AMES	11734
This Is The Moody Blues | MOODY BLUES	1895
This Is The Way | ROSSINGTON COLLINS B...	4133
This Is The Way That I Feel | Marie OSMOND	10349
This Is This | WEATHER REPORT	13767
This Is Tom Jones | Tom JONES	287
This Is Us | The SEARCHERS	7968
This Is Your Life | Norman CONNORS	5343
This Is Your Time | CHANGE	11437
This Kind Of Lovin' | The WHISPERS	8267
This Love For You | Al MARTINO	7645
This Moment In Time | Engelbert HUMPERDINC...	12008
This Mother's Daughter | Nancy WILSON	7796
This Note's For You | Neil YOUNG	5446
This Old Heart Of Mine | ISLEY BROTHERS	11011
This One's For You | Barry MANILOW	431
This One's For You | Teddy PENDERGRASS	5952
This Side Of Paradise | Ric OCASEK	3842
This Time | Al JARREAU	2321
This Time It's For R... | SOUTHSIDE JOHNNY & T...	7485
This Time We Mean It | REO SPEEDWAGON	6777
This Was | JETHRO TULL	4565
This Woman | K.T. OSLIN	3604
This Years Model | Elvis COSTELLO & The...	3589
The Thomas Crown Affair | SOUNDTRACK-MOVIE	11713
The Thom Bell Sessions | Elton JOHN	4436
The Best Of The Thompson T... | THOMPSON TWINS	12201
The Thorn In Mrs. Rose's Side | Biff ROSE	5624

Title | Act	Rank
Thoroughbred | Carole KING	1029
Thoroughfare Gap | Stephen STILLS	9225
Thoroughly Modern Millie | SOUNDTRACK-MOVIE	1428
Those Glorious...Show Boat... | SOUNDTRACK-MOVIE	12275
Those Glorious MG...Singin'... | SOUNDTRACK-MOVIE	11899
Those Of You With Or Without C... | Bill COSBY	4639
Those Southern Knights | The CRUSADERS	3764
Those Were The Days | BAJA MARIMBA BAND	7607
Those Were The Days | EXOTIC GUITARS	9372
Those Were The Days | Johnny MATHIS	3970
Those Were The Days | Percy FAITH His Orch...	6323
Those Were The Days | Pete FOUNTAIN	11641
Thoughts Of Movin' On | LIGHTHOUSE	11047
Thrash Zone | D.R.I.	9242
Threads Of Glory - 200 Ye... | VARIOUS ARTISTS	13238
3 | POUSETTE-DART BAND	11402
3 | VIOLENT FEMMES	7822
Three | Bob JAMES	3269
3 + 3 | ISLEY BROTHERS	1270
The Three Degrees | 3° DEGREES	3573
Three Degrees Live | 3° DEGREES	13820
Three Dog Night | THREE DOG NIGHT	477
3 Feet High And Rising | DE LA SOUL	2634
Three For Love | SHALAMAR	2395
Three Friends | GENTLE GIANT	12878
Three Hearts | Bob WELCH	3447
Three Hearts In The Happy Endi... | Daryl HALL	3816
360 Degrees Of Billy Paul | Billy PAUL	2160
Three Lock Box | Sammy HAGAR	1915
Three O'Clock In The... | Bert KAEMPFERT And H...	4539
Three Of A Perfect Pair | KING CRIMSON	5916
Three Piece Suite | Ramsey LEWIS	11056
Three Quartets | Chick COREA	12345
Three's A Crowd | TARNEY/SPENCER Band	12359
3 Ships | Jon ANDERSON	12296
Three Sides Live | GENESIS	2166
Three Times In Love | Tommy JAMES And The ...	9791
III Wishes | SHOOTING STAR	8714
Thriller | Michael JACKSON	3
Thriller! | COLD BLOOD	7193
Throbbing Python Of Love | Robin WILLIAMS	9559
Through The Eyes Of Love | Ray CHARLES	11550
Through The Eyes Of Love | The FROST	13666
Through The Fire [A] | Kenny AARONSON	4835
Through The Fire [A] | Michael SHRIEVE	4835
Through The Fire [A] | Neal SCHON	4835
Through The Fire [A] | Sammy HAGAR	4835
Through The Looking ... | SIOUXSIE & The BANSH...	13311
Through The Past, Darkly (... | ROLLING STONES	609
Through The Storm | Aretha FRANKLIN	5926
Throwin' Down | Rick JAMES	2562
Thrust | Herbie HANCOCK	2087
Thru The Years | John MAYALL	10758
Thunder | Andy TAYLOR	5124
Thunder And Lightning | THIN LIZZY	11588
Thunderball | SOUNDTRACK-MOVIE	1933
Thunderbox | HUMBLE PIE	5430
Thunder In My Heart | Leo SAYER	5828
Thunder Island | Jay FERGUSON	6553
Thunder In The East | LOUDNESS	5526
Thunder Seven | TRIUMPH	3055
Thundersteel | RIOT	9965
Ticket To Ride | CARPENTERS	7562
Tiffany | TIFFFANY	260
Tiger In The Rain | Michael FRANKS	5321
Tigers Will Survive | Ian MATTHEWS	13324

Title | Act	Rank
Tighten Up | Archie BELL & The DR...	9398
Tighten Up Vol. '88 | BIG AUDIO DYNAMITE	8193
Tightrope | Steve KHAN	11039
Tight Shoes | FOGHAT	8048
Till | Jerry VALE	6534
Till | The VOGUES	2578
Till I Loved You | Barbra STREISAND	1769
Till The End Of Time | Jerry VALE	4066
Tim | The REPLACEMENTS	12387
The Time | The TIME	3176
Time | ELECTRIC LIGHT ORCHE...	2288
Time | POZO-SECO SINGERS	10042
Time After Time | Chris MONTEZ	7692
Time Alone Will Tell | Jerry VALE	10854
Time & Charges | The BUCKINGHAMS	5125
Time And Tide | BASIA	1495
Time And Tide | SPLIT ENZ	5720
Time Changes | Dave BRUBECK Quartet	8569
Time Exposure | LITTLE RIVER BAND	1642
Time Exposure | Stanley CLARKE	9654
Time Fades Away | Neil YOUNG	3639
Time For Another | ACE	10733
Time For Livin' | YOUNG AMERICANS	12551
A Time For Living, A Time For Hop... | Ed AMES	7149
A Time For Love | Percy FAITH His Orch...	13707
A Time For Love | Tony BENNETT	5314
A Time For Singing | ORIGINAL CAST	12740
A Time For Us | Donny OSMOND	6071
A Time For Us | Jack JONES	12454
The Time Has Come | CHAMBERS BROTHERS	740
Time In A Bottle/Jim Croce's Gr... | Jim CROCE	12547
The Time Is Near | KEEF HARTLEY BAND	13126
Timeless | Frankie VALLI	12015
Time Loves A Hero | LITTLE FEAT	3611
Time Odyssey | Vinnie MOORE	10879
The Time Of My Life! | John DAVIDSON	2543
Time Out For Smokey ... | The MIRACLES/Smokey ...	2530
Time Passages | Al STEWART	1269
Time Peace/The Rasca... | RASCALS/YOUNG RAS...	139
Time Pieces -- The Best Of E... | Eric CLAPTON	7941
Times Have Changed | The IMPRESSIONS	13562
Times Of Our Lives | Judy COLLINS	12765
Times Of Your Life | Paul ANKA	2029
Times Square | SOUNDTRACK-MOVIE	4226
The Times They Are A-Changin' | Bob DYLAN	3939
Time, Time | Ed AMES	5088
A Time To Keep: 1963 | Chet HUNTLEY & David...	9912
Time To Think | KINGSTON TRIO	3405
Time Won't Let Me | The OUTSIDERS	4626
Tim Moore | Tim MOORE	8766
Timothy B. | Timothy B. SCHMIT	8690
Tim Weisberg Band | Tim WEISBERG Band	7249
Tim Weisberg 4 | Tim WEISBERG	7856
Tina Live In Europe | Tina TURNER	8402
Tinderbox | SIOUXSIE & The BANSH...	7312
Tin Machine | TIN MACHINE	4515
The Tin Man Was A Dreamer | Nicky HOPKINS	8297
Tinsel Town Rebellion | Frank ZAPPA	6310
Tin Tin | TIN TIN	13798
Tiny Bubbles | Don HO and the ALIIS	1869
Tippy Toeing | HARDEN Trio	11075
Tirami Su | Al Di MEOLA	13802
TNT | Tanya TUCKER	4484
Tobacco Road | SPOOKY TOOTH	9916
To Be Continued | Isaac HAYES	755
To Be Continued... | The TEMPTATIONS	4824

Title	Act	Rank
To Be True	Harold MELVIN And Th...	1699
To Be With You	DAWN/Tony ORLANDO	8650
To Bonnie From Delan...	DELANEY & BONNIE & F...	5927
Toby	The CHI-LITES	12094
Toby Beau	TOBY BEAU	4126
Today	Bobby GOLDSBORO	5156
Today	Elvis PRESLEY	5471
Today	Marty ROBBINS	11720
Today	NEW CHRISTY MINSTREL...	1645
Today	STATLER BROTHERS	12972
Today	TODAY	5878
Today-My Way	Nancy WILSON	2537
Today's Best	Glen GRAY & The CASA...	6722
Today's Great Hits	Lawrence WELK	9635
Today's Romantic Hits/...	Jackie GLEASON	9636
Today's Romantic Hits/...Vol. 2	Jackie GLEASON	8102
Today's Themes For Y...	Percy FAITH His Orch...	7054
Today, Tomorrow, Forever	Nancy WILSON	1619
Todd	Todd RUNDGREN	4890
Todd Rundgren's Utopia	UTOPIA	4119
Todd Rundgren's Utopia/Another Liv...	UTOPIA	6891
To Each His Own	Frankie LAINE	9319
2XS	NAZARETH	9288
Together [A]	Edgar WINTER	7124
Together [A]	Johnny WINTER	7124
Together [A]	Marvin GAYE	5468
Together [A]	Mary WELLS	5468
Together	Anne MURRAY	8632
Together	Charles WRIGHT And T...	9902
Together	COUNTRY JOE & The Fl...	3327
Together	Diana ROSS & The SUP...	3413
Together	Jesse Colin YOUNG	10831
Together	McCoy TYNER	6924
Together	OAK RIDGE BOYS	11253
Together Again	The TEMPTATIONS	7003
Together Again! [A]	Brother Jack McDUFF	11404
Together Again! [A]	Willis JACKSON	11404
Together Again!	Benny GOODMAN	8145
Together Again...Liv...	B.B. KING & Bobby BL...	5726
Together Again / My Heart Skip...	Buck OWENS	6889
Together: A New Chuck Mang...	Chuck MANGIONE	12849
Together Brothers (S...	LOVE UNLIMITED ORCHE...	8008
Together Forever	MARSHALL TUCKER Band	3293
Together For The Fir...	B.B. KING & Bobby BL...	4236
Together In Concert [A]	Arlo GUTHRIE	12469
Together In Concert [A]	Pete SEEGER	12469
Togetherness	L.T.D.	1958
Together On Broadway	Steve LAWRENCE & Eyd...	10812
To Hell With The Devil	STRYPER	1655
To Know You Is To Love You	B.B. KING	4978
Told U So	NU SHOOZ	7411
Toledo Window Box	George CARLIN	2713
To Lefty From Willie	Willie NELSON	7271
To Live And Die In L.A. (Sound...	WANG CHUNG	6794
To Love Again	Diana ROSS	4092
To Lovers Everywhere U.S.A.	MANTOVANI	9435
Tom	Tom JONES	1351
Tom Cat	Tom SCOTT & The L.A....	2369
Tomcattin'	BLACKFOOT	4351
Tom Cochrane & Red Rider	Tom COCHRANE/RED R...	8485
Tom Fogerty	Tom FOGERTY	11925
Tom Jones	SOUNDTRACK-MOVIE	3872
The Tom Jones Fever Zone	Tom JONES	717
Tom Jones Greatest Hits(2)	Tom JONES	13102
Tom Jones' Greatest Hits	Tom JONES	12800
Tom Jones Live!	Tom JONES	611

Title	Act	Rank
Tom Jones Live At Caesars Palac...	Tom JONES	5068
Tom Jones Live In Las Vegas	Tom JONES	226
Tommy	SOUNDTRACK-MOVIE	517
Tommy	The WHO	64
Tommy	VARIOUS ARTISTS	1211
Tommy Page	Tommy PAGE	12474
Tommy Tutone	TOMMY TUTONE	6202
Tommy Tutone-2	TOMMY TUTONE	2570
Tom Paxton 6	Tom PAXTON	12658
Tom Petty And The He...	Tom PETTY And The HE...	3095
Tom Rush	Tom RUSH	5397
Tom Scott & The L.A....	Tom SCOTT & The L.A....	7521
Tom Tom Club	TOM TOM CLUB	2322
Tongue In Chic	CHIC	12404
Tongue Twister	SHOES	9862
A Tonic For The Troops	BOOMTOWN RATS	6977
Tonight!	FOUR TOPS	3754
Tonight	David BOWIE	2426
Tonight	France JOLI	12776
Tonight I'll Say A Prayer	Eydie GORME	7182
Tonight I'm Yours	Rod STEWART	1196
The Tonight Show Ban...	Doc SEVERINSEN And T...	5047
Here's Johnny--Magic Moment...	SOUNDTRACK-TV	4622
Tonight's The Night	Neil YOUNG	3889
Tonight You're Mine	Eric CARMEN	11349
Tons Of Sobs	FREE	13541
Tony Bennett's All-Time Grea...	Tony BENNETT	11143
Tony Bennett's Greatest Hits...	Tony BENNETT	10605
Tony Bennett's "Something"	Tony BENNETT	13512
Tony Carey [I Won't Be Home To...	Tony CAREY	11016
Tony Joe White	Tony Joe WHITE	12346
Tony Makes It Happen!	Tony BENNETT	11937
Tony Mottola's Guitar Factor...	Tony MOTTOLA	13256
Tony Orlando & Dawn II	DAWN/Tony ORLANDO	11375
Tony's Greatest Hits, Volume...	Tony BENNETT	1718
Tony Sings The Great Hits Of...	Tony BENNETT	8998
Too	S.O.S. BAND	10051
Too Far To Whisper	SHADOWFAX	7922
Too Fast For Love	MÖTLEY CRÜE	3459
Too Good To Stop Now	John SCHNEIDER	8819
2-Hot!	PEACHES & HERB	397
Too Hot To Handle	HEATWAVE	1253
Too Hot To Sleep	SURVIVOR	13549
Too Hot To Sleep	SYLVESTER	11672
Too Hot To Stop	The BAR-KAYS	4422
Too Hot To Stop It	The MANHATTANS	11991
Too Late The Hero	John ENTWISTLE	7246
Too Late To Cry	WIDOWMAKER	9673
Too Long In The Wasteland	James McMURTRY	9880
Too Low For Zero	Elton JOHN	1803
Too Many Rivers	Brenda LEE	5272
Too Much!	Lou RAWLS	2203
Too Much Pressure	The SELECTER	12302
Too Old To Rock 'N' Roll: Too...	JETHRO TULL	2393
Too-Rye-Ay	DEXYS MIDNIGHT RUNNE...	2378
Too Stuffed To Jump	AMAZING RHYTHM ACES	10339
Tooth And Nail	DOKKEN	2408
Too Tough	Angela BOFILL	3510
Too Tough To Die	The RAMONES	12069
Tootsie	SOUNDTRACK-MOVIE	9878
To Our Children's Children's ...	MOODY BLUES	1333
Too Young	Donny OSMOND	1433
Too Young To Feel This O...	McKENDREE SPRING	13227
The Top	The CURE	12905
Top Gun	SOUNDTRACK-MOVIE	197
The Top Hits Of 1963	Bobby RYDELL	7911

Title	Act	Rank
Topkapi	Jimmy McGRIFF	13055
Topkapi	SOUNDTRACK-MOVIE	13052
Top Of The World	Lynn ANDERSON	12951
Top Priority	Rory GALLAGHER	11085
Top Ten	Jimmy RUFFIN	9177
The Top Ten Hits	Elvis PRESLEY	10156
Torch	Carly SIMON	4216
Tormato	YES	2527
Tornado	The RAINMAKERS	7355
Torn Between Two Lovers	Mary MacGREGOR	2794
To Russell, My Brother, Whom I...	Bill COSBY	879
To Sir With Love	LULU	3368
To Sir, With Love	SOUNDTRACK-MOVIE	2401
Total Devo	DEVO	13294
Total Eclipse	Billy COBHAM	4275
Totally Connected	T-CONNECTION	13084
Totally Hot	Olivia NEWTON-JOHN	1015
Totally Out Of Control	HUDSON BROTHERS	12519
To The Door Of The Sun	Al MARTINO	9340
To The Heart	MARK-ALMOND	7646
To The Hilt	GOLDEN EARRING	11633
To The Limit	Joan ARMATRADING	8433
To The Max	CON FUNK SHUN	6066
To The Power Of Three	3	8532
Toto	TOTO	776
Toto IV	TOTO	239
Toucan Do It Too	AMAZING RHYTHM ACES	8131
The Touch	ALABAMA	4309
Touch	CON FUNK SHUN	4130
Touch	EURYTHMICS	1045
Touch	Gladys KNIGHT & The ...	8791
Touch	John KLEMMER	4945
Touch	Laura BRANIGAN	5608
Touch	Sarah McLACHLAN	9732
Touch	The SUPREMES	6874
Touch And Go	FORCE M.D.'S	6507
Touch And Gone	Gary WRIGHT	8699
Touch Dance	EURYTHMICS	8494
Touchdown	Bob JAMES	2972
Touch 'Em With Love	Bobbie GENTRY	11576
Touching Home	Jerry Lee LEWIS	11959
Touching You Touching Me	Neil DIAMOND	2152
Touch Me	Samantha FOX	3002
Touch Me	The TEMPTATIONS	10184
Touch Me In The Morning	Diana ROSS	1251
Touch Me Tonight-The Best O...	SHOOTING STAR	11192
Touch My Heart	Ray PRICE	8358
A Touch Of Gold	Johnny RIVERS	2027
A Touch Of Today	Nancy WILSON	2239
A Touch On The Rainy Sid...	Jesse WINCHESTER	10121
Touch The Sky	Carole KING	8294
Touch The Sky	Smokey ROBINSON	5864
Touch The World	EARTH, WIND & FIRE	3258
Touch You	Jimmy HALL	13360
Tough	Kurtis BLOW	11981
Tough All Over	John CAFFERTY & The ...	3092
Tougher Than Leather	RUN-D.M.C.	1824
Tougher Than Leather	Willie NELSON	4552
Tough Guys (Soundtrack)	Isaac HAYES	9895
Toulouse Street	DOOBIE BROTHERS	939
Tour De Farce American ...	SMOTHERS BROTHERS	6014
Tour De Force	.38 SPECIAL	1713
Tour De Force - "Live"	Al Di MEOLA	11580
Tourist In Paradise	The RIPPINGTONS	7579
The Towering Inferno	SOUNDTRACK-MOVIE	12020
Tower of Power	TOWER OF POWER	2373

Title | Act	Rank
To Whom It May Concern | BEE GEES	4439
To Whom It May Concern | The PASADENAS	7742
To You Honey, Honey With Lov... | David HUDSON	13356
To You With Love, Donny | Donny OSMOND	1239
Toys In The Attic | AEROSMITH	240
The Toys sing "A Lover's Concerto | The TOYS	8860
TP | Teddy PENDERGRASS	1215
T'Pau | T'PAU	3958
Traces | Andre KOSTELANETZ An...	13611
Traces | CLASSICS IV	3606
Traces/Memories | The LETTERMEN	4176
Traces Of Love | Bert KAEMPFERT And H...	9401
Tracie Spencer | Tracie SPENCER	7834
Track Of The Cat | Dionne WARWICK	7680
Track Record | Joan ARMATRADING	9280
Tracy | CUFF LINKS	8864
Tracy Chapman | Tracy CHAPMAN	220
Tracy Nelson | Tracy NELSON	10838
Trade Winds | Earl GRANT	11834
Trafalgar | BEE GEES	3555
Traffic | TRAFFIC	1975
Traffic-On The Road | TRAFFIC	3576
Tragedy/A Million To One | Brian HYLAND	10868
Trammps | The TRAMMPS	11762
Trammps III | The TRAMMPS	7339
A Tramp Shining | Richard HARRIS	1002
Trans | Neil YOUNG	3516
Trans-Europe Express | KRAFTWERK	8684
Transformer | Lou REED	2482
Transition | Kenny ROGERS & The F...	12139
Trapped By A Thing Called ... | Denise LaSALLE	8921
Trash | ALICE COOPER (Solo)	1349
T.R.A.S.H. (Tubes Rarities And ... | The TUBES	10633
Trash It Up | SOUTHSIDE JOHNNY & T...	11435
Travelin' | Tommy JAMES And The ...	7869
Travelin' At The Speed Of Thou... | The O'JAYS	3726
Travels | PAT METHENY GROUP	6043
Travolta Fever | John TRAVOLTA	10474
TRB Two | Tom ROBINSON Band	10911
Treacherous: A History O... | NEVILLE BROTHERS	13142
Treasure Chest | Herbie HANCOCK	12165
A Treasury Of Great Conte... | VARIOUS ARTISTS	9237
Treat Her Right | TREAT HER RIGHT	7611
Treat Me Right | Roy HEAD	9496
Treemonisha | ORIGINAL CAST	13714
Tres Hombres | ZZ TOP	581
Trevor Rabin | Trevor RABIN	12941
T-Rex | T. REX	12442
Trial By Fire: Live In L... | Yngwie MALMSTEEN	10774
The Trial Of Billy Jack | SOUNDTRACK-MOVIE	8895
Triangle | BEAU BRUMMELS	13761
Tribute [A] | Ozzy OSBOURNE	1658
Tribute [A] | Randy RHOADS	1658
A Tribute To Jack Johnson (So... | Miles DAVIS	10787
A Tribute To The All-Time G... | Lawrence WELK	11082
A Tribute To The Best Damn ... | Merle HAGGARD	6379
A Tribute To Woody Guthrie - Part 1 | VARIOUS ARTISTS	13347
A Tribute To Woody Guthrie - Part 2 | VARIOUS ARTISTS	13495
A Trick Of The Tail | GENESIS	3256
Trick Or Treat (Soundtrack) | FASTWAY	10503
Trident | McCoy TYNER	13686
Trilogy | EMERSON, LAKE & PALM...	841
Trilogy | Yngwie MALMSTEEN	4917
Trilogy: Past, Present And ... | Frank SINATRA	2105
Greatest Hits | TRINERE & FRIENDS	13768
Trini | Trini LOPEZ	5908

Title | Act	Rank
Trini Lopez In London | Trini LOPEZ	10187
Trini Lopez - Now! | Trini LOPEZ	11523
The Trinity Session | COWBOY JUNKIES	2591
Trio [A] | Dolly PARTON	1476
Trio [A] | Emmylou HARRIS	1476
Trio [A] | Linda RONSTADT	1476
Trip To Heaven | Freddie HART	12249
Triumph | JACKSON 5	1181
Triumph And Agony | WARLOCK	5194
Triumvirate [A] | DR. JOHN	7988
Triumvirate [A] | John Paul HAMMOND	7988
Triumvirate [A] | Mike BLOOMFIELD	7988
Trombipulation | PARLIAMENT	7586
Tron | SOUNDTRACK-MOVIE	11722
Troop | TROOP	9757
Tropea | TROPEA	10078
Tropico | Gato BARBIERI	8811
Tropico | Pat BENATAR	2136
Troubadour | J.J. CALE	6273
Trouble In Paradise | Randy NEWMAN	6739
Trouble In Paradise | SOUTHER, HILLMAN, FU...	4861
The Troublemaker | Willie NELSON	6896
Troublemaker | Ian McLAGAN	9431
Trouble Man | Marvin GAYE	2091
Trouble Walkin' | Ace FREHLEY	9690
Truce [A] | Jack BRUCE	9581
Truce [A] | Robin TROWER	9581
Truckload Of Lovin' | Albert KING	11103
Truck Stop | Jerry SMITH	13663
Truck Turner (Soundtrack) | Isaac HAYES	10074
True | SPANDAU BALLET	2467
True Blue | Hank CRAWFORD	13009
True Blue | MADONNA	162
True Colors | Cyndi LAUPER	977
True Colours | SPLIT ENZ	3110
True Confessions | BANANARAMA	2501
True Democracy | STEEL PULSE	8920
True Grit | SOUNDTRACK-MOVIE	5893
True Love | Crystal GAYLE	8553
True Love Ways | PETER And GORDON	6301
True Stories: A Film By Dav... | TALKING HEADS	2215
True Stories And Other Dream... | Judy COLLINS	3780
True To Life | Ray CHARLES	6211
Truly Fine Citizen | MOBY GRAPE	10280
Truly For You | The TEMPTATIONS	3945
Trust | Elvis COSTELLO & The...	3863
Truth | Jeff BECK	1383
Truth And Soul | FISHBONE	11276
Truthdare Doubledare | BRONSKI BEAT	11363
Truth In Disguise | Denise LOPEZ	12917
Truth Is On Its Way | Nikki GIOVANNI	8910
Truth Of Truths - A Conte... | VARIOUS ARTISTS	11819
Try A Little Kindness | Glen CAMPBELL	1849
Try A Little Love | Sam COOKE	9978
Tryin' To Get The Feelin' | Barry MANILOW	548
Try It Out | KLIQUE	7033
Try My Love | Tata VEGA	10736
Try Too Hard | Dave CLARK Five	7324
Try To Remember | BROTHERS FOUR	6635
T Shirt | Loudon WAINWRIGHT II...	12763
The Tubes | The TUBES	6784
Tubular Bells | Mike OLDFIELD	599
Tuckerized | MARSHALL TUCKER Band	9620
Tuff Darts! | TUFF DARTS	10840
Tuff Enuff | FABULOUS THUNDERBIRD...	1009
Tug Of War | Paul McCARTNEY	836

Title | Act	Rank
Tumbleweed Connection | Elton JOHN	578
Tuneweaving | DAWN/Tony ORLANDO	2873
Tunnel Of Love | Bruce SPRINGSTEEN	506
Tupelo Honey | Van MORRISON	2546
Turbo | JUDAS PRIEST	2096
Turn! Turn! Turn! | The BYRDS	2194
Turn Around Look At ... | Ray CONNIFF & His Or...	4335
Turn Around, Look At Me | Lenny DEE	13629
Turn Around, Look At Me | The VOGUES	2438
Turn Back | TOTO	5287
Turn Back The Clock | JOHNNY HATES JAZZ	4348
Turn Back The Hands Of Time | Tyrone DAVIS	7162
The Turning Point | John MAYALL	1560
Turnin' On | HIGH INERGY	2827
The Turn Of A Friend... | Alan PARSONS PROJECT	734
Turn Of The Cards | RENAISSANCE	5586
Turn Of The Screw | DIRTY LOOKS	8683
Turn On Some Happy! | Danny DAVIS And The ...	12719
(Turn On) The Music Machine | MUSIC MACHINE	6308
Turnstiles | Billy JOEL	7625
Turn The Hands Of Time | Peabo BRYSON	6991
Turn The World Around | Eddy ARNOLD	3581
Turn This Mutha Out | Idris MUHAMMAD	7130
Turn Up The Music | MASS PRODUCTION	11153
Turn Your Radio On | Ray STEVENS	10844
Turtle Bay | Herbie MANN	9742
The Turtles! Golden Hits | The TURTLES	1235
The Turtles! More Golden Hits | The TURTLES	9703
The Turtles' Greatest Hits/Ha... | The TURTLES	12087
Turtle Soup | The TURTLES	8167
The Turtles Present The Battl... | The TURTLES	8505
Tusk | FLEETWOOD MAC	591
Tutu | Miles DAVIS	10504
Tuxedo Junction | TUXEDO JUNCTION	3738
The Twain Shall Meet | The ANIMALS/Eric BUR...	4375
Twang Bar King | Adrian BELEW	10862
Twangin... | Dave EDMUNDS	5214
"Twangin'" Up A Storm! | Duane EDDY	8900
12 | Bob JAMES	10248
Twelve Dreams Of Dr. Sardonicus | SPIRIT	5905
12 Greatest Hits Vol. II | Neil DIAMOND	4191
12 In A Roe/A Collection Of Tom... | Tommy ROE	1758
12 String Guitar! | The FOLKSWINGERS	11393
12 x 5 | ROLLING STONES	1308
Twennynine With Lenny White | TWENNYNINE	9231
25th Anniversary | The SUPREMES/Diana R...	7601
25th Anniversary | The TEMPTATIONS	8619
A 25th Anniversary In Show Bu... | Ray CHARLES	8822
21st Century Man | Billy THORPE	11146
25 Miles | Edwin STARR	5670
25 #1 Hits From 25 Years | VARIOUS ARTISTS	4662
2525 (Exordium & Terminus) | ZAGER & EVANS	3488
25 Years Of Grammy Greats | VARIOUS ARTISTS	9082
24 Carrots | Al STEWART	4684
2400 Fulton St. | JEFFERSON AIRPLANE/S...	10084
24/7 | DINO	2404
20 Golden Hits | MAMAS & The PAPAS	12846
20 Granite Creek | MOBY GRAPE	11662
20 Greatest Hits | The BEATLES	4451
Twenty Greatest Hits | Kenny ROGERS	2456
21 At 33 | Elton JOHN	2237
2112 | RUSH	4990
20 Original Winners Of 19... | VARIOUS ARTISTS	5299
2300 Jackson St. | JACKSON 5	6714
20/20 | 20/20	8444
20/20 | BEACH BOYS	6059

Title	Act	Rank
20/20	George BENSON	4024
20/20 Twenty No.1 Hits Fr...	VARIOUS ARTISTS	10688
22B3	DEVICE	6916
20 Years Of Jethro Tull	JETHRO TULL	7658
Twice As Sweet	A TASTE OF HONEY	3078
Twice Removed From Yesterday	Robin TROWER	6446
...Twice Shy	GREAT WHITE	847
Twice The Fire	PEACHES & HERB	3444
Twice The Love	George BENSON	7687
Twilley	Dwight TWILLEY	8786
Twilley Don't Mind	Dwight TWILLEY	6469
Twin Hype	TWIN HYPE	9717
Twin Peaks	MOUNTAIN	9569
Twins	SOUNDTRACK-MOVIE	9913
Twin Sons Of Different Mothers [A]	Dan FOGELBERG	973
Twin Sons Of Different Mothers [A]	Tim WEISBERG	973
Twisting By The Pool	DIRE STRAITS	5942
Twist Of Shadows	XYMOX	11133
Twitch	MINISTRY	13508
Two	Bob JAMES	6249
Two	GQ	4279
Two All-Time Great S...	Paul REVERE And The ...	11648
2:00 A.M. Paradise Cafe	Barry MANILOW	3888
Two B's Please	Robbin THOMPSON Band	10690
2 X 4	GUADALCANAL DIARY	12018
Two For The Road (So...	Henry MANCINI and hi...	13186
Two For The Show	KANSAS	3448
Two Great Experiences T... [A]	Lonnie YOUNGBLOOD	10806
Two Great Experiences Togeth... [A]	Jimi HENDRIX	10806
Two Hearts	MEN AT WORK	6226
Two Hot For Love!	THP ORCHESTRA	5380
200 M.P.H.	Bill COSBY	1662
2 Hype	KID 'N PLAY	3852
Two Lane Highway	PURE PRAIRIE LEAGUE	3579
2 Live Crew Is What We Are	2 LIVE CREW	6946
Two Of A Kind (Soundtrac...	SOUNDTRACK-MOVIE	3315
Two Of A Kind	Bob JAMES & Earl KLU...	3677
Two Of A Kind	Porter WAGONER and D...	11976
The Two Of Us [A]	Nancy WILSON	10322
The Two Of Us [A]	Ramsey LEWIS	10322
The Two Of Us	Marilyn McCOO & Bill...	7347
The Two Of Us	SONNY & CHER	7776
The Two Of Us	YARBROUGH & PEOPLES	2140
Two Places At The Sa...	Ray PARKER Jr./RAYDI...	3271
The Two Ring Circus	ERASURE	13289
Two's Company	AZTEC TWO STEP	12542
Two Sides Of Leonard Nimoy	Leonard NIMOY	7301
Two Sides Of Peter Banks	Peter BANKS	10242
Two Sides Of The Moon	Keith MOON	11912
2000 And Thirteen	Carl REINER & Mel BR...	9016
2001: A Space Odyssey	SOUNDTRACK-MOVIE	660
2001: A Space Odyssey (V...	SOUNDTRACK-MOVIE	9898
2010	SOUNDTRACK-MOVIE	12448
Two Tons O' Fun	WEATHER GIRLS	7857
Two Wheels Good	PREFAB SPROUT	12511
2 Years On	BEE GEES	3877
Tycoon	TYCOON	4641
Typical American Boys	Chad MITCHELL Trio	12104
Tyrannosaurus Rex (A Beginning)	T. REX	7551
Tyranny And Mutation	BLUE ÖYSTER CULT	8052
Tyrone Davis	Tyrone DAVIS	11248
U		
'U'	INCREDIBLE STRING BA...	12925
UB40	UB40	3954
Ugly Ego	CAMEO	6941
UHF/Original Motion P...	"Weird Al" YANKOVIC	11916
Uh-Huh	John MELLENCAMP	512
U.K.	U.K.	5659
UK Jive	The KINKS	10151
Ultimate	ULTIMATE	9222
The Ultimate Sin	Ozzy OSBOURNE	1271
Ultimate Spinach	ULTIMATE SPINACH	3254
Ultra Wave	BOOTSY'S RUBBER BAND	7078
Ummagumma	PINK FLOYD	4504
Um, Um, Um, Um, Um, Um/The Be...	Major LANCE	9019
Unbelievable	Billy STEWART	10617
Unborn Child	SEALS & CROFTS	1298
Unchain My Heart	Joe COCKER	5237
Uncle Charlie & His ...	NITTY GRITTY DIRT BA...	3772
Uncle Jam Wants You	FUNKADELIC	3505
Uncle Meat	Frank ZAPPA	4893
Unconditionally Guar...	CAPTAIN BEEFHEART & ...	12982
Undead	TEN YEARS AFTER	7158
Under A Raging Moon	Roger DALTREY	4145
Undercover	ROLLING STONES	1862
Undercover Lover	Debbie JACOBS	10265
Underdog	ATLANTA RHYTHM SECTI...	2795
Underground	ELECTRIC PRUNES	12426
Underground Fire	The VENTURES	8018
Underground Gold	VARIOUS ARTISTS	13543
Under Lock And Key	DOKKEN	2221
Underneath The Radar	UNDERWORLD	7597
Understanding	Bobby WOMACK	1731
Under The Big Black Sun	X	6906
Under The Blade	TWISTED SISTER	9132
Under The Blue Moon	NEW EDITION	4561
Under The Boardwalk	The DRIFTERS	4328
Under The Gun	POCO	4814
Under The Influence	OVERKILL	8913
Under The Influence Of...	LOVE UNLIMITED	862
Under The Volcano	ROCK And HYDE	7229
The Undertones	The UNDERTONES	10649
Undertow	FIREFALL	6264
Under Wraps	JETHRO TULL	7656
Under Wraps	Shaun CASSIDY	4399
The Undisputed Truth	UNDISPUTED TRUTH	4023
Unfinished Business	EPMD	5856
Unfinished Business	The BLACKBYRDS	3100
Unfinished Music No. 1...	John LENNON & Yoko O...	8387
Unfinished Music No.2...	John LENNON & Yoko O...	10589
Unforgettable	Nat King COLE	2460
The Unforgettable Fire	U2	670
The Unforgiven	The UNFORGIVEN	13580
Unguarded	Amy GRANT	2663
The Unicorn	IRISH ROVERS	1814
Union	Toni CHILDS	3231
Union Jacks	The BABYS	3706
United	Marvin GAYE & Tammi ...	3539
United	The COMMODORES	7631
United States Live	Laurie ANDERSON	13086
The United States Of...	UNITED STATES OF AME...	11160
United We Stand	BROTHERHOOD OF MAN	10849
Unity	SHINEHEAD	13018
Universal Consciousness	Alice COLTRANE	13505
Universal Love	MFSB	5358
Universal Rhythm	Ralph MacDONALD	8809
Unleashed In The East (Live ...	JUDAS PRIEST	6313
Unlimited!	ROGER	3466
Unlimited Touch	UNLIMITED TOUCH	10180
Unmistakably Lou	Lou RAWLS	3781
Unorthodox Behaviour	BRAND X	13098
Unpredictable	Natalie COLE	1315
Unreal	BLOODSTONE	5783
Unrequited	Loudon WAINWRIGHT II...	10959
The Unsinkable Molly Bro...	SOUNDTRACK-MOVIE	2017
Unsung Heroes	DIXIE DREGS	5871
Unsung Heroes	The CRUSADERS	9537
Untold Passion	Neal SCHON & Jan HAM...	9075
Untouchables	LAKESIDE	5443
Up	Le ROUX	10418
Up And Down	OPUS	6134
Upendo Ni Pamoja	Ramsey LEWIS Trio	4923
The Up Escalator	Graham PARKER And Th...	4688
Up In Smoke (Soundtrack)	CHEECH & CHONG	10835
Uplift Mofo Party Pl...	RED HOT CHILI PEPPER...	8560
Upon The Wings Of Music	Jean-Luc PONTY	11343
Up Pops Ramsey Lewis	Ramsey LEWIS	3964
Uprising	Bob MARLEY And The W...	3567
Upstairs At Eric's	YAZ	5958
Up The Creek	SOUNDTRACK-MOVIE	13224
Up The Yellow Brick Roa...	SALSOUL Orchestra	8956
Uptight (Soundtrack)	BOOKER T. & The M.G....	4955
Up-Tight Everything's Alrig...	Stevie WONDER	3379
Up To Date	PARTRIDGE FAMILY	346
Uptown	NEVILLE BROTHERS	10746
Uptown Festival	SHALAMAR	5162
Up Up And Away	BOSTON POPS Orchestr...	9863
Up, Up And Away	5TH DIMENSION	1113
Up, Up And Away	Johnny MATHIS	5226
Up With People!	UP WITH PEOPLE	6343
Up Your Alley	Joan JETT & The BLAC...	1279
Urban Beaches	CACTUS WORLD NEWS	12565
Urban Chipmunk	The CHIPMUNKS	3412
Urban Cowboy	SOUNDTRACK-MOVIE	479
Urban Cowboy II	SOUNDTRACK-MOVIE	9927
Urban Daydreams	David BENOIT	7808
Urban Desire	Genya RAVAN	10777
Urban Renewal	TOWER OF POWER	3103
Urgh! A Music War	VARIOUS ARTISTS	12667
Uriah Heep	URIAH HEEP	12832
Uriah Heep Live	URIAH HEEP	3283
USA	KING CRIMSON	10079
U.S.A. For M.O.D.	M.O.D.	12045
USA Union	John MAYALL	3067
Used To Be	CHARLENE	11504
U.S. 1	HEAD EAST	9956
UTFO	UTFO	6030
Utopia	UTOPIA	6506
Under A Blood Red Sky	U2	915
V		
V	ZAPP	12325
Vacation	The GO-GO'S	1936
A Valentine Gift For You	Elvis PRESLEY	12613
Valerie Simpson	Valerie SIMPSON	10830
Valerie Simpson Exposed	Valerie SIMPSON	10857
Valley Hi	Ian MATTHEWS	11481
Valley Of The Dolls	Dionne WARWICK	1017
Valley Of The Dolls	SOUNDTRACK-MOVIE	2151
Valotte	Julian LENNON	1036
Vandenberg	VANDENBERG	6401
Van Go	BEAT FARMERS	10543
Van Halen	VAN HALEN	406
Van Halen II	VAN HALEN	686
Vanilla Fudge	VANILLA FUDGE	353
Vanity 6	VANITY	4036
Van-Zant	Johnny Van ZANT Band	11172

Title | Act	Rank
Variations | Eddie RABBITT	10144
Vaudeville! | Eric ROGERS & His Or...	11359
Veedon Fleece | Van MORRISON	6152
Vehicle | IDES OF MARCH	5425
The Velveteen Rabbit [A] | George WINSTON	13001
The Velveteen Rabbit [A] | Meryl STREEP	13001
Velvet Kiss, Lick Of The... | LIONS AND GHOSTS	13373
The Velvet Underground | VELVET UNDERGROUND	13778
The Velvet Underground... | VELVET UNDERGROUND	10542
Velvet Voices And Bold... | Anita KERR Singers	12412
Venice Blue | Bobby DARIN	11512
The Ventures A Go-Go | The VENTURES	1899
The Ventures/Batman Theme | The VENTURES	4647
The Ventures Knock Me Out! | The VENTURES	3548
The Ventures On Stage | The VENTURES	3018
The Ventures 10th Anniversar... | The VENTURES	5176
Venus And Mars | Paul McCARTNEY & WIN...	419
Venusian Summer | Lenny WHITE	12619
Verities & Balderdash | Harry CHAPIN	873
Vertical Smiles | BLACKFOOT	12333
The Very Best Of Connie Fr... | Connie FRANCIS	5491
The Very Best Of Dave Mason | Dave MASON	12525
The Very Best Of Gordon ... | Gordon LIGHTFOOT	10709
The Very Best Of Poco | POCO	7887
The Very Best Of Ray Stevens | Ray STEVENS	12303
The Very Best Of Roy Orbison | Roy ORBISON	8463
Very Dionne | Dionne WARWICK	3130
Very Greasy | David LINDLEY	12076
Very Special | Debra LAWS	4338
A Very Special Christmas | VARIOUS ARTISTS	2730
Very Special Love Songs | Charlie RICH	2076
Very Together | DEODATO	7309
Very Young And Early Songs | Cat STEVENS	7628
Vesta 4 U | VESTA	9387
Vibrations | Roy AYERS UBIQUITY	6601
Vices | KICK AXE	8077
Vicki Sue Robinson | Vicki Sue ROBINSON	5023
Victim Of Love | Elton JOHN	4993
Victims Of The Fury | Robin TROWER	4160
Victims Of The Future | Gary MOORE	12237
The Victors | SOUNDTRACK-MOVIE	12292
Victor/Victoria | SOUNDTRACK-MOVIE	12756
Victory | JACKSON 5	1451
Victory | Larry GRAHAM/GRAHAM ...	12566
Victory | Narada Michael WALDE...	8418
Victory Day | Tom COCHRANE/RED RID...	9108
Vienna | ULTRAVOX	10067
View From The Ground | AMERICA	3409
A View To A Kill | SOUNDTRACK-MOVIE	5204
Vikki! | Vikki CARR	5208
Vikki Carr's Love Story | Vikki CARR	5305
The Village Caller! | Johnny LYTLE	12783
Village People | VILLAGE PEOPLE	1541
Vincebus Eruptum | BLUE CHEER	1988
Vinnie Vincent Invas... | Vinnie VINCENT INVAS...	4125
Vintage-Canned Heat | CANNED HEAT	11563
Vintage Dead | GRATEFUL DEAD	8489
Vintage '78 | Eddie KENDRICKS	12920
Vintage 74 | Sergio MENDES And BR...	11858
The Vintage Years | The IMPRESSIONS	13711
Vintage Years | FLEETWOOD MAC	9407
Vinton | Bobby VINTON	5587
Vinyl Confessions | KANSAS	3425
Violation | STARZ	7956
Visage | VISAGE	12407
Vision Quest | SOUNDTRACK-MOVIE	2431

Title | Act	Rank
Visions | Gladys KNIGHT & The ...	2812
Visions | Grant GREEN	9640
Visions Of A New Worl... | Lonnie Liston SMITH	6187
Visions Of The Emera... | John McLAUGHLIN/MAHA...	6367
Visions Of The Lite | SLAVE	12255
The Visitor | Mick FLEETWOOD	4961
The Visitors | ABBA	3920
Visitors | AUTOMATIC MAN	8746
Visual Lies | LIZZY BORDEN	11120
Vital Idol | Billy IDOL	1605
Vital Signs | SURVIVOR	1018
Viva! Roxy Music | ROXY MUSIC	8050
Viva Hate | MORRISSEY	4645
Viva Santana | SANTANA	11017
Viva Terlingua! | Jerry Jeff WALKER	9836
Viva Tirado | EL CHICANO	4949
Vive Le Rock | Adam ANT	10635
Vivid | LIVING COLOUR	586
Vixen | VIXEN	2574
VOA | Sammy HAGAR	2400
Vocalese | MANHATTAN TRANSFER	4660
The Vogues' Greatest Hits | The VOGUES	9943
The Voice Of Africa | Miriam MAKEBA	11497
Voice Of America | LITTLE STEVEN	5547
The Voice Of Scott McKenzi... | Scott McKENZIE	9626
Voices | Daryl HALL & John OA...	380
Voices & Images | CAMOUFLAGE	7632
Voices Carry | 'TIL TUESDAY	2216
Voices In The Rain | Joe SAMPLE	4844
Voices In The Sky-Best Of The... | MOODY BLUES	9758
Voices Of Babylon | The OUTFIELD	5051
Voices Of The Heart | CARPENTERS	5129
Volcanic Action Of My Soul | Ray CHARLES	4666
Volcano | Jimmy BUFFETT	2035
Volume VIII | AVERAGE WHITE BAND/A...	13313
Volume 1 | TRAVELING WILBURYS	366
Volume One | The HONEYDRIPPERS	1098
Volunteer Jam | VARIOUS ARTISTS	10643
Volunteer Jam VII | VARIOUS ARTISTS	11284
Volunteer Jam VI | VARIOUS ARTISTS	8266
Volunteers | JEFFERSON AIRPLANE/S...	1197
Voulez-Vous | ABBA	1961
Vox Humana | Kenny LOGGINS	3637
Voyage | VOYAGE	4256
Voyage Of The Acolyte | Steve HACKETT	12877
Voyager | Dexter WANSEL	9841
Voyager | Roger WHITTAKER	9173
Voyeur | David SANBORN	3596
Voyeur | Kim CARNES	4947
V.S.O.P. | Herbie HANCOCK	8064
VU | VELVET UNDERGROUND	7456
Vulture Culture | Alan PARSONS PROJECT	4727
W	
Wack Wack | YOUNG-HOLT UNLIMITED	10223
Wade In The Water | Ramsey LEWIS	1722
Waiata | SPLIT ENZ	3979
Wait For Night | Rick SPRINGFIELD	10902
Waitin' For The Sun To Shine | Ricky SKAGGS	5112
Waiting | FUN BOY THREE	9490
Waiting For Columbus | LITTLE FEAT	1945
Waiting For Spring | David BENOIT	13376
Waiting For The Sun | The DOORS	444
Waiting On You | BRICK	12124
Waitress In The Donut Shop | Maria MULDAUR	2368
Waka/Jawaka - Hot Rats | Frank ZAPPA	10539

Title | Act	Rank
Wake Me When It's Over | FASTER PUSSYCAT	3213
Wake Of The Flood | GRATEFUL DEAD	3325
Wake Up Everybody | Harold MELVIN And Th...	1632
Waking & Dreaming | ORLEANS	3671
Waking Up With The House On ... | CULTURE CLUB	3300
The Walk | The CURE	11386
Walkabout | The FIXX	3626
Walk A Fine Line | Paul ANKA	10876
Walk Away | Matt MONRO	12033
Walk Away - Collector's Edit... | Donna SUMMER	5556
Walk Away Renee/Pretty Balleri... | LEFT BANKE	7240
Walk, Don't Run, Vol. 2 | The VENTURES	3142
Walker's Collectibles | Jerry Jeff WALKER	9191
Walking In Space | Quincy JONES	2659
Walking Man | James TAYLOR	2034
Walking On New Grass | Wayne NEWTON	13262
Walking The Dog | Rufus THOMAS	12245
Walkin' The Razor's Edge | HELIX	6670
Walking Through Fire | APRIL WINE	12922
Walking Wild | NEW ENGLAND	12443
Walking With A Panther | LL COOL J	1683
Walkin' In Love Land | Eddy ARNOLD	6190
Walkin' In The Sunshine | Roger MILLER	9179
Walk On The Wild Side-The Best O... | Lou REED	10807
Walk Under Ladders | Joan ARMATRADING	4580
The Wall | PINK FLOYD	52
Walls And Bridges | John LENNON	924
Wall To Wall | RENÉ & ANGELA	8726
Walter Carlos' Clockwork Or... | Walter CARLOS	9477
The Waltons' Christmas Albu... | SOUNDTRACK-TV	11922
The Wanderer | Donna SUMMER	2584
The Wandering Minstr... | NEW CHRISTY MINSTREL...	9408
Wanna Be A Star | CHILLIWACK	4677
Wanted | Richard PRYOR	3463
Wanted! The Outlaws [A] | Jessi COLTER	1254
Wanted! The Outlaws [A] | Tompall GLASER	1254
Wanted! The Outlaws [A] | Waylon JENNINGS	1254
Wanted! The Outlaws [A] | Willie NELSON	1254
Wanted Dead Or Alive | David BROMBERG	11830
Wanted Dead Or Alive (Ban... | Joe CUBA Sextet	10237
Wanted Dread & Alive | Peter TOSH	6994
War | U2	678
War | WAR	12062
War & Peace | Edwin STARR	5310
War And Peace | SOUNDTRACK-MOVIE	13050
War Babies | Daryl HALL & John OA...	7068
War Child | JETHRO TULL	391
Warehouse: Songs And Stories | HUSKER DU	9442
War Heroes | Jimi HENDRIX	4669
War Live! | WAR	1376
Warm | Herb ALPERT & The TI...	2335
Warm | The LETTERMEN	5554
Warm And Tender | Olivia NEWTON-JOHN	8905
Warm And Tender | Petula CLARK	12734
Warm & Tender Soul | Percy SLEDGE	11840
Warm And Wonderful | Bert KAEMPFERT And H...	12520
Warmer | Randy VANWARMER	7674
Warmer Communication... | AVERAGE WHITE BAND/...	3410
The Warmer Side Of Cool | WANG CHUNG	10210
Warm Leatherette | Grace JONES	8576
A Warm Shade Of Ivor... | Henry MANCINI and hi...	695
The Warmth Of Eddy | Eddy ARNOLD	8529
Warm Thoughts | Smokey ROBINSON	1989
Warner Brothers Presents Montros... | MONTROSE	8380
The Warning | QUEENSRYCHE	5384
War Of The Gods | Billy PAUL	5756

Title | Act	Rank
The War Of The Worlds | VARIOUS ARTISTS	5304
Warren Zevon | Warren ZEVON	13390
Warrior | SCANDAL	1852
Warrior On The Edge Of Time | HAWKWIND	11130
The Warriors | SOUNDTRACK-MOVIE	8908
War, War, War | COUNTRY JOE & The Fl...	12620
Was Captured Live At The ... | THREE DOG NIGHT	369
Washington County | Arlo GUTHRIE	3848
Washington Square | New Band of Spike JONES	11234
Washington Square | VILLAGE STOMPERS	1676
Wasn't That A Party | IRISH ROVERS	10236
Wasn't Tomorrow Wonderful? | The WAITRESSES	4107
W.A.S.P. | W.A.S.P.	5442
Watch | MANFRED MANN'S EARTH...	8903
Watching You, Watching Me | Bill WITHERS	10705
Watch Out! | Patrice RUSHEN	6522
Watch Out! | BAJA MARIMBA BAND	3199
Watchout! | MARTHA & The VANDELL...	8850
Water Babies | Miles DAVIS	13429
Waterbed | Herbie MANN	7354
Waterbeds In Trinidad! | The ASSOCIATION	12812
Waterfall | IF	13066
Waterfront | WATERFRONT	8334
The Watergate Comedy Hour | VARIOUS ARTISTS	5894
Waterloo | ABBA	9781
Watermark | Art GARFUNKEL	2821
Watermark | ENYA	1985
Water Sign | Jeff LORBER	8062
Watertown | Frank SINATRA	7765
Watt | TEN YEARS AFTER	2754
Watts In A Tank | DIESEL	5476
Wattstax: The Living Wor... | SOUNDTRACK-MOVIE	3797
Wattstax 2: The Living W... | SOUNDTRACK-MOVIE	11391
Wave | Antonio Carlos JOBIM	8747
Wave | Patti SMITH	2733
Wavelength | Van MORRISON	2965
Wa Wa Nee | WA WA NEE	7731
Wax Museum | JAY & The AMERICANS	7603
The Way It Is | Bruce HORNSBY And Th...	244
The Way It Was - The Way It Is | Lou RAWLS	4474
Waylon | Waylon JENNINGS	13511
Waylon & Willie | Waylon JENNINGS & Willie NELSON	1830
Waylon "Live" | Waylon JENNINGS	4615
Wayne Cochran! | Wayne COCHRAN	12365
Wayne Newton - Now! | Wayne NEWTON	5558
The Way Of Love | Jim NABORS	9922
Way Out West | Mae WEST	10484
The Ways To Love A Man | Tammy WYNETTE	6920
The Way To Become The Sen... | VARIOUS ARTISTS	12261
The Way We Were | Barbra STREISAND	921
The Way We Were | SOUNDTRACK-MOVIE	3266
The Way We Were | Willis JACKSON	12857
W. C. Fields On Radio | W.C. FIELDS	13552
Wcyaya | OSIBISA	5184
We All Have A Star | Wilton FELDER	9268
We All Know Who We Are | CAMEO	4653
Weapons Of Love | The TRUTH	9715
We Are Family | SISTER SLEDGE	799
We Are One | MANDRILL	8688
We Are One | MAZE Featuring Frank...	3391
We Are One | PIECES OF A DREAM	8161
We Are The World | USA For AFRICA	1322
Wear Your Love Like Heaven | DONOVAN	5991
Weasels Ripped My Flesh | Frank ZAPPA	13090
Weather Report(2) | WEATHER REPORT	6901
Weather Report | WEATHER REPORT	12720

Title | Act	Rank
We Came To Play | The PERSUASIONS	12975
We Came To Play | TOWER OF POWER	8202
We Can Fly | The COWSILLS	8016
We Can Fly! Up-Up And... | Johnny MANN Singers	4732
We Can Make Music | Tommy ROE	9911
We Can't Go Wrong | COVER GIRLS	7373
We Could | Al MARTINO	5604
Wedding Album | John LENNON & Yoko ONO	12625
Wedding Album | Leon & Mary RUSSELL	3077
We'd Like To Teach The World ... | NEW SEEKERS	4651
Wednesday Morning, 3 AM | SIMON & GARFUNKEL	3628
We Don't Talk Anymore | Cliff RICHARD	6982
Weekend In L.A. | George BENSON	702
Weekend In London | Dave CLARK Five	3932
Weekend Warriors | Ted NUGENT	2664
Wee Tam | INCREDIBLE STRING BA...	12498
We Go A Long Way Back | BLOODSTONE	8242
We Go Together [A] | George JONES	10952
We Go Together [A] | Tammy WYNETTE	10952
We Gotta Start Lovin' | Bobby GOLDSBORO	8168
We Got The Rhythm | PEOPLE'S CHOICE	12593
We Got To Live Together | Buddy MILES	3428
"Weird Al" Yankovic | "Weird Al" YANKOVIC	10288
"Weird Al" Yankovic I... | "Weird Al" YANKOVIC	2586
Weird Scenes Inside The Gold Mi... | The DOORS	6003
Weird Science | SOUNDTRACK-MOVIE	8776
Welcome | SANTANA	2864
Welcome Back | John SEBASTIAN	7145
Welcome Back, My Fri... | EMERSON, LAKE & PALM...	1479
Welcome Home | Carole KING	8475
Welcome Home | OSIBISA	13734
Welcome Home | 'TIL TUESDAY	4209
Welcome To My Love | Nancy WILSON	7165
Welcome To My Nightma... | ALICE COOPER (Solo)	748
Welcome To My World | Dean MARTIN	1510
Welcome To My World | Elvis PRESLEY	3747
Welcome To My World | Ray PRICE	10646
Welcome To Our World | MASS PRODUCTION	9148
Welcome To The Canteen | TRAFFIC	3025
Welcome To The Club | Ian HUNTER	5862
Welcome To The Dance | SONS OF CHAMPLIN	12587
Welcome To The LBJ Ranch! | VARIOUS ARTISTS	1601
Welcome To The Pleas... | FRANKIE GOES TO HOLL...	2056
Welcome To The Ponderosa | Lorne GREENE	4841
Welcome To The Real World | MR. MISTER	445
Welcome To The Wrecking Ball | Grace SLICK	5286
Welcome Two Missouri | MISSOURI	12326
We'll Cry Together | Maxine BROWN	13554
Well Kept Secret | James LAST	12540
The Well-Tempered Synthesiz... | Walter CARLOS	13705
We Made It Happen | Engelbert HUMPERDINC...	2052
We Must Be Doing Somethin... | Joe CUBA Sextet	11554
We Must Believe In Magic | Crystal GAYLE	1594
Wendy And Lisa | WENDY and LISA	7503
We Only Make Believe | Conway TWITTY & Loretta Lynn	6172
We're All In This Together | CHOCOLATE MILK	11429
We're An American Ban... | GRAND FUNK RAILROAD	752
We're A Winner | The IMPRESSIONS	3167
We're Gonna Get Together [A] | Buck OWENS	10975
We're Gonna Get Together [A] | Susan RAYE	10975
We're Gonna Make It | LITTLE MILTON	7753
We Remember Sam Cooke | The SUPREMES/Diana ...	5838
We're Movin' Up | ATLANTIC STARR	10593
We're Only In It For The Mone... | Frank ZAPPA	3933
We're The Best Of Friends [A] | Natalie COLE	4033
We're The Best Of Friends [A] | Peabo BRYSON	4033

Title | Act	Rank
We Shall Overcome | Pete SEEGER	3211
We Should Be Together | Crystal GAYLE	9224
We Sold Our Souls For Rock ... | BLACK SABBATH	5776
Westbound #9 | FLAMING EMBER	13078
Western Union | FIVE AMERICANS	8583
We Still Ain't Got No Ban... | The PERSUASIONS	12890
West Meets East [A] | Ravi SHANKAR	11076
West Meets East [A] | Yehudi MENUHIN	11076
West Side Highway | Stanley TURRENTINE	6067
West Side Story | Leonard BERNSTEIN	6159
We Sure Can Love Each Other | Tammy WYNETTE	8051
Wet | Barbra STREISAND	1119
We Too Are One | EURYTHMICS	2904
The Wetter The Better | WET WILLIE	9598
We've Got A Live One... | COMMANDER CODY & His...	12499
We've Got To Get It On A... | ADDRISI BROTHERS	11778
We've Got Tonight | Kenny ROGERS	2779
We've Only Just Begu... | Ray CONNIFF & His Or...	7544
We Want Miles | Miles DAVIS	11220
We Went To Different Schools ... | The JAGGERZ	5977
Whale Meat Again | Jim CAPALDI	13220
Whales & Nightingales | Judy COLLINS	1232
Whammy! | The B-52s	3568
The Wham Of That Memphis Man! | Lonnie MACK	9029
Wha'ppen | ENGLISH BEAT	9511
What About Me? | Kenny ROGERS	3006
What About Me | QUICKSILVER MESSENGE...	3202
What About Today? | Barbra STREISAND	3779
What About You! | Stanley TURRENTINE	7409
What A Diff'rence A Day M... | Esther PHILLIPS	3549
What A Feelin' | Irene CARA	4063
What A Life! | DIVINYLS	7120
What A Long Strange Trip It... | GRATEFUL DEAD	9097
What Becomes A Semi-Legend Mo... | Joan RIVERS	3815
What Can You Do To Me Now | Willie NELSON	13280
What Cha' Gonna Do For Me | Chaka KHAN	2522
What Cha Gonna Do...With ... | Stephanie MILLS	2054
Whatcha See Is Whatcha Get | The DRAMATICS	2278
What Did You Do In T... | Henry MANCINI and hi...	12761
What Does It Take To... | Jr. WALKER & The ALL...	5414
What Do You Want From Live | The TUBES	7793
Whatever | FRIENDS OF DISTINCTI...	12655
What Ever Happened To Benny San... | Chris REA	5318
Whatever Turns You On | WEST, BRUCE & LAING	7478
What Goes Around | The HOLLIES	8524
What Goes Around Comes Ar... | Waylon JENNINGS	3695
What If | DIXIE DREGS	12417
What If | Tommy SHAW	8682
What Is Beat? | ENGLISH BEAT	6007
What Is This | WHAT IS THIS	13080
What It Was, Was Lov... | Steve LAWRENCE & Eyd...	9683
What Love Has...Join... | The MIRACLES/Smokey ...	7097
What Makes Sammy Run? | ORIGINAL CAST	5661
What More Can I Say? | AUDIO TWO	12892
What Now My Love | Herb ALPERT & The Tl...	54
What Price Paradise | CHINA CRISIS	8609
What's Going On | Marvin GAYE	388
What's My Name | STEADY B	11214
What's New | Linda RONSTADT	451
What's New!!! | Sonny STITT	13198
What's New Pussycat? | SOUNDTRACK-MOVIE	2903
What's New Pussycat? | Tom JONES	10568
What's Next | MAHOGANY RUSH	7928
What's Up Front That-Counts | The COUNTS	13609
What's Up, Tiger Lily? (S... | LOVIN' SPOONFUL	9018
What's Wrong With This Pictur... | Andrew GOLD	6921

Title | Act	Rank
What The World Is Comin' To | Dexter WANSEL	12377
What The World Needs Now Is Love | Tom CLAY	9348
What The World Needs Now Is Lo... | Jack JONES	11760
What Time Is It? | The TIME	3165
What Up, Dog? | WAS (NOT WAS)	3312
What Were Once Vices Are ... | DOOBIE BROTHERS	308
What You Don't Know | EXPOSÉ	2176
What You Need | SIDE EFFECT	7541
Wheatfield Soul | GUESS WHO	3551
The Wheel | ASLEEP AT THE WHEEL	11715
Wheelin' And Dealin' | ASLEEP AT THE WHEEL	12664
The Wheel Of Hurt | Margaret WHITING	8909
Wheels | RESTLESS HEART	5646
Wheels Are Turnin' | REO SPEEDWAGON	944
Wheels Of Fire | CREAM	188
When A Guitar Plays The Blue... | Roy BUCHANAN	9835
When All The Pieces Fit | Peter FRAMPTON	11394
When A Man Loves A Woman | Percy SLEDGE	4078
Whenever You Need Somebody | Rick ASTLEY	542
When Harry Met Sally (S... | Harry CONNICK Jr.	1696
When I Die | MOTHERLODE	6822
When I Dream | Crystal GAYLE	3320
When I Need You | Roger WHITTAKER	9727
When In Rome | WHEN IN ROME	5528
When I Was A Kid | Bill COSBY	7452
When Lights Are Low | Tony BENNETT	8039
When Love Comes Calling | Deniece WILLIAMS	8135
When Love Is New | Billy PAUL	7483
When Seconds Count | SURVIVOR	4230
When The Boys Meet The Gir... | Connie FRANCIS	7706
When The Eagle Flies | TRAFFIC	1850
When The Going Gets Tough, Th... | BOW WOW WOW	7267
When The Night Comes | Lou RAWLS	12247
When The Snow Is On The Roses | Ed AMES	2858
When The Snow Is On The Roses | Sonny JAMES	12671
When The Sun Goes Down | RED 7	13049
When The Whistle Blows Any... | SOUL SURVIVORS	8340
When Will I See You Again | Johnny MATHIS	6785
When Will I See You Again | The O'JAYS	11340
When You Hear Lou, You've Heard... | Lou RAWLS	2476
When You're Hot, You're Hot | Jerry REED	3707
When You're In Love The W... | VARIOUS ARTISTS	3934
When You're # 1 | Gene CHANDLER	12000
Where Are You Now, My Son? | Joan BAEZ	9687
Where Can You Go For A Bro... | George MAHARIS	8990
Where Did Our Love G... | The SUPREMES/Diana R...	269
Where Did Our Love Go | Donnie ELBERT	9787
Where Does Love Go | Charles BOYER	12987
Where Do We Go From Here | Michael DAMIAN	5268
Where Do You Go When You Drea... | Anne MURRAY	4925
Where Have I Known You ... | RETURN TO FOREVER	3415
Where I'm Coming From | Stevie WONDER	3518
Where I Should Be | Peter FRAMPTON	3012
Where Is Love? | Jack JONES	13222
Where Love Has Gone | Jack JONES	5666
Where's The Money? | Dan HICKS & His HOT ...	11742
Where's The Party? | Eddie MONEY	5790
Where's The Playground Susie? | Jerry VALE	12091
Where The Action Is | The VENTURES	3847
Where The Beat Meets... | BOBBY And The MIDNIT...	12723
Where The Happy People Go | The TRAMMPS	3616
Where There's Smoke | Smokey ROBINSON	1581
Where To Now | Charlie DORE	10476
Where We All Belong | MARSHALL TUCKER Band	5075
Which One's Willie | WET WILLIE	10120
Which Way You Goin' Billy? | POPPY FAMILY	6610

Title | Act	Rank
While The City Sleeps... | George BENSON	5754
Whiplash Smile | Billy IDOL	1213
Whipped Cream & Othe... | Herb ALPERT & The TI...	8
Whirlwinds | DEODATO	5409
Whisper In Your Ear | The WHISPERS	9564
The Whispers | The WHISPERS	954
Whispers | Jackie WILSON	9433
Whispers And Promises | Earl KLUGH	11805
The Whispers' Love Story | The WHISPERS	13420
Whisper Tames The Lion | DRIVIN' N' CRYIN'	8936
Whistle Rymes | John ENTWISTLE	8393
Whistle Stopping With Jo... | Jonathan WINTERS	13085
Whistling Down The W... | David CROSBY/Graham ...	3009
White Bird | David LAFLAMME	11190
White Christmas | John SCHNEIDER	10875
White City - A Novel | Pete TOWNSHEND	2661
White Feathers | KAJAGOOGOO	4311
White Gold | LOVE UNLIMITED ORCHE...	2540
White Hot | ANGEL	5199
White Hot & Blue | Johnny WINTER	10981
The White Knight | Cledus MAGGARD And ...	9238
White Knuckle Ride | DUKE JUPITER	8568
White Light/White Heat | VELVET UNDERGROUND	13774
White Mansions | VARIOUS ARTISTS	12335
White Nights | SOUNDTRACK-MOVIE	2472
White Noise | Jay FERGUSON	12310
White On White | Danny WILLIAMS	11110
White Rock (Soundtrack) | Rick WAKEMAN	9738
A Whiter Shade Of Pale | MUNICH MACHINE	13139
White Shoes | Emmylou HARRIS	8173
Whitesnake | WHITESNAKE	74
White Winds | Andreas VOLLENWEIDER	4553
Whitney | Whitney HOUSTON	78
Whitney Houston | Whitney HOUSTON	17
Who? | TONY! TONI! TONE!	3924
Who Are You | The WHO	846
Who Came First | Pete TOWNSHEND	5342
Who Can I Turn To | Tony BENNETT	4775
Who Do We Think We Are! | DEEP PURPLE	1272
Who Do Ya (Love) | KC And The SUNSHINE ...	3836
Who I Am | David RUFFIN	2308
Who Is This Bitch, Anyway? | Marlena SHAW	11260
Who Knows Where The Time Goe... | Judy COLLINS	1799
Whole Lotta Love | C.C.S.	13583
The Whole Story | Kate BUSH	5483
The Whole Thing Started With... | Ray MANZAREK	10412
The Whole World's Dancing | The TRAMMPS	13395
Who Loves You | 4 SEASONS	2633
Who Made Who (Soundtrack) | AC/DC	2612
Whomp That Sucker | SPARKS	13304
(Who's Afraid Of?) The Art O... | ART OF NOISE	7279
Who's Afraid Of Virginia Wool... | Jimmy SMITH	2141
Who's Afraid Of Virginia... | SOUNDTRACK-MOVIE	10406
The Who Sell Out | The WHO	4995
Who's Foolin' Who | ONE WAY	4573
Who's Greatest Hits | The WHO	8349
Who's Last | The WHO	6953
Who's Making Love... | Johnnie TAYLOR	3846
Who's Missing | The WHO	10337
Who's Next | The WHO	562
Who's Sorry Now | Marie OSMOND	10424
Who's That Girl (Soundtrack) | MADONNA	1858
Who's To Bless...And Who... | Kris KRISTOFFERSON	7794
Who's Zoomin' Who? | Aretha FRANKLIN	835
Who Will Answer? And Other Songs ... | Ed AMES	1289
Why Am I Treated So ... | "Cannonball" ADDERLE...	9330

Title | Act	Rank
Why Can't We Be Friends? | WAR	1021
Why Can't We Live Together | Timmy THOMAS	5350
Why Do Fools Fall In Love | Diana ROSS	1268
Why Dontcha | WEST, BRUCE & LAING	3205
Why Is There Air? | Bill COSBY	255
Why Lady Why | Gary MORRIS	11629
Why Not Me | Fred KNOBLOCK	12114
Why Not Me | The JUDDS	5338
Why You Been Gone So Long | Johnny DARRELL	12334
Wichita Lineman | Glen CAMPBELL	87
The Wicked Pickett | Wilson PICKETT	3543
Wide Awake In America | U2	5949
Wide Awake In Dreamland | Pat BENATAR	2870
Wide Receiver | Michael HENDERSON	3897
Wild! | ERASURE	5498
Wild! Wild! Wild! Wild! | WILD MAN STEVE	13176
Wild & Blue | John ANDERSON	6493
A Wild And Crazy Guy | Steve MARTIN	587
Wild And Free | DAZZ BAND	8451
Wild & Loose | OAKTOWN'S 3.5.7	7975
Wild And Peaceful | KOOL & The GANG	1648
Wild And Peaceful | Teena MARIE	5649
The Wild Angels (Sou... | Davie ALLAN And The ...	1112
The Wild Angels, Vol... | Davie ALLAN And The ...	6636
Wild Animal | VANITY	5619
The Wild Bunch | SOUNDTRACK-MOVIE	13424
Wild Cherry | WILD CHERRY	1010
Wilder | TEARDROP EXPLODES	12489
Wilderness | C.W. McCALL	11101
Wildest Organ In Town! | Billy PRESTON	9963
Wild Exhibitions | Walter EGAN	13586
Wild-Eyed Dream | Ricky Van SHELTON	4358
Wild-Eyed Southern Boys | .38 SPECIAL	970
Wildflowers | Judy COLLINS	583
Wild Frontier | Gary MOORE	8933
Wild Gift | X	11303
The Wild Heart | Stevie NICKS	706
Wild Heart Of The Young | Karla BONOFF	3335
Wild Honey | BEACH BOYS	3492
Wild Honey & 20/20 | BEACH BOYS	5492
Wild Horses/Rock Steady | Johnny HAMMOND	11483
Wild In The Streets | HELIX	13461
Wild In The Streets | SOUNDTRACK-MOVIE	1538
Wild Is The Wind | Nina SIMONE	8586
Wild Life | Paul McCARTNEY & WIN...	1901
The Wild Places | Duncan BROWNE	11729
Wild Planet | The B-52s	2385
Wild Romance | Herb ALPERT	10305
Wildside | LOVERBOY	4592
Wild Streak | Hank WILLIAMS Jr.	4769
Wild Tales | Graham NASH	4508
The Wild, The Innocent ... | Bruce SPRINGSTEEN	4006
The Wild The Willing And The Innocent | UFO	7205
Wild Thing | The TROGGS	5046
Wild Things! | The VENTURES	3464
Wild Things Run Fast | Joni MITCHELL	3578
Wild Weekend | NRBQ	13578
Wild West | Dottie WEST	7835
Wild, Wild West | ESCAPE CLUB	2211
Will And The Kill | WILL And The KILL	9885
William Russo: Three ... [A] | SIEGEL-SCHWALL Band	7278
William Russo: Three... [A] | SAN FRANCISCO Symph...	7278
Willie & The Poor Bo... | WILLIE & The POOR BO...	8210
Willie Mitchell Live | Willie MITCHELL	11923
Willie Nelson And Family Li... | Willie NELSON	2202
Willie Nelson Live | Willie NELSON	10828

Title | Act	Rank
Willie Nelson's Greatest Hi... | Willie NELSON	1243
Willie Nelson Sings Kristof... | Willie NELSON	3307
Willie Nile | Willie NILE	10468
Willie Remembers.. | RARE EARTH	5722
Will O' The Wisp | Leon RUSSELL	2083
Will Power | Joe JACKSON	10185
Will The Circle Be Unbrok... | NITTY GRITTY DIRT BA...	3791
Will The Circle Be Unbroken Vol. 2 | NITTY GRITTY DIR...	7979
Will To Power | WILL TO POWER	4813
Willy And The Poorbo... | CREEDENCE CLEARWATER...	279
Will You Be Staying Af... | PEPPERMINT RAINBOW	7554
Wilmer & The Dukes | WILMER And The DUKES	12444
Wilson Pickett In Philadel... | Wilson PICKETT	5031
Wilson Pickett's Greatest ... | Wilson PICKETT	11348
Winchester Cathedral | Lawrence WELK	1359
Winchester Cathedral | NEW VAUDEVILLE BAND	1223
Winchester Cathedral | PALM BEACH BAND BOYS	13501
Wind & Wuthering | GENESIS	2678
Windfall | Rick NELSON	12880
Windham Hill Piano Sampler | VARIOUS ARTISTS	10922
Windham Hill Records Sampler '84 | VARIOUS ARTI...	6333
Windham Hill Records Sampler '86 | VARIOUS ARTI...	6827
Windham Hill Records Sampler '88 | VARIOUS ARTI...	7891
Windham Hill Records Sampler '89 | VARIOUS ARTI...	12640
The Wind In The Willo... | WIND IN THE WILLOWS	13235
Windjammer | Freddie HUBBARD	7316
The Windmills Are Weakening | Bob NEWHART	10927
The Windmills Of You... | Billy VAUGHN and His...	5697
The Windmills Of Your Mind | Ed AMES	10759
Windmills Of Your Mi... | Percy FAITH His Orch...	12657
Windmills Of Your Mind | Jimmie RODGERS	12298
Wind Of Change | Peter FRAMPTON	11675
Wind On The Water | David CROSBY/Graham ...	1276
Window Of A Child | SEAWIND	9745
Windows | Charlie DANIELS Band	3825
Windows And Walls | Dan FOGELBERG	2376
The Windows Of The World | Dionne WARWICK	2973
Winds Of Change | JEFFERSON AIRPLANE/S...	2347
Winds Of Change | The ANIMALS/Eric BUR...	4670
Windsong | John DENVER	236
Windsong | Randy CRAWFORD	10000
Winelight | Grover WASHINGTON Jr...	504
Winger | WINGER	758
Wingless Angels | John STEWART	10659
Wings At The Speed O... | Paul McCARTNEY & WIN...	138
Wings Greatest | Paul McCARTNEY & WIN...	3617
Wings Of Love | The TEMPTATIONS	3079
Wings Over America | Paul McCARTNEY & WIN...	528
Wings Upon Your Horns | Loretta LYNN	9060
Win, Lose Or Draw | ALLMAN BROTHERS Band	1827
Winner In You | Patti LaBELLE	819
Winners | BROTHERS JOHNSON	5496
Winners | KLEEER	9512
Winners | VARIOUS ARTISTS	7881
Winner Takes All | ISLEY BROTHERS	2548
Winning Combination | Donny & Marie OSMOND	7921
The Winning Hand | VARIOUS ARTISTS	8216
Winter Into Spring | George WINSTON	6964
A Winter's Solstice | VARIOUS ARTISTS	7112
A Winter's Solstice II | VARIOUS ARTISTS	9468
Winter World Of Love | Billy VAUGHN and His...	13464
Winwood | Steve WINWOOD	7710
Wipe The Windows-Che... | ALLMAN BROTHERS Band	7252
Wired | Jeff BECK	1956
Wired For Sound | Cliff RICHARD	11008
Wire Fire | SAVOY BROWN	10334

Title | Act	Rank
Wise Guy | KID CREOLE & The COC...	9712
Wishbone Four | WISHBONE ASH	4895
Wishes | Jon BUTCHER AXIS	5206
Wishful Thinking | Earl KLUGH	5313
Wish It Would Rain | The TEMPTATIONS	1335
Wish Me A Rainbow | Gunter KALLMANN Chor...	9465
Wish Someone Would Care | Irma THOMAS	9334
Wish You Were Here | BADFINGER	10374
Wish You Were Here | PINK FLOYD	543
Witch Doctor | INSTANT FUNK	7784
Witchdoctor | SIDEWINDERS	12260
Witch Queen | WITCH QUEEN	11108
With A Little Help From My Fri... | Joe COCKER	2184
With A Lot O' Soul | The TEMPTATIONS	1391
With A Taste Of Honey | Morgana KING	7685
With Everything I Feel In... | Aretha FRANKLIN	5345
With Friends And Neighbors | Alex TAYLOR	13412
With Love | Bobby VINTON	9540
With Love | Roger WHITTAKER	13148
With Love | Tony BENNETT	9168
With Love, Bobby | Bobby SHERMAN	2065
With Love - Cher | CHER	5540
With Love, From Lynn | Lynn ANDERSON	13532
With Love, Jerry Vale | Jerry VALE	13451
...With Love/The Seductive... | Boots RANDOLPH	5027
Without A Song | Willie NELSON	4282
Without Her | Jack JONES	10333
Without You | Robert GOULET	6778
Without You In My Life | Tyrone DAVIS	12152
With Sympathy | MINISTRY	7986
With The Naked Eye | Greg KIHN Band	8160
With You | Stacy LATTISAW	4855
Witness | SPOOKY TOOTH	7889
Wives And Lovers | Jack JONES	1284
The Wiz | ORIGINAL CAST	4253
The Wiz | SOUNDTRACK-MOVIE	4076
A Wizard/A True Star | Todd RUNDGREN	6429
Wizard Island | Jeff LORBER	8665
The Wizard Of Oz | MECO	6298
Wolf Creek Pass | C.W. McCALL	9083
The Womack "Live" | Bobby WOMACK	12430
Woman | PETER And GORDON	6297
Woman Across The River | Freddie KING	10420
Woman In Flames | CHAMPAIGN	13202
The Woman In Red (Soundtrac... | Stevie WONDER	947
A Woman Needs Love | Ray PARKER Jr./RAYDI...	1400
Woman Of The World / To Make... | Loretta LYNN	11325
Woman Of The Year | ORIGINAL CAST	13618
Woman Out Of Control | Ray PARKER Jr./RAYDI...	4041
A Woman's Got The Power | The A's	10703
A Woman's Point Of View | Shirley MURDOCK	8982
Woman To Woman | Shirley BROWN	7828
Woman, Woman | Gary PUCKETT And The...	2291
Woman, Woman | Robert GOULET	8612
Women And Children First | VAN HALEN	1082
The Womenfolk | The WOMENFOLK	10668
Women's Love Rights | Laura LEE	8166
Wonderful | Rick JAMES	10947
Wonderful! Wonderful! | Lawrence WELK	4143
Wonderfulness | Bill COSBY	208
The Wonderful World Of Andy... | Andy WILLIAMS	1920
The Wonderful World ... | Antonio Carlos JOBIM	6327
The Wonderful World Of Julie... | Julie LONDON	11611
The Wonderful World Of Make... | Johnny MATHIS	8370
Wonderland | BIG COUNTRY	6947
The Wonder Of You | The SANDPIPERS	12434

Title | Act	Rank
Wonders Of The Wine | David HOUSTON	12492
Wonderwall Music | George HARRISON	4229
Wonderworld | URIAH HEEP	4304
The Wondrous World Of Sonny ... | SONNY & CHER	3786
Won't Be Blue Anymore | Dan SEALS	6546
Woodstock | SOUNDTRACK-MOVIE	75
Woodstock Two | SOUNDTRACK-MOVIE	1941
Woody Allen | Woody ALLEN	7405
Woody Herman: 1964 | Woody HERMAN	12977
Wooly Bully | SAM THE SHAM And The...	4290
The Word Is Out | Jermaine STEWART	7892
Word Of Mouth | Jaco PASTORIUS	12263
Word Of Mouth | MERRYWEATHER & FRIEN...	13619
Word Of Mouth | The KINKS	4976
Word Of Mouth | Toni BASIL	2536
Word Pictures Featuring A... | Bobby GOLDSBORO	7016
Words And Music | Roger MILLER	7669
Words Of Earnest | GOOSE CREEK SYMPHONY	10497
Words We Can Dance To | Steve GOODMAN	12161
Word Up! | CAMEO	927
Workbook | Bob MOULD	8687
Workers Playtime | Billy BRAGG	13837
Working Class Dog | Rick SPRINGFIELD	321
Working Girl | SOUNDTRACK-MOVIE	5387
Workingman's Dead | GRATEFUL DEAD	2296
Working My Way Back To You | 4 SEASONS	5642
Workin' It Back | Teddy PENDERGRASS	7096
Workin' On A Groovy Thin... | Mongo SANTAMARIA	13522
Workin' Overtime | Diana ROSS	10231
Workin' Together | Ike & Tina TURNER	2008
The Works | QUEEN	3245
Works | PINK FLOYD	7958
Works, Volume 1 | EMERSON, LAKE & PALM...	1527
Works, Volume 2 | EMERSON, LAKE & PALM...	4593
The World According To Me | Jackie MASON	10173
World Anthem | MAHOGANY RUSH	13298
World In Motion | Jackson BROWNE	5186
The World Is A Ghetto | WAR	242
World Machine | LEVEL 42	2057
The World Of Boots Randolp... | Boots RANDOLPH	10013
World Of Country Music | VARIOUS ARTISTS	9735
The World Of Johnny Cash | Johnny CASH	3709
The World Of Lynn Anderson | Lynn ANDERSON	12265
The World Of Mantovani | MANTOVANI	6348
The World Of Miriam Makeba | Miriam MAKEBA	8368
A World Of Our Own | The SEEKERS	10316
The World Of Tammy Wynette | Tammy WYNETTE	12401
World Of Wonders | Bruce COCKBURN	10411
Worlds Apart | SAGA	2280
Worlds Away | PABLO CRUISE	855
The World's Greatest... | Doug E. FRESH & The ...	7560
The World's Greatest Interna... | Petula CLARK	9565
The World We Knew | Bert KAEMPFERT And H...	9892
Elvis-World Wide 50 Gold Aw... | Elvis PRESLEY	3173
World Wide Live | SCORPIONS	1522
The World Within | Stix HOOPER	11652
A World Without Love | PETER And GORDON	4866
The Worm | Jimmy McGRIFF	7472
The Worst Of Jeffers... | JEFFERSON AIRPLANE/S...	1281
Worth The Wait | PEACHES & HERB	9695
Would You Lay With Me (In A ... | Tanya TUCKER	11200
Would You Take Another Ch... | Jerry Lee LEWIS	7416
Wovoka | REDBONE	5854
Wow! | BANANARAMA	4329
Wow | MOBY GRAPE	2637
Wrabit | WRABIT	10511

Title	Act	Rank
Wrap Around Joy	Carole KING	974
Wrap Your Arms Around Me	Agnetha FALTSKOG	8456
Wrap Your Body	ONE WAY	11091
The Wrestling Album	VARIOUS ARTISTS	6501
Writer: Carole King	Carole KING	4497
Wrong End Of The Rainbow	Tom RUSH	8345
WWII	Waylon JENNINGS & Wi...	5059
Wynton Marsalis	Wynton MARSALIS	11891

X

Title	Act	Rank
Xanadu (Soundtrack) [A]	ELECTRIC LIGHT ORCHE...	793
Xanadu (Soundtrack) [A]	Olivia NEWTON-JOHN	793
XL-1	Pete SHELLEY	11796
X-Multiplies	YELLOW MAGIC ORCHEST...	13187
X-Periment	The SYSTEM	12627
X-Rated	BLACK OAK ARKANSAS	6703
X-Static	Daryl HALL & John OA...	2900
X2	TIMES TWO	9329
XYZ	XYZ	6440

Y

Title	Act	Rank
Yakety Revisited	Boots RANDOLPH	6509
Y'all Come Back Saloon	OAK RIDGE BOYS	8845
The Yama Yama Man	George SEGAL	13783
The Yardbirds/Featuring Per...	The YARDBIRDS	11094
Yardbirds Greatest Hits	The YARDBIRDS	2474
The Yard Went On Forever.....	Richard HARRIS	3089
Yeah!	BROWNSVILLE STATION	7053
Yeah!!!	Aretha FRANKLIN	9119
Yearbooks And Yesterdays	Jeannie C. RILEY	12133
Year Of Sunday	SEALS & CROFTS	6871
Year Of The Cat	Al STEWART	590
Years Ago	STATLER BROTHERS	8093
Years Gone By	Albert KING	10531
The Years Of Decay	OVERKILL	11291
The Year 2000	The O'JAYS	4498
Yeh Yeh	Georgie FAME	12228
The Yellow And Black Attack	STRYPER	6535
Yellow Fever	HOT TUNA	8459
Yellow Magic Orchest...	YELLOW MAGIC ORCHEST...	5835
Yellow Moon	NEVILLE BROTHERS	4938
Yellow River	CHRISTIE	8407
The Yellow Rolls-Royce	SOUNDTRACK-MOVIE	8107
Yellow Submarine (Soundtrack)	The BEATLES	899
Ye-Me-Le	Sergio MENDES And BR...	6010
Yentl (Soundtrack)	Barbra STREISAND	2015
Yer' Album	JAMES GANG	4702
The Yes Album	YES	2103
Yes, Giorgio	Luciano PAVAROTTI	12528
Yes, I'm Ready	Barbara MASON	9723
Yes It's You Lady	Smokey ROBINSON	4352
Yesshows	YES	5469
Yessongs	YES	1884
"Yesterday" And Today	The BEATLES	790
Yesterday Once More	CARPENTERS	10613
Yesterdays	YES	3274
Yesterday's Dreams	FOUR TOPS	6230
Yesterday's Gone	CHAD & JEREMY	2497
Yesterday's Love Songs/Today...	Nancy WILSON	994
Yesterday, Today & Tomorrow	SPINNERS	4449
Yesterday, When I Was Young	Roy CLARK	4192
Yestergroovin'	Chet ATKINS	10754
The Yiddish Are Coming! T...	VARIOUS ARTISTS	12040
Yipes!!	YIPES!!	12389
Yo! Bum Rush The Show	PUBLIC ENEMY	8681
Yo Frankie	DION	7400

Title	Act	Rank
Yoko Ono/Plastic Ono Band	Yoko ONO	12944
You	Aretha FRANKLIN	6806
You Ain't Heard Noth...	Danny DAVIS And The ...	7123
You Ain't Woman Enough	Loretta LYNN	10034
You And I	O'BRYAN	6129
You & Me	Jerry BUTLER	12058
You And Me	Rockie ROBBINS	5892
You And Me Both	YAZ	7141
You Are Beautiful	The STYLISTICS	7388
You Are My Starship	Norman CONNORS	3612
You Are The Sunshine...	Ray CONNIFF & His Or...	12205
You Are What You Is	Frank ZAPPA	8790
You Asked For It!	FERRANTE & TEICHER	5039
You Bought It-You Name It	Joe WALSH	5765
You Break It...You B...	Michael STANLEY Band	12903
You Broke My Heart In 17 Pl...	Tracey ULLMAN	4047
You Broke My Heart So I Bust...	SPOOKY TOOTH	6576
You Can Dance	MADONNA	2386
You Can't Argue With A Sick Min...	Joe WALSH	2671
You Can't Fight Fash...	Michael STANLEY Band	6031
You Can't Stop Rock 'N' Ro...	TWISTED SISTER	8648
You Can Tune A Piano But Y...	REO SPEEDWAGON	2265
You Could Have Been With Me	Sheena EASTON	2588
You Devil You	Flip WILSON	9949
You Don't Bring Me Flowers	Neil DIAMOND	1217
You Don't Have To Be A Bab...	The CARAVELLES	11347
You Don't Have To Be Jewi...	VARIOUS ARTISTS	1948
(You Don't Have To) ...	Gary LEWIS And The P...	6510
You Don't Have To Say Y...	Dusty SPRINGFIELD	7655
You Don't Have To Say You Love...	Jerry VALE	11188
You Don't Know Me	Mickey GILLEY	11227
You Don't Mess Around With Jim	Jim CROCE	117
You Don't Stand A Ch...	Jimmy JAMES & The VA...	7827
You Fooled Me	GREY And HANKS	8041
You Gave Me A Mountain	Frankie LAINE	5225
You Got-ta Have A License	Porter WAGONER	13468
You Gotta Say Yes To Another Excess	YELLO	12995
You Gotta Wash Your Ass	Redd FOXX	7224
You Got What It Takes	Dave CLARK Five	12289
You Had To Be There	Jimmy BUFFETT	5334
You Know How To Love Me	Phyllis HYMAN	4258
You Lay So Easy On My Mind	Andy WILLIAMS	11285
You Light Up My Life	Debby BOONE	1464
You Light Up My Life	Johnny MATHIS	1571
You Light Up My Life	SOUNDTRACK-MOVIE	3500
You'll Never Know	Rodney FRANKLIN	7527
You'll Never Walk Alone	Elvis PRESLEY	6235
You'll Never Walk Alone	The LETTERMEN	7342
You Make Me Feel So ...	Ray CONNIFF & His Or...	6791
You, Me And He	MTUME	6863
You Need Someone To ...	NEW CHRISTY MINSTREL...	13557
You Never Know Who Your Friends...	Al KOOPER	9906
Young Americans	David BOWIE	825
Young And Rich	The TUBES	4746
Youngblood	SOUNDTRACK-MOVIE	12102
Youngblood	WAR	8367
The Youngbloods	The YOUNGBLOODS	10239
Younger Girl	The CRITTERS	12741
Younger Than Yesterday	The BYRDS	3676
Youngest In Charge	SPECIAL ED	4942
The Youngest Teenager	Moms MABLEY	12423
Young Frankenstein	SOUNDTRACK-MOVIE	8707
Young, Gifted And Black	Aretha FRANKLIN	1258
Young Girl	Gary PUCKETT And The...	1714
Young Hearts Run Free	Candi STATON	7083
Young, Loud And Snotty	DEAD BOYS	12748

Title	Act	Rank
Young Man Running	Corey HART	9631
The Young Mods' Forgotten...	The IMPRESSIONS	5867
The Young Rascals	RASCALS/YOUNG RASCAL...	1399
You Only Live Twice	SOUNDTRACK-MOVIE	3270
Your All-Time Country Favorites	John GARY	6767
Your All-Time Favorite Songs	John GARY	3496
Your Cheatin' Heart (So...	Hank WILLIAMS Jr.	2285
You're A Big Boy Now (Sou...	LOVIN' SPOONFUL	11509
You're A Good Man, Charlie ...	ORIGINAL CAST	11735
You're All I Need	Marvin GAYE & Tammi ...	4682
You Really Got Me	The KINKS	3819
You're Gettin' Even While I...	J. GEILS Band	7802
You're Gonna' Get It	Tom PETTY And The HE...	2597
You're Good For Me	Lou RAWLS	11673
You're My Man	Lynn ANDERSON	6316
You're Never Alone With A Schi...	Ian HUNTER	2756
You're Not Alone	Roy BUCHANAN	9093
You're Only Lonely	J.D. SOUTHER	4157
You're So Beautiful	Charles WRIGHT And T...	8290
You're The One For Me	"D" TRAIN	9672
You're Under Arrest	Miles DAVIS	9163
Your Good Thing	Lou RAWLS	13709
Your Mama Won't Like Me	Suzi QUATRO	10566
Your Mother's Prayer	Buck OWENS	13693
Your Move	AMERICA	7491
Your Saving Grace	Steve MILLER Band	4072
Yours Forever	ATLANTIC STARR	6161
Yours Forever More	FOREVER MORE	12965
Your Squaw Is On The Warpath	Loretta LYNN	11031
Yours Truly	Tom BROWNE	6967
Your Tender Loving Care	Buck OWENS	11631
Your Wish Is My Command	LAKESIDE	4787
You Send Me	Roy AYERS	5123
You Shouldn't-Nuf Bit Fish	George CLINTON	7313
You Smile-The Song B...	Herb ALPERT & The TI...	6339
The Youth Of Today	MUSICAL YOUTH	3468
Youthquake	DEAD OR ALIVE	3763
You Turn Me On!	Ian WHITCOMB	8291
You've Got A Friend	Andy WILLIAMS	5411
You've Got A Friend	Johnny MATHIS	7006
You've Got A Friend	Mark LINDSAY	13121
You've Got A Good Love Comi...	Lee GREENWOOD	8452
You've Got It Bad Girl	Quincy JONES	5459
You've Got The Power	THIRD WORLD	5094
You've Lost That Lovin...	RIGHTEOUS BROTHERS	848
You've Made Me So Very Happy	Lou RAWLS	12731
You've Never Been This Far ...	Conway TWITTY	9120
You Wanna Dance With Me?	Jody WATLEY	7638
You Want It, You Got It	Bryan ADAMS	8053
You Want It, You Got It	DETROIT EMERALDS	6372
You Were Only Fooling	Vic DAMONE	8044
You Were On My Mind	WE FIVE	3473
You Won't Believe Your Ears	Wes HARRISON	10032
YoYo	BOURGEOIS TAGG	6140
Y U I Orta [A]	Ian HUNTER	8159
Y U I Orta [A]	Mick RONSON	8159
Yusef Lateef's Detroit	Yusef LATEEF	12004
Yvonne	Yvonne ELLIMAN	11636

Z

Title	Act	Rank
Z	SOUNDTRACK-MOVIE	9228
The Zagora	LOOSE ENDS	6644
Zapp	ZAPP	3047
Zappa In New York	Frank ZAPPA	6932
Zapp III	ZAPP	5038
Zapp II	ZAPP	3914

Title | Act	Rank
Zebop! | SANTANA	806
Zebra | ZEBRA	3440
Zeno | ZENO	8663
Zenyatta Mondatta | The POLICE	153
Zephyr | ZEPHYR	3323

Title | Act	Rank
Ziggy Stardust-The Motion Pic... | David BOWIE	7285
Zig Zag | The HOOTERS	7418
Zigzagging Through Ghostlan... | The RADIATORS	9138
Zig-Zag Walk | FOGHAT	13715
Zodiac: Cosmic Sounds, Th... | VARIOUS ARTISTS	9327

Title | Act	Rank
The Zombies | The ZOMBIES	4605
Zoot Allures | Frank ZAPPA	5806
Zorba | ORIGINAL CAST	10944
Zorba The Greek | SOUNDTRACK-MOVIE	1051
Zuma | Neil YOUNG	2809

The Albums Special Lists

100 Highest Charting Movie Soundtracks

50 Highest Charting Original Cast

200 Highest Charting Greatest Hits/Compilations

200 Highest Charting Live Albums

50 Highest Charting Various Artists

100 Weeks or More On Chart

20 Weeks or More in Top 10

40 Weeks or More in Top 40

Top 100 Albums Entering Each Year

Top 50 Albums By Raw Score In Each Year

Most Points Only From Weeks in Top 5 or Top 10

Number 1 Albums by Weeks

50 Highest Charting Albums to Miss the Weekly Top 5

50 Lowest Scoring Number 1 Albums

Week-to-Week Lifecycle Charts of Top 25 Albums

100 Highest Charting Soundtracks

Rank. Title - Act (Entry Year)	Score
1. **The Sound Of Music** - Soundtrack (65)	29435
2. **Doctor Zhivago** - Soundtrack (66)	21854
3. **Saturday Night Fever** - Bee Gees (77)	19144
4. **Dirty Dancing** - Soundtrack (87)	16684
5. **Mary Poppins** - Soundtrack (64)	14811
6. **Grease** - Soundtrack (78)	13745
7. **Purple Rain** - Prince And The Revolution (84)	13717
8. **The Graduate** - Simon & Garfunkel (68)	11898
9. **Woodstock** - Soundtrack (70)	11782
10. **My Fair Lady** - Soundtrack (64)	9912
11. **Flashdance** - Soundtrack (83)	9902
12. **That's The Way Of The World** - Earth, Wind & Fire (75)	9789
13. **Romeo & Juliet** - Soundtrack (69)	9730
14. **A Hard Day's Night** - The Beatles (64)	9013
15. **A Star Is Born** - Barbra Streisand & Kris Kristofferson (76)	8852
16. **Easy Rider** - Soundtrack (69)	8708
17. **Shaft** - Isaac Hayes (71)	8587
18. **The Jazz Singer** - Neil Diamond (80)	8275
19. **Top Gun** - Soundtrack (86)	8187
20. **Magical Mystery Tour** - The Beatles (67)	8172
21. **Beaches** - Bette Midler (89)	8076
22. **Footloose** - Soundtrack (84)	7852
23. **Funny Girl** - Barbra Streisand (68)	7627
24. **The Sting** - Marvin Hamlisch (74)	7349
25. **Help!** - The Beatles (65)	6986
26. **Let It Be** - The Beatles (70)	6889
27. **A Man And A Woman** - Soundtrack (66)	6866
28. **Goldfinger** - Soundtrack (64)	6654
29. **Beverly Hills Cop** - Soundtrack (85)	6652
30. **Superfly** - Curtis Mayfield (72)	6533
31. **Love Story** - Soundtrack (71)	6436
32. **American Graffiti** - Soundtrack (73)	6407
33. **Cocktail** - Soundtrack (88)	6310
34. **My Name Is Barbra** - Barbra Streisand (65)	6304
35. **Lady Sings The Blues** - Diana Ross (72)	6201
36. **Miami Vice** - TV Soundtrack (85)	6180
37. **Chariots Of Fire** - Vangelis (81)	6161
38. **Star Wars** - Soundtrack (77)	6071
39. **TCB** - Diana Ross & The Supremes And The Temptations (68)	6057
40. **Rattle And Hum** - U2 (88)	5894
41. **More Dirty Dancing** - Soundtrack (88)	5578
42. **Urban Cowboy** - Soundtrack (80)	5546
43. **The Big Chill** - Soundtrack (83)	5525
44. **The Pink Panther** - Henry Mancini And His Orchestra (64)	5336
45. **Tommy** - Soundtrack (75)	5315
46. **Mad Dogs & Englishmen** - Joe Cocker (70)	4992
47. **Butch Cassidy And The Sundance Kid** - Soundtrack (69)	4935
48. **Batman** - Prince (89)	4618
49. **2001: A Space Odyssey** - Soundtrack (68)	4561
50. **Camelot** - Soundtrack (67)	4487
51. **The Good, The Bad And The Ugly** - Soundtrack (68)	4465
52. **Fame** - Soundtrack (80)	4319
53. **La Bamba** - Los Lobos (87)	4269
54. **Oliver!** - Soundtrack (68)	4128
55. **Rocky** - Soundtrack (77)	4092
56. **Xanadu** - Olivia Newton-John/Electric Light Orchestra (80)	4087
57. **Midnight Cowboy** - Soundtrack (69)	3978
58. **Jonathan Livingston Seagull** - Neil Diamond (73)	3874
59. **The Song Remains The Same** - Led Zeppelin (76)	3843
60. **The Rose** - Bette Midler (79)	3819
61. **Yellow Submarine** - The Beatles (69)	3755
62. **Fiddler On The Roof** - Soundtrack (71)	3657
63. **The Empire Strikes Back** - Soundtrack (80)	3643
64. **The Woman In Red** - Stevie Wonder (84)	3577
65. **Eddie & The Cruisers** - John Cafferty & The Beaver Brown Band (83)	3552
66. **Color Me Barbra** - Barbra Streisand (66)	3524
67. **Roustabout** - Elvis Presley (64)	3337
68. **Zorba The Greek** - Soundtrack (65)	3295
69. **Charade** - Henry Mancini And His Orchestra (63)	3236
70. **Sgt. Pepper's Lonely Hearts Club Band** - Soundtrack (78)	3219
71. **The Wild Angels** - Davie Allan And The Arrows (66)	3165
72. **Parade: Music From The Motion Picture Under The Cherry Moon** - Prince And The Revolution (86)	3097
73. **Cabaret** - Soundtrack (72)	3000
74. **FM** - Soundtrack (78)	2902
75. **Pretty In Pink** - Soundtrack (86)	2899
76. **Fun In Acapulco** - Elvis Presley (63)	2835
77. **Thank God It's Friday** - Soundtrack (78)	2815
78. **Honeysuckle Rose** - Willie Nelson & Family (80)	2735
79. **Ghostbusters** - Soundtrack (84)	2711
80. **Thoroughly Modern Millie** - Soundtrack (67)	2607
81. **American Gigolo** - Soundtrack (80)	2595
82. **All In The Family** - TV Soundtrack (71)	2564
83. **Beverly Hills Cop II** - Soundtrack (87)	2457
84. **Paint Your Wagon** - Soundtrack (69)	2453
85. **Wild In The Streets** - Soundtrack (68)	2424
86. **Funny Lady** - Barbra Streisand (75)	2399
87. **The Godfather** - Soundtrack (72)	2381
88. **Good Morning, Vietnam** - Soundtrack (88)	2363
89. **Girl Happy** - Elvis Presley (65)	2361
90. **Stop Making Sense** - Talking Heads (84)	2336
91. **The Sesame Street Book & Record** - TV Soundtrack (70)	2333
92. **The Kids Are Alright** - The Who (79)	2320
93. **Endless Love** - Soundtrack (81)	2231
94. **When Harry Met Sally** - Harry Connick Jr. (89)	2220
95. **Heavy Metal** - Soundtrack (81)	2195
96. **Kissin' Cousins** - Elvis Presley (64)	2182
97. **Rocky IV** - Soundtrack (85)	2167
98. **Pat Garrett & Billy The Kid** - Bob Dylan (73)	2130
99. **Breakin'** - Soundtrack (84)	2129
100. **Staying Alive** - Bee Gees (83)	2100

50 Highest Charting Original Casts

Rank. Title - Act (Entry Year)	Score
1. **Hair** - Original Cast (68)	18698
2. **Hello, Dolly!** - Original Cast (64)	10990
3. **Fiddler On The Roof** - Original Cast (64)	9072
4. **Funny Girl (Original Cast)** - Barbra Streisand (64)	6318
5. **Man Of La Mancha** - Original Cast (66)	4961
6. **The Phantom Of The Opera** - Original London Cast Recording (87)	4006
7. **Godspell** - Original Cast Recording (71)	3506
8. **Mame** - Original Cast (66)	2733
9. **Dreamgirls** - Original Cast (82)	2076
10. **Cabaret** - Original Cast (67)	1286
11. **On A Clear Day You Can See Forever** - Original Cast (65)	871
12. **Annie** - Original Cast (77)	784
13. **The Roar Of The Greasepaint-The Smell Of The Crowd** - Original Cast (65)	761
14. **The Wiz** - Original Cast (75)	746
15. **A Chorus Line** - Original Cast (75)	710
16. **The Girl Who Came To Supper** - Original Cast (64)	570
17. **No, No, Nanette** - Original Cast (71)	565
18. **Golden Boy** - Original Cast (64)	564
19. **Jesus Christ Superstar** - Original Broadway Cast Recording (72)	560
20. **Cats** - Original Broadway Cast Recording (83)	536
21. **110 In The Shade** - Original Cast (64)	511
22. **Here's Love** - Original Cast (63)	503
23. **What Makes Sammy Run?** - Original Cast (64)	453
24. **Cats** - Original London Cast (82)	451
25. **High Spirits** - Original Cast (64)	384
26. **Promises, Promises** - Original Cast (69)	372
27. **I Do! I Do!** - Original Cast (67)	362
28. **La Cage Aux Folles** - Original Cast (83)	352
29. **Evita** - Original Cast (80)	332
30. **Sweet Charity** - Original Cast (66)	322
31. **Sweeney Todd-The Demon Barber Of Fleet Street** - Original Cast (79)	288
32. **Chicago** - Original Cast (75)	275
33. **A Little Night Music** - Original Cast (73)	259
34. **The Catherine Wheel (Original Cast)** - David Byrne (81)	237
35. **Half A Sixpence** - Original Cast (65)	220
36. **Les Miserables** - Original London Cast Recording (87)	211
37. **42nd Street** - Original Cast (81)	195
38. **Do I Hear A Waltz?** - Original Cast (65)	182
39. **The Apple Tree** - Original Cast (66)	175
40. **Dear World** - Original Cast (69)	172
41. **Hamlet** - Original Cast (64)	171
42. **Lena Horne: The Lady And Her Music (Original Cast)** - Lena Horne (81)	166
43. **Pippin** - Original Cast (73)	159
44. **Cats** - Selections from Original Broadway Cast (83)	137
45. **Flora, The Red Menace** - Original Cast (65)	136
46. **Annie Get Your Gun** - Original Cast (66)	135
47. **Fade Out-Fade In** - Original Cast (64)	133
48. **Les Miserables** - Original Broadway Cast Recording (87)	125
49. **Sunday In The Park With George** - Original Broadway Cast Recording (84)	122
50. **Skyscraper** - Original Cast (66)	116

200 Highest Charting Greatest Hits/Compilations

Rank. Title - Act (Entry Year)	Score
1. **John Denver's Greatest Hits** - John Denver (73)	15297
2. **Kenny Rogers' Greatest Hits** - Kenny Rogers (80)	12108
3. **Their Greatest Hits 1971-1975** - Eagles (76)	12106
4. **Diana Ross And The Supremes Greatest Hits** - Diana Ross & The Supremes (67)	11993
5. **The Temptations Greatest Hits** - The Temptations (66)	10179
6. **Hot Rocks 1964-1971** - The Rolling Stones (72)	9918
7. **Time Peace/The Rascals' Greatest Hits** The Rascals (68)	9593
8. **Elton John's Greatest Hits** - Elton John (74)	9369
9. **Greatest Hits** - Sly & The Family Stone (70)	8278
10. **The Beatles 1967-1970** - The Beatles (73)	8202
11. **Donovan's Greatest Hits** - Donovan (69)	7771
12. **Chicago IX: Chicago's Greatest Hits** - Chicago (75)	7717
13. **The Best Of The Animals** - The Animals (66)	7333
14. **Golden Bisquits** - Three Dog Night (71)	6926
15. **Endless Summer** - The Beach Boys (74)	6903
16. **The Best Of Bread** - Bread (73)	6903
17. **Greatest Hits** - The Association (68)	6883
18. **The Beatles 1962-1966** - The Beatles (73)	6830
19. **On The Radio: Greatest Hits: Volumes I & II** - Donna Summer (79)	6739
20. **History/America's Greatest Hits** - America (75)	6466
21. **The Best Of Herman's Hermits** - Herman's Hermits (65)	5995
22. **Best Of Cream** - Cream (69)	5962
23. **Big Hits (High Tide And Green Grass)** - The Rolling Stones (66)	5844
24. **Simon And Garfunkel's Greatest Hits** - Simon & Garfunkel (72)	5831
25. **The Four Tops Greatest Hits** - Four Tops (67)	5647
26. **Greatest Hits** - Linda Ronstadt (76)	5314
27. **Barbra Streisand's Greatest Hits, Volume 2** - Barbra Streisand (78)	5226
28. **Hey Jude** - The Beatles (70)	4999
29. **The Best Of The Lovin' Spoonful** - The Lovin' Spoonful (67)	4907
30. **Through The Past, Darkly (Big Hits Vol. 2)** - The Rolling Stones (69)	4827
31. **The Singles 1969-1973** - Carpenters (73)	4680
32. **Farewell To The First Golden Era** - The Mamas & The Papas (67)	4665
33. **Best Of The Doobies** - The Doobie Brothers (76)	4564
34. **Elvis' Golden Records Volume 3** - Elvis Presley (63)	4515
35. **Dionne Warwick's Golden Hits, Part One** - Dionne Warwick (67)	4514
36. **The Doors Greatest Hits** - The Doors (80)	4507
37. **Bee Gees Greatest** - Bee Gees (79)	4406
38. **The Best Of The Guess Who** - The Guess Who (71)	4389
39. **Photographs & Memories/ His Greatest Hits** - Jim Croce (74)	4349
40. **The 5th Dimension/Greatest Hits** - The 5th Dimension (70)	4338
41. **Living In The Past** - Jethro Tull (72)	4299
42. **Best Of Bee Gees** - Bee Gees (69)	4241
43. **Flowers** - The Rolling Stones (67)	4192
44. **Bob Dylan's Greatest Hits** - Bob Dylan (67)	4188
45. **Greatest Hits Vol. I & II** - Billy Joel (85)	4119
46. **"Yesterday" And Today** - The Beatles (66)	4104
47. **The Best Of Charley Pride** - Charley Pride (69)	4079
48. **The Best Of Earth, Wind & Fire, Vol. I** - Earth, Wind & Fire (78)	4044
49. **Olivia's Greatest Hits, Vol. 2** - Olivia Newton-John (82)	4032
50. **Smash Hits** - The Jimi Hendrix Experience (69)	4007
51. **History Of Eric Clapton** - Eric Clapton (72)	4002
52. **Greatest Hits** - Waylon Jennings (79)	3978
53. **Greatest Hits** - Barry Manilow (78)	3851
54. **Memories** - Barbra Streisand (81)	3838
55. **Greatest Hits** - Air Supply (83)	3820
56. **Golden Hits** - Roger Miller (65)	3805
57. **Rock 'N Soul Part 1** - Daryl Hall & John Oates (83)	3750
58. **The 4 Seasons' Gold Vault of Hits** - The 4 Seasons (65)	3741
59. **Temptations Greatest Hits II** - The Temptations (70)	3633
60. **Rock 'N' Roll Music** - The Beatles (76)	3564
61. **History Of Otis Redding** - Otis Redding (67)	3564
62. **Best Of The Beach Boys** - The Beach Boys (66)	3529
63. **Cat Stevens Greatest Hits** - Cat Stevens (75)	3509
64. **Helen Reddy's Greatest Hits** - Helen Reddy (75)	3481
65. **Journey's Greatest Hits** - Journey (88)	3252
66. **So Far** - Crosby, Stills, Nash & Young (74)	3250
67. **Greatest Hits** - Paul Revere & The Raiders (67)	3215
68. **The Dave Clark Five's Greatest Hits** - The Dave Clark Five (66)	3166
69. **Ann Murray's Greatest Hits** - Anne Murray (80)	3147
70. **Bob Dylan's Greatest Hits, Vol. II** - Bob Dylan (71)	3021
71. **The Kinks Greatest Hits!** - The Kinks (66)	2978
72. **The Turtles! Golden Hits** - The Turtles (67)	2929
73. **Willie Nelson's Greatest Hits (& Some That Will Be)** - Willie Nelson (81)	2922
74. **The Worst Of Jefferson Airplane** - Jefferson Airplane (70)	2830
75. **Spirit Of America** - The Beach Boys (75)	2808
76. **Golden Greats** - Gary Lewis And The Playboys (66)	2733
77. **The Best Of Al Hirt** - Al Hirt (65)	2719
78. **Greatest Hits** - Seals & Crofts (75)	2708
79. **Dance!...Ya Know It!** - Bobby Brown (89)	2707
80. **Gold & Platinum** - Lynyrd Skynyrd (79)	2678
81. **Greatest Hits** - War (76)	2664
82. **Jackson 5 Greatest Hits** - The Jacksons (72)	2634
83. **The Byrds' Greatest Hits** - The Byrds (67)	2607
84. **Dean Martin's Greatest Hits! Vol. 1** - Dean Martin (68)	2602
85. **Ten Years Of Gold** - Kenny Rogers (78)	2566
86. **The Best Of Luther Vandross... The Best Of Love** - Luther Vandross (89)	2564
87. **The Best Of Jim Reeves** - Jim Reeves (64)	2545
88. **Creedence Gold** - Creedence Clearwater Revival (72)	2531
89. **Greatest Hits, Vol. 2** - Smokey Robinson & The Miracles (68)	2524
90. **Aretha's Gold** - Aretha Franklin (69)	2486
91. **Changesonebowie** - David Bowie (76)	2467
92. **A Man And His Music** - Frank Sinatra (65)	2377
93. **More Hot Rocks (Big Hits & Fazed Cookies)** - The Rolling Stones (72)	2367
94. **Vital Idol** - Billy Idol (87)	2338
95. **Golden Grass** - The Grass Roots (68)	2292
96. **Crash Landing** - Jimi Hendrix (75)	2260
97. **Greatest Hits** - The Cars (85)	2244
98. **The Hollies' Greatest Hits** - The Hollies (67)	2243
99. **Golden Hits Of The 4 Seasons** - The 4 Seasons (63)	2218
100. **Legend** - Bob Marley And The Wailers (84)	2209
101. **10 Years Together/ The Best Of Peter, Paul And Mary** - Peter, Paul & Mary (70)	2209
102. **The George Benson Collection** - George Benson (81)	2205

Rank. Title - Act (Entry Year)	Score
103. **Tony's Greatest Hits, Volume III** - Tony Bennett (65)	2192
104. **Diana Ross' Greatest Hits** - Diana Ross (76)	2188
105. **The Best Of Tommy James & The Shondells** - Tommy James And The Shondells (69)	2162
106. **12 In A Roe/A Collection Of Tommy Roe's Greatest Hits** - Tommy Roe (69)	2145
107. **The Best Of Sonny & Cher** - Sonny & Cher (67)	2144
108. **2nd Vault Of Golden Hits** - The 4 Seasons (66)	2127
109. **Made In The Shade** - The Rolling Stones (75)	2123
110. **Greatest Hits/Live** - Heart (80)	2112
111. **Stevie Wonder's Original Musiquarium I** - Stevie Wonder (82)	2112
112. **Greatest Hits** - Queen (81)	2106
113. **Alice Cooper's Greatest Hits** - Alice Cooper (74)	2081
114. **Dan Fogelberg/Greatest Hits** - Dan Fogelberg (82)	2056
115. **Aretha's Greatest Hits** - Aretha Franklin (71)	2043
116. **Steppenwolf Gold/Their Great Hits** - Steppenwolf (71)	2035
117. **Olivia Newton-John's Greatest Hits** - Olivia Newton-John (77)	2002
118. **This Is The Moody Blues** - The Moody Blues (74)	2000
119. **Tammy's Greatest Hits** - Tammy Wynette (69)	1964
120. **Ole ELO** - Electric Light Orchestra (76)	1908
121. **Bobby Vinton's Greatest Hits** - Bobby Vinton (64)	1869
122. **Hits!** - Boz Scaggs (80)	1868
123. **Substance** - New Order (87)	1864
124. **A Touch Of Gold** - Johnny Rivers (69)	1863
125. **Times Of Your Life** - Paul Anka (75)	1862
126. **Santana's Greatest Hits** - Santana (74)	1831
127. **Shaved Fish** - John Lennon/Plastic Ono Band (75)	1819
128. **Greatest Hits** - Tony Orlando & Dawn (75)	1816
129. **Greatest Hits** - ABBA (76)	1814
130. **Then & Now... The Best Of The Monkees** - The Monkees (86)	1814
131. **John Denver's Greatest Hits, Volume 2** - John Denver (77)	1792
132. **Burning Love And Hits From His Movies, Volume 2** - Elvis Presley (72)	1789
133. **Records** - Foreigner (82)	1785
134. **Every Breath You Take-The Singles** - The Police (86)	1778
135. **M.U. The Best Of Jethro Tull** - Jethro Tull (76)	1768
136. **Neil Diamond/His 12 Greatest Hits** - Neil Diamond (74)	1754
137. **Greatest Hits On Earth** - The 5th Dimension (72)	1753
138. **Greatest Hits** - Alabama (86)	1740
139. **Greatest Hits** - James Taylor (76)	1710
140. **Metamorphosis** - The Rolling Stones (75)	1693
141. **Greatest Hits** - Fleetwood Mac (88)	1681
142. **Meaty Beaty Big And Bouncy** - The Who (71)	1680
143. **More Of Roy Orbison's Greatest Hits** - Roy Orbison (64)	1665
144. **Al Green/Greatest Hits** - Al Green (75)	1639
145. **Joy To The World-Their Greatest Hits** - Three Dog Night (74)	1638
146. **Mark, Don & Mel 1969-71** - Grand Funk Railroad (72)	1625
147. **You Can Dance** - Madonna (87)	1585
148. **The Best Of The Lettermen** - The Lettermen (66)	1573
149. **The Best Of Carly Simon** - Carly Simon (75)	1571
150. **Smashes, Thrashes & Hits** - KISS (88)	1558
151. **Greatest Hits** - Mary Wells (64)	1555
152. **Bert Kaempfert's Greatest Hits** - Bert Kaempfert And His Orchestra (66)	1545
153. **Greatest Hits, Etc.** - Paul Simon (77)	1544
154. **Twenty Greatest Hits** - Kenny Rogers (83)	1524
155. **Greatest Hits** - Ronnie Milsap (80)	1516
156. **Yardbirds Greatest Hits** - The Yardbirds (67)	1513
157. **The Best Of Wilson Pickett** - Wilson Pickett (67)	1510
158. **Dionne Warwick's Golden Hits, Part 2** - Dionne Warwick (69)	1504
159. **Greatest Hits** - The Judds (88)	1503
160. **Coda** - Led Zeppelin (82)	1495
161. **The Best Of Eddy Arnold** - Eddy Arnold (67)	1493
162. **Greatest Hits 1974-78** - The Steve Miller Band (78)	1469
163. **Elton John's Greatest Hits, Volume II** - Elton John (77)	1459
164. **The Partridge Family At Home With Their Greatest Hits** - The Partridge Family (72)	1437
165. **Blood, Sweat & Tears Greatest Hits** - Blood, Sweat & Tears (72)	1413
166. **Greatest Hits, Volume 2** - Linda Ronstadt (80)	1391
167. **Johnny Rivers' Golden Hits** - Johnny Rivers (66)	1388
168. **Greatest Hits From The Beginning** - The Miracles (65)	1381
169. **Greatest Hits** - Steely Dan (78)	1375
170. **Odds & Sods** - The Who (74)	1359
171. **The Best Of Herman's Hermits, Volume 2** - Herman's Hermits (66)	1339
172. **Love Songs** - The Beatles (77)	1319
173. **The Best Of Blondie** - Blondie (81)	1318
174. **Greatest Hits** - Stevie Wonder (68)	1317
175. **Dionne Warwick's Greatest Motion Picture Hits** - Dionne Warwick (69)	1296
176. **Standing On A Beach -- The Singles** - The Cure (86)	1287
177. **Barry White's Greatest Hits** - Barry White (75)	1277
178. **Recollections** - Judy Collins (69)	1273
179. **An Anthology** - Duane Allman (72)	1263
180. **By Request (The Best of Billy Vera & The Beaters)** - Billy Vera & The Beaters (86)	1239
181. **Chronicles** - Steve Winwood (87)	1238
182. **Greatest Hits** - Little River Band (82)	1237
183. **A Collection: Greatest Hits... And More** - Barbra Streisand (89)	1234
184. **Johnny Cash's Greatest Hits, Volume I** - Johnny Cash (67)	1231
185. **Commodores' Greatest Hits** - Commodores (78)	1220
186. **Diana Ross & The Supremes Greatest Hits, Volume 3** - Diana Ross & The Supremes (70)	1218
187. **Mrs. Miller's Greatest Hits** - Mrs. Miller (66)	1217
188. **13** - The Doors (70)	1204
189. **Best Of B.T.O. (So Far)** - Bachman-Turner Overdrive (76)	1203
190. **Greatest Hits** - The Righteous Brothers (67)	1203
191. **Andy Williams' Newest Hits** - Andy Williams (66)	1185
192. **Glen Campbell's Greatest Hits** - Glen Campbell (71)	1166
193. **The Best Of The Doors(2)** - The Doors (87)	1157
194. **Edizione D'Oro (The 4 Seasons Gold Edition-29 Gold Hits)** - The 4 Seasons (68)	1140
195. **Greatest Hits Of All Times** - Gene Pitney (66)	1138
196. **All The Great Hits** - Diana Ross (81)	1126
197. **Double Platinum** - KISS (78)	1125
198. **All The Best Cowboys Have Chinese Eyes** - Pete Townshend (82)	1124
199. **Rod Stewart Greatest Hits** - Rod Stewart (79)	1118
200. **Elvis-World Wide 50 Gold Award Hits, Vol. 1** - Elvis Presley (70)	1117

200 Highest Charting Live Albums

Rank. Title - Act (Entry Year)	Score
1. **Frampton Comes Alive!** - Peter Frampton (76)	20521
2. **Johnny Cash At San Quentin** - Johnny Cash (69)	11537
3. **Live And More** - Donna Summer (78)	8386
4. **Tom Jones Live In Las Vegas** - Tom Jones (69)	7828
5. **Johnny Cash At Folsom Prison** - Johnny Cash (68)	7728
6. **4 Way Street** - Crosby, Stills, Nash & Young (71)	6910
7. **Gratitude** - Earth, Wind & Fire (75)	6844
8. **Here At Last...Bee Gees...Live** - Bee Gees (77)	6803
9. **Barry Manilow Live** - Barry Manilow (77)	6736
10. **Cheap Trick At Budokan** - Cheap Trick (79)	6482
11. **Was Captured Live At The Forum** - Three Dog Night (69)	6338
12. **Beach Boys Concert** - The Beach Boys (64)	6309
13. **The Concert For Bangla Desh** - George Harrison and Friends (72)	6165
14. **Eat A Peach** - The Allman Brothers Band (72)	5683
15. **Live At Leeds** - The Who (70)	5677
16. **Lou Rawls Live** - Lou Rawls (66)	5676
17. **Live Album** - Grand Funk Railroad (70)	5403
18. **Alive!** - KISS (75)	5270
19. **Band Of Gypsys** - Jimi Hendrix (70)	5259
20. **Wings Over America** - Paul McCartney And Wings (76)	5248
21. **Chicago At Carnegie Hall** - Chicago (71)	5202
22. **An Evening With John Denver** - John Denver (75)	5194
23. **The Kingsmen In Person** - The Kingsmen (64)	5152
24. **Just One Night** - Eric Clapton (80)	5135
25. **Hot August Night** - Neil Diamond (72)	5024
26. **Mad Dogs & Englishmen (Soundtrack)** - Joe Cocker (70)	4992
27. **Nine Tonight** - Bob Seger & The Silver Bullet Band (81)	4899
28. **The In Crowd** - Ramsey Lewis Trio (65)	4876
29. **Tom Jones Live!** - Tom Jones (69)	4814
30. **Briefcase Full Of Blues** - Blues Brothers (78)	4763
31. **Made In Japan** - Deep Purple (73)	4753
32. **Marvin Gaye Live At The London Palladium** - Marvin Gaye (77)	4450
33. **Weekend In L.A.** - George Benson (78)	4426
34. **Aloha From Hawaii Via Satellite** - Elvis Presley (73)	4378
35. **Fandango!** - ZZ Top (75)	4374
36. **Aretha Live At Fillmore West** - Aretha Franklin (71)	4367

Rank. Title - Act (Entry Year)	Score
37. **Neil Diamond/Gold** - Neil Diamond (70)	4353
38. **Miles Of Aisles** - Joni Mitchell (74)	4070
39. **The London Chuck Berry Sessions** - Chuck Berry (72)	4034
40. **Steppenwolf 'Live'** - Steppenwolf (70)	4000
41. **Peter, Paul And Mary In Concert** - Peter, Paul & Mary (64)	3909
42. **Bruce Springsteen & The E Street Band Live 1975-1985** - Bruce Springsteen (86)	3897
43. **On Stage** - Loggins & Messina (74)	3837
44. **Under A Blood Red Sky** - U2 (83)	3718
45. **Live** - Kenny G (89)	3642
46. **Commodores Live!** - Commodores (77)	3522
47. **Journey To The Centre Of The Earth** - Rick Wakeman With The London Symphony Orchestra & The English Chamber Choir (74)	3498
48. **One More From The Road** - Lynyrd Skynyrd (76)	3462
49. **Joplin In Concert** - Janis Joplin (72)	3439
50. **'Live' Bullet** - Bob Seger & The Silver Bullet Band (76)	3359
51. **Donny Hathaway Live** - Donny Hathaway (72)	3318
52. **Procol Harum Live In Concert with the Edmonton Symphony Orchestra** - Procol Harum (72)	3272
53. **Captured** - Journey (81)	3197
54. **Eagles Live** - Eagles (80)	3172
55. **Carlos Santana & Buddy Miles! Live!** - Carlos Santana & Buddy Miles (72)	3157
56. **The Lettermen!!!...And "Live!"** - The Lettermen (67)	3145
57. **At Fillmore East** - The Allman Brothers Band (71)	3136
58. **Joan Baez In Concert, Part 2** - Joan Baez (63)	3108
59. **The Supremes At The Copa** - The Supremes (65)	3076
60. **Elvis As Recorded At Madison Square Garden** - Elvis Presley (72)	3063
61. **Elvis** - TV Special - Elvis Presley (68)	3062
62. **Alive II** - KISS (77)	3023
63. **Glen Campbell** - "Live" - Glen Campbell (69)	2936
64. **Rock Of Ages** - The Band (72)	2929
65. **One For The Road** - The Kinks (80)	2816
66. **'Get Yer Ya-Ya's Out!'** - The Rolling Stones (70)	2715
67. **Sinatra At The Sands** - Frank Sinatra With Count Basie And The Orchestra (66)	2712
68. **War Live!** - War (74)	2702
69. **Before The Flood** - Bob Dylan/The Band (74)	2697
70. **The Plastic Ono Band** - Live Peace In Toronto 1969 - The Plastic Ono Band (70)	2690

Rank. Title - Act (Entry Year)	Score
71. **Marvin Gaye Live!** - Marvin Gaye (74)	2663
72. **Arena** - Duran Duran (84)	2637
73. **Temptations Live!** - The Temptations (67)	2619
74. **Four Tops Live!** - Four Tops (66)	2605
75. **Songs In The Attic** - Billy Joel (81)	2554
76. **Welcome Back, My Friends, To The Show That Never Ends - Ladies and Gentlemen** - Emerson, Lake & Palmer (74)	2531
77. **The Beatles At The Hollywood Bowl** - The Beatles (77)	2503
78. **Curtis/Live!** - Curtis Mayfield (71)	2481
79. **Got Live If You Want It!** - The Rolling Stones (66)	2455
80. **World Wide Live** - Scorpions (85)	2451
81. **Candles In The Rain** - Melanie (70)	2416
82. **Kenny Loggins Alive** - Kenny Loggins (80)	2402
83. **The Turning Point** - John Mayall (69)	2398
84. **11/17/1970** - Elton John (71)	2371
85. **The Osmonds "Live"** - The Osmonds (72)	2368
86. **From Memphis To Vegas / From Vegas To Memphis** - Elvis Presley (69)	2345
87. **Live At The Copa** - The Temptations (69)	2337
88. **Stop Making Sense** - Talking Heads (84)	2336
89. **Leon Live** - Leon Russell (73)	2331
90. **The Kids Are Alright (Soundtrack)** - The Who (79)	2320
91. **Here And There** - Elton John (76)	2275
92. **Johnny Rivers At The Whisky A Go Go** - Johnny Rivers (64)	2271
93. **Tribute** - Ozzy Osbourne/Randy Rhoads (87)	2266
94. **The Concert In Central Park** - Simon & Garfunkel (82)	2249
95. **Live! Bootleg** - Aerosmith (78)	2223
96. **Paris** - Supertramp (80)	2219
97. **The Cowsills In Concert** - The Cowsills (69)	2183
98. **Absolutely Live** - The Doors (70)	2183
99. **Donovan In Concert** - Donovan (68)	2162
100. **Live From Earth** - Pat Benatar (83)	2147
101. **Amazing Grace** - Aretha Franklin (72)	2145
102. **Live At The Bijou** - Grover Washington Jr. (78)	2135
103. **Near The Beginning** - Vanilla Fudge (69)	2128
104. **Greatest Hits/Live** - Heart (80)	2112
105. **On Stage-February, 1970** - Elvis Presley (70)	2088
106. **Pictures At An Exhibition** - Emerson, Lake & Palmer (72)	2084
107. **Moonflower** - Santana (77)	2061
108. **Aretha In Paris** - Aretha Franklin (68)	2053

Rank. Title - Act (Entry Year)	Score
109. Exit...Stage Left - Rush (81)	2016
110. Performance-Rockin' The Fillmore - Humble Pie (71)	2010
111. Yessongs - Yes (73)	2009
112. David Live - David Bowie (74)	1991
113. Live Rust - Neil Young With Crazy Horse (79)	1985
114. For Once In My Life - Vikki Carr (69)	1978
115. Swiss Movement - Les McCann & Eddie Harris (69)	1948
116. Waiting For Columbus - Little Feat (78)	1946
117. Getz Au Go Go - The New Stan Getz Quartet Featuring Astrud Gilberto (64)	1938
118. Hendrix In The West - Jimi Hendrix (72)	1932
119. Foghat Live - Foghat (77)	1928
120. The Live Adventures Of Mike Bloomfield And Al Kooper - Mike Bloomfield/Al Kooper (69)	1918
121. Live At The Sahara Tahoe - Isaac Hayes (73)	1914
122. Live In Cook County Jail - B.B. King (71)	1908
123. One Voice - Barbra Streisand (87)	1848
124. Still Life (American Concert 1981) - The Rolling Stones (82)	1847
125. Love You Live - The Rolling Stones (77)	1840
126. Live At The Apollo, Volume II - James Brown (68)	1809
127. Love At The Greek - Neil Diamond (77)	1780
128. Delicate Sound Of Thunder - Pink Floyd (88)	1759
129. Live Cream - Cream (70)	1759
130. Three Sides Live - Genesis (82)	1758
131. Sonny & Cher Live - Sonny & Cher (71)	1756
132. Live Concert At The Forum - Barbra Streisand (72)	1749
133. Hang On Ramsey! - Ramsey Lewis Trio (66)	1732
134. Willie Nelson And Family Live - Willie Nelson (78)	1726
135. Happy Trails - Quicksilver Messenger Service (69)	1713
136. Mercy, Mercy, Mercy! - "Cannonball" Adderley Quintet (67)	1705
137. Robin Trower Live! - Robin Trower (76)	1702
138. Live In Australia (With The Melbourne Symphony Orchestra) - Elton John (87)	1685
139. Live At Carnegie Hall/What You Hear Is What You Get - Ike & Tina Turner (71)	1685
140. A Happening In Central Park - Barbra Streisand (68)	1678
141. Double Live Gonzo! - Ted Nugent (78)	1657
142. The Nancy Wilson Show! - Nancy Wilson (65)	1643
143. Elvis In Concert - Elvis Presley (77)	1640
144. Spinners Live! - Spinners (75)	1636
145. Betty Wright Live - Betty Wright (78)	1624
146. Okie From Muskogee - Merle Haggard And The Strangers (70)	1623
147. Living The Blues - Canned Heat (68)	1612
148. The O'Jays Live In London - The O'Jays (74)	1577
149. Sex Machine - James Brown (70)	1538
150. Pure Dynamite! Live At The Royal - James Brown (64)	1525
151. Fleetwood Mac Live - Fleetwood Mac (80)	1524
152. Sam Cooke At The Copa - Sam Cooke (64)	1517
153. Around The World With Three Dog Night - Three Dog Night (73)	1513
154. Monterey International Pop Festival - Otis Redding/ The Jimi Hendrix Experience (70)	1502
155. Bob Dylan At Budokan - Bob Dylan (79)	1495
156. The Kingsmen, Volume II - The Kingsmen (64)	1490
157. Roadwork - Edgar Winter's White Trash (72)	1487
158. Elvis-That's The Way It Is - Elvis Presley (70)	1454
159. The Last Waltz (Soundtrack) - The Band (78)	1452
160. Horowitz at Carnegie Hall - An Historic Return - Vladimir Horowitz (65)	1418
161. You Can't Argue With A Sick Mind - Joe Walsh (76)	1384
162. Derek & The Dominos In Concert - Derek & The Dominos (73)	1350
163. Europe '72 - Grateful Dead (72)	1340
164. Early Steppenwolf - Steppenwolf (69)	1339
165. Speak Of The Devil - Ozzy Osbourne (82)	1334
166. Charley Pride: In Person - Charley Pride (69)	1331
167. No Nukes/The MUSE Concerts For A Non-Nuclear Future - Various Artists (79)	1322
168. An Evening Of Magic - Chuck Mangione Live At The Hollywood Bowl - Chuck Mangione (79)	1318
169. Iron Butterfly Live - Iron Butterfly (70)	1298
170. Deliverin' - Poco (71)	1294
171. Robert Goulet In Person - Robert Goulet (63)	1292
172. On The Move - Trini Lopez (64)	1277
173. Live - George Thorogood & The Destroyers (86)	1273
174. Live After Death - Iron Maiden (85)	1244
175. Live/Johnny Winter And - Johnny Winter (71)	1240
176. Jethro Tull Live - Bursting Out - Jethro Tull (78)	1229
177. Stars & Stripes Forever - Nitty Gritty Dirt Band (74)	1215
178. Live & Well - B.B. King (69)	1199
179. The Ventures On Stage - The Ventures (65)	1192
180. Welcome To The Canteen - Traffic, Etc. (71)	1188
181. Live At London's Talk Of The Town - The Temptations (70)	1188
182. Queen Live Killers - Queen (79)	1183
183. Live In New Orleans - Maze Featuring Frankie Beverly (81)	1181
184. The Byrds (Untitled) - The Byrds (70)	1166
185. More Trini Lopez At PJ's - Trini Lopez (63)	1165
186. E.C. Was Here - Eric Clapton (75)	1158
187. Pat Travers Band Live! Go For What You Know - Pat Travers Band (79)	1151
188. Belafonte At The Greek Theatre - Harry Belafonte (64)	1149
189. Rare Earth In Concert - Rare Earth (72)	1137
190. Alive She Cried - The Doors (83)	1135
191. Revolution Of The Mind - Live At The Apollo, Volume III - James Brown (71)	1114
192. Otis Redding Live In Europe - Otis Redding (67)	1113
193. Rock N Roll Animal - Lou Reed (74)	1104
194. The Beach Boys In Concert - The Beach Boys (73)	1104
195. Pack Up The Plantation - Live! - Tom Petty And The Heartbreakers (85)	1104
196. Live And Sleazy - Village People (79)	1074
197. Person To Person - Average White Band (77)	1074
198. Uriah Heep Live - Uriah Heep (73)	1071
199. Bring It Back Alive - The Outlaws (78)	1068
200. I'm The Man – Anthrax	1066

50 Highest Charting Various Artists

Rank. Title (Entry Year)	Score
1. Jesus Christ Superstar (1970)	18456
2. Tommy (1972)	2970
3. The Super Hits (1967)	2829
4. Welcome To The LBJ Ranch! (1965)	2345
5. You Don't Have To Be Jewish (1965)	1942
6. A Very Special Christmas (1987)	1351
7. No Nukes/The MUSE Concerts For A Non-Nuclear Future (1979)	1322
8. A Night At Studio 54 (1979)	1295
9. Themes Like Old Times (1969)	1158
10. Dick Clark/20 Years Of Rock N' Roll (1973)	1028
11. Free To Be...You And Me (1973)	929
12. The Super Hits, Vol. 2 (1968)	861
13. When You're In Love The Whole World Is Jewish (1966)	841
14. Mickey Mouse Disco (1980)	815
15. Nadia's Theme (The Young And The Restless) (1976)	794
16. Fillmore: The Last Days (1972)	752
17. Opening Nights At The Met (1966)	745
18. The Secret Policeman's Other Ball (1982)	710
19. 1988 Summer Olympics-One Moment In Time (1988)	676
20. The Big Sounds Of The Drags! (1963)	655
21. 25 #1 Hits From 25 Years (1983)	641
22. Concerts For The People Of Kampuchea (1981)	610
23. Chess (1985)	589
24. The Super Hits, Vol. 3 (1968)	583
25. Our Wedding Album or The Great Society Affair (1966)	565

Rank. Title (Entry Year)	Score
26. Happy Anniversary, Charlie Brown (1989)	534
27. 16 Original Big Hits, Volume 5 (1966)	522
28. 20 Original Winners Of 1964 (1965)	514
29. The War Of The Worlds (1978)	513
30. Apollo Saturday Night (1964)	480
31. Oldies But Goodies, Vol. 6 (1964)	478
32. Casino Lights (1982)	457
33. Greenpeace/Rainbow Warriors (1989)	443
34. Music To Read James Bond By (1965)	430
35. Television's Greatest Hits (1985)	429
36. First Great Rock Festivals Of The Seventies: Isle Of Wight/Atlanta Pop Fest (1971)	427
37. The Watergate Comedy Hour (1973)	419
38. Hot Rod Rally (1963)	409
39. 16 Original Big Hits, Volume 6 (1967)	377
40. Exposed/A Cheap Peek At Today's Provocative New Rock (1981)	376
41. Joseph And The Amazing Technicolor Dreamcoat (1971)	370
42. Windham Hill Records Sampler '84 (1984)	361
43. The Greatest Hits From England (1967)	349
44. The Wrestling Album (1985)	343
45. 16 Original Big Hits, Volume 7 (1967)	336
46. Great Voices Of The Century (1964)	315
47. Requiem (1985)	311
48. Windham Hill Records Sampler '86 (1986)	306
49. Solid Gold Soul (1966)	302
50. The New First Family, 1968 (1966)	288

Albums 100 Weeks or More On Chart

Title - Act (Entry Year)	Weeks
The Dark Side Of The Moon - Pink Floyd (73)	741
Tapestry - Carole King (71)	302
Led Zeppelin IV - Led Zeppelin (71)	259
The Phantom Of The Opera - Original London Cast Recording (87)	255
Hot Rocks 1964-1971 - The Rolling Stones (72)	243
The Sound Of Music - Musical (65)	233
Fiddler On The Roof - Original Cast (64)	206
Soul Provider - Michael Bolton (89)	202
Whipped Cream & Other Delights - Herb Alpert's Tijuana Brass (65)	185
Nick Of Time - Bonnie Raitt (89)	185
Eliminator - ZZ Top (83)	183
Kenny Rogers' Greatest Hits - Kenny Rogers (80)	181
Under A Blood Red Sky - U2 (83)	180
War - U2 (83)	179
December - George Winston (83)	178
Beaches - Bette Midler (89)	176
Forever Your Girl - Paula Abdul (88)	175
Sgt. Pepper's Lonely Hearts Club Band - The Beatles (67)	175
John Denver's Greatest Hits - John Denver (73)	175
Chicago Transit Authority - Chicago (69)	171
Off The Wall - Michael Jackson (79)	169
The Beatles 1967-1970 - The Beatles (73)	169
Van Halen - Van Halen (78)	169
Madonna - Madonna (83)	168
Man Of La Mancha - Original Cast (66)	167
!!Going Places!! - Herb Alpert & The Tijuana Brass (65)	164
Face Value - Phil Collins (81)	164
The Beatles 1962-1966 - The Beatles (73)	164
South Of The Border - Herb Alpert & The Tijuana Brass (65)	163
Whitney Houston - Whitney Houston (85)	162
Feels So Right - Alabama (81)	161
The Big Chill - Various Artists (83)	161
Can't Slow Down - Lionel Richie (83)	160
Sports - Huey Lewis & The News (83)	158
Doctor Zhivago - Instrumental (66)	157
Rapture - Anita Baker (86)	157
Endless Summer - The Beach Boys (74)	156
The Beatles [White Album] - The Beatles (68)	155
'Live' Bullet - Bob Seger & The Silver Bullet Band (76)	154
1999 - Prince (82)	153
Zenyatta Mondatta - The Police (80)	153
Why Is There Air? - Bill Cosby (65)	152
Hair - Original Cast Recording (68)	151
Fleetwood Mac - Fleetwood Mac (75)	148
The End Of The Innocence - Don Henley (89)	148
Appetite For Destruction - Guns N' Roses (87)	147
Escape - Journey (81)	146

Title - Act (Entry Year)	Weeks
Parsley, Sage, Rosemary And Thyme - Simon & Garfunkel (66)	145
Bella Donna - Stevie Nicks (81)	143
Killin' Time - Clint Black (89)	143
The Sea - The San Sebastian Strings (67)	143
Sounds Of Silence - Simon & Garfunkel (66)	141
Hello, I Must Be Going! - Phil Collins (82)	141
In-A-Gadda-Da-Vida - Iron Butterfly (68)	140
Lionel Richie - Lionel Richie (82)	140
I Started Out As A Child - Bill Cosby (64)	140
Born In The U.S.A. - Bruce Springsteen (84)	139
The Cars - The Cars (78)	139
The Stranger - Billy Joel (77)	137
On The Threshold Of A Dream - The Moody Blues (69)	136
Rumours - Fleetwood Mac (77)	134
Chicago - Chicago (70)	134
Hysteria - Def Leppard (87)	133
Their Greatest Hits 1971-1975 - Eagles (76)	133
Hangin' Tough - New Kids On The Block (88)	132
Boston - Boston (76)	132
The Unforgettable Fire - U2 (84)	132
Back In Black - AC/DC (80)	131
The Kingsmen In Person - The Kingsmen (64)	131
What Now My Love - Herb Alpert & The Tijuana Brass (66)	129
Abbey Road - The Beatles (69)	129
Rio - Duran Duran (82)	129
Bill Cosby Is A Very Funny Fellow, Right! - Bill Cosby (64)	128
Toys In The Attic - Aerosmith (75)	128
The Grand Illusion - Styx (77)	127
Simon And Garfunkel's Greatest Hits - Simon & Garfunkel (72)	127
Tommy - The Who (69)	126
Sergio Mendes & Brasil '66 - Sergio Mendes & Brasil '66 (66)	126
No Jacket Required - Phil Collins (85)	123
The Wall - Pink Floyd (79)	123
Infinity - Journey (78)	123
Thriller - Michael Jackson (82)	122
Get Lucky - Loverboy (81)	122
Johnny Cash At Folsom Prison - Johnny Cash (68)	122
Live - Kenny G (89)	122
In The Heat Of The Night - Pat Benatar (79)	122
When Harry Met Sally - Harry Connick Jr. (89)	122
The Doors - The Doors (67)	121
The Temptations Greatest Hits - The Temptations (66)	120
Saturday Night Fever - Bee Gees (77)	120
Jane Fonda's Workout Record - Jane Fonda (82)	120
2001: A Space Odyssey - Instrumental (68)	120
The Best Of Bread - Bread (73)	119
Toulouse Street - The Doobie Brothers (72)	119

Title - Act (Entry Year)	Weeks
Release Me - Engelbert Humperdinck (67)	118
Machine Head - Deep Purple (72)	118
Stop Making Sense - Talking Heads (84)	118
Stardust - Willie Nelson (78)	117
Christopher Cross - Christopher Cross (80)	116
Pyromania - Def Leppard (83)	116
Band On The Run - Paul McCartney And Wings (73)	116
Silk Degrees - Boz Scaggs (76)	115
The Jazz Singer - Neil Diamond (80)	115
Greatest Hits - Waylon Jennings (79)	115
Mary Poppins - Musical (64)	114
Mountain Music - Alabama (82)	114
The Best Of The Animals - The Animals (66)	113
Foreigner - Foreigner (77)	113
Legend - Bob Marley And The Wailers (84)	113
Sittin' In - Kenny Loggins With Jim Messina (72)	113
The Gambler - Kenny Rogers (78)	112
My Fair Lady - Musical (64)	111
An Innocent Man - Billy Joel (83)	111
Don't Say No - Billy Squier (81)	111
Shout At The Devil - Mötley Crüe (83)	111
Big Bambu - Cheech & Chong (72)	111
Pump - Aerosmith (89)	110
Against The Wind - Bob Seger & The Silver Bullet Band (80)	110
Stranger In Town - Bob Seger & The Silver Bullet Band (78)	110
Alive! - KISS (75)	110
Born To Run - Bruce Springsteen (75)	110
Blood, Sweat & Tears - Blood, Sweat & Tears (69)	109
Dr. Feelgood - Mötley Crüe (89)	109
Summer Breeze - Seals & Crofts (72)	109
Ghost In The Machine - The Police (81)	109
Talking Book - Stevie Wonder (72)	109
Janet Jackson's Rhythm Nation 1814 - Janet Jackson (89)	108
Like A Virgin - Madonna (84)	108
Santana - Santana (69)	108
Funny Girl - Barbra Streisand (68)	108
Crosby, Stills & Nash - Crosby, Stills & Nash (69)	107
Hotel California - Eagles (76)	107
The River - Bruce Springsteen (80)	107
Control - Janet Jackson (86)	106
Are You Experienced? - The Jimi Hendrix Experience (67)	106
Private Dancer - Tina Turner (84)	106
Wonderfulness - Bill Cosby (66)	106
American Fool - John Cougar (82)	106
Days Of Future Passed - The Moody Blues With The London Festival Orchestra (68)	106
High 'N' Dry - Def Leppard (81)	106
Break Out - The Pointer Sisters (83)	105
If You Can Believe Your Eyes And Ears - The Mamas & The Papas (66)	105

Title - Act (Entry Year)	Weeks
Behind Closed Doors - Charlie Rich (73)	105
The Best Of Herman's Hermits - Herman's Hermits (65)	105
Loverboy - Loverboy (81)	105
Honey In The Horn - Al Hirt (63)	104
Elton John's Greatest Hits - Elton John (74)	104
Lost In Love - Air Supply (80)	104
Blizzard Of Ozz - Ozzy Osbourne (81)	104
Memories - Barbra Streisand (81)	104
Love Will Keep Us Together - Captain & Tennille (75)	104

Title - Act (Entry Year)	Weeks
7800 Degrees Fahrenheit - Bon Jovi (85)	104
Ten Years Of Gold - Kenny Rogers (78)	104
Billy Idol - Billy Idol (82)	104
The Joshua Tree - U2 (87)	103
Goodbye Yellow Brick Road - Elton John (73)	103
Always & Forever - Randy Travis (87)	103
Breakin' Away - Al Jarreau (81)	103
Parallel Lines - Blondie (78)	103
Sweet Baby James - James Taylor (70)	102
The Monkees - The Monkees (66)	102

Title - Act (Entry Year)	Weeks
Duotones - Kenny G (86)	102
The Captain And Me - The Doobie Brothers (73)	102
Stand! - Sly & The Family Stone (69)	102
Jesus Christ Superstar - Various Artists (70)	101
Hi Infidelity - REO Speedwagon (80)	101
Look What The Cat Dragged In - Poison (86)	101
Voices - Daryl Hall & John Oates (80)	100
Dreamboat Annie - Heart (76)	100
Reggatta De Blanc - The Police (79)	100
Storms Of Life - Randy Travis (86)	100

Albums 20 Weeks or More in Top 10

Title - Act (Entry Year)	Wks
The Sound Of Music - Soundtrack (65)	109
Born In The U.S.A. - Bruce Springsteen (84)	84
Thriller - Michael Jackson (82)	78
Hysteria - Def Leppard (87)	78
Doctor Zhivago - Soundtrack (66)	71
Forever Your Girl - Paula Abdul (88)	64
Whipped Cream & Other Delights - Herb Alpert's Tijuana Brass (65)	61
Can't Slow Down - Lionel Richie (83)	59
Frampton Comes Alive! - Peter Frampton (76)	52
Rumours - Fleetwood Mac (77)	52
Appetite For Destruction - Guns N' Roses (87)	52
Faith - George Michael (87)	51
Blood, Sweat & Tears - Blood, Sweat & Tears (69)	50
In-A-Gadda-Da-Vida - Iron Butterfly (68)	49
Mary Poppins - Soundtrack (64)	48
!!Going Places!! - Herb Alpert & The Tijuana Brass (65)	48
Dirty Dancing - Soundtrack (87)	48
Tapestry - Carole King (71)	46
Whitney Houston - Whitney Houston (85)	46
Slippery When Wet - Bon Jovi (86)	46
Don't Be Cruel - Bobby Brown (88)	45
Hangin' Tough - New Kids On The Block (88)	45
Sports - Huey Lewis & The News (83)	42
Jesus Christ Superstar - Various Artists (70)	41
Girl You Know It's True - Milli Vanilli (89)	41
Whitesnake - Whitesnake (87)	41
Synchronicity - The Police (83)	40
Reckless - Bryan Adams (84)	40
Bad - Michael Jackson (87)	39
Private Dancer - Tina Turner (84)	39
Escape - Journey (81)	38
Pyromania - Def Leppard (83)	38
Fleetwood Mac - Fleetwood Mac (75)	37
Brothers In Arms - Dire Straits (85)	37
Heart - Heart (85)	37
Control - Janet Jackson (86)	37
Goodbye Yellow Brick Road - Elton John (73)	36
Hello, Dolly! - Original Cast (64)	35
Songs In The Key Of Life - Stevie Wonder (76)	35
Saturday Night Fever - Bee Gees (77)	35
The Joshua Tree - U2 (87)	35
Janet Jackson's Rhythm Nation 1814 - Janet Jackson (89)	35
4 - Foreigner (81)	34
Full Moon Fever - Tom Petty (89)	34
Like A Virgin - Madonna (84)	33
Sgt. Pepper's Lonely Hearts Club Band - The Beatles (67)	33
H2O - Daryl Hall & John Oates (82)	33
Chicago - Chicago (70)	33
What Now My Love - Herb Alpert & The Tijuana Brass (66)	32
The Monkees - The Monkees (66)	32
Purple Rain - Prince And The Revolution (84)	32
Songs From The Big Chair - Tears For Fears (85)	32

Title - Act (Entry Year)	Wks
Band On The Run - Paul McCartney And Wings (73)	32
Are You Experienced? - The Jimi Hendrix Experience (67)	32
Business As Usual - Men At Work (82)	31
No Jacket Required - Phil Collins (85)	31
Whitney - Whitney Houston (87)	31
Heartbeat City - The Cars (84)	31
Abraxas - Santana (70)	30
Hi Infidelity - REO Speedwagon (80)	30
Colour By Numbers - Culture Club (83)	30
Fly Like An Eagle - Steve Miller Band (76)	30
Boston - Boston (76)	30
My Fair Lady - Soundtrack (64)	30
Disraeli Gears - Cream (67)	30
An Innocent Man - Billy Joel (83)	30
Pump - Aerosmith (89)	30
Grease - Soundtrack (78)	29
Crimes Of Passion - Pat Benatar (80)	29
Scarecrow - John Mellencamp (85)	29
Off The Wall - Michael Jackson (79)	29
In The Wind - Peter, Paul & Mary (63)	28
Hair - Original Cast (68)	28
John Denver's Greatest Hits - John Denver (73)	28
Hotel California - Eagles (76)	28
A Hard Day's Night - The Beatles (64)	28
Santana - Santana (69)	28
The Dark Side Of The Moon - Pink Floyd (73)	27
The Wall - Pink Floyd (79)	27
Paradise Theater - Styx (81)	27
Asia - Asia (82)	27
The Raw & The Cooked - Fine Young Cannibals (89)	27
Abbey Road - The Beatles (69)	27
1984 (MCMLXXXIV) - Van Halen (84)	27
Double Vision - Foreigner (78)	27
The Lonesome Jubilee - John Mellencamp (87)	27
The Graduate - Simon & Garfunkel (68)	26
Breakfast In America - Supertramp (79)	26
Bella Donna - Stevie Nicks (81)	26
Fore! - Huey Lewis & The News (86)	26
Open Up And Say...Ahh! - Poison (88)	26
Invisible Touch - Genesis (86)	26
More Of The Monkees - The Monkees (67)	25
Time Peace/The Rascals' Greatest Hits - The Rascals (68)	25
Glass Houses - Billy Joel (80)	25
Flashdance - Soundtrack (83)	25
Make It Big - Wham! (84)	25
True Blue - Madonna (86)	25
Diana Ross And The Supremes Greatest Hits - Diana Ross & The Supremes (67)	24
Led Zeppelin II - Led Zeppelin (69)	24
Woodstock - Various Artists (70)	24
Carpenters - Carpenters (71)	24
Ghost In The Machine - The Police (81)	24
Ram - Paul & Linda McCartney (71)	24
Honey In The Horn - Al Hirt (63)	24
Graceland - Paul Simon (86)	24
Deja Vu - Crosby, Stills, Nash & Young (70)	23
Back Home Again - John Denver (74)	23
Some Girls - The Rolling Stones (78)	23

Title - Act (Entry Year)	Wks
The Way It Is - Bruce Hornsby & The Range (86)	23
Back In Black - AC/DC (80)	23
Goldfinger - Soundtrack (64)	22
Wichita Lineman - Glen Campbell (68)	22
Still Crazy After All These Years - Paul Simon (75)	22
52nd Street - Billy Joel (78)	22
Against The Wind - Bob Seger & The Silver Bullet Band (80)	22
Double Fantasy - John Lennon & Yoko Ono (80)	22
Tattoo You - The Rolling Stones (81)	22
American Fool - John Cougar (82)	22
Beverly Hills Cop - Soundtrack (85)	22
Tiffany - Tiffany (87)	22
New Jersey - Bon Jovi (88)	22
Funny Girl (Original Cast) - Barbra Streisand (64)	22
The Doors - The Doors (67)	22
Frontiers - Journey (83)	22
Kick - INXS (87)	22
Volume 1 - Traveling Wilburys (88)	22
Toto IV - Toto (82)	22
Cosmic Thing - The B-52s (89)	22
The Third Album - Barbra Streisand (64)	22
People - Barbra Streisand (64)	21
Headquarters - The Monkees (67)	21
That's The Way Of The World - Earth, Wind & Fire (75)	21
Red Octopus - Jefferson Starship (75)	21
The Long Run - Eagles (79)	21
The Game - Queen (80)	21
Meet The Beatles! - The Beatles (64)	21
Wings At The Speed Of Sound - Wings (76)	21
Lionel Richie - Lionel Richie (82)	21
Soul Provider - Michael Bolton (89)	21
She's So Unusual - Cyndi Lauper (83)	21
Zenyatta Mondatta - The Police (80)	21
Beach Boys Concert - The Beach Boys (64)	20
If You Can Believe Your Eyes And Ears - The Mamas & The Papas (66)	20
Bookends - Simon & Garfunkel (68)	20
Wheels Of Fire - Cream (68)	20
Johnny Cash At San Quentin - Johnny Cash (69)	20
Every Picture Tells A Story - Rod Stewart (71)	20
Kenny Rogers' Greatest Hits - Kenny Rogers (80)	20
Footloose - Soundtrack (84)	20
Top Gun - Soundtrack (86)	20
Dancing On The Ceiling - Lionel Richie (86)	20
Third Stage - Boston (86)	20
...But Seriously - Phil Collins (89)	20
Mud Slide Slim And The Blue Horizon - James Taylor (71)	20
Damn The Torpedoes - Tom Petty And The Heartbreakers (79)	20
Surrealistic Pillow - Jefferson Airplane (67)	20
Aja - Steely Dan (77)	20

Albums 40 Weeks or More in Top 40

Title - Act (Entry Year)	Weeks
The Sound Of Music - Soundtrack (65)	161
Whipped Cream & Other Delights - Herb Alpert's Tijuana Brass (65)	141
Doctor Zhivago - Instrumental (66)	115
!!Going Places!! - Herb Alpert & The Tijuana Brass (65)	107
Born In The U.S.A. - Bruce Springsteen (84)	96
Hysteria - Def Leppard (87)	96
Thriller - Michael Jackson (82)	91
In-A-Gadda-Da-Vida - Iron Butterfly (68)	87
Eliminator - ZZ Top (83)	82
Christopher Cross - Christopher Cross (80)	81
Forever Your Girl - Paula Abdul (88)	78
Can't Slow Down - Lionel Richie (83)	78
Appetite For Destruction - Guns N' Roses (87)	78
Mary Poppins - Soundtrack (64)	78
Whitney Houston - Whitney Houston (85)	78
Control - Janet Jackson (86)	77
Janet Jackson's Rhythm Nation 1814 - Janet Jackson (89)	77
My Fair Lady - Soundtrack (64)	77
Are You Experienced? - The Jimi Hendrix Experience (67)	76
Sports - Huey Lewis & The News (83)	72
Rapture - Anita Baker (86)	72
Hangin' Tough - New Kids On The Block (88)	71
No Jacket Required - Phil Collins (85)	70
The Stranger - Billy Joel (77)	70
Faith - George Michael (87)	69
Don't Be Cruel - Bobby Brown (88)	69
Dirty Dancing - Soundtrack (87)	68
Tapestry - Carole King (71)	68
Fleetwood Mac - Fleetwood Mac (75)	68
Blood, Sweat & Tears - Blood, Sweat & Tears (69)	66
Reckless - Bryan Adams (84)	66
Honey In The Horn - Al Hirt (63)	66
Jesus Christ Superstar - Various Artists (70)	65
Kick - INXS (87)	65
The Temptations Greatest Hits - The Temptations (66)	65
Break Out - The Pointer Sisters (83)	65
Sgt. Pepper's Lonely Hearts Club Band - The Beatles (67)	63
The Dark Side Of The Moon - Pink Floyd (73)	63
Richard Marx - Richard Marx (87)	63
Private Dancer - Tina Turner (84)	62
An Innocent Man - Billy Joel (83)	62
She's So Unusual - Cyndi Lauper (83)	62
Girl You Know It's True - Milli Vanilli (89)	61
Invisible Touch - Genesis (86)	61
Rumours - Fleetwood Mac (77)	60
Slippery When Wet - Bon Jovi (86)	60
What Now My Love - Herb Alpert & The Tijuana Brass (66)	60

Title - Act (Entry Year)	Weeks
Parsley, Sage, Rosemary And Thyme - Simon & Garfunkel (66)	60
Back In The High Life - Steve Winwood (86)	60
Fiddler On The Roof - Original Cast (64)	60
Hair - Original Cast (68)	59
Escape - Journey (81)	58
Pyromania - Def Leppard (83)	58
Heart - Heart (85)	58
Hello, Dolly! - Original Cast (64)	58
The Joshua Tree - U2 (87)	58
In The Wind - Peter, Paul & Mary (63)	58
Innervisions - Stevie Wonder (73)	58
The End Of The Innocence - Don Henley (89)	58
Their Greatest Hits 1971-1975 - Eagles (76)	57
Skid Row - Skid Row (89)	57
1999 - Prince (82)	57
Suddenly - Billy Ocean (84)	57
Make It Big - Wham! (84)	56
Frampton Comes Alive! - Peter Frampton (76)	55
Brothers In Arms - Dire Straits (85)	55
Songs From The Big Chair - Tears For Fears (85)	55
Dr. Feelgood - Mötley Crüe (89)	55
Why Is There Air? - Bill Cosby (65)	55
Whitesnake - Whitesnake (87)	54
Bad - Michael Jackson (87)	54
Saturday Night Fever (Soundtrack) - Bee Gees (77)	54
Pump - Aerosmith (89)	54
Flashdance - Soundtrack (83)	54
Sweet Baby James - James Taylor (70)	54
Wonderfulness - Bill Cosby (66)	54
Chicago - Chicago (70)	53
The Doors - The Doors (67)	53
Silk Degrees - Boz Scaggs (76)	53
Exposure - Exposé (87)	53
4 - Foreigner (81)	52
Like A Virgin - Madonna (84)	52
Off The Wall - Michael Jackson (79)	52
1984 (MCMLXXXIV) - Van Halen (84)	52
True Blue - Madonna (86)	52
Graceland - Paul Simon (86)	52
New Jersey - Bon Jovi (88)	52
Aja - Steely Dan (77)	52
Close To You - Carpenters (70)	52
South Of The Border - Herb Alpert & The Tijuana Brass (65)	52
Permanent Vacation - Aerosmith (87)	52
Full Moon Fever - Tom Petty (89)	51
Whitney - Whitney Houston (87)	51
Open Up And Say...Ahh! - Poison (88)	51
Get Lucky - Loverboy (81)	51
The Best Of The Animals - The Animals (66)	51
Emergency - Kool & The Gang (84)	51
Synchronicity - The Police (83)	50

Title - Act (Entry Year)	Weeks
Hi Infidelity - REO Speedwagon (80)	50
Disraeli Gears - Cream (67)	50
Soul Provider - Michael Bolton (89)	50
...But Seriously - Phil Collins (89)	50
Getz/Gilberto - Stan Getz And Joao Gilberto Featuring Antonio Carlos Jobim (64)	50
Led Zeppelin - Led Zeppelin (69)	50
The Monkees - The Monkees (66)	49
Boston - Boston (76)	49
Diana Ross And The Supremes Greatest Hits - Diana Ross & The Supremes (67)	49
Night Songs - Cinderella (86)	49
Raising Hell - Run-D.M.C. (86)	49
Business As Usual - Men At Work (82)	48
Heartbeat City - The Cars (84)	48
Fly Like An Eagle - Steve Miller Band (76)	48
Scarecrow - John Mellencamp (85)	48
Breakfast In America - Supertramp (79)	48
People - Barbra Streisand (64)	48
Hello Dolly! - Louis Armstrong (64)	48
Where Did Our Love Go - The Supremes (64)	48
Let It Loose - Gloria Estefan & Miami Sound Machine (87)	48
The Graduate (Soundtrack) - Simon & Garfunkel (68)	47
The Second Barbra Streisand Album - Barbra Streisand (63)	47
Look What The Cat Dragged In - Poison (86)	47
Tommy - The Who (69)	47
Repeat Offender - Richard Marx (89)	47
So - Peter Gabriel (86)	47
H2O - Daryl Hall & John Oates (82)	46
Tracy Chapman - Tracy Chapman (88)	46
My Name Is Barbra (Soundtrack) - Barbra Streisand (65)	46
September Of My Years - Frank Sinatra (65)	46
Out Of Order - Rod Stewart (88)	46
John Denver's Greatest Hits - John Denver (73)	45
Bella Donna - Stevie Nicks (81)	45
More Of The Monkees - The Monkees (67)	45
Back In Black - AC/DC (80)	45
Dear Heart - Andy Williams (65)	45
Out Of The Blue - Debbie Gibson (87)	45
Different Light - The Bangles (86)	45
Songs In The Key Of Life - Stevie Wonder (76)	44
Chicago 17 - Chicago (84)	44
A New World Record - Electric Light Orchestra (76)	44
Tango In The Night - Fleetwood Mac (87)	44
Tea For The Tillerman - Cat Stevens (71)	44
A Man And A Woman - Instrumental (66)	44
Jody Watley - Jody Watley (87)	44
Goodbye Yellow Brick Road - Elton John (73)	43

Title - Act (Entry Year)	Weeks
Against The Wind - Bob Seger & The Silver Bullet Band (80)	43
One Of These Nights - Eagles (75)	43
Foreigner - Foreigner (77)	43
Strangers In The Night - Frank Sinatra (66)	43
Purple Rain (Soundtrack) - Prince And The Revolution (84)	42
Santana - Santana (69)	42
The Way It Is - Bruce Hornsby & The Range (86)	42
Frontiers - Journey (83)	42
Toto IV - Toto (82)	42
The Third Album - Barbra Streisand (64)	42
You Don't Mess Around With Jim - Jim Croce (72)	42
The Final Countdown - Europe (86)	42
The Pink Panther (Soundtrack) - Henry Mancini And His Orchestra (64)	42
Feels So Right - Alabama (81)	42
Chicago Transit Authority - Chicago (69)	42
Fore! - Huey Lewis & The News (86)	41
Cosmic Thing - The B-52s (89)	41
Headquarters - The Monkees (67)	41
Somewhere My Love - Ray Conniff & His Orchestra & Chorus (66)	41
Seven And The Ragged Tiger - Duran Duran (83)	41
Duotones - Kenny G (86)	41
Easy Rider - Soundtrack (69)	41
Cuts Both Ways - Gloria Estefan (89)	41
American Graffiti - Soundtrack (73)	41
Tender Lover - Babyface (89)	41
Band On The Run - Paul McCartney And Wings (73)	40
Abraxas - Santana (70)	40
A Hard Day's Night (Soundtrack) - The Beatles (64)	40
The Raw & The Cooked - Fine Young Cannibals (89)	40
American Fool - John Cougar (82)	40
Funny Girl (Original Cast) - Barbra Streisand (64)	40
Beach Boys Concert - The Beach Boys (64)	40
Bookends - Simon & Garfunkel (68)	40
Crosby, Stills & Nash - Crosby, Stills & Nash (69)	40
Gentle On My Mind - Glen Campbell (67)	40
Nick Of Time - Bonnie Raitt (89)	40

100 Highest Charting Albums Entering Each Year

Rank. Title - Act Peak (Peak Wks) Score

1964

1. **Mary Poppins** - Soundtrack 1 (14) 14811
2. **Hello, Dolly!** - Original Cast 1 (1) 10990
3. **My Fair Lady** - Soundtrack 4 (2) 9912
4. **Fiddler On The Roof** - Original Cast 7 (2) 9072
5. **A Hard Day's Night (Soundtrack)** - The Beatles 1 (14) 9013
6. **Meet The Beatles!** - The Beatles 1 (11) 8283
7. **Hello Dolly!** - Louis Armstrong 1 (6) 8075
8. **People** - Barbra Streisand 1 (5) 7751
9. **Where Did Our Love Go** - The Supremes 2 (4) 7153
10. **Getz/Gilberto** - Stan Getz And Joao Gilberto Featuring Antonio Carlos Jobim 2 (2) 7098
11. **Goldfinger** - Soundtrack 1 (3) 6654
12. **The Third Album** - Barbra Streisand 5 (8) 6437
13. **Funny Girl (Original Cast)** - Barbra Streisand 2 (3) 6318
14. **Beach Boys Concert** - The Beach Boys 1 (4) 6309
15. **Everybody Loves Somebody** - Dean Martin 2 (4) 5739
16. **Something New** - The Beatles 2 (9) 5426
17. **The Pink Panther (Soundtrack)** - Henry Mancini And His Orchestra 8 (2) 5336
18. **Introducing...The Beatles** - The Beatles 2 (9) 5276
19. **The Beatles' Second Album** - The Beatles 1 (5) 5191
20. **The Kingsmen In Person** - The Kingsmen 20 (1) 5152
21. **Bill Cosby Is A Very Funny Fellow, Right!** - Bill Cosby 21 (1) 5024
22. **All Summer Long** - The Beach Boys 4 (5) 4899
23. **Cotton Candy** - Al Hirt 6 (2) 4430
24. **Peter, Paul And Mary In Concert** - Peter, Paul & Mary 4 (3) 3909
25. **The Academy Award Winning "Call Me Irresponsible"** - Andy Williams 5 (3) 3722
26. **I Started Out As A Child** - Bill Cosby 32 (1) 3629
27. **Yesterday's Love Songs/Today's Blues** - Nancy Wilson 4 (1) 3448
28. **Roustabout (Soundtrack)** - Elvis Presley 1 (1) 3337
29. **Joan Baez/5** - Joan Baez 12 (2) 3336
30. **Glad All Over** - The Dave Clark Five 3 (1) 3158
31. **Sugar Lips** - Al Hirt 9 (2) 2984
32. **The Great Songs From "My Fair Lady" And Other Broadway Hits** - Andy Williams 5 (2) 2848
33. **Keep On Pushing** - The Impressions 8 (2) 2831
34. **12 x 5** - The Rolling Stones 3 (4) 2795
35. **How Glad I Am** - Nancy Wilson 4 (2) 2768
36. **Shut Down, Volume 2** - The Beach Boys 13 (2) 2630
37. **The Best Of Jim Reeves** - Jim Reeves 9 (1) 2545
38. **My Love Forgive Me** - Robert Goulet 5 (2) 2442
39. **Today, Tomorrow, Forever** - Nancy Wilson 10 (3) 2325
40. **Today** - The New Christy Minstrels 9 (2) 2283
41. **Johnny Rivers At The Whisky A Go Go** - Johnny Rivers 12 (1) 2271
42. **Kissin' Cousins (Soundtrack)** - Elvis Presley 6 (3) 2182
43. **Encore** - John Gary 16 (3) 2020
44. **There! I've Said It Again** - Bobby Vinton 8 (2) 1993
45. **The Dave Clark Five Return!** - The Dave Clark Five 5 (1) 1986
46. **The Wonderful World Of Andy Williams** - Andy Williams 9 (3) 1973
47. **Tender Is The Night** - Johnny Mathis 13 (3) 1962
48. **Getz Au Go Go** - The New Stan Getz Quartet Featuring Astrud Gilberto 24 (2) 1938
49. **The Serendipity Singers** - The Serendipity Singers 11 (1) 1915
50. **It Might As Well Be Swing** - Frank Sinatra & Count Basie 13 (1) 1904
51. **Rag Doll** - The 4 Seasons 7 (1) 1894
52. **The Door Is Still Open To My Heart** - Dean Martin 9 (3) 1884
53. **Something Special For Young Lovers** - Ray Charles Singers 11 (1) 1871
54. **The Unsinkable Molly Brown** - Soundtrack 11 (2) 1870
55. **Bobby Vinton's Greatest Hits** - Bobby Vinton 12 (1) 1869
56. **England's Newest Hit Makers/The Rolling Stones** - The Rolling Stones 11 (1) 1808
57. **Who's Afraid Of Virginia Woolf?** - Jimmy Smith 16 (2) 1774
58. **Dawn (Go Away) And 11 Other Great Songs** - The 4 Seasons 6 (2) 1679
59. **The Animals** - The Animals 7 (3) 1667
60. **More Of Roy Orbison's Greatest Hits** - Roy Orbison 19 (3) 1665
61. **Living A Lie** - Al Martino 13 (1) 1616
62. **Days Of Wine And Roses, Moon River, And Other Academy Award Winners** - Frank Sinatra 10 (2) 1588
63. **Greatest Hits** - Mary Wells 18 (2) 1555
64. **Pure Dynamite! Live At The Royal** - James Brown 10 (1) 1525
65. **The Cat** - Jimmy Smith 12 (2) 1520
66. **Sam Cooke At The Copa** - Sam Cooke 29 (1) 1517
67. **Sweet & Sour Tears** - Ray Charles 9 (2) 1499
68. **Yesterday's Gone** - Chad & Jeremy 22 (1) 1499
69. **The Kingsmen, Volume II** - The Kingsmen 15 (1) 1490
70. **Rick Nelson Sings "For You"** - Rick Nelson 14 (2) 1487
71. **Dream With Dean** - Dean Martin 15 (2) 1384
72. **"Pops" Goes The Trumpet** - Al Hirt & Boston Pops Orchestra 18 (1) 1383
73. **I Don't Want To Be Hurt Anymore** - Nat King Cole 18 (2) 1375
74. **Softly, As I Leave You** - Frank Sinatra 19 (1) 1352
75. **The Beatles' Story** - The Beatles 7 (4) 1335
76. **The Beatles Song Book** - The Hollyridge Strings 15 (1) 1300
77. **On The Move** - Trini Lopez 32 (1) 1277
78. **Licorice Stick** - Pete Fountain 48 (1) 1260
79. **American Tour** - The Dave Clark Five 11 (1) 1233
80. **The Latin Album** - Trini Lopez 18 (2) 1229
81. **Shangri-La** - Robert Maxwell His Harp And Orchestra 17 (1) 1227
82. **The Incomparable Mantovani** - Mantovani 37 (1) 1218
83. **The Sidewinder** - Lee Morgan 25 (3) 1153
84. **Belafonte At The Greek Theatre** - Harry Belafonte 17 (1) 1149
85. **The Many Moods Of Tony** - Tony Bennett 20 (2) 1139
86. **Walk, Don't Run, Vol. 2** - The Ventures 17 (2) 1134
87. **Invisible Tears** - Ray Conniff & His Orchestra & Chorus 23 (1) 1127
88. **The Chipmunks Sing The Beatles Hits** - The Chipmunks 14 (1) 1091
89. **From Russia With Love** - Soundtrack 27 (1) 1036
90. **It Must Have Been Something I Said!** - The Smothers Brothers 23 (2) 1022
91. **Time To Think** - The Kingston Trio 18 (2) 1022
92. **A Bit Of Liverpool** - The Supremes 21 (3) 1016
93. **Roger And Out** - Roger Miller 37 (2) 1015
94. **The Best Of Mancini** - Henry Mancini And His Orchestra 42 (1) 1007
95. **Meet The Searchers/Needles & Pins** - The Searchers 22 (2) 999
96. **Another Side Of Bob Dylan** - Bob Dylan 43 (1) 985
97. **So Tenderly** - John Gary 42 (1) 945
98. **Reflecting** - The Chad Mitchell Trio 29 (1) 928
99. **Moonlight And Roses** - Jim Reeves 30 (2) 922
100. **Be My Love** - Jerry Vale 26 (2) 911

1965

1. **The Sound Of Music** - Soundtrack 1 (2) 29435
2. **Whipped Cream & Other Delights** - Herb Alpert's Tijuana Brass 1 (8) 22164
3. **!!Going Places!!** - Herb Alpert & The Tijuana Brass 1 (6) 17192
4. **South Of The Border** - Herb Alpert & The Tijuana Brass 6 (1) 7622
5. **Why Is There Air?** - Bill Cosby 19 (1) 7355
6. **Help! (Soundtrack)** - The Beatles 1 (9) 6986
7. **Beatles '65** - The Beatles 1 (9) 6884
8. **Rubber Soul** - The Beatles 1 (6) 6749
9. **My Name Is Barbra (Soundtrack)** - Barbra Streisand 2 (3) 6304
10. **September Of My Years** - Frank Sinatra 5 (2) 6107
11. **The Best Of Herman's Hermits** - Herman's Hermits 5 (3) 5995

Rank. Title - Act Peak (Peak Wks) Score
12. **Out Of Our Heads** - The Rolling Stones 1 (3) 5973
13. **Dear Heart** - Andy Williams 4 (3) 5727
14. **Look At Us** - Sonny & Cher 2 (8) 5119
15. **My Name Is Barbra, Two...** - Barbra Streisand 2 (3) 5109
16. **Beatles VI** - The Beatles 1 (6) 4898
17. **The In Crowd** - Ramsey Lewis Trio 2 (1) 4876
18. **Introducing Herman's Hermits** - Herman's Hermits 2 (4) 4748
19. **Herman's Hermits On Tour** - Herman's Hermits 2 (6) 4648
20. **Bringing It All Back Home** - Bob Dylan 6 (1) 4566
21. **The Beach Boys Today!** - The Beach Boys 4 (6) 4482
22. **The Rolling Stones, Now!** - The Rolling Stones 5 (2) 4325
23. **My World** - Eddy Arnold 7 (3) 4040
24. **Blue Midnight** - Bert Kaempfert And His Orchestra 5 (1) 3936
25. **You've Lost That Lovin' Feelin'** - The Righteous Brothers 4 (4) 3910
26. **The Return Of Roger Miller** - Roger Miller 4 (2) 3884
27. **Golden Hits** - Roger Miller 6 (2) 3805
28. **The 4 Seasons' Gold Vault of Hits** - The 4 Seasons 10 (2) 3741
29. **Highway 61 Revisited** - Bob Dylan 3 (1) 3582
30. **Summer Days (And Summer Nights!!)** - The Beach Boys 2 (1) 3318
31. **Zorba The Greek** - Soundtrack 26 (2) 3295
32. **L-O-V-E** - Nat King Cole 4 (3) 3271
33. **Sinatra '65** - Frank Sinatra 9 (1) 3267
34. **December's Children (And Everybody's)** - The Rolling Stones 4 (3) 3215
35. **The Supremes At The Copa** - The Supremes 11 (1) 3076
36. **A Song Will Rise** - Peter, Paul & Mary 8 (3) 2954
37. **Going To A Go-Go** - Smokey Robinson & The Miracles 8 (2) 2801
38. **The Best Of Al Hirt** - Al Hirt 13 (1) 2719
39. **More Hits By The Supremes** - The Supremes 6 (2) 2713
40. **Just Once In My Life...** - The Righteous Brothers 9 (3) 2570
41. **Temptin' Temptations** - The Temptations 11 (1) 2552
42. **That Was The Year That Was** - Tom Lehrer 18 (1) 2499
43. **A Man And His Music** - Frank Sinatra 9 (2) 2377
44. **(Remember Me) I'm The One Who Loves You** - Dean Martin 12 (1) 2362
45. **Girl Happy (Soundtrack)** - Elvis Presley 8 (2) 2361
46. **Houston** - Dean Martin 11 (1) 2347
47. **Welcome To The LBJ Ranch!** - Various Artists 3 (3) 2345
48. **Tony's Greatest Hits, Volume III** - Tony Bennett 20 (1) 2192
49. **Mr. Tambourine Man** - The Byrds 6 (3) 2014
50. **The Ventures A Go-Go** - The Ventures 16 (1) 1996

Rank. Title - Act Peak (Peak Wks) Score
51. **Beach Boys' Party!** - The Beach Boys 6 (1) 1962
52. **Thunderball** - Soundtrack 10 (1) 1962
53. **You Don't Have To Be Jewish** - Various Artists 9 (1) 1942
54. **Downtown** - Petula Clark 21 (2) 1803
55. **My Cherie** - Al Martino 19 (1) 1791
56. **Marianne Faithfull** - Marianne Faithfull 12 (1) 1789
57. **Coast To Coast** - The Dave Clark Five 6 (1) 1773
58. **See What Tomorrow Brings** - Peter, Paul & Mary 11 (1) 1750
59. **Elvis For Everyone!** - Elvis Presley 10 (1) 1740
60. **Your Cheatin' Heart (Soundtrack)** - Hank Williams Jr. 16 (1) 1666
61. **The Nancy Wilson Show!** - Nancy Wilson 24 (2) 1643
62. **Dear Heart** - Jack Jones 11 (1) 1642
63. **Harum Scarum (Soundtrack)** - Elvis Presley 8 (2) 1634
64. **The Nearness Of You** - John Gary 11 (2) 1604
65. **Kinks-Size** - The Kinks 13 (1) 1542
66. **Organ Grinder Swing** - Jimmy Smith 15 (1) 1532
67. **Unforgettable** - Nat King Cole 30 (1) 1519
68. **Dear Heart And Other Songs About Love** - Henry Mancini And His Orchestra And Chorus 11 (1) 1504
69. **Cast Your Fate To The Wind** - Sounds Orchestral 11 (2) 1484
70. **Today-My Way** - Nancy Wilson 7 (1) 1472
71. **The 3rd Time Around** - Roger Miller 13 (2) 1472
72. **The Genius Of Jankowski!** - Horst Jankowski 18 (1) 1460
73. **Dean Martin Hits Again** - Dean Martin 13 (1) 1425
74. **Back To Back** - The Righteous Brothers 16 (1) 1425
75. **Horowitz at Carnegie Hall - An Historic Return** - Vladimir Horowitz 22 (2) 1418
76. **Four Tops Second Album** - Four Tops 20 (2) 1384
77. **The Hit Sounds Of The Lettermen** - The Lettermen 13 (1) 1382
78. **Greatest Hits From The Beginning** - The Miracles 21 (1) 1381
79. **Red Roses For A Blue Lady** - Vic Dana 13 (1) 1373
80. **Ferry Cross The Mersey (Soundtrack)** - Gerry And The Pacemakers 13 (1) 1357
81. **Having A Wild Weekend** - The Dave Clark Five 15 (1) 1332
82. **A Little Bit Of Heaven** - John Gary 17 (2) 1308
83. **Farewell, Angelina** - Joan Baez 10 (1) 1298
84. **All I Really Want To Do** - Cher 16 (2) 1280
85. **Right Now!** - The Righteous Brothers 11 (2) 1264
86. **Gentle Is My Love** - Nancy Wilson 17 (1) 1261
87. **Some Blue-Eyed Soul** - The Righteous Brothers 14 (2) 1260
88. **What's New Pussycat?** - Soundtrack 14 (1) 1253

Rank. Title - Act Peak (Peak Wks) Score
89. **Papa's Got A Brand New Bag** - James Brown 26 (2) 1247
90. **Pearly Shells** - Billy Vaughn And His Orchestra 18 (1) 1224
91. **The Ventures On Stage** - The Ventures 27 (1) 1192
92. **That Honey Horn Sound** - Al Hirt 28 (3) 1185
93. **The Folk Album** - Trini Lopez 18 (1) 1177
94. **Do You Believe In Magic** - The Lovin' Spoonful 32 (1) 1170
95. **Moon Over Naples** - Billy Vaughn And His Orchestra 31 (2) 1130
96. **Chim Chim Cher-ee** - The New Christy Minstrels 22 (1) 1123
97. **The Magic Music Of Far Away Places** - Bert Kaempfert And His Orchestra 27 (1) 1099
98. **The Mantovani Sound** - Big Hits From Broadway And Hollywood - Mantovani 26 (1) 1039
99. **Hush, Hush, Sweet Charlotte** - Patti Page 27 (1) 1028
100. **Red Roses For A Blue Lady** - Wayne Newton 17 (1) 1028

1966

Rank. Title - Act Peak (Peak Wks) Score
1. **Doctor Zhivago** - Soundtrack 1 (1) 21854
2. **The Monkees** - The Monkees 1 (13) 13494
3. **What Now My Love** - Herb Alpert & The Tijuana Brass 1 (9) 12888
4. **Parsley, Sage, Rosemary And Thyme** - Simon & Garfunkel 4 (2) 10665
5. **The Temptations Greatest Hits** - The Temptations 5 (2) 10179
6. **S.R.O.** - Herb Alpert & The Tijuana Brass 2 (6) 8579
7. **Wonderfulness** - Bill Cosby 7 (1) 8093
8. **If You Can Believe Your Eyes And Ears** - The Mamas & The Papas 1 (1) 7986
9. **The Best Of The Animals** - The Animals 6 (3) 7333
10. **Somewhere My Love** - Ray Conniff & His Orchestra & Chorus 3 (4) 7273
11. **Strangers In The Night** - Frank Sinatra 1 (1) 6964
12. **A Man And A Woman** - Soundtrack 10 (2) 6866
13. **Revolver** - The Beatles 1 (6) 6808
14. **The Supremes A' Go-Go** - The Supremes 1 (2) 6652
15. **The Mamas & The Papas** - The Mamas & The Papas 4 (7) 6311
16. **Sergio Mendes & Brasil '66** - Sergio Mendes & Brasil '66 7 (1) 5896
17. **Big Hits (High Tide And Green Grass)** - The Rolling Stones 3 (3) 5844
18. **Lou Rawls Live** - Lou Rawls 4 (1) 5676
19. **Sounds Of Silence** - Simon & Garfunkel 21 (2) 5415
20. **Man Of La Mancha** - Original Cast 31 (3) 4961
21. **Aftermath** - The Rolling Stones 2 (2) 4649
22. **Ballads Of The Green Berets** - SSgt Barry Sadler 1 (5) 4543
23. **Born Free** - Roger Williams 7 (2) 4216
24. **"Yesterday" And Today** - The Beatles 1 (5) 4104
25. **That's Life** - Frank Sinatra 6 (3) 4016

Rank. Title - Act Peak (Peak Wks) Score
26. Lou Rawls Soulin' - Lou Rawls 7 (1) 3955
27. Spanish Eyes - Al Martino 8 (2) 3743
28. Best Of The Beach Boys - The Beach Boys 8 (1) 3529
29. Color Me Barbra (Soundtrack) - Barbra Streisand 3 (2) 3524
30. Boots - Nancy Sinatra 5 (3) 3329
31. And Then...Along Comes The Association - The Association 5 (1) 3303
32. The Dave Clark Five's Greatest Hits - The Dave Clark Five 9 (1) 3166
33. The Wild Angels (Soundtrack) - Davie Allan And The Arrows 17 (2) 3165
34. The Shadow Of Your Smile - Andy Williams 6 (2) 3103
35. The Kinks Greatest Hits! - The Kinks 9 (1) 2978
36. Winchester Cathedral - The New Vaudeville Band 5 (3) 2950
37. Just Like Us! - Paul Revere & The Raiders 5 (1) 2924
38. The Spirit Of '67 - Paul Revere & The Raiders 9 (3) 2863
39. Pet Sounds - The Beach Boys 10 (1) 2810
40. The Impossible Dream - Jack Jones 9 (1) 2802
41. Midnight Ride - Paul Revere & The Raiders 9 (1) 2770
42. Mame - Original Cast 23 (2) 2733
43. Golden Greats - Gary Lewis And The Playboys 10 (4) 2733
44. Winchester Cathedral - Lawrence Welk 12 (2) 2716
45. Sinatra At The Sands - Frank Sinatra With Count Basie And The Orchestra 9 (1) 2712
46. Soul & Inspiration - The Righteous Brothers 7 (2) 2668
47. The Young Rascals - The Young Rascals 15 (1) 2658
48. Four Tops Live! - Four Tops 17 (1) 2605
49. I Hear A Symphony - The Supremes 8 (3) 2599
50. The Shadow Of Your Smile - Johnny Mathis 9 (1) 2530
51. Got Live If You Want It! - The Rolling Stones 6 (2) 2455
52. Gettin' Ready - The Temptations 12 (2) 2397
53. Jim Nabors Sings Love Me With All Your Heart - Jim Nabors 24 (2) 2391
54. Je M'appelle Barbra - Barbra Streisand 5 (2) 2334
55. Rhapsodies For Young Lovers - Midnight String Quartet 17 (1) 2273
56. Herb Alpert's Tijuana Brass, Volume 2 - Herb Alpert's Tijuana Brass 17 (1) 2265
57. Blonde On Blonde - Bob Dylan 9 (1) 2252
58. Crying Time - Ray Charles 15 (1) 2251
59. Wade In The Water - Ramsey Lewis 16 (2) 2188
60. 2nd Vault Of Golden Hits - The 4 Seasons 22 (2) 2127
61. I'll Remember You - Roger Williams 24 (2) 2126
62. Tiny Bubbles - Don Ho 15 (1) 2021
63. Sunshine Superman - Donovan 11 (1) 2000
64. Guantanamera - The Sandpipers 13 (1) 1942

Rank. Title - Act Peak (Peak Wks) Score
65. Peter, Paul And Mary Album - Peter, Paul & Mary 22 (1) 1924
66. Daydream - The Lovin' Spoonful 10 (1) 1900
67. The Movie Song Album - Tony Bennett 18 (2) 1804
68. Spinout (Soundtrack) - Elvis Presley 18 (3) 1755
69. Turn! Turn! Turn! - The Byrds 17 (1) 1737
70. Hang On Ramsey! - Ramsey Lewis Trio 15 (2) 1732
71. A Touch Of Today - Nancy Wilson 15 (1) 1697
72. Rain Forest - Walter Wanderley 22 (1) 1682
73. Animalization - The Animals 20 (2) 1672
74. The Best Of The Lettermen - The Lettermen 17 (1) 1573
75. Bert Kaempfert's Greatest Hits - Bert Kaempfert And His Orchestra 30 (1) 1545
76. Hums Of The Lovin' Spoonful - The Lovin' Spoonful 14 (2) 1525
77. Distant Drums - Jim Reeves 21 (1) 1514
78. Don't Go To Strangers - Eydie Gorme 22 (2) 1472
79. Hold On! (Soundtrack) - Herman's Hermits 14 (2) 1471
80. The Time Of My Life! - John Davidson 19 (2) 1469
81. Mr. Music...Mantovani - Mantovani 27 (2) 1396
82. Johnny Rivers' Golden Hits - Johnny Rivers 29 (2) 1388
83. The Exciting Wilson Pickett - Wilson Pickett 21 (1) 1379
84. Breakout...!!! - Mitch Ryder And The Detroit Wheels 23 (1) 1345
85. The Best Of Herman's Hermits, Volume 2 - Herman's Hermits 20 (2) 1339
86. Born Free - Soundtrack 42 (1) 1322
87. Fifth Dimension - The Byrds 24 (2) 1288
88. Paradise, Hawaiian Style (Soundtrack) - Elvis Presley 15 (2) 1246
89. Got My Mojo Workin' - Jimmy Smith 28 (2) 1222
90. I Want To Go With You - Eddy Arnold 26 (1) 1219
91. Psychedelic Lollipop - Blues Magoos 21 (1) 1219
92. Mrs. Miller's Greatest Hits - Mrs. Miller 15 (1) 1217
93. Andy Williams' Newest Hits - Andy Williams 23 (1) 1185
94. Mantovani Magic - Mantovani 23 (1) 1172
95. Greatest Hits Of All Times - Gene Pitney 61 (2) 1138
96. Changes - Johnny Rivers 33 (2) 1137
97. Watch Out! - Baja Marimba Band 54 (1) 1103
98. Music - A Part Of Me - David McCallum 27 (1) 1095
99. Projections - The Blues Project 52 (2) 1092
100. Frankie And Johnny (Soundtrack) - Elvis Presley 20 (1) 1086

1967

Rank. Title - Act Peak (Peak Wks) Score
1. Sgt. Pepper's Lonely Hearts Club Band - The Beatles 1 (15) 17889
2. More Of The Monkees - The Monkees 1 (18) 12541
3. Are You Experienced? - The Jimi Hendrix Experience 5 (1) 12140
4. Diana Ross And The Supremes Greatest Hits - Diana Ross & The Supremes 1 (5) 11993
5. The Doors - The Doors 2 (2) 11218
6. Disraeli Gears - Cream 4 (2) 9811
7. Headquarters - The Monkees 1 (1) 8689
8. Magical Mystery Tour (Soundtrack) - The Beatles 1 (8) 8172
9. Blooming Hits - Paul Mauriat And His Orchestra 1 (5) 7252
10. I Never Loved A Man The Way I Love You - Aretha Franklin 2 (3) 6978
11. Gentle On My Mind - Glen Campbell 5 (1) 6843
12. Sounds Like... - Herb Alpert & The Tijuana Brass 1 (1) 6677
13. Vanilla Fudge - Vanilla Fudge 6 (4) 6459
14. Revenge - Bill Cosby 2 (1) 6405
15. Surrealistic Pillow - Jefferson Airplane 3 (1) 6325
16. Born Free - Andy Williams 5 (2) 6101
17. The Mamas & The Papas Deliver - The Mamas & The Papas 2 (7) 6067
18. Release Me - Engelbert Humperdinck 7 (3) 6029
19. Pisces, Aquarius, Capricorn, And Jones Ltd. - The Monkees 1 (5) 5738
20. The Four Tops Greatest Hits - Four Tops 4 (1) 5647
21. By The Time I Get To Phoenix - Glen Campbell 15 (4) 5471
22. The Best Of The Lovin' Spoonful - The Lovin' Spoonful 3 (2) 4907
23. Strange Days - The Doors 3 (4) 4773
24. My Cup Runneth Over - Ed Ames 4 (3) 4722
25. Farewell To The First Golden Era - The Mamas & The Papas 5 (3) 4665
26. Alice's Restaurant - Arlo Guthrie 17 (2) 4547
27. Dionne Warwick's Golden Hits, Part One - Dionne Warwick 10 (2) 4514
28. Camelot - Soundtrack 11 (4) 4487
29. Between The Buttons - The Rolling Stones 2 (4) 4292
30. Insight Out - The Association 8 (1) 4254
31. Flowers - The Rolling Stones 3 (6) 4192
32. Bob Dylan's Greatest Hits - Bob Dylan 10 (1) 4188
33. Groovin' - The Young Rascals 5 (1) 4184
34. Herb Alpert's Ninth - Herb Alpert & The Tijuana Brass 4 (2) 4113
35. A Day In The Life - Wes Montgomery 13 (2) 4035
36. The Sea - The San Sebastian Strings 52 (1) 3867
37. Their Satanic Majesties Request - The Rolling Stones 2 (6) 3838
38. Aretha Arrives - Aretha Franklin 5 (5) 3756
39. Album 1700 - Peter, Paul & Mary 15 (2) 3755
40. Ode To Billie Joe - Bobbie Gentry 1 (2) 3754
41. Collections - The Young Rascals 14 (1) 3678

Rank. Title - Act Peak (Peak Wks) Score
42. History Of Otis Redding - Otis Redding 9 (2) 3564
43. Claudine - Claudine Longet 11 (3) 3541
44. Greatest Hits - Paul Revere & The Raiders 9 (2) 3215
45. Up, Up And Away - The 5th Dimension 8 (2) 3162
46. The Lettermen!!!...And "Live!" - The Lettermen 10 (5) 3145
47. Bee Gees' 1st - Bee Gees 7 (1) 3047
48. The Turtles! Golden Hits - The Turtles 7 (3) 2929
49. The Super Hits - Various Artists 12 (2) 2829
50. The Supremes Sing Holland-Dozier-Holland - The Supremes 6 (2) 2805
51. Here Where There Is Love - Dionne Warwick 18 (2) 2757
52. It Must Be Him - Vikki Carr 12 (2) 2756
53. With A Lot O' Soul - The Temptations 7 (1) 2677
54. Fresh Cream - Cream 39 (1) 2650
55. Temptations Live! - The Temptations 10 (1) 2619
56. The Byrds' Greatest Hits - The Byrds 6 (3) 2607
57. Thoroughly Modern Millie - Soundtrack 16 (2) 2607
58. Four Tops Reach Out - Four Tops 11 (4) 2530
59. The Temptations In A Mellow Mood - The Temptations 13 (1) 2492
60. The Last Waltz - Engelbert Humperdinck 10 (2) 2478
61. Welcome To My World - Dean Martin 20 (1) 2465
62. There's A Kind Of Hush All Over The World - Herman's Hermits 13 (2) 2311
63. Love, Andy - Andy Williams 8 (2) 2267
64. The Hollies' Greatest Hits - The Hollies 11 (3) 2243
65. The Best Of Sonny & Cher - Sonny & Cher 23 (1) 2144
66. Georgy Girl - The Seekers 10 (2) 2096
67. Incense And Peppermints - Strawberry Alarm Clock 11 (3) 1854
68. Equinox - Sergio Mendes & Brasil '66 24 (2) 1836
69. Simply Streisand - Barbra Streisand 12 (3) 1808
70. Too Much! - Lou Rawls 18 (2) 1724
71. Mercy, Mercy, Mercy! - "Cannonball" Adderley Quintet 13 (2) 1705
72. Bill Cosby Sings/Silver Throat - Bill Cosby 18 (2) 1688
73. Lou Rawls Carryin' On! - Lou Rawls 20 (2) 1676
74. I'll Take Care Of Your Cares - Frankie Laine 16 (2) 1670
75. This Is My Song - Ray Conniff & His Orchestra & Chorus 30 (2) 1582
76. To Sir, With Love - Soundtrack 16 (4) 1569
77. Boots With Strings - Boots Randolph 36 (2) 1533
78. Cowboys & Colored People - Flip Wilson 34 (2) 1514

Rank. Title - Act Peak (Peak Wks) Score
79. Yardbirds Greatest Hits - The Yardbirds 28 (1) 1513
80. Moby Grape - Moby Grape 24 (1) 1512
81. The Best Of Wilson Pickett - Wilson Pickett 35 (2) 1510
82. How Great Thou Art - Elvis Presley 18 (1) 1505
83. The Best Of Eddy Arnold - Eddy Arnold 34 (2) 1493
84. Gone With The Wind - Soundtrack 24 (1) 1418
85. Rewind - Johnny Rivers 14 (2) 1352
86. In The Arms Of Love - Andy Williams 21 (1) 1306
87. Cabaret - Original Cast 37 (1) 1286
88. When The Snow Is On The Roses - Ed Ames 24 (1) 1277
89. After Bathing At Baxter's - Jefferson Airplane 17 (2) 1263
90. The Supremes Sing Rodgers & Hart - The Supremes 20 (3) 1262
91. These Are My Songs - Petula Clark 27 (2) 1245
92. Johnny Cash's Greatest Hits, Volume I - Johnny Cash 82 (1) 1231
93. Francis Albert Sinatra & Antonio Carlos Jobim - Frank Sinatra & Antonio Carlos Jobim 19 (2) 1222
94. The Windows Of The World - Dionne Warwick 22 (2) 1218
95. Electric Music For The Mind And Body - Country Joe & The Fish 39 (3) 1210
96. Happy Together - The Turtles 25 (2) 1203
97. Greatest Hits - The Righteous Brothers 21 (1) 1203
98. Sugar - Nancy Sinatra 18 (1) 1188
99. Let's Fall In Love - Peaches & Herb 30 (1) 1183
100. Gallant Men - Senator Everett McKinley Dirksen 16 (2) 1182

1968

Rank. Title - Act Peak (Peak Wks) Score
1. Hair - Original Cast 1 (13) 18698
2. In-A-Gadda-Da-Vida - Iron Butterfly 4 (1) 18683
3. The Beatles [White Album] - The Beatles 1 (9) 13693
4. The Graduate (Soundtrack) - Simon & Garfunkel 1 (9) 11898
5. Wichita Lineman - Glen Campbell 1 (5) 11245
6. Cheap Thrills - Big Brother And The Holding Company 1 (8) 10453
7. Bookends - Simon & Garfunkel 1 (7) 10281
8. Time Peace/The Rascals' Greatest Hits - The Rascals 1 (1) 9593
9. Wheels Of Fire - Cream 1 (4) 8375
10. Feliciano! - Jose Feliciano 2 (3) 7730
11. Johnny Cash At Folsom Prison - Johnny Cash 13 (2) 7728
12. Funny Girl (Soundtrack) - Barbra Streisand 12 (1) 7627
13. Beat Of The Brass - Herb Alpert & The Tijuana Brass 1 (2) 7403
14. Greatest Hits - The Association 4 (3) 6883
15. Aretha: Lady Soul - Aretha Franklin 2 (2) 6779
16. The Second - Steppenwolf 3 (1) 6505
17. Days Of Future Passed - The Moody Blues With The London Festival Orchestra 3 (5) 6396
18. TCB (Soundtrack) - Diana Ross & The Supremes And The Temptations 1 (1) 6057
19. Look Around - Sergio Mendes & Brasil '66 5 (2) 5796
20. Waiting For The Sun - The Doors 1 (4) 5773
21. Electric Ladyland - The Jimi Hendrix Experience 1 (2) 5633
22. Wildflowers - Judy Collins 5 (1) 4954
23. Steppenwolf - Steppenwolf 6 (3) 4857
24. John Wesley Harding - Bob Dylan 2 (4) 4807
25. 2001: A Space Odyssey - Soundtrack 24 (1) 4561
26. A Man Without Love - Engelbert Humperdinck 12 (2) 4524
27. Diana Ross & The Supremes Join The Temptations - Diana Ross & The Supremes And The Temptations 2 (1) 4480
28. The Good, The Bad And The Ugly - Soundtrack 4 (2) 4465
29. Honey - Bobby Goldsboro 5 (3) 4427
30. The Tom Jones Fever Zone - Tom Jones 14 (1) 4358
31. The Time Has Come - The Chambers Brothers 4 (2) 4290
32. Realization - Johnny Rivers 5 (5) 4252
33. Aretha Now - Aretha Franklin 3 (2) 4130
34. Oliver! - Soundtrack 20 (2) 4128
35. Fool On The Hill - Sergio Mendes & Brasil '66 3 (1) 4126
36. The Birds, The Bees & The Monkees - The Monkees 3 (4) 4110
37. Axis: Bold As Love - The Jimi Hendrix Experience 3 (3) 4033
38. To Russell, My Brother, Whom I Slept With - Bill Cosby 7 (2) 3821
39. The Dock Of The Bay - Otis Redding 4 (3) 3733
40. Bobbie Gentry & Glen Campbell - Bobbie Gentry & Glen Campbell 11 (2) 3701
41. Honey - Andy Williams 9 (2) 3600
42. A Tramp Shining - Richard Harris 4 (3) 3427
43. Valley Of The Dolls - Dionne Warwick 6 (2) 3381
44. Music From "A Fistful Of Dollars" & "For A Few Dollars More" & "The Good, The Bad And The Ugly" - Hugo Montenegro, His Orchestra And Chorus 9 (1) 3176
45. Beggars Banquet - The Rolling Stones 5 (3) 3171
46. Elvis - TV Special - Elvis Presley 8 (3) 3062
47. Promises, Promises - Dionne Warwick 18 (1) 2942
48. Crown Of Creation - Jefferson Airplane 6 (2) 2849
49. Who Will Answer? And Other Songs Of Our Time - Ed Ames 13 (1) 2821
50. Wish It Would Rain - The Temptations 13 (2) 2761
51. Goin' Out Of My Head - The Lettermen 13 (1) 2723
52. The Crazy World Of Arthur Brown - The Crazy World Of Arthur Brown 7 (2) 2702
53. Truth - Jeff Beck 15 (1) 2689

Rank. Title - Act Peak (Peak Wks) Score
54. **Nancy & Lee** - Nancy Sinatra & Lee Hazlewood 13 (1) 2606
55. **Dean Martin's Greatest Hits! Vol. 1** - Dean Martin 26 (1) 2602
56. **Boogie With Canned Heat** - Canned Heat 16 (2) 2552
57. **Greatest Hits, Vol. 2** - Smokey Robinson & The Miracles 7 (2) 2524
58. **Wild In The Streets** - Soundtrack 12 (2) 2424
59. **Super Session** - Mike Bloomfield/ Al Kooper/Steve Stills 12 (1) 2396
60. **Golden Grass** - The Grass Roots 25 (2) 2292
61. **Harper Valley P.T.A.** - Jeannie C. Riley 12 (2) 2265
62. **200 M.P.H.** - Bill Cosby 16 (1) 2263
63. **Hey, Little One** - Glen Campbell 26 (1) 2254
64. **Once Upon A Dream** - The Rascals 9 (2) 2202
65. **Young Girl** - Gary Puckett And The Union Gap 21 (2) 2196
66. **Late Again** - Peter, Paul & Mary 14 (2) 2174
67. **Donovan In Concert** - Donovan 18 (2) 2162
68. **Hickory Holler Revisited** - O.C. Smith 19 (2) 2145
69. **Cycles** - Frank Sinatra 18 (1) 2141
70. **Honey** - Ray Conniff & His Orchestra & Chorus 22 (1) 2135
71. **The Papas & The Mamas** - The Mamas & The Papas 15 (1) 2131
72. **Who Knows Where The Time Goes** - Judy Collins 29 (2) 2111
73. **The Unicorn** - The Irish Rovers 24 (2) 2090
74. **Jungle Book** - Soundtrack 19 (2) 2083
75. **Aretha In Paris** - Aretha Franklin 13 (2) 2053
76. **The Mason Williams Phonograph Record** - Mason Williams 14 (2) 1993
77. **Renaissance** - Vanilla Fudge 20 (2) 1979
78. **Bonnie And Clyde** - Soundtrack 12 (3) 1955
79. **Traffic** - Traffic 17 (2) 1909
80. **Vincebus Eruptum** - Blue Cheer 11 (3) 1897
81. **God Bless Tiny Tim** - Tiny Tim 7 (2) 1886
82. **Idea** - Bee Gees 17 (3) 1886
83. **Incredible** - Gary Puckett And The Union Gap 20 (1) 1854
84. **In Search Of The Lost Chord** - The Moody Blues 23 (1) 1837
85. **The Hurdy Gurdy Man** - Donovan 20 (1) 1832
86. **Reflections** - Diana Ross & The Supremes 18 (2) 1832
87. **Live At The Apollo, Volume II** - James Brown 32 (1) 1809
88. **Love Child** - Diana Ross & The Supremes 14 (1) 1803
89. **Creedence Clearwater Revival** - Creedence Clearwater Revival 52 (1) 1789
90. **Valley Of The Dolls** - Soundtrack 11 (2) 1769
91. **It Must Be Him** - Ray Conniff & His Orchestra & Chorus 25 (1) 1710
92. **Love Is Blue** - Johnny Mathis 26 (1) 1700
93. **The Promise Of A Future** - Hugh Masekela 17 (1) 1681
94. **A Happening In Central Park** - Barbra Streisand 30 (2) 1678
95. **The Beat Goes On** - Vanilla Fudge 17 (4) 1677
96. **Woman, Woman** - The Union Gap Featuring Gary Puckett 22 (2) 1662

Rank. Title - Act Peak (Peak Wks) Score
97. **Living The Blues** - Canned Heat 18 (2) 1612
98. **The Electrifying Eddie Harris** - Eddie Harris 36 (1) 1604
99. **A New Place In The Sun** - Glen Campbell 24 (1) 1569
100. **Shades Of Deep Purple** - Deep Purple 24 (1) 1555

1969

Rank. Title - Act Peak (Peak Wks) Score
1. **Blood, Sweat & Tears** - Blood, Sweat & Tears 1 (7) 23126
2. **Abbey Road** - The Beatles 1 (11) 15679
3. **Led Zeppelin II** - Led Zeppelin 1 (7) 13989
4. **Santana** - Santana 4 (6) 12586
5. **Tommy** - The Who 4 (2) 12174
6. **Johnny Cash At San Quentin** - Johnny Cash 1 (4) 11537
7. **Chicago Transit Authority** - Chicago 17 (2) 11343
8. **Crosby, Stills & Nash** - Crosby, Stills & Nash 6 (3) 10638
9. **Led Zeppelin** - Led Zeppelin 10 (1) 10151
10. **Bayou Country** - Creedence Clearwater Revival 7 (1) 9860
11. **Romeo & Juliet** - Soundtrack 2 (2) 9730
12. **Green River** - Creedence Clearwater Revival 1 (4) 9555
13. **The Age Of Aquarius** - The 5th Dimension 2 (2) 8929
14. **Easy Rider** - Soundtrack 6 (1) 8708
15. **Nashville Skyline** - Bob Dylan 3 (4) 8062
16. **Tom Jones Live In Las Vegas** - Tom Jones 3 (5) 7828
17. **Donovan's Greatest Hits** - Donovan 4 (4) 7771
18. **Hot Buttered Soul** - Isaac Hayes 8 (3) 7331
19. **Blind Faith** - Blind Faith 1 (2) 7080
20. **Willy And The Poorboys** - Creedence Clearwater Revival 3 (6) 7040
21. **This Is Tom Jones** - Tom Jones 4 (3) 6974
22. **Stand!** - Sly & The Family Stone 13 (1) 6820
23. **Help Yourself** - Tom Jones 5 (2) 6408
24. **Was Captured Live At The Forum** - Three Dog Night 6 (7) 6338
25. **Best Of Cream** - Cream 3 (1) 5962
26. **Get Ready** - Rare Earth 12 (3) 5848
27. **Suitable For Framing** - Three Dog Night 16 (4) 5812
28. **Galveston** - Glen Campbell 2 (1) 5663
29. **Joe Cocker!** - Joe Cocker 11 (3) 5627
30. **Cloud Nine** - The Temptations 4 (1) 5561
31. **Three Dog Night** - Three Dog Night 11 (1) 5552
32. **The Band** - The Band 9 (1) 5473
33. **On The Threshold Of A Dream** - The Moody Blues 20 (1) 5328
34. **Puzzle People** - The Temptations 5 (2) 5097
35. **Let It Bleed** - The Rolling Stones 3 (2) 5094
36. **Ball** - Iron Butterfly 3 (1) 5063
37. **Butch Cassidy And The Sundance Kid** - Soundtrack 16 (2) 4935
38. **Through The Past, Darkly (Big Hits Vol. 2)** - The Rolling Stones 2 (2) 4827
39. **Tom Jones Live!** - Tom Jones 13 (4) 4814

Rank. Title - Act Peak (Peak Wks) Score
40. **A Warm Shade Of Ivory** - Henry Mancini And His Orchestra 5 (1) 4446
41. **Goodbye** - Cream 2 (2) 4361
42. **Best Of Bee Gees** - Bee Gees 9 (1) 4241
43. **Switched-On Bach** - Walter Carlos 10 (1) 4085
44. **The Best Of Charley Pride** - Charley Pride 24 (1) 4079
45. **Smash Hits** - The Jimi Hendrix Experience 6 (2) 4007
46. **Midnight Cowboy** - Soundtrack 19 (2) 3978
47. **The Soft Parade** - The Doors 6 (2) 3805
48. **Yellow Submarine (Soundtrack)** - The Beatles 2 (2) 3755
49. **Everybody Knows This Is Nowhere** - Neil Young & Crazy Horse 34 (2) 3638
50. **I Got Dem Ol' Kozmic Blues Again Mama!** - Janis Joplin 5 (3) 3427
51. **Crimson & Clover** - Tommy James And The Shondells 8 (4) 3415
52. **Memphis Underground** - Herbie Mann 20 (1) 3383
53. **Bobby Sherman** - Bobby Sherman 11 (1) 3166
54. **From Elvis In Memphis** - Elvis Presley 13 (2) 3133
55. **Volunteers** - Jefferson Airplane 13 (2) 3005
56. **At Your Birthday Party** - Steppenwolf 7 (2) 2980
57. **Monster** - Steppenwolf 17 (2) 2957
58. **Glen Campbell - "Live"** - Glen Campbell 13 (1) 2936
59. **Hawaii Five-O** - The Ventures 11 (3) 2935
60. **Happy Heart** - Andy Williams 9 (2) 2702
61. **Soulful Strut** - Young-Holt Unlimited 9 (2) 2672
62. **Feliciano/10 To 23** - Jose Feliciano 16 (2) 2654
63. **Aretha Franklin: Soul '69** - Aretha Franklin 15 (2) 2593
64. **On Time** - Grand Funk Railroad 27 (1) 2581
65. **It's A Beautiful Day** - It's A Beautiful Day 47 (2) 2563
66. **Engelbert** - Engelbert Humperdinck 12 (2) 2547
67. **Aretha's Gold** - Aretha Franklin 18 (1) 2486
68. **Good Morning Starshine** - Oliver 19 (1) 2471
69. **The Ice Man Cometh** - Jerry Butler 29 (1) 2455
70. **Paint Your Wagon** - Soundtrack 28 (2) 2453
71. **Gentle On My Mind** - Dean Martin 14 (1) 2434
72. **Closing The Gap** - Michael Parks 35 (1) 2433
73. **Make It Easy On Yourself** - Burt Bacharach 51 (2) 2425
74. **The Turning Point** - John Mayall 32 (2) 2398
75. **Stand Up** - Jethro Tull 20 (1) 2387
76. **From Memphis To Vegas / From Vegas To Memphis** - Elvis Presley 12 (3) 2345
77. **Live At The Copa** - The Temptations 15 (1) 2337
78. **Hurt So Bad** - The Lettermen 17 (1) 2311
79. **Soulful** - Dionne Warwick 11 (2) 2188
80. **The Cowsills In Concert** - The Cowsills 16 (2) 2183
81. **The Best Of Tommy James & The Shondells** - Tommy James And The Shondells 21 (1) 2162

Rank. Title - Act Peak (Peak Wks) Score
82. The Family That Plays Together - Spirit 22 (2) 2156
83. 12 In A Roe/A Collection Of Tommy Roe's Greatest Hits - Tommy Roe 21 (1) 2145
84. Peter, Paul And Mommy - Peter, Paul & Mary 12 (3) 2132
85. Near The Beginning - Vanilla Fudge 16 (2) 2128
86. The Original Voice Tracks From His Greatest Movies - W.C. Fields 30 (1) 2088
87. A Group Called Smith - Smith 17 (2) 2072
88. My Way - Frank Sinatra 11 (2) 1986
89. For Once In My Life - Vikki Carr 29 (2) 1978
90. Odessa - Bee Gees 20 (3) 1972
91. Tammy's Greatest Hits - Tammy Wynette 37 (1) 1964
92. Swiss Movement - Les McCann & Eddie Harris 29 (1) 1948
93. The Live Adventures Of Mike Bloomfield And Al Kooper - Mike Bloomfield/Al Kooper 18 (2) 1918
94. A Touch Of Gold - Johnny Rivers 26 (1) 1863
95. Beck-Ola - Jeff Beck Group 15 (3) 1841
96. Let Us Go Into The House Of The Lord - The Edwin Hawkins Singers 15 (1) 1835
97. Touching You Touching Me - Neil Diamond 30 (1) 1768
98. Cold Blood - Cold Blood 23 (1) 1750
99. With A Little Help From My Friends - Joe Cocker 35 (2) 1745
100. Brave New World - The Steve Miller Band 22 (2) 1738

1970

Rank. Title - Act Peak (Peak Wks) Score
1. Jesus Christ Superstar - Various Artists 1 (3) 18456
2. Abraxas - Santana 1 (6) 14731
3. Chicago - Chicago 4 (5) 14299
4. Woodstock - Soundtrack 1 (4) 11782
5. Bridge Over Troubled Water - Simon & Garfunkel 1 (10) 11307
6. Sweet Baby James - James Taylor 3 (4) 11267
7. Deja Vu - Crosby, Stills, Nash & Young 1 (1) 11184
8. Close To You - Carpenters 2 (1) 10928
9. Cosmo's Factory - Creedence Clearwater Revival 1 (9) 10485
10. Greatest Hits - Sly & The Family Stone 2 (1) 8278
11. The Partridge Family Album - The Partridge Family 4 (2) 7904
12. First Take - Roberta Flack 1 (5) 7872
13. All Things Must Pass - George Harrison 1 (7) 7410
14. McCartney - Paul McCartney 1 (3) 7209
15. Led Zeppelin III - Led Zeppelin 1 (4) 6898
16. Let It Be (Soundtrack) - The Beatles 1 (4) 6889
17. Third Album - The Jackson 5 4 (3) 6084
18. Closer To Home - Grand Funk Railroad 6 (4) 5948
19. The Isaac Hayes Movement - Isaac Hayes 8 (1) 5908
20. Live At Leeds - The Who 4 (3) 5677
21. After The Gold Rush - Neil Young 8 (5) 5639
22. Blood, Sweat & Tears 3 - Blood, Sweat & Tears 1 (2) 5566
23. Elton John - Elton John 4 (1) 5452
24. Live Album - Grand Funk Railroad 5 (2) 5403
25. Band Of Gypsys - Jimi Hendrix 5 (4) 5259
26. Hey Jude - The Beatles 2 (4) 4999
27. Mad Dogs & Englishmen (Soundtrack) - Joe Cocker 2 (1) 4992
28. Pendulum - Creedence Clearwater Revival 5 (1) 4865
29. ABC - The Jackson 5 4 (2) 4817
30. Naturally - Three Dog Night 14 (2) 4797
31. Layla And Other Assorted Love Songs - Derek & The Dominos 16 (1) 4748
32. Chapter Two - Roberta Flack 33 (1) 4728
33. A Question Of Balance - The Moody Blues 3 (1) 4666
34. American Woman - The Guess Who 9 (4) 4539
35. It Ain't Easy - Three Dog Night 8 (2) 4535
36. Diana Ross Presents The Jackson 5 - The Jackson 5 5 (1) 4519
37. Engelbert Humperdinck - Engelbert Humperdinck 5 (2) 4394
38. Stephen Stills - Stephen Stills 3 (3) 4358
39. Neil Diamond/Gold - Neil Diamond 10 (2) 4353
40. The 5th Dimension/Greatest Hits - The 5th Dimension 5 (2) 4338
41. Raindrops Keep Fallin' On My Head - B.J. Thomas 12 (2) 4324
42. To Be Continued - Isaac Hayes 11 (2) 4236
43. Grand Funk - Grand Funk Railroad 11 (2) 4140
44. Steppenwolf 'Live' - Steppenwolf 7 (2) 4000
45. John Barleycorn Must Die - Traffic 5 (2) 3781
46. Temptations Greatest Hits II - The Temptations 15 (2) 3633
47. Ecology - Rare Earth 15 (5) 3565
48. Curtis - Curtis Mayfield 19 (1) 3351
49. Psychedelic Shack - The Temptations 9 (2) 3327
50. Mountain Climbing! - Mountain 17 (2) 3285
51. Tap Root Manuscript - Neil Diamond 13 (2) 3215
52. Hello, I'm Johnny Cash - Johnny Cash 6 (1) 3209
53. Morrison Hotel - The Doors 4 (4) 3197
54. Here Comes Bobby - Bobby Sherman 10 (2) 3180
55. For The Good Times - Ray Price 28 (3) 3115
56. Portrait - The 5th Dimension 20 (2) 2967
57. Still Waters Run Deep - Four Tops 21 (1) 2937
58. Whales & Nightingales - Judy Collins 17 (1) 2934
59. John Lennon/Plastic Ono Band - John Lennon/Plastic Ono Band 6 (1) 2885
60. The Worst Of Jefferson Airplane - Jefferson Airplane 12 (1) 2830
61. Them Changes - Buddy Miles 35 (2) 2822
62. James Gang Rides Again - The James Gang 20 (1) 2788
63. To Our Children's Children's Children - The Moody Blues 14 (3) 2762
64. Benefit - Jethro Tull 11 (2) 2733
65. Tom - Tom Jones 6 (2) 2733
66. 'Get Yer Ya-Ya's Out!' - The Rolling Stones 6 (2) 2715
67. The Plastic Ono Band - Live Peace In Toronto 1969 - The Plastic Ono Band 10 (2) 2690
68. Black Sabbath - Black Sabbath 23 (2) 2645
69. Stage Fright - The Band 5 (1) 2635
70. Sit Down Young Stranger - Gordon Lightfoot 12 (2) 2614
71. Self Portrait - Bob Dylan 4 (2) 2600
72. Frijid Pink - Frijid Pink 11 (4) 2597
73. "The Devil Made Me Buy This Dress" - Flip Wilson 17 (1) 2590
74. New Morning - Bob Dylan 7 (1) 2443
75. Candles In The Rain - Melanie 17 (3) 2416
76. Bloodrock 2 - Bloodrock 21 (3) 2334
77. The Sesame Street Book & Record - Soundtrack-TV 23 (1) 2333
78. This Girl's In Love With You - Aretha Franklin 17 (2) 2306
79. Diana Ross - Diana Ross 19 (2) 2261
80. 10 Years Together/The Best Of Peter, Paul And Mary - Peter, Paul & Mary 15 (3) 2209
81. Share The Land - The Guess Who 14 (2) 2202
82. Absolutely Live - The Doors 8 (1) 2183
83. Eric Burdon Declares "War" - Eric Burdon And War 18 (3) 2173
84. Ladies Of The Canyon - Joni Mitchell 27 (3) 2113
85. I'll Never Fall In Love Again - Dionne Warwick 23 (2) 2099
86. On The Waters - Bread 12 (2) 2097
87. On Stage-February, 1970 - Elvis Presley 13 (1) 2088
88. Cricklewood Green - Ten Years After 14 (2) 2062
89. Try A Little Kindness - Glen Campbell 12 (2) 2051
90. Fire And Water - Free 17 (2) 2029
91. Workin' Together - Ike & Tina Turner 25 (1) 1877
92. John B. Sebastian - John Sebastian 20 (2) 1865
93. Eric Clapton - Eric Clapton 13 (2) 1847
94. We Made It Happen - Engelbert Humperdinck 19 (2) 1843
95. With Love, Bobby - Bobby Sherman 20 (2) 1837
96. Alone Together - Dave Mason 22 (2) 1830
97. Gasoline Alley - Rod Stewart 27 (1) 1802
98. Sugarloaf - Sugarloaf 24 (2) 1782
99. Live Cream - Cream 15 (1) 1759
100. Blows Against The Empire - Paul Kantner/Jefferson Starship 20 (3) 1714

1971

Rank. Title - Act Peak (Peak Wks) Score
1. Tapestry - Carole King 1 (15) 25830
2. Led Zeppelin IV - Led Zeppelin 2 (4) 13899
3. Every Picture Tells A Story - Rod Stewart 1 (4) 10659
4. Carpenters - Carpenters 2 (2) 10448
5. American Pie - Don McLean 1 (7) 9002
6. Teaser And The Firecat - Cat Stevens 2 (1) 8980
7. Pearl - Janis Joplin 1 (9) 8905
8. Sticky Fingers - The Rolling Stones 1 (4) 8853

Rank. Title - Act Peak (Peak Wks) Score
9. **Mud Slide Slim And The Blue Horizon** - James Taylor 2 (4) 8844
10. **Ram** - Paul & Linda McCartney 2 (2) 8807
11. **Shaft (Soundtrack)** - Isaac Hayes 1 (1) 8587
12. **Aqualung** - Jethro Tull 7 (7) 8099
13. **Tea For The Tillerman** - Cat Stevens 8 (3) 7879
14. **Santana III** - Santana 1 (5) 7577
15. **Music** - Carole King 1 (3) 7352
16. **Golden Bisquits** - Three Dog Night 5 (4) 6926
17. **4 Way Street** - Crosby, Stills, Nash & Young 1 (1) 6910
18. **Chicago III** - Chicago 2 (2) 6848
19. **Up To Date** - The Partridge Family 3 (3) 6505
20. **Poems, Prayers & Promises** - John Denver 15 (5) 6479
21. **Love Story** - Soundtrack 2 (6) 6436
22. **What's Going On** - Marvin Gaye 6 (3) 6199
23. **Every Good Boy Deserves Favour** - The Moody Blues 2 (3) 6059
24. **Paranoid** - Black Sabbath 12 (3) 5864
25. **Imagine** - John Lennon/Plastic Ono Band 1 (1) 5713
26. **Nilsson Schmilsson** - Nilsson 3 (3) 5228
27. **Chicago At Carnegie Hall** - Chicago 3 (1) 5202
28. **Who's Next** - The Who 4 (2) 5051
29. **There's A Riot Goin' On** - Sly & The Family Stone 1 (2) 5000
30. **Tumbleweed Connection** - Elton John 5 (4) 4966
31. **Madman Across The Water** - Elton John 8 (2) 4698
32. **Survival** - Grand Funk Railroad 6 (1) 4577
33. **The Best Of The Guess Who** - The Guess Who 12 (2) 4389
34. **Aretha Live At Fillmore West** - Aretha Franklin 7 (2) 4367
35. **The Cry Of Love** - Jimi Hendrix 3 (2) 4351
36. **The Partridge Family Sound Magazine** - The Partridge Family 9 (2) 4266
37. **Love Story** - Andy Williams 3 (1) 4207
38. **L.A. Woman** - The Doors 9 (1) 4180
39. **Killer** - Alice Cooper 21 (2) 4153
40. **Master Of Reality** - Black Sabbath 8 (2) 4105
41. **All Day Music** - War 16 (3) 3774
42. **Harmony** - Three Dog Night 8 (2) 3761
43. **Fiddler On The Roof** - Soundtrack 30 (2) 3657
44. **E Pluribus Funk** - Grand Funk Railroad 5 (2) 3651
45. **Maybe Tomorrow** - The Jackson 5 11 (2) 3527
46. **Godspell** - Original Cast 34 (1) 3506
47. **Quiet Fire** - Roberta Flack 18 (2) 3375
48. **Emerson, Lake & Palmer** - Emerson, Lake & Palmer 18 (2) 3365
49. **The Low Spark Of High Heeled Boys** - Traffic 7 (2) 3342
50. **The Donny Osmond Album** - Donny Osmond 13 (1) 3214
51. **Gypsys, Tramps & Thieves** - Cher 16 (1) 3158
52. **At Fillmore East** - The Allman Brothers Band 13 (1) 3136
53. **"5th"** - Lee Michaels 16 (1) 3084
54. **Black Moses** - Isaac Hayes 10 (2) 3071
55. **A Nod Is As Good As A Wink...To A Blind Horse** - Faces 6 (4) 3065

Rank. Title - Act Peak (Peak Wks) Score
56. **Cheech And Chong** - Cheech & Chong 28 (3) 3041
57. **Bob Dylan's Greatest Hits, Vol. II** - Bob Dylan 14 (1) 3021
58. **(For God's Sake) Give More Power To The People** - The Chi-Lites 12 (1) 3014
59. **Osmonds** - The Osmonds 14 (3) 3012
60. **Sky's The Limit** - The Temptations 16 (1) 2951
61. **To You With Love, Donny** - Donny Osmond 12 (3) 2927
62. **The Stylistics** - The Stylistics 23 (1) 2783
63. **Tarkus** - Emerson, Lake & Palmer 9 (2) 2751
64. **Stoney End** - Barbra Streisand 10 (4) 2716
65. **Barbra Joan Streisand** - Barbra Streisand 11 (2) 2697
66. **Gather Me** - Melanie 15 (1) 2640
67. **All In The Family** - Soundtrack-TV 8 (1) 2564
68. **Rose Garden** - Lynn Anderson 19 (3) 2483
69. **Curtis/Live!** - Curtis Mayfield 21 (1) 2481
70. **Thirds** - The James Gang 27 (2) 2465
71. **Blue** - Joni Mitchell 15 (2) 2459
72. **Stones** - Neil Diamond 11 (2) 2428
73. **B, S & T; 4** - Blood, Sweat & Tears 10 (2) 2413
74. **Blessed Are ...** - Joan Baez 11 (2) 2387
75. **Bark** - Jefferson Airplane 11 (2) 2382
76. **11/17/1970** - Elton John 11 (1) 2371
77. **The Silver Tongued Devil And I** - Kris Kristofferson 21 (2) 2314
78. **Leon Russell & The Shelter People** - Leon Russell 17 (1) 2296
79. **Stephen Stills 2** - Stephen Stills 8 (2) 2174
80. **Homemade** - The Osmonds 22 (2) 2172
81. **This Is A Recording** - Lily Tomlin 15 (1) 2097
82. **Burt Bacharach** - Burt Bacharach 18 (2) 2088
83. **Songs For Beginners** - Graham Nash 15 (3) 2087
84. **Goin' Back To Indiana** - The Jackson 5 16 (1) 2052
85. **Aretha's Greatest Hits** - Aretha Franklin 19 (2) 2043
86. **Steppenwolf Gold/Their Great Hits** - Steppenwolf 24 (2) 2035
87. **Performance-Rockin' The Fillmore** - Humble Pie 21 (1) 2010
88. **A Space In Time** - Ten Years After 17 (1) 2003
89. **Love It To Death** - Alice Cooper 35 (2) 1999
90. **Wild Life** - Wings 10 (2) 1994
91. **Elvis Country ("I'm 10,000 Years Old")** - Elvis Presley 12 (1) 1982
92. **Rainbow Bridge (Soundtrack)** - Jimi Hendrix 15 (1) 1976
93. **Manna** - Bread 21 (3) 1963
94. **One World** - Rare Earth 28 (1) 1962
95. **Woodstock Two** - Soundtrack 7 (1) 1948
96. **It's Impossible** - Perry Como 22 (2) 1909
97. **Live In Cook County Jail** - B.B. King 25 (3) 1908
98. **Summer Of '42** - Peter Nero 23 (2) 1829
99. **Chase** - Chase 22 (1) 1820
100. **The Point!** - Nilsson 25 (1) 1819

Rank. Title - Act Peak (Peak Wks) Score
1972
1. **You Don't Mess Around With Jim** - Jim Croce 1 (5) 10154
2. **Hot Rocks 1964-1971** - The Rolling Stones 4 (2) 9918
3. **Talking Book** - Stevie Wonder 3 (3) 8080
4. **Harvest** - Neil Young 1 (2) 7962
5. **Honky Château** - Elton John 1 (5) 7808
6. **The World Is A Ghetto** - War 1 (2) 7568
7. **Big Bambu** - Cheech & Chong 2 (1) 7459
8. **Chicago V** - Chicago 1 (9) 7391
9. **No Secrets** - Carly Simon 1 (5) 7375
10. **America** - America 1 (5) 6744
11. **Summer Breeze** - Seals & Crofts 7 (3) 6716
12. **Superfly (Soundtrack)** - Curtis Mayfield 1 (4) 6533
13. **Machine Head** - Deep Purple 7 (2) 6452
14. **Catch Bull At Four** - Cat Stevens 1 (3) 6321
15. **Seventh Sojourn** - The Moody Blues 1 (5) 6301
16. **Lady Sings The Blues (Soundtrack)** - Diana Ross 1 (2) 6201
17. **The Concert For Bangla Desh** - George Harrison and Friends 2 (6) 6165
18. **They Only Come Out At Night** - The Edgar Winter Group 3 (1) 6108
19. **Thick As A Brick** - Jethro Tull 1 (2) 5915
20. **Simon And Garfunkel's Greatest Hits** - Simon & Garfunkel 5 (4) 5831
21. **Fragile** - Yes 4 (7) 5692
22. **Eat A Peach** - The Allman Brothers Band 4 (2) 5683
23. **Rhymes & Reasons** - Carole King 2 (5) 5586
24. **Exile On Main St.** - The Rolling Stones 1 (4) 5537
25. **Never A Dull Moment** - Rod Stewart 2 (3) 5459
26. **All Directions** - The Temptations 2 (2) 5346
27. **Baby I'm-A Want You** - Bread 3 (1) 5112
28. **Rocky Mountain High** - John Denver 4 (3) 5091
29. **The Divine Miss M** - Bette Midler 9 (2) 5034
30. **Hot August Night** - Neil Diamond 5 (3) 5024
31. **I'm Still In Love With You** - Al Green 4 (2) 5005
32. **Let's Stay Together** - Al Green 8 (2) 4963
33. **Carney** - Leon Russell 2 (4) 4705
34. **Moods** - Neil Diamond 5 (3) 4630
35. **Roberta Flack & Donny Hathaway** - Roberta Flack & Donny Hathaway 3 (2) 4421
36. **Living In The Past** - Jethro Tull 3 (3) 4299
37. **Still Bill** - Bill Withers 4 (3) 4281
38. **Paul Simon** - Paul Simon 4 (2) 4225
39. **I Am Woman** - Helen Reddy 14 (4) 4068
40. **The London Chuck Berry Sessions** - Chuck Berry 8 (3) 4034
41. **History Of Eric Clapton** - Eric Clapton 6 (2) 4002
42. **Trilogy** - Emerson, Lake & Palmer 5 (1) 3937
43. **Seven Separate Fools** - Three Dog Night 6 (2) 3787
44. **A Song For You** - Carpenters 4 (3) 3786
45. **School's Out** - Alice Cooper 2 (3) 3734

Rank. Title - Act Peak (Peak Wks) Score
46. Toulouse Street - The Doobie Brothers 21 (2) 3618
47. Joplin In Concert - Janis Joplin 4 (2) 3439
48. A Lonely Man - The Chi-Lites 5 (1) 3349
49. Donny Hathaway Live - Donny Hathaway 18 (2) 3318
50. Ben - Michael Jackson 5 (3) 3309
51. Procol Harum Live In Concert with the Edmonton Symphony Orchestra - Procol Harum 5 (1) 3272
52. Manassas - Stephen Stills/Manassas 4 (2) 3270
53. Close To The Edge - Yes 3 (1) 3249
54. Can't Buy A Thrill - Steely Dan 17 (1) 3203
55. Lookin' Through The Windows - The Jackson 5 7 (1) 3181
56. Caravanserai - Santana 8 (2) 3161
57. Carlos Santana & Buddy Miles! Live! - Carlos Santana & Buddy Miles 8 (3) 3157
58. Elvis As Recorded At Madison Square Garden - Elvis Presley 11 (2) 3063
59. Smokin' - Humble Pie 6 (1) 3010
60. Cabaret - Soundtrack 25 (1) 3000
61. Loggins And Messina - Loggins & Messina 16 (1) 2971
62. Tommy - Various Artists 5 (3) 2970
63. Rock Of Ages - The Band 6 (2) 2929
64. Graham Nash/David Crosby - Graham Nash/David Crosby 4 (3) 2912
65. FM & AM - George Carlin 13 (3) 2901
66. Homecoming - America 9 (4) 2887
67. Young, Gifted And Black - Aretha Franklin 11 (2) 2870
68. One Man Dog - James Taylor 4 (2) 2862
69. Sittin' In - Kenny Loggins With Jim Messina 70 (1) 2771
70. Portrait Of Donny - Donny Osmond 6 (1) 2647
71. Jackson 5 Greatest Hits - The Jacksons 12 (1) 2634
72. All I Ever Need Is You - Sonny & Cher 14 (2) 2618
73. Gilbert O'Sullivan-Himself - Gilbert O'Sullivan 9 (2) 2604
74. Too Young - Donny Osmond 11 (2) 2602
75. Baby Don't Get Hooked On Me - Mac Davis 11 (2) 2594
76. Back Stabbers - The O'Jays 10 (2) 2577
77. Phoenix - Grand Funk Railroad 7 (2) 2563
78. Creedence Gold - Creedence Clearwater Revival 15 (1) 2531
79. Phase-III - The Osmonds 10 (1) 2523
80. Son Of Schmilsson - Nilsson 12 (2) 2432
81. Black Sabbath, Vol. 4 - Black Sabbath 13 (1) 2382
82. The Godfather - Soundtrack 21 (2) 2381
83. Malo - Malo 14 (1) 2371
84. The Osmonds "Live" - The Osmonds 13 (2) 2368
85. More Hot Rocks (Big Hits & Fazed Cookies) - The Rolling Stones 9 (3) 2367
86. Bealtitude: Respect Yourself - The Staple Singers 19 (1) 2328
87. For The Roses - Joni Mitchell 11 (2) 2227
88. Saint Dominic's Preview - Van Morrison 15 (3) 2203

Rank. Title - Act Peak (Peak Wks) Score
89. Demons And Wizards - Uriah Heep 23 (2) 2202
90. Guitar Man - Bread 18 (1) 2192
91. Got To Be There - Michael Jackson 14 (2) 2185
92. Understanding - Bobby Womack 43 (2) 2180
93. Class Clown - George Carlin 22 (2) 2176
94. Amazing Grace - Aretha Franklin 7 (1) 2145
95. Music Of My Mind - Stevie Wonder 21 (1) 2134
96. Something/Anything? - Todd Rundgren 29 (2) 2116
97. Pictures At An Exhibition - Emerson, Lake & Palmer 10 (2) 2084
98. Space Oddity - David Bowie 16 (1) 2014
99. The Rise And Fall Of Ziggy Stardust And The Spiders From Mars - David Bowie 75 (1) 2014
100. Round 2: The Stylistics - The Stylistics 32 (2) 2006

1973

Rank. Title - Act Peak (Peak Wks) Score
1. The Dark Side Of The Moon - Pink Floyd 1 (1) 23108
2. John Denver's Greatest Hits - John Denver 1 (3) 15297
3. Goodbye Yellow Brick Road - Elton John 1 (8) 12843
4. Band On The Run - Paul McCartney And Wings 1 (4) 11152
5. Innervisions - Stevie Wonder 4 (1) 9362
6. Houses Of The Holy - Led Zeppelin 1 (2) 9285
7. The Beatles 1967-1970 - The Beatles 1 (1) 8202
8. Brothers And Sisters - The Allman Brothers Band 1 (5) 7279
9. Don't Shoot Me I'm Only The Piano Player - Elton John 1 (2) 7076
10. The Captain And Me - The Doobie Brothers 7 (2) 7061
11. Chicago VI - Chicago 1 (5) 6934
12. The Best Of Bread - Bread 2 (1) 6903
13. The Beatles 1962-1966 - The Beatles 3 (2) 6830
14. Diamond Girl - Seals & Crofts 4 (1) 6512
15. American Graffiti - Soundtrack 10 (1) 6407
16. Los Cochinos - Cheech & Chong 2 (1) 6317
17. Behind Closed Doors - Charlie Rich 8 (1) 6008
18. Life And Times - Jim Croce 7 (2) 5513
19. Maria Muldaur - Maria Muldaur 3 (3) 5319
20. Goats Head Soup - The Rolling Stones 1 (4) 5266
21. The Joker - The Steve Miller Band 2 (1) 5132
22. I Got A Name - Jim Croce 2 (2) 5040
23. Tres Hombres - ZZ Top 8 (1) 4957
24. Billion Dollar Babies - Alice Cooper 1 (1) 4898
25. Tubular Bells - Mike Oldfield 3 (2) 4893
26. Imagination - Gladys Knight And The Pips 9 (1) 4850
27. There Goes Rhymin' Simon - Paul Simon 2 (2) 4781
28. Made In Japan - Deep Purple 6 (2) 4753
29. The Singles 1969-1973 - Carpenters 1 (1) 4680
30. Let's Get It On - Marvin Gaye 2 (1) 4642

Rank. Title - Act Peak (Peak Wks) Score
31. Ringo - Ringo Starr 2 (2) 4551
32. Aloha From Hawaii Via Satellite - Elvis Presley 1 (1) 4378
33. Red Rose Speedway - Paul McCartney And Wings 1 (3) 4375
34. The Smoker You Drink, The Player You Get - Joe Walsh 6 (2) 4294
35. We're An American Band - Grand Funk 2 (2) 4245
36. Now & Then - Carpenters 2 (1) 4176
37. Living In The Material World - George Harrison 1 (5) 4174
38. Quadrophenia - The Who 2 (1) 3945
39. Jonathan Livingston Seagull (Soundtrack) - Neil Diamond 2 (1) 3874
40. Under The Influence Of... - Love Unlimited 3 (2) 3858
41. Killing Me Softly - Roberta Flack 3 (2) 3825
42. Dueling Banjos - Eric Weissberg & Steve Mandell 1 (3) 3805
43. Foreigner - Cat Stevens 3 (1) 3640
44. Brain Salad Surgery - Emerson, Lake & Palmer 11 (1) 3512
45. Long Hard Climb - Helen Reddy 8 (3) 3510
46. Ship Ahoy - The O'Jays 11 (1) 3438
47. Moving Waves - Focus 8 (2) 3393
48. Deliver The Word - War 6 (2) 3392
49. A Passion Play - Jethro Tull 1 (1) 3303
50. Call Me - Al Green 10 (2) 3301
51. Full Sail - Loggins & Messina 10 (1) 3243
52. Fantasy - Carole King 6 (3) 3155
53. Fresh - Sly & The Family Stone 7 (1) 2971
54. Laid Back - Gregg Allman 13 (1) 2934
55. Touch Me In The Morning - Diana Ross 5 (2) 2899
56. Head To The Sky - Earth, Wind & Fire 27 (1) 2882
57. 3 + 3 - The Isley Brothers 8 (1) 2841
58. Who Do We Think We Are! - Deep Purple 15 (3) 2840
59. Prelude - Deodato 3 (1) 2782
60. I've Got So Much To Give - Barry White 16 (2) 2762
61. Angel Clare - Art Garfunkel 5 (1) 2638
62. Masterpiece - The Temptations 7 (2) 2636
63. Stone Gon' - Barry White 20 (1) 2562
64. Bloodshot - The J. Geils Band 10 (1) 2546
65. The Pointer Sisters - The Pointer Sisters 13 (1) 2503
66. Shoot Out At The Fantasy Factory - Traffic 6 (1) 2471
67. Bette Midler - Bette Midler 6 (1) 2369
68. Lynyrd Skynyrd (pronounced leh-nerd skin-nerd) - Lynyrd Skynyrd 27 (2) 2368
69. Leon Live - Leon Russell 9 (1) 2331
70. Neither One Of Us - Gladys Knight And The Pips 9 (1) 2326
71. Mind Games - John Lennon 9 (3) 2321
72. Wild And Peaceful - Kool & The Gang 33 (1) 2282
73. Aerosmith - Aerosmith 21 (2) 2229
74. Desperado - Eagles 41 (1) 2133
75. Pat Garrett & Billy The Kid (Soundtrack) - Bob Dylan 16 (2) 2130

Rank. Title - Act Peak (Peak Wks) Score
76. **The Six Wives Of Henry VIII** - Rick Wakeman 30 (1) 2130
77. **Birds Of Fire** - The Mahavishnu Orchestra 15 (2) 2128
78. **Farewell Andromeda** - John Denver 16 (2) 2083
79. **Jeff Beck, Tim Bogert, Carmine Appice** - Beck, Bogert & Appice 12 (1) 2019
80. **Yessongs** - Yes 12 (1) 2009
81. **Spectrum** - Billy Cobham 26 (1) 1990
82. **Beginnings** - The Allman Brothers Band 25 (1) 1945
83. **Muscle Of Love** - Alice Cooper 10 (2) 1921
84. **Live At The Sahara Tahoe** - Isaac Hayes 14 (2) 1914
85. **Don't Cry Now** - Linda Ronstadt 45 (1) 1894
86. **Joy** - Isaac Hayes 16 (1) 1890
87. **Deodato 2** - Deodato 19 (1) 1875
88. **Dawn's New Ragtime Follies** - Dawn Featuring Tony Orlando 43 (1) 1852
89. **Jesus Christ Superstar** - Soundtrack 21 (1) 1818
90. **Spinners** - Spinners 14 (1) 1782
91. **Eddie Kendricks** - Eddie Kendricks 18 (1) 1772
92. **Back To The World** - Curtis Mayfield 16 (2) 1745
93. **Green Is Blues** - Al Green 19 (1) 1707
94. **Ol' Blue Eyes Is Back** - Frank Sinatra 13 (1) 1676
95. **Over-Nite Sensation** - The Mothers 32 (1) 1629
96. **In The Right Place** - Dr. John 24 (2) 1606
97. **The Marshall Tucker Band** - The Marshall Tucker Band 29 (1) 1606
98. **Bachman-Turner Overdrive** - Bachman-Turner Overdrive 70 (1) 1602
99. **Tower of Power** - Tower Of Power 15 (1) 1596
100. **All American Boy** - Rick Derringer 25 (1) 1586

1974

Rank. Title - Act Peak (Peak Wks) Score
1. **Back Home Again** - John Denver 1 (1) 11102
2. **Elton John's Greatest Hits** - Elton John 1 (10) 9369
3. **Chicago VII** - Chicago 1 (1) 7973
4. **Court And Spark** - Joni Mitchell 2 (4) 7427
5. **The Sting (Soundtrack)** - Marvin Hamlisch 1 (5) 7349
6. **Caribou** - Elton John 1 (4) 7168
7. **Not Fragile** - Bachman-Turner Overdrive 1 (1) 7020
8. **Endless Summer** - The Beach Boys 1 (1) 6903
9. **Bachman-Turner Overdrive II** - Bachman-Turner Overdrive 4 (2) 6892
10. **What Were Once Vices Are Now Habits** - The Doobie Brothers 4 (1) 6848
11. **Buddha And The Chocolate Box** - Cat Stevens 2 (3) 6219
12. **War Child** - Jethro Tull 2 (3) 6168
13. **Heart Like A Wheel** - Linda Ronstadt 1 (1) 5903
14. **Sundown** - Gordon Lightfoot 1 (2) 5326
15. **On The Border** - Eagles 17 (1) 5317
16. **Fire** - Ohio Players 1 (1) 5305

Rank. Title - Act Peak (Peak Wks) Score
17. **AWB** - Average White Band 1 (1) 5109
18. **Bad Company** - Bad Company 1 (1) 5083
19. **If You Love Me Let Me Know** - Olivia Newton-John 1 (1) 5055
20. **Fullfillingness First Finale** - Stevie Wonder 1 (2) 5002
21. **Phoebe Snow** - Phoebe Snow 4 (1) 4909
22. **461 Ocean Boulevard** - Eric Clapton 1 (4) 4705
23. **Holiday** - America 3 (1) 4445
24. **Photographs & Memories/His Greatest Hits** - Jim Croce 2 (2) 4349
25. **Body Heat** - Quincy Jones 6 (1) 4311
26. **Perfect Angel** - Minnie Riperton 4 (1) 4299
27. **Shinin' On** - Grand Funk 5 (2) 4246
28. **Serenade** - Neil Diamond 3 (2) 4131
29. **Skin Tight** - Ohio Players 11 (3) 4072
30. **Miles Of Aisles** - Joni Mitchell 2 (1) 4070
31. **Can't Get Enough** - Barry White 1 (1) 3956
32. **It's Only Rock 'N Roll** - The Rolling Stones 1 (1) 3928
33. **On Stage** - Loggins & Messina 5 (2) 3837
34. **Planet Waves** - Bob Dylan with The Band 1 (4) 3836
35. **Verities & Balderdash** - Harry Chapin 4 (1) 3835
36. **Bridge Of Sighs** - Robin Trower 7 (1) 3733
37. **Do It ('Til You're Satisfied)** - B.T. Express 5 (1) 3720
38. **The Way We Were** - Barbra Streisand 1 (2) 3692
39. **Walls And Bridges** - John Lennon 1 (1) 3671
40. **Hotcakes** - Carly Simon 3 (1) 3664
41. **Head Hunters** - Herbie Hancock 13 (1) 3602
42. **Wrap Around Joy** - Carole King 1 (1) 3499
43. **Journey To The Centre Of The Earth** - Rick Wakeman With The London Symphony Orchestra & The English Chamber Choir 3 (2) 3498
44. **Pretzel Logic** - Steely Dan 8 (1) 3468
45. **So Far** - Crosby, Stills, Nash & Young 1 (1) 3250
46. **Open Our Eyes** - Earth, Wind & Fire 15 (2) 3222
47. **Second Helping** - Lynyrd Skynyrd 12 (2) 3205
48. **Apostrophe (')** - Frank Zappa 10 (1) 3152
49. **Stop And Smell The Roses** - Mac Davis 13 (2) 3144
50. **Barry Manilow II** - Barry Manilow 9 (1) 3088
51. **Love Is The Message** - MFSB 4 (1) 3069
52. **Free And Easy** - Helen Reddy 8 (1) 3045
53. **Anka** - Paul Anka 9 (2) 3025
54. **Eldorado** - Electric Light Orchestra 16 (2) 2969
55. **Unborn Child** - Seals & Crofts 14 (2) 2815
56. **Al Green Explores Your Mind** - Al Green 15 (1) 2759
57. **Sedaka's Back** - Neil Sedaka 23 (1) 2755
58. **I Feel A Song** - Gladys Knight And The Pips 17 (3) 2750
59. **Mother Lode** - Loggins & Messina 8 (1) 2707
60. **War Live!** - War 13 (1) 2702
61. **Before The Flood** - Bob Dylan/The Band 3 (2) 2697
62. **Marvin Gaye Live!** - Marvin Gaye 8 (2) 2663

Rank. Title - Act Peak (Peak Wks) Score
63. **Love Song For Jeffrey** - Helen Reddy 11 (1) 2630
64. **Rags To Rufus** - Rufus 4 (1) 2614
65. **Tales From Topographic Oceans** - Yes 6 (2) 2614
66. **Nightbirds** - Labelle 7 (3) 2605
67. **Sun Goddess** - Ramsey Lewis 12 (1) 2592
68. **Goodnight Vienna** - Ringo Starr 8 (2) 2581
69. **Welcome Back, My Friends, To The Show That Never Ends - Ladies and Gentlemen** - Emerson, Lake & Palmer 4 (1) 2531
70. **Mighty Love** - Spinners 16 (1) 2520
71. **Dark Horse** - George Harrison 4 (1) 2480
72. **Diamond Dogs** - David Bowie 5 (2) 2476
73. **Sheer Heart Attack** - Queen 12 (2) 2420
74. **Moontan** - Golden Earring 12 (2) 2405
75. **Late For The Sky** - Jackson Browne 14 (2) 2401
76. **Burn** - Deep Purple 9 (1) 2392
77. **I Can Stand A Little Rain** - Joe Cocker 11 (1) 2387
78. **Dragon Fly** - Jefferson Starship 11 (1) 2371
79. **New And Improved** - Spinners 9 (1) 2351
80. **That Nigger's Crazy** - Richard Pryor 29 (1) 2290
81. **Rhapsody In White** - Love Unlimited Orchestra 8 (2) 2231
82. **Cheech & Chong's Wedding Album** - Cheech & Chong 5 (1) 2222
83. **Sabbath Bloody Sabbath** - Black Sabbath 11 (1) 2195
84. **Shock Treatment** - The Edgar Winter Group 13 (1) 2159
85. **ButterFly** - Barbra Streisand 13 (1) 2119
86. **Souvenirs** - Dan Fogelberg 17 (2) 2116
87. **Alice Cooper's Greatest Hits** - Alice Cooper 8 (1) 2081
88. **All The Girls In The World Beware!!!** - Grand Funk 10 (1) 2054
89. **When The Eagle Flies** - Traffic 9 (1) 2051
90. **It'll Shine When It Shines** - Ozark Mountain Daredevils 19 (1) 2033
91. **Flying Start** - The Blackbyrds 30 (1) 2018
92. **Relayer** - Yes 5 (1) 2003
93. **This Is The Moody Blues** - The Moody Blues 11 (1) 2000
94. **David Live** - David Bowie 8 (1) 1991
95. **Let's Put It All Together** - The Stylistics 14 (2) 1986
96. **Let Me In Your Life** - Aretha Franklin 14 (1) 1918
97. **Live It Up** - The Isley Brothers 14 (2) 1914
98. **Crime Of The Century** - Supertramp 38 (2) 1891
99. **The Souther, Hillman, Furay Band** - The Souther, Hillman, Furay Band 11 (1) 1884
100. **Caught Up** - Millie Jackson 21 (1) 1877

1975

Rank. Title - Act Peak (Peak Wks) Score
1. **Fleetwood Mac** - Fleetwood Mac 1 (1) 18198
2. **Red Octopus** - Jefferson Starship 1 (4) 10755
3. **One Of These Nights** - Eagles 1 (5) 10702
4. **That's The Way Of The World (Soundtrack)** - Earth, Wind & Fire 1 (3) 9789

Rank. Title - Act Peak (Peak Wks) Score
5. **Captain Fantastic And The Brown Dirt Cowboy** - Elton John 1 (7) 8391
6. **Still Crazy After All These Years** - Paul Simon 1 (1) 8118
7. **Chicago IX: Chicago's Greatest Hits** - Chicago 1 (5) 7717
8. **Windsong** - John Denver 1 (2) 7642
9. **Toys In The Attic** - Aerosmith 11 (1) 7586
10. **The Dream Weaver** - Gary Wright 7 (3) 6852
11. **Gratitude** - Earth, Wind & Fire 1 (3) 6844
12. **Between The Lines** - Janis Ian 1 (1) 6807
13. **Love Will Keep Us Together** - Captain & Tennille 2 (1) 6501
14. **History/America's Greatest Hits** - America 3 (6) 6466
15. **Physical Graffiti** - Led Zeppelin 1 (6) 6436
16. **Venus And Mars** - Wings 1 (1) 5972
17. **Born To Run** - Bruce Springsteen 3 (2) 5889
18. **The Heat Is On** - The Isley Brothers 1 (1) 5866
19. **A Night At The Opera** - Queen 4 (3) 5738
20. **Have You Never Been Mellow** - Olivia Newton-John 1 (1) 5700
21. **Tommy** - Soundtrack 2 (1) 5315
22. **Alive!** - KISS 9 (4) 5270
23. **An Evening With John Denver** - John Denver 2 (2) 5194
24. **Wish You Were Here** - Pink Floyd 1 (2) 5152
25. **Tryin' To Get The Feelin'** - Barry Manilow 5 (2) 5128
26. **Chicago VIII** - Chicago 1 (2) 5049
27. **Honey** - Ohio Players 2 (1) 5039
28. **Blood On The Tracks** - Bob Dylan 1 (2) 4750
29. **KC And The Sunshine Band** - KC And The Sunshine Band 4 (2) 4590
30. **Rufus Featuring Chaka Khan** - Rufus And Chaka Khan 7 (1) 4562
31. **Face The Music** - Electric Light Orchestra 8 (1) 4530
32. **Main Course** - Bee Gees 14 (1) 4461
33. **Fandango!** - ZZ Top 10 (1) 4374
34. **Welcome To My Nightmare** - Alice Cooper 5 (1) 4253
35. **Young Americans** - David Bowie 9 (2) 3974
36. **Rock Of The Westies** - Elton John 1 (3) 3949
37. **Hearts** - America 4 (1) 3874
38. **Diamonds & Rust** - Joan Baez 11 (1) 3801
39. **Family Reunion** - The O'Jays 7 (1) 3525
40. **Cat Stevens Greatest Hits** - Cat Stevens 6 (2) 3509
41. **Helen Reddy's Greatest Hits** - Helen Reddy 5 (3) 3481
42. **Breakaway** - Art Garfunkel 7 (2) 3474
43. **Daryl Hall & John Oates** - Daryl Hall & John Oates 17 (1) 3473
44. **Why Can't We Be Friends?** - War 8 (1) 3374
45. **A Song For You** - The Temptations 13 (1) 3279
46. **Gorilla** - James Taylor 6 (1) 3257
47. **Prisoner In Disguise** - Linda Ronstadt 4 (3) 3251
48. **Cut The Cake** - Average White Band 4 (1) 3219
49. **Pick Of The Litter** - Spinners 8 (3) 3195
50. **Mister Magic** - Grover Washington Jr. 10 (1) 3167

Rank. Title - Act Peak (Peak Wks) Score
51. **Straight Shooter** - Bad Company 3 (1) 3006
52. **Melissa** - Melissa Manchester 12 (1) 2971
53. **Wind On The Water** - David Crosby/Graham Nash 6 (2) 2837
54. **Stampede** - The Doobie Brothers 4 (2) 2821
55. **The Salsoul Orchestra** - The Salsoul Orchestra 14 (2) 2820
56. **Spirit Of America** - The Beach Boys 8 (2) 2808
57. **Judith** - Judy Collins 17 (1) 2761
58. **Rufusized** - Rufus And Chaka Khan 7 (1) 2759
59. **Blue Sky-Night Thunder** - Michael Murphey 18 (1) 2744
60. **Inseparable** - Natalie Cole 18 (1) 2731
61. **Blow By Blow** - Jeff Beck 4 (1) 2731
62. **Fool For The City** - Foghat 23 (2) 2711
63. **Greatest Hits** - Seals & Crofts 11 (2) 2708
64. **Autobahn** - Kraftwerk 5 (1) 2679
65. **The Who By Numbers** - The Who 8 (2) 2563
66. **The Hissing Of Summer Lawns** - Joni Mitchell 4 (3) 2504
67. **Ted Nugent** - Ted Nugent 28 (2) 2458
68. **Love To Love You Baby** - Donna Summer 11 (2) 2422
69. **Rhinestone Cowboy** - Glen Campbell 17 (2) 2409
70. **Funny Lady (Soundtrack)** - Barbra Streisand 6 (1) 2399
71. **Atlantic Crossing** - Rod Stewart 9 (1) 2387
72. **City Life** - The Blackbyrds 16 (1) 2376
73. **Eric Carmen** - Eric Carmen 21 (2) 2361
74. **The Hungry Years** - Neil Sedaka 16 (2) 2358
75. **Survival** - The O'Jays 11 (1) 2341
76. **Four Wheel Drive** - Bachman-Turner Overdrive 5 (2) 2340
77. **For Earth Below** - Robin Trower 5 (2) 2314
78. **Wake Up Everybody** - Harold Melvin And The Blue Notes 9 (1) 2307
79. **Desolation Boulevard** - The Sweet 25 (2) 2306
80. **No Way To Treat A Lady** - Helen Reddy 11 (1) 2270
81. **Nuthin' Fancy** - Lynyrd Skynyrd 9 (2) 2261
82. **Crash Landing** - Jimi Hendrix 5 (1) 2260
83. **To Be True** - Harold Melvin And The Blue Notes 26 (1) 2217
84. **Before The Next Teardrop Falls** - Freddy Fender 20 (1) 2213
85. **Rock 'N' Roll** - John Lennon 6 (1) 2182
86. **Five-A-Side (An Ace Album)** - Ace 11 (1) 2156
87. **Made In The Shade** - The Rolling Stones 6 (2) 2123
88. **Bay City Rollers** - Bay City Rollers 20 (2) 2107
89. **Win, Lose Or Draw** - The Allman Brothers Band 5 (2) 2076
90. **So What** - Joe Walsh 11 (1) 2050
91. **Feels So Good** - Grover Washington Jr. 10 (1) 2039
92. **Save Me** - Silver Convention 10 (1) 2031
93. **Mellow Madness** - Quincy Jones 16 (2) 2019
94. **Movin' On** - Commodores 29 (1) 2007
95. **Hair Of The Dog** - Nazareth 17 (2) 2005
96. **Frampton** - Peter Frampton 32 (2) 1990
97. **The Original Soundtrack** - 10cc 15 (2) 1986
98. **Cold On The Shoulder** - Gordon Lightfoot 10 (1) 1965

Rank. Title - Act Peak (Peak Wks) Score
99. **The Basement Tapes** - Bob Dylan And The Band 7 (2) 1964
100. **Empty Sky** - Elton John 6 (1) 1955

1976

Rank. Title - Act Peak (Peak Wks) Score
1. **Frampton Comes Alive!** - Peter Frampton 1 (10) 20521
2. **Songs In The Key Of Life** - Stevie Wonder 1 (14) 16923
3. **Boston** - Boston 3 (6) 14152
4. **Hotel California** - Eagles 1 (8) 12868
5. **Their Greatest Hits 1971-1975** - Eagles 1 (5) 12106
6. **Fly Like An Eagle** - The Steve Miller Band 3 (2) 11974
7. **Silk Degrees** - Boz Scaggs 2 (5) 11882
8. **Wings At The Speed Of Sound** - Wings 1 (7) 9726
9. **A Star Is Born (Soundtrack)** - Barbra Streisand & Kris Kristofferson 1 (6) 8852
10. **Breezin'** - George Benson 1 (2) 8344
11. **A New World Record** - Electric Light Orchestra 5 (2) 8133
12. **A Night On The Town** - Rod Stewart 2 (5) 7129
13. **Chicago X** - Chicago 3 (1) 6723
14. **Dreamboat Annie** - Heart 7 (2) 6018
15. **Bigger Than Both Of Us** - Daryl Hall & John Oates 13 (1) 5998
16. **Desire** - Bob Dylan 1 (5) 5953
17. **This One's For You** - Barry Manilow 6 (2) 5876
18. **Part 3** - KC And The Sunshine Band 13 (1) 5842
19. **Rocks** - Aerosmith 3 (3) 5740
20. **Night Moves** - Bob Seger & The Silver Bullet Band 8 (1) 5606
21. **Spitfire** - Jefferson Starship 3 (6) 5588
22. **Children Of The World** - Bee Gees 8 (3) 5355
23. **Greatest Hits** - Linda Ronstadt 6 (1) 5314
24. **Wings Over America** - Paul McCartney And Wings 1 (1) 5248
25. **Spirit** - Earth, Wind & Fire 2 (2) 4953
26. **Year Of The Cat** - Al Stewart 5 (3) 4916
27. **Leftoverture** - Kansas 5 (4) 4802
28. **Black And Blue** - The Rolling Stones 1 (4) 4733
29. **Best Of The Doobies** - The Doobie Brothers 5 (1) 4564
30. **Look Out For #1** - The Brothers Johnson 9 (2) 4485
31. **Hot On The Tracks** - Commodores 12 (3) 4400
32. **Hasten Down The Wind** - Linda Ronstadt 3 (3) 4346
33. **Rock And Roll Over** - KISS 11 (2) 4256
34. **Presence** - Led Zeppelin 1 (2) 4218
35. **Beautiful Noise** - Neil Diamond 4 (3) 4132
36. **Summertime Dream** - Gordon Lightfoot 12 (2) 4127
37. **Song Of Joy** - Captain & Tennille 9 (2) 4113
38. **The Pretender** - Jackson Browne 5 (3) 3859
39. **The Song Remains The Same (Soundtrack)** - Led Zeppelin 2 (3) 3843
40. **Destroyer** - KISS 11 (1) 3772
41. **Diana Ross (II)** - Diana Ross 5 (1) 3743
42. **Rock 'N' Roll Music** - The Beatles 2 (2) 3564

Rank. Title - Act Peak (Peak Wks) Score
43. Station To Station - David Bowie 3 (2) 3525
44. One More From The Road - Lynyrd Skynyrd 9 (3) 3462
45. Firefall - Firefall 28 (2) 3446
46. Wild Cherry - Wild Cherry 5 (2) 3397
47. Endless Flight - Leo Sayer 10 (2) 3371
48. I Want You - Marvin Gaye 4 (1) 3363
49. Thoroughbred - Carole King 3 (3) 3360
50. 'Live' Bullet - Bob Seger & The Silver Bullet Band 34 (1) 3359
51. Blue Moves - Elton John 3 (3) 3289
52. Dr. Buzzard's Original Savannah Band - Dr. Buzzard's Original Savannah Band 22 (2) 3237
53. Spirit - John Denver 7 (2) 3216
54. Mothership Connection - Parliament 13 (2) 3129
55. Run With The Pack - Bad Company 5 (2) 3069
56. Anyway You Like It - Thelma Houston 11 (2) 3022
57. Brass Construction - Brass Construction 10 (1) 3002
58. Takin' It To The Streets - The Doobie Brothers 8 (1) 2991
59. All Things In Time - Lou Rawls 7 (2) 2947
60. Wanted! The Outlaws - Waylon Jennings, Willie Nelson, Jessi Colter, Tompall Glaser 10 (2) 2890
61. Car Wash - Rose Royce 14 (2) 2828
62. Harvest For The World - The Isley Brothers 9 (2) 2792
63. Eargasm - Johnnie Taylor 5 (2) 2713
64. Greatest Hits - War 6 (3) 2664
65. Natalie - Natalie Cole 13 (1) 2646
66. Nights Are Forever - England Dan & John Ford Coley 17 (1) 2640
67. Rastaman Vibration - Bob Marley And The Wailers 8 (2) 2535
68. Soul Searching - Average White Band 9 (1) 2478
69. Changesonebowie - David Bowie 10 (1) 2467
70. 15 Big Ones - The Beach Boys 8 (1) 2437
71. The Roaring Silence - Manfred Mann's Earth Band 10 (2) 2423
72. Here And There - Elton John 4 (2) 2275
73. Amigos - Santana 10 (2) 2247
74. Diana Ross' Greatest Hits - Diana Ross 13 (2) 2188
75. Agents Of Fortune - Blue Öyster Cult 29 (1) 2186
76. No Reason To Cry - Eric Clapton 15 (3) 2173
77. Manhattans - The Manhattans 16 (1) 2147
78. The Royal Scam - Steely Dan 15 (2) 2133
79. Alice Cooper Goes To Hell - Alice Cooper 27 (1) 2077
80. In The Pocket - James Taylor 16 (1) 2054
81. Contradiction - Ohio Players 12 (2) 2029
82. Happiness Is Being With The Spinners - Spinners 25 (2) 1974
83. Thirty Three & 1/3 - George Harrison 11 (2) 1965
84. Wired - Jeff Beck 16 (1) 1931
85. Aftertones - Janis Ian 12 (2) 1910
86. Ole ELO - Electric Light Orchestra 32 (1) 1908
87. Tales Of Mystery & Imagination - The Alan Parsons Project 38 (1) 1902

Rank. Title - Act Peak (Peak Wks) Score
88. Sparkle (Soundtrack) - Aretha Franklin 18 (3) 1899
89. Silver Convention - Silver Convention 13 (1) 1891
90. I Hope We Get To Love In Time - Marilyn McCoo & Billy Davis Jr. 30 (1) 1875
91. Come On Over - Olivia Newton-John 13 (1) 1869
92. Sky High! - Tavares 24 (2) 1862
93. After The Lovin' - Engelbert Humperdinck 17 (2) 1851
94. Hideaway - America 11 (3) 1839
95. Jailbreak - Thin Lizzy 18 (2) 1839
96. Get Closer - Seals & Crofts 37 (1) 1828
97. Struttin' My Stuff - Elvin Bishop 18 (2) 1815
98. Greatest Hits - ABBA 48 (1) 1814
99. M.U. The Best Of Jethro Tull - Jethro Tull 13 (2) 1768
100. Starland Vocal Band - Starland Vocal Band 20 (2) 1758

1977

Rank. Title - Act Peak (Peak Wks) Score
1. Rumours - Fleetwood Mac 1 (31) 27526
2. Saturday Night Fever (Soundtrack) - Bee Gees 1 (24) 19144
3. The Stranger - Billy Joel 2 (6) 14610
4. Foreigner - Foreigner 4 (5) 9882
5. Aja - Steely Dan 3 (7) 9774
6. Simple Dreams - Linda Ronstadt 1 (5) 8545
7. The Grand Illusion - Styx 6 (2) 8016
8. Slowhand - Eric Clapton 2 (5) 7923
9. Commodores - Commodores 3 (3) 7441
10. Feels So Good - Chuck Mangione 2 (2) 7254
11. Foot Loose & Fancy Free - Rod Stewart 2 (6) 7013
12. Point Of Know Return - Kansas 4 (2) 6810
13. Here At Last...Bee Gees...Live - Bee Gees 8 (1) 6803
14. Barry Manilow Live - Barry Manilow 1 (1) 6736
15. Book Of Dreams - The Steve Miller Band 2 (2) 6696
16. All 'N All - Earth, Wind & Fire 3 (6) 6106
17. Star Wars - Soundtrack 2 (3) 6071
18. Shaun Cassidy - Shaun Cassidy 3 (2) 5827
19. Anytime...Anywhere - Rita Coolidge 6 (4) 5275
20. Bat Out Of Hell - Meat Loaf 14 (1) 5240
21. News Of The World - Queen 3 (2) 5213
22. JT - James Taylor 4 (5) 5169
23. Out Of The Blue - Electric Light Orchestra 4 (4) 5045
24. CSN - Crosby, Stills & Nash 2 (4) 4989
25. I'm In You - Peter Frampton 2 (4) 4671
26. French Kiss - Bob Welch 12 (2) 4546
27. Little Queen - Heart 9 (2) 4503
28. Marvin Gaye Live At The London Palladium - Marvin Gaye 3 (3) 4450
29. Rocky - Soundtrack 4 (6) 4092
30. I Robot - The Alan Parsons Project 9 (3) 3902
31. Moody Blue - Elvis Presley 3 (3) 3887
32. Flowing Rivers - Andy Gibb 19 (4) 3832
33. Rejoice - The Emotions 7 (3) 3823
34. Changes In Latitudes, Changes In Attitudes - Jimmy Buffett 12 (2) 3750

Rank. Title - Act Peak (Peak Wks) Score
35. Right On Time - The Brothers Johnson 13 (3) 3695
36. Streisand Superman - Barbra Streisand 3 (4) 3602
37. Commodores Live! - Commodores 3 (2) 3522
38. In Flight - George Benson 9 (2) 3477
39. Go For Your Guns - The Isley Brothers 6 (2) 3468
40. Street Survivors - Lynyrd Skynyrd 5 (2) 3443
41. Even In The Quietest Moments... - Supertramp 16 (2) 3418
42. Little Criminals - Randy Newman 9 (2) 3124
43. Animals - Pink Floyd 3 (3) 3108
44. I Remember Yesterday - Donna Summer 18 (1) 3051
45. I'm Glad You're Here With Me Tonight - Neil Diamond 6 (2) 3041
46. Let's Get Small - Steve Martin 10 (2) 3035
47. Alive II - KISS 7 (2) 3023
48. A Place In The Sun - Pablo Cruise 19 (2) 2997
49. Rose Royce II/In Full Bloom - Rose Royce 9 (2) 2948
50. Thankful - Natalie Cole 16 (1) 2927
51. A Rock And Roll Alternative - Atlanta Rhythm Section 11 (1) 2926
52. Too Hot To Handle - Heatwave 11 (1) 2892
53. Nether Lands - Dan Fogelberg 13 (1) 2848
54. Cat Scratch Fever - Ted Nugent 17 (1) 2820
55. Love Gun - KISS 4 (2) 2788
56. Unpredictable - Natalie Cole 8 (2) 2786
57. Funkentelechy Vs. The Placebo Syndrome - Parliament 13 (1) 2705
58. Here You Come Again - Dolly Parton 20 (2) 2682
59. Born Late - Shaun Cassidy 6 (3) 2635
60. Carolina Dreams - The Marshall Tucker Band 23 (1) 2565
61. You Light Up My Life - Debby Boone 6 (3) 2560
62. Songs From The Wood - Jethro Tull 8 (2) 2518
63. The Beatles At The Hollywood Bowl - The Beatles 2 (2) 2503
64. Something To Love - L.T.D. 21 (2) 2471
65. Izitso - Cat Stevens 7 (2) 2460
66. Works, Volume 1 - Emerson, Lake & Palmer 12 (2) 2442
67. Down Two Then Left - Boz Scaggs 11 (2) 2430
68. Village People - Village People 54 (2) 2422
69. Going For The One - Yes 8 (2) 2421
70. Floaters - The Floaters 10 (2) 2403
71. Barry White Sings For Someone You Love - Barry White 8 (2) 2402
72. We Must Believe In Magic - Crystal Gayle 12 (2) 2354
73. Teddy Pendergrass - Teddy Pendergrass 17 (3) 2327
74. Ol' Waylon - Waylon Jennings 15 (2) 2323
75. Once Upon A Time... - Donna Summer 26 (2) 2318
76. Chicago XI - Chicago 6 (2) 2251
77. Brick - Brick 15 (1) 2241
78. Arrival - ABBA 20 (2) 2238
79. A Real Mother For Ya - Johnny Guitar Watson 20 (2) 2149

Rank. Title - Act Peak (Peak Wks) Score
80. Ahh... The Name Is Bootsy, Baby - Bootsy's Rubber Band 16 (4) 2108
81. Moonflower - Santana 10 (4) 2061
82. Ask Rufus - Rufus And Chaka Khan 12 (2) 2013
83. Olivia Newton-John's Greatest Hits - Olivia Newton-John 13 (2) 2002
84. Slave - Slave 22 (1) 1934
85. Celebrate Me Home - Kenny Loggins 27 (1) 1932
86. Foghat Live - Foghat 11 (1) 1928
87. Exodus - Bob Marley And The Wailers 20 (5) 1910
88. Star Wars & Other Galactic Funk - Meco 13 (2) 1899
89. Galaxy - War 15 (2) 1878
90. Lights Out - UFO 23 (2) 1861
91. Baby It's Me - Diana Ross 18 (2) 1845
92. Chic - Chic 27 (1) 1842
93. Love You Live - The Rolling Stones 5 (3) 1840
94. A Day At The Races - Queen 5 (1) 1797
95. Player - Player 26 (2) 1794
96. John Denver's Greatest Hits, Volume 2 - John Denver 6 (1) 1792
97. Livin' On The Fault Line - The Doobie Brothers 10 (3) 1792
98. Burnin' Sky - Bad Company 15 (2) 1784
99. Love At The Greek - Neil Diamond 8 (2) 1780
100. Draw The Line - Aerosmith 11 (3) 1694

1978

Rank. Title - Act Peak (Peak Wks) Score
1. Grease - Soundtrack 1 (12) 13745
2. 52nd Street - Billy Joel 1 (8) 10703
3. Some Girls - The Rolling Stones 1 (2) 10361
4. Double Vision - Foreigner 3 (8) 10010
5. Minute By Minute - The Doobie Brothers 1 (5) 9288
6. Live And More - Donna Summer 1 (1) 8386
7. Stranger In Town - Bob Seger & The Silver Bullet Band 4 (2) 8305
8. The Cars - The Cars 18 (2) 7689
9. Pieces Of Eight - Styx 6 (1) 7036
10. Blondes Have More Fun - Rod Stewart 1 (3) 6671
11. Running On Empty - Jackson Browne 3 (2) 6523
12. Natural High - Commodores 3 (8) 6240
13. The Gambler - Kenny Rogers 12 (3) 6142
14. 2-Hot! - Peaches & Herb 2 (6) 6131
15. Van Halen - Van Halen 19 (2) 6065
16. Cruisin' - Village People 3 (4) 6026
17. Parallel Lines - Blondie 6 (3) 5717
18. Even Now - Barry Manilow 3 (3) 5474
19. Don't Look Back - Boston 1 (2) 5419
20. Barbra Streisand's Greatest Hits, Volume 2 - Barbra Streisand 1 (3) 5226
21. City To City - Gerry Rafferty 1 (1) 5110
22. Earth - Jefferson Starship 5 (7) 5106
23. Darkness On The Edge Of Town - Bruce Springsteen 5 (3) 4951
24. A Wild And Crazy Guy - Steve Martin 2 (6) 4946
25. C'est Chic - Chic 4 (4) 4931
26. London Town - Wings 2 (6) 4850

Rank. Title - Act Peak (Peak Wks) Score
27. Living In The U.S.A. - Linda Ronstadt 1 (1) 4804
28. Briefcase Full Of Blues - Blues Brothers 1 (1) 4763
29. Weekend In L.A. - George Benson 5 (3) 4426
30. Toto - Toto 9 (2) 4137
31. Shadow Dancing - Andy Gibb 7 (5) 4069
32. The Best Of Earth, Wind & Fire, Vol. I - Earth, Wind & Fire 6 (1) 4044
33. Infinity - Journey 21 (1) 3957
34. Who Are You - The Who 2 (2) 3916
35. Worlds Away - Pablo Cruise 6 (3) 3880
36. Greatest Hits - Barry Manilow 7 (1) 3851
37. Macho Man - Village People 24 (2) 3831
38. Dog And Butterfly - Heart 17 (1) 3764
39. Champagne Jam - Atlanta Rhythm Section 7 (2) 3722
40. Fantasy Love Affair - Peter Brown 11 (2) 3524
41. Twin Sons Of Different Mothers - Dan Fogelberg/Tim Weisberg 8 (3) 3504
42. Backless - Eric Clapton 8 (3) 3494
43. Stardust - Willie Nelson 30 (1) 3488
44. Nightwatch - Kenny Loggins 7 (5) 3483
45. Totally Hot - Olivia Newton-John 7 (2) 3388
46. "But Seriously Folks..." - Joe Walsh 8 (2) 3226
47. Sgt. Pepper's Lonely Hearts Club Band - Soundtrack 5 (6) 3219
48. Destiny - The Jacksons 11 (2) 3181
49. A Taste Of Honey - A Taste Of Honey 6 (2) 3180
50. Sleeper Catcher - Little River Band 16 (2) 3077
51. Boys In The Trees - Carly Simon 10 (3) 3027
52. You Don't Bring Me Flowers - Neil Diamond 4 (3) 2963
53. The Album - ABBA 14 (2) 2946
54. Come Get It! - Rick James 13 (1) 2904
55. FM - Soundtrack 5 (2) 2902
56. Legend - Poco 14 (2) 2856
57. Blue Lights In The Basement - Roberta Flack 8 (1) 2852
58. Time Passages - Al Stewart 10 (1) 2841
59. Showdown - The Isley Brothers 4 (3) 2838
60. Thank God It's Friday - Soundtrack 10 (3) 2815
61. So Full Of Love - The O'Jays 6 (2) 2763
62. Brother To Brother - Gino Vannelli 13 (3) 2750
63. Smooth Talk - Evelyn "Champagne" King 14 (2) 2726
64. Life Is A Song Worth Singing - Teddy Pendergrass 11 (2) 2687
65. Comes A Time - Neil Young 7 (2) 2660
66. Let's Keep It That Way - Anne Murray 12 (1) 2589
67. Ten Years Of Gold - Kenny Rogers 33 (2) 2566
68. Children Of Sanchez - Chuck Mangione 14 (2) 2562
69. Excitable Boy - Warren Zevon 8 (2) 2546
70. You Light Up My Life - Johnny Mathis 9 (3) 2385
71. Central Heating - Heatwave 10 (2) 2341
72. Hot Streets - Chicago 12 (1) 2337
73. Get Off - Foxy 12 (1) 2286

Rank. Title - Act Peak (Peak Wks) Score
74. Blam!! - The Brothers Johnson 7 (3) 2283
75. More Songs About Buildings And Food - Talking Heads 29 (1) 2250
76. Son Of A Son Of A Sailor - Jimmy Buffett 10 (2) 2228
77. Live! Bootleg - Aerosmith 13 (2) 2223
78. ...And Then There Were Three... - Genesis 14 (1) 2200
79. Jazz - Queen 6 (2) 2182
80. Songbird - Barbra Streisand 12 (2) 2155
81. Is It Still Good To Ya - Ashford & Simpson 20 (1) 2148
82. Live At The Bijou - Grover Washington Jr. 11 (2) 2135
83. Nicolette - Nicolette Larson 15 (2) 2121
84. Eddie Money - Eddie Money 37 (2) 2099
85. Street Player - Rufus And Chaka Khan 14 (2) 2079
86. Waylon & Willie - Waylon Jennings & Willie Nelson 12 (1) 2075
87. Energy - The Pointer Sisters 13 (3) 2026
88. Octave - The Moody Blues 13 (1) 2006
89. Waiting For Columbus - Little Feat 18 (2) 1946
90. Togetherness - L.T.D. 18 (1) 1929
91. Mixed Emotions - Exile 14 (2) 1927
92. Move It On Over - George Thorogood & The Destroyers 33 (1) 1895
93. Sounds...And Stuff Like That!! - Quincy Jones 15 (1) 1846
94. Life Beyond L.A. - Ambrosia 19 (2) 1840
95. Gene Simmons - Gene Simmons(2) 22 (2) 1803
96. Chaka - Chaka Khan 12 (3) 1800
97. Bobby Caldwell - Bobby Caldwell 21 (2) 1758
98. Ace Frehley - Ace Frehley 26 (3) 1749
99. Willie Nelson And Family Live - Willie Nelson 32 (2) 1726
100. Inner Secrets - Santana 27 (2) 1716

1979

Rank. Title - Act Peak (Peak Wks) Score
1. Breakfast In America - Supertramp 1 (6) 13764
2. Off The Wall - Michael Jackson 3 (3) 13427
3. The Wall - Pink Floyd 1 (15) 13311
4. The Long Run - Eagles 1 (9) 11205
5. Bad Girls - Donna Summer 1 (6) 8577
6. In Through The Out Door - Led Zeppelin 1 (7) 8553
7. Spirits Having Flown - Bee Gees 1 (6) 8229
8. Damn The Torpedoes - Tom Petty And The Heartbreakers 2 (7) 8108
9. Get The Knack - The Knack 1 (5) 7540
10. Cornerstone - Styx 2 (1) 6989
11. On The Radio: Greatest Hits: Volumes I & II - Donna Summer 1 (1) 6739
12. Cheap Trick At Budokan - Cheap Trick 4 (4) 6482
13. Midnight Magic - Commodores 3 (2) 6387
14. Candy-O - The Cars 3 (4) 6067
15. Desolation Angels - Bad Company 3 (2) 5595
16. In The Heat Of The Night - Pat Benatar 12 (2) 5547
17. Phoenix - Dan Fogelberg 3 (2) 5420
18. Dire Straits - Dire Straits 2 (1) 5417

Rank. Title - Act Peak (Peak Wks) Score
19. **I Am** - Earth, Wind & Fire 3 (3) 5406
20. **Kenny** - Kenny Rogers 5 (2) 5370
21. **Rickie Lee Jones** - Rickie Lee Jones 3 (2) 5217
22. **Tusk** - Fleetwood Mac 4 (3) 4913
23. **Evolution** - Journey 20 (2) 4507
24. **Van Halen II** - Van Halen 6 (3) 4482
25. **Bee Gees Greatest** - Bee Gees 1 (1) 4406
26. **Discovery** - Electric Light Orchestra 5 (2) 4323
27. **Head Games** - Foreigner 5 (3) 4255
28. **Ladies' Night** - Kool & The Gang 13 (4) 4088
29. **We Are Family** - Sister Sledge 3 (2) 4071
30. **Greatest Hits** - Waylon Jennings 28 (1) 3978
31. **Rise** - Herb Alpert 6 (1) 3939
32. **Million Mile Reflections** - The Charlie Daniels Band 5 (3) 3838
33. **The Rose (Soundtrack)** - Bette Midler 12 (3) 3819
34. **Love Tracks** - Gloria Gaynor 4 (2) 3789
35. **Keep The Fire** - Kenny Loggins 16 (2) 3776
36. **Rust Never Sleeps** - Neil Young & Crazy Horse 8 (2) 3716
37. **Dionne(2)** - Dionne Warwick 12 (1) 3593
38. **Eat To The Beat** - Blondie 17 (3) 3570
39. **Journey Through The Secret Life Of Plants** - Stevie Wonder 4 (5) 3272
40. **Highway To Hell** - AC/DC 17 (2) 3255
41. **Wet** - Barbra Streisand 7 (4) 3155
42. **Disco Nights** - GQ 13 (1) 3146
43. **Slow Train Coming** - Bob Dylan 3 (4) 3127
44. **Freedom At Point Zero** - Jefferson Starship 10 (1) 3057
45. **Teddy** - Teddy Pendergrass 5 (2) 2994
46. **Flirtin' With Disaster** - Molly Hatchet 19 (2) 2838
47. **The Boss** - Diana Ross 14 (2) 2825
48. **One Voice** - Barry Manilow 9 (3) 2784
49. **Livin' Inside Your Love** - George Benson 7 (2) 2783
50. **Street Life** - The Crusaders 18 (1) 2774
51. **Enlightened Rogues** - The Allman Brothers Band 9 (4) 2714
52. **Bombs Away Dream Babies** - John Stewart 10 (1) 2711
53. **Reggatta De Blanc** - The Police 25 (2) 2694
54. **First Under The Wire** - Little River Band 10 (3) 2687
55. **Gold & Platinum** - Lynyrd Skynyrd 12 (2) 2678
56. **Go West** - Village People 8 (3) 2579
57. **Morning Dance** - Spyro Gyra 27 (3) 2545
58. **Dream Police** - Cheap Trick 6 (2) 2528
59. **Bustin' Out Of L Seven** - Rick James 16 (3) 2430
60. **Risque** - Chic 5 (2) 2414
61. **Dynasty** - KISS 9 (3) 2407
62. **Masterjam** - Rufus And Chaka Khan 14 (3) 2405
63. **Where There's Smoke** - Smokey Robinson 17 (2) 2370
64. **The Kids Are Alright (Soundtrack)** - The Who 8 (2) 2320
65. **Armed Forces** - Elvis Costello 10 (2) 2310
66. **Back To The Egg** - Wings 8 (2) 2258
67. **Outlandos D'Amour** - The Police 23 (1) 2233
68. **Instant Funk** - Instant Funk 12 (1) 2198

Rank. Title - Act Peak (Peak Wks) Score
69. **Songs Of Love** - Anita Ward 8 (2) 2164
70. **The B-52's** - The B-52s 59 (2) 2154
71. **Reality... What A Concept** - Robin Williams 10 (2) 2118
72. **Flag** - James Taylor 10 (1) 2110
73. **Deguello** - ZZ Top 24 (3) 2062
74. **Look Sharp!** - Joe Jackson 20 (2) 2057
75. **Eve** - The Alan Parsons Project 13 (2) 2057
76. **Live Rust** - Neil Young With Crazy Horse 15 (2) 1985
77. **One On One** - Bob James/Earl Klugh 23 (3) 1967
78. **Monolith** - Kansas 10 (2) 1948
79. **Voulez-Vous** - ABBA 19 (2) 1925
80. **Big Fun** - Shalamar 23 (2) 1879
81. **Volcano** - Jimmy Buffett 14 (1) 1857
82. **Prince** - Prince 22 (2) 1850
83. **Low Budget** - The Kinks 11 (2) 1846
84. **What Cha Gonna Do...With My Lovin'?** - Stephanie Mills 22 (2) 1842
85. **Life For The Taking** - Eddie Money 17 (2) 1842
86. **Night In The Ruts** - Aerosmith 14 (2) 1808
87. **Communique** - Dire Straits 11 (2) 1787
88. **Angel Of The Night** - Angela Bofill 34 (1) 1773
89. **Secrets** - Robert Palmer 19 (1) 1736
90. **Partners In Crime** - Rupert Holmes 33 (2) 1717
91. **George Harrison** - George Harrison 14 (1) 1708
92. **Identify Yourself** - The O'Jays 16 (2) 1633
93. **Fear Of Music** - Talking Heads 21 (1) 1626
94. **Head First** - The Babys 22 (2) 1615
95. **Mingus** - Joni Mitchell 17 (1) 1561
96. **The Muppet Movie: Original Soundtrack Recording** - Soundtrack 32 (2) 1544
97. **Sheik Yerbouti** - Frank Zappa 21 (1) 1539
98. **Knock On Wood** - Amii Stewart 19 (1) 1535
99. **I'm The Man** - Joe Jackson 22 (1) 1521
100. **Bob Dylan At Budokan** - Bob Dylan 13 (2) 1495

1980

Rank. Title - Act Peak (Peak Wks) Score
1. **Hi Infidelity** - REO Speedwagon 1 (15) 16076
2. **Christopher Cross** - Christopher Cross 6 (3) 12682
3. **Kenny Rogers' Greatest Hits** - Kenny Rogers 1 (2) 12108
4. **Glass Houses** - Billy Joel 1 (6) 11662
5. **Against The Wind** - Bob Seger & The Silver Bullet Band 1 (6) 11583
6. **Crimes Of Passion** - Pat Benatar 2 (5) 11064
7. **Back In Black** - AC/DC 4 (3) 10402
8. **Double Fantasy** - John Lennon & Yoko Ono 1 (8) 9397
9. **Guilty** - Barbra Streisand 1 (3) 9281
10. **Zenyatta Mondatta** - The Police 5 (6) 9097
11. **The Game** - Queen 1 (5) 9015
12. **The Jazz Singer (Soundtrack)** - Neil Diamond 3 (7) 8275
13. **Diana** - Diana Ross 2 (2) 7266
14. **Emotional Rescue** - The Rolling Stones 1 (7) 7106
15. **The River** - Bruce Springsteen 1 (4) 6583
16. **Hold Out** - Jackson Browne 1 (1) 6411
17. **Voices** - Daryl Hall & John Oates 17 (1) 6297
18. **Hotter Than July** - Stevie Wonder 3 (7) 6054
19. **Urban Cowboy** - Soundtrack 3 (2) 5546
20. **Winelight** - Grover Washington Jr. 5 (7) 5367
21. **Just One Night** - Eric Clapton 2 (6) 5135
22. **Mad Love** - Linda Ronstadt 3 (4) 4864
23. **Autoamerican** - Blondie 7 (5) 4533
24. **The Doors Greatest Hits** - The Doors 17 (2) 4507
25. **Give Me The Night** - George Benson 3 (2) 4441
26. **Lost In Love** - Air Supply 22 (3) 4355
27. **Fame** - Soundtrack 7 (2) 4319
28. **The Turn Of A Friendly Card** - The Alan Parsons Project 13 (2) 4304
29. **Celebrate!** - Kool & The Gang 10 (2) 4159
30. **Pretenders** - The Pretenders 9 (2) 4145
31. **Xanadu (Soundtrack)** - Olivia Newton-John/ Electric Light Orchestra 4 (3) 4087
32. **Empty Glass** - Pete Townshend 5 (3) 3960
33. **Middle Man** - Boz Scaggs 8 (2) 3683
34. **The Empire Strikes Back** - Soundtrack 4 (4) 3643
35. **Gaucho** - Steely Dan 9 (3) 3629
36. **One Step Closer** - The Doobie Brothers 3 (3) 3578
37. **The Whispers** - The Whispers 6 (2) 3555
38. **Departure** - Journey 8 (2) 3453
39. **Duke** - Genesis 11 (2) 3426
40. **Light Up The Night** - The Brothers Johnson 5 (2) 3294
41. **Women And Children First** - Van Halen 6 (5) 3216
42. **Sweet Sensation** - Stephanie Mills 16 (2) 3213
43. **Eagles Live** - Eagles 6 (4) 3172
44. **Horizon** - Eddie Rabbitt 19 (2) 3151
45. **Ann Murray's Greatest Hits** - Anne Murray 16 (5) 3147
46. **Let's Get Serious** - Jermaine Jackson 6 (3) 3133
47. **Mouth To Mouth** - Lipps Inc. 5 (5) 3106
48. **Permanent Waves** - Rush 4 (3) 3066
49. **Heroes** - Commodores 7 (3) 3045
50. **Triumph** - The Jacksons 10 (4) 3024
51. **Freedom Of Choice** - Devo 22 (2) 3023
52. **Panorama** - The Cars 5 (4) 2985
53. **TP** - Teddy Pendergrass 14 (3) 2966
54. **9 To 5 And Odd Jobs** - Dolly Parton 11 (2) 2959
55. **The Gap Band III** - The Gap Band 16 (2) 2856
56. **McCartney II** - Paul McCartney 3 (5) 2823
57. **One For The Road** - The Kinks 14 (4) 2816
58. **Super Trouper** - ABBA 17 (3) 2763
59. **Love Stinks** - The J. Geils Band 18 (2) 2737
60. **Honeysuckle Rose (Soundtrack)** - Willie Nelson & Family 11 (3) 2735
61. **Anytime, Anyplace, Anywhere** - The Rossington Collins Band 13 (3) 2669
62. **American Gigolo** - Soundtrack 7 (3) 2595
63. **Making Movies** - Dire Straits 19 (3) 2553
64. **Bebe Le Strange** - Heart 5 (2) 2426
65. **Kenny Loggins Alive** - Kenny Loggins 11 (2) 2402

Rank. Title - Act Peak (Peak Wks) Score
66. **Go All The Way** - The Isley Brothers 8 (4) 2369
67. **Foolish Behaviour** - Rod Stewart 12 (5) 2330
68. **Full Moon** - The Charlie Daniels Band 11 (2) 2276
69. **Fantastic Voyage** - Lakeside 16 (2) 2242
70. **Paris** - Supertramp 8 (2) 2219
71. **The Pleasure Principle** - Gary Numan 16 (2) 2216
72. **One-Trick Pony** - Paul Simon 12 (2) 2214
73. **Peter Gabriel (III)** - Peter Gabriel 22 (2) 2135
74. **Gideon** - Kenny Rogers 12 (2) 2123
75. **Scary Monsters** - David Bowie 12 (2) 2118
76. **Greatest Hits/Live** - Heart 13 (3) 2112
77. **Fun And Games** - Chuck Mangione 8 (4) 2095
78. **Nothin' Matters And What If It Did** - John Cougar 37 (2) 2032
79. **Faces** - Earth, Wind & Fire 10 (2) 1942
80. **One Eighty** - Ambrosia 25 (1) 1910
81. **Warm Thoughts** - Smokey Robinson 14 (2) 1895
82. **The Blues Brothers (Soundtrack)** - Blues Brothers 13 (2) 1874
83. **Hits!** - Boz Scaggs 24 (6) 1868
84. **S.O.S.** - The S.O.S. Band 12 (3) 1865
85. **Ray, Goodman & Brown** - Ray, Goodman & Brown 17 (2) 1827
86. **Trilogy: Past, Present And Future** - Frank Sinatra 17 (2) 1804
87. **Love Approach** - Tom Browne 18 (2) 1795
88. **September Morn** - Neil Diamond 10 (3) 1793
89. **The Two Of Us** - Yarbrough & Peoples 16 (2) 1775
90. **London Calling** - The Clash 27 (3) 1770
91. **Remain In Light** - Talking Heads 19 (2) 1717
92. **21 At 33** - Elton John 13 (2) 1698
93. **Roses In The Snow** - Emmylou Harris 26 (2) 1665
94. **Crash And Burn** - Pat Travers Band 20 (1) 1651
95. **This Time** - Al Jarreau 27 (2) 1635
96. **Cameosis** - Cameo 25 (3) 1618
97. **After Midnight** - The Manhattans 24 (2) 1600
98. **Barry** - Barry Manilow 15 (2) 1599
99. **Wild Planet** - The B-52s 18 (1) 1586
100. **Scream Dream** - Ted Nugent 13 (2) 1565

1981

Rank. Title - Act Peak (Peak Wks) Score
1. **Escape** - Journey 1 (1) 17166
2. **4** - Foreigner 1 (10) 15590
3. **Bella Donna** - Stevie Nicks 1 (1) 12532
4. **Paradise Theater** - Styx 1 (3) 10999
5. **Tattoo You** - The Rolling Stones 1 (9) 9921
6. **Get Lucky** - Loverboy 7 (2) 9866
7. **Beauty And The Beat** - Go-Go's 1 (6) 9856
8. **Ghost In The Machine** - The Police 2 (6) 8836
9. **Freeze-Frame** - The J. Geils Band 1 (4) 8234
10. **Face Value** - Phil Collins 7 (4) 8163
11. **Feels So Right** - Alabama 16 (2) 8135
12. **Don't Say No** - Billy Squier 5 (3) 8125
13. **Street Songs** - Rick James 3 (2) 7134
14. **Mistaken Idenity** - Kim Carnes 1 (4) 6959
15. **Long Distance Voyager** - The Moody Blues 1 (3) 6873
16. **Moving Pictures** - Rush 3 (3) 6817
17. **Working Class Dog** - Rick Springfield 7 (2) 6754
18. **Precious Time** - Pat Benatar 1 (1) 6605
19. **Private Eyes** - Daryl Hall & John Oates 5 (3) 6383
20. **The Dude** - Quincy Jones 10 (1) 6231
21. **Chariots Of Fire (Soundtrack)** - Vangelis 1 (4) 6161
22. **Arc Of A Diver** - Steve Winwood 3 (6) 5990
23. **Dirty Deeds Done Dirt Cheap** - AC/DC 3 (6) 5829
24. **The Innocent Age** - Dan Fogelberg 6 (6) 5782
25. **I Love Rock 'N Roll** - Joan Jett & the Blackhearts 2 (3) 5608
26. **Physical** - Olivia Newton-John 6 (7) 5534
27. **Juice** - Juice Newton 22 (3) 5505
28. **Hooked On Classics** - Royal Philharmonic Orchestra Conducted By Louis Clark 4 (6) 5342
29. **Abacab** - Genesis 7 (1) 5305
30. **Breakin' Away** - Al Jarreau 9 (3) 5128
31. **The One That You Love** - Air Supply 10 (4) 5042
32. **Nine Tonight** - Bob Seger & The Silver Bullet Band 3 (4) 4899
33. **Something Special** - Kool & The Gang 12 (2) 4669
34. **Blizzard Of Ozz** - Ozzy Osbourne 21 (1) 4478
35. **For Those About To Rock (We Salute You)** - AC/DC 1 (3) 4377
36. **Loverboy** - Loverboy 13 (2) 4338
37. **Hard Promises** - Tom Petty And The Heartbreakers 5 (2) 4235
38. **Diary Of A Madman** - Ozzy Osbourne 16 (4) 4170
39. **Zebop!** - Santana 9 (4) 4051
40. **Shake It Up** - The Cars 9 (4) 3973
41. **Share Your Love** - Kenny Rogers 6 (2) 3955
42. **Quarterflash** - Quarterflash 8 (3) 3953
43. **Memories** - Barbra Streisand 10 (6) 3838
44. **Raise!** - Earth, Wind & Fire 5 (8) 3652
45. **In The Pocket** - Commodores 13 (2) 3539
46. **Wild-Eyed Southern Boys** - .38 Special 18 (2) 3509
47. **Pirates** - Rickie Lee Jones 5 (2) 3376
48. **Face Dances** - The Who 4 (4) 3313
49. **Being With You** - Smokey Robinson 10 (2) 3208
50. **Captured** - Journey 9 (4) 3197
51. **High 'N' Dry** - Def Leppard 38 (1) 3096
52. **Fancy Free** - The Oak Ridge Boys 14 (1) 3024
53. **Tonight I'm Yours** - Rod Stewart 11 (4) 3006
54. **Willie Nelson's Greatest Hits (& Some That Will Be)** - Willie Nelson 27 (1) 2922
55. **Why Do Fools Fall In Love** - Diana Ross 15 (6) 2846
56. **Another Ticket** - Eric Clapton And His Band 7 (2) 2816
57. **A Woman Needs Love** - Ray Parker Jr. & Raydio 13 (2) 2655
58. **Fair Warning** - Van Halen 5 (3) 2642
59. **Dad Loves His Work** - James Taylor 10 (3) 2592
60. **Songs In The Attic** - Billy Joel 8 (3) 2554
61. **Give The People What They Want** - The Kinks 15 (2) 2399
62. **Never Too Much** - Luther Vandross 19 (2) 2394
63. **Nightwalker** - Gino Vannelli 15 (4) 2311
64. **Time Exposure** - Little River Band 21 (1) 2288
65. **Allied Forces** - Triumph 23 (1) 2287
66. **Black & White** - The Pointer Sisters 12 (2) 2271
67. **Modern Times** - Jefferson Starship 26 (3) 2256
68. **Endless Love** - Soundtrack 9 (2) 2231
69. **Stars On Long Play** - Stars On 9 (4) 2230
70. **The George Benson Collection** - George Benson 14 (2) 2205
71. **Heavy Metal** - Soundtrack 12 (2) 2195
72. **Controversy** - Prince 21 (3) 2142
73. **The Nature Of The Beast** - April Wine 26 (1) 2119
74. **Greatest Hits** - Queen 14 (6) 2106
75. **If I Should Love Again** - Barry Manilow 14 (3) 2058
76. **Exit...Stage Left** - Rush 10 (3) 2016
77. **Mecca For Moderns** - The Manhattan Transfer 22 (4) 2009
78. **Fire Of Unknown Origin** - Blue Öyster Cult 24 (2) 1923
79. **Skyy Line** - Skyy 18 (2) 1892
80. **Seven Year Ache** - Rosanne Cash 26 (1) 1880
81. **Every Home Should Have One** - Patti Austin 36 (8) 1862
82. **El Loco** - ZZ Top 17 (2) 1836
83. **Sheena Easton** - Sheena Easton 24 (1) 1828
84. **On The Way To The Sky** - Neil Diamond 17 (2) 1772
85. **Carol Hensel's Exercise And Dance Program** - Carol Hensel 56 (1) 1759
86. **Pretenders II** - The Pretenders 10 (3) 1727
87. **Step By Step** - Eddie Rabbitt 23 (1) 1720
88. **It Must Be Magic** - Teena Marie 23 (1) 1680
89. **Time** - Electric Light Orchestra 16 (3) 1665
90. **Imagination** - The Whispers 23 (2) 1662
91. **Rockihnroll** - Greg Kihn Band 32 (1) 1636
92. **Tom Tom Club** - Tom Tom Club 23 (1) 1635
93. **Three For Love** - Shalamar 40 (2) 1577
94. **Franke & The Knockouts** - Franke & The Knockouts 31 (1) 1518
95. **There Goes The Neighborhood** - Joe Walsh 20 (1) 1499
96. **The Clarke/Duke Project** - Stanley Clarke & George Duke 33 (4) 1491
97. **What Cha' Gonna Do For Me** - Chaka Khan 17 (2) 1482
98. **Evangeline** - Emmylou Harris 22 (3) 1480
99. **It's Time For Love** - Teddy Pendergrass 19 (2) 1462
100. **You Could Have Been With Me** - Sheena Easton 47 (1) 1443

1982

Rank. Title - Act Peak (Peak Wks) Score
1. **Thriller** - Michael Jackson 1 (37) 25933
2. **Business As Usual** - Men At Work 1 (15) 12719
3. **Lionel Richie** - Lionel Richie 3 (7) 9861
4. **Asia** - Asia 1 (9) 9795

Rank. Title - Act Peak (Peak Wks) Score
5. **American Fool** - John Cougar 1 (9) 9588
6. **H2O** - Daryl Hall & John Oates 3 (15) 9556
7. **1999** - Prince 9 (7) 8588
8. **Built For Speed** - Stray Cats 2 (15) 7957
9. **Toto IV** - Toto 4 (4) 7593
10. **Mirage** - Fleetwood Mac 1 (5) 6695
11. **Always On My Mind** - Willie Nelson 2 (4) 6455
12. **Combat Rock** - The Clash 7 (5) 5485
13. **Jane Fonda's Workout Record** - Jane Fonda 15 (4) 5318
14. **Rio** - Duran Duran 6 (7) 5168
15. **Emotions In Motion** - Billy Squier 5 (8) 4779
16. **Mountain Music** - Alabama 14 (2) 4690
17. **Night And Day** - Joe Jackson 4 (6) 4503
18. **Hello, I Must Be Going!** - Phil Collins 8 (5) 4492
19. **Get Nervous** - Pat Benatar 4 (5) 4128
20. **Dare** - The Human League 3 (3) 4081
21. **Eye Of The Tiger** - Survivor 2 (4) 4056
22. **Olivia's Greatest Hits, Vol. 2** - Olivia Newton-John 16 (4) 4032
23. **Tug Of War** - Paul McCartney 1 (3) 3951
24. **Success Hasn't Spoiled Me Yet** - Rick Springfield 2 (3) 3922
25. **Abracadabra** - The Steve Miller Band 3 (6) 3819
26. **The Nylon Curtain** - Billy Joel 7 (4) 3773
27. **Daylight Again** - Crosby, Stills & Nash 8 (5) 3714
28. **A Flock Of Seagulls** - A Flock Of Seagulls 10 (3) 3417
29. **Diver Down** - Van Halen 3 (3) 3394
30. **Eye In The Sky** - The Alan Parsons Project 7 (6) 3372
31. **Spring Session M** - Missing Persons 17 (6) 3181
32. **Aldo Nova** - Aldo Nova 8 (6) 3135
33. **Blackout** - Scorpions 10 (2) 3091
34. **Long After Dark** - Tom Petty And The Heartbreakers 9 (3) 3020
35. **Screaming For Vengeance** - Judas Priest 17 (8) 2965
36. **Pictures At Eleven** - Robert Plant 5 (6) 2950
37. **"...Famous Last Words..."** - Supertramp 5 (7) 2901
38. **Gap Band IV** - The Gap Band 14 (5) 2837
39. **Heartlight** - Neil Diamond 9 (3) 2817
40. **Picture This** - Huey Lewis & The News 13 (4) 2810
41. **Chicago 16** - Chicago 9 (5) 2792
42. **Good Trouble** - REO Speedwagon 7 (9) 2702
43. **Midnight Love** - Marvin Gaye 7 (5) 2691
44. **Nebraska** - Bruce Springsteen 3 (4) 2563
45. **The Lexicon Of Love** - ABC 24 (10) 2473
46. **High Adventure** - Kenny Loggins 13 (3) 2457
47. **All Four One** - The Motels 16 (2) 2453
48. **Non-Stop Erotic Cabaret** - Soft Cell 22 (1) 2367
49. **Special Forces** - 38 Special 10 (3) 2351
50. **The Concert In Central Park** - Simon & Garfunkel 6 (2) 2249
51. **If That's What It Takes** - Michael McDonald 6 (6) 2160
52. **Friend Or Foe** - Adam Ant 16 (3) 2159

Rank. Title - Act Peak (Peak Wks) Score
53. **I Can't Stand Still** - Don Henley 24 (7) 2131
54. **It's Hard** - The Who 8 (5) 2131
55. **Stevie Wonder's Original Musiquarium I** - Stevie Wonder 4 (3) 2112
56. **Keep It Live** - Dazz Band 14 (4) 2100
57. **Dreamgirls** - Original Cast 11 (3) 2076
58. **Billy Idol** - Billy Idol 45 (1) 2061
59. **Dan Fogelberg/Greatest Hits** - Dan Fogelberg 15 (4) 2056
60. **No Control** - Eddie Money 20 (3) 2013
61. **Signals** - Rush 10 (1) 1996
62. **Great White North** - Bob & Doug McKenzie 8 (2) 1984
63. **Three Lock Box** - Sammy Hagar 17 (2) 1980
64. **Vacation** - Go-Go's 8 (5) 1956
65. **Forever, For Always, For Love** - Luther Vandross 20 (5) 1945
66. **Quiet Lies** - Juice Newton 20 (2) 1875
67. **The Other Woman** - Ray Parker Jr. 11 (2) 1850
68. **Still Life (American Concert 1981)** - The Rolling Stones 5 (4) 1847
69. **Standing Hampton** - Sammy Hagar 28 (2) 1836
70. **All This Love** - DeBarge 24 (2) 1789
71. **Records** - Foreigner 10 (4) 1785
72. **The Nightfly** - Donald Fagen 11 (4) 1763
73. **Three Sides Live** - Genesis 10 (3) 1758
74. **Hooked On Swing** - Larry Elgart And His Manhattan Swing Orchestra 24 (5) 1729
75. **No Fun Aloud** - Glenn Frey 32 (3) 1696
76. **Jump Up!** - Elton John 17 (3) 1675
77. **Worlds Apart** - Saga 29 (5) 1669
78. **Winds Of Change** - Jefferson Starship 26 (6) 1616
79. **Hey Ricky** - Melissa Manchester 19 (5) 1614
80. **Peter Gabriel (Security)** - Peter Gabriel 28 (9) 1598
81. **Donna Summer** - Donna Summer 20 (5) 1550
82. **The Number Of The Beast** - Iron Maiden 33 (2) 1510
83. **Coda** - Led Zeppelin 6 (3) 1495
84. **Special Beat Service** - The English Beat 39 (3) 1477
85. **Word Of Mouth** - Toni Basil 22 (7) 1472
86. **Throwin' Down** - Rick James 13 (4) 1459
87. **Dawn Patrol** - Night Ranger 38 (4) 1458
88. **Tommy Tutone-2** - Tommy Tutone 20 (3) 1453
89. **Heartbreaker** - Dionne Warwick 25 (3) 1452
90. **Now And Forever** - Air Supply 25 (3) 1443
91. **Cut** - Golden Earring 24 (2) 1364
92. **Pelican West** - Haircut One Hundred 31 (3) 1363
93. **Love Over Gold** - Dire Straits 19 (3) 1361
94. **As One** - Kool & The Gang 29 (4) 1353
95. **Straight From The Heart** - Patrice Rushen 14 (2) 1343
96. **Rocky III** - Soundtrack 15 (5) 1334
97. **Speak Of The Devil** - Ozzy Osbourne 14 (4) 1334
98. **Jump To It** - Aretha Franklin 23 (4) 1328
99. **Shango** - Santana 22 (3) 1288
100. **Eddie Murphy** - Eddie Murphy 52 (5) 1275

Rank. Title - Act Peak (Peak Wks) Score
1983
1. **Can't Slow Down** - Lionel Richie 1 (3) 17509
2. **Sports** - Huey Lewis & The News 1 (1) 15377
3. **Synchronicity** - The Police 1 (17) 13507
4. **Eliminator** - ZZ Top 9 (1) 11592
5. **Pyromania** - Def Leppard 2 (2) 11178
6. **An Innocent Man** - Billy Joel 4 (5) 11007
7. **Flashdance** - Soundtrack 1 (2) 9902
8. **She's So Unusual** - Cyndi Lauper 4 (4) 9304
9. **Break Out** - The Pointer Sisters 8 (2) 9038
10. **Frontiers** - Journey 2 (9) 8070
11. **Colour By Numbers** - Culture Club 2 (6) 8038
12. **Metal Health** - Quiet Riot 1 (1) 7033
13. **Madonna** - Madonna 8 (3) 6893
14. **Let's Dance** - David Bowie 4 (1) 6138
15. **Seven And The Ragged Tiger** - Duran Duran 8 (5) 5895
16. **What's New** - Linda Ronstadt & The Nelson Riddle Orchestra 3 (5) 5736
17. **The Big Chill** - Soundtrack 17 (2) 5525
18. **Kissing To Be Clever** - Culture Club 14 (10) 5493
19. **Uh-Huh** - John Mellencamp 9 (1) 5328
20. **Rebel Yell** - Billy Idol 6 (3) 5290
21. **Cargo** - Men At Work 3 (5) 4751
22. **Midnight Madness** - Night Ranger 15 (10) 4751
23. **Shout At The Devil** - Mötley Crüe 17 (2) 4698
24. **War** - U2 12 (1) 4509
25. **Reach The Beach** - The Fixx 8 (2) 4454
26. **90125** - Yes 5 (4) 4449
27. **The Wild Heart** - Stevie Nicks 5 (7) 4401
28. **Cuts Like A Knife** - Bryan Adams 8 (3) 4109
29. **Kilroy Was Here** - Styx 3 (2) 3996
30. **No Parking On The Dance Floor** - Midnight Star 27 (2) 3986
31. **The Distance** - Bob Seger & The Silver Bullet Band 5 (6) 3858
32. **Genesis** - Genesis 9 (1) 3843
33. **Greatest Hits** - Air Supply 7 (1) 3820
34. **Eyes That See In The Dark** - Kenny Rogers 6 (4) 3792
35. **Rock 'N Soul Part 1** - Daryl Hall & John Oates 7 (2) 3750
36. **Under A Blood Red Sky** - U2 28 (3) 3718
37. **Speaking In Tongues** - Talking Heads 15 (2) 3554
38. **Eddie & The Cruisers (Soundtrack)** - John Cafferty & The Beaver Brown Band 9 (5) 3552
39. **Stay With Me Tonight** - Jeffrey Osborne 25 (1) 3485
40. **Living In Oz** - Rick Springfield 12 (3) 3368
41. **Keep It Up** - Loverboy 7 (5) 3349
42. **December** - George Winston 54 (1) 3285
43. **The Closer You Get** - Alabama 10 (1) 3270
44. **The Principle Of Moments** - Robert Plant 8 (1) 3102
45. **Sweet Dreams (Are Made Of This)** - Eurythmics 15 (3) 3056
46. **Duran Duran** - Duran Duran 10 (1) 3007
47. **Faster Than The Speed Of Night** - Bonnie Tyler 4 (1) 2933
48. **Labour Of Love** - UB40 14 (1) 2783

Rank. Title - Act Peak (Peak Wks) Score
49. Julio - Julio Iglesias 32 (1) 2545
50. The Crossing - Big Country 18 (2) 2443
51. Piece Of Mind - Iron Maiden 14 (1) 2309
52. Future Shock - Herbie Hancock 43 (2) 2229
53. She Works Hard For The Money - Donna Summer 9 (1) 2220
54. Lawyers In Love - Jackson Browne 8 (3) 2216
55. Tour De Force - 38 Special 22 (2) 2197
56. Killer On The Rampage - Eddy Grant 10 (3) 2188
57. In Heat - The Romantics 14 (1) 2167
58. Live From Earth - Pat Benatar 13 (2) 2147
59. Jarreau - Al Jarreau 13 (2) 2144
60. Too Low For Zero - Elton John 25 (1) 2107
61. Staying Alive (Soundtrack) - Bee Gees 6 (2) 2100
62. Undercover - The Rolling Stones 4 (2) 2032
63. The Final Cut - Pink Floyd 6 (2) 1966
64. Rhythm Of Youth - Men Without Hats 13 (3) 1887
65. Alpha - Asia 6 (4) 1881
66. Yentl (Soundtrack) - Barbra Streisand 9 (2) 1871
67. Outside Inside - The Tubes 18 (1) 1846
68. The Golden Age Of Wireless - Thomas Dolby 13 (2) 1799
69. Another Page - Christopher Cross 11 (5) 1765
70. Born To Love - Peabo Bryson & Roberta Flack 25 (1) 1749
71. State Of Confusion - The Kinks 12 (1) 1739
72. Cold Blooded - Rick James 16 (1) 1717
73. In Your Eyes - George Benson 27 (1) 1711
74. Pipes Of Peace - Paul McCartney 15 (1) 1698
75. In The Heart - Kool & The Gang 29 (2) 1676
76. Too-Rye-Ay - Dexys Midnight Runners 14 (2) 1589
77. Blinded By Science - Thomas Dolby 20 (4) 1559
78. Rant 'N' Rave With The Stray Cats - Stray Cats 14 (2) 1548
79. Busy Body - Luther Vandross 32 (4) 1534
80. Twenty Greatest Hits - Kenny Rogers 22 (2) 1524
81. Gap Band V- Jammin' - The Gap Band 28 (1) 1519
82. Powerlight - Earth, Wind & Fire 12 (4) 1518
83. True - Spandau Ballet 19 (1) 1516
84. Poncho & Lefty - Merle Haggard/Willie Nelson 37 (1) 1509
85. Bark At The Moon - Ozzy Osbourne 19 (3) 1506
86. Headhunter - Krokus 25 (2) 1468
87. Flick Of The Switch - AC/DC 15 (2) 1466
88. In A Special Way - DeBarge 36 (1) 1448
89. Lick It Up - KISS 24 (2) 1444
90. Kihnspiracy - Greg Kihn Band 15 (2) 1424
91. Never Surrender - Triumph 26 (2) 1416
92. Fascination! - The Human League 22 (1) 1400
93. Listen - A Flock Of Seagulls 16 (2) 1383
94. Naked Eyes - Naked Eyes 32 (2) 1339
95. Punch The Clock - Elvis Costello And The Attractions 24 (1) 1334
96. Infidels - Bob Dylan 20 (5) 1332

Rank. Title - Act Peak (Peak Wks) Score
97. We've Got Tonight - Kenny Rogers 18 (1) 1326
98. Eddie Murphy: Comedian - Eddie Murphy 35 (1) 1323
99. After Eight - Taco 23 (2) 1311
100. Visions - Gladys Knight And The Pips 34 (2) 1303

1984

Rank. Title - Act Peak (Peak Wks) Score
1. Born In The U.S.A. - Bruce Springsteen 1 (7) 23827
2. Purple Rain (Soundtrack) - Prince And The Revolution 1 (24) 13717
3. Private Dancer - Tina Turner 3 (11) 11671
4. Reckless - Bryan Adams 1 (2) 11440
5. Like A Virgin - Madonna 1 (3) 10496
6. Make It Big - Wham! 1 (3) 9851
7. 1984 (MCMLXXXIV) - Van Halen 2 (5) 9001
8. Heartbeat City - The Cars 3 (1) 8802
9. Footloose - Soundtrack 1 (10) 7852
10. Suddenly - Billy Ocean 9 (2) 6704
11. Chicago 17 - Chicago 4 (1) 6572
12. Emergency - Kool & The Gang 13 (1) 5376
13. Big Bam Boom - Daryl Hall & John Oates 5 (2) 4851
14. Love At First Sting - Scorpions 6 (2) 4637
15. The Unforgettable Fire - U2 12 (3) 4535
16. Out Of The Cellar - Ratt 7 (4) 4307
17. Building The Perfect Beast - Don Henley 13 (5) 4238
18. New Edition - New Edition 6 (2) 4038
19. Wheels Are Turnin' - REO Speedwagon 7 (1) 3592
20. The Woman In Red (Soundtrack) - Stevie Wonder 4 (3) 3577
21. Learning To Crawl - The Pretenders 5 (4) 3545
22. Into The Gap - Thompson Twins 10 (2) 3487
23. Vital Signs - Survivor 16 (3) 3378
24. Valotte - Julian Lennon 17 (2) 3339
25. 1100 Bel Air Place - Julio Iglesias 5 (2) 3337
26. Touch - Eurythmics 7 (3) 3314
27. Stay Hungry - Twisted Sister 15 (3) 3275
28. Ice Cream Castle - The Time 24 (3) 3275
29. Street Talk - Steve Perry 12 (4) 3214
30. Volume One - The Honeydrippers 4 (2) 3186
31. No Brakes - John Waite 10 (1) 2827
32. Ghostbusters - Soundtrack 6 (3) 2711
33. A Private Heaven - Sheena Easton 15 (2) 2682
34. Arena - Duran Duran 4 (3) 2637
35. The Allnighter - Glenn Frey 22 (2) 2635
36. Victory - The Jacksons 4 (3) 2571
37. Jermaine Jackson - Jermaine Jackson 19 (3) 2569
38. Roll On - Alabama 21 (2) 2447
39. Stop Making Sense - Talking Heads 41 (4) 2336
40. I Feel For You - Chaka Khan 14 (3) 2332
41. Swept Away - Diana Ross 26 (1) 2303
42. Self Control - Laura Branigan 23 (2) 2270
43. Bon Jovi - Bon Jovi 43 (2) 2265
44. Legend - Bob Marley And The Wailers 54 (2) 2209
45. Talk Show - Go-Go's 18 (3) 2131

Rank. Title - Act Peak (Peak Wks) Score
46. Breakin' - Soundtrack 8 (2) 2129
47. Camouflage - Rod Stewart 18 (2) 2113
48. Animalize - KISS 19 (1) 2076
49. Warrior - Scandal Featuring Patty Smyth 17 (3) 2050
50. Signs Of Life - Billy Squier 11 (4) 2034
51. Perfect Strangers - Deep Purple 17 (2) 2024
52. Grace Under Pressure - Rush 10 (4) 1905
53. Body And Soul - Joe Jackson 20 (4) 1868
54. The Glamorous Life - Sheila E. 28 (2) 1845
55. Welcome To The Pleasure Dome - Frankie Goes To Hollywood 33 (5) 1841
56. Defenders Of The Faith - Judas Priest 18 (4) 1785
57. Tropico - Pat Benatar 14 (4) 1780
58. Breaking Hearts - Elton John 20 (5) 1779
59. Slide It In - Whitesnake 40 (2) 1759
60. ...All The Rage - General Public 26 (2) 1712
61. Against All Odds - Soundtrack 12 (4) 1684
62. Ammonia Avenue - The Alan Parsons Project 15 (1) 1684
63. Somebody's Watching Me - Rockwell 15 (2) 1634
64. Chinese Wall - Philip Bailey 22 (3) 1633
65. Escape - Whodini 35 (1) 1624
66. Reckoning - R.E.M. 27 (5) 1613
67. Windows And Walls - Dan Fogelberg 15 (3) 1593
68. VOA - Sammy Hagar 32 (3) 1571
69. Tooth And Nail - Dokken 49 (2) 1562
70. First Offense - Corey Hart 31 (3) 1550
71. Tonight - David Bowie 11 (2) 1546
72. Lush Life - Linda Ronstadt 13 (2) 1541
73. Hard To Hold (Soundtrack) - Rick Springfield 16 (3) 1538
74. Phantoms - The Fixx 19 (3) 1488
75. The Last In Line - Dio 23 (2) 1475
76. Emotion - Barbra Streisand 19 (3) 1464
77. Solid - Ashford & Simpson 29 (2) 1459
78. "Weird Al" Yankovic In 3-D - "Weird Al" Yankovic 17 (3) 1444
79. Couldn't Stand The Weather - Stevie Ray Vaughan And Double Trouble 31 (3) 1443
80. Don't Stop - Jeffrey Osborne 39 (4) 1412
81. Points On The Curve - Wang Chung 30 (3) 1405
82. Condition Critical - Quiet Riot 15 (3) 1402
83. Milk And Honey - John Lennon & Yoko Ono 11 (1) 1381
84. Amadeus (Soundtrack) - Neville Marriner 56 (2) 1365
85. Bananarama - Bananarama 30 (5) 1349
86. Run D.M.C. - Run-D.M.C. 53 (2) 1346
87. Starchild - Teena Marie 31 (2) 1315
88. Beat Street - Soundtrack 14 (2) 1313
89. Powerslave - Iron Maiden 21 (3) 1313
90. About Face - David Gilmour 32 (3) 1288
91. Giuffria - Giuffria 26 (2) 1272
92. Let The Music Play - Shannon 32 (2) 1253
93. What About Me? - Kenny Rogers 31 (3) 1199
94. Planetary Invasion - Midnight Star 32 (2) 1191
95. Love Life - Berlin 28 (2) 1186
96. Thunder Seven - Triumph 35 (2) 1173

Rank. Title - Act Peak (Peak Wks) Score
97. **Lights Out** - Peter Wolf 24 (2) 1151
98. **Nuclear Furniture** - Jefferson Starship 28 (4) 1140
99. **Love Language** - Teddy Pendergrass 38 (4) 1095
100. **The Works** - Queen 23 (1) 1088

1985

Rank. Title - Act Peak (Peak Wks) Score
1. **Whitney Houston** - Whitney Houston 1 (14) 18282
2. **No Jacket Required** - Phil Collins 1 (7) 14141
3. **Brothers In Arms** - Dire Straits 1 (9) 11915
4. **Heart** - Heart 1 (1) 11541
5. **Songs From The Big Chair** - Tears For Fears 1 (5) 11182
6. **Scarecrow** - John Mellencamp 2 (3) 9110
7. **The Dream Of The Blue Turtles** - Sting 2 (6) 7101
8. **Beverly Hills Cop** - Soundtrack 1 (2) 6652
9. **Miami Vice** - Soundtrack-TV 1 (11) 6180
10. **Promise** - Sade 1 (2) 5873
11. **Welcome To The Real World** - Mr. Mister 1 (1) 5753
12. **Around The World In A Day** - Prince And The Revolution 1 (3) 5561
13. **Afterburner** - ZZ Top 4 (3) 5557
14. **Centerfield** - John Fogerty 1 (1) 5442
15. **The Broadway Album** - Barbra Streisand 1 (3) 5422
16. **Riptide** - Robert Palmer 8 (1) 4955
17. **Diamond Life** - Sade 5 (2) 4672
18. **In Square Circle** - Stevie Wonder 5 (2) 4553
19. **Knee Deep In The Hoopla** - Starship 7 (3) 4436
20. **Rock Me Tonight** - Freddie Jackson 10 (1) 4250
21. **Play Deep** - The Outfield 9 (1) 4156
22. **Greatest Hits Vol. I & II** - Billy Joel 6 (2) 4119
23. **Nervous Night** - Hooters 12 (1) 4059
24. **Primitive Love** - Miami Sound Machine 21 (1) 4048
25. **The Power Station** - The Power Station 6 (2) 3972
26. **Who's Zoomin' Who?** - Aretha Franklin 13 (1) 3951
27. **Agent Provocateur** - Foreigner 4 (3) 3946
28. **Theatre Of Pain** - Mötley Crüe 6 (1) 3895
29. **7 Wishes** - Night Ranger 10 (3) 3665
30. **Once Upon A Time** - Simple Minds 10 (5) 3400
31. **Little Creatures** - Talking Heads 20 (3) 3390
32. **Be Yourself Tonight** - Eurythmics 9 (1) 3357
33. **Dream Into Action** - Howard Jones 10 (1) 3115
34. **Ready For the World** - Ready For The World 17 (5) 3043
35. **Listen Like Thieves** - INXS 11 (1) 3022
36. **Lovin' Every Minute Of It** - Loverboy 13 (5) 3011
37. **Southern Accents** - Tom Petty And The Heartbreakers 7 (2) 2944
38. **Hunting High And Low** - a-ha 15 (2) 2928
39. **7800 Degrees Fahrenheit** - Bon Jovi 37 (3) 2896

Rank. Title - Act Peak (Peak Wks) Score
40. **Meeting In The Ladies Room** - Klymaxx 18 (3) 2800
41. **We Are The World** - USA For Africa 1 (3) 2778
42. **Invasion Of Your Privacy** - Ratt 7 (1) 2750
43. **The Secret Of Association** - Paul Young 19 (6) 2699
44. **Rhythm Of The Night** - DeBarge 19 (2) 2623
45. **Mike + The Mechanics** - Mike + The Mechanics 26 (6) 2589
46. **Rock A Little** - Stevie Nicks 12 (1) 2539
47. **Crazy From The Heat** - David Lee Roth 15 (4) 2528
48. **As The Band Turns** - Atlantic Starr 17 (2) 2457
49. **World Wide Live** - Scorpions 14 (1) 2451
50. **The Night I Fell In Love** - Luther Vandross 19 (3) 2435
51. **Here's To Future Days** - Thompson Twins 20 (1) 2347
52. **Boy In The Box** - Corey Hart 20 (7) 2253
53. **Greatest Hits** - The Cars 12 (4) 2244
54. **Rocky IV** - Soundtrack 10 (1) 2167
55. **Nightshift** - Commodores 12 (3) 2071
56. **Power Windows** - Rush 10 (2) 2056
57. **Maverick** - George Thorogood & The Destroyers 32 (1) 1995
58. **All For Love** - New Edition 32 (1) 1967
59. **The Firm** - The Firm 17 (2) 1884
60. **How To Be A...Zillionaire!** - ABC 30 (2) 1871
61. **Only Four You** - Mary Jane Girls 18 (2) 1841
62. **Friends** - Dionne Warwick 12 (2) 1836
63. **Contact** - The Pointer Sisters 24 (1) 1809
64. **St. Elmo's Fire** - Soundtrack 21 (2) 1793
65. **Back To The Future** - Soundtrack 12 (2) 1783
66. **Pictures For Pleasure** - Charlie Sexton 15 (3) 1753
67. **Jesse Johnson's Revue** - Jesse Johnson's Revue 43 (5) 1738
68. **Voices Carry** - 'Til Tuesday 19 (1) 1712
69. **Under Lock And Key** - Dokken 32 (3) 1710
70. **She's The Boss** - Mick Jagger 13 (1) 1708
71. **Fables Of The Reconstruction** - R.E.M. 28 (2) 1668
72. **Asylum** - KISS 20 (1) 1639
73. **Street Called Desire** - René & Angela 64 (4) 1585
74. **King Of Rock** - Run-D.M.C. 52 (3) 1556
75. **Vision Quest** - Soundtrack 11 (1) 1542
76. **Katrina And The Waves** - Katrina And The Waves 25 (2) 1525
77. **Tao** - Rick Springfield 21 (2) 1524
78. **Crush** - Orchestral Manoeuvres In The Dark 38 (2) 1514
79. **White Nights** - Soundtrack 17 (2) 1513
80. **The Breakfast Club** - Soundtrack 17 (2) 1501
81. **White City - A Novel** - Pete Townshend 26 (3) 1391
82. **Unguarded** - Amy Grant 35 (1) 1391
83. **The Dream Academy** - The Dream Academy 20 (1) 1369
84. **Magic Touch** - Stanley Jordan 64 (2) 1345
85. **Strength** - The Alarm 39 (3) 1304
86. **How Could It Be** - Eddie Murphy 26 (1) 1285
87. **Lisa Lisa & Cult Jam With Full Force** - Lisa Lisa And Cult Jam With Full Force 52 (2) 1280

Rank. Title - Act Peak (Peak Wks) Score
88. **Sign In Please** - Autograph 29 (2) 1278
89. **Live After Death** - Iron Maiden 19 (1) 1244
90. **40 Hour Week** - Alabama 28 (3) 1203
91. **Animotion** - Animotion 28 (1) 1200
92. **Brother Where You Bound** - Supertramp 21 (2) 1176
93. **Tough All Over** - John Cafferty & The Beaver Brown Band 40 (3) 1156
94. **Sacred Heart** - Dio 29 (4) 1116
95. **Rockin' With The Rhythm** - The Judds 66 (1) 1113
96. **Soul To Soul** - Stevie Ray Vaughan And Double Trouble 34 (2) 1106
97. **Pack Up The Plantation - Live!** - Tom Petty And The Heartbreakers 22 (2) 1104
98. **That's Why I'm Here** - James Taylor 34 (3) 1103
99. **Hounds Of Love** - Kate Bush 30 (1) 1088
100. **Behind The Sun** - Eric Clapton 34 (1) 1065

1986

Rank. Title - Act Peak (Peak Wks) Score
1. **Slippery When Wet** - Bon Jovi 1 (8) 14801
2. **Control** - Janet Jackson 1 (2) 12415
3. **Rapture** - Anita Baker 11 (2) 9452
4. **Invisible Touch** - Genesis 3 (2) 9040
5. **True Blue** - Madonna 1 (5) 8991
6. **Graceland** - Paul Simon 3 (1) 8543
7. **Top Gun** - Soundtrack 1 (5) 8187
8. **Licensed To Ill** - Beastie Boys 1 (7) 7721
9. **The Way It Is** - Bruce Hornsby & The Range 3 (4) 7530
10. **Back In The High Life** - Steve Winwood 3 (2) 7480
11. **Fore!** - Huey Lewis & The News 1 (1) 7433
12. **Raising Hell** - Run-D.M.C. 3 (3) 7388
13. **So** - Peter Gabriel 2 (3) 7120
14. **Look What The Cat Dragged In** - Poison 3 (2) 6911
15. **Night Songs** - Cinderella 3 (3) 6880
16. **5150** - Van Halen 1 (3) 6636
17. **Different Light** - The Bangles 2 (2) 6569
18. **Dancing On The Ceiling** - Lionel Richie 1 (2) 6483
19. **Duotones** - Kenny G 6 (2) 6209
20. **Third Stage** - Boston 1 (4) 6153
21. **The Final Countdown** - Europe 8 (2) 5668
22. **Like A Rock** - Bob Seger & The Silver Bullet Band 3 (4) 5287
23. **Love Zone** - Billy Ocean 6 (7) 4661
24. **Raised On Radio** - Journey 4 (2) 4605
25. **The Bridge** - Billy Joel 7 (4) 4352
26. **Winner In You** - Patti LaBelle 1 (1) 4001
27. **Bruce Springsteen & The E Street Band Live 1975-1985** - Bruce Springsteen 1 (7) 3897
28. **Word Up!** - Cameo 8 (1) 3662
29. **Give Me The Reason** - Luther Vandross 14 (1) 3534
30. **True Colors** - Cyndi Lauper 4 (2) 3490
31. **Eat 'Em And Smile** - David Lee Roth 4 (2) 3485
32. **Tuff Enuff** - The Fabulous Thunderbirds 13 (3) 3398
33. **The Jets** - The Jets 21 (2) 3252
34. **Break Every Rule** - Tina Turner 4 (1) 3207

Rank. Title - Act Peak (Peak Wks) Score
35. **Strong Persuader** - The Robert Cray Band 13 (3) 3174
36. **Parade: Music From The Motion Picture Under The Cherry Moon (Soundtrack)** - Prince And The Revolution 3 (3) 3097
37. **The Other Side Of Life** - The Moody Blues 9 (4) 3087
38. **Life, Love & Pain** - Club Nouveau 6 (1) 3075
39. **Crowded House** - Crowded House 12 (1) 3074
40. **Please** - Pet Shop Boys 7 (1) 3061
41. **Can't Hold Back** - Eddie Money 20 (3) 3034
42. **Whiplash Smile** - Billy Idol 6 (1) 2968
43. **Pretty In Pink** - Soundtrack 5 (4) 2899
44. **Just Like The First Time** - Freddie Jackson 23 (2) 2850
45. **The Ultimate Sin** - Ozzy Osbourne 6 (2) 2840
46. **Falco 3** - Falco 3 (1) 2764
47. **Georgia Satellites** - The Georgia Satellites 5 (1) 2752
48. **Picture Book** - Simply Red 16 (3) 2549
49. **The Thin Red Line** - Glass Tiger 27 (2) 2531
50. **Dirty Work** - The Rolling Stones 4 (2) 2422
51. **To Hell With The Devil** - Stryper 32 (2) 2270
52. **Strength In Numbers** - 38 Special 17 (1) 2220
53. **Solitude/Solitaire** - Peter Cetera 23 (1) 2156
54. **Somewhere In Time** - Iron Maiden 11 (1) 2136
55. **Revenge** - Eurythmics 12 (1) 2090
56. **GTR** - GTR 11 (2) 2069
57. **Notorious** - Duran Duran 12 (1) 1997
58. **Belinda** - Belinda Carlisle 13 (1) 1971
59. **World Machine** - Level 42 18 (2) 1841
60. **Shake You Down** - Gregory Abbott 22 (1) 1838
61. **Then & Now...The Best Of The Monkees** - The Monkees 21 (2) 1814
62. **Turbo** - Judas Priest 17 (2) 1811
63. **Every Breath You Take-The Singles** - The Police 7 (1) 1778
64. **Music From The Edge Of Heaven** - Wham! 10 (2) 1761
65. **Greatest Hits** - Alabama 24 (3) 1740
66. **True Stories: A Film By David Byrne, The Complete Soundtrack** - Talking Heads 17 (3) 1713
67. **Forever** - Kool & The Gang 25 (1) 1651
68. **Aretha (II)** - Aretha Franklin 32 (2) 1604
69. **Master Of Puppets** - Metallica 29 (2) 1587
70. **Lives In The Balance** - Jackson Browne 23 (3) 1582
71. **Lifes Rich Pageant** - R.E.M. 21 (2) 1563
72. **Stand By Me** - Soundtrack 31 (6) 1541
73. **True Confessions** - Bananarama 15 (2) 1497
74. **Robbie Nevil** - Robbie Nevil 37 (2) 1460
75. **Get Close** - The Pretenders 25 (3) 1457
76. **Especially For You** - The Smithereens 51 (1) 1438
77. **Storms Of Life** - Randy Travis 85 (2) 1430
78. **Heartbeat** - Don Johnson 17 (2) 1426
79. **Who Made Who (Soundtrack)** - AC/DC 33 (4) 1419
80. **Emerson, Lake, & Powell** - Emerson, Lake & Powell 23 (3) 1419
81. **Boomtown** - David & David 39 (2) 1413
82. **Chicago 18** - Chicago 35 (2) 1402
83. **Dancing Undercover** - Ratt 26 (2) 1372
84. **Poolside** - Nu Shooz 27 (2) 1359
85. **Headed For The Future** - Neil Diamond 20 (1) 1336
86. **Standing On A Beach -- The Singles** - The Cure 48 (2) 1287
87. **El DeBarge** - El DeBarge 24 (3) 1280
88. **Live** - George Thorogood & The Destroyers 33 (3) 1273
89. **Back In Black** - Whodini 35 (2) 1272
90. **By Request (The Best of Billy Vera & The Beaters)** - Billy Vera & The Beaters 15 (1) 1239
91. **Crash** - The Human League 24 (2) 1236
92. **Double Vision** - Bob James/David Sanborn 50 (2) 1216
93. **Touch Me** - Samantha Fox 24 (2) 1202
94. **August** - Eric Clapton 37 (2) 1193
95. **Emotional** - Jeffrey Osborne 26 (1) 1155
96. **QR III** - Quiet Riot 31 (2) 1142
97. **Into The Light** - Chris de Burgh 25 (2) 1127
98. **Mosaic** - Wang Chung 41 (2) 1118
99. **Big World** - Joe Jackson 34 (2) 1053
100. **Fahrenheit** - Toto 40 (2) 1052

1987

Rank. Title - Act Peak (Peak Wks) Score
1. **Hysteria** - Def Leppard 1 (6) 19758
2. **Appetite For Destruction** - Guns N' Roses 1 (5) 17811
3. **Dirty Dancing** - Soundtrack 1 (18) 16684
4. **Faith** - George Michael 1 (12) 16081
5. **Bad** - Michael Jackson 1 (6) 13217
6. **The Joshua Tree** - U2 1 (9) 12139
7. **Whitesnake** - Whitesnake 2 (10) 11814
8. **Whitney** - Whitney Houston 1 (11) 11594
9. **Kick** - INXS 3 (4) 10126
10. **Tiffany** - Tiffany 1 (2) 7298
11. **Let It Loose** - Gloria Estefan & Miami Sound Machine 6 (2) 6903
12. **Richard Marx** - Richard Marx 8 (2) 6799
13. **Out Of The Blue** - Debbie Gibson 7 (2) 6673
14. **The Lonesome Jubilee** - John Mellencamp 6 (7) 6213
15. **Bad Animals** - Heart 2 (3) 6177
16. **Tango In The Night** - Fleetwood Mac 7 (3) 5973
17. **Permanent Vacation** - Aerosmith 11 (4) 5898
18. **Tunnel Of Love** - Bruce Springsteen 1 (1) 5349
19. **Indtroducing The Hardline According To Terence Trent D'Arby** - Terence Trent D'Arby 4 (2) 5202
20. **A Momentary Lapse Of Reason** - Pink Floyd 3 (1) 5195
21. **Jody Watley** - Jody Watley 10 (1) 4882
22. **Exposure** - Exposé 16 (2) 4850
23. **Girls, Girls, Girls** - Mötley Crüe 2 (1) 4702
24. **Bigger And Deffer** - LL Cool J 3 (1) 4537
25. **Pride** - White Lion 11 (1) 4513
26. **La Bamba (Soundtrack)** - Los Lobos 1 (2) 4269
27. **Spanish Fly** - Lisa Lisa And Cult Jam 7 (3) 4194
28. **Heaven On Earth** - Belinda Carlisle 13 (2) 4078
29. **The Phantom Of The Opera** - Original London Cast 33 (1) 4006
30. **Always & Forever** - Randy Travis 19 (1) 3934
31. **...Nothing Like The Sun** - Sting 9 (4) 3861
32. **Crushin'** - Fat Boys 8 (3) 3405
33. **Sign 'O' The Times** - Prince 6 (2) 3322
34. **Into The Fire** - Bryan Adams 7 (1) 3091
35. **Cloud Nine** - George Harrison 8 (1) 3080
36. **In The Dark** - Grateful Dead 6 (2) 2807
37. **Once Bitten** - Great White 23 (2) 2769
38. **R.E.M. No. 5: Document** - R.E.M. 10 (1) 2688
39. **Coming Around Again** - Carly Simon 25 (2) 2616
40. **Trio** - Dolly Parton, Linda Ronstadt, Emmylou Harris 6 (1) 2543
41. **Surfing With The Alien** - Joe Satriani 29 (4) 2477
42. **Beverly Hills Cop II** - Soundtrack 8 (1) 2457
43. **Actually** - Pet Shop Boys 25 (1) 2421
44. **One Heartbeat** - Smokey Robinson 26 (2) 2397
45. **Vital Idol** - Billy Idol 10 (1) 2338
46. **Solitude Standing** - Suzanne Vega 11 (2) 2315
47. **Inside Information** - Foreigner 15 (1) 2306
48. **Tribute** - Ozzy Osbourne/Randy Rhoads 6 (2) 2266
49. **Back For The Attack** - Dokken 13 (1) 2188
50. **In My Tribe** - 10,000 Maniacs 37 (1) 2156
51. **Kiss Me, Kiss Me, Kiss Me** - The Cure 35 (4) 2063
52. **Crazy Nights** - KISS 18 (1) 2060
53. **Who's That Girl (Soundtrack)** - Madonna 7 (2) 2038
54. **Big Generator** - Yes 15 (3) 2009
55. **Characters** - Stevie Wonder 17 (3) 1959
56. **Keep Your Eye On Me** - Herb Alpert 18 (3) 1954
57. **Hot, Cool And Vicious** - Salt-N-Pepa 26 (4) 1947
58. **All In The Name Of Love** - Atlantic Starr 18 (1) 1929
59. **Magic** - The Jets 35 (1) 1898
60. **Hold Your Fire** - Rush 13 (2) 1873
61. **Substance** - New Order 36 (1) 1864
62. **One Voice** - Barbra Streisand 9 (2) 1848
63. **Broadcast** - Cutting Crew 16 (2) 1795
64. **Everlasting** - Natalie Cole 42 (2) 1792
65. **Cher(2)** - Cher 32 (3) 1727
66. **It's Better To Travel** - Swing Out Sister 40 (1) 1716
67. **Just Gets Better With Time** - The Whispers 22 (2) 1710
68. **Mechanical Resonance** - Tesla 32 (2) 1704
69. **Live In Australia (With The Melbourne Symphony Orchestra)** - Elton John 24 (2) 1685
70. **I Never Said Goodbye** - Sammy Hagar 14 (1) 1636
71. **How Ya Like Me Now** - Kool Moe Dee 35 (1) 1604
72. **The Return Of Bruno** - Bruce Willis 14 (3) 1592
73. **You Can Dance** - Madonna 14 (1) 1585
74. **Running In The Family** - Level 42 23 (1) 1525
75. **Life As We Know It** - REO Speedwagon 28 (2) 1504

Rank. Title - Act Peak (Peak Wks) Score
76. **Hearsay** - Alexander O'Neal 29 (1) 1492
77. **Music For The Masses** - Depeche Mode 35 (2) 1461
78. **No Protection** - Starship 12 (1) 1442
79. **Let Me Up (I've Had Enough)** - Tom Petty And The Heartbreakers 20 (2) 1401
80. **Man Of Colours** - Icehouse 43 (1) 1358
81. **If I Were Your Woman** - Stephanie Mills 30 (1) 1353
82. **A Very Special Christmas** - Various Artists 20 (3) 1351
83. **Bangin'** - The Outfield 18 (1) 1345
84. **Lost Boys** - Soundtrack 15 (1) 1302
85. **Babylon And On** - Squeeze 36 (2) 1284
86. **Electric** - The Cult 38 (3) 1278
87. **Midnight To Midnight** - Psychedelic Furs 29 (2) 1246
88. **Chronicles** - Steve Winwood 26 (1) 1238
89. **Born To Boogie** - Hank Williams Jr. 28 (1) 1235
90. **Crest Of A Knave** - Jethro Tull 32 (1) 1219
91. **I'm No Angel** - The Gregg Allman Band 30 (3) 1183
92. **Robbie Robertson** - Robbie Robertson 38 (2) 1181
93. **The Best Of The Doors(2)** - The Doors 32 (1) 1157
94. **The Hunger** - Michael Bolton 46 (1) 1145
95. **The $5.98 E.P.: Garage Days Re-Revisited** - Metallica 28 (2) 1117
96. **Ready Or Not** - Lou Gramm 27 (1) 1094
97. **Touch The World** - Earth, Wind & Fire 33 (1) 1083
98. **Less Than Zero** - Soundtrack 31 (2) 1080
99. **Canciones de Mi Padre** - Linda Ronstadt 42 (1) 1069
100. **I'm The Man** - Anthrax 53 (1) 1066

1988

Rank. Title - Act Peak (Peak Wks) Score
1. **Forever Your Girl** - Paula Abdul 1 (10) 19418
2. **Don't Be Cruel** - Bobby Brown 1 (6) 15398
3. **Hangin' Tough** - New Kids On The Block 1 (2) 14550
4. **New Jersey** - Bon Jovi 1 (4) 9744
5. **Open Up And Say...Ahh!** - Poison 2 (1) 9336
6. **Tracy Chapman** - Tracy Chapman 1 (1) 7949
7. **OU812** - Van Halen 1 (4) 6971
8. **G N' R Lies** - Guns N' Roses 2 (1) 6434
9. **Volume 1** - Traveling Wilburys 3 (6) 6396
10. **Giving You The Best That I Got** - Anita Baker 1 (4) 6333
11. **Cocktail** - Soundtrack 2 (1) 6310
12. **Rattle And Hum (Soundtrack)** - U2 1 (6) 5894
13. **Roll With It** - Steve Winwood 1 (1) 5737
14. **Long Cold Winter** - Cinderella 10 (5) 5711
15. **More Dirty Dancing** - Soundtrack 3 (5) 5578
16. **Out Of Order** - Rod Stewart 20 (2) 5537
17. **Whenever You Need Somebody** - Rick Astley 10 (2) 5157
18. **...And Justice For All** - Metallica 6 (2) 4977
19. **Vivid** - Living Colour 6 (2) 4950
20. **Now And Zen** - Robert Plant 6 (1) 4702
21. **He's The D.J., I'm The Rapper** - D.J. Jazzy Jeff & The Fresh Prince 4 (1) 4651

Rank. Title - Act Peak (Peak Wks) Score
22. **Shooting Rubberbands At The Stars** - Edie Brickell & New Bohemians 4 (2) 4620
23. **Make It Last Forever** - Keith Sweat 15 (1) 4409
24. **Heart Break** - New Edition 12 (1) 4305
25. **Tell It To My Heart** - Taylor Dayne 21 (1) 4302
26. **Silhouette** - Kenny G 8 (1) 4280
27. **Winger** - Winger 21 (3) 4224
28. **Green** - R.E.M. 12 (3) 3841
29. **Lap Of Luxury** - Cheap Trick 16 (1) 3824
30. **Simple Pleasures** - Bobby McFerrin 5 (3) 3562
31. **Stronger Than Pride** - Sade 7 (2) 3456
32. **Savage Amusement** - Scorpions 5 (1) 3456
33. **Diesel And Dust** - Midnight Oil 21 (3) 3447
34. **In Effect Mode** - Al B. Sure! 20 (1) 3363
35. **Lita** - Lita Ford 29 (4) 3280
36. **Journey's Greatest Hits** - Journey 10 (2) 3252
37. **Let's Get It Started** - MC Hammer 30 (1) 3114
38. **Scenes From The Southside** - Bruce Hornsby & The Range 5 (1) 3112
39. **Guy** - Guy 27 (5) 3108
40. **Heavy Nova** - Robert Palmer 13 (3) 3027
41. **Skyscraper** - David Lee Roth 6 (6) 3013
42. **Pebbles** - Pebbles 14 (1) 2973
43. **It Takes Two** - Rob Base & D.J. E-Z Rock 31 (1) 2923
44. **Karyn White** - Karyn White 19 (1) 2905
45. **Up Your Alley** - Joan Jett & the Blackhearts 19 (1) 2833
46. **Everything** - The Bangles 15 (2) 2818
47. **Melissa Etheridge** - Melissa Etheridge 22 (1) 2781
48. **Eazy-Duz-It** - Eazy-E 41 (1) 2665
49. **Any Love** - Luther Vandross 9 (1) 2513
50. **Time And Tide** - Basia 36 (1) 2498
51. **Good Morning, Vietnam** - Soundtrack 10 (2) 2363
52. **All That Jazz** - Breathe 34 (3) 2350
53. **Reg Strikes Back** - Elton John 16 (1) 2304
54. **Hold An Old Friend's Hand** - Tiffany 17 (4) 2282
55. **Conscious Party** - Ziggy Marley And The Melody Makers 23 (1) 2220
56. **Kingdom Come** - Kingdom Come 12 (1) 2156
57. **Till I Loved You** - Barbra Streisand 10 (1) 2133
58. **Living Years** - Mike + The Mechanics 13 (2) 2127
59. **Tougher Than Leather** - Run-D.M.C. 9 (1) 2081
60. **See The Light** - The Jeff Healey Band 22 (3) 2041
61. **Tear Down These Walls** - Billy Ocean 18 (1) 2012
62. **Small World** - Huey Lewis & The News 11 (2) 1851
63. **19** - Chicago 37 (2) 1846
64. **Blow Up Your Video** - AC/DC 12 (1) 1815
65. **No Rest For The Wicked** - Ozzy Osbourne 13 (1) 1774
66. **Reach For The Sky** - Ratt 17 (1) 1768
67. **Delicate Sound Of Thunder** - Pink Floyd 11 (1) 1759
68. **Blow My Fuse** - Kix 46 (1) 1757
69. **Wild, Wild West** - The Escape Club 27 (3) 1716

Rank. Title - Act Peak (Peak Wks) Score
70. **Greatest Hits** - Fleetwood Mac 14 (1) 1681
71. **American Dream** - Crosby, Stills, Nash & Young 16 (1) 1667
72. **The Innocents** - Erasure 49 (1) 1638
73. **Information Society** - Information Society 25 (1) 1635
74. **Seventh Son Of A Seventh Son** - Iron Maiden 12 (1) 1631
75. **Never Die Young** - James Taylor 25 (2) 1606
76. **Smashes, Thrashes & Hits** - KISS 21 (2) 1558
77. **Big Thing** - Duran Duran 24 (2) 1528
78. **Bulletboys** - BulletBoys 34 (3) 1504
79. **Greatest Hits** - The Judds 76 (2) 1503
80. **The Right Stuff** - Vanessa Williams 38 (1) 1476
81. **Vixen** - Vixen 41 (1) 1452
82. **Britny Fox** - Britny Fox 39 (2) 1441
83. **Starfish** - The Church 41 (2) 1426
84. **Out Of This World** - Europe 19 (1) 1396
85. **The Lion And The Cobra** - Sinead O'Connor 36 (3) 1345
86. **Lovesexy** - Prince 11 (1) 1341
87. **Naked** - Talking Heads 19 (1) 1340
88. **Old 8 x 10** - Randy Travis 35 (1) 1338
89. **Messages From The Boys** - The Boys 33 (2) 1335
90. **Ooh Yeah!** - Daryl Hall & John Oates 24 (2) 1295
91. **Wide Awake In Dreamland** - Pat Benatar 28 (2) 1272
92. **Operation: Mindcrime** - Queensryche 50 (2) 1266
93. **I Wanna Have Some Fun** - Samantha Fox 37 (1) 1231
94. **Born To Be Bad** - George Thorogood & The Destroyers 32 (3) 1214
95. **Even Worse** - "Weird Al" Yankovic 27 (1) 1209
96. **It Takes A Nation Of Millions To Hold Us Back** - Public Enemy 42 (2) 1159
97. **Union** - Toni Childs 63 (1) 1092
98. **2nd Wave** - Surface 56 (2) 1080
99. **The Lover In Me** - Sheena Easton 44 (4) 1067
100. **What Up, Dog?** - Was (Not Was) 43 (2) 1057

1989

Rank. Title - Act Peak (Peak Wks) Score
1. **Girl You Know It's True** - Milli Vanilli 1 (7) 14650
2. **Janet Jackson's Rhythm Nation 1814** - Janet Jackson 1 (4) 13746
3. **Soul Provider** - Michael Bolton 3 (3) 12887
4. **The Raw & The Cooked** - Fine Young Cannibals 1 (7) 10227
5. **...But Seriously** - Phil Collins 1 (4) 9734
6. **Full Moon Fever** - Tom Petty 3 (2) 9020
7. **Nick Of Time** - Bonnie Raitt 1 (3) 8820
8. **Pump** - Aerosmith 5 (3) 8649
9. **Dr. Feelgood** - Mötley Crüe 1 (2) 8619
10. **Skid Row** - Skid Row 6 (1) 8481
11. **The End Of The Innocence** - Don Henley 8 (1) 8388
12. **Like A Prayer** - Madonna 1 (6) 8128
13. **Beaches (Soundtrack)** - Bette Midler 2 (3) 8076

Rank. Title - Act Peak (Peak Wks) Score
14. Repeat Offender - Richard Marx 1 (1) 7671
15. Cosmic Thing - The B-52s 4 (1) 7172
16. Storm Front - Billy Joel 1 (1) 6443
17. Electric Youth - Debbie Gibson 1 (5) 6295
18. Cuts Both Ways - Gloria Estefan 8 (2) 5235
19. Loc-ed After Dark - Tone-Loc 1 (1) 5062
20. Dirty Rotten Filthy Stinking Rich - Warrant 10 (3) 4909
21. Steel Wheels - The Rolling Stones 3 (4) 4806
22. Cry Like A Rainstorm, Howl Like The Wind - Linda Ronstadt (Featuring Aaron Neville) 7 (1) 4767
23. Tender Lover - Babyface 14 (1) 4740
24. Batman (Soundtrack) - Prince 1 (6) 4618
25. Keep On Movin' - Soul II Soul 14 (4) 4558
26. Stone Cold Rhymin' - Young M.C. 9 (1) 4442
27. Heart Of Stone - Cher 10 (2) 4398
28. As Nasty As They Wanna Be - The 2 Live Crew 29 (1) 3974
29. ...Twice Shy - Great White 9 (1) 3912
30. Heart Shaped World - Chris Isaak 7 (4) 3876
31. Killin' Time - Clint Black 31 (1) 3718
32. Disintegration - The Cure 12 (3) 3656
33. Live - Kenny G 16 (1) 3642
34. Look Sharp! - Roxette 23 (2) 3575
35. Journeyman - Eric Clapton 16 (1) 3472
36. New Kids On The Block - New Kids On The Block 25 (3) 3437
37. Can't Fight Fate - Taylor Dayne 25 (1) 3361
38. The Great Radio Controversy - Tesla 18 (1) 3201
39. Back On The Block - Quincy Jones 9 (2) 3185
40. Pump Up The Jam - The Album - Technotronic 10 (1) 3107
41. Mystery Girl - Roy Orbison 5 (2) 3024
42. Big Tyme - Heavy D & The Boyz 19 (3) 2838
43. Bad English - Bad English 21 (2) 2809
44. Sonic Temple - The Cult 10 (6) 2792
45. Straight Outta Compton - N.W.A. 37 (3) 2777

Rank. Title - Act Peak (Peak Wks) Score
46. Trash - Alice Cooper 20 (2) 2735
47. Dance!...Ya Know It! - Bobby Brown 9 (3) 2707
48. Slip Of The Tongue - Whitesnake 10 (1) 2611
49. Pickin' On Nashville - The Kentucky Headhunters 41 (1) 2571
50. The Best Of Luther Vandross...The Best Of Love - Luther Vandross 26 (2) 2564
51. Life Is...Too Short - Too Short 37 (2) 2412
52. Blind Man's Zoo - 10,000 Maniacs 13 (1) 2375
53. The Seeds Of Love - Tears For Fears 8 (3) 2355
54. Sleeping With The Past - Elton John 23 (1) 2337
55. A New Flame - Simply Red 22 (1) 2305
56. Walking With A Panther - LL Cool J 6 (1) 2231
57. When Harry Met Sally (Soundtrack) - Harry Connick Jr. 42 (2) 2220
58. Larger Than Life - Jody Watley 16 (2) 2129
59. Big Daddy - John Mellencamp 7 (1) 2048
60. Martika - Martika 15 (1) 2041
61. Crossroads - Tracy Chapman 9 (2) 2020
62. Merry, Merry Christmas - New Kids On The Block 9 (1) 2001
63. Love And Rockets - Love And Rockets 14 (1) 1984
64. Watermark - Enya 25 (4) 1899
65. After 7 - After 7 35 (1) 1864
66. Flying In A Blue Dream - Joe Satriani 23 (3) 1863
67. The Little Mermaid - Soundtrack 32 (2) 1861
68. What You Don't Know - Exposé 33 (2) 1752
69. Big Game - White Lion 19 (2) 1730
70. Indigo Girls - Indigo Girls 22 (3) 1704
71. Flowers In The Dirt - Paul McCartney 21 (3) 1694
72. Brave And Crazy - Melissa Etheridge 22 (1) 1683
73. The Great Adventures Of Slick Rick - Slick Rick 31 (3) 1609

Rank. Title - Act Peak (Peak Wks) Score
74. 24/7 - Dino 34 (3) 1569
75. The Other Side Of The Mirror - Stevie Nicks 10 (1) 1562
76. In Step - Stevie Ray Vaughan And Double Trouble 33 (1) 1544
77. No One Can Do It Better - The D.O.C. 20 (2) 1531
78. Presto - Rush 16 (2) 1481
79. Nothing Matters Without Love - Seduction 36 (1) 1477
80. Cocked & Loaded - L.A. Guns 38 (1) 1459
81. The Trinity Session - Cowboy Junkies 26 (1) 1441
82. March - Michael Penn 31 (1) 1417
83. Cycles - The Doobie Brothers 17 (1) 1414
84. 3 Feet High And Rising - De La Soul 24 (2) 1407
85. Spike - Elvis Costello 32 (1) 1380
86. Hold Me In Your Arms - Rick Astley 19 (3) 1365
87. Hot In The Shade - KISS 29 (1) 1344
88. Ghostbusters II - Soundtrack 14 (1) 1340
89. Mother's Milk - Red Hot Chili Peppers 52 (1) 1311
90. No Holdin' Back - Randy Travis 33 (1) 1311
91. We Too Are One - Eurythmics 34 (2) 1252
92. A Collection: Greatest Hits...And More - Barbra Streisand 26 (3) 1234
93. 11 - The Smithereens 41 (1) 1219
94. Absolute Torch And Twang - k.d. lang & The Reclines 69 (1) 1203
95. Legacy - Poco 40 (2) 1198
96. Technique - New Order 32 (1) 1165
97. Knowledge Is King - Kool Moe Dee 25 (2) 1142
98. The Disregard Of Timekeeping - Bonham 38 (1) 1131
99. Freedom - Neil Young 35 (2) 1127
100. Paul's Boutique - Beastie Boys 14 (2) 1118

50 Highest Charting Albums By Raw Score In Each Year

Rank. **Title** - Act YrPeak (YrWks) YrScr

1964

1. **Hello, Dolly!** - Original Cast 1 (45) 22738
2. **Meet The Beatles!** - The Beatles 1 (48) 20504
3. **Honey In The Horn** - Al Hirt 3 (52) 19405
4. **A Hard Day's Night (Soundtrack)** - The Beatles 1 (24) 19376
5. **In The Wind** - Peter, Paul & Mary 2 (52) 17539
6. **Hello Dolly!** - Louis Armstrong 1 (33) 17351
7. **Funny Girl (Original Cast)** - Barbra Streisand 2 (35) 15806
8. **The Third Album** - Barbra Streisand 5 (44) 15513
9. **Introducing...The Beatles** - The Beatles 2 (47) 14260
10. **The Beatles' Second Album** - The Beatles 1 (36) 13658
11. **Getz/Gilberto** - Stan Getz And Joao Gilberto Featuring Antonio Carlos Jobim 2 (30) 12463
12. **The Singing Nun** - The Singing Nun (Soeur Sourire) 1 (31) 12087
13. **Something New** - The Beatles 2 (21) 12050
14. **The Second Barbra Streisand Album** - Barbra Streisand 3 (52) 12017
15. **Everybody Loves Somebody** - Dean Martin 2 (20) 11500
16. **The Pink Panther (Soundtrack)** - Henry Mancini And His Orchestra 8 (38) 10827
17. **Cotton Candy** - Al Hirt 6 (32) 10399
18. **All Summer Long** - The Beach Boys 4 (22) 9655
19. **People** - Barbra Streisand 1 (13) 9337
20. **Yesterday's Love Songs/Today's Blues** - Nancy Wilson 4 (42) 9331
21. **Glad All Over** - The Dave Clark Five 3 (30) 9020
22. **The Academy Award Winning "Call Me Irresponsible"** - Andy Williams 5 (34) 8554
23. **Charade (Soundtrack)** - Henry Mancini And His Orchestra 6 (41) 8308
24. **The Kingsmen In Person** - The Kingsmen 20 (50) 7988
25. **Shut Down, Volume 2** - The Beach Boys 13 (38) 7567
26. **Bach's Greatest Hits** - Swingle Singers 15 (52) 7435
27. **Peter, Paul And Mary In Concert** - Peter, Paul & Mary 4 (20) 7424
28. **Wives And Lovers** - Jack Jones 18 (52) 7258
29. **Joan Baez In Concert, Part 2** - Joan Baez 7 (32) 7236
30. **Fun In Acapulco (Soundtrack)** - Elvis Presley 3 (22) 7197
31. **Catch A Rising Star** - John Gary 19 (52) 7159
32. **Little Deuce Coupe** - The Beach Boys 4 (38) 6906
33. **Today, Tomorrow, Forever** - Nancy Wilson 10 (30) 6803
34. **How Glad I Am** - Nancy Wilson 4 (17) 6753
35. **Today** - The New Christy Minstrels 9 (34) 6631

Rank. **Title** - Act YrPeak (YrWks) YrScr

36. **Kissin' Cousins (Soundtrack)** - Elvis Presley 6 (30) 6280
37. **Keep On Pushing** - The Impressions 8 (21) 5961
38. **The Dave Clark Five Return!** - The Dave Clark Five 5 (22) 5733
39. **Ramblin' Featuring Green, Green** - The New Christy Minstrels 22 (52) 5619
40. **Johnny Rivers At The Whisky A Go Go** - Johnny Rivers 12 (28) 5516
41. **Encore** - John Gary 16 (45) 5449
42. **Beach Boys Concert** - The Beach Boys 1 (8) 5407
43. **There! I've Said It Again** - Bobby Vinton 8 (28) 5366
44. **Something Special For Young Lovers** - Ray Charles Singers 11 (33) 5361
45. **Sugar Lips** - Al Hirt 9 (19) 5344
46. **The Wonderful World Of Andy Williams** - Andy Williams 9 (24) 5340
47. **Tender Is The Night** - Johnny Mathis 13 (28) 5312
48. **The Serendipity Singers** - The Serendipity Singers 11 (29) 5254
49. **Who's Afraid Of Virginia Woolf?** - Jimmy Smith 16 (31) 5152
50. **Rag Doll** - The 4 Seasons 7 (21) 5095

1965

1. **Mary Poppins** - Soundtrack 1 (52) 33720
2. **The Sound Of Music** - Soundtrack 1 (41) 23875
3. **My Fair Lady** - Soundtrack 4 (52) 19675
4. **Beatles '65** - The Beatles 1 (52) 19387
5. **Goldfinger** - Soundtrack 1 (52) 18503
6. **Where Did Our Love Go** - The Supremes 2 (52) 16429
7. **Fiddler On The Roof** - Original Cast 7 (52) 14119
8. **Whipped Cream & Other Delights** - Herb Alpert's Tijuana Brass 1 (33) 13807
9. **My Name Is Barbra (Soundtrack)** - Barbra Streisand 2 (32) 13451
10. **Beach Boys Concert** - The Beach Boys 2 (52) 13291
11. **Dear Heart** - Andy Williams 4 (38) 13018
12. **Help! (Soundtrack)** - The Beatles 1 (18) 12916
13. **Introducing Herman's Hermits** - Herman's Hermits 2 (40) 12864
14. **The Beach Boys Today!** - The Beach Boys 4 (40) 12494
15. **Herman's Hermits On Tour** - Herman's Hermits 2 (28) 12451
16. **Beatles VI** - The Beatles 1 (27) 12399
17. **Bringing It All Back Home** - Bob Dylan 6 (35) 11888
18. **People** - Barbra Streisand 8 (52) 11637
19. **The Rolling Stones, Now!** - The Rolling Stones 5 (41) 11081
20. **Out Of Our Heads** - The Rolling Stones 1 (21) 10913

Rank. **Title** - Act YrPeak (YrWks) YrScr

21. **Blue Midnight** - Bert Kaempfert And His Orchestra 5 (49) 10720
22. **The Return Of Roger Miller** - Roger Miller 4 (47) 10672
23. **Look At Us** - Sonny & Cher 2 (19) 10130
24. **You've Lost That Lovin' Feelin'** - The Righteous Brothers 4 (49) 9963
25. **The In Crowd** - Ramsey Lewis Trio 2 (20) 9017
26. **L-O-V-E** - Nat King Cole 4 (38) 8988
27. **A Song Will Rise** - Peter, Paul & Mary 8 (38) 8341
28. **Summer Days (And Summer Nights!!)** - The Beach Boys 2 (23) 8273
29. **Joan Baez/5** - Joan Baez 12 (52) 8084
30. **The Best Of Al Hirt** - Al Hirt 13 (43) 7613
31. **Getz/Gilberto** - Stan Getz And Joao Gilberto Featuring Antonio Carlos Jobim 17 (52) 7535
32. **Hello, Dolly!** - Original Cast 13 (45) 7081
33. **My Love Forgive Me** - Robert Goulet 5 (28) 7070
34. **Roustabout (Soundtrack)** - Elvis Presley 1 (20) 6750
35. **Girl Happy (Soundtrack)** - Elvis Presley 8 (31) 6669
36. **Just Once In My Life...** - The Righteous Brothers 9 (31) 6633
37. **A Hard Day's Night (Soundtrack)** - The Beatles 5 (27) 6608
38. **Sinatra '65** - Frank Sinatra 9 (26) 6368
39. **Getz Au Go Go** - The New Stan Getz Quartet Featuring Astrud Gilberto 24 (44) 5679
40. **12 x 5** - The Rolling Stones 3 (31) 5504
41. **Hello Dolly!** - Louis Armstrong 23 (41) 5418
42. **Highway 61 Revisited** - Bob Dylan 3 (13) 5346
43. **Honey In The Horn** - Al Hirt 20 (37) 5278
44. **Coast To Coast** - The Dave Clark Five 6 (21) 5217
45. **More Hits By The Supremes** - The Supremes 6 (19) 5212
46. **Zorba The Greek** - Soundtrack 26 (35) 5156
47. **Marianne Faithfull** - Marianne Faithfull 12 (30) 5084
48. **Mr. Tambourine Man** - The Byrds 6 (27) 5078
49. **Everybody Loves Somebody** - Dean Martin 12 (29) 4914
50. **Downtown** - Petula Clark 21 (36) 4913

1966

1. **Whipped Cream & Other Delights** - Herb Alpert's Tijuana Brass 6 (53) 29737
2. **!!Going Places!!** - Herb Alpert & The Tijuana Brass 6 (47) 28428
3. **The Sound Of Music** - Soundtrack 3 (38) 27731
4. **What Now My Love** - Herb Alpert & The Tijuana Brass 1 (29) 22446
5. **Doctor Zhivago** - Soundtrack 5 (50) 20800
6. **Rubber Soul** - The Beatles 1 (32) 17597

Rank. Title - Act YrPeak (YrWks) YrScr
7. If You Can Believe Your Eyes And Ears - The Mamas & The Papas 5 (53) 15166
8. South Of The Border - Herb Alpert & The Tijuana Brass 1 (18) 14036
9. The Best Of The Animals - The Animals 3 (25) 13465
10. Big Hits (High Tide And Green Grass) - The Rolling Stones 4 (35) 12326
11. Strangers In The Night - Frank Sinatra 5 (40) 12257
12. September Of My Years - Frank Sinatra 1 (26) 11915
13. Ballads Of The Green Berets - SSgt Barry Sadler 2 (26) 11734
14. The Best Of Herman's Hermits - Herman's Hermits 1 (13) 11505
15. Revolver - The Beatles 7 (32) 11441
16. Somewhere My Love - Ray Conniff & His Orchestra & Chorus 7 (47) 10869
17. Lou Rawls Live - Lou Rawls 6 (50) 10292
18. My Name Is Barbra, Two... - Barbra Streisand 19 (53) 10130
19. "Yesterday" And Today - The Beatles 3 (36) 9908
20. Aftermath - The Rolling Stones 8 (46) 9870
21. The Monkees - The Monkees 5 (42) 9789
22. Wonderfulness - Bill Cosby 1 (15) 9494
23. My World - Eddy Arnold 10 (53) 9354
24. Golden Hits - Roger Miller 11 (49) 9311
25. Why Is There Air? - Bill Cosby 5 (43) 9301
26. Color Me Barbra (Soundtrack) - Barbra Streisand 9 (45) 9219
27. Spanish Eyes - Al Martino 4 (30) 8605
28. Boots - Nancy Sinatra 8 (35) 8556
29. The Supremes A' Go-Go - The Supremes 11 (47) 8373
30. The 4 Seasons' Gold Vault of Hits - The 4 Seasons 6 (34) 8337
31. Mary Poppins - Soundtrack 7 (32) 7980
32. Just Like Us! - Paul Revere & The Raiders 10 (32) 7685
33. The Dave Clark Five's Greatest Hits - The Dave Clark Five 4 (14) 7572
34. December's Children (And Everybody's) - The Rolling Stones 11 (32) 7455
35. Going To A Go-Go - Smokey Robinson & The Miracles 21 (42) 7115
36. The Supremes At The Copa - The Supremes 9 (31) 7093
37. The Shadow Of Your Smile - Andy Williams 9 (38) 7031
38. Soul & Inspiration - The Righteous Brothers 9 (30) 6834
39. Pet Sounds - The Beach Boys 8 (37) 6648
40. The Mamas & The Papas - The Mamas & The Papas 24 (47) 6524
41. Temptin' Temptations - The Temptations 17 (51) 6418
42. Bill Cosby Is A Very Funny Fellow, Right! - Bill Cosby 18 (43) 6381
43. A Man And His Music - Frank Sinatra 15 (36) 6325
44. The Shadow Of Your Smile - Johnny Mathis 8 (24) 6296

Rank. Title - Act YrPeak (YrWks) YrScr
45. Midnight Ride - Paul Revere & The Raiders 5 (20) 6277
46. I Hear A Symphony - The Supremes 37 (53) 6271
47. My Fair Lady - Soundtrack 12 (26) 6177
48. Herb Alpert's Tijuana Brass, Volume 2 - Herb Alpert's Tijuana Brass 16 (44) 5989
49. That Was The Year That Was - Tom Lehrer 11 (26) 5815
50. Crying Time - Ray Charles 9 (19) 5786

1967

Rank. Title - Act YrPeak (YrWks) YrScr
1. More Of The Monkees - The Monkees 1 (48) 25738
2. Doctor Zhivago - Soundtrack 3 (52) 24230
3. Sgt. Pepper's Lonely Hearts Club Band - The Beatles 1 (28) 23709
4. The Sound Of Music - Soundtrack 4 (52) 20309
5. The Monkees - The Monkees 1 (52) 19951
6. S.R.O. - Herb Alpert & The Tijuana Brass 2 (52) 16941
7. Headquarters - The Monkees 1 (30) 15925
8. The Temptations Greatest Hits - The Temptations 5 (52) 15644
9. The Doors - The Doors 2 (41) 15098
10. I Never Loved A Man The Way I Love You - Aretha Franklin 2 (39) 13542
11. Surrealistic Pillow - Jefferson Airplane 3 (41) 13535
12. Whipped Cream & Other Delights - Herb Alpert's Tijuana Brass 9 (52) 13341
13. A Man And A Woman - Soundtrack 10 (52) 13257
14. The Mamas & The Papas Deliver - The Mamas & The Papas 2 (42) 13063
15. Sounds Like... - Herb Alpert & The Tijuana Brass 1 (31) 12515
16. !!Going Places!! - Herb Alpert & The Tijuana Brass 6 (52) 11702
17. Revenge - Bill Cosby 2 (34) 11570
18. The Best Of The Lovin' Spoonful - The Lovin' Spoonful 3 (42) 10693
19. Born Free - Andy Williams 5 (34) 10648
20. Diana Ross And The Supremes Greatest Hits - Diana Ross & The Supremes 1 (14) 10579
21. Between The Buttons - The Rolling Stones 2 (46) 9779
22. Wonderfulness - Bill Cosby 12 (52) 9612
23. That's Life - Frank Sinatra 6 (52) 9299
24. Flowers - The Rolling Stones 3 (24) 9053
25. My Cup Runneth Over - Ed Ames 4 (44) 8918
26. Born Free - Roger Williams 7 (52) 8425
27. What Now My Love - Herb Alpert & The Tijuana Brass 16 (52) 8388
28. Release Me - Engelbert Humperdinck 7 (29) 8282
29. Collections - The Young Rascals 14 (50) 7884
30. Ode To Billie Joe - Bobbie Gentry 1 (16) 7852
31. The Mamas & The Papas - The Mamas & The Papas 10 (52) 7794
32. Groovin' - The Young Rascals 5 (21) 7684
33. Aretha Arrives - Aretha Franklin 5 (19) 7280
34. Claudine - Claudine Longet 11 (38) 6979

Rank. Title - Act YrPeak (YrWks) YrScr
35. The Supremes A' Go-Go - The Supremes 9 (45) 6971
36. Insight Out - The Association 8 (24) 6928
37. Bob Dylan's Greatest Hits - Bob Dylan 10 (35) 6901
38. The Spirit Of '67 - Paul Revere & The Raiders 9 (32) 6791
39. Sergio Mendes & Brasil '66 - Sergio Mendes & Brasil '66 20 (52) 6749
40. Greatest Hits - Paul Revere & The Raiders 9 (34) 6579
41. Somewhere My Love - Ray Conniff & His Orchestra & Chorus 14 (45) 6500
42. The Supremes Sing Holland-Dozier-Holland - The Supremes 6 (29) 6403
43. Why Is There Air? - Bill Cosby 22 (52) 6391
44. Man Of La Mancha - Original Cast 31 (52) 6313
45. Bill Cosby Is A Very Funny Fellow, Right! - Bill Cosby 30 (52) 6230
46. Winchester Cathedral - The New Vaudeville Band 5 (27) 6028
47. Vanilla Fudge - Vanilla Fudge 6 (16) 6027
48. Here Where There Is Love - Dionne Warwick 18 (52) 6006
49. Are You Experienced? - The Jimi Hendrix Experience 7 (19) 5887
50. Parsley, Sage, Rosemary And Thyme - Simon & Garfunkel 7 (52) 5881

1968

Rank. Title - Act YrPeak (YrWks) YrScr
1. The Graduate (Soundtrack) - Simon & Garfunkel 1 (42) 23726
2. Are You Experienced? - The Jimi Hendrix Experience 5 (52) 19430
3. Disraeli Gears - Cream 4 (52) 19371
4. Bookends - Simon & Garfunkel 1 (36) 18375
5. Magical Mystery Tour (Soundtrack) - The Beatles 1 (52) 16195
6. Blooming Hits - Paul Mauriat And His Orchestra 1 (47) 15828
7. Aretha: Lady Soul - Aretha Franklin 2 (45) 15114
8. Time Peace/The Rascals' Greatest Hits - The Rascals 1 (25) 14779
9. Diana Ross And The Supremes Greatest Hits - Diana Ross & The Supremes 3 (52) 14442
10. Parsley, Sage, Rosemary And Thyme - Simon & Garfunkel 5 (52) 13820
11. Beat Of The Brass - Herb Alpert & The Tijuana Brass 1 (34) 13767
12. Wheels Of Fire - Cream 1 (25) 13549
13. Cheap Thrills - Big Brother And The Holding Company 1 (18) 12633
14. Look Around - Sergio Mendes & Brasil '66 5 (43) 12199
15. Feliciano! - Jose Feliciano 2 (24) 12066
16. Sgt. Pepper's Lonely Hearts Club Band - The Beatles 5 (52) 10637
17. John Wesley Harding - Bob Dylan 2 (49) 10510
18. The Good, The Bad And The Ugly - Soundtrack 4 (47) 9944
19. Doctor Zhivago - Soundtrack 6 (52) 9929
20. Waiting For The Sun - The Doors 1 (21) 9733

Rank. Title - Act YrPeak (YrWks) YrScr
21. By The Time I Get To Phoenix - Glen Campbell 15 (52) 9386
22. Gentle On My Mind - Glen Campbell 5 (40) 9218
23. The Doors - The Doors 11 (52) 9133
24. Axis: Bold As Love - The Jimi Hendrix Experience 3 (47) 8913
25. Honey - Bobby Goldsboro 5 (37) 8758
26. Herb Alpert's Ninth - Herb Alpert & The Tijuana Brass 4 (47) 8739
27. The Time Has Come - The Chambers Brothers 4 (46) 8630
28. The Dock Of The Bay - Otis Redding 4 (41) 8093
29. Vanilla Fudge - Vanilla Fudge 20 (52) 7981
30. Steppenwolf - Steppenwolf 6 (43) 7963
31. The Sound Of Music - Soundtrack 7 (52) 7913
32. The Birds, The Bees & The Monkees - The Monkees 3 (34) 7855
33. Dionne Warwick's Golden Hits, Part One - Dionne Warwick 11 (52) 7828
34. To Russell, My Brother, Whom I Slept With - Bill Cosby 7 (39) 7755
35. Their Satanic Majesties Request - The Rolling Stones 2 (28) 7746
36. Camelot - Soundtrack 11 (52) 7654
37. History Of Otis Redding - Otis Redding 9 (45) 7612
38. Farewell To The First Golden Era - The Mamas & The Papas 8 (52) 7577
39. Valley Of The Dolls - Dionne Warwick 6 (43) 7377
40. Aretha Now - Aretha Franklin 3 (25) 7307
41. In-A-Gadda-Da-Vida - Iron Butterfly 5 (24) 7301
42. Music From "A Fistful Of Dollars" & "For A Few Dollars More" & "The Good, The Bad And The Ugly" - Hugo Montenegro, His Orchestra And Chorus 9 (39) 7225
43. Realization - Johnny Rivers 5 (27) 7174
44. Pisces, Aquarius, Capricorn, And Jones Ltd. - The Monkees 3 (41) 7094
45. The Temptations Greatest Hits - The Temptations 20 (52) 7073
46. The Four Tops Greatest Hits - Four Tops 21 (52) 6854
47. The Lettermen!!!...And "Live!" - The Lettermen 10 (42) 6704
48. Sounds Of Silence - Simon & Garfunkel 21 (44) 6688
49. Wildflowers - Judy Collins 5 (52) 6611
50. A Day In The Life - Wes Montgomery 13 (52) 6584

1969

Rank. Title - Act YrPeak (YrWks) YrScr
1. Blood, Sweat & Tears - Blood, Sweat & Tears 1 (48) 30061
2. Hair - Original Cast Recording 1 (52) 27425
3. In-A-Gadda-Da-Vida - Iron Butterfly 4 (52) 22365
4. The Beatles [White Album] - The Beatles 1 (52) 15889
5. Wichita Lineman - Glen Campbell 1 (39) 15116
6. Johnny Cash At San Quentin - Johnny Cash 1 (26) 14856
7. Romeo & Juliet - Soundtrack 2 (47) 14319
8. Bayou Country - Creedence Clearwater Revival 7 (47) 14034
9. Led Zeppelin - Led Zeppelin 10 (46) 13700
10. Donovan's Greatest Hits - Donovan 4 (45) 13012
11. Nashville Skyline - Bob Dylan 3 (35) 12795
12. Green River - Creedence Clearwater Revival 1 (16) 10942
13. Greatest Hits - The Association 4 (52) 10627
14. Blind Faith - Blind Faith 1 (20) 10346
15. This Is Tom Jones - Tom Jones 4 (29) 10328
16. Help Yourself - Tom Jones 5 (46) 10225
17. Crosby, Stills & Nash - Crosby, Stills & Nash 6 (27) 10170
18. The Age Of Aquarius - The 5th Dimension 2 (31) 9970
19. TCB (Soundtrack) - Diana Ross & The Supremes And The Temptations 1 (33) 9969
20. Cloud Nine - The Temptations 4 (40) 9441
21. Abbey Road - The Beatles 1 (11) 9344
22. Galveston - Glen Campbell 2 (37) 9267
23. Best Of Cream - Cream 3 (24) 8762
24. Funny Girl (Soundtrack) - Barbra Streisand 12 (52) 8629
25. Three Dog Night - Three Dog Night 11 (49) 8527
26. Ball - Iron Butterfly 3 (44) 8411
27. Tom Jones Live! - Tom Jones 13 (42) 7407
28. Hot Buttered Soul - Isaac Hayes 8 (25) 7263
29. Goodbye - Cream 2 (26) 7245
30. A Warm Shade Of Ivory - Henry Mancini And His Orchestra 5 (35) 7113
31. Johnny Cash At Folsom Prison - Johnny Cash 30 (52) 7107
32. Tommy - The Who 7 (30) 7003
33. Through The Past, Darkly (Big Hits Vol. 2) - The Rolling Stones 2 (16) 6990
34. Diana Ross & The Supremes Join The Temptations - Diana Ross & The Supremes And The Temptations 2 (27) 6468
35. Chicago Transit Authority - Chicago 17 (33) 6358
36. The Tom Jones Fever Zone - Tom Jones 14 (47) 6351
37. Smash Hits - The Jimi Hendrix Experience 6 (22) 6333
38. The Second - Steppenwolf 3 (39) 6295
39. Switched-On Bach - Walter Carlos 10 (48) 6282
40. Cheap Thrills - Big Brother And The Holding Company 6 (48) 6248
41. The Soft Parade - The Doors 6 (21) 6206
42. Yellow Submarine (Soundtrack) - The Beatles 2 (24) 6188
43. Fool On The Hill - Sergio Mendes & Brasil '66 3 (26) 5908
44. Suitable For Framing - Three Dog Night 16 (25) 5898
45. Best Of Bee Gees - Bee Gees 9 (23) 5837
46. Stand! - Sly & The Family Stone 13 (36) 5831
47. Santana - Santana 4 (16) 5819
48. Gentle On My Mind - Glen Campbell 12 (32) 5647
49. Crimson & Clover - Tommy James And The Shondells 8 (35) 5565
50. Oliver! - Soundtrack 20 (52) 5187

1970

Rank. Title - Act YrPeak (YrWks) YrScr
1. Chicago - Chicago 4 (46) 20112
2. Bridge Over Troubled Water - Simon & Garfunkel 1 (46) 18609
3. Woodstock - Soundtrack 1 (30) 18326
4. Deja Vu - Crosby, Stills, Nash & Young 1 (39) 17303
5. Led Zeppelin II - Led Zeppelin 1 (52) 17179
6. Cosmo's Factory - Creedence Clearwater Revival 1 (23) 16218
7. Abbey Road - The Beatles 1 (52) 14924
8. Santana - Santana 4 (52) 13241
9. McCartney - Paul McCartney 1 (34) 12919
10. Sweet Baby James - James Taylor 3 (42) 11937
11. Willy And The Poorboys - Creedence Clearwater Revival 3 (52) 11715
12. Let It Be (Soundtrack) - The Beatles 1 (31) 11611
13. Easy Rider - Soundtrack 6 (52) 10704
14. Abraxas - Santana 1 (12) 10218
15. Live At Leeds - The Who 4 (31) 9958
16. Blood, Sweat & Tears 3 - Blood, Sweat & Tears 1 (24) 9826
17. The Isaac Hayes Movement - Isaac Hayes 8 (37) 9587
18. Tom Jones Live In Las Vegas - Tom Jones 3 (44) 9580
19. Was Captured Live At The Forum - Three Dog Night 6 (52) 9446
20. Get Ready - Rare Earth 12 (51) 9428
21. Hey Jude - The Beatles 2 (33) 9306
22. Closer To Home - Grand Funk Railroad 6 (25) 9202
23. Band Of Gypsys - Jimi Hendrix 5 (35) 8596
24. ABC - The Jackson 5 4 (30) 8403
25. American Woman - The Guess Who 9 (46) 8346
26. Diana Ross Presents The Jackson 5 - The Jackson 5 5 (32) 8345
27. Joe Cocker! - Joe Cocker 11 (47) 8291
28. Tommy - The Who 4 (37) 8172
29. It Ain't Easy - Three Dog Night 8 (35) 8064
30. Engelbert Humperdinck - Engelbert Humperdinck 5 (41) 8017
31. Butch Cassidy And The Sundance Kid - Soundtrack 16 (52) 7984
32. Led Zeppelin III - Led Zeppelin 1 (10) 7897
33. Raindrops Keep Fallin' On My Head - B.J. Thomas 12 (41) 7889
34. Let It Bleed - The Rolling Stones 3 (35) 7604
35. Mad Dogs & Englishmen (Soundtrack) - Joe Cocker 2 (17) 7332
36. Blood, Sweat & Tears - Blood, Sweat & Tears 7 (52) 7296
37. The 5th Dimension/Greatest Hits - The 5th Dimension 5 (33) 7118
38. Grand Funk - Grand Funk Railroad 11 (48) 7092

Rank. Title - Act YrPeak (YrWks) YrScr
39. **Steppenwolf 'Live'** - Steppenwolf 7 (37) 6910
40. **Third Album** - The Jackson 5 4 (14) 6702
41. **In-A-Gadda-Da-Vida** - Iron Butterfly 11 (52) 6650
42. **Close To You** - Carpenters 2 (15) 6610
43. **John Barleycorn Must Die** - Traffic 5 (25) 6433
44. **Crosby, Stills & Nash** - Crosby, Stills & Nash 8 (52) 6370
45. **Mountain Climbing!** - Mountain 17 (39) 6172
46. **Psychedelic Shack** - The Temptations 9 (30) 6131
47. **Hello, I'm Johnny Cash** - Johnny Cash 6 (30) 6078
48. **Morrison Hotel** - The Doors 4 (27) 6048
49. **The Band** - The Band 9 (38) 5807
50. **Ecology** - Rare Earth 15 (25) 5651

1971

Rank. Title - Act YrPeak (YrWks) YrScr
1. **Jesus Christ Superstar** – Various Artists 1 (52) 27930
2. **Tapestry** - Carole King 1 (38) 25720
3. **Pearl** - Janis Joplin 1 (42) 16006
4. **Abraxas** - Santana 2 (52) 15466
5. **Every Picture Tells A Story** - Rod Stewart 1 (28) 15024
6. **Mud Slide Slim And The Blue Horizon** - James Taylor 2 (34) 14511
7. **Ram** - Paul & Linda McCartney 2 (30) 14449
8. **Sticky Fingers** - The Rolling Stones 1 (33) 14178
9. **Carpenters** - Carpenters 2 (30) 13923
10. **Close To You** - Carpenters 8 (52) 12452
11. **All Things Must Pass** - George Harrison 1 (36) 12322
12. **Chicago III** - Chicago 2 (48) 11975
13. **Tea For The Tillerman** - Cat Stevens 8 (47) 11967
14. **4 Way Street** - Crosby, Stills, Nash & Young 1 (36) 11815
15. **Love Story** - Soundtrack 2 (39) 11576
16. **Golden Bisquits** - Three Dog Night 5 (44) 11386
17. **Aqualung** - Jethro Tull 7 (33) 11144
18. **The Partridge Family Album** - The Partridge Family 4 (52) 10789
19. **Up To Date** - The Partridge Family 3 (39) 10744
20. **Shaft (Soundtrack)** - Isaac Hayes 1 (19) 10413
21. **Greatest Hits** - Sly & The Family Stone 4 (52) 10088
22. **Paranoid** - Black Sabbath 12 (45) 9527
23. **What's Going On** - Marvin Gaye 6 (29) 9200
24. **Sweet Baby James** - James Taylor 12 (52) 8932
25. **Tumbleweed Connection** - Elton John 5 (37) 8878
26. **Every Good Boy Deserves Favour** - The Moody Blues 2 (19) 8701
27. **Pendulum** - Creedence Clearwater Revival 5 (41) 8492
28. **Santana III** - Santana 1 (11) 8346

Rank. Title - Act YrPeak (YrWks) YrScr
29. **Live Album** - Grand Funk Railroad 5 (52) 7893
30. **Survival** - Grand Funk Railroad 6 (35) 7835
31. **Naturally** - Three Dog Night 14 (52) 7734
32. **The Cry Of Love** - Jimi Hendrix 3 (39) 7699
33. **Elton John** - Elton John 4 (38) 7671
34. **Love Story** - Andy Williams 3 (33) 7552
35. **Imagine** - John Lennon/Plastic Ono Band 1 (15) 7535
36. **Who's Next** - The Who 4 (20) 7330
37. **Aretha Live At Fillmore West** - Aretha Franklin 7 (30) 7231
38. **The Best Of The Guess Who** - The Guess Who 12 (37) 7224
39. **L.A. Woman** - The Doors 9 (34) 7172
40. **Poems, Prayers & Promises** - John Denver 15 (37) 6544
41. **To Be Continued** - Isaac Hayes 11 (52) 6445
42. **Chicago Transit Authority** - Chicago 25 (52) 6390
43. **Teaser And The Firecat** - Cat Stevens 2 (12) 6188
44. **Chapter Two** - Roberta Flack 34 (52) 6084
45. **Emerson, Lake & Palmer** - Emerson, Lake & Palmer 18 (42) 6058
46. **Maybe Tomorrow** - The Jackson 5 11 (35) 5894
47. **Stephen Stills** - Stephen Stills 3 (34) 5731
48. **Chicago** - Chicago 12 (52) 5698
49. **The Partridge Family Sound Magazine** - The Partridge Family 9 (18) 5575
50. **Osmonds** - The Osmonds 14 (43) 5413

1972

Rank. Title - Act YrPeak (YrWks) YrScr
1. **Harvest** - Neil Young 1 (41) 15203
2. **American Pie** - Don McLean 1 (41) 14838
3. **First Take** - Roberta Flack 1 (42) 14412
4. **Honky Château** - Elton John 1 (29) 14086
5. **Chicago V** - Chicago 1 (23) 13385
6. **America** - America 1 (40) 13060
7. **Tapestry** - Carole King 6 (53) 12693
8. **Music** - Carole King 1 (41) 12361
9. **The Concert For Bangla Desh** - George Harrison and Friends 2 (41) 11847
10. **Thick As A Brick** - Jethro Tull 1 (33) 11387
11. **Hot Rocks 1964-1971** - The Rolling Stones 4 (52) 11244
12. **Fragile** - Yes 4 (44) 10893
13. **Exile On Main St.** - The Rolling Stones 1 (30) 10817
14. **Eat A Peach** - The Allman Brothers Band 4 (42) 10562
15. **Never A Dull Moment** - Rod Stewart 2 (21) 10156
16. **Big Bambu** - Cheech & Chong 2 (27) 9756
17. **Led Zeppelin IV** - Led Zeppelin 2 (52) 9744
18. **Baby I'm-A Want You** - Bread 3 (48) 9731
19. **Superfly (Soundtrack)** - Curtis Mayfield 1 (19) 9571
20. **Nilsson Schmilsson** - Nilsson 3 (42) 9440
21. **Teaser And The Firecat** - Cat Stevens 3 (52) 9426
22. **Let's Stay Together** - Al Green 8 (47) 9341
23. **Carney** - Leon Russell 2 (25) 9147
24. **Roberta Flack & Donny Hathaway** - Roberta Flack & Donny Hathaway 3 (34) 8835

Rank. Title - Act YrPeak (YrWks) YrScr
25. **Moods** - Neil Diamond 5 (25) 8433
26. **Still Bill** - Bill Withers 4 (33) 8254
27. **Paul Simon** - Paul Simon 4 (36) 8228
28. **All Directions** - The Temptations 2 (20) 7899
29. **History Of Eric Clapton** - Eric Clapton 6 (38) 7776
30. **School's Out** - Alice Cooper 2 (27) 7440
31. **Simon And Garfunkel's Greatest Hits** - Simon & Garfunkel 5 (27) 7377
32. **Madman Across The Water** - Elton John 8 (46) 7264
33. **Trilogy** - Emerson, Lake & Palmer 5 (23) 7161
34. **Catch Bull At Four** - Cat Stevens 1 (12) 7152
35. **The London Chuck Berry Sessions** - Chuck Berry 8 (30) 7137
36. **A Song For You** - Carpenters 4 (26) 6981
37. **Joplin In Concert** - Janis Joplin 4 (27) 6975
38. **Killer** - Alice Cooper 21 (50) 6930
39. **A Lonely Man** - The Chi-Lites 5 (36) 6843
40. **Manassas** - Stephen Stills/Manassas 4 (30) 6682
41. **Procol Harum Live In Concert with the Edmonton Symphony Orchestra** - Procol Harum 5 (28) 6635
42. **All Day Music** - War 16 (43) 6551
43. **Days Of Future Passed** - The Moody Blues With The London Festival Orchestra 3 (17) 6539
44. **Seven Separate Fools** - Three Dog Night 6 (23) 6485
45. **Lookin' Through The Windows** - The Jackson 5 7 (31) 6471
46. **Donny Hathaway Live** - Donny Hathaway 18 (38) 6337
47. **Carlos Santana & Buddy Miles! Live!** - Carlos Santana & Buddy Miles 8 (26) 6121
48. **Elvis As Recorded At Madison Square Garden** - Elvis Presley 11 (26) 6004
49. **Chicago At Carnegie Hall** - Chicago 3 (26) 5946
50. **Graham Nash/David Crosby** - Graham Nash/David Crosby 4 (26) 5941

1973

Rank. Title - Act YrPeak (YrWks) YrScr
1. **The Dark Side Of The Moon** - Pink Floyd 1 (42) 19148
2. **Houses Of The Holy** - Led Zeppelin 1 (38) 15044
3. **The World Is A Ghetto** - War 1 (52) 14221
4. **No Secrets** - Carly Simon 1 (52) 13972
5. **Don't Shoot Me I'm Only The Piano Player** - Elton John 1 (47) 13469
6. **Talking Book** - Stevie Wonder 3 (52) 12622
7. **Brothers And Sisters** - The Allman Brothers Band 1 (19) 12146
8. **Lady Sings The Blues (Soundtrack)** - Diana Ross 1 (48) 11982
9. **Chicago VI** - Chicago 1 (25) 11475
10. **They Only Come Out At Night** - The Edgar Winter Group 3 (52) 11252
11. **Diamond Girl** - Seals & Crofts 4 (37) 11237
12. **The Captain And Me** - The Doobie Brothers 7 (40) 10711
13. **The Beatles 1967-1970** - The Beatles 1 (38) 10616
14. **The Best Of Bread** - Bread 2 (40) 10029

Rank. Title - Act YrPeak (YrWks) YrScr
15. **Billion Dollar Babies** - Alice Cooper 1 (42) 9845
16. **Goodbye Yellow Brick Road** - Elton John 1 (11) 9582
17. **Made In Japan** - Deep Purple 6 (37) 9537
18. **There Goes Rhymin' Simon** - Paul Simon 2 (32) 9415
19. **Red Rose Speedway** - Paul McCartney And Wings 1 (31) 9234
20. **The Divine Miss M** - Bette Midler 9 (52) 8897
21. **Living In The Material World** - George Harrison 1 (26) 8809
22. **Hot August Night** - Neil Diamond 5 (52) 8709
23. **Goats Head Soup** - The Rolling Stones 1 (14) 8687
24. **The Beatles 1962-1966** - The Beatles 3 (38) 8616
25. **Aloha From Hawaii Via Satellite** - Elvis Presley 1 (36) 8531
26. **Now & Then** - Carpenters 2 (31) 8373
27. **Machine Head** - Deep Purple 7 (52) 8123
28. **Dueling Banjos** - Eric Weissberg & Steve Mandell 1 (25) 8120
29. **Los Cochinos** - Cheech & Chong 2 (17) 8078
30. **Seventh Sojourn** - The Moody Blues 1 (37) 8008
31. **Summer Breeze** - Seals & Crofts 7 (52) 7987
32. **Rocky Mountain High** - John Denver 4 (37) 7928
33. **Innervisions** - Stevie Wonder 4 (20) 7820
34. **I Am Woman** - Helen Reddy 14 (52) 7738
35. **We're An American Band** - Grand Funk 2 (20) 7699
36. **Life And Times** - Jim Croce 7 (46) 7488
37. **The Smoker You Drink, The Player You Get** - Joe Walsh 6 (28) 7205
38. **Moving Waves** - Focus 8 (38) 7154
39. **Let's Get It On** - Marvin Gaye 2 (16) 6896
40. **Rhymes & Reasons** - Carole King 2 (22) 6669
41. **Call Me** - Al Green 10 (33) 6659
42. **I'm Still In Love With You** - Al Green 4 (52) 6529
43. **A Passion Play** - Jethro Tull 1 (24) 6395
44. **Can't Buy A Thrill** - Steely Dan 17 (52) 6387
45. **Foreigner** - Cat Stevens 3 (23) 6338
46. **Fantasy** - Carole King 6 (28) 6115
47. **Killing Me Softly** - Roberta Flack 3 (18) 6029
48. **Who Do We Think We Are!** - Deep Purple 15 (49) 5987
49. **Prelude** - Deodato 3 (26) 5865
50. **Touch Me In The Morning** - Diana Ross 5 (25) 5864

1974

Rank. Title - Act YrPeak (YrWks) YrScr
1. **John Denver's Greatest Hits** - John Denver 1 (52) 22515
2. **Band On The Run** - Paul McCartney And Wings 1 (52) 21027
3. **Goodbye Yellow Brick Road** - Elton John 2 (52) 15431
4. **The Sting (Soundtrack)** - Marvin Hamlisch 1 (41) 14492
5. **Court And Spark** - Joni Mitchell 2 (47) 14259
6. **Back Home Again** - John Denver 1 (27) 13918
7. **Chicago VII** - Chicago 1 (40) 13213
8. **Bachman-Turner Overdrive II** - Bachman-Turner Overdrive 4 (50) 12978
9. **You Don't Mess Around With Jim** - Jim Croce 1 (48) 12647
10. **Caribou** - Elton John 1 (26) 11754
11. **Buddha And The Chocolate Box** - Cat Stevens 2 (36) 11579
12. **Innervisions** - Stevie Wonder 11 (52) 10624
13. **Sundown** - Gordon Lightfoot 1 (42) 10444
14. **Maria Muldaur** - Maria Muldaur 3 (41) 9846
15. **Tubular Bells** - Mike Oldfield 3 (37) 9719
16. **I Got A Name** - Jim Croce 2 (50) 9489
17. **Behind Closed Doors** - Charlie Rich 8 (52) 9322
18. **American Graffiti** - Soundtrack 10 (42) 9169
19. **Not Fragile** - Bachman-Turner Overdrive 1 (18) 9000
20. **461 Ocean Boulevard** – Eric Clapton 1 (24) 8527
21. **If You Love Me Let Me Know** - Olivia Newton-John 1 (30) 8090
22. **Shinin' On** - Grand Funk 5 (29) 7898
23. **Bad Company** - Bad Company 1 (23) 7654
24. **The Singles 1969-1973** - Carpenters 1 (39) 7617
25. **Body Heat** - Quincy Jones 6 (32) 7528
26. **Planet Waves** - Bob Dylan with The Band 1 (21) 7503
27. **Fullfillingness First Finale** - Stevie Wonder 1 (21) 7385
28. **Head Hunters** - Herbie Hancock 13 (47) 7271
29. **Hotcakes** - Carly Simon 3 (35) 7184
30. **The Way We Were** - Barbra Streisand 1 (31) 7131
31. **What Were Once Vices Are Now Habits** - The Doobie Brothers 8 (33) 7063
32. **Skin Tight** - Ohio Players 11 (36) 7041
33. **Bridge Of Sighs** - Robin Trower 7 (31) 7006
34. **Imagination** - Gladys Knight & The Pips 15 (43) 6906
35. **On Stage** - Loggins & Messina 5 (31) 6883
36. **Holiday** - America 3 (25) 6819
37. **Tres Hombres** - ZZ Top 8 (49) 6727
38. **Brain Salad Surgery** - Emerson, Lake & Palmer 11 (44) 6709
39. **Pretzel Logic** - Steely Dan 8 (36) 6450
40. **Ship Ahoy** - The O'Jays 11 (40) 6447
41. **Journey To The Centre Of The Earth** - Rick Wakeman With The London Symphony Orchestra & The English Chamber Choir 3 (27) 6404
42. **Endless Summer** - The Beach Boys 1 (24) 6347
43. **Under The Influence Of...** - Love Unlimited 3 (27) 6252
44. **Love Is The Message** - MFSB 4 (35) 6208
45. **Can't Get Enough** - Barry White 1 (17) 6205
46. **On The Border** - Eagles 17 (37) 6136
47. **Open Our Eyes** - Earth, Wind & Fire 15 (37) 5992
48. **The Dark Side Of The Moon** - Pink Floyd 22 (42) 5920
49. **The Joker** - The Steve Miller Band 4 (27) 5882
50. **Apostrophe (')** - Frank Zappa 10 (37) 5769

1975

Rank. Title - Act YrPeak (YrWks) YrScr
1. **That's The Way Of The World (Soundtrack)** - Earth, Wind & Fire 1 (42) 16383
2. **Captain Fantastic And The Brown Dirt Cowboy** - Elton John 1 (30) 15342
3. **Red Octopus** - Jefferson Starship 1 (24) 14960
4. **One Of These Nights** - Eagles 1 (27) 14747
5. **Physical Graffiti** - Led Zeppelin 1 (28) 11038
6. **Between The Lines** - Janis Ian 1 (41) 10758
7. **The Heat Is On** - The Isley Brothers 1 (29) 10483
8. **Have You Never Been Mellow** - Olivia Newton-John 1 (31) 10342
9. **Heart Like A Wheel** - Linda Ronstadt 1 (47) 9779
10. **Elton John's Greatest Hits** - Elton John 1 (52) 9769
11. **Tommy** - Soundtrack 2 (35) 9526
12. **Windsong** - John Denver 1 (13) 9169
13. **Chicago VIII** - Chicago 1 (29) 9061
14. **Venus And Mars** - Wings 1 (29) 9007
15. **An Evening With John Denver** - John Denver 2 (43) 8994
16. **Blood On The Tracks** - Bob Dylan 1 (24) 8547
17. **AWB** - Average White Band 1 (28) 8148
18. **Love Will Keep Us Together** - Captain & Tennille 2 (29) 7834
19. **Wish You Were Here** - Pink Floyd 1 (14) 7798
20. **Fire** - Ohio Players 1 (23) 7570
21. **Welcome To My Nightmare** - Alice Cooper 5 (37) 7467
22. **Fandango!** - ZZ Top 10 (33) 7448
23. **Honey** - Ohio Players 2 (19) 7027
24. **Hearts** - America 4 (39) 6736
25. **War Child** - Jethro Tull 2 (21) 6524
26. **Toys In The Attic** - Aerosmith 11 (36) 6519
27. **Miles Of Aisles** - Joni Mitchell 2 (19) 6496
28. **Phoebe Snow** - Phoebe Snow 4 (36) 6378
29. **Young Americans** - David Bowie 9 (38) 6343
30. **Born To Run** - Bruce Springsteen 3 (16) 6302
31. **Diamonds & Rust** - Joan Baez 11 (33) 6155
32. **Why Can't We Be Friends?** - War 8 (26) 6019
33. **Back Home Again** - John Denver 4 (52) 5996
34. **Gorilla** - James Taylor 6 (27) 5972
35. **A Song For You** - The Temptations 13 (36) 5901
36. **Perfect Angel** - Minnie Riperton 4 (27) 5844
37. **Cut The Cake** - Average White Band 4 (24) 5832
38. **Cat Stevens Greatest Hits** - Cat Stevens 6 (25) 5773
39. **KC And The Sunshine Band** - KC And The Sunshine Band 4 (22) 5772
40. **Do It ('Til You're Satisfied)** - B.T. Express 5 (25) 5732
41. **Pick Of The Litter** - Spinners 8 (21) 5660
42. **Rock Of The Westies** - Elton John 1 (8) 5609
43. **Mister Magic** - Grover Washington Jr. 10 (34) 5569
44. **What Were Once Vices Are Now Habits** - The Doobie Brothers 4 (29) 5561
45. **Straight Shooter** - Bad Company 3 (33) 5512
46. **Melissa** - Melissa Manchester 12 (41) 5244

Rank. Title - Act YrPeak (YrWks) YrScr
47. **Stampede** - The Doobie Brothers 4 (25) 5210
48. **Fleetwood Mac** - Fleetwood Mac 9 (22) 5003
49. **Blue Sky-Night Thunder** - Michael Murphey 18 (38) 4979
50. **Judith** - Judy Collins 17 (34) 4955

1976

Rank. Title - Act YrPeak (YrWks) YrScr
1. **Frampton Comes Alive!** - Peter Frampton 1 (48) 31780
2. **Fleetwood Mac** - Fleetwood Mac 1 (52) 22273
3. **Wings At The Speed Of Sound** - Wings 1 (38) 17943
4. **Their Greatest Hits 1971-1975** - Eagles 1 (43) 16286
5. **Silk Degrees** - Boz Scaggs 2 (41) 13769
6. **Breezin'** - George Benson 1 (37) 13103
7. **Fly Like An Eagle** - The Steve Miller Band 3 (31) 11877
8. **Desire** - Bob Dylan 1 (35) 11205
9. **Songs In The Key Of Life** - Stevie Wonder 1 (11) 11000
10. **The Dream Weaver** - Gary Wright 7 (51) 10885
11. **Chicago X** - Chicago 3 (26) 10545
12. **Gratitude** - Earth, Wind & Fire 1 (50) 10517
13. **A Night At The Opera** - Queen 4 (46) 10284
14. **Still Crazy After All These Years** - Paul Simon 2 (30) 10079
15. **Chicago IX: Chicago's Greatest Hits** - Chicago 1 (47) 9434
16. **History/America's Greatest Hits** - America 3 (52) 9326
17. **Spitfire** - Jefferson Starship 3 (25) 9206
18. **Rocks** - Aerosmith 3 (31) 9132
19. **Black And Blue** - The Rolling Stones 1 (24) 8592
20. **Look Out For #1** - The Brothers Johnson 9 (38) 8072
21. **A Night On The Town** - Rod Stewart 2 (24) 7987
22. **Presence** - Led Zeppelin 1 (25) 7880
23. **Dreamboat Annie** - Heart 7 (38) 7735
24. **Rufus Featuring Chaka Khan** - Rufus And Chaka Khan 7 (28) 7483
25. **Beautiful Noise** - Neil Diamond 4 (26) 7192
26. **Diana Ross (II)** - Diana Ross 5 (32) 7007
27. **Hasten Down The Wind** - Linda Ronstadt 3 (18) 6729
28. **Station To Station** - David Bowie 3 (32) 6525
29. **Rock 'N' Roll Music** - The Beatles 2 (27) 6296
30. **Thoroughbred** - Carole King 3 (21) 6220
31. **I Want You** - Marvin Gaye 4 (26) 6220
32. **Face The Music** - Electric Light Orchestra 8 (38) 6217
33. **Hot On The Tracks** - Commodores 12 (25) 6209
34. **Summertime Dream** - Gordon Lightfoot 12 (27) 6131
35. **Song Of Joy** - Captain & Tennille 9 (41) 6000
36. **Spirit** - Earth, Wind & Fire 2 (11) 5992
37. **Tryin' To Get The Feelin'** - Barry Manilow 5 (42) 5917
38. **Wild Cherry** - Wild Cherry 5 (23) 5873
39. **Boston** - Boston 3 (14) 5834

Rank. Title - Act YrPeak (YrWks) YrScr
40. **Mothership Connection** - Parliament 13 (37) 5771
41. **Run With The Pack** - Bad Company 5 (28) 5666
42. **Brass Construction** - Brass Construction 10 (35) 5559
43. **Helen Reddy's Greatest Hits** - Helen Reddy 5 (46) 5481
44. **Takin' It To The Streets** - The Doobie Brothers 8 (39) 5400
45. **All Things In Time** - Lou Rawls 7 (30) 5250
46. **Family Reunion** - The O'Jays 7 (29) 5097
47. **Eargasm** - Johnnie Taylor 5 (28) 5063
48. **Harvest For The World** - The Isley Brothers 9 (26) 5049
49. **The Salsoul Orchestra** - The Salsoul Orchestra 14 (40) 5019
50. **Daryl Hall & John Oates** - Daryl Hall & John Oates 17 (51) 5014

1977

Rank. Title - Act YrPeak (YrWks) YrScr
1. **Rumours** - Fleetwood Mac 1 (45) 40126
2. **Hotel California** - Eagles 1 (53) 23458
3. **Songs In The Key Of Life** - Stevie Wonder 1 (53) 18797
4. **A Star Is Born (Soundtrack)** - Barbra Streisand & Kris Kristofferson 1 (48) 16804
5. **Boston** - Boston 3 (53) 16355
6. **Foreigner** - Foreigner 4 (41) 13722
7. **Commodores** - Commodores 3 (40) 13071
8. **Simple Dreams** - Linda Ronstadt 1 (15) 11956
9. **A New World Record** - Electric Light Orchestra 5 (53) 11456
10. **Book Of Dreams** - The Steve Miller Band 2 (33) 10242
11. **Barry Manilow Live** - Barry Manilow 1 (32) 10075
12. **Star Wars** - Soundtrack 2 (29) 9867
13. **Fly Like An Eagle** - The Steve Miller Band 5 (53) 9542
14. **Wings Over America** - Paul McCartney And Wings 1 (53) 9400
15. **CSN** - Crosby, Stills & Nash 2 (26) 9172
16. **Night Moves** - Bob Seger & The Silver Bullet Band 8 (53) 8934
17. **Shaun Cassidy** - Shaun Cassidy 3 (28) 8668
18. **I'm In You** - Peter Frampton 2 (28) 8659
19. **JT** - James Taylor 4 (26) 8572
20. **Anytime...Anywhere** - Rita Coolidge 6 (40) 8424
21. **Greatest Hits** - Linda Ronstadt 6 (53) 8357
22. **Marvin Gaye Live At The London Palladium** - Marvin Gaye 3 (26) 8120
23. **Little Queen** - Heart 9 (32) 8017
24. **Leftoverture** - Kansas 5 (34) 7901
25. **Rocky** - Soundtrack 4 (34) 7739
26. **Here At Last...Bee Gees...Live** - Bee Gees 8 (31) 7603
27. **Silk Degrees** - Boz Scaggs 15 (53) 7516
28. **Part 3** - KC And The Sunshine Band 19 (53) 7352
29. **Moody Blue** - Elvis Presley 3 (24) 7196
30. **Changes In Latitudes, Changes In Attitudes** - Jimmy Buffett 12 (42) 7049
31. **Rejoice** - The Emotions 7 (28) 7049
32. **Year Of The Cat** - Al Stewart 5 (36) 6926

Rank. Title - Act YrPeak (YrWks) YrScr
33. **This One's For You** - Barry Manilow 6 (41) 6797
34. **Streisand Superman** - B arbra Streisand 3 (25) 6793
35. **Right On Time** - The Brothers Johnson 13 (31) 6765
36. **In Flight** - George Benson 9 (35) 6536
37. **Aja** - Steely Dan 3 (12) 6489
38. **Go For Your Guns** - The Isley Brothers 6 (34) 6312
39. **Frampton Comes Alive!** - Peter Frampton 7 (49) 6268
40. **Bigger Than Both Of Us** - Daryl Hall & John Oates 20 (39) 6265
41. **Rock And Roll Over** - KISS 11 (39) 6182
42. **I Robot** - The Alan Parsons Project 9 (25) 6073
43. **Even In The Quietest Moments...** - Supertramp 16 (35) 5959
44. **Anyway You Like It** - Thelma Houston 11 (36) 5890
45. **Animals** - Pink Floyd 3 (28) 5860
46. **Endless Flight** - Leo Sayer 10 (46) 5833
47. **Best Of The Doobies** - The Doobie Brothers 5 (51) 5782
48. **A Rock And Roll Alternative** - Atlanta Rhythm Section 11 (39) 5701
49. **A Place In The Sun** - Pablo Cruise 19 (44) 5620
50. **Their Greatest Hits 1971-1975** - Eagles 21 (53) 5570

1978

Rank. Title - Act YrPeak (YrWks) YrScr
1. **Saturday Night Fever (Soundtrack)** - Bee Gees 1 (52) 32198
2. **Grease** - Soundtrack 1 (33) 21489
3. **The Stranger** - Billy Joel 2 (52) 20798
4. **Some Girls** - The Rolling Stones 1 (28) 15243
5. **Slowhand** - Eric Clapton 2 (52) 14159
6. **Double Vision** - Foreigner 3 (26) 14060
7. **Running On Empty** - Jackson Browne 3 (52) 12865
8. **Feels So Good** - Chuck Mangione 2 (52) 12381
9. **Aja** - Steely Dan 5 (48) 12187
10. **Natural High** - Commodores 3 (32) 11570
11. **Stranger In Town** - Bob Seger & The Silver Bullet Band 4 (32) 10778
12. **Even Now** - Barry Manilow 3 (45) 10413
13. **Foot Loose & Fancy Free** - Rod Stewart 2 (41) 10301
14. **Rumours** - Fleetwood Mac 1 (52) 9833
15. **The Grand Illusion** - Styx 6 (52) 9766
16. **All 'N All** - Earth, Wind & Fire 3 (42) 9684
17. **Point Of Know Return** - Kansas 4 (39) 9680
18. **Earth** - Jefferson Starship 5 (34) 9385
19. **City To City** - Gerry Rafferty 1 (35) 9297
20. **London Town** - Wings 2 (28) 9103
21. **Weekend In L.A.** - George Benson 5 (38) 8589
22. **Don't Look Back** - Boston 1 (18) 8521
23. **Live And More** - Donna Summer 1 (16) 8444
24. **News Of The World** - Queen 3 (31) 8306
25. **Bat Out Of Hell** - Meat Loaf 14 (52) 8290
26. **52nd Street** - Billy Joel 1 (10) 7922

Rank. Title - Act YrPeak (YrWks) YrScr
27. **Out Of The Blue** - Electric Light Orchestra 4 (52) 7139
28. **Fantasy Love Affair** - Peter Brown 11 (44) 7118
29. **Darkness On The Edge Of Town** - Bruce Springsteen 5 (29) 7002
30. **Champagne Jam** - Atlanta Rhythm Section 7 (40) 6915
31. **Who Are You** - The Who 2 (17) 6747
32. **Living In The U.S.A.** - Linda Ronstadt 1 (13) 6561
33. **Shadow Dancing** - Andy Gibb 7 (29) 6547
34. **Nightwatch** - Kenny Loggins 7 (24) 6353
35. **Worlds Away** - Pablo Cruise 6 (29) 6168
36. **French Kiss** - Bob Welch 12 (33) 6017
37. **"But Seriously Folks..."** - Joe Walsh 8 (27) 5874
38. **Blue Lights In The Basement** - Roberta Flack 8 (32) 5866
39. **A Taste Of Honey** - A Taste Of Honey 6 (27) 5795
40. **Sgt. Pepper's Lonely Hearts Club Band** - Soundtrack 5 (21) 5763
41. **The Album** - ABBA 14 (41) 5726
42. **Boys In The Trees** - Carly Simon 10 (29) 5700
43. **Infinity** - Journey 21 (47) 5483
44. **Thankful** - Natalie Cole 16 (35) 5432
45. **FM** - Soundtrack 5 (24) 5416
46. **Showdown** - The Isley Brothers 4 (21) 5345
47. **Funkentelechy Vs. The Placebo Syndrome** - Parliament 13 (32) 5253
48. **Thank God It's Friday** - Soundtrack 10 (27) 5228
49. **Macho Man** - Village People 24 (41) 5202
50. **So Full Of Love** - The O'Jays 6 (28) 5179

1979

Rank. Title - Act YrPeak (YrWks) YrScr
1. **Breakfast In America** - Supertramp 1 (40) 22836
2. **Minute By Minute** - The Doobie Brothers 1 (52) 17264
3. **Spirits Having Flown** - Bee Gees 1 (46) 15761
4. **Bad Girls** - Donna Summer 1 (34) 15551
5. **Get The Knack** - The Knack 1 (27) 13697
6. **Blondes Have More Fun** - Rod Stewart 1 (35) 13056
7. **In Through The Out Door** - Led Zeppelin 1 (17) 12932
8. **Cheap Trick At Budokan** - Cheap Trick 4 (45) 12620
9. **2-Hot!** - Peaches & Herb 2 (40) 11800
10. **52nd Street** - Billy Joel 1 (43) 11687
11. **Dire Straits** - Dire Straits 2 (41) 10645
12. **Desolation Angels** - Bad Company 3 (37) 10624
13. **The Long Run** - Eagles 1 (11) 10514
14. **I Am** - Earth, Wind & Fire 3 (29) 9816
15. **Rickie Lee Jones** - Rickie Lee Jones 3 (36) 9803
16. **Candy-O** - The Cars 3 (27) 9783
17. **Briefcase Full Of Blues** - Blues Brothers 1 (27) 9279
18. **The Cars** - The Cars 18 (52) 9078
19. **Midnight Magic** - Commodores 3 (20) 8968
20. **The Gambler** - Kenny Rogers 12 (52) 8586
21. **Cruisin'** - Village People 3 (34) 8479
22. **Van Halen II** - Van Halen 6 (38) 8094
23. **We Are Family** - Sister Sledge 3 (33) 8031
24. **Discovery** - Electric Light Orchestra 5 (28) 7986
25. **Parallel Lines** - Blondie 6 (52) 7887
26. **C'est Chic** - Chic 4 (43) 7624
27. **Love Tracks** - Gloria Gaynor 4 (34) 7445
28. **Barbra Streisand's Greatest Hits, Volume 2** - Barbra Streisand 1 (41) 7191
29. **Off The Wall** - Michael Jackson 5 (18) 7034
30. **Million Mile Reflections** - The Charlie Daniels Band 5 (34) 6940
31. **Cornerstone** - Styx 2 (12) 6908
32. **Live And More** - Donna Summer 12 (52) 6904
33. **Pieces Of Eight** - Styx 19 (52) 6733
34. **Evolution** - Journey 20 (38) 6547
35. **The Best Of Earth, Wind & Fire, Vol. I** - Earth, Wind & Fire 6 (52) 6360
36. **Toto** - Toto 9 (37) 6325
37. **Totally Hot** - Olivia Newton-John 7 (35) 6266
38. **Rust Never Sleeps** - Neil Young & Crazy Horse 8 (24) 6175
39. **Destiny** - The Jacksons 11 (38) 6114
40. **Disco Nights** - GQ 13 (35) 5912
41. **Slow Train Coming** - Bob Dylan 3 (17) 5844
42. **Teddy** - Teddy Pendergrass 5 (28) 5650
43. **Head Games** - Foreigner 5 (14) 5620
44. **On The Radio: Greatest Hits: Volumes I & II** - Donna Summer 2 (9) 5373
45. **Legend** - Poco 14 (46) 5360
46. **Greatest Hits** - Barry Manilow 7 (43) 5319
47. **Livin' Inside Your Love** - George Benson 7 (26) 5276
48. **Dionne(2)** - Dionne Warwick 12 (30) 5222
49. **The Boss** - Diana Ross 14 (29) 5174
50. **Enlightened Rogues** - The Allman Brothers Band 9 (24) 5145

1980

Rank. Title - Act YrPeak (YrWks) YrScr
1. **The Wall** - Pink Floyd 1 (52) 24529
2. **Glass Houses** - Billy Joel 1 (41) 21125
3. **Against The Wind** - Bob Seger & The Silver Bullet Band 1 (42) 19982
4. **Off The Wall** - Michael Jackson 3 (52) 15287
5. **The Game** - Queen 1 (24) 14569
6. **Christopher Cross** - Christopher Cross 6 (46) 13843
7. **Damn The Torpedoes** - Tom Petty And The Heartbreakers 2 (46) 13664
8. **Emotional Rescue** - The Rolling Stones 1 (24) 12844
9. **Diana** - Diana Ross 2 (29) 12531
10. **The Long Run** - Eagles 2 (46) 11279
11. **Hold Out** - Jackson Browne 1 (24) 11261
12. **Urban Cowboy** - Soundtrack 3 (33) 10669
13. **Just One Night** - Eric Clapton 2 (31) 10383
14. **Phoenix** - Dan Fogelberg 3 (35) 10041
15. **Mad Love** - Linda Ronstadt 3 (36) 9691
16. **Guilty** - Barbra Streisand 1 (12) 9383
17. **On The Radio: Greatest Hits: Volumes I & II** - Donna Summer 1 (30) 8126
18. **Empty Glass** - Pete Townshend 5 (30) 8115
19. **The Rose (Soundtrack)** - Bette Midler 12 (43) 7984
20. **Crimes Of Passion** - Pat Benatar 5 (19) 7972
21. **Back In Black** - AC/DC 4 (19) 7862
22. **In The Heat Of The Night** - Pat Benatar 12 (52) 7748
23. **Pretenders** - The Pretenders 9 (49) 7744
24. **Give Me The Night** - George Benson 3 (21) 7660
25. **The Empire Strikes Back** - Soundtrack 4 (28) 7465
26. **Middle Man** - Boz Scaggs 8 (33) 7364
27. **The Whispers** - The Whispers 6 (35) 7346
28. **Xanadu (Soundtrack)** - Olivia Newton-John/ Electric Light Orchestra 4 (25) 7116
29. **Duke** - Genesis 11 (31) 6975
30. **Kenny Rogers' Greatest Hits** - Kenny Rogers 1 (11) 6657
31. **Kenny** - Kenny Rogers 5 (39) 6600
32. **The River** - Bruce Springsteen 1 (9) 6533
33. **Light Up The Night** - The Brothers Johnson 5 (30) 6493
34. **Women And Children First** - Van Halen 6 (31) 6428
35. **Departure** - Journey 8 (40) 6390
36. **Fame** - Soundtrack 7 (30) 6350
37. **Let's Get Serious** - Jermaine Jackson 6 (29) 6323
38. **Mouth To Mouth** - Lipps Inc. 5 (26) 6210
39. **Sweet Sensation** - Stephanie Mills 16 (35) 6107
40. **Cornerstone** - Styx 3 (35) 6082
41. **Permanent Waves** - Rush 4 (28) 6054
42. **Heroes** - Commodores 7 (27) 5748
43. **Bee Gees Greatest** - Bee Gees 1 (25) 5715
44. **McCartney II** - Paul McCartney 3 (19) 5644
45. **Tusk** - Fleetwood Mac 8 (28) 5470
46. **One For The Road** - The Kinks 14 (27) 5313
47. **Love Stinks** - The J. Geils Band 18 (34) 5313
48. **Panorama** - The Cars 5 (17) 5262
49. **One Step Closer** - The Doobie Brothers 3 (12) 5249
50. **American Gigolo** - Soundtrack 7 (25) 5126

1981

Rank. Title - Act YrPeak (YrWks) YrScr
1. **Hi Infidelity** - REO Speedwagon 1 (52) 29558
2. **Paradise Theater** - Styx 1 (48) 20929
3. **Double Fantasy** - John Lennon & Yoko Ono 1 (52) 16634
4. **4** - Foreigner 1 (23) 16632
5. **Escape** - Journey 1 (21) 13332
6. **Tattoo You** - The Rolling Stones 1 (16) 13113
7. **Crimes Of Passion** - Pat Benatar 2 (52) 12762
8. **The Jazz Singer (Soundtrack)** - Neil Diamond 3 (52) 12679
9. **Mistaken Idenity** - Kim Carnes 1 (35) 12608
10. **Kenny Rogers' Greatest Hits** - Kenny Rogers 3 (52) 12419
11. **Long Distance Voyager** - The Moody Blues 1 (29) 12383
12. **Moving Pictures** - Rush 3 (43) 12147
13. **Arc Of A Diver** - Steve Winwood 3 (43) 11956
14. **Bella Donna** - Stevie Nicks 1 (20) 11424
15. **Zenyatta Mondatta** - The Police 5 (52) 11183
16. **Street Songs** - Rick James 3 (35) 11099
17. **Back In Black** - AC/DC 4 (52) 10750
18. **Precious Time** - Pat Benatar 1 (23) 10538

Rank. Title - Act YrPeak (YrWks) YrScr
19. **Christopher Cross** - Christopher Cross 17 (52) 10476
20. **Dirty Deeds Done Dirt Cheap** - AC/DC 3 (37) 10058
21. **Winelight** - Grover Washington Jr. 5 (45) 10019
22. **Don't Say No** - Billy Squier 5 (35) 9700
23. **Face Value** - Phil Collins 7 (40) 9642
24. **Guilty** - Barbra Streisand 2 (37) 9095
25. **Working Class Dog** - Rick Springfield 7 (42) 8859
26. **Autoamerican** - Blondie 7 (31) 8168
27. **Hard Promises** - Tom Petty And The Heartbreakers 5 (31) 8041
28. **Hotter Than July** - Stevie Wonder 3 (33) 7703
29. **Feels So Right** - Alabama 16 (40) 7589
30. **Zebop!** - Santana 9 (32) 7569
31. **Voices** - Daryl Hall & John Oates 17 (52) 7472
32. **The Turn Of A Friendly Card** - The Alan Parsons Project 13 (51) 7270
33. **Nine Tonight** - Bob Seger & The Silver Bullet Band 3 (14) 6760
34. **The One That You Love** - Air Supply 10 (29) 6553
35. **Juice** - Juice Newton 25 (43) 6533
36. **The Dude** - Quincy Jones 14 (39) 6474
37. **Celebrate!** - Kool & The Gang 10 (33) 6363
38. **Pirates** - Rickie Lee Jones 5 (21) 6299
39. **Ghost In The Machine** - The Police 2 (10) 6188
40. **Gaucho** - Steely Dan 9 (32) 6163
41. **Face Dances** - The Who 4 (20) 6119
42. **Wild-Eyed Southern Boys** - .38 Special 18 (42) 6076
43. **Being With You** - Smokey Robinson 10 (28) 5950
44. **Share Your Love** - Kenny Rogers 6 (25) 5907
45. **Loverboy** - Loverboy 13 (40) 5794
46. **In The Pocket** - Commodores 13 (25) 5752
47. **The Innocent Age** - Dan Fogelberg 6 (16) 5718
48. **The Gap Band III** - The Gap Band 16 (36) 5700
49. **9 To 5 And Odd Jobs** - Dolly Parton 11 (30) 5646
50. **Breakin' Away** - Al Jarreau 9 (19) 5588

1982

Rank. Title - Act YrPeak (YrWks) YrScr
1. **Asia** - Asia 1 (39) 21989
2. **American Fool** - John Cougar 1 (34) 18194
3. **Escape** - Journey 2 (52) 17313
4. **Get Lucky** - Loverboy 7 (52) 16373
5. **Freeze-Frame** - The J. Geils Band 1 (52) 15707
6. **Mirage** - Fleetwood Mac 1 (24) 15567
7. **Beauty And The Beat** - Go-Go's 1 (50) 15540
8. **4** - Foreigner 1 (49) 14032
9. **Chariots Of Fire (Soundtrack)** - Vangelis 1 (46) 12395
10. **Always On My Mind** - Willie Nelson 2 (41) 11974
11. **I Love Rock 'N Roll** - Joan Jett & the Blackhearts 2 (52) 11892
12. **Business As Usual** - Men At Work 1 (26) 11505
13. **Ghost In The Machine** - The Police 2 (52) 10774
14. **Bella Donna** - Stevie Nicks 6 (52) 10642
15. **Hooked On Classics** - Royal Philharmonic Orchestra Conducted By Louis Clark 4 (52) 9939
16. **Tug Of War** - Paul McCartney 1 (29) 9912
17. **Eye Of The Tiger** - Survivor 2 (27) 9484
18. **Dare** - The Human League 3 (38) 9340
19. **Success Hasn't Spoiled Me Yet** - Rick Springfield 2 (35) 9256
20. **Abracadabra** - The Steve Miller Band 3 (27) 9250
21. **Physical** - Olivia Newton-John 6 (48) 8586
22. **Toto IV** - Toto 4 (36) 8512
23. **Combat Rock** - The Clash 10 (29) 8321
24. **Private Eyes** - Daryl Hall & John Oates 5 (47) 7965
25. **Built For Speed** - Stray Cats 2 (26) 7874
26. **Emotions In Motion** - Billy Squier 5 (21) 7810
27. **Eye In The Sky** - The Alan Parsons Project 7 (28) 7685
28. **For Those About To Rock (We Salute You)** - AC/DC 1 (27) 7422
29. **Diver Down** - Van Halen 3 (34) 7369
30. **Quarterflash** - Quarterflash 8 (43) 7345
31. **A Flock Of Seagulls** - A Flock Of Seagulls 10 (32) 7103
32. **Daylight Again** - Crosby, Stills & Nash 8 (24) 7067
33. **Aldo Nova** - Aldo Nova 8 (37) 6961
34. **Abacab** - Genesis 12 (46) 6945
35. **Shake It Up** - The Cars 9 (36) 6885
36. **Tattoo You** - The Rolling Stones 5 (42) 6835
37. **Mountain Music** - Alabama 14 (42) 6829
38. **Good Trouble** - REO Speedwagon 7 (24) 6757
39. **Something Special** - Kool & The Gang 17 (52) 6731
40. **Diary Of A Madman** - Ozzy Osbourne 16 (52) 6678
41. **Pictures At Eleven** - Robert Plant 5 (24) 6358
42. **Chicago 16** - Chicago 9 (27) 6356
43. **Night And Day** - Joe Jackson 4 (24) 6297
44. **Blackout** - Scorpions 10 (40) 6243
45. **The Innocent Age** - Dan Fogelberg 15 (46) 5908
46. **Screaming For Vengeance** - Judas Priest 17 (23) 5789
47. **Picture This** - Huey Lewis & The News 13 (35) 5663
48. **All Four One** - The Motels 16 (36) 5586
49. **Special Forces** - 38 Special 10 (31) 5547
50. **Gap Band IV** - The Gap Band 14 (29) 5491

1983

Rank. Title - Act YrPeak (YrWks) YrScr
1. **Thriller** - Michael Jackson 1 (53) 42551
2. **Synchronicity** - The Police 1 (27) 23144
3. **Pyromania** - Def Leppard 2 (48) 23140
4. **Flashdance** - Soundtrack 1 (36) 19702
5. **H2O** - Daryl Hall & John Oates 3 (53) 19456
6. **Business As Usual** - Men At Work 1 (53) 19281
7. **Frontiers** - Journey 2 (46) 18554
8. **Lionel Richie** - Lionel Richie 3 (53) 14064
9. **1999** - Prince 9 (53) 13584
10. **Let's Dance** - David Bowie 4 (36) 13267
11. **Metal Health** - Quiet Riot 1 (37) 12112
12. **Built For Speed** - Stray Cats 2 (48) 11703
13. **Kissing To Be Clever** - Culture Club 14 (52) 11498
14. **Cargo** - Men At Work 3 (35) 11101
15. **Eliminator** - ZZ Top 9 (37) 10882
16. **Kilroy Was Here** - Styx 3 (34) 10304
17. **The Distance** - Bob Seger & The Silver Bullet Band 5 (39) 10197
18. **Rio** - Duran Duran 6 (53) 10046
19. **An Innocent Man** - Billy Joel 4 (20) 9743
20. **The Wild Heart** - Stevie Nicks 5 (27) 9296
21. **Toto IV** - Toto 8 (46) 9291
22. **Cuts Like A Knife** - Bryan Adams 8 (46) 9269
23. **Reach The Beach** - The Fixx 8 (32) 9269
24. **Get Nervous** - Pat Benatar 4 (40) 8278
25. **Jane Fonda's Workout Record** - Jane Fonda 15 (53) 7672
26. **Keep It Up** - Loverboy 7 (27) 7569
27. **Hello, I Must Be Going!** - Phil Collins 8 (47) 7158
28. **Speaking In Tongues** - Talking Heads 15 (28) 7131
29. **The Closer You Get** - Alabama 10 (41) 7062
30. **Living In Oz** - Rick Springfield 12 (36) 7055
31. **War** - U2 12 (42) 6946
32. **The Principle Of Moments** - Robert Plant 8 (23) 6609
33. **Greatest Hits** - Air Supply 7 (20) 6515
34. **Faster Than The Speed Of Night** - Bonnie Tyler 4 (22) 6431
35. **Can't Slow Down** - Lionel Richie 1 (8) 6165
36. **Duran Duran** - Duran Duran 10 (46) 5966
37. **Long After Dark** - Tom Petty And The Heartbreakers 9 (26) 5837
38. **Eyes That See In The Dark** - Kenny Rogers 6 (15) 5769
39. **Spring Session M** - Missing Persons 17 (29) 5739
40. **What's New** - Linda Ronstadt & The Nelson Riddle Orchestra 3 (14) 5703
41. **Sweet Dreams (Are Made Of This)** - Eurythmics 15 (32) 5666
42. **Combat Rock** - The Clash 7 (32) 5471
43. **Killer On The Rampage** - Eddy Grant 10 (30) 5439
44. **Olivia's Greatest Hits, Vol. 2** - Olivia Newton-John 33 (53) 5346
45. **Jarreau** - Al Jarreau 13 (38) 5257
46. **She Works Hard For The Money** - Donna Summer 9 (25) 5211
47. **Staying Alive (Soundtrack)** - Bee Gees 6 (25) 5191
48. **Three Lock Box** - Sammy Hagar 17 (33) 5147
49. **Night And Day** - Joe Jackson 4 (33) 4964
50. **Piece Of Mind** - Iron Maiden 14 (30) 4912

1984

Rank. Title - Act YrPeak (YrWks) YrScr
1. **Can't Slow Down** - Lionel Richie 2 (52) 28838
2. **Sports** - Huey Lewis & The News 1 (52) 27658
3. **Thriller** - Michael Jackson 1 (52) 24570
4. **Purple Rain (Soundtrack)** - Prince And The Revolution 1 (25) 23782

Rank. Title - Act YrPeak (YrWks) YrScr
5. **Born In The U.S.A.** - Bruce Springsteen 1 (28) 21500
6. **1984 (MCMLXXXIV)** - Van Halen 2 (49) 20899
7. **Footloose** - Soundtrack 1 (46) 18934
8. **Heartbeat City** - The Cars 3 (39) 17988
9. **She's So Unusual** - Cyndi Lauper 4 (52) 17668
10. **Colour By Numbers** - Culture Club 2 (50) 16709
11. **An Innocent Man** - Billy Joel 6 (52) 14839
12. **Private Dancer** - Tina Turner 3 (29) 14218
13. **Eliminator** - ZZ Top 10 (52) 14066
14. **Break Out** - The Pointer Sisters 8 (52) 13651
15. **Seven And The Ragged Tiger** - Duran Duran 8 (52) 13523
16. **Rebel Yell** - Billy Idol 6 (52) 11669
17. **Midnight Madness** - Night Ranger 15 (52) 10825
18. **Madonna** - Madonna 8 (52) 10688
19. **Love At First Sting** - Scorpions 6 (42) 10568
20. **Uh-Huh** - John Mellencamp 9 (44) 10132
21. **Synchronicity** - The Police 4 (48) 10052
22. **Out Of The Cellar** - Ratt 7 (41) 9597
23. **90125** - Yes 5 (48) 9375
24. **Learning To Crawl** - The Pretenders 5 (42) 9210
25. **Touch** - Eurythmics 7 (37) 8611
26. **Shout At The Devil** - Mötley Crüe 17 (52) 8379
27. **Into The Gap** - Thompson Twins 10 (42) 8183
28. **What's New** - Linda Ronstadt & The Nelson Riddle Orchestra 3 (52) 7895
29. **Chicago 17** - Chicago 9 (31) 7493
30. **1100 Bel Air Place** - Julio Iglesias 5 (18) 7123
31. **Rock 'N Soul Part 1** - Daryl Hall & John Oates 7 (37) 6983
32. **The Big Chill** - Soundtrack 17 (52) 6634
33. **Ghostbusters** - Soundtrack 6 (26) 6459
34. **Victory** - The Jacksons 4 (24) 6358
35. **Street Talk** - Steve Perry 12 (36) 6353
36. **The Woman In Red (Soundtrack)** - Stevie Wonder 4 (15) 6256
37. **Stay Hungry** - Twisted Sister 15 (26) 6209
38. **Genesis** - Genesis 13 (38) 6058
39. **Eddie & The Cruisers (Soundtrack)** - John Cafferty & The Beaver Brown Band 9 (22) 5927
40. **No Brakes** - John Waite 10 (25) 5827
41. **Roll On** - Alabama 21 (47) 5747
42. **No Parking On The Dance Floor** - Midnight Star 27 (52) 5667
43. **Metal Health** - Quiet Riot 5 (44) 5375
44. **Self Control** - Laura Branigan 23 (36) 5368
45. **Breakin'** - Soundtrack 8 (23) 5221
46. **Talk Show** - Go-Go's 18 (32) 5186
47. **Jermaine Jackson** - Jermaine Jackson 19 (33) 5137
48. **Stay With Me Tonight** - Jeffrey Osborne 25 (52) 5002
49. **Signs Of Life** - Billy Squier 11 (22) 4991
50. **Camouflage** - Rod Stewart 18 (27) 4899

1985

Rank. Title - Act YrPeak (YrWks) YrScr
1. **Born In The U.S.A.** - Bruce Springsteen 1 (52) 30298
2. **No Jacket Required** - Phil Collins 1 (43) 25911
3. **Reckless** - Bryan Adams 1 (52) 24040
4. **Like A Virgin** - Madonna 1 (52) 22466
5. **Songs From The Big Chair** - Tears For Fears 1 (39) 21847
6. **Make It Big** - Wham! 1 (52) 21331
7. **Brothers In Arms** - Dire Straits 1 (30) 17879
8. **Beverly Hills Cop** - Soundtrack 1 (51) 17160
9. **Private Dancer** - Tina Turner 5 (52) 14163
10. **Centerfield** - John Fogerty 1 (49) 14096
11. **Around The World In A Day** - Prince And The Revolution 1 (34) 13740
12. **Whitney Houston** - Whitney Houston 2 (40) 13450
13. **The Dream Of The Blue Turtles** - Sting 2 (25) 12994
14. **Suddenly** - Billy Ocean 12 (52) 12216
15. **Emergency** - Kool & The Gang 13 (52) 11860
16. **Heart** - Heart 1 (25) 10986
17. **Building The Perfect Beast** - Don Henley 13 (52) 10364
18. **Agent Provocateur** - Foreigner 4 (45) 10350
19. **Miami Vice** - Soundtrack 1 (12) 10079
20. **The Power Station** - The Power Station 6 (38) 9818
21. **Purple Rain (Soundtrack)** - Prince And The Revolution 1 (47) 9737
22. **Diamond Life** - Sade 5 (45) 9699
23. **Scarecrow** - John Mellencamp 2 (16) 8722
24. **Chicago 17** - Chicago 4 (41) 8622
25. **Wheels Are Turnin'** - REO Speedwagon 7 (43) 8523
26. **New Edition** - New Edition 6 (42) 8387
27. **Break Out** - The Pointer Sisters 11 (47) 8253
28. **Greatest Hits Vol. I & II** - Billy Joel 6 (24) 8179
29. **Be Yourself Tonight** - Eurythmics 9 (32) 8011
30. **Big Bam Boom** - Daryl Hall & John Oates 7 (41) 7889
31. **7 Wishes** - Night Ranger 10 (30) 7693
32. **Dream Into Action** - Howard Jones 10 (37) 7602
33. **Vital Signs** - Survivor 16 (47) 7450
34. **Southern Accents** - Tom Petty And The Heartbreakers 7 (32) 7365
35. **Theatre Of Pain** - Mötley Crüe 6 (25) 7253
36. **Rock Me Tonight** - Freddie Jackson 10 (32) 7252
37. **We Are The World** - USA For Africa 1 (22) 6924
38. **Can't Slow Down** - Lionel Richie 12 (52) 6907
39. **Crazy From The Heat** - David Lee Roth 15 (33) 6604
40. **Invasion Of Your Privacy** - Ratt 7 (27) 6532
41. **The Secret Of Association** - Paul Young 19 (32) 6475
42. **Valotte** - Julian Lennon 17 (38) 6462
43. **Rhythm Of The Night** - DeBarge 19 (41) 6445
44. **She's So Unusual** - Cyndi Lauper 9 (42) 6388
45. **Sports** - Huey Lewis & The News 11 (52) 6243
46. **Who's Zoomin' Who?** - Aretha Franklin 13 (23) 6147
47. **Little Creatures** - Talking Heads 20 (26) 5792
48. **The Night I Fell In Love** - Luther Vandross 19 (39) 5561
49. **The Unforgettable Fire** - U2 16 (52) 5457
50. **Nightshift** - Commodores 12 (37) 5408

1986

Rank. Title - Act YrPeak (YrWks) YrScr
1. **Whitney Houston** - Whitney Houston 1 (52) 27456
2. **Control** - Janet Jackson 1 (43) 17840
3. **Heart** - Heart 2 (52) 17099
4. **Top Gun** - Soundtrack 1 (30) 16820
5. **5150** - Van Halen 1 (38) 15652
6. **Promise** - Sade 1 (44) 14758
7. **Scarecrow** - John Mellencamp 3 (52) 14300
8. **True Blue** - Madonna 1 (24) 13453
9. **Like A Rock** - Bob Seger & The Silver Bullet Band 3 (37) 12263
10. **Brothers In Arms** - Dire Straits 6 (52) 11871
11. **Raising Hell** - Run-D.M.C. 3 (29) 11736
12. **Welcome To The Real World** - Mr. Mister 1 (40) 11697
13. **The Broadway Album** - Barbra Streisand 1 (32) 11660
14. **So** - Peter Gabriel 2 (29) 11253
15. **Invisible Touch** - Genesis 3 (27) 11110
16. **Afterburner** - ZZ Top 5 (52) 11006
17. **Riptide** - Robert Palmer 8 (52) 10614
18. **Love Zone** - Billy Ocean 6 (33) 10605
19. **Play Deep** - The Outfield 9 (48) 10308
20. **Winner In You** - Patti LaBelle 1 (30) 10266
21. **Slippery When Wet** - Bon Jovi 1 (16) 10161
22. **Dancing On The Ceiling** - Lionel Richie 1 (18) 9566
23. **Fore!** - Huey Lewis & The News 1 (16) 9444
24. **Back In The High Life** - Steve Winwood 3 (24) 9211
25. **Primitive Love** - Miami Sound Machine 21 (52) 9078
26. **Knee Deep In The Hoopla** - Starship 7 (37) 8883
27. **No Jacket Required** - Phil Collins 15 (52) 8542
28. **Third Stage** - Boston 1 (11) 8441
29. **Raised On Radio** - Journey 4 (34) 8359
30. **Tuff Enuff** - The Fabulous Thunderbirds 13 (42) 8321
31. **Different Light** - The Bangles 12 (48) 8103
32. **Eat 'Em And Smile** - David Lee Roth 4 (23) 7966
33. **Parade: Music From The Motion Picture Under The Cherry Moon (Soundtrack)** - Prince And The Revolution 3 (28) 7736
34. **The Other Side Of Life** - The Moody Blues 9 (33) 7655
35. **Please** - Pet Shop Boys 7 (31) 7645
36. **The Bridge** - Billy Joel 7 (20) 7406
37. **The Ultimate Sin** - Ozzy Osbourne 6 (39) 7371
38. **Pretty In Pink** - Soundtrack 5 (27) 7236
39. **Once Upon A Time** - Simple Minds 10 (34) 7183
40. **Born In The U.S.A.** - Bruce Springsteen 8 (52) 7026
41. **In Square Circle** - Stevie Wonder 7 (39) 6944
42. **Falco 3** - Falco 3 (27) 6898
43. **Miami Vice** - Soundtrack 1 (22) 6887

Rank. Title - Act YrPeak (YrWks) YrScr
44. **Listen Like Thieves** - INXS 11 (46) 6847
45. **Mike + The Mechanics** - Mike + The Mechanics 26 (47) 6573
46. **Rapture** - Anita Baker 12 (37) 6543
47. **Songs From The Big Chair** - Tears For Fears 10 (43) 6338
48. **Dirty Work** - The Rolling Stones 4 (25) 6129
49. **Nervous Night** - Hooters 12 (42) 6124
50. **Rock A Little** - Stevie Nicks 12 (32) 6037

1987

Rank. Title - Act YrPeak (YrWks) YrScr
1. **Slippery When Wet** - Bon Jovi 1 (52) 27590
2. **The Joshua Tree** - U2 1 (39) 23781
3. **Whitesnake** - Whitesnake 2 (37) 22110
4. **Licensed To Ill** - Beastie Boys 1 (52) 20606
5. **Whitney** - Whitney Houston 1 (27) 19378
6. **Graceland** - Paul Simon 3 (52) 16236
7. **Look What The Cat Dragged In** - Poison 3 (52) 15215
8. **The Way It Is** - Bruce Hornsby & The Range 3 (45) 13886
9. **The Final Countdown** - Europe 8 (52) 13682
10. **Control** - Janet Jackson 5 (52) 13087
11. **Bad Animals** - Heart 2 (29) 12967
12. **Rapture** - Anita Baker 11 (52) 12890
13. **Duotones** - Kenny G 6 (52) 12867
14. **Invisible Touch** - Genesis 4 (52) 12631
15. **Night Songs** - Cinderella 3 (46) 12156
16. **Bad** - Michael Jackson 1 (14) 11842
17. **Tango In The Night** - Fleetwood Mac 7 (35) 11478
18. **Girls, Girls, Girls** - Mötley Crüe 2 (29) 10693
19. **Dirty Dancing** - Soundtrack 1 (15) 10442
20. **Fore!** - Huey Lewis & The News 5 (45) 10418
21. **Back In The High Life** - Steve Winwood 10 (52) 10130
22. **True Blue** - Madonna 6 (52) 10060
23. **Bigger And Deffer** - LL Cool J 3 (28) 10046
24. **Spanish Fly** - Lisa Lisa And Cult Jam 7 (34) 9572
25. **La Bamba (Soundtrack)** - Los Lobos 1 (23) 9173
26. **Hysteria** - Def Leppard 4 (19) 9077
27. **Different Light** - The Bangles 2 (34) 9073
28. **Third Stage** - Boston 3 (39) 8781
29. **Exposure** - Exposé 23 (45) 8316
30. **Strong Persuader** - The Robert Cray Band 13 (47) 8216
31. **Life, Love & Pain** - Club Nouveau 6 (42) 8056
32. **Crowded House** - Crowded House 12 (47) 7896
33. **Into The Fire** - Bryan Adams 7 (33) 7709
34. **Jody Watley** - Jody Watley 10 (41) 7638
35. **Give Me The Reason** - Luther Vandross 14 (42) 7516
36. **Crushin'** - Fat Boys 8 (29) 7464
37. **Dancing On The Ceiling** - Lionel Richie 7 (40) 7408
38. **Raising Hell** - Run-D.M.C. 12 (42) 6968
39. **Sign 'O' The Times** - Prince 6 (37) 6967
40. **A Momentary Lapse Of Reason** - Pink Floyd 3 (14) 6820
41. **Georgia Satellites** - The Georgia Satellites 5 (33) 6711

Rank. Title - Act YrPeak (YrWks) YrScr
42. **The Lonesome Jubilee** - John Mellencamp 6 (15) 6648
43. **Just Like The First Time** - Freddie Jackson 23 (44) 6460
44. **In The Dark** - Grateful Dead 6 (23) 6414
45. **So** - Peter Gabriel 16 (47) 6274
46. **Beverly Hills Cop II** - Soundtrack 8 (26) 6220
47. **Word Up!** - Cameo 12 (40) 6180
48. **Trio** - Dolly Parton, Linda Ronstadt, Emmylou Harris 6 (38) 6032
49. **Tunnel Of Love** - Bruce Springsteen 1 (10) 5976
50. **Bruce Springsteen & The E Street Band Live 1975-1985** - Bruce Springsteen 1 (21) 5964

1988

Rank. Title - Act YrPeak (YrWks) YrScr
1. **Faith** - George Michael 1 (53) 34530
2. **Hysteria** - Def Leppard 1 (53) 30503
3. **Dirty Dancing** - Soundtrack 1 (53) 30330
4. **Appetite For Destruction** - Guns N' Roses 1 (53) 26816
5. **Kick** - INXS 3 (53) 21690
6. **Bad** - Michael Jackson 2 (53) 19472
7. **Tiffany** - Tiffany 1 (49) 14879
8. **Out Of The Blue** - Debbie Gibson 7 (53) 14319
9. **Tracy Chapman** - Tracy Chapman 1 (36) 14236
10. **OU812** - Van Halen 1 (29) 13721
11. **Open Up And Say...Ahh!** - Poison 2 (33) 13359
12. **Indtroducing The Hardline According To Terence Trent D'Arby** - Terence Trent D'Arby 4 (50) 12512
13. **Let It Loose** - Gloria Estefan & Miami Sound Machine 6 (53) 12175
14. **More Dirty Dancing** - Soundtrack 3 (42) 12100
15. **Richard Marx** - Richard Marx 8 (53) 11994
16. **Roll With It** - Steve Winwood 1 (26) 11225
17. **Whenever You Need Somebody** - Rick Astley 10 (50) 11051
18. **Permanent Vacation** - Aerosmith 12 (52) 10578
19. **Now And Zen** - Robert Plant 6 (43) 10209
20. **Cocktail** - Soundtrack 3 (21) 10071
21. **He's The D.J., I'm The Rapper** - D.J. Jazzy Jeff & The Fresh Prince 4 (37) 9963
22. **Whitney** - Whitney Houston 7 (53) 9790
23. **The Lonesome Jubilee** - John Mellencamp 6 (38) 9158
24. **Make It Last Forever** - Keith Sweat 15 (52) 8966
25. **New Jersey** - Bon Jovi 1 (13) 8817
26. **Rattle And Hum (Soundtrack)** - U2 1 (10) 8371
27. **Long Cold Winter** - Cinderella 10 (24) 8264
28. **Don't Be Cruel** - Bobby Brown 6 (24) 8031
29. **Lap Of Luxury** - Cheap Trick 16 (35) 8013
30. **Heaven On Earth** - Belinda Carlisle 13 (41) 7980
31. **Pride** - White Lion 11 (53) 7772
32. **Savage Amusement** - Scorpions 5 (35) 7696
33. **Tunnel Of Love** - Bruce Springsteen 8 (35) 7643
34. **Diesel And Dust** - Midnight Oil 21 (47) 7393
35. **Whitesnake** - Whitesnake 4 (39) 7357

Rank. Title - Act YrPeak (YrWks) YrScr
36. **Stronger Than Pride** - Sade 7 (31) 7271
37. **Simple Pleasures** - Bobby McFerrin 5 (37) 7252
38. **Scenes From The Southside** - Bruce Hornsby & The Range 5 (27) 7018
39. **Tell It To My Heart** - Taylor Dayne 21 (49) 6780
40. **The Joshua Tree** - U2 13 (53) 6727
41. **Heart Break** - New Edition 12 (26) 6718
42. **Skyscraper** - David Lee Roth 6 (27) 6665
43. **...Nothing Like The Sun** - Sting 11 (43) 6640
44. **In Effect Mode** - Al B. Sure! 20 (34) 6578
45. **Pebbles** - Pebbles 14 (38) 6577
46. **Giving You The Best That I Got** - Anita Baker 1 (9) 6265
47. **Cloud Nine** - George Harrison 8 (25) 6134
48. **A Momentary Lapse Of Reason** - Pink Floyd 6 (42) 6110
49. **Out Of Order** - Rod Stewart 21 (31) 6070
50. **Heavy Nova** - Robert Palmer 13 (25) 5917

1989

Rank. Title - Act YrPeak (YrWks) YrScr
1. **Don't Be Cruel** - Bobby Brown 1 (52) 27180
2. **Forever Your Girl** - Paula Abdul 1 (52) 24387
3. **Hangin' Tough** - New Kids On The Block 1 (52) 24242
4. **Girl You Know It's True** - Milli Vanilli 1 (41) 22975
5. **The Raw & The Cooked** - Fine Young Cannibals 1 (43) 21779
6. **Like A Prayer** - Madonna 1 (39) 16977
7. **Appetite For Destruction** - Guns N' Roses 1 (52) 15778
8. **Full Moon Fever** - Tom Petty 3 (34) 15075
9. **New Jersey** - Bon Jovi 4 (52) 14569
10. **G N' R Lies** - Guns N' Roses 2 (47) 14423
11. **Electric Youth** - Debbie Gibson 1 (47) 14300
12. **Repeat Offender** - Richard Marx 1 (33) 14247
13. **Skid Row** - Skid Row 6 (47) 14202
14. **Beaches (Soundtrack)** - Bette Midler 2 (50) 12751
15. **Volume 1** - Traveling Wilburys 3 (39) 12318
16. **Loc-ed After Dark** - Tone-Loc 1 (40) 11607
17. **Vivid** - Living Colour 6 (52) 11074
18. **Batman (Soundtrack)** - Prince 1 (26) 10949
19. **Hysteria** - Def Leppard 4 (52) 10349
20. **Janet Jackson's Rhythm Nation 1814** - Janet Jackson 1 (13) 9353
21. **Dirty Rotten Filthy Stinking Rich** - Warrant 10 (44) 9325
22. **...Twice Shy** - Great White 9 (35) 9205
23. **Shooting Rubberbands At The Stars** - Edie Brickell & New Bohemians 4 (39) 9051
24. **Giving You The Best That I Got** - Anita Baker 1 (33) 8688
25. **Winger** - Winger 21 (48) 8308
26. **Disintegration** - The Cure 12 (33) 8220
27. **Steel Wheels** - T he Rolling Stones 3 (16) 8057
28. **Dr. Feelgood** - Mötley Crüe 1 (15) 7801
29. **Open Up And Say...Ahh!** - Poison 3 (37) 7694
30. **The End Of The Innocence** - Don Henley 8 (25) 7311
31. **Green** - R.E.M. 12 (34) 7290

Rank. Title - Act YrPeak (YrWks) YrScr
32. Sonic Temple - The Cult 10 (33) 7081
33. Mystery Girl - Roy Orbison 5 (27) 6956
34. Keep On Movin' - Soul II Soul 14 (26) 6953
35. Silhouette - Kenny G 10 (46) 6753
36. Out Of Order - Rod Stewart 20 (41) 6520
37. ...And Justice For All - Metallica 21 (52) 6503
38. Pump - Aerosmith 5 (14) 6345
39. Heart Of Stone - Cher 10 (24) 6329
40. Karyn White - Karyn White 19 (42) 6242
41. Let's Get It Started - MC Hammer 30 (52) 6240
42. Cuts Both Ways - Gloria Estefan 8 (23) 6167
43. Cosmic Thing - The B-52s 6 (24) 6140
44. Blind Man's Zoo - 10,000 Maniacs 13 (28) 5903
45. Guy - Guy 27 (47) 5712
46. Rattle And Hum (Soundtrack) - U2 2 (28) 5586
47. Everything - The Bangles 15 (33) 5510
48. Cocktail - Soundtrack 2 (40) 5502
49. Storm Front - Billy Joel 1 (9) 5481
50. Journey's Greatest Hits - Journey 10 (45) 5478

Points Only From Weeks in the Top 5 or Top 10

Rank. Title - Act	Top 5 Wks
1. **Thriller** - Michael Jackson	71
2. **Born In The U.S.A.** - Bruce Springsteen	66
3. **The Sound Of Music** - Soundtrack	73
4. **Rumours** - Fleetwood Mac	46
5. **Dirty Dancing** - Various Artists	43
6. **Doctor Zhivago** - Instrumental	47
7. **Slippery When Wet** - Bon Jovi	38
8. **Purple Rain (Soundtrack)** - Prince And The Revolution	30
9. **Forever Your Girl** - Paula Abdul	40
10. **Frampton Comes Alive!** - Peter Frampton	35
11. **Faith** - George Michael	33
12. **Appetite For Destruction** - Guns N' Roses	37
13. **Bad** - Michael Jackson	38
14. **Mary Poppins** - Soundtrack	32
15. **Can't Slow Down** - Lionel Richie	38
16. **Saturday Night Fever (Soundtrack)** - Bee Gees	26
17. **Whipped Cream & Other Delights** - Herb Alpert's Tijuana Brass	33
18. **Songs In The Key Of Life** - Stevie Wonder	32
19. **Synchronicity** - The Police	29
20. **Sgt. Pepper's Lonely Hearts Club Band** - The Beatles	29
21. **Whitney Houston** - Whitney Houston	30
22. **4** - Foreigner	32
23. **Girl You Know It's True** - Milli Vanilli	31
24. **Hysteria** - Def Leppard	33
25. **Blood, Sweat & Tears** - Blood, Sweat & Tears	30
26. **Janet Jackson's Rhythm Nation 1814** - Janet Jackson	32
27. **Whitesnake** - Whitesnake	35
28. **Escape** - Journey	34
29. **Hi Infidelity** - REO Speedwagon	25
30. **Business As Usual** - Men At Work	27
31. **The Monkees** - The Monkees	25
32. **Tapestry** - Carole King	25
33. **Jesus Christ Superstar** - Various Artists	31
34. **Hotel California** - Eagles	26
35. **The Wall** - Pink Floyd	23
36. **Hair** - Original Cast Recording	23
37. **Don't Be Cruel** - Bobby Brown	27
38. **What Now My Love** - Herb Alpert & The Tijuana Brass	27
39. **!!Going Places!!** - Herb Alpert & The Tijuana Brass	28
40. **Sports** - Huey Lewis & The News	29
41. **A Hard Day's Night (Soundtrack)** - The Beatles	22
42. **Grease** - Soundtrack	23
43. **More Of The Monkees** - The Monkees	19
44. **No Jacket Required** - Phil Collins	23
45. **Asia** - Asia	24
46. **Abbey Road** - The Beatles	21
47. **The Graduate (Soundtrack)** - Simon & Garfunkel	22
48. **Led Zeppelin II** - Led Zeppelin	21
49. **Breakfast In America** - Supertramp	22
50. **Glass Houses** - Billy Joel	22

Rank. Title - Act	Top 10 Wks
1. **Thriller** - Michael Jackson	78
2. **The Sound Of Music** - Soundtrack	109
3. **Born In The U.S.A.** - Bruce Springsteen	84
4. **Rumours** - Fleetwood Mac	52
5. **Hysteria** - Def Leppard	78
6. **Doctor Zhivago** - Soundtrack	71
7. **Forever Your Girl** - Paula Abdul	64
8. **Whipped Cream & Other Delights** - Herb Alpert's Tijuana Brass	61
9. **Dirty Dancing** - Various Artists	48
10. **Faith** - George Michael	51
11. **Can't Slow Down** - Lionel Richie	59
12. **Frampton Comes Alive!** - Peter Frampton	52
13. **Appetite For Destruction** - Guns N' Roses	52
14. **Mary Poppins** - Soundtrack	48
15. **Slippery When Wet** - Bon Jovi	46
16. **Blood, Sweat & Tears** - Blood, Sweat & Tears	50
17. **Whitney Houston** - Whitney Houston	46
18. **Tapestry** - Carole King	46
19. **Synchronicity** - The Police	40
20. **Saturday Night Fever (Soundtrack)** - Bee Gees	35
21. **Purple Rain (Soundtrack)** - Prince And The Revolution	32
22. **!!Going Places!!** - Herb Alpert & The Tijuana Brass	48
23. **Don't Be Cruel** - Bobby Brown	45
24. **Girl You Know It's True** - Milli Vanilli	41
25. **Bad** - Michael Jackson	39
26. **Sgt. Pepper's Lonely Hearts Club Band** - The Beatles	33
27. **Songs In The Key Of Life** - Stevie Wonder	35
28. **Jesus Christ Superstar** - Various Artists	41
29. **Whitesnake** - Whitesnake	41
30. **4** - Foreigner	34
31. **Sports** - Huey Lewis & The News	42
32. **The Monkees** - The Monkees	32
33. **Hi Infidelity** - REO Speedwagon	30
34. **Hangin' Tough** - New Kids On The Block	45
35. **Escape** - Journey	38
36. **Janet Jackson's Rhythm Nation 1814** - Janet Jackson	35
37. **Business As Usual** - Men At Work	31
38. **Brothers In Arms** - Dire Straits	37
39. **The Joshua Tree** - U2	35
40. **In-A-Gadda-Da-Vida** - Iron Butterfly	49
41. **The Wall** - Pink Floyd	27
42. **No Jacket Required** - Phil Collins	31
43. **What Now My Love** - Herb Alpert & The Tijuana Brass	32
44. **Hair** - Original Cast Recording	28
45. **A Hard Day's Night (Soundtrack)** - The Beatles	28
46. **Hotel California** - Eagles	28
47. **Goodbye Yellow Brick Road** - Elton John	36
48. **Grease** - Soundtrack	29
49. **Heart** - Heart	37
50. **Whitney** - Whitney Houston	31

Number 1 Albums By Weeks

Title – Act (Entry Yr)	#1 Wks
Thriller - Michael Jackson (82)	37
Rumours - Fleetwood Mac (77)	31
Saturday Night Fever (Soundtrack) - Bee Gees (77)	24
Purple Rain (Soundtrack) - Prince And The Revolution (84)	24
Dirty Dancing - Various Artists (87)	18
More Of The Monkees - The Monkees (67)	18
Synchronicity - The Police (83)	17
Tapestry - Carole King (71)	15
Sgt. Pepper's Lonely Hearts Club Band - The Beatles (67)	15
Business As Usual - Men At Work (82)	15
Hi Infidelity - REO Speedwagon (80)	15
The Wall - Pink Floyd (79)	15
Mary Poppins - Musical (64)	14
Whitney Houston - Whitney Houston (85)	14
Songs In The Key Of Life - Stevie Wonder (76)	14
A Hard Day's Night (Soundtrack) - The Beatles (64)	14
The Monkees - The Monkees (66)	13
Hair - Original Cast Recording (68)	13
Faith - George Michael (87)	12
Grease - Musical (78)	12
Whitney - Whitney Houston (87)	11
Abbey Road - The Beatles (69)	11
Meet The Beatles! - The Beatles (64)	11
Miami Vice - Various Artists (85)	11
Forever Your Girl - Paula Abdul (88)	10
Frampton Comes Alive! - Peter Frampton (76)	10
4 - Foreigner (81)	10
Footloose - Various Artists (84)	10
The Singing Nun - The Singing Nun (Soeur Sourire) (63)	10
Bridge Over Troubled Water - Simon & Garfunkel (70)	10
Elton John's Greatest Hits - Elton John (74)	10
Brothers In Arms - Dire Straits (85)	9
The Joshua Tree - U2 (87)	9
What Now My Love - Herb Alpert & The Tijuana Brass (66)	9
Asia - Asia (82)	9
The Graduate (Soundtrack) - Simon & Garfunkel (68)	9
Tattoo You - The Rolling Stones (81)	9
American Fool - John Cougar (82)	9
The Long Run - Eagles (79)	9
Cosmo's Factory - Creedence Clearwater Revival (70)	9
Beatles '65 - The Beatles (65)	9
Pearl - Janis Joplin (71)	9
Help! (Soundtrack) - The Beatles (65)	9
The Beatles [White Album] - The Beatles (68)	9
Chicago V - Chicago (72)	9
Whipped Cream & Other Delights - Herb Alpert's Tijuana Brass (65)	8
Slippery When Wet - Bon Jovi (86)	8
Goodbye Yellow Brick Road - Elton John (73)	8
Hotel California - Eagles (76)	8
52nd Street - Billy Joel (78)	8
Double Fantasy - John Lennon & Yoko Ono (80)	8
Cheap Thrills - Big Brother And The Holding Company (68)	8
Magical Mystery Tour (Soundtrack) - The Beatles (67)	8
My Son, The Nut - Allan Sherman (63)	8
Born In The U.S.A. - Bruce Springsteen (84)	7
Blood, Sweat & Tears - Blood, Sweat & Tears (69)	7
Girl You Know It's True - Milli Vanilli (89)	7
No Jacket Required - Phil Collins (85)	7
The Raw & The Cooked - Fine Young Cannibals (89)	7
Led Zeppelin II - Led Zeppelin (69)	7
Wings At The Speed Of Sound - Wings (76)	7
Bookends - Simon & Garfunkel (68)	7
Licensed To Ill - Beastie Boys (86)	7
In Through The Out Door - Led Zeppelin (79)	7
American Pie - Don McLean (71)	7
Captain Fantastic And The Brown Dirt Cowboy - Elton John (75)	7
All Things Must Pass - George Harrison (70)	7
Emotional Rescue - The Rolling Stones (80)	7
Bruce Springsteen & The E Street Band Live 1975-1985 - Bruce Springsteen (86)	7
Hysteria - Def Leppard (87)	6
!!Going Places!! - Herb Alpert & The Tijuana Brass (65)	6
Don't Be Cruel - Bobby Brown (88)	6
Bad - Michael Jackson (87)	6
Abraxas - Santana (70)	6
Breakfast In America - Supertramp (79)	6
Glass Houses - Billy Joel (80)	6
Against The Wind - Bob Seger & The Silver Bullet Band (80)	6
Hello Dolly! - Louis Armstrong (64)	6
Spirits Having Flown - Bee Gees (79)	6
A Star Is Born (Soundtrack) - Barbra Streisand & Kris Kristofferson (76)	6
Bad Girls - Donna Summer (79)	6
Like A Prayer - Madonna (89)	6
Beauty And The Beat - Go-Go's (81)	6
Rattle And Hum (Soundtrack) - U2 (88)	6
Rubber Soul - The Beatles (65)	6
Revolver - The Beatles (66)	6
Beatles VI - The Beatles (65)	6
Physical Graffiti - Led Zeppelin (75)	6
Batman (Soundtrack) - Prince (89)	6
Appetite For Destruction - Guns N' Roses (87)	5
Songs From The Big Chair - Tears For Fears (85)	5
In The Wind - Peter, Paul & Mary (63)	5
True Blue - Madonna (86)	5
Diana Ross And The Supremes Greatest Hits - Diana Ross & The Supremes (67)	5
Wichita Lineman - Glen Campbell (68)	5
People - Barbra Streisand (64)	5
The Game - Queen (80)	5
Top Gun - Various Artists (86)	5
You Don't Mess Around With Jim - Jim Croce (72)	5
Honky Château - Elton John (72)	5
One Of These Nights - Eagles (75)	5
Mirage - Fleetwood Mac (82)	5
Simple Dreams - Linda Ronstadt (77)	5
Minute By Minute - The Doobie Brothers (78)	5
Brothers And Sisters - The Allman Brothers Band (73)	5
The Sting (Soundtrack) - Marvin Hamlisch (74)	5
Get The Knack - The Knack (79)	5
The Beatles' Second Album - The Beatles (64)	5
Blooming Hits - Paul Mauriat And His Orchestra (67)	5
First Take - Roberta Flack (70)	5
No Secrets - Carly Simon (72)	5
America - America (72)	5
Chicago IX: Chicago's Greatest Hits - Chicago (75)	5
Desire - Bob Dylan (76)	5
Electric Youth - Debbie Gibson (89)	5
Pisces, Aquarius, Capricorn, And Jones Ltd. - The Monkees (67)	5
Seventh Sojourn - The Moody Blues (72)	5
Their Greatest Hits 1971-1975 - Eagles (76)	5
Santana III - Santana (71)	5
Ballads Of The Green Berets - SSgt Barry Sadler (66)	5
Chicago VI - Chicago (73)	5
"Yesterday" And Today - The Beatles (66)	5
Living In The Material World - George Harrison (73)	5
Janet Jackson's Rhythm Nation 1814 - Janet Jackson (89)	4
Band On The Run - Paul McCartney And Wings (73)	4
Woodstock - Various Artists (70)	4
New Jersey - Bon Jovi (88)	4
Red Octopus - Jefferson Starship (75)	4
Beach Boys Concert - The Beach Boys (64)	4
Wheels Of Fire - Cream (68)	4

Title – Act (Entry Yr)	#1 Wks
Johnny Cash At San Quentin - Johnny Cash (69)	4
Every Picture Tells A Story - Rod Stewart (71)	4
Third Stage - Boston (86)	4
...But Seriously - Phil Collins (89)	4
Freeze-Frame - The J. Geils Band (81)	4
Giving You The Best That I Got - Anita Baker (88)	4
OU812 - Van Halen (88)	4
Green River - Creedence Clearwater Revival (69)	4
Sticky Fingers - The Rolling Stones (71)	4
Led Zeppelin III - Led Zeppelin (70)	4
Caribou - Elton John (74)	4
Chariots Of Fire (Soundtrack) - Vangelis (81)	4
Mistaken Idenity - Kim Carnes (81)	4
Exile On Main St. - The Rolling Stones (72)	4
Superfly (Soundtrack) - Curtis Mayfield (72)	4
Goats Head Soup - The Rolling Stones (73)	4
Let It Be (Soundtrack) - The Beatles (70)	4
Waiting For The Sun - The Doors (68)	4
461 Ocean Boulevard - Eric Clapton (74)	4
Black And Blue - The Rolling Stones (76)	4
The River - Bruce Springsteen (80)	4
Planet Waves - Bob Dylan with The Band (74)	4
Can't Slow Down - Lionel Richie (83)	3
Jesus Christ Superstar - Various Artists (70)	3
Like A Virgin - Madonna (84)	3
John Denver's Greatest Hits - John Denver (73)	3
Paradise Theater - Styx (81)	3
Make It Big - Wham! (84)	3
Goldfinger - Instrumental (64)	3
That's The Way Of The World (Soundtrack) - Earth, Wind & Fire (75)	3
Guilty - Barbra Streisand (80)	3
The Broadway Album - Barbra Streisand (85)	3
Out Of Our Heads - The Rolling Stones (65)	3
Music - Carole King (71)	3
Blondes Have More Fun - Rod Stewart (78)	3
Around The World In A Day - Prince And The Revolution (85)	3
5150 - Van Halen (86)	3
McCartney - Paul McCartney (70)	3
Gratitude - Earth, Wind & Fire (75)	3
Catch Bull At Four - Cat Stevens (72)	3
Long Distance Voyager - The Moody Blues (81)	3
For Those About To Rock (We Salute You) - AC/DC (81)	3
Barbra Streisand's Greatest Hits, Volume 2 - Barbra Streisand (78)	3
Nick Of Time - Bonnie Raitt (89)	3
Tug Of War - Paul McCartney (82)	3
Red Rose Speedway - Paul McCartney And Wings (73)	3
Dueling Banjos - Eric Weissberg & Steve Mandell (73)	3
Rock Of The Westies - Elton John (75)	3
We Are The World - USA For Africa (85)	3
The Sound Of Music - Musical (65)	2

Title – Act (Entry Yr)	#1 Wks
Hangin' Tough - New Kids On The Block (88)	2
Reckless - Bryan Adams (84)	2
Control - Janet Jackson (86)	2
Flashdance - Various Artists (83)	2
Some Girls - The Rolling Stones (78)	2
Beverly Hills Cop - Various Artists (85)	2
Tiffany - Tiffany (87)	2
Kenny Rogers' Greatest Hits - Kenny Rogers (80)	2
Dancing On The Ceiling - Lionel Richie (86)	2
Beat Of The Brass - Herb Alpert & The Tijuana Brass (68)	2
Harvest - Neil Young (72)	2
The World Is A Ghetto - War (72)	2
Windsong - John Denver (75)	2
Promise - Sade (85)	2
The Supremes A' Go-Go - The Supremes (66)	2
Breezin' - George Benson (76)	2
Blind Faith - Blind Faith (69)	2
Houses Of The Holy - Led Zeppelin (73)	2
Lady Sings The Blues (Soundtrack) - Diana Ross (72)	2
Blood, Sweat & Tears 3 - Blood, Sweat & Tears (70)	2
Chicago VIII - Chicago (75)	2
Don't Look Back - Boston (78)	2
La Bamba (Soundtrack) - Los Lobos (87)	2
Dr. Feelgood - Mötley Crüe (89)	2
Ode To Billie Joe - Bobbie Gentry (67)	2
There's A Riot Goin' On - Sly & The Family Stone (71)	2
Thick As A Brick - Jethro Tull (72)	2
Electric Ladyland - The Jimi Hendrix Experience (68)	2
Don't Shoot Me I'm Only The Piano Player - Elton John (73)	2
Blood On The Tracks - Bob Dylan (75)	2
Wish You Were Here - Pink Floyd (75)	2
Presence - Led Zeppelin (76)	2
Sundown - Gordon Lightfoot (74)	2
Fullfillingness First Finale - Stevie Wonder (74)	2
The Way We Were - Barbra Streisand (74)	2
Doctor Zhivago - Instrumental (66)	1
Sports - Huey Lewis & The News (83)	1
Escape - Journey (81)	1
Fleetwood Mac - Fleetwood Mac (75)	1
Heart - Heart (85)	1
Hello, Dolly! - Original Cast (64)	1
The Dark Side Of The Moon - Pink Floyd (73)	1
Bella Donna - Stevie Nicks (81)	1
Fore! - Huey Lewis & The News (86)	1
Time Peace/The Rascals' Greatest Hits - The Rascals (68)	1
Deja Vu - Crosby, Stills, Nash & Young (70)	1
Back Home Again - John Denver (74)	1
Still Crazy After All These Years - Paul Simon (75)	1
Headquarters - The Monkees (67)	1
If You Can Believe Your Eyes And Ears - The Mamas & The Papas (66)	1

Title – Act (Entry Yr)	#1 Wks
Storm Front - Billy Joel (89)	1
On The Radio: Greatest Hits: Volumes I & II - Donna Summer (79)	1
Tracy Chapman - Tracy Chapman (88)	1
Metal Health - Quiet Riot (83)	1
Shaft (Soundtrack) - Isaac Hayes (71)	1
Not Fragile - Bachman-Turner Overdrive (74)	1
Centerfield - John Fogerty (85)	1
Strangers In The Night - Frank Sinatra (66)	1
Chicago VII - Chicago (74)	1
Precious Time - Pat Benatar (81)	1
Roll With It - Steve Winwood (88)	1
4 Way Street - Crosby, Stills, Nash & Young (71)	1
Briefcase Full Of Blues - Blues Brothers (78)	1
Bee Gees Greatest - Bee Gees (79)	1
Hold Out - Jackson Browne (80)	1
Roustabout (Soundtrack) - Elvis Presley (64)	1
Sounds Like... - Herb Alpert & The Tijuana Brass (67)	1
Imagine - John Lennon/Plastic Ono Band (71)	1
Have You Never Been Mellow - Olivia Newton-John (75)	1
Live And More - Donna Summer (78)	1
Welcome To The Real World - Mr. Mister (85)	1
Winner In You - Patti LaBelle (86)	1
Loc-ed After Dark - Tone-Loc (89)	1
Repeat Offender - Richard Marx (89)	1
Heart Like A Wheel - Linda Ronstadt (74)	1
The Heat Is On - The Isley Brothers (75)	1
Barry Manilow Live - Barry Manilow (77)	1
TCB (Soundtrack) - Diana Ross & The Supremes And The Temptations (68)	1
The Beatles 1967-1970 - The Beatles (73)	1
Wings Over America - Paul McCartney And Wings (76)	1
Fire - Ohio Players (74)	1
Tunnel Of Love - Bruce Springsteen (87)	1
Billion Dollar Babies - Alice Cooper (73)	1
The Singles 1969-1973 - Carpenters (73)	1
AWB - Average White Band (74)	1
Between The Lines - Janis Ian (75)	1
Living In The U.S.A. - Linda Ronstadt (78)	1
Bad Company - Bad Company (74)	1
City To City - Gerry Rafferty (78)	1
Venus And Mars - Wings (75)	1
Aloha From Hawaii Via Satellite - Elvis Presley (73)	1
Can't Get Enough - Barry White (74)	1
It's Only Rock 'N Roll - The Rolling Stones (74)	1
A Passion Play - Jethro Tull (73)	1
If You Love Me Let Me Know - Olivia Newton-John (74)	1
Endless Summer - The Beach Boys (74)	1
Walls And Bridges - John Lennon (74)	1
So Far - Crosby, Stills, Nash & Young (74)	1
Wrap Around Joy - Carole King (74)	1

50 Highest Charting Albums to Miss the Weekly Top 5

Rank.	Title	Act	[Enter]	Peak(Wks)	T10	T40	Tot Wks	Score
59.	CHRISTOPHER CROSS	Christopher Cross	[16Feb80]	6(3)	15	81	116	12682
79.	ELIMINATOR	ZZ Top	[23Apr83]	9(1)	4	82	183	11592
84.	CHICAGO TRANSIT AUTHORITY	Chicago	[17May69]	17(2)	0	42	171	11343
105.	CROSBY, STILLS & NASH	Crosby, Stills & Nash	[28Jun69]	6(3)	17	40	107	10638
118.	LED ZEPPELIN	Led Zeppelin	[15Feb69]	10(1)	1	50	95	10151
126.	GET LUCKY	Loverboy	[14Nov81]	7(2)	14	51	122	9866
128.	BAYOU COUNTRY	Creedence Clearwater Revival	[08Feb69]	7(1)	13	37	88	9860
143.	RAPTURE	Anita Baker	[19Apr86]	11(2)	0	72	157	9452
154.	FIDDLER ON THE ROOF	Original Cast	[31Oct64]	7(2)	3	60	206	9072
156.	BREAK OUT	The Pointer Sisters	[26Nov83]	8(2)	6	65	105	9038
173.	EASY RIDER	Soundtrack	[06Sep69]	6(1)	6	41	72	8708
177.	1999	Prince	[20Nov82]	9(7)	11	57	153	8588
184.	SKID ROW	Skid Row	[11Feb89]	6(1)	11	57	78	8481
186.	THE END OF THE INNOCENCE	Don Henley	[15Jul89]	8(1)	5	58	148	8388
199.	FACE VALUE	Phil Collins	[14Mar81]	7(4)	10	26	164	8163
200.	FEELS SO RIGHT	Alabama	[28Mar81]	16(2)	0	42	161	8135
207.	AQUALUNG	Jethro Tull	[15May71]	7(7)	16	32	76	8099
208.	WONDERFULNESS	Bill Cosby	[28May66]	7(1)	5	54	106	8093
215.	THE GRAND ILLUSION	Styx	[30Jul77]	6(2)	12	37	127	8016
223.	TEA FOR THE TILLERMAN	Cat Stevens	[06Feb71]	8(3)	6	44	79	7879
231.	JOHNNY CASH AT FOLSOM PRISON	Johnny Cash	[15Jun68]	13(2)	0	39	122	7728
234.	THE CARS	The Cars	[01Jul78]	18(2)	0	37	139	7689
237.	FUNNY GIRL (SOUNDTRACK)	Barbra Streisand	[28Sep68]	12(1)	0	31	108	7627
238.	SOUTH OF THE BORDER	Herb Alpert & The Tijuana Brass	[16Jan65]	6(1)	3	52	163	7622
240.	TOYS IN THE ATTIC	Aerosmith	[26Apr75]	11(1)	0	30	128	7586

Rank.	Title	Act	[Enter]	Peak(Wks)	T10	T40	Tot Wks	Score
255.	WHY IS THERE AIR?	Bill Cosby	[28Aug65]	19(1)	0	55	152	7355
258.	THE BEST OF THE ANIMALS	The Animals	[12Feb66]	6(3)	7	51	113	7333
259.	HOT BUTTERED SOUL	Isaac Hayes	[12Jul69]	8(3)	4	36	81	7331
278.	THE CAPTAIN AND ME	The Doobie Brothers	[31Mar73]	7(2)	3	33	102	7061
280.	PIECES OF EIGHT	Styx	[30Sep78]	6(1)	8	28	92	7036
297.	LET IT LOOSE	Gloria Estefan & Miami Sound Machine	[20Jun87]	6(2)	9	48	97	6903
299.	MADONNA	Madonna	[03Sep83]	8(3)	5	36	168	6893
306.	A MAN AND A WOMAN	Soundtrack	[19Nov66]	10(2)	2	44	93	6866
307.	THE DREAM WEAVER	Gary Wright	[23Aug75]	7(3)	8	35	75	6852
313.	STAND!	Sly & The Family Stone	[26Apr69]	13(1)	0	24	102	6820
318.	HERE AT LAST...BEE GEES...LIVE	Bee Gees	[04Jun77]	8(1)	4	31	90	6803
319.	RICHARD MARX	Richard Marx	[20Jun87]	8(2)	4	63	86	6799
321.	WORKING CLASS DOG	Rick Springfield	[14Mar81]	7(2)	5	38	73	6754
327.	SUMMER BREEZE	Seals & Crofts	[02Sep72]	7(3)	5	33	109	6716
328.	SUDDENLY	Billy Ocean	[25Aug84]	9(2)	2	57	86	6704
332.	OUT OF THE BLUE	Debbie Gibson	[05Sep87]	7(2)	13	45	89	6673
351.	POEMS, PRAYERS & PROMISES	John Denver	[17Apr71]	15(5)	0	31	80	6479
353.	VANILLA FUDGE	Vanilla Fudge	[16Sep67]	6(4)	11	39	80	6459
355.	MACHINE HEAD	Deep Purple	[15Apr72]	7(2)	6	30	118	6452
363.	AMERICAN GRAFFITI	Soundtrack	[01Sep73]	10(1)	1	41	60	6407
369.	WAS CAPTURED LIVE AT THE FORUM	Three Dog Night	[29Nov69]	6(7)	11	24	72	6338
380.	VOICES	Daryl Hall & John Oates	[16Aug80]	17(1)	0	35	100	6297
383.	THE DUDE	Quincy Jones	[04Apr81]	10(1)	1	26	80	6231
385.	THE LONESOME JUBILEE	John Mellencamp	[19Sep87]	6(7)	27	37	53	6213
386.	DUOTONES	Kenny G	[06Sep86]	6(2)	10	41	102	6209

50 Lowest Scoring Number 1s

Rank.	Title	Act	[Enter]	Peak(Wks)	T10	T40	Tot Wks	Score
1322.	**WE ARE THE WORLD**	USA For Africa	[20Apr85]	1(3)	7	11	22	2778
1071.	**SO FAR**	Crosby, Stills, Nash & Young	[07Sep74]	1(1)	5	12	27	3250
1049.	**A PASSION PLAY**	Jethro Tull	[21Jul73]	1(1)	6	14	32	3303
1038.	**ROUSTABOUT (SOUNDTRACK)**	Elvis Presley	[14Nov64]	1(1)	12	20	27	3337
974.	**WRAP AROUND JOY**	Carole King	[28Sep74]	1(1)	5	13	29	3499
924.	**WALLS AND BRIDGES**	John Lennon	[12Oct74]	1(1)	6	11	35	3671
921.	**THE WAY WE WERE**	Barbra Streisand	[16Feb74]	1(2)	6	12	31	3692
901.	**ODE TO BILLIE JOE**	Bobbie Gentry	[16Sep67]	1(2)	10	18	30	3754
885.	**DUELING BANJOS**	Eric Weissberg & Steve Mandell	[27Jan73]	1(3)	9	14	25	3805
872.	**PLANET WAVES**	Bob Dylan with The Band	[09Feb74]	1(4)	7	12	21	3836
851.	**BRUCE SPRINGSTEEN & THE E STREET BAND LIVE 1975-1985**	Bruce Springsteen	[29Nov86]	1(7)	11	15	26	3897
844.	**IT'S ONLY ROCK 'N ROLL**	The Rolling Stones	[02Nov74]	1(1)	7	11	20	3928
837.	**ROCK OF THE WESTIES**	Elton John	[08Nov75]	1(3)	7	9	26	3949
836.	**TUG OF WAR**	Paul McCartney	[15May82]	1(3)	9	18	29	3951
831.	**CAN'T GET ENOUGH**	Barry White	[07Sep74]	1(1)	7	13	38	3956
819.	**WINNER IN YOU**	Patti LaBelle	[24May86]	1(1)	12	19	30	4001
790.	**"YESTERDAY" AND TODAY**	The Beatles	[09Jul66]	1(5)	9	15	31	4104
768.	**LIVING IN THE MATERIAL WORLD**	George Harrison	[16Jun73]	1(5)	7	15	26	4174
759.	**PRESENCE**	Led Zeppelin	[24Apr76]	1(2)	9	13	30	4218
743.	**LA BAMBA (SOUNDTRACK)**	Los Lobos	[25Jul87]	1(2)	11	19	44	4269
713.	**RED ROSE SPEEDWAY**	Paul McCartney And Wings	[12May73]	1(3)	9	16	31	4375
712.	**FOR THOSE ABOUT TO ROCK (WE SALUTE YOU)**	AC/DC	[12Dec81]	1(3)	12	16	30	4377
711.	**ALOHA FROM HAWAII VIA SATELLITE**	Elvis Presley	[24Feb73]	1(1)	7	19	52	4378
705.	**BEE GEES GREATEST**	Bee Gees	[17Nov79]	1(1)	13	17	32	4406
666.	**BALLADS OF THE GREEN BERETS**	SSgt Barry Sadler	[26Feb66]	1(5)	10	20	32	4543
653.	**BATMAN (SOUNDTRACK)**	Prince	[08Jul89]	1(6)	10	17	34	4618
639.	**THE SINGLES 1969-1973**	Carpenters	[01Dec73]	1(1)	9	17	49	4680
632.	**461 OCEAN BOULEVARD**	Eric Clapton	[20Jul74]	1(4)	9	14	25	4705
629.	**BLACK AND BLUE**	The Rolling Stones	[08May76]	1(4)	9	14	24	4733
625.	**BLOOD ON THE TRACKS**	Bob Dylan	[08Feb75]	1(2)	9	14	24	4750
621.	**BRIEFCASE FULL OF BLUES**	Blues Brothers	[23Dec78]	1(1)	13	16	29	4763
614.	**LIVING IN THE U.S.A.**	Linda Ronstadt	[07Oct78]	1(1)	9	17	32	4804
598.	**BEATLES VI**	The Beatles	[26Jun65]	1(6)	13	21	41	4898
597.	**BILLION DOLLAR BABIES**	Alice Cooper	[17Mar73]	1(1)	10	23	50	4898
573.	**THERE'S A RIOT GOIN' ON**	Sly & The Family Stone	[13Nov71]	1(2)	10	18	31	5000
572.	**FULLFILLINGNESS FIRST FINALE**	Stevie Wonder	[10Aug74]	1(2)	7	11	65	5002
563.	**CHICAGO VIII**	Chicago	[12Apr75]	1(2)	11	15	29	5049
561.	**IF YOU LOVE ME LET ME KNOW**	Olivia Newton-John	[08Jun74]	1(1)	6	19	61	5055
560.	**LOC-ED AFTER DARK**	Tone-Loc	[18Feb89]	1(1)	12	23	42	5062
558.	**BAD COMPANY**	Bad Company	[27Jul74]	1(1)	8	15	64	5083
552.	**AWB**	Average White Band	[21Sep74]	1(1)	9	17	43	5109
551.	**CITY TO CITY**	Gerry Rafferty	[06May78]	1(1)	8	23	49	5110
543.	**WISH YOU WERE HERE**	Pink Floyd	[27Sep75]	1(2)	9	15	39	5152
539.	**THE BEATLES' SECOND ALBUM**	The Beatles	[25Apr64]	1(5)	15	26	55	5191
532.	**BARBRA STREISAND'S GREATEST HITS, VOLUME 2**	Barbra Streisand	[02Dec78]	1(3)	11	17	46	5226
528.	**WINGS OVER AMERICA**	Paul McCartney And Wings	[25Dec76]	1(1)	11	18	86	5248
526.	**GOATS HEAD SOUP**	The Rolling Stones	[29Sep73]	1(4)	11	19	37	5266
519.	**FIRE**	Ohio Players	[23Nov74]	1(1)	10	19	29	5305
513.	**SUNDOWN**	Gordon Lightfoot	[02Feb74]	1(2)	8	23	42	5326
508.	**MY SON, THE NUT**	Allan Sherman	[17Aug63]	1(8)	12	24	32	5346

The Albums: Lifecycle Graphs

The Lifecycle Graphs of the Top 25 Albums show week-to-week chart ranks from the first entry of the album to its final exit. Additionally, the week-to-week rankings of the singles derived from these albums are superimposed.

In many cases, it's clear that successful singles drive album success—the album rank tends to fall off as the charted singles stop. In some cases, the album either returns to the chart or gets a boost from a later album by the same act. To avoid cluttering the graph I did not include the full lifecycle of subsequent albums, however the peak date for each is marked with a dashed line, and the peak rank is in parentheses.

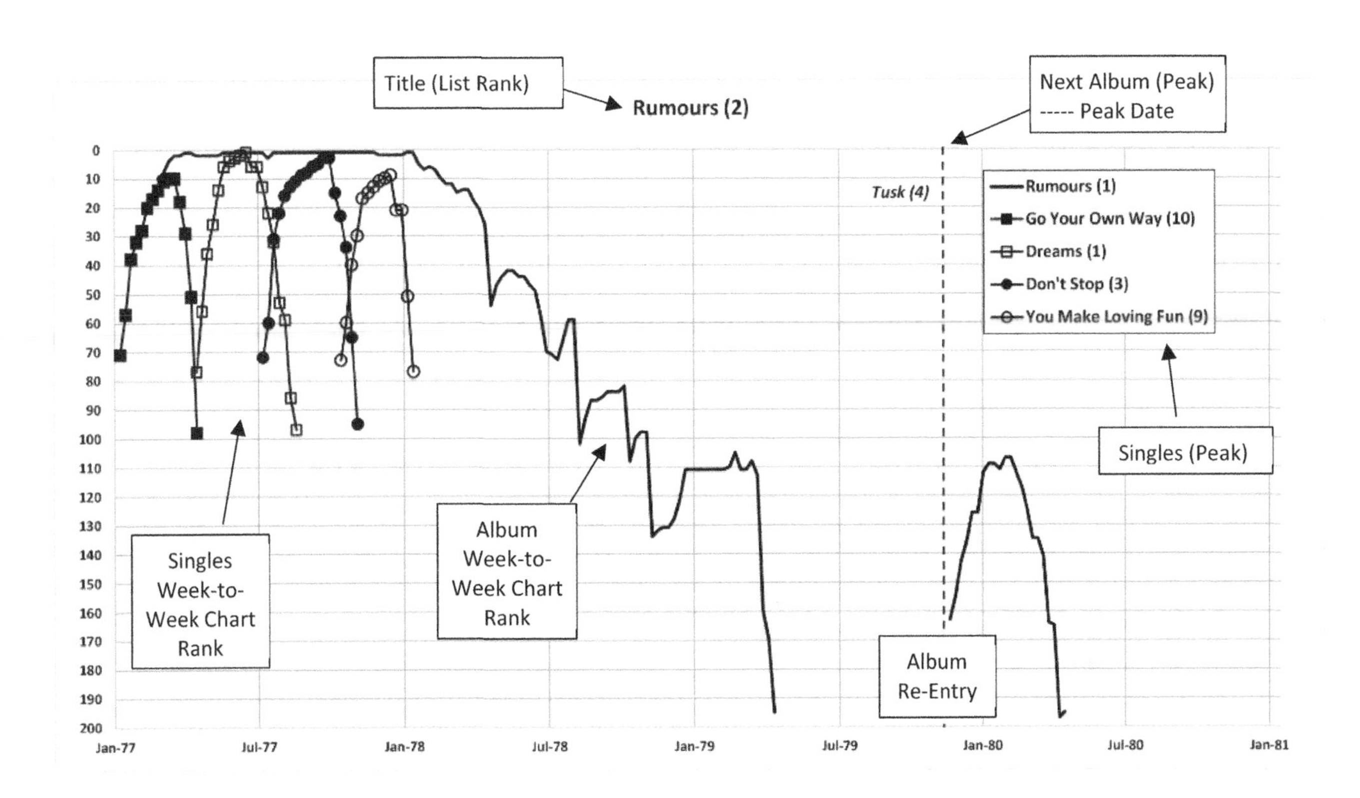

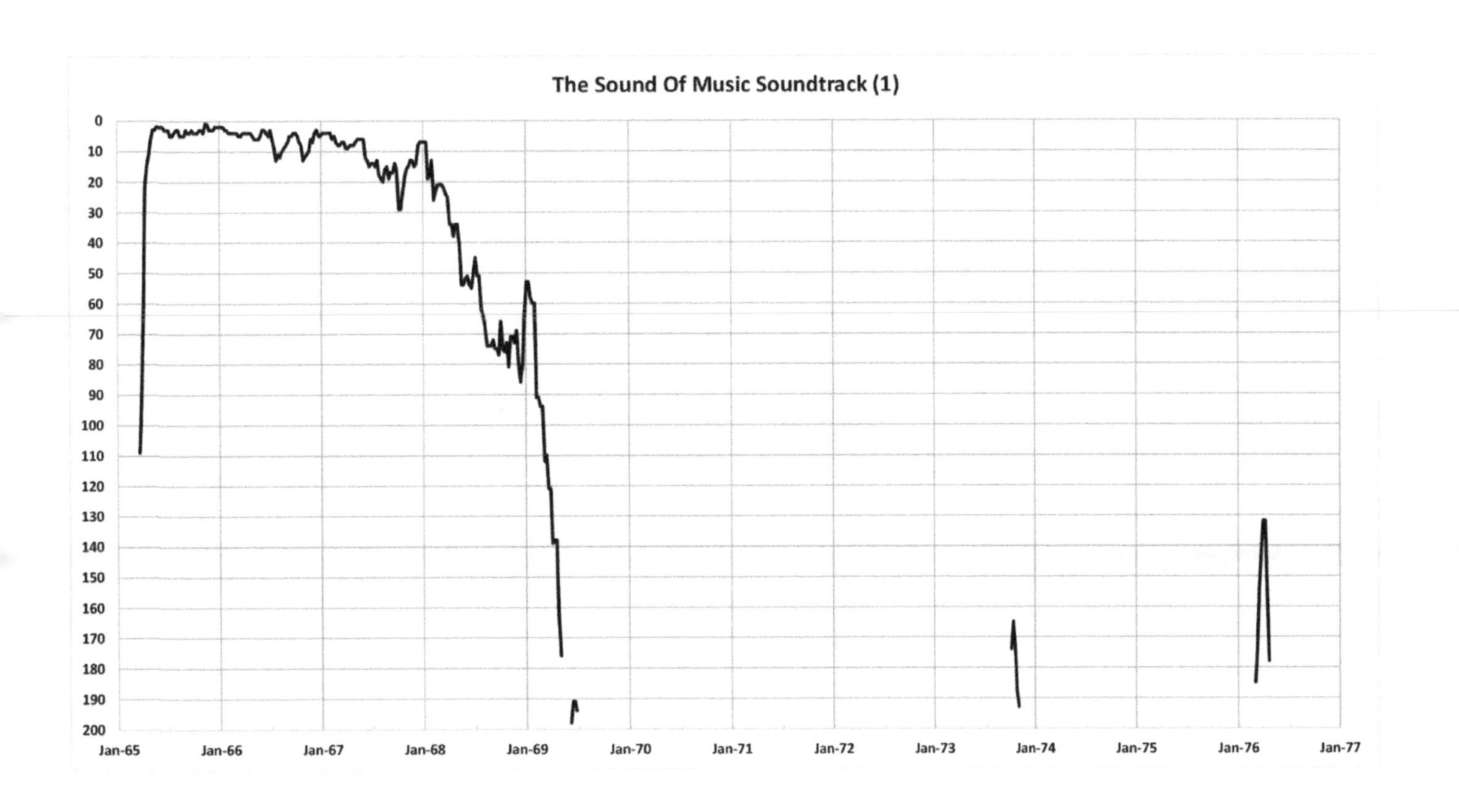
The Sound Of Music Soundtrack (1)
0
10
20
30
40
50
60
70
80
90
100
110
120
130
140
150
160
170
180
190
200
Jan-65
Jan-66
Jan-67
Jan-68
Jan-69
Jan-70
Jan-71
Jan-72
Jan-73
Jan-74
Jan-75
Jan-76
Jan-77

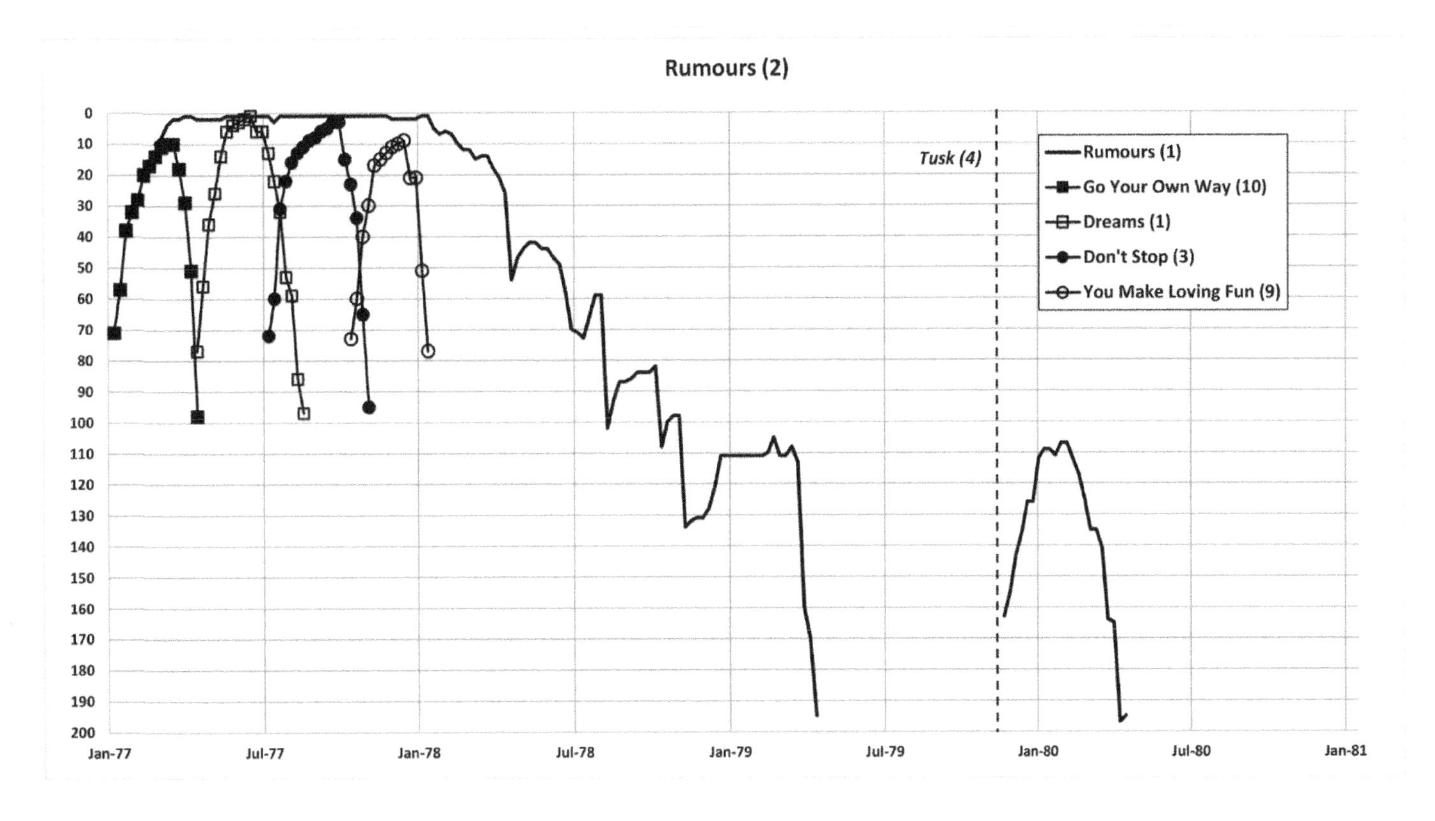
Rumours (2)
Tusk (4)
Rumours (1)
Go Your Own Way (10)
Dreams (1)
Don't Stop (3)
You Make Loving Fun (9)
0
10
20
30
40
50
60
70
80
90
100
110
120
130
140
150
160
170
180
190
200
Jan-77
Jul-77
Jan-78
Jul-78
Jan-79
Jul-79
Jan-80
Jul-80
Jan-81

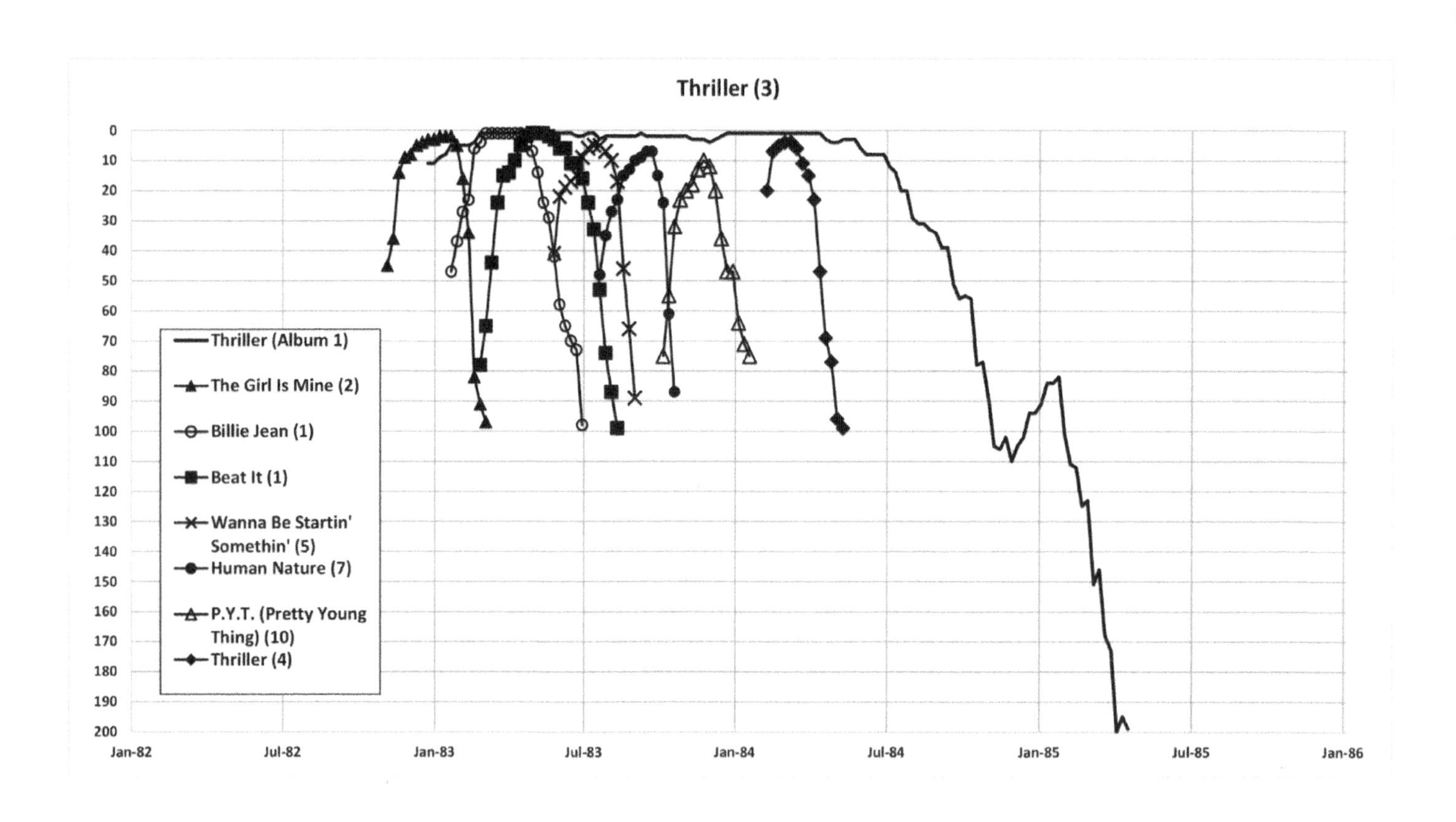
Thriller (3)
Thriller (Album 1)
The Girl Is Mine (2)
Billie Jean (1)
Beat It (1)
Wanna Be Startin' Somethin' (5)
Human Nature (7)
P.Y.T. (Pretty Young Thing) (10)
Thriller (4)
0
10
20
30
40
50
60
70
80
90
100
110
120
130
140
150
160
170
180
190
200
Jan-82
Jul-82
Jan-83
Jul-83
Jan-84
Jul-84
Jan-85
Jul-85
Jan-86

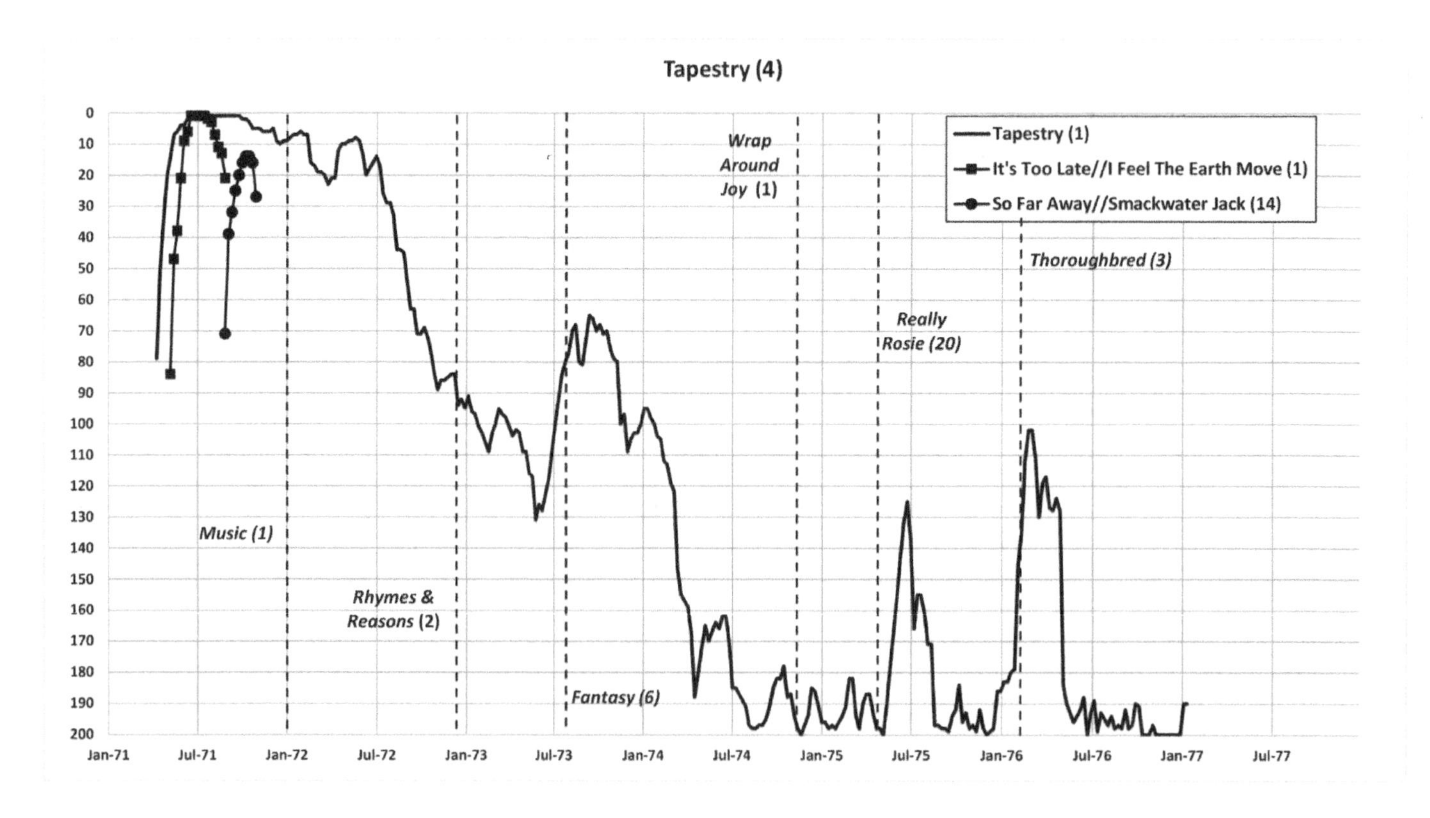
Tapestry (4)
Tapestry (1)
It's Too Late//I Feel The Earth Move (1)
So Far Away//Smackwater Jack (14)
Music (1)
Rhymes & Reasons (2)
Fantasy (6)
Wrap Around Joy (1)
Really Rosie (20)
Thoroughbred (3)
0
10
20
30
40
50
60
70
80
90
100
110
120
130
140
150
160
170
180
190
200
Jan-71
Jul-71
Jan-72
Jul-72
Jan-73
Jul-73
Jan-74
Jul-74
Jan-75
Jul-75
Jan-76
Jul-76
Jan-77
Jul-77

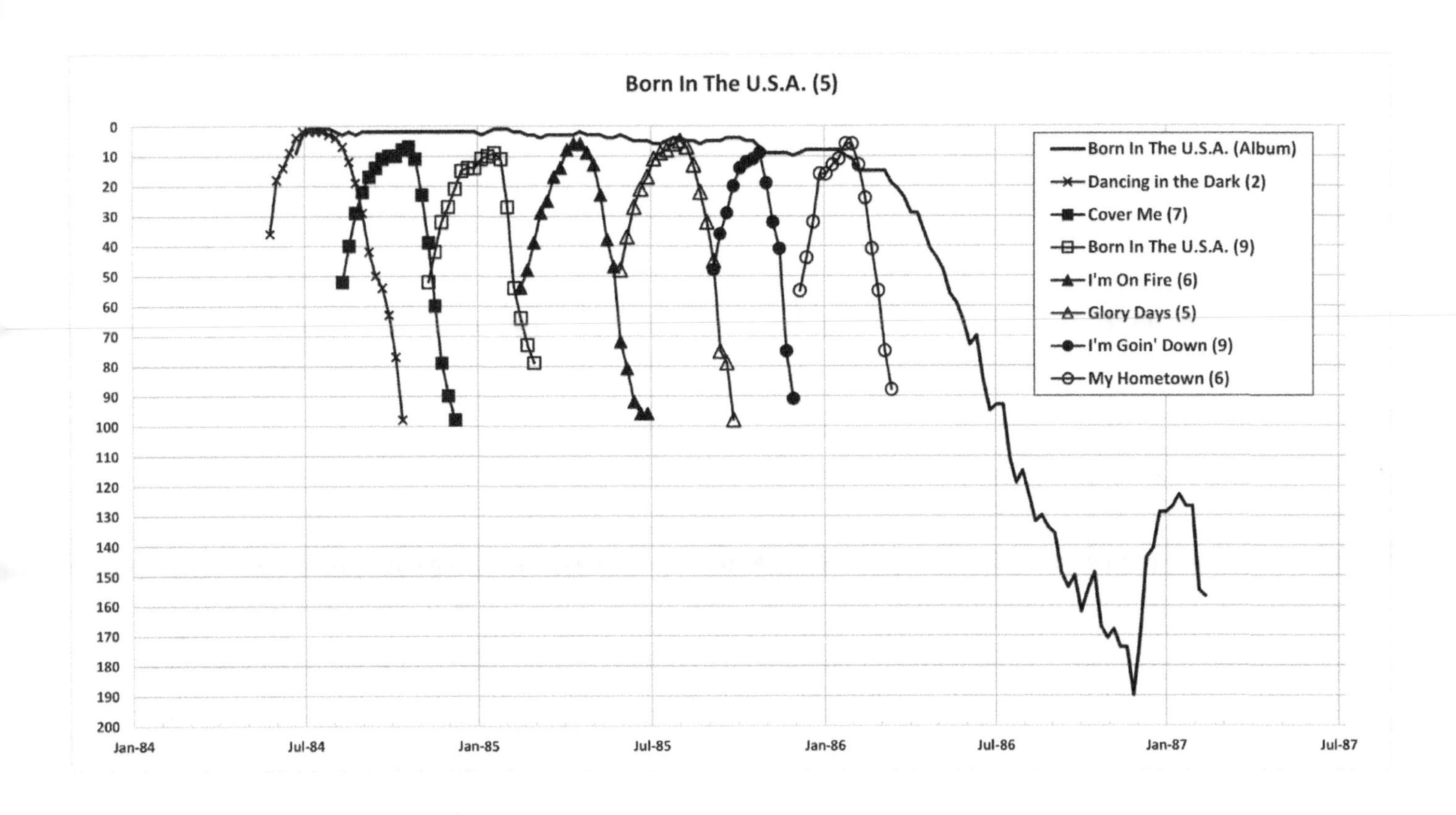
Born In The U.S.A. (5)
Born In The U.S.A. (Album)
Dancing in the Dark (2)
Cover Me (7)
Born In The U.S.A. (9)
I'm On Fire (6)
Glory Days (5)
I'm Goin' Down (9)
My Hometown (6)
0
10
20
30
40
50
60
70
80
90
100
110
120
130
140
150
160
170
180
190
200
Jan-84
Jul-84
Jan-85
Jul-85
Jan-86
Jul-86
Jan-87
Jul-87

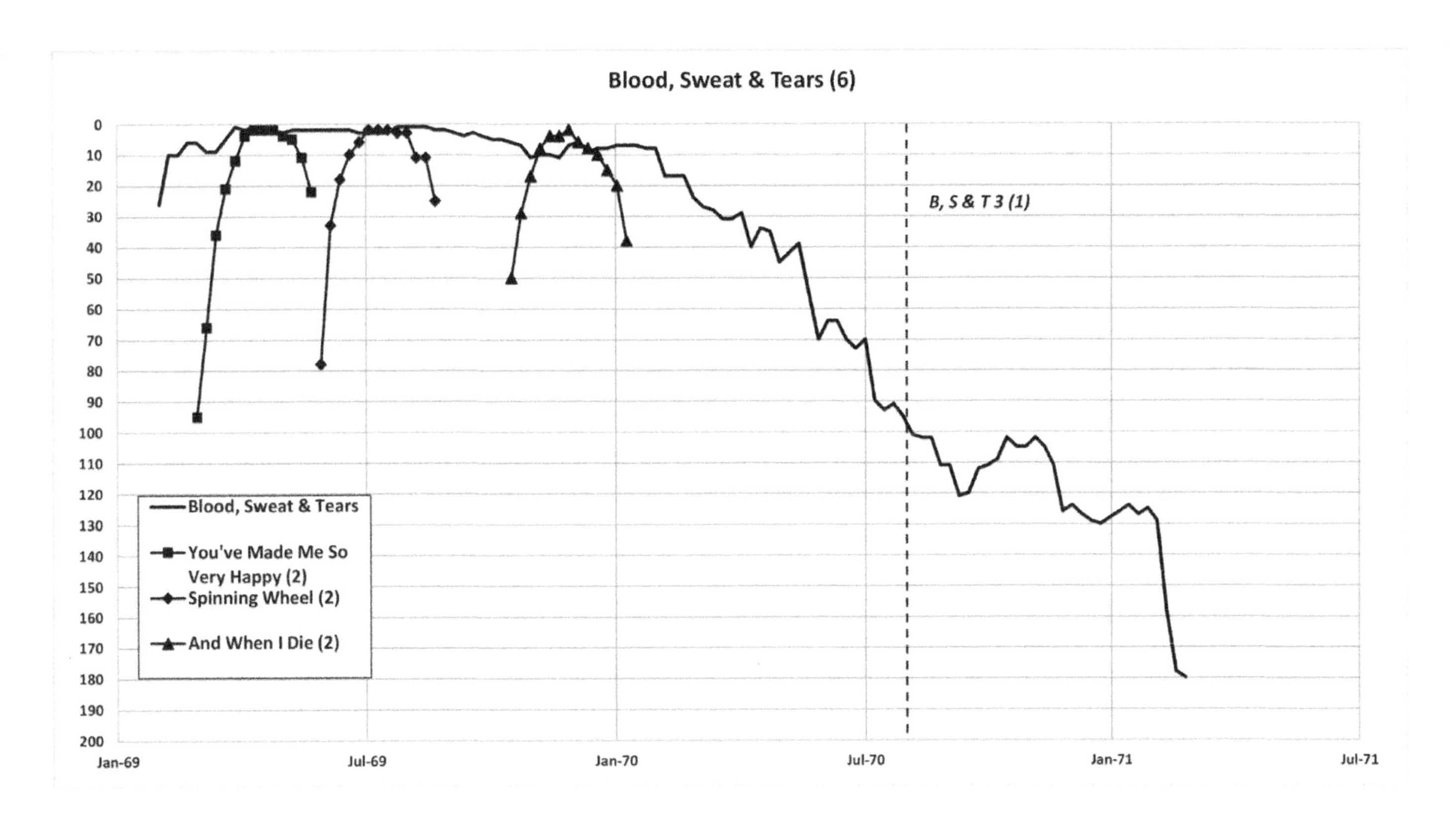
Blood, Sweat & Tears (6)
B, S & T 3 (1)
Blood, Sweat & Tears
You've Made Me So Very Happy (2)
Spinning Wheel (2)
And When I Die (2)
0
10
20
30
40
50
60
70
80
90
100
110
120
130
140
150
160
170
180
190
200
Jan-69
Jul-69
Jan-70
Jul-70
Jan-71
Jul-71

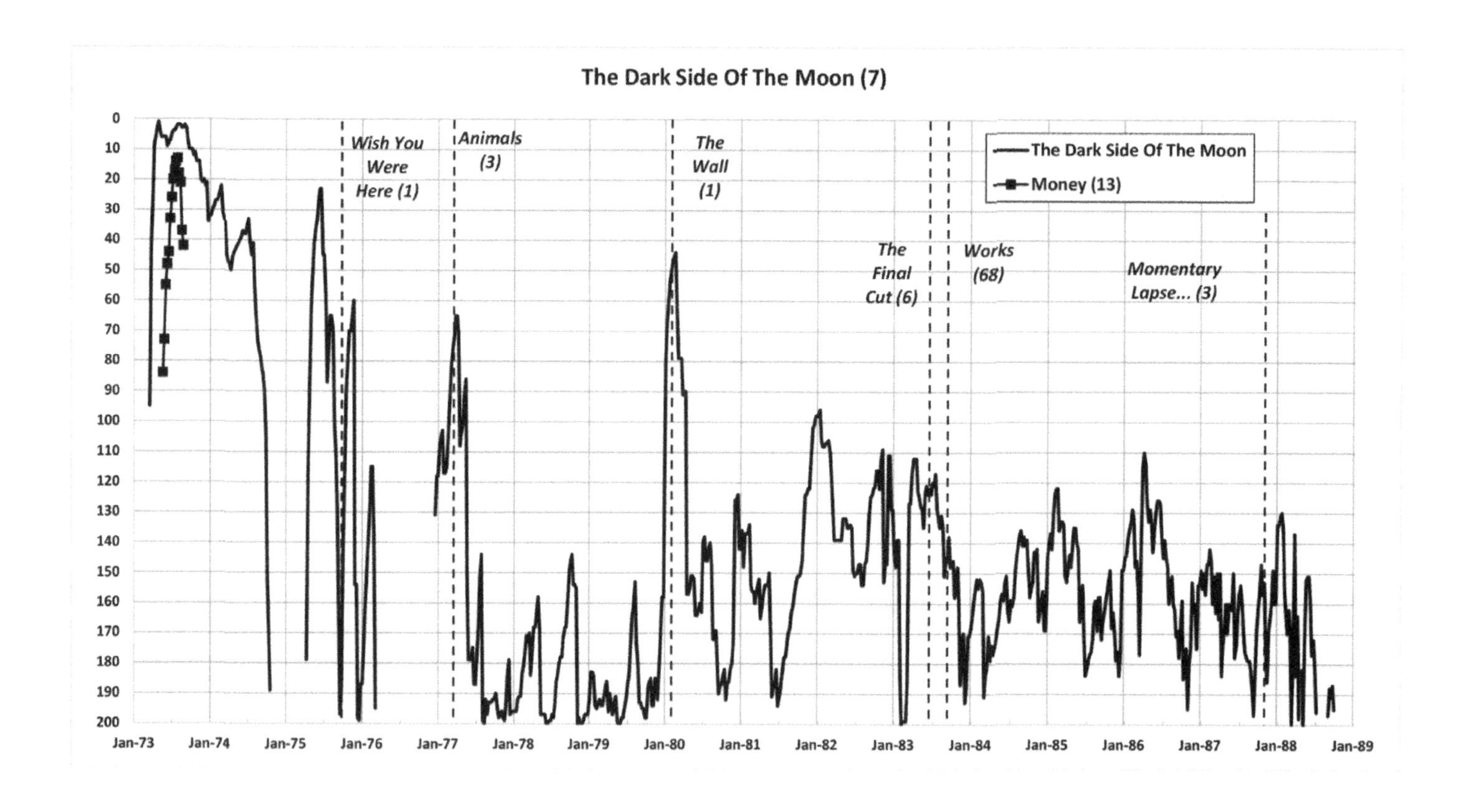
The Dark Side Of The Moon (7)
Wish You Were Here (1)
Animals (3)
The Wall (1)
The Final Cut (6)
Works (68)
Momentary Lapse... (3)
The Dark Side Of The Moon
Money (13)
Jan-73
Jan-74
Jan-75
Jan-76
Jan-77
Jan-78
Jan-79
Jan-80
Jan-81
Jan-82
Jan-83
Jan-84
Jan-85
Jan-86
Jan-87
Jan-88
Jan-89

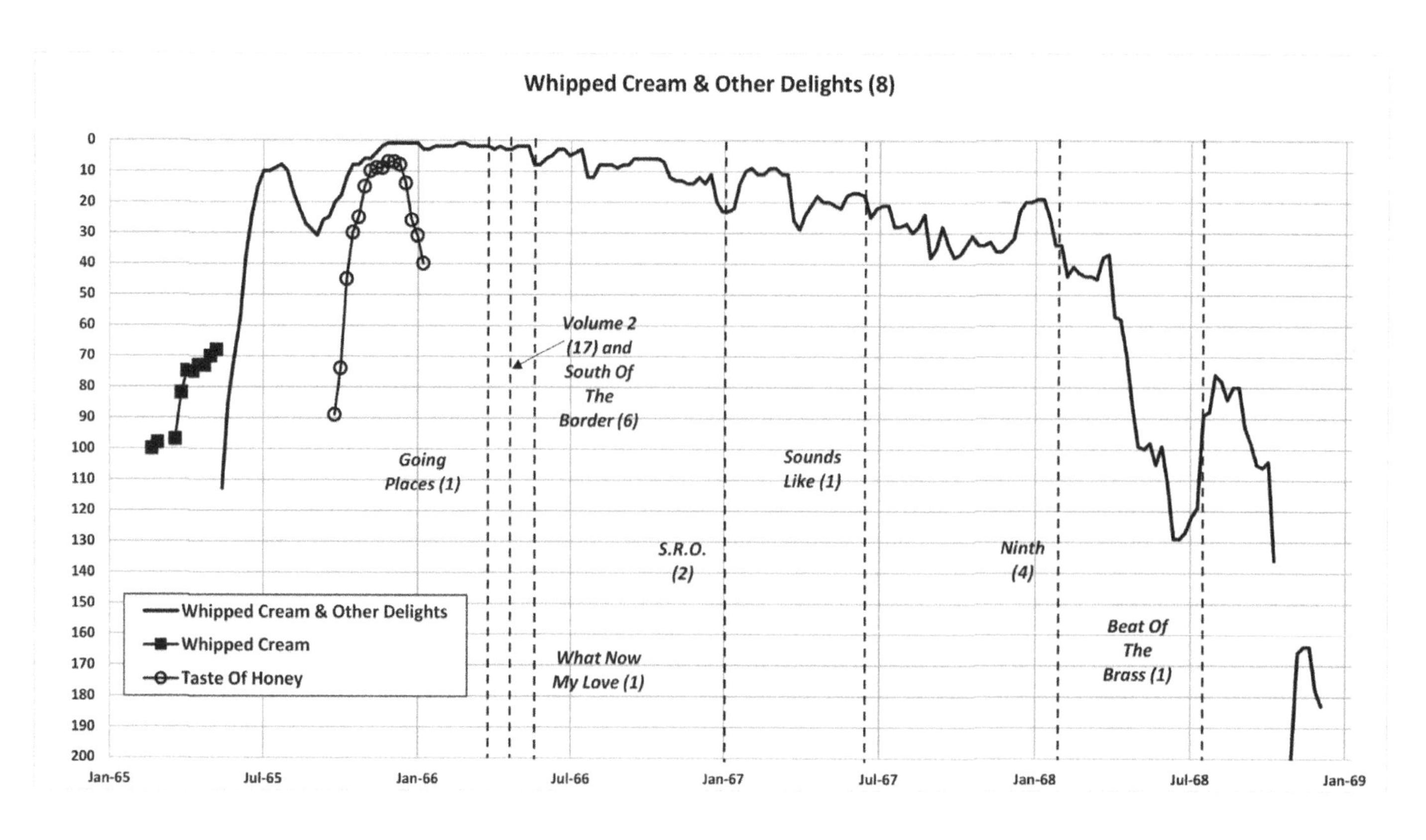
Whipped Cream & Other Delights (8)
Volume 2 (17) and South Of The Border (6)
Going Places (1)
Sounds Like (1)
S.R.O. (2)
Ninth (4)
Beat Of The Brass (1)
What Now My Love (1)
Whipped Cream & Other Delights
Whipped Cream
Taste Of Honey
Jan-65
Jul-65
Jan-66
Jul-66
Jan-67
Jul-67
Jan-68
Jul-68
Jan-69

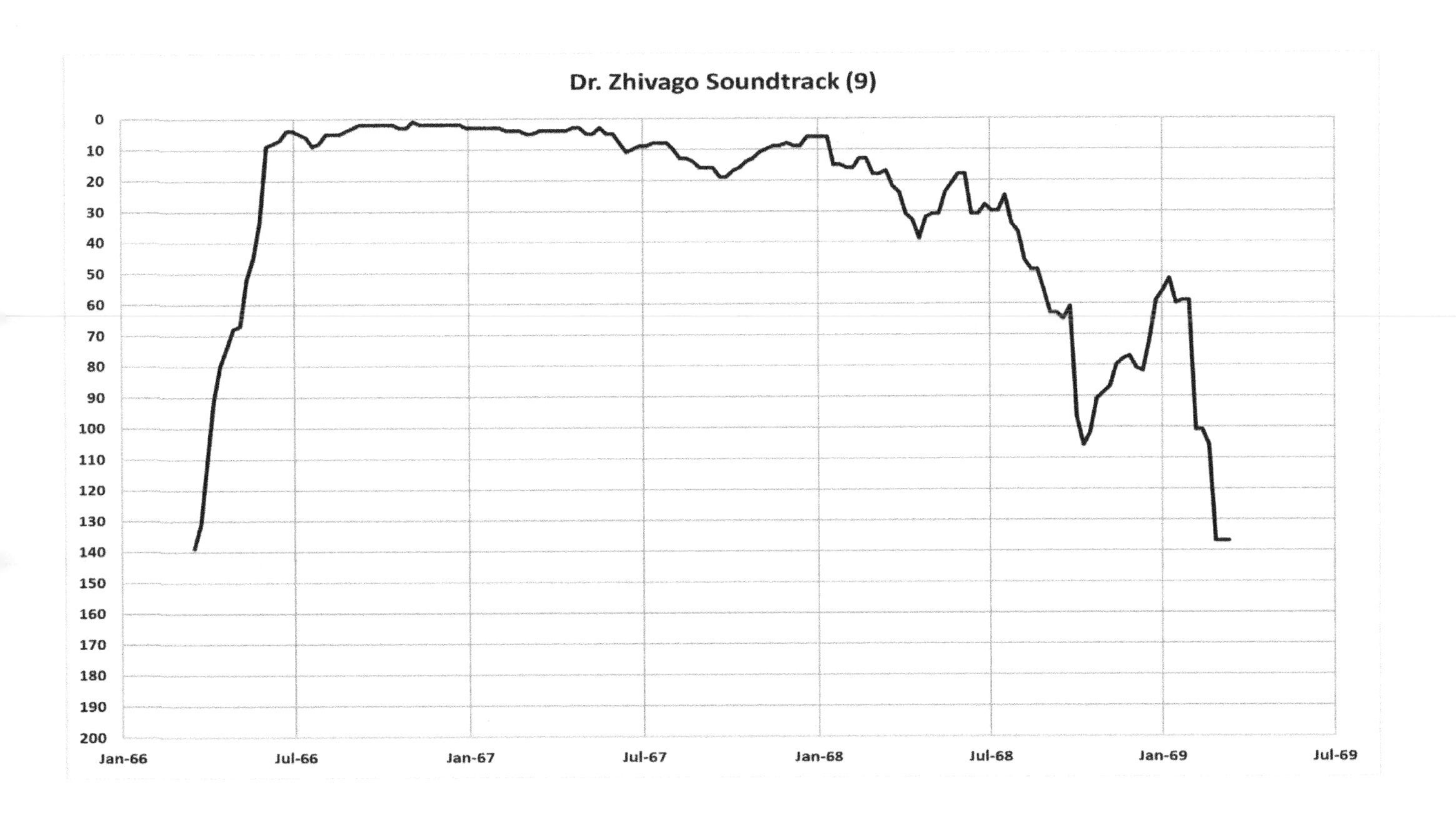
Dr. Zhivago Soundtrack (9)
0
10
20
30
40
50
60
70
80
90
100
110
120
130
140
150
160
170
180
190
200
Jan-66
Jul-66
Jan-67
Jul-67
Jan-68
Jul-68
Jan-69
Jul-69

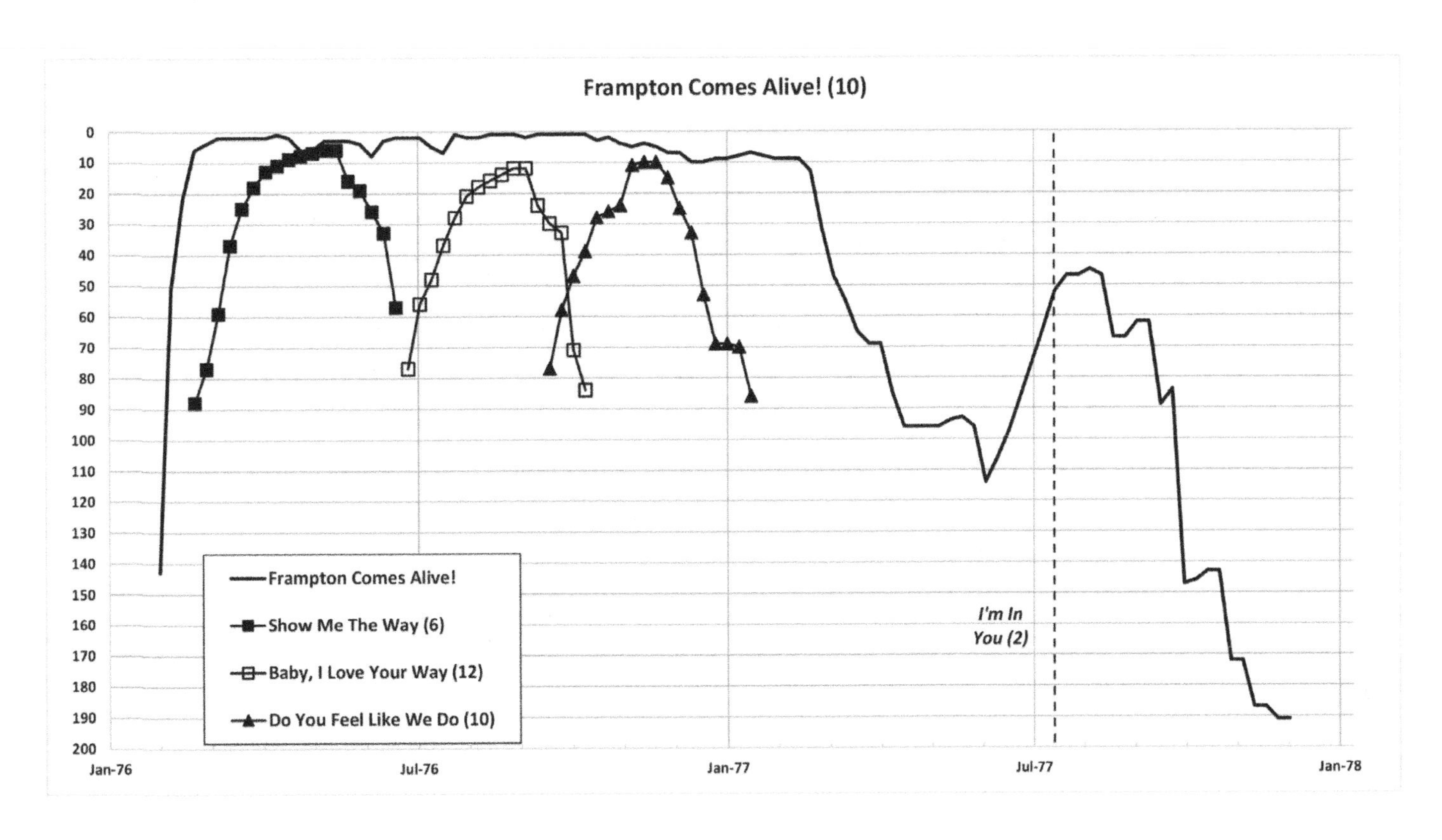
Frampton Comes Alive! (10)
0
10
20
30
40
50
60
70
80
90
100
110
120
130
140
150
160
170
180
190
200
Frampton Comes Alive!
Show Me The Way (6)
Baby, I Love Your Way (12)
Do You Feel Like We Do (10)
I'm In
You (2)
Jan-76
Jul-76
Jan-77
Jul-77
Jan-78

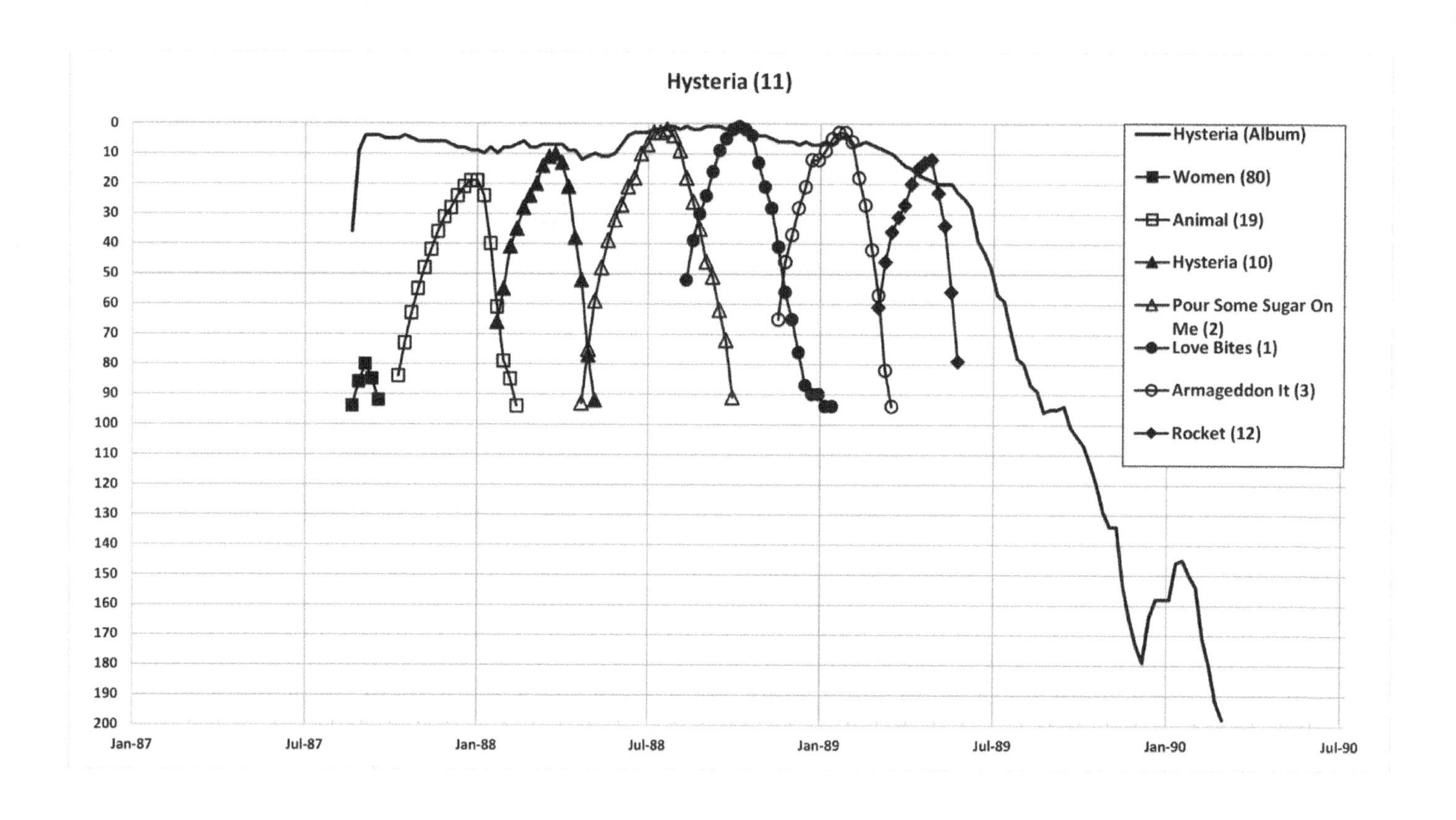
Hysteria (11)
Hysteria (Album)
Women (80)
Animal (19)
Hysteria (10)
Pour Some Sugar On Me (2)
Love Bites (1)
Armageddon It (3)
Rocket (12)
0
10
20
30
40
50
60
70
80
90
100
110
120
130
140
150
160
170
180
190
200
Jan-87
Jul-87
Jan-88
Jul-88
Jan-89
Jul-89
Jan-90
Jul-90

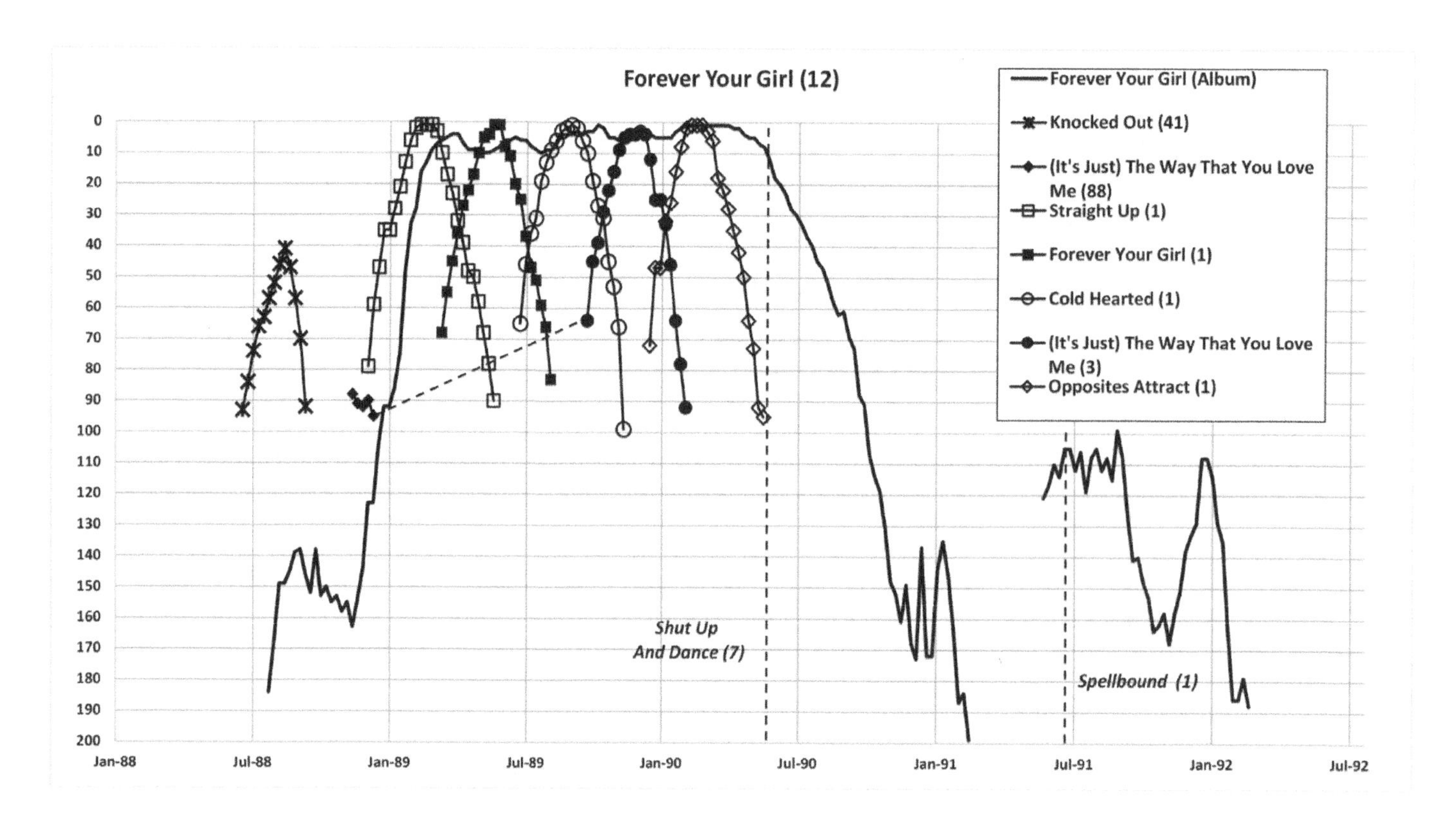
Forever Your Girl (12)
Forever Your Girl (Album)
Knocked Out (41)
(It's Just) The Way That You Love Me (88)
Straight Up (1)
Forever Your Girl (1)
Cold Hearted (1)
(It's Just) The Way That You Love Me (3)
Opposites Attract (1)
Shut Up
And Dance (7)
Spellbound (1)
0
10
20
30
40
50
60
70
80
90
100
110
120
130
140
150
160
170
180
190
200
Jan-88
Jul-88
Jan-89
Jul-89
Jan-90
Jul-90
Jan-91
Jul-91
Jan-92
Jul-92

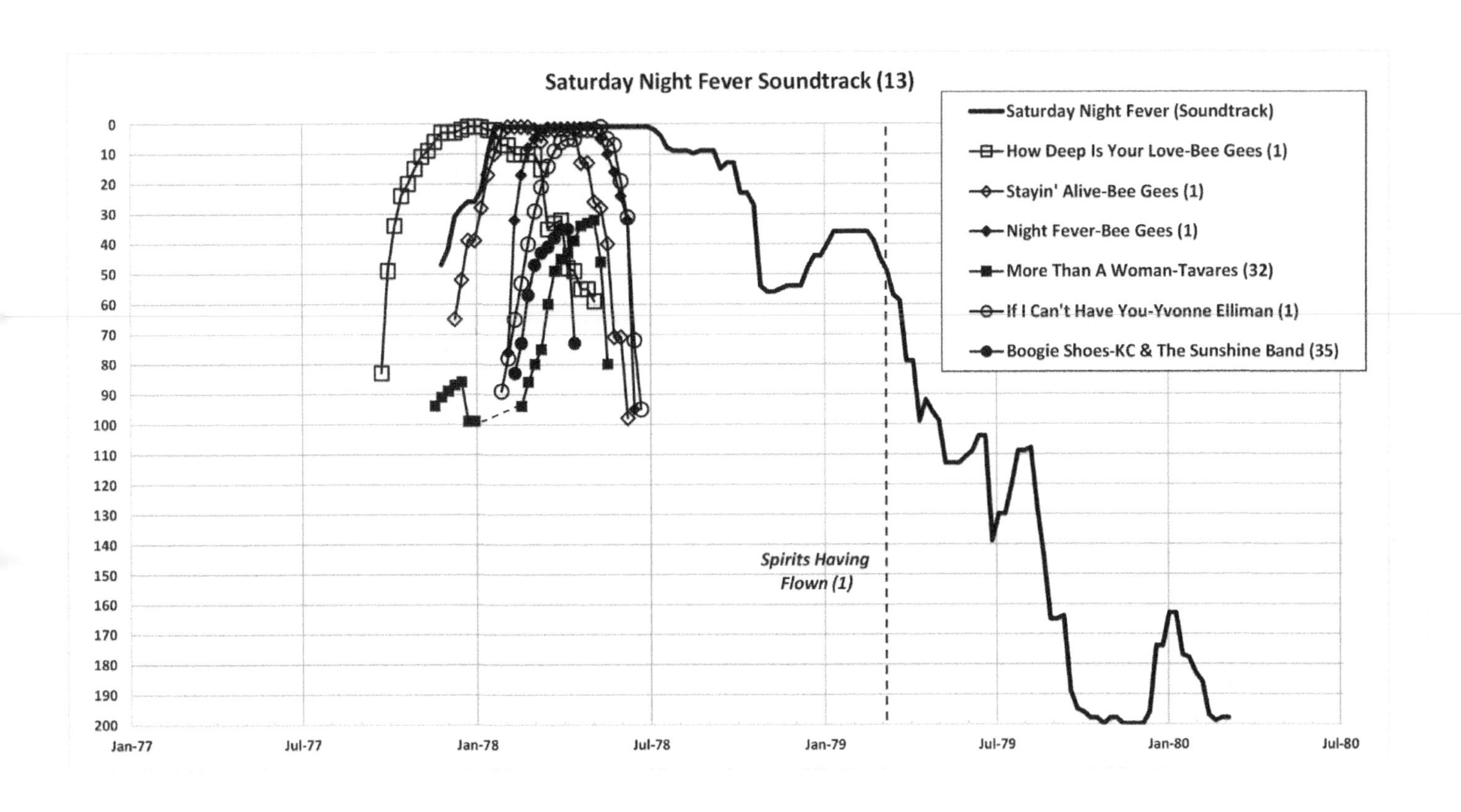
Saturday Night Fever Soundtrack (13)
Saturday Night Fever (Soundtrack)
How Deep Is Your Love-Bee Gees (1)
Stayin' Alive-Bee Gees (1)
Night Fever-Bee Gees (1)
More Than A Woman-Tavares (32)
If I Can't Have You-Yvonne Elliman (1)
Boogie Shoes-KC & The Sunshine Band (35)
Spirits Having Flown (1)
0 10 20 30 40 50 60 70 80 90 100 110 120 130 140 150 160 170 180 190 200
Jan-77 Jul-77 Jan-78 Jul-78 Jan-79 Jul-79 Jan-80 Jul-80

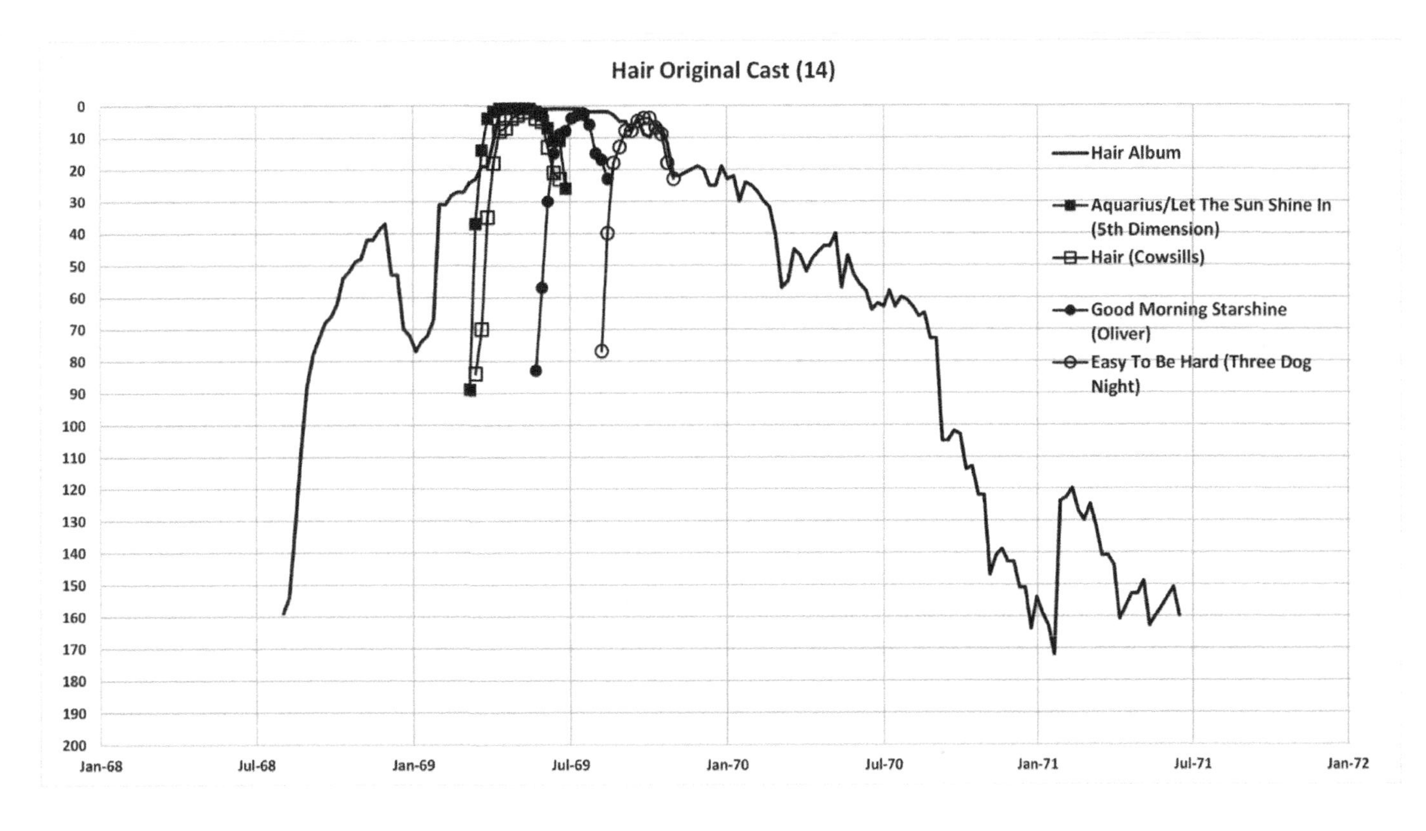
Hair Original Cast (14)
Hair Album
Aquarius/Let The Sun Shine In (5th Dimension)
Hair (Cowsills)
Good Morning Starshine (Oliver)
Easy To Be Hard (Three Dog Night)
0 10 20 30 40 50 60 70 80 90 100 110 120 130 140 150 160 170 180 190 200
Jan-68 Jul-68 Jan-69 Jul-69 Jan-70 Jul-70 Jan-71 Jul-71 Jan-72

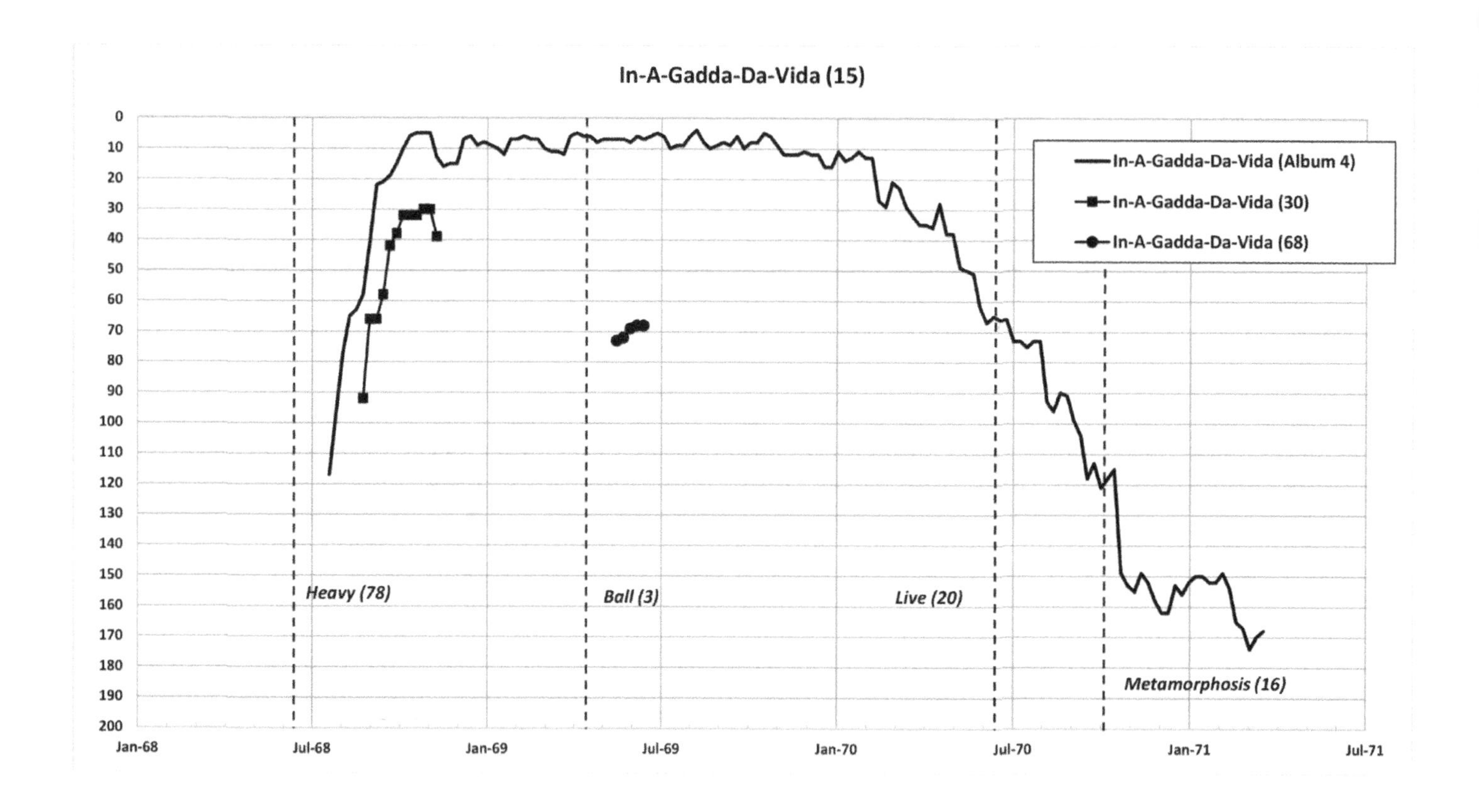
In-A-Gadda-Da-Vida (15)
In-A-Gadda-Da-Vida (Album 4)
In-A-Gadda-Da-Vida (30)
In-A-Gadda-Da-Vida (68)
Heavy (78)
Ball (3)
Live (20)
Metamorphosis (16)
Jan-68
Jul-68
Jan-69
Jul-69
Jan-70
Jul-70
Jan-71
Jul-71

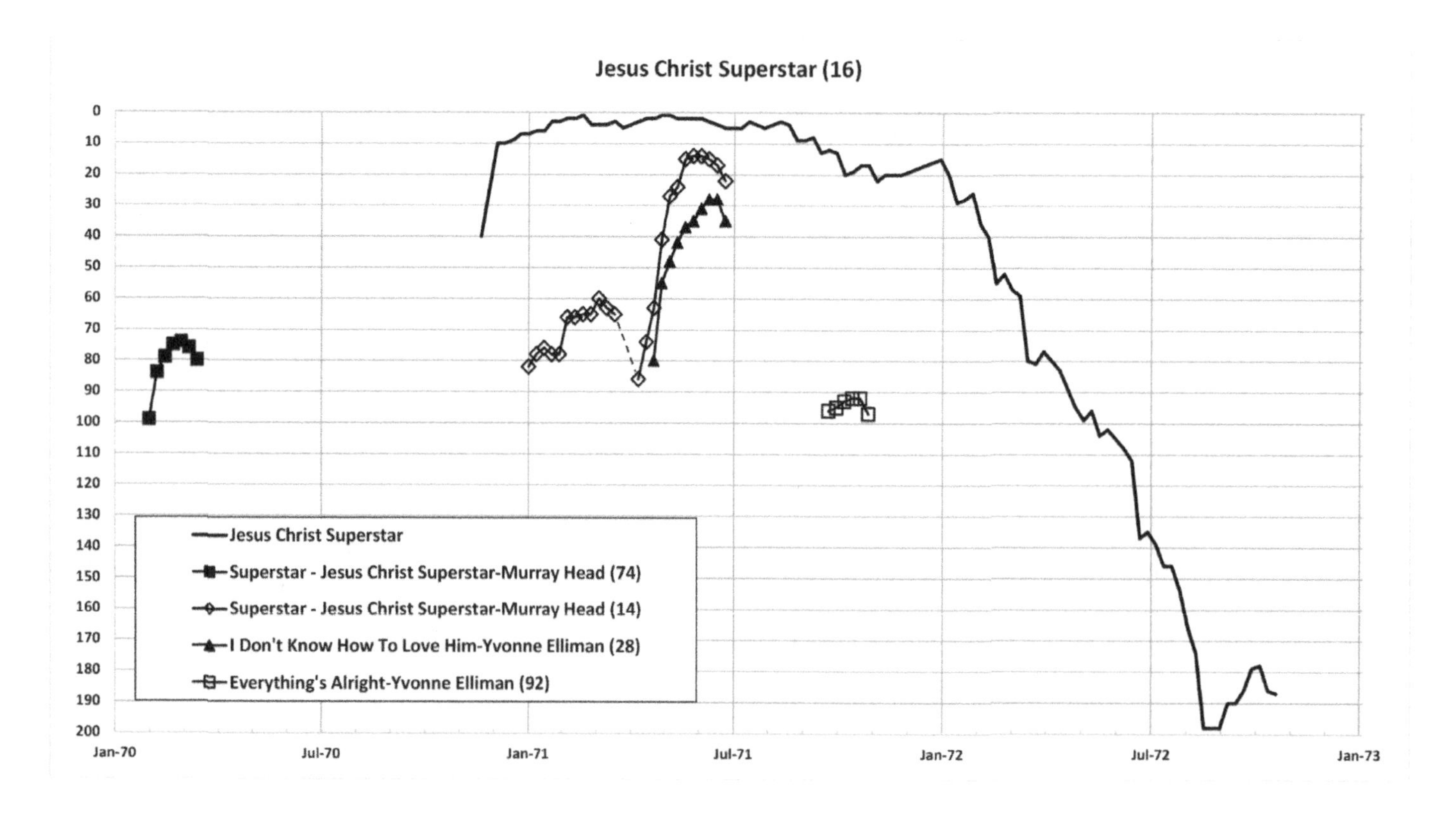
Jesus Christ Superstar (16)
Jesus Christ Superstar
Superstar - Jesus Christ Superstar-Murray Head (74)
Superstar - Jesus Christ Superstar-Murray Head (14)
I Don't Know How To Love Him-Yvonne Elliman (28)
Everything's Alright-Yvonne Elliman (92)
Jan-70
Jul-70
Jan-71
Jul-71
Jan-72
Jul-72
Jan-73

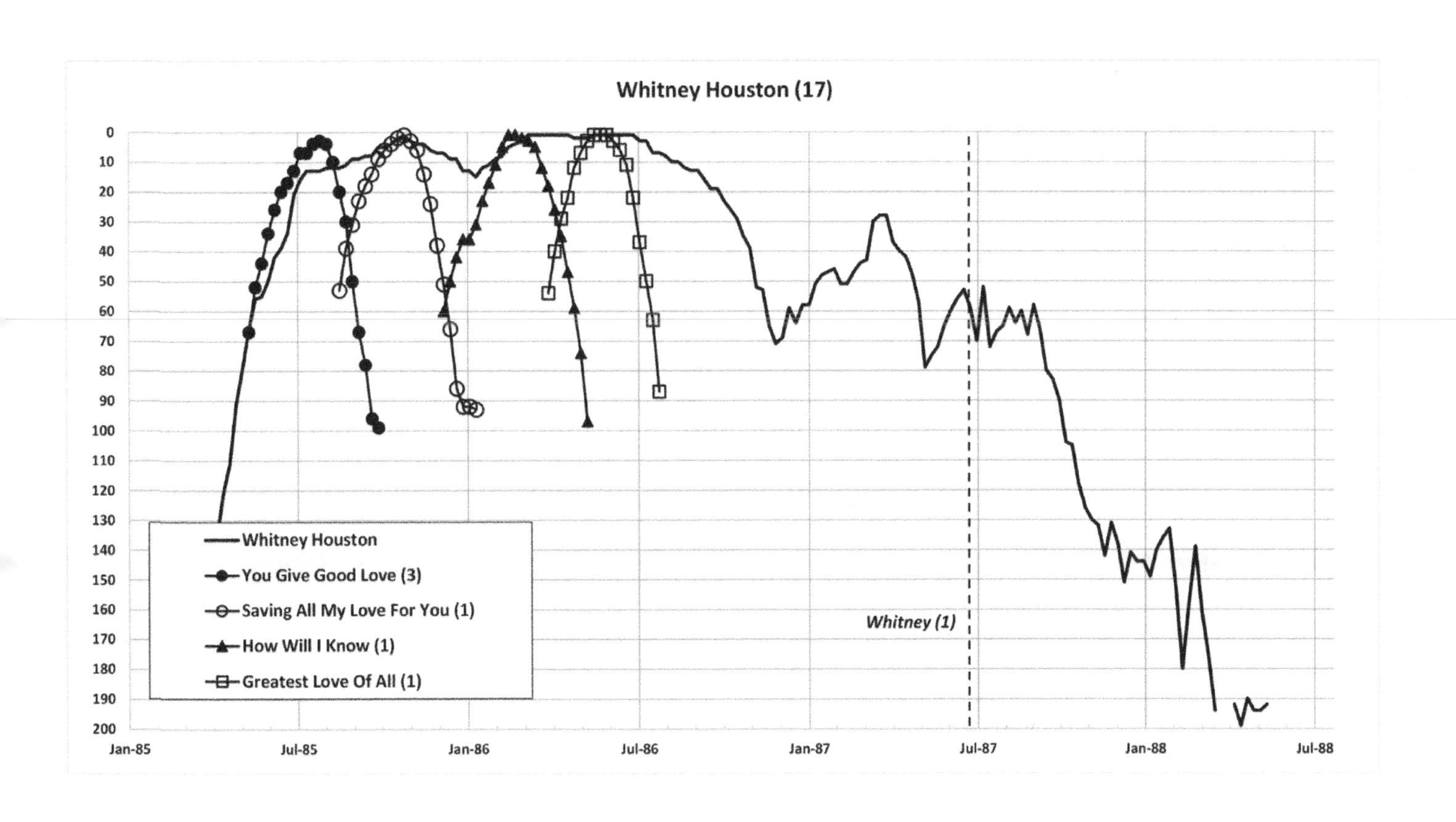
Whitney Houston (17)
0
10
20
30
40
50
60
70
80
90
100
110
120
130
140
150
160
170
180
190
200
Jan-85
Jul-85
Jan-86
Jul-86
Jan-87
Jul-87
Jan-88
Jul-88
Whitney Houston
You Give Good Love (3)
Saving All My Love For You (1)
How Will I Know (1)
Greatest Love Of All (1)
Whitney (1)

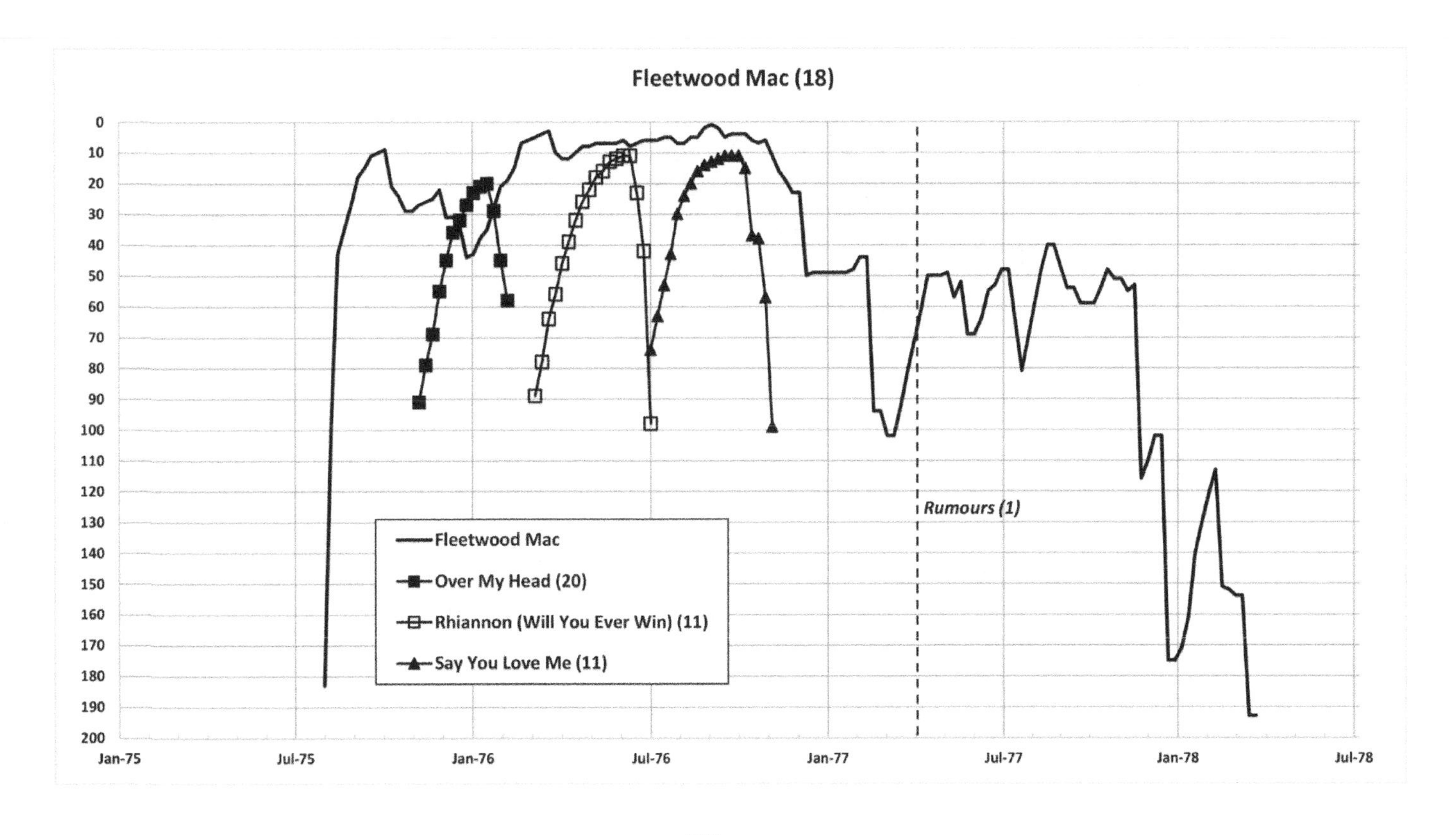
Fleetwood Mac (18)
0
10
20
30
40
50
60
70
80
90
100
110
120
130
140
150
160
170
180
190
200
Jan-75
Jul-75
Jan-76
Jul-76
Jan-77
Jul-77
Jan-78
Jul-78
Fleetwood Mac
Over My Head (20)
Rhiannon (Will You Ever Win) (11)
Say You Love Me (11)
Rumours (1)

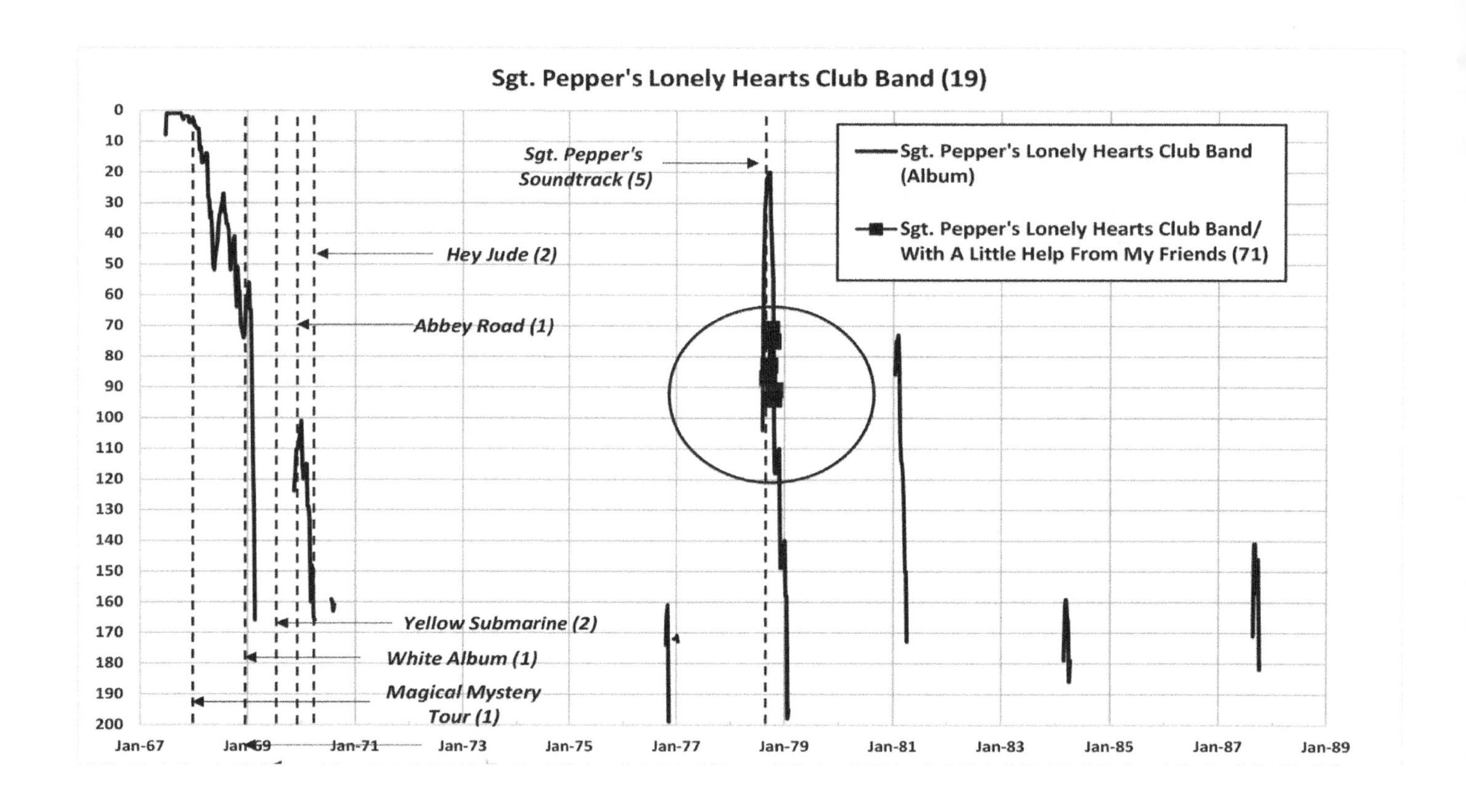

Sgt. Pepper's Lonely Hearts Club Band (19)
Sgt. Pepper's Soundtrack (5)
Hey Jude (2)
Abbey Road (1)
Yellow Submarine (2)
White Album (1)
Magical Mystery Tour (1)
Sgt. Pepper's Lonely Hearts Club Band (Album)
Sgt. Pepper's Lonely Hearts Club Band/ With A Little Help From My Friends (71)
Jan-67
Jan-69
Jan-71
Jan-73
Jan-75
Jan-77
Jan-79
Jan-81
Jan-83
Jan-85
Jan-87
Jan-89

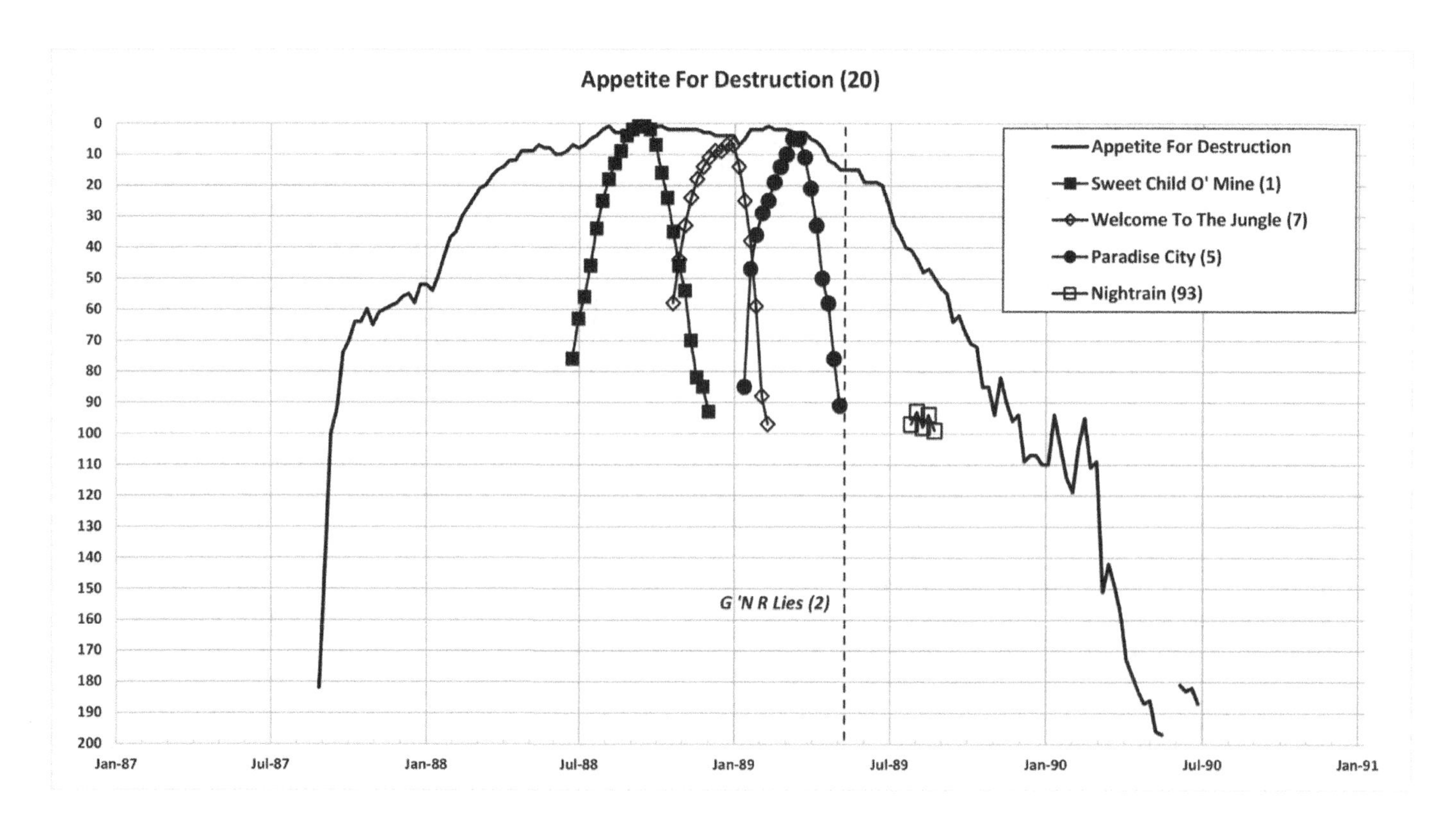

Appetite For Destruction (20)
Appetite For Destruction
Sweet Child O' Mine (1)
Welcome To The Jungle (7)
Paradise City (5)
Nightrain (93)
G 'N R Lies (2)
Jan-87
Jul-87
Jan-88
Jul-88
Jan-89
Jul-89
Jan-90
Jul-90
Jan-91

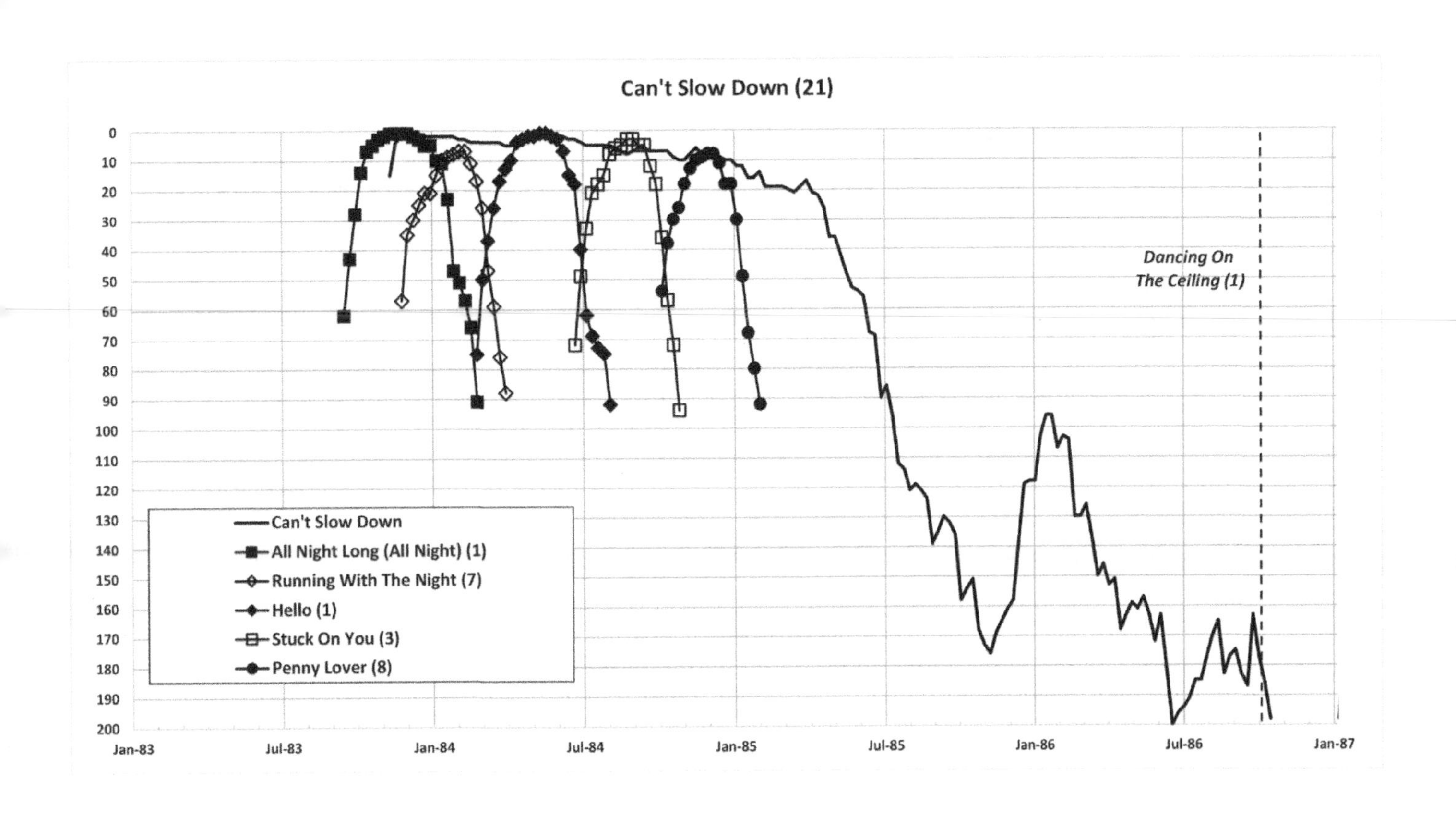
Can't Slow Down (21)
Dancing On
The Ceiling (1)
Can't Slow Down
All Night Long (All Night) (1)
Running With The Night (7)
Hello (1)
Stuck On You (3)
Penny Lover (8)
0
10
20
30
40
50
60
70
80
90
100
110
120
130
140
150
160
170
180
190
200
Jan-83
Jul-83
Jan-84
Jul-84
Jan-85
Jul-85
Jan-86
Jul-86
Jan-87

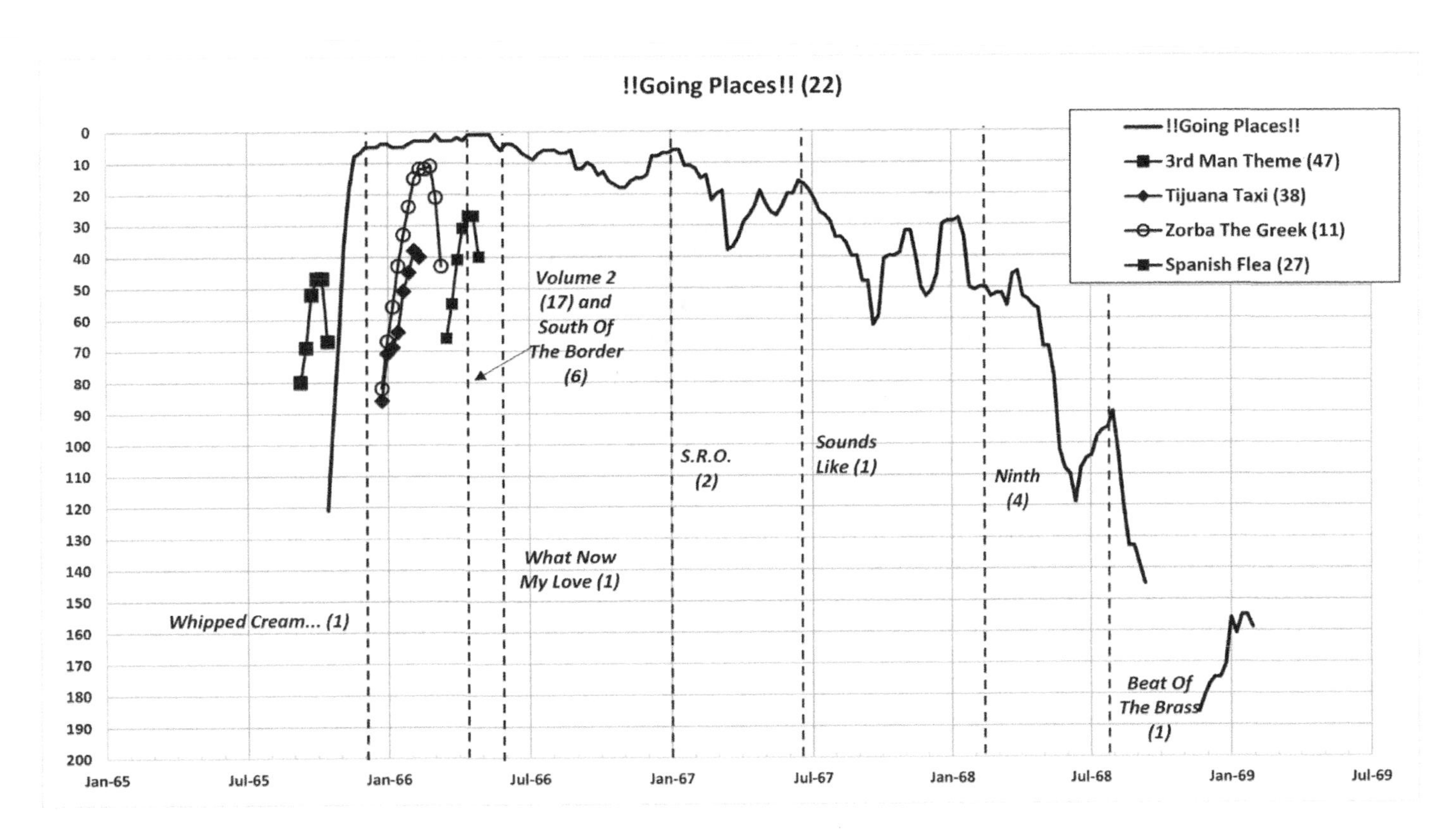
!!Going Places!! (22)
!!Going Places!!
3rd Man Theme (47)
Tijuana Taxi (38)
Zorba The Greek (11)
Spanish Flea (27)
Volume 2
(17) and
South Of
The Border
(6)
S.R.O.
(2)
Sounds
Like (1)
Ninth
(4)
What Now
My Love (1)
Whipped Cream... (1)
Beat Of
The Brass
(1)
0
10
20
30
40
50
60
70
80
90
100
110
120
130
140
150
160
170
180
190
200
Jan-65
Jul-65
Jan-66
Jul-66
Jan-67
Jul-67
Jan-68
Jul-68
Jan-69
Jul-69

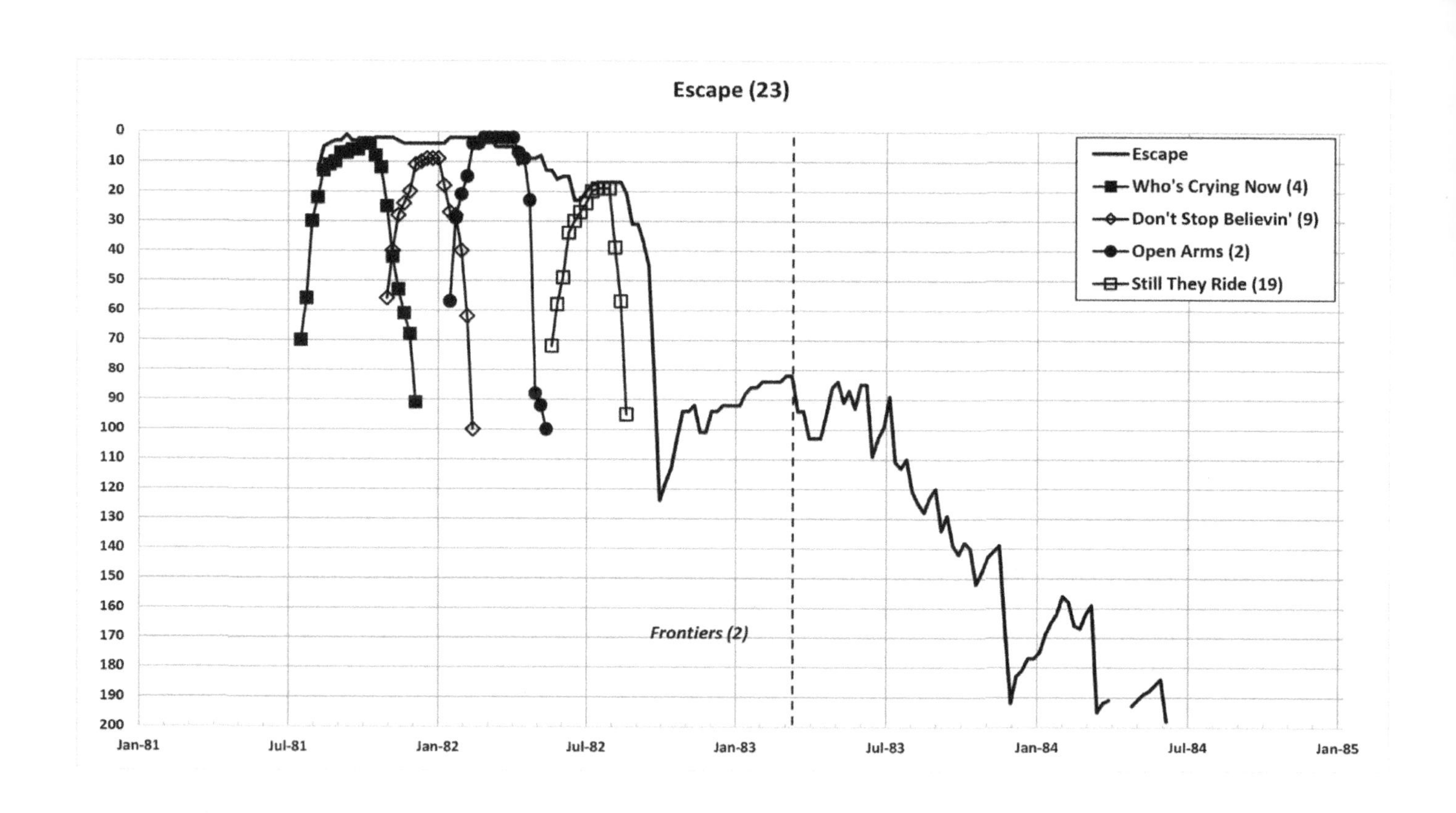
Escape (23)
Escape
Who's Crying Now (4)
Don't Stop Believin' (9)
Open Arms (2)
Still They Ride (19)
Frontiers (2)
0
10
20
30
40
50
60
70
80
90
100
110
120
130
140
150
160
170
180
190
200
Jan-81
Jul-81
Jan-82
Jul-82
Jan-83
Jul-83
Jan-84
Jul-84
Jan-85

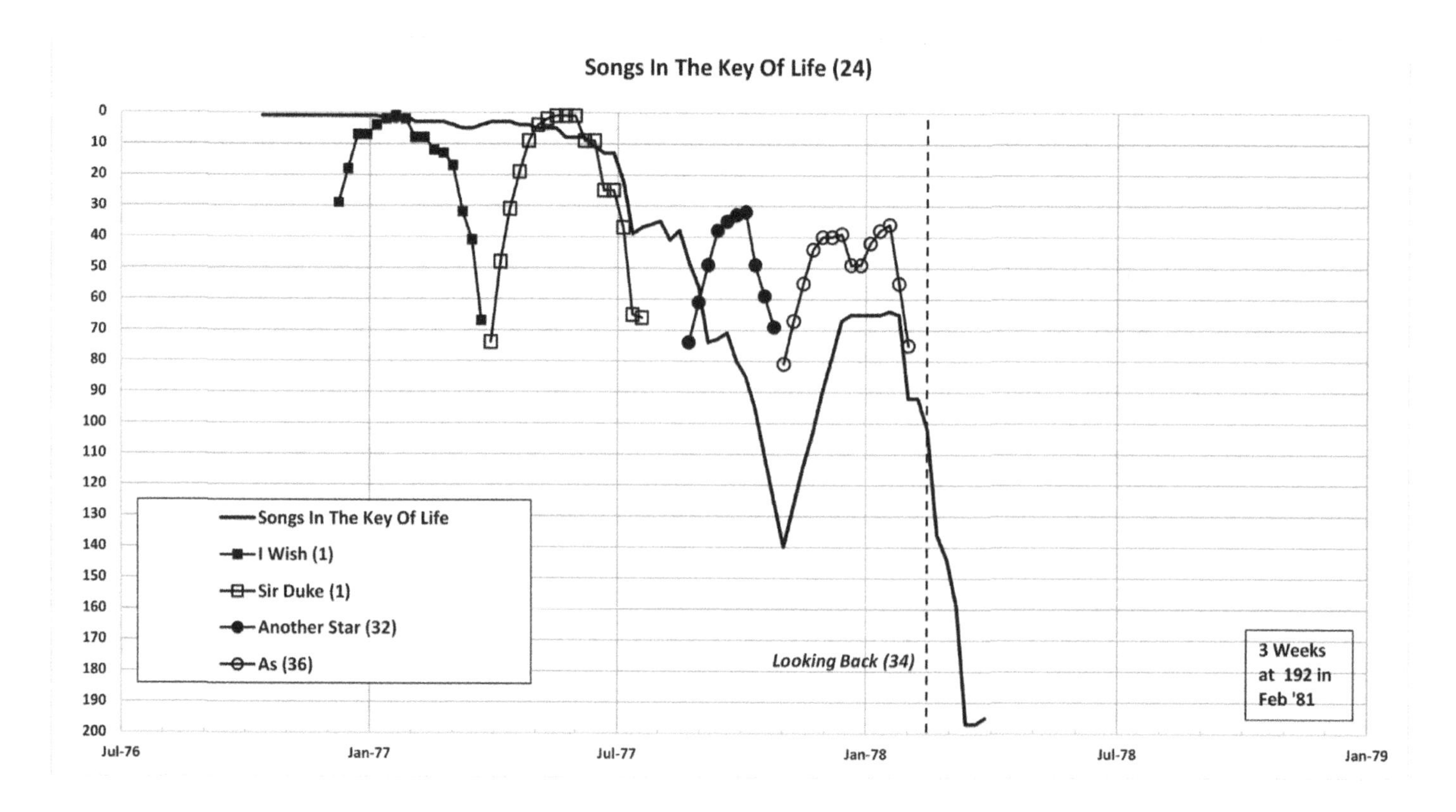
Songs In The Key Of Life (24)
Songs In The Key Of Life
I Wish (1)
Sir Duke (1)
Another Star (32)
As (36)
Looking Back (34)
3 Weeks
at 192 in
Feb '81
0
10
20
30
40
50
60
70
80
90
100
110
120
130
140
150
160
170
180
190
200
Jul-76
Jan-77
Jul-77
Jan-78
Jul-78
Jan-79

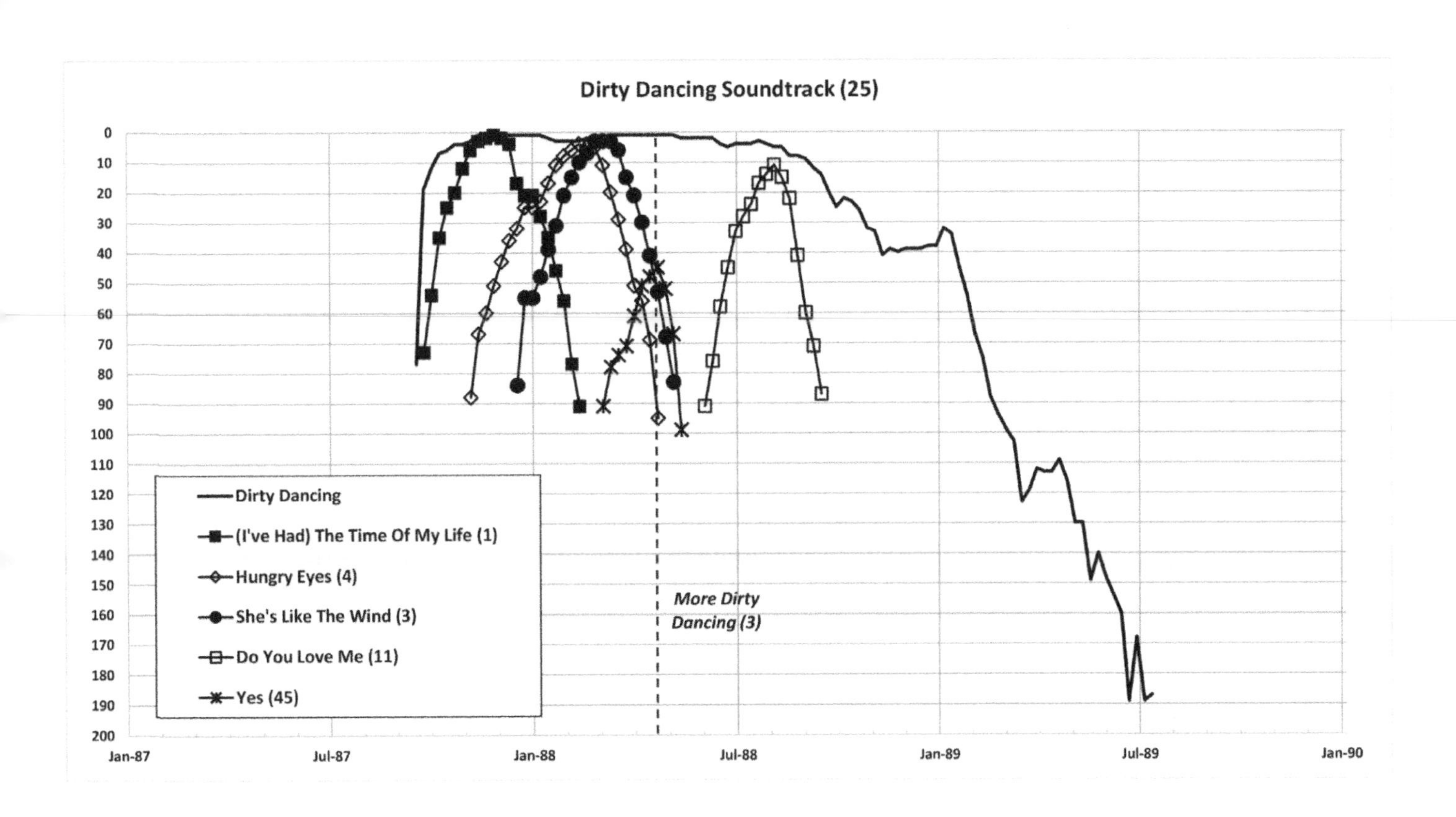

Dirty Dancing Soundtrack (25)
0
10
20
30
40
50
60
70
80
90
100
110
120
130
140
150
160
170
180
190
200
Jan-87
Jul-87
Jan-88
Jul-88
Jan-89
Jul-89
Jan-90
Dirty Dancing
(I've Had) The Time Of My Life (1)
Hungry Eyes (4)
She's Like The Wind (3)
Do You Love Me (11)
Yes (45)
More Dirty Dancing (3)

Ranking The Acts

For Acts 1-1250

Act Rank and Name [Highest Peak of any Album]

The BEATLES [1]
23 (331); 27 (618); 37 (1849)

Top Ten Entries (Top Ten Weeks); Top 40 Entries (Top 40 Weeks); Total Entries (Total Weeks) Score

For Acts 1251-3542

Rank. Act [Highest Peak of any Album] Entries (Total Weeks) Score

1252. Robert MAXWELL [17] 1 (24) 1227

Ranking The Acts: 1-1250

Rank. Act [Hi Peak] T10s (Wks); T40s (Wks); Entries (Wks)	Score
1. The BEATLES [1] 23 (331); 27 (618); 37 (1849)	169751
2. ROLLING STONES [1] 31 (290); 33 (603); 35 (1512)	145643
3. Barbra STREISAND [1] 21 (240); 34 (656); 40 (1475)	126028
4. Elton JOHN [1] 13 (145); 26 (391); 30 (1131)	102732
5. CHICAGO [1] 12 (155); 18 (385); 20 (1047)	98583
6. Herb ALPERT & The TIJUANA BRASS [1] 8 (201); 11 (505); 18 (1070)	93850
7. LED ZEPPELIN [1] 10 (120); 10 (239); 10 (769)	78767
8. The TEMPTATIONS [2] 8 (60); 24 (364); 37 (1093)	72959
9. Billy JOEL [1] 9 (147); 12 (329); 14 (736)	72919
10. Elvis PRESLEY [1] 11 (70); 27 (306); 71 (1248)	71798
11. Stevie WONDER [1] 9 (116); 16 (284); 22 (784)	71559
12. FLEETWOOD MAC [1] 5 (129); 8 (237); 19 (652)	70927
13. Bob DYLAN [1] 12 (92); 27 (334); 31 (852)	69964
14. BEE GEES [1] 8 (89); 15 (263); 25 (808)	69117
15. Neil DIAMOND [2] 12 (90); 21 (284); 32 (990)	66597
16. John DENVER [1] 7 (96); 14 (233); 21 (779)	65149
17. JEFFERSON AIRPLANE/STARSHIP [1] 7 (87); 21 (299); 27 (757)	63716
18. Aretha FRANKLIN [2] 6 (58); 21 (295); 36 (878)	61975
19. Rod STEWART [1] 6 (76); 16 (280); 21 (668)	61323
20. EAGLES [1] 5 (86); 7 (215); 9 (600)	59933
21. BEACH BOYS [1] 12 (96); 18 (310); 38 (1034)	59702
22. PINK FLOYD [1] 6 (88); 9 (181); 17 (1236)	59509
23. Michael JACKSON [1] 4 (152); 5 (224); 11 (491)	59268
24. SIMON & GARFUNKEL [1] 6 (92); 8 (242); 8 (698)	58590
25. Linda RONSTADT [1] 10 (96); 13 (219); 23 (770)	57697
26. SANTANA [1] 7 (88); 14 (212); 17 (545)	56859
27. Bruce SPRINGSTEEN [1] 7 (139); 7 (206); 9 (630)	54719
28. Carole KING [1] 6 (96); 8 (161); 15 (594)	53533
29. EARTH, WIND & FIRE [1] 8 (93); 13 (202); 18 (568)	53194
30. MOODY BLUES [1] 6 (54); 14 (199); 16 (693)	50515
31. The MONKEES [1] 5 (99); 7 (186); 13 (513)	49833
32. The SUPREMES/ Diana ROSS And The SUPREMES [1] 6 (73); 14 (250); 21 (673)	49628
33. CREEDENCE CLEARWATER REVIVAL [1] 5 (74); 7 (159); 13 (559)	49421
34. JOURNEY [1] 6 (78); 8 (208); 12 (777)	49037

Rank. Act [Hi Peak] T10s (Wks); T40s (Wks); Entries (Wks)	Score
35. JETHRO TULL [1] 7 (67); 17 (214); 22 (551)	48841
36. Glen CAMPBELL [1] 3 (46); 14 (198); 25 (633)	48249
37. FOREIGNER [1] 6 (101); 7 (204); 7 (430)	47775
38. Daryl HALL & John OATES [3] 4 (69); 13 (254); 16 (628)	47738
39. The WHO [2] 9 (80); 12 (189); 20 (548)	47372
40. THREE DOG NIGHT [5] 5 (35); 12 (221); 14 (556)	47366
41. Paul McCARTNEY & WINGS/ WINGS [1] 8 (98); 9 (160); 9 (449)	46521
42. The DOORS [1] 7 (60); 12 (192); 18 (597)	45576
43. James TAYLOR [2] 7 (61); 12 (208); 14 (467)	45567
44. Kenny ROGERS [1] 4 (43); 15 (187); 23 (842)	45527
45. PRINCE [1] 6 (80); 9 (196); 11 (551)	45278
46. Andy WILLIAMS [3] 10 (72); 14 (255); 26 (679)	45079
47. DOOBIE BROTHERS [1] 8 (54); 11 (179); 12 (625)	44835
48. Diana ROSS [1] 4 (44); 16 (213); 26 (647)	44648
49. Frank SINATRA [1] 7 (44); 18 (272); 31 (713)	44458
50. Eric CLAPTON [1] 6 (58); 16 (206); 19 (524)	44038
51. Bob SEGER [1] 6 (77); 7 (173); 12 (682)	43818
52. Bill COSBY [2] 3 (21); 10 (229); 22 (877)	43693
53. Barry MANILOW [1] 7 (35); 13 (183); 18 (674)	43066
54. The COMMODORES [3] 5 (61); 12 (198); 16 (455)	43008
55. GRAND FUNK RAILROAD [2] 8 (53); 12 (183); 16 (499)	42926
56. VAN HALEN [1] 7 (89); 8 (190); 8 (524)	42406
57. Cat STEVENS [1] 7 (66); 9 (188); 13 (421)	42184
58. JACKSON 5 [4] 6 (48); 14 (191); 20 (538)	42109
59. Donna SUMMER [1] 4 (47); 12 (171); 15 (489)	41664
60. STYX [1] 5 (81); 7 (160); 11 (490)	40950
61. AEROSMITH [3] 2 (40); 10 (209); 14 (674)	40371
62. Tom JONES [3] 4 (44); 8 (136); 18 (536)	40204
63. Neil YOUNG [1] 4 (34); 16 (160); 23 (589)	39694
64. HEART [1] 5 (65); 10 (197); 10 (426)	39475
65. Isaac HAYES [1] 4 (27); 9 (164); 21 (554)	39251
66. CARPENTERS [1] 5 (61); 7 (162); 14 (395)	39187
67. David BOWIE [3] 6 (36); 15 (164); 28 (674)	38179
68. The POLICE [1] 4 (89); 6 (143); 6 (526)	38145

SOUNDTRACK-TV [1]
2 (21); 7 (64); 25 (350) 18674

SOUNDTRACK-MOVIE [1]
39 (663); 111 (1910); 371 (7299) 442594

ORIGINAL CAST [1]
3 (66); 15 (256); 78 (1869) 72783

VARIOUS ARTISTS [1]
4 (55); 19 (185); 188 (2128) 69190

Rank. Act [Hi Peak] T10s (Wks); T40s (Wks); Entries (Wks)	Score
69. MADONNA [1] 5 (82); 6 (196); 6 (485)	38131
70. Steve MILLER Band [2] 4 (68); 10 (155); 18 (480)	37817
71. KISS [4] 4 (20); 16 (181); 20 (663)	37030
72. Dionne WARWICK [6] 2 (7); 14 (151); 33 (780)	36632
73. Phil COLLINS [1] 4 (68); 4 (167); 4 (518)	36530
74. BLOOD, SWEAT & TEARS [1] 3 (63); 5 (109); 10 (306)	35654
75. DEF LEPPARD [1] 2 (116); 3 (157); 5 (424)	35547
76. Olivia NEWTON-JOHN [1] 5 (46); 12 (158); 16 (481)	35230
77. John MELLENCAMP [1] 5 (84); 6 (179); 7 (407)	35005
78. QUEEN [1] 5 (50); 12 (154); 15 (363)	34591
79. ELECTRIC LIGHT ORCHESTRA [4] 5 (37); 10 (164); 14 (435)	34118
80. CREAM [1] 4 (71); 7 (129); 8 (342)	34066
81. Pat BENATAR [1] 3 (55); 8 (160); 9 (440)	34030
82. Lionel RICHIE [1] 3 (100); 3 (155); 3 (358)	33853
83. Marvin GAYE [2] 6 (46); 11 (136); 26 (529)	33535
84. U2 [1] 2 (49); 6 (133); 8 (740)	32944
85. The CARS [3] 4 (56); 7 (165); 7 (401)	32798
86. ZZ TOP [4] 4 (22); 7 (197); 9 (499)	32519
87. Tom PETTY And The HEARTBREAKERS [2] 5 (75); 8 (166); 9 (344)	32417
88. YES [3] 7 (50); 13 (150); 16 (396)	31781
89. ISLEY BROTHERS [1] 6 (30); 12 (134); 23 (446)	31661
90. George HARRISON [1] 6 (50); 10 (126); 14 (262)	31599
91. PETER, PAUL & MARY [1] 3 (41); 9 (183); 11 (445)	31221
92. Paul SIMON [1] 4 (65); 8 (156); 9 (319)	31217
93. George BENSON [1] 5 (43); 7 (116); 18 (441)	30929
94. AC/DC [1] 3 (47); 8 (125); 13 (493)	30779
95. GENESIS [3] 4 (38); 8 (171); 13 (407)	30643

Rank. Act [Hi Peak]	T10s (Wks); T40s (Wks); Entries (Wks)	Score
96. Peter FRAMPTON [1]	2 (64); 4 (80); 11 (287)	29896
97. REO SPEEDWAGON [1]	3 (47); 6 (104); 13 (436)	29876
98. Whitney HOUSTON [1]	2 (77); 2 (129); 2 (247)	29875
99. BON JOVI [1]	2 (68); 3 (117); 4 (360)	29706
100. AMERICA [1]	5 (42); 8 (111); 14 (350)	29659
101. Johnny CASH [1]	2 (24); 3 (91); 22 (504)	29361
102. KOOL & The GANG [10]	1 (2); 8 (169); 20 (565)	29155
103. Joni MITCHELL [2]	3 (30); 12 (123); 15 (358)	29015
104. MAMAS & The PAPAS [1]	4 (59); 5 (120); 9 (386)	28671
105. Roberta FLACK [1]	4 (32); 8 (127); 12 (408)	28482
106. Willie NELSON [2]	2 (17); 11 (85); 33 (873)	28455
107. WAR [1]	4 (30); 8 (121); 15 (359)	28429
108. Dean MARTIN [2]	2 (19); 11 (140); 21 (524)	28226
109. Engelbert HUMPERDINCK [5]	3 (18); 9 (120); 16 (501)	28050
110. STEPPENWOLF [3]	4 (28); 8 (113); 14 (392)	27952
111. IRON BUTTERFLY [3]	2 (57); 4 (119); 7 (291)	27778
112. Huey LEWIS And The NEWS [1]	2 (68); 4 (139); 4 (308)	27471
113. Carly SIMON [1]	4 (26); 10 (104); 15 (410)	27298
114. 5TH DIMENSION [2]	3 (17); 8 (105); 14 (443)	27257
115. Janet JACKSON [1]	2 (72); 2 (154); 4 (245)	26849
116. Jimi HENDRIX EXPERIENCE [1]	4 (56); 5 (132); 6 (268)	26797
117. STEELY DAN [3]	3 (29); 8 (137); 9 (311)	26790
118. James BROWN [10]	1 (1); 14 (78); 48 (712)	26659
119. ALLMAN BROTHERS Band [1]	4 (35); 8 (99); 16 (350)	26611
120. Nancy WILSON [4]	4 (21); 11 (144); 31 (567)	26555
121. SUPERTRAMP [1]	3 (36); 6 (106); 9 (333)	26526
122. BOSTON [1]	3 (61); 3 (91); 3 (227)	25724
123. Jackson BROWNE [1]	4 (39); 6 (97); 9 (308)	25712
124. DEEP PURPLE [6]	3 (18); 9 (120); 18 (461)	25711
125. RUSH [3]	6 (29); 11 (132); 17 (413)	25584
126. Jim CROCE [1]	4 (42); 4 (109); 6 (297)	25550
127. SLY & THE FAMILY STONE [1]	3 (31); 5 (92); 9 (285)	24976
128. Al GREEN [4]	3 (14); 8 (115); 15 (416)	24854
129. ALABAMA [10]	1 (1); 6 (114); 12 (613)	24744
130. RASCALS/YOUNG RASCALS [1]	3 (41); 6 (109); 10 (353)	24629
131. DIRE STRAITS [1]	2 (50); 5 (109); 8 (270)	24314
132. GUNS N' ROSES [1]	2 (70); 2 (111); 2 (200)	24245
133. Al HIRT [3]	3 (38); 7 (175); 12 (379)	24139
134. Dan FOGELBERG [3]	3 (23); 9 (127); 10 (325)	24135
135. Johnny MATHIS [9]	2 (5); 10 (80); 44 (682)	23738
136. SEALS & CROFTS [4]	2 (17); 6 (106); 12 (398)	23363
137. Quincy JONES [6]	3 (9); 6 (96); 13 (380)	23227
138. Steve WINWOOD [1]	3 (41); 6 (143); 8 (262)	23159
139. CROSBY, STILLS, NASH & YOUNG [1]	3 (41); 4 (87); 4 (188)	23012
140. BLACK SABBATH [8]	1 (5); 10 (112); 16 (386)	22920
141. MÖTLEY CRÜE [1]	3 (32); 4 (127); 5 (400)	22918
142. FOUR TOPS [4]	1 (7); 8 (103); 24 (522)	22847
143. Bette MIDLER [2]	3 (18); 6 (100); 11 (414)	22820
144. Lou RAWLS [4]	3 (16); 6 (99); 22 (450)	22767
145. Gladys KNIGHT & The PIPS [9]	2 (6); 9 (78); 25 (522)	22628
146. The O'JAYS [6]	3 (12); 10 (103); 17 (368)	22620
147. The KINKS [9]	1 (3); 10 (88); 32 (501)	22538
148. POINTER SISTERS [8]	1 (6); 7 (131); 16 (373)	22249
149. Joan BAEZ [7]	2 (9); 9 (99); 22 (436)	22203
150. DONOVAN [4]	1 (14); 10 (107); 20 (336)	22162
151. Henry MANCINI and his Orchestra [5]	3 (16); 6 (101); 27 (481)	22072
152. PARTRIDGE FAMILY [3]	3 (23); 5 (98); 7 (217)	22023
153. EMERSON, LAKE & PALMER [4]	4 (16); 8 (101); 11 (265)	22001
154. Helen REDDY [5]	3 (14); 7 (91); 10 (329)	21797
155. HERMAN'S HERMITS [2]	3 (51); 6 (104); 10 (318)	21602
156. Grover WASHINGTON Jr. [5]	3 (10); 9 (88); 17 (392)	21353
157. Boz SCAGGS [2]	2 (14); 4 (102); 10 (260)	21311
158. LOVERBOY [7]	2 (21); 4 (112); 6 (332)	21227
159. OHIO PLAYERS [1]	2 (18); 5 (78); 16 (290)	21127
160. Stevie NICKS [1]	3 (38); 4 (95); 4 (251)	21034
161. Alan PARSONS PROJECT [7]	2 (11); 7 (99); 11 (357)	20991
162. DURAN DURAN [4]	4 (34); 6 (119); 8 (399)	20851
163. BACHMAN-TURNER OVERDRIVE [1]	3 (30); 5 (82); 11 (273)	20790
164. GRATEFUL DEAD [6]	1 (7); 13 (92); 25 (402)	20748
165. Ray CONNIFF & His Orch. & Chorus [3]	1 (17); 7 (88); 29 (537)	20729
166. BAD COMPANY [1]	4 (33); 6 (79); 9 (267)	20639
167. The LETTERMEN [10]	1 (5); 8 (74); 28 (507)	20616
168. LYNYRD SKYNYRD [5]	3 (12); 8 (86); 11 (355)	20576
169. Judy COLLINS [5]	1 (6); 8 (76); 16 (394)	20457
170. Sergio MENDES & BRASIL '66/'77 [3]	3 (17); 5 (87); 15 (364)	20448
171. J. GEILS Band [1]	2 (20); 7 (77); 15 (334)	20369
172. BREAD [2]	2 (18); 7 (86); 8 (304)	20310
173. CHEECH & CHONG [2]	3 (27); 5 (74); 8 (303)	20297
174. NEW KIDS ON THE BLOCK [1]	2 (48); 3 (102); 3 (240)	19989
175. CROSBY, STILLS & NASH [2]	3 (33); 3 (90); 5 (198)	19840
176. KANSAS [4]	3 (22); 7 (93); 13 (281)	19810
177. Paul McCARTNEY [1]	3 (29); 7 (84); 9 (228)	19611
178. Joe COCKER [2]	1 (8); 5 (62); 14 (348)	19573
179. Paula ABDUL [1]	1 (64); 1 (78); 1 (175)	19418
180. Gordon LIGHTFOOT [1]	2 (9); 7 (84); 16 (287)	19172
181. TALKING HEADS [15]	0 (0); 8 (102); 10 (438)	19104
182. Bryan ADAMS [1]	3 (51); 3 (113); 4 (218)	18844
183. ALICE COOPER (Grp) [1]	4 (20); 6 (80); 7 (224)	18831
184. Rick SPRINGFIELD [2]	2 (17); 6 (101); 9 (282)	18828
185. LOGGINS & MESSINA [5]	3 (14); 6 (75); 9 (339)	18720
186. TRAFFIC [5]	4 (15); 8 (85); 12 (258)	18515
187. Bobby BROWN [1]	2 (50); 2 (86); 3 (147)	18363
188. Jimi HENDRIX [3]	3 (18); 5 (67); 17 (279)	18349
189. RUFUS [4]	3 (13); 6 (87); 11 (236)	18333
190. Rick JAMES [3]	1 (12); 6 (84); 11 (284)	18183
191. The VENTURES [11]	0 (0); 11 (82); 25 (493)	18179
192. The ASSOCIATION [4]	3 (21); 6 (76); 10 (299)	18121
193. The BAND [5]	3 (12); 8 (83); 10 (236)	17981
194. CHEAP TRICK [4]	2 (17); 7 (91); 11 (251)	17889
195. MEN AT WORK [1]	2 (45); 2 (71); 3 (152)	17845
196. Paul REVERE And The RAIDERS [5]	4 (17); 6 (88); 14 (341)	17747
197. Anne MURRAY [12]	0 (0); 7 (50); 24 (468)	17584
198. RIGHTEOUS BROTHERS [4]	3 (18); 10 (106); 15 (350)	17573
199. Ozzy OSBOURNE [6]	2 (14); 7 (104); 8 (333)	17459
200. Curtis MAYFIELD [1]	1 (11); 6 (71); 15 (275)	17360
201. Barry WHITE [1]	2 (10); 7 (68); 14 (314)	17306
202. 4 SEASONS [6]	3 (12); 8 (73); 20 (429)	17241
203. Janis JOPLIN [1]	3 (28); 4 (57); 6 (139)	17145
204. Frank ZAPPA [10]	1 (1); 9 (54); 33 (453)	17113
205. Luther VANDROSS [9]	1 (3); 7 (115); 7 (306)	16919
206. CHER [10]	1 (2); 7 (75); 18 (341)	16854

Rank. Act [Hi Peak]	T10s (Wks); T40s (Wks); Entries (Wks)	Score
207. WHITESNAKE [2]	2 (42); 3 (76); 6 (229)	16712
208. Chuck MANGIONE [2]	2 (16); 4 (55); 17 (325)	16569
209. SPINNERS [8]	2 (7); 8 (81); 17 (266)	16544
210. VILLAGE PEOPLE [3]	2 (14); 4 (52); 7 (257)	16445
211. GUESS WHO [9]	1 (7); 4 (58); 15 (278)	16289
212. POISON [2]	2 (43); 2 (98); 2 (171)	16247
213. Gloria ESTEFAN/ MIAMI SOUND MACHINE [6]	2 (13); 3 (123); 3 (241)	16186
214. Natalie COLE [8]	1 (4); 5 (56); 13 (322)	16168
215. George MICHAEL [1]	1 (51); 1 (69); 1 (87)	16081
216. Johnny RIVERS [5]	1 (9); 8 (75); 16 (356)	16072
217. TOTO [4]	2 (24); 4 (67); 8 (252)	15986
218. Tina TURNER [3]	2 (45); 3 (84); 5 (193)	15981
219. BLONDIE [6]	2 (14); 5 (73); 6 (240)	15962
220. Anita BAKER [1]	1 (18); 2 (100); 3 (210)	15908
221. SCORPIONS [5]	3 (22); 4 (82); 9 (298)	15852
222. AIR SUPPLY [7]	2 (12); 5 (86); 6 (283)	15837
223. Teddy PENDERGRASS [5]	1 (5); 7 (72); 11 (283)	15817
224. Billy SQUIER [5]	2 (16); 3 (81); 6 (235)	15757
225. Al MARTINO [8]	2 (5); 6 (75); 22 (404)	15663
226. Donny OSMOND [6]	1 (4); 6 (69); 11 (251)	15478
227. The ANIMALS/ Eric BURDON & The ANIMALS [6]	2 (11); 4 (82); 17 (363)	15402
228. CULTURE CLUB [2]	1 (30); 4 (91); 4 (184)	15345
229. Smokey ROBINSON [10]	1 (2); 6 (64); 16 (351)	15341
230. Kenny LOGGINS [7]	1 (7); 5 (68); 7 (227)	15306
231. The MIRACLES/ Smokey ROBINSON & The MIRACLES [7]	2 (6); 5 (59); 18 (335)	15173
232. Leon RUSSELL [2]	2 (14); 8 (64); 12 (246)	15035
233. Waylon JENNINGS [10]	1 (2); 6 (37); 17 (452)	15018
234. Charley PRIDE [22]	0 (0); 4 (27); 17 (361)	14897
235. Dave CLARK Five [3]	4 (27); 8 (103); 13 (259)	14893
236. AVERAGE WHITE BAND/ AWB [1]	3 (20); 8 (58); 10 (197)	14891
237. Ray CHARLES [2]	2 (16); 4 (57); 23 (408)	14823
238. TEARS FOR FEARS [1]	2 (35); 2 (72); 3 (185)	14793
239. KENNY G [6]	2 (19); 3 (89); 5 (314)	14770
240. Don HENLEY [8]	1 (5); 3 (108); 3 (246)	14758
241. INXS [3]	1 (22); 2 (81); 6 (204)	14731
242. MILLI VANILLI [1]	1 (41); 1 (61); 1 (78)	14650
243. SONNY & CHER [2]	1 (14); 5 (58); 12 (291)	14615
244. Jimmy BUFFETT [10]	1 (2); 6 (53); 16 (329)	14581
245. Christopher CROSS [6]	1 (15); 2 (92); 3 (153)	14517
246. BROTHERS JOHNSON [5]	3 (16); 4 (76); 7 (163)	14486
247. Richard MARX [1]	2 (16); 2 (110); 2 (152)	14470
248. Ted NUGENT [13]	0 (0); 7 (66); 13 (279)	14453
249. Michael BOLTON [3]	1 (21); 1 (50); 3 (256)	14229
250. RARE EARTH [12]	0 (0); 4 (61); 9 (238)	14173
251. Joe WALSH [6]	2 (10); 5 (62); 10 (216)	14162
252. EURYTHMICS [7]	2 (9); 5 (88); 8 (246)	14127
253. Otis REDDING [4]	2 (10); 5 (54); 15 (343)	14072
254. CAPTAIN & TENNILLE [2]	2 (12); 4 (47); 6 (246)	14057
255. SADE [1]	3 (32); 3 (75); 3 (172)	14002
256. Billy IDOL [6]	3 (11); 3 (77); 5 (330)	13945
257. The GO-GO'S [1]	2 (24); 3 (66); 3 (132)	13943
258. The BYRDS [6]	2 (8); 8 (64); 15 (295)	13819
259. Billy OCEAN [6]	2 (14); 3 (98); 5 (184)	13737
260. José FELICIANO [2]	1 (19); 4 (47); 10 (186)	13682
261. ABBA [14]	0 (0); 5 (60); 10 (277)	13632
262. Cyndi LAUPER [4]	2 (27); 3 (89); 3 (161)	13582
263. The OSMONDS [10]	1 (1); 5 (59); 12 (224)	13441
264. Bonnie RAITT [1]	1 (11); 4 (52); 9 (312)	13284
265. Robin TROWER [5]	3 (11); 8 (60); 13 (221)	13240
266. KC And The SUNSHINE BAND [4]	1 (7); 3 (55); 7 (211)	13222
267. The B-52s [4]	1 (22); 4 (60); 7 (236)	13148
268. Joe JACKSON [4]	1 (7); 5 (73); 11 (258)	13137
269. R.E.M. [10]	1 (1); 6 (82); 8 (263)	13110
270. John LENNON/PLASTIC ONO BAND [1]	3 (18); 4 (48); 4 (142)	13107
271. MARSHALL TUCKER Band [15]	0 (0); 8 (52); 12 (276)	13081
272. Peter GABRIEL [2]	1 (12); 4 (75); 8 (217)	12998
273. VANILLA FUDGE [6]	1 (11); 5 (70); 5 (186)	12984
274. Debbie GIBSON [1]	2 (26); 2 (70); 2 (140)	12968
275. Robert PALMER [8]	1 (4); 3 (63); 11 (280)	12949
276. Van MORRISON [15]	0 (0); 6 (37); 20 (328)	12778
277. LITTLE RIVER BAND [10]	1 (3); 4 (48); 9 (291)	12752
278. CINDERELLA [3]	2 (20); 2 (81); 2 (136)	12591
279. The PRETENDERS [5]	3 (17); 5 (66); 6 (212)	12453
280. The CRUSADERS [18]	0 (0); 6 (40); 18 (315)	12409
281. Al JARREAU [9]	1 (4); 3 (37); 10 (330)	12394
282. RUN-D.M.C. [3]	2 (16); 2 (63); 4 (220)	12371
283. John GARY [11]	0 (0); 5 (66); 14 (324)	12365
284. Eddy ARNOLD [7]	1 (6); 5 (42); 17 (361)	12308
285. .38 SPECIAL [10]	1 (3); 5 (72); 8 (251)	12291
286. WHAM! [1]	2 (27); 2 (67); 3 (152)	12152
287. The SUPREMES And The TEMPTATIONS [1]	2 (19); 4 (38); 4 (96)	12112
288. ASIA [1]	2 (32); 2 (46); 3 (106)	12094
289. CAMEO [8]	1 (3); 4 (56); 13 (290)	12075
290. Herbie HANCOCK [13]	0 (0); 4 (37); 18 (289)	12075
291. POCO [14]	0 (0); 4 (20); 20 (325)	12029
292. Bobby VINTON [8]	1 (5); 6 (50); 21 (283)	11983
293. Kris KRISTOFFERSON [1]	1 (18); 3 (46); 11 (228)	11961
294. John LENNON & Yoko ONO [1]	1 (22); 2 (37); 7 (141)	11923
295. Don McLEAN [1]	1 (17); 3 (39); 6 (117)	11891
296. Charlie RICH [8]	1 (6); 4 (54); 12 (257)	11834
297. Robert PLANT [5]	3 (24); 4 (65); 4 (160)	11787
298. ALICE COOPER (Solo) [5]	1 (10); 3 (46); 10 (203)	11705
299. Eddie MONEY [17]	0 (0); 5 (52); 8 (260)	11661
300. NILSSON [3]	1 (12); 3 (40); 13 (200)	11646
301. NEW EDITION [6]	1 (6); 3 (81); 5 (208)	11484
302. BIG BROTHER And The HOLDING COMPANY [1]	1 (19); 1 (29); 5 (109)	11287
303. Jack JONES [9]	1 (2); 5 (62); 17 (307)	11267
304. Emmylou HARRIS [6]	1 (3); 6 (55); 17 (301)	11224
305. TEN YEARS AFTER [14]	0 (0); 5 (35); 12 (220)	11163
306. Dolly PARTON [6]	1 (3); 6 (55); 17 (302)	11130
307. Charlie DANIELS Band [5]	1 (5); 5 (37); 12 (228)	11056
308. Joan JETT & The BLACKHEARTS [2]	1 (12); 3 (48); 6 (183)	11020
309. IRON MAIDEN [11]	0 (0); 6 (65); 8 (281)	10997
310. PARLIAMENT [13]	0 (0); 5 (59); 8 (174)	10992
311. Janis IAN [1]	1 (9); 3 (38); 8 (162)	10971
312. STING [2]	2 (23); 2 (63); 2 (110)	10962
313. FINE YOUNG CANNIBALS [1]	1 (27); 1 (40); 2 (91)	10909
314. FOGHAT [11]	0 (0); 7 (33); 13 (262)	10900

Rank. Act [Hi Peak]	T10s (Wks); T40s (Wks); Entries (Wks)	Score
315. Stephen STILLS [3]	2 (13); 6 (50); 10 (178)	10877
316. Edgar WINTER [3]	1 (9); 3 (47); 8 (176)	10742
317. Roger MILLER [4]	2 (17); 4 (61); 9 (212)	10727
318. Jeff BECK [4]	1 (4); 7 (61); 8 (181)	10683
319. NIGHT RANGER [10]	1 (3); 4 (65); 5 (209)	10661
320. Rickie Lee JONES [3]	2 (16); 4 (43); 5 (127)	10651
321. Bruce HORNSBY And The RANGE [3]	2 (30); 2 (61); 2 (100)	10643
322. PROCOL HARUM [5]	1 (5); 6 (49); 11 (174)	10625
323. JUDAS PRIEST [17]	0 (0); 7 (59); 10 (224)	10585
324. Ed AMES [4]	1 (10); 3 (45); 13 (266)	10582
325. Ray PARKER Jr./RAYDIO [11]	0 (0); 4 (42); 10 (209)	10580
326. Roger WILLIAMS [7]	1 (4); 3 (38); 18 (331)	10549
327. The WHISPERS [6]	1 (9); 5 (47); 13 (248)	10547
328. The STYLISTICS [14]	0 (0); 3 (35); 10 (239)	10541
329. Ringo STARR [2]	2 (13); 5 (48); 9 (135)	10520
330. MANTOVANI [23]	0 (0); 4 (26); 20 (378)	10488
331. Bob MARLEY And The WAILERS [8]	1 (4); 2 (25); 14 (307)	10462
332. RATT [7]	2 (15); 4 (64); 5 (184)	10425
333. Patti LaBELLE [1]	2 (16); 3 (32); 12 (227)	10378
334. CHIC [4]	2 (18); 4 (45); 7 (144)	10365
335. Jimmy SMITH [12]	0 (0); 6 (59); 18 (300)	10320
336. Jermaine JACKSON [6]	1 (5); 3 (41); 11 (221)	10083
337. John LENNON [1]	3 (15); 5 (44); 7 (130)	10083
338. B.B. KING [25]	0 (0); 3 (16); 21 (305)	10066
339. Stephanie MILLS [16]	0 (0); 4 (45); 9 (250)	10060
340. Elvis COSTELLO & The ATTRACTIONS [10]	1 (2); 8 (52); 11 (199)	9978
341. Tracy CHAPMAN [1]	2 (22); 2 (60); 2 (87)	9969
342. LOVIN' SPOONFUL [3]	2 (10); 4 (52); 9 (173)	9888
343. ATLANTA RHYTHM SECTION [7]	1 (5); 3 (36); 10 (179)	9842
344. The BANGLES [2]	1 (9); 2 (64); 3 (154)	9839
345. BLUE ÖYSTER CULT [22]	0 (0); 5 (32); 14 (230)	9809
346. QUIET RIOT [1]	1 (17); 3 (55); 4 (147)	9745
347. Al STEWART [5]	2 (6); 4 (42); 6 (140)	9727
348. GAP BAND [14]	0 (0); 3 (41); 9 (239)	9708
349. STRAY CATS [2]	1 (18); 2 (47); 4 (117)	9692
350. Andy GIBB [7]	1 (9); 3 (40); 4 (144)	9669
351. Bert KAEMPFERT And His Orchestra [5]	1 (5); 4 (45); 15 (241)	9590
352. TIFFANY [1]	1 (22); 2 (54); 2 (98)	9580
353. Tony BENNETT [18]	0 (0); 4 (46); 21 (289)	9576
354. Ramsey LEWIS [12]	0 (0); 2 (27); 22 (293)	9551
355. Melissa MANCHESTER [12]	0 (0); 4 (30); 13 (234)	9466
356. Phoebe SNOW [4]	1 (5); 3 (39); 7 (161)	9372
357. The CLASH [7]	1 (10); 3 (53); 8 (166)	9264
358. Dave MASON [22]	0 (0); 4 (22); 14 (238)	9253
359. Bobby SHERMAN [10]	1 (2); 3 (35); 6 (140)	9243
360. Shaun CASSIDY [3]	2 (15); 3 (41); 3 (107)	9172
361. Steve MARTIN [2]	2 (12); 3 (35); 4 (120)	9151
362. DAWN/Tony ORLANDO [16]	0 (0); 5 (26); 11 (204)	9150
363. JAMES GANG [20]	0 (0); 3 (33); 11 (228)	9136
364. Sheena EASTON [15]	0 (0); 4 (41); 7 (221)	9075
365. SPYRO GYRA [19]	0 (0); 2 (19); 13 (263)	9067
366. David Lee ROTH [4]	2 (16); 3 (57); 3 (96)	9025
367. The KNACK [1]	1 (15); 2 (31); 3 (60)	9019
368. HUMBLE PIE [6]	1 (4); 4 (33); 9 (172)	9007
369. SURVIVOR [2]	1 (12); 2 (46); 7 (169)	8985
370. George CARLIN [13]	0 (0); 5 (41); 9 (164)	8926
371. Paul MAURIAT And His Orchestra [1]	1 (14); 1 (25); 9 (132)	8880
372. BEASTIE BOYS [1]	1 (19); 2 (45); 2 (83)	8839
373. Wes MONTGOMERY [13]	0 (0); 2 (24); 10 (268)	8834
374. Kim CARNES [1]	1 (12); 1 (23); 6 (128)	8833
375. NEW CHRISTY MINSTRELS [9]	1 (2); 3 (51); 8 (194)	8821
376. Arlo GUTHRIE [17]	0 (0); 2 (26); 11 (239)	8808
377. Paul & Linda McCARTNEY [2]	1 (24); 1 (28); 1 (37)	8807
378. Nancy SINATRA [5]	1 (8); 4 (52); 9 (205)	8806
379. Rita COOLIDGE [6]	1 (7); 2 (26); 10 (171)	8806
380. Gino VANNELLI [13]	0 (0); 4 (35); 9 (186)	8771
381. Gary WRIGHT [7]	1 (8); 2 (44); 5 (123)	8756
382. Lou REED [10]	1 (2); 3 (17); 18 (231)	8712
383. PABLO CRUISE [6]	1 (4); 4 (38); 6 (141)	8695
384. PEACHES & HERB [2]	1 (13); 3 (34); 7 (125)	8645
385. ASHFORD & SIMPSON [20]	0 (0); 4 (33); 14 (233)	8599
386. Hank WILLIAMS Jr. [16]	0 (0); 2 (16); 20 (415)	8574
387. TRIUMPH [23]	0 (0); 5 (39); 9 (222)	8542
388. Bob JAMES [37]	0 (0); 2 (4); 17 (338)	8517
389. SKID ROW [6]	1 (11); 1 (57); 1 (78)	8481
390. METALLICA [6]	1 (5); 3 (49); 6 (253)	8469
391. Bill WITHERS [4]	1 (4); 3 (28); 11 (185)	8442
392. Mac DAVIS [11]	0 (0); 3 (33); 11 (183)	8426
393. Sammy HAGAR [14]	0 (0); 4 (48); 11 (206)	8404
394. The IMPRESSIONS [8]	1 (6); 3 (35); 18 (247)	8403
395. Richard PRYOR [12]	0 (0); 5 (33); 10 (177)	8377
396. The CHI-LITES [5]	1 (6); 2 (30); 10 (152)	8284
397. Ramsey LEWIS Trio [2]	1 (15); 2 (48); 7 (148)	8241
398. Pete TOWNSHEND [5]	1 (9); 4 (43); 9 (150)	8239
399. The FIXX [8]	1 (10); 3 (46); 6 (180)	8231
400. L.T.D. [18]	0 (0); 4 (38); 6 (154)	8221
401. MAZE Featuring Frankie BEVERLY [25]	0 (0); 6 (24); 9 (228)	8199
402. Minnie RIPERTON [4]	1 (6); 4 (34); 6 (126)	8198
403. Randy TRAVIS [19]	0 (0); 3 (30); 5 (300)	8181
404. The CURE [12]	0 (0); 2 (34); 7 (231)	8100
405. Trini LOPEZ [11]	0 (0); 6 (40); 13 (210)	8087
406. The KINGSMEN [15]	0 (0); 3 (44); 5 (211)	8080
407. Louis ARMSTRONG [1]	1 (19); 1 (48); 1 (74)	8075
408. Johnny WINTER [22]	0 (0); 4 (22); 15 (196)	8027
409. Art GARFUNKEL [5]	2 (10); 3 (37); 6 (99)	7994
410. Juice NEWTON [20]	0 (0); 2 (42); 5 (162)	7920
411. George THOROGOOD & The DESTROYERS [32]	0 (0); 4 (36); 7 (225)	7915
412. Herb ALPERT [6]	1 (7); 3 (40); 8 (155)	7901
413. URIAH HEEP [23]	0 (0); 5 (31); 15 (214)	7871
414. Freddie JACKSON [10]	1 (1); 2 (62); 3 (143)	7863
415. LL COOL J [3]	2 (18); 2 (37); 3 (112)	7817
416. Petula CLARK [21]	0 (0); 3 (29); 14 (228)	7803
417. John MAYALL [22]	0 (0); 3 (11); 16 (223)	7682
418. Robert GOULET [5]	1 (8); 5 (44); 13 (195)	7680
419. Taylor DAYNE [21]	0 (0); 2 (68); 2 (124)	7663
420. Buddy MILES [8]	1 (8); 2 (19); 9 (208)	7634
421. MELANIE [15]	0 (0); 3 (29); 10 (151)	7615
422. ATLANTIC STARR [17]	0 (0); 3 (36); 8 (212)	7569
423. Richard HARRIS [4]	1 (5); 4 (36); 6 (119)	7542
424. B.J. THOMAS [12]	0 (0); 1 (23); 10 (176)	7507

Rank. Act [Hi Peak]	T10s (Wks); T40s (Wks); Entries (Wks)	Score
425. Harry CHAPIN [4]	1 (7); 1 (17); 11 (160)	7478
426. Nat King COLE [4]	1 (5); 3 (40); 10 (190)	7466
427. Lawrence WELK [12]	0 (0); 3 (24); 19 (256)	7461
428. MOUNTAIN [16]	0 (0); 3 (32); 8 (141)	7419
429. Jeffrey OSBORNE [25]	0 (0); 3 (38); 5 (211)	7415
430. The BLACKBYRDS [16]	0 (0); 3 (20); 8 (180)	7415
431. Marvin HAMLISCH [1]	1 (15); 1 (23); 2 (46)	7401
432. Maria MULDAUR [3]	1 (11); 2 (27); 4 (99)	7400
433. ROSE ROYCE [9]	1 (3); 3 (33); 5 (112)	7384
434. Rick WAKEMAN [3]	1 (6); 3 (35); 7 (115)	7357
435. David CROSBY/Graham NASH [4]	2 (13); 3 (32); 5 (84)	7327
436. Gary PUCKETT And The UNION GAP [20]	0 (0); 3 (29); 6 (153)	7325
437. Harold MELVIN And The BLUE NOTES [9]	1 (2); 2 (24); 7 (151)	7299
438. GREAT WHITE [9]	1 (4); 2 (44); 5 (140)	7283
439. Chaka KHAN [12]	0 (0); 3 (33); 7 (146)	7266
440. Roy ORBISON [5]	1 (8); 3 (34); 12 (183)	7260
441. Jody WATLEY [10]	1 (1); 2 (61); 3 (127)	7245
442. CANNED HEAT [16]	0 (0); 3 (25); 11 (189)	7227
443. Donny HATHAWAY [3]	1 (8); 2 (44); 5 (136)	7219
444. Paul ANKA [9]	1 (3); 3 (28); 13 (151)	7180
445. Allan SHERMAN [1]	1 (12); 3 (35); 5 (93)	7160
446. THOMPSON TWINS [10]	1 (2); 3 (52); 7 (147)	7153
447. HUMAN LEAGUE [3]	1 (9); 3 (39); 5 (112)	7148
448. Tommy JAMES And The SHONDELLS [8]	1 (5); 2 (24); 10 (146)	7134
449. BLUES BROTHERS [1]	1 (13); 2 (28); 4 (63)	7128
450. MANHATTAN TRANSFER [22]	0 (0); 2 (17); 11 (232)	7104
451. BLIND FAITH [1]	1 (14); 1 (20); 1 (45)	7080
452. EUROPE [8]	1 (10); 2 (53); 2 (103)	7064
453. TOWER OF POWER [15]	0 (0); 3 (18); 10 (170)	7063
454. Herbie MANN [20]	0 (0); 2 (20); 22 (216)	7044
455. John FOGERTY [1]	1 (15); 2 (34); 4 (92)	7021
456. VANGELIS [1]	1 (14); 1 (20); 2 (96)	7000
457. Belinda CARLISLE [13]	0 (0); 3 (53); 3 (110)	6991
458. Vikki CARR [12]	0 (0); 2 (23); 12 (183)	6983
459. The HOLLIES [11]	0 (0); 4 (23); 13 (174)	6950
460. LITTLE FEAT [18]	0 (0); 7 (33); 7 (141)	6911
461. ROYAL PHILHARMONIC Orchestra [4]	1 (9); 2 (29); 4 (131)	6873
462. Neil SEDAKA [16]	0 (0); 3 (23); 8 (149)	6870
463. Eddie RABBITT [19]	0 (0); 3 (30); 7 (163)	6832
464. Bobby WOMACK [29]	0 (0); 2 (7); 13 (210)	6777
465. The OUTLAWS [13]	0 (0); 4 (20); 10 (166)	6766
466. Leo SAYER [10]	1 (2); 4 (29); 6 (132)	6752
467. CHAMBERS BROTHERS [4]	1 (10); 2 (23); 6 (128)	6750
468. Julio IGLESIAS [5]	1 (11); 2 (30); 8 (177)	6749
469. Merle HAGGARD [37]	0 (0); 1 (1); 20 (313)	6727
470. FIREFALL [27]	0 (0); 3 (26); 7 (154)	6727
471. SINGING NUN [1]	1 (18); 1 (22); 2 (53)	6724
472. QUICKSILVER MESSENGER SERVICE [25]	0 (0); 4 (23); 9 (164)	6702
473. Jerry VALE [22]	0 (0); 5 (24); 18 (236)	6646
474. Gary LEWIS And The PLAYBOYS [10]	1 (4); 3 (23); 9 (177)	6616
475. EXPOSÉ [16]	0 (0); 2 (59); 2 (124)	6602
476. Gerry RAFFERTY [1]	1 (8); 2 (29); 3 (79)	6588
477. The BAR-KAYS [35]	0 (0); 1 (4); 12 (232)	6588
478. Wilson PICKETT [21]	0 (0); 2 (15); 14 (233)	6543
479. PET SHOP BOYS [7]	1 (6); 3 (46); 4 (110)	6535
480. Rick ASTLEY [10]	1 (2); 2 (49); 2 (83)	6522
481. CON FUNK SHUN [30]	0 (0); 2 (12); 10 (208)	6517
482. Crystal GAYLE [12]	0 (0); 2 (15); 11 (191)	6506
483. Todd RUNDGREN [29]	0 (0); 2 (10); 12 (194)	6505
484. Deniece WILLIAMS [19]	0 (0); 4 (27); 8 (172)	6497
485. FAT BOYS [8]	1 (4); 2 (26); 7 (178)	6422
486. WHITE LION [11]	0 (0); 2 (44); 3 (126)	6411
487. TRAVELING WILBURYS [3]	1 (22); 1 (32); 1 (53)	6396
488. SHALAMAR [23]	0 (0); 4 (18); 8 (177)	6358
489. OAK RIDGE BOYS [14]	0 (0); 2 (19); 11 (189)	6346
490. DOKKEN [13]	0 (0); 3 (24); 5 (204)	6337
491. Teena MARIE [23]	0 (0); 3 (21); 8 (180)	6330
492. B.T. EXPRESS [5]	1 (5); 2 (26); 6 (82)	6286
493. Billy PRESTON [17]	0 (0); 3 (20); 10 (167)	6260
494. Bobbie GENTRY [1]	1 (10); 2 (31); 6 (112)	6220
495. Larry GRAHAM/ GRAHAM CENTRAL STATION [22]	0 (0); 2 (15); 11 (159)	6208
496. DEODATO [3]	1 (5); 2 (23); 9 (135)	6207
497. MR. MISTER [1]	1 (12); 1 (34); 3 (82)	6196
498. WEATHER REPORT [30]	0 (0); 2 (9); 15 (171)	6193
499. HEATWAVE [10]	1 (2); 3 (27); 5 (101)	6175
500. D.J. JAZZY JEFF & THE FRESH PRINCE [4]	1 (10); 2 (30); 3 (110)	6158
501. The EMOTIONS [7]	1 (7); 2 (24); 6 (101)	6150
502. Howard JONES [10]	1 (1); 2 (27); 5 (155)	6130
503. Bobby GOLDSBORO [5]	1 (9); 1 (22); 10 (130)	6129
504. SISTER SLEDGE [3]	1 (9); 2 (24); 5 (99)	6121
505. Jim NABORS [24]	0 (0); 2 (10); 12 (243)	6119
506. Chuck BERRY [8]	1 (7); 3 (25); 8 (133)	6114
507. DEREK And The DOMINOS [16]	0 (0); 2 (28); 2 (98)	6098
508. SAN SEBASTIAN Strings [20]	0 (0); 1 (4); 7 (228)	6092
509. AMBROSIA [19]	0 (0); 3 (24); 5 (119)	6084
510. The OUTFIELD [9]	1 (6); 2 (40); 3 (110)	6062
511. Los LOBOS [1]	1 (11); 1 (19); 4 (114)	6046
512. MOLLY HATCHET [19]	0 (0); 3 (28); 7 (167)	6021
513. MIDNIGHT STAR [27]	0 (0); 2 (37); 4 (170)	6014
514. Evelyn "Champagne" KING [14]	0 (0); 4 (29); 7 (142)	6007
515. Gloria GAYNOR [4]	1 (9); 2 (20); 7 (103)	6007
516. DEVO [22]	0 (0); 2 (22); 8 (145)	5999
517. NAZARETH [17]	0 (0); 2 (16); 13 (180)	5984
518. Ronnie MILSAP [31]	0 (0); 3 (10); 14 (233)	5944
519. MEAT LOAF [14]	0 (0); 1 (28); 3 (103)	5922
520. DeBARGE [19]	0 (0); 3 (36); 3 (136)	5860
521. SIMPLY RED [16]	0 (0); 3 (37); 3 (125)	5859
522. Claudine LONGET [11]	0 (0); 3 (33); 4 (111)	5858
523. Stevie Ray VAUGHAN And DOUBLE TROUBLE [31]	0 (0); 4 (23); 5 (182)	5856
524. Peabo BRYSON [35]	0 (0); 2 (6); 11 (201)	5792
525. Bob WELCH [12]	0 (0); 2 (34); 4 (76)	5780
526. BAY CITY ROLLERS [20]	0 (0); 4 (27); 6 (102)	5777
527. SMALL FACES/FACES [6]	1 (6); 3 (26); 8 (110)	5746
528. LISA LISA And CULT JAM [7]	1 (7); 1 (29); 3 (127)	5726
529. The MANHATTANS [16]	0 (0); 2 (22); 11 (138)	5649
530. Joan ARMATRADING [28]	0 (0); 2 (8); 11 (213)	5610
531. GRASS ROOTS [25]	0 (0); 2 (12); 7 (156)	5597
532. Stan GETZ [2]	1 (16); 2 (67); 5 (151)	5590
533. FOCUS [8]	1 (4); 2 (25); 8 (120)	5588

Rank. Act [Hi Peak]	T10s (Wks); T40s (Wks); Entries (Wks)	Score
534. Terence Trent D'ARBY [4]	1 (8); 1 (32); 2 (75)	5579
535. Eddie KENDRICKS [18]	0 (0); 3 (14); 9 (171)	5569
536. Jim REEVES [9]	1 (3); 3 (30); 6 (126)	5560
537. Laura BRANIGAN [23]	0 (0); 3 (33); 5 (161)	5558
538. BOOTSY'S RUBBER BAND [16]	0 (0); 2 (22); 6 (100)	5537
539. UB40 [14]	0 (0); 2 (18); 6 (166)	5531
540. Jane FONDA [15]	0 (0); 1 (27); 3 (137)	5515
541. The TIME [24]	0 (0); 2 (42); 3 (122)	5509
542. Johnnie TAYLOR [5]	1 (6); 1 (11); 10 (122)	5485
543. Ronnie LAWS [24]	0 (0); 2 (8); 7 (149)	5485
544. BRASS CONSTRUCTION [10]	1 (1); 2 (22); 8 (114)	5473
545. Burt BACHARACH [18]	0 (0); 1 (12); 5 (187)	5460
546. David SANBORN [45]	0 (0); 0 (0); 10 (272)	5444
547. Randy NEWMAN [9]	1 (3); 2 (20); 7 (116)	5441
548. The DRAMATICS [20]	0 (0); 2 (14); 9 (149)	5438
549. Mike OLDFIELD [3]	1 (12); 1 (23); 6 (78)	5431
550. Billy VAUGHN and His Orchestra [18]	0 (0); 2 (15); 17 (196)	5387
551. ABC [24]	0 (0); 2 (35); 4 (119)	5377
552. Ray PRICE [28]	0 (0); 1 (16); 9 (171)	5359
553. Joe SATRIANI [23]	0 (0); 2 (23); 3 (140)	5352
554. Earl KLUGH [38]	0 (0); 1 (3); 16 (247)	5335
555. Lee MICHAELS [16]	0 (0); 1 (12); 6 (107)	5285
556. Millie JACKSON [21]	0 (0); 2 (19); 14 (184)	5269
557. The JETS [21]	0 (0); 2 (31); 3 (127)	5263
558. The HOOTERS [12]	0 (0); 2 (35); 3 (116)	5253
559. NITTY GRITTY DIRT BAND [28]	0 (0); 1 (6); 12 (182)	5205
560. PURE PRAIRIE LEAGUE [24]	0 (0); 4 (15); 9 (135)	5203
561. Glenn FREY [22]	0 (0); 3 (32); 3 (122)	5192
562. KING CRIMSON [28]	0 (0); 2 (11); 11 (149)	5190
563. ROXY MUSIC [23]	0 (0); 3 (14); 11 (149)	5188
564. Flip WILSON [17]	0 (0); 2 (14); 5 (154)	5155
565. RAINBOW [30]	0 (0); 3 (13); 10 (141)	5147
566. SALSOUL Orchestra [14]	0 (0); 1 (14); 8 (133)	5134
567. SPIRIT [22]	0 (0); 2 (15); 9 (132)	5128
568. Jerry BUTLER [29]	0 (0); 1 (6); 15 (183)	5118
569. The TUBES [18]	0 (0); 2 (18); 9 (142)	5104
570. MISSING PERSONS [17]	0 (0); 1 (26); 4 (114)	5098
571. A TASTE OF HONEY [6]	1 (5); 2 (18); 4 (84)	5093
572. Jean-Luc PONTY [35]	0 (0); 2 (6); 12 (180)	5091
573. UFO [23]	0 (0); 1 (12); 10 (136)	5089
574. 2 LIVE CREW [29]	0 (0); 1 (31); 3 (156)	5065
575. TONE-LOC [1]	1 (12); 1 (23); 1 (42)	5062
576. The MOTELS [16]	0 (0); 3 (25); 5 (103)	5060
577. Perry COMO [22]	0 (0); 2 (16); 10 (145)	5055
578. Ike & Tina TURNER [25]	0 (0); 2 (19); 12 (144)	5053
579. A FLOCK OF SEAGULLS [10]	1 (3); 2 (36); 3 (83)	5042
580. Donald BYRD [33]	0 (0); 2 (5); 8 (140)	4991
581. The TURTLES [7]	1 (6); 2 (23); 7 (117)	4987
582. BLOODROCK [21]	0 (0); 2 (16); 6 (108)	4956
583. TAVARES [24]	0 (0); 2 (16); 10 (148)	4955
584. LIVING COLOUR [6]	1 (8); 1 (28); 1 (76)	4950
585. FUNKADELIC [16]	0 (0); 2 (15); 12 (157)	4948
586. SQUEEZE [32]	0 (0); 2 (11); 7 (159)	4918
587. WARRANT [10]	1 (3); 1 (33); 1 (65)	4909
588. TESLA [18]	0 (0); 2 (24); 2 (128)	4905
589. QUARTERFLASH [8]	1 (4); 2 (25); 3 (78)	4884
590. Billy COBHAM [23]	0 (0); 3 (16); 9 (119)	4879
591. CLIMAX BLUES Band [27]	0 (0); 2 (8); 9 (158)	4875
592. Tammy WYNETTE [37]	0 (0); 1 (2); 12 (177)	4799
593. PAT METHENY GROUP [44]	0 (0); 0 (0); 11 (204)	4798
594. John CAFFERTY & The BEAVER BROWN BAND [9]	1 (6); 2 (27); 3 (100)	4782
595. Angela BOFILL [34]	0 (0); 2 (11); 5 (134)	4774
596. KINGSTON TRIO [7]	1 (4); 3 (25); 7 (109)	4774
597. Jesse Colin YOUNG [26]	0 (0); 3 (10); 8 (125)	4771
598. BABYFACE [14]	0 (0); 1 (41); 1 (61)	4740
599. Warren ZEVON [8]	1 (4); 2 (21); 6 (87)	4725
600. MIKE + THE MECHANICS [13]	0 (0); 2 (34); 2 (90)	4715
601. DR. HOOK [41]	0 (0); 0 (0); 10 (200)	4711
602. SIMPLE MINDS [10]	1 (5); 1 (27); 5 (107)	4711
603. BOOKER T. & The M.G.'s [35]	0 (0); 1 (4); 10 (163)	4711
604. SLAVE [22]	0 (0); 1 (12); 8 (136)	4710
605. LOVE UNLIMITED [3]	1 (5); 1 (17); 4 (86)	4693
606. FERRANTE & TEICHER [35]	0 (0); 1 (6); 22 (209)	4679
607. Pat TRAVERS [20]	0 (0); 3 (18); 7 (121)	4672
608. Bob DYLAN And The BAND [3]	2 (9); 2 (19); 2 (33)	4661
609. SILVER CONVENTION [10]	1 (1); 2 (20); 4 (71)	4658
610. Corey HART [20]	0 (0); 2 (21); 4 (108)	4644
611. The CULT [10]	1 (6); 2 (24); 3 (99)	4643
612. Edie BRICKELL & NEW BOHEMIANS [4]	1 (8); 1 (28); 1 (54)	4620
613. Frank SINATRA & Count BASIE [9]	1 (2); 2 (30); 2 (75)	4616
614. Greg KIHN Band [15]	0 (0); 3 (21); 8 (122)	4606
615. The BABYS [22]	0 (0); 2 (14); 6 (108)	4600
616. SSgt Barry SADLER [1]	1 (10); 1 (20); 2 (35)	4592
617. Robert CRAY Band [13]	0 (0); 2 (33); 5 (131)	4577
618. LAKESIDE [16]	0 (0); 1 (12); 7 (138)	4570
619. Bonnie TYLER [4]	1 (7); 2 (26); 4 (62)	4566
620. SOUL II SOUL [14]	0 (0); 1 (36); 1 (51)	4558
621. MFSB [4]	1 (4); 2 (16); 5 (79)	4550
622. Thomas DOLBY [13]	0 (0); 3 (27); 4 (96)	4541
623. Sammy DAVIS Jr. [11]	0 (0); 3 (22); 7 (95)	4538
624. 10,000 MANIACS [13]	0 (0); 2 (21); 2 (105)	4531
625. John McLAUGHLIN/ MAHAVISHNU ORCHESTRA [15]	0 (0); 1 (11); 8 (118)	4470
626. Miles DAVIS [35]	0 (0); 1 (4); 24 (225)	4469
627. 10cc [15]	0 (0); 2 (15); 9 (106)	4465
628. Melissa ETHERIDGE [22]	0 (0); 2 (24); 2 (123)	4464
629. YOUNG M.C. [9]	1 (4); 1 (30); 1 (48)	4442
630. STAPLE SINGERS [19]	0 (0); 2 (20); 6 (101)	4439
631. KRAFTWERK [5]	1 (5); 1 (11); 7 (110)	4428
632. Peter NERO [23]	0 (0); 3 (15); 14 (151)	4413
633. Keith SWEAT [15]	0 (0); 1 (27); 1 (67)	4409
634. MANFRED MANN'S EARTH BAND [10]	1 (2); 2 (13); 10 (129)	4400
635. LOVE UNLIMITED ORCHESTRA [8]	1 (3); 2 (13); 5 (85)	4356
636. SMOTHERS BROTHERS [13]	0 (0); 3 (19); 7 (129)	4351
637. TWISTED SISTER [15]	0 (0); 1 (26); 5 (104)	4349
638. Julian LENNON [17]	0 (0); 2 (33); 3 (79)	4347
639. Roger DALTREY [22]	0 (0); 2 (11); 7 (117)	4338
640. The JUDDS [51]	0 (0); 0 (0); 6 (246)	4334
641. Walter CARLOS [10]	1 (1); 1 (17); 4 (74)	4296
642. DIO [23]	0 (0); 2 (20); 5 (129)	4291

Rank. Act [Hi Peak]	T10s (Wks); T40s (Wks); Entries (Wks)	Score
643. COUNTRY JOE & THE FISH [23]	0 (0); 2 (10); 10 (135)	4289
644. Jeff BECK Group [15]	0 (0); 2 (17); 3 (63)	4285
645. The SWEET [25]	0 (0); 2 (13); 6 (98)	4273
646. Adam ANT [16]	0 (0); 1 (16); 5 (125)	4268
647. John Fitzgerald KENNEDY [5]	2 (6); 4 (22); 10 (88)	4268
648. READY FOR THE WORLD [17]	0 (0); 2 (35); 3 (84)	4267
649. OZARK MOUNTAIN DAREDEVILS [19]	0 (0); 2 (12); 7 (101)	4267
650. GOLDEN EARRING [12]	0 (0); 2 (25); 8 (90)	4250
651. APRIL WINE [26]	0 (0); 2 (15); 6 (121)	4241
652. Stephen STILLS & MANASSAS [4]	1 (7); 2 (21); 2 (48)	4240
653. STRYPER [32]	0 (0); 2 (17); 4 (193)	4229
654. WINGER [21]	0 (0); 1 (35); 1 (64)	4224
655. BRICK [15]	0 (0); 2 (17); 5 (79)	4216
656. DEPECHE MODE [35]	0 (0); 1 (3); 8 (211)	4189
657. John WAITE [10]	1 (1); 2 (20); 4 (94)	4189
658. The DELLS [29]	0 (0); 1 (5); 12 (156)	4187
659. KROKUS [25]	0 (0); 2 (14); 7 (140)	4185
660. S.O.S. BAND [12]	0 (0); 1 (11); 7 (112)	4170
661. SWINGLE SINGERS [15]	0 (0); 1 (24); 3 (97)	4147
662. MOTT THE HOOPLE [23]	0 (0); 3 (15); 7 (102)	4121
663. DAZZ BAND [14]	0 (0); 1 (11); 7 (146)	4120
664. Eddie MURPHY [26]	0 (0); 2 (13); 4 (132)	4105
665. IT'S A BEAUTIFUL DAY [28]	0 (0); 1 (5); 5 (126)	4105
666. Michael MURPHEY [18]	0 (0); 1 (13); 8 (92)	4099
667. BANANARAMA [15]	0 (0); 2 (18); 5 (118)	4094
668. Patti SMITH [18]	0 (0); 2 (15); 5 (82)	4089
669. SAVOY BROWN [34]	0 (0); 2 (8); 11 (134)	4086
670. Boots RANDOLPH [36]	0 (0); 1 (4); 12 (162)	4040
671. George WINSTON [54]	0 (0); 0 (0); 4 (258)	4037
672. MANDRILL [28]	0 (0); 1 (8); 9 (130)	4018
673. FABULOUS THUNDERBIRDS [13]	0 (0); 1 (25); 4 (82)	4014
674. Tommy ROE [21]	0 (0); 2 (21); 5 (69)	4009
675. GQ [13]	0 (0); 1 (19); 3 (63)	3982
676. WILD CHERRY [5]	1 (8); 1 (15); 3 (47)	3979
677. POWER STATION [6]	1 (11); 1 (25); 1 (44)	3972
678. Michael PARKS [24]	0 (0); 2 (11); 4 (76)	3947
679. Elvin BISHOP [18]	0 (0); 2 (10); 5 (92)	3923
680. Hugo MONTENEGRO [9]	1 (6); 1 (17); 4 (68)	3897
681. Chris ISAAK [7]	1 (7); 1 (21); 2 (76)	3886
682. T. REX [17]	0 (0); 2 (16); 5 (85)	3869
683. CHAD & JEREMY [22]	0 (0); 2 (14); 8 (128)	3866
684. Patrice RUSHEN [14]	0 (0); 3 (13); 7 (122)	3852
685. George DUKE [25]	0 (0); 2 (10); 14 (129)	3850
686. CROWDED HOUSE [12]	0 (0); 2 (26); 2 (77)	3847
687. Bobby McFERRIN [5]	1 (7); 1 (16); 2 (74)	3846
688. The COWSILLS [16]	0 (0); 2 (17); 6 (77)	3844
689. Stanley CLARKE [34]	0 (0); 2 (7); 8 (121)	3828
690. Kenny ROGERS & The FIRST EDITION [26]	0 (0); 1 (6); 8 (110)	3818
691. Eric CARMEN [21]	0 (0); 1 (8); 6 (111)	3817
692. BADFINGER [28]	0 (0); 2 (8); 8 (97)	3810
693. Sam COOKE [29]	0 (0); 2 (8); 9 (153)	3803
694. Johnny Guitar WATSON [20]	0 (0); 1 (13); 7 (91)	3778
695. Rob BASE [31]	0 (0); 1 (8); 2 (107)	3771
696. WHODINI [30]	0 (0); 3 (15); 3 (109)	3761
697. ENGLAND DAN & John Ford COLEY [17]	0 (0); 1 (12); 5 (74)	3750
698. DR. BUZZARD'S ORIGINAL "SAVANNAH" BAND [22]	0 (0); 2 (21); 2 (58)	3742
699. Clint BLACK [31]	0 (0); 1 (6); 1 (143)	3718
700. BIG COUNTRY [18]	0 (0); 1 (18); 5 (94)	3673
701. Thelma HOUSTON [11]	0 (0); 1 (16); 4 (66)	3651
702. SKYY [18]	0 (0); 1 (11); 7 (106)	3643
703. Lita FORD [29]	0 (0); 1 (23); 2 (78)	3642
704. Aldo NOVA [8]	1 (8); 1 (16); 2 (57)	3623
705. Carlos SANTANA [8]	1 (8); 3 (25); 7 (102)	3621
706. Tom SCOTT & The L.A. EXPRESS [18]	0 (0); 1 (8); 9 (127)	3615
707. UTOPIA [32]	0 (0); 2 (7); 10 (116)	3612
708. NEW ORDER [32]	0 (0); 2 (13); 4 (131)	3596
709. Graham PARKER And The RUMOUR [40]	0 (0); 2 (3); 9 (124)	3585
710. ROXETTE [23]	0 (0); 1 (21); 1 (71)	3575
711. The SUPREMES [25]	0 (0); 1 (6); 7 (97)	3572
712. Joao GILBERTO [2]	1 (16); 1 (50); 1 (96)	3549
713. The SMITHEREENS [41]	0 (0); 0 (0); 3 (119)	3547
714. THIN LIZZY [18]	0 (0); 2 (12); 9 (103)	3532
715. Peter BROWN [11]	0 (0); 1 (19); 1 (44)	3524
716. Jerry Lee LEWIS [37]	0 (0); 1 (3); 21 (180)	3517
717. Davie ALLAN And The ARROWS [17]	0 (0); 1 (13); 3 (91)	3515
718. MIDNIGHT OIL [21]	0 (0); 1 (26); 3 (66)	3511
719. Gilbert O'SULLIVAN [9]	1 (4); 1 (14); 3 (58)	3507
720. The CHIPMUNKS [14]	0 (0); 2 (17); 5 (99)	3507
721. David RUFFIN [31]	0 (0); 2 (13); 6 (73)	3506
722. O.C. SMITH [19]	0 (0); 1 (10); 5 (85)	3498
723. PSYCHEDELIC FURS [29]	0 (0); 1 (11); 7 (119)	3498
724. ROSSINGTON COLLINS BAND [13]	0 (0); 2 (18); 3 (49)	3494
725. Lynn ANDERSON [19]	0 (0); 1 (12); 10 (94)	3488
726. Elvis COSTELLO [28]	0 (0); 3 (19); 3 (75)	3466
727. LEVEL 42 [18]	0 (0); 2 (23); 3 (77)	3464
728. Paul YOUNG [19]	0 (0); 1 (24); 3 (83)	3453
729. Freddy FENDER [20]	0 (0); 1 (11); 5 (82)	3446
730. FREE [17]	0 (0); 1 (11); 7 (78)	3428
731. Karla BONOFF [31]	0 (0); 1 (8); 3 (101)	3427
732. ORCHESTRAL MANOEUVRES IN THE DARK [38]	0 (0); 1 (5); 6 (129)	3422
733. SWITCH [37]	0 (0); 2 (8); 5 (104)	3404
734. LIPPS INC. [5]	1 (7); 1 (13); 2 (35)	3403
735. Brian AUGER [41]	0 (0); 0 (0); 11 (112)	3393
736. HOT TUNA [30]	0 (0); 1 (5); 8 (102)	3393
737. NEW RIDERS Of The PURPLE SAGE [33]	0 (0); 2 (8); 8 (97)	3393
738. Gregg ALLMAN [13]	0 (0); 1 (17); 2 (51)	3392
739. The VOGUES [29]	0 (0); 2 (10); 5 (78)	3376
740. The ALARM [39]	0 (0); 1 (3); 6 (153)	3365
741. AL B. SURE! [20]	0 (0); 1 (25); 1 (54)	3363
742. Mitch RYDER And The DETROIT WHEELS [23]	0 (0); 3 (14); 5 (92)	3346
743. Jr. WALKER & The ALL STARS [43]	0 (0); 0 (0); 10 (145)	3316
744. "Weird Al" YANKOVIC [17]	0 (0); 2 (20); 6 (81)	3313
745. A-HA [15]	0 (0); 1 (25); 3 (73)	3302
746. RETURN TO FOREVER [32]	0 (0); 4 (11); 6 (87)	3297
747. Wayne NEWTON [17]	0 (0); 2 (13); 10 (113)	3280
748. Stanley TURRENTINE [63]	0 (0); 0 (0); 14 (144)	3278
749. MOBY GRAPE [20]	0 (0); 2 (13); 5 (76)	3271
750. Nicolette LARSON [15]	0 (0); 1 (12); 4 (80)	3266
751. Les McCANN & Eddie HARRIS [29]	0 (0); 1 (5); 2 (65)	3249

Rank. Act [Hi Peak] T10s (Wks); T40s (Wks); Entries (Wks)	Score
752. The YARDBIRDS [28] 0 (0); 1 (8); 6 (111)	3246
753. FOXY [12] 0 (0); 2 (18); 2 (43)	3240
754. NEW BIRTH [31] 0 (0); 1 (4); 8 (106)	3238
755. Donny & Marie OSMOND [35] 0 (0); 1 (4); 6 (108)	3215
756. Steve PERRY [12] 0 (0); 1 (18); 1 (60)	3214
757. KLYMAXX [18] 0 (0); 1 (15); 2 (98)	3213
758. MECO [13] 0 (0); 1 (9); 6 (76)	3209
759. Tom BROWNE [18] 0 (0); 2 (11); 5 (77)	3204
760. Rick NELSON [14] 0 (0); 2 (17); 6 (71)	3203
761. John STEWART [10] 1 (1); 1 (14); 7 (59)	3199
762. LOVE AND ROCKETS [14] 0 (0); 1 (17); 3 (84)	3195
763. RENAISSANCE [46] 0 (0); 0 (0); 8 (101)	3192
764. CLUB NOUVEAU [6] 1 (7); 1 (18); 2 (50)	3188
765. The HONEYDRIPPERS [4] 1 (10); 1 (18); 1 (31)	3186
766. Eydie GORME [22] 0 (0); 1 (9); 7 (112)	3164
767. GEORGIA SATELLITES [5] 1 (5); 1 (20); 3 (68)	3156
768. SHEILA E. [28] 0 (0); 1 (9); 3 (91)	3150
769. Ziggy MARLEY & The MELODY MAKERS [23] 0 (0); 2 (24); 2 (60)	3140
770. MIDNIGHT STRING QUARTET [17] 0 (0); 1 (12); 5 (107)	3140
771. Billy PAUL [17] 0 (0); 1 (9); 9 (118)	3126
772. ANTHRAX [30] 0 (0); 1 (5); 4 (130)	3124
773. KOOL MOE DEE [25] 0 (0); 2 (12); 3 (94)	3121
774. MC HAMMER [30] 0 (0); 1 (23); 1 (80)	3114
775. GUY [27] 0 (0); 1 (13); 1 (70)	3108
776. TECHNOTRONIC [10] 1 (1); 1 (22); 1 (55)	3107
777. HEAVY D & The BOYZ [19] 0 (0); 1 (14); 2 (67)	3106
778. Richie HAVENS [29] 0 (0); 1 (7); 13 (117)	3105
779. XTC [41] 0 (0); 0 (0); 7 (112)	3095
780. Michael HENDERSON [35] 0 (0); 2 (7); 7 (94)	3094
781. Lily TOMLIN [15] 0 (0); 1 (11); 3 (53)	3085
782. HUDSON And LANDRY [30] 0 (0); 2 (8); 3 (58)	3073
783. The SANDPIPERS [13] 0 (0); 1 (10); 7 (101)	3060
784. BUFFALO SPRINGFIELD [42] 0 (0); 0 (0); 5 (86)	3058
785. FALCO [3] 1 (6); 1 (18); 2 (40)	3057
786. Samantha FOX [24] 0 (0); 2 (15); 3 (87)	3044
787. MALO [14] 0 (0); 1 (14); 4 (59)	3043
788. The RAMONES [44] 0 (0); 0 (0); 12 (124)	3030
789. SCANDAL [17] 0 (0); 2 (17); 2 (73)	3024
790. Mason WILLIAMS [14] 0 (0); 1 (8); 4 (78)	2989
791. Grace JONES [32] 0 (0); 1 (4); 9 (128)	2986
792. Gene PITNEY [42] 0 (0); 0 (0); 9 (131)	2982
793. HIROSHIMA [51] 0 (0); 0 (0); 6 (150)	2977
794. PEBBLES [14] 0 (0); 1 (19); 1 (38)	2973
795. SALT-N-PEPA [26] 0 (0); 2 (18); 2 (84)	2970
796. Paul BUTTERFIELD Blues Band [52] 0 (0); 0 (0); 10 (126)	2967
797. BLACKFOOT [42] 0 (0); 0 (0); 5 (91)	2967
798. Laura NYRO [32] 0 (0); 1 (3); 8 (88)	2953
799. NEW VAUDEVILLE BAND [5] 1 (7); 1 (17); 1 (31)	2950
800. Graham NASH [15] 0 (0); 2 (14); 4 (50)	2947
801. BERLIN [28] 0 (0); 2 (15); 3 (84)	2939
802. ZAPP [19] 0 (0); 3 (15); 5 (90)	2936
803. WANG CHUNG [30] 0 (0); 1 (6); 4 (97)	2930
804. The ROMANTICS [14] 0 (0); 1 (15); 5 (71)	2930
805. Eddie HARRIS [36] 0 (0); 1 (1); 11 (125)	2913
806. The MIRACLES [33] 0 (0); 1 (10); 6 (72)	2910
807. Karyn WHITE [19] 0 (0); 1 (17); 1 (54)	2905
808. SOFT CELL [22] 0 (0); 1 (18); 3 (63)	2899
809. Bob JAMES & Earl KLUGH [23] 0 (0); 1 (13); 2 (62)	2889
810. BLACK OAK ARKANSAS [52] 0 (0); 0 (0); 10 (125)	2887
811. Ian HUNTER [35] 0 (0); 1 (6); 7 (101)	2872
812. Ray CHARLES Singers [11] 0 (0); 1 (15); 4 (81)	2860
813. BAJA MARIMBA BAND [54] 0 (0); 0 (0); 10 (154)	2846
814. GLASS TIGER [27] 0 (0); 1 (28); 2 (66)	2842
815. The FIRM [17] 0 (0); 2 (23); 2 (52)	2841
816. Marianne FAITHFULL [12] 0 (0); 1 (15); 7 (90)	2840
817. PLAYER [26] 0 (0); 2 (8); 3 (64)	2838
818. QUEENSRYCHE [47] 0 (0); 0 (0); 4 (118)	2832
819. Liza MINNELLI [19] 0 (0); 2 (13); 7 (76)	2830
820. Percy FAITH His Orchestra And Chorus [80] 0 (0); 0 (0); 20 (167)	2817
821. YOUNG-HOLT UNLIMITED [9] 1 (2); 1 (14); 3 (42)	2816
822. BAD ENGLISH [21] 0 (0); 1 (22); 1 (52)	2809
823. OLIVER [19] 0 (0); 1 (10); 2 (51)	2803
824. Yngwie MALMSTEEN [40] 0 (0); 1 (2); 5 (120)	2794
825. COLD BLOOD [23] 0 (0); 1 (6); 6 (79)	2785
826. USA For AFRICA [1] 1 (7); 1 (11); 1 (22)	2778
827. N.W.A. [37] 0 (0); 1 (9); 1 (81)	2777
828. The SEEKERS [10] 1 (2); 1 (12); 5 (63)	2767
829. MARY JANE GIRLS [18] 0 (0); 1 (11); 2 (79)	2765
830. The TRAMMPS [46] 0 (0); 0 (0); 6 (98)	2761
831. John SEBASTIAN [20] 0 (0); 1 (7); 5 (66)	2761
832. Suzanne VEGA [11] 0 (0); 1 (16); 2 (63)	2760
833. NEKTAR [19] 0 (0); 2 (9); 5 (69)	2757
834. Kate BUSH [30] 0 (0); 1 (6); 5 (97)	2754
835. GERRY And The PACEMAKERS [13] 0 (0); 2 (17); 5 (70)	2753
836. BLUE CHEER [11] 0 (0); 1 (11); 4 (62)	2748
837. Peter CETERA [23] 0 (0); 1 (17); 3 (70)	2743
838. Buck OWENS [43] 0 (0); 0 (0); 16 (143)	2743
839. FRIJID PINK [11] 0 (0); 1 (12); 2 (42)	2738
840. Gary NUMAN [16] 0 (0); 1 (14); 4 (54)	2737
841. Ray STEVENS [35] 0 (0); 1 (3); 10 (113)	2737
842. Al KOOPER [12] 0 (0); 2 (20); 9 (97)	2719
843. Nils LOFGREN [32] 0 (0); 2 (5); 7 (77)	2716
844. Ace FREHLEY [26] 0 (0); 1 (10); 3 (57)	2715
845. JAN & DEAN [22] 0 (0); 3 (6); 8 (104)	2712
846. Crazy World Of Arthur BROWN [7] 1 (7); 1 (10); 1 (24)	2702
847. 'TIL TUESDAY [19] 0 (0); 1 (12); 3 (76)	2702
848. Rosanne CASH [26] 0 (0); 1 (9); 5 (92)	2695
849. Phyllis HYMAN [50] 0 (0); 0 (0); 6 (118)	2689
850. EAZY-E [41] 0 (0); 0 (0); 1 (90)	2665
851. Linda CLIFFORD [22] 0 (0); 2 (13); 5 (58)	2644
852. Waylon JENNINGS & Willie NELSON [12] 0 (0); 1 (9); 2 (51)	2636
853. Michael McDONALD [6] 1 (6); 1 (11); 2 (47)	2631
854. Tim WEISBERG [8] 1 (5); 1 (13); 8 (88)	2630
855. Debby BOONE [6] 1 (6); 1 (10); 2 (42)	2629
856. Tom LEHRER [18] 0 (0); 1 (19); 2 (59)	2615
857. Amy GRANT [35] 0 (0); 1 (4); 4 (104)	2613
858. ROGER [26] 0 (0); 2 (11); 3 (63)	2610
859. INSTANT FUNK [12] 0 (0); 1 (13); 4 (48)	2606

Rank. Act [Hi Peak]	T10s (Wks); T40s (Wks); Entries (Wks)	Score
860. Stacy LATTISAW [44]	0 (0); 0 (0); 7 (107)	2605
861. SYLVESTER [28]	0 (0); 1 (6); 7 (91)	2595
862. ORLEANS [30]	0 (0); 2 (10); 3 (61)	2587
863. Eddy GRANT [10]	1 (3); 1 (15); 2 (47)	2578
864. KENTUCKY HEADHUNTERS [41]	0 (0); 0 (0); 1 (96)	2571
865. KINGDOM COME [12]	0 (0); 1 (12); 2 (44)	2570
866. Carol HENSEL [56]	0 (0); 0 (0); 3 (95)	2563
867. David FRYE [19]	0 (0); 1 (8); 4 (52)	2542
868. The FLOATERS [10]	1 (2); 1 (13); 2 (33)	2539
869. Maynard FERGUSON [22]	0 (0); 1 (7); 8 (74)	2538
870. MAIN INGREDIENT [52]	0 (0); 0 (0); 9 (109)	2531
871. SPLIT ENZ [40]	0 (0); 1 (2); 4 (74)	2526
872. Joe TEX [17]	0 (0); 1 (11); 9 (85)	2525
873. Eric BURDON & WAR [18]	0 (0); 1 (13); 3 (41)	2522
874. CHANGE [29]	0 (0); 1 (7); 5 (78)	2509
875. ICEHOUSE [43]	0 (0); 0 (0); 4 (89)	2508
876. MEN WITHOUT HATS [13]	0 (0); 1 (14); 3 (55)	2504
877. John KLEMMER [51]	0 (0); 0 (0); 10 (122)	2503
878. BASIA [36]	0 (0); 1 (3); 1 (77)	2498
879. Dan HILL [21]	0 (0); 1 (8); 5 (80)	2493
880. Chad MITCHELL Trio [29]	0 (0); 2 (5); 5 (94)	2492
881. Joe SAMPLE [56]	0 (0); 0 (0); 5 (99)	2487
882. Michael FRANKS [45]	0 (0); 0 (0); 9 (132)	2483
883. SOUTHER, HILLMAN, FURAY Band [11]	0 (0); 2 (12); 2 (33)	2483
884. Hugh MASEKELA [17]	0 (0); 1 (10); 7 (76)	2471
885. PETER And GORDON [21]	0 (0); 1 (5); 7 (92)	2456
886. Patti AUSTIN [36]	0 (0); 1 (11); 4 (79)	2452
887. The SMITHS [55]	0 (0); 0 (0); 6 (140)	2442
888. IRISH ROVERS [24]	0 (0); 1 (11); 4 (64)	2442
889. Jeannie C. RILEY [12]	0 (0); 1 (12); 3 (39)	2440
890. "Cannonball" ADDERLEY Quintet [13]	0 (0); 1 (9); 9 (83)	2434
891. Jesse JOHNSON [43]	0 (0); 0 (0); 3 (76)	2433
892. SPOOKY TOOTH [44]	0 (0); 0 (0); 8 (89)	2418
893. Pete FOUNTAIN [48]	0 (0); 0 (0); 8 (104)	2414
894. TOO SHORT [37]	0 (0); 1 (8); 1 (78)	2412
895. L.A. GUNS [38]	0 (0); 1 (1); 2 (89)	2410
896. SMITH [17]	0 (0); 1 (11); 2 (40)	2410
897. Andreas VOLLENWEIDER [52]	0 (0); 0 (0); 5 (130)	2399
898. STARS ON [9]	1 (5); 1 (8); 3 (36)	2396
899. Isao TOMITA [49]	0 (0); 0 (0); 7 (83)	2395
900. David GILMOUR [29]	0 (0); 2 (16); 2 (46)	2390
901. Frankie VALLI [34]	0 (0); 1 (2); 7 (81)	2384
902. Mick JAGGER [13]	0 (0); 1 (12); 2 (49)	2376
903. Roberta FLACK & Peabo BRYSON [25]	0 (0); 1 (14); 2 (61)	2374
904. Frankie LAINE [16]	0 (0); 1 (9); 4 (51)	2356
905. ERASURE [49]	0 (0); 0 (0); 5 (89)	2351
906. BREATHE [34]	0 (0); 1 (8); 1 (51)	2350
907. SOUTHSIDE JOHNNY & The ASBURY JUKES [48]	0 (0); 0 (0); 10 (98)	2348
908. Dave EDMUNDS [46]	0 (0); 0 (0); 7 (84)	2334
909. SLADE [33]	0 (0); 1 (4); 7 (92)	2312
910. Lonnie Liston SMITH [58]	0 (0); 0 (0); 8 (96)	2311
911. HOT CHOCOLATE [31]	0 (0); 1 (4); 5 (66)	2310
912. Leif GARRETT [34]	0 (0); 2 (8); 4 (72)	2299
913. Glenn YARBROUGH [35]	0 (0); 1 (3); 10 (120)	2297
914. CHASE [22]	0 (0); 1 (10); 3 (48)	2289
915. JAY & The AMERICANS [21]	0 (0); 1 (5); 6 (77)	2284
916. Don HO and the ALIIS [15]	0 (0); 1 (8); 6 (71)	2284
917. VILLAGE STOMPERS [5]	1 (2); 1 (14); 2 (33)	2281
918. BOX TOPS [45]	0 (0); 0 (0); 4 (71)	2276
919. SERENDIPITY SINGERS [11]	0 (0); 1 (18); 3 (46)	2264
920. Jessi COLTER [10]	1 (2); 1 (14); 5 (113)	2261
921. Dwight YOAKAM [55]	0 (0); 0 (0); 4 (118)	2260
922. ACE [11]	0 (0); 1 (11); 3 (30)	2260
923. Van McCOY [12]	0 (0); 1 (9); 5 (53)	2255
924. FRIENDS OF DISTINCTION [35]	0 (0); 1 (3); 5 (62)	2243
925. Robin WILLIAMS [10]	1 (2); 1 (12); 2 (31)	2239
926. Roy AYERS UBIQUITY [51]	0 (0); 0 (0); 6 (80)	2232
927. David CASSIDY [15]	0 (0); 1 (8); 2 (40)	2232
928. ENGLISH BEAT [39]	0 (0); 1 (3); 4 (86)	2223
929. Marilyn McCOO & Billy DAVIS JR. [30]	0 (0); 1 (7); 3 (52)	2222
930. Harry CONNICK Jr. [42]	0 (0); 0 (0); 1 (122)	2220
931. Norman CONNORS [39]	0 (0); 1 (1); 8 (82)	2216
932. W.A.S.P. [48]	0 (0); 0 (0); 5 (100)	2209
933. DR. JOHN [24]	0 (0); 1 (9); 6 (80)	2207
934. BLUE MAGIC [45]	0 (0); 0 (0); 4 (64)	2206
935. RAY, GOODMAN & BROWN [17]	0 (0); 1 (11); 3 (42)	2198
936. RITCHIE FAMILY [30]	0 (0); 1 (7); 5 (65)	2196
937. BLOODSTONE [30]	0 (0); 1 (7); 5 (83)	2189
938. Roy AYERS [33]	0 (0); 1 (3); 7 (73)	2189
939. Cheryl LYNN [23]	0 (0); 1 (6); 5 (72)	2184
940. SANTA ESMERALDA [25]	0 (0); 1 (8); 3 (43)	2178
941. J.J. CALE [51]	0 (0); 0 (0); 7 (96)	2169
942. John DAVIDSON [19]	0 (0); 1 (10); 6 (66)	2169
943. Anita WARD [8]	1 (4); 1 (10); 1 (19)	2164
944. Brenda LEE [36]	0 (0); 2 (3); 8 (88)	2156
945. Bobby CALDWELL [21]	0 (0); 1 (10); 3 (59)	2149
946. The ARCHIES [66]	0 (0); 0 (0); 5 (85)	2136
947. Philip BAILEY [22]	0 (0); 1 (11); 3 (60)	2136
948. SWING OUT SISTER [40]	0 (0); 1 (1); 2 (62)	2136
949. FATBACK [44]	0 (0); 0 (0); 8 (83)	2135
950. Chris De BURGH [25]	0 (0); 1 (8); 3 (73)	2135
951. LAST POETS [29]	0 (0); 1 (7); 3 (51)	2135
952. Shirley BASSEY [60]	0 (0); 0 (0); 10 (111)	2134
953. Gil SCOTT-HERON & Brian JACKSON [30]	0 (0); 1 (3); 6 (65)	2128
954. Lee RITENOUR [26]	0 (0); 1 (7); 9 (79)	2128
955. MANNHEIM STEAMROLLER [36]	0 (0); 1 (4); 4 (96)	2122
956. Jerry GARCIA [35]	0 (0); 1 (3); 5 (56)	2121
957. Vicki Sue ROBINSON [45]	0 (0); 0 (0); 3 (64)	2107
958. W.C. FIELDS [30]	0 (0); 1 (11); 2 (31)	2101
959. ICE-T [35]	0 (0); 2 (8); 3 (88)	2096
960. DELANEY & BONNIE & FRIENDS [29]	0 (0); 1 (6); 5 (59)	2086
961. KATRINA & The WAVES [25]	0 (0); 1 (9); 3 (56)	2082
962. Steve FORBERT [20]	0 (0); 1 (6); 4 (56)	2074
963. SUGARLOAF [24]	0 (0); 1 (10); 3 (44)	2070
964. GTR [11]	0 (0); 1 (17); 1 (26)	2069
965. FRANKIE GOES TO HOLLYWOOD [33]	0 (0); 1 (14); 2 (54)	2056
966. George STRAIT [68]	0 (0); 0 (0); 8 (139)	2051
967. Rick DERRINGER [25]	0 (0); 1 (8); 5 (61)	2050
968. Michael STANLEY Band [64]	0 (0); 0 (0); 7 (96)	2047
969. Jeff HEALEY Band [22]	0 (0); 1 (8); 1 (69)	2041

Rank. Act [Hi Peak]	T10s (Wks); T40s (Wks); Entries (Wks)	Score
970. MARTIKA [15]	0 (0); 1 (12); 1 (39)	2041
971. TOM TOM CLUB [23]	0 (0); 1 (10); 3 (57)	2038
972. Dick HYMAN [30]	0 (0); 1 (8); 5 (55)	2035
973. Nick LOWE [31]	0 (0); 1 (7); 4 (53)	2030
974. Mary WELLS [18]	0 (0); 1 (12); 4 (69)	2022
975. YARBROUGH & PEOPLES [16]	0 (0); 1 (11); 2 (40)	2020
976. SAGA [29]	0 (0); 1 (13); 3 (55)	2008
977. ONE WAY [51]	0 (0); 0 (0); 8 (102)	2007
978. LOBO [37]	0 (0); 1 (7); 5 (71)	2007
979. STARLAND VOCAL BAND [20]	0 (0); 1 (10); 2 (38)	2006
980. CLASSICS IV [45]	0 (0); 0 (0); 4 (50)	2001
981. Betty WRIGHT [26]	0 (0); 1 (7); 4 (61)	1995
982. Ry COODER [43]	0 (0); 0 (0); 9 (83)	1995
983. COMMANDER CODY & His LOST PLANET AIRMEN [58]	0 (0); 0 (0); 8 (93)	1988
984. Bob & Doug McKENZIE [8]	1 (4); 1 (13); 1 (21)	1984
985. SPANDAU BALLET [19]	0 (0); 1 (8); 2 (53)	1980
986. Al Di MEOLA [52]	0 (0); 0 (0); 8 (80)	1979
987. Dickey BETTS [19]	0 (0); 2 (9); 4 (37)	1973
988. David CROSBY [12]	0 (0); 1 (10); 2 (28)	1973
989. Johnny NASH [23]	0 (0); 1 (8); 3 (49)	1971
990. Henry GROSS [26]	0 (0); 1 (3); 3 (58)	1971
991. FRANKE AND THE KNOCKOUTS [31]	0 (0); 1 (5); 2 (45)	1968
992. Stephen BISHOP [34]	0 (0); 2 (7); 2 (51)	1965
993. GENERAL PUBLIC [26]	0 (0); 1 (11); 2 (55)	1964
994. Jeff LORBER [68]	0 (0); 0 (0); 7 (103)	1962
995. Gregory ABBOTT [22]	0 (0); 1 (16); 2 (45)	1961
996. Hubert LAWS [42]	0 (0); 0 (0); 8 (82)	1959
997. Chick COREA [42]	0 (0); 0 (0); 8 (68)	1957
998. BRITNY FOX [39]	0 (0); 1 (2); 2 (60)	1956
999. Dave GRUSIN [52]	0 (0); 0 (0); 10 (110)	1948
1000. Edwin HAWKINS Singers [15]	0 (0); 1 (8); 3 (35)	1940
1001. TRIUMVIRAT [27]	0 (0); 1 (5); 3 (42)	1937
1002. Larry ELGART And His MANHATTAN SWING Orchestra [24]	0 (0); 1 (15); 2 (55)	1934
1003. RASPBERRIES [36]	0 (0); 1 (4); 5 (63)	1932
1004. EXILE [14]	0 (0); 1 (8); 1 (26)	1927
1005. Charlie SEXTON [15]	0 (0); 1 (13); 2 (43)	1926
1006. Mike BLOOMFIELD [12]	0 (0); 2 (20); 4 (74)	1922
1007. Gregg ALLMAN Band [30]	0 (0); 1 (6); 3 (51)	1918
1008. Eric WEISSBERG [1]	1 (9); 1 (14); 2 (27)	1908
1009. Sergio MENDES [27]	0 (0); 1 (10); 3 (59)	1904
1010. Steve MANDELL [1]	1 (9); 1 (14); 1 (25)	1902
1011. HIGH INERGY [28]	0 (0); 1 (7); 3 (43)	1900
1012. ENYA [25]	0 (0); 1 (13); 1 (39)	1899
1013. Los INDIOS TABAJARAS [7]	1 (2); 1 (11); 2 (41)	1896
1014. Gary (U.S.) BONDS [27]	0 (0); 1 (7); 2 (37)	1893
1015. TINY TIM [7]	1 (2); 1 (10); 1 (32)	1886
1016. Leo KOTTKE [45]	0 (0); 0 (0); 9 (89)	1883
1017. Horst JANKOWSKI [18]	0 (0); 1 (12); 3 (46)	1881
1018. WISHBONE ASH [44]	0 (0); 0 (0); 10 (94)	1881
1019. MEGADETH [28]	0 (0); 1 (6); 2 (70)	1870
1020. Sir MIX-A-LOT [67]	0 (0); 0 (0); 2 (99)	1866
1021. AFTER 7 [35]	0 (0); 1 (4); 1 (72)	1864
1022. BLUES PROJECT [52]	0 (0); 0 (0); 4 (70)	1857
1023. Bobbi HUMPHREY [30]	0 (0); 1 (4); 4 (58)	1856
1024. STRAWBERRY ALARM CLOCK [11]	0 (0); 1 (13); 1 (24)	1854
1025. CUTTING CREW [16]	0 (0); 1 (10); 2 (51)	1853
1026. TOMMY TUTONE [20]	0 (0); 1 (8); 3 (46)	1852
1027. Gato BARBIERI [66]	0 (0); 0 (0); 6 (78)	1850
1028. C.W. McCALL [12]	0 (0); 1 (8); 3 (32)	1850
1029. ARGENT [23]	0 (0); 1 (7); 5 (47)	1843
1030. THIRD WORLD [55]	0 (0); 0 (0); 8 (93)	1842
1031. Alexander O'NEAL [29]	0 (0); 1 (8); 4 (68)	1842
1032. INDIGO GIRLS [22]	0 (0); 1 (11); 2 (49)	1821
1033. Lindsey BUCKINGHAM [32]	0 (0); 1 (6); 2 (40)	1817
1034. SPANKY And OUR GANG [56]	0 (0); 0 (0); 4 (64)	1816
1035. KIX [46]	0 (0); 0 (0); 2 (68)	1812
1036. FASTWAY [31]	0 (0); 1 (6); 4 (68)	1806
1037. Duane ALLMAN [28]	0 (0); 1 (6); 2 (42)	1804
1038. Gene SIMMONS [22]	0 (0); 1 (12); 1 (22)	1803
1039. K.D. LANG [69]	0 (0); 0 (0); 2 (81)	1778
1040. Jimmy CASTOR Bunch [27]	0 (0); 1 (6); 4 (53)	1775
1041. Dennis COFFEY [36]	0 (0); 1 (4); 4 (52)	1775
1042. K.T. OSLIN [68]	0 (0); 0 (0); 2 (84)	1774
1043. Walter MURPHY [15]	0 (0); 1 (6); 2 (32)	1772
1044. Donald FAGEN [11]	0 (0); 1 (10); 1 (27)	1763
1045. Gloria LYNNE [27]	0 (0); 1 (10); 3 (51)	1757
1046. ROCKWELL [15]	0 (0); 1 (12); 2 (39)	1753
1047. AUTOGRAPH [29]	0 (0); 1 (12); 3 (59)	1753
1048. The BLASTERS [36]	0 (0); 1 (4); 4 (65)	1750
1049. RENÉ & ANGELA [64]	0 (0); 0 (0); 2 (78)	1749
1050. Ric OCASEK [28]	0 (0); 2 (14); 2 (39)	1743
1051. FLASH [33]	0 (0); 1 (5); 3 (50)	1743
1052. Connie FRANCIS [61]	0 (0); 0 (0); 8 (90)	1741
1053. Grace SLICK [32]	0 (0); 1 (4); 6 (62)	1737
1054. Robbie NEVIL [37]	0 (0); 1 (3); 2 (67)	1736
1055. Kris KRISTOFFERSON & Rita COOLIDGE [26]	0 (0); 1 (6); 3 (54)	1729
1056. HEAD EAST [65]	0 (0); 0 (0); 7 (80)	1728
1057. PLEASURE [67]	0 (0); 0 (0); 6 (78)	1727
1058. Roger WHITTAKER [31]	0 (0); 1 (5); 6 (56)	1722
1059. ANIMOTION [28]	0 (0); 1 (7); 3 (61)	1720
1060. Vladimir HOROWITZ [22]	0 (0); 1 (8); 3 (50)	1719
1061. Rupert HOLMES [33]	0 (0); 1 (12); 1 (31)	1717
1062. ESCAPE CLUB [27]	0 (0); 1 (14); 1 (38)	1716
1063. SAM & DAVE [45]	0 (0); 0 (0); 4 (58)	1712
1064. Danny DAVIS And The NASHVILLE BRASS [78]	0 (0); 0 (0); 8 (86)	1709
1065. Bryan FERRY [63]	0 (0); 0 (0); 5 (71)	1708
1066. Harry BELAFONTE [17]	0 (0); 1 (10); 8 (64)	1697
1067. KASHIF [51]	0 (0); 0 (0); 4 (87)	1692
1068. Justin HAYWARD [16]	0 (0); 2 (11); 3 (44)	1690
1069. Stanley JORDAN [64]	0 (0); 0 (0); 3 (93)	1685
1070. Walter WANDERLEY [22]	0 (0); 1 (9); 1 (41)	1682
1071. VANITY [45]	0 (0); 0 (0); 3 (74)	1680
1072. WET WILLIE [41]	0 (0); 0 (0); 8 (69)	1678
1073. ERIC B. & RAKIM [22]	0 (0); 1 (7); 2 (54)	1667
1074. Shawn PHILLIPS [50]	0 (0); 0 (0); 4 (54)	1666
1075. VOYAGE [40]	0 (0); 1 (2); 2 (48)	1664
1076. HOLLYRIDGE STRINGS [15]	0 (0); 1 (9); 5 (46)	1657
1077. Marvin GAYE & Tammi TERRELL [60]	0 (0); 0 (0); 4 (70)	1657
1078. Suzi QUATRO [37]	0 (0); 1 (5); 6 (68)	1657

Rank. Act [Hi Peak] T10s (Wks); T40s (Wks); Entries (Wks)	Score
1079. SEA LEVEL [31] 0 (0); 1 (3); 4 (53)	1657
1080. DEAD OR ALIVE [31] 0 (0); 1 (6); 4 (56)	1656
1081. ELECTRIC FLAG [31] 0 (0); 1 (5); 2 (47)	1654
1082. Dwight TWILLEY [39] 0 (0); 1 (3); 5 (68)	1652
1083. LEVERT [32] 0 (0); 1 (7); 3 (58)	1649
1084. Y&T [46] 0 (0); 0 (0); 5 (71)	1646
1085. ODYSSEY [36] 0 (0); 1 (5); 4 (52)	1646
1086. Bruce COCKBURN [45] 0 (0); 0 (0); 6 (84)	1646
1087. Dorothy MOORE [29] 0 (0); 1 (7); 2 (36)	1642
1088. The BUCKINGHAMS [53] 0 (0); 0 (0); 5 (64)	1640
1089. INFORMATION SOCIETY [25] 0 (0); 1 (9); 1 (38)	1635
1090. Brenda RUSSELL [49] 0 (0); 0 (0); 3 (56)	1635
1091. Freddie HART [37] 0 (0); 1 (4); 4 (51)	1625
1092. The SYLVERS [58] 0 (0); 0 (0); 6 (76)	1624
1093. Conway TWITTY [65] 0 (0); 0 (0); 8 (86)	1623
1094. SURFACE [55] 0 (0); 0 (0); 2 (58)	1623
1095. GIUFFRIA [26] 0 (0); 1 (7); 2 (43)	1621
1096. Stanley CLARKE & George DUKE [33] 0 (0); 1 (8); 2 (33)	1615
1097. Andy KIM [21] 0 (0); 1 (6); 3 (37)	1613
1098. NU SHOOZ [27] 0 (0); 1 (8); 2 (46)	1612
1099. SLICK RICK [31] 0 (0); 1 (5); 1 (40)	1609
1100. ART OF NOISE [53] 0 (0); 0 (0); 4 (66)	1604
1101. MTUME [26] 0 (0); 1 (7); 4 (53)	1603
1102. Donnie IRIS [57] 0 (0); 0 (0); 5 (85)	1596
1103. Vic DANA [13] 0 (0); 1 (11); 3 (35)	1594
1104. Peter WOLF [24] 0 (0); 1 (8); 2 (41)	1593
1105. Bruce WILLIS [14] 0 (0); 1 (11); 1 (29)	1592
1106. DEXYS MIDNIGHT RUNNERS [14] 0 (0); 1 (12); 1 (24)	1589
1107. Joe SIMON [71] 0 (0); 0 (0); 7 (75)	1585
1108. MILLS BROTHERS [21] 0 (0); 1 (10); 4 (40)	1581
1109. BLUES MAGOOS [21] 0 (0); 1 (5); 2 (48)	1578
1110. Placido DOMINGO [18] 0 (0); 1 (8); 3 (44)	1577
1111. Loretta LYNN [80] 0 (0); 0 (0); 10 (86)	1571
1112. DINO [34] 0 (0); 1 (6); 1 (48)	1569
1113. Rex SMITH [19] 0 (0); 1 (8); 3 (26)	1564
1114. Donna FARGO [47] 0 (0); 0 (0); 2 (54)	1564
1115. Mongo SANTAMARIA [62] 0 (0); 0 (0); 8 (79)	1561
1116. FASTER PUSSYCAT [48] 0 (0); 0 (0); 2 (76)	1561
1117. Cliff RICHARD [76] 0 (0); 0 (0); 5 (75)	1554
1118. Tom RUSH [68] 0 (0); 0 (0); 8 (69)	1554
1119. BREWER And SHIPLEY [34] 0 (0); 1 (3); 4 (46)	1553
1120. Tom COCHRANE/RED RIDER [65] 0 (0); 0 (0); 6 (78)	1551
1121. Jennifer WARNES [43] 0 (0); 0 (0); 3 (62)	1550
1122. The CHURCH [41] 0 (0); 0 (0); 2 (47)	1542
1123. UNDISPUTED TRUTH [43] 0 (0); 0 (0); 6 (55)	1539
1124. Jerry REED [45] 0 (0); 0 (0); 7 (56)	1537
1125. Amii STEWART [19] 0 (0); 1 (9); 1 (23)	1535
1126. Edwin STARR [52] 0 (0); 0 (0); 5 (55)	1533
1127. Esther PHILLIPS [32] 0 (0); 1 (6); 6 (63)	1532
1128. THE D.O.C. [20] 0 (0); 1 (10); 1 (34)	1531
1129. HONEYMOON SUITE [60] 0 (0); 0 (0); 3 (62)	1523
1130. NAKED EYES [32] 0 (0); 1 (4); 2 (52)	1523
1131. Rodney DANGERFIELD [36] 0 (0); 1 (3); 2 (39)	1520
1132. Lou GRAMM [27] 0 (0); 1 (7); 2 (49)	1519
1133. Kim WILDE [40] 0 (0); 1 (2); 4 (64)	1516
1134. LULU [24] 0 (0); 1 (10); 3 (44)	1514
1135. SHANNON [32] 0 (0); 1 (4); 2 (53)	1511
1136. Burton CUMMINGS [30] 0 (0); 1 (7); 2 (26)	1507
1137. Marshall CRENSHAW [50] 0 (0); 0 (0); 3 (59)	1506
1138. BULLETBOYS [34] 0 (0); 1 (5); 1 (47)	1504
1139. SHA NA NA [38] 0 (0); 1 (2); 7 (75)	1504
1140. Morris DAY [37] 0 (0); 1 (3); 2 (46)	1501
1141. Jerry Jeff WALKER [60] 0 (0); 0 (0); 8 (72)	1494
1142. OSIBISA [55] 0 (0); 0 (0); 6 (57)	1494
1143. The CALL [64] 0 (0); 0 (0); 4 (80)	1485
1144. RED HOT CHILI PEPPERS [52] 0 (0); 0 (0); 2 (60)	1485
1145. SOUNDS ORCHESTRAL [11] 0 (0); 1 (9); 1 (28)	1484
1146. SEDUCTION [36] 0 (0); 1 (7); 1 (47)	1477
1147. Vanessa WILLIAMS [38] 0 (0); 1 (4); 1 (55)	1476
1148. Toni BASIL [22] 0 (0); 1 (9); 1 (30)	1472
1149. The SEARCHERS [22] 0 (0); 1 (8); 6 (54)	1472
1150. DIXIE DREGS [56] 0 (0); 0 (0); 5 (63)	1470
1151. MARK-ALMOND [73] 0 (0); 0 (0); 6 (80)	1463
1152. Emitt RHODES [29] 0 (0); 1 (7); 3 (25)	1458
1153. FIRESIGN THEATRE [50] 0 (0); 0 (0); 8 (58)	1457
1154. VIXEN [41] 0 (0); 0 (0); 1 (40)	1452
1155. Alicia BRIDGES [33] 0 (0); 1 (7); 1 (32)	1450
1156. NAJEE [56] 0 (0); 0 (0); 2 (66)	1449
1157. Lee OSKAR [29] 0 (0); 1 (4); 3 (42)	1445
1158. Kenny RANKIN [63] 0 (0); 0 (0); 5 (77)	1445
1159. Kate SMITH [36] 0 (0); 1 (5); 5 (49)	1441
1160. COWBOY JUNKIES [26] 0 (0); 1 (9); 1 (29)	1441
1161. CHAMPAIGN [53] 0 (0); 0 (0); 3 (47)	1437
1162. Jimmy PAGE [26] 0 (0); 1 (6); 2 (30)	1427
1163. Don JOHNSON [17] 0 (0); 1 (11); 1 (27)	1426
1164. The YOUNGBLOODS [80] 0 (0); 0 (0); 8 (86)	1419
1165. EMERSON, LAKE & POWELL [23] 0 (0); 1 (12); 1 (26)	1419
1166. FIVE STAR [57] 0 (0); 0 (0); 2 (72)	1419
1167. Roger WATERS [31] 0 (0); 1 (7); 2 (37)	1417
1168. Michael PENN [31] 0 (0); 1 (8); 1 (34)	1417
1169. The DELFONICS [61] 0 (0); 0 (0); 5 (60)	1416
1170. DAVID & DAVID [39] 0 (0); 1 (2); 1 (38)	1413
1171. Melba MOORE [91] 0 (0); 0 (0); 9 (111)	1411
1172. Billy VERA & The BEATERS [15] 0 (0); 1 (10); 2 (36)	1411
1173. DE LA SOUL [24] 0 (0); 1 (10); 1 (29)	1407
1174. WEST, BRUCE & LAING [26] 0 (0); 1 (6); 3 (36)	1406
1175. BOSTON POPS Orchestra/ Arthur FIEDLER [18] 0 (0); 1 (12); 11 (93)	1402
1176. John SCHNEIDER [37] 0 (0); 1 (3); 3 (41)	1401
1177. Iggy POP [72] 0 (0); 0 (0); 7 (74)	1394
1178. STARPOINT [60] 0 (0); 0 (0); 3 (69)	1392
1179. DREAM ACADEMY [20] 0 (0); 1 (9); 2 (40)	1391
1180. Morris ALBERT [37] 0 (0); 1 (2); 2 (38)	1389
1181. George CLINTON [40] 0 (0); 1 (1); 5 (73)	1386
1182. Rory GALLAGHER [101] 0 (0); 0 (0); 9 (88)	1385
1183. Jonathan BUTLER [50] 0 (0); 0 (0); 3 (71)	1385
1184. Regina BELLE [63] 0 (0); 0 (0); 2 (59)	1384
1185. Mary HOPKIN [28] 0 (0); 1 (7); 1 (20)	1373
1186. Jermaine STEWART [32] 0 (0); 1 (5); 3 (48)	1373
1187. James INGRAM [46] 0 (0); 0 (0); 2 (51)	1372
1188. ROCKPILE [27] 0 (0); 1 (10); 1 (19)	1371

Rank. Act [Hi Peak] T10s (Wks); T40s (Wks); Entries (Wks)	Score
1189. Don Williams [57] 0 (0); 0 (0); 4 (57)	1366
1190. Neville MARRINER [56] 0 (0); 0 (0); 1 (78)	1365
1191. Roy CLARK [50] 0 (0); 0 (0); 8 (66)	1364
1192. GENTLE GIANT [48] 0 (0); 0 (0); 7 (56)	1364
1193. HAIRCUT ONE HUNDRED [31] 0 (0); 1 (7); 1 (37)	1363
1194. Stevie B [75] 0 (0); 0 (0); 2 (67)	1356
1195. Peter TOSH [59] 0 (0); 0 (0); 6 (70)	1355
1196. The ROCKETS [53] 0 (0); 0 (0); 3 (46)	1348
1197. Jean Michel JARRE [52] 0 (0); 0 (0); 4 (59)	1348
1198. Sinead O'CONNOR [36] 0 (0); 1 (5); 1 (38)	1345
1199. BROOKLYN BRIDGE [54] 0 (0); 0 (0); 2 (38)	1344
1200. David McCALLUM [27] 0 (0); 1 (8); 2 (36)	1344
1201. Gene CHANDLER [47] 0 (0); 0 (0); 6 (58)	1344
1202. HUES CORPORATION [20] 0 (0); 1 (7); 2 (23)	1342
1203. MONTROSE [65] 0 (0); 0 (0); 6 (57)	1335
1204. The BOYS [33] 0 (0); 1 (7); 1 (36)	1335
1205. FREDDIE And The DREAMERS [19] 0 (0); 1 (7); 3 (41)	1329
1206. 3° DEGREES [28] 0 (0); 1 (5); 5 (39)	1329
1207. LONE JUSTICE [56] 0 (0); 0 (0); 2 (55)	1327
1208. PUBLIC ENEMY [42] 0 (0); 0 (0); 2 (63)	1326
1209. Roy BUCHANAN [86] 0 (0); 0 (0); 10 (86)	1325
1210. LOVE [57] 0 (0); 0 (0); 7 (66)	1325
1211. MAHOGANY RUSH [74] 0 (0); 0 (0); 9 (71)	1324
1212. Ronnie DOVE [35] 0 (0); 1 (6); 4 (52)	1322
1213. Wynton MARSALIS [90] 0 (0); 0 (0); 6 (92)	1317
1214. JO JO GUNNE [57] 0 (0); 0 (0); 4 (47)	1316
1215. Mary MacGREGOR [17] 0 (0); 1 (7); 1 (19)	1316
1216. Leon REDBONE [38] 0 (0); 1 (4); 4 (43)	1313
1217. John TRAVOLTA [39] 0 (0); 1 (4); 3 (38)	1311
1218. TACO [23] 0 (0); 1 (11); 1 (24)	1311
1219. Lee HAZLEWOOD [13] 0 (0); 1 (18); 1 (44)	1303
1220. Randy MEISNER [50] 0 (0); 0 (0); 2 (44)	1301
1221. CORNELIUS BROTHERS & SISTER ROSE [29] 0 (0); 1 (6); 1 (25)	1299
1222. John Lee HOOKER [62] 0 (0); 0 (0); 4 (73)	1296
1223. Sam HARRIS [35] 0 (0); 1 (3); 2 (43)	1295
1224. GIPSY KINGS [57] 0 (0); 0 (0); 2 (61)	1293
1225. Jon BUTCHER AXIS [66] 0 (0); 0 (0); 5 (71)	1287
1226. McFADDEN & WHITEHEAD [23] 0 (0); 1 (8); 2 (23)	1286
1227. Meli'sa MORGAN [41] 0 (0); 0 (0); 2 (55)	1284
1228. Dusty SPRINGFIELD [62] 0 (0); 0 (0); 7 (63)	1283
1229. El DeBARGE [24] 0 (0); 1 (11); 1 (23)	1280
1230. Norman GREENBAUM [23] 0 (0); 1 (5); 1 (25)	1276
1231. COVER GIRLS [64] 0 (0); 0 (0); 2 (80)	1271
1232. Nick GILDER [33] 0 (0); 1 (5); 2 (28)	1270
1233. TALK TALK [42] 0 (0); 0 (0); 3 (55)	1268
1234. Charles Randolph GREAN Sounde [23] 0 (0); 1 (5); 1 (15)	1266
1235. Billy SWAN [21] 0 (0); 1 (7); 1 (16)	1265
1236. Daryl HALL [29] 0 (0); 1 (6); 2 (38)	1262
1237. MADNESS [41] 0 (0); 0 (0); 4 (50)	1259
1238. Richard "Dimples" FIELDS [33] 0 (0); 1 (4); 2 (37)	1258
1239. Garland JEFFREYS [59] 0 (0); 0 (0); 6 (51)	1257
1240. BE BOP DELUXE [65] 0 (0); 0 (0); 4 (49)	1254
1241. MC5 [30] 0 (0); 1 (3); 2 (30)	1254
1242. MONTY PYTHON [48] 0 (0); 0 (0); 6 (53)	1252
1243. Yvonne ELLIMAN [40] 0 (0); 1 (2); 3 (39)	1241
1244. Michelle SHOCKED [73] 0 (0); 0 (0); 2 (61)	1238
1245. Pat COOPER [82] 0 (0); 0 (0); 3 (58)	1236
1246. STRAWBS [47] 0 (0); 0 (0); 7 (59)	1236
1247. Ralph MacDONALD [57] 0 (0); 0 (0); 4 (53)	1236
1248. MASS PRODUCTION [43] 0 (0); 0 (0); 5 (51)	1235
1249. Leon & Mary RUSSELL [34] 0 (0); 1 (4); 2 (33)	1235
1250. Steve EARLE [56] 0 (0); 0 (0); 2 (48)	1231

Rank. Act [Hi Peak] Entries (Wks)	Score
1251. MARILLION [47] 4 (63)	1229
1252. Robert MAXWELL [17] 1 (24)	1227
1253. BIG AUDIO DYNAMITE [85] 4 (83)	1227
1254. T-CONNECTION [51] 6 (62)	1225
1255. Brook BENTON [27] 4 (31)	1223
1256. Lee MORGAN [25] 3 (36)	1223
1257. Christine McVIE [26] 2 (33)	1223
1258. Senator Everett McKinley DIRKSEN [16] 2 (19)	1222
1259. The DEELE [54] 3 (52)	1222
1260. Chris MONTEZ [33] 2 (35)	1220
1261. SAM THE SHAM And The PHARAOHS [26] 3 (42)	1219
1262. Major HARRIS [28] 2 (28)	1218
1263. Mrs. MILLER [15] 1 (17)	1217
1264. Mark LINDSAY [36] 3 (31)	1216
1265. Irene CARA [76] 2 (54)	1213
1266. Patti PAGE [27] 3 (38)	1212
1267. DISCO TEX & The SEX-O-LETTES [36] 1 (22)	1210
1268. Ricky Van SHELTON [76] 2 (65)	1208
1269. CACTUS [54] 5 (52)	1206
1270. ZEBRA [29] 2 (39)	1202
1271. STATLER BROTHERS [103] 13 (87)	1196
1272. B.B. KING & Bobby BLAND [43] 2 (34)	1193
1273. SYLVIA (2) [56] 4 (59)	1192
1274. X [76] 6 (73)	1192
1275. Dan HARTMAN [55] 3 (49)	1189
1276. Paul DAVIS [52] 4 (57)	1185
1277. CHERRELLE [36] 3 (53)	1185
1278. POINT BLANK [80] 5 (66)	1183
1279. Robbie ROBERTSON [38] 1 (34)	1181
1280. JONES GIRLS [50] 3 (55)	1180
1281. Paul CARRACK [67] 3 (63)	1180
1282. Leonard COHEN [63] 4 (47)	1179
1283. ENCHANTMENT [46] 3 (48)	1179
1284. Vinnie VINCENT INVASION [64] 2 (44)	1179
1285. Kurtis BLOW [71] 6 (74)	1175
1286. WAS (NOT WAS) [43] 2 (46)	1174
1287. O'BRYAN [64] 3 (60)	1172
1288. BOOGIE DOWN PRODUCTIONS [36] 2 (40)	1170
1289. MYSTIC MOODS Orchestra [63] 12 (86)	1170
1290. ECHO & The BUNNYMEN [51] 6 (71)	1170
1291. Frank MILLS [21] 2 (25)	1167
1292. LOOSE ENDS [46] 3 (48)	1166
1293. SEATRAIN [48] 3 (36)	1160
1294. Carl CARLTON [34] 3 (33)	1159
1295. Taj MAHAL [84] 9 (72)	1156
1296. Paul STANLEY [40] 1 (18)	1149
1297. Antonio Carlos JOBIM [19] 4 (55)	1148
1298. Luciano PAVAROTTI [77] 5 (63)	1146
1299. Delbert McCLINTON [34] 3 (43)	1146
1300. ANGEL [55] 6 (50)	1139
1301. Debbie HARRY [25] 3 (33)	1138
1302. BRAM TCHAIKOVSKY [36] 3 (36)	1137
1303. John McLAUGHLIN [14] 4 (48)	1136
1304. Randy RHOADS [6] 1 (23)	1133
1305. Joe SOUTH [60] 3 (48)	1131
1306. BONHAM [38] 1 (29)	1131
1307. LeRoy HOLMES and His Orchestra [42] 2 (37)	1129
1308. CHARLIE [60] 4 (48)	1128
1309. Dennis DeYOUNG [29] 2 (33)	1127
1310. Percy SLEDGE [37] 5 (44)	1124

Rank. Act [Hi Peak] Entries (Wks)	Score
1311. SOULFUL STRINGS [59] 5 (63)	1121
1312. SHOOTING STAR [82] 5 (66)	1119
1313. Sammi SMITH [33] 2 (23)	1119
1314. Pete SEEGER [42] 2 (40)	1116
1315. Marty BALIN [35] 2 (29)	1114
1316. U.K. [45] 3 (32)	1109
1317. MUSICAL YOUTH [23] 2 (34)	1107
1318. Henry LEE SUMMER [56] 2 (40)	1104
1319. EVERLY BROTHERS [38] 5 (52)	1102
1320. John PRINE [66] 8 (63)	1101
1321. The JAM [72] 7 (69)	1101
1322. Enoch LIGHT & The LIGHT BRIGADE [78] 13 (80)	1098
1323. ULTIMATE SPINACH [34] 2 (26)	1098
1324. Lenny WILLIAMS [87] 4 (62)	1094
1325. Toni CHILDS [63] 1 (45)	1092
1326. Big Daddy KANE [33] 2 (49)	1091
1327. BELL And JAMES [31] 2 (23)	1089
1328. The PROCLAIMERS [31] 1 (37)	1089
1329. Jack WAGNER [44] 3 (52)	1089
1330. KEEL [53] 3 (52)	1089
1331. Barbara MANDRELL [86] 8 (71)	1088
1332. Debbie REYNOLDS [23] 2 (28)	1088
1333. STORIES [29] 2 (28)	1087
1334. Neneh CHERRY [40] 1 (35)	1083
1335. Narada Michael WALDEN [74] 4 (49)	1082
1336. Alison MOYET [45] 2 (42)	1079
1337. Reba McENTIRE [78] 5 (79)	1077
1338. Peter CRISS [43] 1 (20)	1076
1339. Tanya TUCKER [54] 5 (46)	1076
1340. OINGO BOINGO [77] 8 (75)	1074
1341. Ben E. KING [33] 2 (35)	1063
1342. BROTHERS FOUR [56] 5 (51)	1057
1343. ROYAL GUARDSMEN [44] 3 (35)	1052
1344. J.D. SOUTHER [41] 2 (33)	1051
1345. WE FIVE [32] 2 (36)	1051
1346. ZEPHYR [48] 1 (26)	1050
1347. TIMBUK 3 [50] 2 (43)	1045
1348. John LODGE [16] 2 (32)	1044
1349. GAMMA [65] 3 (48)	1042
1350. Clarence CARTER [44] 6 (34)	1040
1351. Keith RICHARDS [24] 1 (23)	1040
1352. ARCADIA [23] 1 (17)	1039
1353. SPARKS [63] 6 (58)	1038
1354. GRIM REAPER [73] 3 (62)	1036
1355. JON And VANGELIS [64] 3 (56)	1035
1356. AFTER THE FIRE [25] 1 (20)	1034
1357. Chet ATKINS [64] 11 (75)	1034
1358. Paul KANTNER [20] 3 (44)	1034
1359. The FLOCK [48] 2 (29)	1034
1360. BOY MEETS GIRL [50] 2 (37)	1034
1361. Kiki DEE [28] 2 (23)	1027
1362. Mary TRAVERS [71] 5 (46)	1027
1363. The OUTSIDERS [37] 3 (36)	1025
1364. The SYSTEM [62] 3 (53)	1024
1365. REDBONE [66] 4 (45)	1021
1366. Ravi SHANKAR [43] 5 (40)	1020
1367. Ian MATTHEWS [72] 4 (49)	1019
1368. The NYLONS [43] 3 (50)	1019
1369. Tyrone DAVIS [89] 7 (56)	1019
1370. Rod McKUEN [96] 9 (69)	1017
1371. John MAYALL'S BLUESBREAKERS [59] 2 (33)	1011
1372. Astrud GILBERTO [41] 2 (36)	1007

Rank. Act [Hi Peak] Entries (Wks)	Score
1373. Carla THOMAS [36] 6 (61)	1005
1374. Frank FONTAINE [44] 2 (37)	1004
1375. Moms MABLEY [48] 6 (49)	1003
1376. Johnny MANN Singers [51] 3 (42)	1002
1377. Jennifer HOLLIDAY [31] 2 (36)	1001
1378. Freda PAYNE [60] 3 (39)	1000
1379. NAZZ [80] 2 (41)	999
1380. Dana DANE [46] 1 (32)	998
1381. UTFO [67] 4 (52)	994
1382. ZAGER & EVANS [30] 1 (13)	992
1383. David SOUL [40] 2 (29)	989
1384. BEAU BRUMMELS [24] 3 (26)	989
1385. The SUGARCUBES [54] 2 (38)	988
1386. LITTLE STEVEN [55] 3 (47)	987
1387. Maxine NIGHTINGALE [45] 3 (31)	987
1388. Leonard BERNSTEIN [53] 2 (40)	985
1389. KING CURTIS [54] 9 (62)	982
1390. CHILLIWACK [78] 4 (57)	982
1391. EPMD [53] 2 (37)	982
1392. The WAITRESSES [41] 3 (39)	979
1393. BREAKFAST CLUB [43] 1 (30)	978
1394. The ZOMBIES [39] 2 (30)	977
1395. CALIFORNIA RAISINS [60] 2 (51)	976
1396. POCKETS [57] 2 (30)	975
1397. The DRIFTERS [40] 3 (36)	974
1398. Billy THORPE [39] 2 (28)	972
1399. IAN & SYLVIA [70] 6 (59)	972
1400. DYNASTY [43] 2 (25)	972
1401. GYPSY [44] 2 (28)	971
1402. CHANSON [41] 1 (21)	970
1403. McGUINN, CLARK & HILLMAN [39] 2 (26)	970
1404. ACCEPT [74] 4 (58)	968
1405. Bertie HIGGINS [38] 1 (25)	966
1406. Jim STAFFORD [55] 1 (33)	961
1407. Jonathan EDWARDS [42] 2 (29)	960
1408. Biz MARKIE [66] 2 (48)	960
1409. Patsy CLINE [29] 2 (30)	957
1410. Richard SIMMONS [44] 1 (40)	954
1411. Jack BRUCE [37] 6 (43)	954
1412. Lalo SCHIFRIN [47] 1 (31)	953
1413. J.J. FAD [49] 1 (30)	953
1414. Paul WILLIAMS [95] 6 (68)	950
1415. Don RICKLES [54] 2 (33)	947
1416. EL CHICANO [51] 5 (58)	945
1417. GO WEST [60] 2 (44)	944
1418. Michael SCHENKER Group [81] 4 (53)	940
1419. Tom WAITS [89] 9 (63)	938
1420. STYLE COUNCIL [56] 5 (54)	938
1421. MARTHA & The VANDELLAS [50] 7 (51)	937
1422. Luther INGRAM [39] 2 (32)	936
1423. Robert GORDON [106] 5 (51)	935
1424. France JOLI [26] 2 (20)	934
1425. Alvin LEE [65] 7 (54)	931
1426. Le ROUX [64] 4 (46)	929
1427. SLY FOX [31] 1 (22)	928
1428. Shirley MURDOCK [44] 2 (41)	928
1429. Peggy LEE [55] 6 (42)	924
1430. Buddy RICH [91] 5 (62)	924
1431. NEW ENGLAND CONSERVATORY CHORUS [65] 1 (36)	923
1432. WORLD PARTY [39] 1 (31)	923
1433. Kylie MINOGUE [53] 1 (28)	922
1434. STARGARD [26] 2 (15)	922

Rank. Act [Hi Peak] Entries (Wks)	Score
1435. TIERRA [38] 1 (21)	919
1436. Ricky SKAGGS [61] 4 (51)	918
1437. Larry CARLTON [99] 7 (70)	912
1438. SUN [69] 2 (32)	910
1439. BRONSKI BEAT [36] 2 (31)	908
1440. HAMILTON, JOE FRANK & REYNOLDS [59] 3 (33)	907
1441. TUXEDO JUNCTION [56] 1 (32)	905
1442. Spencer DAVIS Group [54] 3 (37)	902
1443. SCRITTI POLITTI [50] 2 (36)	900
1444. Carl DOUGLAS [37] 1 (17)	900
1445. 3rd BASS [55] 1 (30)	897
1446. Joshua RIFKIN [75] 3 (37)	895
1447. NEW SEEKERS [37] 4 (34)	893
1448. AURRA [38] 2 (28)	893
1449. Tommy SHAW [50] 2 (34)	892
1450. Bob WEIR [68] 2 (31)	891
1451. Freddie HUBBARD [85] 9 (56)	890
1452. Tim CURRY [53] 2 (32)	890
1453. MERCY [38] 1 (15)	889
1454. Walter EGAN [44] 3 (39)	887
1455. David BYRNE [44] 4 (49)	885
1456. PRISM [53] 3 (38)	883
1457. Joan RIVERS [22] 1 (21)	880
1458. The VAPORS [62] 2 (37)	879
1459. FORCE M.D.'S [67] 3 (45)	877
1460. BLOW MONKEYS [35] 2 (26)	876
1461. Cal TJADER [52] 2 (36)	876
1462. Billie HOLIDAY [85] 3 (46)	870
1463. HEAVEN 17 [68] 3 (44)	870
1464. SNIFF 'N' The TEARS [35] 2 (19)	870
1465. Charlie McCOY [98] 3 (44)	869
1466. The REPLACEMENTS [57] 3 (45)	869
1467. Randy CRAWFORD [71] 6 (58)	867
1468. KID 'N PLAY [96] 1 (47)	865
1469. DANGEROUS TOYS [65] 1 (36)	863
1470. Marie OSMOND [59] 4 (44)	858
1471. Jon ANDERSON [47] 4 (34)	858
1472. MAMA CASS [49] 5 (38)	856
1473. John HANDY [43] 2 (23)	854
1474. Jane OLIVOR [58] 4 (38)	854
1475. Nina SIMONE [99] 9 (61)	854
1476. Johnny Van ZANT Band [48] 4 (39)	853
1477. Miriam MAKEBA [74] 5 (51)	853
1478. ROTARY CONNECTION [37] 2 (36)	849
1479. STACEY Q [59] 2 (50)	848
1480. RHYTHM HERITAGE [40] 2 (23)	848
1481. SIOUXSIE & The BANSHEES [68] 4 (45)	845
1482. Dennis EDWARDS [48] 1 (27)	845
1483. BUCKNER And GARCIA [24] 1 (16)	844
1484. TONY! TONI! TONE! [69] 1 (46)	844
1485. JASON & The SCORCHERS [91] 3 (57)	841
1486. BODEANS [86] 3 (52)	839
1487. FRIDA [41] 1 (28)	839
1488. Laurie ANDERSON [60] 5 (60)	834
1489. Dave DAVIES [42] 2 (22)	831
1490. T'PAU [31] 1 (24)	831
1491. LOUDNESS [64] 3 (44)	827
1492. Terri GIBBS [53] 1 (25)	822
1493. JIVE BUNNY & The MASTERMIXERS [26] 1 (19)	818
1494. PLANET P [42] 2 (37)	818
1495. BOOMTOWN RATS [103] 4 (41)	814
1496. Robbie DUPREE [51] 2 (29)	813
1497. BANG TANGO [58] 1 (39)	813
1498. David ESSEX [32] 1 (21)	812
1499. DOUBLE [30] 1 (21)	809
1500. Roger HODGSON [46] 2 (28)	807
1501. Lyle LOVETT [62] 2 (35)	805
1502. ROYAL SCOTS DRAGOON GUARDS [34] 1 (15)	804
1503. Tracey ULLMAN [34] 1 (20)	803
1504. SWEET SENSATION (2) [63] 1 (32)	799
1505. BRECKER BROTHERS [82] 4 (38)	794
1506. Chuck BROWN & The SOUL SEARCHERS [31] 1 (14)	794
1507. The ILLUSION [69] 1 (27)	792
1508. METAL CHURCH [75] 2 (38)	792
1509. Roland SHAW Orchestra [38] 2 (30)	790
1510. KLAATU [32] 2 (18)	787
1511. Tony Joe WHITE [51] 3 (23)	786
1512. TOBY BEAU [40] 1 (23)	781
1513. RHINOCEROS [105] 3 (37)	779
1514. Martin BRILEY [55] 2 (32)	777
1515. SA-FIRE [79] 1 (46)	773
1516. MODERN ENGLISH [70] 3 (47)	772
1517. THEM [54] 3 (40)	771
1518. Ronnie DYSON [55] 2 (25)	769
1519. SYREETA [73] 5 (52)	769
1520. PSEUDO ECHO [54] 1 (27)	769
1521. Andrew Dice CLAY [94] 1 (47)	767
1522. Andrea TRUE Connection [47] 1 (17)	764
1523. LITTLE ANTHONY And The IMPERIALS [74] 4 (45)	764
1524. BOW WOW WOW [67] 4 (46)	762
1525. Lee GREENWOOD [73] 4 (62)	761
1526. Charles EARLAND [108] 4 (47)	759
1527. Jim MESSINA [58] 2 (25)	758
1528. Jimmy DURANTE [30] 1 (19)	756
1529. KAJAGOOGOO [38] 2 (24)	755
1530. Chris REA [49] 2 (25)	755
1531. Nicky HOPKINS [33] 2 (21)	753
1532. SLAYER [57] 2 (37)	752
1533. McCoy TYNER [66] 8 (48)	749
1534. C.J. & CO. [60] 1 (23)	747
1535. NENA [27] 1 (14)	747
1536. The TROGGS [52] 2 (25)	747
1537. TORA TORA [47] 1 (33)	746
1538. CHARLENE [36] 2 (27)	746
1539. HONEY CONE [72] 3 (32)	745
1540. Ginger BAKER's Air Force [33] 1 (15)	745
1541. ULTRAVOX [61] 4 (41)	742
1542. Conway TWITTY & Loretta LYNN [78] 3 (37)	741
1543. SHOCKING BLUE [31] 1 (17)	737
1544. EXODUS [82] 2 (37)	737
1545. Lesley GORE [95] 6 (49)	734
1546. Brian SETZER [45] 2 (26)	733
1547. Eric BURDON Band [51] 2 (21)	733
1548. LIGHTHOUSE [80] 5 (47)	726
1549. ARTISTS UNITED AGAINST APARTHEID [31] 1 (18)	726
1550. Debra LAWS [70] 1 (27)	726
1551. STEALERS WHEEL [50] 2 (25)	725
1552. Muddy WATERS [70] 5 (33)	724
1553. AMAZING RHYTHM ACES [114] 6 (45)	724
1554. George McCRAE [38] 2 (20)	724
1555. GRANDMASTER FLASH And The FURIOUS FIVE [53] 2 (27)	724
1556. JOHNNY HATES JAZZ [56] 1 (25)	723
1557. John HIATT [98] 2 (48)	723
1558. Rich LITTLE [29] 1 (13)	723
1559. Tompall GLASER [10] 1 (51)	723
1560. BADLANDS [57] 1 (26)	720
1561. Tony CAREY [60] 2 (33)	719
1562. STEEL BREEZE [50] 1 (28)	719
1563. Joe PERRY PROJECT [47] 2 (23)	719
1564. NEVILLE BROTHERS [66] 4 (39)	719
1565. KING FAMILY [34] 2 (19)	719
1566. FIVE STAIRSTEPS [83] 6 (37)	717
1567. Lenny KRAVITZ [61] 1 (28)	715
1568. Leonard NIMOY [83] 2 (38)	715
1569. FESTIVAL [50] 1 (18)	711
1570. BOOGIE BOYS [53] 3 (37)	710
1571. CAMEL [118] 5 (46)	707
1572. TWENNYNINE [54] 3 (29)	706
1573. Paul STOOKEY [42] 1 (15)	706
1574. The MARKETTS [37] 2 (26)	705
1575. JIGSAW [55] 1 (19)	705
1576. Jack GREENE [66] 2 (33)	705
1577. Flora PURIM [59] 6 (36)	704
1578. SAILCAT [38] 1 (14)	704
1579. MOTHER'S FINEST [123] 4 (45)	703
1580. Brenda K. STARR [58] 1 (24)	700
1581. Jackie GLEASON [71] 6 (37)	697
1582. TA MARA & The SEEN [54] 1 (25)	695
1583. MANFRED MANN [35] 3 (27)	694
1584. PIECES OF A DREAM [90] 4 (48)	694
1585. John PARR [48] 1 (26)	693
1586. ENUFF Z'NUFF [74] 1 (34)	693
1587. Samantha SANG [29] 1 (14)	692
1588. Jay FERGUSON [72] 3 (33)	692
1589. John ENTWISTLE [71] 5 (39)	692
1590. PUBLIC IMAGE LIMITED [106] 5 (56)	691
1591. SIDE EFFECT [86] 3 (36)	690
1592. David HOUSTON [57] 4 (30)	690
1593. Jim CARROLL Band [73] 2 (30)	688
1594. David BROMBERG [104] 7 (43)	687
1595. YAZ [69] 2 (45)	686
1596. George HOWARD [109] 5 (53)	685
1597. SYNERGY [66] 3 (35)	685
1598. Les CRANE [32] 1 (11)	680
1599. RAM JAM [34] 1 (12)	680
1600. Rafael CAMERON [67] 2 (30)	680
1601. AMBOY DUKES [74] 4 (34)	680
1602. Jim STEINMAN [63] 1 (17)	676
1603. TIN MACHINE [28] 1 (17)	676
1604. FEVER TREE [83] 3 (40)	675
1605. Carmen APPICE [12] 1 (27)	673
1606. Tim BOGERT [12] 1 (27)	673
1607. Ronnie WOOD [45] 3 (24)	670
1608. "Groove" HOLMES [89] 3 (35)	668
1609. Sonny JAMES [83] 10 (45)	668
1610. KLEEER [81] 3 (34)	666
1611. The KINGS [74] 2 (30)	665
1612. George JONES [115] 7 (57)	665
1613. Angela WINBUSH [81] 2 (45)	662
1614. DINO, DESI & BILLY [51] 2 (30)	661
1615. Waldo DE LOS RIOS [53] 1 (16)	659
1616. Barry McGUIRE [37] 1 (21)	656
1617. WING And A PRAYER FIFE And DRUM CORPS. [47] 1 (16)	655
1618. SHADOWFAX [114] 4 (60)	655
1619. PACIFIC GAS AND ELECTRIC [91] 4 (39)	654
1620. Neal HEFTI [41] 1 (21)	652
1621. The FUGS [95] 3 (40)	652
1622. Oran 'Juice' JONES [44] 1 (22)	651
1623. Marty ROBBINS [117] 6 (52)	650
1624. WALL OF VOODOO [45] 2 (25)	650
1625. TYCOON [41] 1 (17)	648
1626. CROW [69] 2 (28)	648
1627. Rev. Martin Luther KING Jr. [69] 7 (37)	647
1628. MORRISSEY [48] 1 (20)	647
1629. Bonnie POINTER [63] 2 (29)	644
1630. Andrew GOLD [81] 3 (32)	643
1631. LIMAHL [41] 1 (20)	642
1632. DION [128] 6 (49)	642
1633. SANFORD/TOWNSEND Band [57] 2 (23)	639

Rank. Act [Hi Peak] Entries (Wks)	Score
1634. CRUZADOS [76] 2 (39)	636
1635. BOX OF FROGS [45] 2 (23)	635
1636. Larry GATLIN/GATLIN BROTHERS Band [102] 6 (44)	634
1637. The SPECIALS [84] 2 (26)	632
1638. T.S. MONK [64] 2 (30)	630
1639. ATOMIC ROOSTER [90] 3 (32)	629
1640. The RECORDS [41] 1 (14)	629
1641. Rusty WARREN [52] 2 (25)	627
1642. Gil SCOTT-HERON [106] 3 (42)	625
1643. Sam KINISON [43] 2 (22)	625
1644. HELIX [69] 4 (39)	624
1645. Dan HICKS & HIS HOT LICKS [67] 4 (34)	624
1646. Sandy NELSON [118] 6 (44)	622
1647. Buffy SAINTE-MARIE [97] 6 (44)	622
1648. The ANGELS [33] 1 (14)	621
1649. Yoko ONO [49] 5 (31)	620
1650. Marlena SHAW [62] 3 (23)	620
1651. Gino SOCCIO [79] 2 (27)	619
1652. Victor BUONO [66] 1 (17)	619
1653. MR. BIG [46] 1 (18)	618
1654. ROMEO VOID [68] 3 (38)	617
1655. The FIREBALLS/Jimmy GILMER And The FIREBALLS [26] 1 (14)	617
1656. Tanita TIKARAM [59] 1 (23)	616
1657. DANGER DANGER [88] 1 (42)	615
1658. Etta JAMES [82] 4 (36)	614
1659. RESTLESS HEART [73] 2 (36)	614
1660. HURRICANE [92] 1 (36)	611
1661. STARCASTLE [95] 3 (29)	610
1662. VIOLENT FEMMES [84] 2 (37)	610
1663. BACK STREET CRAWLER [85] 3 (28)	609
1664. Bobby BLAND [119] 7 (48)	609
1665. WILL TO POWER [68] 1 (29)	609
1666. Dobie GRAY [64] 3 (28)	606
1667. LONDON SYMPHONY Orchestra [62] 4 (31)	606
1668. MUSIQUE [62] 1 (17)	605
1669. RE-FLEX [53] 1 (28)	604
1670. The INTRUDERS [112] 3 (33)	604
1671. ICICLE WORKS [40] 1 (18)	604
1672. Lorne GREENE [35] 1 (19)	604
1673. GEORGIO [117] 1 (52)	603
1674. APOLLO 100 [47] 1 (16)	603
1675. Robert FRIPP [79] 3 (27)	603
1676. SUGARHILL GANG [50] 1 (18)	601
1677. Hamilton BOHANNON [58] 1 (19)	601
1678. Nona HENDRYX [83] 3 (39)	601
1679. ISLEY JASPER ISLEY [77] 2 (36)	600
1680. John DENVER & The MUPPETS [26] 1 (12)	600
1681. The RAINMAKERS [85] 2 (41)	599
1682. King Sunny ADE & His AFRICAN BEATS [91] 2 (39)	598
1683. SEAWIND [83] 4 (34)	596
1684. Bud SHANK [56] 1 (21)	596
1685. DEL FUEGOS [132] 3 (62)	596
1686. GIANT [80] 1 (36)	595
1687. LOVE AND KISSES [85] 2 (31)	595
1688. JANE'S ADDICTION [103] 1 (35)	595
1689. Judy GARLAND & Liza MINELLI [41] 2 (22)	591
1690. NEW ENGLAND [50] 2 (21)	591
1691. Carole Bayer SAGER [60] 1 (22)	590
1692. Wilton FELDER [81] 3 (43)	590
1693. STARZ [89] 3 (30)	589
1694. GODLEY & CREME [37] 1 (15)	589
1695. CURIOSITY KILLED THE CAT [55] 1 (29)	587
1696. HELLOWEEN [104] 3 (44)	586
1697. MOM & DADS [85] 2 (29)	585
1698. KINGFISH [50] 2 (19)	583
1699. SPECIAL ED [73] 1 (28)	583
1700. JOY OF COOKING [100] 3 (30)	583
1701. Mickey NEWBURY [58] 3 (23)	583
1702. Peter SCHILLING [61] 1 (23)	582
1703. Hurricane SMITH [53] 1 (18)	582
1704. Mick FLEETWOOD [43] 1 (14)	581
1705. EXTREME [80] 1 (32)	580
1706. Michael JOHNSON [81] 2 (29)	580
1707. CAT MOTHER & The ALL NIGHT NEWS BOYS [55] 1 (15)	577
1708. SHADOWS OF KNIGHT [46] 1 (18)	576
1709. Bill SUMMERS & SUMMERS HEAT [92] 2 (31)	576
1710. Jim CAPALDI [82] 5 (38)	576
1711. The McCOYS [44] 1 (19)	576
1712. SARAYA [79] 1 (39)	574
1713. B.W. STEVENSON [45] 1 (14)	569
1714. Gary MOORE [114] 5 (49)	569
1715. NATIONAL LAMPOON [107] 3 (33)	568
1716. Chet ATKINS/BOSTON POPS Orchestra [62] 2 (27)	568
1717. ARMORED SAINT [108] 3 (47)	565
1718. The CYRKLE [47] 2 (17)	564
1719. Doc SEVERINSEN And The TONIGHT SHOW Orchestra [65] 1 (26)	563
1720. Albert KING [133] 8 (47)	563
1721. Archie BELL & The DRELLS [95] 3 (31)	562
1722. PHANTOM, ROCKER & SLICK [61] 2 (25)	561
1723. WILLIE, WAYLON, JOHNNY & KRIS [92] 1 (35)	561
1724. Livingston TAYLOR [82] 3 (35)	560
1725. Long John BALDRY [83] 2 (24)	559
1726. Eddie FISHER [52] 3 (23)	556
1727. BLACK 'N BLUE [110] 3 (40)	556
1728. Paul HARDCASTLE [63] 1 (25)	551
1729. Henry MANCINI & Doc SEVERINSEN [74] 2 (22)	550
1730. FABULOUS POODLES [61] 2 (20)	549
1731. Andy TAYLOR [46] 1 (17)	549
1732. The WATERBOYS [76] 1 (26)	548
1733. Mel CARTER [62] 2 (23)	547
1734. Gale GARNETT [43] 1 (22)	544
1735. Godfrey CAMBRIDGE [42] 2 (22)	541
1736. CERRONE [118] 4 (36)	540
1737. Nik KERSHAW [70] 2 (30)	539
1738. BEACON STREET UNION [75] 2 (26)	535
1739. WARLOCK [80] 1 (27)	534
1740. David JOHANSEN [90] 4 (37)	534
1741. TANGERINE DREAM [96] 7 (36)	533
1742. Van STEPHENSON [54] 1 (20)	533
1743. Greg LAKE [62] 1 (17)	533
1744. Keith CARRADINE [61] 1 (17)	528
1745. The DILLARDS [79] 1 (18)	528
1746. TNT [100] 2 (33)	524
1747. The RIPPINGTONS [85] 2 (27)	522
1748. Biff ROSE [75] 2 (21)	521
1749. Johnny KEMP [68] 1 (19)	521
1750. BOYS DON'T CRY [55] 1 (19)	520
1751. Michael DAMIAN [61] 1 (27)	520
1752. Kenny ROGERS & Dottie WEST [82] 2 (26)	520
1753. FIONA [71] 2 (34)	519
1754. REAL LIFE [58] 2 (27)	518
1755. KING DIAMOND [89] 3 (33)	516
1756. Maureen McGOVERN [77] 2 (26)	515
1757. The BACHELORS [70] 4 (29)	515
1758. Count BASIE [69] 8 (54)	515
1759. Matt MONRO [86] 2 (25)	513
1760. Benny MARDONES [65] 1 (24)	511
1761. HARPERS BIZARRE [76] 2 (20)	510
1762. USA-EUROPEAN CONNECTION [66] 1 (19)	510
1763. HOTHOUSE FLOWERS [88] 1 (33)	507
1764. Timmy THOMAS [53] 1 (15)	506
1765. KBC BAND [75] 1 (24)	506
1766. Arthur PRYSOCK [97] 5 (39)	505
1767. The STANDELLS [52] 1 (16)	505
1768. SAINT TROPEZ [65] 2 (21)	504
1769. SPIRAL STARECASE [79] 1 (16)	503
1770. FREHLEY'S COMET [81] 2 (23)	503
1771. Rachel SWEET [97] 3 (27)	502
1772. THP ORCHESTRA [65] 1 (19)	502
1773. Noel POINTER [95] 4 (32)	502
1774. Rockie ROBBINS [71] 2 (22)	501
1775. Walter JACKSON [113] 3 (28)	501
1776. Orson WELLES [66] 1 (16)	499
1777. Tony SANDLER And Ralph YOUNG [85] 4 (28)	499
1778. Patrick HERNANDEZ [61] 1 (15)	498
1779. HOODOO GURUS [101] 3 (35)	497
1780. Jan HAMMER Group [23] 1 (15)	497
1781. Leontyne PRICE [66] 3 (25)	496
1782. Leslie WEST [72] 2 (20)	496
1783. Al WILSON [70] 3 (26)	495
1784. The INMATES [49] 1 (17)	495
1785. Willie HUTCH [114] 5 (38)	495
1786. PEOPLE'S CHOICE [56] 2 (18)	494
1787. The NEWBEATS [56] 2 (23)	494
1788. IDES OF MARCH [55] 1 (12)	494
1789. David LINDLEY [83] 2 (24)	493
1790. Dave LOGGINS [54] 1 (16)	493
1791. Rocky BURNETTE [53] 1 (14)	491
1792. The SUPREMES & FOUR TOPS [113] 3 (28)	490
1793. Jerry HARRISON: CASUAL GODS [78] 1 (20)	489
1794. HOUSE OF LORDS [78] 1 (27)	489
1795. The ROCHES [58] 3 (21)	488
1796. Steve HACKETT [103] 5 (31)	488
1797. Nat ADDERLEY Sextet [75] 1 (20)	488
1798. DIESEL [68] 1 (24)	486
1799. Les DUDEK [100] 2 (23)	486
1800. Vicki LAWRENCE [51] 1 (14)	485
1801. FIRST CHOICE [103] 4 (31)	485
1802. FLASH & THE PAN [80] 2 (22)	484
1803. SHOES [50] 2 (19)	482
1804. COCK ROBIN [61] 2 (22)	481
1805. The HAPPENINGS [61] 4 (24)	480
1806. Henry PAUL Band [107] 3 (28)	480
1807. Clarence CLEMONS [62] 2 (23)	480
1808. Bunny SIGLER [77] 2 (22)	479
1809. LEAPY LEE [71] 1 (12)	476
1810. Kevin PAIGE [107] 1 (31)	476
1811. Tommy GARRETT [94] 5 (27)	475
1812. WHEN IN ROME [84] 1 (24)	475
1813. EL COCO [82] 1 (23)	475
1814. Tommy BOLIN [96] 2 (22)	474
1815. TESTAMENT [77] 2 (26)	473
1816. Moon MARTIN [80] 2 (26)	470
1817. Keith JARRETT [117] 8 (35)	470
1818. TAKE 6 [71] 1 (19)	470
1819. HOWLIN' WOLF [79] 1 (15)	468
1820. SAD CAFÉ [94] 3 (25)	468
1821. JONZUN CREW [66] 1 (20)	467
1822. BRIDES OF FUNKENSTEIN [70] 2 (20)	467
1823. Jimmy BARNES [104] 2 (31)	466
1824. PIXIES [98] 1 (27)	464
1825. FAZE-O [98] 2 (20)	463
1826. HIPSWAY [55] 1 (18)	462

Rank. Act [Hi Peak] Entries (Wks)	Score
1827. NEWCLEUS [74] 1 (28)	460
1828. Lou DONALDSON [141] 7 (39)	460
1829. Jane WIEDLIN [105] 2 (27)	459
1830. Johnny BRISTOL [82] 2 (28)	459
1831. BOURGEOIS TAGG [84] 2 (28)	457
1832. The MARVELETTES [84] 2 (24)	456
1833. OCEAN [60] 1 (13)	455
1834. Billy J. KRAMER with The DAKOTAS [48] 1 (15)	455
1835. BeBe & CeCe WINANS [95] 1 (25)	453
1836. The FAMILY [62] 1 (22)	452
1837. Cassius CLAY [61] 1 (20)	452
1838. Dave BRUBECK Quartet [81] 6 (28)	451
1839. BABYLON A.D. [88] 1 (28)	450
1840. SONS OF CHAMPLIN [117] 5 (34)	449
1841. CHAIRMEN OF THE BOARD [117] 3 (29)	449
1842. Mike DOUGLAS [46] 1 (15)	448
1843. The POGUES [88] 2 (25)	448
1844. MENUDO [100] 2 (31)	447
1845. YELLOW MAGIC ORCHESTRA [81] 2 (23)	447
1846. GENE LOVES JEZEBEL [108] 2 (41)	447
1847. BALTIMORA [49] 1 (17)	446
1848. Rebbie JACKSON [63] 1 (18)	445
1849. SYBIL [75] 1 (24)	445
1850. Grayson HUGH [71] 1 (24)	445
1851. Charles WRIGHT And The WATTS 103rd STREET Band [140] 4 (30)	445
1852. Matthew WILDER [49] 1 (16)	443
1853. GARY'S GANG [42] 1 (10)	440
1854. Andy PRATT [90] 3 (23)	440
1855. SUICIDAL TENDENCIES [100] 3 (30)	440
1856. DETROIT EMERALDS [78] 3 (20)	438
1857. David GATES [102] 3 (23)	436
1858. Floyd CRAMER [107] 5 (34)	436
1859. ALCATRAZZ [128] 3 (44)	434
1860. MOUTH & MACNEAL [77] 1 (16)	434
1861. Tommy CONWELL And The YOUNG RUMBLERS [103] 1 (28)	434
1862. QUESTION MARK & The MYSTERIANS [66] 1 (15)	434
1863. Mike POST [70] 2 (20)	434
1864. Johnny TILLOTSON [48] 2 (17)	434
1865. CROWN HEIGHTS AFFAIR [121] 2 (29)	431
1866. GALLERY [75] 1 (15)	431
1867. David BENOIT [101] 3 (31)	430
1868. Patty SMYTH [66] 1 (20)	428
1869. Tim BUCKLEY [81] 3 (19)	428
1870. NUCLEAR ASSAULT [126] 2 (35)	426
1871. BLUE MURDER [69] 1 (21)	425
1872. The MINDBENDERS [58] 2 (18)	422
1873. TODAY [86] 1 (22)	421
1874. Kenny NOLAN [78] 1 (16)	421
1875. AXE [81] 2 (26)	421
1876. Frankie SMITH [54] 1 (10)	420
1877. Adrian BELEW [82] 3 (27)	420
1878. CAPTAIN BEYOND [90] 3 (24)	419
1879. RAVEN [81] 2 (25)	419
1880. DIFFORD & TILBROOK [55] 1 (15)	418
1881. Edward BEAR [63] 2 (22)	416
1882. BUS BOYS [85] 2 (22)	416
1883. Chico DeBARGE [90] 1 (30)	416
1884. Brian WILSON [54] 1 (13)	415
1885. Margie JOSEPH [67] 2 (17)	414
1886. The THE [89] 2 (30)	414
1887. ELECTRIC PRUNES [113] 3 (29)	413
1888. ARPEGGIO [75] 1 (16)	413
1889. The COMMUNARDS [90] 2 (25)	413
1890. Candi STATON [129] 3 (22)	413
1891. Buddy HOLLY [55] 1 (12)	412
1892. FLESH FOR LULU [89] 1 (24)	412
1893. PRELUDE [94] 2 (21)	411
1894. JUNIOR [71] 2 (22)	411
1895. VANDENBERG [65] 2 (25)	410
1896. Michael COOPER [98] 1 (25)	409
1897. The JAGGERZ [62] 1 (11)	408
1898. ANNETTE [39] 1 (13)	408
1899. MOTHER EARTH [95] 3 (19)	408
1900. SIR DOUGLAS Quintet [81] 2 (15)	408
1901. Cleo LAINE [138] 6 (41)	407
1902. Julian COPE [105] 3 (31)	406
1903. D.C. LaRUE [115] 2 (24)	405
1904. Albert HAMMOND [77] 2 (19)	405
1905. Danny O'KEEFE [87] 2 (25)	404
1906. IMPELLITTERI [91] 1 (20)	404
1907. Dan REED Network [95] 2 (25)	403
1908. Benjamin ORR [86] 1 (22)	402
1909. BLOWFLY [82] 1 (20)	401
1910. Steve HOWE [63] 2 (15)	401
1911. Johnny PAYCHECK [72] 1 (14)	399
1912. BLUE SWEDE [80] 1 (17)	398
1913. Brian ENO [44] 3 (24)	398
1914. Frankie MILLER(1) [124] 3 (31)	397
1915. Jesse WINCHESTER [115] 4 (30)	396
1916. STARBUCK [78] 2 (16)	396
1917. Jean KNIGHT [60] 2 (15)	395
1918. Rusty WIER [103] 2 (23)	395
1919. Ray THOMAS [68] 2 (16)	393
1920. Nia PEEPLES [97] 1 (21)	393
1921. Bobby VEE [66] 3 (21)	392
1922. KING'S X [123] 2 (29)	392
1923. CONCRETE BLONDE [96] 2 (34)	392
1924. CYMANDE [85] 2 (21)	392
1925. MUNGO JERRY [64] 1 (11)	390
1926. STUFF [61] 2 (16)	390
1927. The WINSTONS [78] 1 (12)	388
1928. T.G. SHEPPARD [119] 3 (28)	388
1929. Robyn HITCHCOCK And The EGYPTIANS [111] 2 (24)	388
1930. 9.9 [79] 1 (22)	387
1931. John ANDERSON [58] 2 (17)	387
1932. FLYING BURRITO BROTHERS [138] 6 (35)	386
1933. ORION THE HUNTER [57] 1 (14)	386
1934. BROWNSVILLE STATION [98] 3 (32)	385
1935. OPUS [64] 1 (16)	385
1936. John WAYNE [66] 1 (16)	383
1937. LET'S ACTIVE [111] 3 (37)	383
1938. DELEGATION [84] 1 (16)	382
1939. SHERIFF [60] 1 (14)	381
1940. Chris SQUIRE [69] 1 (12)	380
1941. Gilda RADNER [69] 1 (12)	380
1942. RIP CHORDS [56] 1 (17)	380
1943. Mica PARIS [86] 1 (23)	380
1944. Deborah ALLEN [67] 1 (20)	379
1945. Bernadette PETERS [114] 2 (23)	378
1946. Eddie HOLMAN [75] 1 (13)	377
1947. Steve ARRINGTON'S HALL OF FAME [101] 3 (31)	377
1948. Lyle MAYS [50] 1 (21)	377
1949. Pat METHENY [50] 1 (21)	377
1950. JESUS AND MARY CHAIN [105] 4 (36)	377
1951. Redd FOXX [87] 3 (24)	377
1952. CLANCY BROTHERS AND Tommy MAKEM [60] 2 (18)	376
1953. Phil SEYMOUR [64] 1 (16)	376
1954. SUTHERLAND BROTHERS And QUIVER [77] 3 (22)	376
1955. John MILES [93] 2 (19)	375
1956. Johnny LEE [132] 2 (29)	375
1957. The JB'S [77] 2 (16)	375
1958. CAMPER VAN BEETHOVEN [124] 2 (29)	374
1959. William BELL [63] 1 (12)	373
1960. Jackie DeSHANNON [81] 2 (17)	372
1961. 20/20 [127] 2 (25)	371
1962. MANDRE [64] 1 (13)	371
1963. BLUES IMAGE [112] 2 (22)	370
1964. Mick RONSON [103] 3 (34)	369
1965. Marc BENNO [70] 2 (28)	369
1966. The TRASHMEN [48] 1 (15)	369
1967. PURSUIT OF HAPPINESS [93] 1 (21)	368
1968. Alton McCLAIN & DESTINY [88] 1 (16)	368
1969. MODELS [84] 1 (18)	368
1970. DETECTIVE [103] 2 (21)	366
1971. WENDY and LISA [88] 2 (21)	365
1972. ORPHEUS [119] 3 (27)	365
1973. MUSIC MACHINE [76] 1 (16)	364
1974. Judi Sheppard MISSETT [117] 1 (20)	364
1975. Nino TEMPO & April STEVENS [48] 1 (14)	364
1976. DeFRANCO FAMILY [109] 2 (23)	364
1977. Les McCANN [141] 5 (30)	363
1978. Maurice WHITE [61] 1 (19)	363
1979. Robert JOHN [68] 1 (14)	363
1980. Claudja BARRY [101] 2 (20)	363
1981. The METERS [108] 4 (22)	361
1982. MISSION U.K. [108] 2 (28)	361
1983. Lonnie MACK [103] 2 (30)	361
1984. UP WITH PEOPLE [61] 1 (14)	360
1985. SHOTGUN MESSIAH [99] 1 (23)	358
1986. Bobby DARIN [98] 4 (22)	358
1987. GONZALEZ [67] 1 (14)	355
1988. DIRTY LOOKS [118] 2 (25)	355
1989. Leon HAYWOOD [92] 2 (23)	355
1990. Jimmy McGRIFF [130] 3 (27)	353
1991. VELVET UNDERGROUND [85] 4 (30)	353
1992. The GODFATHERS [91] 2 (22)	353
1993. HAWKWIND [110] 3 (25)	353
1994. Roger McGUINN [92] 3 (20)	352
1995. SPLINTER [81] 1 (14)	352
1996. D.R.I. [116] 2 (27)	352
1997. The PRIMITIVES [106] 2 (24)	352
1998. CRAZY HORSE [84] 2 (17)	351
1999. LEMON PIPERS [90] 1 (18)	351
2000. Bo DONALDSON And The HEYWOODS [97] 1 (16)	351
2001. GORKY PARK [80] 1 (21)	350
2002. Andy SUMMERS & Robert FRIPP [60] 2 (16)	350
2003. XYZ [99] 1 (24)	350
2004. The BELLS [90] 1 (14)	350
2005. Loudon WAINWRIGHT III [102] 3 (22)	349
2006. BABE RUTH [75] 3 (19)	349
2007. Barbara MASON [95] 3 (22)	349
2008. APOLLONIA 6 [62] 1 (17)	348
2009. STEEL PULSE [120] 3 (32)	347
2010. THEY MIGHT BE GIANTS [89] 1 (19)	346
2011. FULL FORCE [126] 3 (32)	346
2012. RIOT [99] 3 (27)	345
2013. Ivan NEVILLE [107] 1 (23)	345
2014. Ella FITZGERALD [69] 5 (31)	345
2015. Maggie BELL [122] 2 (21)	344
2016. The PERSUASIONS [88] 4 (21)	344
2017. Tim WEISBERG Band [108] 2 (18)	344
2018. RED ROCKERS [71] 1 (16)	343
2019. LITTLE MILTON [101] 3 (23)	342
2020. PILOT [82] 1 (14)	342
2021. Rita PAVONE [60] 1 (14)	341
2022. Pat PAULSEN [71] 1 (10)	339
2023. BIONIC BOOGIE [88] 1 (16)	339
2024. Brother Jack McDUFF [81] 3 (24)	339

Rank. Act [Hi Peak] Entries (Wks)	Score
2025. Papa John CREACH [94] 1 (14)	339
2026. Bing CROSBY [98] 3 (24)	339
2027. Dan SEALS [59] 1 (15)	338
2028. LAID BACK [67] 1 (15)	338
2029. OMAR And The HOWLERS [81] 1 (19)	338
2030. TANGIER [91] 1 (17)	338
2031. Peter ALLEN [123] 3 (29)	336
2032. STEAM [84] 1 (13)	335
2033. BRADY BUNCH [108] 1 (19)	335
2034. MINISTRY [96] 4 (31)	335
2035. Lou CHRISTIE [103] 2 (20)	335
2036. LORD SUTCH And HEAVY FRIENDS [84] 1 (13)	335
2037. The SHERBS [100] 1 (16)	334
2038. HILLSIDE SINGERS [71] 1 (16)	334
2039. FANTASTIC FOUR [99] 1 (16)	333
2040. LIZZY BORDEN [133] 4 (33)	333
2041. FATES WARNING [111] 3 (26)	333
2042. The MARMALADE [71] 1 (13)	332
2043. Richard TORRANCE And EUREKA [107] 1 (17)	331
2044. POZO-SECO SINGERS [81] 2 (16)	331
2045. POPPY FAMILY [76] 1 (11)	330
2046. JOBOXERS [70] 1 (15)	330
2047. BIG PIG [93] 1 (17)	330
2048. CRACK THE SKY [124] 4 (24)	330
2049. Tom JOHNSTON [100] 2 (20)	329
2050. Richard THOMPSON [102] 4 (29)	328
2051. Nick LOWE And His COWBOY OUTFIT [113] 2 (24)	328
2052. Mason RUFFNER [80] 1 (16)	327
2053. Lene LOVICH [94] 3 (22)	327
2054. The REDDINGS [106] 3 (29)	327
2055. LEATHERWOLF [105] 2 (20)	327
2056. LaToya JACKSON [116] 3 (22)	323
2057. MIKE CURB CONGREGATION [105] 3 (15)	323
2058. John Paul YOUNG [119] 1 (18)	322
2059. BELLAMY BROTHERS [69] 1 (12)	320
2060. The STOOGES [106] 2 (14)	320
2061. DEAD MILKMEN [101] 2 (30)	319
2062. HUMAN BEINZ [65] 1 (10)	319
2063. PASSPORT [137] 5 (24)	318
2064. Glen GRAY & The CASA LOMA Orchestra [69] 1 (15)	318
2065. SISTERS OF MERCY [101] 1 (16)	317
2066. Manu DIBANGO [79] 1 (13)	317
2067. LENNON SISTERS [77] 1 (18)	317
2068. AMERICAN FLYER [87] 2 (15)	316
2069. TEN WHEEL DRIVE With Genya RAVAN [151] 3 (29)	316
2070. Neal SCHON & Jan HAMMER [115] 2 (20)	316
2071. Rob JUNGKLAS [102] 1 (22)	315
2072. Herman BROOD [122] 1 (19)	315
2073. Julia FORDHAM [118] 1 (25)	315
2074. The RUTLES [63] 1 (9)	313
2075. Alec R. COSTANDINOS [92] 1 (17)	313
2076. BRITISH LIONS [83] 1 (15)	313
2077. Gunter KALLMANN Chorus [97] 2 (18)	311
2078. SAVATAGE [116] 2 (30)	311
2079. J. Frank WILSON and The CAVALIERS [54] 1 (14)	311
2080. LOOKING GLASS [113] 1 (18)	310
2081. Jerry JORDAN [79] 1 (12)	310
2082. Earl SCRUGGS Revue [104] 3 (19)	310
2083. Midge URE [88] 1 (16)	310
2084. SUSAN of SESAME STREET [86] 1 (13)	309
2085. Philip GLASS [91] 2 (19)	309
2086. Ali THOMSON [99] 1 (15)	308
2087. TEXAS [88] 1 (16)	308

Rank. Act [Hi Peak] Entries (Wks)	Score
2088. The RUBBERBANDITS [116] 2 (14)	308
2089. HORSLIPS [98] 2 (18)	308
2090. Johnny HAMMOND [125] 2 (20)	307
2091. MOTHERLODE [93] 1 (12)	307
2092. R.B. GREAVES [85] 1 (14)	307
2093. Bill WYMAN [99] 2 (16)	307
2094. Burl IVES [65] 1 (15)	307
2095. Howard HEWETT [110] 2 (28)	306
2096. Little Jimmy OSMOND [105] 1 (14)	306
2097. Porter WAGONER and Dolly PARTON [137] 5 (21)	306
2098. 1910 FRUITGUM CO. [147] 3 (28)	304
2099. AUTOMATIC MAN [109] 2 (15)	303
2100. Billy VAUGHN Singers [114] 2 (25)	302
2101. Major LANCE [100] 3 (18)	302
2102. KIDS FROM FAME [98] 3 (23)	301
2103. Gloria LORING [61] 1 (14)	300
2104. Tom T. HALL [137] 4 (23)	299
2105. SATURDAY NIGHT BAND [125] 1 (17)	299
2106. SYLVIA [70] 1 (12)	298
2107. PARIS [103] 2 (15)	297
2108. Bernard WRIGHT [116] 1 (14)	297
2109. DEVICE [73] 1 (16)	296
2110. Michael SHRIEVE [42] 2 (30)	296
2111. Tony MOTTOLA [85] 3 (19)	296
2112. Al Di MEOLA/John McLAUGHLIN/ Paco De LUCIA [97] 2 (18)	295
2113. Billy Joe ROYAL [96] 2 (16)	295
2114. Steve LAWRENCE [73] 3 (16)	295
2115. Eric ANDERSEN [113] 2 (20)	294
2116. Barry YOUNG [67] 1 (12)	294
2117. Teri DeSARIO [80] 1 (13)	292
2118. ANIMAL LOGIC [106] 1 (21)	292
2119. SKYLARK [102] 1 (16)	292
2120. Gabor SZABO [140] 5 (26)	291
2121. David WERNER [65] 1 (11)	290
2122. Rodney CROWELL [105] 3 (23)	290
2123. Roger GLOVER [101] 2 (20)	290
2124. The SEEDS [87] 2 (15)	290
2125. Peter McCANN [82] 1 (12)	289
2126. FAITH, HOPE AND CHARITY [100] 1 (14)	288
2127. CHUNKY A [71] 1 (13)	288
2128. The PLASMATICS [134] 3 (22)	288
2129. Shawn COLVIN [111] 1 (24)	287
2130. Warren KIME [89] 2 (19)	287
2131. Billy CRYSTAL [65] 1 (13)	286
2132. BARDEUX [104] 2 (19)	286
2133. Louise GOFFIN [87] 1 (13)	286
2134. Patrick SIMMONS [52] 1 (11)	286
2135. KLIQUE [70] 1 (14)	285
2136. LAKE [92] 1 (15)	285
2137. Jim WEATHERLY [94] 1 (14)	285
2138. Glenn JONES [94] 1 (17)	284
2139. PRETTY THINGS [104] 2 (15)	284
2140. Deon ESTUS [89] 1 (15)	284
2141. EXOTIC GUITARS [155] 3 (22)	284
2142. Bobby RYDELL [67] 2 (13)	283
2143. Géza ANDA [115] 1 (17)	283
2144. KANE GANG [115] 1 (20)	282
2145. The MOMENTS (2) [132] 3 (23)	282
2146. YELLO [92] 3 (23)	282
2147. Arthur CONLEY [93] 3 (17)	281
2148. L.A. BOPPERS [85] 1 (11)	281
2149. LORDAN [37] 1 (16)	281
2150. The RADIATORS [122] 2 (27)	281
2151. DANNY WILSON [79] 1 (16)	280
2152. MC LYTE [86] 1 (20)	280
2153. Gavin CHRISTOPHER [74] 1 (15)	278
2154. Diane RENAY [54] 1 (11)	277
2155. DIVINYLS [91] 1 (18)	277

Rank. Act [Hi Peak] Entries (Wks)	Score
2156. McKENDREE SPRING [118] 4 (20)	277
2157. Rodney FRANKLIN [104] 3 (19)	276
2158. Idris MUHAMMAD [127] 1 (19)	276
2159. Raymond LEFEVRE And His Orchestra [117] 1 (16)	275
2160. FOOLS GOLD [100] 1 (13)	274
2161. ANDREWS SISTERS [126] 4 (20)	274
2162. The SURFARIS [94] 2 (16)	273
2163. FOTOMAKER [88] 1 (13)	272
2164. KAYAK [117] 3 (18)	271
2165. BOYS CLUB [93] 1 (16)	271
2166. SAXON [130] 4 (29)	271
2167. John EDDIE [83] 1 (15)	271
2168. Soupy SALES [80] 2 (14)	269
2169. 8TH DAY [131] 1 (16)	269
2170. Frank BARBER Orchestra [94] 1 (16)	269
2171. INCREDIBLE STRING BAND [161] 7 (26)	269
2172. Graeme EDGE Band [107] 2 (13)	269
2173. Glenn MEDEIROS [83] 1 (17)	269
2174. MOTORHEAD [150] 4 (30)	269
2175. SEX PISTOLS [106] 1 (12)	268
2176. Morgana KING [118] 2 (20)	267
2177. ROCK And HYDE [94] 1 (15)	267
2178. Duke ELLINGTON [78] 3 (23)	267
2179. NEW YORK DOLLS [116] 2 (17)	267
2180. MACHO [101] 1 (14)	266
2181. LEFT BANKE [67] 1 (11)	266
2182. ADDRISI BROTHERS [118] 2 (17)	266
2183. The T-BONES [75] 1 (12)	265
2184. HOT [125] 1 (15)	265
2185. Jean BEAUVOIR [93] 1 (15)	265
2186. David PEASTON [113] 1 (18)	264
2187. Jimmy ROSELLI [96] 4 (19)	264
2188. Mario LANZA [87] 1 (15)	264
2189. Keith WHITLEY [115] 2 (21)	262
2190. CAPTAIN BEEFHEART [66] 2 (17)	262
2191. Billy STEWART [97] 2 (16)	262
2192. SKY [125] 2 (18)	262
2193. CITY BOY [115] 3 (16)	261
2194. Lowell GEORGE [71] 1 (9)	260
2195. CHOCOLATE MILK [161] 4 (24)	259
2196. Steve EARLE And The DUKES [90] 1 (14)	259
2197. The BRANDOS [108] 1 (19)	258
2198. The FOUNDATIONS [92] 1 (11)	255
2199. David PORTER [104] 2 (19)	255
2200. Robert WINTERS and FALL [71] 1 (8)	255
2201. MISTRESS [100] 1 (14)	254
2202. SWINGIN' MEDALLIONS [88] 1 (12)	253
2203. Woody ALLEN [63] 1 (11)	253
2204. Maxi PRIEST [108] 1 (17)	253
2205. Michael MORALES [113] 1 (20)	253
2206. Ian GOMM [104] 1 (12)	253
2207. Terry REID [147] 3 (21)	252
2208. Benny GOODMAN [90] 2 (17)	251
2209. The FROST [148] 3 (20)	250
2210. The LIMELITERS [73] 2 (13)	250
2211. Jimmy CLIFF [122] 4 (18)	248
2212. Michael ZAGER Band [120] 1 (13)	248
2213. Pete DRAKE [85] 1 (14)	247
2214. Pia ZADORA [113] 1 (20)	247
2215. The SANDALS [110] 1 (13)	247
2216. K-9 POSSE [98] 1 (14)	247
2217. Carroll O'CONNOR [118] 1 (13)	247
2218. MASKED MARAUDERS [114] 1 (12)	247
2219. RARE BIRD [117] 2 (15)	246
2220. Vincent BELL [75] 1 (8)	246
2221. Alan PRICE [117] 2 (17)	245
2222. BOSTON SYMPHONY Orchestra [82] 1 (12)	244
2223. Ronnie LANE [45] 1 (12)	244

Rank. Act [Hi Peak] Entries (Wks)	Score
2224. Len BARRY [90] 1 (13)	244
2225. The HEADBOYS [113] 1 (15)	244
2226. Carrie LUCAS [119] 4 (21)	244
2227. PEARL HARBOR And The EXPLOSIONS [107] 2 (14)	243
2228. Bobby HEBB [103] 1 (12)	243
2229. FIVE AMERICANS [121] 2 (15)	242
2230. Miles JAYE [125] 2 (21)	242
2231. PEPPERMINT RAINBOW [106] 1 (9)	242
2232. Nanci GRIFFITH [99] 1 (14)	242
2233. Doug E. FRESH & The GET FRESH CREW [88] 1 (13)	241
2234. Terry JACKS [81] 1 (9)	241
2235. CLIMIE FISHER [120] 1 (16)	240
2236. Feargal SHARKEY [75] 1 (11)	240
2237. ASLEEP AT THE WHEEL [136] 4 (17)	240
2238. Joyce KENNEDY [79] 1 (13)	240
2239. Myron COHEN [102] 1 (13)	239
2240. Jean CARN [122] 3 (19)	239
2241. Jimmy RUFFIN [133] 4 (22)	238
2242. UNDERWORLD [139] 1 (19)	237
2243. COCTEAU TWINS [109] 1 (18)	236
2244. 24-7 SPYZ [113] 1 (16)	236
2245. TREAT HER RIGHT [127] 1 (18)	236
2246. OFF BROADWAY USA [101] 1 (11)	236
2247. Carl ANDERSON [87] 1 (12)	235
2248. Hagood HARDY [112] 1 (14)	235
2249. CAMOUFLAGE [100] 1 (14)	235
2250. Terry KNIGHT And The PACK [127] 2 (16)	234
2251. Carol DOUGLAS [139] 3 (19)	233
2252. Marilyn MARTIN [72] 1 (11)	232
2253. Bob NEWHART [113] 2 (16)	232
2254. Randy VANWARMER [81] 1 (10)	232
2255. ISLE OF MAN [110] 1 (18)	231
2256. Marvin SEASE [114] 1 (17)	231
2257. HUSKER DU [117] 2 (20)	231
2258. The ASTRONAUTS [100] 2 (14)	230
2259. KWAMÉ & A NEW BEGINNING [114] 1 (18)	229
2260. The CAPITOLS [95] 1 (12)	229
2261. WA WA NEE [123] 1 (17)	228
2262. SRC [134] 2 (13)	228
2263. EYE TO EYE [99] 1 (15)	228
2264. Maria McKEE [120] 1 (15)	227
2265. The PASADENAS [89] 1 (12)	227
2266. Gwen GUTHRIE [89] 1 (13)	227
2267. Roger TAYLOR [121] 1 (10)	226
2268. VOIVOD [114] 1 (16)	226
2269. Peter MURPHY [135] 1 (19)	226
2270. Michael NESMITH [143] 3 (16)	225
2271. Eugene WILDE [97] 1 (15)	225
2272. Lenny WELCH [73] 2 (12)	225
2273. The RUMOUR [124] 2 (13)	225
2274. FACE TO FACE [126] 2 (23)	224
2275. Bob CREWE Generation [100] 1 (11)	224
2276. Michel POLNAREFF [117] 1 (13)	223
2277. OVERKILL [142] 3 (22)	222
2278. ELECTRIC INDIAN [104] 1 (9)	222
2279. MOVING PICTURES [101] 1 (16)	222
2280. Joe ELY [135] 2 (14)	222
2281. Jody MILLER [117] 2 (14)	222
2282. GREY And HANKS [97] 2 (14)	222
2283. HEINTJE [108] 1 (11)	221
2284. Michel LEGRAND [127] 2 (22)	221
2285. Barry GOUDREAU [88] 1 (8)	220
2286. Jimmy JAMES & The VAGABONDS [139] 1 (16)	220
2287. Shirley BROWN [98] 1 (11)	220
2288. John HARTFORD [137] 2 (13)	220
2289. Tracie SPENCER [146] 1 (21)	220
2290. Dottie WEST [126] 1 (15)	220
2291. Eric GALE [148] 2 (17)	220
2292. Donald BYRD And 125th STREET N.Y.C. [93] 1 (10)	220
2293. Patty DUKE [90] 1 (12)	220
2294. George BAKER Selection [107] 2 (13)	219
2295. WEATHER GIRLS [91] 1 (11)	219
2296. Steve LAWRENCE & Eydie GORME [136] 3 (15)	218
2297. Kim MITCHELL [106] 1 (15)	218
2298. GUADALCANAL DIARY [132] 2 (20)	218
2299. Miki HOWARD [145] 2 (22)	217
2300. LITTLE AMERICA [102] 1 (14)	216
2301. SUAVE [101] 1 (12)	215
2302. James LAST [148] 3 (16)	215
2303. BRAINSTORM [145] 1 (16)	214
2304. Colonel ABRAMS [75] 1 (11)	214
2305. David GRISMAN [108] 3 (21)	214
2306. Timothy B. SCHMIT [106] 2 (16)	213
2307. John KILZER [110] 1 (15)	213
2308. ANGEL CITY [133] 3 (18)	213
2309. Ray BRYANT [111] 2 (15)	213
2310. Martha VELEZ [153] 1 (17)	212
2311. OSCAR PETERSON TRIO [81] 1 (12)	212
2312. Groucho MARX [155] 2 (18)	212
2313. SNEAKER [149] 1 (17)	211
2314. George BURNS [93] 1 (10)	211
2315. Lena HORNE [112] 2 (19)	211
2316. DR. J.R. KOOL and The OTHER ROXANNES [113] 1 (13)	210
2317. PHOTOGLO [119] 2 (14)	210
2318. BOY GEORGE [126] 2 (16)	210
2319. The HIGHWAYMEN [79] 1 (9)	210
2320. OAKTOWN'S 3.5.7 [126] 1 (16)	209
2321. ZODIAC MINDWARP & The LOVE REACTION [132] 1 (15)	209
2322. REDEYE [113] 1 (12)	209
2323. OLD & IN THE WAY [99] 1 (8)	209
2324. Stomu YAMASHTA [60] 2 (18)	209
2325. ROMAN HOLLIDAY [116] 2 (17)	209
2326. Zubin MEHTA/LOS ANGELES PHILHARMONIC Orchestra [130] 2 (18)	207
2327. Jim Ed BROWN [81] 1 (9)	207
2328. Chubby CHECKER [104] 3 (16)	206
2329. Tom ROBINSON Band [144] 2 (15)	206
2330. The TYMES [117] 2 (14)	205
2331. CHINA CRISIS [114] 2 (16)	205
2332. Vic DAMONE [86] 1 (10)	205
2333. MINK DE VILLE [126] 4 (15)	205
2334. BATDORF & RODNEY [140] 2 (17)	204
2335. Queen LATIFAH [124] 1 (17)	204
2336. Don RAY [113] 1 (11)	203
2337. Alan O'DAY [109] 1 (9)	203
2338. BRAND X [125] 3 (17)	203
2339. Tony TERRY [151] 1 (20)	203
2340. Genya RAVAN [106] 2 (12)	202
2341. KICK AXE [126] 1 (15)	202
2342. MASON PROFFIT [177] 3 (27)	202
2343. AZTEC CAMERA [129] 4 (22)	202
2344. SNAIL [135] 2 (14)	202
2345. 5 SPECIAL [118] 1 (11)	201
2346. Steve MORSE Band [101] 2 (15)	201
2347. KING TEE [125] 1 (15)	200
2348. FANNY [135] 2 (13)	200
2349. Terry STAFFORD [81] 1 (11)	199
2350. BEAT FARMERS [131] 3 (20)	199
2351. Trevor RABIN [111] 2 (14)	199
2352. Laura LEE [117] 1 (11)	197
2353. RENÉ & RENÉ [129] 1 (9)	197
2354. TOOTS And The MAYTALS [157] 2 (18)	197
2355. The KORGIS [113] 1 (12)	197
2356. RHYTHM CORPS [104] 1 (14)	197
2357. Patrick JUVET [125] 1 (14)	197
2358. Glenn MILLER Orchestra [115] 1 (9)	196
2359. Stan KENTON [146] 1 (14)	196
2360. CLANNAD [131] 2 (17)	195
2361. BRASS RING [109] 3 (13)	195
2362. 7 SECONDS [153] 1 (19)	194
2363. Pigmeat MARKHAM [109] 1 (9)	194
2364. WILLIE & The POOR BOYS [96] 1 (12)	194
2365. John HALL Band [147] 2 (18)	194
2366. Merry CLAYTON [146] 2 (19)	194
2367. THREE TIMES DOPE [122] 1 (18)	194
2368. Tom KIMMEL [104] 1 (15)	194
2369. The HOUSEMARTINS [124] 2 (20)	194
2370. TROPEA [138] 2 (14)	193
2371. LIVING IN A BOX [89] 1 (13)	193
2372. Jimmie WALKER [130] 1 (12)	193
2373. Clint HOLMES [122] 1 (12)	192
2374. The GENTRYS [99] 1 (10)	192
2375. FIFTH ANGEL [117] 1 (13)	192
2376. Tom PAXTON [120] 4 (15)	192
2377. Stevie WOODS [153] 1 (25)	192
2378. SILVER CONDOR [141] 1 (12)	191
2379. Gwen McCRAE [121] 1 (10)	191
2380. John KAY [113] 2 (13)	191
2381. FLATT & SCRUGGS [134] 4 (19)	191
2382. Cheryl LADD [129] 2 (14)	190
2383. SWEET THUNDER [125] 1 (11)	190
2384. Benjamin BRITTEN [68] 1 (8)	190
2385. SHRIEKBACK [145] 3 (21)	190
2386. Ian WHITCOMB [125] 1 (13)	189
2387. Tim MOORE [119] 2 (12)	189
2388. NIGHT [113] 1 (10)	189
2389. Russ BALLARD [147] 3 (19)	189
2390. TASTE [133] 1 (9)	189
2391. DOUBLE EXPOSURE [129] 1 (11)	188
2392. JUNKYARD [105] 1 (11)	188
2393. Elliot EASTON [99] 1 (11)	188
2394. CHAKACHAS [117] 1 (11)	188
2395. Mike RUTHERFORD [145] 2 (17)	187
2396. JELLYBEAN [101] 1 (11)	187
2397. WATERFRONT [103] 1 (13)	187
2398. Pete SHELLEY [121] 2 (15)	187
2399. SOUL SURVIVORS [123] 1 (13)	187
2400. Telly SAVALAS [117] 1 (8)	187
2401. BLODWYN PIG [96] 2 (10)	186
2402. Barry De VORZON [133] 1 (12)	185
2403. Horace SILVER Quintet [95] 2 (12)	185
2404. FAT MATTRESS [134] 1 (10)	185
2405. FROZEN GHOST [107] 1 (13)	185
2406. NATURE'S DIVINE [91] 1 (8)	185
2407. L'TRIMM [132] 1 (16)	184
2408. Le PAMPLEMOUSSE [116] 1 (11)	184
2409. MAC Band [109] 1 (14)	184
2410. CLEAR LIGHT [126] 1 (13)	184
2411. Nancy AMES [133] 2 (12)	183
2412. Andre KOSTELANETZ And His Orchestra [68] 4 (13)	183
2413. CHRISTIE [115] 1 (10)	183
2414. Kiri TE KANAWA [136] 1 (16)	183
2415. Sam NEELY [147] 2 (17)	183
2416. Phil OCHS [149] 4 (16)	183
2417. SHANICE [149] 1 (18)	183
2418. MAGNIFICENT MEN [89] 2 (11)	182
2419. Willie NILE [145] 2 (14)	182
2420. Jackie WILSON [108] 3 (14)	182
2421. Robben FORD [120] 1 (13)	182
2422. Del SHANNON [123] 1 (14)	182

Rank. Act [Hi Peak] Entries (Wks)	Score
2423. NORMA JEAN [134] 1 (11)	181
2424. Robert HAZARD [102] 1 (11)	181
2425. Barry GIBB [72] 1 (8)	181
2426. Dennis WILSON [96] 1 (8)	181
2427. HEADHUNTERS [126] 1 (10)	180
2428. 707 [129] 2 (15)	180
2429. Agnetha FALTSKOG [102] 1 (11)	180
2430. Johnny RODRIGUEZ [156] 2 (18)	179
2431. Duane EDDY [93] 2 (10)	178
2432. Michael SEMBELLO [80] 1 (10)	178
2433. Chaz JANKEL [126] 1 (14)	178
2434. George HAMILTON IV [77] 1 (8)	177
2435. AMERICAN BREED [99] 1 (10)	177
2436. Kate TAYLOR [88] 1 (8)	177
2437. Lamont DOZIER [136] 2 (15)	177
2438. Mireille MATHIEU [118] 1 (8)	176
2439. Jerry WALLACE [96] 2 (15)	176
2440. Jackie LEE [85] 1 (9)	176
2441. 3 [97] 1 (10)	175
2442. RAGING SLAB [113] 1 (15)	174
2443. JAY And The TECHNIQUES [129] 1 (13)	174
2444. Dave ALVIN [116] 1 (13)	174
2445. Gertrude BERG [131] 1 (12)	174
2446. No Artist [96] 1 (9)	174
2447. Dick DALE and The DEL-TONES [106] 1 (11)	174
2448. BONEY M [134] 1 (10)	174
2449. HELLO PEOPLE [145] 1 (13)	174
2450. DUKE JUPITER [122] 1 (12)	173
2451. Tommy KEENE [148] 1 (17)	173
2452. M.O.D. [151] 3 (19)	173
2453. SCARLETT & BLACK [107] 1 (11)	173
2454. Adam Clayton POWELL [112] 1 (9)	173
2455. BLACK IVORY [158] 2 (18)	172
2456. Doc SEVERINSEN [133] 4 (14)	172
2457. KINGS OF THE SUN [136] 1 (16)	172
2458. SPIDER [130] 2 (12)	172
2459. Joey SCARBURY [104] 1 (9)	172
2460. Tim HARDIN [129] 2 (9)	171
2461. RED 7 [105] 2 (13)	171
2462. ERUPTION [133] 1 (13)	170
2463. FLYING LIZARDS [99] 1 (8)	170
2464. Martha DAVIS [127] 1 (13)	170
2465. NEW COLONY SIX [157] 3 (17)	170
2466. ODETTA [75] 1 (8)	169
2467. Sue SAAD And The NEXT [131] 1 (12)	169
2468. Sammy JOHNS [148] 1 (12)	169
2469. DREAMS SO REAL [150] 1 (18)	169
2470. ZENO [107] 1 (10)	168
2471. OHIO EXPRESS [126] 2 (13)	168
2472. The CRETONES [125] 1 (10)	167
2473. STAGE DOLLS [118] 1 (12)	167
2474. JOE & EDDIE [119] 2 (11)	167
2475. Jimmy 'Bo' HORNE [122] 1 (10)	167
2476. Bob MOULD [127] 1 (14)	167
2477. DISNEYLAND AFTER DARK [116] 1 (11)	167
2478. Jeanne PRUETT [122] 1 (9)	166
2479. Maria CALLAS [87] 1 (8)	166
2480. Amy HOLLAND [146] 1 (14)	165
2481. Barbara Ann AUER [145] 1 (15)	165
2482. ELEVENTH HOUSE [163] 2 (15)	164
2483. ROUGH DIAMOND [103] 1 (8)	164
2484. Cheryl Pepsii RILEY [128] 1 (11)	164
2485. BROOKLYN, BRONX & QUEENS Band [109] 1 (9)	164
2486. WAX [101] 1 (11)	164
2487. Andre PREVIN [130] 3 (17)	164
2488. The WAIKIKIS [93] 1 (9)	163
2489. Bob McGRATH [126] 1 (11)	163
2490. BUCKWHEAT ZYDECO [104] 2 (12)	163

Rank. Act [Hi Peak] Entries (Wks)	Score
2491. Bobby WHITLOCK [140] 2 (13)	162
2492. ROACHFORD [109] 1 (12)	162
2493. M [79] 1 (8)	162
2494. BAKER GURVITZ ARMY [140] 2 (12)	161
2495. The WINANS [109] 1 (11)	161
2496. CARAVAN [124] 1 (10)	161
2497. Levon HELM [142] 1 (10)	160
2498. Fontella BASS [93] 1 (8)	160
2499. BOOKER T. & PRISCILLA [106] 2 (10)	160
2500. Richie FURAY Band [130] 1 (8)	159
2501. KaSANDRA [142] 1 (8)	159
2502. Debbie JACOBS [153] 2 (15)	159
2503. MADHOUSE [107] 1 (11)	159
2504. Ellen FOLEY [137] 2 (10)	158
2505. P.F.M. [151] 2 (14)	158
2506. Joey HEATHERTON [154] 1 (13)	158
2507. Los BRAVOS [93] 1 (7)	158
2508. TROUBLE FUNK [121] 1 (14)	157
2509. Steve STEVENS ATOMIC PLAYBOYS [119] 1 (12)	157
2510. The TOYS [92] 1 (8)	157
2511. CUFF LINKS [138] 1 (11)	156
2512. KALEIDOSCOPE [139] 1 (8)	156
2513. SIGUE SIGUE SPUTNIK [96] 1 (10)	156
2514. Donna ALLEN [133] 1 (13)	156
2515. Bernie LEADON-Michel GEORGIADES Band [91] 1 (6)	156
2516. Sylvain SYLVAIN [123] 1 (8)	156
2517. Margaret WHITING [109] 1 (8)	154
2518. Nikki GIOVANNI [165] 1 (13)	154
2519. Webster LEWIS [114] 1 (9)	154
2520. Denise LaSALLE [120] 1 (9)	154
2521. POUSETTE-DART BAND [143] 2 (12)	153
2522. George MARTIN & His Orchestra [111] 1 (10)	153
2523. HUDSON BROTHERS [165] 3 (14)	153
2524. DRIVIN' N' CRYIN' [130] 1 (12)	153
2525. Valerie SIMPSON [159] 2 (12)	152
2526. DYNAMIC SUPERIORS [130] 1 (10)	152
2527. Billy RANKIN [119] 1 (11)	152
2528. Joe CUBA Sextet [119] 2 (9)	152
2529. RED SIREN [124] 1 (12)	152
2530. Curtis KNIGHT [75] 1 (12)	152
2531. Terry BOZZIO [49] 1 (18)	152
2532. Tony HYMAS [49] 1 (18)	152
2533. MANTRONIX [108] 1 (8)	152
2534. ADC BAND [139] 1 (9)	151
2535. Kenny AARONSON [42] 1 (18)	151
2536. Neal SCHON [42] 1 (18)	151
2537. NOEL [126] 1 (13)	151
2538. David OLIVER [128] 1 (8)	150
2539. George MAHARIS [77] 1 (7)	150
2540. Earl GRANT [139] 4 (13)	150
2541. Ian DURY And The BLOCKHEADS [126] 2 (10)	150
2542. The NITE-LITERS [167] 2 (15)	149
2543. KONGAS [120] 1 (8)	149
2544. NEW YORK CITY [122] 1 (10)	149
2545. Steve HILLAGE [130] 1 (9)	149
2546. Tané CAIN [121] 1 (10)	149
2547. Sammy KAYE & His Orchestra [97] 1 (9)	149
2548. Willie MITCHELL [151] 3 (14)	149
2549. Carl REINER & Mel BROOKS [150] 1 (12)	149
2550. Chuckii BOOKER [116] 1 (10)	148
2551. FAIRPORT CONVENTION [143] 3 (12)	148
2552. SOUL CHILDREN [154] 2 (12)	148
2553. Jackie LOMAX [145] 1 (9)	148
2554. SO [124] 1 (9)	148
2555. Dexter WANSEL [139] 2 (9)	148

Rank. Act [Hi Peak] Entries (Wks)	Score
2556. David FOSTER [111] 2 (11)	147
2557. Bill BLACK'S Combo [139] 4 (13)	147
2558. Shelley BERMAN [88] 1 (8)	147
2559. PEOPLE [128] 1 (8)	147
2560. McCRARYS [138] 1 (9)	147
2561. PRETTY POISON [104] 1 (8)	146
2562. Doug SAHM And Band [125] 1 (10)	146
2563. SWINGING BLUE JEANS [90] 1 (9)	146
2564. WHITE WOLF [137] 2 (15)	145
2565. TRAPEZE [146] 2 (12)	145
2566. D.L. BYRON [133] 1 (10)	145
2567. CAPTAIN SKY [157] 1 (12)	145
2568. YELLOWJACKETS [145] 3 (16)	144
2569. Jerry KNIGHT [146] 2 (13)	144
2570. SUNSHINE COMPANY [126] 1 (10)	143
2571. Doris DAY [102] 1 (8)	143
2572. The FOOLS [151] 2 (12)	143
2573. CRYAN' SHAMES [156] 3 (18)	143
2574. Alex BUGNON [127] 1 (11)	142
2575. Toni TENNILLE [142] 2 (13)	142
2576. Hank CRAWFORD [143] 3 (12)	141
2577. Rick DANKO [119] 1 (8)	141
2578. Harvey MASON [149] 2 (11)	141
2579. BUD And TRAVIS [126] 2 (10)	141
2580. Billy BUTTERFIELD [85] 1 (13)	141
2581. Ray CONNIFF [85] 1 (13)	141
2582. HEAR 'N AID [80] 1 (7)	140
2583. John BRANNEN [156] 1 (14)	140
2584. The RONETTES [96] 1 (8)	139
2585. Skitch HENDERSON [103] 1 (8)	139
2586. The FORTUNES [134] 1 (10)	138
2587. Alice COLTRANE [79] 2 (10)	138
2588. BLACK PEARL [130] 2 (7)	138
2589. Sharon BRYANT [139] 1 (13)	138
2590. ULTIMATE [157] 1 (11)	138
2591. Jennifer RUSH [118] 1 (10)	137
2592. Cledus MAGGARD And The CITIZEN's BAND [135] 1 (8)	137
2593. Keith SYKES [147] 1 (11)	137
2594. EVERY MOTHERS' SON [117] 1 (10)	136
2595. PAPER LACE [124] 1 (8)	136
2596. Ritchie VALENS [100] 1 (10)	136
2597. Tony WILLIAMS [113] 1 (7)	135
2598. The CHIEFTAINS [102] 2 (17)	135
2599. FIVE MAN ELECTRICAL BAND [148] 2 (11)	135
2600. Red SOVINE [119] 1 (6)	134
2601. TKA [135] 1 (11)	134
2602. KID CREOLE & The COCONUTS [145] 2 (14)	134
2603. BALANCE [133] 1 (12)	134
2604. Beverly BREMERS [124] 1 (8)	134
2605. BLACKJACK [127] 1 (7)	133
2606. Michael PINDER [133] 1 (8)	133
2607. TIMES TWO [137] 1 (11)	133
2608. Irma THOMAS [104] 1 (8)	132
2609. SAN FRANCISCO Symphony [105] 1 (15)	132
2610. SIEGEL-SCHWALL Band [105] 1 (15)	132
2611. Louise TUCKER [127] 1 (10)	132
2612. Tom CLAY [92] 1 (5)	132
2613. Jimmie RODGERS [145] 3 (12)	132
2614. Steve GOODMAN [144] 2 (10)	132
2615. STEALIN HORSES [146] 1 (12)	131
2616. STONE CITY BAND [122] 1 (8)	130
2617. David LANZ [125] 2 (18)	130
2618. Bob GELDOF [130] 1 (12)	129
2619. VESTA [131] 1 (10)	129
2620. BREAKWATER [141] 2 (10)	129

Rank. Act [Hi Peak] Entries (Wks)	Score
2621. Frank CHACKSFIELD And His Orchestra [120] 1 (9)	129
2622. Bill QUATEMAN [129] 1 (8)	128
2623. LARSEN-FEITEN BAND [142] 1 (10)	128
2624. Andre CYMONE [121] 2 (12)	128
2625. Shirley JONES [128] 1 (10)	128
2626. KING HARVEST [136] 1 (10)	128
2627. The KINGBEES [160] 1 (12)	127
2628. Ian McLAGAN [125] 1 (9)	127
2629. TRANSVISION VAMP [115] 1 (8)	127
2630. Jack GREEN [121] 1 (8)	127
2631. The INDEPENDENTS [127] 1 (9)	127
2632. STONE FURY [144] 1 (12)	127
2633. BOSTON POPS Orchestra/ John WILLIAMS [155] 2 (14)	127
2634. Jud STRUNK [138] 1 (9)	126
2635. Stewart COPELAND [148] 2 (13)	126
2636. JETBOY [135] 1 (10)	126
2637. DANZIG [125] 1 (9)	126
2638. Paul WINTER [138] 1 (11)	125
2639. GOLDDIGGERS [142] 1 (7)	125
2640. KITARO [141] 3 (13)	125
2641. Solomon BURKE [140] 2 (7)	125
2642. Noel HARRISON [135] 1 (9)	125
2643. Ofra HAZA [130] 1 (9)	124
2644. Rufus THOMAS [138] 2 (8)	124
2645. Brian MAY [125] 1 (9)	124
2646. SPINAL TAP [121] 1 (10)	124
2647. FUN BOY THREE [104] 1 (7)	124
2648. The PERSUADERS [141] 2 (11)	124
2649. Roy HEAD [122] 1 (8)	124
2650. Danny Joe BROWN [120] 1 (7)	123
2651. Sergio FRANCHI [97] 2 (11)	123
2652. Z.Z. HILL [165] 3 (16)	123
2653. The PLATTERS [100] 1 (6)	123
2654. GLASS MOON [148] 1 (9)	123
2655. Annie HASLEM [167] 1 (13)	123
2656. Sandy POSEY [129] 2 (11)	123
2657. Kirk WHALUM [142] 1 (10)	122
2658. CATE BROS. [158] 2 (11)	122
2659. Freddy WELLER [144] 1 (7)	122
2660. MAGIC ORGAN [135] 1 (7)	122
2661. Daniel BOONE [142] 1 (9)	121
2662. FAIRGROUND ATTRACTION [137] 1 (11)	121
2663. ALPHAVILLE [174] 2 (21)	120
2664. The NICE [152] 2 (13)	120
2665. Paul RODGERS [135] 1 (10)	120
2666. Pharoah SANDERS [163] 3 (12)	120
2667. Tommy BOYCE & Bobby HART [109] 2 (6)	120
2668. Anita KERR Singers [162] 2 (9)	120
2669. Ernie WATTS [161] 1 (12)	120
2670. Bobbi MARTIN [127] 2 (10)	120
2671. Kinky FRIEDMAN [132] 1 (6)	120
2672. The HEADPINS [114] 1 (9)	119
2673. Sensational Alex HARVEY Band [100] 2 (5)	119
2674. MIGHTY CLOUDS OF JOY [165] 2 (11)	119
2675. ANN-MARGRET [83] 2 (13)	118
2676. Dickie GOODMAN [144] 1 (8)	118
2677. William DeVAUGHN [165] 1 (11)	118
2678. Kathy SMITH [144] 1 (13)	118
2679. Scott McKENZIE [127] 1 (7)	118
2680. James COTTON Band [146] 2 (11)	118
2681. Beverly SILLS [113] 1 (6)	118
2682. Grant GREEN [151] 1 (9)	118
2683. HOT BUTTER [137] 1 (7)	118
2684. Marc ALMOND [144] 1 (11)	118
2685. SOFT MACHINE [160] 1 (9)	117
2686. "D" TRAIN [128] 1 (9)	117
2687. WIDOWMAKER [150] 1 (9)	117
2688. SWEET INSPIRATIONS [90] 1 (6)	117
2689. IRONHORSE [153] 1 (10)	116
2690. Eloise LAWS [156] 2 (12)	116
2691. DALE & GRACE [100] 1 (7)	116
2692. The TRUTH [115] 1 (8)	115
2693. TWIN HYPE [140] 1 (11)	115
2694. Sarah McLACHLAN [132] 1 (12)	115
2695. Bobby BARE [119] 2 (8)	115
2696. The THREE O'CLOCK [125] 1 (10)	114
2697. MAMA'S BOYS [151] 2 (14)	114
2698. SAWYER BROWN [140] 1 (11)	114
2699. WIRE TRAIN [150] 2 (13)	114
2700. REGINA [102] 1 (8)	114
2701. Brian HYLAND [160] 2 (9)	114
2702. TROOP [133] 1 (9)	114
2703. The TREMELOES [119] 1 (8)	113
2704. MUSCLE SHOALS HORNS [154] 1 (8)	113
2705. SWEET TEE [169] 1 (13)	113
2706. John FRED & His PLAYBOY BAND [154] 1 (10)	113
2707. Chi COLTRANE [148] 1 (10)	113
2708. Charlie BYRD [129] 2 (8)	113
2709. GRIN [180] 3 (16)	113
2710. Donnie ELBERT [153] 1 (9)	112
2711. Willie BOBO [137] 1 (8)	112
2712. TEARDROP EXPLODES [156] 2 (10)	112
2713. ACE SPECTRUM [138] 1 (7)	112
2714. David CLAYTON-THOMAS [159] 2 (11)	112
2715. CREATIVE SOURCE [152] 1 (10)	111
2716. MIRABAI [128] 1 (6)	111
2717. Giorgio MORODER [130] 1 (7)	111
2718. NITRO [140] 1 (9)	111
2719. QUAZAR [121] 1 (5)	111
2720. Kathi McDONALD [156] 1 (11)	111
2721. Freddy ROBINSON [133] 1 (7)	111
2722. GRINDER SWITCH [144] 1 (8)	110
2723. The MONROES [109] 1 (9)	110
2724. WICHITA TRAIN WHISTLE [144] 1 (7)	110
2725. Marc TANNER BAND [140] 1 (8)	109
2726. Lou Ann BARTON [133] 1 (9)	109
2727. Jimmie SPHEERIS [135] 1 (6)	109
2728. James McMURTRY [125] 1 (9)	109
2729. David T. WALKER [166] 2 (13)	109
2730. WILL And The KILL [129] 1 (8)	109
2731. SPYS [138] 1 (10)	109
2732. L.A. DREAM TEAM [138] 2 (11)	108
2733. Chet HUNTLEY & David BRINKLEY [115] 1 (7)	108
2734. Tony MacALPINE [146] 1 (11)	108
2735. DEATH ANGEL [143] 1 (11)	107
2736. DILLMAN Band [145] 2 (9)	107
2737. Porter WAGONER [161] 3 (11)	107
2738. Ahmad JAMAL Trio [168] 2 (13)	107
2739. PEPSI and SHIRLIE [133] 1 (9)	107
2740. Jimmy DAVIS & JUNCTION [122] 1 (8)	107
2741. Howard JOHNSON [122] 1 (9)	106
2742. LeBLANC & CARR [145] 1 (7)	106
2743. Barbara LEWIS [118] 1 (7)	106
2744. McGUINNESS FLINT [155] 2 (10)	106
2745. Colin James HAY [126] 1 (9)	105
2746. AZTECA [151] 1 (9)	105
2747. Chris HILLMAN [152] 2 (9)	105
2748. The SILENCERS [147] 1 (11)	105
2749. Neil LARSEN [139] 1 (7)	105
2750. Cecil HOLMES SOULFUL SOUNDS [141] 1 (10)	105
2751. BANG [164] 1 (10)	104
2752. CASHFLOW [144] 1 (11)	104
2753. DORO [154] 1 (11)	104
2754. Bill BRUFORD [123] 2 (7)	104
2755. XAVIER [129] 1 (7)	104
2756. UNICORN [129] 1 (5)	103
2757. Wes HARRISON [83] 1 (5)	103
2758. James GALWAY [150] 2 (11)	103
2759. Jon ASTLEY [135] 1 (10)	103
2760. PAUL HYDE AND THE PAYOLAS [144] 1 (10)	103
2761. WET WET WET [123] 1 (7)	103
2762. KOKOMO [159] 2 (11)	102
2763. KGB [124] 1 (6)	102
2764. Joe Lynn TURNER [143] 1 (12)	102
2765. BOBBY And The MIDNITES [158] 2 (11)	102
2766. THUNDERCLAP NEWMAN [161] 1 (10)	102
2767. Jake HOLMES [135] 1 (6)	102
2768. PENTANGLE [183] 5 (13)	101
2769. Ann PEEBLES [155] 2 (10)	101
2770. Judy GARLAND [136] 3 (8)	101
2771. Billy STRANGE [135] 2 (8)	101
2772. The SHANGRI-LAS [109] 1 (6)	101
2773. FUSE ONE [139] 1 (8)	101
2774. BARRABAS [149] 1 (7)	101
2775. Stan RIDGWAY [131] 1 (9)	101
2776. Garnet MIMMS & The ENCHANTERS [91] 1 (5)	101
2777. Steve WALSH [124] 1 (6)	100.1
2778. Josie COTTON [147] 1 (12)	99.9
2779. EUROGLIDERS [140] 1 (11)	99.9
2780. OXO [117] 1 (7)	99.8
2781. WIRE [135] 1 (10)	99.8
2782. COUNT FIVE [122] 1 (6)	99.8
2783. Wanda ROBINSON [186] 1 (13)	99.6
2784. Patrick MORAZ [132] 1 (5)	99.6
2785. King FLOYD [130] 1 (5)	99.6
2786. FLAMIN' GROOVIES [142] 1 (7)	99.5
2787. TORONTO [162] 2 (14)	99.2
2788. SWEAT BAND [150] 1 (8)	99.1
2789. Martin DENNY [123] 1 (7)	99.0
2790. RAIL [143] 1 (10)	98.9
2791. FACTS OF LIFE [146] 1 (7)	98.8
2792. V.S.O.P [123] 1 (5)	98.6
2793. Harvey MANDEL [169] 3 (10)	98.5
2794. Robert Ellis ORRALL [146] 1 (9)	98.5
2795. MILLIONS LIKE US [171] 1 (12)	98.4
2796. Jackie MASON [146] 1 (9)	98.4
2797. UNLIMITED TOUCH [142] 1 (7)	97.8
2798. EGYPTIAN LOVER [146] 1 (10)	97.6
2799. BULLDOG [176] 1 (12)	97.5
2800. FIREBALLET [151] 1 (8)	97.1
2801. Dee Dee BRIDGEWATER [170] 2 (11)	97.0
2802. HOUSE OF FREAKS [154] 1 (10)	96.8
2803. SHOTGUN [163] 2 (9)	96.7
2804. CENTRAL LINE [145] 1 (9)	96.6
2805. Alphonse MOUZON [146] 1 (11)	96.0
2806. JOY DIVISION [146] 1 (8)	95.9
2807. KING SWAMP [159] 1 (14)	95.8
2808. Peter BANKS [152] 1 (8)	95.8
2809. RUBICON [147] 1 (7)	95.3
2810. Shel SILVERSTEIN [155] 1 (8)	95.2
2811. Peter YARROW [163] 1 (8)	94.5
2812. STATUS QUO [148] 1 (7)	94.5
2813. DOUCETTE [159] 1 (8)	94.5
2814. Bill MEDLEY [152] 2 (8)	94.4
2815. Judson SPENCE [168] 1 (13)	94.3
2816. Nina HAGEN [151] 2 (11)	93.4
2817. STEELEYE SPAN [143] 2 (9)	93.2
2818. Mickey GILLEY [170] 2 (9)	93.0
2819. AORTA [167] 1 (8)	92.6
2820. FAMILY [177] 2 (12)	92.1
2821. MAZARATI [133] 1 (8)	92.0

Rank. Act [Hi Peak] Entries (Wks)	Score
2822. The PYRAMIDS [119] 1 (6)	91.3
2823. SILVER [142] 1 (6)	91.3
2824. MOCEDADES [152] 1 (7)	91.2
2825. David ACKLES [167] 1 (10)	91.2
2826. TAXXI [161] 1 (11)	91.1
2827. Paul SPEER [125] 1 (12)	91.0
2828. AFRIQUE [152] 1 (8)	90.9
2829. MEMPHIS HORNS [163] 1 (9)	90.8
2830. Mick TAYLOR [119] 1 (5)	90.8
2831. TUCK & PATTI [162] 1 (11)	90.5
2832. Ray MANZAREK [150] 1 (6)	90.2
2833. ATLANTA [140] 1 (7)	90.1
2834. Freddie KING [158] 1 (8)	89.8
2835. Betty EVERETT [102] 1 (11)	89.8
2836. Stephane GRAPELLI [108] 1 (10)	89.7
2837. Dianne REEVES [172] 1 (12)	89.5
2838. KING [140] 1 (9)	89.5
2839. JOHNNY And The DISTRACTIONS [152] 1 (9)	89.2
2840. PROPHET [137] 1 (7)	88.8
2841. SCREAMING BLUE MESSIAHS [172] 1 (11)	88.8
2842. Theo VANESS [145] 1 (6)	88.8
2843. Mort SAHL [149] 1 (7)	88.5
2844. CASHMAN & WEST [168] 2 (10)	88.2
2845. SUPERSAX [169] 2 (10)	88.1
2846. Charlie DORE [145] 1 (7)	88.0
2847. AIRTO [114] 1 (9)	88.0
2848. DAVE & SUGAR [157] 2 (8)	87.9
2849. KEITH [124] 1 (5)	87.9
2850. DOCTOR And The MEDICS [125] 1 (8)	87.8
2851. Mae WEST [116] 1 (5)	87.7
2852. John HUNTER [148] 1 (9)	87.4
2853. BOOK OF LOVE [156] 1 (10)	87.3
2854. GOOSE CREEK SYMPHONY [167] 1 (8)	87.3
2855. WRABIT [157] 1 (8)	86.9
2856. STREETS [166] 1 (11)	86.8
2857. BULGARIAN STATE RADIO & T.V. FEMALE CHOIR [165] 1 (10)	86.8
2858. DREAMBOY [168] 1 (11)	86.6
2859. MOOG MACHINE [170] 1 (8)	86.6
2860. BROOKLYN DREAMS [151] 1 (7)	86.6
2861. Lee DORSEY [129] 1 (5)	86.3
2862. FLOTSAM AND JETSAM [143] 1 (8)	86.1
2863. Carlene CARTER [139] 1 (6)	85.7
2864. M + M [163] 3 (11)	85.6
2865. ATLANTA DISCO BAND [172] 1 (9)	85.4
2866. Jane SIBERRY [149] 1 (8)	85.4
2867. Bobby NUNN [148] 1 (8)	85.2
2868. The LEAVES [127] 1 (5)	85.2
2869. ILLINOIS SPEED PRESS [144] 1 (4)	84.5
2870. The GRACES [147] 1 (9)	84.5
2871. Woody HERMAN [136] 2 (6)	84.4
2872. RONNY And The DAYTONAS [122] 1 (6)	84.4
2873. GANG OF FOUR [168] 4 (11)	84.2
2874. Carla CAPUANO [152] 1 (8)	84.0
2875. AQUARIAN DREAM [154] 1 (6)	83.5
2876. Connie SMITH [105] 1 (5)	83.3
2877. HEARTSFIELD [159] 1 (7)	83.0
2878. 100 PROOF AGED IN SOUL [151] 1 (7)	82.9
2879. The UNDERTONES [154] 1 (7)	82.6
2880. FREE MOVEMENT [167] 1 (8)	82.3
2881. Diane SCHUUR [170] 1 (10)	82.2
2882. The ADVENTURES [144] 1 (9)	82.1
2883. The WOMENFOLK [118] 1 (6)	82.1
2884. The CONTROLLERS [146] 1 (6)	82.1
2885. SWEET SENSATION [163] 1 (7)	82.0
2886. EZO [150] 1 (9)	81.9
2887. The PRESIDENTS [158] 1 (6)	81.7
2888. VAIN [154] 1 (8)	81.5

Rank. Act [Hi Peak] Entries (Wks)	Score
2889. Johnny CASH And The TENNESSEE TWO/THREE [181] 4 (11)	81.5
2890. Robert TEPPER [144] 1 (8)	81.5
2891. Robbin THOMPSON Band [168] 1 (11)	81.5
2892. Joe FARRELL [100] 1 (8)	81.2
2893. The A's [146] 1 (7)	80.9
2894. Bo HANSSON [154] 1 (8)	80.5
2895. Leroy HUTSON [170] 1 (8)	80.5
2896. ARMAGEDDON [151] 1 (6)	80.4
2897. Dinah WASHINGTON [130] 1 (6)	80.4
2898. Billy "Crash" CRADDOCK [142] 1 (5)	80.2
2899. Richard CLAYDERMAN [160] 1 (9)	80.1
2900. The FLAME [147] 1 (5)	80.0
2901. DFX2 [143] 1 (8)	80.0
2902. The WAILERS [127] 1 (6)	79.9
2903. Tata VEGA [170] 1 (8)	79.8
2904. Gene CLARK [144] 1 (5)	79.8
2905. Kenny BURRELL [108] 3 (8)	79.7
2906. NITZINGER [170] 1 (8)	79.5
2907. Albert COLLINS [124] 2 (20)	79.1
2908. DAMITA JO [121] 2 (6)	79.0
2909. EBONEE WEBB [157] 1 (7)	79.0
2910. Don HARRISON Band [159] 1 (6)	78.7
2911. Mojo NIXON & Skid ROPER [151] 2 (9)	78.7
2912. E.U. [158] 1 (9)	78.6
2913. DREAMS [146] 1 (6)	78.5
2914. Barbara ACKLIN [146] 1 (5)	78.5
2915. Melvin JAMES [146] 1 (8)	78.4
2916. TEE SET [158] 1 (6)	78.2
2917. Bob KUBAN And The IN-MEN [129] 1 (5)	77.8
2918. BLACK UHURU [146] 1 (7)	77.7
2919. DIXIE CUPS [112] 1 (5)	77.6
2920. Fats DOMINO [130] 2 (6)	77.1
2921. Herschel BERNARDI [138] 1 (5)	77.0
2922. IF [171] 3 (9)	76.9
2923. Tracy NELSON [145] 1 (5)	76.5
2924. TUFF DARTS [156] 1 (6)	76.5
2925. BROTHERHOOD OF MAN [168] 1 (8)	76.1
2926. The O'KAYSIONS [153] 1 (4)	75.9
2927. Pope JOHN PAUL II [126] 1 (4)	75.7
2928. Malcolm McLAREN [173] 2 (12)	75.5
2929. The RIVIERAS [115] 1 (5)	75.4
2930. DON And The GOODTIMES [109] 1 (4)	75.3
2931. The UNTOUCHABLES [162] 1 (9)	74.8
2932. Vinnie MOORE [147] 1 (7)	74.7
2933. Nigel OLSSON [140] 1 (5)	74.4
2934. The PIPKINS [132] 1 (4)	74.4
2935. Charles LLOYD Quartet [171] 2 (11)	74.2
2936. The CHRISTIANS [158] 1 (8)	74.1
2937. David MATTHEWS [169] 1 (7)	73.9
2938. The PLIMSOULS [153] 2 (8)	73.9
2939. Sonny CHARLES [136] 1 (7)	73.4
2940. Gil TRYTHALL [157] 1 (6)	73.4
2941. Joe BECK [140] 1 (5)	73.4
2942. ILLUSION [163] 1 (7)	73.3
2943. Desmond CHILD and ROUGE [157] 1 (6)	73.0
2944. Sandie SHAW [100] 1 (4)	72.8
2945. FOUR JACKS And A JILL [155] 1 (6)	72.8
2946. Paul DESMOND [129] 2 (8)	72.6
2947. Greg GUIDRY [147] 1 (7)	72.4
2948. The KNICKERBOCKERS [134] 1 (5)	72.2
2949. Georgie FAME [137] 2 (7)	72.1
2950. Janey STREET [145] 1 (6)	72.0
2951. Wynn STEWART [158] 1 (8)	72.0
2952. DARLING CRUEL [160] 1 (8)	72.0
2953. RANKING ROGER [151] 1 (7)	71.8
2954. TARNEY/SPENCER Band [174] 2 (8)	71.8
2955. Robert JOHNSON [174] 1 (8)	71.8
2956. GAYLORD & HOLIDAY [180] 1 (8)	71.7
2957. The TOKENS [134] 2 (8)	71.3

Rank. Act [Hi Peak] Entries (Wks)	Score
2958. Bobby SHORT [169] 1 (8)	71.0
2959. Nick DeCARO [165] 1 (5)	70.6
2960. BUBBLE PUPPY [176] 1 (6)	70.5
2961. John CALE [154] 1 (5)	70.4
2962. BADGER [167] 1 (8)	70.4
2963. BILLY SATELLITE [139] 1 (6)	70.3
2964. STEADY B [149] 2 (8)	70.2
2965. Foster SYLVERS [159] 1 (7)	70.1
2966. Johnny CLEGG & SAVUKA [155] 1 (7)	70.0
2967. OTHER ONES [139] 1 (6)	70.0
2968. REVERBERI [169] 1 (7)	69.8
2969. The MOVE [172] 1 (8)	69.8
2970. Steve KHAN [157] 1 (5)	69.7
2971. John PHILLIPS [181] 1 (9)	69.6
2972. John Paul HAMMOND [105] 1 (12)	69.5
2973. Stanky BROWN Group [192] 3 (10)	68.9
2974. The CONNELLS [163] 1 (10)	68.9
2975. Ronnie ALDRICH [169] 1 (6)	68.9
2976. SKY (2) [160] 1 (6)	68.6
2977. HARDEN Trio [146] 1 (5)	68.5
2978. WILD MAN STEVE [179] 2 (8)	68.3
2979. Roy ETZEL [140] 1 (5)	68.3
2980. Karen BETH [171] 1 (6)	68.2
2981. SAVAGE GRACE [182] 1 (8)	67.8
2982. MANCHILD [154] 1 (6)	67.7
2983. The MOTORS [174] 1 (8)	67.6
2984. 4 BY FOUR [141] 1 (7)	67.6
2985. WITCH QUEEN [158] 1 (6)	67.5
2986. Danny WILLIAMS [122] 1 (5)	67.4
2987. MARIACHI BRASS [120] 1 (4)	67.3
2988. Durell COLEMAN [155] 1 (7)	67.2
2989. GRANDMASTER FLASH [145] 2 (7)	67.2
2990. Jane MORGAN [134] 1 (4)	67.0
2991. Danny WILDE [176] 1 (9)	67.0
2992. Johnny COPELAND [124] 1 (18)	67.0
2993. STAMPEDERS [172] 1 (6)	66.8
2994. XYMOX [165] 1 (10)	66.8
2995. COMPANY B [143] 1 (6)	66.7
2996. David FREIBERG [120] 1 (12)	66.5
2997. Robbie PATTON [162] 1 (6)	66.5
2998. Miguel RIOS [140] 1 (4)	66.1
2999. CAPTAIN BEEFHEART & The MAGIC BAND [191] 2 (11)	66.1
3000. UNITED STATES OF AMERICA [181] 1 (9)	66.1
3001. POTLIQUOR [168] 1 (7)	65.9
3002. Fee WAYBILL [146] 1 (6)	65.9
3003. Glen BURTNICK [147] 1 (6)	65.9
3004. Millie SMALL [132] 1 (5)	65.7
3005. Jumpin' Gene SIMMONS [132] 1 (5)	65.6
3006. David LAFLAMME [159] 1 (6)	65.6
3007. Jorma KAUKONEN & VITAL PARTS [163] 1 (6)	65.5
3008. PHILADELPHIA Orchestra [136] 1 (8)	65.2
3009. NRBQ [162] 2 (7)	65.0
3010. Kristy And Jimmy McNICHOL [116] 1 (4)	64.7
3011. New Band of Spike JONES [113] 1 (4)	64.3
3012. COLD CHISEL [171] 1 (6)	64.0
3013. Dick GREGORY [182] 1 (8)	64.0
3014. Elisa FIORILLO [163] 1 (8)	63.7
3015. NOVO COMBO [167] 1 (6)	63.5
3016. FETCHIN BONES [175] 1 (8)	63.4
3017. Rick DEES [157] 1 (5)	63.4
3018. FISHBONE [153] 1 (9)	63.3
3019. Martin MULL [157] 2 (5)	63.1
3020. FEMME FATALE [141] 1 (5)	63.0
3021. FLYING MACHINE [179] 1 (7)	63.0
3022. Jim GILSTRAP [179] 1 (7)	62.9
3023. EARTH QUAKE [151] 1 (4)	62.8
3024. FUNKADELIC(2) [151] 1 (4)	62.7
3025. PRETTY MAIDS [165] 1 (8)	62.4

Rank. Act [Hi Peak] Entries (Wks)	Score
3026. Slim WHITMAN [175] 2 (7)	62.4
3027. CLIMAX [177] 1 (7)	61.9
3028. Don DIXON [162] 1 (8)	61.9
3029. The RINGS [164] 1 (6)	61.8
3030. Ken HENSLEY [173] 1 (7)	61.5
3031. The CARAVELLES [127] 1 (4)	61.5
3032. DARK ANGEL [159] 1 (6)	61.5
3033. CLEVELAND Orchestra [152] 1 (4)	61.3
3034. Eric ROGERS & His Orchestra [114] 1 (3)	61.2
3035. SHAKTI With John McLAUGHLIN [168] 2 (6)	60.8
3036. OZONE [152] 1 (6)	60.6
3037. Itzhak PERLMAN [149] 1 (9)	60.6
3038. Anna MOFFO [97] 1 (7)	60.4
3039. The FOLKSWINGERS [132] 1 (4)	60.4
3040. Gene PAGE [156] 1 (4)	60.3
3041. The RAES [161] 1 (5)	60.2
3042. HOUSE OF LOVE [156] 1 (7)	60.2
3043. SMOKIE [173] 1 (6)	60.1
3044. FOSTER & LLOYD [142] 1 (6)	60.0
3045. MEL And TIM [175] 1 (7)	59.9
3046. Howie MANDEL [148] 1 (6)	59.6
3047. The HONDELLS [119] 1 (4)	59.5
3048. SEA HAGS [163] 1 (7)	59.3
3049. BALLIN' JACK [180] 1 (8)	59.3
3050. Shuggie OTIS [181] 3 (10)	59.1
3051. Lonnie JORDAN [158] 1 (5)	59.0
3052. Anita BRYANT [146] 1 (4)	58.9
3053. Jose JIMENEZ [128] 1 (4)	58.9
3054. SOUNDS OF SUNSHINE [187] 1 (8)	58.8
3055. AKA The MAX DEMIAN Band [159] 1 (5)	58.8
3056. Nana MOUSKOURI [124] 1 (8)	58.8
3057. Paul HUMPHREY & The COOL AID CHEMISTS [170] 1 (6)	58.8
3058. CHEQUERED PAST [151] 1 (6)	58.5
3059. LORDS Of The NEW CHURCH [158] 1 (7)	58.2
3060. Hoyt AXTON [171] 2 (6)	58.1
3061. Mary Chapin CARPENTER [183] 1 (10)	57.7
3062. Ian DURY [168] 1 (5)	57.5
3063. STACKRIDGE [191] 1 (9)	57.5
3064. Michael MONROE [161] 1 (8)	56.8
3065. Willis JACKSON [137] 2 (7)	56.8
3066. Keith BARBOUR [163] 1 (4)	56.6
3067. Gary GLITTER [186] 1 (8)	56.5
3068. ALIVE 'N KICKIN' [129] 1 (3)	56.5
3069. DB'S [171] 1 (8)	56.4
3070. Sarah DASH [182] 1 (7)	56.4
3071. Nick MASON [154] 2 (8)	56.3
3072. Myron LeFEVRE [138] 1 (8)	56.3
3073. CRABBY APPLETON [175] 1 (6)	56.3
3074. Bobby BLOOM [126] 1 (3)	56.1
3075. D.J. ROGERS [175] 1 (5)	56.0
3076. Linda FRATIANNE [174] 1 (7)	55.7
3077. STALLION [191] 1 (9)	55.6
3078. PARTLAND BROTHERS [146] 1 (5)	55.2
3079. Branford MARSALIS [164] 1 (7)	55.1
3080. Julie LONDON [136] 1 (4)	54.9
3081. DETROIT [176] 1 (6)	54.7
3082. Julie BROWN [168] 1 (7)	54.4
3083. Gary MORRIS [174] 1 (8)	54.3
3084. Carl PERKINS [87] 1 (12)	54.0
3085. FABULOUS RHINESTONES [193] 2 (9)	53.9
3086. Stix HOOPER [166] 1 (5)	53.6
3087. Ruben BLADES [156] 1 (6)	53.6
3088. Pete BARDENS [148] 1 (5)	53.6
3089. BUZZCOCKS [163] 1 (6)	53.4
3090. John CONLEE [166] 1 (6)	53.4
3091. Simon TOWNSHEND [169] 1 (7)	53.0
3092. Freddie MERCURY [159] 1 (6)	52.8

Rank. Act [Hi Peak] Entries (Wks)	Score
3093. PAVLOV'S DOG [181] 1 (6)	52.6
3094. TEXTONES [176] 1 (8)	52.5
3095. RAMATAM [182] 1 (7)	52.5
3096. CANNIBAL And The HEADHUNTERS [141] 1 (4)	52.2
3097. Bonnie BRAMLETT [168] 1 (5)	52.1
3098. Lenny DEE [189] 3 (8)	52.0
3099. Don FELDER [178] 1 (8)	52.0
3100. Duncan BROWNE [174] 1 (5)	51.9
3101. Johnny GILL [139] 1 (8)	51.8
3102. Desmond DEKKER And The ACES [153] 1 (3)	51.7
3103. Susan RAYE [154] 2 (8)	51.7
3104. KILLER DWARFS [165] 1 (6)	51.6
3105. The RUNAWAYS [172] 2 (6)	51.6
3106. The ORIGINALS [174] 2 (6)	51.5
3107. LOVE CHILDS AFRO CUBAN BLUES Band [168] 1 (5)	51.5
3108. LOVE AND MONEY [175] 1 (7)	51.2
3109. SUSAN [169] 1 (5)	51.0
3110. SUNNY & The SUNLINERS [142] 2 (4)	51.0
3111. CELI BEE And The BUZZY BUNCH [169] 1 (5)	51.0
3112. Syd BARRETT [163] 1 (4)	50.9
3113. David PEEL & The LOWER EAST SIDE [186] 2 (6)	50.8
3114. VIO-LENCE [154] 1 (6)	50.7
3115. Frank IFIELD [104] 1 (6)	50.7
3116. John O'BANION [164] 1 (4)	50.7
3117. BUCKWHEAT [179] 1 (6)	50.2
3118. CALDERA [159] 1 (4)	50.1
3119. Terri Lyne CARRINGTON [169] 1 (7)	49.9
3120. BAUHAUS [169] 1 (6)	49.8
3121. Lou JACOBI [134] 1 (3)	49.7
3122. SCRUFFY THE CAT [177] 1 (8)	49.6
3123. The GODZ [189] 2 (7)	49.6
3124. Sarah VAUGHAN [173] 1 (12)	49.3
3125. ASWAD [173] 1 (7)	49.1
3126. MARLEY MARL [163] 1 (5)	49.0
3127. The BUGGLES [161] 1 (5)	48.9
3128. WHITE PLAINS [166] 1 (4)	48.9
3129. The LARKS [143] 1 (4)	48.9
3130. Jerry GOODMAN & Jan HAMMER [150] 1 (3)	48.7
3131. POP WILL EAT ITSELF [169] 1 (6)	48.7
3132. ASHTON, GARDNER & DYKE [178] 1 (6)	48.7
3133. The BEARS [159] 1 (5)	48.6
3134. Pete WINGFIELD [165] 1 (5)	48.5
3135. Roy WOOD [176] 1 (6)	47.8
3136. Keith MOON [155] 1 (3)	47.8
3137. Jonathan WINTERS [145] 2 (4)	47.7
3138. Tom FOGERTY [180] 1 (6)	47.6
3139. Razzy BAILEY [176] 2 (6)	47.4
3140. THEE PROPHETS [163] 1 (3)	47.1
3141. Jan AKKERMAN [192] 3 (8)	47.0
3142. TYZIK [172] 1 (6)	47.0
3143. Valerie CARTER [182] 1 (5)	47.0
3144. BLUE MERCEDES [165] 1 (5)	46.8
3145. Cory DAYE [171] 1 (5)	46.8
3146. Cliff NOBLES & Co. [159] 1 (3)	46.5
3147. MAX Q [182] 1 (8)	46.4
3148. The MAR-KEYS [98] 1 (4)	46.4
3149. Demis ROUSSOS [184] 1 (6)	46.3
3150. Chico HAMILTON [145] 1 (4)	46.3
3151. BAND Of The BLACK WATCH [164] 1 (4)	46.2
3152. PYTHON LEE JACKSON [182] 1 (6)	46.2
3153. AUDIENCE [175] 1 (5)	46.1
3154. Marlon JACKSON [175] 1 (7)	46.1
3155. Tim FINN [161] 1 (5)	45.8
3156. Dave VALENTIN [184] 2 (6)	45.8

Rank. Act [Hi Peak] Entries (Wks)	Score
3157. Yusef LATEEF [183] 1 (5)	45.7
3158. Tony BANKS [171] 1 (5)	45.6
3159. David STEINBERG [182] 1 (6)	45.5
3160. LITTLE RICHARD [184] 2 (7)	45.5
3161. COUCHOIS [170] 1 (4)	45.4
3162. GUCCI CREW II [173] 1 (6)	45.3
3163. Martin L. GORE [156] 1 (5)	44.9
3164. Cal SMITH [170] 2 (5)	44.8
3165. TROUBADOURS Du ROI BAUDOUIN [184] 1 (5)	44.8
3166. CHECKMATES, LTD. [178] 1 (4)	44.8
3167. 999 [177] 2 (5)	44.5
3168. Thelonious MONK [127] 1 (3)	44.5
3169. Don GIBSON [134] 1 (3)	44.4
3170. CANDLEMASS [174] 1 (6)	44.1
3171. The LITTER [175] 1 (5)	43.9
3172. Art LINKLETTER [143] 1 (3)	43.8
3173. RUNNER [167] 1 (4)	43.8
3174. FARRENHEIT [179] 1 (7)	43.8
3175. The FLESHTONES [174] 1 (5)	43.8
3176. Fred KNOBLOCK [179] 1 (5)	43.5
3177. John COLTRANE [186] 2 (6)	43.4
3178. Taka BOOM [171] 1 (4)	43.3
3179. INSIDERS [167] 1 (5)	43.3
3180. Jean-Pierre RAMPAL & Claude BOLLING [173] 1 (4)	43.2
3181. LATIMORE [181] 1 (5)	43.1
3182. Billy Edd WHEELER [132] 1 (3)	43.1
3183. Little Peggy MARCH [139] 1 (3)	43.0
3184. The NIGHTHAWKS [166] 1 (4)	42.9
3185. Dean FRIEDMAN [192] 1 (6)	42.9
3186. MADAME X [162] 1 (5)	42.9
3187. Franklin D. ROOSEVELT [109] 1 (5)	42.8
3188. UNDERGROUND SUNSHINE [161] 1 (3)	42.6
3189. The CHIFFONS [149] 1 (3)	42.2
3190. Coke ESCOVEDO [190] 3 (6)	42.1
3191. Robin LANE & The CHARTBUSTERS [172] 1 (4)	41.9
3192. APPALOOSA [178] 1 (4)	41.6
3193. Bob HOPE [175] 1 (4)	41.6
3194. Sue THOMPSON [134] 1 (3)	41.3
3195. Fred WESLEY & The HORNY HORNS [181] 1 (5)	40.7
3196. Q [140] 1 (2)	40.6
3197. BROS [171] 1 (5)	40.0
3198. YUTAKA [174] 1 (4)	39.8
3199. SIDEWINDERS [169] 1 (5)	39.8
3200. Jaco PASTORIUS [161] 1 (3)	39.7
3201. LINX [175] 1 (4)	39.5
3202. Jack BLANCHARD & Misty MORGAN [185] 1 (5)	39.5
3203. Freddie NORTH [179] 1 (5)	39.4
3204. RANK AND FILE [165] 1 (5)	39.3
3205. The SELECTER [175] 1 (4)	39.0
3206. Bunny DeBARGE [172] 1 (5)	38.8
3207. Lonnie YOUNGBLOOD [127] 1 (4)	38.8
3208. WILBURN BROTHERS [143] 1 (2)	38.7
3209. EARTH OPERA [181] 1 (4)	38.7
3210. David JONES [185] 1 (6)	38.6
3211. MISSOURI [174] 1 (4)	38.5
3212. Esther SATTERFIELD [180] 1 (4)	38.5
3213. Peter GREEN [186] 1 (5)	38.4
3214. Johnny DARRELL [172] 1 (3)	38.4
3215. INNER CITY [162] 1 (4)	37.8
3216. Wayne COCHRAN [167] 1 (4)	37.8
3217. Sally FIELD [172] 1 (4)	37.7
3218. The FEELIES [173] 1 (5)	37.5
3219. DAVE DEE, DOZY, BEAKY, MICK And TICH [155] 1 (3)	37.4
3220. Spyder TURNER [158] 1 (3)	37.4

Rank. Act [Hi Peak] Entries (Wks)	Score
3221. YIPES!! [177] 1 (4)	37.3
3222. Johnny BOND [142] 1 (3)	37.2
3223. KALYAN [173] 1 (4)	37.1
3224. SHIRLEY (& COMPANY) [169] 1 (3)	37.1
3225. VISAGE [178] 1 (4)	36.9
3226. Christopher SCOTT [175] 1 (3)	36.7
3227. GREEN ON RED [177] 1 (6)	36.6
3228. Lenny BRUCE [178] 2 (4)	36.4
3229. Ron CARTER [178] 2 (4)	36.2
3230. TROOPER [182] 1 (4)	36.2
3231. Frank WARING [116] 1 (7)	36.1
3232. WILMER And The DUKES [173] 1 (3)	36.1
3233. ROCKIN' SIDNEY [166] 1 (4)	35.7
3234. Tommy PAGE [166] 1 (5)	35.3
3235. MALICE [177] 1 (6)	35.3
3236. Lori LIEBERMAN [192] 1 (6)	34.9
3237. GOANNA [179] 1 (5)	34.9
3238. Stanley BLACK [148] 1 (3)	34.5
3239. PREFAB SPROUT [178] 1 (5)	34.5
3240. Roger VOUDOURIS [171] 1 (3)	34.4
3241. BIDDU Orchestra [170] 1 (3)	34.4
3242. Yehudi MENUHIN [161] 1 (7)	34.2
3243. Larry ELGART [128] 1 (5)	34.1
3244. Les ELGART [128] 1 (5)	34.1
3245. DEJA [186] 1 (6)	33.7
3246. Joe DOLCE [181] 1 (4)	33.7
3247. Bill CHAMPLIN [178] 1 (4)	33.5
3248. AZTEC TWO STEP [181] 1 (4)	33.5
3249. Bobby "Boris" PICKETT [173] 1 (4)	33.4
3250. The WOODENTOPS [185] 1 (6)	33.4
3251. YOUNG AMERICANS [178] 1 (3)	33.3
3252. CACTUS WORLD NEWS [179] 1 (5)	33.0
3253. DREAM SYNDICATE [171] 1 (4)	32.8
3254. Gerald ALBRIGHT [181] 1 (5)	32.7
3255. David Allan COE [179] 1 (5)	32.7
3256. Odell BROWN & THE ORGAN-IZERS [173] 1 (4)	32.7
3257. Peggy SCOTT & Jo Jo BENSON [196] 1 (5)	32.6
3258. The EASYBEATS [180] 1 (5)	32.6
3259. ESQUIRE [165] 1 (4)	32.3
3260. HUGO & LUIGI [125] 1 (2)	32.2
3261. BARCLAY JAMES HARVEST [174] 1 (3)	32.2
3262. Robert Francis KENNEDY [187] 1 (4)	32.1
3263. LACE [187] 1 (5)	31.9
3264. LEROI BROS. [181] 1 (5)	31.7
3265. Lenny WHITE [177] 1 (3)	31.6
3266. Lana CANTRELL [166] 1 (2)	31.3
3267. Danny DAVIS [150] 1 (5)	31.3
3268. Gary STEWART [165] 1 (3)	31.3
3269. GIANT STEPS [184] 1 (5)	31.3
3270. Gary TOMS Empire [178] 1 (3)	31.2
3271. GIRLSCHOOL [182] 1 (5)	31.0
3272. The STRANGLERS [172] 1 (4)	30.9
3273. The CLIQUE [177] 1 (3)	30.9
3274. McGUFFEY LANE [193] 1 (6)	30.9
3275. The ARBORS [144] 1 (2)	30.9
3276. Eddie SCHWARTZ [195] 1 (6)	30.9
3277. RATCHELL [176] 1 (3)	30.9
3278. Bobby RUSSELL [183] 1 (3)	30.6
3279. Link WRAY & His RAY MEN [186] 1 (4)	30.1
3280. Sonny TERRY & Brownie McGHEE [185] 1 (5)	30.1
3281. Joanie GREGGAINS [177] 1 (4)	30.0
3282. BURNING SENSATIONS [175] 1 (4)	29.9
3283. Steve JONES [169] 1 (4)	29.9
3284. Pete SINFIELD [190] 1 (5)	29.7
3285. Marilyn SCOTT [189] 1 (4)	29.5
3286. RED FLAG [178] 1 (4)	29.4
3287. WRATHCHILD AMERICA [190] 1 (6)	29.2
3288. Mavis STAPLES [188] 1 (4)	29.1
3289. The CRITTERS [147] 1 (2)	29.0
3290. HOLLY And The ITALIANS [177] 1 (3)	29.0
3291. DEAD BOYS [189] 1 (4)	28.9
3292. Della REESE [149] 1 (2)	28.8
3293. SYNDICATE OF SOUND [148] 1 (2)	28.8
3294. The STRIKERS [174] 1 (3)	28.8
3295. AREA CODE 615 [191] 1 (4)	28.7
3296. Jenny BURTON [181] 1 (4)	28.7
3297. Chris JAGGER [186] 1 (4)	28.6
3298. JULUKA [186] 1 (5)	28.4
3299. Johnny LYTLE [141] 1 (2)	28.3
3300. Alicia MYERS [186] 1 (5)	28.1
3301. FELONY [185] 1 (5)	28.1
3302. Johnny SEA [147] 1 (2)	28.0
3303. Carmen McRAE [150] 1 (2)	27.9
3304. Nick HEYWARD [178] 1 (4)	27.9
3305. Joe VITALE [181] 1 (3)	27.8
3306. Keith EMERSON [183] 1 (3)	27.8
3307. Wayne SHORTER [183] 1 (3)	27.5
3308. YACHTS [179] 1 (3)	27.5
3309. Terence BOYLAN [181] 1 (3)	27.4
3310. Carolyne MAS [172] 1 (3)	27.4
3311. T-Bone BURNETT [188] 1 (5)	27.3
3312. Dave BRUBECK [167] 1 (5)	27.3
3313. The HOMBRES [180] 1 (4)	27.1
3314. Bobby FULLER Four [144] 1 (2)	27.0
3315. The STRANGELOVES [141] 1 (2)	26.9
3316. EBN-OZN [185] 1 (4)	26.6
3317. The PRODUCERS [163] 1 (2)	26.5
3318. Oscar TONEY, Jr. [192] 1 (5)	26.5
3319. Phil MANZANERA [176] 1 (3)	26.3
3320. The VISCOUNTS [144] 1 (2)	26.3
3321. AUDIO TWO [185] 1 (4)	26.2
3322. Les Paul [172] 1 (5)	26.2
3323. SHARKS [189] 1 (4)	26.0
3324. Mickey HART [190] 1 (4)	26.0
3325. Little Johnny TAYLOR [140] 1 (2)	25.9
3326. Denise LOPEZ [184] 1 (4)	25.8
3327. The CASINOS [187] 1 (4)	25.8
3328. Merl SAUNDERS [197] 1 (5)	25.8
3329. Merrilee RUSH [196] 1 (4)	25.7
3330. The KIMBERLYS [169] 1 (4)	25.6
3331. DYKE And The BLAZERS [186] 1 (4)	25.5
3332. Billy LARKIN & The DELEGATES [148] 1 (2)	25.5
3333. BALTIMORE And OHIO MARCHING BAND [177] 1 (3)	25.5
3334. Wayne TOUPS & ZYDECAJUN [183] 1 (4)	25.4
3335. Bob LIND [148] 1 (2)	25.4
3336. Scott BAIO [181] 1 (4)	25.2
3337. VICTORY [182] 1 (5)	25.2
3338. Tom VERLAINE [177] 1 (3)	25.1
3339. GREASE BAND [190] 1 (3)	25.0
3340. The CORPORATION [197] 1 (4)	25.0
3341. Gary McFARLAND [189] 1 (3)	24.9
3342. FOREVER MORE [180] 1 (3)	24.9
3343. NATURAL FOUR [182] 1 (3)	24.9
3344. BALAAM AND THE ANGEL [174] 1 (3)	24.6
3345. David COURTNEY [194] 1 (4)	24.6
3346. ELECTRONIC CONCEPT ORCHESTRA [175] 1 (2)	24.5
3347. Eddie RAMBEAU [148] 1 (2)	24.5
3348. Ethel ENNIS [147] 1 (2)	24.4
3349. Charles BOYER [148] 1 (2)	24.4
3350. GILLAN [183] 1 (3)	24.3
3351. WILD ONES [149] 1 (2)	24.1
3352. Joe PISCOPO [168] 1 (3)	24.1
3353. CYMARRON [187] 1 (3)	24.0
3354. SHINEHEAD [185] 1 (4)	23.8
3355. Rubin MITCHELL [164] 1 (2)	23.7
3356. KANO [189] 1 (4)	23.3
3357. EGG CREAM [197] 1 (4)	23.2
3358. The MOONGLOWS [193] 1 (4)	22.9
3359. The HONEYCOMBS [147] 1 (2)	22.9
3360. Fannie FLAGG [183] 1 (3)	22.8
3361. Gene AMMONS [174] 1 (2)	22.7
3362. VOICES OF EAST HARLEM [191] 1 (3)	22.6
3363. FLAMING EMBER [188] 1 (3)	22.5
3364. WHAT IS THIS [187] 1 (4)	22.5
3365. Jimmy WITHERSPOON [176] 1 (2)	22.4
3366. MAD LADS [180] 1 (2)	22.3
3367. Chris JASPER [182] 1 (3)	22.0
3368. Kathy DALTON [190] 1 (3)	21.9
3369. COLOSSEUM [192] 1 (3)	21.8
3370. Larry CORYELL [196] 1 (3)	21.8
3371. Rick FENN [154] 1 (5)	21.8
3372. KEEF HARTLEY BAND [191] 1 (3)	21.7
3373. SCHOOLLY D [180] 1 (3)	21.6
3374. BRENDA & The TABULATIONS [191] 1 (4)	21.6
3375. THRILLS [199] 1 (4)	21.6
3376. MUNICH MACHINE [190] 1 (3)	21.5
3377. Doc WATSON [193] 1 (3)	21.3
3378. MONTANA Orchestra [195] 1 (4)	21.2
3379. Angelo BOND [179] 1 (2)	20.9
3380. ART IN AMERICA [176] 1 (3)	20.9
3381. Steve CROPPER [171] 1 (5)	20.7
3382. Pop STAPLES [171] 1 (5)	20.7
3383. FANTASY [194] 1 (3)	20.4
3384. The CANDYMEN [195] 1 (4)	20.4
3385. Sonny STITT [172] 1 (2)	20.4
3386. PLASTIC COW [184] 1 (2)	20.3
3387. DAMNATION OF ADAM BLESSING [181] 1 (2)	20.2
3388. Mike THEODORE Orchestra [178] 1 (2)	20.1
3389. James DARREN [187] 1 (3)	20.0
3390. GLASS HARP [192] 1 (3)	20.0
3391. Moe BANDY [170] 1 (4)	20.0
3392. Joe STAMPLEY [170] 1 (4)	20.0
3393. TKO [181] 1 (2)	20.0
3394. The FUZZ [196] 1 (3)	19.9
3395. Hank WILLIAMS Sr. [139] 1 (3)	19.8
3396. DA'KRASH [184] 1 (3)	19.7
3397. WIND IN THE WILLOWS [195] 1 (3)	19.6
3398. VITAMIN Z [183] 1 (3)	19.5
3399. Mick JONES [184] 1 (3)	19.4
3400. FARQUAHR [195] 1 (3)	19.3
3401. Kim FOWLEY [198] 1 (3)	19.2
3402. Letta MBULU [192] 1 (3)	19.1
3403. The KLOWNS [184] 1 (2)	19.0
3404. Brad SWANSON [185] 1 (2)	19.0
3405. Father Guido SARDUCCI [179] 1 (2)	18.9
3406. SILVER APPLES [193] 1 (3)	18.9
3407. Virgil FOX [183] 1 (2)	18.8
3408. ROSE GARDEN [176] 1 (2)	18.8
3409. Gayle McCORMICK [198] 1 (3)	18.8
3410. Don NIX [197] 1 (3)	18.6
3411. Anthony PHILLIPS [191] 1 (3)	18.5
3412. WILD TURKEY [193] 1 (3)	18.2
3413. Bill DEAL & The RHONDELS [185] 1 (2)	18.0
3414. Nancy MARTINEZ [178] 1 (3)	17.9
3415. Luis GASCA [195] 1 (3)	17.8
3416. Robert KLEIN [191] 1 (3)	17.7
3417. The PAUPERS [178] 1 (2)	17.5
3418. Gram PARSONS [195] 1 (3)	17.4
3419. Carl WILSON [185] 1 (2)	17.4
3420. Gary MYRICK [186] 1 (3)	17.4
3421. Henson CARGILL [179] 1 (2)	17.3
3422. GIBSON BROTHERS [185] 1 (2)	17.3

Rank.	Act [Hi Peak] Entries (Wks)	Score
3423.	Bruce WOOLLEY & The CAMERA CLUB [184] 1 (2)	17.2
3424.	David HUDSON [184] 1 (2)	17.2
3425.	Jimmy HALL [183] 1 (2)	17.1
3426.	Lonnie SMITH [186] 1 (2)	17.0
3427.	LIONS AND GHOSTS [187] 1 (3)	17.0
3428.	RACING CARS [198] 1 (3)	16.9
3429.	MUSIC EXPLOSION [178] 1 (2)	16.9
3430.	Johnny CASH & June CARTER [194] 1 (3)	16.8
3431.	The HESITATIONS [193] 1 (3)	16.7
3432.	Rick GRECH [195] 1 (3)	16.6
3433.	Larry GROCE [187] 1 (2)	16.6
3434.	SILK [191] 1 (2)	16.6
3435.	Lillo THOMAS [186] 1 (3)	16.5
3436.	Alex TAYLOR [190] 1 (2)	16.2
3437.	BANGOR FLYING CIRCUS [190] 1 (2)	16.2
3438.	ROSE TATTOO [197] 1 (3)	16.1
3439.	PRATT & McCLAIN [190] 1 (2)	16.0
3440.	Duke PEARSON [193] 1 (2)	16.0
3441.	MAD RIVER [192] 1 (2)	16.0
3442.	The CARNIVAL [191] 1 (2)	15.8
3443.	Loleatta HOLLOWAY [187] 1 (2)	15.8
3444.	Wilbert HARRISON [190] 1 (2)	15.7
3445.	Paul KOSSOFF [191] 1 (2)	15.5
3446.	The AQUARIANS [192] 1 (2)	15.4
3447.	Brenton WOOD [184] 1 (2)	15.2
3448.	TANTRUM [199] 1 (3)	15.1
3449.	MADURA [186] 1 (2)	15.0
3450.	PEANUT BUTTER CONSPIRACY [196] 1 (3)	14.9
3451.	BEAST [195] 1 (2)	14.7
3452.	PALM BEACH BAND BOYS [149] 1 (1)	14.5
3453.	Liz DAMON'S ORIENT EXPRESS [190] 1 (2)	14.1
3454.	Dennis WEAVER [191] 1 (2)	13.9
3455.	RODNEY O & Joe COOLEY [187] 1 (2)	13.8
3456.	TSOL [184] 1 (2)	13.7
3457.	The DICTATORS [193] 1 (2)	13.6
3458.	Maxine BROWN [195] 1 (2)	13.4
3459.	"Tennessee" Ernie FORD [192] 1 (2)	13.4
3460.	AMERICAN DREAM [194] 1 (2)	13.3
3461.	KING BISCUIT BOY [194] 1 (2)	13.3
3462.	SOUTHERN COMFORT [196] 1 (2)	13.3
3463.	The UNFORGIVEN [185] 1 (2)	13.0
3464.	C.C.S. [197] 1 (2)	13.0
3465.	CIRCUS OF POWER [185] 1 (2)	12.9
3466.	WAYSTED [185] 1 (2)	12.9
3467.	Big Mama THORNTON [198] 1 (2)	12.8
3468.	PURE LOVE & PLEASURE [195] 1 (2)	12.7
3469.	The MERRY-GO-ROUND [190] 1 (2)	12.7
3470.	ARMADA Orchestra [196] 1 (2)	12.6
3471.	CONEY HATCH [186] 1 (2)	12.6
3472.	FUNKY COMMUNICATION COMMITTEE [192] 1 (2)	12.6
3473.	Steve WARINER [187] 1 (2)	12.6
3474.	The COUNTS [193] 1 (2)	12.6
3475.	THIRD POWER [194] 1 (2)	12.5
3476.	JADE WARRIOR [194] 1 (2)	12.5
3477.	Jane BIRKIN & Serge GAINSBOURG [196] 1 (2)	12.5
3478.	MERRYWEATHER & FRIENDS [199] 1 (2)	12.4
3479.	ELEPHANT'S MEMORY [200] 1 (2)	12.4
3480.	Erma FRANKLIN [199] 1 (2)	12.4
3481.	The SPORTS [194] 1 (2)	12.3
3482.	HARDY BOYS [199] 1 (2)	12.3
3483.	MINOR DETAIL [187] 1 (2)	12.3
3484.	Wild Bill DAVIS [148] 1 (2)	12.3
3485.	Johnny HODGES [148] 1 (2)	12.3
3486.	Sir Lord BALTIMORE [198] 1 (2)	12.1

Rank.	Act [Hi Peak] Entries (Wks)	Score
3487.	Meryl STREEP [180] 1 (4)	12.1
3488.	SMOKESTACK LIGHTNIN' [200] 1 (2)	12.1
3489.	The RENAISSANCE [198] 1 (2)	12.0
3490.	SWEETWATER [200] 1 (2)	11.9
3491.	ROMEO'S DAUGHTER [191] 1 (2)	11.9
3492.	BILLION DOLLAR BABIES [198] 1 (2)	11.8
3493.	Jerry SMITH [200] 1 (2)	11.8
3494.	Sandy DENNY [197] 1 (2)	11.8
3495.	The RUSTIX [200] 1 (2)	11.8
3496.	SOPWITH "CAMEL" [191] 1 (2)	11.8
3497.	PEARLS BEFORE SWINE [200] 1 (2)	11.7
3498.	SPIDERS FROM MARS [197] 1 (2)	11.5
3499.	The ROAD [199] 1 (2)	11.3
3500.	INCREDIBLE BONGO BAND [197] 1 (2)	11.3
3501.	Michael CRAWFORD [192] 1 (2)	11.2
3502.	BELLE STARS [191] 1 (2)	11.2
3503.	ICON [190] 1 (2)	11.2
3504.	Manny KELLEM, His Orchestra And Voices [197] 1 (2)	11.0
3505.	KWICK [197] 1 (2)	10.9
3506.	Carol BURNETT [199] 1 (2)	10.9
3507.	Eric MARTIN Band [191] 1 (2)	10.8
3508.	Robert KNIGHT [196] 1 (2)	10.8
3509.	Paul DEAN [195] 1 (2)	10.6
3510.	EDEN'S CHILDREN [196] 1 (2)	10.5
3511.	BONZO DOG BAND [199] 1 (2)	10.3
3512.	Michael ANDERSON [194] 1 (2)	10.3
3513.	ANVIL [191] 1 (2)	10.2
3514.	CROSS COUNTRY [198] 1 (2)	10.1
3515.	Jerry JAYE [195] 1 (2)	10.1
3516.	Steven WRIGHT [192] 1 (2)	10.0
3517.	The NAILS [194] 1 (2)	10.0
3518.	Kasim SULTON [197] 1 (2)	10.0
3519.	KING RICHARD'S FLUEGEL KNIGHTS [198] 1 (2)	9.9
3520.	TRINERE & FRIENDS [196] 1 (2)	9.6
3521.	ARABIAN PRINCE [193] 1 (2)	9.6
3522.	SHY [193] 1 (2)	9.5
3523.	Ray LYNCH [197] 1 (2)	9.4
3524.	Boris GREBENSHIKOV [198] 1 (2)	9.2
3525.	GOLDEN GATE Strings [200] 1 (2)	8.8
3526.	George SEGAL [199] 1 (2)	8.7
3527.	Ian McCULLOCH [179] 1 (1)	8.0
3528.	Mark KNOPFLER [180] 1 (1)	7.5
3529.	OSBORNE BROTHERS [193] 1 (1)	6.9
3530.	TIN TIN [197] 1 (1)	6.8
3531.	Johnny & Jonie MOSBY [197] 1 (1)	6.7
3532.	John ROWLES [197] 1 (1)	6.5
3533.	R. Dean TAYLOR [198] 1 (1)	6.1
3534.	The KAY-GEES [199] 1 (1)	5.9
3535.	DELIVERANCE [196] 1 (2)	5.8
3536.	Albert FINNEY [199] 1 (1)	5.5
3537.	Pat McLAUGHLIN [195] 1 (1)	5.4
3538.	KILLING JOKE [194] 1 (1)	5.1
3539.	Billy BRAGG [198] 1 (1)	4.6
3540.	The ROBBS [200] 1 (1)	4.5
3541.	MC SHY D [197] 1 (1)	4.5
3542.	BOBBY JIMMY & The CRITTERS [200] 1 (1)	3.6

Acts Alphabetically

This is an alphabetical listing of all the acts, along with act rankings. See also the Acts with Albums section for more information, organized by act.

Act	Rank
A	
Kenny AARONSON	2535
ABBA	261
Gregory ABBOTT	995
ABC	551
Paula ABDUL	179
Colonel ABRAMS	2304
ACCEPT	1404
AC/DC	94
ACE	922
ACE SPECTRUM	2713
David ACKLES	2825
Barbara ACKLIN	2914
Bryan ADAMS	182
ADC BAND	2534
Nat ADDERLEY Sextet	1797
"Cannonball" ADDERLEY Quintet	890
ADDRISI BROTHERS	2182
King Sunny ADE & His AFRICAN BEATS	1682
The ADVENTURES	2882
AEROSMITH	61
AFRIQUE	2828
AFTER 7	1021
AFTER THE FIRE	1356
A-HA	745
AIR SUPPLY	222
AIRTO	2847
Jan AKKERMAN	3141
ALABAMA	129
The ALARM	740
Morris ALBERT	1180
Gerald ALBRIGHT	3254
AL B. SURE!	741
ALCATRAZZ	1859
Ronnie ALDRICH	2975
ALICE COOPER (Grp)	183
ALICE COOPER (Solo)	298
ALIVE 'N KICKIN'	3068
Davie ALLAN And The ARROWS	717
Deborah ALLEN	1944
Donna ALLEN	2514
Peter ALLEN	2031
Woody ALLEN	2203
Duane ALLMAN	1037
Gregg ALLMAN	738
Gregg ALLMAN Band	1007
ALLMAN BROTHERS Band	119
Marc ALMOND	2684
Herb ALPERT	412
Herb ALPERT & The TIJUANA BRASS	6
ALPHAVILLE	2663
Dave ALVIN	2444
AMAZING RHYTHM ACES	1553
AMBOY DUKES	1601
AMBROSIA	509
AMERICA	100
AMERICAN BREED	2435
AMERICAN DREAM	3460
AMERICAN FLYER	2068
Ed AMES	324
Nancy AMES	2411
Gene AMMONS	3361
Géza ANDA	2143
Eric ANDERSEN	2115
Carl ANDERSON	2247
John ANDERSON	1931
Jon ANDERSON	1471
Laurie ANDERSON	1488
Lynn ANDERSON	725
Michael ANDERSON	3512
ANDREWS SISTERS	2161
ANGEL	1300
ANGEL CITY	2308
The ANGELS	1648
ANIMAL LOGIC	2118
The ANIMALS/ Eric BURDON & The ANIMALS	227
ANIMOTION	1059
Paul ANKA	444
ANNETTE	1898
ANN-MARGRET	2675
Adam ANT	646
ANTHRAX	772
ANVIL	3513
AORTA	2819
APOLLONIA 6	2008
APOLLO 100	1674
APPALOOSA	3192
Carmen APPICE	1605
APRIL WINE	651
AQUARIAN DREAM	2875
The AQUARIANS	3446
ARABIAN PRINCE	3521
The ARBORS	3275
ARCADIA	1352
The ARCHIES	946
AREA CODE 615	3295
ARGENT	1029
ARMADA Orchestra	3470
ARMAGEDDON	2896
Joan ARMATRADING	530
ARMORED SAINT	1717
Louis ARMSTRONG	407
Eddy ARNOLD	284
ARPEGGIO	1888
Steve ARRINGTON'S HALL OF FAME	1947
ART IN AMERICA	3380
ARTISTS UNITED AGAINST APARTHEID	1549
ART OF NOISE	1100
The A's	2893
ASHFORD & SIMPSON	385
ASHTON, GARDNER & DYKE	3132
ASIA	288
ASLEEP AT THE WHEEL	2237
The ASSOCIATION	192
Jon ASTLEY	2759
Rick ASTLEY	480
The ASTRONAUTS	2258
ASWAD	3125
Chet ATKINS	1357
Chet ATKINS/ BOSTON POPS Orchestra	1716
ATLANTA	2833
ATLANTA DISCO BAND	2865
ATLANTA RHYTHM SECTION	343
ATLANTIC STARR	422
ATOMIC ROOSTER	1639
AUDIENCE	3153
AUDIO TWO	3321
Barbara Ann AUER	2481
Brian AUGER	735
AURRA	1448
Patti AUSTIN	886
AUTOGRAPH	1047
AUTOMATIC MAN	2099
AVERAGE WHITE BAND/AWB	236
AXE	1875
Hoyt AXTON	3060
Roy AYERS	938
Roy AYERS UBIQUITY	926
AZTECA	2746
AZTEC CAMERA	2343
AZTEC TWO STEP	3248
B	
BABE RUTH	2006
BABYFACE	598
BABYLON A.D.	1839
The BABYS	615
Burt BACHARACH	545
The BACHELORS	1757
BACHMAN-TURNER OVERDRIVE	163
BACK STREET CRAWLER	1663
BAD COMPANY	166
BAD ENGLISH	822
BADFINGER	692
BADGER	2962
BADLANDS	1560
Joan BAEZ	149
Philip BAILEY	947
Razzy BAILEY	3139
Scott BAIO	3336
BAJA MARIMBA BAND	813
Anita BAKER	220
MARIACHI BRASS	2987
George BAKER Selection	2294
Ginger BAKER's Air Force	1540
BAKER GURVITZ ARMY	2494
BALAAM AND THE ANGEL	3344
BALANCE	2603
Long John BALDRY	1725
Marty BALIN	1315
Russ BALLARD	2389
BALLIN' JACK	3049
BALTIMORA	1847
BALTIMORE And OHIO MARCHING BAND	3333
BANANARAMA	667
The BAND	193
BAND Of The BLACK WATCH	3151
Moe BANDY	3391
BANG	2751
The BANGLES	344
BANGOR FLYING CIRCUS	3437
BANG TANGO	1497
Peter BANKS	2808
Tony BANKS	3158
Frank BARBER Orchestra	2170
Gato BARBIERI	1027
Keith BARBOUR	3066
BARCLAY JAMES HARVEST	3261
Pete BARDENS	3088
BARDEUX	2132
Bobby BARE	2695
The BAR-KAYS	477
Jimmy BARNES	1823
BARRABAS	2774
Syd BARRETT	3112
Claudja BARRY	1980
Len BARRY	2224
Lou Ann BARTON	2726
BASIA	878
Count BASIE	1758
Toni BASIL	1148
Fontella BASS	2498
Shirley BASSEY	952
BATDORF & RODNEY	2334
BAUHAUS	3120
BAY CITY ROLLERS	526
BEACH BOYS	21
BEACON STREET UNION	1738
The BEARS	3133
BEAST	3451
BEASTIE BOYS	372
BEAT FARMERS	2350
The BEATLES	1
BEAU BRUMMELS	1384
Jean BEAUVOIR	2185
BE BOP DELUXE	1240
Jeff BECK	318
Jeff BECK Group	644
Joe BECK	2941
BEE GEES	14
Harry BELAFONTE	1066
Adrian BELEW	1877
Archie BELL & The DRELLS	1721
Maggie BELL	2015
Vincent BELL	2220
William BELL	1959
BELLAMY BROTHERS	2059
BELL And JAMES	1327
Regina BELLE	1184
BELLE STARS	3502
The BELLS	2004
Pat BENATAR	81
Tony BENNETT	353
Marc BENNO	1965
David BENOIT	1867
George BENSON	93
Brook BENTON	1255
Gertrude BERG	2445
BERLIN	801
Shelley BERMAN	2558
Herschel BERNARDI	2921
Leonard BERNSTEIN	1388
Chuck BERRY	506
Karen BETH	2980

Act	Rank
Dickey BETTS	987
The B-52s	267
BIDDU Orchestra	3241
BIG AUDIO DYNAMITE	1253
BIG BROTHER And The HOLDING COMPANY	302
BIG COUNTRY	700
BIG PIG	2047
BILLION DOLLAR BABIES	3492
BILLY SATELLITE	2963
BIONIC BOOGIE	2023
Jane BIRKIN & Serge GAINSBOURG	3477
Elvin BISHOP	679
Stephen BISHOP	992
Biz MARKIE	1408
Bill BLACK'S Combo	2557
Clint BLACK	699
Stanley BLACK	3238
The BLACKBYRDS	430
BLACKFOOT	797
BLACK IVORY	2455
BLACKJACK	2605
BLACK 'N BLUE	1727
BLACK OAK ARKANSAS	810
BLACK PEARL	2588
BLACK SABBATH	140
BLACK UHURU	2918
Ruben BLADES	3087
Jack BLANCHARD & Misty MORGAN	3202
Bobby BLAND	1664
The BLASTERS	1048
BLIND FAITH	451
BLODWYN PIG	2401
BLONDIE	219
BLOODROCK	582
BLOODSTONE	937
BLOOD, SWEAT & TEARS	74
Bobby BLOOM	3074
Mike BLOOMFIELD	1006
Kurtis BLOW	1285
BLOWFLY	1909
BLOW MONKEYS	1460
BLUE CHEER	836
BLUE MAGIC	934
BLUE MERCEDES	3144
BLUE MURDER	1871
BLUE ÖYSTER CULT	345
BLUES BROTHERS	449
BLUES IMAGE	1963
BLUES MAGOOS	1109
BLUES PROJECT	1022
BLUE SWEDE	1912
BOBBY And The MIDNITES	2765
BOBBY JIMMY & The CRITTERS	3542
Willie BOBO	2711
BODEANS	1486
Angela BOFILL	595
Tim BOGERT	1606
Hamilton BOHANNON	1677
Tommy BOLIN	1814
Michael BOLTON	249
Angelo BOND	3379
Johnny BOND	3222
Gary (U.S.) BONDS	1014
BONEY M	2448
BONHAM	1306
BON JOVI	99
Karla BONOFF	731
BONZO DOG BAND	3511
BOOGIE BOYS	1570

Act	Rank
BOOGIE DOWN PRODUCTIONS	1288
Chuckii BOOKER	2550
BOOKER T. & PRISCILLA	2499
BOOKER T. & The M.G.'s	603
BOOK OF LOVE	2853
Taka BOOM	3178
BOOMTOWN RATS	1495
Daniel BOONE	2661
Debby BOONE	855
BOOTSY'S RUBBER BAND	538
BOSTON	122
BOSTON POPS Orchestra/ Arthur FIEDLER	1175
BOSTON POPS Orchestra/ John WILLIAMS	2633
BOSTON SYMPHONY Orchestra	2222
BOURGEOIS TAGG	1831
David BOWIE	67
BOW WOW WOW	1524
BOX OF FROGS	1635
BOX TOPS	918
Tommy BOYCE & Bobby HART	2667
Charles BOYER	3349
BOY GEORGE	2318
Terence BOYLAN	3309
BOY MEETS GIRL	1360
The BOYS	1204
BOYS CLUB	2165
BOYS DON'T CRY	1750
Terry BOZZIO	2531
BRADY BUNCH	2033
Billy BRAGG	3539
BRAINSTORM	2303
Bonnie BRAMLETT	3097
BRAM TCHAIKOVSKY	1302
The BRANDOS	2197
BRAND X	2338
Laura BRANIGAN	537
John BRANNEN	2583
BRASS CONSTRUCTION	544
BRASS RING	2361
BREAD	172
BREAKFAST CLUB	1393
BREAKWATER	2620
BREATHE	906
BRECKER BROTHERS	1505
Beverly BREMERS	2604
BRENDA & The TABULATIONS	3374
BREWER And SHIPLEY	1119
BRICK	655
Edie BRICKELL & NEW BOHEMIANS	612
BRIDES OF FUNKENSTEIN	1822
Alicia BRIDGES	1155
Dee Dee BRIDGEWATER	2801
Martin BRILEY	1514
Johnny BRISTOL	1830
BRITISH LIONS	2076
BRITNY FOX	998
Benjamin BRITTEN	2384
David BROMBERG	1594
BRONSKI BEAT	1439
Herman BROOD	2072
BROOKLYN BRIDGE	1199
BROOKLYN, BRONX & QUEENS Band	2485
BROOKLYN DREAMS	2860
BROS	3197
BROTHERHOOD OF MAN	2925
BROTHERS FOUR	1342
BROTHERS JOHNSON	246

Act	Rank
Crazy World Of Arthur BROWN	846
Bobby BROWN	187
Chuck BROWN & The SOUL SEARCHERS	1506
Danny Joe BROWN	2650
James BROWN	118
Jim Ed BROWN	2327
Julie BROWN	3082
Maxine BROWN	3458
Odell BROWN & THE ORGAN-IZERS	3256
Peter BROWN	715
Shirley BROWN	2287
Duncan BROWNE	3100
Jackson BROWNE	123
Tom BROWNE	759
BROWNSVILLE STATION	1934
Dave BRUBECK	3312
Dave BRUBECK Quartet	1838
Jack BRUCE	1411
Lenny BRUCE	3228
Bill BRUFORD	2754
Anita BRYANT	3052
Ray BRYANT	2309
Sharon BRYANT	2589
Peabo BRYSON	524
B.T. EXPRESS	492
BUBBLE PUPPY	2960
Roy BUCHANAN	1209
Lindsey BUCKINGHAM	1033
The BUCKINGHAMS	1088
Tim BUCKLEY	1869
BUCKNER And GARCIA	1483
BUCKWHEAT	3117
BUCKWHEAT ZYDECO	2490
BUD And TRAVIS	2579
BUFFALO SPRINGFIELD	784
Jimmy BUFFETT	244
The BUGGLES	3127
Alex BUGNON	2574
BULGARIAN STATE RADIO & T.V. FEMALE CHOIR	2857
BULLDOG	2799
BULLETBOYS	1138
Victor BUONO	1652
Eric BURDON Band	1547
Eric BURDON & WAR	873
Solomon BURKE	2641
Carol BURNETT	3506
T-Bone BURNETT	3311
Rocky BURNETTE	1791
BURNING SENSATIONS	3282
George BURNS	2314
Kenny BURRELL	2905
Glen BURTNICK	3003
Jenny BURTON	3296
BUS BOYS	1882
Kate BUSH	834
Jon BUTCHER AXIS	1225
Jerry BUTLER	568
Jonathan BUTLER	1183
Billy BUTTERFIELD	2580
Paul BUTTERFIELD Blues Band	796
BUZZCOCKS	3089
Charlie BYRD	2708
Donald BYRD	580
Donald BYRD And 125th STREET N.Y.C.	2292
The BYRDS	258
David BYRNE	1455
D.L. BYRON	2566

C

Act	Rank
CACTUS	1269
CACTUS WORLD NEWS	3252
John CAFFERTY & The BEAVER BROWN BAND	594
Tané CAIN	2546
CALDERA	3118
Bobby CALDWELL	945
J.J. CALE	941
John CALE	2961
CALIFORNIA RAISINS	1395
The CALL	1143
Maria CALLAS	2479
Godfrey CAMBRIDGE	1735
CAMEL	1571
CAMEO	289
Rafael CAMERON	1600
CAMOUFLAGE	2249
Glen CAMPBELL	36
CAMPER VAN BEETHOVEN	1958
CANDLEMASS	3170
The CANDYMEN	3384
CANNED HEAT	442
CANNIBAL And The HEADHUNTERS	3096
Lana CANTRELL	3266
Jim CAPALDI	1710
The CAPITOLS	2260
CAPTAIN & TENNILLE	254
CAPTAIN BEEFHEART	2190
CAPTAIN BEEFHEART & The MAGIC BAND	2999
CAPTAIN BEYOND	1878
CAPTAIN SKY	2567
Carla CAPUANO	2874
Irene CARA	1265
CARAVAN	2496
The CARAVELLES	3031
Tony CAREY	1561
Henson CARGILL	3421
George CARLIN	370
Belinda CARLISLE	457
Walter CARLOS	641
Carl CARLTON	1294
Larry CARLTON	1437
Eric CARMEN	691
Jean CARN	2240
Kim CARNES	374
The CARNIVAL	3442
Mary Chapin CARPENTER	3061
CARPENTERS	66
Vikki CARR	458
Paul CARRACK	1281
Keith CARRADINE	1744
Terri Lyne CARRINGTON	3119
Jim CARROLL Band	1593
The CARS	85
Carlene CARTER	2863
Clarence CARTER	1350
Mel CARTER	1733
Ron CARTER	3229
Valerie CARTER	3143
Johnny CASH	101
Johnny CASH & June CARTER	3430
Johnny CASH And The TENNESSEE TWO/THREE	2889
Rosanne CASH	848
CASHFLOW	2752
CASHMAN & WEST	2844

Act	Rank
The CASINOS	3327
David CASSIDY	927
Shaun CASSIDY	360
Jimmy CASTOR Bunch	1040
CATE BROS.	2658
CAT MOTHER & The ALL NIGHT NEWS BOYS	1707
C.C.S.	3464
CELI BEE And The BUZZY BUNCH	3111
CENTRAL LINE	2804
CERRONE	1736
Peter CETERA	837
Frank CHACKSFIELD And His Orchestra	2621
CHAD & JEREMY	683
CHAIRMEN OF THE BOARD	1841
CHAKACHAS	2394
CHAMBERS BROTHERS	467
CHAMPAIGN	1161
Bill CHAMPLIN	3247
Gene CHANDLER	1201
CHANGE	874
CHANSON	1402
Harry CHAPIN	425
Tracy CHAPMAN	341
CHARLENE	1538
Ray CHARLES	237
Ray CHARLES Singers	812
Sonny CHARLES	2939
CHARLIE	1308
CHASE	914
CHEAP TRICK	194
Chubby CHECKER	2328
CHECKMATES, LTD.	3166
CHEECH & CHONG	173
CHEQUERED PAST	3058
CHER	206
CHERRELLE	1277
Neneh CHERRY	1334
CHIC	334
CHICAGO	5
The CHIEFTAINS	2598
The CHIFFONS	3189
Desmond CHILD and ROUGE	2943
Toni CHILDS	1325
The CHI-LITES	396
CHILLIWACK	1390
CHINA CRISIS	2331
The CHIPMUNKS	720
CHOCOLATE MILK	2195
The CHRISTIANS	2936
CHRISTIE	2413
Lou CHRISTIE	2035
Gavin CHRISTOPHER	2153
CHUNKY A	2127
The CHURCH	1122
CINDERELLA	278
CIRCUS OF POWER	3465
CITY BOY	2193
C.J. & CO.	1534
CLANCY BROTHERS AND Tommy MAKEM	1952
CLANNAD	2360
Eric CLAPTON	50
Dave CLARK Five	235
Gene CLARK	2904
Petula CLARK	416
Roy CLARK	1191
Stanley CLARKE	689
Stanley CLARKE & George DUKE	1096
The CLASH	357
CLASSICS IV	980
Andrew Dice CLAY	1521
Cassius CLAY	1837
Tom CLAY	2612
Richard CLAYDERMAN	2899
Merry CLAYTON	2366
David CLAYTON-THOMAS	2714
CLEAR LIGHT	2410
Johnny CLEGG & SAVUKA	2966
Clarence CLEMONS	1807
CLEVELAND Orchestra	3033
Jimmy CLIFF	2211
Linda CLIFFORD	851
CLIMAX	3027
CLIMAX BLUES Band	591
CLIMIE FISHER	2235
Patsy CLINE	1409
George CLINTON	1181
The CLIQUE	3273
CLUB NOUVEAU	764
Billy COBHAM	590
Wayne COCHRAN	3216
Tom COCHRANE/RED RIDER	1120
Bruce COCKBURN	1086
Joe COCKER	178
COCK ROBIN	1804
COCTEAU TWINS	2243
David Allan COE	3255
Dennis COFFEY	1041
Leonard COHEN	1282
Myron COHEN	2239
COLD BLOOD	825
COLD CHISEL	3012
Nat King COLE	426
Natalie COLE	214
Durell COLEMAN	2988
Albert COLLINS	2907
Judy COLLINS	169
Phil COLLINS	73
COLOSSEUM	3369
Jessi COLTER	920
Alice COLTRANE	2587
Chi COLTRANE	2707
John COLTRANE	3177
Shawn COLVIN	2129
COMMANDER CODY & His LOST PLANET AIRMEN	983
The COMMODORES	54
The COMMUNARDS	1889
Perry COMO	577
COMPANY B	2995
CONCRETE BLONDE	1923
CONEY HATCH	3471
CON FUNK SHUN	481
John CONLEE	3090
Arthur CONLEY	2147
The CONNELLS	2974
Harry CONNICK Jr.	930
Ray CONNIFF	2581
Ray CONNIFF & His Orchestra & Chorus	165
Norman CONNORS	931
The CONTROLLERS	2884
Tommy CONWELL And The YOUNG RUMBLERS	1861
Ry COODER	982
Sam COOKE	693
Rita COOLIDGE	379
Michael COOPER	1896
Pat COOPER	1245
Julian COPE	1902
Johnny COPELAND	2992
Stewart COPELAND	2635
Chick COREA	997
CORNELIUS BROTHERS & SISTER ROSE	1221
The CORPORATION	3340
Larry CORYELL	3370
Bill COSBY	52
Alec R. COSTANDINOS	2075
Elvis COSTELLO	726
Elvis COSTELLO & The ATTRACTIONS	340
James COTTON Band	2680
Josie COTTON	2778
COUCHOIS	3161
COUNT FIVE	2782
COUNTRY JOE & The FISH	643
The COUNTS	3474
David COURTNEY	3345
COVER GIRLS	1231
COWBOY JUNKIES	1160
The COWSILLS	688
CRABBY APPLETON	3073
CRACK THE SKY	2048
Billy "Crash" CRADDOCK	2898
Floyd CRAMER	1858
Les CRANE	1598
Hank CRAWFORD	2576
Michael CRAWFORD	3501
Randy CRAWFORD	1467
Robert CRAY Band	617
CRAZY HORSE	1998
Papa John CREACH	2025
CREAM	80
CREATIVE SOURCE	2715
CREEDENCE CLEARWATER REVIVAL	33
Marshall CRENSHAW	1137
The CRETONES	2472
Bob CREWE Generation	2275
Peter CRISS	1338
The CRITTERS	3289
Jim CROCE	126
Steve CROPPER	3381
Bing CROSBY	2026
David CROSBY	988
David CROSBY/Graham NASH	435
CROSBY, STILLS & NASH	175
CROSBY, STILLS, NASH & YOUNG	139
Christopher CROSS	245
CROSS COUNTRY	3514
CROW	1626
CROWDED HOUSE	686
Rodney CROWELL	2122
CROWN HEIGHTS AFFAIR	1865
The CRUSADERS	280
CRUZADOS	1634
CRYAN' SHAMES	2573
Billy CRYSTAL	2131
Joe CUBA Sextet	2528
CUFF LINKS	2511
The CULT	611
CULTURE CLUB	228
Burton CUMMINGS	1136
MIKE CURB CONGREGATION	2057
The CURE	404
CURIOSITY KILLED THE CAT	1695
Tim CURRY	1452
CUTTING CREW	1025
CYMANDE	1924
CYMARRON	3353
Andre CYMONE	2624
The CYRKLE	1718
D	
DA'KRASH	3396
Dick DALE and The DEL-TONES	2447
DALE & GRACE	2691
Kathy DALTON	3368
Roger DALTREY	639
Michael DAMIAN	1751
DAMITA JO	2908
DAMNATION OF ADAM BLESSING	3387
Liz DAMON'S ORIENT EXPRESS	3453
Vic DAMONE	2332
Vic DANA	1103
Dana DANE	1380
DANGER DANGER	1657
Rodney DANGERFIELD	1131
DANGEROUS TOYS	1469
Charlie DANIELS Band	307
Rick DANKO	2577
DANNY WILSON	2151
DANZIG	2637
Terence Trent D'ARBY	534
Bobby DARIN	1986
DARK ANGEL	3032
DARLING CRUEL	2952
Johnny DARRELL	3214
James DARREN	3389
Sarah DASH	3070
DAVE & SUGAR	2848
DAVE DEE, DOZY, BEAKY, MICK And TICH	3219
DAVID & DAVID	1170
John DAVIDSON	942
Dave DAVIES	1489
Danny DAVIS	3267
Danny DAVIS And The NASHVILLE BRASS	1064
Jimmy DAVIS & JUNCTION	2740
Mac DAVIS	392
Martha DAVIS	2464
Miles DAVIS	626
Paul DAVIS	1276
Sammy DAVIS Jr.	623
Spencer DAVIS Group	1442
Tyrone DAVIS	1369
Wild Bill DAVIS	3484
DAWN/Tony ORLANDO	362
Doris DAY	2571
Morris DAY	1140
Cory DAYE	3145
Taylor DAYNE	419
DAZZ BAND	663
DB'S	3069
DEAD BOYS	3291
DEAD MILKMEN	2061
DEAD OR ALIVE	1080
Bill DEAL & The RHONDELS	3413
Paul DEAN	3509
DEATH ANGEL	2735
DeBARGE	520
Bunny DeBARGE	3206
Chico DeBARGE	1883
El DeBARGE	1229
Chris De BURGH	950
Nick DeCARO	2959

Act	Rank
Kiki DEE	1361
Lenny DEE	3098
The DEELE	1259
DEEP PURPLE	124
Rick DEES	3017
DEF LEPPARD	75
DeFRANCO FAMILY	1976
DEJA	3245
Desmond DEKKER And The ACES	3102
DELANEY & BONNIE & FRIENDS	960
DE LA SOUL	1173
DELEGATION	1938
The DELFONICS	1169
DEL FUEGOS	1685
DELIVERANCE	3535
The DELLS	658
Martin DENNY	2789
Sandy DENNY	3494
John DENVER	16
John DENVER & The MUPPETS	1680
DEODATO	496
DEPECHE MODE	656
DEREK And The DOMINOS	507
Rick DERRINGER	967
Teri DeSARIO	2117
Jackie DeSHANNON	1960
Paul DESMOND	2946
DETECTIVE	1970
DETROIT	3081
DETROIT EMERALDS	1856
William DeVAUGHN	2677
DEVICE	2109
DEVO	516
Barry De VORZON	2402
DEXYS MIDNIGHT RUNNERS	1106
Dennis DeYOUNG	1309
DFX2	2901
Neil DIAMOND	15
Manu DIBANGO	2066
The DICTATORS	3457
DIESEL	1798
DIFFORD & TILBROOK	1880
The DILLARDS	1745
DILLMAN Band	2736
Al Di MEOLA	986
Al Di MEOLA/John McLAUGHLIN/ Paco De LUCIA	2112
DINO	1112
DINO, DESI & BILLY	1614
DIO	642
DION	1632
DIRE STRAITS	131
Senator Everett McKinley DIRKSEN	1258
DIRTY LOOKS	1988
DISCO TEX & The SEX-O-LETTES	1267
DISNEYLAND AFTER DARK	2477
DIVINYLS	2155
DIXIE CUPS	2919
DIXIE DREGS	1150
Don DIXON	3028
D.J. JAZZY JEFF & THE FRESH PRINCE	500
THE D.O.C.	1128
DOCTOR And The MEDICS	2850
DR. BUZZARD'S ORIGINAL "SAVANNAH" BAND	698
DR. HOOK	601
DR. JOHN	933
DR. J.R. KOOL and The OTHER ROXANNES	2316

Act	Rank
DOKKEN	490
Thomas DOLBY	622
Joe DOLCE	3246
Placido DOMINGO	1110
Fats DOMINO	2920
Bo DONALDSON And The HEYWOODS	2000
Lou DONALDSON	1828
DON And The GOODTIMES	2930
DONOVAN	150
DOOBIE BROTHERS	47
The DOORS	42
Charlie DORE	2846
DORO	2753
Lee DORSEY	2861
DOUBLE	1499
DOUBLE EXPOSURE	2391
DOUCETTE	2813
Doug E. FRESH & The GET FRESH CREW	2233
Carl DOUGLAS	1444
Carol DOUGLAS	2251
Mike DOUGLAS	1842
Ronnie DOVE	1212
Lamont DOZIER	2437
Pete DRAKE	2213
The DRAMATICS	548
DREAM ACADEMY	1179
DREAMBOY	2858
DREAMS	2913
DREAMS SO REAL	2469
DREAM SYNDICATE	3253
D.R.I.	1996
The DRIFTERS	1397
DRIVIN' N' CRYIN'	2524
"D" TRAIN	2686
Les DUDEK	1799
George DUKE	685
Patty DUKE	2293
DUKE JUPITER	2450
Robbie DUPREE	1496
DURAN DURAN	162
Jimmy DURANTE	1528
Ian DURY	3062
Ian DURY And The BLOCKHEADS	2541
DYKE And The BLAZERS	3331
Bob DYLAN	13
Bob DYLAN And The BAND	608
DYNAMIC SUPERIORS	2526
DYNASTY	1400
Ronnie DYSON	1518
E	
EAGLES	20
Charles EARLAND	1526
Steve EARLE	1250
Steve EARLE And The DUKES	2196
EARTH OPERA	3209
EARTH QUAKE	3023
EARTH, WIND & FIRE	29
Elliot EASTON	2393
Sheena EASTON	364
The EASYBEATS	3258
EAZY-E	850
EBN-OZN	3316
EBONEE WEBB	2909
ECHO & The BUNNYMEN	1290
John EDDIE	2167

Act	Rank
Duane EDDY	2431
EDEN'S CHILDREN	3510
Graeme EDGE Band	2172
Dave EDMUNDS	908
Edward BEAR	1881
Dennis EDWARDS	1482
Jonathan EDWARDS	1407
Walter EGAN	1454
EGG CREAM	3357
EGYPTIAN LOVER	2798
8TH DAY	2169
Donnie ELBERT	2710
EL CHICANO	1416
EL COCO	1813
ELECTRIC FLAG	1081
ELECTRIC INDIAN	2278
ELECTRIC LIGHT ORCHESTRA	79
ELECTRIC PRUNES	1887
ELECTRONIC CONCEPT ORCHESTRA	3346
ELEPHANT'S MEMORY	3479
ELEVENTH HOUSE	2482
Larry ELGART	3243
Larry ELGART And His MANHATTAN SWING Orchestra	1002
Les ELGART	3244
Yvonne ELLIMAN	1243
Duke ELLINGTON	2178
Joe ELY	2280
Keith EMERSON	3306
EMERSON, LAKE & PALMER	153
EMERSON, LAKE & POWELL	1165
The EMOTIONS	501
ENCHANTMENT	1283
ENGLAND DAN & John Ford COLEY	697
ENGLISH BEAT	928
Ethel ENNIS	3348
Brian ENO	1913
John ENTWISTLE	1589
ENUFF Z'NUFF	1586
ENYA	1012
EPMD	1391
ERASURE	905
ERIC B. & RAKIM	1073
ERUPTION	2462
ESCAPE CLUB	1062
Coke ESCOVEDO	3190
ESQUIRE	3259
David ESSEX	1498
Gloria ESTEFAN/ MIAMI SOUND MACHINE	213
Deon ESTUS	2140
Melissa ETHERIDGE	628
Roy ETZEL	2979
E.U.	2912
EUROGLIDERS	2779
EUROPE	452
EURYTHMICS	252
Betty EVERETT	2835
EVERLY BROTHERS	1319
EVERY MOTHERS' SON	2594
EXILE	1004
EXODUS	1544
EXOTIC GUITARS	2141
EXPOSÉ	475
EXTREME	1705
EYE TO EYE	2263
EZO	2886

Act	Rank
F	
FABULOUS POODLES	1730
FABULOUS RHINESTONES	3085
FABULOUS THUNDERBIRDS	673
FACE TO FACE	2274
FACTS OF LIFE	2791
Donald FAGEN	1044
FAIRGROUND ATTRACTION	2662
FAIRPORT CONVENTION	2551
Percy FAITH His Orchestra And Chorus	820
Marianne FAITHFULL	816
FAITH, HOPE AND CHARITY	2126
FALCO	785
Agnetha FALTSKOG	2429
Georgie FAME	2949
FAMILY	2820
The FAMILY	1836
FANNY	2348
FANTASTIC FOUR	2039
FANTASY	3383
Donna FARGO	1114
FARQUAHR	3400
Joe FARRELL	2892
FARRENHEIT	3174
FASTER PUSSYCAT	1116
FASTWAY	1036
FATBACK	949
FAT BOYS	485
FATES WARNING	2041
FAT MATTRESS	2404
FAZE-O	1825
The FEELIES	3218
Don FELDER	3099
Wilton FELDER	1692
José FELICIANO	260
FELONY	3301
FEMME FATALE	3020
Freddy FENDER	729
Rick FENN	3371
Jay FERGUSON	1588
Maynard FERGUSON	869
FERRANTE & TEICHER	606
Bryan FERRY	1065
FESTIVAL	1569
FETCHIN BONES	3016
FEVER TREE	1604
Sally FIELD	3217
Richard "Dimples" FIELDS	1238
W.C. FIELDS	958
FIFTH ANGEL	2375
5TH DIMENSION	114
FINE YOUNG CANNIBALS	313
Tim FINN	3155
Albert FINNEY	3536
FIONA	1753
Elisa FIORILLO	3014
FIREBALLET	2800
The FIREBALLS/Jimmy GILMER And The FIREBALLS	1655
FIREFALL	470
FIRESIGN THEATRE	1153
The FIRM	815
FIRST CHOICE	1801
FISHBONE	3018
Eddie FISHER	1726
Ella FITZGERALD	2014
FIVE AMERICANS	2229

Act	Rank
FIVE MAN ELECTRICAL BAND	2599
5 SPECIAL	2345
FIVE STAIRSTEPS	1566
FIVE STAR	1166
The FIXX	399
Roberta FLACK	105
Roberta FLACK & Peabo BRYSON	903
Fannie FLAGG	3360
The FLAME	2900
FLAMING EMBER	3363
FLAMIN' GROOVIES	2786
FLASH	1051
FLASH & THE PAN	1802
FLATT & SCRUGGS	2381
Mick FLEETWOOD	1704
FLEETWOOD MAC	12
FLESH FOR LULU	1892
The FLESHTONES	3175
The FLOATERS	868
The FLOCK	1359
A FLOCK OF SEAGULLS	579
FLOTSAM AND JETSAM	2862
King FLOYD	2785
FLYING BURRITO BROTHERS	1932
FLYING LIZARDS	2463
FLYING MACHINE	3021
FOCUS	533
Dan FOGELBERG	134
John FOGERTY	455
Tom FOGERTY	3138
FOGHAT	314
Ellen FOLEY	2504
The FOLKSWINGERS	3039
Jane FONDA	540
Frank FONTAINE	1374
The FOOLS	2572
FOOLS GOLD	2160
Steve FORBERT	962
FORCE M.D.'S	1459
Lita FORD	703
Robben FORD	2421
"Tennessee" Ernie FORD	3459
Julia FORDHAM	2073
FOREIGNER	37
FOREVER MORE	3342
The FORTUNES	2586
David FOSTER	2556
FOSTER & LLOYD	3044
FOTOMAKER	2163
The FOUNDATIONS	2198
Pete FOUNTAIN	893
4 BY FOUR	2984
FOUR JACKS And A JILL	2945
4 SEASONS	202
FOUR TOPS	142
Kim FOWLEY	3401
Samantha FOX	786
Virgil FOX	3407
Redd FOXX	1951
FOXY	753
Peter FRAMPTON	96
Sergio FRANCHI	2651
Connie FRANCIS	1052
FRANKE AND THE KNOCKOUTS	991
FRANKIE GOES TO HOLLYWOOD	965
Aretha FRANKLIN	18
Erma FRANKLIN	3480
Rodney FRANKLIN	2157
Michael FRANKS	882
Linda FRATIANNE	3076

Act	Rank
John FRED & His PLAYBOY BAND	2706
FREDDIE And The DREAMERS	1205
FREE	730
FREE MOVEMENT	2880
Ace FREHLEY	844
FREHLEY'S COMET	1770
David FREIBERG	2996
Glenn FREY	561
FRIDA	1487
Dean FRIEDMAN	3185
Kinky FRIEDMAN	2671
FRIENDS OF DISTINCTION	924
FRIJID PINK	839
Robert FRIPP	1675
The FROST	2209
FROZEN GHOST	2405
David FRYE	867
The FUGS	1621
Bobby FULLER Four	3314
FULL FORCE	2011
FUN BOY THREE	2647
FUNKADELIC	585
FUNKADELIC(2)	3024
FUNKY COMMUNICATION COMMITTEE	3472
Richie FURAY Band	2500
FUSE ONE	2773
The FUZZ	3394
G	
Peter GABRIEL	272
Eric GALE	2291
Rory GALLAGHER	1182
GALLERY	1866
James GALWAY	2758
GAMMA	1349
GANG OF FOUR	2873
GAP BAND	348
Jerry GARCIA	956
Art GARFUNKEL	409
Judy GARLAND	2770
Judy GARLAND & Liza MINELLI	1689
Gale GARNETT	1734
Leif GARRETT	912
Tommy GARRETT	1811
John GARY	283
GARY'S GANG	1853
Luis GASCA	3415
David GATES	1857
Larry GATLIN/ GATLIN BROTHERS Band	1636
Marvin GAYE	83
Marvin GAYE & Tammi TERRELL	1077
Crystal GAYLE	482
GAYLORD & HOLIDAY	2956
Gloria GAYNOR	515
J. GEILS Band	171
Bob GELDOF	2618
GENE LOVES JEZEBEL	1846
GENERAL PUBLIC	993
GENESIS	95
GENTLE GIANT	1192
Bobbie GENTRY	494
The GENTRYS	2374
Lowell GEORGE	2194
GEORGIA SATELLITES	767
GEORGIO	1673
GERRY And The PACEMAKERS	835
Stan GETZ	532

Act	Rank
GIANT	1686
GIANT STEPS	3269
Andy GIBB	350
Barry GIBB	2425
Terri GIBBS	1492
Debbie GIBSON	274
Don GIBSON	3169
GIBSON BROTHERS	3422
Astrud GILBERTO	1372
Joao GILBERTO	712
Nick GILDER	1232
Johnny GILL	3101
GILLAN	3350
Mickey GILLEY	2818
David GILMOUR	900
Jim GILSTRAP	3022
Nikki GIOVANNI	2518
GIPSY KINGS	1224
GIRLSCHOOL	3271
GIUFFRIA	1095
Philip GLASS	2085
GLASS HARP	3390
GLASS MOON	2654
GLASS TIGER	814
Tompall GLASER	1559
Jackie GLEASON	1581
Gary GLITTER	3067
Roger GLOVER	2123
GOANNA	3237
The GODFATHERS	1992
GODLEY & CREME	1694
The GODZ	3123
Louise GOFFIN	2133
The GO-GO'S	257
Andrew GOLD	1630
GOLDDIGGERS	2639
GOLDEN EARRING	650
GOLDEN GATE Strings	3525
Bobby GOLDSBORO	503
Ian GOMM	2206
GONZALEZ	1987
Benny GOODMAN	2208
Dickie GOODMAN	2676
Jerry GOODMAN & Jan HAMMER	3130
Steve GOODMAN	2614
GOOSE CREEK SYMPHONY	2854
Robert GORDON	1423
Lesley GORE	1545
Martin L. GORE	3163
GORKY PARK	2001
Eydie GORME	766
Barry GOUDREAU	2285
Robert GOULET	418
GO WEST	1417
GQ	675
The GRACES	2870
Larry GRAHAM/ GRAHAM CENTRAL STATION	495
Lou GRAMM	1132
GRAND FUNK RAILROAD	55
GRANDMASTER FLASH	2989
GRANDMASTER FLASH And The FURIOUS FIVE	1555
Amy GRANT	857
Earl GRANT	2540
Eddy GRANT	863
Stephane GRAPELLI	2836
GRASS ROOTS	531
GRATEFUL DEAD	164
Dobie GRAY	1666

Act	Rank
Glen GRAY & The CASA LOMA Orchestra	2064
Charles Randolph GREAN Sounde	1234
GREASE BAND	3339
GREAT WHITE	438
R.B. GREAVES	2092
Boris GREBENSHIKOV	3524
Rick GRECH	3432
Al GREEN	128
Grant GREEN	2682
Jack GREEN	2630
Peter GREEN	3213
Norman GREENBAUM	1230
Jack GREENE	1576
Lorne GREENE	1672
GREEN ON RED	3227
Lee GREENWOOD	1525
Joanie GREGGAINS	3281
Dick GREGORY	3013
GREY And HANKS	2282
Nanci GRIFFITH	2232
GRIM REAPER	1354
GRIN	2709
GRINDER SWITCH	2722
David GRISMAN	2305
Larry GROCE	3433
Henry GROSS	990
Dave GRUSIN	999
GTR	964
GUADALCANAL DIARY	2298
GUCCI CREW II	3162
GUESS WHO	211
Greg GUIDRY	2947
GUNS N' ROSES	132
Arlo GUTHRIE	376
Gwen GUTHRIE	2266
GUY	775
GYPSY	1401
H	
Steve HACKETT	1796
Sammy HAGAR	393
Nina HAGEN	2816
Merle HAGGARD	469
HAIRCUT ONE HUNDRED	1193
Daryl HALL	1236
Daryl HALL & John OATES	38
Jimmy HALL	3425
John HALL Band	2365
Tom T. HALL	2104
Chico HAMILTON	3150
George HAMILTON IV	2434
HAMILTON, JOE FRANK & REYNOLDS	1440
Marvin HAMLISCH	431
Jan HAMMER Group	1780
Albert HAMMOND	1904
Johnny HAMMOND	2090
John Paul HAMMOND	2972
Herbie HANCOCK	290
John HANDY	1473
Bo HANSSON	2894
The HAPPENINGS	1805
Paul HARDCASTLE	1728
HARDEN Trio	2977
Tim HARDIN	2460
Hagood HARDY	2248
HARDY BOYS	3482
HARPERS BIZARRE	1761

Act	Rank
Eddie HARRIS	805
Emmylou HARRIS	304
Major HARRIS	1262
Richard HARRIS	423
Sam HARRIS	1223
Don HARRISON Band	2910
George HARRISON	90
Jerry HARRISON: CASUAL GODS	1793
Noel HARRISON	2642
Wes HARRISON	2757
Wilbert HARRISON	3444
Debbie HARRY	1301
Corey HART	610
Freddie HART	1091
Mickey HART	3324
John HARTFORD	2288
KEEF HARTLEY BAND	3372
Dan HARTMAN	1275
Sensational Alex HARVEY Band	2673
Annie HASLEM	2655
Donny HATHAWAY	443
Richie HAVENS	778
Edwin HAWKINS Singers	1000
HAWKWIND	1993
Colin James HAY	2745
Isaac HAYES	65
Justin HAYWARD	1068
Leon HAYWOOD	1989
Ofra HAZA	2643
Robert HAZARD	2424
Lee HAZLEWOOD	1219
Roy HEAD	2649
The HEADBOYS	2225
HEAD EAST	1056
HEADHUNTERS	2427
The HEADPINS	2672
Jeff HEALEY Band	969
HEAR 'N AID	2582
HEART	64
HEARTSFIELD	2877
Joey HEATHERTON	2506
HEATWAVE	499
HEAVEN 17	1463
HEAVY D & The BOYZ	777
Bobby HEBB	2228
Neal HEFTI	1620
HEINTJE	2283
HELIX	1644
HELLO PEOPLE	2449
HELLOWEEN	1696
Levon HELM	2497
Michael HENDERSON	780
Skitch HENDERSON	2585
Jimi HENDRIX	188
Jimi HENDRIX EXPERIENCE	116
Nona HENDRYX	1678
Don HENLEY	240
Carol HENSEL	866
Ken HENSLEY	3030
Woody HERMAN	2871
HERMAN'S HERMITS	155
Patrick HERNANDEZ	1778
The HESITATIONS	3431
Howard HEWETT	2095
Nick HEYWARD	3304
John HIATT	1557
Dan HICKS & His HOT LICKS	1645
Bertie HIGGINS	1405
HIGH INERGY	1011
The HIGHWAYMEN	2319

Act	Rank
Dan HILL	879
Z.Z. HILL	2652
Steve HILLAGE	2545
Chris HILLMAN	2747
HILLSIDE SINGERS	2038
HIPSWAY	1826
HIROSHIMA	793
Al HIRT	133
Robyn HITCHCOCK And The EGYPTIANS	1929
Don HO and the ALIIS	916
Johnny HODGES	3485
Roger HODGSON	1500
Billie HOLIDAY	1462
Amy HOLLAND	2480
Jennifer HOLLIDAY	1377
The HOLLIES	459
Loleatta HOLLOWAY	3443
Buddy HOLLY	1891
HOLLY And The ITALIANS	3290
HOLLYRIDGE STRINGS	1076
Eddie HOLMAN	1946
Cecil HOLMES SOULFUL SOUNDS	2750
Clint HOLMES	2373
"Groove" HOLMES	1608
Jake HOLMES	2767
LeRoy HOLMES and His Orchestra	1307
Rupert HOLMES	1061
The HOMBRES	3313
The HONDELLS	3047
The HONEYCOMBS	3359
HONEY CONE	1539
The HONEYDRIPPERS	765
HONEYMOON SUITE	1129
HOODOO GURUS	1779
John Lee HOOKER	1222
Stix HOOPER	3086
The HOOTERS	558
Bob HOPE	3193
Mary HOPKIN	1185
Nicky HOPKINS	1531
Jimmy 'Bo' HORNE	2475
Lena HORNE	2315
Bruce HORNSBY And The RANGE	321
Vladimir HOROWITZ	1060
HORSLIPS	2089
HOT	2184
HOT BUTTER	2683
HOT CHOCOLATE	911
HOTHOUSE FLOWERS	1763
HOT TUNA	736
The HOUSEMARTINS	2369
HOUSE OF FREAKS	2802
HOUSE OF LORDS	1794
HOUSE OF LOVE	3042
David HOUSTON	1592
Thelma HOUSTON	701
Whitney HOUSTON	98
George HOWARD	1596
Miki HOWARD	2299
Steve HOWE	1910
HOWLIN' WOLF	1819
Freddie HUBBARD	1451
David HUDSON	3424
HUDSON And LANDRY	782
HUDSON BROTHERS	2523
HUES CORPORATION	1202
Grayson HUGH	1850
HUGO & LUIGI	3260
HUMAN BEINZ	2062

Act	Rank
HUMAN LEAGUE	447
HUMBLE PIE	368
Engelbert HUMPERDINCK	109
Bobbi HUMPHREY	1023
Paul HUMPHREY & The COOL AID CHEMISTS	3057
Ian HUNTER	811
John HUNTER	2852
Chet HUNTLEY & David BRINKLEY	2733
HURRICANE	1660
HUSKER DU	2257
Willie HUTCH	1785
Leroy HUTSON	2895
Paul HYDE And The PAYOLAS	2760
Brian HYLAND	2701
Dick HYMAN	972
Phyllis HYMAN	849
Tony HYMAS	2532

I

Act	Rank
Janis IAN	311
IAN & SYLVIA	1399
ICEHOUSE	875
ICE-T	959
ICICLE WORKS	1671
ICON	3503
IDES OF MARCH	1788
Billy IDOL	256
IF	2922
Frank IFIELD	3115
Julio IGLESIAS	468
ILLINOIS SPEED PRESS	2869
ILLUSION	2942
The ILLUSION	1507
IMPELLITTERI	1906
The IMPRESSIONS	394
INCREDIBLE BONGO BAND	3500
INCREDIBLE STRING BAND	2171
The INDEPENDENTS	2631
INDIGO GIRLS	1032
INFORMATION SOCIETY	1089
James INGRAM	1187
Luther INGRAM	1422
The INMATES	1784
INNER CITY	3215
INSIDERS	3179
INSTANT FUNK	859
The INTRUDERS	1670
INXS	241
Donnie IRIS	1102
IRISH ROVERS	888
IRON BUTTERFLY	111
IRONHORSE	2689
IRON MAIDEN	309
Chris ISAAK	681
ISLE OF MAN	2255
ISLEY BROTHERS	89
ISLEY JASPER ISLEY	1679
IT'S A BEAUTIFUL DAY	665
Burl IVES	2094

J

Act	Rank
Terry JACKS	2234
Freddie JACKSON	414
Janet JACKSON	115
Jermaine JACKSON	336
Joe JACKSON	268
LaToya JACKSON	2056

Act	Rank
Marlon JACKSON	3154
Michael JACKSON	23
Millie JACKSON	556
Rebbie JACKSON	1848
Walter JACKSON	1775
Willis JACKSON	3065
JACKSON 5	58
Lou JACOBI	3121
Debbie JACOBS	2502
JADE WARRIOR	3476
Chris JAGGER	3297
Mick JAGGER	902
The JAGGERZ	1897
The JAM	1321
Ahmad JAMAL Trio	2738
Bob JAMES	388
Bob JAMES & Earl KLUGH	809
Etta JAMES	1658
Jimmy JAMES & The VAGABONDS	2286
Melvin JAMES	2915
Rick JAMES	190
Sonny JAMES	1609
Tommy JAMES And The SHONDELLS	448
JAMES GANG	363
JAN & DEAN	845
JANE'S ADDICTION	1688
Chaz JANKEL	2433
Horst JANKOWSKI	1017
Jean Michel JARRE	1197
Al JARREAU	281
Keith JARRETT	1817
JASON & The SCORCHERS	1485
Chris JASPER	3367
JAY & The AMERICANS	915
JAY And The TECHNIQUES	2443
Jerry JAYE	3515
Miles JAYE	2230
The JB'S	1957
JEFFERSON AIRPLANE/STARSHIP	17
Garland JEFFREYS	1239
JELLYBEAN	2396
Waylon JENNINGS	233
Waylon JENNINGS & Willie NELSON	852
JESUS AND MARY CHAIN	1950
JETBOY	2636
JETHRO TULL	35
The JETS	557
Joan JETT & The BLACKHEARTS	308
JIGSAW	1575
Jose JIMENEZ	3053
JIVE BUNNY & The MASTERMIXERS	1493
J.J. FAD	1413
Antonio Carlos JOBIM	1297
JOBOXERS	2046
JOE & EDDIE	2474
Billy JOEL	9
David JOHANSEN	1740
Elton JOHN	4
Robert JOHN	1979
JOHNNY And The DISTRACTIONS	2839
JOHNNY HATES JAZZ	1556
Sammy JOHNS	2468
Don JOHNSON	1163
Howard JOHNSON	2741
Jesse JOHNSON	891
Michael JOHNSON	1706
Robert JOHNSON	2955
Tom JOHNSTON	2049
JO JO GUNNE	1214
France JOLI	1424

Act	Rank
JON And VANGELIS	1355
David JONES	3210
George JONES	1612
Glenn JONES	2138
Grace JONES	791
Howard JONES	502
Jack JONES	303
Mick JONES	3399
Oran 'Juice' JONES	1622
Quincy JONES	137
Rickie Lee JONES	320
Shirley JONES	2625
New Band of Spike JONES	3011
Steve JONES	3283
Tom JONES	62
JONES GIRLS	1280
JONZUN CREW	1821
Janis JOPLIN	203
Jerry JORDAN	2081
Lonnie JORDAN	3051
Stanley JORDAN	1069
Margie JOSEPH	1885
JOURNEY	34
JOY DIVISION	2806
JOY OF COOKING	1700
JUDAS PRIEST	323
The JUDDS	640
JULUKA	3298
Rob JUNGKLAS	2071
JUNIOR	1894
JUNKYARD	2392
Patrick JUVET	2357

K

Act	Rank
Bert KAEMPFERT And His Orchestra	351
KAJAGOOGOO	1529
KALEIDOSCOPE	2512
Gunter KALLMANN Chorus	2077
KALYAN	3223
Big Daddy KANE	1326
KANE GANG	2144
KANO	3356
KANSAS	176
Paul KANTNER	1358
KaSANDRA	2501
KASHIF	1067
KATRINA & The WAVES	961
Jorma KAUKONEN & VITAL PARTS	3007
John KAY	2380
KAYAK	2164
Sammy KAYE & His Orchestra	2547
The KAY-GEES	3534
KBC BAND	1765
KC And The SUNSHINE BAND	266
KEEL	1330
Tommy KEENE	2451
KEITH	2849
Manny KELLEM, His Orchestra And Voices	3504
Johnny KEMP	1749
Eddie KENDRICKS	535
John Fitzgerald KENNEDY	647
Joyce KENNEDY	2238
Robert Francis KENNEDY	3262
KENNY G	239
Stan KENTON	2359
KENTUCKY HEADHUNTERS	864
Anita KERR Singers	2668
Nik KERSHAW	1737

Act	Rank
KGB	2763
Chaka KHAN	439
Steve KHAN	2970
KICK AXE	2341
KID CREOLE & The COCONUTS	2602
KID 'N PLAY	1468
KIDS FROM FAME	2102
Greg KIHN Band	614
KILLER DWARFS	3104
KILLING JOKE	3538
John KILZER	2307
Andy KIM	1097
The KIMBERLYS	3330
Warren KIME	2130
Tom KIMMEL	2368
KING	2838
Albert KING	1720
B.B. KING	338
B.B. KING & Bobby BLAND	1272
Ben E. KING	1341
Carole KING	28
Evelyn "Champagne" KING	514
Freddie KING	2834
Morgana KING	2176
Rev. Martin Luther KING Jr.	1627
The KINGBEES	2627
KING BISCUIT BOY	3461
KING CRIMSON	562
KING CURTIS	1389
KING DIAMOND	1755
KINGDOM COME	865
KING FAMILY	1565
KINGFISH	1698
KING HARVEST	2626
KING RICHARD'S FLUEGEL KNIGHTS	3519
The KINGS	1611
The KINGSMEN	406
KINGS OF THE SUN	2457
KINGSTON TRIO	596
KING SWAMP	2807
KING'S X	1922
KING TEE	2347
Sam KINISON	1643
The KINKS	147
KISS	71
KITARO	2640
KIX	1035
KLAATU	1510
KLEEER	1610
Robert KLEIN	3416
John KLEMMER	877
KLIQUE	2135
The KLOWNS	3403
Earl KLUGH	554
KLYMAXX	757
The KNACK	367
The KNICKERBOCKERS	2948
Curtis KNIGHT	2530
Gladys KNIGHT & The PIPS	145
Jean KNIGHT	1917
Jerry KNIGHT	2569
Robert KNIGHT	3508
Terry KNIGHT And The PACK	2250
K-9 POSSE	2216
Fred KNOBLOCK	3176
Mark KNOPFLER	3528
KOKOMO	2762
KONGAS	2543
KOOL & The GANG	102

Act	Rank
KOOL MOE DEE	773
Al KOOPER	842
The KORGIS	2355
Paul KOSSOFF	3445
Andre KOSTELANETZ And His Orchestra	2412
Leo KOTTKE	1016
KRAFTWERK	631
Billy J. KRAMER with The DAKOTAS	1834
Lenny KRAVITZ	1567
Kris KRISTOFFERSON	293
Kris KRISTOFFERSON & Rita COOLIDGE	1055
KROKUS	659
Bob KUBAN And The IN-MEN	2917
KWAMÉ & A NEW BEGINNING	2259
KWICK	3505

L

Act	Rank
Patti LaBELLE	333
L.A. BOPPERS	2148
LACE	3263
Cheryl LADD	2382
L.A. DREAM TEAM	2732
David LAFLAMME	3006
L.A. GUNS	895
LAID BACK	2028
Cleo LAINE	1901
Frankie LAINE	904
LAKE	2136
Greg LAKE	1743
LAKESIDE	618
Major LANCE	2101
Robin LANE & The CHARTBUSTERS	3191
Ronnie LANE	2223
K.D. LANG	1039
David LANZ	2617
Mario LANZA	2188
Billy LARKIN & The Delegates	3332
The LARKS	3129
Neil LARSEN	2749
LARSEN-FEITEN BAND	2623
Nicolette LARSON	750
D.C. LaRUE	1903
Denise LaSALLE	2520
James LAST	2302
LAST POETS	951
Yusef LATEEF	3157
LATIMORE	3181
Stacy LATTISAW	860
Cyndi LAUPER	262
Steve LAWRENCE	2114
Steve LAWRENCE & Eydie GORME	2296
Vicki LAWRENCE	1800
Debra LAWS	1550
Eloise LAWS	2690
Hubert LAWS	996
Ronnie LAWS	543
Bernie LEADON-Michel GEORGIADES Band	2515
LEAPY LEE	1809
LEATHERWOLF	2055
The LEAVES	2868
LeBLANC & CARR	2742
LED ZEPPELIN	7
Alvin LEE	1425
Brenda LEE	944
Jackie LEE	2440
Johnny LEE	1956

Act	Rank
Laura LEE	2352
Peggy LEE	1429
Myron LeFEVRE	3072
Raymond LEFEVRE And His Orchestra	2159
LEFT BANKE	2181
Michel LEGRAND	2284
Tom LEHRER	856
LEMON PIPERS	1999
John LENNON	337
John LENNON & Yoko ONO	294
John LENNON/PLASTIC ONO BAND	270
Julian LENNON	638
LENNON SISTERS	2067
Le PAMPLEMOUSSE	2408
LEROI BROS.	3264
Le ROUX	1426
LET'S ACTIVE	1937
The LETTERMEN	167
LEVEL 42	727
LEVERT	1083
Barbara LEWIS	2743
Gary LEWIS And The PLAYBOYS	474
Huey LEWIS And The NEWS	112
Jerry Lee LEWIS	716
Ramsey LEWIS	354
Ramsey LEWIS Trio	397
Webster LEWIS	2519
Lori LIEBERMAN	3236
Enoch LIGHT & The LIGHT BRIGADE	1322
Gordon LIGHTFOOT	180
LIGHTHOUSE	1548
LIMAHL	1631
The LIMELITERS	2210
Bob LIND	3335
David LINDLEY	1789
Mark LINDSAY	1264
Art LINKLETTER	3172
LINX	3201
LIONS AND GHOSTS	3427
LIPPS INC.	734
LISA LISA And CULT JAM	528
The LITTER	3171
Rich LITTLE	1558
LITTLE AMERICA	2300
LITTLE ANTHONY And The IMPERIALS	1523
LITTLE FEAT	460
LITTLE MILTON	2019
LITTLE RICHARD	3160
LITTLE RIVER BAND	277
LITTLE STEVEN	1386
LIVING COLOUR	584
LIVING IN A BOX	2371
LIZZY BORDEN	2040
LL COOL J	415
Charles LLOYD Quartet	2935
LOBO	978
John LODGE	1348
Nils LOFGREN	843
Dave LOGGINS	1790
Kenny LOGGINS	230
LOGGINS & MESSINA	185
Jackie LOMAX	2553
Julie LONDON	3080
LONDON SYMPHONY Orchestra	1667
LONE JUSTICE	1207
Claudine LONGET	522
LOOKING GLASS	2080
LOOSE ENDS	1292

Act	Rank
Denise LOPEZ	3326
Trini LOPEZ	405
Jeff LORBER	994
LORDAN	2149
LORDS Of The NEW CHURCH	3059
LORD SUTCH And HEAVY FRIENDS	2036
Gloria LORING	2103
Los BRAVOS	2507
Los INDIOS TABAJARAS	1013
Los LOBOS	511
LOUDNESS	1491
LOVE	1210
LOVE AND KISSES	1687
LOVE AND MONEY	3108
LOVE AND ROCKETS	762
LOVE CHILDS AFRO CUBAN BLUES Band	3107
LOVERBOY	158
Lyle LOVETT	1501
LOVE UNLIMITED	605
LOVE UNLIMITED ORCHESTRA	635
Lene LOVICH	2053
LOVIN' SPOONFUL	342
Nick LOWE	973
Nick LOWE And His COWBOY OUTFIT	2051
L.T.D.	400
L'TRIMM	2407
Carrie LUCAS	2226
LULU	1134
Ray LYNCH	3523
Cheryl LYNN	939
Loretta LYNN	1111
Gloria LYNNE	1045
LYNYRD SKYNYRD	168
Johnny LYTLE	3299
M	2493

M

Act	Rank
Moms MABLEY	1375
Tony MacALPINE	2734
MAC Band	2409
Ralph MacDONALD	1247
Mary MacGREGOR	1215
MACHO	2180
Lonnie MACK	1983
MADAME X	3186
MADHOUSE	2503
MAD LADS	3366
MADNESS	1237
MADONNA	69
MAD RIVER	3441
MADURA	3449
Cledus MAGGARD And The CITIZEN's BAND	2592
MAGIC ORGAN	2660
MAGNIFICENT MEN	2418
Taj MAHAL	1295
George MAHARIS	2539
MAHOGANY RUSH	1211
MAIN INGREDIENT	870
Miriam MAKEBA	1477
MALICE	3235
Yngwie MALMSTEEN	824
MALO	787
MAMA CASS	1472
MAMAS & The PAPAS	104
MAMA'S BOYS	2697
Melissa MANCHESTER	355
MANCHILD	2982

Act	Rank
Henry MANCINI & Doc SEVERINSEN	1729
Henry MANCINI and his Orchestra	151
Harvey MANDEL	2793
Howie MANDEL	3046
Steve MANDELL	1010
MANDRE	1962
Barbara MANDRELL	1331
MANDRILL	672
MANFRED MANN	1583
MANFRED MANN'S EARTH BAND	634
Chuck MANGIONE	208
The MANHATTANS	529
MANHATTAN TRANSFER	450
Barry MANILOW	53
Herbie MANN	454
Johnny MANN Singers	1376
MANNHEIM STEAMROLLER	955
MANTOVANI	330
MANTRONIX	2533
Phil MANZANERA	3319
Ray MANZAREK	2832
Little Peggy MARCH	3183
Benny MARDONES	1760
Teena MARIE	491
MARILLION	1251
MARK-ALMOND	1151
The MARKETTS	1574
The MAR-KEYS	3148
Pigmeat MARKHAM	2363
Bob MARLEY And The WAILERS	331
Ziggy MARLEY & The MELODY MAKERS	769
MARLEY MARL	3126
The MARMALADE	2042
Neville MARRINER	1190
Branford MARSALIS	3079
Wynton MARSALIS	1213
MARSHALL TUCKER Band	271
M + M	2864
MARTHA & The VANDELLAS	1421
MARTIKA	970
Bobbi MARTIN	2670
Dean MARTIN	108
Eric MARTIN Band	3507
George MARTIN & His Orchestra	2522
Marilyn MARTIN	2252
Moon MARTIN	1816
Steve MARTIN	361
Nancy MARTINEZ	3414
Al MARTINO	225
The MARVELETTES	1832
Groucho MARX	2312
Richard MARX	247
MARY JANE GIRLS	829
Carolyne MAS	3310
Hugh MASEKELA	884
MASKED MARAUDERS	2218
Barbara MASON	2007
Dave MASON	358
Harvey MASON	2578
Jackie MASON	2796
Nick MASON	3071
MASON PROFFIT	2342
MASS PRODUCTION	1248
Mireille MATHIEU	2438
Johnny MATHIS	135
David MATTHEWS	2937
Ian MATTHEWS	1367
Paul MAURIAT And His Orchestra	371

Act	Rank
AKA The MAX DEMIAN Band	3055
MAX Q	3147
Robert MAXWELL	1252
Brian MAY	2645
John MAYALL	417
John MAYALL'S BLUESBREAKERS	1371
Curtis MAYFIELD	200
Lyle MAYS	1948
MAZARATI	2821
MAZE Featuring Frankie BEVERLY	401
Letta MBULU	3402
MC5	1241
MC HAMMER	774
MC LYTE	2152
MC SHY D	3541
C.W. McCALL	1028
David McCALLUM	1200
Les McCANN	1977
Les McCANN & Eddie HARRIS	751
Peter McCANN	2125
Paul McCARTNEY	177
Paul & Linda McCARTNEY	377
Paul McCARTNEY & WINGS/WINGS	41
Alton McCLAIN & DESTINY	1968
Delbert McCLINTON	1299
Marilyn McCOO & Billy DAVIS JR.	929
Gayle McCORMICK	3409
Charlie McCOY	1465
Van McCOY	923
The McCOYS	1711
George McCRAE	1554
Gwen McCRAE	2379
McCRARYS	2560
Ian McCULLOCH	3527
Kathi McDONALD	2720
Michael McDONALD	853
Brother Jack McDUFF	2024
Reba McENTIRE	1337
McFADDEN & WHITEHEAD	1226
Gary McFARLAND	3341
Bobby McFERRIN	687
Maureen McGOVERN	1756
Bob McGRATH	2489
Jimmy McGRIFF	1990
McGUFFEY LANE	3274
Roger McGUINN	1994
McGUINN, CLARK & HILLMAN	1403
McGUINNESS FLINT	2744
Barry McGUIRE	1616
Maria McKEE	2264
McKENDREE SPRING	2156
Bob & Doug McKENZIE	984
Scott McKENZIE	2679
Rod McKUEN	1370
Sarah McLACHLAN	2694
Ian McLAGAN	2628
Malcolm McLAREN	2928
John McLAUGHLIN	1303
John McLAUGHLIN/MAHAVISHNU ORCHESTRA	625
Pat McLAUGHLIN	3537
Don McLEAN	295
James McMURTRY	2728
Kristy And Jimmy McNICHOL	3010
Carmen McRAE	3303
Christine McVIE	1257
MEAT LOAF	519
MECO	758
Glenn MEDEIROS	2173
Bill MEDLEY	2814

Act	Rank
MEGADETH	1019
Zubin MEHTA/LOS ANGELES PHILHARMONIC Orchestra	2326
Randy MEISNER	1220
MEL And TIM	3045
MELANIE	421
John MELLENCAMP	77
Harold MELVIN And The BLUE NOTES	437
MEMPHIS HORNS	2829
MEN AT WORK	195
Sergio MENDES	1009
Sergio MENDES And BRASIL '66/'77	170
MENUDO	1844
Yehudi MENUHIN	3242
MEN WITHOUT HATS	876
Freddie MERCURY	3092
MERCY	1453
The MERRY-GO-ROUND	3469
MERRYWEATHER & FRIENDS	3478
Jim MESSINA	1527
METAL CHURCH	1508
METALLICA	390
The METERS	1981
Pat METHENY	1949
PAT METHENY GROUP	593
MFSB	621
George MICHAEL	215
Lee MICHAELS	555
Bette MIDLER	143
MIDNIGHT OIL	718
MIDNIGHT STAR	513
MIDNIGHT STRING QUARTET	770
MIGHTY CLOUDS OF JOY	2674
MIKE + THE MECHANICS	600
Buddy MILES	420
John MILES	1955
Frankie MILLER(1)	1914
Glenn MILLER Orchestra	2358
Jody MILLER	2281
Mrs. MILLER	1263
Roger MILLER	317
Steve MILLER Band	70
MILLIONS LIKE US	2795
MILLI VANILLI	242
Frank MILLS	1291
Stephanie MILLS	339
MILLS BROTHERS	1108
Ronnie MILSAP	518
Garnet MIMMS & The ENCHANTERS	2776
The MINDBENDERS	1872
MINISTRY	2034
MINK DE VILLE	2333
Liza MINNELLI	819
Kylie MINOGUE	1433
MINOR DETAIL	3483
MIRABAI	2716
The MIRACLES/Smokey ROBINSON & The MIRACLES	231
The MIRACLES	806
Judi Sheppard MISSETT	1974
MISSING PERSONS	570
MISSION U.K.	1982
MISSOURI	3211
MR. BIG	1653
MR. MISTER	497
MISTRESS	2201
Chad MITCHELL Trio	880
Joni MITCHELL	103

Act	Rank
Kim MITCHELL	2297
Rubin MITCHELL	3355
Willie MITCHELL	2548
MOBY GRAPE	749
MOCEDADES	2824
M.O.D.	2452
MODELS	1969
MODERN ENGLISH	1516
Anna MOFFO	3038
MOLLY HATCHET	512
MOM & DADS	1697
The MOMENTS (2)	2145
Eddie MONEY	299
T.S. MONK	1638
Thelonious MONK	3168
The MONKEES	31
Matt MONRO	1759
Michael MONROE	3064
The MONROES	2723
MONTANA Orchestra	3378
Hugo MONTENEGRO	680
Chris MONTEZ	1260
Wes MONTGOMERY	373
MONTROSE	1203
MONTY PYTHON	1242
MOODY BLUES	30
MOOG MACHINE	2859
Keith MOON	3136
The MOONGLOWS	3358
Dorothy MOORE	1087
Gary MOORE	1714
Melba MOORE	1171
Tim MOORE	2387
Vinnie MOORE	2932
Michael MORALES	2205
Patrick MORAZ	2784
Jane MORGAN	2990
Lee MORGAN	1256
Meli'sa MORGAN	1227
Giorgio MORODER	2717
Gary MORRIS	3083
Van MORRISON	276
MORRISSEY	1628
Steve MORSE Band	2346
Johnny & Jonie MOSBY	3531
The MOTELS	576
MOTHER EARTH	1899
MOTHERLODE	2091
MOTHER'S FINEST	1579
MÖTLEY CRÜE	141
MOTORHEAD	2174
The MOTORS	2983
Tony MOTTOLA	2111
MOTT THE HOOPLE	662
Bob MOULD	2476
MOUNTAIN	428
Nana MOUSKOURI	3056
MOUTH & MACNEAL	1860
Alphonse MOUZON	2805
The MOVE	2969
MOVING PICTURES	2279
Alison MOYET	1336
MTUME	1101
Idris MUHAMMAD	2158
Maria MULDAUR	432
Martin MULL	3019
MUNGO JERRY	1925
MUNICH MACHINE	3376
Shirley MURDOCK	1428
Michael MURPHEY	666

Act	Rank
Eddie MURPHY	664
Peter MURPHY	2269
Walter MURPHY	1043
Anne MURRAY	197
MUSCLE SHOALS HORNS	2704
MUSICAL YOUTH	1317
MUSIC EXPLOSION	3429
MUSIC MACHINE	1973
MUSIQUE	1668
Alicia MYERS	3300
Gary MYRICK	3420
MYSTIC MOODS Orchestra	1289

N

Act	Rank
Jim NABORS	505
The NAILS	3517
NAJEE	1156
NAKED EYES	1130
Graham NASH	800
Johnny NASH	989
NATIONAL LAMPOON	1715
NATURAL FOUR	3343
NATURE'S DIVINE	2406
NAZARETH	517
NAZZ	1379
Sam NEELY	2415
NEKTAR	833
Rick NELSON	760
Sandy NELSON	1646
Tracy NELSON	2923
Willie NELSON	106
NENA	1535
Peter NERO	632
Michael NESMITH	2270
Robbie NEVIL	1054
Ivan NEVILLE	2013
NEVILLE BROTHERS	1564
The NEWBEATS	1787
NEW BIRTH	754
Mickey NEWBURY	1701
NEW CHRISTY MINSTRELS	375
NEWCLEUS	1827
NEW COLONY SIX	2465
NEW EDITION	301
NEW ENGLAND	1690
NEW ENGLAND CONSERVATORY CHORUS	1431
Bob NEWHART	2253
NEW KIDS ON THE BLOCK	174
Randy NEWMAN	547
NEW ORDER	708
NEW RIDERS Of The PURPLE SAGE	737
NEW SEEKERS	1447
Juice NEWTON	410
Wayne NEWTON	747
Olivia NEWTON-JOHN	76
NEW VAUDEVILLE BAND	799
NEW YORK CITY	2544
NEW YORK DOLLS	2179
The NICE	2664
Stevie NICKS	160
NIGHT	2388
The NIGHTHAWKS	3184
Maxine NIGHTINGALE	1387
NIGHT RANGER	319
Willie NILE	2419
NILSSON	300
Leonard NIMOY	1568
999	3167
9.9	1930
1910 FRUITGUM CO.	2098
The NITE-LITERS	2542
NITRO	2718
NITTY GRITTY DIRT BAND	559
NITZINGER	2906
Don NIX	3410
Mojo NIXON & Skid ROPER	2911
No Artist	2446
Cliff NOBLES & Co.	3146
NOEL	2537
Kenny NOLAN	1874
NORMA JEAN	2423
Freddie NORTH	3203
Aldo NOVA	704
NOVO COMBO	3015
NRBQ	3009
NUCLEAR ASSAULT	1870
Ted NUGENT	248
Gary NUMAN	840
Bobby NUNN	2867
NU SHOOZ	1098
N.W.A.	827
The NYLONS	1368
Laura NYRO	798

O

Act	Rank
OAK RIDGE BOYS	489
OAKTOWN'S 3.5.7	2320
John O'BANION	3116
O'BRYAN	1287
Ric OCASEK	1050
OCEAN	1833
Billy OCEAN	259
Phil OCHS	2416
Carroll O'CONNOR	2217
Sinead O'CONNOR	1198
Alan O'DAY	2337
ODETTA	2466
ODYSSEY	1085
OFF BROADWAY USA	2246
OHIO EXPRESS	2471
OHIO PLAYERS	159
OINGO BOINGO	1340
The O'JAYS	146
The O'KAYSIONS	2926
Danny O'KEEFE	1905
OLD & IN THE WAY	2323
Mike OLDFIELD	549
OLIVER	823
David OLIVER	2538
Jane OLIVOR	1474
Nigel OLSSON	2933
OMAR And The HOWLERS	2029
Alexander O'NEAL	1031
100 PROOF AGED IN SOUL	2878
ONE WAY	977
Yoko ONO	1649
OPUS	1935
Roy ORBISON	440
ORCHESTRAL MANOEUVRES IN THE DARK	732
The ORIGINALS	3106
ORION THE HUNTER	1933
ORLEANS	862
ORPHEUS	1972
Benjamin ORR	1908
Robert Ellis ORRALL	2794
Jeffrey OSBORNE	429
OSBORNE BROTHERS	3529
Ozzy OSBOURNE	199
OSIBISA	1142
Lee OSKAR	1157
K.T. OSLIN	1042
Donny OSMOND	226
Donny & Marie OSMOND	755
Little Jimmy OSMOND	2096
Marie OSMOND	1470
The OSMONDS	263
Gilbert O'SULLIVAN	719
OTHER ONES	2967
Shuggie OTIS	3050
The OUTFIELD	510
The OUTLAWS	465
The OUTSIDERS	1363
OVERKILL	2277
Buck OWENS	838
OXO	2780
OZARK MOUNTAIN DAREDEVILS	649
OZONE	3036

P

Act	Rank
PABLO CRUISE	383
PACIFIC GAS AND ELECTRIC	1619
Gene PAGE	3040
Jimmy PAGE	1162
Patti PAGE	1266
Tommy PAGE	3234
Kevin PAIGE	1810
PALM BEACH BAND BOYS	3452
Robert PALMER	275
PAPER LACE	2595
PARIS	2107
Mica PARIS	1943
Graham PARKER And The RUMOUR	709
Ray PARKER Jr./RAYDIO	325
Michael PARKS	678
PARLIAMENT	310
John PARR	1585
Alan PARSONS PROJECT	161
Gram PARSONS	3418
PARTLAND BROTHERS	3078
Dolly PARTON	306
PARTRIDGE FAMILY	152
The PASADENAS	2265
PASSPORT	2063
Jaco PASTORIUS	3200
Robbie PATTON	2997
Billy PAUL	771
Henry PAUL Band	1806
Les PAUL	3322
Pat PAULSEN	2022
The PAUPERS	3417
Luciano PAVAROTTI	1298
PAVLOV'S DOG	3093
Rita PAVONE	2021
Tom PAXTON	2376
Johnny PAYCHECK	1911
Freda PAYNE	1378
PEACHES & HERB	384
PEANUT BUTTER CONSPIRACY	3450
PEARL HARBOR And The EXPLOSIONS	2227
PEARLS BEFORE SWINE	3497
Duke PEARSON	3440
David PEASTON	2186
PEBBLES	794
Ann PEEBLES	2769

Act	Rank
David PEEL & The LOWER EAST SIDE	3113
Nia PEEPLES	1920
Teddy PENDERGRASS	223
Michael PENN	1168
PENTANGLE	2768
PEOPLE	2559
PEOPLE'S CHOICE	1786
PEPPERMINT RAINBOW	2231
PEPSI and SHIRLIE	2739
Carl PERKINS	3084
Itzhak PERLMAN	3037
Joe PERRY PROJECT	1563
Steve PERRY	756
The PERSUADERS	2648
The PERSUASIONS	2016
PETER And GORDON	885
PETER, PAUL & MARY	91
Bernadette PETERS	1945
OSCAR PETERSON TRIO	2311
PET SHOP BOYS	479
Tom PETTY And The HEARTBREAKERS	87
P.F.M.	2505
PHANTOM, ROCKER & SLICK	1722
PHILADELPHIA Orchestra	3008
Anthony PHILLIPS	3411
Esther PHILLIPS	1127
John PHILLIPS	2971
Shawn PHILLIPS	1074
PHOTOGLO	2317
Bobby "Boris" PICKETT	3249
Wilson PICKETT	478
PIECES OF A DREAM	1584
PILOT	2020
Michael PINDER	2606
PINK FLOYD	22
The PIPKINS	2934
Joe PISCOPO	3352
Gene PITNEY	792
PIXIES	1824
PLANET P	1494
Robert PLANT	297
The PLASMATICS	2128
PLASTIC COW	3386
The PLATTERS	2653
PLAYER	817
PLEASURE	1057
The PLIMSOULS	2938
POCKETS	1396
POCO	291
The POGUES	1843
POINT BLANK	1278
Bonnie POINTER	1629
Noel POINTER	1773
POINTER SISTERS	148
POISON	212
The POLICE	68
Michel POLNAREFF	2276
Jean-Luc PONTY	572
Iggy POP	1177
Pope JOHN PAUL II	2927
POPPY FAMILY	2045
POP WILL EAT ITSELF	3131
David PORTER	2199
Sandy POSEY	2656
Mike POST	1863
POTLIQUOR	3001
POUSETTE-DART BAND	2521
Adam Clayton POWELL	2454

Act	Rank
POWER STATION	677
POZO-SECO SINGERS	2044
Andy PRATT	1854
PRATT & McCLAIN	3439
PREFAB SPROUT	3239
PRELUDE	1893
The PRESIDENTS	2887
Elvis PRESLEY	10
Billy PRESTON	493
The PRETENDERS	279
PRETTY MAIDS	3025
PRETTY POISON	2561
PRETTY THINGS	2139
Andre PREVIN	2487
Alan PRICE	2221
Leontyne PRICE	1781
Ray PRICE	552
Charley PRIDE	234
Maxi PRIEST	2204
The PRIMITIVES	1997
PRINCE	45
John PRINE	1320
PRISM	1456
The PROCLAIMERS	1328
PROCOL HARUM	322
The PRODUCERS	3317
PROPHET	2840
Jeanne PRUETT	2478
Richard PRYOR	395
Arthur PRYSOCK	1766
PSEUDO ECHO	1520
PSYCHEDELIC FURS	723
PUBLIC ENEMY	1208
PUBLIC IMAGE LIMITED	1590
Gary PUCKETT And The UNION GAP	436
PURE LOVE & PLEASURE	3468
PURE PRAIRIE LEAGUE	560
Flora PURIM	1577
PURSUIT OF HAPPINESS	1967
The PYRAMIDS	2822
PYTHON LEE JACKSON	3152
Q	3196

Q

Act	Rank
QUARTERFLASH	589
Bill QUATEMAN	2622
Suzi QUATRO	1078
QUAZAR	2719
QUEEN	78
Queen LATIFAH	2335
QUEENSRYCHE	818
QUESTION MARK & The MYSTERIANS	1862
QUICKSILVER MESSENGER SERVICE	472
QUIET RIOT	346

R

Act	Rank
Eddie RABBITT	463
Trevor RABIN	2351
RACING CARS	3428
The RADIATORS	2150
Gilda RADNER	1941
The RAES	3041
Gerry RAFFERTY	476
RAGING SLAB	2442
RAIL	2790
RAINBOW	565

Act	Rank
The RAINMAKERS	1681
Bonnie RAITT	264
RAMATAM	3095
Eddie RAMBEAU	3347
RAM JAM	1599
The RAMONES	788
Jean-Pierre RAMPAL & Claude BOLLING	3180
Boots RANDOLPH	670
RANK AND FILE	3204
Billy RANKIN	2527
Kenny RANKIN	1158
RANKING ROGER	2953
RARE BIRD	2219
RARE EARTH	250
RASCALS/YOUNG RASCALS	130
RASPBERRIES	1003
RATCHELL	3277
RATT	332
Genya RAVAN	2340
RAVEN	1879
Lou RAWLS	144
Don RAY	2336
Susan RAYE	3103
RAY, GOODMAN & BROWN	935
Chris REA	1530
READY FOR THE WORLD	648
REAL LIFE	1754
The RECORDS	1640
REDBONE	1365
Leon REDBONE	1216
Otis REDDING	253
The REDDINGS	2054
Helen REDDY	154
REDEYE	2322
RED FLAG	3286
RED HOT CHILI PEPPERS	1144
RED ROCKERS	2018
RED 7	2461
RED SIREN	2529
Dan REED Network	1907
Jerry REED	1124
Lou REED	382
Della REESE	3292
Dianne REEVES	2837
Jim REEVES	536
RE-FLEX	1669
REGINA	2700
Terry REID	2207
Carl REINER & Mel BROOKS	2549
R.E.M.	269
RENAISSANCE	763
The RENAISSANCE	3489
Diane RENAY	2154
RENÉ & ANGELA	1049
RENÉ & RENÉ	2353
REO SPEEDWAGON	97
The REPLACEMENTS	1466
RESTLESS HEART	1659
RETURN TO FOREVER	746
REVERBERI	2968
Paul REVERE And The RAIDERS	196
Debbie REYNOLDS	1332
RHINOCEROS	1513
Randy RHOADS	1304
Emitt RHODES	1152
RHYTHM CORPS	2356
RHYTHM HERITAGE	1480
Buddy RICH	1430

Act	Rank
Charlie RICH	296
Cliff RICHARD	1117
Keith RICHARDS	1351
Lionel RICHIE	82
Don RICKLES	1415
Stan RIDGWAY	2775
Joshua RIFKIN	1446
RIGHTEOUS BROTHERS	198
Cheryl Pepsii RILEY	2484
Jeannie C. RILEY	889
The RINGS	3029
Miguel RIOS	2998
Waldo DE LOS RIOS	1615
RIOT	2012
RIP CHORDS	1942
Minnie RIPERTON	402
The RIPPINGTONS	1747
RITCHIE FAMILY	936
Lee RITENOUR	954
Joan RIVERS	1457
Johnny RIVERS	216
The RIVIERAS	2929
ROACHFORD	2492
The ROAD	3499
Rob BASE	695
Marty ROBBINS	1623
Rockie ROBBINS	1774
The ROBBS	3540
Robbie ROBERTSON	1279
Freddy ROBINSON	2721
Smokey ROBINSON	229
Tom ROBINSON Band	2329
Vicki Sue ROBINSON	957
Wanda ROBINSON	2783
The ROCHES	1795
ROCK And HYDE	2177
The ROCKETS	1196
ROCKIN' SIDNEY	3233
ROCKPILE	1188
ROCKWELL	1046
Jimmie RODGERS	2613
Paul RODGERS	2665
RODNEY O & Joe COOLEY	3455
Johnny RODRIGUEZ	2430
Tommy ROE	674
ROGER	858
D.J. ROGERS	3075
Eric ROGERS & His Orchestra	3034
Kenny ROGERS	44
Kenny ROGERS & Dottie WEST	1752
Kenny ROGERS & The FIRST EDITION	690
ROLLING STONES	2
ROMAN HOLLIDAY	2325
The ROMANTICS	804
ROMEO'S DAUGHTER	3491
ROMEO VOID	1654
The RONETTES	2584
RONNY And The DAYTONAS	2872
Mick RONSON	1964
Linda RONSTADT	25
Franklin D. ROOSEVELT	3187
Biff ROSE	1748
ROSE GARDEN	3408
Jimmy ROSELLI	2187
ROSE ROYCE	433
ROSE TATTOO	3438
Diana ROSS	48
ROSSINGTON COLLINS BAND	724
ROTARY CONNECTION	1478

Act	Rank
David Lee ROTH	366
ROUGH DIAMOND	2483
Demis ROUSSOS	3149
John ROWLES	3532
ROXETTE	710
ROXY MUSIC	563
Billy Joe ROYAL	2113
ROYAL GUARDSMEN	1343
ROYAL PHILHARMONIC Orchestra	461
ROYAL SCOTS DRAGOON GUARDS	1502
The RUBBERBANDITS	2088
RUBICON	2809
David RUFFIN	721
Jimmy RUFFIN	2241
Mason RUFFNER	2052
RUFUS	189
The RUMOUR	2273
The RUNAWAYS	3105
Todd RUNDGREN	483
RUN-D.M.C.	282
RUNNER	3173
RUSH	125
Jennifer RUSH	2591
Merrilee RUSH	3329
Tom RUSH	1118
Patrice RUSHEN	684
Bobby RUSSELL	3278
Brenda RUSSELL	1090
Leon RUSSELL	232
Leon & Mary RUSSELL	1249
The RUSTIX	3495
Mike RUTHERFORD	2395
The RUTLES	2074
Bobby RYDELL	2142
Mitch RYDER And The DETROIT WHEELS	742
S	
Sue SAAD And The NEXT	2467
SAD CAFÉ	1820
SADE	255
SSgt Barry SADLER	616
SA-FIRE	1515
SAGA	976
Carole Bayer SAGER	1691
Mort SAHL	2843
Doug SAHM And Band	2562
SAILCAT	1578
Buffy SAINTE-MARIE	1647
SAINT TROPEZ	1768
Soupy SALES	2168
SALSOUL Orchestra	566
SALT-N-PEPA	795
SAM & DAVE	1063
Joe SAMPLE	881
SAM THE SHAM And The PHARAOHS	1261
David SANBORN	546
The SANDALS	2215
Pharoah SANDERS	2666
Tony SANDLER And Ralph YOUNG	1777
The SANDPIPERS	783
SANFORD/TOWNSEND Band	1633
SAN FRANCISCO Symphony	2609
Samantha SANG	1587
SAN SEBASTIAN Strings	508
SANTA ESMERALDA	940
Mongo SANTAMARIA	1115
SANTANA	26

Act	Rank
Carlos SANTANA	705
SARAYA	1712
Father Guido SARDUCCI	3405
Joe SATRIANI	553
Esther SATTERFIELD	3212
SATURDAY NIGHT BAND	2105
Merl SAUNDERS	3328
SAVAGE GRACE	2981
Telly SAVALAS	2400
SAVATAGE	2078
SAVOY BROWN	669
SAWYER BROWN	2698
SAXON	2166
Leo SAYER	466
Boz SCAGGS	157
SCANDAL	789
Joey SCARBURY	2459
SCARLETT & BLACK	2453
Michael SCHENKER Group	1418
Lalo SCHIFRIN	1412
Peter SCHILLING	1702
Timothy B. SCHMIT	2306
John SCHNEIDER	1176
Neal SCHON	2536
Neal SCHON & Jan HAMMER	2070
SCHOOLLY D	3373
Diane SCHUUR	2881
Eddie SCHWARTZ	3276
SCORPIONS	221
Christopher SCOTT	3226
Marilyn SCOTT	3285
Peggy SCOTT & Jo Jo BENSON	3257
Tom SCOTT & The L.A. EXPRESS	706
Gil SCOTT-HERON	1642
Gil SCOTT-HERON & Brian JACKSON	953
SCREAMING BLUE MESSIAHS	2841
SCRITTI POLITTI	1443
SCRUFFY THE CAT	3122
Earl SCRUGGS Revue	2082
Johnny SEA	3302
SEA HAGS	3048
SEA LEVEL	1079
Dan SEALS	2027
SEALS & CROFTS	136
The SEARCHERS	1149
Marvin SEASE	2256
SEATRAIN	1293
SEAWIND	1683
John SEBASTIAN	831
Neil SEDAKA	462
SEDUCTION	1146
The SEEDS	2124
Pete SEEGER	1314
The SEEKERS	828
George SEGAL	3526
Bob SEGER	51
The SELECTER	3205
Michael SEMBELLO	2432
SERENDIPITY SINGERS	919
Brian SETZER	1546
707	2428
7 SECONDS	2362
Doc SEVERINSEN	2456
Doc SEVERINSEN And The TONIGHT SHOW Orchestra	1719
SEX PISTOLS	2175
Charlie SEXTON	1005
Phil SEYMOUR	1953
SHADOWFAX	1618
SHADOWS OF KNIGHT	1708

Act	Rank
SHAKTI With John McLAUGHLIN	3035
SHALAMAR	488
SHA NA NA	1139
The SHANGRI-LAS	2772
SHANICE	2417
Bud SHANK	1684
Ravi SHANKAR	1366
SHANNON	1135
Del SHANNON	2422
Feargal SHARKEY	2236
SHARKS	3323
Marlena SHAW	1650
Roland SHAW Orchestra	1509
Sandie SHAW	2944
Tommy SHAW	1449
SHEILA E.	768
Pete SHELLEY	2398
Ricky Van SHELTON	1268
T.G. SHEPPARD	1928
The SHERBS	2037
SHERIFF	1939
Allan SHERMAN	445
Bobby SHERMAN	359
SHINEHEAD	3354
SHIRLEY (& COMPANY)	3224
Michelle SHOCKED	1244
SHOCKING BLUE	1543
SHOES	1803
SHOOTING STAR	1312
Bobby SHORT	2958
Wayne SHORTER	3307
SHOTGUN	2803
SHOTGUN MESSIAH	1985
SHRIEKBACK	2385
Michael SHRIEVE	2110
SHY	3522
Jane SIBERRY	2866
SIDE EFFECT	1591
SIDEWINDERS	3199
SIEGEL-SCHWALL Band	2610
Bunny SIGLER	1808
SIGUE SIGUE SPUTNIK	2513
The SILENCERS	2748
SILK	3434
Beverly SILLS	2681
SILVER	2823
Horace SILVER Quintet	2403
SILVER APPLES	3406
SILVER CONDOR	2378
SILVER CONVENTION	609
Shel SILVERSTEIN	2810
Gene SIMMONS	1038
Jumpin' Gene SIMMONS	3005
Patrick SIMMONS	2134
Richard SIMMONS	1410
Carly SIMON	113
Joe SIMON	1107
Paul SIMON	92
SIMON & GARFUNKEL	24
Nina SIMONE	1475
SIMPLE MINDS	602
SIMPLY RED	521
Valerie SIMPSON	2525
Frank SINATRA	49
Frank SINATRA & Count BASIE	613
Nancy SINATRA	378
Pete SINFIELD	3284
SINGING NUN	471
SIOUXSIE & The BANSHEES	1481
SIR DOUGLAS Quintet	1900

Act	Rank
Sir Lord BALTIMORE	3486
Sir MIX-A-LOT	1020
SISTER SLEDGE	504
SISTERS OF MERCY	2065
Ricky SKAGGS	1436
SKID ROW	389
SKY	2192
SKY (2)	2976
SKYLARK	2119
SKYY	702
SLADE	909
SLAVE	604
SLAYER	1532
Percy SLEDGE	1310
Grace SLICK	1053
SLICK RICK	1099
SLY & THE FAMILY STONE	127
SLY FOX	1427
Millie SMALL	3004
SMALL FACES/FACES	527
SMITH	896
Cal SMITH	3164
Connie SMITH	2876
Frankie SMITH	1876
Hurricane SMITH	1703
Jerry SMITH	3493
Jimmy SMITH	335
Kate SMITH	1159
Kathy SMITH	2678
Lonnie SMITH	3426
Lonnie Liston SMITH	910
O.C. SMITH	722
Patti SMITH	668
Rex SMITH	1113
Sammi SMITH	1313
The SMITHEREENS	713
The SMITHS	887
SMOKESTACK LIGHTNIN'	3488
SMOKIE	3043
SMOTHERS BROTHERS	636
Patty SMYTH	1868
SNAIL	2344
SNEAKER	2313
SNIFF 'N' The TEARS	1464
Phoebe SNOW	356
SO	2554
Gino SOCCIO	1651
SOFT CELL	808
SOFT MACHINE	2685
SONNY & CHER	243
SONS OF CHAMPLIN	1840
SOPWITH "CAMEL"	3496
S.O.S. BAND	660
David SOUL	1383
SOUL CHILDREN	2552
SOULFUL STRINGS	1311
SOUL SURVIVORS	2399
SOUL II SOUL	620
SOUNDS OF SUNSHINE	3054
SOUNDS ORCHESTRAL	1145
Joe SOUTH	1305
J.D. SOUTHER	1344
SOUTHER, HILLMAN, FURAY Band	883
SOUTHERN COMFORT	3462
SOUTHSIDE JOHNNY & The ASBURY JUKES	907
Red SOVINE	2600
SPANDAU BALLET	985
SPANKY And OUR GANG	1034
SPARKS	1353

Act	Rank
SPECIAL ED	1699
The SPECIALS	1637
Paul SPEER	2827
Judson SPENCE	2815
Tracie SPENCER	2289
Jimmie SPHEERIS	2727
SPIDER	2458
SPIDERS FROM MARS	3498
SPINAL TAP	2646
SPINNERS	209
SPIRAL STARECASE	1769
SPIRIT	567
SPLINTER	1995
SPLIT ENZ	871
SPOOKY TOOTH	892
The SPORTS	3481
Dusty SPRINGFIELD	1228
Rick SPRINGFIELD	184
Bruce SPRINGSTEEN	27
SPYRO GYRA	365
SPYS	2731
SQUEEZE	586
Billy SQUIER	224
Chris SQUIRE	1940
SRC	2262
STACEY Q	1479
STACKRIDGE	3063
Jim STAFFORD	1406
Terry STAFFORD	2349
STAGE DOLLS	2473
STALLION	3077
STAMPEDERS	2993
Joe STAMPLEY	3392
The STANDELLS	1767
STANKY BROWN Group	2973
Michael STANLEY Band	968
Paul STANLEY	1296
Mavis STAPLES	3288
Pop STAPLES	3382
STAPLE SINGERS	630
STARBUCK	1916
STARCASTLE	1661
STARGARD	1434
STARLAND VOCAL BAND	979
STARPOINT	1178
Brenda K. STARR	1580
Edwin STARR	1126
Ringo STARR	329
STARS ON	898
STARZ	1693
STATLER BROTHERS	1271
Candi STATON	1890
STATUS QUO	2812
STEADY B	2964
STEALERS WHEEL	1551
STEALIN HORSES	2615
STEAM	2032
STEEL BREEZE	1562
STEELEYE SPAN	2817
STEEL PULSE	2009
STEELY DAN	117
David STEINBERG	3159
Jim STEINMAN	1602
Van STEPHENSON	1742
STEPPENWOLF	110
Cat STEVENS	57
Ray STEVENS	841
Steve STEVENS ATOMIC PLAYBOYS	2509
B.W. STEVENSON	1713
Stevie B	1194

Act	Rank
Al STEWART	347
Amii STEWART	1125
Billy STEWART	2191
Gary STEWART	3268
Jermaine STEWART	1186
John STEWART	761
Rod STEWART	19
Wynn STEWART	2951
Stephen STILLS	315
Stephen STILLS & MANASSAS	652
STING	312
Sonny STITT	3385
STONE CITY BAND	2616
STONE FURY	2632
The STOOGES	2060
Paul STOOKEY	1573
STORIES	1333
George STRAIT	966
Billy STRANGE	2771
The STRANGELOVES	3315
The STRANGLERS	3272
STRAWBERRY ALARM CLOCK	1024
STRAWBS	1246
STRAY CATS	349
Meryl STREEP	3487
Janey STREET	2950
STREETS	2856
Barbra STREISAND	3
The STRIKERS	3294
Jud STRUNK	2634
STRYPER	653
STUFF	1926
STYLE COUNCIL	1420
The STYLISTICS	328
STYX	60
SUAVE	2301
The SUGARCUBES	1385
SUGARHILL GANG	1676
SUGARLOAF	963
SUICIDAL TENDENCIES	1855
Kasim SULTON	3518
Donna SUMMER	59
Henry LEE SUMMER	1318
Andy SUMMERS & Robert FRIPP	2002
Bill SUMMERS & SUMMERS HEAT	1709
SUN	1438
SUNNY & The SUNLINERS	3110
SUNSHINE COMPANY	2570
SUPERSAX	2845
SUPERTRAMP	121
Diana ROSS & The SUPREMES And The TEMPTATIONS	287
The SUPREMES & FOUR TOPS	1792
The SUPREMES/ Diana ROSS And The SUPREMES	32
The SUPREMES	711
SURFACE	1094
The SURFARIS	2162
SURVIVOR	369
SUSAN	3109
SUSAN of SESAME STREET	2084
SUTHERLAND BROTHERS And QUIVER	1954
Billy SWAN	1235
Brad SWANSON	3404
Keith SWEAT	633
SWEAT BAND	2788
The SWEET	645
Rachel SWEET	1771
SWEET INSPIRATIONS	2688

Act	Rank
SWEET SENSATION	2885
SWEET SENSATION (2)	1504
SWEET TEE	2705
SWEET THUNDER	2383
SWEETWATER	3490
SWINGING BLUE JEANS	2563
SWINGIN' MEDALLIONS	2202
SWINGLE SINGERS	661
SWING OUT SISTER	948
SWITCH	733
SYBIL	1849
Keith SYKES	2593
Sylvain SYLVAIN	2516
Foster SYLVERS	2965
The SYLVERS	1092
SYLVESTER	861
SYLVIA	2106
SYLVIA (2)	1273
SYNDICATE OF SOUND	3293
SYNERGY	1597
SYREETA	1519
The SYSTEM	1364
Gabor SZABO	2120

T

Act	Rank
TACO	1218
TAKE 6	1818
TALKING HEADS	181
TALK TALK	1233
TA MARA & The SEEN	1582
TANGERINE DREAM	1741
TANGIER	2030
Marc TANNER BAND	2725
TANTRUM	3448
TARNEY/SPENCER Band	2954
TASTE	2390
A TASTE OF HONEY	571
TAVARES	583
TAXXI	2826
Alex TAYLOR	3436
Andy TAYLOR	1731
James TAYLOR	43
Johnnie TAYLOR	542
Kate TAYLOR	2436
Little Johnny TAYLOR	3325
Livingston TAYLOR	1724
Mick TAYLOR	2830
R. Dean TAYLOR	3533
Roger TAYLOR	2267
The T-BONES	2183
T-CONNECTION	1254
TEARDROP EXPLODES	2712
TEARS FOR FEARS	238
TECHNOTRONIC	776
TEE SET	2916
Kiri TE KANAWA	2414
Nino TEMPO & April STEVENS	1975
The TEMPTATIONS	8
10cc	627
Toni TENNILLE	2575
10,000 MANIACS	624
TEN WHEEL DRIVE With Genya RAVAN	2069
TEN YEARS AFTER	305
Robert TEPPER	2890
Sonny TERRY & Brownie McGHEE	3280
Tony TERRY	2339
TESLA	588
TESTAMENT	1815

Act	Rank
Joe TEX	872
TEXAS	2087
TEXTONES	3094
The THE	1886
THEE PROPHETS	3140
THEM	1517
Mike THEODORE Orchestra	3388
THEY MIGHT BE GIANTS	2010
THIN LIZZY	714
3rd BASS	1445
THIRD POWER	3475
THIRD WORLD	1030
.38 SPECIAL	285
B.J. THOMAS	424
Carla THOMAS	1373
Irma THOMAS	2608
Lillo THOMAS	3435
Ray THOMAS	1919
Rufus THOMAS	2644
Timmy THOMAS	1764
Richard THOMPSON	2050
Robbin THOMPSON Band	2891
Sue THOMPSON	3194
THOMPSON TWINS	446
Ali THOMSON	2086
Big Mama THORNTON	3467
George THOROGOOD & The DESTROYERS	411
Billy THORPE	1398
THP ORCHESTRA	1772
3	2441
3° DEGREES	1206
THREE DOG NIGHT	40
The THREE O'CLOCK	2696
THREE TIMES DOPE	2367
THRILLS	3375
THUNDERCLAP NEWMAN	2766
TIERRA	1435
TIFFFANY	352
Tanita TIKARAM	1656
Johnny TILLOTSON	1864
'TIL TUESDAY	847
TIMBUK 3	1347
The TIME	541
TIMES TWO	2607
TIN MACHINE	1603
TIN TIN	3530
TINY TIM	1015
Cal TJADER	1461
TKA	2601
TKO	3393
TNT	1746
TOBY BEAU	1512
TODAY	1873
The TOKENS	2957
Isao TOMITA	899
Lily TOMLIN	781
TOMMY TUTONE	1026
Gary TOMS Empire	3270
TOM TOM CLUB	971
TONE-LOC	575
Oscar TONEY, Jr.	3318
TONY! TONI! TONE!	1484
TOO SHORT	894
TOOTS And The MAYTALS	2354
TORA TORA	1537
TORONTO	2787
Richard TORRANCE And EUREKA	2043
Peter TOSH	1195
TOTO	217

Act	Rank
Wayne TOUPS & ZYDECAJUN	3334
TOWER OF POWER	453
Pete TOWNSHEND	398
Simon TOWNSHEND	3091
The TOYS	2510
T'PAU	1490
TRAFFIC	186
The TRAMMPS	830
TRANSVISION VAMP	2629
TRAPEZE	2565
The TRASHMEN	1966
TRAVELING WILBURYS	487
Mary TRAVERS	1362
Pat TRAVERS	607
Randy TRAVIS	403
John TRAVOLTA	1217
TREAT HER RIGHT	2245
The TREMELOES	2703
T. REX	682
TRINERE & FRIENDS	3520
TRIUMPH	387
TRIUMVIRAT	1001
The TROGGS	1536
TROOP	2702
TROOPER	3230
TROPEA	2370
TROUBADOURS Du ROI BAUDOUIN	3165
TROUBLE FUNK	2508
Robin TROWER	265
Andrea TRUE Connection	1522
The TRUTH	2692
Gil TRYTHALL	2940
TSOL	3456
The TUBES	569
TUCK & PATTI	2831
Louise TUCKER	2611
Tanya TUCKER	1339
TUFF DARTS	2924
Ike & Tina TURNER	578
Joe Lynn TURNER	2764
Spyder TURNER	3220
Tina TURNER	218
Stanley TURRENTINE	748
The TURTLES	581
TUXEDO JUNCTION	1441
TWENNYNINE	1572
24-7 SPYZ	2244
20/20	1961
Dwight TWILLEY	1082
TWIN HYPE	2693
TWISTED SISTER	637
Conway TWITTY	1093
Conway TWITTY & Loretta LYNN	1542
2 LIVE CREW	574
TYCOON	1625
Bonnie TYLER	619
The TYMES	2330
McCoy TYNER	1533
TYZIK	3142

U

Act	Rank
UB40	539
UFO	573
U.K.	1316
Tracey ULLMAN	1503
ULTIMATE	2590
ULTIMATE SPINACH	1323
ULTRAVOX	1541
UNDERGROUND SUNSHINE	3188
The UNDERTONES	2879
UNDERWORLD	2242
UNDISPUTED TRUTH	1123
The UNFORGIVEN	3463
UNICORN	2756
UNITED STATES OF AMERICA	3000
UNLIMITED TOUCH	2797
The UNTOUCHABLES	2931
UP WITH PEOPLE	1984
Midge URE	2083
URIAH HEEP	413
USA-EUROPEAN CONNECTION	1762
USA For AFRICA	826
UTFO	1381
UTOPIA	707
U2	84

V

Act	Rank
VAIN	2888
Jerry VALE	473
Ritchie VALENS	2596
Dave VALENTIN	3156
Frankie VALLI	901
VANDENBERG	1895
Luther VANDROSS	205
Theo VANESS	2842
VANGELIS	456
VAN HALEN	56
VANILLA FUDGE	273
VANITY	1071
Gino VANNELLI	380
Randy VANWARMER	2254
Johnny Van ZANT Band	1476
The VAPORS	1458
Sarah VAUGHAN	3124
Stevie Ray VAUGHAN And DOUBLE TROUBLE	523
Billy VAUGHN and His Orchestra	550
Billy VAUGHN Singers	2100
Bobby VEE	1921
Suzanne VEGA	832
Tata VEGA	2903
Martha VELEZ	2310
VELVET UNDERGROUND	1991
The VENTURES	191
Billy VERA & The BEATERS	1172
Tom VERLAINE	3338
VESTA	2619
VICTORY	3337
VILLAGE PEOPLE	210
VILLAGE STOMPERS	917
Vinnie VINCENT INVASION	1284
Bobby VINTON	292
VIO-LENCE	3114
VIOLENT FEMMES	1662
VISAGE	3225
The VISCOUNTS	3320
Joe VITALE	3305
VITAMIN Z	3398
VIXEN	1154
The VOGUES	739
VOICES OF EAST HARLEM	3362
VOIVOD	2268
Andreas VOLLENWEIDER	897
Roger VOUDOURIS	3240
VOYAGE	1075
V.S.O.P.	2792

W

Act	Rank
Jack WAGNER	1329
Porter WAGONER	2737
Porter WAGONER and Dolly PARTON	2097
The WAIKIKIS	2488
The WAILERS	2902
Loudon WAINWRIGHT III	2005
John WAITE	657
The WAITRESSES	1392
Tom WAITS	1419
Rick WAKEMAN	434
Narada Michael WALDEN	1335
David T. WALKER	2729
Jerry Jeff WALKER	1141
Jimmie WALKER	2372
Jr. WALKER & The ALL STARS	743
Jerry WALLACE	2439
WALL OF VOODOO	1624
Joe WALSH	251
Steve WALSH	2777
Walter WANDERLEY	1070
WANG CHUNG	803
Dexter WANSEL	2555
WAR	107
Anita WARD	943
Steve WARINER	3473
Frank WARING	3231
WARLOCK	1739
Jennifer WARNES	1121
WARRANT	587
Rusty WARREN	1641
Dionne WARWICK	72
Dinah WASHINGTON	2897
Grover WASHINGTON Jr.	156
WAS (NOT WAS)	1286
W.A.S.P.	932
The WATERBOYS	1732
WATERFRONT	2397
Muddy WATERS	1552
Roger WATERS	1167
Jody WATLEY	441
Doc WATSON	3377
Johnny Guitar WATSON	694
Ernie WATTS	2669
WA WA NEE	2261
WAX	2486
Fee WAYBILL	3002
John WAYNE	1936
WAYSTED	3466
WEATHER GIRLS	2295
Jim WEATHERLY	2137
WEATHER REPORT	498
Dennis WEAVER	3454
WE FIVE	1345
Bob WEIR	1450
Tim WEISBERG	854
Tim WEISBERG Band	2017
Eric WEISSBERG	1008
Bob WELCH	525
Lenny WELCH	2272
Lawrence WELK	427
Freddy WELLER	2659
Orson WELLES	1776
Mary WELLS	974
WENDY and LISA	1971
David WERNER	2121
Fred WESLEY & The HORNY HORNS	3195
Dottie WEST	2290
Leslie WEST	1782
Mae WEST	2851
WEST, BRUCE & LAING	1174
WET WET WET	2761
WET WILLIE	1072
Kirk WHALUM	2657
WHAM!	286
WHAT IS THIS	3364
Billy Edd WHEELER	3182
WHEN IN ROME	1812
The WHISPERS	327
Ian WHITCOMB	2386
Barry WHITE	201
Karyn WHITE	807
Lenny WHITE	3265
Maurice WHITE	1978
Tony Joe WHITE	1511
WHITE LION	486
WHITE PLAINS	3128
WHITESNAKE	207
WHITE WOLF	2564
Margaret WHITING	2517
Keith WHITLEY	2189
Bobby WHITLOCK	2491
Slim WHITMAN	3026
Roger WHITTAKER	1058
The WHO	39
WHODINI	696
WICHITA TRAIN WHISTLE	2724
WIDOWMAKER	2687
Jane WIEDLIN	1829
Rusty WIER	1918
WILBURN BROTHERS	3208
WILD CHERRY	676
Danny WILDE	2991
Eugene WILDE	2271
Kim WILDE	1133
Matthew WILDER	1852
WILD MAN STEVE	2978
WILD ONES	3351
WILD TURKEY	3412
WILL And The KILL	2730
Andy WILLIAMS	46
Danny WILLIAMS	2986
Deniece WILLIAMS	484
Don WILLIAMS	1189
Hank WILLIAMS Jr.	386
Hank WILLIAMS Sr.	3395
Lenny WILLIAMS	1324
Mason WILLIAMS	790
Paul WILLIAMS	1414
Robin WILLIAMS	925
Roger WILLIAMS	326
Tony WILLIAMS	2597
Vanessa WILLIAMS	1147
WILLIE & The POOR BOYS	2364
WILLIE, WAYLON, JOHNNY & KRIS	1723
Bruce WILLIS	1105
WILL TO POWER	1665
WILMER And The DUKES	3232
Al WILSON	1783
Brian WILSON	1884
Carl WILSON	3419
Dennis WILSON	2426
Flip WILSON	564
Jackie WILSON	2420
J. Frank WILSON and The CAVALIERS	2079

Act	Rank
Nancy WILSON	120
The WINANS	2495
BeBe & CeCe WINANS	1835
Angela WINBUSH	1613
Jesse WINCHESTER	1915
WIND IN THE WILLOWS	3397
WING And A PRAYER FIFE And DRUM CORPS.	1617
WINGER	654
Pete WINGFIELD	3134
George WINSTON	671
The WINSTONS	1927
Edgar WINTER	316
Johnny WINTER	408
Paul WINTER	2638
Jonathan WINTERS	3137
Robert WINTERS and FALL	2200
Steve WINWOOD	138
WIRE	2781
WIRE TRAIN	2699
WISHBONE ASH	1018
WITCH QUEEN	2985
Bill WITHERS	391
Jimmy WITHERSPOON	3365
Peter WOLF	1104
Bobby WOMACK	464
The WOMENFOLK	2883
Stevie WONDER	11
Brenton WOOD	3447

Act	Rank
Ronnie WOOD	1607
Roy WOOD	3135
The WOODENTOPS	3250
Stevie WOODS	2377
Bruce WOOLLEY & The CAMERA CLUB	3423
WORLD PARTY	1432
WRABIT	2855
WRATHCHILD AMERICA	3287
Link WRAY & His RAY MEN	3279
Bernard WRIGHT	2108
Betty WRIGHT	981
Charles WRIGHT And The WATTS 103rd STREET Band	1851
Gary WRIGHT	381
Steven WRIGHT	3516
Bill WYMAN	2093
Tammy WYNETTE	592
X	
X	1274
XAVIER	2755
XTC	779
XYMOX	2994
XYZ	2003

Act	Rank
Y	
YACHTS	3308
Stomu YAMASHTA	2324
Y&T	1084
"Weird Al" YANKOVIC	744
Glenn YARBROUGH	913
YARBROUGH & PEOPLES	975
The YARDBIRDS	752
Peter YARROW	2811
YAZ	1595
YELLO	2146
YELLOWJACKETS	2568
YELLOW MAGIC ORCHESTRA	1845
YES	88
YIPES!!	3221
Dwight YOAKAM	921
Barry YOUNG	2116
Jesse Colin YOUNG	597
John Paul YOUNG	2058
Neil YOUNG	63
Paul YOUNG	728
YOUNG AMERICANS	3251
Lonnie YOUNGBLOOD	3207
The YOUNGBLOODS	1164
YOUNG-HOLT UNLIMITED	821
YOUNG M.C.	629
YUTAKA	3198

Act	Rank
Z	
Pia ZADORA	2214
Michael ZAGER Band	2212
ZAGER & EVANS	1382
ZAPP	802
Frank ZAPPA	204
ZEBRA	1270
ZENO	2470
ZEPHYR	1346
Warren ZEVON	599
ZODIAC MINDWARP & The LOVE REACTION	2321
The ZOMBIES	1394
ZZ TOP	86

The Acts Special Lists

50 Highest Charting Acts By Raw Score Within Each Year

	1964	1965	1966	1967	1968
1	The BEATLES	The BEATLES	Herb ALPERT/TJB	Herb ALPERT/TJB	SIMON & GARFUNKEL
2	Barbra STREISAND	BEACH BOYS	The BEATLES	The MONKEES	Herb ALPERT/TJB
3	Al HIRT	Barbra STREISAND	Frank SINATRA	Bill COSBY	CREAM
4	BEACH BOYS	ROLLING STONES	ROLLING STONES	ROLLING STONES	Jimi HENDRIX EXPERIENCE
5	Nancy WILSON	HERMAN'S HERMITS	Bill COSBY	The BEATLES	Glen CAMPBELL
6	PETER, PAUL & MARY	The SUPREMES	Barbra STREISAND	MAMAS & The PAPAS	The BEATLES
7	Henry MANCINI/Orch	RIGHTEOUS BROTHERS	The SUPREMES	The TEMPTATIONS	Aretha FRANKLIN
8	Elvis PRESLEY	Al HIRT	MAMAS & The PAPAS	(Diana ROSS)/SUPREMES	The DOORS
9	Andy WILLIAMS	Andy WILLIAMS	HERMAN'S HERMITS	Aretha FRANKLIN	RASCALS
10	Dave CLARK Five	Herb ALPERT/TJB	The ANIMALS	The DOORS	The MONKEES
11	Louis ARMSTRONG	Elvis PRESLEY	BEACH BOYS	Frank SINATRA	Diana ROSS/SUPREMES
12	Dean MARTIN	Dean MARTIN	Paul REVERE/RAIDERS	Lou RAWLS	Bill COSBY
13	John GARY	Bob DYLAN	Lou RAWLS	YOUNG RASCALS	The TEMPTATIONS
14	NEW CHRISTY MINSTRELS	Roger MILLER	RIGHTEOUS BROTHERS	FOUR TOPS	Otis REDDING
15	4 SEASONS	Nat King COLE	Eddy ARNOLD	Paul REVERE/RAIDERS	Paul MAURIAT/Orch
16	SINGING NUN	PETER, PAUL & MARY	Al MARTINO	Andy WILLIAMS	Dionne WARWICK
17	Johnny MATHIS	Bert KAEMPFERT/Orch	Andy WILLIAMS	LOVIN' SPOONFUL	Sergio MENDES/BRASIL '66
18	Al MARTINO	Frank SINATRA	The TEMPTATIONS	JEFFERSON AIRPLANE	VANILLA FUDGE
19	Jimmy SMITH	Nancy WILSON	SSgt Barry SADLER	Roger WILLIAMS	MAMAS & The PAPAS
20	Jack JONES	Dave CLARK Five	Dean MARTIN	HERMAN'S HERMITS	Engelbert HUMPERDINCK
21	Trini LOPEZ	Henry MANCINI/Orch	Ray CONNIFF/Orch/Chor	The ASSOCIATION	STEPPENWOLF
22	The KINGSMEN	Robert GOULET	Elvis PRESLEY	Ray CONNIFF/Orch/Chor	BIG BROTHER/ HOLDING COMPANY
23	John Fitzgerald KENNEDY	SONNY & CHER	4 SEASONS	Sergio MENDES/BRASIL '66	The LETTERMEN
24	Joan BAEZ	Joan BAEZ	Dave CLARK Five	Eric BURDON/ANIMALS	Bob DYLAN
25	The IMPRESSIONS	The VENTURES	The VENTURES	Ed AMES	Andy WILLIAMS
26	SWINGLE SINGERS	John GARY	Nancy SINATRA	Dionne WARWICK	José FELICIANO
27	Bobby VINTON	Ramsey LEWIS Trio	Bob DYLAN	Claudine LONGET	Ed AMES
28	Ray CHARLES	Stan GETZ	SIMON & GARFUNKEL	Engelbert HUMPERDINCK	Wes MONTGOMERY
29	Frank SINATRA	The KINGSMEN	The MONKEES	Dean MARTIN	CHAMBERS BROTHERS
30	Jim REEVES	Trini LOPEZ	Ramsey LEWIS Trio	Bobbie GENTRY	Ray CONNIFF/Orch/Chor
31	ROLLING STONES	Jack JONES	Roger MILLER	The BYRDS	DONOVAN
32	The VENTURES	The KINKS	LOVIN' SPOONFUL	Eddy ARNOLD	Gary PUCKETT/UNION GAP
33	SMOTHERS BROTHERS	The LETTERMEN	Johnny MATHIS	4 SEASONS	Bobby GOLDSBORO
34	Ray CHARLES Singers	Tony BENNETT	Nancy WILSON	Elvis PRESLEY	IRON BUTTERFLY
35	Johnny RIVERS	Jimmy SMITH	Tony BENNETT	Bob DYLAN	FOUR TOPS
36	Stan GETZ	Petula CLARK	The BYRDS	Lawrence WELK/Orch	ROLLING STONES
37	Joao GILBERTO	Sam COOKE	Smokey ROBINSON/ MIRACLES	Johnny RIVERS	JEFFERSON AIRPLANE
38	KINGSTON TRIO	CHAD & JEREMY	Ray CHARLES	Davie ALLAN/ARROWS	BEE GEES
39	SERENDIPITY SINGERS	MANTOVANI	The KINKS	MIDNIGHT STRING QUARTET	Smokey ROBINSON/ MIRACLES
40	James BROWN	Bobby VINTON	Gary LEWIS/PLAYBOYS	The HOLLIES	Dean MARTIN
41	Mary WELLS	Petula CLARK	Tom LEHRER	SIMON & GARFUNKEL	Richard HARRIS
42	Jerry VALE	Sam COOKE	Roger WILLIAMS	SONNY & CHER	Hugo MONTENEGRO
43	Lawrence WELK/Orch	CHAD & JEREMY	PETER, PAUL & MARY	NEW VAUDEVILLE BAND	Barbra STREISAND
44	Bob DYLAN	MANTOVANI	Bert KAEMPFERT/Orch	VANILLA FUDGE	Johnny RIVERS
45	Chad MITCHELL Trio	Bobby VINTON	SONNY & CHER	Jimi HENDRIX EXPERIENCE	Judy COLLINS
46	HOLLYRIDGE STRINGS	Johnny RIVERS	Jimmy SMITH	PETER, PAUL & MARY	CANNED HEAT
47	Tony BENNETT	Billy VAUGHN/Orch	James BROWN	BEACH BOYS	Johnny CASH
48	Frank SINATRA/Count BASIE	GERRY/PACEMAKERS	The ASSOCIATION	Jim NABORS	Vikki CARR
49	Allan SHERMAN	The IMPRESSIONS	FOUR TOPS	Wes MONTGOMERY	The TURTLES
50	Roy ORBISON	Louis ARMSTRONG	JACK JONES	Mitch RYDER/ DETROIT WHEELS	Nancy SINATRA

	1969	1970	1971	1972	1973
1	Tom JONES	The BEATLES	Carole KING	Carole KING	Elton JOHN
2	Glen CAMPBELL	CREEDENCE CLEARWATER	PARTRIDGE FAMILY	Roberta FLACK	DEEP PURPLE
3	The BEATLES	LED ZEPPELIN	CHICAGO	ROLLING STONES	Stevie WONDER
4	IRON BUTTERFLY	CHICAGO	CARPENTERS	Elton JOHN	LED ZEPPELIN
5	BLOOD, SWEAT & TEARS	SANTANA	SANTANA	CHICAGO	WAR
6	CREEDENCE CLEARWATER	JACKSON 5	James TAYLOR	Cat STEVENS	PINK FLOYD
7	Johnny CASH	THREE DOG NIGHT	Elton JOHN	YES	The BEATLES
8	The TEMPTATIONS	GRAND FUNK RAILROAD	THREE DOG NIGHT	JETHRO TULL	SEALS & CROFTS
9	CREAM	SIMON & GARFUNKEL	GRAND FUNK RAILROAD	Neil YOUNG	Diana ROSS
10	LED ZEPPELIN	Tom JONES	Isaac HAYES	Don McLEAN	Neil DIAMOND
11	Diana ROSS/SUPREMES/ TEMPTATIONS	The WHO	Cat STEVENS	Al GREEN	Al GREEN
12	STEPPENWOLF	CROSBY, STILLS, NASH & YOUNG	BLACK SABBATH	CHEECH & CHONG	ROLLING STONES
13	DONOVAN	BLOOD, SWEAT & TEARS	Rod STEWART	ALICE COOPER (Grp)	ALLMAN BROTHERS Band
14	THREE DOG NIGHT	Johnny CASH	Janis JOPLIN	NILSSON	Carole KING
15	Jimi HENDRIX EXPERIENCE	Joe COCKER	SLY & THE FAMILY STONE	AMERICA	Carly SIMON
16	ROLLING STONES	The TEMPTATIONS	ROLLING STONES	Donny OSMOND	Helen REDDY
17	Bob DYLAN	Isaac HAYES	CROSBY, STILLS, NASH & YOUNG	Rod STEWART	DOOBIE BROTHERS
18	The ASSOCIATION	RARE EARTH	Paul & Linda McCARTNEY	MOODY BLUES	Elvis PRESLEY
19	Dionne WARWICK	5TH DIMENSION	JACKSON 5	JACKSON 5	BREAD
20	Elvis PRESLEY	Engelbert HUMPERDINCK	MOODY BLUES	The OSMONDS	Jim CROCE
21	Barbra STREISAND	Paul McCARTNEY	CREEDENCE CLEARWATER	GRAND FUNK RAILROAD	CHICAGO
22	Aretha FRANKLIN	MOODY BLUES	The WHO	ALLMAN BROTHERS Band	John DENVER
23	BLIND FAITH	James TAYLOR	George HARRISON	George HARRISON	JETHRO TULL
24	CROSBY, STILLS & NASH	ROLLING STONES	John LENNON/ PLASTIC ONO BAND	CARPENTERS	Cat STEVENS
25	BEE GEES	STEPPENWOLF	Jimi HENDRIX	Neil DIAMOND	CHEECH & CHONG
26	5TH DIMENSION	Neil DIAMOND	JETHRO TULL	BREAD	Edgar WINTER
27	Judy COLLINS	IRON BUTTERFLY	EMERSON, LAKE & PALMER	EMERSON, LAKE & PALMER	MOODY BLUES
28	Frank SINATRA	Bobby SHERMAN	Aretha FRANKLIN	Aretha FRANKLIN	Marvin GAYE
29	José FELICIANO	GUESS WHO	The DOORS	THREE DOG NIGHT	CARPENTERS
30	Sergio MENDES/BRASIL '66	Charley PRIDE	GUESS WHO	Donny HATHAWAY	ALICE COOPER (Grp)
31	The DOORS	The DOORS	Neil DIAMOND	The TEMPTATIONS	David BOWIE
32	SIMON & GARFUNKEL	The BAND	JEFFERSON AIRPLANE	Curtis MAYFIELD	LOGGINS & MESSINA
33	James BROWN	B.J. THOMAS	Elvis PRESLEY	Elvis PRESLEY	FOCUS
34	Henry MANCINI/Orch	Elvis PRESLEY	Stephen STILLS	Isaac HAYES	Paul McCARTNEY/WINGS
35	Engelbert HUMPERDINCK	Neil YOUNG	Marvin GAYE	Michael JACKSON	Bette MIDLER
36	Isaac HAYES	Glen CAMPBELL	The OSMONDS	LED ZEPPELIN	The TEMPTATIONS
37	The WHO	SLY & THE FAMILY STONE	Andy WILLIAMS	Leon RUSSELL	Paul SIMON
38	Andy WILLIAMS	Jimi HENDRIX	5TH DIMENSION	HUMBLE PIE	DEODATO
39	Diana ROSS /SUPREMES	Bob DYLAN	Barbra STREISAND	SANTANA	GRAND FUNK RAILROAD
40	The LETTERMEN	TRAFFIC	Curtis MAYFIELD	The CHI-LITES	George HARRISON
41	RASCALS	Aretha FRANKLIN	The TEMPTATIONS	Bill WITHERS	Gladys KNIGHT & The PIPS
42	CHICAGO	PETER, PAUL & MARY	JAMES GANG	Eric CLAPTON	STEELY DAN
43	Walter CARLOS	JETHRO TULL	Donny OSMOND	Paul SIMON	Joe WALSH
44	BIG BROTHER/ HOLDING COMPANY	Barbra STREISAND	LED ZEPPELIN	PARTRIDGE FAMILY	Curtis MAYFIELD
45	VANILLA FUDGE	CARPENTERS	Gordon LIGHTFOOT	George CARLIN	Leon RUSSELL
46	Bill COSBY	Michael PARKS	Roberta FLACK	Chuck BERRY	TRAFFIC
47	Tommy JAMES/SHONDELLS	CROSBY, STILLS & NASH	John DENVER	SONNY & CHER	URIAH HEEP
48	Charley PRIDE	John MAYALL	Ike & Tina TURNER	WAR	J. GEILS Band
49	SLY & THE FAMILY STONE	MOUNTAIN	Neil YOUNG	SIMON & GARFUNKEL	Roberta FLACK
50	SANTANA	MELANIE	STEPPENWOLF	Janis JOPLIN	Isaac HAYES

	1974	1975	1976	1977
1	John DENVER	Elton JOHN	Peter FRAMPTON	FLEETWOOD MAC
2	Elton JOHN	John DENVER	FLEETWOOD MAC	EAGLES
3	Jim CROCE	EAGLES	EAGLES	Linda RONSTADT
4	BACHMAN-TURNER OVERDRIVE	EARTH, WIND & FIRE	Paul McCARTNEY/WINGS	Barry MANILOW
5	Stevie WONDER	JEFFERSON STARSHIP	CHICAGO	Steve MILLER Band
6	Paul McCARTNEY/WINGS	OHIO PLAYERS	AEROSMITH	Stevie WONDER
7	CHICAGO	CHICAGO	EARTH, WIND & FIRE	KISS
8	Charlie RICH	Linda RONSTADT	George BENSON	The COMMODORES
9	LOGGINS & MESSINA	AVERAGE WHITE BAND/AWB	LED ZEPPELIN	BOSTON
10	Joni MITCHELL	LED ZEPPELIN	Boz SCAGGS	Barbra STREISAND
11	Marvin Hamlisch	Olivia NEWTON-JOHN	JEFFERSON STARSHIP	Peter FRAMPTON
12	Cat STEVENS	DOOBIE BROTHERS	John DENVER	ELECTRIC LIGHT ORCHESTRA
13	Gladys KNIGHT & The PIPS	PINK FLOYD	Bob DYLAN	BEE GEES
14	Barry WHITE	Janis IAN	AMERICA	Elvis PRESLEY
15	EMERSON, LAKE & PALMER	ISLEY BROTHERS	Steve MILLER Band	FOREIGNER
16	Maria MULDAUR	JETHRO TULL	David BOWIE	HEART
17	Neil DIAMOND	AMERICA	ELECTRIC LIGHT ORCHESTRA	KANSAS
18	Gordon LIGHTFOOT	ROLLING STONES	Stevie WONDER	James TAYLOR
19	DOOBIE BROTHERS	SPINNERS	The BEATLES	Shaun CASSIDY
20	Herbie HANCOCK	BEACH BOYS	Daryl HALL & John OATES	Paul McCARTNEY/WINGS
21	Mike OLDFIELD	Paul McCARTNEY/WINGS	KISS	Bob SEGER
22	SEALS & CROFTS	Bob DYLAN	Elton JOHN	Kris KRISTOFFERSON
23	Bob DYLAN	BACHMAN-TURNER OVERDRIVE	Diana ROSS	George BENSON
24	CHEECH & CHONG	DAWN/Tony ORLANDO	Gary WRIGHT	CROSBY, STILLS & NASH
25	OHIO PLAYERS	Barbra STREISAND	QUEEN	DOOBIE BROTHERS
26	The O'JAYS	Minnie RIPERTON	Barry MANILOW	Daryl HALL & John OATES
27	Olivia NEWTON-JOHN	Al GREEN	BEE GEES	Boz SCAGGS
28	BEACH BOYS	Bruce SPRINGSTEEN	Paul SIMON	ROSE ROYCE
29	Marvin GAYE	B.T. EXPRESS	CAPTAIN & TENNILLE	Rita COOLIDGE
30	Barbra STREISAND	Joni MITCHELL	Rod STEWART	Donna SUMMER
31	Frank ZAPPA	AEROSMITH	The COMMODORES	Rod STEWART
32	GRAND FUNK RAILROAD	Helen REDDY	ROLLING STONES	Marvin GAYE
33	ROLLING STONES	CAPTAIN & TENNILLE	Linda RONSTADT	The EMOTIONS
34	Helen REDDY	ZZ TOP	Helen REDDY	PINK FLOYD
35	PINK FLOYD	Grover WASHINGTON Jr.	BROTHERS JOHNSON	Jimmy BUFFETT
36	Eric CLAPTON	Barry MANILOW	PARLIAMENT	KC And The SUNSHINE BAND
37	David BOWIE	David BOWIE	Donna SUMMER	The BEATLES
38	EARTH, WIND & FIRE	ALICE COOPER (Solo)	HEART	SUPERTRAMP
39	CARPENTERS	George HARRISON	OHIO PLAYERS	BROTHERS JOHNSON
40	LYNYRD SKYNYRD	Neil SEDAKA	Natalie COLE	Al STEWART
41	BAD COMPANY	BAD COMPANY	Neil DIAMOND	ISLEY BROTHERS
42	AMERICA	The TEMPTATIONS	RUFUS	Thelma HOUSTON
43	Quincy JONES	Cat STEVENS	The O'JAYS	Alan PARSONS PROJECT
44	Carly SIMON	Phoebe SNOW	DOOBIE BROTHERS	CHICAGO
45	John LENNON	Joan BAEZ	Carole KING	Leo SAYER
46	DEEP PURPLE	FLEETWOOD MAC	Gordon LIGHTFOOT	STEELY DAN
47	Carole KING	WAR	BEACH BOYS	Ted NUGENT
48	Robin TROWER	KC And The SUNSHINE BAND	Marvin GAYE	Waylon JENNINGS
49	ALICE COOPER (Grp)	James TAYLOR	SEALS & CROFTS	John DENVER
50	LOVE UNLIMITED	LYNYRD SKYNYRD	BRASS CONSTRUCTION	PABLO CRUISE

	1978	1979	1980	1981
1	BEE GEES	Donna SUMMER	PINK FLOYD	REO SPEEDWAGON
2	Billy JOEL	SUPERTRAMP	Bob SEGER	Pat BENATAR
3	FOREIGNER	BEE GEES	Billy JOEL	AC/DC
4	Chuck MANGIONE	The CARS	Kenny ROGERS	STYX
5	The COMMODORES	VILLAGE PEOPLE	Pat BENATAR	JOURNEY
6	Eric CLAPTON	DOOBIE BROTHERS	Michael JACKSON	Kenny ROGERS
7	ROLLING STONES	CHEAP TRICK	QUEEN	The POLICE
8	STYX	EARTH, WIND & FIRE	Tom PETTY/HEARTBREAKERS	ROLLING STONES
9	Barry MANILOW	Billy JOEL	ROLLING STONES	FOREIGNER
10	STEELY DAN	LED ZEPPELIN	Christopher CROSS	John LENNON & Yoko ONO
11	Jackson BROWNE	STYX	EAGLES	RUSH
12	Linda RONSTADT	Rod STEWART	Diana ROSS	Neil DIAMOND
13	Donna SUMMER	DIRE STRAITS	Barbra STREISAND	Kim CARNES
14	Bob SEGER	The KNACK	Donna SUMMER	MOODY BLUES
15	EARTH, WIND & FIRE	Kenny ROGERS	Linda RONSTADT	Daryl HALL & John OATES
16	VILLAGE PEOPLE	Barbra STREISAND	Jackson BROWNE	Steve WINWOOD
17	KANSAS	PEACHES & HERB	Eric CLAPTON	Stevie NICKS
18	Andy GIBB	CHIC	Dan FOGELBERG	Rick JAMES
19	Rod STEWART	VAN HALEN	Willie NELSON	Grover WASHINGTON Jr.
20	FLEETWOOD MAC	BAD COMPANY	AC/DC	Christopher CROSS
21	Paul McCARTNEY/WINGS	FOREIGNER	The CARS	AIR SUPPLY
22	BOSTON	EAGLES	The COMMODORES	Barbra STREISAND
23	QUEEN	BLONDIE	Bette MIDLER	Bob SEGER
24	JEFFERSON STARSHIP	The COMMODORES	JOURNEY	Billy SQUIER
25	Gerry RAFFERTY	Rickie Lee JONES	Boz SCAGGS	Phil COLLINS
26	George BENSON	Barry MANILOW	Kenny LOGGINS	BLONDIE
27	MEAT LOAF	BLUES BROTHERS	Pete TOWNSHEND	KOOL & The GANG
28	ELECTRIC LIGHT ORCHESTRA	Bob DYLAN	Bruce SPRINGSTEEN	Rick SPRINGFIELD
29	Natalie COLE	ELECTRIC LIGHT ORCHESTRA	Stevie WONDER	Tom PETTY/HEARTBREAKERS
30	Shaun CASSIDY	Neil YOUNG	The PRETENDERS	Alan PARSONS PROJECT
31	Steve MARTIN	Gloria GAYNOR	George BENSON	Stevie WONDER
32	Peter BROWN	SISTER SLEDGE	VAN HALEN	ALABAMA
33	HEART	JOURNEY	The WHISPERS	SANTANA
34	Bruce SPRINGSTEEN	TOTO	GENESIS	The WHO
35	Barbra STREISAND	Michael JACKSON	STYX	Diana ROSS
36	ATLANTA RHYTHM SECTION	Charlie DANIELS Band	BLONDIE	QUEEN
37	The WHO	Olivia NEWTON-JOHN	DOOBIE BROTHERS	LOVERBOY
38	Kenny LOGGINS	Rick JAMES	Smokey ROBINSON	Ozzy OSBOURNE
39	Roberta FLACK	LITTLE RIVER BAND	LIPPS INC.	Willie NELSON
40	Joe WALSH	JACKSON 5	SUPERTRAMP	Juice NEWTON
41	Dolly PARTON	Teddy PENDERGRASS	KOOL & The GANG	Quincy JONES
42	ABBA	Steve MARTIN	Jermaine JACKSON	The PRETENDERS
43	PABLO CRUISE	GQ	Waylon JENNINGS	Rickie Lee JONES
44	Bob WELCH	The WHO	BROTHERS JOHNSON	Billy JOEL
45	HEATWAVE	Joe JACKSON	RUSH	STEELY DAN
46	Grover WASHINGTON Jr.	Paul McCARTNEY/WINGS	FLEETWOOD MAC	Eddie RABBITT
47	A TASTE OF HONEY	Eric CLAPTON	Teddy PENDERGRASS	.38 SPECIAL
48	Neil DIAMOND	POCO	BEE GEES	Bruce SPRINGSTEEN
49	KISS	FLEETWOOD MAC	Stephanie MILLS	Smokey ROBINSON
50	Carly SIMON	Diana ROSS	HEART	The COMMODORES

	1982	1983	1984	1985
1	ASIA	Michael JACKSON	Lionel RICHIE	Bruce SPRINGSTEEN
2	The GO-GO'S	MEN AT WORK	PRINCE	Phil COLLINS
3	LOVERBOY	DEF LEPPARD	Michael JACKSON	MADONNA
4	JOURNEY	The POLICE	Huey LEWIS/NEWS	PRINCE
5	John MELLENCAMP	Daryl HALL & John OATES	VAN HALEN	Bryan ADAMS
6	J. GEILS Band	JOURNEY	Bruce SPRINGSTEEN	TEARS FOR FEARS
7	FLEETWOOD MAC	Lionel RICHIE	CULTURE CLUB	WHAM!
8	Willie NELSON	DURAN DURAN	DURAN DURAN	DIRE STRAITS
9	FOREIGNER	STRAY CATS	The CARS	Tina TURNER
10	Joan JETT/BLACKHEARTS	CULTURE CLUB	Cyndi LAUPER	John FOGERTY
11	Rick SPRINGFIELD	Billy JOEL	Billy JOEL	Whitney HOUSTON
12	The POLICE	David BOWIE	Billy IDOL	STING
13	Daryl HALL & John OATES	PRINCE	ZZ TOP	POINTER SISTERS
14	Billy SQUIER	Kenny ROGERS	Tina TURNER	Billy OCEAN
15	ROLLING STONES	QUIET RIOT	POINTER SISTERS	KOOL & The GANG
16	VANGELIS	ALABAMA	MADONNA	HEART
17	ROYAL PHILHARMONIC	Pat BENATAR	The POLICE	Billy JOEL
18	ALABAMA	Stevie NICKS	NIGHT RANGER	Don HENLEY
19	Olivia NEWTON-JOHN	LOVERBOY	SCORPIONS	FOREIGNER
20	MEN AT WORK	The FIXX	Daryl HALL & John OATES	SADE
21	GENESIS	ZZ TOP	John MELLENCAMP	Daryl HALL & John OATES
22	Stevie NICKS	Bob SEGER	Julio IGLESIAS	POWER STATION
23	Ozzy OSBOURNE	STYX	MÖTLEY CRÜE	U2
24	AC/DC	TOTO	EURYTHMICS	MÖTLEY CRÜE
25	SURVIVOR	Bryan ADAMS	RATT	NEW EDITION
26	Steve MILLER Band	Willie NELSON	YES	John MELLENCAMP
27	Paul McCARTNEY	Thomas DOLBY	Kenny ROGERS	TALKING HEADS
28	HUMAN LEAGUE	PINK FLOYD	The PRETENDERS	CHICAGO
29	Neil DIAMOND	Jane FONDA	U2	EURYTHMICS
30	REO SPEEDWAGON	Phil COLLINS	Linda RONSTADT	REO SPEEDWAGON
31	KOOL & The GANG	U2	QUIET RIOT	Stevie WONDER
32	TOTO	Robert PLANT	ALABAMA	NIGHT RANGER
33	The CLASH	Rick SPRINGFIELD	THOMPSON TWINS	Howard JONES
34	Juice NEWTON	TALKING HEADS	CHICAGO	Lionel RICHIE
35	STRAY CATS	AIR SUPPLY	Elton JOHN	Tom PETTY/HEARTBREAKERS
36	Alan PARSONS PROJECT	John MELLENCAMP	TWISTED SISTER	SURVIVOR
37	Dan FOGELBERG	Linda RONSTADT	DEF LEPPARD	RATT
38	VAN HALEN	Bonnie TYLER	JACKSON 5	Freddie JACKSON
39	QUARTERFLASH	MISSING PERSONS	Jeffrey OSBORNE	USA For AFRICA
40	AIR SUPPLY	Al JARREAU	Steve PERRY	DeBARGE
41	Kenny ROGERS	IRON MAIDEN	Stevie WONDER	David Lee ROTH
42	A FLOCK OF SEAGULLS	Tom PETTY/HEARTBREAKERS	Barbra STREISAND	Paul YOUNG
43	CROSBY, STILLS & NASH	Donna SUMMER	GENESIS	Julian LENNON
44	Aldo NOVA	Joe JACKSON	MIDNIGHT STAR	Cyndi LAUPER
45	Diana ROSS	EURYTHMICS	John CAFFERTY/ BEAVER BROWN BAND	Huey LEWIS/NEWS
46	The CARS	The CLASH	John WAITE	Aretha FRANKLIN
47	RUSH	Eddy GRANT	Laura BRANIGAN	George THOROGOOD/ DESTROYERS
48	CHICAGO	ASIA	Billy SQUIER	SCORPIONS
49	Robert PLANT	Olivia NEWTON-JOHN	Rick SPRINGFIELD	ZZ TOP
50	Joe JACKSON	Sammy HAGAR	The GO-GO'S	Luther VANDROSS

	1986	1987	1988	1989
1	Whitney HOUSTON	BON JOVI	George MICHAEL	NEW KIDS ON THE BLOCK
2	Janet JACKSON	U2	DEF LEPPARD	GUNS N' ROSES
3	SADE	Whitney HOUSTON	GUNS N' ROSES	Bobby BROWN
4	HEART	WHITESNAKE	INXS	Paula ABDUL
5	MADONNA	BEASTIE BOYS	Michael JACKSON	MILLI VANILLI
6	VAN HALEN	Paul SIMON	TIFFFANY	FINE YOUNG CANNIBALS
7	John MELLENCAMP	MADONNA	POISON	MADONNA
8	Bob SEGER	POISON	U2	Debbie GIBSON
9	Bruce SPRINGSTEEN	Bruce HORNSBY/RANGE	Debbie GIBSON	Tom PETTY/HEARTBREAKERS
10	ZZ TOP	EUROPE	Tracy CHAPMAN	BON JOVI
11	RUN-D.M.C.	HEART	VAN HALEN	Richard MARX
12	BON JOVI	Janet JACKSON	Steve WINWOOD	SKID ROW
13	DIRE STRAITS	Anita BAKER	Terence Trent D'ARBY	Bette MIDLER
14	Barbra STREISAND	KENNY G	Gloria ESTEFAN/ MIAMI SOUND MACHINE	TRAVELING WILBURYS
15	MR. MISTER	GENESIS	Richard MARX	TONE-LOC
16	Peter GABRIEL	Bruce SPRINGSTEEN	Rick ASTLEY	LIVING COLOUR
17	Phil COLLINS	CINDERELLA	AEROSMITH	PRINCE
18	GENESIS	Michael JACKSON	BON JOVI	DEF LEPPARD
19	Billy OCEAN	FLEETWOOD MAC	D.J. JAZZY JEFF/FRESH PRINCE	Janet JACKSON
20	Lionel RICHIE	Los LOBOS	Whitney HOUSTON	WARRANT
21	Robert PALMER	Steve WINWOOD	Robert PLANT	GREAT WHITE
22	Patti LaBELLE	MÖTLEY CRÜE	Anita BAKER	Anita BAKER
23	The OUTFIELD	Huey LEWIS/NEWS	John MELLENCAMP	ROLLING STONES
24	Huey LEWIS/NEWS	LL COOL J	Keith SWEAT	Edie BRICKELL/NEW BOHEMIANS
25	Steve WINWOOD	LISA LISA And CULT JAM	Elton JOHN	WINGER
26	Gloria ESTEFAN/ MIAMI SOUND MACHINE	BOSTON	CINDERELLA	Roy ORBISON
27	BOSTON	DEF LEPPARD	WHITE LION	The CURE
28	JEFFERSON AIRPLANE/STARSHIP	The BANGLES	PINK FLOYD	MÖTLEY CRÜE
29	Billy JOEL	Robert CRAY Band	Bobby BROWN	POISON
30	JOURNEY	Billy IDOL	CHEAP TRICK	Tracy CHAPMAN
31	FABULOUS THUNDERBIRDS	EXPOSÉ	Belinda CARLISLE	R.E.M.
32	The MONKEES	PINK FLOYD	SCORPIONS	Don HENLEY
33	The BANGLES	CLUB NOUVEAU	WHITESNAKE	KENNY G
34	David Lee ROTH	CROWDED HOUSE	Bruce SPRINGSTEEN	Melissa ETHERIDGE
35	PRINCE	FAT BOYS	Randy TRAVIS	The CULT
36	MOODY BLUES	Bryan ADAMS	MIDNIGHT OIL	SOUL II SOUL
37	PET SHOP BOYS	Jody WATLEY	SADE	WHITE LION
38	TALKING HEADS	Lionel RICHIE	Bobby McFERRIN	Rod STEWART
39	Ozzy OSBOURNE	Luther VANDROSS	Bruce HORNSBY/RANGE	Gloria ESTEFAN/ MIAMI SOUND MACHINE
40	SIMPLE MINDS	Randy TRAVIS	Taylor DAYNE	AEROSMITH
41	Stevie WONDER	RUN-D.M.C.	NEW EDITION	METALLICA
42	FALCO	PRINCE	KENNY G	CHER
43	INXS	John MELLENCAMP	David Lee ROTH	Karyn WHITE
44	MIKE + THE MECHANICS	GEORGIA SATELLITES	STING	MC HAMMER
45	Anita BAKER	Freddie JACKSON	AL B. SURE!	The B-52s
46	TEARS FOR FEARS	GRATEFUL DEAD	PEBBLES	10,000 MANIACS
47	Tina TURNER	Peter GABRIEL	SALT-N-PEPA	U2
48	ROLLING STONES	CAMEO	George HARRISON	GUY
49	The HOOTERS	Gloria ESTEFAN/ MIAMI SOUND MACHINE	Rod STEWART	Jody WATLEY
50	Stevie NICKS	R.E.M.	Joe SATRIANI	The BANGLES

100 Highest Charting Acts By Raw Score Each Decade

1963-1969
1 The BEATLES
2 Herb ALPERT & The TIJUANA BRASS
3 Barbra STREISAND
4 ROLLING STONES
5 The SUPREMES/Diana ROSS And The SUPREMES
6 BEACH BOYS
7 The MONKEES
8 Bill COSBY
9 The TEMPTATIONS
10 Frank SINATRA
11 Andy WILLIAMS
12 SIMON & GARFUNKEL
13 Elvis PRESLEY
14 Bob DYLAN
15 PETER, PAUL & MARY
16 Dean MARTIN
17 Glen CAMPBELL
18 MAMAS & The PAPAS
19 Al HIRT
20 Nancy WILSON
21 Aretha FRANKLIN
22 CREAM
23 HERMAN'S HERMITS
24 Jimi HENDRIX EXPERIENCE
25 The DOORS
26 RASCALS/YOUNG RASCALS
27 Henry MANCINI and his Orchestra
28 Tom JONES
29 RIGHTEOUS BROTHERS
30 Dionne WARWICK
31 Ray CONNIFF & His Orchestra & Chorus
32 The VENTURES
33 Dave CLARK Five
34 The LETTERMEN
35 IRON BUTTERFLY
36 Sergio MENDES And BRASIL '66/'77
37 Al MARTINO
38 4 SEASONS
39 The ANIMALS/Eric BURDON & The ANIMALS
40 Paul REVERE And The RAIDERS
41 DONOVAN
42 Lou RAWLS
43 Johnny CASH
44 Johnny RIVERS
45 Johnny MATHIS
46 FOUR TOPS
47 The ASSOCIATION
48 John GARY
49 BLOOD, SWEAT & TEARS
50 James BROWN

1963-1969
51 Ray CHARLES
52 STEPPENWOLF
53 Eddy ARNOLD
54 Joan BAEZ
55 Engelbert HUMPERDINCK
56 Roger MILLER
57 Jack JONES
58 CREEDENCE CLEARWATER REVIVAL
59 The MIRACLES/Smokey ROBINSON & The MIRACLES
60 VANILLA FUDGE
61 Jimmy SMITH
62 JEFFERSON AIRPLANE/STARSHIP
63 Otis REDDING
64 Roger WILLIAMS
65 Bert KAEMPFERT And His Orchestra
66 The BYRDS
67 SONNY & CHER
68 NEW CHRISTY MINSTRELS
69 LOVIN' SPOONFUL
70 BEE GEES
71 Ed AMES
72 MANTOVANI
73 Louis ARMSTRONG
74 Tony BENNETT
75 Trini LOPEZ
76 The KINGSMEN
77 José FELICIANO
78 Bobby VINTON
79 The IMPRESSIONS
80 Robert GOULET
81 Nat King COLE
82 BIG BROTHER And The HOLDING COMPANY
83 Ramsey LEWIS Trio
84 5th DIMENSION
85 Diana ROSS And The SUPREMES And The TEMPTATIONS
86 Judy COLLINS
87 Wes MONTGOMERY
88 LED ZEPPELIN
89 Paul MAURIAT And His Orchestra
90 SINGING NUN
91 Allan SHERMAN
92 Petula CLARK
93 Nancy SINATRA
94 The KINKS
95 Jerry VALE
96 Lawrence WELK
97 Gary LEWIS And The PLAYBOYS
98 THREE DOG NIGHT
99 Jim REEVES
100 Billy VAUGHN and His Orchestra

1970s
1 Elton JOHN
2 CHICAGO
3 LED ZEPPELIN
4 John DENVER
5 ROLLING STONES
6 FLEETWOOD MAC
7 BEE GEES
8 EAGLES
9 Carole KING
10 Paul McCARTNEY & WINGS/WINGS
11 Stevie WONDER
12 Neil DIAMOND
13 The BEATLES
14 SANTANA
15 Rod STEWART
16 EARTH, WIND & FIRE
17 JETHRO TULL
18 Cat STEVENS
19 GRAND FUNK RAILROAD
20 Barbra STREISAND
21 James TAYLOR
22 DOOBIE BROTHERS
23 CARPENTERS
24 THREE DOG NIGHT
25 Elvis PRESLEY
26 JACKSON 5
27 Linda RONSTADT
28 JEFFERSON AIRPLANE/STARSHIP
29 Bob DYLAN
30 The WHO
31 Barry MANILOW
32 Isaac HAYES
33 MOODY BLUES
34 CREEDENCE CLEARWATER REVIVAL
35 The TEMPTATIONS
36 The COMMODORES
37 WAR
38 Neil YOUNG
39 Donna SUMMER
40 PINK FLOYD
41 Peter FRAMPTON
42 Eric CLAPTON
43 Steve MILLER Band
44 AMERICA
45 ELECTRIC LIGHT ORCHESTRA
46 Billy JOEL
47 Jim CROCE
48 Diana ROSS
49 Roberta FLACK
50 George HARRISON

1970s
51 David BOWIE
52 Al GREEN
53 ALLMAN BROTHERS Band
54 Marvin GAYE
55 Joni MITCHELL
56 KISS
57 SEALS & CROFTS
58 ISLEY BROTHERS
59 STEELY DAN
60 FOREIGNER
61 YES
62 Olivia NEWTON-JOHN
63 Carly SIMON
64 Aretha FRANKLIN
65 EMERSON, LAKE & PALMER
66 Helen REDDY
67 AEROSMITH
68 DEEP PURPLE
69 PARTRIDGE FAMILY
70 BACHMAN-TURNER OVERDRIVE
71 BREAD
72 CHEECH & CHONG
73 STYX
74 The O'JAYS
75 George BENSON
76 OHIO PLAYERS
77 CROSBY, STILLS, NASH & YOUNG
78 SLY & THE FAMILY STONE
79 Paul SIMON
80 QUEEN
81 ALICE COOPER (Grp)
82 LOGGINS & MESSINA
83 BLACK SABBATH
84 BEACH BOYS
85 Gladys KNIGHT & The PIPS
86 SIMON & GARFUNKEL
87 BAD COMPANY
88 Gordon LIGHTFOOT
89 SUPERTRAMP
90 BOSTON
91 Curtis MAYFIELD
92 Jimi HENDRIX
93 Barry WHITE
94 LYNYRD SKYNYRD
95 HEART
96 KANSAS
97 5TH DIMENSION
98 BLOOD, SWEAT & TEARS
99 Jackson BROWNE
100 Bob SEGER

1980s
1 Michael JACKSON
2 PRINCE
3 Bruce SPRINGSTEEN
4 Billy JOEL
5 MADONNA
6 JOURNEY
7 DEF LEPPARD
8 John MELLENCAMP
9 Lionel RICHIE
10 U2
11 The POLICE
12 VAN HALEN
13 Daryl HALL & John OATES
14 BON JOVI
15 Whitney HOUSTON
16 Kenny ROGERS
17 Pat BENATAR
18 Huey LEWIS And The NEWS
19 PINK FLOYD
20 Phil COLLINS
21 ROLLING STONES
22 Barbra STREISAND
23 Bob SEGER
24 GUNS N' ROSES
25 Tom PETTY And The HEARTBREAKERS
26 AC/DC
27 REO SPEEDWAGON
28 HEART
29 GENESIS
30 ALABAMA
31 FOREIGNER
32 DURAN DURAN
33 ZZ TOP
34 Steve WINWOOD
35 KOOL & The GANG
36 The CARS
37 Bryan ADAMS
38 LOVERBOY
39 Stevie WONDER
40 RUSH
41 Stevie NICKS
42 FLEETWOOD MAC
43 MEN AT WORK
44 Linda RONSTADT
45 MÖTLEY CRÜE
46 Janet JACKSON
47 DIRE STRAITS
48 STYX
49 George MICHAEL
50 Neil DIAMOND

1980s
51 Tina TURNER
52 Rick SPRINGFIELD
53 CULTURE CLUB
54 POISON
55 Anita BAKER
56 Diana ROSS
57 INXS
58 Luther VANDROSS
59 Bobby BROWN
60 WHITESNAKE
61 Ozzy OSBOURNE
62 POINTER SISTERS
63 TALKING HEADS
64 Rod STEWART
65 Cyndi LAUPER
66 TEARS FOR FEARS
67 SADE
68 Elton JOHN
69 Billy IDOL
70 Willie NELSON
71 AIR SUPPLY
72 Billy SQUIER
73 EURYTHMICS
74 Billy OCEAN
75 SCORPIONS
76 Gloria ESTEFAN/MIAMI SOUND MACHINE
77 Dan FOGELBERG
78 JEFFERSON AIRPLANE/STARSHIP
79 NEW KIDS ON THE BLOCK
80 R.E.M.
81 CHICAGO
82 CINDERELLA
83 Debbie GIBSON
84 Richard MARX
85 QUEEN
86 AEROSMITH
87 RUN-D.M.C.
88 WHAM!
89 Christopher CROSS
90 Paul SIMON
91 The GO-GO'S
92 KENNY G
93 David BOWIE
94 ASIA
95 .38 SPECIAL
96 Peter GABRIEL
97 Paul McCARTNEY
98 Alan PARSONS PROJECT
99 NEW EDITION
100 The PRETENDERS

Yearly Highest Charting Acts Year by Year

This list of 529 acts includes all that finished in the top 50 for any year. The scoring is raw points and only points scored in that year. Places 1-50 are noted by number. Places 51-100 are designated A and greater than 100 designated B. A blank indicates no scoring that year. Number of charted albums, 1955-63 and in the 1990s are also noted.

Act (Rank)	*Pre*	'64	'65	'66	'67	'68	'69	'70	'71	'72	'73	'74	'75	'76	'77	'78	'79	'80	'81	'82	'83	'84	'85	'86	'87	'88	'89	*'90s*
ABBA (261)												B	B	B	A	**42**	A	B	A	B	B							*1*
Paula ABDUL (179)																										B	**4**	*3*
AC/DC (94)															B	B	A	**20**	**3**	**24**	A	B	B	A	B	A		*1*
Bryan ADAMS (182)																				B	**25**	B	**5**	A	**36**			*5*
AEROSMITH (61)											B	B	**31**	**6**	A	A	A	A	B	B	B		B	B	A	**17**	**40**	*3*
AIR SUPPLY (222)																		A	**21**	**40**	**35**	B	B	B				
ALABAMA (130)																		B	**32**	**18**	**16**	**32**	A	A	B	B	B	*3*
AL B. SURE! (741)																										**45**	B	*2*
ALICE COOPER (Grp) (183)							B		A	**13**	**30**	**49**	B															
ALICE COOPER (Solo) (298)													**38**	B	B	B	B	B	B					B	B	B	A	*2*
Davie ALLAN And The ARROWS (717)				B	**38**	B																						
ALLMAN BROTHERS Band (119)								B	A	**22**	**13**	B	A	B	B		A	B	B								B	*2*
Herb ALPERT/TIJUANA BRASS (6)	*1*		**10**	**1**	**1**	**2**	A	A	B	B	B	B	B									B						
AMERICA (100)										**15**	A	**42**	**17**	**14**	B	B	B	B		B	B	B						
Ed AMES (324)				B	**25**	**27**	B	B	B																			
The ANIMALS/Eric BURDON&... (227)		A	A	**10**	**24**	A	B				B				B						B	B						
Louis ARMSTRONG (407)	*2*	**11**	**45**																									
Eddy ARNOLD (284)	*1*		A	**15**	**32**	A	B	B	B																			
ASIA (288)																				**1**	**48**	B	B	B				
The ASSOCIATION (192)				**48**	**21**	A	**18**	B	B	B																		
Rick ASTLEY (480)																										**16**	A	*2*
ATLANTA RHYTHM SECTION (343)												B	B	B	A	**36**	A	B	B	B								
AVERAGE WHITE BAND/AWB (236)												B	**9**	A	A	B	B	B										
BACHMAN-TURNER OVERDRIVE (163)											B	**4**	**23**	A	B	B	B					B						
BAD COMPANY (166)												**41**	**41**	A	A		**20**			B	B			B		B	B	*4*
Joan BAEZ (149)	*4*	**24**	**24**	A	A	B	A	B	A	B	B		**45**	B	B	B	B											
Anita BAKER (220)																					B	B		**45**	**13**	**22**	**22**	*2*
The BAND (193)						A	A	**32**	B	A	B	B	B	B	B	B												*1*
The BANGLES (344)																						B	B	**33**	**28**	B	**50**	*1*
BEACH BOYS (21)	*4*	**4**	**2**	**11**	**47**	A	B	B	B	B	B	**28**	**20**	**47**	B	B	B	B	B	B			B	B			B	*1*
BEASTIE BOYS (372)																								B	**5**	B	B	*7*
The BEATLES (1)		**1**	**1**	**2**	**5**	**6**	**3**	**1**	B		**7**	A		**19**	**37**	A	B	B	A	B	B	B		B	B	B		*4*
BEE GEES (14)					A	**38**	**25**	B	A	B	B	B	B	**27**	**13**	**1**	**3**	**48**	B	B	A	B			B		B	*1*
Pat BENATAR (81)																	B	**5**	**2**	A	**17**	A	A	B		A	B	*3*
Tony BENNETT (353)	*4*	**47**	**34**	**35**	B	B	B	B	B	B	B													B				*6*
George BENSON (93)							B					B	B	**8**	**23**	**26**	A	**31**	B	A	A	B	B	B	B	B	B	*1*
Chuck BERRY (506)	*1*	A	B		B					**46**	B																	
The B-52s (267)																	B	A	B	B	B			B	B		**45**	*3*
BIG BROTHER/HOLDING... (302)					B	**22**	**44**	B	B																			
BLACK SABBATH (140)								B	**12**	A	B	A	B	B	B	B	B	B	B	B	B	B		B	B	B	B	*3*
BLIND FAITH (451)							**23**	B							B													
BLONDIE (219)																B	**23**	**36**	**26**	B								*1*
BLOOD, SWEAT & TEARS (74)						B	**5**	**13**	A	A	B	B	B	B														
BLUES BROTHERS (449)																B	**27**	A	B	B								*1*
BON JOVI (99)																						A	A	**12**	**1**	**18**	**10**	*5*
BOSTON (123)														A	**9**	**22**	B							**27**	**26**			*2*
David BOWIE (67)										B	**31**	**37**	**37**	**16**	A	B	B	A	B	B	**12**	A	B	B	B		B	*4*
Laura BRANIGAN (537)																				B	A	**47**	B		B	B		*1*
BRASS CONSTRUCTION (544)														**50**	B	B	B	B		B	B							
BREAD (172)							B	A	A	**26**	**19**	A	B		B													
Edie BRICKELL/NEW BOHEM...(612)																										B	**24**	*2*

Act (Rank)	Pre	'64	'65	'66	'67	'68	'69	'70	'71	'72	'73	'74	'75	'76	'77	'78	'79	'80	'81	'82	'83	'84	'85	'86	'87	'88	'89	'90s
BROTHERS JOHNSON (246)														35	39	A	B	44	B		B	B						
Bobby BROWN (187)																								B	B	29	3	2
James BROWN (118)	1	40	A	47	A	A	33	A	A	A	A	A	B	B	B	B	B	B						B		B		
Peter BROWN (715)																32												
Jackson BROWNE (124)										B	B	A	B	B	A	11	B	16	B		A	B		A			B	3
B.T. EXPRESS (492)												B	29	B	B	B		B										
Jimmy BUFFETT (244)												B	B	B	35	A	A	B	B	B	B	B	B	B		B	B	8
The BYRDS (258)			47	36	31	A	B	B	B	B	B																	1
John CAFFERTY/BEAVER...(594)																					B	45	A	B			B	
CAMEO (289)															B	B	B	A	B	B	B	B	B	A	48	B	B	1
Glen CAMPBELL (36)					B	5	2	36	A	B	B	B	A	B	B	B	B		B									
CANNED HEAT (442)					B	46	A	B	B	B																		
CAPTAIN & TENNILLE (254)													33	29	A	B	B	B										
George CARLIN (370)										45	A	B	B	B	B		B		B	B		B						
Belinda CARLISLE (457)																								A	B	31	B	
Walter CARLOS (641)							43	B		B																		
Kim CARNES (374)																		B	13	B	B	B	B	B				
CARPENTERS (66)								45	4	24	29	39	A	B	B	B	B		B		B	B	B					1
Vikki CARR (458)		B			A	48	A	B	B	B	B	B																
The CARS (85)																B	4	21	B	46		9	A	A	B	B		
Johnny CASH (101)	3	A	B	B	B	47	7	14	B	B	B													B				4
Shaun CASSIDY (360)															19	30												
CHAD & JEREMY (683)		B	38	A	B																							
CHAMBERS BROTHERS (467)						29	B	B	B	B																		
Tracy CHAPMAN (341)																										10	30	2
Ray CHARLES (237)	13	28	B	38	A	A	B	B	B	B	B		B	B	B	B							B					1
Ray CHARLES Singers (812)		34	A																									
CHEAP TRICK (194)															B	B	7	A	B	A	B		B	B		30	B	4
CHEECH & CHONG (173)									B	12	25	24	B	B		B	B	B					B					
CHER (206)			A	A	B	B	B		A	A	B	B	B				B								B	A	42	4
CHIC (334)															B	A	18	B	B	B	B							
CHICAGO (5)							42	4	3	5	21	7	7	5	44	B	B	B	B	48	B	34	28	B	B	A	B	5
The CHI-LITES (396)							B		A	40	B	B						B	B	B	B							
CINDERELLA (278)																								A	17	26	A	2
Eric CLAPTON (50)								A	B	42	A	36	A	B	B	6	47	17	A	B	A		B	B	A	B	B	9
Dave CLARK Five (235)		10	20	24	B																							1
Petula CLARK (416)			36	A	A	A	B	B	B																			
The CLASH (357)																	B	A	B	33	46		B	B		B		1
CLUB NOUVEAU (764)																								B	33	B		
Joe COCKER (178)							A	15	B	B	B	B	B	B	B	B				B		B		B	B	B	B	2
Nat King COLE (426)	18	A	15	B		B	B																					1
Natalie COLE (214)													B	40	A	29	B	B	B		B		B		B	A	B	7
Judy COLLINS (169)		B	B		B	45	27	B	A	B	B		A	B	B	B	B	B		B								
Phil COLLINS (73)																			25	B	30	B	2	17	B		B	4
The COMMODORES (54)												B	A	31	8	5	24	22	50	B	B		A	B	B			
Ray CONNIFF/Orch. & Chor. (165)	20	A	48	21	22	30	B	B	B	B	B																	
Sam COOKE (693)	4	A	37	B																			B	B				
Rita COOLIDGE (379)									B	B	B	B	B	B	29	A	B	B	B									
Bill COSBY (52)		B	A	5	3	12	46	B	B	B	B			B						B	B			B				
Robert CRAY Band (617)																								B	29	B	B	6
CREAM (80)					A	3	9	A		B					B													
CREEDENCE CLEARWATER... (33)						B	6	2	21	A	A	B		B				B	B					B	B			
Jim CROCE (127)										A	20	3	B	B	B													
CROSBY, STILLS & NASH (175)							24	47	B						24	B			B	43	A							3
CROSBY, STILLS, NASH&YOUNG (139)								12	17	B		A	B		B											B	B	1
Christopher CROSS (245)																		10	20	B	A	B	B	B				
CROWDED HOUSE (686)																								B	34	B		2
The CULT (611)																							B	B	A		35	2
CULTURE CLUB (228)																					10	7	B	B				2
The CURE (404)																					B	B	B	A	A	B	27	6
Charlie DANIELS Band (307)											B	B	B	B	B	B	36	A	B	B	B					B	B	1
Terence Trent D'ARBY (534)																									B	13	B	2
DAWN/Tony ORLANDO (362)								B	B		A	B	24	B														
Taylor DAYNE (419)																										40	A	1
DeBARGE (520)																				B	A	B	40	B				
DEEP PURPLE (125)						A	B	B	B	A	2	46	B	B	B			B				B	A		B	B		2

Act (Rank)	*Pre*	'64	'65	'66	'67	'68	'69	'70	'71	'72	'73	'74	'75	'76	'77	'78	'79	'80	'81	'82	'83	'84	'85	'86	'87	'88	'89	*'90s*
DEF LEPPARD (75)																		B	B	B	3	37			27	2	18	*5*
John DENVER (16)							B	B	47	A	22	1	2	12	49	B	B	B	B	B	B	B	B					*3*
DEODATO (496)											38	B	B	B		B		B										
Neil DIAMOND (15)				B	B	B	B	26	31	25	10	17	B	41	A	48	A	A	12	29	A	B	B	A	B	B	B	*5*
DIRE STRAITS (132)																	13	B	A	B	B	B	8	13	B	B	B	*2*
D.J. JAZZY JEFF/FRESH PRINCE (500)																									B	19	B	*3*
Thomas DOLBY (622)																					27	B				B		
DONOVAN (150)			A	A	A	31	13	A	B		B	B	B	B														
DOOBIE BROTHERS (47)										B	17	19	12	44	25	B	6	37	A	B	B						A	*1*
The DOORS (42)					10	8	31	31	29	B	B					B	B	B	A	B	B	B	B		B	B		*3*
DURAN DURAN (162)																				B	8	8	A	B	A	B	B	*5*
Bob DYLAN (13)	*1*	44	13	27	35	24	17	39	A	A	A	23	22	13		A	28	B	B		B	B	B	B		B	B	*8*
EAGLES (20)										A	A	A	3	3	2	B	22	11	A	B	B							*1*
EARTH, WIND & FIRE (29)									B	B	A	38	4	7	A	15	8	B	A	A	A	B			B	B		*2*
ELECTRIC LIGHT ORCHESTRA (79)										B	B	A	A	17	12	28	29	A	A	B	B			B				
EMERSON, LAKE & PALMER (153)									27	27	B	15	B		A	B	B	B	B									*1*
The EMOTIONS (501)														B	33	B	B	B	B									
Gloria ESTEFAN/MIAMI SOUND MACHINE (213)																							B	26	49	14	39	*8*
Melissa ETHERIDGE (628)																										B	34	*3*
EUROPE (452)																								B	10	A	B	
EURYTHMICS (252)																					45	24	29	A	B	B	B	*2*
EXPOSÉ (475)																									31	A	A	*1*
FABULOUS THUNDERBIRDS (673)																			B					31	B		B	
Marianne FAITHFULL (816)			46	B			B											B	B		B							*1*
FALCO (785)																					B			42				
FAT BOYS (485)																							A	B	35	A	B	
José FELICIANO (260)						26	29	A	B	B	B	B	B															
5TH DIMENSION (114)					A	A	26	19	38	A	B		B															
FINE YOUNG CANNIBALS (313)																								B			6	
The FIXX (399)																				B	20	A	B	B	B		B	*1*
Roberta FLACK (105)								B	46	2	49	B	B			39		B	B	B							B	*1*
FLEETWOOD MAC (12)						B	B	B	B	B	B	B	46	2	1	20	49	46	A	7	B				19	A	A	*2*
A FLOCK OF SEAGULLS (579)																				42	A	B						
FOCUS (533)											33	B	B		B													
Dan FOGELBERG (122)												B	A	B	A	A	B	18	A	37	A	A	B		B			*2*
John FOGERTY (455)											B		B										10	B	B			*2*
Jane FONDA (540)																				A	29	B						
FOREIGNER (37)															15	3	21	B	9	9	A		19		B	A		*3*
4 SEASONS (202)	*4*	15	B	23	33	B	B	B					B	B	B													
FOUR TOPS (142)			A	49	14	35	B	A	B	B	A	B	B	B	B				B	B			B			B		
Peter FRAMPTON (96)										B	B	B	B	1	11	B	B		B	B				B			B	
Aretha FRANKLIN (18)	*1*	B	B	B	9	7	22	41	28	28	B	A	B	A	B	B	B	B	B	B	B		46	A	A	B	B	*3*
Peter GABRIEL (272)															B	B		A	B	B	B		B	16	47		B	*3*
John GARY (283)	*1*	13	26	A	A	B	B																					
Marvin GAYE (83)		A	B	B	B	B	A	B	35	B	28	29	B	48	32		B		B	B	A	B	B	B				
Gloria GAYNOR (515)													B	B	B		31	B										
J. GEILS Band (171)									B	B	48	B	B	B	B	B	B	A	B	6	B	B	B					
GENESIS (95)											B	B	B	B	B	A		34	A	21	A	43		18	15	B		*4*
Bobbie GENTRY (494)					30	A	B	B																				
GEORGIA SATELLITES (767)																								B	44	B	B	
GERRY And The PACEMAKERS (835)		A	43																									
Stan GETZ (532)	*3*	36	28	B	B								B															
Andy GIBB (350)															B	18	B	B	B									
Debbie GIBSON (274)																									B	9	8	*2*
Joao GILBERTO (712)		37	A	B																								
The GO-GO'S (257)																			A	2	B	50						*1*
Bobby GOLDSBORO (503)					B	33	B	B	B		B	B																
Robert GOULET (418)	*5*	A	22	A	B	B	B	B																				
GQ (675)																	43	B	B	B								
GRAND FUNK RAILROAD (55)							B	8	9	21	39	32	A	B					B									
Eddy GRANT (862)																					47	B						
GRATEFUL DEAD (164)					B	B	B	A	A	B	A	A	B	B	B	B	B	B	B						46	B	B	*8*
GREAT WHITE (438)																						B		B	A	A	21	*4*
Al GREEN (129)									B	11	11	A	27	B	B	B									B			*1*
GUESS WHO (211)							B	29	30	B	B	B	B		B													
GUNS N' ROSES (133)																									B	3	2	*4*

Act (Rank)	Pre	'64	'65	'66	'67	'68	'69	'70	'71	'72	'73	'74	'75	'76	'77	'78	'79	'80	'81	'82	'83	'84	'85	'86	'87	'88	'89	'90s
GUY (775)																										B	48	1
Sammy HAGAR (393)															B	B	B	B		A	50	A	B		A			3
Daryl HALL & John OATES (38)												B	B	20	26	B	B	A	15	13	5	20	21	B		A		2
Marvin Hamlisch (431)												11																
Herbie HANCOCK (290)					B						B	20	B	B	B	B	B	B	B	B	B	A						
Richard HARRIS (423)						41	B		B	B	B	B	B															
George HARRISON (90)							B	B	23	23	40	B	39	B	A		A		B	B	B				B	48	B	
Donny HATHAWAY (443)									B	30	B																	
Isaac HAYES (65)							36	17	10	34	50	B	B	B	B	B	B	B										
HEART (64)														38	16	33	A	50	A	B	B	B	16	4	11	B		5
HEATWAVE (499)															A	45	B	B	B	B								
Jimi HENDRIX (188)					B		38	25	A	B			A	B		B	B	B		B		B		B				10
Jimi HENDRIX EXPERIENCE (116)					45	4	15	B	B																	B	B	1
Don HENLEY (240)																				A	B	B	18	B			32	1
HERMAN'S HERMITS (155)			5	9	20	B																						
Al HIRT (134)	7	3	8	A	B	B																						
The HOLLIES (459)				B	40	B		B	B	B	B	B	B								B							
HOLLYRIDGE STRINGS (1076)		46	B	B																								
The HOOTERS (558)																							A	49	B	B	B	
Bruce HORNSBY And The RANGE (321)																								A	9	39		4
Thelma HOUSTON (701)														B	42	B			B									
Whitney HOUSTON (98)																							11	1	3	20	B	4
HUMAN LEAGUE (447)																				28	A	B		B	B			
HUMBLE PIE (368)									A	38	A	B	B					B	B									
Engelbert HUMPERDINCK (109)					28	20	35	20	A	B	B	B	B	B	B	B	B											
Janis IAN (311)					A	B						B	14	A	B	B			B									
Billy IDOL (256)																			B	B	A	12	B	B	30	B		2
Julio IGLESIAS (468)																					B	22	B			B		2
The IMPRESSIONS (394)	1	25	44	B	B	A	B		B	B		B	B	B	B													
INXS (241)																					B	B	B	43	B	4	B	6
IRON BUTTERFLY (111)						34	4	27	B	B			B															
IRON MAIDEN (309)																			B	B	41	A	B	A	B	A		6
ISLEY BROTHERS (89)	1			B			A		B	A	A	A	15	A	41	A	B	A	B	B	B		B	B	B		B	2
Freddie JACKSON (414)																							38	A	45	B	B	4
Janet JACKSON (115)																				B	B	B		2	12	B	19	3
Jermaine JACKSON (336)										B	B			B	B			42	B	B		A	B	B		B		
Joe JACKSON (268)																	45	B	B	50	44	A		B	B	B	B	1
Michael JACKSON (23)										35	B		B				35	6	B	B	1	3	B		18	5	B	3
JACKSON 5 (58)								6	19	19	B	B	B	B	B	B	40	A	A	B		38	B			B		
Rick JAMES (190)																A	38	B	18	A	A	B	B	B		B		1
Tommy JAMES/SHONDELLS (448)				B	B	B	47	A	B									B										
JAMES GANG (363)							B	A	42	B	B	B	B															
Al JARREAU (281)														B	B	B	B	B	A	A	40	B	B	B	B	B	B	2
JEFFERSON AIRPLANE/STARSHIP (17)				B	18	37	A	A	32	A	B	B	5	11	B	24	A	A	A	B	B	A	A	28	A	B	B	
Waylon JENNINGS (233)							B	B			B	B	B	A	48	B	A	43	B	B	B							2
JETHRO TULL (35)							A	43	26	8	23	A	16	A	A	A	B	B		B		B	B		B	B	B	4
Joan JETT & The BLACKHEARTS (308)																			B	10	B	B	B	B	B	A	B	1
Billy JOEL (9)												A	B	B	B	2	9	3	44	A	11	11	17	29	A	B	A	2
Elton JOHN (4)								B	7	4	1	2	1	22	A	B	B	A	B	A	B	35	B	B	B	25	B	6
Howard JONES (502)																						B	33	A	B		B	
Jack JONES (303)	2	20	31	50	A	B	B																					
Quincy JONES (137)	1						B	A	B	B	B	43	A	B	B	A			41	A							B	2
Rickie Lee JONES (320)																	25		43	B	B	B	B				B	4
Tom JONES (62)			B		B	B	1	10	A	B	B	B			B				B									
Janis JOPLIN (203)							A	B	14	50	B		B							B								
JOURNEY (34)													B	B	B	A	33	24	5	4	6	B		30	A	B	A	2
Bert KAEMPFERT And His Orch. (351)	6	B	17	44	A	B	B	B	B																			
KANSAS (176)												B	B	B	17	17	A	B	B	B	B	B		B	B	B		
KC And The SUNSHINE BAND (266)													48	A	36	B	B	B				B						
John Fitzgerald KENNEDY (647)		23	B	B																								
KENNY G (239)																						B	B	B	14	42	33	6
Carole KING (28)									1	1	14	47	A	45	B	B	B	B		B							B	1
The KINGSMEN (406)		22	29	A																								
KINGSTON TRIO (596)	17	38	A				B																					
The KINKS (147)		B	32	39	A	B	B	B	B	B	B	B	B	B	B	B	A	A	A	B	A	B	B	B	B	B	B	1
KISS (71)												B	A	21	7	49	A	B	B	B	A	A	A	B	B	A	A	6

Act (Rank)	Pre	'64	'65	'66	'67	'68	'69	'70	'71	'72	'73	'74	'75	'76	'77	'78	'79	'80	'81	'82	'83	'84	'85	'86	'87	'88	'89	'90s
The KNACK (367)																	14	A	B									
Gladys KNIGHT & The PIPS (145)					B	B	B	B	B	B	41	13	A	B	B	B		B	B		B	B	B		B	B		2
KOOL & The GANG (102)									B	B	B	A	B	B	B	B	A	41	27	31	B	A	15	B	A	B		
Kris KRISTOFFERSON (293)									A	B	A	B	B	B	22	B						B						
Patti LaBELLE (333)												B	A	B	B	B	B	B	B			B	B	22			B	5
Cyndi LAUPER (262)																					B	10	44	A	A		B	3
LED ZEPPELIN (7)							10	3	44	36	4	A	10	9	B		10	A		B	B		B		B			5
Tom LEHRER (856)			B	41																								
John LENNON (337)											B	45	A						B	B	B			B		B	B	2
John LENNON & Yoko ONO (294)							B			B								B	10	B		A						
John LENNON/PLASTIC ONO BAND (270)								A	24	B			B	B					B									
Julian LENNON (638)																						B	43	B			B	
The LETTERMEN (167)		A	33	A	A	23	40	B	B	B	B	B																
Gary LEWIS And The PLAYBOYS (474)			49	40	A	B																						
Huey LEWIS And The NEWS (112)																				A	B	4	45	24	23	A	B	3
Ramsey LEWIS Trio (397)	1	B	27	30			B			B																		
Gordon LIGHTFOOT (180)							B	B	45	B	B	18	A	46	B	B		B		B	B			B				
LIPPS INC. (734)																		39										
LISA LISA And CULT JAM (528)																							B	B	25	B	B	1
LITTLE RIVER BAND (277)														B	B	A	39	B	B	B	A		B					
LIVING COLOUR (584)																										B	16	3
LL COOL J (415)																								B	24	B	A	5
Kenny LOGGINS (230)															A	38	B	26	B	A	B		B			B		6
LOGGINS & MESSINA (185)										B	32	9	A	B	B													
Claudine LONGET (522)					27	A	B																					
Trini LOPEZ (405)	2	21	30	A	B																							
Los LOBOS (511)																						B	B		20	B		5
LOVERBOY (158)																			37	3	19	B	A	A	B	B	B	
LOVE UNLIMITED (605)										B	B	50	B		B													
LOVIN' SPOONFUL (342)			B	32	17	B								B														
LYNYRD SKYNYRD (168)											B	40	50	A	A	A	B	A	B	B	B				B	B		6
MADONNA (69)																					B	16	3	5	7	A	7	6
MAMAS & The PAPAS (104)				8	6	19	B	B	B		B																	
Henry MANCINI/Orchestra (151)	11	7	21	A	B	B	34	B	A	B				B	B										B			
Chuck MANGIONE (208)									B	B	B	B	B	B	B	4	A	A	B	B	B	B						
Barry MANILOW (53)												B	36	26	4	9	26	B	A	B	A	B	B	B	B	B	B	7
MANTOVANI (330)	26	A	39	A	A	A	B	B	B	B																		
Dean MARTIN (108)	4	12	12	20	29	40	A	B	B	B																		
Steve MARTIN (361)															A	31	42	B	B									
Al MARTINO (225)	3	18	A	16	A	A	B	B	B	B			B															
Richard MARX (247)																									A	15	11	4
Johnny MATHIS (135)	19	17	A	33	B	A	A	A	B	B	B	B	B	B	B	A	B	B	B	B		B			B			
Paul MAURIAT/Orchestra (371)					B	15	B	B	B																			
John MAYALL (417)						B	A	48	B	B	B		B															
Curtis MAYFIELD (200)								A	40	32	44	B	B	B	B		B	B										1
MC HAMMER (774)																										B	44	4
Paul McCARTNEY (177)								21	B									A	B	27	B	A	B	B	B	B	B	10
Paul & Linda McCARTNEY (377)									18	B																		
Paul McCARTNEY/WINGS (41)									B	A	34	6	21	4	20	21	46											
Bobby McFERRIN (687)																									B	38	B	2
Don McLEAN (295)									B	10	B	B	B						B	B								
MEAT LOAF (519)															B	27	B		B				B					3
MELANIE (421)							B	50	B	A	B	B																
John MELLENCAMP (77)																	B	B	B	5	36	21	26	7	43	23	A	7
MEN AT WORK (195)																				20	2	B	B					
Sergio MENDESBRASIL'66/'77 (170)				A	23	17	30	B	B	B	B	B		B	B													
METALLICA (390)																						B	B	A	A	A	41	6
George MICHAEL (215)																									B	1	A	4
Bette MIDLER (143)										B	35	A		B	B	B	B	23	B		B		B	B			13	6
MIDNIGHT OIL (718)																						B	B			36	B	4
MIDNIGHT STAR (513)																					A	44	A	B		B	B	
MIDNIGHT STRING QUARTET (770)				B	39	B																						
MIKE + THE MECHANICS (600)																							B	44		B	A	1
Roger MILLER (317)		A	14	31	B	B	B	B																				
Steve MILLER Band (70)						B	A	A	B	B	A	A		15	5	B	B		B	26	B	B	B	B	B	B		1
MILLI VANILLI (242)																											5	1

Act (Rank)	*Pre*	'64	'65	'66	'67	'68	'69	'70	'71	'72	'73	'74	'75	'76	'77	'78	'79	'80	'81	'82	'83	'84	'85	'86	'87	'88	'89	*'90s*
Stephanie MILLS (339)																	A	**49**	B	B	B	B	B	B	A	B	B	
The MIRACLES/Smokey ROBINSON & The MIRACLES (231)	*1*	B	A	**37**	A	**39**	A	B	B	B	B	B																
MISSING PERSONS (570)																				A	**39**	B		B				
MR. MISTER (497)																						B	B	**15**	B	B		
Chad MITCHELL Trio (880)	*5*	**45**	B																									
Joni MITCHELL (103)						B	B	A	A	B	A	**10**	**30**	A	B	B	B	B	B	B	B		B	B		B		*4*
The MONKEES (31)				**29**	**2**	**10**	A	B						B										**32**	B			
Hugo MONTENEGRO (680)				A		**42**	B																					
Wes MONTGOMERY (373)			B	A	**49**	**28**	B	B																				
MOODY BLUES (30)						A	A	**22**	**20**	**18**	**27**	B	B		B	A	B		**14**	B	B	B	B	**36**	B	B	B	*3*
MÖTLEY CRÜE (141)																					B	**23**	**24**	B	**22**	B	**28**	*4*
MOUNTAIN (428)								**49**	A	B	B	B											B					
Maria MULDAUR (432)											B	**16**	B	B		B												
Jim NABORS (505)				B	**48**	B	B	A	B	B																		
Willie NELSON (106)													B	A	B	A	A	**19**	**39**	**8**	**26**	A	B					*8*
NEW CHRISTY MINSTRELS (375)		**14**	A	B				B																				
NEW EDITION (301)																					B	B	**25**	A	B	**41**	A	*2*
NEW KIDS ON THE BLOCK (174)																										B	**1**	*3*
Juice NEWTON (410)																			**40**	**34**	B	B						
Olivia NEWTON-JOHN (76)									B		B	**27**	**11**	A	A	B	**37**	A	A	**19**	**49**	B	B	B		B	B	*2*
NEW VAUDEVILLE BAND (799)				B	**43**																							
Stevie NICKS (160)																			**17**	**22**	**18**	B	B	**50**			A	*3*
NIGHT RANGER (319)																				B	A	**18**	**32**	B	B	B		
NILSSON (300)							B		A	**14**	B	B	B	B	B	B												
Aldo NOVA (704)																				**44**	B	B						*1*
Ted NUGENT (248)													B	A	**47**	A	A	A	B	B		B		B		B		*1*
Billy OCEAN (259)																			B			A	**14**	**19**	B	A	B	
OHIO PLAYERS (159)										B	B	**25**	**6**	**39**	B	B	B		B									
The O'JAYS (146)										A	B	**26**	A	**43**	B	A	B	B		B	B		B	B	B	B	B	*3*
Mike OLDFIELD (549)											B	**21**	B	B					B	B						B		
Roy ORBISON (440)	*2*	**50**	A	B																				B			**26**	*2*
Jeffrey OSBORNE (429)																				B	A	**39**	B	B		B		*1*
Ozzy OSBOURNE (199)																			**38**	**23**	A	A		**39**	B	A	B	*6*
Donny OSMOND (226)									**43**	**16**	A	B	B	B	B												B	*1*
The OSMONDS (263)									**36**	**20**	B	B	B	B	B	B												
The OUTFIELD (510)																							B	**23**	A		B	*1*
PABLO CRUISE (383)													B	B	**50**	**43**	B	B	B									
Robert PALMER (275)													B	B	B	B	A	B	B	B	B		B	**21**	B	A	B	*2*
Michael PARKS (678)							B	**46**	B																			
PARLIAMENT (310)													B	**36**	B	A	B	B	B									
Alan PARSONS PROJECT (161)														B	**43**	A	A	B	**30**	**36**	B	A	B	B	B			*1*
Dolly PARTON (306)							B	B	B						B	**41**	B	B	A	B	B	B	B		B	B		*10*
PARTRIDGE FAMILY (152)								A	**2**	**44**	B																	
PEACHES & HERB (384)					A	B										B	**17**	B	B									
PEBBLES (794)																										**46**		*1*
Teddy PENDERGRASS (223)															A	A	**41**	**47**	A	B		A	B	B		B		*3*
Steve PERRY (756)																						**40**	B					*1*
PETER, PAUL & MARY (91)	*3*	**6**	**16**	**43**	**46**	A	A	**42**	B							B									B			
PET SHOP BOYS (479)																								**37**	B	A	B	*7*
Tom PETTY/HEARTBREAKERS (87)															B	A	B	**8**	**29**	B	**42**		**35**	B	A		**9**	*5*
PINK FLOYD (22)					B	B		B	B	B	**6**	**35**	**13**	B	**34**	B	B	**1**	B	A	**28**	B	B	B	**32**	**28**	A	*2*
Robert PLANT (297)																				**49**	**32**	B	B			**21**	B	*4*
POCO (291)							B	B	A	B	B	B	B	B	B	B	**48**	B	B	B		B					B	
POINTER SISTERS (148)											A	B	B	B	B	B	A	B	A	B	B	**15**	**13**	B	B	B		
POISON (212)																								B	**8**	**7**	**29**	*3*
The POLICE (68)																	A	A	**7**	**12**	**4**	**17**		B	A			*2*
POWER STATION (677)																							**22**	B				
Elvis PRESLEY (10)	*23*	**8**	**11**	**22**	**34**	A	**20**	**34**	**33**	**33**	**18**	A	B	B	**14**	B	B	B	B	B	B	B	B	B	B			*4*
The PRETENDERS (279)																		**30**	**42**	B		**28**		B	B	B		*4*
Charley PRIDE (234)						B	**48**	**30**	A	A	B				B				B	B								
PRINCE (45)																B	B	A	B	A	**13**	**2**	**4**	**35**	**42**	A	**17**	*18*
Gary PUCKETT And The UNION GAP (436)						**32**	B	B	B																			
QUARTERFLASH (589)																			B	**39**	B		B					
QUEEN (78)											B	B	A	**25**	A	**23**	A	**7**	**36**	A		B		B			B	*6*
QUIET RIOT (346)																					**15**	**31**	B	B	B	B	B	

Act (Rank)	Pre	'64	'65	'66	'67	'68	'69	'70	'71	'72	'73	'74	'75	'76	'77	'78	'79	'80	'81	'82	'83	'84	'85	'86	'87	'88	'89	'90s
Eddie RABBITT (463)																B	B	B	46	B	B							
Gerry RAFFERTY (476)																25	B	B										
RARE EARTH (250)							B	18	A	B	B		B		B	B												
RASCALS/YOUNG RASCALS (131)				A	13	9	41	B	B	B																		
RATT (332)																						25	37	B	B	B	B	3
Lou RAWLS (144)	1			13	12	B	B	B	B	B				A	B	B	B	B	B		B							
Otis REDDING (253)		B	B	A	A	14	B	B	B	B																		
Helen REDDY (154)									B	B	16	34	32	34	B													
Jim REEVES (536)		30	A	A	B																							
R.E.M. (269)																					B	A	A	A	50	A	31	6
REO SPEEDWAGON (97)												B	B	B	B	B	B	B	1	30		B	30		A	B		1
Paul REVERE And The RAIDERS (196)			B	12	15	A	B	B	A	B																		
Charlie RICH (296)											A	8	B	B	B													
Lionel RICHIE (82)																				A	7	1	34	20	38			3
RIGHTEOUS BROTHERS (198)			7	14	A	B	B					B																3
Minnie RIPERTON (402)												B	26		B		B	B										
Johnny RIVERS (216)		35	41	A	37	44	A	B	B	B	B		B			B												
Smokey ROBINSON (229)											B	B	B	B	B	B	B	38	49	B	B	B		B	A	B		2
Kenny ROGERS (44)															B	A	15	4	6	41	14	27	B	B	B		B	5
ROLLING STONES (2)		31	4	4	4	36	16	24	16	3	12	33	18	32	A	7	A	9	8	15	B	A		48			23	6
Linda RONSTADT (25)					B	B		B		B	B	A	8	33	3	12	B	15	B	B	37	30	A	B	A	B	A	7
ROSE ROYCE (433)														B	28	B	B		B									
Diana ROSS (48)								A	A	B	9	A		23	A	B	50	12	35	45	A	B	A	B	B		B	4
David Lee ROTH (366)																							41	34	B	43		4
ROYAL PHILHARMONIC Orch. (461)								B											B	17	B							
RUFUS (189)											B	A	A	42	A	A	B	B	B	B	B	B						
RUN-D.M.C. (282)																						B	A	11	41	A		3
RUSH (126)												B	B	B	B	B	B	45	11	47	B	A	B	B	A	B	A	5
Leon RUSSELL (232)								B	A	37	45	B	B	B	B	B	B		B									
Mitch RYDER/DETROIT WHEELS (742)				B	50	B															B							
SADE (255)																							20	3		37	B	2
SSgt Barry SADLER (616)				19																								
SALT-N-PEPA (795)																									B	47	B	3
SANTANA (26)							50	5	5	39	A	A	B	A	A	B	A	B	33	B	B		B		B	B		4
Joe SATRIANI (553)																									B	50	A	5
Leo SAYER (466)													B	B	45	B		B	B									
Boz SCAGGS (157)									B	B		B		10	27	A		25	A							B		2
SCORPIONS (221)																	B	B		A	B	19	48	B		32	B	3
SEALS & CROFTS (136)								B	B	A	8	22	A	49	B	B												
Neil SEDAKA (462)	1											B	40	A	B			B										
Bob SEGER (51)							B	B		B	B		B	B	21	14	A	2	23	B	22			8	B			2
SERENDIPITY SINGERS (919)		39	B																									
Allan SHERMAN (445)	3	49	A	B																								
Bobby SHERMAN (359)							B	28	A	B																		
Carly SIMON (113)									A	A	15	44	A	A		50	B	B	B	B	B	B	B		A	B		4
Paul SIMON (92)										43	37	B	A	28	B	B		A	B		B	B		A	6	B	B	4
SIMON & GARFUNKEL (24)				28	41	1	32	9	A	49	B	B	B	B						A	B							
SIMPLE MINDS (602)																					B	B	B	40	B		B	2
Frank SINATRA (49)	23	29	18	3	11	B	28	B	B	B	B	B	B					A	B	B		B						8
Frank SINATRA & Count BASIE (613)	1	48	B	A	B																							
Nancy SINATRA (378)				26	A	50	B	B																				
SINGING NUN (471)		16																										
SISTER SLEDGE (504)																	32	B	B	B	B							
SKID ROW (389)																											12	3
SLY & THE FAMILY STONE (128)						B	49	37	15	A	A	B	B	B			B											
Jimmy SMITH (335)	3	19	35	46	B	B	B	B																				
SMOTHERS BROTHERS (636)	4	33	A	A		B																						
Phoebe SNOW (356)												B	44	A	B	B			B								B	
SONNY & CHER (243)			23	45	42	B			B	47	B	B																
SOUL II SOUL (620)																											36	2
SPINNERS (209)								B			A	A	19	A	B	B	B	B	B	B	B							
Rick SPRINGFIELD (184)										B									28	11	33	49	A			B		1
Bruce SPRINGSTEEN (27)													28	B		34	B	28	48	A	B	6	1	9	16	34		7
Billy SQUIER (224)																		B	24	14	A	48	B	B	B		B	1
STEELY DAN (117)										B	42	A	B	A	46	10	B	B	45	B								1
STEPPENWOLF (110)						21	12	25	50	B	B	B	B												B			

Act (Rank)	*Pre*	'64	'65	'66	'67	'68	'69	'70	'71	'72	'73	'74	'75	'76	'77	'78	'79	'80	'81	'82	'83	'84	'85	'86	'87	'88	'89	*'90s*
Cat STEVENS (57)									**11**	**6**	**24**	**12**	**43**	B	A	B	B					B	B					
Al STEWART (347)												B	B	B	**40**	A	B	B	B	B								
Rod STEWART (19)							B	B	**13**	**17**	A	B	A	**30**	**31**	**19**	**12**	B	A	A	B	A	B	B		**49**	**38**	*6*
Stephen STILLS (315)						B	B	B	**34**				B	B	B	B						B						
STING (312)																							**12**	A	A	**44**		*7*
STRAY CATS (349)																				**35**	**9**	B		B			B	
Barbra STREISAND (3)	*2*	**2**	**3**	**6**	A	**43**	**21**	**44**	**39**	B	A	**30**	**25**	B	**10**	**35**	**16**	**13**	**22**	A	A	**42**	A	**14**	A	B	A	*6*
STYX (60)												B	B	B	A	**8**	**11**	**35**	**4**	B	**23**	B						*4*
Donna SUMMER (59)													B	**37**	**30**	**13**	**1**	**14**	B	A	**43**	B	B		B		B	
SUPERTRAMP (121)												B	B	B	**38**	B	**2**	**40**	B	A	A		A		B	B		
Diana ROSS And The SUPREMES And The TEMPTATIONS (287)						B	**11**	B																				
The SUPREMES/Diana ROSS And The SUPREMES (32)		A	**6**	**7**	**8**	**11**	**39**	A				B												B				
SURVIVOR (369)																		B	B	**25**	B	B	**36**	B	B	B		
Keith SWEAT (633)																										**24**	B	*5*
SWINGLE SINGERS (661)	*1*	**26**	B																									
TALKING HEADS (181)															B	A	A	B	B	B	**34**	A	**27**	**38**	B	A		*1*
A TASTE OF HONEY (571)																**47**	B	B	B	B								
James TAYLOR (43)								**23**	**6**	B	A	A	**49**	A	**18**	B	A		A				B	B		A		*3*
TEARS FOR FEARS (238)																					B		**6**	**46**			A	*3*
The TEMPTATIONS (8)		B	A	**18**	**7**	**13**	**8**	**16**	**41**	**31**	**36**	B	**42**	A	B	B		B	B	B	B	B	B	B	B	B		*2*
10,000 MANIACS (624)																									B	A	**46**	*4*
.38 SPECIAL (285)															B			B	**47**	A	B	A		A	B	B	B	*1*
B.J. THOMAS (424)							B	**33**	B	B			B		B						B							
THOMPSON TWINS (446)																				B	B	**33**	B	A	B	B	B	
George THOROGOOD...(411)																B	A	B	B	B	B		**47**	B	B	B		*3*
THREE DOG NIGHT (40)							**14**	**7**	**8**	**29**	A	B	B	B														
TIFFFANY (352)																									A	**6**	A	
TONE-LOC (575)																											**15**	
TOTO (217)																B	**34**	B	B	**32**	**24**	B	B	B	B	B		*1*
Pete TOWNSHEND (398)										B	B				B			**27**		B	B		B	A	B		B	*1*
TRAFFIC (186)						B	A	**40**	A	A	**46**	A	B															*1*
TRAVELING WILBURYS (487)																										A	**14**	*1*
Randy TRAVIS (403)																								B	**40**	**35**	A	*9*
Robin TROWER (265)											B	**48**	A	A	B	B		B	B	B	B			B	B	B		
Ike & Tina TURNER (578)			B				B	B	**48**	B	B	B											B					
Tina TURNER (218)													B									**14**	**9**	**47**	A	B	B	*3*
The TURTLES (581)			B	B	A	**49**	B	B				B	B															
TWISTED SISTER (637)																					B	**36**	B	B	B			
Bonnie TYLER (619)																B	B				**38**	B		B				
URIAH HEEP (413)								B	B	A	**47**	B	B	B	B	B				B	B							
USA For AFRICA (826)																							**39**					
U2 (84)																			B	B	**31**	**29**	**23**	A	**2**	**8**	**47**	*5*
Jerry VALE (473)		**42**	A	A	B	B	B	B		B																		
Luther VANDROSS (205)																			B	A	B	A	**50**	B	**39**	A	A	*7*
VANGELIS (456)																			B	**16**				B	B			
VAN HALEN (56)																A	**19**	**32**	A	**38**	B	**5**	B	**6**	B	**11**	B	*5*
VANILLA FUDGE (273)					**44**	**18**	**45**	B																				
Billy VAUGHN/Orchestra (550)	*18*	A	**42**	A	B	B	B	B																				
The VENTURES (191)	*13*	**32**	**25**	**25**	A	A	A	B	B	B																		
VILLAGE PEOPLE (210)	*3*														B	**16**	**5**	B	B									
Bobby VINTON (292)		**27**	**40**	B	B	A	A	B		B	B	B	B	B	B													*1*
John WAITE (657)																				B		**46**	B		B			
Joe WALSH (251)										B	**43**	B	A	B		**40**			A		B		B		B			*1*
WAR (107)									B	**48**	**5**	A	**47**	A	B	A	B	B		B	B				B			*1*
WARRANT (587)																											**20**	*2*
Dionne WARWICK (72)		A	B	A	**26**	**16**	**19**	A	A	B	B		B	B	B		A	A	B	B	B	B	B	A	B	B	B	*1*
Grover WASHINGTON Jr. (156)										B	B		**35**	B	B	**46**	B	A	**19**	B	B	B	B		B			*2*
Jody WATLEY (441)																									**37**	A	**49**	*2*
Bob WELCH (525)															B	**44**	B	B										
Lawrence WELK/Orchestra (427)	*23*	**43**	A	B	**36**	B	B	B	B	B	B																	
Mary WELLS (974)	*1*	**41**	B																									
WHAM! (286)																					B	B	**7**	A	B			
The WHISPERS (327)										B				B	B	B	B	**33**	A	B	B	B	B		A	B		*12*
Barry WHITE (201)											A	**14**	A	B	A	B	B	B		B					B	B		*4*
Karyn WHITE (807)																										B	**43**	*2*

Act (Rank)	Pre	'64	'65	'66	'67	'68	'69	'70	'71	'72	'73	'74	'75	'76	'77	'78	'79	'80	'81	'82	'83	'84	'85	'86	'87	'88	'89	'90s
WHITE LION (486)																									B	27	37	1
WHITESNAKE (207)																		B	B			B	B		4	33	B	1
The WHO (39)					B	B	37	11	22	B	A	A	A	B		37	44	B	34	A	B	B	B	B				3
Andy WILLIAMS (46)	5	9	9	17	16	25	38	A	37	A	B	B	B															1
Hank WILLIAMS Jr. (386)			50			B	B											B	B	B	B	B	B	B	A	B	B	9
Roger WILLIAMS (326)	19	A	B	42	19	B	B		B	B																		
Nancy WILSON (120)	4	5	19	34	A	A	B	B	B	B		B	B	B	B							B						
WINGER (654)																										B	25	2
Edgar WINTER (316)								B	B	A	26	A	B	B														
Steve WINWOOD (138)									B					B	B				16	B	B			25	21	12	B	2
Bill WITHERS (391)									B	41	B	B	B	B	B	B	B		B				B					
Stevie WONDER (11)	1			A	B	A	A	A	B	A	3	5	B	18	6	B	A	29	31	A		41	31	41	B	A		2
Gary WRIGHT (381)													B	24	B	B	B		B									
YES (88)									B	7	A	A	A		A	B	B	B	B	B	B	26	B	B	B	B	B	6
Neil YOUNG (63)							B	35	49	9	A	B	B	B	B	A	30	A	B	B	A		B	B	B	B	B	8
Paul YOUNG (728)																						B	42	B	B			1
Frank ZAPPA (204)					A	B	B	B	B	B	B	31	B	B	B	B	A	B	B	B	B			B				
ZZ TOP (86)										B	A	A	34	B	A	B	B	A	A	B	21	13	49	10	B			5

Acts With 200 Or More Weeks on Chart

Act [Act Rank]	Wks
The BEATLES [1]	1849
ROLLING STONES [2]	1512
Barbra STREISAND [3]	1475
Elvis PRESLEY [10]	1248
PINK FLOYD [22]	1236
Elton JOHN [4]	1131
The TEMPTATIONS [8]	1093
Herb ALPERT & The TIJUANA BRASS [6]	1070
CHICAGO [5]	1047
BEACH BOYS [21]	1034
Neil DIAMOND [15]	990
Aretha FRANKLIN [18]	878
Bill COSBY [52]	877
Willie NELSON [106]	873
Bob DYLAN [13]	852
Kenny ROGERS [44]	842
BEE GEES [14]	808
Stevie WONDER [11]	784
Dionne WARWICK [72]	780
John DENVER [16]	779
JOURNEY [34]	777
Linda RONSTADT [25]	770
LED ZEPPELIN [7]	769
JEFFERSON AIRPLANE/ STARSHIP [17]	757
U2 [84]	740
Billy JOEL [9]	736
Frank SINATRA [49]	713
James BROWN [118]	712
SIMON & GARFUNKEL [24]	698
MOODY BLUES [30]	693
Bob SEGER [51]	682
Johnny MATHIS [135]	682
Andy WILLIAMS [46]	679
Barry MANILOW [53]	674
AEROSMITH [61]	674
David BOWIE [67]	674
The SUPREMES/Diana ROSS And The SUPREMES [32]	673
Rod STEWART [19]	668
KISS [71]	663
FLEETWOOD MAC [12]	652
Diana ROSS [48]	647
Glen CAMPBELL [36]	633
Bruce SPRINGSTEEN [27]	630
Daryl HALL & John OATES [38]	628
DOOBIE BROTHERS [47]	625
ALABAMA [130]	613
EAGLES [20]	600
The DOORS [42]	597
Carole KING [28]	594
Neil YOUNG [63]	589
EARTH, WIND & FIRE [29]	568

Act [Act Rank]	Wks
Nancy WILSON [120]	567
KOOL & The GANG [102]	565
CREEDENCE CLEARWATER REVIVAL [33]	559
THREE DOG NIGHT [40]	556
Isaac HAYES [65]	554
JETHRO TULL [35]	551
PRINCE [45]	551
The WHO [39]	548
SANTANA [26]	545
JACKSON 5 [58]	538
Ray CONNIFF & His Orchestra & Chorus [165]	537
Tom JONES [62]	536
Marvin GAYE [83]	529
The POLICE [68]	526
Eric CLAPTON [50]	524
VAN HALEN [56]	524
Dean MARTIN [108]	524
FOUR TOPS [142]	522
Gladys KNIGHT & The PIPS [145]	522
Phil COLLINS [73]	518
The MONKEES [31]	513
The LETTERMEN [167]	507
Johnny CASH [101]	504
Engelbert HUMPERDINCK [109]	501
The KINKS [147]	501
GRAND FUNK RAILROAD [55]	499
ZZ TOP [86]	499
AC/DC [94]	493
The VENTURES [191]	493
Michael JACKSON [23]	491
STYX [60]	490
Donna SUMMER [59]	489
MADONNA [69]	485
Olivia NEWTON-JOHN [76]	481
Henry MANCINI and His Orchestra [151]	481
Steve MILLER Band [70]	480
Anne MURRAY [197]	468
James TAYLOR [43]	467
DEEP PURPLE [125]	461
The COMMODORES [54]	455
Frank ZAPPA [204]	453
Waylon JENNINGS [233]	452
Lou RAWLS [144]	450
Paul McCARTNEY & WINGS/WINGS [41]	449
ISLEY BROTHERS [89]	446
PETER, PAUL & MARY [91]	445
5TH DIMENSION [114]	443
George BENSON [93]	441
Pat BENATAR [81]	440

Act [Act Rank]	Wks
TALKING HEADS [181]	438
REO SPEEDWAGON [97]	436
Joan BAEZ [149]	436
ELECTRIC LIGHT ORCHESTRA [79]	435
FOREIGNER [37]	430
4 SEASONS [202]	429
HEART [64]	426
DEF LEPPARD [75]	424
Cat STEVENS [57]	421
Al GREEN [129]	416
Hank WILLIAMS Jr. [386]	415
Bette MIDLER [143]	414
RUSH [126]	413
Carly SIMON [113]	410
Roberta FLACK [105]	408
Ray CHARLES [237]	408
John MELLENCAMP [77]	407
GENESIS [95]	407
Al MARTINO [225]	404
GRATEFUL DEAD [164]	402
The CARS [85]	401
MÖTLEY CRÜE [141]	400
DURAN DURAN [162]	399
SEALS & CROFTS [136]	398
YES [88]	396
CARPENTERS [66]	395
Judy COLLINS [169]	394
STEPPENWOLF [110]	392
Grover WASHINGTON Jr. [156]	392
MAMAS & The PAPAS [104]	386
BLACK SABBATH [140]	386
Quincy JONES [137]	380
Al HIRT [134]	379
MANTOVANI [330]	378
POINTER SISTERS [148]	373
The O'JAYS [146]	368
Sergio MENDES And BRASIL '66/'77 [170]	364
QUEEN [78]	363
The ANIMALS/ Eric BURDON & The ANIMALS [227]	363
Charley PRIDE [234]	361
Eddy ARNOLD [284]	361
BON JOVI [99]	360
WAR [107]	359
Lionel RICHIE [82]	358
Joni MITCHELL [103]	358
Alan PARSONS PROJECT [161]	357
Johnny RIVERS [216]	356
LYNYRD SKYNYRD [168]	355

Act [Act Rank]	Wks
RASCALS/ YOUNG RASCALS [131]	353
Smokey ROBINSON [229]	351
AMERICA [100]	350
ALLMAN BROTHERS Band [119]	350
RIGHTEOUS BROTHERS [198]	350
Joe COCKER [178]	348
Tom PETTY And The HEARTBREAKERS [87]	344
Otis REDDING [253]	343
CREAM [80]	342
Paul REVERE And The RAIDERS [196]	341
CHER [206]	341
LOGGINS & MESSINA [185]	339
Bob JAMES [388]	338
DONOVAN [150]	336
The MIRACLES/ Smokey ROBINSON & The MIRACLES [231]	335
J. GEILS Band [171]	334
SUPERTRAMP [121]	333
Ozzy OSBOURNE [199]	333
LOVERBOY [158]	332
Roger WILLIAMS [326]	331
Billy IDOL [256]	330
Al JARREAU [281]	330
Helen REDDY [154]	329
Jimmy BUFFETT [244]	329
Van MORRISON [276]	328
Dan FOGELBERG [134]	325
Chuck MANGIONE [208]	325
POCO [291]	325
John GARY [283]	324
Natalie COLE [214]	322
Paul SIMON [92]	319
HERMAN'S HERMITS [155]	318
The CRUSADERS [280]	315
Barry WHITE [201]	314
KENNY G [239]	314
Merle HAGGARD [469]	313
Bonnie RAITT [264]	312
STEELY DAN [117]	311
Huey LEWIS And The NEWS [112]	308
Jackson BROWNE [124]	308
Jack JONES [303]	307
Bob MARLEY And The WAILERS [331]	307
BLOOD, SWEAT & TEARS [74]	306
Luther VANDROSS [205]	306
B.B. KING [338]	305
BREAD [172]	304
CHEECH & CHONG [173]	303

Act [Act Rank]	Wks
Dolly PARTON [306]	302
Emmylou HARRIS [304]	301
Jimmy SMITH [335]	300
Randy TRAVIS [403]	300
The ASSOCIATION [192]	299
SCORPIONS [221]	298
Jim CROCE [127]	297
The BYRDS [258]	295
Ramsey LEWIS [354]	293
IRON BUTTERFLY [111]	291
SONNY & CHER [243]	291
LITTLE RIVER BAND [277]	291
OHIO PLAYERS [159]	290
CAMEO [289]	290
Herbie HANCOCK [290]	289
Tony BENNETT [353]	289
Peter FRAMPTON [96]	287
Gordon LIGHTFOOT [180]	287
SLY & THE FAMILY STONE [128]	285
Rick JAMES [190]	284
AIR SUPPLY [222]	283
Teddy PENDERGRASS [223]	283
Bobby VINTON [292]	283
Rick SPRINGFIELD [184]	282
KANSAS [176]	281
IRON MAIDEN [309]	281
Robert PALMER [275]	280
Jimi HENDRIX [188]	279
Ted NUGENT [248]	279
GUESS WHO [211]	278
ABBA [261]	277
MARSHALL TUCKER Band [271]	276
Curtis MAYFIELD [200]	275
BACHMAN-TURNER OVERDRIVE [163]	273
David SANBORN [546]	272
DIRE STRAITS [132]	270
Jimi HENDRIX EXPERIENCE [116]	268
Wes MONTGOMERY [373]	268
BAD COMPANY [166]	267

Act [Act Rank]	Wks
SPINNERS [209]	266
Ed AMES [324]	266
EMERSON, LAKE & PALMER [153]	265
R.E.M. [269]	263
SPYRO GYRA [365]	263
George HARRISON [90]	262
Steve WINWOOD [138]	262
FOGHAT [314]	262
Boz SCAGGS [157]	260
Eddie MONEY [299]	260
Dave CLARK Five [235]	259
TRAFFIC [186]	258
Joe JACKSON [268]	258
George WINSTON [671]	258
VILLAGE PEOPLE [210]	257
Charlie RICH [296]	257
Michael BOLTON [249]	256
Lawrence WELK/ Orchestra [427]	256
METALLICA [390]	253
TOTO [217]	252
Stevie NICKS [160]	251
CHEAP TRICK [194]	251
Donny OSMOND [226]	251
.38 SPECIAL [285]	251
Stephanie MILLS [339]	250
The WHISPERS [327]	248
Whitney HOUSTON [98]	247
The IMPRESSIONS [394]	247
Earl KLUGH [554]	247
Leon RUSSELL [232]	246
Don HENLEY [240]	246
EURYTHMICS [252]	246
CAPTAIN & TENNILLE [254]	246
The JUDDS [640]	246
Janet JACKSON [115]	245
Jim NABORS [505]	243
Gloria ESTEFAN/MIAMI SOUND MACHINE [213]	241
Bert KAEMPFERT And His Orchestra [351]	241

Act [Act Rank]	Wks
NEW KIDS ON THE BLOCK [174]	240
BLONDIE [219]	240
The STYLISTICS [328]	239
GAP BAND [348]	239
Arlo GUTHRIE [376]	239
RARE EARTH [250]	238
Dave MASON [358]	238
RUFUS [189]	236
The BAND [193]	236
The B-52s [267]	236
Jerry VALE [473]	236
Billy SQUIER [224]	235
Melissa MANCHESTER [355]	234
ASHFORD & SIMPSON [385]	233
Wilson PICKETT [478]	233
Ronnie MILSAP [518]	233
MANHATTAN TRANSFER [450]	232
The BAR-KAYS [477]	232
Lou REED [382]	231
The CURE [404]	231
BLUE ÖYSTER CULT [345]	230
WHITESNAKE [207]	229
Paul McCARTNEY [177]	228
Kris KRISTOFFERSON [293]	228
Charlie DANIELS Band [307]	228
JAMES GANG [363]	228
Maze Featuring Frankie BEVERLY [401]	228
Petula CLARK [416]	228
SAN SEBASTIAN Strings [508]	228
BOSTON [123]	227
Kenny LOGGINS [230]	227
Patti LaBELLE [333]	227
George THOROGOOD & The DESTROYERS [411]	225
Miles DAVIS [626]	225
ALICE COOPER (Grp) [183]	224
The OSMONDS [263]	224
JUDAS PRIEST [323]	224
John MAYALL [417]	223

Act [Act Rank]	Wks
TRIUMPH [387]	222
Robin TROWER [265]	221
Jermaine JACKSON [336]	221
Sheena EASTON [364]	221
RUN-D.M.C. [282]	220
TEN YEARS AFTER [305]	220
Bryan ADAMS [182]	218
PARTRIDGE FAMILY [152]	217
Peter GABRIEL [272]	217
Joe WALSH [251]	216
Herbie MANN [454]	216
URIAH HEEP [413]	214
Joan ARMATRADING [530]	213
The PRETENDERS [279]	212
Roger MILLER [317]	212
ATLANTIC STARR [422]	212
KC And The SUNSHINE BAND [266]	211
The KINGSMEN [406]	211
Jeffrey OSBORNE [429]	211
DEPECHE MODE [656]	211
Anita BAKER [220]	210
Trini LOPEZ [405]	210
Bobby WOMACK [464]	210
NIGHT RANGER [319]	209
Ray PARKER Jr./ RAYDIO [325]	209
FERRANTE & TEICHER [606]	209
NEW EDITION [301]	208
Buddy MILES [420]	208
CON FUNK SHUN [481]	208
Sammy HAGAR [393]	206
Nancy SINATRA [378]	205
INXS [241]	204
DAWN/Tony ORLANDO [362]	204
DOKKEN [490]	204
PAT METHENY GROUP [593]	204
ALICE COOPER (Solo) [298]	203
Peabo BRYSON [524]	201
GUNS N' ROSES [133]	200
NILSSON [300]	200
DR. HOOK [601]	200

Acts With 10 Or More Chart Entries

Act [Act Rank]	Ent
Elvis PRESLEY [10]	71
James BROWN [118]	48
Johnny MATHIS [135]	44
Barbra STREISAND [3]	40
BEACH BOYS [21]	38
The BEATLES [1]	37
The TEMPTATIONS [8]	37
Aretha FRANKLIN [18]	36
ROLLING STONES [2]	35
Dionne WARWICK [72]	33
Willie NELSON [106]	33
Frank ZAPPA [204]	33
Neil DIAMOND [15]	32
The KINKS [147]	32
Bob DYLAN [13]	31
Frank SINATRA [49]	31
Nancy WILSON [120]	31
Elton JOHN [4]	30
Ray CONNIFF & His Orchestra & Chorus [165]	29
David BOWIE [67]	28
The LETTERMEN [167]	28
JEFFERSON AIRPLANE/ STARSHIP [17]	27
Henry MANCINI and His Orchestra [151]	27
Andy WILLIAMS [46]	26
Diana ROSS [48]	26
Marvin GAYE [83]	26
BEE GEES [14]	25
Glen CAMPBELL [36]	25
Gladys KNIGHT & The PIPS [145]	25
GRATEFUL DEAD [164]	25
The VENTURES [191]	25
FOUR TOPS [142]	24
Anne MURRAY [197]	24
Miles DAVIS [626]	24
Linda RONSTADT [25]	23
Kenny ROGERS [44]	23
Neil YOUNG [63]	23
ISLEY BROTHERS [89]	23
Ray CHARLES [237]	23
Stevie WONDER [11]	22
JETHRO TULL [35]	22
Bill COSBY [52]	22
Johnny CASH [101]	22
Lou RAWLS [144]	22
Joan BAEZ [149]	22
Al MARTINO [225]	22
Ramsey LEWIS [354]	22
Herbie MANN [454]	22
FERRANTE & TEICHER [606]	22
John DENVER [16]	21
Rod STEWART [19]	21

Act [Act Rank]	Ent
The SUPREMES/ Diana ROSS And The SUPREMES [32]	21
Isaac HAYES [65]	21
Dean MARTIN [108]	21
Bobby VINTON [292]	21
B.B. KING [338]	21
Tony BENNETT [353]	21
Jerry Lee LEWIS [716]	21
CHICAGO [5]	20
The WHO [39]	20
JACKSON 5 [58]	20
KISS [71]	20
KOOL & The GANG [102]	20
DONOVAN [150]	20
4 SEASONS [202]	20
Van MORRISON [276]	20
POCO [291]	20
MANTOVANI [330]	20
Hank WILLIAMS Jr. [386]	20
Merle HAGGARD [469]	20
Percy FAITH And His Orchestra [820]	20
FLEETWOOD MAC [12]	19
Eric CLAPTON [50]	19
Lawrence WELK/ Orchestra [427]	19
Herb ALPERT & The TIJUANA BRASS [6]	18
EARTH, WIND & FIRE [29]	18
The DOORS [42]	18
Barry MANILOW [53]	18
Tom JONES [62]	18
Steve MILLER Band [70]	18
George BENSON [93]	18
DEEP PURPLE [125]	18
CHER [206]	18
The MIRACLES/ Smokey ROBINSON & The MIRACLES [231]	18
The CRUSADERS [280]	18
Herbie HANCOCK [290]	18
Roger WILLIAMS [326]	18
Jimmy SMITH [335]	18
Lou REED [382]	18
The IMPRESSIONS [394]	18
Jerry VALE [473]	18
PINK FLOYD [22]	17
SANTANA [26]	17
RUSH [126]	17
The O'JAYS [146]	17
Grover WASHINGTON Jr. [156]	17
Jimi HENDRIX [188]	17
Chuck MANGIONE [208]	17
SPINNERS [209]	17

Act [Act Rank]	Ent
The ANIMALS/ Eric BURDON & The ANIMALS [227]	17
Waylon JENNINGS [233]	17
Charley PRIDE [234]	17
Eddy ARNOLD [284]	17
Jack JONES [303]	17
Emmylou HARRIS [304]	17
Dolly PARTON [306]	17
Bob JAMES [388]	17
Billy VAUGHN and His Orchestra [550]	17
MOODY BLUES [30]	16
Daryl HALL & John OATES [38]	16
The COMMODORES [54]	16
GRAND FUNK RAILROAD [55]	16
Olivia NEWTON-JOHN [76]	16
YES [88]	16
Engelbert HUMPERDINCK [109]	16
ALLMAN BROTHERS Band [119]	16
BLACK SABBATH [140]	16
POINTER SISTERS [148]	16
OHIO PLAYERS [159]	16
Judy COLLINS [169]	16
Gordon LIGHTFOOT [180]	16
Johnny RIVERS [216]	16
Smokey ROBINSON [229]	16
Jimmy BUFFETT [244]	16
John MAYALL [417]	16
Earl KLUGH [554]	16
Buck OWENS [838]	16
Carole KING [28]	15
Donna SUMMER [59]	15
QUEEN [78]	15
Joni MITCHELL [103]	15
WAR [107]	15
Carly SIMON [113]	15
Al GREEN [129]	15
Sergio MENDES And BRASIL '66/'77 [170]	15
J. GEILS Band [171]	15
RIGHTEOUS BROTHERS [198]	15
Curtis MAYFIELD [200]	15
GUESS WHO [211]	15
Otis REDDING [253]	15
The BYRDS [258]	15
Bert KAEMPFERT And His Orchestra [351]	15
Johnny WINTER [408]	15
URIAH HEEP [413]	15
WEATHER REPORT [498]	15
Jerry BUTLER [568]	15
Billy JOEL [9]	14
THREE DOG NIGHT [40]	14

Act [Act Rank]	Ent
James TAYLOR [43]	14
AEROSMITH [61]	14
CARPENTERS [66]	14
ELECTRIC LIGHT ORCHESTRA [79]	14
George HARRISON [90]	14
AMERICA [100]	14
STEPPENWOLF [110]	14
5TH DIMENSION [114]	14
Joe COCKER [178]	14
Paul REVERE And The RAIDERS [196]	14
Barry WHITE [201]	14
John GARY [283]	14
Bob MARLEY And The WAILERS [331]	14
BLUE ÖYSTER CULT [345]	14
Dave MASON [358]	14
ASHFORD & SIMPSON [385]	14
Petula CLARK [416]	14
Wilson PICKETT [478]	14
Ronnie MILSAP [518]	14
Millie JACKSON [556]	14
Peter NERO [632]	14
George DUKE [685]	14
Stanley TURRENTINE [748]	14
The MONKEES [31]	13
CREEDENCE CLEARWATER REVIVAL [33]	13
Cat STEVENS [57]	13
AC/DC [94]	13
GENESIS [95]	13
REO SPEEDWAGON [97]	13
Quincy JONES [137]	13
KANSAS [176]	13
Natalie COLE [214]	13
Dave CLARK Five [235]	13
Ted NUGENT [248]	13
Robin TROWER [265]	13
CAMEO [289]	13
NILSSON [300]	13
FOGHAT [314]	13
Ed AMES [324]	13
The WHISPERS [327]	13
Melissa MANCHESTER [355]	13
SPYRO GYRA [365]	13
Trini LOPEZ [405]	13
Robert GOULET [418]	13
Paul ANKA [444]	13
The HOLLIES [459]	13
Bobby WOMACK [464]	13
NAZARETH [517]	13
Richie HAVENS [778]	13
STATLER BROTHERS [1271]	13
Enoch LIGHT & The LIGHT BRIGADE [1322]	13

Act [Act Rank]	Ent
JOURNEY [34]	12
DOOBIE BROTHERS [47]	12
Bob SEGER [51]	12
Roberta FLACK [105]	12
ALABAMA [130]	12
Al HIRT [134]	12
SEALS & CROFTS [136]	12
TRAFFIC [186]	12
Leon RUSSELL [232]	12
SONNY & CHER [243]	12
The OSMONDS [263]	12
MARSHALL TUCKER Band [271]	12
Charlie RICH [296]	12
TEN YEARS AFTER [305]	12
Charlie DANIELS Band [307]	12
Patti LaBELLE [333]	12
Roy ORBISON [440]	12
Vikki CARR [458]	12
The BAR-KAYS [477]	12
Todd RUNDGREN [483]	12
Jim NABORS [505]	12
NITTY GRITTY DIRT BAND [559]	12
Jean Luc PONTY [572]	12
Ike & Tina TURNER [578]	12
FUNKADELIC [585]	12
Tammy WYNETTE [592]	12
The DELLS [658]	12
Boots RANDOLPH [670]	12
The RAMONES [788]	12
MYSTIC MOODS Orch. [1289]	12
Michael JACKSON [23]	11
PRINCE [45]	11
STYX [60]	11
PETER, PAUL & MARY [91]	11
Peter FRAMPTON [96]	11
Bette MIDLER [143]	11

Act [Act Rank]	Ent
EMERSON, LAKE & PALMER [153]	11
Alan PARSONS PROJECT [161]	11
BACHMAN-TURNER OVERDRIVE [163]	11
LYNYRD SKYNYRD [168]	11
RUFUS [189]	11
Rick JAMES [190]	11
CHEAP TRICK [194]	11
Teddy PENDERGRASS [223]	11
Donny OSMOND [226]	11
Joe JACKSON [268]	11
Robert PALMER [275]	11
Kris KRISTOFFERSON [293]	11
PROCOL HARUM [322]	11
Jermaine JACKSON [336]	11
Elvis COSTELLO & The ATTRACTIONS [340]	11
DAWN/Tony ORLANDO [362]	11
JAMES GANG [363]	11
Arlo GUTHRIE [376]	11
Bill WITHERS [391]	11
Mac DAVIS [392]	11
Sammy HAGAR [393]	11
Harry CHAPIN [425]	11
CANNED HEAT [442]	11
MANHATTAN TRANSFER [450]	11
Crystal GAYLE [482]	11
OAK RIDGE BOYS [489]	11
Larry GRAHAM/GRAHAM CENTRAL STATION [495]	11
Peabo BRYSON [524]	11
The MANHATTANS [529]	11
Joan ARMATRADING [530]	11
KING CRIMSON [562]	11
ROXY MUSIC [563]	11
PAT METHENY GROUP [593]	11
SAVOY BROWN [669]	11

Act [Act Rank]	Ent
Brian AUGER [735]	11
Eddie HARRIS [805]	11
BOSTON POPS Orchestra/ Arthur FIEDLER [1175]	11
Chet ATKINS [1357]	11
LED ZEPPELIN [7]	10
HEART [64]	10
BLOOD, SWEAT & TEARS [74]	10
RASCALS/ YOUNG RASCALS [131]	10
Dan FOGELBERG [134]	10
Helen REDDY [154]	10
HERMAN'S HERMITS [155]	10
Boz SCAGGS [157]	10
TALKING HEADS [181]	10
The ASSOCIATION [192]	10
The BAND [193]	10
AVERAGE WHITE BAND/ AWB [236]	10
Joe WALSH [251]	10
José FELICIANO [260]	10
ABBA [261]	10
Al JARREAU [281]	10
ALICE COOPER (Solo) [298]	10
Stephen STILLS [315]	10
JUDAS PRIEST [323]	10
Ray PARKER Jr./RAYDIO [325]	10
The STYLISTICS [328]	10
ATLANTA RHYTHM SECTION [343]	10
Wes MONTGOMERY [373]	10
Rita COOLIDGE [379]	10
Richard PRYOR [395]	10
The CHI-LITES [396]	10
MELANIE [421]	10
B.J. THOMAS [424]	10
Nat King COLE [426]	10
Tommy JAMES And The SHONDELLS [448]	10

Act [Act Rank]	Ent
TOWER OF POWER [453]	10
The OUTLAWS [465]	10
CON FUNK SHUN [481]	10
Billy PRESTON [493]	10
Bobby GOLDSBORO [503]	10
Johnnie TAYLOR [542]	10
David SANBORN [546]	10
RAINBOW [565]	10
UFO [573]	10
Perry COMO [577]	10
TAVARES [583]	10
DR. HOOK [601]	10
BOOKER T. & The M.G.'s [603]	10
MANFRED MANN'S EARTH BAND [634]	10
COUNTRY JOE & THE FISH [643]	10
John Fitzgerald KENNEDY [647]	10
UTOPIA [707]	10
Lynn ANDERSON [725]	10
Jr. WALKER & The ALL STARS [743]	10
Wayne NEWTON [747]	10
Paul BUTTERFIELD Blues Band [796]	10
BLACK OAK ARKANSAS [810]	10
BAJA MARIMBA BAND [813]	10
Ray STEVENS [841]	10
John KLEMMER [877]	10
SOUTHSIDE JOHNNY & The ASBURY JUKES [907]	10
Glenn YARBROUGH [913]	10
Shirley BASSEY [952]	10
Dave GRUSIN [999]	10
WISHBONE ASH [1018]	10
Loretta LYNN [1111]	10
Roy BUCHANAN [1209]	10
Sonny JAMES [1609]	10

Acts With 1 Or More Top 10 Entries

Act [Act Rank]	Ent
ROLLING STONES [2]	31
The BEATLES [1]	23
Barbra STREISAND [3]	21
Elton JOHN [4]	13
BEACH BOYS [21]	12
Neil DIAMOND [15]	12
Bob DYLAN [13]	12
CHICAGO [5]	12
Elvis PRESLEY [10]	11
Andy WILLIAMS [46]	10
Linda RONSTADT [25]	10
LED ZEPPELIN [7]	10
The WHO [39]	9
Stevie WONDER [11]	9
Billy JOEL [9]	9
GRAND FUNK RAILROAD [55]	8
DOOBIE BROTHERS [47]	8
Paul McCARTNEY & WINGS/WINGS [41]	8
EARTH, WIND & FIRE [29]	8
BEE GEES [14]	8
The TEMPTATIONS [8]	8
Herb ALPERT & The TIJUANA BRASS [6]	8
YES [88]	7
Cat STEVENS [57]	7
VAN HALEN [56]	7
Barry MANILOW [53]	7
Frank SINATRA [49]	7
James TAYLOR [43]	7
The DOORS [42]	7
JETHRO TULL [35]	7
Bruce SPRINGSTEEN [27]	7
SANTANA [26]	7
JEFFERSON AIRPLANE/ STARSHIP [17]	7
John DENVER [16]	7
RUSH [126]	6
George HARRISON [90]	6
ISLEY BROTHERS [89]	6
Marvin GAYE [83]	6
David BOWIE [67]	6
JACKSON 5 [58]	6
Bob SEGER [51]	6
Eric CLAPTON [50]	6
PRINCE [45]	6
FOREIGNER [37]	6
JOURNEY [34]	6
The SUPREMES/Diana ROSS And The SUPREMES [32]	6
MOODY BLUES [30]	6
Carole KING [28]	6
SIMON & GARFUNKEL [24]	6
PINK FLOYD [22]	6
Rod STEWART [19]	6
Aretha FRANKLIN [18]	6

Act [Act Rank]	Ent
AMERICA [100]	5
George BENSON [93]	5
Tom PETTY And The HEARTBREAKERS [87]	5
ELECTRIC LIGHT ORCHESTRA [79]	5
QUEEN [78]	5
John MELLENCAMP [77]	5
Olivia NEWTON-JOHN [76]	5
MADONNA [69]	5
CARPENTERS [66]	5
HEART [64]	5
STYX [60]	5
The COMMODORES [54]	5
THREE DOG NIGHT [40]	5
CREEDENCE CLEARWATER REVIVAL [33]	5
The MONKEES [31]	5
EAGLES [20]	5
FLEETWOOD MAC [12]	5
Dave CLARK Five [235]	4
Paul REVERE And The RAIDERS [196]	4
TRAFFIC [186]	4
ALICE COOPER (Grp) [183]	4
BAD COMPANY [166]	4
DURAN DURAN [162]	4
EMERSON, LAKE & PALMER [153]	4
Jim CROCE [127]	4
Jackson BROWNE [124]	4
Nancy WILSON [120]	4
ALLMAN BROTHERS Band [119]	4
Jimi HENDRIX EXPERIENCE [116]	4
Carly SIMON [113]	4
STEPPENWOLF [110]	4
WAR [107]	4
Roberta FLACK [105]	4
MAMAS & The PAPAS [104]	4
GENESIS [95]	4
Paul SIMON [92]	4
ZZ TOP [86]	4
The CARS [85]	4
CREAM [80]	4
Phil COLLINS [73]	4
KISS [71]	4
Steve MILLER Band [70]	4
The POLICE [68]	4
Isaac HAYES [65]	4
Neil YOUNG [63]	4
Tom JONES [62]	4
Donna SUMMER [59]	4
Diana ROSS [48]	4
Kenny ROGERS [44]	4
Daryl HALL & John OATES [38]	4

Act [Act Rank]	Ent
Michael JACKSON [23]	4
John LENNON [337]	3
Robert PLANT [297]	3
The PRETENDERS [279]	3
John LENNON/ PLASTIC ONO BAND [270]	3
Robin TROWER [265]	3
Billy IDOL [256]	3
SADE [255]	3
BROTHERS JOHNSON [246]	3
AVERAGE WHITE BAND/ AWB [236]	3
SCORPIONS [221]	3
Janis JOPLIN [203]	3
4 SEASONS [202]	3
RIGHTEOUS BROTHERS [198]	3
The BAND [193]	3
The ASSOCIATION [192]	3
RUFUS [189]	3
Jimi HENDRIX [188]	3
LOGGINS & MESSINA [185]	3
Bryan ADAMS [182]	3
Paul McCARTNEY [177]	3
KANSAS [176]	3
CROSBY, STILLS & NASH [175]	3
CHEECH & CHONG [173]	3
Sergio MENDES And BRASIL '66/'77 [170]	3
LYNYRD SKYNYRD [168]	3
BACHMAN-TURNER OVERDRIVE [163]	3
Stevie NICKS [160]	3
Grover WASHINGTON Jr. [156]	3
HERMAN'S HERMITS [155]	3
Helen REDDY [154]	3
Dan FOGELBERG [134]	3
PARTRIDGE FAMILY [152]	3
Henry MANCINI and His Orchestra [151]	3
The O'JAYS [146]	3
Lou RAWLS [144]	3
Bette MIDLER [143]	3
MÖTLEY CRÜE [141]	3
CROSBY, STILLS, NASH & YOUNG [139]	3
Steve WINWOOD [138]	3
Quincy JONES [137]	3
Al HIRT [134]	3
RASCALS/ YOUNG RASCALS [131]	3
Al GREEN [129]	3
SLY & THE FAMILY STONE [128]	3
DEEP PURPLE [125]	3
BOSTON [123]	3
SUPERTRAMP [121]	3

Act [Act Rank]	Ent
STEELY DAN [117]	3
5TH DIMENSION [114]	3
Engelbert HUMPERDINCK [109]	3
Joni MITCHELL [103]	3
REO SPEEDWAGON [97]	3
AC/DC [94]	3
PETER, PAUL & MARY [91]	3
Lionel RICHIE [82]	3
Pat BENATAR [81]	3
BLOOD, SWEAT & TEARS [74]	3
Bill COSBY [52]	3
Glen CAMPBELL [36]	3
John Fitzgerald KENNEDY [647]	2
Bob DYLAN And The BAND [608]	2
David CROSBY/ Graham NASH [435]	2
LL COOL J [415]	2
Art GARFUNKEL [409]	2
David Lee ROTH [366]	2
Steve MARTIN [361]	2
Shaun CASSIDY [360]	2
Al STEWART [347]	2
LOVIN' SPOONFUL [342]	2
Tracy CHAPMAN [341]	2
CHIC [334]	2
Patti LaBELLE [333]	2
RATT [332]	2
Ringo STARR [329]	2
Bruce HORNSBY And The RANGE [321]	2
Rickie Lee JONES [320]	2
Roger MILLER [317]	2
Stephen STILLS [315]	2
STING [312]	2
ASIA [288]	2
Diana ROSS And The SUPREMES And The TEMPTATIONS [287]	2
WHAM! [286]	2
RUN-D.M.C. [282]	2
CINDERELLA [278]	2
Debbie GIBSON [274]	2
Cyndi LAUPER [262]	2
Billy OCEAN [259]	2
The BYRDS [258]	2
The GO-GO'S [257]	2
CAPTAIN & TENNILLE [254]	2
Otis REDDING [253]	2
EURYTHMICS [252]	2
Joe WALSH [251]	2
Richard MARX [247]	2
KENNY G [239]	2
TEARS FOR FEARS [238]	2

Act [Act Rank]	Ent
Ray CHARLES [237]	2
Leon RUSSELL [232]	2
The MIRACLES/Smokey ROBINSON & The MIRACLES [231]	2
The ANIMALS/Eric BURDON & The ANIMALS [227]	2
Al MARTINO [225]	2
Billy SQUIER [224]	2
AIR SUPPLY [222]	2
BLONDIE [219]	2
Tina TURNER [218]	2
TOTO [217]	2
Gloria ESTEFAN/MIAMI SOUND MACHINE [213]	2
POISON [212]	2
VILLAGE PEOPLE [210]	2
SPINNERS [209]	2
Chuck MANGIONE [208]	2
WHITESNAKE [207]	2
Barry WHITE [201]	2
Ozzy OSBOURNE [199]	2
MEN AT WORK [195]	2
CHEAP TRICK [194]	2
Bobby BROWN [187]	2
Rick SPRINGFIELD [184]	2
Gordon LIGHTFOOT [180]	2
NEW KIDS ON THE BLOCK [174]	2
BREAD [172]	2
J. GEILS Band [171]	2
Alan PARSONS PROJECT [161]	2
OHIO PLAYERS [159]	2
LOVERBOY [158]	2
Boz SCAGGS [157]	2
Joan BAEZ [149]	2
Gladys KNIGHT & The PIPS [145]	2
SEALS & CROFTS [136]	2
Johnny MATHIS [135]	2
GUNS N' ROSES [133]	2
DIRE STRAITS [132]	2
Janet JACKSON [115]	2
Huey LEWIS And The NEWS [112]	2
IRON BUTTERFLY [111]	2
Dean MARTIN [108]	2
Willie NELSON [106]	2
Johnny CASH [101]	2
BON JOVI [99]	2
Whitney HOUSTON [98]	2
Peter FRAMPTON [96]	2
U2 [84]	2
DEF LEPPARD [75]	2
Dionne WARWICK [72]	2
AEROSMITH [61]	2
Tompall GLASER [1559]	1
Randy RHOADS [1304]	1
TINY TIM [1015]	1

Act [Act Rank]	Ent
Los INDIOS TABAJARAS [1013]	1
Steve MANDELL [1010]	1
Eric WEISSBERG [1008]	1
Bob & Doug McKENZIE [984]	1
Anita WARD [943]	1
Robin WILLIAMS [925]	1
Jessi COLTER [920]	1
VILLAGE STOMPERS [917]	1
STARS ON [898]	1
The FLOATERS [868]	1
Eddy GRANT [863]	1
Debby BOONE [855]	1
Michael McDONALD [853]	1
Crazy World Of Arthur BROWN [846]	1
The SEEKERS [828]	1
USA For AFRICA [826]	1
YOUNG-HOLT UNLIMITED [821]	1
NEW VAUDEVILLE BAND [799]	1
FALCO [785]	1
TECHNOTRONIC [776]	1
GEORGIA SATELLITES [767]	1
The HONEYDRIPPERS [765]	1
CLUB NOUVEAU [764]	1
John STEWART [761]	1
LIPPS INC. [734]	1
Gilbert O'SULLIVAN [719]	1
Joao GILBERTO [712]	1
Carlos SANTANA [705]	1
Aldo NOVA [704]	1
Bobby McFERRIN [687]	1
Chris ISAAK [681]	1
Hugo MONTENEGRO [680]	1
POWER STATION [677]	1
WILD CHERRY [676]	1
John WAITE [657]	1
Stephen STILLS & MANASSAS [652]	1
Walter CARLOS [641]	1
LOVE UNLIMITED ORCHESTRA [635]	1
MANFRED MANN'S EARTH BAND [634]	1
KRAFTWERK [631]	1
YOUNG M.C. [629]	1
MFSB [621]	1
Bonnie TYLER [619]	1
SSgt Barry SADLER [616]	1
Frank SINATRA & Count BASIE [613]	1
Edie BRICKELL & NEW BOHEMIANS [612]	1
The CULT [611]	1
SILVER CONVENTION [609]	1
LOVE UNLIMITED [605]	1
SIMPLE MINDS [602]	1
Warren ZEVON [599]	1
KINGSTON TRIO [596]	1

Act [Act Rank]	Ent
John CAFFERTY And The BEAVER BROWN BAND [594]	1
QUARTERFLASH [589]	1
WARRANT [587]	1
LIVING COLOUR [584]	1
The TURTLES [581]	1
A FLOCK OF SEAGULLS [579]	1
TONE-LOC [575]	1
A TASTE OF HONEY [571]	1
Mike OLDFIELD [549]	1
Randy NEWMAN [547]	1
BRASS CONSTRUCTION [544]	1
Johnnie TAYLOR [542]	1
Jim REEVES [536]	1
Terence Trent D'ARBY [534]	1
FOCUS [533]	1
Stan GETZ [532]	1
LISA LISA And CULT JAM [528]	1
SMALL FACES/FACES [527]	1
Gloria GAYNOR [515]	1
Los LOBOS [511]	1
The OUTFIELD [510]	1
Chuck BERRY [506]	1
SISTER SLEDGE [504]	1
Bobby GOLDSBORO [503]	1
Howard JONES [502]	1
The EMOTIONS [501]	1
D.J. JAZZY JEFF & THE FRESH PRINCE [500]	1
HEATWAVE [499]	1
MR. MISTER [497]	1
DEODATO [496]	1
Bobbie GENTRY [494]	1
B.T. EXPRESS [492]	1
TRAVELING WILBURYS [487]	1
FAT BOYS [485]	1
Rick ASTLEY [480]	1
PET SHOP BOYS [479]	1
Gerry RAFFERTY [476]	1
Gary LEWIS And The PLAYBOYS [474]	1
SINGING NUN [471]	1
Julio IGLESIAS [468]	1
CHAMBERS BROTHERS [467]	1
Leo SAYER [466]	1
ROYAL PHILHARMONIC Orchestra [461]	1
VANGELIS [456]	1
John FOGERTY [455]	1
EUROPE [452]	1
BLIND FAITH [451]	1
BLUES BROTHERS [449]	1
Tommy JAMES And The SHONDELLS [448]	1
HUMAN LEAGUE [447]	1
THOMPSON TWINS [446]	1
Allan SHERMAN [445]	1
Paul ANKA [444]	1
Donny HATHAWAY [443]	1

Act [Act Rank]	Ent
Jody WATLEY [441]	1
Roy ORBISON [440]	1
GREAT WHITE [438]	1
Harold MELVIN And The BLUE NOTES [437]	1
Rick WAKEMAN [434]	1
ROSE ROYCE [433]	1
Maria MULDAUR [432]	1
Marvin Hamlisch [431]	1
Nat King COLE [426]	1
Harry CHAPIN [425]	1
Richard HARRIS [423]	1
Buddy MILES [420]	1
Robert GOULET [418]	1
Freddie JACKSON [414]	1
Herb ALPERT [412]	1
Louis ARMSTRONG [407]	1
Minnie RIPERTON [402]	1
The FIXX [399]	1
Pete TOWNSHEND [398]	1
Ramsey LEWIS Trio [397]	1
The CHI-LITES [396]	1
The IMPRESSIONS [394]	1
Bill WITHERS [391]	1
METALLICA [390]	1
SKID ROW [389]	1
PEACHES & HERB [384]	1
PABLO CRUISE [383]	1
Lou REED [382]	1
Gary WRIGHT [381]	1
Rita COOLIDGE [379]	1
Nancy SINATRA [378]	1
Paul & Linda McCARTNEY [377]	1
NEW CHRISTY MINSTRELS [375]	1
Kim CARNES [374]	1
BEASTIE BOYS [372]	1
Paul MAURIAT And His Orchestra [371]	1
SURVIVOR [369]	1
HUMBLE PIE [368]	1
The KNACK [367]	1
Bobby SHERMAN [359]	1
The CLASH [357]	1
Phoebe SNOW [356]	1
TIFFANY [352]	1
Bert KAEMPFERT And His Orchestra [351]	1
Andy GIBB [350]	1
STRAY CATS [349]	1
QUIET RIOT [346]	1
The BANGLES [344]	1
ATLANTA RHYTHM SECTION [343]	1
Elvis COSTELLO & The ATTRACTIONS [340]	1
Jermaine JACKSON [336]	1
Bob MARLEY And The WAILERS [331]	1

Act [Act Rank]	Ent
The WHISPERS [327]	1
Roger WILLIAMS [326]	1
Ed AMES [324]	1
PROCOL HARUM [322]	1
NIGHT RANGER [319]	1
Jeff BECK [318]	1
Edgar WINTER [316]	1
FINE YOUNG CANNIBALS [313]	1
Janis IAN [311]	1
Joan JETT & The BLACKHEARTS [308]	1
Charlie DANIELS Band [307]	1
Dolly PARTON [306]	1
Emmylou HARRIS [304]	1
Jack JONES [303]	1
BIG BROTHER And The HOLDING COMPANY [302]	1
NEW EDITION [301]	1
NILSSON [300]	1
ALICE COOPER (Solo) [298]	1

Act [Act Rank]	Ent
Charlie RICH [296]	1
Don McLEAN [295]	1
John LENNON & Yoko ONO [294]	1
Kris KRISTOFFERSON [293]	1
Bobby VINTON [292]	1
CAMEO [289]	1
.38 SPECIAL [285]	1
Eddy ARNOLD [284]	1
Al JARREAU [281]	1
LITTLE RIVER BAND [277]	1
Robert PALMER [275]	1
VANILLA FUDGE [273]	1
Peter GABRIEL [272]	1
R.E.M. [269]	1
Joe JACKSON [268]	1
The B-52s [267]	1
KC And The SUNSHINE BAND [266]	1
Bonnie RAITT [264]	1
The OSMONDS [263]	1

Act [Act Rank]	Ent
José FELICIANO [260]	1
Michael BOLTON [249]	1
Christopher CROSS [245]	1
Jimmy BUFFETT [244]	1
SONNY & CHER [243]	1
MILLI VANILLI [242]	1
INXS [241]	1
Don HENLEY [240]	1
Waylon JENNINGS [233]	1
Kenny LOGGINS [230]	1
Smokey ROBINSON [229]	1
CULTURE CLUB [228]	1
Donny OSMOND [226]	1
Teddy PENDERGRASS [223]	1
Anita BAKER [220]	1
Johnny RIVERS [216]	1
George MICHAEL [215]	1
Natalie COLE [214]	1
GUESS WHO [211]	1
CHER [206]	1

Act [Act Rank]	Ent
Luther VANDROSS [205]	1
Frank ZAPPA [204]	1
Curtis MAYFIELD [200]	1
Rick JAMES [190]	1
Paula ABDUL [179]	1
Joe COCKER [178]	1
Judy COLLINS [169]	1
The LETTERMEN [167]	1
Ray CONNIFF & His Orchestra & Chorus [165]	1
GRATEFUL DEAD [164]	1
DONOVAN [150]	1
POINTER SISTERS [148]	1
The KINKS [147]	1
FOUR TOPS [142]	1
BLACK SABBATH [140]	1
ALABAMA [130]	1
James BROWN [118]	1
KOOL & The GANG [102]	1

Acts With 5 Or More Top 40 Entries

Act [Act Rank]	Ent
Barbra STREISAND [3]	34
ROLLING STONES [2]	33
Bob DYLAN [13]	27
Elvis PRESLEY [10]	27
The BEATLES [1]	27
Elton JOHN [4]	26
The TEMPTATIONS [8]	24
Aretha FRANKLIN [18]	21
JEFFERSON AIRPLANE/ STARSHIP [17]	21
Neil DIAMOND [15]	21
Frank SINATRA [49]	18
BEACH BOYS [21]	18
CHICAGO [5]	18
JETHRO TULL [35]	17
KISS [71]	16
Neil YOUNG [63]	16
Eric CLAPTON [50]	16
Diana ROSS [48]	16
Rod STEWART [19]	16
Stevie WONDER [11]	16
David BOWIE [67]	15
Kenny ROGERS [44]	15
BEE GEES [14]	15
James BROWN [118]	14
Dionne WARWICK [72]	14
JACKSON 5 [58]	14
Andy WILLIAMS [46]	14
Glen CAMPBELL [36]	14
The SUPREMES/ Diana ROSS And The SUPREMES [32]	14
MOODY BLUES [30]	14
SANTANA [26]	14
John DENVER [16]	14
GRATEFUL DEAD [164]	13
YES [88]	13
Barry MANILOW [53]	13
Daryl HALL & John OATES [38]	13
EARTH, WIND & FIRE [29]	13
Linda RONSTADT [25]	13
Joni MITCHELL [103]	12
ISLEY BROTHERS [89]	12
QUEEN [78]	12
Olivia NEWTON-JOHN [76]	12
Donna SUMMER [59]	12
GRAND FUNK RAILROAD [55]	12
The COMMODORES [54]	12
James TAYLOR [43]	12
The DOORS [42]	12
THREE DOG NIGHT [40]	12

Act [Act Rank]	Ent
The WHO [39]	12
Billy JOEL [9]	12
The VENTURES [191]	11
RUSH [126]	11
Nancy WILSON [120]	11
Dean MARTIN [108]	11
Willie NELSON [106]	11
Marvin GAYE [83]	11
DOOBIE BROTHERS [47]	11
Herb ALPERT & The TIJUANA BRASS [6]	11
RIGHTEOUS BROTHERS [198]	10
DONOVAN [150]	10
The KINKS [147]	10
The O'JAYS [146]	10
BLACK SABBATH [140]	10
Johnny MATHIS [135]	10
Carly SIMON [113]	10
George HARRISON [90]	10
ELECTRIC LIGHT ORCHESTRA [79]	10
Steve MILLER Band [70]	10
HEART [64]	10
AEROSMITH [61]	10
Bill COSBY [52]	10
LED ZEPPELIN [7]	10
Frank ZAPPA [204]	9
Grover WASHINGTON Jr. [156]	9
Joan BAEZ [149]	9
Gladys KNIGHT & The PIPS [145]	9
DEEP PURPLE [125]	9
Dan FOGELBERG [134]	9
Engelbert HUMPERDINCK [109]	9
PETER, PAUL & MARY [91]	9
Isaac HAYES [65]	9
Cat STEVENS [57]	9
PRINCE [45]	9
Paul McCARTNEY & WINGS/ WINGS [41]	9
PINK FLOYD [22]	9
Elvis COSTELLO & The ATTRACTIONS [340]	8
MARSHALL TUCKER Band [271]	8
Robin TROWER [265]	8
The BYRDS [258]	8
AVERAGE WHITE BAND/ AWB [236]	8
Dave CLARK Five [235]	8
Leon RUSSELL [232]	8

Act [Act Rank]	Ent
Johnny RIVERS [216]	8
SPINNERS [209]	8
4 SEASONS [202]	8
The BAND [193]	8
TRAFFIC [186]	8
TALKING HEADS [181]	8
Judy COLLINS [169]	8
LYNYRD SKYNYRD [168]	8
The LETTERMEN [167]	8
EMERSON, LAKE & PALMER [153]	8
FOUR TOPS [142]	8
Al GREEN [129]	8
ALLMAN BROTHERS Band [119]	8
STEELY DAN [117]	8
5TH DIMENSION [114]	8
STEPPENWOLF [110]	8
WAR [107]	8
Roberta FLACK [105]	8
KOOL & The GANG [102]	8
AMERICA [100]	8
GENESIS [95]	8
AC/DC [94]	8
Paul SIMON [92]	8
Tom PETTY And The HEARTBREAKERS [87]	8
Pat BENATAR [81]	8
Tom JONES [62]	8
VAN HALEN [56]	8
JOURNEY [34]	8
Carole KING [28]	8
SIMON & GARFUNKEL [24]	8
FLEETWOOD MAC [12]	8
LITTLE FEAT [460]	7
JUDAS PRIEST [323]	7
Jeff BECK [318]	7
FOGHAT [314]	7
Ted NUGENT [248]	7
Teddy PENDERGRASS [223]	7
CHER [206]	7
Luther VANDROSS [205]	7
Barry WHITE [201]	7
Ozzy OSBOURNE [199]	7
Anne MURRAY [197]	7
CHEAP TRICK [194]	7
Gordon LIGHTFOOT [180]	7
Paul McCARTNEY [177]	7
KANSAS [176]	7
BREAD [172]	7
J. GEILS Band [171]	7
Ray CONNIFF & His Orchestra & Chorus [165]	7

Act [Act Rank]	Ent
Alan PARSONS PROJECT [161]	7
Helen REDDY [154]	7
POINTER SISTERS [148]	7
Al HIRT [134]	7
George BENSON [93]	7
ZZ TOP [86]	7
The CARS [85]	7
CREAM [80]	7
CARPENTERS [66]	7
STYX [60]	7
Bob SEGER [51]	7
FOREIGNER [37]	7
CREEDENCE CLEARWATER REVIVAL [33]	7
The MONKEES [31]	7
Bruce SPRINGSTEEN [27]	7
EAGLES [20]	7
Trini LOPEZ [405]	6
Maze Featuring Frankie BEVERLY [401]	6
Jimmy SMITH [335]	6
PROCOL HARUM [322]	6
Stephen STILLS [315]	6
IRON MAIDEN [309]	6
Dolly PARTON [306]	6
Emmylou HARRIS [304]	6
Bobby VINTON [292]	6
The CRUSADERS [280]	6
Van MORRISON [276]	6
R.E.M. [269]	6
Jimmy BUFFETT [244]	6
Waylon JENNINGS [233]	6
Smokey ROBINSON [229]	6
Donny OSMOND [226]	6
Al MARTINO [225]	6
Curtis MAYFIELD [200]	6
Paul REVERE And The RAIDERS [196]	6
The ASSOCIATION [192]	6
Rick JAMES [190]	6
RUFUS [189]	6
LOGGINS & MESSINA [185]	6
Rick SPRINGFIELD [184]	6
ALICE COOPER (Grp) [183]	6
BAD COMPANY [166]	6
DURAN DURAN [162]	6
HERMAN'S HERMITS [155]	6
Henry MANCINI and His Orchestra [151]	6
Lou RAWLS [144]	6
Bette MIDLER [143]	6
Steve WINWOOD [138]	6
Quincy JONES [137]	6

Act [Act Rank]	Ent
SEALS & CROFTS [136]	6
RASCALS/ YOUNG RASCALS [131]	6
ALABAMA [130]	6
Jackson BROWNE [124]	6
SUPERTRAMP [121]	6
REO SPEEDWAGON [97]	6
U2 [84]	6
John MELLENCAMP [77]	6
MADONNA [69]	6
The POLICE [68]	6
Jerry VALE [473]	5
Robert GOULET [418]	5
URIAH HEEP [413]	5
Richard PRYOR [395]	5
TRIUMPH [387]	5

Act [Act Rank]	Ent
George CARLIN [370]	5
DAWN/Tony ORLANDO [362]	5
BLUE ÖYSTER CULT [345]	5
John LENNON [337]	5
Ringo STARR [329]	5
The WHISPERS [327]	5
PARLIAMENT [310]	5
Charlie DANIELS Band [307]	5
TEN YEARS AFTER [305]	5
Jack JONES [303]	5
Eddie MONEY [299]	5
.38 SPECIAL [285]	5
Eddy ARNOLD [284]	5
John GARY [283]	5
The PRETENDERS [279]	5

Act [Act Rank]	Ent
VANILLA FUDGE [273]	5
Joe JACKSON [268]	5
The OSMONDS [263]	5
ABBA [261]	5
Otis REDDING [253]	5
EURYTHMICS [252]	5
Joe WALSH [251]	5
SONNY & CHER [243]	5
The MIRACLES/ Smokey ROBINSON & The MIRACLES [231]	5
Kenny LOGGINS [230]	5
AIR SUPPLY [222]	5
BLONDIE [219]	5
Natalie COLE [214]	5
Jimi HENDRIX [188]	5

Act [Act Rank]	Ent
Joe COCKER [178]	5
CHEECH & CHONG [173]	5
Sergio MENDES And BRASIL '66/'77 [170]	5
BACHMAN-TURNER OVERDRIVE [163]	5
OHIO PLAYERS [159]	5
PARTRIDGE FAMILY [152]	5
DIRE STRAITS [132]	5
SLY & THE FAMILY STONE [128]	5
Jimi HENDRIX EXPERIENCE [116]	5
MAMAS & The PAPAS [104]	5
BLOOD, SWEAT & TEARS [74]	5
Michael JACKSON [23]	5

Acts With More Than 100 Consecutive Weeks On The Chart

Act	Weeks
PINK FLOYD	618
The BEATLES	385
The TEMPTATIONS	344
Carole KING	302
Willie NELSON	272
Andy WILLIAMS	269
BEE GEES	262
Elton JOHN	254
Dean MARTIN	254
ALABAMA	252
John DENVER	251
The SUPREMES/ Diana ROSS And The SUPREMES	247
MADONNA	244
Nancy WILSON	230
Dionne WARWICK	229
Daryl HALL & John OATES	214
Barry MANILOW	213
ROLLING STONES	212
Herb ALPERT & The TIJUANA BRASS	210
Cat STEVENS	202
ZZ TOP	202
Aretha FRANKLIN	201
The VENTURES	200
Bill COSBY	199
STEPPENWOLF	197
U2	195
Barbra STREISAND	195
FLEETWOOD MAC	194
JOURNEY	189
Van MORRISON	189
Kenny ROGERS	187
GRAND FUNK RAILROAD	184
THREE DOG NIGHT	177
Charley PRIDE	176
CREAM	176
EAGLES	174
Stevie WONDER	174
Bette MIDLER	173
Reba McENTIRE	172
Isaac HAYES	170
Glen CAMPBELL	169
PRINCE	169
BREAD	169
CREEDENCE CLEARWATER REVIVAL	168
RASCALS/YOUNG RASCALS	167
Frank SINATRA	167
ELECTRIC LIGHT ORCHESTRA	167
Donna SUMMER	165
FOREIGNER	164
SLY & THE FAMILY STONE	164
CHICAGO	163
STYX	162
The ANIMALS/ Eric BURDON & The ANIMALS	162
KISS	160
MOODY BLUES	159

Act	Weeks
DURAN DURAN	158
AEROSMITH	157
JACKSON 5	157
Bruce SPRINGSTEEN	153
Dave CLARK Five	153
IRON BUTTERFLY	153
MAMAS & The PAPAS	152
Ray CONNIFF & His Orchestra & Chorus	152
Al GREEN	152
John GARY	151
Randy TRAVIS	149
CHEECH & CHONG	148
SANTANA	148
Sergio MENDES And BRASIL '66/'77	147
HERMAN'S HERMITS	146
Pat BENATAR	146
Paul McCARTNEY & WINGS/WINGS	145
MÖTLEY CRÜE	145
Johnny CASH	144
PETER, PAUL & MARY	144
Paul REVERE And The RAIDERS	144
The COMMODORES	144
George STRAIT	144
SIMON & GARFUNKEL	142
Al MARTINO	142
The CARS	142
Billy JOEL	141
VAN HALEN	141
The CURE	141
The MONKEES	140
BEACH BOYS	135
CARPENTERS	135
TALKING HEADS	135
Olivia NEWTON-JOHN	135
AMERICA	134
LOGGINS & MESSINA	133
Roger MILLER	133
DEF LEPPARD	133
Neil DIAMOND	132
Jimi HENDRIX EXPERIENCE	132
Wes MONTGOMERY	131
FOUR TOPS	130
Roberta FLACK	130
Al JARREAU	129
DOKKEN	129
DEEP PURPLE	128
Gary LEWIS And The PLAYBOYS	128
Helen REDDY	127
Bonnie RAITT	125
SAN SEBASTIAN Strings	124
LOVERBOY	124
METALLICA	123
POINTER SISTERS	123
R.E.M.	123
DOOBIE BROTHERS	122
Michael JACKSON	122
The POLICE	121

Act	Weeks
LED ZEPPELIN	119
Elvis PRESLEY	119
Steve MILLER Band	119
Joe COCKER	119
BLOOD, SWEAT & TEARS	119
Al HIRT	118
Donny OSMOND	118
Jim CROCE	118
The KINGSMEN	117
Engelbert HUMPERDINCK	116
Gladys KNIGHT & The PIPS	116
5TH DIMENSION	116
The ASSOCIATION	116
Bob SEGER	115
BACHMAN-TURNER OVERDRIVE	115
Waylon JENNINGS	115
Jimi HENDRIX	115
Boz SCAGGS	115
Henry MANCINI and his Orchestra	114
SEALS & CROFTS	113
EARTH, WIND & FIRE	113
The DOORS	112
CAPTAIN & TENNILLE	112
Eddy ARNOLD	111
Billy SQUIER	111
The OSMONDS	111
UB40	111
Chuck MANGIONE	110
The LETTERMEN	109
Billy IDOL	109
JETHRO TULL	109
Tanya TUCKER	109
Julio IGLESIAS	108
RIGHTEOUS BROTHERS	107
BLONDIE	107
REO SPEEDWAGON	106
Ozzy OSBOURNE	106
Tina TURNER	106
4 SEASONS	105
Charlie RICH	105
James TAYLOR	105
WAR	105
Peter FRAMPTON	105
The WHO	104
Jack JONES	103
VANILLA FUDGE	103
Linda RONSTADT	103
Trini LOPEZ	102
The PRETENDERS	102
KENNY G	102
Ed AMES	101
LYNYRD SKYNYRD	101
VILLAGE PEOPLE	101
HEART	100
CROSBY, STILLS & NASH	100
Jeffrey OSBORNE	100

Acts With Most Albums On The Chart Simultaneously

9 Albums	Wks	Dates
LED ZEPPELIN	2	27-Oct-79 - 03-Nov-79
8 Albums	**Wks**	**Dates**
The BEATLES	2	02-Jan-65 - 09-Jan-65
Herb ALPERT & The TIJUANA BRASS	4	11-May-68 - 01-Jun-68
7 Albums	**Wks**	**Dates**
Bill COSBY	6	24-Feb-68; 06-Apr-68 - 04-May-68
CHICAGO	7	07-Sep-74 - 19-Oct-74
The MONKEES	3	08-Nov-86 - 22-Nov-86
John Fitzgerald KENNEDY	2	08-Feb-64 - 15-Feb-64
U2	22	25-Apr-87 - 19-Sep-87
6 Albums	**Wks**	**Dates**
Elvis PRESLEY	8	29-Oct-77 - 17-Dec-77
ROLLING STONES	3	11-Oct-80 - 25-Oct-80
Marvin GAYE	2	12-May-84 - 19-May-84
Johnny CASH	2	11-Oct-69 - 18-Oct-69
John DENVER	5	20-Dec-75 - 17-Jan-76
Tom JONES	18	14-Jun-69 - 15-Nov-69
REO SPEEDWAGON	2	07-Mar-81 - 14-Mar-81
Julio IGLESIAS	4	15-Sep-84 - 06-Oct-84
Kenny ROGERS	1	10-May-80
5 Albums	**Wks**	**Dates**
BEACH BOYS	5	31-Jul-76 - 28-Aug-76
Neil DIAMOND	1	27-Feb-71
Glen CAMPBELL	12	16-Nov-68 - 01-Feb-69
FLEETWOOD MAC	1	27-Sep-75
Barry MANILOW	8	28-May-77 - 16-Jul-77
Engelbert HUMPERDINCK	1	7-Feb-70
AC/DC	13	19-Dec-81 - 13-Mar-82
JOURNEY	11	15-Aug-81 - 26-Sep-81; 14-Nov-81 - 05-Dec-81
Al HIRT	11	13-Mar-65 - 22-May-65
Mac DAVIS	1	15-Feb-75
RASCALS/YOUNG RASCALS	3	13-Jul-68 - 27-Jul-68
Bruce SPRINGSTEEN	11	22-Nov-80 - 20-Dec-80; 12-Jan-85 - 16-Feb-85
SIMON & GARFUNKEL	11	15-Jun-68 - 10-Aug-68; 25-Jan-69 - 01-Feb-69
Rev. Martin Luther KING	1	8-Jun-68
The POLICE	33	27-Aug-83 - 07-Apr-84

4 Albums	Weeks
Johnny MATHIS	4
Barbra STREISAND	24
The TEMPTATIONS	13
Aretha FRANKLIN	1
Dionne WARWICK	5
Willie NELSON	6
Bob DYLAN	4
Frank SINATRA	24
Nancy WILSON	3
Elton JOHN	34
David BOWIE	7
Henry MANCINI and his Orchestra	10
Andy WILLIAMS	3
BEE GEES	6
Gladys KNIGHT & The PIPS	10
Lou RAWLS	17
Al MARTINO	5
The SUPREMES Diana ROSS And The SUPREMES	26
Dean MARTIN	7
KISS	29
4 SEASONS	2
The DOORS	8
PINK FLOYD	8
Jack JONES	4
GRAND FUNK RAILROAD	2
Billy JOEL	2
THREE DOG NIGHT	5
AEROSMITH	11
STEPPENWOLF	10
5TH DIMENSION	8
CREEDENCE CLEARWATER REVIVAL	48
Cat STEVENS	2
Ed AMES	5
DOOBIE BROTHERS	8
Bob SEGER	23
ALABAMA	11
SEALS & CROFTS	8
Charlie RICH	18
PRINCE	21
STYX	26
LYNYRD SKYNYRD	3
DAWN/Tony ORLANDO	4
Nat King COLE	12
EAGLES	21
Paul McCARTNEY & WINGS/WINGS	6
MAMAS & The PAPAS	18
Ozzy OSBOURNE	2
IRON MAIDEN	2
FOREIGNER	5
VILLAGE PEOPLE	6
MADONNA	3
MÖTLEY CRÜE	3

100 Acts with Highest Average Album Score

Highest average score per album, across the entire catalog, with a minimum of 5 albums. Since the average album overall = 1000 points, these acts' entire catalog averages more than twice the average album.

Rank. Act - Avg Score/Entries
1. LED ZEPPELIN - 7877/10
2. SIMON & GARFUNKEL - 7324/8
3. DEF LEPPARD - 7109/5
4. FOREIGNER - 6825/7
5. EAGLES - 6659/9
6. The POLICE - 6358/6
7. MADONNA - 6355/6
8. Bruce SPRINGSTEEN - 6080/9
9. Michael JACKSON - 5388/11
10. VAN HALEN - 5301/8
11. Herb ALPERT & The TIJUANA BRASS - 5214/18
12. Billy JOEL - 5209/14
13. Paul McCARTNEY & WINGS/ WINGS - 5169/9
14. John MELLENCAMP - 5001/7
15. CHICAGO - 4929/20
16. The CARS - 4685/7
17. The BEATLES - 4588/37
18. MÖTLEY CRÜE - 4584/5
19. Jimi HENDRIX EXPERIENCE - 4466/6
20. Jim CROCE - 4258/6
21. CREAM - 4258/8
22. ROLLING STONES - 4161/35
23. U2 - 4118/8
24. PRINCE - 4116/11
25. JOURNEY - 4086/12
26. IRON BUTTERFLY - 3968/7
27. CROSBY, STILLS & NASH - 3968/5
28. HEART - 3947/10
29. The MONKEES - 3833/13
30. CREEDENCE CLEARWATER REVIVAL - 3802/13
31. Pat BENATAR - 3781/9
32. DOOBIE BROTHERS - 3736/12
33. FLEETWOOD MAC - 3733/19
34. STYX - 3723/11
35. Bob SEGER - 3652/12
36. ZZ TOP - 3613/9
37. Tom PETTY And The HEARTBREAKERS - 3602/9
38. Carole KING - 3569/15
39. BLOOD, SWEAT & TEARS - 3565/10
40. LOVERBOY - 3538/6
41. PINK FLOYD - 3501/17
42. Paul SIMON - 3469/9
43. Elton JOHN - 3424/30
44. THREE DOG NIGHT - 3383/14
45. SANTANA - 3345/17
46. James TAYLOR - 3255/14
47. Stevie WONDER - 3253/22
48. Cat STEVENS - 3245/13
49. Tina TURNER - 3196/5
50. MAMAS & The PAPAS - 3186/9
51. MOODY BLUES - 3157/16
52. Barbra STREISAND - 3151/40
53. PARTRIDGE FAMILY - 3146/7
54. John DENVER - 3102/21
55. DIRE STRAITS - 3039/8
56. Daryl HALL & John OATES - 2984/16
57. STEELY DAN - 2977/9
58. EARTH, WIND & FIRE - 2955/18
59. KENNY G - 2954/5
60. SUPERTRAMP - 2947/9
61. Rod STEWART - 2920/21
62. Steve WINWOOD - 2895/8
63. AEROSMITH - 2884/14
64. Janis JOPLIN - 2857/6
65. Jackson BROWNE - 2857/9
66. PETER, PAUL & MARY - 2838/11
67. CARPENTERS - 2799/14
68. Billy IDOL - 2789/5
69. WHITESNAKE - 2785/6
70. Donna SUMMER - 2778/15
71. SLY & THE FAMILY STONE - 2775/9
72. BEE GEES - 2765/25
73. Billy OCEAN - 2747/5
74. Peter FRAMPTON - 2718/11
75. ALICE COOPER (Grp) - 2690/7
76. The COMMODORES - 2688/16
77. GRAND FUNK RAILROAD - 2683/16
78. BLONDIE - 2660/6
79. AIR SUPPLY - 2639/6
80. Billy SQUIER - 2626/6
81. DURAN DURAN - 2606/8
82. VANILLA FUDGE - 2597/5
83. BREAD - 2539/8
84. CHEECH & CHONG - 2537/8
85. The DOORS - 2532/18
86. Linda RONSTADT - 2509/23
87. RASCALS/YOUNG RASCALS - 2463/10
88. INXS - 2455/6
89. ELECTRIC LIGHT ORCHESTRA - 2437/14
90. Luther VANDROSS - 2417/7
91. Dan FOGELBERG - 2414/10
92. Barry MANILOW - 2393/18
93. Roberta FLACK - 2374/12
94. The WHO - 2369/20
95. AC/DC - 2368/13
96. The SUPREMES/Diana ROSS And The SUPREMES - 2363/21
97. JEFFERSON AIRPLANE/ STARSHIP - 2360/27
98. GENESIS - 2357/13
99. VILLAGE PEOPLE - 2349/7
100. CAPTAIN & TENNILLE - 2343/6

Acts With #1 Albums

Act	Num (Wk)
The BEATLES	15 (119)
ROLLING STONES	9 (38)
Elton JOHN	7 (39)
LED ZEPPELIN	6 (28)
Herb ALPERT & The TIJUANA BRASS	5 (26)
CHICAGO	5 (22)
Barbra STREISAND	5 (16)
Paul McCARTNEY & WINGS/WINGS	5 (16)
The MONKEES	4 (37)
EAGLES	4 (27)
Bruce SPRINGSTEEN	4 (19)
FLEETWOOD MAC	3 (37)
PRINCE	3 (33)
BEE GEES	3 (31)
SIMON & GARFUNKEL	3 (26)
Carole KING	3 (19)
PINK FLOYD	3 (18)
Billy JOEL	3 (15)
MADONNA	3 (14)
Bob DYLAN	3 (11)
Donna SUMMER	3 (8)
Linda RONSTADT	3 (7)
John DENVER	3 (6)
CROSBY, STILLS, NASH & YOUNG	3 (3)
Michael JACKSON	2 (43)
Stevie WONDER	2 (16)
U2	2 (15)
CREEDENCE CLEARWATER REVIVAL	2 (13)
BON JOVI	2 (12)
George HARRISON	2 (12)
Phil COLLINS	2 (11)
SANTANA	2 (11)
BLOOD, SWEAT & TEARS	2 (9)
MOODY BLUES	2 (8)
Rod STEWART	2 (7)
The SUPREMES/ Diana ROSS And The SUPREMES	2 (7)
VAN HALEN	2 (7)
BOSTON	2 (6)
EARTH, WIND & FIRE	2 (6)
Janet JACKSON	2 (6)
Paul McCARTNEY	2 (6)
BEACH BOYS	2 (5)
Lionel RICHIE	2 (5)
JETHRO TULL	2 (3)
Elvis PRESLEY	2 (2)
Huey LEWIS And The NEWS	2 (2)
Olivia NEWTON-JOHN	2 (2)
The POLICE	1 (17)
MEN AT WORK	1 (15)
REO SPEEDWAGON	1 (15)
Whitney HOUSTON	1 (14)
George MICHAEL	1 (12)

Act	Num (Wk)
FOREIGNER	1 (10)
Paula ABDUL	1 (10)
Peter FRAMPTON	1 (10)
SINGING NUN	1 (10)
ASIA	1 (9)
DIRE STRAITS	1 (9)
Janis JOPLIN	1 (9)
John MELLENCAMP	1 (9)
Allan SHERMAN	1 (8)
BIG BROTHER And The HOLDING COMPANY	1 (8)
John LENNON & Yoko ONO	1 (8)
BEASTIE BOYS	1 (7)
Don McLEAN	1 (7)
FINE YOUNG CANNIBALS	1 (7)
MILLI VANILLI	1 (7)
Barbra STREISAND & Kris KRISTOFFERSON	1 (6)
Bob SEGER	1 (6)
Bobby BROWN	1 (6)
DEF LEPPARD	1 (6)
Louis ARMSTRONG	1 (6)
SUPERTRAMP	1 (6)
The GO-GO'S	1 (6)
ALLMAN BROTHERS Band	1 (5)
AMERICA	1 (5)
Carly SIMON	1 (5)
Debbie GIBSON	1 (5)
DOOBIE BROTHERS	1 (5)
Glen CAMPBELL	1 (5)
GUNS N' ROSES	1 (5)
Jim CROCE	1 (5)
Marvin Hamlisch	1 (5)
Paul MAURIAT And His Orchestra	1 (5)
PETER, PAUL & MARY	1 (5)
QUEEN	1 (5)
Roberta FLACK	1 (5)
SSgt Barry SADLER	1 (5)
TEARS FOR FEARS	1 (5)
The KNACK	1 (5)
Anita BAKER	1 (4)
CREAM	1 (4)
Curtis MAYFIELD	1 (4)
Eric CLAPTON	1 (4)
J. GEILS Band	1 (4)
JEFFERSON AIRPLANE/STARSHIP	1 (4)
Johnny CASH	1 (4)
Kim CARNES	1 (4)
The DOORS	1 (4)
VANGELIS	1 (4)
AC/DC	1 (3)
Bonnie RAITT	1 (3)
Cat STEVENS	1 (3)
Eric WEISSBERG & Steve MANDELL	1 (3)

Act	Num (Wk)
STYX	1 (3)
USA For AFRICA	1 (3)
WHAM!	1 (3)
BLIND FAITH	1 (2)
Bobbie GENTRY	1 (2)
Bryan ADAMS	1 (2)
Diana ROSS	1 (2)
George BENSON	1 (2)
Gordon LIGHTFOOT	1 (2)
Jimi HENDRIX EXPERIENCE	1 (2)
Kenny ROGERS	1 (2)
Los LOBOS	1 (2)
MÖTLEY CRÜE	1 (2)
Neil YOUNG	1 (2)
NEW KIDS ON THE BLOCK	1 (2)
SADE	1 (2)
SLY & THE FAMILY STONE	1 (2)
TIFFFANY	1 (2)
WAR	1 (2)
ALICE COOPER (Grp)	1 (1)
AVERAGE WHITE BAND/AWB	1 (1)
BACHMAN-TURNER OVERDRIVE	1 (1)
BAD COMPANY	1 (1)
Barry MANILOW	1 (1)
Barry WHITE	1 (1)
BLUES BROTHERS	1 (1)
CARPENTERS	1 (1)
Frank SINATRA	1 (1)
Gerry RAFFERTY	1 (1)
HEART	1 (1)
Isaac HAYES	1 (1)
ISLEY BROTHERS	1 (1)
Jackson BROWNE	1 (1)
Janis IAN	1 (1)
John FOGERTY	1 (1)
John LENNON	1 (1)
John LENNON/PLASTIC ONO BAND	1 (1)
JOURNEY	1 (1)
MAMAS & The PAPAS	1 (1)
MR. MISTER	1 (1)
OHIO PLAYERS	1 (1)
Pat BENATAR	1 (1)
Patti LaBELLE	1 (1)
Paul SIMON	1 (1)
QUIET RIOT	1 (1)
RASCALS/YOUNG RASCALS	1 (1)
Richard MARX	1 (1)
Steve WINWOOD	1 (1)
Stevie NICKS	1 (1)
Diana ROSS And The SUPREMES And The TEMPTATIONS	1 (1)
TONE-LOC	1 (1)
Tracy CHAPMAN	1 (1)

100 Highest Scoring Acts with No Weekly Top 5

This list comprises the highest scoring acts never to have a top 5 album, minimum of 5 albums.

Rank. Act (Act Rank) Peak [T10 I T40 I Tot]	Score
1. Dionne WARWICK (72) Pk: 6 [2 I 14 I 33]	36632
2. KOOL & The GANG (102) Pk: 10 [1 I 8 I 20]	29155
3. James BROWN (118) Pk: 10 [1 I 14 I 48]	26659
4. DEEP PURPLE (125) Pk: 6 [3 I 9 I 18]	25711
5. ALABAMA (130) Pk: 10 [1 I 6 I 12]	24744
6. Johnny MATHIS (135) Pk: 9 [2 I 10 I 44]	23738
7. Quincy JONES (137) Pk: 6 [3 I 6 I 13]	23227
8. BLACK SABBATH (140) Pk: 8 [1 I 10 I 16]	22920
9. Gladys KNIGHT & The PIPS (145) Pk: 9 [2 I 9 I 25]	22628
10. The O'JAYS (146) Pk: 6 [3 I 10 I 17]	22620
11. The KINKS (147) Pk: 9 [1 I 10 I 32]	22538
12. POINTER SISTERS (148) Pk: 8 [1 I 7 I 16]	22249
13. Joan BAEZ (149) Pk: 7 [2 I 9 I 22]	22203
14. LOVERBOY (158) Pk: 7 [2 I 4 I 6]	21227
15. Alan PARSONS PROJECT (161) Pk: 7 [2 I 7 I 11]	20991
16. GRATEFUL DEAD (164) Pk: 6 [1 I 13 I 25]	20748
17. The LETTERMEN (167) Pk: 10 [1 I 8 I 28]	20616
18. TALKING HEADS (181) Pk: 15 [0 I 8 I 10]	19104
19. The VENTURES (191) Pk: 11 [0 I 11 I 25]	18179
20. Anne MURRAY (197) Pk: 12 [0 I 7 I 24]	17584
21. Ozzy OSBOURNE (199) Pk: 6 [2 I 7 I 8]	17459
22. 4 SEASONS (202) Pk: 6 [3 I 8 I 20]	17241
23. Frank ZAPPA (204) Pk: 10 [1 I 9 I 33]	17113
24. Luther VANDROSS (205) Pk: 9 [1 I 7 I 7]	16919
25. CHER (206) Pk: 10 [1 I 7 I 18]	16854
26. SPINNERS (209) Pk: 8 [2 I 8 I 17]	16544
27. GUESS WHO (211) Pk: 9 [1 I 4 I 15]	16289
28. Natalie COLE (214) Pk: 8 [1 I 5 I 13]	16168
29. BLONDIE (219) Pk: 6 [2 I 5 I 6]	15962
30. AIR SUPPLY (222) Pk: 7 [2 I 5 I 6]	15837
31. Al MARTINO (225) Pk: 8 [2 I 6 I 22]	15663
32. Donny OSMOND (226) Pk: 6 [1 I 6 I 11]	15478
33. The ANIMALS/Eric BURDON & The ANIMALS (227) Pk: 6 [2 I 4 I 17]	15402
34. Smokey ROBINSON (229) Pk: 10 [1 I 6 I 16]	15341
35. Kenny LOGGINS (230) Pk: 7 [1 I 5 I 7]	15306
36. The MIRACLES/Smokey ROBINSON & The MIRACLES (231) Pk: 7 [2 I 5 I 18]	15173
37. Waylon JENNINGS (233) Pk: 10 [1 I 6 I 17]	15018
38. Charley PRIDE (234) Pk: 22 [0 I 4 I 17]	14897
39. KENNY G (239) Pk: 6 [2 I 3 I 5]	14770
40. Jimmy BUFFETT (244) Pk: 10 [1 I 6 I 16]	14581
41. Ted NUGENT (248) Pk: 13 [0 I 7 I 13]	14453
42. RARE EARTH (250) Pk: 12 [0 I 4 I 9]	14173
43. Joe WALSH (251) Pk: 6 [2 I 5 I 10]	14162
44. EURYTHMICS (252) Pk: 7 [2 I 5 I 8]	14127
45. Billy IDOL (256) Pk: 6 [3 I 3 I 5]	13945
46. The BYRDS (258) Pk: 6 [2 I 8 I 15]	13819
47. Billy OCEAN (259) Pk: 6 [2 I 3 I 5]	13737
48. ABBA (261) Pk: 14 [0 I 5 I 10]	13632
49. The OSMONDS (263) Pk: 10 [1 I 5 I 12]	13441
50. R.E.M. (269) Pk: 10 [1 I 6 I 8]	13110
51. MARSHALL TUCKER Band (271) Pk: 15 [0 I 8 I 12]	13081
52. VANILLA FUDGE (273) Pk: 6 [1 I 5 I 5]	12984
53. Robert PALMER (275) Pk: 8 [1 I 3 I 11]	12949
54. Van MORRISON (276) Pk: 15 [0 I 6 I 20]	12778
55. LITTLE RIVER BAND (277) Pk: 10 [1 I 4 I 9]	12752
56. The CRUSADERS (280) Pk: 18 [0 I 6 I 18]	12409
57. Al JARREAU (281) Pk: 9 [1 I 3 I 10]	12394
58. John GARY (283) Pk: 11 [0 I 5 I 14]	12365
59. Eddy ARNOLD (284) Pk: 7 [1 I 5 I 17]	12308
60. .38 SPECIAL (285) Pk: 10 [1 I 5 I 8]	12291
61. CAMEO (289) Pk: 8 [1 I 4 I 13]	12075
62. Herbie HANCOCK (290) Pk: 13 [0 I 4 I 18]	12075
63. POCO (291) Pk: 14 [0 I 4 I 20]	12029
64. Bobby VINTON (292) Pk: 8 [1 I 6 I 21]	11983
65. Charlie RICH (296) Pk: 8 [1 I 4 I 12]	11834
66. Eddie MONEY (299) Pk: 17 [0 I 5 I 8]	11661
67. NEW EDITION (301) Pk: 6 [1 I 3 I 5]	11484
68. Jack JONES (303) Pk: 9 [1 I 5 I 17]	11267
69. Emmylou HARRIS (304) Pk: 6 [1 I 6 I 17]	11224
70. TEN YEARS AFTER (305) Pk: 14 [0 I 5 I 12]	11163
71. Dolly PARTON (306) Pk: 6 [1 I 6 I 17]	11130
72. IRON MAIDEN (309) Pk: 11 [0 I 6 I 8]	10997
73. PARLIAMENT (310) Pk: 13 [0 I 5 I 8]	10992
74. FOGHAT (314) Pk: 11 [0 I 7 I 13]	10900
75. NIGHT RANGER (319) Pk: 10 [1 I 4 I 5]	10661
76. JUDAS PRIEST (323) Pk: 17 [0 I 7 I 10]	10585
77. Ray PARKER Jr./RAYDIO (325) Pk: 11 [0 I 4 I 10]	10580
78. Roger WILLIAMS (326) Pk: 7 [1 I 3 I 18]	10549
79. The WHISPERS (327) Pk: 6 [1 I 5 I 13]	10547
80. The STYLISTICS (328) Pk: 14 [0 I 3 I 10]	10541
81. MANTOVANI (330) Pk: 23 [0 I 4 I 20]	10488
82. Bob MARLEY And The WAILERS (331) Pk: 8 [1 I 2 I 14]	10462
83. RATT (332) Pk: 7 [2 I 4 I 5]	10425
84. Jimmy SMITH (335) Pk: 12 [0 I 6 I 18]	10320
85. Jermaine JACKSON (336) Pk: 6 [1 I 3 I 11]	10083
86. B.B. KING (338) Pk: 25 [0 I 3 I 21]	10066
87. Stephanie MILLS (339) Pk: 16 [0 I 4 I 9]	10060
88. Elvis COSTELLO & The ATTRACTIONS (340) Pk: 10 [1 I 8 I 11]	9978
89. ATLANTA RHYTHM SECTION (343) Pk: 7 [1 I 3 I 10]	9842
90. BLUE ÖYSTER CULT (345) Pk: 22 [0 I 5 I 14]	9809
91. GAP BAND (348) Pk: 14 [0 I 3 I 9]	9708
92. Tony BENNETT (353) Pk: 18 [0 I 4 I 21]	9576
93. Ramsey LEWIS (354) Pk: 12 [0 I 2 I 22]	9551
94. Melissa MANCHESTER (355) Pk: 12 [0 I 4 I 13]	9466
95. The CLASH (357) Pk: 7 [1 I 3 I 8]	9264
96. Dave MASON (358) Pk: 22 [0 I 4 I 14]	9253
97. Bobby SHERMAN (359) Pk: 10 [1 I 3 I 6]	9243
98. DAWN/Tony ORLANDO (362) Pk: 16 [0 I 5 I 11]	9150
99. JAMES GANG (363) Pk: 20 [0 I 3 I 11]	9136
100. Sheena EASTON (364) Pk: 15 [0 I 4 I 7]	9075

The Acts: Chronologies

The Chronologies show the entry date and relative strength of the entire catalog of albums of the Top 25 acts.

This is an example of the headings:

The BEATLES ▶ 1 (37) 169751

That is, **the Act, its rank (Number of Entries) Total Act Points**.
In the stories that accompany the graphs, mention is made of the "Top X%" of albums. The upper percentiles relate to score as follows

Percentile	Score
Top 1%	>9592
Top 2.5%	>6505
Top 5%	>4454
Top 10%	>2688
Top 25%	>1000

Thus, as discussed in the Methodology in the Appendix, an "average" song score actually places a song at the top 25%, not the top half.
The Time scale for each of the chronologies is kept the same to allow comparisons among them. However the Score scale is changed for each chronology in order to give better granularity to the view. In some cases where there are wide disparities in score, insets may be used.
In some chronologies a line is used to show the entire time a record was on the chart. In those cases, a solid line means the record charted continuously in that period; a dashed line means there were times it was off the chart between it entry and ultimate exit. A number in parentheses after the name of an album on the graph denotes the album ranking for the top 100.

The BEATLES ▶ 1 (37) 169751

The Beatles' US album career started less than six months after Billboard switched to the consolidated Mono and Stereo chart, so all their albums are included here. Three of the 13 main catalog albums, that is the Capitol/Apple albums, scored in the Top 50 for this period—of that catalog, only *"Yesterday" And Today* fell out of the top 5%.

Sgt. Pepper's logged 175 weeks on the chart, on and off over a span of twenty years, finally exiting in October of 1987. The *White Album* and *Abbey Road* stayed on for 155 and 129 weeks respectively, but their longevity was surpassed by the first "greatest hits" collections: Beatles 1962-1966 and Beatles 1967-1970 at 164 and 169 weeks respectively. All of those efforts are well into the top 1% of all records.

The Beatles were on the charts for 385 consecutive weeks, second only to Pink Floyd, for a total of 1849 weeks, the most of any act. In January of 1965 eight of their albums were on the chart simultaneously in the days of the 150-position chart—qualifying at least for an asterisk in the record book, since Led Zeppelin charted 9 in 1979 but on the 200-position chart. They appeared in the Top 50 acts for the year in eight of the years between 1964 and 1973.

Looking at all their releases, however, the Beatles were not the most efficient group, ranking 17th with an average score of 4588; however, their 37 chart entries (tied for sixth highest) in the period included some lesser works released in the early days to capitalize on their skyrocket and anthologies released 10-20 years after their heyday.

It's incredible to think that they could crank out music of that chart popularity, and that quality at an average rate of one album every six months or so over a period of about six years.

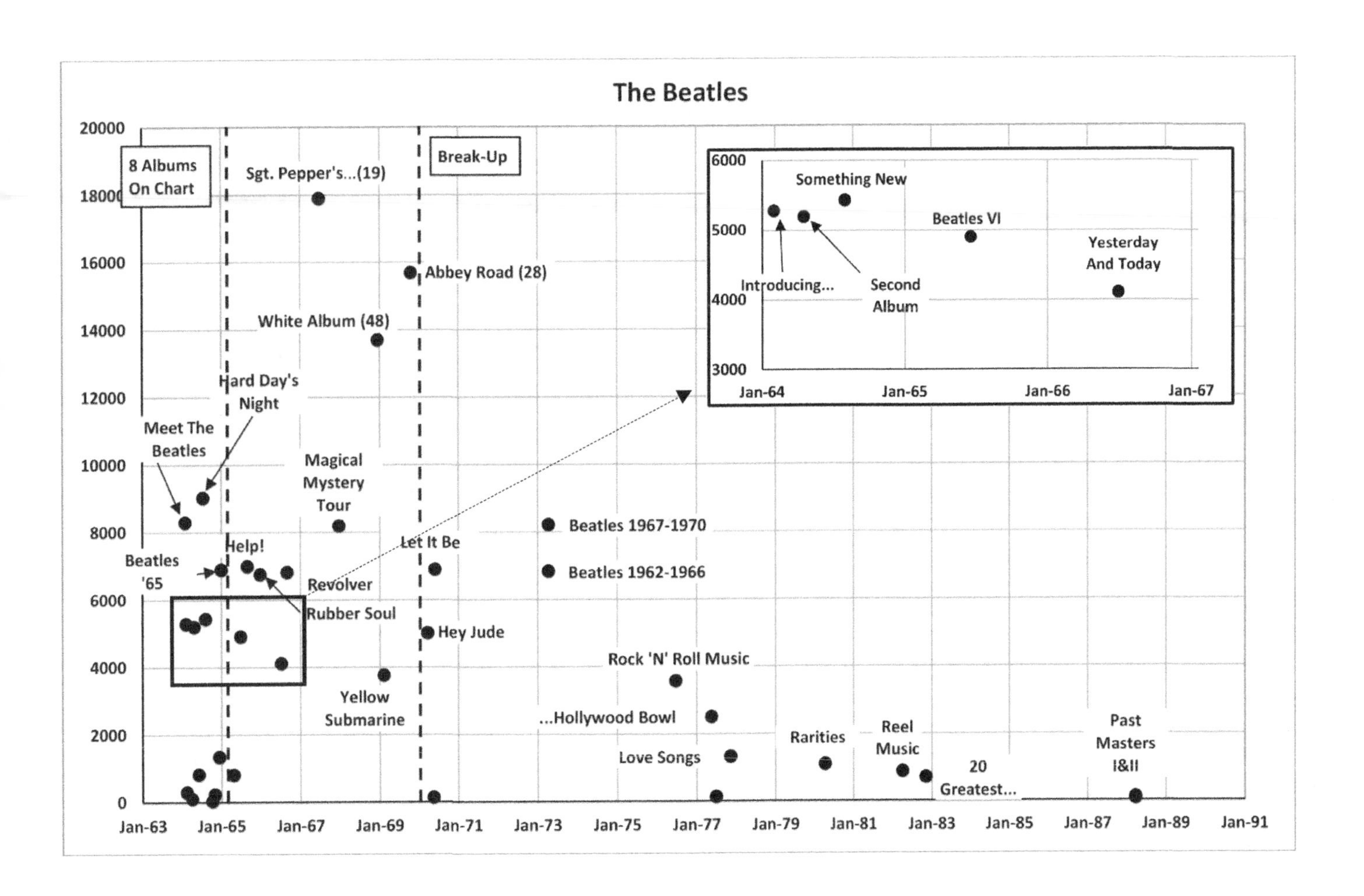

The Individual Beatles

The story would be incomplete without some discussion of the solo albums. *Wonderwall Music*, by Harrison was the first solo album effort to chart, in January of 1969 before the band officially broke up. Clearly, Paul McCartney was the most successful in all his manifestations (McCartney(s)/Wings, 74939—if combined would place 7th for the period. The McCartney entities scored nearly as much as the other three combined: Lennon/Ono/Plastic Ono Band, 35113; Harrison, 31599; Starr 10520) but all four were in the top 10% of the acts charting in this period. It's surprising to see how close George Harrison's chart score is to John Lennon's. What's more, the sum of the parts was nearly as much as the whole—152171 as individuals vs 169751 as The Beatles

Only one of those albums scored in the top 1%--*Band On The Run*, with its 116 weeks and 32 in the top 10—although *Wings At The Speed Of Sound* and *Double Fantasy* were close. Perhaps it is either tragic or ironic that Lennon's biggest success came after his death.

McCartney and Wings were the 13th most efficient act of those charting 5 albums or more, averaging 5169 points over 9 entries. Harrison was well down the list at 2257.

The individual histories take the same shape as the band's history. After peaking with *Sgt. Pepper's*, they all had a gradual fall-off for the rest of the period. Still, some McCartney entity charted every year between 1970 and 1989, and he placed in the top 50 acts for the year ten times.

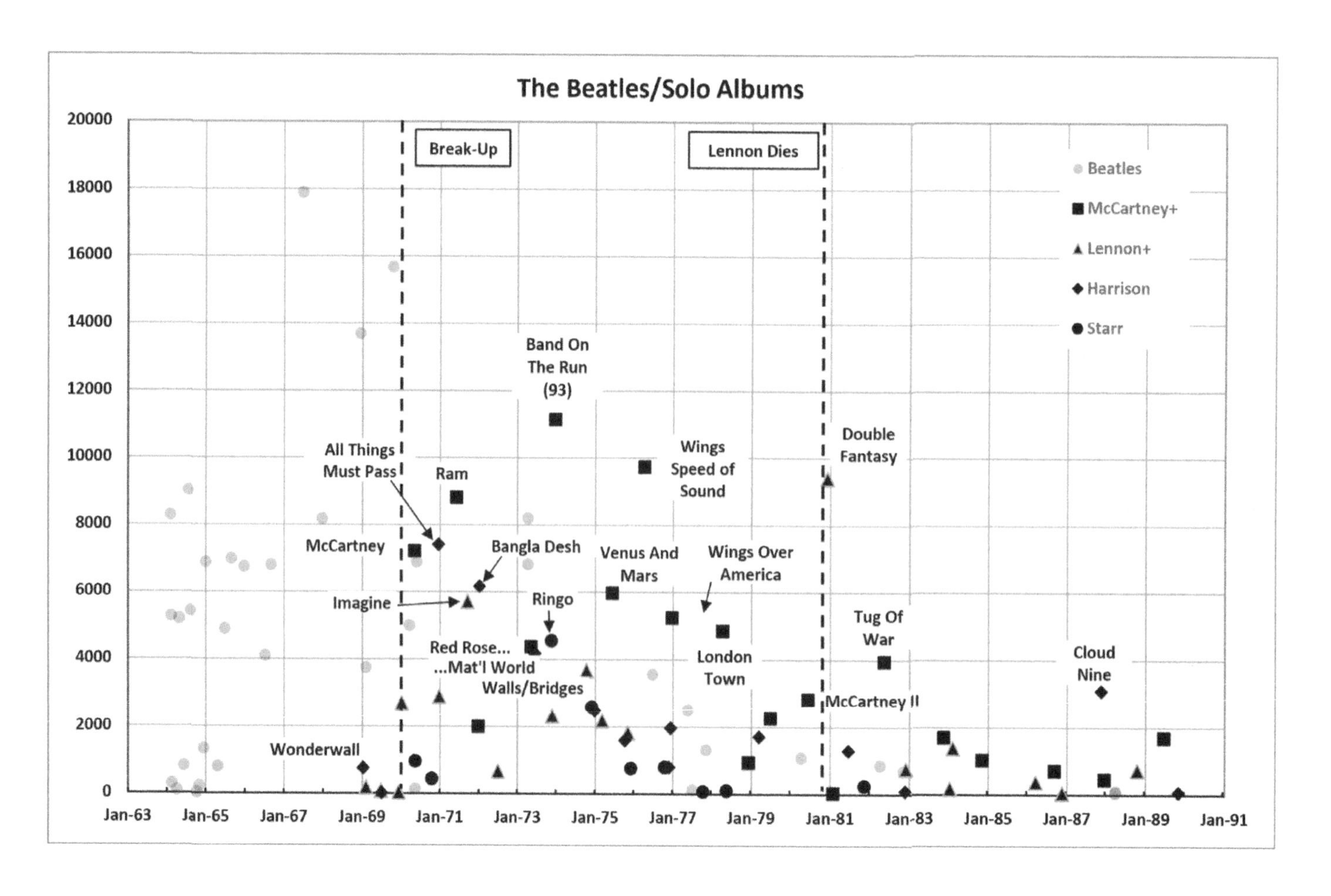

ROLLING STONES ► 2 (35) 145643

It seems very strange that one of the vanguard bands of the British Invasion would not hit its apex of chart performance until nearly 15 years later. Up to 1971, the Stones seemed to have the profile of a singles band with its best-performing album a greatest hits collection, with album performance falling off after that. But *Some Girls* and *Tattoo You* fell into the top 1% of album performers, and *Emotional Rescue* in the Top 2%.

What caused the resurgence? Patrick Byron writing in Medium about *Some Girls* attributes it to three things. First, the addition of Ron Wood to replace Mick Taylor. Second, a good sense for the times—*Miss You*—which Jagger described as disco without being disco. Third, at the dawn of punk, attitude paired with musicality.

Tattoo You almost seems like an accidental success. It consists of fragments and outtakes with new vocals and overdubs which could be promoted on their epic 1981-82 US and European tour. Richards noted, "There was no time to make a whole new album and go out on tour."

The Stones were a top 50 act for the year in 19 of the 26 years of this period. *Hot Rocks* logged 243 weeks on the chart, fifth most, but that was their only album to chart for more than 100 weeks. However, in total chart weeks they are second with 1512.

None of the Stones' records broke into the all-time Top 100. Maybe that's the most interesting question: why weren't *Let It Bleed* (peaked at number 3), *Sticky Fingers* and *Exile On Main Street* (number 1 four weeks each) more popular?

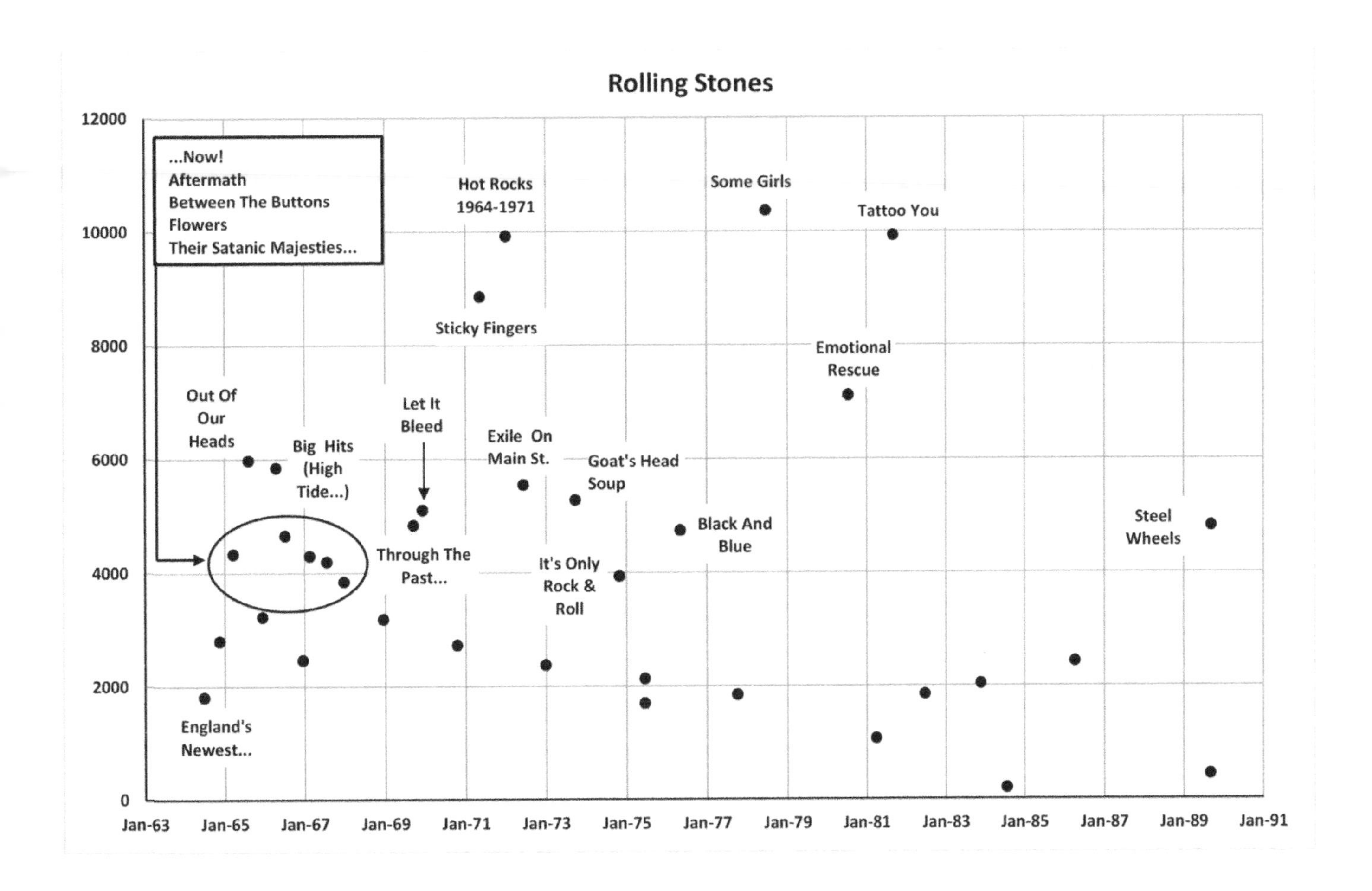

BARBRA STREISAND ▶ 3 (40) 126028

Barbra Streisand's debut album, entering April 13, 1963, predates the combined chart, but like her albums 2-9 (including three soundtracks) it peaked in the top 10. Streisand came from the same musical incubator as Neil Diamond, Erasmus High School, one of four high schools in Brooklyn whose alumni shaped popular music for decades to come.

Those first ten albums were heavy on show tunes and standards, but her albums showed declining chart scores as rock albums moved to the fore. *What About Today* (1969) was an attempt to pivot to more current material, including Beatles and Simon And Garfunkel. It was her poorest chart performance for a studio album.

A switch to other writers for *Stoney End* (Laura Nyro, Randy Newman) and *Barbra Joan Streisand* (Carole King, John Lennon) started a resurgence which lasted through the '70s. As with the Rolling Stones, the apex of her chart success in this era came nearly 20 years after her debut, with *A Star Is Born* and the entirely Barry Gibb-written and produced *Guilty*. The latter two fall just short of the top 1%.

More evidence of her rising trajectory is the relative success of her Greatest Hits albums. The first, released in February, 1970 scored 1001 points—an average album. *Greatest Hits Volume 2*, which chronologically starts with Stoney End, scored 5226, over five times the average record of its time.

Of her 21 studio albums in the period, 13 reached the top 10; 21 of 40 overall. She charted in every year between 1964 and 1989, placing in the top 50 in 16 of those years. Overall, her 1475 chart weeks for the period place her third. Only one of her studio albums since 1990 has failed to make the Billboard top 10.

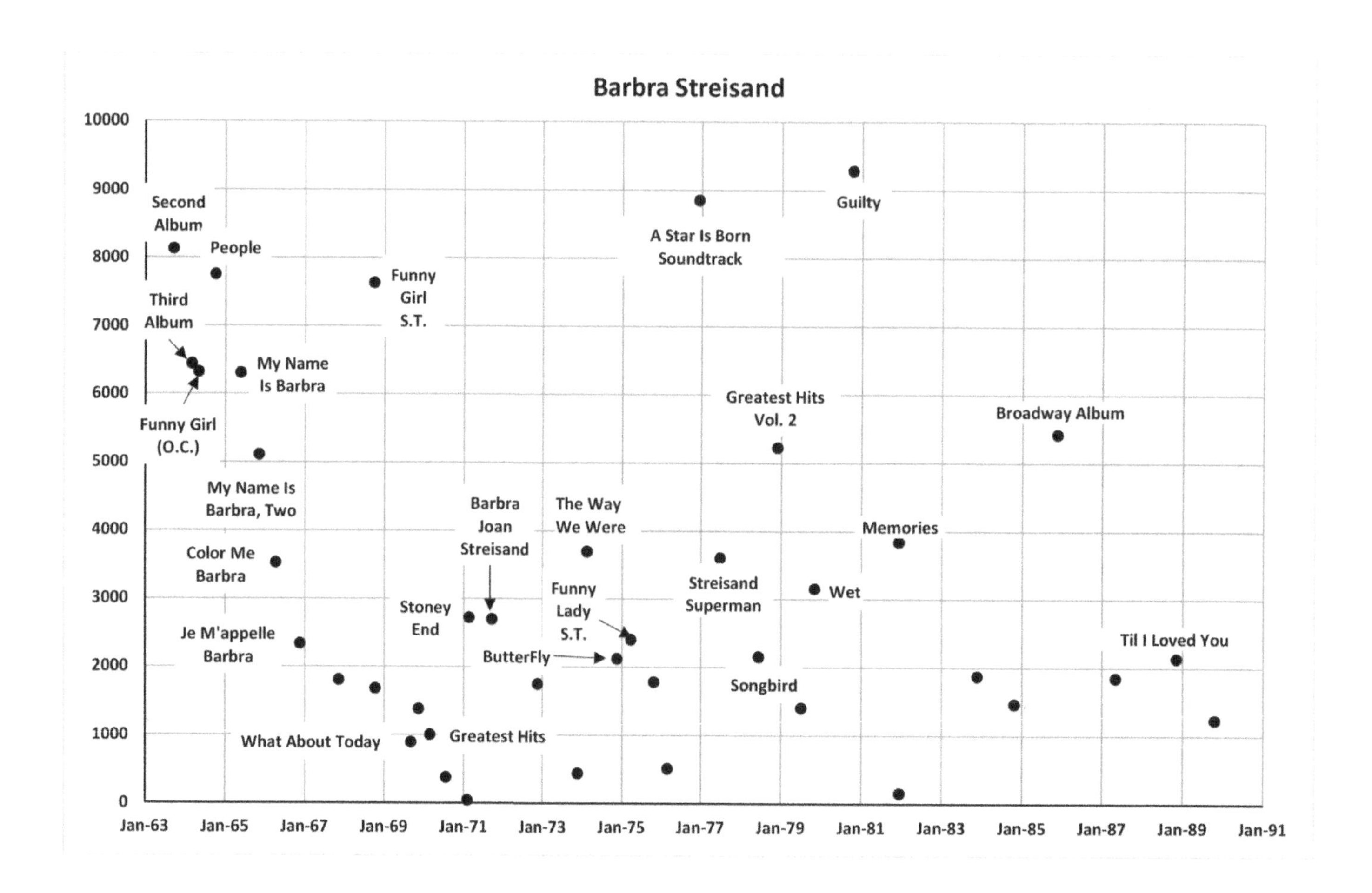

ELTON JOHN ▶ 4 (30) 102732

Since the movie *Rocketman*, it seems there are no more secrets to learn about Elton John; all the inside information is now out. His first album, *Empty Sky*, was released in the UK in 1969 but not in the US until 1975. His real debut was *Elton John*, released in April 1970 and which started a chart arc that reached its apex three years later with *Goodbye Yellow Brick Road*. That album ranks 57 in this set with nearly 13,000 points amassed over 103 chart weeks, 36 in the top 10. While his next album, *Caribou*, only achieved about half that success, *Elton John's Greatest Hits*, released in November of 1974, stayed on the charts for 104 weeks, nearly making the top 1%.

Factoid: Elton John had two consecutive albums debut at number 1 on the Billboard 200 chart: *Captain Fantastic* and *Rock Of The Westies*; While *Captain Fantastic* had an outstanding chart run into the top 2%, the graph is clear that his trajectory as an artist had changed. An interesting indicator is the relative success of Greatest Hits Volumes I, II and III, going from 9369 to 1459 to 324 points.

The last album in this group, *Sleeping With The Past* is the first album since *Captain Fantastic* written totally with Taupin with no other writing credits. This was at the beginning of his journey to sobriety, which would take substantially longer. The album remained on the chart for over a year.

Elton John is sixth in cumulative chart weeks with 1131 and was on the charts for 254 consecutive weeks. In 1973-1975 he was first, second and first in the top 50 acts of the year.

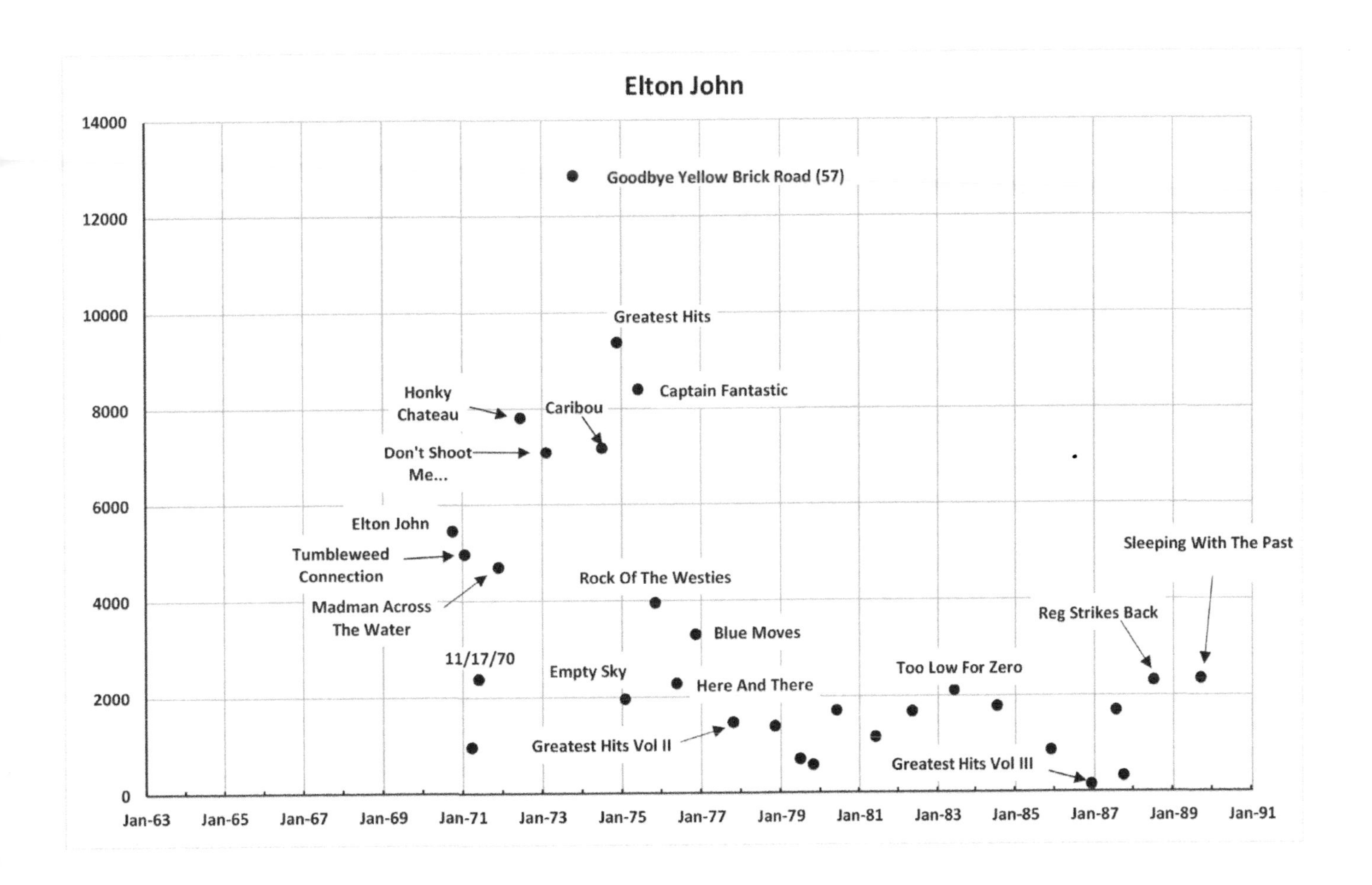

CHICAGO ▶ 5 (20) 98583

Chicago was the king of the double album. It takes a lot of confidence in a band to release a debut double album—well, and maybe a lower list price and a band agreement to take less in royalties--but Columbia made a good call with that one: over the course of its run, *Chicago Transit Authority* logged over 11000 points, ranking 84 on this list, even though it only peaked at number 17. The score was derived from its durability: It stayed on the charts for 171 weeks, 148 consecutively. Not quite so gutsy a move to release the follow-up as a double album; in fact, *Chicago* was even more successful—peaking at number 4 but charting for 134 weeks, 33 of which were in the top 10 and amassing 14299 points.

Six out of the next eight albums rose to the top 2% of records in this era, but none came close to the success of the first two.

Despite some singles success in the mid-70s, the albums were not charting as well. Internal tensions between manager and producer James Guercio and the band came to a head in 1978 and they split. Additionally, guitarist Terry Kath died of an accidental gunshot wound. And the sound had changed. And nobody was happy. By 1982, Columbia had bought out their contract.

Bill Champlin joined the group in 1982 and introduced them to David Foster, who produced the next three albums, co-wrote many of the songs, and fueled the Chicago ballad era—yet another sound change. *Chicago 17* was their highest selling album, if not the strongest charting. *Chicago 19* yielded three top ten singles, but the 20th album was another Greatest Hits collection, signaling the end of that era.

Chicago had 1047 cumulative chart weeks in this period, and charted in every year from 1969 on, including 12 in the top 50 acts. Eighteen of their 20 charted albums made the top 40, and for seven weeks in 1974 had seven albums—the entire catalog—on the chart simultaneously.

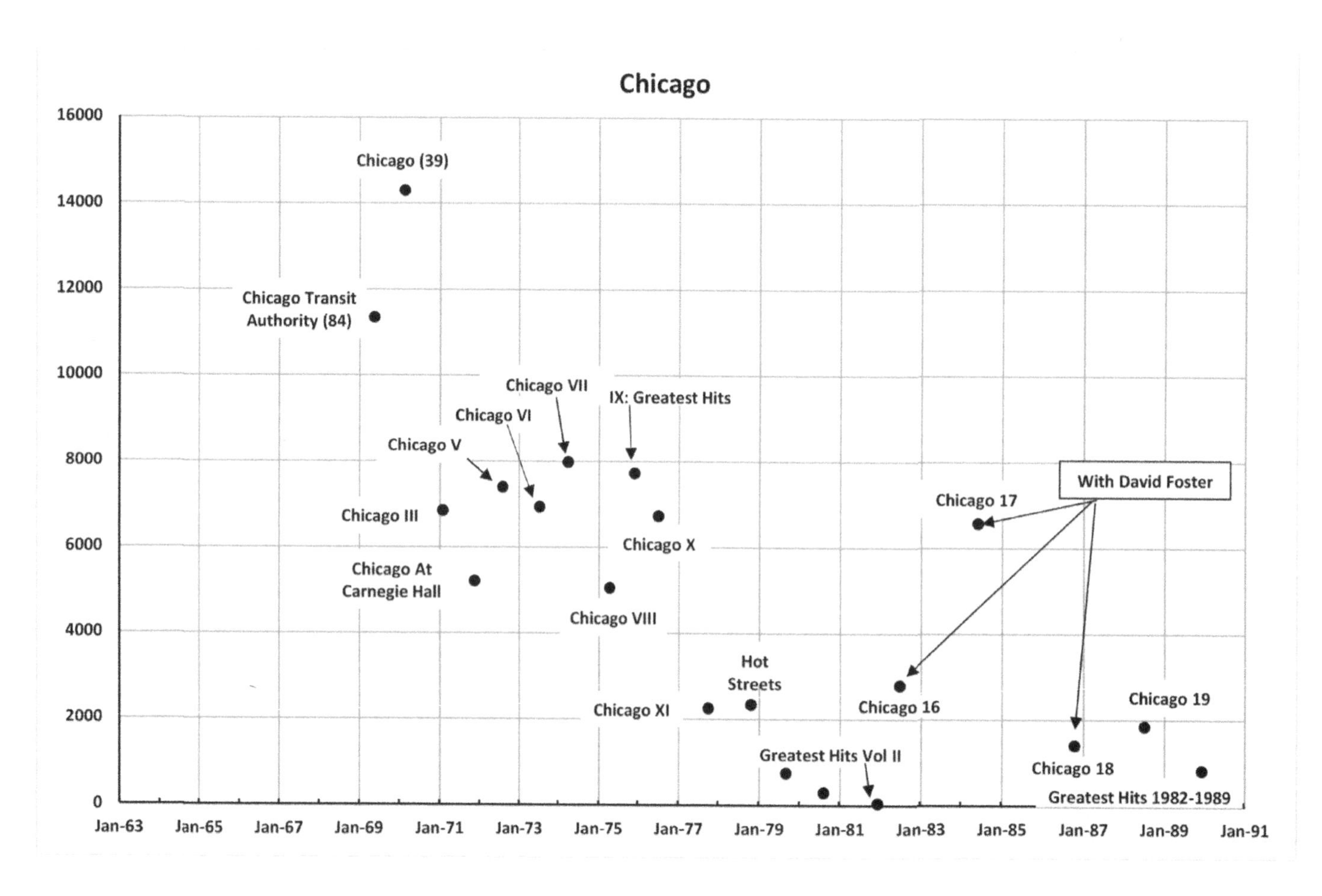

HERB ALPERT & THE TIJUANA BRASS ▶ 6 (18) 95830

Herb Alpert was a founder of A&M records before he was the Tijuana Brass. And on *The Lonely Bull* single, he WAS the Tijuana Brass, overdubbing his own trumpet lines. After the success of the single, he assembled Wrecking Crew members to create an album—*The Lonely Bull*-- which charted for 157 weeks after entering in December, 1962. It peaked at number 10.

Eventually the demand for live appearances necessitated a real band, and the resulting review-style show became enormously popular. TV specials came soon after. While the Tijuana Brass singles were moderately popular—the biggest being *A Taste Of Honey*, featuring Hal Blaine's signature kick bass line--the albums were through the roof.

Volume 2 was originally released in 1963 but entered the charts in 1966. The next eight albums went to the top ten; four to number one. Four charted for over 100 weeks.

While *South Of The Border* was a big hit, it would be hard to extrapolate that to the performance of *Whipped Cream And Other Delights*—released just four months later—which would spend eight weeks at number 1, 61 weeks in the top 10, 141 in the top 40 and a total of 185 weeks, becoming the number 8 record of this period. The cover, of course, didn't hurt sales but the music had to hold up as well.

The Beat Of The Brass was TJB's last number 1 album. *Whipped Cream, Going Places* and *What Now My Love* all reside in the top 1%. As shown on the graph, in May, 1968 the act had eight albums on the chart simultaneously.

The Tijuana Brass was disbanded in 1969 but at various times, newer versions were assembled to release an album. Herb Alpert recorded as a solo in the late '70s and '80s. His album *Rise* peaked at number 6.

The TJB had 1070 cumulative chart weeks, and were on the charts 210 weeks consecutively. In 1966-68 they were the number 1, 1, and 2 acts in the top 50.

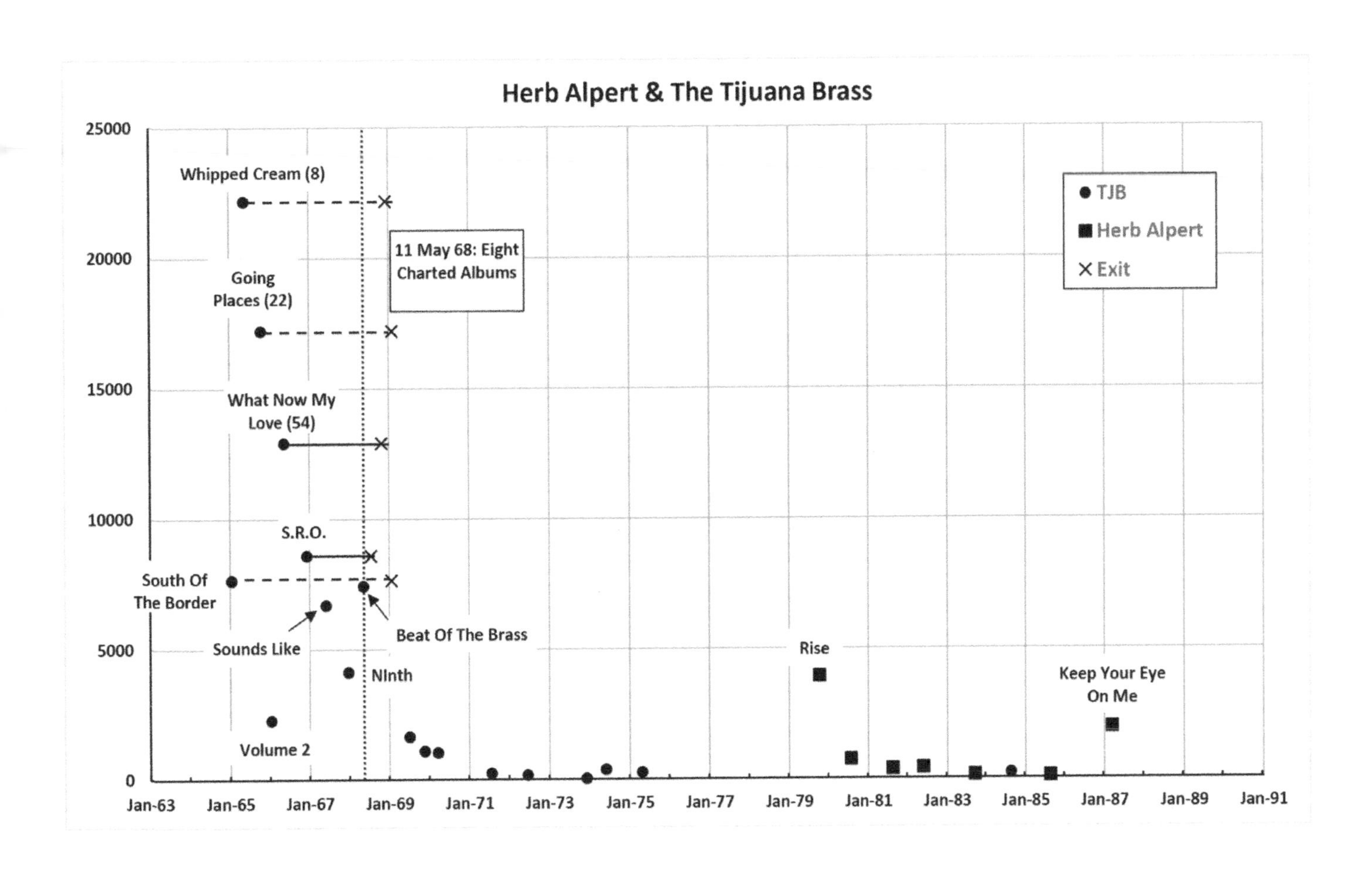

LED ZEPPELIN ▶ 7 (10) 78767

There is a big scoring gap between acts 6 and 7 in this list; however, Led Zeppelin far and away is the most efficient act on this list. Ten entries, ten top tens, six number 1s. Those ten entries averaged 7877 points—which if distributed in that way would put all their albums in the top 2%. As shown below, for two weeks, Oct. 27 and Nov. 3, 1979, all nine albums in their contemporaneous catalog charted simultaneously.

Led Zeppelin IV, ranked 43, charted 259 weeks—number 3 in duration--on and off the charts between November, 1971 and July 1987; incredibly, it peaked only at number 2. *Led Zeppelin* (118), *Led Zeppelin II* (42) and *Houses Of The Holy* (150) charted for over 90 weeks each.

By December 1990, *Led Zeppelin IV* was certified 10 times platinum by RIAA; by December 1990, *Led Zeppelin II* was certified 5 times platinum. Their chart scores to that time are virtually identical, showing the increase in total album sales over the course of the '70s and '80s. The same chart performance in those latter days required many more sales.

Led Zeppelin charted 759 aggregate weeks and placed in the top 50 acts seven out of eight years between 1969 and 1976. While their aggregate numbers are not so staggering as higher ranked acts, it is remarkable to remember that they only charted eight studio albums.

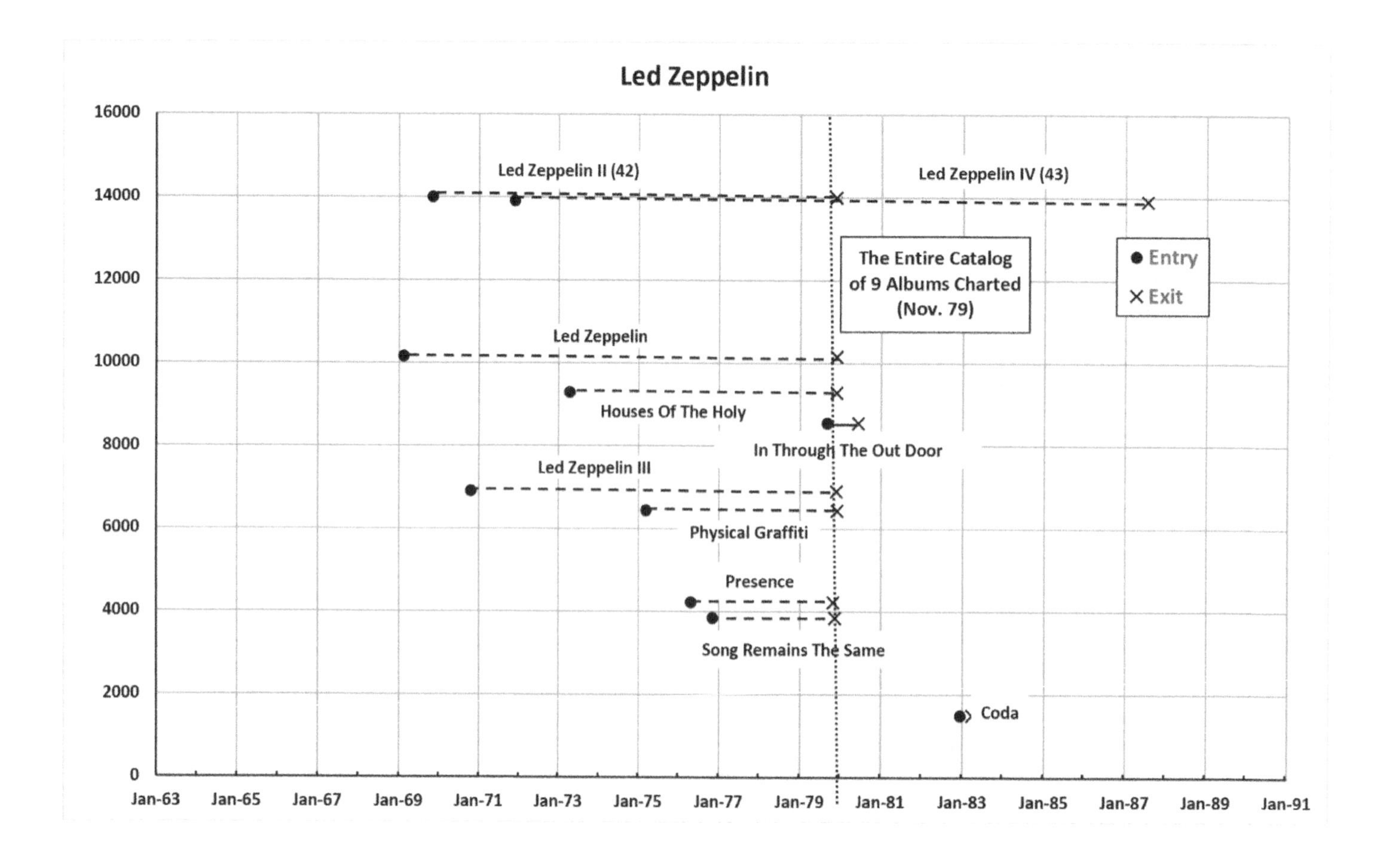

THE TEMPTATIONS ▶ 8 (37) 72959

The Temptations first charted a single on the Bubbling Under chart in December, 1962 for one week. Their real debut came in February, 1964 with *The Way You Do The Things You Do.* Their first album, *Meet The Temptations*, which hit the chart in May, 1964, included that song and peaked at number 95.

The graph below suggests that the Temptations were really a singles act rather than an album act, at least until the advent of psychedelic soul in 1969. Their regular albums prior to 1969 attracted some attention at about twice the chart strength of an average album, but none really making a mark. Their *Greatest Hits* was only their fifth album.

There were two things going on in that period, particularly prior to *Sgt. Pepper.* First, the album market was changing from an adult market to a teen market. Second, the record market overall was changing from singles-centric to album-centric. The Beatles may have been strong in the mid-'60s, but Barbra Streisand, Herb Alpert, Al Hirt and soundtracks owned it. Of the Motown acts, only The Supremes cracked the top 10 album acts in a year prior to 1967.

Early Motown was a product of its time—a singles-centric operation until the end of the '60s. But that was the plan. Berry Gordy, based on his experience working an auto assembly line, founded it to be an assembly line for songs and performance.

Of the top 453 singles 1963-1969 (top 10%), Motown had 44; of the top 302 albums of the same period (top 10%), Motown had only 14. The label's top 2 were greatest hits collections and number 5 was the Supremes-Temptations TV special *TCB.*

The Temptations made it to the number 8 ranking by flooding the zone. Their efficiency, at 1972 for 37 albums, is 135th; one way to make a lot of shots is to take a lot of shots. And they were present on the charts for most of the period, ranking in the top 50 acts for 9 of the 10 years 1966-75, but not cracking the top 100 after 1976.

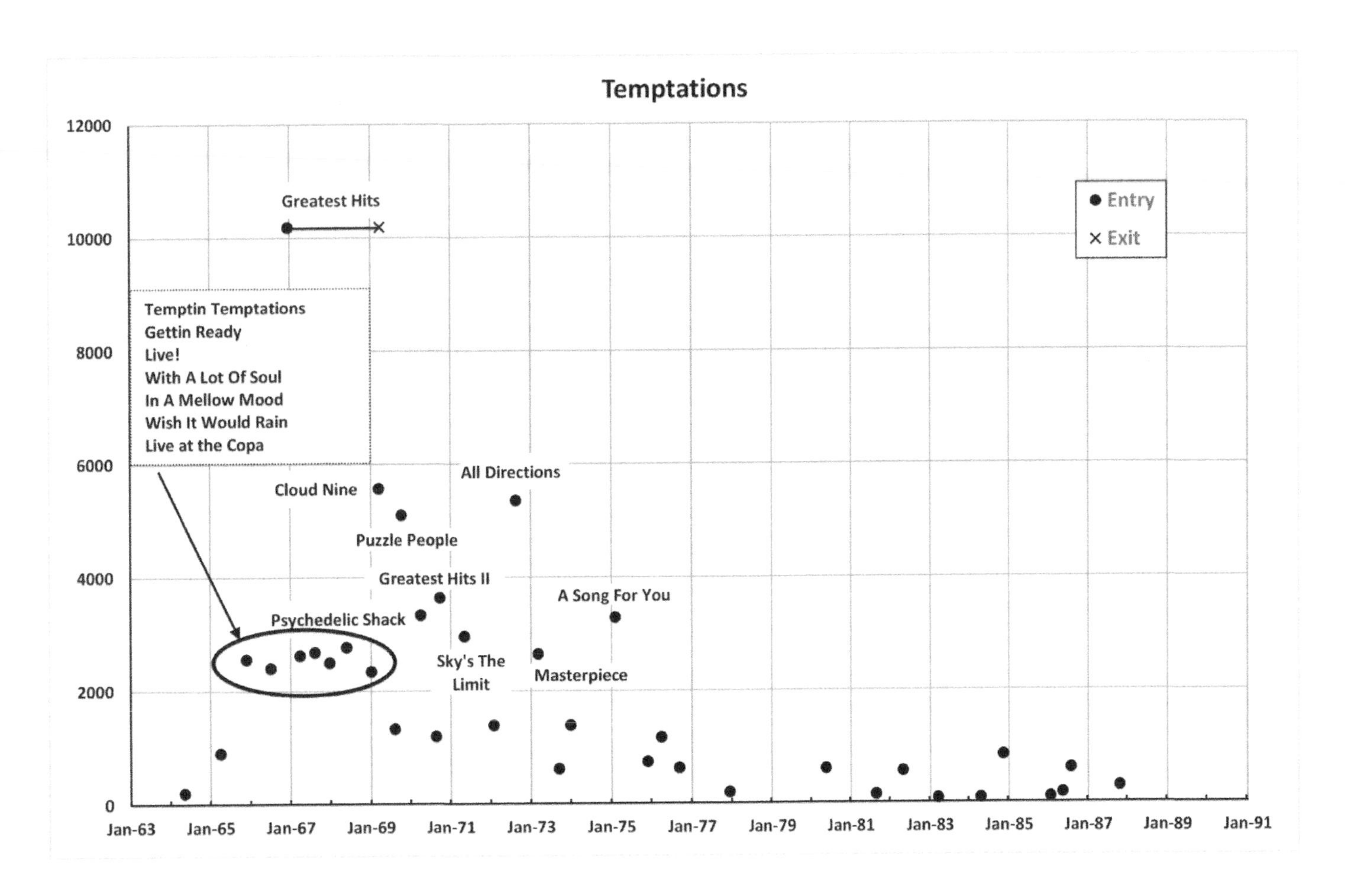

BILLY JOEL ▶ 9 (14) 72919

Billy Joel, in a virtual tie with The Temptations, was their opposite as an act. Although his singles were eventually successful, he was an album-oriented act in an album-oriented era. He averaged about one entry per year rather than close to two.

Cold Spring Harbor, his first album, appears out of chronological order. After it was recorded, it was transferred to vinyl at the wrong speed. Billy Joel said it made him sound like a Chipmunk. The album noted in the graph is a remastered sweetened version. He wasn't crazy about the new version either.

His album *Greatest Hits Volume I & II* is notable. During the eight years after its release it achieved good success, selling about 5 million copies; however, in the next seven years, 1994-2000 it sold 15 million more copies while never hitting the Top 200 chart. It now stands as certified 23 times platinum by RIAA as of 2011. By comparison, *The Stranger* is certified 10 times platinum, and its last certification was in 2003.

After only moderate success for his first three albums, Joel followed with four skyrockets out of his next five studio albums of new material, placing *52nd Street, Glass Houses* and *An Innocent Man* in the top 1% and *The Stranger* at number 37 for the period. This placed him in the top 50 acts for eight of the nine years following release of *The Stranger.*

He has 736 total chart weeks—good for 26th place and surprisingly low for his high position in total points. On the other hand, his record efficiency is 5209—relatively high for someone with so many entries.

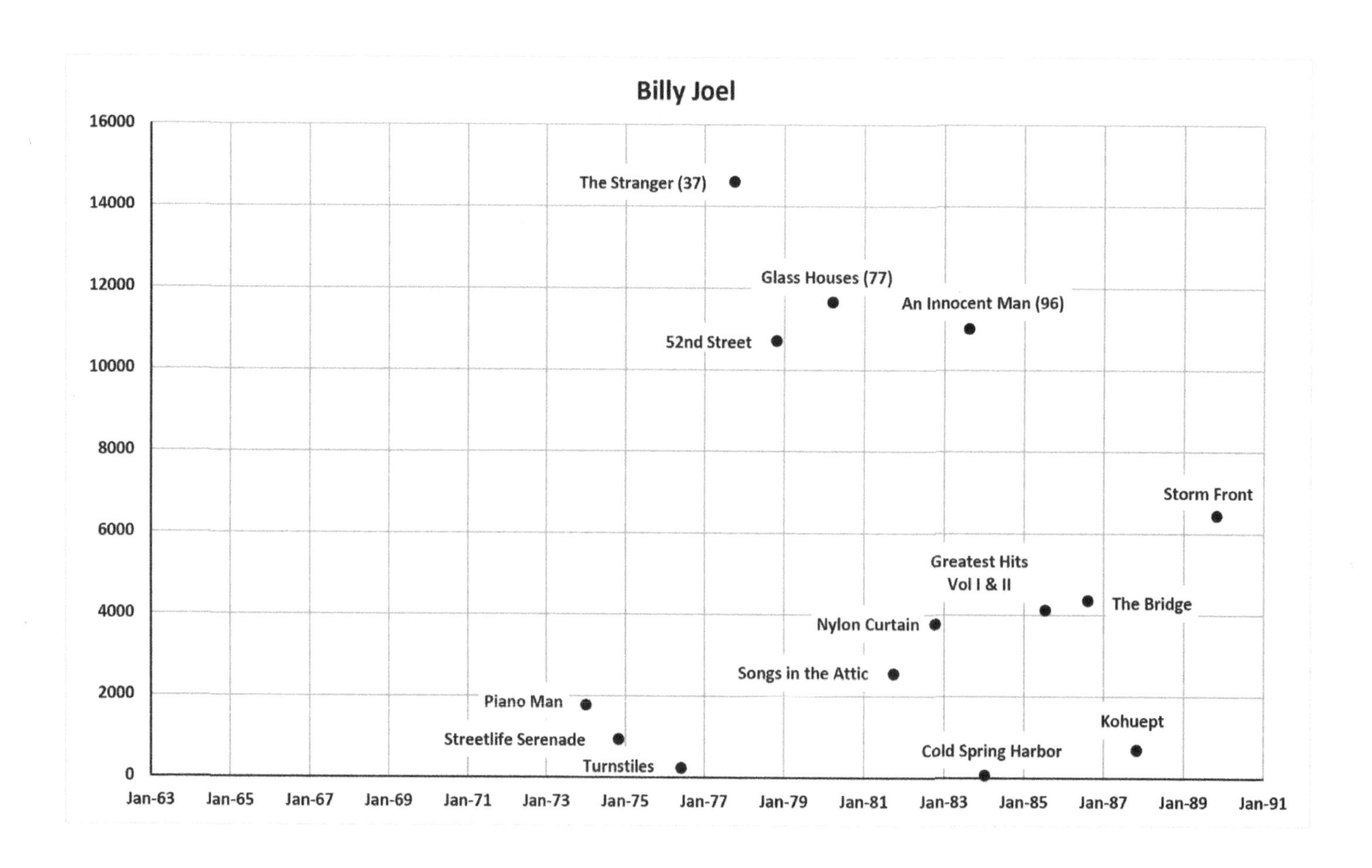

ELVIS PRESLEY ▶ 10 (71) 71798

In a way, this ranking is terribly unfair to Elvis. It's obvious from the graph below—which I have kept at similar scale to those with higher scores—that he is on a glide path. The only real exceptions are *Aloha From Hawaii* which was a live TV special, and *Moody Blue*, his last studio album, released just before he died. In addition to being on a glide path, there was very little new studio material to work with and a lot of soundtrack and compilations.

It's worth a note on what his trajectory might have looked like if we included albums reaching back to 1956, his real breakout year. Prior to August, 1963, Elvis charted 19 albums: eight studio, eight soundtracks, two compilation, two religious and one Christmas album. Of those, seven peaked at number 1, seven more peaked in the top 5, and four peaked in the top 20 of the mono chart. The two strongest, *GI Blues* and *Blue Hawaii* were number 1 for 10 and 20 weeks respectively and on the chart for 111 and 79 weeks respectively.

How strong were those albums? A reasonably close analogy in the early '60s is the Mary Poppins soundtrack, charting at number 1 for 14 weeks and 114 weeks on the chart. It scored 14811 points and ranked 33rd. It seems clear that his collection of twelve albums in the top 5 would have comprised a tall front wave to the declining curve we see.

Elvis charted 71 albums in this period. Obviously the 20 that came after his death were compilations, repackages or archived, and none of them scored very well. His efficiency is quite low at 1011 points, just about average for all records, but albums like those last 20 diluted his score significantly. Even so, he had 1248 weeks on the chart, good for fourth. He had 11 top 10s and 27 top 40s, good for ninth and fourth respectively. He was in the top 50 acts nine of the ten years from 1964 to 1973.

It's a reasonable guess that if all the data were available, Elvis would probably have been at the top of the acts for albums as he was for singles—or very close to it.

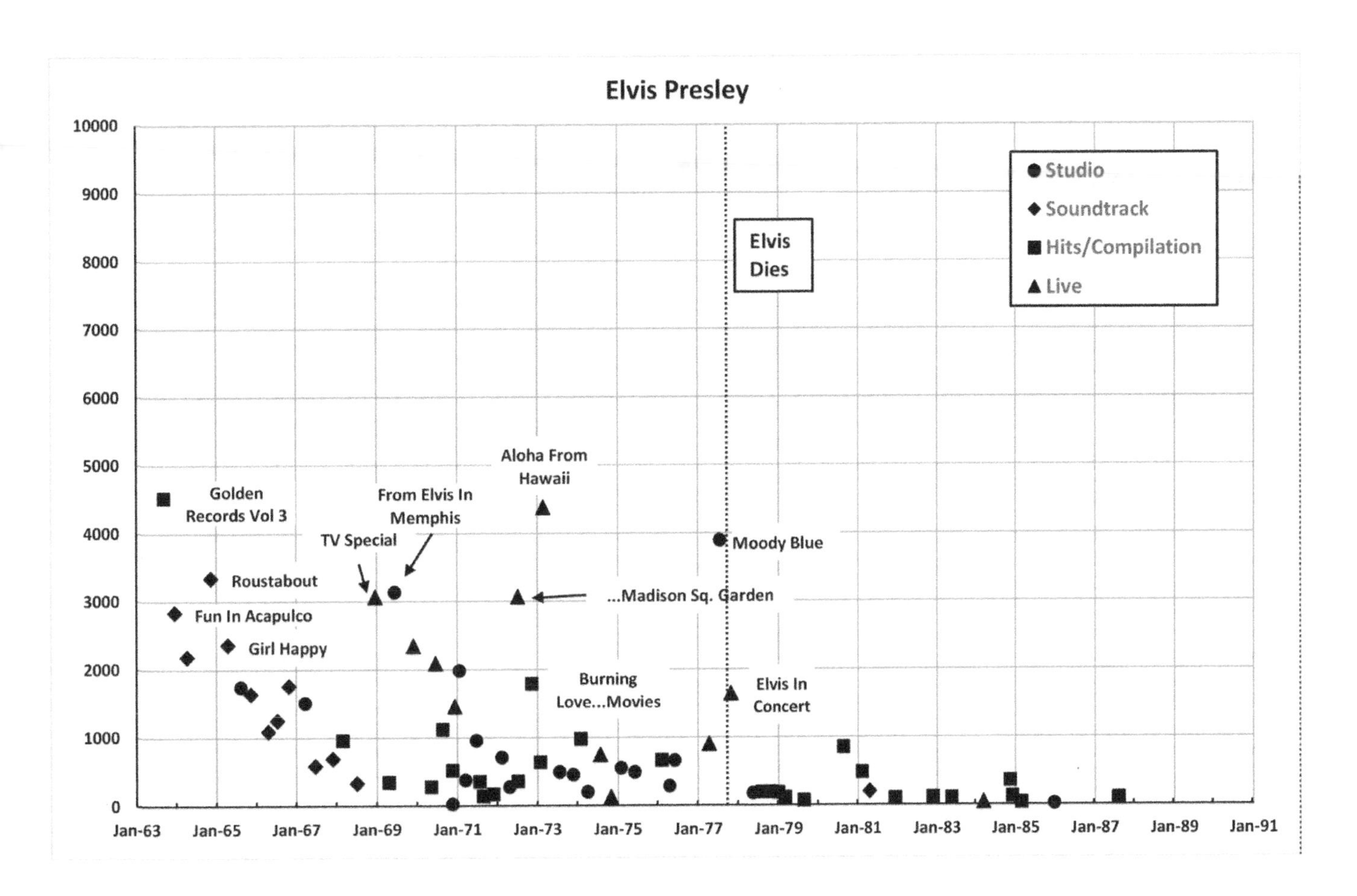

STEVIE WONDER ▶ 11 (22) 71559

The entry of Stevie Wonder's first album predates the combined charts by one month: *The Twelve-Year Old Genius* was number 1 for one week, spent 20 weeks on the chart, and was his strongest album for the next nine years. In a way, his graph looks a little like Fleetwood Mac at the beginning: a number of not terribly spectacular offerings, in no way suggesting what was to come. In Stevie's case, even the Greatest Hits albums didn't attract much attention.

Where I'm Coming From, his first album after his marriage to Syreeta Wright, was meant to be more of a social statement than the albums before, and was compared at the time to Marvin Gaye's *What's Going On*—not always favorably—but it contained a new sounding single: *If You Really Love Me*. It was a springboard to his so-called Classic Period, which began with *Music Of My Mind*, followed by *Talking Book*. The next three albums, *Innervisions, Fulfillingness First Finale* and *Songs In The Key Of Life* all won Grammys for Album of the Year.

Songs In The Key Of Life was an odd package—two LPs and an EP. It debuted at number 1 and remained for 14 weeks, and was the apex of his chart arc—16923 points, good for number 24. *Talking Book*, *Innervisions* and *Hotter Than July* all placed in the top 3%.

Stevie Wonder charted for 784 weeks, ranking a bit lower than his points rank of 11. He had nine top 10s and 16 top 40s. He charted in 20 of the 26 years, and made the top 50 nine times.

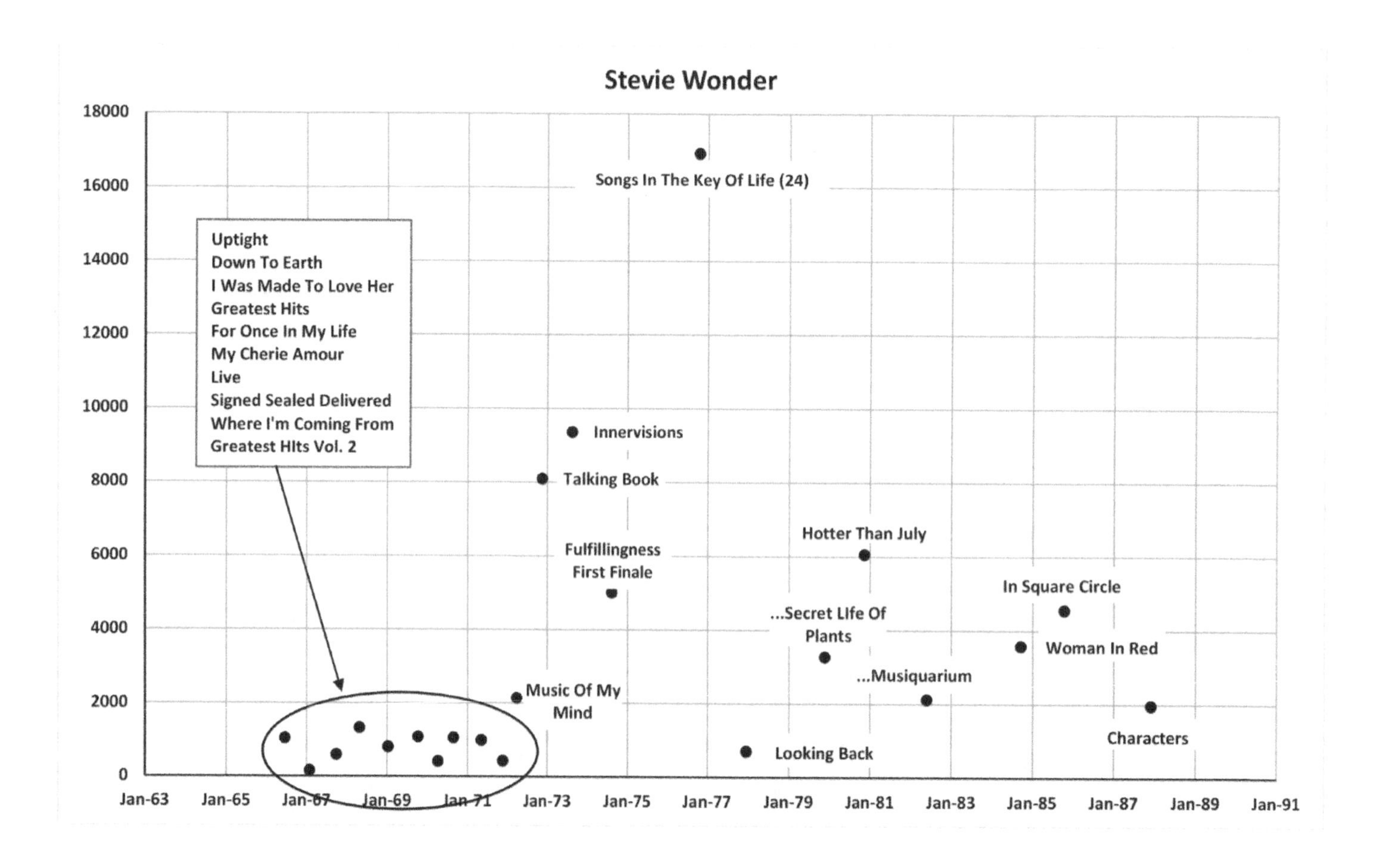

FLEETWOOD MAC ▶ 12 (19) 70921

Fleetwood Mac was actually a number of bands over the years due to the changing personnel. From 1967 to 1974 a number of players shuttled in and out around the core of Mick Fleetwood and John McVie, and slightly later Christine McVie. But with the addition of free agents Lindsey Buckingham and Stevie Nicks, a pleasant but average charting group became a dynamo. Their first album together was actually the second one named *Fleetwood Mac* (18198 points, #18) which was only a first step to *Rumours*, (27526 points, #2). Those two albums comprised 64% of their total career points earned in 19 entries.

Because those two albums scored so high, the graph looks as though the albums that followed were of minor significance. That's an optical illusion due to the scale. In fact, *Tusk*, *Mirage* and *Tango In The Night* all placed in the top 5%. In a way, it's surprising that the *Live* album and the *Greatest Hits* album performed relatively poorly; perhaps everyone already owned the two skyrockets, making *Greatest Hits* superfluous.

Because of that rocky start, for its final ranking Fleetwood Mac underperforms in most statistics including weeks on (652) and numbers of albums in the top 10 or 40, but the band appeared in the top 50 acts six consecutive years in the 1970s and 1980s, achieving number 2 in 1975 and number 1 in 1976. They had five albums on the charts simultaneously on September 27, 1975, and logged 194 consecutive weeks on the chart.

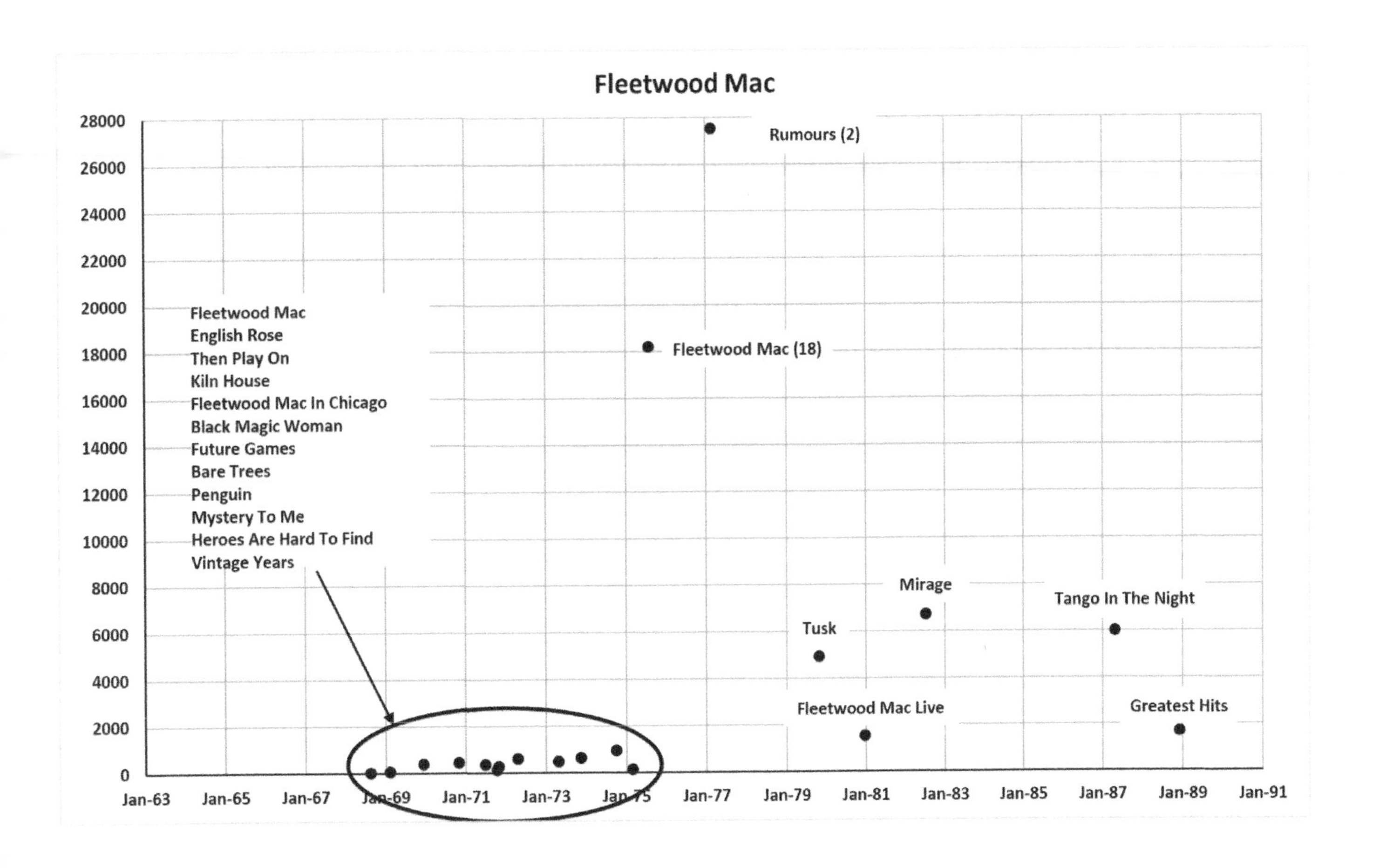

BOB DYLAN ▶ 13 (31) 69964

Bob Dylan's chart history from the beginning to the end of the '80s is captured here, from *The Freewheelin'*... to *Oh Mercy*. Note that his first album, *Bob Dylan*, released in 1962, did not chart. Recently, as *Rough And Rowdy Ways* went to number 1, he became the first artist with a top 40 album in seven decades. He received the Nobel Prize for Literature in 2016.

Bob Dylan became the early prototype for the singer-songwriter. As the '60s and '70s progressed, numerous "new Dylans" were anointed among pithy writers and singers—some deserving (Bruce Springsteen, for example) and some not. There is even a band called The New Dylans. But the greatest New Dylan of them all is Bob Dylan who reinvented himself at least twice in the 1960s alone and returned from the dead numerous times, perhaps both literally and figuratively.

If Fleetwood Mac was meteoric, Bob Dylan was consistent, at least through the end of the '70s, averaging 3054 points for his first 20 albums. However, none of those albums makes the top 1%; only Nashville Skyline makes even the top 2%. He has 852 weeks on the chart with 12 top 10 entries and 27 top 40 entries—the latter tied for third most with Elvis Presley and the Beatles.

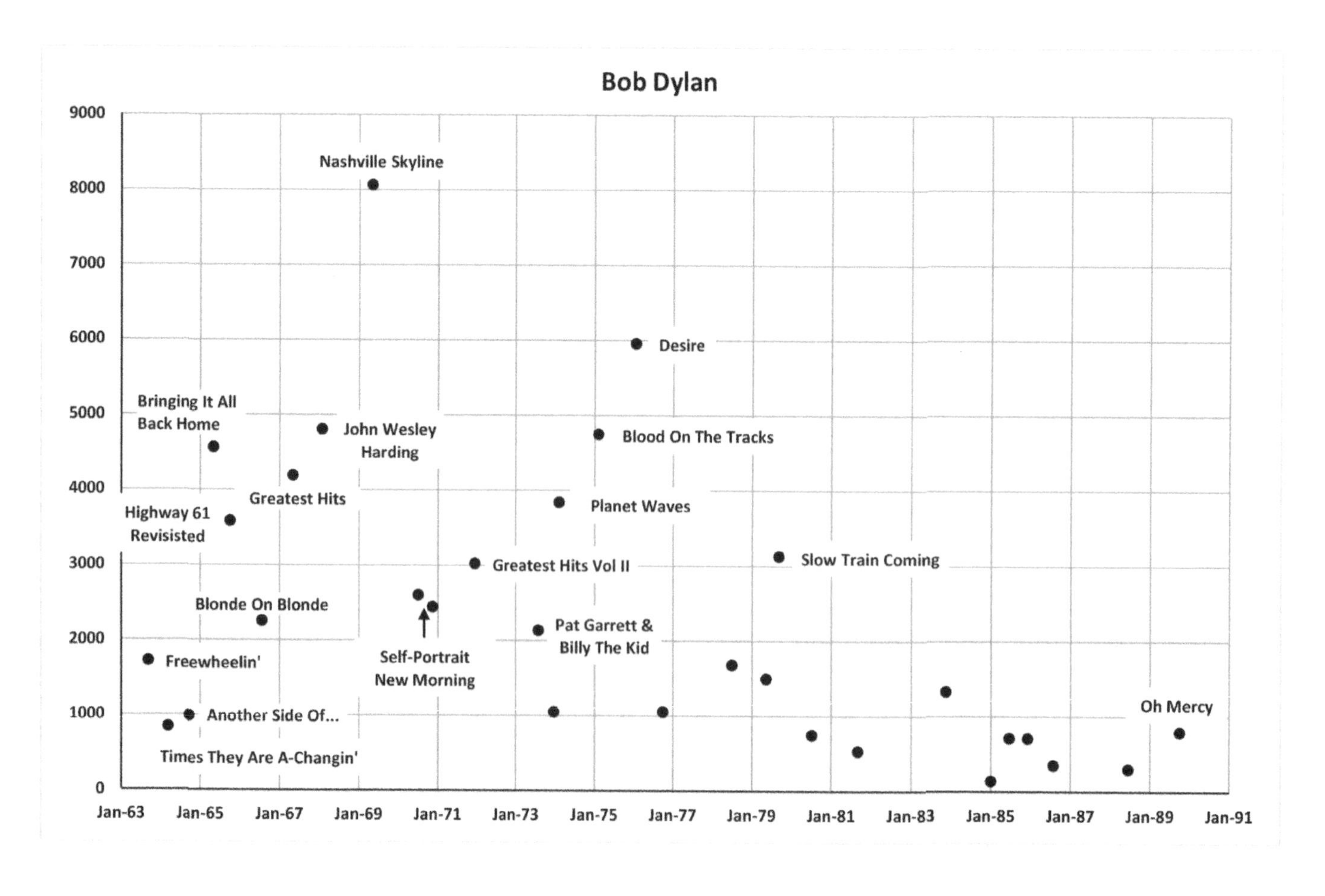

BEE GEES ▶ 14 (25) 69117

A crude hypothesis: When an anthology collection is more popular than the underlying albums, it suggests the act is a singles act; when the opposite is true, it suggests people already own the underlying albums (and could create their own mixtape). The first case is the early Temptations; the second case is Fleetwood Mac. The Bee Gees exemplify both cases: *Best Of Bee Gees* is the first type and *Bee Gees Greatest* is the second.

Bee Gees 1st had moderate success, but the first anthology, *Best Of Bee Gees*, issued after four more albums of declining popularity outcharted them all—suggesting people liked the singles and wanted them all in one place. More relatively pedestrian albums followed until the beginnings of disco and a change in their writing style from ballads to dance music. It's hard not to hear bits of *Superstition* in *Jive Talkin'*, and *Main Course* started a five-year run of chart success. *Bee Gees Gold Vol. 1* was essentially the same record as *Best Of Bee Gees*; *Bee Gees Greatest* was a two record set that concentrated on Main Course and later. It did not chart as well as the underlying records.

The *Saturday Night Fever Soundtrack*, (19144 points, number 13) was written mostly in one weekend at the request of Robert Stigwood at the Honky Château (Château d'Hérouville). It is also where Elton John wrote and recorded *Goodbye Yellow Brick Road* in a similarly concentrated recording process.

The first three singles from Spirits Having Flown—Too Much Heaven, Tragedy and Love You Inside And Out—all went to number 1, giving them a run of six consecutive singles to do so. The album spent six weeks at number 1 and 55 weeks on the chart.

The Bee Gees have 808 weeks total on the chart with eight top 10s and fifteen top 40s of their 25 entries. They appeared in the top 50 acts in 1968-69 and 1976-80. They had 262 consecutive weeks on the chart, seventh-most but due to those early efforts efficiency per record is low at 2765 (72nd).

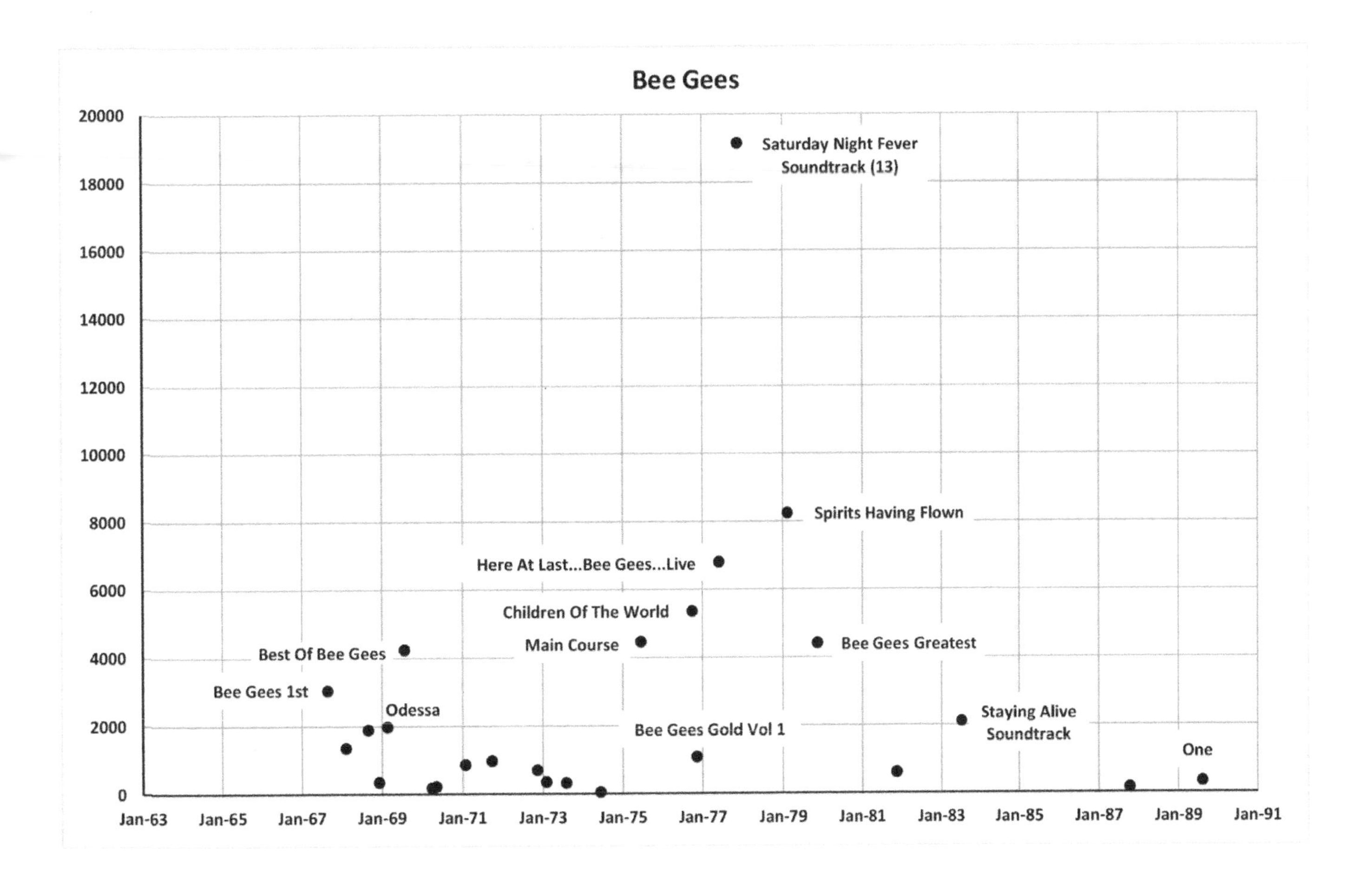

NEIL DIAMOND ▶ 15 (32) 66597

Neil Diamond is the second alumnus of Erasmus High School, Brooklyn to make this list of top album acts (Barbra Streisand is the other). He started as a Brill Building writer for Lieber and Stoller, and when he asked for a raise, they canned him. He was eventually signed by Jeff Barry and Ellie Greenwich more for his performance talent than his writing.

He had great early success as a writer—but with songs performed by others such as *I'm A Believer* and *A Little Bit Me/A Little Bit You* by the Monkees. Gradually his recordings of his songs charted more strongly, and a chart arc rising through *Tap Root Manuscript* which included the experimental *African Trilogy*--peaked in the live double album *Hot August Night*, recorded at the Greek Theatre in Los Angeles. Albums that followed had reasonable chart performance gradually declining through the '80s.

Then there was *The Jazz Singer*, his acting debut, derived from the 1920s-era play and movie. While the film was a disappointment, the soundtrack yielded three top 10 singles: *Love On The Rocks*, *Hello Again* and *America* and was his greatest chart success, peaking at number 3.

Neil Diamond's 32 entries ties him for thirteenth, his 12 top 10s and 21 top 40s also overachieve for his 15th rank. He logged 990 weeks on the chart. He was in the top 50 acts in nine years, but never higher than 10th. On Feb 27, 1971 he had five albums on the chart simultaneously. *The Jazz Singer* logged 115 weeks on the chart and *Hot August Night* 78.

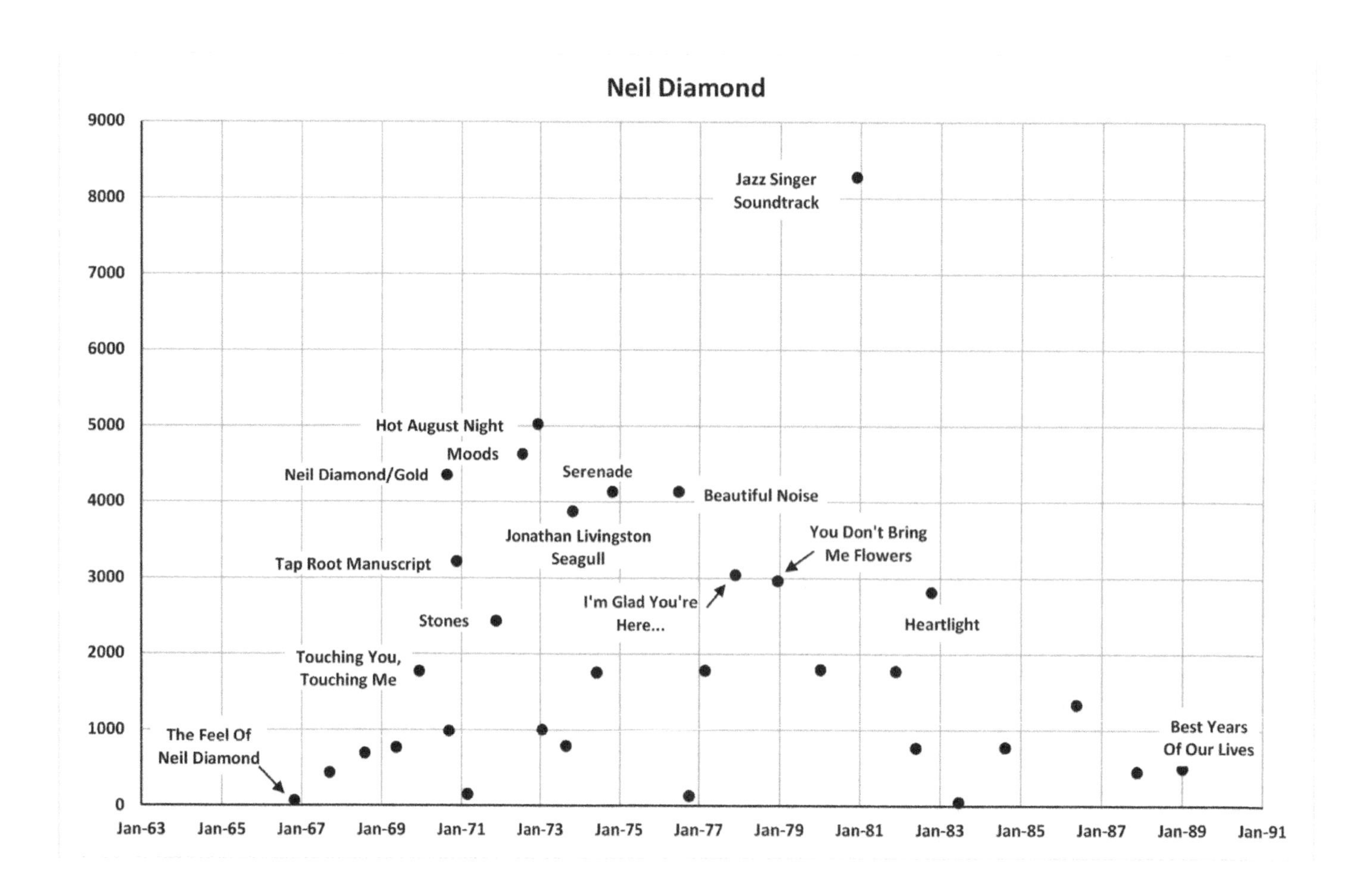

JOHN DENVER ▶ 16 (21) 65149

Henry John Deutschendorf, Jr. joined the Mitchell Trio in 1965, replacing founder Chad Mitchell. He first charted as the writer of *Babe I Hate To Go*—later retitled *Leaving On A Jet Plane*. It was recorded by Peter, Paul and Mary in 1969 and became their last charted record—which went to #1.

Poems, Prayers & Promises was his breakthrough, with *Take Me Home Country Roads*. It peaked at 15, but had 80 weeks on the chart. *Rocky Mountain High* peaked at number 4, but only charted for 53 weeks. *John Denver's Greatest Hits* included newly recorded versions of the songs from previous albums.

There doesn't seem to be a good explanation for his huge success between 1973 and 1977 other than that he had the right thing at the right time. It was a period when Motown was in decline, the singer-songwriter was winding down, disco was not yet entrenched and music was in flux. The top 10 songs of 1974 included *I Honestly Love You* by Olivia Newton-John, *The Streak* by Ray Stevens and *Kung Fu Fighting* by Carl Douglas—as well as Denver's *Annie's Song*. There was no dominant genre in a year where there was a new number 1 single nearly every week.

John Denver's Greatest Hits and *Back Home Again* rank in the top 1%--32 and 94 respectively—and six albums rank in the top 5%. His 21 chart entries are relatively few for his score ranking but he had 779 weeks on the chart, 251 consecutively—largely due to 175 weeks of *John Denver's Greatest Hits* and 96 of *Back Home Again*. He had 7 top 10s and 14 top 40s. He made the top 50 acts only 6 times but was number 1 in 1974 and number 2 in 1975. He charted six albums simultaneously in December of 1975 and January of 1976.

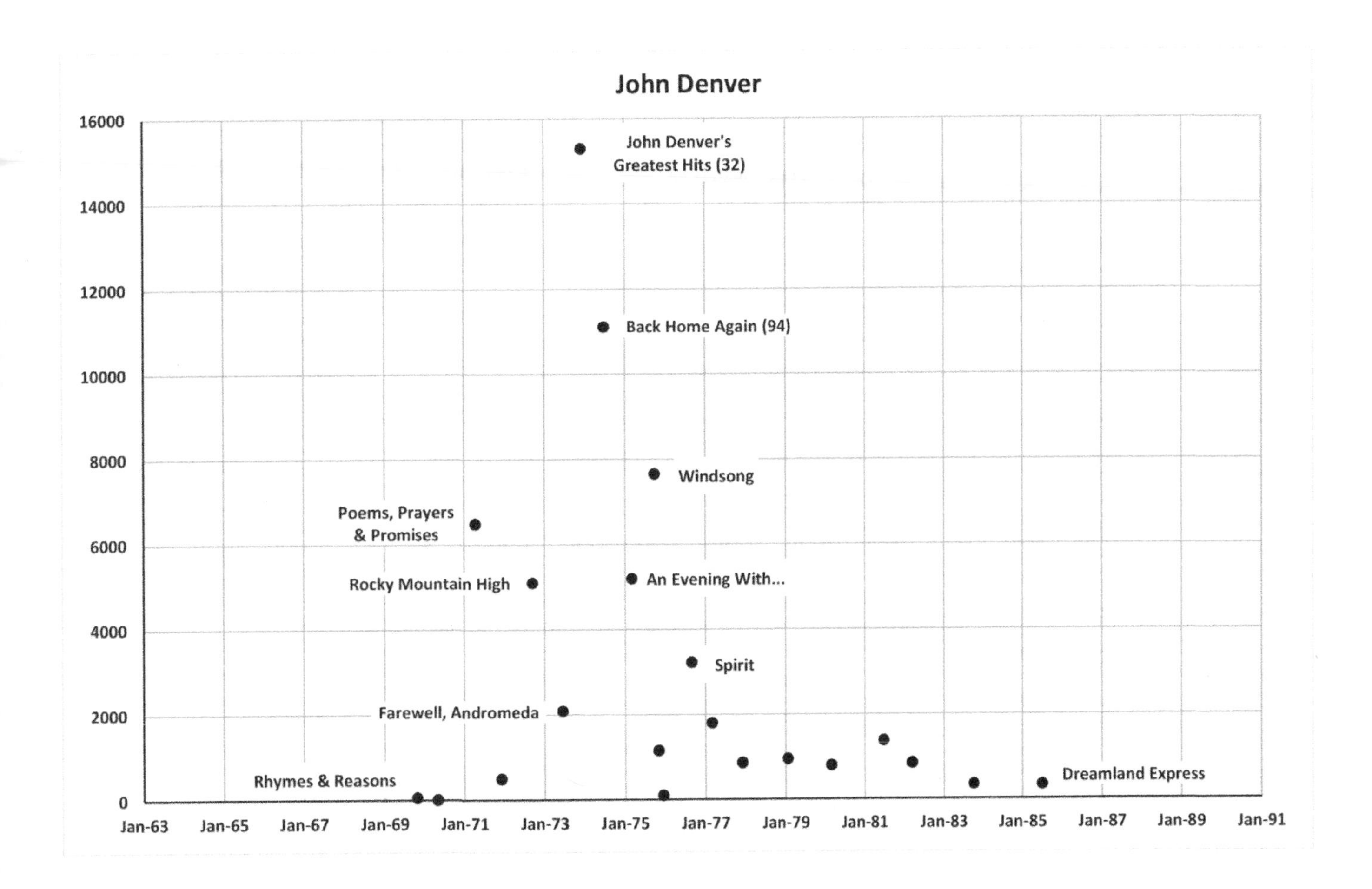

JEFFERSON AIRPLANE/JEFFERSON STARSHIP/STARSHIP ▶ 17 (27) 63716

This truly is the history of three bands. In some ways, it's a similar story to the personnel shuffling history of Fleetwood Mac. Jefferson Airplane/Starship's chart history looks like Neil Diamond's. And maybe that's the way you get to the top teens of acts in this list. Have a reasonable career and add to it one skyrocket. For Jefferson Starship, that skyrocket was *Red Octopus*. And for *Red Octopus*, the rocket engine was *Miracles*, a single that peaked at number 3. For Starship, the chart high water mark—something short of a skyrocket--was *Knee Deep In The Hoopla*.

Jefferson Airplane had a similar single skyrocket surrounded by other albums with more pedestrian chart histories: *Surrealistic Pillow*; the difference, of course, is that *Surrealistic Pillow* is an icon of the psychedelic era and in the Grammy Hall of Fame, which also scores in the top 3% of this era.

The personnel of *Surrealistic Pillow* was Grace Slick, Spencer Dryden, Marty Balin, Jorma Kaukonen, Jack Casady and Paul Kantner. On *Red Octopus* Slick, Kantner and Balin were the only three who remained. On *Knee Deep In The Hoopla*, only Grace Slick remained, although Craig Chaquico and Pete Sears were Jefferson Starship holdovers. These three were the same act in the same way that the carpenter has the same hammer after replacing the head twice and the handle three times. There is not much continuity in the music.

Surrealistic Pillow peaked at number 3 and spent 56 weeks on the chart. *Red Octopus* peaked at number 1 for four discontinuous weeks and remained for 87 weeks. *Knee Deep* peaked at number 7 and spent 50 weeks on.

Jefferson Airplane/Starship had 757 total chart weeks. The 27 entries included 7 top 10s but a surprising 21 top 40s. It made the top 50 acts of the year 7 times; its best showing was at number 5 in 1975.

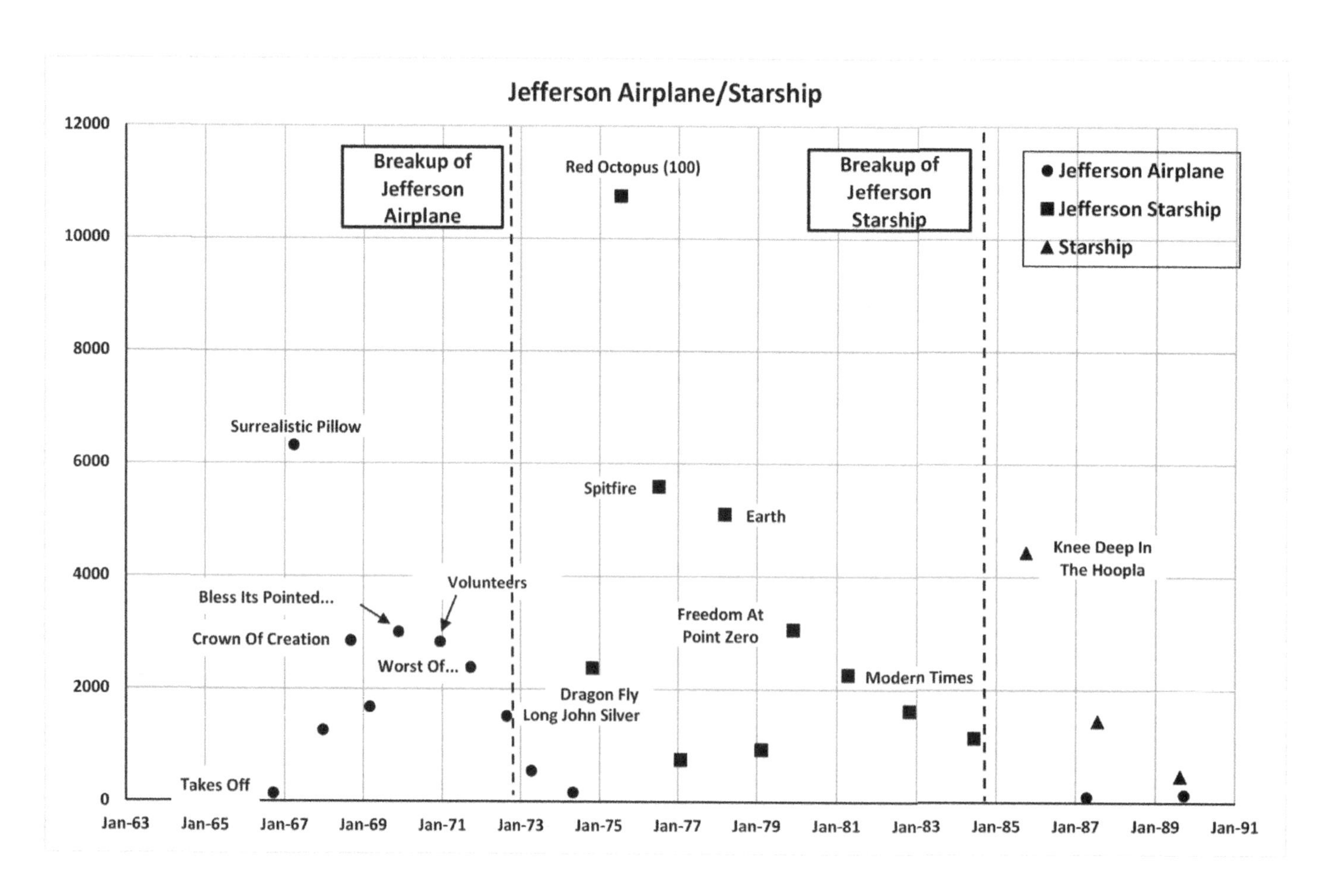

ARETHA FRANKLIN ▶ 18 (36) 61975

Aretha Franklin's first charted album, 1962's, *The Tender, The Moving, The Swinging Aretha Franklin* predates the combined Billboard chart. After three lesser albums and a Greatest Hits album for punctuation, Aretha changed from Columbia to Atlantic.

I Never Loved A Man The Way I Love You was her Atlantic debut album. In addition to the title cut, the album contained Sam Cooke's *A Change Is Gonna Come, Do Right Woman-Do Right Man* and her signature, Otis Redding's *Respect*. The album spent three weeks at number 2 behind *More Of The Monkees* and 79 total on the chart.

Aretha Arrives followed; but *Aretha: Lady Soul* was the second of her biggest three studio albums, containing *Chain Of Fools, (You Make Me Feel Like) A Natural Woman, Since You've Been Gone (Sweet Sweet Baby)* and *Ain't No Way*. It also peaked at number 2 for two weeks behind Paul Mauriat's *Blooming Hits* and spent 52 weeks in total. *Aretha Now* peaked at number 3 and spent 35 weeks; on it were Think and I Say a Little Prayer.

The albums that followed *Aretha Live At Fillmore West* had solid chart history but the time trend was downward. Part of that trend as the '70s progressed was the departure of Jerry Wexler. She left Atlantic for Arista.

Clive Davis felt that Aretha had regrettably gotten away from Columbia, before he took the helm in the late '60. When she left Atlantic, they developed a personal relationship; Davis took a deep interest in getting her the right material to take advantage of a historic voice. And Aretha wanted hits.

Her 30th album, *Who's Zoomin' Who*? was done with a new producer, Narada Michael Walden, who wanted to give her a younger sound. The lead single, *Freeway Of Love* and the title track were top 10 singles, and it became her first platinum album.

Her 36 chart entries places her eighth, with six top 10s and 21 top 40s; she charted a total of 878 weeks, 201 consecutively. She charted in every year but 1984 and appeared in the top 50 seven times with two top 10s.

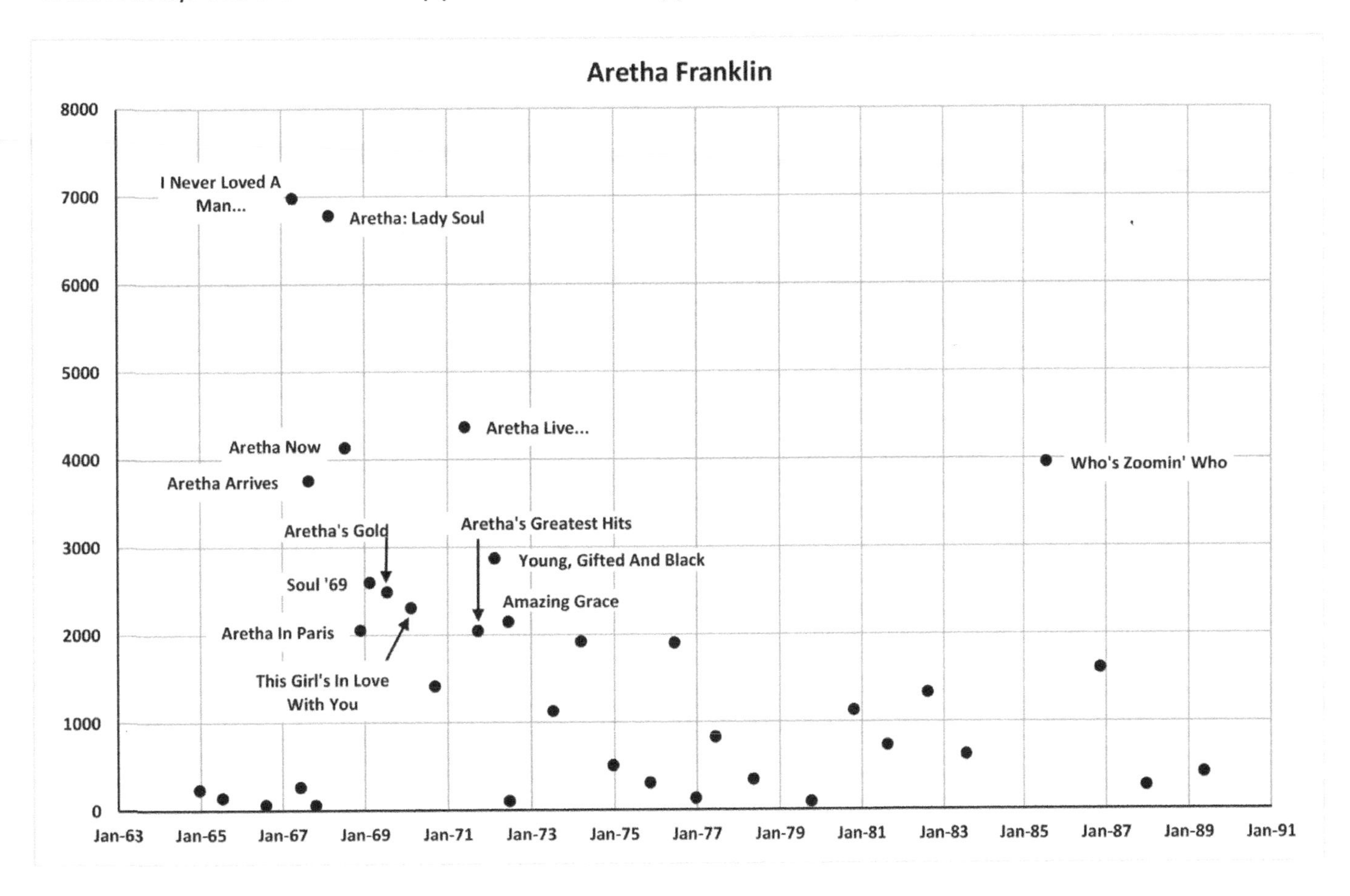

ROD STEWART ▶ 19 (21) 61323

Rod Stewart maintained a pretty stable career of top 5% albums. He has had a top 20 album in every decade from the '70s to the '10s and has almost taken on a Tony Bennett-like agelessness as a singer of standards.

Riding on top of that is his magnum opus, *Every Picture Tells A Story*, driven by the two-sided hit *Maggie May/Reason To Believe*. Interestingly, *Maggie May* was the B side, but became the bigger hit. Reaching number 1 for four weeks and 52 weeks on the chart, *Every Picture* sits at number 104 with 10659 points. It was released in May, 1971.

During this period, the lines between Rod Stewart and Faces and for that matter Small Faces and Faces blurred a bit. The members of Faces played on this album, and Rod acknowledges them as "...my old associates and colleagues, The Faces" although they would collaborate for a time going forward. Some of the other credits are odd: "The mandolin was played by the mandolin player in Lindisfarne. The name slips my mind." One wonders if the rush to release the album precluded a phone call or two.

Before getting to his full-time solo career, Stewart earned his spurs with Long John Baldry, as a member of Steampacket (which included Brian Auger and Julie Driscoll) and the Jeff Beck Group before coming to Faces in 1970. He also sang guest vocals for an Australian group called Python Lee Jackson.

His time with Faces and his then-growing solo career was coming to conflict and they split in 1975. *Atlantic Crossing* was released soon after, accompanied by a move from Mercury to Warner.

Stewart had 668 weeks on the chart, somewhat fewer than his rank at 19 would suggest. Of his 21 entries, 6 were top 10s and 16 were top 40s. His canon includes two number 1 albums and three number 2's. He placed in the top 50 acts in eight years, but his highest rank was 12 in 1979.

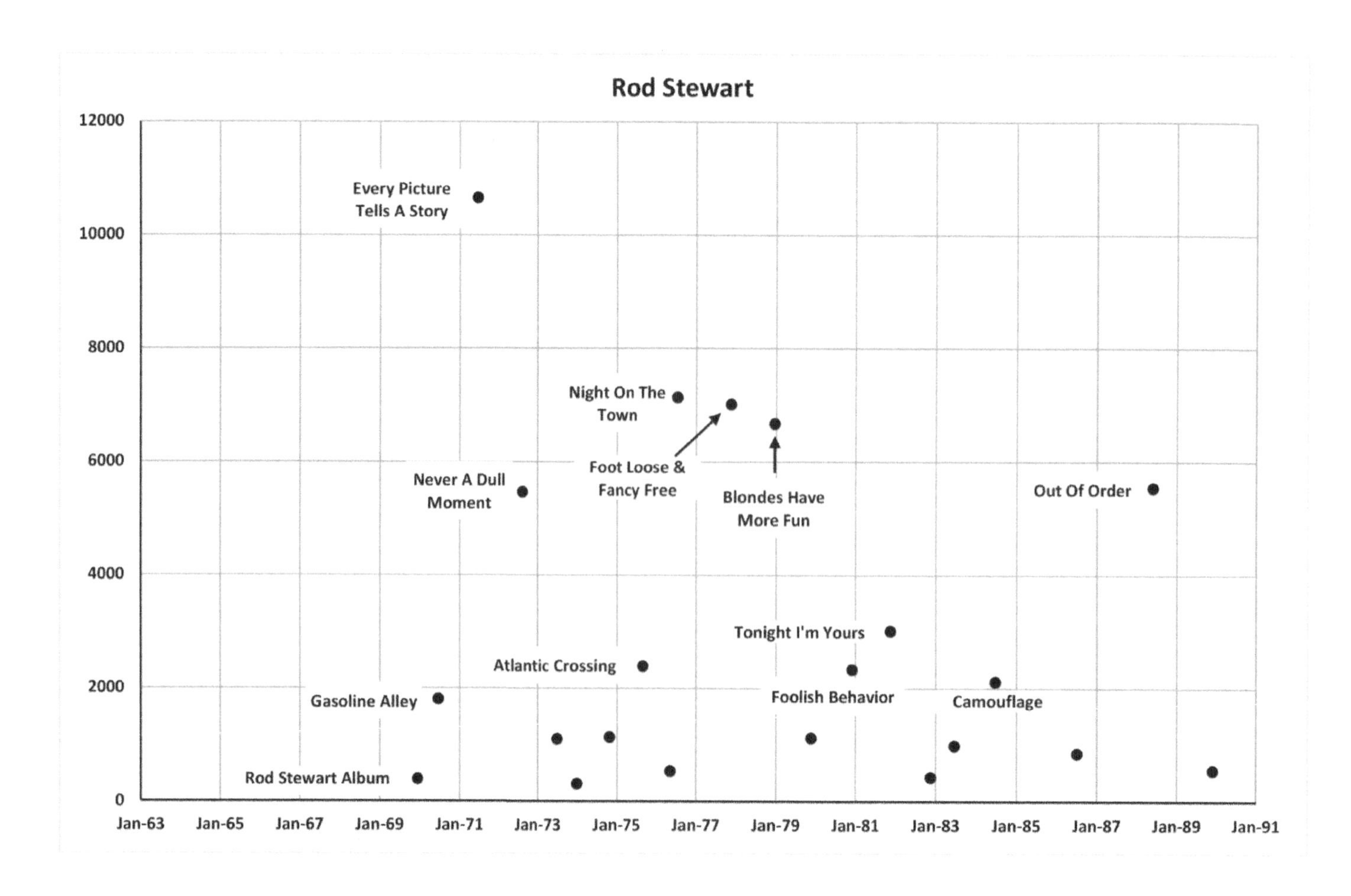

EAGLES ▶ 20 (9) 59933

Eagles have their roots as backup for Linda Ronstadt and formed as a discreet band in 1971, originally Glen Frey, Don Henley, Bernie Leadon and Randy Meisner. Their first album, *Eagles*, appeared in 1972 and included *Take It Easy*. Twice the average record is not a bad debut.

The trajectory was up from there—a little with *Desperado* and somewhat more with *On The Border* when Don Felder was added to the group and the music tended more toward rock. *One Of These Nights* was the first of their sequence of number 1 albums. Bernie Leadon left the group in December, 1975, and was replaced by Joe Walsh. This change in personnel apparently prompted release of *Their Greatest Hits 1971-1975*, which was followed by *Hotel California,* released in December, 1976.

Meisner left the band after their 1977 tour and was replaced by Timothy B. Schmit. Work on *The Long Run* also began in 1977 and took two years to complete. Not the commercial success of *Hotel California*, it still gave rise to three top ten singles. *Eagles Live* and *Greatest Hits Volume 2* were contract obligations and the band went on hiatus until 1994.

Eagles are a particularly good example of the vagaries of the Billboard Top 200 chart rules, as described in the methodology. *Greatest Hits Volume 2* peaked at number 52 and was on the chart for 15 weeks originally. Billboard.com lists that it has had 5 post-2000 chart weeks; yet by November, 2002 it was certified to have 11 million sales. The situation with *Greatest Hits 1971-1975*: prior to 2000 it charted for 133 weeks. Billboard.com now lists it with 333 weeks as of July 2020, and was certified to have 38 million sales in August 2018. It is the largest selling record of all time in the US. *Hotel California* is third, with 26 million, certified at the same time.

Eagles had nine charted records in this era, five top 10s and seven top 40s for 600 total weeks, 174 consecutively. For the years 1975-77 they were acts ranked 3, 3 and 2 and charted four albums simultaneously for 21 weeks. They were the fifth most efficient group on a per record basis, averaging 6659 points.

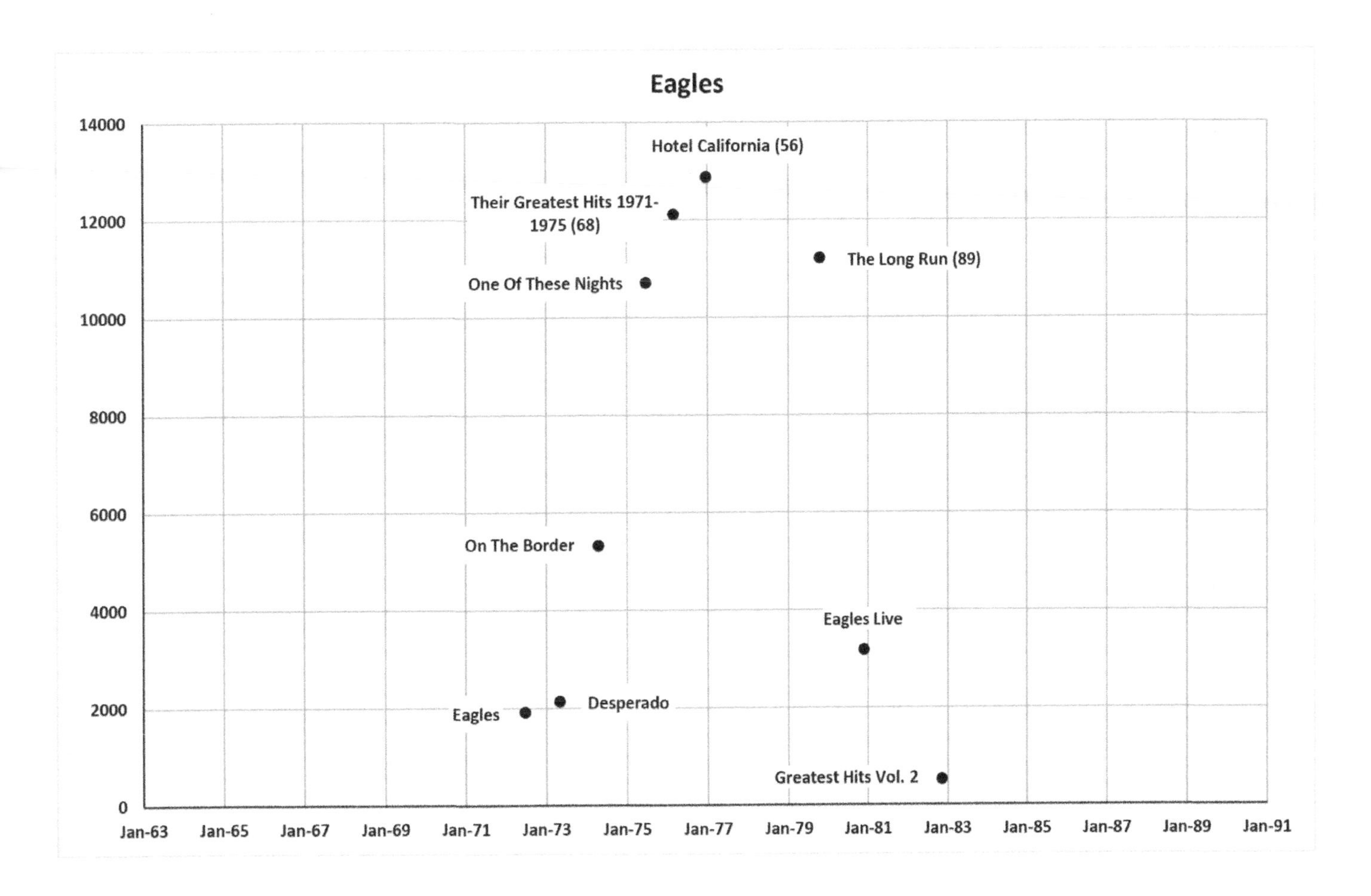

BEACH BOYS ▶ 21 (38) 59702

The Beach Boys first two albums, *Surfin' Safari* and *Surfin' USA* predate the combined chart; *Surfin' Safari*, peaking at 32 and 37 weeks on would have been no better than the average 1000 points, while *Surfin' USA* would have been significant, peaking at number 2 for two weeks and 78 weeks on the chart—probably scoring somewhere between *All Summer Long* and *Beach Boys Concert*.

It's interesting that their two highest scoring albums—and both are around the top 2-3%--are not new studio work; *Beach Boys Concert* is live and *Endless Summer* is an anthology. Additionally, virtually all their chart strength comes from the period 1963-1966, including *Endless Summer* which mines that period. This is the same period of their hit singles. The inevitable conclusion is that the Beach Boys were the ultimate singles band, and only albums driven by those singles charted well.

So how did they end up the 21st album act? Five or six reasonable hit albums and the brute force of 32 more entries, most of which mined the singles territory. In the period 1963-66 they charted eight studio albums. Beyond that, ten of the 30 remaining entries were anthologies; three were live.

Their 38 entries places them fifth, as does their 12 top 10s; their 18 top 40s is 12th. Their 1034 weeks on the chart is tenth; however, their efficiency is 180th with an average of 1571 points per record.

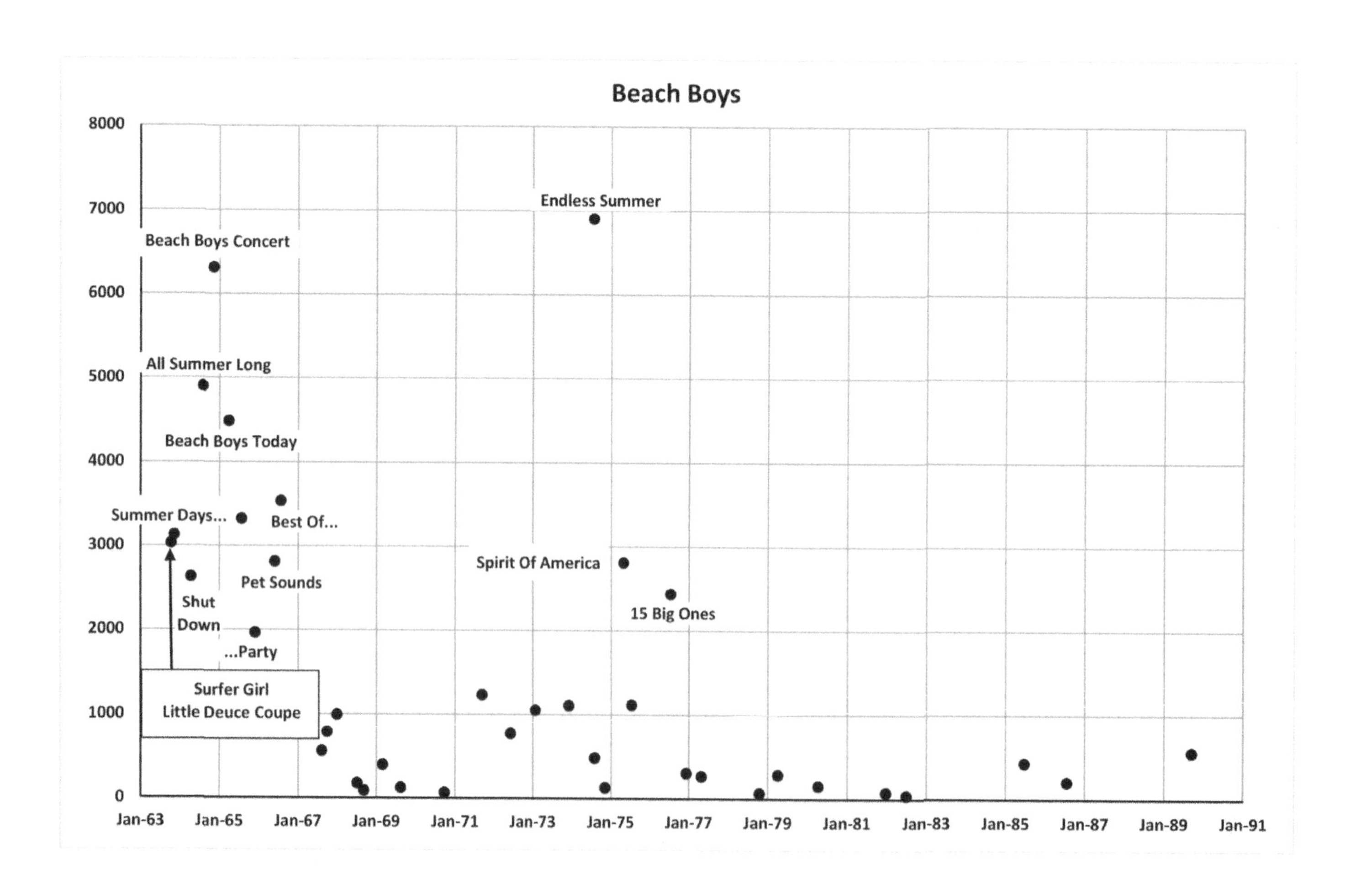

PINK FLOYD ► 22 (17) 59509

Chart-wise, Pink Floyd is a slightly above average band with two monstrous claps of thunder and two smaller echoes. In that sense, their graph looks a lot like Fleetwood Mac's. *The Dark Side Of The Moon* and *The Wall* account for 61% of the act's points over 22 years. Two other top 5% records, *Wish You Were Here* and *Momentary Lapse Of Reason* account for another 17%.

Roger Waters wrote all of the songs for *Dark Side Of The Moon*, and the band toured it while it was being recorded, refining it as they went. The album scored as it did because of longevity, not brute chart strength. It spent 741 weeks on the chart in this period, 592 consecutively between 1976 and 1988, and has sold over 15 million copies in the US. It peaked at number 1 for one week in April, 1973.

Wish You Were Here also had a conceptual theme and was totally written by Waters. It peaked at number 1 for two weeks and remained on the chart for 46 weeks, ultimately selling over six million copies in the US.

The Wall was also conceived by Waters, and is the last album to feature Pink Floyd as a quartet. Some outtakes from *The Wall* sessions were used in their album *The Final Cut*. *The Wall* peaked at number 1 for 15 weeks and spent 123 weeks on the chart, 27 in the top 10.

For *A Momentary Lapse Of Reason*, Roger Waters was out and Richard Wright was back. There was also considerable fighting about who owned the Pink Floyd name. The album peaked at number 3 and remained on the charts for 56 weeks.

As an act, Pink Floyd had 1236 chart weeks, good for fifth most—nearly three quarters of which were those two albums. Six of its 17 albums made the top 10 and nine made the top 40. It appeared in the top 50 acts eight times, Including number 1 in 1980.

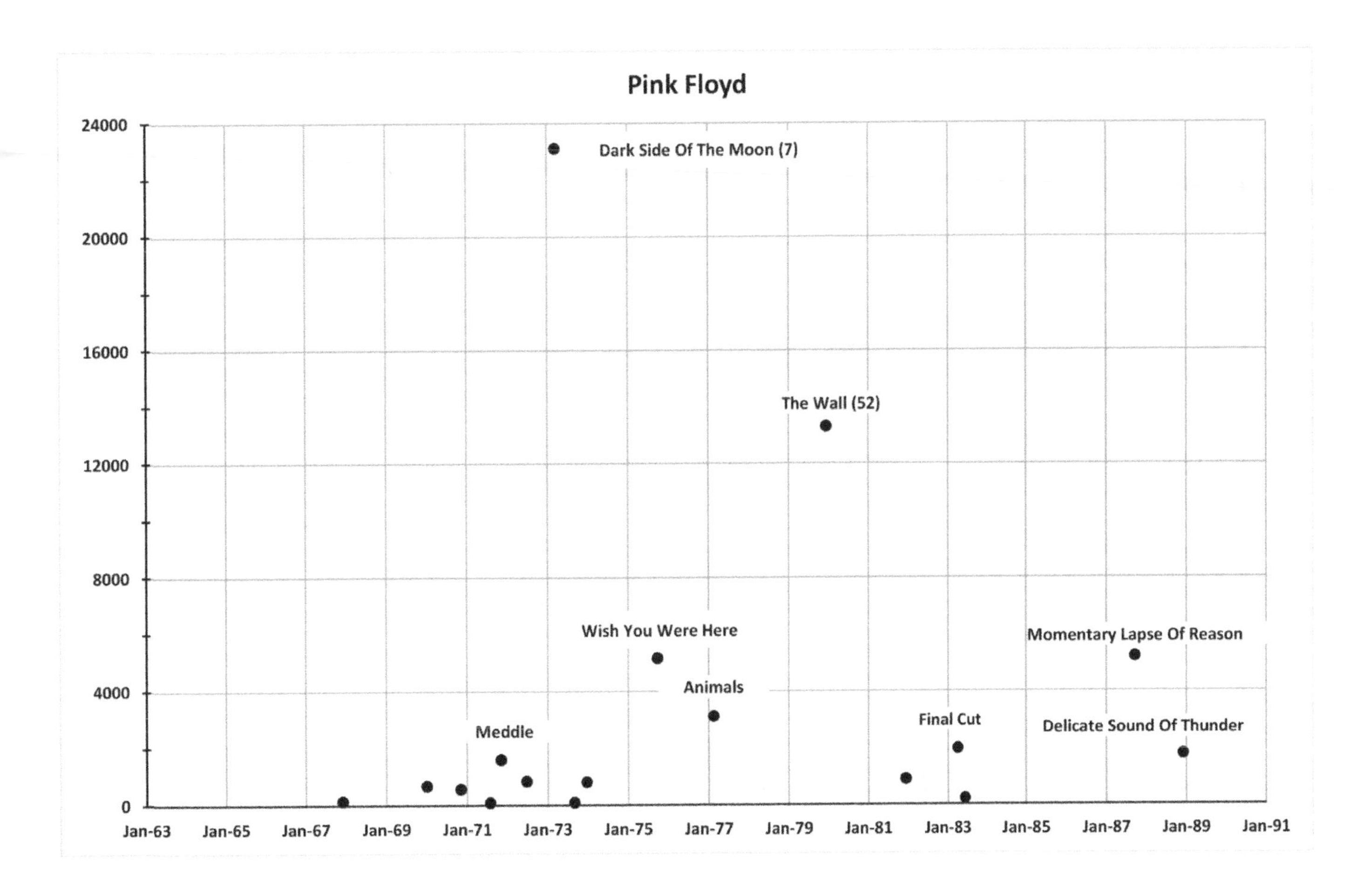

MICHAEL JACKSON ▶ 23 (11) 59268

Michael Jackson's album career can be divided into two parts: the kid part, which includes *Got To Be There* and *Ben* and the adult part that starts with *Off The Wall*. There are two important albums released after the period of this book but before his death: *Dangerous* and *Invincible*; however, neither of those measures up to the three pillars of the adult Michael Jackson, all produced by Quincy Jones: *Off The Wall*, *Thriller* and *Bad*.

Off The Wall was intended to be an artistic break from the Jackson 5. It peaked at number 3, spawned two number 1 and two top 10 singles, and was certified at 8 million US copies in 2009. It charted 169 weeks in this period.

What to say about *Thriller*? 1982 was an odd time—not unlike 1974. Disco was over and punk on the decline and no one genre dominated. But MTV was coming into its own and the videos, especially for *Billie Jean*, *Beat It* and *Thriller* crystallized the medium and drove the album sales, which were certified at 33 million in the US in 2017. *Thriller* charted for 122 weeks in this period including 37 at number 1 and 78 in the top 10. It also gave rise to seven top ten singles.

Thus, the bar was set high for *Bad*. It came five years after *Thriller*, had a harder musical edge and was a year in the making. It charted for 87 weeks in this period including six at number 1 and was certified at 10 million US sales in 2017. Sales of all three albums took off again after Jackson's death.

Michael Jackson had only 11 entries with two number 1s, four top tens and five top 40s for 491 chart weeks, but much of his chart career would come after this period. He was in the top 50 acts for seven years, including number 1 in 1983. He had three albums in the top 0.5% (*Thriller*-3; *Off The Wall*-51; *Bad*-53).

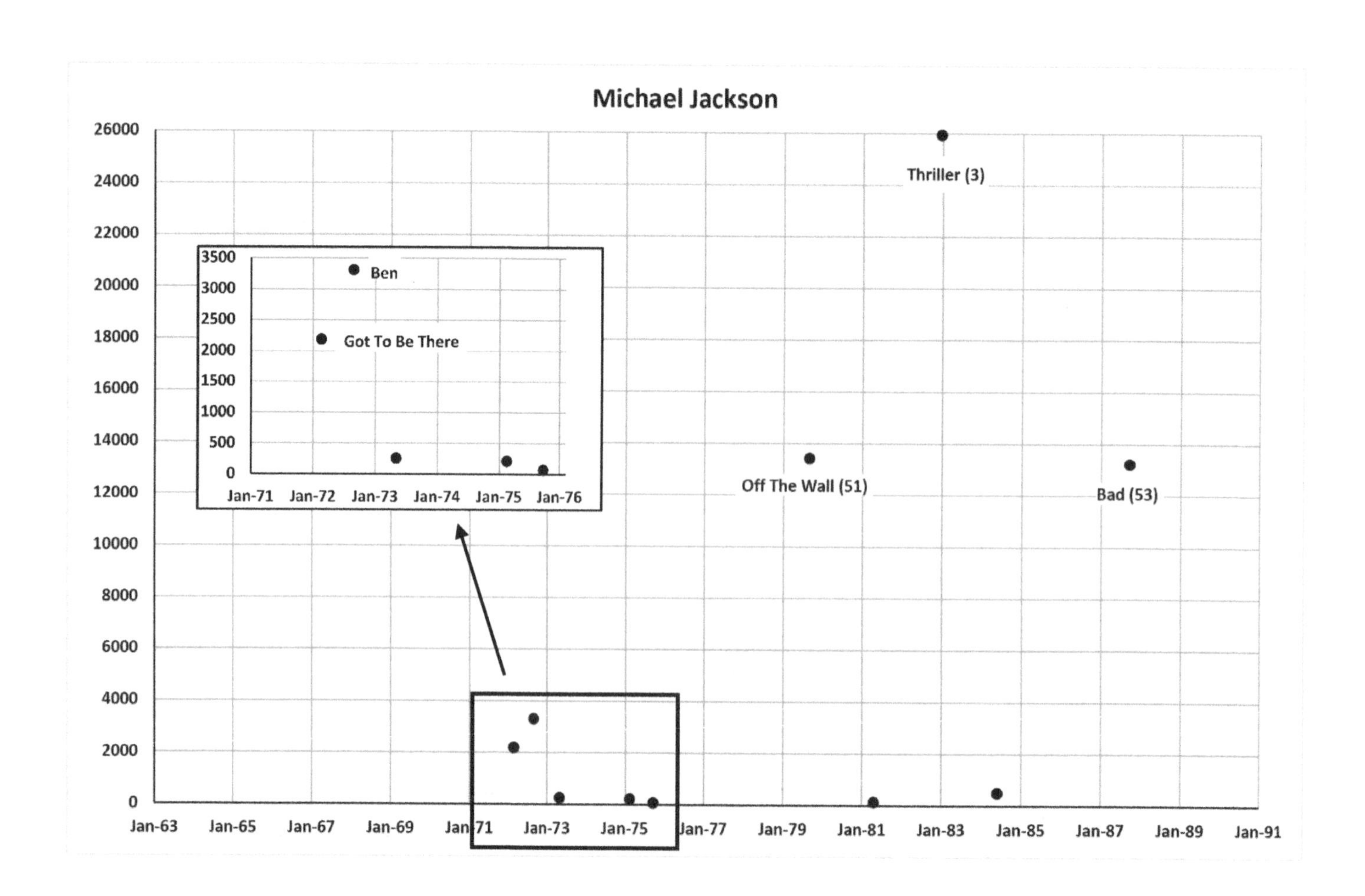

SIMON & GARFUNKEL ▶ 24 (8) 58590

Paul Simon and Art Garfunkel started working together in the '50s as Tom & Jerry, split until 1963, recorded a folk album, *Wednesday Morning 3 AM*, which stiffed, and split again. It included an acoustic version of *Sounds Of Silence*.

Famously, while Paul was in England, Tom Wilson created a new version of *Sounds Of Silence* by adding electric guitar and some percussion, and speeding it up a bit. His goal was folk-rock in the new style of Dylan and the Byrds. The single went to number 1 and an album was rushed out to capitalize. The *Sounds Of Silence* album peaked at 21 and spent nearly three years on the chart. The single dragged *Wednesday Morning 3 AM* along and peaked at 30.

Parsley, Sage, Rosemary and Thyme took nine months to record and entered the chart November of 1966, peaking at number 4 with 145 weeks duration on the chart. *The Graduate* soundtrack came next, after repeated requests from Director Mike Nichols to Paul Simon to do music for the film, and spent nine weeks at number 1 in a 69-week run.

Bookends was a bit like *Magical Mystery Tour*, in that one side was unambiguously new material and the other collected previously charted singles and reprised *Mrs. Robinson* from *The Graduate* soundtrack. It shipped as a Gold Record, spent seven weeks at number 1 and 66 weeks on the chart.

Bridge Over Troubled Water was their final studio album recorded at the time they were on the verge of solo careers. It spent 10 weeks at number 1 and 87 weeks on the chart. Their final two albums, *Greatest Hits* and *The Concert In Central Park* peaked at five and six respectively; *Greatest Hits* had a 127 week run in this period and has sold over 14 million copies in the US.

Simon & Garfunkel's eight entries—three number 1s, five top 10s and all top 40s-- logged 698 chart weeks. They were in the top 50 acts for six years and number 1 in 1968. They were the second most efficient act next to Led Zeppelin averaging 7324 points per album

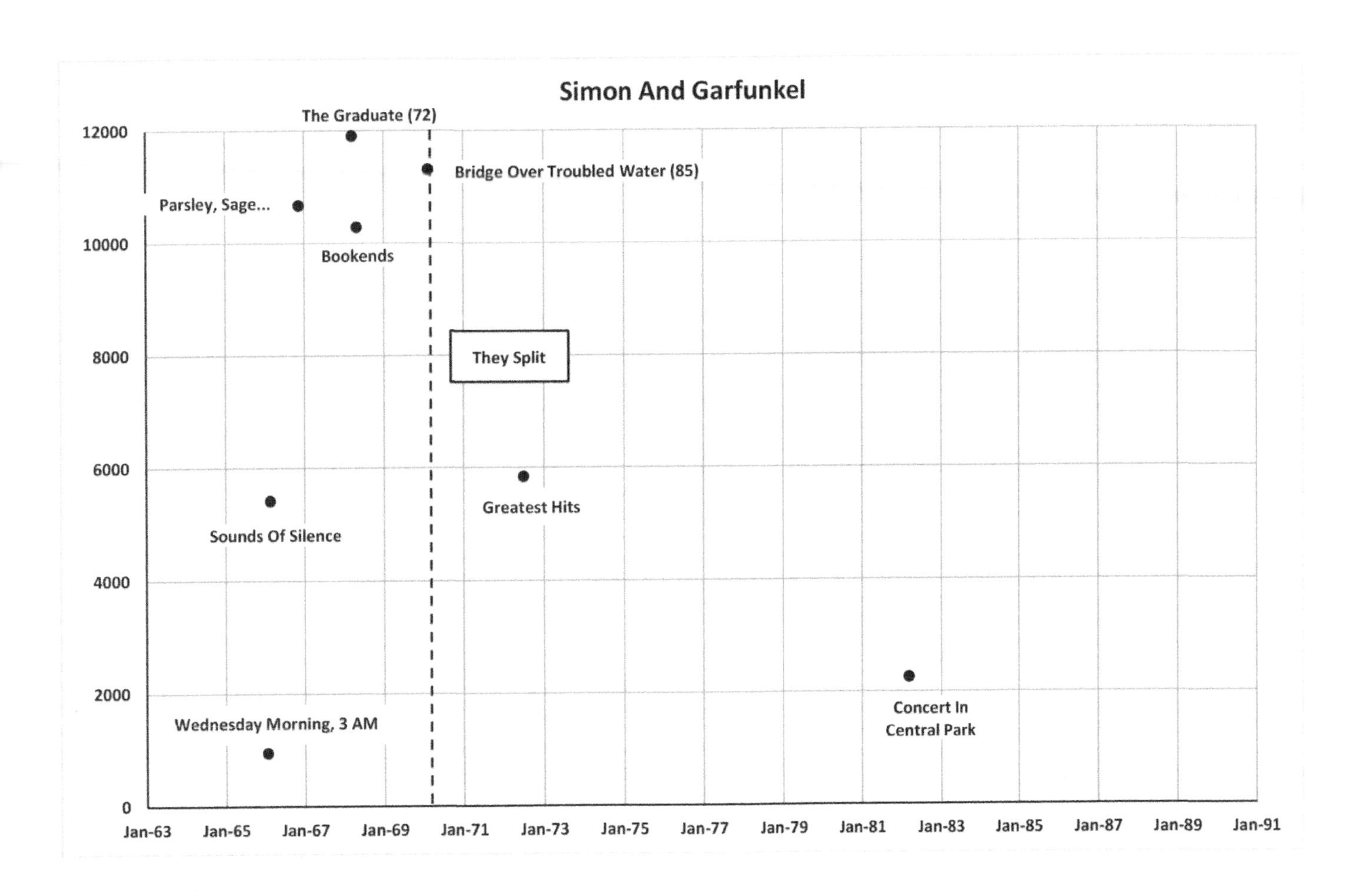

LINDA RONSTADT ▶ 25 (8) 57697

Everyone knows Linda Ronstadt started with the Stone Poneys, who had one charted album called *Evergreen Vol. 2*. Her first solo effort was *Hand Sown...Home Grown*, which did not chart. *Silk Purse* was released in 1970.

Don't Cry Now was her fourth effort and the first to show chart life. She toured that album as opening act for Neil Young's *Time Fades Away* tour. *Heart Like A Wheel*, driven by her version of Clint Ballard's *You're No Good*, spent a week at number 1 and 51 weeks on the chart. Her next two albums, *Prisoner In Disguise* and *Hasten Down The Wind* were also successes, rising to the top 5.

After a *Greatest Hits* album that peaked at number 6 but eventually sold more than seven million US copies, came her biggest album, *Simple Dreams*. It gave rise to four top 40 singles; *Blue Bayou* and *It's So Easy* peaked at number 3 and number 5 and occupied the top 5 at the same time. The album spent five weeks at number 1; 47 weeks on the chart.

Living In The USA and *Mad Love* saw Ronstadt at the top of her appeal. The first was her third number 1; the second spent four weeks at number 3. *Get Closer* broke the string only going to number 31.

Ronstadt's mind changed about musical choices after Get Closer. Her next three albums were made with Nelson Riddle, and were done to remake standards from The Great American Songbook. *What's New*, *Lush Life* and *For Sentimental Reasons* all sold over a million copies, but chart performance declined with each of the trilogy. *Canciones de Mi Padre* was an album of traditional Mexican folk songs.

She returned to pop music for *Cry Like A Rainstorm-Howl Like The Wind*. It included duets with Aaron Neville and returned her to the top 10.

Of her 23 entries, 10 made the top 10 and 13 made the top 40, for a total of 770 chart weeks. She made the top 50 acts in six years; number 3 in 1977.

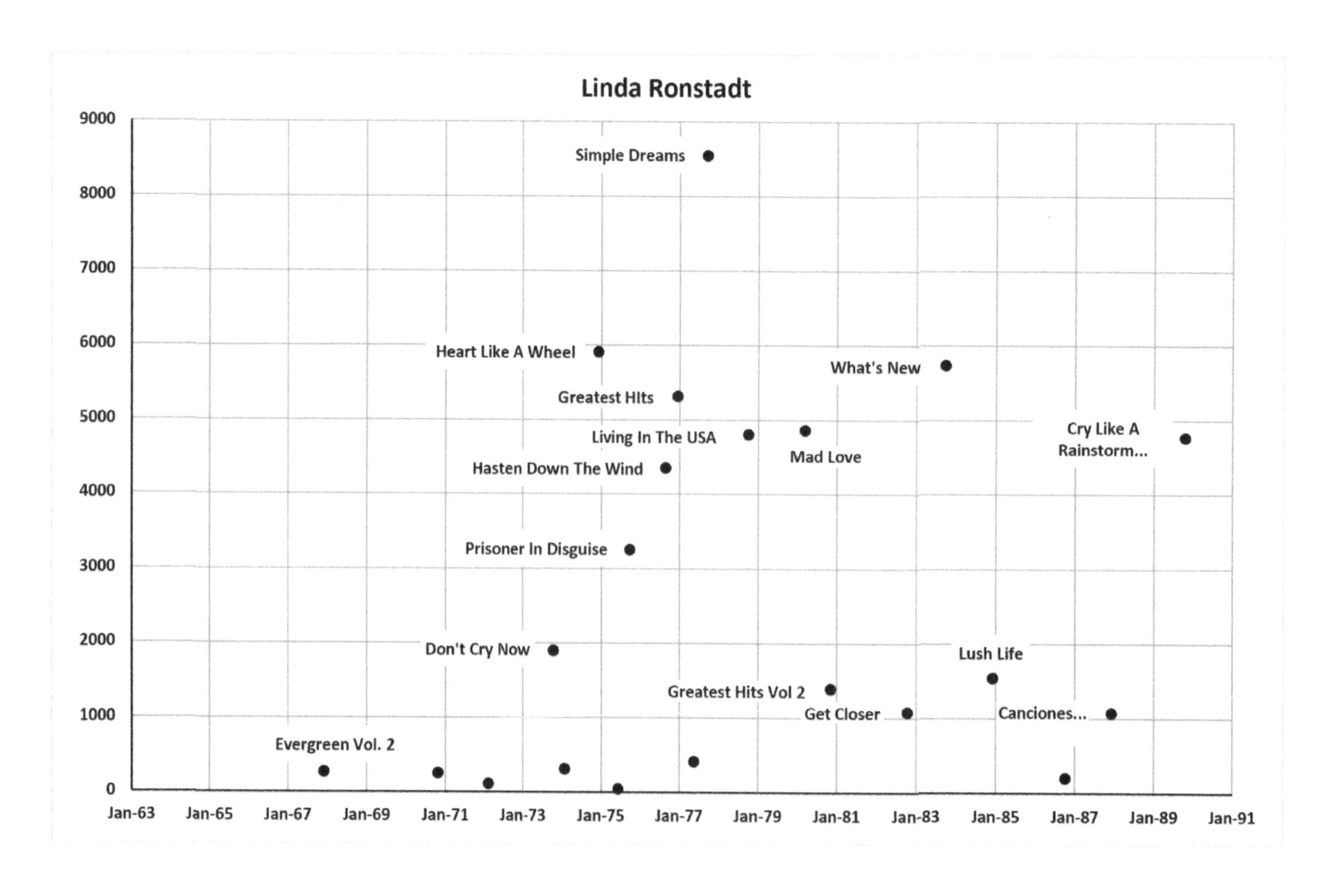

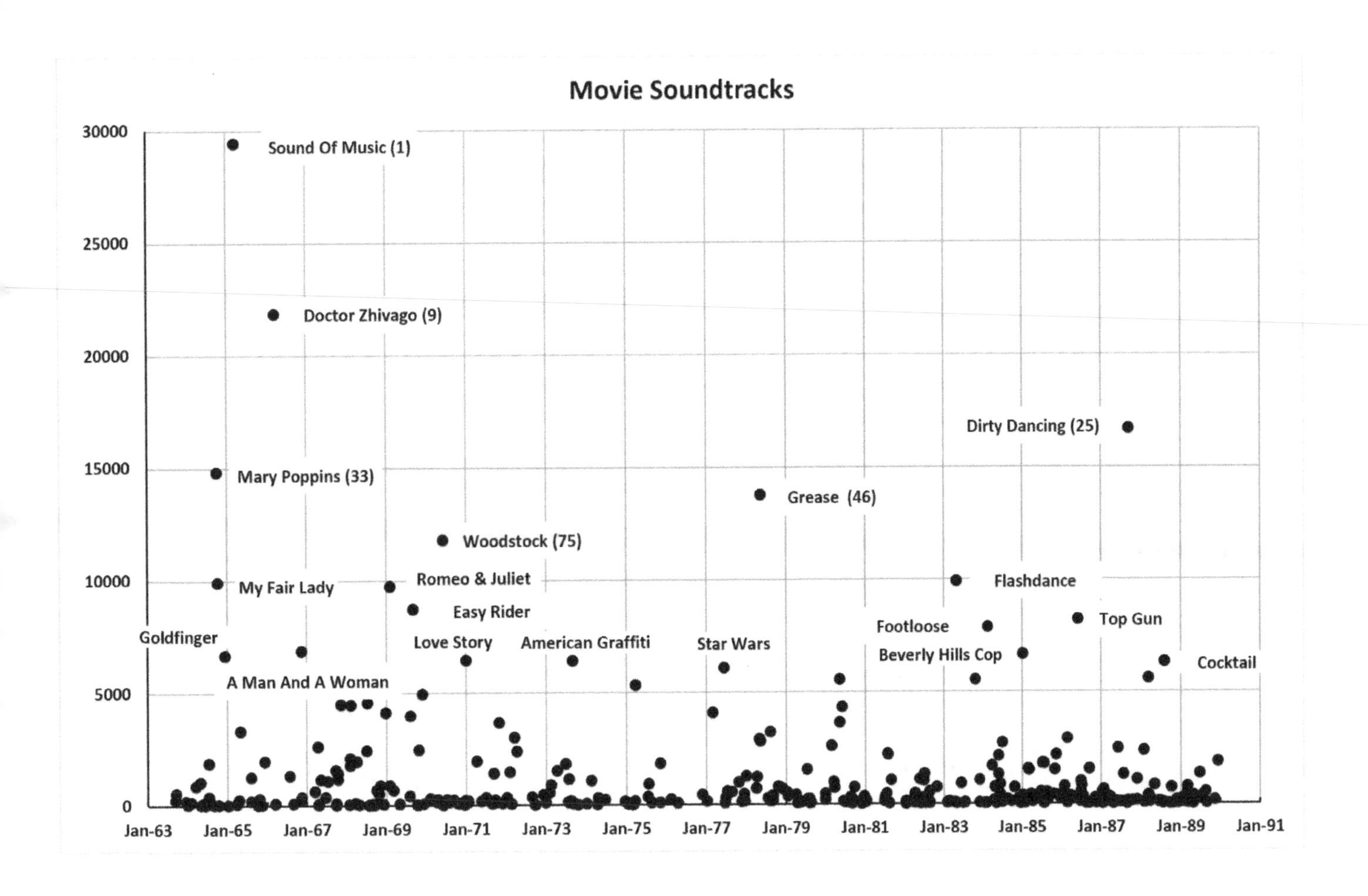
Movie Soundtracks
30000
25000
20000
15000
10000
5000
0
Jan-63
Jan-65
Jan-67
Jan-69
Jan-71
Jan-73
Jan-75
Jan-77
Jan-79
Jan-81
Jan-83
Jan-85
Jan-87
Jan-89
Jan-91
Sound Of Music (1)
Doctor Zhivago (9)
Dirty Dancing (25)
Mary Poppins (33)
Grease (46)
Woodstock (75)
My Fair Lady
Romeo & Juliet
Flashdance
Easy Rider
Footloose
Top Gun
Goldfinger
Love Story
American Graffiti
Star Wars
Beverly Hills Cop
Cocktail
A Man And A Woman

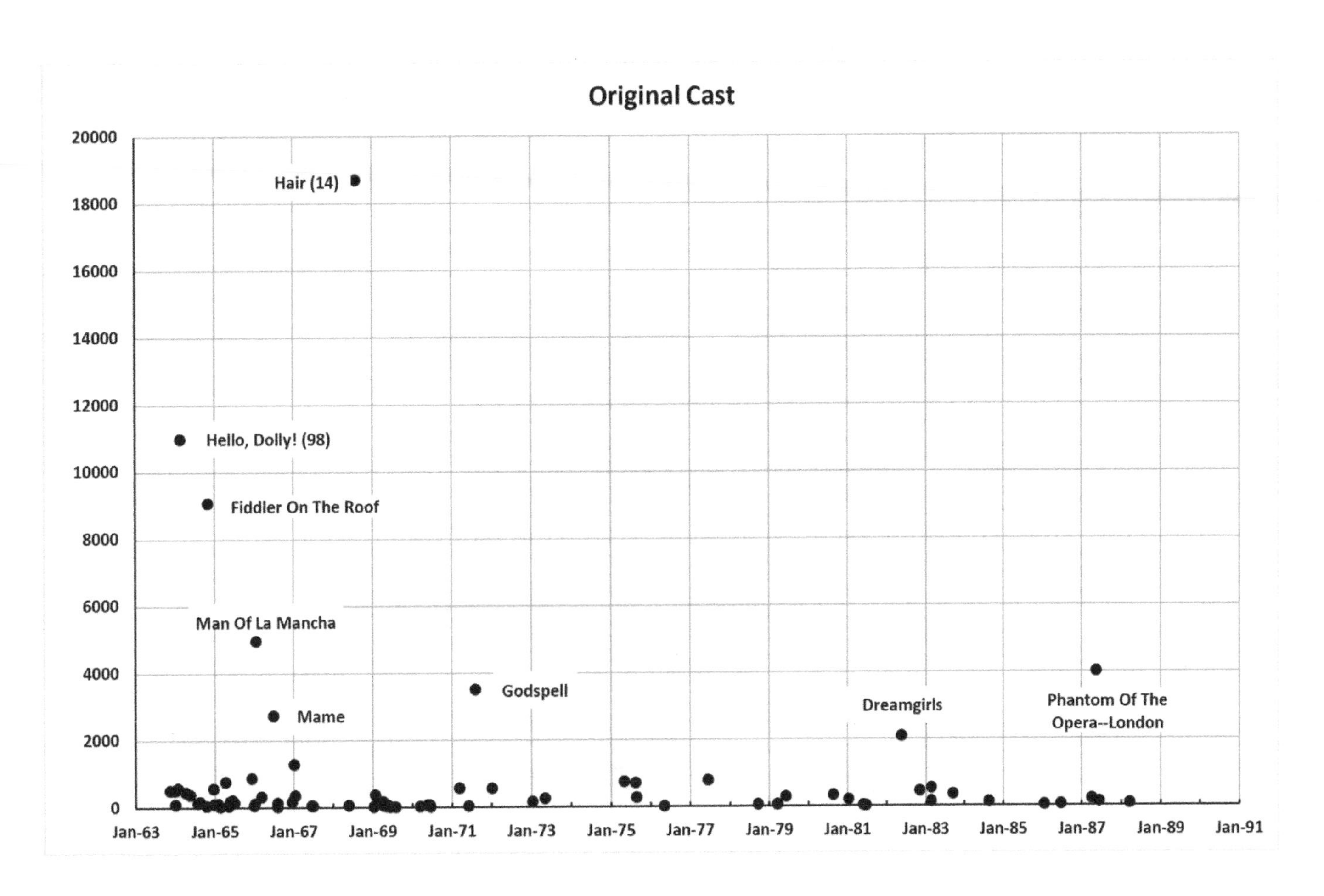
Original Cast
20000
18000
16000
14000
12000
10000
8000
6000
4000
2000
0
Jan-63
Jan-65
Jan-67
Jan-69
Jan-71
Jan-73
Jan-75
Jan-77
Jan-79
Jan-81
Jan-83
Jan-85
Jan-87
Jan-89
Jan-91
Hair (14)
Hello, Dolly! (98)
Fiddler On The Roof
Man Of La Mancha
Godspell
Mame
Dreamgirls
Phantom Of The
Opera--London

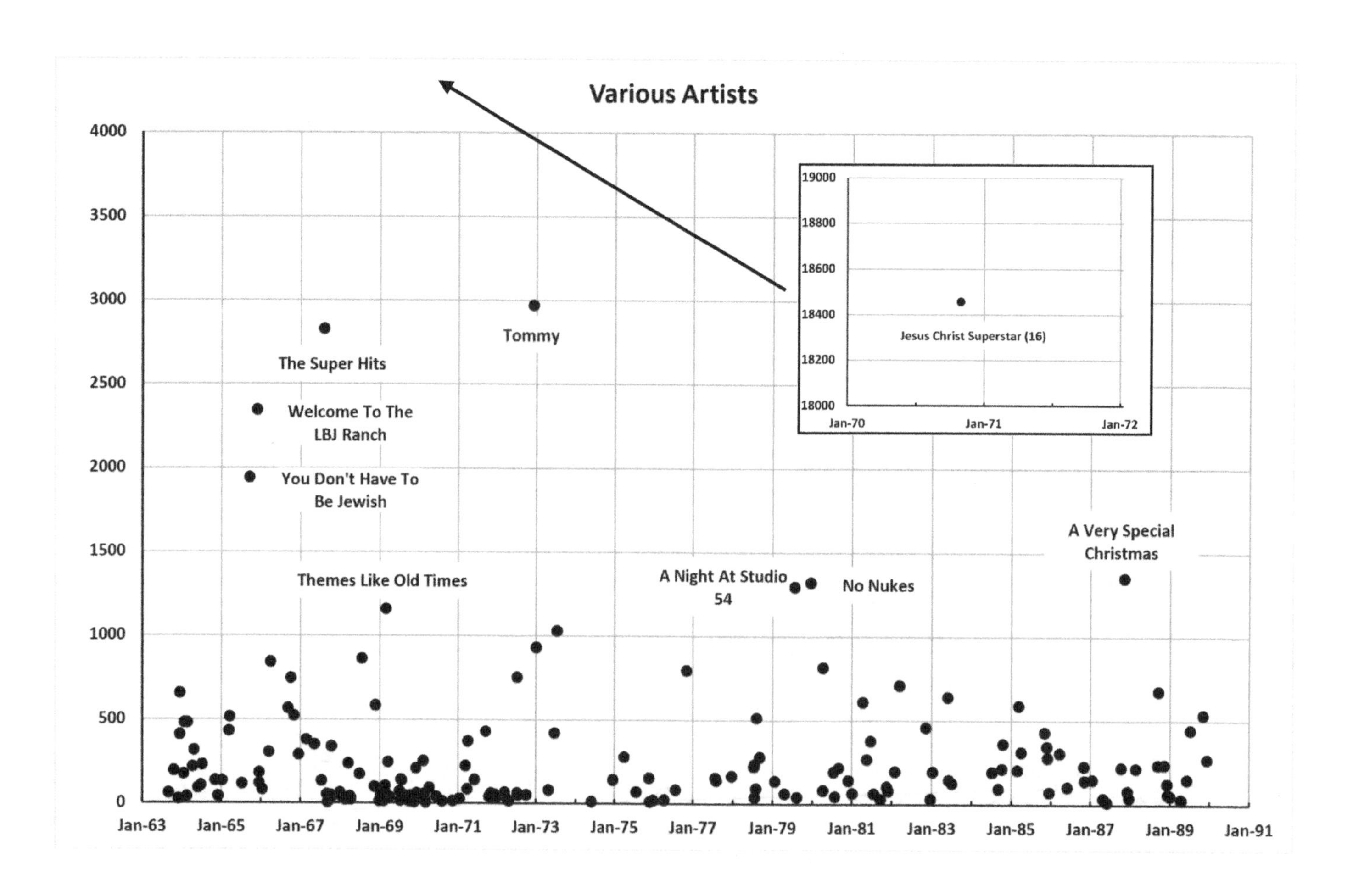
Various Artists
4000
3500
3000
2500
2000
1500
1000
500
0
Jan-63
Jan-65
Jan-67
Jan-69
Jan-71
Jan-73
Jan-75
Jan-77
Jan-79
Jan-81
Jan-83
Jan-85
Jan-87
Jan-89
Jan-91
The Super Hits
Tommy
Welcome To The LBJ Ranch
You Don't Have To Be Jewish
Themes Like Old Times
A Night At Studio 54
No Nukes
A Very Special Christmas
19000
18800
18600
18400
18200
18000
Jan-70
Jan-71
Jan-72
Jesus Christ Superstar (16)

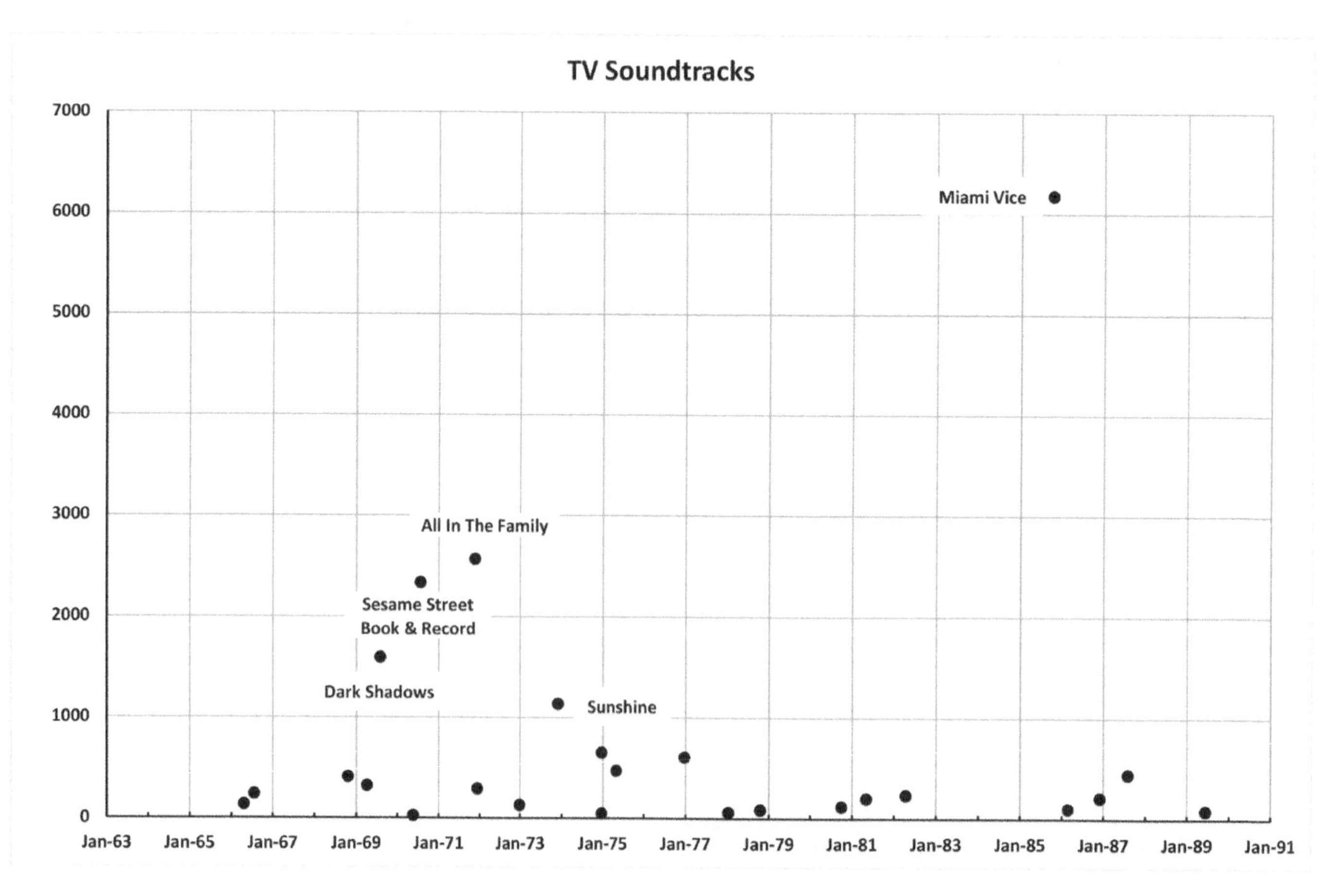
TV Soundtracks
7000
6000
5000
4000
3000
2000
1000
0
Jan-63
Jan-65
Jan-67
Jan-69
Jan-71
Jan-73
Jan-75
Jan-77
Jan-79
Jan-81
Jan-83
Jan-85
Jan-87
Jan-89
Jan-91
Miami Vice
All In The Family
Sesame Street Book & Record
Dark Shadows
Sunshine

Appendix

Methodology

Albums with Allocated Act Credit

Top 5 Albums of the Year 1956-1963

Acknowledgements

Epilog: My Vinyl Romance

About the Author

Methodology

Time Period Studied

The Billboard consolidated albums chart called *Top LPs* debuted August 17, 1963. Prior to that date Billboard had separate charts for mono and stereo albums: the mono charts were 150 records and stereo charts were 50. At the time of the changeover, Billboard explained it adopted the new methodology because the sales of stereo albums was approaching parity with mono albums; by the end of the decade mono was virtually non-existent.

This book covers the records that entered the Billboard album chart--*Top LPs* and successors--from August 17, 1963 to December 31, 1989. While the middle of 1963 might seem like an odd and arbitrary time to start this study, I saw no legitimate way of harmonizing the mono and stereo charts to produce comparable prior data. Moreover, those of us of a certain age truly began our album-collecting careers with the advent of the Beatles. Memorable albums prior to that time were those our parents owned—mostly because our allowances made a $3.98 album a multi-week savings project, and singles provided more nearly instant gratification.

In the period covered, the preferences of the buying public evolved as popular albums migrated from soundtracks to folk to easy listening to rock. Additionally, by the end of the 1960s, the single was in decline and the album became the preferred mode for record collecting for most of us.

So why end in 1989? By that time the vinyl album was all but dead, having been supplanted by cassettes and finally CDs. The end of the decade seemed to be a good stopping point; moreover, in the nineties, data collection would change making it difficult to compare that decade to the ones that came before it.

This book, however, does not cover the complete lifecycle for all the albums included. It does include all data up to the end of 1999, and none of the albums included charted in the 1994-1999 period. There are a number of Billboard chart methodology changes that occurred over the years in addition to the use of SoundScan for data acquisition in 1991.

At some point after 1989, the Billboard 200 was reserved for records newer than 18 months from release that also charted in the top 100 positions. Albums older than 18 months charting below 100 were called catalog albums. In 2003 the Billboard Comprehensive Albums chart was created, which was based solely on current sales and included the catalog albums. It was not published in the magazine.

The Wikipedia entry for the Billboard Comprehensive Albums chart notes:

> The issue dated July 11, 2009 was the first time any catalog album outsold the number-one album on the *Billboard* 200. Three of Michael Jackson's albums (*Number Ones*, *The Essential Michael Jackson* and *Thriller*) claimed positions 1-3 respectively on *Top Pop Catalog Albums* and *Top Comprehensive Albums* in the week following Jackson's death.

In November of that year, the rules for the Billboard 200 were changed to include catalog albums. In order to treat the studied albums on an apples-to-apples basis, only data prior to 2000 is used herein.

So this book covers from *My Son, the Nut* to *Rhythm Nation 1814* and allows for a reasonable comparison of most of the '60s, '70s and '80s. But there are a number of enormously popular albums of the late 1950s and early 1960s that are not covered here because they entered the charts prior to the chart consolidation.

For example, *Johnny Mathis' Greatest Hits* amassed 490 weeks on the charts, and the Original Cast of *My Fair Lady*, 480 weeks; records that entered the charts in 1958 and 1956 respectively. The *West Side Story* Soundtrack spent 198 weeks on the chart—54 at Number 1. Most of the lifecycle of those albums came prior to the consolidated chart.[1] Consequently, early parts of the career of many artists who are included in this study are absent for the same reason. Elvis Presley is probably the most outstanding example.

Attribution of Act (Artist)

In most cases the act attribution is unambiguous. Where there is a question, generally, the label credit is used as first determinant. In some cases where label and album cover differ, I simply used my best judgment. Others might have made different choices. I apologize for any egregious violations of common sense.

Where there are different configurations of essentially the same entity, they are grouped: i.e., Bob Seger, The Bob Seger System, and Bob Seger and the Silver Bullet Band are all grouped under Bob Seger. However, actual label attribution is also noted in the description of each record.

As a general rule, artists who are listed as "with" the primary artist are generally not credited unless they receive similar size type font billing on the label and the jacket. Those who are listed as "and" are credited.

Many collaborations are stable and long term, even if the individuals occasionally record under their own names; i.e., Daryl Hall and John Oates. On the other hand there are unusual and temporary collaborations of otherwise established artists; i.e., The Supremes and The Temptations.

Generally, for one-off collaborations of this type; i.e. Dylan And The Dead, credit is divided based on the number of collaborating acts (in this case, 2). This is referred to as allocated credit, and there is a list of the albums for which credit is allocated in the Appendix. A few one-offs are credited explicitly: *Ram* by Paul and Linda McCartney is an example. In order to allocate credit, an entry for Linda McCartney would have had to be created, so that collaboration was made its own entry. Similarly, Blind Faith is treated as a discreet entity and not allocated to the members.

There are three special cases: Soundtracks, Original Cast, and Various Artists. Where a soundtrack is not explicitly assigned on the label or the jacket to a particular act (i.e., The Graduate Soundtrack to Simon and Garfunkel) the act assignment is Soundtrack, and all such Soundtracks are grouped together, either as movie or TV soundtracks. Original Casts are treated similarly.

Records designated Various Artists are those where there is not a predominance of one act on the record. On the other hand, if a majority of cuts is assignable to a main act, the record is designated for that act. In fact, many soundtracks are also various artist recordings.

When "(II)" appears after an album name it signifies a second and different album with the same name. When "(2)" appears after the name it signifies a slightly modified re-release of the original.

Scoring.

Ranking involves scoring, and chart scoring systems involve two parameters: chart position value and time. The first parameter defines the relative value of achievement of a specific chart rank. Many systems award points equal to the length of the chart for #1, declining to 1 point for the last in the list. Thus, for a list of 200, awarding 200 points for #1, 199 for #2 and so on to one point for #200. This system is called "Reverse Rank."

Some systems value only peak achievement as in "That record went to number 1." For most analysts, that is not sufficient granularity and some time value is included. For example, "That record was number 1 for four weeks."

---

[1] A list of the Billboard top five albums for each year 1956-1963 appears in the Appendix.

Other systems award peak achievement with a value for peak points and add a bonus for number of weeks at that peak and/or number of weeks on the chart. Such a system can be constructed from a less-than-complete chart history for a record. For example: 100 points for number 1; 10 points for each additional week at number 1 and one point for each week on the charts.

Most systems, however, involve giving points for performance each week of the record lifecycle, then summing those points to obtain a final score. This is called an "area under the curve" system.

Reverse Rank has shortcomings. As an example, the difference between Number 1 and Number 2 is the same as the difference between Number 199 and Number 200; intuitively, and based on sales data, the rewards should be higher and more spread out near the top of the chart. Most systems use this kind of spread-out scale,[2] which may be based in some logical methodology or may be totally empirical. Such scales assign significantly greater value for higher achievement. Figure 1 shows two area under the curve approaches: Reverse Rank and the system used in this book for a hypothetical record. While Reverse Rank gives substantial relative score to lower ranks, the current system highly rewards the top ten places. Note the difference in scale.

Figure 1. Comparison of Reverse Rank Scoring with the scoring system used in this book. Horizontal legend is actual chart rank.

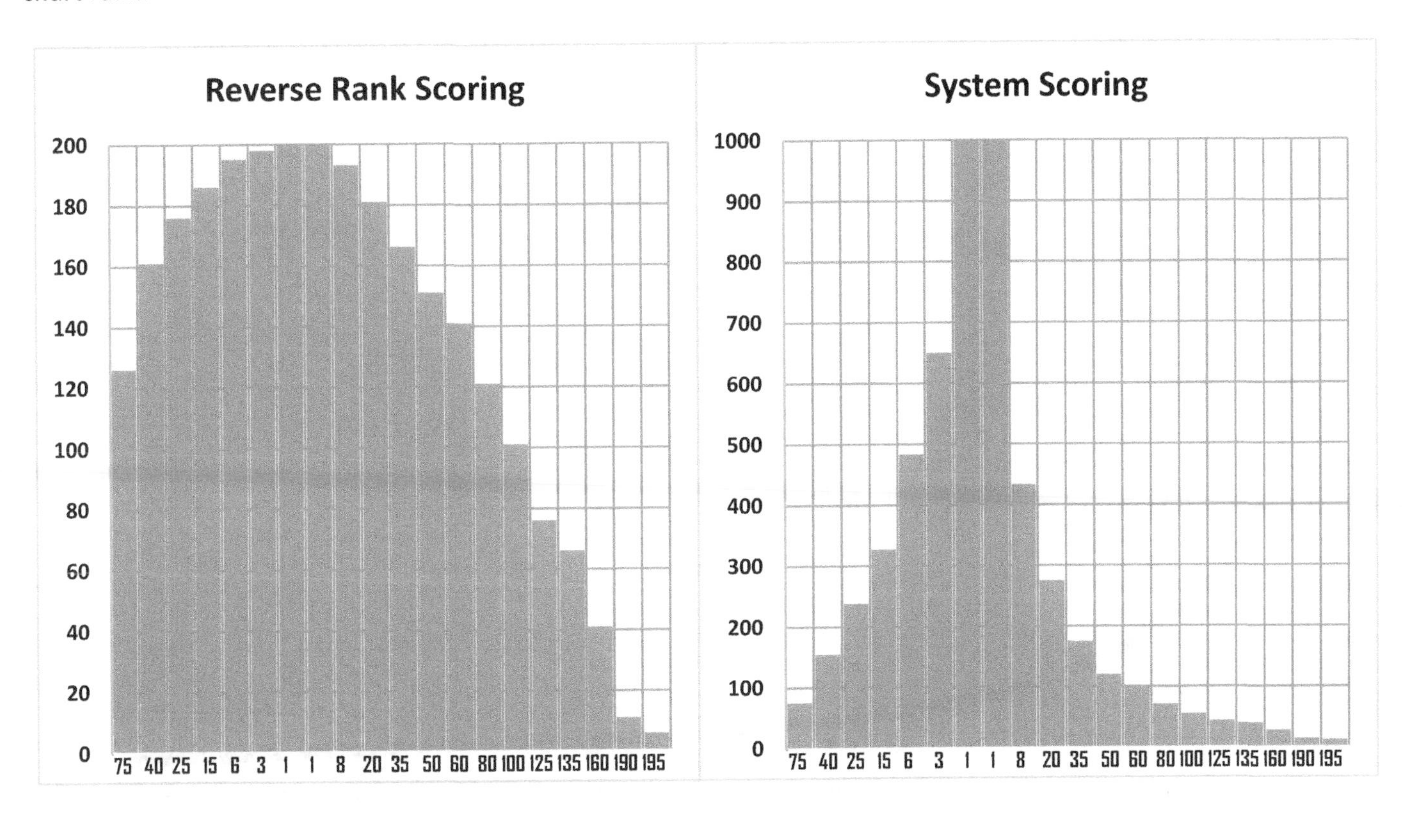

While there are numerous systems for ranking chart performance of singles, few systems have been devised to score albums. Joel Whitburn[3] awards points for peak, bonuses for additional weeks at peaks number 1, 2 and 3, and points for weeks charted. Billboard Magazine compiled annual lists of top LPs, and was generally not transparent about methodology.

---

[2] Carroll, William F., Jr. "Not So Lonely At The Top: Billboard #1s and a New Methodology for Comparing Records, 1958-1975." Popular Music And Society 38, 586-610 (2015) DOI: 10.1080/03007766.2014.991188. Published Online 20 Dec 2014. http://dx.doi.org/10.1080/03007766.2014.991188.

[3] Joel Whitburn, "Top Pop Albums, 1955-2016" © 2018, Record Research, Inc., P.O. Box 200, Menomonee Falls, WI

The methodology for this book begins with sales of the top ten albums by year, which could be retrieved for 1991-2019 from the Nielsen Music Year-End Reports. Sales for the top album of the year was scaled at 1000 and positions 2-10 were scaled accordingly. Averages for 2-10 were computed over the period and are shown in Table 1. The rest of the positions 11-200 were calculated empirically to produce a smooth scoring curve, which is shown in Figure 2.

Table 1. Rank and average scaled scores based on top ten album sales, 1991-2019.

Rank	Score	Rank	Score
1	1000	6	483
2	757	7	457
3	650	8	433
4	567	9	410
5	520	10	392

Figure 2. Scoring by rank used for this book.

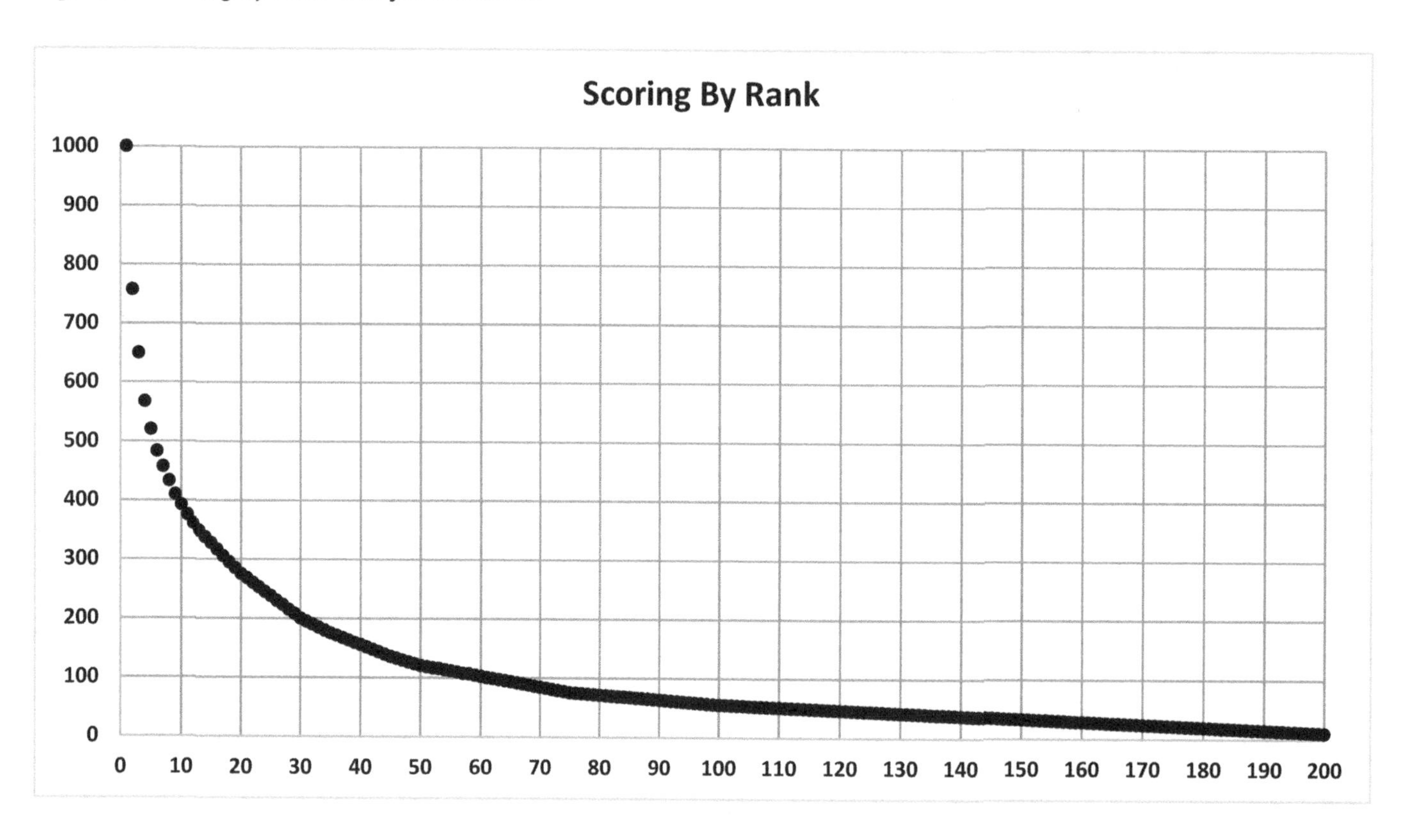

The shape of the curve in Figure 2 is analogous in shape to the area under the curve systems used in previous books for ranking the weekly top 100 singles.[4,5]

---

[4] Dann Isbell and Bill Carroll "Ranking the '70s: A Complete Compilation of the Chart Songs and Acts from Pop's Eclectic Decade" © 2015 Jefrian Books, Dallas, TX.

[5] Bill Carroll "Ranking the Rock Writers" © 2018 Carroll Applied Science, LLC Dallas, TX

To calculate scores, weekly rankings for each album were obtained from Billboard Magazine, either archived hardcopy or the website (https://www.billboard.com/charts/billboard-200). The historical information from the chart is used to create this derivative work product. The charts themselves are not reproduced. After the debut of *Top LPs* as a 150 record chart, on March 25, 1967, the chart was increased to 165, then to 175 on April 8, 1967, and on May 13, 1967 the 200-record format was introduced, which remains the standard today.

Normalization for Era.

One of the most difficult parts of compiling any "Greatest Of All Time" list is the challenge of comparing performances in different eras. In sports, different eras can mean different equipment, different rules, different conditioning and different lengths of seasons, among other things. Ranking greatness over time requires a methodology for taking all those variables into account.

In the sciences, datasets that have been gathered at different times can sometimes be made to work together through a process called normalization. In normalization, these datasets are scaled to a common standard and the data are cautiously used together as a single dataset.

The charts are really no different than sports statistics. Music eras change. Aggregate sales change up and down. Editorial philosophies change. Methodologies change. The underlying data for how charts were constructed is unavailable, so the only information is a date, a title, an act and a chart rank week-to-week.

My philosophy in ranking records is to highlight performances that are *transcendent in their time*, rather than absolute score; this means those that stood out most from the competition around them. To do this, I determine the average record score for a given time and then compare each individual record performance against that average.

Specifically, this means dividing the score of every record by the average score of all the records that enter the charts three months before it to one year after it. This span is arbitrary but is intended to include sensitivity to the environment into which the record was released, and a long tail for sensitivity to the long chart life of high scoring records.

The purpose of normalizing to that era average is to remove dependencies of record score on externalities; the average at the time is an internal standard, and an "average" record always has a score of 1. Additionally, the average of all normalized scores for a year should be very close to 1, and a record with a score of 10 always has ten times the chart presence of an average record.

As a chart is constructed, there are a fixed number of ranks, each of which is awarded each week. The total points awarded per year remains the same year to year (although there is an occasional 53rd chart due to calendar considerations). But the number of records entering the charts varies from year to year. In some cases, this is because of editorial preference to keep the charts fresh with new material. In other cases, it could be due to an abundance or shortage of quality material or exceptional promotion. Whatever the reason, Entries per Year varies, and because the points awarded per year does not vary, the score of an average charted record also varies.

A plot of Raw Score vs Entry Date is shown in Figure 3. Note the number of very high scores (>40,000) in the periods 1964-1966 and 1983-1989.

Figure 3. Raw scores for 1963-1989.

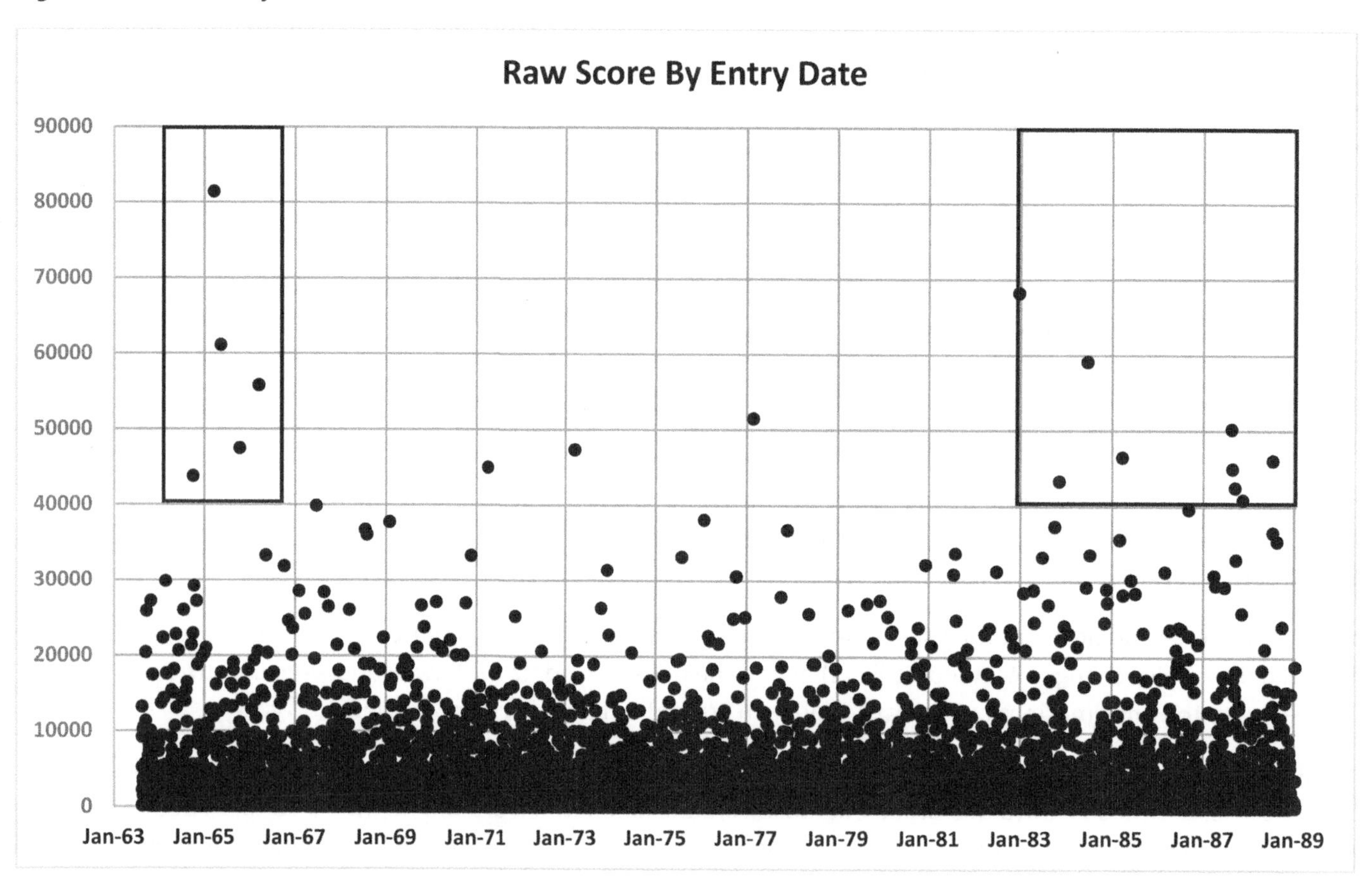

Trends for this period can be seen more easily in Figures 4 and 5.

From the inception of the combined chart through mid-1967 there were fewer than 200 records on the chart per week, and as a result the fewest Entries per Year were in this period. Generally, when Entries Per Year are low, average scores are high, and vice versa. The plots of Entries per Year and Average Raw Score are virtually mirror images. The year 1969 is anomalous in that there were a number of weeks with exceptionally high numbers of new entries, leading to a large number of entries in that year.

Two other charts, Figure 6 and 7, show the interdependency of Raw Score, Entries, and Weeks on Chart. In Figure 6, 1964, 1965 and 1966 lie above the line and are outliers. This is because a 150-position chart awards 20520 points per week, and those years divided those points among the fewest Entries. In 1968, the first full year of the 200-position chart, there were 20% more entries but only about 5% more points awarded per week for positions 151-200 (21576 total) thus average scores are lower in that year. Fewer average weeks on the chart after the advent of the longer chart may be explained by the lack of 50 lower ranks to extend a chart run while not adding many score points.

Figure 4. Average Record Raw Score by Year

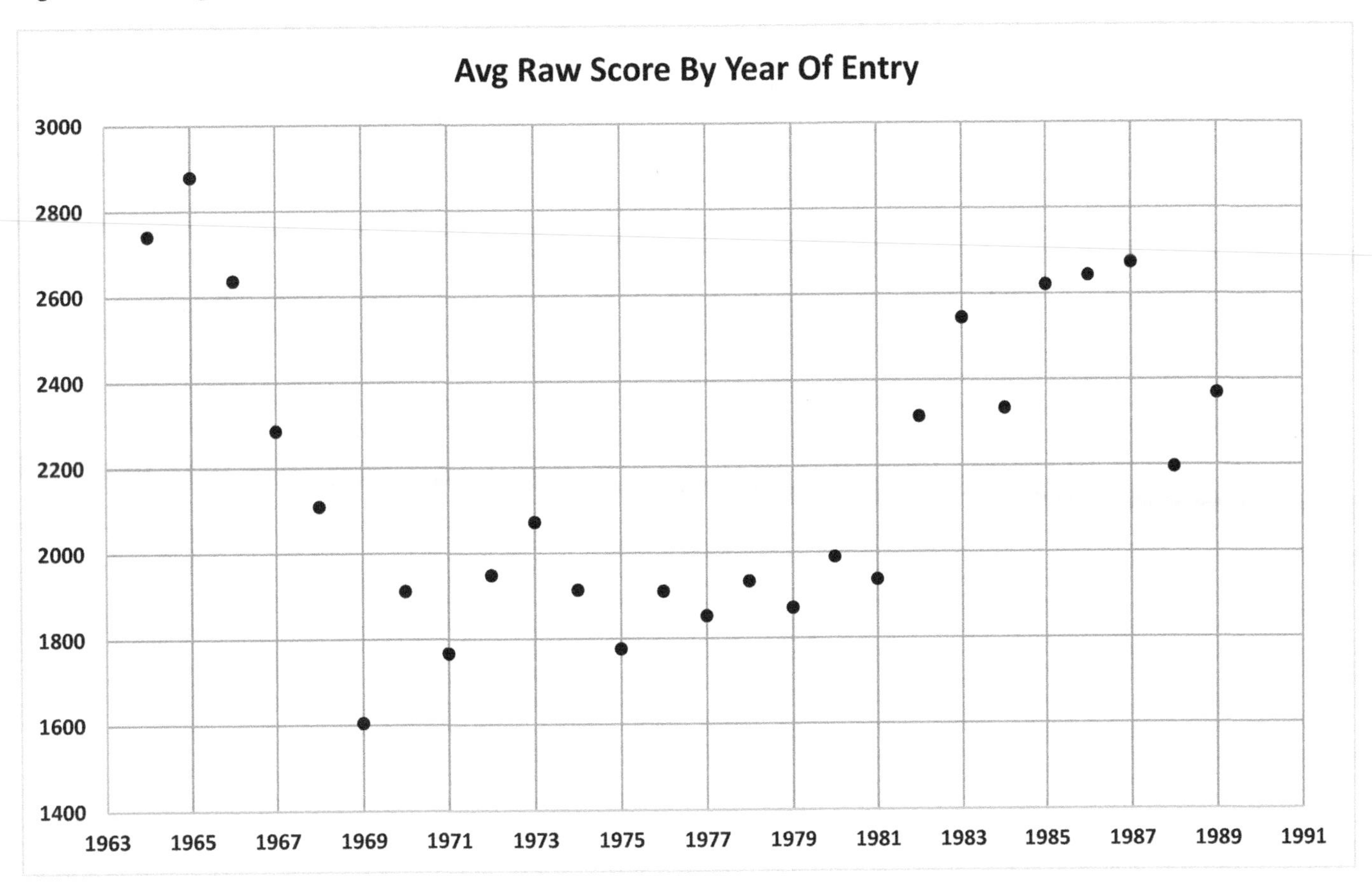

Figure 5. Entries per Year.

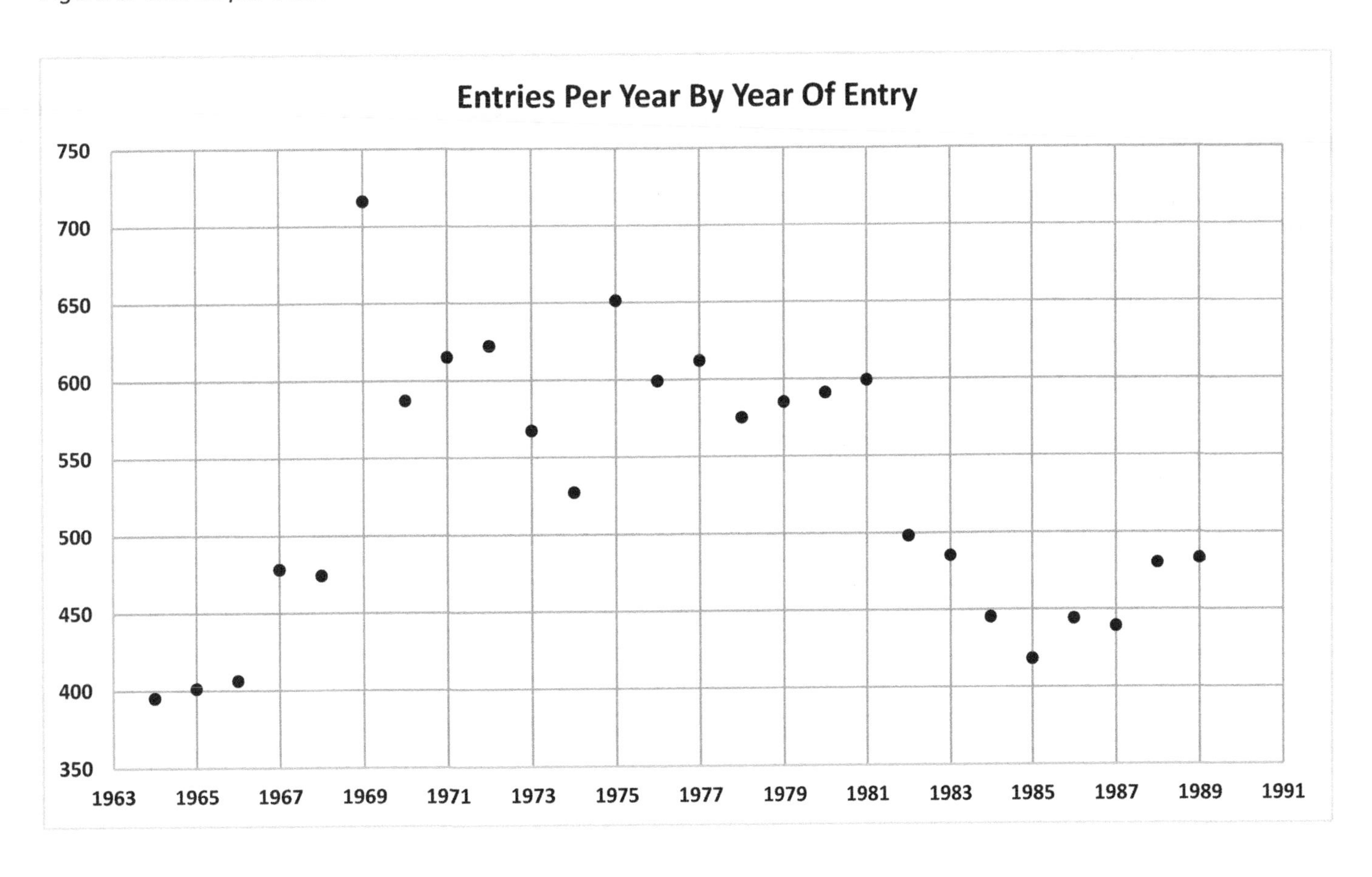

Figure 6. Average Raw Score Vs. Average Weeks On Chart. Each point represents one year.

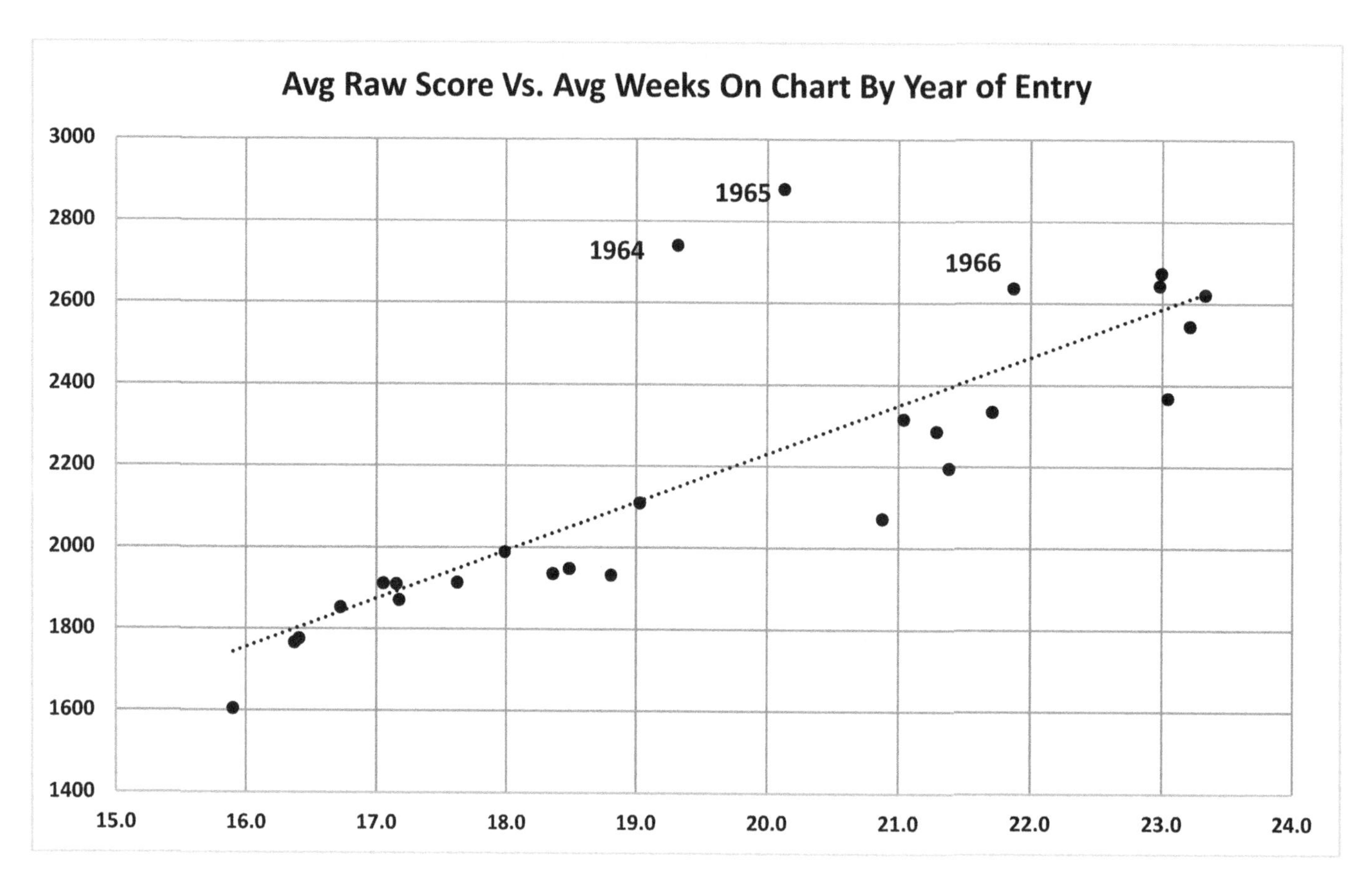

Figure 7. Average Raw Score by Entries Per Year. Each point represents one year.

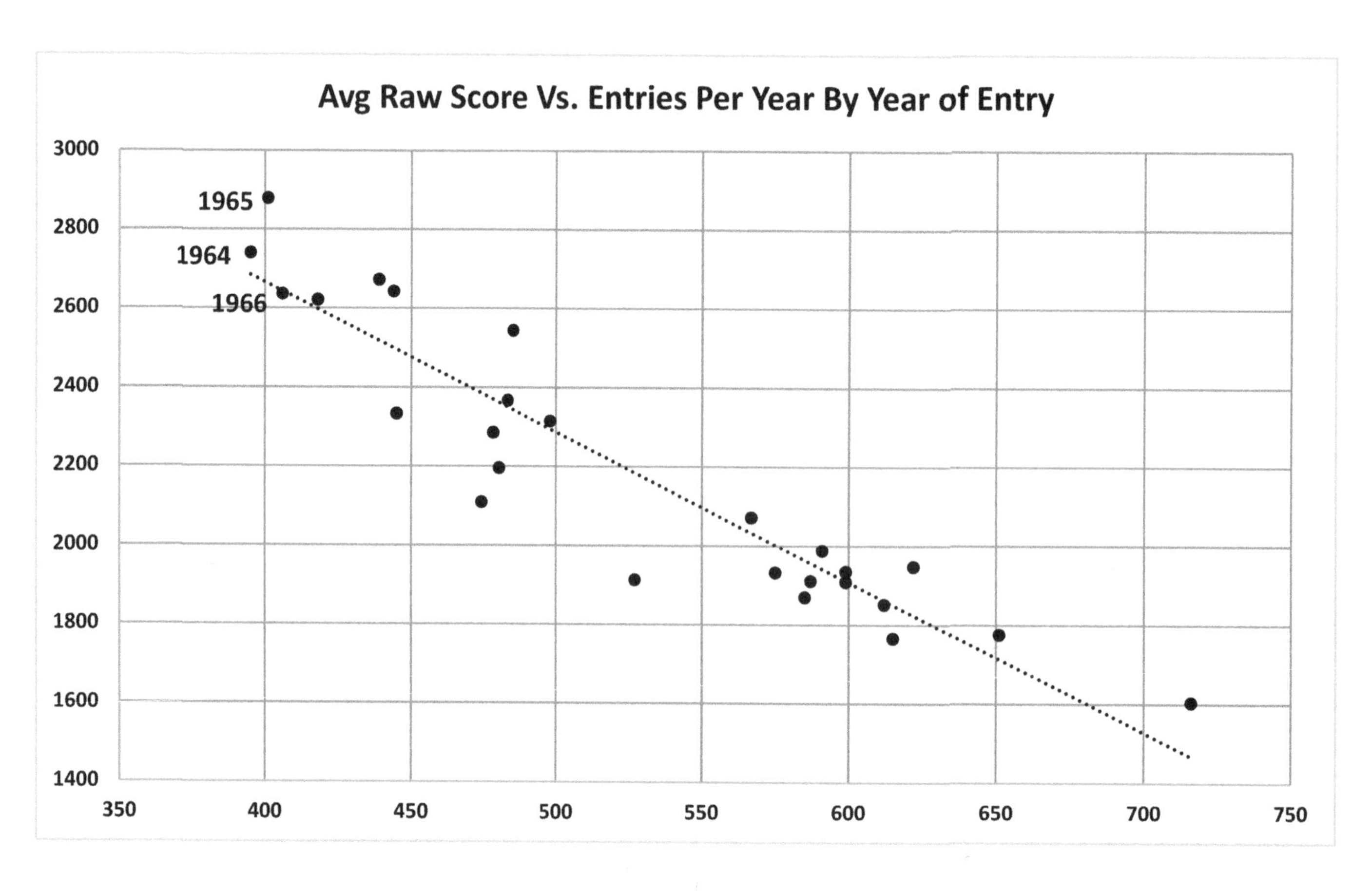

Figure 8. Average Normalized Score by Year

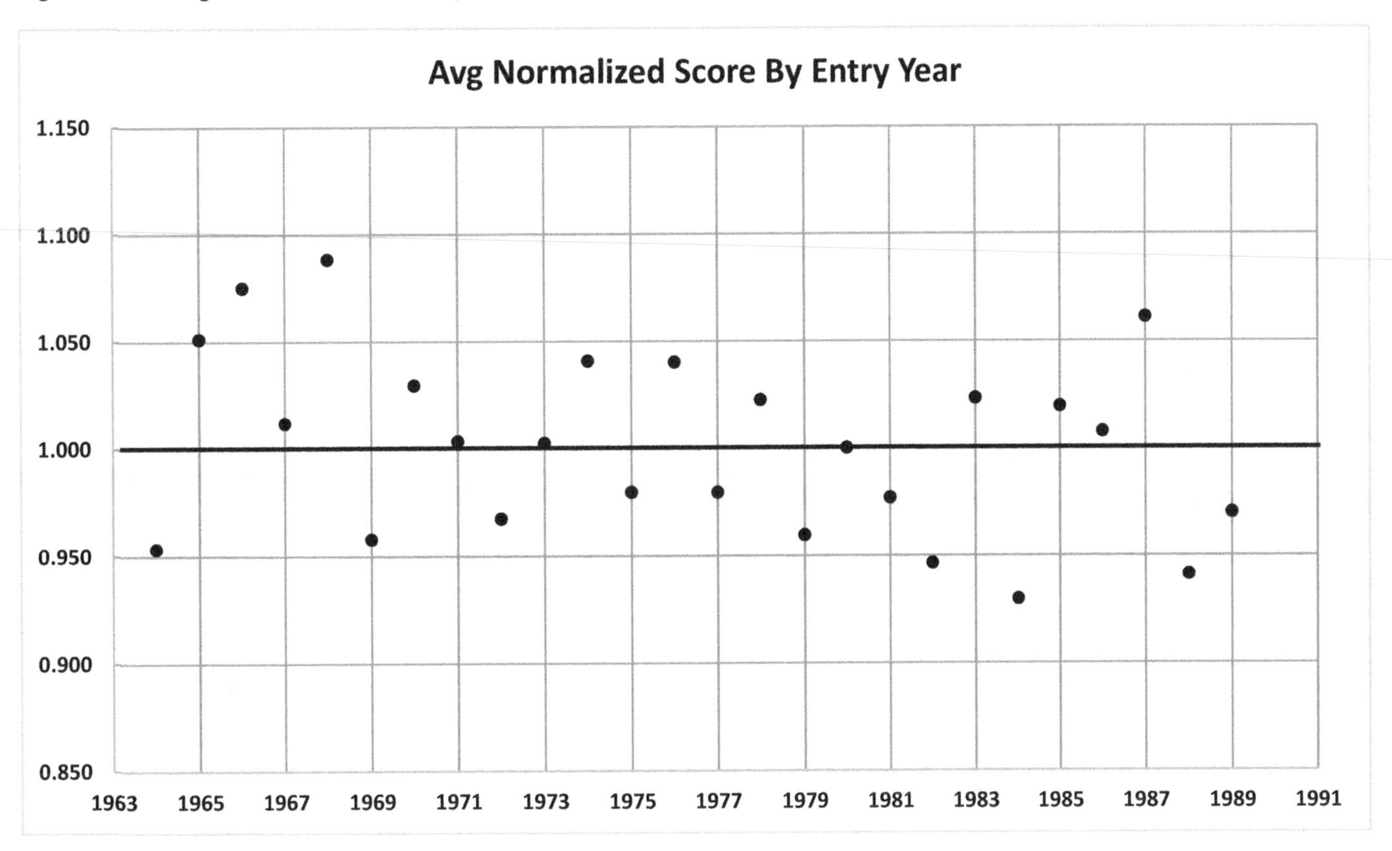

Figure 9. Average Normalized Score by Weeks On Chart. Each point represents one year.

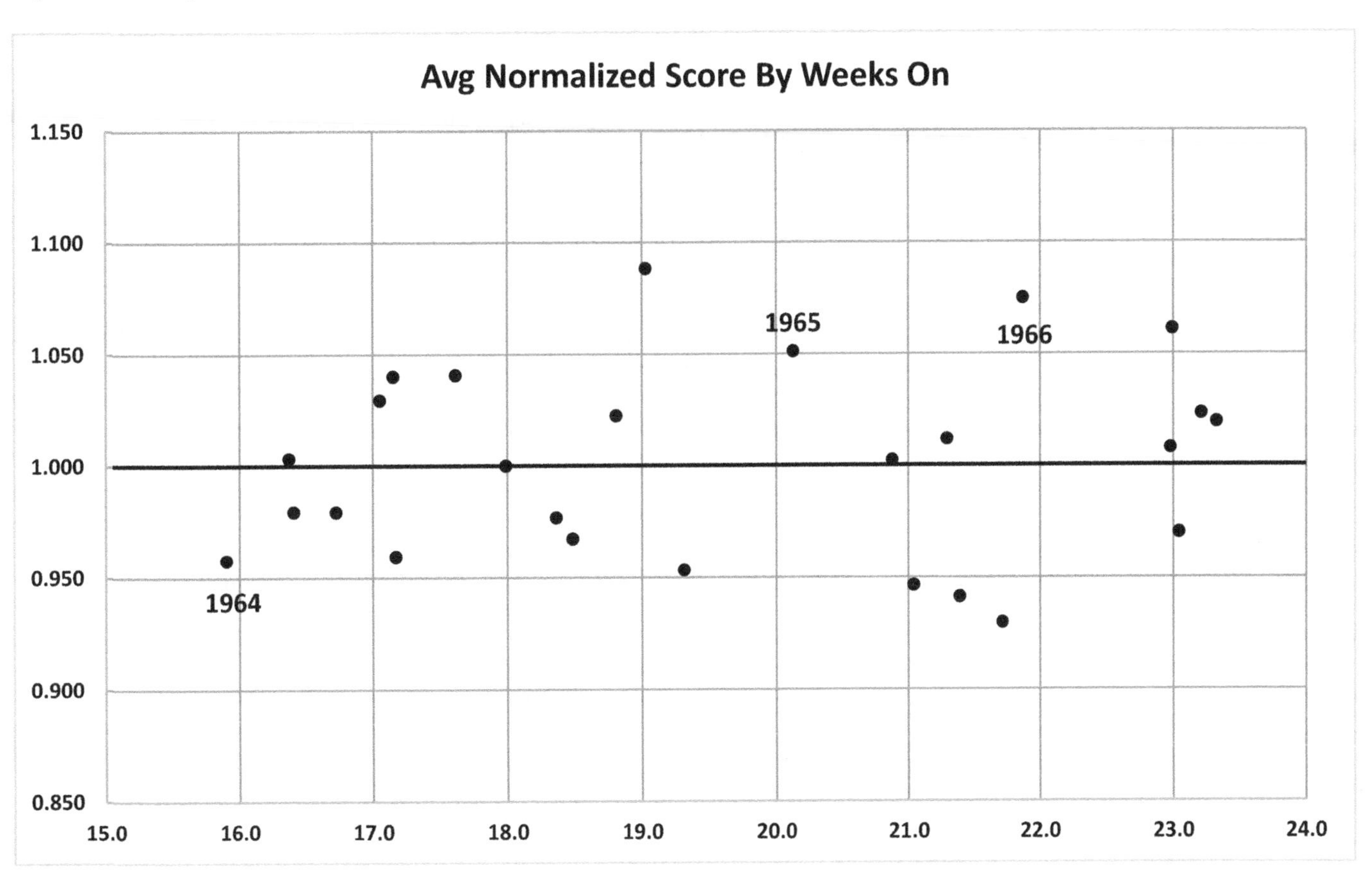

Figure 10. Average Normalized Score by Weeks On Chart. Each Point represents one year.

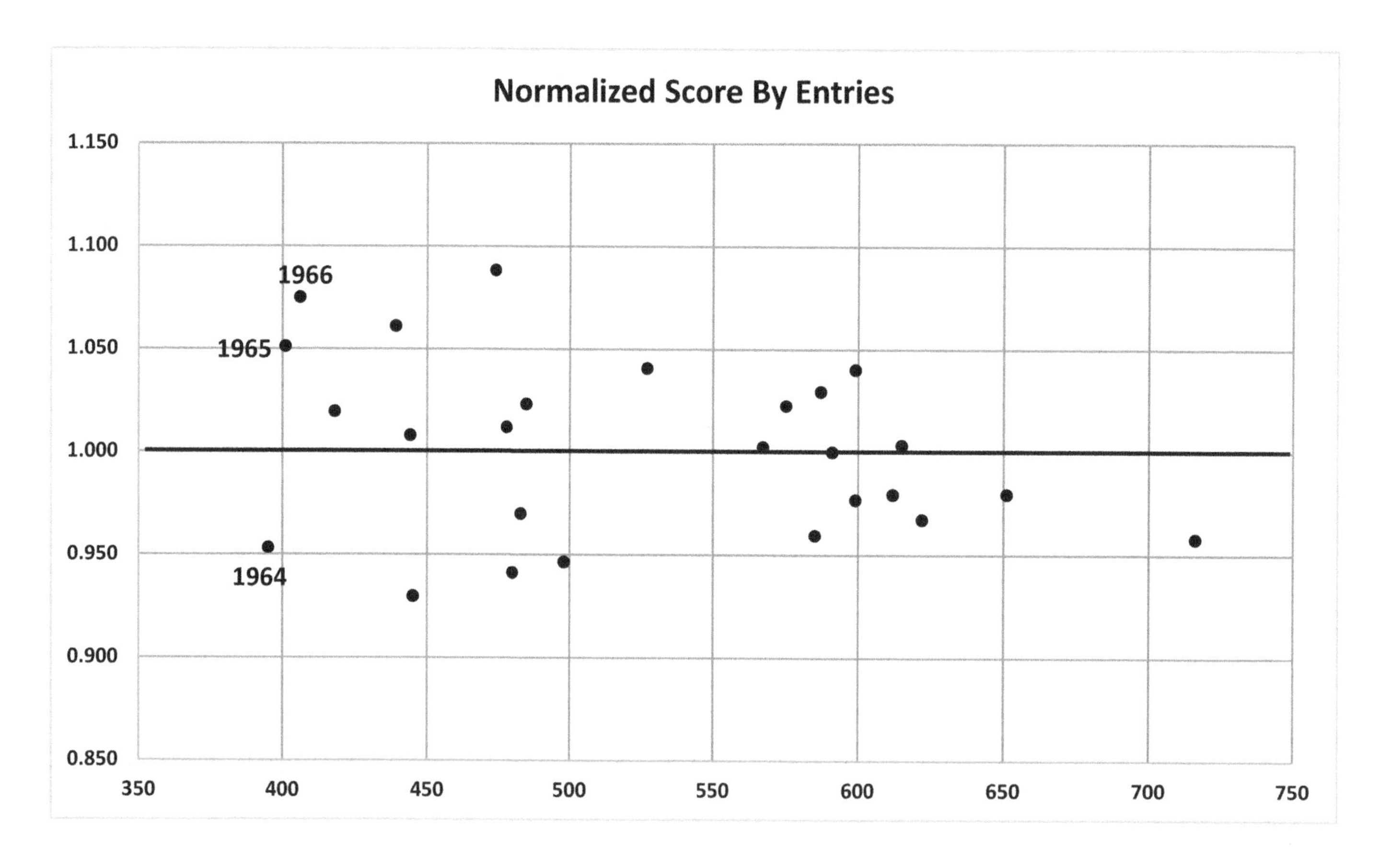

Figure 8 shows that after normalization there is no remaining year dependency, only variation around 1.0. Figures 9 and 10 show little or no correlation between normalized score and either number of entries or average weeks on the chart as was apparent in Figures 6 and 7.

For purposes of readability, in this book normalized scores are multiplied by 1000.

Normalized scores in series

For those who are interested in statistics, Figure 11 shows all the normalized album scores in numerical order from smallest to largest, vs. the percentage of the distribution. In normalizing, there is a choice between using the median or the average of the normalizing set of data. Each has practical consequences.

Average is used rather than median for normalization because the average is more responsive (that is, it rises) in eras of high scores (Figure 3). Using the median would not necessarily bring into account the different skewness of the data in a particular era. Skewness in this case means the difference between an era characterized by very large and very small scores versus one where scores tend more toward the middle range. The average does reflect the difference between those two distributions, but it means that an "average" record is not the median—in fact an average record represents the top 25 percent of this distribution. I've chosen to use the average in order to reflect different skewness over time, and ask the reader to recognize that an "average" song—scoring 1000 points--is still in the upper part of the distribution, and the charts are mainly populated with low performing records. The median for this overall data set is about 300. (Figure 11)

Figure 11. Percentile distribution of Normalized Scores.

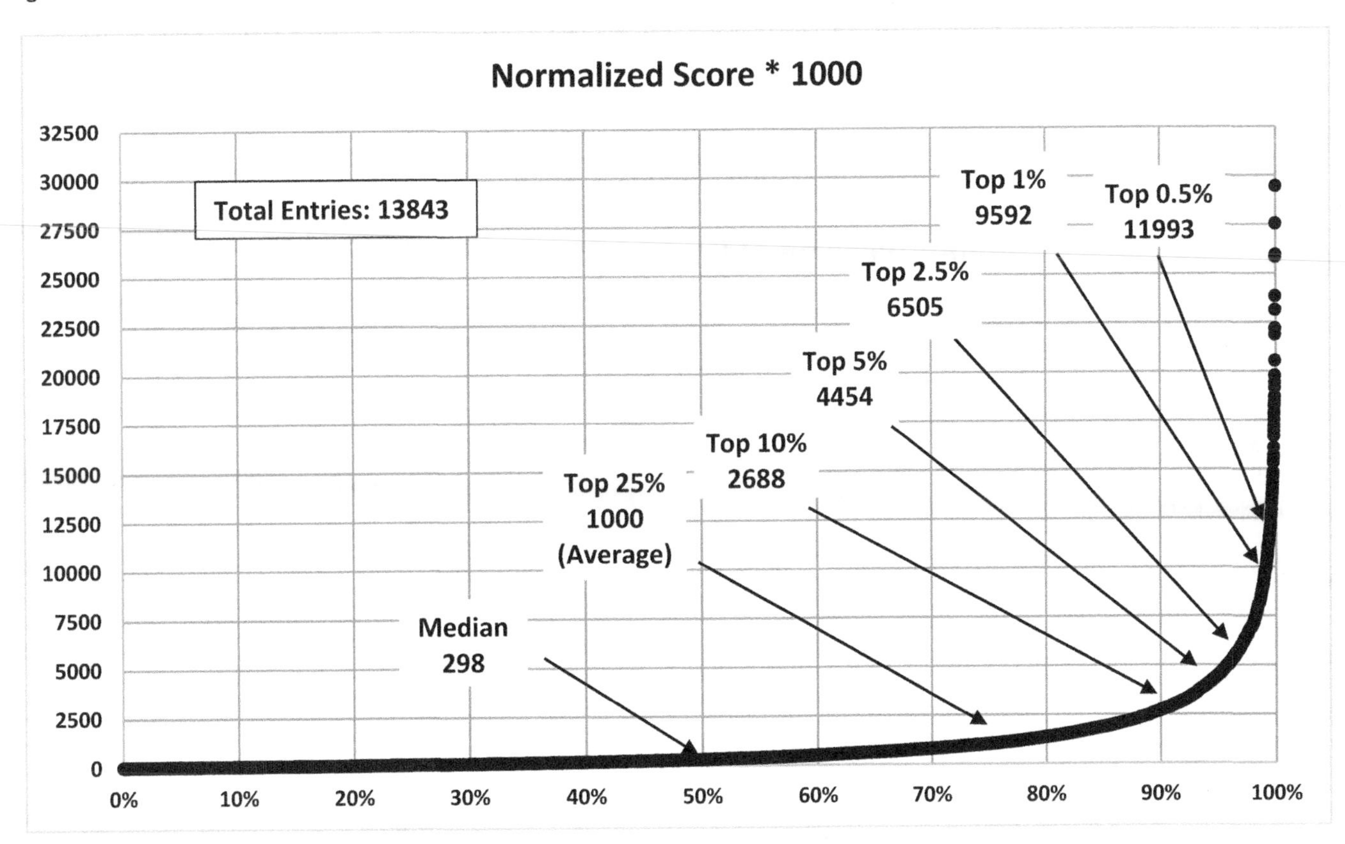

As an example, Table 2 shows performance of a sample of albums that score at about 1000 points, the average. Those records tend to peak in the 30s and have a chart life on the order of 25 weeks. Table 3 shows records that score near the median of 300. Those records tend to peak in the 60s with a chart life of about ten weeks,

Table 2. Albums scoring near the average (1000 points).

Rank. Name Act	Peak (Wks)	Weeks on	Score
3463. WANTED Richard Pryor	32 (2)	20	1002
3464. WILD THINGS! The Ventures	33 (1)	26	1001
3465. BARBRA STREISAND'S GREATEST HITS Barbra Streisand	32 (1)	30	1001
3466. UNLIMITED! Roger	35 (1)	24	1000
3467. MEET THE SEARCHERS/NEEDLES & PINS The Searchers	22 (2)	21	999
3468. THE YOUTH OF TODAY Musical Youth	23 (4)	22	999
3469. DANA DANE WITH FAME Dana Dane	46 (2)	32	998

Table 3. Albums scoring near the median (298 points)

Rank. Name Act	Peak (Wks)	Weeks on	Score
6896. THE TROUBLEMAKER Willie Nelson	60 (1)	7	298
6897. MECHANIX UFO	82 (1)	14	298
6898. 1980 Gil Scott-Heron & Brian Jackson	82 (1)	12	298
6899. PILLOW TALK Sylvia	70 (1)	12	298
6900. JOHNNY THE FOX Thin Lizzy	52 (1)	11	298
6901. WEATHER REPORT(2) Weather Report	68 (1)	11	298
6902. PLAYING TO WIN LRB	75 (3)	14	298

Finally, the distribution of peak positions for albums is similar to that of singles and is shown in Figure 12. That is, the most likely peak position for an album is number 1. More than twice as many albums peak there as at any other rank.[1]

Figure 12. Peak position frequency in per cent.

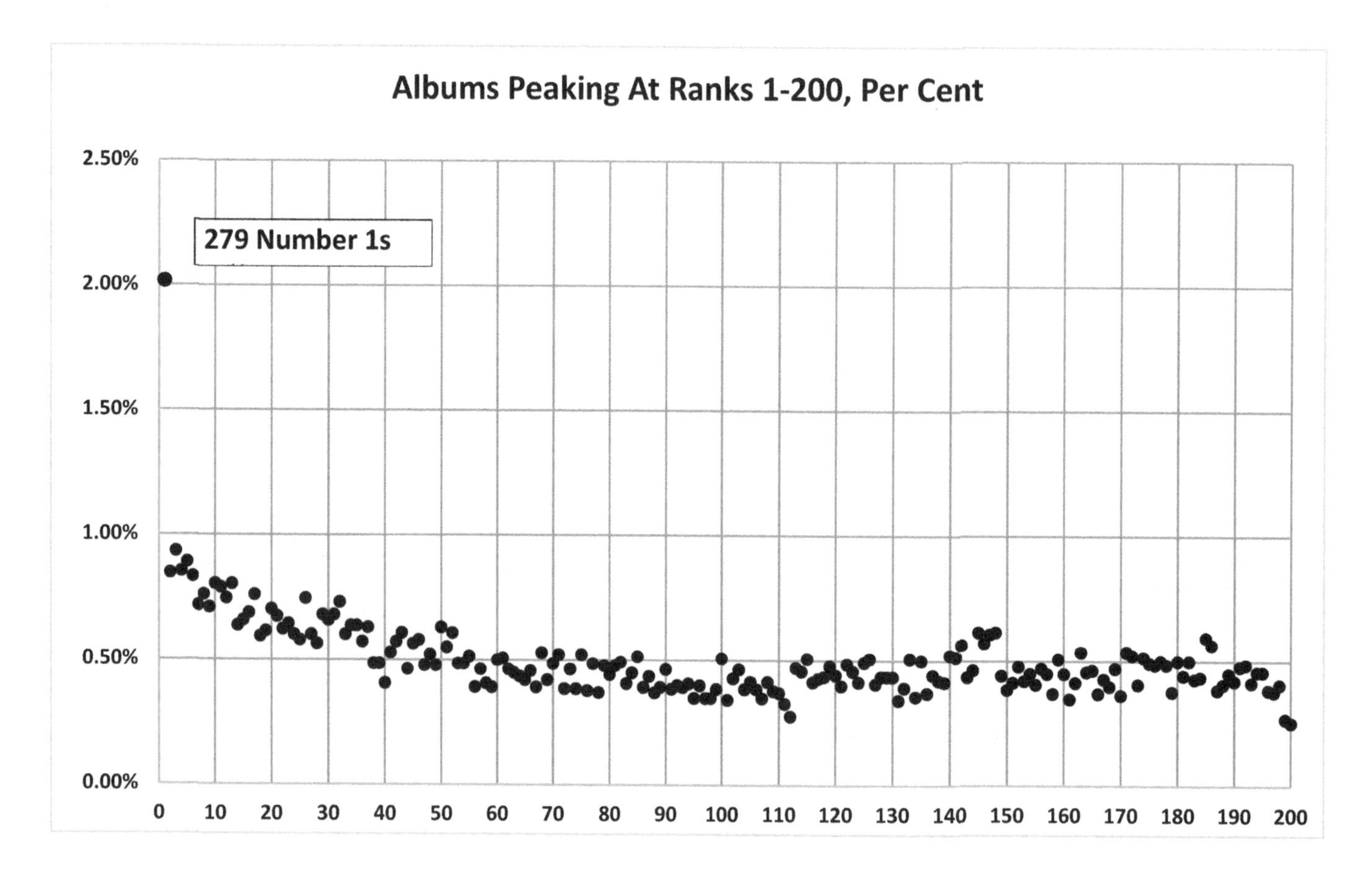

Albums with Credit Allocated to Underlying Acts

"Pops" Goes The Trumpet (64)-Al Hirt & Boston Pops Orchestra
14 Greatest Hits (84)-Michael Jackson & The Jackson 5
1975: The Duets (76)-Dave Brubeck And Paul Desmond
A Different Kind Of Blues (81)-Itzhak Perlman & Andre Previn
A Man And A Woman (77)-Isaac Hayes & Dionne Warwick
A Star Is Born (Soundtrack) (76)-Barbra Streisand & Kris Kristofferson
A Taste Of Yesterday's Wine (82)-Merle Haggard/ George Jones
Actual Speeches Of Franklin D. Roosevelt And John F. Kennedy (64)-Franklin D. Roosevelt And John F. Kennedy
America, I Hear You Singing (64)-Frank Sinatra/ Bing Crosby/Frank Waring
An Evening With Belafonte/Makeba (65)- Harry Belafonte & Miriam Makeba
An Evening With Belafonte/Mouskouri (66)- Harry Belafonte & Nana Mouskouri
An Evening With Chick Corea & Herbie Hancock (79)- Chick Corea & Herbie Hancock
An Evening With Herbie Hancock And Chick Corea (79)- Herbie Hancock And Chick Corea
Anne Murray / Glen Campbell (71)-Anne Murray & Glen Campbell
Arthur Prysock/Count Basie (66)-Arthur Prysock/ Count Basie
As Falls Wichita, So Falls Wichita Falls (81)- Pat Metheny & Lyle Mays
Asylum Choir II (71)-Leon Russell & Marc Benno
B.L.T. (81)-Jack Bruce/Bill Lordan/Robin Trower
Back To Back (67)- The Mar-Keys/Booker T. & The MG's
Back To Back (67)-The Tokens/The Happenings
Baron Von Tollbooth & The Chrome Nun (73)- Paul Kantner, Grace Slick & David Freiberg
Beauty And The Beard (64)-Al Hirt & Ann-Margret
Benny And Us (77)-Average White Band & Ben E. King
Benson & Farrell (76)-George Benson & Joe Farrell
Billy Preston & Syreeta (81)-Billy Preston & Syreeta
Blows Against The Empire (70)-Paul Kantner/ Jefferson Starship
Blue Bash! (63)-Kenny Burrell/Jimmy Smith
Blue Jays (75)-Justin Hayward & John Lodge
Blue Rabbit (65)-Johnny Hodges/Wild Bill Davis
Bobbie Gentry & Glen Campbell (68)-Bobbie Gentry & Glen Campbell
Bongo Fury (75)-Frank Zappa/Captain Beefheart/ The Mothers
Carlos Santana & Buddy Miles! Live! (72)-Carlos Santana & Buddy Miles
Chester & Lester (76)-Chet Atkins And Les Paul
Class Of '55 (86)-Carl Perkins, Jerry Lee Lewis, Roy Orbison, & Johnny Cash
Classical Gas (87)-Mason Williams & Mannheim Steamroller
Collaboration (87)-George Benson/Earl Klugh
Command Performance! Les & Larry Elgart Play The Great Dance Hits (64)-Les & Larry Elgart
Concerto For Group And Orchestra (70)-Deep Purple/ The Royal Philharmonic Orchestra
Country-Folk (69)-Waylon Jennings & The Kimberlys
Danny Davis & Willie Nelson With The Nashville Brass (80)-Danny Davis And Willie Nelson With The Nashville Brass
Dave Mason & Cass Elliot (71)-Dave Mason & Cass Elliot

David Bowie Narrates Prokofiev's "Peter And The Wolf" (78)-David Bowie/Philadelphia Orchestra/ Eugene Ormandy
David Merrick Presents Hits From His Broadway Hits (64)- John Gary/Ann-Margret
Delicious Together (64)-Betty Everett & Jerry Butler
Diana & Marvin (73)-Diana Ross & Marvin Gaye
Double Vision (86)-Bob James/David Sanborn
Dueling Banjos (73)-Eric Weissberg & Steve Mandell
Dylan And The Dead (89)-Bob Dylan & The Grateful Dead
Ella And Basie! (63)-Ella & Basie
Father & Son (65)-Hank Williams Sr. & Hank Williams Jr.
For The First Time (68)-Brenda & Pete
Francis A. & Edward K. (68)-Frank Sinatra & Duke Ellington
Francis Albert Sinatra & Antonio Carlos Jobim (67)- Frank Sinatra & Antonio Carlos Jobim
Gene & Jerry - One & One (71)-Gene Chandler & Jerry Butler
George Jones & Gene Pitney (65)-George Jones & Gene Pitney
Get That Feeling (67)-Jimi Hendrix and Curtis Knight
Getz/Gilberto (64)-Stan Getz And Joao Gilberto Featuring Antonio Carlos Jobim
Go (76)-Stomu Yamashta/Steve Winwood/ Michael Shrieve
Half & Half (70)-Frankie Valli & The 4 Seasons
Harlequin (85)-Dave Grusin & Lee Ritenour
Herb Alpert/Hugh Masekela (78)-Herb Alpert/ Hugh Masekela
Hey Joe, Hey Moe (81)-Moe Bandy & Joe Stampley
Hooker 'N Heat (71)-Canned Heat And John Lee Hooker
How To Beat The High Cost Of Living (Soundtrack) (80)- Hubert Laws And Earl Klugh
I Am My Brother's Keeper (70)-The Ruffin Brothers (Jimmy & David)
Illuminations (74)-Devadip Carlos Santana & Turiya Alice Coltrane
In Concert (74)-Deodato/Airto
Irish Heartbeat (88)-Van Morrison & The Chieftains
Jammed Together (69)-Albert King, Steve Cropper, Pop Staples
Jeff Beck With The Jan Hammer Group Live (77)-Jeff Beck With The Jan Hammer Group
Jeff Beck, Tim Bogert, Carmine Appice (73)-Beck, Bogert & Appice
Jeff Beck's Guitar Shop (89)-Jeff Beck With Terry Bozzio & Tony Hymas
Jimmy & Wes The Dynamic Duo (67)-Jimmy Smith & Wes Montgomery
Jolly What! The Beatles & Frank Ifield (64)- The Beatles/Frank Ifield
Just Kiddin' Around (63)-Ray Conniff & Billy Butterfield
King & Queen (67)-Otis Redding & Carla Thomas
Kooper Session (70)-Al Kooper/Shuggie Otis
Leather And Lace (81)-Waylon Jennings & Jessi Colter
Lena & Gabor (70)-Lena Horne & Gabor Szabo
Live (81)-Stephane Grappelli/David Grisman
Live - On Tour In Europe (76)-Billy Cobham/ George Duke Band
Long May You Run (76)-Stills-Young Band
Love Devotion Surrender (73)-Carlos Santana & Mahavishnu John McLaughlin
Manufacturers Of Soul (68)-Jackie Wilson And Count Basie
Meant For Each Other (84)-Barbara Mandrell & Lee Greenwood
Monterey International Pop Festival (70)-Otis Redding/The Jimi Hendrix Experience

Music From Songwriter (Soundtrack) (84)-Willie Nelson & Kris Kristofferson
My Life In The Bush Of Ghosts (81)-Brian Eno - David Byrne
Nancy & Lee (68)-Nancy Sinatra & Lee Hazlewood
Natural States (88)-David Lanz & Paul Speer
Nero Goes "Pops" (65)-Peter Nero/Boston Pops Orchestra
On The Road To Freedom (74)-Alvin Lee & Myron LeFevre
Once Upon A Christmas (84)-Kenny Rogers & Dolly Parton
One For The Road (79)-Willie Nelson And Leon Russell
Our Shining Hour (65)-Sammy Davis-Count Basie
Perfect Combination (84)-Stacy Lattisaw & Johnny Gill
Peter And The Commissar (64)-Allan Sherman/Boston Pops Orchestra/Arthur Fiedler
Poncho & Lefty (83)-Merle Haggard/Willie Nelson
Porgy & Bess (76)-Ray Charles And Cleo Laine
Profiles (85)-Nick Mason & Rick Fenn
Roberta Flack & Donny Hathaway (72)-Roberta Flack & Donny Hathaway
Rod Stewart/Faces Live - Coast To Coast Overture And Beginners (74)-Rod Stewart/Faces
Rough Mix (77)-Pete Townshend & Ronnie Lane
Royal Rappin's (79)-Millie Jackson & Isaac Hayes
Rural Free Delivery (73)-Eric Weissberg & Deliverance
San Antonio Rose (80)-Willie Nelson & Ray Price
Sarah Vaughan/Michel Legrand (72)-Sarah Vaughan/Michel Legrand
Showdown! (86)-Albert Collins, Robert Cray, Johnny Copeland
Sometimes When We Touch (80)-Cleo Laine & James Galway
Sunfighter (71)-Grace Slick and Paul Kantner
Super Session (68)-Mike Bloomfield/Al Kooper/Steve Stills
That's What Friends Are For (78)-Johnny Mathis & Deniece Williams
The Beatles vs. The Four Seasons (64)-The Beatles/Four Seasons
The Board Of Directors (68)-Count Basie & The Mills Brothers
The Dells vs. The Dramatics (74)-The Dells/The Dramatics
The Dream Duet (64)-Anna Moffo & Sergio Franchi
The Duke At Tanglewood (66)-Duke Ellington/Boston Pops Orchestra/Arthur Fiedler
The Electric Horseman (Soundtrack) (80)-Willie Nelson/Dave Grusin
The Hollywood Musicals (87)-Johnny Mathis & Henry Mancini
The Live Adventures Of Mike Bloomfield And Al Kooper (69)-Mike Bloomfield/Al Kooper
The Right Combination (80)-Linda Clifford & Curtis Mayfield
The Two Of Us (84)-Ramsey Lewis & Nancy Wilson
The Velveteen Rabbit (85)-Meryl Streep & George Winston
Thelma & Jerry (77)-Thelma Houston & Jerry Butler
Through The Fire (84)-Hagar, Schon, Aaronson, Shrieve
Together (64)-Marvin Gaye & Mary Wells
Together (76)-Johnny & Edgar Winter
Together Again! (66)-Willis Jackson & Jack McDuff
Together In Concert (75)-Pete Seeger/Arlo Guthrie
Tribute (87)-Ozzy Osbourne/Randy Rhoads
Trio (87)-Dolly Parton, Linda Ronstadt, Emmylou Harris
Triumvirate (73)-Mike Bloomfield/John Paul Hammond/Dr. John
Truce (82)-Jack Bruce & Robin Trower
Twin Sons Of Different Mothers (78)-Dan Fogelberg/ Tim Weisberg

Two Great Experiences Together! (71)-Jimi Hendrix & Lonnie Youngblood

Wanted! The Outlaws (76)-Waylon Jennings, Willie Nelson, Jessi Colter, Tompall Glaser

We Go Together (71)-Tammy Wynette & George Jones

We're Gonna Get Together (70)-Buck Owens & Susan Raye

We're The Best Of Friends (79)-Natalie Cole & Peabo Bryson

West Meets East (67)-Yehudi Menuhin & Ravi Shankar

William Russo: Three Pieces For Blues Band And Symphony Orchestra (73)-San Francisco Symphony/Siegel-Schwall Band

Xanadu (Soundtrack) (80)-Olivia Newton-John/ Electric Light Orchestra

Y U I Orta (89)-Ian Hunter/ Mick Ronson

Billboard Top 5 Albums of the Year: 1956-63

This list is compiled from the Wikipedia article "List of Best-Selling Albums By Year in the United States"

https://en.wikipedia.org/wiki/List_of_best-selling_albums_by_year_in_the_United_States#cite_note-1

The underlying data is obtained from archived Billboard pages available on the site. The numbers in parentheses are the rankings given those albums In Joel Whitburn's list: The Top 100 Albums 1955-2016.[6]

Title	Act	1956	1957	1958	1959	1960	1961	1962	1963
Calypso (4)	Harry Belafonte	1							
My Fair Lady (21)	Original Cast	2	1	1					
The King And I	Soundtrack	3	5						
The Eddie Duchin Story	Soundtrack	4							
Elvis Presley (60)	Elvis Presley	5							
Hymns	Tennessee Ernie Ford		2						
Oklahoma!	Soundtrack		3						
Around The World In 80 Days (57)	Soundtrack		4						
The Music Man (42)	Original Cast			2					
Johnny's Greatest Hits	Johnny Mathis			3					
South Pacific (3)	Soundtrack			4	3				
Come Fly With Me	Frank Sinatra			5					
Music From "Peter Gunn" (61)	Henry Mancini				1				
Gigi (58)	Soundtrack				2				
...From the Hungry I	Kingston Trio				4				
The Kingston Trio At Large (25)	Kingston Trio				5				
The Sound Of Music (17)	Original Cast					1	4	5	
Inside Shelley Berman	Shelley Berman					2			
The Button-Down Mind Of Bob Newhart (30)	Bob Newhart					3			
Sixty Years Of Music America Loves Best Volume I	Various Artists					4			
Here We Go Again	Kingston Trio					5			
Camelot	Original Cast						1		
Great Motion Picture Themes	Various Artists						2		
Never On Sunday	Soundtrack						3		
Exodus (31)	Soundtrack						5		
West Side Story (1)	Soundtrack							1	1
Breakfast At Tiffany's (44)	Soundtrack							2	
Blue Hawaii (11)	Elvis Presley							3	
West Side Story	Original Cast							4	
Peter, Paul And Mary	Peter, Paul And Mary								2
Moving	Peter, Paul And Mary								3
Joan Baez In Concert	Joan Baez								4
I Left My Heart In San Francisco	Tony Bennett								5

Whitburn places 31 albums from the pre-consolidated chart era into his Top 100 (1955-2016); over twice as many as would be expected based on the number of years. This points up the limited nature of the album market in those years and the need at the very least for normalization to place those albums on an equal footing with those that came later–if a valid comparison can be made at all. Top 50 Whitburn albums that did not make these Top 5 lists include *The Days Of Wine And Roses* by Andy Williams (19), *Modern Sounds In Country And Western Music* by Ray Charles (33), *Persuasive Percussion* Soundtrack (35), *Judy At Carnegie Hall* by Judy Garland (37), *Sold Out* by The Kingston Trio (46) and *The First Family* by Vaughn Meader (48). All these are post-1960 releases.

---

[6] Joel Whitburn, "Top Pop Albums, 1955-2016" © 2018, Record Research, Inc., P.O. Box 200, Menomonee Falls, WI

ACKNOWLEDGEMENTS

Thanks to Doug Heatherly, Ph.D. for tech support on cover art and file uploading. Doug has been a part of the Ranking team from the beginning.

Thanks to my writing colleague Dann Isbell—the founder of the *Ranking* franchise--who I met online nearly the first day I started this line of work in July, 2013. Through *Ranking the '70s*, he taught me how to create a book like this one. He got me engaged in another album project last winter, from which the idea for this book came. He is a marvelous sounding board, proofreader, ground wire and friend.

Thanks for encouragement and facilitation to Lou Simon of Sirius XM who maintains an oasis on satellite radio called The Diner, where music fans of all ages congregate once a week to talk about the music they love. Out of that common interest has grown a community of people who have also found ways to meet and care for one another in the real world. Few people could have created such a community out of the void using nothing but warmth and personality. Lou did.

Thanks to Rich Appel, professor and radio entrepreneur, a source of information, support and friendship since I started chart work in earnest. In that time, he has harpooned his white whale—bringing *That Thing with Rich Appel* to life on over 100 stations, where he is heard weekly, literally around the world.

Thanks to Fred Bronson, writer of Billboard's Chart Beat and a number of books for his great Foreword to this opus. Fred has forgotten more about the charts than I will ever know. I am in awe of him because he is a wonderful resource and a great guy.

Finally, and saving the best for last, I want to thank my wife Mary, daughter Allison and sons Will and Quin. They have been kind enough to only roll their eyes when they thought I wasn't looking, enduring the gestation and birth of three books over the past six years. They didn't scream when I hijacked interesting conversations on other topics to describe this work to poor souls who were unable to chew a leg off to escape the trap. My late brother Jim provided the first impetus to start the work by bequeathing me his collection of chart books. My sister Mary Ellen still runs rings around me musically. I can't hear "Dancing Queen" without a fond remembrance of my late sister Kate.

My closet, with a thousand albums, 500 CDs and boxes of 45s—a small collection among those of the Diner crowd, but one that has been accumulating over 60 years—demonstrates that you don't own your stuff, your stuff owns you.

August, 2020

Epilog: My Vinyl Romance

I remember where I was the day Billboard published its first consolidated mono and stereo album chart. That date was August 17, 1963. I was in the seventh grade at St. Mary's School in Crown Point, Indiana, and I was going to my first dance. It is memorable not because I was a fat kid who had no earthly idea how to dance but because I heard *Surfer Girl* and *Little Deuce Coupe* for the first time. They would not chart in Chicago for a couple of weeks yet.

It was a singles-centric world in Crown Point in 1963, for at least two reasons. First, we lived by Top 40 radio, and radio played singles. Second, mono albums cost $3.98 at Blanchard's Record Store—way more than the 98 cents a single cost—and you could never be sure you'd like the non-singles. In my family, most albums were soundtracks, with the exception of a couple of comedy albums like Allan Sherman's *My Son, The Nut* and *The First Family,* which it seemed everybody owned. Eleven-year-old me may have influenced those latter purchases.

The first music album I **bought** was *The Beatles Song Book Volume 2* by the Hollyridge Strings. Early on, my relationship with the Beatles was complicated. Of course they were huge, but I didn't want to ride a bandwagon. So I was kind of a Beatles denier, and this was a way of having the Beatles music without having them. I bought the single *Yesterday*. Album-wise, I finally caved at *Help*.

But the first music album I **owned** was *Beach Boys Concert,* which my cousin got me for my 13th birthday. She called me a couple of weeks before and said she was doing a survey of the boys in the class about which groups they liked. I took the survey ruse seriously for about 15 seconds. Subterfuge was not her long suit.

And then there was **the one that got away**. I couldn't bring myself to pull the trigger on buying *All Summer Long* by the Beach Boys, despite looking at it in the store numerous times. Looking back, I wish I had. I'd have loved all those cuts I didn't recognize.

As the '60s progressed, albums seemed to make more and more sense. I liked Simon and Garfunkel and bought both *Sounds of Silence* and *Parsley, Sage Rosemary and Thyme*. Then, I took a chance on their first album, *Wednesday Morning, 3 AM*, which didn't sell very well initially. It was way different. Folk rock, hold the rock. Still liked it, though, which is what you do if you're a fan.

My transition from singles to albums was accelerated by the advent of underground FM radio around 1968 in Chicago. As I remember, WOPA and WLS-FM were two early adopters and it was there you could be exposed to the 17-minute version of *In-A-Gadda-Da-Vida* and the 17 minute version of far less musically complex songs. But there was no getting that 17-minute version on a single.

Well, and in many cases, not on a single album either. My first double album was *Wheels of Fire*, with the Beatles *White Album* not far behind. Although, my all-time favorite double album is *Chicago Transit Authority*. I remember it as having a low list price—maybe $5.98—which for two records was a bargain, even if there was about 17 minutes of random instrumental noodling. It was hot when I graduated from Crown Point High in 1969.

When I went to college, I discovered Record Club of America. When you joined, you paid a small membership fee and got X free albums from their catalog, and you never actually had to buy anything ever again. What's more, if you signed a friend up, he paid a small membership fee, got X free albums, and YOU got X free albums too. My summer job was selling used cars. Selling free albums was shooting fish in a barrel, and I shot a LOT of fish.

Of course, sometimes you hadn't used up all your free albums, and you already owned everything in the catalog you recognized. Which is how I ended up with *One Stormy Night* by the Mystic Moods Orchestra.

For the popular albums, Record Club of America licensed the record and pressed its own copies on vinyl that was half ground-up shower curtains and half dirt. But then again, I didn't have a great stereo either so it was hard to tell exactly why it sounded like listening to music through the phone.

By the early '70s, I was fully in "buy the album for that one cut" mode. *Steam* comes to mind, and it didn't even dawn on me to buy the single of *Na Na Hey Hey Kiss Him Goodbye*. So why did I buy an awful album? I think because changing records every 2:45 was just too much trouble. Maybe you could stand to listen to the side with the single for 18:00.

Sometimes I'd even buy the album for no cuts because I wanted an artist's complete collection. In fact, I have two copies of *The Secret Life Of J. Eddy Fink* by Janis Ian. I bought the second one because I forgot that the one I needed was *Who Really Cares?*

Later, I discovered used record and cutout stores where filling in bits of a collection for $2.99 seemed like you were actually making money. My favorite thing to do in the late '70s was buy the album of the singer-songwriters who wrote for more popular acts like Barry Manilow and Helen Reddy. I have a lot of Randy Edelman, David Pomeranz, Bruce Johnston, Alan O'Day and Harriet Schock. Those were the days I fancied myself a budding singer-songwriter. Fortunately, I had chemistry to fall back on.

Maybe it was fate that as a voracious consumer of records I spent the last few years of the LP era working for a company that made vinyl record compound. Records are made from a complex mixture of plastic, wax, softener, soot, extender, heat stabilizer and fairy dust. And squishing a biscuit of that stuff into a functioning record is as much art as science.

And it was a dying business. We went from decent volume to virtually zero in the period 1986-1989. Cassettes took out one engine and CDs finished us off. And I had to admit—CDs seemed better. No pops, no hiss, no scratches. I switched to CDs—my first was *The Best Of The Alan Parsons Project*, although *Brothers In Arms* was not far behind.

If you get to be old enough you get to see it all again—like the rebirth of vinyl. What drew us to CDs is now the major flaw. They have no pops, no hiss, no scratches. LPs now seem warm and real, and CDs seem cold and sterile.

As a mid-generation Baby Boomer, that's OK. I grew up with Stereo LPs and I'm glad they're back. They were dear to me then and they are dear to me now.

About The Author

BILL CARROLL, Ph.D. is an Adjunct Professor of Chemistry at Indiana University, Bloomington, IN and lives with his wife Mary in Dallas, TX. They have three children, Allison, Will and Quin.
Bill has been President and Chair of the Board of the American Chemical Society, the world's largest single-discipline scientific professional organization with over 150,000 members.
In 2015, Bill retired after a 37-year career in industry and now spends his time as a globally recognized industrial chemistry consultant through his company, Carroll Applied Science, LLC. His first love for 60 years, however, has been the pop charts. As an author of peer-reviewed articles, the massive *Ranking the Rock Writers* and co-author with Dann Isbell of the highly-rated *Ranking the '70s*, he is fulfilling his dream of applying science-based data analytics to popular music.